ENVIRONMENTAL LAW AND POLICY: NATURE, LAW, AND SOCIETY

ENVIRONMENTAL LAW AND POLICY: NATURE, LAW, AND SOCIETY

Third Edition

Zygmunt J.B. Plater
Boston College Law School

Robert H. Abrams
Wayne State University Law School

William Goldfarb
Department of Environmental Sciences
Cook College, Rutgers University

Robert L. Graham
Jenner & Block, Chicago

Lisa Heinzerling
Georgetown University Law Center

David A. Wirth
Boston College Law School

PUBLISHERS

111 Eighth Avenue, New York, NY 10011
www.aspenpublishers.com

About Aspen Publishers

Aspen Publishers, headquartered in New York City, is a leading information provider for attorneys, business professionals, and law students. Written by preeminent authorities, our products consist of analytical and practical information covering both U.S. and international topics. We publish in the full range of formats, including updated manuals, books, periodicals, CDs, and online products.

Our proprietary content is complemented by 2,500 legal databases, containing over 11 million documents, available through our Loislaw division. Aspen Publishers also offers a wide range of topical legal and business databases linked to Loislaw's primary material. Our mission is to provide accurate, timely, and authoritative content in easily accessible formats, supported by unmatched customer care.

To order any Aspen Publishers title, go to *www.aspenpublishers.com* or call 800-638-8437.

To reinstate your manual update service, call 800-638-8437.

For more information on Loislaw products, go to *www.loislaw.com* or call 800-364-2512.

For Customer Care issues, e-mail *CustomerCare@aspenpublishers.com*; call 800-234-1660; or fax 800-901-9075.

Aspen Publishers
a Wolters Kluwer business

To our families

and to all who act to protect this fragile planet

Summary of Contents

Environmentalists are like misers. They are hard to live with, but make great ancestors.

— The India Times

Contents

REFERENCE MATERIALS

There is hardly a political question in the United States which does not sooner or later turn into a judicial one.

— Alexis de Tocqueville, Democracy in America, 1848

PREFACE

"When we try to pick out anything by itself, we find it hitched to everything else in the universe," John Muir, founder of the Sierra Club, once said.[1] Indeed, "Everything is connected to everything else" is the First Law of Ecology. This is depressing news for anyone designing a coursebook on environmental law. It means that it is impossible to capture in one book a field that ultimately takes on the entire planet as its subject matter.

This is primarily a book about environmental law. Environmental law necessarily includes environmental science, environmental economics, and environmental policy as essential elements of its analysis. Even so, environmental law itself has become so extensive and complex that courses in the subject run the risk of bogging down, a danger that has encouraged us to use a different approach to organizing the field.

How then does this coursebook handle the numbing complexity and detail of modern environmental law? Rather than organizing the book around physical science categories, such as air, water, toxics, wildlife, etc., we organize it around legal categories. The way the legal system works, not the intricacy of some media-specific physical science area, is our primary concern. Using this legal process structure, the book probes every nook and cranny of the legal system, exploring ways in which environmental attorneys in and out of government have attempted to understand the fascinating complexities of environmental problems in the real world — both human and ecological — and to use law imaginatively and competently to address them.

The materials here aim to prepare interested and concerned students to be active participants in the processes that shape their environmental future. In addition to teaching students about the substance of environmental laws , the book pursues the broader goal of teaching about how the legal system functions in an area of vital public concern. In short, this book aims to give students analytical skills and a solid doctrinal footing in environmental law, along with encouraging a taste for the pleasures of creative lawyering in meeting the challenges of human governance in the ecological context. Ultimately we are guardedly optimistic that our society's environmental dilemmas can be resolved, and that law will be a sensitive part of the solution.

THE THIRD EDITION OF *ENVIRONMENTAL LAW AND POLICY: NATURE, LAW, AND SOCIETY*

Revisions incorporated in this third edition are designed to reinforce the book's focus on the evolving structure and process of environmental law. How do various legal standards and mechanisms integrate civic environmental values into the complexities of a modern industrial democracy, and how do these systems change over time?

---

1. J. Muir, My First Summer in the Sierra 211 (1911).

In this third edition, we have added new coverage, commentary, and questions in every chapter. In addition there are two new chapters — Chapter 8 on how international legal norms enter into domestic environmental law, and Chapter 13 on the use of cost-benefit analysis as a prescriptive standard for regulation.

We have expanded the book's coverage of market-enlisting approaches and government-industry partnerships for achieving environmental quality beyond command-and-control, and the political history of environmental law — contrasting the eras of energetic development of environmental protection law with the periods of reaction and resistance during the Reagan Administration, the 104th Congress, and the George W. Bush Administration, with an eye to the rest of the twenty-first century.

A number of significant new cases and materials appear here for the first time — the Supreme Court's regulatory takings decisions in Palazzolo v. Rhode Island and *Tahoe-Sierra Preservation Council*, and the new law of takings they have created — the *American Trucking* case, validating an embattled delegation of power to EPA and refusing to impose cost-benefit analysis requirements — the *Norfolk & Western Ry.* decision on cancerphobia and joint and several liability — the first-time ever congressional veto of agency safety rules, overturning the OSHA ergonomic stress regulations — *Laidlaw Environmental Services* and newly clarified citizen standing law — the *Solid Waste Agency of Northern Cook County* case, and *Borden Ranch*, asserting new definitions of federal jurisdiction under the Clean Water Act — the international arbitral decisions under NAFTA in the Metalclad and Methanex (MTBE) arbitrations, and the first successful citizen-initiated fact-finding procedures in the Migratory Bird Treaty Act inquiry — the federal-state jurisdictional clash over CAA implementation in the 2004 *Alaska Dept. of Envtl. Conservation* case — and in addition we suspect this is the first environmental law coursebook to look into the messy problem of mad cow disease.

This book is used for the first, and often students' only, course in environmental law, and we therefore feel obligated to leave students with a well-rounded legal overview. Not all professors design their course syllabus in similar layouts. This book, consistent with its legal process approach to organizing the large and unwieldy field, therefore offers teachers a menu of shorter chapters with which to design and build each individual course, and to suit different ways of approaching the subject. Some courses have chosen to focus on and follow one chosen problem area throughout the semester (typically air or water pollution, or toxics), or kept track of an ongoing local controversy — a particular hazardous waste disposal case, wildlife or park management issue, mining, dredging, or dam project. Others have assigned short individual research papers, class presentations, field visits, and so on, and each of these has been valuable in providing reinforcing feedback to the analyses and techniques of environmental law set out broadly in the book.

A number of additional materials are listed and available on the coursebook's Web site: http//www.bc.edu/schools/law/library/coursebook/envtlaw

NOTE ON EDITING CONVENTIONS USED IN THIS BOOK

In editing materials for this book we have tried to make the text as smooth as possible to the reader's eye, and to keep the amount of text as short as possible, while covering this dauntingly broad and expansive field. This has required quite a bit of editorial surgery on text and excerpted materials.

Within excerpts, many internal citations (especially string citations) are simply excised, with no indication by ellipsis, or are dropped to footnotes. (In some cases in the text itself, when discussing general scientific or other nonlegal data, only limited citations are supplied.) Footnotes in excerpted materials, when they remain, do not have their original numbers unless a footnote holds special importance to subsequent commentators. Judicial opinions are often drastically cut and edited, indicated only by simple ellipsis, and in a few cases portions of text are reordered to make the presentation flow more smoothly. As with most casebooks, if the reader wishes to delve into a particular case or text, the excerpts here should serve to get the inquiry started, but there is no substitute for going back to the original full text.

Various departures from literary convention and Blue Book style have been incorporated throughout the book to improve scansion (as in eliminating brackets on [i]nitial capitalization changes, or our simplified *infra* and *supra* references). Case opinion excerpts, however, usually retain the originating court's stylistic idiosyncrasies.

Gender-sensitivity was a virtually unknown editing concept until the 1960s. Accordingly many classic cases, and some modern texts as well, address all significant parties as male. In this book the pronouns "he" and "she" when used generically should be understood to refer inclusively to all persons regardless of gender (although in retrospect it seems most polluters still appear here as male).

HELP! ACRONYMS!

Swarms of acronyms have invaded environmental law — EISs, NIMBY, LULUs, PSD, SARA, ToSCA, TMDLs, ad infinitum. To give students a sobering welcome to the field, and to save trees, we use acronyms throughout the book after their first appearance in these pages. To facilitate readers' coping with those acronyms, the back reference pages (which contain all reference sections except the Contents) also include a glossary of acronyms & abbreviations with initial page notations, which you may want to tab for easy reference.

GOING BEYOND THE BOOK

An environmental law course is broad in scope. The text and commentary in this book often incorporate analysis of source material, cases, and issues extending far beyond the excerpted textual material. The excerpted material often serves to supplement the text, rather than vice-versa as in most law books. To provide more depth and familiarity with detail, some professors choose to add other components to the coursework.

A number of offerings have integrated one or more regulatory simulations into the course, giving students an experience of the art and skills of regulatory practice, which characterizes so much of modern law. For many this may be the only chance they'll have in law school to pick up this critical knowledge. Several good sources of hands-on exercises are available; we have used Anderson & Hirsch's excellent Environmental Law Practice: Problems and Exercises for Skills Development (2003) to good effect.

Some very fine on-line and loose-leaf services provide information updates on a regular, often daily, basis: Greenwire; the Environmental Law Reporter (cases and analyses by The Environmental Law Institute); the BNA Environment Reporter (cases, statutes, and current developments by the Bureau of National Affairs); the BNA International Environmental Reporter; the BNA Chemical Regulation Reporter; the BNA Toxics Law Reporter; and the BNA Asbestos Abatement Reporter. Student subscriptions to activist listservs and newsletters are also available and valuable: The Amicus Journal, Natural Resources Defense Council, 122 E. 42d St., Suite 4500, NYC 10168; Earth Island Institute's E.I. Journal, 300 Broadway, San Francisco CA 94133; Environmental Defense's monthly newsletter, 257 Park Ave. S, NYC 10010; Not Man Apart, Friends of the Earth, 530 7th St. SE, Washington DC 20003; the National Wildlife Federation's Weekly News Report, 1416 P. St. NW, Washington DC 20036; resolve, published by Center for Environmental Dispute Resolution, World Wildlife Fund and The Conservation Foundation, 1250 24th St. NW, Washington, DC 20037; and the Sierra Club National Newsletter, 320 Pennsylvania Ave. SE, Washington, DC 20003. The National Wildlife Federation's Conservation Directory is a useful catalogue of hundreds of environmental organizations; the Federation also has a congressional hotline recording for legislative updates, at 202-797-6655. Many industry organizations also publish newsletters and are pleased to provide extensive materials in support of their positions. A number of excellent law reviews specialize in environmental law. A plethora of useful Web sites has also developed and can be explored in virtually every part of the field. Several publishers produce useful annual statutory compilations. Background books on environmental analysis provide helpful orientation in this sprawling field. Worthwhile classics include Eugene Odum's Fundamentals of Ecology, Rachel Carson's Silent Spring, Barry Commoner's The Closing Circle, Theo Colborn, Dianne Dumanoski & John Myers's Our Stolen Future, Diane Muir's Reflections in Bullough's Pond, and Aldo Leopold's Sand County Almanac. Joseph Sax's Defending the Environment (1971) continues to be a vivid introduction and guide to the use of law in resolving the pervasive social, economic, and ecological governance problems we call "environmental."

ACKNOWLEDGMENTS

This book sometimes seems to have evolved with as much biodiversity of input as any marsh or rainforest. Dozens of people have helped shape and reshape it over the years. For all who know the work of Professor Joseph Sax, now at Berkeley, the mark of his thinking and advice on our efforts will be discernible throughout these pages. In its earliest form the book derives from materials prepared by a committee of law students at the University of Michigan in the early 1970s, including two of the present authors, for a course called Nature, Law, and Society offered to graduate and undergraduate students. In that original group Peter Schroth served not only as a major contributor but also as administrator of the course, a thankless and demanding task; without his energetic work the whole project might well have died a-borning. The Nature, Law, and Society project was supported and advised by Joe Sax and the late Professor William Stapp of the School of Natural Resources; they served graciously and well as mentors and midwives. Bill is missed by us and hundreds of other alumni of his environmental courses. Prior to its first publication in 1992, this book went through repeated reincarnations at a succession of schools at which we taught — Boston College Law School, Harvard Law School, the University of Michigan Law School, Rutgers, the University of Tennessee College of Law, and Wayne State Law School. Before the first edition and since then we have greatly benefited from suggestions and comments gratefully received from students and colleagues around the country. Very helpful contributions have come from our colleagues Glenn Adelson, Harry Bader, Michael Blumm, John Dernbach, Jeffrey Haynes, Oliver Houck, Casey Jarman, John Kostyack, Patrick Parenteau, Beth Perkins, Jon Witten, and Mary Wood, as well, of course, as the two new collaborators who have stepped in to help carry major burdens as co-authors on this third edition.

Among the many students who contributed to this edition we want to thank especially Brian Crossman, Rachel Donn, Una Kang, Amy Kullenberg, Jeremy McDiarmid, Rebecca Rich, Trevor Wiessman, and the members of the Boston College Law School Environmental Law Society who compiled the tables of cases and authorities under deadline pressures.[2] The Boston College Law School Library staff repeatedly has provided indispensable detective work and support, receiving fiendish eleventh-hour requests and calmly coming through for us: Liza Miller Arend, Karen Beck, Irene Good, Ann MacDonald, Michael Mitsukawa, Connie Sellers, Joan Shear, Mark Sullivan, Susan Sullivan, and Mo Truong. Support staffers Anne Marie Dolan, Donna Gattoni, Theresa Kachmar, Jeannie Kelly, Alice Lyons, and Donna McDermott, responded energetically and well to crisis calls for help. As for the many authors and publishers who graciously granted us permission to reprint portions of their works, a complete listing follows immediately after the text.

We also owe a debt to the remarkable group associated with Aspen Publishers who welcomed and coddled this edition — especially Carol McGeehan, Melody Davies, Barbara Roth, Elsie Starbecker, and copyeditor extraordinaire Lisa Wehrle — and to the computers (and eyes and brains) of Michael Kitchen of the PixelAntics Electronic Design Studio for design and typesetting wizardry.

Ultimately, our greatest warm thanks and appreciation must be reserved for all our families, who naïvely expressed pleasure when they first heard of this project.

Z.J.B.P.   R.H.A.   W.G.   R.L.G.   L.H.   D.A.W.

May 2004

---

2. The Environmental Law Society volunteers who worked late hours on this project were Katherine Conrad, Robert Creamer, David Galalis, Marc Gilmore, Andrew Hughes, Joseph Iole, Philip Jordan, Marco Quina, Eli Scheiman, and Elizabeth Treadaway.

INTRODUCTION

We travel together, passengers on a little space ship, dependent on its vulnerable resources of air and soil, all committed for our safety to its security and peace, preserved from annihilation only by the care, the work, and, I will say, the love we bestow on our fragile craft.

— Adlai Stevenson, at the United Nations, 1965

SPACESHIP EARTH[1]

David Brower — one of the founding elders of the twentieth century American environmental movement, who held the title role in Encounters with the Archdruid, John McPhee's book about environmentalism in America[2] — was standing on a lakeshore talking to an environmental law class. White-haired and raw-boned with piercing blue eyes, Brower stretched out his arm, with thumb and forefinger held about two inches apart, and said:

> Imagine if you will our entire planet reduced to this, the size of an egg.... If the planet Earth were reduced to the size of an egg, what do you think, proportionally, all its air, its atmosphere, would be? And what would be the total volume of the water that, along with air and sunlight, sustains life on this Earth?... According to the computations I've seen, the sum total of atmosphere veiled around this egg planet Earth would be equivalent to no more than the volume of a little pea wrapped around the globe. And the water? That would be no more than a match-head, a tiny volume spread thin enough to fill the oceans, rivers and lakes of the world.[3]

Looking at the students, Brower asked,

> Thinking of those limits, can you any longer not believe that our planet is a tremendously vulnerable little system, totally dependent on this fragile tissue of air and water, a thin fabric of life support made up of all the air and water the Earth will ever have?[4]

Like the astronauts who reported dramatic and startling personal reactions to their first glimpse down upon planet Earth from outer space, the images of Brower's egg and Stevenson's Spaceship Earth force us to recognize our interrelatedness with all other human and natural systems that make up the planet. The Earth is indeed one small,

1. See Kenneth Boulding, The Economics of Spaceship Earth, in Environmental Quality in a Growing Economy 3–14 (1971), arguing that the economy of the future will be like a space craft with closed-cycle limited resources.

2. McPhee, Encounters with the Archdruid (1971).

3. In fact, the relative scale of the mass of atmosphere and water to the planet Earth is apparently even more dramatic. According to Dr. Heinrich Holland of Harvard's geology department, taking the relative *masses* of Earth's air and water (as opposed to spatial volume which is a misleading construct), the atmosphere constitutes less than one-millionth of the planet's mass, and the water less than one-thousandth.

4. Brower was speaking on a beach on Mission Point Peninsula, Grand Traverse Bay, Michigan, October 1977.

limited, totally self-contained entity, a single natural system (albeit made up of many interconnected and interdependent systems) containing great richness, diversity, and vulnerability.

As the First Law of Ecology says, everything is connected to everything else. Environmentalists tend to be conservative at least in this regard: out of utilitarian caution as well as ethical impulse they tend to value the dynamic natural systems that have evolved over millennia, and they distrust the wholesale human intrusions on these systems that have occurred particularly since the arrival of the industrial age. Every act of technology or human behavior is likely to have direct and indirect results, some quite drastic, unpredictable, and long-term in their effects. Who but environmentalists would have foreseen that the choice of coalburning methods in the Midwest would hurt maple sugar producers in Vermont, and leach lead into the water supplies of eastern New England homes 700 miles away? Yet acid rain was a natural chemical reaction just waiting to be triggered. It is important, environmentalists say, to look wide and long before we leap.

Unfortunately, the "long view," looking out for long-term negative consequences, does not seem instinctive to the human brain. Quite the contrary. If it can, the human species will consistently overlook ecological repercussions and other long-term problems, and instead focus on the more upbeat realm of short-term payoffs. The supposition is that as problems start piling up one can ignore them, get around them, pass them off or away downstream and downwind, or one can move on to new frontiers. Brower's egg planet reminds us that there are no such frontiers left; everything goes somewhere and remains within the grand system in which we must continue to live.

Environmental law attempts to build foresight into the human decisional system, along with an awareness of costs and values that are typically invisible because, though real, they exist outside the formal market economy. Often environmental law works after the fact, attempting to force accountings for depredations that have already occurred, in hopes of deterring future repetitions. Environmental law has also developed elaborate doctrines attempting to anticipate and prevent environmental disruptions. The goal is to incorporate a process of fair, overall, comprehensive accounting of real societal costs, benefits, and alternatives into major public and private decisionmaking.

Over the past several decades there has been a dramatic change in the stature of the field. It is no longer dismissable as the fad of a disgruntled minority. It is now the stuff of presidential campaigns and national public opinion poll majorities. There are now more environmental lawyers in the United States than labor lawyers.[5] Given these toeholds and the reality of environmental problems, the field inevitably will continue to grow ever more intricate, challenging, and important.

---

5. The private environmental bar parallels the remarkable development of staff and law in the environmental agencies. The federal Environmental Protection Agency (EPA) alone employs more than fifteen thousand people, with its major environmental statutes filling a book of more than 600 pages, and its regulations filling a dozen volumes and almost 10,000 pages of the Code of Federal Regulations. EPA's operating programs are funded at a level of more than $4 billion annually. See Reitze, Environmental Policy — It Is Time for a New Beginning, 14 Colum. J. Envtl. L. 111 (1988).

THE BOOK'S PERSPECTIVE

This book is designed to track through environmental law according to the structure of the legal process. It uses some of the classic cases and materials of environmental law as well as some of the most recent.

There are a few further necessary comments — our bias, for example. Every book has its bias, usually unacknowledged. If it isn't already, we wish to make this book's clear. We believe that to understand the realities of environmental law one must take straightforward account of the political contexts and agendas that swirl around the field. We view most environmental problems as arising from a fundamental human tension between short-term marketplace interests and the larger civic-societal public interest. In a dynamic logic that has built the greatest economy the world has ever known, individual human actors, including ourselves, behave rationally to maximize their own short-term best interests, with insufficient consideration or accounting for the natural and societal consequences of their actions. The ecological and civic-societal values affected by such human actions will be most efficiently addressed if they can be brought into the marketplace economy, but the altruism of market players cannot be relied upon to do that job. Environmental law therefore seeks to force these public values into the markets of daily life, in spite of the natural and powerful resistance of market forces. The powerful tension between marketplace dynamics and public civic values remains a consistent day-by-day reality within the legal process.

In large part the corporate marketplace, we believe, has come to accept and internalize public environmental values, not necessarily as a result of civic instincts but rather because of the credible prospect today of environmental enforcement by agencies and an active citizenry. This book therefore approaches many, though not all, environmental cases from the perspective of those who enforce environmental laws — citizens, public interest groups, and agencies. Our approach will often be "how can this problem be appropriately managed and corrected within the legal system?" presuming in most cases that the problem does exist. Through changing cycles of environmental law — with government sometimes more protective, sometimes less — a societal constant is the necessity for nongovernmental citizen environmentalists' continuing oversight and active participation. This book thus makes particular effort to include consideration of the role of citizens, as well as governmental officials, in the environmental legal process.

This approach seems realistic and useful as well as defensible. To understand environmental law one must understand environmental plaintiffs, especially the individuals and professionalized groups who make up the active environmental "movement." (Environmental defendants generally do not offer similarly broad countervailing legal theories of environmental defense.[6]) So to get deeper into the

---

6. Legal defenses typically amount to a series of attempts to avoid the issue — "the facts aren't sufficiently shown," "the plaintiffs don't have the right to be heard in this court," "the matter has continued for so long that the law is estopped from changing the status quo," "enforcement of the law would violate our constitutional rights," in short "the law should not be applied." To the extent that the law-and-economics movement has aspired to provide countervailing legal theories as well as market-oriented policy arguments, it has generally been unsuccessful.

swamps of environmental law, in practical terms one must follow the environmental enforcement trail, which often means citizen enforceability. Whether readers ultimately view the field from the point of view of plaintiffs or defense, an understanding of the plaintiffs' perspective is indispensable to a recognition of what's going on, and how it could be done better.

STRUCTURE

As reflected in the tables of contents, this coursebook surveys environmental law issues throughout the vast range of the American legal process — with additional consideration of international environmental law principles, which have developed extensively in the past two decades, often on the American model.

Most books on environmental law have fallen into an organization by physical science categories — air, water, toxics, wildlife, groundwater, energy, etc. — not by legal categories, which often leads them to duplicative legal analysis. This book contains material from each such area, but takes its organization from the elements of the legal system itself, building upon a base of common law and constitutional law, and continuing on to statutory and administrative law. We find that this approach is a faster and more efficient path into technical and structural questions of environmental law. In large part the aim is not to present hyper-technical details of current law, like specific regulatory parts-per-million hydrocarbon standards for automobile tailpipe emissions, and so on. The details of most areas of modern environmental law change and evolve too quickly to be fixed in a static course of study. We aim, rather, to show the design and structure of the different areas of the field, and how they work in practice.

Part One of the book explores major themes in modern environmental law analysis — an evolution of ecological science, legal techniques and mechanisms, environmental politics, economics, and risk assessment, and the growing (if sometimes reluctant) systemic acceptance of the legitimacy of environmental controls. It briefly examines the statutory history of the field and introduces the public trust doctrine, which is one of environmental law's most dramatic contributions to the modern legal system. Based on this review and orientation, the book explores the current legal structures and remedies of the common law upon which environmental law doctrines originally developed and continue to flourish today. The common law context also serves to underscore how individual citizens in a modern democrcy, primarily as environmental plaintiffs, can serve to integrate overlooked public values into the economic and political marketplace.

Part Two explores different levels and sovereignties in modern public law — the development of statutory and regulatory law in the administrative state as an overlay upon the common law. The chapters include an introduction to basic regulatory structure, to the fundamental structural questions raised in U.S. environmental law by the complexities of federal-state relations, a basic chapter on the administrative law of environmental law useful even for students who have not studied the world of agencies, and finally a chapter introducing the imminent reality of international law principles entering into domestic U.S. environmental law. Look under the surface of almost any significant environmental case and you will find yourself dealing with basic questions of modern democratic governance.

Part Three's chapters present a "taxonomy" of public law statutes, beginning with the National Environmental Policy Act, a broad-brush procedural and substantive compliance statute, and and the statutory strategy of forced informationn disclosure. Subsequent chapters examine one-by-one a variety of different approaches that can be selected by legislatures and administrative agencies to define, and then to apply, specific regulatory standards. The different standard-setting approaches, which often have application in multiple statutory structures, are viewed here in the context of the major command-and-control industrial pollution regulatory systems — harm-based ambient standards in the Clean Air Act, best-available-technology-based standards in the Clean Water Act, and recent theories for using cost-benefit analysis in standard-setting. Part Three continues with an examination of different designs and strategies of regulatory structures created by legislatures to apply environmental standards to the practical realities of the marketplace. These different implementation approaches — in addition to the classic command-and-control model for pollution control — include a new generation of approaches that attempt to enlist market dynamics into the environmental protection process, technology-forcing standards in automobile pollution and atmospheric chlorofluorocarbons, the roadblock (and regulatory "slippage") model represented by the Endangered Species Act, and the special designs and strategies of modern toxics statutes.

In Part Four the focus is on compliance, enforcement, and dispute resolution mechanisms, both civil and criminal, with enforcement initiatives coming from agencies, citizens, and, increasingly, from industries themselves. ADR (Alternative Dispute Resolution) methods provide a further evolving realm of nonmandatory mechanisms for environmental protection.

Part Five wrestles with conflicts between societal rights and responsibilities and private rights and responsibilities, leading off with the Public Trust doctrine and constitutional rights, public resource management and its special constraints and clienteles, and the political and legal tensions between public interests and private due process property rights.

Part Six acknowledges the accelerating globalization and convergence in international legal practice as well as in technology and commerce. A knowledge of comparative law techniques in understanding foreign nations' internal law is increasingly necessary for attorneys in the twenty-first century, and the recent flowering of international environmental law has changed the way many economies do business, as well as modifying some governmental behaviors and providing some collective hopes for the future.

Finally, don't be daunted by the "numbing complexity and detail"[7] of some sectors of environmental law. Because everything is connected to everything else, if one just picks up a trail and follows it, it will lead to all there is to know.

---

7. See Sax, Environmental Law in the Law Schools: What We Teach and How We Feel about It, 19 ELR 10251 (1989).

All thinking worthy of the name must now be ecological.

— Lewis Mumford, the Pentagon of Power, 1970

ENVIRONMENTAL LAW AND POLICY:
NATURE, LAW, AND SOCIETY

Never doubt that a small group of committed citizens can change the world. Indeed, it's the only thing that ever does.

— Margaret Mead

PART ONE
BEGINNINGS...

BASIC THEMES AND THE
COMMON LAW CONTEXT
OF ENVIRONMENTAL LAW

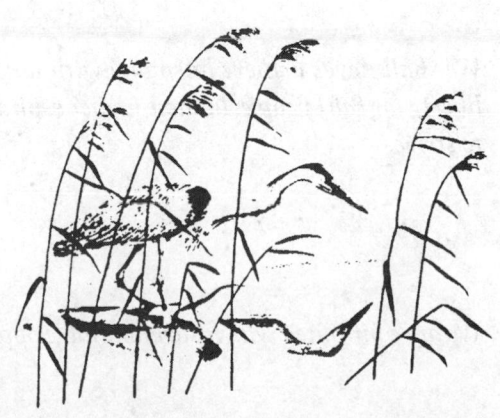

"*To secure our common future, we need a new international vision based on cooperation and a new environmental ethic, based on the realization that the issues with which we wrestle are globally interconnected. This is not only a moral ethic but also a practical one — the only way we can pursue our own self interests on a small and closely-knit planet.*"

— Gro Harlem Brundtland

We shall never achieve harmony with land, any more than we shall achieve justice and liberty for [all] people. In these higher aspirations, the important thing is not to achieve, but to strive.

— Aldo Leopold, Sand County Almanac, at 72

We are confronted with insurmountable opportunities.

— Pogo

Chapter 1

BASIC THEMES IN THE LEGAL PROCESS OF ENVIRONMENTAL LAW

A. *The Environmental Perspective*
B. *The Problem of the Commons*
C. *A Salty Paradigm: Road Salt, a Problem that Has Not Yet Met Its Legal Process*

A. THE ENVIRONMENTAL PERSPECTIVE

Section 1. THE BREADTH AND SCOPE OF ENVIRONMENTAL LAW

The ecological future of the planet is constantly being shaped by its geophysical history — by continuing natural forces of sun, rain, wind, water, seismics, vulcanism, the carbon cycle, and the diverse onrolling biological evolution built upon them — and by humans, corporations, and governments. These latter three items are very recent arrivals on the global scene and are relatively trivial in mass. They have proved, however, to have a remarkable capacity for causing planetary effects, for good and ill, and it is upon them that environmental law focuses in doing its work.

Environmental law was born in controversy and has developed in cycles alternating between flourishing growth and retrenchment under bitter counterattack. Since 1960 it has become a major sector of our legal system and a vivid mirror of the political evolution of our society, operating across a remarkably broad horizon.

If you made a mental list of the amazing diversity of situations that are considered environmental law issues, it might include the following:

- Factories discharging liquid wastes from their drainpipes and smoke from their stacks
- Chemical wastes buried in suburban fields
- Seal puppies clubbed to death on floating ice packs in the Gulf of St. Lawrence
- Uranium fuel rods being shipped thousands of miles to nuclear plants in South Carolina, or India, or North Korea
- A government highway agency cutting a path for an interstate through a park and low-income neighborhood in Memphis
- Schools of fish dying in coastal waters from bacterial toxins triggered by wastes dumped by upland hog and chicken farmers
- Toxic gases spreading from chemical plants, poisoning surrounding low-income neighborhoods in Italy, India, and Louisiana

- Sprawl development creating towns that resemble residential parking lots more than communities
- A single-hulled oil tanker more than three football fields long, with an exhausted crew, running at high speed through icebergs in a narrow rocky channel at night
- The imminent extinction of an endangered snapdragon plant in Maine
- Hairdressing salons in Yosemite National Park
- Decisions to put toxic waste sites and incinerators in the midst of low-income minority neighborhoods
- Carcinogenic chemical fire retardants in infant sleepwear
- The cutting of shade trees along rural roads
- A Tennessee river and its fertile valley eliminated by a federal agency's recreational dam project
- A centuries-old church bulldozed for a parking lot, and a host of other historic preservation issues
- Nonreturnable bottles lying along highways and in urban trash
- Disappearing rainforests and desertification in the Third World
- New Jersey's refusal to permit Philadelphia's garbage to be disposed of in New Jersey landfills
- Chlorinated hydrocarbons from consumer products and pesticides disrupting hormones, lowering sperm counts, and harming child development around the world
- Children exposed to rat bites and lead poisoning in an urban slum
- Redwood trees turned into tomato stakes and our remnant ancient forests cut for subsidized export
- An internationally-known 10 million-year-old paleontological fossil site in Colorado being bulldozed for a resort subdivision
- Asbestos dust in local elementary schools
- The construction of a new federal prison breaking apart a cohesive low-income neighborhood in New York City
- Chlorofluorocarbons thinning stratospheric ozone, causing increased ultraviolet radiation hazards on earth
- A primitive tribe in Panama threatened by extension of the Pan-American Highway through their jungle territory
- Changing weather patterns and rising sea levels across the entire planet, caused in substantial part by global warming from human-generated greenhouse gases
- And hundreds more

Is this parade of challenges just *one* field of law? It seems so. All of these widely diverse situations have been identified as "environmental." For each of them (and hundreds of others), activists identified as "environmentalists" have taken legal action to try to improve the situation, often with a good deal of success. Each case involves a highly individualized set of economic and political issues, scientific facts, private or governmental actors, and social and natural consequences. Many of them have no obvious connection with others on the list beyond their "environmental" label. The different areas of environmental law have become so voluminously complex that they become compartmentalized and unwieldy. An expert working on water pollution law typically has little time to do anything else. A person studying the science and law of endangered plants may have no special knowledge of any other environmental area and no ties to individuals working on other kinds of environmental cases. Given this diversity, the term "environmental" may seem uselessly broad, describing nothing in particular. At worst, the environmental label can give each of these situations a quixotic implication that can detract from serious public consideration of the merits, though this is changing.

What do these "environmental" examples all have in common? It may be that what makes issues "environmental" is that they all reflect a characteristic battle between two very different ways of looking at the world:

One perspective is the traditional instinctive way most human enterprises operate, especially in Western industrial democracies, with each individual person, agency, or corporate actor tending to seek to achieve the best for itself, measuring the costs and benefits in its own individualized terms and not worrying about "extraneous" consequences. The implicit or explicit assumption is that in the marketplace of national life the sum total of all such entrepreneurial strivings will be a dynamic economy and the greatest net gain for society overall. This perspective has a good deal of accomplishment to back it up. Based on this world-view, modern Western technology and commerce have built a superstructure of unprecedented wealth, dynamism, and technical progress.

The environmental perspective is a good deal more complicated than that. It starts from the premise of interconnectedness — that all human enterprises exist within one vast shared common context in which actions have collateral consequences that are relevant and should be considered, even if ignored by the market economy and official agencies. The environmental perspective is that human actions should be carefully considered and rational decisions made in terms of the full real scope of values and consequences, not just in the limited terms of those individuals who may be making particular decisions.

Instead of an image of individual self-contained enterprises all floating like separate planets and stars in the ether, the environmental perspective conceptualizes all human enterprises existing within one large system of interconnected systems. All of these systems, human and physical, ultimately draw upon the natural world that supports them with air, water, and resources. All of them have consequences, positive and negative, that impact upon the surrounding mega-context. No [hu]man is an island. In virtually every case like the inventory of issues listed above, the environmental problems we deal with are caused by instrumental human actions or development decisions that fail to take adequate account of their full direct and indirect consequences, human and eco-physical. If a negative consequence doesn't have a direct market cost, it is too often ignored. As a result, the environmental law process is typically motivated by a desire for broadened accountings, in terms of ecology and public values, of the full consequences of human decisionmaking in the political and economic marketplace of everyday life. The logic is that if human decisions are planned and made with a fuller overview, society will ultimately end up better off overall. If individual enterprises, private and public, are required to anticipate and are held to account for their serious real consequences, they will tend to avoid or mitigate their negative effects, ultimately achieving greater efficiency and societal good.

Environmental law is the legal manifestation of the Environmental Movement, which operates in both reactive and proactive modes. In its reactive mode, environmentalism attempts to counteract four counterproductive mythologies: (1) that humans are dominant over and independent of the natural world; (2) that technological change is always a good thing, a corollary of the myth of inevitable progress; (3) that the present is always superior to the past; and (4) that quantity of tangible objects, materialism, is more important than intangible qualities of life. Since modern Western society typically embraces all of these mythologies, either consciously or unconsciously, environmentalists often find themselves opponents of the status quo.

Almost every environmental case starts in response to someone's decision to do something: a new product or technology; a construction project; the start, continuation, or cessation of various programs that affect the physical world.[1] A common complaint of the environmental camp is that most people who make project proposals do not adequately consider their projects' problematic aspects. The resulting decisions thus are predicated on irrationally and unrealistically narrow grounds, unwisely ignoring facts, costs, and impacts on social and natural values that have real importance to the well-being of the community and natural systems. Unfortunately the environmental perspective often surfaces relatively late in the game, long after the planning stages and well into the implementation stages — that is, at the last minute when citizens see bulldozers rolling. And environmentalists, because of their instinctive tendency to look for overlooked problems and their often-skeptical view of claimed benefits, often end up sounding chronically negative. It need not be so.

Take the example of the Memphis superhighway, studied in the *Overton Park* case.[2] The federal and state highway planners wanted to locate a stretch of Interstate 40 along a route that would minimize the costs of land acquisition and the inconvenience of lawsuits. With that strategy in mind, they planned to run the road straight through an urban park and a low-income minority neighborhood. The local citizen environmentalists argued that this official decision took no account of the natural and social value of parkland, especially a park serving low-income communities that had no other open-space options. It was argued that the highway officials' cost considerations, based only upon the cost of condemning land and constructing the roadway, ignored the considerable social values inherent in a stable, cohesive, lower-income urban neighborhood. Furthermore, if the full costs and values were taken into account, alternative routes existed that were preferable and available. The citizens found some tactical law — as it turned out, an environmental statute limiting highway impacts on parklands —

---

1. With regard to some of the largest geophysical issues, of course — such as deforestation or, especially, overpopulation, which produces circumstances where basic natural resources are simply incapable of supporting the geometrically increasing numbers of dependent humans thrust upon them — the operative human decisions are not made consciously but by tradition, atavistic drives, inertia, and default.

2. Citizens to Preserve Overton Park v. Volpe, 401 U.S. 402 (1971), in Chapter 7.

that made their point and won the issue. That citizen-generated legal precedent has subsequently resulted in substantial improvements in the official foresight and planning given to major highway projects around the nation.

But environmental activists' confrontational legal tactics often feed the caricature of environmentalists as meddling negativistic outsiders.[3] The natural tendency of the individuals and authorities whose decisions are being questioned is to resent and resist. Environmentalists often must build their lawsuits on technicalities and a healthy dose of emotion, so that it can be hard to see their efforts as seeking a comprehensive rational analysis of challenged projects or programs. And urgent calls for rationality, for that matter, do not consistently build public respect, accord, or political momentum.

Sustainability. Modern environmentalism, despite its critics, isn't a nature-worshipping regression. Rather, it seeks to implement the concept of "sustainability" — a truly conservative doctrine — as its societal goal.[4] It's a hopeful conceptual approach, holding that thoughtfulness, planning, and luck will enable successive future generations of humankind to sustain and improve our society's collective quality of life in this global setting that supports us. As Professor Dernbach has noted, environmentalism has proactive goals that range far beyond mere defensiveness.[5]

> We often say that the purpose of environmental law is to protect the environment. But it is much more complicated than that. To begin with, environmental law has never been aimed simply at protecting the environment. Environmental law has at least nine major purposes,[6] the most prominent of which is protection of human health. Environmental law also has objectives that are plainly essential to sustainable development, including intergenerational equity and protection of the resource base upon which society rests. Other goals of environmental law include efficiency, national security, preservation or aesthetics or recreation, community stability, biocentrism, and pursuit of scientific knowledge and technology. With the possible exception of national security, citizen suit plaintiffs are seeking to enforce one or more of these objectives.

> Sustainable development concepts are embedded in environmental law. The nine purposes of environmental law can be organized under the four broad goals of sustainable development:

Natural Resources Protection	Economic Development
• Preservation for Aesthetics or Recreation	• Efficient Production of Goods & Services
• Biocentrism	• Pursuit of Scientific Knowledge and Technology
• Sustainability of Resource Base	

---

3. Environmental plaintiffs are often compelled to accomplish their ends by legal indirection, using doctrines originally intended for application in other situations. There is a political hazard involved in using legal technicalities as leverage for larger issues. Conspicuous examples are the snail darter and spotted owl endangered species cases chronicled in Chapter 16, where the solid merits of an environmental argument can be overshadowed by the tactical choice of legal tools.

4. "Sustainability" has become the central principle of the international consensus first enunciated in "Our Common Future," the 1987 Report of the World Commission on Environment and Development, echoed since then in the 1992 and 2002 Earth Summits and a succession of international and domestic declarations of policy and law. The concept makes intuitive good sense despite its susceptibility to varying interpretations.

5. Dernbach, Citizen Suits and Sustainability, 11 Widener L. Rev. No.2 (2004).

6. C. Campbell-Mohn, Objectives and Tools of Environmental Law, in Environmental Law: From Resources to Recovery §4.1 (C. Campbell-Mohn et al. eds., 1993).

Social Well-being, or "Equity"[7]

- Protection of Human Health
- Intergenerational Equity
- Community Stability

Peace and Security

- National Security [which includes effects of protecting sustainability of quality-of-life for populations in less-developed countries]

A context of struggle. The "established" players in government — not to mention the business establishment — are typically slow to welcome environmentalists and environmental laws into the system. Environmentalist citizens generally are "outsiders" who win legislative battles only when they are able to mobilize public opinion outside the political capitals, and then they are forced to defend each victory against a process of political erosion. Since environmental statutes and regulations often have come rather late and in a watered-down condition, citizen environmentalists early on became experts in blending combinations of law drawn from different sources — common law, administrative procedure, and other relevant subject areas as well as strictly environmental statutes — to serve the purposes of environmental advocacy. It is a skill and orientation that continues to characterize environmental law.

Nevertheless, due in large part to the potential for citizen enforcement in most federal environmental statutes, in the years since the original Earth Day in 1970 environmental law itself has become "established." Ecology and related sciences have developed sophistication and depth. Many manufacturing industries and businesses have reconciled themselves and adapted to basic environmental requirements, seeking to achieve cost-effective compliance, especially when federal enforcement is credible. Today, many environmental lawyers work for industry seeking to achieve rather than evade regulatory compliance. Flourishing secondary "environmental control" industries have developed. Regulatory agencies have gained in expertise and delegated authority. Public polling reveals generic support for environmental protection.

Entering the twenty-first century, modern environmental law had matured a great deal as an established body of doctrine and had become an accepted part of the structure of societal governance in the United States and abroad, no longer denigrated by even the most callow critics as a fad. The 2000 national election, however, brought into office an industry-centered antiregulatory administration that undertook a comprehensive agenda restricting mandatory environmental protections. The current assaults on the established body of environmental law are being felt and, at least to some extent, contested in virtually every corner of the field. As the federal administration has retreated from its regulatory role, some state governments have attempted to hold the line, particularly in air pollution and toxics. Environmental law continues to be inescapably political, and over the years, as a bellwether of societal governance, will undoubtedly continue to reflect the evolving path of American democracy.

---

7. To the three functions listed in this category could well be added a fourth, "Citizen Empowerment," in recognition of the normative and practical importance of citizen law enforcement in building environmental law, the right to information and pluralistic public participation, women's rights, the rights of indigenous peoples, and other fundamental rights reflected in the Rio Declaration of 1992. [Eds.]

Section 2. **THE ECOLOGICAL AND ETHICAL BASES OF ENVIRONMENTAL LAW**

Environmental economics and politics play their role in environmental law, as we will see, but other important analytical filters are provided at the threshold by ecology, the environmental sciences, and environmental ethics.

a. The science of ecology (MICRO and MACRO)

Law draws many lessons and arguments from ecology and the other flourishing environmental sciences. Modern environmentalists have drawn particular inspiration and momentum from Rachel Carson and Aldo Leopold, two giants in the field. Here are two brief examples of their work.

Aldo Leopold, A Sand County Almanac
214–220 (1968 ed.)

The image commonly employed in conservation education is "the balance of nature." For reasons too lengthy to detail here, this figure of speech fails to describe accurately what little we know about the land mechanism. A much truer image is the one employed in ecology: the biotic pyramid.... Plants absorb energy from the sun. This energy flows through a circuit called the biota, which may be represented by a pyramid consisting of layers. The bottom layer is the soil. A plant layer rests on the soil, an insect layer on the plants, a bird and rodent layer on the insects, and so on up through various animal groups to the apex layer, which consists of the larger carnivores....

In the beginning, the pyramid of life was low and squat; the food chains short and simple. Evolution has added layer after layer, link after link. Man is one of thousands of accretions to the height and complexity of the pyramid. Science has given us many doubts, but it has given us at least one certainty: the trend of evolution is to elaborate and diversify the biota. Land, then, is not merely soil; it is a fountain of energy flowing through soils, plants, and animals. Food chains are the living channels which conduct energy upward; death and decay return to the soil. The circuit is not closed; some energy is dissipated in decay, some is added by absorption from the air, some is stored in soils, peats, and long-lived forests; but it is a sustained circuit, like a slowly augmented revolving fund of life....

The velocity and character of the upward flow of energy depend on the complex structure of the plant and animal community, much as the upward flow of sap in a tree depends on its complex cellular organization. Without this complexity, normal circulation would presumably not occur. Structure means the characteristic numbers, as well as the characteristic kinds and functions, of the component species. This interdependence between the complex structure of the land and its smooth functioning as an energy unit is one of its basic attributes.

When a change occurs in one part of the circuit, many other parts must adjust themselves to it. Change does not necessarily obstruct or divert the flow of energy; evolution is a long series of self-induced changes, the net result of which has been to elaborate the flow mechanism and to lengthen the circuit. Evolutionary changes, however, are usually slow and local. Man's invention of tools has enabled him to make changes of unprecedented violence, rapidity, and scope.... The combined evidence of history and ecology seems to support one general deduction: the less violent the man-made changes, the greater the probability of successful readjustment in the pyramid.... This deduction runs counter to our current philosophy, which assumes that because a small increase in density enriched human life, that an indefinite increase will enrich it indefinitely. Ecology knows of no density relationship that holds for indefinitely wide limits. All gains from density are subject to a law of diminishing returns.

Rachel Carson, Silent Spring
54–57, 61 (1962)

There are few studies more fascinating, and at the same time more neglected, than those of the teeming populations that exist in the dark realms of the soil. Perhaps the most essential organisms in the soil are the smallest — the invisible hosts of bacteria and threadlike fungi. Statistics of their abundance take us at once into astronomical figures. A teaspoonful of topsoil may contain billions of bacteria. In spite of their minute size, the total weight of this host of bacteria in the top foot of a single acre of fertile soil may be as much as a thousand pounds. Ray fungi, bacteria, [and] small green cells called algae, these make up the microscopic plant life of the soil [and are] the principal agents of decay, reducing plant and animal residues to their component minerals. The vast cyclic movements of chemical elements such as carbon and nitrogen through soil and air and living tissue could not proceed without these microplants. Without the nitrogen-fixing bacteria, for example, plants would starve for want of nitrogen, though surrounded by a sea of nitrogen-containing air. Other organisms form carbon dioxide, which, as carbonic acid, aids in dissolving rock. Still other soil microbes perform various oxidations and reductions by which minerals such as iron, manganese, and sulfur are transformed and made available to plants.

Also present in prodigious numbers are microscopic mites and primitive wingless insects called springtails. Despite their small size they play an important part in breaking down the residues of plants, aiding in the slow conversion of the litter of the forest floor to soil. The specialization of some of these minute creatures for their task is almost incredible. Several species of mites, for example, can begin life only within the fallen needles of a spruce tree. Sheltered here, they digest out the inner tissues of the needle. When the mites have completed their development only the outer layer of the cells remains. The truly staggering task of dealing with the tremendous amount of plant material in the annual leaf fall belongs to some of the small insects of the soil and the forest floor. They macerate and digest the leaves, and aid in mixing the decomposed matter with surface soil.

Besides all this horde of minute but ceaselessly toiling creatures there are of course many larger forms, for soil life runs the gamut from bacteria to mammals. Some are permanent residents of the dark subsurface layers; some hibernate or spend definite parts of their life cycles in underground chambers; some freely come and go between their burrows and the upper world. In general the effect of all this habitation of the soil is to aerate it and improve both its drainage and the penetration of water throughout the layers of plant growth.

Of all the larger inhabitants of the soil, probably none is more important than the earthworm. Over three quarters of a century ago, Charles Darwin...gave the world its first understanding of the fundamental role of earthworms as geologic agents for the transport of soil — a picture of surface rocks being gradually covered by fine soil brought up from below by the worms, in annual amounts running from many tons to the acre in most favorable areas.[8] At the same time, quantities of organic matter contained in leaves and grass (as much as 20 pounds to the square yard in six months) are drawn down into the burrows and incorporated in soil. Darwin's calculations showed that the toil of earthworms might add a layer of soil an inch to inch and a half thick in a ten-year period. And this is by no means all they do: their burrows

---

8. C. Darwin, The Formation of Vegetable Mould, through the Action of Worms, with Observations on Their Habits (1897).

aerate the soil, keep it well drained, and aid the penetration of plant roots.... The soil community, then, consists of a web of interwoven lives, each in some way related to the others — the living creatures depending on the soil, but the soil in turn a vital element of the earth only so long as this community within it flourishes.

The problem that concerns us here is one that has received little consideration: What happens to these incredibly numerous and vitally necessary inhabitants of soil when poisonous chemicals are carried down into their world, either introduced directly as soil "sterilants" or borne on the rain that has picked up a lethal contamination as it filters through the leaf canopy of forest and orchard cropland? Is it reasonable to suppose that we can apply a broad-spectrum insecticide to kill the burrowing larval stages of a crop-destroying insect, for example, without also killing the "good" insects whose function may be the essential one of breaking down matter? Or can we use a nonspecific fungicide without also killing the fungi that inhabit the roots of many trees in a beneficial association that aids the tree in extracting nutrients from the soil?...

Chemical control of insects seems to have proceeded on the assumption that the soil could and would sustain any amount of...poisons without striking back. The very nature of the world of the soil has been largely ignored.... A group of specialists who met to discuss the ecology of the soil...summed up the hazards of using such potent and little understood tools.... "A few false moves on the part of man may result in destruction of soil productivity, and the arthropods may well take over."

COMMENTARY & QUESTIONS

1. **Leopold, ecology, and the romantic misnomer of "natural equilibrium."** In the years since 1948, when Aldo Leopold first wrote Sand County Almanac, the observations and interconnections he discovered in the Wisconsin countryside helped nurture the new-old science of ecology. The study of organisms as they actually live and interact in living networks over time offers important advantages over the reductionistic study of a creature or compound or its genetic building blocks isolated on a slide or lab table. The multifactored effects of industrial activities on the people and environments they impact are not realistically predictable through traditional scientific disciplines. For lawyers in the field, a survey course in ecology and environmental science techniques is a good investment of time. The University of Maryland's environmental law program has published a short course book on "Environmental Science for Lawyers." There are also useful books that help to illustrate the breadth and depth of modern ecological sciences and explain how to ask intelligent questions about them. See, e.g., K. S. Shrader-Frechette & E. D. McCoy, Method in Ecology (1993).

As Leopold noted, the image commonly employed of "the balance of nature" fails to describe accurately what we now know about ecology. It now is generally conceded that the natural world is composed of dynamic ongoing systems, not of static balances. There is no ideal historical "balance of nature" from which today's environment came and to which natural communities can or should be returned, despite the classical rhetoric of some environmentalists.

> "Equilibrium" was the source of the "balance of nature" premise.... It was understood that populations of organisms could swing from low to high in accordance with the seasons and the system's other cycles, but its "equilibrium" levels [supposedly] remained constant over time and the system's pattern did not change.

"Briefly stated, the Balance of Nature myth has three basic features: First, Nature, undisturbed by human influences, achieves a permanency of form and structure that persists indefinitely. Second, this permanent condition is the best condition for Nature: best for other creatures, best for the environment, and best for humans. Third, when disturbed from this natural state, Nature is capable of returning to it."[9]

The balance of nature premise has been described as the ecological justification for what was once the dominant principle in environmental law — "let nature be."[10] Equilibrium theory no longer governs ecological thinking. Instead, [it is now understood that] ecosystems…do not reach a climax state…[but] continue to evolve and change….

"Although some may endure, apparently unchanged, for periods that are long in comparison with the human lifespan, [ecosystems] must and do change eventually. Species come and go, climates change, plant and animal communities adapt to altered circumstances, and when examined in fine detail such adaptation and consequent change can be seen to be taking place constantly. The 'balance of nature' is a myth. Our planet is dynamic, and so are the arrangements by which its inhabitants live together."[11] Pardy, Changing Nature: The Myth of the Inevitability of Ecosystem Management, 20 Pace Envtl. L. Rev. 675, 687 (2003).[12]

Everything in nature is continually adapting, but the rate and character of evolving changes in natural systems around us have encountered rapid disruptions from human impacts in the past 100 years that are unprecedented in scale and disruptive consequences. Ecology and the Law, 25 IIT/Chi.-Kent L. Rev. 847–985 (1994). Environmental law parallels the changing dynamics of human and ecological interconnections.

2. **The broad reverberations of Rachel Carson's microcosm.** Rachel Carson's perceptive observations revealed a systemic deficiency in the way mid-twentieth-century humans made decisions. Carson changed the way many Americans viewed their world.[13] Reflecting the traditional instinctive perspective of human enterprises, most people plan projects or solve problems using one-shot technology — insulated, narrow, and unidimensional.

"You got bugs? So go get a pesticide." …

Zap.

"Now you've got what you wanted. Dead bugs. The End."

---

9. Botkin, Adjusting Law to Nature's Discordant Harmonies, 7 Duke Envtl. L. & Pol'y F. 25, 26 (1996).

10. Tarlock, The Nonequilibrium Paradigm in Ecology and the Partial Unraveling of Environmental Law, 27 Loy. L.A. L. Rev. 1121, 1122 (1994). This principle was adopted by legislators, regulators, resource managers, and lawyers, and gradually replaced the progressive conservation movement's ethic of multiple use. Tarlock cites D. L. Feldman, Water Resources Management: In Search of an Environmental Ethic (1991), as providing a good case study of this evolution.

11. M. Allaby, Basics of Environmental Science 154 (1996).

12. (Quoting Botkin and Allaby.) Prof. Pardy's article explores the policy allegation that, since there is no such thing as natural equilibrium to act as a moral and legal touchstone, human "ecosystem management" activities impacting natural systems do not thereby violate any norm of natural systems, but rather are just one more form of change. But this assertion "is a policy choice masquerading as an inevitability. Neither nonequilibrium nor the absence of pristine systems demands that ecosystems be changed to suit human preferences…. Natural is possible. Whether it is preferable is a different debate." Pardy, 20 Pace Envtl. L. Rev. at 691.

13. It is remarkable in retrospect how three books written at virtually the same historical moment so powerfully reshaped so much of modern American society's view of life — Jane Jacobs, The Death and Life of Great American Cities (1961); Rachel Carson, Silent Spring (1962); Betty Friedan, The Feminine Mystique (1963). What is it they have in common?

But that is not the end of it. There is no such thing as a simple one-shot technology. Everything has continuing long-term consequences. Pesticides don't just disappear after they have killed the target bugs. They linger on and on, blowing in the wind, leaching into groundwater, eliminating the rich, interconnected communities that had naturally evolved in the land to give it its fertility in the first place, moving up through ecological food chains, and diffusing far and wide through the air currents of the hemisphere.[14]

The lessons Carson drew from DDT pesticides are readily applied to many other settings as well — to other kinds of pollution, to resource management issues such as timber and grazing, to highway and transportation planning, to pharmaceuticals and health technology, and, by extension, to many other areas of national policy. The kind of narrowed human thinking that ignores the consequences of pesticides has been applied in cutting timber from fragile mountainsides or discharging wastes from industrial factories.

Carson showed that the particular desired result of any human action is typically not all that happens. Predictable problems follow when official players, both corporate and governmental, make decisions in traditional terms, seeking short-term benefits with a narrowed, insulated field of vision. Although humans may not take account of the real social and ecological costs of their actions, nature keeps a comprehensive tab, and real consequences follow. Western societies traditionally have tended to view human actors as the central players in the life of the planet, with nature as a subservient and pliant backdrop, but Nature is not "outside" our human economy or our jurisprudence.[15] Carson demonstrated through an ecological lens that the natural backdrop to human activity may be far larger in scale and importance than the human figures pirouetting in the foreground. The earth's environment has developed richly diverse and dynamic interconnected natural systems, communities of communities spread around the planet providing services previously unrecognized and fulfilling important productive functions previously taken for granted. These natural communities, intimately linked

---

14. See T. Colborn, D. Dumanoski & J. P. Myers, Our Stolen Future: Are We Threatening Our Fertility, Intelligence, and Survival? — A Scientific Detective Story (1997).

15. Professor David Westbrook has expressed some frustration at the difficulty of defining a coherent philosophy of environmental jurisprudence. He tried to build a liberal conceptual overview upon the perspectives of individual human rights, collective aggregated rights, and markets but was unable to fit some sectors of environmental law into those realms.

Norms protecting endangered species, for instance, seemed to come from an alien, less human-centered domain. See generally D. A. Westbrook, Liberal Environmental Jurisprudence, 27 U.C. Davis L. Rev. 619 (1994). As he has commented:

> Most of our law may be (must be) articulable in some liberal language. But the Endangered Species Act cannot be, not really.... At some point liberalism's concern for the internal (autonomy, choice), fails to capture environmentalism's sense of the external (ecosystems, nature, etc.). At the end of the day, you cannot explain the outside in terms of the inside. Westbrook, e-mail posting to Envprofs listserv, from dwestbro@acsu.buffalo.edu to envlawprofs@darkwing.uoregon.edu (Nov. 6, 2001).

Conceptualizing the existence of three interlinked economies, however, explains that environmental jurisprudence operates on the realistic foundation that there is no external outside. Environmental law's high purpose and aspiration is to make sense of the First Law of Ecology, that everything is connected to everything else. Environmental law, like all law, ultimately must function in the real world, a world made up of multiple interlocking systems. We humans individually and collectively are indeed significant components of many of these multiple systems. But we are not hermetically separated from the systemic elements and networks that don't operate on our own terms, just as we are not disconnected from the consequences of our own actions.

to the human communities that share the environment with them, are capable of causing broadly destructive systemic consequences when they are disrupted or destroyed.

The "Precautionary Principle" asserts this utilitarian perspective: Unless you collectively are pretty sure that the negative consequences are foreseeable, minor, and mitigatable, and that fundamentally important interconnections will not be disrupted, you had better be sure that what somebody proposes to do is worth the potential costs. It is generally safer not to take casual risks with the escalating domino consequences that may follow. In this regard, Carson showed that moving from a human-centered master-of-nature perspective to the holistic human-species-as-constituent-part-of-nature view is not just an ethical idea — it is fundamentally practical and utilitarian as well.

Talbot Page, A Generic View of Toxic Chemicals and Similar Risks
7 Ecology Law Quarterly 207 (1978)

...Relative costs: false negatives and false positives. By definition, the potential costs of environmental risks are great and the benefits are generally modest. Correspondingly, there is asymmetry in the costs of making wrong decisions. For classical pollutants, the asymmetry of potential costs and benefits, and hence the potential costs of wrong decisions, are likely to be less pronounced than for environmental risk problems.

The concept of false negatives and false positives helps to illustrate this distinction. In criminal law, two basic kinds of mistakes can occur: the jury (or judge) can find a guilty man innocent or an innocent man guilty. Testing chemicals for toxicity presents the same problem. Test results may indicate that a toxic chemical is not toxic or that a non-toxic chemical is toxic. The former type of error is called a false negative and the latter a false positive....

[In environmental risk situations] the cost of a false negative — deciding that the benign hypothesis is true when it is not — is much higher than the cost of a false positive — deciding that the catastrophic hypothesis is true when it is not.... Catastrophic results more than offset the modest benefits of erroneously accepting the benign hypothesis....

Difficulties in the management of environmental risk... *1. Acceptable risk...* Even if the probability of an environmental risk were well defined, our legal, regulatory, and economic institutions must still decide what degree of risk is acceptable. Although there are several approaches for defining acceptable risk, there is little agreement on what is the best approach. This ambiguity presents a major difficulty in managing environmental risk. A few of the approaches are discussed below....

2. Limiting false positives. The most common approach for risks subject to governmental regulation and court proceedings, starts with the assumption that there is no risk and requires that a hazard be proved beyond some standard. Under this approach [of limiting false positives], by definition, if the standard of proof is not met, then the risk is acceptable. The burden of proof is placed on those seeking precautionary action.... However, the approach of limiting false positives, although often effective in defining acceptable risk for classical problems, has questionable value for the management of environmental risk....

3. Limiting false negatives. Limiting false positives is the guiding principle of criminal law. The objective is to limit the chance of a false conviction. The common-sense justification for this objective is that it is better to free a hundred guilty men than to convict one innocent one....

A comparison of criminal law with environmental risk, however, suggests an important difference. The costs of false negatives and false positives are asymmetric for environmental risk as well, but the asymmetry is in reverse order. For environmental risk, the asymmetrically high cost arises from a false negative; in criminal law from a false positive. Similarly, just as a primary good, liberty, is an important concern in criminal law, so another primary good, health, is an important concern in environmental risk management, but again the roles are reversed. Typically, public health is adversely affected under a false negative for environmental risk, while liberty is adversely affected under a false positive for criminal law.

The analogy between criminal law and environmental risk requires that the roles of negatives and positives be reversed. If the emphasis on limiting false positives for criminal law is sensible and based on the asymmetry of costs of wrong decisions and the possible deprivation of a public good, then the implication is that a decision procedure based on limiting false negatives is more appropriate for environmental risk than one based on limiting false positives....

Focusing more attention on the need to limit false negatives brings us back to the importance of modeling the risks and hypotheses, including "credible" worst case modeling. It is clearly infeasible to take precautionary action for each conceivable environmental risk; there would be too many. Requiring some sort of model of the risk provides an entrance barrier against the flood of conceivable risks for which precautionary action should be evaluated. Because of the nature of environmental risk it is senseless to require proof of actual harm; the barrier should be no more than a reasonable basis within the context of the model for believing that there is a risk of harm. The risk itself may be small.

4. *Balancing false positives and false negatives.* [Page then recommends a decisionmaking mechanism, which he calls "the expected value approach," that balances the cost of a false negative, weighted by its probability of occurrence, against the cost of a false positive, weighted by its probability of occurrence, and chooses the alternative with the lower weighted cost.[16] Page recognizes the importance and intransigence of "outrage" factors in risk management.]

The hard part is to uncover a social consensus on the appropriate amount of risk aversion and then to build this amount into the institutions which manage environmental risks.

The expected value approach does not require that each environmental risk be regulated, or not regulated, on the sole basis of a detailed and quantified cost-benefit analysis. For example, the internal transfer of benefits tends to be associated with a sharply focused group of proponents of the environmental risk taking, while the external transfer of the potential costs, both spatially and temporally, is associated with a broader but less focused group of opponents.[17] This imbalance in interests, for and against, is likely to lead to an imbalance in decision making, even for an ostensibly neutral cost-benefit analysis, unless the imbalance in interests is recognized and offset by the design of the decision making institutions. Alternatively, in order to come closer to a minimum expected cost of wrong decisions, it is necessary to adjust the rules of the decision process — the standards and burdens of proof, the rules of liability, the incentives for the generation and valuation of information, and so on. For instance, when the potential adverse effects of an environmental risk are many times greater than the potential benefits, a proper standard of proof of danger under the expected cost minimization criterion may be that there is only "at least a reasonable doubt" that the adverse effect will occur, rather than requiring a greater probability, such as "more likely than not," that the effect will occur.

---

16. Once the concepts of "minimizing false negatives" and "minimizing false positives" have been learned, it might be simpler to refer to them as the "proactive" and "reactive" approaches to risk management. The proactive approach is also linked to the "Precautionary Principle" explored in Chapter 26. [Eds.]

17. This is one of the central tenets of "public choice theory." [Eds.]

COMMENTARY & QUESTIONS

1. **"Classical pollution" and "environmental risk."** In the same article, Dr. Page recommended that the legal system manage risks caused by pollution and resource depletion based on where a particular risk falls on a continuum between what he terms "Classical Pollution" and "Environmental Risk." The former presents the more humdrum problem of dealing with relatively well-understood and innocuous effluent streams and their effects on the environment. The latter is more complex. Page defines "Environmental Risk" in terms of nine characteristics, four dealing with the uncertainties surrounding environmental decisionmaking, and five bearing on institutional problems encountered in environmental management. Environmental problems differ as to how intensely they exhibit these characteristics. The first four characteristics of "Environmental Risk" are

1. ignorance of mechanism (i.e., scientific uncertainty as to the generation and transmission of hazards, as well as their environmental impacts),

2. relatively modest benefits,

3. potentially catastrophic costs, and

4. relatively low probability of occurrence of catastrophic outcomes.

Hazards manifesting these characteristics often present the "Zero-Infinity Dilemma"— a virtually zero probability of occurrence of a virtually infinite catastrophe. The remaining characteristics are

5. internal benefits,

6. external costs,

7. collective risk,

8. latency (e.g., carcinogenic effects may not manifest themselves until 20 or 30 years after exposure), and

9. irreversibility of effects.

2. **Environmental risk and environmental justice.** Since Dr. Page wrote this article, environmental justice has emerged as a matter of concern. With that in mind, distributional inequality might qualify as a tenth characteristic of environmental risk. Environmental risks are imposed disproportionately on the least politically powerful members of our society — minorities, the poor, children, and the sick and disabled. The toxic effects of pesticides, for example, are most intensely experienced by farm workers. Most hazardous waste disposal facilities have been located in neighborhoods occupied by disadvantaged groups. Is that form of environmental injustice a form of racism?

3. **Species eradication as a catastrophic ecological cost.** The importance of biodiversity, both as a necessity for human survival and as an end in itself, is better understood today than it was even a generation ago. Managing environmental risks entails factoring ecological effects of human behavior into environmental decisionmaking. Extinction is the most profoundly irreversible phenomenon on this planet. How should risks of species extinction be managed? The Endangered Species Act is studied in Chapter 16.

4. **External cost transfers and political power.** Note how heavily Page, in his definition of environmental risk, relies on the theory of "externalities." Internalization of economic benefits among a focused, knowledgeable, and politically powerful group of producers and consumers leads to concentrated political power that tends to outweigh the weaker political influence exercised by a diffuse, disorganized, unaware, and often politically powerless class of polluted public (which, in theory, includes future generations, which cannot directly participate in the political process). Furthermore, it is difficult to organize members of the general public to oppose the imposition of a collective risk because of the "transaction costs" (e.g., time and money) of participation and the "free rider problem" (i.e., the human tendency to believe that someone else will solve the problem). This political asymmetry is another reason for minimizing false negatives. It also explains the need for politically strong environmental groups to counterbalance the influence of powerful producer and consumer constituencies.

5. **Burdens of proof and liability rules in environmental risk management decision-making.** Page clearly recognizes the importance of burdens of proof (burdens of going forward and burdens of ultimate persuasion) and liability rules in the legal system's management of environmental risk. As cases studied in Chapter 4 demonstrate, legal rules regarding burdens of proof and liability have been modified to some degree to accommodate legal claims made by victims of pollution. Of particular relevance to the management of environmental risk, courts are divided regarding the burden of proof in toxic exposure cases. Some courts require plaintiff to prove only that exposure to a toxic substance was a "substantial factor" causing her damage, whereas other courts adhere to a standard more nearly like the usual standard in civil cases that requires plaintiff to prove it is more likely than not that her injury would not have occurred "but for" the exposure.

6. **Risk assessment and risk management.** Regulators typically have divided environmental risk analysis into "risk assessment" and "risk management" phases: Risk assessment is seen as scientific, objective, and quantitative, whereas risk management considers the social, economic, and political factors involved in determining acceptable risk. The accuracy and utility of this distinction have been questioned by several commentators. In fact, because of the profound scientific uncertainties and measurement variabilities involved in determining environmental risk, assessors rely on conservative "default assumptions," combinations of science and policy that are sometimes referred to as "trans-science." For example, with regard to most carcinogenic substances, there is not certain knowledge that threshold dose levels (i.e., levels of exposure) exist below which an exposed individual would not contract cancer. Thus to protect public health, cancer risk assessors assume that "one hit" of a carcinogenic substance can cause cancer. (Would Page agree with this approach?) For a useful review of the literature on risk assessment, as well as the methodology of cancer risk assessment, see Shere, The Myth of Meaningful Environmental Risk Assessment, 19 Harv. Envtl. L. Rev. 409 (1995). Commentators differ, however, about the importance of the trans-scientific elements of risk assessment. Contrast Shere ("the hard fact is that quantitative risk assessment generates numbers that are meaningless," 19 Harv. Envtl. L. Rev. at 414) with the Presidential/Congressional Commission on Risk Assessment and Risk

Management, Final Report (1997) (risk assessments are useful for setting upper-bound estimates of risk and setting priorities for environmental regulation).

7. The classic *Reserve Mining* case. Reserve Mining v. EPA, 514 F.2d 492 (8th Cir. 1975), is a classic early risk management case. Reserve was mining low-grade iron ore (taconite) in Minnesota and processing it into iron-rich pellets at facilities bordering Lake Superior. The residues of this process were the discharge of taconite tailings into Lake Superior and the emission of taconite particles into the air near several Minnesota towns. (It was proven at the trial that taconite is structurally identical to amosite asbestos.) In light of seemingly dramatic risks to public health, but also of the profound uncertainties in the epidemiological and toxicological evidence regarding the toxicity of taconite, the court ordered Reserve to cease its water discharge "within a reasonable time" and to "promptly...use such available technology as will reduce the asbestos fiber count in the ambient air...below a medically significant level." Asbestos, however, is a zero-tolerance carcinogen — one exposure can trigger mortal disease — so the court's risk standard is ambiguous. Reserve moved to land disposal of tailings in 1980 and closed down several years later, not because of burdensome pollution control requirements but because of the general decline of the U.S. steel industry in the face of foreign competition.

Reserve Mining is also a classic case of corporate intransigence on pollution control. For ten years, Reserve was able to frustrate federal, state, and citizen efforts to abate its dischargers. An entire legal process course could be taught out of the *Reserve Mining* case, which involved federal and state statutory and common law; federal, state, and private plaintiffs against corporate defendants and their labor and municipal supporters; carcinogenic pollutants and the aesthetics of a pristine Great Lake; air and water pollution; convoluted industrial economics; and much chemistry and technological debate.[18]

G. Tyler Miller, Living in the Environment: Principles, Connections, and Solutions
105, 247–248 (11th ed. 1999)

None of us live apart from nature.... Ecosystems provide us and other species with a number of natural services; ecosystem services, which constitute earth capital, support life on

---

18. Reserve Mining required nine trips to the federal district court (one hearing lasting nine months), two to the state courts, four to the Eighth Circuit, one to the Supreme Court in an unsuccessful petition to revoke a stay; injunctions, stays, modified injunctions, mandamus orders (also stayed, and reinstated); an elaborate permit and standard-setting administrative system; counterclaims by industry for tort damages owing to "negligently-issued permits"; a federal statute that, after 60 years of dormancy, suddenly imposed new prohibitions through a twist of statutory interpretation; plus an appellate order forcing the district judge to recuse himself for bias formed in the course of trial. See Reserve Mining Co. v. Minnesota Pollution Control Agency, 434 F. Supp. 1191 (D. Minn. 1976); United States v. Reserve Mining Co., 417 F. Supp. 791 (D. Minn. 1976); 417 F. Supp. 789 (D. Minn.), aff'd, 543 F.2d 1210 (8th Cir. 1976); 412 F. Supp. 705 (D. Minn. 1976); 408 F. Supp. 1212 (D. Minn. 1976); 394 F. Supp. 233 (D. Minn. 1974), modified sub nom. Reserve Mining Co. v. EPA, 514 F.2d 492 (8th Cir. 1975), modified en banc sub nom. Reserve Mining Co. v. Lord, 529 F.2d 181 (8th Cir. 1976) (recusal order); 380 F. Supp. 11 (D. Minn.), stayed, 498 F.2d 1073 (8th Cir.), motion to vacate stay denied, 418 U.S. 911, motion to vacate or modify stay denied, 419 U.S. 802 (1974) (Douglas, J., dissenting). See also Reserve Mining Co. v. Herbst, 256 N.W.2d 808 (Minn. 1977); Reserve Mining Co. v. Minnesota Pollution Control Agency, 200 N.W.2d 142 (Minn. 1972); see N.Y. Times, Apr. 25, 1982, at 31, col. 1; Bartlett, The *Reserve Mining* Controversy (1980); and Farber, Risk Regulation in Perspective: *Reserve Mining* Revisited, 21 Envtl. L. 1321 (1991).

the earth and are essential to the quality of human life and to the functioning of the world's economies....[19]

Ecosystems...

- Control and moderate climate
- Provide us with and renew air, water, and soil
- Recycle vital nutrients through chemical cycling
- Provide us with renewable and nonrenewable energy sources and nonrenewable minerals
- Furnish us with food, fiber, medicines, timber, and paper
- Pollinate crops and other plant species
- Absorb, dilute, or detoxify many pollutants and toxic chemicals
- Help control populations of pests and disease organisms
- Slow soil erosion and help prevent flooding
- Provide the biodiversity of genes and species needed to adapt to ever-changing environmental conditions through evolution and genetic engineering.

All natural and human-altered ecosystems that have their functional integrity intact provide some or all of these services free of charge....

What can we learn from nature about living sustainably? After billions of years of trial and error, the rest of nature has solved the problem of dynamic sustainability by being able to change and adapt to new conditions through the biological evolution of populations. But there is growing concern that humans, as newcomers on the scene, are beginning to threaten this substantially for our own species and millions of others.

Living systems have six key features, *interdependence, diversity, resilience, adaptability, unpredictability, and limits*.... Here are some basic ecological lessons from nature.

Most ecosystems use sunlight as their primary source of energy....

Soil, water, air, plants, and animals are renewed through natural processes.

Energy is always required to produce or maintain an energy flow or to recycle chemicals.

Biodiversity takes various forms in different parts of the world,...species diversity, genetic diversity, and ecological diversity having evolved over billions of years under different environmental conditions.

Complex networks of positive and negative feedback loops give organisms and populations information and control mechanisms for adapting, within limits, to changing conditions.

The population size and growth rate of all species are controlled by their interactions with other species and with their nonliving environment. In nature there are always limits to population growth.

Organisms, except perhaps humans, generally use only what they need (not merely want) to survive, stay healthy, and reproduce.

Currently, humans are violating these principles of sustainability. No one knows how long we can continue doing this. Biologists have formulated several important principles that can

---

19. "An ecosystem is a community of different species interacting with one another and with their nonliving environment of matter and energy The [expanse] of an ecosystem is somewhat arbitrary; it is defined by the...unit of study,...small and particular...or large and generalized.... All of the earth's ecosystems together make up what we call the ecosphere or biosphere...." Id. at 83.

help guide us in our search for more suitable lifestyles: We are part of, not apart from, the earths' dynamic web of life…. Our lives, lifestyles, and economics are totally dependent on the sun and the earth…. We can never do merely one thing…. The first law of human ecology [is that] everything is connected to everything else: we are all in it together. We are connected to all living organisms through the long evolutionary history contained in our DNA. We are connected to the earth through our interactions with air, water, soil, and other living organisms making up the ever-changing web of life. The destiny of all species is a shared one. The primary goal of ecology is to discover which connections in nature are the strongest, most important, and most vulnerable to disruption.

We need not — and indeed cannot — stop growing food or building cities. Indeed, concentrating people in cities and increasing food supplies by raising the yields per area of cropland are both ways to help protect much of the earth's biodiversity from being destroyed or degraded, as long as the harmful environmental side effects of such activities are kept under control. The key lesson is that we need earth wisdom, care, restraint, humility, cooperation, and love as we alter the ecosphere to meet our needs and wants. Earth care is self-care, and we can change our ways. According to environmentalist David Brower, we need to focus on "global CPR… conservation, preservation, and restoration." This means (1) building societies based on conservation, not waste, (2) preserving what we can't replace, and (3) working with nature to help restore what we have degraded or destroyed.

COMMENTARY & QUESTIONS

1. **The concept of "ecosystems."** You cannot make sense of any piece of nature if you observe it in isolation. Ecology forces us to look beyond just a single bacterium, a cubic centimeter of soil, an earthworm, a tuft of grass, a cow, a wolf, a rancher. An understanding of context, including physical settings and interrelationships with surrounding individuals and communities, is fundamental to understanding reality and the science of ecology.

Most ecosystems are complex communities in which all the elements exist and interact in multiple interrelationships characterized overall by extremely high efficiency and relatively high stability so long as fundamental changes do not occur. Disruptions and dislocations cause immediate reverberating effects through the system, leading to adaptive changes and new accommodations, though perhaps with decreased richness in surviving numbers of component species and lowered net productivity. Some elements may be more significant than others. One species may have only a small role in a particular ecosystem, while others may be "indicator species," whose welfare is a barometer for the health of the entire ecosystem, or "keystone species," which if they are removed or altered will force systemic changes throughout the ecosystem. The greater the complexity and biodiversity of the ecosystem, the higher the net primary productivity and adaptive resilience are likely to be.

2. **Can the ecosystems metaphor be applied to human systems?** The ecosystems metaphor seems applicable to many human social structures such as corporations or political capitals, but it is probably more accurate to say that we humans, whether we like it or not, are part of the ecosystems and biosphere in which we live, uniquely able to observe and manage the way we impact our base and the other systems with which we coexist. To remain ignorant of these systems of ecosystems is, in many cases at least,

likely to be costly and dangerous. Think how staphylococci are increasingly resistant to antibiotics, agricultural soils are losing their fertility and natural regeneration ability, and ocean fish stocks around the world are in precipitous decline.

Thomas Sancton, What on Earth Are We Doing?
Time, January 2, 1989, at 24–30

"One generation passeth away, and another generation cometh: but the earth abideth forever." Ecclesiastes.

...Not forever. At the outside limit, the earth will probably last another 4 billion to 5 billion years. By that time, scientists predict, the sun will have burned up so much of its own hydrogen fuel that it will expand and incinerate the surrounding planets, including the earth. A nuclear cataclysm, on the other hand, could destroy the earth tomorrow. Somewhere within those extremes lies the life expectancy of this wondrous, swirling globe. How long it endures and the quality of life it can support do not depend alone on the immutable laws of physics. For man has reached a point in his evolution where he has the power to affect, for better or worse, the present and future state of the planet....

By 1800 there were 1 billion human beings bestriding the planet. That number had doubled by 1930 and doubled again by 1975. If current birthrates hold, the world's present population of 5.1 billion will double again in 40 more years.... 40,000 babies die of starvation each day in Third World countries.... Smokestacks have disgorged noxious gases into the atmosphere, factories have dumped toxic wastes into rivers and streams, automobiles have guzzled irreplaceable fossil fuels and fouled the air with their detritus in the name of progress, forests have been denuded, lakes poisoned with pesticides, underground aquifers pumped dry.... Changing weather patterns could make huge areas infertile or uninhabitable, touching off refugee movements unprecedented in history....

Whatever the validity of this or that theory, the earth will not remain as it is now. Says Harvard biologist E. O. Wilson: "The extinctions ongoing worldwide promise to be as least as great as the mass extinction that occurred at the end of the age of dinosaurs...." Increasingly, technology has come up against the law of unexpected consequences.... Advances in health care have lengthened life-spans, lowered infant mortality rates and, thus, aggravated the population problem. The use of pesticides increased crop yields but polluted water supplies. The invention of automobiles and jet planes revolutionized travel but sullied the atmosphere.... Let there be no illusions.... Both the causes and effects of the problems that threaten the earth are global, and they must be attacked globally....

COMMENTARY & QUESTIONS

1. **The depressing perspectives of global ecology and the law.** To observers like Sancton, the global challenges can be met only through a basic change in attitudes toward use and preservation of natural resources that would dramatically change lifestyles in virtually all parts of the world. What role, if any, would law play in that process? Laws can prohibit directly and indirectly some forms of environmental carnage, as with attempts to protect endangered species. The effectiveness of such attempts, however, remains an open question. Finding laws that seem capable of effecting larger behavioral changes, such as reducing global emissions of greenhouse gases produced by fossil fuel consumption and deforestation, remains more problematic.

Environmental law often adopts Abbie Hoffman's compromise advice to "think globally, act locally."

Arnold Reitze, in a penetrating article reviewing 20 years of environmental efforts,[20] dourly noted that virtually all global environmental degradation can be traced back to three major human phenomena — population, wasteful resource consumption, and pollution — all of which are out of control.[21] Of these, he said, the most devastating is population pressure. Relentless population growth undercuts the hopes of nation-builders and those who try to apply industrial, social, economic, and legal technology to alleviate the ills of humankind and the planet. It may be that the world's population is in the process of leveling off by 2050 at 12 billion, twice the current total, but dehumanizing poverty, hunger, homelessness, and lack of opportunity are still increasing in both relative and absolute terms. Individuals and nations who can do so strive to increase their wealth and consumption rather than ratcheting down to allow the earth's resource base to carry more souls, so the numbers and problems of abject underclasses tend to grow rather than shrink. Society, instead of moving toward global cooperation, often seems to be degenerating into mutually antagonistic tribes. These human conditions can themselves be considered "environmental" problems. And they have the disastrous further consequence of reducing the terms of human decisionmaking to purely short-term coping and survival, so that long-term ecological rationality seems a wistful impossibility. Urban decay, children having children, desertification, desperate exploitation of resources — these are products of population pressures and it is far from clear what law can do about it. In fact, Reitze noted, governments find the problems of population and resource consumption so hard to handle that they tend to ignore them and focus instead on pollution, which, though serious, is the least important of the major causes of environmental degradation.

This book, to some extent, incorporates that mistake. It is far easier to study legal remedies for controlling pollution than for controlling population and resource consumption patterns. This coursebook does look beyond pollution, however, and the legal process approaches examined here can be flexibly extended as far as environmental analysis can go. Law will be a participant in the mission to bring humankind and the planet into some dynamic equilibrium, even if that sometimes appears to be a quixotic quest.

2. **A need for integrated environmental management?** Reality exists in the holistic, integrated overview, but knowledge and the capacity to manage discrete problems build from the bottom, from a narrow, incisive, specialized focus. Several strategy reports prepared by the U.S. Environmental Protection Agency[22] begin with a

---

20. Reitze, Environmental Policy — It Is Time for a New Beginning, 14 Colum. J. Envtl. L. 111 (1989).

21. Observing where we are today, we might add that there are *four* systemic problems (setting up an egregious pun — the "Four Horsemen of the Ecopalypse" — see Environmental Law as a Mirror of the Future, 23 B.C. Envtl. Aff. L. Rev. 733 (1996)). The fourth horseman is the gap between what we know and what we do. Despite a truly amazing expansion of ecological knowledge — about pollution, population, resource losses, and the interconnectedness of human and natural systems — and the ability to communicate that knowledge globally at the speed of light, it is distressing to observe the difference between knowledge and practice. Our capacity to implement what we know about these serious threats consistently falls short, often because of political marketplace resistance.

22. L. Thomas, Environmental Progress and Challenges: EPA Update (1988).

fundamental declaration that EPA should take an overall "systems approach" that views the environment as an integrated whole and should coordinate all protection strategies on that basis. The proposal has global implications, which are considered in the last chapter of this book. Perhaps ironically, however, the rest of the EPA report was organized on a medium-by-medium approach — air, water, toxics, noise, land use, and so on. Is it practically inevitable that bureaucrats, legislators, lawyers, litigants, and humans generally will focus on narrow slices of the environmental dilemma? In an increasingly specialized world, how do we keep our eyes open to the whole?

b. Environmental ethics

Aldo Leopold, A Sand County Almanac
129–130, 203, 224–225 (1968 ed.)

Thinking Like a Mountain... Only the mountain has lived long enough to listen objectively to the howl of a wolf.... My own conviction on this score dates from the day I saw a wolf die. We were eating lunch on a high rimrock, at the foot of which a turbulent river elbowed its way. We saw what we thought was a doe fording the torrent, her breast awash in white water. When she climbed the bank toward us and shook out her tail, we realized our error: it was a wolf. A half-dozen others, evidently grown pups, sprang from the willows and all joined in a welcoming mêlée of wagging tails and playful maulings. What was literally a pile of wolves writhed and tumbled in the center of an open flat at the foot of our rimrock.

In those days we had never heard of passing up a chance to kill a wolf. In a second we were pumping lead into the pack, but with more excitement than accuracy.... When our rifles were empty, the old wolf was down, and a pup was dragging a leg into impassable slide-rocks. We reached the old wolf in time to watch a fierce green fire dying in her eyes. I realized then, and have known ever since, that there was something new to me in those eyes — something known only to her and to the mountain. I was young then, and full of trigger-itch; I thought that because fewer wolves meant more deer, that no wolves would mean hunters' paradise. But after seeing the green fire die, I sensed that neither the wolf nor the mountain agreed with such a view....

The Land Ethic... There is as yet no ethic dealing with man's relation to land and to the animals and plants which grow upon it.... The extension of ethics to this...element in human environment is, if I read the evidence correctly, an evolutionary possibility and an ecological necessity.... The "key-log" which must be moved to release the evolutionary process for an ethic is simply this: quit thinking about decent land-use as solely an economic problem. Examine each question in terms of what is ethically and esthetically right, as well as what is economically expedient. A thing is right when it tends to preserve the integrity, stability, and beauty of the biotic community. It is wrong when it tends otherwise.

An Environmental Ethic Beyond Utilitarianism? Leopold's lyrical ecology has inspired generations of environmental scientists and a vigorous ongoing ethical debate. Isn't the environment more than a commodity and medium for human designs? Shouldn't there be a recognized moral and ethical standard extending beyond pure human self-interest, recognizing the normative rights of the planet and of nature itself?

It is true, of course, that many environmentalists (like most chapters of this book) do indeed focus on utilitarian arguments for environmental quality: Basic human self-interest, health, and economics should force society not to ignore ecological consequences. Even Leopold himself is ambiguous. He continues the wolf-killing story by showing how wolves are important for controlling populations of deer and other foraging animals that otherwise would strip the forests bare and turn cattle ranges to dustbowls. When he later criticizes current land use policy because "it assumes, falsely, I think, that the economic parts of the biotic clock will function without the uneconomic parts," he is again making a utilitarian argument.

But the fire dying in the she-wolf's eyes, that is something else.

Could it be that humans are not indeed the measure of all things? Are we instead only one part of a larger ecological community, with responsibilities accompanying our undoubted powers and rights? Is there, in other words, a moral-legal basis for environmentalism beyond utilitarianism? This question increasingly reappears in environmental law cases. When a project is stopped because it threatens extinction for some endangered insect or a court considers awards of natural resource damages for ecosystems destroyed by oil spills, the law must reach beyond the normal justifications founded upon net human benefit.

Should we declare that the wolf herself has legal rights, rights that, although not absolute, must nevertheless be substantively weighed in the legal process? Impressive work has been devoted to animal rights and natural rights theories.[23] Nagging problems arise, however, in drawing lines. Is sentiency the litmus? If not, shouldn't plants, rocks, and hills as well be able to claim these rights?[24] Unless the broader view prevails, the ethic ignores the rights of ecosystems. If natural rights can be defined, moreover, who defines them and determines when and how they are to be applied and weighed against human rights and the rights of other entities in the system?

Taking another approach, can it be argued that there is a God who commands ecological sensitivity? Many have criticized the Bible's call for humans to conquer nature:

> Be the terror and dread of all the wild beasts and all the birds of heaven, of everything that crawls on the ground and all the fish of the sea; they are handed over to you.... Teem over the earth and be lord of it. Genesis 9:1–2, 7.[25]

But other strands in Judeo-Christian theology and other religious cultures cast humans in a less domineering role. Primitive humans were probably animists. The mountains and rivers had spirits, and humans spoke with the trees and animals they

---

23. See Roderick Nash's Rights of Nature: A History of Environmental Ethics (1989); H. Rolston, Environmental Ethics: Duties to and Values in the Natural World (1988); R. Nozick, Anarchy, State and Utopia 35–42 (1975); and the active literature of environmental ethics including the journal *Environmental Ethics*.

24. See C. Stone, Should Trees Have Standing? (1972). Cf. the view from the self-styled "wise use" movement, noted further at the end of the next section: "Environmentalism is the new paganism, trees are worshipped and humans sacrificed at its altar.... It is evil...and we intend to destroy it." Ron Arnold, chairman of the Center for the Defense of Free Enterprise, One Man's Land Is Another's Pollution, Wash. Post, Feb. 23, 1992 at C7.

25.Calvin and many other Christian theologians have argued that God "created all things for man's sake." Institutes of Religion 182; bk.1, ch. 14, 22 (Battles ed. 1961); see generally J. A. Passmore, Man's Responsibility for Nature (1974).

were about to kill for their use. In many Eastern and Native American[26] cultures, gods are intimately linked with nature; humans are merely a part of the web, the Tao. Human disruption of nature is deplored as having destroyed "the age of perfect virtue, when men lived in common with birds and beasts, as forming one family."[27] The Dalai Lama, speaking of his Buddhism, said "We have always considered ourselves as part of our environment."[28] The great Jewish philosopher Maimonides dramatically recanted his early Greek-inspired view of human primacy: "It should not be believed that all things exist for the sake of the existence of man. On the contrary, all the other beings, too, have been intended for their own sakes and not for the sake of something else."[29]

Christianity, whose God became human, has been more resistant to the diminution of human-centeredness. The Protestant ethic, when it appeared, fit nicely with the Industrial Revolution's conquest of nature. Fundamentalist Christians' resistance to the notion that humans evolved as part of the natural world demonstrates a continuing need to see humans as separate and distinct from nature. But others can now read the Old Testament, particularly the Noah story, as affirming the sanctity and uniqueness of every living species and setting humans the task of preserving the earth's natural heritage. Some new Christian scholarship urges an active ethic of human "stewardship" over all Creation.[30] These theological debates between human-centered and more inter-relational metaphysics have been paralleled in the dialogues of nonreligious philosophy as well.[31]

Without a clearly divine or natural source of a moral ethic for the environment, the ethic, if it is to exist, must come from humans. Much of any human-based environmental ethic, of course, will continue to be based on utilitarianism — if we want our species' descendants to survive on the planet, we must take the sensitive, cautious long view. But beyond self-interest, further distinctions can extend the ethic. We may indeed currently be the dominant species on the earth, possessing earth-changing knowledge, technology, and physical powers, but along with these powers may come ethical

---

26. "Human beings are not superior to the rest of creation. If human beings were to drop out of the cycle of life, the earth would heal itself and go on. But if any of the other elements would drop out — air, water, animal or plant life — human beings and the earth itself would end." Audrey Shenandoan, Onandaga tribe, N.Y. This echoes the "Gaia" hypothesis that the planet Earth itself is a living, self-regulating organism; disruptions will modify the system, and life as we know it may disappear, though the planet will ultimately strike a new balance. J. Lovelock, The Ages of Gaia (1988); A. Miller, Gaia Connections (1991). In this sense, the planet Earth may not be so "fragile."

27. Chuang Tsu, 4th c. B.C., in Passmore, note 25 above, at 7–8. "When humans interfere with the Tao, the sky becomes filthy, the equilibrium crumbles, creatures become extinct." Lao-tzu, Tao Te Ching (500 B.C.).

28. He continues, "Our scriptures speak of the container and the contained. The world is the container — our house — and we are the contained — the contents of the container.... As a boy studying Buddhism I was taught the importance of a caring attitude toward the environment. Our practice of nonviolence applies not just to human beings but to all sentient beings.... In Buddhist practice we get so used to this idea of nonviolence and the ending of all suffering that we become accustomed to not harming or destroying anything indiscriminately. Although we do not believe that trees or flowers have minds, we treat them also with respect. Thus we share a sense of universal responsibility for both mankind and nature." H.H. the 14th Dalai Lama & G. Rowell, My Tibet 79–80 (1990).

29. See Passmore, note 25 above, at 12.

30. Fellows of the Calvin Center for Christian Scholarship, Earthkeeping: Christian Stewardship of Natural Resources (1980); P. Riesenberg, The Inalienability of Sovereignty in Medieval Political Thought (1956), explores medieval concepts of human (and royal) stewardship.

31. Goethe and Henry More were early outposts in the resistance to the human-centeredness of Bacon, Descartes, and even Kant. See generally Passmore, note 25 above, at 16–23.

responsibilities. Perhaps these are responsibilities to past generations and to the future, to steward and pass on the extraordinary legacy we have received. A classic legal algorithm holds that for every power there is a countervailing responsibility. The ability to destroy surely does not carry with it the moral right to do so, tempered only by the limitations of self-interest against self-inflicted wounds. That would be too primitive a norm for a species that has been maturing for 2 million years.

From the fact of human intellectual development come other bases for an environmental ethic. On one hand are the arguments that proceed from our superiorities, like the claim for an ecological *noblesse oblige* — because we humans uniquely have been able, in some settings at least, to move beyond the bare demands of food, shelter, and survival to build an abstract culture and to understand the effects of our actions upon the planet, our species has a high calling to protect the less powerful parts of the ecological community in which we live. Aesthetic principles, also a unique human development, likewise argue for an extended stewardship.

On the other hand lie the arguments from humility. The more one knows, the more one realizes one does not know. The greater the expansion of our knowledge and technology, the vaster the realm of the unknown. When we look into the she-wolf's eyes with Leopold, some of what we feel may be anthropomorphic sympathy. But the fire dying there may also spark a recognition that we will never know the world she knows, and that should make us hesitant to make ourselves the measure of it all. Ultimately humans may be impelled to honor an environmental ethic protecting the planet's ecology for the same reason that they are impelled to climb Mt. Everest: because it is there. The very existence — the "is-ness" — of the wolf and her rivers and mountains, separate from humans, makes the ethic fitting and proper for recognition.

When the question arises, as it continually does in legislatures and agencies, courts, and saloons, "Why protect such-and-such particular part of the environment?" environmentalists undoubtedly will continue to argue practically, "Because it may turn out to be important to us or to hurt us if we lose it." But often, when the setting and the light are right, won't many of us also feel a further pull, coming from something more than the stark counsels of daily human utility?

COMMENTARY & QUESTIONS

1. **The public trust doctrine.** This preceding mix of ethical and practical reasoning is also incorporated within the public trust doctrine. The public trust, studied later in Chapter 22, is a potentially powerful legal doctrine derived from ancient principles that echo environmental law's current mantra of "sustainability." Society must protect certain resources that are owned by humankind through the generations, a legacy received from the past to be stewarded in the present and assured for the future. As Emperor Justinian declared, "By the law of nature, these things are common to humankind: the air, running water, the sea, and…the shores of the sea…."[32] Further public trust rights have been acknowledged over the years — in wildlife, in parks, even

---

32. Institutes of Emperor Justinian, 2.1.1 (a.d. 529).

in fossils and human cultural artifacts. The public trust doctrine includes both the utilitarian perspective that protecting the environment protects human health and welfare, and further resource protections that go beyond strict human utility.

The public trust applies in three different settings — providing equitable remedies (1) where government agencies inappropriately attempt to sell a public trust resource into private hands ("alienation"), (2) where government agencies attempt to shift a trust from one public use into an inappropriate new public use ("diversion," as when parkland is converted into a municipal parking lot), and (3) where trust uses are being polluted or destroyed ("derogation").

2. **Beyond strict utility.** The public trust doctrine's direct human utilitarianism is evident when it is applied to protect the quality of drinking water[33] or public access to a river, harbor, or beach. Why is it, however, that environmental law protects groundwater aquifers from pollution *even if they may never be used by anyone* and are not connected to other water bodies? Why do we protect endangered species even when we are virtually certain a particular species will never have any human usefulness? Why do we protect clean environments against minor lowering of air or water quality when some polluting development projects could generate huge economic profits with no danger of reaching the maximum legal levels of harm to health or property?[34] Why do we try to make strip miners in the mountains of Appalachia restore hillsides to premining conditions, when the cost of remediation is ten times the market value of the land per acre before or after the restoration? Protecting a pristine waterfall, an endangered species, a unique prairie, or a wilderness virgin grove of trees in the face of commercial development apparently serves some further societal objectives. How and why does the law assert abstract "legacy" values in addition to utilitarian environmental goals that protect human welfare? The answer in U.S. law, and in emerging international law doctrines such as "intergenerational equity" and the "common heritage of humankind," as we will see, lies in the public trust doctrine.

Environmental law generally has drawn upon standard preexisting legal tools and doctrines to build a body of law incorporating its new perspective, but the public trust doctrine is an exception. It is environmental law's own special ancient and innovative contribution to our legal system.

B. THE PROBLEM OF THE COMMONS

Life is not a cow pasture nor a salty highway. These two images that follow below, however, present fundamental illustrations of how human beings act in ways that pose problems for the environment and for democratic governance. Fortunately or unfortunately, much of the natural world is a commons — air, water, wildlife — which puts it on a collision course with dynamics of human behavior that are based on individually based rational choices.

---

33. See Tenn. Code Ann. §§70.324 et seq. (Tennessee Water Pollution Control Act, expressly incorporating the authority of the public trust).

34. PSD rules have been instituted in a number of areas for the "prevention of significant deterioration."

Garrett Hardin, The Tragedy of the Commons
162 Science 1243, 1243–1248 (1968)

The tragedy of the commons develops this way. Picture a pasture open to all. It is to be expected that each herdsman will try to keep as many cattle as possible on the commons. Such an arrangement may work reasonably satisfactorily for centuries because tribal wars, poaching, and disease keep the numbers of both man and beast well below the carrying capacity of the land. Finally, however, comes the day of reckoning, that is, the day when the long-desired goal of social stability becomes a reality. At this point, the inherent logic of the commons remorselessly generates tragedy.

As a rational being, each herdsman seeks to maximize his gain. Explicitly or implicitly, more or less consciously, he asks, "What is the utility to me of adding one more animal to my herd?" This utility has one negative and one positive component:

1. The positive component is a function of the increment of one animal. Since the herdsman receives all the proceeds from the sale of the additional animal, the positive utility is nearly +1.

2. The negative component is a function of the additional overgrazing created by one more animal. Since, however, the effects of overgrazing are shared by all the herdsmen, the negative utility for any particular decision-making herdsman is only a fraction of -1.

Adding together the component partial utilities, the rational herdsman concludes that the only sensible course for him to pursue is to add another animal to his herd. And another; and another.... But his is the conclusion reached by each and every rational herdsman sharing a commons. Therein is the tragedy. Each man is locked into a system that compels him to increase his herd without limit — in a world that is limited. Ruin is the destination toward which all men rush, each pursuing his own best interest in a society that believes in the freedom of the commons. Freedom in a commons brings ruin to all.

Some would say that this is a platitude. Would that it were! In a sense, it was learned thousands of years ago, but natural selection favors the forces of psychological denial. The individual benefits as an individual from his ability to deny the truth even though society as a whole, of which he is a part, suffers. Education can counteract the natural tendency to do the wrong thing, but the inexorable succession of generations requires that the basis for this knowledge be constantly refreshed....

In an approximate way, the logic of the commons has been understood for a long time, perhaps since the discovery of agriculture or the invention of private property in real estate. But it is understood mostly only in special cases which are not sufficiently generalized. Even at this late date, cattlemen leasing national land on the western ranges demonstrate no more than an ambivalent understanding, in constantly pressuring federal authorities to increase the head count to the point where overgrazing produces erosion and weed dominance. Likewise, the oceans of the world continue to suffer from the survival of the philosophy of the commons. Maritime nations still respond automatically to the shibboleth of the "freedom of the seas." Professing to believe in the "inexhaustible resources of the oceans," they bring species after species of fish and whales closer to extinction.

The National Parks present another instance of the working out of the tragedy of the commons. At present, they are open to all, without limit. The parks themselves are limited in extent — there is only one Yosemite Valley — whereas population seems to grow without limit. The values that visitors seek in the parks are steadily eroded. Plainly, we must soon cease to treat the parks as commons or they will be of no value to anyone.

What shall we do? We have several options. We might sell them off as private property. We might keep them as public property, but allocate the right to enter them. The allocation might be on the basis of wealth, by the use of an auction system. It might be on the basis of merit, as defined by some agreed-upon standards. It might be by lottery. Or it might be on a first-come, first-served basis, administered to long queues. These, I think, are all the reasonable possibilities. They are all objectionable. But we must choose — or acquiesce in the destruction of the commons that we call our National Parks.

Pollution... In a reverse way, the tragedy of the commons reappears in problems of pollution. Here it is not a question of taking something out of the commons, but of putting something in — sewage, or chemical, radioactive, and heat wastes into water; noxious and dangerous fumes into the air; and distracting and unpleasant advertising signs into the line of sight. The calculations of utility are much the same as before. The rational man finds that his share of the cost of the wastes he discharges into the commons is less than the cost of purifying his wastes before releasing them. Since this is true for everyone, we are locked into a system of "fouling our own nest," so long as we behave only as independent, rational, free-enterprisers.

The tragedy of the commons as a food basket is averted by private property, or something formally like it. But the air and waters surrounding us cannot readily be fenced, and so the tragedy of the commons as a cesspool must be prevented by different means, by coercive laws or taxing devices that make it cheaper for the polluter to treat his pollutants than to discharge them untreated. We have not progressed as far with the solution of this problem as we have with the first. Indeed, our particular concept of private property, which deters us from exhausting the positive resources of the earth, favors pollution. The owner of a factory on the bank of a stream — whose property extends to the middle of the stream — often has difficulty seeing why it is not his natural right to muddy the waters flowing past his door. The law, always behind the times, requires elaborate stitching and fitting to adapt it to this newly perceived aspect of the commons.

The pollution problem is a consequence of population. It did not much matter how a lonely American frontiersman disposed of his waste. "Flowing water purifies itself every 10 miles," my grandfather used to say, and the myth was near enough to the truth when he was a boy, for there were not too many people. But as population became denser, the natural chemical and biological recycling processes became overloaded, calling for a redefinition of property rights.

How to Legislate Temperance?... Analysis of the pollution problem as a function of population density uncovers a not generally recognized principle of morality, namely: the morality of an act is a function of the state of the system at the time it is performed....

The laws of our society follow a complex, crowded, changeable world. Our epicyclic solution is to augment statutory law with administrative law. Since it is practically impossible to spell out all the conditions under which it is safe to burn trash in the back yard or to run an automobile without smog-control, by law we delegate the details to [agencies]. The result is administrative law, which is rightly feared for an ancient reason — *Quis custodiet ipsos custodes?* — "Who shall watch the watchers themselves?"... Administrators, trying to evaluate the morality of acts in the total system, are singularly liable to corruption, producing a government by men, not laws.

Prohibition is easy to legislate (though not necessarily to enforce); but how do we legislate temperance? Experience indicates that it can be accomplished best through the mediation of administrative law.... The great challenge facing us now is to invent the corrective feedbacks that are needed to keep custodians honest. We must find ways to legitimate the needed authority of both the custodians and the corrective feedbacks.

Pathogenic Effects of Conscience... The long-term disadvantage of an appeal to conscience [as a means to mitigate the tragedy of the commons] should be enough to condemn it, but it has serious short-term disadvantages as well. If we ask a man who is exploiting a commons to desist "in the name of conscience," what are we saying to him?... Two communications, and they are contradictory: (i) (the intended communication) "If you don't do as we ask, we will openly condemn you for not acting like a responsible citizen"; (ii) (the unintended communication) "If you do behave as we ask, we will secretly condemn you for a simpleton who can be shamed into standing aside while the rest of us exploit the commons." Every man then is caught in what Bateson has called a "double bind."...

Mutual Coercion Mutually Agreed Upon... "Responsibility...is the product of definite social arrangements." The social arrangements that produce responsibility are arrangements that create coercion, of some sort. Consider bank-robbing. The man who takes money from a bank acts as if the bank were a commons. How do we prevent such action? Certainly not by trying to control his behavior solely by a verbal appeal to his sense of responsibility. Rather than rely on propaganda we...insist that a bank is not a commons; we seek the definite social arrangements that will keep it from becoming a commons. That this would infringe on the freedom of would-be robbers we neither deny nor regret....

To say that we mutually agree to coercion is not to say that we are required to enjoy it, or even to pretend we enjoy it. Who enjoys taxes? We all grumble about them. But we accept compulsory taxes because we recognize that voluntary taxes would favor the conscienceless. We institute and (grumblingly) support taxes and other coercive devices to escape the horror of the commons.

An alternative to the commons need not be perfectly just to be preferable. With real estate and other material goods, the alternative we have chosen is the institution of private property coupled with legal inheritance. Is this system perfectly just? As a genetically trained biologist I deny that it is. It seems to me that, if there are to be differences in individual inheritance, legal action should be perfectly correlated with biological inheritance — that those who are biologically more fit to be the custodians of property and power should legally inherit more. But...an idiot can inherit millions, and a trust fund can keep his estate intact. We must admit that our legal system of private property plus inheritance is unjust — but we put up with it because we are not convinced, at the moment, that anyone has invented a better system....

But we can never do nothing. That which we have done for thousands of years is also action. It also produces evils. Once we are aware that the status quo is action, we can then compare its discoverable advantages and disadvantages with the predicted advantages and disadvantages of the proposed reform, discounting as best we can for our lack of experience. On the basis of such a comparison, we can make a rational decision which will not involve the unworkable assumption that only perfect systems are tolerable.

Recognition of Necessity... Perhaps the simplest summary of this analysis of man's population problems is this: the commons, if justifiable at all, is justifiable only under conditions of low-population density. As the human population has increased, the commons has had to be abandoned in one aspect after another.

First we abandoned the commons in food gathering, enclosing farm land and restricting pastures and hunting and fishing areas. These restrictions are still not complete throughout the world.

Somewhat later we saw that the commons as a place for waste disposal would also have to be abandoned. Restrictions on the disposal of domestic sewage are widely accepted in the Western world; we are still struggling to close the commons to pollution by automobiles, factories, insecticide sprayers, fertilizing operations, and atomic energy installations.

In a still more embryonic state is our recognition of the evils of the commons in matters of pleasure. There is almost no restriction on the propagation of sound waves in the public medium. The shopping public is assaulted with mindless music, without its consent.... Advertisers muddy the airwaves of radio and television and pollute the view of travelers. We are a long way from outlawing the commons in matters of pleasure....

Every new enclosure of the commons involves the infringement of somebody's personal liberty. Infringements made in the distant past are accepted because no contemporary person complains of a loss. It is the newly proposed infringements that we vigorously oppose; cries of "rights" and "freedom" fill the air. But what does "freedom" mean? When men mutually agreed to pass laws against robbing, mankind became more free, not less so. Individuals locked into the logic of the commons are free only to bring on universal ruin; once they see the necessity of mutual coercion, they become free to pursue other goals. I believe it was Hegel who said, "Freedom is the recognition of necessity."

COMMENTARY & QUESTIONS

1. **Common resources, environmental damage, and the "rational maximizer."** Looking at the beleaguered cow pasture, Hardin's central metaphor reveals a basic motivation driving each human actor to add to the "tragedy": Operating as self-contained individuals, all human actors instinctively seek to harvest and hold onto the maximum amount of benefits from their actions for themselves. This simplistic model of human behavior is frequently employed in economic analysis. If environmental social costs can be passed on into the commons where they will not be clearly visible or traceable, the human actors who cause the negative consequences will not be easily called to account for them — thus the entrepreneurial tendency toward "externalization[35] of social costs." On that model of human behavior, what can be done to alter the calculus of those choosing to use the commons? Environmental law's answer has been to seek accounting of those costs back to the people who caused them — "reinternalization" of the costs, or the polluter-pays principle. If the people who are making harmful decisions have to pay for or physically remedy them, the theory goes, over time they will cease their harmful activity or find a more efficient and benign way of doing it.

2. **Extrapolating to global scale.** Does Hardin's analysis apply beyond the cow pasture to the continental air masses or the oceans? The uses of all these commons are so diverse and diffuse that it is often difficult to demonstrate who is causing what effects. Even when individual actions hurting the common resource are invisible, diffuse, or unaccountable, however, cumulatively they can be critical. There tend to be two separate scenarios that demonstrate the tend toward "tragedy." One is pollution of the commons, where the private positive benefit is waste disposal and the externalized cost is a small decrease in resource quality. The second paradigm is in overuse via harvesting of the commons: the grass of the cow pasture, the fish in the ocean. In the latter

---

35. If an individual enterprise absorbs a cost, the cost payment is perceived as "internal" to its business. If it can pass it outside the business where it doesn't have to pay for it, that's "external." The Nobel laureate Ronald Coase relied on the rational actor concept underlying Hardin's tragedy of the commons, that individuals are driven to externalize costs.

paradigm, the private benefit is captured by either a pragmatic (cows eating the grass) or legal rule of capture (granting exclusive property rights to one who catches the fish). Don't the incentives facing the rational maximizer change if, for example, the individual owns the entirety of the resource base? If owners will suffer the losses as well as the benefits, their behavioral calculus will be quite different from an open-access commons. Are there ways in which legal rules can be established to force a group of users of the resource to act as a single owner would? The law has evolved in this way in at least one setting, hydrocarbon development, where the owners of land overlying an oil and gas formation are forced to "unitize" the field, extracting oil or gas as if they were a single owner and then sharing the profits of the whole field. This results in greater total production and therefore a greater total benefit to the class of owners than does the wasteful race to capture the resource that occurs in the absence of legally coerced collective action. Some industry advocates have therefore argued that other resources — national forests, fish stocks, minerals on public lands, even national parks — should be "privatized," turned over to single corporate ownership for the sake of efficiency. Many environmental problems, such as pollution and global warming, are of a scale that refutes privatization.[36] The difficulty of the grand scale lies in discovering the true measure of public costs and what controls may avert the logic of the tragedy, a problem that is nowhere more difficult than in the area Hardin targeted, global population control. Environmental law addresses many different problems of cumulative effects in a wide variety of ways, at different scales. The behavioral logic of the tragedy of the commons, however, permeates virtually all environmental issues.

3. **John Locke and a political philosophy of the tragedy of the commons.** Under Lockean political theory, if we lived under Eden-like conditions of plenty, there would be no competition for resources, and property law would not be necessary because all desired items would be sufficiently abundant. With increasing populations and limited resources, however, a means for allocating available goods had to be found. To Locke, the institution of exclusive individual property fit nicely with his sense of the order of God's universe and also responded to social needs.[37] Private property induces people to work by granting them ownership of all or some of the fruits of their labors. Nonexclusive rights to property fail to produce work incentives. Like the rational choice theories of modern economics, Locke presumed that human actors generally act in their own rational self-interest. For private property's relationship to a commons, this means that owners will do whatever will maximize their advantage in regard to their own property.

In the old days prior to 1960, individual enterprises lived in a version of the frontier myth, where each could operate independently on its own terrain, and the negative consequences that individual actions generated would disappear away into an all-absorbing tolerant vacuum. Rachel Carson showed us, however, that this tendency is

---

36. It should be noted, however, that Coase's Theorem is based on a sort of privatization proposition: that, for efficiency purposes, plenary rights to pollute could be transferred to polluters, thereafter leaving it up to "consumers" of pollution to try to bargain in the marketplace for the amount of clean air they desired.

37. For a more thorough discussion of John Locke's view of private property, see Sanders, The Lockean Proviso, 10 Harv. J.L. & Pub. Pol'y 401 (1988).

dominated by short-term individualized thinking and can be quite dysfunctional. Externalized costs don't disappear, even if they are ignored. The "free" absorption of negatives by the commons, or the destruction of resources that do not in the commons have to be paid for, are not in reality "free goods" in terms of a societal accounting. These externalities have serious accumulated consequences that can end up dwarfing the short-term logic that spawned them.

4. **The pessimism and optimism of the commons.** Does Hardin seem too optimistic about the chances for reforming the tragedy of the commons? Some who have considered the matter find Hardin's view — that necessity will induce us to accept protections based on "mutual coercion, mutually agreed upon"— grossly over-optimistic. See W. Ophuls, Ecology and the Politics of Scarcity 145–165 (1977). At the opposite pole are the "cornucopialists." Susan Cox, for example, argues that problems of the commons are not of the magnitude that Hardin fears, and humans will always find new resources and technologies to cope. In her assessment, society has adequately managed such problems through the ages, with the major lapses coming only in times of cultural shifts. See Cox, No Tragedy of the Commons, 7 Envtl. Ethics 49 (1985).

5. **The commons and positive outcomes.** How do you decide what things should be maintained in common ownership rather than being reduced to a form of exclusive private property? Locke, Jeremy Bentham, and Adam Smith all noted how private property ownership and the right to exclude others play a crucial role in motivating political and economic life. As Professor Carol Rose writes:

> The right to exclude others has often been cited as the most important characteristic of private property. This right, it is said, makes private property fruitful by enabling owners to capture the full value of their individual investments, thus encouraging everyone to put time and labor into the development of the resources. Moreover, exclusive control makes it possible for owners to identify other owners, and for all to exchange the fruits of their labors until these things arrive in the hands of those who value them most highly — to the great cumulative advantage of all.[38]

What kinds of things are better suited to public ownership and communal use? Professor Rose cites public libraries and public highways as examples of successful commons. What of lakes and rivers? Forests? Antarctica? In most of the world, private landowners do not own resources beneath their land; the public retains the right to determine their use and development.

6. **Measuring sustainability.** Another fundamental problem with the commons is defining the level of sustainability. It isn't easy to define the point where cows exceed the sustainable carrying capacity of the commons. It is far harder to define the acceptable level of imposition on a common resource such as air or water ("assimilative capacity") or an ocean fishery. Is anything less than purity a negative burden on the commons? What constitutes tolerable depreciation, and what constitutes Hardin's downward spiral to disaster? The different approaches to defining and setting appropriate environmental standards is the subject of the chapters in Part Three of this coursebook.

---

38. Rose, The Comedy of the Commons, 53 U. Chi. L. Rev. 711, 711–712 (1986).

7. Law as mutual coercion. Assuming that much of the commons paradigm is relevant to analyzing environmental policy, note how Hardin sets up a critical role for the law but doesn't specify its operation. If nonmandatory policies or physical privatization are unlikely to work on a pollution commons (are they?), what kinds of legal intervention are likely to be effective and appropriate to avoiding the tragedy of the commons? Criminal sanctions, taxes, individual lawsuits, administrative bureaucracies? The choice is not easy. In practice, as this book repeatedly notes, environmental law has developed an amazing biodiversity of statutory design models, whether by accident or pragmatic plan — producing a wide range of legal approaches to environmental protection.

8. The Coase theorem. One influential argument holds that law's purpose here is to create property rights that are capable of being traded via market exchange. A famous article by Nobel laureate Ronald Coase argues that — assuming the reality of a universal tendency to externalize costs — the same outcomes will be reached, through bargaining starting from a clear legal rule of entitlement, irrespective of which of two different parties holds the legal entitlement. See The Problem of Social Cost, 3 J.L. & Econ. 1 (1960). Coase's demonstration relies on assumptions about equal resources, equal access of all participants to information, and the absence of transaction costs. Perhaps efficiency-maximizing bargaining seems likely to occur in a simple and limited dispute between a neighboring rancher and farmer over fencing (Coase's hypothetical). Is bargaining toward an efficient solution likely to be easy when a large number of parties are joint holders of a legal right, as in the case of a commons used and enjoyed by many? The difficulties of organizing groups of victims of pollution to bargain collectively (a form of "transaction costs") poses one problem. Would the bargaining go better if the initial legal right were assigned to the polluter? If that is the case, might some members of the group choose to become "free riders," refusing to participate in the belief that they will be able to reap the shared benefit without active participation? Is there another explanation for why victims of pollution might refuse to bargain with their polluter? See Farnsworth, Do Parties to Nuisance Cases Bargain After Judgment? A Glimpse Inside the Cathedral, 66 U. Chi. L. Rev. 373 (1999) (empirical study of 20 "Coasian" lawsuits in which parties to nuisance cases refused to bargain with their adversaries after a legal judgment, as a result of the enmity between the parties and their conviction that legal entitlements were not an appropriate subject of bargaining).

9. The view from "free market" advocates. Juxtaposed against an environmental economics overview is the traditional view of nature as a resource base for dynamic human enterprise. This marketplace logic of industrial and development interests casts resource exploitation and pollution externalities in a far more upbeat light. Here is part of a manifesto from the self-styled "Wise Use" movement:

> Humans, like all organisms, must use natural resources to survive. This fundamental truth is never addressed by environmentalists.... If environmentalism were to acknowledge our necessary use of the earth, its ideology would lose its meaning. To recognize the legitimacy of the human use of the earth would be to accept the unavoidable environmental damage that is the price of our survival. Once that price is acceptable, the moral framework of environmentalist ideology becomes

> irrelevant and the issues become technical and economic.... The earth and its life are tough and resilient, not fragile and delicate. Environmentalists tend to be catastrophists, believing that any human use of the earth is "damage" and massive human use of the earth is "a catastrophe." An environmentalist motto is "We all live downstream," the viewpoint of helpless or vengeful victims. Wise-users, on the other hand, tend to be cornucopians.... A wise-use motto is "We all live upstream," the viewpoint of responsible and concerned individuals....

The only way we humans can learn about our surroundings is through trial and error.... Environmental ideology fetishizes nature to the point that eco-activists will not permit others to make errors with the environment, dead-ending in no trials and no learning.... Our limitless imaginations can break through natural limits to make earthly goods and carrying capacity virtually infinite. Just as settled agriculture increased goods and carrying capacity vastly beyond hunting and gathering, so our imaginations can find ways to increase total productivity by superseding one level of technology after another.... Man's reworking of the earth is revolutionary, problematic and ultimately benevolent.... Ron Arnold, What Do We Believe?[39]

Where is the commons in this rhetorical context? The marketplace's optimistic focus on the ongoing achievements of human enterprise comes from a totally different way of seeing the world, a perspective from which most environmental regulations based on ecological and civic concepts of the commons appear dismally negativistic, unnecessary, and obstructive. Both perspectives cannot be right.

C. A SALTY PARADIGM: ROAD SALT, A PROBLEM THAT HAS NOT YET MET ITS LEGAL PROCESS

The prosaic environmental controversy that follows has as yet hardly been noticed by the legal system. It nevertheless illustrates a classic environmental law conundrum, with elements that recur throughout the field.[40] Readers in Snow Belt states are living in the midst of this exercise. For readers in Sun Belt states, it offers a bemusing and instructive opportunity to observe from a safe distance. The contaminant is highway de-icing salt, which in its own ways can spread as widely as harmful chemicals, with some serious human effects including even death.

---

39. Arnold is a principal spokesman of the "Wise Use" movement and chairman of the Center for the Defense of Free Enterprise, part of the marketplace coalition that attempted to roll back environmental regulation across the board in the 104th Congress; text from http://www.cdfe.org/wiscusc.html. Started in the late 1980s in the West, funded by mining, timber, grazing, and other environment-related industries, Wise Users create coalitions of local and regional groups loudly opposing federal environmental regulation. "Wise use" is a slogan hijacked from the conservation creed developed by the eminent conservationist Gifford Pinchot, father of the Forest Service, who used the phrase to emphasize the necessity of tighter sustainability restrictions on resource use.

40. Few environmental issues are as uncomplicated as the salt example — where easily identified externalities and self-interests sustain practices that tend to erode overall societal welfare, with the political context of our governance system making it extremely difficult to change those dysfunctional practices even when the facts are clear. The current opponents of hydrogen-based energy innovations, usually representatives of the traditional coal, oil, and gas industry, echo the salt industry's criticism of innovative de-icing alternatives. Coal, oil, and natural gas are dominant in the marketplace over environmentally more sustainable renewable energy sources in major part because so many costs are externalized, with both short-term social costs and long-term ecological risks (including global climate change). They also have built up major subsidies that protect the price advantage of traditional energy companies, beginning with tax code provisions that give credits for resource depletion to less direct expenditures for national security policies that appear related to protecting access to sources of supply.

Like King Lear, one can learn much from salt. A few years ago, EPA prepared a major analysis of the effects of highway salt, based on more than 300 prior research projects and reports.[41] Dr. Charles Wurster, of the State University of New York's Marine Sciences Research Center, published the following summary (which in retrospect is even more sobering because virtually nothing has changed since he wrote it).

Charles Wurster, Of Salt . . .
New York Times, March 4, 1978, at A21

The use of salt on roads for snow and ice removal has increased in the years [since the early 1960s]. About nine million tons, more than 10 percent of all salt produced in the world, are applied annually to American highways in snowy states.

The benefits of salt for road de-icing — and its costs — are rarely questioned. A recent report of the EPA, which weighed the costs and benefits of the practice, includes surprises.

The costs of salting begin with $200 million for the salt and its application. Roadside vegetation destroyed by salt, particularly shade trees, was estimated by EPA to add another $150 million. Underground water mains, telephone cables and electric lines are corroded by salt seepage, adding another $10 million in damages. The Consolidated Edison Company, which owns the world's largest underground electrical system, estimated that road salt did $5 million in damages during [a single] winter....

Salt finds its way into drinking-water supplies, especially ground-water aquifers, thereby becoming a health hazard. Recent research implicates salt intake as a causative factor in hypertension, heart disease and other circulatory problems, as well as various liver, kidney and metabolic disorders. It is estimated that at least 20 percent of Americans should restrict salt intake.

Individuals can control the salt that is added to foods, but salt in drinking water is harder to manage. About 27 percent of the drinking water supplies in Massachusetts are contaminated with road salt, and New Hampshire has a state-financed system for replacing contaminated wells. Long Island is especially vulnerable, since its sole drinking water is ground water recharged by precipitation, including highway runoff.

The EPA estimated that 25 percent of the population in the Snow Belt drinks water contaminated with road salt. The cost of providing pure water for these people was put at $150 million, but no objective cost was ascribed to health damage.

Salt damages bridges and other highway structures, best exemplified by the deterioration and collapse of New York City's West Side Highway. Corrosion by salt is believed to have been a major cause of the failure. The EPA estimated the national annual cost of damage to highway structures by salt at $500 million.

But the largest and most obvious cost of road salt is automobile corrosion, estimated by the EPA at $2 billion annually, or an average of about $34 per car per year in the Snow Belt. Heavy salting of highways hastens auto depreciation by about 20 percent. Telephone company vehicles last twice as long in the South as they do in New England.

Although they are usually assumed without question, the benefits of road salting have proven elusive to substantiate. At temperatures near or slightly below freezing, salt hastens melting and increases traction. But at lower temperatures, salt makes dry snow shiny and more slippery, and causes it to stick on windshields hampering vision. Salt also prolongs street wetness, reducing the friction.

---

41. EPA Document 600/2-76-105 (May 1976).

Solid evidence of increased safety is lacking, because inadequate studies have been confounded by too many variables. The effects of salting are often inseparable from the effects of plowing and sanding. A Michigan study found fewer accidents during years when salt was used, but the number of storms and quantity of snowfall were ignored. Other studies showed no effects on accident rates.

Salt usually permits faster driving which would benefit emergency vehicles but is a mixed blessing for others. In snow, people tend to drive slowly and have "fender benders," but after salt applications they tend to drive faster and have more serious accidents.

The benefits of salt in preventing accidents, if any, are small. Not surprisingly, this conclusion is disputed by the salt industry, which claims great benefits from its use.

An interesting benefit-cost analysis results. Whereas benefits are uncertain but apparently small (except to the salt and automobile industries), costs total nearly $3 billion per year. Only a small amount of the cost is the salt itself, 93 percent consisting of indirect costs, borne especially by owners of motor vehicles.

Road salting should be re-examined. Reduced salting, combined with increased plowing, tire modifications, and driver education in snow driving might yield better results at lower costs.

The EPA report summarized by Dr. Wurster contains many other fascinating details:

- The State of Alaska manages to maintain its highways without any use of road salt.
- The citizens of Michigan, leading the world in auto production, also lead in auto corrosion, losing $198,630,000 each year in salt-caused depreciation, which almost matches the total cost of salt application in the nation.
- Urban shade trees are vulnerable to salt and have substantial monetizable values[42] (a 15" diameter tree was valued at $1767; if a tree starts showing leaf damage from salt, it is beyond saving).
- So much salt has spilled into the Great Lakes that parts of the Lake Michigan depths now have a marine saltwater ecology, including marine fish such as flounder.
- Salt infiltrates through concrete and sets up a powerful pressure reaction with reinforcing steel bars, causing overpass damage and potholes on roadways, (as well as pitted sidewalks and crumbling concrete steps when applied by individuals for residential use[43]).
- All things being equal, people favor the "bare pavement" look of salted roads because the visual impression is misleadingly clearer than that of a scraped and sanded roadway.
- Salt intake is a critical factor in many health afflictions including hypertension, cardiovascular diseases, renal and liver diseases, and metabolic disorders, with

---

42. The words "monetized" and "marketized" are used in this text in the informal sense of "having been attributed a market value," not in the technical economics sense of converting to legal obligation.

43. A consumer-protection vignette: Some salt manufacturers, marketing their product for residential de-icing, label their product as **"Safe for application to concrete and cement! when used as directed,"** thereafter stating in the directions' fine print, "In order to avoid harm to concrete and cement, remove slush and moisture associated with this product within 30 minutes of application," a caveat that practically nullifies the premise.

likely linkages to increased mortalities, but no studies have focused on the wide-spread effects of highway salt on drinking water supplies.

- The report also notes that highway salt can be harmful to fish and wildlife but doesn't pursue these costs.

- The report makes extensive cost comparisons with a "scrape, sand, and selective salting" alternative model. (The net cost of the unlimited salting model was almost twice that of the restricted model.)

- The report doesn't review any of the available salt substitutes for de-icing such as organic CMA (calcium magnesium acetate).

COMMENTARY & QUESTIONS

1. **Evaluating the benefits, costs, and alternatives to salting.** Is salt an "environmental" problem? Although it involves potential damages to public health, vegetation, fish, and wildlife, these are precisely the areas that are least covered in the report, although they are potentially quite significant in terms of tangible costs. They lie at the end of an indirect chain of causation and are the hardest to prove and least quantifiable in money terms. The presence of these interconnected human and natural effects, and the narrowed basis upon which the salt decision is made, make it an issue typical of the environmental realm.

Salting is a classic example of how humans typically think in terms of "one-shot" technology. Who wants to bother with thinking about where the salt goes after the zap? Out of sight, out of mind. Environmental science, however, reminds us that everything goes somewhere and has residual consequences. We will live in a natural system with those residuals long after the ice and snow are gone.

Dr. Wurster's article demonstrates the elements of a classic environmental policy analysis, in which a program decision is made that wastefully impacts the natural and human environment — and it's a government agency that makes the decision in virtually the same terms as would a polluting private corporate factory owner. Note the decision-maker's calculus: The nation's road commissions decide to put salt on roads because, for them, it is a completely logical benefit-cost-alternatives decision; they get the *benefits* of bare roads,[44] paying only $200 million a year. But note that this marketplace decision ignores billions, at least 93% of the true *costs* as seen by environmentalists, and ignores some far better *alternatives*.

2. **Costs, economic and natural.** Environmentalists typically argue that the costs of a proposal are far greater than the limited costs considered by those who make the decision. Here are the conservative EPA estimates of some of the total yearly costs of road salting that can be monetized:[45]

---

44. The highly specific traditional goal definition of highway agencies is to "achieve highway user satisfaction" in terms of "mobility, productivity, and safety," to this end using snow and ice treatments to avoid weather-caused roadway congestion and to "maintain core highway operations priorities."

45. All salt figures in the EPA Report and the text discussion are given in 1976 dollars. Since 1976, no comprehensive report has been issued to update these cumulative national cost estimates.

ESTIMATED YEARLY COSTS

Salt Purchase & Application	$ 200.00 million
Highway Structures	500.00 million
Water Supplies	150.00 million
Vehicles	2000.00 million
Utilities	10.00 million
Vegetation	50.00 million
TOTAL:	ca. $2.91 billion

This set of costs, of course, is not complete. Remarkably, the analyzed costs completely excluded health costs, beyond a factor based on substitute drinking water supply. Given the severe risks of heart disease posed by salt in water supplies, this would appear to be a strong candidate for application of the "Precautionary Principle," the environmental principle reflected in many international and domestic regulatory fields — if a thing is potentially very dangerous and alternatives exist, why wait until all studies are complete before acting to limit exposures?[46] The report also does not include any fish and wildlife or other environmental values, nor the costs that occur at the source of the salt, such as harms caused by mining, which typically include local water pollution from mine runoff and leachate. As is often the case in environmental matters, many costs are indirect and borne in small amounts by a large, dispersed class of adversely affected individuals.

The point, of course, is that most of these kinds of costs are hidden from direct public view and not chargeable to the persons who decide to impose them. In societal terms the question should be: How many of these costs should rationally be considered as part of the systemic decision to apply or continue applying salt? In operative terms, however, the actual question will be: How many of the salt costs listed above will have to be paid by the road commissions that choose to use salt? If the answer is little or none, then those costs will receive little or no consideration.

3. **Benefits.** The classic environmental response to a proposal's claimed benefits is to doubt them. The official decisionmakers in the marketplace have decided to go ahead for their own direct market reasons, but is it really necessary that the proposed project or program be done, or done in this particular way?

In the case of highway salt, the environmental argument would focus initially on the lack of proof of benefits from the "bare pavement" model. What is the value of a road that appears to be clear, especially if it retains an icy film? What is the value of faster-moving traffic, especially in light of the evidence that accidents on salted road systems

---

46. Serious salt-caused problems for pedestrians (avoidable by use of salt substitutes) have been reported, from bleeding ulceration of the paws of guide dogs for blind pedestrians to electrocution deaths of humans as well. "Hot spots [of leaking voltage on wet streets and sidewalks] are not uncommon this time of year because the salt used to de-ice the sidewalks serves as a conductor. The salt…has been known to eat through wiring and electrify metal grates — as it did recently in the death of a New York woman…. The electrical line that triggered Oscar's death runs 2 or 3 feet underground and carries about 120 volts." Bennett & Abel, Stray Street Voltage Electrocutes Dog, Boston Globe, Feb. 5, 2004 at B1.

are more likely to be fatal than the scrape-and-sand model's "fender-benders"? The environmentalist would admit the benefits of time saved and disruptions avoided by highway salting, but would argue that these benefits should be weighed against the foreseeable costs to figure out how best to do the job. In practice, however, the decision will be made by highway commissioners whose intuitive judgment is that the "bare-pavement" result of salting is worth more to them than their own yearly $200 million cost of buying and applying salt, and that is the only calculus that they consider. In this and other cases where valuation is difficult, moreover, the public tends to leave the calculations to official administrative discretion and the marketplace.

4. **Available alternatives: CMA and more.** The analysis of a proposal's benefits and costs is meaningless unless it is linked to a comparison of alternatives. Environmentalists can accurately be regarded as narrow-minded negativists if they merely attack proposals without reviewing alternative courses of action. One alternative in every case, of course, is the "no-action" alternative. When developers planned to build a dam that would flood part of the Grand Canyon for power and water supply, environmentalists were able to show that those benefits were not needed at that time and place, in light of the social costs. The better option was to do nothing.

Often the analysis of alternatives turns upon whether the action can better take place with a different design, location, timing, process, and so on. A particular factory might be a better neighbor, for example, if it installed pollution-control mechanisms, used a higher temperature process, or located itself downwind. Beverage bottles would cause less litter and save energy and raw materials if they were returnable. In the Memphis highway case, the citizens argued for location and construction designs that were feasible and prudent alternatives to going through the middle of their park.

In the case of salt, the purpose of the proposed action — removal of snow from the highways so as to allow traffic to move — is clearly necessary. Only the most troglodytic environmentalist would argue that traffic should come to a halt when the snow falls. Rather, the analysis should turn to a comparison of realistic alternatives. Installation of infrared electric melting devices in highway pavements might be effective and avoid all the indirect costs of salting, but the direct costs would be outrageous.

Excellent alternatives to salt exist, however — salt substitutes with the same snow melting characteristics as salt yet lacking its destructive characteristics. CMA (calcium magnesium acetate), invented by Chevron, is a prime example.[47] It can be made from readily available materials including recycled corn wastes or milk whey, it has none of the destructive effects of salt, and in fact it actually rebuilds salt-damaged soils by replacing stripped magnesium and calcium.[48] In 1994 the State of Oregon made a generic switch to using de-icing chemicals including CMA based on an overall analysis of direct and indirect costs, with special consideration of corrosion effects and

---

47. Another benign alternative is potassium acetate, which has long been used as a de-icer for runways (and is FAA approved for that purpose), and on bridges and other areas especially sensitive to corrosion. Although potassium acetate has the same environmental benefits and risks as CMA, while often being less expensive, CMA has a larger share of the alternative market.

48. See Horner & Brenner, Environmental Evaluation of Calcium Magnesium Acetate for Highway Deicing Applications, 7 Resources, Conservation & Recycling 213–237 (1992).

environmental effects, particularly to the state's protected salmon runs.[49] Even ignoring the public health costs that were not accounted for in the EPA study, it appears reasonable that nonsalt alternatives such as CMA might realize savings of almost $2 billion per year when compared with continued use of salt. This would be true even if the direct costs for de-icing increased fivefold, from $200 million to $1 billion. The actual overall public costs would still drop more than $1.9 billion.

CMA, however, costs the highway officials who budget for roads between $200 and $1000 per ton, as opposed to salt's $20 to $70.[50] "The problem," says Chevron's Dan Walter, "is that the benefit of CMA does not go back to the governmental agency that pays for de-icers, typically state maintenance departments. If a bridge on an interstate highway must be replaced, the federal government will pay 80% of the cost. Therefore the highway department cannot justify paying $600 per ton for CMA."[51] The way the commercial-political marketplace is set up, no one and no forum is in a position to bring the overall public economics to bear upon the operative decisions.

5. **The political context.** So assume now that a careful study conclusively proved that the United States loses a net $2 billion or more each year, destructively and unnecessarily, because of the use of road salt instead of benign alternatives. What corrective response can we expect to occur?

Perhaps none. As so often, the important question is who if anyone will take up the problem and resolve it? Will the industry itself, and the marketplace economy, take on the problem and solve it? Not likely. Will some government agency do so of its own initiative? Not likely. If not, will activist members of the public do so in the classic process that created environmental law — through media efforts, politics, and creative use of the legal system? Not yet.

The next chapter of this book explores the political context that sustains the kind of governmental and marketplace behavior we're describing, along with more issues from highway salting, and exploration of a number of other themes encountered throughout environmental law.

Meanwhile, the salt goes on.

---

49. See D. Keep & D. Parker, Tests Clear Snow, Path for Use of Liquid Anti-icing in Northwest, Roads & Bridges (Aug. 1995), reporting significant overall governmental savings (including cleanup costs).

50. In 2002, a survey by one of our research assistants revealed that the majority of road commissions could buy salt for $29.76 per ton. While CMA sold for $200 to $1000 per ton, the similar road treatment, potassium acetate, sold for $330 to $700 per ton.

51. U.S. Water News, Jan. 1990, at 11. If a road commission simply could not find the cash to pay for a 100% switch to CMA, 20 to 60% CMA-to-salt blends are available that buffer much of the salt's negatives but still cost two to three times as much as salt.

Chapter 2

CROSS-CUTTING THEMES IN ENVIRONMENTAL LAW

A. *A Milestone Pollution Case in Historical Context:*
   Allied Chemical and Kepone Pesticide
B. *Beyond Kepone: Tracking Several Decades of Environmental Law Development*
C. *Themes, Contexts, and Arguments for Change: Politics, Economics, and Tactics*

A. A MILESTONE POLLUTION CASE IN HISTORICAL CONTEXT: ALLIED CHEMICAL AND KEPONE PESTICIDE

For more than 300 years of our national development, there was little or nothing of environmental law. This is not to say that serious, cumulative environmental problems did not exist. They did, increasing throughout the pre-environmental law years in number and severity. Today's environmental law came together in a blur of activity during the 1960s and 1970s and has grown in depth and breadth since then.

This section invites you to survey the history of the field and to examine the Allied Chemical Kepone disaster — a milestone case in that historical development process.

A quick overview of the evolution of U.S. environmental law helps to orient the materials in this coursebook. From the start, environmental law has consistently reflected larger issues of science, politics, and social policy (for example, the changing social conceptions of government and the relative shifts in the balance between the individual and the community). A sense of the history of it gives you a more sophisticated understanding of the case law and public law of the past, present, and future.[1]

Section 1. A SHORT HISTORICAL SKETCH OF THE EVOLUTION OF U.S. ENVIRONMENTAL LAW

In the following sketch history, the different epochs are not given names. As you go through this historical summary you might consider: What labels would you assign to each?

1600s–1890s. Discharges of all forms of pollution are an established disposal practice, resource exploitation is almost completely unrestrained, and neither are recognized as systemic problems. If addressed at all by law, the issues we now call *environmental* are handled opportunistically and rather crudely by individuals under

---

1. For a beautifully done evolutionary chronicle of U.S. economic and environmental development from colonial times to the present, see D. Muir, Reflections in Bullough's Pond: Economy and Ecosystem in New England (2000).

common law, primarily the tort law of neighbors. There are a few scattered occurrences of public law, often at the level of local ordinances on sewage practices, grazing rights, and the like.[2]

Late 1800s–1914. Corporate enterprises build the structures and dynamics of a rapidly expanding modern industrial economy. Pollution continues to be standard operating procedure, and resource exploitation remains largely unconstrained. Some industries successfully assert dominant common law positions owing to the societal importance of industrial enterprise.[3] Other cases strike more subtle common law balances between industry and neighbors.[4] Population pressures are felt in various settings. A few citizen movements come into being: The celebration-of-nature Preservationist Movement is reflected in groups such as John Muir's Sierra Club and the Audubon Society, and echoed in Congress's creation of Yellowstone National Park (1872) and other national forests, parks, and monuments, especially during Teddy Roosevelt's presidency. Some regulatory agencies begin to wield limited authority in fields now identified as environmental: for example, local health departments and federal resource regulation, beginning with rudimentary U.S. Forest Service rules on grazing and timbercutting.

1914–1960. Whatever legal constraints are applied continue to be largely uncoordinated common law actions between neighbors, low-level public law regulations operating primarily through local health ordinances exercising limited powers delegated under generic state health codes, or primitive state air and water laws. The Public Health Movement, which includes some pollution control aims, gets underway with limited success. Natural resource management, typified by Gifford Pinchot and Aldo Leopold, becomes an established profession linked to the generally *non*-preservationist Conservation Movement. Business practices of discharging pollution and chemical products into the environment, however, and largely unrestricted resource exploitation patterns (except during wartime) continue to be the norm as postwar economic growth surges. State regulation is generally lax as state governments compete for industrial payrolls. Federal administrative regulation of business expands greatly starting in the 1920s — on the standard bipolar regulatory model in which government agencies are designed to counterweigh the excesses of the marketplace[5] — but little regulation

---

2. Until the late 1800s, the private marketplace was the dominant "government" of the United States. (In some senses it still is, for, in a society that is basically structured by the private corporate market, the vast majority of daily actions and personal incentives are shaped by private economic decisions.) In the trust-busting era of the 1890s, however, the laissez-faire theory of governance began to be supplemented by selective government regulation.

3. See Pennsylvania Coal Co. v. Sanderson, 6 A. 453, 459 (1886) (riparians' common law rights to unpolluted water "must yield to the necessities of a great public industry").

4. See Madison v. Ducktown Sulphur, Copper & Iron Co., 83 S.W. 658 (Tenn. 1904).

5. *Bipolar* means that governance has two primary sectors: the commerce-industry sector and the official agencies created to correct "market failures" when the marketplace economy, left to itself, cannot adequately handle major external considerations that society must address. Government intervention was seen to be necessary in order to impose certain nonmarket values upon the market, through laws on child labor, antitrust, worker safety, consumer fraud, and so on. Only later, with the appearance of citizen and nongovernmental organizations' active role in governance, does the legal system become "multipolar" or "polycentric." The "bipolar/multipolar" distinction draws upon Professor Lon Fuller's analysis of judicial roles in a report of the Joint Conference on Professional Responsibility, 44 A.B.A. J. 1159 (1958), republished in the posthumously assembled work that appeared as Fuller, The Forms and Limits of Adjudication, 92 Harv. L. Rev. 353, 383 (1978). See Langbein, The German Advantage in Civil Procedure, 52 U. Chi. L. Rev. 823 (1985).

occurs in the environmental area. The administrative law bar develops an array of doctrines under the 1946 Administrative Procedures Act (APA) for counteracting governmental agency regulation. The first federal efforts to address air and water pollution in the 1950s, drafted in consultation with industry representatives, provide funds for pollution research (with some funding for state and local pollution programs) and, in the absence of meaningful federal enforcement mechanisms, they direct the states to address the regulation of this pollution.

1960–1970. Rachel Carson's book *Silent Spring* galvanizes broad public recognition of systemic environmental problems. The Johnson Administration is the first to support substantive federal environmental statutes — the Wilderness Act of 1964, parkland and scenic protections in Federal Highway Acts. Business-sponsored nonmandatory federal laws, however, are still the norm. Federal air, water, endangered species, and pesticide laws continue to seek voluntary compliance, defer broadly to state statutes whatever they may be, and focus federal activity on funding "research" into problems and possible solutions. Possibilities for federal enforcement are limited almost exclusively to instances of pollution crossing state lines. State regulation still reflects a "race-to-the-bottom," a competition of laxity between states vying to attract industry. Citizen litigation builds momentum in re-energized uses of common law, including public and private nuisance, and in new applications of generic administrative law.[6] The older citizen movements dedicated to nature preservation, conservation, and public health pollution abatement begin to come together in a series of large citizen coalitions now dominated by the new Environmental Movement. The pioneering *Scenic Hudson* case and a subsequent series of similar lawsuits allow citizens for the first time to apply the same judicial review and administrative law tactics used by business. This pluralistic access to the legal system forcibly opens the prevailing bipolar regulatory model, which had become a fairly unresponsive "Establishment" through the "agency capture" phenomenon, to start internalizing public interest concerns. Building upon the structures and energies of the Civil Rights and Antiwar Movements, Earth Day 1970 attracts massive public attention, encourages a wide range of citizen-based organizations and initiatives, and coalesces substantial political momentum.

1970–1980. Starting just before Earth Day 1970 an unprecedented series of more than two dozen environmental statutes pours forth from Congress during the presidency of Richard Nixon,[7] replacing diffuse and generally ineffective state environmental regulation with credible substantive federal minimum standards. The new laws are backed by the creation and expansion of complex federal regulatory agencies and implementation programs to be administered by state agencies under federal supervision — "cooperative federalism." Major media stories about notorious pollution incidents — Los Angeles killer smogs, New York State's Love Canal neighborhood built on a chemical dump, Pennsylvania's Donora air pollution deaths, Virginia's Allied

---

6. The Bible of the early environmental law field became Joseph Sax's Defending the Environment: A Strategy for Citizen Action (1970). Sax's article, The Public Trust Doctrine in Natural Resource Law: Effective Judicial Intervention, 68 Mich. L. Rev. 471, 489–502 (1970), likewise launched a remarkable resurrection of the public trust doctrine in the 1970s.

7. By our count, 34 important federal environmental statutes were passed in the three years after NEPA, which became effective January 2, 1970. See the chronological statutory appendix on the coursebook Web site.

Chemical Kepone contamination — lead directly to such innovations as the Clean Air Act (CAA) autopollution controls, toxics control statutes, and a new Clean Water Act (CWA). The standard regulatory model involves comprehensive prescriptive federal standards — sometimes labeled "command-and-control" in the most complexly regulated sectors of the law — with enforcement authority given to the federal agencies, to state agencies via delegation, and to citizens. Environmental initiatives in the United States trigger an international response, with 113 nations represented at the 1972 Stockholm Conference on the Environment, which lays the groundwork for a variety of follow-up efforts including a Law of the Sea conference process. A few years into the 1970s, Nixon starts to retreat from the issue (telling his Cabinet that it is time to "get off the environment kick"[8]), media attention begins to drift, and traditional Establishment linkages between business and bureaucracy tend to constrain active enforcement of the laws. Citizen action in the Environmental Movement, however, forges the new laws into a powerful new sector of the legal system. Hundreds of citizen interventions in agency process and citizen enforcement actions in federal court (using the new statutes' citizen suit provisions originally modeled on civil rights laws) secure and expand the federal regulatory structures during the Ford and Carter Administrations. Industry begins coordinated efforts to counteract environmental regulation. The Powell Memorandum,[9] characterizing environmentalism and other social causes as anti-American "subversive" movements, prompts the National Association of Manufacturers, the U.S. Chamber of Commerce, oil and timber interests, and others to create the richly funded Heritage Foundation and a number of other academic think-tanks and lobbying centers committed to building a political reaction against these public interest movements and the regulatory systems that incorporated their public interest values. The number of environmental attorneys — plaintiff, defense, and government — surpasses the number of attorneys in the labor law bar.

1980–1988. The first major assault on federal environmental laws comes during the Reagan years. Industry lobbyists dominate the President's policies, and presidential appointees openly seek to diminish environmental regulatory systems built up over the past 20 years. Interior Secretary James Watt proposes to sell off almost 100 national park segments. The OSHA Administrator announces that OSHA should be repealed. EPA and Interior officials implement indictable deregulatory sweetheart deals with

8. J. B. Flippen, The Nixon Administration, Politics, and the Environment, 316–317 (Ph.D. diss. submitted to University of Maryland, 1994), in R. J. Lazarus, The Making of Environmental Law (2004).

9. The Powell Memorandum was prepared by Lewis Powell for the U.S. Chamber of Commerce in 1971, shortly before he went onto the Supreme Court. In it he decried the creeping socialism dominating America, as exemplified by civil rights, consumerism, and environmentalism, and he called for business to begin funding academic and representational programs and foundations to counteract the 1960s "public-interest" ideologies in American society. The memorandum led directly to the founding of a number of copiously funded corporate initiatives — the creation of the Heritage Foundation and similar "free enterprise" think-tanks; industry-funded "public interest law firms" such as the Pacific Legal Foundation opposing environmentalism and bringing the anti-regulatory agenda into courts across the country; the Federalist Society instilling the business perspective on campuses; the "Wise Use" Movement in the rural West; the Law-and-Economics Movement funding faculty research critical of regulation; programs bringing pressure on textbooks to "restor[e] the balance…of fair and factual treatment of our system of government and our enterprise system"; coordinated efforts to appoint anti-regulatory federal judges; and a newly sophisticated approach to the media designed to build "confidence in business and free enterprise" and encourage media skepticism of critics of corporate management. See L. F. Powell, Jr., Confidential Memorandum: Attack on American Free Enterprise System (Aug. 23, 1971) (available on the coursebook's Web site).

industries they regulate. President Reagan famously lectures audiences that smog is caused by trees; as to redwood trees, "you've see one, you've seen 'em all." (Criminal prosecutions of environmental violators, however, paradoxically increase dramatically, though mostly of small-time scofflaws.) Many anti-environmental White House initiatives are ultimately curtailed by extensive criticism from media watchdogs and by criminal indictments of a number of Administration environmental officials.

1988–1994 — Consolidation. The Bush I and early Clinton Administrations consolidate environmental law and policy. Faced with public skepticism about Reagan environmental policy, Bush makes improved environmental protection part of his election campaign. In office, his Administration returns agency regulatory agendas back toward environmental protection. In the 1992 UNCED Conference in Rio, attended by 140 heads of state, the Bush I Administration is supportive of international environmental law "sustainability" principles. Thereafter, the Clinton Administration builds on the Bush agenda by proposing increased air and water protections, although policy accommodates more toward New Democrat trade and business principles than toward Vice President Gore's avowed environmental agenda. Industry lobbying becomes extremely sophisticated, avoiding the crude assaults launched during the Reagan years. "Responsible corporate partnership" seeking "balanced" environmental policy accommodations with regulatory government is a theme of business lobbying. Arguments for new approaches to regulation — for example, information disclosure mandates, cost-benefit and risk analysis, and market-enlisting strategies including trading schemes — offer real potential for improving the effectiveness of the prescriptive-standards systems. But these same approaches may undercut and avoid environmental protections, depending on who adopts them. Other regulatory reform arguments — to engineer a "devolution" of most environmental regulation back to the states, to narrow the terms of delegation of regulatory power to agencies, and to expand the basis for finding regulations to be invalid confiscatory takings of private property rights — are clearly aimed at undercutting regulatory effectiveness.

1994–2000. The second major assault on environmental laws is launched by the 104th "Contract With America" Congress. It ultimately fails, leaving a solidified structure of environmental laws. In 1994, led by Newt Gingrich, the Republican Party coordinates voter resentments against big government, continued economic doldrums, social engineering, and protection of minorities to take over both houses of Congress. Business lobbyists, coordinated as "Project Relief," an anti-regulatory coalition of 300+ industry lobbies, are invited to legislate wholesale changes. Congressional offices and the legislative process are opened up to direct drafting of statutes and amendments that aim to repeal or dilute more than a dozen federal statutes or return them back to the states. (The Reagan-era initiative had been more regulatory in focus.) But facing public outcry generated by media coverage, and with the stalwart defense of environmental statutes by GOP Senator John Chaffee of Rhode Island and environmental control technology industries, most attempts to undercut federal environmental statutes fail. By the late 1990s, environmental law appears to have become a political "third rail" — hit it, and the media and public opinion will zap you. Clinton Administration policy is able to restore momentum to moderate but incrementally substantial federal regulatory programs, with credible federal oversight of "cooperative federalism" state regulatory programs. EPA under Carol Browner and Interior under Bruce Babbitt, the two main federal environmental agencies, are brought to high levels of morale and enforcement credibility.

2000 to the present. The third broad-scale initiative against federal environmental laws is launched when the Bush II Administration takes the White House. Unlike the Reagan (1980s) and Contract With America (1994–1995) initiatives, those of the Bush II Administration influence both chambers of Congress for most of Bush's tenure. Bush campaigns as a moderate but, once in office, follows the lead of anti-regulatory neoconservatives in domestic regulatory policy as well as in foreign policy. Legal initiatives by Administration officials working closely with industrial lobbies — such as oil and gas, mining and timber, and heavy manufacturing — reflect a sophisticated, radical, coordinated agenda to reverse the trend of environmental protection laws in virtually every nook and cranny of the legal process. Administration officials advance this agenda in Congress and the agencies, through courtroom challenges (in cooperation with anti-regulatory state governments and industry), and by deftly managing the press.[10] The United States' international environmental cooperation comes to a virtual standstill with rejection of the Kyoto Protocol on Global Warming that is anathema to the oil and gas industry, and unilateral intransigence at the Rio-plus-10 conference in Johannesburg in 2002. Given the Iraqi war and official invocations of a predominating need to fight terrorism, media coverage and public reactions to the Administration's dramatic environmental and other national policy shifts are initially disjointed and quite muted. Opposition candidates fail to mobilize popular recognition of threats to the environment. A major attempt to weaken environmental protection policy appears to be underway, with its consequences uncertain. And while the environmental policy of the subsequent Administration is likely to be more protective, it is likewise hard to predict.

COMMENTARY & QUESTION

Layers of legal history. In the developmental history of environmental law, what different variables have shaped the changing profile of public environmental awareness and national policy? Here are a few that emerge from the preceding sketch history:

- Increasing knowledge of science and of the cumulative consequences of cost externalizing behaviors
- Shifts in the degree of industry influence on presidential policy, congressional affairs, and state governments
- Shifts in concepts of the social responsibility and civil obligations of individuals and corporations
- Shifts in the ability of citizens to sue in court and to intervene in agency proceedings

---

10. The general semantic strategy of the Administration, in which, for instance, the program to roll back air pollution controls would be called the "Clear Skies Initiative" and increased clearcutting of national forests would be called the "Healthy Forests Initiative," was revealed in a leaked memorandum. The document, the "Luntz Memorandum," written by consultant Frank Luntz, is available on the coursebook Web site.

- Accumulation of applicable legal doctrine, with the common law supplemented over time by public law statutes and regulation
- Oscillations in the relative organizational strength of business lobbies, individual governing figures, and citizen alliances and networks
- Shifts in the predominating level of government — federal versus state
- The degree to which the media actively investigates and covers public interest issues

All of these elements figure in the classic pollution case that follows.

Section 2. ALLIED CHEMICAL'S KEPONE PESTICIDE POLLUTION DISASTER

The Kepone incident in Hopewell, Virginia, a notorious case from the first generation of modern environmental law in the 1970s, set off a media avalanche that galvanized public and regulatory attention and subsequently helped push Congress into making major overhauls of federal environmental statutes. The case illustrates many of the classic determinants of industrial market behavior that made environmental law necessary in the first place. The Kepone disaster, however, differs from most major environmental incidents in that it did not result in reported court decisions telling the story of what had happened.[11] (Most court cases were settled by the company before they got to a verdict.) The facts presented here were gathered from a wide variety of field and archival sources. As you read the narrative, note the different kinds of serious negative externalities — to occupational health conditions within the factories; to air, water, and environmental quality outside the plants; and to ultimate consumers exposed to pesticides — and consider how the corporate and legal systems should or could have taken account of them.

Kepone: A Case Study[12]

Hopewell (population approximately 24,000) is a blue-collar industrial town located on the banks of the James River in southern Virginia. Naming itself "the Chemical Capital of the South," Hopewell actively recruited large chemical manufacturers to come to the area. Firestone,

---

11. Within the limited case law reported, some details about the case can be gleaned from a Tax Court decision rejecting Allied's attempt to write off an in-lieu-of-penalties contribution to an environmental trust fund. Allied-Signal v. Commissioner, 1992 Tax Ct. Memo LEXIS 204, 241 (T.C. 1992). Personal injury cases such as Gilbert v. Allied Chem., 411 F. Supp. 505 (E.D. Va. 1976, on a collateral motion), never resulted in a reported decision. A federal criminal prosecution resulted in a court-ordered criminal settlement. United States v. Allied Chem., 420 F. Supp. 122 (E.D. Va. 1976). A lawsuit filed by fishermen and seafood processors hurt by closure of the James River and Chesapeake Bay has interesting remedy issues, see Chapter 3, but gives little background on the case. Pruitt v. Allied Chem. Corp., 523 F. Supp. 975 (E.D. Va. 1981). An OSHA administrative penalty case focuses primarily on whether Moore and Hundtofte were personally liable for penalties. Moore, Hundtofte & LSP v. Occupational Safety & Health Rev. Comm'n, 591 F.2d 991 (4th Cir. 1979) (they were held personally liable). A major retrospective symposium on the *Kepone* incident appears in 29 U. Rich. L. Rev. 493 (1995). See Goldfarb, Kepone: A Case Study, 8 Envtl. L. 645 (1978), and Goldfarb, Changes in the Clean Water Act since Kepone, 29 U. Rich. L. Rev. 603 (1995); Zim, Allied Chemical's $20–Million Ordeal with Kepone, Fortune, Sept. 11, 1978, at 82; Stone, A Slap on the Wrist for the Kepone Mob, 22 Bus. & Soc'y Rev. 4-11 (1977), reprinted in Corporate Violence 121 (S. L. Hills ed., 1977); Mintz & Klaidman, Creative Settlement or Improper Deal?, Legal Times, May 11, 1992, at 1; and Facing a Time of Counter-Revolution — The Kepone Incident and a Review of First Principles, 29 U. Rich. L. Rev. 657 (1995).

12. This text is primarily drawn from Goldfarb, Kepone: A Case Study, 8 Envtl. L. 645 (1978), and incorporates material from Goldfarb, Changes in the Clean Water Act since Kepone, 29 U. Rich. L. Rev. 603 (1995).

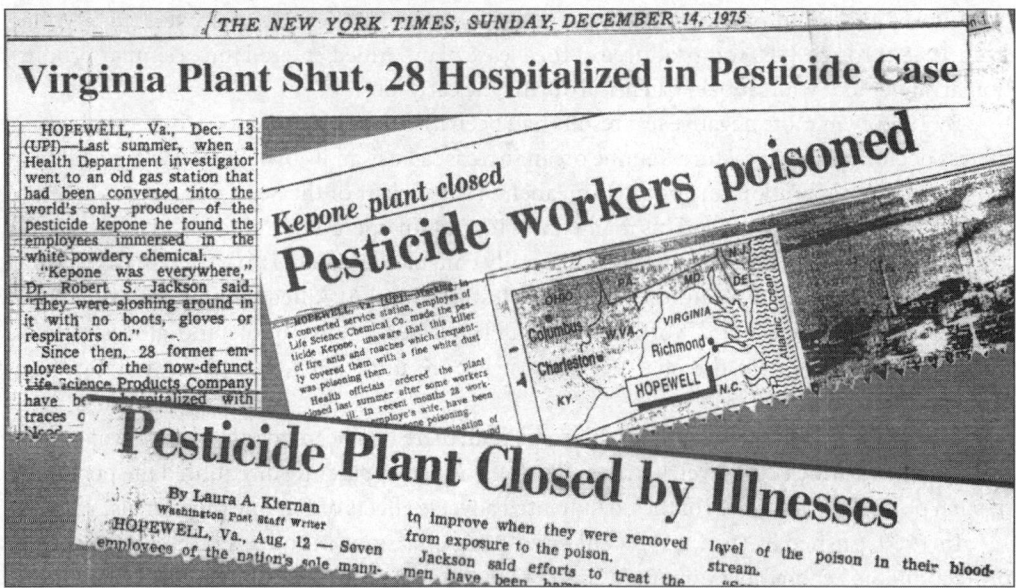

THE NEW YORK TIMES, SUNDAY, DECEMBER 14, 1975

Virginia Plant Shut, 28 Hospitalized in Pesticide Case

HOPEWELL, Va., Dec. 13 (UPI)—Last summer, when a Health Department investigator went to an old gas station that had been converted into the world's only producer of the pesticide kepone he found the employees immersed in the white powdery chemical.

"Kepone was everywhere," Dr. Robert S. Jackson said. "They were sloshing around in it with no boots, gloves or respirators on."

Since then, 28 former employees of the now-defunct Life Science Products Company have been hospitalized with traces o...

Kepone plant closed

Pesticide workers poisoned

Pesticide Plant Closed by Illnesses

By Laura A. Kiernan
Washington Post Staff Writer

HOPEWELL, Va., Aug. 12 — Seven employees of the nation's sole manu...

...to improve when they were removed from exposure to the poison.

Jackson said efforts to treat the men have been ham...

...level of the poison in their bloodstream.

Hercules, Continental Can, and Allied Chemical (now known as Allied-Signal), with $3 billion in annual sales in the 1970s, located some of their chemical plants in Hopewell.

Allied Chemical opened its Hopewell plant in 1928, the first industrial plant capable of utilizing atmospheric nitrogen for the production of ammonia and nitrogen fertilizer. Eventually Allied's Hopewell plant became the Hopewell "complex," which in 1975 was Hopewell's largest employer, with 4,000 workers.

The initial batch of 500 pounds of a pesticide named Kepone was produced by Allied in 1949. Two patents for the process were awarded to it in 1952.

Kepone is a chlorinated hydrocarbon pesticide, a chemical relative of DDT, Aldrin/Dieldrin, and Mirex (all of which have now been banned by the EPA). As such, Kepone is a contact poison, capable of being absorbed through the skin or cuticle; it is lipophilic (fat soluble), but insoluble in water; it is persistent in the environment; and it will bioaccumulate in the fatty tissues of the body. The exact mechanism by which chlorinated hydrocarbons kill target pests is uncertain. What is known is that they are nerve poisons, interfering with the transmission of electrical impulses along nerve channels.

Before moving to commercial production, Allied subjected Kepone to toxicity tests necessary in order to obtain registration under the federal pesticide laws for use in the USA.[13] The results of this research revealed Kepone to be highly toxic to all species tested: it caused cancer, liver damage, reproductive system failure, and inhibition of growth and muscular coordination in fish, mammals, and birds. Upon being presented with the test results, Allied voluntarily withdrew its petition to the Food and Drug Administration for the establishment of Kepone residue tolerances for agricultural products, so that the pesticide could only be sold for application outside the USA. Despite the unfavorable toxicity test results, Allied deemed Kepone ready for commercial production for overseas sales, and contracted with the Nease Chemical Company of State College, Pennsylvania, to produce it for them.

Allied did not consider Kepone to be a major pesticide. With less than $200,000 in annual sales over a 16 year period, Kepone production never exceeded 0.1 percent of America's total pesticide production. Kepone was primarily exported to South America to control the Banana

---

13. Registration was required under the precursor statute to the present Federal Insecticide, Fungicide, and Rodenticide Act (FIFRA) (now codified at 7 U.S.C. §§135–136 (1976)). [Eds.]

Root Borer and to Europe for use against potato beetles. The Kepone sold overseas by Allied from 1958 through 1960 was produced at the Nease plant. Allied entered into a similar production arrangement with Hooker Chemical during the early '60s.

By 1966 even more negative test results had been associated with Kepone, but Allied nevertheless decided to manufacture Kepone on an increased basis in its own Semi-Works facility in Hopewell. In preparation for production, an area supervisor of the Semi-Works was asked to develop a production manual. This manual was to contain operating and safety instructions for the production process. The supervisor naturally consulted available toxicity research results, and his recommended precautions reflect the test findings. At Allied, Kepone spills and dust were closely controlled, and workers wore safety glasses, rubber boots and gloves. Allied's Kepone operations were directed by William Moore until 1968, and thereafter by Virgil Hundtofte.

Prior to preparation of the production manual, there had been no recorded case of human exposure of Kepone to the level of acute poisoning. Allied apparently discounted the possibility of such poisoning, regardless of the documented adverse effects of Kepone on animals.

In 1969, pushed by the first rush of citizen organizations mobilizing for environmental protection, the Federal government resurrected the 1899 Refuse Act requirement that all industries discharging wastes into navigable waters must obtain permits from the U.S. Army Corps of Engineers.[14] The Allied complex at Hopewell had three pipes discharging directly into a stream called Gravelly Run, a tributary of the James River. One of these pipes originated at the Semi-Works where Kepone was manufactured. The Refuse Act permit application was discussed by Allied's plant managers and their assistants, who found themselves on the horns of a dilemma. Allied was discharging Kepone process wastes without treatment of any kind, and the installation of pollution control equipment would be quite expensive. Moreover there were plans to build a municipal sewage treatment plant which hopefully would treat the wastes of all industries in Hopewell, but the treatment plant would not be completed before 1975. What should Allied do during the interim period?

Allied decided to list the Semi-Works discharges as "temporary, to be discontinued within two years." The short form Refuse Act application for such "temporary discharges" did not require identification of the substance being dumped. Thus, neither Kepone nor two plastics products (TAIC and THEIC) also manufactured at the Semi-Works were listed by Allied on its Refuse Act application, even though Allied quite clearly did not intend to terminate production at Hopewell and had no plans to treat the wastes until publicly funded treatment would become available five or more years later.

In 1972 the Refuse Act permit program was taken over by EPA, the federal Environmental Protection Agency created in 1970, under the Federal Water Pollution Control Act Amendments of 1972 (FWPCA, soon to be renamed the Clean Water Act). The new permit program was called the National Pollutant Discharge Elimination System (NPDES), and its permits would all be issued in Washington D.C. until such time as EPA certified a state's regulatory program as adequate to exercise the federal law's "cooperative federalism" authority.[15] In Virginia the state government did not immediately move to win certification.

---

14. The Refuse Act is a subsection of the 1899 Rivers and Harbors Appropriation Act, 30 Stat. §1151 (1899), 33 U.S.C. §407, and is discussed in Chapter 20. In the late 1960s, Representative Henry Reuss of Wisconsin, prodded by early environmental activists, pressured the Corps to interpret industrial pollution as illegal "refuse." For a time thereafter the Refuse Act was the most effective federal water pollution law; it still has enforceable effect in a number of settings. [Eds.]

15. 33 U.S.C. §§1251–1376 (Supp. V 1973); §1342(a)(1) (Supp. V 1975). The federal CWA is studied in Chapter 12. [Eds.]

So in mid-1972 EPA requested data on the nature, volume, and strength of Allied's discharges, and again Allied faced a dilemma about complying. One of Allied's plant managers prepared an option memorandum outlining three strategies which Allied might follow: (1) to do nothing and hope for a lack of enforcement by EPA; (2) to divert the Semi-Works effluent to another outfall pipe for which a permit had been obtained; or (3) to tell EPA about the Kepone discharges and try to strike a deal, making minor improvements to the Semi-Works effluent to "buy time" until completion of the municipal treatment plant. Ultimately Allied chose a fourth option, submitting sketchy data to the federal government, as in 1970, not revealing the composition of the raw Kepone and plastics waste discharges and describing them only as "unmetered, unsampled, temporary outfalls."

In 1973 Allied underwent a corporate reorganization, during which control of the Semi-Works facility was transferred from the Agricultural Division to the Plastics Division. The transfer took place in expectation of the Agriculture Division's impending move to new facilities in Baton Rouge, Louisiana, an area eagerly competing for chemical plants. Virgil Hundtofte, plant manager of Allied's Agricultural Division at Hopewell, and William Moore, Research Director, made plans to retire from the company rather than relocate. (Hundtofte had been with Allied in Hopewell since 1965, and Moore since 1948.)

One effect of the reorganization was a reorientation of production priorities among the products manufactured at the Semi-Works. Kepone production had decreased steadily, but THEIC plastic, which had been manufactured in small quantities for eighteen years, suddenly found a lucrative market calling for a doubling of production. THEIC and Kepone shared certain production equipment, and with the surge in demand for THEIC a decision was made in 1973 to "toll" Kepone production. Tolling is a common arrangement in the chemical industry whereby another company performs processing work for a fee or "toll" and then returns the final product to the originating company for subsequent sale on the open market. The keynote of a tolling arrangement is that during the processing period legal title to the materials and product remains in the supplier, in this case Allied. (More recently, many U.S. companies have entered into similar tolling agreements with "maquiladora" companies they set up across the border in Mexico to take advantage of looser environmental and labor standards.)

In January, 1973, when the decision to toll Kepone was divulged, William Moore saw his opportunity to remain in Virginia and continue in the Kepone manufacturing business. He immediately contacted Hundtofte, who had recently resigned from Allied and gone to work for a fuel oil distributor. Moore and Hundtofte agreed to form a corporation and bid for the Kepone tolling contract. On November 9, 1973, Life Science Products Company (LSP) was incorporated under the laws of the Commonwealth of Virginia. Moore and Hundtofte were the only shareholders, directors, and officers of LSP. Less than a month later, the tolling agreement between Allied and LSP was signed. Allied had solicited bids from Hooker Chemical, Nease Chemical, Velsicol and LSP, but LSP's bid was by far the lowest: 54 cents per pound for 500,000 pounds of Kepone. Nease Chemical (which had manufactured Kepone for Allied from 1958 through 1960) declined to bid, but responded that if it chose to bid on the contract, just disposing of the waste properly would cost Nease 30 cents per pound. Hooker Chemical bid $3.00 per pound.

LSP began producing Kepone for Allied in mid-1973. The details of the tolling agreement are important because the question of Allied's responsibility for LSP's illegal acts affects most subsequent issues of liability. The contract provided that Allied would supply — at its own expense — all of the raw materials for Kepone production, with the title to remain in Allied. Within certain broad limits, Allied would determine the monthly production rate of Kepone, which would be packed in Allied containers and transported in Allied trucks. Allied also agreed to pay LSP's taxes, other than corporate income taxes. LSP was to receive between 32 and 38

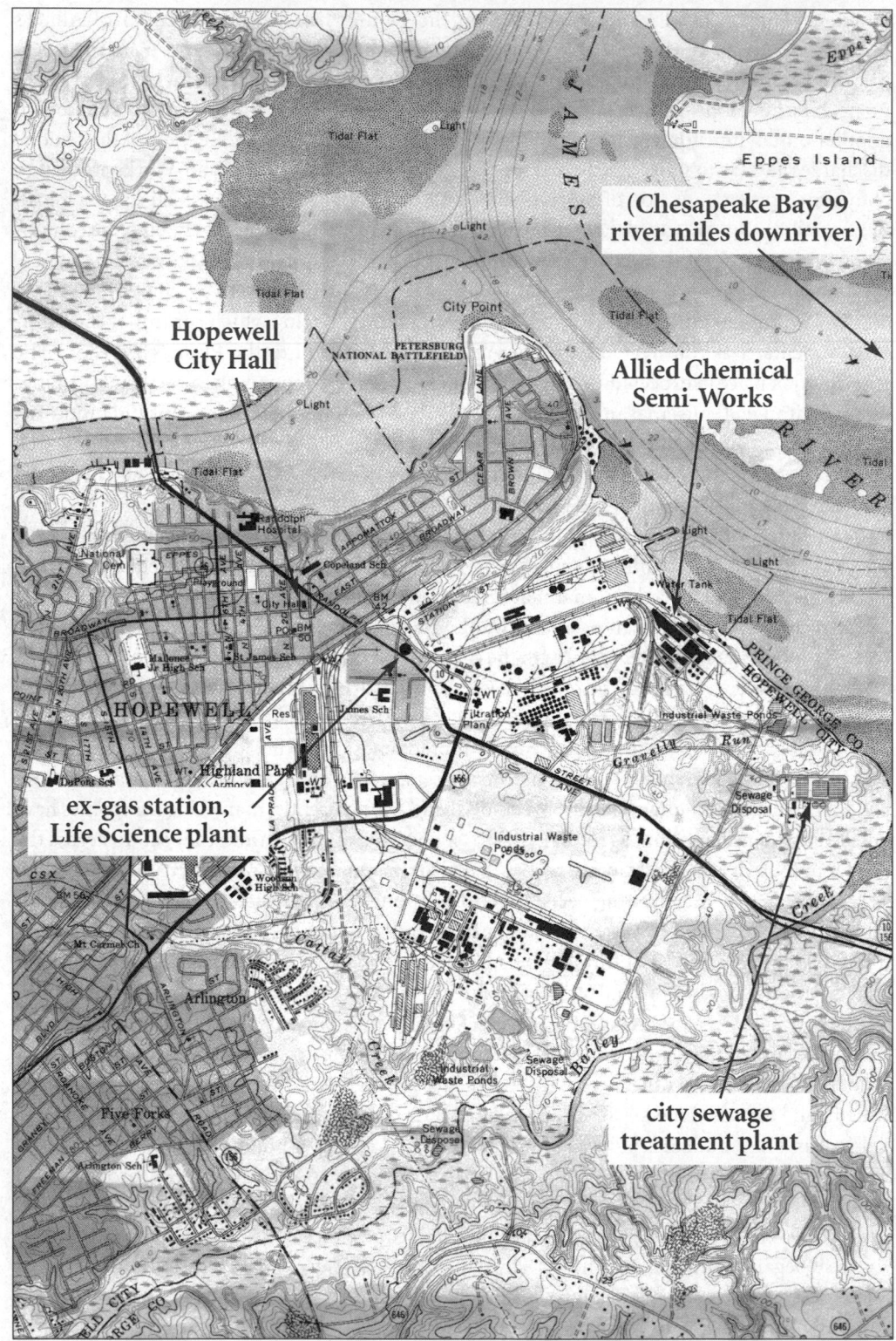

ADAPTED FROM USGS MAP NO. 37077-C3-TF-024 HOPEWELL QUADRANGLE

FIGURE 2-1
Schematic overview of the Allied Chemical Semi-Works and Life Science Products Co. in Hopewell, Virginia, site of the Kepone pesticide waste contamination controversy.

cents per pound for 650,000 pounds or more of Kepone. Through a capital surcharge arrangement, Allied was to pay for all of LSP's approved capital expenditures, whether for production or pollution control, except for land and building. If LSP was closed for pollution violations during the first year of the contract, Allied had the option to purchase LSP's assets for $25,000. And if the contract was terminated by either party for any reason, LSP agreed to refrain from producing Kepone for anyone else.

The relationship between Allied and LSP was only partially defined by the tolling agreement. Moore and Hundtofte further promised Allied that they would not dispose of their shares in LSP without Allied's consent. Moreover, Allied assisted LSP in many ways — in obtaining equipment and loans from outside sources (including the mortgage to buy the abandoned gas station in which Kepone would be made), in meeting temporary cash deficits, in augmenting fuel supplies during the oil embargo, and in attaining greater efficiency by the use of Allied facilities. Most importantly, LSP's effluent was sampled and analyzed by Allied personnel after Virginia began to order such testing in October 1974. Before that LSP had "tested" its effluent only by a visual check — if the effluent was cloudy, the presence of suspended Kepone was indicated.

Allied officials regularly toured the LSP plant, and were also informed by mail of the waste disposal problems which LSP faced almost from its inception. Allied had discharged the residues of its Kepone production process directly into Gravelly Run Brook which flows into the James River. LSP at first discharged into a disposal pit on Allied's property, as well as tank-trucking some wastes to the Hopewell landfill. As the possibility increased of inspection by either the state or federal agency, or both, it was decided that LSP would discharge into the Hopewell sewer system, despite the fact that the treatment plant was still unfinished. By this means LSP would avoid having to apply for an NPDES permit to discharge through a pipe "point source." ("Indirect dischargers" into POTWs — publicly-owned treatment works — are not considered point sources and so don't need a NPDES permit.[16]) Having made the decision to "plug in" to the Hopewell system, LSP contacted C.L. Jones, Director of Hopewell's Department of Public Works, for permission. At the time, Hopewell possessed only a "primary" level waste treatment plant — a series of filters and settling tanks without any biological or chemical treatment other than disinfection and sludge digestion. Such a rudimentary system would not degrade Kepone, but would merely divide Kepone effluent between outfall pipe and sludge. Jones, who had been Plant Manager of Allied's Semi-Works prior to Hundtofte, recommended to Hopewell's City Manager that LSP be permitted to discharge. Permission was granted in November of 1973. (LSP was asked by Hopewell to meet a pretreatment standard of three parts per million of Kepone.) Thus, LSP became the only industry in Hopewell allowed to discharge into the municipal sewerage system. Allied Chemical's attorneys participated in these negotiations and agreed to pay for the pollution control equipment that Life Science would require in order to meet the pretreatment standard.

Problems developed as soon as LSP began diverting Kepone wastes into Hopewell's treatment plant. In October 1974 a state inspector discovered that the sludge digester at the plant was inoperative, and his investigation revealed LSP to be the source of contamination. Prior to the plant breakdown, the State was apparently unaware that Kepone was being discharged into the Hopewell system because Hopewell's application for an NPDES permit for its treatment plant (filed a month before plug-in permission was granted to LSP) made no mention of any industrial discharge into the municipal system.[17] LSP's discharges were not halted when the State

---

16. 33 U.S.C. §1317(b) (Supp. V 1975), as amended by CWA of 1977. Pub. L. No. 95-217, 33 U.S.C. §1317(b); 49 C.F.R. §125.4(a) (1977).

17. The Virginia State Water Control Board was by this time administering the NPDES program pending formal delegation by EPA, under 33 U.S.C. §1342(b). [Eds.]

brought the situation to the attention of LSP and Hopewell officials, even though the pretreatment standard was being violated. Instead, a "study" was commenced to determine a "safe" effluent limit for Kepone.

In September 1974 an LSP employee complained to the Occupational Safety and Health Administration (OSHA) of excessive pesticide fumes and dust in the LSP plant, but based on a phone call to Hundtofte, with no on-site inspection, OSHA found insufficient evidence to support the charge and dismissed it.

In March 1975 the EPA accepted the Commonwealth of Virginia's application for certification to take over by delegation the role of issuing and enforcing NPDES permits governing the discharge of pollutants into navigable waters within the Commonwealth. In June of 1975, the state set a pretreatment standard for LSP (.5 parts per billion) that was weaker than EPA wished but stricter than prior standards. EPA, which had been informed of the situation, agreed to this compromise. In order to meet this standard LSP was supposed to further pretreat its wastes and hold its discharges in "equalization" tanks until such time as discharge would not violate the pretreatment standard (i.e. to even-out the flow). Allied had participated in the negotiations among LSP, Hopewell, Virginia, and EPA, and Allied opted to pay for the necessary pollution control equipment. Allied and LSP then began to discuss the capital costs of expanding Kepone production to 2,500,000 pounds per year in order to meet an increasing demand in the European market. (From the inception of LSP, Allied had constantly requested increased Kepone production.) However, even after the new equipment was installed, the pretreatment standard was violated in 19 out of 21 samplings, though local and state officials appear to have taken no action on the violations.

On July 7, 1975, as LSP was preparing for increased Kepone production, one of its employees visited Dr. Chou, a Hopewell internist, complaining of tremors, weight loss, quickened pulse rate, unusual eye movements, and a tender, enlarged liver. Such symptoms were not unusual among LSP employees, but by now were generally tolerated as a necessary price to be paid for the $5.00 per hour wage they received. Although about twenty physicians had been consulted during the sixteen months of LSP's existence, only Dr. Chou suggested a connection between the ailments and the workplace environment. After questioning his patient and taking a blood sample, Dr. Chou forwarded the sample to the Center for Disease Control in Atlanta, where an analysis for Kepone could be performed. The tests disclosed that the blood sample contained 7.5 parts per million of Kepone, an astounding concentration to be found in human blood. The federal doctors then contacted the Virginia State Epidemiologist, Dr. Robert Jackson, who immediately asked for a meeting with Hundtofte and Moore.[18]

It quickly became clear that Kepone pollution was poisoning workers at the site and contaminating their families with dust brought home in workers' clothing and hair. As a chlorinated hydrocarbon, Kepone can be absorbed through the skin as well as breathed in or swallowed. As it accumulates in the body it generates neurological symptoms, including eye tremors, slurred speech, hand tremors, and serious liver dysfunction, and apparently was the cause of a number of workers' sterility.

When State Epidemiologist Jackson toured the plant he was appalled: Conditions within the LSP workplace were "incredible,…might have shocked Charles Dickens," "Kepone dust was

---

18. Meetings had previously been requested by the Virginia State Department of Labor and Industry, but LSP had been successful in postponing them. Only one Federal official, an EPA pesticide inspector, visited LSP before 1973; but he was not authorized to enter the production area. EPA jurisdiction over air and water pollution had been delegated to state officials. At various times representatives of the Virginia Air Pollution Control Board, Water Pollution Control Board, and State Health Department had all visited LSP, but they were not responsible for inspecting LSP's working conditions.

everywhere,…flying through the air…saturating the workers' clothing, getting…into sandwiches they munched…."[19] Workers were "virtually swimming in the stuff," were not required to wear protective equipment even when it was available, and no warning signs were posted. Seven out of ten production workers present had "the shakes" so severely that they required immediate hospitalization.[20] One worker, Del White, like many others, now reported that he began to develop tremors within a month of the time he started at LSP. "I thought it was just me, but then I noticed everyone was shaking." He had gone to Moore and Hundtofte and "they assured me that there was nothing in Kepone which could hurt humans…. When they told us it wouldn't hurt us, I went back to work." If Kepone had been dangerous, workers reported, they assumed government health officials would require precautions.

On July 25, 1975, LSP voluntarily ended its operations under threat of a closure order by the Virginia Department of Health. In January 1976, the National Cancer Institute released a report implicating Kepone as a possible carcinogen in humans. Investigations revealed seventy-five cases of acute Kepone poisoning among LSP workers and high levels of Kepone in the blood of some of their family members. Some workers showed dramatically lowered sperm counts and low sperm motility.

Outside the plant there was found to be massive contamination of air, soil, and especially water, with the Kepone contamination plume extending 100 miles downstream in the James River. Shellfish and finfish in Chesapeake Bay had dangerous levels of toxic residue. As a result, the State of Virginia closed the James and portions of Chesapeake Bay to fishing. (Parts of the river and bay remained closed to fishing until 1980.) EPA reported Kepone particulates in the atmosphere as far away as Richmond. Serious levels of Kepone contaminated the Life Science plant, a neighboring building, the soil at the plant site, a section of the Hopewell landfill, and a lagoon adjacent to the Hopewell waste treatment facility. Life Science had declared insolvency as soon as the plant closed, and the officers announced the firm was financially incapable of remedying any consequences of the Kepone contamination.

The *Kepone* case thrust a dramatic new message into the national consciousness. For a dozen years the new environmental movement had been echoing Rachel Carson's *Silent Spring* warning that chemicals in the environment threatened the nation's soils and wildlife. Citizen lawsuits had been filed challenging DDT and other chlorinated hydrocarbon pesticides for their effects on populations of birds like eagles and brown pelicans.[21] The chemical industry had mounted a wide-ranging counter-attack, slighting Carson's scientific credentials, spreading rumors about her personal lifestyle, and characterizing chemical manufacturing as a benign economic enterprise being criticized by an elitist bunch of birdwatcher extremists. Middle America remained skeptical about tree-huggers' warnings about harms to nature. But now suddenly the *Kepone* story, coming in a week of summer news-lull, carried the heartbreaking

---

19. See Harvard Business School, "Allied Chemical Corporation Case" 5 (1979, written by Joseph L. Bodaracco). Interestingly, the HBS case study essentially ignores the role of Allied managers in the Kepone affair, treating contamination as the result of isolated renegade acts of the Life Sciences company, which was identified only as a small Allied "supplier," thereby finessing the point that the tolling contract was a carefully considered corporate externalization by Allied itself.

20. In late 1974, the federal Occupational Safety and Health Agency (OSHA) had received a complaint from an LSP worker who claimed to have been fired for refusing to work in the Kepone-laden work setting. OSHA informed the worker that since he was no longer an employee he had no standing to complain under the Act. Miller, Occupational Safety and Health Act, Environmental Law Handbook 517 (17th Ed., 2003). OSHA did send a written inquiry to LSP, but after receiving a mollifying response closed the file without making an on-site inspection.

21. The citizens' pesticide lawsuits, beginning in Long Island, NY, launched the Environmental Defense Fund, a pioneering public interest environmental law organization which now has global activities. See Yannacone v. Dennison, 285 N.Y.S.2d 476 (N.Y. App. 1967) (subsequently settled out of court), EDF v. Hardin, 428 F.2d 1093 (D.C. Cir. 1970) (inducing cancellation proceedings), EDF, Inc. v. Ruckelshaus, 142 U.S. App. D.C. 74 (1971).

images — of *humans*, ordinary people, suffering neurological shaking and sterility from exposures to chlorinated hydrocarbon pesticide dust — to TV sets across the nation. The story broadened national skepticism about the human consequences of chemical exposures and about the corporate executives who managed the nation's industrial production. In covering the story the local and national press consistently laid the blame for the *Kepone* incident on Allied. Some news reports and editorials described Life Science as a front for Allied's Kepone manufacture, while others ignored Life Science's role altogether, laying full responsibility directly upon Allied. On December 14, 1975, the CBS program "60 Minutes" aired damaging interviews with Allied officials, tricking them into acknowledging their internal decisions, and sharply criticized the company for creating the *Kepone* incident.

After councilling with industry colleagues about how to address the horrific adverse publicity arising from the *Kepone* incident, Allied planned a major advertising campaign that would attempt to portray it as a good and concerned corporate citizen. Facing the prospect of significant litigation, however, as well as persistent negative stories on Allied's role in the *Kepone* incident, Allied postponed the advertising campaign. Allied's board of directors took a high level of interest in senior management's responses to the *Kepone* incident and to the negative publicity and litigation that Allied faced. At its February 1976 meeting, the board was informed that Allied's outside auditors had identified the *Kepone* incident as having a potentially significant impact on Allied's financial statements. The auditors' opinion with respect to Allied's financial statements for 1976 was "qualified" because of the inability to predict what additional costs from pending lawsuits and other exposure Allied would incur as a result of the *Kepone* incident.

What about law and the legal repercussions of the *Kepone* story? Under the common law, hundreds of personal injury and other damage claims were filed against Allied. Tort claims by Life Science employees, their families, and others aggregated approximately $85 million. Approximately 400 fishermen, alleging that their livelihood was impaired by the closing of the James River and Chesapeake Bay, filed tort claims against Allied aggregating $24 million. In addition, a class action suit was brought against Allied on behalf of some 10,000 fishermen and other members of the Bay-area seafood industry, claiming economic damages of $25 billion.

In terms of public law, OSHA, the Occupational Health and Safety Administration, assessed an administrative fine of $16,500 against LSP for hazards to its workers, which LSP could not pay.[22] As to water pollution, the Virginia Water Control Board brought suit directly against Allied for $3.5 million in civil penalties under the terms of both state and federal statutes. The Commonwealth of Virginia, the City of Hopewell, the EPA, the Army Corps of Engineers, and other governmental agencies involved in the investigation of the *Kepone* incident and its subsequent cleanup also requested reimbursement from Allied for expenses incurred or expected to be incurred in the cleanup. In the aggregate, these cleanup expenses could have exceeded $20 million.

Although the Ford Administration's EPA deferred to the state's civil penalties lawsuit, it decided to file federal criminal charges in the case. In early 1976 the United States Attorney for the Northern District of Virginia obtained grand jury criminal indictments against Allied, LSP, Hundtofte, Moore, and the City of Hopewell under the federal water pollution act and the Refuse Act. In the summer of 1976, Judge Robert Mehrige presided over a criminal trial given so much passionate public attention that it had to be moved to West Virginia. [The *Kepone* criminal case is discussed in Chapter 20.]

---

22. It appears that Hundtofte and Moore then were personally assessed the penalties. See Moore, Hundtofte & LSP v. Occupational Safety and Health Review Commission, 591 F.2d 991 (4th Cir. 1979).

Testimony and graphic presentations from the *Kepone* debacle were featured in a series of 1976 congressional hearings, leading to passage of two toxics statutes in 1976, RCRA and ToSCA, and the Clean Water Act of 1977 (CWA) establishing the fundamental structure of current federal water pollution law.

Responding to the continuing international sales of stockpiled Kepone and similar hazardous substances, President Jimmy Carter issued an Executive Order prohibiting the overseas export of unregistered chemicals and pharmaceuticals found to be too dangerous to be approved for use in the United States.[23]

COMMENTARY & QUESTIONS

1. **Why did the *Kepone* disaster happen?** How did this dramatic widespread poisoning — of workers and their families, neighbors, water, wildlife, air, and soil — come to pass? Was Allied a rogue corporation or just following the business norms of the time? The chronology of the *Kepone* story in the years following Allied's 1949 invention of the compound involved dozens of conscious management decisions. It seems clear that the corporate players were not ignorant of Kepone's dangers and the hazardous externalities that Allied and Life Science's operations imposed on the workplace, the surrounding environment, and human exposures including consumers overseas. To what extent did the corporate and legal systems incline them toward ignoring those externalized costs?

For Allied's executives in the 1970s, passing the costs of toxic wastes into the environment was probably a normal, economically rational, matter-of-fact business decision that just went sour in this particular case because Life Science's pollution became a dramatic public story. But in ignoring the foreseeable costs to human health, water quality, fisheries resources, and the like, were Allied and LSP being shortsighted, or evil? Most industries, at least before the mid-1970s, regarded pollution as a standard industrial by-product. "Pollution is the price of progress." "That smoke smells like money." "Out of sight, out of mind." Still today, the basic logic of cost externalization — the inherent incentive to avoid paying for anything that doesn't return net private benefits — means that, in the absence of some public reckoning system such as reliable environmental law accounting or negative publicity in the press, industry still tries to pass much of its waste disposal costs and consequences into the public commons.

Wouldn't the fear of legal liability change the corporate executives' calculus? In the *Kepone* era, the prospect of legal accountability was quite unlikely. Who could be expected to keep a close eye on Kepone production? The federal agencies? The local city government? The Commonwealth of Virginia? The working poor of Hopewell? Effective public law requires that appropriate standards, regulatory structures, and

---

23. 46 Fed. Reg. 4659 (Jan. 19, 1981). The first Federal Register order published in the name of President Ronald Reagan was a one-sentence Executive Order reversing the Carter ban on export of unregisterable substances: "By the authority vested in me as President by the Constitution of the United States of America, and in order to ensure that the Export Administration Act of 1979 is implemented with the minimum regulatory burden, Executive Order No. 12264 of January 15, 1981, entitled 'On Federal Policy Regarding the Export of Banned or Significantly Restricted Substances,' is hereby revoked." /s/ R. Reagan, 02/17/1981. 46 Fed. Reg. 12,943 (Feb. 19, 1981). By 1982, 30% of the nation's chemical pesticide exports were of substances unregisterable in the United States.

enforcement policy are in place and operating. The common law does not readily apply before actual injuries occur. In the *Kepone* case, no one acted until a foreign-born outsider doctor blew the whistle. This suggests that then, as now, (1) the practicalities involved in enforcing law, including institutional follow-through, are as vital as the substantive standards on the books; and (2) the realistic prospect of legal accountability is important to the cost-externalizing calculus of business decisionmakers and can vary with the political winds.

2. **Attempts to reform corporate power.** Plainly, not all environmental regulation of corporate behavior is good. Equally plainly, modern corporate structures still externalize social costs and resist attempts to apply civic controls. It is interesting to note a growing revisionist discussion contemplating minor or major overthrows of the corporation as a dominant entity in modern society. This initiative includes attempts to force more accurate accounting of public costs, to require tighter interpretations of corporate charters, and to change the constitutional status of corporations, which since 1886 have been allowed to claim most of the constitutionally protected rights of natural persons.[24] See Estes, The Public Cost of Private Corporations, 6 Advances Pub. Int. Acct. 329–351 (1995); and articles prepared by the Program on Corporations, Law, and Democracy (POCLAD) as part of the Ending Corporate Dominance Alliance, available at http://www.poclad.org. While these initiatives may be regarded as quixotic, note that they have had increasing populist echoes in election campaign and talk show rhetoric, from both left and right. Their appeal may grow even more in the wake of the vast corporate accounting scandals such as that involving Enron uncovered in the early 2000s.

3. **Allied's "tolling" agreement with LSP.** Do you see how the tolling agreement for LSP to produce Kepone for Allied produced mutual benefits? As with the *maquiladora* factories along the U.S.-Mexico border, corporations arrange such "independent subcontracting" relationships not only for production cost-cutting but also to limit potential liability for environmental, labor, and other legal consequences.

4. **A state tendency toward laxity?** In *Kepone*, the state's administrative inattention to pollution problems contributed to the scope and severity of contamination. The laxity of the Virginia agencies reflects the interstate competition for industry and jobs that originally prompted Hopewell to advertise itself as "the Chemical Capital of the South." That pressure to compete for jobs undercuts the vigilance of local and state officials. The race-to-the-bottom continues to be a powerful competitive tendency within the political marketplace at all levels, nibbling away at state regulations as well as the federal laws that attempt to provide a national floor. In most areas of the field, one continues to

---

24. One of the most important Supreme Court decisions shaping American society was also one of the most casual. In Santa Clara County v. Southern Pac. R.R., 118 U.S. 394 (1886), a railroad wished to challenge its property tax assessments on equal protection grounds. To do so it had to assert that a corporation could demand the same civil rights as a natural person. Although the parties had prepared extensive arguments on this issue — "[whether] Corporations are persons within the meaning of the Fourteenth Amendment to the Constitution of the United States" — before the Supreme Court argument could begin, Chief Justice Waite announced: "The court does not wish to hear argument on the question whether the provision in the Fourteenth Amendment to the Constitution, which forbids a State to deny to any person within its jurisdiction the equal protection of the laws, applies to these corporations. We are all of opinion that it does." 118 U.S. at 394–395. Thus occurred a major milestone in the evolution of constitutional doctrine, consolidating the presence of marketplace structures within the public law.

see arguments of federalism and devolution to the states as a recurring theme of industrial politics.

5. **The legal repercussions of the *Kepone* disaster.** As noted in the narrative, one of the major legal consequences of the *Kepone* debacle was congressional action. The legislative debates leading to the 1976 toxics statutes and the 1977 CWA repeatedly invoked the *Kepone* disaster, and four major provisions in the new water act derived from specific reactions against Allied's Hopewell contamination.[25] Regulatory responses were evident too, as federal and state agencies were prompted by the *Kepone* case's notoriety to tighten reporting and enforcement practices against industries around the nation under state and federal pollution laws.

In terms of civil litigation, the sum total of Allied's ultimate liability is not known because of confidential sealed settlements. We do know how much the state and local governments collected: $5,250,000 to settle all of the claims of the Commonwealth of Virginia and the City of Hopewell for Kepone-related costs that these governmental bodies had incurred, as well as administrative penalties assessed by the Virginia Water Control Board. Embarrassed by the *Kepone* debacle, EPA and the Virginia agency also entered into administrative negotiations with Allied to force the cleanup of contaminated areas. During the latter half of 1975, Allied Chemical voluntarily decontaminated the Life Science plant site at a cost of close to a million dollars. (There were no federal civil recoveries, the federal toxic cleanup statutes not yet having become law.)

Allied also sponsored health tests for former Life Science workers and conducted intensive research on methods of retrieving Kepone from the James River and incinerating Kepone residuals. In early 1976, Allied Chemical donated $88,000 to the Medical College of Virginia for monitoring and treating former Life Science employees who had been severely affected by Kepone. (As a result of these studies, the college's medical team perfected a technique for accelerating elimination of Kepone from the human body, thereby speeding the recovery of those persons who had suffered from Kepone poisoning.)

As to civil litigation filed by individual plaintiffs for personal injuries, little was officially reported about the cases or the amounts of damages paid out to private victims of the toxic exposures. After several cases had proceeded through initial stages of tort litigation,[26] in which the most effective cause of action surprisingly turned out to be product liability-based claims for failure to warn (see Figure 2-2, excerpts from plaintiffs' Complaint in Civ. Action 75-0469-R), Allied adopted a policy of settling all suits out of court, each with a strict settlement stipulation that no information ever be provided on the amount of payments.[27] According to one insider, the personal injury

25. See Goldfarb, Changes in the Clean Water Act since Kepone, 29 U. Rich. L. Rev. 603, 612–615 (1995), describing Kepone's explicit role in Congress's "mid-course corrections" of water pollution law.

26. A chutzpah common law action filed by LSP's president, William Moore, against Allied alleging "intentional infliction of emotional distress" and "failure to warn" for not telling him of Kepone's dangers unsurprisingly failed. Moore v. Allied, 480 F. Supp. 364, 480 F. Supp. 377 (E.D. Va. 1979).

27. In most legal settlement agreements, a standard provision decrees that no details of the settlement are ever to be revealed on pain of forfeiting the cash; some also require plaintiff's attorney to refrain from such representations in the future. The facts of settled cases, however, including investigative research, could be important in warning other injured persons and helping to pursue legal remedies. As a matter of social policy, should such

settlements totaled about $5 million. The only civil damage action to go to verdict, a suit filed by ten classes of fishermen and other users of Chesapeake Bay who suffered economic losses, resulted in damages awarded to two of the plaintiff classes likewise in the neighborhood of $5 million. (That court decision, Pruitt v. Allied Chemical, is noted in Chapter 3.)

In a separate criminal trial before Judge Robert Merhige, Moore and Hundtofte were both convicted of conspiracy to furnish false information to the federal government, conspiracy relating to LSP's discharge of Kepone, and 79 counts under the FWPCA for Kepone discharges into the Hopewell sewer system, for which they were fined $25,000 each. Hopewell was fined $10,000 because, as Judge Merhige stated, "heavy fines would serve no purpose, [taking] money from one pocket of the taxpayer to another." Allied pleaded nolo contendere, was convicted of 940 counts of violating the federal water act, and was fined $13.3 million. (Following up on an indirect suggestion by Judge Merhige, Allied then proposed to set up an $8 million fund for a Virginia Environmental Endowment, a nonprofit corporation that would perform research and implement programs to mitigate the environmental effects of Kepone. As a result, Allied's penalty was reduced to $5 million. Allied's attempt to write off this $8 million as a nonpenal ordinary business expense deduction on its taxes was denied by the Internal Revenue Service.[28]) No one got jail time in the *Kepone* incident.[29]

For the *Kepone* event as a whole, Allied's total outlay was reported by a company attorney to have approached $30 million.

To what extent did Allied have to account for the *totality* of the costs its decisions had caused? What about natural resources damages? The judge noted in the *Pruitt* fisheries case that "the costs...of Kepone pollution...were borne most directly by the *wildlife* of Chesapeake Bay," but no natural resources damages or restoration orders were ever issued in a Kepone case. Are there other legal accountings that could have occurred in this process? The natural resources damages section of Chapter 3 and the public trust materials of Chapter 22 explore those possibilities.

6. **Is *Kepone* a tragedy of the commons?** To what extent does the *Kepone* story parallel Garrett Hardin's tragedy of the commons (see Chapter 1)? The waters of the James River and Chesapeake Bay and the air in Hopewell are indeed commons in the sense that they are resources that are used by all and are owned by none, and these commons undoubtedly were polluted by the actions of Allied and Life Science. *Kepone* and other pollution and resource depletion situations typically do reflect the *behavioral* aspects of Hardin's cow pasture tragedy — the entrepreneurial tendency of each individual actor to pass diffuse harms into the commons to avoid facing their full cost. Pollution cases

---

information be open? See Twomey, Breaking the Silence: Examining the Enforceability of Private Settlements Which Conceal Environmental Hazards, 4 New Eng. Envtl. L.F. 109 (1997); Gibeaut, Secret Justice, A.B.A. J., April 1998, at 50 (reporter fined $500,000 for revealing $36 million settlement amount in pollution class action suit against Conoco Inc.).

28. Allied-Signal v. Commissioner, 1992 Tax Ct. Memo LEXIS 204, 241 (T.C. 1992).

29. Early in the trial, Judge Merhige commented "nobody is going to jail in this case," thereby dampening the prosecutors' attempts to persuade some defendants to turn state's evidence. The criminal case was Crim. Act. No. 76-0129-R, U.S. District Court for the Eastern District of Virginia, Richmond Div. (1977, unreported).

```
                        UNITED STATES DISTRICT COURT
                        EASTERN DISTRICT OF VIRGINIA
                            Richmond Division
DALE F. GILBERT, DELBERT R. WHITE,
EVERETTE L. MESSER, NICKEY F. SHOWN,
JAMES O. ROGERS, JR., JOHN EDWARD COX,        CIVIL ACTION NO. CA-75-0469-R
MELVIN L. RUSSELL, ROBERT W. NEWMAN,               FILED : Sep 19 1973
FRANK M. ARRIGO
             Plaintiffs,
          v.
ALLIED CHEMICAL CORPORATION,
a New York corporation,...
                  Defendants
```

<u>COUNT 1</u>   <u>COMPLAINT</u>

   1. Plaintiffs are all citizens of the Commonwealth of Virginia. Defendant, Allied Chemical Corporation, hereinafter referred to as "Allied", is a New York corporation and has its principal place of business in the State of New Jersey;... The matter in controversy..., exclusive of interest and costs, exceeds the sum of Ten Thousand Dollars ($10,000.00).

   2. **That defendants...beginning in about March, 1974, furnished, sold or supplied certain chemicals to Life Science Products Company of Hopewell, Virginia...which were used by Life Science in the manufacture or production of a chemical substance sold under the Allied trade name of Kepone; that defendants knew or should have known that the said chemicals are imminently and inherently dangerous to life or property, yet defendants negligently supplied said chemicals to Life Science without notice or warning of the defect or danger to the plaintiffs who were users of said chemicals; that defendants failed to exercise a high degree of care and vigilance in dealing with these dangerous chemicals; that it was reasonably foreseeable to the defendants that their failure to warn, explain, instruct and apprise the plaintiffs of the dangers involved would result in serious injuries to them.**

   3. **As a proximate result of the defendants' negligent failure to warn and/or to adequately warn the plaintiffs of the dangers involved, the plaintiffs have suffered severe and permanent injuries** to their health, bodies and minds, including, but not limited to, tremors, opisclonus, memory deficits, pleuritic and joint pains, liver damage, cataracts, and injuries to their reproductive systems, and did suffer and will suffer in the future, loses due to being prevented from following their usual course of affairs and the expenditure of large <u>sums of money</u> for medical treatment in an effort to be cured....

<u>COUNT 2</u>...

...WHEREFOR, plaintiffs demand judgment against Allied...in the sums opposite their respective names, together with costs and interest from date of injury:

Gilbert, Three Million Dollars	$3,000,000.00
White, Three Million Dollars	$3,000,000.00
Messer, Two Million Five Hundred Thousand Dollars	$2,500,000.00
Shown, Three Million Dollars	$3,000,000.00
Rogers, Two Million Five Hundred Thousand Dollars	$2,500,000.00
Cox, Two Million Three Hundred Thousand Dollars	$2,300,000.00
Price, Two Million Three Hundred Thousand Dollars	$2,300,000.00
Russell, Two Million Three Hundred Thousand Dollars	$2,300,000.00
Newman, Two Million Dollars	$2,000,000.00
Arrigo, Two Million Dollars	$2,000,000.00

TRIAL BY JURY IS DEMANDED.   By:_____, Counsel

                              Edward W. Taylor, James D. Hundley
                              HUNDLEY, TAYLOR & GLASS
                              P.O. Box 518, Richmond, Virginia 23204

FIGURE 2-2

Excerpts from a personal injury Complaint filed in the aftermath of the Kepone incident. Three other counts added to the factual allegations of Count 1 by including claims for negligent supervision of Life Sciences, strict liability personal injury, and strict liability failure to warn. All such private complaints were withdrawn prior to trial on the basis of off-the-record nondisclosure settlements.

likewise illustrate the strong practical pressures in the competitive marketplace to continue doing so. The commons metaphor emphasizes basic drives in human nature that produce externalized costs and demonstrates tensions between the management dynamics of privately owned enterprises and the optimal management needed for common resources.

But in other ways the Kepone on the banks of the James River is quite different from Hardin's cow pasture. In Hardin's pasture metaphor, the degradation of the resource — destruction of the grassland — would ultimately force each of the herdsmen to face the practical consequences of his actions. So far as we know, however, neither Kepone factory ever faced internal production problems from self-polluted air or water supplies, so the "comes-back-around" feature of Hardin's tragedy was missing.[30] Likewise, in many pollution settings, no physical feedback enforces a practical reckoning upon the actors. Unlike overfishing a marine commons, which destroys the industry itself, the physical consequences of chemical pollution do not usually come back through natural physical processes to burden the polluters. Water polluting factories such as Allied are less likely to locate on enclosed lakes where their pollution is drawn back into their own intake pipes than on rivers where their dumped wastes flow away downstream. Given the different positions of parties in relation to the common, and the disparity of power they represent, if there is to be an accounting it probably will have to be imposed by the artifices of law, or the press, or politics. The resulting political context is examined later in this chapter.

7. *Kepone* **and the role of lawyers.** Many of the critical corporate decisions in the *Kepone* case, as in most business enterprises, undoubtedly involved corporate attorneys. Allied's attorneys worked on the patents, franchise and tolling agreements, withdrawn domestic pesticide application, export permits, occupational health regulations, disposal practices, Refuse Act and NPDES applications, and other critical actions. Could and should they have raised the hazards issues?

Environmental cases continually present true moral dilemmas and tough questions of legal ethics. What is the attorney's role and duty upon discovering a significant environmental hazard created by a client that the client refuses to report or correct?

> Despite the threat of harm, the rules of ethics bind you to remain silent if the danger arises from negligence rather than a criminal act.... Which duty should predominate — the duty to maintain the confidences of the client or the duty to avert a danger to the community?... The applicable rule of ethics [Rule 1.6 of the ABA Model Rules of Professional Conduct in its currently diluted form] appears to allow an attorney to remain silent despite significant danger to the public or an individual.... Society has a critical interest in the balance struck between these conflicting duties and in encouraging lawyers to assess environmental dangers rather than blindly adhering to an ethic of silence.[31] Russell, Cries and Whispers: Environmental Hazards, Model Rule 1.6, and the Attorney's Conflicting Duties to Clients and Others, 72 Wash. L. Rev. 409, 411–415 (1997).

---

30. Prior to the revelation of Kepone contamination, probably the only self-pollution cost Allied faced was whatever minimal worker health costs it had to absorb through workers' sick pay or company doctors' fees.

31. In her extended analysis of this dilemma, Professor Russell also notes that there is a growing countervailing risk of tort liability to victims for attorneys who fail to warn nonclients of such dangers.

For an attorney to raise such sensitive issues is not necessarily conducive to job security, at least not until the risks of huge future liabilities that may follow are acknowledged.

8. *Kepone* **and environmental justice.** Looking at the map of Hopewell (see Figure 2-1), it perhaps isn't surprising to learn that the residential areas most directly exposed to air and water toxics from the plants that produced Kepone were poor minority neighborhoods. "Poor people and people of color bear the brunt of environmental dangers, from pesticides to air pollution to toxics to occupational hazards. At the same time, poor people and people of color also have the fewest resources to cope with these dangers, legally, medically or politically."[32] The Hopewell neighbors appear to have had only an absorptive role in the story.

Issues of environmental justice — the way race, low income, and political disenfranchisement are reflected in environmental impacts — appear in a number of places in this coursebook. The text does not regularly note the income and political character of plaintiff groups or their racial composition. Yet it is increasingly clear that many environmental burdens are especially likely to be visited upon communities of color or communities marked by low-level incomes and limited political clout. The burdens range from loss of critical urban amenities and quality of life issues to rat bites and pollution exposure effects.[33] In the ongoing discourse about environmental justice (or "environmental racism"), it is toxics exposure that has provided the focusing images of the phenomenon: It seems that many hazardous substance facilities are sited where the neighboring communities are poor or of color, or both.

In the years following the *Kepone* case, many people began to see a pattern in the distribution of toxic harms and the characteristics of the people who were most often exposed to them. The correlation was first highlighted in Charles Lee's 1987 study "Toxic Wastes and Race in the United States," sponsored by the United Church of Christ Commission for Racial Justice, followed by Dr. Robert Bullard's *Dumping in Dixie. Race, Class & Environmental Quality* (1990). In these and subsequent studies, racial minorities' and low-income groups' risk of exposure to environmental hazards appeared to be both quantitatively and qualitatively greater than that of the general public.

Recognition of disproportionate exposure patterns has produced a number of serious attempts to mobilize the tools of environmental law to rectify the phenomenon of

---

32. Cole, Empowerment as a Key to Environmental Protection: The Need for Environmental Poverty Law, 19 Ecology L.Q. 619 (1992). See S. Bonorris, Ed., Environmental Justice For All: A Fifty-State Survey of Legislation, Policies and Initiatives (2003). Hill & Targ, The Link Between Protecting Natural Resources and the Issue of Environmental Justice, 28 B.C. Envtl. Aff. L. Rev. 1 (2000).

33. Among the current catalog of environmental justice settings are these:
   - The physical location of hazardous-waste treatment, storage, and disposal facilities
   - Eminent domain of low-income and/or minority communities, as in the *Poletown* and *Overton Park* cases
   - The effects of pesticides on migrant workers in the California grape-growing regions
   - Disproportionate environmental exportation of toxic and other wastes to Third World countries for disposal
   - Discrimination against indigenous peoples of an area, as in the James Bay HydroQuebec Power Project
   - The frequency of heavy industrial facilities located in or near low-income/racial minority neighborhoods
   - Accusations of racism within the environmental movement, including predominately white, middle and upper class membership in environmental organizations; hiring biases within environmental agencies and organizations; and claims that the Environmental Movement is a movement out of touch with the people it should be working with and for on a daily basis

environmental injustice. Lawsuits have attempted to prove intentional discrimination on the basis of race and poverty in pollution management decisions, tracking an equal protection analysis. Whether because of the times or the circumstances, however, this approach has not been highly successful in court,[34] leading to other approaches, including attempts to use Title VI of the 1964 Civil Rights Act.[35]

Environmental justice issues are often quite ambiguous, however. In most cases, the decision to locate hazardous waste activities is not clearly motivated by invidious discriminatory intent. Land in poor areas is cheaper and effective political opposition less likely, so straightforward economic and political marketplace considerations favor such siting. Professor Vicki Been has argued that even if the original decision for siting toxic facilities is totally free of discrimination, with the site placed in a well-off white area, it is altogether likely that normal market effects will soon shift the surrounding neighborhood toward a population of color and lower income.[36] Siting thus is only one problem of many.

In addition to increasingly active environmental citizens groups,[37] environmental justice has received federal government attention, including President Clinton's 1994 Executive Order 12,898, "Federal Actions to Address Environmental Justice in Minority Populations and Low-Income Populations." The Clinton EPA issued a guidance document as well as Title VI regulations to permit the integration of environmental justice issues into the agency's implementation of a variety of statutes. This focus was continued in the Bush II Administration by Christine Todd Whitman while she was EPA Administrator.[38] Addressing the distributional inequities in different communities' differing levels of environmental quality would seem to be a civic and social necessity for a society attempting to achieve long-term sustainability.

9. **A first-generation regulatory setting.** The Allied *Kepone* case illustrates a relatively uncomplicated stage in the modern history of environmental regulation. Initially, at the time Allied began manufacturing Kepone in Hopewell in 1966, it was regulated only under the common law and the State of Virginia's water pollution statute, which was a permissive, 1940s-style law that apparently imposed no significant constraint on the

---

34. See East Bibb Twiggs Neighborhood Ass'n v. Macon-Bibb County Planning & Zoning Comm'n, 706 F. Supp. 880 (M.D. Ga. 1989); Bean v. Southwestern Waste Mgmt. Corp., 482 F. Supp. 673 (S.D. Tex. 1979).

35. See Chester Residents v. Pennsylvania DEP, 132 F.3d 925 (3d Cir. 1997). The Title VI attempts appear to have been brought to a halt by Justice Scalia in Alexander v. Sandoval, 532 U.S. 275 (2001).

36. Been, Locally Undesirable Land Uses in Minority Neighborhoods: Disproportionate Siting or Market Dynamics?, 103 Yale L.J. 1383 (1994).

37. Environmental justice activism started in local citizen groups, some of which have allied with law school programs, including Alternatives for Community and Environment (ACE) at Boston College Law School, and environmental justice clinics at Berkeley and Georgetown. Pointed criticism of established national environmental groups as lily-white, middle class enterprises have prompted serious soul-searching and extensive efforts to integrate more minority and low-income individuals and groups into the mainstream environmental organizations and alliances that built the successes of environmentalism in the United States: the "Group of Ten" (the Sierra Club, Earth Justice Legal Defense Fund, Friends of the Earth, Wilderness Society, National Audubon Society, Natural Resources Defense Council, Environmental Defense Fund, National Wildlife Federation, Izaak Walton League, and National Parks and Conservation Association).

38. An excellent periodical resource on issues of environmental justice is Race, Poverty & the Environment, a quarterly newsletter published by the California Rural Legal Assistance Foundation and the Earth Island Institute Urban Habitat Program, 436 14th Street, Oakland, CA 94612. Information about Race, Poverty & the Environment is available at http://urbanhabitat.org/Publications.htm.

industry's behavior until it was too late. The federal Refuse Act, an 1890s criminal law that coincidentally fit the needs of environmentalists, rediscovered in the late 1960s, appears to have been the first federal environmental statute to force significant modification in corporate behavior.[39] The Refuse Act provisions were relatively primitive, however, requiring only a simple permit from the U.S. Army Corps of Engineers, and the statutory standards for issuing permits were unclear.

When Congress passed the comprehensively amended FWPCA[40] in 1972, reacting to the race-to-the-bottom, it required each industrial discharge "point source" to obtain a NPDES permit set at levels based on Best Available Technology (BAT) standards. (Under federal water law, because of extensive lobbying from the farm states, "nonpoint sources" such as agricultural runoff and erosion comprise huge volumes of pollution but are not required to have permits, and are thus largely unregulated.) EPA's issuance of point source standards began in 1972 and dragged on for years. Until a state received "cooperative federalism" certification to apply the NPDES program, EPA also had the job of applying its defined pollution standards through federal permits for every point source — every pipe, drain, and drainage channel — in the state. Most states, including Virginia, eventually sought EPA approval to take over implementation of the federal law, often apparently in order to moderate the strictness anticipated under the federal program. Under the provisions of the FWPCA, citizens can bring enforcement actions against violations,[41] but in the *Kepone* case, no citizen actions were filed. In subsequent years, however, citizen enforcement became a major force in shaping and applying pollution standards. At first it was not clear how workable and credible the federal water program would be. Within a few years, in part because of citizen enforcement, it became an accepted regulatory reality.

Without question, the first generation of active federal environmental regulation during the *Kepone* years looked haphazard and unsophisticated. That soon changed. The first generation of any statute's implementation looks different from the later stages of that law's evolution. Each regulatory statute begins its life as an unfinished product. Unclear initially how it will work in practice, it evolves over time according to the quality of the enforcement, compliance, political support, and resistance it encounters.

B. BEYOND *KEPONE*: TRACKING SEVERAL DECADES OF ENVIRONMENTAL LAW DEVELOPMENT

The *Kepone* incident captured a moment early in the development of the statutory public law of environmental protection. Although a half-dozen or more significant statutes had been put on the books by 1975, they were then only in their first hesitant

---

39. The strict, simple terms of the Refuse Act's criminal provisions are noted in Chapter 20.

40. 33 U.S.C. §1251ff. The new law set federal minimum standards without which, it is thought, an intense interstate competition for jobs and revenues powerfully induces states to lower their environmental standards. States that enforce environmental protections tend to lose their industries to states that require fewer restrictions. Pollution, moreover, is an interstate problem. More than 20 states receive more than 50% of their water pollution from other states, and an additional 15 states receive between 25 and 50% from other states.

41. See citizen enforcement of FWPCA and CWA §515, noted further in Chapters 7 and 21.

stages of implementation. The extent, seriousness, and complexity of statutory systems regulating pollution have grown dramatically in the decades after *Kepone* and Love Canal.

The CWA, for one example, has continued to expand beyond the 1977 amendments prompted by the *Kepone* scare. Amendments in 1987 tightened toxic pollutant controls, industrial stormwater management, industrial pretreatment, sewage sludge disposal, "placed-based" environmental protection (also called "ecosystem management," "watershed management," or "bioregionalism," which the Act applied with special emphasis on Chesapeake Bay), and expanded and strengthened the CWA's criminal enforcement mechanisms. Judges now possess stronger criminal sanctions with which to punish knowing violators of the CWA: "knowing endangerment" that "places another person in imminent danger of death or serious bodily injury" can lead to fines of $250,000 or 15 years imprisonment, doubled for second convictions. 33 U.S.C. §1319.

Kepone also reflected an early period in the development of corporate responses to the new legal restraints on pollution. Allied Chemical's illegal behavior was flagrant, its assimilation of the new legal norms primitive. In some ways, its conduct seems to come from a bygone era. It is important to realize, however, that wrongful corporate conduct of the Allied Chemical variety still occurs. Consider the case of workers in a uranium facility in Paducah, Kentucky, exposed into the 1990s to plutonium, without their knowledge or consent, while the owners of the facility knew of the hazards.[42] Or consider industry decisions to allow widespread asbestos exposure as noted in the next chapter. The examples could be multiplied, and they do not come only from bygone eras. Nevertheless, it is also true that many companies have significantly modified their behavior in response to the modern environmental laws. Yet they have not simply accepted stringent environmental restrictions as a way of life. Rather, their efforts to resist often appear in earlier stages of the legal process, resulting in active lobbying of legislators to reject new (or dilute old) environmental laws, aggressive pressuring of agency regulators to do the same, and sophisticated think-tank and trade association networks aimed, often, at undermining the case for stringent environmental protection of any kind. Many of the proposals for reform introduced later in this chapter grew out of these networks.

Section 1. A MODERN STATUTORY ARRAY

Federal Statutes. One way to track the evolution of environmental statutes is to see how many now apply. If, for example, Allied Chemical decided today to construct a factory to manufacture a twenty-first-century pesticide (hypothetically, perhaps, NeoPone), it would trigger consideration under virtually all 17 of the federal statutes

---

42. In January 2000, Bill Richardson, Secretary of Energy, accepted after decades of denials that thousands of workers at Paducah "had been exposed to radiation and chemicals that produced cancer and early death." Most of the victims displayed symptoms similar to Gulf War veterans, particularly chronic fatigue and joint pain. The workers had been handling uranium contaminated with plutonium and neptunium. Paducah was designed to handle uranium, not plutonium, which is about 100,000 times more radioactive per gram. See Warrick, Study Finds More Hazards at Paducah, Discord Greets Draft Report on Uranium Workers' Radiation Exposure, Wash. Post, Oct. 5, 2000, at A03.

listed below. Most of these statutes also have a state or local counterpart regulation. Consider this list as a short primer on current statutes, and, looking at the map of Allied's Hopewell location (see Figure 2-1), consider how each might indeed apply to a new Allied Semi-Works. (For a fuller description of these and other significant state and federal environmental statutes and their operation, see the Statutory Capsule Appendix in the Reference Materials at the back of this coursebook.)

1. **CWA:** The federal Clean Water Act,[43] administered by EPA. As already seen, CWA is a federal-state partnership where EPA sets permissible levels of discharge for different industrial categories based on the performance of BAT; states with approved laws and programs issue NPDES permits based on the federal standards, backed up by on-site ambient water quality requirements; and state enforcement of permits is backed up by the federal EPA. Criminal prosecutions under the CWA and other laws, with jail time, have increased from zero in the days of *Kepone*. Lying on pollution reports, as well as "knowing endangerment," can send an executive to jail.[44]

2. **CWA §404:** The federal dredge-and-fill regulation program also falls under CWA, restricting the elimination of wetlands; EPA and the U.S. Army Corps of Engineers also require permits for installing in-stream structures if Allied installs sewerage outfalls.

3. **CAA:** The federal Clean Air Act,[45] administered by EPA. Like the CWA, CAA is a federal-state partnership, has special provisions regulating hazardous air pollutants, and holds new air pollution sources to the cleanliness levels of BAT. The basic CAA structure requires enforcement of state implementation plans (SIPs) to prevent overall ambient levels of pollution from exceeding federal "primary standards" set according to harm-based safety criteria.

4. **FFDCA:** The Federal Food, Drug, and Cosmetics Act,[46] administered by EPA and the Department of Health and Human Services. This statute provides, among others, protections for food quality by setting permissible tolerances for chemical residues such as pesticides in food products and by monitoring compliance. This obviously would be a significant regulatory constraint for registration of NeoPone for use on foods to be consumed in the United States.

5. **EPCRA:** The federal Emergency Planning and Community Right-to-Know Act,[47] passed in 1986 after the Bhopal disaster, administered by EPA. EPCRA requires mandatory public reporting by industry of the nature and characteristics of certain hazardous materials and requires states to establish statewide and local emergency response plans. Hopewell's city government would receive this information, and regular TRIs (toxic release inventory reports) would have to be filed.

6. **RCRA:** The federal Resource Conservation and Recovery Act,[48] a 1976 update of the Solid Waste Disposal Act (SWDA), administered by EPA. RCRA regulates waste disposal in general and certain hazardous wastes (via Subtitle C) in particular,

---

43. 33 U.S.C. §1251 (1972, 1977).

44. It was under these enhanced federal charges that a corporate executive for Smithfield Foods was sentenced on eight counts of destroying records and rendering false information about discharges into the Chesapeake Bay watershed, serving a 30-month prison term starting in January 1997. United States v. Smithfield Foods, 965 F. Supp. 769; 972 F. Supp. 338 (E.D. Va. 1997).

45. 42 U.S.C. §§7521 et seq. (1970).

46. 21 U.S.C. §§301 et seq. (1954, as amended).

47. 42 U.S.C. §§1101 et seq. (1986).

48. 42 U.S.C. §§6901 et seq. (1976).

tracking the wastes (not the original chemicals) beginning with their generation and ending with their treatment, storage, or disposal (somewhat imprecisely dubbed "cradle to grave" regulation). RCRA also authorizes EPA to take corrective actions to prevent or remedy contamination; special provisions apply to leaking underground storage tanks and medical wastes.

7. **CERCLA:** The 1980 federal Comprehensive Environmental Response, Compensation, and Liability Act (or "Superfund" Act),[49] administered by EPA. The statute provides for EPA investigations and supervised cleanups of hazardous contaminated sites, paid for by the parties who own or contaminated the sites, with backup funding from a federal Superfund combining taxes from chemical production, penalties, and taxpayer dollars.

8. **SDWA:** The federal Safe Drinking Water Act,[50] administered by EPA. It sets water quality standards for drinking water suppliers and protection of underground drinking water sources and regulates the deep well injection of wastes, a common industrial practice of pumping chemicals into old wells and drill holes as a method of disposal.

9. **OSHA:** The federal Occupational Safety and Health Act,[51] administered by the Occupational Health and Safety Administration (likewise called OSHA). OSHA addresses safety conditions within industrial workplaces and other work settings. The agency sets general industry standards and monitors and enforces them through agency inspections.

10. **CZMA:** The federal Coastal Zone Management Act,[52] administered by the National Oceanic and Atmospheric Administration (NOAA) in the Department of Commerce. CZMA encourages comprehensive state planning and siting controls in coastal and tidal regions. (A close look at the Hopewell map in Figure 2-1 reveals that the James River is still "tidal" 100 miles inland.) Federal reinforcement is provided through the requirement that federal actions be "consistent" with state standards.

11. **NEPA:** The National Environmental Policy Act,[53] a generic procedural statute administered by the President's Council on Environmental Quality. NEPA does not stipulate any pollution control measures, nor any direct regulation of any private industry, but levies the significant, litigatable requirement that all federal agencies must prepare an environmental impact statement (EIS) before taking any "major federal action significantly affecting the human environment." Some agency permits, such as permits for Allied's installation of outfall pipes under CWA §404, thus probably would have to go through the EIS process.

12. **PPA:** The 1990 federal Pollution Prevention Act,[54] administered by EPA. This statute is mainly an exhortation to industry to reduce, recycle, or prevent pollution through internal planning, design, and technology adaptations. EPA has the power, however, to impose PPA requirements as permit conditions or as part of violation penalty orders.

---

49. 42 U.S.C. §§9601 et seq. (1980), as amended by the Superfund Amendments and Reauthorization Act of 1986 (SARA).
50. 42 U.S.C. §3007 et seq. (1974, as amended).
51. 29 U.S.C. §§651 et seq. (1970).
52. 16 U.S.C. §1451 et seq. (1970).
53. 42 U.S.C. §§4321 et seq. (1970).
54. 42 U.S.C. §§13101 et seq. (1990).

13. **ESA:** The federal Endangered Species Act,[55] administered by the U.S. Department of Interior Fish and Wildlife Service (FWS) and NOAA. ESA prohibits harms to endangered and threatened species; if a listed species is present in an ecosystem, pollution discharge permits and construction projects can be forced to go through significant modification procedures or be blocked. Harms caused by private actions are subject to criminal penalties.

14. **ToSCA:** The 1976 federal Toxic Substances Control Act,[56] administered by EPA. This "market access" regulation authorizes the agency to require manufacturers to test chemical substances for hazards to human health and the environment before they are permitted to be manufactured and sold. Failure of EPA to act to restrict use of a substance acts like a grant of a permit, although with a new pesticide like NeoPone, EPA is unlikely to fail to scrutinize.

15. **FIFRA:** The 1975 Federal Insecticide, Fungicide, and Rodenticide Act,[57] administered by EPA. FIFRA requires persons distributing, selling, offering, or receiving any pesticide to register the poison with EPA after testing for "unreasonable risks to humans and the environment, taking into account the economic, social, and environmental costs and benefits of the pesticide's intended use"; the "market access" registration, once granted with practicable tolerance levels, is akin to a perpetual license to market the product, though registrations can be canceled or suspended.

16. **HMTA:** The 1980 federal Hazardous Materials Transportation Act,[58] administered by the U.S. Department of Transportation. This statute provides for extensive regulation of hazardous substances in transit, with requirements for spill control and prevention, and central reporting in the event of spills of toxic or hazardous substances, and invites concurrent state regulation.

17. **The hazardous materials export controls statute:** One provision of a larger consumer safety statute,[59] this statute requires that a party intending to export a banned hazardous substance notify the Consumer Product Safety Commission at least 30 days prior to exportation. The Commission notifies the government of the country to which the substance is to be exported and informs it of the reasons for which the substance was banned. Regulation, if any, is then solely the responsibility of the receiving country.

At least a dozen additional federal statutes are commonly encountered in environmental practice,[60] including a long list of natural resources management statutes, statutes limiting ocean dumping and export of misbranded products, laws protecting parks and marine sanctuaries, historic preservation regulations, transportation planning requirements, the market disclosure requirements of the SEC and the FTC, significant IRS tax code provisions, and so on.

State and Local Regulatory Systems. To the above federal laws one must add their state corollaries as well as an array of state laws in areas not covered by federal statutes: land use controls and siting, groundwater protection, recycling and noise regulations, landfill regulations beyond toxics and industrial wastes, toxic product standards, land

---

55. 16 U.S.C. §§1531 et seq. (1973, as amended).

56. 15 U.S.C. §§2601 et seq. (1976).

57. 7 U.S.C. §§136 et seq. (1973).

58. 49 U.S.C. §§1801 et seq. (1980).

59. 15 U.S.C. §1273 (1993).

60. For a chronological index of federal statutes in the environmental field promulgated since the late 1800s, see the Chronological Appendix of Statutes on the coursebook Web site.

sale disclosure laws, and more.[61] There is a lot of law here. The following chart shows the kind of state and local permits that might be required in setting up a plant like Allied's Semi-Works today:

AGENCY:	REGULATORY REQUIREMENT:
State air, water, natural resources	[FEDERAL-ANALOG PERMITS: More than a dozen permits commissions directly analogous to the federal regulatory systems noted above]
plus	
State Department of Health	• Approval of sanitary sewer system
State Department of Natural Resources	• Permit for dredging and filling as required on site
	• Permit for construction in zone close to major bodies of water
	• Soil erosion and sedimentation permit
	• Inland streams alteration permit
State Water Resources Commission	• Permit for alteration of channels or floodplains, or any drains
	• Permit for use of water during plant construction, operation, and sewage treatment (in addition to state water pollution control, or NPDES permit)
State Air Pollution Commission	• Permit for boilers and diesel generators
State Police	• Approval for above-ground storage of flammable liquids
State Department of Aeronautics	• Permit for construction of high smokestacks
State Department of Labor	• Permit for boiler installation
	• Permit for any elevators involved in a plant
State Public Utilities Commission	• Permit for construction of high voltage electric transmission lines
	• Permission for connection to high voltage electric transmission lines
	• Railroad spur construction, alteration, and connection to existing railroad spurs
	• Permits for building grade crossings across railroad tracks
	• Construction permit for operation of electrical substation
State Department of Highways	• Permit for alteration of highway access
County Health Commission	• Permit for alteration of any drains
	• Approval of sewer system
County Road Commission	• Permit for altering or temporary closing of highways for construction
County, and Local Municipality	• Zoning permits
Local Township	• Building, electrical, and plumbing permits
Local Township	• Permits for water use and sewerage

---

61. A number of these state laws are noted in the Statutory Capsule Appendix in the Reference Materials at the back of this coursebook, including California's Proposition 65 toxic product labeling law, New Jersey's land transfer disclosure requirements, and waste minimization laws. As for the local level of government, the rapid growth of environmental law in the local realm is chronicled in J. Nolon, New Ground: The Advent of Local Environmental Law (2003).

COMMENTARY & QUESTIONS

1. **A biodiversity of public law statutes.** The federal and state environmental agency structures and their regulations and guidelines have proliferated since the early 1970s into a body of public law that is now far more complex and voluminous than the Internal Revenue Code and its rules. Regulatory standards and court enforcement today, moreover, are not preoccupied only with preventing human disasters but look also at the diffused ecological effects of pollution. A modern pollution case similar to *Kepone* would likely mention effects on vegetation and wildlife as well as effects on humans because today the linkage is clear: Disruptions of the natural economy can have serious effects within the societal economy as well.[62]

But do not make the mistake of thinking that this parade of statutes follows a common design. Each statute has its own story. Some statutes are purely procedural, some have substantive teeth, some represent a strong initial consensus, some are ragtag pragmatic compromises that pleased no one, some embody a cynical legislative decision to create an empty false impression of action, and so on.[63] Each is typically hatched into law by legislators in response to the public's short-term focused concern about some perceived disaster, then developed over time through a vagarious process of opportunistic administrative and judicial action. The passage of a bill is like the launching of an unguided missile. Only after it has been flying for a while, buffeted this way and that by the forces that continue to act upon it, does it become clearer where it is going and what it may do, with what impact.

Upon promulgation each of these statutes possesses whatever words the legislatures happen to have grafted into them, and they rarely have a clear, immediate, automatic effect. In virtually all cases we have to wait for agency and judicial interpretation. In most statutes like those listed above, the first step in shaping the statute's implementation is an agency's internal planning about how the law is to be implemented, then usually the issuance of facilitational regulations in the Federal Register or the state equivalent (normally by notice-and-comment rulemaking, in which a proposed rule is published, attracting a cascade of comments from friends and foes, then proceeding with revisions to final publication in the Federal Register). Every significant statute and its regulations inevitably go to court to be further interpreted, enforced, or attacked by someone. The buzzing political contexts that constantly encircle each law from its conception as a bill until it reaches its end (or achieves a stable niche, having become established consensus wisdom, a sort of emeritus statutory stud standing out to pasture) guarantee that each statute's development is incremental, fractionalized and usually fractious, and idiosyncratically different from others.

In Europe, these statutes probably would be collected into one large environmental law "code," a general law drafted by a sober, rational expert law commission, with uniform

---

62. See, for example, United States v. Smithfield Packing Co., 965 F. Supp. 769, 972 F. Supp. 338 (E.D. Va. 1997), a water pollution case on a river leading into the Chesapeake Bay, like the *Kepone* setting.

63. For example, it could be argued that the PPA can be categorized as purely procedural, the CAA as containing both substantive and procedural requirements, the Wilderness Act as a strong (though narrow) consensus, the Superfund Act as a mishmash that was no one's idea of a good bill, and NEPA as a law that was quite clearly designed to be a ringing but unenforceable statement of a toothless idealistic policy.

standard-setting and enforcement procedures, and specialized subparts reserved for the unique features of each area. This is America, however, so our statutes remain a menagerie of different laws reflecting the diversity and happenstance of events that created them and enforced by a variety of agencies in a variety of different ways.

2. **Getting a handle on statutes: statutory "taxonomy."** Practicing attorneys usually develop extensive checklists of existing statutes and regulations to help them orient their analyses of a major project or program, like the construction of a new chemical factory. In addition, given the different kinds of statute and regulatory systems, in order to develop practical understanding of each relevant statute, it is useful to learn to think about them like biologists, who analyze different creatures according to taxonomy categories based on their structural elements and essential design.

A variety of discernible statutory taxonomies can be identified in these regulatory systems. Some statutes focus on the threshold of the problem area such as the initial point of market access, others on the production process itself, and still others at the back end of production with waste disposal regulation. Some require permits; others require inspections, reactive enforcement, or just planning procedures. Some set regulatory standards based on BAT; others base standards on harm to humans and nature, on politically desired technology-forcing, on participant negotiations, or on industry self-regulatory standards. Some statutes avoid command regulation in favor of the carrot of subsidies or market-enlisting procedures such as pollution credit trading. Given the complexity of modern environmental public law, this book's Part Three teaches the "taxonomy" approach, exploring different statutes from the perspective of these descriptive designs and elements in order to organize, simplify, and deepen the regulatory analysis.

3. **The standard default regulatory design — the comprehensive "prescriptive-federal-standards" model.** Although every statute is different, in the most basic terms most major modern regulatory systems use a standard conceptual design. As illustrated best by the big federal pollution control statutes and regulations studied in Chapters 11 and 12, the model can be described as setting up comprehensive "prescriptive-federal-standards" regulatory programs. According to this default model, the federal government dictates the minimum nationwide standards that must be met, standards are administered through federal permits obtained from federal agencies or delegated state agencies for each regulated source, and standards enforcement comes from agencies or citizens. The federal standards and the means for enforcing them must be sufficiently precise and mandatory that they are evenly and effectively enforced across the country despite differences in local political cultures or persistent efforts by corporations and states that seek to soften or avoid them.

These prescriptive-federal-standards programs began in the early 1970s with the CAA and CWA and were naturally echoed in basic terms in the toxics and other regulatory systems that followed. As sophisticated science issues and enforcement practicalities required more and more administrative detail, however, and industry lawyers demanded more and more clarity about technical requirements, these regulatory systems became extremely complex administrative apparatuses subject to criticism as insensitive to local nuance and insufficiently agile to cope with complex situations. The pejorative term "command-and-control" has been quite successfully stuck onto the prescriptive-federal-standards programs by the industrial lobby, evoking an image of heavy-handed totalitarian diktats issuing from Washington. On the other hand, those prescriptive-federal-standards programs have created a system of credible deterrents to pollution and have been remarkably effective in cleaning up the environment.

Efforts to reform the major prescriptive-federal-standards programs, as noted below, sometimes seek to supplement and improve their efficiency and sometimes are disingenuous attempts to undercut them.

4. **Citizen enforcement as part of modern environmental law.** In the years after *Kepone* (in which, remember, there was no citizen statutory enforcement), the fact of citizen participation in environmental public law has completely permeated the system, both in litigation and in informal and formal participation in agency practice. As noted further in Chapters 7 and 21, every major federal environmental law since 1970 has included a specific authorization for enforcement by citizens, with the possibility of reimbursement of enforcement costs. Citizen litigation subsequently has shaped every part of the public law structure. Agencies, it turns out, often lack the resources to enforce statutes or are not inclined to constrain industries that pay the bills. In a lesson that has begun to spread to the rest of the world, U.S. practice has shown that if you really want to have a public law enforced, it is sensible to provide for supplemental private enforcement by those who are personally affected and hence have a personal incentive to do so. This not only enlists the efforts of "private attorneys general," but it also means that in many cases the mere looming potential for citizen enforcement impels agencies into enforcement that otherwise would be stalled by political inertia. So citizen groups in general have tended to take on the same kind of enforcement actions that government agencies are authorized to undertake.

Citizens' enforcement action often are motivated by the conviction that state pollution agencies are not very interested in enforcement. Citizens may try to persuade EPA to enforce or do it themselves. If a state agency is systematically undercutting the national water pollution control system or another cooperative federalism system, citizens may also push EPA (which obviously does not relish the task of taking over state pollution controls) to consider decertifying the delegation of federal pollution control powers to the state.

Citizen intervention has been the major element in shifting social governance in environmental law from the old bipolar model (where government agencies hold the sole responsibility for counterbalancing the excesses of corporate business) to a Jeffersonian multicentric pluralism where a diversity of affected interests is actively involved in the legal process to assure that public and individual values do not get lost in the tangles of the political-economic marketplace. Citizen enforcement often acts as the strategic force pushing implementation of public interest statutes through the snarls and blandishments of marketplace politics into practical service to the civic economy.

Eliminating the possibility of citizen enforcement is one of the main elements in the resistance to environmental law.

5. **Biodiversity of law: the common law's continuing roles.** Modern public law remedies, based on state and nationwide regulatory systems, do have advantages over common law actions in terms of scale (broad-scale comprehensiveness) and applicability (e.g., requiring no proof of causation of unreasonable harms).

The common law, however, remains a fundamentally important part of modern environmental law. Public law remedies build upon and supplement the common law, but common law stands as the foundational underpinning of the legal system. It is a traditionally open legal forum for affected individuals and often is more flexible and creative in integrating public civic values into new and significant settings.

Consider Alaska's *Exxon-Valdez* oil spill, for example. In that extraordinary case of negligence by the Alyeska pipeline consortium and Exxon Corporation, a cataclysmic contamination poured out over one of the nation's richest ecosystems, threatening billions of dollars of commercial fisheries, not to mention priceless natural and cultural resources not valued by the market economy (see Chapter 3). After the wreck of the *Exxon-Valdez* in 1989, the majority of legal claims filed by the State of Alaska and thousands of individuals hurt by the spill proceeded on common law theories of public and private nuisance and marine tort, not on public law.

Common law cases continue to be the numerical majority of environmental actions each year, as neighborhoods face or suffer harm from a local polluter or individuals are exposed to environmental contamination. When public agencies are not responsive or when the machinery of statutory enforcement is too complex, hampered by administrative discretion, or too static to respond to novel problems, many environmental controversies turn to the classic and flexible remedies of the common law.

Common law litigation imposes potentially heavy costs and burdens on its participants, although the availability of damages and counterclaims provides funding in some settings. Because of its costs and occasional imprecision, the common law is often a backup to public law, but in some settings it provides necessary legal remedies that are found nowhere else.

6. **Generational differences: new expectations, new remedies, new science.** Much has changed since the *Kepone* years. Today's pollution statutes are essentially a strict liability system: Fault need not be proved in order to assess penalties for pollution, and mere recordkeeping violations are subject to serious penalties, including jail. More than two decades after *Kepone* and the first generation of major pollution law enforcement actions, administrative and judicial pollution prosecutions are more numerous now than during the 1970s. But often they are quite different in character, turning on subtleties of administrative implementation of statutes and regulations.

There are also unsubtle differences between the first generation of environmental law and now. In *Kepone*, no one went to jail. Today, dozens of individual and corporate defendants have been convicted of criminal offenses for harming the environment. Chapter 20 reviews the increasing number of criminal prosecutions since the 1970s.

In the *Kepone* cases, very little scientific data on the off-site poisoning effects of Kepone were ever collected. Nor was a comprehensive quantification made of natural resources damages. No reported *Kepone* case explored the scientific questions that today would be part of the record: How does Kepone enter and affect human metabolisms? How does it react when released into air and water? How does it cumulate in aquatic ecosystems, with what results to fish high on the food chain and humans who eat them? Since the 1970s, environmental sciences and assessment technologies have expanded dramatically. These more sophisticated epidemiological sciences make it possible to measure a wide range of ecological disruptions, to trace their interconnections through different natural systems, and, in many cases, to craft remedies that can help injured resources to recover. For example, under natural resources damage provisions of the CWA and other statutes, and under innovative new common law theories of "restoration" and the public trust, pollution defendants can now be assessed damages beyond permit penalties to provide funding for resource remediation.

7. **New kinds of concerns.** In the twenty-first century, many of the most pressing environmental problems do not even remotely resemble the pollution discharge cases that typified the first generation of environmental law. In those earlier cases, some definable individuals chose to dump or spew harmful materials directly into a lake, river, or the air. How different that is from the global CO_2 buildup changing Earth's climate or the chlorinated hydrocarbons seeping out of consumer products, plastics, and aerosols into the water and atmosphere, causing hormone disruption, lowered sperm counts throughout broad populations, and other gender and fertility effects.[64] These recently recognized "pollution sources" are systemic, number in the millions or billions, and have cumulative effects on a far wider scale but with far less individual assignability of fault.

> The challenges we confront today — atmospheric buildup of carbon dioxide and other greenhouse gases, the potential environmental impacts of genetically modified organisms, and the risk of exposure to trace residues of pesticides that might disrupt endocrine cycles within a human body — were not even contemplated by first-generation environmental laws…. Since the time of Earth Day in 1970, we have cleaned up thousands of the "big dirties" through the use of pioneering federal legislation designed to take direct action against these threats to air, water, and land. Now, a generation later, we must confront environmental problems that are subtler, less visible, and more difficult to address: fertilizer runoff from thousands of farms and millions of yards; emissions from gas stations, bakeries, and dry cleaners; and smog produced by tens of millions of motor vehicles. Like nature itself, the size and shape of environmental problems constantly evolve; so too must the strategies, approaches, institutions, and tools chosen to address them. Chertow & Esty, Environmental Policy: The Next Generation, Issues Sci. & Tech., Fall 1997, at 73.[65]

8. **International convergences.** Just as problems of environmental pollution and resource depletion spread across international boundaries, so too do the responsive mechanisms of environmental law, through international conventions and evolving principles of responsibility for sustainability.

---

64. See T. Colborn, D. Dumanoski & J. P. Myers, Our Stolen Future: Are We Threatening Our Fertility, Intelligence, and Survival? A Scientific Detective Story (1997).

65. Marian Chertow and Daniel Esty are the editors of Thinking Ecologically: The Next Generation of Environmental Policy (1997).

Chapter 8 tracks a number of international legal ramifications upon the practice of environmental law domestically in the United States. The pesticide issue reflects this globalization process, with its own dynamics and complexities. The public policy debate at first focused on exports of chemicals and pesticides prohibited for use in the United States, often to countries with little or no regulatory infrastructure that were ill equipped to police their borders. In addition to the ethical and moral considerations inherent in a double standard, with one test for domestic commerce and another for international trade, the "circle of poison" that allowed prohibited pesticides to be exported and then reimported as residues on foods also attracted considerable attention. Industry responded that importing countries ought to be able decide for themselves what pesticides to import, some of which, such as DDT, might be useful for purposes such as malaria control, for which there was no need in the United States. In the mid-1970s, Congress passed several provisions requiring exporters to notify foreign governments when domestically banned or regulated chemicals and pesticides are being shipped to their ports. In an eleventh-hour executive order issued mere days before leaving office, the Carter Administration banned overseas shipments of some particularly harmful substances. The Reagan Administration, after assuming power, withdrew the Carter executive order just as quickly, leaving it as one of the shortest-lived in history.

As other countries began to become concerned about the "export of hazard," the locus of policy action shifted to international organizations, including the Organization for Economic Cooperation and Development (OECD) — a club of 24 industrialized countries — and the United Nations Environment Program (UNEP) — a global organization. At the insistence of industrialized exporting countries, both the OECD and UNEP in the mid-1980s adopted notification requirements similar to the weakened U.S. regulations. Developing countries protested, however, leading to the adoption of "prior informed consent" (PIC) as a more rigorous minimum international requirement for toxic pesticides, banned chemicals, and hazardous wastes. Under the PIC scheme, shipments cannot be exported until the government of the importing state consents in writing, a regulatory structure that creates more control for developing countries. Preceded by nonbinding international "good practice standards," PIC was codified in binding multilateral agreements for hazardous wastes in 1989 (the Basel Convention on the Control of Transboundary Movements of Hazardous Wastes and Their Disposal) and for chemicals and pesticides in 1998 (the Rotterdam Convention on the Prior Informed Consent Procedure for Certain Hazardous Chemicals and Pesticides in International Trade).

More recently, it has become apparent that international trade in chemicals and pesticides is only a piece of the larger international problem. Long-lived chemicals and pesticides — "persistent organic pollutants" (POPs) such as DDT and PCBs, typically containing chlorine as part of their chemical makeup — accumulate in fat, concentrate at higher levels of the food chain, and are often transported literally thousands of miles from the point of their release. While cancer was the greatest concern in earlier years, new evidence has emerged that by mimicking estrogen these same chemicals can disrupt hormonal messages at early stages of human development, even in the womb.

In response to these and other concerns, and building on years of work by international nongovernmental organizations to target a "Dirty Dozen" list of pesticides and industrial chemicals, the Stockholm Convention on Persistent Organic Pollutants was adopted in 2001. The POPs Convention adds to existing international agreements by targeting nine chemicals and categories of chemicals for elimination: the pesticides aldrin, chlordane, dieldrin, endrin, heptachlor, mirex, and toxaphene; and the chemicals hexachlorobenzene and PCBs. The agreement also strictly limits the use of DDT to controlling disease-carrying insects and requires governments to limit unintentional releases of PCBs, hexachlorobenzene, dioxins, and furans. Although international efforts on chemical pesticides give reason for cautious optimism, there are still significant threats requiring multilateral cooperation.

9. **The legal skill of comparative law.** Reading statutes and regulations is a necessary process that doesn't necessarily get you very far. Part of the art of modern environmental law is the contextual analysis skill of comparative law, noted in Chapter 26. Approaching any environmental case — be it on the massive scale of a Love Canal, the *Kepone* incident, or a disaster such as Bhopal's gas cloud in 1984, Chernobyl's radiation poisoning in 1986, or the *Exxon-Valdez* oil spill in 1989, or on a much smaller scale — attorneys must survey not only the physical facts and causations but also the legal culture of the locale. What law is on the books, and how does it work in practice? Responding to any environmental event requires a "culturally relative" and incisive analysis of the regulatory systems existing at the time of the incident, the politics, and the range of public and private law remedies available. In the *Kepone* case, this analysis would also take into account the differing (sometimes reluctant) regulatory abilities of state and federal agencies before and after the disaster, and the different avenues of statutory and nonstatutory liability and remedies that could be tried. An analysis of these practicalities, and of the differing types of relationship among agencies, citizens, and courts, provides a more competent basis for planning a party's legal course of action.[66] The same comparative process recurs, in varying degrees, whenever attorneys deal with situations outside their home jurisdiction.

C. THEMES, CONTEXTS, AND ARGUMENTS FOR CHANGE: POLITICS, ECONOMICS, AND TACTICS

Section 1. POLITICAL CONTEXT

Environmental law's development has never been a simple, steady progression. Environmental law was born in battle and likely will continue to draw its sword because it so directly embodies a fundamental conflict in human society — between the natural tendency of almost all private and public human actors to perceive costs and benefits in individual terms, and the overarching ecophysical reality that everything is

---

66. The comparative overview also allows the examiner to gauge larger societal themes, noting in the Bhopal case, for example, how a holistic ideology like those in a number of Asian cultures may subordinate the individual to society, while an individualistic ideology of the sort that often characterizes the West tends to subordinate society to the individual in its emphasis on personal initiative and autonomy.

interconnected. Until a thorough consensus emerges supporting the operative reality of interconnectedness, however, it is hard to imagine an environmental law process that does not involve opposing parties, mutual suspicions and disgruntlement, and compromises and provisional structures constantly subject to revisionist reengineering and political assault. Viewed from this perspective, it's remarkable that the field has grown so consistently in volume and permanence and that public support for environmental protection, as measured by opinion polls over the years, has remained so constant and strong.

The basis of the contentious political context starts with Hardin's tragedy of the commons. As noted earlier, unlike Hardin's simplified cow pasture where every participant ultimately faces the same cumulative harm from resource destruction, in reality common resources such as rivers and the air involve players with differential stakes. This creates political consequences. Take the example of a river into which factories are dumping their pollution. Each factory will tend to locate in places where the increasing degree of pollution is not a problem for itself and, absent the artifices of law, will pass on its waste disposal costs into the downstream commons. A factory that needs pure water for its production will tend to locate higher up the river where the input water is clean and will send its pollution output downstream. Factories that can use dirtier water will tend to locate further downstream, perhaps closer to their customers or suppliers. In these circumstances, all the factories may be quite satisfied with the resulting situation.

But a commons resource like a river has hundreds of other participants and many critical roles to play beyond "factory-process-input" and "disposal-of-factory-waste-output." A river is used by swimmers, boaters, farmers, water-drinkers and gazers, and by tadpoles, diatoms, waterplants, fish, ospreys, and myriad other players in our sprawling human and nonhuman ecosystems. The commons is inhabited and used by units that have very different interests and circumstances. The most substantial economic players — the factories — may not have such a pressing need to keep the river clean, but most of the river's other users do.

Politics enters the picture in this river example when factory owner decisionmakers act to further their own particular cost-benefit positions, very different from the positions of the public users and ecological inhabitants of the commons. The industries naturally will work individually and together to avoid being forced to contribute to any cleanup of the river that is "unnecessary and unreasonable" in their terms. Even if the full real public costs of having the river polluted far outweigh the benefits, the costs are diffused out into the river commons or are unmarketized values, and thus difficult to collect and invoice in market terms. That is why we push governments to impose "artificial" regulatory constraints on the marketplace. But the factories' economic position, which includes the focused economic gains from not cleaning up, produces focused political power as well. Over time this can mean that even if government regulation is imposed on the polluting industries, they will be able to wield significant leverage to modify or avoid accounting for the full scope of the cost externalities they impose on the common resource. This helps explain Allied Chemical's longtime ability to avoid meaningful government regulation (and why highway salt, discussed in Chapter 1, continues to be basically unregulated).

The three basic blocs of participants — industry and its adherents, government regulatory agencies, and active environmental citizen coalitions — live in a basic tension that continues to exist today throughout environmental law. Industry and commerce have highly focused lobbying structures bent on maximizing their short-term gains and avoiding as many costs as possible. The environmental nongovernmental organizations (NGOs) and other active citizens seek to represent the public interest by arguing for fuller forced accountings of all the real social costs. And government agencies, the third bloc of players in the political context of a modern industrial democracy, are pulled and shoved in both directions, damned by industry if they enforce their regulatory civic mandates too attentively and by citizens when they don't.

These three categories of players are not tidily delineated one from another. When, for instance, the 104th Congress attempted to undercut the CAA and CWA in 1994, a number of industrial lobbies representing new businesses that design and sell cleanup technology to primary industries understandably stood with the environmental NGOs in defense of the laws. At the same time, some citizens groups, including industry-funded "Wise Users" and a few labor unions, stood with industry in calling for rollbacks in environmental regulation. Some sectors of government, such as the Army Corps of Engineers and parts of the Energy Department, routinely align themselves with industry and fight fiercely behind the scenes to help weaken environmental statutes while others fought to protect them. Changes in administration, too, can noticeably shift the orientation of government departments closer to or farther from the perspectives of industry and commerce and blur the delineations. And the media, itself a fourth branch of government, unpredictably shifts its whirling ephemeral attentions from one perspective to another, or sometimes ignores all perspectives entirely.

The pressures against environmental regulation coming from regulated market place interests are always present in the modern political context. They achieve special decisiveness when they gain the White House or both chambers of Congress. In this political context, moreover, the role of media is critical. If the press covers the details of initiatives against environmental law, public opinion typically generates a backlash. If the media does not get a handle on anti-environmental campaigns, they have a far better chance of prevailing.

The politics of environment is de facto quite partisan. The League of Conservation Voters is a citizen monitoring group that resolutely attempts to be nonpartisan. It nurtures and cherishes its opportunities to support environmentally progressive Republicans, however, because the annual legislative scorecards show so few members of the GOP at that environmental protection end of the spectrum. Where the congressional GOP membership typically has annual scores averaging less than 20%, and its leadership close to 0%, the Democrats' average is above 80%, with its leaders at 83%.[67]

---

67. In the 2001 League of Conservation Voters' Scorecard, for example, Democrats in the Senate averaged 82% and Republicans 9%; Democrats in the House averaged 81% and Republicans 16%. The senior Democratic leadership averaged 84% in the Senate and 83% in the House; the senior GOP leaders averaged 0% in the Senate and 0% in the House. The highest-scoring GOP legislator scored 93%. There were 72 Democrats with scores of 100%. There were 128 Republicans, no Democrats, with scores of 0%. League of Conservation Voters, 2001 National Environmental Scorecard 6, 8-10 (2002). The LCV scorecards are based each year on a comprehensive tabulation of between 15 and 20 key congressional votes. The annotated statistical abstracts are available annually at http://www.lcv.org.

Although no political party openly espouses an anti-environmental agenda, history tends to validate the caricature of the GOP as the party reflecting corporate enterprise's routinely regressive opposition to environmental protection regulations.

In Chapter 1, we examined the instructive problematics of highway salting (public highway agencies consistently avoiding alternative technologies that would save the public billions in annual property and ecological damages). Earlier in this chapter, we did the same using the *Kepone* pesticide case (corporate executives systematically ignoring pollution harms to workers, neighbors, and natural resources). The reluctance of enterprises to account for externalizable costs has not dissipated over the past 30 years of environmental law. Allied-Signal and the rest of the chemical industry, along with the majority of American business, indeed has accepted the inevitability of some environmental regulation. Through a powerful and pervasive lobbying presence in the bureaucracy, legislative branch, and media, however, industry is consistently able to shape, blunt, or dilute many of the regulatory mandates, as reflected in subsequent regulatory chapters of this coursebook. The balance of power in most environmental issue areas is quite lopsided, with the regulated industry consistently in a strong position even when the national administration and Congress are not in the hands of industry-oriented blocs. And as to highway salting, our symptomatic initial case study, virtually no accounting for consequences has occurred over 30 years, readily available alternatives continue to be ignored, and in fact the application of salt has dramatically increased.

The typically dominant position of commerce and industry derives from its sophisticated networks of communication and influence, campaign financing, and the obvious daily societal importance of the enterprises that generate the nation's economic revenues. In the modern political context, every industry consistently focuses on the governmental processes and public relations issues that can affect it.[68] The hundreds of individual industry trade associations have well-funded, full-time

---

68. Soon after initial publication of this coursebook, the authors received a letter from Richard L. Hanneman, President of the Salt Institute, the salt industry's national lobbying association, strongly complaining about this book's Chapter 1 analysis of the road salt industry. Mr. Hanneman touted a study released by the Transportation Research Board, an arm of the National Research Council, concluding that calcium magnesium acetate (CMA) was not — or at least not yet — a sufficiently economical substitute for highway de-icing to justify a switch away from rock salt. Mr. Hanneman's letter ended by saying that

> there is a strong relationship between the application of de-icing salt and the prevention of about 80 percent of the fatalities and serious injuries that would otherwise occur on untreated highways....
> [The report shows that] using highway de-icing salt may prevent huge numbers of tort recoveries, but it still (sic) might be of interest to aspiring attorneys.

Upon examination, however, the cited report actually found that the unaccounted external costs of salting exceeded $2 billion by an undetermined amount. But the report concluded that the preponderate advantage of salt substitutes could not yet be accurately established. On its own terms the report suffered from some serious exclusions from its research. In comparing salt and CMA, using an overall economic accounting approach and monetary estimations, the analysis completely excluded from its calculus certain public costs that indeed seem significant — notably human health problems, particularly those from salt infiltration into drinking water supplies, and "environmental damages" — both of potentially large magnitude and both excluded on grounds of "insufficient information." As to safety statistics, moreover, it would seem that untreated highways were not the appropriate comparison to salted highways. The citation for the report is Transportation Research Board, Highway De-icing: Comparing Salt and Calcium Magnesium Acetate, Special Report 235 (1991). Follow-up government research reports seem warranted but have not been done.

The Chemical Manufacturers Association led the counterattack on Rachel Carson in the 1960s and on the 1997 book Our Stolen Future, and keeps constant watch and pressure on the half-dozen federal agencies that can promote or restrict chemical usage.

lobbying and media operations with public relations savvy[69] and resources that often dwarf those of even the few largest citizen environmental groups. On many issues, the trade associations work together in large networked coalitions, as notably demonstrated in the Project Relief Movement in the 104th Congress that linked more than 300 lobbies in attempts to roll back environmental protection law.

Government agencies, which in the bipolar model of government are tasked with the primary role in controlling the excesses of the marketplace, typically have been constrained by their political context. Some government agencies are inherently aligned with kindred enterprises — state and federal highway commissions with the salt and other industries linked to road building and maintenance, and agricultural departments with pesticide and fertilizer industries. Other agencies are more regulatory in function, but over time they too often tend to come ever closer to the corporate entities they regulate, a process political scientists describe as "agency capture."[70]

Environmental politics have forced the creation of a third sector. The comfortable bipolar structure of government was wedged open starting in the late 1960s by an energetic multicentric pluralism —the active participation of many different civic interest groupings, notably the energetic presence of nonmarketplace NGOs. Public interest environmental citizen groups have reinvigorated a process of active pluralistic democracy and have been the dominant enforcers of many environmental statutes. At one pole, the environmentalists include ecoguerrillas of the EarthFirst! Movement, "Greens," and "deep ecologists" dedicated to iconoclastic political action. The opposite pole lies rightward across a wide spectrum of groups and programs all the way to the silk-stockinged salons of Brahmin conservationists. Environmentalism today includes citizens from a wide range of income levels and racial backgrounds.[71] At every point across the spectrum stand environmental lawyers and legal advocacy groups. The players in this third sector are often volunteers, unfunded by the marketplace or official government, attempting to bring public environmental concerns into market and government processes that so often seem to ignore them.[72] This book repeatedly emphasizes the central role played by citizen activists in the creation and continuing development of modern environmental law. The legal system would have much

---

69. "At their annual meeting at The Greenbrier resort, the Chemical Manufacturers Association (CMA) voted to change its name to the 'American Chemistry Council' (ACC). The new name reflects...significant business changes...and the desire for a more positive reputation.... The public still reacts with fear and negative feelings to the word 'chemical....' For some reason, the word 'chemistry' generates milder, even favorable responses." Association of Consulting Chemists & Chemical Engineers Newsletter, The Chemical Consultant, Volume 12, Number 5&6, May/June 2000.

70. See Stewart, The Reformation of American Administrative Law, 88 Harv. L. Rev. 1669, 1684–1687 (1975).

71. The early predominance of white, upper middle income activists is changing due to outreach by national environmental organizations and the grassroots efforts of groups such as Highlander Center, New Market, Tennessee; Citizens for a Better America, Halifax, Virginia; Native Americans for a Clean Environment, Tahlequah, Oklahoma; Tools for Change, San Francisco; ACE: Alternatives for Community and Environment, Boston; Urban Habitat, San Francisco; and West Harlem Environmental Action, New York City.

72. Legislative hearings, agency proceedings on regulation of an industry, or court enforcement actions against large polluters typically reflect the dominant position of industry in all but the most highly publicized cases. The relative weakness of environmentalists in absolute terms would be justified if their concerns were trivial. (Often volunteer environmentalists *don't* do their homework well enough.) But the environmental accounting approach is not trivial, and environmentalists have necessarily become more expert in science, economics, politics, and law. Of the vast array of challengeable projects, only a tiny handful, typically the worst in economic and ecological terms, can be challenged, and of these most will survive environmental attack. It would not be so if the environmental side of the debate were funded in any rough parity with the marketplace.

dimmer prospects in its efforts at conserving the planet without the informed participation of citizen environmentalists.

Section 2. THE TACTICAL LOGIC OF CITIZEN ENFORCEMENT OF ENVIRONMENTAL LAW

How, in this political context, can citizens attempt to play an effective role in holding enterprises accountable for the real consequences of their actions? The highway
salting and *Kepone* stories illustrate the potential importance of citizens playing an
active role.

Marketplace Remedies. Theoretically, citizens can work within the private marketplace
— petitioning the players, buying out the salt producers, mobilizing boycotts, or advertising salt's harms sufficiently to dry up the market. A brief reflection on practicalities in
the modern marketplace reveals the limits of this approach. And then there is ADR,
negotiation, mediation, and the like. Avoiding the battlefield mode of dispute resolution
is a growing and desirable trend, and probably 90% of legal controversies are ultimately
settled out of court. The problem is that, without the portent of legal battle, it is highly
unlikely that market players will willingly sit down to negotiate any compromises.

Public Law Remedies: Petitioning the Agencies, or Interventions. Administrative
agencies theoretically can be induced to act through citizen petitions for enforcement
action, rulemaking petitions, and requests for administrative hearings. As the highway
salting and *Kepone* cases indicate, however, for a host of reasons environmental protection agencies often cannot be relied upon to undertake enforcement efforts in adequate
fashion. (Where ongoing agency actions are lackluster, timid, collusive, or otherwise
inadequate, citizens theoretically have the legal ability to file interventions in these
matters, even in informal proceedings.[73] Having a citizen group representative in the
administrative process, with advance notice and the opportunity to observe and participate in interactions between agency and industry, can dramatically change the nature
of the process. Citizens rarely file interventions in informal agency proceedings,
however, perhaps because they may not be warmly welcomed when they do.)

Petitioning the Legislature. Legislatures present tactical opportunities for citizen
initiatives, particularly at the local level where petitions and testimony may represent
sufficient potential votes to command attention. There are limitations of scale,
however. In the highway salt setting, a local ordinance would have quite limited practical effects, and state or federal legislation is exponentially harder to achieve. In any
legislative setting in which citizens face industrial opposition, which is the case in the
salting and chemical plant cleanup settings as in a majority of environmental issues,
there is a pronounced imbalance in political and financial resources. To get legislative

---

73. See, e.g., §555(b) of the Administrative Procedure Act: "So far as the orderly conduct of public business
permits, an interested person may appear before an agency or its responsible employees for the presentation,
adjustment, or determination of an issue, request, or controversy in a proceeding…or in connection with an
agency function." 5 U.S.C. §555(b).

attention environmentalists often need a vivid crisis, an altruistic legislative crusader, or a blockbusting TV exposé.

The Media. The media have often and accurately been called a branch of government. Media attention on an issue is often extremely effective, making politicians respond for reasons that lie in the theatrical nature of the governing process as well as in the quest for votes. The media attention focused on Allied's Kepone contamination was decisively important in inducing corrective actions and strengthening legal initiatives in court and Congress. But actual media coverage is too often just "info-tainment," hard to mobilize and keep focused. An effective media strategy is highly contingent upon citizens' ability to interest the media in the issue, to transmit sufficient detail to reporters (and most environmental analyses are quite complex, in comparison to straightforward marketplace arguments that "salt clears roads," and "this chemical production supports the local economy and our nation's technology needs"), to focus coverage on the relevant governmental target, and perhaps hardest, to keep the media on the story as long as required.

Sue Them. Notice that most of the prior tactical options focus upon rational persuasion. Realistically, however, many environmental cases must turn to the force of law to give practical effect to their arguments — the threat of court action to force negotiated consideration of public environmental values or the actuality of legal action when threats are not enough.

If a fundamental problem of our economic system is that decisionmakers won't take account of many of the real costs they impose unless they themselves have to account for them,[74] then environmental law fundamentally is the art of presenting the bill for environmental social costs, most often by litigation.

The legal weaponry available to environmental activists in the United States is remarkably broad. Most of the available legal actions are based on actions in court. Although there are often useful opportunities to intervene directly in agency proceedings, most such interventions are backed up by the litigation option. In this country, courts have their fingers in the widest array of pies.

Here are some available lawsuits, all of which have possible applications to the salt and *Kepone* problems:

- *Tort actions:* The most compelling tort claims in the *Kepone* case were for the personal injuries to workers, their families, and the industry's neighbors. Most environmental cases include property claims as well for injury to homes, farms, and personal property. A number of creative tort theories are available, including public nuisance, posing interesting procedural problems but offering the potential of money damages or injunctions in individual or class actions.[75]

---

74. This is the basic "cost-externalization" syndrome. The managers of a factory, for example, often try to pass on to others ("externalize") as much of the costs of their operations as they can, while holding onto, or "internalizing," maximum benefits (i.e., income) to their corporate entity.

75. In novel settings even tort law may take time to develop. In the highway salting context, for example, only a very few such cases have been reported to date. See Morash v. Commonwealth, 296 N.E.2d 461 (Mass. 1973); Mueller v. Brunn, 313 N.W.2d 790 (Wis. 1982).

- *Constitutional claims:* Particular actions by government officials may run afoul of the federal or state constitution by violating due process rights, taking property without compensation, unlawfully restricting interstate commerce, and so on. In some settings, for instance, salt damage might be the subject of an inverse condemnation claim.

- *Public trust theories:* In many environmental settings, major impacts are imposed upon resources that potentially raise public trust issues, which are sometimes the base of direct equitable claims or suits to compel the public trust actions by government to protect water quality, wildlife, and other natural resources.

- *Statutorily-based actions:* As noted earlier in the chapter, dozens of statutes provide for citizen enforcement. Citizens would have several federal statutory claims that could be directly litigated in the settings of both *Kepone* and highway salting, after giving 60-day notice to the offending industry and the federal agency that has primary enforcement authority.[76]

- *Administrative law litigation:* Administrative law offers a number of judicial review formats for pressuring regulatory agencies on environmental claims. Such reviews seek to compel agency action against a problem (e.g., by injunction or mandamus to obtain EPA enforcement of the CWA in particular cases) or to force improvement in agency regulations. In a number of settings, citizens file suit against those agencies that are the direct cause of problems (in the salting example, suit might be filed against state highway commissions for the "arbitrary and capricious" irrationality of their administrative decision to salt or directly against them as the dumpers of salt into the environment).

- *International law:* This field covers international treaties and conventions, as well as transboundary pollution cases. In the *Kepone* example, Allied's entire market for this neurotoxin so hazardous to humans was overseas. Under a number of conventions and principles of international law, there are ways in which liability and disapprobation might be attached to different aspects of overseas marketing of such products. As to international implications of highway salting, it is clearly possible, for example, that Canadian waters would be injured by cumulative salt infiltration into the Great Lakes drainage system, with possible arbitral and litigative remedies. See Chapters 8 and 26.

The list of modes of citizen legal action goes on, each avenue raising a sequence of technical and procedural problems as well — standing to sue, class actions, estoppel, how to finance lawsuits, and so on. Some litigation approaches are quite limited in their direct effects, and some quite far-reaching (with their impact extended by class actions or the effect of precedent in subsequent litigation and negotiations). Most of these

---

76. Highway salting, for instance, might give rise to CAA issues. Or it might qualify as "point-source" pollution under the CWA when the salt is discharged from salting trucks onto highways, from which salt foreseeably passes through drains into roadside watercourses, which then would require road commissions to get permits and use BATs. This possibility depends on how highway runoffs are regulatorily defined as stormwater discharges. As a result of a pair of California lawsuits brought by the NRDC against several cities and the state Department of Transportation for failure to comply with general permits issued by state Water Quality Boards, the court required comprehensive stormwater control systems to control runoff, a precedent that could be applied in the salting setting as well. See 25 BNA Env't Rep. Curr. Devs. 1492 (1994).

citizen interventions encounter industry or governmental resistance, from the former because economic interests are affected and from the latter because attitudes are that law enforcement should be left to official agency processes.[77]

Citizen litigation continues to be strategically important. A study by Prof. James May shows that in the first years of the twenty-first century three out of every four judicial opinions in civil environmental cases in the United States were the result of a citizen suit. See May, Now More Than Ever: Trends in Environmental Citizen Suits at 30, 10 Widener L. Rev. 1 (2003). Ultimately it is necessary to remind ourselves that the genius of the Anglo-American system of law is that it is always in flux, though the process remains the same. Creative use of legal theories has shaped today's environmental law and will continue to do so. Perhaps some day environmental mediation and consensus negotiation will resolve the pressing questions of the day. For now, however, sweet reason and facts alone have insufficient force in the system. They require the support of credible legal leverages, mobilized by citizens to make their point in a vastly complex confrontational system. To give effect to values and analyses, one must know the full array of ways to play the game.

Section 3. ECONOMICS, AND THREE ECONOMIES

A fundamental theme and force in shaping national environmental law, as in most of modern life, is *economics*. We have already considered some of the perspectives of modern resource economics and the internal economic dynamics that drive industrial processes to pollute, to externalize costs out into the commons. Economics constitutes one of the major cross-cutting themes encountered in environmental law.

The word *economics* comes from two Greek words: *oikos*, meaning "household, home, or family estate," and *nomos*, meaning "rules." Thus *economics* literally means "the rules governing the human household." It is easy to see, then, that economics could be considered to include the full range of concerns covered by environmental law itself.[78] Usually, however, economics is given a narrower reach, evoking solely the concerns of the marketplace or the market economy.

But consider a useful new analytical perspective: *three* economies. To understand modern societal dynamics, it is helpful to conceptualize three different intersecting economies: (1) the familiar industrial-commercial marketplace economy and all the structures that support it; (2) a separate economy of natural systems; and (3) a human-

---

77. For example, Justice Scalia has strongly opposed citizen enforcement of environmental laws, writing, "Does what I have said mean that…'important legislative purposes, heralded in the halls of Congress, [can be] lost or misdirected in the vast hallways of the federal bureaucracy?' Of course it does — and a good thing, too…. Lots of once-heralded programs ought to get lost or misdirected, in vast hallways or elsewhere." Scalia, The Doctrine of Standing as an Essential Element of the Separation of Powers, 17 Suffolk U. L. Rev. 881, 897 (1983).

78. On the other hand, the derivation of the word *ecology* connotes a far broader realm — *oikos* again for "home" in the broad figurative sense and *logos*, which means "word" in a sense connoting an all-encompassing sense of thoughtful reckoning narrative, an idea of law and deepened appreciation of reality. As Garrett Hardin has written, it is ecology that should be the meta-discipline, with economics just one of its subsidiary parts. "Logically it is obvious that economics is but a small specialty in the much larger science, ecology. Sociologically, it is quite otherwise: the tail wags the dog." G. Hardin, Sweet-Singing Economists, Exploring New Ethics for Survival: The Voyage of the Spaceship Beagle ch. 9 (1972).

oriented, civic-societal economy comprised of all the societal values, capital, institutions, and infrastructure not included in the marketplace.[79]

Since the marketplace economy, broadly defined, generates virtually all environmental problems, environmental law is understood as a comprehensive attempt to control and guide the dynamics of the marketplace economy on behalf of the other two economies. The three-economies construct provides a useful way to talk about an array of long-established concepts of environmental law (and public policy generally), integrating an analysis of societal necessities and ecological realities with the powerful machinery of market dynamics.[80]

Figure 2-3 offers a schematic view of the three economies. The marketplace economy is the dynamic central core of the three economies' cosmology. It is systematically blind, however, to many important economic elements. For the most part, the marketplace economy deals only with things and services that have a price tag and are bought and sold. It generates waste and externalities as well as profits and products, problems that are massive and real and need to be included as part of societal economic accounting.

The natural economy is the intricate system of living and geophysical systems that sustains dynamic planetary processes, providing resources and a geophysical base for the human economies. The economy of nature gives and takes, and adjusts as best it can to the marketplace's pollution, resource derogation, and disrupted ecosystem dynamics, while passing the effects of many of these externality impacts onward into the civic economy. As economist Herman Daly has reminded us, the marketplace economy exists *within* the economy of nature. The latter is more intricately connected and complex than is the marketplace economy, which can thrive only so long as the

FIGURE 2-3

CENTER SPHERE: *the marketplace economy.*

INTERMEDIARY SPHERE: *the civic-societal economy.*

THE ENCOMPASSING SPHERE: *the economy of nature.*

The rim banding the center sphere represents the governmental role. Relative scale and proportions depend upon observer's perspective.

79. This idea builds on the work of Professor Joseph L. Sax, who argued that environmental law should recognize an economy of nature as well as the marketplace economy. Sax, Property Rights and the Economy of Nature, 45 Stan. L. Rev. 1433 (1993). See also M. Sagoff, The Economy of the Earth (1988), and the work of a respected consultant on fisheries management policy based in Sequim, Washington, James Lichatowich, "It's the *Economies*, Mr. President," 34 Trout No. 3, at 22–23 (Summer 1993). Sax uses the phrase "transformative economy" for marketplace economics; Lichatowich uses "industrial economy."

80. For more on the three economies, see Plater, Environmental Law and Three Economies, 23 Harv. Envtl. L. Rev. 359 (1999); Plater, The Three Economies: An Essay in Honor of Professor Sax, 25 Ecology L.Q. 411 (1998).

economy of nature thrives. The economy of nature has hugely significant value to humans even if it is unacknowledged or undervalued by the marketplace.[81]

Obvious as this may seem, not everyone sees it. While he was Senior Economist at the World Bank, Daly participated in developing the report "Development and the Environment." Here is Daly's account of the evolution of one part of the report:

> An early draft contained a diagram entitled "The Relationship Between the Economy and the Environment." It consisted of a square labeled "economy," with an arrow coming in labeled "inputs" and an arrow going out labeled "outputs" — nothing more. I suggested that the picture failed to show the environment, and that it would be good to have a large box containing the one depicted, to represent the environment. Then the relation between the environment and the economy would be clear — specifically, that the economy is a subsystem of the environment and depends upon the environment both as a source of raw material inputs and as a "sink" for waste outputs.
>
> The next draft included the same diagram and text, but with an unlabeled box drawn around the economy like a picture frame. I commented that the larger box had to be labeled "environment" or else it was merely decorative, and that the text had to explain that the economy is related to the environment as a subsystem within the larger ecosystem and is dependent on it in the ways previously stated. The next draft omitted the diagram altogether.
>
> By coincidence, a few months later the chief economist of the World Bank, Lawrence H. Summers (now President of Harvard University), under whom the report was being written, happened to be on a conference panel at the Smithsonian Institution, discussing the book *Beyond the Limits* (Donella H. Meadows, et al.), which Summers considered worthless. In that book there was a diagram showing the relation of the economy to the ecosystem, a diagram exactly like the one I had suggested.... During the question-and-answer time I asked the chief economist if, looking at that diagram, he felt that the question of the size of the economic subsystem relative to the total ecosystem was an important one, and whether he thought economists should be asking the question, What is the optimal scale of the macro economy relative to the environment? His reply was immediate and definite: "That's not the right way to look at it."[82]

Even beyond Daly's apparent heresy, full economic analysis requires a third conceptual economy. Environmental law did not begin exclusively nor primarily as a defense of nature. The images that launched the environmental law revolution in the 1960s were of pollution directly impinging upon human health. The civic-societal economy comprises the actual social costs, benefits, resources, energy, inputs, outputs,

---

81. Robert Costanza and his colleagues have analyzed the multi-*trillion* dollar values of "natural capital," the resources and services provided free or far below their true value, without which the marketplace and human life would be impossible. Costanza and Daly have come up with very impressive "natural capital" numbers:

> We have estimated the current economic value of 17 ecosystem services for 16 biomes, based on published studies and a few original calculations. For the entire biosphere, the value (most of which is outside the market) is estimated to be in the range of US $16–54 trillion per year.... Because of the nature of the uncertainties, this must be considered a minimum estimate. Global gross national product total is around $18 trillion per year. Costanza et al., The Value of the World's Ecosystem Services, 387 Nature 253 (1997).

See also P. Hawken et al., Natural Capitalism: The Coming Efficiency Revolution (1998); Costanza & Daly, Natural Capital and Sustainable Development, 6 Conservation Biology 37–46 (1992); Hawken, Natural Capitalism, Mother Jones, Mar.–Apr. 1997, at 40.

82. H. Daly, Beyond Growth: The Economics of Sustainable Development 6 (1997).

values, qualities, and consequences that are not accounted for in the marketplace. Where do externalized costs go? They exit the marketplace economy, but they do not thereby drop into oblivion: By the laws of physics, ecology, and logic they are internalized into the fabric of one or both of the other economies. Widespread pesticide use, overgrazing, dumping pollutants like Kepone wastes, highway salting, massive layoffs of corporate workers, or a host of other cost externalizations may make powerfully good sense to market players in the narrow market terms of individual gains but be quite irrational in societal economics terms. Healthy societal economic systems are founded upon healthy and sustainable ecological system cycles of soil, water, air, and living communities. When a resource system is derogated or destroyed, some enterprises may prosper greatly, but society is likely to be far less well off. The societal public economy needs the market economy, but for the sake of its own short- and long-term interests society must somehow contrive to value and incorporate into its governance important elements of civic economic reality that the daily dominant marketplace resists. Toxic spills into watercourses, global warming, lost fisheries, eroded soils, wetlands destruction, pesticide loading, and a multitude of other environmental issues demonstrate important linkages between all three economies.

Where are law and government in the three economies? Government statutes, agencies, and programs are avowedly designed to protect civic-societal interests. Schematically, then, government is strategically positioned in a circling band at the interface between the civic-societal economy and the marketplace economy. Statutes and regulatory systems are primarily positioned to monitor and mediate the marketplace economy, attempting to prevent or correct its dysfunctional impacts upon the other two spheres. Environmental common law is similarly positioned and likewise represents values within the civic and natural economies that it attempts to force entities within the marketplace economy to account for. Public law can lapse and veer, but it remains a major element in the interplay of the three economies.

The importance of a comprehensive accounting for externalized costs has long been acknowledged by academic economists, but it gets overlooked in the day-to-day economic and political pressures of the marketplace. Economic analyses that ignore civic societal economics or the impacts of natural economics on society, however, are naïvely or disingenuously narrow, ignoring substantial realities that inevitably are felt by society. The competent practice of both economics and environmental law (not to mention rational democratic governance) implicitly incorporates and requires an understanding of the reality and interdependence of all three economies.

Section 4. ARGUMENTS FOR REFORMATION OF ENVIRONMENTAL LAW

In a field so complex in terms of science, policy formulation, and economic variables, and simultaneously so politically contentious, it is not surprising that there has been a 30-year history of proposals for large and small reformations of environmental protection law that are examined in many later chapters of this book.[83]

---

83. In this inherently cantankerous setting, the trick is to analyze and realistically weigh the design, intent, and likely contextual effect of each proposal. Some are incremental, merely adding or fine-tuning elements to

The Status Quo. The standard existing model of environmental regulation that has evolved over the past decades — the backdrop against which most reform proposals are made — is the classic regulatory structure often tendentiously called "command-and-control." In this model, statutorily directed prescriptive standards are articulated in uniform national terms and applied through permits issued by federal or federally certified state administrative agencies to each regulated enterprise. These prescriptive standards are enforced through a set progression of procedures that are initiated by citizens as well as agency personnel, leading to civil penalties, injunctions, and agency-initiated criminal penalties. Although the process is quite cumbersome, it has accomplished a great deal in cleaning up the nation's environment.

An Array of Reform Approaches. Here, in no particular order, is a quick summary of an array of reformations that are occasionally or repeatedly proposed for environmental law.

- *"Market-based" options:* "Market-based" reform proposals, many of which Chapter 14 suggests are more accurately defined as "market-enlisting" techniques, include a variety of adjustments to the basic regulatory structure in order to achieve aims most often described as greater efficiency. These market-based propositions are aimed at creating formats where environmental standards are implemented by market voluntarism, that is, by innovative participation from regulated industries themselves rather than by bureaucratic decrees. Environmental law now has programs for trading, netting, and banking of pollution credits, particularly in the air pollution regulatory structure noted in Chapter 14.[84]

- *Voluntarism:* The argument here is for substituting voluntary for mandatory requirements. Modern manifestations of voluntarism arguments are seen in libertarian foundations' calls for "free market environmentalism," the Bush II Administration's enforcement policies in a number of areas where the discovery of violations leads to administrative negotiations rather than judicial or

---

existing environmental protection structures. Some are drastic, suggesting the elimination or creation of entire regulatory programs. Some proposals are bona fide attempts to improve existing environmental law, trying to make it more effective, efficient, fair, and wise. Others are overtly or disingenuously designed to roll back or undercut environmental protections in order to serve other agendas or the proponents' particular interests. By the nature of the setting, most proposals — even those most cynically designed to eliminate environmental protection to maximize individual or corporate gain — are presented and lobbied in terms of civic improvement. Figuring out the intent and probable effects of reform proposals is not always a straightforward process. The authors of this book, who consider efficient, effective sustainability as the societal goal for environmental protection, tend overall to support the accomplishments of the existing uniform regulatory structures, crude though they occasionally may be, and generally regard reform proposals as bearing the burden of proof and persuasion.

84. Some scholars argue that the data show disappointing results for the reform experiments' cost efficiency and innovation rates. See Driesen, Is Emissions Trading an Economic Incentive Program? Replacing the Command and Control/Economic Incentive Dichotomy, 55 Wash. & Lee L. Rev. 289 (1998); Driesen, Does Emissions Trading Encourage Innovation?, 33 Envt'l L. Rep. 10094 (2003); Steinzor, Toward Better Bubbles and Future Lives: A Progressive Response to the Conservative Agenda for Reforming Environmental Law, 32 Envtl. L. Rep. 11421, 11426-11427, 11430, 11435-11437 (2002). Trading systems continue to be popular with post-Clinton New Democrats as well as with Republicans, for international as well as domestic policy, so this debate will continue.

administrative penalty proceedings, and in some recent calls for cooperative partnership between industry and regulators.[85]

- *Self-policing:* Closely related to the calls for voluntarism are proposals for corporate self-policing, according to which companies largely take over the oversight responsibilities of the government by auditing their own compliance with the law and pledging to take steps to correct noncompliance. On the limits of this approach in a post-Enron world, see Flatt, The Enron Story and Environmental Policy, 33 Envtl. L. Rep. 10485 (2003).

- *Privatization:* Especially in natural resources fields, this argument holds that government management is inexpert and lacks incentive. By transferring resources into private corporate hands, the exploiting industry will have an incentive to manage the resource base for long-term sustainable profits rather than short-term profit maximization.[86]

- *Emphasis on common law instead of regulatory law:* Some recent corporation-oriented libertarian writings argue that environmental protection is better achieved through traditional common law causes of action and remedies (explored in Chapters 3 and 4) than through public law regulation.[87]

- *"Tort reform" restraints on common law:* At the same time, strenuous arguments for restricting tort law have been made over the past 20 years by industry critics of the common law liability system. Tort awards, especially punitive and emotional pain and suffering damages, are often very large and quite crude.[88] In the wake of the asbestos and Agent Orange toxic exposure cases, a number

---

85. There is some validity to assertions about an era of government-industry partnership as a "third generation" of environmental law. By the early 1990s, it may be that the framework of federal pollution laws had generally become accepted by the marketplace, shaping internal industry planning and giving rise to the small but vital secondary sector of pollution control business. But how does one then explain the 104th Congress? The dramatic events of the Contract With America Congress in 1994 vividly demonstrated that the inherent instinct of the marketplace to unshackle itself and externalize social costs had not disappeared. Because industry was able to capture the House of Representatives, its Project Relief proceeded to pass bills overturning a broad swath of protective environmental and social welfare laws. Species protection listings under the ESA were subjected to a year-long statutory moratorium. Entrepreneurial human nature had not been reversed by years of industrial accommodation to environmental regulation. Had it not been for the bravery in particular of Republican Senator John Chaffee of Rhode Island, chair of the Senate Environment and Public Works Committee, many more corrosive statutes would have been passed in the 104th Congress. As anti-environmental efforts recur, it is not clear who stands in Chafee's shoes protecting the prior landscape of environmental law.

86. This argument is sometimes overtly based on the further rationale that resource exploitation industries dominate government agencies that are supposed to regulate them, a prime example being the timber industry and the U.S. Forest Service in the Dept. of Agriculture. See Huffman, Public Lands: The Case for Privatization, 6 Lewis & Clark Nat. Res. Law Inst. News, Number 2 at 10 (1995). The physical results of the Mining Law of 1872, 30 U.S.C. §§22 et seq., which for token payments turns over ownership of large blocks of federal land to mining companies, do not provide a very good advertisement for privatization arguments.

87. See, e.g., Bourdreaux & Yandle, Public Bads and Public Nuisance: Common Law Remedies for Environmental Decline, 14 Fordham Envtl. L.J. 55 (2002), Huffman, Markets, Regulation, and Environmental Protection, 55 Mont. L. Rev. 425 (1994). These arguments are generally libertarian in perspective and appear to regard common law as an accepted part of the "free market" system, far more legitimate than regulation (echoing a distinction Justice Scalia relied upon in the *Lucas* case, 505 U.S. 1003, 1027–1028 (1992), noted in Chapter 23). The common law holds an important place in environmental law, but many environmental social costs are not effectively regulated by the common law because they are so broadly diffused, are hampered by transaction causes, and need to prove specific causation of injuries deriving from the defendants' actions, which is often impossible.

88. Since the late 1980s, environmental tort cases have generated the largest jury verdicts awarded, often in the area of toxic exposures. See, e.g., these asbestos verdicts: Coyne v. Celotex Group, 1989 WL 1099878 (D. Mass. 1989) ($152 million verdict); Todak v. Foster Wheeler Corp., 2002 WL 1162452 (Cal. Super. Ct. 2002) ($33.7 million verdict); Dudley v. Owens-Corning Fiberglass Corp., 1994 WL 864863 (Fla. Cir. Ct. 1994) ($19.3 million verdict); Harlow v. Hopeman Bros., Inc., 2003 WL 535927 (Md. Cir. Ct. 2003) ($19.9 million verdict).

of proposals surfaced for managing mass environmental tort cases, though none has been successfully implemented. Several states have legislated caps on tort recoveries,[89] cheered on by business and bitterly criticized by the plaintiffs' bar.

- *Proposals for alternative implementation of environmental standards via Pigouvian taxes:* Sometimes included in inventories of "market-based" approaches to environmental regulation (studied in Chapter 14) are proposals that taxes or fees for pollution are a far better way to force industry to confront the fuller costs of its production. The approach is usually to set Pigouvian taxes at a level that will compensate society for the real cost of cleaning up or the real cost of absorbing the pollution into human metabolisms and the environment.[90] A brief effort to imagine such a system quickly reveals that setting the amount of such taxes inevitably is a highly subjective process. The approach, however, offers analytical attractions and several areas of practical utility.

- *"Economic impact statement" review procedures:* Taking their lead from the effectiveness of the NEPA's requirement of EISs, a number of legislative attempts have been made to attach a similar requirement to the implementation of environmental protection measures.[91] They are generally regarded in the political world as attempts to delay and prevent environmental regulation rather than to improve its efficiency and effectiveness, but there is a seeming symmetry to requiring all agency actions, not just those that pose environmental threats, to go through comprehensive analysis. These review processes, whether so intended, tend to create "paralysis by analysis" in which forward movement is thwarted by endless rounds of discussion and review.

- *Cost-benefit-risk analysis as a prescriptive standard for barring or shaping regulatory decisionmaking:* This initiative attempts to establish market-oriented cost-benefit formulas as determinative procedures in setting and enforcing regulatory standards domestically and abroad.[92] Should agencies be required to prove that regulatory standards are cost-justified before they can be promulgated and applied? Should careful calculations of provable risk be required to justify all regulation? Or are these reform proposals consciously or inadvertently designed to produce "paralysis by analysis"? These issues are studied in depth in Chapter 13. Although cost-benefit analysis has had powerful effect in many lower court decisions as well as national legislative policy, the Supreme Court has ruled that basic regulatory rationality does not require cost-benefit analysis.[93] Since the

---

89. See, e.g., Ala. Code §6-11-21, Fla. Stat. ch. 768.73, Kan. Stat. Ann. §60-3701, Tex. Civ. Prac. & Rem. Code Ann. §41.008, Va. Code Ann. §8.01-38.1. Instead of capping punitive damages, some, like Massachusetts, bar punitive or "exemplary" damages altogether.

90. *See generally,* W. Baumol & W. Oates, The Theory of Environmental Policy (2d ed. 1988); Cavanaugh, On the Road to Incoherence: Congress, Economics, and Taxes, 49 UCLA L. Rev. 685 (2002); Merrill, Explaining Market Mechanisms, 2000 U. Ill. L. Rev. 275.

91. See, e.g., H.R. 1631, 107th Cong. (1st Sess. 2001) (requiring the preparation of an environmental impact statement for activities conducted off the coast of Florida under oil and gas leases); Campbell & Holmes, Going Once, Going Twice, Sold! EPA Auctions Pollution Rights; Market-Based System Permits Sale of Allowances to Emit Sulfur Dioxide, N.Y. L.J., June 7, 1993, at 10 (discussing a 1993 New York legislative proposal to require utilities to prepare environmental impact statements regarding sales of allowances).

92. By its nature, this approach tends to override the precautionary and polluter-pays principles.

93. See American Textile Mfr. Inst. v. Donovan, 452 U.S. 490 (1981) (the "cotton dust" case, Rehnquist, J., dissent); Whitman v. American Trucking Assns., Inc., 531 U.S. 457 (2001).

2000 election, however, a narrow cost-benefit approach has been wielded by John Graham, an anti-regulation activist installed by the Bush II White House as head of the OMB reviewing proposed rules, to dilute or block a wide range of environmental protection measures. This shift in regulatory process is studied in Chapter 13.

• *Devolution back to the states:* Efforts in courts and legislatures to recapture and transfer regulatory primacy back to the states from the federal government have used a selective "federalist" argument to achieve a "divide-and-conquer," "race-to-the-bottom" political logic. The operative premise seems to be that if regulation of the marketplace is devolved to 50 different legal systems, the overall regulatory constraints on industry will decline.[94] Recent manifestations include Bush II Administration suggestions that determinations on required degrees of pollution control should be shifted back to the states that best know their own situations, and recent Supreme Court decisions such as *Lopez, Morrison,* and *SWANCC* that cut back the scope of federal regulatory jurisdiction. On the other hand, where states are more protective of health and environment than the federal government, these advocates shift to the preemption defense. Devolution and the balance between state and federal power are noted in Chapter 6.

• *Risk-based priority-setting, by experts:* Justice Stephen Breyer, among others, has recommended the creation of a centralized federal administrative group that would develop, coordinate, and supervise federal risk regulation through a decisional structure similar to an agency of experts on a military command model. Breyer has decried the lack of an overall agenda for reducing risks. Breyer proposed the development of a system by which regulatory resources could be shifted from areas of minimal risk to fields in which they could achieve the greatest amount of risk reduction for every dollar spent. Such calls for risk-based regulation have been echoed in radio talk shows, the 104th Congress, and a popular collection of anecdotes castigating government regulations as intemperate and disproportionate. See, e.g., Philip Howard's *The Death of Common Sense: How Law Is Suffocating America* (1994), calling, like Justice Breyer, for a body of statistical risk experts to reform regulatory practice.

• *"Sound science" and peer review:* Many proposals for fundamental reform of the way environmental policy is developed do not attack the environmental laws directly but instead target the way the science underlying environmental standards is conducted. Numerous regulatory critics believe that EPA's science is unsound and that the agency tends to overstate environmental risks through such practices as, for example, relying on high-dose animal testing for evidence of carcinogenicity and emphasizing the upper bound estimates in risk assessments. One prominent proposal for reform (embraced by OMB in 2003) is to subject EPA's science to peer review by outside experts — a proposal that threatens further to lengthen already complex and time-consuming regulatory actions.

---

94. The uniform federal minimum regulatory standards of "cooperative federalism" blocks the interstate race-to-the-bottom. That the race-to-the-bottom divide-and-conquer strategy is real, despite a good deal of recent wistful revisionist denial, one need only consider the core attempts in each of the three anti-environmental eras to neuter environmental law by shifting it back to the states. See, e.g., D. McSteety & J. Owens, The Republican Takeover of Congress (1998).

A Further Array of Anti-regulatory Tactics. There is a further range of generic "reform" strategies designed to reduce environmental protection law, regularly advocated by the industrial lobbies in Washington and echoed in anti-regulatory administrations and in the anti-regulatory sector of the judiciary that has been built up since 1981.[95]

- *Restricting citizen enforcement:* The post-1960s pluralism that built environmental law on the foundation of the Civil Rights, Antiwar, and Consumerist Movements focused on citizen action and citizen law enforcement. If citizen enforcement is blocked, then many regulatory laws are ineffective, and "Iron Triangles"[96] — made up of regulated industries, supportive legislators, and suborned agencies — can continue to dominate in the traditional insider-politics fashion. Severe constraints have increasingly been placed on citizen enforcement by legislative riders and judicial holdings, particularly in the area of standing to sue, studied in Chapters 7 and 21. The Supreme Court's 2000 *Laidlaw* decision somewhat abated the siege against citizen standing, though subsequent decisions reflect continuing efforts to constrain citizen suits.

- *Regulatory takings challenges:* These constitutional claims propose that when government regulation "goes too far" in its impact upon private business enterprises, it is void or held to require compensation. The definition of private rights, of public rights, and of when a regulation "goes too far" is an intensely political process, in which private rights initiatives recently have been strongly in the ascendancy, taking property rights to a position of dominance unprecedented in this or any other country. Uncertainty about how private property rights will be weighed — studied in Chapter 23 — serves to chill new regulation as well as to encourage state and local courts to broaden the scope of required compensation for existing regulations. The Supreme Court's *Palazzolo* and *Tahoe-Sierra* cases have dampened this initiative in the judicial setting. This sector of challenges tends to raise fundamental questions about how we conceive of the nature of government. At times, as during the Gingrich revolution of the 104th Congress or in certain opinions expressed by Justice Scalia or radio commentator Rush

---

95. In an extended inquiry into the judicial role in environmental public law, a report discerned and tracked a complex and coordinated campaign by industry-funded groups starting in the Reagan years to appoint federal judges and shape judicial agendas to serve a generally anti-regulatory, anti-environmental agenda:

> The cases…showed remarkable activism by [these] jurists: in many cases, the judges overcame seemingly insurmountable procedural and substantive hurdles to rule in favor of…developers…. The political, more than the judicial or scholarly, background of many of these same judges…resulted, in many instances, from a concerted effort by conservatives and libertarians within the Reagan and Bush [I] administrations to use the court system to further their attack on federal regulations…. More remarkably,…the most activist judges…have attended the same, all-expenses-paid, week-long summer seminars at a Montana resort hosted by a property rights group [funded by] the same conservative foundations that…bankroll [anti-regulatory] litigation before the Federal Circuit. Kendall & Lord, The Takings Project, 25 B.C. Envtl. Aff. L. Rev. 509, 511 (1999).

In 1997 alone, one of the market advocacy foundations reported, 8% of the entire federal judiciary had enjoyed resort holidays at its "issue seminars," making a total until then of 40% of the judiciary. See Marcus, Issues Groups Fund Seminars for Judges, Wash. Post, Apr. 9, 1998, at A1.

96. "Iron Triangles" in the political science rubric are the colluding political blocs formed in a particular area by industry groups in the marketplace, by the agencies that fund or regulate them, and by their congressional supporters. Examples are the timber industry, U.S. Forest Service, and timber states legislators; the barge and shipping industries, the Army Corps of Engineers, and southern delegations; and more. See F. Powledge, *Water: The Nature, Uses, and Future of Our Most Precious and Abused Resource* 285–289 (1982).

Limbaugh, government is depicted as a junior partner to the marketplace, a dubious, barely legitimate necessary evil.[97]

- *Hold it right there. Haven't we done enough already?* Has modern environmental law reached the limit of reasonable returns? One current generalized theory of "reform" is that environmental law doesn't need to be further extended in the United States and other nations that are the leading players in global commerce. A number of media voices have made that argument, echoing the traditional marketplace plaint that the environmental pendulum has swung too far. In his 1995 book *A Moment on the Earth,* Gregg Easterbrook argued that environmentalists "are surely on the right side of history, but increasingly on the wrong side of the present," arguing that environmental protection law had become a sufficiently accepted and implemented societal norm (this at the same moment that industrial lobbyists had just taken over the 104th Congress) that pressure should be taken off Western industry and focus instead on the large-scale environmental problems of the Third World. In 2001 Bjorn Lomborg, a Danish political science statistics professor, published *The Skeptical Environmentalist: Measuring the Real State of the World,* likewise challenging the idea that the global environment is deteriorating. Like Easterbrook, Lomborg argued the environment has actually been rapidly improving and criticized environmentalists for unjustifiably instilling fear in the public. Both books triggered passionate praise and criticism.[98] Lomborg's critics, mostly scientists and environmental organizations, attacked his scientific credibility. Lomborg's supporters, primarily economists and political scientists, praised his numbers-oriented deflationary approach to weighing the necessities of environmental regulation. The advice from pundits like Easterbrook and Lomborg that we should cease tightening environmental standards is quickly pulled into the national policy debate. Their arguments, however, can be accused of missing the point:

> At first blush, many people might conclude from the visible improvements to the environment that we have done our work well and that, except for maintenance, the...government should move on to other pressing priorities. Others would prefer to see a rollback of environmental legislation, as was proposed in the 104th Congress, in the belief that we have simply gone too far. [Others] might feel that the enormous problems of maintaining clean water and air in the world's developing megacities or habitat destruction in Asia or South America are now more important than reforming environmental protection in the United States.... These assessments overlook some important facts. First, many once "quiet" issues are emerging as population densities increase. Second, our understanding of ecological and public health threats continues to change. Substances that were beneficial in direct application, such as

---

97. An interchange between Justices O'Connor and Scalia in the *Palazzolo* case noted in Chapter 23 nicely framed this basal difference in perspective, with Justice O'Connor criticizing Justice Scalia's concept of "Government-as-thief." Palazzolo v. Rhode Island, 533 U.S. 606, 636 at n.4 (2001) (O'Connor, J., concurrence; cf. Scalia, J., dissent, id. at 637).

98. See A Moment of Truth: Correcting the Scientific Errors in Gregg Easterbrook's *A Moment on the Earth* (L. Haimson & B. Goodman eds., 1996). The authors conclude that Easterbrook's account of environmental issues "is replete with errors and misinterpretations of the scientific evidence...especially notable in regard to...habitat loss, global warming, ozone depletion, and species extinction."

Lomborg's Skeptical Environmentalist is analyzed from multiple perspectives in 53 Case W. Res. L. Rev. No. 2 (2002).

chlorofluorocarbons, turn out to be harmful long after they have served their local function. Third, the environmental advances of recent years are not evenly distributed among urban and suburban areas, rich and poor neighborhoods, and geographical regions. Fourth, we are just beginning to appreciate how deeply the environment is intertwined with many other issues such as human health, energy and food production, and international trade. Thus, rather than retrench, we must renew our commitment to environmental protection. Chertow & Esty, Environmental Policy: The Next Generation, Issues Sci. & Tech., Fall 1997, at 73–74.

Reform: A View to the Future. Trying to find common ground, a group of 80 eminent participants from business, government, and citizen environmental groups put together a consensus prescription for future environmental protection:

A VISION FOR THE FUTURE

1. Maintain basic standards of environmental protection, and effectively and efficiently prevent and control threats to human health and the environment;

2. Ensure that all environmental laws and regulations are fairly and consistently enforced;

3. Distribute costs and benefits fairly, accounting for impacts on both present and future generations, and address disproportionate impacts on any group in society, especially low-income individuals, people of color, or other disadvantaged groups;

4. Set and pursue clear environmental goals and milestones for the nation, states, localities, and tribes, and use understandable indicators to measure progress;

5. Adapt and adjust policies, strategies, and systems based on experience and new information;

6. Generate, disseminate, and rely on the best available scientific and economic information;

7. Offer flexibility of means coupled with clarity of responsibility, accountability for performance, and transparency of results;

8. Rely on a broad set of policy tools, including:
   - economic incentives that are aligned with environmental goals, reward superior environmental performance, and stimulate technological innovation,
   - incentives for changes in individual behavior, and
   - disclosure of consistent and accurate source-level performance information;

9. Place authority, responsibility, and accountability at the appropriate level of government;

10. Promote collaborative problem solving and integrated policy making by all branches and levels of government;

11. Promote high levels of environmental stewardship and continuous improvement in environmental performance; and

12. Create decision processes that meaningfully involve affected stakeholders and engage all citizens in protecting the environment. Ruckleshaus, Stepping Stones, Envtl. F., Mar. 1998, at 31.

Is this set of overview prescriptions useful or a collection of ambiguous aspirations? The trick is moving such principles into practicable enforceability in a context fraught with fractious politics and differential political advantages. For the foreseeable future the development of environmental law is likely to remain a process of battle. It is a task as broad as government itself, frustrating, burdensome, never permanently successful or satisfying, altruistic, and practically necessary.

Section 5. A SUMMARY OF CROSS-CUTTING THEMES

Uncertainty, Scientific Complexity, and Risk. These three are endemic problems in environmental policy. Often both the presence and the effects of a harmful human impact are invisible until too late. When chemicals leach through the subsoil killing communities of microscopic soil-building organisms or highway salt poisons the root systems of trees, neither cause nor effect is seen until the soil's productivity crashes or the trees begin to die. When pollution is spread widely through an air or water commons, its concentrations are so diffused that the pollution is not noticed until huge volumes are discharged. When human health begins to show signs of illness and injury from widespread exposures to environmental toxins — sometimes 30 years after the exposure — the individual pathways of contamination and proof of causation are typically so scientifically complicated as to be practically impossible to pin down.

And trying to ascertain and handle "risk," the statistical likelihood of particular perils in particular settings, confronts even greater scientific complexities and subjectivities, as well as psychological and political barriers. Tradeoffs between risks do occur. For example, tradeoffs are made between short-term material welfare and long-term ecological integrity. Some toxic residues can be tolerated in foods in order to have the benefit of crops that are not destroyed by pests; some continuing risks such as global warming are accepted in the short term for the sake of developing economies and consumption desires. Environmentalists, however, continually argue against false tradeoff choices when rational alternatives are available. Is it really true that "You have to choose — either economic progress or environmental quality. You can't have both"? To most modern environmental analysts that universal cliché sounds like the classic false tradeoff. In the long term, both are inseparable; in the short term, they can and, at the very least, must be reconcilable.

Science and law continually work together, but they essentially occupy different worlds. In the complex business of proving "causation," for example — that exposure to chemical X causes malady Y — science requires a certainty level of 95% (a margin of error of no more than 5%), criminal law requires a supermajority ("beyond a reasonable doubt," perhaps somewhat less than 95%), common law requires only 50% plus one ("probable"), and statutory law (which in many cases needs only to be "not arbitrary") can regulate with even less certain proof of causation.[99] This often produces confusion. Navigating the subtle cross-channels of science and law is a continuing challenge.

The Many Meanings of Risk. What is the nature of the risk posed by industrial pollution and toxic chemicals? Can that risk be meaningfully described exclusively by

---

99. Regulatory law often deals with risk situations where government must protect against unproved or unquantified threats, as when it controls releases of genetically-altered organisms into the environment. Sometimes these include "zero-infinity" problems, where public law attempts to control the risks of harms that are close to zero in likelihood of happening but that would be catastrophic in scale of harm if they were to occur.

reference to the numerical probability and magnitude of the physical harms these substances produce? Or is it also helpful, for regulatory purposes, to consider as well the qualitative features of the risks posed by them? For decades, Paul Slovic and other cognitive psychologists have studied risk perceptions and their determinants. They have arrived at a fairly compact list of attributes that tend to make a substance or activity seem risky to ordinary citizens. Involuntariness, uncontrollability, unfamiliarity, inequitable distribution, effects on future generations, catastrophic outcomes — these are among the qualities that make particular hazards especially scary. A fierce debate exists as to whether risk regulation should be controlled by reference to quantitative factors alone or should also be informed by the qualitative features of risk.

Human Nature and the Externalization of Social Costs. Hardin's tragedy of the commons and Coase's descriptions of cost externalization illustrate how individual human actors are powerfully motivated to maximize their own gains at the expense of the public and the commons. These drives have produced the biggest marketplace economy the world has known, with all the blessings that follow it, and all the forlorn consequences that arise from not planning for and dealing with the realities of costs that are externalized onto nature and the public.

Environmental Law Attempts to "Internalize" Social Costs. In effect, Rachel Carson's *Silent Spring* spread a broad intellectual catch-basket beneath the welfare economists' universe of benefit maximizing individual actors, so as to collect and take overall account of their jettisoned "externalized" social costs, even if they are indirect and unmarketized. The role of environmental law has been to attempt through common law, state and federal statutory and regulatory systems, and even constitutional theories to force externalized environmental and social costs back into the politics and economics of the marketplace.

Resistance to Regulation. Business-oriented resistance to regulation tends to be a consistent backdrop to the government process. An economic entity naturally tends to resist cost internalization. Multiply this by tens of thousands of economic entities, and one finds a broad concurrent tendency permeating the governance process. Like flowing water, market forces and the behavioral realities that drive them inherently tend to resist any "artificial" barriers that curtail their externalizations of social costs. To place a single sandbag into the current is difficult and not likely to have significant effect. As other sandbags are added with great effort, the inherent pressures of the market economy still pour around them. When finally a working accumulation of sandbags is secured, the waters may turn to a path of less resistance, but they do not stop trying to infiltrate and undercut the obstacles blocking their maximum satisfaction. Across the entire face of the environmental law dike the pressures are felt. Lobbyists, lawyers, media managers, political action committees, and a host of political players apply subtle, comprehensive pressure within all three branches of government. When citizens attempt to get around the phenomenon of agency capture[100] by bringing private

---

100. On the classic political science phenomenon of "agency capture," see Chapter 7.

enforcement actions in the courts, the forces of the marketplace try to undercut citizen standing and judicial remedies.

Biodiversity — of Nature and Law. From ecological science comes the proposition that natural systems that evolve and maintain a wider diversity of living elements are more likely to be successful in the long run. A rich natural biodiversity means that ecosystems are likely to have more interlocking practical mechanisms and more available adaptive options for coping with ongoing changes.[101] Law too has its biodiversity. A consistent reality in environmental practice is the multiplicity of public law statutes and regulations — not to mention potential common law liabilities — that can come to bear in a particular environmental case. The American legal system has always had as one of its special strengths that it combines statutory, regulatory, constitutional, and common law mechanisms within a single system, and each of these has a rich variety of different approaches and remedies, all employed on occasion by opportunistic environmental law.

The Goal of Environmental Law (and Democratic Governance)? Long-term survivability and success in maintaining civic and social quality of life for present and future human generations is an appropriate goal for a society. Careful consideration and stewardship of natural systems typically contributes to that goal. Because of our human natural history, our species' ethical perceptions, the remarkable qualities of life that flow from contact with natural processes, or the stark utilitarian necessity of not betraying the natural systems that support and nourish us, nature is important. A sensitive ongoing balance between the dynamics of daily life and the past, present, and future richness of human existence, in its complex natural context, will define the successes that environmental law strives to achieve.

Sustainable Development and Intergenerational Equity. Perhaps the phrase that best captures the goal of environmental law and policy is "sustainable development." It was the leitmotif of the Rio Conference on the Environment of 1992, where more than 100 presidents and kings, and hundreds of delegations from around the world, agreed that the momentum and practices of the status quo threaten our common global future and that coherent international planning and action are necessary. "Sustainable development" means many things to different people, but its gravamen seems to be that our societies and legal systems owe it to ourselves and our posterity to live within available resources and not to destroy the environmental birthright of future generations for the needs and profits of today, a theme echoed in the public trust doctrine in Chapter 22 and elsewhere. Development must not be based upon an erosive diminution of global assets, but rather on systems of indefinitely extendable human sustenance and life quality, in balance with the resource capacity of the planet's environments.

Politics. Environmental law inevitably creates political tensions, raising new civic concerns about the human and ecological consequences of marketplace practices.

---

101. See the discussion of biodiversity in Chapter 16.

Governmental regulation is a natural battleground. Industry groups understandably and powerfully fight back. The result is a neverending process of back-and-forth political contention.

Common Law and Public Law. Both common law and statutory public law play a range of potential roles. The structures of the modern administrative state — public law agencies, statutes, and regulations at local, state, and federal levels — are built upon the flexible and evolving foundations of common law. Environmental attorneys often find it necessary to draw upon both systems, sometimes simultaneously.

Laissez-Faire: How Well Does It Work for Long-Term Societal and Environmental Concerns? There is an instinct in most humans' nature, absent government regulation, to maximize individual profits and avoid thinking of diffused public detriments. If nonstatutory law cannot effectively protect the public interests impacted by the market economy, government regulation of some sort will probably be necessary to bring civic concerns into the daily life of business.

Environmental Justice. As in the *Kepone* case, the ultimate location of many potentially dangerous facilities often turns out to be poorer communities or communities of color, the least empowered populations. The reasons include managers' desires to save money and site operations where they will be least likely to face effective environmental opposition; the self-condescension of low-income communities, exhibited in uncritical eagerness to attract jobs at any price; or simple discrimination. Environmental law increasingly has been pressured to take account of environmental justice issues.

The Race-to-the-Bottom: State and Federal Jurisdictions. A basic pressure within environmental law comes from the tendency of states to compete with each other for industrial payrolls by lowering regulatory standards. This race-to-the-bottom is a political kind of tragedy of the commons.[102] Federal statutes have formed the core of environmental law, typically structured to provide federal minimum floors to counter the erosive race-to-the-bottom. Environmental law repeatedly serves as a battleground for economic conflicts in "federalism" debates over the basic allocation of roles between federal and state governments.

Environmental Statutes Evolve. Statutes change over time, for better and worse, in the same way as living species evolve, according to the pressures, experience, and changing contexts they encounter.

Role of Citizen-Initiated Actions in the Legal System. Perhaps the core feature in the evolution of U.S. environmental law has been the critical role played by citizens in initiating, shaping, and shepherding the development of environmental protection case law

---

102. Allied had been persuaded to move some operations to Louisiana, where they became part of a highly polluted industrial area now often known as "Cancer Alley." The concept of race-to-the-bottom is subject to ongoing debate and is explored further in Chapter 5.

and statutes.[103] Legal standing provisions allowing "private attorneys general" to enforce environmental statutes had an immediate and dramatic effect, and imaginative common law actions built a jurisprudence that became a model for the rest of the world. Citizen litigation continues to be a significant component in 75% of environmental civil cases.

Strategic Role of the Media. A critical part of many or most significant environmental issues, as in the *Kepone* story, is the amount and kind of media coverage they receive. Media climate builds the momentum of citizen organizations, often impels corporate acknowledgment of public concerns, and is particularly helpful in making public law mechanisms responsive. Effective public communication of information plays a significant role in social governance.

Systemic Roles of "Outrage." There is a tension between outrage-driven controversies and cool-headed analysis. Environmentalists often find that they must cast their public arguments in terms of outrage and extremes in order to gain and hold official attention and political credibility. Outrage can skew the subtleties of an issue; it can also focus necessary attention on issues the public cares about, whereas cool, less passionate discussions may end up missing the public reality.

Remedy and Enforcement Choices. Both private parties and public agencies have a wide choice of potential legal remedies and make their selections based upon the character of acts and actors, the scope of harms, the parties' own agendas, the climate of public reaction, and more. The common law offers a number of forms of damages and creative equitable remedies. Public law provides a further range of civil remedies, plus the possibility of criminal punishments. Administrative options for civil and criminal remedies, or combinations thereof, add a further level of tactical analysis to the complexities of environmental enforcement. See Chapters 20 and 21.

Global Interconnections. Many environmental issues involve international interconnections and repercussions. In some cases, the linkage is through transboundary spillover effects, international standards or obligations tied to legal conventions, or an international reprise of the race-to-the-bottom when U.S. manufacturers threaten to move operations to less-stringent manufacturing locations overseas. In other cases, it is through international business activities, such as Allied's 20 years of Kepone sales to countries that lacked basic safety testing procedures and made no provisions for limiting human exposures. Potential international liability issues arise as environmental law increasingly reflects interconnections transcending national boundaries.

---

103. In many countries, it is up to a government agency to recover such damages for injured citizens. After 2500 people were killed by methyl-isocyanate in Bhopal, in 1984, it was the government of India that sued Union Carbide, recovering $14,500 per death; after the Seveso dioxin incident in Italy in 1976, the settlement negotiated by the government ended the liability claims. After the Exxon-Valdez oil spill disaster in Alaska in 1989, the state government briefly considered recovering on behalf of its injured citizens, but ultimately deferred to normal Anglo-American custom and left private recoveries up to private litigants.

The Polluter-Pays Principle. As the strict liability character of most of today's pollution legislation shows, a basic premise of most modern regulation here and abroad is that absorbing environmental costs is a responsibility of marketplace industries, not a cost to be absorbed by public subsidies paying for prevention and cleanups, nor by the unpaid subsidy of public toleration of pollution (even if it is more "efficient" to pay industry to end pollution).

Precaution (a/k/a the Precautionary Principle). Environmental problems frequently arise at the cutting edge of human knowledge, areas of vigorous scientific inquiry that may be fraught with uncertainty. Environmental risks in such situations, while not precisely known from a scientific point of view, may represent immense potential for harms, like those from global warming of the earth's climate due to the "greenhouse" effect. Precautionary approaches counsel taking early policy action to avoid uncertain or poorly understood risks, particularly in situations where the consequences may be catastrophic. The concept is frequently espoused in international and domestic law and policy, countered by arguments that disruptive regulations should not be applied to risks until the likelihood of harms and their serious nature have been scientifically established and carefully weighed against the status quo.

Administrative Process. The delegation of pervasive administrative powers to government agencies is a vital part of modern legal process and a part of the perplexing nature of environmental law. Deference to administrative agencies is obviously important in order to allow implementation of public law in a complex world. On the other hand, agencies are vulnerable to the suasions of politics. The skills of managing the administrative process are technically challenging and also raise fundamental questions about democratic governance in modern industrial societies.

Citizen Enforcement, Multicentric Pluralism. A fundamentally important element of the U.S. legal system, increasingly being adopted abroad, is the legal and practical opportunity for participation in regulation and enforcement by directly affected citizens, a shift from the old bipolar regulatory structure dominated by industry and agencies to a multicentric pluralistic process.

A Reaction Against Pluralism. Given that citizen participation and enforcement have been strategically important in achieving compliance with laws constraining the marketplace, it is likewise unsurprising that a major continuing theme of daily politics has been to limit the role of citizens and to return to the past's more insulated relationship between agencies and industries. This market resistance against the pluralization of the U.S. legal system, beginning in the Nixon years, is seen daily in the regulatory process, in legislative attempts to rescind citizen enforcement provisions, and in some federal courts' ongoing attempts to cut back on citizen standing and judicial scrutiny of agency decisionmaking.

Risk and Cost-Benefit Analyses. Part of the ongoing debates about enhancing or decreasing environmental protections will continue to be the relativity questions. Given the costs and uncertainties of trying to achieve high degrees of protection, and alternative demands on precious public and private resources of time and money, it is consistently important to gauge the balance of costs, benefits, and alternatives, though the perspectives of the marketplace economy and the civic economy will cast the balance in very different terms.

The Public Trust Doctrine, and Cultural Values Beyond Market Values. The public trust embodies fundamentally conservative principles. The ultimate measure of a society would seem to be based upon more than just the essential physical needs for survival — to this should be added the full quality of its people's life, and the legacy of ideas, accomplishments, resources, and potentials it seeks to pass on to successor generations. The public trust, whether incorporated in statutes or existing within our nonstatutory jurisprudence, represents and gives legal force to many of the unmarketized present and future social values that often get overlooked in the immediacy of daily life but that are part of the ultimate measure.

Stewardship, Intergenerational Equity, and Sustainability. If a society is to survive and advance over time, like species competing in the Darwinian process of replicating and prolonging their genetic identity over succeeding generations, it must incorporate present realities and the needs of future generations into its present legal norms. Ethical concepts of environmental stewardship described by ecophilosophers evoke concepts of legacy — nations, like most nondysfunctional families, honoring what they have received from the past and trying to pass it on, enhanced, to their posterity. The ancient public trust doctrine thus fits well with modern environmental law's principles and technologies of sustainability.

By conducting ourselves ethically toward all creatures, we enter into a spiritual relationship with the universe.

— Albert Schweitzer

Why all this talk about efficiency? The last thing the "Founding Fathers" were after was efficiency. There were after freedom. And they understood that freedom implied a certain tolerance for messy conflict.

— John Culver, quoted in N.Y Times Mag., 12 March '89, at 101

Chapter 3

THE COMMON LAW IN MODERN ENVIRONMENTAL LAW: NONSTATUTORY CAUSES OF ACTION

A. *Tort Causes of Action in the Environmental Arena*
B. *Defenses in Environmental Tort Suits*
C. *Causation in Conventional Environmental Tort Suits*
D. *Remedies in Environmental Litigation*
E. *Environmental Uses of Other Nonstatutory Causes of Action*

This chapter begins with a brief overview of tort law followed immediately by the classic case of Oscar Boomer and the Atlantic Cement Company. Many students have already encountered the *Boomer* case in a torts or property class, so some aspects of its legal analysis may be familiar. In this coursebook, however, *Boomer* serves as a case study of private intentional nuisance torts, illustrating a wide range of legal strategies, defenses, remedies, and novel approaches used in environmental litigation. *Boomer* also can be a vehicle for developing the ecological, economic, and political accounting that underlies every environmental case. This chapter proceeds from *Boomer* to a more general study of how torts and other nonstatutory causes of action have been adapted to fit environmental cases, leading into Chapter 4 and some special lessons to be drawn from modern toxic chemical cases.

Each year many environmental cases involving localized pollution are filed under common law theories. These local cases undoubtedly make up the numerical majority of environmental cases generally. Even so, when an oil tanker disaster strikes the waters and coastal shores of a state or when a chemical factory's dump-site poisons land and groundwater, the major remedies litigated by injured parties are likewise based almost entirely on common law. After the wreck of the *Exxon-Valdez*, for example, the majority of legal claims filed by the State of Alaska and its citizens relied primarily on tort and public trust theories to respond to that vast catastrophe.[1] The common law is a fertile hunting ground for environmental lawyers trying to get a handle on some of the most modern ecological problems, and the common law thus plays a critical role in shaping private litigation in U.S. environmental law.

The common law also provides the conceptual foundation for most statutes and regulations. Legislatures and agencies rely on the continued existence of common law

---

1. The largest damage awards resulting from the Alaska oil spill were based on common law. Government claims also were filed under criminal and civil provisions of state and federal water laws, and the penalties paid to the governments combined both common law and statutory claims.

to fill gaps in public law and to guide courts and agencies in their interpretation of statutes and rules. Statutes may come and go, but the common law generally rolls on.

Many fundamental issues raised in environmental law, moreover, will continue to be raised first in the common law realm. Questions of proof, uncertainty, balances of risk, fault, liability, foreseeability, standards of care, technological feasibility, causation, long-term residual injuries, remedies, practical deterrence, enforceability, and so on — all these are found first in the common law. Despite the existence of innumerable federal and state environmental statutes and reams of administrative regulations, the common law of environmental protections remains vigorous and important.

A. TORT CAUSES OF ACTION IN THE ENVIRONMENTAL ARENA

Section 1. TRANSFORMING TRADITIONAL COMMON LAW TORTS INTO MODERN ENVIRONMENTAL LAW

To facilitate the study of torts in environmental law, a short review of general tort law principles is helpful. One of the best answers to the question, "What are torts?"[2] was given by Cecil A. Wright, who based his definition in the dynamism of changing community norms regarding redress for injuries:

> Arising out of the various and ever-increasing clashes of the activities of persons living in a common society, carrying on business in competition with fellow members of that society, owning property which may in any of a thousand ways affect the persons or property of others — in short, doing all the things that constitute modern living — there must of necessity be losses, or injuries of many kinds sustained as a result of the activities of others. The purpose of the law of torts is to adjust these losses, and to afford compensation for injuries sustained by one person as the result of the conduct of another.[3]

The field of torts has a long and storied history that reaches back many centuries. Rooted in community norms governing relationships between community members, tort law emerged as the evolving common law court system began to recognize the provision of remedies to suitors who had suffered certain wrongs or injuries. Early on, tort causes of action joined claims based on contract and property at the core of the common law. Over time, the system became highly articulated, where particular claims of injury were raised by pleading them according to a formula that was associated with a particular kind of writ. The use of these particularized writs was required in order to initiate an action in the common law courts. In the modern law of torts, the contemporary counterpart to the antiquated formulary writ is the cause of action. In modern tort practice, there are now distinct causes of action that are affiliated with distinct species of torts. Each cause of action comprises certain specific elements that must be proven in order for a plaintiff to prevail on a claim for that kind of tort.

In addition to this evolution from the writ system to modern tort causes of action, a more recent development makes common law torts an important part of

---

2. See, e.g., W. P. Keeton & W. L. Prosser, Prosser and Keeton on Torts §1 (5th ed. 1984).
3. Wright, Introduction to the Law of Torts, 8 Cambridge L.J. 238 (1944).

environmental law — the adaptation of several well-recognized tort causes of action to provide remedies for pollution-induced and exposure-realted injuries to human health, property rights, and the environment. Losses sustained as a result of pollution and exposure to hazardous substances have become more frequent as the commons everyone shares becomes more congested due to increasing population, industrial activity, and resource exploitation. The law of torts has been adapted to provide remedies for these "environmental" claims and others. Much of what is now seen as standard application of tort law reflects a period of creative use of common law principles by environmental plaintiffs who were able to persuade judges that claims for novel environmental harms were legitimate and should be remedied in accordance with familiar and traditional principles of tort law. The cases and other materials in this chapter will try simultaneously to give a snapshot of tort law as it applies to environmental cases while capturing the adaptive dynamism of tort law in that same context.

Consider a simple working model (one of several that can be constructed) of what can loosely be called *generic tort law*: To prevail in tort, a plaintiff must show three basic things: liability, causation, and damage (L, C, and D for short). With some exceptions that are addressed later in this chapter, the plaintiff has the burden of proof to show each of these items by a preponderance of the evidence, i.e., that each is more likely than not. These three elements of L, C, and D compose what is referred to as a prima facie case, or a case that is enough to win. This chapter analyzes these individual tort elements in the context of environmental litigation and also reveals how these separate elements influence one another.

This model uses the terms L, C, and D in a specific sense:

- Liability addresses the reason for shifting the loss from where it has fallen on Plaintiff (π) to Defendant (Δ). The reasons for loss shifting relate to a societal choice to protect an interest of π because it has been affected by an act of Δ for which, to a varying degree, Δ can be seen as "culpable." The culpability aspect of this inquiry has three distinct variations, some having to do with traditional notions of culpability, but others having less to do with the antisocial aspect of the conduct and more to do with risk management and loss allocation policy. The continuum starts with negligent actions that demonstrate a lack of care by Δ. It moves next to "intentional" actions where Δ is charged with responsibility for the "substantially certain" consequences of any actions that Δ intended to take, even if Δ did not desire that those actions would result in harmful consequences. Finally, the continuum ends with strict liability, where loss allocation policy is the predominant factor at work and the law imposes the loss on Δ solely in relation to the nature of the activity that Δ has undertaken without regard to the qualitative assessment of Δ's conduct while undertaking the activity.

- Causation is the existence of a link between the conduct of Δ and the harm suffered by π. Causation has two distinct aspects: cause-in-fact and proximate cause. Cause-in-fact relates to the popular sense of cause and effect and is frequently expressed in the phrase "but for Δ's action, π would not have suffered the injury." Proximate cause is a qualitative element of linkage, requiring, as the term suggests, proximity rather than attenuation and directness rather than circuitousness. In the end, proximate cause places a limit on just how far the law is willing to go in requiring Δ to make redress to π.

• Damage, in this generic description of tort law, means injury to π. There is a substantiality requirement here captured by the Latin phrase "de minimis non curat lex" — the law will not concern itself with trifles. Thus in order to satisfy the general tort element of damage, π must show an injury that is sufficiently serious to justify the law's attention. It is important to note that the term *damages* is also commonly used in tort parlance to denote the umbrella of remedies that π may be awarded at the conclusion of a tort claim, i.e., after π has established and proved a prima facie case. The law provides several categories of damages — compensatory, consequential, special, or punitive. In addition to damages, π might also seek injunctive relief. In the tort context, injunctive relief usually prevents Δ from beginning or continuing to do something that the law determines to be injurious to π or π's property. The assessment of which kind of remedy will apply in any given case involves a separate analysis that is frequently as complex as the L-C-D analysis used to establish a prima facie tort case. After π has made out a prima facie case, many subtleties remain that affect the amount or measure of compensatory damages awarded, as well as the array of compensable items recognizable under various theories of liability. Moreover, there are additional requirements that determine the availability of injunctive relief and punitive damages.

One aspect of damages is becoming less complicated. Traditional rigidities limited recoverable damages narrowly to harms associated with the core interest of the cause of action (e.g., harms to exclusive possession for trespass; to quiet enjoyment for nuisance; from nonconsensual touching for battery; bodily injury for negligence). These limitations have waned under an expanding concept of what are termed *special* or *consequential* damages. To a considerable degree, common law courts have broadened recoveries, showing less interest in the choice of the underlying cause of action and giving greater regard to providing full compensation for all harms caused by the tortious act.

The L-C-D organizational approach used in this chapter is helpful in terms of understanding how traditional common law theories of tort have been adapted for application in the arena of environmental law. The L-C-D device also helps the student distinguish one species of tort from another. Although the issues and theories associated with the elements of causation and damage tend to be similar for all torts, theories of liability tend to draw boundaries between torts.

Section 2. INVOKING NUISANCE LAW TO REMEDY ENVIRONMENTAL PROBLEMS

Tort law in general, and nuisance in particular, offers an aggrieved plaintiff the possibility of monetary recoveries and a variety of injunctive remedies. With its roots in everyday tort law, private nuisance is a familiar claim to judges and lawyers alike, though somewhat less so than trespass. Nuisance can be described roughly as use of property by one party so as to (a) interfere substantially with the reasonable use, enjoyment, or value of another's property; (b) injure life or health; (c) offend the senses or violate principles of decency; or (d) obstruct free passage or use of highways, navigable streams, public parks and beaches, and other public rights. Nuisance is divided into two distinctive branches: Private nuisance is based on interference with individual plaintiffs' private property rights in land ((a) and (b) above), while public nuisance (studied later in this chapter) stems from violations of "public rights" of varying descriptions (primarily (c) and (d)).

The elements of a prima facie case of private nuisance, when it is brought as an "intentional" tort action as in *Boomer*, merely require plaintiffs to prove that:

(1) they have suffered substantial unreasonable interference with property use,

(2) the interference was caused by defendant's use of its land, and

(3) the defendant acted "intentionally."[4]

An interesting aspect of the nuisance case that follows is that, at the appellate level, the court spent almost no time establishing that a private nuisance existed, taking it to be obvious as well as uncontested on appeal by the defendant. In reading through *Boomer*, however, you should picture the practicalities of litigating the case at trial in terms of the evidence that the plaintiffs needed to introduce to show liability for the intentional tort of private nuisance, causation, and damage. In anticipation of having to decide the ultimate outcome of the case in terms of what will happen on the ground in the future, try to construct an environmental benefit-cost-alternatives analysis that might be applied to the controversy between Mr. Boomer and his industrial neighbor.

Boomer et al. v. Atlantic Cement Company
New York Court of Appeals, 1970
26 N.Y.2d 219, 257 N.E.2d 870, 309 N.Y.S.2d 312

BERGAN, J. Defendant operates a large cement plant near Albany. These are actions for injunction and damages by neighboring land owners alleging injury to property from dirt, smoke and vibration emanating from the plant. A nuisance has been found after trial, temporary damages have been allowed; but an injunction has been denied.

The public concern with air pollution arising from many sources in industry and in transportation is currently accorded ever wider recognition accompanied by a growing sense of responsibility in State and Federal Governments to control it. Cement plants are obvious sources of air pollution in the neighborhoods where they operate.

But there is now before the court private litigation in which individual property owners have sought specific relief from a single plant operation. The threshold question raised by the division of view on this appeal is whether the court should resolve the litigation between the parties now before it as equitably as seems possible; or whether, seeking promotion of the general public welfare, it should channel private litigation into broad public objectives.

A court performs its essential function when it decides the rights of parties before it. Its decision of private controversies may sometimes greatly affect public issues. Large questions of law are often resolved by the manner in which private litigation is decided. But this is normally an incident to the court's main function to settle controversy. It is a rare exercise of judicial power to use a decision in private litigation as a purposeful mechanism to achieve direct public objectives greatly beyond the rights and interests before the court....

---

4. This very traditional statement of the elements of intentional nuisance contains the generic L-C-D pattern, but it is not set out in that same array. The first and third elements noted in the text encompass the L and the D. L is unreasonable interference with the plaintiff's quiet enjoyment (an interest that tort law accords high protection) that was intentional in the sense that it was a natural consequence of an act defendant intended to do. Because the interference is "unreasonable" in its degree, which is more than mere annoyance, it constitutes D.

It seems apparent that the amelioration of air pollution will depend on technical research in great depth; on a carefully balanced consideration of the economic impact of close regulation; and of the actual effect on public health. It is likely to require massive public expenditure and to demand more than any local community can accomplish and to depend on regional and inter-state controls. A court should not try to do this on its own as a by-product of private litigation and it seems manifest that the judicial establishment is neither equipped in the limited nature of any judgment it can pronounce nor prepared to lay down and implement an effective policy for the elimination of air pollution. This is an area beyond the circumference of one private lawsuit. It is a direct responsibility for government and should not thus be undertaken as an incident to solving a dispute between property owners and a single cement plant — one of many — in the Hudson River valley.

The cement making operations of defendant have been found by the court of Special Term to have damaged the nearby properties of plaintiffs in these two actions. That court, as it has been noted, accordingly found defendant maintained a nuisance and this has been affirmed at the Appellate Division. The trial judge had made a simple, direct finding that "the discharge of large quantities of dust upon each of the properties and excessive vibration from blasting deprived each party of the reasonable use of his property and thereby prevented his enjoyment of life and liberty therein." The judge continued, however: "I have given careful consideration to the plea of plaintiffs that an injunction should issue in this action. Although the Supreme Court has the power to grant and enforce an injunction, equity forbids its employment in this instance. The defendant's immense investment in the Hudson River Valley, its contribution to the Capital District's economy and its immediate help to the education of children in the Town of Coeymans through the payment of substantial sums in school and property taxes leads me to the conclusion that an injunction would produce great public...hardship." The total damage to plaintiffs' properties is, however, relatively small in comparison with the value of defendant's operation and with the consequences of the injunction which plaintiffs seek.

The ground for the denial of injunction, notwithstanding the finding both that there is a nuisance and that plaintiffs have been damaged substantially, is the large disparity in economic consequences of the nuisance and of the injunction. This theory cannot, however, be sustained without overruling a doctrine which has been consistently reaffirmed in several leading cases in this court and which has never been disavowed here, namely that where a nuisance has been found and where there has been any substantial damage shown by the party complaining an injunction will be granted.

The rule in New York has been that such a nuisance will be enjoined although marked disparity be shown in economic consequence between the effect of the injunction and the effect of the nuisance. The problem of disparity in economic consequence was sharply in focus in Whalen v. Union Bag & Paper Co., 101 N.E. 805. A pulp mill entailing an investment of more than a million dollars polluted a stream in which plaintiff, who owned a farm, was "a lower riparian owner." The economic loss to plaintiff from this pollution was small. This court...reinstated the injunction [despite] the argument of the mill owner that in view of "the slight advantage to plaintiff and the great loss that will be inflicted on defendant" an injunction should not be granted.... "Although the damage to the plaintiff may be slight as compared with the defendant's expense of abating the condition, that is not a good reason for refusing an injunction."... The rule laid down in that case, then, is that whenever the damage resulting from a nuisance is found not "unsubstantial," viz., $100 a year, injunction would follow....

Although the court [at trial in this case] held that an injunction should be denied, it found that plaintiffs had been damaged in various specific amounts up to the time of the trial and damages to the respective plaintiffs were awarded for those amounts. The effect of this was, injunction having been denied, plaintiffs could maintain successive actions at law for damages thereafter as further damage was incurred. The court also found the amount of permanent damage attributable to each plaintiff, for the guidance of the parties in the event both sides stipulated to the payment and acceptance of such permanent damage as a settlement of all the controversies among the parties. The total of permanent damages to all plaintiffs thus found was $185,000. This basis of adjustment has not resulted in any stipulation by the parties.

This [refusal to enjoin] is a departure from a rule that has become settled; but to follow the rule literally in these cases would be to close down the plant at once. This court is fully agreed to avoid that immediately drastic remedy; the difference in view is how best to avoid it.[5]

One alternative is to grant the injunction but postpone its effect to a specified future date to give opportunity for technical advances to permit defendant to eliminate the nuisance; another is to grant the injunction conditioned on the payment of permanent damages to plaintiffs which would compensate them for the total economic loss to their property present and future caused by defendant's operations. For reasons which will be developed the court chooses the latter alternative. If the injunction were to be granted unless within a short period — e.g., 18 months — the nuisance be abated by improved methods, there would be no assurance that any significant technical improvement would occur.

The parties could settle this private litigation at any time if defendant paid enough money and the imminent threat of closing the plant would build up the pressure on defendant. If there were no improved techniques found, there would inevitably be applications to the court at Special Term for extensions of time to perform on showing of good faith efforts to find such techniques.

Moreover, techniques to eliminate dust and other annoying by-products of cement making are unlikely to be developed by any research the defendant can undertake within any short period, but will depend on the total resources of the cement industry nationwide and throughout the world. The problem is universal wherever cement is made. For obvious reasons the rate of the research is beyond control of defendant. If at the end of 18 months the whole industry has not found a technical solution a court would be hard put to close down this one cement plant if due regard be given to equitable principles.

On the other hand, to grant the injunction unless defendant pays plaintiffs such permanent damages as may be fixed by the court seems to do justice between the contending parties. All of the attributions of economic loss to the properties on which plaintiffs' complaints are based will have been redressed.

The nuisance complained of by these plaintiffs may have other public or private consequences, but these particular parties are the only ones who have sought remedies and the judgment proposed will fully redress them. The limitation of relief granted is a limitation only within the four corners of these actions and does not foreclose public health or other public agencies from seeking proper relief in a proper court.

It seems reasonable to think that the risk of being required to pay permanent damages to injured property owners by cement plant owners would itself be a reasonable effective spur to research for improved techniques to minimize nuisance....

The damage base here suggested is consistent with the general rule in those nuisance cases where damages are allowed. "Where a nuisance is of such a permanent and unabatable character that a single recovery can be had, including the whole damage past and future resulting therefrom, there can be but one recovery" (66 C.J.S. Nuisances §140, 947). It has been said that permanent damages are allowed where the loss recoverable would obviously be small as

---

5. Respondent's investment in the plant is in excess of $45,000,000. There are over 300 people employed there.

compared with the cost of removal of the nuisance (Kentucky-Ohio Gas Co. v. Bowling, 95 S.W.2d 1).... Equity will give full relief in one action and prevent a multiplicity of suits....

Thus it seems fair to both sides to grant permanent damages to plaintiffs which will terminate this private litigation. The theory of damage is the "servitude on land" of plaintiffs imposed by defendant's nuisance. (See United States v. Causby, 328 U.S. 256, 261, 262, 267, where the term "servitude" addressed to the land was used by Justice Douglas relating to the effect of airplane noise on property near an airport.) The judgment, by allowance of permanent damages imposing a servitude on land, which is the basis of the actions, would preclude future recovery by plaintiffs or their grantees. This should be placed beyond debate by a provision of the judgment that the payment by defendant and the acceptance by plaintiffs of permanent damages found by the court shall be in compensation for a servitude on the land.

Although the Trial Term has found permanent damages as a possible basis of settlement of the litigation, on remission the court should be entirely free to examine this subject. It may again find the permanent damage already found, or make new findings.

The orders should be reversed, without costs, and the cases remitted to Supreme Court, Albany County to grant an injunction which shall be vacated upon payment by defendant of such amounts of permanent damage to the respective plaintiffs as shall for this purpose be determined by the court.

JASEN, J., dissenting.... To now change the rule to permit the cement company to continue polluting the air indefinitely upon the payment of permanent damages is, in my opinion, compounding the magnitude of a very serious problem in our State and Nation today.... The harmful nature and widespread occurrence of air pollution have been extensively documented. Congressional hearings have revealed that air pollution causes substantial property damage, as well as being a contributing factor to a rising incidence of lung cancer, emphysema, bronchitis and asthma.

The specific problem faced here is known as particulate contamination because of the fine dust particles emanating from defendant's cement plant. The particular type of nuisance is not new, having appeared in many cases for at least the past 60 years. (See Hulbert v. California Portland Cement Co., 118 P. 928 (Cal. 1911).) It is interesting to note that cement production has recently been identified as a significant source of particulate contamination in the Hudson Valley. This type of pollution, wherein very small particles escape and stay in the atmosphere, has been denominated as the type of air pollution which produces the greatest hazard to human health. We have thus a nuisance which not only is damaging to the plaintiffs, but also is decidedly harmful to the general public....

The majority is, in effect, licensing a continuing wrong. It is the same as saying to the cement company, you may continue to do harm to your neighbors so long as you pay a fee for it. Furthermore, once such permanent damages are assessed and paid, the incentive to alleviate the wrong would be eliminated, thereby continuing air pollution of an area without abatement.... It is clearly established that the cement company is creating a continuing air pollution nuisance primarily for its own private interest with no public benefit. This kind of inverse condemnation may not be invoked by a private person or corporation for private gain or advantage. Inverse condemnation should only be permitted when the public is primarily served in the taking or impairment of property. The promotion of the interests of the polluting cement company has, in my opinion, no public use or benefit. Nor is it constitutionally permissible to impose a servitude on land, without consent of the owner, by payment of permanent damages where the continuing impairment of the land is for a private use....

I would enjoin the defendant cement company from continuing the discharge of dust particles upon its neighbors' properties unless, within 18 months, the cement company abated this nuisance.[6]

It is not my intention to cause the removal of the cement plant from the Albany area, but to recognize the urgency of the problem stemming from this stationary source of air pollution, and to allow the company a specified period of time to develop a means to alleviate this nuisance.

I am aware that the trial court found that the most modern dust control devices available have been installed in defendant's plant, but, I submit, this does not mean that better and more effective dust control devices could not be developed within the time allowed to abate the pollution. Moreover, I believe it is incumbent upon the defendant to develop such devices, since the cement company, at the time the plant commenced production (1962), was well aware of the plaintiffs' presence in the area, as well as the probable consequences of its contemplated operation. Yet, it still chose to build and operate the plant at this site.

In a day when there is a growing concern for clean air, highly developed industry should not expect acquiescence by the courts, but should, instead, plan its operations to eliminate contamination of our air and damage to its neighbors. Accordingly [I would] grant an injunction to take effect 18 months hence, unless the nuisance is abated by improved techniques prior to said date.

COMMENTARY & QUESTIONS

1. ***Boomer* as an environmental case.** Do you think that Oscar Boomer regarded himself as an environmentalist? Mr. Boomer clearly wanted to stop the cement dust falling on him and get compensation, but he may have considered environmentalists to be a bunch of birdwatchers and tree huggers. Note that although there were undoubtedly a number of ecological consequences to natural resources in the area polluted by cement dust, the case is totally silent about these, focusing instead upon injury to plaintiffs' personal and real property. Injury to human health and property remains the primary locus of much environmental litigation; human quality of life is an important part of environmental concern. The law, however, is slowly growing conscious of the tangible importance of ecological natural resource harms as well.

2. **Nuisance basics in *Boomer*.** The *Boomer* case was brought as a common law tort action, based on a complaint by the victims of air pollution against the factory whose emissions were causing an injury to plaintiffs' property. The case exemplifies an action for private nuisance, the doctrine that serves as the basis for suit in the majority of today's nonstatutory environmental law cases. Nuisance protects the interest of a plaintiff in the quiet enjoyment of property against interference with that enjoyment that reaches an unreasonable level. Virtually all reported modern nuisance cases are sued upon as intentional torts, where the defendant is charged with intending the ordinary consequences of an act that was itself taken intentionally. When operating a facility such as a cement plant, one expected consequence is the escape of pollution and the creation of noise and vibration. Even if the defendant did not want to harm the plaintiff as a result of operating the factory, the imposition of that harm is, in the eyes of the law, intentional.

---

6. The issuance of an injunction to become effective in the future is not an entirely new concept. For instance, in Schwarzenbach v. Oneonta Light & Power Co., 100 N.E. 1134, an injunction against the maintenance of a dam spilling water on plaintiff's property was issued to become effective one year hence.

3. ***Boomer* and the cement company's "cost externalization."** Besides its interesting holdings on permanent damages and balancing the equities, many aspects of the *Boomer* case reflect classic environmental perceptions. The case involved a typical industrial setting, with the cement company doing its own internal benefit-cost analysis that made discharging waste dust into the commons the rational disposal option. Absent successful legal action, the company would have had to account for almost none of the pollution's cost, even if the total of actual costs to natural systems, human health, and property in the affected area, extending downwind many miles, were actually greater than the cost of installing better control equipment (or might even have exceeded total net benefits to the company). The problem is that costs to the natural and societal economies are typically spread so far and wide, or are so hard to take account of and quantify in monetary terms, that the overall accounting is rarely done.

4. **The "cost internalizing" effect of the *Boomer* lawsuit.** To the extent that common law litigation like *Boomer* forces a factory to provide relief to plaintiffs, to that same extent the company is forced to internalize some of the negative effects of its pollution as a cost of doing business, to be passed on to its consumers. How much gets internalized here? The *Boomer* decision resulted in internalizing some of the private property damage suffered by the Boomers and their co-plaintiff neighbors. What *Boomer* does not even attempt to do is to trace more carefully all of the negative consumption externalities caused by the pollution. Why not? Does the difficulty lie in cost accounting? Recall from the discussions in Chapters 1 and 2 how difficult it would be to provide an accurate measure of the harms to affected natural resources (forests, wildlife, etc.) or the low-level adverse human health effects of particulate pollution. Oscar Boomer may or may not care deeply about the environment, but it is probably not in his self-interest to spend vast amounts of effort and energy trying to marshal evidence on damages to the commons beyond his own private property. Even if such evidence could be assembled and litigated, it might not be worthwhile or efficient to do so.

Do we have the time or luxury, on the other hand, to consider all the diverse external costs of each industrial operation? The cacophony of voices raised by a host of far-off pollution victims in such efforts might mean that nothing gets done. Some pollution is necessary to progress, say the pragmatists: It has to occur somewhere. The market's accounting dictates that it occur here, in a rural area where only a few relatively low-income people will be affected. There is no complaint about health effects in *Boomer*, so the effects of cement dust pollution may be relatively slight. The benefits of cement are clearly substantial. Does the rough accounting reached in *Boomer* thus suffice? Does society have the luxury of performing an endless analysis of the benefits and costs of every enterprise like the Atlantic Cement Company, or should such scrutiny be reserved for cases of more dramatic environmental impact?

Class actions offer a vehicle for expanded internalization and dramatically increase defendants' incentives to clean up. *Boomer* was not filed as a class action case, although it could have been. Would that have achieved more rational results? See Wright, The Cost-Internalization Case for Class Actions, 21 Stan. L. Rev. 383 (1969), on environmental use of class actions. It could have been filed as a public nuisance, which would also have changed the dynamics of the case as is noted later in this chapter.

5. **Tactics, politics, and the urge to litigate.** If the cement dust pollution was so obvious in this case, why didn't Boomer and his lawyer go straight to the state air pollution agency? Albany, the state capital, was close by, and the official state pollution control agency possessed statutory authority, extensive regulations, public funding appropriated for enforcement, and expertise. What practical advantages in getting relief persuade pollution victims to take on the burdens of litigating in common law courts rather than trusting to the official public law system?

The United States is an unusually litigious society. For that reason, it may seem natural that when the Boomers felt themselves aggrieved by the action of their cement plant neighbor, they resorted to a lawsuit in an effort to obtain redress. Speculating about the reasons for that choice by the Boomers reveals a great deal about the attraction of the common law as a system for environmental governance in American society.

The avenues of potential redress for the Boomers other than a lawsuit were not particularly promising because of the Boomers' lack of access and influence in decisional processes. In the private corporate decision, of course, the Boomers' interests were not likely to be of great concern. But the public law, both state and local, might have been expected to be different.

The construction of a major facility like a cement plant is usually the subject of local governmental land use regulations, most often zoning. If the project was consistent with existing local zoning classifications, there was no opportunity for Boomer to oppose the project in the zoning board forum; if, however, the use was one not initially allowed by the zoning, the project proponents would have had to seek a zoning change in order to construct the plant. Even if the project were consistent with existing zoning, some communities require permits for either the siting or the construction of large facilities.

Are the various local regulatory systems likely to provide people like the Boomers a sympathetic local forum in which to oppose the plant before it is built? The $45 million in equities weigh heavily in the balance. Today, as communities prostrate themselves in efforts to attract the economic benefits that come with major industrial facilities, the pressures to grant needed permits are substantial. Except for immediate neighbors of the plant who may suffer, like the Boomers, most of the community will find its immediate self-interest aligned with having the plant built.

What about the state pollution control system? As studied later, beginning in Chapter 5, the regulatory statutes are highly complex and primarily concerned with the general business of pollution control, not with providing discrete local remedies for relatively small individual claims. The statutes are primarily tools for governmental regulation of polluters, and opportunities for individual citizens to play a significant role in that process are few. The regulators are seldom eager to expand their dialogue with regulated parties into a multi-dimensional process in which citizens seek results that are often at odds with the agency's own view of proper outcome. This is not to say that seeking the aid of public authorities charged with control of pollution is always unavailing, but merely that it is a process over which the private citizen has little control.

Compare the official public law processes to an ordinary common law tort suit. Plaintiffs can hire a lawyer, probably on a contingent fee basis, who seeks relief at the local courthouse where the opportunity to win damages and injunctions provides a strong self-interest incentive to prosecute the case, a flexible scope of remedies, and broad, familiar theories for the judge to apply, without any need for entering the quagmire of administrative proceedings where the outcome can be so heavily influenced by politics and regional economics. Plaintiffs can exercise a measure of control over the litigation, selecting the lawyer and perhaps helping to develop the evidence, and the litigation process to some extent can equalize the parties to the controversy. And unlike the agency regulatory process, of course, the common law can provide damage recoveries for the plaintiff's injuries. There is, moreover, a growing literature in the civil procedure area addressing the psychological benefits of the litigation process. In addition to its various participatory characteristics, litigation usually leads to a definitive end, sometimes providing a personal sense of vindication, and always at least providing closure, itself an important benefit.

6. **Environmental tort remedies.** Tort actions illustrate other advantages of common law remedies in environmental cases. Tort law typically looks to community standards of appropriateness; it provides jury trials on key issues of liability, causation, and monetary damages so that the actual decisionmakers on whether community standards have been met are local citizens themselves. As a means of seeking redress, tort cases demystify the technicalities of environmental cases, reverting to shared community understandings about what is right and what is wrong.

When plaintiffs successfully establish defendant's liability under an environmental tort cause of action, one remedy is automatic: the award of compensatory damages for tort injuries suffered. The well-established checklist of compensatory damage categories includes recoveries for health and property damage, lost profits and earnings, pain and suffering, and the like. Environmental cases occasionally add new remedy theories, noted later. The *Boomer* case concerned only property damages but added the relatively novel permanent damage approach in lieu of an injunction.

After a court awards compensatory damages, typically for past rather than permanent injuries, courts then move to the further question of whether an injunction will be issued. This issue is for the judge, not the jury. Mirroring *Boomer*, the grant of an injunction in virtually all modern courts is never automatic but depends upon a balancing of the equities. Accepting that principle, does an environmental perspective on the *Boomer* case reveal any problems with the court's balance? Would you mention the cement dust's more general public effects? Following Judge Jasen's lead, would you have proposed alternative forms of injunction? These and other issues are developed in Part D on remedies.

7. **A word about public nuisance.** The case that follows is a public nuisance case. Quite unlike private nuisance, public nuisance is descended from criminal offenses against the public peace. Over time public nuisance became a civil action as well, providing remedies for violations of public rights. Traditionally it has applied to cases like the blocking of public rights of way or offenses against public sensitivities and decency, like

boisterous saloons and bawdy houses or, in modern times, pornography shops. In typical public nuisance actions, public prosecutors bring lawsuits seeking injunctions to force cessation of nuisances (often preferring the tort approach even where statutory remedies apply). Public nuisance is usually litigated as an intentional tort, although in some cases involving the release of toxic contaminants into the environment, it is also litigated on a strict liability theory. See Chapter 4 for a discussion of special challenges associated with toxic tort litigation. In some circumstances, public nuisance actions can be brought by private plaintiffs, and public nuisances can simultaneously be private nuisances. In analyzing the following cases, consider the tactical advantages public nuisance offers prosecutors and private plaintiffs.

Village of Wilsonville v. SCA Services, Inc.
Supreme Court of Illinois, 1981
86 Ill. 2d 1, 426 N.E.2d 824

CLARK, J. On April 18, 1977, the plaintiff village of Wilsonville (the village) filed a complaint seeking injunctive relief in the circuit court of Macoupin County. Plaintiffs Macoupin County and the Macoupin County Farm Bureau were granted leave to intervene.... The gravamen of the complaints was that the operation of the defendant's chemical-waste-disposal site presents a public nuisance and a hazard to the health of the citizens of the village, the county and the State. The Attorney General of Illinois filed a complaint on May 26, 1977, seeking an injunction pursuant to the Environmental Protection Act (Ill. Rev. Stat. 1975, ch. 111 1/2).... [The two actions were consolidated for trial and disposition.] Trial began on June 7, 1978, consumed 104 days, and resulted in judgment for the plaintiffs on August 28, 1978. The trial court's judgment order concluded that the site constitutes a nuisance and enjoined the defendant from operating its hazardous-chemical waste landfill in Wilsonville. It ordered the defendant to remove all toxic waste buried there, along with all contaminated soil found at the disposal site as a result of the operation of the landfill. Further, the court ordered the defendant to restore and reclaim the site. The defendant appealed....

The defendant has operated a chemical waste landfill since 1977. The site comprises approximately 130 acres, 90 of which are within the village limits of the plaintiff village. The remaining 40 acres are adjacent to the village. The defendant enters into agreements with generators of toxic chemical waste to haul the waste away from the generators' locations. The defendant then delivers it to the Wilsonville site, tests random samples of chemical waste, and then deposits the waste in trenches. There are seven trenches at the site. Each one is approximately 15 feet deep, 50 feet wide, and 250 to 350 feet long. Approximately 95 percent of the waste materials were buried in 55-gallon steel drums, and the remainder is contained in double-wall paper bags. After the materials are deposited in the trenches, uncompacted clay is placed between groups of containers and a minimum of one foot of clay is placed between the top drum and the top clay level of the trench.

The site is bordered on the east, west, and south by farmland and on the north by the village. The entire site, the village, and much of the surrounding area is located above the abandoned Superior Coal Mine No. 4, which operated from 1917 to 1954. The No. 6 seam of the mine was exploited in this area at a depth of 312 feet. The mining method used to extract coal was the room-and-panel method, whereby about 50 percent of the coal is left in pillars which provide some support for the earth above the mine. There was testimony at trial by Dr. Nolan Augenbaugh, chairman of the Department of Mining, Petroleum and Geological Engineering at the University of Missouri at Rolla, that pillar failure can occur in any mine where there is a readjustment of stress. Also on the defendant's site is a 30- to 40-feet-high pile of "gob," or mine spoil of coal, shale, and clay, which was accumulated over the time the mine was operated. Acid drainage from the mine has seeped into the ground and contaminated three surface drainage channels at the site. The defendant has attempted to remedy this situation by covering the surface of the "gob pile" with excess soil from the trenches.

There are 14 monitoring wells along the perimeter of the site. They are designed to detect liquids which seep through the soil and into the wells. They are not designed to contain liquids, however. In fact, monitoring wells Nos. 5 and 6 are 650 feet apart, which would allow many materials to pass between those two wells and not be discovered. The wells are sampled quarterly by a private laboratory, and test results are submitted to the Illinois Environmental Protection Agency (IEPA). Additional water samples are taken from three surface channels and are tested and reported in the same manner as samples taken from the wells. The surface drainage and the ground-water drainage from the site are to the south, away from the village and toward farmland.

The village has no sewage-treatment plant and no municipally owned sewage system. Most homes are served by septic tanks, and some homes and businesses are connected to private sewers. The water-distribution system is centralized, and water is purchased from Gillespie, Illinois. The system was built in 1952 after the village tried unsuccessfully to find sufficient water by drilling municipal wells in the area. There are still 73 water wells in the village, some of which are used to water gardens or wash cars. At least one well is used to water pets, and another is used for drinking water. South of defendant's site, approximately one-half mile from the gob pile, is the Vassi Spring, the owner of which intends to use it as his water supply when he builds his home. Further south are four more springs used to water livestock.

On February 11, 1976, the defendant applied to the IEPA for a permit to develop and operate the hazardous-waste landfill. A developmental permit was issued by the IEPA on May 19, 1976. After a preoperation inspection was conducted by the IEPA, an operational permit was issued to the defendant on September 28, 1976. Each delivery of waste material to the site must be accompanied by a supplemental permit issued by the IEPA. A supplemental permit specifies the chemical nature and quantity of the waste to be deposited at the sites. Between November 12, 1976, and June 7, 1977, the first day of trial, the defendant had obtained 185 such permits.

The materials deposited at the site include polychlorinated biphenyls (PCBs), a neurotoxic, possibly carcinogenic chemical which it has been illegal to produce in this country since 1979. Due to the extensive use of PCBs in electrical equipment such as transformers, capacitors, and heat-transfer systems, and in hydraulic systems, any PCBs that were produced legally now have to be disposed of when they are no longer in use. PCBs have been stored at the site in liquid, solid and semi-solid form. Additionally, there are a number of now-empty drums which had once contained PCBs, which are also buried at the site. Other materials buried at the site in large quantities are solid cyanide, a substance known as C5, 6, paint sludge, asbestos, pesticides, mercury, and arsenic. Considerable evidence was adduced to show that these and other substances deposited at the site are extremely toxic to human beings. Some of the adverse reactions which could result from exposure to these materials are pulmonary diseases, cancer, brain damage, and birth defects.

The general geologic profile of the site shows a surface layer of about 10 feet of loess (wind-blown silt and clay material), under which lies 40 to 65 feet of glacial till. In the till material there is a thin sand layer of a few inches to approximately two feet. Some ground water has been found in the sand layer. All trenches dug at the site have between 10 to 15 feet of glacial till below them. The glacial till is reported to be very dense and is not very permeable. Thus liquids do not travel through it quickly.

Permeability studies conducted before the site opened by John Mathes, a professional engineer hired by the defendant, indicate permeability results ranging from 7.4 X 10^{-8} centimeters per second to 1.2 X 10^{-8} centimeters per second (cm/sec.). (The larger the negative exponent is, the less permeable the soil. E.g., a finding of 10^{-8} cm/sec. indicates that the soil is less permeable than would a reading of 10^{-4} cm/sec.) After the site opened, Mathes took permeability samples from or near the bottoms of the trenches that had been dug. His second set of results ranged from 1.4 X 10^{-7} cm/sec. to .9 X 10^{-7} cm/sec.

Dr. James Williams, an engineering geologist with the Missouri Geology and Land Survey, also made permeability findings on behalf of the defendant from samples taken from the site after it opened. Dr. Williams' results ranged from 7 X 10^{-6} cm/sec. to 1 X 10^{-7} cm/sec. Dr. Williams testified on cross-examination that the general permeability of the site is considered to be greater than 1 X 10^{-8} cm/sec. and that he would not expect the average permeability of the soil to be as low as that used for samples. In the interim between the opening of the site and the time of trial, the IEPA adopted a suggested permeability standard of 1 X 10^{-8} cm/sec. for hazardous-waste landfills.

Subsidence of the earth underneath the site is another contention raised by the plaintiffs to support their thesis that the site is unsafe and is therefore an enjoinable nuisance. Dr. Nolan Augenbaugh testified extensively at trial. Dr. Augenbaugh took pictures of the area from an airplane as well as at ground level. During his testimony, he pointed out where subsidence occurred in the pictures he had taken. Dr. Augenbaugh stated that he had observed subsidence in a wheat field on the Wilbur Sawyer farm on June 17, 1977. Dr. Augenbaugh also testified that a subsidence basin lies to the northeast of the disposal site. The pictures also indicate, according to Dr. Augenbaugh, fractures in the ground. One picture depicts a fault, which, Dr. Augenbaugh explained, is a "fracture where there's been differential movement of the two blocks. One block has been moved more than the other block." Sawyer, the farmer, told Dr. Augenbaugh the cracks had begun to appear approximately two months before, which would have been spring 1977. Several of these subsidences and fractures are located approximately one-half mile from the western boundary of the lower part of the disposal site. Dr. Augenbaugh testified that, in his opinion, subsidence can and will occur at the disposal site. Further, that ruptures in the earth would occur which, like an open pipe, would act as conduits for artesian water to reach the trenches, thereby contaminating the water.

Dr. Augenbaugh...testified that on March 22, 1978, he...had a trench dug across the subsidence cracks which he had observed earlier. When the digging was completed, there was a trench nine feet long and approximately three feet wide, with a maximum depth of a little over eight feet. Photographs were taken and slides prepared of the operation at the site. As the trench was being dug, water began to seep into the trench at a depth of approximately 4 feet. Dr. Augenbaugh testified that the water flowed from subsidence fractures which were below the surface of the ground. Dr. Augenbaugh then poured some green dye into a surface fracture which was located approximately 10 feet away from the trench. The green dye entered the trench through two openings within 25 minutes. Thomas O. Glover, a mining engineer and liaison officer with the United States Bureau of Mining, Department of the Interior, also testified regarding subsidence. Glover defined subsidence as the settling of the ground, due to the diminution of the underground support structure, and either the pillars pushing into the fine clay bottom below the coal system, or the roof fracturing immediately above the coal seam and continuing to the surface. He stated that subsidence normally can be expected to appear, on the average, 40 years after a mine has closed down. Glover never visited the instant disposal site, but he had examined the information relative to Superior Mine No. 4 and he had witnessed subsidences many times in the field over the course of 27 years as a mining engineer. Glover offered the opinion that there is a possibility of subsidence wherever coal is mined and underground support is removed.

Several of the defendant's expert witnesses, James Douglas Andrews, the designer of the site and a consulting engineer for the defendant, John A. Mathes, an engineer, Steven Hunt, a geologist with the Illinois State Geological Survey (ISGS), and Paul B. DuMontelle, an engineering geologist with ISGS and coordinator of environmental geology for the Survey, testified in summary that there would be subsidence at the site, but that it would not be deep, would close in a short time, and could be repaired by means of engineering techniques.

Another of plaintiffs' witnesses, Dr. Arthur Zahalsky, offered the opinion that an "explosive interaction," resulting in chemical explosions, fires, or emissions of poisonous gases, will occur at the site. Dr. Zahalsky is a professor of biochemistry and head of the laboratory of biochemical parasitology at Southern Illinois University at Edwardsville. He testified in essence that if sufficient oxygen could reach the buried chemicals, and he believed it could, then an explosive interaction of unknown date of occurrence, magnitude, and duration is likely. Moreover, Dr. Zahalsky testified that it is unknown what interactions might occur when the waste materials combine after the deterioration of the steel containers and paper bags.

The defendant challenged Dr. Zahalsky's opinion during cross-examination and requested him to diagram the precise chemical formula which would result in an explosive interaction. Dr. Zahalsky testified that a precise formula could not be diagrammed. He stated that the defendant's trench logs indicate that several of the chemical wastes have flash points less than 80 degrees Fahrenheit. Zahalsky reviewed the trench logs and gave examples of chemicals, such as paranitroaniline, which is a strong oxidizing agent and may be explosive, and also paint sludge, which has a flash point of less than 80 degrees Fahrenheit, which could result in a chemical fire. Dr. Zahalsky offered one scenario in which acidic chlorinated degreasers would interact with waste phenolics, releasing the phenolics so that the flash point would be achieved, thereby setting off the paint sludges which, in turn, would set off paint wastes, which would achieve the temperature sufficient for the ignition and combustion of liquid PCBs. All of these materials are deposited together in trench No. 3.

Finally, considerable testimony was adduced, much of it conflicting, as to dust, odors, and spills of chemical waste which have occurred in the village. Various residents testified that dust emanating from the site blew toward their houses. Also, odors which caused burning eyes, running noses, headaches, nausea, and shortness of breath were mentioned in testimony. The odors themselves were said to resemble, among other things, fertilizer, insecticide, and burning rubber. There was further testimony that the dust and odors interfered with the witnesses' ability to use their yards for gardening or other recreational uses. The defendant presented witnesses who denied that the disposal site was the source of any odors, and that the odors resulted from the local practices of openly burning refuse and dumping sewage into a nearby creek.

There was testimony that trucks carrying the waste materials to the disposal site via Wilson Avenue, the main street of the village, sometimes spilled toxic liquids onto the street. The evidence is undisputed, both from the defendant's receiving reports and testimony from IEPA inspectors, that many drums arrived on the site leaking waste materials....

The defendant has raised several issues on appeal: (1) whether the finding of the circuit and appellate courts that the waste-disposal site is a prospective nuisance is contrary to the manifest weight of the evidence; (2) whether those courts applied the wrong legal standard in finding that the waste-disposal site constitutes a prospective nuisance; (3) whether the circuit and appellate courts erred in failing to balance the equities, either in finding a prospective nuisance or in fashioning relief; (4) whether the courts erred in failing to defer to, or to otherwise weight, the role of the IEPA, the United States Environmental Protection Agency (USEPA), and the Illinois State

Geological Survey (PCB); (5) whether the courts erred in finding that plaintiffs have no adequate remedy at law; (6) whether the courts erred in ordering a mandatory injunction; and, finally, (7) whether the courts' decisions constituted a taking of property without due process of law.

We conclude that the evidence in this case sufficiently establishes by a preponderance of the evidence that the chemical-waste-disposal site is a nuisance both presently and prospectively....

The defendant points out three areas where, it argues, the trial court made erroneous findings of fact. The defendant refers to: (1) Dr. Arthur Zahalsky's opinion testimony concerning an explosive interaction and Dr. Stephen Hall's testimony which concurred in that opinion; (2) evidence concerning soil permeability; and, (3) infiltration of water into the trenches, and of migration out of the defendant's trenches of chemical waste either through the "bathtub effect" or subsidence.

We have reviewed the extensive record compiled in this case. While it is true that the defendant vigorously challenged the evidence concerning an explosive interaction, permeability, and infiltration and migration due to subsidence, the defendant has not overcome the natural and logical conclusions which could be drawn from the evidence. Findings of fact made by the trial court will not be set aside unless they are contrary to the manifest weight of the evidence....

The defendant [to refute the conclusions of Drs. Zahalsky and Hall] particularly relies upon the opinion of Dr. Raymond D. Harbison, a professor of pharmacology at Vanderbilt University, a toxicologist and consultant to the USEPA on toxic-waste handling. Dr. Harbison offered the opinion that the instant site is the most advanced scientific landfill in this country, and that the inventory system and the "absolute confinement" of the materials to the site render the interaction of the chemicals an impossibility.

At bottom, Dr. Harbison's opinion is premised upon his belief that the materials at the site will be sufficiently confined so that they will not pose a threat to the health or lives of the residents of the village. Dr. Harbison's opinions were discounted by the trial court, however, due to the substantial evidence which shows that the soil is more permeable than originally thought; that there is migration of water out of the trenches; and that there is subsidence in the area. Moreover, Dr. Harbison's opinion must be further discounted due to his erroneous statement that the waste materials will be sufficiently confined since "there is no ground water to be contaminated anyway below the particular site." Dr. Harbison later amended that statement to say there was no "usable water supply below the site" in terms of volume. This statement is also erroneous and also ignores evidence that the ground water would flow from beneath the site, thereby transporting any contamination into Cahokia Creek and could eventually flow into the Mississippi River. Thus we will not overturn the trial court's findings on this issue. They are amply supported by the manifest weight of the evidence....

The defendant also contends that the trial court's finding that subsidence warrants closing of the site is erroneous. The defendant argues that, assuming arguendo that subsidence would occur at the site, it could be counteracted by engineering techniques. This issue becomes complicated by the fact that the IEPA adopted a regulation providing that Class I disposal sites (i.e., chemical-waste-disposal sites), must be secure without engineering. The USEPA, however, has recently adopted regulations to require all landfill sites to establish containment-engineering systems to detect and prevent migration of chemicals. Moreover, the General Assembly has, since the inception of this suit, passed a statute prohibiting the placement of a hazardous-waste-disposal site above a shaft or tunneled mine.... The instant disposal site is above an inactive tunneled mine lying partly within the corporate limits of the village of Wilsonville. Without an express statutory provision stating an act is to have retroactive effect, it can only be applied prospectively. Thus, the defendant cannot be thought to be in violation of the foregoing provision. The fact remains, however, that the instant site, which is intended to be permanent, is located above an inactive tunneled mine.

Moreover, Dr. Nolan Augenbaugh testified at great length, supported by many photographs, of the considerable subsidence which has already occurred near the site. In Dr. Augenbaugh's opinion, subsidence will occur at the site itself. The defendant's experts testified that any subsidence would be negligible and shallow and would not present a threat to health or life. Dr. Augenbaugh refuted this testimony. He stated that subsidence would permit chemical-waste materials to seep into the ground water. In addition, Dr. Augenbaugh testified that subsidence would create a "bathtub effect" by permitting water to get into the trenches, eventually rise to the surface, overflow, and contaminate the ground around the site. We think the circuit court was fully justified in giving more weight to Dr. Augenbaugh's well-documented opinion than to the opinions of defendant's experts. We will not disturb that finding.... [A long discussion about the nature of Illinois nuisance law follows.]

Moreover, the trial court did engage in a balancing process.... The Court understands as does counsel that there is a need for disposal of industrial hazardous wastes. However, where disposal of wastes creates a nuisance said disposal site may be closed through legal action. Whether or not a business is useful or necessary or whether or not it contributes to the welfare and/or prosperity of the community are elements to be considered in a serious manner but said elements are not determinative as to whether or not the operation is a nuisance. The importance of an industry to the wealth and prosperity of an area does not as a matter of law give to it rights superior to the primary or natural rights of citizens who live nearby. However, such matters may be considered and have been in this case....

The defendant's next contention is that the courts below were in error when they failed to require a showing of a substantial risk of certain and extreme future harm before enjoining operation of the defendant's site. We deem it necessary to explain that a prospective nuisance is a fit candidate for injunctive relief. Prosser states: "Both public and private nuisances require some substantial interference with the interest involved. Since nuisance is a common subject of equity jurisdiction, the damage against which an injunction is asked is often merely threatened or potential; but even in such cases, there must be at least a threat of a substantial invasion of the plaintiff's interests." (Prosser, Torts §87, at 577 (4th ed. 1971).) The defendant does not dispute this proposition; it does, however, argue that the trial court did not follow the proper standard for determining when a prospective nuisance may be enjoined. The defendant argues that the proper standard to be used is that an injunction is proper only if there is a "dangerous probability" that the threatened or potential injury will occur. (See Restatement (Second) of Torts §933(1), at 561, comment b (1979).) The defendant further argues that the appellate court looked only at the potential consequences of not enjoining the operation of the site as a nuisance and not at the likelihood of whether harm would occur....

In this case there can be no doubt but that it is highly probable that the chemical-waste-disposal site will bring about a substantial injury. Without again reviewing the extensive evidence adduced at trial, we think it is sufficiently clear that it is highly probable that the instant site will constitute a public nuisance if, through either an explosive interaction, migration, subsidence, or the "bathtub effect," the highly toxic chemical wastes deposited at the site escape and contaminate the air, water, or ground around the site. That such an event will occur was positively attested to by several expert witnesses. A court does not have to wait for it to happen before it can enjoin such a result. Additionally, the fact is that the condition of a nuisance is already present at the site due to the location of the site and the manner in which it has been operated. Thus, it is only the damage which is prospective. Under these circumstances, if a court can prevent any damage from occurring, it should do so....

The next issue we consider is whether the trial court erroneously granted a permanent injunction.... Defendant cites Harrison v. Indiana Auto Shredders Co., 528 F.2d 1107 (7th Cir. 1975), for the proposition that the court must balance the relative harm and benefit to the plaintiff and defendant before a court may enjoin a nuisance....

In *Harrison*, an auto shredder operated its business in a residential neighborhood in Indianapolis.... The court concluded in *Harrison* that since the defendant was not in violation of any relevant zoning standards, and since the shredder did not pose an imminent hazard to the public health, the defendant should not be prevented from continuing to operate. The court then ordered that the defendant be permitted a reasonable time to "launder its objectionable features."

This case is readily distinguishable for the reason that the gist of this case is that the defendant is engaged in an extremely hazardous undertaking at an unsuitable location, which seriously and imminently poses a threat to the public health. We are acutely aware that the service provided by the defendant is a valuable and necessary one. We also know that it is preferable to have chemical-waste-disposal sites than to have illegal dumping in rivers, streams, and deserted areas. But a site such as defendant's, if it is to do the job it is intended to do, must be located in a secure place, where it will pose no threat to health or life, now, or in the future. This site was intended to be a permanent disposal site for the deposit of extremely hazardous chemical-waste materials. Yet this site is located above an abandoned tunneled mine where subsidence is occurring several years ahead of when it was anticipated. Also, the permeability-coefficient samples taken by defendant's experts, though not conclusive alone, indicate that the soil is more permeable at the site than expected. Moreover, the spillage, odors, and dust caused by the presence of the disposal site indicate why it was inadvisable to locate the site so near the plaintiff village.

Therefore, we conclude that in fashioning relief in this case the trial court did balance relative hardship to be caused to the plaintiffs and defendant, and did fashion reasonable relief when it ordered the exhumation of all material from the site and the reclamation of the surrounding area. The instant site is akin to Mr. Justice Sutherland's observation that "Nuisance may be merely a right thing in a wrong place — like a pig in the parlor instead of the barnyard." Village of Euclid v. Ambler Realty Co., 272 U.S. 365, 388 (1926).

We are also cognizant of amicus USEPA's suggestion in its brief and affidavits filed with the appellate court which urge that we remand to the circuit court so that alternatives to closure of the site and exhumation of the waste materials may be considered. The USEPA states: "Heavy equipment may damage drums, releasing wastes and possibly causing gaseous emissions, fires, and explosions. Repackaging and transporting damaged drums also risks releasing wastes. Workers performing the exhumation face dangers from contact with or inhalation of wastes; these risks cannot be completely eliminated with protective clothing and breathing apparatus. Nearby residents may also be endangered." It is ironic that the host of horribles mentioned by the USEPA in support of keeping the site open includes some of the same hazards which the plaintiffs have raised as reasons in favor of closing the site....

Accordingly, for all the reasons stated, the judgments of the circuit and appellate courts are affirmed and the cause is remanded to the circuit court to enable it to retain jurisdiction to supervise the enforcement of its order. Affirmed and remanded.

RYAN, J., concurring. While I agree with both the result reached by the majority and the reasoning employed supporting the opinion, I wish to add a brief comment.... Any injunction is, by its very nature, the product of a court's balancing of competing interests, with a result equitably obtained. Prosser, in discussing the law of nuisance...states: "If the possibility [of harm] is merely uncertain or contingent [the plaintiff] may be left to his remedy after the nuisance has occurred." Prosser, Torts §90, at 603 (4th ed. 1971).

Prosser thus recognizes that there are cases in which the possibility of inflicting harm is slight and where the plaintiff may be left to his remedy at law. However, I believe that there are situations where the harm that is potential is so devastating that equity should afford relief even though the possibility of the harmful result occurring is uncertain or contingent. The Restatement's position applicable to preventative injunctive relief in general is that "the more serious the impending harm, the less justification there is for taking the chances that are involved in pronouncing the harm too remote." Restatement (2d) of Torts §933, at 561, comment b (1979). If the harm that may result is severe, a lesser possibility of it occurring should be required to support injunctive relief. Conversely, if the potential harm is less severe, a greater possibility that it will happen should be required. Also, in the balancing of competing interests, a court may find a situation where the potential harm is such that a plaintiff will be left to his remedy at law if the possibility of it occurring is slight. This balancing test allows the court to consider a wider range of factors and avoids the anomalous result possible under a more restrictive alternative where a person engaged in an ultrahazardous activity with potentially catastrophic results would be allowed to continue until he has driven an entire community to the brink of certain disaster. A court of equity need not wait so long to provide relief.

Although the "dangerous probability" test has certainly been met in this case, I would be willing to enjoin the activity on a showing of probability of occurrence substantially less than that which the facts presented to this court reveal, due to the extremely hazardous nature of the chemicals being dumped and the potentially catastrophic results.

COMMENTARY & QUESTIONS

1. ***Wilsonville* as compared to *Boomer*.** What are the salient factual similarities of the two cases? Both involve siting of a facility in a rural area that has low land values, few close neighbors, and proximity to relevant markets for the product or service that the facility provides. These siting choices are not irrational from the project proponents' point of view, nor are they anti-social from a more general societal point of view. So what are their dissimilarities? Boomer is a private individual. The *Wilsonville* plaintiffs are government entities. Does that make a difference? Does the ultimate difference in relief seem more to be a function of the fact that *Wilsonville* was brought as a public nuisance case while *Boomer* is a private nuisance case? Or is some other factor in the case crucial? Recall here the explicit balancing of the equities done by the *Boomer* majority. The Illinois Supreme Court said the trial court needed to balance the equities in *Wilsonville* as well. Assuming that the two balances of the equities were in the service of the same legal doctrine, why did the balance favor injunction and exhumation of waste already deposited in *Wilsonville*, but disfavor any form of injunction in *Boomer*?

2. **Private parties as risk promoters.** The underlying idea and impetus to site the toxic disposal facility in *Wilsonville* came from SCA Services. In an earlier, less regulation-bound era, SCA's private decision regarding the facility might have been dispositive, in the sense that no governmental pre-approval would have been needed. What factors motivated SCA's decision to select the Wilsonville site as a repository for wastes generated primarily in the nearby St. Louis metropolitan area? Most obvious are economic factors, such as low rural land costs and acceptable transportation costs based on

reasonable proximity. Are those factors the same ones that ought to be considered by the IEPA and USEPA (or the courts) in their roles as risk managers?

3. **Local politics, community involvement, and environmental risk management.** It is easy to understand that siting a hazardous waste disposal facility is going to be unpopular. The popular perception is replete with acronyms that make the point — NIMBY (not in my back yard), LULU (locally unwanted land use), and BANANA (build absolutely nothing anywhere near anyone). As one person in the waste industry has said, "Everyone wants us to pick the garbage up, but no one wants us to put it down." SCA Services apparently had gone a step further in angering the local Wilsonville population. At the start, the citizens and officials of Wilsonville apparently had been told that no hazardous wastes would be disposed of in their village and that the landfill would be made into a park. The citizenry was so outraged by the discovery that the wastes were toxic that, before the case came to trial, armed vigilante groups had blockaded the main streets of the village against waste transport vehicles. The Illinois courts, beginning with the (locally elected) judge of the Circuit Court of Macoupin County, assuaged this citizen outrage by ordering the site closed, thoroughly cleaned up (with wastes and contaminated soil to be removed and shipped elsewhere, back to St. Louis as it turned out), and restored. Does the *Wilsonville* case inspire confidence in the judicial system as risk managers? Try to review critically the plaintiff's evidence as to the likelihood of its predictions and the magnitude of harm actually threatened. Should the courts have given more credence to USEPA's suggestion that exhumation and removal would pose a greater risk of explosion, among other things, than "containing" the site (e.g., laying a cement cap over the site to prevent further infiltration, building an underground slurry wall around the site with a leachate monitoring system, and installing "pump-and-treat" technology if toxic leaching into the groundwater ever did occur)? Should the courts have considered the comparative economic costs of both alternatives? In fact, it took one year and cost $5 million — in 1981 dollars — to perform the court-ordered remediation. What about the risks of transporting the wastes offsite and depositing them in another landfill that might pose even greater risks than the Wilsonville site? The Resource Conservation and Recovery Act (RCRA), the federal law requiring that hazardous waste landfills be upgraded in order to protect the environment, had been enacted in 1976 but had not yet been fully implemented on existing sites.[7] To what extent are common law courts capable of determining the overall public interest in the context of lawsuits between specific litigants? The Illinois Supreme Court in *Wilsonville* did not shy away from the challenge.

4. **Administrative agencies as risk managers.** Presumably, expert administrators should be better risk managers than self-interested project proponents, outraged litigants, or inexpert judges and juries. What, then, explains the lackluster performance of the state and federal agencies in the *Wilsonville* case? In the space of just a few years, IEPA granted 185 permits to the SCA facility, and USEPA, although it was aware of the problems at the site, did not intervene or otherwise oversee IEPA action, despite possessing clear legal authority to do so. What explains the willingness of the IEPA to

---

7. RCRA is studied in greater detail in Chapter 18.

support, through the grant of so many permits and other favorable actions, a project that it later came to view as fundamentally flawed, sufficiently so that the State of Illinois filed suit against SCA on IEPA's behalf? The apparent comfort level of the expert agencies with the site and its continued operations appears rather curious. The numerous continuing permits make it incontrovertible that the agencies were aware of the operations at the Wilsonville site. Did the agencies deem the risks associated with the Wisonville site to be not very serious? Or could there be other reasons for the agencies' behavior? As for injecting the state into the suit on behalf of the plaintiffs, the Attorney General may have had a political agenda that is independent of risk management choices made by an expert agency.

5. **Risk, scientific uncertainty, and expert testimony.** A prominent feature of environmental disputes frequently is pervasive scientific uncertainty. Scientific uncertainty makes the assessment and management of risk exceptionally difficult. Are there systematic strategies that should be invoked in cases of scientific uncertainty? See Page, A Generic View of Toxic Chemicals and Similar Risks, 7 Ecology L.Q. 207 (1978) (excerpted in Chapter 1). When scientific data is absent or inconclusive, common law courts resolve questions of fact by considering expert testimony in light of the parties' relative burdens of proof. In the *Wilsonville* case, why were plaintiffs' experts believed rather than defendants' experts? Whose witnesses were better prepared to testify regarding the actual possibilities of release of materials from the Wilsonville site? In the ordinary case where individual citizens sue a large corporate defendant, whom would you expect to present the better qualified and prepared expert witnesses? Did the joinder of the Illinois Attorney General on the plaintiffs' side in this case alter the usual imbalance of resources? The standards for admissibility of expert testimony is, quite evidently, a vital concern in environmental litigation involving complex scientific issues. That topic is addressed in Chapter 4.

6. *Wilsonville* **as environmental injustice.** Apart from the previously identified economic motivation facing SCA Services, are there other factors that might have influenced a decision to site a hazardous waste landfill at this geologically dubious location: Is this a case of environmental injustice? Wilsonville, a poor rural community whose residents included many unemployed ex-miners, had little political leverage compared to that of defendant, its clients (some of whom were highly capitalized hazardous waste generators), and state and federal agencies. If that slant is appropriate, the wonder is that the state's Attorney General intervened to support the town's call for abatement. Most environmental justice cases do not end as this one did. Decisions regarding siting are subjected at times to rigorous state hazardous waste disposal facility siting statutes. These are considered in Chapter 25.

The following public nuisance case shows a state in the role of plaintiff seeking relief for toxic contamination caused by a negligently operated dumpsite in which defendant chemical company had deposited waste several years prior to the litigation. Other aspects of the case appear later in the materials on affirmative defenses to tort liability.

New York v. Schenectady Chemical Company
N.Y. Supreme Court, Rensselaer County, 1983
117 Misc. 2d 960, 459 N.Y.S. 2d 971

The court must decide if the State, either by statute or common law, can maintain an action to compel a chemical company to pay the costs of cleaning up a dump site so as to prevent pollution of surface and ground water when the dumping took place between 15 to 30 years ago at a site owned by an independent contractor hired by the chemical company to dispose of the waste material....

The amended complaint contains the following factual assertions. The action is brought by the State in its role as guardian of the environment against Schenectady Chemicals, Inc. with respect to a chemical dump site located on Mead Road, Rensselaer County, New York (the Loeffel site). Since 1906 Schenectady Chemicals has manufactured paints, alkyl phenols and other chemical products, a byproduct of which is waste, including but not limited to phenol, benzene, toluene, xylene, formaldehyde, vinyl chloride, chlorobenzene, 1,2 dichlorobenzene, 1,4 dichlorobenzene, trichloroethylene, chloroform, ethyl benzene, ethylene chloride, 1,1 dichloroethane, 1,2 dichloroethane, trans-1,2 dichloroethylene, lead, copper, chromium, selenium, and arsenic. These chemical wastes are dangerous to human, animal and plant life, and the defendant was so aware. During the 1950s until the mid-1960s the defendant disposed of its chemical wastes by way of contract with Dewey Loeffel, or one of Mr. Loeffel's corporations. Mr. Loeffel made pick-ups at the defendant's manufacturing plants and disposed of the material by dumping directly into lagoons at the Loeffel site, and in some instances by burying the wastes. It is alleged that with knowledge of the danger of environmental contamination if its wastes were not properly disposed, and knowing of Loeffel's methods, Schenectady Chemicals: (1) hired an incompetent independent contractor to dispose of the wastes; and (2) failed to fully advise Loeffel of the dangerous nature of the waste material and recommend proper disposal methods.

It is alleged that the Loeffel site is approximately 13 acres of low-lying swamp land located in a residential-agricultural area in Rensselaer County with surface soil consisting mainly of gravel and sand. The ground water beneath the site is part of an aquifer which serves as the sole source of water for thousands of area residents and domestic animals. The site drains into two surface streams, one a tributary of the Valatie Kill, and the other a tributary of Nassau Lake. During the period in question approximately 46,300 tons of chemical wastes were deposited at the Loeffel site, of which 17.8 percent, or 8,250 tons, came from defendant. The other material was generated by General Electric Company and Bendix Corporation and has been so inextricably mixed with defendant's as to become indistinguishable....

The complaint alleges that over the years the chemical wastes have migrated into the surrounding air, surface and ground water contaminating at least one area drinking well and so polluting, or threatening to pollute, the area surface and ground water as to constitute an unreasonable threat to the public well-being and a continuing public nuisance. As a result, the Department of Environmental Conservation (DEC) developed a plan to prevent further migration of chemical wastes from the site, and General Electric and Bendix have agreed to pay 82.2 percent of the costs thereof. Defendant's refusal to pay its portion of the clean-up costs gives rise to this suit....

The fourth through eighth causes of action rely upon a nuisance theory. The "term nuisance, which in itself means no more than harm, injury, inconvenience, or annoyance...arises from a series of historical accidents covering the invasion of different kinds of interests and referring to various kinds of conduct on the part of defendants." Nuisances are classified as either private or public. In *Copart*, the Court of Appeals described a public nuisance as:

A public, or as sometimes termed a common, nuisance is an offense against the State and is subject to abatement or prosecution on application of the proper governmental agency. It consists of conduct or omissions which offend, interfere with or cause damage to the public in the exercise of rights common to all in a manner such as to offend public morals, interfere with use by the public of a public place or endanger or injure the property, health, safety or comfort of a consider-able number of persons. 362 N.E.2d at 968....

[The court permitted the public nuisance to be litigated based on both intentional and strict liability theories.] While ordinarily nuisance is an action pursued against the owner of land for some wrongful activity conducted thereon, "everyone who creates a nuisance or partici-pates in the creation or maintenance of a nuisance are liable jointly and severally for the wrong and injury done thereby." Even a non-landowner can be liable for taking part in the creation of a nuisance upon the property of another. Thus, in Hine v. Air-Don Co., 250 N.Y.S. 75, the Third Department held that it was for the jury to decide if the defendant had taken part in the creation of a nuisance so as to render it liable to the injured plaintiff through the act of leaving the unassembled parts of a furnace in a pile upon a public sidewalk. In Caso v. District Council, 350 N.Y.S.2d 173, the defendant, a union of employees working for municipal sewage treatment plants, engaged in an illegal strike resulting in one billion gallons of raw sewage being emitted into the East River. The plaintiffs, officials of Nassau County and affected towns on Long Island, sued on behalf of their governmental units seeking compensatory and punitive damages for injury done to their water and beaches. The union moved to dismiss the complaint, alleging that no such cause of action existed.... The Second Department stated, "A common law cause of action in nuisance would appear to be the appropriate remedy in the instant case." 350 N.Y.S. 2d 177.

The common law is not static. Society has repeatedly been confronted with new inventions and products that, through foreseen and unforeseen events, have imposed dangers upon society (explosives are an example). The courts have reacted by expanding the common law to meet the challenge, in some instances imposing absolute liability upon the party who, either through manufacture or use, has sought to profit from marketing a new invention or product. The modern chemical industry, and the problems engendered through the disposal of its byprod-ucts, is, to a large extent, a creature of the twentieth century. Since the Second World War hundreds of previously unknown chemicals have been created. The wastes produced have been dumped, sometimes openly and sometimes surreptitiously, at thousands of sites across the country. Belatedly it has been discovered that the waste products are polluting the air and water and pose a consequent threat to all life forms. Someone must pay to correct the problem, and the determination of who is essentially a political question to be decided in the legislative arena. As Judge Bergan noted in Boomer v. Atlantic Cement Co., resolution of the issues raised in society's attempt to ameliorate pollution are to a large extent beyond the ken of the judicial branch. Nonetheless, courts must resolve the issues raised by litigants and, in that vein, this court holds that the fourth through seventh causes of action of the amended complaint state viable causes of action sounding in nuisance.

[In subsequent proceedings, the case was settled out of court, with no admission of liability. There was, however, a consent judgment whereby the defendant paid $498,500 in damages. Additionally, the defendant was not excused from paying for future damages if pollution migrated off the site. – Eds.]

COMMENTARY & QUESTIONS

1. **Why public nuisance?** Why did the government prosecutors in this case use common law instead of the elaborate federal and state statutory provisions that were available for decontamination of toxic sites? Does public nuisance provide greater efficiency in establishing liability and obtaining effective remedies? This case also may illustrate how liberal the concept of "intentional" tort can be. What did the defendant know was substantially certain to happen? In a public nuisance action brought by the appropriate public official, the public official acting as plaintiff is clothed with a presumptive authority to speak for the common good. Does that mean that the interests represented by the public official presumptively outweigh the costs to a private nuisance-maker when equities are balanced, or does it merely mean that (unlike in *Boomer*) the public values are allowed onto the scale?

2. **Vicarious liability.** Did Schenectady Chemical create the nuisance in this case or did Loeffel? Here Loeffel and his various companies were independent contractors. Unlike in the employer-employee setting where vicarious liability applies unless the employee is acting outside the scope of his employment,[8] one who hires an independent contractor usually will not be vicariously liable for the contractor's acts. Doctrinally, there are ways that plaintiffs can overcome efforts by parties who try to hide behind the claim that the wrong was done by an independent contractor. One such approach is to claim that the party was negligent in hiring that particular contractor. This has the effect of putting the contractor's credentials on trial, which at times can be very harmful to a defendant if the contractor is plainly unqualified to perform the task at hand. A second doctrine arises in relation to the risks surrounding the task being turned over to an independent contractor. When the court deems that the responsibility of the person hiring the independent contractor for the subject matter involved is sufficiently important to the community, the court will term it a non-delegable duty and hold the hiring party vicariously liable for the failings of the independent contractor. A third possibility is that the plaintiff can try to show collusion — that the party who hired the independent contractor was cooperating in the performance of a wrongful act. In the case at hand, do you think Loeffel's creation of a nuisance should be imputed to Schenectady Chemical? Is your answer based on the law of independent contractors or on a sense that the court is not about to let a large chemical concern hide behind a small (probably bankrupt) disposal firm?

3. **Aquifers attract toxics.** Note the horrendous siting of this toxic dump: in a low-lying wetland with substrata of gravel and sand, precisely the kind of geology that carries groundwater and acts as an aquifer recharge area. Perversely, many dumpers over the years have chosen marshes and gravel quarries as the most convenient dumping spots — out of sight, out of mind. Once within an aquifer, a toxic plume spreads widely, and decontamination of the subsoil is grossly expensive and time-consuming, if not impossible.

---

8. The degree of deviation from the scope of employment that will cut off vicarious liability is captured by the phrase often found in the cases, "frolic and detour."

4. **Public nuisance actions for contamination of public drinking water supplies.** Is there any reason why it might not be a public nuisance for a defendant to contaminate a public drinking water supply? There are not many reported cases, but there is no theoretical reason why such cases should not succeed. The damages can be quite substantial, with at least one reported settlement reaching almost $70 million. See South Tahoe Pub. Util. Dist. v. Atlantic Richfield Co., Cal. Super. Ct., S.F. County, NO. 999128, described at 34 BNA Envtl. Rep. 817 (Apr. 11, 2003).

The following public nuisance case is best known for its surprising remedy that is influenced by the usually disfavored affirmative defense of coming to the nuisance, but the environmental implications of its cause of action are likewise notable.

Spur Industries, Inc. v. Del Webb Development Company
Supreme Court of Arizona, 1972
108 Ariz. 178, 494 P.2d 700

CAMERON, J. The area in question is located in Maricopa County, Arizona, some 14 to 15 miles west of the urban area of Phoenix, on the Phoenix-Wickenburg Highway, also known as Grand Avenue. About two miles south of Grand Avenue is Olive Avenue which runs east and west. 111th Avenue runs north and south as does the Agua Fria River immediately to the west.

Farming started in this area about 1911. In 1929, with the completion of the Carl Pleasant Dam, gravity flow water became available to the property. By 1950, the only urban areas in the vicinity were the agriculturally related communities of Peoria, El Mirage, and Surprise located along Grand Avenue. Along 111th Avenue approximately one mile south of Grand Avenue and 1 1/2 miles north of Olive Avenue, the community of Youngtown was commenced in 1954. Youngtown is a retirement community appealing primarily to senior citizens.

In 1956, Spur's predecessors in interest, H. Marion Welborn and the Northside Hay Mill and Trading Company, developed feedlots about one-half mile south of Olive Avenue. The area is well suited for cattle feeding and in 1959, there were 25 cattle feeding pens or dairy operations within a 7 mile radius of the location.... In April and May of 1959, the Northside Hay Mill was feeding between 6,000 and 7,000 head of cattle and Welborn approximately 1,500 head on a combined area of 35 acres.

In May of 1959, Del Webb began to plan the development of an urban area to be known as Sun City. For this purpose, the Marinette and Santa Fe Ranches, some 20,000 acres of farmland, were purchased for $15,000,000 or $750.00 per acre. This price was considerably less than the price of land located near the urban area of Phoenix, and along with the success of Youngtown was a factor influencing the decision to purchase the property in question.

By September 1959, Del Webb had started construction of a golf course south of Grand Avenue and Spur's predecessors had started to level ground for more feedlot area. In 1960, Spur purchased the property...and began a rebuilding and expansion program extending both to the north and south of the original facilities. By 1962 Spur's expansion program was completed and had expanded from approximately 35 acres to 114 acres.

Accompanied by an extensive advertising campaign, homes were first offered by Del Webb in January 1960 and the first unit to be completed was south of Grand Avenue and approximately two and a half miles north of Spur. By May 2, 1960, there were 450 to 500 houses completed or under construction. At this time, Del Webb did not consider odors from the Spur feed pens a problem. [In 1963 Webb's staff knew of the potential conflict, but decided to

FIGURE 3-1

Inset map from Spur decision, 494 P.2d 702, and two views of feedlot operations like those involved in Spur. Rather than grazing, the cattle have feed and water brought to them. Densities sometimes reach 400+ per acre, with predictable liquid and solid waste and animal health consequences. Note the manure runoff in lower photograph; in some feedlots the wastes do not drain off but accumulate where the cattle stand. (Under a recent EPA regulation, concentrated animal feedlots can now be designated as regulated "point sources" under the CWA. 40 C.F.R. §122.1(b)(2).)

continue its southward development.] By December 1967, Del Webb's property had extended south to Olive Avenue and Spur was within 500 feet of Olive Avenue to the north.... Del Webb continued to develop in a southerly direction until sales resistance became so great that the parcels were difficult if not impossible to sell.... Del Webb filed its original complaint alleging that in excess of 1,300 lots in the southwest portion were unfit for development for sale as residential lots because of the operation of the Spur feedlot.

Del Webb's suit complained that the Spur feeding operation was a public nuisance because of the flies and the odor which were drifting or being blown by the prevailing south to north wind over the southern portion of Sun City. At the time of the suit, Spur was feeding between 20,000 and 30,000 head of cattle, and the facts amply support the finding of the trial court that the pens had become a nuisance to the people who resided in the southern part of Del Webb's development. The testimony indicated that cattle in a commercial feedlot will produce 35 to 40 pounds of wet manure per day, per head, or over a million pounds of wet manure per day for 30,000 head of cattle, and that despite the admittedly good feedlot management and good housekeeping practices by Spur, the resulting odor and flies produced an annoying if not unhealthy situation as far as the senior citizens of southern Sun City were concerned. There is no doubt that some of the citizens of Sun City were unable to enjoy the outdoor living which Del Webb had advertised and that Del Webb was faced with sales resistance from prospective purchasers as well as strong and persistent complaints from the people who had purchased homes in that area....

It is noted, however, that neither the citizens of Sun City nor Youngtown are represented in this lawsuit and the suit is solely between Del Webb Development Company and Spur Industries.... It is clear that as to the citizens of Sun City, the operation of Spur's feedlot was both a public and a private nuisance. They could have successfully maintained an action to abate the nuisance. Del Webb, having shown a special injury in the loss of sales, has standing to bring suit to enjoin the nuisance. The judgment of the trial court permanently enjoining the operation of the feedlot is affirmed.

A suit to enjoin a nuisance sounds in equity and the courts have long recognized a special responsibility to the public when acting as a court of equity: Courts of equity may, and frequently do, go much further both to give and withhold relief in furtherance of the public interest than they are accustomed to go when only private interests are involved. Accordingly, the granting or withholding of relief may properly be dependent upon considerations of public interest.... 27 Am. Jur. 2d, Equity, §104, 626.

In addition to protecting the public interest, however, courts of equity are concerned with protecting the operator of a lawful, albeit noxious, business from the result of a knowing and willful encroachment by others near his business.

In the so-called "coming to the nuisance" cases, the courts have held that the residential landowner may not have relief if he knowingly came into a neighborhood reserved for industrial or agricultural endeavors and has been damaged thereby:

> Plaintiffs chose to live in an area uncontrolled by zoning laws or restrictive covenants and remote from urban development. In such an area plaintiffs cannot complain that legitimate agricultural pursuits are being carried on in the vicinity, nor can plaintiffs, having chosen to build in an agricultural area, complain that the agricultural pursuits carried on in the area depreciate the value of their homes....

Were Webb the only party injured, we would feel justified in holding that the doctrine of "coming to the nuisance" would have been a bar to the relief asked by Webb, and, on the other hand, had Spur located the feedlot near the outskirts of a city and had the city grown toward the feedlot, Spur would have to suffer the cost of abating the nuisance as to those people locating within the growth pattern of the expanding city....

There was no indication in the instant case at the time Spur and its predecessors located in western Maricopa County that a new city would spring up, full blown, alongside the feeding operations and that the developer of that city would ask the court to order Spur to move because of the new city. Spur is required to move not because of any wrongdoing on the part of Spur, but because of a proper and legitimate regard of the courts for the rights and interests of the public.

Del Webb, on the other hand, is entitled to the relief prayed for (a permanent injunction), not because Webb is blameless, but because of the damage to the people who have been encouraged to purchase homes in Sun City. It does not equitably or legally follow, however, that Webb, being entitled to the injunction, is then free of any liability to Spur if Webb has in fact been the cause of the damage Spur has sustained. It does not seem harsh to require a developer, who has taken advantage of the lesser land values in a rural area as well as the availability of large tracts of land on which to build and develop a new town or city in the area, to indemnify those who are forced to leave as a result.

Having brought people to the nuisance to the foreseeable detriment of Spur, Webb must indemnify Spur for a reasonable amount of the cost of moving or shutting down. It should be noted that this relief to Spur is limited to a case wherein a developer has, with foreseeability, brought into a previously agricultural or industrial area the population which makes necessary the granting of an injunction against a lawful business and for which the business has no adequate relief.

It is therefore the decision of this court that the matter be remanded to the trial court for a hearing upon the damages sustained by the defendant Spur as a reasonable and direct result of the granting of the permanent injunction. Since the result of the appeal may appear novel and both sides have obtained a measure of relief, it is ordered that each side will bear its own costs.

COMMENTARY & QUESTIONS

1. **The twist in *Spur*.** On remand, Webb settled, reportedly paying Spur more than $1 million in moving costs. In a subsequent case, the Arizona court also allowed Spur to sue for indemnity, so that Webb would have to reimburse the feedlot for tort damages Spur might have to pay to individual homeowners. Spur v. Superior Ct., 505 P.2d 1377 (Ariz. 1973). The unusual feature of the *Spur* case is not its public nuisance theory but its remedy, conditioning the injunction on plaintiff's payment of moving costs. Is this a case about comparative fault? The court seems to consider that it was the developer's fault that caused the conflict. Is Spur's nuisance therefore based on some kind of no-fault liability? What if the only suit for injunction and damages had been brought by homeowners, not by Webb? What if Webb lacked funds to pay Spur? Doesn't this get the court into judicial land use decisions, as noted below? On a larger scale, it is useful to note that agricultural pollution cases generally can be litigated only under common law theories because the farm lobbies' political strength has successfully inserted blanket exemptions for agriculture into all significant federal and state pollution statutes.

2. **The "right-to-farm" debate.** Common law nuisance claims have long provided a method for many rural and suburban residents to end the noise, odor, and annoyance that accompanies animal production. For farms that use manure and other odiferous fertilizers and for animal producers, injunctive relief granted in favor of their neighbors

often means that they can no longer use existing barns and equipment, creating considerable hardship for members of the farming community. Agricultural interest groups have been able to obtain anti-nuisance "right-to-farm" legislation in roughly 40 states. Do these right-to-farm laws derogate neighbors' common law nuisance rights to such a degree that their enforcement may be considered a taking of property? In Anti-Nuisance Legislation, 30 Envtl. L. Rep. 10253 (2000), Terence Centner analyzes cases including Bormann v. Koussuth County Bd. of Sup'rs, 584 N.W.2d 309 (Iowa 1998), where the Iowa Supreme Court held that a county board's approval of an "agricultural area" that triggered nuisance immunity resulted in condemnation by nuisance of neighbors' property without just compensation, thus making the board's action unconstitutional. This question echoes issues that are seen in the "permit defense" setting later in this chapter.

3. **The tactical advantages of public nuisance.** What advantages did Webb get from suing in public nuisance? Part of Webb's strategy was to get around the coming-to-the-nuisance defense. Did the development company also get a broader basis for nuisance claims than it would have under private nuisance, even class action private nuisance? The court unhesitatingly balanced the overall public interest against Spur. Note, moreover, that there was no proof of personal injury or property damage in *Spur*. The court said that "the odor and flies produced an annoying if not unhealthy situation," and seemed to focus on the aesthetics and quality of life of the community of Sun City. Would Oscar Boomer have gained from filing his case in public nuisance? Aesthetic nuisance litigation, applied to billboards, junkyards, and the like, is typically based on public nuisance.

Public nuisance also opens up otherwise impossible liability claims, such as predecessor liability for land contamination. In most states, a buyer has no action against a seller who has sold property that turns out to be spoiled or hazardous. Caveat emptor. In several cases of contaminated land, however, the courts, though refusing to allow private nuisance claims because the parties did not own different parcels, allowed public nuisance claims. In Nashua Corp. v. Norton Co., 45 BNA Env't Rep. Cas. 1013 (N.D.N.Y. 1997),[9] public nuisance applied because groundwater pollution from the parcel threatened the general public. The plaintiff's response costs and alleged stigma damages qualified as special damages.

4. **A widening role for environmental public nuisance?** Public nuisance traditionally has been applied against actions that injure life or health; offend the senses; violate principles of decency; obstruct free passage or use of highways, navigable streams, public parks, and beaches; and otherwise disrupt public rights. These definitions obviously possess great potential to expand with contemporary sensibilities to incorporate a wide range of environmental values. How far into novel environmental settings can public nuisance be extended? The aesthetic enjoyment of low-tech visitors to a Walden Pond, a desert park, or a wilderness river can be disturbed by just a few individuals with boom boxes or all-terrain vehicles. Are these public nuisances? Is smoking in public

---

9. Plaintiff also filed under CERCLA's and RCRA's private cleanup remedies, but the nuisance claims were filed in order to recover "stigma" damages, unrecoverable under statutory causes of action.

becoming litigatable as public nuisance? Destruction of historic monuments? Could public nuisance injunctions, if the facts had been known, have blocked the importation of alien species such as gypsy moths, poisonous walking catfish, carp, and starlings into the United States? Can public nuisance be used where consequences are potentially disastrous but probabilities are uncertain, as with genetic engineering experimentation with recombinant DNA outside the laboratory? For an ancient doctrine, the flexibility and scope of public nuisance give it remarkable evolutionary potential.

5. **Public nuisance/private plaintiffs.** Public nuisance, deriving from criminal law, is in the first instance supposed to be litigated by public prosecutors, but local and state governments often are not enthusiastic about litigation and are sometimes themselves the defendants in public nuisance actions. Private plaintiffs thus have played a major role in the expansion of public nuisance. Standing of private parties, however, traditionally has posed a procedural barrier: In order to sue in public nuisance, private plaintiffs have to show "special injury" different in kind, and not just in degree, from the public as a whole. In *Spur*, for example, Webb's "sales resistance" is special injury. A homeowner in the neighborhood might or might not be granted special injury standing. A disgusted county resident with no health or property damage traditionally would have no hope of suing in public nuisance. Isn't it somewhat paradoxical that in order to represent public values in public nuisance, which offers wide attractions to environmental plaintiffs, potential public nuisance plaintiffs must prove that they are substantially different from the public? Recent amendments to the Restatement (Second) of Torts §421c attempt to extend standing in public nuisance, for injunctive relief only, to any person "having standing to sue as a representative of the general public, as a citizen in a citizen suit, or class representative in a class action." Many courts have continued to follow the old special injury rule, although a number of states hold that any bodily injury is per se special. Note that public nuisance actions usually seek equitable relief only; private plaintiffs typically cannot recover public nuisance damages (unless special damages as in the *Nashua Corp.* case above), and public plaintiffs normally do not seek damages.

6. **Judicial zoning under public nuisance?** Given the Arizona court's holding in *Spur*, would it have issued an injunction against Webb's southward development if Spur had timely brought such an action in 1962? The court clearly considered the natural and appropriate use for the area to be agricultural rather than urban. In a number of fascinating cases, courts have issued injunctions against, for instance, funeral parlors and gas stations in unzoned residential areas, judicially recognizing their primarily residential character. Powell v. Taylor, 263 S.W.2d 906 (Ark. 1954) (funeral parlor); State v. Feezell, 400 S.W.2d 716 (Tenn. 1966) (crematorium). In Harrison v. Indiana Auto Shredders, 528 F.2d 1102 (7th Cir. 1975), however, the court permitted a noisy, smelly, gas-and-dust emitting automobile shredding and recycling operation to locate in a low-income neighborhood, merely awarding damages, evidently classifying the neighborhood as less deserving of equitable protection. In Bove v. Donner-Hanna Coke Corp., 258 N.Y.S. 229, 233 (1932), the court denied even damages to a woman whose home was polluted by installation of a smelly coke oven, saying that "it is true that...when the plaintiff built her house, the land on which these coke ovens now stand

was a hickory grove. But...this region was never fitted for a residential district; for years it has been peculiarly adapted for factory sites." Recognizing the environmental potential for incorporating evolving public sensibilities into public nuisance, do you nevertheless feel uncomfortable with the role that judges can play in dictating appropriate uses for particular parcels of land?

Section 3. ADAPTING TRESPASS, THE MOST TRADITIONAL OF TORTS

Borland v. Sanders Lead Company
Supreme Court of Alabama, 1979
369 So. 2d 523

JONES, J. This appeal involves the right of a property owner, in an action for trespass, to recover damages for pollution of his property.... J. H. Borland, Sr., and Sarah M. Borland, Appellants, own approximately 159 acres of land, located just south of Troy, Alabama, on Henderson Road. On this property, Appellants raise cattle, grow several different crops, and have a large pecan orchard.

In 1968, the Appellee, Sanders Lead Company, started an operation for the recovery of lead from used automobile batteries...just east of the Borlands' property.... The Appellee's smelter was placed on the west edge of their property, that part nearest to the Appellants' property. The smelter is used to reduce the plates from used automobile batteries. It is alleged by Appellants that the smelting process results in the emission of lead particulates and sulfoxide gases....

Appellee installed a filter system, commonly known as a "bag house," to intercept these lead particulates which otherwise would be emitted into the atmosphere. The "bag house" is a building containing fiber bags. The smoke emitting from the furnace is passed through two cooling systems before passing through the "bag house" so that the fiber bags will not catch fire. If properly installed and used, an efficient "bag house" will recover over 99 percent of the lead emitted. On two occasions, the cooling system at Appellee's smeltering plant has failed to function properly, resulting in the "bag house's" catching fire on both occasions.... Appellants allege that, because of the problems with the "bag house," their property has been damaged by a dangerous accumulation of lead particulates and sulfoxide deposits on their property....

The trial Court was under the mistaken impression that compliance with the Alabama Air Pollution Control Act shielded the Defendant from liability for damages caused by pollutants emitting from its smelter. This is not the law in this State.... Furthermore, the trial Court incorrectly applied the law of this State in concluding that, because there was evidence showing that the Plaintiffs' farm had increased in value as industrial property, due to its proximity to the lead plant, Plaintiffs could not recover of the Defendant. Such a rule, in effect, would permit private condemnation, which, unquestionably, is impermissible...[and] overlooks the fact that the appreciation factor is totally unrelated to the wrongful acts complained of....

Alabama law clearly provides an appropriate remedy for Plaintiffs who have been directly injured by the deleterious effects of pollutants created by another party's acts.... A trespass need not be inflicted directly on another's realty, but may be committed by discharging foreign polluting matter at a point beyond the boundary of such realty.... Restatement, 2d, Torts, §158 recites:

> In order that there may be a trespass under the rule stated in this Section, it is not necessary that the foreign matter should be thrown directly and immediately upon the other's land. It is enough that an act is done with knowledge that it will to a substantial certainty result in entry of foreign matters.

In Martin v. Reynolds Metals Co., 342 P.2d 790 (Or. 1959), a case remarkably similar to the present case, the Plaintiffs sought recovery...for trespass [alleging] that the operation by Defendants of an aluminum reduction plant caused certain fluoride compounds in the form of gases and particulates, invisible to the naked eye, to become airborne and settle on Plaintiffs' property, rendering it unfit for raising livestock. Plaintiffs in the present case allege that the operation of Defendant's lead reduction plant causes an emission of lead particulates, and SO_2, invisible to the naked eye, which emissions have settled on their property, making it unsuitable for raising cattle or growing crops.

The Defendants in *Martin* contended that there had not been a sufficient invasion of Plaintiffs' property to constitute trespass, but, at most, Defendant's acts constituted a nuisance. This would have allowed the Defendants to set up Oregon's two-year statute of limitations applicable to non-possessory injuries to land rather than Oregon's six-year statute for trespass to land. The *Martin* Court pointed out that trespass and nuisance are separate torts for the protection of different interests invaded — trespass protecting the possessor's interest in exclusive possession of property and nuisance protecting the interest in use and enjoyment. The Court noted, and we agree, that the same conduct on the part of defendant may, and often does, result in the actionable invasion of both interests....

The modern action for trespass to land stemmed inexorably from the common law action for trespass which lay when the injury was both direct and substantial. Nuisance, on the other hand, would lie when injuries were indirect and less substantial. A fictitious "dimensional" test arose, which obviated the necessity of determining whether the intrusion was "direct" and "substantial." If the intruding agent could be seen by the naked eye, the intrusion was considered a trespass. If the agent could not be seen, it was considered indirect and less substantial, hence, a nuisance.... The *Martin* Court rejected the dimensional test and substituted in its place a force and energy test, stating:

> The view recognizing a trespassory invasion where there is no "thing" which can be seen with the naked eye undoubtedly runs counter to the definition of trespass expressed in some quarters. It is quite possible that in an earlier day when science had not yet peered into the molecular and atomic world of small particles, the courts could not fit an invasion through unseen physical instrumentalities into the requirement that a trespass can result only from a direct invasion. But in this atomic age even the uneducated know the great and awful force contained in the atom and what it can do to a man's property if it is released. In fact, the now famous equation $E=mc^2$ has taught us that mass and energy are equivalents and that our concept of "things" must be reframed. If these observations on science in relation to the law of trespass should appear theoretical and unreal in the abstract, they become very practical and real to the possessor of land when the unseen force cracks the foundation of his house. The force is just as real if it is chemical in nature.... Viewed in this way we may define trespass as an intrusion which invades the possessor's protected interest in exclusive possession, whether that intrusion is by visible or invisible pieces of matter or by energy which can be measured only by the mathematical language of the physicist. We are of the opinion, therefore, that the intrusion of the fluoride particulates in the present case constituted a trespass.

It might appear, at first blush, from our holding today that every property owner in this State would have a cause of action against any neighboring industry which emitted particulate matter into the atmosphere, or even a passing motorist, whose exhaust emissions come to rest upon another's property. But we hasten to point out that there is a point where the entry is so lacking in substance that the law will refuse to recognize it, applying the maxim de minimis non curat lex — the law does not concern itself with trifles. In the present case, however, we are not faced with a trifling complaint. The Plaintiffs in this case have suffered, if the evidence is believed, a real and substantial invasion of a protected interest.... If the intrusion is direct, then, under our present law, actual damages need not be shown; nominal damages may be awarded and this will support punitive damages....

Under the modern theory of trespass, the law presently allows an action to be maintained in trespass for invasions that, at one time, were considered indirect and, hence, only a nuisance. In order to recover in trespass for this type of invasion (i.e., the asphalt piled in such a way as to run onto plaintiff's property, or the pollution emitting from a defendant's smoke stack, such as in the present case), a plaintiff must show (1) an invasion affecting an interest in the exclusive possession of his property; (2) an intentional doing of the act which results in the invasion; (3) reasonable foreseeability that the act done could result in an invasion of plaintiff's possessory interest; and (4) substantial damages to the res [i.e., unlike direct trespasses which need not show substantial damages]....

If, as a result of the defendant's operation, the polluting substance is deposited upon the plaintiff's property, thus interfering with his exclusive possessory interest by causing substantial damage to the res, then the plaintiff may seek his remedy in trespass, though his alternative remedy in nuisance may co-exist.... Reversed and remanded.

COMMENTARY & QUESTIONS

1. **Trespass and tactics.** As the *Borland* and *Martin* courts both noted, pollution may constitute both a trespass and a nuisance simultaneously, and plaintiffs may seek recovery under one or both legal theories. What are the advantages and disadvantages of nuisance and trespass? Trespass carries a number of internal restrictions, including those noted by the court. Why then would a plaintiff sue in trespass instead of nuisance? One reason is that the statute of limitations, as in *Martin*, often extends further back in time for trespass than for nuisance. Another reason is that trespass actions seem to encourage the grant of injunctions because they emphasize the fact of an unconsented invasion, penetration, or incursion onto private property. Even judges who are normally quite unattuned to environmental issues have acknowledged that "a man's home is his castle" and granted injunctions accordingly.

2. **How far can trespass go?** After *Borland*, Alabama apparently requires actual and substantial injury for an "indirect" trespass such as in a pollution case. Most other states, however, do not. If courts apply $E=mc^2$ to determine whether there has been "physical invasion" of plaintiff's property, is there any limit to how far the trespass action might apply? Noise? Light photons? Low-frequency electromagnetic radiation from high-voltage transmission facilities? An ugly view? The further down this path a court travels, the more its protection of the right of exclusive possession (trespass) and the right of quiet enjoyment (nuisance) becomes coextensive. What are the benefits to a plaintiff in pleading that the same events constitute both a trespass and a nuisance? Is there any downside?

3. **Defenses to trespass and nuisance.** Defenses to tort claims are studied more extensively in Part B. It is good at the outset, however, to see the way courts account for defenses as legal issues separate from whether plaintiff has established a prima facie case. Remember that a prima facie case is a case that is good enough to win unless its

elements are successfully rebutted by the defendant or unless its effect is successfully avoided by defendant establishing an affirmative defense. In *Borland*, note that the defendant unsuccessfully attempted to use the "permit defense." The *Borland* court's reasoning reflects a distinction between the remedial purposes of the common law and the regulatory purposes of the pollution control statutes — the former is concerned with redress for local injuries, and the latter is concerned with minimum public health and welfare standards. Defendant also raised as a partial defense to the assessment of damages the argument that, despite having committed a trespassory invasion, it had caused no loss to the plaintiff because the land had appreciated in value due to its value as commercial property. It is a partial defense because it does not avoid all liability; it merely attempts to limit the remedy that the court may grant. The appellate court rejected the defense. If change in property value is not the measure of damage, what is? Is it possible to base the measure of damages on the change in value of the land as used for purposes desired by the plaintiff? This topic is considered again in Part D.

Section 4. THE ROLE OF NEGLIGENCE IN ENVIRONMENTAL CASES

The development of negligence as a separate tort cause of action emerged in the nineteenth century. Before this, negligence had been treated as a component of other torts — a mental element that operated like intentionality in torts such as battery or nuisance. Eventually, negligence was recognized as a separate and independent tort, and it became the foundation for most suits dealing with accidental (as opposed to intentional) personal injuries.[10] The modern negligence cause of action represents the legal incarnation of the social norm that one who fails to avoid avoidable injuries to others ought to bear the cost of those injuries. Thus negligence jurisprudence is replete with efforts to draw a normative line between avoidable and unavoidable accidents. Somewhat more formally, the translation of this normative line into a cause of action establishes

(1) a standard of conduct that a "reasonable person" (i.e., objective standard) would follow to protect other persons from an unreasonable risk of harm, and

(2) conduct by the defendant that does not satisfy this "reasonable person" standard.

These two requirements are frequently referred to as "duty" and "breach of duty."

The concept of duty imports a relational test to the equation: Duties are owed to someone, and the plaintiff must be among those to whom duties are owed. In a sense, this adds a foreseeability element to the cause of action. The famous case of Palsgraf v. Long Island R.R.[11] is the leading case on the issue of foreseeability in negligence cases. The majority opinion, written by Justice Cardozo, analyzed the case as one of whether the duty was owed to plaintiff and finding it was not because she was not a foreseeable victim of the particular substandard conduct that occurred. The dissent, written by Justice Andrews, argued that the conduct was not reasonable under the circumstances

---

10. See W. P. Keeton & W. L. Prosser, Prosser and Keeton on Torts, 160–161 (5th ed. 1984.)
11. 248 N.Y. 339, 162 N.E. 99 (1928).

and analyzed the case in terms of proximate cause,[12] which he thought had been proved. There are thus two different approaches to raising foreseeability requirements in negligence cases. In modern times, being among those to whom a duty is owed has some effect in limiting recoveries, but the scope of many duties owed has expanded greatly as the population has grown and the public has developed a greater understanding of the broader ramifications of individual actions. This is particularly true in cases involving the eventual harms caused by pollutants released into the environment. Many environmental tort duties thus reach as far as the pollution eventually travels. In addition to duty and breach of duty, a prima facie negligence case requires causation and damage, as noted at the beginning of this chapter.

Traditionally, negligence seldom was the sole theory of recovery in successful environmental cases. Environmental cases tend to involve damage to property as well as damage to person. Historically, achieving remedy for an injury to property required that the suit sound in nuisance or trespass or some other cause of action specifically intended to redress injury to property rights. Correlatively, negligence grew out of a focus on redress for injury to person, and, as a historic matter, in many jurisdictions could not support remedies for damage to property.[13] Despite these observations, there are instances where negligence is the most appropriate claim in a setting of environmental harm alone, as when carelessly performed crop dusting with an herbicide caused contamination of a nearby farm's mint crop with a resultant award of damages.[14]

Negligence often is harder to prove than the intentionality required for trespass or nuisance recoveries. Undertaking deliberate actions, such as to emit pollutants in the act of operating a factory, and then being deemed liable for various types of harms that result as a natural consequence of such pollution makes the imposition of liability straightforward in many environmental cases. Proving a duty owed, and a breach of that duty, comparatively speaking, seems difficult, but plaintiffs attempt it for several reasons, two of which are most prominent — judicial familiarity and the ability to introduce evidence of defendant's misdeeds.

All trial courts are well versed in the law of negligence. They have tried many such cases and intuitively understand that what otherwise might seem to be novel claims of environmental injury constitute a prima facie case of liability (duty and breach), causation, and damage. Strategically, as to liability, the heart of negligence action revolves around proof that defendant's conduct fell below what reasonable citizens can expect. Consider, for example, Hagy v. Allied Chemical, in which defendant chemical company was operating a plant in Los Angeles that produced large amounts of acidic smokestack emissions. On days of thermal inversion, the emissions, including amounts of sulphuric acid, poured down the side of the stack and cast a pall over the neighborhood. Allied instructed its employees to don gas masks during inversions and to ignore

---

12. Proximate cause is discussed in greater detail in Part C.

13. Older personal injury cases litigated on the basis of negligence have occasional environmental overtones. See, e.g., Greyhound v. Blakely, 262 F.2d 401 (9th Cir. 1958) (plaintiff was awarded damages as a result of carbon monoxide poisoning she suffered while riding in defendant's bus).

14. Bella v. Aurora Air Ind., 279 Or. 13, 566 P.2d 489 (1977). See also Rotella v. McGovern, 288 A.2d 258 (R.I. 1972) (negligent sewer maintenance produced sewage flood in basement).

telephone calls from gassed neighbors. The Hagys were gassed while driving by, sued for negligent personal injury instead of public nuisance, and won substantial damages. 265 P.2d 86 (Cal. App. 1953). If tried as a nuisance case, the evidence about gas masks for employees would not have been relevant. The issue of nuisance turns on the degree of harm suffered by the public, and the use of gas masks inside the facility would not be relevant to proving the quality or quantity of emissions released beyond the plant's boundaries. In the negligence action, however, the gas mask evidence is relevant to show a possible standard of care, the foreseeable nature of neighbors and passersby as potential victims of the emissions, and a standard of conduct that defendant itself deemed appropriate for its workforce but neglected to extend to others facing the same danger. Negligence literally puts on trial the issue of whether defendant's conduct is substandard. Even in pollution cases not so egregious as *Hagy*, the addition of a negligence count can be an effective litigation strategy. When negligence is joined to other theories that are likely to prevail (such as nuisance or strict liability), it does not matter greatly whether the jury finds defendant's conduct to be negligent. The evidence offered by plaintiff to establish defendant's negligence inevitably affects how the jury awards damages for the other counts.

COMMENTARY & QUESTIONS

1. **Standards of care.** The general standard of care in a negligence case is captured in a phrase that often appears in jury instructions — that the defendant must exercise "due care and caution for the safety of plaintiff." At a minimum, that standard is based on an objective (i.e., community standard) view of what is reasonable under the circumstances. At times, however, specific standards of conduct can be imported from regulatory contexts and brought to bear on defendant's conduct. Most commonly this is done with safety standards. For example, where a regulation forbids the dispensing of gasoline into non-certified containers, a station that dispensed gas into such containers can be said to have breached the duty set by the statute if the non-standard container leads to a spill, fire, or explosion that causes harm.[15] In the environmental field, particularly in relation to hazardous substances, there are an amazing number of regulations. Even when strict liability is available to a plaintiff, it may still be beneficial for the plaintiff to show that the defendant knowingly violated a safety standard. Most courts, although there is a degree of variation among jurisdictions, will treat proof of violation of a relevant regulatory standard as creating a prima facie case, sometimes stating that plaintiff has established a "rebuttable presumption of negligence." The onus is then on defendant to show why violation of the regulatory standard should not be deemed negligence. Usually this means that defendant must demonstrate why the regulatory standard should not be the standard of care under the circumstances. A few courts take a stronger view of the violation of a regulatory standard in a negligence case. For example, in a case involving eight bellwether or "flagship" plaintiffs, the judge instructed that in order to find negligence the jury had to decide only that federal emissions standards

---

15. Another frequent use of safety standards to prove negligence is made in products liability cases brought in jurisdictions that have narrowed the availability of strict liability for defective products.

were violated. See Hall v. Babcock & Wilcox Co., 69 F. Supp. 2d 716 (W.D. Pa. 1999). The claim arose in Pennsylvania where radiation emissions were associated with extremely high rates of cancer. The judge instructed that the emissions violation would constitute negligence per se. Having shown the violation, the plaintiffs then had to argue damage and causation — that plaintiffs were harmed and that the negligence caused their harm — and the jury so found.

2. **Custom, regulatory compliance, and state of the art as satisfaction of the standard of care.** Negligence begins with examining defendant's conduct to see if it meets the relevant standard of care. Defendants frequently try to show the exercise of due care by proving that their conduct is what is customary, or that their conduct meets the standard set by a regulation, or that it meets the terms of the permit under which they are operating, or, finally, that because they are operating at a "state of the art" level, their conduct is not negligent. These arguments can be offered either as rebuttals to plaintiff's allegations that defendant did not meet a standard of care or as affirmative defenses that may defeat plaintiff's prima facie case. Because these defensive arguments go to the qualitative character of defendant's actions, they are relevant in determining whether defendant was negligent, but they are not relevant in determining liability in intentional torts or strict liability. Although proof of compliance with custom or regulation is relevant and helpful to defendant in negligence cases, it is not always conclusive in defendant's favor. Focusing on what the standard of care represents explains why proof of compliance with custom or regulation is only partial evidence of due care. By contrast, proof that defendant is utilizing state of the art practices to avoid harm is highly probative in negligence cases because care need only be reasonable to be non-negligent, and state of the art is almost by definition the best possible care in the circumstances.

3. **Deterrence, the role of benefit-cost analysis in determining negligence, and cost internalization.** Does the threat of negligence verdicts deter would-be polluters? Surely that threat deters some negligent conduct. In a rational, predictable world, the threat of negligence actions would deter some defendants from negligently causing high-cost harms. Simultaneously, as rational actors, that same threat would not deter them in cases where their conclusion is that the cost of being careful exceeds the cost of increased litigation and compensation to victims. Is there reason to expect that the real-world result is anything close to the optimal amount of deterrence? Optimal deterrence, from a total social cost point of view, would result in duties aligned with that level of care that prevents losses to others in excess of the cost of their prevention.[16] If cost internalization and the "polluter pays" principle is the yardstick, how does negligence measure up when compared to intentional tort and strict liability? Negligence systematically underachieves the goal of full cost internalization. All cases in which defendant prevails on grounds of nonliability and all cases in which plaintiffs choose

---

16. This view of due care as aligned with efficiency is derived from the famous passage penned by Learned Hand in United States v. Carroll Towing Co., 159 F.2d 169, 173 (2d Cir. 1947), describing a vessel owner's duty to guard against it breaking from its moorings as a function of (1) the probability of the event (P), (2) the gravity of the resulting injury (L, as in loss), and (3) the burden of adequate precautions (B). Liability (negligence) is present when B is less than PL.

not to sue due to uncertainty of result on the issue of liability result in less cost internalization being achieved by negligence than comparatively more certain-to-succeed causes of action.

4. **Less obvious tactical advantages of negligence claims.** For plaintiffs, winning in court is not everything. Winning in court and then successfully collecting the judgment is far more vital. If a defendant (picture a thinly capitalized dump operator such as Dewey Loeffel in *Schenectady Chemical*) is "judgment proof," no case is likely to be worth bringing (except for injunctive relief) unless there is insurance available to pay the judgment. Most businesses carry comprehensive general liability (CGL) insurance policies. Historically, those polices tended to cover defendants only for accidental discharges, not for "intentional" pollution, so a negligence judgment is more likely to be covered by insurance and therefore collectable. See, e.g., Technicon Elec. Corp. v. American Home Assur. Co., 542 N.E.2d 1048 (N.Y. 1989). In more recent years, most insurance polices have been written to exclude environmental liabilities using even more demanding terms for policy coverage to apply. See Chapter 19 for a discussion of insurance in the context of CERCLA. Another advantage of the negligence claim lies in suits against governmental defendants. In a few states, statutes waiving governmental sovereign immunity permit suits for negligence but not suits based on intentional torts or strict liability.

Section 5. STRICT LIABILITY

RESTATEMENT (SECOND) OF TORTS (1977) — Division 3: Strict Liability

Chapter 21. Abnormally Dangerous Activities

§519. General Principles

(1) One who carries on an abnormally dangerous activity is subject to liability for harm to the person, land or chattels of another resulting from the activity, although he has exercised the utmost care to prevent such harm.

(2) Such strict liability is limited to the kind of harm, the risk of which makes the activity abnormally dangerous....

§520. Abnormally Dangerous Activities

In determining what constitutes an abnormally dangerous activity, under Restatement §519, the following factors are to be considered:

(a) Whether the activity involves a high degree of risk of some harm to the person, land, or chattels of others;

(b) Whether the gravity of the harm which may result from it is likely to be great;

(c) Whether the risk cannot be eliminated by the exercise of reasonable care;

(d) Whether the activity is not a matter of common usage;

(e) Whether the activity is inappropriate to the place where it is carried on; and

(f) The value of the activity to the community.

Branch v. Western Petroleum, Inc.
Supreme Court of Utah, 1982
657 P.2d 267

STEWART, J. The Branches, the plaintiff property owners, sued for damages for the pollution of their culinary water wells caused by percolation of defendant Western Petroleum's formation waters into the subterranean water system that feeds the wells....

In December 1975, Western purchased forty acres of land in a rural area north of Roosevelt, Utah, which had previously been used as a gravel pit. Western used the property solely for the disposal of formation water, a waste water produced by oil wells while drilling for oil. Formation water contains oil, gas and high concentrations of salt and chemicals, making it unfit for culinary or agricultural uses. The formation water was transported by truck from various oil-producing sites and emptied into the disposal pit with the intent that the toxic water would dissipate through evaporation into the air and percolation into the ground. Alternative sites for disposing of the water were available to Western, but at a greater expense.

In 1976, the Branches purchased a parcel of property immediately adjacent to, and at an elevation of approximately 200 to 300 feet lower than Western's property. The twenty-one acre parcel had on it a "diligence" well, which had been in existence since 1929, some outbuildings, and a home. After acquiring the property, the Branches made some $60,000 worth of improvements to the home and premises. Prior owners of the property used the water from the well for a grade A dairy and later a grade B dairy. Both dairy operations required that the water be approved for fitness and purity by appropriate state agencies. The Branches, as had all prior owners since 1929, used water from the diligence well for culinary purposes. The water from the diligence well was described as being sweet to the taste and of a high quality until December of 1976.

Two months after purchasing the property, the Branches noticed that the well water began to take on a peculiar taste and had the distinctive smell of petroleum products. Soap added to the water would no longer form suds. They observed that polluted water from Western's disposal pit was running onto the surface of the Branches' property and, on one occasion, reached their basement, causing damage to food stored there. After testing the diligence well water and finding it unfit for human consumption, and after their rabbits and one hundred chickens had died, apparently from the polluted water, the Branches began trucking water to their property from outside sources. In November, 1977, the Branches dug an additional well south of their home. Water from the new well was tested and found safe for culinary purposes. But after a few months, the new well also ceased producing potable water, and on advice of the State Health Department, the Branches ceased using the new well for culinary purposes and hauled water to their property almost until the time of trial.

The Branches requested Western to cease dumping formation water in the disposal pit, but Western refused unless the Branches would post a bond to cover the costs....

At trial the major issue was whether and how Western's formation waters caused the pollution of the Branches' wells.... The Branches' expert, Mr. Montgomery, a state geologist who had spent nine years working for the Utah Division of Water Resources, [said] that the subsurface waters consist of shallow groundwater and a deeper aquifer known as the Duchesne Formation.... Water in the disposal pit was percolating into the subsurface waters....

The major substantive dispute is whether the trial court erred in entering judgment against Western on the basis of strict liability for pollution of the Branches' wells. Western argues that other states have based liability for pollution of subterranean waters on either negligence, nuisance, or trespass, and that since the Branches failed to allege nuisance or trespass, "the only accepted theory upon which this case could be based is negligence." Therefore, according to

Western, the trial court erred in entering judgment on the basis of strict liability. Western further submits that since the court did not instruct the jury on proximate cause and comparative negligence, the judgment cannot stand. The Branches, on the other hand, take the position that Western created an abnormally dangerous condition by collecting contaminated water on its land for the purpose of having it seep or percolate into the groundwater and that, therefore, the law of strict liability controls....

In England under the common law, percolating water was considered part of the freehold and subject to private ownership. In American law it is generally recognized that a landowner has no absolute right to pollute percolating waters. In this state, a landowner has no such absolute right because percolating waters belong to the people of the state. For that reason, and because percolating waters are migratory and the rights of the landowners to those waters are correlative, such waters are subject to the maxim that one may not use his land so as to pollute percolating waters to the injury of another.

As Utah is one of the most arid states in the union, the protection of the purity of the water is of critical importance, and the Legislature has enacted laws for the protection of both surface and subterranean waters....

The landmark case of Rylands v. Fletcher, 3 H. & C. 774, 159 Eng. Rep. 737 (1865), rev'd in Fletcher v. Rylands, L.R. 1 Ex. 265 (1866), aff'd in Rylands v. Fletcher, L.R. 3 H.L. 330 (1868), held that one who uses his land in an unnatural way and thereby creates a dangerous condition or engages in an abnormal activity may be strictly liable for injuries resulting from that condition or activity. Whether a condition or activity is considered abnormal is defined in terms of whether the condition or activity is unduly dangerous or inappropriate to the place where it is maintained. That doctrine was the genesis of §519 of the Restatement of Torts (1939), which, however, limited strict liability to "ultrahazardous activities."

Although Rylands v. Fletcher was initially rejected by a number of states, its influence has been substantial in the United States. According to the latest edition of Dean Prosser's treatise on torts, only seven American jurisdictions have rejected the rule of that case, while some thirty jurisdictions have essentially approved the rule. Indeed, the strict liability rule of the Restatement of Torts was broadened in §519 of the Restatement 2d of Torts by making it applicable to "abnormally dangerous activities."

There are two separate, although somewhat related, grounds for holding Western strictly liable for the pollution of the Branches' wells. First, the facts of the case support application of the rule of strict liability because the ponding of the toxic formation water in an area adjacent to the Branches' wells constituted an abnormally dangerous and inappropriate use of the land[17] in

---

17. Several cases on comparable facts have applied strict liability due to the abnormal danger of polluting activity. For example, Mowrer v. Ashland Oil & Refining Co., 518 F.2d 659 (7th Cir. 1975), applied strict liability to the leakage of crude oil and salt water into a fresh water well; Yommer v. McKenzie, 257 A.2d 138 (Md. 1969), applied the same rule to the seepage of gasoline from an underground tank into an adjoining landowner's well; Cities Service Co. v. Florida, 312 So. 2d 799 (Fla. 1975), applied strict liability to the escape of phosphate slime into a creek and river. See also Bumbarger v. Walker, 164 A.2d 144 (Pa. 1960) (strict liability for well pollution caused by defendant's mine blasting). See generally Clark-Aiken Co. v. Cromwell-Wright Co., 323 N.E.2d 876 (Mass. 1975) (strict liability applied to escape of impounded water); Indiana Harbor Belt Railroad Co. v. American Cyanamid Co., 517 F. Supp. 314 (N.D. Ill. 1981) (strict liability applied to spillage of toxic chemical that resulted in property damage and pollution of water supply); W. Prosser, Torts §78 at 512-13 and cases there cited. See also Atlas Chemical Industries, Inc. v. Anderson, 514 S.W.2d 309 (Tex. Civ. App. 6 Dist., 1974), aff'd 524 S.W.2d 681 (1975), where the Texas court, distinguishing a case relied upon by Western, Turner v. Big Lake Oil Co., 96 S.W.2d 221 (Tex. 1936), held the defendant strictly liable for polluting surface streams with industrial wastes. The strict liability rule of Rylands v. Fletcher was held to apply to pollution cases "in which the defendant has set the substance in motion for escape, such as the discharge of the harmful effluent or the emission of a harmful gas or substance." Atlas Chemical, 514 S.W.2d at 314.

light of its proximity to the Branches' property and was unduly dangerous to the Branches' use of their well water.[18]

[Second],...the common law rules of tort liability in pollution cases should be in conformity with the public policy of this state as declared by the Legislature,...[and an] industrial polluter can and should assume the costs of pollution as a cost of doing business rather than charge the loss to a wholly innocent party:

> We know of no acceptable rule of jurisprudence which permits those engaged in important and desirable enterprises to injure with impunity those who are engaged in enterprises of lesser economic significance. The costs of injuries resulting from pollution must be internalized by industry as a cost of production and borne by consumers or shareholders, or both, and not by the injured individual. *Atlas Chemical*, 514 S.W.2d 309.

We think these reasons adequately support application of the rule of strict liability in this case. In sum, the trial court properly ruled that Western was strictly liable for the damage which it caused the Branches....

COMMENTARY & QUESTIONS

1. Why strict liability? Analytically, the *Branch* case could have been brought using other tort theories, such as nuisance, trespass, or negligence. Look closely at Restatement (Second) of Torts §519. Does this explain the advantages of using strict liability as the basis for the claim in *Branch*?

2. "Abnormally dangerous." In *Branch*, what is found to be ultrahazardous or abnormally dangerous under the terms of Restatement (Second) of Torts §§519–520? Is oil really an abnormally dangerous material? Or is storage of oil-drilling wastewater an abnormally dangerous activity? On the facts of *Branch*, the closest analogy to *Rylands* is disposing of formation waters by placing them in an impoundment near a property line or recharge area for local wells.

---

18. Even if Western did not know that the formation water would enter the aquifer and cause damage to plaintiffs' wells, it could have determined the likelihood of that consequence. As Professor Davis has stated:

> A polluter should not be absolved from liability just because he may not be able to anticipate the movement of the polluted groundwater he created. This defense should not be recognized for several reasons. First, the hydrology of groundwater movement is much better understood now than it was when many of the early groundwater pollution cases were decided. Even though precise mapping of groundwater movement in any particular location is still expensive, it is within the reach of any major waste producer which proposes to inject wastes underground. Disposal wells need porous formations for successful waste injection and the appropriate hydrologic tests would insure a successful injection well. Therefore, persons deliberately disposing of wastes underground ought to be required to act in accordance with the information gained by such testing regarding the movement of the injected wastes and their probable effects on neighboring groundwater uses. If they do not make such tests, they should be charged with the information they would have gained had they made them. Second, it is generally known now that liquids placed on the ground will seep into the soil and may enter the body of groundwater percolating beneath the surface. Persons causing groundwater pollution, in ways other than by deliberate underground disposal, should be charged with such knowledge and should not be insulated from liability for groundwater pollution by claiming that they know nothing more about groundwater movement than was known in 1843 when Acton v. Blundell was decided. Although a particular polluter might still legitimately claim he could not predict particular injurious consequences of his activity, he can no longer claim legitimately that the polluting material vanished from the earth once it seeped beneath the surface. He knows it will go somewhere. Such a defense to nuisance liability is not recognized in surface watercourse and air pollution cases. Groundwater pollution cases should not recognize it either. Davis, Groundwater Pollution: Case Law Theories for Relief, 39 Mo. L. Rev. 117, 145–46 (1974). See also Wood v. Picillo, 443 A.2d 1244, 1249 (R.I. 1982).

3. **Foreseeability.** Did Western know that the formation water would reach the wells? It appears that they did not foresee such an occurrence and, even after the fact, disputed its occurrence through the testimony of their expert witness. To what degree is foreseeability relevant under §519? In its footnote, the court relies on Professor Davis's argument to reject the importance of defendant's foreknowledge of events. What is Davis's argument? It first simply charges highly capitalized waste disposers with foreseeing whatever testing would have revealed; it second simply recognizes that liquids tend to percolate down into aquifers, and it charges defendants with that knowledge, something that the law refused to do in an earlier era when less was known about hydrogeology. So stated, would there be sufficient evidence of foreseeability in *Branch* to reflect intent under a nuisance theory?

4. **Strict liability for what harms?** The court points out the nonchalance of Western in its attitude toward the Branches' rights and its lack of inquiry into the pollution laws of Utah. Why is this relevant in a strict liability case? The answer lies with a claim for punitive damages, discussed in Part D on remedies. In Langan v. Valicopters, 567 P.2d 218 (Wash. 1977), an aerial crop-dusting service had allowed its pesticide sprays to drift onto an organic farm. No crops were killed. The plaintiffs' injury claim was based purely on their crops' loss of "organic" certification caused by the spray. The court went step by step through Restatement §§519 and 520 and applied strict liability. Looking at §519(2), would you? If pesticide spraying is indeed an abnormally dangerous activity, what kinds of ecological harms can be recouped, by whom? What other activities might be deemed ultrahazardous? See Koos v. Roth, 293 Or. 670 (1982) (farmer who employed field burning as an agricultural technique was held strictly liable for damages when the fire destroyed neighbor's property). At times the defendant in strict liability will try to fob off the liability on another party who actually engaged in the ultrahazardous activity. As with negligence, the concept of a nondelegable duty applies in the strict liability context as well. See Loe v. Lenhard, 227 Or. 242, 362 P.2d 312 (1961) (liability for extra-hazardous activity is nondelegable; farmer and hired crop duster both liable for damage to neighbor's crops).

5. **Environmental applications of other tort theories.** Beyond the preceding commonly encountered torts, environmental cases filed by creative plaintiffs can be based on theories of "battery" (where pollution is characterized as unconsented intentional physical contact with plaintiffs' bodies), Martin v. National Steel, 607 F. Supp. 1430 (S.D. Ill. 1985); "waste" to land (where degradation of rented land, life estates, or a defeasible fee injures the reversion), United States v. Denver RGR Co., 190 F. 825 (D. Colo. 1911); water-based violations of "reasonable use" (impacting riparian property rights), Thompson v. Enz, 154 N.W.2d 473 (Mich. 1967), and other flexible applications of existing doctrine, each presenting different litigation requirements and potential benefits. Environmental plaintiffs are continually exploring and rethinking old tort options in order to develop new litigation approaches and tactics.

B. DEFENSES IN ENVIRONMENTAL TORT SUITS

There are two principal ways to defend a torts case: The defendant can deny and refute a critical element of the plaintiff's prima facie case or else can try to raise and prove an affirmative defense. As to affirmative defenses, a laundry list of the most common ones is found in Fed. R. Civ. P. 8(c). A quick review of that list shows only a few — contributory negligence, estoppel, laches, discharge in bankruptcy, res judicata, and statute of limitations — that might have a bearing on a typical environmental tort lawsuit. Apart from the standard affirmative defenses, however, environmental lawsuits confront a number of more specialized defenses. In the *Schenectady Chemical* case that was excerpted earlier, the court reviewed an array of defenses.

New York v. Schenectady Chemical Company
N.Y. Supreme Court, Rensselaer County, 1983
117 Misc. 2d 960, 459 N.Y.S.2d 971

[The court first heard the defendant manufacturer's arguments that the elements of a common law cause of action did not exist, and that cleanup costs at the Loeffel site were not recoverable under common law. Finding that these arguments lacked merit, the court turned to an illustrative laundry list composed mostly of affirmative defenses.]

The defendant has raised many additional objections.... It is argued that the action is untimely. The limitation applicable to a nuisance cause of action is the three-year period provided in N.Y. Civ. Prac. L. & R. 214. The rule with respect to an ongoing nuisance, as here alleged, is that the action continually accrues anew upon each day of the wrong although the recovery of money damages is limited to the three-year period immediately prior to suit. Defendant's contention that the limitation period should accrue upon the last day of dumping lacks merit since the law has long been settled that, "the right to maintain an action for...nuisance continues as long as the nuisance exists...."

The argument that [the governmental plaintiff] lacks standing to maintain the action because the waters are private rather than public cannot withstand scrutiny. The amended complaint alleges that the waste has migrated from the Loeffel site into neighboring surface and ground water, including two streams. By statute, "waters" is defined to include "all other bodies of surface or underground water...public or private (except those private waters which do not combine or effect a junction with natural surface or underground waters)...."

[As to an attempted constitutional prescriptive rights defense, the state high court has] rejected [the] claim that protecting water from pollution somehow violated a due process property right, stating that the argument was "untenable since such rights do not attach to water itself and in any event are required to yield to public health and public safety."

Defendant's next contention is that the complaint must be dismissed since the requested relief is speculative and to some degree not authorized or appropriate. A complaint will not be dismissed due to a prayer for inappropriate relief so long as some right to recover is demonstrated.

The court will dismiss the demand for attorney's fees since that relief is not available in the absence of a statute or contract authorizing same.[19]

---

19. This is not necessarily true. A traditional rule of equity is that although the American rule, unlike the English, is that in the absence of contrary statute each party bears its own legal expenses, courts can order "fee-shifting" where the loser pays the prevailing party's expert witness and attorneys' fees when there is a showing of defendant's "bad faith," a "common fund" of value is accrued by the defendant, or the court decides that plaintiffs have

The objection that the complaint is improperly set forth as eight separate and distinct causes of action instead of one is not a basis for relief. While better pled as a single nuisance cause of action, the method employed here does not constitute improper splitting since all claims are contained in a single action.

As to the request for dismissal for failure to join necessary parties, i.e., other alleged tortfeasors guilty of dumping at the site, the rule is that those contributing to a nuisance are liable jointly and severally and "it is fundamental that a plaintiff...is free to choose his defendant." If defendant feels that others may have contributed to plaintiff's damage it should commence the appropriate third-party practice.[20]

The argument that plaintiff has released [co-defendants] General Electric Company and Bendix and thus defendant is released, must fail. First of all the...purported releases have not been furnished, lending credence to plaintiff's assertion that they do not yet exist. More importantly, plaintiff has averred that the language of the proposed releases will specifically reserve its rights against defendant; thus, [defendant] will not be discharged.

The defenses of res judicata and collateral estoppel due to the order and judgment of March 4, 1968 in Ingraham v. Loeffels Oil Removal & Serv. Co. are not available since this action involves different parties upon different causes of action, and defendant's responsibility, if any, was never addressed in the prior action.

Likewise, dismissal is not warranted under N.Y. Civ. Prac. L. & R. 3211 due to "another action pending between the same parties for the same cause of action," since the pending case of Thornton v. General Electric does not involve the identical parties and causes of action.

The defense that the statutory scheme of the Environmental Conservation Law is exclusive and bars common law actions is directly contradicted by §17-1101 of that law....

Likewise, the complaint cannot be dismissed upon defendant's "state of the art" defenses.... The fact that a manufacturer may have complied with the latest industry standards is no defense to an action to abate a nuisance since, as stated earlier with respect to public nuisances and inherently dangerous activities, fault is not an issue, the inquiry being limited to whether the condition created, not the conduct creating it, is causing damage to the public.

The final argument for dismissal worthy of discussion is the contention that by hiring a private contractor licensed to dispose of chemical wastes the defendant has met its legal duty and cannot be held liable for the contractor's wrongdoing. Defendant [however, can] be found liable for Loeffel's acts if: (1) it was negligent in retaining an incompetent contractor; (2) it failed, with knowledge thereof, to remedy or prevent an unlawful act; (3) the work itself was illegal; (4) the work itself was inherently dangerous; or (5) the work involved the creation of a nuisance....

COMMENTARY & QUESTIONS

1. **Evaluating *Schenectady Chemical*'s defenses.** Consider each of the foregoing defensive arguments made by the chemical company. How many of these defenses deserve legitimate attention when environmental cases such as *Schenectady Chemical* go to trial? Although the company's lawyers raised a welter of attempted defenses, there are

---

acted as private attorneys general. This last exception sounds well-suited to environmental cases and remains applicable in many state courts, though it was gutted in federal court practice by the Supreme Court in the Alyeska Pipeline Company case, 421 U.S. 240 (1975). [Eds.]

20. The ability of one tortfeasor to shift or share the loss is considered in the materials on multiple defendants and causation that appears in Part C, §2 of this chapter. [Eds.]

even more categories of potential defenses that could be asserted in environmental litigation. These additional categories are described in the following notes.

2. **The permit defense.** One common line of defense in environmental cases, the "permit defense," is a form of preemption argument based on defendant's assertion that the polluting activity is being conducted under the terms of a valid government permit. (A number of pollution permit systems are explored beginning in Chapter 5.) This defense is consistently rejected unless the statute creating the permit system has expressly repealed the availability of common law remedies in the field. Because environmental activists are keenly aware of this issue, virtually all pollution statutes have specifically rejected industry lobbyists' attempts to preempt common law by making statutory permit enforcement the exclusive pollution remedy. Where a case is argued on a negligence-based theory, including negligently created nuisance, on the other hand, courts have been willing to take notice of permit compliance into account as evidence tending to show that due care was exercised. The converse is also true — that courts treat proof of permit noncompliance as evidence of defendant's negligence. In policy terms, why shouldn't permit compliance always be a valid defense?

The Alaska legislature, prompted by paper mill lobbyists concerned with citizen tort suits, passed a bill in 1994 that prohibits lawsuits for common law private nuisance if defendant corporations are in compliance with state permits. Alaska Stat. §09.45.230 (Michie 1994). The statute, basing its regulation on statewide emission standards, thus tries to preempt common law, which traditionally tailors its protections according to particular local effects on neighbors. Such permit defense statutes raise a fascinating question: Does repeal of traditional common law protections of private property constitute an invalid regulatory taking? See Hasselman, Alaska's Nuisance Statute Revisited: Federal Substantive Due Process Limits to Common Law Abrogation, 24 B.C. Envtl. Aff. L. Rev. 347 (1997), and Chapter 23.

3. **Primary jurisdiction.** The "primary jurisdiction" defense is less dramatic than the permit defense but equally disliked by environmental plaintiffs. Under this defense, the defendant urges the judge to suspend the common law suit in order to await enforcement by the government agency with jurisdiction over the matter. The argument is not that common law remedies do not coexist with the public law remedy, but rather that courts should defer initially to the expertise, official appropriateness, and uniformity function represented by the statutory regulators. Environmental plaintiffs bemoan such remands to the agencies. Why? The fact that polluters want to be sent to the official agencies gives some indication of which forum is more likely to provide effective remedies against them (as well as giving an ironic twist to familiar corporate arguments denouncing the bureaucratic state). Plaintiffs try to resist the primary jurisdiction defense by arguing that the reasons for deference to agencies do not apply in their case, that only a court can offer them damage remedies, that unlike the public law system the common law is designed to deal with localized controversies, and so on.[21] Primary jurisdiction is not a well-understood nor widely litigated defense. It invites interesting environmental arguments on both sides of the question.

---

21. See Comment, Primary Jurisdiction in Environmental Cases, 48 Ind. L.J. 676 (1973).

4. **Is the utility of a facility a defense to liability?** Over the years, many courts have confused the issues of what constitutes a legitimate defense to liability with choice of remedy. This is particularly common in nuisance suits where the defense invokes the social utility of defendant's conduct. Thus there have been some nuisance cases in which courts have denied relief altogether on a "balance of utilities," finding defendants' conduct tolerable (not actionable) under the circumstances, as when major industrial facilities have inflicted substantial damage on nearby houses. In doing so, those courts replicated the oversimplification of an Old English dictum: "Le utility del chose excusera le noisomeness del stink," roughly, "The usefulness of the thing will excuse the foulness of the pollution." The legal French appears to be a version of a line from *Ranketts* case in 1684: "Si home fait Candells deins un vill, per que il caufe un noyfom fent al Inhabitants, uncore ceo neft alcun Nusans, car le needfulnefs de eux difpenfera ove le noifomnefs del fmell." P. 3 Ja. B.R. Rolle's Abridgement, Nusans, 139 (1684). As *Boomer* showed, this may be relevant to the grant or denial of injunctive relief, but it should not affect a finding on the issue of liability.

5. **Statutory preemption of common law?** Marketplace lobbyists often attempt to insert a seemingly innocuous phrase into drafts of environmental regulatory statutes: "The provisions of this title shall constitute the exclusive remedy for the subject matter it covers." What would be the consequence of this provision on pollution torts, for example, if it slipped into law? This effort reflects the marketplace's healthy appreciation of how effective common law remedies can be. In some cases, however, defendants can argue that statutory preemptions of common law are implicit in strict federal regulatory schemes:

> This case requires us to determine whether a state [common law] award of punitive damages arising out of the escape of plutonium from a federally-licensed nuclear facility is pre-empted either because it falls within that forbidden field or because it conflicts with some other aspect of the Atomic Energy Act. Karen Silkwood was a laboratory analyst for Kerr-McGee at its Cimmaron plant near Crescent, Oklahoma. The plant fabricated plutonium fuel pins for use as reactor fuel in nuclear power plants. Accordingly, the plant was subject to licensing and regulation by the Nuclear Regulatory Commission (NRC) pursuant to the Atomic Energy Act. During a three-day period of November 1974, Silkwood was contaminated by plutonium from the Cimmaron plant. Karen's father brought the present diversity action...based on common law tort principles under Oklahoma law...to recover for the contamination injuries....
>
> Congress' decision to prohibit the states from regulating the safety aspects of nuclear development was premised on its belief that the Commission was more qualified to determine what type of safety standards should be enacted in this complex area.... Congress assumed that traditional principles of state tort law would apply with full force unless they were expressly supplanted. Thus, it is Kerr-McGee's burden to show that Congress intended to preclude such awards. Yet, the company is unable to point to anything in the legislative history.... We do not suggest that there could never be an instance in which the federal law would pre-empt the recovery of damages based on state law. But insofar as damages for radiation injuries are concerned, pre-emption should not be judged on the basis that the federal government has so completely occupied the field of safety that state remedies are foreclosed but on whether there is an irreconcilable conflict between

the federal and state standards or whether the imposition of a state standard in a damages action would frustrate the objectives of the federal law. We perceive no such conflict or frustration in the circumstances of this case. White, J., in Silkwood v. Kerr-McGee Corp., 464 U.S. 238 (1984).

If punitive damages are not preempted, clearly compensatory damages are available. What about injunctions?

6. **Statutes of limitation, other time bars, and prescriptive nuisances.** Can statutes of limitations provide a good defense for operators of longstanding nuisances? What if a state has a three-year general torts statute of limitation, and an offending plant commenced operations five years before the suit is brought? Not all state courts have treated the question alike, but the majority position is like *Schenectady Chemical*'s — that if the pollution is a "continuing nuisance," each day is a separate injury, so that a lawsuit can recapture all losses within the period of the statute of limitations. When, however, a nuisance is of a "permanent" nature (loosely defined as a nuisance plainly intended from the first to continue to operate for many years in exactly the same way, for instance, such as one generated by a major electric generation facility), a few court decisions allow the defendant to use the tort statute of limitations to bar untimely suits. In such cases, the statute begins to run from the time at which the cause of action first accrues to the plaintiff. See Goldstein v. Potomac Elec. Power Co., 404 A.2d 1064 (Md. 1979). Do you see that the two different scenarios are not always clearly distinguishable?

Even where a lawsuit is brought within the statute of limitations, a defendant may claim to have acquired a prescriptive private right to pollute, the prescriptive period usually in the 10- to 20-year range. Other estoppel arguments are also available against injunction suits under the equitable defense of laches. As in *Schenectady*, however, public rights usually override such private defenses. At least one state, Alabama, has created a degree of statutory protection for prescriptive nuisances by a law that, in effect, gives prescriptive rights to continue operation against intentional nuisance claims if the new operation is not a nuisance within its first year of operation. See Ala. Code §6-5-127(a) (1975). Causes of action based on other theories, including trespass and negligence are not affected. See Courtaulds Fibers v. Long, 779 So. 2d 198 (Ala. 2000).

7. **Coming to the nuisance.** A few states still recognize a special defense (a form of estoppel defense) called "coming to the nuisance," seen in the *Spur Industries* case. As the name suggests, the thrust of the claim is that the defendant had become established in the area before the plaintiff arrived, so the injury to plaintiff was, in effect, self-inflicted. Would a coming to the nuisance defense have prevailed in *Boomer*? As indicated by its lack of widespread recognition, the defense of coming to the nuisance is flawed analytically. Although the defendant may have begun operations that did no palpable harm to neighboring landowners at the time, with the advent of the injury to plaintiff the question is who enjoys the better right — plaintiff to the quiet enjoyment of her land or defendant to continue the operation of its factory that casts its wastes onto its neighbors' lands? To say, as a defendant does in raising this defense, that plaintiff could have avoided the conflict by settling elsewhere begs the question whether defendant had any legal right to insist that plaintiff do so. In the last analysis, defendant is seeking to use another's land as its disposal site without ever having purchased that

privilege from its neighbor. Most modern courts do not seem fully to understand the defense's internal flaws. Instead they most frequently point to the existence of tight housing markets or zoning ordinances to affirm the primacy of residential uses. The defense accordingly may still be applied in some rural areas.

8. **Releases from liability.** Frequently, as part of a settlement of a dispute, one or both parties will grant releases of liability to the other party in regard to the subject matter of the dispute. Think of a release as the equivalent of a contract between the party giving the release and the party being released. The question that *Schenectady* raises is whether a release, given by the state to General Electric and Bendix in regard to the cleanup, also releases Schenectady Chemical. Here the court rejects that defense on a narrow ground — the failure to show that the releases had actually been given. Assume instead that there are releases and that they are silent as to whether there is a release given to Schenectady Chemical as well as the settling tortfeasors. What should the general rule be? As a hint about how to answer that question, ask first what rule (yes, release; no, no release) is more likely to encourage parties to settle. Section 6 of the Uniform Comparative Fault Act states:

> "A release, covenant not to sue, or similar agreement entered into by a claimant and a person liable discharges that person from all liability for contribution, but it does not discharge any other persons liable upon the same claim unless it so provides. However, the claim of the releasing person against other persons is reduced by the amount of the released person's equitable share of the obligation...."[22]

9. **The best defense is a good offense? "SLAPPs."** One interesting environmental defense tactic is the filing of "SLAPPs" — strategic lawsuits against public participation. When public-interest citizen activists bring actions to enforce the common law or statutory law against polluters, developers, public utilities, ranchers, or other entrepreneurs using federal lands, in at least 100 recent cases defendants have sued or countersued for damages averaging $7.4 million.[23] To get around the First Amendment's petition protection, defense lawyers argue in tort: Plaintiffs' allegations amount to libel, slander, defamation, interference with business advantage, and abuse of judicial process.

On their merits, SLAPPs are overwhelmingly thrown out of court if plaintiffs persevere in resisting them. The fear and burden on volunteer activists of defending against these intimidation suits, however, in practice has resulted in the collapse of many citizen initiatives. Well-heeled defendants can justify spending time and money on SLAPPs as tax-deductible business expenses, knowing that the citizen plaintiffs are likely to be greatly hindered, or halted, in their efforts regardless of the SLAPP's minimal merits. Given the disparate status of the players and the courts' current lack of rigor against attorneys bringing such suits, environmental plaintiffs' ability to obtain sanctions (as

---

22. Section 4 of the Uniform Contribution Among Tortfeasors Act takes the same position.

23. SLAPPs have also issued in response to the filing of petitions and testimony by activists in legislative and executive proceedings. See generally Canan & Pring, Studying Strategic Lawsuits Against Public Participation, 22 Law & Soc'y Rev. 385 (1988:2); Pring, Intimidation Suits Against Citizens: A Risk for Public Policy Advocates, 7 Nat. L.J. 16 (1985); Comment, Counterclaim and Countersuit Harassment of Private Environmental Plaintiffs, 74 Mich. L. Rev. 106 (1975).

allowed under Fed. R. Civ. P. 11) against SLAPP attorneys remains largely theoretical. Note, however, that Rule 11 does not impose limits on the amount the judge may award.[24]

"SLAPP-back" suits, countersuing SLAPPers for damages, are increasing. See Gordon v. Marrone, 590 N.Y.S.2d 649 (1992) (Nature Conservancy recovers $10,000 for developer's harassing lawsuit challenging its tax exemption). For more on SLAPP-backs, see the California anti-SLAPP statute, 1991 Cal. S.B. 341 §425/66(a); Leonardini v. Shell Oil, 216 Cal. App. 3d 547 (1989); Wegis v. J. G. Boswell Co., 1991 Lexis 4641 (Cal. Ct. App. 1991), cert. denied, 502 U.S. 1097 (1992); and the article by the father of SLAPP jurisprudence, Professor George "Rock" Pring, in 7 Pace Envtl. L. Rev. 3 (1989), in a symposium on SLAPPs.

10. **The strategies of environmental defendants.** Environmental defenses are directed predominantly toward blocking plaintiffs' claims from going to trial. Where plaintiffs can prove the factual elements of an intentional tort claim or strict liability, there is no general substantive theory of environmental defense available to polluters for avoiding payment of environmental damages as a cost of doing business. As you go through environmental case law, keep an eye on the various defense strategies that are mobilized. Understandably, they are often attempts to duck the merits or to switch them into forums that are more politically and economically sensitive to defendants' interests.

C. CAUSATION IN CONVENTIONAL ENVIRONMENTAL TORT SUITS

As described in the overview of tort law that opens this chapter, the plaintiff must prove that the injury suffered was caused by the defendant's tortious conduct. This part of the chapter addresses in separate sections the two distinct branches of the causation inquiry: cause-in-fact and proximate cause.[25] Sandwiched in between these two discussions is a section on joint and several liability, a doctrine that alters significantly the standard operation of cause-in-fact principles when the actions of more than one independent tortfeasor combine to cause injury.

Section 1. CAUSATION-IN-FACT

Cause-in-fact in most contexts is a simple concept to grasp at a theoretical level but somewhat harder to work with in practice. In the main, this book contents itself with

---

24. Should courts hold SLAPP plaintiffs to a heightened standard of pleading where litigation chills citizens' First Amendment right to petition government? In Florida Fern Growers Assoc., Inc. v. Concerned Citizens of Putnam County, 616 So. 2d 562 (Fla. Ct. App. 1993), growers charged citizens with "intentional and malicious interference with business relationships" for challenging the issuance of consumptive water permits, but the court held that this did not justify requiring heightened pleadings and sent the case for trial. Given the limited monetary sanctions that can be awarded under many states' procedural rules for instigating frivolous litigation, it is important to public interest groups to have SLAPP suits dismissed as early as possible.

For further reading on SLAPP suits, see Note, Silencing SLAPPS: An Examination of Proposed Legislative Remedies and a Solution for Florida, 20 Fla. St. U. L. Rev. 487 (1992); Note, SLAPP Suits: Weakness in First Amendment Law and in the Courts' Response to Frivolous Litigation, 39 UCLA L. Rev. 979 (1992); Tobias, Environmental Litigation and Rule 11, 33 Wm. & Mary L. Rev. 429 (1992).

25. This book separates cause-in-fact from proximate cause. Some courts and commentators on the subject use the term *proximate cause* to encompass all of the causation issues.

the simple aspects of cause-in-fact and leaves the bulk of the more nuanced material for torts classes. The one exception to this approach is in relation to causation in toxic tort settings, which is explored in detail in the next chapter.

The requirement that defendant's action be the cause-in-fact of the plaintiff's injury is an obvious requisite of tort law. Remembering that the ultimate goal is to provide remedies for some categories of injuries, the cause-in-fact link is the assurance that the loss is being shifted to the appropriate party; i.e., to the one whose act or omission is in some tangible way responsible for the injury, rather than to someone having no part in the chain of events.

The cause-in-fact inquiry purports to be based solely in fact, yet a key aspect of the inquiry requires conjecture about what would have happened in the absence of defendant's action or omission. Indeed, a conclusion that A is a cause of B represents a judgment made by the trier of fact that may be founded alternatively upon experience about the degree of association between A and B, or upon evidence supplied by experts, or even upon mere circumstantial evidence.

COMMENTARY & QUESTIONS

1. **No causation in fact if it would have happened anyway.** Is a failure to fence off a dangerous condition along the roadside the cause-in-fact of an injury that occurred when the plaintiff's vehicle goes out of control and would have crashed through any fence that reasonably might have been constructed? In the environmental torts setting, the "it would have happened anyway" challenge to cause-in-fact is most commonly made in regard to injuries suffered following exposure to toxic substances. Anticipating the next section on joint and several liability, how should cause-in-fact questions be answered when the acts of two independent tortfeasors are each capable of causing the entire injury suffered by plaintiff? Can each claim they are not the but for cause because the injury would have occurred anyway?

2. **Proving too much with "but for."** In general, the cause-in-fact inquiry seeks to establish a but-for relationship — but for the defendant's tortious conduct, the plaintiff's injury would not have happened. While helpful, overemphasizing the but-for inquiry at times obscures proper analysis. A famous example is where defendant driver drives at grossly excessive speeds, and, as a result, plaintiff passengers arrive at destination X just in time to have a wall collapse on them, causing injury. Defendant's negligent conduct in driving so recklessly is indeed a but-for cause of the injury, for otherwise plaintiffs would not have been in the location of the collapsing wall. Nevertheless, for the purposes of tort law, despite the presence of (1) substandard conduct, (2) but-for causation, and (3) injury to plaintiffs, there should be no recovery against defendant driver because the scope of duty owed by the driver does not extend to what befell the passengers when they arrived at their destination. A narrow focus on but-for causation can thus sometimes improperly shift the analysis away from duty, breach, or other tort requirements. A second problem with the but-for analysis lies in the scope of its application and is illustrated by borrowing an example from chaos theory: Because the butterfly flapped its wings in Malaysia, the wind currents reaching the villager carried an extra grain of pollen that caused the villager to sneeze and spill

water into the stream, which altered the flow of the river,…and the cable on the cable car in San Francisco snapped, injuring plaintiff. This problem is addressed by placing limits on the attenuation of causation studied later in the section on proximate cause.

Section 2. **MULTIPLE DEFENDANTS AND THE DOCTRINE OF
JOINT AND SEVERAL LIABILITY**

The traditional analysis of causation in tort is more difficult when more than one defendant is involved in the case. First, the but-for problem rears its head. When the acts of several parties converge to effect a result that injures plaintiff, tort law must find a way to allocate the loss. Traditionally, the plaintiff had to show which of several actors was responsible for the damage and to what extent, or all recovery would be denied. If there were six independent upwind industrial polluters, all using coal for their boiler fuel, the plaintiff would be hard pressed to segregate the emissions of any of them as responsible for the injuries. Gradually, the doctrine of joint and several liability developed to allow the plaintiff to obtain full compensation more easily in such circumstances by making them all liable to the plaintiff for the full amount of the injury and, in effect, allowing the plaintiff to select which defendant or defendants to pursue in court. Once judgment is obtained on this basis, the common law allows the plaintiff to collect the full judgment from any one of the jointly liable defendants (or subset of the group), who then can turn for contribution to other defendants. In an earlier era, the common law generally forbade these defendants from shifting all or a portion of the loss to co-tortfeasors. Modern tort law recoiled at that unfairness and now allows loss shifting and spreading among the tortfeasors in contribution actions, but the problem of loss apportionment in hazardous waste toxic tort cases remains a major area of litigation.[26] The following case explores the imposition of joint and several liability in a conventional pollution setting. The principles enunciated will take on additional importance in the toxic tort area.

Velsicol Chemical Corporation v. Rowe
Supreme Court of Tennessee, 1976
543 S.W.2d 337

[The original plaintiffs, residents and homeowners in the Alton Park area of Chattanooga, sued Velsicol Chemical for damages allegedly caused them by pollutants emitted from its chemical manufacturing plant. The complaint alleged that Velsicol's emissions contaminated the air and water, creating a nuisance and a trespass in depositing quantities of chemicals and other pollutants upon plaintiffs' properties. Because plaintiffs alleged that Velsicol had intentionally disregarded past injunctions, they also asked for punitive damages. Velsicol, however, argued that there were five other chemical polluters in the Alton Park area who could have caused or contributed to plaintiffs' injuries. This raised the question, first, whether plaintiffs could choose to proceed only against Velsicol, and second, if they prevailed, whether Velsicol could then turn and sue the five for contribution in paying damages.]

---

26. Interdefendant loss shifting is considered more fully in Chapter 19 in conjunction with CERCLA.

BROCK, J.... It has been suggested that joint torts be divided into four basic categories, viz., (1) the actors knowingly join in the performance of the tortious act or acts; (2) the actors fail to perform a common duty owed to the plaintiff; (3) there is a special relationship between the parties (e.g., master and servant or joint entrepreneurs); and (4) although there is no concert of action, nevertheless, the independent acts of several actors concur to produce indivisible harmful consequences. 1 Harper & James, Law of Torts, §10.1. While acknowledging that the last category, which may be termed independent, concurring torts, may not fall within the traditional definition of "joint torts," the authors note an increasing tendency in judicial decisions and among legal commentators to impose joint and several liability for such wrongs and thus to establish such torts as "joint" in their practical or legal effect.

The primary concern in dealing with independent, concurring torts is the proper extent of the liability of such wrongdoers, i.e., when should tortfeasors who do not act in concert, but whose acts combine to produce injury to the plaintiff, be held individually liable for the entire damage? It has been suggested that the proper approach should be to look to the combined effect of the several acts:

> If the acts result in separate and distinct injuries, then each wrongdoer is liable only for the damage caused by his acts. However, if the combined result is a single and indivisible injury, the liability should be entire. Thus the distinction to be made is between injuries which are divisible and those which are indivisible. Jackson, Joint Torts & Several Liability, 17 Tex. L. Rev. 399, 406 (1939).

The requirement of "indivisibility" can mean either that the harm is not even theoretically divisible, as death or total destruction of a building, or that the harm, while theoretically divisible, is single in a practical sense in that the plaintiff is not able to apportion it among the wrongdoers with reasonable certainty, as where a stream is polluted as the result of refuse from several factories.

In Landers v. East Texas Salt Water Disposal Co., 248 S.W.2d 731 (Tex. 1952), the plaintiff sued the defendant salt water disposal company and an oil company jointly and severally for the damage resulting when they independently deposited salt water in his lake. The court, apparently assuming that neither defendant acting alone would have caused the entire damage, extended the liability of such wrongdoers by holding them, in effect, to be jointly and severally liable, with the reservation that any one defendant could reduce his liability by showing the amount of damage caused by his acts only, or the amount that was caused by other defendants. The Texas court said:

> Where the tortious acts of two or more wrongdoers join to produce an indivisible injury, that is, an injury which cannot be apportioned with reasonable certainty to the individual wrongdoers, all of the wrongdoers will be held jointly and severally liable for the entire damages and the injured party may proceed to judgment against any one separately or against all in one suit. 248 S.W.2d at 734.

More recently, in Michie v. Great Lakes Steel, 495 F.2d 213 (6th Cir. 1974), residents of LaSalle, Ontario, brought a nuisance action in federal court, claiming that air pollutants from defendants' manufacturing plants across the Detroit River caused diminution of the value of their property, impairment of their health, and interference with the use and enjoyment of their land. Each plaintiff claimed at least $11,000 joint damage against these defendants, charging that the defendants were jointly and severally liable.

Relying upon Michigan automobile cases involving successive collisions, the Court reasoned that in any claim for relief there was a manifest unfairness in "putting on the injured party the impossible burden of proving the specific shares of harm done by each [defendant]," quoting *Landers*. The Court concluded that the Michigan Supreme Court would extend the principle of the automobile collision cases to the *Michie* facts and held that joint and several liability is applicable in nuisance actions. It is our conclusion that the rule stated and applied in the *Landers* and *Michie* cases is…consonant with modern legal thought and pragmatic concepts of justice….

After filing an answer generally denying the plaintiffs' allegations, Velsicol filed a third-party complaint against five third-party defendants, alleging that each of them operated a plant in the Alton Park area, that during the period alleged in the original complaint each of them emitted pollutants of the air and water, and that by reason of these facts the third-party defendants are liable to Velsicol for "whatever amount of recovery is made by said plaintiffs."…

The common law rule was that there could be no contribution between those who were regarded as "joint tortfeasors," when one had discharged the claim of the injured plaintiff…. Prosser, §50 and n. 38. The rule was originally adopted by the English courts in Merryweather v. Nixon, 101 Eng. Rep. (K.B. 1799). Apparently, the basis of the rule was the unwillingness of the court to allow anyone to found a cause of action upon his own deliberate wrong, an aspect of the "unclean hands" doctrine. When, in the United States, the codes of civil procedure permitted joinder of defendants who were merely negligent, such defendants came to be called "joint tortfeasors," and the reason for the rule against contribution was lost to sight. The great majority of American jurisdictions applied the rule of no-contribution to all situations, even those in which independent, but concurrent, acts of negligence had contributed to a single resulting injury. A small minority of states — including Tennessee — eventually came to a contrary conclusion, allowing contribution among joint tortfeasors without the aid of legislation. Davis v. Broad St. Garage, 232 S.W.2d 355 (1950); Huggins v. Graves, 210 F. Supp. 98 (E.D. Tenn. 1962)…. In *Huggins*, the federal district judge concluded that:

> The right of contribution exists under Tennessee law as between joint tortfeasors in a negligence action in the absence of willful or wanton negligence upon the part of the party seeking contribution. Moreover, this result accords with reason and, as stated by the Tennessee Supreme Court in the Davis case, "justice, right, and equity demand this conclusion." 210 F. Supp. at 103.

Any remaining uncertainty regarding the extent of the right of contribution among joint tortfeasors in Tennessee was dispelled by the 1968 enactment of the Tennessee Uniform Contribution Among Tortfeasors Act. TCA §§23-3104, 3105 (1975). Excluding intentional tortfeasors, the Tennessee Uniform Act provides that the right to contribution arises upon the satisfaction of two general conditions. First, there must be "two (2) or more persons…jointly or severally liable in tort for the same injury to person or property…." Secondly, one of those jointly or severally liable must have paid more than his pro rata share of the common liability.

Obviously, the meaning of the phrase "jointly or severally liable" is of primary importance in determining the right of contribution under our law. An early Tennessee case, Swain v. Tennessee Copper Co., 78 S.W. 93 (1903), stated that the test of joint liability is "whether each of the parties is liable for the entire injury done." It would appear that the Court was begging the question:

> If they [the defendants] are joint tortfeasors, each one is responsible for the damage resulting from the acts of all the wrongdoers, and they may all be sued severally or jointly; but, if they are not joint tortfeasors, each is liable only for the injury contributed by him, and can only be sued in a separate action therefor. 78 S.W. at 94.

The factual situation presented in the *Swain* case was markedly similar to that in the instant case. The plaintiff-landowners brought suit against two neighboring copper smelting plants, alleging that the noxious fumes emitted from their respective hearths became "indistinguish-ably mingled," creating "a great nuisance." The Court, however, refused to acknowledge that the harm done to the plaintiffs' land was indivisible. Rather, the Court said:

> Proof of the extent and capacity of the several plants causing the damages complained of, the tonnage of ores treated by each of them, the time each has been in operation, their comparative proximity or distance from the plaintiff's lands, the usual condition of the air currents in that locality, and many other facts and circumstances, will show with substantial certainty the extent of the injury inflicted by each of the defendants.... Id. at 99.

Apparently, the Court was not troubled by the fact that it would be extremely difficult, if not impossible, for the plaintiff to apportion his damages among the defendants. The rationale of the *Swain* decision is shown:

> If it were otherwise...one defendant, however little he might have contributed to the injury, would be liable for all the damages caused by the wrongful acts of all the other defendants, and he would have no remedy against the latter, because no contribution could be enforced by the tortfeasors. Id. at 97, quoting Miller v. Highland Ditch Co., 25 P. 550 (Cal. 1891).

Such was the state of our law regarding contribution among tortfeasors at the time *Swain* was decided. Since that time, however, as above indicated, we have developed not only a common law right of contribution among tortfeasors but the legislature has passed a uniform act specifically granting such a right. Thus, the no-contribution rationale of the *Swain* case has collapsed, so that we look elsewhere for the import of the phrase "jointly or severally liable."

In Waller v. Skelton, 212 S.W.2d 690 (1948), it was no defense for a defendant, who drove over the crest of a hill on the wrong side of the road in the face of congested oncoming traffic and collided with the oncoming car in which plaintiff was riding, that a motorist who was driving behind plaintiff's car negligently collided with plaintiff's car, contributing to the plaintiff's injuries. Since the following motorist's negligence was concurrent with the defendant's negligence, the Court reasoned, each would be jointly and severally liable for all of plaintiff's injury. Relying upon various legal authorities, the Court said:

> A defendant's negligent act, in order to be the proximate or legal cause of plaintiff's injuries, need not have been the whole cause or the only factor in bringing them about. It was enough if such act was a substantial factor in causing them. 212 S.W.2d at 696.

While not relying on the "single, indivisible injury" theory, the Court did decide that where successive impacts with different negligently operated vehicles contributed to or combined to cause the aggregate harm suffered, the plaintiff is entitled to a joint and several recovery against both tortfeasors....

We depart from *Swain*...and adopt the rule of *Landers* and *Michie* for determining joint and several liability when an indivisible injury has been caused by the concurrent, but independent, wrongful acts or omissions of two or more wrongdoers, whether the case be one of negligence or nuisance. We hold that the third-party complaint may stand as a claim for contribution by one tortfeasor from other alleged joint tortfeasors....

COMMENTARY & QUESTIONS

1. **Problems of joint liability.** In *Rowe*, and the *Landers* and *Michie* cases it discusses, is it clear that the plaintiffs have suffered a single harm from the air or water pollution? The plaintiffs have suffered a single type of harm in each of the three instances, but no

single defendant is the cause-in-fact of the entire extent of the harm suffered. What justifies "extending" the liability of each potential defendant? Is the extension effectively offset by the availability of an action for contribution?

2. **The "single bullet" problem.** In each of the cases just mentioned, the court presumes that the injuries probably were caused by multiple defendants, each of whom contributed a part. What if it had been a "single bullet" injury, however? The leading case on this subject is Summers v. Tice, 199 P.2d 1 (Cal. 1948). In *Summers*, two members of a hunting party simultaneously fired shotguns in exactly the same direction. Plaintiff, the third member of the hunting party, unfortunately was hit in the eye by a single pellet. It was impossible to determine which gun had shot that pellet. At a very literal level, this might be a hard case for plaintiff — both defendants are negligent, but only one of them is the cause-in-fact of plaintiff's injury, and plaintiff cannot prove which of the two it was. Moreover, since plaintiff has the burden of proof to show it more likely than not that one defendant or the other was the cause-in-fact, plaintiff cannot meet that burden, since it is a 50-50 proposition as to whose pellet struck the plaintiff. Plaintiff won despite this problem, however, because the *Summers* court shifted the burden of proving cause-in-fact from the plaintiff to the defendants. In other words, instead of requiring the plaintiff to prove affirmatively which defendant actually fired the offending shot, the court instead imputed joint liability to both defendants unless and until one or the other defendant could absolve himself of liability. In *Summers*, where there is one innocent plaintiff and two negligent actors, shifting the cause-in-fact burden from plaintiff to defendants is eminently fair and appealing. Is the logic equally appealing in an environmental tort setting? Take the problem of a landfill holding 1000 unmarked barrels of hazardous waste. If these barrels had been sent to the landfill by seven different waste generators over a multiyear period, what happens if just one of these unidentifiable barrels escapes in a flood and poisons a city's drinking water? Can this problem be answered by the concert of action principles described in *Rowe*? Should *Summers*-type logic lead to the imposition of joint and several liability on the defendants? What evidence would be relevant to an intra-defendant lawsuit trying to allocate the loss among them? See Sindell v. Abbot Labs., 607 P.2d 924 (Cal. 1980) (liability imposed in relation to market share of equivalent generic drugs provided to fill prescriptions in the relevant region during the relevant period). At least in the toxic tort context, the answer that seems to be evolving is a blend of strict liability, concert of action, and enterprise liability, permitting courts to shift the impossible burden of proving which defendant caused the harm from innocent plaintiffs to the class of defendants, all of whom may have been careless or risky in dumping toxic barrels, but only one of whom is likely to have been the source of plaintiff's particular exposure. For an assessment of this practice, see Nesson, Agent Orange Meets the Blue Bus: Factfinding at the Frontier of Knowledge, 66 B.U. L. Rev. 521 (1986).

3. **The power of joint and several liability.** What makes the availability of joint and several liability so important to plaintiffs in environmental tort cases? Consider not only the ability to ease plaintiff's burden of proof regarding causation but litigative strategies as well, e.g., the ability to collect judgments or to coerce defendants to settle

or undertake cleanups. The coercive nature of joint and several liability is reprised in Chapter 19 in relation to CERCLA litigation, especially its use by EPA.

4. **Contribution and indemnity.** Traditionally, contribution and indemnity, when they were allowed at all, were independent causes of action that became available only after a tortfeasor had paid more than its appropriate share of a judgment to the plaintiff. With the rise of more liberal joinder rules, in particular Fed. R. Civ. P. 14 and its state court counterparts, defendants who are sued alone may join potential contributors and indemnitors in the original action. This encourages efficiency by joining more of the issues in a single lawsuit, but it does not alter the plaintiff's option to enforce the ensuing judgment in toto against a single defendant. When is that option important?

Under the common law, the Uniform Contribution Among Tortfeasors Act (UCATA), and the Uniform Comparative Fault Act (UCFA), contribution is usually pro rata unless there is some other provable basis on which to apportion the injury. The emergence and growth of comparative negligence in recent years has led to apportionment in accordance with the respective percentages of negligence. In cases founded on nuisance, trespass, and strict liability, comparative fault would seem to be irrelevant, but there, too, some courts nevertheless divide responsibility according to the UCFA's comparative fault principles. Dole v. Dow Chem., 282 N.E.2d 288 (N.Y. 1972). See Phillips, Contribution and Indemnity in Products Liability, 42 Tenn. L. Rev. 85 (1974). What avenues might a polluter in *Rowe* consider when trying to pay less than a pro rata amount?

5. **Predecessor landowners' liability.** Can the prior owner of a contaminated parcel of land be held liable for common law damages when the toxics are subsequently discovered? Some forms of predecessor liability are straightforwardly available. Within the constraints of statutes of limitation, prior owners who polluted the land are liable to injured neighbors who sue in tort. Similarly, federal and state cleanup statutes generally extend regulatory liability to prior owners (see Chapter 19), but other areas can be more problematic.

What about suits by private individuals who purchase contaminated land? The traditional property doctrine is caveat emptor — buyer beware. Unlike the case of contracts for the sale of goods, traditionally sellers of land are held to no implied warranty that the land will be fit for use. That situation is changing. In some states, statutes now require disclosure of hazards such as lead paint or mold that are known by the seller. A few states have imposed disclosure requirements via judicial expansion of property law concepts. Some jurisdictions, for example, have found the presence of hazardous waste sufficient to constitute an "encumbrance" that, in turn, is sufficient to constitute breach of covenant against encumbrances or is sufficient to constitute unmarketable title. See, e.g., H. M. Holdings, Inc. v. Rankin, 70 F.3d 933 (7th Cir. 1995); Vandervort v. Higginbotham, 222 A.D.2d 831, 634 N.Y.S.2d 800 (1995); see also Comment, Toxic Clouds on Title, 19 B.C. Envtl. Aff. L. Rev. 355 (1991). While awaiting the development of such an implied warranty in other jurisdictions, can landowners sue predecessor owners (particularly those who can be shown to have known about the toxics, not to mention those who actually dumped them) under nuisance theories? In Philadelphia Elec. Co. v. Hercules, 762 F.2d 303 (3d Cir. 1985), the plaintiff alleged claims for both private and public nuisance but could not prevail on either theory. The court held that private nuisance was unavailable because that tort was designed for contemporaneous owners of separate land parcels rather than for successive owners of the same parcel. Plaintiff's claim for public nuisance was dismissed on standing grounds. If the plaintiff in *Hercules* could have shown a special injury, might its public nuisance claim have worked? Would a claim of abnormally dangerous activity have improved plaintiff's chances by adding strict liability to the equation? See T&E Indus. v. Safety Light Corp., 587 A.2d 1249 (N.J. 1991) (court allowed strict liability in favor of landowner against predecessor in title). See also Civins, Environmental Law Concerns in Real Estate Transactions, 43 Sw. L.J. 819 (1990).

Section 3. PROXIMATE CAUSATION

Proximate causation is concerned with the problem of remoteness. At times, but-for causation extends to great distances, perhaps linking defendant's conduct to losses that are beyond the scope of responsibility that defendant should bear. If a highway oil spill negligently caused by defendant's tanker truck causes a traffic jam that delays the delivery van that was carrying a needed part to fix the machine that was to make the widget that the plaintiff had contracted to supply to a customer who had to have it by today, and the cash from the sale was needed to pay the bill to ward off repossession of... etc., somewhere along the line it may be appropriate to limit the availability of remedies for the far-off consequences of wrongful acts, especially where injuries are purely economic. Where is that line?

The following is an excerpt from the only reported civil case decision arising from Chapter 2's Kepone debacle. It raises questions about how far down the chain of but-for causation liability can be extended. Plaintiffs in this case did not allege physical injuries to themselves or their property. Allied quickly settled any and all local physical injury claims. This is a case of increasingly "distant" economic harm.

Pruitt v. Allied Chemical Corporation
United States District Court, Eastern District of Virginia, 1981
523 F. Supp. 975

MERHIGE, D.J. Plaintiffs bring the instant action against Allied Chemical Corporation ("Allied") for Allied's alleged pollution of the James River and Chesapeake Bay with the chemical agent commonly known as Kepone....

Plaintiffs allegedly engage in a variety of different businesses and professions related to the harvesting and sale of marine life from the Chesapeake Bay. All claim to have suffered economic harm from defendant's alleged discharges of Kepone into the James River and thence into the Bay. Plaintiffs assert their right to compensation under each of the dozen counts to their complaint [including claims in negligence and strict liability]....

The general rule both in admiralty and at common law has been that a plaintiff cannot recover for indirect economic harm. The logical basis for this rule is obscure. Although Courts have frequently stated that economic losses are "not foreseeable" or "too remote," these explanations alone are rarely apposite. As one well-respected commentator has noted, "the loss to plaintiff in each case...would be readily recoverable if the test of duty — or remoteness — usually associated with the law of negligence were applied...."[27]

Given the conflicting case law from other jurisdictions, together with the fact that there exists no Virginia law on indirect, economic damages, the Court has considered more theoretical sources in order to find a principled basis for its decision.... Scholars in the field rely on Judge Learned Hand's classic statement of negligence...that a principal purpose of tort law is to maximize social utility: where the costs of accidents exceed the costs of preventing them, the law will impose liability.

The difficulty in the present case is how to measure the cost of Kepone pollution. In the instant action, those costs were borne most directly by the wildlife of the Chesapeake Bay. The fact that no one individual claims property rights to the Bay's wildlife could arguably preclude liability. The Court doubts, however, whether such a result would be just. Nor would a denial of liability serve social utility: many citizens, both directly and indirectly, derive benefit from the Bay and its marine life. Destruction of the Bay's wildlife should not be a costless activity....

Commercial fishermen are entitled to compensation for any loss of profits they may prove to have been caused by defendant's negligence. The entitlement given these fishermen presumably arises from what might be called a constructive property interest in the Bay's harvestable species...within a category established in Union Oil Co. v. Oppen, 501 F.2d 558 (9th Cir. 1974) (the Santa Barbara oil spill case): they "lawfully and directly make use of a resource of the sea."

The use that marina and charterboat owners make of the water, though hardly less legal, is...less direct.... Still less direct, but far from nonexistent, is the link between the Bay and the seafood dealers, restaurants, and tackle shops that seek relief (as do the employees of these establishments).

One meaningful distinction to be made among the various categories of plaintiffs here arises from a desire to avoid double-counting in calculating damages. Any seafood harvested by the commercial fishermen here would have been bought and sold several times before finally being purchased for consumption. Considerations both of equity and social utility suggest that just as defendant should not be able to escape liability for destruction of publicly owned marine life entirely, it should not be caused to pay repeatedly for the same damage. The Court notes, however, that allowance for recovery of plaintiffs' lost profits here would not in all cases result in double-counting of damages. Plaintiff...seafood wholesalers, retailers, processors, distributors and restaurateurs...allegedly lost profits when deprived of supplies of seafood. Those profits represented a return on the investment of each of the plaintiffs in material and labor in their businesses, and thus the independent loss to each would not amount to double-counting.... Employees undoubtedly lost wages and faced a less favorable job market than they would have, but for defendant's acts, and they have thus been harmed by defendant. What is more, the number of parties with a potential cause of action against defendant is hardly exhausted in plaintiffs' complaint. In theory, parties who bought and sold to and from the plaintiffs named here also suffered losses in business, as did their employees. In short, the set of potential plaintiffs seems almost infinite.

Perhaps because of the large set of potential plaintiffs,...some limitation to liability, even when damages are foreseeable, is advisable.... The Court thus finds itself with a perceived need to limit liability, without any articulated reason for excluding any particular set of plaintiffs.

---

27. James, Limitations of Liability for Economic Loss Caused by Negligence: A Pragmatic Appraisal, 25 Vand. L. Rev. 43 (1972). Prof. James has gone on to state that "the prevailing distinction between indirect economic loss and physical damage is probably a crude and unreliable one that may need reexamination if a limitation on liability for pragmatic reasons is to be retained." Id. at 50–51.

Other courts have had to make similar decisions.[28] The Court concludes that [commercial fishermen can recover for their lost profits, but the categories of] plaintiffs who purchased and marketed seafood from commercial fishermen suffered damages that are not legally cognizable, because insufficiently direct.... The Court holds that plaintiff...boat, marina, and tackle and bait shop owners have suffered legally cognizable damages.... Only if some set of surrogate plaintiffs is entitled to press its own claims which flow from the damage to the Bay's sportfishing industry will the proper balance of social forces be preserved.... The Court's conclusion results from consideration of all these factors, and an attempt to tailor justice to the facts of the instant case....

COMMENTARY & QUESTIONS

1. **The rationale for barring indirect damages.** Is there any compelling reason for the traditional tort law rule that forbade recovery of indirect economic losses in the absence of physical injury? Could the reason be institutional, seeking to limit the number of cases in which courts were called upon to make necessarily speculative determinations about the course of future events? Could the reason instead represent an inductive overgeneralization that in a substantial majority of cases lacking physical damage there is likewise no credible economic damage? The bar against indirect recoveries has been widely applied in maritime tort cases under the rule of *Robins Drydock*, 275 U.S. 303 (1927), and has attracted criticism as a major barrier to oil spill plaintiffs in cases such as the *Exxon-Valdez* spill, although statutory exceptions sometimes apply. See Mulhern, Marine Pollution: A Tort Recovery Standard for Pure Economic Losses, 18 B.C. Envtl. Aff. L. Rev. 85 (1990).

2. **Of double-counting and foreseeable losses.** What is the double-counting danger that is raised by defendants? The judge is correct in saying that the sum of the lost profits of the several categories of victims, by definition a net figure, is inherently free of double-counting problems. Is it correct to limit the award to "replacement value of a plaintiff's actual investment"? What if a plaintiff bought a going fishing business at an unreasonably low price? Is there any reason to allow defendant to deprive that victim of the anticipated net income the wise investment would have generated?

The judge draws the line at the water's edge. Is that fair to inland plaintiffs who are foreseeable victims of massive contamination of the Bay? How does a recovery by the commercial fishermen in any way protect the interests of the owners and employees of a cannery that can no longer process fish from the Bay? And are you satisfied with the allowance of sport fishery industry recoveries as a proxy for natural resource damage? How complete an accounting did Allied Chemical face from private litigation?

3. **Proximate cause as loss-shifting policy.** Can there be a valid policy reason for not shifting all of the loss caused by a defendant's tortious conduct back to that responsible defendant? Possible policy justifications include large transaction costs that might be

---

28. See, e.g., Judge Kaufmann's opinion in Petition of Kinsman Transit Co., 388 F.2d 821, 824-25 (2d Cir. 1968), where the court noted that "in the final analysis the circumlocution whether posed in terms of 'foreseeability,' 'duty,' 'proximate cause,' 'remoteness,' etc. seems unavoidable," and then turned to Judge Andrews' well-known statement in Palsgraf v. Long Island R.R. Co., 162 N.E. 99, 104 (N.Y. 1928): "It is all a question of expediency...of fair judgment, always keeping in mind the fact that we endeavor to make a rule in each case that will be practical and in keeping with the general understanding of mankind."

incurred in a "full accounting," conservation of authority (i.e., not calling on the cumbersome civil justice system backed by the authority of the state to redress every last little bit of injury), or maintaining "affordable" prices for goods and services by permitting some degree of cost externalization onto victims by denying them compensation for remote injuries. Assume that some or all of these justifications for limiting liability are embodied in the proximate cause inquiry. Does that provide any predictable standard regarding when the limit will be invoked to prevent recovery? Even if the policy-oriented aspect of the proximate cause inquiry seems almost devoid of a standard that can be clearly articulated, could tort law employ some better mechanism than proximate cause when dealing with those policy concerns?

D. REMEDIES IN ENVIRONMENTAL LITIGATION

Many novel issues arise in the context of environmental law remedies. The following sections explore equitable remedies, damages, restoration remedies, and natural resources remedies. Criminal penalties are considered in Chapter 20 and administrative sanctions in Chapter 21.

Section 1. EQUITY AND INJUNCTIONS

Zygmunt Plater, Statutory Violations and Equitable Discretion
70 California Law Review 524, 533–544, 545–546 (1982)

The exercise of equitable jurisdiction, particularly the availability of injunctions, has increased over the years. The anachronistic requirement of a property interest in order to invoke equity has been scrapped of necessity, and other impediments have been removed. Despite regular protestations to the contrary, the status of the injunction has become a common, widely used judicial remedy precisely because of its ability to fine-tune the requirements of private conduct in a complex, modern society. Its development parallels the expansion of cases [in environmental law and] in civil rights and other constitutional areas, where damage remedies are insufficient or miss the point....

When equity's application in traditional common law cases is subjected to careful analysis, some basic clarifications emerge. Analytically, it can be argued that the umbrella terms "balancing the equities" and "equitable discretion" obscure what are really three separate areas of balancing, three different functions fulfilled by three different types of equitable relativism. The three areas are:

1. *Threshold balancing*, based in both law and equity, tests whether plaintiffs can maintain their actions. This stage includes questions of laches, clean hands, other estoppels, the lack of an adequate remedy at law, proof of irreparable harm, and similar issues.

2. *Determination of contending conducts* ascertains which conduct will be permitted to continue and which will be subordinated. It often involves the question of abatement, a separate issue from the question of liability for past injuries to protected interests.

3. *Discretion in fashioning remedies* involves a process of tailoring remedies to implement the second stage determination of contending conducts.

Consider, for example, the relatively simple field of private nuisance torts where equity has traditionally played an active role. The classic *Ducktown Sulphur* case demonstrates all three of equity's distinctly different roles. In that turn-of-the-century case, 83 S.W. 658 (Tenn. 1904), the court had to deal with an early example of an environmental tradeoff. The smelting industry was getting underway in the foothills of southeastern Tennessee and northern Georgia. It was likely to provide sizable revenues for the entrepreneurs of Atlanta and Chattanooga, jobs for local residents, and copper and other materials for the nation's industrial economy. The copper ore was mined in nearby hills, then smelted in large open-air piles layered with firewood and coal. This firing process, however, produced acidic "sulphurectic" air emissions that eventually turned nearly a hundred square miles of hills into a remarkably stark, denuded desert, its topsoil slowly washing away down sterile, chemical-laden streams. The plaintiffs were farmers whose fields and orchards began to die as the smelting got underway.

The Tennessee high court held that the smelting was a continuing private nuisance, but after long and careful deliberation allowed the defendant industries to continue operations despite their drastic impact upon the plaintiffs' land and livelihood. The court required only that the mills compensate the plaintiffs for their losses. In common parlance, it awarded legal compensatory damages but denied any injunctive remedy, based on a balancing of equities. The *Ducktown* court certainly balanced the equities. Analytically, however, it did so not once but thrice:

Threshold Balancing. The first type of balancing addresses threshold questions which plaintiffs must survive if a cause of action is to be heard. Some issues appear in the guise of affirmative legal defenses: laches and coming to the nuisance, for example, are legal defenses grounded in principles of equitable estoppel. Other issues — clean hands, additional estoppel principles, proof of irreparable harm, and the inadequacy of legal remedies — are more specifically equitable, brought to bear only where the plaintiff seeks equitable remedies. Each of these threshold issues involves comparisons and balances that are part of the longstanding discretionary processes of equity. The *Ducktown* court made several such determinations, excluding some plaintiffs on laches grounds as to certain defendants, confirming their rights to sue as to others, and noting injuries to land that analytically made equitable remedies potentially available on grounds of irreparability.

The Determination of Contending Conducts. After plaintiffs survive equity's threshold gauntlet, nonstatutory litigation moves to the application of rules of conduct. The major discretionary function of the equity court at this second stage is the determination of whether the defendant's conduct will be permitted to continue. To reach this abatement determination, however, courts must first consider issues of liability....

The initial question is whether defendants are liable at all, whether their conduct is "illegal" under the common law.... Plaintiffs in private nuisance cases and in other common law areas seek equitable remedies — particularly injunctions — as well as damages. In such cases, once tort liability is found, the court turns to the different question of whether defendant's conduct will be abated....

The *Ducktown* abatement question focused on the desirability and consequences of the competing forms of conduct, considering relative hardship between the parties, the balance of comparative social utility between the two competing conducts, and the public interest (which usually amounts to the same thing). The court declared:

> A judgment for damages in this class of cases is a matter of absolute right, where injury is shown. A decree for an injunction is a matter of sound legal discretion, to be granted or withheld as that discretion shall dictate, after a full and careful considerations of every element appertaining to the injury.

Citing a series of equity cases in which the utility of defendant's enterprises weighed against injunctions, the court's "careful consideration" began with a question that virtually answered itself:

Shall the complainants be granted, by way of damages, the full measure of relief to which their injuries entitle them or shall we go further, and grant their request to blot out two great mining and manufacturing enterprises, destroy half of the taxable values of a county, and drive more than 10,000 people from their homes?...

The tort debts owed by one party to the other might be decided by uniformly applicable substantive tort principles, but questions of the life and death of farms and smelting plants — of who must stop and who may go on — were left to the flexible hands and heart of equity. In short, courts have used equity to define and exercise a separate judicial role, grounded upon a rational discretion and working beyond the rigid rules of the law.

Tailoring the Remedies.... At this point in a lawsuit, law and equity have determined all the substantive issues, and only the equitable function of implementation remains. If the court had decided in the second stage balance that defendant's conduct may continue, the award of legal damages for past injuries ends the question of remedy. In that situation no equitable remedy is necessary unless required to enforce payment of damages.

When the court determines that defendant's conduct may not continue, on the other hand, a full array of equitable options exists. If defendants agree to abate their activity voluntarily, the court has the option of not issuing any formal equitable remedy at all. This point...is taken for granted in the common law setting: an injunction need not issue if the court finds that the abatement decision will be implemented without it, but will usually issue where there is any doubt on the matter. Between these two extremes lies the declaratory judgment, a remedy slightly more formal and more assertive than the no-injunction option but similarly unenforceable through contempt proceedings. Yet in the case of good faith defendants, a declaratory judgment or less may be all that is necessary to implement the court's abatement decision.

The strength and flexibility of injunctions, however, makes them attractive as the remedy of choice in many cases. Equity courts shape injunctions in multifarious forms: injunctions to halt an enterprise completely, to shut down a particular component activity, to scale down overall activity by a certain percentage, to halt a specific offensive effect, to abate after a lapse of a specific term if certain performance standards are not achieved — these are but a few. Injunctions also serve different tactical ends. They can be wielded to drag a rambunctiously recalcitrant defendant into compliance, to tighten the reins on slipshod defendants whose compliance efforts may be sloppy, or merely to add a final reassuring level of certainty to a good faith defendant's compliance. In short, "the plastic remedies of the chancery are molded to the needs of justice."

COMMENTARY & QUESTIONS

1. **A range of equitable remedies.** The last paragraph offers a reminder that injunctions can be far more subtly crafted than mere cease-and-desist prohibitions. When Oscar Boomer went to his lawyer's office, he undoubtedly wanted to stop that cursed cement dust, and the remedy he instinctively favored for the factory was to shut it down. When most attorneys consider remedies beyond damages they are equally unsubtle; the only injunction they conceive of is an order halting the defendants in their tracks. Environmental attorneys can increase the force and effect of their litigation efforts, however, by considering a range of appropriate, innovative equitable remedies and proposing them to the court. Consider each of the following equity options available as remedies in settings ranging from localized pollution like *Boomer* to massive episodes like coastal oil spills:

- decrees encouraging technological innovation, like Judge Jasen's proposed order in *Boomer*, postponing shutdowns for a set term, to be effective thereafter unless clean technology can be applied;

- decrees ordering, say, a 30% cutback in production until cleaner technology is achieved;

- decrees restricting defendant's activity during times when weather conditions are particularly likely to cause pollution damage;

- decrees requiring ongoing corporate monitoring of offsite pollution;

- decrees requiring that defendants actively clean up their externalized pollution;

- decrees ordering installation of particular specified control technology;

- decrees ordering restitution of profits gained from avoidance of pollution controls;

- decrees requiring periodic reporting to the court;

- decrees ordering "restoration" of trees, soil, personal property, and natural resources;

- appointment of equitable trial masters under Fed. R. Civ. P. 53 for managing complex factual and procedural issues prior to judgment;

- appointment of post-decree monitors to oversee defendants' compliance with court orders, backed by subpoena powers and reporting to the courts;[29]

- environmental receiverships, so that where defendant firms can't or won't comply with environmental requirements, courts will take over and run them through appointed equitable receiverships; and other creative applications of this remarkable judicial power.

Injunctions decree whatever a court chooses to prescribe, and their prescriptive capabilities are given extra credibility by the criminal contempt-of-court penalties they carry with them.

When an injunction commands a halt to a polluting activity, it acts like a decisive statutory prohibition. Is that cost internalization? The more subtle equitable orders noted above can clearly improve the internalization process. In the Oregon aluminum factory cases cited in *Borland*, the courts prescribed precisely which pollution control devices defendants had to install and established strict schedules for the defendants to follow. What about cleanup or restoration orders? There is no doctrinal reason why equity cannot take sensitive account of the natural resource consequences of wrongful acts and remedy them in accord with modern public policy. Defendants' realization that they may have to pay restitution of profits or to clean or replace soil, trees, or other property drastically changes the economic calculus of industrial waste disposal and raises ecological consciousness.

2. **The balance of equities.** The *Boomer* case is perhaps most famous for its rejection of the traditional New York common law rule that an injunction would routinely issue to shut down a continuing nuisance, in favor of the more flexible balancing the equities

---

29. See Feldman, Post-Decree Judicial Agents in Environmental Litigation, 18 B.C. Envtl. Aff. L. Rev. 809 (1991). The classic *Ducktown* case had a court-appointed monitor remedy to police emissions limits, and the monitor was guaranteed full access to defendant's operations. See *Tennessee Copper*, 237 U.S. at 478, and 240 U.S. 650.

doctrine. Was the court undercutting environmental protection and sound policy when it reversed the automatic rule? In legal history terms, would you be surprised to find that for 50 years after the tough *Whalen* rule shut down a paper mill, the tendency of trial courts in New York had been to find no nuisance at all, knowing that any finding of nuisance liability would automatically trigger a complete shutdown of industrial operations?

A fundamental canon of equity law is that an equitable decree must do equity. That means it must be sensitive to public as well as private consequences of proposed restrictions. Under the *Ducktown* principle, it was surely fitting and relevant that the *Boomer* court considered public interests weighing in favor of continued plant operation. But what items were allowed into the balance of equities in *Boomer*? Do they appear to include all relevant information for a full-scale balancing? The court weighed items of both public and private concern affirmatively in favor of the defendant, against the proposed injunction. What did it weigh in favor of the injunction for plaintiffs? A more evenhanded approach might have allowed plaintiffs to present evidence of the cement plant's adverse impacts on the community at large. Why does the majority explicitly remove public health issues from its consideration? In light of the public interest element in equitable balancing, which he himself applied in favor of the defendant, doesn't Justice Bergan's refusal to intrude "broad public objectives" into a simple suit between "individual property owners and a single cement plant" ring hollow? How would you have argued the point?

Would the equities of the case have been different if the Boomers, well before construction of the cement plant, had repeatedly told Atlantic Cement Company that they feared the dust would escape and injure them, only to receive assurances that there would be no problem? See Smith v. Staso Milling Co., 18 F.2d 736 (2d Cir. 1927) (opinion by Learned Hand granting an injunction in such circumstances, under Vermont nuisance law).

Note that when courts balance the equities to determine what kind of order to issue, they are not restricted to facts and values incorporated in the elements of the cause of action, nor even to the evidence adduced on the trial record. This means that in appropriate cases the equitable balancing can include consideration of a broad range of public environmental concerns that could not be directly litigated, including a community's quality of life, ecological consequences to natural resources, and declared public policies of local, state, and federal governments.

3. **Constraints on equitable remedies.** In addition to equity's particular threshold and balancing requirements noted in the equitable discretion article excerpt, equity law presents other constraints to environmental litigants. One of the most interesting is the defense of "prospective" or "anticipatory nuisance" seen in the *Wilsonville* case. The traditional rule was that in order to get an injunction against proposed actions, one had to prove the probability of serious injury or that it was a "nuisance per se"; otherwise the law would "wait and see." But in environmental litigation, plaintiffs are often attempting to stop activities that have no legal track record. In Wallace v. Andersonville Docks, 489 S.W.2d 532 (Tenn. 1972), for example, a court refused on those grounds to

halt a cross-country motorcycle race through a state reserve. Or a case may pose a "zero-infinity" problem — release of a particular chemical or gene-altered organism may have only a small possibility of negative effects, but if they occur they may be catastrophic. As a result, the common law abdicated all such issues to the tender mercies of public authorities. There are signs, as in Judge Ryan's concurrence in *Wilsonville*, that the situation is changing. See Sharp, Rehabilitating the Anticipatory Nuisance Doctrine, 15 B.C. Envtl. Aff. L. Rev. 627 (1988).

4. **Other equitable actions.** The present focus on equitable remedies should not obscure the fact that although equity is usually employed to supply remedies for common law or statutory causes of action, some causes of action are themselves based on the traditional equity jurisdiction. Substantive equitable claims thus may have environmental importance in cases involving fraud, bankruptcy, and trust law. Does equity embody a creative free-floating cause of action? In other words, can a judge issue an injunction whenever she is convinced that a wrong is occurring? Conventional wisdom holds rather that plaintiffs must show injury to a legal right.

5. **Restoration remedies.** Modern environmental cases have brought new and expanded currency to the old remedy of restoration. The restoration concept has great environmental utility, but raises some knotty problems. When and for what kind of case are injunctions or damages based on restoration justified and desirable? Note the potency of the restoration remedy in *Schenectady Chemical* and *Wilsonville* where defendants were forced to remove polluted soils and restore the land. In the right settings, restoration can serve not only to restore the "status quo ante"[30] but also to protect human and ecological safety, and powerfully to deter. In deterrent terms, defendants face the prospect that ill-gotten profits quickly can be dwarfed by the costs of restoration. In a Michigan case, a neighbor, after the plaintiff refused to sell him part of her rural land for a subdivision project, "accidentally" destroyed plaintiff's private arboretum, clearcutting five acres of exotic imported trees. The defendant admitted the wrongful act but argued that damages were purely nominal since he had actually *improved* the plaintiff's development-based market value (a similar claim was made in *Borland*). Though the case never resulted in a reported decision, consider the abrupt change in defendant's position that occurs when a court allows consideration of restoration remedies, for example, a restoration order requiring replanting equivalent mature trees. See Verdiccio, Environmental Restoration Orders, 12 B.C. Envtl. Aff. L. Rev. 171 (1985); Cox, Reforming the Law Applicable to the Award of Restoration Damages as a Remedy for Environmental Torts, 20 Pace Envtl. L. Rev. 777 (2003) (arguing for broader availability of such awards coupled with application of equitable trust principles that could ensure awards are used for restoration and not mere enrichment of plaintiffs).

Equitable restoration orders tend to rehabilitate natural values that would be excluded from the usual monetary interests balanced in legal actions. Consider the effect of an order requiring Allied to cleanse the polluted sediments of the James River and

---

30. One of the traditional aims of legal damages and equitable orders has been to return innocent plaintiffs to the position they had held before the wrongdoing.

Chesapeake Bay or Atlantic Cement to reclaim its cement dust. Restoration provides a compelling deterrent in a variety of environmental settings, such as the killing of fish in a river, the wrongful partial demolition of a historic building lacking market value, and so on. The prospect of forced restoration is a powerful deterrent to discharge of toxics: Thousands of dollars can initially be made or saved by disposing of hazardous wastes carelessly, but the subsequent cost of retrieving and removing those toxics from soil and water can be geometrically more expensive, running into hundreds of thousands or millions of dollars. If you might be caught, it is far cheaper to treat and dispose of chemicals properly at the outset when you have them in one place than to recapture them after they have dispersed and percolated through a mile or more of underground gravel aquifer.

Restoration, however, may be impossible or so grossly expensive that it makes no sense. How does a court decide when to order restoration? In a Louisiana case, a court noted that the polluted property was a swamp, subject to overflowing by the Mississippi River, used seasonally for grazing, hunting and fishing:

> Its value was set at $375 per acre, or slightly over $200,000 for the 550 acres affected.... The restoration of the property, according to plaintiff's witness, would take about seven years, involve the use of 100 trucks running continuously during that time and would cost $170 million. Ewell v. Petro Processors, 364 So. 2d 604, 608 (La. Ct. App. 1978).

The *Ewell* court understandably denied the restoration, instead merely awarding the difference in market value, a remedy that left all the toxins in the ground and ground-water. The judge may have suspected that plaintiffs were using a restoration injunction claim to extort a hefty cash payoff from the defendants or, if restoration damages were granted, might not actually spend them on restoration. Some case law makes likelihood of actual restoration a consideration in the decision. Puerto Rico v. S.S. Zoe Colocotroni, 628 F.2d 652, 676 (1st Cir. 1980). Should courts presume that market value ($375 per acre in *Ewell*) sets an appropriate maximum remedy?

The Restatement (Second) of Torts §929(1)(a) prescribes, as to measure of damages:

> for harm to land resulting from a past invasion and not amounting to a total destruction of value, the damages include compensation for (a) the difference between the value of the land before the harm and the value after the harm, *or at plaintiff's election in an appropriate case, the cost of restoration that has been or may be reasonably incurred....* (Emphasis added.)

In Escamilla v. Asarco, Inc., a restoration case lying in the grey area between equitable remedies and damages, the court ordered a remediation of the top 15 inches of soil in Globeville, a low-income, working class, ethnic minority community in northern Denver contaminated with arsenic and cadmium, even though the cost of restoration was far in excess of market value losses. Applying Restatement §929, the court held:

> If the damage is reparable, and the costs, although greater than original value, are not wholly unreasonable in relation to that value, and if the evidence demonstrates that payment of market value likely will not adequately compensate the property owner for some personal or other special reason, we conclude that the selection of the cost of restoration as the proper measure of damages would be within the

limits of a trial court's discretion.... It is precisely because the market value measure may not adequately compensate land owners that the remediation measure may come into play.

It was undisputed that full use of the property can be restored simply by removing and replacing the contaminated topsoil.... The jury found that it would cost $20,125,000 to remediate Plaintiffs' properties. The jury found that Plaintiffs' properties suffered a diminution in market value of $4,159,000,...the jury found the uncontaminated market value of Plaintiffs' properties to be approximately $17.5 million, and the contaminated value to be approximately $13.4 million. Thus, the remediation costs exceed not only the diminution in market value, but also both the pre- and post-tort market values themselves.... This excess does not necessarily preclude remediation, but does require me to consider carefully whether the remediation costs are "wholly unreasonable" in relation to the proper-ties' market values.... Relative to the total uncontaminated market value..., the excess represents only 13 percent of the total market value,...only $4,600 per class family.... Under all of the circumstances of this case, I cannot say that the remedia-tion costs are "wholly unreasonable" in relation to the market value.

Considering all the factors..., and with due regard for the overarching principles of full and just compensation on the one hand, but no windfalls on the other, I find and conclude: that the losses which Plaintiff class members have suffered to their residences as a result of Defendant's negligence are remediable; that the cost of that remediation, as found by the jury, is not wholly unreasonable in relation to the uncontaminated or "pre-tort" market value of the Plaintiff class members' resi-dences; that the market value measure will not adequately compensate Plaintiff class members for the damage to their residences; that there is no significant risk that the Plaintiff class will be overcompensated by a remediation award,...or that such an award will encourage wasteful expenditures by Plaintiff class members; and therefore that the jury's remediation award is the more appropriate measure of damages to compensate Plaintiff class members for their property losses.... Escamilla v. Asarco, Inc. (D.C. Denver, Colorado, No. 91 CV 5716, Apr. 23, 1993).[31]

When should restoration be ordered? Neither the *Escamilla* court nor the Restatement require a showing of special circumstances, but some special showing seems appropri-ate. A Florida wetlands case set out some guidelines for restoration orders: To establish that restoration is appropriate, "the selected plan must: (1) confer maximum environ-mental benefits, (2) be achievable as a practical matter, and (3) bear an equitable relationship to the degree and kind of wrong which it is intended to remedy."[32]

It would seem important to consider the proportionality between potential land uses and the costs of "Cadillac cleanups," to avoid overreactions in excessive remedies, while acknowledging the array of values beyond market values that restoration can incorpo-rate — protecting community integrity, protecting individual autonomy, recreating natural economy values and human-specific values, punishing malicious actions,

---

31. After this decision, Asarco decided to settle. In the settlement, the plaintiffs agreed to allow the defendant itself to do most of the supervised remediation (i.e., the equivalent of an injunction to restore), reducing the defendant's cost to as little as $11 million (the jury's award of $8 million for "discomfort" was raised to $11 million).

32. United States v. Weissmann, 489 F. Supp. 1331 (M.D. Fla. 1980); the court included an extensive analysis of the values of wetlands. Because the Corps was plaintiff, no showing of plaintiff's circumstances was relevant; Escamilla merely had required a showing that land had been used personally by the plaintiff.

vindicating the innocence of victimized plaintiffs by restoring them as much as possible to their status quo ante in a manner that market value compensation does not achieve.[33] Standards for when and how restoration is to be adopted as a remedy undoubtedly will continue to evolve in environmental law.

6. **Restoration and other injunctive relief as legalized extortion.** Echoing the judge's suspicions in the *Ewell* case, the potential for extortionate injunctions is a topic increasingly recognized by legal scholars. By asking for restoration injunctions or other remedies that would impose large costs on the defendant, plaintiffs may be seeking to set up an extortionate bargaining position for settlement negotiations. In their article "Threatening Inefficient Performance of Injunctions and Contracts," Ian Ayres and Kristin Madison draw attention to this problem, arguing that it produces inefficiency in the form of negotiation costs, failures to reach a bargain, and inefficient ex ante actions. The article considers legal reforms that could undercut extortionate injunction threats by giving defendants two options: an option to make any injunctive relief inalienable and an option to commit to paying higher damages. Ayres and Madison argue that these options would eliminate the threat of undercompensation while reducing the inequitable risk of overcompensation and extortion. Ayres & Madison, Threatening Inefficient Performance of Injunctions and Contracts, 148 U. Pa. L. Rev. 45 (1999).

Section 2. DAMAGES

a. Compensatory damage remedies — past damages

The typical tort plaintiff seeks an award of compensatory damages for past injuries, whether or not an injunction is also being sought. Unlike injunctive relief, compensatory damages follow automatically upon a finding of defendant's liability. Compensatory damages can include sums awarded for all forms of property damage, injuries to the plaintiff's health, loss of consortium, and so on. In *Boomer*, there was little dispute about the amount of damages awarded for past harms. Damages included injury to stored automobiles and other personal property, and, as to real property, the "loss of rental value or loss of usable value," averaging $60 per plaintiff per month. Imputed rental value attempts to gauge the burden imposed by pollution upon the lives of the plaintiffs, assuming that the amount of rent that people would be willing to pay adequately captures the sum total of life-quality values involved. Does it?

Compare the elements of damage allowed in *Boomer* to those found in the typical personal injury lawsuit. In the latter, the plaintiff's recovery is generally made up of two broad categories: (1) compensation for monetary losses such as lost wages, medical

---

33. The Florida Supreme Court found that damages measured by diminution in value were inappropriate to compensate the municipality for the loss of five of its six water wells. The court stated that, in this instance, public policy supported restoration costs as the measure of damages because the court was "dealing with the single most necessary substance for the continuation of life.... Any danger to that primary necessity is ecologically and humanly unacceptable." Indicating that it thought it was diverging from the general rule on damages for wrongful injury, the court stated that extending damages beyond the loss of value of the property was further justified in this case because neither overcompensation nor overlapping of recoveries was likely. Davey Compressor Co. v. Delray Beach, 7 Toxics L. Rep. 97 (Mar. 3, 1994). The *Escamilla* court declined to consider punishment as a reason for a restoration remedy, but because punitive and deterrent considerations issues traditionally can be weighed in equitable balancing, they would seem to be appropriate here as well.

expenses, and automobile repair costs; and (2) compensation for intangibles, especially pain and suffering, but also anxiety and emotional trauma. The *Boomer* damages were limited to the first category. Is there any reason to ignore intangible elements of damage? What if Oscar and June Boomer had long been planning on this farm as their idyllic retreat from the sights and sounds of urban America? "Hedonic damages" offer an interesting new remedy theory. Traditional recoveries compensate for injuries and pain sustained and look to the future only in terms of lost profits or earnings. Hedonics compensate for losses of future quality of life, a broader concept that has obvious applicability in environmental law. See Sherrod v. Berry, 629 F. Supp. 155 (N.D. Ill. 1985), aff'd, 827 F.2d 195 (7th Cir. 1987), rev'd on reh'g, 856 F.2d 802 (7th Cir. 1988).[34] Note, however, that most damage awards make provision only for injuries to human plaintiffs. Possibilities for getting natural resource damages are noted in Section 3 below.

b. Permanent damages

Here is part of the trial court's original opinion in *Boomer*, 287 N.Y.S.2d 112 (1967), in which Judge Herzberg denied an injunction and calculated the proposed (and relatively unusual) alternative of permanent damages:

After reviewing the evidence in this action, I find that an injunction would produce great public hardship.... I find that the reasonable market value of each property as of September 1, 1962 (the date of the commencement of operations by Atlantic), the reasonable market value as of June 1, 1967 (the time of trial), and the permanent loss to each plaintiff, are as follows:

| | REASONABLE MARKET VALUE | | PERMANENT DAMAGES |
	9/1/62	6/1/67	
Oscar H. Boomer and June C. Boomer	25,000	12,500	12,500
Theodore J. Richard and Miriam W. Richard	30,000	12,000	18,000
Avie Kinley, Martha Kinley and Mary Kinley	140,000	70,000	70,000
Kenneth Livengood and Delores Livengood	18,000	7,000	11,000
Floyd W. Millious and Barbara A. Millious	20,000	8,000	12,000
Joseph L. Ventura and Carrie Ventura	25,000	12,500	12,500
James W. McCall	22,000	11,000	11,000
Charles J. Meilak and Angelina Meilak	26,000	12,000	14,000
		Total	**$185,000**

---

34. Though the Seventh Circuit vacated and remanded the lower court's opinion, it did so on other grounds. The Seventh Circuit's prior approval of the hedonic damages, described the testimony on that issue as "invaluable to the jury," 827 F.2d at 206. Subsequently, other courts have awarded hedonic damages. See also McClurg, It's a Wonderful Life: The Case for Hedonic Damages in Wrongful Death Cases, 66 Notre Dame L. Rev. 57 (1990).

COMMENTARY & QUESTIONS

1. **The measure of permanent damages.** Permanent damages are supposed to account for all the named plaintiffs' private property rights lost to cement dust. In theory, these damages ought to be equal in value to the relief that would have been obtained from the denied injunction. Are they? Market values do capture the current best estimate of what the land's future profitable economic uses will be, discounted back into present dollars, in terms of what a willing buyer would pay a willing seller. According to Judge Herzberg's formula, however, what would be the permanent damages if in the years between 1962 and 1967 Boomer's property value, as polluted, had appreciated, along with general land values, back to $24,999?

Even if the accounting is accurately done (subtracting the land's *present* value as polluted from *present* value as it would be without pollution), the net result of the refusal of an injunction and award of permanent damages is to force Boomer unwillingly to sell Atlantic Cement Company an easement to pollute at its market value. Can the court assess an extra amount to account for his unwillingness to sell? On remand, the trial court found the actual loss of market value to be $140,000, and then added a further $35,000, while admitting that it really couldn't define why: "If analogy is found in Newton's experiment with prisms showing that white light is composed of all the colors of the spectrum, each lending its own characteristics to a degree when passed through a prism, all the approaches to valuation entering into the informed mind and sensitive conscience of the court lend to an appropriate degree in the resulting decision." 340 N.Y.S.2d at 108. See also Hiley, Involuntary Sale Damages in Permanent Nuisance Cases: A Bigger Bang from *Boomer*, 14 B.C. Envtl. Aff. L. Rev. 61, 86–91 (1986). How is the court to choose between a forced sale of rights and the possibility that plaintiffs will use defendant's large sunk capital investment to "extort" a grossly exaggerated price for surrender of their rights?

2. **Do permanent damages create private expropriation?** Dissenting Judge Jasen in *Boomer* and some commentators have argued that permanent damages are unconstitutional because they amount to private exercise of the condemnation power, "which, unquestionably, is impermissible," said the *Borland* court. But is it? Defendants in cases like *Boomer* are using common law rather than the police power. There are other precedents for private forced purchases — to get access easements to landlocked parcels, to transport water over neighboring lands, or to build milldams — each justified by theories of public necessity. Are such forced sales justified by theories of efficient use of scarce resources? The right to deposit pollution on neighbors, however, is quite a different kind of claimed "necessity."

3. **The decision to award permanent damages.** Traditionally courts did not award permanent damages but instead permitted the plaintiff to return to court over time to prove a new case. What institutional factors relating to the court system workload and judicial competence militate for and against the old approach? As a litigant in a case like *Boomer*, how valuable to you is the sense of closure that accompanies the award of permanent damages?

4. The future of permanent damages. Despite much discussion in the literature, *Boomer*'s permanent damage remedy has not been applied often by subsequent courts. Is it a remedy that deserves more attention, assuming that standards for measuring the damages can be defined, or is there something organically wrong in a remedy that displaces permanent injunctions and is based on discounted future values? Do permanent damages imply that pollution is acceptable as long as polluters pay?

c. Punitive damages

Punitive damages are extraordinary in a variety of ways. Law in general is conservative about intervening in the private ordering of affairs. Even when an injury that befalls one member of society can be said to have been caused by another member of society, the first impulse of the legal system is to erect relatively high barriers before the power of the state, acting through its courts, will redistribute the loss away from the victim. These barriers are, of course, the various elements of tort, contract, or other causes of action that the plaintiff must be able to prove by a preponderance of the evidence. In tort, the non-strict liability branches all involve culpable conduct. Even strict liability torts involve conduct that has been singled out for special loss-shifting treatment because (in most cases and especially in toxic tort cases) the defendants knowingly engaged in conduct involving great dangers. And even when these barriers are scaled, all that is awarded is compensation designed to make plaintiff whole, restoring the status quo before the defendant's act injured the plaintiff. Permanent damages and past compensatory damages are both pegged to determinations of actual damages suffered.

Punitive damages are based on the egregious wrongfulness of the defendant's conduct. When available, they add a new dimension to damage remedies, serving functions quite different from compensation — retributive punishment and deterrence. Thus in some cases plaintiffs may get $5000 in compensatory damages and $100,000 or more in punitives. Punitive damages find justification in the fact that, as the name implies, they are intended to *punish* fault, or reckless disregard for others, even in cases where fault is not an element of the tort. The 40 or so states permitting awards of punitive damages typically prescribe them for cases where the defendant's conduct was found to be "willful," "wanton," "malicious," or "reckless." Because it is the wrongful character of defendant's conduct that is the issue, historically there needed to be no proportionality between the amount of punitive damages and the actual harm inflicted. Modern cases have made some change in this doctrine on federal constitutional grounds.

Punitive damages also may serve other purposes, including camouflaged compensation. To some environmental attorneys, punitive awards are readily justifiable, not only to force defendants to confront the seriousness of environmental concerns, but more practically as a means of capturing and internalizing some of the unrecovered intangible costs, such as ecological injuries to natural resources and property damages to persons downwind for whom injuries were real but insufficient to justify litigation. In the latter cases, punitives are forms of extended compensation for externalities, or at times can be thought of as a source from which a plaintiff can recoup litigation costs that are not usually recoverable absent an express statutory authorization. Further, punitive awards serve as a bounty incentive for private citizen enforcement of environmental standards, acknowledging that public officials are often unable to do so. Injured plaintiffs may also be especially deserving, having suffered disproportionately. To some observers, punitives raise serious concerns because of their absence of standards for quantification, their potential for duplication in multiple lawsuits, and their lack of direct nexus to the externalities imposed by the defendants.

Branch v. Western Petroleum, Inc.
Supreme Court of Utah, 1982
657 P.2d 267, 277–278

[After discussing strict liability in its opinion excerpted above, the court went on to discuss punitive damages for the oil company's failure to protect groundwater.]

Western's final contention on its appeal challenges the award of punitive damages. It argues that punitive damages are appropriate only when willful and malicious conduct is shown and that the court erred in including the phrase "reckless indifference and disregard" in its instruction on punitive damages. However, punitive damages may be awarded when one acts with reckless indifference and disregard of the law and his fellow citizens:

> This presumed malice or malice in law does not consist of personal hate or ill will of one person towards another but rather refers to that state of mind which is reckless of law and of the legal rights of the citizen in a person's conduct toward that citizen.... In such cases malice in law will be implied from unjustifiable conduct which causes the injury complained of or from a wrongful act intentionally done without cause or excuse. Terry v. Zions Cooperative, 605 P.2d 314, 327 (Utah, 1979).

The evidence in this case meets that standard. Western discharged the waste water into the disposal pit intending that it seep into and percolate through the soil. Thus, the pollution of the percolating waters was willful and carried out in disregard of the rights of the Branches. Moreover, Western compounded the Branches' problems by its trespass on their land, the spraying of waste water over their land and the failure to comply with state law. In addition, Western continued its dumping activities even after notice of the pollution of the diligence well. The punitive damage award was adequately supported by evidence of reckless indifference toward, and disregard of, the Branches' rights.

Furthermore, there is no merit to Western's contention that the award of punitive damages was excessive and influenced by passion or prejudice rather than reason. The jury was properly instructed that the purpose of exemplary damages is to deter defendant and others from engaging in similar conduct....

Fischer v. Johns-Manville Corporation
Supreme Court of New Jersey, 1986
103 N.J. 643, 512 A.2d 466

[Plaintiff in this case was awarded punitive damages for lung injuries caused by exposure to asbestos more than 40 years earlier. The defendant challenged the award on a number of grounds. Only a small excerpt of the court's discussion is reprinted.]

CLIFFORD, J...."Manufacturer misconduct" [justifying punitives has been typed] into five categories: (1) fraudulent-type, affirmative conduct designed to mislead the public, (2) knowing violations of safety standards, (3) inadequate testing and quality-control, manufacturing procedures, (4) failure to warn of known dangers, and (5) post-marketing failures to remedy known dangers. Owen, Punitive Damages in Products Liability Litigation, 74 Mich. L. Rev. at 1329–61 (1976).

We...view [this case] as falling within Professor Owen's categories one and four.... We cannot imagine that the conduct proven in this case would have been viewed as any less egregious in the 1940s, when the exposure commenced, than it is today. In this connection we share the Appellate Division's reaction to defendant's "knowingly and deliberately...subjecting (James Fischer) as an asbestos worker to serious health hazards with utter and reckless disregard of his safety and well-being."

It is indeed appalling to us that Johns-Manville had so much information on the hazards to asbestos workers as early as the mid-1930s and that it not only failed to use that information to protect these workers but, more egregiously, that it also attempted to withhold this information from the public. It is also clear that even though Johns-Manville may have taken some remedial steps decades ago to protect its own employees, it apparently did nothing to warn and protect those who, like plaintiff, were employed by Johns-Manville customers engaged in the manufacture and fabrication of asbestos products....

The corporate personnel who made the decisions at the time of the exposure are no longer with the defendant company, possibly no longer alive. From this fact it is argued that punitive damages are inappropriate because they will not punish the true wrongdoers. But as many courts have observed, this contention ignores the nature of a corporation as a separate legal entity. Although the responsible management personnel may escape punishment, the corporation itself will not.... A primary goal of punitive damages is general deterrence — that is, the deterrence of others from engaging in similar conduct. That purpose is, of course, well served regardless of changes in personnel within the offending corporation.

A related argument, which similarly ignores the legal nature of corporations, is that punitive damages unfairly punish innocent shareholders. This argument has been rejected repeatedly. It is the corporation, not the individual shareholders, that is recognized as an ongoing legal entity engaged in manufacturing and distributing products.... Also, we would not consider it harmful were shareholders to be encouraged by decisions such as this to give close scrutiny to corporate practices in making investment decisions.

Another characteristic of asbestos litigation is found in the startling numbers that reflect the massive amount of litigation generated by exposure to asbestos. Although we are mindful of the fact that the case before us involves one worker, whose exposure to asbestos caused legally compensable injury to him and his wife — it is not a class action, not a "mass" case — nevertheless we would be remiss were we to ignore the society-wide nature of the asbestos problem....

Studies show that between eleven million and thirteen million workers have been exposed to asbestos. More than 30,000 lawsuits have been filed already for damages caused by that exposure, with no indication that there are no more victims who will seek redress. Of the multitude of lawsuits that are faced by asbestos defendants as a group, Johns-Manville alone has been named in more than 11,000 cases. New claims are stayed because Johns-Manville is attempting reorganization under federal bankruptcy law.

Defendant argues that the amount of *compensatory* damages assessed and to be assessed is so great that it will effectively serve the functions of punitive damages — that is, defendants are more than sufficiently punished and deterred. We are not at all satisfied, however, that compensatory damages effectively serve the same functions as punitive damages, even when they amount to staggering sums. Compensatory damages are often foreseeable as to amount.... Anticipation of these damages will allow potential defendants, aware of dangers of a product, to factor those anticipated damages into a cost-benefit analysis and to decide whether to market a particular product. The risk and amount of such damages can, and in some cases will, be reflected in the cost of a product, in which event the product will be marketed in its dangerous condition.

Without punitive damages a manufacturer who is aware of a dangerous feature of its product but nevertheless knowingly chooses to market it in that condition, willfully concealing from the public information regarding the dangers of the product, would be far better off than an innocent manufacturer who markets a product later discovered to be dangerous — this, because both will be subjected to the same compensatory damages, but the innocent manufacturer, unable to anticipate those damages, will not have incorporated the cost of those damages into the cost of the product. All else being equal, the law should not place the innocent manufacturer in a worse position than that of a knowing wrongdoer. Punitive damages tend to meet this need.[35]

Defendant argues further that the cumulative effect of punitive damages in mass-tort litigation is "potentially catastrophic." The Johns-Manville bankruptcy is offered as proof of this effect. We fail to see the distinction, in the case of Johns-Manville, between the effect of compensatory damages and that of punitive damages....

Heretofore the typical setting for punitive damage claims has been the two-party lawsuit in which, more often than not, a punitive damages award was supported by a showing of some element of malice or intentional wrongdoing, directed by a defendant to the specific plaintiff. Even if the actual object of the malicious conduct was unknown to defendant, the conduct nevertheless was directed at a single person or a very limited group of potential plaintiffs.

Punishable conduct in a products liability action, on the other hand, will often affect countless potential plaintiffs whose identities are unknown to defendant at the time of the culpable conduct. We agree with the Illinois court that the mere fact that a defendant, "through outrageous misconduct...manage(s) to seriously injure a large number of persons" should not relieve it of liability for punitive damages. Froud v. Celotex Corp., 437 N.E.2d 910, 913 (1982).

Of greater concern to us is the possibility that asbestos defendants' assets may become so depleted by early awards that the defendants will no longer be in existence and able to pay compensatory damages to later plaintiffs. Again, it is difficult if not impossible to ascertain the additional impact of punitive damages as compared to the impact of mass compensatory damages alone.

Many of the policy arguments against punitive damages in mass tort litigation cases can be traced to Roginsky v. Richardson-Merrell, Inc., 378 F.2d 832 (2d Cir. 1967). The *Roginsky* court denied punitive damages to a plaintiff who suffered cataracts caused by MER/29, an anti-cholesterol drug. Although the denial of punitive damages rested on a determination that the evidence was insufficient to send the matter to the jury, the court expressed several concerns over allowing punitive damages for injuries to multiple plaintiffs. The fear that punitive damages would lead to "overkill" turned out to be unfounded in the MER/29 litigation. Approximately 1,500 claims were made, of which only eleven were tried to a jury verdict. Punitive damages were awarded in only three of those cases, one of which was reversed on appeal. While we do not discount entirely the possibility of punitive damage "overkill" in asbestos litigation, we do recognize that the vast majority of cases settle without trial.

Accepting the possibility of punitive damage "overkill," we turn to means of addressing that problem. Because the problem is nationwide, several possible remedial steps can be effective only on a nationwide basis, and hence are beyond our reach. One such solution is the setting of a

---

35. In addition, it is questionable how much punishment is effected by compensatory damages alone, which, unlike punitives, are generally covered by liability insurance.

cap on total punitive damages against each defendant. Such a cap would be ineffective unless applied uniformly. To adopt such a cap in New Jersey would be to deprive our citizens of punitive damages without the concomitant benefit of assuring the availability of compensatory damages for later plaintiffs. This we decline to do....

At the state court level we are powerless to implement solutions to the nationwide problems created by asbestos exposure and litigation arising from that exposure. That does not mean, however, that we cannot institute some controls over runaway punitive damages. When a defendant manufacturer engages in conduct warranting the imposition of punitive damages, the harm caused may run to countless plaintiffs. Each individual plaintiff can fairly charge that the manufacturer's conduct was egregious as to him and that punitive damages should be assessed in his lawsuit.... Nonetheless, there should be some limits placed on the total punishment exacted from a culpable defendant. We conclude that a reasonable imposition of those limits would permit a defendant to introduce evidence of other punitive damage awards already assessed against and paid by it, as well as evidence of its own financial status and the effect a punitive award would have....

We realize that defendants may be reluctant to alert juries to the fact that other courts or juries have assessed punitive damages for conduct similar to that being considered by the jury in a given case. Although the evidence may convince a jury that a defendant has been sufficiently punished, the same evidence could nudge a jury closer to a determination that punishment is warranted. That is a risk of jury trial. The willingness to accept that risk is a matter of strategy for defendant and its counsel, no different from other strategy choices facing trial lawyers every day.

When evidence of other punitive awards is introduced, trial courts should instruct juries to consider whether the defendant has been sufficiently punished, keeping in mind that punitive damages are meant to punish and deter defendants for the benefit of society, not to compensate individual plaintiffs.

A further protection may be afforded defendants by the judicious exercise of remittitur. Should a trial court determine that an award is "manifestly outrageous" or "grossly excessive," it may reduce that award or order a new trial on punitive damages. In evaluating the excessiveness of challenged punitive damage awards, trial courts are expressly authorized to consider prior punitive damage awards....

COMMENTARY & QUESTIONS

1. **Do all intentional torts deserve punitive damages?** Could Oscar Boomer have gotten punitive damages against Atlantic Cement? Boomer proved that the cement dust pollution was an intentional tort; so wasn't it "willful," justifying punitives? In McElwain v. Georgia Pac. Corp., a pulp mill air pollution case, the court majority allowed punitive damages in a case very much like *Boomer*:

> The intentional disregard of the interest of another is the equivalent of legal malice, and justifies punitive damages for trespass. Where there is proof of an intentional, unjustifiable infliction of harm with deliberate disregard of the social consequences, the question of award of punitive damages is for the jury.

> It is abundantly clear from the record that defendant knew when it decided to construct its [paper] mill in Toledo, that there was danger, if not a probability, that the mill would cause damage to adjoining property.... The jury could have found that during the period involved in this action the defendant had not done everything reasonably possible to eliminate or minimize the damage to adjoining properties by its mill. 421 P.2d 957, 958 (Or. 1966).

The dissenting justice in *McElwain* strongly disagreed, arguing that actual malice was a necessary and desirable requirement for award of punitive damages. Which is right? These and related questions resurface in the toxic tort cases.

2. **The availability and measure of punitives.** Analyzing *Branch*, *McElwain*, and *Fischer*, is the availability of punitive damages restricted to situations where defendants' conduct is extreme and antisocial? What is the proper measure of punitive damages? What checks are imposed? In a jury case, the process by which punitive damages are awarded most often begins with plaintiffs' closing argument urging the jury, in accordance with the judge's charge, to award punitives because the defendant's conduct has been shown to "merit" such an award. Thereafter, a jury instruction will be given to the effect that the prevailing plaintiffs are also entitled to punitive damages if the standard for disregard or indifference to the rights of others is met. Rather less is said in the jury charge about how those awards are to be calculated. Are juries free to vent their spleen?

Caps on punitives have been increasingly proposed. The 104th Congress failed to pass several bills containing caps. (See, e.g., 104 H.R. 956, §201(e).) Then-Texas Governor George W. Bush signed bill S.B. 25 in April 1996 capping punitive damages claims at two times economic damages, plus no more than $750,000 in noneconomic damages or $200,000, whichever is greater. The bill requires a plaintiff to prove fraud or malice and changes the burden of proof from a preponderance of the evidence to clear and convincing evidence.

3. **Proving punitives.** What kind of proof is likely to incite a jury to award punitives? In a book on the asbestos litigation, Paul Brodeur chronicled the industry's 40 year-long "conspiracy of silence" in failing to warn workers or consumers about the fatal dangers of asbestos exposure that it had known about at least since the 1940s. Brodeur quotes a company memo written by Dr. Kenneth W. Smith, Johns-Manville's medical director, after a 1949 study showed that of 708 asbestos workers like Fischer, only 4 did not have asbestosis:

> It must be remembered that although these men have the X-ray evidence of asbestosis, they are working today and definitely are not disabled.... They have not been told of this diagnosis for it is felt that as long as the man feels well, is happy at home and at work, and his physical condition remains good, nothing should be said. When he becomes disabled and sick, then the diagnosis should be made and the claim submitted by the Company. The fibrosis of this disease is irreversible and permanent so that eventually compensation will be paid to each of these men. But as long as the man is not disabled it is felt that he should not be told of his condition so that he can live and work in peace and the Company can benefit by his many years of experience. Should the man be told of his condition today there is a very definite possibility that he would become mentally and physically ill, simply through the knowledge that he has asbestosis.

Another memo from a later year revealed a conversation about a 52-year-old man:

> "Advanced pneumoconiosis," Dr. Smith declared after looking at the patient's medical file.

> "Should we change him?" inquired Sheckler [a safety and health supervisor for the company, who wanted to know if a transfer to a non-dusty area was in order].

> "Won't make any difference," Smith replied.

> "If he hits sixty-five, I will be surprised," Dr. DuBow [a plant physician] said.
>
> On the basis of such advice, Sheckler decided to take no action other than to watch the patient carefully and retire him on disability, if, as he put it, it became "necessary." And as to a woman testing positive for advanced asbestosis, "If she is called in, she will get hysterical, and I am sure you'll have a claim on your hands," so nothing was done. See P. Brodeur, Outrageous Misconduct: The Asbestos Industry on Trial 102–103, 145–146 (1985).

And so contaminated workers were not informed, nor were new employees entering the plant's workforce in succeeding years told of the fatal hazard. Analyze why these items of evidence might have an effect on punitive damages (and why, as in the Kepone case, the system couldn't rely upon the medical profession for warnings and correction).

4. **Punitive problems in mass cases.** The *Fischer* case, involving a single plaintiff, raises many of the problems that have impelled some state legislatures to yield to industry lobbyists and prohibit punitive damages altogether, or to restrict their availability to special cases of malice, or to cap maximum awards. Are you satisfied with the *Fischer* court's rejoinders to these arguments? The facts of environmental cases often arouse anger and outrage in juries. If a defendant has limited funds, or if juries in sequential cases award duplicative punitive damages for a single mass exposure, there is at least the possibility of unfairness to defendants and other potential plaintiffs. If there are restraints imposed on later duplicative punitive awards, doesn't that prompt a race to court? In the 180 *Exxon-Valdez* cases, proposals were made for mandatory certification of one all-inclusive punitive damage claim. Should there be a national clearinghouse coordinating punitive damage claims filed against mass tortfeasors? Or is the risk of an avalanche of punitive-minded juries just part of the game?

5. **The Exxon-sponsored attack on the concept of punitive damages.** The *Exxon-Valdez* oil spill continues to push the cutting edge in environmental law, in this case in the realm of punitive damages theory, where Exxon was hit with punitive damage judgments that ultimately could total $5 to $15 billion. A pitched debate has resulted in the pages of the Georgetown Law Review and elsewhere. In an article funded in part by a grant from Exxon, Professor W. Kip Viscusi argues that punitive damages should be abolished for corporate risk and environmental cases. Using benefit-cost analysis, Viscusi concludes that in these settings punitive damages create more harm than good for society. "There is no deterrence benefit that justifies the chaos and economic disruption inflicted by punitive damages." Viscusi, The Social Costs of Punitive Damages Against Corporations in Environmental and Safety Torts, 87 Geo. L.J. 285 (1998).

Here are the basic components of Viscusi's argument:[36]

> 1. If punitive damages deterred risk-imposing behavior, the 4 states that lack punitive damages should have worse environmental and accident records than the 46 states that have them. But in fact, Michigan, Nebraska, New Hampshire, and Washington do as well or better than the other 46. So punitive damages do not deter.

---

36. The outline is taken from Professor David Luban's rebuttal article, Luban, A Flawed Case Against Punitive Damages, 87 Geo. L.J. 359, at 360 (1998).

2. In any event, it is a bad and fanciful idea to try to bring risk levels down to zero.

3. Juries are irrational, and their irrationality leads them to impose punitive damages on corporations that have not brought risk levels down to zero. This will be the case even when corporations make rational risk decisions; a risk decision that is rational ex ante (that is, at the time it is made) looks unreasonable ex post (that is, at the time the jury looks at it) because of cognitive bias.

4. The capricious character of punitive damages deters corporate innovation and thus harms us all.

5. Compensatory damages plus governmental regulation suffice to ensure an adequate level of safety.

6. Thus, because punitive damages offer no benefits and impose substantial costs, they should be abolished.

Professor David Luban wrote a vehement rebuttal to Viscusi's article, questioning the appropriateness of benefit-cost analysis of punitive damages and systematically disputing the assumptions and data on which Viscusi's argument rests.

Here are the basic components of Luban's rebuttal. Luban, A Flawed Case Against Punitive Damages, 87 Geo. L.J. 359, 379 380 (1998):

1. It [Viscusi's argument] assumes that the aim of punitive damages is entirely to secure good [economic] consequences, ignoring the retributive character of punishment.

2. It assumes that the sole consequentialist aim of punitive damages is deterrence, ignoring the aims of influencing settlement behavior and financing private enforcement of environmental and safety norms.

3. It assumes that punitive damages are "out of control," when the available data show that this is far from the case.

4. It argues from the fact that the four states with no punitive damages have similar environmental and safety-related records to the conclusion that punitive damages have no deterrent effect. This ignores the influence of punitive damages in other states on the safety records of the four states with no punitive damages.

5. It also ignores the fact that punitive damages are an unusual remedy aiming to deter unusual behavior. Even if they perfectly deterred the exceptional behavior they are directed toward, this would create no noticeable change in general accident rates.

6. It argues against pursuing the ideal of zero risk without ever showing that punitive damages are generally awarded on the basis that defendants failed to attain zero risk.

7. It argues that cognitive biases predispose juries to award punitive damages when such awards are not justified, even though the overwhelming evidence shows that juries seldom award punitive damages. Furthermore, the argument ignores the collective and deliberate character of the jury.

8. It ignores the role of cognitive bias in corporate decisionmaking concerning risk. This leads to a false contrast between supposedly irrational juries and supposedly rational corporate decisionmakers.

9. It argues that high liability awards deter innovation, without showing that punitive damages contribute substantially to high liability awards.

10. It argues for government regulation in place of punitive damages, ignoring the limited enforcement capacity of government agencies and the possibility that public law regulatory standards are often too lenient.

11. It argues that one rationale for punitive damages, enforcement error, rarely arises in environmental or accident cases because accidents are readily detected. This ignores the fact that enforcement requires not just detection but the filing of claims, and Americans fail to file claims in 90% of accidents.

12. It argues that another rationale for punitive damages, malicious intent, is irrelevant to corporations, ignoring the equally egregious motive of wanton indifference to safety — a motive that seems quite salient in the business world.

13. It ignores the doctrinal basis for punitive damages, which is punishment for really mean or really stupid behavior.

Luban concludes that Viscusi ultimately "fails to identify all the potential benefits of punitive damages; fails to establish that punitive damages are ineffective deterrents; and fails to exhibit any significant social harms that punitive damages inflict." 87 Geo. L.J. at 380. This debate is likely to continue.

In a column scrutinizing corporate attacks against punitive damages, Russell Mokhiber and Robert Weissman criticize Exxon's ongoing efforts to avoid paying the billions in punitive damages awarded to those who were harmed by the spill. "Exxon's behavior in Prince William Sound was either really mean or really stupid and is deserving of punishment," they argue. Mokhiber & Weissman, Exxon: Mean and Stupid, 20 Multinat'l Monitor 3 (1999).[37] They call upon Exxon to focus on safeguarding against future catastrophes rather than attacking the concept of punitive damages. Mokhiber and Weissman pressed Professor Viscusi to disclose the amount of money Exxon paid him to write his article, but Viscusi told them it was none of their business.

In June 1997, Exxon appealed the *Exxon-Valdez* oil spill punitive damage judgment to the Ninth Circuit Court of Appeals, where remittitur is likely to be the fallback argument, following Exxon's frontal assaults on the concept of punitive damages.[38] There is much controversy over the delay in payment because if the appeal lasts long enough, Exxon will earn enough in interest on $5 billion to recoup the full cost of the award plus interest. Exxon is earning close to $800 million a year on that fund of unpaid punitives, while the plaintiff award will be attributed interest at a mere 5.9% a year, which did not even begin to accrue until two years after the appeal was filed.[39]

6. **Constitutional checks on the award of punitive damages.** The U.S. Supreme Court has decided several cases considering (and eventually imposing) due process limitations on the award of punitive damages. In Pacific Mut. Life Ins. Co. v. Haslip, 499 U.S. 1 (1991), the Court acknowledged that awards of punitive damages in some cases could

---

37. For the full text of this and other "Focus on the Corporation" articles, you can visit the *Multinational Monitor* Web site at http://www.essential.org/monitor.

38. See Clarke, Exxon Appeals Verdict, Anchorage Daily News, June 20, 1997, at B1. Available at http://www.adn.com/evos/stories/EV413.html.

39 See Bardwick, The American Tort System's Response to Environmental Disaster: The Exxon-Valdez Oil Spill as a Case Study, 19 Stan. Envtl. L.J. 259 (2000). See also Phillips, As Appeals Drag, Exxon Banks the Interest, Anchorage Daily News, Aug. 4, 1998; for articles on this and other related *Exxon-Valdez* oil spill issues from the *Anchorage Daily News*, visit http://www.adn.com/evos/index.html, including the four-day feature series "Exxon Valdez — Legacy of a Spill," starting Thursday, May 13, 1999.

violate due process. The jury verdict of $800,000 in *Haslip*, more than four times the compensatory damages in the case, was upheld because the Alabama courts had applied seven test criteria in reviewing the punitives award: (1) the reasonable relationship between the amount awarded and the harm caused or threatened by defendant's action; (2) the reprehensibility, duration, frequency, and consciousness of defendant's conduct; (3) the profitability of the action; (4) the defendant's financial position; (5) the costs of litigation; (6) whether criminal sanctions had been imposed (which would mitigate the punitives award); and (7) whether defendant had had to pay other civil awards.[40] The first Supreme Court decision actually to *strike down* a punitive damages award as a violation of Fourteenth Amendment due process was Honda Motors v. Oberg, 517 U.S. 1219 (1996). Justice Stevens held that judicial review of the size of punitive damages awards is a necessary due process safeguard against excessive awards, and that a state's common law or statutory law must provide a set of standards for the size of a punitive award, providing for possible remission of punitive damages along the lines of the seven tests in *Haslip*. In BMW v. Gore, 517 U.S. 559, 562 (1996), the Court held that "the Due Process Clause of the Fourteenth Amendment prohibits a State from imposing a 'grossly excessive' punishment on a tortfeasor," applying the same factors as in the *Haslip* case. The relevance of due process limits to environmental cases was made clear by the Court's decision in Combustion Eng'g v. Johansen, 517 U.S. 1217 (1996), where the Supreme Court remanded the $15 million punitive damages award in a Georgia strip-mine acid drainage case for review of its due process proportionality

In State Farm Mut. Auto. Ins. Co. v. Campbell, the plaintiffs sued an insurance company for bad faith, fraud, and intentional infliction of emotional distress after State Farm badly mishandled a claim after a serious accident, forcing plaintiffs personally to pay damages four times greater than their insurance coverage. Plaintiffs were awarded a verdict of $1 million in compensatory damages and $145 million in punitive damages by the Utah Supreme Court, and State Farm appealed to the U.S. Supreme Court. State Farm Mut. Auto. Ins. Co. v. Campbell, 123 S. Ct. 1513, 1513 (2003). Stating that the $145 million punitive damages verdict was "neither reasonable nor proportionate" and amounted to "an irrational and arbitrary deprivation of property," the Supreme Court overturned the award against the automobile insurance company. Citing *Gore* for the remittitur order, Justice Kennedy, writing for the majority, said, "It should be presumed a plaintiff has been made whole for his injuries by compensatory damages, so punitive damages should only be awarded if the defendant's culpability, after having paid compensatory damages, is so reprehensible as to warrant the imposition of further sanctions to achieve punishment or deterrence." 123 S. Ct. at 1521. Kennedy's opinion also frowned upon evidence that the punitive damages in this case were meant to punish State Farm not just for conduct related to this case but for other conduct, some of it outside of Utah, that would be illegal in Utah. While the Court declined to state what amount of punitive damages would be acceptable, the majority said: "Few awards exceeding a single-digit ratio…will satisfy due process." 123 S. Ct. at 1524. The Court suggested an award of more than a 4-to-1 ratio of punitive to compensatory damages

---

40. Substantially followed in TXO v. Alliance Res., 509 U.S. 443 (1993).

may be "close to the line of constitutional impropriety." Id. The decision left open the possibility for larger ratios where the plaintiff had suffered physical as opposed to economic harm or the conduct of the defendant had been particularly egregious, while at the same time suggesting that where compensatory damages are high, a 1-to-1 ratio may be the maximum punitive damages that can be awarded without overstepping due process. Id. The court also warned against using punitive damages as a substitute for a criminal remedy: "Punitive damages are not a substitute for the criminal process, and the remote possibility [sic] of a criminal sanction does not automatically sustain a punitive damages award." 123 S. Ct. at 1526. The decision could have negative effects in environmental tort cases where actual damages measured in terms of market value are quite low, but the ecological, social, or cultural damages are large, and the defendant acted with egregious disregard for the latter values. Does *Campbell*'s due process concern impose a limitation on restoration remedies when the cost of restoration far exceeds the market value losses of the plaintiff?

7. **Remittitur.** As the above cases show, appellate (and even trial court) judges can and do at times order a rollback of punitive damage verdicts that they consider excessive, but there are virtually no generally agreed-upon common law judicial standards for remittitur. The Alabama courts' tests in *Haslip* are just a start. How would they tend to apply in environmental cases? Can uncompensated ecological damages be considered? See Garcia, Remittitur in Environmental Cases, 16 B.C. Envtl. Aff. L. Rev. 119 (1988).

8. **Punitive damages and insurance.** Under the typical corporate insurance policy's pollution exclusion clauses, punitive damages usually are not covered. An award to a harmed plaintiff is only as good as the defendant's ability to pay. Some states such as California, however, prohibit insurance coverage for willful or malicious acts on public policy grounds. For other examples of the intricacies of pollution exclusion clauses, see Freedom Gravel Prods. v. Michigan Mut. Ins., 819 F. Supp. 275 (W.D.N.Y. 1993).

9. **Creative accounting in damage remedies: ill-gotten gains and punitive damages.** An intriguing potential for a new theory of damages is presented by 18 U.S.C. §3571 in the criminal law field:

> Alternative fine based on gain or loss. If any person derives pecuniary gain from the offense, or if the offense results in pecuniary loss to a person other than the defendant, the defendant may be fined not more than the greater of twice the gross gain or twice the gross loss, unless the imposition of a fine under this subsection would unduly complicate or prolong the sentencing process.

If, for example, a factory has avoided a million dollars in waste treatment expenses by violating pollution discharge limits, energetic application of this provision can provide a measure of equitable divestment of ill-gotten gains, a dramatically enhanced deterrent to future evasions, and, especially if the public is deemed an injured "person," a more accurate internalization of environmental harm losses to the commons.

To what extent can this same rationale be applied in civil cases under the common law? In a Georgia strip-mine acid drainage case, the jury awarded $15 million in punitive damages, in large part on an ill-gotten gains basis, to 24 plaintiffs whose 1100 acres of land had suffered $47,000 in damages from a strip-mining operation. The punitive award's disproportion was justified in part by the fact that over the span of 11 years of unheeded warnings to correct its waste treatment, defendant had saved a great deal of money by not cleaning up — a saving of $6 million in the last 4 years of operation alone — echoing the *Haslip* test of "profitability of the action." See Combustion Eng'g v. Johansen, 98 F.3d 1351 (11th Cir. 1996).[41] The ill-gotten gains recoupment theory of punitive damage awards is likely to find increasingly active use.

A further theory for disgorgement can be based on the quasi-contract theories of "restitution" of ill-gotten gains or "unjust enrichment." So far the courts have not quite bought the theory: Evans v. Johnstown, 410 N.Y.S.2d 199 (N.Y. Sup. Ct. Fulton Cty., 1978) (municipal sewage treatment plant), County Line Inv. Co. v. Tinney, 933 F.2d 1508 (10th Cir. 1991) (suit against predecessor for landfill remediation by a successor).

Section 3. NATURAL RESOURCES REMEDIES

Because the vast majority of environmental litigation is directed at recouping losses to humans and their property, one tends to lose sight of ecological reality: that human injuries are not necessarily the major consequences of disruptions of the natural equilibrium. As Judge Mehrige said in *Pruitt*, "Kepone pollution...costs were borne most directly by the wildlife of the Chesapeake Bay." 523 F. Supp. at 978. When a wrongdoer destroys or injures natural resources, the law can do an adequate enough job establishing fault or an equivalent basis for liability. The riddle is how to define and apply remedies for injuries beyond damages to humans. Over the past decade, environmental law has committed itself in a variety of ways to answering that question.

The public trust doctrine, explored in Chapter 22, offers a foundation for equitable restoration remedies and government economic recoveries for natural resources damage (NRD). Public nuisance actions also have supplied authority for NRD remedies, as well as a number of state and federal statutes. The CWA, CERCLA, and other federal acts require the federal government to "identify the best available procedures to determine natural resources damages, including both direct and indirect injury, destruction or loss."[42] The evolution of NRD liability theories, evaluation methods, and remedies is occurring concurrently in both common law and public law settings.

The *Exxon-Valdez* oil spill provides a classic example of NRD accounting. Shortly after midnight on March 24, 1989, the single-hulled supertanker *Exxon-Valdez* sliced into the submerged granite of Bligh Reef in Alaska's Prince William Sound. Pushed by northeasterly winds, the 11 million gallons of crude oil that spewed from the wreck

---

41. Johansen v. Combustion Eng'g, No. CV-191-178 (S.D. Ga. June 1993), remitted 98 F.3d 1351 (11th Cir. 1996). The Supreme Court sent the verdict back for reconsideration under the due process remittitur theories of the 1997 *BMW* case. 517 U.S. 1217 (1996).

42. CWA, 33 U.S.C.A. §1321(f)(4)(5); CERCLA, 42 U.S.C.A. §9651(C)(2). The other federal statutes that authorize NRD are the Oil Pollution Act of 1990, 33 U.S.C.A. §§2701, 2702(b)(2)(A) (1990); Trans-Alaska Pipeline Auth. Act, 43 U.S.C.A. §1653 (1973, 1988); Deepwater Port Act, 33 U.S.C.A. §1501 (1974, 1988); Outer Continental Shelf Lands Act Amendments of 1978, 43 U.S.C.A. §§1331-1356 (1978, 1988); Marine Protection, Research, and Sanctuaries Act of 1988, 16 U.S.C.A. §1443 (1988); National Parks Systems Authority Act, 16 U.S.C.A. §19ii (Supp. V 1993). The doctrines of NRD liability and valuation methods are being actively debated and shaped in judicial review of federal agency NRD regulations.

spread out over 1000 miles of coastal waters.[43] The ecosystem hit by the *Exxon-Valdez* spill was extraordinarily rich. Affected species included herring, black cod, cutthroat trout, dolly varden, shark, halibut, rock fish, shell fish, fin fish, several species of salmon, sea otters, fur seals, steller's sea lions, harbor porpoises, dall porpoises, killer whales, hump-back whales, minke whales, fin whales, blue whales, gray whales, deer, fox, coyotes, black bears, brown bears, bald eagles, several species of gulls, hundreds of thousands of sea birds (such as kittiwakes, puffins, hawks, guillemots, murres, murrelets, loons, grebes, and diving ducks), dungeness crabs, pot shrimp, trawl shrimp — and these were just the upper layers of the ecological pyramid. The waters and wildlife of the Gulf of Alaska were among the most fertile coastal communities on earth, built upon a confluence of ocean currents rich in microorganisms, zooplankton, and phytoplankton.

In the aftermath of the *Exxon-Valdez* oil spill, more than 180 civil suits were filed, almost all by people claiming injury to their economic interests. Some of those economic claims are relatively uninteresting — claims for direct property losses and diminution of market value. Others raise some of the questions noted in the preceding section about how far economic recoveries can extend along a chain of "indirect" causation, from commercial fishers, to processors, distributors, ship owners, outfitters, and restauranteurs, none of whom sustained actual physical damage.

The State of Alaska's lawsuit included many predictable economic claims — loss of tourism and recreation; reimbursement for out-of-pocket cleanup efforts by towns, native American tribes, and the State; emotional distress and disruption of citizens' lives; and so on — but the State also asked the trial court to award damages and injunctions that would capture a broader swath of values, based on natural resources losses. As you read the following brief excerpts from the State's 40-page complaint, note the problems faced in defining and separating human and ecological remedies.

IN THE SUPERIOR COURT FOR THE STATE OF ALASKA
THIRD JUDICIAL DISTRICT

THE STATE OF ALASKA, on its own behalf,	)	
and as public trustee and as *parens patriae* for	)	
the citizens of the State, Plaintiff,	)	Case No. 3AN8906852CIV
vs.	)	
EXXON CORPORATION, a New Jersey	)	
corporation; EXXON PIPELINE COMPANY, a	)	
Delaware corporation; EXXON SHIPPING	)	
COMPANY, a Delaware corporation;	)	
ALYESKA PIPELINE SERVICE COMPANY,	)	
a Delaware corporation; et al.	)	
Defendants.	)	

---

43. As to fault, the wreck was an accident waiting to happen, attributable to cost-cutting and complacency within the oil industry, abetted by lassitude within the U.S. Coast Guard and state and federal regulatory agencies. See State of Alaska Oil Spill Comm'n, Spill: The Wreck of the Exxon-Valdez: Lessons for the Safe Transportation of Oil (1990). Disclosure notice: One of the authors worked for the State of Alaska and for the Oil Spill Commission itself on legal responses to the Exxon-Valdez spill.

COMPLAINTS FOR COMPENSATORY AND PUNITIVE DAMAGES, CIVIL PENALTIES AND INJUNCTIVE RELIEF...

20. "Environmental damages" includes, but is not limited to, one or more types of damages to use and enjoyment values derived from State lands, waters, and resources:

(1) Use values, including consumptive and nonconsumptive uses;

(2) Nonuse values, including existence, intrinsic, option, bequest, temporal, and quasi-option values;

(3) Values derived from the existence of management options and the expertise and data to exercise and support same;

(4) Values associated with the necessity or desirability of restoration, replacement, assessment or monitoring;

(5) Other ecosystem existing values....

DAMAGES TO PLAINTIFF

...61. As a result of the oil spill from the EXXON-VALDEZ, over a thousand square miles of State lands, waters, and resources have suffered severe environmental damage. A growing number of coastal and inland sounds and bays, beaches, tidelands, tidal pools, wetlands, estuaries, and other sensitive elements of the ecosystems have been devastated; thousands of mammals, fowl, and fish have been killed or injured; anadromous streams, near shore environments and other fish and wildlife critical habitats have been contaminated; aesthetics and scenic quality have been destroyed or impaired, together with attendant opportunities for recreational experiences; air quality has deteriorated through the escape of evaporating pollutants; commercial fisheries have been sharply curtailed, with adverse biological and economic consequences; the greater ecosystem in the spill area has been deprived of its pristine condition with attendant damage to the condition of, and interrelationship among, living creatures comprising the system; and the management opportunities available through the knowledge and data base generated from prior experience with the ecosystem have been compromised....

RELIEF SOUGHT

WHEREFORE, plaintiff prays that this Court: ...

Award all compensatory and punitive damages authorized under the common law, including, but not limited to, environmental and economic damages.

Award all compensatory and punitive damages authorized under the general maritime law.

Order that the defendants be permanently enjoined to remove all spilled oil and to restore the surface and subsurface lands, wildlife, waters, fisheries, shellfish and associated marine resources, air and other State lands, waters and resources affected directly or indirectly by the spill;

Order immediate and continuing environmental monitoring and assessment of the conditions of the air, waters and subsurface and surface lands, fisheries, shellfish and the associated marine resources and other natural resources...[and]

Award such other and further relief as this Court deems just and proper.

DATED this 15th day of August, 1989.

Douglas B. Baily

Attorney General

COMMENTARY & QUESTIONS

1. **Non-marketplace human-based remedies.** Assuming first that the numerical loss of living resources can be accurately established,[44] natural resources remedies then go beyond the mere commodity-pricing approach of the marketplace. As the appellate court wrote when Ohio challenged the CWA and Superfund natural resource regulations:

> It is the incompleteness of market processes that give rise to the need for [nonmarket valuation].... While it is not irrational to look to market price as one factor in determining the use value of a resource, it is unreasonable to view market price as the *exclusive* factor, or even the predominant one. From the bald eagle to the blue whale and snail darter, natural resources have values that are not fully captured by the market system.... Option and existence values may represent "passive" use, they nonetheless reflect utility derived by humans from a resource, and thus prima facie ought to be included in a damage assessment. Ohio v. U.S. Dept. of Interior, 880 F.2d 432, 462–464 (D.C. Cir. 1989).[45]

Note how the court returns to humans. Likewise, although the Alaska complaint begins its narration of damages with environmental losses, even within the definition of "environmental damages" many if not all of the contentions are for *human*-based economic recovery.[46] The term "use value," for instance, seeks to capture values for things that don't actually trade in the marketplace, but uses an attributed market value. "Consumptive value" attributes a value to lost resource uses of sportsmen and tourists who would have taken wildlife in hunting or fishing pursuits. "Nonconsumptive" uses include the ecosystem's value to photographers, bird watchers, and the like. Some "non-use" values are based on attributed human value: what it means to people just to know the resource is there, even if they never actively use it; it is "option value" if they may use it. "Bequest value" reflects the resource as a legacy passed by the present generation to its children. "Temporal" and "quasi-option" values assess unknown future values foreclosed. There is a wide range of economic methods for estimating or "shadow pricing" some of these values, including travel cost (the amount that people are willing to spend to travel to such places); "hedonic" value, using market activity preferences; implied speculative rent values; and contingent valuation methods (CVM) based on public opinion surveys about willingness to pay (as in a hypothetical tax).[47]

Fundamentally, each of these approaches creates a hypothetical human market for resources, an approach that requires the component fish, wildlife, bugs, and

---

44. Measuring transient living resources that previously came to a particular place and now are absent is often a challenging scientific process. For one of the most awful judicial opinions on this point and generally, see Hampton v. North Carolina Pulp Co., 49 F. Supp. 625 (E.D.N.C. 1943), thankfully rev'd, 139 F.2d 840 (4th Cir. 1943).

45. Ohio v. U.S. Dep't of Interior, 880 F.2d 432, 464 (D.C. Cir. 1989)(emphasis in original). Petition for rehearing *en banc* denied, 897 F. 2d 1151 (D.C. Cir. 1989).

46. Beyond the realm of natural resources, the Alaska complaint also raises environmental questions regarding remedies for the dramatic disruptions to the Alaska Native communities along the coast, where the prior-existing complex and stable subsistence culture may never recover from the onslaughts of oil and oil spill cleanup salaries. The complaint also seeks remedies for non-economic human losses in psychological stresses suffered by many non-Native Alaskans whose lives were severely impacted by the spill.

47. See Cross, Natural Resource Damage Valuation, 42 Vand. L. Rev. 269 (1989); Cicchetti & Peck, Assessing Natural Resource Damages: The Case Against Contingent Value Survey Methods, 4 Nat. Resources & Env't 6 (Spring 1989).

microorganisms of an ecosystem be made sufficiently recognizable and attractive to a human audience to deserve monetary recognition. A growing literature addresses this topic using the concept of "ecosystem services." For an extensive symposium volume on the natural capital represented by ecosystem services supplied to the marketplace economy by Mother Nature, see 20 Stan. Envtl. L.J. 309 (Number 2, 2001).

2. **Natural resources' own intrinsic value?** None of the preceding remedies pretends to assess the value of the resources in and of themselves. It seems presumptuous, however, to argue that humans are the sole measure of what has been lost in an ecological catastrophe (although only humans, of course, are in a position to raise the intrinsic ethical claims). If courts can look beyond human-based values, as both law and ethics may currently be inviting them to do, serious questions arise. Can you talk intelligently about the lost wildlife's value to itself? First, it's dead; second, it's wildlife, not human. The flora and fauna and their ecosystem leave no probate estates for wrongful death recoveries. Who can sue, for what purpose, and for what measure of relief?

Who can sue? Given our legal system, it would be vastly easier to sue for the loss of resources if they were citizens, or someone owned them. In the absence of either, the State of Alaska can file its claims for remedies based on its "parens patriae" and public trustee roles, and environmentalists can sue as public trust beneficiaries (see Chapter 22), but the nature and extent of standing to recover for intrinsic natural resources losses are not self-evident.

What is the purpose of seeking natural resources damages? The dead wildlife cannot be brought back to life. In ordinary tort law, the purpose of damages is a delicate mix of restoring plaintiffs to their prior position and taxing wrongdoers for their wrongdoing. "Destruction of the Bay's wildlife should not be a costless activity," said the judge in the *Pruitt* Kepone case in this chapter. To this extent, the punitive damages sought in the Alaska complaint may be an attempt to capture unquantifiable intrinsic losses and deter future wrongful actions.

But what is the measure of loss? The wildlife and their ecological pyramid had an "existence value" that is gone. The fact that they used to be there, and no longer are, reflects the disruption of an evolved ecological community that didn't just happen to be there but had adapted and developed over thousands and millions of years. What is the value of the components of that system, especially the vast numbers of small rather prosaic protozoans, sea slugs, and the like?[48]

The fundamental problem of damage valuation for the per se loss of wildlife is that the intrinsic worth of natural resources does not conveniently fit the terms of economic accountability.

3. **Natural capital.** Some economists take a different tack in valuing natural resources.

---

48. In some cases, courts have tried to value the wildlife itself in terms of what it would bring at a meat market or pet store. In a case where millions of baby striped bass were sucked into the cooling intakes of a power plant, the court awarded the per pound price of striped bass in the fish market; zoos may have set a special market value by buying animals like sea otters, sometimes for tens of thousands of dollars; sea slugs have a value as delicacies in Japanese restaurants. Does this sound like an appropriate approach for estimating the intrinsic value of ecological losses?

To justify a different mode of valuing natural resources, Robert Costanza, among others, has argued for the concept of valuing the services produced by the world's stock of "natural capital." If his premises and figures are correct, a great deal of the world's output of goods and services is not being accounted for by traditional measures. The services of ecological systems and the natural capital stocks that produce them are critical to the functioning of the Earth's life-support system. They contribute to human welfare, both directly and indirectly, and therefore represent part of the total economic value of the planet. We have estimated the current economic value of 17 ecosystem services for 16 biomes, based on published studies and a few original calculations. For the entire biosphere, the value (most of which is outside the market) is estimated to be in the range of US$16 to $54 trillion per year, with an average of US$33 trillion per year. Because of the nature of the uncertainties, this must be considered a minimum estimate. Global gross national product total is around US$18 trillion per year.[49]

Businessman-turned-author Paul Hawken describes the concept of natural capital in more intuitive terms. He says:

> "Natural capital"...comprises the resources we use, both nonrenewable (oil, coal, metal ore) and renewable (forests, fisheries, grasslands). Although we usually think of renewable resources in terms of desired materials, such as wood, their most important value lies in the services they provide. These services are related to, but distinct from, the resources themselves. They are not pulpwood but forest cover, not food but topsoil. Living systems feed us, protect us, heal us, clean the nest, let us breathe. They are the "income" derived from a healthy environment: clean air and water, climate stabilization, rainfall, ocean productivity, fertile soil, watersheds, and the less-appreciated functions of the environment, such as processing waste — both natural and industrial. Hawken, Natural Capitalism, Mother Jones, Mar/Apr. 1997, at 40.

Where does all of this new economics lead? Critics on the right seem to think it is a smoke-and-mirrors effort to reach an ideologically preferred result by injecting unsupportable numbers into the environmental cost side of the economic analysis. Critics on the left view it even more cynically, as an effort to forestall radical change of a materialistic capitalist economy that is destined to self-destruct. See Cooper, The Myth of Capitalist Sustainability: An Answer to the New Green Economics, Socialist Organizer Rev. 7 (Fall 1997). If natural resources were considered to be a form of scarce capital and valued as such, however, it would routinely be the case that economic evaluations of actions that threatened serious environmental damage would have to be assigned larger costs than they do under present, more conventional economic standards.

4. **Ecological restoration remedies.** The shortcomings in human-based valuations, and the perplexities of awarding intrinsic value natural resources damages, propel the law increasingly toward performance-based relief — restoration or mitigation remedies.

Restoration, as an in-kind ecological remedy, represents two different rationales: first, the aim to put things back as they were before defendants' wrongdoing occurred, a

---

49. Costanza et al., The Value of the World's Ecosystem Services and Natural Capital, 387 Nature 253 (May 15, 1997). See also Costanza & Daly, Natural Capital and Sustainable Development, 6 Conservation Biology 37–46 (1992); P. Hawken et al., Natural Capitalism: Creating the Next Industrial Revolution (1999).

satisfying and understandable objective; second, to provide a performance standard as a proxy for the otherwise difficult task of valuing what has been lost. The court cuts through the riddles of natural resources valuation by ordering that the wrong be undone. If a piece of forest was wrongfully clearcut, how fitting to order soil restoration and replanting of mature trees, shrubs, and undergrowth. As with human-based restoration remedies, natural resources remediation is a way to capture widespread values within judicial relief and raise potent deterrent examples for prospective wrong-doers. Restoration presents serious questions, however, not least the definition of what restoration means.

What does Alaska's complaint mean when it demands restoration? As requested, it is clearly impossible. It is technically and economically infeasible to recapture more than about 20% of any major oil spill. Most is now lodged deep within ocean bottom sediments, traveling in solution through ocean currents, or located within the tissues of coastal and marine wildlife, the strata of coastal beaches, and so on. What would the cost of a partial restoration undertaking be, if it could be done? And might not the removal of oil, through solvents or organic methods, cause more destruction than the oil itself?

In fact, a natural restoration process begins as soon as an oil spill catastrophe occurs. Volatiles evaporate into the air and are diffused; hydrocarbons begin a very slow process of breaking down and becoming ever-more diluted components of the ecosystem. With the action of wind, waves, sun, and time, within 50 years the Gulf of Alaska is likely to be very similar to its condition prior to the oil spill (although several species may be gone). If that is the case, then what is meant by a legally mandated restoration? Various ecosystem components can indeed be added immediately by human actions: Hatcheries can be created to propagate fish, birds, even mayflies and plankton, and those efforts, although they risk a sort of suburban homogenizing of the naturally diverse gene pool, nevertheless can serve a useful function. But if one begins with the curve of natural restoration, apparently the primary rationale of legal restoration remedies is to accelerate, artificially, the rate of natural recovery, a somewhat ambiguous undertaking even if it is feasible.

Restoration can arguably be vastly more expensive than it is worthwhile, which guarantees that it will attract strong resistance. The Clean Water and Superfund Acts both provide for "the restoration or replacement of natural resources damaged or destroyed as a result of discharge of oil or a hazardous substance.... Sums recovered shall be used to restore, rehabilitate, or acquire the equivalent of such natural resources"[50] by the appropriate agencies. As issued by Secretary James Watt, however, the required regulations on natural resources remedies provided that the measure of damages should be "the *lesser* of restoration or replacement costs, or diminution of use values." The *Ohio* court struck down the regulations, declaring that "the Department of Interior erred by establishing a strong presumption in favor of market price,"[51] and emphasized the

---

50. 33 U.S.C.A. §1321(f)(4)(5), echoed in Superfund, 42 U.S.C.A. §9651(c)(2).
51. Ohio v. U.S. Dep't of Interior, 880 F.2d 432, 464 (D.C. Cir. 1989) (emphasis added).

preferability of restoration. The NOAA regulations, with more inclusive NRD accounting, have been upheld.

But cost must play some part in the balance. An army of biologists can be deployed, sopping up oil with sponges and propagating myriad tiny organisms and higher life-forms to rebuild shattered food chains; sands and mud can be imported; floating filtration plants can be installed. The costs would be astronomical, however, and the results uncertain. In a case arising from a Puerto Rican oil spill, the First Circuit had to balance the feasibility and cost of restoration against a statutory restoration mandate. Puerto Rico had asked for removal and replacement of oil-soaked bottom sediments, and replanting of thousands of poisoned mangroves, at a cost of $7 million, or alternatively an award of "replacement value" based on a biologist's estimate that 92 million creatures had been destroyed, and a guesstimate that they averaged a replacement value or cost of $.06 each, totaling $5,526,583.20. The court decided that "the appropriate primary standard for determining damages in a case such as this, is the cost reasonably to be incurred by the sovereign or its designated agency to restore or rehabilitate the environment in the affected area to its pre-existing condition, or as close thereto as is feasible without *grossly disproportionate expenditures*...with attention to such factors as technical feasibility, harmful side effects, compatibility with or duplication of such regeneration as is naturally to be expected, and the extent to which efforts beyond a certain point would become either redundant or disproportionately expensive." The court rejected the government's $7 million remedy as "impractical, inordinately expensive, and unjustifiably dangerous to the healthy mangroves and marine animals still present in the area to be restored," and the second, replacement value theory on the ground that the government was not actually proposing to replace the 92 million creatures into the contaminated bay "which, being contaminated with oil, would hardly support them...."[52] Was this a judgment based on a finding that the cost was "grossly disproportionate" or that actual restoration was infeasible in the circumstances? If restoration is feasible, how does one weigh the cost of natural resources restoration?

5. **Must restoration awards be used to restore?** If Alaska recovers $500 million in damages based on the cost of feasible restoration, could Governor Wally Hickel then take the money and use it to build roads through the wilderness, which, he said, were a more worthwhile project? His road project failed, but approximately $55 million of NRD recovery was put into a Sea Life tourist attraction. Under the law of the case, or the public trust doctrine examined in Chapter 22, it would seem that restoration awards are impressed with a trust for restorative purposes, but it is not clearly so.

6. **NRD precedents from the Alaska oil spill.** The *Exxon-Valdez* spill was a milestone event in national environmental policy debates. See J. S. Picou et al., The *Exxon Valdez* Disaster: Readings on a Modern Social Problem (1997). In NRD terms, by 1992 Exxon was told it could stop further cleanup on the beaches of Prince William Sound because it had reached a point of diminishing returns.[53] The state and federal governments

---

52. Puerto Rico v. S. S. Zoe Colocotroni, 628 F.2d 652, 676, 677 (1st Cir. 1980) (emphasis added).

53. In fact it is questionable whether from the beginning the solvents used to produce clean beaches for the visitor's eye did not do more harm than good, contaminating the microecology of the beaches far down into the substrates. Oil still remains within the subsurface layers.

negotiated a settlement agreement with Exxon for a $125 million criminal penalty, $12 million of which went to the North American Wetlands Conservation Fund, and civil penalties of $900 million to be paid over ten years into a fund administered by a state-federal Trustee Council.[54]

The Trustees' management of the $900 million *Exxon-Valdez* fund constitutes a precedent-setting NRD experiment. The governmental civil penalties were the largest NRD recovery ever. The massive Gulf of Alaska program offers a superb opportunity for comprehensive analysis of NRD remediation. Unfortunately the Trustees' program, launched by the immediacy of the spill, has not produced a clear or comprehensive analysis of the legal regime of NRD. Ensuing study is needed to analyze the full range of NRD options, methodologies, and requirements. At this point, the authority and legal obligations of the Trustees are not clear — either to the Trustees themselves or to observers. Are they trustees under the public trust doctrine generally or trustees only under authority of particular statutes? Are they subject to judicial supervision of their trusteeship upon citizen petition?[55] What are the standards that bind them? The legal history of the Alaska NRD Trusteeship will be instructive. The Trustees have undertaken extensive scientific studies of harms done to the impacted environment, potentially consuming more than half the NRD recovery. Somewhat less than half of the fund has been targeted toward mitigation and restoration expenditures noted below.

(Private litigation for economic harms from the Alaska oil spill have resulted in verdicts exceeding $5 billion, raising issues that will take a decade to be worked out in the courts. Virtually all such recoveries are for human economic losses, however, not for NRD.)

7. **Mitigation and substituted resources.** An early common law suit filed by environmentalists in the Alaska oil spill case, analogizing to CWA provisions, requested the establishment of a fund or foundation for "the acquisition of equivalent [and additional] natural resources" as an alternative remedy where restoration was ecologically or economically infeasible.[56] Is such mitigation-by-acquisition a satisfactory natural resources remedy? In effect it merely secures (as a park or reserve) existing resources that otherwise might face destruction by economic development. Does it add or replace anything beyond what existed in the aftermath of an ecological catastrophe? Anticipatory mitigation was the approach taken in Alaska's Prince William Sound. The Trustees obligated almost $500 million of oil spill NRD to buy up forests surrounding the Sound to prevent the drastic clearcutting that otherwise, laws or no laws, would have choked spawning streams with erosion and debris and altered stream flows and water quality throughout the area.

---

54. The federal trustees are the Secretaries of Agriculture, Commerce, and Interior; state trustees are the Attorney General and the Commissioners of the Alaska Department of Fish and Game and Department of Environmental Conservation. The Trustees' legal status and enforceable duties are basically unclear. 33 U.S.C. §3121(f)(5); 42 U.S.C. §9607(f); 33 U.S.C. §2706(b); Executive Order 12580, 52 Fed. Reg. 2923 (Jan. 29, 1987).

55. This question was raised in regard to whether the Trustees were a federal agency, obliged to release their post-settlement scientific studies under the Freedom of Information Act, a question that ultimately was not clearly answered.

56. National Wildlife Fed'n v. Exxon Corp., Alyeska Pipeline Serv. Co., 3 AN-89-2533 Civ. (Super. Ct. 3d Dist. Alaska 1989).

8. **Prospects.** Ultimately, natural resources remedies are not a neatly quantifiable concept, as they would be if they merely paralleled marketplace assessments. Natural resources remedies are an evolving part of the common law and have been written into statutes, so the evolution of NRD remedies, with their ambiguities and opportunities, will continue in judicial proceedings and administrative agency processes.

E. ENVIRONMENTAL USES OF OTHER NONSTATUTORY CAUSES OF ACTION

Environmental law is where you find it. The dramatic evolution of environmental tort law demonstrates the ability of the legal system to find flexible solutions for modern problems in old doctrines creatively applied and litigated. But tort law is not the only source of this adaptive legal technology. Other nonstatutory fields can be drawn into environmental law cases: trust law in the environmental public trust doctrine, property law, contract law, corporate law, and a variety of other areas of practice. This provides a reminder to modern lawyers facing the challenges of a dynamically evolving field always to scope out broad possibilities within the common law, as well as within specific statutes and regulations on point.

As one of many examples, strip-mining is a highly emotional modern controversy of the "energy v. environment" variety and a classic environmental problem in terms of overview benefit-cost accounting. The market's optimum production method in mountain terrain, "strip and augering,"[57] tends to externalize and thus ignore the serious costs it imposes on neighboring communities and the environment, unless an adequate statute is passed and enforced, which is difficult,[58] or unless plaintiffs can find a relevant nonstatutory cause of action.

Tort law, however, may not apply in this setting because in many places strip-mine companies own subsurface coal rights under "broad form deeds" and claim the right to destroy the surface to get at it:

---

57. Mountains in parts of Appalachia stand like multilayered pyramidal chocolate cakes in which coal seams one to eight feet thick lie flat, one above the other, separated by five to a hundred feet of shale and earth, covered with mountainside ecosystems. Significant amounts of coal can be gotten cheaply with dynamite and bulldozers by carving benches around the sides of the mountains atop the coal outcroppings and pushing the trees and soil "overburden" over the side, clearing the way for front-end loaders to shovel up the coal and drive it away. After an outcrop coal seam has been stripped to the high walls (the point where the overhang of the excavated slope is too unstably high to be cut further inward), and the seams have been augered-drilled sideways further into the hill to salvage as much readily reachable coal as possible, the mountain is so unstable that underground mining is impossible and 70% of a mountain's coal may be permanently unreachable thereafter, at least under today's technology. The mountain is often left a tortured moonscape, descending in ragged steps to the valley below, with sulfuric shale, runoff water, and the rubble of soil and trees sliding down the hillside, filling the valley below, poisoning the streams, covering the bottomland agricultural fields of the mountain communities that remain, and swelling seasonal floods.

58. Both state and federal governments have passed strip-mining controls. At the state level, many regulatory systems have been dominated by the industry. At the federal level, regulation under the Surface Mining Control and Reclamation Act (SMCRA) has had a similarly checkered history, being almost completely diluted during the Reagan years under Interior Secretary James Watt. To many non-Kentucky environmental lawyers, at least, common law remedies often appear to be more practical than public law. In 1974, the Kentucky legislature actually passed a statute requiring strip-mining consent by all who owned any interest in land, but the high court quickly declared it an unconstitutional taking. DNR v. No. 8 Ltd., 528 S.W.2d 684 (Ky. 1975).

[This deed] grants and conveys property, rights and privileges, in, of, to, on, under, concerning...all the coal, minerals and mineral products,...and such of the standing timber as may be by the Grantee, its successors, or assigns be deemed necessary for mining purposes.... Grantee may use and operate the same and surface thereof...in any and every manner that may be deemed necessary or convenient for mining, and therefrom removing minerals,...and in the use of said land and surface thereof by the Grantee, his heirs, successors and assigns, shall be free from, and are, hereby released from liability or claim of damage to the said Grantor, their representatives, heirs and assigns.... There is reserved to the Grantor all the timber upon the said land, except that necessary for mining, and the free use of land for agricultural purposes, so far as such use is consistent with the property, rights and privileges hereby bargained, sold, granted or conveyed to Grantee.[59]

Attempts to assert tort law protections in the face of this deed raise basic questions of contract and deed interpretation — what was conveyed by the document?

The only feasible and economical way to mine the coal in question is by the strip and auger method of mining.... Appellant contends that since all of the coal was conveyed it may be mined by any method, and the appellees' surface rights are subordinate to the rights of the appellant.... The deed by express language did not exclude or include this method of mining, and the proof shows that such mining methods were known and had been used prior to the date of the deed. It seems clear that the parties intended the conveyance of the coal. To deny the right to remove it by the only feasible method is to defeat the principal purpose of the deed....

Two fundamental rules for construction of deeds [govern]: that a deed which grants land and certain specific rights and privileges, there being no ambiguity in the instrument, will be construed according to its terms, and enforced strictly according to its terms, and where there is ambiguity or uncertainty in the deed, it will be construed most strongly against the grantor and in favor of the grantee.... Buchanan v. Watson, 290 S.W.2d at 40.

Here is the contrary argument, also based on contract and deed interpretation grounds:

There has been a long line of cases holding that grantees under "broad form" deeds have a right to use the surface for any purpose "deemed necessary or convenient" by the grantee. However, all those cases involved deep-mining methods, which was the method of mining contemplated by the parties in 1905. Even where a drastic technology was in theory known to exist on the date of execution of a lease, courts should be guided by the implied intention of the parties that minerals should be extracted in the customary manner that prevailed when the lease was executed. The parties to this deed had not contemplated the strip and auger method of mining nor did they contemplate that any portion of the surface of the land would be destroyed or rendered valueless for agricultural purposes or growing timber. Modern courts moreover should not ignore and disregard the rights of the surface owner. Many courts have held that the owner of the coal must leave pillars of coal to support the surface. To permit stripmining in many of these areas would be to allow the dominant estate to destroy the servient estate completely, and that

---

59. From a fee simple coal deed in Buchanan v. Watson, 290 S.W.2d 40 (Ky. 1956), dated May 19, 1903, from Miles Cole and wife to a land company agent, covering 129.47 acres of land in Magoffin County, for less than $3 per acre; similar language exists in some mineral easements and leases.

ZBP

FIGURE 3-2

A stripmine in the Cumberland Mountains near the Kentucky-Tennessee border. Note the results of the primitive blast and scrape method, and its consequences in erosion, mudslides, and disruption of natural water flows. Photograph is taken from the unstable edge of an excavated seam higher up on the mountain. When trees start to lean, it means that the surface of the mountain is beginning to "creep" or slide. Mines on the mountains in the distance extract coal from the same horizontal seams.

diabolical devastation and destruction could not have been the parties' intent or understanding.[60]

COMMENTARY & QUESTIONS

1. **Interpretation of strip-mine broad form deeds.** In applying the canons of interpretation against the grantor of a broad form deed, should courts consider the fact that most such deeds were prepared by *grantees* and that many grantors signed with an X? If the terms of a document are clear, to what extent should courts look to the intention of the parties, given that in the statutory interpretation setting, the clear words govern? Does the subdivision of a parcel of land into two separate estates, surface and subsurface, necessarily imply that a party who owns just one estate cannot destroy the existence of the other? What do you make of the fact that many original subsurface deeds were purchased for $3 an acre, which was often more than the full assessed value of a full fee simple?

2. **The broad reach of private land controls.** Looking beyond review of deeds, note that other private land use concepts — restrictive covenants, conservation easements, and other private land interests — can be given strong environmental applications, incorporating whatever terms and values the private parties want, far beyond the range of governmental regulations. Private land controls can create nonprofit wildlife preserves perpetually excluded from development, dictating the kinds of trees to be maintained, the preservation of buildings; control of developments' style, density, and appearance; the total nondevelopment of some developable areas, and so on. There is no clear legal basis, however, upon which to distinguish desirable private land use planning and controls from capricious restraints on future use of scarce resources.

3. **Prescriptive easements.** "Easements by prescription" can be acquired by using land without permission for a statutory term (typically 5 to 10 years), paralleling doctrines of squatters' rights to title in adverse possession of land. In some cases, prescriptive easements can be used affirmatively to assert environmental rights, as in establishing public rights of access to beaches. In other cases they can set up environmental challenges: A "right to dump" can be an easement, so some polluters have claimed an "easement to pollute" particular streams into which they have discharged waste over the years, thus claiming immunity from private nuisance suits. In the absence of a statute, how do private plaintiffs overcome such polluters' "right to dump"? Prescriptive easements usually are defined fairly strictly in terms of the quantity and quality of use established over the prescriptive term, and squatters' rights are generally not recognized where they are in competition with public rights. See Anneberg v. Kurtz, 28 S.E.2d 769, 773 (Ga. 1944).

4. **Equitable restrictions.** On Shady Mountain in Tennessee, a land developer from Chattanooga had sold ten lots to families who moved in and, pursuant to covenants in

---

60. This argument is paraphrased from Judge Hill's opinion in Martin v. Kentucky Oak Mining Co., 429 S.W.2d 395 (Ky. 1968), a dissent (but reflecting majority holdings in all strip-mining states except Kentucky). The attorney for appellants in *Martin* was the late Harry Caudill, who wrote Night Comes to the Cumberlands (1963) and three other anguishing chronicles of Appalachia and strip-mining.

their deeds, built single-family homes. Thereafter she stopped sales for a while, and later leased lots #11–18 to a coal strip-mining company that had just moved onto the land and was ready to bulldoze and blast. The government control agencies provided no effective constraint on the strip-mining. Some activist law students stopped the strip-mine operation for the families by a property law action based on a negative reciprocal covenant (sometimes confusingly called an "equitable servitude"). When a seller subdivides lots and begins to sell them with a similar or uniform set of restrictions, there is an enforceable implied equitable promise that all lots will similarly be held to the earlier restrictions.

5. **Toxic breach of implied warranty of title.** What happens if a buyer discovers toxic contaminants on the land between the day the contract to purchase was made and the date set for the transfer of title? The law creates an implied warranty that sellers will provide good marketable title at the closing. Will the mere presence of toxics on the land create a "cloud on the title" allowing purchasers to rescind contracts based upon violation of the warranty? The consequences of such a rule would be drastic. Because it would threaten marketability of any affected parcel, it would practically compel environmental assessment audits of all major land purchases. It is not yet clear how pollution per se affects the implied warranty of marketable title (unless the government has slapped a lien on the title). Should buyers be able to rescind in such cases? Note that, having notice, they probably could not claim the "innocent landowner" exception from Superfund liability. (In practice, most residential contracts are made contingent on buyers obtaining financing, so all the buyer has to do in such cases is tell the bank about the chemicals and her financing will be withdrawn, triggering the contract release clause.)

6. **Breach of warranty — products liability.** The Uniform Commercial Code's §2-314, the implied warranty of merchantability warranting that products are fit for ordinary use, also has a potential use in environmental cases. Strangely enough, in the Allied Kepone case studied earlier in this chapter, it was reportedly the products liability cause of action that was most successful in the pretrial process that led to damage settlements. Using warranty theories and strict tort liability defective products cases, plaintiffs have sought remedies for harms from formaldehyde insulation pollution inside mobile homes, for radiation effects from products using radium, for the deleterious effects of cigarettes, and for other environmental situations, with varying results. Brummett v. Skyline Corp., No. C-81-0103-L(B), slip op. (W.D. Ky. June 3, 1985) (formaldehyde); Allen v. U.S. Radium Corp., No. L-013851-84, slip op. (N.J. Super. 1984) (radium radiation); Cipollone v. Liggett Group, Inc., 505 U.S. 504 (1992) (cigarettes, action based on claim of express warranty); Wingo v. Celotex Corp., 834 F.2d 375 (4th Cir. 1987) (asbestos). In other cases, express warranty claims are possible where manufacturers have incorrectly alleged that products are safe or environmentally benign. Contract-based warranty actions, with their opportunity for consequential damages under UCC §2-714, in some cases may offer advantages over tort theories, advantages that are worth exploring.

7. **Environmental breach of federal contract.** Most government-supply contracts made by corporations — and these run into the billions of dollars each year — contain

a standard clause agreeing that suppliers will comply with all relevant statutes and regulations, including environmental protection laws. When a supplier is discovered in violation of such laws, there are potential remedies for breach of contract and misrepresentation. These remedies gain special impetus from the fact that citizens are granted standing under the Federal False Claims Act, 31 U.S.C. §3729, to bring such actions even if the official parties aren't interested in doing so; treble damages are available, with a 25% bounty thereof payable to the individual plaintiffs. Does this bear further investigation?

8. **Other horizons for environmental law.** There are undoubtedly dozens of other situations in which environmental issues can be raised using statutory or nonstatutory legal doctrines drawn from areas of modern practice that have rarely or never before been so applied — from labor, tax, equity, antitrust, public utilities, consumer protection, banking, admiralty, and so on, as well as corporate law, property, trusts, and contract.

The point is, environmental law is where you find it.

They were careless people.... They smashed up things and creatures and then retreated back into their money or their vast carelessness...and let other people clean up the mess they had made....

— F. Scott Fitzgerald, The Great Gatsby (1925)

Of all possible worlds, we only got one.
We gotta ride it
Whatever we've done,
We'll never get far from what we leave behind.
Baby, we can run, run, run, but we can't hide....

— The Grateful Dead
We Can Run
(IceNine Publishing Co., Inc., 1989)

Chapter 4

THE SPECIAL CHALLENGES OF TOXIC TORT LITIGATION

A. *Remedies for Victims of Toxic Contamination*
B. *Proof of Complex Causation*
C. *Law and Science in the Toxic Tort Context*
D. *Litigating Toxic Tort Cases*
E. *Relationships Between Toxic Tort and Public Law*

A. REMEDIES FOR VICTIMS OF TOXIC CONTAMINATION

Nowhere is the continued vitality, flexibility, and relevance of the common law more evident in modern environmental law than in the raucous field of toxic torts. The case reporters reflect this active field, as do the increasing numbers of law schools that offer specialized toxic tort courses.

Toxic tort case settings may be as localized as a single grease pit in a rural junkyard, or as regional or even nationwide in scope as asbestos exposure litigation. The mass tort exposure cases present especially complex legal issues in establishing environmental liability, including fiendishly complex issues of civil procedure, but even smaller scale toxic exposure cases present challenging scientific and litigation issues. Potentially devastating harms to human health are the primary focus of toxic torts. In a modern world containing so many different exposures to so many different kinds of risk, voluntary as well as involuntary, common law toxics cases often face a virtual impossibility in proving that a particular harm was caused by a particular exposure. Proof of causation is difficult not only because of the attenuated pathways by which toxics may travel and combine in a course of exposure, but also by the long-term latencies of environmental illnesses. A chemical may accumulate or lie latent in human bodies over decades before its serious or fatal effects are revealed. The character of toxic threats — typically moving unseen and almost undetectably, occurring almost anywhere, and potentially so harmful — has created energetic social reactions against toxic contaminations.

Given the nature of the modern technological marketplace, toxic exposures present a dilemma. Chemicals, including very powerful compounds, are woven into the fabric of our production and consumption economy. Virtually the entire population is exposed to a lifelong interacting mélange of at least small amounts of potentially harmful compounds (and some harmless compounds that become harmful when synergistically combined). Avoiding exposures is impossible. Remedying the horrors of some exposures is impossible. The amounts in damages that could be assessed against the industries that generated toxins over the past 50 years, if ever the "true" causes of all exposure illnesses could be proved, would be astronomical.

Some assert that the issue of toxic exposures is a fundamental problem of modern societal governance that should be handled by public law processes, not by common law tort.[1] Until the legislatures discover a scientifically, politically, and constitutionally feasible regime to take over the field, however, people who believe they have been or will be harmed by particular toxic events will continue to plunk down their filing fees in court, putting the force of the common law, evolving over seven centuries, to work on toxic torts.

Section 1. LESSONS FROM THE WOBURN TOXICS CIVIL ACTION

To introduce the array of elements in modern toxic tort law, this chapter opens with the Woburn toxics case, a noted case of toxic contamination of groundwater. The following account, written by the plaintiffs' attorney, gives one view of Anderson v. W. R. Grace Co. and Beatrice Foods,[2] and conveys a sense of some of the tasks facing plaintiffs trying to prove causation in complex toxics cases. Many readers will have encountered the story in much greater detail in Jonathan Harr's bestselling book, A Civil Action (1995), and the movie made from it. The elaborate civil procedure history of the case can be traced in Lewis Grossman and Robert Vaughan, A Civil Action: A Civil Procedure Supplement (1999).

Jan Schlichtmann, Eight Families Sue W. R. Grace and Beatrice Foods for Poisoning City Wells with Solvents, Causing Leukemia, Disease, and Death (1987)

The Woburn case began with a mother's horror that her child had leukemia. Anne Anderson had moved to Woburn, Massachusetts, a small city 13 miles north of Boston, with her husband and daughter in 1965. Over the next few years she gave birth to two more children. Although all of the children seemed to have more than their fair share of colds, sore throats, and infections, James, the youngest, seemed to get sick more than the others and recovered slower. In the winter of 1971, when Jimmy did not get over the latest round of flu, the family doctor referred Ms. Anderson to a specialist at Massachusetts General Hospital in Boston. The specialist told Anne that Jimmy had cancer in his bone marrow. Treatment would be long and painful.

Anne Anderson's distress soon gave way to the realization that she was not the only mother in Woburn with a child suffering from leukemia. There were other Woburn mothers who sat quietly in the waiting room at Massachusetts General while their children received chemotherapy — women and children from her neighborhood, whose homes were a block or two from her own.... In May, 1979, two of the city wells were found to be contaminated with toxic industrial

---

1. See Huber, Safety and the Second Best: The Hazards of Public Risk Management in the Courts, excerpted in this chapter's Part E, cited by advocates for "tort reform" arguments seeking to limit the litigatibilty of personal injury cases.

2. Anderson v. W. R. Grace, U.S.D.C. Mass. C.A. No. 82-1672-S (May 1982); Anderson v. W. R. Grace, 628 F. Supp. 1219 (D.C. Mass. 1986) (summary judgment rulings); Anderson v. Cryovac, Inc., 805 F.2d 1 (1st Cir. 1986) (gag order reversed); Anderson v. Beatrice Foods Co., 862 F.2d 910 (1st Cir. 1988); Anderson v. Beatrice Foods Co., 127 F.R.D. 1 (D. Mass. July 1989) and 129 F.R.D. 394 (D. Mass. Dec. 1989); Anderson v. Beatrice Foods Co., 900 F.2d 388 (1st Cir. 1990), cert. denied, 498 U.S. 891 (1990).

The narrative is drawn from an article in ATLA Report: The Woburn Case: Stricken Families Take On a Chemical Giant and Win (Sept. 1987).

(Disclosure notice: one of this casebook's authors and his students worked with plaintiffs on the case.)

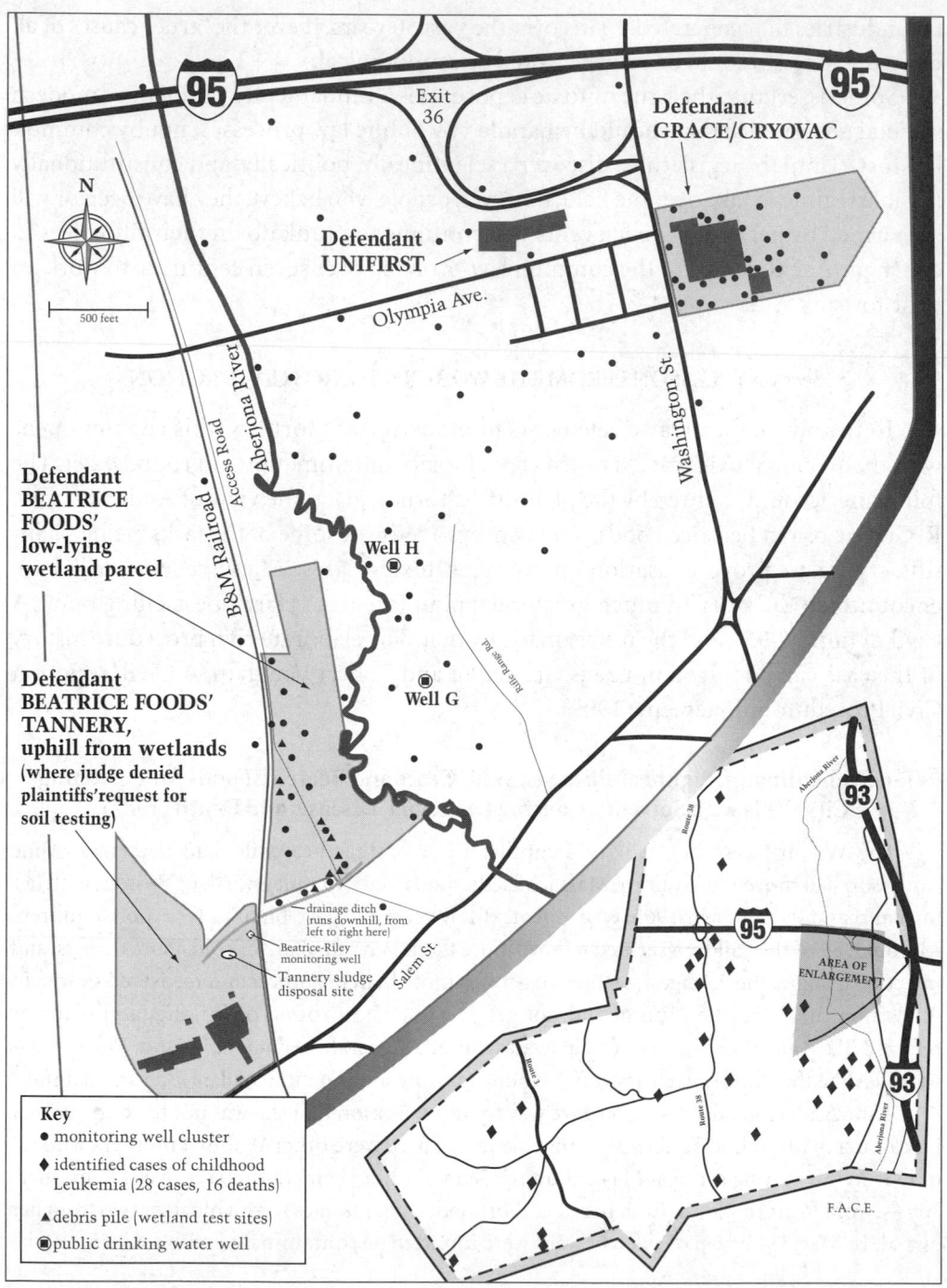

FIGURE 4-1

SMALL OVERVIEW MAP shows the area in Woburn, Massachusetts, served by Wells G & H, and the 28 identified childhood leukemia cases (16 fatal) that occurred there between the time the wells were opened in 1964 and the time of trial. The blow-up ENLARGED MAP AREA shows the properties involved in the lawsuit, Wells G & H, with defendant Grace Cryovac on an upward slope to the northeast of the wells, defendant Beatrice's tannery atop a rise to the southwest, from which a ditch leads downward to the low-lying wetland parcel that was filled with contaminants, and the Aberjona River, a creek winding through the middle of the area.

solvents, including trichloroethylene (TCE) and tetrachloroethylene, suspected carcinogens....
The Center for Disease Control (CDC) and the Massachusetts Department of Public Health
confirmed that the children in Woburn were coming down with leukemia at a rate significantly
higher than would be expected. Within a six block radius of the Anderson home there were
seven other children with leukemia. Many other cases were also documented throughout the
East Woburn community. But the health agencies couldn't say if the contaminated well water
had anything to do with the leukemia in the neighborhood. The EPA and the state environmental agency confirmed that the aquifer feeding the two contaminated city wells was heavily
polluted with industrial solvents but could not say from whose property the contamination was
coming or when the wells had become contaminated.

With the help of a local minister, Ms. Anderson organized members of the community into
a vocal and active citizens' environmental group, For A Cleaner Environment (FACE), to monitor and prod the governmental agencies. Jimmy's death in January, 1981, strengthened her
resolve. She and seven other families hired a tort lawyer.

A review of the work done by the governmental agencies up through 1981 made it clear that
evidence for the case would in large measure have to be obtained by the plaintiffs themselves. In
March, 1982, the EPA issued its report regarding the contamination of the aquifer. It drew no
conclusions concerning the sources of the well contamination. The CDC and State Department
of Health were still unsure of the next step to take.

The EPA field data available as of March, 1982, was reviewed by Robert Harris, a professor
of chemical engineering, who concluded that the likely sources of the well contamination were
the properties of the W. R. Grace Company, twenty-four hundred feet northeast, and a tannery
owned by Beatrice Foods, six hundred feet west of the contaminated wells. In May, 1982, suit
was filed against Grace and Beatrice on behalf of the eight families. In seven of the families a
child had contracted leukemia. Five of those children had died from the disease. In one family an
adult suffered from the disease.

The filing of suit received intense public and media attention. The defendants, especially
Grace, responded by publicly denouncing the suit as baseless. They denied that their plant in
Woburn used the chemicals, or that it could have contributed to the contamination.

In response to the plaintiffs' interrogatories as to chemical use and disposal, Grace moved
to dismiss.... Grace contended that plaintiffs' attorneys had no good faith basis to assert that
Grace used the chemicals found in the wells, that it disposed of them so as to contaminate the
aquifer, or that the chemicals could cause leukemia. The proceedings over Grace's unsuccessful
Rule 11[3] motion to dismiss consumed the entire first year of litigation.

Thereafter, in February, 1983, Grace was forced to answer plaintiffs' interrogatories. In its
answers, Grace admitted that it had used the same type of chemicals found in the wells, and had
disposed of "small quantities" of the chemicals on the ground to the rear of the plant building, as
well as burying several drums in a pit. The grudging revelations by Grace of its chemical use and
disposal practices sharply contrasted with information Grace had previously provided the EPA
during that agency's investigation the year before. The EPA subsequently ordered Grace,
Beatrice, and another company, Unifirst, to conduct on-site investigations of their properties to
determine if their properties were contributing to the pollution of the aquifer. EPA lethargy over
the next two years, however, prompted plaintiffs to conduct their own on-site investigations.

In January, 1984, a year after Grace was ordered to investigate its property and after its
consultant's report documented contamination at the site, Grace moved for summary judgment

---

3. Since its original promulgation, FRCP Rule 11 has provided for the striking of pleadings and the imposition of
disciplinary sanctions on the attorney, the client, or both to check abuses in pleadings and litigation.

on the basis that plaintiffs could not prove that the contaminated water caused the children's leukemia. In support of its motion, Grace submitted the affidavits of two hematologists, Drs. Maloney and Jandl, who asserted that there was no scientific basis for an opinion that the chemicals found in the contaminated wells could cause leukemia.

In the fall of 1983, plaintiffs had retained Dr. Allen S. Levin, an immuno-pathologist, who had a great deal of clinical experience treating people exposed to toxic substances. Dr. Levin was very knowledgeable regarding the effects of toxic exposure on the body's immune system. The plaintiffs' medical records, which had been systematically collected, were reviewed by Dr. Levin. In addition, he ordered blood tests of the surviving family members which were conducted at the Massachusetts General Hospital immuno-pathology lab. The review of the families' medical records revealed a pattern of infection, skin disorders, gastrointestinal problems, genito-urinary problems, and cardiac problems as well as cancer. The blood tests which looked at the absolute numbers and ratios of "T-cells," which are the specialized cells of the immune system, demonstrated striking abnormalities in many of the family members. Also, Harvard scientists examining health survey data from Woburn had concluded that there was an association between certain childhood disorders including leukemia and availability of water from the contaminated wells. This marked the first time that such an association had been shown.[4]

In his affidavit opposing summary judgment, Dr. Levin outlined the scientific methodology he followed in concluding that exposure to the contaminated water caused leukemia in the families. In so doing, he illustrated how a clinician makes use of epidemiological data, like the Harvard health study, not to prove causation in an individual case, but in conjunction with clinical data, history, examination and tests, to assist in forming opinions as to the likely etiology of a patient's disease.

Levin began by discussing the scientific knowledge regarding the capacity of the solvents found in the water to harm the building blocks of the body's cells, DNA and its constituents, making them potentially cancerous. He outlined how solvent exposure can damage the immune system, the role of which is to remove these cancerous elements. By both creating opportunities for cancer and awakening the body's ability to remove it, he explained how solvent exposure can increase a host's susceptibility to cancer. Further, Dr. Levin pointed to scientific studies of animals and human populations showing a statistical relation between solvent exposure and cancer. After establishing the toxic nature of the chemicals, and the mechanism of harm, Dr. Levin turned his attention to the Woburn population exposed to the solvent-contaminated water. The government health studies done in Woburn showed that the community was suffering from an increased incidence of childhood leukemia. The Harvard health study demonstrated that this increased incidence of leukemia and other childhood disorders was associated with exposure to the contaminated water. Their relationship indicated that exposure to the contaminated well water had affected the population's ability to fight disease and cancer. Finally, Dr. Levin discussed the medical histories and test results of individual family members. The histories were consistent with people suffering from chemical exposure, and the blood tests demonstrated that this group of people had been resisting a carcinogen on a chronic basis. For these reasons he concluded that in all probability the exposure to the solvents in the water "substantially contributed" to the family members succumbing to leukemia.

Plaintiffs argued that to overcome Grace's motion for summary judgment it was their burden merely to show that there was factual dispute on the issue of causation. The court's role

---

4. This Harvard study was the fortuitous product of a student-faculty field project at the Harvard School of Public Health, launched when students looking for a fieldwork opportunity heard an informal presentation by several mothers and Schlichtmann. To have paid for the massive door-to-door survey would have been impossible for plaintiffs. [Eds.]

was not to determine which expert's opinion was more persuasive, but rather whether reasonable experts could disagree about whether the exposure to the contaminated water caused the plaintiffs' leukemias. If the court was satisfied that the expert's conclusion regarding the etiology of plaintiffs' disease was based on sound scientific methodology and principles, then the expert's conclusion, even if considered controversial, was sufficient to sustain plaintiffs' burden. The court in a brief opinion determined that the issue of medical causation as to leukemia was "hotly contested" and denied the defendant's motion for summary judgment in an unpublished opinion, July, 1984.

Over the next year and a half plaintiffs' medical condition was extensively examined. In an effort to establish a basis for proving a connection between exposure to the water and leukemia, the impact of toxic exposure on the health of the surviving plaintiffs was brought into sharper focus. The theory of cancer causation based on the toxic effects of the solvents on the body's immune system led to the examination of other organ systems which were known to be affected by solvents, namely the nerves and heart. Complete health histories, examinations, and tests were performed by experts in immunology and internal medicine to establish the overall health and condition of the plaintiffs, and to rule out other causes for their health problems. The plaintiffs were also extensively examined by experts in neurology, neuropsychology, and cardiology. The detailed testing in these specialties provided objective evidence that the surviving plaintiffs had indeed suffered significant damage to these organ systems. In addition, psychiatric examination revealed the interplay between the impact of the exposure on the body and the knowledge of it on the mind.

Because a domestic population had never before been examined and tested so extensively to determine the effects of exposure to solvents contaminating a drinking water supply, the unique findings of the clinicians studying the Woburn population was further supplemented and supported by work of scientists in toxicology, genetics, and epidemiology. The scientific effort included the establishment for the first time of control groups and scientific benchmarks for study of populations exposed to contaminated drinking water....

COMMENTARY & QUESTIONS

1. **Woburn background notes.** The contamination of Wells G & H originally was discovered by happenstance. In May 1979, a midnight dumper dropped leaking barrels of waste along the B&M railroad access road, which scared city officials into testing the wells, at which point they found the four contaminants (none of which had been in the dumped barrels). The case probably never would have been a lawsuit, only a low-profile long-term government cleanup case, had it not been for the extraordinary organizing efforts of the mothers of the affected children. They begged and dragooned Schlichtmann into taking the case against the advice of his colleagues, and suit was filed in May 1982. Schlichtmann was a charismatic young attorney with tactical plans and enthusiasm for litigative battling far beyond his limited resources. Harr's book chronicles the lawsuit's wing-and-a-prayer character, sometimes evident in contingent fee toxic tort cases. Defendants Grace and Beatrice appear to have been surprised by the allegations. Grace's dumping apparently had been done by low-level workers for casual convenience. Beatrice Foods had bought the tannery parcels after most of the dumping had occurred, apparently while the tannery was a small local operation owned by John Riley. Defendants had virtually unlimited resources and, as Harr's book shows, superb attorneys.

2. **Causes of action.** Remarkably little mention is made here or anywhere of the causes of action in the Woburn case. The case's theories of liability were personal injury and public and private nuisance based on negligence, intentional tort, and strict liability. The judge did not distinguish clearly between these theories, usually treating the liability claims in negligence terms. This set up two important legal problems not treated in the Harr book. First was the question of foreseeability under the negligence or intentional culpability theories. The judge was surprised to learn that groundwater could travel under a creek to get from the tannery to the wells, and so he made negligence-style rulings on grounds of unforeseeability. He said Beatrice could not be held liable for contamination that left the tannery property prior to the date that engineering reports of the flow to the wells were received.[5] Shouldn't any dumper know, however, that it is extremely likely that toxics dumped on the ground will go downward, enter the groundwater, and travel along with the groundwater thence to some public well? Whether the underground toxic plume ultimately moves toward Wells G, H, or some other well does not materially change the character of defendants' acts.

If the strict liability theory had been examined, it raises an interesting question in relation to the tannery. Since it was hard to prove the tannery's own dumping, plaintiffs tried to base their claim on the tannery's ownership of the low-lying parcel where a great deal of toxics had been discharged "by persons unknown." Assuming that toxics in the ground are abnormally dangerous, can owners who know of the toxics but cannot be proved to have dumped them or played any other active role nevertheless be held strictly liable for the results of the hazards?[6] Strict liability is frequently the basis of toxic tort litigation, but intentional tort causes of action also are often effective in these cases.

One recent defense-oriented article began with the following introduction:

> The sphere of injuries for which plaintiffs may seek compensation in toxic tort cases is, it seems, bounded only by the ingenuity of counsel and by the human capacity to feel wronged.... To meet these more exotic toxic injury claims, the defense counsel in toxic tort cases must counter ingenious allegations with equally ingenious defenses.[7]

Toxic tort cases present special problems in the scope of liability for damages, including unique claims based on increased risk of contracting an exposure-induced disease, seeking present compensation for future damages that may or may not come to pass. In many cases, as in Anderson v. W. R. Grace, plaintiffs also make claims for fear and emotional distress in the toxic tort setting.

These are hotly contested issues. The stakes are high. Toxic exposures often create mass torts. Potential damages are multiplied by a potentially large number of victims. The

---

5. This ultimately meant that the jury did not have enough specific evidence of groundwater flow within the narrowed time window to find liability. The unreported ruling was made under Restatement (Second) §435(2), discussed below.

6. In some public law statutes, there is an "innocent landowner" or "act of third party" defense, but the common law may allow passive strict liability. In the Woburn case, the plaintiffs found an old Massachusetts case holding that a defendant who owned a stone-walled house that burned out and who passively left it standing there was strictly liable when later the walls toppled on a passerby. That case, however, seems to have based its "strict" liability on an act of omission based on a duty to warn or duty to mitigate, both of which sound in negligence.

7. Pagliaro & Lynch, No Pain, No Gain: Current Trends in Determining Compensable Injury in Toxic Tort Cases, 4 BNA Toxics L. Rep. 271 (1989).

types of damage in dispute are significant items such as increased medical expenses and damages caused by catastrophic diseases. Many of the losses are either uninsured or uninsurable and become major unexpected costs for whoever ends up bearing them. The intensity with which the cases are litigated, coupled with the fact that plaintiffs have been pressing for novel extensions of tort liability, has led to friction between lawyers representing plaintiffs and those representing defendants.

In the Woburn case, a typically broad array of claims for damages was made, although the damages issue was never finally adjudicated. Below is one preliminary skirmish, testing the availability of various emotional distress and risk-of-future-illness damage theories.

Anderson v. W. R. Grace & Co., Beatrice Foods Co., et al.
United States District Court for the District of Massachusetts, 1986
628 F. Supp. 1219

MEMORANDUM AND ORDER ON DEFENDANTS' JOINT MOTION FOR PARTIAL SUMMARY JUDGMENT

SKINNER, D.J. This case arises out of the defendants' alleged contamination of the groundwater in certain areas of Woburn, Massachusetts, with chemicals, including trichloroethylene and tetrachloroethylene. Plaintiffs allege that two of Woburn's water wells, Wells G and H, drew upon the contaminated water until the wells were closed in 1979 and that exposure to this contaminated water caused them to suffer severe injuries.

Of the 33 plaintiffs in this action, five are the administrators of minors who died of leukemia allegedly caused by exposure to the chemicals. They bring suit for wrongful death and conscious pain and suffering. Sixteen of the 28 living plaintiffs are members of the decedents' immediate families. These plaintiffs seek to recover for the emotional distress caused by witnessing the decedents' deaths. Three of the living plaintiffs also contracted leukemia and currently are either in remission or treatment for the disease. The 25 non-leukemic plaintiffs allege that exposure to the contaminated water caused a variety of illnesses and damaged their bodily systems. All of the living plaintiffs seek to recover for their illnesses and other damage, increased risk of developing future illness, and emotional distress.... W. R. Grace & Co. and Beatrice Foods Co. (collectively "defendants"), have jointly moved for partial summary judgment on...plaintiffs' claims [of emotional distress and risk of future illness]....

Claims for Emotional Distress... Defendants move for summary judgment on plaintiffs' claims of emotional distress on the grounds that the non-leukemic plaintiffs' distress was not caused by any physical injury. They also move for summary judgment on the emotional distress claims of plaintiffs who witnessed a family member die of leukemia, arguing that Massachusetts law does not recognize such a claim....

(1) Physical Injury... In seeking summary judgment on the non-leukemic plaintiffs' claims for emotional distress, defendants rely on Payton v. Abbott Labs, 437 N.E.2d 171 (Mass. 1982). In *Payton*, the Supreme Judicial Court answered a certified question as follows:

> In order for...plaintiffs to recover for negligently inflicted emotional distress, [they] must allege and prove [they] suffered physical harm as a result of the conduct which caused the emotional distress. We answer, further, that a plaintiff's physical harm must either cause or be caused by the emotional distress alleged, and that the physical harm must be manifested by objective symptomatology and substantiated by expert medical testimony. (437 N.E.2d at 181.)

Defendants attack plaintiffs' claims of emotional distress at three points: they argue that plaintiffs did not suffer physical harm as a result of defendants' allegedly negligent conduct; that, if the plaintiffs did suffer any harm, it was not "manifested by objective symptomatology"; and that any manifest physical harm did not cause the claimed emotional distress....

Each plaintiff states that exposure to contaminants in the water drawn from Wells G and H "affected my body's ability to fight disease, [and] caused harm to my body's organ systems, including my respiratory, immunological, blood, central nervous, gastro-intestinal, urinary-renal systems...." This alleged harm is sufficient to maintain plaintiffs' claims for emotional distress under *Payton*. As used in that opinion, the term "physical harm" denotes "harm to the bodies of the plaintiffs." 437 N.E.2d at 175 n. 4. In requiring physical harm rather than mere "injury" as an element of proof in a claim for emotional distress, the court required that a plaintiff show some actual physical damage as a predicate to suit.

Defendants argue that plaintiffs' alleged harm is "subcellular" and therefore not the type of harm required to support a claim for emotional distress under *Payton*. I disagree. The Supreme Judicial Court requires that plaintiffs' physical harm be "manifested by objective symptomatology and substantiated by expert medical testimony." 437 N.E.2d at 181. In setting forth this requirement, the court did not distinguish between gross and subcellular harm. Instead, the court drew a line between harm which can be proven to exist through expert medical testimony based on objective evidence and harm which is merely speculative or based solely on a plaintiff's unsupported assertions. Upon review of the pleadings and the affidavits of plaintiffs' expert, I cannot say as a matter of law that this standard will not be met at trial.

The alleged damages to plaintiffs' bodily systems is manifested by the many ailments which plaintiffs claim to have suffered as a result of exposure to the contaminated water. Dr. Levin apparently will testify to the existence of changes in plaintiffs' bodies caused by exposure to the contaminated water. He will base his testimony on objective evidence of these changes, including the maladies listed.... Dr. Levin explicitly states that the changes in plaintiffs' systems have "produced illnesses related to these systems." Although the affidavit does not specifically identify the illnesses suffered by each plaintiff as a result of the changes, nor state that plaintiffs suffered more ailments than the average person would have over the same time span, it is sufficient evidence of harm to support the existence of a factual dispute and bar summary judgment.

Under *Payton*, of course, injury is not sufficient. The harm allegedly caused by defendants' conduct must either have caused or been caused by the emotional distress.... However, certain elements of plaintiffs' emotional distress stem from the physical harm to their immune systems allegedly caused by defendants' conduct and [these] are compensable. Plaintiffs have stated that the illnesses contributed to by exposure to the contaminated water have caused them anxiety and pain. The excerpts from plaintiffs' depositions appended to defendants' motion indicate that plaintiffs are also worried over the increased susceptibility to disease which results from the alleged harm to their immune systems and exposure to carcinogens. As these elements of emotional distress arise out of plaintiffs' injuries, plaintiffs may seek to recover for them.

Defendants contend that plaintiffs' physical harm did not "cause" plaintiffs' distress over their increased susceptibility to disease. They argue that the fear arose out of discussions between plaintiffs and their expert witness, Dr. Levin, in which the expert informed plaintiffs of their suppressed immune systems. Assuming, as I must for purposes of the motion, that Dr. Levin is telling the truth, this argument is frivolous.

Plaintiffs can recover "only for that degree of emotional distress which a reasonable person normally would have experienced under [the] circumstances." 437 N.E.2d at 181. The Supreme Judicial Court has explicitly stated that the reasonableness of a claim for emotional distress is to be determined by the trier of fact. Accordingly, defendants' motion for summary judgment on the non-leukemic plaintiffs' claims for emotional distress is denied.

(2) Witnessing Death of a Family Member... The second issue raised by defendants' motions is whether Massachusetts recognizes a claim for emotional distress for witnessing a family member die of a disease allegedly caused by defendants' conduct. This differs from the question considered in the preceding section because the concern now is whether the plaintiffs can recover for distress caused by witnessing the injuries of others, not by their own condition. The plaintiffs do not claim any physical harm resulted from this emotional distress.

The plaintiffs proceed on alternative theories: (1) that they were in the "zone of danger," Restatement 2d of Torts §313(2), and (2) that they themselves were the victims of an "impact" from the same tortious conduct that caused the death of the children.... The Supreme Judicial Court has [held that] damages may be recovered for emotional distress over injury to a child or spouse when the plaintiff suffers contemporaneous physical injury from the same tortious conduct that caused the injury to the close relative. Cimino v. Milford Keg, Inc., 431 N.E.2d 920, 927 (Mass. 1982)....

Plaintiffs would be entitled to go forward on the basis of *Cimino*, if it were not for three further prudential limitations on recovery of a bystander for emotional distress resulting from injuries to another. These are the requirements of physical proximity to the accident, temporal proximity to the negligent act, and familial proximity to the victim. The plaintiffs in this case were present during the illness and death of the children, and at least 16 of them... are immediate family members of the decedents, but they do not meet the [temporal proximity] test....

For emotional distress to be compensable under Massachusetts law...the distress must result from immediate apprehension of the defendant's negligence or its consequences. In each of the cases in which recovery for the emotional distress of a bystander has been allowed, there has been a dramatic traumatic shock causing immediate emotional distress. Such is not the case here. There is no indication in the Massachusetts cases that liability would be extended to a family member's emotional distress which built over time during the prolonged illness of a child.

Imposition of liability in that case, while logically indistinguishable from the trauma situation, would violate the Massachusetts court's demonstrated prudential inclination to keep the scope of liability within manageable bounds....

Claims for Increased Risk of Future Illness... Plaintiffs seek to recover damages for the increased risk of serious illness they claim resulted from consumption of and exposure to contaminated water.... In Massachusetts,

> a plaintiff is entitled to compensation for all damages that reasonably are to be expected to follow, but not to those that possibly may follow, the injury which he has suffered. He is not restricted to compensation for suffering and expense which by a fair preponderance of the evidence he has proved will inevitably follow. He is entitled to compensation for suffering and expense which by a fair preponderance of the evidence he has satisfied the jury reasonably are to be expected to follow, so far as human knowledge can foretell. Pullen v. Boston Elevated Ry. Co., 94 N.E. 469, 471 (Mass. 1911).

In addition, when there is a "reasonable probability" that future expenses will be required to remedy the consequences of a defendant's negligence, the jury may consider the expense in awarding damages. Menard v. Collins, 9 N.E.2d 387 (Mass. 1937). Plaintiffs argue that these cases indicate that Massachusetts accepts the general rule of tort law that "[o]ne injured by the tort of another is entitled to recover damages for all harm, past, present and prospective, legally caused by the tort." Restatement 2d of Torts §910. I agree, subject to two caveats. First, as is indicated by *Pullen and Menard*, when an injured person seeks to recover for harms that may result in the future, recovery depends on establishing a "reasonable probability" that the harm will occur. See Restatement 2d of Torts §912. Second, recovery for future harm in an action assumes that a cause of action for that harm has accrued at the time recovery is sought. See Restatement 2d of Torts §910....

Defendants argue that the cause of action for any future serious illness, including leukemia and other cancers, has not yet accrued because the injury has not yet occurred.[8] This is the rationale of the discovery rule applied to latent disease cases in Massachusetts under which the injury is equated with the manifestation of the disease. The question thus becomes whether, upon the manifestation of one or more diseases, a cause of action accrues for all prospective diseases so that a plaintiff may seek to recover for physically distinct and separate diseases which may develop in the future.

The answer to this question depends on the connection between the illnesses plaintiffs have suffered and fear they will suffer in the future. Unfortunately, the nature of plaintiffs' claim for increased risk of future illness is unclear on two counts. Nothing in the present record indicates the magnitude of the increased risk, or the diseases which plaintiffs may suffer....

A further reason for denying plaintiffs' damages for the increased risk of future harm in this action is the inevitable inequity which would result if recovery were allowed. To award damages based on a mere mathematical probability would significantly undercompensate those who actually develop cancer and would be a windfall to those who do not. In addition, if plaintiffs could show that they were more likely than not to suffer cancer or other future illness, full recovery would be allowed for all plaintiffs, even though only some number more than half would actually develop the illness. In such a case, the defendant would overcompensate the injured class.

Accordingly, action on plaintiffs' claims for the increased risk of serious future illness, including cancer, must be delayed....

COMMENTARY & QUESTIONS

1. **Physical harm/emotional distress.** What is the relevance of physical harm in a claim for infliction of emotional distress? Is it possible that an individual could be greatly distressed without suffering any injury whatever? The usual rationale for a physical harm requirement is the desire to prevent fictitious claims. It may be underinclusive in those genuine cases where a victim suffers emotionally without physical damage, and it may be overinclusive in allowing claims of emotional distress by unprincipled plaintiffs who suffer no distress at all.

In *Anderson*, satisfaction of the physical harm requirement by subcellular T-cell effects seems to be a needless formality.[9] Are the physical damage requirement and the required causal link between physical injury and emotional distress intended to substitute for a policy debate about whether the defendant's conduct, as a matter of law and policy, should result in liability for this type of injury? Recall that one of the functions

---

8. The weight of authority would deny plaintiffs a cause of action solely for increased risk because no "injury" has occurred.

9. The defendants and the court could entertain no real doubt about the plaintiffs' sufferings. The defendants may think that the plaintiffs are suffering needlessly, i.e., that nothing will come of the exposures, but it is hard to believe that they discredit the claims of fear and anxiety.

of the proximate cause inquiry is to limit the extent of liability that could be imposed using but-for causation carried to extreme lengths. Pruitt v. Allied Chemical Co., in Chapter 3, however, shows that proximate cause analyses also may resort to arbitrary rules to guide their application.

Even if you are hostile to attempts to limit emotional distress claims for those personally victimized by contamination, is the argument for prudential limitations stronger in the case of those who suffer by witnessing the suffering of others? These claims are no less real to their victims, nor are they any less credible, in the context of watching an immediate family member die an agonizing and unnecessary death, than are first party claims for infliction of emotional distress. Are courts, rather than the legislature, deciding that it is simply too expensive to compensate these noneconomic losses and still maintain affordable prices for goods that produce hazardous materials as by-products of their manufacture?

2. **A Civil Action.** The Woburn case has become one of the most famous in modern American annals. Its compelling human interest aspects led to the publication of Jonathan Harr's best-selling book A Civil Action (1995) and the subsequent movie of the same title. An earlier version of the story was P. Brown and E. Mikkelson, No Safe Place (1990). The case's notoriety coupled with a very interesting procedural history has led to its continuing use as a case study for procedure students. See L. Grossman and R. Vaughan, A Civil Action: A Civil Procedure Supplement (1999). The following six Commentary & Questions items draw on material beyond this coursebook. Students may wish to consult the materials mentioned above while working through these items.

3. **Discovery issues.** The judge in the Woburn case repeatedly refused to allow plaintiffs to test for contamination on the site of the tannery itself and in its sludge disposal area (see map of the Woburn site), restricting testing to the wetland parcel downhill from the tannery. It is not clear why this ruling was made. Initially Beatrice's attorneys appeared to resist tannery investigation on the ground that the tannery had been reconveyed back to John Riley and was no longer owned by them. Later the rationale appears to have been that plaintiffs had based their case primarily on the wetland parcel, which they knew to be contaminated, not the tannery for which they had little information. One valid purpose of discovery, however, is to allow plaintiffs to investigate sources of contamination that they have good faith reason to believe are sources, such as the sludge disposal site behind the tannery, in order to build a case. In the meantime, Beatrice took advantage of the exclusion to excavate and clean up the tannery site, including the disposal areas.[10] Later the judge appears to have relented: He would let plaintiffs enter the tannery site if they would use an expert of his choosing. The plaintiffs rejected that belated compromise.

---

10. The closest plaintiffs came to testing on the tannery site, according to plaintiffs' attorney, was the day Schlichtmann played Ivanhoe: When a phone call from a neighbor told him the tannery land was being bulldozed, he raced off to a hardware store, bought a long piece of half-inch conduit pipe, and drove to the site holding the pipe out the window of his girlfriend's Dodge like a knight charging with a lance. Thrusting the pipe through the security fence into a pile of excavated sludge, he was able to retrieve a plug of material from the site before a guard came rushing to intercept him. Although the sample proved to contain traces of the solvents, he was not able to introduce it at trial. This scene, inexplicably, didn't make it into book or movie.

In other toxic tort cases, discovery has been complex and inventive, including the use of physical experimentation on defendants' land, the tracing of smokestack emissions via isotopes or dye markers in groundwater as in the *Wilsonville* case (discussed in Chapter 3), and the like. For environmental plaintiffs, the trick often has been to find probative evidence that can be obtained without great cost.

4. **Novel civil procedure: "polyfurcation."** The major issues of the Woburn toxics case in *Anderson* never went to trial because the judge in February 1986 split the case into four sequential phases. Under Fed. R. Civ. P. 42(b), a judge may phase a trial in the interests of efficiency, so basic questions, such as liability, are raised and litigated first in a separate trial; then consequential issues, such as remedies, are litigated as necessary. The Woburn judge, however, split the liability issue itself three ways. He set Phase 1 to determine whether defendants' contaminants ever reached the public wells, Phase 2 on causation of leukemia, Phase 3 on causation of other injuries to other family members, and Phase 4 on damages. Only the first phase ever went to trial, limited to the question of liability for groundwater flow. Plaintiffs' attorneys generally oppose such multiple phasing because it "cuts the heart out" of the continuity of the story they are trying to present to the jury. The Woburn jury nevertheless came in with a verdict against defendant Grace in Phase 1, and Grace quickly settled for $8 million in damages. Does that outcome reinforce the rationale for phasing or support the plaintiffs' fear of dilution? See Bedecarré, Polyfurcation of Liability Issues in Environmental Tort Cases, 17 B.C. Envtl. Aff. L. Rev. 123 (1989).

5. **Special jury questions.** The Woburn plaintiffs' case encountered another tactical disadvantage when the judge required the jury in the Phase 1 trial, instead of bringing in a simple verdict on whether the defendants' contamination reached the wells, to specify the particular time at which each of four chemicals reached the wells. The questions were so complex that even the jury verdict against Grace was internally inconsistent, and jury members confessed their extreme confusion about the highly technical subquestions they were required to answer. See Pacelle, Contaminated Verdict, Am. Law. (Dec. 1986), at 75; cf. Brodin, Accuracy, Efficiency, and Accountability in the Litigation Process: The Case for the Fact Verdict, 59 U. Cin. L. Rev. 15 (1990). (Confronted with the inconsistencies in the Woburn jury's answers, the judge overturned the verdict and ordered a new trial. Grace's decision, after weighing its options, to settle for $8 million came the same day despite the overturned verdict.)

6. **The "highly extraordinary" defense and its evidentiary consequences.** A critical legal ruling, not noted in the Woburn case's popular chronicles, was an application of Restatement (Second) of Torts §435(2)'s "highly extraordinary" excuse. Section 435(2) allows a judge to excuse liability where "looking back from the harm to the actor's negligent conduct, it appears to the court highly extraordinary that it should have brought about the harm." This grant of discretion to the trial judge was designed to nullify liability where the chains of causation are extremely improbable in statistical terms, as in the classic case of Palsgraf v. Long Island R.R. Co., 162 N.E. 99 (N.Y. 1928). Under Restatement §435, foreseeability is not the issue; rather it is a response to very unlikely Palsgrafian combinations of coincidence in a chain of causation. In the Woburn case, however, the judge used §435(2) to excuse the Beatrice tannery on fore-

seeability grounds from any liability prior to the time when it was told by an engineer that the groundwater under its property flowed laterally 800 feet, under the Aberjona stream, to the public wells. The judge said it was extraordinary to him that groundwater can flow laterally under a stream. How does this square with Professor Davis's analysis cited in a footnote by the court in Branch v. Western Petroleum, excerpted in Chapter 3, that implies that long-distance groundwater pollution flow in fact is not extraordinary? Scientifically, it is axiomatic under the laws of physics that pollutants would be drawn, along with the groundwater, under the creek and to the wells from a broad radius including the tannery's lowland parcel. The evidentiary effects of this ruling were dramatic. Although extensive evidence proved that contaminants came to the wells from Beatrice's property in the same way as from Grace, a point echoed in government assessments of cleanup liability against both, the judge told the jury that it had to ignore prior passage of contaminants from Beatrice's land. Beatrice could be held liable only for flows after the engineer's notice. The jury decided that with the evidence thus restricted, it could not make the required specialized timing findings for chemical exposure in Beatrice's narrowed window of liability, and the case against Beatrice collapsed.

7. **Woburn's other evidentiary rulings.** The judge in *Anderson* made several other evidentiary rulings that were perplexing. At one point, he substituted his own observations for the testimony of chemists who had found tannery compounds in waste piles on the wetlands parcel: "I compared samples of this material with samples of tannery sludge both at the trial and during the recent hearings and found them totally different in color, consistency and odor." 127 F.R.D. 1 (1989). At the end of the trial, he made another surprising finding in light of the established fact of groundwater flows to the wells: "In response to plaintiffs' post-verdict objection to the ambiguous form of the interrogatories, I made a finding of fact under FRCP 49(a): plaintiffs had not proven by a preponderance of the evidence that the complaint chemicals migrated to wells G and H." 129 F.R.D. 394 (1989). (This perhaps meant to say "within the time horizon I had set for liability under Restatement §435(2).")

8. **Fed. R. Civ. P. 11 in the Woburn toxics case.** Fed. R. Civ. P. 11, generally designed to police attorneys' ethical practice, waxes and wanes over the years. In toxic tort cases, including the Woburn case, Rule 11 motions often are made by defendants to challenge plaintiffs for proceeding without traditional proof of causation, when plaintiffs propose to prove their case based on statistical or circumstantial logic or on theories on the frontiers of science. In the *Anderson* case's first Rule 11 hearing, Judge Skinner ruled that plaintiffs had enough of a case on causation to proceed in good faith.

A second Rule 11 hearing, not noted in the movie, was more remarkable, putting the entire civil action into wry context. Shortly after losing the case against Beatrice, Schlictmann discovered by accident that although during discovery he had requested all data on tannery site contamination and had been told there was none, in fact two such reports existed. Known to the tannery attorneys, groundwater studies done in 1983 and 1985 showed the presence of several of the contaminants on the tannery site proper. Plaintiffs eagerly requested a retrial, arguing that these reports would have triggered greater scrutiny of the tannery, perhaps convincing the judge to allow them to test the tannery site and its disposal lagoons. The judge's refusal to reopen the case was reversed and remanded by the First Circuit. Anderson v. Beatrice Foods Co., 862 F.2d 910 (1st Cir. 1988). On remand, the judge did make a finding of "deliberate misconduct" against Mr. Riley and his attorney (although refusing to allow Riley's counsel to introduce evidence implicating Beatrice's attorney in the coverup[11]). But plaintiffs' expectations of a retrial against Beatrice (in which they hoped to overturn the key ruling under Restatement §435(2) that had constricted the timeframe of the tannery's liability) were dashed by the judge's ruling sua sponte that plaintiffs, too, had committed an offsetting Rule 11 violation, so no new trial would be ordered. After reviewing plaintiffs' investigative manual, the judge said he thought that plaintiffs had not had enough evidence at the start of the trial to proceed with the claim that the tannery itself had dumped contaminants. Offsetting Rule 11 sanctions meant that defendants won and plaintiffs lost.

> The honors for sanctionable conduct are about evenly divided.... At least by the close of his investigation and discovery,...plaintiffs' counsel knew that there was no...basis in fact for the assertion that the defendant disposed of the complaint chemicals at the tannery site or on the 15 acres. 129 F.R.D. at 403.

Schlictmann was apoplectic. "I know the joy of a madman! He says we should be sanctioned?!" The reason that plaintiffs at trial had only circumstantial evidence of contamination on the tannery site (which all now knew in retrospect to be true) was the judge's original ruling preventing them from direct testing on the site, and the malfeasance of defense attorneys hiding the contamination data. The judge discounted the circumstantial evidence of tannery-like wastes down in the lower parcel as insufficient to go to a jury. A jury, Schlictmann believed, easily could have found direct tannery liability based on wastes in the ditch leading down from the tannery and from tannery wastes laced with solvents in the wetland. The judge had put plaintiffs into a Catch-22, said Schlictmann. The First Circuit declined to get back into this thicket, and a petition for certiorari to the Supreme Court was denied, 498 U.S. 890 (1990).

At the end of the Woburn tort case, one should ask whether the *Anderson* civil action shows the continued relevance and efficacy of tort law in toxic contamination situations or the opposite. The plaintiffs recovered $8 million from the W. R. Grace Company (which subsequent geological evidence indicates contributed little or no solvents to the wells) and zero from Beatrice (from whose property most of the pollution originated). The trial cost plaintiffs more than $2 million and defendants more than twice that amount. The actual determinations of fact in the litigation process were partial and some of them almost certainly were inaccurate. The government, as noted later in this chapter, had much more effective remedies available and levied penalties of almost $70 million against the defendants. If there were no toxic tort actions available in the legal system in this case, or in general, would society be better off or worse?

---

11. "[Riley's attorney] came forward...with an affidavit asserting communications with defendant's attorneys never before revealed, said to be supported by no less than forty-one documents contradicting defendant's attorneys in several respects. No rule of due process that I know of permits an attorney...to withhold information until such time as it is to her advantage to reveal it.... Such a rule would put a premium on strategic concealment." 129 F.R.D. 394, 409. Plaintiffs, of course, were exasperated that this evidence of defendants' concealment would thus remain concealed, weakening plaintiffs' case for a retrial.

Does the account of the Woburn case give some indication of the enormous burdens imposed on plaintiffs trying to use the common law to redress their injuries in complex circumstances? As with all litigation, students must be reminded that a case does not develop and prove itself at trial. Each step of the litigation involves guesses and gambles, rationing of time and resources, choices made, and viable options foregone. The actions of judges, not to mention attorneys and juries, are not necessarily predictable. Facts and procedural rulings can be slippery. Because of the burdens and complexities of the process, opportunities for appeal may offer no effective redress for mistakes. What ultimately emerges is a potpourri of happenstance that may or may not accord with one's sense of justice. Alternatively, as you study the remainder of this chapter, evaluate the possibility that Woburn is an early evolutionary decision along a path that now offers far more coherent remedial protection to the victims of toxic exposures.

Section 2. COMPENSABLE ELEMENTS OF DAMAGE IN TOXIC TORT CASES

Ayers v. Township of Jackson
Supreme Court of New Jersey, 1987
106 N.J. 557, 525 A.2d 287

STEIN, J. The litigation involves claims for damages sustained because plaintiffs' well water was contaminated by toxic pollutants leaching...from a landfill established and operated by Jackson Township. After an extensive trial, the jury found that the township had created a "nuisance" and a "dangerous condition" by virtue of its operation of the landfill, that its conduct was "palpably unreasonable" [a prerequisite to recovery under N.J.'s sovereign immunity tort claims waiver], and that it was the proximate cause of the contamination of plaintiffs' water supply. The jury verdict resulted in an aggregate judgment of $15,854,392.78, to be divided among the plaintiffs in varying amounts. The jury returned individual awards for each of the plaintiffs that varied in accordance with such factors as proximity to the landfill, duration and extent of the exposure to contaminants, and the age of the claimant.

The verdict provided compensation for three distinct claims of injury: $2,056,480 was awarded for emotional distress caused by the knowledge that they had ingested water contaminated by toxic chemicals for up to six years; $5,396,940 was awarded for the deterioration of their quality of life during the twenty months when they were deprived of running water; and $8,204,500 was awarded to cover the future cost of annual medical surveillance that plaintiffs' expert testified would be necessary because of plaintiffs' increased susceptibility to cancer and other diseases.

...The chemical contamination of their wells was caused by the township's improper operation of the landfill [resulting in infiltration into the wells by] acetone; benzene; chlorobenzene; chloroform; dichlorofluoromethane; ethylbenzene; methylene chloride; methyl isobutyl ketone; 1,1,2,2-tetrachloroethane; tetrahydrofuran; 1,1,1-trichloroethane; and trichloroethylene....

An expert in the diagnosis and treatment of diseases caused by exposure to toxic substances testified that the plaintiffs required annual medical examinations to afford the earliest possible diagnosis of chemically induced illnesses. Her opinion was that a program of regular medical surveillance for plaintiffs would improve prospects for cure, treatment, prolongation of life, and minimization of pain and disability.

A substantial number — more than 150 — of the plaintiffs gave testimony with respect to damages, describing in detail the impairment of their quality of life during the period that they

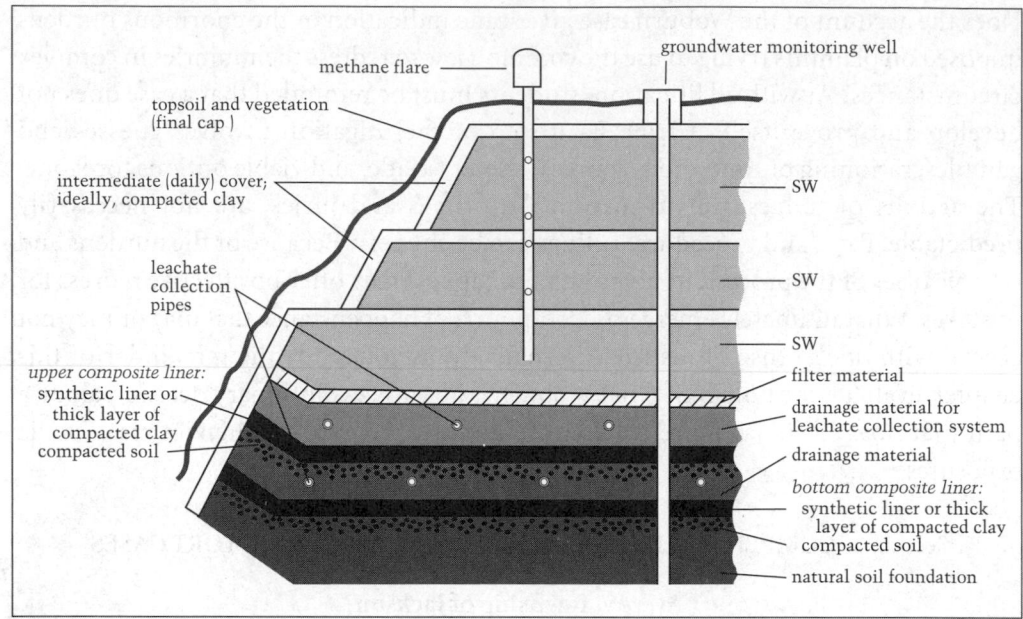

FIGURE 4-2

Schematic cutaway diagram of the corner of a state-of-the-art solid waste landfill, showing protective liner layers, water-repelling capping, and internal drainage and monitoring systems. As in the Ayers case, solid waste landfill operations in practice often are much less fastidious about design and maintenance; moreover, as one state official said, the basic rule of liners is that they all eventually leak.

were without running water, and the emotional distress they suffered. With regard to the emotional distress claims, the plaintiffs' testimony detailed their emotional reactions to the chemical contamination of their wells and the deprivation of their water supply, as well as their fears for the health of their family members. Expert psychological testimony was offered to document plaintiffs' claims that they had sustained compensable psychological damage as a result of the contamination of their wells.

Quality of Life... Residents in need of water tied a white cloth on their mailbox and received a 40 gallon barrel containing a plastic liner filled with water. The filled barrels weighed in excess of 100 pounds.... One witness, who suffered from arthritis, testified to hauling her water for drinking, cooking and bathing up nine steps because, as she said, [t]here was no way that I could get the water upstairs except by hauling pot after pot out of the containers...which was a considerable amount of hauling everyday just to use for drinking and bathing the children and cooking.... Plaintiffs' households...for nearly two years were compelled to obtain water in this primitive manner.

The trial court charged the jury that plaintiffs' claim for "quality of life" damages encompassed "inconveniences, aggravation, and unnecessary expenditure of time and effort related to the use of the water hauled to their homes, as well as to other disruption in their lives, including disharmony in the family unit."...

Emotional Distress... Many of the plaintiffs testified about their emotional reactions to the knowledge that their well-water was contaminated.... Typically, their testimony did not indicate that the emotional distress resulted in physical symptoms or required medical treatment....

Nevertheless, the consistent thrust of the testimony offered by numerous witnesses was that they suffered anxiety, stress, fear, and depression, and that these feelings were directly and causally related to the knowledge that they and members of their family had ingested and been exposed to contaminated water for a substantial time period.

Plaintiffs also presented testimony from an experienced clinical psychologist, Dr. Margaret Gibbs...[who] testified that the sample of 88 plaintiffs she tested manifested abnormally high levels of stress, depression, health concerns, and psychological problems.... The township contended that plaintiffs had not proved that the emotional distress experienced by them was manifested by any discernible physical symptoms or injuries, arguing that proof of related physical symptoms was a prerequisite to recovery.... Our cases no longer require proof of causally-related physical impact to sustain a recovery for emotional distress.... [The N.J. sovereign immunity statute, however, bars emotional injury recoveries.]

Claims for Enhanced Risk, and Medical Surveillance... We concur with the Appellate Division's refusal to recognize plaintiffs' damage claim based on enhanced risk... We disagree with its conclusion that an award for medical surveillance damages cannot be supported by this record.

Our evaluation of the enhanced risk and medical surveillance claims requires that we focus on a critical issue in the management of toxic tort litigation: at what stage in the evolution of a toxic injury should tort law intercede by requiring the responsible party to pay damages?... In the absence of statutory or administrative mechanisms for processing injury claims resulting from environmental contamination, courts have struggled to accommodate common-law tort doctrines to the peculiar characteristics of toxic-tort litigation....

Among the recent toxic tort cases rejecting liability for damages based on enhanced risk is Anderson v. W. R. Grace & Co.... We observe that the overwhelming weight of the scholarship on this issue favors a right of recovery for tortious conduct that causes a significantly enhanced risk of injury.... It is the highly contingent and speculative quality of an unquantified claim based on enhanced risk that renders it novel and difficult to manage and resolve.... On the other hand, denial of the enhanced-risk cause of action may mean that some of these plaintiffs will be unable to obtain compensation for their injury. Those who contract diseases in the future because of their exposure to chemicals in their well water may be unable to prove a causal relationship between such exposure and their disease...because of the difficulty of proving that injuries manifested in the future were not the product of intervening events or causes.... In our view, the speculative nature of an unquantified enhanced risk claim, the difficulties inherent in adjudicating such claims, and the policies underlying the Tort Claims Act argue persuasively against the recognition of this cause of action...for the unquantified enhanced risk of disease.

The claim for medical surveillance expenses stands on a different footing from the claim based on enhanced risk. It seeks to recover the cost of periodic medical examinations intended to monitor plaintiffs' health and facilitate early diagnosis and treatment of disease caused by plaintiffs' exposure to toxic chemicals.... An application of tort law that allows post-injury, pre-symptom recovery in toxic tort litigation for reasonable medical surveillance costs is manifestly consistent with the public interest in early detection and treatment of disease,...to deter polluters, [and] preventing or mitigating serious future illnesses [where an exposed person would otherwise be] unable to pay his own expenses when medical intervention is clearly reasonable and necessary....

Accordingly, we hold that the cost of medical surveillance is a compensable item of damages where the proofs demonstrate, through reliable expert testimony predicated upon the significance and extent of exposure to chemicals, the toxicity of the chemicals, the seriousness of the diseases for which individuals are at risk, the relative increase in the chance of onset of disease in those exposed, and the value of early diagnosis, that such surveillance to monitor the effect of exposure to toxic chemicals is reasonable and necessary...notwithstanding the fact that the extent of plaintiffs' impaired health is unquantified....

COMMENTARY & QUESTIONS

1. **The medical surveillance remedy and latency compensation.** The relatively novel surveillance monitoring fund remedy sought by the attorneys in *Ayers* has been picked up in several other states as a response to the problems of long-term toxic torts' latency. It seems like an appropriate and measured response to the feeling of vulnerability and burden felt by wrongfully exposed persons, who otherwise might not be able to provide themselves rigorous medical attention, while not breaking the bank. Subsequent courts, including New Jersey's, have amended the medical surveillance remedy by setting up a fund rather than awarding a lump sum. "The indeterminate nature of damage claims in toxic-tort litigation suggests...the use of court-supervised funds to pay medical-surveillance claims as they accrue, rather than lump-sum verdicts." *Ayers*, 525 A.2d at 313. Would the *Anderson* court have allowed medical surveillance, although it foreclosed recovery for risk?

2. **The medical monitoring remedy since *Ayers*.** The medical monitoring remedy has made great strides since *Ayers*. A recent comprehensive listing of medical monitoring cases can be found at Martens & Getto, Medical Monitoring and Class Actions, 17 Nat. Resources & Env't 225, 226 (2003). In Paoli R.R. Yard PCB Litig., 916 F.2d 829, 852 (1990), the Third Circuit set out a four-part test for medical monitoring: Courts should grant the medical monitoring remedy if plaintiffs demonstrate that (1) they were significantly exposed to hazardous materials as a result of the negligence of the defendant; (2) as a proximate result of their exposure, they suffer a significantly increased risk of contracting a serious latent disease; (3) the increased risk makes regular medical monitoring and treatment reasonably necessary; and (4) the monitoring and treatment make early detection and/or prevention of the disease possible. In several cases, courts, including the Supreme Court, have indicated a willingness to apply the remedy though declining to do so in the particular case at hand. In an asbestos exposure case, Metro-North Commuter R.R. v. Buckley, 521 U.S. 424 (1997), the Supreme Court declined to award medical monitoring under the Federal Employers' Liability Act (FELA). Though the Court endorsed the *Paoli* tests in principle, it suggested that asymptomatic plaintiffs should be restricted to court-supervised monitoring funds rather than "full-blown lump sum recoveries" and clearly was worried that "tens of millions of individuals may have suffered exposure to substances that might justify some form of substance-exposure-related medical monitoring." 521 U.S. at 442.

3. **Damages for increased risk of future illness.** It is undeniably true that certain exposures to toxics, by their effects (including damage to the immune system), increase the likelihood that a person will suffer serious future illness and earlier death. Can exposed persons sue against identifiable sources of the contamination prior to the onset of disease, not for the disease but for the increased risk? Such damages could be claimed

by a very broad swath of plaintiffs, many of whom in statistical terms surely would never get the illnesses, and would presumably not foreclose future recoveries by those who later actually got sick. Pre-illness claims are inherently enigmatic. On one hand, compensation can mulct defendants of damages even in cases where illness never occurs. This results in a form of systematic overcompensation. On the other hand, to refuse compensation is to ignore the goal of complete compensation because defendant's conduct has made plaintiffs less well off. Consider whether an individual would voluntarily choose to drink contaminated water for several years. See R. Posner, Economic Analysis of Law 149 (6th ed. 2003). Likewise, consider what a prudent insurer of health risks would do if it discovered that an applicant for insurance had suffered a major toxic exposure, as had the plaintiffs in *Ayers*. Are there persuasive rebuttals to these assertions of over- and undercompensation? Is there a further argument that compensation for enhanced risk systematically undercompensates those victims who actually contract the feared disease? To what extent is it necessary to know whether subsequent lawsuits (when diseases actually appear) will be barred by the statute of limitations or by doctrines of res judicata? As a policy matter, the majority in *Ayers* tried to indicate in dicta that New Jersey courts should be receptive to later suits. The court coupled that assurance with its perception that courts are facing only the beginning of a flood of toxic tort litigation, to justify its conservative wait-and-see, wait-and-sue approach to enhanced risk.

4. **Hedonic "quality of life" damages.** What items of damage seem to have been included in the *Ayers* "quality of life" recovery? Hedonic damages, noted in Chapter 3, are recent arrivals in toxic tort law and will require judicial elaboration. Is there any recognition of the stigma of living in a contaminated community? Is there any argument that separates toxic tort cases from ordinary tort cases when it comes to compensation for subjective intangibles? The mass exposure aspect of toxic tort cases implies that defendant's financial exposure may be great. Under what circumstances will that justify modification of the ordinary substantive rules?

5. **Stigma and the new tort of "toxiprox."** Owners of land situated in close proximity to hazardous materials sites frequently find that the market values of their land are adversely affected as a result of the nearby presence of the hazardous materials. This is particularly true in the case of sites at which toxic materials have been released into the environment, but it is also true to a lesser extent where a nearby facility is used for the proper treatment or disposal of hazardous materials, or even where the facility is simply one at which hazardous materials are known to be in use. Would-be buyers discount the value of the parcel in consequence of the proximity of the hazardous materials, often without reference to whether those materials pose even a scintilla of risk of harm to the parcel being offered for sale. Compensation increasingly is being sought for losses that are consequent upon toxic proximity alone. Consider the following situations:

- A New Jersey trial court judge certified a class action lawsuit brought by owners of parcels located in close proximity to an infamous Glouster Environmental Services (GEMS Landfill) hazardous waste site. The principal claim of the suit is that the affected homes are either unsaleable or seriously devalued by their proximity to the contaminated site.[12]

- New York's highest court, in determining how much compensation is due to owners of property condemned for its proximity to high voltage lines, has recognized a compensable interest in favor of property owners who can prove that fear of EMF (electromagnetic field) emissions from high voltage power lines will cause a reduction in the value of their real property, and contemporary cases involving parcel valuation for tax assessment purposes also are beginning to take toxic contamination and its effect on market price into account in valuing the subject parcel.[13]

- In Strawn v. Incollingo, N.J. Super. Ct. App. Div., No. A-4764-91T3 (Feb. 22, 1994), purchasers of homes in a new development were held to have a cause of action against the builder and brokers who sold them houses without disclosing the proximity to a closed landfill suspected of containing toxic waste.

What is the legal theory supporting recovery in these cases? As these claims proliferate, it will be possible to determine whether these cases comprise a new unique toxic tort cause of action or are instead an additional element of damage (similar to fear of cancer claims) being asserted under existing rubrics of negligence, nuisance, and strict liability.

Under New York law, landowners who prove that a neighboring business contaminated their property with hazardous pollutants may be entitled to damages for "stigma" above and beyond the costs of cleaning up the property. In Scribner v. Summers, 138 F.3d 471 (2d Cir. 1998), plaintiffs brought suit under CERCLA and state nuisance laws when defendant's steel treating operation contaminated plaintiffs' property with barium. The district court granted plaintiffs' claims but refused to award permanent damages on the state law claims on the grounds that the CERCLA cleanup would remedy any permanent injury to the property. In a per curiam opinion, the Second Circuit Court of Appeals reversed and remanded the district court decision as to the denial of permanent damages, holding that, while New York law is unsettled on this point, plaintiffs may be able to recover damages for any "stigma" that attaches to the property and depresses its value, even though a full cleanup has occurred. The court indicated that it would be inclined to certify the question to the New York Court of Appeals if it were presented on an adequate record.

Another remedy for these losses is a publicly administered fund established by a tax on landfill operators. See New Jersey Sanitary Landfill Facility Closure and Contingency

---

12. See In re GEMS Landfill Super. Ct. Litig., N.J. Super. Ct., Camden County, No. L-068199-85 (Feb. 2, 1994), as reported at 8 BNA Toxics L. Rep. 1035-1036 (1994). See also Exxon Corp. v. Yarema, 516 A.2d 990 (Md. 1986) (allowing recovery for decreased property value caused by groundwater contamination that did not reach the affected parcel); but see Adkins v. Thomas Solvent, 440 Mich. 293, 487 N.W.2d 715 (1992) (holding that diminished property values caused by negative publicity affecting parcels proximate to, but not themselves subject to, hazardous waste contamination, is a loss without legal injury). A California jury awarded $826,500 to a property owner for postcleanup stigmatization of the property and $400,000 in lost rents. Bixby Ranch Co. v. Spectrol Elec. Corp., Cal. Super. Ct., Los Angeles County, No. BC052566 (Dec. 13, 1993), as reported at 8 BNA Toxics L. Rep. 955-956 (1994).

13. See Criscuola v. Power Auth. of the State of N.Y., 81 N.Y.2d 649, 621 N.E.2d 1195, 602 N.Y.S.2d 588 (1993); Westling v. County of Mille Lacs, 512 N.W.2d 863 (Minn. 1994) (assessment included a deduction for the claimed stigma attached to the property because of the pollution).

Fund Act, N.J.S.A. §§13:1E-100 to 13:1E-116. But see also Citizens for Equity v. New Jersey Dep't of Envtl. Protection, 599 A.2d 507 (1991), where the court upheld a change in administrative rules that cut off recoveries by landowners that previously had been defined by the agency to include: "(1) The cost of restoring, repairing or replacing any real or personal property damaged or destroyed, and *the diminution in fair market value of any real property*." 599 A.2d at 509 (emphasis added by the court). Up until that point, the fund had paid over $5 million in compensation, with more than 95% of that amount going for decreased value in the absence of parcel contamination. Most payments under the law were made to landowners affected by the GEMS Landfill.

6. Statutes of limitation — "I wasted time, and now doth time waste me."[14] Toxic tort cases raise a number of difficult statute of limitations problems. As an initial matter, the discovery by plaintiffs that they are victims of a tort is seldom concurrent with the defendant's tortious conduct. In both *Ayers* and *Anderson*, the groundwater contamination and plaintiffs' exposure to it began long before plaintiffs learned that contamination had occurred and before plaintiffs suffered physical injury.

The courts have adopted two devices for dealing with statutes of limitations problems. The first doctrine, intended to protect courts from the burden of adjudicating unripe controversies, turns on the definition of when a cause of action accrues. Accrual occurs only when all of the elements necessary for successful prosecution of the claim have occurred. A lawsuit cannot be brought by a plaintiff before the basic facts required for a cause of action have happened, and a central element of any tort claim is the injury to the plaintiff. To hold otherwise defies logic, asking plaintiff to act on a legal right not yet in existence.

The second major concept in limitation of actions, offering particular protection to plaintiffs in toxic tort cases, is the so-called discovery rule. It, too, helps to define when a cause of action accrues. In a portion of the *Anderson* opinion addressing the effect of the statute of limitations on wrongful death claims, the court stated the general discovery rule:

> The discovery rule is a method of defining when a cause of action accrues. The principle behind the rule is that "a plaintiff should be put on notice before his or her claim is barred by the passage of time." The notice required by the rule includes knowledge of both the injury and its cause — that plaintiff "has been harmed as a result of defendant's conduct." 628 F. Supp. at 1224.

This particular form of the discovery rule, requiring that the plaintiff must be on actual or constructive notice of the fact of injury and who caused it before the statute starts running, is not a majority rule, although it appears to be gaining. Other states toll the statue of limitations in these toxic tort cases only until discovery of the injury. See Development in the Law — Toxic Waste Litigation, 99 Harv. L. Rev. 1458, 1906–1907 (1986).

---

14. William Shakespeare, Richard II, Act V, Scene V.

"Statutes of repose" have been enacted in some states.[15] Unlike statutes of limitations, statutes of repose expressly disallow the operation of the discovery rule. These statutes appear to be motivated by marketplace concerns for the burdens placed on present-day operators of businesses by large judgments for "ancient torts." Unfortunately, many illnesses caused by wrongful exposures to environmental toxics lie latent for years before surfacing. Marketplace lobbyists argue that often the wrongful acts were committed by officers and employees who have no present relation to the defendant.

The discovery rule addresses the problem of long latency periods intervening between tortious exposure and the onset of disease. If the statute of limitations does not begin to run until the disease is manifest, then plaintiffs will have ample opportunity to bring suit after the onset of the disease. There may be some proof difficulties in reconstructing the events surrounding exposure, but these are the lesser of evils. The principal alternatives to the discovery rule are requiring defendants to compensate *all* exposure victims as if they have developed the disease or abandoning the discovery rule, thereby limiting tort recoveries to just those harms that became manifest within a short time after exposure. *Ayers* recognizes another potential discovery rule problem, the operation of the rules of res judicata (in particular, merger and bar) that the New Jersey court labels "the single controversy rule." In most instances, in order to avoid duplicative and inefficient litigation of a case, all claims must be joined in a single suit. To the extent that claims have been omitted and not placed in issue, the single controversy rule deems them extinguished and "merged" into the original judgment. In cases like *Ayers*, the pitfall of the single controversy rule is that later-initiated claims for matured illness would be allowed by the discovery rule but barred by merger. The New Jersey answer to this problem is to recognize that the policies of the discovery rule would be set at naught if merger and bar were applied. The court pointed out that merger and bar apply only to claims that could have been brought at the time of the first suit, and here, technically speaking, the cause of action for bodily injury would not yet have come into existence.

7. **Sovereign immunity.** Most sovereigns in history have not encouraged their citizens (or anyone else, for that matter) to sue them in the sovereign's own courts. The idea of sovereign immunity has long been a powerful part of the American law. In the nineteenth and twentieth centuries, however, numerous attacks on the unfairness and irrationality of immunity were mounted and, eventually, took their toll. In an era where government is acknowledged to have many similarities to other corporate entities, why,

---

15. See Mass. Gen. L. ch. 260, §2B (-6 years); 735 Ill. Comp. Stat. 5/13-213(b) (-12 years); Va. Code Ann. §8.01-250 (-5 years).

> An action of tort for damages arising out of any deficiency or neglect in the design, planning, construction or general administration of an improvement to real property...shall be commenced only within three years next after the cause of action accrues; *provided, however,* that in no event such actions be commenced more than six years after the earlier of the dates of: (1) the opening of the improvement to use; or (2) substantial completion of the improvement and the taking of possession for occupancy by the owner. Mass. Gen. L. ch. 260, §2B.

Courts have reached different conclusions about the defense's applicability in long-term latency environmental contamination cases. Pitney-Bowes v. Baker Indus., 649 A.2d 1325 (N.J. Ct. App. 1994); Weymouth v. Welch Co., 18 Mass. L. Rptr. 6 (Mass. App. Ct. 1996); Norfolk v. U.S. Gypsum, 360 S.E.2d 325 (Va. 1987); Rowan County v. U.S. Gypsum, 418 S.E.2d 648 (N.C. 1992).

for example, should a pedestrian negligently run down by a government-owned vehicle find her suit barred by governmental immunity when no such bar would encumber a suit against a private company? In the *Ayers* case, for example, why should Jackson Township be any less responsible for harms caused by its dump operations than a private landfill operator?

Over time, the courts, and to a lesser extent legislatures, responded to arguments favoring a partial abolition of governmental immunity. On the common law front, a popular innovation is to distinguish between cases in which the governmental defendant is performing a governmental function, and those in which it is engaging in a mere proprietary function.[16] For example, setting the standard for airborne lead pollution would be governmental in character and would be immune from suit even if the government did it negligently; running a hot dog stand at the public beach or emitting excess pollutants from a furnace at a state-owned office building would be proprietary in character and subject to suit. In between these two examples lie many gray areas. Another popular judicial device for limiting immunity is to grant official immunity for acts that are clothed with discretion (again, standard-setting is a good example), but to hold officials liable for negligence or intentional torts in the performance of mere "ministerial" functions.[17] Some legislatures have taken similar initiatives, while a larger number have codified what the courts have done, sometimes modifying the scope of the judicial abrogation of immunity, other times not.

In recent years, with the advent of widely publicized tort recoveries and a manifold increase in governmental liability insurance costs, a reaction to the liberalized abrogation of immunity has taken place. The statute construed in *Ayers* had reasserted a broader concept of governmental immunity in that state, though creating an exception to that immunity under statutorily defined circumstances. Even in cases where the New Jersey statute waives governmental immunity, however, the statute expressly denies damages for pain and suffering and similar intangible items of damage.

8. **"Cancerphobia."** Cancerphobia and fear of cancer are not one and the same thing. In its more precise clinical medical sense, cancerphobia is a phobic reaction or apprehension experienced by its victim stemming from fear of contracting cancer in the future even in the absence of a specific event that presents an objective danger of contracting cancer. As a medical condition, it requires expert medical testimony to prove its existence, not merely credible lay testimony describing the plaintiff's experience of fear of cancer. See, e.g., Znaniecki, Cancerphobia Damages in Medical Malpractice Claims, 1997 U. Ill. L. Rev. 639, 642. True cancerphobia, as a presently existing and documented medical impairment, is a compensable injury in almost all jurisdictions. Courts, however, are not always cognizant of this distinction and frequently use the term *cancerphobia* to describe cases that are merely claims for emotional distress associated

---

16. *Proprietary* implies that there is no functional difference from a privately owned profit-making enterprise; *governmental* implies a function carried on in satisfaction of a public duty.

17. *Ministerial* implies that the public employee is simply executing explicitly required governmental duties; *discretionary* acts are based on broader, less constrained grants of delegated authority to act.

with fear of cancer. "Mere" fear of cancer cases are, not surprisingly, more common and pose more pointed questions regarding the wisdom of offering compensation for emotional distress in the absence of physical injury.

9. **Fear of cancer.** A growing number of cases have accepted, in various degrees, the concept of recovery for fear of cancer for cases involving emotional distress suffered after exposure to carcinogenic chemicals. For example, one court allowed recovery for fear of cancer risk even though it denied recovery for the risk itself. See Sterling v. Velsicol, 855 F.2d 1188 (6th Cir. 1988). The reluctance of courts to open a floodgate of cases based on fear with no attendant physical injury has led to a high standard in some states. In New Jersey, for instance, the *Ironbound* cases held that the neighbors of an Agent Orange production facility who had been contaminated by that defoliant could not recover for "cancerphobia" because their distress was not sufficiently "severe and substantial." Ironbound Health Rights Advisory Comm'n v. Diamond Shamrock Chems. Co., 578 A.2d 1248 (N.J. Super. 1990); see also Gale and Goyer, Recovery for Cancerphobia and Increased Rick of Cancer, 15 Cumb. L. Rev. 734 (1985).

Part of the courts' hesitancy in the fear of cancer cases, and in other mass tort environmental cases, is that the theories of common law liability prove too much. Eminently reasonable serious fears of chemical contamination can be so widespread that a defendant who pollutes a community might readily face a billion dollars in jury verdicts, and, arguably, the American economy cannot stand the economic dislocations that would follow the imposition of such tort liability. When courts raise the threshold barriers to tort recovery in mass toxic tort cases, are they making a social policy judgment that, for reasons of social utility, the damages for nonphysical injuries must remain where they have fallen? Is that policy judgment analytically different from the judicial role in enforcing the ordinary private nuisance requirement that the interference with plaintiff's quiet enjoyment be "unreasonable"?

10. **Fear of cancer and risk together in California.** In Potter v. Firestone Tire & Rubber Co., 6 Cal. 4th 965, 25 Cal. Rptr. 2d 550 (1993), the Supreme Court of California erected a very high standard for recovery for emotional distress caused by exposure to a carcinogen, in the absence of physical injury. The court accepted as a general rule that

> in the absence of a present physical injury or illness, recovery of damages for fear of cancer in a negligence action should be allowed only if the plaintiff pleads and proves that the fear stems from a knowledge, corroborated by reliable medical and scientific opinion, *that it is more likely than not that the feared cancer will develop* in the future due to the toxic exposure....
>
> [We admit that] a reasonable person who has consumed, cooked with, and bathed in water that has been contaminated by toxic waste is likely to sustain serious emotional distress relating to fear of developing a serious illness in the future, not only when the person's chances of developing an illness is more than 50 percent, but also when his or her chance of developing the illness is considerably lower, for example, "only" 25 or 30 percent. (Emphasis added.)

How great is the possibility of obtaining proof that will satisfy this standard? It may seem difficult based on the materials studied thus far, but materials that follow later in this chapter will show that the task is insurmountable absent extraordinarily acute exposures.[18] Under rather compelling facts that demonstrated the disregard of the defendant for the safety of plaintiffs, the *Potter* court also created "an exception to this general rule...if the toxic exposure that has resulted in the fear of cancer was caused by conduct amounting to 'oppression, fraud, or malice,'" and applied the exception to allow recovery in *Potter* for fears based on less than 50% probability. The *Potter* dissent would have allowed recovery for negligently inflicted emotional distress in toxic exposure cases even more liberally, where in addition to proof of serious emotional distress the plaintiff also proves that (1) the level of toxic substances to which he or she was exposed posed a significant risk that the plaintiff will develop the feared disease or illness (i.e., a risk that is sufficiently substantial that it would result in serious emotional distress in a reasonable, rather than an unusually sensitive, person), and (2) the defendant's negligence substantially increased plaintiff's risk of contracting the disease or illness (so that the plaintiff's serious emotional distress is a condition for which the defendant appropriately should be held responsible). 6 Cal. 4th at 1025, 25 Cal. Rptr. 2d at 591.

11. **Supreme Court allows fear of cancer emotional distress actions under FELA and applies joint and several liability.** In Norfolk & Western Ry. Co. v. Ayers, 123 S. Ct. 1210 (2003), former railroad employees sued the railway under FELA, seeking damages for negligent exposure to asbestos that had caused them to contract asbestosis, as well as damages for mental anguish resulting from the fear of developing cancer. The Supreme Court addressed two questions: (1) whether employees can recover damages for asbestosis-related fear of developing cancer, and (2) whether employees may recover their entire damage award from a railroad whose negligence, together with that of others, jointly caused the injury.

The Court based its reasoning in this statutory FELA case on common law precedents. It found that emotional distress precedents consisted of two categories: stand-alone emotional distress claims not provoked by any physical injury[19] and emotional distress claims brought on by a physical injury.[20] The Court noted that recovery is sharply circumscribed in the first category, but more readily permitted in the second category. In determining that Norfolk & Western fit into the second category, the Court relied on the Restatement (Second) of Torts §456, which states that an actor whose negligence has caused any bodily harm to another is also liable for other emotional disturbance resulting from either the bodily harm or the conduct that causes it. Therefore the Court determined that because the asbestosis that the employees had already contracted arose from the same conduct that created their fear of developing cancer, the employees could recover damages for their fear of cancer, provided they could prove that their fear is genuine and serious. Finally the Court found that, under FELA, an employee who suffers an injury caused in whole or in part by the employer railroad's negligence may

---

18. The difficulty arises through the combination of requirements regarding the methodologies that must be employed by expert witnesses (*Daubert*) and the typical nature of epidemiological studies (*Donaldson* and *Landrigan*). Available scientific evidence usually will be in the form of studies that begin with individuals who have contracted disease and then correlate that group with exposure to a potential causative agent, rather than the reverse.

19. See Metro-North Commuter Ry. v. Buckley, 521 U.S. 424 (1997).

20. See Consolidated Rail Corp. v. Gottshall, 512 U.S. 532 (1994).

recover full damages from the railroad, regardless of whether the injury was also caused in part by the actions of a third party. This finding avoided an apportionment of liability and placed a burden of seeking contribution from other tortfeasors upon the railroad and not upon the employee.

As to apportionment versus joint and several liability, the railroad had argued that "the modern trend is to apportion damages between multiple tortfeasors." The Court rejected the attempt:

> Many States retain full joint and several liability, see Restatement (Third) of Torts, Apportionment of Liability §17, (1999), even more retain it in certain circumstances, and most of the recent changes away from the traditional rule have come through legislative enactments rather than judicial development of common-law principles.... Reading the FELA to require apportionment would handicap plaintiffs and could vastly complicate adjudications.... Once an employer has been adjudged negligent with respect to a given injury, it accords with the FELA's overarching purpose to require the employer to bear the burden of identifying other responsible parties and demonstrating that some of the costs of the injury should be spread to them.... Under the FELA, an employee who suffers an injury caused in whole or in part by the railroad's negligence may recover his or her full damages from the railroad, regardless of whether the injury was also caused in part by the actions of a third party. 123 S. Ct. at 1227–1228.

12. **Distinguishing "community fears" from "rational fears."** In her article, Arguing Public Policy as a Defense to Environmental Toxic Tort Claims, 8 BNA Toxics L. Rep. 505 (1993), Martha Churchill[21] contrasts a community fear standard that relies on "popular anxiety, and even hysteria," with a rationally based fear standard that requires a plaintiff to "prove some objective danger which serves as a basis for the fear." She proposes this distinction as a means to prevent recovery in many fear-of-cancer cases. She views the extent of available compensation to be a matter of policy, and as an initial matter she castigates the legislative branch for not settling the dispute by enacting legislation requiring a rationally based fear standard.

As for the judicial branch, acting in a vacuum of legislative inaction, she suggests that the toxic fear and stigma (toxiprox) cases decided thus far can be grouped into two camps according to which of those two standards a court adopts. The danger, in her view, of using the community fear standard to judge the reasonableness of a claimed toxic fear is that "a community exhibiting irrational or hysterical behavior may be considered 'reasonable' simply on the grounds that its phobia is widely shared." 8 BNA Toxics L. Rep. at 506. Churchill argues that the better public policy is for courts to insist that the fears be rationally based. She states that it is wrong for courts to allow "the reality of the market place [to prevail] over the reality in the groundwater." See id. at 507. From the affected owners' point of view, the loss in the marketplace is still a very real loss even if the groundwater is still clean. Is there any compelling reason why this externality should be treated differently from most?

---

21. In a note, Churchill is described as being the president of Mid-America Legal Foundation, "a non-profit advocacy center devoted to products liability and environmental issues which affect the economy." For an assessment of Churchill's organization, see Houck, With Charity for All, 93 Yale L.J. 1415, 1486 (1984).

B. PROOF OF COMPLEX CAUSATION

In almost every toxic tort case, proof of causation of harm is a difficult litigation hurdle for plaintiffs. The precise mechanism by which toxic exposure results in disease is not well known and is not observable in the same way that a broken bone can be understood and seen to have been caused by an automobile accident. Even where scientific studies are viewed as authoritative because of the large populations studied, and even where previous litigation has been successful in obtaining remedies, proof of causation remains an issue of fact in each case that is likely to be difficult for the plaintiffs. For example, in litigation involving mesothelioma, asbestosis, or other asbestos-related maladies, plaintiffs still must show that their disease was caused by exposure to defendant's asbestos products and not by some other toxic exposure or predisposition to disease.

In the Woburn toxics case, which is more typical, the obstacle of proving causation was immense. The plaintiffs had no prior evidence proving that the subject chemicals caused cancer. Defendants steadfastly denied any such dumping. The victims, like most Americans, were exposed to literally hundreds of possible carcinogens in daily life. The Aberjona creek itself carried the four toxics, though in lesser concentrations than the wellwater.[22] Leukemia has long been linked to radioactivity exposures, and Woburn had several radium watch-dial factories in the old days. (It took serious investigation to exclude the possibility that victims had been exposed to these long-defunct companies' wastes.) When plaintiffs filed (eight days before the three-year statute of limitations was set to expire) the best evidence they had was the EPA field memo from the time the wells were closed, saying that from agency groundwater samples, Grace, Beatrice, and Unifirst were PRPs (potentially responsible parties under CERCLA, or Superfund, studied in Chapter 19).[23] The Centers for Disease Control added their statistical conclusion that the leukemias were caused by abnormal exposure, and the Harvard public health students added evidence that some correlation existed between wellwater and illness, but neither of these data came close to establishing causation by the defendants' chemicals. Even the plaintiffs' tipoff from Al Love, a Grace employee who lived near the Andersons, revealing the solvent-dumping practices at the Grace plant, did little to tie the defendants specifically to the plaintiffs' illnesses. Plaintiffs' attorney Schlichtmann nevertheless was confident he could do so at trial.

Conventional tort law doctrine places the burden of establishing causation on the plaintiff, requiring that the plaintiff be able to prove it is more likely than not that the defendant's tortious conduct is the but-for cause of plaintiff's injury. To carry the burden of proof in a toxic tort bodily injury case, the plaintiff eventually must prove (1) the linkage between exposure and the disease, (2) that defendant is the source of the exposure, and (3) that the exposure was of a magnitude (concentration) sufficient to be consistent with the plaintiff's proof of linkage. None of those three inquiries is simple. The first requires delving deeply into the science of epidemiology, at times seeking to

---

22. If concentrations are greater in groundwater than in an adjoining surface stream, that means the stream cannot be the source of contamination. Materials imported into groundwater do not become more concentrated in groundwater solution; if anything, they diffuse. That basic logic never got incorporated into trial findings.

23. The 1979 EPA memo was paradoxically the trigger that started the statute of limitations running.

prove linkages of toxins and diseases that are sufficiently rare that they have not previously been studied. The second can be complicated by the fungible nature of toxic products (such as asbestos insulation) or the number of possible sources of the contaminants having similar toxic properties. Plaintiff's case becomes more difficult whenever the defendant may not be responsible for all of the relevant exposures. The third requires proof of facts regarding plaintiff's exposure to the toxic substance when, in almost all cases, the plaintiff was unaware that the exposure was occurring and in historic contexts where the extent of the exposure was not being measured.

Donaldson v. Central Illinois Public Service Company
Supreme Court of Illinois, 2002
199 Ill. 2d 63, 767 N.E.2d 314, 262 Ill. Dec. 854

FITZGERALD, J. Plaintiffs are the parents of four children suing, on their own behalf and on behalf of their children, Central Illinois Public Service Company (CIPS), the owner of a former manufactured gas plant in Taylorville, Illinois (Site). The plaintiffs alleged that certain acts or omissions by CIPS and three of its contractors during the cleanup of the Site caused their children to develop neuroblastoma, a rare form of cancer. The litigation spanned six years and included the exchange of hundreds of thousands of documents and more than 250 depositions of numerous witnesses. After a four-month jury trial, at which 77 witnesses testified, a jury returned a $3.2 million verdict for plaintiffs against CIPS. The appellate court affirmed the trial court judgment (730 N.E.2d 68), and we granted CIPS's petition for leave to appeal [and] we now affirm the judgment....

Taylorville, located in Christian County, is a town which recorded 520 live births in 1988. Statistically, a case of neuroblastoma occurs one time every 29 years in a community the size of Taylorville. Between March 1989 and August 1991, during approximately a two-year period, three infants and a teenager in Taylorville were diagnosed with neuroblastoma. Zachary Donaldson was conceived in December 1987 and was born on September 7, 1988. Six months later, in March 1989, Zachary was diagnosed with neuroblastoma. At the time of trial, Zachary was in remission from his illness. Chad Hryhorysak was conceived in April 1989 and was born January 12, 1990. Chad was diagnosed with neuroblastoma six months after his birth, in March 1990. As a result of his illness, Chad is paralyzed from the waist down. Erika May was conceived in February 1989 and was born November 27, 1989. She was diagnosed with neuroblastoma two months later, in January 1990. At the time of trial, she was in remission from her illness. Lastly, Brandon Steele was born on March 17, 1978. On August 9, 1991, at age 13, Brandon was diagnosed with neuroblastoma. Brandon died on January 19, 1993....

Plaintiffs claim that the statistical excess of neuroblastoma cases in Taylorville was caused by their exposure to potent chemical carcinogens released, in part, during the cleanup of the Site. The Donaldsons lived one mile from the Site, the Hryhorysaks lived three miles from the Site, and between 1985 and 1989 the Mays lived in several locations near the Site, the closest one-half mile away and the farthest eight miles away. During his lifetime, Brandon Steele lived two miles from the Site. We now turn to the Site.

[The court reviewed the Site history from 1892, when gas production began. When the plant ceased operations in the 1930s the plant was dismantled, but large underground tanks and containers filled with 50,000 gallons of coal tar, a by-product of the coal gasification process, were left in place. In 1961, CIPS sold the Site without disclosing the residual presence of the buried coal tar. Again, in the early 1980s, after federal laws required disclosure of the toxins, CIPS remained silent, despite its knowledge of a warning in the Handbook on Manufactured

Gas that some chemicals in coal tar "are among the most powerful carcinogens known to exist."]

Aware of the risk, CIPS, through its environmental affairs department, conducted an independent on-site investigation of its manufactured gas plants and drafted a final report discussing the condition of, and potential risk at, each of its abandoned gas-manufacturing sites, including the Site. CIPS forwarded this report to its insurer and applied for "Gradual Environmental Impairment" insurance to cover "potential claims." CIPS did not report the coal tar sites to any state or federal agency or notify current owners of the potential risk.

[In 1985, after the then-current owner discovered the contamination and after that owner disturbed the soil, Taylorville authorities recorded complaints about strange odors near the Site and in the adjacent public park. Shortly thereafter, CIPS finally came forward and disclosed the fact of the contamination to the Illinois Environmental Protection Agency (IEPA) and hired contractors to conduct a "Phase I" study of the site.]

Coal tar may contain up to 10,000 different chemicals; CIPS tested for approximately 190 different compounds. This testing detected the presence of various carcinogenic compounds, including polynuclear organic (aromatic) hydrocarbons (PAHs) and volatile organic compounds (VOCs). … Monitoring revealed extremely high concentrations of volatile chemicals on the Site, in the area surrounding the Site, and in the adjacent public park to the east. In some areas, monitoring detected soil contamination at a depth of 95 feet. A Hanson[24] employee recommended "use of the lot south of the building be immediately prohibited." A second contractor, hired by CIPS to detect and minimize emissions, observed that the presence of such high levels of volatile agents, coupled with the Site's close proximity to residents living to the north, required "a strong effort to detect and reduce these emissions." … Although contained in initial drafts of the Phase I report, risk assessment and health information was deleted from the final report submitted to the IEPA. [In 1986, IEPA ordered CIPS to commence an "immediate removal action."]

As part of the immediate removal action, CIPS implemented an air-monitoring plan to measure particulate emissions and identify the ambient air quality during the excavation. Emissions particles vary in size, such that matter may be small enough to be easily respirable and undetectable to sensory perception such as smell, taste, or sight. Particles, including coal tar chemicals, may bond to soil particles. Moreover, wind speed and temperature influence emissions. Therefore, CIPS approved the use of stationary equipment placed in trailers to monitor emissions 24 hours a day, while technicians also performed spot testing several times a day with portable hand-held instruments. If the ambient air quality reached certain levels, defined within the remediation plan, workers took safety precautions and the Site was shut down.

CIPS initiated air monitoring, in part, to "minimize liability from 'real' or frivolous lawsuits." Internal documents encouraged "minimal data collection necessary to quantitatively document the principal compounds of concern, thus providing a data base for use in response to potential inquiries or claims from the nearby residents or Manners Park [the public park adjacent to the site] users" because "without (emissions data) they (CIPS) have no data if neighbors claim damages." By the time of discovery [in the lawsuit], the computer data base and original data had disappeared. In its place, CIPS offered a summary of the data, prepared internally, called the Air Monitoring Report, as its "best evidence." The report was offered during trial, and to government agencies during final remediation discussions, as a basis to show that exposure did not occur.

CIPS began the remediation on January 20, 1987. Workers removed building debris, an above-ground gas holder, two underground structures (separators), and 9,000 cubic yards of

---

24. Hanson, Parsons, and Haztech are independent contractors hired by CIPS at various stages in the site investigation and remediation efforts undertaken by CIPS. [Eds.]

soil. CIPS required the use of gas masks and protective clothing during removal of the buried structures. Hanson and Parsons, the on-site contractors, recommended relocating residents during removal of the buried structure, but CIPS declined to follow their suggestion. Excavated material and soil were removed from the Site by truck, and soil that was not trucked away at the end of the day was covered with plastic foam.

Air monitoring detected emissions above the National Air Quality Standards (NAAQS) primary health based standard for particulate emissions on seven days during the first three months of excavation. Additionally, on February 8, 1987, a Site security guard reported that high winds blew dust "all over." Two days later, on February 10, 1987, an air-monitoring station reported a NAAQS exceedance, and a local resident was hospitalized with an intense headache, nausea, blurred vision, and convulsions. She was diagnosed with an acute attack caused by some toxic cause. The Site diary indicates that CIPS was advised of the incident. On February 11, 1987, the Site project manager expressed "great concern" about air emissions at the Site, and "wanted to be on record as pushing for shutdown and resident relocation." During this same time, truck drivers removing the soil and waste complained of nausea. As a result, the drivers were advised to wear respirators once they crossed the railroad tracks near the Site. However, residents living in this same area were not warned or relocated. At trial, CIPS maintained that NAAQS exceedances were the result of other sources, such as truck exhaust and burning leaves, and not the excavated soil.

[Once the excavation and removal of soil was completed in early 1987, activity at the Site halted.] CIPS did not backfill the excavation with soil. CIPS and the IEPA disagreed about the scope of further remediation…. During this [two-year] conflict…CIPS covered the hole with styrofoam and plywood sheets to reduce dust emissions and volatilization…[and] discontinued particulate testing and dismantled the air-monitoring program…. Eventually, in April 1989, the IEPA granted CIPS approval to permanently backfill the hole.

The Illinois Department of Public Health (Department) examined the unusually high statistical incidence of neuroblastoma cases in Taylorville. Initially, the Department studied the genetic relatedness between families; scientific testing defeated this theory. In June 1990, the Department prepared a final draft "Preliminary Health Assessment" report for the Site. The report was available to the public for review and made available to CIPS for comment. The report concluded that the Taylorville "population had been exposed to…dust entrained contaminants…largely as the result of limited remedial action on the part of CIPS." Further, the report stated that the Site "is considered to be of potential public health concern because of the risk to human health caused by the possibility of exposure to hazardous substances…. The contaminants are present at the site in large quantities and the presence of significant quantities of contaminated soils represents a source of continuing release to the environment."

CIPS argued to the Department that its report was misleading, stating that more recent CIPS air-monitoring data contradicted the Department's assessment and that the report "should be based on current Site conditions." CIPS maintained that this current data was available in its Air Monitoring Report, the only available source of information regarding ambient air at the Site. Based upon CIPS's Air Monitoring Report, the Department's report was modified to state that "the lack of likely completed exposure pathways makes the CIPS site an unlikely cause of the neuroblastoma excess." The Department's report was finalized as modified despite commentary from the USEPA that because "air emissions occurred during the excavation and likely occurred while the excavation was left open for two years, it appears to be likely that some exposure occurred to residents surrounding the Site."

[Actions were filed in beginning in 1991, containing counts of negligence, nuisance, conspiracy, willful and wanton conduct, spoliation of evidence, conspiracy, and negligent remediation counts. In 1996, after some of the peripheral claims and parties were dismissed or settled, the cases were consolidated in Christian County. Prior to trial] the trial court denied plaintiffs' claims for punitive damages. At trial, plaintiffs called three experts to connect the neuroblastomas to the toxins at the Site. Plaintiffs called Dr. Shira Kramer, an epidemiologist specializing in childhood cancers; Dr. Harlee Sue Strauss, a toxicologist specializing in molecular biology; and Dr. Thomas Winters, a physician specializing in occupational and environmental medicine. CIPS responded with numerous experts and plaintiffs' own treating physicians, all of whom testified that the cause of neuroblastoma is unknown, and that they could not testify within a reasonable degree of medical certainty that exposures from the Site caused the particular neuroblastomas in this case.

At the close of plaintiffs' case, the trial court denied CIPS's motion to strike plaintiffs' expert testimony and its motion for a directed verdict. The jury returned a $3.2 million verdict in favor of plaintiffs against CIPS alone, finding CIPS liable for negligence and public nuisance. The trial court entered judgment on the verdict on March 27, 1998, and CIPS appealed.... The appellate court affirmed the judgment.... This appeal followed....[25]

Causation. CIPS maintains that plaintiffs failed to satisfy their overall burden to show causation. CIPS points to the record as support, and argues that it shows only a "mere possibility" of causation, rather than that causation is "more probably true than not." According to CIPS, a showing of causation includes both "generic causation" — i.e., coal tar is capable of causing neuroblastoma — and "specific causation"— i.e., exposure to coal tar from the Site did in fact occur and actually caused the neuroblastomas. CIPS also argues that in toxic tort litigation, causation also includes a showing of "exposure," which must be quantified with evidence of the level or dose of exposure. CIPS asserts that a plaintiff may establish this exposure requirement with evidence of biological markers, such as trace fibers or particles found in the body, proximity to the defendant's product, or personal or environmental monitoring.

We disagree with defendant's characterization of Illinois law on causation.[26] First, Illinois law does not define causation in terms of "generic" or "specific" causation. Rather, our case law clearly states that in negligence actions, the plaintiff must present evidence of proximate causation, which includes both "cause in fact" and "legal cause."... A plaintiff may show "cause in fact" under the substantial factor test, showing that the defendant's conduct was a material element and substantial factor in bringing about the alleged injury.... "Legal cause" examines the foreseeability of injury — whether the injury is "of a type which a reasonable man would see as a likely result of his conduct." Defendant does not allege that plaintiffs failed to show legal cause.

Turning to "cause in fact," a plaintiff may meet his or her burden of causation with circumstantial evidence — evidence from which a "jury may infer other connected facts which usually and reasonably follow according to...common experience." This is to say, Illinois law does not require unequivocal or unqualified evidence of causation. To the contrary, we have held that where "there exists limited medical knowledge of a malady,...medical testimony pertaining to causation may not be unqualified and unequivocal."

Additionally, we reject CIPS's assertion that causation includes a showing of exposure, which must be quantified. A plaintiff must establish that he or she came into contact with chemicals produced by the defendant. In this context, however, Illinois law does not require that

---

25. A long section on the admissibility of plaintiffs' expert testimony is omitted. That subject is considered in Part C of this chapter. [Eds.]

26. There are terminological differences between Illinois's causation jurisprudence and the generic tort materials set out in Chapter 3. Substantively, the two are similar. This is typical and underscores the reminder that tort law is state common law and the terminology and substance vary slightly from jurisdiction to jurisdiction. [Eds.]

plaintiffs quantify the level of exposure. CIPS relies upon cases that address exposure to asbestos-containing products in an occupational setting. These cases hold that in order to show causation in an asbestos case, a plaintiff must "produce evidence of exposure to a specific product on a regular basis over some extended period of time in proximity to where the plaintiff actually worked," commonly called the "frequency, regularity and proximity" test. ... In this instance, we are not compelled to adopt this rule and depart from traditional concepts of causation. Environmental exposure cases, like the instant case, do not afford litigants the opportunity to specify with such certainty the exact level and dose of exposure. In most instances, the details of exposure, including information of exactly when or where exposure occurred, is not available. ... Accordingly, we review whether there was evidence from which a jury could conclude that CIPS's conduct was a material element and substantial factor in bringing about the neuroblastomas.

Plaintiffs presented testimony from Dr. Winters, an expert in occupational and environmental medicine. Dr. Winters testified that in the case of environmental exposure, like the instant matter, it is difficult to quantify exposure to individual community members. However, his review of evidence in this case, including the IEPA 4(q) immediate removal action plans, Department reports, USEPA reports, family medical histories and interviews, and Site reports that discussed the level of soil contamination and methods of removal, as well as the open and unmonitored status of the Site for two years, led him to conclude that cumulative exposure occurred here.

Further, plaintiffs presented circumstantial evidence of community exposure. The jury heard evidence regarding the potential of particulate matter to travel undetected for several miles. The jury was advised of Taylorville weather conditions during the period of remediation, including high wind and unseasonably warm weather, which facilitate the travel of air-borne contaminants. Plaintiffs offered evidence that during the period of remediation, on-site workers complained of symptoms consistent with exposure to toxic substances. At that same time, the record shows that a local resident, who lived within several hundred feet of the Site, was hospitalized with dizziness, headaches, vomiting, and seizures, and later diagnosed with exposure to an unknown toxic cause. This individual testified that "everything just reeked from it [coal tar]. It even penetrated into the homes." She later added the Site cast a "heavy mist over the whole area, like a fog" and that workers at the Site dressed in protective gear. [The court recounted next the NAAQS violations and "Draft" state-compiled Health Assessment as further evidence that sustained a finding of exposure.]

Plaintiffs presented testimony from Dr. Kramer, an expert witness who testified regarding causation. [The court recounted Dr. Kramer's extraordinary qualifications as an epidemiologist.] Scientists in this field assume that disease is not distributed randomly in a group of individuals and that identifiable subgroups, including those exposed to certain agents, are at increased risk of contracting particular diseases. Dr. Kramer explained that epidemiology concerns whether a particular agent is capable of causing a disease or injury. Further, she testified that an epidemiologist may conduct one of many studies to determine whether an agent is related to the risk of disease or adverse health affects. As she explained, study design varies depending upon the circumstances, including resource limitations, time constraints, or the subject of the study. Both parties agree that under the current scientific literature, several epidemiologic criteria are used to judge the relation between an agent and the risk of disease, including the temporal relationship between the disease and the exposure; the statistical strength of association; the dose-response relationship; the replication of findings; the biologic plausibility; alternative causes; cessation of exposure; the association of exposure with a single disease; and consistency with other knowledge. According to Dr. Kramer, however, scientific literature also explains that the science of epidemiology does not demand satisfaction of each criteria, rather on occasion some may be irrelevant or impossible to determine.

Dr. Kramer testified that the carcinogens contained in coal tar and coal tar related carcinogens from the Site were the most-likely cause of the plaintiffs' neuroblastomas. She later quantified this as a "greater than 50 percent probability." Dr. Kramer admitted that no scientific consensus exists to support the theory that coal tar causes neuroblastoma. However, in great detail she outlined the methodology used to generate her conclusion, including her own published studies on neuroblastoma, scientific literature on risk factors for nervous system cancers, animal studies regarding nervous system cancer, studies regarding the risks of expectant mothers and infants, and her Taylorville case-specific study that was based upon family history questionnaires and Illinois Cancer Registry data. Her research ruled out random variability as the cause for the sudden increase of Taylorville neuroblastoma cases.

Dr. Kramer discussed the temporal relationship between the release of ambient air emissions from the Site and the onset of neuroblastoma. However, Dr. Kramer did not rely solely on an abstract temporal connection. Dr. Kramer also examined the increased incidence of neuroblastoma through standard scientific calculation, and calculated the probability that the onset of neuroblastoma was due to random chance; she concluded that the possibility of chance was one in 10,000. Further, Dr. Kramer discussed that coal tar is a multipotential carcinogen that can cause cancer at multiple sites in the body. Dr. Kramer addressed alternative sources, and determined that although alternative sources are potential causes of neuroblastoma, only the Site was a common risk factor among all plaintiffs. Consistent with the science of epidemiology, Dr. Kramer performed a cancer incidence rate analysis to measure the rate of development of neuroblastoma and adult cancers in Taylorville. The incidence rate examines whether the sudden or dramatic increase in cases is more likely due to chance. In order to complete this study, Dr. Kramer studied the incidence of neuroblastoma in four different comparison groups during the period 1986 through 1991, including: the National Cancer Institute Surveillance Epidemiology and End Results Program Rates (SEER, a national cancer registry), the State of Illinois, demographically similar zip codes without manufactured gas plant sites, and demographically similar zip codes with manufactured gas sites. At the conclusion of her study, Dr. Kramer testified that there was a one in 10,000 probability that chance caused the neuroblastomas in this case. Further, Dr. Kramer discussed fetal nervous system cancers and the increased sensitivity of expectant mothers and young children to carcinogens. Based upon medical research animal studies, she testified that the fetal nervous system is 50 times more sensitive to carcinogens. Dr. Kramer also testified that there is no safe level of exposure to known sensitive populations, and argued that this was a "known scientific fact" cited in the literature.

Plaintiffs also presented Dr. Strauss, a molecular biologist and toxicologist.... Her field of study, toxicology, examines the adverse effects of chemicals on living organisms, and is otherwise called the "science of poisons." Dr. Strauss explained that toxicological studies, by themselves, rarely offer direct evidence that a disease in any one individual was caused by a chemical exposure. However, toxicology can rule out other risk factors known to cause a disease and provide scientific information regarding the increased risk of contracting a disease at any given dose.

Dr. Strauss testified that coal tar and its general chemical constituents were the cause of plaintiffs' neuroblastomas. Dr. Strauss based her conclusions upon animal studies and medical research in the area of nervous system tumors, soil samples from the Site, health and safety diaries from the Site, and air-monitoring logs from the Site. Additionally, Dr. Strauss discussed the volatile potential of coal tar compounds, using studies that discussed manufactured gas plant sites with similar site histories and VOC contamination profiles. From this data, she compiled the potential toxicity of the Site and the cancer potency of the coal tar. Further, Dr. Strauss discussed the complex chemical compounds contained in coal tar, and the "synergistic" effect that occurs when these compounds interact to form more potent compounds. She stated that these same compounds are multipotential, affecting several organ sites, and transplacental, meaning that the carcinogen may pass from the placenta to a developing fetus.

This case presents the classic "battle of the experts" frequently seen in toxic tort litigation. Plaintiffs' experts testified that the Site was a substantial factor in bringing about plaintiffs' neuroblastomas, while defendants' experts testified that medical science does not associate coal tar with neuroblastoma. When viewing this evidence in the light most favorable to the plaintiffs, we do not find that the evidence so overwhelmingly favors CIPS that no contrary verdict based on that evidence could ever stand.[27] Clearly, there was sufficient evidence from which a jury could conclude that CIPS's conduct was a material element and substantial factor in bringing about the alleged injury.

Duty. CIPS next claims that plaintiffs failed to satisfy [their] burden to show CIPS violated any duty. CIPS does not deny the existence of a duty; it argues that the evidence was insufficient to establish that it breached its duty. We find sufficient evidence of a breach.

In their complaint, plaintiffs alleged a breach of duty beginning in 1939 and ending in 1989. Jury instructions incorporated specific acts and omissions alleged in plaintiffs' complaint: (1) the abandonment of coal tar in the underground tanks in 1938; (2) failure to monitor the Site before contaminants migrated off-site and were discovered by local authorities; (3) failure to warn local authorities or residents after CIPS discovered contamination in 1985; (4) failure to control airborne pathways before beginning its immediate removal action in 1987; (5) increasing volatile air and dust emissions during the immediate removal action in 1987; (6) failure to control the volatile air and dust emissions after the immediate removal action between 1987 and 1989; (7) failure to warn residents of any risk to human health resulting from exposure to the Site while it remained open between 1987 and 1989; and (8) failure to provide reliable air monitoring of emissions while the Site remained open between 1987 and 1989. [The court with little discussion found sufficient evidence that a jury could find that CIPS had breached its duty.]

Public Nuisance. Last, CIPS claims that plaintiffs' nuisance claims were defective. … At the time plaintiffs filed their complaint, plaintiffs had a common law right to claim damages for public nuisance. At common law, a public nuisance included:

> an unreasonable interference with a right common to the general public. Earlier cases recognized that the public had a right to clean, unpolluted air and that any deprivation of that right was actionable as a private injury and indictable as a public wrong. However, the notion of pure air has come to mean clean air consistent with the character of the locality and the attending circumstances. Whether smoke, odors, dust or gaseous fumes constitute a nuisance depends on the peculiar facts presented by each case. City of Chicago v. Commonwealth Edison, 321 N.E.2d 412 (1974)….

We find, therefore, that plaintiffs' nuisance claim was proper.

The second issue presented for our review is whether IEPA direction and supervision bar nuisance liability. CIPS maintains that the extension of nuisance liability in this context will

---

27. The latter half of this sentence describes the usual standard appropriate when an appellate court is asked to rule that the trial court erred in failing to grant either a directed verdict or a judgment notwithstanding the verdict. The first half of the sentence is usually associated with the posture to be taken by a trial court (i.e., viewed in the light most favorable to the nonmoving party) in considering materials offered in support and opposition to a motion for summary judgment. [Eds.]

damage State interests by discouraging the private sector from cooperating with the IEPA. At the heart of CIPS's albeit brief argument is the contention that it is "unfair" to reward cooperation with exposure to liability. CIPS warns that if this court permits liability here, it will slow down or reduce future clean-up efforts.

First, we reject CIPS's argument based upon the language of the Illinois Environmental Protection Act §45(a), [which] states that "no existing civil or criminal remedy for any wrongful action shall be excluded or impaired by this Act."... We are, however, compelled to respond further. CIPS was not held liable for the mere release of toxins into the ambient air during remediation. In an industrial society, odors, film, dust, and smoke may exist. This logic is equally true in the case of an environmental remediation. In this instance, however, plaintiffs allege a substantial injury different from the general public, and claim that this injury is not based solely on ordinary clean-up efforts, but rather negligent remedial conduct. We need only look to plaintiffs' allegations: CIPS is liable for the "release of 'coal tar' into the soil, groundwater and air *in violation of the IEPA*; contamination of public water supplies *in violation of the IEPA*; release of airborne carcinogens, clastogens, and mutagens from the Site before its 'Immediate Removal Action'; release of airborne carcinogens, clastogens, and mutagens from the Site during its 'Immediate Removal Action'; release of airborne carcinogens, clastogens, and mutagens after its 'Immediate Removal Action'; maintaining an open pit resulting in erosion of soil and collection of surface water which allowed the further release of volatile air and fugitive dust emissions for two years after its 'Immediate Removal Action.'" (Emphasis added by the court.) We do not find that liability in this case will frustrate future remedial efforts or deter cooperation. To the contrary, it may encourage cooperation with government agencies, and heighten care and concern for public safety during remedial actions. As a final matter, we reject CIPS's argument that it should not be liable because the release of emissions was solely the result of IEPA oversight. The record demonstrates otherwise.... Affirmed. [Concurrence of MCMORROW, J., omitted.]

COMMENTARY & QUESTIONS

1. **Plaintiff's theories and the relevance of defendant's efforts at concealment.** CIPS's behavior demonstrates a consistent pattern of attempting to conceal information about the contamination from the authorities and the public. Why is this concealment relevant? Which legal issues does CIPS's concealment affect? The court relies on the concealment to find a breach of duty, but it also is relevant to plaintiffs' claims for punitive damages. Why did the trial court dismiss plaintiffs' punitive damage claims, and why did the plaintiffs fail to cross-appeal that dismissal? The court also references the concealment evidence in relation to the nuisance claim and plainly finds a *negligently* created public nuisance. But could the court have sustained a nuisance finding based on *intentionality* alone? Recall that the legal rubric for intentionality — that CIPS intended the natural consequences of its acts — is quite straightforward. However, the somewhat harder question is just what should be included among the "nautral consequences." If CIPS's only act had been leaving the coal tar in the ground decades ago, the issue might be a difficult one for plaintiffs. As the events played out, however, the carcinogenicity and amount of coal tar, coupled with the necessity of disturbing the soil to remediate the site, make potential exposures resulting from volatilization and particulate pollution a natural consequence of intended actions. Care in performing the remedial activity, therefore, is not relevant to an intentional tort theory. Likewise, even carrying

out a cleanup according to IEPA requirements that might be evidence of due care in a negligence claim is plainly not relevant if the plaintiffs' claims sound in intentional nuisance or strict liability.

2. **Linking exposure to disease and reaching novel conclusions.** In *Donaldson*, what are the most convincing evidence and testimony linking coal tar exposure to neuroblastomas? Could the jury have found for plaintiffs without the testimony of the epidemiologist? Although it is not yet a universal position, many courts are requiring that plaintiffs be able to produce epidemiological testimony to avoid summary judgment on the issue of causation. See, e.g., Daniels v. Lyondell-Citgo Ref. Co., 99 S.W.3d 722 (Tex. App. 2003) (summary judgment for defendant was properly granted because plaintiff's proferred epidemiological studies did not reach the required standard of statistical significance and thus could not constitute evidence sufficient to establish causation). See also Exxon Corp. v. Makofski, No. 14-00-00763-Cv, 2003 Tex. App. Lexis 6411 (July 24, 2003) (in the absence of epidemiological studies showing a statistically significant doubling of the risk of childhood leukemia or other diseases from exposure to benzene, there was insufficient proof that benzene in the drinking water caused any diseases). An older case that does not require epidemiological testimony is Chevron Chem. Co. v. Ferebee, 736 F.2d 1529 (D.C. Cir. 1984). In *Ferebee*, plaintiff's decedent died of pulmonary fibrosis after extensive exposure to sprayed Paraquat (an insecticide manufactured by defendant), during the course of decedent's employment at a federal agricultural research facility. Neither of plaintiff's testifying experts in *Ferebee* were epidemiologists:

> Chevron argues that there has never been any evidence nor any suggestion that paraquat can cause chronic injury of this sort and that, in any event, Ferebee could not have been exposed to enough paraquat to injure him in this fashion. The short answer to Chevron's argument is that two expert witnesses refuted it and that the jury was entitled to believe those experts. Both Drs. Crystal and Yusuf, who are eminent specialists in pulmonary medicine and who were Ferebee's treating physicians, testified that paraquat poisoning was the cause of Ferebee's illness and death. Both admitted that cases like Ferebee's were rare, but Dr. Crystal identified three other cases he felt were similar to that of Mr. Ferebee. Chevron argues that these cases can be distinguished from Mr. Ferebee's, but it is not our role to decide the merits of Chevron's attempted distinctions; Dr. Crystal thought the cases were similar, and the jury was entitled to believe him. Chevron of course introduced its own experts who were of the view that Ferebee's illness was not caused by paraquat, but the testimony of those witnesses, who did not treat Mr. Ferebee or examine him, can hardly be deemed so substantial that the jury had no choice but to accept it. The experts on both sides relied on essentially the same diagnostic methodology; they differed solely on the conclusions they drew from the test results and other information. The case was thus a classic battle of the experts, a battle in which the jury must decide the victor. 736 F.2d at 1535.

Apart from the lack of epidemiologic testimony, this brief excerpt from *Ferebee* highlights a second common problem for courts in toxic tort cases — novel conclusions drawn by the experts. Chevron, based on its considerable knowledge and experience with Paraquat-related injuries, believed that the data was quite conclusive that the type of Paraquat exposure suffered by Ferebee was not correlated with the type of injury he sustained, and attacked the conclusions of Drs. Crystal and Yusef to the contrary. *Donaldson* addresses this by saying in the portion of the opinion discussing the admissibility of expert testimony (a topic considered more fully in Part C): "Rather, the proper focus of the general acceptance test is on the underlying methodology used to generate the conclusion. If the underlying method used to generate an expert's opinion are reasonably relied upon by the experts in the field, the fact finder may consider the opinion — despite the novelty of the conclusion rendered by the expert." 767 N.E.2d at 324. Returning to the *Ferebee* facts, how would the *Donaldson* court characterize the testimony on causation of two treating lung specialists based on very small samples and their own personal knowledge and experience — as novel conclusions or as flawed and unacceptable methodology?

3. **Litigation involving rare cancers and litigation involving more common cancers.** In light of the importance of epidemiological evidence to proving linkage of exposure and disease, which cases are likely to be easier to litigate, cases involving relatively rare cancers, such as *Donaldson*, or cases involving more prevalent and, therefore, more frequently studied cancers? One variable that affects the answer is resources. If the plaintiff is able to obtain painstaking case-specific research and testimony relating to a rare cancer, such as that done by Dr. Kramer in *Donaldson*, the rarity of the cancer may become a plus. There is likely to be no other research that addresses the subject, thereby reducing the grounds for debating the conclusion of linkage and causation offered by plaintiff's expert. Lacking the resources, however, plaintiff either will have to forgo epidemiological testimony, which could easily result in losing the issue, or rely on testimony that collects and opines on the instant case relying on studies that are not quite on-point. This latter technique is referred to by the experts and the court in *Donaldson* as "extrapolation" and is considered by the court to be a generally accepted methodology where more direct data are not available. Even more confounding for the victim of a rare cancer, could a plaintiff win a case like *Donaldson* if there is only one victim in the locality of the exposure? In such a case, the statistical possibility that the cancer can be explained as a random event is considerable. With more common cancers, there are likely to be more studies. As already noted, that may present equivocality if the studies all do not reach the same results. Additionally, the more extensive research may demonstrate that other hazardous substances, in addition to those for which defendant is responsible, are correlated with the disease. This will make it harder to persuade the trier of fact that the exposure for which defendant is responsible "was a material element and substantial factor in bringing about the alleged injury," to use the language of the *Donaldson* opinion. 199 Ill. 2d at 90. Reconsider this point after you have read the *Landrigan* case and its discussion of relative and attributable risk that follows.

4. **Legal theories in toxic tort cases involving occupational exposures.** All states in the United States have enacted workers' compensation statutes that replace tort suits by employees against their employers with administrative compensation ("Comp") systems. Thus when an employee suffers an on-the-job exposure to a toxic substance, recourse against the employer is limited to Comp, and Comp almost invariably provides a far lesser recovery than would a tort suit. Injured workers in these cases frequently seek to bring tort cases against third parties (i.e., parties other than their

employer) who can in some way be held liable in tort. Third parties targeted in such suits may include independent contractors who are responsible for the exposure or manufacturers of the hazardous materials, who are sued on a defective products strict liability theory. In Chevron Chem. Co. v. Ferebee, 736 F.2d 1529 (D.C. Cir. 1984), discussed above in note 2, Ferebee's claim against Chevron was based on a Maryland products liability law that requires warnings to consumers of a product's known dangers. On a failure to warn theory, the plaintiff must prove all of the causal links from exposure to injury, i.e., that "paraquat proximately caused Mr. Ferebee's illness and death" and also that "the inadequacy of the warning proximately caused Mr. Ferebee's illness and death." Warnings were on the package, but they did not refer to dermal absorption and lung disease. The warning, "CAN KILL IF SWALLOWED, HARMFUL TO THE EYES AND SKIN," certainly indicated that Paraquat isn't an appropriate tonic or skin lotion, but the warning did not specifically mention adverse consequences of dermal contact other than skin irritation. This failure in the warning to disclose consequences of exposure known to Chevron was deemed sufficient by the appellate court to support the jury finding in Ferebee's favor.

Landrigan v. Celotex Corporation
Supreme Court of New Jersey, 1992
127 N.J. 404, 605 A.2d 1079

POLLACK, J. Plaintiff, Angelina Landrigan, sued defendants Owens-Corning Fiberglass Corporation and Owens Illinois, Inc. for the personal injuries and death of her husband, Thomas Landrigan, claiming that exposure to defendants' asbestos had caused his death from colon cancer....

Decedent worked as a maintenance man and pipe insulator at the Bayonne Terminal Warehouse from 1956 until December 1981, when he was diagnosed as suffering from colon cancer. From 1956 until 1972, he allegedly worked with insulation containing asbestos supplied by defendants. In January 1982, he underwent surgery but the cancer spread, and he died in December 1982. The cause of his death was adenocarcinoma, "a malignant adenoma arising from a glandular organ," the most common type of colon cancer. Generally speaking, colorectal cancer is the second most common cancer in the United States, striking 140,000 persons and causing 60,000 deaths annually. In 1984, plaintiff filed this survivorship and wrongful death action, asserting that exposure to asbestos had caused decedent's death.

At the trial in 1989, plaintiff relied on two experts, Dr. Joseph Sokolowski, Jr., a physician who is board certified in both internal medicine and pulmonary medicine, and Dr. Joseph K. Wagoner, an epidemiologist and biostatistician but not a physician. Dr. Sokolowski never treated or examined decedent. He based his conclusions on a review of decedent's history of exposure to asbestos, the absence of other risk factors in decedent's history, and on various epidemiological, animal, and in vitro studies. Stating that physicians regularly rely on epidemiological studies, Dr. Sokolowski testified that asbestos can cause colon cancer in humans. He also described the path asbestos fibers take from inhalation to the gastrointestinal tract. Dr. Sokolowski testified that exposure to asbestos was the cause of decedent's colon cancer...[and] further that decedent would not have contracted colon cancer if he had not been exposed to asbestos.

Plaintiff also offered Dr. Wagoner to testify that asbestos exposure had caused decedent's colon cancer. After conducting a hearing pursuant to Evidence Rule 8, the trial court ruled that as an epidemiologist and not a physician, Dr. Wagoner was not qualified to testify that asbestos had caused decedent's cancer. The court, however, permitted the witness to testify about epidemiological methods and studies linking colon cancer to asbestos exposure. It also allowed Dr. Wagoner to state his opinion that asbestos causes colon cancer in humans.... At the close of plaintiff's case, the trial court granted defendants' motions for a directed verdict.

In recent years, we have sought to accommodate the requirements for the admission of expert testimony with the need for that testimony. Nowhere is that accommodation more compelling than on the issue of causation in toxic-tort litigation concerning diseases of indeterminate origin. Many such injuries remain latent for years, are associated with diverse risk factors, and occur without any apparent cause. Steve Gold, Note, Causation in Toxic Torts: Burdens of Proof, Standards of Persuasion, and Statistical Evidence, 96 Yale L.J. 376, 376 (1986). In that context, proof that a defendant's conduct caused decedent's injuries is more subtle and sophisticated than proof in cases concerned with more traditional torts....

Traditionally, plaintiffs have established a connection between tortious conduct and personal injuries through the testimony of medical experts who testify that the defendant's specific conduct was the cause of the plaintiff's injuries. Toxic torts, however, do not readily lend themselves to proof that is so particularized. Developments in the Law-Toxic Waste Litigation, 99 Harv. L. Rev. 1458, 1620 (1986). Plaintiffs in such cases may be compelled to resort to more general evidence, such as that provided by epidemiological studies. A basic understanding of some fundamentals of epidemiology is essential for an assessment of the admissibility of such evidence.

Simply defined, epidemiology is "the study of disease occurrence in human populations." Gary D. Friedman, Primer of Epidemiology 1 (3d ed. 1987). Epidemiology studies the relationship between a disease and a factor suspected of causing the disease, using statistical methods to determine the likelihood of causation. Bert Black & David E. Lilienfeld, Epidemiologic Proof in Toxic Tort Litigation, 52 Fordham L. Rev. 732, 750 (1984). By comparison to the clinical health sciences, which are directly concerned with diseases in particular patients, epidemiology is concerned with the statistical analysis of disease in groups of patients. The statistical associations may become so compelling, as they did in establishing the correlation between asbestos exposure and mesothelioma, that they raise a legitimate implication of causation. "Statistical associations," however, "do not necessarily imply causation.... It is important, therefore, to have some basis for deciding whether a statistical association derived from an observational study represents a cause-and-effect relationship." Friedman, supra, at 182–183. See Austin B. Hill, The Environment and Disease: Association or Causation?, 58 Proc. Royal Soc. Med. 295 (1965) (criteria to assess likelihood of causal relationship from statistical associations).

At oral argument, defendants, for example, stressed two criteria, among others, that are crucial in determining whether a statistical association will give rise to an inference that a particular substance causes a certain disease in people who are exposed to it. The two criteria are the strength of the association and the consistency of any such association with other knowledge. The argument is sound. As Professor Friedman explains:

> In general, the stronger the association, the more likely it represents a cause-and-effect relationship. Weak associations often turn out to be spurious and explainable by some known, or as yet unknown, confounding variable.... Strength of an association is usually measured by the relative risk or the ratio of the disease rate in those with the factor to the rate in those without. The relative risk of lung cancer in cigarette smokers as compared to nonsmokers is on the order of 10:1, whereas the relative risk of pancreatic cancer is about 2:1. The difference suggests that cigarette smoking is more likely to be a causal factor for lung cancer than for pancreatic cancer.

If the association makes sense in terms of known biological mechanisms or other epidemiologic knowledge, it becomes more plausible as a cause-and-effect relationship. Part of the attractiveness of the hypothesis that a high-saturated fat, high-cholesterol diet predisposes to atherosclerosis is the fact that a biologic mechanism can be invoked. Such a diet increases blood lipids, which may in turn be deposited in arterial walls. A correlation between the number of telephone poles in a country and its coronary heart disease mortality rate lacks plausibility as a cause-and-effect relationship partly because it is difficult to imagine a biologic mechanism whereby telephone poles result in atherosclerosis. [Friedman, *supra*, at 183–184.]

The "attributable risk," by comparison, is the proportion of the disease that is statistically attributable to the factor. Black & Lilienfeld, supra, 52 Fordham L. Rev. at 761. It "is a composite measure that takes into account both the relative risk of disease if exposed and the proportion of the population so exposed."...

Plaintiff's medical expert was Dr. Sokolowski. Initially, he explained that he had examined certain literature on colon cancer, including the landmark study by Dr. Irving Selikoff. See Irving Selikoff, et al., Mortality Experience of Insulation Workers in the United States and Canada, 330 Annals N.Y. Acad. Sci. 91 (1979). The study indicated a relative risk of colon cancer from the exposure to asbestos of 1.55. The attributable risk, which would vary according to the extent and intensity of the exposure, was approximately thirty-five percent. Thus, assuming a causal relationship, the Selikoff study indicates that thirty-five percent of the cases of colon cancer in the population exposed to asbestos can be attributed to that exposure.

Dr. Sokolowski had never treated or examined decedent, but he had reviewed decedent's medical records and plaintiff's answers to interrogatories. Those materials indicated that decedent had been exposed to asbestos in his work. They also indicated the absence of other risk factors such as a family history of colon cancer, a high-fat diet, and the undue consumption of alcohol. Dr. Sokolowski acknowledged that "many studies...show no statistically significant increase in colon cancer in workers exposed to asbestos." Finally, he relied on the results of animal and in vitro studies.

The trial court rejected Dr. Sokolowski's testimony as a "net opinion" unsupported by any facts. Specifically, the court stated that "epidemiological evidence can only be used to show that a defendant's conduct increased a plaintiff's risk of injury to some measurable extent but it cannot be used to answer the critical question did the asbestos cause Mr. Landrigan's colon cancer."

The Appellate Division agreed with that assessment, explaining that Dr. Sokolowski had failed to account for other factors that may have caused decedent's cancer. Although it accepted the validity of the Selikoff study, the court stated that the 1.55 relative risk was insufficient to support Dr. Sokolowski's opinion that decedent's exposure had caused the cancer. Without expressly adopting a specific standard, the court cited with approval several cases that adopted a requirement that an epidemiological study show a relative risk in excess of 2.0 to prove that causation in a specific individual was more probable than not. The significance of a relative risk greater than 2.0 representing a true causal relationship is that the ratio evidences an attributable risk of more than fifty percent, which means that more than half of the cases of the studied disease in a comparable population exposed to the substance are attributable to that exposure. This finding could support an inference that the exposure was the probable cause of the disease in a specific member of the exposed population.

Defense counsel urges that the Appellate Division opinion may be read as requiring that an expert may not rely on an epidemiological study to support a finding of individual causation unless the relative risk is greater than 2.0. At oral argument before us, they agreed that such a requirement may be unnecessary. Counsel acknowledged that under certain circumstances a study with a relative risk of less than 2.0 could support a finding of specific causation. Those circumstances would include, for example, individual clinical data, such as asbestos in or near the tumor or a documented history of extensive asbestos exposure. So viewed, a relative risk of 2.0 is not so much a password to a finding of causation as one piece of evidence, among others, for the court to consider in determining whether the expert has employed a sound methodology in reaching his or her conclusion....

The court must also examine the manner in which experts reason from the studies and other information to a conclusion. As previously indicated, that conclusion must derive from a sound methodology that is supported by some consensus of experts in the field.

In the present case, Dr. Sokolowski began by reviewing the scientific literature to establish both the ability of asbestos to cause colon cancer and the magnitude of the risk that it would cause that result. Next, he assumed that decedent was exposed to asbestos and that his exposure, in both intensity and duration, was comparable to that of the study populations described in the literature. He then assumed that other known risk factors for colon cancer did not apply to decedent. After considering decedent's exposure and the absence of those factors, Dr. Sokolowski concluded that decedent's exposure more likely than not had been the cause of his colon cancer.

Without limiting the trial court on remand, its assessment of Dr. Sokolowski's testimony should include evaluation of the validity both of the studies on which he relied and of his assumption that the decedent's asbestos exposure was like that of the members of the study populations. The court should also verify Dr. Sokolowski's assumption concerning the absence of other risk factors. Finally, the court should ascertain if the relevant scientific community accepts the process by which Dr. Sokolowski reasoned to the conclusion that the decedent's asbestos exposure had caused his cancer. Thus, to determine the admissibility of the witness's opinion, the court, without substituting its judgment for that of the expert, should examine each step in Dr. Sokolowski's reasoning.

Our decision does not necessarily mean that on remand the trial court must reach a different result. Although the diagnosis of decedent's disease and the cause of his death are not in dispute, the parties vigorously contest the probability that decedent's colon cancer was caused by asbestos exposure. The issue posed to both Dr. Wagoner and Dr. Sokolowski was the likelihood that decedent's colon cancer was caused by asbestos exposure. Dr. Wagoner did not rely exclusively on epidemiological studies in addressing that issue. In addition to relying on such studies, he, like Dr. Sokolowski, reviewed specific evidence about decedent's medical and occupational histories. Both witnesses also excluded certain known risk factors for colon cancer, such as excessive alcohol consumption, a high-fat diet, and a positive family history. From statistical population studies to the conclusion of causation in an individual, however, is a broad leap, particularly for a witness whose training, unlike that of a physician, is oriented toward the study of groups and not of individuals. Nonetheless, proof of causation in toxic-tort cases depends largely on inferences derived from statistics about groups. Gold, *supra*, 96 Yale L.J. at 401....[Reversed and remanded.]

COMMENTARY & QUESTIONS

1. **Epidemiology, relative risk, and attributable risk.** Although the *Landrigan* opinion is not very explicit on this point, relative risk (RR) and attributable risk (AR) are, in a sense, reciprocal measures. When the relative risk is 2.0 (sometimes expressed as 2:1), the attributable risk is 50% (.5). What this relative risk of 2.0 or 2:1 means in popular parlance is that a person with that risk factor is twice as likely as someone without the

factor to have the correlated harm occur. The precise equation that relates the two values is RR-1/RR=AR. So, for example, in the cigarette smoking to lung cancer example, where the relative risk is 10, the attributable risk is 90% (.9), i.e., nine of the ten lung cancers that befall smokers are attributable to smoking cigarettes rather than to other factors. In the Selikoff study, the relative risk is 1.55, so the attributable risk is (1.55-1)/1.55=.35, or 35%. For a good introductory discussion to the forms of epidemiological data and its use in toxic tort litigation, see Dintzer & Mosher, Epidemiological Evidence in Toxic Tort Cases, 17 Nat. Resources & Env't 222 (2003).

2. **Legal causation and statistical proof: comparing apples and pears.** What makes a relative risk value of 2.0 appear to be particularly important in the legal arena? A relative risk value in excess of 2.0 makes it appear more likely than not that the risk factor is the operative cause of the injury. This linguistic formulation tracks the standard that the plaintiff must meet to carry the burden of proof on the issue of causation-in-fact. That is, the plaintiff has the burden of persuading the trier of fact that defendant's action is more likely than not the cause of plaintiff's injury. Using the term *attributable risk* makes this linguistically even clearer; when the risk attributable to defendant is more than half (>50%) of the total risk, it is easy to conclude that the defendant's act is more likely than not the cause of the plaintiff's injury.

The court in *Landrigan* makes it very clear that failure to establish a relative risk value in excess of 2.0 is not fatal to a plaintiff's case. Why shouldn't it be? The court's answer is that other factors could be proved in the case that would make it more likely in this particular case that the risk factor for which the defendant is responsible is the operative cause of the particular plaintiff's injury. Examples include specific clinical evidence or proof of extraordinary exposures. What about the flip side of the issue — will proof of a relative risk in excess of 2.0 always result in a decision in plaintiff's favor on the issue of cause-in-fact? It should be obvious that the same type of individualized proof that can allow a plaintiff to win despite a relative risk that does not exceed 2.0 can also allow a defendant to prevail in a case of relative risk higher than 2.0.

3. **Legal causation and statistical significance: comparing apples and pear melba.** When the term *significant* appears in legal discourse, it usually has its lay meanings that speak to the importance of a factor or that contrast the central with the peripheral. In relation to scientific studies that find a correlation significant (as between an exposure and the subsequent onset of disease), the word *significant* is a term of art that describes the reliability of the linkage. To be more precise, the significance of a correlation is the likelihood that the data observed are not the product of mere random chance. In a case of radiation exposure, one judge explained statistical significance this way:

> Where there is an increase of observed cases of a particular cancer or leukemia over the number statistically "expected" to normally appear, the question arises whether it may be rationally inferred that the increase is causally connected to specific human activity. The scientific papers and reports will often speak of whether a deviation from the expected numbers of cases is "statistically significant," supporting a hypothesis of causation, or whether the perceived increase is attributable to random variation in the studied population, i.e., to chance. The mathematical tests of significance commonly used in research tend to be stringent; for an increase to

be considered "statistically significant," the probability that it can be attributed to random chance usually must be five percent or less (p=.05). In other words, if the level of significance chosen by the researcher is p=.05, then an observed correlation is "significant" if there is 1 chance in 20 — or less — that the increase resulted from chance. In scientific practice, levels of significance of .01 or .001 are used providing an even more stringent test of a chosen hypothetical relationship. Allen v. United States, 588 F. Supp. 247, 416 (D. Utah 1984).

Accordingly, from the legal viewpoint, a causal hypothesis that narrowly fails to satisfy a .05 level of statistical significance is not insignificant. For instance, data for which there is only a 1 in 19 chance of its being random fails a .05 significance test but nevertheless evidences a relationship for which "the probability is 94.73 percent or 18 chances out of 19 that the observed relationship is not a random event...[and] the certainty that the observed increase is related to its hypothetical cause rather than mere chance is still far more likely than not." Id. What does all this mean for the trial of toxic tort cases? First, even causal hypotheses that are not statistically significant at traditional p-values used in scientific research may be significant proof that helps establish causation in fact.

4. **The plaintiff's dilemma.** Under the *Landrigan* standard for proving causation, how often can plaintiffs win exposure-induced cancer cases where the epidemiological studies do not evidence a relative risk value in excess of 2.0? What will be the usual impact on available proof of the long latency periods between exposure and the onset of disease? Most likely, the delay will make it difficult for plaintiffs to obtain reliable proof of exposure levels and introduce, in the course of living, many confounding variables, such as other exposures or lifestyle choices, thereby reducing the chance of making the individualizing proofs the *Landrigan* court views as so important.

5. **The pitfalls of probabilistic proof.** A hot debate in the legal literature surrounds the advisability of allowing proof of probabilities to establish causation in fact. There are numerous good articles on this subject, two of the classics being Tribe, Trial by Mathematics: Precision and Ritual in the Legal Process, 84 Harv. L. Rev. 1329 (1971), and Nesson, Agent Orange Meets the Blue Bus: Factfinding at the Frontier of Knowledge, 66 B.U. L. Rev. 521 (1986).

Consider the following hypotheticals:[28] Following exposure to defendant's toxic waste that leached into an aquifer, the cancer rate in a community rises from 10 per year to 19 per year (hypo 1) or 21 per year (hypo 2) and all other possible causes have been ruled out by undisputed expert testimony. If probability is translated uncritically into plaintiffs' failure or success in carrying the burden of proof on the cause-in-fact issue, then in hypo 1 defendant goes free of liability to any of the 19 victims, and in hypo 2 defendant must compensate all 21 victims. Is such a result absurd? Do the hypotheticals make it clear why the *Landrigan* court is chary of making a relative risk of 2.0 a litmus for recovery?

Should plaintiffs be relieved of their usual burden of proof because of these proof problems? In Allen v. United States, 588 F. Supp. 247 (D. Utah 1984), noted above for its discussion of statistical significance, the court fashioned a more lenient standard that

---

28. The hypotheticals are adapted from Delgado, Beyond *Sindell*, 70 Calif. L. Rev. 881, 885 (1982).

adapted the substantial factor doctrine that was developed in the joint and several liability context to allow for proof of cause-in-fact in toxic exposure cases. *Allen* involved very compelling facts: the unannounced atmospheric testing of atomic weapons that resulted in mass exposure of the general public to ionizing radiation from the fallout released by the test. The government's lack of warning and haphazard monitoring of fallout levels made it impossible for citizens to avoid the exposure and, likewise, impossible for them to reliably prove their level of exposure. Still, the relative risk levels (a term not used in the *Allen* litigation) were far lower than 2.0. Although its precise ruling is elusive and not easy to summarize, the court allowed the plaintiffs to shift the burden of proof on the cause-in-fact issue (which the *Allen* court refers to as the factual connection issue) to the defendant by proving that the defendant's conduct was a substantial risk-increasing factor. Once plaintiff makes that showing, the defendant is to come forward with evidence that tries to weaken the factual connection between its acts and the plaintiff's injuries. In the end, no fixed rule is announced: "Whether any of these factual connections will lead to liability is, as Professor Thode reminds us, 'an issue involving *the scope of the legal system's protection afforded to plaintiff* and not an issue of factual causation.' Thode, Tort Analysis: Duty-Risk v. Proximate Cause and the Rational Allocation of Functions Between Judge and Jury, 1977 Utah L. Rev. 1, 6." (Emphasis by the court.) In short, the key issue becomes one of policy regarding the extent of protection offered by the legal system, the very essence of the proximate cause inquiry.

Are there other ways of relaxing the plaintiff's burden on cause-in-fact that are not fraught with unfairness to defendants? Professor Richard Delgado suggests allowing full recovery for the harms caused by defendant (9 persons harmed in hypo 1, 11 in hypo 2) to be shared by the entire class of plaintiffs. This forces defendant to bear its costs, and "probabilities are not used...to establish a causal link between conduct of a certain type and a particular injury." Delgado, Beyond *Sindell*, 70 Cal. L. Rev. 881, 905 (1982).

C. LAW AND SCIENCE IN THE TOXIC TORT CONTEXT

Section 1. COMPETING CONCEPTIONS: LAW, SCIENCE, AND POPULAR PERCEPTION

In a very real sense, law and science are contrasting modes of ascertaining different varieties of truth.

- *Functional Differences.* The major function of the legal system is to resolve disputes efficiently, effectively, and equitably. The major function of science is to make accurate, empirically verifiable predictions about the physical world.

- *Conclusiveness vs. Tentativeness.* Because the primary function of private law (and to a lesser extent public law) is to finally resolve disputes so that they do not fester and threaten social cohesiveness, the legal system places a substantial value on the finality of decisions. Doctrines such as res judicata, collateral estoppel, double jeopardy, statutes of limitations, and the presumption against nonretroactivity of legislation support the need for finality of legal decisions. Science, with a goal of accurate prediction, can afford to wait. It proceeds by way of tentative (and sometimes conflicting) hypotheses that lead to data collection through empirical experiments that seek to verify these hypotheses through replicable tests.

- *Moralistic vs. Value-Free Approaches.* Law is unabashedly moralistic. Although law and morality are not always congruent, law is the formalized, enforceable embodiment of public morality. In its heavily prescriptive endeavors, law deals with concepts such as deterrence, compensation, motive, intent, rights, punishment, and environmental justice. Legal decisionmakers seek to implement "average morality" through principles such as the "reasonable person" standard of tort law and institutions such as the jury system. Science, on the other hand, attempts to banish value preferences from application of the scientific method because the goal of science is the objective prediction of physical phenomena. Values and politics, of course, are rife within the scientific community, but every effort is made to exclude them from scientific method. Science itself — as distinguished from the politics of science or the role of scientists in politics — is descriptive rather than prescriptive.

- *Adversarial vs. Cooperative Mechanisms.* Legal process in general, and private law in particular, is institutionalized combat. Scientists are profoundly uncomfortable when they appear in the legal arena (as expert witnesses or otherwise) because scientists view the pursuit of scientific knowledge as a cooperative effort among members of the scientific community. There is sometimes acrimonious conflict among scientists regarding the reliability of data or the importance of particular research, but the ultimate arbiter of scientific disputes is the independent verifiability of empirical experiments, the results of which are disseminated by publications accessible to other scientists working in the field. Scientists tend to resolve scientific disputes through cooperation among peer researchers at symposia or in committees of scientific bodies, not in courts or administrative proceedings. The legal system possesses no counterpart of the scientific community.

- *Geographic Variability vs. Universality.* Because law is institutionalized morality, and morality is often contextual (situational), legal rules frequently differ among jurisdictions. Scientists find it difficult to deal with this variability because science ("good science" at least) is universal in the sense that it is nonvaluational, noncontextual, and empirically verifiable within the limits of scientific method.

- *Disparate Rates of Change.* Because law is generated by human beings in order to resolve policy issues that are perceived to be important to societies, legal rules can change relatively quickly in response to fluctuations in public opinion. The phenomenal growth of environmental law after 1970 is a prime example of how rapidly legal "paradigm shifts" can occur. Scientists are sometimes uncomfortable with the comparative volatility of the legal system because, in contrast, the pace of fundamental change in scientific theory is glacial.

- *Deductive vs. Inductive Approaches.* Both deductive and inductive patterns of analysis are important in both law and science. Deduction allows the investigator to compare a new set of facts or circumstances against a known body of laws to arrive at a conclusion, whereas induction allows the investigator to expand the current body of knowledge based on a set of observations. On the whole, deduction is more significant in legal reasoning than induction. Scientific method, in contrast, places heavier emphasis on induction than on deduction.

- *Different Conceptions of Causation.* Science accepts statistical evidence (e.g., cigarette smokers contract lung cancer at a rate ten times higher than nonsmokers) as proof of general scientific propositions (e.g., cigarettes cause lung cancer) that facilitate predictability. The common law, with its emphasis on resolving individual disputes in conformance with prevailing social morality, requires particularized proof of causation (e.g., the defendant's cigarettes, in fact, caused plaintiff's cancer).[29] For many years, courts did not accept statistical epidemiological or toxicological data as evidence of individual causation. Nowadays, courts in many jurisdictions accept statistical evidence, but only where plaintiff has also produced individualized evidence of causation (e.g., clinical evidence or negative lifestyle factors). Thus the legal system, in the context of common law tort actions and administrative decisionmaking, may refuse to accept fully general conclusions that are accepted in the scientific community. Conversely, a common law court or administrative agency, compelled to resolve a dispute with the best evidence available, may accept evidence that is not generally accepted in the scientific community. Scientific method requires that "good science" be validated by a 95% confidence level (that might be analogized to the same level of confidence as the law requires for criminal convictions when the standard of proof is "beyond a reasonable doubt"), whereas common law courts require only that plaintiff prove causation by a preponderance of the evidence (a roughly 51% confidence level), and administrative law requires only that administrative decisions pass a "fundamental rationality" test (i.e., they not be "arbitrary and capricious").

———————————

Risk often is defined as a measure of (1) the probability that a particular act will cause damage to human health and the environment, and (2) the severity of any damage that may occur. That is where most technical definitions of risk end, but another dimension to risk involves public perceptions and outrage.

Peter Sandman, Risk Communication: Facing Public Outrage
EPA Journal Vol. 13, No. 9 (Nov. 1987), at 21–22

If you make a list of environmental risks in order of how many people they kill each year, then list them again in order of how alarming they are to the general public, the two lists will be very different. The first list will also be very debatable, of course; we don't really know how many deaths are attributable to, say, geological radon or toxic wastes. But we do know enough to be nearly certain that radon kills more Americans each year than all our Superfund sites combined. Yet...millions who choose not to test their homes for radon are deeply worried about toxic wastes. The conclusion is inescapable: the risks that kill you are not necessarily the risks that anger and frighten you....

The core problem is one of definition. To the experts, risk means expected annual mortality. But to the public (and even to the experts when they go home at night), risk means much more

———————————

29. Causation in the legal arena also has a policy element subsumed in the proximate cause inquiry that limits the consequential reach of cause and effect chains.

than that. Let's redefine terms. Call the death rate (what the experts mean by risk) "hazard." Call all the other factors, collectively, "outrage." Risk, then, is the sum of hazard and outrage. The public pays too little attention to hazard; the experts pay absolutely no attention to outrage. Not surprisingly, they rank risks differently.

Risk perception scholars have identified more than 20 "outrage factors." Here are a few of the main ones:

- *Voluntariness:* A voluntary risk is much more acceptable to people than a coerced risk, because it generates no outrage. Consider the difference between getting pushed down a mountain on slippery sticks and deciding to go skiing.

- *Control:* Almost everybody feels safer driving than riding shotgun. When prevention and mitigation are in the individual's hands, the risk (though not the hazard) is much lower than when they are in the hands of a government agency.

- *Fairness:* People who must endure greater risks than their neighbors, without access to greater benefits, are naturally outraged — especially if the rationale for so burdening them looks more like politics than science. Greater outrage, of course, means greater risk.

- *Process:* Does the agency come across as trustworthy or dishonest, concerned or arrogant? Does it tell the community what's going on before the real decisions are made? Does it listen and respond to community concerns?

- *Morality:* American society has decided over the last two decades that pollution isn't just harmful — it's evil. But talking about cost-risk tradeoffs sounds very callous when the risk is morally relevant. Imagine a police chief insisting that an occasional child-molester is an "acceptable risk."

- *Familiarity:* Exotic, high-tech facilities provoke more outrage than familiar risks (your home, your car, your jar of peanut butter).

- *Memorability:* A memorable incident — Love Canal, Bhopal, Times Beach — makes the risk easier to imagine, and thus (as we have defined the term) more risky. A potent symbol — the 55-gallon drum — can do the same thing.

- *Dread:* Some illnesses are more dreaded than others; compare AIDS and cancer with, say, emphysema. The long latency of most cancers and the undetectability of most carcinogens add to the dread.

- *Diffusion in time and space:* Hazard A kills 50 anonymous people a year across the country. Hazard B has one chance in 10 of wiping out its neighborhood of 5,000 people sometime in the next decade. Risk assessment tells us the two have the same expected annual mortality: 50. "Outrage assessment" tells us A is probably acceptable and B is certainly not.

These "outrage factors" are not distortions in the public's perception of risk. They explain why people worry more about Superfund sites than geological radon, more about industrial emissions of dimethylmeatloaf than aflatoxin peanut butter.

There is a peculiar paradox here. Many risk experts resist the pressure to consider outrage in making risk management decisions; they insist that "the data" alone, not the "irrational" public, should determine policy. But we have two decades of data indicating that voluntariness, control, fairness, and the rest are important components of our society's definition of risk. When a risk manager continues to ignore these factors — and continues to be surprised by the public's response of outrage — it is worth asking whose behavior is irrational.

COMMENTARY & QUESTIONS

1. **Reactions to outrage.** Commentators who accept the legitimacy of outrage as an element of risk generally recommend two strategies for reconciling the discordances between "expert" and "public" definitions of risk: (1) better "risk communication," the two-way process of information exchange between governmental risk managers and the general public; and (2) involvement of "stakeholders," the parties that are affected by the risk management problem, during all stages of the risk definition and management process. See, e.g., Presidential/Congressional Commission on Risk Assessment and Risk Management, Final Report (hereinafter "Commission Report"), Volume 2, Chaps. 1–3 (1997). Others more skeptical of outrage as a genuine element of risk belittle these approaches. See Cross, The Public Role in Risk Control, 24 Envtl. L. 887 (1994) ("A variety of measures could be taken to facilitate the government's use of scientifically accurate measures of risk rather than mistaken public perceptions. Foremost is the reduction in opportunities for public participation in decisionmaking." Id. at 950.).

2. **How EPA considers risk in environmental protection.** As explored later in Chapter 13, risk assessment is a burgeoning field in the realm of environmental regulation. For a summary of the methods of analysis used by the EPA in performing risk assessment, see Coperland & Simpson, Considering Risk in Environmental Protection, 8 Cong. Res. Serv. Rev. (No. 10) 7–9 (1987). That article describes the risk quantification procedure that the federal government uses to evaluate health risks of hazardous substances. The two-fold inquiry first identifies the hazard, usually relying on epidemiologic studies, animal bioassays, short-term bioassays, and chemical structure-activity studies. The second prong of the inquiry attempts to look at the exposure side of the problem, considering the magnitude (frequency and intensity) of the exposure to the substance that will be suffered by the populace and then trying to make an assessment of the likely response of exposed individuals to the exposure. This latter effort is fraught with scientific uncertainty primarily attributable to (1) the unknown physical mechanism that is at work and (2) imperfections in the measurement of the exposure. The results of studies tend to have unusual variability, possibly as a result of the imprecision of the measurements of most human exposure data.

3. **The law and outrage.** Should legal institutions take outrage into account? Is a court better equipped to do so than a politically responsible actor, such as a legislator or an executive branch administrative official? In the materials that appear in this coursebook, observe whether the legal system ignores, represses, assuages (symbolically or authentically), channels into socially productive pathways, or is misdirected by public outrage. In that study, also try to identify whose risk management decision is under review, that of a government regulator or that of a private project proponent.

Section 2. **THE STANDARDS FOR EXPERT TESTIMONY**

The *Daubert* case that follows is the U.S. Supreme Court's most important decision in decades bearing on the relationship between law and science. It addresses in an oblique way the difficulties that cases such as *Ferebee* and *Landrigan* pose regarding the distinction between legal and scientific proof. The dilemma confronting courts arises because cases involving claims of toxic exposure-caused injury must frequently be decided before the scientific community has accumulated sufficient data to establish scientific causation. If courts adopt a scientific standard of causation, then plaintiffs will invariably lose where the cases involve matters "at the frontier of current medical and epidemiological inquiry." If, on the other hand, courts impose no limits on plaintiffs' ability to place a particular theory of causation before the trier of fact (almost always a lay jury in toxic tort cases), then quackery, coincidence, or the sympathy of jurors toward injured parties could lead to findings of causation where the preponderance of credible evidence favors the defendant.

Courts have responded to this dilemma by developing rules governing the admissibility of evidence. In matters of a scientific or technical nature, for example, virtually all courts require that testimony be given only by experts having appropriate qualifications. Although this requirement provides a safeguard of sorts, plaintiffs' and defendants' bars both have developed cadres of qualified expert witnesses skilled in presenting their respective opposing views on toxic injury causation. A growing number of courts are demanding more than mere expertise and are increasingly sophisticated about the difference between legal and scientific proof.

Daubert speaks to the appropriate standard of admissibility for expert scientific evidence. A 1991 decision by the U.S. Court of Appeals for the Ninth Circuit (951 F.2d 1128) had affirmed summary judgment against two families who had alleged the morning sickness drug Bendectin caused their children's limb reduction birth defects. The Ninth Circuit opinion had ruled that the plaintiffs' expert proof was inadmissible because it was not based on methodologies generally accepted in the relevant scientific communities. Without peer-reviewed epidemiological evidence, the court said, the plaintiffs could not prove causation. This position generally is referred to as the *Frye* rule. It derives from an old criminal prosecution for murder in which the defendant attempted to have an expert witness testify to the results of a systolic blood pressure deception (lie detector) test, at that time a relatively novel scientific test. Frye v. United States, 293 F. 1013 (D.C. Cir. 1923). The *Frye* court said:

> Just when a scientific principle or discovery crosses the line between the experimental and demonstrable stages is difficult to define. Somewhere in this twilight zone the evidential force of the principle must be recognized, and while courts will go a long way in admitting expert testimony deduced from a well-recognized scientific principle or discovery, the thing from which the deduction is made must be sufficiently established to have gained general acceptance in the particular field in which it belongs. We think the systolic blood pressure deception test has not yet gained such standing and scientific recognition among physiological and psychological authorities as would justify the courts in admitting expert testimony deduced from the discovery, development, and experiments thus far made. Frye, 293 F. at 1014.

Frye has come under attack on a number of grounds, some having to do with the problem of scientific advancement. Expert testimony founded on new, but not yet recognized, general principles is not admissible under *Frye*. As the argument goes, this either stymies science or at least those who deserve the right to have their cases considered on the basis of new lines of scientific inquiry. By the time of *Daubert*, a third of jurisdictions, federal and state, had repudiated or recanted *Frye*. See Imwinkelreid, Science Takes the Stand: The Growing Misuse of Expert Testimony, The Sciences, Nov./Dec. 1986, at 20, 22.

In *Daubert*, the plaintiffs (petitioners) claimed that the Federal Rules of Evidence controlled the case and would permit their evidence on causation to be heard. As you will see, the Supreme Court agreed and then went on to offer some indication of how it viewed the meaning of the governing evidentiary rules. The relevant Rules of Evidence are these:

> RULE 702. TESTIMONY BY EXPERTS… If scientific, technical, or other specialized knowledge will assist the trier of fact to understand the evidence or to determine a fact in issue, a witness qualified as an expert by knowledge, skill, experience, training, or education, may testify thereto in the form of an opinion or otherwise.

> RULE 703. BASES OF OPINION TESTIMONY BY EXPERTS… The facts or data in the particular case upon which an expert bases an opinion or inference may be those perceived by or made known to the expert at or before the hearing. If of a type reasonably relied upon by experts in the particular field in forming opinions or inferences upon the subject, the facts or data need not be admissible in evidence.

Daubert v. Merrell Dow Pharmaceuticals, Inc.
United States Supreme Court, 1993
509 U.S. 579

BLACKMUN, J. In this case we are called upon to determine the standard for admitting expert scientific testimony in a federal trial.

Petitioners Jason Daubert and Eric Schuller are minor children born with serious birth defects. They and their parents sued respondent in California state court, alleging that the birth defects had been caused by the mothers' ingestion of Bendectin, a prescription anti-nausea drug marketed by respondent. Respondent removed the suits to federal court on diversity grounds.

After extensive discovery, respondent moved for summary judgment, contending that Bendectin does not cause birth defects in humans and that petitioners would be unable to come forward with any admissible evidence that it does. In support of its motion, respondent submitted an affidavit of Steven H. Lamm, physician and epidemiologist, who is a well-credentialed expert on the risks from exposure to various chemical substances. Doctor Lamm stated that he had reviewed all the literature on Bendectin and human birth defects — more than 30 published studies involving over 130,000 patients. No study had found Bendectin to be a human teratogen (i.e., a substance capable of causing malformations in fetuses). On the basis of this review, Doctor Lamm concluded that maternal use of Bendectin during the first trimester of pregnancy has not been shown to be a risk factor for human birth defects.

Petitioners did not (and do not) contest this characterization of the published record regarding Bendectin. Instead, they responded to respondent's motion with the testimony of eight experts of their own, each of whom also possessed impressive credentials. These experts had concluded that Bendectin can cause birth defects. Their conclusions were based upon "in vitro" (test tube) and "in vivo" (live) animal studies that found a link between Bendectin and malformations; pharmacological studies of the chemical structure of Bendectin that purported to show similarities between the structure of the drug and that of other substances known to cause birth defects; and the "reanalysis" of previously published epidemiological (human statistical) studies.

The District Court granted respondent's motion for summary judgment. The court stated that scientific evidence is admissible only if the principle upon which it is based is " 'sufficiently established to have general acceptance in the field to which it belongs.'" The court concluded that petitioners' evidence did not meet this standard. Given the vast body of epidemiological data concerning Bendectin, the court held, expert opinion which is not based on epidemiological evidence is not admissible to establish causation. Thus, the animal-cell studies, live-animal studies, and chemical-structure analyses on which petitioners had relied could not raise by themselves a reasonably disputable jury issue regarding causation. Petitioners' epidemiological analyses, based as they were on recalculations of data in previously published studies that had found no causal link between the drug and birth defects, were ruled to be inadmissible because they had not been published or subjected to peer review.... [Citing Frye v. United States, the United States Court of Appeals for the Ninth Circuit affirmed.]

The Court of Appeals emphasized that other Courts of Appeals considering the risks of Bendectin had refused to admit reanalyses of epidemiological studies that had been neither published nor subjected to peer review. Those courts had found unpublished reanalyses "particularly problematic in light of the massive weight of the original published studies supporting [respondent's] position, all of which had undergone full scrutiny from the scientific community." Contending that reanalysis is generally accepted by the scientific community only when it is subjected to verification and scrutiny by others in the field, the Court of Appeals rejected petitioners' reanalyses as "unpublished, not subjected to the normal peer review process and generated solely for use in litigation." The court concluded that petitioners' evidence provided an insufficient foundation to allow admission of expert testimony that Bendectin caused their injuries and, accordingly, that petitioners could not satisfy their burden of proving causation at trial....

In the 70 years since its formulation in the *Frye* case, the "general acceptance" test has been the dominant standard for determining the admissibility of novel scientific evidence at trial. Although under increasing attack of late, the rule continues to be followed by a majority of courts, including the Ninth Circuit....

The merits of the *Frye* test have been much debated, and scholarship on its proper scope and application is legion. Petitioners' primary attack, however, is not on the content but on the continuing authority of the rule. They contend that the *Frye* test was superseded by the adoption of the Federal Rules of Evidence. We agree.

We interpret the legislatively-enacted Federal Rules of Evidence as we would any statute. Rule 402 provides the baseline: "All relevant evidence is admissible, except as otherwise provided by the Constitution of the United States, by Act of Congress, by these rules, or by other rules prescribed by the Supreme Court pursuant to statutory authority. Evidence which is not relevant is not admissible." "Relevant evidence" is defined as that which has "any tendency to make the existence of any fact that is of consequence to the determination of the action more probable or less probable than it would be without the evidence." Rule 401. The Rule's basic standard of relevance thus is a liberal one....

Here there is a specific Rule [702] that speaks to the contested issue. [See text above.] Nothing in the text of this Rule establishes "general acceptance" as an absolute prerequisite to admissibility. Nor does respondent present any clear indication that Rule 702 or the Rules as a whole were intended to incorporate a "general acceptance" standard. The drafting history makes no mention of *Frye*, and a rigid "general acceptance" requirement would be at odds with the "liberal thrust" of the Federal Rules and their "general approach of relaxing the traditional barriers to 'opinion' testimony." Given the Rules' permissive backdrop and their inclusion of a specific rule on expert testimony that does not mention "general acceptance," the assertion that the

Rules somehow assimilated *Frye* is unconvincing. *Frye* made "general acceptance" the exclusive test for admitting expert scientific testimony. That austere standard, absent from and incompatible with the Federal Rules of Evidence, should not be applied in federal trials.

That the *Frye* test was displaced by the Rules of Evidence does not mean, however, that the Rules themselves place no limits on the admissibility of purportedly scientific evidence. Nor is the trial judge disabled from screening such evidence. To the contrary, under the Rules the trial judge must ensure that any and all scientific testimony or evidence admitted is not only relevant, but reliable.

The primary locus of this obligation is Rule 702, which clearly contemplates some degree of regulation of the subjects and theories about which an expert may testify. "If scientific, technical, or other specialized knowledge will assist the trier of fact to understand the evidence or to determine a fact in issue" an expert "may testify thereto." The subject of an expert's testimony must be "scientific...knowledge." The adjective "scientific" implies a grounding in the methods and procedures of science. Similarly, the word "knowledge" connotes more than subjective belief or unsupported speculation. The term "applies to any body of known facts or to any body of ideas inferred from such facts or accepted as truths on good grounds." Webster's Third New International Dictionary 1252 (1986). Of course, it would be unreasonable to conclude that the subject of scientific testimony must be "known" to a certainty; arguably, there are no certainties in science. But, in order to qualify as "scientific knowledge," an inference or assertion must be derived by the scientific method. Proposed testimony must be supported by appropriate validation — i.e., "good grounds," based on what is known. In short, the requirement that an expert's testimony pertain to "scientific knowledge" establishes a standard of evidentiary reliability.

Rule 702 further requires that the evidence or testimony "assist the trier of fact to understand the evidence or to determine a fact in issue." This condition goes primarily to relevance....

That these requirements are embodied in Rule 702 is not surprising. Unlike an ordinary witness an expert is permitted wide latitude to offer opinions, including those that are not based on first-hand knowledge or observation. Presumably, this relaxation of the usual requirement of first-hand knowledge — a rule which represents "a 'most pervasive manifestation' of the common law insistence upon 'the most reliable sources of information,'" Advisory Committee's Notes on Fed. Rule Evid. 602 — is premised on an assumption that the expert's opinion will have a reliable basis in the knowledge and experience of his discipline.

Faced with a proffer of expert scientific testimony, then, the trial judge must determine at the outset, pursuant to Rule 104(a), whether the expert is proposing to testify to (1) scientific knowledge that (2) will assist the trier of fact to understand or determine a fact in issue. This entails a preliminary assessment of whether the reasoning or methodology underlying the testimony is scientifically valid and of whether that reasoning or methodology properly can be applied to the facts in issue. We are confident that federal judges possess the capacity to undertake this review. Many factors will bear on the inquiry, and we do not presume to set out a definitive checklist or test. But some general observations are appropriate.

Ordinarily, a key question to be answered in determining whether a theory or technique is scientific knowledge that will assist the trier of fact will be whether it can be (and has been) tested. "Scientific methodology today is based on generating hypotheses and testing them to see if they can be falsified; indeed, this methodology is what distinguishes science from other fields of human inquiry."

Another pertinent consideration is whether the theory or technique has been subjected to peer review and publication. Publication (which is but one element of peer review) is not a sine qua non of admissibility; it does not necessarily correlate with reliability, and in some instances well-grounded but innovative theories will not have been published. Some propositions, moreover, are too particular, too new, or of too limited interest to be published. But submission to the scrutiny of the scientific community is a component of "good science," in part because it increases the likelihood that substantive flaws in methodology will be detected. The fact of publication (or lack thereof) in a peer-reviewed journal thus will be a relevant, though not dispositive, consideration in assessing the scientific validity of a particular technique or methodology on which an opinion is premised.

Additionally, in the case of a particular scientific technique, the court ordinarily should consider the known or potential rate of error, and the existence and maintenance of standards controlling the technique's operation.

Finally, "general acceptance" can yet have a bearing on the inquiry. A "reliability assessment does not require, although it does permit, explicit identification of a relevant scientific community and an express determination of a particular degree of acceptance within that community." Widespread acceptance can be an important factor in ruling particular evidence admissible, and "a known technique that has been able to attract only minimal support within the community," may properly be viewed with skepticism.

The inquiry envisioned by Rule 702 is, we emphasize, a flexible one. Its overarching subject is the scientific validity — and thus the evidentiary relevance and reliability — of the principles that underlie a proposed submission. The focus, of course, must be solely on principles and methodology, not on the conclusions that they generate.

Throughout, a judge assessing a proffer of expert scientific testimony under Rule 702 should also be mindful of other applicable rules. Rule 703 provides that expert opinions based on otherwise inadmissible hearsay are to be admitted only if the facts or data are "of a type reasonably relied upon by experts in the particular field in forming opinions or inferences upon the subject." Rule 706 allows the court at its discretion to procure the assistance of an expert of its own choosing. Finally, Rule 403 permits the exclusion of relevant evidence "if its probative value is substantially outweighed by the danger of unfair prejudice, confusion of the issues, or misleading the jury...." Judge Weinstein has explained: "Expert evidence can be both powerful and quite misleading because of the difficulty in evaluating it. Because of this risk, the judge in weighing possible prejudice against probative force under Rule 403 of the present rules exercises more control over experts than over lay witnesses."

We conclude by briefly addressing what appear to be two underlying concerns of the parties and amici in this case. Respondent expresses apprehension that abandonment of "general acceptance" as the exclusive requirement for admission will result in a "free-for-all" in which befuddled juries are confounded by absurd and irrational pseudoscientific assertions. In this regard respondent seems to us to be overly pessimistic about the capabilities of the jury, and of the adversary system generally. Vigorous cross-examination, presentation of contrary evidence, and careful instruction on the burden of proof are the traditional and appropriate means of attacking shaky but admissible evidence.... These conventional devices, rather than wholesale exclusion under an uncompromising "general acceptance" test, are the appropriate safeguards where the basis of scientific testimony meets the standards of Rule 702.

Petitioners and, to a greater extent, their amici exhibit a different concern. They suggest that recognition of a screening role for the judge that allows for the exclusion of "invalid" evidence will sanction a stifling and repressive scientific orthodoxy and will be inimical to the search for truth. It is true that open debate is an essential part of both legal and scientific analyses. Yet there are important differences between the quest for truth in the courtroom and the quest for truth in the laboratory. Scientific conclusions are subject to perpetual revision. Law, on the other hand, must resolve disputes finally and quickly. The scientific project is advanced by broad and wide-ranging consideration of a multitude of hypotheses, for those that are incorrect will eventually be shown to be so, and that in itself is an advance. Conjectures that are probably wrong are of little use, however, in the project of reaching a quick, final, and binding legal judgment — often of great consequence — about a particular set of events in the past. We recognize that in practice, a gatekeeping role for the judge, no matter how flexible, inevitably on occasion will prevent the jury from learning of authentic insights and innovations. That, nevertheless, is the balance that is struck by Rules of Evidence designed not for the exhaustive search for cosmic understanding but for the particularized resolution of legal disputes.

To summarize: "general acceptance" is not a necessary precondition to the admissibility of scientific evidence under the Federal Rules of Evidence, but the Rules of Evidence — especially Rule 702 — do assign to the trial judge the task of ensuring that an expert's testimony both rests on a reliable foundation and is relevant to the task at hand. Pertinent evidence based on scientifically valid principles will satisfy those demands.

The inquiries of the District Court and the Court of Appeals focused almost exclusively on "general acceptance," as gauged by publication and the decisions of other courts. Accordingly, the judgment of the Court of Appeals is vacated and the case is remanded for further proceedings consistent with this opinion. It is so ordered.

COMMENTARY & QUESTIONS

1. **What did *Daubert* decide?** Apart from holding that *Frye* is not controlling in the wake of Evidence Rule 702, can you isolate the meaning of *Daubert*? What seem to emerge are two requirements: that judges employ discretion to ensure that scientific evidence is sufficiently reliable and that they consider a number of nonexclusive factors in making that decision. But the factors, including general acceptance, certainly do resemble the *Frye* rule. *Daubert* does not confront the basic problem that civil suits are based on preponderance and science is based on something very different — resembling criminal law's "beyond a reasonable doubt."

2. **Is *Daubert* a plaintiff's victory?** On remand, what outcome would you predict? The plaintiffs' eight experts were characterized by the Supreme Court as being possessed of "impressive credentials," yet their reanalysis of the epidemiological data was unpublished and did not fit the orthodox interpretation given to that data by the defendant's expert and the literature in the field. Even if the remand does not result in admission of the proffered testimony in *Daubert*, isn't it fairly clear that toxic tort plaintiffs, in general, are far better off having the *Frye* "generally accepted" test declared dead and buried, at least in litigation conducted in federal court?[30] To answer this question, it is useful to recall the role summary judgment plays in the litigation process. The standard for the grant of summary judgment requires that there be no genuine issue of material fact and that the party seeking summary judgment is entitled to judgment as a matter of law. See generally Fed. R. Civ. P. 56. The basic idea is that cases presenting no honestly debatable issue of fact should not be tried. Berry v. Armstrong Rubber Co., discussed in note 4 below, fits this mold. In that case, plaintiffs' experts' testimony was ruled inadmissible. As a result, there remained no credible evidence to support plaintiffs'

---

30. As canvassed in the subsequent notes, post-*Daubert* developments in the courts have clouded the issue whether *Daubert* is a plaintiff's victory. See also Kassirer & Cecil, Inconsistency in the Evidentiary Standards for Medical Testimony: Disorder in the Courts, 288 J. Am. Med. Ass'n 1382, 1383 (2002) (characterizing *Frye* as erecting a "deferential standard" and *Daubert* as being a "more assertive" standard").

affirmative case on causation and damage, so the court ruled that there was no genuine issue of material fact that could be tried to a jury. It granted the motion for summary judgment, thereby preventing a jury from hearing the case at all.

Preventing jury consideration is widely thought to have a major influence on outcomes. Tactically, once a toxic tort case is permitted to be decided by the jury (i.e., where the judge allows the jury to hear and evaluate the weight of the testimony offered by the plaintiffs' experts on the liability and causation issues), the frequently sympathetic nature of the cases (innocent and badly injured victim suing a deep-pocket corporate defendant) makes defending the case very problematic for the defendant and ripe for settlement.

3. **The use of *Frye* in *Donaldson*.** In a major portion of its opinion, the *Donaldson* court applied the *Frye* general acceptance test, as it understands it (and therefore makes it the law of Illinois on the subject), to determine whether the testimony of the plaintiffs' three experts is admissible. In part the court stated:

> The *Frye* standard, commonly called the "general acceptance" test, dictates that scientific evidence is only admissible at trial if the methodology or scientific principle upon which the opinion is based is "sufficiently established to have gained general acceptance in the particular field in which it belongs." *Frye*, 293 F. at 1014. First, "general acceptance" does not concern the ultimate conclusion. Rather, the proper focus of the general acceptance test is on the underlying methodology used to generate the conclusion. If the underlying method used to generate an expert's opinion are reasonably relied upon by the experts in the field, the fact finder may consider the opinion — despite the novelty of the conclusion rendered by the expert. Second, general acceptance of methodologies does not mean "universal" acceptance of methodologies. The medical community may entertain diverse opinions regarding causal relationships, but this diversity of opinion does not preclude the admission of testimony that a causal relationship exists if the expert used generally accepted methodology to develop the conclusion. "In determining whether a novel scientific procedure is 'generally accepted' in the scientific community, the issue is consensus versus controversy over a particular technique.... Moreover, the mere existence of a dispute does not preclude a finding that the procedure is generally accepted." People v. Dalcollo, 669 N.E.2d 378 (1996); see also Chevron Chemical Corp. v. Ferebee, 736 F.2d 1529, 1535–36 ("a cause-effect relationship need not be clearly established by animal or epidemiological studies before a doctor can testify that, in his opinion, such a relationship exists. As long as the basic methodology employed to reach such a conclusion is sound,...products liability law does not preclude recovery until a 'statistically significant' number of people have been injured or until science has had the time and resources to complete sophisticated laboratory studies of the chemical"); *Frye*, 293 F. at 1014 ("Just when a scientific principle or discovery crosses the line between the experimental and demonstrable stages is difficult to define. Somewhere in this twilight zone the evidential force of the principle must be recognized"). Simply stated, general acceptance does not require that the methodology be accepted by unanimity, consensus, or even a majority of experts. A technique, however, is not "generally accepted" if it is experimental or of dubious validity. Thus, the *Frye* rule is meant to exclude methods new to science that undeservedly create a perception of certainty when the basis for the evidence or opinion is actually invalid. *Donaldson*, 199 Ill. 2d at 77–78.

Is this formulation any less liberal than *Daubert*? Is this standard more certain of application and less susceptible to variation resulting from judicial attitudes and experience with expert testimony in the particular field involved?

4. ***Daubert* and bad expert testimony.** Will *Daubert* change the result in cases where the testimony of plaintiffs' experts is unconvincing? Cases that rely on bad expert testimony should, and do, and probably will continue to lose. One recent example of this is Berry v. Armstrong Rubber Co., 989 F.2d 822 (5th Cir. 1993). In consolidated cases, plaintiffs sought recoveries for reduced property values traceable to defendant's long-term waste disposal practices as well as for personal injuries caused by exposure to contaminated drinking water. The Fifth Circuit upheld defendant's summary judgment because of the inadequacy of plaintiff's expert testimony. More specifically, the exclusion of expert testimony under Fed. R. Evid. 703 was held proper where the experts testified in areas in which they were not qualified, offered opinions that were not based on tests that they had performed, or used data and methodology that were not recognized by other experts in the field. For example, significant portions of the testimony were based on data developed at locations other than the plaintiffs' property; the plaintiffs' property was not itself tested. Another expert's testimony (that of Nolan Augenbaugh of the *Wilsonville* case, discussed in Chapter 3) was held properly rejected because it rested on an assumption that groundwater flowed toward plaintiffs' land, despite the lack of any testing by plaintiffs to substantiate that claim and the presence of EPA testing that showed the groundwater flowed in the opposite direction. Correspondingly, medical experts' testimony that relied on Augenbaugh's conclusions about the level of contaminants present at the plaintiffs' property were likewise unfounded.

5. **Expansion of *Daubert* by the Supreme Court.** The U.S. Supreme Court has construed *Daubert* in two significant cases to date. In General Elec. Co. v. Joiner, 522 U.S. 136 (1997), the Court reversed an Eleventh Circuit decision that, in turn, reversed a district court's grant of summary judgment against a municipal electrician who alleged that his exposure to PCBs in the workplace had "promoted" his contraction of lung cancer. Plaintiff was a smoker and there was a family history of lung cancer. With regard to the standard of appellate review, the Supreme Court stated that

> [w]hile the Federal Rules of Evidence allow district courts to admit a somewhat broader range of scientific testimony than would have been admissible under *Frye*, they leave in place the "gatekeeper" role of the trial judge in screening such evidence. A court of appeals applying "abuse of discretion" review to such rulings may not categorically distinguish between rulings allowing expert testimony and rulings which disallow it. We likewise reject respondent's argument that because the granting of summary judgment in this case was "outcome determinative," it should have been subjected to a more searching standard of review. On a motion for summary judgment, disputed issues of fact are resolved against the moving party — here petitioners. But the question of admissibility of expert testimony is not such an issue of fact, and is reviewable under the abuse of discretion standard. 522 U.S. at 142–143.

In addition, the Court held the district court had not erred in excluding the expert testimony in this case. Notably, Justice Rehnquist's opinion for the majority seemed somewhat surprised that the animal studies that are the basis of much modern risk assessment in general, and the animal studies in this case in particular, are so dissimilar to the range of relevant human exposures that are the subject of claims for recovery such as that of plaintiff:

> The studies involved infant mice that had developed cancer after being exposed to PCBs. The infant mice in the studies had had massive doses of PCBs injected directly into their peritoneums or stomachs. Joiner was an adult human being whose alleged exposure to PCBs was far less than the exposure in the animal studies. The PCBs were injected into the mice in a highly concentrated form. The fluid with which Joiner had come into contact generally had a much smaller PCB concentration of between 0–500 parts per million. The cancer that these mice developed was alveologenic adenomas; Joiner had developed small-cell carcinomas. No study demonstrated that adult mice developed cancer after being exposed to PCBs. One of the experts admitted that no study had demonstrated that PCBs lead to cancer in any other species.

> Respondent failed to reply to this criticism. Rather than explaining how and why the experts could have extrapolated their opinions from these seemingly far-removed animal studies, respondent chose "to proceed as if the only issue [was] whether animal studies can ever be a proper foundation for an expert's opinion." *Joiner*, 864 F. Supp. at 1324. Of course, whether animal studies can ever be a proper foundation for an expert's opinion was not the issue. The issue was whether these experts' opinions were sufficiently supported by the animal studies on which they purported to rely. The studies were so dissimilar to the facts presented in this litigation that it was not an abuse of discretion for the District Court to have rejected the experts' reliance on them.... Nothing in either *Daubert* or the Federal Rules of Evidence requires a district court to admit opinion evidence which is connected to existing data only by the ipse dixit of the expert. A court may conclude that there is simply too great an analytical gap between the data and the opinion proffered. This is what the District Court did here, and we hold that it did not abuse its discretion in so doing. 522 U.S. at 144–146.

Under what circumstances, if any, would the majority ever find animal studies involving massive doses administered to laboratory animals sufficiently similar to human exposures? In a concurring opinion, Justice Breyer spoke to the problem of scientifically untrained judges being asked "to make subtle and sophisticated determinations about scientific methodology and its relation to the conclusions an expert witness seeks to offer — particularly when a case arises in an area where the science itself is tentative or uncertain, or where testimony about general risk levels in human beings or animals is offered to prove individual causation." 522 U.S. at 147–148. Justice Breyer recommended resort to "Rule 16's pretrial conference authority to narrow the scientific issues in dispute, pretrial hearings where potential experts are subject to examination by the court, and the appointment of special masters and specially trained law clerks." Id. at 149.

The second major U.S. Supreme Court case construing *Daubert* is Kumho Tire Co. v. Carmichael, 526 U.S. 137 (1999), in which the Court extended the *Daubert* doctrine to testimony by an expert witness trained in engineering:

> We conclude that *Daubert*'s general holding — setting forth the trial judge's general "gatekeeping obligation" — applies not only to testimony based on "scientific"

knowledge, but also to testimony based on "technical" and "other specialized" knowledge. We also conclude that a trial court may consider one or more of the more specific factors that *Daubert* mentioned when doing so will help determine that testimony's reliability. But...the test of reliability is "flexible," and *Daubert*'s list of specific factors neither necessarily nor exclusively applies to all experts or in every case. Rather, the law grants a district court the same broad latitude when it decides how to determine reliability as it enjoys in respect to its ultimate reliability determination. 526 U.S. at 141–142.

For one of several good general discussions of the *Daubert* ruling and its impact, see Kesan, An Autopsy of Scientific Evidence in a Post-*Daubert* World, 84 Geo. L.J. 1985 (1996). For a discussion of the effort to "Daubertize" the administrative law process by employing similar gatekeeper standards for administrative agency procedures of all types, see Raul & Zampa, Deeper Judicial Scrutiny Needed for Agencies' Use of Science, 24 (No. 7) Andrews Asbestos Litig. Rep. 9 (2002); Miller & Rein, "Gatekeeping" Agency Reliance on Scientific and Technical Materials After *Daubert*: Ensuring Relevance and Reliability in the Administrative Process, 17 Touro L. Rev. 297 (2000).

Cases decided by the lower federal courts and states that have adopted the *Daubert* position are not showing the hoped-for consistency and predictability in regard to admissibility of expert testimony. Compare, e.g., Moore v. Ashland Chem. Co., 151 F.3d 269 (5th Cir. 1998) (rejecting pulmonologist's testimony on causation of breathing disorder relying on Material Data Sheet but absent corroborative epidemiological testimony), *with* Westberry v. Gilslaved Gummi AB, 178 F.3d 257 (4th Cir. 1999) (clinician allowed to testify to causation of lung disease relying on Material Data Sheet without epidemiological expert).

6. **Distinguishing innovative explanations of causation from junk science.** In Medical Experts and the Ghost of Galileo, 54 Law & Contemp. Probs. 119 (1991), Peter Huber argues that there are virtually no "Galileos" serving as experts in toxic tort and product liability litigation. The credible scientific discoveries, the ones that identify "real risks," were not ones made and brought to light in the crucible of litigation. Rather, Huber traces the history of scientific evidence that supported liability in regard to asbestos, the Ford Pinto, the Dalkon Shield, Rely tampons, DES, and thalidomide to typical sources within the accepted scientific community — traditional epidemiological research and inquiries prompted and followed up on by administrative agencies concerned with public safety. In contrast, Huber tells the story of incorrect conclusions reached by researchers into traumatic cancer (claims that traumatic injury causes cancer) and cerebral palsy, as cautionary vignettes. He uses these examples to urge the legal system to be wary of the "post hoc fallacy" that arises when researchers seek to identify causes after first observing the result. He criticizes the effort of researchers who observed cancers and thereafter linked them to histories of trauma. He makes his point by repeating one scientist's pithy observation, "Because toads appear after a rain it is not necessary to assume that it has rained toads."[31] Surely, this criticism cuts too broadly, but it should sound a cautionary note. Is Huber correct in asserting that the legal

---

31. 54 Law & Contemp. Probs. at 160, quoting Stewart, Occupational and Post-Traumatic Cancer, 23 Bull. N.Y. Acad. Med. 145 (1947).

system functions best when it follows scientific discovery rather than getting out ahead of it?

7. **The complex but necessary interplay between science and the courts.** In her significant book Science at the Bar: Law, Science, and Technology in America (1995), Professor Sheila Jasanoff argues that science and the legal process are inextricably interconnected:

> The central argument regarding toxic torts is that legally compelling knowledge about toxic properties of chemicals arises not from science alone but through complex interactions between adjudication and scientific activity. Mainstream science does not exist in a pure cognitive domain that courts can reach into at will. Like all other human knowledge, mainstream science is made, and it is made in part through the incremental efforts of the legal system to acquire relevant knowledge. However, to admit this is not to deny that there are defects in the traditional approach to litigating scientific uncertainty: the sometimes gross mismatch between scientific and judicial appraisals of credibility, the often ill-motivated efforts to fit scientific claims to legal concepts of causation, and the discrepant and idiosyncratic results reached in science-intensive litigation in different jurisdictions.

> The belief that mainstream science can dispel most of the legal system's problems in handling sociotechnical conflicts rests upon two fundamental misconceptions about the links between scientific and legal decisionmaking. First, good science is not a commodity that courts can conveniently shop for in some extrasocietal marketplace of pure knowledge. Second, scientific closure and legal controversy do not stand in a predictably linear chronological relationship. Disagreement is endemic in science, and knowledge claims as often as not remain open-ended within the scientific community at times when they must be subjected to further testing in court. Jasanoff, at 137, 207.

In the wake of *Daubert*, Professor Jasanoff recommends "educat[ing] judges, lawyers, and scientific experts in each other's modes of reasoning and discourse." Id. at 68.

8. **Administrative agencies and "good science."** Professor Jasanoff's insight that good science is not always readily identifiable is exemplified by the case of Sierra Club v. Marita, 46 F.3d 606 (7th Cir. 1995). Plaintiff conservation groups sued the U.S. Forest Service, seeking to enjoin timber harvesting, road construction, and the creation of wildlife openings in two national forests in northern Wisconsin. In effect, plaintiffs argued that the Forest Service had violated the National Forest Management Act and the National Environmental Policy Act[32] by utilizing "bad science" in developing its Land and Resource Management Plans for the forests. Plaintiffs alleged that the Forest Service had used scientifically unsupported techniques to address biodiversity concerns in its management plans and had arbitrarily disregarded certain principles of conservation biology in developing those plans. In particular, the Forest Service's approach allegedly generated a plan that tended to allow extensive fragmentation of the forests into small patches, in contravention of the "large block" approach of conservation biology. The court affirmed the district court's granting of summary judgment in favor of the defendant Forest Service:

---

32. The National Environmental Policy Act (NEPA) requires a federal agency proposing to undertake a major action that might have a significant impact on the human environment to prepare and circulate an EIS before proceeding to implement its proposal. See Chapter 9.

> The Service is entitled to use its own methodology, unless it is irrational.... The Service developed an appropriate method of analyzing diversity. The Sierra Club is correct that the Service did not employ conservation biology in its final analysis. However, the Service appropriately considered conservation biology and ultimately determined that science to be uncertain in application.... We cannot conclude from the record that the Service acted irrationally.
>
> In supporting the Sierra Club's allegation that the Service used "bad" science, amici Society for Conservation Biology and the American Institute of Biological Sciences have suggested that we borrow the Supreme Court's test for admissibility of scientific expert testimony as set forth in [Daubert] as a way of determining whether the Service's scientific assertions are owed any deference under NEPA. We decline the suggestion. While such a proposal might assure better documentation of an agency's scientific decisions, we think that forcing an agency to make such a showing as a general rule is intrusive, undeferential, and not required. An EIS is designed to ensure open and honest debate of the environmental consequences of an agency action, not to prove admissibility of testimony in a court of law. 46 F.3d at 621.

Clearly, the "arbitrary and capricious" doctrine of administrative law (see Chapter 7), and the judicial deference to agency decisions that it symbolizes, gives a reviewing court a much less significant "gatekeeper" role, with regard to scientific information, than that performed by a common law court in a toxic tort case.

D. LITIGATING TOXIC TORT CASES

The common law put down its roots in an age where its rigid formal procedures could be applied in lawsuits that might be described as simple binary litigation: one plaintiff, one defendant. The litigation was also bi-polar, having two clearly defined sides on the pivotal issue. Outcomes were likewise all-or-nothing; the plaintiff would either recover fully or not at all. Traditionally, the rigid formalities of English law required the parties to select a single form of action (such as trespass) and thereafter reduce their dispute to a single contested issue (such as whether the emissions of the defendant were the cause-in-fact of the plaintiff's injury). Through intricate and bewildering pleading devices, all other issues were removed from the lawsuit. The rigidity was not a problem in most cases because in a simpler era most tort victims were injured in discrete events, involving clear direct injury to at most a few people at a time. Toxic torts, however, are often mass torts of staggering complexity, often with multiple defendants and involving large classes of victims. Examples include asbestos exposure as in the *Fischer* case in Chapter 3 or the *Landrigan* case above, where literally millions of people may have suffered serious harm; pesticide and herbicide spraying as in the Agent Orange cases;[33] atmospheric nuclear testing in Nevada (Allen v. United States); and all persons who drank water from contaminated public wells (Anderson v. W. R. Grace & Co. and Ayers v. Jackson Township). With their multiplicity of claims and proof of remote causation for long-latent disease, those cases present serious questions

---

33. See P. Schuck, Agent Orange on Trial: Mass Toxic Disasters in the Courts (1988).

about the transaction costs of extended litigation, about defendants' ability to pay, and about the fairness of compensating victims far removed from defendant's action.

Courts have responded to the challenges of complex litigation through procedural innovation. In the environmental law context, the impact of changes in procedure has been absolutely essential to the emergence of meaningful common law remedies for injuries caused by both conventional and toxic tort. The complexity of many environmental cases as to matters of fact, issues of causation, measurement of damage, etc., would have been virtually impossible to litigate in a meaningful fashion without a procedural system that allowed for the concurrent pleading and proof of many theories and issues. Additionally, the advent of procedural devices allowing joinder of claims and joinder of parties has allowed a would-be plaintiff in a case involving great legal difficulty and expense to pool resources with other plaintiffs facing the same problem.[34]

When a toxic substance has entered the environment and when large numbers of potential plaintiffs have been exposed to it, sometimes on a nationwide scale, serious logistical problems confront the legal system. Many of the issues of liability, defenses, and proof will be exactly the same in hundreds and thousands of cases; to litigate them separately or even state by state would be wastefully redundant. Other issues may, however, be highly particular to individual plaintiffs. Litigation costs to plaintiffs and defendants alike become astronomical and themselves become part of the tactical setting.

Compare an air pollution nuisance case of the *Boomer* variety. In that case as litigated, only a small number of individuals sued, each claiming a number of thousands of dollars in damages. They were all aided in their efforts to force the cement company to pay for their damage by the fact that their individual cost of seeking a remedy was reduced by the sharing of litigation expenses with their coplaintiffs. As litigated, however, the *Boomer* case probably did not go as far in this direction as possible. There were numerous individuals owning land at a slightly greater remove from the cement plant who suffered lesser degrees of interference with their quiet enjoyment of their property. While the law of nuisance at some point says insubstantial loss of quiet enjoyment is not a violation of legal rights because the degree of interference is not unreasonable, it remains quite likely that many people suffering unreasonable interference with quiet enjoyment did not sue because the amount of their individual recovery would not justify the expense and hassle of pursuing the litigation. These people may choose to sue later,[35] but they may not. Institutionally for the court system, efficiency is better served if only one lawsuit is brought on behalf of all of the victims of the pollution. In joined or class actions, the court's workload is reduced because the basic underlying facts have to be resolved only once. Economic efficiency is also served because composite lawsuits internalize a greater portion of the costs of the pollution. See Wright, The Cost-Internalization Case for Class Actions, 21 Stan. L. Rev. 383 (1969).

---

34. In the American legal system, absent special equitable considerations or legislation, each party usually must pay its own attorneys' fees and expert witness fees.

35. Subsequent plaintiffs in some cases will benefit by the *Boomer* court's findings. This will depend on their ability to invoke the doctrine of collateral estoppel without mutuality of estoppel. Such parties are "free riders" on *Boomer*'s efforts, but their recovery extends the sum of costs internalized by legal action.

Toxic torts are frequently ideal candidates for joined litigation because they are often mass torts: large numbers of individuals injured through the same pattern of events. One generic pattern involves a toxic release (or a series of releases) that exposes a community to hazardous materials. To some degree, that was the backdrop of the *Kepone* case (discussed in Chapter 2). Two cases considered in this chapter, Anderson v. W. R. Grace & Co. and Ayers v. Jackson Township, also fit that pattern. In these cases, the impetus to group litigation lies both in the commonality of the questions presented for legal resolution and in the economies of scale obtained by pooling resources for litigation.

Modern procedure offers the class action device as an opportunity for bringing all pollution or toxic tort victims into a single lawsuit. In class actions, a large class of persons who are similarly situated in regard to the dispute being litigated are represented in litigation by a single member of the class or by a small group drawn from the class. The procedural rules governing class actions go to considerable lengths to ensure full and fair representation of the members of the class. Rule 23 of the Federal Rules of Civil Procedure is the most prominent of the class action rules, operating in all federal court litigation and serving as a model for the procedural rules of many of the states.

Most environmental class actions are litigated under the following two provisions of Rule 23:

(b)(2) the party opposing the class has acted or refused to act on grounds generally applicable to the class, thereby making appropriate final injunctive relief or corresponding declaratory relief with respect to the class as a whole; or

(b)(3) the court finds that the questions of law or fact common to the members of the class predominate over any questions affecting only individual members, and that a class action is superior to other available methods for the fair and efficient adjudication of the controversy.

The court exercises considerable control over cases that are maintained as a class action. The court decides whether the class action device is appropriate and must consider factors such as the ability of the class representative fully and fairly to represent the class, the interest of individual class member plaintiffs in controlling the prosecution of their own claims, the desirability of concentrating the litigation in a single court and, perhaps most importantly for mass toxic tort cases, "the difficulties likely to be encountered in the management of a class action."

Imagine, for example, the difficulty of a trial that seeks to present all of the health-related claims arising from the widespread use of asbestos as insulating material in this country.[36] Who are the plaintiffs? Looking narrowly, the group still includes millions of construction workers, some who have contracted forms of cancer, others who have not but who are now at far greater risk of developing cancer in the future. Who are the defendants? This second group, again looking narrowly, includes the hundreds

---

36. See, e.g., Jenkins v. Raymark Indus., 782 F.2d 468 (5th Cir. 1986). In *Jenkins*, the court of appeals approved trial court certification of a district-wide class action (the judicial district covered a part of Texas) to determine certain issues of liability against 13 defendant asbestos manufacturers. The class, at the time of certification, included over 1000 plaintiffs and continued to grow as asbestos-related disease manifested itself in additional exposed victims. Of course, if trial of an asbestos case like *Jenkins* appears daunting, consider the alternative of having that same trial 1000+ times over! The total number of American workers exposed to asbestos was estimated by the *Jenkins* court to be "at least 21 million."

(perhaps thousands) of companies that produced and distributed asbestos. Some of these companies were long aware of the harmful nature of contact with the product and concealed that fact; others may have been unaware. And what are the damages? And who is responsible for what share of the damages? And which particular defendant's product caused which particular plaintiff's injury when so much of the material was of a generic type that might be impossible to identify many years after the exposure to the asbestos?

The inescapable conclusion, considering that manageability is an element in class action suitability, is that no one class action can possibly take on so massive a problem, and that class action treatment may be inappropriate generally. Attempts to set up an alternative system with a special fund and arbitrational tribunal for asbestos claims (the "Wellington Agreement") have not succeeded either. While the asbestos problem is close to unique in its scale, it is not unique in displaying horrific manageability problems.

Environmental lawyers have become inventive and adaptive in using various procedural devices to overcome the manageability problems incident to the multiparty nature of many toxic tort cases. Where class actions are likely to be unmanageable, for example, the plaintiffs have in some cases opted to select "flagship" plaintiffs. These plaintiffs are similar to those who would have been selected as class representatives — their claims are among the most typical. If they win, the understanding, made clear to the defendant, is that other claims will follow. At times, courts require these later lawsuits to relitigate the disputed issues from scratch; other courts allow later cases to make collateral use of determinations that were squarely faced in the earlier lawsuit.[37]

COMMENTARY & QUESTIONS

1. **The multiplier effect of multiparty litigation.** To a defendant, what is the impact of procedural devices that result in the joinder of multiple similar claims into a single lawsuit? One obvious result is that the amount at risk in the event of an award of damages may increase manyfold. In the toxic tort area, where the injuries often are serious, this may turn many cases into a "you bet your company" scenario. Is there anything unfair in this? In general, plaintiffs can be expected to meet any such claims by defendants by pointing out that the case arose only because the defendant's actions touched the lives of so many people. Can an individual plaintiff with a marginal case, by turning to a multiparty device, "extort" a handsome settlement of the case? Here it seems more plausible that defendants can make credible claims of unfairness. In this context, the cost of responding to (or settling) marginal claims is a cost faced by virtually all enterprises, not just toxic tort defendants. What may be different in toxic tort cases are the cost, complexity, and uncertainty of maintaining a successful defense.

---

37. The use of the results in prior litigation to foreclose relitigation of claims or issues — res judicata — is subdivided into two branches, one that prevents the relitigation of entire claims (merger and bar) and another that prevents the relitigation of previously decided issues (collateral estoppel). In the successful flagship plaintiff toxic tort setting, later plaintiffs who were not parties of record in the first lawsuit would seek issue preclusion against defendant on issues such as causation or liability for the toxic release. The term that describes this use of the results of prior litigation by a second plaintiff against the common defendant is "offensive use of collateral estoppel without mutuality of estoppel." The leading federal case on the subject is Parklane Hosiery Co. v. Shore, 439 U.S. 322 (1979).

2. **The benefits of using multiparty devices.** There are ways in which the resort to multiparty litigation can make outcomes more just. Initially, to the extent that multiparty litigation reduces the need for repetitive litigation, the cost savings to the parties on both sides make the process preferable. There are at least two other settings in which having all of the claims joined in a single lawsuit holds a potential for making outcomes more just. On the plaintiffs' side, consider what happens when total liability exceeds a defendant's assets. If the litigation occurs in a piecemeal fashion, the early winners will collect their full damages, and later winners may find the defendant bankrupt and unable to pay any part of their claims. If the litigation all takes place in a single lawsuit, the proceeds can be placed in a common fund that is allocated in proportion to the individual entitlements of every deserving party. On the defendants' side, consider punitive damages. Assume that the conduct involved is such that punitive damages are awarded. If the litigation is piecemeal, punitive damages may be imposed numerous times, by numerous juries, each failing to take full account of what other punitive damages have been imposed. If only a single lawsuit is involved, a one-time-for-all award would more accurately measure the extent of punishment that should be imposed on the defendant. As Judge Clifford noted later in the *Fischer* asbestos case, "Perhaps the most likely solution to the problem of cumulative punitive damages lies in the use of a class action for those damages."

3. **Settlements and mass class actions.** In settling class action litigation, the judge has a special responsibility under Fed. R. Civ. P. 23(e) to ensure that the settlement is fair to the nonparty class members. For a case in which that power was used to reject a settlement, with the result that the parties reached a "fairer" result, see Shults v. Champion Int'l Corp., 821 F. Supp. 520 (E.D. Tenn. 1993).

The viability of class action suits in mass toxic tort settings is somewhat problematic at best since the toxic injuries suffered by each individual class member are often highly personalized and unique, and defendants will often argue that the individual causation and damage issues predominate over the common liability issues. Mass toxic tort settlements are even more problematic because of the potential for intra-class conflicts. The Supreme Court has been hostile toward toxic tort settlements of class actions in the asbestos area. In Amchem Prods., Inc. v. Windsor, 521 U.S. 591 (1997), and again in Ortiz v. Fibreboard Corp., 527 U.S. 815 (1999), the Court rejected settlements of asbestos class actions. In each of these instances, the principal issue involved the propriety of class certification for the purposes of settling the case without plenary litigation. In each instance, the Court rejected the "settlement class" device. Justice Souter wrote the majority opinion in *Ortiz* and framed the issue and holding as follows:

> This case turns on the conditions for certifying a mandatory settlement class on a limited fund theory under Federal Rule of Civil Procedure 23(b)(1)(B). We hold that applicants for contested certification on this rationale must show that the fund is limited by more than the agreement of the parties, and has been allocated to claimants belonging within the class by a process addressing any conflicting interests of class members. 527 U.S. at 821.

The majority held that the judge's findings on class inclusiveness and the fact of a truly limited fund were insufficient on the facts of *Ortiz* to allow the class to be certified.

Much of the majority's concern arose from the totally unmanageable nature of the asbestos litigation. Class actions based on group exposures that are not as disparate from one another as they appear to be in the asbestos context might not meet with the same degree of judicial hostility.

E. RELATIONSHIPS BETWEEN TOXIC TORT AND PUBLIC LAW

The common law's private remedies, of course, do not stand alone. Public law — governmental regulatory action — plays an even larger role in environmental law. Like many environmental issues, the mass toxic tort problem is simply too large for adequate control by after-the-fact damage suits and the rare injunction based on prospective nuisance.

The public law statute most readily applicable to the Woburn case was the Comprehensive Environmental Response, Compensation, and Liability Act (CERCLA, popularly known as Superfund), passed in 1980; a second major statute of potential applicability is RCRA, the Resource Conservation and Recovery Act. These are examined in Chapters 19 and 18 respectively. Both laws work to achieve cleanups of contaminated parcels. Neither grants private remedies for bodily injury or compensation for property damage, although CERCLA creates a private cause of action to obtain reimbursement for cleanup costs. On the governmental enforcement side, both laws allow the federal government to issue administrative orders requiring responsible parties to undertake cleanup, and CERCLA requires responsible parties in appropriate cases to pay damages to government for natural resource damages. RCRA also has elaborate requirements that seek to prevent releases of hazardous wastes into the environment in the first place, but events had moved far past that at Woburn by the time RCRA was enacted in 1976.

Section 1. CONTRASTING PRIVATE AND PUBLIC LAW

In the *Anderson* wellwater contamination case, as in many toxic tort controversies, both private law and public law ultimately played extensive roles. Private law and public law tend to be two different and uncoordinated worlds, both absorbing huge amounts of time and resources, and imposing major legal constraints on the industrial marketplace. Given the complex economic, political, and technical context, it is not surprising that systemic questions are constantly being raised whether the two legal régimes are redundant and ought to be rationalized, most often by proposals for limiting or eliminating toxic tort litigation.

The Woburn case offers an opportunity to consider larger questions about the systemic role of tort civil actions against the backdrop of state and federal statutes and regulatory agencies. What observations can be drawn from the following partial chronology of the parallel processes in the Woburn case's public and private law?

A WOBURN TOXICS TIMELINE:

1979   Government agencies (the federal EPA, the state environmental agency, and the local health board) take the first legal actions after testing groundwater around the wellfield: they close the wells, fence the site, and identify potentially responsible parties (PRPs).

1980   EPA began the Superfund process: Preliminary Assessment: site investigation and analysis of the need and method for remediation, under §§106 and 107 of CERCLA (a cleanup process that averages 12 years; see Chapter 19).

1980–   Robbie Robbins, Jimmie Anderson, and Jarrod Aufiero died.
1981

1981   The future plaintiffs ask the federal CDC to study the seeming leukemia cluster, and the CDC affirms that leukemia cluster is extraordinary.

1982   EPA places Wells G & H on the National Priorities List (NPL).

        Lawsuit filed; discovery and other extensive trial preparations begin; Schlichtmann and plaintiffs give presentation at Harvard School of Public Health that launches field study. Grace admits using TCE and begins to undertake voluntary groundwater investigatory work.

1983   EPA Remedial Investigation and Feasibility Study (RIFS) complete.

        EPA issues an Administrative Order to Grace to look for buried drums, excavate them, and install groundwater monitoring wells.

1983–   Plaintiffs' intensive investigation into medical causation of leukemias.
1986

1984   CERCLA implementation process continues; Beatrice and Riley tell EPA they never used subject chemicals; Grace completes testing, inventory, and some drum removal as required by the 1983 Administrative Order.

        Harvard School of Public Health Study published showing local health anomalies.

1985   EPA and USGS conduct a 30-day aquifer test. Plaintiffs' on-site testing accompanied by government investigators.

1986   Anderson et al. v. Grace & Beatrice: Trial on exposure phase begins in February, verdict at end of July: ambiguous verdict against Grace; plaintiffs cannot prove Beatrice tannery's contamination on terms required by court.

        September: Grace settles for $8 million.

1987   Plaintiffs discover Yankee Report in EPA files in September, showing contamination at the tannery site itself in test results.

1987–   Plaintiffs appeal Beatrice verdict and attempt to get a new trial to prove Beatrice's
1990   contamination based on Beatrice's witholding of reports during discovery. First Circuit tells Judge Skinner to review; he does and denies a retrial based on a Rule 11 theory, cert. denied.

1988   EPA begins criminal action against Grace based on its responses to a 1982 information request; Grace agrees to a settlement for appromimately $10,000 on a plea equivalent to nolo contendere.

1989   February: EPA proposes Remedial Design with on-site incineration. Major local opposition during comment period.

        September: EPA finalizes second version of Remedial Design for site remediation, with off-site incineration and some removal of materials to RCRA-approved landfills.

        September 14: EPA final Record of Decision (ROD).

1991   EPA Remedial Action begins with pump tests and pilot study of pump-and-treat system.

        Remediation will take "several years," and will take place only on the property of the individual PRPs. No cleanup is scheduled for the contaminated well sites. EPA negotiates a consent decree with Beatrice, Unifirst, New England Plastics, Grace, and others for cleanup. Estimated cost of $69.5 million, with each party paying its own share. EPA will oversee and charge PRPs for administrative costs.

1992   Pump-and-treat remediation system in full operation; to remain so for indefinite future. Remediation under the modified plan is based on substantial removal of soils to RCRA-certified landfills.

1997   State Dept. of Public Health releases study concluding that the contaminated well-water was the cause of increased likelihood of childhood leukemia in the plaintiffs' Woburn neighborhood.[38]

2000   Final remediation largely achieved for selected contaminated parcels (except well sites); groundwater not to be safe until 2020 at the earliest. The total amount of contaminated soil estimated by EPA for removal and incineration had been seriously underestimated; the final total has not yet been announced.

There is still major contamination of the land in Woburn. EPA has required the cleanup of only some of the contaminated parcels — Grace/Cryovac, New England Plastics (near Grace), Unifirst, Olympia Nominee Trust (land near Unifirst), and Wildwood Conservation (the tannery's low-lying 15-acre parcel). There are three additional sites being cleaned up under a state statute (Whitney Barrel, Aberjona Auto Parts, and Murphy's Waste Oil, all small entities along Salem Street at the bottom of the site map). Massachusetts would sign on to the settlement only if these latter sites were included. EPA had not gone after these sites because they were small and their contamination was predominantly oil, which is not covered under CERCLA. There is no cleanup being done on Well Sites G & H themselves because EPA is waiting to see whether the cleanup of the "contribution sites" will eventually result in a decontamination of the well sites. Note also that the tannery itself is not one of the sites being cleaned up, much of its soil reportedly having been removed informally during the course of the litigation.

COMMENTARY & QUESTIONS

1. **Did public law contribute to the private law civil action and vice versa?** Looking at this chronology, one can ask, "To what degree, if any, did the parallel processes facilitate one another?" Were they all coordinated, or were they moving on two quite separate tracks?

It is clear that EPA's initial studies helped to target plaintiffs' efforts and that the CDC's study confirmed the likelihood of wrongful causation of the leukemias. Governmental findings of cleanup liability might have helped prove some of the elements of tort liability, especially Beatrice's contamination of the wells, and improved the plaintiffs' momentum, but they were not finalized until five years after trial.[39] The state epidemiology study might have helped prove causation, but it was not completed until ten years after trial. During the tort litigation, as is so often the case, government staffers were hesitant to provide active aid to plaintiffs, who only by chance found the 1983 Yankee Report in EPA files.

Did the private litigation aid the government's efforts? Without the plaintiffs, the government agencies probably never would have discovered Al Love, whose testimony

38. Mass. Dept. Pub. Health, Bur. of Envtl. Health Assessment, Woburn Childhood Leukemia Follow-Up Study (July 1997).

39. Tort plaintiffs often seek to go to trial after the government has successfully prosecuted the same defendants for the same acts, riding the coattails of governmental findings of administrative liability or criminal penalties. A conviction or administrative penalty substantially aids private claims, but given uncoordinated statutes of limitations, the timing is often difficult.

about Grace's dumping produced criminal fines for perjury against the company. On several occasions, government field investigators lacked sufficient funds to do ongoing field studies and requested permission to come along when plaintiffs hired backhoes to dig for evidence of contamination. Without the dramatic tort case, is it likely the land and water would still ultimately reach the same level of remediation by EPA? Some government staffers said that the media climate around the case made it easier to negotiate with the corporations and pushed the file with greater internal momentum within the agency. Others denied this. Plaintiffs' evidence tending to show active contamination by the tannery was of no special assistance to the government because in the Woburn defendants' context, the toxic cleanup statutes made mere ownership of contaminated land a basis for strict liability.

2. **Comparative advantages of public law.** For the people of Woburn, the public law's cleanup mechanisms for contaminated land and groundwater presented some substantial advantages over private law. Emergency protective actions can be ordered instantaneously, as were those ordering the well closings. Sophisticated land remediation techniques are applied under expert agency supervision at no expense to the neighborhood, paid for by the responsible corporations. Proof in a public law case can be far easier than in tort law. Unlike private plaintiffs, administrative agencies engaged in environmental protection are not required to prove causation by a preponderance of the evidence. Plaintiffs recovered zero from Beatrice's contamination of wellwater, while EPA got a large part of $69.5 million.[40] The agencies' presumed expertise and authority to protect public health entitle their decisions to great deference from reviewing courts. Courts can overturn agency decisions only where they have been found to be "arbitrary and capricious" or the equivalent. See Chapter 7. When scientific uncertainty and potential danger are both great, reviewing courts show even greater deference and accept administrative records that they would reject under other circumstances. When EPA issued its regulations prohibiting lead in gasoline (suspected to pose particular risks to urban children), for example, the agency admitted that scientific knowledge regarding the harmful effects of lead was highly uncertain. The evidence never would have supported tort liability. In Ethyl Corp. v. EPA, 541 F.2d 1 (D.C. Cir. 1976), however, the court upheld the public law prohibition:

> From extensive and often conflicting evidence, the EPA in this case made numerous factual determinations.... Some of the questions involved in the promulgation of these standards are on the frontiers of scientific knowledge, and consequently as to them insufficient data is presently available to make a fully informed factual determination. Decision making must in that circumstance depend to a greater extent upon policy judgments and less upon purely factual analysis.... We note that many of the issues in this case do not involve "historical" facts subject to the ordinary means of judicial resolution. Indeed, a number of the disputes involve conflicting theories and experimental results, about which it would be judicially presumptuous to offer conclusive findings. In such circumstances, the finder of

---

40. Under the settlement, the companies agreed to pay $58.4 million to clean up polluted soil and groundwater, $5.8 million to fund EPA oversight of the cleanup, $2.7 million to the government for its previous work at the site, and $2.6 million for further studies and cleanup costs. EPA assessed Beatrice for the majority of these costs, based on EPA's determination that Beatrice had been responsible for the majority of the contamination.

fact must accept certain areas of uncertainty, and the findings themselves cannot extend further than attempting to assess or characterize the strengths and weaknesses of the opposing arguments....

Where a statute is precautionary in nature, the evidence difficult to come by, uncertain, or conflicting because it is on the frontiers of scientific knowledge, the regulations designed to protect public health, and the decision that of an expert administrator, we will not demand rigorous step-by-step proof of cause and effect. Of course, we are not suggesting that the Administrator has the power to act on hunches or wild guesses. His conclusions must be rationally justified. However, we do hold that in such cases the Administrator may assess risks.... He may apply his expertise to draw conclusions from suspected, but not completely substantiated, relationships between facts, from trends among facts, from theoretical projections from imperfect data, from probative preliminary data not yet certifiable as "fact," and the like.... Operating within the prescribed [statutory] guidelines, he must consider all the information available to him. Some of the information will be factual, but much of it will be more speculative scientific estimates and "guesstimates" of probable harm, hypotheses based on still-developing data, etc. 541 F.2d at 26–29.

This process of imposing public law liability, needless to say, is totally different from the process of proving legal liability in a tort case like the Woburn setting. As studied later, in Chapters 18 and 19, government hazardous waste remedies have no need to prove specific causation of harm, the scientifically subjective task that overturns most tort plaintiffs. Agencies merely have to show that a responsible party owned the site, or transported, dumped, or arranged for the disposal of toxics at the site. The burden of proof in this context is effectively on the PRP, not the prosecuting agency. It may take an average of 12 years to clean contaminated sites, but government eventually gets the job done.

3. **Comparative advantages of private law.** But private law offers major utilities as well. Public law remedies depend on official decisionmaking, which in some settings can be held back by politics or inertia. At common law, however, if a plaintiff pays the filing fee and has competent proof on point, a court has to hear the case, and if the facts are there, a remedy is likely to issue. Public law produces no compensation for injured citizens. Common law damages are a driving force behind many private law actions against toxic industrial cost externalizations. The self-interest of affected citizens, as in *Boomer*, or in citizen suits authorized by statutes such as the CWA often are a better motivator to bring important issues into the law. Courts in tort actions, moreover, as noted in this and the preceding chapter, also have a variety of equitable remedies to tailor outcomes to public and private needs, a flexibility in available remedies that few agencies know to exercise. (Tort remedies, however, especially punitive damages, may have no necessary proportionality in the burdens they impose. Public remedies, which are developed in standardized administrative procedures, may have greater uniformity and circumspection.) Tort remedies, evolved over centuries and familiar to judges, can sometimes be mobilized more readily and applied more flexibly, without attenuated technical procedures, than can public regulatory law.

Note in the Woburn toxics case a further societal utility of private law: In public law, there is little or no legal obligation of official agencies to investigate and remedy public health threats. The vigilance and perseverance of official agencies in investigating and defending against public toxic exposures depends on a variety of logistical and political conditions. A charged-up media climate is often necessary to attract official response to a diffuse health threat such as a possible leukemia cluster. Private law tort actions can bring health considerations into the central focus of the legal forum and serve to mobilize governmental attention. Public and private law thus operate in two different realms, serving quite different functions.

Do the two realms conflict with one another? On the ground they seem at most to supplement one another. To marketplace industries, however, the two forms of liability understandably seem like duplicative overkill — you can comply with CERCLA and still get sued by the neighbors for an even more stringent common law cleanup order[41] — which leads to calls for "tort reform" relief.

4. **The "tort reform" efficiency debate.** Does the Woburn toxics case throw any light on arguments that complex cases involving scientific subtleties and public risk should be handled in the future by government agencies under public laws rather than by private litigation in courts? Over the years there have been recurring calls (from many academics as well as defense attorneys) for tort reform, based not only on perceptions of the growing size of tort recoveries (the radio talk shows' favorite example probably is the plaintiff who initially was awarded $2 million for burns from spilled coffee) but also on perceptions of the common law's limitations in coping with the problems of mass tort and toxics cases. The plaintiffs' bar responds that the average recovery in tort cases has not increased disproportionately, and that the insurance industry, in decrying the need to raise premiums, focuses on tort payments to the exclusion of its own internal investment policies. That debate is likely to be noisy and continuing.

In recent years, environmental tort cases have regularly provided some of the nation's largest damage recoveries.[42] As to mass toxic torts, a substantial body of scholarship argues that toxic exposure cases are too massive and complex to be left to the common law. The nature of epidemiology, the size of exposed plaintiff classes, the emotional and economic repercussions of litigation, and the problems of latency all combine to recommend statutory and administrative overrides of the tort law. See Trauberman, Statutory Reform of "Toxic Torts," 7 Harv. Envtl. L. Rev. 177, 188–202 (1983). Some scholars thus recommend statutory or administrative mechanisms that would permit compensation to be awarded on the basis of exposure and significant risk of disease, without the necessity of proving the existence of present injury. The size and arcane bureaucratic complexity of proposed public law remedies for mass torts, however, and their alleged vulnerability to political pressure from industry defendants combine to raise substantial doubts about any such preemption of common law. What is the verdict on tort reform to be drawn from Woburn's Civil Action? Tort law is a known commodity that carries its own internal incentives to prosecution of claims. Public law

---

41. That in fact was exactly the situation in the *Escamilla* restoration damages case discussed in Chapter 3.

42. The *Exxon-Valdez* civil damage verdicts, totaling more than $5 billion in suits brought by harmed users of the Gulf of Alaska, takes a prize, but asbestos recoveries often have major price tags as well. Coyne and McCoubrey v. Celotex, (settled), Wall St. J., 9 Feb. 1990, at B1 ($76 million for each of two workers exposed to asbestos).

management cannot easily replicate the tort law's claims-processing mechanisms. For the time being, the legal situation is likely to continue with common law as an active and tangible element in most toxic exposure cases, with supplementary overlays from the public law system. Or is it vice versa?

Section 2. **RISK MANAGEMENT CONCERNS**

In an influential article, excerpts of which follow, Peter Huber (of the "junk science" debate, previously discussed in this chapter) argued that private tort law should be supplanted by a system of public law administered by expert agencies. In his view, tort claims wrongly fixate on public risks, which are only one part of society's risk "portfolio," and this fixation often backfires by increasing total risk through discouraging public risks. As you read the article, consider what Huber might have to say about the comparative advantages of public and private law in the Woburn case.

Peter Huber, Safety and the Second Best: The Hazards of Public Risk Management in the Courts
85 Columbia Law Review 277, 277–281, 301–307, 329–337 (1985)

The devastating chemical plant tragedy in Bhopal, India will do little to reassure skeptics about the advantages of technological innovation and development. Those who already view the chemical, nuclear, pharmaceutical, and other high-tech industries with profound suspicion and fear can now point to the 2200 dead of Bhopal as martyrs to unbridled technological tyranny. And Bhopal will henceforth serve as the shrine of Nemesis for those who would defend the value of high technology.

But Bhopal is only one painfully vivid example in a much larger, longstanding legal debate in this country. The debate reflects a deep division among legal commentators regarding the role of mass production and technological change in the improvement of social welfare. Long before Bhopal, the standard diagnosis in many judicial opinions and in much of our scholarly legal literature has been that our society produces too much "public" risk, through its excessive or unwise use of dangerous new technology and the tools of mass production. The standard prescription has been for lawyers to do something about it. This article argues that the diagnosis is probably wrong, and that the prescription should certainly be rejected.

The legal debate about risks is very much a debate about "public" risks. These are threats to human health or safety that are centrally or mass-produced, broadly distributed, and largely outside the individual risk bearer's direct understanding and control. Public risks usually derive from new or especially complex technology — they are the hazards of large-scale electric power plants, air transport in jumbo jets, mass-produced vaccines, chemical additives and contaminants in food, or recombinant-DNA technology. For many lawyers, "advancements" such as these arouse deep suspicion and concern. "Private risks," by contrast, are discretely produced, localized, personally controlled, or of natural origin. They are the risks of cottage industries, wood stoves, transportation by car, or exposure to natural toxins or pathogens. Typically, private risks arouse little anxiety among legal commentators.

The legal system's almost obsessive preoccupation with public risks is, in my view, entirely misguided.[43] I wish to develop this argument soberly; there can be no technological arrogance in

---

43. [Particularly at the outset, Huber is responding to the work of commentators who argued that public risk is being overproduced. Two articles in particular provoked Huber's attacks: Yellin, High Technology and the

the shadow of Bhopal. But the facts and the regulatory arguments seem plain nonetheless. First, public risks are progressive — they improve the overall state of our risk environment — whenever the incremental risk created is smaller than the quantum of existing privately-created risk that is displaced. The point may seem obvious, but the fact that a large number of judges and legal commentators ignore it suggests otherwise.

Second, the judicial system is, for a variety of reasons, incapable of engaging in the aggregative calculus of risk created and risk averted that progressive public-risk management requires. While it is not my goal to replace an absolutist's aversion to public risk with an absolutist's embrace of it, I will argue that the judicial role sought (and achieved) by many commentators is imprudently biased against many progressive, risk-reducing (though still risky) technologies. This bias significantly hinders our progress towards a healthier, safer environment.

My arguments grow out of a single paradox of the risk economy: greater private safety is often to be found in the greater acceptance of public risk....

The Attack on the Windmill... How much public risk is too much? And who shall decide how much is too much? Most of the legal debate revolves around these two questions. For many legal scholars and judges, the answer to the first question is almost self-evident: we currently bear more public risk than we should, because we have been too ready to accept the hazards of new or mass-production technology. Answers to the second question tend to be longer and more varied, but most have the same general thrust: lawyers and judges are well positioned to assess the problem and supply the additional deterrence that is so plainly needed. It is this pair of answers (both of which are, in my view, quite wrong) that this Part describes....

Excess Public Risk... Life is already unacceptably hazardous, and likely to grow more so as the result of excessively rapid and overwhelming technological change. This is the common starting point in much of the legal commentary. How is the point to be proved? First, by referring to the public's aversion to public risks. Second, by reciting the myriad public terrors already in our midst. Third, by developing the microeconomic and philosophical underpinnings of a case against means of production that entail public hazards.

Lawyers opposed to public risks are in good company. The public consensus, if there is one, seems to be that risk-taking, like abortion, religion, travel, or marriage, should be a private affair. Indeed, consumer hostility to public risk is matched only by consumer affection for private risk. Illustrations of this division of preferences abound. The aerial spraying of malathion in a California program to combat the Mediterranean fruit fly provokes passionate opposition, but consumers eagerly spray tens of thousands of gallons of the same pesticide in their own, private gardens. A proposal to vent small amounts of radioactive gas and water from the damaged nuclear reactor at Three Mile Island in the course of cleaning up that facility — a comparatively minuscule investment in public risk with clear risk-reducing benefits — causes panic. But a proposal to ban saccharin — a proposal to curtail, as these things go, a fairly substantial investment in comparatively "private" patterns of risk taking — precipitates what was described in the New York Times as panic buying of the sweetener. Mass aircraft accidents arouse great concern, and the mandatory use of seat belts in planes is accepted without a murmur. But in the much more hazardous private-risk environment of automobile travel, seat belt interlock systems or mandatory seat belt laws encounter vociferous consumer opposition. Mandatory vaccination programs are vigorously attacked in the courts, but individuals also come to court to insist on

Courts: Nuclear Power and the Need for Institutional Reform, 94 Harv. L. Rev. 489 (1981), and Rosenberg, The Causal Connection in Mass Exposure Cases: A Public Law Vision of the Tort System, 97 Harv. L. Rev. 851 (1984).] [Eds.]

their right to be treated with medical quackery of every description, apricot pits providing a recent and much-publicized example.

Panic, protest, and organized resistance thus greet almost every venture that entails new public risk. Meanwhile, efforts to restrain private risk-taking are denounced as grave attacks on personal freedom. Some litigants have seriously maintained — and some courts have agreed — that the Constitution itself enshrines both the right to bear a private risk and the right not to be exposed to a public one. In short, shared risks, like shared goods, are thought to be almost un-American — a collectivist affront to individual autonomy and self-reliance.

The layperson's aversion to public risks is shared by much of the legal community. Lawyers, for the most part, are convinced that there is too much public risk out there, and they generally begin their indictment of public risks by citing some that they especially dislike. Professor Yellin, for example, uses as his paradigm case the hazards of generating nuclear power, but he also points to chemical pesticides, air and water pollution, occupational hazards, and "complex environmental decisions" of every description — the "ominous, not yet fully understood risks to public health [that] involve decisions that may seriously alter our physical environment." Professor Rosenberg's concern centers on similar targets: the risks accompanying "the production, distribution, marketing, consumption, and disposal of toxic agents." He lists as examples "asbestos, Agent Orange and Agent White, Three-Mile Island, dioxin, and a string of acronyms — DES, PCB, PBB and IUD," drugs, and aircraft disasters. Numerous other commentators have similar lists of concerns, and all supply citations to cases in which judges and juries have echoed these fears.

It is easy enough to clothe a visceral aversion to public risk in the robes of market efficiency or social justice. So easy, in fact, that the exercise has become quite reflexive and mechanical in much of the legal literature.

To the lawyer qua economist, risk is a cost — the cost of confining, disposing of, or simply coexisting with hazardous matter or energy. The cost can, of course, vary enormously, depending on how wisely a particular hazard is managed. It is nevertheless ascertainable. As with all other costs, the lawyer-economist will contend, the creator of a risk must shoulder it if markets are to operate "efficiently." A producer of risk who is not held strictly accountable for the unconsented-to consequences of that risk will generate risk in socially undesirable amounts. The result will be a market failure. Or so the story goes.

The lawyer qua philosopher may reach similar conclusions about public risks on somewhat different grounds. Our libertarian, individualistic, political ideal forbids one person from imposing unconsented-to burdens on another. Burdens that take the form of external threats to health or safety are especially objectionable intrusions on the risk bearer's private space and personal autonomy. Like the lawyer-economist, the lawyer-philosopher is therefore opposed to external risk. The mass producer of a dangerous good, or the operator of a hazardous power plant, acts antisocially. Her conduct is worse than economically inefficient — it is morally wrong. Or so the story goes.

Arguments along these lines are wheeled out, with pedestrian regularity, by those opposed to everything from nuclear power to synthetic sweeteners. Absent the risk bearer's individual, fully informed, and entirely free consent, any activity that creates public risk is, pro tanto, both a threat to market efficiency and an infringement on the just entitlements of the risk bearer. Public risks are an absolute bad. We want as few of them as possible.

The Judicial Role... Though there is somewhat less unanimity about precisely why it is that a nation with a large and powerful government, fifty autonomous state governments, and 650,000 lawyers, has apparently allowed public-risk technology to run so wild, the consensus is that the existing, agency-centered system of risk regulation inadequately deters the production of public risk. Help from the legal community is therefore in order. It may come before the accident, or after it, but in either event its thrust should be to discourage new dangerous technologies and the instrumentalities of mass-produced risks. Professor Yellin's and Professor Rosenberg's proposals typify the two larger schools of thought.

Professor Yellin urges the courts to improve pre-accident decision-making. He advocates closer judicial scrutiny of "broad new regulatory departures." When an agency approves a novel technological venture that entails new public risk, the courts, suitably advised by "a committee of scientists, engineers, and lawyers to act as standing masters," should supply a "second" (read "final") opinion.

Professor Rosenberg, for his part, suggests a greater degree of judicial intervention after the public risk has been approved and is in place. The courts, again advised by "court-appointed experts, special masters, and blue-ribbon juries," should impose tort liability on public risk creators sooner, more often, and in larger amount. To this end, the cost of risk itself, rather than consummated injury, is to be made compensable — when, and only when, it is a "public" or "mass exposure" risk. Questions of legal causation are to be resolved under a relaxed "proportionality" rule, that will hold risk creators liable for the proportion of total injuries attributable to their activities, even when no single plaintiff can accurately claim that her injury was, more likely than not, caused by the defendant's conduct.

The Yellin and Rosenberg prescriptions are complementary in their intended effect on activities that create public risks. More before-the-accident review and stricter after-the-accident liability are mutually reinforcing responses to the same perceived problem — the excess creation of public risks. At first blush, it is hard to think of any reason not to applaud. Indeed, many do, by citation to or by development of Yellin's and Rosenberg's proposals....

[Eds.—Major portions of the article are omitted here, including a segment in which Huber presents a case study of how vaccine development and use has been greatly overdeterred by the cost of paying damage awards to injured victims of the vaccine. Also omitted is a segment that argues against treating damage awards against public risk producers as desirable cost internalization. To internalize those costs, Huber argues, in the absence of imposing corresponding costs against natural risk producers, such as disease, leads to a distortion of risk consumption. He invokes the theory of second best in favor of noninternalization of public risks stating, "patchy, erratic risk internalization may impose greater costs on the safer substitutes within particular markets, and so may encourage a shift in consumption to the more hazardous." Huber claims that the morality of public risks also must be judged with reference to the private risks they retire, not merely on the basis of harms they may inflict. To prove that changes in lifestyle associated with public risk-creating behaviors have made life safer in the aggregate, Huber invokes evidence of decreasing mortality and increases in life expectancy in the last several centuries. He then argues more narrowly that the degree of capitalization and expertise surrounding most public risk ventures are likely to make them more safe than the private risk counterparts that they displace.]

On close, objective examination one almost invariably discovers that public risk alternatives provide goods and services with less risk (per unit of good) than the private-supply substitutes. The reasons are not difficult to discover. Large, centralized, capital-intensive production facilities are easier to operate safely than their small, distributed, labor-intensive alternatives. The very characteristics of mass production and distribution that make public risks possible in the first place also make mass production inherently safer than the private-production alternative. The central- or mass-producers can and do deliver goods and services with much less attendant risk than distributed- or discrete-producers (including Nature) possibly could....

The Judicial Role in Managing Public Risks... The second large question in the public risk debate follows naturally from the first; who should decide how much public risk is enough? Since some measure of public risk is not only inevitable but desirable, some institution must be directed to define the measure and specify its ingredients....

Public control of public risks is therefore necessary, both to prevent the excess generation of public risk and to make possible the acceptance of as much public risk as is socially desirable. The government regulator, a single, central decision-maker, acts as the consumers' collective "broker" in a particular risk market. The regulator — whoever it may be — must perform at least two tasks. One, of course, is to reject unfavorable investments in public risk. The regulator has the resources to proceed against creators of unacceptable public risks. Here we have the more familiar regulator, government, saying "no," placing limits on the risks individuals may create.

But the regulator's second function is to acquiesce in risk creation. To represent his principal effectively, a broker in a risk market, like a broker in any other setting, must be able to buy as well as to sell. A centralized risk-regulatory system must not only reject bad public risk choices but also supply the public's consent to good ones. This is most clearly illustrated in comprehensively regulated industries such as those producing electric power, drugs, pesticides, and many other products of modern technology. In these areas, risk creators start with no freedom to do anything at all until they receive express regulatory permission. The nay-saying regulatory role then effectively disappears; the regulator's task is to serve as a retail deregulator, giving case-by-case consent to new ventures that entail public risks.

The administrative agencies are, of course, the more familiar regulators, wielding authority over public risks of every variety. But the courts are also vigorous regulators, and it is their role that most concerns me here. The courts are pivotal actors in the prospective approval of new technological ventures. They possess considerable authority to review agency approvals of new sources of risk, whether the risk involves a new vaccine, power plant, pesticide, or food additive. And in areas not subject to comprehensive administrative regulation the courts can use injunctions to act as first-tier gatekeepers of the risk environment. The courts are also heavily engaged in the retrospective regulation of public risks. Damage actions sounding in nuisance, negligence, strict liability, and absolute liability are powerful instruments of regulation. Indeed, the legal community invented the "emission fee" for dealing with hazards such as pollution long before the economists had much to say about it. Every risk creator and every risk bearer knows that the damage action, and most particularly an action seeking punitive damages, is potent medicine for regulating public risks.... [Huber's specific attacks on the judicial system as regulator are omitted.]

Private Injury and Public Safety: The Courts and the Agencies... My discussion in the previous Part brings me to two conclusions. First, governmental control of public risks is both necessary and useful. Many public risks should be excluded if they are not yet a part of our environment, or controlled if they already are. Government regulation, moreover, is also needed to fulfill the second half of the regulatory function — to supply our collective consent to public risks that are judged to be good risk investments. Second, the courts are institutionally predisposed to favor regressive public risk choices. The courts systematically prefer old risks to new ones and discretely produced or natural hazards to mass-produced substitutes, and have neither the inclination nor the expertise to distinguish sources of truly "excess" risk from their risky yet risk-reducing counterparts.

Who then should decide how much public risk we will accept and in what areas? The answer is painfully obvious to almost everyone outside the legal community: expert administrative agencies, not lawyers. To make life safer, faster, we need not more scientists in the legal process, but fewer lawyers in the scientific one. The legal system has no special competence to assess and compare public risks, and the legal process is not designed or equipped to conduct the broad-ranging, aggregative inquiries on which sensible public-risk choices are built. Expert administrative agencies, troubled and erratic though they may be, remain best able to regulate public risks in a manner calculated to advance the public health and welfare....

COMMENTARY & QUESTIONS

1. **The benefits of public risk.** Huber is surely correct that credit should be given in the evaluation of public risks for the risks, private or public, that they displace. This is simply good accounting, just like the good accounting that the environmental perspective demands when ecosystem benefits are advanced in support of some regulatory activity, such as wetlands preservation.

Does this mean that Talbot Page, whose views were encountered in Chapter 1, is wrong when he argues that environmental risk situations display the potential for catastrophic costs weighed against relatively modest benefits? Page uses nuclear power generation as a prototypical example of an environmental risk, with regard to which we should minimize false negatives. How might Huber champion nuclear power in preference to fossil fuel generation of electricity? Nuclear power reduces the risk of ecosystem harms due to the emission of sulfur oxides from coal-fired power plants, a major cause of acid precipitation. Likewise, nuclear energy reduces the risk of massive ecological harms that would accompany the global warming threatened by the production of greenhouse gases. Are courts in a position to measure the trade-offs? Huber, in his mocking comparison of wood stoves to nuclear power plants, conveniently omits elaborate discussion about the back end of the nuclear fuel cycle — the extreme difficulties of nuclear waste disposal (including the risk of terrorist diversion of that material) — but even putting all the factors on the table, is it certain that nuclear power generation is a bad choice? Is one subject that Huber should address (but doesn't) the problems of risk assessment in high-uncertainty (sometimes zero-infinity) situations? How do you suppose that Huber would analyze a technology that provided many calculable benefits but also posed a slight chance of destroying a significant part of the world? Should Huber also take public outrage seriously? At present, the American public appears to be unalterably opposed to expanding reliance upon nuclear power, regardless of rational cost-benefit accounting. Would Huber agree with the decision in *Wilsonville*, discussed in Chapter 3?

2. **The opportunity costs of proactive regulation.** A point that Huber did not make, but well could have, is that risk management, by minimizing false negatives, may also adversely affect public health:

> Current risk assessment practice is also one-sided in failing to consider the potential negative health effects that may follow from regulatory costs themselves. Economic studies suggest that regulatory costs may impair public health, a point that has been picked up by some judges. Under this view, every dollar that goes to regulatory costs is unavailable for things that tend to promote health, such as extra medical exams, better neighborhoods, safer cars, shorter work hours, or basic

nutrition. Moreover, investigators report that mortality data show a correlation between health and wealth. They suggest from this data that each $3 million to $7 million spent on regulatory costs may lead to one additional premature death. Shere, The Myth of Meaningful Environmental Risk Assessment, 19 Harv. Envtl. L. Rev. 409, 472 (1995).

Is this an effective argument? Are these costs commensurable? For a critique of the estimates cited by Shere, see Heinzerling & Ackerman, The Humbugs of the Anti-Regulatory Movement, 87 Cornell L. Rev. 648, 666-670 (2002).

3. **Stephen Breyer and other risk reformers.** Huber argued that (1) courts over-deter investment in public risk, and (2) reliance on administrative agencies is more likely to achieve acceptance of the optimal amount of public risk. Justice Stephen Breyer, in a book published shortly before his appointment to the U.S. Supreme Court — Breaking the Vicious Circle: Toward Effective Risk Regulation (1993) — makes similar arguments and recommends the creation of a centralized federal administrative group that would develop, coordinate, and supervise federal risk regulation through a decisional structure similar to an agency of experts on a military command model.

Justice Breyer noted that there was no "detailed federal government list that prioritizes health or safety risk problems so as to create a rational, overall agenda." He decried the "tunnel vision" occurring when an agency "effectively carries single-minded pursuit of a single goal too far," thereby doing more harm than good. He pointed to the EPA ban on asbestos pipe featured in the *Corrosion Proof Fittings* case, discussed in Chapter 13, which allegedly imposed extra costs of $200–300 million in order to save seven or eight lives over 13 years, while in the same period twice as many deaths could be expected from ingested toothpicks! Breyer proposed the development of a system by which regulatory resources could be shifted from areas of minimal risk to fields in which they "could buy the largest amount of safety per dollar."

Such calls for risk-based regulation have been echoed in radio talk shows, the 104th Congress, and a popular collection of anecdotes castigating government regulations as intemperate and disproportionate, like Philip Howard's The Death of Common Sense: How Law Is Suffocating America (1994), calling, like Justice Breyer's book, for a body of statistical risk experts to reform regulatory practice. Analyzing this debate, two scholars have written:

> The "cures" proposed by the ["Contract with America"] Congress...and by Breyer and Howard... — both of them "tyrannies of the rational" —are themselves risky and may very likely be worse than the "disease." Although it may not seem terribly exciting, the best solution may be for the public to demand more rational regulation through existing channels. The give-and-take among the branches of government and with the public may be a necessary, even desirable, characteristic of risk regulation. Democracy and cost-effective, rational regulation are not incompatible....
>
> Pending legislative proposals quite obviously would exacerbate the less desirable aspects of the current system rather than ameliorate them. In context, it is difficult to characterize the use of risk assessment in the legislative vehicles currently proposed as anything other than an abuse of that methodology, designed not to promote regulatory reform but to impede desirable or necessary regulatory activity. Wirth & Silbergeld, Risky Reform, 95 Colum. L. Rev. 1857, 1895 (1995).

Professor Donald Hornstein, after canvassing the virtues of comparative risk analysis, provided an array of arguments against uncritical reliance on comparative risk analysis as anything more than a useful datum in setting environmental protection priorities and policies. See Hornstein, Reclaiming Environmental Law: A Normative Critique of Comparative Risk Analysis, 92 Colum. L. Rev. 562 (1992). The article, marshaling arguments developed in social sciences literature, asserted that (like "efficiency") the comparative risk analysis process is sufficiently problematic that it should not be adopted uncritically as a normative touchstone.

4. **Attacking Huber's assessment of institutional competence.** Professors Clayton Gillette and James Krier, in their article entitled Risk, Courts, and Agencies, 138 U. Pa. L. Rev. 1027 (1990), directly attack Huber's arguments. They propose a method for deciding whether courts are being too generous or too stingy toward plaintiffs who challenge activities involving public risks. There are two lines of inquiry, one into process bias and one into access bias:

> Process bias arises from the interplay of legal doctrine and adjudicative decision-makers. It concerns the ways in which judges and juries interpret and apply the law that defines the rights and liabilities of the parties before them. Access bias, on the other hand, arises from the interplay of legal doctrine, the structure of litigation, and the nature of public risk. It concerns the ways in which victims decide whether (given prevailing doctrine, among other things) litigation is worthwhile, and the ability of victims to initiate claims. Access is anterior to process; only when obstacles to access are overcome, so that claims are actually filed and prosecuted, can process bias come into play. 138 U. Pa. L. Rev. at 1045.

They then focus on the failings of professional risk assessment (i.e., hazard alone) to account for the multidimensional character of the layperson's perception of risk:

> Whatever its motivations, the experts' approach to risk is obviously not senseless. Yet neither is the public's approach. This is why...the problem comes down to one of competing rationalities. Admit this, and it unarguably follows that the choice of approach is an ethical and political one that technical experts have neither the knowledge nor the authority to dictate, because the issue transcends technocratic expertise. Were we to defer to agencies simply on the basis of their technical proficiency, the ethical-political question would be begged entirely. Agencies could be expected to resort to methods the use of which denies the very values at stake (it is, after all, the claim of methodological proficiency that grounds the argument for deference in the first place). And, to return to the idea with which we began this section, methodological proclivities would bias agency risk processing in the direction of too much public risk — as viewed from the public's perspective. 138 U. Pa. L. Rev. at 1085.

Gillette and Krier also conclude that access bias unduly restricts the number of public risk cases heard by the courts and that access bias skews the administrative process in favor of over-acceptance of public risks.

5. **Is everyone crazy (in Huber's sense)?** The number and scope of environmental concerns have burgeoned in recent years, with the result that they cannot all be addressed simultaneously. Even if there were agreement that all environmental problems are worthy of action, to take on all of the perceived problems at once would demand more resources, human and fiscal, than society is willing to commit to the task.

Inevitably, priorities must be set that select some problems for more immediate attention while postponing action on others. Setting those priorities is a vital form of policymaking, but it is not easy. How, for example, do we choose between spending $1 million to clean up contaminated groundwater in Wichita, Kansas, or to remove lead-based paint from aging single family homes in Detroit, Michigan? There does not seem to be a ready common denominator for making such policy decisions. However, at least when the risks involved relate to human health, it seems that setting priorities that maximize risk reduction offers a form of cross-medium comparison. The greatest amount of risk reduction means, in effect, that the aggregate environmental hazard has been reduced by the greatest amount. EPA, in response to demands for consistency and rationality in priority setting, began to embrace risk reduction as a priority-setting mechanism in the late 1980s. In 1987 it published Unfinished Business: A Comparative Assessment of Environmental Problems, which attempted to make relative risk reduction a part of EPA's policymaking process. William Reilly, then EPA Administrator, wrote, "To the extent permitted by our statutory mandates, sound science can help us set priorities based on risk. Indeed, the rigorous analysis of risk is fundamental to all of EPA's regulatory programs. Without some way of determining relative levels of risk, we would quickly become mired in a regulatory swamp, wherein all problems were equally important; all risks would have to be addressed with equal urgency; and accordingly, nothing would get done."[44] A more substantial EPA document soon followed. In Reducing Risk: Setting Priorities and Strategies for Environmental Protection, Report of the Science Advisory Board; Relative Risk Reduction Strategies Committee (RRRSC), Science Advisory Board A101, SAB-EC 90-021, Sept. 1990, EPA found that in some ways its regulatory priorities did not reflect a focus on the greatest risks. EPA found, for example, that risk-based priority setting would support giving more attention to the hazards of indoor air pollution and rather less attention to cleaning up abandoned hazardous waste sites.

6. "Hormesis" — the benefits of toxins? In recent years new arguments have emerged asserting the hormesis hypothesis — that a number of environmental toxins may actually fulfill beneficial functions for human health. At low doses both dioxin and DDT have been shown to reduce some cancers in lab animals. Low doses of cadmium, which can be highly toxic, reduces liver cancer in rats. The implications for standard premises about exposure avoidance and the Precautionary Principle are obvious, but hardly justify calls to retreat from toxics regulation. A toxin that has a beneficial effect on one physical parameter may well cause malignant effects in other areas. Because it so clearly has policy implications, the hormesis theory will doubtlesslessly prompt continuing political arguments as well as scientific debate. See Calabrese & Baldwin, Chemical Hormesis: Its Historical Foundations as a Biological Hypothesis, 27.2 Toxicol. Pathol., 195 (1999). Cf. Heinzerling and Lechleider, Hormesis and the Law, 20 Human Experimental Toxicology No. 3, at 150 (2001).

---

44. William Reilly, Taking Aim Toward 2000: Rethinking the Nation's Environmental Agenda, 21 Envtl. L. 1359, 1361 (1991).

7. **Competing proposals for setting environmental priorities.** Resources for the Future sponsored a national Worst Things First conference on potential uses of risk-based analysis in setting the federal regulatory agenda. Several competing paradigms emerged from that conference.[45] Barry Commoner, director of the Center for the Biology of Natural Systems at Queens College, offered a pollution prevention-based approach to setting priorities. He proposed that the general public should set U.S. environmental priorities, based on what it decides are the most important opportunities to transform industries from polluting to non-polluting. John Graham, professor of health policy at Harvard University, argued that pollution prevention and comparative risk assessment-based approaches are complementary. Robert Bullard, professor of sociology at University of California-Riverside, argued that environmental protection is not a privilege to be doled out but is a right for all individuals. He argued that a strictly risk-based priority system may perpetuate the failure to identify and remediate "hot spots" of environmental risk that exist in communities with significant minority populations. Instead, EPA's priority should be to clean up hazardous waste sites in communities where minorities and the poor face multiple risks from multiple sites and to limit imposition of new risks in these areas. A third alternative, "directed innovation," which focuses on evaluating the causes of environmental problems, was urged by Nicholas Ashford, a professor of technology policy at MIT. He argued that strict regulation, properly designed, can trigger technological innovation that allows for more risk reduction at equal or lower costs. James Wilson of Monsanto, the chemical company, argued that individual companies do not always know when a particular innovation will succeed, and thus it's folly to believe that the federal government can reliably choose targets for directed innovation. Chapter 15 discusses this problem in the context of technology-forcing.

"If seven maids with seven mops,
Swept if for half a year,
Do you suppose, the Walrus said,
That they could get it clear?
I doubt it, said the Carpenter,
And shed a bitter tear."

— Lewis Carroll, Through the Looking Glass, 1871

---

45. Finkel & Golding, eds., Worst Things First? The Debate over Risk-Based National Environmental Priorities (1994); see also K. Arrow et al., Benefit-Cost Analysis in Environmental, Health, and Safety Regulation: A Statement of Principles 3 (1996).

PART TWO

DIFFERENT SOVEREIGNTIES IN MODERN ENVIRONMENTAL LAW

These must be the years when America pays its debs to the past by reclaiming the purity of it air, its water, and our living environment. It is literally now or never.

— Richard Nixon, 1970

For a successful technology, reality must take precedence over public relations, for nature cannot be fooled.

— Richard Feynman

The fight against adequate government control and supervision of...corporate wealth engaged in interstate business is chiefly done under cover, and especially under the cover of an appeal to state's rights.

— Teddy Roosevelt (quoted by Professor Kathleen Sullivan, New York Times Magazine, August 18, 1986 at 36, from Arthur Schlesinger, Cycles of American History and Capitals, at 236).

The simple plan: That they should take, who have the power, and they should keep, who can.

— Meeker v. City of East Orange, 74 A. 379, 385 (N.J. 1909)

Congress made clear that citizen groups are not to be treated as nuisances or troublemakers but rather as welcomed participants in the vindication of environmental interests."

—Friends of the Earth v. Carey, 535 F.2d 165, 172 (2d Cir. 1976)

Chapter 5

THE DEVELOPMENT AND STRUCTURE OF ENVIRONMENTAL PUBLIC LAW

A. *The Evolution of Environmental Regulation*
B. *Why Did the Parade of Tougher Federal Statutes Begin in the 1970s?*
C. *The Conceptual Building Blocks of Regulation*
D. *An Introduction to Cooperative Federalism*
E. *Rethinking Command-and-Control Regulation, the Standard Approach to Environmental Protection*

Common law environmental litigation, as the preceding chapters indicate, continues to play a very important role in the structure of modern environmental protection law. It should be clear from the Woburn case in the previous chapter, however, that many modern environmental problems are so complex and difficult to prove in the courtroom setting that common law cannot be relied upon to serve as society's primary environmental law strategy. Modern environmental protection requires public law — legal structures and mechanisms built upon statutes and administrative regulations.

Here are some reasons public law has been needed to reinforce the common law of environmental protection.

- The common law, in most cases, operates retrospectively. It emphasizes monetary compensation for past injuries. Only in unusual situations can plaintiffs win injunctions inhibiting future conduct without showing that defendants have committed past wrongful acts.

- The range of common law remedies is inadequate to the demands of a public law area. Protecting the environment demands flexible remedies, such as restoration, supplemental project implementation, and fines based on recovery of the economic benefit of noncompliance — all of which are either rarely or never available under common law — as well as possible criminal sanctions, which are only available pursuant to statutes. (See Chapter 20.)

- The common law is sporadic in that common law rules vary among jurisdictions. Thus, the common law cannot furnish the prospective, national applicability of rules that is necessary in order to preclude the interstate competition for polluting facilities that is referred to as the "race to the bottom" or "race of laxity."

- The common law is administered by generalist judges and court administrative personnel, who lack the specialized scientific and engineering knowledge and the programmatic and issue-specific continuity that are necessary for implementation of an environmental protection system. This deficiency was apparent in the *Boomer* case in Chapter 3 and *Woburn* in Chapter 4.

- The burden of proof in common law cases, which requires a plaintiff to prove causation by a preponderance of the evidence, is inapplicable to public law cases where governmental administrators, who are authorized by legislatures to protect the public health and welfare, wield a broad array of regulatory powers that are unconstrained by traditional burdens of proof.

- Common law systems lack the international scope that is becoming increasingly prominent as humankind perceives that the scope of many environmental problems is transnational, regional, and even global. (See Chapters 8 and 26.)

Public law regulation has proven to be the principal modern legal mode for protecting the environment. Regulatory law derives from legislative enabling statutes that delegate authority to administrative agencies to promulgate and enforce regulations of prospective and general applicability. (The notice-and-comment process of promulgating regulations is discussed in Chapter 7; administrative enforcement is covered in Chapter 21.) Administrative agencies also perform quasi-judicial adjudicatory functions with regard to permitting and enforcement.

Environmental public law is constructed from thousands of statutes, ordinances, and regulations that emanate from at least three levels of government — federal, state, and local. (Environmental public law is also generated by substate or interstate regional agencies, such as regional commissions or interstate compacts; in addition, international environmental law is a significant source of national environmental public law — see Chapter 8.)

These public law mechanisms typically are designed to implement public values in ways that avoid many of the limitations of common law. While the forms and methods by which public law attempts to achieve various civic objectives are diverse, almost all of these regulatory approaches stand in marked contrast to private law remedies: For example, regulatory activities are facilitated by a presumption of validity, a lighter burden of proving causation, and frequently a prospective and interjurisdictional scope.

Environmental regulation is actually centuries old. London had smoke-control ordinances in the 1600s. But environmental regulation was neither varied nor sophisticated until the final third of the twentieth century. Since 1970, environmental regulation has broadened its reach in terms of subjects addressed and has developed a rich amalgam of types of regulatory approaches. The standard modern mode of American pollution control regulation has been a Washington-dominated "cooperative federalism" in a "command-and-control" regulatory format. Despite constant efforts to delegitimatize this approach, it appears to have achieved notable successes in some areas. Air and water quality are significantly improved. Fewer hazardous substances are discharged into the environment, and those hazardous residuals that are still discharged must be treated to high levels of quality and publicly reported. Accidental spills and releases of hazardous materials must be reported and immediately contained and cleaned up. Most abandoned hazardous waste disposal sites have already been, or are in the process of being, remediated. Federal activities that might have significant environmental impacts must be documented and publicly disclosed and their alternatives analyzed. Pesticides must be registered and their uses justified. Endangered species, federal public lands, and critical areas such as wetlands and marine sanctuaries have received some legal protection. And several international environmental threats have been addressed (e.g., the phaseout of ozone depleting substances — see Chapter 15). The American environmental regulatory model has been so successful that most other nations have established similar regulatory systems.

Despite these manifest achievements, subsequent chapters will illustrate that many aspects of U.S. environmental regulatory law are inadequate, ineffectual, suboptimal, symbolically reassuring, and even counterproductive. For example, the effectiveness of the federal ESA is compromised by statutory loopholes, political pressures on the administrative agencies that administer the Act, insufficient governmental resources, and systematic nonenforcement. The federal CWA cannot presently be used to address the major remaining sources of water pollution — nonpoint sources — because these dischargers are exempt from the Act's provisions. (See Chapter 12.) Major environmental threats, such as suburban sprawl and climate change, remain virtually unregulated by federal environmental law.

In short, although the United States (and, to some extent, the world community) has made substantial progress in recognizing and controlling environmental pollution and natural resource depletion, there is still a long way to go, and the fight against environmental degradation is perpetual and ever-changing.

A. THE EVOLUTION OF ENVIRONMENTAL REGULATION

Section 1. EARLY EFFORTS AND THEIR LEGACY

Jan Laitos, Legal Institutions and Pollution: Some Intersections between Law and History
15 Natural Resources Journal 423 (1975)

Prior to 1880 the dominant social and economic institution which both affected and implemented choices was the market.... Beginning around 1880, America's legal, political, and economic institutions had to concern themselves with the general organization and effects of power concentrations. The rapid settlement of cities, the growth of urban living, and a large increase in population had led to social configurations that overshadowed individual lives. The startling pace of the industrial revolution had stimulated the growth of factories; men lived in the midst of machinery, mines, railroads, and automobiles....

By the turn of the century changes in America's social and economic condition forced closer attention to the social costs of reckless, unregulated natural resource use. First, the frontier had finally been pushed to the Pacific Ocean. With its disappearance had ended the nineteenth-century [1800 to 1880] assumption of inexhaustible natural resources.... Second, due in part to some of the worst decades of agricultural depression in our nation's history and in part to an unparalleled wave of immigration from Europe, there had been a sudden convergence of people upon America's cities. Water supply and sewage disposal lagged far behind the needs of mushrooming city populations.... Policy makers at last began to acknowledge the existence of social costs.... Due to the natural proclivity of injured parties to seek immediate relief through litigation, the courts were first to respond to twentieth century [1880 to 1930] air pollution.... In the case of air pollution the first legislative bodies to take affirmative action were the common councils of large industrial municipalities. It is not surprising that it was the city, and not the state or federal government, which first responded to air pollution. People saw dirty air as a local problem, not a regional or national concern....

Air pollution ordinances enacted by these late nineteenth century metropolitan common councils typically fell into three categories. Most common were the ordinances that simply declared (1) that the emission of dense smoke from any chimney or smokestack within the city was a public nuisance, and (2) that those who caused the emission of this smoke were liable to a fine, usually not exceeding $100. A second type of ordinance did not merely declare the escape of dense smoke illegal; these more sophisticated laws placed an affirmative duty on polluters, requiring them not only to remove all ashes and cinders from their shops, but also to construct their furnaces "so as to consume smoke arising therefrom...." These ordinances flatly prohibited the importation, sale, use or consumption of any coal containing more than 12 percent ash or 2 percent sulphur....

Although the ordinance typically declared that the emission of thick, dense smoke was a public nuisance, no public official was empowered either to locate or abate these nuisances.... Unfortunately, whatever advantage there was in having dense smoke recognized as a nuisance per se was outweighed by the fact that such a narrowly focused prohibition ignored the more harmful invisible pollutants present in the smoke. Moreover, lawmakers and administrators failed to investigate whether more than just smoke affected the ambient air, and made no effort to define more precisely the acceptable and unacceptable density limits of smoke plumes....

COMMENTARY & QUESTIONS

1. **Why this system failed. Local health commissions were the first stage of pollution regulation, supplementing common law tort actions.** But, for several major reasons, these attempts largely failed: (1) The industries that externalized their costs in the form of pollution continued to grow in both size and political influence, ultimately coming to dominate local governments (through their control over jobs and municipal tax bases) as well as common law courts (through their enhanced access to information, legal assistance, and scientific experts). (2) Comparatively little scientific evidence was available to tie pollution (especially toxic pollution) to specific public health threats. (3) Attempts to control pollution through municipal ordinances and judicial decrees were primitive and ineffectual, incapable of adequately dealing with transboundary impacts, multiple polluter situations, and intransigent polluters.

2. **Scaling upward — first, a shift from municipal to state level.** As the scope, persistence, and intensity of pollution grew and the environmental movement became a potent political force in the 1960s, major pollution control statutes began to emerge from state legislatures. State regulatory systems developed because of persistent and pervasive failure of the marketplace, common law courts, and local governments to deal adequately with the problem of pollution. The political dynamics of the shift from the local to the state level of government, and later from state to federal, were exceedingly complex. Taking water pollution control as an example, during the 1940s and 1950s, local and later state boards of health had the primary role, mostly in constructing and operating sewage treatment plants. The federal presence mainly consisted of federal grants to sewerage authorities. Only later did the federal government move into an active regulatory role.

Section 2. **IN RE: UTILEX, INC.: A CASE STUDY FROM "THE OLD DAYS"—
STATE POLLUTION CONTROL IN THE MID-TWENTIETH CENTURY**

In the evolution of environmental law through the middle of the twentieth century, as the primary forum shifted from the municipal level to the state level, the state regulatory experience was often not encouraging. The Michigan Water Resources Commission Act, as it stood from 1949 to the early 1970s,[1] was a typical example of a mid-century pollution control statute. The basic regulatory design can be described as "review-and-permit." Derived from an older public health statute, the Michigan statute established a seven-member, part-time Water Resources Commission (WRC),[2] "to prohibit the pollution of any waters of the state."[3]

> The commission shall protect and conserve the water resources of the state and shall have control of the pollution of surface or underground waters of the state and the Great Lakes which are or may be affected by waste disposal.... The commission shall enforce this act and shall promulgate rules as considered necessary to carry out its duties under this act. Mich. Comp. Laws. Ann. §323.2(1) (West 1969).

To go along with its broad mandate, the WRC was given investigatory power and the power to bring actions at law and in equity.[4] The legislation in general terms prohibited discharges that harmed public health or destroyed fish life in the water,[5] and granted the WRC the power to regulate discharges into the state's waters by setting and enforcing pollution standards, in terms common to other review-and-permit programs:

> The commission shall establish such pollution standards for lakes, rivers, streams and other waters of the state in relation to the public use to which they are or may be put, as it shall deem necessary.... It shall have the authority to make rules and orders [i.e., permits] restricting the polluting content of any waste material or polluting substance discharged or sought to be discharged into any lake, river, stream or other waters of the state. It shall have the authority to take all appropriate steps to prevent any pollution which is deemed by the commission to be unreasonable and against public interest in view of the existing conditions in any lake, river, stream or other waters of the state. Mich. Comp. Laws. Ann. §323.5 (West 1969).

With the broad authority to implement a review and permit process thus set, the statute also addressed some of the more critical details. Since the first enactment of the statutory plan, the WRC had enjoyed the power to make orders (permits) that would limit discharges. As of 1949, what might be called the "burden of initiation" of action under the WRC Act became explicit. As to existing facilities, the WRC had the burden of initiating standard-setting and permitting procedures. If it did not make standards and apply them to specific polluters, there was no need for the polluters to seek WRC

---

1. The Act has since been amended to satisfy the rigorous requirements for state laws imposed by the federal CWA. See Act 293 of 1972 Mich. Pub. Acts, Mich. Comp. Laws §16.357 (1980).

2. The composition of the commission, as spelled out in the legislation in 1949, comprised the directors of the state departments of natural resources, public health, highways, and agriculture; and three citizens of the state to be appointed by the governor, by and with the advice and consent of the state senate: one from groups representative of industrial management; one from groups representative of municipalities; and one citizen from a group "representative of conservation associations or interests."

3. 1929 Mich. Pub. Acts, No. 245, as amended.

4. Mich. Comp. Laws. Ann. §323.3-4 (West 1969).

5. Id. §323.6.

approval of their practices. As to new or increased discharges only, a mandatory review and permit process was added:

> It shall be the duty of any person...requiring a new or substantial increase over and above the present use now made of the waters of the state for sewage or waste disposal purposes, to file with the commission a written statement setting forth the nature of the enterprise or development contemplated, the amount of water required to be used, its source, the proposed point of discharge of said wastes into the waters of the state, the estimated amount so to be discharged, and a fair statement setting forth the expected bacterial, physical, chemical and other known characteristics of said wastes. Within 60 days of receipt of said statement, it shall be the duty of the commission to make an order stating such minimum restrictions as in the judgment of the commission may be necessary to guard adequately against such unlawful uses of the public waters.... Mich. Comp. Laws. Ann. §323.8(b) (West 1969).

The vague generality of these standards poses two different obstacles to preventing pollution. The first obstacle is interpretive — to the extent that the standards are vague (e.g., "injurious to public health or to the conducting of any industrial enterprise"), the WRC had to come up with more precise enforceable definitions. Recalling that the WRC was not a politically powerful agency — and by its very composition was somewhat sympathetic to industrial and commercial interests — suggests that it would tend not to interpret those terms stringently. Only the clearest cases of injury would be defined by the WRC as violating the threshold of harm that triggered its regulatory powers.

The second obstacle lay in the steps required in going from a case of probable unlawful discharge (i.e., a finding that the application, if granted without conditions, would result in an unlawful discharge) to the regulatory application of adequate permit conditions to prevent the proscribed harm from occurring. The WRC, for political reasons already described, was hesitant to deny permit applications outright. In general, the WRC could be expected to insert permit conditions that would allow the discharger to go forward with the overall project but that would also require that the effluent be treated in some manner before discharge. Here the WRC's lack of staff and technical expertise was a major barrier to effective operation. Industrial permit applicants generally possess engineering expertise and use it well in negotiating permit conditions. The WRC, and most similar agencies or commissions, were, in the period under discussion, simply overmatched in that process.[6]

The third strike against the WRC Act was its under-enforcement.

THE UTILEX CASE FILE

As part of a project undertaken by the University of Michigan Environmental Law Society in the early 1970s, law students examined a typical case file on one particular WRC permit issued to the Utilex Company of Fowlerville, Michigan, a small electro-

---

6. Despite the many shortcomings of the Michigan Water Resources Commission Act, it was in some ways a remarkably enlightened piece of legislation. One noteworthy feature is that it applied to both groundwater and surface water. Few pollution control laws, either past or present (and most notably the CWA), address groundwater contamination. Second, the law applies to water quantity concerns pertaining to the environmental effects of diminished stream flows. This, too, was extraordinary.

plating plant. (The file has been revisited to update the study.) The partial chronology that follows tells its own story.

Michigan Department of Natural Resources Enforcement File # MI 0003727: UTILEX-HOOVER BALL BEARING

[A digest of file entries:]

December, 1952: Utilex Company requests "new use" permit to allow dumping of cyanide, copper, zinc, nickel and other matter, in connection with new plating operations, into the adjoining Looking Glass River.

January, 1953: WRC makes order granting permit, attaching [weak] standards for water quality.

July, 1953: Staff field report: effluent violates permit standards.

September, 1953: Staff field report: effluent violates permit standards.

September, 1954: Staff field report: effluent violates permit standards.

March, 1955: Staff field report: effluent violates permit standards. Staff writes letter to company suggesting new control equipment.

March, 1956: Staff field report: effluent violates permit standards.

November, 1956: Staff field report: effluent violates permit standards.

June, 1957: Violation noted for nickel only.

June, 1959: Staff field report: effluent violates permit standards in all categories.

January, 1960: Staff field report: effluent violates permit standards in all categories.

October, 1960: Staff field report: effluent violates permit standards in all categories.

May, 1961: Staff field report: effluent violates permit standards in all categories. Biological test shows long-term toxic effect; fifteen river miles required for recovery of water quality in river.

June, 1963: Staff field report: effluent violates permit standards.

September, 1963: Staff field report: effluent violates permit standards.

January, 1964: Biological test shows no sign of life to three and one-half miles downstream; near-lethal cyanide levels.

October, 1964: WRC writes company that controls would be "most desirable."

November, 1965: Staff field report: concentrations exceeding standards 9.3 miles downstream.

September, 1966: Citizen complaints [others have apparently been received, but are not copied in file] lead to staff field report: effluent violates permit standards.

November, 1966: University biological test shows complete eradication of life to 4.7 miles downstream.

March, 1968: Staff field report: excess effluents in all categories.

May, 1968: In response to public environmental concern, WRC asks company for stipulation of new standards; company accepts, "prefers to have voluntary stipulation"; no mention of previous violations of permit.

December, 1968:   Excess effluents; company submits plans for control equipment to meet new standards by April, 1969.

July, 1969:   Company fails to install equipment by promised date due to "changed engineering plans." WRC sets new due date: April, 1970.

February, 1970:   Staff field report: effluent violates both old and new standards.

April, 1970:   Staff field report: effluent violates both old and new standards; no equipment installed by due date.

June, 1970:   Company requests postponement of due date; WRC notes the company "is moving expeditiously."

September, 1970:   Equipment installed.

October, 1970:   Staff field report: excess heavy metals in violation of 1953 standards.

December, 1970:   Staff field report: effluent violates permit standards.

Spring, 1971:   Environmental Law Society has been investigating WRC files; at next meeting WRC passes resolution limiting citizen access to its files.

March, 1972:   Staff field report: effluents exceed standards up to two miles downstream. Company writes letter explaining difficulty of cleaning up. Effluents do not meet 1953 permit standards.

[October 1972]:   [Congress passes CWA, requiring states in the National Pollution Discharge Elimination System (NPDES) program to upgrade their state pollution regulatory systems.]

February 28, 1974: NPDES discharge permit issued; includes stricter standards.

August 9, 1974:   NPDES discharge permit issued on 02/28/74 found to be in error.

January 8, 1976:   Monitoring requirements are revised. Verification that cadmium was no longer present in detectable quantities; cadmium monitoring requirement could be deleted.

January 20, 1977:   New NPDES permit is issued to Utilex on nickel and chromium discharges.

January 28, 1977:   Utilex receives an "I" rating for inadequate permit compliance; effluent violates NPDES permit.

February 7, 1977:   A waste water treatment construction project is begun at Utilex.

June 22, 1977:   A sulfuric acid spill occurs at Utilex.

June 30, 1977:   Revised draft permit for Utilex. Standards of original NPDES permit based on Michigan Waste Criteria were more stringent than EPA guidelines. WRC agrees to loosen standards.

July 11, 1977:   Completion of waste water treatment system at Utilex.

July 13, 1977:   A letter from Utilex explaining corrective actions taken in response to the acid spill of 06/22/77. Utilex installed a lining for a retaining wall and replaced storage tanks.

July 29, 1977: Completion of water waste treatment project is confirmed.

September 13, 1977: Field waste water survey done; shows violations of NPDES permit.

October 4, 1977: Notice of non-compliance and Order to Comply sent to Utilex. Utilex found to have exceeded both its chromium and oil & grease maximums during July. Letter of explanation requested.

October 12, 1977: Utilex writes that the parameters set forth by the permit have been attained.

November 8, 1977: Utilex exceeds permit limits on pH acidity, zinc, and copper.

November 9, 1977: Utilex writes that DNR [Department of Natural Resources] limits for chrome, acid, and nickel had been exceeded due to a crack in a pipe sustained during demolition and replacement of roof.

December 6, 1977: Letter from Water Quality Division stating that waste water survey of 09/13/77 indicated that limits on NPDES permit had been exceeded. A letter of explanation is requested.

December 22, 1977: Notice of non-compliance with permit issued on 01/20/77. Chromium and nickel levels exceeded limits during the period from 10/14 to 10/25/77.

1978: Utilex closes, still in violation of standards.

COMMENTARY & QUESTIONS

1. **The administrative explanation.** When asked about the Utilex file in 1972, the WRC Executive Director complained that he "didn't have sufficient manpower and budget to enforce the law" and that his agency also lacked sufficient legal authority. The personnel and budget complaints were, in large measure, well-founded. By 1972, the WRC was administering thousands of permits with a mere handful of staff (although note that staffing was adequate to do almost 20 years of violation reports). The claim of insufficient legal authority seems to be contradicted by the broad grant of enforcement authority set forth in the WRC Act. The WRC, however, had no legal counsel on its own staff, and its only method of seeking enforcement was to refer cases to the offices of the attorney general or local county prosecutors for action. Perhaps ironically, a number of cases like *Utilex* were not referred for prosecution because the WRC staff held the erroneous belief that legally, in order to mount a prosecution, they had to be able to prove fish kills, and, as one field inspector said in the 1970s, "all of the fish were poisoned out of there in the 1950s."

And politics is surely part of the explanation. One staffer told us that "Every time it looked as if maybe our boss was going to let us crack down on Utilex, it seems like the entire male population of Fowlerville — almost all of them worked at Utilex — would come up to our office here in Lansing to talk with the Executive Director about how much they needed that plant. And they'd be accompanied by their state Senator, who made it clear that tightening our enforcement against Utilex would trigger some payback at appropriations time."

2. **The post-1949 mandatory permit system.** Why had the legislature decided to

require a mandatory new and enlarged source permit system for the 1950s? One explanation was that the cumulative effects of pollution on aquatic ecosystems by then were becoming a visible concern, as was the economic impact of deteriorating water quality on all forms of water use. Section 323.6 was expanded from a concern with pollution that endangered public health and fish kills to include pollution that would harm "any fish or migratory bird life or any wild animal or aquatic life." The language formerly addressed to public health alone was expanded to prohibit any water use "which is injurious to the public health or to the conducting of any industrial enterprise or other lawful occupation." Why was this permit process imposed only on new and increased sources? Plainly, this is not a trivial loophole, given that by 1949 existing pollution already was severe enough to be causing readily identifiable undesirable effects. It seems irrational to exclude all existing sources from the permit system; some countervailing political force probably explains that compromise.

3. **The standards to be applied by the WRC.** The 1949 statutory review-and-permit process called for the polluter (the applicant) to furnish information about its anticipated discharge (the application); the WRC then had to evaluate the application (review) and issue an order (permit) that includes restrictions on the discharge. The permit process was subject to subsequent judicial review. What standards did the WRC have to apply in acting on permit applications? Under §323.6 as it stood in 1949, pollution could not be permitted if it would injure public health and welfare or the aquatic ecosystem. In addition, "any pollution which is deemed by the commission to be unreasonable and against public interest" was prohibited under §323.5. Were these standards likely to obtain effective protection of water quality?

4. **Improving the system — standard-setting.** The WRC case study drawn from the *Utilex* file is a paradigm of why enforcement of pollution control laws was problematic during the pre-1970 years of traditional review-and-permit statutes. A number of changes in regulatory approach had to be made if pollution control was to improve significantly, for example, a move toward more definite standards. Chapters 11–13 and 15 are organized as a study of how various standard-setting methods are effectuated and made a part of regulatory regimes.

5. **Improving the system — changing the bipolar paradigm.** This traditional review-and-permit process is strictly "bipolar" — a dialogue between the regulated corporation and the administrative agency alone. Where was the public? The only gesture to other constituencies was in the representative composition of the WRC itself, which might include a sportsman or garden club representative along with industrial appointees. How could the regulatory process be changed to incorporate a broader "multi-polar" conception of the public interest? This question is addressed in later chapters, beginning with the discussion of modern administrative agencies in Chapter 7.

6. **Improving the system — intra-agency changes.** The agencies that administered the mid-century permit systems were the forerunners of modern environmental protection agencies, and they pioneered changes in the bureaucratic landscape. In the case of Michigan and the WRC, the agency added in-house technical expertise. The WRC staff originally was drawn from the DNR, which historically was concerned with fish and

game management, not pollution control. Over time, DNR and similar agencies throughout the nation added staff with environmental and pollution control expertise. These agencies, by introducing a new technocratic class into the regulatory process, heralded a new era in which regulatory agencies possess their own environmental and technical expertise. The commission composition and the Act's cumbersome procedures, however, hampered effective regulation.

B. WHY DID THE PARADE OF TOUGHER FEDERAL STATUTES BEGIN IN THE 1970s?

Donald Elliott, Bruce Ackerman, and John Millian, Toward a Theory of Statutory Evolution: The Federalization of Environmental Law
1 Journal of Law, Economics & Organization 313 (1985)

...An extraordinary outburst of lawmaking related to pollution and the environment occurred at the national level during the 1960s and 1970s as a dozen major federal pollution control statutes were enacted. This network of national statutes — together with a much larger body of implementing regulations — now constitutes one of the most pervasive systems of national regulation known to American law. Today every discharge into the land, water, or air — from the smallest smokestack to the largest landfill for the disposal of toxic chemicals — requires direct or indirect permission from the national government....

What accounts for this "dramatic plunge forward"? After decades of incrementalism and accommodation, why did Congress suddenly enact a series of relatively extreme federal environmental statutes in the early 1970s?...

It is a non sequitur to assert — as lawyers frequently do — that Congress passes statutes "because" policy problems exist. The existence of a real or perceived policy problem may be a necessary condition for the passage of a statute, but the existence of a problem alone does not a statute make; additional conditions must be satisfied, which explains why Congress passes statutes addressed to certain problems while other equally pressing problems go unaddressed. Conversely, when the Clean Air Act was passed [in 1970], at least some air pollution problems were getting better as a result of the gradual substitution of oil for coal during the 1960s....

The first significant statutes regulating air pollution, the Motor Vehicle Pollution Control Act of 1965 and the Air Quality Act of 1967, were not passed because of the political power of environmentalists at the national level but because two well-organized industrial groups, the automobile industry and the soft coal industry, were threatened with a state of affairs even worse from their perspective than federal air pollution regulation — namely, inconsistent and progressively more stringent environmental laws at the state and local level. As a consequence of the structure of our federal lawmaking system, environmentalists were able to organize industry to do their bidding for them. Thus, the first federal legislation regulating air pollution was passed not because environmentalists solved their organizational problems on the national level but because environmentalists exploited the organizational difficulties of their industrial adversaries at the state and local level.

The auto industry and the soft coal industry undoubtedly would have preferred no government regulation of air pollution rather than federal legislation. When faced with the threat of inconsistent and increasingly rigorous state laws, however, they [used] their superior organizational capacities in Washington to preempt or control the environmentalists' legislative victories at the state level....

The first statute which gave the federal government regulatory power over air pollution was the Motor Vehicle Air Pollution Control Act of 1965. The roots of this federal legislation run deep into the California of the 1950s and 1960s.... Through a combination of a cost-externalization strategy by California politicians, auto industry ineptitude, and local environmental organizing, state air pollution legislation had begun to pose a serious threat to the automobile industry by the middle 1960s....

Unlike most other industries, the automobile industry has strong reasons to prefer national legislation over state and local regulation of air pollution. Most manufacturing industries would rather have state and local governments set air pollution standards, because the political and economic costs of controlling their pollution are concentrated at the local level....

The automobile industry is in a very different strategic position, however, because it is geographically concentrated and its product, not its factories, is the main source of pollution. Local politicians can set strict antipollution standards for motor vehicles without fear of being accused of putting their constituents out of work. It is true that pollution controls tend to increase the price of new cars, but the connection between government action and particular price increases is only dimly perceived by voters. And unlike other industries, Detroit could not credibly threaten to stop selling cars in California or other states which established stringent pollution standards. Moreover, differing or inconsistent air pollution standards set at the state and local level were perceived as a serious threat to Detroit's assembly lines. Finally, the companies feared a political domino effect, in which one state legislature after another would set more and more stringent emission standards, without regard to the costs or technical difficulties involved....

During the early 1960s, the automobile industry successfully opposed federal emissions standards for motor vehicles. In mid-1965, however, the industry abruptly reversed its position...: provided that the federal standards would be set by an administrative agency, and provided that they would preempt any state standards more stringent than California's, the industry would support federal legislation.... With auto industry backing, the Motor Vehicle Pollution Control Act of 1965 became the first federal statute regulating air pollution....

[The authors of this article go on to analyze the unprecedentedly stringent provisions of the 1970 CAA — i.e., the requirements that auto manufacturers reduce some auto pollution by 90% within five years, and the mandate that the EPA ignore economic and technological feasibility when setting National Ambient Air Quality Standards[7] — as a function of how pro-environment public opinion played two ambitious politicians (President Richard Nixon and Senator Edmund Muskie) off against each other.] By strategically threatening these political entrepreneurs with the loss of political capital which they had previously worked to build, environmentalists were able to organize them to pass a statute more stringent than the politicians really wanted....

COMMENTARY & QUESTIONS

1. **The eruption of environmentalism.** During the late 1960s and early 1970s, a volcanic outburst of public sentiment against environmental degradation and in favor of strong, national environmental laws swept traditional, well-entrenched political interests away on its molten flow. Three formerly separate but powerful subsets of interest groups —

---

7. See Chapters 11 and 15.

the resource conservationists, the aristocratic wilderness preservationists, and public health protection groups — joined forces with newly-minted Rachel Carson populists to capture the attention of the media and general public as "the environmental movement." This eruption of public opinion was generated by (1) blatant and well-publicized environmental abuses such as Allied's Kepone discharges in Hopewell, Virginia, construction of homes and schools on an abandoned and leaking hazardous waste disposal site in New York's Love Canal neighborhood, water pollution so extreme that Ohio's Cuyahoga River caught fire twice near Cleveland, the fouling of 30 miles of California beaches by a massive oil spill from a blown offshore oil well off Santa Barbara, and air pollution-caused "killer fogs" in London, England, and Donora, Pennsylvania, that killed and injured hundreds of people; (2) the emergence of a credible and persuasive environmentalist literature — notably Carson's 1962 book *Silent Spring* — that identified environmental stressors and recommended reasonable solutions; and (3) an already angry and mistrustful public that was antagonized by the U.S government's involvement in the unpopular war in Vietnam. The American political system tends to accommodate such torrents of public opinion, and great progress followed.

2. **The federalization of environmental law.** A role for the federal government began to take shape in the 1960s as the mid-century primacy of state governments — operating 50+ independent review-and-permit systems (as in the Utilex case study) — increasingly revealed its shortcomings. Some of the shortcomings were technical, posed by the geographic scope and complexity of pollution. Awareness and public arousal regarding environmental quality in this era was focused initially on dramatic events, such as fish kills near a factory's outfall, or fumes and smoke invading a neighborhood, or raw sewage polluting beaches, and so on. Broader public health issues began to surface indicating that pollution appeared not only in isolated hot spots but also affected large areas of the United States. Data from many cities began to show increased incidence of respiratory disease linked to increased air pollution. Fish populations were in decline almost everywhere.

No single city or state was in a position to collect or process the overall data, which could best be done and funded on a national level. In the aftermath of World War II, the national government had taken its first tentative steps in the field. In 1948, Congress had enacted the Federal Water Pollution Control Act,[8] establishing funding for basic water pollution control research and funding some cleanup programs.[9] On the air side, the same evolution was occurring. In 1955, the federal Department of Health, Education and Welfare (HEW) was assigned a major research role into the effects of air pollution.[10] Federal studies of automobile pollution began a few years later,[11] and in the 1963 version of the CAA,[12] HEW was directed to published advisory national air quality criteria. These "criteria" documents, based on epidemiological and other research that

---

8. Act of June 30, 1948, ch. 758, 62 Stat. 1155 (1948).

9. FWPCA's one foray into providing substantive remedies was to establish a convoluted, and ultimately unsuccessful, public nuisance cause of action that could be enforced only by federal officials in cases of proven interstate water pollution.

10. Act of July 14, 1955, ch. 360, 69 Stat. 322 (1955).

11. Act of June 8, 1960, Pub. L. No. 86-493, 74 Stat. 162 (1960).

12. The Clean Air Act of 1963, Pub. L. No. 88-206, 77 Stat. 392 (1963).

correlated levels of air quality with public health effects, later became the federal ambient air quality standards.[13] In 1956, the states successfully lobbied the federal government for larger subsidies for sewage treatment, singled out for federal funding because of the interstate flow of many rivers. Federal expertise and funding were clearly necessary, but a need for federal regulation was also becoming obvious.

State-by-state control of pollution did not address the increasingly serious problem of cross-border spillover effects.[14] Downwind and downstream states had no power, other than persuasion and invocation of the doctrine of comity (voluntary respect by one state for the interests of a sister state) by which to protect themselves from transboundary pollution. The upwind and upstream states had little incentive to use scarce political capital to regulate their near-border polluters whose waste streams would have little or no effect on the state's own citizens. These scenarios also supported a more extensive federal role in environmental regulation.

3. **The race of laxity as a justification for federal regulation.** By the late 1960s, it was also becoming apparent that many states could not or would not regulate pollution adequately, for political reasons. Some of the inadequacies of state programs could be attributed to the generic difficulty of pushing marketplace economic powers toward respecting public needs for environmental quality. In the minds of many, however, the low levels of many state-mandated pollution controls had an even more sinister aspect that argued for federal minimum standards — the "race of laxity," also called the "race to the bottom" or "the Mississippi Syndrome," after the industrial recruitment strategy of the poorest state in the nation.

The race of laxity was perceived as a state-by-state lowering of standards in order to attract new industry. To be sure, environmental laws were but one of several components of state efforts to woo industry, along with hospitable tax rates, labor costs, corporate laws, and so on. Nevertheless, a failure to join in the race of laxity in environmental regulation posed a major threat of lost economic prosperity to those states enforcing more burdensome environmental regulations than those enacted by their sister states.

By the beginning of the 1970s, the conviction that states were being pressured into keeping down their environmental control standards by an invidious race of laxity competition for marketplace economics prompted Congress to initiate a dramatic federal takeover of the job of setting nationwide minimum standards.

Not unsurprisingly, relatively little direct evidence supports the race of laxity's existence.[15] Whether an intentional race of laxity occurred during the mid-century period

---

13. The role of HEW was expanded to include the delineation of air quality control regions in the Air Quality Act of 1967, §108, 81 Stat. 490-497. Also included in that statute was an upgrading of the criteria documents from being merely "advisory" to a status as air quality standards. Three years later, in 1970, these standards became the federal government's nationwide mandatory minimum standards. (See Chapter 11.)

14. Interstate pollution is still a substantial problem, even after the federalization of environmental law. (See Chapters 11 and 12.)

15. A recent governmental report provided evidence demonstrating a continuing race of laxity despite current federal floors designed to prevent it. See USGAO, Differences Among the States in Issuing Permits Limiting the Discharge of Pollutants 9 (1996), and Professor Engel's study discussed below. Anecdotal evidence is abundantly available. In 1965, for example, Governor Ross Barnett of Mississippi gave a speech at Princeton University

is largely beside the point. Standards did vary, and state officials thought and reacted with the presumption that other states were doing it. It is unimaginable that a sophisticated firm considering major plant investment would not at least consider costs of environmental compliance in its decisional process. Most important, members of Congress from the populous and industrialized states worried about interstate competition over pollution. For instance, in debates over the CAA of 1970, which imposed national standards, Representative Vanik of Ohio declared:

> To date, the States have been left to establish their own air quality standards. In all too many areas, there has been delay and foot dragging — and ridiculously low standards set to accommodate local industries and interests. The establishment of national standards will ensure action throughout the Nation on a rapid basis.... National standards of pollution control would prevent another State from attracting any industries because of a greater pollution tolerance. Such competition is unfair and against the public interest. 116 Cong. Rec. 19,218 (91st Cong., 1st Sess., June 10, 1970).

By virtue of their voting strength in Congress, the Senators and Representatives from populous, industrialized states who perceived the face of laxity as a threat could enact laws of nationwide scope that limited the race. Thus arrived the federal laws that marked the end of the mid-century review-and-permit era.

4. **Federal law, the race of laxity, and modern devolutionism.** Fear of a race of laxity among the states motivated Congress to give the federal government a dominant role in environmental regulation, rather than confining it to research, funding, and policing interstate pollution externalizations. During the 1990s a revisionist academic and political debate arose over the question of whether such a race ever existed or, beyond that, whether it leads to negative results. Professor Richard Revesz is the leading revisionist voice. See Revesz, Rehabilitating Interstate Competition: Rethinking the "Race-to-the-Bottom" Rationale for Federal Environmental Regulation, 67 N.Y.U. L. Rev. 1210 (1992):

> Contrary to prevailing assumption, competition among the states for industry should not be expected to lead to a race that decreases social welfare; indeed, as in other areas, such competition can be expected to produce an efficient allocation of industrial activity among the states. It shows, moreover, that federal regulation aimed at dealing with the asserted race to the bottom, far from correcting evils of interstate competition, is likely to produce results that are undesirable. 67 N.Y.U. L. Rev. at 1211–1212.

The argument is important for contemporary environmental policy making. If one agrees with the Revesz analysis, the modern federal role in environmental regulation should be scaled back and returned to the states, changing much of what will be studied in this book (and in all other current environmental law texts) about environmental standard-setting and policy making, shifting it into 50 different systems. This is the "devolution" agenda that has seized upon Revesz's theoretical inquiry. It is instructive

---

(attended by one of this book's authors) in which he lauded the state's lax environmental laws, low tax rates, and weak labor protections to a group of students whom he believed might become future corporate decisionmakers making plant siting decisions.

to note that regulated industries have been throwing their weight on the side of state autonomy.[16]

As is often the case with important conceptual articles, players in the political market-place often pick up ideas selectively, with less-than-full accuracy in noting the original authors' caveats and underlying assumptions. Revesz appends a cautious disclaimer:

> One should not overstate the nature of my claim against the race-to-the-bottom justifications for environmental regulation. The fact that there are no models consistent with race-to-the-bottom claims does not rule out the possibility that further research will yield such models. Modeling, by necessity, involves making strong sets of assumptions.... A theoretical literature evolves as assumptions are relaxed.... Revesz, Rethinking the "Race-to-the-Bottom"..., 67 N.Y.U. L. Rev. at 1211–1212, 1244.

5. **Responding to Revesz.** An extensive reply and counter-argument to Revesz and others questioning the race to the bottom is made in Engel, State Environmental Standard-Setting: Is There a "Race" and Is It "to the Bottom?" 48 Hastings L.J. 271 (1997).[17] Professor Engel's article challenges Revesz' revisionist theory by suggesting that there are already well-established theoretical economic models that do predict a race-to-the-bottom. Her principal criticism of Revesz' theory attacks its reliance on neoclassical economic assumptions of purely competitive behavior. Engel instead argues for the use of game theory in explaining states' strategic behaviors:

> The argument that interstate competition leads to a race-to-the-bottom and the revisionists' argument that it does not are both based on long-standing theoretical traditions. A principal argument for the existence of a race-to-the-bottom is based upon game theory, of which the classic Prisoner's Dilemma model is a simple but frequently cited example. According to this model, competition among a small number of players makes each player worse off than if he or she had not been a player in a game. The argument that interstate competition leads to socially-optimal environmental standards, on the other hand, is based upon competitive neoclassical economics, according to which competition among market partici-pants leads to efficient outcomes for society as a whole.... Despite revisionist claims to the contrary, the argument that interstate competition in environmental stan-dard-setting triggers a race-to-the-bottom is based upon a detailed theoretical literature. The Prisoner's Dilemma was...applied specifically to environmental problems in 1968 by Garrett Hardin. Many scholars have used a game-theoretic approach to model a race-to-the-bottom in interstate competition.... The rejection of game theory in favor of neoclassical competitive economic models as the theo-retical foundation for interstate competition contains a deeper irony, however.

---

16. For example, in the failed attempt to promote and obtain passage of H.R. 961 in the 104th Congress (a bill popularly referred to as the Dirty Water Act), the two groups that drafted and pushed the bill through the House — "Project Relief" and the "Alliance for Reasonable Regulation" — designed the bill to undercut pollu-tion controls primarily by shifting ultimate standard-setting and enforcement to the states. The corporations making up these groups include more than 500 of the nation's largest dischargers of water pollutants.

17. Revesz' article has gathered a number of critics in addition to Professor Engel. See, e.g., Esty, Revitalizing Environmental Federalism, 95 Mich. L. Rev. 570 (1996); Sarnoff, The Continuing Imperative (But Only from a National Perspective) for Environmental Protection, 7 Duke Envtl. L. & Pol'y F. 225 (1997); Swire, The Race of Laxity and the Race to Undesirability: Explaining Failures in Competition Among Jurisdictions in Environmental Law, 14 Yale J. on Reg. 67 (1996). See Revesz in reply, The Race-to-the-Bottom and Federal Environmental Regulation: A Response to Critics, 82 Minn. L. Rev. 535 (1997). The devolution debate is a continuing feature of environmental policy analysis.

Game theory was invented fifty years ago to address shortcomings in traditional neoclassical economics, which could not handle situations in which market participants interacted strategically. Thus, the revisionists' return to the neoclassical economic framework to understand interstate competition, a problem many theorists were already solving through the application of game theory, is, historically speaking, a conceptual step backward. 48 Hastings L.J. at 298–298.

Professor Engel did an empirical survey analysis of state officials and corporate executives. She found very few corporate executives who would say that environmental laxity was a major inducement to their location decisions, but that nevertheless many state officials apparently acted under the assumption that it was so. As a result, "a substantial minority of officials influential in the state standard-setting process concede that their state has relaxed its standards and permit procedures in order to attract or retain industrial firms." 48 Hastings L.J. at 351–352.

6. **Inverting the race of laxity.** Is it possible that states could invert the race of laxity into a race for enhanced environmental quality, a race-to-the-top? For that to happen, states raising their environmental standards would have to provide some offsetting benefits to firms that would more than outweigh the increased cost of doing business there. Is the value of a cleaner, healthier environment a sufficient lure? To some executive decision makers who themselves would be living in the preferred setting, higher environmental standards might be a plus, and perhaps those same benefits would be useful in personnel recruitment. A more likely path by which states can raise environmental standards is market power, such as that enjoyed by California and described in the Elliott et al. excerpts above. California's economy is so large that if it were an independent nation, its economy would be among the ten largest in the world. Most large firms doing business in the United States will act in ways that accommodate California if the alternative is to limit their access to California's market. In the environmental field, that market power has occasionally allowed California to invert the race of laxity to suit its will. For example, California developed its own higher-than-national standards for automobile emissions and had both the market power to force the automakers to manufacture to California standards and the political power to keep Congress from preempting those standards in the CAA. Even more of an inversion of the race of laxity has occurred in the wake of California's Proposition 65 requiring disclosure of use of hazardous chemicals (see Chapter 10). Many producers serving the California market have chosen to adapt their products to meet California's most-stringent-in-the-nation regulation and have made the decision to market the identical products nationwide. The economic logic is built upon economies of scale in having to manufacture and distribute a unitary line of products, rather than separate (but similar) products designed to meet both higher and lower regulatory standards. There are not many states with market power like California's. Moreover, as touched upon in Chapter 6, groups of states cannot act in concert in regulatory matters absent congressional approval under the Compact Clause of Article I, §10, of the U.S. Constitution.

7. **Other issues, other scenarios.** Elliott et al. present one model of statutory growth in which loosely organized coalitions of environmental activists concentrate on passing state legislation that threatens industries with inconsistent state pollution control

standards, to the point where industry itself lobbies for preemptive federal legislation. Although counterintuitive at first glance, in certain situations it is sensible for industry to trade off regulation for an economically level playing field, even if the resulting legislation is stronger than industry might have expected. This model enjoys explanatory force not only in relation to the development of federal legislation such as the Motor Vehicle Air Pollution Control Act of 1965, but also plausibly explains the development of federal pesticide laws and the federal regulations that uniformly phased out phosphate ingredients in laundry detergents and lead in gasoline. It also suggests that environmental groups should focus on state lawmaking in order to eliminate mercury in products, MTBE in gasoline, and carbon dioxide emissions from automobiles (see Chapter 15).

Other environmental regulatory issues exemplify different political dynamics. Elliott et al. concede that the automobile industry is unusual in that it is geographically concentrated and its product, not its factories, is the main source of pollution. In other situations, where a race of laxity is perceived to exist, well-organized environmental groups have lobbied Congress directly in order to pass statutes such as the CWA, RCRA, and CERCLA (see Chapters 12, 18, and 19), by successfully contending that the race of laxity renders states incapable of effectively regulating interstate pollution from large localized industries. Other political paradigms of environmental statutory development involve legislative responses to perceived public health and environmental emergencies (e.g., the SDWA's passage amidst concern about toxic pollutants in the water supplies of major cities, such as New Orleans, which diverts water from the Mississippi River) and the suasive effects of international agreements (e.g., the influence of the Montreal Protocol on national legislation phasing out chemicals that deplete the ozone layer — see Chapter 15).

8. The actors in the environmental political drama. Just as the evolution of federal environmental regulatory law follows several general political patterns, the major political actors in these environmental regulatory issues are predictable, although their political positions on particular environmental issues may not be formulaic.

The U.S. Environmental Protection Agency (EPA) is the major pollution regulatory institution in the United States. It was formed in 1970 by a Reorganization Plan (a type of executive order) that centralized the pollution control functions that had previously resided in several federal agencies. (E.g., prior to 1970, air and water pollution control were under the jurisdiction of separate federal agencies.) EPA is an agency that is headquartered in Washington, D.C., with ten regional offices dispersed throughout the United States. EPA is headed by an Administrator, who is located in the main office in Washington, D.C. Each regional office is run by a Regional Administrator. The relationships among the EPA regions and the main EPA office, and among the regions themselves, are complex. For example, political administrations differ with regard to allocations of administrative authority between central EPA and the regions. As to the regions themselves, some are traditionally more enthusiastic regarding pollution control than are others. Some of the environmental regulatory functions performed by EPA are (1) promulgating pollution control regulations; (2) providing technical assistance and program funding to state pollution control agencies; and (3) issuing permits and performing monitoring (both ambient and compliance monitoring), surveillance, and administrative enforcement activities, where states do not.

EPA also possesses some regulatory authority on the "conservation" (as distinguished from pollution control) side of environmental law (e.g., EPA's authority to protect wetlands and marine sanctuaries), but other federal agencies bear the major responsibility for conservation regulation at the federal level. For example, the U.S. Fish and Wildlife Service and the National Marine Fisheries Service, in the U.S. Department of the Interior, administer the Federal Endangered Species Act (see Chapter 16); the Bureau of Land Management, also located in USDI, administers federal grazing laws (see Chapter 24); and the Forest Service, located in the U.S. Department of Agriculture, administers the National Forest Management Act. Figure 5-1 shows some of the most

FEDERAL STATUTE	ADMINISTERING AGENCY	FEDERAL STATUTE	ADMINISTERING AGENCY
GENERAL		**WILDLIFE & WILDERNESS**	
NEPA	CEQ	ESA	DoI-FWS DoC-NOAA, NMFS
EPCRA	EPA	MMPA	DoC-NOAA DoI-FWS
PPA	EPA	MBTA	DoI-FWS
OSHA	DoL	NWRAA	DoI-FWS
Consumer Prod. Safety Act	CPSC	FWCA	DoI-FWS
National Historic Preservation Act	DoI-NPS	Wilderness Act of 1964	DoI; USDA-USFS
AIR		WSRA FWS; USDA-USFS	DoI-NPS, BLM,
CAA	EPA	**PUBLIC LANDS**	
WATER		FLPMA	DoI-BLM
CWA	EPA; DoD-Army COE	NFMA	USDA-USFS
SDWA	EPA	**MINING**	
MPRSA	EPA; DoC-NOAA	SMCRA	DoI-OSM
CZMA	DoC-NOAA, OOCRM	Mining and Minerals Policy Act	DoI
CBRA	DoI-FWS	Mining Act of 1872	DoI-BLM
OPA	EPA; DoD/DHS-U.S. Coast Guard; DoC-NOAA	Mineral Leasing Act of 1920	DoI-BLM
Refuse Act	DoD-U.S. Army COE	Federal Coal Leasing Amendments of 1975	DoI-BLM
Watershed Act	USDA; DoI	**FARM BILLS**	
HAZARDOUS MATERIALS	**& HAZARDOUS WASTE**	Conservation Reserve Program	USDA
RCRA	EPA	Wetlands Reserves	USDA
CERCLA	EPA	**ENERGY**	
ToSCA	EPA	NWPA	DoE
HMTA	DOT	AEA	DoE-NRC
Pesticides:		PURPA	DoE-FERC
FIFRA	EPA	**TRANSPORTATION**	
FDCA	HHS-FDA	ISTEA	DoT
FQPA	EPA	§4(f) the Parklands Act	Dot-FHWA

FIGURE 5-1

SOME MAJOR FEDERAL ENVIRONMENTAL STATUTES AND THE AGENCIES THAT HAVE MAJOR RESPONSIBILITY FOR THEM

significant environmental statutes and the federal agencies that hold primary responsibility for implementing them.

Each state has established its own set of pollution control and conservation regulatory agencies. In some states, these functions are included in a single agency, but in others they are separated into two or more agencies. The power relationships between federal and state environmental regulatory agencies are governed by the laws relating to American federalism (see Chapter 6), the provisions of particular environmental protection statutes relating to "devolution" of regulatory power to states, and the political climates surrounding particular regulatory issues.

Local environmental protection agencies, at the county and municipal levels of government, perform many environmental regulatory functions relating to local activities, such as permitting and monitoring of onsite septic systems. Having been created by state law, county and municipal governments possess only those regulatory powers that have been delegated to them by state legislative enactments.

At all levels of government, legislative committees with authority to review environmental bills, and the legislators who sponsor or oppose those bills and chair or sit on those committees, are important actors in the environmental political process.

On the nongovernmental side of environmental politics, the major actors at the federal level are the national environmental groups, industry, and organized labor. National environmental groups differ with regard to (1) preferred strategies (e.g., legislative lobbying, electoral politics, media utilization, litigation, cooperative problem-solving with industry, intervention in administrative proceedings, land purchases and leases, political demonstrations); (2) priority issues (e.g., pollution, protection of public lands, protection of fish and wildlife, international issues); and (3) political stridency and willingness to enter into coalitions with other environmental groups and compromise with industry. Industry is also not monolithic in terms of its behavior on environmental regulatory issues. For example, manufacturing industries, which are designated as regulated point sources under the CWA, are sometimes in political conflict with large agricultural operations, which are unregulated nonpoint sources of water pollution, over who should bear the costs of the enhanced water pollution controls that are required by the CWA. Organized labor sometimes sides with industry on environmental regulatory issues, especially where jobs might be threatened by proposed environmental regulation. At other times, unions oppose industry on issues such as workplace health and safety or environmental justice for workers who live in neighborhoods close to existing or proposed industrial facilities.

C. THE CONCEPTUAL BUILDING BLOCKS OF REGULATION

Modern American environmental legislation initially was designed on a medium-by-medium, resource-by-resource basis, often targeting only a single phase of the process that affects the environment. In the pollution regulation lexicon, a *medium* is the carrying or receiving element — air, water, and so on. Surface freshwater, groundwater, marine and estuarine water, wetlands, air, workplaces, and land are all environmental media. A resource is something scarce and valuable, whether it be a natural resource (an old-growth forest) or a human-constructed one (an important cultural site or artifact).

Adopting a media or resource-specific approach, Congress has enacted major (and fundamentally different) regulatory statutes at different times to control pollution of various media and depletion of various resources. On the resource conservation side of environmental law, separate federal statutes govern the management of national forests, national parks, national wildlife refuges, public mining lands, public grazing lands, endangered species, wild and scenic rivers, historic sites, and so on. (See Chapter 24.)

One of the major defects of American environmental law is that its fragmentation contradicts the First Law of Ecology: "Everything is connected to everything else." A media or resource-specific approach deemphasizes intermedia or multiresource impacts, and often precludes the adoption of environmentally holistic and economically efficient solutions to environmental problems. For example, deposition of air pollutants such as acid, nutrients, and toxic chemicals is a major cause of water pollution, but air deposition is covered not at all by the CWA and only indirectly by the CAA. A particular national forest may face threats from excessive logging, uncontrolled mining activities, and destruction of endangered species habitat, each of which is regulated by a different federal statute administered by a different federal agency. See Figure 5-1, above.

Second, this atomistic system confuses environmental regulation because each statute is based on an idiosyncratic combination of philosophies and methodologies of regulation (e.g., harm-based and/or technology-based standard-setting methods), each includes different lists of hazardous and toxic substances to be controlled, and each uses different terminology, sometimes referring to essentially the same things (e.g., a water *discharge*, an air *emission*, and a *release* to land). Third, the media and resource-specific legislative approach to environmental regulation is self-reinforcing and tends to impede effective implementation by erecting artificial organizational divisions both within EPA and among EPA and other federal agencies. Environmental protection responsibilities are dispersed throughout the federal government, among agencies with different mandates, cultures, and clienteles.

The targeted phase of market behavior also varies. For instance, at what point in the chronology of the industrial process, from creation to disposal of an environmental pollutant, should regulatory controls be applied? Some federal statutes attempt to be proactive by regulating the introduction of new chemicals into commerce. These are termed *market access* and *product regulation* statutes (see Chapter 17). In contrast, federal cleanup or restoration statutes (see Chapter 19) are reactive and take effect at the back end of the waste disposal process. Other federal statutes regulate the production and content of public environmental information (see Chapters 9 and 10), and others impose waste treatment requirements on users of certain substances in a manufacturing process (see Chapters 11–13, 15, 18). Only RCRA, discussed in Chapter 18, makes a comprehensive attempt to regulate all phases of a particular means of waste disposal.

Whatever their unique characteristics, however, all regulatory systems under environmental statutes include a series of common elements and issues.

- *Planning and Priority-Setting* — What should be the regulatory goals? What should be the process for setting them? How can they best be achieved within the statutory context? How often should they be reevaluated? How much public participation should be permitted, and at what stages of the planning process? How should planning be related to implementation?
- *Standard-Setting* — Which standard-setting methodology should be (or is statutorily required to be) utilized? Harm-based? Technology-based? Technology-forcing? Benefit-cost analysis? (See Chapters 11–13, 15.)
- *Permitting* — What are the optimum means of achieving these standards by relating them to the legal obligations of users of the environment through the specific provisions of permits, approvals, contracts, leases, or licenses?
- *Monitoring and Surveillance* — What is the most effective system of ambient monitoring in order to determine whether progress is being made toward meeting the standards? What is the best system of compliance monitoring to determine whether permittees are complying with the terms of their permits? What should be the applicable rules for assuring data quality?
- *Enforcement* — Should enforcement be formal or informal? Administrative or judicial? Civil or criminal? When should environmental restoration be required, and under what conditions? Is a citizen suit necessary and legally authorized? (See Chapter 21.)

Each agency implementing these functional regulatory elements must perform them in the context of budget constraints, the uncertain availability of dependable scientific data, a range of different possible regulatory approaches including command-and-control or market-enlisting strategies (see Chapter 14), public acceptability, international implications, and the continuing need to demonstrate programmatic successes, for instance, during congressional oversight or reauthorization hearings.

Particular environmental statutes tend to emphasize one or a number of the regulatory elements and place lesser emphasis on others. For example, the CWA emphasizes planning, with each state administering an elaborate continuing planning process to review water quality standards and implementation efforts. In other environmental statutes, such as FIFRA, planning may consist only of ad hoc advisory committees to comment on narrowly circumscribed issues. In the permitting setting, discharge permits under the CWA, and grazing permits under the FLPMA, are long and highly detailed documents that comprehensively spell out the obligations and liabilities of dischargers into public water bodies and private ranchers grazing their cattle on federal lands. On the other hand, no formal permit is required under the ToSCA. If EPA does not, within a certain time after being informed of impending sale by a manufacturer of a new chemical, promulgate a ToSCA rule requiring further testing of the environmental effects of that chemical, the manufacturer can simply proceed with its sales campaign without a formal authorization from EPA. Cap-and-trade market-enlisting regulatory systems are explicitly authorized under the CAA, but are not mentioned in the CWA. As far as monitoring and surveillance are concerned, some regulatory statutes, such as the CAA and CWA, require permittees to perform detailed and frequent self-monitoring activities — even to the point of installing particular monitoring technologies — and immediately report all exceedances (violations of permit limitations) to governmental agencies. In contrast, no self-monitoring is required of regulated parties under the ESA; when an endangered species has been illegally "taken," enforcement is entirely dependent on timely and effective governmental surveillance. Finally, as described in Chapters 19 and 20, enforcement devices differ from statute to statute. Treble damages and heavy criminal sanctions are available to federal authorities under CERCLA, while only injunctions are available to litigants under NEPA.

COMMENTARY & QUESTIONS

Antidotes to systemic fragmentation. Proposals for ameliorating the media, resource, and phase-specific fragmentation of environmental law range from wholesale reorganization of the field to focused boundary-spanning within the current structural confines of the field. More far-reaching recommendations include replacing the current hodgepodge of sporadically enacted environmental legislation with a consolidated, comprehensive federal environmental statute that applies the same general methodologies and strategies to the protection of all environmental resources. (Clean air and water may also be considered resources in that they are valuable and in short supply.) This suggestion might be theoretically appealing, but political factors militate against its effectuation. Another recommended solution — forming a large, cabinet-level environmental protection agency that would combine the environmental functions of EPA, NOAA, the Forest Service, the U.S. Army Corps of Engineers, and the subagencies in USDI — would likely founder on political shoals in those agencies and Congress. Less ambitious proposals that might be achieved administratively — such as pollution prevention, one-stop permit shopping, facility-wide permitting, comprehensive place-based (e.g., watershed-based) environmental regulation, and combined implementation (permitting, monitoring, and enforcement) of several environmental protection statutes — have been moderately successful and will be discussed in subsequent chapters. Furthermore, market-based systems for trading pollution rights, both intra- and inter-facility, show promise in achieving least-cost, multimedia pollution control.

D. AN INTRODUCTION TO COOPERATIVE FEDERALISM

Cooperative federalism, or the "federal-state partnership," is the legal and institutional model that underlies most environmental regulatory statutes in the United States. Cooperative federalism entails nationwide environmental planning, research and demonstration, and standard-setting at the federal level, with subsequent delegation ("devolution") of legal authority ("primacy") to consenting states to perform localized environmental planning and research, set more stringent standards, administer environmental permit systems, and carry out first-line monitoring, surveillance and enforcement activities within their boundaries. Cooperative federalism includes the concept of "federal floor" standards, whereby a state can set stricter, but not less strict, environmental protection standards than the federally designated "floor" standards. A federal agency will delegate primacy to a state that makes a satisfactory showing that it

possesses the necessary legal authority, financial resources, and political will to effectively and efficiently administer a particular regulatory program. Approximately 75 to
80% of the pollution control permits authorized by federal law are actually issued by
state agencies. After delegation has taken place, the lead federal agency remains in an
oversight capacity — providing program grant funding and technical assistance to state
agencies, supervising state performance, and intervening with regard to permitting,
monitoring and surveillance, and enforcement, only where the state program is shown
to be inadequate in general or in a particular instance. Where a state does not consent to
accept programmatic primacy, the lead federal agency directly administers permitting,
monitoring and surveillance, and enforcement in that state.

In most instances, cooperative federalism operates smoothly to allocate the
elements of the elaborate system of pollution control regulatory activities among the
levels of government that are capable of performing them most efficiently, effectively,
and equitably. The following two case studies, however, illustrate potential pitfalls of
cooperative federalism. They serve as warnings that governmental officials and citizens
alike should be vigilant against abuses of cooperative federalism.

Save the Valley v. U.S. Environmental Protection Agency
United States District Court for the Southern District of Indiana, 2002
223 F. Supp. 2d 997

Plaintiffs...sue the EPA under the Clean Water Act.... Pursuant to the citizen suit provision
of the Act, Plaintiffs seek injunctive relief and a writ of mandamus. Plaintiffs contend that the
EPA possesses actual knowledge that the State of Indiana has failed to adopt and enforce
adequate laws and regulations concerning the discharge of pollutants from concentrated animal
feeding operations ("CAFOs"), particularly industrial hog farms, and has failed to require those
operations to acquire National Pollutant Discharge Elimination System ("NPDES") permits.
Thus, they seek to compel the EPA: (1) to reassume enforcement of Indiana's EPA-authorized
NPDES permitting program..., and (2) to initiate proceedings...to withdraw approval of
Indiana's NPDES program. The state agency responsible for the administration of Indiana's
NPDES program, the Indiana Department of Environmental Management ("IDEM"), has
intervened as a defendant....

Plaintiffs had become concerned that, due to what they perceived to be inadequate state
regulation of CAFOs, Indiana was becoming a popular state in which to open hog farms....
Animals in CAFOs are usually kept in pens within larger buildings. The floors of the pens are
slatted so as to collect the waste excreted by the animals into a holding tank located below the
floor. The waste is then usually piped into storage lagoons, uncovered pits that some have
referred to, not unfairly, as "open air cesspools." From the storage lagoons, waste is transported
to be spread, sprayed, or injected into croplands or pastures.

Manure is the primary source of CAFO pollution....[18] "Animal manure typically contains
nutrients (nitrogen and phosphorus), pathogens, salts, and heavy metals (e.g., copper)." CAFO
pollution can negatively impact surface water, groundwater, air, and soil. Environmental
damage due to CAFOs may occur due to lagoon breakage or spillage or to problems with land
application of manure, among other things. One storage lagoon often holds millions of gallons

---

18. Not all AFOs are CAFOs. AFOs are classified as CAFOs based in part on the number of animal units they
contain. For example, if an AFO contains more than 2,500 swine, it is classified as a CAFO. Only CAFOs are
federally regulated under the CWA. Other AFOs are regulated by the states. [Eds.]

of waste; in the event of a spill or break, thousands of those gallons may flow into creeks, drainage ditches, streams, rivers, or lakes [causing fish kills and contamination of drinking water supplies].... Public and government attention have focused increasingly on the environmental impact of animal feeding operations.[19] In the past twenty years, the trend in the livestock industry has been toward fewer but larger operations. A foreseeable result of this trend has been increased reports of large-scale discharges from these facilities, as well as continued runoff of nutrients.... In Indiana, the number of operating CAFOs is approximately 550 [out of 2,998 AFOs statewide]. In 1997, animal feedlots were responsible for 2,391 spills of manure in Indiana, including one single spill of approximately 9,600 gallons of hog manure....

The Clean Water Act... The Clean Water Act "anticipates a partnership between the States and the Federal Government." This relationship has also been aptly characterized as a "distinctive variety of cooperative federalism." The Act authorizes the EPA to issue NPDES permits,[20] but States may apply for and receive EPA approval to administer their own permit programs, provided they comply with detailed statutory and regulatory requirements. The EPA retains a high level of involvement and authority when a state administers its own NPDES permit program. For instance, the EPA continues to review state water quality standards, retains authority to object to the issuance of particular permits, monitors state programs for continuing compliance with federal directives, and enforces the terms of individual NPDES permits when a State has failed to institute enforcement proceedings.

At issue in the present action are §1319(a)(2) and §1342(c)(3) [of the CWA].... Section 1319(a)(2) states that the EPA Administrator shall assume enforcement of a State's permit program when "the Administrator finds that violations of permit conditions or limitations...are so widespread that such violations appear to result from a failure of a state to enforce such permit conditions or limitations effectively...," Section 1342(c)(3) states that the administrator shall withdraw approval of a State's NPDES program when a State fails to take appropriate corrective action even after being notified by the Administrator that its program is noncompliant.... The act requires the Administrator to make a "finding" under §1319(a)(2) or a "determination" under §1342(c)(3)...when [s]he becomes aware of such violations as articulated in §1319(a)(2).... [This finding or determination initiates formal proceedings, including public notice and public hearings, that could ultimately result in EPA's resumption of enforcement and perhaps even program withdrawal.] Again, the citizen suit provision of the Clean Water Act permits citizens to bring suit to force the Administrator to perform nondiscretionary duties under the Act.

Regulation of CAFOs in Indiana... In January 1975, the EPA approved Indiana's proposed NPDES program.... Indiana regulations prohibit point sources from discharging pollutants into waters of the state unless in conformance with a valid NPDES permit obtained from IDEM prior to the discharge. However, as of January 2002, IDEM had never issued an NPDES permit to a CAFO....

Historically, Indiana has chosen to deal with CAFOs through a system distinct from their NPDES permitting program. In 1971, the state first enacted legislation pertaining to the construction and operation of confined feeding operations, known as the Confined Feeding Control Act. Under Indiana's confined feeding program, IDEM issues approval permits to persons or entities wishing to construct and operate confined feeding operations. The Confined

---

19. See Chapter 12 for a further discussion of CAFO regulation.
20. Under the CWA, any discharge from a point source (discrete pipe, ditch, or other conveyance) is illegal unless it complies with the terms of an EPA-issued NPDES permit or its state equivalent. The Act explicitly defines CAFOs as point sources. [Eds.]

Feeding Control Act defines a confined feeding operation as any operation with confined feeding of more than...600 swine...or any operation with a history of pollution problems. Thus, it covers operations beyond those within the scope of the federal definition of a CAFO.... Approval for a permit is based upon factors outlined in Indiana statutes and regulations. In the past, IDEM also utilized an Indiana Water Pollution Control Board guidance document, known as the Animal Waste 1, or AW-1. The AW-1 specified the supplemental information IDEM required for permit approval. The preamble to AW-1 indicated that it was only a recommendation. So IDEM at times took the position that its requirements were not mandatory. There is some evidence they viewed their approval permits as no more than recommendations for prudent action.... While apparently designed and intended to prevent discharge of manure into waters of the state, it is not clear that the permits actually implemented any effluent limitations.[21] Thus, it is not clear that they were "equivalent" to NPDES permits. Not only did IDEM fail to issue NPDES permits to CAFOs, it appears that IDEM did not inspect CAFOs until 1999. Before 1999, Indiana had never pursued an enforcement action against any CAFO.

In 1997, Indiana began to formulate new rules for confined feeding operations.... On November 14, 2001, the state's Water Pollution Control Board adopted the new rules. IDEM claims that the new rules contain standards "analogous to those contained in [an EPA] Comprehensive Nutrient Management Plan." In addition, between sometime in 1999 and January 2002, IDEM completed over 3300 inspections of confined feeding operations, including inspections of all federally-defined CAFOs. As of February 2002, Indiana had pursued 32 enforcement actions against CAFOs, and had required 18 facilities to apply for individual NPDES permits.[22] The first individual permit for a CAFO in Indiana was publicly noticed in January 2002. However, it bears repeating that as of January 28, 2002, no CAFO in Indiana had ever actually been issued an NPDES permit. While Indiana finally appears to be requiring CAFOs that have been found to discharge pollutants to apply for NPDES permits, it is unclear why IDEM requires only that limited group of CAFOs to obtain permits. Indiana and federal regulations require NPDES permits for point sources that discharge or *propose to discharge*....

Throughout the time that Indiana has been in the process of revising its confined feeding rules, the EPA has been following the state's progress and offering guidance.... In a letter dated July 20, 2001, the EPA told IDEM "it is important for you to understand the need for IDEM to aggressively implement the NPDES program for CAFOs that are subject to existing 25-year old federal regulations." The EPA went on to remind IDEM that "under the Clean Water Act and EPA's 1975 approval of the Indiana NPDES program, IDEM is required to issue NPDES permits to CAFOs, evaluate compliance with NPDES permit requirements by CAFOs, and, when violations are discovered, enforce compliance...." The EPA reiterated IDEM's choices for satisfying its obligations..., which included issuing all federally-required individual permits, issuing one or

---

21. An effluent limitation is a numerical limit on the discharge of a particular pollutant, expressed in terms of either mass or concentration, based either on the volume of wastewater discharged or the amount of product manufactured (or in this case raised) by a particular process. [Eds.]

22. The court explained that "states with authorized NPDES permitting programs may issue either general permits or individual permits in order to address point sources within their boundaries. An individual permit is issued to a specific operation and tailored to its pollution issues. A general permit is written to cover a category of point sources with similar characteristics for a defined area. Every individual discharger expected to be covered by a particular general permit is required to submit a written "notice of intent, which serves as a permit application. The EPA approves of the use of general permits for CAFOs.... CAFOs are particularly suited to coverage by general permits because they "involve similar types of operations, require the same kinds of effluent limitations and operating conditions, and can discharge the same types of pollutants." If a state decides to utilize a general permit, it may still issue individual permits to some operations in the category that are exceptionally large, have a history of compliance problems, or are marked by other exceptional circumstances." 223 F. Supp. 2d at 1007. [Eds.]

more general permits, or submitting the amended rule to EPA as an approvable revision to the Indiana NPDES program. The EPA "strongly urged" IDEM to select one of the available choices "as expeditiously as possible."... IDEM responded to the EPA's letter in a letter dated September 11, 2001.... IDEM stated its belief that its revised program would "yield a comparable level of environmental protection to the strategy outlined by U.S. EPA and U.S. Department of Agriculture." Then, incredibly, IDEM posed the following question to EPA: "Can you please describe the circumstances in which a state may operate a confined feeding approval program without specifically requiring an NPDES individual permit, NPDES general permit, or NPDES permit-by-rule for CAFOs?"

Findings under §342(C)(3)... The most generous interpretation of IDEM's final question to the EPA is that it wanted to know the procedure for submission of the confined feeding rule to the EPA as a revision to Indiana's NPDES program.... Of course, the procedure is outlined in 40 C.F.R. §123.62. Another, and we think more likely, interpretation of IDEM's question is that it believed its program to be sufficiently "comparable" so that, despite being directly and repeatedly informed otherwise by the EPA, circumstances might exist under which it need not develop any rules relating to NPDES permits for CAFOs. It is unclear why IDEM thought it might not need a rule for the NPDES program as it relates to CAFOs.... In any case, it is clear that Indiana's Water Pollution Control Board adopted the new confined feeding rules in November 2001 even though they still did not completely comply with the Clean Water Act and federal regulations concerning CAFOs. At this point, the EPA had been informing IDEM for two years of the requirements for CAFOs that needed to be included in the new rules. Indiana's program had apparently *never* been in compliance....

We agree with Plaintiffs that Indiana's program is not in compliance, and that the evidence shows EPA has known that to be true for some time. Nonetheless we decline ..to compel the EPA to act immediately to withdraw the approval of Indiana's NPDES program.... [Noting that IDEM had already made significant progress in regulating CAFOs, the court then gave IDEM 240 days to bring its program into compliance with federal law and ordered EPA to commence withdrawal proceedings if IDEM did not meet this time limit.] We are acutely aware of the harmful effects that could result from the immediate withdrawal of Indiana's NPDES program. The program regulates municipal wastewater dischargers, wastewater treatment plants, industrial wastewater dischargers, stormwater activities, construction activities, aquaculture and silviculture activities, and more. Withdrawal of the program would impose significant administrative burdens on the EPA.... [For the same reasons, the court also declined to order EPA to take over enforcement of Indiana's NPDES permit program under §1319(a)(2) of the CWA.]

COMMENTARY & QUESTIONS

1. **Were the hogs racing-to-the-bottom in Indiana?** What was going on here? Plaintiffs alleged that IDEM was engaging in a race of laxity to attract hog farms to Indiana, but there is little evidence in the opinion upon which to evaluate this charge. EPA's implication, in its July 20, 2001, letter to IDEM, that Indiana had been slow to implement the 25-year old federal NPDES program for CAFOs, was at least somewhat disingenuous in that EPA itself had placed this program on the back burner until the early 1990s because the agency had previously concentrated on reducing water pollution from other point sources, such as municipal sewage treatment plants and industries. But EPA had resuscitated its CAFO regulatory program after settlement of a citizen suit in 1989 and after increasing public recognition of the impacts of CAFOs on water quality (stimulated by

conspicuous and widely reported incidents of fish kills and well contamination by runoff from CAFOs). See U.S. General Accounting Office, Increased EPA Oversight Will Improve Environmental Program for Concentrated Animal Feeding Operations (2003, GAO-03-285, p. 2) (hereafter cited as "2003 GAO Report"). Indiana's lackluster performance, prior to 1997, in regulating CAFOs was typical of federal and state neglect of this source of water pollution. Indiana's CAFO regulatory activities subsequent to 1997 appear to have been exemplary. The state's departures from EPA's CAFO regulations were relatively technical — the result of Indiana's philosophical conviction that a better approach to federal regulation of CAFOs would be for EPA to remove CAFOs from the NPDES program and instead allow the states to regulate CAFOs under state law, with EPA exerting supervision over state activities through its ability to withhold federal program grants and technical assistance in cases of substandard state programs. Indiana argued that it had achieved the "functional equivalent" of the EPA regulations and, in fact, that part of its program (the minimum number of animals constituting a CAFO) was even stricter than EPA's federal floor regulations, so why should Indiana have to do anything more? EPA, of course, disagreed.

2. **The dynamic tension of cooperative federalism.** Large portions of the *Save the Valley* opinion are reproduced above in order to convey the endemic push and pull of cooperative federalism. *Save the Valley* shows EPA attempting to achieve national regulatory uniformity while simultaneously being cognizant of states as "laboratories of regulatory creativity," where innovative mechanisms can be devised that not only protect a state's environment in accordance with federal standards, but also achieve least-cost solutions that benefit a state's industries and general economic health in accordance with that state's unique geographic, economic, and political situation. Unfortunately, allowing a state the flexibility to allocate pollution within its borders — as well as downwind and downstream — consistent with its social, economic, and political objectives can also result in a race of laxity as well as transboundary pollution. Cooperative federalism is an elaborate, delicate balancing of federal and state interests, with many occasions for disagreement by any of the multiple stakeholder groups.

3. **The environmentalist citizen suit as a goad to administrative agency action.** Chapter 1 noted that the citizen suit is one of environmental law's major contributions to public legal process. On a programmatic level, EPA revived its comparatively dormant CAFO regulatory program during the early 1990s at least partially in response to an environmentalist citizen suit (2003 GAO Report at 2). The *Save the Valley* litigation was instituted by a citizen group, not by EPA. The concerned citizens had grown impatient with IDEM's refusal to fully integrate Indiana's confined animal feeding operation regulatory system with the federal NPDES system, while EPA probably thought that continued dialogue and threats of litigation would bring Indiana into compliance. Was this citizen suit necessary? The bottom line was that Indiana's confined feeding operation program, although apparently effective, was not in compliance with federal law. If IDEM had later decided, because of political factors, to "go easy" on one or more Indiana hog farmers, it would have been much more difficult for EPA to discover and remedy this situation if the Indiana program had not been integrated with EPA's NPDES system. Regulatory system standardization can greatly facilitate federal oversight and

response activities. The court granted a delayed injunction, requiring IDEM to begin the compliance process but postponing program withdrawal so as not to disrupt Indiana's viable water pollution control program, most of which had been subsumed under the NPDES program.

4. **The pitfalls of federal oversight.** The *Save the Valley* court makes clear that delegation withdrawal would not only paralyze Indiana's water pollution control program but also would "impose significant administrative burdens on the EPA." Thus EPA is so reluctant to begin withdrawal proceedings that delegation withdrawal is a virtual paper tiger:

> The reality is that once EPA has delegated a program, it almost never takes it back. All the laws that allow delegation also allow EPA to revoke the delegation, and the agency sometimes threatens to do so. However, because both the political and resource costs would be high, EPA has only once revoked a state permitting program — in 1981, when the Iowa legislature refused to appropriate money for the state drinking water program. EPA returned authority to the state a year later. In 1987, EPA commenced a proceeding to withdraw the authorization of North Carolina's RCRA program but decided in 1990 not to pursue the action.... Davies et al., Reforming Permitting 59 (2001).[23]

EPA admits that "[it] does not have the resources to directly implement the entire [NPDES] permit program in additional states" (2003 GAO Report at 3).

There is evidence that other intended safeguards of environmental cooperative federalism are also inadequate deterrents to substandard state environmental regulation. First, federal program grants to state environmental agencies have declined since 1970. The Economic Council of the States (ECOS) has reported that only about 30% of the resources that states receive for implementing required federal water pollution control programs comes from federal sources. ECOS, State Water Quality Management Resource Analysis — Interim Report on Results (2002). Even where federal program grants constitute a significant portion of a state's environmental regulatory resources, EPA has been reluctant to curtail them for state underperformance because "withholding grant funding would further hamper the states' ability [sic] to effectively implement their programs,..." (2003 GAO Report at 3).

Second, resource constraints have prevented EPA from reviewing more than an average of 10% of state drafted permits (Davies et al., at 61). These same resource limitations preclude EPA from performing backup monitoring and enforcement activities in underperforming states except in unusual, highly visible situations. (See the following note on EPA "overfiling.")

Focusing on the CAFO regulatory program, the GAO concluded that "EPA's limited oversight of the states has contributed to inconsistent and inadequate implementation by the authorized states" (2003 GAO Report at 7). GAO recommended that if EPA is to credibly implement new, and significantly more comprehensive, CAFO regulations (68 Fed. Reg. 7175 (Feb. 12, 2003)), "EPA will need to increase its oversight of state programs to

23. On December 1, 2001, EPA revoked Maryland's air permitting program delegation because the state had failed to afford adequate public participation. Little more than one year later, on January 15, 2003, EPA returned control of this program to state environmental regulators because the state had allegedly cured the program defects. See the Steinzor case study, below, where the Maryland Department of the Environment discouraged public participation with regard to an NPDES permit for a large steel mill, and EPA did not respond. [Eds.]

ensure that the new requirements are adopted and implemented" (2003 GAO Report at 4). Additional EPA oversight, according to the GAO, would require substantially increased funding.

Perhaps withdrawal of an entire NPDES program for inadequate state implementation of only one of its components is so crude an instrument that effective federal oversight is necessarily precluded. Through statutory amendment or regulation, the NPDES program could be subdivided, enabling EPA to withdraw one of its aspects (e.g., a state's CAFO regulatory program) instead of a state's entire point source water pollution control program.

5. **"Overfiling" (and "underfiling").** One of the most controversial aspects of EPA's oversight function is whether EPA has authority to "overfile" a state enforcement lawsuit when the state has been delegated federal enforcement authority. If EPA is skeptical whether state enforcement action is being conducted in good faith (if it suspects, for example, that the state is likely to enter into "sweetheart" consent decrees with violators), is EPA authorized to commence its own enforcement action paralleling the state lawsuit, or is EPA's only remedy to de-certify the state regulatory program, taking over the enforcement job itself? The answer may vary with the particular environmental protection statute involved (see Chapter 21). On the other hand, an alternate possibility exists: What if a state believes EPA itself is making a sweetheart deal with a violator? Can a state then "underfile" EPA's ongoing litigation, commencing its own tougher enforcement action?

6. **"Cooperative federalism" in the environmental permitting setting.** Permits are a crucial link in the environmental regulatory chain. They are frequently the nexus between the administrative agency that administers a particular environmental protection statute and the potential sources of environmental damage. Permitting is the process that makes environmental goals and standards operational by specifying acceptable behavior that, if violated, can subject the permittee to enforcement sanctions. Thus, the permitting phase of environmental regulation is a crucial context for an evaluation of environmental cooperative federalism. The following case study focuses on a water discharge permit for a steel mill in Maryland. Can we derive different conclusions from this situation than we did from the *Save the Valley* case? Is a race of laxity occurring here? Is cooperative federalism working? Is there something unique about environmental permitting that requires a different perspective on environmental cooperative federalism?

Rena Steinzor, EPA and Its Sisters at 30: Devolution, Revolution, or Reform?
31 Environmental Law Reporter 11086 (September 2001)

Let us begin with a cautionary and, unfortunately, true tale. The Bethlehem Steel facility at Sparrow's Point, Maryland, is among the largest integrated steel mills in the country, with multiple production lines and a new $300 million, state-of-art cold rolling mill. With a capacity of 3.7 million tons of steel annually, the plant is a classic "Rust Belt" employer, anchoring Maryland's economy with some 4,000 unionized jobs.

The plant is also the 48th largest discharger of toxic metals to surface waters in the nation, and the second largest discharger of persistent toxic metals to the Chesapeake Bay, with 43,150 pounds reported in the 1997 Toxic Release Inventory.[24] Its effluent travels from the Patapsco River to Baltimore Harbor and from there to the Chesapeake Bay. The Harbor is one of three "toxic hot spots" afflicting the Bay.

In 1985, the State of Maryland, operating under authority delegated by the U.S. Environmental Protection Agency (EPA), issued a National Pollutant Discharge Elimination System (NPDES) permit to the Sparrow's Point plant. The 1985 Permit reflected technology-based standards[25] for a variety of pollutants,... Soon after the 1985 Permit was issued, state regulators signed a consent decree with the company, modifying the permit's limits.... [One effluent limitation was decreased by 20%, while ten other effluent limitations were increased between 120% and 1,635%, thereby allowing the permittee to discharge significantly more toxic pollutants than had been specified under the original permit.]

Under the 1985 Consent Decree, the revised limits were supposed to be effective for three years, in order to give the company time to upgrade its treatment facilities. Once those improvements were complete, and the Maryland Department of the Environment (MDE) made a separate determination regarding the "net credits" to award the facility, the Consent Decree would expire and the 1985 permit would go into effect. MDE never made that determination, and the 1985 Consent Decree's alternative numbers remained in effect until 2001, when a new permit and consent decree were negotiated.[26]

Although the 1985 Consent Decree limits appear outrageous on paper, their true import depends of course on what the company actually discharged over the period during which the inflated standards remained effective. While the company upgraded its treatment facilities as required in 1985, those improvements clearly were not effective. According to the facility's Discharge Monitoring Reports (DMRs),[27] during the period from January 1998 to May 2000, the facility violated the 1985 Permit's daily maximum limit for Total Suspended Solids (TSS) 7 times; its TSS monthly average limit 14 times; and its standard for Dissolved Oxygen 28 times. The 1985 Consent Decree converted these violations into two, none, and one, respectively.

To add insult to injury, the 1985 Consent Decree not only imposed limits more lenient than Best Available Technology for chromium, lead, and zinc,[28] but allowed the company to test its effluent by first filtering out solid particles of the metals and then measuring only the levels of "soluble" metals. This practice violates federal regulations, which require compliance with permit limits to be measured in terms of "total recoverable metals." In fact, [in a case involving another company,] federal prosecutors brought criminal charges against an individual for tampering with samples using the same method that MDE sanctioned for Bethlehem Steel.

The 1985 Permit was issued for a five-year term and expired in 1990. Bethlehem filed an application for renewal that entitled it to continue to operate under the old standards, as modified by the 1985 Consent Decree. The company and state regulators then proceeded to spend more than a decade debating the terms of a new permit.

---

24. See Chapter 10 for a discussion of the TRI, which requires companies to disclose the environmental destinations of hundreds of toxic substances. [Eds.]

25. Compliance with technology-based standards, based on some version of Best Available Technology Economically Achievable, is required of all point source dischargers, such as Bethlehem Steel, under the CWA. (See Chapter 12.) [Eds.]

26. At that point, MDE finally issued the company a new permit, accompanied by a new Consent Decree providing still more time for it to achieve compliance.... [This is footnote 10 in the original. — Eds.]

27. DMRs are the required self-reporting mechanism under the CWA (see Chapter 12). [Eds.]

28. These are listed as toxic heavy metals under the CWA. [Eds.]

Meanwhile, back in the real world, throughout the long process of rewriting the 1985 Permit, Bethlehem conducted business as usual. In 1998, it announced construction of a brand new cold rolling mill that would cost $300 million, eliminate 400 jobs, and put the company back on the worldwide steel-making map. In May 2000, amidst great fanfare, the ribbon was cut on this facility....

The Clean Water Act (CWA) defines a "new source" as "any source, the construction of which is commenced after the publication of proposed regulations" imposing standards on the relevant industrial process. EPA regulations clarify this definition, describing a new source as one that "totally replaces the process or production equipment that causes the discharge of pollutants at an existing source." In 1984, EPA issued New Source Performance Standards (NSPS) for cold rolling mills that would result in pollution reductions of 97.5% for the company's new mill.... Yet Bethlehem flipped the switch on the new mill without first obtaining a permit that incorporates these standards. The company did not notify the MDE permit writer in charge of its renewal application, who assented to the start-up.

In the fall of 2000, for the first time in at least two decades, EPA Region III sent MDE both "general" and "specific" objection letters, the threshold step in a process that could result in the Agency asserting authority to "pull" the Bethlehem Steel permit from state regulatory control in order to draft a different document acceptable to federal regulators. Everyone's attention immediately shifted to Philadelphia, with local environmentalists and the company's top officials meeting with senior federal and state regulators. On the eve of his departure from office at the end of the Clinton Administration, Region III Administrator Bradley Campbell put the finishing touches on a new permit and consent decree endorsed by all of the disparate participants in those negotiations.

Although this particular cautionary tale had a happy ending, the resources required to achieve that result were extraordinary and could not possibly be brought to bear on the dozens of other similar permit disputes now pending. There is no hope of recouping the damage already done to Chesapeake Bay's ecology, which in itself is Maryland's most lucrative commercial enterprise, contributing an estimated $31.6 billion to the Maryland and Virginia region in 1987.... Until fundamental changes are made in the institutional dynamics that produce such fiascos, history will undoubtedly repeat itself, not just in Maryland, but nationwide....

Whether one describes the problem as Agency capture, bureaucratic inertia, failed political will, the tension between job creation and protection of the environment, or the systematic defunding of government at all levels, the theory animating EPA's creation three decades ago was that a system of federal standard-setting and state implementation was the best we could do to keep these destructive influences at bay. If the safeguards of environmental federalism fail us even in the most extreme of situations, and violations of the law are sanctioned by state regulators without anyone noticing for 15 years, we must think twice about diminishing federal authority any further....

COMMENTARY & QUESTIONS

1. **Environmental permitting as "Let's Make a Two-Way Deal."** The various Bethlehem Steel facility permits, as modified by administrative consent decrees, were essentially negotiated between the MDE and the company, with minimal public participation. Other commentators confirm that this bipolar bargaining process is typical of environmental permitting:

Permitting is basically a bargaining process between the permit applicant and the permitting authority. Which side has the advantage depends on a variety of factors, one of the most important of which is whether the applicant seeks a new permit for construction of a facility or a renewal of an operating permit for an existing facility. For new facilities (or modifications of existing facilities), the applicant is motivated to get the permit issued as soon as possible because construction cannot begin without it. There is no such incentive for renewal of existing permits because a facility can continue to operate even if its permit has expired.

The bargaining over the content of permits is less constrained than most other environmental regulatory processes because there is less litigation. Especially when permits for new construction are the issue, industry does not want to sue because it doesn't want to delay issuance of the permit. Because permits are site-specific, national environmental groups do not want to get involved, and local environmental groups usually do not have the money or expertise to litigate permitting decisions. Courts are generally reluctant to enter the arcane thickets of permitting law and regulation. The result is that permitting bargains can be struck that do not have any solid basis in law. Davies et al., at 8.

Professor Steinzor relates these conclusions to the Bethlehem Steel situation:

While I have no way to prove it, I would be shocked to find anyone who would disagree with the assertion that public participation in the process of renewing existing permits is virtually non-existent. Behind the scenes, the process amounts to an uneven struggle between the superior technical resources of the permittee and federal and state bureaucrats barely in control of their workloads. As long as it is cheaper to churn out data and engage in extensive debates about arcane conditions, permittees have only one incentive to bring the process to conclusion: their need to construct and operate new facilities.

In Bethlehem Steel's case, even that incentive failed. State regulators agreed to allow the company to operate a new source, months before a draft permit was issued for public comment, indicating that permit writers...were sufficiently politicized that they did nothing to thwart, and much to encourage, the company's efforts. Steinzor, at 11100–11101.

Maryland environmentalists became aware of the Bethlehem permit problems almost accidentally and comparatively late in the process. Even then the environmentalists, "who were in the rare position of having free legal and technical help to unravel the dense paper record compiled by MDE and the company" (Id. at 11091), were continually frustrated in their attempts to participate: "It took literally hundreds of hours of work over a two-year period to come to grips with the substance of the...dispute. A substantial portion of this time was spent fighting over requests to review documents under the state's Freedom of Information Act" (Id. at 11106).

It is true that environmental permitting, especially where large, multifaceted facilities are concerned, cannot be a formulaic exercise in translating general environmental protection standards into permit conditions for a single unique facility. How, for example, is a permit writer to apply technology-based effluent limitations based on an individual industrial process to a facility that combines this manufacturing process with another that is subject to a different set of technology-based effluent limitations? What about permitting a facility employing a process that generates both toxic water and air pollution, which are regulated by different federal statutes, including different standard-setting mechanisms, monitoring and reporting requirements, and permit systems? Clearly, a permit writer's exercise of "best professional judgment" can be beneficial in such cases in order to devise creative multi-media, least-cost pollution prevention and control strategies. But when the permit applicant is politically influential and the public is excluded from participating in the permit negotiation process, otherwise salutary bargaining can degenerate into "sweetheart deals" crafted behind closed doors, even in an environmentally aware state such as Maryland.

2. **Environmental federalism in the permit setting.** In theory, environmental federalism is a constructive division of labor between the federal and state governments, through which Congress authorizes delegation of program primacy to states to address local environmental problems — with which the states are presumably more familiar than the federal government — by applying rigorous legal requirements for state performance that are undergirded by competent federal oversight. But, in practice, ample evidence indicates that this ideal of environmental cooperative federalism is rarely approximated in real-world environmental regulation. This is especially true at the permitting stage, where bipolar bargaining and enhanced emphasis on access to technical information render informed citizen participation unlikely, in contrast to the relatively unencumbered access to generally unsophisticated public data that the citizen groups in *Save the Valley* exercised.

3. **Improving environmental permitting.** Recommendations for improving the environmental permitting process range from antidotes to the systemic fragmentation of environmental law to more focused recommendations such as funding citizen participation through permit fees and increased reliance on general permits (Davies et al., at 11–12).

Perhaps the most innovative suggestions for reforming environmental permitting involve a strategy called "differential oversight":

> In 1995, the National Academy of Public Administration ("NAPA") published what became an extraordinarily influential report.... Entitled *Setting Priorities, Getting Results*, its most prominent recommendation was that EPA should undertake the "accountable devolution" of national environmental programs, using a system of "differential oversight" that would reduce federal supervision when it is not needed....
>
> The report also recommended that EPA engineer a fundamental shift in the methods it uses to evaluate state performance. Rather than reviewing the details of all of the activities that states undertake as they implement federal programs, EPA should develop "outcome measures" or "performance indicators" that would be used to assess whether those activities actually improve environmental conditions. The states would then be subject to different degrees of scrutiny on the basis of their achievements, with high-performing states rewarded by more autonomy and low-performing states punished by more intensive review. NAPA warned that EPA must maintain a "credible capacity" to deliver the ultimate punishment — withdrawing delegated authority when a state fails to perform — and suggested that EPA consider the deployment of specialized teams that could assume responsibility for specific state programs almost immediately. Steinzor, Devolution and the Public Health, 24 Harv. Envtl. L. Rev. 351, 421 (2001).

Thus far, the scientific and political obstacles to instituting "differential oversight" of state environmental permitting, based on objective indicators of state "performance," have been formidable, if not overwhelming. But even if these hurdles could be cleared, the critical fiscal issues would remain unresolved: Where will EPA find the resources to develop a differential oversight system and its underlying performance indicators, as well as a credible program to withdraw delegation from underperforming states? And how can this process be made transparent, in the sense that public interest groups can afford to participate in effective and informed ways? Requiring permittees to pay reasonable permit fees will defray some of the costs of administering environmental permit programs, but not the overriding costs of instituting an effective system of differential oversight. Unless significant public funding is devoted to improving environmental federalism in general – and in particular the permitting processes that are its essence — environmental regulation in the United States will fail to reach its full potential for achieving environmental progress.

4. **Racing-to-the-bottom via lax enforcement.** Was the State of Maryland — which has been so progressive in devising innovative regulatory controls over stormwater runoff from agriculture and new residential development — engaging in a race of laxity with regard to Bethlehem Steel's Sparrow's Point plant? Again, it is difficult to prove that a state is consciously racing-to-the-bottom in a particular situation, but it is clear that Maryland was attempting to cut a "sweetheart deal" with one of its largest employers and corporate taxpayers. Even with federal floors for standard-setting, states can manipulate highly technical environmental standards to favor particular industries, as Maryland did for Bethlehem Steel. Moreover, states eager to appease industry have other opportunities, particularly in monitoring, surveillance, and enforcement. One of plaintiffs' allegations in *Save the Valley* was that Indiana's monitoring and enforcement was substandard with regard to confined animal feeding operations, but the state had cured these program defects before the lawsuit was instituted. This was not the case with regard to Maryland's favorable treatment of the Sparrow Point facility. Professor Victor Flatt supports his assertion of a race-to-the-bottom resulting from variable enforcement by comparing the CWA enforcement activities of the states of Georgia and Washington. Flatt, A Dirty River Runs Through It (The Failure of Enforcement in the Clean Water Act), 25 B.C. Envtl. Aff. L. Rev. 1 (1997). One easily discerned strategy of the states in these cases is to take weak administrative action or seek lenient consent decrees in enforcement actions, thus forestalling more rigorous enforcement either by EPA or, more often, by citizen enforcers. Compare, e.g., Knee Deep Cattle Co. v. Bindana Inv. Co., 94 F.3d 514 (9th Cir. 1996) (the state did not diligently prosecute a pending state law action for pollution in violation of a NPDES permit, so citizen enforcement was allowed under federal law), with Arkansas Wildlife Fed'n v. ICI Americas, Inc., 29 F.3d 376 (8th Cir. 1994) (a state administrative penalty proceeding was sufficiently prosecuted to bar a citizen suit for violation of an NPDES permit). See also Friends of the Earth, Inc. v. Laidlaw Envtl. Servs., Inc., 528 U.S. 167 (2000), where defendant, in order to head off a citizen suit, requested the state environmental protection agency to commence an enforcement action against it, drafted the complaint and paid the filing fee for the state agency, and then agreed to pay a relatively low civil penalty. This topic is discussed more fully in Chapters 7 and 21.

Environmental attorneys who represent firms in regulatory settings confirm that their clients are very sensitive to the possibility of obtaining less stringent regulation from state regulators than from EPA. In the air pollution setting, a routine strategy of firms that realize they have violations that may be pursued by either state agencies or EPA is to urge the state to file and then negotiate a settlement, on the belief that the state will be more lenient than EPA. Even more pointedly, when EPA files a complaint first, the discharger will often allege that EPA has deliberately "overcharged" them in the case; the discharger will then enlist the state agency to first file its own case and then attempt to persuade EPA to dismiss its lawsuit in deference to the state filing.

E. RETHINKING COMMAND-AND-CONTROL REGULATION, THE STANDARD APPROACH TO ENVIRONMENTAL PROTECTION

Since the mid-1970s, U.S. industry has faced an intensive coordinated system of federal pollution regulation. Prescriptive federal standards applied comprehensively, source-by-source, became the nation's standard regulatory approach, widely referred to (rather pejoratively) as "command-and-control" regulatory structures.

The Latin/Ackerman-Stewart debate, a classic debate between environmental law scholars, laid the groundwork for many subsequent reform arguments on whether prescriptive standards should be applied uniformly to all polluters.

> As critics of the present system, we believe...the present regulatory system wastes tens of billions of dollars every year, misdirects resources, stifles innovation, and spawns massive and often counterproductive litigation. There is a variety of fundamental but practical changes that could be made to improve its environmental and economic performance. Why have such changes not been adopted? Powerful organized interests have a vested stake in the status quo. The congressional committees, government bureaucracies, and industry and environmental groups that have helped to shape the present system want to see it perpetuated. But the current system is also bolstered by an often inarticulate sense that, however cumbersome, it "works," and that complexity and limited information make major improvements infeasible.... The current system does not in fact "work" and its malfunctions, like those of Soviet-style central planning, will become progressively more serious as the economy grows and changes and our knowledge of environmental problems develops.... Economic incentive systems [provide] fundamental alternatives to our current reliance on centralized regulatory commands, [and] economic incentive systems are feasible and effective.... Some of our proposals involve reform of the criteria and procedures which Congress, agencies, and the courts use in setting environmental goals; others involve reform of the means by which the goals (whatever they may be) are implemented in the real world. Ackerman & Stewart, Reforming Environmental Law, 37 Stan. L. Rev. 1333, 1333–1340 (1985).[29]

Professor Latin took the contrary position.

> Prominent legal scholars such as Bruce Ackerman, Steven Breyer, and Richard Stewart have concluded that command-and-control regulation is inefficient

---

29. Copyright © 1985 by the Board of Trustees of Leland Stanford, Junior University. Reprinted by permission of the copyright holder, Fred B. Rothman Co.

and should be replaced by more flexible strategies: ...environmental controls should be tailored to particularized ecological and economic circumstances, regulatory benefits weighed against the costs of environmental protection, and increased reliance placed on economic incentive mechanisms, such as taxes on environmentally destructive activities or transferable pollution rights. Professor Stewart, for example, recently advocated "a more individualized or 'fine-tuning' approach to regulation...." The academic literature on "regulatory reform" reflects an excessive preoccupation with theoretical efficiency, while it places inadequate emphasis on actual decisionmaking costs and implementation constraints.... The critical issue is not which regulatory system aspires to ideal "efficiency" but which is most likely to prove effective.[30]

There are numerous advantages of uniform standards in comparison with more particularized and flexible regulatory strategies. These advantages include decreased information collection and evaluation costs, greater consistency and predictability of results, greater accessibility of decisions to public scrutiny and participation, increased likelihood that regulations will withstand judicial review, reduced opportunities for manipulative behavior by agencies in response to political or bureaucratic pressures, reduced opportunities for obstructive behavior by regulated parties, and decreased likelihood of social dislocation and "forum shopping" resulting from competitive disadvantages between geographical regions or between firms in regulated industries.... Well-intentioned scholars often recommend "fine-tuning" because they focus on ideal efficiency, while [antiregulatory activists] may advocate "fine-tuning" precisely because they believe it will seldom work in practice and would therefore accomplish sub rosa deregulation. Intemperate academic criticisms of command-and-control standards combined with support of unrealistic "fine-tuning" strategies may lend an aura of intellectual credibility to political initiatives designed to achieve less regulation, not better regulation....

Despite its imperfections, command-and-control regulation has fostered significant improvements in environmental quality at a societal cost that has not proved prohibitive.[31] Critics of uniform standards should therefore be required to demonstrate with reasonable assurance that "fine-tuning" approaches can be successfully implemented, and will actually perform better, before the current regulatory system is "reformed." Latin, Ideal versus Real Regulatory Efficiency: Implementation of Uniform Standards and "Fine-Tuning" Regulatory Reforms, 37 Stan. L. Rev. 1267, 1267–1273 (1985).[32]

Note the two different focuses of this debate: (1) How should environmental standards be applied, by bureaucrats or through industry's active participation? (2) Should environmental standard-setting be based on cost-benefit calculations — whether

---

30. There are numerous formal economic definitions of efficiency. See e.g. Coleman, Efficiency, Exchange, and Auction: Philosophic Aspects of the Economic Approach to Law, 68 Calif. L. Rev. 221 (1980); Latin, Environmental Deregulation and Consumer Decisionmaking Under Uncertainty, 6 Harv. Envtl. L. Rev. 187, 191 n.26 (1982).... The important contrast is between an emphasis on ideal or optimal decisionmaking,... denoted by the label "efficiency," and an emphasis on "effective" decisionmaking. See Costle, Environmental Regulation and Regulatory Reform, 57 Wash. L. Rev. 409, 416 (1982) (estimating that pollution control requirements imposed regulatory costs of about 3.3% of GNP and about 3.1% of total industry expenditures on plants and equipment; Costle does admit, however, that "the effects [of environmental costs] on specific industries can be substantial").

31. As noted elsewhere in this book, the phrase "command-and-control" regulation has a pejorative cast with no good substitute. Cf. "comprehensive prescriptive regulation." [Eds.]

32. Copyright © 1985 by the Board of Trustees of Leland Stanford, Junior University. Reprinted by permission of the copyright holder, the author, and Fred B. Rothman Co.

figured on an overall basis or case-by-case to account for localized differences and special circumstances?

On the first point Ackerman and Stewart have won significant political success. Drawing upon work like theirs, Congress passed a major experiment in the 1990 CAA Amendments setting up a power plant sulfur oxides trading system. The CAA's Title IV allows utilities to innovate and trade surplus clean air credits around the country, so that each can adjust the amount of cleanup it wants to pay for, and efficiencies will be rewarded with profit-generating tradable credits. This and other market-enlisting mechanisms studied in Chapter 14, such as netting and banking of pollution credits, have now become part of the air pollution regulatory structure.

The second suggestion advocated by Ackerman and Stewart — prescriptive standard-setting by cost-benefit calculations — has had only limited success to date. It makes fundamental good sense to consider cost, benefits, and alternatives in any endeavor, but to base such analyses exclusively on market-based pricing and to convert them into direct prescriptive standards risks skewing the environmental protection endeavor away from a holistic civic accounting into a business exercise. Should calculations of benefits, costs, and provable risk be required to justify all regulation? Or are such reform proposals inadvertently or consciously designed to produce "paralysis by analysis"? Discretionary administrative action is increasingly importing cost-benefit restrictions into a wide range of settings, and a few cost-benefit provisions have been inserted into a variety of secondary statutory provisions, as studied later in Chapter 13.

The prescriptive "command-and-control" system remains the dominant regulatory paradigm, and has clearly produced significant improvements in the quality of air, water, and control of toxic contamination. Some scholars argue that the empirical data on the economics-based reform experiments' innovation rates show disappointing results, and an uneven record in terms of equity and performance.[33] Trading systems and cost-benefit reasoning, however, continue to be popular with New Democrats as well as Republicans, for international as well as domestic policy, so this debate will continue.

COMMENTARY & QUESTIONS

1. **The pollution prevention strategy.** There is frequent rhetorical support, both from critics and supporters of the current pollution control regulatory system, for efforts to integrate pollution prevention into the environmental protection laws.

Pollution prevention (also known as *P2*, *source reduction*, and *toxic use reduction*) is the use of materials, processes, or practices that reduce or eliminate the creation of pollutants or wastes at the source. Pollution prevention often occurs naturally when industries reasonably fear vigorous enforcement of environmental law, whether public laws or common law liabilities. Governments can also can push industry toward prevention strategies through direct inducements (subsidies), direct requirements for

---

33. See Driesen, Is Emissions Trading an Economic Incentive Program?: Replacing the Command and Control/Economic Incentive Dichotomy, 55 Wash. & Lee L. Rev. 289 (1998); Driesen, Does Emissions Trading Encourage Innovation?, 33 Envtl. L. Rep. 10094 (2003); Steinzor, Toward Better Bubbles and Future Lives: A Progressive Response to the Conservative Agenda for Reforming Environmental Law, 32; Envtl. L. Rep. 11421 (Dec. 2002); Richard Toshiyuki Drury et al., Pollution Trading and Environmental Injustice: Los Angeles' Failed Experiment in Air Quality Policy, 9 Duke Envtl. L. & Pol'y F. 231 (1999).

source reductions, or mere rhetorical exhortations. The Massachusetts TURA statute,[34] for instance, provides financial as well as regulatory incentives for industries to adopt internal pollution reduction planning. TURA is credited with millions of pounds of toxics reduction and substantial though unquantified savings to industry.

Which governmental approach is reflected in the Pollution Prevention Act of 1990? In that statute, 42 U.S.C. §§13101 et seq., Congress declared a national policy

> that pollution should be prevented or reduced at the source whenever feasible, [or otherwise] recycled in an environmentally safe manner whenever feasible, and disposal...employed only as a last resort.

> The United States of America annually produces millions of tons of pollution and spends tens of billions of dollars per year controlling this pollution.... There are significant opportunities for industry to reduce or prevent pollution at the source through cost-effective changes in production, operation, and raw materials use, [offering] industry substantial savings in reduced raw materials, pollution control, and liability costs as well as help protect the environment and reduce risks to worker health and safety.... Existing regulations...focus upon treatment and disposal, rather than source reduction....

> The Environmental Protection Agency must establish a source reduction program which collects and disseminates information, provides financial assistance to States, and implements the other activities provided for in this chapter. 42 U.S.C. §13101.

Professor Michele Ochsner has expressed skepticism about voluntary corporate pollution prevention as the centerpiece of a reformed pollution control system, emphasizing instead that some form of government suasion will often be necessary to encourage systemic pollution prevention efforts:

> The literature is filled with case studies that document impressive savings achieved through pollution prevention at many facilities. However, [industrial] managers find that pollution prevention cannot always be justified in terms of short-term economic benefits. Although the savings achievable through simple changes in procedures (e.g., changes in housekeeping and inventory management) may be obvious, the nature of the investment needed to implement more complex source reduction projects (such as those involving manufacturing technology or product formulas) may be far less clear.... The benefits of the project — such as potential savings on raw materials, greater process efficiency, or the market for a greener product line — may also be difficult to predict....

> Despite the development of programs at the state and federal level[s] designed to encourage pollution prevention, the evidence suggests that the majority of American companies still depend primarily on end-of-pipe controls to achieve desired decreases in emissions.... The existing framework of environmental regulations is an imperfect instrument for fostering innovative, preventive approaches to environmental management. Environmental statutes at the federal and state level[, however, do] make prevention attractive by increasing the costs associated with hazardous by-products of industrial production....

---

34. Massachusetts Toxic Use Reduction Act, Mass. Gen. Laws ch. 21I (1989). The TURA over nine years was credited with reduction of toxic wastes by 275 million pounds,while production increased 40%. Mass. DEP, Bureau of Waste Prevention, TUR Information Release (Spring 2000). The new state administration has nevertheless unaccountably considered abandoning the program.

A number of states have enacted similar statutes mandating that facilities undertake pollution prevention planning, although actual implementation of these plans is basically voluntary.

There is considerable evidence that companies continue to weigh the costs associated with current or anticipated regulatory compliance when they consider undertaking pollution prevention.... The evidence suggests that existing environmental regulations offer important incentives, and significant barriers, to pollution prevention.... A balanced perspective on regulatory barriers should be shaped by an appreciation of regulatory incentives, and an understanding that other, non-regulatory barriers may contribute equally or more in impeding pollution prevention.... Ochsner, Pollution Prevention: An Overview of Regulatory Incentives and Barriers, 6 N.Y.U. Envtl. L.J. 586 (1998).

2. **Pollution prevention as one of many regulatory approaches.** As you explore the public law environmental protection strategies presented in the following chapters, consider whether they utilize proactive, managerial, or reactive approaches to problems of pollution or resource depletion. (See the Talbot Page excerpt in Chapter 1 for a theoretical analysis of these options.) Pollution prevention can be a particularly proactive approach to potential pollution, but it requires practical incentives. A managerial approach to forestalling pollution might be the utilization of better management practices or the installation of pollution control technology. Or reactive approaches — cleanup after the pollution has occurred — can be selected. In the resource depletion area, government might purchase private property that constitutes critical habitat of an endangered species in advance of development proposals; or the development might be permitted subject to precautions with regard to project scope, timing, or intensity; or else species restoration programs might be undertaken subsequent to the development's having caused the eradication of the species in that area. Each of these approaches has advantages and disadvantages in terms of effectiveness, economic efficiency, equity, and environmental protectiveness — and each is repeatedly encountered in environmental public law.[35]

3. **Beware the ghost of *Utilex*.** The *Utilex* case study at the start of this chapter illustrated an ineffective midcentury review-and-permit system that was handicapped by ambiguous standards, unenergetic bipolar negotiations between the state agency and the industry, and selective nonenforcement. Professor Steinzor's *Bethlehem Steel* example warns us that it is just as possible today, despite the federalization of environmental law and the safeguards erected by cooperative federalism. Ambiguous standards, bipolar negotiations, and selective nonenforcement can still cause regulatory failure, although the environmental regulatory system, in general, is significantly more effective than it was 50 years ago. In any reconsideration of environmental law structures as they have evolved to date, the guiding principle must be the *improvement* of current protection regimes, coupled with an awareness of the entropy principle — that the tendencies that required the protections in the first place continually tend to attempt to erode the laws, often deploying the rhetoric of reform. *Utilex* and *Bethlehem Steel* remind us that the investment of citizen energies will continue to be necessary to the successful performance of the standard regulatory system or any of its alternatives.

---

35. For example, see the discussions of encouraging pollution prevention through strict environmental standard-setting (Chapter 12) and through Supplemental Environmental Projects imposed as part of environmental enforcement proceedings (Chapter 21).

Chapter 6

POWER RELATIONSHIPS BETWEEN FEDERAL AND STATE GOVERNMENTS IN ENVIRONMENTAL REGULATION

A. Constitutional Federalism and Environmental Law Controversies
B. Preemption of State Law
C. "Dormant Commerce Clause" Overrides of Subordinate Legislation
D. Limitations on Federal Power

A. CONSTITUTIONAL FEDERALISM AND ENVIRONMENTAL LAW CONTROVERSIES

The historical overview of environmental regulation in Chapter Five noted the distinct and evolving roles of the national and state governments. Those roles, of course, are not derived through happenstance, logic, or necessity alone. Instead, those roles, despite their variation over time, are rooted deeply in the defining elements of American democracy and in the concept of federalism that animates the federal Constitution. Thus the federal government and the states are subject to legally binding limitations that constrain their power. (Several international federal examples exist, notably the European Union with its "subsidiarity" principle, but the different systems share few common legal principles.) This chapter examines the constitutional dimension of federal-state power relations as it relates to environmental law in the United States.

At stake in the disputes explored in this chapter are momentous principles of American constitutional federalism more comfortably studied as part of a constitutional law course. The doctrines and case law that undergird contemporary decisions were crafted to resolve disputes involving subjects as remote as Revolutionary War debts, nineteenth-century steamboat monopolies, and early twentieth-century immigration issues. They continue to have great practical importance for the modern environmental lawyer. In policy circles, "devolution" of authority from the federal government to the states is all the rage. At the same time, since the early 1990s the Supreme Court has struck down more legislation — federal and state — on federalism-related grounds than arguably at any time in its past. Far from being of marginal concern in environmental law, federalism has, with these developments, assumed a central role.

Section 1. THE ROLES OF FEDERALISM IN DETERMINING ENVIRONMENTAL OUTCOMES

In thinking about why the federal-state relationship is important in environmental policy, consider, as a first example, the nuclear power industry. Without a division of power between the federal government and the states, the industry likely would not exist. Nuclear generation is a risk-laden enterprise. Moreover, if a major accident happens, the losses will be astronomical and will create tort liability that would bankrupt virtually any private entity. It is also an industry that faces immense costs of facility construction and operation, which act as further barriers to entry for commercial nuclear power generators. To encourage commercial nuclear generation in the face of those risks and barriers to entry, a government must create a legal environment in which these obstacles are managed efficiently and in which economies of scale are realized. If every single facility has to "reinvent the wheel" to be licensed and built, the undertaking becomes enormously expensive and the redundancies wasteful. Likewise, if all 50 states are free to regulate the industry, the chances are great that their 50 sets of regulations (each influenced by local concerns, such as the in-state coal producers in one state, or a strong antinuclear lobby in another) will read like a crazy quilt that forestalls creation of the industry. It is economically more prudent, under that scenario, to invest in fossil fuel generation or some other means to supply electricity. But American federalism created a way out of that scenario by giving the national government the power to preempt the states from acting. With respect to nuclear power, the national government exercised that power in two ways. First, in 1957, in the Price-Anderson Act,[1] Congress used its affirmative authority to limit the total liability for a nuclear accident to $560 million (peanuts in the post-*Exxon-Valdez* punitive damages world). Under the Supremacy Clause of the U.S. Constitution, no state law can require more. Second, it allowed the industry to realize the economies of scale offered by unitary regulation of reactors, expressly forbidding state regulation of facility design and safety.[2]

In other environmental controversies, American federalism may play a different, but still critical, role. What if a state, through geologic fortuity, is home to the nation's single best and largest hazardous waste disposal site? The site is developed for just that purpose by the nation's largest and most experienced hazardous materials handling firm. The firm is able to do so at a relatively low cost because the site is so geologically favorable. Concurrently, the NIMBY ("not in my back yard") phenomenon is at fever pitch, making it very hard for any other sites to obtain licenses and driving up disposal prices due to the scarcity of disposal sites. As a result of all this, the site is both the safest site in the nation and, by a wide margin, the most economical site in the nation. Can the state withhold from out-of-state generators of hazardous wastes the benefit of using the site for disposal? More shrewdly, can the state allow its own citizens to use the site for a low cost by barely taxing disposal of in-state wastes, while charging the operator more for out-of-state wastes? The answer to this legal question, and many more like it, again

---

1. Pub. L. No. 85-256, 71 Stat. 576 (1957).
2. Atomic Energy Act of 1954, 42 U.S.C. §§2011 et seq., especially §2074. See Northern States Power Co. v. Minnesota, 447 F.2d 1143 (8th Cir. 1971), aff'd, 405 U.S. 1035 (1972).

turns on the intricate division of power between the states and national government — federalism.

As if the environmental disputes that are controlled by the preemption cases and interstate commerce cases are not enough, federalism has even more facets of importance for environmental laws. Not only does our federalism include doctrines that subordinate state power to that of the central government, but whole lines of cases also curtail national power in favor of state power. Even more bewildering, the norm in most areas of environmental regulation is that the controversies — from pollution and licensing of miners to management of wild burros on the public lands — are regulated by *both* the national government and the states. Add to that the uneven efforts of the two governments to work cooperatively, and the possible complexity seems endless.

Rather than decrying that state of affairs, many lawyers find in the complexity and subtlety of federalism an opportunity for making interesting tactical choices. Some of the tactics are fairly straightforward: If the law of the one sovereign is anathema to the client, try to have it invalidated as being in contravention of the constitutional division of authority. In the nuclear and hazardous waste disposal hypotheticals above, the effort was to knock out state law, but the arguments can run the other way. For example, a lawyer representing a would-be land developer whose project is going to be blocked by federal wetland regulation of non-navigable, intrastate waterways might argue that the federal law being used is not a proper exercise of Congress's authority under the Commerce Clause.

More subtle tactical maneuvering occurs in cases in which state and federal regulation overlap. Here, federalism has altered the way in which practicing lawyers represent their clients by raising the possibility of what might be called "forum shopping." A lawyer may try to influence the law's impact on a client by deliberately seeking to have the particular issue handled in one system or the other, either state or federal, depending upon which system is more favorable to the client's interests.

Imagine representing a client who owns a brownfields[3] parcel and wants to clean up the existing contamination and redevelop the parcel for light commercial use. As explored more fully in Chapter 19, there are concurrent federal and state regulations that might apply to the cleanup, imposing standards of how clean the parcel needs to be at the end of the process and the means by which the cleanup is effected. As a strategic matter, the lawyer will consider whether there is a practical advantage to the client that might favor seeking to have the cleanup governed by one sovereign or the other. The advantages might be, for example, a difference in the expected cost or duration of the process. As it turns out, because of the efforts and institutional need of the federal government to work cooperatively with the states in this field (and others), the affected party (i.e., the client) may be able to steer the case into one system or the other. In this way, the federalism superstructure that favors concurrency of regulatory authority becomes a fertile ground for tactical maneuvering by lawyers.

---

3 *Brownfields* is the term given to urban land that has been used in the past and become environmentally degraded, as through the presence of contaminants. Nevertheless, for reasons of location and sound urban policy, many brownfields sites now are being considered for redevelopment. The usual competing option is *greenfields* land, that is, land that lies beyond the urban area in the as-yet-undeveloped surrounding farmland and open space.

The bottom line for these federalism doctrines and structures is that they strongly affect outcomes in the real world. Even that may not be enough to make all of what follows scintillating for everyone.

Section 2. BASIC FEDERALISM PRECEPTS

To begin at the most fundamental level, in a constitutional democracy, as a matter of elementary political theory, whatever is enshrined in the Constitution takes precedence over "mere" legislation or other efforts to alter constitutionally established norms. In the United States, the judiciary is the branch of government that serves as the guardian of constitutional norms. Exercising judicial review, the courts will invalidate laws and regulations that are inconsistent with constitutional requirements. Judicial review relies heavily on discerning the intent of the Framers of the Constitution in interpreting and applying its doctrines to specific cases.

In regard to federal-state relations, the intent of the Framers of the U.S. Constitution is well understood at a general level. The Framers were keenly aware of the potential for conflict between the central government and the states. The document itself established a division of authority that has remained largely intact for two centuries, altered only by a few duly ratified amendments. The core concept is that the federal government is not given general powers, but only specific enumerated powers. If this principle was not made sufficiently clear by a carefully drawn list of powers granted to the central government, the Tenth Amendment, ratified almost as the ink was drying on the original document, stated:

> The powers not delegated to the United States by the Constitution, nor prohibited by it to the States, are reserved to the States respectively, or to the people.

On a structural level, this arrangement reflected the political reality. Although they had need of forming a union to secure their independence from England, at the time of forming the nation, the states were a group of independent sovereigns. For the states, the controlling premise in forming the union was continuation of their sovereignty to the fullest extent, with only a limited cession of power to the newly created national entity. The Tenth Amendment made this explicit; the states ceded only those powers expressly given to the national government and those that were specifically forbidden to the states in the Constitution.[4]

Despite leaving a great deal of power in the states, the constitutional power granted to the federal government was substantial. To avoid a narrow view of the enumerated powers from being an impediment that hamstrung the newly formed entity, the Framers included the "Necessary and Proper Clause," supplementing the enumerated powers with such lesser powers as are needed to effectuate the specifically granted ones.

---

4. This latter concept is less familiar. A well-known prohibition of that latter type forbids the states from coining money. See U.S. Const., Art. I, §10, cl. 1. Another such prohibition forbids the states from entering into compacts (agreements to work together) unless Congress ratifies the action. See U. S. Const., Art. I, §10, cl. 3. This prohibition prevents states from combining with one another to the detriment of other states or the nation. In the environmental and natural resources area, compacts often are made with Congress's blessing regarding the allocation of interstate resources such as rivers.

Even more significant to federal-state relations is the Supremacy Clause of Article VI, which provides:

> This Constitution, and the Laws of the United States which shall be made in Pursuance thereof; and all Treaties made, or which shall be made, under the authority of the United States, shall be the supreme Law of the Land; and the Judges in every State shall be bound thereby, any Thing in the Constitution or Laws of any State to the Contrary notwithstanding.

The supremacy of federal law is of considerable importance for environmental regulation and creates the possibility of tension between the national government and the states. Assume as a starting point, for now, the proposition that environmental regulation fits within the federal government's interstate commerce power.[5] From this alone, because of the Supremacy Clause, Congress is empowered to enact regulation and have that regulation take precedence over state regulation of the same conduct. Recall, however, (1) the retention of as much sovereignty as possible by the states, and (2) the fact that environmental regulation was traditionally a state function at the core of the state police power to regulate for health, safety, and welfare.

The potentially antagonistic concepts of federal supremacy and the continuing sovereignty of the states, can be, and often are, reconciled by creating a presumption in favor of the validity of concurrent regulation by both the federal and state governments. The presumption of concurrency means, most simply, that state regulation is permitted absent additional indications that the federal government intends to employ its supremacy to block concurrent state activity.[6] This presumption does not do violence to the constitutional division of power. Indeed, especially in the environmental field, it would be odd to expect that the mere fact that Congress does some regulating, absent something more, would be enough to completely displace the ability of the states to exercise their traditional police power authority over the same subject. Also, it is only a presumption of concurrency, one that is subject to revision by Congress in the legislative process.

Over time, two lines of cases have emerged that delineate the extent to which federal laws and regulation displace state authority because of federal supremacy. The more general line of cases addresses the subject in terms of "federal preemption." The narrower line of cases applies to state efforts that directly affect the interstate movement of goods and services and is described as involving the "dormant Commerce Clause."

As a doctrinal matter affecting environmental law, there is more to federalism than just preemption and dormant Commerce Clause cases. There are two more pieces to the "power puzzle": (1) defining what falls within the enumerated powers of the United States (and what is beyond those powers) and (2) mapping out the very complex issue of state sovereign immunity in cases that are litigated in the courts of the federal sovereign. These last two topics are addressed at the end of the chapter.

---

5. The scope of the federal commerce power has varied over time. Recent cases, discussed below, raise questions concerning the limits of that federal power.

6. The one generic setting in which additional factors need not be present in finding a denial to the states of concurrent regulatory power is in the judge-made "dormant Commerce Clause" doctrine. For environmental law, the dormant Commerce Clause doctrine affects natural resources and the movement of solid waste.

B. PREEMPTION OF STATE LAW

Establishing concurrent regulation as the norm does not negate the power of supremacy. Thus, for example, if Congress expressly says that there shall be only federal law on an environmental topic, state laws to the contrary are preempted. Congressional action of this type is called *express preemption*. In the environmental field, express preemption is not often used, but there are a few examples, prominent among them express federal preemption of state regulation of nuclear safety through the Atomic Energy Act of 1954. As we saw in Chapter 5, most federal environmental statutes leave room for the states to regulate more stringently than federal law.

Express preemption is not the only way in which the effect of the Supremacy Clause can lead to the invalidation of state environmental regulation. The U.S. Supreme Court, in a case involving pesticide regulation, summarized the general framework of preemption analysis as follows:

> Under the Supremacy Clause, U.S. Const., Art. VI, cl. 2, state laws that "interfere with, or are contrary to the laws of Congress, made in pursuance of the constitution" are invalid. Gibbons v. Ogden, 9 Wheat. 1, 211 (1824, Marshall, C.J.). The ways in which federal law may preempt state law are well established and in the first instance turn on congressional intent. Congress' intent to supplant state authority in a particular field may be express in the terms of the statute. Absent explicit preemptive language, Congress' intent to supersede state law in a given area may nonetheless be implicit if a scheme of federal regulation is "so pervasive as to make reasonable the inference that Congress left no room for the States to supplement it," if "the Act of Congress...touch[es] a field in which the federal interest is so dominant that the federal system will be assumed to preclude enforcement of state laws on the same subject," or if the goals "sought to be obtained" and the "obligations imposed" reveal a purpose to preclude state authority. Rice v. Santa Fe Elevator Corp., 331 U.S. 218, 230 (1947). See Pacific Gas & Electric Co. v. State Energy Resources Conservation and Development Commission, 461 U.S. 190, 203–204 (1983). When considering preemption, "we start with the assumption that the historic police powers of the States were not to be superseded by the Federal Act unless that was the clear and manifest purpose of Congress." *Rice*, 331 U.S. at 230.[7]

Even when Congress has not chosen to occupy a particular field, preemption may occur to the extent that state and federal law actually conflict. Such a conflict arises when "compliance with both federal and state regulations is a physical impossibility," Florida Lime & Avocado Growers, Inc. v. Paul, 373 U.S. 132, 142–143 (1963), or when a state law "stands as an obstacle to the accomplishment and execution of the full purposes and objectives of Congress." Hines v. Davidowitz, 312 U.S. 52 (1941). Naturally enough, the three categories of preemption are known as *express*, *occupation of the field*, and *conflict preemption*. As we will see, while general statements of the law of federal preemption are succinct and appear straightforward, the cases themselves frequently are difficult to understand and turn on very subtle distinctions.

---

7. Wisconsin Public Intervenor v. Mortier, 501 U.S. 597, 605 (1991).

Section 1. EXPRESS PREEMPTION

In principle, the most straightforward case for preemption is one in which Congress explicitly provides that state regulation is superseded by federal law. Even here, however, ambiguities arise. Congress seldom speaks with perfect clarity, and often it seeks to displace some but not all state regulation in a particular area. Add to this the Court's oft-stated (but not always applied) presumption against preemption, and cases can become very complicated indeed.

The prize for creating the longest-running, most contentious environmental preemption disputes must go to the states' efforts to regulate automobile emissions. The Clean Air Act allows only California — the only state that regulated automobile emissions before March 30, 1966 (42 U.S.C. §7543(b)) — to set stricter emissions standards for mobile sources than the federal government sets. Under §177 of the Act, however, other states may "piggyback" onto California's rules, under certain fairly stringent conditions, including the requirement that the other states' programs be "identical to California standards for which a waiver has been granted." In the 1990s, as we discuss in greater detail in Chapter 15, California developed a set of automobile emissions requirements that, among other things, initially imposed a minimum quota on the sales of "zero emission vehicles," or ZEVs. New York and Massachusetts followed suit with their own sales quotas. However, in response to severe pressure from the automobile industry, California abandoned its regulations establishing near-term ZEV quotas and replaced them with MOAs (memoranda of agreement), setting forth the same basic requirements. In one of many such cases in this interminable saga, the automobile manufacturers sued the northeastern states, alleging that their ZEV quotas were preempted by the CAA as a result of California's legal machinations.

Association of International Automobile Manufacturers v. Massachusetts Department of Environmental Protection
208 F.3d 1 (1st Cir. 2000)

TORRUELLA, C.J.... The district court held that the MOAs entered into by California and the automakers are not standards within the meaning of §177, because they are voluntary contractual agreements rather than legislation or formal administrative regulations. The court found that both the language and the legislative history of the CAA suggested that the provisions of §§209 and 177 were intended to govern formal regulations adopted by the states, rather than voluntary and cooperative agreements between the states and automakers.

The district court's ruling is consistent with Supreme Court precedents holding that federal preemption is generally confined to formal state laws and regulations and not applicable to contracts and other voluntary agreements.

Furthermore, this is the general position taken by the EPA in its opinion letter [written in response to an earlier opinion of the court in the same litigation]:

> EPA believes that in general, provisions in voluntary agreements ordinarily should not be considered "standards" subject to section 209(a). The language of the statute appears to indicate that provisions in voluntary agreements should not generally be considered standards under section 209. The legislative history of section 209 also appears to indicate that the prohibition in section 209 is meant to apply to state mandates (regulations and laws), not voluntary agreements.

Moreover, if production requirements in voluntary agreements were generally preempted, then every such requirement in agreements in every state would be preempted.... EPA believes it would be an inappropriate interpretation of section 209(a) to treat all such agreements as prohibited.

Nevertheless, the EPA concluded that the "unique circumstances of this case" supported a determination that these particular MOAs were standards for purposes of §§209 and 177.

We agree with the EPA's general analysis, but not with its specific conclusion in this case. We do not share the agency's willingness to create an exception in this case that would be inconsistent with the statutory language and congressional intent. The EPA concluded that the California MOAs should be considered standards because (1) they replaced the binding ZEV requirements enacted in 1990; (2) the MOAs provided for severe contractual remedies in the event of nonperformance by the automakers; and (3) there were indications that California and the automakers entered into the MOAs intending that other states not be able to copy them under §177 as they could formal regulations. We find these considerations insufficient to support a conclusion at odds with the EPA's general (and, we think, correct) interpretation of the statute. Although we understand the EPA's central concern — that allowing agreements such as the MOAs to escape §177 analysis could interfere with the ability of other states to emulate the regulatory scheme actually in effect in California — we think that our result is dictated by the plain language and intent of the statute. The circumstances of this case provide no sufficient justification, if in fact one could exist, for ignoring the mandates of the Act.

The frustration felt by the EPA and Massachusetts likely stems in part from the fact that Massachusetts' aim in enacting the ZEV mandates was to reduce air pollution, a laudable goal in its own right and, more importantly, the central purpose of the Clean Air Act. However, in enacting §§209 and 177, Congress chose carefully the means by which to implement the Act's purpose, and we are not at liberty to modify Congress's determination....

Because the California MOAs are not "standards" for purposes of §177 of the CAA, Massachusetts' regulations purporting to copy them are not "identical to California standards for which a waiver has been granted" as required by §177. We therefore hold that the Massachusetts ZEV mandates are preempted by the CAA....

COMMENTARY & QUESTIONS

1. **California as super-sovereign?** Notice how unusual the CAA's preemption scheme is, giving a kind of "super-sovereign" status to California as the only state allowed to enact its very own automobile emissions standards. Does this create room for special deals between California and the automobile companies? Is that what happened in this case?

2. **Win some, lose some.** In other cases involving their efforts to adopt the California standards, Massachusetts and New York have enjoyed more success. For example, their rules for non-ZEVs were substantially upheld against a no-holds-barred legal attack by the automobile industry, and these rules are helping to determine the shape of the New York and Massachusetts automobile fleet today. Indeed, the California rules (along with other states' adoption of them) have affected the entire nation's car fleet.

3. **Civil rights for car companies?** After this decision, the automobile companies asked for attorneys' fees for having won this lawsuit. They brought their claim for fees under 42 U.S.C. §1988, which provides for attorneys' fees to prevailing parties in cases involving the violation of, among other statutes, 42 U.S.C. §1983. Section 1983, for its part,

provides a cause of action for persons subjected to "the deprivation of any rights, privileges, or immunities secured by the Constitution...." Since the automobile companies' case was brought under the Constitution's Supremacy Clause, a magistrate hearing their claim was persuaded that it fit within the scope of §1988. The Massachusetts Department of Environmental Protection (DEP) asked the district court to exercise its discretion not to award fees because of the "special circumstances" of the case. The magistrate responded:

> DEP...argues that the Manufacturers' allegedly unsavory lobbying efforts in California resulted in the regulations being moved to the memoranda of understanding for the express purpose of defeating other states' regulations. As DEP puts it, "In view of the automakers' conduct in taking affirmative steps to subvert Massachusetts' legitimate program in pursuance of the Clean Air Act's purpose to protect the public health and environment, the Court should exercise its discretion to deny the application for fees as unjust." DEP's passion is clear. However, a fee petition is not the appropriate forum to argue the "public good" — those issues are best debated in the legislature. Case law mandates that the Manufacturers recover fees and expenses in the instant case. DaimlerChrysler Corp. v. Commissioner, 2001 U.S. Dist. LEXIS 18325, 53 ERC (BNA) 1728 (D. Mass. 2001).

The magistrate recommended that the district judge order Massachusetts to pay the automobile manufacturers approximately a quarter of a million dollars in attorneys' fees. The parties later settled for $100,000.

4. **California's own preemption problems.** Northeastern states aren't the only ones experiencing preemption difficulties. In Central Valley Chrysler Plymouth v. California Air Res. Bd., 2002 U.S. Dist. LEXIS 20403 (E.D. Cal. 2002), the court granted a preliminary injunction against a California regulation that allowed automobile manufacturers to meet California's emissions requirements partly through the use of fuel-efficient automobile technologies (specifically, advanced gasoline hybrid vehicles). Because the car companies had complained that they could not meet the ZEV mandates California had earlier imposed, California had offered the alternative of advanced hybrids as a way of lowering the regulatory burden the car companies faced. But no good deed goes unpunished. Car manufacturers sued, alleging that California's program was preempted by the Energy Conservation Policy Act of 1975, which provides for federal fuel efficiency standards and contains the following preemption clause:

> When an average fuel economy standard prescribed under this chapter is in effect, a State or a political subdivision of a State may not adopt or enforce a law or regulation related to fuel economy standards or average fuel economy standards for automobiles covered by an average fuel economy standard under this chapter.

Because the car companies' ability to take advantage of California's new regulatory alternative turned in part on the fuel efficiency of their cars, the court held that California's program was preempted by the federal fuel efficiency law. The case was settled while an appeal to the Ninth Circuit was pending. Nevertheless, the district court's decision is a cautionary tale for states attempting both to avoid preemption problems and to offer companies the kind of regulatory flexibility for which they have long clamored.

5. **The *Engine Manufacturers* case.** Southern California has long had the worst air

quality in the country (although by some measures, Houston, Texas, has "caught up with" California in this regard). In addition to statewide rules on automobile emissions, discussed previously, the South Coast Air Quality Management District has established "fleet rules" requiring that when certain local operators of car or truck fleets purchase or replace fleet vehicles, they may acquire only certain motor vehicles, identified by the District. Most of the allowable vehicles are alternative-fuel vehicles. The Engine Manufacturers Association challenged the fleet rules, arguing that they were preempted by §209 of the CAA because they were unlawful "standard[s] relating to the control of emissions from new motor vehicles or motor vehicle engines." In Engine Mfrs. Ass'n v. South Coast Air Quality Mgmt. Dist., 158 F. Supp. 2d 1107 (C.D. Cal. 2001), the district court rejected their challenge with the following explanation:

> …The Rules regulate the purchasing and leasing, not the sale, of vehicles by fleet operators. Fleet operators are required to purchase "cleaner" vehicles when adding or replacing fleet vehicles. The Fleet Rules accept as given the existing [California Air Resources Board (CARB)] vehicle standards; they merely require fleet operators to choose from among the least polluting of CARB-certified, available vehicles. The Rules impose no new emission requirements on manufacturers whatsoever, and therefore do not run afoul of Congress's purpose behind motor vehicle preemption: namely, the protection of manufacturers against having to build engines in compliance with a multiplicity of standards.

> Furthermore, the Fleet Rules do not set a "standard relating to the control of emissions." Rather than imposing any numerical control on new vehicles, the rules regulate the purchase of previously-certified vehicles…. The Fleet Rules require purchasers to choose from among a subset of previously certified California vehicles. Where a state regulation does not compel manufacturers to meet a new emissions limit, but rather affects the purchase of vehicles, as the Fleet Rules do, that regulation is not a standard. No restriction on the sale of vehicles is present here. Plaintiffs may continue to sell any vehicle which is otherwise certified in California….

The Ninth Circuit affirmed the district court's opinion without writing a new opinion of its own. The Supreme Court granted certiorari, setting oral argument for the Court's 2003–2004 Term. The United States filed an amicus brief in support of the engine manufacturers' claim of preemption.

6. **Is a state's purpose relevant?** In the environmental area, the case of Huron Portland Cement Co. v. Detroit, 362 U.S. 440 (1960), marked the emergence of a distinctive trend in environmental preemption litigation. That case upheld a local Detroit smoke abatement ordinance that was applied to ships that docked at Detroit. The cement company owned and operated ships whose boilers had to remain fired while in port in order to operate the deck equipment for loading and unloading. The particular boilers in question had operational characteristics that caused them to violate Detroit's Smoke Abatement Code. Those same boilers were regulated by federal law; they were inspected by the Coast Guard and found to meet all applicable federal requirements. The Court stated that the relevant legislation

> make[s] clear that inspection of boilers and related equipment is for the purpose of seeing to it that the equipment "may be safely employed in the service proposed."…
> By contrast, the sole aim of the Detroit ordinance is the elimination of air

pollution to protect the health and enhance the cleanliness of the local community. 362 U.S. at 445.

In *Huron Portland Cement*, it was conceded that the boilers could not easily be retrofitted to meet the Detroit standards and might have to be replaced. Thus the "different purposes" test, as it might be called, does not sit easily alongside the line of cases that invalidate state regulations because of the difficulty or impossibility of complying with both federal and state rules.

Nevertheless, in Pacific Gas & Elec. v. California Energy Res. Conservation & Dev. Comm'n, 461 U.S. 190 (1983), the Court again invoked the "different purposes" test in upholding a state law against a preemption challenge. Utility companies claimed that a California law requiring findings by a state agency that adequate means were available for the storage and disposal of nuclear waste was preempted by the Atomic Energy Act of 1954. California argued that its law was motivated by economic concerns, not safety concerns, and that the Atomic Energy Act had preserved state authority to regulate the economics of electricity production. The Court agreed with California, along the way giving the impression that if a state regulation were inspired by a purpose different from allegedly preemptive federal regulation, the state regulation would stand. Subsequent cases, however, have made clear that this broad reading of *Pacific Gas & Electric* is incorrect. In English v. General Elec. Co., 496 U.S. 72 (1990), the Court explained *Pacific Gas & Electric* as follows: "[E]ven as the Court suggested that part of the pre-empted field is defined by reference to the purpose of the state law in question, it made clear that another part of the field is defined by the state law's actual effect on nuclear safety."

7. **Federal preemption of tort remedies.** In Silkwood v. Kerr-McGee, 464 U.S. 238 (1984), sizable awards of state common law damages, both compensatory and punitive, were upheld against a claim of federal preemption of nuclear safety issues. In English v. General Elec. Co., cited in the preceding note, the Court revisited the subject of preemption of tort remedies in another case involving a nuclear materials processor as defendant. In that case, the plaintiff reported workplace safety violations and eventually was fired by her employer. She sought a statutory remedy under a federal whistleblower's provision but was denied relief on procedural grounds. She subsequently filed a state common law tort suit for intentional infliction of emotional distress and was met with the claim of federal preemption. A unanimous Supreme Court rejected the preemption argument. The Court stated:

> Although the decision in *Silkwood* was based in substantial part on legislative history suggesting that Congress did not intend to include in the preempted field state tort remedies for radiation-based injuries, we think it would be odd, if not irrational, to conclude that Congress intended to include tort actions stemming from retaliation against whistleblowers in the preempted field but intended not to include tort actions stemming from radiation damage suffered as a result of actual safety violations. 496 U.S. at 85.

The Court also rejected the narrower argument that the enactment of a federal whistleblower remedy precluded the availability of additional state law-based remedies that served a similar purpose.

8. Do savings clauses save anything anymore? The savings clause, a tool extensively used by the federal environmental statutes, ostensibly preserves the ability of states to adopt requirements different from — and typically more stringent than — those imposed by the federal program. They attempt to prevent, in other words, the preemption of state requirements by the federal program. Recently, however, the Supreme Court has found some savings clauses inadequate to the task.

In a unanimous decision in United States v. Locke, 529 U.S. 89 (2000), the Court held that federal law preempted Washington State's regulations covering oil tankers in state waters, a law enacted in the oily wake of the *Exxon Valdez*. Washington had earlier adopted similar rules, but the Supreme Court held them preempted by the Ports and Waterways Safety Act of 1972 (PWSA), 86 Stat. 424, in Ray v. Atlantic Richfield Co., 435 U.S. 151 (1978).

Title I of the Oil Pollution Act of 1990 (OPA), 33 U.S.C. §2701, includes several savings clauses that appear to grant states leeway to adopt more stringent standards than those prescribed by OPA. Washington contended that these clauses had altered the preemptive effect given the PWSA in *Ray*. The Court read the clauses narrowly and found that *Ray*'s holding was unaffected by OPA. It found that their placement in a title captioned "Oil Pollution Liability and Compensation" indicated that they were not intended to cover tanker regulation as a whole, but rather were limited to preserving state rules relevant to the subject matter of Title I: "The evident purpose of the savings clauses is to preserve state laws which, rather than imposing substantive regulation of a vessel's primary conduct, establish liability rules and financial requirements relating to oil spills." *Locke*, 529 U.S. at 105. The Court also found the clauses too weak to defeat a long history of comprehensive federal regulation in the field:

> We think it quite unlikely that Congress would use a means so indirect as the savings clauses in Title I of OPA to upset the settled division of authority by allowing states to impose additional unique substantive regulation on the at-sea conduct of vessels. We decline to give broad effect to saving clauses where doing so would upset the careful regulatory scheme established by federal law. Id. at 106.

Later in the same term, in its 5-4 decision in Geier v. American Honda Motor Co., 529 U.S. 861 (2000), the Court took a similarly narrow view of a savings clause, as applied to federal preemption of state tort claims. The Court found that the National Traffic and Motor Vehicle Safety Act of 1966, 15 U.S.C. §1381, preempted a state tort claim alleging a design defect in the omission of a driver's side airbag. The Act expressly preempts "any safety standard" different from a federal standard, 15 U.S.C. §1392(d), but also contains a savings clause that states that "compliance with" a federal standard "does not exempt any person from any liability under common law." 15 U.S.C. §1397(k). The Court held the express preemption provision inapplicable, finding that the savings clause prevented its application to tort actions. The Court nevertheless concluded that the state lawsuit was preempted based on implied conflict preemption principles. Neither the express preemption provision nor the savings clause, the Court reasoned, demonstrated a congressional intention to preclude the operation of conflict preemption doctrine.

The Court embraced the same kind of logic in Buckman Co. v. Plaintiffs' Legal Comm., 531 U.S. 341 (2001). There, the Court held that a state law fraud claim, premised on the assertion that the manufacturer of a medical device had obtained federal approval for its product only through fraudulent representations to the FDA, was impliedly preempted by the federal law governing medical devices due to the conflict state tort law would create with the federal scheme. A preemption clause in the statute arguably afforded the possibility of a narrow interpretation, thus saving the state tort claim, but the Court concluded it need not even look at the preemption clause because it had found a conflict between the state and federal regimes.

These cases may have significant ramifications for interpretation of the federal environmental statutes. Savings clauses are an important part of federal environmental law. First, they protect a state's ability to adopt standards more protective than required by the uniform baseline of environmental quality that the federal statutes purport to guarantee. As *Locke* demonstrates, a narrow reading of a savings clause may prevent states from choosing a level of environmental protection or risk reduction more stringent than that established by federal law. Perhaps more importantly, it undermines a role that the states have played repeatedly in the history of federal environmental law: states as "laboratories" developing regulatory approaches that are subsequently adopted at the national level. The less states are able to exceed federal standards, the less experimentation will be available to inform future iterations of federal policy.

Savings clauses in the environmental statutes also guarantee that those harmed by pollution and other environmental insults may avail themselves of any available state common law remedies. See, e.g., 33 U.S.C. §1365(e) (CWA); 42 U.S.C. §7604(e) (CAA). This sort of clause — similar to that at issue in *Geier* — goes toward preventing pollution hot spots by allowing affected parties to bring tort suits to respond to the distributional elements of pollution that may go unconsidered in programs predicated on ensuring environmental quality at regional, state, and national levels. Here again, if the Court is adopting a sub rosa canon of interpretation that disfavors preemption savings clauses, communities may lose the capacity to respond to these localized environmental threats.

9. **Other environmental preemptions.** Preemption issues have arisen in a variety of other environmental controversies, in which regulated interests have attempted to use federal law to trump state or local regulations (or state law to trump local regulations). The cases include efforts to prevent local town governments from passing ordinances requiring stricter standards of herbicide and pesticide applicators, as in *Mortier*, to industry efforts to prevent states from banning potentially harmful fuel additives. For a sample, see Oxygenated Fuels Ass'n v. Davis, 331 F.3d 665 (9th Cir. 2003) (upholding California's ban on fuel additive MTBE against preemption challenge based on CAA); Boyes v. Shell Oil Prods. Co., 199 F.3d 1260 (5th Cir. 2000) (Florida statute prohibiting individual's suit for remediation of property contaminated with petroleum from nearby service stations preempted by federal Resource Conservation and Recovery Act's citizen suit provision); CSX Transp. v. Public Util. Comm'n of Ohio, 901 F.2d 497 (6th Cir. 1990) (federal rail safety act preempted most of the state hazardous material transport law).

Section 2. **PREEMPTING STATE INTERFERENCE WITH FEDERAL RESOURCE PROGRAMS**

Beginning in the latter half of the nineteenth century with the federal mining acts and the creation of the National Forest system on the federal public lands, Congress established numerous federal resource management programs designed to promote a variety of declared national interests. When states try to regulate the environmental impacts of federal programs and their licensees, thorny preemption issues arise.

Generically, these cases most often raise claims that the state law interferes with the accomplishment of federal objectives. In broad terms, the argument goes like this: The federal agency, by licensing the private activity as part of its resource management program, has affirmatively authorized the activity; state laws that bar or burden the activity therefore conflict with federal law. The counterargument rests on the view that federal licenses or permits are not intended to divest states of their traditional police power authority, including environmental quality regulation.

Frequently, however, cases are complicated by the fact that many federal licensing programs also include their own environmental standards and reviews. If a federal agency imposes environmentally protective conditions on its licensees, the preemption argument against additional state environmental regulation is strengthened. At that point, the additional state environmental review may be redundant and, more tellingly, inconsistent with federal determination of the proper balance between environmental quality and other national programmatic objectives. In this situation, concurrent state regulation arguably constitutes an interference with the federal program.

In California v. Federal Energy Regulatory Comm'n (FERC), 495 U.S. 490 (1990), a proposed hydroelectric facility on a tributary of the American River in California (Rock Creek), threatened to reduce stream flows in a way that would adversely affect fisheries. FERC, as part of its licensing process and pursuant to congressional directives,[8] reviewed information on these issues and granted the applicant a license that prescribed specified minimum stream flows. FERC's minimum flow standard allowed stream flows to decline to less than a third of the state's proposed minimum requirements. The Supreme Court held that FERC's minimal standards governed. The Court applied the arguments of its 1946 decision in First Iowa Hydro-Electric Coop. v. FPC, 328 U.S. 152, interpreting §27 of the FPA, which specifically disclaims any congressional aim to "affect[] or intend[] to affect or in any way to interfere with the laws of the respective States relating to the control, appropriation, use, or distribution of water used in irrigation or for municipal or other uses, or any vested right acquired therein." Faced with the seemingly clear intent of Congress to preserve state water regulatory powers, the First Iowa decision had narrowed the clause's meaning, holding that its preservation of state jurisdiction is "confined to rights of the same nature as those relating to the use of water in irrigation or for municipal purposes." 328 U.S. at 175–176. With this case as its guide, the Supreme Court held in California v. FERC that

---

8. The Electric Consumers Protection Act of 1986, Pub. L. No. 99-495, codified as part of the Federal Power Act at 16. U.S.C. §§797(e) and 808(a), requires FERC to consider fish and wildlife effects in making its licensure determinations, although in practice the statutory standards are neither substantively nor procedurally rigorous.

California could not impose its own more environmentally protective stream flow requirements.[9]

California Coastal Comm'n v. Granite Rock Co., 480 U.S. 572 (1987), presented a similarly subtle preemption problem. Granite Rock had obtained a permit from the U.S. Forest Service to mine for pharmaceutical grade white limestone in a portion of the Los Padres National Forest near Big Sur (California). Due to the land's proximity to the Pacific coast, the area was also within the jurisdiction of the California Coastal Commission (CCC), a state agency having extensive land use planning and environmental protection powers. Despite the existence of the federal permit, CCC directed Granite Rock to apply to it for an additional permit, a request that was met with a lawsuit claiming that the CCC's authority had been preempted.

The Supreme Court rejected Granite Rock's argument that the state process was preempted by federal law, and required Granite Rock to submit to the state permit proceeding. One key to the ruling lay in the language of the Forest Service regulations, several of which called for federal licensees to comply with applicable state environmental quality standards; one regulation specifically mentioned state permits' usefulness for proving such compliance with state regulations. See 36 C.F.R. §§228.5(b), 228.8(a)–(c), (h).

The licensee's second major contention in the Supreme Court was that the CCC's actions were a thinly veiled effort to reverse the Forest Service's choices under its land use planning mandate, contained in the National Forest Management Act of 1976, 16 U.S.C.A. §§1600–1614. Granite Rock claimed that CCC was trying to prohibit mining in an area that the Forest Service had determined was appropriate for mining. The majority found this challenge speculative; CCC had not acted to impose any conditions or requirements on Granite Rock prior to the filing of the lawsuit.

Justice O'Connor's majority opinion also drew a rather fine semantic distinction between land use planning and environmental protection:

> The California Coastal Commission alleges that it will use its permit requirement to impose reasonable environmental regulation.... Federal land use statutes and regulations, while arguably expressing an intent to preempt state land use planning, distinguish environmental regulation from land use planning. 480 U.S. at 593.

COMMENTARY & QUESTIONS

1. **The case for finding preemption.** *Granite Rock* presents a strong case for displacement of state authority. The parallel state authority that is to be exercised affects lands in federal ownership that are part of the National Forest system and that are being managed under an articulated "multiple use" mandate that establishes federal policies

---

9. In Nugget Hydroelectric Co. v. SWRCB, Civs-90-0203 EJG/EM (E.D. Cal. July 9, 1991), the preemptive effect of California v. FERC was extended to divest the California State Water Resource Control Board (SWRCB) of the authority to require the FERC licensee to submit information to the state on issues other than the availability of water. The SWRCB had required Nugget to provide more thorough analyses of the in-stream impacts of its project than those provided to FERC, at which point Nugget withdrew its application for a SWRCB permit and went to federal court seeking a preemption-based order to save it from having to "jump through a never-ending series of hoops [that] relate to matters already reviewed by FERC," adding that "the delay and cost impose a tremendous hardship on plaintiff [Nugget]." The court preempted the SWRCB efforts.

regarding the administration of National Forest tracts. See Chapter 25. To whatever extent the California Coastal Commission (CCC) might thwart a federally approved project, there is both an intrusion upon federal government planning and de facto imposition of state land use controls on federal land. These points motivated a dissent by Justice Powell (joined by Justice Stevens) and a dissent by Justice Scalia (joined by Justice White). Even so, a majority of the Court was willing to support concurrent regulatory control as long as there was no concrete conflict of regulations. What can the CCC now impose by way of conditions that would not be in conflict with the Forest Service plan? Would erosion and dust emission control requirements that forced Granite Rock to keep excavated materials covered during mining operations, or a strict postmining reclamation requirement, be allowed? Does it matter how much compliance with such requirements would cost? What if, for example, the increased cost made the proposed mining project more expensive than other feasible alternative sites?

2. **Local expertise and pluralism.** Do concurrent regulatory authorities make sense? Concurrency almost surely is less efficient, with dual filings, studies, and processing. Congress and the federal agencies have become the de facto primary regulators. But perhaps CCC has better local knowledge and environmental expertise than the federal district ranger? Or does concurrency reflect a salutary measure of respect for states' sovereignty? It may be that the environmental perspective is benefited by concurrency. The theory is that two forums are better than one. The public-interest environmental perspective may receive a more hospitable reception in one place rather than the other, and potentially destructive projects must survive the rigors of both tests. Making concurrency the norm arguably doesn't stalemate the federal agencies; it just places the burden on them to assert primacy when they need to have unilateral control. In the air pollution context, this theory gains support from Alaska Dep't of Envtl. Conservation (ADEC) v. EPA, 2004 U.S. LEXIS 820 (2004), in which the Supreme Court upheld EPA's rejection of ADEC's grant of an air permit to a zinc mine on the ground that ADEC had not adequately justified its failure to require the most effective pollution control technology for the permitted sources.

3. **State regulation of the federal public lands.** As a historical matter in the public lands area, it is only recently that the Property Clause of the U.S. Constitution has been recognized as supporting active federal management authority over federal lands. Nineteenth-century cases frequently regarded that clause merely as an authority to own on the same basis as any other landholder, i.e., subject to state regulation. For an excellent discussion of this topic and many others relating to the federal public lands, see Cowart & Fairfax, Public Lands Federalism: Judicial Theory and Administrative Reality, 15 Ecology L.Q. 375, 439–476 (1988). Cowart and Fairfax criticize the majority opinion in Granite Rock:

> The majority opinion fails to clarify either general preemption doctrine or its application to the public lands. Instead, the decision turns on a presumed fine-grained distinction between land use planning and environmental regulation. That distinction is unclear, unsupported by the public lands statutes and not at all helpful to state and federal legislators and administrators seeking to manage complex intermixed resources. Id. at 463.

Are these criticisms well taken? The distinction is indeed a fine one, but *Pacific Gas* and *Huron Portland Cement* similarly drew distinctions based on the purposes of statutes. It is unfortunate that no clear guide was announced, but is it really within the power of the Court rather than Congress to unravel the complexities of concurrency?

4. **Is preemption analysis better applied on a local or a national level?** Consider the following criticism of the *Granite Rock* approach:

> The Court focused on the preemptive effect of the governing federal statutes and nationwide regulations. Some vehicle was needed, it rightly assumed, to avoid giving the states a veto over federal land uses. But the Court could better have addressed the issue by instead considering the preemption of state law at the lowest level — the preemption that occurs when a federal agency at the local level lawfully acts in a way that causes conflict with a state or local law. So long as federal action preempts at that level, preemption at a higher level is unneeded and, in this setting at least, undesirable. From an institutional perspective, preemption at the lowest level can best foster cooperative land planning on the scene. For a variety of reasons, preemption should occur only when a federal agency concludes, in a site-specific determination made in the course of statutory land-planning processes, that a particular federal use should override contrary state and local rules. Freyfogle, *Granite Rock*: Institutional Competence and the State Role in Federal Land Planning, 59 U. Colo. L. Rev. 475, 477 (1988).

5. **State regulation of federal facilities.** To what extent can states and local governments apply their environmental regulations to federal facilities in their territories? The question has recurred over the years, as military posts allow toxins to leach into groundwater, federal hospitals violate air pollution standards, federal authorities authorize the construction of mammoth power transmission towers or radio transmission towers in historic zones, and so on. The simplest answer seems to be that the federal action trumps state and local regulations unless the basic federal statute accepts state jurisdiction, or unless the federal government has voluntarily agreed to accommodate state and local restraints.

6. **Requirements for federal-state coordination.** Given the numerous opportunities for overlapping federal-state jurisdictions over projects, activities, and regulatory programs, there are obvious advantages to coordinating actions. The federal government often has subscribed to the rhetoric of federal-state coordination and has implemented a succession of formal procedural requirements aimed toward that end. For many years, Circular A-95, issued by the federal Office of Management and Budget (OMB) in 1968, directed federal agencies to provide opportunities for advance consultation with state agencies whenever a federal proposal might affect state interests. If a state was about to be chosen as the site of a federal bombing range, waste dump, or penitentiary, the Governor's office was supposed to get early warning of it through A-95 procedures. Executive Order 12,372, "Intergovernmental Review of Federal Programs" (July 14, 1982), issued early in the Reagan presidency, supplanted A-95 and sought to establish a more responsive process. Supplementing the Intergovernmental Cooperation Act of 1968, 42 U.S.C. §4231(a), E.O. 12,372 states that "federal agencies shall provide opportunities for consultation by elected officials of those State and local

governments that would provide the non-Federal funds for, or that would be directly affected by, proposed Federal financial assistance or direct Federal development."

In promoting federal-state coordination in federal regulatory programs, Executive Order 12,372 has been overshadowed by two executive orders issued by President Clinton — Executive Orders 12,866 and 13,132. E.O. 12,866 is the general regulatory order issued by President Clinton in 1993; this is the executive order that imposes cost-benefit requirements on federal agencies, enforced by the OMB. One of the "Principles of Regulation" set forth in the first section of E.O. 12,866 states:

> Wherever feasible, agencies shall seek views of appropriate State, local, and tribal officials before imposing regulatory requirements that might significantly or uniquely affect those governmental entities. Each agency shall assess the effects of Federal regulations on State, local, and tribal governments, including specifically the availability of resources to carry out those mandates, and seek to minimize those burdens that uniquely or significantly affect such governmental entities, consistent with achieving regulatory objectives. In addition, as appropriate, agencies shall seek to harmonize Federal regulatory actions with related State, local, and tribal regulatory and other governmental functions. 58 Fed. Reg. 51735 (1993).

In 1999, partly in response to the federal Unfunded Mandates Reform Act, President Clinton issued Executive Order 13,132, specifically addressing the topic of federal-state relations in regulatory matters. The Order begins with a sweeping statement of the virtues of states and local governments in our political system. It then creates several requirements for agencies proposing actions that either have "federalism implications" (broadly defined) or would preempt state laws, including a requirement of a "federalism impact statement" and a directive to try to interpret federal laws in a way that does not preempt state laws. 64 Fed. Reg. 43,255 (Aug. 4, 1999). In the Bush II Administration, the OMB has warned agencies that "rulemaking proposals that were not subjected to adequate State and local consultation will be returned to agencies for reconsideration." See Memorandum from John D. Graham to President's Management Council, Sept. 20, 2001, available at http://www.whitehouse.gov/omb/inforeg/oira_review-process.html.

7. **Preemption of local municipal laws, etc.** The preemption arguments between federal and state governments are echoed in many cases where local municipal ordinances are challenged, sometimes for double preemption, i.e., by conflict with both the federal law in violation of the Supremacy Clause, and state law, despite Home Rule. The case law tends to track the same analysis as federal-state preemption arguments. For some attorneys, preemption is one of the best fallback issues; if there appear to be no credible arguments on one's side, look for a preemption claim.

C. "DORMANT COMMERCE CLAUSE" OVERRIDES OF SUBORDINATE LEGISLATION

Preemption cases begin with an affirmative act by Congress. Before the states, the traditional full-purpose sovereigns in the American federal system, can be displaced through preemption, the limited federal government must act using its enumerated powers. That is, the mere fact that the Constitution permits federal action does not, alone, prevent state action. There is one major exception to this precept as it applies to the interstate commerce power, and it is an exception that has application in the environmental and natural resources area.

One of the important goals of the Constitution was to permit the development of a national economy. A common practice in the late eighteenth century (and thereafter) was for nations to erect a variety of barriers to trade with other nations, be it in the form of tariffs, prohibitions on the movement of goods of certain types, pilotage requirements, or other like devices. The states, in the pre-constitutional period and to the present, have engaged in such trade-restrictive efforts, usually with the aim of protecting local industries from outside competition by requiring outside entities to make use of local goods and services or by insuring that certain natural resources or other natural advantages remained at home. Even without the passage of federal legislation in furtherance of the interstate and international commerce power, myriad state and local efforts at economic protectionism can work at cross purposes to a constitutionally established national policy.

Recognizing that state and local laws that burden interstate commerce are contrary to constitutional policy is the first step toward allowing courts to declare such laws unconstitutional. The second step, which is not always stated explicitly in judicial opinions, is more pragmatic: If Congress does not have enough time or resources to pass federal statutes overriding state or local laws whenever the federal interest in commerce requires it, the federal courts can take on the job. When the Commerce Clause has not been used by Congress to preterrnit state legislation, its power still exists, lying "dormant" until the courts apply it to strike down protectionist laws.

But in the courts' hands, the clause has been anything but dormant. State laws that explicitly distinguish between domestic commodities and consumers, and out-of-state commodities and consumers, are almost invariably struck down. States laws that are facially evenhanded but that burden interstate commerce are subject to a somewhat more complicated test. The judicial test of the dormant Commerce Clause validity of state and local laws closely resembles the test of regulatory takings (see Chapter 23): The state or local law must have a proper public purpose, not an improper one (e.g., like protectionism, favoring local businesses); its design must be reasonably related to achieving that purpose; and the burden on interstate commerce must not be "excessive" when balanced against the public interests being protected. Applying these standards is often a subjective process.

Natural resource cases have been a staple of dormant Commerce Clause jurisprudence for at least a century, beginning with a famous opinion by Justice Oliver Wendell Holmes that allowed Connecticut to restrict the export of wild fowl captured by hunters.[10] The formal doctrine in this area is now fairly well settled and permits states very little latitude in attempting to block the interstate movement of goods and services. That, however, has not kept the states from trying, especially in regard to the movement of solid and hazardous waste.

---

10. See Geer v. Connecticut, 161 U.S. 519 (1896), overruled in Hughes v. Oklahoma, 441 U.S. 322 (1979).

Section 1. EVENHANDEDNESS AND THE RULE OF VIRTUAL PER SE INVALIDITY OF DISCRIMINATORY STATE LAWS

For contemporary purposes, the leading Supreme Court decision concerning the dormant Commerce Clause and facially discriminatory state legislation has been City of Philadelphia v. New Jersey, 437 U.S. 617 (1978). In that case, which follows, an effort by New Jersey to forbid out-of-state garbage from its landfill sites was struck down as unconstitutional. Philadelphia v. New Jersey was the first of many such cases involving the interstate movement of solid waste. Parochial legislation that seeks to block waste at the state border is easy to enact. Legislated preferences that provide local benefits at the expense of out-of-state third parties are popular and offer no viable political recourse to those who bear the brunt of the law (but who are not part of the in-state voting electorate). As one waste disposal official said in a federal hearing on the subject, "Everyone wants us to pick up the trash, but no one wants us to put it down." The Commerce Clause, however, also has been deployed to strike down state laws that try to keep waste *in state*, and that is where things start to get tricky.

City of Philadelphia v. New Jersey
United States Supreme Court, 1978
437 U.S. 617

STEWART, J. A New Jersey law prohibits the importation of most "solid or liquid waste which originated or was collected outside the territorial limits of the State...." In this case we are required to decide whether this statutory prohibition violates the Commerce Clause of the United States Constitution.

The statutory provision in question is Chapter 363 of 1973 N.J. Laws, which took effect in early 1974. In pertinent part it provides:

> No person shall bring into this State any solid or liquid waste which originated or was collected outside the territorial limits of the State, except garbage to be fed to swine in the State of New Jersey, until the commissioner [of the State Department of Environmental Protection] shall determine that such action can be permitted without endangering the public health, safety and welfare and has promulgated regulations permitting and regulating the treatment and disposal of such waste in this State. N.J. Stat. Ann. §13:1I–10.

As authorized by Ch. 363, the Commissioner promulgated regulations permitting four categories of waste to enter the State. Apart from these narrow exceptions, however, New Jersey closed its borders to all waste from other States.

Immediately affected by these developments were the operators of private landfills in New Jersey, and several cities in other States that had agreements with these operators for waste disposal....

Although the Constitution gives Congress the power to regulate commerce among the States, many subjects of potential federal regulation under that power inevitably escape congressional attention "because of their local character and their number and diversity." South Carolina State Highway Dept. v. Barnwell Bros., Inc., 303 U.S. 177, 185. In the absence of federal legislation, these subjects are open to control by the States so long as they act within the restraints imposed by the Commerce Clause itself. The bounds of these restraints appear nowhere in the words of the Commerce Clause, but have emerged gradually in the decisions of this Court giving effect to its basic purpose. That broad purpose was well expressed by Mr.

Justice Jackson in his opinion for the Court in H. P. Hood & Sons, Inc. v. Du Mond, 336 U.S. 525, 537–538:

> This principle that our economic unit is the Nation, which alone has the gamut of powers necessary to control of the economy, including the vital power of erecting customs barriers against foreign competition, has as its corollary that the states are not separable economic units. As the Court said in Baldwin v. Seelig, 294 U.S. 511, 527, "What is ultimate is the principle that one state in its dealings with another may not place itself in a position of economic isolation."

The opinions of the Court through the years have reflected an alertness to the evils of "economic isolation" and protectionism, while at the same time recognizing that incidental burdens on interstate commerce may be unavoidable when a State legislates to safeguard the health and safety of its people. Thus, where simple economic protectionism is effected by state legislation, a virtually per se rule of invalidity has been erected. The clearest example of such legislation is a law that overtly blocks the flow of interstate commerce at a State's borders. But where other legislative objectives are credibly advanced and there is no patent discrimination against interstate trade, the Court has adopted a much more flexible approach, the general contours of which were outlined in Pike v. Bruce Church, Inc., 397 U.S. 137, 142:

> Where the statute regulates evenhandedly to effectuate a legitimate local public inter-est, and its effects on interstate commerce are only incidental, it will be upheld unless the burden imposed on such commerce is clearly excessive in relation to the putative local benefits.... If a legitimate local purpose is found, then the question becomes one of degree. And the extent of the burden that will be tolerated will of course depend on the nature of the local interest involved, and on whether it could be promoted as well with a lesser impact on interstate activities....

The crucial inquiry, therefore, must be directed to determining whether Ch. 363 is basically a protectionist measure, or whether it can fairly be viewed as a law directed to legitimate local concerns, with effects upon interstate commerce that are only incidental.

The purpose of Ch. 363 is set out in the statute itself as follows:

> The Legislature finds and determines that...the volume of solid and liquid waste continues to rapidly increase, that the treatment and disposal of these wastes continues to pose an even greater threat to the quality of the environment of New Jersey, that the available and appropriate land fill sites within the State are being diminished, that the environment continues to be threatened by the treatment and disposal of waste which originated or was collected outside the State, and that the public health, safety and welfare require that the treatment and disposal within this State of all wastes generated outside of the State be prohibited.

The New Jersey Supreme Court accepted this statement of the state legislature's purpose. The state court additionally found that New Jersey's existing landfill sites will be exhausted within a few years; that to go on using these sites or to develop new ones will take a heavy environmental toll, both from pollution and from loss of scarce open lands; that new techniques to divert waste from landfills to other methods of disposal and resource recovery processes are under development, but that these changes will require time; and finally, that "the extension of the lifespan of existing landfills, resulting from the exclusion of out-of-state waste, may be of crucial importance in preventing further virgin wetlands or other undeveloped lands from being devoted to landfill purposes." 348 A.2d at 509–512. Based on these findings, the court concluded that Ch. 363 was designed to protect, not the State's economy, but its environment, and that its substantial benefits outweigh its "slight" burden on interstate commerce. 348 A.2d at 515–519.

The appellants strenuously contend that Ch. 363, "while outwardly cloaked 'in the currently fashionable garb of environmental protection,'...is actually no more than a legislative effort to suppress competition and stabilize the cost of solid waste disposal for New Jersey residents...." The appellees, on the other hand, deny that Ch. 363 was motivated by financial concerns or economic protectionism....

This dispute about ultimate legislative purpose need not be resolved, because its resolution would not be relevant to the constitutional issue to be decided in this case. Contrary to the evident assumption of the state court and the parties, the evil of protectionism can reside in legislative means as well as legislative ends. Thus, it does not matter whether the ultimate aim of Ch. 363 is to reduce the waste disposal costs of New Jersey residents or to save remaining open lands from pollution, for we assume New Jersey has every right to protect its residents' pocket-books as well as their environment. And it may be assumed as well that New Jersey may pursue those ends by slowing the flow of all waste into the State's remaining landfills, even though inter-state commerce may incidentally be affected. But whatever New Jersey's ultimate purpose, it may not be accomplished by discriminating against articles of commerce coming from outside the State unless there is some reason, apart from their origin, to treat them differently. Both on its face and in its plain effect, Ch. 363 violates this principle of nondiscrimination.

The Court has consistently found parochial legislation of this kind to be constitutionally invalid, whether the ultimate aim of the legislation was to assure a steady supply of milk by erecting barriers to allegedly ruinous outside competition, or to create jobs by keeping industry within the State, or to preserve the State's financial resources from depletion by fencing out indi-gent immigrants. In each of these cases, a presumably legitimate goal was sought to be achieved by the illegitimate means of isolating the State from the national economy.

Also relevant here are the Court's decisions holding that a State may not accord its own inhabitants a preferred right of access over consumers in other States to natural resources located within its borders. These cases stand for the basic principle that a "State is without power to prevent privately owned articles of trade from being shipped and sold in interstate commerce on the ground that they are required to satisfy local demands or because they are needed by the people of the State." Foster-Fountain Packing Co. v. Haydel, 278 U.S. 1, 10.

The New Jersey law at issue in this case falls squarely within the area that the Commerce Clause puts off limits to state regulation. On its face, it imposes on out-of-state commercial interests the full burden of conserving the State's remaining landfill space. It is true that in our previous cases the scarce natural resource was itself the article of commerce, whereas here the scarce resource and the article of commerce are distinct. But that difference is without conse-quence. In both instances, the State has overtly moved to slow or freeze the flow of commerce for protectionist reasons. It does not matter that the State has shut the article of commerce inside the State in one case and outside the State in the other. What is crucial is the attempt by one State to isolate itself from a problem common to many by erecting a barrier against the movement of interstate trade....

Today, cities in Pennsylvania and New York find it expedient or necessary to send their waste into New Jersey for disposal, and New Jersey claims the right to close its borders to such traffic. Tomorrow, cities in New Jersey may find it expedient or necessary to send their waste into Pennsylvania or New York for disposal, and those States might then claim the right to close their borders. The Commerce Clause will protect New Jersey in the future, just as it protects her neighbors now, from efforts by one State to isolate itself in the stream of interstate commerce from a problem shared by all.

REHNQUIST, J., dissenting.... The Court recognizes that States can prohibit the importation of items "'which, on account of their existing condition, would bring in and spread disease, pestilence, and death, such as rags or other substances infected with the germs of yellow fever or the virus of small-pox, or cattle or meat or other provisions that are diseased or decayed, or otherwise, from their condition and quality, unfit for human use or consumption.'" Bowman v. Chicago & Northwestern R. Co., 125 U.S. 465, 489 (1888). As the Court points out, such "quarantine laws have not been considered forbidden protectionist measures, *even though they were directed against out-of-state commerce.*" (Emphasis added.)

In my opinion, these cases are dispositive of the present one. Under them, New Jersey may require germ-infected rags or diseased meat to be disposed of as best as possible within the State, but at the same time prohibit the *importation* of such items for disposal at the facilities that are set up within New Jersey for disposal of such material generated *within* the State. The physical fact of life that New Jersey must somehow dispose of its own noxious items does not mean that it must serve as a depository for those of every other State. Similarly, New Jersey should be free under our past precedents to prohibit the importation of solid waste because of the health and safety problems that such waste poses to its citizens. The fact that New Jersey continues to, and indeed must continue to, dispose of its own solid waste does not mean that New Jersey may not prohibit the importation of even more solid waste into the State. I simply see no way to distinguish solid waste, on the record of this case, from germ-infected rags, diseased meat, and other noxious items....

COMMENTARY & QUESTIONS

1. **States try other tacks.** Recognizing that simple bans on out-of-state waste were legally doomed, states and local governments became more inventive in their efforts to prevent waste importation. A commonly chosen method was to charge differential tipping fees[11] that discouraged disposal of out-of-state wastes at in-state facilities by charging them higher prices than those charged for in-state wastes. States claimed the differential was justified to offset the costs imposed by the presence of the waste, i.e., the potential environmental harms and cost of remediation if the disposal site did have problems in the future. Put differently, the higher fees were established as an effort to internalize the costs of long-term waste management that were otherwise likely to be borne by the receiving state and its citizens. In Chemical Waste Mgmt., Inc. v. Hunt, 504 U.S. 334 (1992), and again in Oregon Waste Sys., Inc. v. Oregon Dep't of Envtl. Quality, 511 U.S. 93 (1994), differential tipping fees were held unconstitutional. In both instances, the Court treated the regulations as "discriminatory" and therefore prohibited under Philadelphia's virtual per se rule of invalidity. Undeterred, states attempted to erect other barriers to the entry of out-of-state wastes. Michigan, for example, erected a comprehensive statewide waste management system that gave local officials an optional veto power over nonlocal wastes. This was invalidated by the Supreme Court in Fort Gratiot Sanitary Landfill Inc. v. Michigan Dep't of Natural Res., 504 U.S. 353 (1992). The Supreme Court quoted *Philadelphia* in stating that, "the evil of protection can reside in the legislative means as well as the legislative ends." 504 U.S. at 360.

---

11. A tipping fee is paid by a waste disposer seeking to dump at a disposal facility. Usually these fees are levied on a per ton basis. Calling them fees is a bit of a misnomer in this context since the charges under constitutional scrutiny are more akin to taxes — they are legislatively imposed and inure to the benefit of the government as an addition to the amounts received by the facility operator for disposal.

2. **Criticism of the nondiscrimination principle.** Few judges or legal scholars have questioned the Supreme Court's nondiscrimination principle, requiring the almost automatic invalidation of state or local laws that facially discriminate against out-of-state commodities. Here is one dissenting view:

> [T]he nondiscrimination principle serves none of the objectives commonly cited in favor of it — neither economic efficiency, representation reinforcement, nor national unity.... Where, as here, the dominant justification for invalidating state and local legislation is that this practice serves important purposes, purposelessness alone would warrant reconsideration of the Court's doctrine. Nonetheless, the nondiscrimination principle is imperiled not only by what it does not achieve, but by what it does: a mandated preference for markets over regulation, where "regulation" is identified by an interference with the market as shaped by common-law entitlements. Thus the nondiscrimination principle is not an unassuming rule designed to rein in outlaw state and local governments, but a *Lochner*-style incursion on their legislative autonomy.
>
> The cases applying the nondiscrimination principle to invalidate the political judgments of state and local governments are not the only examples of the current Court's usurpation of the legislative function. Some have also seen a repetition of *Lochner*'s mistakes in the Court's recent decisions on takings, standing, and the scope of Congressional power under the Commerce Clause. With *Lochner* everywhere, it is perhaps not surprising that it should appear even in such a seemingly mundane and uncontroversial setting as the Court's review of laws that discriminate against interstate commerce. What is more surprising is that its presence there has gone largely unremarked. Heinzerling, The Commercial Constitution, 1995 Sup. Ct. Rev. 217, 275–276.

3. **Presumptions of invalidity and congressional authorization of discrimination.** An interesting way to characterize the contrast between preemption and dormant Commerce Clause cases is to say that the presumption of concurrency is reversed. In preemption cases, the presumption, applied in most cases, is that the state law is to coexist with the federal interest; in dormant Commerce Clause cases the presumption is that the state law is to be invalidated if it overtly adversely affects the national interest. In the former case, courts defer to state efforts if there is any basis on which to avoid preemption, and Congress has to step in to alter that outcome if it wishes to do so. In dormant Commerce Clause cases, courts do not defer to state efforts if they discriminate against interstate commerce, and Congress has to step in to alter that outcome if it wishes to do so. Congress occasionally does act to authorize state laws that otherwise would violate the dormant Commerce Clause. The power to do so is inherent in Congress's plenary control over interstate commerce. The authorization claim is occasionally made in environmental dormant Commerce Clause cases but usually fails. See, e.g., South-Central Timber Dev. Co. v. Wunnicke, 467 U.S. 82 (1984) (rejecting claim that ban on export of raw timber was authorized by Congress).

4. **Evenhanded legislation and legislative purpose.** Regulation that is not deemed facially discriminatory against interstate commerce is subjected to the test set forth in the quotation from Pike v. Bruce Church that appeared in the Philadelphia case. The purpose of the legislation must be legitimate (in furtherance of local public interest), and the burden on interstate commerce must be only "incidental."

5. **The dormant Commerce Clause's balance of burdens.** Even when a state passes the first part of the *Pike* test, the burden on interstate commerce must be weighed against local benefits in a fairly complex calculus that seeks to account for the importance of the local benefit and the extent of the burden on interstate commerce. In Minnesota v. Clover Leaf Creamery Co., 449 U.S. 456 (1981), an attack on state legislation contended that it was prompted by mixed environmental and protectionist motives. The Minnesota statute restricting plastic milk containers arguably favored pulpwood manufacturers (a major Minnesota industry) and disfavored plastics manufacturers (a non-Minnesota industry). The Court found that the statute was not discriminatory and proceeded to measure the burdens on interstate commerce under the *Pike* test, eventually concluding that "even granting that the out-of-state plastics industry is burdened...we find that this burden is not 'clearly excessive' in light of the substantial state interest in promoting conservation of energy and other natural resources and easing solid waste disposal problems...."

The process of balancing is as subjective as it is important to determining validity. The case of Procter & Gamble v. Chicago, 509 F.2d 69 (7th Cir. 1975), tested whether Chicago could ban the sale in the city of all phosphate detergents in order to protect water quality. After a long and detailed balancing process, the court upheld the city ordinance:

> The burden is so slight compared to the important and properly local objective that the presumption [of validity]...should apply. We will accept the City's determination that this phosphate ban is a reasonable means of achieving the elimination and prevention of nuisance algae unless we find that the plaintiffs have presented clear and convincing proof to the contrary [and they haven't].

Notice how important the lawyer's role is in fleshing out the interests to be balanced on both sides of this equation. Articulating and weighing the dormant Commerce Clause balance between burdens on commerce and regulatory benefits presents quite a challenge. Lawyers for the regulated entities will want not only to show how they are burdened in the state or locality that has chosen to regulate, but also to hypothesize about what would happen to the national market if other states, maybe even all states, decided to regulate, too. Suppose, for example, that the CAA's Title II did *not* preempt different states' regulation of automobile emissions beyond the California regulatory scheme. If Massachusetts, New York, California, and other states all decided to strike out on their own in regulating auto pollution, wouldn't the automobile manufacturers have a plausible dormant Commerce Clause claim against the state programs? What would the national market for cars look like if there were such a variety of state rules? On the other side, the attorneys for state or local governments will (as in the regulatory takings tests) try to weigh the countervailing public harms that are being regulated into the balance. Shouldn't the *Pike* balance tip in favor of states or local governments if they are protecting their citizens against direct threats to health and safety? When states are regulating mainly to protect relatively intangible public interests — improving visibility, say, or achieving other aesthetic aims — won't they be at a disadvantage in Commerce Clause litigation against industry interests that are complaining about concrete economic burdens? In the subjective judicial balancing process, which side should be presumptively favored?

6. **"A barrier is a barrier is a barrier," or is it sometimes a quarantine?** Does it make any difference for dormant Commerce Clause purposes whether Philadelphia v. New Jersey is an import ban (blocking the import of waste) or an export ban (blocking the export of landfill space)? In a word, the simple answer would seem to be, "No." State efforts to exclude undesirable items and to hoard valuable ones equally interfere with treating the nation as "one economic unit." Even so, the Court in *Philadelphia* was careful to distinguish the situation there from what it viewed as valid state quarantine laws. The Court found the two situations different because quarantine laws "did not discriminate against interstate commerce as such, but simply prevented traffic in noxious articles, whatever their origin." 437 U.S. at 629. The states have not experienced success in limiting waste movement on quarantine theories. In C&A Carbone v. Town of Clarkstown, 511 U.S. 383, 389 (1994), the Supreme Court showed how little it thought of the quarantine theory as applied to solid waste:

> The town says that its ordinance reaches only waste within its jurisdiction and is in practical effect a quarantine: It prevents garbage from entering the stream of interstate commerce until it is made safe. This reasoning is premised, however, on an outdated and mistaken concept of what constitutes interstate commerce.

In only one case has the Court upheld an environmental embargo based on a quarantine theory. The case, Maine v. Taylor, 477 U.S. 131 (1986), was exceptional when the case was decided and remains so today. The Court upheld a naked import ban on out-of-state seined baitfish, based on very favorable fact-finding that will be difficult to replicate in other cases. The trial court found, and the Supreme Court accepted the finding, that the import ban was necessary to prevent introduction of nonnative parasites into the Maine ecosystem.

7. **Insisting on cleaner, leaner garbage.** Pike v. Bruce Church's more relaxed scrutiny of evenhanded state regulation, allowing justification for discrimination such as that approved in Maine v. Taylor, opens the door a crack to state laws that have the effect of discriminating against out-of-state interests. Can these "exceptions" to the pattern of invalidation of commerce-restricting state laws be adapted to aid the states in their "garbage wars" efforts to enforce differential tipping fees or otherwise disfavor out-of-state waste? There is, of course, very little that distinguishes an in-state pile of garbage from an out-of-state pile of garbage unless something has been done to the in-state garbage that makes it either safer or more economical to manage. Suppose a state, by statute, requires predisposal treatment of waste as a precondition to disposal or as a basis for obtaining a lower tipping fee. Pretreatment could include mandatory recycling (to reduce volume) or segregation of waste streams to eliminate the presence of small-volume hazardous materials such as household batteries and noncommercial volumes of paints and solvents. Are such laws evenhanded? Do they remain evenhanded if the state also makes pretreatment mandatory within its borders? National Solid Waste Mgmt. Ass'n v. Meyer, 63 F.3d 652 (7th Cir. 1995), squarely considered a provision requiring mandatory recycling as a precondition to Wisconsin disposal of solid waste and invalidated it on a variety of grounds. The key flaw, in the court's view, inhered in the fact that if any waste in an out-of-state community was Wisconsin-bound, all of the waste in that community had to be pretreated to satisfy the Wisconsin law. That

amounted to impermissible extraterritorial regulation. The court found the law discriminatory against out-of-state waste haulers "simply because [their waste] comes from a community whose ways are not Wisconsin's ways." 63 F.3d at 662. Finally, even under a nondiscriminatory *Pike* analysis, the court found that Wisconsin had available to it less commerce-burdensome alternatives, such as having nonrecycled out-of-state wastes subject to disposal after first being taken to a recycling facility.

Section 2. THE MARKET PARTICIPANT DOCTRINE AND LEGISLATED OVERCHARGES TO THE CITIZENRY

While the persistent efforts of the states to impede the interstate flow of waste have had little success, one line of cases does allow states and localities to disadvantage interstate competitors. It is called the market participant doctrine.

Swin Resource Systems Inc. v. Lycoming County [Pennsylvania]
United States Circuit Court of Appeals for the Third Circuit, 1989
883 F.2d 245, cert. denied, 493 U.S. 1077

[The operator of a solid waste processing facility brought suit against a county that operated a landfill, challenging on dormant Commerce Clause grounds regulations giving the county residents preference in use of the landfill.]

BECKER, C.J.... Swin contends that Lycoming's attempt to preserve its landfill's capacity for local residents by charging a higher price to dispose of distant waste in the landfill (and limiting the volume of distant waste accepted by the landfill) constitutes an impermissible interference with and discrimination against interstate commerce in violation of the commerce clause. The district court granted the defendants' motion to dismiss the commerce clause claim on the ground that Lycoming had acted as a "market participant." Under the market participant doctrine, a state or state subdivision that acts as a market participant rather than a market regulator "is not subject to the restraints of the Commerce Clause." White v. Massachusetts Council of Construction Employers, Inc., 460 U.S. 204, 208 (1983)....

No court, to our knowledge, has ever suggested that the commerce clause requires city-operated garbage trucks to cross state lines in order to pick up the garbage generated by residents of other states. If a city may constitutionally limit its trucks to collecting garbage generated by city residents, we see no constitutional reason why a city cannot also limit a city-operated dump to garbage generated by city residents. With respect to municipal garbage trucks and municipal garbage dumps, application of the market participant doctrine enables "the people [acting through their local government] to determine as conditions demand what services and functions the public welfare requires." Reeves Inc. v. Stake, 447 U.S. 429, 438 n. 11 (1980). The residents who reside within the jurisdiction of a county or municipality are unlikely to pay for local government services if they must bear the cost but the entire nation may receive the benefit....

COMMENTARY & QUESTIONS

1. **The dissent in *Swin*.** The majority opinion in *Swin* raised a vigorous dissent by Chief Judge Gibbons. He argued that the market participant doctrine is premised on economic unreality:

Under any realistic view, the Lycoming landfill in private hands would never have hindered its ability to sell space to the highest bidder by erecting a differential rate structure that discriminated against waste the further its point of origin. If anything, it would have created a fee structure that did precisely the opposite. A vendor of landfill space hoping to attract business, as do genuine market partici-pants, would logically attempt to lure large volume purchasers concerned with transportation costs through a discount, especially when it appeared that customers dealing in local waste could not themselves provide sufficient business. As an exercise toward the political end of saving space for county waste, Lycoming County's price structure makes good regulatory sense. As an essay in market participation, it is aberrant and the majority's application of the label "market participant" to Lycoming County is an economic jest. 883 F.2d at 262.

2. **When economic unreality resembles indirect taxation.** There can be little doubt that Chief Judge Gibbons has correctly analyzed the economically irrational nature of the local preference aspect of Lycoming County's fee schedule, but is the market partic-ipant doctrine bottomed on the expectation that governmental entities will act in an economically rational fashion? Is a more plausible basis for the doctrine captured in the phrase that the state has "put its money where its mouth is." That is, the state has entered the market to buy the privilege of running a business by its own terms. The state, when it spends its money, has not merely commanded via regulation that some-one else, whose assets the state did not purchase in the marketplace, run her business in a way that favors the state's residents and discriminates against interstate commerce.

3. **Flow control that keeps garbage at home.** Now, in many states, *keeping local trash at home* — rather than keeping nonlocal trash out — is the object of numerous laws and regulations. One scenario is presented by the case of C.A. Carbone, Inc. v. Town of Clarkstown, 511 U.S. 383 (1994). In that case, the old landfill was in violation of state law and had to be closed. To replace the local dump, the town opted for a solid waste transfer station that would receive solid waste, separate recyclable from nonrecyclable materials, and send the waste on to its appropriate destination. To induce a private operator to build the transfer station and, after five years, deed it over to the town, Clarkstown passed an ordinance having two principal features. First, the ordinance required all Clarkstown trash be taken to the transfer station (thereby generating a predictable volume), and second, the ordinance specified an above market rate of $81 per ton as the tipping fee to be paid at the facility. In that way, the private facility opera-tor would be guaranteed of profits sufficient to justify a $1.4 million investment and the town would cure its violation of state law and end up with a paid-for facility. Carbone, a Clarkstown-based recycler that imported trash bound for elsewhere, was required to send its waste to the facility and pay the above-market rate. Carbone challenged the ordinance on dormant Commerce Clause grounds. By a 6–3 vote, the U.S. Supreme Court invalidated the ordinance, finding flow control indistinguishable from the trash embargo laws and differential tipping fees that it had previously struck down. Justice Souter's dissent argued that the case should be analyzed as a market participant case because the ordinance conveyed a privilege on the municipal government alone in its role as a market participant providing services to its citizens. For a critical perspective on the Court's decision in *Carbone* (and other Commerce Clause cases, dormant and

otherwise), see Klein, The Environmental Commerce Clause, 27 Harv. Envtl. L. Rev. 1 (2003).

Do the very different results in *Swin* and *Carbone* potentially put brakes on the large trend toward privatization of governmental services?

D. LIMITATIONS ON FEDERAL POWER

In the same way that the Constitution prescribes enforceable limitations on state authority, it also imposes limits on federal authority. In this latter regard, two doctrinal lines exist. The first grows from the fundamental precept that the federal government is one of limited powers, and powers not granted are withheld. This doctrinal line is often associated with the Tenth Amendment, which makes that limitation explicit, although it is certainly implicit in the body of the Constitution. A related development in this area is a newly increased willingness on the part of the U.S. Supreme Court and lower federal courts to find that the actions of Congress, purportedly taken pursuant to the enumerated power over interstate commerce, in fact exceed Congress's authority. The second doctrinal line also is associated with an amendment to the Constitution, in this case the Eleventh Amendment, that enacts a limitation on the federal judicial power that is bound up with the larger question of how much sovereign immunity was surrendered by the states when they entered into the Union.

Section 1. THE TENTH AMENDMENT

There has long been debate as to whether the Tenth Amendment alters, in any way, the power relation between the states and the federal government established by the Supremacy Clause. The Tenth Amendment, in relevant part, declares that "powers not delegated to the United States by the Constitution, nor prohibited by it to the States, are reserved to the States.,,." The claim made for giving the Tenth Amendment some bite in the matter of federal-state relations is that somehow the amendment erects an area of inviolate state sovereignty that cannot be encroached upon by the federal government.

The conventional wisdom and the vast majority of cases reject that claim. The rejection is captured in a phrase, often repeated in cases raising the issue: "[The Tenth Amendment] states but a truism that all is retained which has not been surrendered." United States v. Darby, 312 U.S. 100, 124 (1941). The "truism" confirms federal supremacy (within the sphere of the federal government's enumerated powers) and some abdication of state sovereignty as being surrendered on nationhood, but notes the fact that the remainder of state sovereignty was unaffected. Nevertheless, the idea of state sovereignty is an important one in the federal system, and there are occasional cases in which the Supreme Court has been willing to restrict the federal government's encroachment on the states, even when the federal government is pursuing national objectives that are within its sphere of constitutional competence. Importantly for the study of environmental law, the Tenth Amendment argument is made at times in environmental cases.

In the case that follows, the Tenth Amendment argument was used to limit one facet of the Low-Level Radioactive Waste Policy Amendments Act of 1985, Pub. L. No. 99–240, 99 Stat. 1842, 42 U.S.C. §§2021b et seq. The litigation grew out of Congress's attempt to respond to the declining number of low-level radioactive waste disposal sites nationwide and the threat of a total absence of such sites in the future. Congress sought to spur the siting by the states of low-level radioactive waste facilities, preferably on a collaborative basis, where several states would send their waste to a regional facility. To ensure action by the states, Congress used a mix of incentives and penalties, three of which were challenged by the State of New York on Tenth Amendment and other grounds. The challenged provisions included what the Court characterized as "monetary incentives," "access incentives," and the "take title provision." The monetary incentives revolved around a series of federal disposal surcharges on wastes generated outside of the disposal state. The surcharges would create a fund that would be used to reward states that achieved specific milestones in the process of establishing disposal facilities. The access incentives potentially limited disposal to wastes generated in states participating in the programs that Congress sought to encourage. Finally, the take title provision, as a sort of last resort, required states that were not participating in the programs to take title to the waste involved.

New York v. United States
United States Supreme Court, 1992
505 U.S. 144

O'CONNOR, J. This case implicates one of our Nation's newest problems of public policy and perhaps our oldest question of constitutional law. The public policy issue involves the disposal of radioactive waste.... The constitutional question is as old as the Constitution: it consists of discerning the proper division of authority between the Federal Government and the States. We conclude that while Congress has substantial power under the Constitution to encourage the States to provide for the disposal of the radioactive waste generated within their borders, the Constitution does not confer upon Congress the ability simply to compel the States to do so.

These questions [of state and federal authority] can be viewed in either of two ways. In some cases the Court has inquired whether an Act of Congress is authorized by one of the powers delegated to Congress in Article I of the Constitution. In other cases the Court has sought to determine whether an Act of Congress invades the province of state sovereignty reserved by the Tenth Amendment. In a case like this one, involving the division of authority between federal and state governments, the two inquiries are mirror images of each other. If a power is delegated to Congress in the Constitution, the Tenth Amendment expressly disclaims any reservation of that power to the States; if a power is an attribute of state sovereignty reserved by the Tenth Amendment, it is necessarily a power the Constitution has not conferred on Congress.

It is in this sense that the Tenth Amendment "states but a truism that all is retained which has not been surrendered." As Justice Story put it, "[t]his amendment is a mere affirmation of what, upon any just reasoning, is a necessary rule of interpreting the constitution. Being an instrument of limited and enumerated powers, it follows irresistibly, that what is not conferred, is withheld, and belongs to the state authorities." J. Story, 3 Commentaries on the Constitution of the United States 752 (1833). This has been the Court's consistent understanding: "The States unquestionably do retai[n] a significant measure of sovereign authority to the extent that the

Constitution has not divested them of their original powers and transferred those powers to the Federal Government."

Congress exercises its conferred powers subject to the limitations contained in the Constitution. Thus, for example, under the Commerce Clause Congress may regulate publishers engaged in interstate commerce, but Congress is constrained in the exercise of that power by the First Amendment. The Tenth Amendment likewise restrains the power of Congress, but this limit is not derived from the text of the Tenth Amendment itself, which, as we have discussed, is essentially a tautology. Instead, the Tenth Amendment confirms that the power of the Federal Government is subject to limits that may, in a given instance, reserve power to the States. The Tenth Amendment thus directs us to determine, as in this case, whether an incident of state sovereignty is protected by a limitation on an Article I power.

Petitioners do not contend that Congress lacks the power to regulate the disposal of low level radioactive waste. Space in radioactive waste disposal sites is frequently sold by residents of one State to residents of another. Regulation of the resulting interstate market in waste disposal is therefore well within Congress' authority under the Commerce Clause. Petitioners likewise do not dispute that under the Supremacy Clause Congress could, if it wished, preempt state radioactive waste regulation. Petitioners contend only that the Tenth Amendment limits the power of Congress to regulate in the way it has chosen. Rather than addressing the problem of waste disposal by directly regulating the generators and disposers of waste, petitioners argue, Congress has impermissibly directed the States to regulate in this field.

As an initial matter, Congress may not simply "commandee[r] the legislative processes of the States by directly compelling them to enact and enforce a federal regulatory program." Hodel v. Virginia Surface Mining & Reclamation Assn., Inc., 452 U.S. 264, 288 (1981). In *Hodel*, the Court upheld the Surface Mining Control and Reclamation Act of 1977 precisely because it did not "commandeer" the States into regulating mining. The Court found that "the States are not compelled to enforce the steep-slope standards, to expend any state funds, or to participate in the federal regulatory program in any manner whatsoever. If a State does not wish to submit a proposed permanent program that complies with the Act and implementing regulations, the full regulatory burden will be borne by the Federal Government."

This is not to say that Congress lacks the ability to encourage a State to regulate in a particular way, or that Congress may not hold out incentives to the States as a method of influencing a State's policy choices. Our cases have identified a variety of methods, short of outright coercion, by which Congress may urge a State to adopt a legislative program consistent with federal interests. Two of these methods are of particular relevance here.

First, under Congress' spending power, "Congress may attach conditions on the receipt of federal funds." Second, where Congress has the authority to regulate private activity under the Commerce Clause, we have recognized Congress' power to offer States the choice of regulating that activity according to federal standards or having state law preempted by federal regulation.

With these principles in mind, we turn to the three challenged provisions of the Low-Level Radioactive Waste Policy Amendments Act of 1985.

[The opinion had little difficulty in concluding that monetary and access incentives in the legislation passed muster as rather straightforward examples of the federal power to tax and spend and the direct regulation of interstate commerce.]

The take title provision is of a different character. This third so-called "incentive" offers States, as an alternative to regulating pursuant to Congress' direction, the option of taking title to and possession of the low level radioactive waste generated within their borders and becoming liable for all damages waste generators suffer as a result of the States' failure to do so promptly. In this provision, Congress has crossed the line distinguishing encouragement from coercion.

The take title provision offers state governments a "choice" of either accepting ownership of waste or regulating according to the instructions of Congress. Respondents do not claim that the Constitution would authorize Congress to impose either option as a freestanding requirement. On one hand, the Constitution would not permit Congress simply to transfer radioactive waste from generators to state governments. Such a forced transfer, standing alone, would in principle be no different than a congressionally compelled subsidy from state governments to radioactive waste producers. The same is true of the provision requiring the States to become liable for the generators' damages. Standing alone, this provision would be indistinguishable from an Act of Congress directing the States to assume the liabilities of certain state residents. Either type of federal action would "commandeer" state governments into the service of federal regulatory purposes, and would for this reason be inconsistent with the Constitution's division of authority between federal and state governments. On the other hand, the second alternative held out to state governments — regulating pursuant to Congress' direction — would, standing alone, present a simple command to state governments to implement legislation enacted by Congress. As we have seen, the Constitution does not empower Congress to subject state governments to this type of instruction.

Because an instruction to state governments to take title to waste, standing alone, would be beyond the authority of Congress, and because a direct order to regulate, standing alone, would also be beyond the authority of Congress, it follows that Congress lacks the power to offer the States a choice between the two.

States are not mere political subdivisions of the United States. State governments are neither regional offices nor administrative agencies of the Federal Government. The positions occupied by state officials appear nowhere on the Federal Government's most detailed organizational chart. The Constitution instead "leaves to the several States a residuary and inviolable sovereignty," The Federalist No. 39, p. 245 (C. Rossiter ed. 1961), reserved explicitly to the States by the Tenth Amendment.

Whatever the outer limits of that sovereignty may be, one thing is clear: The Federal Government may not compel the States to enact or administer a federal regulatory program. The Constitution permits both the Federal Government and the States to enact legislation regarding the disposal of low level radioactive waste. The Constitution enables the Federal Government to preempt state regulation contrary to federal interests, and it permits the Federal Government to hold out incentives to the States as a means of encouraging them to adopt suggested regulatory schemes. It does not, however, authorize Congress simply to direct the States to provide for the disposal of the radioactive waste generated within their borders. While there may be many constitutional methods of achieving regional self-sufficiency in radioactive waste disposal, the method Congress has chosen is not one of them. The judgment of the Court of Appeals is accordingly affirmed in part and reversed in part.

COMMENTARY & QUESTIONS

1. **The lines of dissent.** Justices White, Blackmun, and Stevens dissented from the invalidation of the take title provision. The thrust of their objection was based on estoppel (New York had reaped the benefits of the law) and the view that the precedents cited by the majority did not establish so great a limitation on congressional choice of means.

2. **The new "truism."** Has the old "truism" taken on a new meaning? Historically, the issue in Tenth Amendment cases was that of federal competence: Was the action within federal power? Chief Justice Rehnquist and others have been advocating a concept of

independent limitation of federal power derived from a notion of inviolable state sovereignty that survived the framing of the U.S. Constitution. A phrase associated with this idea is that the federal government is disabled from enacting legislation that seeks to regulate the "states qua states." To what extent is that view established as a general principle in the opinion and then applied to strike down the take title provision?

3. **Incentives and the dormant Commerce Clause.** Interestingly, for federalism purposes, among the incentives that Congress used (and the Court upheld) to spur the siting of regional facilities was granting those facilities the right to exclude waste from states not a party to the agreement governing the regional facility and allowing those facilities to charge differential waste disposal fees for out-of-state waste. The power of exclusion and charging differential fees for disposal, absent congressional authorization, would violate the dormant Commerce Clause.

4. **Commanding state execution of fedcral law.** Can Congress require the states, or state officials, to take action in furtherance of federal law? In a post-*New York* case involving the Brady Handgun Violence Prevention Act, a closely divided Supreme Court held unconstitutional a requirement that state law enforcement officers maintain files and do background checks on applicants for gun licenses as directed by that federal statute. See Printz v. United States, 521 U.S. 898 (1997). Justice Scalia's majority opinion in *Printz* observed that there is no constitutional provision that specifically addresses the structural question of Congress's ability to direct state officers to execute federal laws. He found, further, that despite longstanding patterns and practices of Congress calling on state judges to enforce federal law, the imposition of federal tasks on other state officials was accomplished by implied consent. Finally, he concluded that the system of "dual sovereignty" that ensures the states a residuary and inviolable sovereignty controlled the issue, making the involuntary imposition of federal duties on state officials unconstitutional.

In Reno v. Condon, 528 U.S. 141 (2000), the unanimous Court upheld the Driver's Privacy Protection Act of 1994, 18 U.S.C. §2721, which restricted states' ability to market their driver's registration records without drivers' consent. *Condon* confirms that the scope of the Tenth Amendment's substantive limitation on congressional power is limited to cases of "commandeering," in which the federal government directs the executive or legislative branch of state government to take some particular governmental action with respect to its own citizens. Unlike the statutes involved in *New York* and *Printz*, the Court held, the driver's privacy law did not direct states to regulate its own citizens in any particular way, but rather regulated the states themselves.

The new logic of the Tenth Amendment, as reflected in these cases, may be relevant to a number of environmental laws. For example, the Emergency Community Planning and Right-to-Know Act (see Chapter 10) requires states and localities to promulgate various emergency plans. Can this planning requirement be differentiated from the requirements struck down in *New York* and *Printz*? Thus far, however, attempts to use the logic of "commandeering" to invalidate federal environmental imposed on states have not met with success (with an exception discussed in the next note). See, e.g.,

Nebraska v. EPA, 331 F.3d 995, 999 (D.C. Cir. 2003) (upholding SDWA because it regulated "states only in their capacity as public water system owners"); City of Abilene v. EPA, 325 F.3d 657 (5th Cir. 2003) (CWA's imposition of conditions on city's storm water discharges did not violate Tenth Amendment because city had choice of compliance options under the Act); Environmental Defense Ctr., Inc. v. EPA, 319 F.3d 398 (9th Cir. 2003) (likewise upholding stormwater regulation issued under CWA); Strahan v. Coxe, 127 F.3d 155 (1st Cir. 1997) (rejecting Tenth Amendment challenge to district court's injunction, based on finding of violation of ESA, against state issuance of licenses for gillnets and lobster pot fishing).

5. **Curbing congressionally mandated environmental remedial programs.** To what extent do New York v. United States and *Printz* limit the ability of Congress to require the states to take action to abate environmental hazards? In 1988, Congress enacted the Lead Contamination Control Act (LCCA), 42 U.S.C. §300j-21 to 300j-26, as an amendment to the federal SDWA, a law that sets health protective standards for drinking water supplies. Pursuant to §300j-24(d), the states are required to establish remedial action programs for the removal of lead contaminants from school drinking water systems within a period of months following the statute's effective date in 1988. In ACORN v. Edwards, 81 F.3d 1387 (5th Cir. 1996), a citizens' group sued Louisiana for violation of the federal requirement, and the state claimed the law violated the Tenth Amendment. The court agreed with the state. Concluding that the challenged law gave the states no choice but to regulate according to Congress's dictates, the court invalidated the law under the Tenth Amendment.

6. **The Unfunded Mandates Reform Act.** The Unfunded Mandates Reform Act of 1995, Pub. L. No. 104-4, 109 Stat. 48, codified principally at 2 U.S.C. §§658 and 1501 et seq., is an amendment to general laws regarding federal spending. If the amounts involved are large enough — in most instances, $50 million for a mandate affecting state, local, and tribal governments, $100 million for a mandate affecting the private sector — the Act's more specific provisions apply. The Act defines a mandate as

> any provision in legislation, statute, or regulation that...would impose an enforceable duty upon State, local, or tribal governments [or the private sector,] or would place caps upon, or otherwise decrease, the Federal Government's responsibility to provide funding to State, local, or tribal governments under a program. §101.

In Congress itself, unfunded mandates can be the subject of a point of order, which means that any member of Congress can, as a parliamentary procedure, seek to have discussion of a bill containing an unfunded mandate deemed out of order if that legislation does not provide new budget authority to defray or cover the cost. See §101(a)(2). Somewhat more onerously, agencies issuing regulations of any sort must prepare an unfunded mandates report detailing "the future compliance costs of the Federal mandate" that include "disproportionate budgetary effects" on governments or the private sector, "estimates by the agency of the effect on the national economy," and, if the agency finds those effects "relevant and material," the agency must also describe its "prior consultation" with affected governments See §202(A)(3). For agency regulations that meet the relevant monetary thresholds, the agency shall identify and consider a reasonable number of regulatory alternatives, and from those alternatives select the least costly, most cost-effective, or least burdensome alternative that achieves the objectives of the rule. Id.

As sanctions for failure to obey the Act, a court may, as a remedy, compel an agency to prepare the written statement required by the Act. §401(a)(2)(B). There are, however, limitations on seeking judicial review that state that

...no provision of this Act shall be construed to create any right or benefit, substantive or procedural, enforceable by any person in any administrative or judicial action. §401(b)(2).

Where does that leave the Act — is it a potent limitation on Congress and the federal agencies, or just an unenforceable gesture? Plainly, the Act expresses a congressional sentiment about agency rulemaking, and agencies that do not abide by the terms of the Act risk losing favor with Congress, which controls their appropriations. But efforts to obtain reversals of agencies' decisions under the Act have so far been unavailing. See Allied Local & Reg'l Mfrs. Caucus v. EPA, 215 F.3d 61 (D.C. Cir. 2000) (refusing to second guess EPA's judgment that the costs of its challenged rule did not cross $100 million threshold of Unfunded Mandates Reform Act); American Trucking Ass'ns, Inc. v. EPA, 175 F.3d 1027 (D.C. Cir. 1999) (declining to entertain possibility that EPA's failure to perform unfunded mandates impact analysis rendered EPA's air quality standards for soot and smog arbitrary and capricious, since the information in the analysis would be about economic costs and EPA was not allowed to consider costs in setting the standards).

7. **Circumventing *Printz* and the Unfunded Mandates Reform Act for federal environmental statutes?** If federal statutes cannot just require state governments to do certain things, because of Printz or the Unfunded Mandates Reform Act, can Congress validly accomplish the same ends by offering states a choice: saying they theoretically can choose not to do what the federal statute requests, but if so they will lose federal funding for various programs? If, for instance, a federal statute says a state will lose all federal highway funds if it refuses to set up a state water pollution control system under the CWA's national permit system, or a hazardous materials inventory and emergency planning council under the Emergency Planning and Community Right-to-Know Act, the statute arguably is not "mandatory" on the state. (The Unfunded Mandates Reform Act does not consider it a "mandate" where compliance is only a condition of federal funding.) The Supreme Court has long recognized, however, that at some point permissible inducements can become impermissible coercion. South Dakota v. Dole, 483 U.S. 203 (1987).

Section 2. THE COMMERCE CLAUSE AND LIMITATIONS ON FEDERAL POWER

American federalism, because it is so intimately bound to the Constitution, is often given meaning by the judicial branch in its exercise of judicial review. This fact makes the legal rules in this area subject to a unique degree of reconsideration when changes in judicial philosophy occur. The period beginning in 1992, when the Supreme Court decided New York v. United States, is a period in which reconsideration is taking place.

A bit of background may be helpful in understanding these developments: Coming out of the Great Depression, a major shift in judicial philosophy established that the breadth of the commerce power was sufficient to support the New Deal legislation then being passed by Congress. That view rejected an earlier prevailing view that had led to invalidation of numerous efforts at federal regulation of economic practices. With that shift, constitutionally permissible federal legislation, at times, reached deep into the states, regulating what were arguably local transactions. For example, the Agricultural Adjustment Act of 1938 sought to protect against actions that would depress commodity prices. One feature of the law limited the acreage a farmer could plant. That limitation on planting was challenged in Wickard v. Filburn, 317 U.S. 111 (1942), as being in excess of the interstate commerce power. Mr. Filburn was an Ohio farmer who was forbidden from producing crops on his own farm that would be consumed by his own farm animals without ever entering the stream of commerce. The law was sustained as a valid commerce power enactment because, in the aggregate, on-farm consumption of the crops reduced demand for the products moving in interstate commerce. In later decades, when Congress turned its attention to other national issues such as civil rights and the environment, the commerce power was the principal ground upon which Congress based its regulatory authority. The Court routinely upheld Congress's power in these areas. The case that follows has opened the possibility that some federal environmental laws, in specific applications, can exceed the limits of the commerce power.

Lopez v. United States
United States Supreme Court, 1995
514 U.S. 549

[This case involved a federal law making it a crime "for any individual knowingly to possess a firearm at a place that the individual knows, or has reasonable cause to believe, is a school zone." Defendant Lopez was convicted under that statute, the Gun-Free School Zones Act of 1990, 18 U.S.C. §922(q)(1)(A) (1988 ed., Supp. V). The Court reviewed his constitutional challenge to the law in which Lopez claimed that Congress had exceeded the limits of the interstate commerce power in enacting a law that regulated intrastate activity that did not affect commerce.]

REHNQUIST, C.J. Consistent with [the constitutional] structure, we have identified three broad categories of activity that Congress may regulate under its commerce power. First, Congress may regulate the use of the channels of interstate commerce. Second, Congress is empowered to regulate and protect the instrumentalities of interstate commerce, or persons or things in interstate commerce, even though the threat may come only from intrastate activities. Finally, Congress' commerce authority includes the power to regulate those activities having a substantial relation to interstate commerce, those activities that substantially affect interstate commerce.

Within this final category, admittedly, our case law has not been clear whether an activity must "affect" or "substantially affect" interstate commerce in order to be within Congress' power to regulate it under the Commerce Clause. We conclude, consistent with the great weight of our case law, that the proper test requires an analysis of whether the regulated activity "substantially affects" interstate commerce.

We now turn to consider the power of Congress, in the light of this framework, to enact §922(q). The first two categories of authority may be quickly disposed of: §922(q) is not a regulation of the use of the channels of interstate commerce, nor is it an attempt to prohibit the interstate transportation of a commodity through the channels of commerce; nor can §922(q) be justified as a regulation by which Congress has sought to protect an instrumentality of interstate commerce or a thing in interstate commerce. Thus, if §922(q) is to be sustained, it must be under the third category as a regulation of an activity that substantially affects interstate commerce.

First, we have upheld a wide variety of congressional Acts regulating intrastate economic activity where we have concluded that the activity substantially affected interstate commerce. Examples include the regulation of intrastate coal mining, intrastate extortionate credit transactions, restaurants utilizing substantial interstate supplies, inns and hotels catering to interstate guests, and production and consumption of home-grown wheat. These examples are by no means exhaustive, but the pattern is clear. Where economic activity substantially affects interstate commerce, legislation regulating that activity will be sustained....

Section 922(q) is a criminal statute that by its terms has nothing to do with "commerce" or any sort of economic enterprise, however broadly one might define those terms.[12] Section 922(q) is not an essential part of a larger regulation of economic activity, in which the regulatory scheme could be undercut unless the intrastate activity were regulated. It cannot, therefore, be sustained under our cases upholding regulations of activities that arise out of or are connected with a commercial transaction, which viewed in the aggregate, substantially affects interstate commerce.

To uphold the Government's contentions here, we would have to pile inference upon inference in a manner that would bid fair to convert congressional authority under the Commerce Clause to a general police power of the sort retained by the States. Admittedly, some of our prior cases have taken long steps down that road, giving great deference to congressional action. The broad language in these opinions has suggested the possibility of additional expansion, but we decline here to proceed any further. To do so would require us to conclude that the Constitution's enumeration of powers does not presuppose something not enumerated, and that there never will be a distinction between what is truly national and what is truly local. This we are unwilling to do. [Lopez' federal conviction was reversed.]

COMMENTARY & QUESTIONS

1. *Lopez* and environmental law. The vast majority of federal environmental legislation, from the major laws such as the CAA and CWA, to lesser known statutes such as the SDWA, is enacted pursuant to the commerce power, as was the Gun-Free School Zones Act of 1990. Does *Lopez* raise any serious doubt as to the constitutionality of those environmental laws? Environmental laws typically bear a clear linkage to the national economy. Consider here the majority's "three broad categories of activity that Congress may regulate under its commerce power." Initially, it is more than a mere debaters' game to try to cast the nation's waters and airsheds in the first or second categories of "channels" or "instrumentalities" of commerce. Historically, water was the principal medium for interstate commerce. The earliest pollution control legislation, the Rivers and Harbors Act of 1899, had as a concern the impacts of pollution on commercial navigation. Environmental legislation such as the Toxic Substance Control Act and the Federal Insecticide, Fungicide, and Rodenticide Act, directly affect the marketing of

---

12. Under our federal system, the "States possess primary authority for defining and enforcing the criminal law."

products in the national economy. Support for an even broader array of federal environmental legislation lies in the third prong, "activities having a substantial relation to interstate commerce." At bedrock, much of the regulation in the CWA and CAA is directed toward the interstate economics of pollution control. The so-called race of laxity is a worry solely because states with lax regulation would provide a comparative economic benefit to firms that locate there. Finally, even the majority in *Lopez* cites with approval Hodel v. Virginia Surface Mining & Reclamation Ass'n, Inc., 452 U.S. 264 (1981), a case involving commerce power-based regulation of intrastate strip mining activities. Likewise, the Supreme Court has not renounced the aggregation principle of Wickard v. Filburn — that the cumulative interstate economic effect of numerous local actions can support regulation of local activities. Federal regulation of even small polluters appears to remain within the Court's vision of permissible Commerce Clause regulation.

2. **The legal process question in *Lopez*.** Which branch of government ought to decide whether federal legislation affects commerce? The Supreme Court, at least since the famous case of Marbury v. Madison in 1803, has the responsibility to exercise judicial review to ascertain whether Congress's enactments are within constitutional bounds, including whether the statutes are passed in pursuance of an enumerated power. Congress's view of its own actions, however, historically has been entitled to considerable deference. As the majority opinion in *Lopez* concedes, "as part of our independent evaluation of constitutionality under the Commerce Clause we of course consider legislative findings, and indeed even congressional committee findings, regarding the effect on interstate commerce...." Justice Breyer's dissent made even more of the deference argument, as did Justice Souter's dissent, which cited the *Hodel* strip mining case mentioned above: "In reviewing congressional legislation under the Commerce Clause, we defer to what is often a merely implicit congressional judgment that its regulation addresses a subject substantially affecting interstate commerce if there is any rational basis for such a finding." 514 U.S. 549 at 603.

3. **Violence against women.** Despite the *Lopez* Court's nod in the direction of deference to legislative findings, legislative findings did not fare very well in United States v. Morrison, 529 U.S. 598 (2000). There, the Court held that Congress lacked authority under the Commerce Clause (or under §5 of the Fourteenth Amendment) to enact the Violence Against Women Act (VAWA), 42 U.S.C. §13981. VAWA created a civil cause of action in federal court for persons harmed by violent crimes "motivated by gender." 42 U.S.C. §13981(c). VAWA, the Court concluded, could not be sustained under the Commerce Clause because it did not fall within any of the three categories of permissible state regulation described in *Lopez*. The Court focused its attention on whether violence against women had a substantial effect on interstate commerce. Sweeping aside voluminous congressional findings on the economic consequences of violence against women, the Court concluded that VAWA's connection to interstate commerce was too attenuated because it did not directly target commercial activity and its connection to any such activity was too remote.

> Gender-motivated crimes of violence are not, in any sense of the phrase, economic
> activity. While we need not adopt a categorical rule against aggregating the effects

of any noneconomic activity in order to decide these cases, thus far in our Nation's history our cases have upheld Commerce Clause regulation of intrastate activity only where that activity is economic in nature.

In contrast with the lack of congressional findings that we faced in *Lopez*, §13981 is supported by numerous findings regarding the serious impact that gender-motivated violence has on victims and their families. But the existence of congressional findings is not sufficient, by itself, to sustain the constitutionality of Commerce Clause legislation. As we stated in *Lopez*, "'Simply because Congress may conclude that a particular activity substantially affects interstate commerce does not necessarily make it so.'" 514 U.S. at 557, n. 2 (quoting Hodel, 452 U.S. at 311 (Rehnquist, J., concurring in judgment)). Rather, "'whether particular operations affect interstate commerce sufficiently to come under the constitutional power of Congress to regulate them is ultimately a judicial rather than a legislative question, and can be settled finally only by this Court.'" 514 U.S. at 557, n. 2 (quoting Heart of Atlanta Motel, 379 U.S. at 273 (Black, J., concurring)).

In these cases, Congress' findings are substantially weakened by the fact that they rely so heavily on a method of reasoning that we have already rejected as unworkable if we are to maintain the Constitution's enumeration of powers. Congress found that gender-motivated violence affects interstate commerce

> by deterring potential victims from traveling interstate, from engaging in employment in interstate business, and from transacting with business, and in places involved in interstate commerce,...by diminishing national productivity, increasing medical and other costs, and decreasing the supply of and the demand for interstate products. H.R. Conf. Rep. No. 103–711, at 385.

Given these findings and petitioners' arguments, the concern that we expressed in Lopez that Congress might use the Commerce Clause to completely obliterate the Constitution's distinction between national and local authority seems well founded. The reasoning that petitioners advance seeks to follow the but-for causal chain from the initial occurrence of violent crime (the suppression of which has always been the prime object of the States' police power) to every attenuated effect upon interstate commerce. If accepted, petitioners' reasoning would allow Congress to regulate any crime as long as the nationwide, aggregated impact of that crime has substantial effects on employment, production, transit, or consumption....

We accordingly reject the argument that Congress may regulate noneconomic, violent criminal conduct based solely on that conduct's aggregate effect on interstate commerce. The Constitution requires a distinction between what is truly national and what is truly local.... The regulation and punishment of intrastate violence that is not directed at the instrumentalities, channels, or goods involved in interstate commerce has always been the province of the States....

4. **Legislative record review.** Numerous legal scholars have criticized the Court's increasingly dismissive treatment of legislative findings. In an excellent article, Professors William Buzbee and Robert Shapiro summarize some of the difficulties posed by the Court's new attitude:

> Legislative record review...represents a novel mode of judicial review that limits congressional power in crucial respects. This kind of review threatens to impose procedural and substantive constraints on legislative action that have no support in precedent or in constitutional text or structure. Moreover, the Court's reliance on the concept of "the legislative record," in the sense of a comprehensive set of

documents reflecting the full scope of congressional deliberations underlying a statute, is fundamentally flawed on the most basic level. This kind of "legislative record" simply does not exist. The entire concept of a legislative record constitutes an inappropriate importation from different institutional settings of the expectation that a written record will justify a legal judgment. Congress acts on the basis of a wide variety of information, concerns, and interests. Informal contacts and latent policy judgments serve as key determinants of legislative conduct. The Court's new legislative record review seeks to reduce the legislative crucible to a written, comprehensive record. Such a process will not be "legislative" as we currently understand that term. In short, "the legislative record" is fundamentally incoherent. To render the concept coherent would require a transformation of legislation. Buzbee & Shapiro, Legislative Record Review, 54 Stan. L. Rev. 87 (2001).

5. Which environmental activities are "economic activities"? In *Morrison*, the Court declined to aggregate individual effects on interstate commerce into a "substantial" whole unless those effects came from commercial activities. Identifying which activity is relevant for purposes of aggregation can matter a great deal. The narrower the relevant category, the lower the federal government's chances of showing substantial effects on interstate commerce become. Suppose a developer wants to build a landfill in a wetland. Is the relevant activity construction of all kinds? Construction of disposal facilities? Construction in wetlands? Construction or other activities that affect migratory birds? These are the kinds of questions asked, but not answered, in the case that follows.

Solid Waste Agency of Northern Cook County v. U.S. Army Corps of Engineers
Supreme Court of the United States, 2001
531 U.S. 159

[A consortium of suburban Chicago municipalities (SWANCC) wanted to build a disposal facility for nonhazardous solid waste on the site of an abandoned sand and gravel pit. Over time, the site's excavation trenches had become permanent and seasonal ponds. SWANCC received approval from the relevant state and local agencies, and initially was assured by the Army Corps of Engineers (Corps) that the site did not contain wetlands and thus did not fall within the Corps's power to regulate wetlands under the CWA. After migratory birds were observed at the site, however, the Corps reversed course based on its so-called migratory bird rule, which interpreted the Act to extend jurisdiction to intrastate waters that serve as habitats for migratory birds. Ultimately the Corps denied approval for the project under §404 of the CWA, which gives the Corps the authority to issue permits "for the discharge of dredged or fill material into the navigable waters at specified disposal sites." 33 U.S.C. §1344(a). SWANCC sued, alleging that the Corps had no jurisdiction over the project because (1) the CWA's definition of "navigable waters" did not apply to this site, and (2) if it did, the application of the Act's requirements to an intrastate, isolated, nonnavigable wetland would violate the Commerce Clause. The Supreme Court held that SWANCC's site did not come within the meaning of "navigable waters." In addressing the Corps's argument that its interpretation of the Act, even if not the only plausible one, should at least be given deference under Chevron U.S.A. Inc. v. Natural Resources Defense Council, Inc., 467 U.S. 837 (1984), the Court had the following to say about the limits of the Commerce Clause.]

REHNQUIST, C.J.... Where an administrative interpretation of a statute invokes the outer limits of Congress' power, we expect a clear indication that Congress intended that result. This requirement stems from our prudential desire not to needlessly reach constitutional issues and our assumption that Congress does not casually authorize administrative agencies to interpret a statute to push the limit of congressional authority. This concern is heightened where the administrative interpretation alters the federal-state framework by permitting federal encroachment upon a traditional state power. Thus, "where an otherwise acceptable construction of a statute would raise serious constitutional problems, the Court will construe the statute to avoid such problems unless such construction is plainly contrary to the intent of Congress." Edward J. DeBartolo Corp. v. Florida Gulf Coast Building & Constr. Trades Council, 485 U.S. 568, 575 (1988).

Twice in the past six years we have reaffirmed the proposition that the grant of authority to Congress under the Commerce Clause, though broad, is not unlimited. Respondents argue that the "Migratory Bird Rule" falls within Congress' power to regulate intrastate activities that "substantially affect" interstate commerce. See United States v. Morrison, 529 U.S. 598 (2000); United States v. Lopez, 514 U.S. 549 (1995). They note that the protection of migratory birds is a "national interest of very nearly the first magnitude," Missouri v. Holland, 252 U.S. 416, 435 (1920), and that, as the Court of Appeals found, millions of people spend over a billion dollars annually on recreational pursuits relating to migratory birds. These arguments raise significant constitutional questions. For example, we would have to evaluate the precise object or activity that, in the aggregate, substantially affects interstate commerce. This is not clear, for although the Corps has claimed jurisdiction over petitioner's land because it contains water areas used as habitat by migratory birds, respondents now, *post litem motam*, focus upon the fact that the regulated activity is petitioner's municipal landfill, which is "plainly of a commercial nature." But this is a far cry, indeed, from the "navigable waters" and "waters of the United States" to which the statute by its terms extends.

These are significant constitutional questions raised by respondents' application of their regulations, and yet we find nothing approaching a clear statement from Congress that it intended §404(a) to reach an abandoned sand and gravel pit such as we have here. Permitting respondents to claim federal jurisdiction over ponds and mudflats falling within the "Migratory Bird Rule" would result in a significant impingement of the States' traditional and primary power over land and water use. Rather than expressing a desire to readjust the federal-state balance in this manner, Congress chose to "recognize, preserve, and protect the primary responsibilities and rights of States...to plan the development and use...of land and water resources..." 33 U.S.C. §1251(b). We thus read the statute as written to avoid the significant constitutional and federalism questions raised by respondents' interpretation, and therefore reject the request for administrative deference....

STEVENS, J., joined by SOUTER, GINSBURG, and BREYER, JJ., dissenting.... The Corps' exercise of its §404 permitting power over "isolated" waters that serve as habitat for migratory birds falls well within the boundaries set by this Court's Commerce Clause jurisprudence.

In United States v. Lopez, 514 U.S. 549, 558-559 (1995), this Court identified "three broad categories of activity that Congress may regulate under its commerce power": (1) channels of interstate commerce; (2) instrumentalities of interstate commerce, or persons and things in interstate commerce; and (3) activities that "substantially affect" interstate commerce. The migratory bird rule at issue here is properly analyzed under the third category. In order to constitute a proper exercise of Congress' power over intrastate activities that "substantially affect" interstate commerce, it is not necessary that each individual instance of the activity substantially affect commerce; it is enough that, taken in the aggregate, the *class of activities* in question has such an effect.

The activity being regulated in this case (and by the Corps' §404 regulations in general) is the discharge of fill material into water. The Corps did not assert jurisdiction over petitioner's land simply because the waters were "used as habitat by migratory birds." It asserted jurisdiction because petitioner planned to *discharge fill* into waters "used as habitat by migratory birds." Had petitioner intended to engage in some other activity besides discharging fill (i.e., had there been no activity to regulate), or, conversely, had the waters not been habitat for migratory birds (i.e., had there been no basis for federal jurisdiction), the Corps would never have become involved in petitioner's use of its land. There can be no doubt that, unlike the class of activities Congress was attempting to regulate in United States v. Morrison, 529 U.S. 598, 613 (2000) ("gender-motivated crimes"), and *Lopez*, 514 U.S. at 561 (possession of guns near school property), the discharge of fill material into the Nation's waters is almost always undertaken for economic reasons.[13]

Moreover, no one disputes that the discharge of fill into "isolated" waters that serve as migratory bird habitat will, in the aggregate, adversely affect migratory bird populations. Nor does petitioner dispute that the particular waters it seeks to fill are home to many important species of migratory birds, including the second-largest breeding colony of Great Blue Herons in northeastern Illinois, and several species of waterfowl protected by international treaty and Illinois endangered species laws.

In addition to the intrinsic value of migratory birds, it is undisputed that literally millions of people regularly participate in birdwatching and hunting and that those activities generate a host of commercial activities of great value.[14] The causal connection between the filling of wetlands and the decline of commercial activities associated with migratory birds is not "attenuated," *Morrison*, 529 U.S. at 612; it is direct and concrete. Cf. Gibbs v. Babbitt, 214 F.3d 483, 492–493 (4th Cir. 2000) ("The relationship between red wolf takings and interstate commerce is quite direct — with no red wolves, there will be no red wolf related tourism....").

Finally, the migratory bird rule does not blur the "distinction between what is truly national and what is truly local." *Morrison*, 529 U.S. at 617–618. Justice Holmes cogently observed in Missouri v. Holland that the protection of migratory birds is a textbook example of a *national* problem. 252 U.S. 416, 435 (1920) ("It is not sufficient to rely upon the States [to protect migratory birds]. The reliance is vain...."). The destruction of aquatic migratory bird habitat, like so many other environmental problems, is an action in which the benefits (e.g., a new landfill) are disproportionately local, while many of the costs (e.g., fewer migratory birds) are widely dispersed and often borne by citizens living in other States. In such situations, described by economists as involving "externalities," federal regulation is both appropriate and necessary. Identifying the Corps' jurisdiction by reference to waters that serve as habitat for birds that migrate over state lines also satisfies this Court's expressed desire for some "jurisdictional element" that limits federal activity to its proper scope.

The power to regulate commerce among the several States necessarily and properly includes the power to preserve the natural resources that generate such commerce. Migratory birds, and the waters on which they rely, are such resources. Moreover, the protection of migratory birds is

---

13. The fact that petitioner can conceive of some people who may discharge fill for noneconomic reasons does not weaken the legitimacy of the Corps' jurisdictional claims. As we observed in Perez v. United States, 402 U.S. 146 (1971), "where the *class of activities* is regulated and that *class* is within the reach of federal power, the courts have no power to excise, as trivial, individual instances of the class."

14. In 1984, the U.S. Congress Office of Technology Assessment found that, in 1980, 5.3 million Americans hunted migratory birds, spending $638 million. More than 100 million Americans spent almost $14.8 billion in 1980 to watch and photograph fish and wildlife. Of 17.7 million birdwatchers, 14.3 million took trips in order to observe, feed, or photograph waterfowl, and 9.5 million took trips specifically to view other water-associated birds, such as herons like those residing at petitioner's site.

a well-established federal responsibility. As Justice Holmes noted in Missouri v. Holland, the federal interest in protecting these birds is of "the first magnitude." Because of their transitory nature, they "can be protected only by national action."

Whether it is necessary or appropriate to refuse to allow petitioner to fill those ponds is a question on which we have no voice. Whether the Federal Government has the power to require such permission, however, is a question that is easily answered. If, as it does, the Commerce Clause empowers Congress to regulate particular "activities causing air or water pollution, or other environmental hazards that may have effects in more than one State," Hodel v. Indiana, 452 U.S. 314, 282 (1981), it also empowers Congress to control individual actions that, in the aggregate, would have the same effect.[15] There is no merit in petitioner's constitutional argument....

COMMENTARY & QUESTIONS

1. *SWANCC* **and the CWA.** In deciding that the wetlands in this case did not fall within the CWA's jurisdiction, the Court emphasized that these wetlands were intrastate, isolated from other waters, and nonnavigable, and that the presence of migratory birds at the site, standing alone, did not bring the site within the Act's ambit. This holding may have huge consequences for the future scope of the Act. Chapter 12 provides more details.

2. **The Commerce Clause as a principle of statutory interpretation.** Notice the role that the constitutional issue played in this case: The Court deployed the Commerce Clause, not for purposes of invalidating any portion of the CWA but for purposes of justifying its refusal to grant deference, under *Chevron*, to the longstanding interpretation of the Act embraced by the agencies charged with implementing it. Congress should have spoken more clearly, the Court said, if it wanted to go to the limits of its constitutional authority. Some have suggested that using the Constitution as an interpretive principle creates a "penumbral" Constitution, giving too much power to judges. Judge Easterbrook has written:

> The canon about avoiding constitutional decisions, in particular, must be used with care, for it is a closer cousin to invalidation than to interpretation. It is a way to enforce the constitutional penumbra, and therefore an aspect of constitutional law proper. Constitutional decisions breed penumbras, which multiply questions. Treating each as justification to construe laws out of existence too greatly enlarges the judicial power. United States v. Marshall, 908 F.2d 1312 (7th Cir. 1990).

3. **Aggregating effects from commercial activities.** As promised in our note preceding the case, *SWANCC* illustrates how difficult it can be to figure out which activity is relevant for purposes of aggregation. Jonathan Adler has argued that wetlands regulation does not involve economic activity and thus cannot be aggregated to produce a substantial effect on interstate commerce:

> Much of the activity that the Corps seeks to regulate in wetlands is noncommercial — the building of an extension on one's own house, the planting of a garden, and so on. The Corps's regulation is not a regulation of commercial development per se, it is a regulation of any activity, save those specifically exempted by Congress,

---

15. Justice Thomas is the only Member of the Court who has expressed disagreement with the "aggregation principle." United States v. Lopez, 514 U.S. 549, 600 (1995) (concurring opinion).

that could impact wetlands in a particular manner. Indeed, that the activity in any given case is commercial in nature is completely incidental to the Corps's assertion of jurisdiction. That is the defect. This is also what differentiates the regulation of wetlands from the regulation of mining activity sustained in *Hodel*. Mining per se is a commercial activity. The filling of wetlands, however, is not. Many wetland permits concern nothing more than a family's effort to expand its home. Moreover, the Corps has asserted that it could regulate "walking, bicycling or driving a vehicle through a wetland," if it so chose, because such activities could result in the "discharge of dredged material." Clearly, regulatory authority of this scope extends far beyond the regulation of purely commercial activity, and is therefore constitutionally suspect. Adler, Commerce Clause Jurisprudence and the Limits of Federal Wetlands Protection, 29 Envtl. L. 1 (1999).

4. **The viability of state regulation.** While the Supreme Court's decision in *SWANCC* does not prevent states from protecting isolated waters through administrative or legislative action, will the states do so? At present, very few states provide such protection. Only approximately one-third of the states currently have programs that are designed to protect isolated wetlands, and many of those states fail to regulate wetlands on federal land. In fact, very little protection is provided in states with some of the largest isolated wetlands. And, in any event, where one state cannot protect migratory birds that travel from within its borders to other states, Justice Holmes's observations in Missouri v. Holland still ring true today: Migratory birds "can be protected only by national action in concert with that of another power. The subject-matter is only transitorily within the State and has no permanent habitat therein. But for [the laws challenged here] there might soon be no birds for any powers to deal with. We see nothing in the Constitution that compels the Government to sit by while a food supply is cut off and the protectors of our forests and our crops are destroyed." 252 U.S. 416 at 435.

5. **The federal government's reaction to *SWANCC*.** Just before President Clinton left office, the Corps and the EPA attempted to limit *SWANCC*'s reach. They withdrew their joint guidance on isolated, intrastate waters and put in its place a memorandum advising the agencies' district offices how to apply the Supreme Court's decision. The agencies all but limited the Court's decision to its facts, asserting that there was federal jurisdiction over all waters unless they were nonnavigable, isolated, and intrastate, and there was no argument for federal jurisdiction other than the waters' use by migratory birds.

The federal government's eagerness to limit *SWANCC*'s reach cooled considerably during the second President Bush's tenure. In January 2003, EPA and the Corps issued yet another guidance reacting to the decision, but by this time the agencies had become considerably more willing to see the potential depth and breadth of *SWANCC*. At the same time, the agencies issued an Advanced Notice of Proposed Rulemaking in which they sought counsel from the public on their proper course in a post-*SWANCC* world. The notice drew some 133,000 comments, ranging from proposals that the agencies limit *SWANCC* to its narrow facts, to arguments that the agencies have no jurisdiction over any body of water too small for an ocean liner. In late 2003, EPA withdrew its proposal to write a new rule, citing massive opposition to the proposal as expressed in public comments.

6. **The courts' struggles with** *SWANCC*. The Court's decision in *SWANCC* has been keeping the lower courts busy. Defendants in wetlands cases have asked courts to modify or vacate consent decrees in civil cases (see, e.g., United States v. Deaton, 332 F.3d 698 (4th Cir. 2003)), to vacate guilty pleas in criminal actions (see, e.g., United States v. Rapanos, 339 F.3d 447 (6th Cir. 2003)), and to dismiss pending cases (see, e.g., Pax Christi Mem'l Gardens, Inc. v. United States, 52 Fed. Cl. 318 (2002)), on the authority of *SWANCC*. In one dramatic case, a defendant pled guilty to criminal charges under the CWA just "hours" before *SWANCC* was handed down. The district court refused to allow the defendant to withdraw his guilty plea, concluding that the federal government had the power to prosecute him under the CWA, even though the creek in which his activities occurred took place in a tributary of a river, some 200 miles from where the river is navigable-in-fact, and even though the court conceded that the debris from defendant's activities would likely never reach waters that were navigable-in-fact. United States v. Buday, 138 F. Supp. 2d 1282 (D. Mont. 2001). Likewise, in United States v. Deaton, 332 F.3d 698 (4th Cir. 2003), the court concluded that the Army Corps of Engineers' assertion of jurisdiction over a nonnavigable tributary of a navigable water "fit…comfortably within Congress's authority to regulate navigable waters." The court stated that "Congress's power over the channels of interstate commerce, unlike its power to regulate activities with a substantial relation to interstate commerce, reaches beyond the regulation of activities that are purely economic in nature," and that "Congress's authority over the channels of commerce is…broad enough to allow it to legislate, as it did in the Clean Water Act, to prevent the use of navigable waters for injurious purposes. For example, Congress may outlaw the use of navigable waters as dumping grounds for fill material." Id. at 707. Judge Michaels's opinion for the Fourth Circuit panel was joined by Judge Luttig, who had authored the Fourth Circuit's opinion invalidating the VAWA in the lower court precursor to *Morrison*. Brzonkala v. Virginia Polytechnic Inst. & State Univ., 169 F.3d 820 (4th Cir. 1999).

7. **What's next? Superfund?** Much nervous (or giddy, depending on your point of view) anticipation surrounds the question of which environmental statute might be next on the Commerce Clause chopping block. Several years ago, a district court in Alabama created a stir when it held that the Commerce Clause prohibited the federal government from ordering a cleanup of a contaminated piece of land in Alabama pursuant to the Comprehensive Environmental Response, Cleanup, and Liability Act (CERCLA). The court found that the contamination was limited to soil and groundwater that would not migrate far enough to affect any areas beyond the immediate Alabama locale, and thus did not justify federal jurisdiction over the site under the Commerce Clause. United States v. Olin Corp., 927 F. Supp. 1502 (S.D. Ala. 1996). The court of appeals reversed, concluding that "CERCLA reflects Congress's recognition that both on-site and off-site disposal of hazardous waste threaten interstate commerce." United States v. Olin Corp., 107 F.3d 1506, 1511 (11th Cir. 1997).

In considering other, perhaps more direct, interstate economic effects on commerce in this setting, it is interesting to advert to some of the furor surrounding the legislative efforts to change the liability scheme in CERCLA, detailed in Chapter 19. One group strongly opposed to eliminating retroactive liability is composed of parties who have cleaned sites and "paid the price" under CERCLA. This group is afraid that their competitors who have not yet done so will escape liability and gain a competitive advantage in (plainly interstate) commerce. For a case citing such a competitive advantage in upholding a federal regulatory scheme against a Commerce Clause challenge, see United States v. Ho, 311 F.3d 589 (5th Cir. 2002) (upholding federal asbestos removal requirements).

8. The Commerce Clause and endangered species. Commerce Clause challenges to federal endangered species protections have prompted a variety of judicial theories in support of federal authority. In National Ass'n of Home Builders v. Babbitt, 130 F.3d 1041 (D.C. Cir. 1997), a builders' association and others including local governments challenged the ESA as it affected certain lands located solely in California. The land involved was designated as critical habitat of the Delhi Sands Flower-Loving Fly, a fly whose known habitat is restricted to a few hundred square miles in the San Bernadino area. ESA §9 prohibits actions that "take" a listed endangered species (see Chapter 16), and in this case it had the effect of forcing substantial design changes for the layout of a new hospital and its access roads. In response to the constitutional claim, the court stated:

> It is clear that, in this instance, §9(a)(1) of the ESA is not a regulation of the instrumentalities of interstate commerce or of persons or things in interstate commerce. As a result, only the first and the third categories of activity discussed in *Lopez* will be examined. In evaluating whether ESA §9(a)(1) is a regulation of the use of the channels of interstate commerce or of activity that substantially affects interstate commerce, we may look not only to the effect of the extinction of the individual endangered species at issue in this case, but also to the aggregate effect of the extinction of all similarly situated endangered species. As the *Lopez* Court explained, "'where a general regulatory statute bears a substantial relation to commerce, the de minimis character of individual instances arising under the statute is of no consequence.'" *Lopez*, 514 U.S. at 558. If a statute regulates "a class of activities...within reach of the federal power," the courts have "no power 'to excise, as trivial, individual instances' of the class," id. Because §9(a)(1) of the ESA regulates a class of activities — takings of endangered species — that is within Congress' Commerce Clause power under both the first and third *Lopez* categories, application of §9(a)(1) to the Fly is constitutional.

In Rancho Viejo v. Norton, 323 F.3d 1062 (D.C. Cir. 2003), the D.C. Circuit reaffirmed its holding in *National Association of Home Builders* in rejecting a challenge to the application of the ESA to a housing development that would jeopardize the arroyo southwestern toad. The court wrote:

> *Morrison* instructs that "the proper inquiry" is whether the challenge is to "a *regulation of activity* that substantially affects interstate commerce." Similarly, SWANCC declares that what is required is an evaluation of "*the precise object or activity* that, in the aggregate, substantially affects interstate commerce." When, as directed, we turn our attention to the precise activity that is regulated in this case, there is no question but that it is economic in nature.

> That regulated activity is Rancho Viejo's planned commercial development, not the arroyo toad that it threatens. The ESA does not purport to tell toads what they may or may not do. Rather, §9 limits the taking of listed species, and its prohibitions and corresponding penalties apply to the persons who do the taking, not to

the species that are taken. In this case, the prohibited taking is accomplished by commercial construction, and the unlawful taker is Rancho Viejo.

Judge Ginsburg concurred based on this understanding of the court's rationale:

> With respect to a species that is not an article in interstate commerce and does not affect interstate commerce, a take can be regulated if — but only if — the take itself substantially affects interstate commerce. The large-scale residential development that is the take in this case clearly does affect interstate commerce. Just as important, however, the lone hiker in the woods, or the homeowner who moves dirt in order to landscape his property, though he takes the toad, does not affect interstate commerce.

In GDF Realty Invs. v. Norton, 326 F.3d 622 (5th Cir. 2003), the Fifth Circuit also brushed back a Commerce Clause challenge to the ESA, but on quite different grounds from those embraced by the D.C. Circuit. In *GDF Realty*, the Fifth Circuit found the necessary "substantial effect" on interstate commerce by aggregating the economic effects of all "takes" of species, rather than by considering the economic effects of the particular activity (there, real estate development) that would achieve the "take." For an impressive variety of approaches to the federal authority issue, see Gibbs v. Babbitt, 214 F.3d 483 (4th Cir. 2000), in which the court found the following sources of commerce clause authority for protecting endangered red wolves in the Southeastern U.S.: the tourism the red wolves generated substantially affected interstate commerce; the regulation of red wolf takings was closely connected to a second interstate market — scientific research; the taking of red wolves was connected to interstate markets for agricultural products and livestock (and if their population rebounded, their pelts could be sold in interstate commerce!); and, perhaps most notably, the regulation was tied to interstate commerce by the very fact that it was part of a comprehensive nationwide federal program for the protection of endangered species. Judicial deference to the judgment of the democratic branches was therefore appropriate.

Section 3. **THE ELEVENTH AMENDMENT THICKET**

In a 1996 decision, Seminole Tribe v. Florida, 517 U.S. 44, Justice Rehnquist reopened a cantankerous debate with environmental consequences over the meaning and effect of the Eleventh Amendment, which provides:

> The Judicial power of the United States shall not be construed to extend to any suit in law or equity, commenced or prosecuted against one of the United States by Citizens of another State, or by Citizens or Subjects of any Foreign State.

By its terms, the amendment would seem to be a relatively narrow limitation on the judicial jurisdiction of the federal courts when one of the several states is sued by a party fitting the description given in the amendment. Through a series of arcane decisions the amendment has not been limited to its terms.[16] The amendment now describes a broader principle of state sovereign immunity to suit in federal court (and elsewhere, under the most recent cases), playing a large role in a resurgent debate about federalism in this country.

---

16. In Hans v. Louisiana, 134 U.S. 1 (1890), the scope of the Eleventh Amendment was expanded from its literal language interpreting suits brought by citizens of other states or foreign nations to include citizens of the defendant state as well.

The relevance of the Eleventh Amendment to environmental law was, before *Seminole*, quite modest. The sole major environmental case raising a serious Eleventh Amendment issue was Pennsylvania v. Union Gas, 491 U.S. 1 (1989). There, the Court, by a 5–4 vote that produced no majority opinion, only a majority result, upheld the creation by Congress (using its commerce power to enact CERCLA) of a right for private parties to recover monetary relief in federal court from states found to be liable for cleanup costs under federal law. With *Union Gas* on the books, Congress had a relatively free hand in authorizing remedies against states that violated federal law. For example, as noted in the next chapter, many federal environmental laws expressly authorize citizen suits as a supplement to governmental enforcement. Under those laws, a state or local government that operated a polluting facility could be sued in federal court on the same basis as any other potential defendant. Likewise, Congress could permit a private suit against a state in federal court to compel the state to perform obligations it had undertaken with respect to environmental regulation.

Seminole, involving Indian casinos, not environmental laws, expressly overruled *Union Gas* and employed broad reasoning in doing so:

> We have understood the Eleventh Amendment to stand not so much for what it says, but for the presupposition...which it confirms. That presupposition...has two parts: first, that each State is a sovereign entity in our federal system; and second, that it is inherent in the nature of sovereignty not to be amenable to the suit of an individual without its consent....

> [In this statute] Congress clearly intended to abrogate the States' sovereign immunity.... In overruling Union Gas today, we reconfirm...the background principle of state sovereign immunity embodied in the Eleventh Amendment.... Even when the Constitution vests in Congress complete law-making authority over a particular area, the Eleventh Amendment prevents congressional authorization of suits by private parties against unconsenting States. The Eleventh Amendment restricts the judicial power under Article III, and Article I cannot be used to circumvent the constitutional limitations placed upon federal jurisdiction. Petitioner's suit against the State of Florida must be dismissed for a lack of jurisdiction. 517 U.S. at 54, 57, 72–73 (1996).

With *Union Gas* overruled, the effect is to prevent private enforcement suits, limiting enforcement to agencies in the political process. Congress loses the ability to enlist private federal court enforcement as a deterrent to state violations of federal environmental law. (The federal government can still bring its own lawsuits against the states in federal court because those are pretty clearly not affected by the Eleventh Amendment.) *Seminole* takes what might be described as a strict chronological approach to parsing out the federal-state power relationship in this area. Justice Rehnquist's opinion, which commanded five votes, took the position that the Eleventh Amendment creates a right of states to be free from private citizens' suits in federal court to recover monetary relief. Congress is not, despite the Supremacy Clause, free to change this under most of its enumerated powers because these powers were granted before the ratification of the Eleventh Amendment.[17] The exception to this general rule would be legislation passed

---

17. The federal law involved in *Seminole* was enacted pursuant to the commerce power as it applies to Indian tribes.

pursuant to the enumerated powers granted to Congress by the post-Civil War amendments, because they came after the Eleventh Amendment and, therefore, are not subject to Eleventh Amendment limitation.

COMMENTARY & QUESTIONS

1. **A short, simplified view of Eleventh Amendment jurisprudence for those who really want to know.** Almost since its enactment, the meaning of the Eleventh Amendment has been shrouded in uncertainty. There is a fair amount of agreement that the amendment was designed to overrule Chisholm v. Georgia, 2 Dall. 419 (1793). In that case, a South Carolina citizen brought a federal lawsuit to recover money owed on a debt incurred by the State of Georgia as part of its Revolutionary War effort. The Court held that Congress could authorize such suits against states by foreigners or citizens of other states. *Chisholm* prompted fears that British nationals and American Tories would file federal lawsuits seeking to collect Revolutionary War debts of the states, and claims of wartime expropriation. The new Eleventh Amendment therefore removed Congress's power to authorize such claims from the federal Article III judicial power.

Things got murkier after the 1890 case of Hans v. Louisiana, 134 U.S. 1. In *Hans* the Court extended the Eleventh Amendment, with no textual support whatever, to suits brought by citizens of a state against that state, stating that to do otherwise would be "anomalous." Professor Erwin Chemerinsky notes the three very different views that followed. One theory is that the Eleventh Amendment puts a general limitation on the power of the federal courts. This view relies on *Hans* as demonstrating the greater breadth of the amendment and "affirms that the fundamental principle of [state] sovereign immunity limits the grant of [federal] judicial authority in Article III." The second major view of the Eleventh Amendment is that it reinstates the common law sovereign immunity of the states. This plays out into three general subprinciples that can be used to understand the array of decisions that have since followed: (a) states are free to consent to suit and, therefore, can waive their immunity; (b) Congress is free to authorize federal jurisdiction in suits against states (which may then opt to waive their immunity); and (c) because the immunity is grounded in common law, Congress can abrogate that immunity via statute. The third view is that the Eleventh Amendment restricts the diversity jurisdiction of the federal courts, when the basis for jurisdiction is the different citizenship of the parties to the lawsuit. On this view, Congress is unfettered in authorizing suits and abrogating the immunity of the states when the case is one based on federal law (or any jurisdictional basis other than diversity of citizenship). Chemerinsky, Federal Jurisdiction 4th ed., at §7.3 (2003).

Other issues have been tacked onto the Eleventh Amendment. Federalism arguments have produced theories of statutory construction requiring explicit congressional intent to allow suit against the state in the first place. Second are cases like Ex parte Young, 209 U.S. 123 (1908), that bypass the Eleventh Amendment by saying that suits against a state "may be brought in federal court by naming the state officer as the defendant." Chemerinsky, at §7.5. The continuing convoluted legal and political nuances of

Eleventh Amendment caselaw will be quite relevant to environmental law. See Strahan v. Coxe, 127 F.3d 155 (1st Cir. 1997) (state officials, sued for licensing fishing gear that harms endangered right whales, claimed, unsuccessfully, that federal government cannot require it to protect whales).

2. *Seminole*'s holding in its Eleventh Amendment context. *Seminole*'s five-member majority is comprised of the four Union Gas dissenters plus Justice Thomas. The majority opts for the first of the three visions of the Eleventh Amendment described in the previous note, that the amendment limits the subject matter jurisdiction of the federal courts (except for cases arising under legislation passed pursuant to the later-in-time Fourteenth Amendment). In this way, *Seminole* has the effect of preventing Congress from abrogating state immunity, even when it legislates pursuant to an enumerated power. Particularly when the majority's Ex parte Young discussion is added in, the *Seminole* majority has painted with a very broad brush. In an effort to blunt criticism that the majority was disregarding precedent in overruling *Union Gas*, Justice Rehnquist observed that the principle of stare decisis has never been slavishly followed by the Supreme Court in areas where the controlling precedents were "unworkable." He then adds, "Our willingness to reconsider our earlier decisions has been particularly true in constitutional cases, because in such cases 'correction through legislative action is practically impossible.'" This latter addition is ironic. Before *Seminole*, Congress, the political and electorally responsible branch, by ordinary legislation, controlled the extent and degree of state sovereign immunity to suits in federal court that redressed violations of federal law. Congress was "aided" in being sensitive to state sovereignty by the numerous interpretive doctrines that the Court had established that, in effect, disfavored the abrogation of state immunity. After *Seminole*, and the nonliteral, textually unsupported view of the Eleventh Amendment that it contains, only constitutional amendment can alter its allocation of power between the Congress and the states.

3. *Seminole*'s holding in its environmental law context. The *Seminole* decision addresses only cases in which federal suit is brought against a state by a private party. This leaves unaffected federal court enforcement of federal law in suits brought by the United States. The dissenters are quite explicit in making this point, and the majority also, although it is less directly stated, subscribes to that view as well. This can be inferred from the cases that the majority opinion uses to support its position. For example, in a key passage, Justice Rehnquist quotes a phrase from the Federalist, No. 81, that had been quoted in a previous Eleventh Amendment case: "[i]t is inherent in the nature of sovereignty not to be amenable to the suit of an *individual* without its consent" (emphasis added by editor). As another example, in discussing the breadth of the Eleventh Amendment bar to federal suit as not being a function of the remedy sought in a particular case, the majority says, "The Eleventh Amendment does not exist solely in order to preven[t] federal court judgments that must be paid out of a State's treasury," it also serves to "avoid the indignity of subjecting a State to the coercive process of federal judicial tribunals at the instance of *private parties*." (Emphasis added by editor, the Court quoting (for the second part) Puerto Rico Aqueduct & Sewer Auth. v. Metcalf & Eddy, Inc., 506 U.S. 139, 146 (1993).)

The impact of *Seminole* on environmental law may be significant. Potentially, *Seminole* applies to all private efforts to enforce federal law-based environmental obligations in federal court against states, state entities, and state officers. Such suits are common, if not ubiquitous. For example, states operate large numbers of facilities that are regulated by the CAA or the CWA. Violations of permits required by those federal acts (and others) can be raised by private parties under the statutes' citizen suit provisions. More generally, many of those same laws impose requirements on the states as regulators who can be sued by citizens to spur enforcement. Private party suits in federal court against nonconsenting states are precluded by *Seminole*.

4. **Getting around *Seminole* by going to state court: not anymore!** There is nothing in *Seminole* (or anything in the text of the Eleventh Amendment) that limits the ability of private suits against states in *state* court. But in Alden v. Maine, 527 U.S. 706 (1999), the Court held that the amendment prohibited a state probation officer from suing in a Maine state court to enforce remedies granted by the federal Fair Labor Standards Act relating to overtime pay. Justice Kennedy, writing for the majority, ruled that Congress could not subject the state to such a suit in state court without state consent.

5. **Getting around *Seminole* in federal court: not anymore!** *Seminole* does not apply if the state involved in a particular case waives its immunity. Politically, states wishing to project a favorable image on environmental issues may be willing to be sued in these cases. Alternatively, Congress may be able to induce the states to waive their immunity, although this avenue around *Seminole* is complicated by the twists and turns of pre-*Seminole* Eleventh Amendment doctrine. One early way around the amendment was thought to be "constructive waiver." The idea here was that if a state entered into a field that Congress had regulated and in which Congress had prescribed federal judicial remedies, the state, by entering the field, "consented" to be sued. See Parden v. Terminal Ry. of Ala. State Docks Dep't, 377 U.S. 184 (1964). *Parden* is another victim of the Court's recent reworking of Eleventh Amendment doctrine. In College Sav. Bank v. Florida Prepaid Postsecondary Educ. Expense Bd., 527 U.S. 666, 676 (1999), the five-member majority referred to *Parden* as an "elliptical opinion that stands at the nadir of our waiver (and, for that matter, sovereign immunity) jurisprudence." So much for the constructive waiver theory.

6. **State waivers of their own immunity.** What remains possible is where states expressly waive their Eleventh Amendment immunity. Congress, in the wake of *Seminole*, may well begin to require such express waivers as a condition precedent to the receipt of federal funds. For example, a waiver of immunity could be a precondition to receipt of federal funds for the construction of POTWs, mass-transit systems, highways, and so on. The problem with this approach is twofold. First, it requires some lead time for Congress to act. In the interim, the environment may suffer. Second, it requires some political will on the part of Congress. It is important to remember that one facet of federal environmental law remains unchanged in all this: Under the wording of the Eleventh Amendment, the federal government remains free to bring suits in its own name to enforce federal environmental laws against states. The only limits on this power are a function of federal enforcement resources and the will to use them.

7. **Changes in the federal-state power structure, changes for environmental law.**
Before the Court's recent Eleventh Amendment cases, the dominant constitutional
precept had been the Supremacy Clause of Article VI. Under that precept, federal legislation that created potential state liability was considered the paramount law. State
sovereign immunity was relevant only insofar as it colored interpretations of federal
court jurisdiction in Eleventh Amendment settings. Congress's paramount authority
was checked by the requirement that Congress be acting pursuant to an enumerated
power when it regulated the states. Federal supremacy was softened further by
presumptions that Congress, in general, does not intend to encroach on state sovereignty unless that intent is clear. The recent cases have apparently changed all of that.
States are no longer subject to monetary damage suits by private citizens in the absence
of state consent by waiver of sovereign immunity.

The relevance of this to environmental law is many-fold. Most obviously, citizen suits
against state entity defendants that seek money damages are now possible only where
the state consents. Thus, for example, a state-run office facility, such as a waste incinerator, would not be subject to damage remedies in citizen suits absent a waiver of
immunity. The various dissenting opinions asserted that federal enforcement of federal
law against an unconsenting state is not affected by these cases. Strictly speaking, that
issue is not presented, but Justice Kennedy's *Alden* opinion in several places discussed
the states' "immunity from private suit." The dissenters took note of the window of
opportunity for Congress to create remedies for the state left open by that possibility.
Justice Breyer, for example, said:

> I recognize the possibility that Congress may achieve its objectives in other ways.
> Ex parte Young, 209 U.S. 123 (1908), is still available, though effective only where
> damages remedies are not important. Congress, too, might create a federal
> damages-collecting "enforcement" bureaucracy charged with responsibilities that
> Congress would prefer to place in the hands of States or private citizens; see also
> Printz v. United States, 521 U.S. 898, 977 (1997) (Breyer, J., dissenting). Or perhaps
> Congress will be able to achieve the results it seeks (including decentralization) by
> embodying the necessary state "waivers" in federal funding programs — in which
> case, the Court's decisions simply impose upon Congress the burden of rewriting
> legislation, for no apparent reason.

Justice Breyer, however, followed that passage with the glum assessment, "But none of
these alternatives is satisfactory."

In the environmental context, the key role of citizen enforcement and the threat of citizen enforcement has been instrumental in making existing laws effective. Thus even if
federal environmental laws can be enforced against unconsenting states by federal
government agencies, it is hard to imagine EPA or any other federal plaintiff being able
to take up the full burden of enforcing all of the many cases of federal environmental
law violations involving state defendants, even if a federal agency could marshal the
political capital to do so.

8. **Implications for environmental justice.** In Kimel v. Florida Bd. of Regents, 528 U.S.
62 (2000), the Court found that, in enacting the Age Discrimination in Employment
Act, 29 U.S.C. §621, Congress plainly intended to abrogate the states' Eleventh
Amendment immunity for private suits alleging violations of the Act. The Court
concluded, however, that such abrogation was not within Congress's authority under

§5 of the Fourteenth Amendment. The Court found that the Act was a proper exercise of congressional power under the Commerce Clause, not under §5 of the Fourteenth Amendment, because age is not a "suspect" classification that would justify enhanced scrutiny under the Court's established equal protection jurisprudence.

Kimel reiterates that Congress may authorize private suits against the states only where it does so under §5 of the Fourteenth Amendment and consistently with the Supreme Court's application of the Fourteenth Amendment. Kimel consequently calls into question the constitutionality of private lawsuits to enforce Title VI of the Civil Rights Act of 1964 against states whose programs allegedly impose disparate environmental impacts on communities of color. See, e.g., Chester Residents Concerned for the Quality of Living v. Seif, 132 F.3d 925 (3d Cir. 1997), vacated, 524 U.S. 974 (1998). (*Chester Residents* and like cases are discussed in Chapter 11.) Such suits would be inconsistent with the Court's holdings that require discriminatory *intent* to justify suit under the Fourteenth Amendment's Equal Protection Clause. See, e.g., Village of Arlington Heights v. Metropolitan Housing Dev. Corp., 429 U.S. 252, 265 (1977). Requiring a showing of intentional discrimination would effectively preclude such suits.

9. **Analogues to federalism in the European Union: subsidiarity.** The European Union provides a rough analogy to a federal state such as the United States. Legal authority or "competence" is divided between Union-level organs, on one hand, that have the capacity to legislate throughout the EU, and the 15 (soon to be 25) member states on the other. In response to concerns that the EU was headed in the direction of becoming a federal state — a "United States of Europe" — the principle of "subsidiarity" has played an important role in EU law and policy in recent years. According to the Treaty on European Union, "in areas which do not fall within its exclusive competence, the Community shall take action...only if and insofar as the objectives of the proposed action cannot be sufficiently achieved by the Member States and can therefore, by reason of the scale or effects of the proposed action, be better achieved by the Community." In other words, other things being equal, the principle of subsidiarity states a preference for taking governmental action at the most local level of political organization, that closest to the public. At least until recently, the U.S. presumption has been quite the opposite. The European principle of subsidiarity, in addition to providing a counterweight to the centralizing tendency of the EU organs, is also a response to the perceived "democratic deficit" in the Union's organs, most of which are located in Brussels, Belgium. Notwithstanding the principle of subsidiarity, however, the European Union has adopted extensive legislation at the EU level on many of the same issues that have prompted federal action in the U.S. — air, surface water, waste, to name a few — as well as some that have no analogue such as consumer packaging. Although the principle of subsidiarity has legal content and provides a basis for judicial review in the European Court of Justice, the Court has been quite deferential to political decisions taken by the law-making organs of the EU as to the appropriate distribution of competence between the Union and the member states. Is a centralized perspective presumptively more rational in some environmental areas? Taken together with insights into the U.S. legal system in this chapter, what broad conclusions could you draw about the appropriate level for environmental legislation in federal and quasi-federal systems?

Chapter 7

THE ADMINISTRATIVE LAW OF ENVIRONMENTAL LAW

A. THE EVOLUTION OF THE ADMINISTRATIVE PROCESS

Looking back over the history of the administrative process in America, it can be divided analytically into at least six different stages.[1]

• **The passive era.** The first stage would begin at the birth of the republic, or earlier, before the Revolution, when, it can be argued, the private marketplace economy was in fact the predominant "government" of America. Many historians argue that the Revolution was more an economic than a political phenomenon: The colonies and their economies matured "like ripe fruit," and when the colonies had become self-sufficient market entities they dropped away from Great Britain. In terms of domestic governance the colonial structures, and then the state, federal, and local governments, initially merely attended to minor governmental chores, and their major early role was to facilitate the private marketplace. Government agencies built roads, canals, and a postal system, and provided a defense of borders and international trade.

• **1880+** The second stage, the advent of regulatory agencies, can be traced to the 1880s, when federal and state governments reacted to the perceived excesses of the Industrial Revolution's unregulated marketplace, including child labor, railroad gouging of farmers and shippers, and the like. Society discovered that there was a civic realm beyond the structures of the marketplace economy. Regulatory agencies were invented to correct "market failures," by imposing a bipolar theory of social governance: The marketplace on one hand would supply economic strength, and government on the other would protect citizens and society from the excesses of the marketplace in specific regulated areas. Reaction against governmental regulation, coming from the marketplace's major players, was immediate and passionate in the 1890s, and continues in much the same

---

1. This historical analysis builds upon ideas in Stewart, The Reformation of American Administrative Law, 88 Harv. L. Rev. 1669 (1975).

rhetorical terms today. From the beginning, however, private regulated interests in the marketplace did not merely oppose governmental regulatory agencies; they also moved to co-opt them. As the Attorney General of the United States wrote to the president of a railroad in 1892 in response to the latter's plea for abolition of the Interstate Commerce Commission as a "socialistic" federal regulatory agency:

> The Commission...is or can be made of great use to the railroads. It satisfies the popular clamor for government supervision of railroads, at the same time that the supervision is almost entirely nominal. Further, the older such a commission gets to be, the more inclined it would be found to take the business and railroad view of things. It thus becomes a sort of barrier between the railroad corporations and the people, and a sort of protection against hasty and crude legislation hostile to railroad interests.... The part of wisdom is not to destroy the Commission, but to utilize it.[2]

In any event, in this era government involvement in the economy remained the exception, not the rule. As Calvin Coolidge is supposed to have said in 1925, "The business of government is business."

• **1930+** The third stage, in the 1930s, marked a shift from regulatory agencies as mere occasional correctives, to the theory that agencies can be given a primary directive role in the economy, at least during national traumas such as the Great Depression and the Second World War. The New Deal produced a host of agencies that were managers as well as regulators. It was at this point that the "administrative state" became a tangible entity. The powers of government reached into areas never before regulated. (This is not to say that the process was systematically rational or even that government became the dominant factor in American society. The relatively unfettered private economy remained the preeminent force in the daily life of the nation.)

• **1946+** In 1946, a reaction against regulatory agency high-handedness resulted in the passage of the federal Administrative Procedures Act (APA),[3] copied in many states. There had always been a reaction against governmental interference with the marketplace because so much human energy and passion is invested in private property and income-generating activities, and government tends to get in the way. The APA's clear and dominating purpose was to prevent the exercise of agency peremptory power through required procedures and judicial control of the agency process.

Nevertheless the United States, faced with all the postwar complexities of life as a great power, melting pot, social experiment, and economic dynamo, continued to develop its administrative substructure at every level of government. By 1968 the federal agencies comprised more than 130 agencies and 2 million civil servants.

• **1960s+** The next phase in the evolution of administrative law is quite closely linked to the growth of environmentalism: It was a 1960s shift from the bipolar model — regulatory agency versus regulated industry — to a far more realistic pluralistic, multicentric model. Citizen outsiders began to use the legal tools created by industry for challenging

---

2. Letter from Attorney General Richard Olney to Charles Perkins, in Jaffe, The Effective Limits of the Administrative Process, 67 Harv. L. Rev. 1105, 1109 (1954).

3. 5 U.S.C. §§501 et seq. (1946).

government agency powers, but deployed them against defendants who now were often agencies and industries working together (the "Establishment" that was targeted by 1960s activists). Beginning in 1966, the federal courts in particular began to be much more open to citizens — to environmentalists, consumers, civil rights activists, and so on — and the administrative process, responding to the courts, began to follow suit. From that pluralistic opening-up of the administrative law system came many of the significant social changes of the second half of the twentieth century.

• **1976+** The year 1976, however, provided early steps in an initiative of retrenchment against pluralistic democratic involvement in the administrative process. The *Vermont Yankee* case later in this chapter was a major contribution to this trend. The Supreme Court has since moved in a variety of ways to limit opportunities for citizens to involve themselves in judicial challenges of agencies and regulated interests, themes echoed in occasional post-1980 campaigns for deregulation.

These stages in the evolution of administrative law overlap one another, so that in modern society one can still simultaneously see a tendency to turn to governmental agencies to handle newly identified societal problems, a reaction against governmental agencies, a pluralistic tendency toward a continuing democratization of the administrative process, and counter-tendencies attempting to limit outsider citizen participation.

This quick excursion through history gives a sense of how environmental law, which has consistently been shaped by private citizens' activist efforts, reflects major cross-currents in the development of American government. The administrative state, built upon a foundation of common law, forces environmentalists to deal with all the varied advantages and disadvantages of the government process.

Because environmentalism has been so ready to rock the boat — persistently trying to force an evasive status quo to confront a broad range of important concerns in the civic-societal economy, about pollution, chemical exposures, and dwindling resources — environmental law has tended to be on the cutting edge of a wide range of fields, including equity, tort, civil procedure, and others already encountered. Administrative law is a prime example on this list. A modern administrative law course could be taught using environmental cases exclusively.

This chapter, however, does not purport to be a course in administrative law. It is a glimpse at the field, one meant to inform subsequent consideration of various environmental regulatory programs in later chapters.

B. ADMINISTRATIVE PROCESS AND ADMINISTRATIVE LAW IN A NUTSHELL

Practical questions of administrative law boil down to three broad areas of inquiry, analyzing:

   • The process by which government agencies (at all levels — local, state, federal, and perhaps even international) receive the powers that they apply in their various regulatory settings — this is the *delegation* issue.

• The methods by which they exercise their powers in particular cases. The three primary modes of agency action that impact upon third parties outside government are — *monitoring*, including data collection, *rulemaking*, and *adjudication*; all three can be undertaken by *formal*, *trial-type*, or *informal* procedures.

• How such agency exercises of power can be mobilized, demobilized, directed, overturned, or circumvented (by judicial review litigation second-guessing particular agency decisions, but also by the process of applying pressures within the legislative and executive branches of government, before or after decisions are made).

The Source of Power: Delegation. Agencies are just that: agents. Their only reason for existence, since they are not provided for in the federal Constitution or most state constitutions, is that the constitutionally created branches of government had more detailed work to do than they could conveniently do themselves. The constitutionally created branches accordingly delegated some of their powers to standing agents in order to spread the workload and drudgery of performing investigations, day-to-day oversight, and the hands-on administrative tasks of running a society.

This reality reflects the utilitarian assumption, common to all modern nations, that government has to take an active part in running a modern society. The market and various social relationships are incapable of managing the full scope and complexity of modern life. Without the external imposition of governmental powers into the market system, some important needs and values would not be adequately addressed. Without government, there would not be adequate machinery for defending our borders against enemies and building roads and schools for all. Without government, factories might well still be using the labor of children (which in localized market terms made compelling good sense) and disposing of pollution by dumping it willy-nilly.

Most government programs, therefore, originate in recognition of market failure, when the marketplace and processes of social accommodation have failed to do a job that a politically significant number of people think need doing. But virtually all such tasks turn out to be too much for the constitutionally established officials (a couple thousand or so legislators and judges in the federal government, and a handful of executives) to handle. So they create agents. (And then, of course, more can be done, so then even more new tasks can be undertaken by government, so then more agents have to be created, and then — but that's another issue.)

Agencies can be created by each branch of government, acting alone. Courts can set up "special masters" to handle administrative tasks; legislatures can set up their own budget-analysis and investigatory offices (CBO, GAO, OTA); chief executives can set up councils of economic advisors, security advisors, budget advisors, and environmental advisors. But in the vast majority of cases where an agency is set up to manage affairs that directly affect people outside of government, including most agencies affecting the environment, the agency will be created by an act of the legislature signed into law by the chief executive, and will be placed more or less into the bailiwick of the executive branch.

The powers and duties of most agencies, therefore, must be set out in the statutes that create them (their respective "organic acts"). Agencies hold only subsidiary powers; they can make only subsidiary rules. Their actions must be authorized by and conform to the requirements of the statutes (and, beyond the statutes, to the Constitution).

Delegation has often provided fertile ground for attacks on agency actions, especially at the state level, and especially rulemaking. Judges who dislike an agency action may turn to the "non-delegation doctrine" to void it: Did the statute give the agency the particular power it is attempting to exercise? Do the legislature and the chief executive have the right to delegate a particular role or power to an agent? Is the legislature's delegating language too broad or vague to give adequate definition of the powers for guidance of the agency and reviewing courts? In some cases, delegations to agencies have been voided under the separation of powers theory: The statute has impermissibly delegated legislative or judicial power to an agent that is a non-legislature and non-court. In some cases, agency actions have been struck down under the ultra vires ("beyond the powers") principle: The delegating statute did not grant a power specifically enough or extend it broadly enough to cover the particular kind of thing that the agency is attempting to do.

In the vast majority of federal cases, however, the non-delegation doctrine now is only a minor background constraint on agency action. After a number of attempts to use non-delegation to strike down environmental regulations for lack of a sufficiently clear delegated definition of "safety," even Justice Rehnquist rejected the non-delegation argument in the 2001 *American Trucking* decision, thereby substantially reducing its utility as a weapon against agencies.[4]

The Exercise of Agency Powers. An administrative agency is an ongoing, functioning organism. As such, it exercises a variety of powers, both internally, within the agency, and externally, impacting upon people outside the agency. The external powers include the power to investigate, require submission of information, etc., and these can be important. Day in and day out, however, the primary exercises of an agency's external powers occur in two ways — rulemaking (the issuance of regulations[5]), and adjudication (the process of making operative agency decisions by applying legal standards set out in statutes or regulations to the facts of particular cases). Most agencies are delegated the power to act in both ways, often according to their own choice of how best to proceed.

The life of the administrative state can be tracked through millions of reams of official paper each year. The RCRA statute, which is 96 pages long, for instance, has been arduously articulated through more than 150 pages of regulations. Each rulemaking reflects hundreds of hours of agency process and disputation. Administrative "adjudications" — which includes the process of applying statutes and rules to tens of

---

4. See Industrial Union Dep't, AFL-CIO v. American Petroleum Inst., 448 U.S. 607 (1980) (the Benzene case, Rehnquist, J., concurring opinion); American Textile Mfg. Inst. v. Donovan, 452 U.S. 490 (1981) (the Cotton Dust case, Rehnquist dissent). What would happen if courts held legislatures to a strict rule that the terms of all statutes must be "as precise as feasible"? In *American Trucking* (examined in depth in Chapter 11), however, the Court, including Justices Rehnquist and Scalia, emphatically overrode the circuit court's attempt to void a major EPA pollution standard with that restrictive delegation logic. Whitman v. American Trucking Assocs., 531 U.S. 457 (2001).

5. Rules and regulations: What is the difference between a rule and a regulation? Nothing.

thousands of cases each year — multiply the scope geometrically. And a large number of these agency processes are controversial, which makes their details important to lawyers. APA is the blueprint of modern federal administrative law, used almost universally as a model by the states as well. It sets out many (although not all) of the basic definitions and prescriptions for how an agency is to run itself — how to promulgate rules, how to give notice to the public, how hearings examiners (administrative law judges) are to proceed, and so on. Chapter 7 of the APA[6] prescribes the basis for judicial review of challenged agency actions.

Both rulemaking and agency adjudication can be accomplished "formally," that is, they can be done with full trial-type process — discovery, motions, production of evidence, cross-examination, stenographic record, and a decisionmaker bound to decide in a reasoned judgment only on the basis of the record produced. Both can also be undertaken "informally" through less than formal procedures and without full trial-type process. They also can be "hybrid," part trial-type process and part informal procedure. Hybrid procedures are not prescribed in the APA; they are applied when required by some other particular statute, by the voluntary decision of the agency itself, or, in some cases, by court order.

The following sections of the APA set out partial prescriptions for how these functions will be exercised; state codes have similar provisions.

	RULEMAKING	ADJUDICATION
Informal	§553, notice-and-comment, or less	(no prescribed process)
(hybrid, in-between)	§553, plus selected parts of §§556–557	(no prescribed process)
Formal	§553, plus full §§556–557 trial-type procedures, "TTP"	§554, plus full §§556–557 trial-type procedures, "TTP"

FIGURE 7-1

A matrix chart of the Administrative Procedure Act's prescriptions for agency process.

APA §553 says that informal rulemaking, when it affects parties outside government, at a minimum must provide for public notice and opportunity to comment prior to publication of a rule in the Federal Register.[7] Sections 556 and 557 are the add-ons for formal trial-type process — discovery, cross-examination, a reasoned decision on the full record, and so on — that can be added on to either adjudication or rulemaking. Section 554 is the prescription for formal adjudication, which always triggers the formal trial-type processes of §§556–557. There is no required process for informal adjudications, even though these are certainly the vast majority of agency actions.

---

6. 5 U.S.C. §§701-706.

7. Rulemaking typically moves through a series of public notice stages before a regulation becomes law. After having been developed within a labyrinth of internal agency procedures, a draft rule is finally published in the Federal Register in a Notice of Proposed Rulemaking, with an explanation of what formal or informal procedures will be applied. At minimum, the public has the opportunity to send in comments by mail. After at least 30 days, the agency can process the comments received and publish a Notice of Final Rulemaking in the Federal Register, along with its summarized reactions to public comments received. Every year or so, regulations are codified into the Code of Federal Regulations (CFR) (a woefully poorly organized compilation; thankfully, regulations can now be searched through Westlaw and Lexis, and Federal Register notices through Hein-on-Line).

Where an agency, for example, says "Yes, you may build a house there," or "No, you may not drain a swamp," or "Yes, you may treat pollution abatement as a tax-deductible business expense," or "No, you may not file a late application" — all these are typically informal adjudications, applying law to facts without trial-type procedures.

Battles are often fought between agencies and regulated parties, or intervening parties, about which kind of procedure the agency should follow, since often there is no express statutory requirement that an agency act through formal or informal rulemaking or adjudication. Sometimes parties want rulemaking rather than adjudication (because then an agency directive can be prospective only). More often parties try to get more formalized trial-type procedures, regardless of whether the agency is proceeding in rulemaking or adjudication. (Attorneys apparently consider that, at least in most cases, the more procedure they get, the better the ultimate deal they'll get for their clients.)

The arguments for more procedure usually come down to one of a couple constitutional issues. Procedural due process is the prime argument, though it is not easy to force an agency to give procedure it doesn't want to give.[8] The other constitutional argument is grounded upon the basic judicial review jurisdiction of Article III of the U.S. Constitution: It is reflected in holdings that a court should require more procedure in a given case for the sake of the integrity of its own judicial review role, in order to produce a sufficient body of data (on a formal or informal agency record) to permit it to make an adequately incisive, though deferential, review of the agency action.

Contending Forces — Four Blocs. In order to understand the realities of modern environmental law's policy and practice, one must take note of the various political players that shape the outcomes of particular issues in the governance process. In operative terms, on any given issue there are typically four significant blocs that are likely to be actively involved and to play significant roles in the determination of administrative outcomes — *industrial-commercial interests* acting individually or through their various organizations, the *administrative agency* or agencies, the *activist citizen associations*, and the *courts*, which typically have the final say. (To these could be added the legislature and the media, although these purport to play less directive adjunct roles in the process, and the White House itself which often finds itself at odds with its federal agencies.) In every administrative law case, diagramming out these blocs of players and their potential positions and tactical agendas, whether obvious or latent, is a sage practical reconnaissance process that usually makes attorneys much more effective.

Pressuring Agencies. There are very few significant legal or economic issues that do not turn in substantial part upon the decisions of governmental agencies — local, state, or federal. Since agencies wield such broad-ranging powers in modern society, pressuring them in one direction or another has become a fundamental task of hundreds of thousands of attorneys and other citizens, most concerned with particular private and corporate interests but a significant number serving avowed public interests. Pressure

---

8. The basic three-point balancing argument comes from Mathews v. Eldridge, 424 U.S. 319 (1976) — a court reviewing how much procedure an agency must constitutionally give a claimant should weigh (1) the hardship to the claimant in not receiving additional process, (2) the hardship to the government in having to provide additional process, and (3) the risk of error in not having particular additional procedures apply.

can be applied before or after a particular agency decision in a variety of forums. Agencies respond to lobbying, to the media, to internal or external politicking, and of course to the legislature that created them and annually can cut them down through the budget process, oversight hearings, and amendments to agencies' statutory authority.

Regulatory Agency Action — Rulemaking. In the regulatory setting, the first stage of official agency action often is the issuance of a regulation detailing permissible behaviors under a statute — for instance, setting out the maximum allowable discharge of particular pollutants. Some statutes are enforceable without further elaboration of details, but most aren't, and even in such cases adjectival rules are usually issued, procedural and substantive. Notices of Proposed Rulemaking are published in the Federal Register, followed by a time for at least written public comment, then a Notice of Final Rulemaking accompanied by written agency responses to comments received, with the rule later codified in the CFR.[9] But what initiates this rulemaking? In some cases, the base statute mandates rulemaking within certain deadlines, but more often the agency has to be prompted to start the rulemaking. Sometimes the initiation comes from within the agency leadership or staff, sometimes from industries and other lobbies that will be benefited by a rule if it is drafted in their favor. Sometimes agency rulemaking is forced by citizens, as in Chapter 11's NRDC v. Train, in which EPA was court-ordered to commence rulemaking and ultimately issue air pollution standards for lead.[10]

Regulations occupy a median position between statutes and mere agency guidelines. In the hierarchy of laws, the *U.S. Constitution* comes first, then *statutes*, then *regulations* that are issued by agencies as adjectival to statutes and that cannot contradict or exceed the terms of the statute. Below regulations are *guidelines* (or, more commonly, *guidance* in current EPA rubric). Guidance documents are issued to set out agency definitions and procedures that affect parties outside the agency, but they are deemed not to be binding. They are generally followed by the agency, however, and have been occasionally forced into §553 rulemaking by judges who believe they are de facto regulations.[11]

Regulatory Agency Action — "Adjudication." The concept of administrative adjudication does not necessarily involve anything resembling a court's procedure. Since it covers any occasion upon which agency staffers apply a morsel of their operative law —

---

9. Learning to move through the forest of regulatory materials is a complicated but necessary part of being an effective attorney. An excellent guidebook to this process is J. Anderson & D. Hirsch, Environmental Law Practice (2d ed. 2003), especially pages 6-52, which carry you through an administrative definition problem and provide a primer on using online databases for researching administrative materials.

10. NRDC v. Train, 545 F.2d 320 (D.C. Cir. 1976). Under APA §553(e), any person has a right to petition an agency for promulgation of a rule, and, especially if the petition actually proposes a title and draft language, this can be tactically very useful. If the agency declines, its basis for declining to move forward with the rule can then be challenged in court under APA §§555(e) and 706. See Baur v. Veneman, 352 F.3d 625 (2d Cir. 2003) (plaintiff who filed §553(e) petition seeking USDA rule banning processing of sick "downer" cows into consumer food products is entitled to judicial review of agency's refusal to do so).

11. See General Elec. Co. v. EPA, 290 F.3d 377, 379 (D.C. Cir. 2002) ("On its face the Guidance Document imposes binding obligations upon applicants to submit applications that conform to the Document and upon the Agency not to question an applicant's use of the 4.0 (mg/kg/day) -1 total toxicity factor. This is sufficient to render it a legislative rule [i.e., requiring notice-and-comment rulemaking if it is to be valid].").

from statutes, regulations, agency practices, common sense — to a set of facts presented to them, it can be very informal indeed.

Enforcement of environmental statutes, usually under the terms of regulations issued under the statutes, is initiated by agency staffers in a variety of formal or informal internal administrative procedures or directly in judicial proceedings. If agencies fail to enforce legal standards against violators, citizens can initiate enforcement themselves, for practical reasons, almost always in court. (See notes on congressional grants of standing for citizen enforcement later in this chapter.)

Lawsuits Against Agencies. Agencies are taken to court in two very different settings — cases in which a court is *reviewing* an agency decision and cases in which the agency is a defendant because of its programmatic actions. Consider the difference between the following two cases.

(1) *Rybachek v. EPA.* After 32 months processing comments from industry and the public on its Notice of Proposed Rulemaking for setting mining industry water pollution standards, EPA issued a 12-page rule establishing water pollution limitations for the placer mining industry (subsequently incorporated into 40 C.F.R. §440) including the following subsection excerpt:

ENVIRONMENTAL PROTECTION AGENCY
Notice of Final Rulemaking
53 Federal Register 18764 (May 24, 1988)

Ore Mining and Dressing; Point Source Category; Effluent Limitations Guidelines, Pretreatment Standards, and New Source Performance Standards....

§440.143 Effluent limitations representing the degree of effluent reduction attainable by the application of the best available technology economically achievable (BAT).... Any existing point source subject to this subpart must achieve the following effluent limitations....

(b) The volume of process wastewater which may be discharged from a dredge plant site shall not exceed: *Settleable solids:* 0.2 ml/liter ...

The Alaska placer mining industry then challenged the rule in court (in a case explored at length in Chapter 12):

Rybachek v. U.S. Environmental Protection Agency
United States Court of Appeals for the Ninth Circuit, 1990
904 F.2d 1276

O'SCANNLAIN, J. The Alaska Miners Association and Stanley and Rosalie Rybachek timely petitioned this court for review of the EPA's regulations...promulgating final effluent-limitation...standards.... [As to settleable solids:] The EPA determined that the settleable solids level achievable with settling ponds was 0.2 ml/l. The Rybacheks assert that the EPA has inadequate support for this determination and was required to set instead a higher level.... Between 1983 and 1986, the EPA took 73 samples of full-scale settling ponds at 39 different gold placer mines; 50 of these samples indicated levels of settleable solids at or below 0.2 ml/l after treatment...; ponds not achieving this level had discernible design or operating deficiencies.... Because...the proper factors were considered, and because...the EPA's determination of the 0.2 ml/l level [and each of the rule's other challenged effluent limitations] is supportable by the record, we uphold the EPA's determination.

(2) Hill v. TVA. Now compare the following judicial challenge, which is like literally thousands of U.S. cases since 1970 in which citizen plaintiffs have enforced federal environmental laws against private and public violators. This case ultimately came to the Supreme Court, an opinion that is excerpted in Chapter 16.

Hiram Hill, et al. v. Tennessee Valley Authority
United States District Court for the Eastern District of Tennessee, 1976
419 F. Supp. 753, 763-764

TAYLOR, J. Plaintiffs, the Association of Southeastern Biologists, the Audubon Council of Tennessee, Hiram Hill, Zygmunt Plater and Donald Cohen seek to enjoin the completion of the Tellico Dam and consequent impoundment of the Little Tennessee River. Plaintiffs allege that defendant TVA, a wholly-owned corporation of the United States, is acting in violation of §7 of the Endangered Species Act of 1973, 16 U.S.C. §1536, by bulldozing and clear-cutting trees and foliage along the banks of the Little Tennessee River and by proceeding with plans to impound the river.... We conclude that TVA has not acted arbitrarily, capriciously or otherwise not in accordance with the law in continuing further implementation of the Tellico Project. It has acted within the scope of authority given it by Congress and... has consulted with other agencies about the problem.... It is ordered that the plaintiffs' request for a permanent injunction in this action be, and hereby is, denied...[and] that the action be, and hereby is, dismissed on the merits....

In the first example, clearly the agency defendant's regulatory action is being subjected to *judicial review*, and in the second, the agency is itself straightforwardly the *statutory defendant*. As noted below, the distinction often can and should make a difference in the posture of the case and the amount of deference the court pays to the agency.

Judicial Review. Judicial review, however, is the most visible and commonly encountered constraint on agency freedom of action. Disgruntled persons in most cases can readily request judicial review of particular agency actions, as in *Rybachek* above, and judicial review can operate to cramp an agency's style even if ultimate reversal of the agency decision is not usually likely.

Judicial review of federal agency action operates under Chapter 7 of the APA. The challenging party must show standing, and reviewability under §702, and fulfill a few other judge-made requirements (ripeness for review, exhaustion of agency remedies, etc.). Section 706 then sets out a catalogue of challenges on the merits:[12] the "arbitrary, capricious, or abuse of discretion" test (for informal rulemaking or adjudication) or the

---

12. §706... To the extent necessary to decision and when presented, the reviewing court shall decide all relevant questions of law, interpret constitutional and statutory provisions, and determine the meaning or applicability of the terms of an agency action. The reviewing court shall—

(1) compel agency action unlawfully withheld or unreasonably delayed; and

(2) hold unlawful and set aside agency action, findings, and conclusions found to be—

requirement of "substantial evidence" supporting the decision (in the case of most formal proceedings).

Most substantive challenges of agency decisions turn on the latter two standards, reviewing the rather subjective question of whether the agency's decision was reasonable in the circumstances. In some environmental cases, to be sure, challenges to agency action come down to straightforward application and interpretation of statutes: Did the agency violate a provision of some particular law? In far more cases, however, the question is not so easy, instead turning on the assertion that the agency has exercised bad judgment. Courts understandably do not usually like to second-guess agencies, instead preferring to defer to agency discretion and expertise. But their Article III judicial mandate requires them to review cases presented.

Degrees of Deference. Issues constantly arise about what "standard of review" should be applied. In challenges to agency findings of fact, the judicial scrutiny can range from the rather minimal "arbitrary" test all the way to judicial takeover of the question (trial de novo). A little-remarked threshold question, noted above, is what is the agency's role that has brought it to court? Analytically there is a distinction between whether the agency's action is merely being *reviewed* or whether the agency is itself being sued as a direct defendant. As self-taught "citizen attorney general" Richard "Max" Strahan once said:

> Hey, why is the judge deferring to the Coast Guard's judgment about how to run their boats in the whales' critical habitat? We're not talking here about the agency as a regulator. Here we're talking about the agency as a perpetrator violating a federal statute by killing whales! Shouldn't that make a difference?[13]

When an agency is being sued for its allegedly illegal physical or programmatic actions rather than reviewed for its regulatory decisions, the posture of the case would seem to indicate less judicial deference to the agency. In *Overton Park*, which follows, the Supreme Court seems to regard the agency as a project construction agency rather than a regulator, and shows little deference. It is difficult, however, to find courts directly discussing this sliding-scale deference issue. Whether the agency is acting as regulator or alleged perpetrator, court challenges may confront issues about the scope

---

(A) arbitrary, capricious, an abuse of discretion, or otherwise not in accordance with law;

(B) contrary to constitutional right, power, privilege, or immunity;

(C) in excess of statutory jurisdiction, authority, or limitations, or short of statutory right;

(D) without observance of procedure required by law;

(E) unsupported by substantial evidence in a case subject to sections 556 and 557 of this title or otherwise reviewed on the record of an agency hearing provided by statute; or

(F) unwarranted by the facts to the extent that the facts are subject to trial de novo by the reviewing court.

In making the foregoing determinations, the court shall review the whole record or those parts of it cited by a party, and due account shall be taken of the rule of prejudicial error.

13. See Strahan v. Linnon, 966 F. Supp. 111 (D. Mass. 1997), Strahan v. Linnon, 1998 U.S. App. LEXIS 16314 (1st Cir. 1998). Non-lawyer "Max, the Prince of Whales" Strahan has spent more than two decades as an intelligent, persistent, annoying, endangered species activist litigating cases (usually pro se, by leave of court) that have gone as far as the Supreme Court. Strahan v. Coxe, 939 F. Supp. 963 (D. Mass. 1996), mostly aff'd in Strahan v. Coxe, 127 F.3d 155 (1st Cir. 1997), cert. denied sub nom. Coates v. Strahan, 525 U.S. 978 (1998). A long-time graduate student in physics, he is the transient public citizen agitator who filed the petition with the FWS that forced the listing of the northern spotted owl as an endangered species; he has obtained injunctions against practices threatening northern right whales and other endangered whales, and inspired the fictional character portrayed by Joe Pesci in the movie *With Honors*. See Allen, Devil Doing Angels' Work? Irascible Environmentalist Winning Battles in His War to Save the Right Whale, Boston Globe, Jan. 13, 1997, at C1.

of agency discretion. Discretion and deference are often paired in administrative law, but they are different concepts, not always exactly congruent.

Most court cases against agencies, however, are couched in terms of judicial *review*. In these cases the question is how deeply will the court pry into the particulars of a decision, especially when it realizes that the closer it looks, the more it is second-guessing and taking over the agency's decisional process? In all but the de novo cases, the question usually comes down to the same judicial determination: Could a reasonable agency official have reached this decision on this record of facts? The practical difference between various standards of judicial review comes down to differences in degrees and moods of deference to agencies in each case, reflecting different sensitivities to separation of powers issues. In the minuet of contending powers, moreover, courts can use the choice of different standards of review — arbitrary for loose review, substantial evidence for tougher — to effectuate a result that they personally prefer. Politics and ideology in this way insinuate themselves into judicial review of agency action.

In challenges to agency interpretations of law, the same sort of scale applies, although a bit less predictably. Judges often don't seem quite so inclined to defer to agencies' decisions of law (the agencies' interpretation of what a statute or regulation requires) as they do to agencies' decisions about questions of fact. See *Chevron* and *Mead* below.

Issues also arise on "scope of review": How broadly will the court look in scrutinizing the agency action? How much data and "record" will it require? Will it allow new evidence to be introduced in court proceedings that was not brought before the agency? Normally the scope of judicial review is limited to the record of whatever was compiled and presented in the challenged agency proceedings. In some cases, a court may say that its necessary scope of review requires more evidence to be prepared and presented.

Remedies. Finally there are questions of remedies. If an enforcement action reaches a successful end in the agency or in court, what remedy should be issued — penalties, fees, criminal penalties,[14] injunctive orders? If judicial review of an agency action finds it to be faulty, what sanction should the reviewing court apply against the agency — injunction, declaratory judgment, remand to the agency, or something else? Environmental administrative cases have sometimes fashioned quite creative remedy packages.

Summary. As this quick excursion should make clear, administrative law and administrative process make up a separate legal ecosystem that is intricately intertwined with hundreds of important environmental and jurisprudential issues, and differs in many regards from the standard litigation model that dominates the law school curriculum.

Whatever substantive area of practice a case arises in, it should by now be evident that a familiarity with underlying administrative law principles is a basic requirement of legal literacy. In no area is this truer than in environmental law.

---

14. One of the authors once briefly researched the possibility of convicting an agency head on a statutory felony charge. Some of the legal reasons, beyond politics, why such attempts are quixotic are set out in Smith, Shields for the King's Men: Official Immunity and Other Obstacles to Effective Prosecution of Federal Officials for Environmental Crimes, 16 Colum. J. Envtl. L. 1 (1991).

C. *OVERTON PARK* — A JUDICIAL REVIEW PARADIGM

The administrative agencies are intimately woven into the power fabric of the nation, and accordingly are linked to most of the environmental issues discovered and decried over the past few decades by environmentalists. Within themselves, agencies mirror many of the forces, procedures, and vested interests that cause environmental problems. It therefore comes as no surprise that environmentalists often find them-selves launching challenges against agency actions at all three levels of government — federal, state, and local. Because of their political context, citizen interventions often get short shrift in the agency process,[15] so citizen activists end up going to court.

In administrative law lawsuits, environmental plaintiffs are usually not asking the court to take over the matter and make the "right" decision itself. Rather, when a court is asked to look at an agency decision in most cases it is only applying judicial review, and that limitation has consequences. Judicial review of agency actions differs from review of decisions made by lower court judges or juries. An agency is a creature of a different branch of government, so more deference is required. Too much deference, however, would mean that courts abdicate their judicial role. So the critical question of administrative law is how, and how much, the court will scrutinize what an official agency has done.

Plaintiffs seeking judicial review of administrative action must first successfully pass a series of threshold obstacles — standing, reviewability, ripeness, exhaustion, and others. The reviewing court then turns to scrutiny of the procedural and substantive merits of the government actions being challenged.

Section 1. THE *OVERTON PARK* CASE

In the following case, note the plaintiffs' array of arguments: that they did not receive adequate procedures, that the agency decision was substantively wrong, and that the Court should extend the most probing, least deferential, level of scrutiny to the agency's fact-finding and decisions of law. They lost on all these battle points but won their road war.

The Road

I think that I have never knowed, a sight as lovely as a road.

A road upon whose concrete tops, the flow of traffic never stops;

A road that costs a lot to build, just as the City Council willed;

A road the planners say we need, to get the cars to greater speed;

We've let the contracts so dig in, and let the chopping now begin;

Somebody else can make a tree, but roads are made by guys like me.

— Mike Royko[16]

---

15. In the *Pigeon River* case, for instance, the citizens were rebuffed by the agency, which considered itself the rightful public representative in deciding whether the forest reserve should be drilled for oil, and they had to face the agency standing alongside the oil company when they went to court. West Mich. Envtl. Action Council v. NRC, 275 N.W. 2d 538 (Mich. 1979).

16. For further evidence of the inspirational qualities of trees, see Fisher v. Lowe, 333 N.W.2d 67 (Mich. Ct. App. 1983).

Citizens to Preserve Overton Park, Inc. v. Volpe
Supreme Court of the United States, 1971
401 U.S. 402

[The Parkland Act, §4(f) of the Department of Transportation Act of 1966 and §138 of the Federal Aid to Highways Act of 1968,[17] provides as follows:]

> §4(f)... It is hereby declared to be the national policy that special effort should be made to preserve the natural beauty of the countryside and public park and recreation lands, wildlife and waterfowl refuges, and historic sites. The Secretary of Transportation... shall not approve any program or project which requires the use of any publicly owned land from a public park, recreation area, or wildlife and waterfowl refuge of national, State, or local significance as determined by the Federal, State, or local officials having jurisdiction thereof, or any land from an historic site of national, State, or local significance...unless (1) there is no feasible and prudent alternative to the use of such land, and (2) such program includes all possible planning to minimize harm to such park, recreational area, wildlife and waterfowl refuge, or historic site resulting from such use.

MARSHALL, J. The growing public concern about the quality of our natural environment has prompted Congress in recent years to enact legislation designed to curb the accelerating destruction of our county's natural beauty. We are concerned in this case with §4(f) of the Department of Transportation Act of 1966, as amended, and [§138] of the Federal-Aid Highway Act of 1968.

Petitioners, private citizens as well as local and national conservation organizations, contend that the Secretary has violated these statutes by authorizing the expenditure of federal funds for the construction of a six-lane interstate highway through a public park in Memphis, Tennessee....

Overton Park is a 342-acre city park located near the center of Memphis. The park contains a zoo, a nine-hole municipal golf course, an outdoor theater, nature trails, a bridle path, an art academy, picnic areas, and 170 acres of forest. The proposed highway, which is to be a six-lane high-speed expressway, will sever the zoo from the rest of the park. Although the roadway will be depressed below ground level except where it crosses a small creek, 26 acres of the park will be destroyed. The highway is to be a segment of Interstate Highway I-40, part of the National System of Interstate and Defense Highways. I-40 will provide Memphis with a major east-west expressway which will allow easier access to downtown Memphis from the residential areas on the eastern edge of the city.

Although the route through the park was approved by the Bureau of Public Roads in 1956 and by the Federal Highways Administration [FHWA] in 1966, the enactment of §4(f) of the Department of Transportation Act prevented distribution of federal funds for the section of the highway designated to go through Overton Park until the Secretary of Transportation determined whether the requirements of §4(f) had been met. Federal funding for the rest of the project was, however, available, and the state acquired a right-of-way on both sides of the park. In April 1968, the Secretary announced that he concurred in the judgment of local officials that I-40 should be built through the park. And in September 1969 the State acquired the right-of-way inside Overton Park from the city. Final approval for the project — the route as well as the design — was not announced until November 1969, after Congress had reiterated in §138 of the Federal-Aid Highway Act that highway construction through public parks was to be restricted. Neither announcement approving the route and design of I-40 was accompanied by a statement

---

17. 49 U.S.C. §1653(f) and 23 U.S.C. §138. The two sections embody exactly the same language.

of the Secretary's factual findings. He did not indicate why he believed there were no feasible and prudent alternative routes or why design changes could not be made to reduce the harm to the park.

Petitioners contend that the Secretary's action is invalid without such formal findings and that the Secretary did not make an independent determination but merely relied on the judgment of the Memphis City Council. They also contend that it would be "feasible and prudent" to route I-40 around Overton Park either to the north or to the south. And they argue that if these alternative routes are not "feasible and prudent," the present plan does not include "all possible" methods for reducing harm to the park. Petitioners claim that I-40 could be built under the park by using either of two possible tunneling methods,[18] and the claim that, at a minimum, by using advanced drainage techniques the expressway could be depressed below ground level along the entire route through the park including the section that crosses the small creek.

Respondent [FHWA argues] that it was unnecessary for the Secretary to make formal findings, and that he did, in fact, exercise his own independent judgment which was supported by the facts. In the District Court, respondents introduced affidavits, prepared specifically for this litigation, which indicated that the Secretary had made the decision and that the decision was supportable....

We agree that formal findings were not required. But we do not believe that in this case judicial review based solely on litigation affidavits was adequate.

A threshold question — whether petitioners are entitled to any judicial review — is easily answered. Section 701 of the APA provides that the action of "each authority of the Government of the United States," which includes the Department of Transportation, is subject to judicial review except where there is a statutory prohibition on review or where "agency action is committed to agency discretion by law." In this case, there is no indication that Congress sought to prohibit judicial review and there is most certainly no "showing of 'clear and convincing evidence' of a...legislative intent" to restrict access to judicial review. Abbott Laboratories v. Gardner, 387 U.S. 136, 141 (1967).

Similarly, the Secretary's decision here does not fall within the exception for action "committed to agency discretion." This is a very narrow exception. The legislative history of the APA indicates that it is applicable in those rare instances where "statutes are drawn in such broad terms that in a given case there is no law to apply." S. Rep. No. 752, 79th Cong., 1st Sess., 26 (1945).

Section 4(f) of the Department of Transportation Act and §138 of the Federal-Aid Highway Act are clear and specific directives. Both [Acts] provide that the Secretary "shall not approve any program or project" that requires the use of any public parkland "unless (1) there is no feasible and prudent alternative to the use of such land, and (2) such program includes all possible planning to minimize harm to such park...." This language is a plain and explicit bar to the use of federal funds for construction of highways through parks — only the most unusual situations are exempted.

Despite the clarity of the statutory language, respondents argue that the Secretary has wide discretion. They recognize that the requirement that there be no "feasible" alternative route admits of little administrative discretion. For this exemption to apply the Secretary must find that as a matter of sound engineering it would not be feasible to build the highway along any other route. Respondents argue, however, that the requirement that there be no other "prudent" route requires the Secretary to engage in a wide-ranging balancing of competing interests. They

---

18. Petitioners argue that either a bored tunnel or a cut-and-cover tunnel, which is a fully depressed route covered after construction, could be built. Respondents contend that the construction of a tunnel by either method would greatly increase the cost of the project, would create safety hazards, and because of increase in air pollution would not reduce harm to the park.

contend that the Secretary should weigh the detriment resulting from the destruction of parkland against the cost of other routes, safety considerations, and other factors, and determine on the basis of the importance that he attaches to these other factors whether, on balance, alternative feasible routes would be "prudent."

But no such wide-ranging endeavor was intended. It is obvious that in most cases considerations of cost, directness of route, and community disruption will indicate that parkland should be used for highway construction whenever possible. Although it may be necessary to transfer funds from one jurisdiction to another, there will always be a smaller outlay required from the public purse when parkland is used since the public already owns the land and there will be no need to pay for right-of-way. And since people do not live or work in parks, if a highway is built on parkland no one will have to leave his home or give up his business. Such factors are common to substantially all highway construction. Thus, if Congress intended these factors to be on an equal footing with preservation of parkland there would have been no need for the statutes.

Congress clearly did not intend that cost and disruption of the community were to be ignored by the Secretary. But the very existence of the statute indicates that protection of parkland was to be given paramount importance. The few green havens that are public parks were not to be lost unless there were truly unusual factors present in a particular case or the cost or community disruption resulting from alternative routes reached extraordinary magnitudes. If the statutes are to have any meaning, the Secretary cannot approve the destruction of parkland unless he finds that alternative routes present unique problems.

Plainly, there is "law to apply" and thus the exemption for action "committed to agency discretion" is inapplicable. But the existence of judicial review is only the start: the standard for review must also be determined. For that we must look to §706, which provides that a "reviewing court shall...hold unlawful and set aside agency action, findings, and conclusions found" not to meet six separate standards. In all cases agency action must be set aside if the action was "arbitrary, capricious, an abuse of discretion, or otherwise not in accordance with law," or if the action failed to meet statutory, procedural, or constitutional requirements. In certain narrow, specifically limited situations, the agency action is to be set aside if the action was not supported by "substantial evidence." And in other equally narrow circumstances the reviewing court is to engage in a de novo review of the action and set it aside if it was "unwarranted by the facts."

Petitioners argue that the Secretary's approval of the construction of I-40 through Overton Park is subject to one or the other of these later two standards of limited applicability..., Neither of these standards is, however, applicable.

Review under the substantial-evidence test is authorized only when the agency action is...based on a [trial-type] hearing. See 5 U.S.C. §§556, 557. The Secretary's decision to allow the expenditure of federal funds to build I-40 through Overton Park was plainly not an exercise of a rulemaking function. And the only hearing that is required by either the APA or the statutes regulating the distribution of federal funds for highway construction is a public hearing conducted by local officials for the purpose of informing the community about the proposed project and eliciting community views on the design and route. 23 U.S.C. §128. The hearing is nonadjudicatory, quasi-legislative in nature. It is not designed to produce a record that is to be the basis of agency action — the basic requirement for substantial-evidence review.

Petitioners' alternative argument also fails. De novo review of whether the Secretary's decision was "unwarranted by the facts" is authorized by §706(2)(F) in only two circumstances. First, such de novo review is authorized when the action is adjudicatory in nature and the agency factfinding procedures are inadequate. And, there may be independent judicial factfinding when issues that were not before the agency are raised in a proceeding to enforce nonadjudicatory agency action. Neither situation exists here.

Even though there is no de novo review in this case and the Secretary's approval of the route of I-40 does not have ultimately to meet the substantial-evidence test, the generally applicable standards of §706 require the reviewing court to engage in a substantial inquiry. Certainly, the Secretary's decision is entitled to a presumption of regularity. But that presumption is not to shield his action from a thorough, probing, in-depth review.

The court is first required to decide whether the Secretary acted within the scope of his authority. This determination naturally begins with a delineation of the scope of the Secretary's authority and discretion. As has been shown, Congress has specified only a small range of choices that the Secretary can make. Also involved in this initial inquiry is a determination of whether on the facts the Secretary's decision can reasonably be said to be within that range. The reviewing court must consider whether the Secretary properly construed his authority to approve the use of parkland as limited to situations where there are no feasible alternative routes or where feasible alternative routes involve uniquely difficult problems. And the reviewing court must be able to find that the Secretary could have reasonably believed that in this case there are no feasible alternatives or that alternatives...involve unique problems.

Scrutiny of the facts does not end, however, with the determination that the Secretary has acted within the scope of his statutory authority. Section 706(2)(A) requires a finding that the actual choice made was not "arbitrary, capricious, an abuse of discretion, or otherwise not in accordance with law." To make this finding the court must consider whether the decision was based on a consideration of the relevant factors and whether there has been a clear error of judgment. Although this inquiry into the facts is to be searching and careful, the ultimate standard of review is a narrow one. The court is not empowered to substitute its judgment for that of the agency.

The final inquiry is whether the Secretary's action followed the necessary procedural requirements. Here the only procedural error alleged is the failure of the Secretary to make formal findings and state his reason for allowing the highway to be built through the park.

Undoubtedly, review of the Secretary's action is hampered by his failure to make such findings, but the absence of formal findings does not necessarily require that the case be remanded to the Secretary. Neither the Department of Transportation Act nor the Federal-Aid Highway Act requires such formal findings. Moreover, the APA requirements that there be formal findings in certain rulemaking and adjudicatory proceedings do not apply to the Secretary's action here. See 5 U.S.C. §§553(a)(2), 554(a). And, although formal findings may be required in some cases in the absence of statutory directives when the nature of the agency action is ambiguous, those situations are rare. Plainly, there is no ambiguity here; the Secretary has approved the construction of I-40 through Overton Park and has approved a specific design for the project.

Petitioners contend that although there may not be a statutory requirement that the Secretary make formal findings and even though this may not be a case for the reviewing court to impose a requirement that findings be made, Department of Transportation regulations require them. This argument is based on DOT Order 5610.1, which requires the Secretary to make formal findings when he approves the use of parkland for highway construction but which was issued after the route for I-40 was approved. Petitioners argue that even though the order was not intended to have retrospective effect the order represents the law at the time of this Court's decision and under Thorpe v. Housing Authority, 393 U.S. 268, 281-282 (1969), should be applied to this case.... The general rule [when government rules change in favor of private individuals] is "that an appellate court must apply the law in effect at the time it renders its decision." 393 U.S. at 281. While we do not question that DOT Order 5610.1 constitutes the law in effect at the time of our decision, we do not believe that Thorpe compels us to remand for the Secretary to make formal findings. Here, unlike the situation in Thorpe, there has been a change in circumstances — additional right-of-way has been cleared and the 26-acre right-of-way inside Overton Park has been purchased by the State. Moreover, there is an administrative record that allows the full, prompt review of the Secretary's action...without additional delay which would result from having a remand to the Secretary.

That administrative record is not, however, before us. The lower courts based their review on the litigation affidavits that were presented. These affidavits were merely "post hoc" rationalizations, which have traditionally been found to be an inadequate basis for review. Burlington Truck Lines v. United States, 371 U.S. 156, 168-169 (1962). And they clearly do not constitute the "whole record" compiled by the agency, the basis for review required by APA §706.

Thus it is necessary to remand this case to the District Court for plenary review of the Secretary's decision. That review is to be based on the full administrative record that was before the Secretary at the time he made his decision. But since the bare record may not disclose the factors that were considered or the Secretary's construction of the evidence it may be necessary for the District Court to require some explanation in order to determine if the Secretary acted within the scope of his authority and if the Secretary's action was justifiable under the applicable standard.

The court may require the administrative officials who participated in the decision to give testimony explaining their action. Of course, such inquiry into the mental processes of administrative decision-makers is usually to be avoided. United States v. Morgan, 313 U.S. 409, 422 (1941). And where there are administrative findings that were made at the same time as the decision, as was the case in *Morgan*, there must be a strong showing of bad faith or improper behavior before such inquiry may be made. But here there are no such formal findings and it may be that the only way there can be effective judicial review is by examining the decision-makers themselves. See Shaughnessy v. Accardi, 349 U.S. 280 (1955).

The District Court is not, however, required to make such an inquiry. It may be that the Secretary can prepare formal findings including the information required by DOT Order 5610.1 that will provide an adequate explanation for his action. Such an explanation will, to some extent, be a "post hoc rationalization" and thus must be viewed critically. If the District Court decides that additional explanation is necessary, that court should consider which method will prove the most expeditious so that full review may be had as soon as possible. Reversed and remanded.

BLACK, J., joined by BRENNAN, J., concurring separately... I agree with the Court that the judgment of the Court of Appeals is wrong and that its action should be reversed. I do not agree that the whole matter should be remanded to the District Court. I think the case should be sent back to the Secretary of Transportation. It is apparent from the Court's opinion today that the Secretary of Transportation completely failed to comply with the duty imposed upon him by Congress not to permit a federally financed public highway to run through a public park "unless (1) there is no feasible and prudent alternative to the use of such land, and (2) such program includes all possible planning to minimize harm to such park...." That congressional command should not be taken lightly by the Secretary or by this Court. It represents a solemn determination of the highest law-making body of this Nation that the beauty and health-giving facilities of our parks are not to be taken away for public roads without hearings, factfindings, and policy determinations under the supervision of a Cabinet officer — the Secretary of Transportation....

I regret that I am compelled to conclude for myself that, except for some too-late formulations, apparently coming from the Solicitor General's office, this record contains not one word to indicate that the Secretary raised even a finger to comply with the command of Congress. It is our duty, I believe, to remand this whole matter back to the Secretary of Transportation for him to give this matter the hearing it deserves in full good-faith obedience to the Act of Congress. That Act was obviously passed to protect our public parks from forays by road builders except in the most extraordinary and imperative circumstances. This record does not demonstrate the existence of such circumstances. I dissent from the Court's failure to send the case back to the Secretary, whose duty has not yet been performed.

BLACKMUN, J., concurring. I fully join the Court in its opinion and in its judgment. I merely wish to state the obvious: (1) The case comes to this Court as the end product of more than a decade of endeavor to solve the interstate highway problem at Memphis. (2) The administrative decisions under attack here are not those of a single Secretary; some were made by the present Secretary's predecessor and, before him, by the Department of Commerce's Bureau of Public Roads. (3) The 1966 Act and the 1968 Act have cut across former methods and here have imposed new standards and conditions upon a situation that already was largely developed. This undoubtedly is why the record is sketchy and less than one would expect if the project were one which had been instituted after the passage of the 1966 Act....

JUSTICE DOUGLAS took no part in the consideration or decision of this case.

COMMENTARY & QUESTIONS

1. **Threshold administrative law issues in citizen suits.** Before plaintiffs can get to the merits of challenges to agency decisions, they must pass a number of threshold tests.

(a) *Reviewability.* When challenged by citizen suits, agency attorneys often (as in the *Overton Park* case) initially argue that their challenged agency decisions are unreviewable because they contain discretionary elements. The courts, however, have demonstrated extreme hesitation in finding non-reviewability, often citing the words of Abbott Laboratories:

> The enactment of the Administrative Procedures Act...embodies the basic presumption of judicial review to one "suffering legal wrong because of agency action...." The legislative material...manifests a congressional intention that it cover a broad spectrum of administrative actions, and this Court has echoed that theme by noting that the...Act's "generous review provision" must be given a "hospitable" interpretation.... Only upon a showing of "clear and convincing evidence" of a contrary legislative intent should the courts restrict access to judicial review. Abbott Labs. v. Gardner, 387 U.S. 136, 141 (1967).

Sovereign immunity barriers to reviewability of federal agency actions were specifically removed in 1976 by amendments to APA §702.

(b) *Standing.* In *Overton Park*, as in many environmental cases, there is no problem with standing. Some or all of the Tennessee plaintiffs would be directly affected by the consequences of the agency decision. It has long been established that plaintiffs' "injury in fact" necessitated by Article III's case-or-controversy requirement does not have to be economic or legal but can extend to recreational, aesthetic, and other injuries.[19] If particular persons are not injured, or are injured only to the same extent as millions of other citizens, the courts may deny standing. Occasionally, however, in part to allow

---

19. Sierra Club v. Morton, 405 U.S. 727, 734 (1972).

troublesome environmental questions to be debated, the Supreme Court has allowed fairly broad standing to sue.[20]

(c) *Exhaustion of remedies and ripeness.* In *Overton Park*, the legal issues were clearly ready for review when plaintiffs went to court. In some environmental cases, it is argued that citizens should exhaust internal remedies within the agency before going to court; in other cases, the argument is that an agency decision, though it has been made, is not yet ripe for judicial review because it has not actually been applied or is not yet completely final. These arguments generally have not been successful defenses against environmental litigation. Courts often seem to reflect the legal system's interest in resolving important legal questions at an efficient early stage, before major investments and commitments of resources are wasted. But not always. Does it seem likely that the *Overton Park* plaintiffs could have succeeded in getting an injunction against the earlier highway activities — the condemnation of land and highway construction up to the edge of the park[21] — as a violation of §4(f)? Probably not. The defense would have been that the issue was not yet ripe, the law not yet violated.[22]

2. **The administrative law of *Overton Park*: tactics and standard of review.** Note how easily the Court in *Overton Park* accepts the plaintiffs' threshold showings allowing them to get into court. As to procedure, however, the plaintiffs did not succeed in their request for formal findings, nor did they get hearings before the Secretary. Both of these procedures obviously would have been helpful in sharpening their case against the highway through the park and obtaining closer judicial review of the subsequent decision. (The Supreme Court opinion, like many lawyers, seems to consider that all agency "adjudications" are formal adjudications, when in fact informal adjudications constitute the vast majority of government agency decisions.)

As to the substantive standard of review to be applied to the agency's factual decision, the plaintiffs didn't get de novo review, the toughest standard, nor even the substantial evidence test. They got only review, under the arbitrary and capricious test, and they never got a judicial ruling that the Secretary had indeed been arbitrary and capricious in approving the parkland route.

So why didn't the Department of Transportation win? While the Court says that "the ultimate standard of review is a narrow one," thus adopting a continued deference to the agency's expertise on fact-finding, it nevertheless recognizes that judges need to see enough facts to "be able to find that the Secretary could reasonably have believed that in this case there are no feasible alternatives," and orders a plenary review on remand to build such a record.

---

20. See, e.g., United States v. SCRAP, 412 U.S. 669 (1973); Duke Power v. Carolina Envtl. Study Group, 438 U.S. 59 (1978).

21. Just as the *Overton Park* plaintiffs were able to bootstrap an injunction against the highway based on the thinness of the agency record, the defendants and their allies had attempted physical bootstrapping: Prior to the filing of the case, the citizens had attempted to argue for alternative routes north and south of Overton Park. The highway authorities, however, proceeded to condemn homes, bulldoze them, and build the highway right-of-way right up to the boundary of the park. They also built a multimillion dollar bridge across the Mississippi River on the park highway alignment. It was only then that they turned to the Secretary to ask approval for the park route on the grounds that there was no longer any feasible and prudent alternative.

22. A NEPA suit might offer better prospects (see Chapter 9).

If environmental lawyers can convince reviewing judges that the factual evidence considered by an agency would not be enough to allow the judges themselves to make intelligent decisions on critical points, then the judges are likely to send the case back to the agency, even if they are not ready to declare that the agency decision was indeed arbitrary. This invites environmental attorneys to search out points of decision that do not appear to be adequately supported by the agency's formal or informal record, and to leverage these thin areas into an argument for remand. In the tactics of lawyering, a remand on technical points is not as good as a substantive victory, but is far from a hollow victory. The challenger is perceived to have beaten the agency in court, an accomplishment in itself. Additionally, the challenger now gets another bite at the bureaucratic apple, presenting an opportunity for bringing political and public opinion pressures to bear.

3. **Interpreting the statutory language: who does it and how to have applied an incorrect interpretation of the statutory words "feasible and prudent."** Are you satisfied with the Court's interpretation of the statutory language? Shouldn't judges defer to expert agencies in its interpretation of law to the same extent they do on fact-finding? In part, it may be that judges consider themselves the experts in interpretation of law, and if a statute's meaning seems obvious to the judges, that is the interpretation the court will require. The "plain meaning" rule is an old maxim of statutory interpretation founded upon the assumption that in some cases the words of a statute are unambiguously clear and hence must be effectuated, whatever their results, because each word of a statute (as opposed to common law terms) is binding law. Ambiguity, however, is the norm. See the *Chevron* discussion in Part E below. Could it also be, as Justice Black implies, that courts will defer less to those agencies that demonstrate institutional resistance to statutory requirements?

4. **"Arbitrary and capricious"?** Like many courts that decide to overturn a particular agency decision, the *Overton Park* Court did not want to declare the Secretary's decision arbitrary and capricious, and so it remanded the case for development of a better record supporting the decision. Could it have found the decision "arbitrary"?

The answer depends on what the term "arbitrary" means. The courts have applied the term to a confusingly wide range of substantive and procedural holdings.[23] Applied as a test of the substantive merits of a decision, it is best defined in terms of rationality: "Does the agency decision have rational support on the record reviewed by the court?" or "could a rational official have reached that decision on this record?"[24]

Even limited to application as a test of substantive rationality, analytically the arbitrary and capricious test can be applied in at least five different settings:

(a) where the agency has no legal standard to apply to the evidence, or uses an incorrect standard;

---

23. See Plater & Norine, Through the Looking Glass of Eminent Domain: Exploring the "Arbitrary and Capricious" Test and Substantive Rationality Review of Governmental Decisions, 16 B.C. Envtl. Aff. L. Rev. 661, 712–722 (1989).

24. Thus, viewed conceptually, the arbitrary and capricious test and the stricter-sounding "substantial evidence" test come down to the same thing; the latter may just require a greater quantum of evidence to prove the point. Id. at 716–718.

(b) where the agency may have had enough evidence back home in its files to support a decision, but just didn't show it to the court;

(c) where the agency did not have enough evidence to support its decision;

(d) where the agency had enough evidence to support its decision rationally, if it were accurate, but plaintiffs prove that the evidence is wrong;

(e) where the agency failed to consider the "relevant factors" set by the statute, or based its decision on irrelevant factors.

In Motor Vehicles Mfrs. Ass'n v. State Farm Mutual Life Ins. Co., 463 U.S. 29 (1983), for instance, the Supreme Court declared a DOT reversal of the prior administration's seat belt and air bag rule arbitrary and capricious because the agency hadn't considered, and failed to present to the Court, evidence supporting the need for a new rule. This would seem to fit the (b) or (c) definitions of arbitrary. Which would have applied to *Overton Park*? The Court could probably have used one or more of the first three of these tests. In other cases, after examining the record basis of agency decisions, plaintiffs can sometimes prove the fourth.[25]

Challenging agency actions under the arbitrary and capricious test, however, is no easy task because judges consider it such a deferential standard of review. In practical terms, in most cases, when a court begins reviewing an agency action under the arbitrary and capricious test, that means that the agency decision is shortly going to be upheld. Even if their case convinces the court, attorneys can reasonably expect that the agency, instead of being declared arbitrary, will receive the kind of face-saving remand that defendants got in *Overton Park* (although that proved to be enough for plaintiffs).

5. **"Feasible and prudent" as a public trust standard.** The "feasible and prudent" standard captures well the idea of a strong presumption in favor of protection, to be factored into decisions about how parkland public trust resources should be developed. By extension it can be read into the public trust generally. But what does it mean? Does it mean that questions of cost are not to be considered at all? Presumably there is always an alternative, if cost is no object. But "prudent" implies some attention to money factors.[26] If money is to be considered, how is it to be weighed against intangible natural values? Money tends to be an all-or-nothing factor. If you consider cost, going through parks will virtually always be the preferable option, and a test that incorporates the prudence of cost saving negates the protective purpose and effect. The Court suggests that only an "extraordinary magnitude" of expense would justify going through the park. What would that mean? Is part of the balance of feasible and prudent the question whether the project should be built at all? Might a decision not to build an interstate highway through Memphis be a feasible and prudent alternative?

6. **The subsequent history of *Overton Park*.** After the Supreme Court's ruling, the case bounced around in the lower courts for a few more years. Finally, after new hearings and an EIS, Secretary Volpe announced in January 1973 that he could not find that

---

25. See Motor Vehicle Mfrs. Ass'n of U.S. v. EPA, 768 F.2d 385 (D.C. Cir. 1985) (by granting a methanol use permit based on a failed test, and tests of three dissimilar gas additives, EPA acted arbitrarily).

26. Note that the standard is *feasible* as well as prudent; agencies thus would want to argue that this includes economic feasibility, in order to expand their range of discretion.

there was no feasible and prudent alternative to going through the park. The Tennessee Department of Transportation thereupon challenged his decision, demanding that he tell them what the feasible and prudent alternative was, but the Sixth Circuit upheld the Secretary's ruling as it stood and the Supreme Court denied certiorari.[27] Congress has not disturbed the judicial results, so I-40 apparently will never be built through Overton Park. Today the original interstate highway corridor comes to an ignominious, disruptive halt at the edge of the park. A loop bypass to the north now carries I-40's through traffic.

7. **Tradeoffs.** Memphis had already purchased 160 acres of private land in the northern part of the city to be made into parks to replace the 26 acres of Overton Park used for the highway and indicated that it probably would acquire still more. Doesn't this mean there would have been a lot more parkland with the highway project through the park than without it? Should that have ended the question?

Was mass transit an available alternative to the through-city expressway? The civic leaders and agency officials who promote such highways traditionally assume that putting an Interstate through the middle of the metropolis will relieve traffic jams and bring added prosperity. The experience of many cities, however, has been that added highway mileage is rapidly congested by traffic newly generated by its existence and travelers lured away from mass transit, and arteries into the hearts of cities often serve to empty the center city of a stable mixed residential and economic basis by accelerating commuting and a shift to the suburbs.

D. CITIZEN ENFORCEMENT IN THE COURTS

Section 1. THE IMPORTANCE OF CITIZEN ENFORCEMENT

Woven through much of this book are examples of the central role of active citizen efforts (often resisted at each step by public and private entities) in creating and shaping environmental law, whether through common law strategies or public law pressuring.

In the *Overton Park* setting, who would have enforced the federal statute if a bunch of low-income citizens had not rallied to carry the case up through the federal courts? The FHWA? The Governor of Tennessee? The Congress that had passed the Parklands Act? No.[28] Within the administrative processes that constitute the bulk of positive law in the administrative state, citizen efforts have been critically important.

Environmentalists operate within the administrative process in two basic ways: (1) by "intervention," formal or informal, in ongoing agency procedures; and (2) by

---

27. Citizens to Preserve Overton Park v. Brinegar, 494 F.2d 1212 (6th Cir. 1974), cert. denied, Citizens to Preserve Overton Park v. Smith, 421 U.S. 991 (1975).

28. The point is that enforcement of public law provisions by the official organs of government is often highly unlikely. Perhaps the Sierra Club, NRDC, or another national group could have picked up the immense burdens of litigating the case (and in fact national environmental groups did help in the later stages of the litigation), but these organizations' capabilities are severely limited. They litigate only a fraction of the deserving cases referred to them each year. That means that most cases deserving judicial attention either never get launched or founder along the way.

bringing agency actions to court for judicial review. Once a state or federal wetlands act, for instance, is passed on the strength of citizen lobbying, it can be neutered, or strengthened, depending on the regulations and administrative implementation given to it by the administering agency. Agency officials hear persistently and powerfully from regulated vested interests. Within the day-to-day administrative process, agencies now often also hear a great deal from concerned citizen activists. If rigorous, enforceable wetlands regulations are produced, it is altogether likely that citizen expertise and political pressure helped produce them. If environmental groups think agency regulations subvert the legislative mandate, they can sue, seeking to hold the agency to the original terms of the statute.

Likewise in the federal arena. The federal air and water acts studied in Chapters 11 and 12, for example, were not only created through extraordinary citizen pressures on Congress, spearheaded by a few notable congressional leaders, but their voluminous subsequent anti-pollution regulatory programs have also been fundamentally shaped by citizen groups, through extensive interventions and litigation.[29]

Knowing the Players. In order to understand any administrative process litigation, one has to figure out the respective roles and status of the various competing participants.

The plaintiffs in the *Overton Park* case were exceptional in that they were a small group of disgruntled neighbors who were able to hold the case together all the way to the U.S. Supreme Court. Far more typical are national environmental citizen organizations designed for sophisticated advocacy in courts, agencies, and the legislature.

Faced with resistance from industry lobbyists and hesitancy on the part of federal regulators, a "shadow government" has sprung up, including notably the Natural Resources Defense Council, EarthLaw, Environmental Defense, the National Wildlife Federation, National Audubon Society, Friends of the Earth, and EarthJustice[30] — national public interest law groups that commit themselves to monitor, negotiate, litigate, and lobby for rigorous, enforceable regulatory programs. Beginning in 1970, a few young law graduates, many from Yale, laid the foundations for such groups, attempting to hold federal government agencies to the terms of the environmental statutes so painfully won in the halls of Congress. The groups evolved to enroll thousands of subscribing members, with legal staffs and budgets of sufficient depth and strength to allow them to play an oversight role in many important administrative programs. The critical role these organizations have played in the securing of environmental protection in the United States is impressive, and their example is now being followed around the world, as the international environmental law movement begins to develop 20 years behind the U.S. lead.

---

29. For instance, in the early stages of the CAA, the federal EPA decided over environmental protests to write rules allowing polluting industry to comply with the CAA by moving to clean air states like Wyoming and Idaho that had pristine air quality, thereby spreading pollution around but not abating it. It was only because of citizen litigation and negotiation that a nationwide "non-deterioration" policy was established. Sierra Club v. Ruckleshaus, 344 F. Supp. 253 (D.D.C.), aff'd, 412 U.S. 541 (1973). (Note in this controversy the interstate replay of a scene from the tragedy of the commons.)

30. This list covers most of the most frequent environmental litigation groups; there are other significant groups as well.

As to defendants, note how in many of these environmental cases there is no clear distinction between the regulatory agency entrusted with the environmental protection mandate and the industry and regulated interests that it is assigned to supervise. In the atomic energy field, for instance, the alignment of the Atomic Energy Commission (AEC) with the nuclear industry was so incestuous that Congress ultimately split the agency into two parts, the promotional Energy Research and Development Agency (ERDA), and the protective Nuclear Regulatory Commission (NRC). The environmental community does not necessarily believe that such organizational splits end the affinity of regulator and regulatee. In any event, it is noteworthy that the original bipolar design of the regulatory state noted in Chapter 2 — regulated industries on one hand and government charged with defending the public interest on the other — has now evolved, under pressure from citizen activists, into a highly articulated and energetic pluralistic democracy, where courts and many agencies are open to a wide variety of differing points of view from a potpourri of citizen intervenors.

Of the Iron Triangle, the Pork Barrel, and the Establishment. The *Overton Park* case reminds environmental observers that environmental quality initiatives, even when they are backed by statutory provisions, run into the opposition of vested interests, public as well as private. Some environmentalists call it the "pork barrel," others the "iron triangle" — in either case referring to the interlocking structure and political process linking private construction and industrial interests, government agencies that service the industry, and congressional delegations that want to attract particular public expenditures into their backyards. The momentum of that combination makes the pork barrel one of the most consistently powerful and resistant forces of environmental alteration. Environmentalists are often underfinanced, politically powerless neighborhood agitators who come along late in the game seeking to stop the momentum of the good ol' boys establishment steamroller.

In the *Overton Park* setting, for example, it was not only that interstate highways required just 10% contribution from state and local government, while 90% of costs would be tapped directly from federal taxpayers and the federal Highway Trust Fund. The attraction of parklands to the highway establishment is even more seductive: Parklands are already owned by government. If Tennessee contributes 26 acres of parkland to the highway project, it gets to value that parkland as if it were a cash contribution based on its fair market value: the value of 26 acres of downtown urban land. For this reason, parks attract their own destruction, and it is for precisely that reason that environmentalists had found it so necessary to fight to put §4(f) into the highway legislation.[31]

By successfully, against the odds, putting the Parklands Act onto the federal books, environmentalists did not automatically succeed in enlisting the federal government as a whole on the side of parkland preservation. Quite the contrary; federal program agencies often adopt a recalcitrant posture toward statutes that limit their standard operating procedures. Agencies that measure their success in terms of accomplishing

---

31. Thus the official argument in *Overton Park* for overriding §4(f), based on "prudent" limiting of acquisition costs, replayed the problem that required §4(f) in the first place.

their mission in pouring concrete and building road mileage understandably treat conservation legislation as a technicality, an annoyance, and often as a frustrating and contradictory obstacle that must be overridden in order to do their jobs.

The need to observe and identify the roles, powers, and predilections of the contesting parties, needless to say, is a recurring reality in analyses of environmental controversies under both public and private law.

The "Capture" Phenomenon. Environmentalists repeatedly identify the problem of governmental agencies' "capture" by market forces as a disturbing backdrop to many administrative process cases. A regulatory agency created in the fervor of a popular movement to regulate some designated problem may begin its life energetically pursuing the overall public interest, but over time its initiative gradually may be eroded into narrower views, intimately linked with the industry and problems it was intended to solve.

Richard Stewart, The Reformation of American Administrative Law
88 Harvard Law Review 1669, 1684–1687 (1975)

Critics have repeatedly asserted...that in carrying out broad legislative directives, agencies unduly favor organized interests, especially the interests of regulated or client business firms and other organized groups at the expense of diffuse, comparatively unorganized interests such as consumers, environmentalists, and the poor. In the midst of a "growing sense of disillusion with the role which regulatory agencies play," many legislators, judges, and legal and economic commentators have accepted the thesis of persistent bias in agency policies. At its crudest, this thesis is based on the "capture" scenario, in which administrations are systematically controlled, sometimes corruptly, by the business firms within their orbit of responsibility, whether regulatory or promotional. But there are more subtle explanations of industry orientation, which include the following:

First — The division of responsibility between the regulated firms, which retain primary control over their own affairs, and the administrator, whose power is essentially negative and who is dependent on industry cooperation in order to achieve his objectives, places the administrator in an inherently weak position. The administrator will, nonetheless, be held responsible if the industry suffers serious economic dislocation. For both of these reasons, he may pursue conservative policies.

Second — The regulatory bureaucracy becomes "regulation minded." It seeks to elaborate and perfect the controls it exercises over the regulated industry. The effect of this tendency, particularly in a regime of limited entry, is to eliminate actual and potential competition and buttress the position of the established firms.

Third — The resources — in terms of money, personnel, and political influence — of the regulatory agency are limited in comparison to those of regulated firms. Unremitting maintenance of an adversary posture would quickly dissipate agency resources. Hence, the agency must compromise with the regulated industry if it is to accomplish anything of significance.

Fourth — Limited agency resources imply that agencies must depend on outside sources of information, policy development, and political support. This outside input comes primarily from organized interests, such as regulated firms, that have a substantial stake in the substance of agency policy and the resources to provide such input. By contrast, the personal stake in agency policy of an individual member of an unorganized interest, such as a consumer, is normally too small to justify such representation. Effective representation of unorganized interests might be possible if a means of pooling resources to share the costs of underwriting collective representation were available. But this seems unlikely since the transaction costs of creating an organization of interest group members increase disproportionately as the size of the group increases. Moreover, if membership in such an organization is voluntary, individuals will not have a strong incentive to join, since if others represent the interests involved, the benefits will accrue not only to those participating in the representation, but to nonparticipants as well, who can, therefore, enjoy the benefits without incurring any of the costs (the free rider effect). As a somewhat disillusioned James Landis wrote in 1960, the result is industry dominance in representation, which has a "daily machine-gun like impact on both [an] agency and its staff" that tends to create an industry bias in the agency's outlook.

These various theses of systematic bias in agency policy are not universally valid. Political pressures and judicial controls may force continuing agency adherence to policies demonstrably inimical to the interests of the regulated industry.... Moreover, the fact that agency policies may tend to favor regulated interests does not in itself demonstrate that such policies are unfair or unjustified, since protection of regulated interests may be implicit in the regulatory scheme established by Congress. Nonetheless, the critique of agency discretion as unduly favorable to organized interests — particularly regulated or client firms — has sufficient power and verisimilitude to have achieved widespread contemporary acceptance.

COMMENTARY & QUESTION

The context of citizen environmental enforcement. The context in which environmental law developed, as noted in Chapter 2, was a shift away from the old bipolar regime in which government agencies were presumed to be the preclusive primary defenders of the public interest. Starting in the 1960s, it became clear that agencies could not exclusively be relied upon to fulfill that role. When the Woodstock Generation accused agencies of being part of the industrial economy's "Establishment,"[32] were they just being paranoid? Agencies in a bipolar system often have tended to resist citizens' calls for rigorous enforcement of laws against the excesses of the marketplace. The history of environmental law can be traced in the oscillating willingness of agencies to enforce statutory standards, as in the 1970s, or to defer to industry, as in the Bush II Administration's OMB/OIRA programs examined later in Chapter 13. Since the beginning of the environmental era, the agencies' various stances have been played out against a backdrop of citizen initiatives pushing agencies to enforce statutes stringently or taking over the enforcement role themselves.

Section 2. STANDING AND THE INSTITUTIONALIZATION
OF CITIZEN ENFORCEMENT

Standing, one of the threshold constitutional and statutory tests citizens have to meet in order to obtain judicial review, is ultimately a judicial doctrine. It is courts that

---

32. The "Establishment" rubric appears to have been coined by Henry Fairlie, writing in *The Spectator* in the 1950s:

> By the "Establishment" I do not mean only the centres of official power — though they are certainly part of it — but rather the whole matrix of official and social relations within which power is exercised. The exercise of power...cannot be understood unless it is recognised that it is exercised socially. Fairlie, The Establishment at Work, Spectator, Sept. 23, 1955.

The label soon was picked up to describe official players being opposed by citizen civil rights activists, and subsequently by environmental activists.

determine when citizens can claim standing and when they cannot, even under statutory grants of standing. In most cases, the plaintiffs' premise in environmental standing cases is that the government agency is not eager to enforce the law or itself has violated the law, and so there will be no enforcement unless the courts support the citizens' standing to sue. The practical motivation of anti-standing advocates seems to reflect precisely the same premise as its intended result. Standing principles can be broadened to permit litigation on issues for which judges want to have dispositive determinations, and conversely can be narrowed to nip off challenges that courts would rather not have to decide.

The law of standing in recent years has often been made through environmental cases. In all standing cases, plaintiffs' standing to sue will be tested under:

• Article III's case or controversy clause (primarily a claim of injury, but also whatever other elements the Court holds to be constitutionally required); plus

• "prudential limitations" invented by the Supreme Court to restrict standing based on judicial discretion, not applicable if a statute overrides them (prudential principles included "no standing to enforce rights of third parties," a requirement of "imminent" injury, the likelihood of "redressability" of plaintiff's harm by judicial order, and so on, but new ones continue to be added, and the Rehnquist Court has converted some to "constitutional" Article III status so that statutory grants of standing cannot override them); and either

• statutory requirements for judicial review in the specific statute being applied, like "aggrieved" under §313(b) of the Federal Power Act in *Scenic Hudson* below (typically no more than the Article III requirements) or special citizen-enforcement authorizations for "any person" who files a 60-day notice (included in many environmental statutes as noted below, they are far more liberal than the Article III "injury" requirement and override prudential limitations); or

• the general statutory requirements for standing under definitions of APA §702's "person adversely affected or aggrieved...within the meaning of a relevant statute" (much the same as Article III but subject to prudential principles).

The law of standing for citizens, in courts and agencies, lies at the heart of the evolution of environmental law and is often the target for latter-day marketplace reactions against environmental protections. The condensed chronology of standing cases that follows reflects the changing context of the field.

The *Storm King* Case (1966). The first major milestone for environmental citizens' participation in administrative law and process — involving citizen enforcement of federal statutes, and citizen standing in agency proceedings as well as in subsequent judicial review of agency decisions — occurred in the mid-1960s in the shadow of Storm King Mountain, on the shores of New York's Hudson River. The Consolidated Edison Company and the Federal Power Commission (FPC) had been planning Con Ed's construction of a "pumped storage" hydroelectric project, cutting a crater reservoir out of the top of Storm King Mountain so that water could be pumped up in hours of slack electricity use, to be released through generator turbines (as "peaking power") when energy needs were greatest. Disturbed by the prospect, a group of local citizens formed the Scenic Hudson Preservation Conference and began to question the utility company and the agency about the project's negative effects — loss of a beautiful mountain, scour, sedimentation, and other impacts on fish and the river when huge volumes of water were sucked up and down through turbines. Neither Con Ed nor the federal agency wanted the citizens to participate in the various permit procedures required to license the Storm King project. The agency eventually allowed the citizens a limited intervention but would not allow them to put several studies on the project's negative consequences on the agency record.

When the Storm King license was granted, the citizens went to court. In a remarkable Second Circuit opinion, Judge Hays had to weigh the project's troubling facts against the agency's demand for deference. As a threshold matter, he first had to consider the agency's argument that the citizens had no right to judicial review because they were not aggrieved parties under the relevant statutory requirements for judicial review or under Article III's case or controversy clause.

Scenic Hudson Preservation Conference v. Federal Power Commission
United States Court of Appeals for the Second Circuit, 1965
354 F.2d 608, cert. denied, 384 U.S. 941 (1966)

HAYS, J.... The Storm King project is to be located in an area of unique beauty and major historical significance. The highlands and gorge of the Hudson offer one of the finest pieces of river scenery in the world.... Respondents argue that "petitioners do not have standing to obtain review" because they make no claim of any personal economic injury resulting from the Commission's action...." [but only aesthetic injuries and thus are not "aggrieved" within the meaning of administrative law standing requirements.] The Commission takes a narrow view of the meaning of "aggrieved party."... The Supreme Court has observed that the law of standing is a "complicated specialty of Federal jurisdiction, the solution of whose problems is in any event more or less determined by the specific circumstances of individual situations...." The "case or controversy" requirement of Article III §2 of the Constitution does not require that an "aggrieved" or "adversely effected" party have a personal economic interest.... In order to insure that the Federal Power Commission will adequately protect the public interest in the aesthetic, conservational, and recreational aspects of power development, those who by their activities and conduct have exhibited a special interest in such areas must be held to be included in the class of "aggrieved" parties under §313(b) [of the Federal Power Act]....

We see no justification for the Commission's fear that our determination will encourage "literally thousands" to intervene and seek review in future proceedings. We rejected a similar contention in Associated Industries v. Ickes, 134 F.2d 694, 707 (1943), noting that "no such horrendous possibilities" exist. Our experience with public actions confirms the view that the expense and vexation of legal proceedings [are] not lightly undertaken.... [The citizens were acting as "private attorneys-general," enforcing the terms of statute in partnership with the agency, and thus should have been given a hospitable reception in the agency.]

A party acting as a "private attorney-general" can raise issues that are not personal to it.... Especially in a case of this type, where public interest and concern is so great, the Commission refusal to receive the [citizens' power study] testimony, as well as proffered information on fish protection devices and underground transmission facilities, exhibits a disregard of the statute and of judicial mandates instructing the Commission to probe all feasible alternatives....

In this case as in many others the Commission has claimed to be the representative of the public interest. This role does not permit it to act as an umpire blandly calling balls and strikes for adversary groups appearing before it; the right of the public must receive active and affirmative protection at the hands of the Commission.

[Reasoning that the agency decision was not rationally supported on the record — absent full citizen participation and agency follow-up on the citizens' substantiated concerns — the court set aside the license and remanded the Storm King project to the district court and the Commission, where it died.[33]]

Mineral King (1972). The first major Supreme Court case encouraging citizen participation through expanded judicial standing was Sierra Club v. Morton, 405 U.S. 727 (1972) (basing the standing question only on the Article III and APA "aggrieved" standard, with no specific grants of standing and no mention of prudential limitations). The Walt Disney Corporation sought to develop ski runs, lodges, and a winter resort on national forest public lands at Mineral King Mountain in the California Sierras. The environmental plaintiffs, trying to enforce federal conservation statutes, asked to be heard based only on their general interest in environmental protection, with no claim of individual injury.[34] The environmentalists argued that a real case or controversy clearly existed between the parties; they would clearly commit substantial effort to litigating the issues fully. Previously the Supreme Court had extended standing only to persons who had a clearly defined economic injury or a "legal interest" specifically protected by statute or constitution. Justice Stewart wrote for the Court:

> The complaint alleged that the development "would destroy or otherwise adversely affect the scenery, natural and historic objects and wildlife of the park and would impair the enjoyment of the park for future generations." We do not question that this type of harm may amount to an "injury in fact" sufficient to lay the basis for standing.... The trend of cases arising under the APA and other statutes authorizing judicial review of federal agency action has been toward recognizing that injuries other than economic harm are sufficient to bring a person within the meaning of the statutory language, and toward discarding the notion that an injury that is widely shared is ipso facto not an injury sufficient to provide the basis for judicial review.... The interest alleged to have been injured "may reflect aesthetic, conservational, and recreational, as well as economic values...." Aesthetic and environmental well-being, like economic well-being, are important ingredients of the quality of life in our society, and the fact that particular environmental interests are shared by the many rather than the few does not make them less deserving of legal protection through the judicial process. *Mineral King*, 405 U.S. at 734, 738.[35]

---

33. A number of books and law review articles have commented on *Scenic Hudson*. See, e.g., A. Talbot, Power Along the Hudson: The Storm King Case & the Birth of Environmentalism (1972). The full case deserves reading by anyone interested in the history of environmental law. For a strident criticism of the case in terms of its putative anti-democratic élitism, see Tucker, Environmentalism and the Leisure Class, 255 Harpers Magazine 49–56, 73–80 (Dec. 1977).

34. This broad commitment to environmental protection had been part of the Scenic Hudson group's successful argument for generalized standing, based on the environmentalists' "activities and conduct [exhibiting] a special interest in such areas." One of the more intriguing issues raised in environmental law has been the attempt to extend standing to non-living things. Could the plaintiffs have filed the lawsuit in the name of the park itself? In a ringing dissent in the *Mineral King* case, Justice Douglas urged the adoption of Professor Chris Stone's argument that standing should be granted to organizations that speak knowingly and will commit resources in defense of inanimate trees, mountains, or wildlife. C. Stone, Should Trees Have Standing? (1974). Why might the Sierra Club have wanted to have the mountain itself as the plaintiff? To some extent, such attempts may reflect a philosophical stance, an attempt to focus attention on the real long-term issues. In part, such a claim might reflect the fact that members do not always live or hike in areas where citizen enforcement efforts are necessary, as in Arctic tundra threatened by oil drilling or in outer space where some energy planners suggest dumping radioactive wastes.

35. Citing dicta in Assoc. of Data Processing Servs. v. Camp, 397 U.S. 150, 154 (1970). The Court did not buy Professor Chris Stone's argument that "trees should have standing," see 45 S. Cal. L. Rev. 450 (1972), and so human plaintiffs need not prove human injury to represent claims of nature, as guardians or next-friends.

The *Mineral King* Court, however, declined to adopt the broadest definition of private attorneys general set out in Scenic Hudson, instead requiring the Sierra Club to allege member injuries from the proposed government action, which on remand it quickly did.[36] Proof of a specific harm, however small, was confirmed as the simplistic test of standing. Note how the *Mineral King* Court nevertheless greatly extended the constitutionally cognizable injuries that could be the basis of citizen lawsuits. The decision firmly established that citizens no longer needed to show an economic injury or violation of a constitutional right.

SCRAP **(1973).** Several years later, a group of law students in Washington, D.C., decided to challenge ICC rate-making decisions that discouraged use of recycled materials by assigning lower transport tariffs to raw materials. United States v. Students Challenging Regulatory Agency Procedures (SCRAP), 412 U.S. 669 (1973). The Court, in another Stewart opinion, found that SCRAP had alleged sufficient individual harm to get standing:

> The challenged agency action in this case is applicable to substantially all of the Nation's railroads.... All persons who utilize the scenic resources of the country, and indeed all who breathe its air, could claim harm similar to that alleged by the environmental groups here. But we have already made it clear that standing is not to be denied simply because many people suffer the same injury.... To deny standing to persons who are in fact injured simply because many others are also injured would mean that the most injurious and widespread Government actions could be questioned by nobody. We cannot accept that conclusion.
>
> But the injury alleged here is [not] direct and perceptible.... Here, the court was asked to follow a far more attenuated line of causation to the eventual injury of which the appellees complained — a general rate increase would allegedly cause increased use of nonrecyclable commodities as compared to recyclable goods, thus resulting in the need to use more natural resources to produce such goods,...resulting in more refuse that might be discarded [along hiking trails used by the students] in national parks in the Washington area....
>
> Of course, pleadings must be something more than an ingenious academic exercise in the conceivable. A plaintiff must allege that he has been or will in fact be perceptibly harmed by the challenged agency action, not that he can imagine circumstances in which he could be affected by the agency's action. And it is equally clear that the allegations must be true and capable of proof at trial.... If proved, [however, plaintiffs' allegations] would place them squarely among those persons injured in fact by the Commission's action. [Standing was granted.] *SCRAP*, 412 U.S. at 687–690.

Understandably, *SCRAP* was viewed as an expansion of citizens' rights to sue against governmental abuses. Potential harms to plaintiffs had to be alleged, but the linkage of such harms to challenged agency actions could be quite indirect. Plaintiffs did not have to prove that they were "within the zone of interests" of a relevant

---

36. On remand, the Club readily supplied available evidence of direct use of the mountain by its members and got standing. Were the original pleadings badly designed or a grab for the brass ring?

statute,[37] nor did plaintiffs have to show a likelihood that the court's orders would "redress" the harms. Citizens could go to court to enforce statutes and the public values they embodied even where official enforcement agencies had been rendered quiescent by the politics of the marketplace. Citizen standing, and the pluralistic democracy it represented, provided a powerful mechanism for protecting civic and environmental interests, counteracting the marketplace's neutralizing pressures upon regulatory programs. In the absence of citizen action, many government agencies could not or would not do a sufficient job of enforcing federal law.

Congressional Grants of Standing for Citizen Enforcement. Though not involved in *Mineral King* or *SCRAP*, more than a dozen environmental statutes passed since the early 1970s, picking up on Martin Luther King's use of citizen enforcement provisions under nineteenth-century civil rights laws, specifically authorized citizen standing,[38] acknowledging the importance of citizen enforcement where citizens can step in and take on the task of enforcing federal statutes when official agencies fail to do so. In the legal systems of other industrial nations, similar provisions are unusual. In the federal CWA's §505, a fairly typical provision, Congress said:

§505(a) ...Any citizen may commence a civil action on his own behalf — (A)...(1) against any person (including (i) the United States, and (ii) any other government instrumentality or agency...) who is alleged to be in violation of (A) an effluent standard or limitation under this chapter or (B) an order issued by the Administrator or State with respect to such a standard or limitation, or (2) against the Administrator where there is alleged a failure of the Administrator to perform any act or duty under this chapter which is not discretionary with the Administrator....

§505(b) No action may be commenced — (1)... (A) prior to sixty days after the plaintiff has given notice of the alleged violation (i) to the Administrator, (ii) to the State in which the alleged violation occurs, and (iii) to any alleged violator of the

---

37. The "zone of interests" test is drawn from words in APA §702, not from Article III constitutional grounds, and has generally been liberally interpreted:

The [APA] should be construed "not grudgingly but as serving a broad remedial purpose."... The "zone of interest" formula [originally mentioned in *Data Processing*, 397 U.S. 153 (1970)] has not proved self-explanatory, but significant guidance can be drawn from that opinion. First, the Court interpreted the phrase "a relevant statute" in §702 quite broadly (indeed even using a different statute from the one sued under).... Second, the Court approved the "trend...toward [the] enlargement of the class of people who may protest administrative action."... The test is not meant to be especially demanding; in particular there need be no indication of congressional purpose to benefit the would-be plaintiff. Clarke v. Securities Indus. Ass'n, 479 U.S. 388, 395–400 (1987).

38. See Toxic Substances Control Act §§19(d), 20(c)(2), 15 U.S.C. §§2618(d), 2619; Endangered Species Act of 1973 §11(g)(4), 16 U.S.C. §1540(g)(4); Surface Mining Control and Reclamation Act of 1977, 30 U.S.C. §1270(d); Deep Seabed Hard Mineral Resources Act §117(c), 30 U.S.C. §1427(c); Clean Water Act (Federal Water Pollution Control Act Amendments of 1972 §505), 33 U.S.C. §1365(d); Marine Protection, Research, and Sanctuaries Act, 33 U.S.C. §1415(g)(4); Deepwater Port Act of 1974, 33 U.S.C. §1515(d); Safe Drinking Water Act §1449(d), 42 U.S.C. §300j-8(d); Noise Control Act of 1972 §12(d), 42 U.S.C. §4911(d); Energy Sources Development Act, 42 U.S.C. §5851(e)(2); Energy Policy and Conservation Act, 42 U.S.C. §6305(d); Solid Waste Disposal Act, 42 U.S.C. §6972(e); Clean Air Act §304, 42 U.S.C. §§7604, 7607(f); Powerplant and Industrial Fuel Act, 42 U.S.C. §8435(d); Ocean Thermal Energy Conservation Act, 42 U.S.C. §9124(d); Outer Continental Shelf Lands Act, 43 U.S.C. §1349(a)(5). The Marine Mammal Protection Act, however, lacks such a provision.

Significantly, most of these grants of enforcement standing also provide for attorney and expert witness fee awards if plaintiffs prevail. See Chapter 21 and each of the sections cited hereabove.

standard, limitation, or order,[39] or (B) if the Administrator or State has commenced and is diligently prosecuting a civil or criminal action in a court of the United States or a State to require compliance with the standard, limitation, or order, but in any such action in a court of the United States any citizen may intervene as a matter of right.... 33 U.S.C. §1365 (1972).

The federal courts have been quite attentive to these citizen suit provisions, generally acknowledging the strength of the congressional intent to encourage citizen enforcement as a parallel national strategy for achieving implementation of federal regulatory programs.[40] Starting in the late 1970s, however, Supreme Court decisions inclined toward rolling back citizen enforcement, retreating to the narrowed industry/agency terms of traditional administrative process.[41]

Retrenchment in the Rehnquist-Scalia Court. In the years immediately following *SCRAP*, standing doctrine initially shifted toward *SCRAP*'s accommodating terms, and then the Court began a steady retrenchment against citizen enforcement.[42] Almost as soon as he was put on the Court, Justice Scalia began to play a dominant role in restricting citizen standing. In a 1983 law review article, he had sharply criticized citizen enforcement of environmental protection laws as the sort of élitism that "met with approval in the classrooms of Cambridge and New Haven, but not in the factories of Detroit and the mines of West Virginia." Reacting to the language of Judge J. Skelly Wright in the classic *Calvert Cliffs* decision noted in Chapter 9 — which asserted that the goal of citizen suits was to assure that important congressional intentions to reduce pollution not be "lost or misdirected in the vast hallways of the federal bureaucracy" — Justice Scalia asked:

> Does what I have said mean that…"important legislative purposes, heralded in the halls of Congress, [can be] lost or misdirected in the vast hallways of the federal bureaucracy?" Of course it does — and a good thing, too.... Lots of once-heralded programs ought to get lost or misdirected, in vast hallways or elsewhere.... Scalia, The Doctrine of Standing as an Essential Element of the Separation of Powers, 17 Suffolk U. L. Rev. 881, 897 (1983).

---

39. The 60-day waiting period does not apply in cases of toxic and pretreatment standards or national performance standards. Environmentalists have argued that waivers to the 60-day waiting period should also be granted or liberalized in other settings where the public interest and congressional policy require it. Irvin, When Survival Is at Stake: A Proposal for Expanding the Emergency Exception to the Sixty-Day Notice Requirement of the Endangered Species Act's Citizen Suit Provision, 14 Harv. Envtl. L. Rev. 343 (1990) (the article presents interesting examples of the necessity for citizen enforcement where industry and government remain passive).

40. "[Where the] only public entities that might have brought suit…[are] named as defendants…and vigorously [oppose] plaintiffs,…only private citizens can be expected to guard the guardians." La Raza Unida v. Volpe, 57 F.R.D. 94, 101 (N.D. Cal. 1972). The nation's "regrettably slow progress in controlling air pollution is blamed on [both] the scarcity of skilled personnel available to enforce control measures and on a lack of aggressiveness by EPA's predecessor agency.... The public suit seems particularly instrumental in the statutory scheme [in cases forcing agency compliance], for only the public — certainly not the polluter — has the incentive to complain if the EPA falls short...." NRDC v. EPA, 484 F.2d 1331 (1st Cir. 1973).

41. Hallstrom v. Tillamook County, 493 U.S. 20 (1989); Gwaltney of Smithfield v. Chesapeake Bay Found., 484 U.S. 49 (1987). *Gwaltney*'s holding — that citizen suits can be filed only where an ongoing violation continues when the lawsuit is filed, but not for past violations — was specifically overridden by Congress as to the CAA. The 1990 CAA Amendments provided for citizen lawsuits upon evidence that past violations have been repeated. Pub. L. No. 101–549, §707(g) (amending §304(a) of the CAA, 42 U.S.C. §7410).

42. Sometimes generous standing rulings, as in Duke Power v. Carolina Envtl. Study Group, 438 U.S. 59 (1978), have reflected the Supreme Court's apparent desire to hear an environmental argument so as to dispose of it permanently in order to remove uncertainty from the marketplace. 438 U.S. at 78.

With Justice Scalia's vote and pen, new majority opinions followed several strategies — applying broadened prudential limitations where Congress has not granted specific standing rights,[43] requiring that plaintiffs be within "the zone of interests" that the statute was intended to protect,[44] holding statutory grants of citizen standing to their narrowest terms,[45] and adding more restrictive principles as constitutional requirements so as to overrride statutory grants and tighten standing generally.[46]

***Gwaltney of Smithfield* (1987).** In Gwaltney of Smithfield v. Chesapeake Bay Found., 484 U.S. 49 (1987), the Court narrowed citizen enforcement standing by strict construction of the statutory grant. In a case where a defendant swine-processing plant had been violating water pollution standards for years but had stopped its discharges shortly after the environmental plaintiffs filed their 60-day notice letter (though not because of it), the Court said the statutory text required an ongoing violation or proof of future likelihood of violations for citizens to have standing. CWA §505(a), noted above, grants standing to "any citizen...against any person...who is alleged to *be in violation* of...an effluent standard or limitation" (emphasis added). This interpretation cast a shadow over citizen suits by raising the possibility that groups taking on the extensive efforts of preparing an enforcement action might find themselves non-suited, with no prospect of regaining expert witness and attorneys' fees, by defendants who move into compliance at the last moment under threat of the citizen suit.

***Lujan I* (1990).** In *Lujan I*, Lujan v. National Wildlife Fed'n, 497 U.S. 871 (1990), the Court used constitutional arguments on standing to require environmentalists challenging agency actions to allege highly particularized injuries, and made suits against alleged programmatic violations extremely difficult. In denying plaintiffs' standing in a suit (based on the APA, not on a specific statutory grant of standing) against Interior Secretary James Watt's agency-industry proposal to open western public lands to grazing, timber, and mining operations, Justice Scalia scrutinized plaintiffs' claimed injuries closely:

> To support the [plaintiffs' standing] the Court of Appeals pointed to the affidavits of two of respondent's members, Peggy Kay Peterson and Richard Erman, which claimed use of land "in the vicinity" of the land covered by two of the listed actions.... There is no showing that Peterson's recreational use and enjoyment extends to the particular 4500 acres covered by the decision to terminate classification.... Erman's affidavit was substantially the same.... Respondent alleges that violation of the law is rampant within this program — failure to revise land use

---

43. For example, the proposition that plaintiffs cannot claim injury from harm to third parties was launched in Warth v. Seldin, 422 U.S. 490 (1975).

44. See Air Courier Conference v. American Postal Workers Union, 498 U.S. 517 (1991) (Rehnquist, J., denying standing).

45. See *Gwaltney*, 484 U.S. 49, 52 (1987), and The Steel Co. v. Citizens for a Better Env't, 523 U.S. 83 (1998).

46. "The constitutional component of standing doctrine incorporates concepts concededly not susceptible of precise definition. The injury alleged must be, for example, 'distinct and palpable,' and not 'abstract' or 'conjectural' or 'hypothetical.' The injury must be 'fairly' traceable to the challenged action, and relief from the injury ['redressability'] must be 'likely' to follow from a favorable decision." Allen v. Wright, 468 U.S. 737 (1984). *SCRAP*, in other words, is history. By calling these tests constitutional rather than prudential, the Court can use them to limit congressional standing grants.

plans in proper fashion, failure to submit certain recommendations to Congress, failure to consider multiple use, inordinate focus upon mineral exploitation, failure to provide adequate environmental impact statements. Perhaps so. But respondent cannot seek wholesale improvement of this program by court decree.... The flaws in the entire "program" — consisting principally of the many individual actions referenced in the complaint, and presumably actions yet to be taken as well — cannot be laid before the courts for wholesale correction under the APA, simply because one of them that is ripe for review adversely affects one of respondent's members. Respondent must seek such programmatic improvements from the BLM or Congress. *Lujan I*, 497 U.S. 871 (1990).

***Lujan II* (1992).** In *Lujan II*, Justice Scalia extended his stringent theories of Article III standing even to cases where Congress had specifically authorized citizen standing. Environmentalists were trying to apply the protections of the federal ESA to overseas projects of U.S. agencies that ignored ecological issues and endangered species. The Act's §7 forbids agencies to jeopardize species or destroy their habitat (see Chapter 16) and requires formal consultations when there is a risk. ESA §11 authorizes "any person" to enforce the Act in court. In 1986, the Reagan Administration had issued a regulation relieving federal agencies from any duty to comply with ESA §7(a)(2) when participating in projects in other countries:

> The Court of Appeals focused on the affidavits of two Defenders' members.... Ms. Skilbred averred that she traveled to Sri Lanka in 1981 and "observed th[e] habitat" of "endangered species such as the Asian elephant and the leopard" at what is now the site of the Mahaweli Project funded by the Agency for International Development (AID) [which] "will seriously reduce endangered, threatened, and endemic species habitat including areas that I visited"...but confessed that she had no current plans...to go back to Sri Lanka:... "There is a civil war going on right now."... These affidavits...contain no facts...showing how damage to the species will produce [the] "imminent" injury to Ms. Skilbred...that our cases require.

> Besides failing to show injury, respondents failed to demonstrate redressability....[47] Since the agencies funding the projects were not parties to the case, the District Court could accord relief only against the Secretary: He could be ordered to revise his regulation to require consultation for foreign projects. But this would not remedy respondents' alleged injury unless the funding agencies were bound by the Secretary's regulation, which is very much an open question....

> The Court of Appeals found that respondents had standing for an additional reason: because they had suffered a "procedural injury." The so-called "citizen-suit" provision of the ESA provides, in pertinent part, that "any person may commence a civil suit...to enjoin any person, including...any...governmental instrumentality or agency...who is alleged to be in violation."... This is not a case where plaintiffs are seeking to enforce a procedural requirement the disregard of which could impair a separate concrete interest of theirs.... Nor...is it the unusual case in which Congress has created a concrete private interest in the outcome of a suit against a private party for the government's benefit, by providing a cash bounty for the victorious plaintiff. Rather, the court held that the injury-in-fact

---

47. This paragraph is from segment IIIB of the opinion, which drew only four votes: Scalia, Rehnquist, White, and Thomas. The redressability concept had been launched in Simon v. Eastern Ky. Welfare Rights Org., 426 U.S. 26, 38, 41 (1976). [Eds.]

requirement had been satisfied by congressional conferral upon all persons of an abstract, self-contained, noninstrumental "right" to have the Executive observe the procedures required by law. We reject this view.... Vindicating the public interest (including the public interest in government observance of the Constitution and laws) is the function of Congress and the Chief Executive.... To permit Congress to convert the undifferentiated public interest in executive officers' compliance with the law into an "individual right" vindicable in the courts is to permit Congress to transfer from the President to the courts the Chief Executive's most important constitutional duty, to "take Care that the Laws be faithfully executed." Lujan v. Defenders of Wildlife, 504 U.S. at 568–578 (1992) (*Lujan II*).

The *Lujan II* decision was strongly criticized for undercutting the Court's previous acceptance of congressional definitions of generalized injury as a base of citizen standing.[48] Justice Blackmun, joined by Justice O'Connor, dissented, saying, "I cannot join the Court on what amounts to a slash-and-burn expedition through the law of environmental standing." In subsequent years, however, Justice Scalia was not uniformly restrictive of citizen standing. When two cattle ranchers sought to challenge the Department of Interior's enforcement of the ESA on the Klamath River, the Court, in an opinion by Justice Scalia, gave the ranchers standing. Bennett v. Spear, 520 U.S. 15 (1997).

The Steel Company (1998). Standing was again further restricted, however, when citizens sued in a case involving a factory that had long failed to file information required by EPCRA on its use of toxics, but filed the reports under threat of the citizens' 60-day enforcement letter. Do citizens suffer a sufficient specific and concrete Article III injury from a polluter's monitoring and reporting violations? In The Steel Co. v. Citizens for a Better Env't, 523 U.S. 83 (1998), noted later in Chapter 21, the Court framed the question but did not decide it: "We have not had occasion to decide whether being deprived of information that is supposed to be disclosed under EPCRA...is a concrete injury in fact that satisfies Article III. We need not reach that question in the present case." 523 U.S. at 105. The Court decided that the citizens' injury, if it existed, had already been redressed by the late reports and so would not be further redressed by a court order; hence, standing was barred. To environmentalist plaintiffs, the *Steel Company* decision, like *Gwaltney*, undercut an important purpose of each citizen enforcement case — to provide a deterrent example of effective citizen prosecution to other violators.

Laidlaw (2000). To the pleasant surprise of many environmentalists who had glumly watched a succession of constrictive standing decisions, in 2000 citizen standing received a strong affirmation from the Court, over Justices Scalia and Thomas's fervent dissent. In Friends of the Earth v. Laidlaw Envtl. Servs., Inc., 528 U.S. 167 (2000), the majority opinion applied a broader, commonsense definition of Article III injury and scrutinized the political realities of a state agency's collusion with an industrial defendant, in order to allow citizen prosecution to go forward.

---

48. Sunstein, What's Standing after *Lujan*?, 91 Mich. L. Rev. 163 (1992); Nichol, Justice Scalia, Standing, and Public Law Litigation, 42 Duke L.J. 1141 (1993); Pierce, Lujan v. Defenders, 42 Duke L.J. 1170 (1993).

A South Carolina hazardous waste incinerating plant had been repeatedly violating its CWA permit by dumping excess toxic wastes including mercury into the Tyger River on 489 occasions over an eight-year span. Echoed by Justice Scalia's dissent, the corporation argued that plaintiffs' enforcement action should be dismissed on four standing grounds:

- There had been no proof of substantial ecological harms from the dumping, so if the environment wasn't injured there was no Article III injury.
- Since there was no demonstrated health or environmental harm, plaintiffs had no personal cognizable injury.
- Because the company had quickly reached a small settlement with the state agency as soon as the citizens filed their 60-day notice letter, the citizen suit was foreclosed under CWA §505(b), above, which bars suits where the agency "has commenced and is diligently prosecuting a civil or criminal action."
- Because, since the plant's operations had subsequently shut down and plaintiffs were not seeking injunctive relief, the plaintiffs' request that the company pay penalties to EPA would do nothing to redress their claimed harms.

Any one of these arguments could previously have been expected to doom the citizens' suit. Remarkably, however, a strong body of scholarship had begun to emerge scrutinizing the tightening line of standing decisions and clarifying the basic principles that underlie the Article III inquiry. Influential studies of standing jurisprudence raised serious questions about whether increased restrictions on standing were the result of evolving doctrinal interpretation or organic agenda-driven decisionmaking.[49] To many scholars, standing decisions were an embarrassing departure from neutral principles for defining what constituted an Article III case or controversy, seeming to turn more upon which team was at bat than upon principle. As Professors Davis and Pierce asked:

> Why does the Court sometimes use a…test that is impossible to meet? What distinguishes these cases from the many cases in which the Court uses a logical and pragmatic test for determining [standing]? Those questions seem easy to answer, though the answer bears no logical relationship to standing. The Court uses standing…to preclude federal courts from intervening in disputes [a majority] considers inappropriate for federal judicial intervention. K. C. Davis & R. Pierce, Administrative Law Treatise §16.5 at 38–39 (1994).[50]

In *Laidlaw*, writing for a new Court majority in an opinion that reads like a primer on citizen standing, Justice Ginsburg rejected all four arguments, in each case directly refuting the assertions being made in dissent by Justice Scalia:.

• As to the purported lack of standing because there had been no proof of harm to the environment from Laidlaw's mercury discharge violations:

---

49. Is the Rehnquist-Scalia line of restrictive holdings "conservative"? Note that they insulate big government agencies from judicial review. The insulation admittedly is not against marketplace players but against citizens, without whom there is no practical likelihood that actions supported by agency-industry coalitions — like the exploitation of western lands in *Mineral King* and *Lujan I*, or destructive public works projects in *Scenic Hudson*, *Lujan II*, and many other cases — will ever be held accountable for ongoing violations of law.

50. See Echeverria & Zeidler, Barely Standing: The Erosion of Citizen "Standing" to Sue and Enforce Environmental Law, Geo. Envtl. L. & Pol'y Inst. (1999); Buzbee, Expanding the Zone, Tilting the Field: Zone of Interests and Article III Standing Analysis After Bennett v. Spear, 49 Admin. L. Rev. 764 (1997); Carlson, Standing for the Environment, 45 UCLA L. Rev. 932 (1998); Coplan, Refracting the Spectrum of Clean Water Act Standing in Light of Lujan v. Defenders of Wildlife, 22 Colum. J. Envtl. L. 170 (1997).

The relevant showing for purposes of Article III standing, however, is not injury to the environment but injury to the plaintiff....

• As to the purported lack of sufficient injury to plaintiffs:

The affidavits and testimony presented by FOE in this case assert that Laidlaw's discharges...directly affected those affiants' recreational, aesthetic, and economic interests.... Kenneth Lee Curtis averred...that he lived a half-mile from Laidlaw's facility; that he occasionally drove over the North Tyger River, and that it looked and smelled polluted; and that he would like to fish, camp, swim, and picnic in and near the river...as he did when he was a teenager, but would not do so because he was concerned that the water was polluted by Laidlaw's discharges.... Unlike the dissent, we see nothing "improbable" about the proposition that a company's continuous and pervasive illegal discharges of pollutants into a river would cause nearby residents to curtail their recreational use of that waterway and would subject them to other economic and aesthetic harms. The proposition is entirely reasonable, the district court found it was true in this case, and that is enough for injury in fact....

• As to the claim that the state's settlement barred the citizens' suit:

Plaintiff-petitioners [FOE]...sent a letter to Laidlaw notifying the company of their intention to file a citizen suit against it under §505(a) of the Act after the expiration of the requisite 60-day notice period.... Laidlaw's lawyer then contacted DHEC [the state enforcement agency] to ask whether DHEC would consider filing a lawsuit against Laidlaw...to bar FOE's proposed citizen suit through [§505](b)(1)(B)[diligent prosecution]. DHEC agreed to file a lawsuit against Laidlaw; the company's lawyer then drafted the complaint for DHEC and paid the filing fee. On June 9, 1992, the last day before FOE's 60-day notice period expired, DHEC and Laidlaw reached a settlement requiring Laidlaw to pay $100,000 in civil penalties and to make "every effort" to comply with its permit obligations.... In imposing the civil penalty of $100,000 against Laidlaw, DHEC failed to recover, or even to calculate, the economic benefit that Laidlaw received by not complying with its permit.... Laidlaw had gained a total economic benefit of $1,092,581 as a result of its extended period of noncompliance with the mercury discharge limit in its permit.... After [the state settlement], but before the district court rendered judgment, Laidlaw violated the mercury discharge limitation in its permit 13 times [and] committed 13 monitoring and 10 reporting violations.... The district court held that DHEC's action against Laidlaw ["entered into with unusual haste, without giving the Plaintiffs the opportunity to intervene"] had not been "diligently prosecuted"; consequently, the court [properly] allowed FOE's citizen suit to proceed....

• And finally, as to mootness and a lack of redressability for the plaintiffs, because now the plant had closed and remedies were limited to payment of penalties to the government:

Penalties in Clean Water Act cases do more than promote immediate compliance by limiting the defendant's economic incentive to delay its attainment of permit limits; they also deter future violations.... "The legislative history of the Act reveals that Congress wanted the district court to consider the need for retribution and deterrence, in addition to restitution, when it imposed civil penalties.... To the extent that civil penalties encourage defendants to discontinue current violations and deter them from committing future ones, they afford redress to citizen plaintiffs who are injured or threatened with injury as a consequence of ongoing unlawful conduct.

COMMENTARY & QUESTIONS

1. *Laidlaw*: **A home run for citizen standing?** Looking over this undulating line of decisions, culminating in *Laidlaw*, where have we come? Do citizens now have a re-opened
road to judicial review of agency actions? Has the standing inquiry now turned to a
realistic basis for assessing whether there is a genuine non-collusive legal case or
controversy that will be competently presented for the court to decide, which after all is
what Article III seeks?

Not exactly. The Court did not back away from the simplistic traditional focus on the
need to prove an injury, any injury, nor from the *Lujan II* requirement that it must be a
present specific discrete harm or risk of harm to the plaintiff, not just a "likely, possibly
in the future" harm. The Court gave significant weight to the plaintiffs' claims that they
would use and enjoy the river "but for" and seemed to be impressed that some of the
plaintiffs had done so before the pollution. The "I-might-go-back-someday-to-see-
the-endangered-animals" of *Lujan II* is probably still too remote a claim of harm.

(Note that *Laidlaw* is a citizen enforcement suit, not a citizen suit seeking judicial
review of agency action, but for standing purposes this does not seem to make any
difference.)

2. **How much harm must a plaintiff now show?** Would a trivial $5 bounty do it? The
Laidlaw majority accepted the sufficiency of standing allegations when plaintiffs said
they would like to use a specifically affected resource located close to where they lived.
But the definition of sufficient Article III standing interest or injury is nebulous in part
because it looks only to the existence of a linkage between the plaintiff and the thing,
not gauging the weightiness of the interest. Not that adding such a subjective relative
balancing test would be a good idea.

But the current state of the law allows the constitutional threshold to be determined by
trivialities. According to the Scalia opinion in *Lujan II*, constitutional standing would
exist "[where] Congress has created a concrete private interest in the outcome of
a suit[51]...by providing a cash bounty for the victorious plaintiff." So if Congress
authorized payment of a $5 pecuniary reward for successful law enforcement, even
Justice Scalia would apparently allow standing — which makes the injury-based standing test seem rather superficial, disingenuous, and beside the point.

If a small money bounty would be sufficient to give a citizen Article III standing in the
Lujan terms, then why not likewise the authorizations for prevailing parties to collect
attorneys' fees and expert witness fees? Those provisions already exist in almost every
major environmental statute's grant of citizen enforcement standing as noted above for
CWA §505. Especially where plaintiffs are public interest attorneys groups, the prospect
of recovering tens of thousand dollars for their labors enforcing the law would seem to
be a tangible enough interest to assure a solid controversy.

And here's an analytic brain-tickler: How do government agencies satisfy Justice Scalia's
specific interest or injury standard? We all assume that when Congress passes a statute

---

51. The quote says "a suit against a private party," but it is difficult to see any Article III difference between suits
against private and public defendants.

and gives an independent federal agency the authority to prosecute it, the agency has Article III standing — for example, the CPSC is given authority to prosecute antitrust violations and is assumed to have standing to do so. Why? What is the CPSC's constitutional injury or interest[52] if it is not the enforcement standing created by Congress's delegation to the agency?

If Congress can delegate statutory enforcement authority to the CPSC, then why can't it also delegate that authority to private organizations similarly dedicated to enforcing public law? (In administrative law, there is no bar preventing delegations to private parties, so that is not the distinction.) Could Justice Scalia be wrong in asserting that a congressionally created procedural interest is not sufficient for standing, especially if he admits that a paltry bounty would support standing? Professor Sunstein has called into question the focus on "injury" as the necessary and sufficient threshold test for standing. "At least in general," Sunstein advises, "standing depends on whether any source of law has created a cause of action." If Congress can create new causes of action, it would seem that it generally could also create standing for their enforcement as it chooses and deny standing when it likes. Sunstein, What's Standing after *Lujan*? — Of Citizen Suits, "Injuries," and Article III, 91 Mich. L. Rev. 163 (1992).

3. **Redressability.** The concept of redressability — asking whether the harms claimed by plaintiffs as a basis for standing are likely to be resolved by a judicial remedy — was previously considered a court-made "prudential principle" subject to being overridden by congressional mandates expanding standing, not an Article III requirement that must be met even if a statute purports to grant standing without it. When injunctions are sought, "Equity will not order a vain thing." Declaratory judgments, however, are thought to guide defendants generally, and particularly where in *Lujan II* the defendants were federal agencies, isn't it likely that the court's rulings would be followed? Is redressability an invitation to political science predictions? After *Laidlaw*, it appears that the Court has at least widened the concept of redressability.

4. **Standing and the "diligent prosecution" jurisdictional defense?** Note how on the facts of *Laidlaw*, the Court did not even deign to consider the "diligently prosecuting" jurisdictional bar to standing. *Laidlaw* illustrates the judiciary's ability to look critically at the quality of state enforcement of environmental laws and to reject state enforcement if it is weak. Considering Laidlaw's transparently disingenuous use of alleged state agency "enforcement" as a shield, what conclusions do you draw about the importance of citizen suits in undercutting the race-to-the-bottom, not to mention the ethics of legal practice reflected in *Laidlaw*?

5. **Ripeness, exhaustion, financing, and other barriers to citizen enforcement.** The extended analysis of standing issues here should not obscure the fact that virtually every tactical issue in administrative law plays a frequent role in environmental litigation. "Ripeness" is a prime example — the question whether the agency has made a sufficiently final decision to be reviewed. See the Supreme Court's ripeness decision in Ohio Forestry v. Sierra Club, 523 U.S. 726 (1998) (agency planning would not be ripe

---

52. The CPSC is an independent agency and thus could not say it has constitutional standing as an executive subordinate of the President who holds the Article II duty to see that the laws are faithfully executed.

for review on whether it conformed with NFMA planning requirements until the plan actually authorized particular trees to be cut). "Exhaustion of remedies" is another, asking whether citizens should seek all appropriate remedies in an agency before trying to pull the issues into court.[53] As to the tactics of financing litigation, when citizens embark as "private attorneys general" attempting to enforce existing law in agencies and courts, they often face substantial administrative and financial burdens, against opponents who are either public officials or well-financed corporate entities writing off expenses against revenues. Expert witnesses and attorneys cost money. For plaintiff groups like the citizens in *Overton Park*, this often means having to raise funds through bake sales, raffles, logo t-shirt sales, or passing the hat. In Chapter 21, which discusses practical issues of statutory enforcement, there is an extended analysis of recovery of attorneys' fees and other practical issues in the logistics of litigation.

6. **Is citizen standing a mistake? — what about prosecutorial discretion?** One of the most ancient elements of governmental power is the grace to *withhold* punishment. Prosecutorial discretion allows appropriate governmental officials to decide where best the society's enforcement efforts should be focused, and what violations should be overlooked for reasons of policy or of fairness (echoing Aristotle's *aequitas* — asserting that to provide for the occasions when laws apply harshly or unwisely there must be an avenue for selective absolution). The Court in Heckler v. Chaney[54] confirmed that federal agencies enjoy a fundamental power of prosecutorial discretion. What happens to that agency discretion if citizens using statutory standing grants can decide to enforce environmental statutes and regulations against violators? Some violations undoubtedly do not deserve active prosecution. Some environmentalists — we'll name no names here — can clearly be loose cannons, undermining the credibility of environmental positions in national policy debates. Literal enforcement of every provision on the statute books is pretty clearly not a good idea. On the other hand, a significant lesson of the twentieth century was that agencies cannot be relied upon to be driven by the public interest in the face of the focused suasions and resistance of the marketplace. How to winnow the wheat from the chaff? The cost of litigating is an unreliable filter to screen out improvident litigation, but why is the Court's rather haphazard harm-based standing criterion any more rational? This argues for the proposition that organized citizen efforts must continue to be a significant part of a modern industrial democracy — and legal standing in court probably is citizens' single most significant institutional instrumentality for guaranteeing their public interest commitments an active role in governance.

---

53. See EDF v. Hardin, 428 F.2d 1093 (D.C. Cir. 1970), where both issues arose in an environmental group's attempt to get an agency to curtail DDT as a pesticide.

54. 470 U.S. 821 (1985). The facts of the *Heckler* case are bemusing. FDA rules prohibit use of pharmaceuticals unless they have been tested for pain and "safety" for a particular use. Drugs used to euthanize animals have to be so certified. In *Heckler*, death row inmates sought to apply the rules to bar the use of drugs used for human lethal injections, which had not been so tested and certified. The Court, however, said the Secretary of Health and Human Services could exercise prosecutorial discretion deciding whether such enforcement would happen.

Agency claims for unreviewability are more likely to be successful in cases of agencies declining to enforce, a central issue in Southern Utah Wilderness Alliance v. Norton, 301 F.3d 1217 (10th Cir. 2002), cert. granted 124 S. Ct. 462 (2003). The FLPMA statute directs the agency "to manage [wilderness study areas]...so as not to impair such areas," but citizen plaintiffs showed that the Bush Administration's BLM declined to prevent ORVs from entering and degrading the areas. The Administration argued that any statutory violation was unreviewable because the agency action was discretionary (was it?), or not yet ripe for review under §706.

Section 3. **POLITICAL RESISTANCE TO CITIZEN ENFORCEMENT: REMOVING COURTS' ABILITY TO GRANT RELIEF TO CITIZENS**

Department of Interior and Related Agencies Appropriations Act, 1990
Public Law Number 101–121 (1989)

§318(g)... No restraining order or preliminary injunction shall be issued by any court of the United States with respect to any decision to prepare, advertise, offer, award, or operate...timber sales in fiscal year 1990 from the thirteen national forests in Oregon and Washington and Bureau of Land Management lands in Western Oregon known to contain northern spotted owls. The provisions of 5 U.S.C. §705 [authorizing courts to stay agency actions] shall not apply to any challenge to such a timber sale. Provided, that the courts shall have authority to [issue permanent injunctions for timber sales found to be] arbitrary, capricious, or otherwise not in accordance with law....

[Other provisions of this appropriations rider required the agencies to sell off increased annual quotas of timber; restricted the cutting of certain "ecologically significant old growth forest stands" except as necessary to meet the sales quotas; directed the Forest Service to prepare a new spotted owl plan and have it in place by September 30, 1990; insulated from judicial review Forest Service and Bureau of Land Management (BLM) decisions shown to be based on outdated information; and made quasi-judicial findings to reverse two injunctions against timbercutting.[55] In recent years, similar riders have surfaced fairly regularly.]

COMMENTARY & QUESTIONS

1. **The spotted owl appropriations rider.** What's going on here? The preceding language was inserted into a Department of Interior appropriations bill in reaction to environmentalists' successes in protecting the northern spotted owl under a variety of environmental statutes. Environmentalists had repeatedly been able to demonstrate that the endangered owl was threatened by illegal clearcutting operations in various old-growth national forests in the Pacific Northwest. The appropriations rider was intended to end the citizens' disruption of ongoing practices.

What is the theory of such riders? They are the legislative parallel to judicial attempts to restrict citizen enforcement standing so that business can go on as usual. They do not repeal or amend laws that stand in the way of promoters' enterprises. (Repeals or amendments are straightforward legislative alternatives available to Congress, but they can be difficult to pass.) Instead riders such as §318 merely remove the citizens' ability to get preliminary injunctions (and foreclose permanent injunctions except in

---

55. See §§314, 318(b)(6), 103 Stat. at 743, 747. In practice, these timber sales typically auction off the public forests at below-cost subsidized prices. Section 318's quasi-judicial findings were held unconstitutional on separation of powers grounds, Seattle Audubon v. Robertson, 914 F.2d 1311 (9th Cir. 1990), rev'd, 503 U.S. 429 (1992).

Section 318 is a "rider" because it was tacked onto the on-rolling spending bill. In fact, attaching such substantive law provisions onto appropriations bills violates House Rule 23 and Senate Rule 16, but through parliamentary maneuvers the rules were not applied.

Timber lobbyists rather cynically tacked a similar rider onto the Oklahoma bombing disaster relief bill, and it stayed in force for 18 months before dying in ill repute. Emergency Supplemental Appropriations for Additional Disaster Assistance, for Anti-Terrorism Initiatives, for Assistance in the Recovery from the Tragedy that Occurred at Oklahoma City, and Rescissions Act, 1995, Pub. L. No. 104–19, 109 Stat. 194, 240 (1995). See Oregon Nat. Res. Council v. Jack Ward Thomas, 92 F.3d 792 (9th Cir. 1996); Northwest Forest Res. Council, 82 F.3d 825 (9th Cir. 1996).

extraordinary cases where citizens are able to prove on the restricted merits that agency action was arbitrary, capricious, etc.).[56]

Isn't the rider's approach quite revealing? Its obvious rationale is that — absent citizen enforcement — neither the private industry logging the lands nor the two federal agencies supervising the logging will comply with federal laws. In order to nullify the laws, one doesn't have to repeal them (and they didn't have the votes to do that), but needs only to eliminate the citizen enforcers.

2. **Can Congress foreclose judicial review?** Beyond the question of legislating on appropriations bills, is there any constitutional limit to the ability of special interest riders to foreclose judicial review of targeted agency practices? After a broad-ranging review of such provisions overriding judicial review, a recent study ended its constitutional and statutory analysis with the plaint that "it is crucial that courts apply a heightened standard of review in examining measures that limit judicial review.... Judicial review is fundamental to the 'very essence of liberty' [citing Marbury v. Madison, 5 U.S. 137, 163 (1803)]. The Supreme Court has held that any 'statutory preclusion of judicial review must be demonstrated clearly and convincingly.'"[57] If Congress doesn't change the law, but removes judicial jurisdiction to consider violations in whole or in part, does that violate the Article III judicial power and the separation of powers doctrine? Absent a clear constitutional barrier to such legislative shortcuts, special interest attempts to foreclose citizen enforcement will undoubtedly continue, pressuring Congress to write specific exemptions from judicial review so that statutes will go unenforced.

Section 4. CITIZENS' ATTEMPTS TO EXPAND AGENCY PROCEDURES

In *Overton Park*, the plaintiffs were unsuccessful in persuading the courts to grant extended procedural opportunities to challenge the highway project within the agency or to require formal findings. In subsequent years, many federal courts, led by the D.C. Circuit, began to expand the procedures owed to citizen challengers — sometimes on claims of individual due process, especially in matters of "Great Public Import," and sometimes based on the review needs of courts. The following case involved both. Note the tone of the Supreme Court opinion, the political alignments among the various parties, and how the citizen environmentalists focused their arguments on procedural claims as much as, or more than, attacking the substantive agency decision.

---

56. In the timing of such citizen efforts, practically speaking, preliminary injunctions are the entire battle. If preliminary relief staying the agency action is not ordered, the forest is stripped bare before plaintiffs can get to trial on the permanent injunctions. Such appropriations riders are effective federal law for only one fiscal year, although when lobbyists successfully add them to an appropriations bill for one year, they tend to reappear thereafter.

After 458 law professors from 61 schools in 41 states and the District of Columbia sent a letter to leaders of the House and Senate protesting §318 as a "dangerous precedent" for undermining protective federal laws, however, §318 was not re-promulgated for the following fiscal year. The fight was successfully led by Senators Baucus and Chaffee, who not coincidentally were the ranking members of the standing committees bypassed by the appropriations stratagem and by the Sierra Club.

57. Sher & Hunting, Eroding the Landscape, Eroding the Laws: Congressional Exemptions from Judicial Review of Environmental Laws, 15 Harv. Envtl. L. Rev. 435, 481 (1991) (citing NLRB v. United Food & Comm'l Wkrs. Union, 484 U.S. 112, 131 (1987)).

Vermont Yankee Nuclear Power Corp. v. Natural Resources Defense Council
Supreme Court of the United States, 1978
435 U.S. 519

REHNQUIST, J. In 1946, Congress enacted the Administrative Procedure Act, which as we have noted elsewhere was not only "a new, basic and comprehensive regulation of procedures in many agencies," Wong Yang Sung v. McGrath, 339 U.S. 33 (1950), but was also a legislative enactment which settled "long-continued and hard-fought contentions, and enacts a formula upon which opposing social and political forces have come to rest."... Interpreting [§4 of the Act, now codified as §553] in United States v. Allegheny-Ludlum Steel Corp., 406 U.S. 742 (1972), and United States v. Florida East Coast Ry. Co., 410 U.S. 224 (1973), we held that generally speaking this section of the Act established the maximum procedural requirements which Congress was willing to have the courts impose upon agencies in conducting rulemaking procedures. Agencies are free to grant additional procedural rights in the exercise of their discretion, but reviewing courts are generally not free to impose them if the agencies have not chosen to grant them. This is not to say necessarily that there are no circumstances which would ever justify a court in overturning agency action because of a failure to employ procedures beyond those required by the statute. But such circumstances, if they exist, are extremely rare....

We granted certiorari to review [a judgment] of the Court of Appeals for the District of Columbia Circuit because of our concern that [the court] had seriously misread or misapplied this statutory and decisional law cautioning reviewing courts against engrafting their own notions of proper procedures upon agencies entrusted with substantive functions by Congress. We conclude that the Court of Appeals has done just that....

Under the Atomic Energy Act of 1954, as amended, 42 U.S.C. §2011 et seq., the Atomic Energy Commission was given broad regulatory authority over the development of nuclear energy. Under the terms of the act, a utility seeking to construct and operate a nuclear power plant must obtain a separate permit or license at both the construction and the operation stage of the project. In order to obtain the construction permit, the utility must file a preliminary safety analysis report, an environmental report, and certain information regarding the antitrust implications of the proposed project. This application then undergoes exhaustive review by the Commission's staff and by the Advisory Committee on Reactor Safe-guards (ACRS), a group of distinguished experts in the field of atomic energy....

In December 1967, after the mandatory adjudicatory hearing and necessary review, the Commission granted petitioner Vermont Yankee a permit to build a nuclear power plant in Vernon, Vt. Thereafter, Vermont Yankee applied for an operating license. Respondent Natural Resources Defense Council (NRDC) objected to the granting of a license, however, and therefore a hearing on the application commenced on August 10, 1971. Excluded from consideration at the hearings, over NRDC's objection, was the issue of the environmental effects of operations to reprocess fuel or dispose of wastes resulting from the reprocessing operations. This ruling was affirmed by the Appeal Board in June 1972.

In November 1972, however, the Commission, making specific reference to the Appeal Board's decision with respect to the Vermont Yankee License, instituted rulemaking proceedings "that would specifically deal with the question of consideration of environmental effects associated with the uranium fuel cycle in the individual cost-benefit analyses for light water cooled nuclear power reactors." [I.e., the rule would stipulate a waste storage evaluation factor that thereafter could be incorporated into formal plant licensing proceedings without re-opening the whole messy question in each licensing.] The notice of proposed rulemaking offered two alternatives, both predicated on a report prepared by the commission's staff entitled Environmental Survey of the Nuclear Fuel Cycle. The first would have required no quantitative evaluation of the environmental hazards of fuel reprocessing or disposal because the Environmental Survey had found them to be slight. The second would have specified numerical values for the environmental impact of this part of the fuel cycle, which values would then be incorporated into a table, along with the other relevant factors, to determine the overall cost-benefit balance for each operating license.

Much of the controversy in this case revolves around the procedures used in the rulemaking hearing which commenced in February 1973.... All participants would be given a reasonable opportunity to present their position and could be represented by counsel if they so desired. Written and, time permitting, oral statements would be received and incorporated into the record.... More than 40 individuals and organizations representing a wide variety of interests submitted written comments....

The Licensing Board forwarded its report to the Commission without rendering any decision [identifying] as the principal procedural question the propriety of declining to use full formal adjudicatory procedures [in the rulemaking]. [Note: the word "adjudicatory" is used throughout the opinion as a synonym for "trial-type process."] The major substantive issue was the [rulemaking choice between the two hazard evaluation options in] the Environmental Survey.

In April 1974, the Commission issued a rule which adopted the second of the two proposed alternatives.... The Commission also approved the procedures used at the hearing, and indicated that the record, including the Environmental Survey, provided an "adequate data base for the regulation adopted.".... Respondents appealed from both the Commission's adoption of the rule and its decision to grant Vermont Yankee's license to the Court of Appeals for the District of Columbia Circuit.

The court...examined the rulemaking proceedings and, despite the fact that it appeared that the agency employed all the procedures required by 5 U.S.C. §553 and more, the court determined the proceedings to be inadequate and overturned the rule. Accordingly, the Commission's determination with respect to Vermont Yankee's license was... remanded for further proceedings.

Petitioner Vermont Yankee first argues that the Commission should grant a license to operate a nuclear reactor without any consideration of waste disposal and fuel reprocessing. We find, however, that this issue is no longer presented by the record in this case.... Vermont Yankee will produce annually well over 100 pounds of radioactive wastes, some of which will be highly toxic.... Many of these substances must be isolated for anywhere from 600 to hundreds of thousands of years. It is hard to argue that these wastes do not constitute "adverse environmental effects which cannot be avoided should the proposal be implemented," or that by operating nuclear power plants we are not making "irreversible and irretrievable commitments of resources." [These are requirements from NEPA §102.]...

We next turn to the invalidation of the fuel cycle rule.... The Court of Appeals struck down the rule because of the perceived inadequacies of the procedures employed in the rulemaking proceedings. The court first determined the intervenors' primary argument to be "that the decision to preclude 'discovery or cross-examination' denied them a meaningful opportunity to participate in the proceedings as guaranteed by due process." The court then went on to frame the issue for decision thus: "Thus, we are called upon to decide whether the procedures provided by the agency were sufficient to ventilate the issues." The court conceded that absent extraordinary circumstances it is improper for a reviewing court to prescribe the procedural format an agency must follow, but it likewise clearly thought it entirely appropriate to "scrutinize the record as a whole to insure that genuine opportunities to participate in a meaningful way were provided...." The court also refrained from actually ordering the agency to follow any specific procedures, but there is little doubt in our minds that the…court's decision is that the procedures afforded during the hearings were inadequate. This conclusion is particularly buttressed by the fact that after the court examined the record, particularly the testimony of Dr. Pittman, and declared it insufficient, the court proceeded to discuss at some length the necessity for further procedural devices or a more "sensitive" application of those devices employed during the proceedings….

In prior opinions we have intimated that even in a rulemaking proceeding when an agency is making a "quasi-judicial" determination by which a very small number of persons are "'exceptionally affected, in each case upon individual grounds,'" in some circumstances additional [trial-type] procedures may be required in order to afford the aggrieved individuals due process. United States v. Florida East Coast R. Co., 410 U.S. at 242, 245 (quoting from Bi-Metallic Investment Co. v. State Board of Equalization, 239 U.S. 441, 446 (1915)). It might also be true, although we do not think the issue is presented in this case and accordingly do not decide it, that a totally unjustified departure from well-settled agency procedures of long standing might require judicial correction.

But this much is absolutely clear. Absent constitutional constraints or extremely compelling circumstances the "administrative agencies 'should be free to fashion their own rules of procedure and to pursue methods of inquiry capable of permitting them to discharge their multitudinous duties.'" FCC v. Schreiber, 381 U.S. 279, 290 (1965).

We have continually repeated this theme through the years…. In determining the proper scope of judicial review of agency action under the Natural Gas Act, we held that…the agency should normally be allowed to "exercise its administrative discretion in deciding how, in light of internal organization considerations, it may best proceed to develop the needed evidence…." We went on to emphasize: "At least in the absence of substantial justification for doing otherwise, a reviewing court may not, after determining that additional evidence is requisite for adequate review, proceed by dictating to the agency the methods, procedures, and time dimension of the needed inquiry and ordering the results to be reported to the court without opportunity for further consideration on the basis of the new evidence by the agency. Such a procedure clearly runs the risk of 'propel[ling] the court into the domain which Congress has set aside exclusively for the administrative agency.' SEC v. Chenery Corp., 332 U.S. 194, 196 (1947)."

Respondent NRDC argues that [§553] of the Administrative Procedure Act merely establishes lower procedural bounds and that a court may routinely require more than the minimum when an agency's proposed rule addresses complex or technical factual issues or "Issues of Great Public Import."…

Our decisions reject this view…. We also think the legislative history…does not bear out its contention. The Senate Report explains what eventually became [§553] thus: "This subsection states…the minimum requirements of public rule making procedure short of statutory hearing. Under it agencies might in addition confer with industry advisory committees, consult organizations, hold informal 'hearings,' and the like. Considerations of practicality, necessity, and public interest…will naturally govern the agency's determination of the extent to which public proceedings should go. Matters of great import, or those where the public submission of facts will be either useful to the agency or a protection to the public, should naturally be accorded more elaborate public procedures." S. Rep. No. 752, 79th Cong., 1st Sess., 14-15 (1945)…. The Attorney General's Manual on the Administrative Procedure Act 31, 35 (1947), a contemporaneous interpretation previously given some deference by this Court because of the role played by the Department of Justice in drafting the legislation, further confirms that view…. All of this leaves little doubt that Congress intended that the discretion of the agencies and not that of the courts be exercised in determining when extra procedural devices should be employed….

If courts continually review agency proceedings to determine whether the agency employed procedures which were, in the court's opinion, perfectly tailored to reach what the court perceives to be the "best" or "correct" result, judicial review would be totally unpredictable. And the agencies, operating under this vague injunction to employ the "best" procedures and facing the threat of reversal if they did not, would undoubtedly adopt full adjudicatory procedures in every instance. Not only would this totally disrupt the statutory scheme,...but all the inherent advantages of informal rulemaking would be totally lost. [The circuit court's] Monday morning quarterbacking not only encourages but almost compels the agency to conduct all rulemaking proceedings with the full panoply of procedural devices normally associated only with adjudicatory hearings....

The court below uncritically assumed that additional procedures will automatically result in a more adequate record because it will give interested parties more of an opportunity to participate and contribute to the proceedings.... The adequacy of the "record" in this type of proceeding is not correlated directly to the type of procedural devices employed, but rather turns on whether the agency has followed the statutory mandate of the Administrative Procedure Act or other relevant statutes....

In short, nothing in the APA,...the circumstances of this case, the nature of the issues being considered, past agency practice, or the statutory mandate under which the Commission operates, permitted the court to review and overturn the rulemaking proceeding on the basis of the procedural devices employed (or not employed) by the Commission so long as the Commission employed at least the statutory minima, a matter about which there is no doubt in this case.

There remains, of course, the question of whether the challenged rule finds sufficient justification in the administrative proceedings that it should be upheld by the reviewing court. Judge Tamm, concurring in the result reached by the majority of the Court of Appeals, thought that it did not. There are also intimations in the majority opinion which suggest that the judges who joined it likewise may have thought the administrative proceedings an insufficient basis upon which to predicate the rule in question. We accordingly remand so that the Court of Appeals may review the rule as the Administrative Procedure Act provides.... The court should...not stray beyond the judicial province to explore the procedural format or to impose upon the agency its own notion of which procedures are "best" or most likely to further some vague, undefined public good....

[The procedural obstacles posed by the court of appeals] border on the Kafkaesque. Nuclear energy may some day be a cheap, safe source of power or it may not. But Congress has made a choice to at least try nuclear energy, establishing a reasonable review process in which courts are to play only a limited role. The fundamental policy questions appropriately resolved in Congress and in the state legislatures are not subject to reexamination in the federal courts under the guise of judicial review of agency action. Time may prove wrong the decision to develop nuclear energy,[58] but it is Congress or the States within their appropriate agencies which must eventually make that judgment. Reversed and remanded.

COMMENTARY & QUESTIONS

1. **Tactics: in procedural terms, what was the NRC attempting to do in *Vermont Yankee*?** By shifting the safety and radiation waste disposal questions into an informal rulemaking proceeding, thereafter to be published as a regulation that could be simply incorporated by reference, the agency would avoid having to face questioning and

---

58. What does this latter clause imply? Cf. Chapter 6 on preemption of state nuclear regulations. [Eds.]

cross-examination on the issue in future formal adjudications when utilities sought operating licenses. If the nuclear waste disposal question remained part of each licensing case, it would be subject to all the trial type procedures: full notice, full discovery, full cross-examination, full right to present contrary evidence. In this particular rule-making proceeding, the agency did in fact allow some hybrid procedures, more than mere notice-and-comment rulemaking, but it prohibited discovery and much cross-examination. Would those really have made much difference to the agency's ultimate decision? After the *Vermont Yankee* decision, can agencies push environmental inter-venors back into the closet, or do the continuing requirements of judicial review keep the intervenors as active players despite Justice Rehnquist's opinion?

2. **What was the holding of *Vermont Yankee*?** *Vermont Yankee* is a ringing denunciation of the court of appeal's requirement of agency procedures to benefit citizen environmental intervenors. Justice Rehnquist successfully argued that the APA's procedural minimum requirements for agencies were now also the maximum procedures that courts could require. (Ironically, in doing so he cited cases such as *Wong Yang Sung* in which the Court had actually granted extended procedures far beyond statutory requirements in order to protect individuals against agency excesses.) What narrow exceptions to the new rule against court-expanded procedures would the Rehnquist opinion allow? He notes several situations in which courts may force agencies to grant more process.[59] But note the penultimate paragraph in the *Vermont Yankee* excerpt. The entire case was sent back for further review on the adequacy of the factual record: whether the NRC had shown enough facts so that a court could determine that reasonable NRC officials could or could not have decided as they did. This is a second kind of procedural argument — that for the courts' own sake, rather than for citizens, agencies must produce a sufficient formal or informal review record to permit judges to apply whatever standard of substantive review applies to the decision. The needs of Article III judicial review thus can still become the tail that wags the dog (as in *Overton Park*).

3. **The substantive question on the *Vermont Yankee* record.** The factual issue that triggered the *Vermont Yankee* remand appears to have been the shakiness of the report by Dr. Pittman, which was the basis of the NRC decision. Dr. Pittman had devoted most of his report to proposed federal repositories for above-ground waste storage, and less than two pages to the problem of geologic waste disposal. The NRC subsequently abandoned above-ground storage and turned to geologic disposal solutions (although these have also been almost impossible to site). The further problem was that the Pittman report, upon which the NRC rule was based, had been produced without an extensive research effort. Might cross-examination, if it had been available, have usefully revealed the thinness of this particular piece of evidence?

4. ***Vermont Yankee*, remand and back.** What ultimately happened with the nuclear waste rule? The NRC prepared a revised rule with further documentation and research, reasserting its determination of an extremely low risk factor, based on an assumption

---

59. One he doesn't note is the entire sector of agency adjudications. Since the APA provides no standards for less-than-formal adjudications, courts are not limited by the *Vermont Yankee* rationale in their ability to require that various procedures be added to agencies' informal adjudications.

that nuclear wastes would never be released into the environment. When the case returned to the Court it upheld this optimistic determination against skeptical citizen challenge:

> The zero-release assumption — a policy judgment concerning one line in a conservative Table designed for the limited purpose of individual licensing decisions — is within the bounds of reasoned decisionmaking. It is not our task to determine what decision we, as Commissioners, would have reached. Our only task is to determine whether the Commission has considered the relevant factors and articulated a rational connection between the facts found and the choice made. Under this standard, we think the Commission's zero-release assumption, within the context of Table S-3 as a whole, was not arbitrary and capricious. Baltimore Gas & Elec. v. NRDC, 462 U.S. 87 (1983).

5. **The "hard look" doctrine.** Prior to *Vermont Yankee*, and subsequent to the decision as well, federal courts have enunciated what is called the "hard look" doctrine: When Congress has set a statutory standard for agencies to apply, courts must see enough evidence on the record to be satisfied that the agency itself took a "hard look" at all relevant facts and the statutory standards that applied to them. The "hard look" determination is obviously subjective. Does *Vermont Yankee* do anything to dampen the courts' scrutiny of an agency's hard look?

6. **Rulemaking/adjudication: tactical considerations.** Other settings illustrate other tactical uses of the rulemaking/adjudication distinction. In some cases, unlike the NRC in *Vermont Yankee*, an agency will seek to proceed by adjudication, rather than by rulemaking, because subsequent courts do not hold agencies to the terms of their adjudicative precedents as strictly as they do to published rules. Conversely, regulated parties sometimes want to have rulemaking on a matter because, unlike adjudication, rulemaking is prospective and cannot penalize past activities. Regulated parties, on the other hand, sometimes prefer adjudication because of the formal trial-type procedures that normally accompany agency adjudicative processes.

Yet another twist shows judicial use of the rulemaking/adjudication distinction. In New York v. Thomas, 802 F.2d 1443 (D.C. Cir. 1986), then-Judge Scalia used the argument of mandatory rulemaking to nullify an environmental injunction on acid rain. According to §115 of the CAA (the result of a strenuous compromise between environmentalists and polluters), once EPA made a formal determination that transboundary international air pollution is occurring and that the foreign country (i.e., Canada) grants reciprocal standing to injured Americans, then EPA was statutorily obliged to require state air pollution plans to restrict sources of acid precipitation. Section 115 was used by Ontario and several downwind states, including New York and Massachusetts, to try to abate acid rain coming from midwestern states. Just before he left office, President Carter's EPA Administrator, Douglas Costle, made a formal finding under §115, dubbed the "Costle hand grenade," requiring certain states to clean up their acid rain emissions. Judge Scalia overturned the trial court's injunction, arguing that what Costle had done was "rulemaking" (because, like a rule under the APA definition, it had "future effect") and therefore was void because EPA had not gone through notice-and-comment rulemaking before acting.[60] Wouldn't this unprecedented argument overrule *Overton Park*? There the Secretary's §4(f) decision clearly had future force and effect. If the *Thomas* opinion were followed more broadly, it would be a potent administrative law weapon for environmentalists and polluters alike, requiring any administrative decision that has future effect to go through notice-and-comment rulemaking, a possibility that would effectively bring most government to a halt. It was probably just an opportunistic anomaly.

The distinctions between rulemaking and adjudication, and their tactical consequences, emphasize that administrative law is surprisingly young and evolving. Interesting administrative law issues arise in many areas of environmental law and will be repeatedly encountered in later chapters.[61]

7. **Citizens intervening in agency proceedings.** In *Vermont Yankee*, the citizen group understandably wanted to participate in the heart of the agency process. Section 6 of the APA, 5 U.S.C. §555(b), provides that "so far as the orderly conduct of the public business permits, an interested person may appear before an agency or its responsible employees for the presentation, adjustment, or determination, request, or controversy in [any] proceeding." Section 555(b), however, has not been extensively developed, at least in non-formal non-trial-type proceedings. What does the "orderly conduct of public business" limitation mean, and who is legally an "interested" party? *Scenic Hudson* presumed the validity of citizen participation in FPC proceedings. Since *Scenic Hudson*, permission for citizen intervention in agency proceedings seems to have become the norm, if only because agencies realize that judicial review standing has expanded, so that if intervention is denied within agency procedures, court review will nevertheless occur and be tougher.[62] Some agencies, nevertheless, are known for their resistance to citizen intervention. See In the Matter of Edlow Int'l Co., 3 NRC 563 (NRC 1976), dismissed as moot, NRDC v. NRC, 580 F.2d 698 (D.C. Cir. 1987).

Intervention is a vital part of citizen involvement in the administrative process, allowing a pluralist debate to begin early in the process rather than later in retrospective judicial review. The future development of APA §555(b) will reflect the evolution of intervention in informal as well as formal proceedings. The arguments of environmentalists to be allowed to intervene in ongoing agency proceedings will continue to be reinforced by the fact that courts in subsequent review often consider that a record made without active participation is not sufficiently comprehensive and does not cover certain critical features sufficiently to support the agency action in judicial review.

---

60. The Supreme Court has never specified when an agency must proceed by rulemaking as opposed to adjudication. The Scalia opinion found little precedent and directed most of its analysis to a question not presented, whether policy rulemaking could be done without notice and comment, an argument that presumed the principal question.

61. Chapter 16, for instance, considers whether, when citizen environmentalists have proved a statutory violation, courts may permit violations to continue, based on traditional common law balancing of the equities (i.e., which party's interests and which policy considerations are more important). The Supreme Court, with one dissent, has said that judges can override legislation they consider to be outweighed by other judicial considerations.

62. As a noted administrative law practitioner observed, "today, at least in my experience, intervention is seldom denied.... In light of the role that the courts have carved out for intervenors, and the risks inherent in denying interested citizens the right to be heard, intervention has assumed the proportions of a right, even where the applicable statute or rules are phrased permissively." Butzel, Intervention and Class Actions Before the Agencies and the Courts, 25 Admin. L. Rev. 135, 136 (1973).

8. **Standing in courts and agencies.** In a notable case expanding citizens' rights to intervene in agency proceedings, then-Judge Warren Burger wrote that "all parties seem to consider that the same standards are applicable to determining standing before the Commission and standing to appeal a Commission decision to this court. We have, therefore, used the cases dealing with standing in the two tribunals interchangeably."[63] Judge Burger took note of the expanding law of standing in federal courts and required expanded intervention standing in the agency. Analytically are the two tribunals the same? They are doing two very different tasks. A citizen's right to intervene in an agency, under APA §555(b) or otherwise is arguably broader than standing for judicial review, because administrative agency process is not constitutionally limited by Article III's "case or controversy" requirement.

9. **The role of an agency when citizens intervene.** Note that in the *Scenic Hudson* standing case excerpted in the previous section, the court criticized the agency for treating citizen intervention not as a helpful contribution, but as a resented disruption; the commission had stepped back and acted like "an umpire blandly calling balls and strikes" between the industry and the small ad hoc group of citizen intervenors. Responding to the same problem in the case noted in the preceding comment, Judge Burger roundly criticized the agency proceedings that had followed his prior order on remand:

> The examiner seems to have regarded [the citizen] appellants as "plaintiffs" and the licensee as "defendant," with burdens of proof allocated accordingly.... We did not intend that intervenors representing a public interest be treated as interlopers. Rather...a "public intervenor" is seeking no license or private right and is, in this context, more nearly like a complaining witness who presents evidence to police or a prosecutor whose duty it is to conduct an affirmative and objective investigation.... In our view the entire hearing was permeated by...the pervasive impatience — if not hostility — of the examiner...which made fair and impartial consideration impossible.... The public intervenors, who were performing a public service under a mandate of this court, were entitled to a more hospitable reception in the performance of that function. As we view the record the examiner tended to impede the exploration of the very issues which we would reasonably expect the Commission itself would have initiated; an ally was regarded as an opponent.... The administrative conduct reflected in this record is beyond repair. [The agency decision was revoked and the proceedings remanded to the agency.] Office of Communication of United Church of Christ v. FCC, 425 F.2d 543, 546–550 (D.C. Cir. 1969).

10. **Citizens' access to information: FOIA.** Information is power, or, at least, it is clear that without basic specific information, interested parties and intervenors will not be effective. In 1966, Congress dramatically reversed the prior widespread agency presumption that government information should be withheld unless there was specific legal authority for its release. The Freedom of Information Act (FOIA), 5 U.S.C. §552, provides that

> each agency upon any request for records which...reasonably describes such records and [follows certain simple procedures] shall make the records promptly available to any person. 5 U.S.C. §552(a)(3).

---

63. Office of Communication, United Church of Christ v. FCC, 359 F.2d 994, 1000 (D.C. Cir. 1966).

FOIA restricts permissible withholding to nine fairly narrow exceptions. 5 U.S.C. §552(b)(1)-(9). Environmentalists have often found FOIA critically helpful in obtaining agency information through formal requests or, perhaps even more usefully, in prompting informal release of information. Federal courts have applied the Act with stringency in a number of environmental cases,[64] although the development of the Act's disclosure mandate, and its provisions for waiving data retrieval fees for requests "primarily benefiting the public interest,"[65] are still evolving, often facing marked official resistance.[66]

11. **Official public participation policies.** In mid-2003, Christine Todd Whitman, then-U.S. EPA Administrator, issued EPA's Public Involvement Policy, which had been initiated by the Clinton Administration and developed through three years of review and comment. The new Policy applies to all EPA environmental programs and seeks to provide guidance to EPA staff on effective ways to involve the public in EPA's regulatory and program implementation decisions, offering seven basic suggestions for effective public involvement. With Whitman's departure it became uncertain how the Policy would translate into practice. The Policy, the framework for its implementation, and EPA's response to comments received are available at http://www.epa.gov/public-involvement/policy2003/index.htm.

12. **"Internalizing costs" through public law?** In approaching pollution and other environmental harms caused by private individuals and industries, environmental law often follows the strategy of cost internalization, attempting to force private decision-makers to account for environmental costs in their economic market behavior. Is there an equivalent accounting strategy in the public law setting, where decisionmakers are not involved in a market enterprise? In *Vermont Yankee*, the environmentalists' ultimate aim was to make the agency take full account of the daunting and potentially overwhelming costs and risks of nuclear waste storage.

To an extent, government decisionmakers often seem to share the functional frame of reference of private corporate entrepreneurs. To the minds of promoters, whether private or public, accounting for negative external consequences is dysfunctional, hence to be avoided, because it gets in the way of the enterprise's mission. Development agencies, however, may tend to be institutionally less sensitive to cost accounting. Their projects are paid for with taxpayer dollars.

How are agency officials practically induced to consider consequential public costs in their internal calculus? One approach is political. The currency of the bureaucratic marketplace is politics — who has power, who has momentum, who is under fire.

64. See Soucie v. David, 448 F.2d 1067 (D.C. Cir. 1971) (negative reports on the predicted effects of a supersonic transport plane must be released); cf. National Parks & Conservation Ass'n v. Morton, 498 F.2d 765 (D.C. Cir. 1974) (financial data from national park concessionaires need not be released).

65. 5 U.S.C. §552(a)(4)(A). The Act's serious intent to compel an open governmental process is underscored by its provisions for advancing FOIA cases to the top of federal court dockets, 5 U.S.C. §552(a)(4)(D); for award of attorneys' fees against the agencies, 5 U.S.C. §552(a)(4)(E); and for personal accountability, see next note.

66. Official reluctance to make proceedings open and disclose document on request long predates the Department of Homeland Security and the Patriot Act, but recent years have seen renewed barriers. See Echeverria & Kaplan, Poisonous Procedural "Reform": In Defense of Environmental Right to Know, Geo. Envtl. L. & Pol'y Inst. (2002).

Agencies can foresee that if they attract severe media criticism, or legislative committee oversight hearings, or negative reactions from an executive office, they will feel the heat, and so they act accordingly. Another internalizing approach is personal accountability, a rarity in government except at the highest levels. FOIA's §552(a) provides:

> Whenever the court orders the production of any agency records improperly with-held from the complainant...and...issues a written finding that the circumstances surrounding the withholding raise questions whether agency personnel acted arbitrarily...with respect to the withholding, the Special Counsel [of the Civil Service merit system review process] shall promptly initiate a proceeding to deter-mine whether disciplinary action is warranted.... 5 U.S.C. §552(a)(4)(F).

Such personal sanctions catch and hold bureaucratic attention but are infrequent. Ultimately it is legal constraints — in practical terms, this means legal constraints that will be enforced against agencies, in many cases only by citizen efforts — that constitute the backbone of administrative accountability.

E. STATUTORY INTERPRETATION: HOW, BY WHOM?

Section 1. JUDICIAL REVIEW OF AGENCY INTERPRETATIONS OF LAW

Chevron U.S.A., Inc. v. Natural Resources Defense Council
Supreme Court of the United States, 1984
467 U.S. 837

[Section 111 of the CAA,[67] requires that tougher permit standards, based on Best Available Technology (BAT) (see Chapter 11), must be applied to any "new source" of pollution in areas that violate existing air quality standards. A "source" was defined in the statute as "any building, structure, facility, or installation which emits or may emit any air pollutant." In 1980, the latter statutory phrase had been interpreted by EPA to mean that every new sub-unit or smokestack of a factory was a source that had to meet those higher standards. In 1981, however, the agency changed its definition by a rulemaking applying a regulatory "bubble"[68] concept: The new regu-lation defined the statutory term "source" to mean "all of the pollutant-emitting activities which belong to the same industrial grouping, are located on one or more contiguous or adjacent properties, and are under the control of the same person or persons." The result was that EPA could now view an entire industrial site as a single source. If a company could offset new emis-sions within a plant by closing old dirtier units, there would be no net increase of pollutants coming from within the bubble, so new construction did not count as a new source and did not have to meet the tougher standards. The NRDC sued.]

STEVENS, J. The question presented by this case is whether EPA's decision to allow states to treat all of the pollution-emitting devices within the same industrial grouping as though they were encased within a single "bubble" is based on a reasonable construction of the statutory term "stationary source."

When a court reviews an agency's construction of the statute which it administers, it is confronted with two questions.

---

67. 42 U.S.C. §7411, as amended in 1977 and 1990.
68. Air pollution "bubbles" are considered in Chapters 11 and 14.

First, always, is the question whether Congress has directly spoken to the precise question at issue. If the intent of Congress is clear, that is the end of the matter; for the court, as well as the agency, must give effect to the unambiguously expressed intent of Congress.[69]

If, however, the court determines Congress has not directly addressed the precise question at issue, the court does not simply impose its own construction on the statute, as would be necessary in the absence of an administrative interpretation. Rather, if the statute is silent or ambiguous with respect to this specific issue, the question for the court is whether the agency's answer is based on a permissible construction of the statute.[70] "The power of an administrative agency to administer a congressionally created...program necessarily requires the formulation of policy in the making of rules to fill any gap left, implicitly or explicitly, by Congress."

The principle of deference to administrative interpretations has been consistently followed by this Court whenever decision as to the meaning or reach of the statute has involved reconciling conflicting policies, and a full understanding of the force of the statutory policy on the given situation has depended upon more than ordinary knowledge respecting the matters subjected to agency regulations. *Hearst*, 322 U.S. 111 (1944).... "If this choice represents accommodation of conflicting policies that were committed to the agency's care by the statute, we should not disturb it unless it appears from the statute or its a legislative history that the accommodation is not one that Congress would have sanctioned...." United States v. Shimer, 367 U.S. 374, 382 (1961).

Our review of the EPA's varying interpretations of the word "source" — both before and after the 1977 amendments — convinces us that the agency primarily responsible for administering this important legislation has consistently interpreted it flexibly — not in a sterile textual vacuum, but in the context of implementing policy decisions in a technical and complex arena.... When a challenge to an agency construction of a statutory provision, fairly conceptualized, really centers on the wisdom of the agency's policy, rather than whether it is a reasonable choice within a gap left open by Congress, the challenge must fail. In such a case, federal judges — who have no constituency — have the duty to respect legitimate policy choices made by those who do. Responsibilities for assessing the wisdom of such policy choices and resolving the struggle between competing views of the public interests are not judicial ones: "Our Constitution vests such responsibilities in the political branches." TVA v. Hill, 437 U.S. 153, 195 (1978). Reversed.

COMMENTARY & QUESTIONS

1. **The strategics of definitions.** Note how critical differences can often turn on agency interpretations of key statutory terms — "source" in *Chevron*, "feasible and prudent" in *Overton Park*, "aggrieved" in *Scenic Hudson*, "point source" in the CWA, and so on. In one famous example, the Reagan Administration's EPA concurrently improved the average gas mileage of the Chrysler Corporation's "passenger vehicle" and "light truck" fleets by re-defining minivans as the latter, not the former, thereby shifting them from embarrassment in one category to enhancement of another. Independent judicial

---

69. The judiciary is the final authority on issues of statutory construction and must recheck administrative constructions which are contrary to clear congressional intent. If a court, employing traditional tools of statutory construction, ascertains that Congress had an intention on the precise question at issue, that intention is the law and must be given effect [as a matter of the judges' own statutory interpretation]. [This is footnote 9 in the original opinion.]

70. The Court need not conclude that the agency construction was the only one it permissibly could have adopted to uphold the construction, or even the reading the court would have reached if the question had initially arisen in a judicial proceeding.

scrutiny of these interpretations obviously can make significant differences for good and ill.

In *Chevron* the interpretation of the term "source" as incorporating air pollution "bubbles" had immediate and far-reaching effects on U.S. industry and air quality. The agency had strong arguments in favor of the bubble interpretation. Do you see how a bubble might result in cleaner air, despite allowing lower standards? If an industry considering upgrading its physical facilities knows it will be held to the highest standards, might it decide not to add new plant modifications at all? The question in every case is whether the agency's interpretation is to be second-guessed by the courts or be deferred to.

2. **Judicial deference to agency interpretations of law, in *Chevron*.** Does *Chevron* set out a principle of general deference to agency interpretations of statutes, or just for agency gap-filling? The Court holds that the agency can so interpret the term "source," "making...rules to fill any gap left, implicitly or explicitly, by Congress," because EPA is following Congress's overall statutory mandate to clean up the air and there is no evidence of any congressional intention on the particular question of bubbling. The *Chevron* rule has spread far beyond gap-filling, however, and is often used as a general deference rule.

The standard analysis drawn from *Chevron* has two steps, with a great deal of room for fudging in each:

- Step One: Given the statutory language, is the intent of Congress (in the eyes of the reviewing court) clear? If so, the court will itself declare that interpretation, whether the agency agrees or not.

- Step Two: If the court decides the meaning is not clear, then the court must review the agency's interpretation deferentially, upholding it if the court thinks the agency's answer is based on "a permissible construction of the statute."

In Step One, great flexibility lies in the judicial determination whether Congress has "directly spoken" to the "precise question at issue" or "unambiguously expressed" its intent. There is even more flexibility in what courts will look at in deciding whether the congressional intent is clear or ambiguous: Will a court look only at the specific words of the challenged statutory provision standing alone, or also at other relevant language in the statute, or at the provision in the full context of the statute, or at the legislative history of the provision in Congress, or at congressional policy on point, or is it open to all the other contextual analysis tools used in statutory interpretation? If courts close their eyes to anything but the specific words, they are in an irrational vacuum, but if they open their eyes to all that is relevant to determining intent, deference is quite diluted.

In Step Two, the question whether the agency's answer is based on "a permissible construction of the statute," likewise incorporates highly subjective weighing. Courts tend to go through all the traditional elements anyway, replicating a full judicial interpretation process, in order to see if the agency's interpretation is "permissible."[71] Judges tend to believe that courts are always competent to interpret statutes. Deference is

---

71. That in fact was what was done in the leading administrative law case declaring deference to agency interpretations of statutes, Hearst v. NLRB, 322 U.S. 111 (1944), and in a recent such case, Holly Farms v. NLRB, 517

decided case by case by the deferrers themselves. And what of the widely varying relationships between particular agencies and particular statutes? In his post-*Chevron* analysis, Professor Colin Diver noted that still "the decision to grant deference depends on various attributes of the agency's legal authority and functions, and of the administrative interpretation at issue."[72] Should courts defer to interpretations of the FWHA, as in *Overton Park*, where the §4(f) parkland environmental protection provision was an unwelcome burr under the agency's bureaucratic saddle, to the same degree as they defer to EPA on toxicity definitions? Even after *Chevron*, would it not be a permissible argument against judicial deference to an agency interpretation that waters down a statutory provision, to show the court that the same agency, disliking that particular provision's strictness, had given extensive testimony against its passage in the first place?

3. **Post-*Chevron* judicial review of agency interpretations of law, and the *Mead* addendum.** The *Chevron* second step is the principle most used by courts when they wish to defer broadly to agency interpretations of law. The *Chevron* first step is the most common approach when courts themselves take over the question, finding that a statutory meaning is sufficiently clear that the court can determine it correctly on its own. Since *Chevron*, the Supreme Court has repeatedly demonstrated that it will dictate its own interpretation of statutory meaning, not deferring to agencies' interpretations, if it believes that standard norms of statutory construction, as interpreted by the court, would lead to a different answer. See INS v. Cardoza-Fonseca, 480 U.S. 421 (1987). The line between deference and judicial takeover of the fundamental decision can thus get quite hazy.

Deference to agencies' legal interpretations is most likely where a legislative scheme seems highly technical, with a wide range of details delegated to the agency's special expertise. *Chevron*, with its intricate air pollution technicalities, was a particularly apt subject for deference to the agency on legal as well as factual matters. The less daunting the legal provisions faced by the courts, however, the less likely they are to be deferential on questions of law. Within judicial chambers, the tendency is to apply the familiar judicial methods to reach an interpretation, then to consider whether the agency's interpretation agrees with the judge's view of the term's meaning, plain or fancy.[73]

The *Chevron* deference formulation nevertheless continues to be one of the most-cited holdings in modern administrative law generally, not just in the environmental field. State and federal courts use it continually as a general touchstone for deferring to agency determinations (including some judges not deeply familiar with administrative law who apply it to agency decisions of fact as well as of law).

U.S. 392 (1996). In *Holly Farms*, the Court said, "Administrators and reviewing courts must take care to assure that exemptions...are not so expansively interpreted as to deny protection...the Act was designed to reach." Note that this implies that if the agency *broadened* the exemptions, courts could appropriately, on a *policy* analysis, defer much less to the agency interpretations. The Court also said, "courts...must respect the judgment of the agency empowered to apply the law to varying fact patterns, even if the issue 'with nearly equal reason [might] be resolved one way rather than another.'" The word "even" missed the point. Can courts *decline* to defer when the interpretations are *not* "nearly equal"? In this labor case, at least, Justices Rehnquist, Scalia, O'Connor, and Thomas declared in dissent that "the deference owed to an expert tribunal cannot be allowed to slip into a judicial inertia...."

72. Diver, Statutory Interpretation in the Administrative State, 133 U. Pa. L. Rev. 549, 562 (1985).

73. Id.

United States v. Mead Corp., 533 U.S. 218 (2001), has somewhat changed the *Chevron* field. In *Mead*, a non-environmental case that nonetheless has importance for its potential shift in the administrative law of judicial review, the Court declined to apply *Chevron* deference in a case involving a Customs Service classification ruling. Under Treasury rules and regulations, the Customs Service issued an administrative "ruling" (apparently a form of informal adjudication) reclassifying Mead's imported three-ring binder day planners as "diaries, bound," subjecting the products to a 4% tariff, instead of the prior 1989 classification as "miscellaneous other," which required no tariff.

In *Mead* the Court held that *Chevron* deference was not appropriate and told the lower court to interpret the statutory definition of products itself, taking account of the agency's advice and expertise on the matter. The Court's decision to reject the *Chevron* standard turned primarily on the premise that Congress had not intended the administrative classifications to have the legal force of regulations. The Court did suggest, however, that the agency rulings may receive some deference under Skidmore v. Swift & Co., 323 U.S. 134 (1944), if the classification decision, made within a highly detailed regulatory scheme, "brought the benefit of specialized agency experience on the subtle questions of the case." While the decision did not provide a narrow guideline for assessing the appropriate degree of judicial deference for various regulatory mechanisms, it explicitly acknowledged a continuum of deference.

Deference will be greatest, using *Chevron*, where Congress has expressed an intent to delegate broad authority to the agency to carry out the goals of the enabling legislation or when strong evidence suggests such an implicit congressional delegation. Yet, even when the *Chevron* standard is inapplicable, the Court will consider the circumstances under which the agency is administering its own statute, such as the "degree of the agency's care, its consistency [note that in *Mead* the agency had changed its position], formality, and relative expertness, and…the persuasiveness of the agency's position." 533 U.S. at 228. This would seem to reopen the door to extended arguments over whether agency determinations of law in a particular case should receive great, medium, or light deference in future judicial reviews.

4. **The "plain meaning" finesse.** It is interesting to see how courts since *Chevron* can avoid deferring to agency interpretations of law when they disagree with them. One of the approaches is the "plain meaning" theory — that if the legal meaning of a term is clear to a court on the face of a statute or regulation, then the court will apply that interpretation regardless of the expert agency's differing opinion.[74] A CERCLA case example of this dealt with §120(h) of the 1986 Superfund Amendments and Reauthorization Act (SARA), which imposed notice-and-covenant requirements on federal agencies that transfer real property contaminated by hazardous substances. Section 120(h)(1) provides in relevant part that

> the head of such department, agency, or instrumentality shall include in such contract notice of the type and quantity of such hazardous substance and notice of the time at which such storage, release or disposal took place, to the extent such information is available on the basis of a complete search of agency files.

---

74. See Murphy, Old Maxims Never Die: The Plain Meaning Rule and Statutory Interpretation in Modern Federal Courts, 75 Colum. L. Rev. 1299 (1975).

In its regulations, however, EPA applied the notice requirements of §120(h)(1) only to real property on which hazardous substances were stored, released, or disposed of "during the time the property was owned by the United States." EPA believed Congress was primarily concerned with federal facilities (chiefly military bases and nuclear weapons facilities) whose own operations involved the storage, release, or disposal of hazardous substances, and that §120(h) therefore was not intended to apply where contamination occurred prior to the government's acquisition of the property. This interpretation, it concluded, was "more appropriate..." and would avoid imposing unfair and unmanageable obligations on federal agencies that had no role in the storage, release or disposal of hazardous substances. The reviewing court held differently:

> By its terms, §120(h) requires agencies to disclose all information of the kind specified (namely, the "type and quantity" of hazardous substances on the property and "the time at which [the] storage, release or disposal took place") to the extent the information is contained in the agency's files, and the plain meaning of Congress's words thus extends the government's notice obligations to properties [contaminated] by prior owners.... Where, as here, the statute's language is plain, "the sole function of the courts is to enforce it according to its terms." We therefore need not look beyond the words of the statute to the legislative history for guidance. Hercules v. EPA, 938 F.2d 276, 280, 281 (D.C. Cir. 1991).

To get the "plain meaning," the *Hercules* court nevertheless reviewed legislative history, contextual analysis, policy analysis of congressional intent in the Act, the statute's broad remedial purposes, the limited agency burdens that would be imposed by the notice requirement, and the legislative purpose of dealing fairly with subsequent purchasers. This typical exercise in statutory interpretation demonstrates how ready courts are to embark on the familiar task of interpreting legal language, going far beyond plain meaning.

5. **Differential deference? How much deference for guidance documents?** To improve its internal efficiency, speed up regulatory management adjustments, and free up its regulatory hands, EPA often avoids official §553 rulemaking and sets out informal standards via guidance documents.[75] In 2004, the Court had to determine the relative authority of interpretations of the CAA made by a state agency and EPA. In Alaska Dep't of Envtl. Conservation (ADEC) v. EPA, 2004 U.S. LEXIS 820 (2004), the state agency had interpreted an air pollution requirement for BACT (Best Available Control Technology) more leniently than EPA. EPA relied on a prior guidance to show its continuing right to intervene to assure that state interpretations are "based on a reasoned analysis." With its strong states-rights advocates, would the Court extend deference to the federal agency's interpretation if EPA was overriding a state agency? Writing for the majority, over a dissent by Justices Rehnquist, Scalia, and Thomas, Justice Ginsburg said:

> We "normally accord particular deference to an agency interpretation of 'long-standing' duration," recognizing that "well-reasoned views" of an expert administrator rest on "a body of experience and informed judgment to which courts and litigants may properly resort for guidance" [quoting Skidmore v. Swift & Co., 323 U.S. 134, 139–140 (1944)]. We have previously accorded dispositive effect to EPA's interpretation of an ambiguous CAA provision. See *Chevron* and

---

75. Sometimes courts reject EPA's use of guidance on the theory that they have too much practical binding effect and therefore require §553 rulemaking, the holding in General Elec. Co. v. EPA, 290 F.3d 377, 379 (D.C. Cir. 2002), footnoted earlier in note 11.

Union Electric [excerpted in Chapter 11]. The Agency's interpretation in this case, presented in internal guidance memoranda, however, does not qualify for the dispositive force described in *Chevron*. "Interpretations such as those in…policy statements, agency manuals, and enforcement guidelines, all of which lack the force of law — do not warrant *Chevron*-style deference"; accord, United States v. Mead Corp. Cogent "administrative interpretations…not [the] products of formal rulemaking… nevertheless warrant respect." We accord EPA's reading of the relevant statutory provisions…that measure of respect. Slip Opinion at 49–50.

Analyzing the basis of the EPA guidance and the statutory scheme, the Court majority accepted the position of the EPA guidance and approved the override of the state standard. What remains unclear in such cases is how and how much deference is given to the guidance, since the Court's decision may well have been largely based on its own interpretation of the statutory language and context.

6. **Organic decisionmaking?** The *Chevron* tests can operate to insulate government agencies' interpretations of key statutory provisions from judicial scrutiny. If judges incline toward overriding an agency interpretation, on the other hand, under *Chevron* they can find a "plain meaning" for the statutory term that differs from the agency's, and override. The process of finding that "plain meaning," moreover, apparently does not have to take place on the face of the text but can be based on the full range of judicial statutory interpretation techniques.

Flexibility exists, moreover, beyond the terms of *Chevron* analysis. If a court dislikes an agency position on an ambiguous term but cannot say that an agency's interpretation is not a "permissible" reading of the statute, the court can utilize the old "delegation doctrine" restriction on agency actions. See Justice Rehnquist's arguments in the OSHA benzene and cotton dust cases, attempting to reject OSHA's definition of "unsafe" environmental exposures on delegation grounds — that Congress had not given the agency sufficient details on how to regulate — in effect rejecting the agency's gap-filling function.[76]

7. **Administrative law as a crap game?** As this chapter's descriptive and analytical materials reflect, administrative law principles provide judges with a wide range of opportunities to fudge decisions toward outcomes they prefer. A court's rulings on judicial review issues are often discretionary and usually outcome-determinative — particularly as to the validity and definition of delegation, standing, exhaustion, ripeness, standard of review, scope of review, procedural quibbles, and tailoring of remedies. Is this an indictment of the field, or a realistic assessment that reinforces the desirability of understanding the complex elements of each issue and scoping out the political and programmatic contexts in which these cases arise? Administrative law demands both technical acuity and consciousness of political context, and the issues it deals with go deep. In the environmental administrative law area, as in environmental law generally, scratch away at almost any case and you soon find yourself contemplating fundamental issues of democratic governance.

---

76. Industrial Union Dept., AFL-CIO v. American Petroleum Inst., 448 U.S. 607 (1980) (Rehnquist, J., concurring opinion); American Textile Mfg. Inst. v. Donovan, 452 U.S. 490 (1981) (Rehnquist, dissent) (both opinions arguing that the agency had too much leeway filling gaps in the regulatory definition). For delegation arguments from the opposite pole, see Schoenbrod, The Delegation Doctrine: Could the Court Give It Substance?, 83 Mich. L. Rev. 1223 (1985).

Chapter 8

INTERNATIONAL AGREEMENTS AS DOMESTIC ENVIRONMENTAL LAW

A. *Shared Natural Resources: Bilateral Treaties*
B. *Protecting the Global Commons: Multilateral Treaties and Executive Agreements*
C. *International Trade Agreements: The Trade and Environment Problem*

As anyone who has picked up a newspaper or turned on the television in the last decade and a half knows, we are living in a world that is rapidly globalizing. Greater interconnectedness in a worldwide marketplace brings benefits for business and consumers in the form of greater access to goods. Globalization may equally encourage widespread dispersion of environmentally harmful "bads," including invasive species, pollution from the transportation of products over great distances, unwitting importation of contaminated food, and the migration of industry to jurisdictions with less stringent environmental policies.

Just as realizing the benefits of international economic activity requires coordinated action among the countries of the planet, there is now a critical need for international cooperation to combat the increasingly lengthy list of environmental hazards that threaten the future of the planet, including

- depletion of the stratospheric ozone layer, which protects life on earth from harmful levels of ultraviolet radiation;

- global warming from the "greenhouse" effect, which threatens the habitability of the planet over the next century;

- massive loss of species of a magnitude unprecedented in human history;

- wholesale conversion of productive land in developing countries to desert;

- global dispersion of pollutants that threaten human health and reproduction;

- acid rain, which endangers lakes and forests in North America, Europe, and other continents;

- and many more, some likely yet to be discovered.

Environmental problems like these, truly global in scope, demand a global response. No single country can prevent catastrophe by itself. Nor, if acting alone, are individual countries likely to find it in their national self-interest to do so on their own unless they are confident that others will act in accordance with a coordinated plan. These global hazards cry out for legal structures and institutions that respond effectively to the next generation of environmental challenges threatening us in the new century.

Although environmental awareness is relatively new to international politics, there has long been interaction and cooperation among the nations of the world. Since the mid-seventeenth century, international law — very different from domestic or national law — has evolved to govern and mold these relationships. The principal actors in this system are typically referred to in international jurisprudence as "states" — not the constituent states of the United States but sovereign nations or countries. Co-equal sovereign states are both the primary and the highest legal authority in the international legal order, with no international legislature or court of general jurisdiction superior to that of the state. A legal structure in which independent states not only make the law, but also interpret and apply it to themselves and each other, requires legal approaches different from those found in most municipal legal systems.

We now live in a legal world in which international norms play an increasing role, not just in the rarefied realm of international relations, but increasingly in domestic law and litigation as well. The call to "think globally, but act locally" presents a challenge for environmental lawyers, who must develop a toolbox for transferring global expectations into domestic law and vice versa. International and domestic law can influence each other in complex ways, often reinforcing each other but sometimes conflicting. An American environmental lawyer therefore now needs to be familiar not only with the operation of statutes and regulations adopted by domestic legislatures and agencies, but also with international agreements that the United States concludes with other states.

This chapter analyzes how the domestic legal system of the United States applies international agreements on the environment by addressing several international environmental issues of pressing current importance — safeguards for migratory birds, international cooperation to save whales, and conflicts with trade agreements. As part of that analysis, we canvass a variety of legal instruments until recently rarely thought to concern domestic lawyers — bilateral and multilateral treaties, executive agreements, and congressional-executive agreements. These issues are as broad as the planet, and the policy tools for tackling them are gateways to international legal concepts of increasing sophistication and burgeoning importance to environmental law in the twenty-first century.

A. SHARED NATURAL RESOURCES: BILATERAL TREATIES

Demystified and stripped of the arcane language of diplomacy, an international agreement is nothing more than a contractual deal between sovereign states. As in any deal making, both parties expect to be better off as a result of the bargain. Both sides are likely to have to make compromises to meet the needs of the treaty partners while pursuing their own self-interest. Political scientists often speak of international treaties as designed to overcome "collective action problems" in which states that are unlikely to take action by themselves are willing to do so in collaboration with others. In the environmental field, for example, arguments are often made against costly unilateral action to control pollution on the theory that competitive disadvantages will result. If, by contrast, two states, all the countries in a region, or the entire international community make pollution control investments on the same schedule, then competitive distortions are reduced or eliminated.

By negotiating an international agreement, states can establish rules governing each other's behavior, much as parties to a private contract can memorialize the terms of a deal in writing. Also in much the same manner as a contract, the rules contained in an agreement between states are legally binding on the states that are party to it and enforceable under international law.[1] To carry the private contract analogy even further, one often speaks of a treaty as establishing a flow of rights and obligations. Important differences, of course, exist between private contracts and international agreements. For example, there is no court of general jurisdiction in the international legal system, which means that in the event of a dispute or breach, no neutral, third-party tribunal automatically has the authority to adjudicate the controversy. In many important respects, however, principles of contract law carry over in a form that readily applies to treaties.

Section 1. MIGRATORY BIRDS IN NORTH AMERICA

Natural resources that span the borders between states, including migratory animals and lakes and rivers that straddle or cross an international border, have long been appreciated as ready candidates for international environmental cooperation. Natural watersheds and patterns of air flow occupy ecological zones that do not necessarily correspond to the arbitrary political boundaries drawn by human hands and may require coordinated action by more than one state for their protection. One state's lackadaisical policies with respect to a shared natural resource can adversely affect or even destroy the benefits provided by the resource to the other, whether economic, ecological, or aesthetic.

The United States has made treaties to protect one kind of shared resource, migratory birds, with a variety of other countries. These include an agreement concluded with Mexico in 1936, with Japan in 1972, and with Russia in 1976. All these pacts are modeled on a 1916 convention (a somewhat lofty term for treaty) on migratory birds with Canada, on whose behalf the agreement was concluded by Great Britain. Consistent with standard international practice, the text of the Convention for the Protection of Migratory Birds was agreed upon between the U.S. representative, Robert Lansing, Secretary of State of the United States, and the British negotiator, Cecil Spring Rice, the British Ambassador to the United States, in Washington on August 16, 1916. The two men certified the terms and authenticity of the text they had settled upon by signing it, very much as they might a private contract.

An editorial from the *New York Times* of September 2, 1916, praises the agreement as "the first of its kind ever negotiated by the United States.... This shows commendable progress in a movement that is distinctly for the benefit of the American people." The piece is surprisingly contemporary in identifying the need for the agreement and its approach to addressing the problems of migratory birds:

---

1. While international agreements are a principal source of international law, particularly from the point of view of its domestic relevance, international law operates in a number of other settings as well, as discussed in Chapter 26.

The chief purpose of...the treaty...is to save from extinction the migratory game birds, whose number has been reduced by more than one-half in the last forty years, and to protect those birds which help the farmer by eating the insects that prey upon his crops.... It has been estimated by the Department of Agriculture that the American farmer's annual loss which is due to insects exceeds $800,000,000. Protection is given by the law and the treaty to the insectivorous birds whose presence in the fields tends to prevent a part of this loss. They aid the farmer, and thus are friends of the consumer....

Notwithstanding the Convention, the fate of migratory birds continues to be a serious environmental concern. According to the Defenders of Wildlife, nearly 80% of the 313 species considered "at risk" in Canada either migrate or range across the U.S.–Canada border.

The content of the 1916 migratory bird treaty with Canada is remarkably modern in tone. The introductory preamble voices concern for "species...of great value as a source of food or in destroying insects which are injurious to forests and forage plants...[and] agricultural crops...but nevertheless are in danger of extermination through lack of adequate protection during the nesting season or while on their way to and from their breeding grounds." The agreement establishes certain dates for closed seasons on migratory birds, prohibits the taking of nests or eggs of migratory birds, prohibits hunting insect-eating birds, and allows the two governments to issue special permits authorizing the killing of migratory birds that have been determined to be harmful to agriculture.

From the point of view of domestic law, however, the agreement has substantial gaps and holes. Most of the harm to migratory birds was expected to be inflicted by hunters and poachers. The agreement does not spell out the form of domestic implementation, which could differ substantially in the United States and Canada, nor would it be expected to deal with domestic matters that are neither part of the international deal nor of any concern to the other treaty partner.

As is common in such situations, the U.S. Congress in 1918 adopted the Migratory Bird Treaty Act (MBTA), 16 U.S.C. §§703-711, as "implementing legislation" to give domestic life to the convention with Canada. The MBTA defines the offenses of taking, killing, and possessing migratory birds. The Act makes violation of the statute a federal crime and in certain cases a felony. Traps and other equipment may be confiscated by the Department of the Interior, whose agents are given the authority to make warrantless arrests to prevent a violation in progress. As domestic legislation, the MBTA is among the more powerful tools available for the protection of wildlife in the United States.

Section 2. THE CONSTITUTIONAL LAW OF TREATY FORMATION

As a matter of domestic U.S. law, the President of the United States — and only the President — as head of the executive branch has the authority to negotiate international agreements. In practice, this means that negotiations are conducted on behalf of the United States by the Department of State — the Cabinet department that represents the interests of the United States abroad and serves as a conduit for communications from foreign governments — together with other executive branch agencies that may have an interest in the subject matter. Article II §2 of the Constitution confirms that the President "shall have Power...to make Treaties...." That same section also limits the President's power, specifying that treaties must be adopted "by and with the Advice and Consent of the Senate...provided two thirds of the Senators present concur...."

The Framers of the Constitution purposely divided treaty power between the President and the Senate, in part because the treaty-making process reverses the usual roles for the President and the Congress. Instead of Congress's adopting legislation subject to the President's approval, as for a statute, the President as treaty negotiator holds the pen as the drafter of new law. The President — or, in practice, executive branch agencies as represented by the State Department — negotiates the treaty for the United States and then presents it as a concluded agreement to the Senate for its subsequent advice and consent prior to ratification. The President may then ratify the agreement, perfecting the obligations in it.[2] At this point, and only at this point, does the treaty become binding as a matter of both international and domestic law.

From the point of view of the effective and efficient conduct of foreign relations, it is sensible to give an authoritative President the capacity to deal confidently and free of domestic discord to foreign powers, some of which may be hostile. The Framers had also experienced the unsatisfactory precedent of the Articles of Confederation, under which Congress had done a poor job of handling foreign relations. If, however, a treaty could take effect without Congress's participation, the President, in effect, could make domestic law through his power to negotiate treaties with no checks and balances. The Framers consequently specified that treaties would take effect for the United States only after the subsequent confirmation or "ratification" of their terms. The requirement for a supermajority of two-thirds in the Senate in theory assures that the President strikes deals that are responsive to the interests of the states and the public. The process of ratification based on domestic legal processes was also well understood in international practice at the time, so the Constitution meshes smoothly with international law as well.

Consistent with the U.S. Constitution, Article IX of the migratory bird treaty with Canada states that the signatures on the text are provisional only, subject to subsequent ratification. The Senate gave its advice and consent to ratification by a two-thirds vote on August 29, 1916, and the President ratified the agreement on September 1. Great Britain ratified the Convention for Canada on October 20, and the parties exchanged instruments of ratification (documents perfecting the obligations in the agreement) on December 7. As specified in the agreement, the contractual rights and obligations of the two treaty partners became effective — "entered into force" — as of that date.

Any treaty, including an environmental pact, has domestic legal effect similar to a federal statute. An international agreement fully ratified by the federal government is

---

2. The President, and only the President, may ratify a treaty on behalf of the United States. Even though frequently encountered, the statement that "the Senate ratifies treaties" is consequently incorrect. Occasionally, the Senate gives its advice and consent, but the President nonetheless withholds ratification. The Basel Convention on the Control of Transboundary Movements of Hazardous Wastes and Their Disposal is one such example in which the Executive refrained from ratifying due to the lack of implementing legislation and active opposition from industry.

both binding under international law and, like federal legislation, operates as "the supreme Law of the Land" through the Supremacy Clause of the Constitution. The "federalization" of policy on migratory birds, however, ran counter to U.S. tradition, in which the regulation of hunting has been generally thought to be a matter of state and local concern. The legal effect of the migratory bird convention with Canada was challenged in the following famous case, arguably the most important Supreme Court decision on the domestic legal effect not just of environmental agreements, but of treaties on any subject matter.

Missouri v. Holland
United States Supreme Court, 1920
252 U.S. 416

HOLMES, J., delivered the opinion of the Court. This is a bill in equity brought by the State of Missouri to prevent a game warden of the United States [Holland] from attempting to enforce the Migratory Bird Treaty Act of July 3, 1918, 40 Stat. 755, and the regulations made by the Secretary of Agriculture in pursuance of the same. The ground of the bill is that the statute is an unconstitutional interference with the rights reserved to the States by the Tenth Amendment, and that the acts of the defendant done and threatened under that authority invade the sovereign right of the State and contravene its will manifested in statutes.... A motion to dismiss was sustained by the District Court on the ground that the Act of Congress is constitutional.... The State appeals.

On December 8, 1916, a treaty between the United States and Great Britain was proclaimed by the President. It recited that many species of birds in their annual migrations traversed many parts of the United States and of Canada, that they were of great value as a source of food and in destroying insects injurious to vegetation, but were in danger of extermination through lack of adequate protection. It therefore provided for specified closed seasons and protection in other forms, and agreed that the two powers would take or propose to their lawmaking bodies the necessary measures for carrying the treaty out. 39 Stat. 1702. The above mentioned act of July 3, 1918, [intended] to give effect to the convention, prohibited the killing, capturing or selling any of the migratory birds included in the terms of the treaty except as permitted by regulations compatible with those terms, to be made by the Secretary of Agriculture. Regulations were proclaimed on July 31, and October 25, 1918. It is unnecessary to go into any details, because, as we have said, the question raised is the general one whether the treaty and statute are void as an interference with the rights reserved to the States.

To answer this question it is not enough to refer to the Tenth Amendment, reserving the powers not delegated to the United States, because by Article 2, Section 2, the power to make treaties is delegated expressly, and by Article 6 treaties made under the authority of the United States, along with the Constitution and laws of the United States made in pursuance thereof, are declared the supreme law of the land. If the treaty is valid there can be no dispute about the validity of the statute under Article 1, Section 8, as a necessary and proper means to execute the powers of the Government. The language of the Constitution as to the supremacy of treaties being general, the question before us is narrowed to an inquiry into the ground upon which the present supposed exception is placed.

It is said that a treaty cannot be valid if it infringes the Constitution, that there are limits, therefore, to the treaty-making power, and that one such limit is that what an act of Congress could not do unaided, in derogation of the powers reserved to the States, a treaty cannot do. An earlier act of Congress that attempted by itself and not in pursuance of a treaty to regulate the killing of migratory birds within the States had been held bad in the District Court. United States v. Shauver, 214 Fed. 154. United States v. McCullagh, 221 Fed. 288. Those decisions were supported by arguments that migratory birds were owned by the States in their sovereign capacity for the benefit of their people, and that under cases like Geer v. Connecticut, 161 U.S. 519, this control was one that Congress had no power to displace. The same argument is supposed to apply now with equal force.

Whether the two cases cited were decided rightly or not they cannot be accepted as a test of the treaty power. Acts of Congress are the supreme law of the land only when made in pursuance of the Constitution, while treaties are declared to be so when made under the authority of the United States. It is open to question whether the authority of the United States means more than the formal acts prescribed to make the convention. We do not mean to imply that there are no qualifications to the treaty-making power; but they must be ascertained in a different way. It is obvious that there may be matters of the sharpest exigency for the national well being that an act of Congress could not deal with but that a treaty followed by such an act could, and it is not lightly to be assumed that, in matters requiring national action, "a power which must belong to and somewhere reside in every civilized government" is not to be found.... When we are dealing with words that also are a constituent act, like the Constitution of the United States, we must realize that they have called into life a being the development of which could not have been foreseen completely by the most gifted of its begetters. It was enough for them to realize or to hope that they had created an organism; it has taken a century and has cost their successors much sweat and blood to prove that they created a nation. The case before us must be considered in the light of our whole experience and not merely in that of what was said a hundred years ago. The treaty in question does not contravene any prohibitory words to be found in the Constitution. The only question is whether it is forbidden by some invisible radiation from the general terms of the Tenth Amendment. We must consider what this country has become in deciding what that amendment has reserved....

Here a national interest of very nearly the first magnitude is involved. It can be protected only by national action in concert with that of another power. The subject matter is only transitorily within the State and has no permanent habitat therein. But for the treaty and the statute there soon might be no birds for any powers to deal with. We see nothing in the Constitution that compels the Government to sit by while a food supply is cut off and the protectors of our forests and our crops are destroyed. It is not sufficient to rely upon the States. The reliance is vain, and were it otherwise, the question is whether the United States is forbidden to act. We are of opinion that the treaty and statute must be upheld.

COMMENTARY & QUESTIONS

1. **Migratory birds and states' rights.** Missouri v. Holland continues to be controversial because of its strong suggestion that the federal government can supersede state prerogatives through the treaty power when an identical statute would unconstitutionally exceed Congress's power to preempt state law through legislation. In other words, Missouri v. Holland means that the President, with a two-thirds vote of the Senate, can cut a deal with a foreign government that represents an unconstitutional intrusion on the reserved powers of the states if attempted by legislation enacted by Congress. If so, the case raises the possibility that the President need merely find a willing foreign power as a pretext for disrupting domestic principles of federalism. The magnitude of the controversy is a little difficult for us in the modern era to appreciate, since nowadays

the MBTA likely would be widely regarded as a valid exercise of congressional authority under the Commerce Clause. Recent Commerce Clause cases including Lopez v. United States, however, in which the Supreme Court has curtailed Congress's constitutional authority to supersede state law, might indicate a greater federal need for the doctrine of Missouri v. Holland in the future.

2. Avoiding a "flap" with Canada — are wild geese a matter of national security? If both treaties and domestic statutes must operate within constitutional limits, what justification is there for distinguishing between the reach of these two forms of lawmaking? What other, perhaps somewhat more compelling, situations might Justice Holmes have in mind when he states, "here a national interest of very nearly the first magnitude is involved"? Are wild geese really that important? Suppose the case had come out the other way — that is, holding that the federal government did *not* have the power to enter into the Convention with Canada. What adverse consequences might there be for national security? What unusual difficulties might courts encounter in reviewing the treaty to determine whether it exceeds constitutional limits? Who should decide this question, and what standards should courts apply in addressing it? Are the benefits to national security from Justice Holmes's position worth the potential interference with the domestic legal order of the 50 states?

Under the doctrine of the "supremacy of international law," even if the Supreme Court were to hold that the Convention with Canada exceeded the treaty power under the Constitution, that agreement would still remain in force as a matter of international law. How does this doctrine affect the outcomes available to Justice Holmes? What unpleasant political and legal consequences could you imagine if the Court were to hold for the State of Missouri and conclude that the agreement exceeded constitutional limits? How would you expect Canada to react? If you are the President, what does that scenario imply to you in terms of practical, real-world dealings with Canada and other foreign powers?

3. The long-range impact of migratory birds. In the early 1950s, Senator Bricker of Ohio proposed a constitutional amendment to overrule the preemptive effect of Missouri v. Holland on state law. A floor vote in the Senate in February 1954 on a version of the Bricker Amendment was 60 to 31 in favor of the amendment, one vote shy of the two-thirds requirement in Article V of the Constitution. Although the Bricker Amendment was never adopted, the federal government has tended to avoid preempting state law through treaties as a policy matter where possible. Is the doctrine of Missouri v. Holland environment-friendly or hostile to goals of environmental protection? As a Senator opposed to the Bricker Amendment, how would you argue that the Bricker Amendment is either unnecessary or a bad idea?

4. Comparative law: the Canadian take on the Migratory Bird Convention. As discussed in Chapter 26, the discipline of comparative law addresses the treatment of analogous questions in other domestic legal systems. Canada, like the United States, is a federal state, and legislative action by Parliament gave domestic legal effect to the Convention in the form of the Migratory Birds Convention Act, S.C. 1994, c. 22. Canada generally has a weaker form of federalism than the United States, and the

Canadian subnational units — the provinces — have greater retained authority than the U.S. states. As might be expected from the U.S. experience with Missouri v. Holland, questions of federalism have featured in domestic implementation in Canada. After the Convention entered into force, a conviction under the Migratory Birds Convention Act was upheld by the Manitoba Court of Appeal, notwithstanding earlier cases holding that the regulation of hunting did not fall within the powers of the federal government. King v. Stuart, [1925] 1 D.L.R. 12. In 1966, the Supreme Court of Canada, reversing the rulings of two lower courts, held that a Native American defendant could be convicted for violations of the Act and the Convention for shooting two ducks for food on an Indian Reserve. Regina v. George, [1966] S.C.R. 267. Based on these insights, would you say that a doctrine like that of Missouri v. Holland is a necessary component of a federal system? Could the aims of the Convention be accomplished domestically if the federal government does not have the capacity to supersede state law?

5. **Missouri triumphant?** In *SWANCC*, noted in Chapters 6 and 12, the MBTA again made a cameo appearance. The Corps of Engineers, a federal agency, denied a permit for solid waste dumping under the CWA on the grounds that the site was frequented by migratory birds, including those protected under the convention with Canada and the MBTA. The Court held that the Corps' extension of jurisdiction to include intrastate waters used as habitat by migratory birds exceeded its statutory authority under the CWA but ducked the question whether federal jurisdiction could have been found under the Treaty. Could you have argued an international law basis for this domestic legal jurisdiction?

6. **One amendment to the Convention lays an egg, another takes flight.** Canada and the United States signed an agreement on January 30, 1979, to amend the Convention to allow subsistence hunting of waterfowl outside of the normal hunting season, but the amendment was never ratified by the Senate and consequently never entered into force. The Convention was amended again in 1995 to allow subsistence hunters — Native Americans in Alaska and Aboriginal people in Canada — to take a quota of migratory birds. This time the Senate gave its advice and consent to the amendment in November 1997, and that amendment entered into force in 1999. As demonstrated by these two examples, under international law an amendment to a treaty is a new agreement binding the parties only if they affirmatively agree to accept the obligations in it. Similarly, the amendment may require ratification through domestic legal processes before taking effect as either international or domestic law. What are the practical and legal consequences of this rule? The advantages? The disadvantages? Consider in particular a situation in which a treaty has not just two parties like the bilateral migratory bird conventions but a multilateral treaty with multiple states as parties.

B. PROTECTING THE GLOBAL COMMONS: MULTILATERAL TREATIES AND EXECUTIVE AGREEMENTS

Why do we think of shared natural resources such as boundary waters or migratory species, as well as shared "bads" in the form of pollution, as international issues? The physical entity concerned — water, an animal, or a pollutant — is either localized on the boundary between countries or moves across that boundary. As for migratory birds, a solution may lie in a bilateral treaty or a regional agreement in which the parties may be more than two states but are limited to a definite geographic region. While a bilateral or regional approach is helpful in dealing with many problems that are geographically localized, environmental threats to areas beyond national jurisdiction, such as the high seas, or those that are truly global in nature present additional challenges.

International law has addressed marine resources from the beginning. Every international lawyer knows the name of Grotius, often described as the "father of international law," who vigorously advocated freedom of the seas.[3] Inherent in the notion of the high seas is the existence of an area beyond the national jurisdiction of any state, the first global commons. Difficulties in managing the resources of the high seas stem not only from the law but also from the physical reality that many marine resources require common management schemes for effective conservation. The alternative all too often is rapacious overexploitation. As Garrett Hardin wrote, "the oceans of the world continue to suffer from the survival of the philosophy of the commons. Maritime nations still respond automatically to the shibboleth of the 'freedom of the seas.' Professing to believe in the 'inexhaustible resources of the oceans,' they bring species after species of fish and whales closer to extinction."[4]

The international law of the sea, framed in terms of rights and obligations of states, poorly reflects the need for collective action to conserve marine biological resources. States nevertheless have evolved a number of mechanisms to overcome collective action problems of the sort described by Hardin, principal among them the multilateral treaty. Unlike the U.S.-Canada migratory bird treaty, multilateral agreements may have numerous parties. In addressing global commons issues, typically every state on the planet is eligible to become party, in which case the agreement is said to be "universal." In principle, a multilateral treaty consists of a huge number of bilateral relationships among the various parties, with a flow of rights and obligations among them. In practice, however, multilateral agreements tend have much more of a legislative character, establishing norms of expected behavior for the parties to them.

Despite their undoubted utility, multilateral treaties present their own impediments to efficacious management of shared or common resources. Multilateral treaties are similar to the bilateral U.S.-Canada migratory bird treaty in terms of formalities such as signature and ratification. Most multilateral agreements have formal procedures for signature of the text as a preliminary indication of an intent to be bound, followed by subsequent ratification that perfects the obligations for a particular party. But treaty negotiations with a large number of participants risk delay or may even collapse. Treaties by definition apply only to those states that indicate their affirmative intent to be bound by those obligations, a system that often rewards free riders, holdouts, scofflaws, and laggards. In contrast to law-making techniques in many municipal legal systems, the texts of multilateral treaties are ordinarily adopted by consensus,

---

3. See generally Hugo Grotius, The Freedom of the Seas (Mare Liberum) (J. Brown Scott ed. & R. van Deman Margoffin trans., 1916) (1633).
4. Hardin, The Tragedy of the Commons, 162 Science 1243, 1245 (1968).

meaning unanimity. Even after acquiescing in the agreement's adoption, any state may decline to be bound by most multilateral agreements merely by withholding approval in a subsequent domestic ratification process. International treaty-making characterized by these multiple junctures at which the consent of states is necessary can produce disappointingly diluted, "least common denominator" obligations determined by the more reluctant, rather than the more ambitious, participants.

Entry into force for a multilateral treaty tends to be somewhat more complex than in a bilateral situation. Consistent with a contractual theory of treaties, a treaty must have a minimum of two parties. While Zen Buddhism might entertain the possibility of the sound of one hand clapping, under international law there can be no such thing as a treaty with only one party. Many multilateral treaties establish a higher threshold, usually phrased as a number of ratifications that serve as a "trigger" or condition precedent for entry into force. While not a legal necessity, the policy motivation for relatively rigorous numerical conditions for entry into force is often strong. States entering into potentially costly obligations may well be prepared to accept those constraints only if potential treaty partners do the same, particularly when the potential for competitive disadvantage is strong. On the other hand, raising the bar for entry into force may increase the time lag until the required critical mass of ratifications is obtained, an effect sometimes known as the "slowest boat" phenomenon.

Section 1. MULTILATERAL TREATIES TO PREVENT THE TRAGEDY OF THE COMMONS: SAVING THE WHALES

Preservation of whales is a classic tragedy of the commons. It is ultimately probably in the best interests of all to prevent the extinction of whales, but because every market participant can make short-term profit by ignoring long-term resource destruction, and none trusts the others to forebear, the resource is exploited in a downward spiral. In the case of many endangered species, moreover, the rarer the remaining individuals, the higher the unit price that is likely to be offered for them, which only accelerates the extinction.

The following excerpt describes the International Convention for the Regulation of Whaling. Originally crafted as a vehicle for divvying up the global pie in whales as a resource, the Convention has metamorphosed into the principal international instrument for protecting these unique creatures. The Convention was adopted on December 2, 1946, in Washington. The Senate subsequently gave its advice and consent to ratification on July 2, 1947. The United States was consequently one of the initial parties to the Convention when it entered into force on November 10, 1948. The Whaling Convention Act of 1949, 16 U.S.C. §§916-916*l*, implements the Convention in U.S. law.

Patricia Birnie, Whaling: End of an Era (1985)

Concerned by a decline in whale stocks...during the 1930s the antarctic whaling nations entered into several voluntary agreements designed to protect whales. Some of them — including the Geneva Convention of 1931, the eight-nation London Agreement of 1937 and a British-German-Norwegian agreement signed the following year — succeeded in reducing the number of whale catchers and limiting the time periods for hunting some species. But none of those agreements stopped the whales' decline. Several whaling nations set up the International Whaling Commission (IWC) in 1946 to try to safeguard the whales and keep the industry alive.... [The IWC] was the first international body given the power to grant complete protection to endangered species and set up yearly hunting quotas for the other species. In addition, the IWC could limit whaling to specific seasons and ban the taking of nursing whales, whale calves, and adults under certain sizes. The commission also carries on regular inspections of whaling operations.... Nearly everyone agrees that the IWC has failed to achieve either goal. "It is widely known that the International Whaling Commission...presided during the first 20 years of its existence over the depletion of nearly all the world's whale populations," British biologist Sidney Holt, a longtime international fisheries expert, asserted. "And the whaling industry, instead of enjoying an orderly development, experienced a disorderly, though long drawn-out collapse."

A resurgence of whaling followed World War II, but by the early 1960s only the Soviet Union and Japan maintained extensive whaling operations. Those two nations, along with Norway, Iceland, Brazil, South Korea, Denmark, Peru, Spain and the Philippines, are the only countries with commercial whaling industries today. A drop in whale oil prices during the worldwide Depression of the 1930s accounted for some of the decline. But the more important factor by far was the decimation of virtually every species of antarctic whale. The relatively slow-swimming humpback was the first to be hunted — and the first to be overharvested. Antarctic whalers killed so many humpbacks beginning in 1904 that they all but disappeared by 1916. Then the blue whale was hunted practically to extinction. "When there were too few blue whales to hunt, the whalers turned to the next largest species, the fin whale, then to the sei [in the mid-1960s], and finally to the little minke [in the mid-1970s]," Richard Ellis noted....

Under the terms of the IWC charter, nations that file formal objections to commission rulings do not have to abide by them. Japan, Norway and the Soviet Union — the nations with the largest commercial whaling operations — promptly filed the requisite formal complaints. Japan and Norway claimed that the ban was not based on scientific evidence and would wipe out profitable domestic whaling industries. The Soviet Union said that "political considerations," not scientific information, motivated the whaling ban. Japan, Norway, and the Soviet Union, however, indicated they would end their commercial ocean whaling operations by 1988.... "The handwriting is on the wall for commercial whaling," Patricia Forkan of the Humane Society of the United States commented....

It is generally conceded that, despite its unprecedented powers, the IWC did little to safeguard diminishing whale species until the 1970s. Still, unlike its predecessors, the commission continued to operate. The IWC "is really a remarkable organization in that it's managed to hold together through all these years and still has a certain amount of legitimacy. It actually seems to function," biologist Scott Krauss of the New England Aquarium in Boston said. "It may not function to my liking, but it does still function." Under increasing pressure from conservationists, the IWC in the late 1970s began cutting quotas and working toward implementing a total moratorium on commercial whaling. This led to the total ban that the commission adopted at its 1982 meeting....

Article VII of the 1946 International Convention for the Regulation of Whaling gives countries the right to kill whales "for the purposes of scientific research." Thus far Iceland and South Korea have officially notified the IWC that they intend to carry out comparatively widescale whaling for scientific purposes.... Whalers in Japan and Brazil reportedly are pushing for those nations to undertake "scientific whaling" as well. Iceland planned to kill 80 fin whales, 80 minke whales and 40 sei whales annually from 1986 to 1989. South Korea said it would take 200 minkes a year.

Icelandic and South Korean officials maintain that the whales will be taken solely for research studies. But conservationists say those nations are actually trying to circumvent the IWC ban on commercial whaling. Conservationists point out that Iceland plans to export the meat from its whales to Japan. "Iceland has made no bones about the fact that they intend to sell [the whale meat] to Japan," Forkan said. "What we are looking at is the potential to make $30 million or so over the four years for a million and a half dollars' worth of research. We think that's commercial whaling."

The IWC allows another exception to its whaling bans, including those on catching totally protected species. IWC regulations permit the taking of whales so long as "the meat and products are to be used exclusively for local consumption by the aborigines." Aboriginal whaling has been permitted in recent years in Greenland where the Eskimos kill fin and humpback whales, in the Soviet Union where Siberian Eskimos take gray whales, and in the United States where Alaskan Eskimos kill bowheads. Conservationists have strenuously objected to these aboriginal whaling activities, alleging that the meat of the gray whales killed in Siberia is used illegally to feed animals on fur farms and that the Eskimos in Greenland and Alaska are killing too many of the rare humpbacks and bowheads.

"U.S. Eskimos are wreaking havoc on the bowhead stocks," Frank Potter said. The problem is not so much the number of whales killed, but the much larger number of those struck and not killed, nearly 90 percent of which die. "The number of whales struck and not landed skyrocketed in the late '70s, early '80s," Potter said. "Given the very low population estimates of these bowhead whales, there is great concern that [the Eskimos] are clearly taking more animals than are being reproduced each year. If you've only got a couple of thousand, it doesn't take long to extinct the species." Some IWC scientists have pushed to end Alaskan bowhead aboriginal whaling. The U.S. government, under pressure from the Alaska Eskimo whaling commission, requested that the IWC allocate 35 bowhead strikes for 1985. The commission eventually allocated the Eskimos 26 strikes a year for 1985, 1986, and 1987.

COMMENTARY & QUESTIONS

1. **Consensus as gridlock: should multilateral agreements find an alternative way?** Like the process of drafting multilateral treaties, most international organizations, whose members are states as represented by their governments, operate by consensus, which in practice means unanimity. One consequence of this rule — which is a principle of international relations not required by international law — is that any one state with sufficient motivation or enough political clout can block or impede the entire process. If the rule of consensus has such an adverse effect on the rigor of international obligations, what, if any, benefits can you identify from such an approach? Majority voting has been proposed as one alternative to the downward drag of the rule of consensus. The ICRW is one of the still relatively few international instruments that incorporate majority voting. After establishing the IWC, of which all parties to the Convention are members, Article III, paragraph 2 proclaims that "Decisions of the Commission shall be taken by a simple majority of those members voting except that a three-fourths majority of those members voting shall be required for action in pursuance of Article V." Article V, which deals with procedures for adopting the all-important catch limitations, sets out a simplified mechanism for adopting supposedly technical requirements that require approval by only a qualified majority of states. As noted by Birnie, after a specified "opt-out" period, those actions then become binding

on all states that have not objected to them. Why do you think the opt-out clause was included in the agreement? What consequences would there be if it had not been? If states can easily shed their obligations by opting out, why even bother to include a majority voting rule in the first place?

2. **The Whaling Convention as paper tiger.** The opt-out provisions in the Whaling Convention have been the subject of stinging criticism from the conservation community. "Most of the [Whaling Convention's] difficulty in regulating the whaling industry can be attributed to the immunity granted whaling countries by the objection (opt-out) clause and the [Convention's] inability to sanction noncomplying nations." Smith, The International Whaling Commission: An Analysis of the Past and Reflections on the Future, 16 Nat'l Res. L. 543, 559 (1984). Others have praised these and similar provisions in other agreements as an improvement on the "pure" consensus model. According to this view, the necessity for a public and visible objection to, for example, an IWC catch limitation is a strong disincentive that tends to discourage such action — the "mobilization of shame." What do you think of the "opt-out" model? Why would states have built this possibility into the ICRW? Is there anything good to be said for it? Can you come up with something better?

3. **Problems of enforcement.** In the decentralized world of public international law, states are the principal if not sole actors. One consequence of this structure is that there is no international legislature. While multilateral treaties may be the rough analogue of international legislation, there is a significant difference because treaties bind only those states that accept the obligations in them, and there is no coercive authority to force states to accept or to abide by obligations to which they object. Similarly, there is no court of general jurisdiction in the international legal system. International tribunals, including the International Court of Justice, require the consent of the states concerned before they can exercise jurisdiction. Despite the name, such binding third-party dispute settlement institutions are much more like arbitral tribunals in the sense that the parties to a dispute consent to the exercise of jurisdiction in advance. Given these twin dead weights of consent and consensus, enforcement, as noted by both Birnie and Smith, is a serious problem. What more effective mechanisms can you imagine to assure that parties to the Whaling Convention are living up to their obligations?

Section 2. EXECUTIVE AGREEMENTS: TENSIONS WITH STATUTORY MANDATES

Although Patricia Birnie's trenchant criticisms of the International Convention for the Regulation of Whaling may have been lost on that multilateral institution, at least one country, the United States, took them to heart by enacting domestic legislation to buttress the Whaling Convention and to enhance the international momentum for compliance. The Pelly and Packwood Amendments, federal statutory requirements, reinforce the Whaling Convention on the domestic level by requiring the Secretary of Commerce to monitor the whaling activities of foreign nationals and to investigate potential violations of the Whaling Convention. Upon completion of this investigation, the Secretary must promptly decide whether to certify conduct by foreign nationals that "diminishes the effectiveness" of the Whaling Convention. After certification by the Secretary, the Packwood Amendment directs the Secretary of State to reduce the offending nation's fishing allocation within the United States' fishery conservation zone by at least 50%. This unilateral strategy relies on a more vigorous domestic statutory framework that emphasizes negative disincentives or punishments for violations of IWC quotas, even if the offending state has opted out of them.

In 1981, the IWC established a zero quota for harvests of sperm whales. During the next year, the Commission ordered a five-year moratorium on commercial whaling to begin in the 1985–1986 season and to continue until 1990. Japan filed timely objections that effectively relieved it, as an international legal matter, from compliance with the sperm whale quotas for 1982 through 1984. Nonetheless, the potential sanction under the Pelly and Packwood Amendments by the United States threatened Japanese whaling for the 1984–1985 season. In response to this situation, the executive branch concluded an executive agreement with Japan, which entered into force without Senate advice and consent, in which that country agreed to abide by the spirit but not the letter of multilaterally agreed whaling quotas, implementing the international prohibitions on a more protracted schedule than contemplated by the IWC. Japan agreed to catch no more than 400 sperm whales in each of the 1984 and 1985 seasons and to stop commercial whaling by 1988, three years after the date specified by the IWC. The United States in return promised that it would not impose its domestic statutory sanctions so long as Japan was adhering to the executive agreement, regardless of Japan's violation of the IWC quotas. Several environmental organizations brought suit to compel the Secretary of Commerce to certify Japan.

The crucial point in this scenario is that the agreement with Japan was concluded with no express congressional participation and, in particular, without Senate advice and consent by a two-thirds majority. Not every international agreement concluded by the United States receives Senate advice and consent under Article II §2 of the Constitution. Notwithstanding the constitutional requirement for Senate advice and consent to ratification, fewer than 10% of international agreements are ever submitted to the Senate.[5] These instruments, done unilaterally by the executive branch, are known as "executive agreements." Although the text of the Constitution makes no reference to such a possibility, the practice of concluding some international agreements without Senate approval has been accepted since soon after the adoption of the Constitution.

International law makes no distinction among domestic processes for implementation of international compacts, all of which are binding and enforceable under international law. Foreign relations lawyers for this reason generally prefer the term "international agreements" when referring to all agreements governed by international law, reserving the term "treaty" to describe the subset that are submitted to the Senate. The term "executive agreement" has purely domestic significance and does not affect the instrument's status in international law.

Circumventing Senate advice and consent and eliminating the possibility for delay or rejection might have substantial appeal from a political point of view. An

---

5. Between 1930 and 1992, 891 international agreements were concluded as treaties in the constitutional sense after Senate advice and consent. By contrast, during the same period, the Executive entered into 13,178 executive agreements — nearly 15 times as many instruments. Congressional Research Service, Treaties and Other International Agreements (Senate Print 103-5 1993).

environmentally conscious President, having negotiated an international agreement, would see his policies implemented immediately, arguably to the benefit of the environment. For example, the United States may never become party to the Kyoto Protocol on global warming (discussed in Chapter 26), negotiated and signed by the Clinton Administration, for lack of Senate advice and consent. The UN Convention on Biological Diversity, adopted in 1992 and signed by the Clinton Administration in 1993, has languished in the Senate for a decade.

Despite their expediency, executive agreements – which on the domestic level are similar to executive orders issued by the President without congressional approval — can raise substantial legal questions. The Constitution directs the President to "take Care that the Laws be faithfully *executed*," while reserving "all legislative powers" to the Congress. Starting from the proposition that every action of the President must be supported by some domestic legal authority, the black letter rule is that executive agreements must find legal support in: (1) statutes enacted by Congress; (2) an Article II §2 treaty, which has the same force as a statute thanks to Senate advice and consent; or (3) the President's own constitutional powers. See 1 Restatement of the Foreign Relations Law of the United States §303 (1987). In environmental matters typically governed by detailed statutory schemes, the first of these options is the most likely.

The test for choosing the form of an international agreement — known as the "choice of instrument" problem — is whether there is legal authority for the agreement absent Senate advice and consent to ratification. While legal considerations play a role in this decision, political factors also come into play. Congress does not always explicitly authorize the Executive to enter into international agreements. The executive branch also enters into some executive agreements that rely on existing statutory authority but are neither expressly authorized by statute nor approved by the Congress after the fact. In situations like the executive agreement with Japan on whaling, the authority to enter into the agreement with a foreign power is implied and the obligations in any resulting agreement may not exceed the statutory boundaries. As a structural matter, the President is in the driver's seat, controlling the decision whether to submit an agreement to the Senate and consequently the form of the agreement.

The dispute that arose over the agreement with Japan on whales is a volatile mix of an Article II treaty, an executive agreement, and a domestic statute, each expressing differing and sometimes competing policies for protecting endangered whales. As you read the opinion, think about how the executive agreement's relationship to the statute would be described (a) by the plaintiffs, an organization dedicated to preserving whales; and (b) by the executive branch, the defendant in the case.

Japan Whaling Association v. American Cetacean Society
United States Supreme Court, 1986
478 U.S. 221

WHITE, J. The issue before us is whether, in the circumstances of these cases, either the Pelly or Packwood Amendment required the Secretary to certify Japan for refusing to abide by the IWC whaling quotas. We have concluded that certification was not necessary and hence reject the Court of Appeals' holding and respondents' submission that certification is mandatory whenever a country exceeds its allowable take under the ICRW Schedule.

Under the Packwood Amendment, certification is neither permitted nor required until the Secretary makes a determination that nationals of a foreign country "are conducting fishing operations or engaging in trade or taking which diminishes the effectiveness" of the ICRW. It is clear that the Secretary must promptly make the certification decision, but the statute does not define the words "diminish the effectiveness of" or specify the factors that the Secretary should consider in making the decision entrusted to him alone. Specifically, it does not state that certification must be forthcoming whenever a country does not abide by IWC Schedules, and the Secretary did not understand or interpret the language of the Amendment to require him to do so. Had Congress intended otherwise, it would have been a simple matter to say that the Secretary must certify deliberate taking of whales in excess of IWC limits....

The Secretary, of course, may not act contrary to the will of Congress when exercised within the bounds of the Constitution. If Congress has directly spoken to the precise issue in question, if the intent of Congress is clear, that is the end of the matter. Chevron U.S.A. Inc. v. Natural Resources Defense Council, Inc., 467 U.S. 837, 843 (1984). But as the courts below and respondents concede, the statutory language itself contains no direction to the Secretary automatically and regardless of the circumstances to certify a nation that fails to conform to the IWC whaling Schedule. The language of the Pelly and Packwood Amendments might reasonably be construed in this manner, but the Secretary's construction that there are circumstances in which certification may be withheld, despite departures from the Schedules and without violating his duty, is also a reasonable construction of the language used in both Amendments. We do not understand the Secretary to be urging that he has carte blanche discretion to ignore and do nothing about whaling in excess of IWC Schedules. He does not argue, for example, that he could refuse to certify for any reason not connected with the aims and conservation goals of the Convention, or refuse to certify deliberate flouting of schedules by members who have failed to object to a particular schedule. But insofar as the plain language of the Amendments is concerned, the Secretary is not forbidden to refuse to certify for the reasons given in these cases. Furthermore, if a statute is silent or ambiguous with respect to the question at issue, our long-standing practice is to defer to the "executive department's construction of a statutory scheme it is entrusted to administer," Chevron, unless the legislative history of the enactment shows with sufficient clarity that the agency construction is contrary to the will of Congress.

Contrary to the Court of Appeals' and respondents' views, we find nothing in the legislative history of either Amendment that addresses the nature of the Secretary's duty and requires him to certify every departure from the IWC's scheduled limits on whaling.... The discussion on the floor of the House by Congressman Pelly and other supporters of the Amendment...demonstrates that Congress' primary concern in enacting the Pelly Amendment was to stave off the possible extermination of both the Atlantic salmon as well as the extinction of other heavily fished species, such as whales, regulated by international fishery conservation programs. 117 Cong. Rec. 34752–34754 (1971) (remarks of Reps. Pelly, Wylie, Clausen, and Hogan). The comments of Senator Stevens, acting Chairman of the reporting Senate Committee and the only speaker on the bill during the Senate debate, were to the same effect. See id., at 47054 (if countries continue indiscriminately to fish on the high seas, salmon may become extinct). Testimony given during congressional hearings on the Pelly Amendment also supports the conclusion that Congress had no intention to require the Secretary to certify every departure from the limits set by an international conservation program....

Enactment of the Packwood Amendment did not negate the Secretary's view that he is not required to certify every failure to abide by IWC's whaling limits. There were hearings on the proposal but no Committee Reports. It was enacted as a floor amendment. It is clear enough, however, that it was designed to remove executive discretion in imposing sanctions once certification had been made — as Senator Packwood put it, "to put real economic teeth into our whale conservation efforts," by requiring the Secretary of State to impose severe economic sanctions until the transgression is rectified. 125 Cong. Rec. 21742 (1979). But Congress specifically retained the identical certification standard of the Pelly Amendment, which requires a determination by the Secretary that the whaling operations at issue diminish the effectiveness of the ICRW. 16 U.S.C. §1821(e)(2)(A)(i). See 125 Cong. Rec. 21743 (1979) (remarks of Sen. Magnuson); id., at 22083 (remarks of Rep. Breaux); id., at 22084 (remarks of Rep. Oberstar). We find no specific indication in this history that henceforth the certification standard would require the Secretary to certify each and every departure from IWC's whaling Schedules....

We conclude that the Secretary's construction of the statutes neither contradicted the language of either Amendment, nor frustrated congressional intent. See Chevron U.S.A. Inc. v. Natural Resources Defense Council, Inc., 467 U.S., at 842–843. In enacting these Amendments, Congress' primary goal was to protect and conserve whales and other endangered species. The Secretary furthered this objective by entering into the agreement with Japan, calling for that nation's acceptance of the worldwide moratorium on commercial whaling and the withdrawal of its objection to the IWC zero sperm whale quota, in exchange for a transition period of limited additional whaling. Given the lack of any express direction to the Secretary that he must certify a nation whose whale harvest exceeds an IWC quota, the Secretary reasonably could conclude, as he has, that, "a cessation of all Japanese commercial whaling activities would contribute more to the effectiveness of the IWC and its conservation program than any other single development."

We conclude, therefore, that the Secretary's decision to secure the certainty of Japan's future compliance with the IWC's program through the 1984 executive agreement, rather than rely on the possibility that certification and imposition of economic sanctions would produce the same or better result, is a reasonable construction of the Pelly and Packwood Amendments. Congress granted the Secretary the authority to determine whether a foreign nation's whaling in excess of quotas diminishes the effectiveness of the IWC, and we find no reason to impose a mandatory obligation upon the Secretary to certify that every quota violation necessarily fails that standard. Accordingly, the judgment of the Court of Appeals is reversed.

MARSHALL, J., with whom BRENNAN, BLACKMUN, and REHNQUIST, JJ., join, dissenting.... I would affirm the judgment below on the ground that the Secretary has exceeded his authority by using his power of certification, not as a means for identifying serious whaling violations, but as a means for evading the constraints of the Packwood Amendment. Even focusing, as the Court does, upon the distinct question whether the statute prevents the Secretary from determining that the effectiveness of a conservation program is not diminished by a substantial transgression of whaling quotas, I find the Court's conclusion utterly unsupported. I am troubled that this Court is empowering an officer of the executive branch, sworn to uphold and defend the laws of the United States, to ignore Congress' pointed response to a question long pondered: "whether Leviathan can long endure so wide a chase, and so remorseless a havoc; whether he must not at last be exterminated from the waters, and the last whale, like the last man, smoke his last pipe, and then himself evaporate in the final puff." H. Melville, Moby Dick 436 (Signet ed. 1961).

COMMENTARY & QUESTIONS

1. **Unilateral action versus multilateralism.** The Pelly and Packwood Amendments are examples of unilateral domestic law measures taken to reinforce and to fill gaps in the

multilateral Whaling Convention. In response to failures of political will and structural barriers to the effective preservation of common resources like whales, environmental groups have advocated unilateral self-help to create incentives for more effective international cooperation. These unilateral measures generally identify a juncture at which governmental action by one state leverages performance by another. One sometimes hears the criticism that these unilateral measures are "inconsistent with multilateralism" — in other words that a state like the United States should seek action from international bodies like the IWC and refrain from resorting to the international version of vigilantism. Are the Pelly and Packwood Amendments just an example of the U.S. throwing its weight around under a cloak of global altruism? Under what circumstances might such unilateral actions be appropriate? Necessary? Inappropriate? Remember that Japan had no international legal obligation to refrain from taking whales.

2. **Executive branch scare tactics.** Because international law makes no distinction between a treaty in the constitutional sense and an executive agreement like the one challenged in this case, the agreement with Japan would remain binding as an international legal matter regardless of the outcome — an unusual twist on the frequent perception that international instruments have less legal force than domestic statutes. In a case like *Japan Whaling* challenging the legality of an executive agreement, the executive branch — the defendant in the case — will often expressly or impliedly raise the specter of judicial disruption of foreign affairs. If the conservation organization plaintiff were to win, the United States would still be obliged to refrain from sanctioning Japan, while at the same time the Executive would be subject to a judicial order directing it to impose sanctions. Arguments about the lack of judicial competence in foreign affairs and the constitutional separation of powers in which the President is the sole voice of the nation in foreign relations are often tossed in for good measure. Based on the extraordinarily low number of cases in which courts have held executive agreements to lack domestic legal authority, these arguments are quite a powerful weapon in discouraging judicial intervention. At the same time, recall that the President makes the choice of form as between a treaty and an executive agreement, and judicial deference to that choice undoubtedly invites abuse by the Executive. If the President had chosen to submit the bilateral agreement with Japan to the Senate for its advice and consent, there would have been no dispute because the Senate's action would have provided the necessary legal authority. On behalf of the plaintiff conservation organization, how would you respond to the government's argument? Why do you think the deal with Japan was concluded as an executive agreement and not a treaty in the constitutional sense? Suppose the Court had held for the conservation organization and declined to give legal effect to the agreement with Japan. What response would you expect from the Japanese government?

3. **Lessons for Congress.** As a member of Congress, would you view the result in *Japan Whaling*, in which the Court seemed to interpret the statutory mandates in light of unilateral executive branch action, as constructive engagement with the needs of Japan, or as a disingenuous sell-out of environmental values? The texts of the Pelly and Packwood Amendments specifically tie those enactments to the multilateral Whaling

Convention, suggesting that Congress not only meant what it said but also clearly said what it meant. If you were a member of Congress, or advising one, how would you frame amendments to Pelly and Packwood that would prevent the problem encountered in *Japan Whaling* from arising in the future? What actions short of adoption of new legislation could Congress take to alter the outcome? In actuality, only Senator Packwood of the 535 members of Congress took the trouble to object to the bilateral agreement.

C. INTERNATIONAL TRADE AGREEMENTS: THE TRADE AND ENVIRONMENT PROBLEM

As long ago as the early nineteenth century, the British economist David Ricardo, reacting to the prevalent mercantilist and colonialist views of the time, hypothesized that countries that reciprocally open their borders to foreign trade will inevitably be better off than countries that impede or prohibit trade. Ricardo observed that free trade in goods (not to be confused with trading of emissions allowances discussed in Chapter 14) encourages specialization and global economic efficiency, both of which benefit the public. The Ricardo theory of comparative advantage is alive and well today in modern trade agreements, including the General Agreement on Tariffs and Trade (GATT),[6] the agreement creating the World Trade Organization (WTO),[7] and the North American Free Trade Agreement (NAFTA).[8]

Section 1. MULTILATERAL AGREEMENTS ON TRADE: THE WTO

The obligations in international trade agreements — including the GATT, WTO agreements, and NAFTA — are basically ones of nondiscrimination and are expressed legally in three principal ways. The first of the principal obligations or "disciplines" found in international trade agreements is the requirement for most favored nation (MFN) treatment. For countries that have MFN status with the United States, the United States has promised to not treat those countries' goods differently from the goods of other MFN nations. So, if the United States is carrying on trade relations with the fictional countries of Fredonia and Ruritania, and both have MFN status, the United States is obliged to treat Ruritania no less well than it treats Fredonia, and vice versa. The second principal discipline — the national treatment obligation — requires treatment of imported products no less well than similar, domestically manufactured products. If the United States imports widgets from Fredonia, it must treat the imported Fredonian widgets no less well than it treats the domestically manufactured widgets.

The national treatment requirement, taken together with the MFN obligation, results in a kind of equal protection clause for goods in international trade. A third

---

6. General Agreement on Tariffs and Trade, Oct. 30, 1947, 61 Stat. (5), (6), T.I.A.S. No. 1700, 55 U.N.T.S. 194, 4 General Agreement on Tariffs and Trade, Basic Instruments and Selected Documents (1969).

7. Agreement Establishing the World Trade Organization, Apr. 15, 1994, 33 I.L.M. 1144.

8. North American Free Trade Agreement, Dec. 8, 11, 14 & 17, 1992, U.S.-Canada-Mexico, 32 I.L.M. 296, 612.

discipline, the prohibition on quantitative restrictions, can be thought of as a corollary to the national treatment obligation. If a country does not have restrictions on the quantity of a certain product that can be produced domestically, it cannot place numerical limits on imported versions of that product. Collectively, these three nondiscrimination obligations operate something like the "dormant Commerce Clause" under the U.S. Constitution, which domestically restricts the capacity of a state as a subnational unit of the United States to regulate in ways that interferes with interstate trade within the United States.

International trade agreements in legal form are similar to multilateral environmental agreements like the Montreal Protocol, but the dynamics of the negotiating process are quite different. Assume both Ruritania and Fredonia have trade barriers of whatever kind — tariffs, embargoes, regulations — that impede the free movement of goods between the two countries. Neither of them acting on its own is likely to lower those trade barriers, a classic collective action problem. Ricardo teaches that if Ruritania and Fredonia collaborate by promising to reduce their trade barriers reciprocally, those states and the public in both countries will both be better off. Each side agrees to reduce its trade barriers in return for a promise from the other side to lower its obstacles to trade. Large multilateral trade agreements, including the WTO suite of agreements, are somewhat more complicated but in principle have a similar structure.

The obligations in these reciprocal trade agreements are significant for a state's economic well-being. If Ruritania agrees to lower its trade barriers in return for similar promises from Fredonia, Fredonia has a legitimate expectation that Ruritania will perform on those obligations. The possibility that Ruritania might not perform raises the need to craft effective means for settling disputes in some binding third party process like a court proceeding. In response to this concern, the GATT eventually created a dispute settlement mechanism in which complaints can be forwarded to a panel of three experts, typically trade specialists, for a hearing. One of the principal innovations in the WTO in 1995 was to strengthen dispute settlement procedures by creating a standing Appellate Body, consisting of seven members.

Section 2. DOMESTIC IMPLEMENTATION OF INTERNATIONAL TRADE AGREEMENTS: CONGRESSIONAL-EXECUTIVE AGREEMENTS

From a constitutional perspective, even the mere phrase "international trade agreement" presents something of a conundrum. The Constitution divides authority over international trade between Congress, on the one hand, and the President on the other. Under Article I §8 of the Constitution, Congress has the exclusive power to regulate international trade. For example, Congress can put tariffs — fees on imported goods — in place by legislation. Congress can also prohibit the importation of foreign goods in whole or in part, or allow importation only under certain circumstances. But without the power to negotiate with other states to overcome the collective action problems that characterize international trade, Congress is poorly positioned to engage in international bargains. Article II §2 of the Constitution, on the other hand, gives the President the exclusive authority to conduct foreign relations and to make treaties. But the President does not have the unilateral power to legislate. So, in the usual case, the

President negotiates an international agreement, brings it home, and presents it to the Senate for its advice and consent to ratification by a two-thirds majority as specified in the Constitution.

From the point of view of international trade policy there are significant problems with this approach. First, the Senate can tinker with an agreement brokered by the president and alter its terms through the ratification process. Given the content of most trade agreements, which are designed to reduce or eliminate protectionist trade barriers including tariffs and subsidies, it is well nigh inevitable that some provisions will negatively affect some domestic constituency. The whole point of trade agreements is to lower trade barriers for the benefit of the public as a whole, but industries and other constituencies that benefit from trade barriers — often pejoratively dubbed "protectionists" — are likely to object to their removal. The result is a high probability that a trade agreement may be subject to significant revision in the Senate. A second criticism of the Article II §2 treaty approach is that it would leave out the House of Representatives, which ordinarily would have a say in legislation affecting trade.

To remedy these difficulties, the executive and legislative branches have crafted an innovation called a "congressional-executive agreement," which is the form in which trade agreements have been adopted since 1974. Congress, exercising its Article I §8 powers, authorizes the President, by prior statute, to negotiate an international trade agreement on general terms, provided that the agreement not enter into force until Congress adopts subsequent implementing legislation. The President carries out the negotiations, brings home an agreement, and then presents the agreement to Congress, along with implementing legislation that is typically drafted by the executive branch.

The principal innovation in this scheme is the last step, in which implementing legislation is adopted on the "fast track" (now known as "trade promotion authority"), which allows for no amendments and only limited public participation. Although most constitutional scholars believe that congressional-executive agreements are fully the equivalent of treaties that have gone through the Senate advice-and-consent process, the agreements in fact provide Congress with a much smaller role. Under fast-track procedures, Congress has only one very unattractive remedy if it does not like an agreement — disapprove it altogether. Congress has essentially forgone the normal domestic statutory processes, thereby substantially increasing the executive's role in the lawmaking function with respect to international trade.[9]

Section 3. TRADE AND THE ENVIRONMENT: COLLISION WITH DOMESTIC ENVIRONMENTAL LAW?

What does all this mean for the environment? International obligations on trade are almost exclusively "negative" in the sense that they place constraints on governmental action. Trade agreements encourage liberalized or free trade through obligations

---

9. In a case seeking compliance with the National Environmental Policy Act for the negotiation of NAFTA, the D.C. Circuit held that the judicial branch has no role in reviewing the fast-track trade agreement process. Public Citizen v. Office of the United States Trade Representative, 5 F.3d 549 (D.C. Cir. 1993), cert. denied, 510 U.S. 104 (1994). So, in addition to Congress's reduced role, the courts essentially are cut out of the process, further enhancing the presidential prerogative.

that limit governmental intrusion into what otherwise would be a free market. From an environmental point of view, this phenomenon is the equivalent of deregulation — in the sense of reducing the level of governmental intrusion in the market — and trade agreements by virtue of their negative obligations are inherently deregulatory. This deregulatory momentum largely explains the phenomenon of globalization, at least as it has been defined for the past decade or so: getting governments out of the business of impeding private interactions and transactions, thereby facilitating their global reach.

Environmental protection anticipates affirmative governmental interventions in the marketplace to offset market failures. That in a nutshell is the clash between the two approaches: one operates to disable governmental action, the other depends on invigorating government. Obligations in trade agreements *proscribe* certain governmental behavior that impede trade, while environmental statutes *prescribe* other governmental actions to protect public health and ecosystems. International environmental agreements operate in a similar way. The Montreal Protocol requires ratifying states to intervene in their domestic jurisdictions to accomplish certain concrete results in the form of prohibitions on private actions. Trade agreements therefore generally create no affirmative rule making authority. Unlike international trade agreements, in domestic legal systems such as the U.S. Constitution, there is normally some affirmative governmental regulatory authority to offset the externalities created by market liberalization.

One regulation challenged in this way was a rule, promulgated in 1994 by the EPA under the CAA, dealing with "reformulated" gasoline. The regulations specify the composition of reformulated gasoline and require reductions in the emissions of certain pollutants. For gasoline to qualify as reformulated it must be compared to a baseline, unreformulated state. In its rule, EPA specified that domestic refiners could choose from a variety of baselines. Because there were fewer data about foreign refiners, making enforcement much more difficult, EPA did not give foreign refiners a choice but instead assigned them a baseline. The Venezuelan national oil company, Petroleos de Venezuela (PDVSA), protested that the EPA rules discriminated against imported gasoline in violation of the United States' WTO obligations. As a matter of trade law, this was a relatively easy case of facial discrimination for the newly created Appellate Body of the WTO in its very first case.[10]

The real issue, however, was what happened after the WTO dispute settlement panel report on the rule came out. As a matter of domestic U.S. law, dispute settlement panel reports have no domestic legal effect. To be implemented domestically, the WTO Appellate Body's report had to go back to EPA for remedial action. The agency subsequently started a new rule-making process by publishing a notice of proposed rule making, soliciting comments, and the like. At the same time that the rule making was going on, another part of the executive branch, the U.S. Trade Representative, was reassuring Venezuela that the new regulation would comply with the WTO report. This tended to attenuate, if not entirely undermine, the rights of public participation that we are accustomed to in the ordinary administrative process and that have given domestic environmental law such vigor. Later, the amended rule, promulgated in 1997, was

---

10. United States — Standards for Reformulated and Conventional Gasoline, 35 I.L.M. 603 (1996).

challenged by a coalition of domestic refiners and environmental organizations in the following case.

George E. Warren Corp. v. EPA
United States Court of Appeals for the District of Columbia Circuit, 1998
159 F.3d 616

GINSBURG, J.: The petitioners argue the rule is beyond the EPA's statutory authority because (1) allowing foreign refiners the option to petition the EPA for an individual baseline may result in a degradation of air quality; [and] (2) in promulgating the rule the EPA considered factors other than air quality, namely (a) the WTO's decision that the 1994 rule was inconsistent with the GATT, and (b) the likely effect of regulation upon the price and supply of gasoline in the U.S. market....

Because the EPA is charged with administering the Clean Air Act, we evaluate a challenge to its statutory authority under the familiar two-step analysis of Chevron U.S.A., Inc. v. NRDC, 467 U.S. 837 (1984). Under *Chevron* step one the court asks "whether Congress has directly spoken to the precise question at issue," id. at 842; if so, then we "must give effect to the unambiguously expressed intent of Congress. " Id. at 843. If the Congress has not addressed the issue, however, then under *Chevron* step two we will defer to the agency's interpretation if it is reasonable in light of the structure and purpose of the statute. See id.

We review a challenge to the agency's actions as arbitrary and capricious under the same standards that we apply when reviewing a rule pursuant to the Administrative Procedure Act. As we have pointed out before, this inquiry may overlap with our analysis under step two of *Chevron*, see Republican Nat'l Comm. v. FEC, 76 F.3d 400, 407 (1996); so it does to some extent in this case.

The petitioners base all their challenges to the EPA's statutory authority upon the premise that any rule that does not guarantee the maintenance or improvement of air quality violates the anti-dumping provision of 42 U.S.C. §7545(k)(8). For this they rely upon our remark in American Petroleum Institute (API) v. EPA, 52 F.3d 1113, 1119 (1995), that the "sole purpose of the [reformulated gasoline] program is to reduce air pollution." In doing so, however, the petitioners misjudge the applicability of that precedent.

The overall goal of the reformulated gasoline program is, of course, to improve air quality by reducing air pollution; the means chosen to achieve that end are, first, requiring that only reformulated gasoline be sold in nonattainment areas, and second, prohibiting the transfer of pollutants in the refining process from reformulated to conventional gasoline.... In sum, although the general purpose of the antidumping provision is to maintain average emissions per gallon from conventional gasoline at no more than 1990 levels, the specific approach adopted by the Congress makes full achievement of that goal less than certain. This result apparently reflects a legislative compromise between two potentially conflicting goals — avoiding degradation of air quality and not disrupting the market for conventional gasoline....

Again proceeding from the mistaken premise that the maintenance or improvement of air quality is the sole focus of the anti-dumping provision, the petitioners argue that the EPA may not consider factors other than air quality in promulgating rules under §7545(k)(8). Thus do they challenge the EPA's consideration both of the WTO's decision interpreting the GATT and of the comments of the Department of Energy concerning the economic effects of the alternatives before the agency.... The EPA responds that nothing in the statute precludes consideration of such factors, and that its approach is congruent with that employed by the Congress when it enacted the anti-dumping provision.

The petitioners do not direct our attention to anything in the text or structure of the statute to indicate that the Congress intended to preclude the EPA from considering the effects a proposed rule might have upon the price and supply of gasoline and the treaty obligations of the United States. Under step two of *Chevron*, therefore, we must defer to the agency's construction if it is reasonable....

Under step two of *Chevron*, we think the agency's interpretation is permissible. Section 7545(k)(8) specifically allows foreign refiners that produced dirtier than average gasoline in 1990 to continue importing gasoline of that quality, presumably in order to prevent the disruption that might ensue were those refiners forced to choose between producing cleaner gasoline than they did in 1990 or quitting the U.S. market. The agency, following the lead of the Congress, similarly sought to prevent its rule from disrupting the market.

In the particular circumstances of this case our usual reluctance to infer from congressional silence an intention to preclude the agency from considering factors other than those listed in a statute is bolstered by the decision of the WTO lurking in the background. "Since the days of Chief Justice Marshall, the Supreme Court has consistently held that congressional statutes must be construed wherever possible in a manner that will not require the United States 'to violate the law of nations.'" South African Airways v. Dole, 817 F.2d 119, 125 (D.C. Cir. 1987) (quoting The Schooner Charming Betsy, 6 U.S. (2 Cranch.) 64, 118, 2 L. Ed. 208 (1804)); see also Vimar Seguros y Reaseguros, S.A. v. M/V Sky Reefer, 515 U.S. 528, 539 (1995) ("If the United States is to be able to gain the benefits of international accords and have a role as a trusted partner in multilateral endeavors, its courts should be most cautious before interpreting its domestic legislation in such manner as to violate international agreements").

In sum, we conclude the EPA's consideration of factors other than air quality is not precluded by anything in §7545(k)(8); in this case, moreover, that consideration appears to be congruent with both the congressional purpose not to disrupt the market for imported gasoline and the Supreme Court's instruction to avoid an interpretation that would put a law of the United States into conflict with a treaty obligation of the United States. For these reasons we deem the EPA's interpretation of the anti-dumping provision a reasonable one; pursuant to Chevron step two, therefore, we must uphold it.

COMMENTARY & QUESTIONS

1. **Judicial review in a foreign policy setting.** As implicitly recognized by the court in the *Warren* case, adverse reports of WTO dispute settlement panels and its Appellate Body have no domestic legal effect. The Appellate Body's report from a legal point of view is a non-event and cannot affect the statutory mandate in the CAA. To that extent, this case has a similar posture to *Japan Whaling*. Nonetheless, the D.C. Circuit seemed to give that report considerable weight. Exactly what was the legal significance of the report, and how did it play a role in the decision from an analytical point of view? Is the D.C. Circuit's approach a good or bad thing from a principled point of view? Is it likely to foster or hinder efforts to protect the environment? What if anything does this case add to your understanding of the *Chevron* rule? Was this an appropriate case for application of the *Chevron* approach?

2. **The WTO and the rule of law.** Although it did not expressly say so, the D.C. Circuit seems to have relied on a general inclination of the courts to defer to the executive in matters of foreign relations. One of the motivations behind the creation of the WTO

was to shift toward a more rule-based system than in the old GATT, with the creation of the Appellate Body a principal component of that agenda. While removal of the governmental action — the "measure" in the parlance of trade agreements — is the preferred remedy, there is disagreement even among eminent trade scholars as to whether there is a legal obligation to do so. WTO panels have the power to award compensation to the prevailing party, suggesting that WTO member states may instead choose to maintain the measure and to subject themselves to retaliatory trade measures imposed by the winning party. What arguments would you make to the D.C. Circuit on behalf of your clients, U.S. environmental groups and domestic petroleum refiners, in support of the proposition that the court should give effect to the domestic statutory mandate notwithstanding the foreign policy consequences?

3. **Trade-based measures to protect the environment.** Environmental measures that employ trade sanctions have been a particular focus of concern under the WTO regime. These include unilateral measures such as the Pelly Amendment, as well as multilateral ones. Do you see why these might be considered to violate the basic GATT/WTO disciplines — MFN, national treatment, and the prohibition on quantitative restrictions? To deal with such situations, the GATT contains exceptions in Article XX, an "escape clause" that in effect authorize states to maintain measures even if they violate the trade disciplines. Two paragraphs of Article XX are of particular relevance to environmental measures:

> Subject to the requirement that such measures are not applied in a manner which would constitute a means of arbitrary or unjustifiable discrimination between countries where the same conditions prevail, or a disguised restriction on international trade, nothing in this Agreement shall be construed to prevent the adoption or enforcement by any contracting party of measures:
>
> > (b) necessary to protect human, animal or plant life or health; [or]
> >
> > (g) relating to the conservation of exhaustible natural resources if such measures are made effective in conjunction with restrictions on domestic production or consumption.

Can you argue on behalf of an environmental group that trade restrictions adopted under the Pelly Amendment meet this test? How would you formulate an argument on behalf of a government challenging U.S. restrictions under Pelly? Can you make similar arguments for the trade restrictions in the Montreal Protocol on Substances that Deplete the Ozone Layer (discussed in Chapter 15), which provide trade advantages to states party to the Protocol and discriminate against non-parties? Based on the text of Article XX, can you make an argument that multilateral measures such as those in the Protocol ought to be more likely to meet the test for application of the exceptions than unilateral measures, including sanctions under the Pelly Amendment?

Section 4. THE NAFTA ENVIRONMENTAL SIDE AGREEMENT: CITIZEN SUBMISSIONS ON ENFORCEMENT

The public debate over NAFTA was fierce. From the environmental side, concerns arose over the vulnerability of environmental regulations like that on reformulated gasoline, the potential for a "race to the bottom" as environmental regulations are relaxed, the lack of institutional capability on environmental matters, and the possibility that even multilateral environmental agreements such as the Montreal Protocol might face trade-based challenges. From the trade point of view, there were symmetrical worries over the abuse of environmental measures for protectionist purposes, the deployment of unilateral trade-based actions including the Pelly Amendment to address international environmental challenges, and the consideration of trade measures in multilateral instruments or by multilateral bodies dealing with environmental hazards. The implication of much of the public policy discussion was that there was a zero-sum set of tradeoffs between the two.

Although NAFTA was negotiated by the first Bush Administration, Congress had not adopted implementing legislation before the expiration of his term. Presidential candidate Bill Clinton voiced strong support for NAFTA, provided that environmental and labor concerns were addressed. Upon assuming office as President, Clinton declined to renegotiate the NAFTA text, instead advocating the adoption of new "side agreements" on environment and labor. The resulting North American Agreement on Environmental Cooperation (NAAEC, the "Side Agreement")[11] did not alter, amend, or clarify the NAFTA text. Instead, the NAAEC establishes a trilateral Commission for Environmental Cooperation (CEC) headed by a council consisting of the environment ministers of the three NAFTA states, which in the case of the United States is the Administrator of the EPA. The CEC is serviced by a professional secretariat in Montreal and advised by a committee of Canadian, Mexican, and U.S. nationals appointed in their personal capacities.

According to President Clinton, the principal environmental concern was not a divergence in national standards among the three NAFTA countries and a potential "race to the bottom." According to the three governments negotiating the Side Agreement, the more pressing need was to provide effective enforcement mechanisms for fully implementing existing national laws. The Side Agreement consequently assigned the CEC Secretariat the responsibility to receive and process citizen submissions alleging that one of the NAFTA parties has failed effectively to enforce its domestic law, as specified in Articles 14 and 15 of the agreement. The CEC citizen submission process is a major innovation in public international law, which ordinarily is confined to articulating a flow of rights and obligations among states and acknowledges no role for individuals, environmental organizations, and corporations that are not "subjects" of international law.

The NAFTA Article 14/15 process begins when a nongovernmental organization or individual lodges a submission with the CEC Secretariat alleging that one of the three NAFTA governments "is failing to effectively enforce its environmental law." The Secretariat first conducts an initial consideration of the admissibility of the submission, determines whether the submission warrants developing a factual record, and transmits its recommendation to the CEC Council. The Council, by two-thirds vote, then instructs the Secretariat whether to prepare a factual record. After the Secretariat

11. Sept. 8–14, 1993, U.S.-Can.-Mex., 32 I.L.M. 1482 (1993). The NAAEC was not authorized by the fast-track legislation that preceded negotiation of NAFTA, leading some to question the legal authority for the Side Agreement's inclusion in the NAFTA package submitted to Congress.

prepares a factual record the Council, by two-thirds vote, decides whether to make the factual record public.

At the time of the negotiations on the Side Agreement, the emphasis on enforcement and implementation was primarily directed at Mexico. In the years since, however, there have been several high-profile cases against Canada, including one alleging that the government of Canada had failed to ensure the protection of fish and fish habitat in British Columbia's rivers from environmental damage caused by hydroelectric dams. The first submission against the United States was filed in 1999. Bringing the subject matter of this chapter full circle, that submission alleges that the U.S. government is failing to effectively enforce §703 of the MBTA, which prohibits the killing of migratory birds without a permit.

Final Factual Record for Submission SEM-99-002
(Migratory Birds) (2003)
<http://www.cec.org/files/pdf/sem/MigratoryBirds-FFR_EN.pdf>

The first case involved the destruction of a great blue heron rookery near Arcata, California, in April 1996. The logging took place under the direction of the owner of the land containing the rookery and it destroyed at least five great blue heron nests, at least some of which contained eggs, plus at least one fledgling great blue heron. A registered professional forester [named Scott Feller] prepared a Notice of Conversion Exemption Timber Operations on the basis that the timber harvest involved less than three acres, but the Notice was not approved by the California Department of Forestry and Fire Protection (CDF) prior to the logging, as required by California law. Consistent with state law, the Notice required that no sites of rare, threatened or endangered plants or animals or species of special concern, such as great blue herons, be disturbed, threatened or damaged during the logging.

After neighbors contacted state wildlife enforcement authorities, the CDF and the [California Department of Fish and Game (CDFG)] launched an investigation on 10 April 1996. These neighbors later sent the [federal Fish and Wildlife Service (FWS), an agency of the Department of the Interior] a letter, dated 16 April 1996, regarding the rookery destruction. The FWS did not participate in the investigation, but the CDFG investigating officer was a deputized US deputy game warden with authority to investigate both state and federal violations of law, including violations of MBTA §703. After the landowner pleaded no contest to six misdemeanor violations of state law, the district attorney recommended the maximum sentence of six months in jail and a $2,700 fine. The county probation office recommended that the landowner be ordered to pay $310,000 in restitution as well. On 9 December 1998, the landowner was sentenced to 120 days in county jail, a fine of $540 and three years' probation, with no order of restitution....

The FWS first became aware of the destruction of the great blue heron rookery upon receipt of the 16 April 1996 letter from the landowners' neighbors. The FWS had no MBTA permitting program that applied to the logging activity that took place, and had no ongoing program for inspecting or monitoring logging operations to determine compliance with the MBTA....

In the view of the FWS, once the state's prosecution of the landowner was completed, it was inappropriate for the FWS to seek federal prosecution under the United States Department of Justice's "Petite Policy." The Petite Policy establishes guidelines for deciding whether to bring a federal prosecution based on conduct involved in a prior state or federal proceeding. The Petite Policy provides an explanation for why the United States believes federal enforcement would have been inappropriate. The United States informed the Secretariat that the Petite Policy was applicable to the landowner, who was convicted and sentenced in a state proceeding. By contrast, it is not clear that the Petite Policy was applicable in connection with the registered professional forester, as to whom the state dismissed criminal charges and sought administrative sanctions.

Under the Petite Policy, for federal prosecution to have proceeded following completion of the state's action against the landowner, the federal government would have had to determine that the case involved a substantial federal interest, that the state prosecution left that interest demonstrably unvindicated, that the landowner's conduct constituted a federal offense, and that he could be convicted on admissible evidence. In addition, the Assistant Attorney General for Environment and Natural Resources, U.S. Department of Justice, would have had to approve a federal prosecution. Last, federal prosecutors would still retain discretion not to pursue the case.

In regard to whether the case involved a substantial federal interest, one might consider the FWS's conclusion that the case was a high priority for investigation because it involved a wild population of a species protected under the MBTA. One might also consider the view of FWS officials that great blue herons are likely to be given special consideration in regard to enforcement of the MBTA because they are colonial nesters.

Regarding whether the state prosecution left the federal interest in protecting migratory birds demonstrably unvindicated, one might consider the district attorney's opinion that the maximum punishment available under state law is insufficient given the nature of the crime in assessing whether additional federal penalties could or should have been sought under the MBTA. Although significant penalties were imposed in MBTA cases that the United States describes as similar, it is not clear that significant additional punishment could have been obtained against the landowner with an MBTA prosecution. The United States and the CDF believe that the state enforcement action adequately addressed the landowner's conduct.

As to the likelihood of success, the evidence that led to the landowner's conviction under state charges might have supported a federal MBTA prosecution as well. The United States asserts that the case would have been a high priority for investigation and that logging that kills birds will be prosecuted in appropriate circumstances when a violation of the MBTA can be proven. However, a federal MBTA prosecution might have raised significant legal issues. As far as the United States is aware, a prosecution against the landowner would have been the first MBTA §703 prosecution ever sought in connection with a logging operation since the MBTA was enacted in 1918. One possible outcome would be a broad ruling that the MBTA does not apply to any unintentional, yet direct takes, contrary to the United States' successful prosecutions, none involving logging, of unintentional takes resulting from otherwise lawful activities. Such an outcome would be a significant setback to the FWS's overall program for enforcing the MBTA. The law in the United States on the applicability of the MBTA to unintentional takings, as opposed to intentional takings resulting from activities such as hunting, is conflicting and unsettled, at least in the context of timber harvesting....

The cases interpreting §703 of the MBTA have unanimously rejected the proposition that habitat modification or loss alone is sufficient to amount to a violation of the taking prohibition. The cases are split, however, on the question of whether §703 of the MBTA prohibits unintentional as well as intentional takes, at least in the context of logging....

A central assertion in submission SEM-99-002 is that it is the unofficial policy and practice of the United States government not to enforce §703 of the MBTA in connection with logging operations. The Submitters rely chiefly on responses to Freedom of Information Act (FOIA) requests indicating that the United States has never sought a prosecution under MBTA in connection with a logging operation, and on an unsigned, unofficial memorandum from the Chief of the FWS that states:

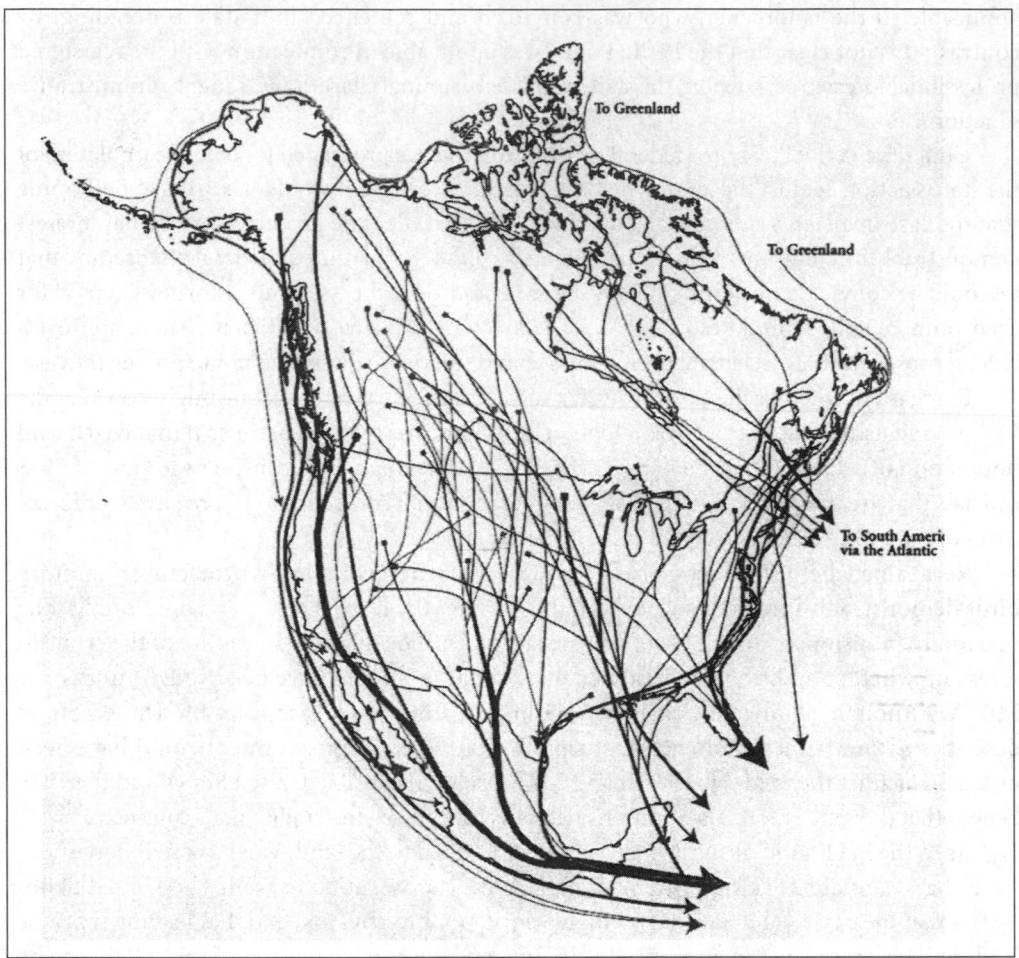

FIGURE 8-1
The migratory bird flyways of North America, including the flyways of land birds, birds of prey, waterfowl, seabirds, shorebirds, and wading birds. Source: North American Commission for Environmental Cooperation, State of the Environment Report (2002).

The [FWS] has had a longstanding, unwritten policy relative to the MBTA that no enforcement or investigative action should be taken in incidents involving logging operations that result in the taking of non-endangered, non-threatened migratory birds and/or their nests.... The Service will continue to enforce the MBTA in accordance with this longstanding policy.

The United States informed the Secretariat that to the best of its knowledge, the United States has never sought to prosecute under the MBTA an incident involving a logging operation. The United States confirms that in response to FOIA requests, it found no record of any such prosecutions. Representatives of the United States also informed the Secretariat that, to the best of their knowledge, federal prosecutions of either of the two cases referenced in Council Resolution 01-10 would have been the first ever prosecution of the MBTA in connection with a logging operation. The United States asserts that the absence to date of any federal prosecutions of the MBTA in connection with logging operations reflects an exercise of prosecutorial discretion and allocation of resources to higher enforcement priorities....

On one hand, the United States asserts that logging that kills birds will be prosecuted in appropriate circumstances when a violation of the MBTA can be proven. The United States informed the Secretariat that "appropriate circumstances" are more likely in cases involving the taking of colonial nesters such as great blue herons, or destruction of their nests or eggs. As noted above, the evidence might have supported a successful federal MBTA prosecution against Wallace [the landowner] as well, putting aside the legal issues that might have been raised. Therefore, the Wallace case might have provided an opportunity to set a precedent in regard to enforcement of the MBTA in connection with logging operations. The district attorney's conclusion that the state's case against Feller lacked sufficient evidence linking Feller with the taking of birds might be taken into account in considering the likelihood of a successful MBTA case against Feller.

Evidentiary considerations aside, a federal MBTA action against Wallace would have been, as far as the United States is aware, the first case ever brought under the MBTA in connection with a logging operation. As noted above, the United States explains that the lack to date of any MBTA prosecutions in connection to logging operations is the result of enforcement discretion.... These examples are consistent with the federal government's record to date of never having enforced the MBTA in regard to logging operations....

COMMENTARY & QUESTIONS

1. **"Factual records" on "failures to enforce": law, fact, or paper tigers?** As this NAAEC blue heron file excerpt indicates, NAFTA's Side Agreement provides, as a remedy, the production of a "factual record" in response to allegations that one of the three government parties to the agreement "is failing to effectively enforce its environmental law." The blue heron factual record demonstrates the tension inherent in this formulation. The Secretariat collects "facts" concerning effective enforcement but is constrained from reaching a conclusion by reference to the legal test of "failing effectively to enforce." The Secretariat phrases its findings by preceding them with the apparently tepid observation "one might...." The last section of the migratory birds factual record is not entitled "Conclusion," but merely "Closing Note." Is this likely an oversight on the part of the drafters of the NAAEC? In the United States, an allegation of failure to enforce the law is very difficult to prove in a suit for judicial review of administrative action. Although regulatory norms governing the behavior of private parties established by administrative agencies such as the Fish and Wildlife Service can be attacked, the government's exercise of its enforcement discretion is largely shielded from review. As demonstrated by the MBTA factual record, the Article 14/15 process, by contrast, anticipates at least modest inquiries into this sensitive area in which the CEC Secretariat evaluates the effectiveness of enforcement efforts and reflects on their likely outcome. Does the NAAEC Article 14/15 process provide an effective vehicle for closing this gap in domestic law? Does the MBTA factual record succeed in convincing you one way or the other as to the effectiveness of U.S. enforcement despite the fact that it does not come to a formal conclusion on this point?

2. **Assuring the effectiveness of the NAAEC.** The independence of the professional Secretariat, which in principle reports to the trilateral Commission and not to individual governments, and the three governments' attempts to constrain or micromanage the process of preparing a factual record, has been an ongoing theme in the implemen-

tation of the citizen submission process. The process is particularly susceptible to political manipulation at the interim step at which the three governments decide whether to authorize the Secretariat to move to the next phase, the preparation of a factual record. In the MBTA case, the United States refused to authorize a wide-ranging inquiry into its alleged failure to enforce the statute, instead confining the Secretariat to examining only those specific instances that had been identified in the submission. Can you explain why the process might have been drafted to put representatives of the three NAFTA parties in this crucial gatekeeping role? As an advocate representing a citizen submitter in the Article 14/15 process, what actions would you take to improve the likelihood that the three ministers comprising the CEC Council would authorize the Secretariat to prepare a factual record?

3. **Safe harbors for delinquent governments.** The NAAEC provides a number of jurisdictional exceptions for

- "any statute or regulation...directly related to worker safety or health" (Article 45(2)(a)(iii)); and
- domestic measures "the primary purpose of which is managing the commercial harvest or exploitation...of natural resources" (Article 45(2)(b)).

There are other defenses, invoked by the United States in the MBTA case, available to governments that justify non-enforcement in a situation that

- "reflects a reasonable exercise of...discretion in respect of investigatory, prosecutorial, regulatory or compliance matters" (Article 45(1)(a)); or
- "results from bona fide decisions to allocate resources to enforcement in respect of environmental matters determined to have higher priorities" (Article 45(1)(b)).

Governments may rely on these criteria as a basis for explaining their own decisions to vote against the preparation of a factual record. Assuming a factual record is prepared, the Secretariat then applies these defenses related to the exercise of enforcement discretion and allocation of enforcement resources. One might think that these defenses would justify almost any action and that the Article 14/15 process would consequently be a "nothing-burger." The information related to those justifications, however, is almost exclusively in the hands of governments, which may then find themselves in something of a Catch-22: either provide sensitive enforcement information to the Secretariat for its evaluation as to whether the governmental decisions were "reasonable" and "bona fide," or withhold it and forgo the defense. If you were representing a government alleged to be failing to effectively enforce its domestic environmental law in a situation like the MBTA case, how would you structure your client's case in light of these considerations? What constraints would you expect to encounter, both from the text of the NAAEC and from the broader institutional and political setting? As a representative of one of the organizations that sponsored the submission, how could you put these insights to use in structuring your case?

4. **What's it good for anyway?** A factual record in an Article 14/15 case has no domestic legal force. Under what circumstances might this channel serve as a useful advocacy tool? Is there anything going on here beyond the "mobilization of shame"? If you were

representing one of the organizations that sponsored the submission in the MBTA case, how, and in what institutional settings, could you use the Secretariat's factual record in your efforts as a policy advocate on behalf of the environment?

5. Do NAAEC factual records return home to roost as supplements to domestic law? As noted in Chapter 7, obtaining judicial review of executive branch enforcement is not always easy. Against this backdrop, an Article 14/15 factual record dealing with the United States serves the very useful purpose of providing an external, independent evaluation of agencies' enforcement of environmental laws that can rarely, if ever, be obtained under domestic law. A CEC factual record could be interpreted as filling a gap in our national legal system by providing an international remedy where the domestic counterpart is inadequate or lacking — a well-accepted approach supported by the United States in such areas as human rights. Although the agreement is silent as to subsequent follow-up, viewed in this light the NAAEC would complement domestic environmental statutes in a meaningful way by providing a standard against which environmental groups, Congress, and the public can measure executive branch performance on environmental enforcement.

This issue came to a head in September 2003 when the CEC Working Group on Environmental Enforcement and Compliance Cooperation was preparing a strategic plan to shape its future efforts. One of this coursebook's authors, a member of a federal advisory committee overseeing the work of the CEC, suggested in a formal comment that the Working Group should itself keep track of and publicize the subsequent implementation of factual records by the NAFTA countries. The Working Group declined to do so on the theory that appropriate follow-up for factual records was up to national governments and not the multilateral CEC. The U.S. Justice Department stated that it intended to follow up on factual records with relevant agencies, but only "informally" and with no explanation to the public. Does this mean that the whole CEC Article 14/15 process is a waste of time?

Since the 1999 filing of the Migratory Bird submission — the first and only submission against the United States to proceed to a full factual record — there have been no further factual records undertaken against non-enforcement by the United States. The governments of the other NAFTA countries, however, appear to have been more responsive to the embarrassment, pressure, and leverage created by a factual record, a factor that may account for the larger number of submissions against them. As of this writing, there have been 19 submissions concerning Mexico, resulting in three factual records with two more in preparation. Fourteen submissions against Canada have resulted in four published factual records on a number of sensitive resource-based issues such as fishing, mining, and logging. The evolving domestic effect of this international law process will continue to be interesting and relevant.

Regulations, the wisdom, necessity, and validity of which, as applied to existing conditions, are…apparent,…a century ago or even a half a century ago probably would have been rejected as arbitrary and oppressive.… While the meaning of the constitutional guaranties never varies, the scope of their application must expand or contract to meet the new and different conditions which are constantly coming within the field of their operation. In a changing world it is impossible that it should be otherwise.

— Sutherland, J., in Euclid v. Ambler, 272 U.S. 365, 387 (1926)

PART THREE

A VARIETY OF STATUTORY APPROACHES

AN INTRODUCTION TO THE NEXT ELEVEN CHAPTERS' "TAXONOMY" OF ENVIRONMENTAL STATUTORY DESIGNS

The next eleven chapters set out an analytical structure for studying modern environmental statutes, which are remarkable for their number and diversity. (The Statutory Capsule Appendix in the Reference Materials at the back of this coursebook catalogues fifty major statutes, and many more than that play significant roles in particular cases.) No book can cover all environmental statutes — the Clean Air Act, Clean Water Act, or Superfund could each more than fill an entire semester of readings. The compromise chosen here is to study selected statutes — analyzing their structures, processes, and enforcement mechanisms, their successes and failures — to facilitate the analysis and understanding of other statutes to be encountered. Each chapter focuses on one specific legislative design and approach to environmental protection, with most chapters focusing on a primary statutory example.

The chapters are organized around a set of analytical categories, each emphasizing a particular strategy for defining and then implementing environmental standards, each presenting tactical advantages and disadvantages. Every statute's actual performance, of course, is also affected to a major degree by its context in the politics and economics of its day.

By understanding a taxonomy of statutory types, environmental lawyers can improve the depth, breadth, and speed of their analyses of new statutes, as well as their command of issues arising in established statutory fields. The categories set out in the taxonomy used here, of course, are not airtight. Much overlapping exists among different statutory types, and some statutes contain multiple approaches and functions. The Resource Conservation and Recovery Act in Chapter 18, for example, is a composite of many of the strategies analyzed elsewhere in Chapters 9 to 19.

HERE IS A BRIEF DIGEST of the next eleven chapters, illustrating this coursebook's "taxonomic" approach to statutory analysis —

CHAPTER 9. FEDERAL AGENCY DISCLOSURE: NEPA'S STOP-AND-THINK LOGIC, AND THE POWER OF INFORMATION. "Information is power" in environmental law as well as in business. The statutory design strategy of mandatory disclosure of official information, enforced by citizen lawsuits, can raise the political and economic visibility of agencies' environmentally degrading activities. The premise is that improved information will lead to improved enforcement, resource conservation, and pollution prevention, as well as improved political acknowledgment of the problems presented. The National Environmental Policy Act is the prime example.

CHAPTER 10. CORPORATE DISCLOSURE: SHAPING PRIVATE RESPONSE BY REQUIRED PRODUCTION OF INFORMATION. The information-disclosure statutory strategy is also applied in the corporate setting and is thought by some observers to be one of the most effective forms of shaping corporate behavior. The chapter explores the Emergency Planning and Community Right-to-Know Act and California's Proposition 65, two different types of corporate disclosure statutes.

CHAPTER 11. HARM-BASED AMBIENT STANDARDS: THE CLEAN AIR ACT. This chapter examines the first of the major command-and-control comprehensive prescriptive federal regulatory systems. The Clean Air Act of 1970 and its reiterations undertake the definition of nationwide federal air quality emissions standards, primarily based on a complex process of measuring potential harm to human health from different levels of ambient air pollution, deriving minimum federal baselines for safe levels of emissions, and then implementing them through complex regulatory structures in every state.

CHAPTER 12. TECHNOLOGY-BASED STANDARD-SETTING: THE CLEAN WATER ACT. The 1972 CWA is a command-and-control system quite different from the CAA. The CWA is a sophisticated regulatory system in which the basic federal standards, to be applied nationwide, are defined by an EPA review of each category of industry that discharges pollution, in order to determine which pollution control technologies are available and economically achievable. Performance standards, based on the results of adopting those best technologies, are then set each category of dischargers and included in discharge permits.

CHAPTER 13. STANDARD-SETTING VIA COST-BENEFIT PROCEDURES. Broad contextual consideration of costs, benefits, and alternatives has always been part of the basic logic of environmental policy positions, although numerical analysis has always been an erratic, imperfect art. Although the public harms and the benefits of regulation are difficult to quantify, it is relatively easy for industry to come up with numbers for the costs that regulation places upon them. In recent years, a number of initiatives, primarily sponsored by industry interests, have sought to establish cost-benefit numerical calculations as the prescriptive basis of regulatory standards.

CHAPTER 14. MARKET-ENLISTING STATUTORY STRATEGIES: POLLUTION TRADING AND OTHER ECONOMIC INCENTIVES. The basic command-and-control environmental regulatory systems have been very effective but often have aroused criticism, not just from resistant industries, for their tendency toward ponderousness and rigidity. Market-enlisting mechanisms are becoming increasingly important in environmental law as supplements to command-and-control approaches. The marketplace is historically a superb mechanism for shaping behavior and getting things done, and the new approaches are designed to invite active industry participation — not as a governmental abdication of regulatory function to the private marketplace but rather as a practical strategy for enlisting its devices in attempts to improve the adjustability and effectiveness of regulation. Taxes, subsidies, preferential governmental purchasing, trading, and other market mechanisms are examined, with special emphasis on the Clean Air Act's program of tradeable sulphur dioxide emissions rights.

CHAPTER 15. TECHNOLOGY-FORCING STANDARDS. In cases where pollution threats are unmistakable, imminent, and serious, legislatures sometimes set standards at levels so stringent that they cannot be achieved with available technology. Target polluters must either develop new pollution control technology or prevent pollution by product reformulation or process changes. The CAA's auto pollution control provisions and the international phaseout of chlorofluorocarbons are studied as illustrations of successful technology-forcing.

CHAPTER 16. ROADBLOCK STRATEGIES: STARK PROHIBITIONS AND THEIR VIABILITY. Statutory roadblocks, such as the Endangered Species Act's stark prohibition on federal activities that are likely to jeopardize the continued existence of an endangered species or substantially modify its critical habitat, are prominent features of environmental law. But statutory detours — means of avoiding these absolute prohibitions — are necessary to ensure the political acceptability of roadblocks. The ESA's evolution is traced in order to show the legal and political interplay between roadblocks and their detours.

CHAPTER 17. PRODUCT REGULATION AND MARKET-ACCESS STRATEGIES: PESTICIDES AND TOXICS. Product regulation is an efficient means of regulating large manufacturers. Requiring governmental approval before potentially dangerous products can be sold is an effective, proactive way to protect human health and the environment. But product regulation and restrictions on market access run squarely against the grain of the American free market economic system. Consequently, the two environmental statutes that fundamentally incorporate this strategy — the Federal Insecticide, Fungicide, and Rodenticide Act and the Toxic Substances Control Act — have been, at best, only moderately successful.

CHAPTER 18. LIFE-CYCLE WASTE CONTROL STRATEGIES: RCRA'S "CRADLE-TO-GRAVE" REGULATION. The Resource Conservation and Recovery Act regulates hazardous wastes from creation to ultimate disposal. It is also a composite of all the taxonomic statutory strategies presented in the surrounding chapters. Special attention is paid to the criteria for determining whether a waste is "hazardous" and to RCRA's roadblock "land ban" that prohibits the disposal of hazardous wastes on land unless they have been treated to technology-based standards.

CHAPTER 19. REMEDIAL LIABILITY STRATEGIES: TOXIC CLEANUPS AND THEIR FUNDING UNDER CERCLA AND STATE PROGRAMS. Cleanup statutes constitute a deterrent to pollution, as well as ensuring that contaminated sites will be remediated so as not to pose a threat to current and future generations of humans and their environments. But cleanup statutes, as represented by the Comprehensive Environmental Response, Compensation, and Liability Act, pose difficult policy questions with regard to liability, cost-allocation, funding, implementation, and cleanup goals.

Chapter 9

FEDERAL AGENCY DISCLOSURE: NEPA'S STOP-AND-THINK LOGIC, AND THE POWER OF INFORMATION

A. *NEPA, the National Environmental Policy Act*
B. *NEPA in Court: The First Generation*
C. *NEPA's International Implications*

This chapter focuses on the broadest, most coherent, and best-known statutory model of an environmental disclosure statute — the National Environmental Policy Act (NEPA) — which tries to induce federal agencies to stop and think before launching projects that harm the environment. NEPA enforces that objective with environmental impact statement (EIS) information-disclosure procedures that repeatedly have been enforced by citizen litigation.

NEPA is by no means the only environmental statute to have an information-disclosure element, although it is more central in NEPA than in many others. Much of environmental law is concerned with obtaining information, organizing it, and directing it to where it can do the most legal and political good. "Information Is Power" in environmental policymaking because if the media and the public have critical information on the negatives of a dubious proposal, the public inclinations toward environmental protection often will produce a corrective decision in court or in the political arena. Getting strategic information into open public debate is often more than half the battle, especially where the availability of direct citizen enforcement mechanisms can make information regarding environmental threats actionable by members of the public, without the intervention of governmental agencies.

Thus information-disclosure components can be found in many environmental statutes, especially federal. The biological assessment mechanism of §7 of the ESA pressures federal wildlife agencies to examine and publish the factual biological vulnerabilities of endangered species populations, forcing many potential conflicts into the open that otherwise would be lost in bureaucratic bogs. Pollution statutes often are linked to public information, requiring submission of data to governmental agencies with a strong presumption in favor of public availability.[1] Product regulation and market access statutes typically require the intensive development and production of information regarding product safety as a core regulatory element. Market-enlisting statutes can succeed or fail depending on the availability of good data on the physical conditions to be addressed as well as the economic and financial impacts of taxes and

---

1. See, e.g., CWA §308(a), 33 U.S.C. §1318(a).

incentives. Effective enforcement and informal dispute resolution demand reliable data of all varieties. The public trust doctrine in part operates to discourage low-visibility decisionmaking by requiring public ventilation of information and consideration of it by responsible political or legal institutions. And international law often operates far more by information generation and production than by mandate.

A. NEPA, THE NATIONAL ENVIRONMENTAL POLICY ACT

NEPA[2] is a statute that provokes a wide diversity of reactions. To some it is a paper tiger, of awesome but toothless aspect. To others, it is a ringing statutory declaration of environmental protection and rational human governance that sets a precedent of international significance. To some it is an unproductive attempt to intrude on productive public-private enterprises. To others, it is a legislative accident (whether fortunate or unfortunate) that was created and continues to evolve by happenstance. As usual, there is probably some truth in each of these perspectives.

Ultimately, NEPA's successes may be impossible to measure, in part because its effectiveness includes the anonymous thousands of destructive federal projects that are withdrawn, or never proposed in the first place, in anticipation of NEPA scrutiny.

In taxonomic form, a distinct new model of statutory regulation can be discerned within NEPA's provisions: NEPA is a broad stop-and-think, disclose-to-the-public administrative law. It is general in its statutory commands — a broad, simple set of directives that apply across the board to all federal agencies. Its operative terms require agencies to contemplate the context and consequences of their actions before acting, in effect mandating a particularized process of program planning, intended to begin early in the genesis of agency decisions. Public disclosure is NEPA's complementary mandate: Agencies must produce a publicly reviewable physical document reflecting the required internal project analysis. Preparation of this document is supposed to ensure that the agency has given "good faith consideration" to the environmental consequences of its proposed action and its reasonable alternatives, but, in practice, this assumption is frequently false.

The rationality of this requirement — requiring documented formal consideration of negatives and alternatives as well as benefits before acting — may be obvious, but NEPA was its pioneer. Its logic has subsequently been adopted in many international and domestic systems. The potent nonenvironmental forces that NEPA attempts to control, however, have kept up a running resistance to its statutory mandates, with some successes over the years.

NEPA at its best becomes a component of the administrative process, shaping the environmentally related content of the administrative decisionmaking record on proposals for major federal actions that might produce significant environmental consequences. Compliance with NEPA strengthens federal agency decisions against potential judicial invalidation for arbitrary and capricious failures to consider relevant environmental factors or because agencies have not adequately explained the

2. 42 U.S.C. §§4321 et seq., Pub. L. No. 91-190 (1970).

environmental implications of their decisionmaking process. Beyond NEPA there are a number of other important information-forcing statutes (see Chapter 10).

Here is the text of NEPA as it was signed into law by Richard Nixon on January 1, 1970. As you read it, note its terms, its style, its poetry, and the regulatory approaches it consciously or unconsciously incorporated.

Public Law 91-190 (1970)

AN ACT: To establish a national policy for the environment, to provide for the establishment of a Council on Environmental Quality, and for other purposes.

Be it enacted by the Senate and House of Representatives of the United States of America in Congress assembled, that this Act may be cited as the "National Environmental Policy Act of 1969."

Title I. Declaration of National Environmental Policy

Sec. 101 (a) The Congress, recognizing the profound impact of man's activity on the interrelations of all components of the natural environment, particularly the profound influences of population growth, high-density urbanization, industrial expansion, resource exploitation, and new and expanding technological advances and recognizing further the critical importance of restoring and maintaining environmental quality to the overall welfare and development of man, declares that it is the continuing policy of the Federal Government, in cooperation with State and local governments, and other concerned public and private organizations, to use all practicable means and measures, including financial and technological assistance, in a manner calculated to foster and promote the general welfare, to create and maintain conditions under which man and nature can exist in productive harmony, and fulfill the social, economic, and other requirements of present and future generations of Americans.

(b) In order to carry out the policy set forth in this Act, it is the continuing responsibility of the Federal Government to use all practicable means, consistent with other essential considerations of national policy, to improve and coordinate Federal plans, functions, programs, and resources to the end that the Nation may—

(1) fulfill the responsibilities of each generation as trustee of the environment for succeeding generations; (2) assure for all Americans safe, healthful, productive, and esthetically and culturally pleasing surroundings; (3) attain the widest range of beneficial uses of the environment without degradation, risk to health or safety, or other undesirable and unintended consequences; (4) preserve important historic, cultural, and natural aspects of our national heritage, and maintain, wherever possible, an environment which supports diversity and variety of individual choice; (5) achieve a balance between population and resource use which will permit high standards of living and a wide sharing of life's amenities; and (6) enhance the quality of renewable resources and approach the maximum attainable recycling of depletable resources.

(c) The Congress recognizes that each person should enjoy a healthful environment and that each person has a responsibility to contribute to the preservation and enhancement of the environment.

Sec. 102. The Congress authorizes and directs that, to the fullest extent possible:

(1) The policies, regulations, and public laws of the United States shall be interpreted and administered in accordance with the policies set forth in this Act, and

(2) all agencies of the Federal Government shall—

(A) utilize a systematic, interdisciplinary approach which will insure the integrated use of the natural and social sciences and the environmental design arts in planning and in decisionmaking which may have an impact on man's environment;

(B) identify and develop methods and procedures, in consultation with the Council on Environmental Quality established by title II of this Act, which will insure that presently unquantified environmental amenities and values may be given appropriate consideration in decisionmaking along with economic and technical considerations;

(C) include in every recommendation or report on proposals for legislation and other major Federal actions significantly affecting the quality of the human environment, a detailed statement by the responsible official on —

(i) the environmental impact of the proposed action,

(ii) any adverse environmental effects which cannot be avoided should the proposal be implemented,

(iii) alternatives to the proposed action,

(iv) the relationship between local short-term uses of man's environment and the maintenance and enhancement of long-term productivity, and

(v) any irreversible and irretrievable commitments of resources which would be involved in the proposed action should it be implemented.

Prior to making any detailed statement, the responsible Federal official shall consult with and obtain the comments of any Federal agency which has jurisdiction by law or special expertise with respect to any environmental impact involved. Copies of such statement and the comments and views of the appropriate Federal, State, and local agencies, which are authorized to develop and enforce environmental standards shall be made available to the President, the Council on Environmental Quality and to the public as provided by section 552 of Title 5, United States Code, and shall accompany the proposal through the existing agency review processes;

(D) study, develop, and describe appropriate alternatives to recommended courses of action in any proposal which involves unresolved conflicts concerning alternative uses of available resources;

(E) recognize the worldwide and long-range character of environmental problems and, where consistent with the foreign policy of the United States, lend appropriate support to initiatives, resolutions, and programs designed to maximize international cooperation in anticipating and preventing a decline in the quality of mankind's world environment;

(F) make available to States, counties, municipalities, institutions, and individuals, advice and information useful in restoring, maintaining, and enhancing the quality of the environment;

(G) initiate and utilize ecological information in the planning and development of resource-oriented projects; and

(H) assist the Council on Environmental Quality established by title II of this Act.

Sec. 103. All agencies of the Federal Government shall review their present statutory authority, administrative regulations, and current polices and procedures for the purpose of determining whether there are any deficiencies or inconsistencies therein which prohibit full compliance with the purposes and provisions of this Act....

Sec. 104. Nothing in Section 102 or 103 shall in any way affect the specific statutory obligations of any Federal agency (1) to comply with criteria or standards of environmental quality, (2) to coordinate or consult with any other Federal or State agency, or (3) to act, or refrain from acting contingent upon the recommendations or certification of any other Federal or State agency.

Sec. 105. The policies and goals set forth in this Act are supplementary to those set forth in existing authorizations of Federal agencies.

[Title II establishes the President's Council on Environmental Quality (CEQ), which gathers information and conducts studies on environmental trends and conditions, reviews federal government programs in light of NEPA's substantive goals, and recommends national policies for environmental improvement. By executive order, the CEQ issues regulations for coordinating federal agency compliance with NEPA. Exec. Order No. 11514 (1970), as amended by Exec. Order No. 11991 (1977).[3]]

---

3. 40 C.F.R. §§1500–1508. These regulations are the most complete guide to the interpretation of NEPA; when an important NEPA court decision is handed down, it is customarily codified here.

COMMENTARY & QUESTIONS

1. **NEPA as paper tiger.** Note that NEPA, as finally passed, contains a great deal of poetic language and precious little that is mandatory. There are ringing hortatory declarations of policy, and wistful commitments to processes of scientific rationality, especially in §101, and in most of §102. Does all this amount to anything? Is there anything in §101, purportedly the primary (i.e., "substantive") section of NEPA, that has any legal effect? Professor Oliver Houck concludes that §101 is not lawmaking in the ordinary sense: "Motivational as [the NEPA policies] may be, they lack the precision that would allow someone in our system, ultimately a reviewing court, to say, 'this is over the line.'" Houck, Is That All?, 11 Duke Envtl. L. & Pol'y F. 173, 180–181 (2000) (reviewing Lynton Keith Caldwell, National Environmental Policy Act, An Agenda for the Future (1998)).

There is, of course, the small matter of §102(2)(C) — NEPA's "procedural" subsection. Note that even that subsection is filled with vague verbiage; the instrumental words are limited to a couple of dozen out of two hundred. If you parse it carefully, however, §102(2)(C) levies a sole, narrow, statutory requirement: An EIS shall be prepared for all major federal actions significantly affecting the quality of the human environment. That deceptively simple requirement has produced virtually all NEPA case law. Nevertheless, even though there may be an enforceable EIS requirement, it seems merely procedural and does not purport to dictate substantive results. In other words, NEPA provides a right to information, not particular programmatic actions. Observing the course of application of NEPA to the intricate internal mechanisms of federal agencies, and the market forces with which they are linked, many observers have said that this procedural restraint is relatively meaningless. As Professor Sax wrote about NEPA, "I think the emphasis on the redemptive quality of procedural reform is about nine parts myth and one part coconut oil...,"[4] A sustained process in some federal courts, and many federal agencies over the years, has held NEPA to purely procedural terms and minimal formal compliance.

In continuing through these NEPA materials, therefore, note that they may chronicle a statutory program that some consider a symbolic assurance sham, not worth the extensive time and energies invested in it.

2. **NEPA as international milestone and state model.** NEPA can also be categorized as a remarkable, internationally pioneering declaration of a national policy of environmental sensitivity. Beyond the high principle of its declaration of policy, moreover, NEPA's EIS requirement is a novel strategic assertion of an all-too-obvious truth: Government agencies, like all other human actors, are prone to tunnel vision. The realities of a complex world require an institutionalized comprehensive stop-and-think review process within the governmental system itself. The NEPA model has been emulated by more than 25 states and over 80 countries around the world, and serves as a model for environmental impact assessments for such global institutions as the World Bank.[5]

---

4. Sax, The (Unhappy) Truth about NEPA, 26 Okla. L. Rev. 239 (1973).

5. Council on Environmental Quality, The National Environmental Policy Act: A Study of Its Effectiveness After Twenty-five Years (1997) (noted later in this chapter). See Robinson, International Trends in Environmental Impact Assessment, 19 B.C. Envtl. Aff. L. Rev. 591 (1991), and Robinson, SEQRA's Siblings: Precedents from Little NEPA's in the Sister States, 46 Alb. L. Rev. 1155 (1982) (state EIS development in the dozen years after NEPA).

In following the NEPA model, these other governmental entities have treated the impact statement process as an apt mechanism for achieving practical enforcement of the broad declarations of environmental policy that accompany it, and as a caveat to the administrative state that it look before it leaps.

3. **NEPA as accidental legislation.** The political reality underlying NEPA's legislative history was an extraordinary post-*Silent Spring*, late-1960s groundswell of popular attention to problems of environmental quality. Facing upcoming by-elections, Congress and President Nixon hastened to adjust to the issue. "The 1970s must be the years that America pays its debts to the past by reclaiming the purity of its air, its water, and our living environment. It is literally now or never," said Nixon. A number of legislative details, however, reveal the moderate intent of the President and Congress. As the various draft bills that became NEPA moved through the legislature in 1969 (as S. 1075 and H.R. 12549, 91st Cong., 1st Sess.), they initially were quite innocuous. Section 101 read then much as it does now; §102 merely called for governmental funding for environmental studies. Where teeth seemed to exist, they were pulled. Section 101(c) originally read: "The Congress recognizes that each person has a fundamental and inalienable *right* to a healthful environment...." and that was changed. Representative Wayne Aspinall of Colorado, a stalwart friend of the mining and lumber industries, was able to insert a provision into the House bill that "Nothing in this act shall increase, decrease, or change any responsibility or authority of any federal official or agency created by other provision of law.... " What was the effect of this provision? (It was changed in conference committee to read as in §§103–105, over Aspinall's objection.) And what does the actual title of the act tell you?

On April 16, 1969, however, in one of a seemingly endless series of small committee hearings, Professor Lynton Caldwell, a political scientist from Indiana University, mentioned in testimony before Senator Jackson's Interior Committee that he "would urge that in the shaping of such policy it have an action-forcing, operational aspect...." Chairman Jackson, to the surprise of his staff, picked up on this: "I agree with you that realistically what is needed in restructuring the governmental side of this problem is to legislatively create those situations that will bring about an action-forcing procedure that departments must comply with. Otherwise these lofty declarations are nothing more than that.... I am wondering if I may broaden the policy provision in the bill so as to lay down a general requirement that would be applicable to all agencies?"[6] Based on this brief interchange, Caldwell sat down with several staffers and drafted the text of the present §102. The underlying mood of Congress continued to be felt, however. Jackson accepted an amendment inserting the phrase "to the fullest extent possible" into §102, a phrase apparently intended to modify the otherwise strict command of its first sentence. In §102(2)(C), Jackson's language originally read that there had to be an environmental finding by the responsible official, a term that was amended to read

---

6. National Environmental Policy Act, 1969: Hearings on S. 1075, S. 233, and S. 1752 before the Senate Comm. on Interior and Insular Affairs, 91st Cong., 1st Sess. 116–117 (1969) (statement of Lynton Caldwell, Professor of Government, University of Indiana).

"statement," apparently to avoid the implication that there might be required findings of fact that would be judicially reviewable.[7]

Imagine the shock of Richard Nixon and many members of Congress when, early in 1970, they discovered that these apparently innocuous words of §102 could be the basis of very real lawsuits. Section 102, like a snake in the grass, contained the hidden but potent EIS requirement. Since then there have been thousands of NEPA lawsuits,[8] affecting federal projects and programs running into billions of dollars. Why didn't Congress recognize this potential? If Congress didn't recognize NEPA's potential, can courts nevertheless enforce the statute to give it precisely the judicial effect that Congress had tried to eliminate?

In the years immediately following NEPA's passage, almost 200 bills were introduced to weaken or repeal it. None passed. This indicates that, once passed, a "motherhood" statute is no less sacred for having been unintended. Isn't it likely, however, that Congress would have passed almost any proposed environmental statute, and that it was only an accident of the legislative process that produced a statute with some teeth? What does that say about the process?

4. **NEPA's de facto statutory strategy.** Despite NEPA's unintended, rather serendipitous legislative history, one can still analyze the provisions that emerged from Congress as embodying a novel de facto statutory strategy, as noted earlier.

First, whatever NEPA requires is government-wide, not a series of directives specifically tailored to particular governmental agencies. This umbrella approach provides strengths as well as weaknesses. Second, NEPA asserts a strong general declaration of policy that might be made relevant to a wide range of substantive interpretations and applications of various statutes, although this has not noticeably been the case. Third, the EIS procedure requires an internal process of overview accounting, specifying a detailed analysis of agency proposals. It pins down this required process with the EIS, a specific work product that provides tangible, reviewable evidence of the agency's compliance. The notion, moreover, that the EIS will accompany proposals through the decisional process may impose a practical timing requirement bringing environmental impact accounting into the earlier project stages.

There is no enforcement mechanism on the face of NEPA. Caldwell and the committee staff presumed that NEPA would be actively enforced by the President, acting through the Office of Management and Budget (OMB) and the Council of Environmental Quality (CEQ), and by Congress. In reality, as we shall soon see, enforcement, if it was to come, had to come from somewhere else.

Nevertheless, the statutory framework can be viewed as incorporating a coherent and quite novel regulatory logic. Through its provisions, even low-visibility agency decisions that might significantly impact the environment would have to be "ventilated"

---

7. For a complete history of NEPA's legislative genesis, see R. N. L. Andrews, Environmental Policy and Administrative Change (1976).

8. An analysis, by one of the authors, of BNA Environment Reporter Cases, Volumes 50-54, covering the years 2000-2002, reveals 63 reported NEPA decisions, comprising over 10% of all reported federal environmental law decisions during that period.

within and outside the agency, and made accessible in published form to the President, Congress, other relevant federal agencies, and the public for their review and response.

5. **The political science of NEPA.** Note that the only legally-specific section of NEPA targeted its environmental protection efforts upon the federal agencies, not upon the corporate polluters who previously had been the primary focus of public attention. Federal agencies, however, happen to be intimately involved with a host of major production and development activities across the face of the economy and the territory of the United States. Federal agencies are involved in the logging of national forests, in water resources, minerals and mining, the construction of highways and airports, urban redevelopment, the oil industry and offshore oil development, and the like. As the extent of potential NEPA litigation has become more obvious, the targeting of NEPA on federal agencies has provided a broad handle on a very broad range of environmental problems. NEPA applies not only to federal construction activities, but also to federal regulations, leases, contracts, permits, purchases, and other proposed actions that might have a significant impact on the human environment.

6. **The role of citizens.** The history of each statute is unique. NEPA was written in broad terms, achieved support, and passed through Congress as a product of its unique times. It is impossible to overestimate the importance of public opinion in pushing NEPA into law. NEPA would never have moved beyond its first drafts without the environmental fervor of hundreds of thousands of citizens in the late 1960s.

Even more than most statutes, however, NEPA was only an incipient force when it was signed in January 1970. Its growth and development once again depended upon citizens' efforts, this time in the courts. Turning to NEPA in the courts, it is important to remember a basic irony: When the terms of a statute require interpretation, courts put their primary reliance upon the intention of the legislature, but in the case of NEPA there really *wasn't* any discernible intent beyond a vague articulation of environmental goals accompanied by an incompletely defined mandatory process lacking an explicit enforcement mechanism. Thus NEPA jurisprudence is primarily judge-made, decisional law (referred to as the "common law of NEPA"), as refined and codified by the CEQ in its regulations.

B. NEPA IN COURT: THE FIRST GENERATION

Whenever a new statute is legislated, an elaborate series of further questions must be answered. Has it created a new cause of action? If so, who can file lawsuits? Against what defendants? What is the statute of limitations? What actions can be attacked? What are potential defendants required to do under the Act? What do plaintiffs have to show in their complaint and at trial? What defenses are available? What remedies are provided for? The evolving answers to these questions create a common law of the statute. Depending upon how they are answered in court, a statute can flourish or wither on the vine.

NEPA litigation, from the beginning, has focused upon the one clear requirement of the Act — a proposal for a major federal action significantly affecting the human environment must be accompanied by an EIS. Tracing some of the issues raised in the cases over the years not only clarifies the law of NEPA but also illuminates the process by which courts shape the flight of the statutory "missile" after the legislature launches it. In the case of NEPA's EIS requirement, the fact that Congress pretty clearly did not intend to create any new cause of action has had remarkably little effect on the growth of the statute in court cases over time.

Section 1. NEPA IN THE JUDICIAL PROCESS: THE *CHICOD CREEK* CONTROVERSY

No case can be a "typical" NEPA case, because of the remarkable diversity of NEPA lawsuits over the years. The legal and practical elements of the *Chicod Creek* decisions, however, offer a broadly instructive blueprint of NEPA litigation generally, as well as a fascinating example of how NEPA, which was not intended to be litigable, quickly became a highly functional cause of action when plaintiffs dragged it before federal judges.

Natural Resources Defense Council v. Grant (*Chicod Creek*)
United States District Court for the Eastern District of North Carolina, 1972
341 F. Supp. 356

LARKINS, J.... Chicod Creek Watershed, located in mideastern North Carolina, covers an area of 35,100 acres of which 29,625 acres are in Pitt County and 5,475 acres in Beaufort County. Plans for solving flooding, water management, and other resources problems have been prepared with the concurrence of local sponsors and with federal assistance under the the provisions of P.L. 566. The sponsoring local organizations are the Pitt Soil and Water Conservation District, Beaufort Soil and Water Conservation District, Pitt County Board of Commissioners, and Pitt County Drainage District Number Nine. Under the Chicod Creek Watershed Work Plan and Supplements, the local organizations assume all local responsibilities for the installation, operation and maintenance of planned structural works.

The topography of the watershed is nearly level to gently sloping. The outer perimeter is flat and well drained and the flood plains are broad swamps. Land use in the watershed consists of 15,600 acres of cropland; 15,550 acres of woodland; 350 acres of grassland; and 3,600 acres of miscellaneous uses. Approximately 10,000 acres of crop and pasture land are subject to flooding.... A loss of at least 50 percent is sustained on the crops grown on land subject to flooding about once each five years. [Such flooding] causes interrupted traffic, blocked school bus and mail delivery routes, interrupted feeding schedules of farm animals, and additional maintenance and repair on the roads. Excessive rainfall and flooding create a health hazard. Septic tanks, nitrification lines, and approved pit-privies overflow to the surface of the soil after excessive rainfall. Poor drainage often results in low quality crops and high unit cost of production.

The population of the watershed is approximately 3,000 people. The entire population is classified as rural with 25 percent being non-farm. Agriculture is the principal enterprise in the watershed. The chief cash crops are tobacco, corn, soybeans, and cotton. Livestock production, consisting of beef cattle and swine, make up 10 percent of the cash farm receipts. Value of farm products sold was under $10,000 for 77.6 percent of the 250 farms in the watershed. Fifty-five percent of the families make less than $3,000 income per year.

Chicod Creek originates about 6 miles south of Grimesland and flows generally (about 10 miles) north to its confluence with the Tar River. Cow Swamp and Juniper Branch are the two largest tributaries and they enter Chicod Creek from the west. Chicod Creek and the surrounding area has significant value for numerous waterfowl, fur bearers and other wetland wildlife species. The streams have substantial resident fish population and support a significant spawning run of herring during the spring.

The project was developed for the purposes of flood prevention, drainage, and conservation, development, and improvement of agricultural tracts of land. These objects are to be achieved by land treatment measures and structural measures. The land treatment measures will include conservation cropping systems, cover crops, crop residue use, minimum tillage, grasses and legumes, and tile and open drains. Also, 300 acres of open land will be reforested, while 1,350 acres of land will be subject to thinning and removal of trees. Structural improvements will consist of approximately 66 miles (comprising the main stream and all the various tributaries) of channel enlargement or "stream channelization." Mitigation measures to reduce the adverse effects on fish and wildlife resources are (1) 73 acres of wildlife wetland preservation area, (2) a 12 acre warm-water impoundment area, (3) 11 channel pools, and (4) 30 swamp drainage control structures. These mitigation measures are designed to mitigate for the disruption to the fish caused by the construction of the channels and to offset the wildlife habitat destroyed by the channels and spoil areas. Certain groups feel that these mitigation measures do not sufficiently lessen the adverse effects of the project on the environment. A letter [from] the Fish and Wildlife Service [FWS], dated September 10, 1971, reflects such an opinion: "It is the opinion of the Service that the original mitigation measures plus the additional measures do *not* significantly lessen the adverse effects of the project on the ecosystem of the watershed."

The Watershed Work Plan and an agreement for the implementation thereof were executed on behalf of [the local] Soil and Water Conservation District...organizations, who are parties to the agreement and plan, and before execution by the Soil Conservation Service [SCS],[9] the plan was reviewed by the Corps of Engineers of the United States Department of the Army and the United States Department of the Interior, and other federal agencies...and approved by the Committees on Agriculture [both House and Senate]....

Pursuant to the provisions of NEPA and the [CEQ regulations], the Administrator of the SCS, through the issuance of Environment Memorandum 1 and Watersheds Memorandum 108, the Chicod Creek Watershed project was placed in Group 2, i.e., those projects having some adverse effect which can be eliminated by minor project modification.... After consideration of environmental concerns, including the unfavorable comments of the FWS, officials of the SCS determined that the project as modified was not a major federal action significantly affecting the quality of human environment and that the project should proceed.

The present action was instituted to enjoin the defendants from financing and participating in the construction of the Chicod Creek Watershed Project. The total installation cost of the project is estimated to be $1,503,831. Public Law 566 funds are to pay $706,684 and other funds will provide $797,147. There has been extensive preparation by the defendants and the intervenors for this project. The landowners have incurred approximately $13,000 of debts to create the drainage district. Easements and rights-of-way have been obtained on 282 tracts of land involving 230 landowners. The local sponsors have procured a Farmers Home Administration loan. The SCS has incurred substantial expenses on the project, having expended $50,000 for planning and $159,176 for engineering, design, and land treatment. The SCS will suffer expenses as a result of the delay caused by this action. The projected cost of delay amounts to $7,650 per month, representing salaries and increased construction costs. The cost of preparing impact statements is approximately $7,500 per project....

---

9. The Soil Conservation Service, in the U.S. Department of Agriculture, was renamed the Natural Resource Conservation Service in 1994. [Eds.]

COMMENTARY & QUESTIONS

1. **The factual setting.** Can you figure out what is going on here? Physically, these SCS channelization projects involve cutting a swath of trees (here about 10% of the area's woodland) along a watercourse and then, using power-scoopers called "draglines," cutting a wide open-banked canal in a straight line through the watershed. The natural meandering stream is thus replaced by a broad ditch. The judge does not seem particularly aware of what "adverse effects" might result. What kind of ecological evidence would you have brought to the hearing on a preliminary injunction to demonstrate the facts?

What were the purposes of the project? "Flood prevention" clearly does not mean protection of lives and property from rampaging floodwaters. Rather, the flood problem appears to be drainage, and the purpose of the project is largely to promote agriculture (although traffic and sanitation consequences are mentioned). By channelizing the watershed and adding open ditches and tile drains, the project would not only have reduced seasonal drainage problems but also have created new arable land out of "useless marshes." About 17% of the benefitted acreage was owned by the Weyerhaeuser Lumber Company.

Economically, it is Public Law 566 that pushes the project along. Watershed Protection Act, 16 U.S.C. §§1001–1009 (1970). The court notes that $706,684 out of the $1,503,831 total cost is to be contributed by federal taxpayers. The "local" contribution is typically not wholly paid in dollars. By donating land rights (i.e., easements of access for the dragline, rights-of-way for ditches), landowners are credited with economic contributions toward the local share. The remainder is made up by assessments in the drainage district. As a result, local agriculture gets a construction project subsidy five to ten times its own dollar outlay (the federal contribution rate varies depending upon how much can be called "flood protection" (75%) rather than drainage (50%)). Does the fact that the private market does not build these projects on its own show that they are not cost-effective without federal subsidies?

2. **The political setting.** The political organization of SCS projects is part of the NEPA story. Originally the SCS was an erosion-control agency whose motto was "stop the raindrop where it falls" through contour plowing and other methods. The agency was so successful that it worked itself out of a job. Accordingly, the SCS shifted its focus to carrying water away from the land, an about-face that naturally brought it into the business of managing small streams since the Corps had carved out its jurisdiction over rivers. Annually, huge sums of federal money are appropriated by the congressional agricultural appropriations subcommittees for distribution around the nation to SCS projects. At the local level, agribusiness and individual farmers, who will ultimately benefit from the subsidies, are organized into Drainage Districts through the efforts of the county or regional agent who administers the local-level SCS Soil Conservation District. The drainage districts are basically state-chartered quasi-governmental units with the power to contract for construction and to assess fees. A project is proposed by one of the participants (often the local SCS agent, whose career advancement typically is linked to success in getting such projects underway). A majority of affected

KARL SCHURR

FIGURE 9-1

Stream channelization involves bulldozing or draglining the natural contours and meanders of a stream into straight-line trapezoidal cross-section ditches. The trees and shrubs naturally clustered along the streambanks are stripped away and burned or left in spoil piles. Water flows change dramatically from natural flows in terms of temperature, volume, velocity, erosion, and water quality. The pre-existing populations of fish and other aquatic life typically decline severely. In this photograph, the dragline is re-dredging a silted-in channelization done approximately five years prior.

landowners (measured by acreage rather than per capita) must approve the project; if approved, all must subsequently contribute. The project is then transmitted by the SCS's "State Conservationist" to Washington where it is "authorized" for construction by the SCS and the FHA, and the Secretary of Agriculture. (The SCS and the TVA are rare examples of agencies that have been given extraordinary powers to self-authorize projects without a congressional vote.) Appropriated money is then released to the District for sequential planning, design, and construction. Low-interest loans, moreover, are granted to finance part of the local share. The participants, throughout this process, are linked in an identity of interests. The SCS owes its existence to the continuation of the drainage function; the congressional appropriations committees derive their political power from the ability to deliver dollars throughout the country; the Department of Agriculture and its subdepartments likewise; state and local government officials may be incorporated into the District funding process; and private individuals receive direct financial benefits, some from the project's subsidized land modifications, others from the award of construction contracts. The various private and public participants have their nationwide organizations, with annual conventions, newsletters, and Washington-based lobbyists, all to assure the system's smooth functioning.

Outside the network of drainage-oriented interests are other public and private bodies. The North Carolina Wildlife Commission had received a report from its expert, George Burdick, noting the drastic ecological effects of channelization and had tried to persuade the SCS to terminate the program. The SCS told the state agency that Chicod Creek was being pushed by local landowners and was beyond SCS control. ("Meantime," said one state official, "the SCS agents were whooping it up with the local people telling them what they wanted where.") In controversial matters like this, a state agency usually will not sue to achieve its objectives, nor even complain administratively over the SCS officer's head. The state commission did not insist on its position but did take part in some planning "at a time when the SCS had already established the design"; it did follow the litigation closely, however, and participated in subsequent negotiations. The federal FWS volunteered the letter cited, noting adverse effects. But the FWS had no legal basis to participate in the decision even if it had wanted to interfere with a sister agency. In sum, from top to bottom, no governmental body existed to defend environmental interests. This gap left things up to the local sporting and conservation groups, which happened to find out about the project and got organized in time to persuade the NRDC, a private entity, to take on the expensive task of litigating this, out of hundreds of other potential cases.

3. **Judicial attitudes towards NEPA challenges.** How do you interpret the mood of Judge Larkins at this stage of the case? Do you notice the inevitability implied in the phrasing (so common in NEPA cases) that "1350 acres of land will be [deforested]," etc.?

4. **Financial commitments and delay costs.** The judge notes the amounts of money committed to date and the cost of delay if an injunction were granted. This information is regularly emphasized by environmental defendants to show that too much project expenditure has occurred before trial to permit the project reasonably to be stopped. Has the $130,000 been spent? Were easements paid for? Can the FHA loan be returned? Do any of the SCS expenditures, for "land treatment," etc., have value irrespective of project completion? How much of this financial commitment took place after NEPA became law in January 1970? As to delay, is it relevant that the majority of costs that would inflate over the course of the suit would ultimately be paid in federal tax dollars that have likewise inflated in revenue terms? In light of the $7,500 cost of an SCS EIS, what relevance do all these numbers seem to have for the judge?

Natural Resources Defense Council v. Grant *(continued)*

Conclusions of Law: Jurisdiction. This Court has jurisdiction of this matter pursuant to 28 U.S.C. §1331 (federal question) and 5 U.S.C. §702 (Administrative Procedure Act).

NEPA requires all federal agencies, in performing their respective functions, to be responsive to possible environmental consequences of their actions. The Act makes it the "continuing" responsibility of the federal government to "use all practicable means and measures" to carry out the national policy of restoring and maintaining a quality environment....

Retroactivity. [Judge Larkins, as most other judges in the early development of NEPA, held that NEPA was applicable to ongoing projects, like the Chicod Creek channelization, on which substantial actions remained to be taken.[10]]

---

10. But see Oregon Nat. Res. Council v. Bureau of Reclamation, 49 F.3d 1441 (9th Cir. 1994) (agency's lowering water levels and applying aquatic herbicides in a federal impoundment is not a "major federal action" because these activities were ongoing in 1970).

Requirements of §102(2)(C) of NEPA. Section 102(2)(C) directs all agencies of the federal government to prepare an EIS for every major federal action significantly affecting the environment. The defendants contend that even though they have not filed an EIS, "a particular form," that in substance they have fulfilled all of the requirements of §102(2)(C). In support they assert that a detailed statement has been prepared and circulated; that the environmental impact has been considered by the SCS and agencies of both state and federal government; that adverse effects which cannot be avoided have been considered and weighed against the total benefit of going on with the project; that alternatives have been considered and some have been adopted; that there have been consultations with other federal agencies and with state and local agencies; and that the project has been open to and has received public comment. According to the record and the testimony received at the motion hearing on January 5, 1972, this cannot be disputed. But the fact remains that an EIS has not been prepared and filed for the Chicod Creek Watershed Project. Mr. Hollis Williams, Deputy Administrator of Watersheds, SCS, at the motion hearing testified to the effect: "We had the belief and still do, that an EIS is not needed in the Chicod Creek Project." An EIS must be filed for every major federal action significantly affecting the quality of the human environment. The District of Columbia Circuit noted in Calvert Cliffs v. AEC, 449 F.2d 1109 (D.C. Cir. 1971) that "...the §102 duties are not inherently flexible. They must be complied with to the fullest extent, unless there is a conflict of statutory authority. Considerations of administrative difficulty, delay or economic cost will not suffice to strip the section of its fundamental importance...."

Administrative Discretion. It is contended that the determination of whether a project is (1) "a major Federal action" and (2) "significantly affecting the quality of the human environment" is within the discretion of the Administrator of the SCS, and that an administrative determination should not be reversed by this Court in the absence of a strong showing that it was arbitrary, capricious, or clearly erroneous. In the case at bar the administrator, with the advice of scientists and specialists, made the determination that the project as modified could not significantly affect the quality of the human environment within the meaning and intent of NEPA, and as such "going forward with the project as modified" was in compliance with the requirements of NEPA. Certainly, an administrative agency like the SCS may make a decision that a particular project is not major, or that it does not significantly affect the quality of the human environment, and, that, therefore, the agency is not required to file an impact statement. However, when the failure to file an impact statement is challenged, it is the court that must construe the statutory standards of "major federal action" and "significantly affecting the quality of the human environment," and having construed them, then apply them to the particular project, and decide whether the agency's failure violates the Congressional command.

Statutory Standards. A "major federal action" is federal action that requires substantial planning, time, resources, or expenditure. The Chicod Creed Watershed Project is a "major federal action." This project calls for sixty-six miles of channelization and the expenditure of $1,503,831, $706,684 of which is to be federally funded. The project has been in the planning and preparation stages for several years. Many persons and agencies have become involved and concerned with this project, and the construction of this project will require a substantial amount of time and labor. Certainly this can be considered to be a "major federal action."

The standard "significantly affecting the quality of the human environment" can be construed as having an important or meaningful effect, direct or indirect, upon a broad range of aspects of the human environment. The cumulative impact with other projects must be considered. Any action that substantially affects, beneficially or detrimentally, the depth or course of streams, plant life, wildlife habitats, fish and wildlife, and the soil and air "significantly affects the quality of the human environment." This project will require sixty-six miles of stream channelization. As a result of such channelization there will be a substantial reduction (ninety percent) in the fish population. As a result of drainage and the clearing of right of ways, there will be significant lossage [sic] in wetland habitat which is vital to waterfowl and forest game. The Chicod Creek Watershed Project as presently proposed will have a cumulative effect upon the environment in the eastern plains of North Carolina. There are a total of forty Soil Conservation projects either authorized for construction, under construction, or completed, representing 1562 miles of stream channelization, affecting over 100,000 acres of wetlands, and having very serious repercussions upon fish and wildlife in the Coastal Plains of North Carolina. The Chicod Creek Watershed Project "significantly affects the quality of the human environment."

It is interesting to note that one of the SCS's own biologists, prior to the implementation of any mitigation, concluded that this project would have significant effects upon the environment. Also noteworthy is the fact that subsequent to Watersheds Memorandum 108, the SCS placed this project in Group 2, a category established by the Watersheds Memorandum indicating that projects placed in this group could have some adverse effect upon the environment. After certain mitigation measures were implemented, this project was placed in Group 1, signifying minor or no known adverse effect upon the environment. It is the opinion of this Court that an EIS should have been issued when this project was placed in Group 2.

Standing. It is contended that the plaintiffs lack standing to pursue this action on the grounds that they have not suffered a legal wrong and have not been adversely affected by agency action.,... The plaintiffs have standing to maintain this action as they have alleged injury to conservational interests and that such interests are within the zone of interests protected by NEPA.

Laches. The mere lapse of time does not constitute laches. Laches is determined in light of all the existing circumstances and requires all delay to be unreasonable and cause prejudice to the adversary. This project has been in the planning and preliminary stages for several years. However, NEPA became effective only on January 1, 1970. The plaintiffs instituted this action on November 30, 1971. At that date no construction contract had been let or had any construction on the installation of the project taken place. Therefore, it appears to this Court that there was no unreasonable delay in the commencement of this action, and even assuming such, there does not appear to be any prejudice to the defendants or intervenors as construction of the project has yet to begin.

Injunction. The plaintiffs seek a preliminary injunction to enjoin construction of the Chicod Creek Watershed Project on the grounds that an EIS has not been issued as required by NEPA. The tests for granting such relief were recently restated by the Fourth Circuit:

> In the exercise of its discretion (to issue a preliminary injunction) it is sufficient if a court is satisfied that there is a probable right and a probable danger and that the right may be defeated, unless the injunction is issued, and considerable weight is given to the need of protection to the plaintiff as contrasted with the probable injury to the defendant.... W. Virginia Highlands Conservancy v. Island Creek Coal, 441 F.2d 232, 235 (4th Cir. 1971).

In summary, the movants are entitled to preliminary injunctive relief if they demonstrate (a) a substantial likelihood that they will prevail on the merits, and (b) that a balancing of the equities favors the granting of such relief. Here, the plaintiffs have shown more than a substantial likelihood that they will prevail on the merits upon final determination of their NEPA EIS claim as NEPA requires that an EIS be filed for "major federal actions significantly affecting the quality of the human environment." The plaintiffs have shown that this project is a "major federal action significantly affecting the quality of the human environment," and that an impact statement has not been filed.

The question as to the balancing of the equities gravely concerns this Court. Basically, there are three different interests represented in this action: the conservationists, the SCS, and the landowners. In considering the various interests the public interest is a relevant consideration. This project was designed to enable the landowners to control severe drainage problems and to increase farm productivity. These farmers have spent much time, effort, and money in preparation for this project with the expectation of federal aid. This has been no easy task for farmers in an area in which fifty-five percent of the families make less than $3,000 income per year. These farmers have given up much in expectation of innumerable benefits resulting from the project.... It was only when the preparations had been made and construction ready to begin that this action was initiated to enjoin the project. The Soil Conservation Service's...primary concern in this action seems to be that if it has to issue an impact statement for this project, it will have to do the same for many other ongoing projects. This will cause delay and, in many cases, duplicity [sic]. The projected cost per project for issuing an impact statement is approximately $7,500. This cost is minute indeed in comparison to the equity of the farmers and the effect that this project will have on the environment. The conservationists are organizations dedicated to the laudable cause of conservation and preservation of our environment. They have shown that this project will have a significant effect on the environment. It is to the public's welfare that any project significantly affecting the environment comply with the procedures established by NEPA so there can be assurance that the environmental aspects have been fully considered. It would constitute irreparable damage for this project to proceed without the environmental aspects being properly considered as required by NEPA. Therefore, the equitable considerations favor the environment, the public, and the plaintiffs and require that the construction of the Chicod Creek Watershed Project be enjoined until the requirements of NEPA are satisfied.

The defendants shall have thirty days within which to prepare and file a "full disclosure" EIS. The preliminary injunction shall remain in effect thereafter until all of the procedures of NEPA have been complied with. The plaintiffs shall file a bond for the payment of costs and damages as may be suffered by any party who is found to have been wrongfully restrained herein. The amount of bond shall be commensurate to the possible damages incurred by the defendants and the intervenors as a result of the injunction. Over $200,000 has already been expended on this project by the SCS and $130,000 of debt has been incurred by the intervenors. The projected cost of delay to the SCS resulting from the institution of this suit is approximately $7,650 per month. Taking into consideration the amounts that have been expended, the costs of delay, and that other amounts are obligated, this Court sets the bond at $75,000.

Now therefore, in accordance with the foregoing, it is *ordered*, that the defendants and their agents, employees, and persons in active concert and participation with them who receive actual notice hereof, be and the same are hereby restrained and enjoined from taking any further steps to authorize, finance, or commence construction or installation of the Chicod Creek Watershed Project until an EIS is filed and circulated according to the requirements of NEPA; and, *Further ordered*, that the defendants prepare and file a "full disclosure" EIS within thirty (30) days from the filing of this Order; and, *Further ordered*, that plaintiffs file a bond for the payment of costs and damages as may be suffered by any party who is found to have been wrongfully or unlawfully restrained herein, in the amount of, or security equivalent to, $75,000.... Let this Order be entered forthwith.

COMMENTARY & QUESTIONS

1. **Standing and ripeness.** Note how little trouble the court had in finding standing to challenge agency action, despite the fact that NEPA had not explicitly given such a right. Purely economic interests, however, have consistently been held not to provide standing under NEPA. See, e.g., Region 8 Forest Serv. Timber Purchasers Council v. Alcock, 993 F.2d 800 (11th Cir. 1993). Moreover, a split has developed among federal circuit courts of appeals regarding standing to assert violations of NEPA where the proposed federal action would not immediately produce site-specific environmental impacts (i.e., proposals for rulemaking, planning, or policy changes). Compare Florida Audubon Soc'y v. Bentsen, 94 F.3d 658 (D.C. Cir. 1996) (en banc) (denying individuals standing to contest the failure of the Secretary of the Treasury to comply with NEPA prior to promulgating a final rule to allow a tax credit for an alternative fuel additive; plaintiffs had not demonstrated an increased risk of serious environmental harm that actually threatened their particular interests), with Citizens for Better Forestry v. Agriculture Dep't, 341 F.3d 961 (9th Cir. 2003) (rejecting the *Bentsen* standing analysis and holding that environmental plaintiffs, asserting a procedural right, can establish standing without meeting the normal standards for immediacy, and need only establish the reasonable probability of the challenged action's threat to their concrete interests; environmental plaintiffs have standing, under NEPA, to challenge not only site-specific proposals, but also higher-level planning regulations). Lack of ripeness for review has not posed a problem for NEPA plaintiffs. But challenges to Land and Resource Management Plans under the NFMA have been dismissed for lack of ripeness on the theory that plaintiffs would have an opportunity to contest future site-specific proposals based on those plans. See Sierra Club v. Thomas, 523 U.S. 726 (1998), discussed in Chapter 24.

2. **A cause of action?** The court presumes, with the other courts that encountered NEPA, that §102 must be actionable because it plainly set up a legal duty — all agencies shall prepare statements — that sounds enforceable, and if Congress had not meant that as a requirement, surely it would not have said that. This amounts to the principle of statutory interpretation that "the Emperor must be wearing clothes."

3. **Laches.** Owing to its casual congressional history, NEPA had no statute of limitations; the equitable doctrine of laches will prevent injunction suits that are "unreasonably delayed." Here, would the judge have decided differently if a construction contract had been let? Should the doctrine of laches be waived for public interest plaintiffs?

4. **The bureaucratic temptation to minimize.** NEPA's enforceability was initially unclear, and some construction agencies tended to minimize its requirements. The following is reportedly the text, in its entirety, of an EIS as it was first published by the Bureau of Reclamation as its compliance with NEPA:

> Palmetto Bend Project, Jackson County, Tex. Proposed construction of a 12.3-mile long, 64-foot high earthfill dam on the Navidad River. The purpose of the project is the supply of industrial and municipal water. Approximately 18,400 acres (11,300 of which will be inundated) will be committed to the project; 40 miles of free-flowing stream will be inundated; nine families will be displaced; fresh water inflow to the Matagorda estuary will be altered; fish and shellfish nursery areas will be

impaired; habitat for such endangered species as the Texas red wolf, the American alligator, the Southern bald eagle, the Peregrine falcon, and the Attwater prairie chicken will be lost.

(The Bureau subsequently realized that more was required, and the project was ultimately subjected to a full formal EIS preparation and review process.)

5. **The classic *Calvert Cliffs* case.** Part of the legal backdrop to Judge Larkins's review of the *Chicod Creek* case was a forceful decision from the D.C. Circuit that became the most important of all early NEPA cases. Calvert Cliffs Coordinating Comm. v. AEC, 449 F.2d 1109 (D.C. Cir. 1971), confronted the Atomic Energy Commission's ingenious refusals to consider environmental issues in its nuclear power plant construction program until after the projects were under construction. In his admonitory and ironic majority opinion, excerpts from which are reproduced below, Judge Skelley Wright "took a stick to the federal agencies" and served notice that NEPA would have to be taken seriously:

> In these cases, we must for the first time interpret the broadest and most important of the recent [environmental] statutes: the National Environmental Policy Act. We must assess claims that one of the agencies charged with its administration has failed to live up to the congressional mandate. Our duty, in short, is to see that important legislative purposes, heralded in the halls of Congress, are not lost or misdirected in the vast hallways of the federal bureaucracy.... The Commission contends that the vagueness of the NEPA mandate and delegation leaves much room for discretion.... We find the policies embodied in NEPA to be a good deal clearer and more demanding than does the Commission. We conclude that the Commission's procedural rules do not comply with the congressional policy. Hence we remand these cases for further rulemaking....

> Of course, all of the §102 duties are qualified by the phrase "to the fullest extent possible." We must stress as forcefully as possible that this language does not provide an escape hatch for footdragging agencies; it does not make NEPA's procedural requirements somehow "discretionary." Congress did not intend the Act to be such a paper tiger. Indeed, the requirement of environmental consideration "to the fullest extent possible" sets a high standard for the agency, a standard which must be rigorously enforced by the reviewing courts....

> NEPA makes only one specific reference to consideration of environmental values in agency review processes. Section 102(2)(c) provides that copies of the staff's "detailed statement" and comments thereon "shall accompany the proposal through the existing agency review process."... The question here is whether the Commission is correct in thinking that its NEPA responsibilities may "be carried out *in toto* outside the hearing process" — whether it is enough that environmental data and evaluations merely "accompany" an application through the review process, but receive no consideration whatever from the hearing board. We believe that the Commission's crabbed interpretation of NEPA makes a mockery of the Act. What possible purpose could there be in the requirement...if "accompany" means no more than physical proximity — mandating no more than the physical act of passing certain folders and papers, unopened, to reviewing officials along with other folders and papers? What possible purpose could there be in requiring the "detailed statement" to be before hearing boards, if the boards are entitled to ignore entirely the contents of the statement? NEPA was meant to do more than regulate the flow of papers in the federal bureaucracy. The word "accompany"

must not be read so narrowly as to make the Act ludicrous. It must, rather, be read to indicate a congressional intent that environmental factors, as compiled in the "detailed statement," be considered through agency review processes.

The rationale of the Commission's limitation of environmental issues to hearings in which parties affirmatively raise those issues may have been one of economy. It may have been supposed that, whenever there are serious environmental costs overlooked or uncorrected by the staff, some party will intervene to bring those costs to the hearing board's attention.... NEPA establishes environmental protection as an integral part of the Atomic Energy Commission's basic mandate. The primary responsibility for fulfilling that mandate lies with the Commission. Its responsibility is not simply to sit back, like an umpire, and resolve adversary contentions at the hearing stage. Rather, it must itself take the initiative of considering environmental values at every distinctive and comprehensive stage of the process beyond the staff's evaluation and recommendation.

[As to the AEC's dilatory and grudging interpretation of NEPA], strangely, the Commission has principally relied on...pragmatic arguments. It seems an unfortunate affliction of large organizations to resist new procedures and to envision massive roadblocks to their adoption.... The introduction of environmental matters cannot have presented a radically unsettling problem. And, in any event, the obvious sense of urgency on the part of Congress should make clear that a transition, however "orderly," must proceed at a pace faster than a funeral procession.

As to [multiple statutory mandates, NEPA] clearly requires obedience to standards set by other [statutes]. But obedience does not imply total abdication.... It does not suggest that other "specific statutory obligations" will entirely replace NEPA....

We hold that...the Commission must revise its rules governing consideration of environmental issues. We do not impose a harsh burden on the Commission. For we require only an exercise of substantive discretion which will protect the environment "to the fullest extent possible." No less is required if the grand congressional purposes underlying NEPA are to become a reality. 449 F.2d at 1111–1124.

6. **What is a "major federal action"?** Is the Chicod Creek channelization project federal? The entire project is to be undertaken by the local District. Yet federal dollars are being spent and "many persons and agencies have become involved." Does that mean that every expenditure of federal revenue-sharing funds requires an EIS?

Note the following excerpt from the CEQ regulations, 40 C.F.R. §§1501 et seq., on the meaning and implementation of NEPA:

§1508.18 Major Federal Action. Major federal action includes actions with effects that may be major and which are potentially subject to Federal control and responsibility. Major reinforces but does not have a meaning independent of significantly (§1508.27). Actions include the circumstance where the responsible officials fail to act and that failure to act is reviewable by courts or administrative tribunals under the Administrative Procedure Act or other applicable law as agency action.

(a) Actions include new and continuing activities, including projects and programs entirely or partly financed, assisted, conducted, regulated, or approved by federal agencies; new or revised agency rules, regulations, plans, policies, or procedures; and legislative proposals. Actions do not include funding assistance solely in the form of general revenue sharing funds, distributed under the State and Local Fiscal Assistance Act of 1972, 31 U.S.C. §1221 et seq., with no Federal agency control over the subsequent use of such funds. Actions do not include bringing judicial or administrative civil or criminal enforcement actions.

In addition, §1508.18 explains that federal actions tend to involve the adoption of official policy, formal plans, or programs, or the approval of specific projects. Courts also have held federal permits, licenses, contracts, or leases given to private parties to be federal actions.

As to whether it is a "major" action, isn't the Chicod Creek project's $706,684 cost a trifling amount in the federal context? Conceptual rather than financial definitions obviously are part of the decision, which depends on an analysis of surrounding circumstances. Is an armed forces plan to launch an amphibious practice assault on a beach in Maine's Acadia National Park a "major" action? What about the installation of an incinerator on a federal hospital? The courts answered "no" and "yes," respectively, perhaps making a distinction based upon short-term versus long-term actions. If Chicod Creek were only 4 miles long, would the project be "major"? Can you take notice of *cumulative* effects in order to judge whether an action is "major" or of significant effect? See 40 C.F.R. §1508.27(b)(7) in Note 8 below.

7. **The "small handle" problem.** Consider this not-so-hypothetical: Several Japanese and Korean corporations plan to open 17 wood-chipping installations throughout the southeastern United States, designed to process trees and vegetation stripped from hundreds of thousands of acres of private forests. The companies will ship the chips by barge and freighter to the Far East as raw material for paper and laminates. This activity would affect the biological and climatological character of major portions of six southern states. Assume that the only federal permit required is an Army Corps of Engineers wharf-building permit for the barge-loading facilities. With that federal permit, the operation will take place; without it, it will not. The corporate proponents and the Corps can argue, however, that a barge wharf is too minor a structure to require an EIS.

This is the small handle problem. Courts disagree on whether, in such cases, the NEPA EIS requirement is triggered by the entire factual consequences of a federal action or focuses exclusively on the effects of the federal component of the project. In Winnebago Tribe v. REA, 621 F.2d 269 (8th Cir. 1980), the court held that a federal river-crossing permit necessary for construction of a 67-mile high-tension power line was not sufficient federal involvement to require an EIS. Some courts have been more willing to note the actual effect of federal actions. Colorado River Indian Tribes v. Marsh, 605 F. Supp. 1425 (C.D. Cal. 1985), held that a Corps permit for riverbank reinforcement (a practical precondition for a proposed large rural commercial and residential development) required an EIS covering the entire actual impact deriving from the federal action. NEPA, the court held, implicitly incorporates reasonable forecasting of consequential and environmental effects. In a Maine case, where construction of a major oil terminal on Sears Island depended upon grant of a Corps permit for an access road causeway, the court required an EIS covering the entire development, taking into account the "reasonably foreseeable indirect effects" of consequential industrial development because the causeway was a necessary part of the larger plan. Sierra Club v. Marsh, 769 F.2d 868, 877 (1st Cir. 1985).

8. **"Significantly affecting the human environment."** This standard echoes the preceding issues. "Significance" similarly varies according to context. What if the project allegedly has net beneficial effects? One SCS official argued that this was so in stream channelization cases, adding that "Conservation is our middle name!" NEPA is clearly aimed at adverse environmental effects (and the present CEQ regulations so direct the EIS procedure); if adverse effects exist, the courts generally have not permitted the counterbalancing of alleged benefits in order to avoid NEPA.[11] The CEQ regulations describe "significantly" in terms of "context" and "intensity":

§1508.27 Significantly. Significantly as used in NEPA requires considerations of both context and intensity:

(a) *Context.* This means that the significance of an action must be analyzed in several contexts such as society as a whole (human, national), the affected region, the affected interests, and the locality. Significance varies with the setting of the proposed action. For instance, in the case of a site-specific action, significance would usually depend upon the effects in the locale rather than in the world as a whole. Both short- and long-term effects are relevant.

(b) *Intensity.* This refers to the severity of impact. Responsible officials must bear in mind that more than one agency may make decisions about partial aspects of a major action. The following should be considered in evaluating intensity:

(1) Impacts that may be both beneficial and adverse. A significant effect may exist even if the Federal agency believes that on balance the effect will be beneficial.

(2) The degree to which the proposed action affects public health or safety.

(3) Unique characteristics of the geographic area such as proximity to historic or cultural resources, park lands, prime farmlands, wetlands, wild and scenic rivers, or ecologically critical areas.

(4) The degree to which the effects on the quality of the human environment are likely to be highly controversial.

(5) The degree to which the possible effects on the human environment are highly uncertain or involve unique or unknown risks.

(6) The degree to which the action may establish a precedent for future actions with significant effects or represents a decision in principle about a future consideration.

(7) Whether the action is related to other actions with individually insignificant but cumulatively significant impacts. Significance exists if it is reasonable to anticipate a cumulatively significant impact on the environment. Significance cannot be avoided by terming an action temporary or by breaking it down into small component parts.

(8) The degree to which the action may adversely affect districts, sites, highways, structures, or objects listed in or eligible for listing in the National Register of Historic Places or may cause loss or destruction of significant scientific, cultural, or historical resources.

(9) The degree to which the action may adversely affect an endangered or threatened species or its habitat that has been determined to be critical under the Endangered Species Act of 1973.

---

11. After an agency has complied with NEPA, issuing an adequate EIS, it may still decide to proceed based on a balance of environmental and nonenvironmental issues (unless going forward can be shown to be "arbitrary").

(10) Whether the action threatens a violation of Federal, State, or local law or requirements imposed for the protection of the environment.

9. FONSIs and mitigation. The *Chicod Creek* case offers an example of another tack: The SCS Administrator made a "negative declaration" or "FONSI" ("finding of no significant impact"), a declaration that the project would cause no significant environmental effect. A FONSI must be based upon an initial Environmental Assessment (EA) in which the agency briefly discusses the need for the proposal as well as the "environmental impacts of, and alternatives to, the proposal."[12] The CEQ defines the FONSI and EA as follows:

> §1508.9 Environmental Assessment. Environmental assessment (a) means a concise public document for which a Federal agency is responsible that serves to: (1) briefly provide sufficient evidence and analysis for determining whether to prepare an environmental impact statement or a finding of no significant impact. (2) aid an agency's compliance with the Act when no environmental impact statement is necessary. (3) facilitate preparation of a statement when one is necessary. (b) shall include brief discussions of the need for the proposal, of alternatives..., of the environmental impacts of the proposed action and alternatives, and a listing of agencies and persons consulted.

> §1508.13 Finding of no significant impact. Finding of no significant impact means a document by a Federal agency briefly presenting the reasons why an action...will not have a significant effect on the human environment and for which an environmental impact statement therefore will not be prepared. It shall include the environmental assessment or a summary of it and shall note any other environmental documents related to it....

An EA is a threshold document and is held to a lower degree of analysis than an EIS. Judge Larkins rejected the SCS's argument that its decision to prepare an EA and FONSI, instead of a full-scale EIS, had to be upheld unless it was arbitrary and capricious. After many years of division among the federal circuit courts on this issue, the Supreme Court settled the matter in Marsh v. Oregon Nat. Res. Council, 490 U.S. 360 (1989) (reviewing courts must apply the "arbitrary and capricious" standard in reviewing agency decisions on "significance"). Nevertheless, federal courts — especially in the Ninth Circuit — frequently hold that an agency must prepare an EIS rather than an EA. See, e.g., Idaho Sporting Congress v. U.S. Forest Serv., 137 F.3d 1146 (9th Cir. 1998) (Forest Service must prepare an EIS for a proposed timber sale).

In *Chicod Creek*, the SCS claimed that its mitigation measures obviated a full EIS, an argument that Judge Larkins did not accept. In fact, according to the CEQ's study, "The National Environmental Policy Act: A Study of Its Effectiveness after Twenty-five Years" (1997) (hereafter "1997 CEQ Study"), the "mitigated FONSI" has become the agencies' primary means of limiting their procedural burdens under NEPA:

> Since NEPA was passed, the role of the EA has evolved to the point where it is the predominant way agencies conduct NEPA analyses. Conceived as a brief analysis to

---

12. An agency may designate a category of actions that do not individually or cumulatively have a significant effect on the human environment for a "categorical exclusion" from NEPA, meaning that neither an EA nor an EIS is necessary. 40 C.F.R. §1508.4. However, a categorical exclusion cannot be utilized to evade NEPA compliance responsibilities. See, e.g., Rhodes v. Johnson, 153 F.3d 785 (7th Cir. 1998) (U.S. Forest Service must prepare an EA on proposed controlled burns because these activities cannot be categorically excluded from NEPA).

determine the significance of environmental effects, the EA today increasingly includes mitigation measures that reduce adverse effects below significant levels. With the increased use of EA's, often to the overall benefit of the environment, comes the danger than public involvement will be diminished and that individually minor actions will have major cumulative effects.... There is a great deal of confusion about what public involvement is required, appropriate, or allowed in the preparation of EAs, because NEPA regulations and guidance are primarily oriented to the preparation of EISs.... Some states, citizen groups, and businesses believe that certain EAs are prepared to avoid public involvement.... The preparation of an EA, rather than an EIS, is the most common source of conflict under NEPA....

All signs point to a significant increase in EAs and a decrease in EISs. The annual number of draft, revised, supplemental, and final EISs prepared has declined from approximately 2,000 in 1973 to 608 in 1995, averaging 508 annually between 1990-1995. By 1993, a CEQ survey of federal agencies estimated that about 50,000 EAs were being prepared annually. That survey also found that five federal agencies — the U.S. Forest Service, the Bureau of Land Management, the Department of Housing and Urban Development, the U.S. Army Corps of Engineers, and the Federal Highway Administration — produce more than 80% of the EAs. While some federal agencies...provide for a public comment period on EAs, many do not.

Another significant trend is that of agencies increasingly identifying and proposing measures to mitigate adverse effects of proposed actions during the preparation of EAs.... If an agency finds that such mitigation will prevent a project from having significant impacts on the environment, the agency can conclude the NEPA process by issuing a FONSI, rather than preparing an EIS. The result is a "mitigated FONSI." While mitigated FONSIs are a good way to integrate NEPA into planning..., not all EAs resulting in mitigated FONSIs are meeting the spirit and intent of NEPA. When the EIS process is viewed as merely a compliance requirement rather than a tool to improve decision-making, mitigated FONSIs may be used simply to prevent the expense and time of the more in-depth analysis required by an EIS. The result is likely to be less rigorous scientific analysis, little or no public involvement, and consideration of fewer alternatives, all of which are at the very core of NEPA's strengths. Moreover, not all agencies that commit to mitigation monitor to determine whether the mitigation was actually implemented or whether it was effective.[13] 1997 CEQ Study at 19–20.

Nevertheless, EAs must also take a "hard look" at a reasonable range of alternatives and their environmental consequences. For an example of a mitigated FONSI that was upheld by a federal circuit court of appeals, see Tillamook County v. Army Dep't, 288 F.3d 1140 (9th Cir. 2002) ("While the Corps was required to develop the proposed mitigation measures 'to a reasonable degree,' it was not required to develop a complete mitigation plan detailing the 'precise nature...of the mitigation measures' nor were the measures required to 'completely compensate for adverse environmental impacts.'" 288 F.3d at 1142, citing Wetlands Action Network v. U.S. Army Corps of Eng'rs, 222 F.3d 1105, 1121 (9th Cir. 2000), cert. denied, 534 U.S. 815 (2001)). But see National Parks &

---

13. Although the CEQ regulations require that mitigation measures be implemented (§1505.3), the U.S. Supreme Court has held that NEPA does not require an agency to either include a mitigation plan in an EA or EIS, or to actually implement identified implementation measures. Robertson v. Director of U.S. Forest Serv., 490 U.S. 332 (1989).

Conservation Ass'n v. Interior Dep't, 241 F.3d 722 (9th Cir. 2001), cert. denied, 534 U.S. 1104 (2002) (mitigated FONSI by National Park Service with regard to a proposal to increase vessel traffic in Glacier Bay National Park held to be arbitrary and capricious).

10. **Formal compliance vs. "functional equivalence."** The judge scarcely listened to the SCS's claim that even though it had not filed a formally prepared EIS, it had substantially complied with the various requirements of an EIS; yet Congress appears to have drafted the phrase "statement" instead of "formal finding" precisely in order to avoid formal requirements. This court simply says, however, that "an EIS has not been prepared and filed for the Chicod Creek Watershed Project."

In several early NEPA cases, polluters tried to use the statute against EPA itself, and courts began to develop an exception for environmental protection agencies whose procedures provide the "functional equivalent" of NEPA. "[The courts have seen] little need in requiring a NEPA statement from an agency whose raison d'etre is the protection of the environment and whose decision...is necessarily infused with the environmental considerations so pertinent to Congress in designing the statutory framework. To require a 'statement,' in addition to a decision setting forth the same considerations, would be a legalism carried to the extreme." International Harvester Co. v. Ruckelshaus, 478 F.2d 615, 650 n. 130 (D.C. Cir. 1973); Texas Comm. on Nat. Res. v. Bergland, 573 F.2d 201, 207 (5th Cir. 1979). How similar to the EPA procedures do other agency procedures need to be in order to be deemed "functionally equivalent" to NEPA? Agencies such as the Forest Service and the Bureau of Land Management, which consider environmental protection along with other multiple-use criteria, are not exempt from NEPA under the "functional equivalent" doctrine; but federal circuit courts have split about whether designations of critical habitat under the ESA are the functional equivalent of NEPA. Contrast Douglas County v. Babbitt, 48 F.3d 1495 (9th Cir. 1994) (ESA procedures are the functional equivalent of NEPA), with Catron County Bd. of Comm'rs v. FWS, 75 F.3d 1429 (10th Cir. 1996) (ESA and NEPA serve different purposes). What are the consequences of this judge-made doctrine? In Alabama ex rel. Siegelman v. EPA, 911 F.2d 499 (11th Cir. 1990), EPA issued a permit to allow the ChemWaste Co. to open the nation's largest hazardous waste disposal facility at Emelle, Alabama, a low-income community of color, without preparing an EIS. The court held that the RCRA permit process was the functional equivalent of an EIS.

Does the "functional equivalence" doctrine adequately address the role of public involvement and comment in the EIS procedure under NEPA? The procedures mapped out in the CEQ's NEPA regulations include extensive provisions requiring agencies to make diligent efforts to solicit information from the public and from other agencies with relevant expertise, to provide adequate notice of NEPA-related hearings, and to respond to comments in the final EIS. Were the SCS procedures in *Chicod Creek* the functional equivalent of NEPA?

11. **Conflicting statutory mandates.** Courts have recognized a narrow exception to NEPA's EIS requirement where compliance with NEPA would result in a "clear and fundamental conflict of statutory duty." Flint Ridge Dev. Co. v. Scenic Rivers Ass'n, 426 U.S. 776, 791 (1976). In *Flint Ridge*, the Court held that the Secretary of HUD was not

required to prepare an EIS before allowing disclosure notices for large-scale rural subdivisions to be filed, even if the developments would significantly affect the environment. Because the Interstate Land Sales Full Disclosure Act required the Secretary to allow accurate and complete notices to go into effect within 30 days of filing, the Court found that it would be impossible simultaneously to prepare an EIS and to respond adequately to comments. While acknowledging that NEPA requires that agencies comply "to the fullest extent possible," the Court reasoned that NEPA was not intended to "repeal by implication any other statute." The Court also, however, quoted statements from House Conferees involved in drafting §102, providing that "no agency shall utilize an excessively narrow construction of its existing statutory authorization to avoid compliance [with NEPA]."

Courts have been unwilling to apply the *Flint Ridge* exception liberally. In Jones v. Gordon, 621 F. Supp. 7 (D. Alaska 1985), the district court held that the National Marine Fisheries Service (NMFS) could not issue a permit for the taking of up to 100 orca whales without preparing an EIS. The court rejected the argument that the 90-day time limit for issuing such permits under the Marine Mammal Protection Act rendered NMFS compliance with NEPA impossible. Instead, the court held that "in the rare cases where an EIS may be required, the NMFS can create time in the application process by delaying initial publication of the notice of the application in the Federal Register." The court found the conflict between statutes in this case to be minor and ultimately reconcilable. But an irreconcilable conflict was found in Westlands Water Dist v. NRDC, 43 F.3d 457 (9th Cir. 1994) (Congress dictated that conservation releases from federal dams take place "upon enactment").

The SCS in *Chicod Creek* was clearly not prevented by conflicting statutory mandates from complying with NEPA.

12. **Emergency exemptions from NEPA.** To what extent can agencies ignore NEPA in situations that they deem to be "emergencies" (recognizing that such a loophole could invite self-serving agency evasions of their mandates)? 40 C.F.R. §1506.11 provides that the requirements of NEPA can be bypassed in emergencies. In Crosby v. Young, 512 F. Supp. 1363 (E.D. Mich. 1981), a district court upheld the claim that Detroit's use of federal funds to raze the Poletown community in order to build a Cadillac plant (see Chapter 23) was an emergency precluding the application of NEPA. The same result occurred in Hester v. National Audubon Soc'y, 801 F.2d 405 (9th Cir. 1986), where the FWS was granted leave, without an EIS, to capture the last 26 surviving California condors for zoo propagation. Although common sense indicates that in some situations the requirements of NEPA must be inapplicable, how do courts or the CEQ fashion such exceptions to a clear legislative mandate? The crop and infrastructure flooding proposed to be addressed by the *Chicod Creek* project lacked the emergency quality that might have exempted this proposal from NEPA.

13. **NEPA and national security.** NEPA does not provide for a national security exception. The Supreme Court, however, has refused to review Defense Department compliance with NEPA where to do so inevitably would result in the disclosure of confidential matters regarding national security. Weinberger v. Catholic Action of Haw., 454

U.S. 139 (1981), involved a NEPA challenge to the Navy's construction of nuclear weapon storage structures. The Navy's regulations prohibited it from either admitting or denying that nuclear weapons were actually stored at the facility. The complaint claimed that the Navy's determination that no significant environmental hazards were present failed to take into account the enhanced risks of a nuclear accident and the potential effects of radiation from the storage of nuclear weapons in a populated location. The Court held that the Navy could not be made to disclose the military secret regarding whether it proposed to store nuclear weapons on Hawaii, even in confidential judicial chambers ex parte, and thus the entire matter was beyond judicial scrutiny.

Subsequent cases have held that some NEPA claims involving national security are justiciable. In *NO GWEN* Alliance of Lane County, Inc. v. Aldridge, 841 F.2d 946 (9th Cir. 1988), the appeals court held that a lawsuit claiming that the Air Force did not discuss environmental impacts of installing radio towers designed to send war messages to U.S. strategic forces in the event of nuclear war raised justiciable questions. See also Romer v. Carlucci, 847 F.2d 463 (8th Cir. 1988) (review of EIS for compliance with NEPA is justiciable under political question doctrine, in connection with proposed deployment and peacetime operations of MX missiles in minuteman silos). While both the Eighth and Ninth Circuits pointed out that there is no national security exemption from NEPA, the *Carlucci* court refused to require the Army EIS to discuss alternative basing modes or alternative weapons systems since such strategic considerations would "involve review of intricate and sensitive defense policy information." In addition, the *NO GWEN* court ultimately did not require the Air Force to prepare an EIS on the grounds that its EA adequately addressed non-nuclear effects and that the nexus between constructing the radio towers and nuclear war was too attenuated to trigger NEPA requirements of discussing environmental effects of nuclear war. In this post-9/11 world, the national security exemption from NEPA inevitably will become the subject of increased litigation. Should anti-terrorism military training activities held on an environmentally fragile beach require compliance with NEPA?

14. **The "human environment"?** What does that phrase mean? Chicod Creek is not human, but without much questioning courts have interpreted the phrase to cover natural environmental qualities that affect humans. What about an Army decision to close down a military depot, which will have major socioeconomic dislocation impacts on humans? See Breckinridge v. Rumsfeld, 537 F.2d 864 (6th Cir. 1976) (no compliance necessary because closure is a secondary, socioeconomic impact without a primary physical impact on the environment).

The Supreme Court confronted the question about NEPA's application to the human environment in Metropolitan Edison v. PANE, 460 U.S. 766 (1983). The worst nuclear accident Americans have yet experienced occurred on March 28, 1979, at Three Mile Island (TMI), south of Harrisburg, Pennsylvania. After the accident, the two nuclear reactors at the plant were shut down. Only one of them, however, had been damaged in the accident. After a lengthy investigation and public hearings, the Nuclear Regulatory Commission (NRC) decided to allow restart of the undamaged reactor (TMI-1). During the hearings, the NRC consistently refused to consider neighboring residents' claims that NEPA required it to study the psychological distress that allegedly would accompany the restart. People Against Nuclear Energy (PANE), a group composed primarily of neighbors of TMI, sought judicial review.

Note the definition of "human environment" articulated in the CEQ regulations:

> §1508.14 Human environment. Human environment shall be interpreted comprehensively to include the natural and physical environment and the relationship of people with that environment.... This means that economic or social effects are not intended by themselves to require preparation of an environmental impact statement. When an environmental impact statement is prepared and economic or social and natural or physical environmental effects are interrelated, then the environmental impact statement will discuss all of these effects on the human environment.

The NRC argued that NEPA requires only that effects on the "natural environment" must be studied. Psychological stress in this case is a product of area residents' fear of a second accident at Three Mile Island, and is not a product of physical changes in the environment. "Peoples' anxiety has very little to do with the environment," the NRC said. Did the psychological effects of restarting the reactor mean that it would be an "action significantly affecting the human environment"? Justice Rehnquist answered that the NRC need not consider PANE's contentions:

> First, §102(2)(C) does not require an agency to assess every impact or effect of its proposed action, but only impacts or effects on the environment. The statute's context shows that Congress was talking about the physical environment. Although NEPA states its goals in sweeping terms of human health and welfare, these goals are ends that Congress has chosen to pursue by means of protecting the physical environment.

> Second, NEPA does not require agencies to evaluate the effects of risk *qua* risk. The terms "environmental effects" and "environmental impact" in §102(2)(C) should be read to include a requirement of a reasonably close causal relationship between a change in the physical environment and the effect at issue. Here, the federal action that affects the environment is permitting renewed operation of TMI-1. The direct effects of this action include release of low-level radiation, increased fog, and the release of warm water into the Susquehanna River, all of which are effects the NRC has considered. The NRC has also considered the risk of a nuclear accident, but a risk of an accident is not an effect on the physical environment. In a causal chain from renewed operation of TMI-1 to psychological health damage, the element of risk and its perception by PANE's members are necessary middle links. That element of risk lengthens the causal chain beyond NEPA's reach. Regardless of the gravity of the harm alleged by PANE, if a harm does not have a sufficiently close connection to the physical environment, NEPA does not apply.

> Finally, the fact that PANE's claim was made in the wake of the accident at TMI-2 is irrelevant. NEPA is not directed at the effects of past accidents and does not create a remedial scheme for past federal actions. 460 U.S. at 778–779.

Are these conclusions self-evident? What happened to the word "human" in the phrase "human environment"? Is the opinion nevertheless correct in holding that there must be some limits upon NEPA coverage of effects that occur far down a chain of indirect causation? Or does the gravity of potential harms, or NEPA's logic in general, argue for consideration of all real consequential effects? Compare the *Pruitt* case's consideration of long-distance liability in the *Kepone* affair, in Chapter 3.

15. **The injunction.** Quite simply, the Chicod Creek project had no EIS, so NEPA was violated. Note, however, that injunctive relief was not automatic; the court traditionally balances the equities before deciding to issue an injunction. How does the judge weigh the value of NEPA compliance against the financial costs involved? In some NEPA cases, judges have permitted the agency to continue construction while preparing an EIS on the question of whether the project should be built. EDF v. Ellis Armstrong, 487 F.2d 814 (9th Cir. 1973) (New Melones Dam). How does a court determine whether an injunction is justified for an ongoing project that does not have an EIS? In another context, the Supreme Court has said that, once having found a statutory violation, it had no discretion but to see that the law was complied with. TVA v. Hill, 437 U.S. 153 (1978). As to NEPA violations, however, the Court has appeared less ready to hold defendants strictly to compliance. Amoco Prod. Co. v. Village of Gambell, 480 U.S. 531 (1987); cf. Sierra Club v. Marsh, 872 F.2d 497, 500 (1st Cir. 1989). Does failure to consider environmental consequences in agency decisionmaking constitute irreparable harm?

16. **A bond requirement?** Finally, having won everything at issue, the citizens unexpectedly were faced with Judge Larkins's requirement of a $75,000 bond. Such bonds are common in commercial litigation. Why not here?

Natural Resources Defense Council v. Grant
United States Court of Appeals for the Fourth Circuit, 1972
2 Environmental Law Reporter 20,555 (1972)

HAYNSWORTH, J. In this ecology case, the District Judge issued a preliminary injunction because no environmental impact statement had been filed. It was conditioned, however, upon the filing by the plaintiffs of a bond in the amount of $75,000. The bond was not filed, and the District Judge withdrew the preliminary injunction on that account. Meanwhile, however, an EIS had been filed, substantially changing the posture of the case.

The controversy is far from ended. The plaintiffs intend to attack the adequacy of the EIS and they seek a continuing injunction against commencement of the project until that question is determined. That is a question initially for the District Court, not for us, but the plaintiffs, organizations interested in conservation and having no financial interest in this controversy, are fearful that any further injunctive order will again be conditioned upon their posting a large bond.

Thus, they seek to prosecute an appeal and have requested a stay of the order dissolving the injunction. The defendants have countered with a suggestion of mootness.

Under all the circumstances, we think an immediate remand of this case to the District Court appropriate.

Any further preliminary injunctive order should not be issued unless the District Judge, after examination of the EIS, is of the opinion that it is probably deficient, and that the plaintiffs more likely than not will prevail. If he satisfies himself on that score, there seems little or no reason for requiring more than a nominal bond of these plaintiffs, who are acting much as private attorneys general. If he finds no apparent deficiencies in the statement and little probability that the plaintiffs will ultimately prevail, he should deny all interim relief and await the conclusion of the hearing on the merits.

COMMENTARY & QUESTIONS

The bond. Note the court's discussion of the only point the citizens care about, the possibility of another $75,000 bond. Does Judge Haynsworth's opinion reflect economic reality? On the other hand, what would be the result of a blanket requirement that environmental plaintiffs seeking to enforce federal laws must post bonds sufficient to cover potential damages to defendants wrongfully restrained?[14]

The case then went back to Judge Larkins's court for review of the SCS's newly prepared EIS. The citizen plaintiffs again sued for a preliminary injunction, alleging that even though there now was an EIS, it was inadequate under the terms of NEPA.

Natural Resources Defense Council v. Grant
United States District Court for the Eastern District of North Carolina, 1973
355 F. Supp. 280

LARKINS, J.:

> The River...is the living symbol of all the life it sustains or nourishes — fish, aquatic insects, water ouzels, otter, fisher, deer, elk, bear, and all other animals, including man, who are dependent upon it or who enjoy it for its sight, its sound or its life. Justice William O. Douglas, dissenting in Sierra Club v. Morton, 405 U.S. 727 (1972)....

Findings of Fact and Conclusions of Law. There is a substantial probability that the provisions of NEPA are not satisfied by the Chicod Creek Watershed EIS.

A. Scope of Judicial Review of the EIS. As the Court views this case, the ultimate decisions must not be made by the judiciary but by the executive and legislative branches of our government. This court does not intend to substitute its judgment as to what would be the best use of Chicod Creek and its environs for that of the Congress or those administrative departments of the executive branch which are charged by the Congress with the duty of carrying out its mandate. The Court's function is to determine whether the environmental effects of the proposed action and reasonable alternatives are sufficiently disclosed, discussed, and that conclusions are substantiated by supportive opinion and data.

B. Requirements of NEPA. Section 102(2)(C) of NEPA requires, first, that federal agencies make full and accurate disclosure of the environmental effects of proposed action and alternatives to such action; and, second, that the agencies give full and meaningful consideration to these effects and alternatives in their decision-making. "At the very least, NEPA is an environmental full disclosure law...intended to make...decision-making more responsive and responsible. The 'detailed statement' required by 102(2)(C) should, at a minimum, contain such information as will alert the President, the Council on Environmental Quality, the public, and indeed, the Congress to all known possible consequences of proposed agency action."

But NEPA requires more than full disclosure of environmental consequences and project alternatives. NEPA requires full consideration of the same in agency decision-making. Calvert Cliffs Coordinating Committee v. Atomic Energy Commission, 449 F.2d 1109 (D.C. Cir. 1971).

----

14. See Calderon, Bond Requirements Under FRCP 65(c): An Emerging Equitable Exemption for Public Interest Litigants, 13 B.C. Envtl. Aff. L. Rev. 125 (1985).

The EIS "must be written in language that is understandable to the nontechnical minds and yet contains enough scientific reasoning to alert specialists to particular problems within the field of their expertise."

C. The Final Statement Omits and Misrepresents a Number of Important Environmental Effects of the Project.

(1) The Statement Misrepresents the Adverse Environmental Effects of the Project upon Fish Habitat. The final Statement concedes that the Project will greatly increase the quantities of sediment carried downstream from the project area into the lower reaches of Chicod Creek and the Tar River. Immediately after construction, annual sediment deposit in the lower Chicod will be 11,670 tons. Sediment yield at the confluence of the Tar River is expected to be 730 tons annually. On the assumption that the banks will stabilize in two years, sedimentation will still be increased to 4,010 tons deposited annually in Chicod Creek and 250 tons in the Tar River.... While disclosing the fact of this increase in sediment load, the statement contains no discussion of its downstream effects. The statement merely concludes, without supportive scientific data and opinion that "No significant reduction in quality of the waters of the Tar River, Pamlico River, and Pamlico Sound is expected." Credible evidence suggests the opposite conclusion. Having conceded a massive increase in sedimentation, the Statement disposes of its environmental effects in one conclusory statement unsupported by empirical or experimental data, scientific authorities or explanatory information of any kind....

(2) The Statement Misrepresents the Effect of the Project upon Fish Resources. The Statement is not at all clear on the effect of the Project on the fishery resources in Chicod Creek. It suggests that there will be effects upon the resident and anadromous fish in Chicod Creek, but the Statement does not define the effects. Yet the Statement without any supportive data declares "Most of the fishery resources within the watershed will not be affected by the project's works of improvement or will be mitigated." This falls far short of the standards of NEPA.

(3) The Statement Ignores the Effect of the Project on Potential Eutrophication Problems in the Tar-Pamlico Estuary. Eutrophication problems occur in waterways which accumulate an excess of nutrients such as nitrogen and phosphorous. Nutrients may be introduced in the waterways from several sources including agricultural runoff and swamp drainage. At the present time the nearby Chowan River is suffering from a very serious eutrophication problem.... Eutrophication is a problem that needs extensive study and research. Yet the Statement is silent on eutrophication. This is a violation of the "full disclosure" requirements of NEPA.

*(4) The Statement Fails to Disclose the Maintenance History of P.L. 566 Projects....*Evidence indicated that local sponsors have failed to adequately perform their maintenance responsibilities in the past.... The Statement should disclose the history of success and failure of similar projects.

(5) The Statement Ignores the Serious Environmental Consequences of the Proposed Use of Kudzu. Although one may not know what it is called, a person does not have to be a scientist to recognize kudzu.... It can be seen growing on banks, stretching over shrubs and underbrush, engulfing trees, small and large, short and tall, slowly destroying and snuffing out the life of its unwilling host. Even manmade structures are susceptible to the vine — the tall slender green tree may be your telephone pole. However, if controlled, kudzu may have erosion preventing value. The defendants propose to plant one row of kudzu at the top edge of the channel slope in cultivated areas — along 23.5 miles of the new channels. As to the use of kudzu, the Statement merely discloses, "one row of kudzu will be planted at the very top edge of the channel slope through cultivated areas. The growth of kudzu will be controlled by mechanical methods." The Statement fails to disclose how the growth of kudzu can be controlled by mechanical or any other methods and in this respect fails to satisfy the requirements of NEPA.

(6) The Statement Misrepresents and Fails to Disclose Other Important Environmental Effects of the Project. The Statement fails to disclose that over 17 percent of the acreage to be benefited by the Project is held by the Weyerhaeuser Company, a large lumber company. The Statement does not contain an adequate discussion of the possible adverse effects of the Project upon downstream flooding.

D. The Statement Does not Disclose or Discuss the Cumulative Effects of the Project.... The [Regulations] of the CEQ focus attention upon the "overall cumulative impact of the action proposed (and further actions contemplated)," since the effect of decision about a project or a complex of projects "can be individually limited but cumulatively considerable." Yet, the Defendants have failed to consider fully in the final Statement the cumulative impact of the Chicod Creek Watershed Project and other channelization projects on the environmental and economic resources of Eastern North Carolina.... The cumulative effect of sedimentation is ignored in the Statement. There is no discussion of the potential adverse effects of long-term accumulation of nutrients caused by this and other channelization projects in the Tar-Pamlico River Basin. There is no discussion of the cumulative impact of drainage projects upon hardwood timber or groundwater resources.... Such effects should be assessed and disclosed in the environmental impact statement.

E. The Statement Does Not Fully Disclose or Adequately Discuss Alternatives to the Project. The "full disclosure" impact statement required by NEPA must contain a full and objective discussion of (1) reasonable alternatives to the proposed project and (2) the environmental impacts of each alternative. The Statement falls far short of satisfying these important and essential standards. Several critical reasonable alternatives are not discussed at all in the Statement. The recommendation of the Bureau of Sport Fisheries and Wildlife that seven miles of channelization be deleted from the most productive portion of the Chicod ecosystem is not discussed as an alternative to the Project. The Statement fails to discuss the alternative of deferral of the Project. Deferral is particularly appropriate in view of differing opinions about the environmental effects of the Project and §102(2)(A) of NEPA which "makes the completion of an adequate research program a prerequisite to agency action." Many of the conclusions in the Statement as to the potential adverse effects of the Project are not supported by references to scientific or other sources. The Statement omits any discussion of the recommendation of the North Carolina Department of Natural and Economic Resources that vertical drainage and water level control structures be discussed in the alternatives section, specifically as they mitigate any adverse ground water effects of the proposed project.

Alternatives are discussed only superficially, and nowhere are the environmental impacts of the alternatives discussed. The Statement thus does not provide "information sufficient to permit a reasoned choice of alternatives so far as environmental aspects are concerned." *Natural Resources Defense Council v. Morton.* It is not the "full disclosure" statement required by NEPA.

F. Conclusions. This Court finds as a fact that the final Chicod Creek Watershed Environmental Statement does not fully and adequately disclose the adverse environmental effects of the Chicod Creek Watershed Project; nor does the Statement adequately disclose or discuss reasonable alternatives to the Project; and, therefore, there is a substantial probability that the Plaintiffs will be able to demonstrate at trial on the merits that the final Statement is not the "full disclosure" statement required by this Court's Order of March 16, 1972, and NEPA. A preliminary injunction barring further action on the Project pending a full hearing on the merits is thus appropriate....

COMMENTARY & QUESTIONS

1. **Agencies and EISs — a shotgun marriage?** What apparently was the nature and tone of the Chicod Creek EIS? Most agencies have an understandable inclination to build their projects as conveniently as possible, and EISs do not serve this end. The central problem of the §102 EIS requirement is that it presents federal agencies (especially "construction" agencies and regulatory agencies with a high level of market involvement, such as the NRC and the Department of Agriculture) with conflicting mandates. On one hand, they have specific statutory missions, backed by the elaborate reward structure of supportive congressional committees, money, and the support of the related private industries and organizations with which they work. On the other hand, they have the vague, generalized values and directives of NEPA, for which there is no affirmative administrative reward system (beyond the satisfaction of a job well done in environmental terms). At the end of a year, agency officials tend to measure their accomplishments in terms of how many miles of river were dammed or channelized or how many reactors licensed — it must be harder to measure institutional success in terms of how many wetlands have not been disrupted or how many rivers left as they are. Yet EISs, by illuminating facts and concerns that previously had no legal place in the institutional decisionmaking process, now can show, in some cases, that the country would be better off without the agency's projects. A straightforward EIS may militate against building the project at all or may indicate a less destructive way of constructing it, for the sake of newly declared ecological values that do not square with the agency's own specific mandate.

Little wonder, then, that there is a marked tendency to write EISs in a manner that is consistent with agencies' program missions. Pick up any recent EIS, review its content and prose, and you will probably be confronted with the predictable agency reaction to contradictory statutory mandates.

So the temptation is great to make the EIS a "post hoc rationalization" that is supportive of the decision the agency has already effectively made. Sometimes, project benefits are stressed, negative effects are briefly noted and rated "manageable," "mitigation" is discussed, and alternatives are cursorily noted and dismissed. Other times, the agency's strategy is to prepare an excessively long, hypertechnical, and unreadable EIS that is calculated to prevent public scrutiny. The CEQ regulations require that EISs be prepared using an interdisciplinary approach (§1502.6), that they not exceed approximate page limitations (§1502.7), and that they be written in "plain language" (§1502.8); but these commands are rarely followed and never enforced. The CEQ itself has admitted that

> frequently NEPA takes too long and costs too much, agencies make decisions before hearing from the public, documents are too long and technical for many people to use, and training for agency officials, particularly senior leadership, is inadequate. The EIS process is still frequently viewed as merely a compliance requirement rather than as a tool to effect better decision-making. Because of this, millions of dollars, years of time, and tons of paper have been spent on documents that have little effect on decision-making. 1997 CEQ Study at 7.

Courts rarely mention the reality of this administrative inclination to write self-justifying FONSIs or impact statements, but in the *Chicod Creek* case the court seems skeptical of the SCS's sincerity. In judicial review of agency decisions under NEPA and other environmental laws, can environmental lawyers ask judges to take account of political science and be less deferential, where applicable laws were designed to constrain the agencies' single-mindedness? Do they already do so implicitly? A number of courts have explicitly noted that deference is less when the statute, like NEPA, is directed to all agencies, not just the subject agency.[15]

2. **Judicial psychology.** Do you detect a change in Judge Larkins's tone? What happened? There is no mention now of the alleged project benefits to small farmers; rather the opinion is a catalog of the project's negative effects. Can you discern which pieces of evidence at trial got through to the judge most dramatically? How sophisticated would the various pieces of plaintiff's evidence have to be on eutrophication, sedimentation, fisheries, and kudzu? What about Weyerhaeuser's ownership? Problems of past maintenance? How do environmental plaintiffs get around a judge's natural inclination to defer to official expertise?

3. **The EIS: what must it contain?** Note the array of requirements for the preparation of EISs set out in §102 as it was drafted by Professor Caldwell. Is there any real difference between (i) "environmental impacts," (ii) "adverse environmental effects which cannot be avoided," (iii) "the relationship between short-term uses and maintenance of long-term productivity(?)"; and (iv) "irretrievable commitments of resources"? Some EISs dutifully separate out multiple sections to cover each of these, but analytically it seems that §102 just requires a statement of *effects* — §102(2)(C)(i), (ii), (iv) & (v) and *alternatives* — (C)(ii) and (D) — prepared in consultation with other relevant agencies.

Judge Larkins's opinion follows this approach by looking at only two categories, effects and alternatives. Note the kinds of effects that were left out, insufficiently disclosed, or, worse, "misrepresented" in the EIS. What effects must be discussed, and to what extent, in order to comply with whatever it is that §102 is supposed to do? Effects on human sport? The aesthetics of a scraped-off linear canal? Slight thermal changes in the local microclimate? Is a short description of sedimentation enough to disclose the existence of a problem to whomever is intended by NEPA to read the EIS? Here, as in other areas of NEPA interpretation, courts have adopted a "rule of reason" in fashioning the common law of NEPA. However, what is reasonable to one judge or panel of judges may not be reasonable to another. Thus NEPA jurisprudence, like the common law, tends to be variable among jurisdictions — in this case, federal circuit courts of appeals. Forum shopping may be advantageous in NEPA litigation.

To what extent must environmental effects be analyzed and discussed in the EIS? The Chicod Creek EIS discussed eutrophication, for example, but not extensively enough

---

15. "The agency's NEPA determination 'is not entitled to the deference that courts must accord to an agency's interpretation of its governing statute' and is instead 'a question of law, subject to de novo review.'" Mineral Policy Center v. Norton, 292 F. Supp. 2d 30, 70 (D.D.C. 2003) (reviewing a FONSI). See also Citizens Against Rails-to-Trails, 267 F.3d 1144, 1150-1151 (D.C. Cir. 2001) ("The court owes no deference to the FAA's interpretation of NEPA or [of] the CEQ regulations because NEPA is addressed to all federal agencies and Congress did not entrust administration of NEPA to the FAA alone"); Grand Canyon Trust v. FAA, 290 F.3d 339, 342 (D.C. Cir. 2002). The premise appears to be that statutes that apply to all agencies are intended to restrict those agencies' behavior, making deference to the agencies' restriction-avoidance determinations less appropriate.

for Judge Larkins. If, as some courts have said, the purpose is to bring the project's consequences to the attention of the agency decisionmaker, mere disclosure may be enough. If, on the other hand, the EIS is intended to demonstrate to the environmentally concerned public and a court that the agency gave "full consideration" to the impact, *Calvert Cliffs*, 449 F.2d at 1128, then more analysis must be reflected in the EIS itself. A middle ground definition was given by the Ninth Circuit: "reasonably thorough discussion of the significant aspects of the probable environmental consequences is all that is required by an EIS," said the court in Trout Unltd. v. Morton, 509 F.2d 1276, 1283 (9th Cir. 1974) (the decision that allowed the construction of the Teton Dam in spite of environmentalists' safety warnings; the dam collapsed, killing more than 100 people). This is another manifestation of the "rule of reason" that courts apply in interpreting most aspects of NEPA.

4. **Alternatives.** Alternatives have been part of our environmental analysis from the beginning of this book and are a critical part of NEPA's EIS requirement. Judge Larkins found that the SCS's EIS did not fully disclose or adequately discuss reasonable alternatives to the project, such as reduction in the scope of the project or project deferral. In some SCS EISs, and those of other agencies, the agency refused to consider the "do-nothing," "no-action," or "zero" alternative. Why? Other agencies refused to consider any alternatives that they themselves could not build or manage. NRDC v. Morton, 458 F.2d 827 (D.C. Cir. 1972), set those arguments to rest: The Interior Department had to consider all practical alternative sources of energy, regardless of whether they were within the agency's control, before deciding to lease offshore oil deposits. Note the relationship between discussions of alternatives and of environmental consequences required by the CEQ regulations:

> §1502.14 Alternatives including the proposed action. This section is the heart of the environmental impact statement.... [I]t should present the environmental impacts of the proposal and the alternatives in comparative form, thus sharply defining the issues and providing a clear basis of choice among options by the decision maker and the public. In this section agencies shall:
>
> (a) Rigorously explore and objectively evaluate all reasonable alternatives and for alternatives which were eliminated from detailed study, briefly discuss the reasons for their having been eliminated.
>
> (b) Devote substantial treatment to each alternative considered in detail including the proposed action so that reviewers may evaluate their comparative merits.
>
> (c) Include reasonable alternatives not within the jurisdiction of the lead agency.
>
> (d) Include the alternative of no action....
>
> §1502.16 Environmental consequences. ...The discussion will include the environmental impacts of the alternatives including the proposed action, any adverse environmental effects which cannot be avoided...and any irreversible or irretrievable commitments of resources which would be involved in the proposal should it be implemented....

Section 1502.16 also provides that the EIS will include discussions of direct and indirect effects and their significance; possible conflicts between the proposed action and the objectives of land use plans, policies, and controls for the area concerned; and the energy and resource requirements and conservation potential of the various alternatives. An EIS also must address urban quality, historic and cultural resources, and measures to mitigate adverse environmental impacts.

If courts did not require consideration of rational alternatives, the stop-and-think process would be neutralized. In Citizens Against Burlington v. Busey, 938 F.2d 190 (D.C. Cir.), cert. denied, 502 U.S. 994 (1991), for instance, an air freight carrier wanted permission to shift its operations 80 miles from Fort Wayne to a Toledo air field, increasing night traffic there from 400 to more than 11,700 flights per year, in order to save operating expenses. The Federal Aviation Administration's EIS considered only the two options advanced by the corporation — the proposed facility or nothing — ignoring the citizens' evidence that operations could be improved at the original facility. Writing for the D.C. Circuit, Judge (now Justice) Clarence Thomas permitted this circumscribing of EIS alternatives.[16] Writing in dissent, Judge James Buckley, a conservative Reagan appointee, complained that the Thomas opinion allowed nonfederal parties "to define the limits of the EIS inquiry and thus to frustrate one of the principal safeguards of the NEPA process, the mandatory consideration of reasonable alternatives." 938 F.2d at 209.

5. **Interagency consultation.** Section 102(2)(C) does not merely require EIS preparation; it also requires that, in this case, the SCS "consult with and obtain the comments of any Federal agency [involved relevant to environmental issues]," and those comments must "accompany the proposal through existing agency review processes." One reason for Judge Larkins's rejection of the Chicod Creek EIS was the SCS's disregard of the project reduction recommendations of the Federal Bureau of Sport Fisheries and Wildlife (since renamed the Fish and Wildlife Service). Federal agencies possess different, and sometimes conflicting, statutory missions. For example, the U.S. Army Corps of Engineers, located in the Defense Department, is primarily a construction and development agency, while the Fish and Wildlife Service, located in the U.S. Department of the Interior, is fundamentally mandated to protect and conserve natural resources. The FWS has no legal power over the activities of its sister agency, but it can effectively influence the SCS decisionmaking process by commenting (in this case unfavorably) on an EIS. State agencies must also be invited to comment (40 C.F.R. §1503.1(2)). Project mitigation recommendations by the North Carolina Department of Natural and Economic Resources were also omitted in the EIS. Citizen plaintiffs in NEPA cases frequently acquire their most convincing evidence of EIS deficiency from federal and state agency comments, and judges — as in this case — are impressed by the credibility of these comments. If the SCS had tried to solicit comments of other agencies, but received none, could the plaintiffs have demanded an injunction until such consultation did occur? In fact, a consulted federal agency has no duty to comment: It may reply with a "no comment" (40 C.F.R. §1503.2).

6. **Treatment of responsible opposing views.** Section 1502.9(b) of the NEPA regulations provides that an agency "shall discuss at appropriate points in the final statement

---

16. Judge Thomas also declined to require noise mitigation measures required under §509(b)(5) of the Airport & Aviation Import Act (AAIA), 49 U.S.C. §2208(b)(5).

any responsible opposing view which was not adequately discussed in the draft statement and shall indicate the agency's response to the issues raised." In Center for Biological Diversity v. U.S. Forest Serv., 349 F.3d 1157 (9th Cir. 2003), the court invalidated the Forest Service's final EIS (FEIS) covering its proposal to set guidelines for maintaining northern goshawk habitat in the Southwestern Region because the Forest Service's key assumption — that northern goshawks are habitat generalists — was persistently challenged by the Arizona and New Mexico wildlife management agencies, as well as the FWS. The agencies had submitted that goshawks prefer to forage in mature, close-canopied forests; and these comments were not disclosed or discussed in either the draft EIS (DEIS) or FEIS. See the critique, in Chapter 24, of the Forest Service's "garbage-in-garbage-out" planning style. In Utahns for Better Transp. v. U.S. Dep't of Transp., 305 F.3d 1152 (10th Cir. 2002), the court, finding that DOT had failed to respond to comments submitted by environmental group appellants regarding allegedly underestimated highway cost estimates contained in the FEIS as well as potential public transit alternatives to the highway, struck down an agency FEIS for the proposed Legacy Parkway, near Salt Lake City.

7. **Epilogue to *Chicod Creek*.** What did finally happen in our North Carolina case? As one state official put it, "Old John Larkins saw he was going to make some enemies either way he decided this thing, so he called in the attorneys for both sides and said 'Boys, we've gone through this stuff long enough now, why don't you go settle it between yourselves?' And because the handwriting was on the wall, the SCS agreed to a compromise." Confidential interview, Feb. 1981. No channelizing, channel straightening, or major tree-cutting was allowed; silt removal was permitted in the upper stretches. The lower six to seven miles of the creek were cleaned of snags and silt, but no draglines were permitted. As a result, the stream and its tributaries were, to a great degree, returned to the quality of the days before intensive agriculture, with a meandering wooded course and restored swimming holes. The redesigned project was so successful that the North Carolina legislature passed a Stream Restoration Act in 1979, mandating consultation with the State Wildlife Resources Commission for all such projects. Is this a success story? What about the poor families that Judge Larkins wrote of in his first opinion? No new subsidized farmland was created. Is this another example of élite conservationists oppressing poor folks?

The result in the *Chicod Creek* case is a typical outcome of NEPA citizen litigation: The proposal is finally implemented, but in a modified, mitigated, or redesigned manner that is less destructive of environmental values than its predecessor. Frequently, the compromise proposal completely satisfies neither the plaintiff nor the defendant but is minimally acceptable to ("satisfices") both sides. The Trans-Alaska Pipeline provides an example of this outcome. The oil industry, and the Bureau of Land Management in the Interior Department, which is authorized to permit pipeline routes over federal lands, first proposed the simplest and cheapest possible pipeline — flat against the tundra with no internal compartments. Conservation groups categorically opposed the construction of any such pipeline on the grounds not only that its environmental impacts (potential damage to permafrost by leaks, obstruction of wildlife migration routes, creation of polluting boom towns, possibility of oil spills by loaded tankers bound from the port of Valdez, the pipeline's terminus,[17] etc.) were unacceptable, but also that North Slope Alaskan oil was unnecessary for the fulfillment of America's legitimate energy needs. After years of NEPA litigation and congressional reconsideration, the Trans-Alaska Pipeline was finally constructed in a more environmentally protective form — including internal bulkheads that could be shut in case of a spill, thus minimizing leakage; elevated sections over migration routes; restricted access by outsiders and closely controlled management of worker villages; and other mitigation measures. Does NEPA promote beneficial compromises or suboptimal, least-common-denominator outcomes?

Section 2. RECURRENT ISSUES IN IMPLEMENTING NEPA

Especially when a statute is written in such general and enigmatic terms as NEPA, and passed with so little relevant legislative history, it is inevitable that a parade of questions will have to be answered before the statute's shape and substance become clear in practice. The position to which NEPA has evolved over the years, almost entirely as a function of citizen litigation, was certainly not preordained. As the *Chicod Creek* case demonstrated, NEPA could have become merely a footnote of judicial deference to agency action, but didn't. With few exceptions, the federal courts took NEPA seriously. NEPA could also have become a super-statute, imposing strict court-enforced substantive controls on the administrative process. That didn't happen either.

The following materials review some of the basic questions raised in the judicial and administrative implementation of NEPA. In the course of this development, NEPA became what it is today — a useful, mixed proposition, a milestone statute in the emerging evolution of national (and international) environmental policy. As you read this section, consider how a federal agency can exploit these issues in order to minimize its NEPA compliance responsibilities.

Segmentation. One agency strategy for avoiding the full effect of NEPA has been segmentation. If an entire project raises major environmental questions, divide it into smaller segments, and build the least destructive segment first, with an EIS (or less, an EA with a FONSI) limited to that segment. Then the later segments will draw momentum from the approval and construction of the first. Some courts have rejected these EISs on the grounds that the segmentation did not have "independent utility" or, implicitly, that this was an attempt to evade NEPA through coercive construction "bootstrapping." Other courts have allowed the strategy. Swan v. Brinegar, 542 F.2d 364 (7th Cir. 1976); Sierra Club v. Callaway (Wallisville Dam), 499 F.2d 982 (5th Cir. 1974); Indian Lookout Alliance v. Volpe, 484 F.2d 11 (8th Cir. 1973). In either event, "independent utility" appears to have emerged as the universal test for determining whether an agency proposal is a separate project or merely a segment of a larger project that is either planned or undergoing construction. Is this a meaningful test? Two proposed dams in a single watershed may have independent utility, but their impacts interact so

---

17. The predicted catastrophic oil spill, of course, actually did occur — at 11:56 p.m., March 23, 1989 — when the *Exxon-Valdez* struck a reef in Prince William Sound (see Chapter 3).

dynamically that both dam proposals should be considered together. Segmentation of a larger project into several components is one variation of the cumulative impacts issue, which is discussed below.

Would it be legal for the builders of a highway to take one portion of the project that is environmentally destructive — say the portion of the highway that runs through a wetlands — and have the state road department build that without federal dollars, thereby trying to "de-federalize" the wetlands stretch of road and avoiding an EIS that would reveal major negative impacts? See Village of Los Ranchos de Albuquerque v. Barnhart, 906 F.2d 1477 (10th Cir. 1990), where the court permitted segmentation by de-federalization; contra Ross v. Federal Highway Admin., 162 F.3d 1046 (10th Cir. 1998).

NEPA and Scientific Uncertainty. One of the recurring themes of environmental law and policy is how to make policy decisions under conditions of pervasive scientific uncertainty. Before 1986, the CEQ regulations required a "worst-case analysis" in such situations, but, during the Reagan Administration, these regulations were amended to read as follows:

> §1502.22 Incomplete or unavailable information. When an agency is evaluating reasonably foreseeable significant adverse effects on the human environment...and there is incomplete or unavailable information, the agency shall always make clear that such information is lacking.
>
> (a) If the incomplete information...is essential to a reasonable choice among alternatives and the overall costs of obtaining it are not exorbitant, the agency shall include the information in the environmental impact statement.
>
> (b) If the information...cannot be obtained because the overall costs of obtaining it are exorbitant, or the means to obtain it are not known, the agency shall include within the environmental impact statement:
>
> (1) A statement that such information is incomplete or unavailable; (2) a statement of the relevance of the incomplete or unavailable information...; (3) a summary of existing credible scientific evidence...; and (4) the agency's evaluation of such impacts based upon theoretical approaches or research methods generally accepted in the scientific community. For the purposes of this section, "reasonably foreseeable" includes impacts which have catastrophic consequences, even if their probability of occurrence is low, provided that the analysis of the impacts is supported by credible scientific evidence, and is within the rule of reason.

In Robertson v. Methow Valley Citizens' Council, 490 U.S. 332 (1989), the Supreme Court upheld the CEQ's abandonment of the "worst-case analysis" requirement.

Who determines whether information is incomplete, unavailable, or only available at "exorbitant" cost? Since NEPA is a full-disclosure statute, should judges give less deference to agency decisions regarding uncertainty than would be entailed by the "arbitrary and capricious" standard of judicial review? Should agency analysis be limited to "theoretical approaches or research methods generally accepted in the scientific community"? (See Chapter 4.) What is "credible scientific evidence"? The CEQ's insistence that the impacts analysis should be consistent with the "rule of reason" and not be based on "pure conjecture" is consistent with judicial interpretations of NEPA. But judicial applications of the reasonableness standard to proffered scientific evidence may differ widely.

As discussed in Chapter 26, the question of scientific uncertainty has now assumed considerable prominence in international environmental law and policy. The accepted international standard, as formulated in the 1992 Rio Declaration on Environment and Development, states that "Where there are threats of serious or irreversible damage, lack of full scientific certainty shall not be used as a reason for postponing cost-effective measures to prevent environmental degradation." To what extent does §1502.22 meet this test?

Where relevant new information becomes available after the EIS is adopted, the lead agency may be required to prepare and circulate a supplemental EIS (SEIS), 40 C.F.R. §1502.9(c). An SEIS may also be required when substantial changes are made in the project after original NEPA compliance. An agency decision whether to prepare an SEIS is reviewable under the "arbitrary and capricious" standard. Marsh v. Oregon Nat. Res. Council, 490 U.S. 360 (1989). See Idaho Sporting Congress v. U.S. Forest Serv., 222 F.3d 562 (9th Cir. 2000) (Forest Service improperly used Supplemental Information Reports to correct deficiencies in previously prepared EISs without preparing Supplemental EAs or EISs).

The wide latitude afforded agencies in defining acceptable scientific data during the NEPA process presents a paradox: In order to convince a court of legitimate doubt regarding the environmental aspects of a proposed project, plaintiffs must ascertain in advance much of the information they are asking the agency to develop during NEPA compliance. This requires private plaintiffs to come up with a lot of expensive expert testimony and, to some extent, mixes up the players' roles.

Who Really Prepares the EIS? Who prepares the EIS? NEPA says "the responsible official," and in a number of early cases the courts had to deal with EISs that were drafted at the local level by state officials or other project proponents and merely fronted by the relevant federal agencies. Citizen plaintiffs successfully urged the courts to require the EISs to be prepared by the federal agencies themselves, on the ground that NEPA was designed to inform the federal decision as it was being made. Greene County Planning Bd. v. FPC, 455 F.2d 412 (2d Cir.), cert. denied, 409 U.S. 849 (1972). What premises are reflected in such lawsuits about the relative bias within and outside the federal agency? Congress amended NEPA in 1975 to permit preparation of the EIS by state agencies that receive federal grants for particular projects. In practice today, many agencies hire consultant firms to prepare "winning" EISs for them, which may set up yet another bias problem. If several federal agencies are involved in a proposal, NEPA compliance is the primary responsibility of a "lead agency," with the assistance of "cooperating agencies." The CEQ resolves disputes among federal agencies over which will be the lead agency (§§1501.5, 1501.6).

Are Agency Promises in an EIS Enforceable? What if an agency prepares an EA or EIS that promises extensive mitigation work (setting up new wetland reserves, wildlife enhancement, etc.) to offset negative project effects, defeats a citizen lawsuit on this basis, and then announces that it will not undertake the promised work (because it has insufficient funds or whatever)? In Robertson v. Methow Valley Citizens' Council, 490 U.S. 332 (1989), the Supreme Court made it clear that courts cannot compel agencies to implement mitigation measures discussed in EISs. The lower courts have uniformly held that the citizens have no remedy if promises made (or implied) in an EIS are not kept. NOE v. Metropolitan Atlanta Transit Auth., 485 F. Supp. 501 (N.D. Ga. 1980); Ogunquit Village Corp. v. Davis, 553 F.2d 243 (1st Cir. 1977). Even if the plaintiffs prove agency bad faith, a court will weigh the value of the requested compliance against the costs. EDF v. Marsh, 651 F.2d 983 (5th Cir. 1981).

Rational Decisionmaking and NEPA's Substantive Effect. The earliest chapters of this book set out the analytical basis of questions now raised by NEPA: A sound, rational decision requires consideration of all the significant effects of a proposal, and of its *alternatives*, as well as its real benefits. When these have finally been disclosed in an adequate EIS, however, can a court force the agency to make its substantive decision consistent with the EIS? Could Judge Larkins, for example, have forbidden the Chicod Creek project if the final EIS showed major sedimentation, eutrophication, wildlife and drainage disruption, and also showed that the countervailing benefits to farming were estimated at less than $100 per acre?

Put another way, does NEPA have an enforceable substantive requirement — that is, that agency decisions must be environmentally sound — as well as the bare procedural requirement that an EIS be prepared and circulated? If it is only the latter, then NEPA appears superficial, allowing an agency to go ahead with major destructive projects if only it first accurately catalogs the destructive effects in an EIS document. If, on the other hand, courts can enforce a substantive application of NEPA's broad principles upon an unwilling agency, what limit is there to the judicial power? Suppose Judge Larkins was deeply convinced, at the end of the trial on the merits, that the *Chicod Creek* case was ludicrously negative on an overall balance of effects. What could he do? Justice Rehnquist, writing for the Supreme Court in Vermont Yankee Nuclear Power Corp. v. NRDC, 435 U.S. 519, 558 (1978), stated that while NEPA "establishes significant substantive goals for the Nation," its actual requirements for the agencies are "essentially procedural." The Supreme Court reiterated its view that NEPA does not demand particular substantive results in Marsh v. Oregon Nat. Res. Council, 490 U.S. 360 (1989) ("NEPA merely prohibits uninformed — rather than unwise — agency decisions"), and Robertson v. Methow Valley Citizens' Council, 490 U.S. 332 (1989). In its Record of Decision, at the conclusion of the NEPA process, an agency must identify the environmentally preferable alternative, but it does not have to choose this alternative (§1505.2).

Judicial Review: The Arbitrary and Capricious Test. Even if courts do not have direct substantive review powers under NEPA, they have some ability to review the decisions of federal agencies under APA's §706, which prohibits actions that are "arbitrary, capricious, or an abuse of discretion." What does this test mean? There have been several interpretations in NEPA cases:

> The test is whether the balance of cost and benefits that was struck was arbitrary or clearly gave insufficient weight to environmental values. *Calvert Cliffs*, 449 F.2d at 1115.

> Our review will perforce be a narrow one, limited to ensuring that the Commission has adequately explained the fact and policy concerns it relied on [and that these]

considerations could by themselves lead a reasonable person to make the judgment that the Agency has made. NRDC v. SEC, 606 F.2d 1031, 1053 (D.C. Cir. 1979).

[The role of the court is to ensure that] the agency made a good faith balancing of environmental benefits and costs. EDF v. TVA, 339 F. Supp. at 810 (1972).

[The reviewing court must insure that] the agency has taken a "hard look" at environmental consequences. Kleppe v. Sierra Club, 427 U.S. 390, 410 n. 21 (1976).

Each of these tests permits a court to review the agency's substantive decision to some degree. Strycker's Bay Neighborhood Council v. Karlen, 444 U.S. 223 (1980), however, considerably clouded the issue. A low-income housing unit that was determined to have serious environmental consequences (including social and economic ghettoization) was proposed for a site in Manhattan. (Courts have consistently held that the urban environment is within the purview of NEPA.) The EIS showed alternative sites available, which did not have such adverse environmental effects, but each alternative would have required a two-year delay to shift the project. The agency chose to build as planned in order to save time. The Second Circuit said that in light of NEPA's policy, the two-year time factor could not be treated as "an overriding factor"; "environmental factors...should be given determinable [sic] weight." 590 F.2d at 44. The Supreme Court reversed, saying "once an agency has made a decision subject to NEPA's procedural requirements, the only role for a court is to insure that the agency has *considered* the environmental consequences." What then is the test? The Court cannot mean that an agency can ignore the environmental evidence after considering it. Even the defendant agency in *Strycker's Bay* conceded that its decision would be arbitrary if it gave little or no decisional weight to environmental factors. Because of the high court's opinion, however, the lower court could no longer give superior weight to environmental factors. So how about equal weight? Does that simplify the question? If the costs of a two-year delay closely balance the negative environmental effects, the agency can be expected to tilt in favor of its original plans, and that decision will not be "arbitrary." But who is to say the opposing factors (apples and oranges?) are or are not closely balanced? If the courts can do so, are they necessarily making part of the substantive decision? This is an enduring problem in NEPA, where an adequate EIS is presumptive evidence of "good faith consideration" by the proposing agency. Ironically, a legally adequate EIS generally insulates the agency from judicial review on the basis of not having considered relevant factors, not explaining its decision satisfactorily, or not having provided a reviewable record.

Circulation and Public Comment. The standard course of the EIS's circulation as a public document follows the APA rulemaking model: The agency prepares a DEIS (analogous to a notice of proposed rulemaking); the DEIS is opened for public comment; the agency prepares the FEIS (analogous to a final rulemaking) with an appendix of comments received on the draft and the agency's responses thereto. 40 C.F.R. §1506. (Note that there is no requirement that agencies hold hearings on DEISs or FEISs.) Finally, the agency prepares and distributes a Record of Decision, stating the alternatives considered, including the environmentally preferable alternative, the nonenvironmental factors that the agency balanced against environmental factors, and "whether all practicable means to avoid or minimize harm from the alternative selected have been adopted, and if not, why they were not." 40 C.F.R. §1505.2. The agency must not make an "irreversible or irretrievable commitment of resources" (NEPA §102 (C)(v)) in furtherance of the proposed action until NEPA compliance has been accomplished (see discussion below).

Once EPA has published notice that an EIS has been filed, an agency cannot make a decision sooner than 90 days after publication, for a DEIS, or 30 days after publication, for a FEIS. If the periods overlap, the later of the two cutoff dates applies. Agencies must allow at least 45 days for comments on draft statements. 40 C.F.R. §1506.11. The lead agency may set time limits consistent with these parameters. In setting such time limits, the regulations suggest that the agency consider factors such as the scope of the action, the potential environmental risks, the consequences of delay, and the degree to which the proposed action is controversial. Are these time parameters realistic, given the long lead time customarily involved in planning agency projects, not to mention the length and complexity of modern EIS preparation? Do members of the public have sufficient time to verify the information included in the EIS or uncover information that the agency may have omitted?

Scoping and Timing. The NEPA regulations also introduce the process of "scoping." 40 C.F.R. §1501.7. At an early stage in the decisional process, an agency must review the breadth of project effects and alternatives, invite comments from the public and other governmental agencies, and prepare a comprehensive plan for addressing all significant issues. The intent is clearly to facilitate EIS preparation and forestall controversy by ventilating major issues and establishing a dialogue with concerned citizens before an EA or EIS is prepared. What would its effect have been on the Chicod Creek EIS? The CEQ, however, points out that scoping cannot be expected to change an agency's preconceptions:

> Citizens are frustrated when they are treated as adversaries rather than welcome participants in the NEPA process. When they are invited to a formal scoping meeting to discuss a well-developed project about which they have heard little, they may feel that they have been invited too late in the process. In addition, public "hearings" at times are seen as parties "talking past each other," with very little listening. Some citizens complain that their time and effort spent providing good ideas is not reflected in changes to proposals or satisfying explanations for why suggestions were not incorporated. Citizens report that they often feel overwhelmed by the resources available to proponents and agencies. As a consequence, litigation can be seen as the only means to affect environmental decisions significantly. 1997 CEQ Study at 18.

Note also if the agency doesn't scope, its failure to do so can't be raised until after the final EIS has been released.

When in a project's life history should the EIS be prepared? The *SIPI* case, Scientists Inst. for Pub. Info. v. Atomic Energy Comm'n, 481 F.2d 1079 (D.C. Cir. 1973), presented a demand for an EIS for the federal fast breeder reactor research program, a sequentially evolving enterprise with millions of dollars in present expenditures, leading to billions in future expenditures, with great potential environmental costs. The question of when in this process an EIS must be presented was poignantly put in the trial judge's question:

There comes a time, we start with $E=MC^2$, we both agree you don't have to have the impact statement then. Then there comes a time when there are a thousand of these breeder plants in existence all over the country. Sometime before that, surely...there has to be an impact statement, and a long time before that, actually. But the question is, exactly where in this chain do we have to have an impact statement? 481 F.2d at 1093.

The appeals court set up a four-factor balancing test designed to require an EIS at the point where binding decisions are being made. The factors were (1) the program's likelihood of practical feasibility, and how soon; (2) the availability of data on the technology and its alternatives, and their effects; (3) the likelihood that irretrievable commitments are being made and options foreclosed as the program continues; and (4) the potential seriousness of environmental effects. Based on these criteria, the court of appeals required an EIS, which exposed the issues of plutonium radiation hazards and runaway costs, and led to Congress's de-authorization of the reactor. What was *SIPI*'s premise? That if an EIS is truly to inform governmental decisionmaking, it has to occur sufficiently early in the process to make a meaningful difference, rather than as a last-step afterthought. As §102(2)(C) says, the DEIS "shall accompany the proposal through the existing agency review [decisionmaking?] process." In a very different setting in the following case, among other major NEPA issues, the Supreme Court had the opportunity to consider the timing of EIS preparation.

Kleppe v. Sierra Club
United States Supreme Court, 1976
427 U.S. 390

POWELL, J.... Respondents, several organizations concerned with the environment, brought this suit in July 1973 in the United States District Court for the District of Columbia. The defendants in the suit, petitioners here, were the officials of the Department [of Interior] and other federal agencies responsible for issuing coal leases, approving mining plans, granting rights-of-way and taking...other actions necessary to enable private companies and public utilities to develop coal reserves on land owned or controlled by the Federal Government. Citing widespread interest in the reserves of a region identified as the "Northern Great Plains region," and an alleged threat from coal-related operations to their members' enjoyment of the region's environment, respondents claimed that the federal officials could not allow further development without preparing a "comprehensive environmental impact statement" under §102(2)(C) on the entire region.... [Plaintiffs lost in the district court, but the court of appeals reversed and granted an injunction.]

The "Northern Great Plains region" identified in respondents' complaint encompasses portions of four States — northeastern Wyoming, eastern Montana, western North Dakota and western South Dakota. There is no dispute about its richness in coal, nor about the waxing interest in developing that coal, nor about the critical role the federal petitioners will play due to the significant percentage of the coal to which they control access....

The major issue [is] whether NEPA requires petitioners to prepare an EIS on the entire Northern Great Plains region. Petitioners, arguing the negative, rely squarely on the facts of the case and the language of §102(2)(C) of NEPA. We find their reliance well placed....

Respondents can prevail only if there has been a report or recommendation on a proposal for major federal action with respect to the Northern Great Plains region. Our statement of the relevant facts shows there has been none; instead, all proposals are for actions of either local or national scope.... The Court of Appeals...concluded nevertheless that the petitioners "contemplated" a regional plan or program....

The Court of Appeals recognized that the mere "contemplation" of certain action is not sufficient to require an impact statement. But it believed the statute nevertheless empowers a court to require the preparation of an impact statement to begin at some point prior to the formal recommendation or report on a proposal. The Court of Appeals accordingly devised its own four-part "balancing test" for determining when, during the contemplation of a plan or other type of federal action, an agency must begin a statement. The factors to be considered were [based on *SIPI*:] the likelihood and imminence of the program's coming to fruition, the extent to which information is available on the effects of implementing the expected program and on alternatives thereto, the extent to which irretrievable commitments are being made and options precluded "as refinement of the proposal progresses," and the severity of the environmental effects should the action be implemented....

The Court's reasoning and action find no support in the language or legislative history of NEPA. The statute clearly states when an impact statement is required, and mentions nothing about a balancing of factors. Rather...the moment at which an agency must have a final statement ready "is the time at which it makes a recommendation or report on a *proposal* for federal action." The procedural duty imposed upon agencies by this section is quite precise and the role of the courts in enforcing that duty is similarly precise. A court has no authority to depart from the statutory language and, by a balancing of court-devised factors, determine a point during the germination process of a potential proposal at which an impact statement *should be prepared*. Such an assertion of judicial authority would leave the agencies uncertain as to their procedural duties under NEPA, would invite judicial involvement in the day-to-day decision making process of the agencies, and would invite litigation....

Respondents [further] insist that, even without a comprehensive federal plan for the development of the Northern Great Plains, a "regional" impact statement nevertheless is required on all coal-related projects in the region because they are intimately related....

We begin by stating our general agreement with respondents' basis premise that §102(2)(C) may require a comprehensive impact statement in certain situations where several proposed actions are pending at the same time.... Thus, when several proposals for coal-related actions that will have a cumulative or synergistic environmental impact upon a region are pending concurrently before an agency, their environmental consequences must be considered together[18]....

Respondents conceded at oral argument that to prevail they must show that petitioners have acted arbitrarily in refusing to prepare one comprehensive statement on this entire region, and we agree. The determination of the region, if any, with respect to which a comprehensive statement is necessary requires the weighting of a number of factors, including the extent of the interrelationship among proposed actions and practical considerations of feasibility. Resolving those issues requires a high level of technical expertise and is properly left to the informed discretion of the responsible federal agencies. Absent a showing of arbitrary action, we must assume that the agencies have exercised this discretion appropriately. Respondents have made no showing to the contrary.

---

18. At some points in their brief respondents appear to seek a comprehensive ["programmatic"] impact statement covering contemplated projects in the region as well as those that already have been proposed. The statute, however, speaks solely in terms of proposed actions; it does not require an agency to consider the possible environmental impacts of less imminent actions when preparing the impact statement on proposed actions. Should contemplated actions later reach the stage of actual proposals, impact statements on them will take into account the effect of their approval upon the existing environment; and the condition of that environment presumably will reflect earlier proposed actions and their effects.

MARSHALL, J., concurring in part and dissenting in part. While I agree with much of the Court's opinion, I must dissent from [that part] which holds that the federal courts may not remedy violations of [NEPA] — no matter how blatant — until too late for an adequate remedy to be formulated. As the Court today recognizes, NEPA contemplates agency consideration of environmental factors throughout the decisionmaking process. Since NEPA's enactment, however, litigation has been brought primarily at the end of that process — challenging agency decisions to act made without adequate EISs or without any statements at all. In such situations, the courts have had to content themselves with the largely unsatisfactory remedy of enjoining the proposed federal action and ordering the preparation of an adequate impact statement. This remedy is insufficient because, except by deterrence, it does nothing to further early consideration of environmental factors. And, as with all after-the-fact remedies, a remand for the preparation of an impact statement after the basic decision to act has been made invites post hoc rationalizations, rather than the candid and balanced environmental assessments envisioned by NEPA. Moreover, the remedy is wasteful of resources and time, causing fully developed plans for action to be laid aside while an impact statement is prepared.

Nevertheless, until this lawsuit, such belated remedies were all the federal courts had had the opportunity to impose under NEPA. In this case, confronted with a situation in which, according to respondents' allegations, federal agencies were violating NEPA prior to their basic decision to act, the Court of Appeals...seized the opportunity to devise a different and effective remedy....

The Court begins its rejection of the [court of appeals'] four-part test by announcing that the procedural duty imposed on the agencies by §102(2)(C) is "quite precise" and leaves a court "no authority to depart from the statutory language." Given the history and wording of NEPA's impact statement requirement, this statement is baffling. A statute that imposes a complicated procedural requirement on all "proposals" for "major federal actions significantly affecting the quality of the human environment" and then assiduously avoids giving any hint, either expressly or by way of legislative history, of what is meant by a proposal for a "major federal action" can hardly be termed precise. In fact, this vaguely worded statute seems designed to serve as no more than a catalyst for development of a "common law" of NEPA. To date, the courts have responded in just that manner and have created such a "common law." Indeed, that development is the source of NEPA's success. Of course, the Court is correct that the courts may not depart from NEPA's language. They must, however, give meaning to that language if there is to be anything in NEPA to enforce at all.

COMMENTARY & QUESTIONS

1. **Programmatic impact statements.** The reality of agency behavior is that individual projects are often part of broad ongoing programs. The CEQ regulations provide two rationales underlying the requirement that agencies prepare "programmatic" EISs where appropriate. 40 C.F.R. §§1502.4, 1502.20. For the agency, preparation of a programmatic EIS can greatly streamline the EIS process for all of the subsequent specific projects that derive from it. A programmatic EIS on nuclear waste disposal, for example, can be done once and then merely incorporated by reference in subsequent nuclear power plant EIS proceedings. For environmentalists, a timely programmatic EIS can raise fundamental issues and shape basic agency decisions at a sufficiently early stage to improve or block a program before it is cast in bureaucratic stone. A programmatic EIS can facilitate the analysis of cumulative impacts and serve as an antidote to improper segmentation of a project. But as with other NEPA threshold decisions, an agency's decision on whether to

prepare a programmatic EIS can be overturned only if it is arbitrary and capricious. Churchill County v. Department of the Interior, 376 F.3d 1060, amended and reh'g denied, 382 F.3d 1055 (9th Cir. 2001).

2. **Tiering of EISs.** Plaintiffs-respondents wanted a full complement of impact statements on the federal coal-leasing program: a national (programmatic, or generic) EIS; a regional EIS; and impact documents for each local coal lease and right-of-way granted by the Department. This hierarchy of impact documents is called "tiering." See 40 C.F.R. §1508.28. How informative could the national EIS and the local impact statements be without a regional EIS integrating them? Regional, or "ecosystem," planning is currently seen as the most efficient, effective prelude to intelligent environmental management:

> An ecosystem, or place-based approach to strategic planning through NEPA can provide a framework for evaluating the environmental status quo and the combined cumulative impacts of individual projects. Analyzing similar but individual projects on a watershed basis, for example, can be very efficient, reducing the number of analyses and documents, and allowing agencies to focus on cumulative impacts within a geographic area. 1997 CEQ Study at 14.

Was the Court suggesting that the Northern Great Plains Resources Program was the "functional equivalent" of a regional EIS?

3. **To plan or not to plan.** Is the *Kleppe* decision a disincentive to comprehensive planning? After all, from the standpoint of a federal agency, if you don't plan, you then don't have to go public with an EIS; thus do you avoid public controversy until the action has become a self-fulfilling prophecy. If this is so, doesn't *Kleppe* contradict NEPA's emphasis on early planning in order to forestall irretrievable commitments of resources to environmentally damaging projects?

The CEQ regulations suggest that the EIS should indeed be a planning tool:

> §1502.1 Purpose. The primary purpose of an environmental impact statement is to serve as an action-forcing device to insure that the policies and goals defined in [NEPA] are infused into the ongoing programs and actions of the Federal Government.... *An environmental impact statement is more than a disclosure document. It shall be used by Federal officials in conjunction with other relevant material to plan actions and make decisions.* [Emphasis added.]

> §1505.1 Agency decisionmaking procedures. Agencies shall adopt procedures to ensure that decisions are made in accordance with the policies and purposes of the Act. Such procedures shall include... (d) Requiring that relevant environmental documents, comments, and responses accompany the proposal through existing agency review processes *so that agency officials use the statement in making decisions.* [Emphasis added.]

> §1502.2 Implementation.... (f) Agencies shall not commit resources prejudicing selection of alternatives before making a final decision.

> §1502.5 Timing. The [EIS] shall be prepared early enough so that it can serve practically as an important contribution to the decision making process and will not be used to rationalize or justify decisions already made.[19]

---

19. In the *Chicod Creek* case, the EIS was drafted after the SCS had decided exactly what it wanted to do. Should Judge Larkins have ordered the SCS to *reopen* the entire question while the EIS was being drafted? If NEPA is interpreted as a directive to include environmental concerns in the actual decisionmaking process, that question

4. **When is there a proposal?** *Kleppe* stands for the rule that a proposal only comes into existence when the agency declares it, unless the agency has been arbitrary and capricious in not making a proposal. The CEQ regulations (§1508.23) state that a proposal may exist in fact even if it is not explicitly made. Should CEQ or the courts have the last word in interpreting NEPA? On one hand, courts should defer to an agency's interpretation of its own enabling act, but this presumption does not apply where the agency interpretation violates the plain language of the statute. Do you agree with Justice Powell or Justice Marshall about how strictly the language of NEPA should be interpreted?

In effect, the *Kleppe* Court holds that the agency itself must determine when a "proposal" is being made, and a court should only overturn this decision if it is arbitrary. Under the *Kleppe* ruling, environmental plaintiffs find it difficult to establish the existence of "de facto proposals." (Cf. 40 C.F.R. §1508.23.) Is the *Kleppe* interpretation consistent with NEPA's goal of factoring environmental analysis into federal agency planning at the earliest possible time? What could the NRC now do in a *SIPI* situation if it wanted to begin a breeder reactor research program with minimal public scrutiny?

Agency rulemaking can constitute a NEPA-triggering proposal. Agencies can voluntarily couple an EIS process with their rulemaking, which can change the ordinary course of rulemaking. See Funk, NEPA at Energy: An Exercise in Legal Narrative, 20 Envtl. L. 759 (1990), discussing three different rules at the Department of Energy that went through NEPA review and the lessons to be learned from each. When agencies refuse to undertake NEPA procedures, citizen action can sometimes force it upon them, See Citizens for Better Forestry v. Forest Serv. (9th Cir. No. 02-16009, Aug. 28, 2003) (in which the Western Environmental Law Center and students from the environmental clinic at the University of Oregon School of Law won a ruling that the Forest Service must comply with NEPA when amending its regulations implementing the NFMA). Cf. Defenders of Wildlife v. Andrus, 627 F.2d 1238 (D.C. Cir. 1980) (NEPA compliance unnecessary where the Secretary of the Interior did not act to prevent the State of Alaska from killing wolves on federal lands). It is not easy to persuade a court that an agency has been arbitrary and capricious because it hasn't done something that you claim it should have done.

5. **The "irreversible and irretrievable commitment of resources" test.** An agency must refrain from making an "irreversible and irretrievable commitment of resources" before complying with NEPA. Metcalf v. Daley, 214 F.3d 1135 (9th Cir. 2000), involved a proposal by the Department of Commerce to petition the International Whaling Commission for an exemption from the international whaling moratorium (see Chapter 26) on behalf of the Makah, a Native American tribe residing in Washington State with a tradition of hunting California gray whales. In 1996, the National Oceanographic and Atmospheric Administration (NOAA is a sub-agency of the Commerce Department) entered into a contract with the Makah under which NOAA committed to (1) making a formal proposal to the IWC for a quota of gray whales for

---

necessarily arises. If NEPA is primarily considered a disclosure requirement (to whom? Congress? the President? the public? the courts?), then courts need not pretend that it will change the minds of agencies, but rather can insist on full EISs for reasons external to the agency process.

subsistence and ceremonial use by the Makah, and (2) participating in the management of the harvest. Soon thereafter the United States presented a formal proposal to the IWC, but it was withdrawn when several IWC member nations objected to the exemption. NOAA envisioned the withdrawal as a tactical retreat until it could develop international support for the proposal through informal negotiations. In 1997, conservationists demanded that NOAA comply with NEPA with regard to the IWC proposal. Shortly thereafter, NOAA distributed a draft EA for public comment. Three months later, NOAA and the Makah reaffirmed their contract, and four days after that NOAA issued a final EA and FONSI. The Makah quota was again submitted to the IWC, but this time the quota was approved after the United States and the Russian Federation had negotiated quotas not only for the Makah but also for the Chukota, a Siberian aboriginal group.

Two members of a three-judge panel of the Ninth Circuit Court of Appeals concluded that NOAA did not engage the NEPA process "at the earliest possible time" (quoting from Andrus v. Sierra Club, 442 U.S. 347, 351 (1979)). The "point of commitment" was considered to be the 1996 contract between NOAA and the Makah. "By the time the Federal Defendants completed the final EA in 1997, the die already had been cast." The panel majority held that NOAA had violated NEPA by making an irreversible and irretrievable commitment of resources before commencing the NEPA process. However, the majority modulated its decision as follows:

> We want to make it clear, however, that this case does not stand for the general proposition that an agency cannot begin preliminary consideration of an action without preparing an EA, or that an agency must always prepare an EA before it can lend support to any proposal.... NEPA does not require that agency officials be "subjectively impartial." The statute does require, however, that projects be objectively evaluated. NEPA assumes as inevitable an institutional bias...and erects the procedural requirements of §102 to insure [that the decisionmaker understands the environmental consequences and alternatives of the proposed action]. Rather, our holding here is limited to the unusual facts and circumstances of this case.... 214 F.3d at 1145.

Judge Kleinfeld dissented on the grounds that "(1)[the majority opinion] imposes a novel version of the 'objectivity' requirement that cannot be applied in a predictable, consistent manner by panels in other cases; (2) it misconstrues the regulation that controls the time when an environmental assessment ought to be prepared; [and] (3) it requires that a new environmental assessment be prepared without finding anything wrong with the old one." 214 F.3d at 1147. In Judge Kleinfeld's view, "the value of the environmental assessments and impact statements comes mostly after the agency has settled on a policy choice. The process of preparing them mobilizes groups that may generate political exposure sufficient to defeat the executive initiative. Exploration of the alternatives, and the facts brought out in preparation, may educate the agency, so that the initiative is modified in a useful way...." Id. Which side is correct in this debate? The majority appears to believe that a governmental agency is educable during the germination of its proposal, but Judge Kleinfeld disagrees, apparently feeling that the proposal will be made on political grounds but that it can be modified afterwards by the political currents that NEPA compliance may generate. Thus, for Judge Kleinfeld, it doesn't matter how late in the agency's original decisionmaking process NEPA analysis is begun because at this stage the agency's decision cannot be influenced by environmental factors. Judge Kleinfeld's view is in the minority, not only in this case but also with regard to NEPA case law and the CEQ regulations. But is Judge Kleinfeld politically realistic rather than unduly cynical? And is the majority opinion politically naive? Is there some truth in both views? Or are the facts of this case really so atypical that this debate is merely academic?

6. **Cumulative impacts and NEPA.** Do you agree with the Court that the cumulative impacts of potential activities in the surrounding area cannot be considered in impact documents until the activities have actually been proposed? Doesn't this lead to fragmented, reactive planning? Even if you consider only the impacts of proposed projects, how helpful is it to consider them in each local, site-specific impact document? Once again, the CEQ regulations appear to conflict with the Supreme Court's interpretation of NEPA (see §1508.7, 25(a), 28):

> §1508.7 Cumulative impact. "Cumulative impact" is the impact on the environment which results from the incremental impact of the action when added to other past, present, and *reasonably foreseeable* future actions regardless of what agency…or person undertakes such other actions. Cumulative impacts can result from individually minor but collectively significant actions taking place over a period of time. [Emphasis added.]

The Ninth Circuit has held that both an EA and an EIS must consider the cumulative impacts of a proposed action, as well as reasonably foreseeable connected and similar actions. Kern v. Bureau of Land Mgmt., 284 F.3d 1062 (9th Cir. 2002) (BLM should have considered other reasonably foreseeable timber sales in its EA for a proposed timber sale).

7. **Hard cases make bad law.** Should the Sierra Club have decided not to file this action under this set of facts? After all, it's not as if the Department hadn't done any planning for utilization of the Northern Great Plains coal reserves. The Sierra Club simply disagreed with Interior about what the relevant planning area should have been.

8. **NEPA as post hoc rationalization.** Is Justice Marshall correct when he charges that a NEPA lawsuit usually comes too late in the agency decisionmaking process to be effective? Has the agency already invested too much money and political capital to change its plans? Or, on the other hand, does the specter of a NEPA suit that would expose substantial waste and shoddy planning inspire agency officials to give prudent consideration to environmental problems early in the process? Is Justice Marshall's reservation about NEPA answered by the CEQ's "scoping" suggestions? See 40 C.F.R. §1501.7 (discussed above).

9. **NEPA in the Supreme Court.** The *Kleppe* decision is merely one example of the generally unsympathetic treatment that NEPA has received in the Supreme Court. (Many lower federal courts, on the other hand, have interpreted NEPA much less restrictively.) Professor Oliver Houck has commented:

> It is hard to imagine a venue more hostile to NEPA — to any aspect of NEPA — than the Supreme Court has proven to be. Of the twenty-two cases raising NEPA to the Court over the last thirty years, none — not one — has been decided in a fashion that favored the application of the statute to the facts at hand. The odds of 22–0

are not explained by any random pattern known to science:... Nor are they explainable as correcting aberrations in the law, as each case had been decided in an opposite fashion by at least one lower federal court.... Houck, Is That All?, 11 Duke Envtl. L. & Pol'y F. 173, 186 (2000) (reviewing Lynton Keith Caldwell, National Environmental Policy Act, An Agenda for the Future (1998)).

Why is the Supreme Court so uncomfortable with NEPA? Is it because NEPA is such an atypical statute? Is it NEPA's aspirational quality and vagueness? Or is there in the Supreme Court an ideological hostility to NEPA?[20]

10. **Where is NEPA's overview?** Observing the scene that has followed the *Kleppe* decision, Professor Houck remarks that

> NEPA is missing the point. It is producing lots of little statements on highway segments, timber sales, and other foregone conclusions; it isn't even present, much less effective, when the major decisions on a national energy policy and a national transportation policy are made. On the most pivotal development questions of our time, NEPA comes in late in the fourth quarter, in time to help tidy up.[21]

The Clinton CEQ repeated this critique:

> The NEPA process is often triggered too late to be fully effective. Generally, agency and private sector planning processes begin long before the NEPA process. By the time an environmental impact analysis is started, alternatives and strategic choices are foreclosed. Congress envisioned that federal agencies would use NEPA as a planning tool to integrate environmental, social, and economic concerns directly into projects and programs. However, during the 25 years of NEPA, application has focused on decisions related to site-specific construction, development, or resource extraction projects. NEPA is virtually ignored in formulating specific policies and often is skirted in developing programs, usually because agencies believe that NEPA cannot be applied within the time available or without a detailed proposal. Instead, agencies tend to examine project-level environmental effects in microscopic detail. The reluctance to apply NEPA analysis to programs and policies reflects the fear that microscopic detail will be expected, even when such depth of analysis is not possible that early in the project development stage. 1997 CEQ Study at 12.

Do you think that federal agencies really do not employ NEPA as a long-range, programmatic planning tool because they are afraid of being compelled to divulge too much detail too early? Or do agencies find it difficult to resist making low-visibility decisions that may be more responsive to political influences?

11. **Has NEPA been worth the effort?** In The (Unhappy) Truth about NEPA, 26 Okla. L. R. 239 (1973), where he concluded that NEPA's procedural reform is "nine parts myth and one part coconut oil," Joseph Sax argued that the Act was unlikely to change the nature of agency decisionmaking. Here are his five basic rules of the game:

---

20. Justice Scalia, while a law professor, once commented, "does [the absence of judicial enforcement of NEPA] mean that important legislative purposes, heralded in the halls of Congress, are lost or misdirected in the vast hallways of the federal bureaucracy? Yes it does, and a good thing too." Scalia, The Doctrine of Standing as an Essential Element of the Separation of Powers, 17 Suffolk L. Rev. 881, 897 (1983) (quoted by Professor Houck in his Book Review at 185). (Note the ironic echoes of language from the *Calvert Cliffs* decision, discussed above.)

21. Letter to Michael Deland, Chairman, CEQ, Feb. 19, 1991. Houck urges that CEQ not focus on making each EIS "a 'succinct review for a single project'...[but] rather, to make NEPA work for legislative proposals and for programs that all but conclusively determine what the subsequent projects will be."

1. Don't expect hired experts to undermine their employers.

2. Don't expect people to believe legislative declarations of policy. The practical working rule is what the legislature will fund is what the legislature's policy is.

3. Don't expect agencies to abandon their traditional friends.

4. Expect agencies to back up their subordinates and professional colleagues.

5. Expect agencies to go for the least risky options (even where risk means performing their missions).

Consider, however, the latent effect of NEPA that is likely to affect virtually all agency actions that faced citizen challenge after the *Chicod Creek* case. Ultimately, for instance, it was the potential disclosure process of NEPA that prevented construction of the environmentally threatening, excessively expensive nuclear fast breeder reactor. The 1997 CEQ Study quoted a former Secretary of Energy as saying, about his decision to defer selection of a tritium production technology, "Thank God for NEPA, because there were so many pressures to make a selection for a technology that might have been forced upon us, and that would have been wrong for the country." 1997 CEQ Study at 13.

In fact, information has a power of its own, even in the absence of substantive review mechanisms. Human beings and their institutions are averse to being embarrassed by public exposure of their nonconformity with generally accepted behavioral norms. The fundamental currency of politics is not money, but "image." International law is the clearest example of this phenomenon. When international agreements are effective, it is not because they threaten sanctions by central enforcement authorities, but because they require parties to produce compliance information, the withholding or clear distortion of which will hold the offending party up to obloquy among its peers in the international community. Indeed, "Information Is Power."

Professor Houck expresses the opinion of many environmental law practitioners and scholars when he concludes that

...NEPA lives on in agency practice and litigation, and — far more often — in the threat of litigation, nipping at the heels of federal decision-making, surfacing greener alternatives, employing its own cadre in every federal agency, and providing access for thousands of individuals and community groups who count on the impact statement process to give them notice and a fighting chance.... Agencies know NEPA is out there, and they fear it. And that has been salutary....

NEPA's great contribution — and it is both magnificent in its simplicity and deceptive in its power — is the environmental impact statement. It is not what the statement says that is important. It is in what comes before, in what agencies have to investigate and learn and listen to, in what they have to fear from other agencies and from environmental groups, the press and reviewing courts, and in the everyday responses and accommodations that they have to make. This was blockbuster stuff in the United States circa 1969, and it remains very difficult stuff in areas like genetic engineering, bio-prospecting, international lending, World Trade Organization commitments, and the new horizon of the year 2000. The NEPA ideas of disclosure, public participation, alternatives, and judicial review are blockbuster stuff as well for the developed countries of Europe and absolutely revolutionary stuff for developing nations in Latin America and the Far East.... NEPA has been the largest environmental success in the world. 11 Duke Envtl. L. & Pol'y F. at 188.

12. **NEPA in the twenty-first century.** Contrary to the view in some quarters that NEPA is old hat, litigation rages on, largely because of the potential constraints the statute imposes on governmental decisionmaking. A recent study analyzed all reported NEPA cases in the first two years of the Bush II Administration — almost 200 — in which the Administration had presented legal arguments.[22] The report suggests that erosive efforts by the Administration have not been consistently successful in the courts:

> Remarkably, when the Bush Administration presented NEPA-hostile arguments, it lost 73 out of 94 cases, or 78% of the time. This very low success rate is fairly astonishing given the high degree of deference that the federal courts employ in reviewing federal agency decisions. However, when the Bush Administration presented NEPA-consistent arguments, it was successful in 75 out of 78 cases, or 96% of the time....

> The NEPA challenges brought during the current Bush Administration can be placed into three categories. The first category includes those cases where the Bush Administration skipped NEPA analysis altogether or has taken positions in litigation that will allow it to avoid NEPA review in the future. The second category includes cases brought where the Bush Administration prepared an EA and unjustifiably failed to prepare a full EIS. The third category includes cases brought where the Bush Administration has prepared a NEPA document but failed to adequately address the environmental impacts of the federal action in question. In all three categories the same [agencies] frequently engaged: the U.S. Forest Service...lost 25 of its NEPA-hostile arguments, the U.S. Department of the Interior lost 15, and the U.S. Department of Transportation...lost 11.... Snape & Carter, Weakening NEPA: How the Bush Administration Uses the Judicial System to Weaken Environmental Protections, 33 Envtl. L. Rep. 10682, 10685–10686, 10695 (2003).

What does this data suggest about the continued utility of NEPA as an action-and-information-forcing mechanism? What signal does it send to executive branch agencies, such as the Forest Service, the Department of the Interior, and the Department of Transportation, that are frequent defendants in NEPA cases?

Early in the Bush II Administration, its CEQ began an interagency NEPA task force review process dubbed "Modernizing NEPA," which produced an extensive preliminary report in 2003 containing a variety of ambiguous but potentially NEPA-hostile recommendations, such as increasing the use of categorical exclusions from NEPA compliance and the use of EAs and FONSIs instead of preparing full EISs. Draft regulations within federal resource management agencies have proposed measures to make NEPA more "efficient"— including rules being prepared for the Forest Service by Under Secretary Mark Rey that would eliminate requirements for the Service to do NEPA documentation at the overall planning stage, limiting the formal NEPA process to individual timbercutting contracts.

---

22. Snape & Carter, Weakening NEPA: How the Bush Administration Uses the Judicial System to Weaken Environmental Protections, 33 Envtl. L. Rep. 10682 (2003). The study was produced by the Defenders of Wildlife Judicial Accountability Project, undertaken with the assistance of the Vermont Law School Clinic for Environmental Law and Policy. See also Carter, Leahy, & Snape, Cutting Science, Ecology, and Transparency Out of National Forest Management: How the Bush Administration Uses the Judicial System to Weaken Environmental Protections, 33 Envtl. L. Rep. 10695 (2003).

C. NEPA'S INTERNATIONAL IMPLICATIONS

NEPA had a profound effect internationally, where it catalyzed a methodology generally known outside the United States as "environmental impact assessment," (EIA). For example, the Rio Declaration on Environment and Development (see Chapter 26), which states that "Environmental impact assessment, as a national instrument, shall be undertaken for proposed activities that are likely to have a significant adverse impact on the environment and are subject to a decision of a competent national authority," is clearly built upon the basic principles of NEPA. Many foreign nations, including a large number of developing countries, the European Union, and international organizations with operational responsibilities such as the World Bank have adopted EIA methodologies. Numerous treaties require EIA as a component of national decisionmaking processes, or in areas of the global commons like Antarctica and the high seas.

In the United States, the applicability of NEPA to activities with international implications remain the last frontier. Actions undertaken by the government of the United States, the last remaining superpower, have truly global implications. The presence and activities of the nation's overseas military bases, for example, can have a profound effect on the environment, and the United States enters into scores of international agreements each year, many of which have environmental implications. Controversial as NEPA may be in a domestic setting, when foreign affairs are involved the stakes are routinely perceived as even higher. When a proposed action with potentially adverse environmental consequences also has implications for the conduct of the nation's foreign policy, NEPA's prescriptions are much more frequently perceived as intruding into the executive branch's monopoly on the conduct of foreign affairs, as in the following case.

Public Citizen v. U.S. Department of Transportation
United States Court of Appeals for the Ninth Circuit, 2003
316 F.3d 1002

[Foreign trucks are permitted to enter the United States only if specifically authorized to do so. As a result of a series of legislative enactments and presidential orders, beginning in 1982 trucks from Mexico were prohibited from entering the United States except within certain areas contiguous to the border. In 2001, a dispute settlement panel constituted under the North American Free Trade Agreement (NAFTA) concluded that the United States' continued refusal to allow Mexican trucks to enter the United States violates that agreement. In response, the President rescinded the moratorium on Mexican trucks and the Department of Transportation (DOT) amended three regulations dealing with foreign truck applications, safety monitoring, and the certification of safety auditors. DOT prepared EAs and issued FONSIs with respect to two of the rules and concluded that the third fell within the agency's regulations identifying categorical exclusions. A coalition of environmental and labor organizations petitioned for review of the amended rules, asserting a failure to prepare an EIS.]

WARDLAW, C.J. The reviewing court must determine that agency actions are not "arbitrary, capricious, an abuse of discretion, or otherwise not in accordance with the law." 5 U.S.C. §706(2)(A). In considering whether an agency acted in an arbitrary and capricious manner, a court "must determine whether the agency articulated a rational connection between the facts found and the choice made." Furthermore, courts must "carefully review the record to 'ensure that agency decisions are founded on a reasoned evaluation of the relevant factors,'" and may not "'rubber-stamp...administrative decisions that they deem inconsistent with a statutory mandate or that frustrate the congressional policy underlying a statute.'"

We [now] determine whether DOT acted in an arbitrary and capricious manner when it failed to prepare an EIS.... DOT alleges that the effects of the Application and Safety Rules are limited to the increased diesel emissions of Mexican trucks during the road-side inspections and safety monitoring mandated by the regulations. It thus predicts that there will be no increase in Mexican truck traffic resulting from the regulations. DOT's analysis goes on to suggest that even if such an increase might occur, its effects would not require consideration because it would be a result of presidential rescission of the moratorium, not the regulations themselves. This novel parsing of the regulations' effects fails to meet NEPA standards.

The CEQ regulations make clear that the "effects" of federal actions include "indirect effects, which are caused by the action and are later in time...but are still reasonably foreseeable," 40 C.F.R. §1508.8(b), as well as "cumulative impact...which results from the incremental impact of the action when added to other...reasonably foreseeable future actions regardless of what agency (Federal or non-Federal) or person undertakes such other actions," id. §1508.7. We have already concluded that the President's rescission of the moratorium was "reasonably foreseeable" at the time the EA was prepared and the decision not to prepare an EIS was made.... To restrict consideration of the regulations' "effects" in the way DOT proposes would contravene not only the plain language of the CEQ regulations, but also the statutory command of NEPA, that environmental effects of government action be considered "to the fullest extent possible."

The CEQ regulations explain that the proposed federal action must be analyzed with regard to several contexts — national, regional, and local — as well as by looking at the short- and long-term effects of the proposed action. Measured against this standard, DOT's EA is woefully inadequate. The EA calculates likely emissions increases if the Application and Safety Rules are implemented. It dismisses those increases as insignificant, however, because they are "very small relative to national levels of emissions." It does not conduct any analysis regarding whether these increases may be localized in certain areas near the Mexican border, including such likely destinations as Southern California or Texas.

The law requires DOT to consider the most likely localities to be affected by increased Mexican truck traffic and to perform more localized analyses for these areas. Indeed, comments submitted...during the notice-and-comment period analyzed publicly available government data to predict, not surprisingly, that major cities near the Mexican border would likely suffer the greatest environmental impact as a result of the regulations. The fact that commenters performed such an analysis does not indicate that their analysis was correct, but rather that it was possible to conduct such an analysis. DOT's failure to do so indicates that it did not take a sufficiently "hard look" at the environmental effects of its actions or at the public comments it received.

Furthermore, DOT failed to address adequately the long-term effects of its actions. In conducting its EA, DOT limited its analysis to the environmental impact of Mexican trucks in the year 2002. This is anomalous in itself, considering that the regulations were scheduled to become effective only as of May 3, 2002. More significantly, the EA offered no projections of the increase (or decrease) in Mexican truck traffic after 2002, though the regulations were certainly expected to continue in effect beyond the end of last year; indeed they would be in effect now absent this action.

[Amicus] ATA contends that increases in Mexican truck traffic in years subsequent to 2002 would be attributable to the "success of NAFTA," rather than to the regulations themselves. This argument is beside the point, as it is impossible to separate increases in truck traffic due to the opening of the border from increases in truck traffic due to successful international trade; it is precisely this desired increase in international trade that prompted DOT to issue regulations facilitating cross-border truck traffic in the first place.

If the environmental effects of a proposed agency action are uncertain, the agency must usually prepare an EIS.... There are a number of areas of uncertainty regarding DOT's EA that merit additional investigation. The most significant of these is whether, and to what extent, cross-border Mexican truck traffic will increase if DOT implements the regulations. A related question is whether, and to what extent, such increased Mexican truck traffic will consist of trucks producing more dangerous emissions than their United States counterparts....

Thus, the EA — assuming no increase in Mexican truck traffic, making an arbitrary assumption about the percentage of newer, "cleaner" Mexican trucks on the roads, and failing to take account of future increasing discrepancies in emissions rules — conducted an environmental analysis that found no increase in emissions due to the regulations' implementation. Our law mandates that an agency complete an EIS "where uncertainty may be resolved by further collection of data, or where the collection of such data may prevent 'speculation on potential... effects.'" Petitioners raise many uncertainties about the EA, as does amicus the Attorney General of the State of California, and there is no suggestion that these uncertainties do not lend themselves to quantification. (Indeed, Petitioners have submitted a number of studies attempting precisely what DOT should have done.)...

"Controversy" sufficient to require preparation of an EIS [under the CEQ regulation defining "significantly"[23]] occurs "when substantial questions are raised as to whether a project...may cause significant degradation of some human environmental factor, or there is a substantial dispute [about] the size, nature, or effect of the major Federal action." The evidence establishing such a controversy must be brought to the agency's attention while the agency is conducting its deliberations, not post hoc. Thus, the controversy requirement is two-fold: Petitioners must show that there was a "substantial dispute" about DOT's actions and that this dispute raised "substantial questions" about their validity. The burden then shifts to DOT to provide a "convincing" explanation why no controversy exists.

Petitioners' claim satisfies the first requirement. We have held that an "'outpouring of public protest'" — where, for example, 85% of public comments opposed the proposed agency action — constitutes a substantial dispute. Here, "over 90 percent of the comments opposed" DOT's regulations. DOT timely received these comments, and duly noted their existence in the comments accompanying the final regulations.

Petitioners' claim also satisfies the second requirement. A substantial portion of the negative comments offered real criticism of DOT's action and its failure to adequately assess its environmental impact. These comments, several of which were made by the future litigants here, as well as by other national environmental organizations, describe many of the defects discussed above. Because many of these criticisms have merit, and DOT failed to adequately account for its failure to act on them, its action is "controversial" under the CEQ regulations and requires preparation of an EIS.

---

23. "Significantly" as used in NEPA requires considerations of both context and intensity:... (b) Intensity. This refers to the severity of impact.... The following should be considered in evaluating intensity:... (2) The degree to which the proposed action affects public health or safety.... (4) The degree to which the effects on the quality of the human environment are likely to be highly controversial.... (5) The degree to which the possible effects on the human environment are highly uncertain or involve unique or unknown risks.... 40 C.F.R. §1508.27.

COMMENTARY & QUESTIONS

1. **The President and NEPA.** The Supreme Court in Franklin v. Massachusetts, 505 U.S. 788 (1992), held that the President is not an "agency" for the purposes of APA. This suggests that at least some actions taken by the President, perhaps including lifting the moratorium on Mexican trucks, might not be reviewable for compliance with NEPA. Note how DOT cleverly — although unsuccessfully — attempted to exploit this loophole in the law by attributing the negative environmental impacts to the President's action and not to the agency's regulations, which are reviewable. The doctrine of *Franklin* had a considerably greater influence on the outcome in Public Citizen v. Office of the U.S. Trade Rep., 5 F.3d 549 (D.C. Cir. 1993), cert. denied, 510 U.S. 104 (1994), in which public interest organizations claimed the need for an EIS to accompany NAFTA. Although the CEQ regulations clearly identify "treaties and international conventions or agreements" as "major federal actions," the President's role in the statutorily prescribed process for adopting and implementing NAFTA was held to insulate the agreement from NEPA's requirements.

2. **NEPA abroad.** A lengthy and ongoing controversy concerns the application of NEPA to major federal actions with impacts overseas — for instance, disposal of hazardous wastes on one of the numerous U.S. military bases around the world, drug eradication involving aerial spraying of pesticides in foreign countries, or cooperative programs with foreign governments to incinerate chemical weapons. As a practical and policy matter, what sorts of additional difficulties do these "NEPA abroad" situations raise that are not found in domestic application of NEPA? Why might governmental officials find NEPA's requirements particularly intrusive in situations with foreign impacts? What legal questions would such cases raise, and how would you address them? The executive branch has strenuously maintained that NEPA does not apply to extraterritorial impacts. Consistent with that view, in 1979 President Carter promulgated Exec. Order No. 12,114, 44 Fed. Reg. 1957, that "furthers the purpose of" NEPA while setting out a watered-down version of the statute and, notably, purporting to preclude judicial review. In EDF v. Massey, 986 F.2d 528 (D.C. Cir. 1993), NEPA was held to apply to the incineration of wastes at McMurdo Station in Antarctica. Anecdotal reports suggest that President Clinton himself made the decision not to petition the Supreme Court for certiorari, which might have reconsidered one of the few cases actually to hold that NEPA applies overseas. See Wirth, International Decisions, 87 Am. J. Int'l L. 626 (1993).

3. **NEPA and foreign policy.** The *Public Citizen* case is similar to George E. Warren Corp. v. EPA, excerpted in Chapter 8, in that both involved judicial review of a regulation promulgated to implement the international obligations of the United States under a trade agreement. The outcomes, however, are different, with the *Warren Corp.* court deferring to the executive branch's interpretation of a statute for foreign policy reasons while the *Public Citizen* court shows little hesitation in setting aside the executive branch's action in a similar setting. Can you think of a principled way to distinguish these two seemingly similar cases?

4. **Comparative law: EIA.** While a great deal of NEPA law and lore has been accepted by foreign countries adopting EIA methodologies, two of the principal building blocks of

NEPA have been less warmly welcomed abroad: public participation and judicial review. Can you imagine why these two aspects of NEPA might be controversial? Suppose the federal courts soon after the adoption of the statute had concluded that the application of NEPA was not reviewable by a court, but that the statute instead was — in the words of George Will — "less a law than a gesture or sentiment." What does the preeminence of judge- and court-made law under NEPA tell you about the nature of environmental law and policy in the United States? Other countries, such as Great Britain, have adopted a version of EIA that does not provide for the consideration of alternatives. What implications would omission of this requirement have for NEPA-like processes?

I know of no safe repository of the ultimate powers of the society but the people themselves; and if we think them not enlightened enough to exercise their discretion; the remedy is not to take it from them, but to inform their discretion.

— Thos. Jefferson to William Charles Jarvis, 28 September 1820

I have no quarrel with…what I believe to be the intent of NEPA…I do have a quarrel with those who, ever since its enactment, have used NEPA to obstruct the orderly progress of obtaining the power supply this region must have if we are to continue to provide for a reasonable lifestyle for ourselves, our children, and the generations to come…. The anti-producers who are abusing the National Environmental Policy Act by using it as a sword have an avowed purpose – to stop growth in our society. They say "Write the environmental impact statement, then they claim it is inadequate and take us to court anyway. If they lose, they appeal. In the meantime, the "development based on planned growth"…is delayed, and thereby the full benefit of the planning is lost.

— "The Prophets of Shortage," Speech by Don Hodel,
past Administrator of the Bonneville Power Administration,
who presided over utility over-building that brought about
the WPPSS bankruptcy, who later was a high-ranking
member of the Reagan administration, Portland, Oregon,
City Club, July 11 1975.

Chapter 10

CORPORATE DISCLOSURE: SHAPING PRIVATE RESPONSE BY REQUIRED PRODUCTION OF INFORMATION

A. *The Emergency Planning and Community Right-to-Know Act*
B. *California's Proposition 65*
C. *Legal Challenges to Regulating Information: The First Amendment*

In principle, almost everyone agrees that protecting public health and the environment through requiring better information from corporations and others who put health and the environment at risk is a good idea. Indeed, few regulatory strategies enjoy support as broad-based as informational mechanisms generally do. Information allows consumers to make better-informed decisions, enables citizens to make better-informed choices in the political arena, and gives everyone (including corporations) the chance to learn more about the kinds of harms they might be causing. "Transparency" principles underlie many of the innovative management theories followed by corporations seeking to demonstrate modern civic responsibilities. See Chapter 21. It is hard to find a policy analyst who rejects informational transparency strategies on theoretical grounds.

In practice, however, debates abound about exactly what kind of information should be required, to whom it should be disclosed, in what format it should appear, and so forth. Controversies also simmer over whether information should displace or merely supplement conventional command-and-control regulation, to what extent information should be curtailed in light of security concerns in the post-9/11 world, and to what extent the First Amendment places limits on the government's ability to require or to prohibit information pertaining to health and the environment.

This chapter introduces you to these issues by discussing two of the most prominent informational statutes: the federal Emergency Planning and Community Right-to-Know Act (EPCRA) and California's Proposition 65 (more formally known as the Safe Drinking Water and Toxic Enforcement Act of 1986). It then examines First Amendment issues that have arisen in response to laws like these, which attempt to use information as a means of regulating threats to health and the environment.

A. THE EMERGENCY PLANNING AND COMMUNITY RIGHT-TO-KNOW ACT

Community right-to-know laws attempt to improve corporate environmental performance by (1) forcing companies to audit their processes and emissions systematically, thus revealing opportunities to prevent pollution and probably save money by doing so; (2) providing information to that increasing segment of the American public that practices "green consumerism," giving a company that achieves pollution prevention a competitive public relations advantage; and (3) informing corporate shareholders, who can use their votes to stimulate corporate environmental performance to achieve positive gains and avoid potential negative costs and liabilities. Where companies fail to prevent pollution, governmental agencies utilize these data to design and implement enforcement programs. Citizen activists use the information from right-to-know laws to (1) lobby legislatures and agencies for stricter pollution control requirements, (2) supervise compliance with emissions permits and bring citizen suits where violations are occurring, and (3) perform "environmental justice" analyses to determine whether members of racial, ethnic, or economic minority groups are being disproportionately exposed to toxic chemicals.

EPCRA[1] embodies each of these goals and possibilities. It was enacted in 1986 in response to media coverage of a tragic series of toxic chemical releases, especially the methyl isocyanate release in Bhopal, India, that killed 2000 people. Section 313 of the Act establishes the Toxic Release Inventory (TRI). TRI requires certain facilities that "manufacture..., process..., or otherwise use..." listed toxic chemicals in amounts above designated thresholds, and that employ ten or more full-time workers, to file annual reports with EPA. EPCRA §§313(a)(1)(A), 313(b)(2). TRI reports detail the use and release of any of approximately 650 listed toxic chemicals above yearly threshold amounts.[2] A facility submits its TRI information on a so-called Form R, which must include the following information:

> (i) Whether the toxic chemical at the facility is manufactured, processed, or otherwise used, and the general category or categories of use of the chemical. (ii) An estimate of the maximum amounts (in ranges) of the toxic chemical present at the facility at any time during the preceding calendar year. (iii) For each waste stream, the waste treatment or disposal methods employed, and an estimate of the treatment efficiency typically achieved by such methods for that waste stream. (iv) The annual quantity of the toxic chemical entering each environmental medium. EPCRA §313(g).

Facilities must also report offsite transfers of TRI chemicals (e.g., to sewage treatment plants or hazardous waste TSD facilities), as well as source reduction, recycling, and waste minimization efforts. More than 20,000 U.S. corporate facilities file Form Rs annually. EPA's Form R compilation is made available to the general public through

---

1. 42 U.S.C. §§11001-11050 (1986).

2. See generally Clay, The EPA's Proposed Phase-III Expansion of the TRI Reporting Requirements: Everything and the Kitchen Sink, 15 Pace Envtl. L. Rev. 293 (1997).

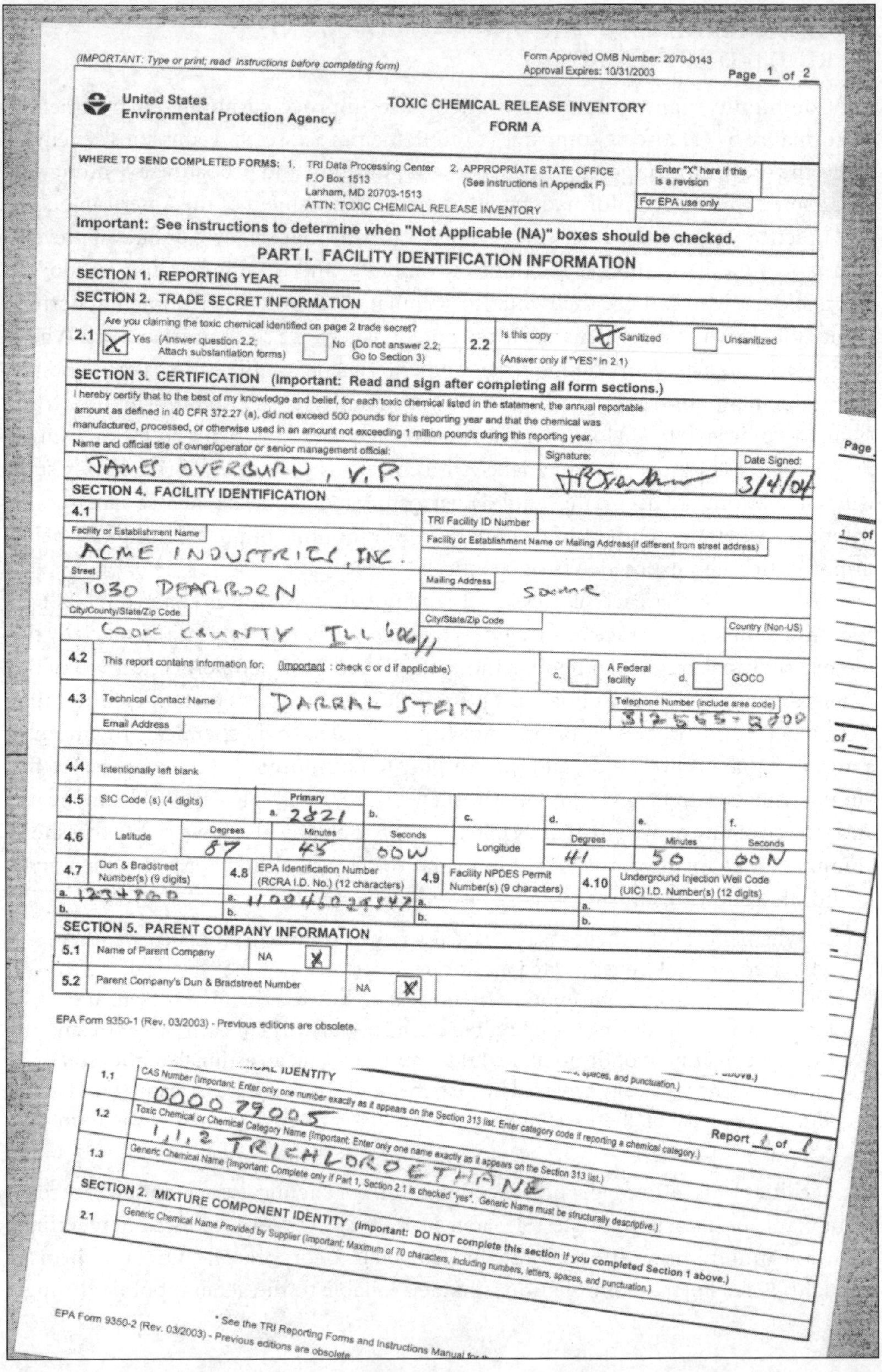

(IMPORTANT: Type or print; read instructions before completing form)

Form Approved OMB Number: 2070-0143
Approval Expires: 10/31/2003

Page 1 of 2

United States Environmental Protection Agency

TOXIC CHEMICAL RELEASE INVENTORY
FORM A

WHERE TO SEND COMPLETED FORMS: 1. TRI Data Processing Center P.O Box 1513 Lanham, MD 20703-1513 ATTN: TOXIC CHEMICAL RELEASE INVENTORY
2. APPROPRIATE STATE OFFICE (See instructions in Appendix F)

Enter "X" here if this is a revision

For EPA use only

Important: See instructions to determine when "Not Applicable (NA)" boxes should be checked.

PART I. FACILITY IDENTIFICATION INFORMATION

SECTION 1. REPORTING YEAR ______

SECTION 2. TRADE SECRET INFORMATION

2.1 Are you claiming the toxic chemical identified on page 2 trade secret?
[X] Yes (Answer question 2.2; Attach substantiation forms) [ ] No (Do not answer 2.2; Go to Section 3)

2.2 Is this copy [X] Sanitized [ ] Unsanitized
(Answer only if "YES" in 2.1)

SECTION 3. CERTIFICATION (Important: Read and sign after completing all form sections.)

I hereby certify that to the best of my knowledge and belief, for each toxic chemical listed in the statement, the annual reportable amount as defined in 40 CFR 372.27 (a), did not exceed 500 pounds for this reporting year and that the chemical was manufactured, processed, or otherwise used in an amount not exceeding 1 million pounds during this reporting year.

Name and official title of owner/operator or senior management official: JAMES OVERBURN, V.P.

Signature:

Date Signed: 3/4/04

SECTION 4. FACILITY IDENTIFICATION

4.1

TRI Facility ID Number

Facility or Establishment Name: ACME INDUSTRIES, INC.

Facility or Establishment Name or Mailing Address(if different from street address)

Street: 1030 DEARBORN

Mailing Address: Same

City/County/State/Zip Code: COOK COUNTY ILL 60611

City/State/Zip Code

Country (Non-US)

4.2 This report contains information for: (Important : check c or d if applicable) c. [ ] A Federal facility d. [ ] GOCO

4.3 Technical Contact Name: DARRAL STEIN

Telephone Number (include area code): 312-555-2700

Email Address

4.4 Intentionally left blank

4.5 SIC Code (s) (4 digits): Primary a. 2821 b. c. d. e. f.

4.6 Latitude: Degrees 87 Minutes 45 Seconds 00W; Longitude: Degrees 41 Minutes 50 Seconds 00N

4.7 Dun & Bradstreet Number(s) (9 digits): a. 1234700 b.

4.8 EPA Identification Number (RCRA I.D. No.) (12 characters): a. 11004602534? b.

4.9 Facility NPDES Permit Number(s) (9 characters): a. b.

4.10 Underground Injection Well Code (UIC) I.D. Number(s) (12 digits): a. b.

SECTION 5. PARENT COMPANY INFORMATION

5.1 Name of Parent Company NA [X]

5.2 Parent Company's Dun & Bradstreet Number NA [X]

EPA Form 9350-1 (Rev. 03/2003) - Previous editions are obsolete.

Report 1 of 1

1.1 CAS Number (Important: Enter only one number exactly as it appears on the Section 313 list. Enter category code if reporting a chemical category.) 000079005

1.2 Toxic Chemical or Chemical Category Name (Important: Enter only one name exactly as it appears on the Section 313 list.) 1,1,2 TRICHLOROETHANE

1.3 Generic Chemical Name (Important: Complete only if Part 1, Section 2.1 is checked "yes". Generic Name must be structurally descriptive.)

SECTION 2. MIXTURE COMPONENT IDENTITY (Important: DO NOT complete this section if you completed Section 1 above.)

2.1 Generic Chemical Name Provided by Supplier (Important: Maximum of 70 characters, including numbers, letters, spaces, and punctuation.)

EPA Form 9350-2 (Rev. 03/2003) - Previous editions are obsolete

* See the TRI Reporting Forms and Instructions Manual for ...

FIGURE 10-1
A TRI report filed by a Midwestern manufacturing plant.

published reports and an online database system (TOXNET) available via the Internet.[3] Published TRI information is organized by total releases and transfers, chronological trends, geographic distributions, and industry-by-industry comparisons. There has historically been a two-year lag, however, between submissions of Form Rs and EPA's published TRI reports.

In addition to the community right-to-know functions listed above, Congress explicitly intended EPCRA to make citizens aware of health and safety risks in their communities in order to facilitate emergency planning and notification procedures to cope with potential chemical releases. Consequently, local police and fire departments, public health officials, and citizen participants, organized into local emergency planning committees, are significant users of TRI material. Local citizen groups also use TRI data to establish cooperative relationships with local industries so as to promote pollution prevention, obtain limited community surveillance and inspection of facilities, and improve community warning systems.

COMMENTARY & QUESTIONS

1. **Evaluating EPCRA.** EPCRA, according to many observers, has been remarkably successful in reducing emissions of toxic chemicals without resort to full-fledged command-and-control regulatory systems. Reported toxic chemical emissions have decreased between 40 and 50% since 1988. While some of this decrease has been caused by more accurate reporting and stringent regulation, there is broad agreement among industry and environmentalists that most of the reduction is due to EPCRA and other disclosure laws. According to the U.S. General Accounting Office (GAO), the public availability of TRI data, which assures that year-to-year changes in a firm's environmental performance are transparent, is a key factor in stimulating firms to use pollution prevention and improve community and public relations. GAO, EPA Should Strengthen Its Efforts to Measure and Encourage Pollution Prevention (01-283) (2001).

On the negative side, EPCRA, like NEPA, is plagued by the major flaw in all mandatory disclosure strategies: The entities that are required to disclose the data have an inherent incentive either not to disclose or to disclose inaccurate or misleading information. Violations of TRI reporting obligations are allegedly widespread. Enforcement of TRI reporting requirements is difficult because agencies and citizen groups seldom know enough about facility operations to form a basis for asserting with confidence that mandated disclosures are missing or incomplete. Limitations on citizen suits, such as the need to allege "continuing violations," have hampered citizen efforts to enforce EPCRA.[4]

---

3. EPA's comprehensive TRI database is available at http://toxnet.nlm.nih.gov. In addition, Environmental Defense (ED) has installed an online database, called the "Chemical Scorecard," that links chemical release and toxicology data with maps locating facilities that use certain chemicals. A user need only enter a zip code in order to see a map highlighting local sources of pollution. More than 150 public databases are linked to create this database, which has drawn over 200,000 "hits" per day. ED's Chemical Scorecard is available at http://www.scorecard.org.

4. See the discussion in Citizens for a Better Env't v. Steel Co., noted in Chapters 7 and 21, holding that environmental plaintiffs must allege continuing violations of EPCRA reporting requirements in order to bring citizen suits.

Also on the downside, it has been argued that the TRI mechanism, in its present form,

> does not and cannot achieve its ostensible goal of accurately informing the public about toxic releases. It omits many environmentally significant chemicals and focuses on [large] sources that account for a small fraction of releases. It largely fails to note distinctions between more and less risky pollutants and modes of release. Finally, EPA has administered TRI in isolation, without coordination with other programs that might correct its defects. As a result, TRI fails to portray accurately the extent and the possible impacts of the chemical releases it purports to cover or to provide a basis for comparing those impacts with other uncovered risks. Pedersen, Regulation and Information Disclosure: Parallel Universes and Beyond, 25 Harv. Envtl. L. Rev. 151, 152 (2001).

2. **Should "materials accounting" data be reported?** On October 1, 1996, EPA issued an Advance Notice of Proposed Rulemaking (ANPR) announcing its intention to expand the TRI requirements to include "materials accounting" data. 61 Fed. Reg. 51,322. Materials accounting would involve a complete analysis of toxic chemicals, identifying the amounts of TRI chemicals (1) coming into the facility; (2) being transformed into products and wastes; and (3) leaving the facility as products, releases, and offsite transfers. New Jersey and Massachusetts require materials accounting data under their state community right-to-know statutes.[5]

Is disclosure of materials accounting data necessary to identify opportunities for pollution prevention and protect against nondisclosure and inaccurate disclosure? Or is it a superfluous, inappropriate intrusion on a facility's confidential business information? Some observers argue that "the collection of [materials accounting] data is an unjustified, fundamental change in the TRI program that is not in harmony with the intent or purpose of EPCRA." Clay, The EPA's Proposed Phase-III Expansion of the Toxic Release Inventory (TRI) Reporting Requirements, 15 Pace Envtl. L. Rev. 293, 297 (1997). EPA received over 40,000 responses to its ANPR, and the materials accounting issue has not, to say the least, been resolved quickly.

3. **Does the TRI convey misleading data?** Critics of EPCRA argue that the disclosure of toxic release data, in terms of total amounts of chemicals released, can lead to media campaigns that distort the actual public risks caused by these releases. As an example, they point to the National Wildlife Federation's "Toxic 500 List" that identifies the 500 "worst" polluters in the United States. On the other hand, it could be argued that EPA has corroborated the toxicity of these chemicals by listing them and their reportable quantities for TRI purposes, and "more" is certainly not "better."

4. **TRI and performance benchmarking.** TRI marks a watershed, pioneering the use of performance monitoring and benchmarking as regulatory tools. By creating an objective performance metric, TRI compels firms to self-monitor even as it enables them to benchmark performance among operating units and against their competitors. For an article exploring the strengths and limitations of this innovative approach, and its implications for future environmental regulation, see Karkkainen, Information as Environmental Regulation: TRI and Performance Benchmarking, Precursor to a New Paradigm?, 89 Geo. L.J. 257 (2001).

---

5. Mass. Gen. Laws Ann. ch. 211 §§1–23, and N.J. Stat. Ann. §§34:5A-1 to 34:5A-31.

5. **Is green golden?** Firms with lower TRI emissions generally outperform their competitors in the stock market. Moreover, abnormally negative market performance typically follows a firm's initial announcement of its TRI releases. Apparently, investors lose confidence in a company with high TRI releases because of the probability of future pollution-related expenditures or liabilities. TRI releases may also be perceived as a waste of resources or a result of mismanagement. The possibility of negative effects of green consumerism may also cause a decline in a firm's stock price after TRI releases are announced. Konar & Cohen, Information as Regulation: The Effect of Community Right to Know Laws on Toxic Emissions, 32 J. Envtl. Econ. & Mgmt. 109 (1997).

6. **International right-to-know.** Right-to-know transparency principles are reflected internationally in a number of settings. The North American Commission for Environmental Cooperation established by the environmental side agreement to NAFTA (Chapters 8 and 26) has been working on the issue of pollutant release and transfer registers, of which the U.S. TRI is one example. The U.S. and Canada have already "harmonized" their programs, making them compatible with each other. Mexico, however, has lagged behind. Unlike the U.S. and Canadian efforts, Mexico's requirements are voluntary rather than mandatory, apply only to facilities regulated by the federal government and not the states, do not guarantee public access, and require reporting in terms of production figures instead of environmental discharges. One of the issues during the NAFTA negotiations was the potential for a "race-to-the-bottom" in a situation such as this, in which those countries with higher standards make them compatible with those of others by relaxing their domestic requirements. To protect against this dynamic, the Commission's governing treaty specifies that "each Party shall ensure that its laws and regulations provide for high levels of environmental protection and shall strive to continue to improve those laws and regulations." While that is perhaps a useful sentiment, what problems might you expect to encounter in implementing it in practice? For example, how would the governments of Canada and the U.S. encourage Mexico to "harmonize up"? What does harmonizing up mean in any event? How does one compare regulations in situations in which the metrics are incommensurable? For instance, Mexico might well argue that reporting production of hazardous chemicals as opposed to discharges is in fact a more meaningful measure, on the theory that measurement of discharges is subject to error or misrepresentation.

Public right-to-know issues are also an important component of the European Union's directive 82/501/EEC on the major accident hazards of certain industrial activities, adopted after one of Europe's most serious industrial accidents. In 1976 a chemical factory in Seveso, Italy released a cloud of dioxin-laced gas that caused widespread harm and catalyzed new European regulations. Even after the World Trade Center and Pentagon attacks on September 11, 2001 heightened concern about the potential for disasters at chemical plants, U.S. requirements still appear to be less stringent than the EU's. As an environmental advocate, how might you use the EU's standards as a basis to encourage the U.S. to "harmonize up"?

7. **Information disclosure and national security.** One of the potential drawbacks of a disclosure strategy is that it arguably might disclose too much. Under CAA §112(r), 42 U.S.C. §7412(r), more than 65,000 companies were required to submit accident

prevention and response plans ("risk management plans"), including "worst-case accident scenarios," to EPA by mid-1999. EPA announced, however, that this data would not be placed on the Internet because of the possibility that terrorists might use the information to plan attacks on vulnerable sites. The data will, however, be made available to local emergency response officials and also to members of the public through FOIA requests. On August 5, 1999, President Clinton signed S. 880, which for one year suspended FOIA disclosures of information on off-site consequences associated with risk management plans required under CAA §112(r). Certain public officials continue to have access to this information.

Concerns about the security implications of disclosure have only intensified in the post-9/11 world. The government has pulled many previously available documents discussing toxic chemical releases and locations from the Web. (For a list, see http://www.mapcruzin.com/news/rtkpost911.htm.) Some have argued, on the other hand, that the possibility of terrorist attacks on chemical plants should strengthen our resolve to gather information about chemical releases and to reduce use of toxic chemicals. A study by the Surgeon General of the Army conducted shortly after September 11 found that as many as 2.4 million people could be killed or injured in a terrorist attack on a chemical plant in a densely populated area in the United States. See Pianin, Study Assesses Risk of Attack on Chemical Plant, Wash. Post, Mar. 12, 2002, at A8. In 2003, Senator Jon Corzine (D-N.J.) sponsored a bill to enact the Chemical Security Act, which would require chemical plants to take steps to reduce the amount of toxics they used. The bill passed the Senate Committee on Environment and Public Works but stalled due to industry opposition.

B. CALIFORNIA'S PROPOSITION 65

In the same year that EPCRA was enacted, California voters approved the Safe Drinking Water and Toxic Enforcement Act of 1986,[6] an initiative popularly known as Proposition 65. Unlike EPCRA, which mandates disclosure only of toxic chemical releases and transfers, Proposition 65 requires that companies provide warnings with regard to consumer product exposures, occupational exposures, and environmental exposures to toxic chemicals.

Proposition 65 coverage extends to almost 700 listed carcinogens and reproductive toxicants.[7] Like EPCRA, Proposition 65 applies to private businesses with ten or more

---

6. Cal. Health & Safety Code §§25249.5-25249.13. In addition, Environmental Defense (ED) has installed an online database, called the "Chemical Scorecard," that links chemical release and toxicology data with maps locating facilities that use certain chemicals. A user need only enter a zip code in order to see a map highlighting local sources of pollution. More than 150 public databases are linked to create this database, which has drawn over 200,000 "hits" per day. ED's Chemical Scorecard is available at http://www.scorecard.org.

7. Here we have yet another list of toxic or hazardous materials that creates legal obligations. Other such lists exist under EPCRA, CWA, CAA, RCRA, as well as under other states' laws. These lists are not uniform and are frequently inconsistent, leading to regulatory inefficiencies and a "toxic shell game," where a pollutant is discharged to the medium of least regulatory supervision. See Dernbach, The Unfocused Regulation of Toxic and Hazardous Pollutants, 21 Harv. Envtl. L. Rev. 1 (1997). Professor Dernbach recommends that Congress or EPA adopt a common list of the most toxic substances, based on the EPCRA list, that would become the basis of a facility-wide and cross-media pollution prevention program.

employees, but its ambit is considerably broader since all businesses are covered, not just designated facilities. Proposition 65 contains exceptions for carcinogens that pose "no significant risk" of contracting cancer (administratively defined as less than one excess cancer case per 100,000 persons exposed for a lifetime) and reproductive toxicants below 1/1000th of the No Observable Effect Level (NOEL) for that chemical.

The following case concerns the potential application of Proposition 65 to naturally occurring carcinogens in foods.

Nicolle-Wagner v. Deukmejian
California Court of Appeal, 1991
230 Cal. App. 3d 652

GRIGNON, J.... At issue is whether a regulation promulgated by the Health and Welfare Agency pursuant to [Proposition 65] conflicts with the language of the act, and whether that regulation is reasonably necessary to effectuate the purposes of the act.... The trial court determined, as a matter of law, that the regulation at issue was reasonable, was the product of fair administrative procedures, and that the Health and Welfare Agency acted within the scope of its statutory authority in enacting the regulation. We affirm.

Proposition 65 was a ballot measure entitled "Restrictions on Toxic Discharge into Drinking Water; Requirement of Notice of Persons' Exposure to Toxics." Its purpose was to identify chemicals known to cause cancer or birth defects, and to prevent exposure to those chemicals through our water supplies, in the workplace, and by other means. Passage of Proposition 65 added §§25249.5-25249.13 to the Health and Safety Code, effective January 1, 1987. Section 25249.5 is a prohibition on contaminating drinking water with chemicals known to cause cancer or reproductive toxicity. Section 25249.6 requires a "clear and reasonable" warning before one may lawfully expose a person to chemicals which are known to cause cancer or reproductive toxicity. That section provides:

> No person in the course of doing business shall knowingly and intentionally expose any individual to a chemical known to the state to cause cancer or reproductive toxicity without first giving clear and reasonable warning to such individual, except as provided in §25249.10....

The Governor was charged with the duty to publish a list of chemicals known to the state to cause cancer or reproductive toxicity. In 1988, almost 300 chemicals were on the list.... The Governor designated the Health and Welfare Agency (the Agency) as the "lead agency" for purposes of Proposition 65.

On April 29, 1987, a petition was submitted to the Agency by 20 different groups, including amicus curiae herein, the Grocery Manufacturers of America, Inc. [seeking] to exempt from §25249.6's "clear and reasonable" warning requirement all food products which comply with certain federal safety regulations. The petition included a compilation of the extent to which various food products contain naturally occurring carcinogens or reproductive toxins. The compilation lists over 300 types of foods which, according to the 16 referenced scientific articles, contain some amount of listed chemicals such as arsenic, chromium, lead, selenium, nickel, cadmium, benzene, benz(a)pyrene, or benz(a)anthracene. Some of these chemicals, like arsenic, selenium, nickel, and cadmium are essential for human nutrition at low levels. In addition, the petition emphasized that some food products contain a naturally occurring carcinogen, aflatoxin, despite existing regulatory efforts. Aflatoxin is a mold that grows in grains and peanuts in storage. It is produced by two common fungi, *Aspergillus flavus* and *A. parasiticus*. The federal government has established an "acceptable level" for aflatoxin....

[In response to the industry petition the Agency issued] §12501 [which] provides that, "Human consumption of a food shall not constitute an 'exposure' for purposes of Health and Safety Code §25249.6…to the extent that the person responsible for the contact can show that the chemical is naturally occurring in the food." A chemical is considered "naturally occurring" if "it is a natural constituent of a food, or if it is present in a food solely as a result of absorption or accumulation of the chemical which is naturally present in the environment in which the food is raised, or grown, or obtained…." The chemical is not naturally occurring to the extent that it is the result of any human activity or failure to observe "good agricultural or good manufacturing practices," such as the "addition of chemicals to irrigation water applied to soil or crops." Even where the chemical is a naturally occurring one, the regulations require that the producer, manufacturer, distributor, or holder of the food at all times utilize measures to reduce that chemical to the lowest level currently feasible.

Following the adoption of §12501, plaintiff filed [this lawsuit] seeking a determination that the [exemption] regulation is unlawful. Plaintiff contends that Proposition 65 created no categorical exemption for naturally occurring carcinogens or naturally occurring reproductive toxins, which are as threatening to health as man-made toxins. Plaintiff maintains that there is no scientific basis for distinguishing between man-made and naturally occurring substances, and that Proposition 65 did not sanction such distinctions…. Following a hearing…, judgment was entered against plaintiff and in favor of defendant….

The sole issue on appeal is whether §12501 is in conflict with or is not reasonably necessary to effectuate the statutory purpose of Health and Safety Code §25249.5 et seq. Our task is to determine whether the Agency "reasonably interpreted its legislative mandate" in adopting that regulation. "Where a statute empowers an administrative agency to adopt regulations, such regulations 'must be consistent, not in conflict with the statute, and reasonably necessary to effectuate its purpose.'"…

Is the Regulation in Conflict with the Governing Statutes? …Plaintiff contends that the Agency regulation is in conflict with the statute because the statute…makes no exception for naturally occurring chemicals. Defendants contend, on the other hand, that while it is true that the statute purports to regulate all listed chemicals, warnings are required only when a business "exposes" an individual to a listed chemical. The term "exposes" is not defined by the statute….

Proposition 65, and the corresponding sections of the Health and Safety Code, are silent on the subject of naturally occurring carcinogens and reproductive toxins. We must search then, for whatever more subtle expressions of the electorate's intent may exist in the language of the statute, as well as the ballot arguments both for and against the proposition. Those sources indicate that Proposition 65 sought to regulate toxic substances which are deliberately added or put into the environment by human activity. The controlling language of the Proposition, now Health and Safety Code §25249.6, provides that "no person in the course of doing business shall knowingly and intentionally expose any individual," thereby suggesting that some degree of human activity which results in toxins being added to the environment is required.

Of course, one could argue that furnishing foods to consumers which are known to contain naturally occurring carcinogens or reproductive toxins might constitute a "knowing and intentional" exposure of individuals to the chemicals. However, the ballot argument in favor of Proposition 65 explains that "[Proposition 65] will not take anyone by surprise. [It] applies only to businesses that know they are putting one of the chemicals out into the environment…." A chemical is not "put" into the environment if it is naturally occurring in, for example, fruits and vegetables….

To be sure, one could find some support for plaintiff's position that no exemption for naturally occurring chemicals was intended.... The ballot proposition itself stated, by way of introduction, that:

> The people of California find that hazardous chemicals pose a serious threat to their health and well-being [and] that state government agencies have failed to provide them with adequate protection.... The people therefore declare their rights:... (b) To be informed about exposures to chemicals that cause cancer, birth defects, or other reproductive harm.

Similarly, the list of chemicals to be controlled...makes no distinction between man-made and naturally occurring substances....

We are persuaded, on balance, that the better view is that the electorate did not intend naturally occurring substances to be controlled by Proposition 65. Use of terms such as "knowingly and intentionally" and "putting" implies that human conduct which results in toxins being added to the environment is the activity to be controlled.... We find that §12501 is consistent with the governing statutes.

Does the Regulation Reasonably Effectuate the Statutory Purpose? We also find that substantial evidence was presented that the regulation reasonably effectuates the statutory purpose.... Most food products contain at least trace amounts of carcinogens and reproductive toxins which appear on the Governor's list.... We all presume, to some extent, that foods that have been eaten for thousands of years are healthful, despite the presence of small amounts of naturally occurring toxins. Were these substances not exempted from Health and Safety Code §25249.6's warning requirements, the manufacturer or seller of such products would bear the burden of proving, under subdivision (c) of Health and Safety Code §25249.10, that the exposure poses no "significant risk" to individuals. The administrative record in this matter indicates that such evidence largely does not exist. Thus, grocers and others would be required, in order to avoid liability under these statutes, to post a warning label on most, if not all, food products.... Since one of the principal purposes of the statutes in question is to provide "clear and reasonable warning" of exposure to carcinogens and reproductive toxins, such warnings would be diluted to the point of meaninglessness if they were to be found on most or all food products.

The [exemption rule's] final statement of reasons also [recognizes] the historical desire to preserve naturally occurring foods in the American food supply, despite the presence in those foods of small amounts of potentially deleterious substances, as well as to recognize the general safety of unprocessed foods as a matter of consumer experience. This exemption, therefore, will further the statutory purpose in safeguarding the effectiveness of warnings which are given, and in removing from regulatory scrutiny those substances which pose only an "insignificant risk" of cancer or birth defects, within the meaning of the statute.

The regulation is also narrowly drawn. It is applicable only to naturally occurring chemicals in foodstuffs and not other products, such as pharmaceuticals and cosmetics.... A chemical is "naturally occurring" only if it is a natural constituent of food or if it is present solely as a result of the absorption or accumulation of chemicals which are naturally present in the environment [and even then] it is not deemed to be "naturally occurring," under the regulation, to the extent it is avoidable by good agricultural or manufacturing techniques. Natural chemical contaminants must be reduced to the "lowest level currently feasible."

We hold that the actions of the Agency in promulgating §12501 were not arbitrary or capricious, or lacking in evidentiary support, and that the Agency considered all relevant factors. We further hold that the regulation...is not in conflict with and reasonably promotes the statutory purposes of Proposition 65.

COMMENTARY & QUESTIONS

1. **Too little information?** If the purpose of Proposition 65 is to inform consumers about carcinogens to which they are exposed, does it make any sense to exempt naturally occurring carcinogens from the law's requirements? Bruce Ames, a scientist at the University of California at Berkeley, has criticized stringent regulation of synthetic chemicals on the ground that most of the carcinogens to which we are exposed are naturally occurring. See, e.g., Ames et al., Dietary Pesticides (99.9% all natural), 87 Proc. Nat'l Acad. Sci. 7777 (1990). Does Ames's argument also suggest that if we are going to require labeling of carcinogens, we should require labeling for natural carcinogens, too?

2. **Too much information?** Professor Sunstein argues that Proposition 65 perhaps requires too much information, leading paradoxically to a less informed citizenry:

> A central difficulty [with disclosure requirements] is that people have limited ability to process information. They have a notoriously difficult time in thinking about low-probability events. Sometimes they discount such events to zero; sometimes they treat them as much more dangerous than they actually are. If people are told, for example, that a certain substance causes cancer, they may think it is far more dangerous than it is in fact. But some carcinogenic substances pose little risk.

> For example, California's Proposition 65, an initiative designed to promote citizen awareness of risk levels, requires warnings for exposure to carcinogens. At first glance, the requirement seems unexceptionable, indeed an important advance.... But Proposition 65 has in some cases been counterproductive or even worse. Consumers appear to think that twelve of every 100 users of a product with the required warning will die from cancer. This estimate exceeds reality by a factor of 1000 or more. The presence of the warning makes people more confused rather than more aware. Sunstein, Informing America: Risk, Disclosure, and the First Amendment, 20 Fla. St. U. L. Rev. 653 (1993).

3. **"Clear and reasonable" warnings.** The text of Proposition 65 specifies only that warnings be "clear and reasonable"; it does not explicitly designate the form of consumer product, occupational, and environmental exposure warnings. Even legible, conspicuous, clear, and informative warnings might be unsuccessful in alerting recipients to the risks associated with the products or activities to which the warnings refer. Professor Rechtschaffen points out that

> Consumers may lack the time or interest to seek out information. Many may have difficulty understanding certain information, especially information about risks. In particular, less educated and limited-English speaking individuals are less likely to be able to read, understand, and use warning information. Even when individuals read and comprehend warnings, they often do not change their behavior in response to the information they receive. Workers, for instance, may disregard the seriousness of the risks to which they are exposed when they perceive the risks as involuntary or out of their control.... Moreover, persons exposed to chemicals in the environment have no traditional "market" in which they can express their preferences. Additionally, conveying information about environmental exposures is much more difficult because there is no single point of purchase, as with consumer products, or even a single point of exposure, as in the workplace. Despite these limitations...only a small number of motivated persons — e.g., attentive, information-seeking consumers, unions, or environmental organizations — actually

needs to use information to accomplish some of the desire benefits of information disclosure laws. Rechtschaffen, The Warning Game: Evaluating Warnings Under California's Proposition 65, 23 Ecology L.Q. 303, 316–318 (1996).

In fact, a significant percentage of Proposition 65 warnings have been inconspicuous, uninformative, misleading, and confusing. For example, consumer product warnings have been placed on the backs of product labels or in small print on the fronts of already crowded labels, on the underside or inside lids of product containers, or in insignificant signs on store shelves or checkout counters. Warnings state that the product "contains" a toxic chemical, not that the product will "expose" the consumer to that chemical. Disclaimers frequently counteract or minimize the warning language. Some products carry the label: "Warning: this product contains materials known to the State of California to cause cancer." Warnings can be found in small signs placed on the grounds of polluting facilities or buried in the "Legal Notices" sections of local newspapers.

4. **Results.** Notably, Proposition 65 appears to have achieved its purposes in spite of the inadequacies of many warnings. Here is Professor Rechtschaffen again:

> Proposition 65's warning requirement has stimulated significant consumer-product reformulation, due to a combination of industry concerns about [tort] liability and consumer reaction to warnings. In some instances, the reformulations have been close to industry-wide, reflecting the competitive pressures that arise once a portion of the industry alters its products. Almost all reformulated products are sold nationwide, giving the statute national effect. Moreoever, the reported product reformulations probably represent only a portion of the private businesses' actions. As one business columnist suggests, "most of the good arising from Proposition 65 remains hidden, in the form of companies that quietly assess what they're doing, and presumably clean up their act to avoid the brouhaha that might arise from having to tell all the neighbors they're being poisoned.... Enforcement actions have triggered many product reformulations.... [With regard to environmental exposure warnings], enforcement actions have stimulated some of the most notable reductions, as prosecuting parties have traded large penalties in exchange for emissions cutbacks.... 23 Ecology L.Q. at 341, 348.

5. **EPCRA and Proposition 65: a one-two punch.** According to David Roe, an attorney who helped to draft Proposition 65, emissions of chemicals for which disclosure is required under both Proposition 65 and EPCRA dropped in California by 85%, from 1988–1997, as compared with a decrease of about 50% in the rest of the country. California has issued numerical risk-based standards for 282 chemicals in less than five years, not one of which has been challenged in litigation. According to Roe, Proposition 65 has been successful because the onus of proving absence of significant risk is on industry, which has the incentive and the resources to resolve scientific uncertainty. Progress in regulating hazardous substances at the federal level has been much slower because EPA lacks the resources to overcome scientific uncertainty, and must defend its actions, in both courts and the political arena, against almost inevitable industry opposition. 2000 BNA Envtl. Rep. Curr. Dev. 2603–2605. Cf. ToSCA and FIFRA procedures studied in Chapter 17.

6. **The interstate effects of state product regulation.** When California enacted Proposition 65, businesses began to include informational warnings on products sold throughout the United States. By and large, industry cannot afford to sell different

forms of the same product, or the same product in different packaging, in different jurisdictions. When Chicago and several other cities, counties, and states enacted bans on the sale of phosphate detergents within their boundaries, detergent manufacturers reformulated their products to eliminate phosphates. Automobile manufacturers lobbied hard for a National Low-Emissions Vehicle (NLEV), rather than sell "California cars" in some states and different low-emission vehicles in other states. See Chapter 15. Industry's need for national uniformity in the marketplace gives enhanced importance to state laws that affect consumer products.

7. **Are mandatory disclosure laws "self-executing"?** This category of statutes does avoid some of the typical accoutrements of command-and-control regulation, such as permitting. But mandatory disclosure laws are far from self-executing. Lists of toxic substances must be prepared, and standards and reportable quantities established. Governmental agencies must perform monitoring and surveillance to ensure that regulated parties are complying with the law. And enforcement programs must be effective, efficient, predictable, and credible if voluntary compliance is to be achieved among a majority of the regulated community. The success of Proposition 65, in spite of the manifold inadequacies of the warning mechanism, can be attributed partly to vigorous enforcement by governmental and private plaintiffs.

8. **The Federal Trade Commission's "Green Guides."** Another variety of mandatory disclosure statute prevents the communication of false and deceptive environmental marketing claims. "Green marketing" has become so lucrative that some unscrupulous businesspersons invent environmental advantages for their products in order to appeal to green consumers who cannot readily determine whether the products possess the advertised attributes. How, for example, can a consumer verify whether an aerosol spray she uses will deplete the ozone layer or contribute to smog? The FTC enforces §5 of the FTC Act, 15 U.S.C. §57a, which generally prohibits "unfair or deceptive acts of practices," including advertising or labeling that is false or misleading. Sporadic state legislation in the area of false environmental advertising has been effectively replaced by the FTC's Guides for the Use of Environmental Marketing Claims (1992), commonly known as the "Green Guides." These guides were issued as policy interpretations, not promulgated as regulations, but industry treats them as authoritative because the FTC uses them as a basis for its enforcement actions. (When dealing with green consumers, who are adept at formal and informal product boycotts, public notice of specious environmental claims can be commercially disastrous.) The Green Guides specify that all express and implied claims about objective product attributes must be substantiated by competent and reliable scientific evidence before they are made. For example, a manufacturer of coffee filters included the phrase "recycled paper" on the side of the box, which could mean, to a reasonable consumer, that both the cardboard box and the coffee filters were made from recycled content. One of the settlements negotiated by the FTC arose from its allegation that it was deceptive to fail to indicate whether the claim referred to the product or the package, because, although the box was made of recycled materials, the filters were not. The Green Guides identify the types of substantiation required and the standard disclaimers that should be included when using terms such as "environmentally safe," "environmentally friendly," "degradable," "recyclable,"

"source reduction," and "ozone friendly." They also cover alleged third party certification claims, such as environmental seals of approval and "green globe" logos. From all indications, industry is voluntarily complying with the Green Guides, and the number of deceptive environmental claims has been reduced.

9. **Consumer notification under the Safe Drinking Water Act.** The SDWA of 1974 required operators of public water systems to notify their customers each time their systems failed to meet one of the maximum contaminant levels for drinking water established by EPA. 42 U.S.C. §300g-3(c). This requirement was more often honored in the breach than the observance. GAO, Drinking Water: Consumers Often Not Well-Informed of Potentially Serious Violations (RCED-92-135) (1992). The 1996 SDWA Amendments strengthened the SDWA's disclosure provisions by requiring that consumers of public water supplies be given more accurate and timely information about violations and that this information be disclosed in a form that is more understandable and useful. A violation with potential to have serious adverse effects on human health must be followed by immediate individual notification of the violation, its potential health effects, the steps that the purveyor is taking to remedy the violation, and the necessity of seeking alternative water supplies during the violation period. If appropriate, additional notification must be made by broadcast or print media or even by posting door-to-door notices. 42 U.S.C. §300g-3(c)(C). Purveyors must also issue annual "Consumer Confidence Reports" that include information on the source of the water, violations of any federal drinking water standards, potential sources of these violations, and contaminants that were detected and their related health effects. These reports must be prepared in plain, understandable language (English only), with all legal and technical terms intelligibly defined. 42 U.S.C. §300g-3(c)(E)(4).

How useful do you suppose these reports will be to the average drinking water consumer? Consider the following statement, which EPA requires to appear in consumer confidence reports regarding drinking water that contains arsenic at a measurable but legal level:[8]

> While your drinking water meets EPA's standard for arsenic, it does contain low levels of arsenic. EPA's standard balances the current understanding of arsenic's possible health effects against the costs of removing arsenic from drinking water. EPA continues to research the health effects of low levels of arsenic which is a mineral known to cause cancer in humans at high concentrations and is linked to other health effects such as skin damage and circulatory problems.

> Some people who drink water containing arsenic in excess of the [maximum contaminant level] over many years could experience skin damage or problems with their circulatory system, and may have an increased risk of getting cancer.

If you received this information in the mail along with your drinking water bill, how would you respond to it?

---

8. For more on EPA's new standard for arsenic in drinking water, see Chapter 13.

C. LEGAL CHALLENGES TO REGULATING INFORMATION: THE FIRST AMENDMENT

Not surprisingly, one of the first legal obstacles encountered by laws that compel disclosure of information is the First Amendment. Firms faced with disclosure requirements point out that the First Amendment protects against compelled speech just as surely as it guards against prohibitions on speech. The following case highlights such a claim.

International Dairy Foods Association v. Amestoy
United States Court of Appeals for the Second Circuit, 1996
92 F.3d 67

ALTIMARI, J. Plaintiffs-appellants International Dairy Foods Association, Milk Industry Foundation (MIF), International Ice Cream Association, National Cheese Institute, Grocery Manufacturers of America, Inc. and National Food Processors Association (collectively "appellants" or "dairy manufacturers") appeal from a decision of the district court, 898 F. Supp. 246, 250 (D. Vt. 1995), denying their motion for a preliminary injunction. The dairy manufacturers challenged the constitutionality of Vermont Stat. Ann. tit. 6, §2754(c), which requires dairy manufacturers to identify products which were, or might have been, derived from dairy cows treated with a synthetic growth hormone used to increase milk production. The dairy manufacturers alleged that the statute violated the United States Constitution's First Amendment....

In 1993, the federal Food and Drug Administration ("FDA") approved the use of recombinant Bovine Somatotropin ("rBST") (also known as recombinant Bovine Growth Hormone ("rBGH")), a synthetic growth hormone that increases milk production by cows. It is undisputed that the dairy products derived from herds treated with rBST are indistinguishable from products derived from untreated herds; consequently, the FDA declined to require the labeling of products derived from cows receiving the supplemental hormone.

In April 1994, defendant-appellee the State of Vermont enacted a statute requiring that "if rBST has been used in the production of milk or a milk product for retail sale in this state, the retail milk or milk product shall be labeled as such." Vt. Stat. Ann. tit. 6, §2754(c). The State of Vermont's Commissioner of Agriculture subsequently promulgated regulations giving those dairy manufacturers who use rBST four labeling options, among them the posting of a sign to the following effect in any store selling dairy products:

> rBST INFORMATION — THE PRODUCTS IN THIS CASE THAT CONTAIN OR MAY CONTAIN MILK FROM rBST-TREATED COWS EITHER (1) STATE ON THE PACKAGE THAT rBST HAS BEEN OR MAY HAVE BEEN USED, OR (2) ARE IDENTIFIED BY A BLUE SHELF LABEL LIKE THIS [BLUE RECTANGLE] OR (3) A BLUE STICKER ON THE PACKAGE LIKE THIS. [BLUE DOT]
> The United States Food and Drug Administration has determined that there is no significant difference between milk from treated and untreated cows. It is the law of Vermont that products made from the milk of rBST-treated cows be labeled to help consumers make informed shopping decisions.

Failure to comply with the statute and companion regulations subjects manufacturers to civil as well as criminal penalties....

Irreparable Harm. Focusing principally on the economic impact of the labeling regulation, the district court found that appellants had not demonstrated irreparable harm to any right protected by the First Amendment. We disagree.

Irreparable harm is "injury for which a monetary award cannot be adequate compensation." It is established that "the loss of First Amendment freedoms, for even minimal periods of time, unquestionably constitutes irreparable injury." Because the statute at issue requires appellants to make an involuntary statement whenever they offer their products for sale, we find that the statute causes the dairy manufacturers irreparable harm....

Ordinarily, it is the purposeful suppression of speech which constitutes irreparable harm. Compliance with the Vermont Labeling Law does not prohibit the plaintiffs from disseminating a message. Instead, it requires the plaintiffs to truthfully disclose the method used in producing their product....

The right not to speak inheres in political and commercial speech alike, and extends to statements of fact as well as statements of opinion. If, however, as Vermont maintains, its labeling law compels appellants to engage in purely commercial speech, the statute must meet a less rigorous test.... Agreeing with Vermont, the district court found that the speech was commercial in nature....

Even assuming that the compelled disclosure is purely commercial speech, appellants have amply demonstrated that the First Amendment is sufficiently implicated to cause irreparable harm. The dairy manufacturers have clearly done more than simply "assert" their First Amendment rights: The statute in question indisputably requires them to speak when they would rather not.... Because the dairy manufacturers challenge government action taken in the public interest, they must also show a likelihood of success on the merits. We find that such success is likely.

In Central Hudson Gas & Elec. Corp. v. Public Serv. Comm'n, 447 U.S. 557 (1980), the Supreme Court articulated a four-part analysis for determining whether a government restriction on commercial speech is permissible....

Under *Central Hudson*, we must determine: (1) whether the expression concerns lawful activity and is not misleading; (2) whether the government's interest is substantial; (3) whether the labeling law directly serves the asserted interest; and (4) whether the labeling law is no more extensive than necessary. Furthermore, the State of Vermont bears the burden of justifying its labeling law. As the Supreme Court has made clear, "this burden is not satisfied by mere speculation or conjecture; rather, a governmental body seeking to sustain a restriction on commercial speech must demonstrate that the harms it recites are real and that its restriction will in fact alleviate them to a material degree." Edenfield v. Fane, 507 U.S. 761 at 770-771 (1993).

In our view, Vermont has failed to establish the second prong of the *Central Hudson* test, namely that its interest is substantial.... As the district court made clear, Vermont "does not claim that health or safety concerns prompted the passage of the Vermont Labeling Law," but instead defends the statute on the basis of "strong consumer interest and the public's 'right to know....'" These interests are insufficient to justify compromising protected constitutional rights.[9]

Vermont's failure to defend its constitutional intrusion on the ground that it negatively impacts public health is easily understood. After exhaustive studies, the FDA has "concluded that rBST has no appreciable effect on the composition of milk produced by treated cows, and that there are no human safety or health concerns associated with food products derived from cows treated with rBST."... It is undisputed that neither consumers nor scientists can

---

9. Although the dissent suggests several interests that if adopted by the state of Vermont may have been substantial, the district court opinion makes clear that Vermont adopted no such rationales for its statute.... The district court...explained, "Vermont has determined that its consumers want to know whether rBST has been used in the production of their milk and milk products."... Unfortunately, mere consumer concern is not, in itself, a substantial interest.

distinguish rBST-derived milk from milk produced by an untreated cow [and] the record in this case contains no scientific evidence…that rBST has any impact at all on dairy products. It is thus plain that Vermont could not justify the statute on the basis of "real" harms.

We do not doubt that Vermont's asserted interest, the demand of its citizenry for such information, is genuine; reluctantly, however, we conclude that it is inadequate. We are aware of no case in which consumer interest alone was sufficient to justify requiring a product's manufacturers to publish the functional equivalent of a warning about a production method that has no discernable impact on a final product.

Although the Court is sympathetic to the Vermont consumers who wish to know which products may derive from rBST-treated herds, their desire is insufficient to permit the State of Vermont to compel the dairy manufacturers to speak against their will. Were consumer interest alone sufficient, there is no end to the information that states could require manufacturers to disclose about their production methods. For instance, with respect to cattle, consumers might reasonably evince an interest in knowing which grains herds were fed, with which medicines they were treated, or the age at which they were slaughtered. Absent, however, some indication that this information bears on a reasonable concern for human health or safety or some other sufficiently substantial governmental concern, the manufacturers cannot be compelled to disclose it. Instead, those consumers interested in such information should exercise the power of their purses by buying products from manufacturers who voluntarily reveal it.

Accordingly, we hold that consumer curiosity alone is not a strong enough state interest to sustain the compulsion of even an accurate, factual statement, in a commercial context….

LEVAL, J., dissenting: I respectfully dissent. Vermont's regulation requiring disclosure of use of rBST in milk production was based on substantial state interests, including worries about rBST's impact on human and cow health, fears for the survival of small dairy farms, and concerns about the manipulation of nature through biotechnology. The objective of the plaintiff milk producers is to conceal their use of rBST from consumers. The policy of the First Amendment, in its application to commercial speech, is to favor the flow of accurate, relevant information. The majority's invocation of the First Amendment to invalidate a state law requiring disclosure of information consumers reasonably desire stands the Amendment on its ear….

Many of the most important facts of this case are omitted from the majority's opinion…. Recent advances in genetic technologies led to the development of a synthetically isolated metabolic protein hormone known as recombinant bovine somatotropin (rBST), which, when injected into cows, increases their milk production. Monsanto Company, an amicus in this action on the side of the plaintiff milk producers, has developed the only commercially approved form of rBST and markets it under the brand name "Posilac." This is, of course, at the frontiers of bio-science. A…government study of rBST describes it as "one of the first major commercial biotechnology products to be used in the U.S. food and agricultural sector and the first to attract significant attention." The FDA and others have studied rBST extensively…, concluding that "milk and meat from [rBST-treated] cows is safe" for human consumption.

The impending use of rBST caused substantial controversy throughout the country. The Federal Study [reported] that consumers favor the labeling of milk produced by use of rBST. In Vermont, a state highly attuned to issues affecting the dairy industry, use of rBST was the subject of frequent press commentary and debate, and provoked considerable opposition. In response to public pressure, the state of Vermont enacted [this labeling] law….

The interests which Vermont sought to advance by its statute and regulations were explained in the Agriculture Department's Economic Impact Statement accompanying its regulations. The Statement reported that consumer interest in disclosure of use of rBST was based on "concerns about FDA determinations about the product as regards health and safety or about recombinant gene technology"; concerns "about the effect of the product on bovine health"; and "concerns about the effect of the product on the existing surplus of milk and in the dairy farm industry's economic status and well-being." This finding was based on "consumer comments to Vermont legislative committees" and to the Department, as well as published reports and letters to the editors published in the press.... Comments by Vermont citizens who had heard or read about rBST were overwhelmingly negative. The most prevalent responses to rBST use included: "Not natural," "More research needs to be done/Long-term effects not clear," "Against additives added to my milk," "Worried about adverse health effects," "Unhealthy for the cow," "Don't need more chemicals," "It's a hormone/Against hormones added to my milk," "Hurts the small dairy farmer," "Producing enough milk already."

On the basis of this evidence the district court found that a majority of Vermonters "do not want to purchase milk products derived from rBST-treated cows," and that the reasons included:

(1) They consider the use of a genetically-engineered hormone in the production unnatural; (2) they believe that use of the hormone will result in increased milk production and lower milk prices, thereby hurting small dairy farmers; (3) they believe that the use of rBST is harmful to cows and potentially harmful to humans; and, (4) they feel that there is a lack of knowledge regarding the long-term effects of rBST.

The court thus understandably concluded that "Vermont has a substantial interest in informing consumers of the use of rBST in the production of milk and dairy products sold in the state."

In the face of this evidence and these explicit findings by the district court, the majority oddly concludes that Vermont's sole interest in requiring disclosure of rBST use is to gratify "consumer curiosity," and that this alone "is not a strong enough state interest to sustain the compulsion of even an accurate factual statement." The majority...disregards the evidence of Vermont's true interests and the district court's findings recognizing those interests. Nowhere does the majority opinion discuss or even mention the evidence or findings regarding the people of Vermont's concerns about human health, cow health, biotechnology, and the survival of small dairy farms.

Second, the majority...relies substantially on Judge Murtha's statement that Vermont..."bases its justification...on strong consumer interest and the public's 'right to know.'" The majority takes this passage out of context. The district court's opinion went on...to explain...that the interests of the citizenry that led to the passage of the law include health and safety concerns, among others.[10]... When [the trial judge] asserted that Vermont's rule was passed to vindicate "strong consumer interest and the public's right to know," this could not mean that the public's interest was based on nothing but "curiosity," because the judge expressly found that the consumer interest was based on health, economic, and ethical concerns.

Third, the majority suggests that, because the FDA has not found health risks in this new procedure, health worries could not be considered "real" or "cognizable." I find this proposition alarming and dangerous; at the very least, it is extraordinarily unrealistic. Genetic and biotechnological manipulation of basic food products is new and controversial. Although I have no reason to doubt that the FDA's studies of rBST have been thorough, they could not cover

---

10. Indeed...a finding [that health and safety were not motivating concerns] would be unsupportable in view of the evidence that the concerns of the citizenry were communicated to the legislature. When the citizens of a state express concerns to the legislature and the state's lawmaking bodies then pass disclosure requirements in response to those expressed concerns, it seems clear (without need for a statutory declaration of purpose) that the state is acting to vindicate the concerns expressed by its citizens, and not merely to gratify their "curiosity." Vermont need not, furthermore, take the position that rBST is harmful to require its disclosure because of potential health risks. The mere fact that it does not know whether rBST poses hazards is sufficient reason to justify disclosure by reason of the unknown potential for harm.

long-term effects of rBST on humans.[11] Furthermore, there are many possible reasons why a government agency might fail to find real health risks, including inadequate time and budget for testing, insufficient advancement of scientific techniques, insufficiently large sampling populations, pressures from industry, and simple human error. To suggest that a government agency's failure to find a health risk in a short-term study of a new genetic technology should bar a state from requiring simple disclosure of the use of that technology where its citizens are concerned about such health risks would be unreasonable and dangerous. Although the FDA's conclusions may be reassuring, they do not guarantee the safety of rBST.

Forty years ago, when I (and nearly everyone) smoked, no one told us that we might be endangering our health. Tobacco is but one of many consumer products once considered safe, which were subsequently found to cause health hazards. The limitations of scientific information about new consumer products were well illustrated in a 1990 study produced at the request of Congress by the General Accounting Office. Looking at various prescription drugs available on the market, the study examined the risks associated with the drugs that became known only after they were approved by the FDA, and concluded:

> Even after approval, many additional risks may surface when the general population is exposed to a drug. These risks, which range from relatively minor (such as nausea and headache) to serious (such as hospitalization and death) arise from the fact that preapproval drug testing is inherently limited.... In studying the frequency and seriousness of risks identified after approval, GAO found that of the 198 drugs approved by FDA between 1976 and 1985 for which data were available, 102 (or 51.5 percent) had serious postapproval risks, as evidenced by labeling changes or withdrawal from the market.... The serious postapproval risks are adverse reactions that could lead to hospitalization...severe or permanent disability, or death. GAO Report, FDA Drug Review: Postapproval Risks, 1976–85, April 1990, at 2–3.

As startling as its results may seem, this study merely confirms a common sense proposition: namely, that a government agency's conclusion regarding a product's safety, reached after limited study, is not a guarantee and does not invalidate public concern for unknown side effects. In short, the majority has no valid basis for its conclusion that Vermont's regulation advances no interest other than the gratification of consumer curiosity, and involves neither health concerns nor other substantial interests.

Substantial State Interests. Freedom of speech is not an absolute right, particularly in the commercial context. In *Central Hudson* the Supreme Court announced standards for governmental regulation of commercial speech. [Even if] it is not misleading..., it is nonetheless subject to regulation if the government has a substantial interest in regulating the speech, the regulation directly advances that interest, and it is no more intrusive than necessary to accomplish its goal....

The sole issue is whether Vermont had a substantial interest in compelling the disclosure of use of rBST in milk production. In my view, Vermont's multifaceted interest...is altogether

---

11. One of Vermont's experts, a specialist in medical information and the review of scientific literature, stated in an affidavit:

> It is not reasonable to conclude that there is uniform agreement that milk from rBST treated cows is 100% safe for human consumption.... Longitudinal studies have been called for to establish the long-term health effects of the use of rBST on cows, and until the results of these studies are published, disagreement on the effects of rBST will likely continue.... Milk from rBST treated cows is generally considered safe by the Food and Drug Administration and some scientists, while the General Accounting Office and other scientists feel that more research is needed before a universal agreement can be reached. Affidavit of Dr. Julie McGowan, at 26–27.

substantial. Consumer worries about possible adverse health effects from consumption of rBST, especially over a long term, [are] unquestionably a substantial interest. As to health risks to cows, the concern is supported by the warning label on Posilac, which states that cows injected with the product are at an increased risk for: various reproductive disorders, "clinical mastitis [udder infections] (visibly abnormal milk)," "digestive disorders such as indigestion, bloat, and diarrhea," "enlarged hocks and lesions," and "swellings" that may be permanent. As to the economic impact of increased milk production, caused by injection of rBST, upon small dairy farmers, the evidence included a U.S. Department of Agriculture economist's written claim that, "if rBST is heavily adopted and milk prices are reduced, at least some of the smaller farmers that do not use rBST might be forced out of the dairy business, because they would not be producing economically sufficient volumes of milk."...

These concerns..., taken together, undoubtedly constitute a substantial governmental justification for Vermont's labeling law....

The text posted by retailers under Vermont's law is innocuous. Apart from enabling the consumer to tell which products derive from rBST-treated cows, the only additional required text states [that] "The United States Food and Drug Administration has determined that there is no significant difference between milk from treated and untreated cows. It is the law of Vermont that products made from the milk of rBSt-treated cows be labeled to help consumers make informed shopping decisions."[12]... It is quite clear that the producers' real objection is to the mandatory revelation of the use of rBST, which many Vermonters disfavor, and not to the bland sentence announcing that products are labeled "to help consumers make informed shopping decisions."

Disclosure v. Concealment. Notwithstanding their self-righteous references to free expression, the true objective of the milk producers is concealment. They do not wish consumers to know that their milk products were produced by use of rBST because there are consumers who, for various reasons, prefer to avoid rBST. Vermont, on the other hand, has established a labeling requirement whose sole objective (and whose sole effect) is to inform Vermont consumers whether milk products offered for sale were produced with rBST.[13] The dispute under the First Amendment is over whether the milk producers' interest in concealing their use of rBST from consumers will prevail over a state law designed to give consumers the information they desire. The question is simply whether the First Amendment prohibits government from requiring disclosure of truthful relevant information to consumers.

In my view, the interest of the milk producers has little entitlement to protection under the First Amendment. The caselaw that has developed under the doctrine of commercial speech has repeatedly emphasized that the primary function of the First Amendment in its application to commercial speech is to advance truthful disclosure — the very interest that the milk producers seek to undermine....

The application of these principles to the case at bar yields a clear message. The benefit the First Amendment confers in the area of commercial speech is the provision of accurate, non-misleading, relevant information to consumers. Thus, regulations designed to prevent the

---

12. Indeed, a statistical sampling shows that this labeling makes milk from rBST-treated cows more acceptable to Vermont consumers. Before reading this sign, 86% of respondents preferred milk from untreated cows; after reading the sign, preference for milk from untreated cows fell to 73%.

13. I disagree with the majority's contention, that voluntary labeling by producers who do not use rBST can be relied on to effectuate Vermont's purpose. There is evidence that, notwithstanding the FDA's determination to permit such voluntary labeling, certain states, no doubt influenced by the rBST lobby, will "not allow any labeling concerning rBST." Affidavit of Ben Cohen, at 3–4. This effectively prevents multistate distributors from including such labeling on their packaging....

flow of such information are disfavored; regulations designed to provide such information are not.

The milk producers' invocation of the First Amendment for the purpose of concealing their use of rBST in milk production is entitled to scant recognition. They invoke the Amendment's protection to accomplish exactly what the Amendment opposes. And the majority's ruling deprives Vermont of the right to protect its consumers by requiring truthful disclosure on a subject of legitimate public concern....

COMMENTARY & QUESTIONS

1. **Agribusiness on the offensive: Watch your mouth: dis a cabbage, go to jail.** At the behest of agribusiness interests, according to one report, 11 states have passed laws prohibiting "food disparagement" — Alabama, Arizona, Colorado, Florida, Georgia, Idaho, Louisiana, Mississippi, Oklahoma, South Dakota, and Texas. Similar "vegetable libel" bills have been proposed for California, Delaware, Illinois, Iowa, Minnesota, Ohio, Oregon, Pennsylvania, South Carolina, and Washington. Rauber, Food for Thought: Vegetable Hate Crimes, Sierra, Nov. 1995. Given the robust free speech protection applied even in commercial settings like *Amestoy*, aren't statutes repressing individual citizens' comments about industrial foods facially unconstitutional? The "beef defamation" suits filed against Oprah Winfrey when she and her guests excoriated the practice of "ruminant-to-ruminant" feeding of animal parts to cattle, which could lead to "mad cow" disease outbreaks (see notes at end of Chapter 17) were dismissed on nonconstitutional grounds. See Texas Beef Group v. Winfrey, 11 F. Supp. 2d 858, 861 (N.D. Tex. 1998), and Engler Cactus Feeders v. Winfrey, 201 F.3d 680 (5th Cir. 2000) (suits filed under Texas Civ. Prac. & Rem. Code Ann. §96.01 (1997)); and Hagy, Let Them Eat Beef: The Constitutionality of the Texas False Disparagement of Perishable Food Products Act, 29 Tex. Tech L. Rev. 851 (1998) (concluding that the Texas statute, which may be limited to egregiously false statements, might be constitutional, but that most such statutes are not).[14]

As the *Amestoy* dissent noted, even voluntary labeling comes under attack. The Monsanto Chemical Corporation, which markets rBST, sued a Maine dairy arguing that it was misleading consumers through its label announcing "OUR PLEDGE — NO ARTIFICIAL HORMONES." Monsanto thought the label misleadingly suggested that the milk from cows not treated with rBST was safer than milk from cows treated with the hormone. Monsanto wanted the dairy to include a recognition of the FDA's 1993 finding that there was no significant difference between milk from treated and untreated cows. The reaction of the dairy's owner, Stanley Bennett: "We are in the business of marketing milk, not Monsanto's drugs." Leeds, Got Hormones? Time, Dec. 22, 2003, at 52. Nevertheless, the dairy settled with Monsanto in December 2003, agreeing to refer to the FDA's finding in its "no hormones" pledge. In late 2003, the Bush II Administration's FDA itself warned four dairies that their "no-hormones" labels were misleading, in violation of the federal FFDCA. (The FDA's press release is available at http://www.fda.gov/bbs/topics/NEWS/2003/NEW00943.html.)

---

14. Cf. Kuran & Sunstein, Availability Cascades and Risk Regulation, 51 Stan. L. Rev. 683, 705–736 (1999) (suggesting that such laws may not be a bad idea).

2. **Mercury and the First Amendment.** In National Elec. Mfrs. Ass'n v. Sorrell, 272 F.3d 104 (2d Cir. 2001), the Second Circuit vacated a preliminary injunction forbidding enforcement of a Vermont statute requiring the labeling of certain products (including lamps) containing mercury. The court concluded that the industry plaintiffs' commercial free speech challenge was unlikely to succeed on the merits, distinguishing the Amestoy ruling in the following terms:

> Our [*Amestoy*] decision was expressly limited to cases in which a state disclosure requirement is supported by no interest other than the gratification of "consumer curiosity." The disclosure statute at issue here, however, is based on Vermont's substantial interest in protecting human health and the environment from mercury poisoning. 272 F.3d at 115 n. 6.

The court also noted "the potentially wide-ranging implications" of the First Amendment claim in the mercury case, citing several federal and state laws requiring information disclosure. "To hold that the Vermont statute is insufficiently related to the state's interest in reducing mercury pollution," the court said, "would expose these long-established programs to searching scrutiny by unelected courts. Such a result is neither wise nor constitutionally required." 272 F.3d at 116.

3. **Nike's speech.** One much-anticipated case involving commercial speech and the First Amendment fizzled when the Supreme Court dismissed as improvidently granted the writ of certiorari in Nike v. Kasky, 123 S. Ct. 2554 (2003). The case involved a California citizen's claim that Nike's public relations campaign in response to complaints about its labor practices abroad was deceptive and thus violated California's consumer protection law. The dispute generated considerable interest from all sides, with some arguing that a judgment in favor of citizen Kasky would spell the end of commercial speech freedom for corporations, and others arguing that a judgment in favor of Nike would doom consumers' interest in truthful commercial speech. The case settled for a reported $1.5 million (to be given to the Fair Labor Association) several months after the Supreme Court's dismissal had the effect of sending the case back to the California courts for a trial on the merits.

4. **Citizen information initiatives in the securities marketplace?** Here's another twist on the information disclosure issue: When citizens attempting to block the reopening of the A-J Mine in a wilderness area near Juneau, Alaska, got little support from government agencies, they decided to take their concerns to Wall Street. The mining company, a subsidiary of a Fortune 500 conglomerate, proposed to extract gold by dumping cyanide-laced acids onto raw ore, sluicing the post-extraction wastes into a nearby creek. It turned out that a pollution permit could not be issued for such discharges, so the company proposed instead to dam up the creek and dump the wastes into the impoundment, designating it as a "waste treatment lagoon" under CWA regulations; the Bush I EPA approved the maneuver. As an experiment in information-leveraging, the citizens then sent a detailed information packet to more than 50 Wall Street securities analysis firms explaining the company's plan and suggesting that investors should be made aware that the project was subject to serious litigation challenges. Several securities analysts wrote thanking the citizens for their "very relevant information" which never would have become known through normal market information channels.

Perhaps in part because of the data feedback loop, the A-J Mine project was subsequently shelved. But some other analysts huffily told the citizens that the information packets were "inappropriate," and raised the possibility that the citizens could be sued for "business defamation," especially if their packets contained any fact that was not accurate. If markets run on information, and citizens want to bring relevant public interest information into the marketplace of ideas, to what extent do they have to fear SLAPP suits filed under tort theories of libel, defamation, and "interference with business advantage"?

Chapter 11

HARM-BASED AMBIENT STANDARDS: THE CLEAN AIR ACT

A. *The Clean Air Act: History and Structure*
B. *Ambient Standards, the Commons, and American Federalism*
C. *Harm as the Threshold of Regulation*
D. *Moving from Identifying Harm to Regulating Polluters: Implementation Plans*
E. *Prescribing the Path to Attainment*
F. *Transboundary Airflows*

The National Ambient Air Quality Standards (NAAQSs) form the centerpiece of what many consider to be this country's single most important environmental program, the Clean Air Act (CAA), 42 U.S.C. §§7401 et seq. (1970). These standards protect public health by governing the quality of the outdoor air throughout the nation. They address the pollutants that are among the best studied, most pervasive, and most diversely harmful of the by-products of industrial society. A large part of the federal regulation that takes place under the CAA, and most of the state regulation, has as its objective the attainment of air quality consistent with the NAAQS.

The CAA's NAAQS program is one of the signal success stories of American environmental law. Emissions of most of the pollutants regulated by this program have decreased dramatically in the 30 years the program has been in place, despite substantial increases in the size of our population and in the amount of economic activity.[1] In a peer-reviewed, retrospective study of the CAA's first 20 years, EPA concluded that the Act had produced almost $22 *trillion* more in benefits than it had imposed in costs, and EPA believed that even this dazzling amount probably understated the benefits of the statute.[2] This result was corroborated in 2003 by none other than the Office of Information and Regulatory Affairs (OIRA) within the Office of Management and Budget (OMB), an office not known for pro-regulatory views, in a report that concluded that federal regulations from 1992–2002 produced from $146–230 billion in annual quantified benefits, while imposing from $36–42 billion in annual quantified costs. OIRA attributed the majority of the quantified benefits to "a handful of clean-air

---

1. See R. N. L. Andrews, Managing the Environment, Managing Ourselves — A History of American Environmental Policy 280 (1999) (citing U.S. Council on Environmental Quality, Environmental Quality: 25th Annual Report — 1994–95, at 179, 182 (1997)).
2. EPA, Office of Air and Radiation, The Benefits and Costs of the Clean Air Act, 1970 to 1990 ES-8 (Oct. 1997). This report focused almost exclusively on the consequences of the NAAQS program.

rules" issued under the 1990 Amendments to the CAA.[3] A widely cited survey of EPA managers conducted in the late 1980s concluded that the air pollution addressed by the NAAQS program should be placed first on a list of environmental problems ranked according to the risks they posed to human health, welfare, and ecosystems.[4]

Nevertheless, as we shall see, critics remain. The ink was barely dry on the 1970 statute creating the NAAQS program when critics began charging that the program was too rigid, too strict, too expensive, and too cumbersome. These charges, and more, continue to this day.

This chapter uses the NAAQS program as its central case study of "harm-based" pollution standards governing ambient air quality. Relying on harm-based ambient standards entails two major, foundational decisions. First, statutory drafters must choose how, and how stringently, to set the standards for ambient environmental quality. In the case of air pollution, for example, the regulators must decide how clean the air should be. Then a choice must be made about how to allocate allowable emissions within the commons so that the end result is attainment of the ambient standard. It may sound simple, but it's not.

The NAAQS program is the leading example of this harm-based approach. These standards, which are uniform throughout the country, are harm-based because they are set based on scientific evidence of the harm to human health and welfare caused by air pollution and because they are set at a level designed to avert such harm. The pollutants currently regulated by this program are sulfur dioxide (SO_2), nitrogen dioxide (NO_2), particulate matter (PM), carbon monoxide (CO), ozone, and lead. These pollutants, called the "criteria" pollutants for reasons explained shortly, are the most ubiquitous and best understood air pollutants in the United States. Many of the regulatory requirements imposed by the CAA are aimed at achieving and maintaining compliance with the NAAQSs. This chapter explains not only how regulators go about setting harm-based ambient standards under the Act, but also how they go about achieving compliance with them through a complex network of federal and state regulatory requirements.

A. THE CLEAN AIR ACT: HISTORY AND STRUCTURE

The harm-based regulation of conventional air pollutants in the CAA is a part of a larger undertaking. The CAA offers a veritable smorgasbord of regulatory techniques:

- *Harm-based:* Title I, §107, §108, §109, and §110, taken together create the basic regulatory system for control of the most commonly produced and significant air pollutants. These sections apply a harm-based ambient quality regulatory approach that constitutes this chapter's primary focus.
- *Technology-forcing:* Title II, discussed in Chapter 15's analysis of technology-forcing standards, sets specific and strict congressional standards for

---

3. OIRA, OMB, Informing Regulatory Decisions: 2003 Report to Congress on the Costs and Benefits of Federal Regulations and Unfunded Mandates on State, Local, and Tribal Entities (Sept. 2003).

4. EPA, Unfinished Business: A Comparative Assessment of Environmental Priorities 58 (1987). The opening paragraphs in this chapter draw heavily on Heinzerling, Clean Air and the Constitution, 20 St. Louis U. Pub. L. Rev. 121, 121–122 (2001).

across-the-board rollbacks of automobile and truck tailpipe emissions and provides that EPA may periodically make these standards even stricter.

- *Best Available Technology:* Section 111, which applies to "new [stationary] sources" of air pollution, establishes a system of "best-technology" emissions requirements, following a technology-based standard-setting approach. The technology-based regulatory technique is explored more fully in Chapter 12, which uses the CWA as its principal example. CAA §112, which regulates hazardous air pollutants such as benzene, arsenic, and many others, employs a similar Best Available Technology (BAT) approach.[5] Statutory provisions aimed at achieving and maintaining the NAAQSs also include variations on BAT, such as requirements that major new and modified sources of air pollution install the Best Available Control Technology (BACT).

- *Market-enlisting:* Title IV of the Act creates an innovative emissions trading program, primarily for SO_2. This program — which has become the paradigm for a host of proposals for shifting environmental regulations into market-trading systems — is discussed in detail in Chapter 14.

These different regulatory techniques did not all appear at once. On the contrary, the evolution of regulatory strategies used by the CAA has occurred over a period of several decades, in three primary stages.

Stage 1 — 1970. The CAA as we know it today was first enacted in 1970. Although technically an amendment to previous air pollution legislation, the 1970 Act fundamentally reshaped the federal government's approach to regulating air pollution. Whereas previous legislation had relied on essentially voluntary efforts by states to reduce air pollution to tolerable levels, the 1970 Act swept voluntarism aside by providing for nationally uniform air quality standards, to be achieved by the states by a deadline set by Congress. The 1970 Act also set strict national standards for automobile emissions and required new stationary sources of air pollution to meet BACT standards as determined by the EPA.

In regard to the "criteria" pollutants, Congress in 1970 chose a "harm-based" approach to deciding how clean the air should be. For the widely emitted and harmful criteria pollutants, the "primary" standards were to be set at a level "adequate to protect the public health" after "allowing an adequate margin of safety."

Congress made other fundamental decisions in 1970 as well. It divided the universe of sources of pollution into two major categories, stationary sources and mobile sources, with the latter more subject to state-by-state control (CAA Title I), and the former subject mostly to direct nationwide federal regulation (CAA Title II). In some ways, the dichotomy is an obvious one. Even though there are millions of mobile sources, there are only a handful of producers of motor vehicles, and the design of a car or truck calls for an integrated pollution control system that is best built into every vehicle at the time of manufacture. Moreover, there are tremendous economies of scale in the mass production of motor vehicles and to allow each of the 50 states to set its

---

5. Originally, this section employed a harm-based approach, but this effort did not work, and in 1990 Congress shifted to a technology-based strategy for regulating hazardous air pollutants.

own standards for motor vehicles threatened to wreak havoc on the auto industry. With an exception for California, where motor vehicle pollution controls already existed and where air pollution problems were recognized as requiring more stringent regulation than elsewhere in the nation, there was to be a single national standard for motor vehicle emissions.

Stationary sources, on the other hand, are often custom-built installations, and their variety makes a nationally uniform standard at once less necessary and potentially more inefficient. Thus, for stationary sources, the 1970 CAA made a different choice: It allowed the states, which in principle are in better touch with the economic and pollution control realities of their industries, to make many of the choices about how to get the emissions reductions needed to achieve the NAAQSs. The statutory mechanism that Congress chose was to require the states to adopt state implementation plans (SIPs), which were, in large part, a prescription for how the state would regulate its stationary sources. The federal EPA would review each state's SIP for each of the criteria pollutants, to determine if it would work. If EPA disapproved of a SIP, the state would have to redraft it until EPA approved. If a state refused to draft an adequate SIP, EPA could impose a federal implementation plan (FIP), a fate most of the states felt would be the worst of all possible regulatory worlds. Apart from reflexive opposition to yielding control to the national government, the states feared that EPA would be insensitive to their particular needs and desires.

Congress, however, did not leave all regulation of stationary sources completely to the states. For major new pollution sources, Congress directed EPA to develop New Source Performance Standards (NSPSs), which were to require new stationary sources to employ BAT for a facility of its kind. In this way, Congress softened the potential for a race of laxity in which areas in compliance with the NAAQSs would try to draw new business from states that had not yet achieved the NAAQSs.

The 1970 Act's division of authority had a profound effect on the states' efforts to attain and maintain the NAAQSs. Three of the criteria pollutants — CO, nitrogen oxides (NOx), and ozone — are major by-products of motor vehicle use. (Lead was in that category for a time, but with the elimination of lead from gasoline, motor vehicles have ceased having an effect on lead air emissions.) If states cannot regulate mobile source pollution, their flexibility and effectiveness in attaining the NAAQSs are greatly undermined. For this reason, as we saw in Chapter 6's discussion of federal preemption, a number of states have taken advantage of authority given to them under the 1977 Amendments to the Act to "piggyback" onto California's strict mobile source standards. Even under the 1970 law, states could indirectly influence air pollution from mobile sources by encouraging car pooling and mass transit, insisting that the federally required pollution controls installed on mobile sources be inspected and properly maintained, and so on. These types of controls were unpopular and seldom employed voluntarily. In addition, EPA's early effort to reduce air pollution by rationing gasoline, embodied in a southern California FIP, was allowed by a federal court[6] but then rejected by Congress in a CAA amendment forbidding EPA to impose transportation controls in FIPs.

---

6. City of Santa Rosa v. EPA, 534 F.2d 150 (9th Cir. 1976).

Finally, the 1970 Act also created a program, in §112, for the regulation of so-called hazardous air pollutants. (Criteria pollutants such as SO_2 and CO are themselves hazardous air pollutants, but §112's hazardous category included pollutants that were acutely toxic even in small amounts.) The original §112, like the NAAQS program itself, was harm-based: Congress directed EPA to set a level for hazardous air pollutants that would protect public health with an "ample margin of safety."

The basic outline of the CAA of 1970: Congress decided that the air throughout the country must be safe to breathe; EPA would identify the air pollution levels consistent with this goal; states for the most part would choose the means of achieving the goal of clean air; and mobile sources would be regulated primarily by the federal government while stationary sources would be regulated primarily by the states.

Stage 2 — 1977. Seven years later, Congress revisited the basic questions of how clean the nation's air should be and how quickly clean air should be achieved. As for the first question, although the 1970 Act had addressed how *clean* the air in "dirty" areas — those that had not attained the NAAQSs — should be, it had not addressed how *dirty* the air in "clean" areas could be allowed to become. Would it suffice, for example, for a relatively clean air region simply to keep its air clean enough to maintain the NAAQSs — that is, could such an area allow pollution up to the level of the NAAQSs? In a remarkable decision based on quite cryptic statutory language, a citizen suit in 1972 won a decision that the preamble to the 1970 Act, which declared that one purpose of the Act was "to protect and enhance the quality of the Nation's air resources," prohibited EPA from approving SIPs in relatively clean areas that would allow such areas to pollute their air to the level of the NAAQSs.[7] Thus was born the Prevention of Significant Deterioration (PSD) program. In the 1977 Amendments to the Act, Congress codified and refined this judicially inspired program. The key regulatory initiative was the imposition of a lower ceiling for allowable pollution that, in effect, superseded the NAAQSs as the federally mandated quality level. The new ceiling was calculated by measuring current air quality as a baseline and then allowing only a relatively small incremental amount of pollution to be added to that baseline. The 1977 Amendments also required major new (and modified) sources in PSD areas to use BAT.

As for the timing of NAAQS compliance, the 1970 Act, by today's standards, had extremely tight deadlines for compliance: "As expeditiously as practicable" but, in any event, no later than three years after having its SIP approved by EPA, a state was supposed to achieve compliance with the NAAQSs. By 1977, however, it was clear that some states had missed the deadline and were not even within sight of achieving the NAAQSs. For nonattainment areas, which included most of the nation's industrial centers, political influences called a retreat from the NAAQSs as rigid short-term requirements and transformed the NAAQSs into goals toward which only "reasonable further progress" was required. At the same time, however, Congress strengthened requirements for stationary sources and for the inspection and maintenance of automobiles in nonattainment areas. All existing sources were required to employ

---

7. Sierra Club v. Ruckelshaus, 344 F. Supp. 253, 255 (D.C. Cir. 1972), aff'd by an equally divided Court, Fri v. Sierra Club, 412 U.S. 541(1973).

Reasonable Available Control Technologies (RACT). All major new sources were required to achieve the Lowest Achievable Emissions Rate (LAER) and to "offset" — by more than a 1 to 1 ratio — their new pollution, by arranging pollution reductions at other facilities in the area.

Stage 3 — 1990. For more than a decade, the CAA muddled through in its 1977 configuration, making relatively little further progress toward attainment in nonattainment areas and making virtually no progress in regulating hazardous air pollutants. Additionally, the well-known but largely unregulated problem of long-range transport of pollutants was attracting attention, particularly in regard both to ground-level ozone and to acid deposition, which was poisoning the lakes and forests of northeastern states. The statute was being criticized on all fronts: Some claimed it was too expensive in achieving the results it did obtain, others claimed it was inadequate because the air in hundreds of localities inhabited by tens of millions of people was not yet safe.

Congress took extraordinary action in 1990, making major revisions on all these fronts. As to the basic NAAQS attainment issue, Congress again set strict compliance dates and stricter requirements for SIPs, as well as tightening standards for mobile sources. As to hazardous air pollutants, Congress abandoned the harm-based approach in favor of a technology-based approach that called for the installation of the Maximum Available Control Technology (MACT). As to long-range deposition, Congress created new devices to limit ozone transport and (in CAA Title IV) established an elaborate emissions trading scheme seeking to reduce SO_2 emissions by 10 million tons from 1980 levels in a decade, thereby almost halving emissions of the most significant precursor to acid rain. The statute also strengthened controls on NOx emissions.

Stage 4 — The new millennium. Since 1990, all of the significant CAA action has been undertaken by the executive branch or the states rather than by Congress. In the late 1990s, EPA strengthened the NAAQSs for ozone and particulate matter and ended up defending the new rules in the Supreme Court; developed a massive program to reduce interstate ozone pollution; for the first time required light trucks to meet the same emission standards as cars; required significant reductions in diesel emissions; and brought a series of lawsuits challenging companies that allegedly evaded the Act's technology-based permit requirements for modified sources of air pollution (the so-called New Source Review (NSR) requirements). During the same period, states began to take the opportunity to opt in to California's stringent emission rules for new automobiles.

In the new millennium, however, EPA has issued rules substantially narrowing the scope of the NSR program; has announced that it will drop investigations pending against some 50 power plants for violations of the former NSR rules; and has proposed that companies be allowed to trade emissions of mercury, a highly toxic substance. The federal government has also now formally declared that greenhouse gases, implicated in climate change, are not to be considered "air pollutants" within the meaning of the CAA and that state efforts to regulate greenhouse gases are preempted by the federal law on fuel efficiency. At the same time, however, EPA has proposed a new interstate air quality rule that, if fully implemented, would cut SO_2 and NOx emissions by 70% and

65%, respectively, while using an emissions trading program modeled after the successful acid rain program created in the 1990 Amendments. We have indeed entered a new stage, but it is too early to tell where it will lead or when it will end.

B. AMBIENT STANDARDS, THE COMMONS, AND AMERICAN FEDERALISM

Air and water are sometimes referred to as "pollution sinks," implying that airsheds and waterbodies are like large vats into which pollutants are thrown as a form of disposal. It is possible, perhaps even probable, that air and water can assimilate some man-made pollution without significant detriment to the natural systems of which they are a part. Whether exploiting this assimilative capacity is a good idea is a subject unto itself, but in the regulation of the criteria pollutants under the CAA, Congress made a pragmatic choice to "use" that assimilative capacity up to the limit of damage to human health and the environment.

Ambient standards do not exist in a vacuum but are a function of whatever purpose the resource base serves. Although the bulk of the material in this chapter focuses on the use of ambient standards in the CAA, the link between ambient quality standards and intended uses of resources is more easily grasped by an example involving water as the pollution sink. Water in a receiving body is used for a variety of purposes, such as drinking, bathing, supporting aquatic life, pleasure boating, industrial process source water, commercial navigation, effluent transport, and so on. The quality of the water necessary to support these uses varies greatly, and therefore the ambient water quality standards for that body of water may also vary greatly. Such standards are harm-based. Drinking water that causes illness or death if ingested harms the intended user. A harm-based ambient quality standard, therefore, is set at a level sufficient to avoid the harm that otherwise would result.

The resort to ambient receiving body quality standards can be understood as a response to the tragedy of the commons (see Chapter 1). Here, imagine that the commons is a receiving body, such as a lake surrounded by several industrial facilities that emit effluents into the lake. To any one industrialist, the cost of avoiding pollution of the lake creates an incentive to pollute the lake. To forgo pollution might avoid costs of reduced receiving body quality, such as the need to treat water drawn from that source for industrial use, but the common pool nature of the receiving body vitiates that possible benefit of avoiding pollution. In the absence of regulatory intervention or comprehensive private agreement, there is no guarantee that the benefit of cleaner water will be obtained by any one of the firms because the other firms bordering the lake still may elect to dump their wastes into the commons.

Setting and maintaining ambient quality levels attacks the commons problem by outlawing the untoward result of harmful deterioration in quality. In this way, an ambient standards approach initially addresses the problem of the commons at a collective level — it defers the intractable problem of translating a prescription about collective results into a series of controls on the behavior of individuals. Note that the choice of means for controlling the individual contributions to ambient quality is wholly independent of adopting an ambient standards approach. From an environmental quality standpoint, as long as the desired ambient quality level is achieved, the choice of who has to reduce emissions by how much is irrelevant. More realistically, however, the choice among possible means of individual control is important because of the economic and political ramifications of that choice.

COMMENTARY & QUESTIONS

1. **Air, water, and what else?** Would harm-based standards be a valuable regulatory technique in fields other than air and water pollution? Harm-based standards are ubiquitous in other fields of regulation involving, for example, product safety for consumer goods and drugs, but in those settings no commons is involved and therefore *ambient* standards are not required. Noise regulation, if it relies on setting maximum allowable levels based on avoidance of harm, is another possible example of a harm-based ambient standard.

2. **The federal-state partnership under the CAA stationary source program.** The principal sections of the CAA that create the harm-based NAAQS program are §§107–110, 42 U.S.C. §§7407–7410. Section 107(a) admirably summarizes the overall concept:

> §107(a)... Each State shall have the primary responsibility for assuring air quality within the entire geographic area comprising such State by submitting an implementation plan for such State which will specify the manner in which national primary and secondary standards will be achieved and maintained within each air quality control region in such State.

Harm-based ambient standards and state plans for achieving them are a good example of cooperative federalism. The states have the freedom and the responsibility to make the difficult and multifaceted determinations about how to limit pollution to the allowable federal NAAQS limits, managing and accommodating the competing interests of their constituents.

3. **State primacy.** Why should "primary responsibility" for air quality be lodged with the states? Does the national interest in the solution of the problem of air pollution end with the attainment of acceptable ambient quality? A decision by an upwind state to require tall smokestacks and location of polluting facilities near the downwind state line might result in satisfactory ambient air quality in the upwind state, but it hardly seems consistent with sound national policy. The national interest can be protected in this sort of a case by the power of the federal government to reject such SIPs as inadequate. Section 110(a)(2)(D) requires SIPs to

> contain adequate provisions (i) prohibiting...any source or other type of emissions activity within the State from emitting any air pollutant in amounts which will (I) contribute significantly to nonattainment in, or interfere with maintenance by, any other State with respect to any such national primary or secondary ambient air quality standard, or (II) interfere with...the applicable implementation plan for any other State...to prevent significant deterioration of air quality.

The federal government has used the power conferred by this section to impose substantial controls on NOx emissions, which lead to long-range ozone transport, in 22 states.

Despite the statutory language regarding state primacy, who is really in control, the states or the federal government? Recalling the concept of federal supremacy, this is a game that the states have no choice but to play. The third prong of the federal role — "FIPping," imposing FIPs on states that do not have adequate regulations — is anathema to the states. No state wants the federal bureaucracy making decisions that may have calamitous statewide economic repercussions, such as forcing major manufacturing facilities to shut down or relocate due to the imposition of stringent pollution control requirements. Through its power to refuse to approve SIPs and through funding cutoffs, EPA can influence how any SIP is drawn.

4. **Preventing significant deterioration.** As we have seen, although the 1970 Congress addressed the question of how clean the air in dirty places must become, it did not address the issue of how dirty the air in clean places could be allowed to become. This consideration received its most careful attention in the PSD program of the 1977 Amendments, 42 U.S.C. §§7470–7491. In basic terms, the PSD program limits the incremental amount of pollution allowed in clean air areas, with smaller increments allowed in areas where there are special national or state interests served by limiting increases in pollution.

The PSD process begins by classifying all attainment Air Quality Control Regions (AQCRs), or parts thereof, into three categories: Class I areas include international and national parks, wilderness areas, and national memorial parks that exceed a prescribed acreage. Class II areas are, in essence, all remaining attainment areas. No Class III areas are established by the legislation, but the states have the ability to redesignate areas downward (to Class III) according to a process set out in §7474. With classification comes an allowable increment, that is, a statutorily or administratively set upper limit on the amount of increase in ambient concentrations of pollutants that can be added to the region's air. The next step in the PSD process is to establish the baseline upon which the allowable increment can be added — a step that can be far more contentious and complex than one might imagine. To provide additional protection for national parks and other areas that obtain Class I designation because of the presence of a federal enclave to which visibility is essential, special visibility protection requirements are even more stringent than the basic PSD provisions.

5. **Exceeding the federal requirements.** The CAA, although less explicitly than CWA §510, gives the states latitude to do more to limit air pollution than the minimum required by federal law. This is manifest in the PSD reclassification program that allows states to designate all areas other than Indian reservations as Class I areas. (Tribes have authority over the classification of reservation airsheds.) Likewise, states in their SIPs and their permitting of polluting facilities (except for mobile sources such as cars and planes) are free to be as stringent as they like. EPA review insures only that the SIPs and permits granted thereunder do not fail to meet the NAAQSs.

6. **Federalism and PSD.** The very nature of the PSD program takes a degree of autonomy away from the states. The level of allowable growth in Class I areas is limited by the stringent PSD increments, and the option of redesignation is limited by the presence of various types of federal lands. Should the federal sites of importance, the Yosemites and Grand Canyons, be insulated against loss of amenity value that is at times obtained at

the expense of economic development in the host state? Even more generally, the PSD program restricts development in less-developed or later developing states by taking away the potential advantage of less expensive pollution control requirements.

7. **Ambient air quality standards and the race of laxity.** Do harm-based ambient standards eliminate the race of laxity among the states? Areas with cleaner-than-required air can still run in the race and attract new industry with lax pollution control programs. Their race, however, will be a short one, and their victory may be Pyrrhic. The NAAQSs limit how long the race can be run, and the PSD program shortens the race still further by setting ceilings on incremental increases in pollution in areas that enjoy especially clean air. Nevertheless, with a substantial percentage of AQCRs still out of compliance with at least one of the NAAQSs, one might say that the race of laxity is still on; it's just not officially sanctioned.

C. HARM AS THE THRESHOLD OF REGULATION

Section 1. WHICH POLLUTANTS ARE COVERED BY THE NAAQSs?

In the absence of identifiable or threatened harm, there is no warrant for regulating conduct under most contemporary theories of social and political organization. In general, no social benefits result from the regulation of such conduct, and regulation bears a cost in terms of both loss of individual autonomy and whatever resources are devoted to enforcement of, and compliance with, regulation. At the same time, few disagree that government is authorized to act to prevent widespread harms caused by the activities of its citizens — to apply Garrett Hardin's "mutual coercion, mutually agreed upon." One must go on to decide what harms are sufficiently serious to justify regulation and how strong the causal connection between the hazard (here, air pollution) and harm must be.

The CAA has approached the multiplicity of harmful agents that might be present in the air by labelling a small number of "criteria pollutants" and an additional set as hazardous air pollutants. Much goes unregulated.[8]

Prior to the 1970 CAA, air quality criteria[9] had already been promulgated for five pollutants: sulfur oxides (SOx), PM, CO, photochemical oxidants (ozone), and hydrocarbons. Section 109(a)(1)(A) required the Administrator to use the existing air quality criteria to establish NAAQSs for these pollutants. Shortly after the 1970 Act was passed, EPA published criteria for NOx and established NAAQSs for them as well.

Remarkably, since that time, only one pollutant — lead — has been added to the list of criteria pollutants.[10] It was added to the list as a consequence of the following

---

8. For an eye-opening discussion of the gaps left by even the 1990 CAA Amendments' strengthened regulation of hazardous air pollutants and of the primitive regulatory structure that governs the pollutants left out of the federal scheme, see N. Morag-Levine, Chasing the Wind: Regulating Air Pollution in the Common Law State (2003).

9. The term *criteria pollutants* derives from the pre-1970 federal air law. Pub. L. No. 88-206, §3(c)(2)(1963).

10. In 1983, the EPA dropped the NAAQS for hydrocarbons because hydrocarbons do not directly affect human health and their contribution to ozone is already regulated through the ozone NAAQS. The hydrocarbon NAAQS had been created to help states decide how much they needed to reduce hydrocarbon emissions in order to meet the ozone NAAQS. Because EPA could not find a consistent quantitative relationship between ozone concentrations and hydrocarbon levels, it decided that a separate NAAQS for hydrocarbons was no longer justified. 48 Fed. Reg. 628 (Jan. 5, 1983).

citizen lawsuit. The Natural Resources Defense Council (NRDC) claimed that because EPA had acknowledged that lead endangers human health and welfare, in regulating lead as a fuel additive under §211 of the Act, EPA therefore had an obligation to regulate lead under the NAAQS program as well.

Natural Resources Defense Council v. Train
United States Court of Appeals for the Second Circuit, 1976
545 F.2d 320

[CAA §108(a)(1) provides: "The [EPA] Administrator shall publish, and shall from time to time thereafter revise, a list, which includes each air pollutant (A) emissions of which, in his judgment, cause or contribute to air pollution which may reasonably be anticipated to endanger public health or welfare; (B) the presence of which in the ambient air results from numerous or diverse mobile or stationary sources; and (C) for which air quality criteria had not been issued before December 31, 1970, but for which he plans to issue air quality criteria under this section."]

SMITH, J. The Environmental Protection Agency and its Administrator, Russell Train, appeal from an order of the United States District Court for the Southern District of New York...requiring the Administrator of the EPA, within thirty days, to place lead on a list of air pollutants under §108(a)(1) of the Clean Air Act. We affirm the order of the district court.

The EPA concedes that lead meets the conditions of §§108(a)(1)(A) and (B) — that it has an adverse effect on public health and welfare, and that the presence of lead in the ambient air results from numerous or diverse mobile or stationary sources. The EPA maintains, however, that under §108(a)(1)(C) of the Act, the Administrator retains discretion whether to list a pollutant, even though the pollutant meets the criteria of §§108(a)(1)(A) and (B). The Agency regards the listing of lead under §108(a)(1) and the issuance of ambient air quality standards as one of numerous alternative control strategies for lead available to it. Listing of substances is mandatory, the EPA argues, only for those pollutants for which the Administrator "plans to issue air quality criteria." He may, it is contended, choose not to issue, i.e., not "plan to issue" such criteria, and decide to control lead solely by regulating emission at the source, regardless of the total concentration of lead in the ambient air. The Administrator argues that if he chooses to control lead (or other pollutants) under §211 [relating to regulation of fuel additives, such as lead], he is not required to list the pollutant under §108(a)(1) or to set air quality standards....

The issue is one of statutory construction. We agree with the district court and with appellees that the interpretation of the Clean Air Act advanced by the EPA is contrary to the structure of the Act as a whole, and that if accepted, it would vitiate the public policy underlying the enactment of the 1970 Amendments as set forth in the Act and in its legislative history.

Section 108(a)(1) contains mandatory language. It provides that "the Administrator *shall*...publish...a list..." (emphasis added). If the EPA interpretation were accepted and listing were mandatory only for substances "for which [the Administrator] plans to issue air quality criteria...," then the mandatory language of §108(a)(1)(A) would become mere surplusage. The determination to list a pollutant and to issue air quality criteria would remain discretionary with the Administrator, and the rigid deadlines of §108(a)(2), §109, and §110 for attaining air quality standards could be bypassed by him at will. If Congress had enacted §211 as an alternative to, rather than as a supplement to, §§108–110, then one would expect a similar fixed timetable for implementation of the fuel control section. The absence of such a timetable for the enforcement of §211 lends support to the view that fuel controls were intended by Congress as a means for attaining primary air quality standards rather than as an alternative to the promulgation of such standards....

Because state planning and implementation under the Air Quality Act of 1967 had made little progress by 1970, Congress reacted by "taking a stick to the States in the form of the Clean Air Amendments of 1970...." Train v. NRDC, 421 U.S. 60, 64 (1975). It enacted §108(a)(1) which provides that the Administrator of the Environmental Protection Agency "shall" publish a list which includes each air pollutant which is harmful to health and originates from specified sources. Once a pollutant is listed under §108(a)(1), §§109 and 110 are to be automatically invoked, and promulgation of national air quality standards and implementation thereof by the states within a limited, fixed time schedule becomes mandatory....

In the legislative history of the 1970 Amendments to the Act,...the summary of the provisions of the conference agreement...by Senator Muskie contained the following language:

> The agreement requires issuance of remaining air quality criteria for major pollutants within 13 months of date of enactment.... Within the 13-month deadline, the Congress expects criteria to be issued for nitrogen oxides, fluorides, lead, polynuclear organic matter, and odors, though others may be necessary.[11]

While the literal language of §108(a)(1)(C) is somewhat ambiguous, this ambiguity is resolved when this section is placed in the context of the Act as a whole and in its legislative history. The deliberate inclusion of a specific timetable for the attainment of ambient air quality standards incorporated by Congress in §§108-110 would become an exercise in futility if the Administrator could avoid listing pollutants simply by choosing not to issue air quality criteria. The discretion given to the Administrator under the Act pertains to the review of state implementation plans under §110, and to §211 which authorizes but does not mandate the regulation of fuel or fuel additives. It does not extend to the issuance of air quality standards for substances derived from specified sources which the Administrator had already adjudged injurious to health....

The Congress sought to eliminate, not perpetuate, opportunity for administrative foot-dragging. Once the conditions of §§108(a)(1)(A) and (B) have been met, the listing of lead and the issuance of air quality standards for lead become mandatory. The order of the district court is affirmed.

COMMENTARY & QUESTIONS

1. **The criteria pollutants.** As already noted, the CAA currently lists six criteria pollutants. This list has not been expanded since lead was added in 1976. In light of the generic statutory definition and the mandatory nature of EPA's obligation to add new criteria pollutants, does the brevity of the list surprise you? What do you suppose happened to the other pollutants mentioned by Senator Muskie, such as fluorides and odors?

2. **Does overregulation lead to underregulation?** In part, the small number of criteria pollutants may reflect the fact that hazardous air pollutants are regulated separately by CAA §112. Might it not reflect other factors as well? Consider that for every listed pollutant, EPA must prepare comprehensive criteria documents (which can run into thousands of pages) and use the scientific data from these documents to develop air quality standards to govern the nation as a whole. In setting these standards, EPA is

---

11. Legislative History, Clean Air Amendments, Vol. 1 at 430, 432 (1974).

forbidden, as we shall see, to take economic cost and technological feasibility into account. Once EPA has set the standards, all 50 states must draw up separate SIPs for attaining or maintaining the NAAQSs. Might a busy (or cost-sensitive) agency be reluctant to start this ball rolling in the first place? For the seminal statement of the "overregulation leads to underregulation" thesis, see J. Mendeloff, The Dilemma of Toxic Substance Regulation: How Overregulation Causes Underregulation at OSHA (1988).

3. **EPA's better way to control lead emissions.** EPA raised two types of arguments against the addition of lead as a criteria pollutant. The first set of arguments claimed general discretion in the selection of criteria pollutants; the second set used what might be termed lead-specific arguments. Although its claims for a general discretion may have seemed a bit lame, EPA had what it believed were strong reasons in support of its lead-specific arguments. EPA studies had shown that almost 90% of lead emissions into the environment were traceable to motor vehicles, an air pollution source that EPA was empowered to regulate both directly and through the regulation of fuel additives. EPA felt the most effective means for limiting lead emissions to safe levels was to force the removal of lead from gasoline. Might EPA's position make good sense, but still be a violation of the statutory command?

4. **Greenhouse gases as criteria pollutants.** Despite the well-publicized denials of a handful of "climate change skeptics," a firm consensus of the world's leading scientists holds that the buildup of greenhouse gases, such as carbon dioxide (CO_2), is contributing and will continue to contribute to large-scale and widespread changes in the earth's climate. Humans have played a significant role in this phenomenon, since CO_2 is emitted when fossil fuels are burned — when power plants burn coal to produce electricity or when cars use gasoline to keep running. Thus, at first blush, one might conclude that CO_2 is an excellent candidate for the list of criteria pollutants that are described in §108(a)(1) of the Act: Emitted by "numerous or diverse stationary or mobile sources," the pollutant can "reasonably be anticipated to endanger public health or welfare" (especially since "welfare" itself is defined to include effects on climate, 42 U.S.C. §7602(h)). Reasoning along these lines, several northeastern states petitioned EPA to include CO_2 on the list of criteria pollutants. In response to a related petition, the Bush II EPA asserted that CO_2 was not an "air pollutant" within the meaning of the statute and that therefore the agency could not regulate it under the CAA. Fabricant, Memorandum: EPA's Authority to Impose Mandatory Controls to Address Global Climate Change under the Clean Air Act, Aug. 28, 2003, available at http://www.epa.gov/airlinks/co2petitiongcmemo8-28.pdf. EPA determined that the CAA does not authorize regulation to address climate change and that, accordingly, CO_2 cannot be considered a pollutant under the CAA. Fabricant, EPA's general counsel, stated that "It is clear that an administrative agency properly awaits congressional direction on a fundamental policy issue such as global climate change, instead of searching for an existing statute that was not designed or enacted to deal with that issue." Lee, EPA Says It Lacks Power to Regulate Some Gases, N.Y. Times, Aug. 29, 2003.

Several states and environmental groups have now teamed up to sue EPA for its failure to regulate greenhouse gases under the Act. Johnson, Three States Sue E.P.A. to Regulate Emissions of Carbon Dioxide, N.Y. Times, June 5, 2003.

In light of what you already know about the NAAQS program — that it sets national, harm-based standards for air quality to be achieved by each of the individual states — is this program a sensible way of addressing the problems posed by greenhouse gases?

Section 2. WHAT ARE THE STANDARDS FOR SETTING
THE NAAQSs?

Few regulatory judgments have as widespread economic and political ramifications as do decisions about how strict the NAAQSs would be, and yet few statutory standards are described quite as tersely. The CAA simply tells EPA that the primary NAAQSs shall be standards "the attainment and maintenance of which in the judgment of the Administrator, based on such criteria and allowing an adequate margin of safety, are requisite to protect the public health." 42 U.S.C. §7409(b)(1). The Act requires EPA to review the existing NAAQSs every five years, 42 U.S.C. §7409(d)(1), and instructs the agency to revise the standards "in the same manner as promulgated." 42 U.S.C. §7409(b)(1).

One of the longest-running and most polarizing debates in the first three decades of the CAA was whether EPA was required or even allowed to consider economic costs in setting or revising the NAAQSs. The issue first arose in the legal challenge to the NAAQS for lead, which was set following the addition of lead as a criteria pollutant. In Lead Indus. Ass'n v. EPA, 647 F.2d 1130 (D.C. Cir. 1980), the court upheld EPA's refusal to consider cost or technological feasibility in setting the NAAQS for lead. The court reasoned that whereas other CAA provisions expressly directed EPA to consider economic and technological feasibility in setting standards, §109(b) did not even mention costs or feasibility. The court also found support for its holding in the Act's legislative history, which the court thought demonstrated Congress's impatience with the failure to achieve progress in addressing air pollution under prior legislation.

Industry groups asked the Supreme Court to review the holdings in *Lead Industries* and three subsequent cases reaffirming it, to no avail. Then, in 1999, the D.C. Circuit set the regulatory world on fire by issuing the ruling that follows.

EPA in 1997 had revised the NAAQSs for ozone and PM, lowering the ozone standard from 0.12 parts per million (ppm) to 0.08 ppm (while changing the averaging period from one hour to eight hours, which dampened the effect of the more stringent ozone level). The agency also set an entirely new PM standard for fine particulates of 2.5 micrometers or less in diameter; the old standard had regulated only coarser particles of 10 micrometers or less.

The inevitable legal challenge ensued. The D.C. Circuit's decision on the challenge did not overturn *Lead Industries* but instead did something even more surprising: It held that the CAA, as long interpreted by EPA to forbid consideration of costs in setting the NAAQSs, violated the constitutional nondelegation doctrine. This decision ultimately led the Supreme Court, in a decision a year and a half after the per curiam circuit opinion that follows, finally to grant review of the longstanding issue of the relevance of costs under the Act and to affirm EPA's long-held view.

American Trucking Associations, Inc. v. U.S. Environmental Protection Agency
United States Court of Appeals for the D.C. Circuit, 1999
175 F.3d 1027

PER CURIAM. We find that the construction of the Clean Air Act on which EPA relied in promulgating the NAAQS at issue here effects an unconstitutional delegation of legislative power. See U.S. Const. art. I §1 ("All legislative powers herein granted shall be vested in a Congress of the United States."). We remand the cases for EPA to develop a construction of the act that satisfies this constitutional requirement....

Although the factors EPA uses in determining the degree of public health concern associated with different levels of ozone and PM are reasonable, EPA appears to have articulated no "intelligible principle" to channel its application of these factors; nor is one apparent from the statute. The nondelegation doctrine requires such a principle. See J. W. Hampton, Jr. & Co. v. United States, 276 U.S. 394, 409 (1928). Here it is as though Congress commanded EPA to select "big guys," and EPA announced that it would evaluate candidates based on height and weight, but revealed no cut-off point. The announcement, though sensible in what it does say, is fatally incomplete. The reasonable person responds, "How tall? How heavy?"

EPA regards ozone definitely, and PM likely, as non-threshold pollutants, i.e., ones that have some possibility of some adverse health impact (however slight) at any exposure level above zero. For convenience, we refer to both as non-threshold pollutants; the indeterminacy of PM's status does not affect EPA's analysis, or ours.

Thus the only concentration for ozone and PM that is utterly risk-free, in the sense of direct health impacts, is zero. Section 109(b)(1) says that EPA must set each standard at the level "requisite to protect the public health" with an "adequate margin of safety." 42 U.S.C. §7409(b)(1). These are also the criteria by which EPA must determine whether a revision to existing NAAQSs is appropriate. For EPA to pick any non-zero level it must explain the degree of imperfection permitted. The factors that EPA has elected to examine for this purpose in themselves pose no inherent nondelegation problem. But what EPA lacks is any determinate criterion for drawing lines. It has failed to state intelligibly how much is too much.

We begin with the criteria EPA has announced for assessing health effects in setting the NAAQSs for non-threshold pollutants.... EPA basically considers severity of effect, certainty of effect, and size of population affected. These criteria, long ago approved by the judiciary, see Lead Industries Ass'n v. EPA, 647 F.2d 1130, 1161 (D.C. Cir. 1980), do not themselves speak to the issue of degree.

Read in light of these factors, EPA's explanations for its decisions amount to assertions that a less stringent standard would allow the relevant pollutant to inflict a greater quantum of harm on public health, and that a more stringent standard would result in less harm. Such arguments only support the intuitive proposition that more pollution will not benefit public health, not that keeping pollution at or below any particular level is "requisite" or not requisite to "protect the public health" with an "adequate margin of safety," the formula set out by §109(b)(1)....

EPA frequently defends a decision not to set a standard at a lower level on the basis that there is greater uncertainty that health effects exist at lower levels than the level of the standard. The dissent's defense of the fine particulate matter standard cites exactly such a justification. But the increasing-uncertainty argument is helpful only if some principle reveals how much uncertainty is too much. None does....Where (as here) statutory language and an existing agency interpretation involve an unconstitutional delegation of power, but an interpretation without the constitutional weakness is or may be available, our response is not to strike down the statute but to give the agency an opportunity to extract a determinate standard on its own. Doing so serves at least two of three basic rationales for the nondelegation doctrine. If the agency develops determinate, binding standards for itself, it is less likely to exercise the delegated authority arbitrarily. And such standards enhance the likelihood that meaningful judicial review will prove feasible. A remand of this sort of course does not serve the third key function of non-delegation doctrine, to "ensure to the extent consistent with orderly governmental administration that important choices of social policy are made by Congress, the branch of our Government most responsive to the popular will," Industrial Union Dep't, AFL-CIO v. American Petroleum Inst., 448 U.S. 607, 685 (1980) ("Benzene") (Rehnquist, J., concurring). The agency will make the fundamental policy choices. But the remand does ensure that the courts not hold unconstitutional a statute that an agency, with the application of its special expertise, could salvage. In any event, we do not read current Supreme Court cases as applying the strong form of the nondelegation doctrine voiced in Justice Rehnquist's concurrence. See Mistretta v. United States, 488 U.S. 361, 377–379 (1989). What sorts of "intelligible principles" might EPA adopt? Cost-benefit analysis...is not available under decisions of this court. Our cases read §109(b)(1) as barring EPA from considering any factor other than "health effects relating to pollutants in the air." *Lead Industries*, 647 F.2d at 1148.

In theory, EPA could make its criterion the eradication of any hint of direct health risk. This approach is certainly determinate enough, but it appears that it would require the agency to set the permissible levels of both pollutants here at zero. No party here appears to advocate this solution, and EPA appears to show no inclination to adopt it.[12]

EPA's past behavior suggests some readiness to adopt standards that leave non-zero residual risk. For example, it has employed commonly used clinical criteria to determine what qualifies as an adverse health effect. See Ozone Staff Paper at 59–60 (using American Thoracic Society standards to determine threshold for "adverse health effect" from ozone). On the issue of likelihood, for some purposes it might be appropriate to use standards drawn from other areas of the law, such as the familiar "more probable than not" criterion.

Of course a one-size-fits-all criterion of probability would make little sense. There is no reason why the same probability should govern assessments of a risk of thousands of deaths as against risks of a handful of people suffering momentary shortness of breath. More generally, all the relevant variables seem to range continuously from high to low: the possible effects of pollutants vary from death to trivialities, and the size of the affected population, the probability of an effect, and the associated uncertainty range from "large" numbers of persons with point estimates of high probability, to small numbers and vague ranges of probability. This does not seem insurmountable. Everyday life compels us all to make decisions balancing remote but severe harms against a probability distribution of benefits; people decide whether to proceed with an operation that carries a 1/1000 possibility of death, and (simplifying) a 90% chance of cure and a 10% chance of no effect, and a certainty of some short-term pain and nuisance. To be sure, all that requires is a go/no-go decision, while a serious effort at coherence under §109(b)(1) would need to be more comprehensive. For example, a range of ailments short of death might need to be assigned weights. Nonetheless, an agency wielding the power over American life possessed by EPA should be capable of developing the rough equivalent of a generic unit of harm that takes

---

12. A zero-risk policy might seem to imply de-industrialization, but in fact even that seems inadequate to the task (and even if the calculus is confined to direct risks from pollutants, as opposed to risks from the concomitant poverty). First, PM (at least) results from almost all combustion, so only total prohibition of fire or universal application of some heretofore unknown control technology would reduce manmade emissions to zero. Second, the combustion associated with pastoral life appears to be rather deadly. See World Bank, World Development Report 1992: Development and the Environment 52 (1992) (noting that "biomass" fuels (i.e., wood, straw, or dung) are often the only fuels that "poor households, mostly in rural areas" can obtain or afford, and that indoor smoke from biomass burning "contributes to acute respiratory infections that cause an estimated 4 million deaths annually among infants and children.").

into account population affected, severity and probability. Possible building blocks for such a principled structure might be found in the approach Oregon used in devising its health plan for the poor. In determining what conditions would be eligible for treatment under its version of Medicaid, Oregon ranked treatments by the amount of improvement in "Quality-Adjusted Life Years" [QALYs] provided by each treatment, divided by the cost of the treatment.[13] Here, of course, EPA may not consider cost, and indeed may well find a completely different method for securing reasonable coherence. Alternatively, if EPA concludes that there is no principle available, it can so report to the Congress, along with such rationales as it has for the levels it chose, and seek legislation ratifying its choice. [Dissent by TATEL, J., omitted.]

COMMENTARY & QUESTIONS

1. **CAA unconstitutional?** What could EPA do in the wake of Judge Williams's opinion other than seeking en banc rehearing or seeking Supreme Court review? (It did both; the Supreme Court's opinion follows.) EPA's difficult task is to set standards for tolerable adverse health effects that relate to some larger normative principle, when Congress in the statute has articulated none except in broad terms of health and safety. If this opinion had remained good law, could EPA ever have implemented its health-safety mission without violating the nondelegation principle, if Congress is unable or unwilling in most complex regulatory settings to set out safety standards in explicit terms?

2. **Who is in charge?** Is there a sense in which Judge Williams is being disingenuous when he, an unelected, generalist judge, trots out anti-delegation — essentially a separation of powers type argument — to block the primary agency's action and replace it with inaction? As a matter of proper allocation of function, even though EPA has not justified its line-drawing choice by reference to a firm definition of acceptable risk, neither has the court, by reference to any apparently congressionally endorsed policy,

---

13. The "quality" of various health states was determined by poll, and medical professionals determined the probabilities and durations of various health states with and without the treatment in question.

Oregon was twice forced to revise its system because the United States Department of Health & Human Services determined that the original proposal and a revision violated the Americans with Disabilities Act, 42 U.S.C. §§12101-12213. The reason given for this determination was that both versions undervalued the lives of persons with disabilities: The original plan measured quality of life according to the attitudes of the general population rather than the attitudes of persons with disabilities. See HHS, Analysis Under the Americans with Disabilities Act ("ADA") of the Oregon Reform Demonstration (Aug. 3, 1992), reprinted in 9 Issues L. & Med. 397, 410 (1994). The revised plan ranked treatments leaving the patient in a "symptomatic" state lower than those leaving the patient asymptomatic, and certain disabling conditions were considered "symptoms." See Letter from Timothy B. Flanagan, Assistant Attorney General, to Susan K. Zagame, Acting General Counsel, HHS (Jan. 19, 1993), reprinted in 9 Issues L. & Med. 397, 418, 421 (1994). The Department's determination was extensively criticized when issued. See Mehlman et al., When Do Health Care Decisions Discriminate Against Persons with Disabilities? 22 J. Health Pol., Pol'y & L. 1385, 1390 (1997) (HHS's "decision provoked a storm of disbelief and denunciation").

We take no position on whether HHS's view was correct, or if the underlying norm also governs EPA's decisions under §109(b)(1). An affirmative answer, however, would not seem to preclude use of some of Oregon's approach. The first step would be giving appropriate weight to the views of persons with disabilities. The second might be measuring the seriousness of a pollution-induced health effect by the absolute level of well-being that the effect brings about, not by the decrease in level that the effect causes. In other words, if the maximum well-being level is 100 and the average asthmatic whose asthma constitutes a disability has a well-being of 80 in the absence of air pollution (according to a measure that appropriately considers asthmatics' own assessments of their condition), then a response to air pollution that reduces the asthmatics' well-being to 70 could be counted as an effect of magnitude 30 (the difference from full health), rather than 10 (the difference from the level without the pollution). That approach would ensure that effects on persons with disabilities were not underestimated, even in the broad sense of that term apparently adopted by HHS.

justified its action of exposing the citizenry to greater health risks. Does it seem a bit odd that the nondelegation principle here applied had never before succeeded as a ground for attacking EPA's setting of an NAAQS, and that the *J.W. Hampton* case relied upon as authority was decided more than seven decades before? Is the underlying thrust of this line of attack a means by which the judiciary could force Congress or EPA to engage in systematic implementation of risk ranking and management by relative risk principles?

3. **Would cost-benefit analysis take care of the problem?** The court suggests that its concerns about nondelegation would be solved if the statute were interpreted to require cost-benefit analysis in setting the NAAQSs, but it also notes that this option is foreclosed by the court's precedents. Would cost-benefit analysis indeed give EPA less discretion in setting the standards? Cass Sunstein, an enthusiastic supporter of cost-benefit analysis, has argued in the context of EPA's decision regulating arsenic in drinking water under the SDWA that plausible evidence would have supported benefits findings ranging from $0 to approximately half a billion dollars. See Sunstein, The Arithmetic of Arsenic, 90 Geo. L.J. 2255 (2002). Does this finding support the court's endorsement of cost-benefit analysis as a way out of the dilemma of agency discretion? Chapter 13 discusses the arguments in favor of and against cost-benefit analysis in detail.

4. **Are QALYs the answer?** Does the opinion adequately defend QALYs against the charge of discrimination? May EPA, under the CAA, use QALYs in setting the NAAQS? Consider the fact that in *Lead Industries*, the D.C. Circuit upheld EPA's decision to protect especially sensitive subpopulations — in that case, very young children — from the harms of air pollution.

Whitman v. American Trucking Associations
Supreme Court of the United States, 2001
531 U.S. 457

SCALIA, J.... Section 109(b)(1) instructs the EPA to set primary ambient air quality standards "the attainment and maintenance of which...are requisite to protect the public health" with "an adequate margin of safety." 42 U.S.C. §7409(B)(1). Were it not for the hundreds of pages of briefing respondents have submitted on the issue, one would have thought it fairly clear that this text does not permit the EPA to consider costs in setting the standards. The language, as one scholar has noted, "is absolute." D. Currie, Air Pollution: Federal Law and Analysis 4–15 (1981). The EPA, "based on" the information about health effects contained in the technical "criteria" documents compiled under §108(a)(2), 42 U.S.C. §7408(a)(2), is to identify the maximum airborne concentration of a pollutant that the public health can tolerate, decrease the concentration to provide an "adequate" margin of safety, and set the standard at that level. Nowhere are the costs of achieving such a standard made part of that initial calculation.

Against this most natural of readings, respondents make a lengthy, spirited, but ultimately unsuccessful attack. They begin with the object of §109(b)(1)'s focus, the "public health." When the term first appeared in federal clean air legislation — in the Act of July 14, 1955 (1955 Act), which expressed "recognition of the dangers to the public health" from air pollution — its ordinary meaning was "the health of the community." Webster's New International Dictionary (2d ed. 1950). Respondents argue, however, that §109(b)(1), as added by the Clean Air Amendments of 1970 (1970 Act), meant to use the term's secondary meaning: "the ways and means of conserving the health of the members of a community, as by preventive medicine, organized care of the sick, etc." Id. Words that can have more than one meaning are given content, however, by their surroundings, and in the context of §109(b)(1) this second definition makes no sense. Congress could not have meant to instruct the Administrator to set NAAQSs at a level "requisite to protect" "the art and science dealing with the protection and improvement of community health." We therefore revert to the primary definition of the term: the health of the public.

Even so, respondents argue, many more factors than air pollution affect public health. In particular, the economic cost of implementing a very stringent standard might produce health losses sufficient to offset the health gains achieved in cleaning the air — for example, by closing down whole industries and thereby impoverishing the workers and consumers dependent upon those industries. That is unquestionably true, and Congress was unquestionably aware of it. Thus, Congress had commissioned in the Air Quality Act of 1967 "a detailed estimate of the cost of carrying out the provisions of this Act; a comprehensive study of the cost of program implementation by affected units of government; and a comprehensive study of the economic impact of air quality standards on the Nation's industries, communities, and other contributing sources of pollution." The 1970 Congress, armed with the results of this study, not only anticipated that compliance costs could injure the public health, but provided for that precise exigency. Section 110(f)(1) of the CAA permitted the Administrator to waive the compliance deadline for stationary sources if, inter alia, sufficient control measures were simply unavailable and "the continued operation of such sources is *essential...to the public health* or welfare." Other provisions explicitly permitted or required economic costs to be taken into account in implementing the air quality standards. Section 111(b)(1)(B), for example, commanded the Administrator to set "standards of performance" for certain new sources of emissions that as specified in §111(a)(1) were to "reflect the degree of emission limitation achievable through the application of the best system of emission reduction which (taking into account the cost of achieving such reduction) the Administrator determines has been adequately demonstrated." Section 202(a)(2) prescribed that emissions standards for automobiles could take effect only "after such period as the Administrator finds necessary to permit the development and application of the requisite technology, giving appropriate consideration to the cost of compliance within such period." Subsequent amendments to the CAA have added many more provisions directing, in explicit language, that the Administrator consider costs in performing various duties. We have therefore refused to find implicit in ambiguous sections of the CAA an authorization to consider costs that has elsewhere, and so often, been expressly granted....

To prevail in their present challenge, respondents must show a textual commitment of authority to the EPA to consider costs in setting NAAQSs under §109(b)(1). And because §109(b)(1) and the NAAQSs for which it provides are the engine that drives nearly all of Title I of the CAA, that textual commitment must be a clear one. Congress, we have held, does not alter the fundamental details of a regulatory scheme in vague terms or ancillary provisions — it does not, one might say, hide elephants in mouseholes.

Respondents'...first claim is that §109(b)(1)'s terms "adequate margin" and "requisite" leave room to pad health effects with cost concerns.... We find it implausible that Congress would give to the EPA through these modest words the power to determine whether implementation costs should moderate national air quality standards.[14]

---

14. None of the sections of the CAA in which the District of Columbia Circuit has found authority for the EPA to consider costs shares §109(b)(1)'s prominence in the overall statutory scheme.

The same defect inheres in respondents'…arguments that…the Administrator's judgment…need not be based *solely* on those criteria, and that those criteria themselves are not necessarily *limited* to "effects on public health or welfare which may be expected from the presence of such pollutant in the ambient air."… Even if we were to concede those premises, we still would not conclude that one of the unenumerated factors that the agency can consider in developing and applying the criteria is cost of implementation. That factor is *both* so indirectly related to public health *and* so full of potential for canceling the conclusions drawn from direct health effects that it would surely have been expressly mentioned in §§108 and 109 had Congress meant it to be considered. Yet while those provisions describe in detail how the health effects of pollutants in the ambient air are to be calculated and given effect, they say not a word about costs.

Respondents point, finally, to a number of provisions in the CAA that *do* require attainment cost data to be generated…. Respondents argue that these provisions make no sense unless costs are to be considered in setting the NAAQS. That is not so. These provisions enable the Administrator to assist the States in carrying out their statutory role as primary *implementers* of the NAAQSs. It is to the States that the Act assigns initial and primary responsibility for deciding what emissions reductions will be required from which sources. It would be impossible to perform that task intelligently without considering which abatement technologies are most efficient, and most economically feasible — which is why we have said that "the most important forum for consideration of claims of economic and technological infeasibility is before the state agency formulating the implementation plan." Union Elec. Co. v. EPA, 427 U.S. 246 (1976)…. That Congress chose…to assist States in choosing the means through which they would implement the standards is perfectly sensible, and has no bearing upon whether cost considerations are to be taken into account in formulating the standards.[15]…

The text of §109(b), interpreted in its statutory and historical context and with appreciation for its importance to the CAA as a whole, unambiguously bars cost considerations from the NAAQS-setting process, and thus ends the matter for us as well as the EPA.[16] …

Section 109(b)(1) of the CAA instructs the EPA to set "ambient air quality standards the attainment and maintenance of which in the judgment of the Administrator, based on the criteria documents of §108 and allowing an adequate margin of safety, are requisite to protect the public health." The Court of Appeals held that this section as interpreted by the Administrator did not provide an "intelligible principle" to guide the EPA's exercise of authority in setting NAAQSs. "The EPA," it said, "lacked any determinate criteria for drawing lines. It has failed to state intelligibly how much is too much." The court hence found that the EPA's interpretation (but not the statute itself) violated the nondelegation doctrine. We disagree.

We agree with the Solicitor General that the text of §109(b)(1) of the CAA at a minimum requires that "for a discrete set of pollutants and based on published air quality criteria that reflect the latest scientific knowledge, the EPA must establish uniform national standards at a level that is requisite to protect public health from the adverse effects of the pollutant in the ambient air." Requisite, in turn, "means sufficient, but not more than necessary." These limits on the EPA's discretion are strikingly similar to the ones we approved in Touby v. United States, 500

---

15. Respondents scarcely mention in their arguments the *secondary* NAAQS required by §109(b)(2), 42 U.S.C. §7409(b)(2). For many of the same reasons described in the body of the opinion, as well as the text of §109(b)(2), which instructs the EPA to set the standards at a level "requisite to protect the public welfare from any known or anticipated adverse effects *associated with the presence of such air pollutant in the ambient air*," we conclude that the EPA may not consider implementation costs in setting the secondary NAAQS.

16. Respondents' speculation that the EPA is secretly considering the costs of attainment without telling anyone is irrelevant to our interpretive inquiry. If such an allegation could be proved, it would be grounds for vacating the NAAQS, because the Administrator had not followed the law. It would not, however, be grounds for this Court's changing the law.

U.S. 160 (1991), which permitted the Attorney General to designate a drug as a controlled substance for purposes of criminal drug enforcement if doing so was "necessary to avoid an imminent hazard to the public safety." They also resemble the Occupational Safety and Health Act provision requiring the agency to "set the standard which most adequately assures, to the extent feasible, on the basis of the best available evidence, that no employee will suffer any impairment of health" — which the Court upheld in Industrial Union Department, AFL-CIO v. American Petroleum Institute, 448 U.S. 607, 646 (1980), and which even then Justice Rehnquist, who alone in that case thought the statute violated the nondelegation doctrine, would have upheld if, like the statute here, it did not permit economic costs to be considered.

It is true enough that the degree of agency discretion that is acceptable varies according to the scope of the power congressionally conferred.... We have never demanded, as the Court of Appeals did here, that statutes provide a "determinate criterion" for saying "how much of the regulated harm is too much."

We therefore reverse the judgment of the Court of Appeals remanding for reinterpretation that would avoid a supposed delegation of legislative power....

BREYER, J., concurring in part and concurring in the judgment. ...Regulators must often take account of all of a proposed regulation's adverse effects, at least where those adverse effects clearly threaten serious and disproportionate public harm. Hence, I believe that, other things being equal, we should read silences or ambiguities in the language of regulatory statutes as permitting, not forbidding, [consideration of costs]. In this case, however, other things are not equal. Here, legislative history, along with the statute's structure, indicates that §109's language reflects a congressional decision not to delegate to the agency the legal authority to consider economic costs of compliance....

Contrary to the suggestion of the Court of Appeals and of some parties, this interpretation of §109 does not require the EPA to eliminate every health risk, however slight, at any economic cost, however great, to the point of "hurtling" industry over "the brink of ruin," or even forcing "deindustrialization." The statute, by its express terms, does not compel the elimination of *all* risk; and it grants the Administrator sufficient flexibility to avoid setting ambient air quality standards ruinous to industry.

Section 109(b)(1) directs the Administrator to set standards that are "requisite to protect the public health" with "an adequate margin of safety." But these words do not describe a world that is free of all risk — an impossible and undesirable objective. Nor are the words "requisite" and "public health" to be understood independent of context. We consider football equipment "safe" even if its use entails a level of risk that would make drinking water "unsafe" for consumption. And what counts as "requisite" to protecting the public health will similarly vary with background circumstances, such as the public's ordinary tolerance of the particular health risk in the particular context at issue. The Administrator can consider such background circumstances when "deciding what risks are acceptable in the world in which we live."

The statute also permits the Administrator to take account of comparative health risks.....A rule likely to cause more harm to health than it prevents is not a rule that is "requisite to protect the public health." For example, as the Court of Appeals held and the parties do not contest, the Administrator has the authority to determine to what extent possible health risks stemming from reductions in tropospheric ozone (which, it is claimed, helps prevent cataracts and skin cancer) should be taken into account in setting the ambient air quality standard for ozone.

The statute ultimately specifies that the standard set must be "requisite to protect the public health" "*in the judgment of the Administrator*," a phrase that grants the Administrator considerable discretionary standard-setting authority.

The statute's words, then, authorize the Administrator to consider the severity of a pollutant's potential adverse health effects, the number of those likely to be affected, the distribution of the adverse effects, and the uncertainties surrounding each estimate. They permit the Administrator to take account of comparative health consequences. They allow her to take account of context when determining the acceptability of small risks to health. And they give her considerable discretion....

EPA, in setting standards that "protect the public health" with "an adequate margin of safety," retains discretionary authority to avoid regulating risks that it reasonably concludes are trivial in context...[and] a standard demanding the return of the Stone Age would not prove "requisite to protect the public health."...

COMMENTARY & QUESTIONS

1. **An anticlimactic ruling?** The decision in *American Trucking* was one of the most anxiously awaited regulatory decisions in many years. After a long fight about the appropriate method for achieving NAAQSs, spurred by private industries' belief that greater efforts were needed to control the high cost of complying with the CAA, industrialists, environmentalists, and EPA staffers all held their breath awaiting the decision from the Supreme Court. The Court's opinion itself was arguably anticlimactic. While concluding that the relevant portions of the CAA preclude consideration of cost, and while refusing to invoke the nondelegation doctrine, the Court, perhaps not surprisingly, delivered a scholarly and lawyerly opinion but left many open issues for another day.

2. **Unresolved questions after *American Trucking*.** In its ruling, the Supreme Court left in place, for now, a number of lower court decisions allowing agencies to consider costs unless Congress concludes otherwise. Are these lower court decisions all "good law"? Moreover, the Court does not preclude challenges, on nonconstitutional grounds, to PM standards, to ozone standards, or to ambient air quality standards. For more on these open questions, see Sunstein, Regulating Risks After *ATA*, 2001 Sup. Ct. Rev. 1.

3. **Justice Breyer's concurrence on risk regulation.** What does Justice Breyer's concurrence mean? Should it really be a dissent on the statutory issue — that is, is Breyer suggesting that EPA actually may look at costs in setting the NAAQSs? If he's not saying that, what is he saying?

4. ***American Trucking* on remand to the D.C. Circuit.** The Supreme Court remanded the *American Trucking* case to the D.C. Circuit to determine if EPA abused its discretion by setting new NAAQSs for fine PM and ozone. Employing a deferential standard, the circuit court held that the new standards implemented by EPA met the requirements prescribed by the Supreme Court. In denying opposite challenges to the standards by industry representatives and environmentalists, the court held that: (1) EPA's adoption of annual and daily NAAQSs for fine PM was not arbitrary or capricious; (2) absent a showing that the reduction of one pollutant would necessarily lead to an increase in another, EPA was not required to determine how the regulation of one pollutant would affect levels of others prior to setting NAAQSs; (3) EPA was not required to publish the data underlying studies upon which it relied in setting primary NAAQSs; and (4) EPA's adoption of primary and secondary NAAQSs for ozone were not arbitrary or capricious in light of the scientific evidence.

5. **The next stop for industry.** In light of the Supreme Court's ruling and the ruling on remand, many in industry have concluded that the time to take an active role is during the state level notice-and-comment rulemaking process when states draw up implementation plans. At the state level, costs determine the appropriate implementation, and the Supreme Court itself recognized that states can and do consider the economic feasibility of implementation: "The most important forum for consideration of claims of economic and technological infeasibility is before the state agency formulating the implementation plan." *American Trucking*, 531 U.S. at 470, quoting Union Elec. Co. v. EPA, 427 U.S. 246, 266 (1976). By interjecting itself in the state agency rulemaking process, industry will likely seek to influence how the agency assesses the cost feasibility of such plans.

6. **Setting the NAAQSs under conditions of uncertainty.** Now that the Supreme Court has laid to rest questions about whether economic costs and technological feasibility are to play a role in setting the NAAQSs, other issues that arise in setting the NAAQSs can take center stage. One of these issues concerns the role of scientific uncertainty. Standard-setting requires judgments about the causal effects of exposure to varying concentrations of pollutants. In *Lead Industries*, the D.C. Circuit recognized that EPA may act despite uncertainty:

> It may be...LIA's [Lead Industry Association] view that the Administrator must show that there is a "medical consensus that [the effects on which the standards were based] are harmful...." If so, LIA is seriously mistaken. This court has previously noted that some uncertainty about the health effects of air pollution is inevitable. And we pointed out that "awaiting certainty will often allow for only reactive, not preventive regulat[ory action]." *Ethyl*, 541 F.2d 1, 25 (D.C. Cir. 1976). Congress apparently shares this view; it specifically directed the Administrator to allow an adequate margin of safety to protect against effects which have not yet been uncovered by research and effects whose medical significance is a matter of disagreement. This court has previously acknowledged the role of the margin of safety requirement. In EDF v. EPA, 598 F.2d 62, 81 (D.C. Cir. 1978), we pointed out that "If administrative responsibility to protect against unknown dangers presents a difficult task, indeed, a veritable paradox...calling as it does for knowledge of that which is unknown...then, the term 'margin of safety' is Congress' directive that means be found to carry out the task and to reconcile the paradox." Moreover, it is significant that Congress has recently acknowledged that more often than not the "margins of safety" that are incorporated into air quality standards turn out to be very modest or nonexistent, as new information reveals adverse health effects at pollution levels once thought to be harmless. See H.R. Rep. No. 95-294 at 103–117. Congress' directive to the Administrator to allow an "adequate margin of safety" alone plainly refutes any suggestion that the Administrator is only authorized to set primary air quality standards which are designed to protect against health effects that are known to be clearly harmful....

> As we read the statutory provisions and the legislative history, Congress directed the Administrator to err on the side of caution in making the necessary decisions. We see no reason why this court should put a gloss on Congress' scheme by requiring the Administrator to show that there is a medical consensus that the effects on which the lead standards were based are "clearly harmful to health." All that is required by the statutory scheme is evidence in the record which substantiates his conclusions about the health effects on which the standards were based.

> Accordingly, we reject LIA's claim that the Administrator exceeded his statutory authority. *LIA*, 647 F.2d at 1154–1156.

The one aspect of the CAA in which the problems of scientific uncertainty eventually gained the upper hand on the harm-based approach was in regard to the regulation of hazardous air pollutants. In that realm, the difficulties of standard-setting totally compromised the program, and in 1990, after 20 years of regulatory failure — see NRDC v. EPA, 824 F. 2d 1146 (D.C. Cir. 1987) (vinyl chloride) — Congress repealed the old §112 that regulated hazardous air pollutants and replaced it with a technology-based system.

7. **Protecting vulnerable subpopulations from subclinical effects.** Another important issue that has dogged the NAAQS program from the start is what effects are harmful enough to justify designing a NAAQS so as to avoid them. The court in *Lead Industries* also had something to say about this issue. It rejected arguments that EPA was forbidden from considering mere "subclinical effects" from lead exposure rather than the onset of disease as the threshold of relevant harm, and that EPA could not base its regulation on achieving levels that would protect the health of the most sensitive population, urban children.

8. **How much harm is too much?** During the 1980s and 1990s, scientific evidence that the existing NAAQS for SO_2 caused harms to sensitive populations (especially asthmatics) began to accumulate. Studies showed that short-term, "high-level bursts" of SO_2 could cause respiratory difficulties for asthmatics; these problems ranged from having to cease strenuous outdoor activity, to taking medication, to seeking medical attention. Despite considerable pressure from the American Lung Association to promulgate a "high-level burst" exposure NAAQS for SO_2, EPA refused to do so. EPA's Clean Air Scientific Advisory Committee had concluded that the respiratory difficulties experienced by asthmatics as a consequence of these "bursts" were transitory and reversible, and that they also were within the range of adverse reactions experienced by asthmatics due to causes other than pollution. Later, however, EPA offered a different explanation for refusing to set a new short-term NAAQS for SO_2. EPA stated that while the respiratory difficulties were adverse and significant if they occurred repeatedly, and while the agency estimated that over 40,000 people would be subject to repeated instances of such effects in the absence of a stricter standard, the agency thought a new standard was not necessary because the adverse effects were "localized, infrequent, and site-specific." The D.C. Circuit failed to see a rational connection between EPA's finding that the health effects were adverse and significant and its decision not to set a new NAAQS to prevent them. The court remanded the case to the agency. American Lung Ass'n v. EPA, 134 F.3d 388, 392 (D.C. Cir. 1998). EPA has not responded to the remand.

9. **Risk-risk tradeoffs.** Even if EPA may not consider economic costs and technological feasibility in setting the NAAQS, may it consider potential adverse health and welfare effects arising from the standards themselves? In *American Trucking*, the D.C. Circuit said "yes." There, EPA argued that it was not required to consider the claim that a stricter ozone standard would harm health and welfare by diluting the layer of ground-level ozone that, the argument went, helped to protect people from the adverse effects of the

thinning of the stratospheric ozone layer. The court held that EPA was obliged to consider the potentially adverse health and welfare effects of the NAAQS. On remand, EPA concluded that the "protective" features of ozone pollution were too speculative to warrant basing the NAAQS on them.

In a related vein, industry groups have argued that EPA must consider the adverse health and welfare effects caused by the high economic costs of the NAAQSs. High regulatory costs cause unemployment, the theory runs, and unemployment leads to adverse health consequences. The D.C. Circuit has rejected this argument, relying on the language of the CAA that directs EPA's attention to an air pollutant's adverse effects arising from the "presence of such pollutant in the ambient air," 42 U.S.C. §7408(a)(2). NRDC v. EPA, 902 F.2d 962 (D.C. Cir. 1990). Has Justice Breyer also rejected this argument?

10. **The §112 experience.** Section 112 of the CAA regulates hazardous air pollutants (HAPs). Criteria pollutants regulated under §§108 and 109 are, of course, hazardous too, but the pollutants regulated under §112 are generally emitted from fewer sources and cause special health concerns, such as being linked to cancer. HAPs are defined as pollutants other than criteria pollutants, the exposure to which is "reasonably anticipated to result in an increase in mortality, or an increase in serious irreversible, or incapacitating irreversible illness." 42 U.S.C. §7412(a)(1).

Section 112 as it originally appeared in the 1970 Act was harm-based. However, unlike the Act's treatment of conventional pollutants, §112 did not rely on the NAAQS process to set National Emissions Standards for Hazardous Air Pollutants (NESHAPs). Instead, EPA was required to compile a list of HAPs and promulgate emission standards directly applicable to sources that emitted the hazardous pollutants in question. Those NESHAPs were to be set at a level that in the judgment of EPA "provides an ample margin of safety to protect the public health from such hazardous air pollutant." 42 U.S.C. §7412(b)(1)(B).

Experience has shown that a harm-based standards approach is not easily applied to the problems of HAPs. In general, these pollutants threaten to cause very grave health effects at minimal exposure levels. Many are considered to be "nonthreshold" pollutants, meaning that no human exposure to them is safe. Despite agreement on the danger of even low exposures, establishing standards for exposure is a task often shrouded in uncertainty because the available data on exposure and response tend to be quite sketchy. Thus, as a first-level problem, standard-setting is both difficult and uncertain.

Even after a "safe" exposure (ambient concentration) level is established for HAPs, meeting the standard is frequently difficult. Some ambient standards are so stringent, due to the low levels of allowable exposure, that the controls needed to achieve the standard are exceedingly expensive. In some cases, control technologies that would prevent excessive emissions are not yet known. In either event, the enforcement of NESHAPs holds a significant possibility of causing economic dislocation, either through the cost or impossibility of compliance. The desire to avoid those consequences is heightened in cases where scientific uncertainty undermines confidence that the standard need be set at so stringent a level.

Perhaps for these reasons, EPA was slow to embark on the hazardous pollutant standard-setting task Congress had set for it. When it did come forth with regulations, they were immediately attacked on both sides: Industry groups found the standards too exacting and expensive; public interest advocates claimed that the standards failed to provide the statutorily mandated "ample margin for safety." Under §112, as under the NAAQS program, the question arose whether economic costs and technological feasibility could be considered in setting the standards. The D.C. Circuit issued two opinions on this issue in the 1980s, one a panel opinion authored by then-Judge Bork and one an en banc opinion reversing the panel opinion, surprisingly also authored by Judge Bork. (In the interval between the two decisions, Bork had been nominated by President Reagan for the Supreme Court.)

In the first decision, Judge Bork upheld EPA's decision to consider cost and feasibility in setting the §112 standard for vinyl chloride and, specifically, to require technology-based controls for this pollutant:

> We believe that the agency in this case has made a reasonable interpretation.... The EPA has not taken the position that it may consider cost and technological feasibility to set a standard that allows a level of emission at or above which evidence has indicated adverse health effects to occur. Perhaps if the evidence positively demonstrated that a given substance had ill effects and endangered the public health in trace amounts, the EPA could permit no emissions of that pollutant. Only when an area of uncertainty exists does the Administrator "reconcile the paradox" of having to protect against dangers he cannot know by setting standards as strict as possible given both available technology and the requirement that the cost of reduction not be grossly disproportionate to the level achieved. That the area of uncertainty, as with vinyl chloride, covers all non-zero levels of emission does not alter our conclusion.
>
> Since the Administrator has no way of knowing health effects in the range of uncertainty, such considerations as technological and economic feasibility seem natural, perhaps inevitable, choices to inform the Administrator's decision whether he has amply provided for a reasonable degree of safety from the unknown. By emphasizing available technology, the EPA has ensured the maximum regulation against uncertainty without the economic and social displacements that would accompany the closing of an industry or any substantial part of an industry. By ensuring that costs do not become grossly disproportionate to the level of reduction achieved, the EPA guarantees that the consuming public does not pay an excessive price for the marginal benefits of increasing increments of protection against the unknown. We cannot say that this represents an unreasonable weighing of values, especially when no other value readily suggests itself and petitioner supplies none apart from health effects, which in the range of uncertainty are by definition unknowable. NRDC v. EPA, 804 F.2d 710, 722–723 (D.C. Cir. 1986).

In his subsequent opinion for the en banc court, however, Judge Bork concluded that in setting the standards for NESHAPs, EPA must first identify a "safe" level for the HAP in question, based exclusively on health considerations and not on cost or feasibility. Then, the agency was to set a margin of safety to provide protection beyond the "safe" level. In this second step, the agency was allowed to consider cost and feasibility in figuring out how large the margin of safety was to be. NRDC v. EPA, 824 F.2d 1146 (D.C. Cir. 1987).

The ruling prompted a quite complicated response from EPA, setting out the process by which EPA would make decisions on NESHAPs. See 53 Fed. Reg. 28,496 (July 28, 1988).

Even after the vinyl chloride decision, EPA regulation in this area continued at a crawl. By 1990, the agency had managed to promulgate standards for only seven hazardous air pollutants, had listed and was in the process of proposing standards for a handful of additional substances, and was proposing to list another ten. In 1990, Congress largely abandoned the harm-based approach to HAPs and substituted a technology-based approach that called for the employment of MACT. The legislation identified some 180 substances to be regulated by that method. Emitting sources were given eight years to install MACT, with EPA thereafter obligated to enact further measures to avoid unacceptable residual risks. This latter provision is, of course, a return to a harm-based approach — but only after MACT has been installed on the relevant facilities.

In addition, however, §112(d) provides that where a health threshold has been established for a HAP, "the Administrator may consider such threshold level, with an ample margin of safety, when establishing emission standards" for HAPs. 42 U.S.C. §7412(d). EPA has proposed using the authority of §112(d) not only to exempt facilities emitting threshold HAPs in below-threshold amounts from the technology-based requirements of §112, but also to exempt facilities emitting nonthreshold pollutants from these requirements if the risks are low enough. See EPA, National Emission Standards for Hazardous Air Pollutants from Stationary Combustion Turbines; Proposed Rule, 68 Fed. Reg. 1888 (Jan. 14, 2003). Does this bring §112 closer to the harm-based approach rejected by Congress in the 1990 Amendments? Is EPA's new approach authorized by §112(d)?

11. **Mercury MACT or mercury trading?** Following a lawsuit brought by the NRDC, EPA agreed to propose a MACT rule for mercury. On January 30, 2004, EPA offered for public comment two options: one to require MACT for utility units that emit mercury and one to create an interstate trading regime for mercury under §111 of the Act, which requires NSPSs for major polluting facilities. EPA explained its proposal under §111 by saying that MACT regulation under §112(n)(1)(A) required a finding by the agency that regulation of mercury from electric utility steam generating units was both "appropriate and necessary," and EPA thought that MACT regulation was not necessary because the trading regime EPA would create under §111 would be far superior to a MACT program for mercury. EPA, Proposed National Emission Standards for Hazardous Air Pollutants; and, in the Alternative, Proposed Standards of Performance for New and Existing Stationary Sources: Electric Utility Steam Generating Units; Proposed Rule, 69 Fed. Reg. 4652 (Jan. 30, 2004). This will undoubtedly provoke some interesting questions.

D. MOVING FROM IDENTIFYING HARM TO REGULATING POLLUTERS: IMPLEMENTATION PLANS

Once the NAAQSs are set, attention shifts to ensuring that they are attained (in "nonattainment" areas) and maintained (in "attainment" areas). At this stage, primary responsibility shifts from the federal government to the states and their SIPs. Nevertheless, the federal government retains several significant roles: It reviews the SIPs and, if they are not up to snuff, may devise implementation plans of its own, the dreaded FIPs; it sets technology-based standards for mobile sources and for major new sources of air pollution; and it brokers disputes between the states about interstate air pollution that might interfere with downwind states' ability to meet the NAAQSs.

When a NAAQS is first established or revised, all 50 states must revise their SIPs to ensure attainment, maintenance, and enforcement of the NAAQS. The process is complex, to say the least. In basic terms, however, it involves three steps. First, the state must take an inventory of the emissions of the pollution sources within its borders. Second, the state must try to predict what future emissions in the state will be, so that it can determine whether it will achieve (or maintain) compliance with the NAAQS by the deadline set by the federal government. This step involves quite complicated exercises in air quality modeling. Finally, the state must seek pollution reductions from individual sources as necessary to come into or stay in compliance with the NAAQSs.

All the while, the state must steer clear of EPA's disapproval of its efforts. We begin our discussion of the implementation process with this topic.

Section 1. THE FEDERAL-STATE RELATIONSHIP IN THE IMPLEMENTATION PROCESS

The *American Trucking* case was emphatic in ruling that economic feasibility had no role to play in the standard-setting process under a harm-based ambient quality approach. That position was supported by the statute's language and structure. Once the court identifies the approach as harm-based, it has no authority to inject the pragmatic concerns that economic and technologic feasibility embody. The reason for this limit on the court is simultaneously simple and politically sophisticated — because Congress said so. Considered as a matter of pure logic, the irrelevance of cost and feasibility is even more clear: The scientific question of how stringent the standard must be to avoid harm has nothing to do with whether the standard is achievable or cost-effective.

As a pragmatic, political matter, however, it is not reasonable to believe that Congress could bar all consideration of cost and feasibility from the system used to regulate the most commonly produced air emissions. Those considerations, or other similar ones, must have a home somewhere in the CAA. The following case explains where.

Union Electric Company v. U.S. Environmental Protection Agency
Supreme Court of the United States, 1976
427 U.S. 246

[Shortly after passage of the CAA, Missouri, like all of the states, was required to adopt a SIP. Under the Missouri SIP, three plants operated by Union Electric Company were made subject to regulations that Union claimed were impossible to meet on technical and/or financial grounds. Union pressed that objection in its negotiations with Missouri to no avail. Missouri presented the SIP to EPA for approval, and approval was granted on May 31, 1972. Union took no action at that time to challenge the Missouri SIP. Instead, Union sought, and Missouri issued, variances for each of the three plants as allowed by the CAA, granting Union additional time to reduce their emissions to the limits specified in the Missouri SIP. In 1974, after two of the three variances had expired and Union had done nothing to reduce its emissions, EPA gave notice to

Union that the company was in violation of the SO$_2$ limitations for it contained in the Missouri SIP. Union sued EPA, and despite Union's having chosen a wrong procedural avenue for raising its claims of economic and technologic infeasibility, the Supreme Court addressed the merits of the claims.]

MARSHALL, J. Since a reviewing court regardless of when the petition for review is filed may consider claims of economic and technological infeasibility only if the Administrator may consider such claims in approving or rejecting a state implementation plan, we must address ourselves to the scope of the Administrator's responsibility. The Administrator's position is that he has no power whatsoever to reject a state implementation plan on the ground that it is economically or technologically infeasible, and we have previously accorded great deference to the Administrator's construction of the Clean Air Act. See Train v. NRDC, 421 U.S., at 75. After surveying the relevant provisions of the CAA Amendments of 1970 and their legislative history, we agree that Congress intended claims of economic and technological infeasibility to be wholly foreign to the Administrator's consideration of a state implementation plan.

As we have previously recognized, the 1970 CAA Amendments were a drastic remedy to what was perceived as a serious and otherwise uncheckable problem of air pollution. The Amendments place the primary responsibility for formulating pollution control strategies on the States, but nonetheless subject the States to strict minimum compliance requirements. These requirements are of a "technology-forcing character" and are expressly designed to force regulated sources to develop pollution control devices that might at the time appear to be economically or technologically infeasible.

This approach is apparent on the face of §110(a)(2). The provision sets out eight criteria that an implementation plan must satisfy, and provides that if these criteria are met and if the plan was adopted after reasonable notice and hearing, the Administrator "shall approve" the proposed state plan. The mandatory "shall" makes it quite clear that the Administrator is not to be concerned with factors other than those specified and none of the eight factors appears to permit consideration of technological or economic infeasibility.[17] Nonetheless, if a basis is to be found for allowing the Administrator to consider such claims, it must be among the eight criteria, and so it is here that the argument is focused.

It is suggested that consideration of claims of technological and economic infeasibility is required by the first criterion that the primary air quality standards be met "as expeditiously as practicable but...in no case later than three years" and that the secondary air quality standards be met within a "reasonable time." §110(a)(2)(A). The argument is that what is "practicable" or "reasonable" cannot be determined without assessing whether what is proposed is possible. This argument does not survive analysis.

Section 110(a)(2)(A)'s three-year deadline for achieving primary air quality standards is central to the Amendments' regulatory scheme and, as both the language and the legislative history of the requirement make clear, it leaves no room for claims of technological or economic infeasibility. The 1970 congressional debate on the Amendments centered on whether technology forcing was necessary and desirable in framing and attaining air quality standards sufficient to protect the public health, standards later termed primary standards. The House version of the Amendments was quite moderate in approach, requiring only that health-related standards be

---

17. Comparison of the eight criteria of §110(a)(2) with other provisions of the Amendments bolsters this conclusion. Where Congress intended the Administrator to be concerned about economic and technological infeasibility, it expressly so provided. Thus, §§110(a), 110(f), 111(a)(1), 202(a), 211(c)(2)(A), and 231(b) of the Amendments all expressly permit consideration, e.g., "of the requisite technology, giving appropriate consideration to the cost of compliance." Section 110(a)(2) contains no such language.

met "within a reasonable time." The Senate bill, on the other hand, flatly required that, possible or not, health-related standards be met "within three years."

The Senate's stiff requirement was intended to foreclose the claims of emission sources that it would be economically or technologically infeasible for them to achieve emission limitations sufficient to protect the public health within the specified time. As Senator Muskie, manager of the Senate bill, explained to his chamber:

> The first responsibility of Congress is not the making of technological or economic judgments or even to be limited by what is or appears to be technologically or economically feasible. Our responsibility is to establish what the public interest requires to protect the health of persons. This may mean that people and industries will be asked to do what seems to be impossible at the present time. 116 Cong. Rec. 32901–32902 (1970).

This position reflected that of the Senate committee:

> In the Committee discussions, considerable concern was expressed regarding the use of the concept of technical feasibility as the basis of ambient air standards. The Committee determined that 1) the health of people is more important than the question of whether the early achievement of ambient air quality standards protective of health is technically feasible; and 2) the growth of pollution load in many areas, even with application of available technology, would still be deleterious to public health.

Therefore, the Committee determined that existing sources of pollutants either should "meet the standard of the law or be closed down...." S. Rep. No. 91–1196, pp. 2–3 (1970).

The Conference Committee and, ultimately, the entire Congress accepted the Senate's three-year mandate for the achievement of primary air quality standards, and the clear import of that decision is that the Administrator must approve a plan that provides for attainment of the primary standards in three years even if attainment does not appear feasible.

Secondary air quality standards, those necessary to protect the public welfare, were subject to [the lesser] requirement that they be met within a "reasonable time." ...

[The Court then addressed the claim that the power to engage in technology-forcing is available to the states under the CAA. Here the utility's argument was that the second criterion for plan approval allowed plans to contain only such control devices "as may be necessary."]

We read the "as may be necessary" requirement of §110(a)(2)(B) to demand only that the implementation plan submitted by the State meet the "minimum conditions" of the Amendments.[18] Beyond that, if a State makes the legislative determination that it desires a particular air quality by a certain date and that it is willing to force technology to attain it or lose a certain industry if attainment is not possible such a determination is fully consistent with the structure and purpose of the Amendments, and §110(a)(2)(B) provides no basis for the EPA Administrator to object to the determination on the ground of infeasibility.[19]

In sum, we have concluded that claims of economic or technological infeasibility may not be considered by the Administrator in evaluating a state requirement that primary ambient air

---

18. Economic and technological factors may be relevant in determining whether the minimum conditions are met. Thus, the Administrator may consider whether it is economically or technologically possible for the state plan to require more rapid progress than it does. If he determines that it is, he may reject the plan as not meeting the requirement that primary standards be achieved "as expeditiously as practicable" or as failing to provide for attaining secondary standards within "a reasonable time."

19. In a literal sense, of course, no plan is infeasible since offending sources always have the option of shutting down if they cannot otherwise comply with the standard of the law. Thus, there is no need for the Administrator to reject an economically or technologically "infeasible" state plan on the ground that anticipated noncompliance will cause the State to fall short of the national standards. Sources objecting to such a state scheme must seek their relief from the State.

quality standards be met in the mandatory three years. And, since we further conclude that the States may submit implementation plans more stringent than federal law requires and that the Administrator must approve such plans if they meet the minimum requirements of §110(a)(2), it follows that the language of §110(a)(2)(B) provides no basis for the Administrator ever to reject a state implementation plan on the ground that it is economically or technologically infeasible. Accordingly, a court of appeals reviewing an approved plan under §307(b)(1) cannot set it aside on those grounds, no matter when they are raised.

Perhaps the most important forum for consideration of claims of economic and technological infeasibility is before the state agency formulating the implementation plan. So long as the national standards are met, the State may select whatever mix of control devices it desires and industries with particular economic or technological problems may seek special treatment in the plan itself. Moreover, if the industry is not exempted from, or accommodated by, the original plan, it may obtain a variance, as petitioner did in this case; and the variance, if granted after notice and a hearing, may be submitted to the EPA as a revision of the plan. §110(a)(3)(A), 42 U.S.C. §1857c-5(a)(3)(A) (1970 ed., Supp. IV). Lastly, an industry denied an exemption from the implementation plan, or denied a subsequent variance, may be able to take its claims of economic or technological infeasibility to the state courts.

While the State has virtually absolute power in allocating emission limitations so long as the national standards are met, if the state plan cannot meet the national standards, the EPA is implicated in any postponement procedure. There are two ways that a State can secure relief from the EPA for individual emission sources, or classes of sources, that cannot meet the national standards. [The opinion here identifies two explicit statutory methods for obtaining short extensions of the date for compliance by an affected emitter, such as Union.]

The Amendments offer ample opportunity for consideration of claims of technological and economic infeasibility. Always, however, care is taken that consideration of such claims will not interfere substantially with the primary goal of prompt attainment of the national standards. Allowing such claims to be raised by appealing the Administrator's approval of an implementation plan, as petitioner suggests, would frustrate congressional intent. It would permit a proposed plan to be struck down as infeasible before it is given a chance to work, even though Congress clearly contemplated that some plans would be infeasible when proposed. And it would permit the Administrator or a federal court to reject a State's legislative choices in regulating air pollution, even though Congress plainly left with the States, so long as the national standards were met, the power to determine which sources would be burdened by regulation and to what extent. Technology forcing is a concept somewhat new to our national experience and it necessarily entails certain risks. But Congress considered those risks in passing the 1970 Amendments and decided that the dangers posed by uncontrolled air pollution made them worth taking. Petitioner's theory would render that considered legislative judgment a nullity, and that is a result we refuse to reach.

COMMENTARY & QUESTIONS

1. **EPA review of SIPs that do consider economic and technologic feasibility.** In this case, the Court said EPA cannot disapprove a SIP on the ground that it does not take economic and technologic feasibility into account. Can EPA disapprove of a SIP that does take feasibility into account? Although the Court doesn't say so in those precise words, it is clear that EPA can approve of SIPs that allow some industries relief on feasibility grounds so long as the allowance of feasibility in allocating plant-specific

emissions limitations in one economic sector does not prevent attainment of the mandated ambient air quality. In fact, the Court virtually invites the states, as a part of SIP formulation, to take feasibility into account when it points to the state SIP formulation process as the principal forum for feasibility arguments.

Must EPA approve SIPs that allow feasibility to be taken into account as long as those SIPs will result in timely attainment of the relevant NAAQS? Technically, the answer is "no." EPA has discretion to reject feasibility allowances in SIPs if, in EPA's judgment, the SIPs do not achieve attainment as quickly as would still be practicable with less allowance for feasibility. Realistically, EPA will not refuse approval of a SIP on that basis. As a matter of federalism, to do so would seem to intrude on the primacy of the state envisioned in the SIP process.

2. **States as pollution allocation brokers.** What happens when states take advantage of their ability to consider economic and technologic feasibility in SIP formulation? Arguably, they open themselves up to horrific lobbying pressure from their most influential industries, all of which can probably make a colorable claim that imposing stringent pollution control requirements on them exceeds their financial or technological abilities. Is there anything wrong with this? One argument is that the political allocation of pollution control burdens will almost certainly be sub-optimal in terms of achieving attainment in a least-cost manner. Viewing the grant of dispensations based on feasibility as a sort of political patronage gives rise to the likelihood that political allocation will tend to result in SIPs that try to achieve attainment by the smallest margin possible. After all, what politician would not dole out as much patronage as possible? How cogent are these criticisms if EPA still insists on NAAQS attainment? Does EPA's watchdog role become more difficult when the states are trying to draw SIPs that are as close to painless as possible?

3. **EPA oversight of states' permitting decisions.** Another example of the federal government's role as watchdog comes from Alaska Dep't of Envtl. Conservation (ADEC) v. EPA, 2004 U.S. LEXIS 820 (2004), in which the Supreme Court upheld EPA orders that effectively overruled a PSD permit granted by ADEC to a zinc mining facility. ADEC issued a PSD permit under its SIP to a zinc mine for both a new and a modified source of NOx emissions. EPA objected that the permit did not require the firm to employ Selective Catalytic Reduction (SCR), the performance standard EPA thought constituted BACT as required by the CAA. ADEC found that this technology was not economically feasible or cost-effective for this firm, while conceding that it lacked site-specific data to support this conclusion. EPA disagreed with ADEC's conclusion, noting that ADEC's cost-effectiveness estimate for SCR was "well within the range that EPA considers reasonable," and also emphasizing ADEC's lack of specific evidence to the contrary. EPA thereafter issued orders that, in effect, vitiated the state action and rendered the state permit ineffective. In a 5–4 decision, the Supreme Court upheld EPA's general authority to oversee state BACT determinations and, in addition, upheld the agency's specific decision in this case. In dissent, Justice Kennedy charged that the Court's ruling would disrupt the federal-state balance contemplated by the Clean Air Act.

Section 2. REVERSE ENGINEERING FROM STANDARDS TO ALLOCATIONS: AIR QUALITY MODELING AND AGENCY EXPERTISE

Although the setting of harm-based ambient standards calls for difficult scientific judgments, an equally difficult process attends the decisions made in writing the prescription for attaining these standards. Under the CAA, these latter decisions are made in the SIP process. As to stationary sources, the SIP requirements usually are put in the form of a permit that dictates how the plant may operate in regard to emitting pollution. The stationary source permits work together with the other parts of the SIP. Those might include transportation planning, vehicle inspection and maintenance, mandatory installation of hoods or vapor recovery systems at gasoline stations, ozone action alerts recommending that citizens refrain from refueling vehicles or using lawn-mowers on days having particular climatic conditions, and so on. Together, all parts of the plan must produce a net effect that allows all of the NAAQSs to be met at virtually all times[20] throughout the state. If a SIP will not have that result, EPA cannot approve it. If the state is unable or unwilling to propose a SIP that EPA approves, EPA must take over the process and write a FIP. As the *Cleveland Electric* case that follows demonstrates, a good deal of science and art is involved in determining whether a proposed implementation plan will result in satisfactory ambient air quality.

The SIP writing process is a form of reverse engineering that moves from a desired result to a plan for attaining the result. Drafters of the SIP must predict the movement of emitted pollutants in the airshed, a task accomplished by creating computer-based airshed models. This is a monumental task because the dispersion of pollutants is affected by local topographic, climatic, and atmospheric conditions and because the predictions have to be made for both long-term average concentrations of pollutants and ambient pollution levels under short-term extraordinary conditions. A substantial degree of precision is required, both to predict confidently that a particular set of allowed emissions will satisfy ambient quality standards and to identify a set of appropriate pollution controls. The airshed modeling is hotly contested because the choice of the model and the assumptions made in modeling directly affect the amount of emissions allowed under the SIP and the pollution control costs that various firms will be forced to incur. The battle lines are numerous. The affected states usually are at odds with EPA because they seek a model that will allow a higher level of emissions. Individual polluters within the airshed have interests adverse to one another because their allowable emissions will often vary depending on what model is used and what assumptions are made in modeling.

Procedurally, the contours of the SIP process are fixed by the CAA itself. A good summary of the statutory deadlines and the process by which EPA oversees the states appears in NRDC v. Train, 545 F.2d 320 (2d Cir. 1976). The key element is the statute's mandated fixed schedule, which begins when a pollutant is added to the list of criteria pollutants and ends with the deadline when states must have credible programs in place to limit emissions of that pollutant enough to attain the primary ambient air quality standard. The "hammer" that gives EPA an ability to insist that the states go forward is

---

20. Some of the NAAQS do allow one or more annual exceedances.

TABLE 1.—EFFECTS THRESHOLD, BEST CHOICE SIGNIFICANT RISK LEVELS AND SAFETY MARGINS CONTAINED IN PRIMARY AMBIENT AIR QUALITY STANDARDS

| Pollutant | Lowest best judgment estimate for effects threshold and best choice for significant risk levels | | Adverse health effect | U.S. primary air quality standard | Margin of safety* (percent) |
	Concentration	Averaging time			
Sulfur dioxide	300 to 400 ug/m³	24 hour	Mortality increase	365 ug/m³	None
	91 ug/m³	Annual	Increased frequency of acute respiratory disease	80 ug/m³	14
Total suspended particulates	250 to 300 ug/m³	24 hour	Mortality increase	260 ug/m³	None
	100 ug/m³	do	Aggravation of respiratory disease	260 ug/m³	None
	70 to 250 ug/m³	Annual	Increased frequency of chronic bronchitis	75 ug/m³	33
Suspended sulfates	10 ug/m³	24 hour	Increased infections in asthmatics	None	None
	15 ug/m³	Annual	Increased lower respiratory infections in children	None	None
Nitrogen dioxide	140 ug/m³	do	Increased severity of acute respiratory illness in children	100 ug/m³	40
Carbon monoxide	23 ug/m³	8 hour	Diminished exercise tolerance in heart patients	10 ug/m³	**130
	73 ug/m³	1 hour	Diminished exercise tolerance in heart patients	40 ug/m³	**82
Photochemical oxidants	200 ug/m³	do	Increased susceptibility to infection	160 ug/m³	25

* Safety margin equals effects threshold minus standard divided by standard X 100.
** Safety margins based upon carboxyhemoglobin levels would be 100 percent for the 8 hour standard and 67 percent for the 1 hour standard.

TABLE 2.—THRESHOLD AND ILLUSTRATIVE HEALTH RISKS FOR SELECTED AMBIENT LEVELS OF SUSPENDED SULFATES

| Adverse health effect | Threshold concentration and exposure duration | Illustrative health risk | | |
		Definition	Level	Sulfur dioxide equivalent
Increase in daily mortality	25 ug/m³ for 24 hr or longer	2½ percent increase in daily mortality	38 ug/m³ for 24 hr	600 ug/m³ for 24 hr.
Aggravation of heart and lung disease in the elderly	9 ug/m³ for 24 hr or longer	50 per cent increase in symptom aggravation	48 ug/m³ for 24 hr	750 ug/m³ for 24 hr.
Aggravation of asthma	6 to 10 ug/m³ for 24 hr	75 percent increase in frequency of asthma attacks.	30 ug/m³ for 24 hr	450 ug/m³ for 24 hr.
Excess acute lower respiratory disease in children.	13 ug/m³ for several yr	50 percent increase in frequency	20 ug/m³ annual average.	100 to 250 ug/m³ annual average.
Excess risk for chronic bronchitis	10 to 15 ug/m³ for up to 10 yr.	50 percent increase in risk	15 to 20 ug/m³ annual average	100 to 250 ug/m³ annual average.

FIGURE 11-1

Tables from Cleveland Electric, *showing the primary NAAQSs for the criteria air pollutants as they were then. Today's chart would add lead, replace photochemical oxidants with ozone, and replace the "suspended" NAAQSs with PM-10 (particulate matter <10 microns) and PM-2.5. The nonmandatory secondary standards are typically ignored, or defined as equal to primary standards.*

the threat that the agency itself will adopt a plan should the states fail to meet the statutory requirements. Under that threat, most states have managed to draft SIPs that have garnered EPA approval. (States also undoubtedly are influenced by EPA's power to prohibit federal highway funding for, and to require pollution offsets in, states that fail to achieve the NAAQSs.) The case that follows is an example of a state that failed to do so, whereupon EPA was forced to draft a FIP to control SO$_2$ emissions in the State of Ohio.[21]

Cleveland Electric Illuminating Company v. U.S. Environmental Protection Agency
United States Court of Appeals for the Sixth Circuit, 1978
572 F.2d 1150

EDWARDS, J. This court now has before it 23 petitions involving 32 companies filed against the United States Environmental Protection Agency which levy a variety of complaints against the federal agency's imposition of a sulfur dioxide (SO$_2$) pollution control plan for industrial discharges into Ohio's ambient air. The issues, which have been extensively briefed and argued, divide into general legal and procedural complaints which might be applicable to any one of the petitioners and a wider variety of specific complaints about the application of the EPA controls to particular power generating or industrial plants.

The major issues dealt with in this opinion are:...intervenor, the State of Ohio, claims that this court should disapprove the federal plan as irrational and arbitrary and rely upon Ohio to come forward with a more rational plan sometime in the future[,] and petitioners claim that the major model employed by the United States Environmental Protection Agency in establishing specific emission limitations for particular plants is invalid both intrinsically and as applied. This model is termed the "Real-Time Air-Quality-Simulator Model" (hereinafter RAM).

National air quality standards for sulfur dioxide, one of the most important pollutants of the ambient air, were set by EPA in 1973 as follows:

> 40 C.F.R. §50.4 — National primary ambient air-quality standards for sulfur oxides (sulfur dioxide). The national primary ambient air quality standards for sulfur oxides measured as sulfur dioxide by the reference method described in Appendix A to this part, or by an equivalent method, are: (a) 80 micrograms per cubic meter (0.03 p.p.m.) — annual arithmetic mean; (b) 365 micrograms per cubic meter (0.14 p.p.m.) — Maximum 24-hour concentration not to be exceeded more than once per year.

Acute episodes of high pollution have clearly resulted in mortality and morbidity. Often the effects of high pollutant concentrations in these episodes have been combined with other environmental features such as low temperatures or epidemic diseases (influenza) which may in themselves have serious or fatal consequences. This has sometimes made it difficult to determine to what extent pollution and temperature extremes are responsible for the effects. Nevertheless, there is now no longer any doubt that high levels of pollution sustained for periods of days can kill. Those aged 45 and over with chronic diseases, particularly of the lungs or heart, seem to be predominantly affected. In addition to these acute episodes, pollutants can attain daily levels which have been shown to have serious consequences to city dwellers.

There is a large and increasing body of evidence that significant health effects are produced by long-term exposures to air pollutants. Acute respiratory infections in children, chronic respiratory diseases in adults, and decreased levels of ventilatory lung function in both children and

---

21. The case has an extensive prior history of litigation concerning SO$_2$ emission controls in Ohio. See Buckeye Power, Inc. v. EPA, 481 F.2d 162 (6th Cir. 1973) (*Buckeye Power I*), and Buckeye Power, Inc. v. EPA, 525 F.2d 80 (6th Cir. 1975) (*Buckeye Power II*).

adults have been found to be related to concentrations of SO_2 and particulates, after apparently sufficient allowance has been made for such confounding variables as smoking and socioeconomic circumstances. Rall, Review of the Health Effects of Sulfur Oxides, 8 Envtl. Health Perspectives 97, 99 (1974).

It appears that present national air quality standards have been set with little or no margin of safety. Adverse health effects are set forth in the NAAQS chart in this section, in which the scanty margins of safety are set out (see Figure 11-1).

The major sources of sulfur dioxide pollution of the ambient air are coal-fired plants — exemplified by power plants operated by some of the petitioners in this case.

The State of Ohio's Petition... On July 13, 1977, the State of Ohio belatedly moved for leave to intervene in this proceeding. Its motion attacked the EPA sulfur dioxide emission control plan as having an adverse impact on the Ohio coal industry, and the Ohio economy as a whole. The motion also asserted that the State was developing a sulfur dioxide plan which would eliminate excessive abatement requirements which Ohio perceived to exist in the federal regulations. This court granted the motion for leave to intervene and has considered the brief and the reply brief filed by Ohio. Under this first disposition heading we consider only Ohio's suggestion that this court reject the United States Environmental Protection Agency's sulfur dioxide control plan and rely upon Ohio's implied promise to promulgate a state sulfur dioxide plan sometime in the future.

We reject this suggestion on the basis of a record of delay and default which has left Ohio in the position of being the only major industrialized state lacking an enforceable plan for control of sulfur dioxide. It was clearly the intention of Congress to have a plan for control of sulfur dioxide emissions in place in all states in need of such control by the year 1972. Clean Air Act §§109(a), 110(a). It was equally clearly the intention of Congress that the preferred mechanism for establishment of such a plan was through the establishment and operation of a state environmental agency. §107(a). [Here the court summarized the sorry history of Ohio's efforts to adopt a SO_2 SIP.] Clearly, the State of Ohio has failed to submit an implementation plan for sulfur dioxide for which a national ambient air quality primary standard has been prescribed. Equally clearly, five years have now elapsed beyond the date when such an implementation plan was called for under the Clean Air Act. Under these circumstances, we find no warrant, consistent with the purposes of the federal legislation, for giving heed to Ohio's petition for further delay....

The "RAM" Model... The petitioners in these cases center most of their criticisms upon the United States EPA's use of the Real-Time Air-Quality-Simulation Model ("RAM") which was employed by the agency in preparation of the Ohio sulfur dioxide control plan. RAM is a dispersion model which evaluates the interaction of a variety of facts in order to make predictions concerning the contribution to the pollution of the ambient air by specific plants. Its formula takes into account the capacity of each plant on a stack-by-stack basis and adds thereto smokestack height, surrounding terrain, and weather conditions. The model is operated on the assumption that the plants concerned operate 24 hours a day at full capacity and predictions are made for every day of the year. The ultimate standards are set according to the predicted second-worst day in terms of pollution results shown.

In comparison to all other prior methods of controlling pollution, RAM starts with a solid, ascertainable data base. This is the established design capacity of the power plants in question related to the sulfur content of the fuel used by each. From these factors the "emissions data" for each plant are developed.

When stack height, wind, weather, terrain, land use, etc., are figured in, the RAM model has the additional value of allowing its user to predict with considerable accuracy the relative contributions of specific power plant stacks to the points of maximum concentration of pollution of the ambient air.

The RAM model was actually developed as a result of the United States EPA's public hearings on the proposed plan for Ohio after five days of hearings on said proposed plan in Columbus, Cleveland, Cincinnati, and Steubenville at which petitioners involved in this current litigation were given an opportunity (which most accepted) to appear, testify, or submit comments. At those hearings the major source of criticism from industries, including some of the present petitioners, was that the plan then under consideration did not determine limitations by individual stacks to a sufficient degree. EPA in its brief in this case compares the "rollback" model employed in the preparation of the first Ohio plan to dispersion models like RAM, which is now the source of present controversy.

Unlike the rollback model, the dispersion models used in developing the promulgated plan allow a determination of the cause-effect relationship between the SO_2 emissions of the pollution sources in an area and the resulting ambient air quality. Therefore, it is possible to determine the proportion by which each source must reduce emissions to meet ambient standards. With the use of the rollback model, in contrast, each source's emissions in the region, whether or not they contributed to a pollution problem, were required to be reduced. Through dispersion modeling, emission limitations can now be set with increased precision. Overcontrol is minimized, so that the plan will still insure attainment and maintenance of the air quality standards, but at a much reduced cost to the sources. This is most clearly demonstrated by comparing emission limitations for power plants under the various plans. Power plants account for approximately 80 percent of the sulfur dioxide emissions in the State.

However, achievement of this added precision requires a massive analytical task. Tremendous amounts of data are required for each source analyzed. In addition to the emissions data for each source, dispersion modeling requires detailed information on all the factors that affect the dispersion of emissions. These include the height of the source's stack (or usually stacks), the spatial orientation of the sources to each other, the topography of the area and the effects it will have on dispersion, and, of crucial importance, detailed weather data for the area.

All this information is needed so that the computer analysis reflects actual conditions. For example, a gaseous pollutant emitted over a grassy field will disperse much differently than if the pollutant is emitted over a large urban area. There the dispersion will be affected not only by the local weather conditions but also by the greater turbulence caused by the different types of surface areas and heat sources throughout a city.

EPA goes on to point out that there are more than 1,000 point sources in the State of Ohio and more than 2,000 area sources,[22] and that in relation to emission data, United States EPA utilized (among other sources) the data base on sulfur dioxide required to be reported to the State of Ohio under [Ohio law].

It is, of course, no part of the responsibility of this court to determine whether the RAM model represents the best possible approach to determining standards or the control of sulfur dioxide emissions. Our standard of review of the actions of United States EPA is whether or not the action of the agency is "arbitrary, capricious, an abuse of discretion, or otherwise not in accordance with law." Thus, we are required to affirm if there is a rational basis for the agency

---

22. An area source is a small source of emissions that is not a large industrial facility. Examples include dry cleaning establishments, gasoline stations, wood-burning stoves and, most relevant in this case, small combustion units.

action and we are not "empowered to substitute [our] judgment for that of the agency." Citizens to Preserve Overton Park v. Volpe, 401 U.S. 402 (1971).

Our review of this record convinces us that we cannot properly hold that United States EPA's adoption of the RAM model for predicting sulfur dioxide emissions and for fixing maximum levels of sulfur dioxide emissions by specific sources was arbitrary and capricious or beyond the agency's authority under the Clean Air Act. The factors cited below support EPA's argument that the RAM model is supported by sufficient evidence so that EPA's adoption cannot be held arbitrary and capricious:

(1) United States EPA's use of the "rollback" model — the principal basis of its first plan on which five days of public hearings were conducted in Ohio — was strenuously objected to by representatives of many of the present petitioners because it was not source-specific and, as a consequence, tended to require more stringent sulfur dioxide controls than would be required if plant capacity, fuel, population, smokestack height, wind and climate were all taken into account. Thus John R. Martin, of Smith & Singer Meteorologists, Inc., commented on behalf of Ohio utilities on the first United States EPA plan as follows:

> More sophisticated modeling is necessary in all seven of the urban counties that use the proportional rollback. In this way, the federal air quality standards can be attained without unnecessary SO_2 emission restrictions being imposed upon sources that do not contribute to SO_2 problem.... We recommended that new strategies be tested which will more fairly identify and control SO_2 sources that create SO_2 problems.

Similarly, Dr. Howard M. Ellis, of Enviroplan, Inc., said on behalf of Ohio power plants:

> In developing an SO_2 control program for this plant, Region V did not consider economically efficient alternatives to constant uniform emission standards — alternatives such as utilizing a supplementary control system to achieve air quality standards or using separate SO_2 emission standards by stack in accordance with each stack's contribution to ground-level SO_2 concentrations. Separate emission standards by stack can reduce considerably the cost of achieving air quality standards.

(2) EPA responded to these arguments favorably by devising and adopting the RAM model which did employ all of these source-specific factors.

(3) Further, as shown on [charts that are not reprinted here], the United States EPA 1976-1977 SO_2 control plan (principally based upon the RAM and MAX-24 models) shows less stringent regulation on a county-by-county basis when compared to the Ohio SO_2 control plans originally promulgated in 1972 and 1974. In addition, when the comparison is limited to petitioners involved in this litigation, but including all of their facilities which were subjected to RAM modeling (and which are identified in this record), we find the plan slightly less strict than the Ohio 1974 plan by a count of 23 to 20.

These comparisons do not, of course, necessarily demonstrate RAM's accuracy. Rather, the comparison with Ohio's previous plans (based upon the earlier rollback model which was used and accepted nationwide) tends simply to show that the choice of RAM modeling lay within administrative discretion.

(4) While this court has currently before it some 32 petitioners protesting the United States EPA's plan for SO_2 emission control for Ohio, it must be remembered that Ohio is estimated to have over 1,000 point sources and over 2,000 area sources of SO_2 pollution.

(5) The RAM model is a general formula which can be applied to many individual sources of pollution to derive specific estimates of SO_2 emission rates for each. It employs a wider, more complete and more accurate data base than any prior model yet employed in devising a sulfur dioxide control strategy for a state or county. The crucial data with which the RAM model starts

are the design capacity figure, plus the fuel sulfur content, from which is computed the SO_2 emission rate for each of the heating or power plants sought to be controlled. Thus at the outset the RAM model starts with ascertainable specific figures for each source where disputes can be resolved by inspection of the equipment or fuel concerned. Many of the additional components such as stack height, wind direction, physical relationship of sources to each other, and topography of the area are similarly ascertainable as matters of fact. With the enormous financial stakes involved in this litigation, every effort to avoid disputes about the accuracy of the data base should be made. This record shows that United States EPA's design of the RAM model was brought about at least in large part by Ohio industry's requests for greater specificity and hence lower costs of compliance with National Air Quality Standards.

(6) While there may yet be developed (and hopefully will be) a better method of establishing a control strategy for sulfur dioxide emissions than the RAM model, no one has yet come forward with such....

(7) We recognize that this record does not present positive proofs of the accuracy of RAM's predictions. Thus far technology has not developed foolproof methods for validating predictions concerning pollution of the ambient air absent years of collection of monitoring data with far more monitors and far more personnel than have thus far been available....

[The court here compared predicted and actual monitor readings for a small number of monitoring sites in Dayton, Ohio:]

SITE NO.	2D HIGHSET 24-HR RAM-PREDICTED CONCENTRATION IN UG PER M/3	1972	1973	1974	1975	1976
1	195	*	*	219	*	*
2	201	73	438	181	163	81
3	83	*	*	117	62	57
4	109	*	*	151	109	17
5	161	57	198	*	68	41
6	207	*	13	66	110	73

Our analysis of these data shows that the yearly second-highest concentration of SO_2 pollution (for a 24-hour average) actually recorded on available monitors exceeded the RAM model prediction for each location once in a five-year period at five out of six locations. This analysis certainly falls short of showing RAM's predictive perfection. But it certainly tends to show that the EPA's use of RAM, if conservative, cannot be held to be arbitrary and capricious.

(8) Finally, as we pointed out at the beginning of this opinion, SO_2 emissions have a direct impact upon the health and the lives of the population of Ohio — particularly its young people, its sick people, and its old people. If the RAM model did overpredict emission rates, such a conservative approach in protection of health and life was apparently contemplated by Congress in requiring that EPA plans contain "emission limitations...necessary to *insure* attainment and maintenance" of national ambient air standards. 42 U.S.C. §1857c-5(a)(2)(B) (1970). (Emphasis added.)

In sum...the record indicates that the Administrator's control regulations for Ohio through use of the RAM model was a rational choice which was well within the discretion committed to him and his agency. We decline petitioners' requests to set the disputed orders aside on the ground that they are arbitrary and capricious....

COMMENTARY & QUESTIONS

1. **Technical complexity and the competence of courts.** Does a case like *Cleveland Electric* prove that the technical complexity of airshed modeling is so great that a judicial forum is inappropriate? Should there instead be a technological decisionmaking body? For years, various regulatory observers have intermittently promoted the development of a "science court." Under current practice, the abuse of discretion standard of review provides a significant safeguard that matters of technical expertise will be decided by an expert decisionmaker, subject only to review that no gross misjudgments have been made. Is there any indication that the court is overmatched by the technical matters involved in this case? Is there any reason to believe that a specialized court would do a better job with the science than EPA?

2. **How far does deference go?** How much stronger would the petitioners' case have been if the chart correlating RAM-predicted pollution concentrations had exceeded actual observed results in every year at every monitoring station? At some degree of error, model failure becomes equivalent to model irrationality. In Ohio v. EPA, 784 F.2d 224, 230 (6th Cir. 1986), in an unusually unforgiving moment, the court held an EPA air quality model to be arbitrary and capricious where EPA had not empirically validated the model for use at the two electric utility sites in question and where the model had made an "unimpressive showing" in validation studies regarding other sites.

Air quality models might also err in their assumptions. In Appalachian Power Co. v. EPA, 249 F.3d 1032, 1053 (D.C. Cir. 2001), the court held that EPA's implicit assumption of "a baseline of negative growth in electricity generation over the course of a decade appear[s] arbitrary, and the EPA can point to nothing in the record to dispel this appearance." EPA's erroneous assumption was embodied in a model used to allocate pollution reduction obligations in EPA's massive NOx SIP call and is discussed later in this chapter.

3. **Advice to modelers and agencies.** In Legal Aspects of the Regulatory Use of Environmental Modeling, 33 Envtl. L. Rep. 10751 (2003), Thomas O. McGarity and Wendy E. Wagner provide a comprehensive analysis of EPA's modeling exercises and their reception in the courts. Based on these authors' research, they offer three pieces of advice for agencies anxious to defend their models in court: (1) "An ounce of ex ante explanation is worth a pound of post-hoc rationalization." (2) "If the model doesn't fit, don't wear it." (3) "Reality usually trumps a model's representation of reality." Id. at 10771.

4. **Where's the margin of safety?** The court observes that the RAM model underestimated 24-hour SO_2 concentrations at five out of six locations over a five-year period. In all other cases, the RAM model *over*estimated SO_2 concentrations. The court calls the model "conservative," presumably because the model tends, if anything, to predict worse pollution — and thus to support more stringent pollution controls — than will actually occur. But couldn't an environmental group challenge the RAM model on the ground that it is not conservative enough? As noted, the model did underestimate emissions in a substantial number of cases (which would lead, in practice, to undercontrolling pollution sources). Moreover, in one case, actual emissions even exceeded the

SO_2 standard itself. (See 1973 concentration at site 2 — at 438 ug per m/3, the site's SO_2 concentrations exceeded the NAAQS of 365 ug per m/3.) Do these observations help to justify the court's deferential attitude?

5. **Amending the emissions limitations later.** If post-implementation monitor readings demonstrate that the RAM over-predicted pollution levels by a significant degree, assume that EPA is willing to adjust the RAM model to make its predictive capacity more accurate and to revise upward allowable emissions from many of the regulated polluters. Is that a satisfactory method of proceeding? Why will the regulated petitioners claim that is an inadequate remedy? What becomes of their investment in pollution control equipment that is no longer necessary or their lost profits due to higher operating costs in the interim? The amount of "overinvestment" in pollution control might be significant. The opinion pointed out that large sums of money were involved in meeting the EPA-imposed limitations. As a general rule, the cost of emissions reduction is not a linear function. The first few units of reduction are usually inexpensive to achieve, but additional improvements are ever more expensive. Is Ohio harmed in the same way? In the interim, its citizens have enjoyed cleaner air and, if it elects to continue emissions controls at their existing levels of stringency on the polluters, it is in a position to introduce new sources of emissions without forcing new cutbacks by the current polluters.

6. **Overriding state sovereignty and state resentment of federally imposed plans.** The court's opinion is sharply critical of Ohio's foot-dragging in implementing SO_2 standards. In the absence of the federal mandate provided by §110, is it likely that the court's attitude would have been the same? Can Ohio fairly claim that the federal act has usurped too much of its traditional power to control local matters? *Cleveland Electric* offers an indication of why states feel threatened by FIPs. Due to the economic burdens to be placed on Ohio industries (especially its coal mining and electric generating industries), Ohio seems opposed to any SO_2 control without regard to whose plan it is. That degree of opposition may be aberrational. The usual state fear of EPA-imposed plans is that EPA might impose the burdens of pollution control in ways that are politically unpopular. For example, EPA has frequently tried to insist that SIPs include regional transportation plans that discourage the use of automobiles by commuters or that reduce emissions by the vehicles that are in service. Requirements for carpool lanes, increased spending on mass transit, and mandatory motor vehicle emissions testing and maintenance are all tools in this approach. These programs have proven very unpopular, and their imposition, even though ordered by EPA, has sometimes been the death knell of local political careers. There is a kindred fear that EPA may seek reductions in a way that is insensitive to the needs and ability to pay of local polluting firms.

7. **Using tall stacks and intermittent controls to meet NAAQS requirements.** In an effort to limit their costs of compliance with the SIP that would eventually emerge, the Ohio utilities were urging Ohio to allow the use of tall smokestacks and intermittent pollution control devices as part of the older (pre-1977) versions of the Ohio SIP. Tall stacks are among the least-cost solutions to meeting ambient air quality standards. They operate in two ways to help attain or maintain NAAQS compliance. First, they lead

to wider dispersion of the pollutants they emit, which means that the concentrations of the pollutant are lower than they would be in areas near the emitting facility if shorter stacks were employed. In effect, the use of taller stack leads to more diluted emissions that cover a wider geographic area. Second, the use of tall stacks makes possible the export of pollution beyond the boundary of the state, turning the pollution into some-one else's problem. Tall stacks are also less expensive than state-of-the-art pollution control technology, which reduces emissions rather than dispersing them more widely. As a result, "utility companies in the 1970s responded to increasingly stringent control of local air pollution by building tall stacks that could project pollution plumes into the upper atmosphere, sending the pollution long distances. More than 175 stacks higher than 500 feet were constructed after enactment of the 1970 Act. This practice was terminated by §123 of the 1977 Amendments, but not before utility companies had constructed the 111 'big dirties' that are the primary sources of acid rain in the eastern United States." R. Percival et al., Environmental Regulation: Law, Science, and Policy 541 (4th ed. 2003).

Intermittent controls are also a lower cost method of meeting the national standards because they are less expensive than comparable continuous controls. Intermittent controls are employed when receiving body air quality is at or near the allowable NAAQS; these controls are not used when receiving body conditions are favorable, i.e., when there is a low concentration of pollutants in the receiving ambient air. A very simple example of an intermittent control would be a plan that called for turning off an electrostatic precipitator that traps emissions in the stack when the local air is clean. The savings to the firm of this practice result from reduced operating and maintenance costs (because large energy costs are avoided during periods when the precipitator is not needed and the device itself will require less maintenance if it is used less often) and reduced capital costs (because the useful life of the device will be extended). An even more dramatic form of intermittent control is to cease production when receiving body conditions are unfavorable and operate with no controls when receiving body condi-tions permit. Using intermittent controls as opposed to continuous controls results in an increase in total emissions by allowing greater emissions when conditions permit.

What is objectionable about SIPs that rely on tall stacks and intermittent controls to meet the NAAQS? The export of pollution (externalizing the cost) to another state is obviously antithetical to notions of equity and responsibility for one's own deeds. The devices embedded in the CAA to deter export of pollution are discussed below. A second objection to tall stacks and intermittent controls turns on the fact that they increase the aggregate amount of pollution that can be emitted without violating the NAAQS. Is that bad? If the NAAQSs are set at levels that are sufficiently protective of health, welfare, and the environment, the criticism loses part of its force. A final objec-tion to tall stacks is that the long-range transport of air pollutants leads to their transformation into even more harmful substances; SO_2 and NOx, for example, become very fine particles of sulfates and nitrates and acids. Fine particulates are the most lethal kinds of PM because they can lodge deep in the lungs, and the acids formed by long-range pollution transport reach our forests, lakes, and streams in the form of acid deposition. In these ways, the tall stacks built to deal with one kind of pollution problem under the 1970 Act (local effects of criteria air pollutants) created a whole new kind of pollution problem future Congresses were forced to confront.[23]

The CAA Amendments of 1977 specifically addressed tall stacks and intermittent controls and limited their attractiveness as control devices. Section 123 explicitly allows firms to increase stack heights and to employ "other dispersion technique[s]" (defined to include intermittent controls), but the degree of emission control attributable to the excessive height of the stack or the use of dispersion techniques does not count toward meeting emission control limitations set by the relevant SIP. For a discussion of this provision and the motivation of Congress in passing it, see Sierra Club v. EPA, 719 F.2d 436, 440–441 (D.C. Cir. 1983). The arguments for limiting dispersion centered on export and the unreliability and lack of enforceability of intermittent controls.

Section 3. TRANSLATING STATUTORY OBLIGATIONS INTO PERMITS

Permits are a recurrent fact of life in studying environmental regulation. They have already figured prominently in cases and case studies such as *Wilsonville* and the *Utilex* saga. Permits are critically important in the next chapter's study of the CWA and in numerous places throughout the materials on regulation and enforcement. It is therefore appropriate and worthwhile to isolate permits here for brief treatment. In the 1990 CAA Amendments, Congress added an entire Title V devoted to permits. That section is closely modeled on the National Pollution Discharge Elimination System (NPDES) permits of the CWA. In describing NPDES, the U.S. Supreme Court outlined the function of all permits to discharge waste materials into the environment:

> Under NPDES, it is unlawful for any person to discharge a pollutant without obtaining a permit and complying with its terms. A NPDES permit serves to transform generally applicable effluent limitations and other standards — including those based on water quality — into the obligations (including a timetable for compliance) of the individual discharger, and the [CWA] provide[s] for direct administrative and judicial enforcement of permits. With few exceptions, for enforcement purposes a discharger in compliance with the terms and conditions of an NPDES permit is deemed to be in compliance with those sections of the [statute] on which permit conditions are based. In short, the permit defines, and facilitates compliance with and enforcement of, a preponderance of a discharger's obligations under the [statute]. EPA v. California, 426 U.S. 200, 205 (1976).

The individual permit process begins with an application in which the applicant gives the permitting authority basic information. For example, the information presented by an air permit applicant includes such things as the product manufactured, the raw materials, the fuels used, the manufacturing process utilized, the locations of stacks, the predicted contents of air emissions, the type and effectiveness of current or planned air pollution control devices, information on current plant equipment, and details of the applicant's current monitoring regime. Once a permit application is complete, the permitting authority must decide whether to deny the permit or to prepare a draft permit. A draft permit must be accompanied by a fact sheet and a public

---

23. Initially, EPA Administrator William Ruckelshaus approved of tall stacks as a way for states to meet their SIP obligations, but his position was rejected by the courts. NRDC v. EPA, 489 F.2d 390 (5th Cir. 1974).

notice that specifies how comments can be made and how a public hearing can be obtained if there is sufficient public interest. If a state is the permitting authority, the draft permit must be sent to EPA for comments or potential veto. Once a decision is made to issue a permit, the permitting agency must issue a final written decision that responds to comments. Interested persons who have filed comments may take an administrative appeal if they are dissatisfied with the terms of the final permit. Unlike the public hearing, this administrative hearing is "on the record"; that is, limited cross-examination is permitted and a formal record of the proceedings is kept. Further appeals may be taken to the head of the relevant permitting agency and to state or federal courts, depending on whether the permitting authority is EPA or a state.

Environmental waste discharge permits contain three major sections: (1) discharge standards, (2) compliance schedules, and (3) monitoring and reporting requirements.

- Discharge standards are detailed, quantified descriptions of allowable emissions.

- Compliance schedules set interim requirements to assure that the ultimate compliance date is met. Each interim step is independently enforceable. Interim requirements may include retaining a consultant, contracting for installation of equipment, installing equipment on schedule, and attaining interim standards.

- Self-monitoring and reporting requirements are the key aspects of enforcing environmental discharge permits. A permittee is required to monitor its releases with the monitoring technology and at the frequencies set out in the permit. All violations of permit standards (called "excursions" or "exceedances") must immediately be reported to the permitting authority. A permittee must also submit periodic reports, signed under oath by a senior plant official, to the permitting authority. These reports must contain all monitoring and sampling data and must include a list of excursions. Monitoring data is public information and cannot be retained as trade secrets. False or inadequate reporting exposes responsible corporate officials to potential criminal enforcement.

Permits may also contain clauses relating to "variances" or "planning." For example, air or water discharge permits frequently include variances or exceptions for "upsets" (temporary noncompliance because of factors beyond the control of the permittee, such as an unpredictable catastrophic storm) or "bypasses" (e.g., shutting down pollution control equipment for unanticipated repairs). A water permit might allow excursions due to intake water variations (permittees are responsible only for pollutants that they add to intake water). Planning requirements may include written preparations for dealing with accidental spills of pollutants at the plant.

With regard to the permittee, a permit operates as both a sword and a shield. Because a permittee is required to monitor in accordance with permit conditions and report its own permit violations, the permit is a sharp sword in the hands of the permitting authority in an enforcement proceeding or a member of the public bringing a citizen suit. There are virtually no defenses — except for the variances included in the permit — to permit enforcement actions based on the permittee's self-monitoring and excursion reports. These will be treated as records kept by the permittee in the ordinary course of business, and can support a grant of summary judgment in the liability phase of a typical enforcement action. On the other hand, the permit can be used to shield the permittee from enforcement of alleged obligations that are not included in the permit.

For example, if in its permit application an applicant for a water discharger permit accurately discloses all of its wastewater discharges, and the permitting authority does not see fit to include discharge standards for one of these substances in the permit, then no enforcement action can be brought against the permittee based upon an alleged unpermitted discharge of that substance. See Atlantic States Legal Found. v. Eastman Kodak, excerpted in Chapter 12.

Permits are issued for periods of time set by statute. For example, CWA discharge permits are issued for a maximum of five years. Before a permit expires, the permittee must apply for renewal, specifying whether any changes in production or wastewater discharge have occurred since the original permit application was filed. The old permit remains in effect until the renewal is granted. Once a new permit is issued, a discharger is bound by its terms, even if the discharger is contesting these conditions in the permitting agency or in court. Permits may be modified or revoked and reissued during the permit period. Common grounds for modification or revocation and reissuance are alterations to permitted facilities, new information, supervening federal regulations (this is generally contained in a permit's so-called reopener clause), unforeseen events, or procurement of a variance. Permits may also be terminated before the expiration date because of nondisclosure or noncompliance.

COMMENTARY & QUESTIONS

1. **Does more formal permitting make the system work better?** Operationally, is a more formal permit system likely to help or hinder the effectiveness of a pollution control system? Cumbersome and confusing processes and shifting demands for information as part of the application process will grind its gears.

2. **Using permits as enforcement mechanisms.** Using lessons learned from the CWA, Title V of the CAA employs the permit process as the key to enforcement. Before the passage of Title V, enforcing the CAA was difficult. The idea is really quite simple: Establish specific emission limits in the permit, require monitoring in the permit, require reporting of the monitoring, and then allow both agency and citizen lawsuits that rely on the comparison of the reports to the permitted limits. See Buente, Citizen Suits and the Clean Air Act Amendments of 1990: Closing the Enforcement Loop, 21 Envtl. L. 2233 (1991).

3. **Blurring the nice distinctions: the CAM rules.** Do not take too seriously the boundaries of categorization used to describe permits, such as distinguishing "compliance" from "monitoring." Administratively, EPA is actively attempting to meld them. For example, a significant innovation under CAA Title V is the Compliance Assurance Monitoring (CAM) rule. First published on August 13, 1996, the CAM rule replaced a proposed "enhanced-monitoring rule." The functionality of the proposed CAM rule was described as follows:

> In contrast to the proposed enhanced-monitoring rule, which was designed to use monitoring as a method for directly determining continuous compliance with applicable requirements, the CAM rule takes the indirect approach of considering the operation of emission-control measures at a facility. These control measures include air-pollution control devices, process modifications, and operating

limitations. The CAM rule essentially requires a facility that employs control measures: to evaluate and document that the control measures are continuously operating within specific performance ranges that have been designed to assure compliance with applicable requirements; to indicate any excursions from these ranges; and to adequately respond to the data so that the excursions are corrected. Van Cleve & Hamilton, Promise and Reality in the Enforcement of the Amended Clean Air Act Part I: EPA's "Any Credible Evidence" and "Compliance Assurance Monitoring" Rules, 27 Envtl. L. Rep. 10097, 10110 (1997).

Section 4. **WHICH SOURCES MAY BE PERMITTED, UNDER WHAT CONDITIONS?**

The specific requirements that must be embodied in permits for pollution sources depend on the attainment status of the area in which the source is or will be located. Requirements are stricter, not surprisingly, for sources in nonattainment areas.

Under the 1977 Amendments, and still more emphatically after the 1990 Amendments, new major sources in nonattainment areas not only must avoid increasing pollution, their introduction of new emissions must be accompanied by more than offsetting reductions in existing emissions from other sources. Historically, as the following case demonstrates, the means for calculating offsets at times can frustrate the spirit of the nonattainment provisions.

Citizens Against the Refinery's Effects (CARE) v.
U.S. Environmental Protection Agency
United States Court of Appeals for the Fourth Circuit, 1981
643 F.2d 183

[A permit to operate a new major pollution source can be granted only if "by the time the source is to commence operation, sufficient offsetting emissions reductions have been obtained, such that total allowable emissions from existing sources in the region, from new or modified sources which are not major emitting facilities, and from the proposed source will be sufficiently less than total emissions from existing sources...prior to the application...so as to represent...reasonable further progress [toward attainment of required air standards]." CAA §173(a)(1)(A).]

HALL, J.... Citizens Against the Refinery's Effects (CARE) appeals from a final ruling by the Administrator of the Environmental Protection Agency (EPA) approving the Virginia State Implementation Plan (SIP) for reducing hydrocarbon pollutants. The plan requires the Virginia Highway Department to decrease usage of a certain type of asphalt, thereby reducing hydrocarbon pollution by more than enough to offset expected pollution from the Hampton Roads Energy Company's (HREC) proposed refinery. We affirm the action of the administrator in approving the state plan....

[Before the 1977 Amendments] the Clean Air Act created a no-growth environment in areas where the clean air requirements had not been attained. EPA recognized the need to develop a program that encouraged attainment of clean air standards without discouraging economic growth. Thus the agency proposed an Interpretive Ruling in 1976 which allowed the states to develop an "offset program" within the State Implementation Plans. 41 Fed. Reg. 55524 (1976). The offset program, later codified by Congress in the 1977 Amendments to the Clean Air Act, permits the states to develop plans which allow construction of new pollution sources where accompanied by a corresponding reduction in an existing pollution source. 42 U.S.C.

§7502(b)(6) and §7503.[24] In effect, a new emitting facility can be built if an existing pollution source decreases its emissions or ceases operations as long as a positive net air quality benefit occurs.

If the proposed factory will emit carbon monoxide, sulfur dioxide, or particulates, the EPA requires that the offsetting pollution source be within the immediate vicinity of the new plant. The other two pollutants, hydrocarbons and nitrogen oxide, are less "site-specific," and thus the ruling permits the offsetting source to locate anywhere within a broad vicinity of the new source.

The offset program has two other important requirements. First, a base time period must be determined in which to calculate how much reduction is needed in existing pollutants to offset the new source. This base period is defined as the first year of the SIP or, where the state has not yet developed a SIP, as the year in which a construction permit application is filed. Second, the offset program requires that the new source adopt the Lowest Achievable Emissions Rate (LAER) using the most modern technology available in the industry.

HREC proposes to build a petroleum refinery and off-loading facility in Portsmouth, Virginia. Portsmouth has been unable to reduce air pollution enough to attain the national standard for one pollutant, photochemical oxidants, which is created when hydrocarbons are released into the atmosphere and react with other substances. Since a refinery is a major source of hydrocarbons, the Clean Air Act prevents construction of the HREC plant until the area attains the national standard.

In 1975, HREC applied to the Virginia State Air Pollution Control Board (VSAPCB) for a refinery construction permit. The permit was issued by the VSAPCB on October 8, 1975, extended and reissued on October 5, 1977 after a full public hearing, modified on August 8, 1978, and extended again on September 27, 1979. The VSAPCB, in an effort to help HREC meet the clean air requirements, proposed to use the offset ruling to comply with the Clean Air Act.

On November 28, 1977, the VSAPCB submitted a State Implementation Plan to EPA which included the HREC permit. The Virginia Board proposed to offset the new HREC hydrocarbon pollution by reducing the amount of cutback asphalt[25] used for road paving operations in three highway districts by the Virginia Department of Highways.[26] By switching from "cutback" to "emulsified" asphalt, the state can reduce hydrocarbon pollutants by the amount necessary to offset the pollutants from the proposed refinery.... [The plan was eventually approved by EPA.]

CARE raises four issues regarding the state plan. First, they argue that the geographic area used as the base for the offset was arbitrarily determined and that the area as defined violates the regulations. Second, CARE contends that EPA should have used 1975 instead of 1977 as the base year to compare usage of cutback asphalt. Third, CARE insists that the offset plan should have been disapproved since the state is voluntarily reducing usage of cutback asphalt anyway. Fourth, CARE questions the approval of the plan without definite Lowest Achievable Emissions Rates (LAER) as required by the statute. We reject the CARE challenges to the state plan....

CARE contends that the state plan should not have been approved by EPA since the three highway-district area where cutback usage will be reduced to offset refinery emissions was artificially developed by the state. The ruling permits a broad area (usually within one AQCR) to be used as the offset basis....

The agency action in approving the use of three highway districts was neither arbitrary, capricious, nor outside the statute. First, Congress intended that the states and the EPA be given

---

24. After the 1990 Amendments, §§172(b)(4) and 173(a)(1) & (c) are the relevant provisions. [Eds.]

25. "Cutback" asphalt has a petroleum base which gives off great amounts of hydrocarbons. "Emulsified" asphalt uses a water base which evaporates, giving off no hydrocarbons.

26. The three highway districts so designated comprise almost the entire eastern one-third of the state. The area cuts across four of the seven Virginia Air Quality Control Regions (AQCR).

flexibility in designing and implementing SIPs. Such flexibility allows the states to make reasoned choices as to which areas may be used to offset new pollution and how the plan is to be implemented. Second, the offset program was initiated to encourage economic growth in the state. Thus a state plan designed to reduce highway department pollution in order to attract another industry is a reasonable contribution to economic growth without a corresponding increase in pollution. Third, to be sensibly administered the offset plan had to be divided into districts which could be monitored by the highway department. Use of any areas other than highway districts would be unwieldy and difficult to administer. Fourth, the scientific understanding of ozone pollution is not advanced to the point where exact air transport may be predicted. Designation of the broad area in which hydrocarbons may be transported is well within the discretion and expertise of the agency.

Asphalt consumption varies greatly from year to year, depending upon weather and road conditions. Yet EPA must accurately determine the volume of hydrocarbon emissions from cutback asphalt. Only then can the agency determine whether the reduction in cutback usage will result in an offset great enough to account for the new refinery pollution. To calculate consumption of a material where it constantly varies, a base year must be selected. In this case, EPA's Interpretive Ruling establishes the base year as the year in which the permit application is made. EPA decided that 1977 was an acceptable base year. CARE argues that EPA illegally chose 1977 instead of 1975.

Considering all of the circumstances, including the unusually high asphalt consumption in 1977, the selection by EPA of that as the base year was within the discretion of the agency. Since the EPA Interpretive Ruling allowing the offset was not issued until 1976, 1977 was the first year after the offset ruling and the logical base year in which to calculate the offset. Also, the permit issued by the VSAPCB was reissued in 1977 with extensive additions and revisions after a full hearing. Under these circumstances 1977 appears to be a logical choice of a base year.

For several years Virginia has pursued a policy of shifting from cutback asphalt to the less expensive emulsified asphalt in road-paving operations. The policy was initiated in an effort to save money, and was totally unrelated to a State Implementation Plan. Because of this policy CARE argues that hydrocarbon emissions were decreasing independent of this SIP and therefore are not a proper offset against the refinery. They argue that there is not, in effect, an actual reduction in pollution.

The Virginia voluntary plan is not enforceable and therefore is not in compliance with the 1976 Interpretive Ruling which requires that the offset program be enforceable. The EPA, in approving the state plan, obtained a letter from the Deputy Attorney General of Virginia in which he stated that the requisites had been satisfied for establishing and enforcing the plan with the Department of Highways. Without such authority, no decrease in asphalt-produced pollution is guaranteed. In contrast to the voluntary plan, the offset plan guarantees a reduction in pollution resulting from road paving operations....

In approving the state plan EPA thoroughly examined the data, requested changes in the plan, and approved the plan only after the changes were made. There is no indication that the agency acted in an arbitrary or capricious manner or that it stepped beyond the bounds of the Clean Air Act. We affirm the decision of the administrator in approving the state plan.

COMMENTARY & QUESTIONS

1. **Insisting on "reasonable further progress."** Was EPA too permissive with Virginia in this case, so permissive that it violated the statutory "reasonable further progress" requirement? Couldn't EPA have gotten both the switch to the less polluting asphalt

plus additional offsets if it had taken a more aggressive stance regarding what is reasonable progress for Virginia under the circumstances?

2. **Reasonably Available Control Measures (RACM) requirements.** CAA §172(c)(1) requires that nonattainment SIPs apply RACM[27] to all sources in nonattainment areas as expeditiously as possible. Plainly that language authorizes EPA to refuse to approve SIPs or SIP revisions for nonattainment areas when those plans do not include RACT or RACM. For example, in Navistar Int'l Transp. Co. v. EPA, 941 F.2d 1339 (6th Cir. 1991), EPA disapproved a proposed Ohio nonattainment volatile organic compound (VOC) SIP revision that would have relaxed VOC emission requirements at a truck manufacturer's plant. One ground EPA advanced (and the court approved) in support of its decision was that the relaxation would violate the requirement of implementing RACT as expeditiously as possible. Note that the *Navistar* case is not inconsistent with *CARE*. In *Navistar*, EPA was claiming that Ohio was seeking to employ less than RACT, while in *CARE*, EPA was supporting Virginia's claim that it was making reasonable further progress. Deferential standards of review allow each decision of the agency to be upheld.

When "weasel words" such as "reasonably available" are conjoined with a deferential standard of review, courts are very unlikely to reverse the agency determination. For example, EPA issued a rule regarding Transportation Control Measures (TCMs). This was a topic that Congress had addressed in the 1990 Amendments by requiring transportation planning and by requiring EPA to provide information on TCMs, which were listed in §108(f). Many of the TCMs in the legislation are nontechnical and site-independent, such as ride sharing, employer programs for flexible commuting, and so on. The old EPA position had been that TCMs were RACMs. In 1992, however, EPA decided that TCMs are not RACMs for all nonattainment areas. 57 Fed. Reg. 13498 (Apr. 16, 1992). That rule was upheld in Ober v. EPA, 84 F.3d 304 (9th Cir. 1996).

3. **Transportation conformity.** Considerably less wiggle room is provided by §176(c) of the Act, which states:

> No department, agency, or instrumentality of the Federal government shall engage in, support in any way or provide financial assistance for, license or permit, or approve, any activity which does not conform to an implementation plan after it has been approved or promulgated under §7410 of this title.... Conformity to an implementation plan means — (A) conformity to an implementation plan's purpose of eliminating or reducing the severity and number of violations of the national ambient air quality standards and achieving expeditious attainment of such standards; and (B) that such activities will not — (i) cause or contribute to any new violation of any standard in any area; (ii) increase the frequency or severity of any existing violation of any standard in any area; or (iii) delay timely attainment of any standard or any required interim emission reductions or other milestones in any area. 42 U.S.C. §7506(c).

The clarity and force of this language has not been lost on courts faced with EPA's efforts to soften §176(c)'s requirements. In Sierra Club v. EPA, 129 F.3d 137 (D.C. Cir.

---

27. RACM by its express language includes RACT when it comes to pollution control devices that might be prescribed for stationary sources.

1997), EPA was held to lack authority to provide a 12-month grace period during which transportation activities in nonattainment areas would be exempt from the transportation conformity requirements of §176(c). Likewise, in Environmental Defense Club v. EPA, 167 F.3d 641 (D.C. Cir. 1999), the court ruled that the EPA regulations applying grandfathering waivers to the CAA's provisions for conformity of federal transportation projects with state SIPs were inconsistent with the CAA.

Perhaps most dramatic is the Ninth Circuit's decision in Public Citizen v. Department of Transportation (DOT), 316 F.3d 1002 (9th Cir. 2003). There, the court faced a challenge to DOT's regulations permitting Mexican-domiciled trucks to operate in the United States beyond the border zones to which they had been previously confined. The regulations came after an arbitral panel had concluded that confining Mexican trucks to the border areas violated NAFTA. Public Citizen challenged DOT's failure to prepare an EIS under NEPA and a conformity determination under the CAA; the court agreed with Public Citizen on both counts. Most important for present purposes, the court held that DOT was required to perform an in-depth analysis of whether allowing Mexican-domiciled trucks beyond the border areas would increase emissions beyond the point allowed by the agency's regulations on transportation conformity. The court told DOT to perform this analysis on a local and regional (not merely national) level. The court also rejected DOT's arguments that rulemaking proceedings were categorically exempt from the requirement to determine transportation conformity. In 2003, the Supreme Court granted certiorari to decide the following question presented by DOT: "Whether a presidential foreign-affairs action that is otherwise exempt from environmental-review requirements under the National Environmental Policy Act, 42 U.S.C. 4321 et seq., and Clean Air Act, 42 U.S.C. 7506(c)(1), became subject to those requirements because an executive agency promulgated administrative rules concerning implementation of the President's action."

4. **Offsets pro and con.** Are offsets a good method of accommodating further development while still seeking improvement of ambient air quality in nonattainment areas? In the absence of state intervention in aid of the new source, either like that given in the *CARE* case or in the form of placing tighter controls on existing sources, which emissions reductions will be realized first? Presumably, the operator of the new source will have to purchase the retirement of pollution sources. The least expensive retirements will involve taking marginally profitable enterprises out of production or paying for pollution control improvements at those sites where the least expenditure produces the greatest reduction. To the extent that practice mirrors the prediction of theory, offsets obtain the apparently optimal result of reducing pollution at the lowest possible cost. Are there social costs that are overlooked in that assessment? What about the dislocation of workers who lose their jobs when the marginal firms are bought out and closed? It is arguable that, for many of them, their firm's survival was unlikely in any event. ("Bubbles," a technique related to offsets whereby all emitting sources at a single facility are treated as a single point source for the purpose of regulation, are discussed in Chapter 14.)

5. **NSPS as a "protection" of nonattainment area economic growth potential.** Congress clearly recognized as a national concern the hardship that would be imposed on dirty

air areas if they were subjected to a total ban on initiating new industrial activity. To allow those areas to compete for industrial growth and development, as demonstrated in the *CARE* case, the nonattainment area provisions allow new sources to obtain permits so long as they employ LAER (the most demanding technology-based standard) and obtain offsets so that "reasonable further progress" toward attainment is maintained. At the same time as it made the location of major new sources in nonattainment areas possible, Congress took steps that lessened the comparative attractiveness of locating a major emitting facility in a clean air area. Congress imposed technology-based standards for pollution controls on all new major emitting sources, wherever they are located, through the NSPS requirements. (In addition, the PSD program shortens the race of laxity by limiting the ability of clean air areas to relax pollution controls as an inducement to new firms to locate there.)

The NSPS program is mandated by §111 of the Act, 42 U.S.C. §7411. In general, the NSPS provisions require that all new or modified emitting sources employ the Best Adequately Demonstrated Pollution Control Technology (BADT) for their type of facility. This standard is defined in the Act and commands EPA to take "into consideration the cost of achieving such emission reduction." By requiring a uniform technology-based performance standard to be employed nationwide, the potential for a race of laxity in permitting new sources is greatly reduced, although not entirely eliminated. Major new sources that emit more than a specified tonnage of pollutants are regulated even more tightly, using technology-based standards. In PSD areas, major new emitting sources must employ the Best Available Control Technology (BACT) (42 U.S.C. §7475(a)(4)).

6. **New Source Review.** As applied to new facilities, the NSR program is closely related to the NSPS program. NSR requirements apply (with differing details) in both attainment and PSD areas. The basic idea is to require BACT for new major sources of air pollution. NSR also applies, however, to existing sources of pollution when they are modified in such a way as to increase their emissions above a certain, statutorily defined limit. When the NSR program was created, Congress chose to grandfather existing plants — not to require them to install BACT immediately — but also to require them to come "up to code" when they undertook significant physical modifications. The application of technology-based requirements to existing sources of pollution has stirred the greatest amount of controversy.

As applied to existing facilities, the NSR program was intended to ensure modernization of pollution control at existing industrial facilities by requiring that modifications of those plants meet the same technology-based standard as the construction of new plants. The premise was that old plants, usually the dirtiest and most polluting, were also likely to be the least efficient and would either be retired or upgraded. NSR kicks in either way to oversee the construction of new facilities or major modifications to existing ones. Theory and practice have not completely coincided. The NSR process is so costly and time-consuming that industry charged that it deterred change of practice, thereby encouraging firms to continue to utilize the worst polluting plants. Similarly, the cleavage between NSR and non-NSR events is of sufficient economic significance to the regulated entities that a cottage industry within the CAA has sprung up on how to change operations at a facility without triggering NSR review. The EPA regulations that long defined when a plant modification triggered NSR review were frequently evaded by various stratagems on the part of industry. Also, the practice of "netting" (see Chapter 14) grew up as a frequent means of avoiding NSR.

Shortly after coming into office, the Bush II Administration made NSR reform a top regulatory priority, as announced in the energy policy developed by Vice President Cheney's task force on energy.[28] OMB likewise made NSR reform a priority by placing the NSR program on an infamous industry-suggested "hit list" of regulations. The expected reforms came in two phases, in late 2002 and mid-2003. The combined reforms ranged from quite arcane adjustments to the rules for determining emissions baselines to a new definition of routine repair and maintenance that would exempt a source from complying with NSR requirements so long as modifications to the source do not cost more than 20% of the total cost of the facility. Few physical modifications of existing plants exceed this threshold. EPA's reforms have been challenged by numerous states and environmental groups.

EPA's reforms to the NSR program came just as the program was beginning to bear fruit in terms of substantial emissions reductions. In 1999, the Justice Department, on behalf of EPA, had brought suits against seven utilities and the Tennessee Valley Authority (TVA) for violating the CAA. EPA alleged that the utilities made major modifications to 17 power plants without installing BACT as required by the Act. The defendants' failure to install the equipment led to the release of massive excess amounts of pollution. Indeed, a 2002 report by Abt Associates, Inc., concluded that pollution emissions from these 17 plants caused between 4800 and 5600 premature deaths in 2001. Abt also estimated that over 3000 hospital admissions or emergency room visits, 930,000 lost work days, 111,000 asthma attacks, and other health effects were associated with these emissions. As cases began to settle, the Bush II Administration announced its intention to reform the NSR program. Needless to say, the announcement put a damper on companies' enthusiasm for settling these cases.

Meanwhile, in the cases that had already reached a judicial forum by the time EPA's reforms were announced, the results have been mixed. The Eleventh Circuit, for example, ruled that the quite unusual administrative process used by EPA in a case brought against the TVA violated due process; therefore the agency's administrative compliance order to TVA was not a final agency act, and the court had no jurisdiction to hear the case until after the EPA sued TVA in district court and proved TVA's violations of the law. TVA v. Whitman, 336 F.3d 1236 (11th Cir. 2003). In a case alleging NSR violations at power plants owned by Ohio Edison, on the other hand, the district court found that the power company had indeed made major modifications at its facilities without complying with NSR permitting requirements. While criticizing EPA for its failure to enforce NSR requirements for years prior to the initiation of this lawsuit, the court nevertheless rejected the company's arguments that the agency had changed its views

---

28. The Vice President's efforts to keep the details of the task force's proceedings secret have led to several lawsuits, one of which was taken up by the Supreme Court in its 2003-2004 Term. In re Cheney, 334 F.3d 1096 (D.C. Cir. 2003), cert. granted, Cheney v. U.S. District Court, 72 U.S.L.W. 3406 (U.S. Dec. 15, 2003).

about the meaning of the CAA and that the agency's enforcement about-face deprived the company of fair notice of the CAA's requirements. See United States v. Ohio Edison, 276 F. Supp. 2d 829 (S.D. Ohio 2003).

7. A mandatory retirement age for grandfathers? In a 2003 report commissioned by Congress, an expert panel convened by the National Academy of Public Administration (NAPA) came to the following conclusions:

> The complicated NSR program has been effective in controlling air pollution from newly built industrial facilities and utilities, but it has performed poorly in reducing pollution from the nation's oldest and dirtiest factories and power plants. The result is unfair to facilities that have invested in upgrading their equipment to reduce pollution while others have avoided controlling their pollution. NSR's unpredictable and lengthy permitting process is also detrimental to facilities that must change operations quickly to compete effectively. Finally, NSR is not having the positive effect on the health of individuals, or on the quality of the nation's air, that Congress intended....
>
> NSR is fundamentally two programs, both requiring permits for releasing air pollution. The first requires that new major sources be built with modern, cleaner equipment to minimize air pollution. The second requires that similar upgrades be installed when existing plants are modified in ways that may significantly increase their emissions.
>
> The Panel's research indicates that the NSR permitting process works as Congress intended for new industrial facilities. Pre-construction permits for newly built sources have promoted development and installation of cleaner technologies in various industry sectors throughout the country, and those cleaner facilities have helped to protect air quality. The Panel believes the success of the program for new sources is primarily due to two factors: fairly straightforward decisions about whether a proposed new source is covered by NSR; and an early EPA lawsuit to enforce NSR's requirement for pre-construction permits at brand new sources.
>
> But NSR has not been as effective in reducing air pollution when changes at existing sources are likely to increase emissions. Instead — contrary to Congressional intent — many large, highly polluting facilities have continued to operate and have expanded their production (and pollution) over the past 25 years without upgrading to cleaner technologies. This avoidance of NSR requirements has delayed the reduction in emissions that Congress expected to result eventually from the NSR program. The result: thousands of premature human deaths, and many thousand additional cases of acute illnesses and chronic diseases caused by air pollution....
>
> NAPA, A Breath of Fresh Air: Reviving the New Source Review Program (2003), available at http://www.napawash.org.

NAPA's first recommendation for reform was for Congress to "end grandfathering": "Congress should end grandfathering of major sources with high emission levels as soon as possible. Within the next ten years, all major sources that have not obtained an NSR permit since 1977 should upgrade their equipment and lower their emissions to levels that are equivalent to the reductions achieved by the current BACT or LAER performance standards."

Section 5. ADDING ENVIRONMENTAL JUSTICE CONCERNS TO THE PERMIT PROGRAM

Title VI of the Civil Rights Act of 1964[29] prohibits intentional racial discrimination by recipients of federal funds. In 1994, President Clinton issued Executive Order 12,898 (Federal Actions to Address Environmental Justice in Minority Populations and Low-Income Populations)[30] and an accompanying presidential memorandum, which direct federal agencies to ensure that federal actions that substantially affect human health or the environment do not have discriminatory effects based on race, color, or national origin. In 1998, EPA issued an interim guidance designed to provide a structure for the agency's Office of Civil Rights in responding to complaints about environmental permitting filed under Title VI.[31] The reception to the interim guidance was less than enthusiastic. State officials were particularly critical. Michigan's Governor John Engler called the interim guidance "reckless" and "ill-defined" — a "jobkiller," he said.[32] EPA went back to the drawing board and came up with a new draft revised guidance, excerpts of which follow.[33]

U.S. Environmental Protection Agency, Draft Revised Guidance for Investigating Title VI Administrative Complaints Challenging Permits
65 Fed. Reg. 39650 (June 27, 2000)

...The goal of the Civil Rights Act of 1964 is to eliminate discrimination in several areas of American society.... Title VI of the Act, which prohibits discrimination on the basis of race, color, and national origin in all federally-assisted programs and activities, applies to the recipients of an estimated $900 billion in federal assistance distributed annually by approximately 27 federal agencies. When submitting the Civil Rights Act to Congress, President Kennedy stated that "[s]imple justice requires that public funds, to which all taxpayers of all races contribute, not be spent in any fashion, which encourages, entrenches, subsidizes, or results in racial discrimination."[34]

Title VI itself prohibits intentional discrimination. In addition, the Supreme Court has stated that Title VI authorizes agencies to adopt implementing regulations that also prohibit discriminatory effects. This is often referred to as reaching actions that have an unjustified adverse disparate impact. EPA in 1973 promulgated regulations that implement Title VI and revised them in 1984. Under EPA's Title VI implementing regulations, agencies receiving EPA financial assistance are prohibited, among other things, from using "criteria or methods of administering its program which have the effect of subjecting individuals to discrimination because of their race, color, [or] national origin." As applied to the permitting process, recipients of EPA financial assistance may not issue permits that are intentionally discriminatory or have a discriminatory effect based on race, color, or national origin....

---

29. 42 U.S.C. §§2000d–2000d-7 (as amended).

30. Exec. Order No. 12,898, 3 C.F.R. 859 (1994), reprinted at 42 U.S.C. §4321 (note).

31. EPA, Office of Enforcement and Compliance Assurance, Interim Guidance for Investigating Title VI Administrative Complaints Challenging Permits (Feb. 1998), available at http://www.epa.gov/civilrights/docs/interim.pdf.

32. Michigan Governor Blames EPA Policy for Company Decision to Scrap Factory Plan, 29 BNA Env't Rep. 995 (Sept. 18, 1998).

33. The agency also provided a draft revised guidance for recipients of federal funds in the same document, but most attention has focused on the guidance for Title VI investigations.

34. H.R. Doc. No. 124, 88th Cong., 1st Sess. (1963), reprinted in 1963 U.S.C.C.A.N. 1534.

Title VI is inapplicable to EPA actions, including EPA's issuance of permits, because it only applies to the programs and activities of recipients of federal financial assistance, not to federal agencies.[35]... Nonetheless, EPA is committed to a policy of nondiscrimination in its own permitting programs. The equal protection guarantee in the Due Process Clause of the U.S. Constitution prohibits the federal government from engaging in intentional discrimination. Moreover, §2-2 of Executive Order 12898, "Federal Actions To Address Environmental Justice in Minority Populations and Low-Income Populations,"[36] directs federal agencies to ensure, in part, that federal actions substantially affecting human health or the environment do not have discriminatory effects based on race, color, or national origin. Consequently, EPA intends to conduct itself in a manner consistent with EPA's Title VI regulations....

This guidance provides a detailed framework explaining how OCR [EPA's Office of Civil Rights] intends to process and investigate allegations about discriminatory effects resulting from environmental permitting decisions. In particular, OCR generally expects to use this guidance for complaints involving allegations related to environmental permits, such as Clean Air Act permits, Clean Water Act discharge permits, Safe Drinking Water Act permits, underground injection permits, and Resource Conservation and Recovery Act permits for treatment, storage, and disposal.... The primary administrative remedy described in the regulations involves the termination of EPA assistance to the recipient.... EPA encourages the use of *informal resolution* to address Title VI complaints whenever possible....

The statements in this document are intended solely as guidance. This document is not intended, nor can it be relied upon, to create any rights or obligations enforceable by any party in litigation....

Roles and Opportunities to Participate... The investigation of Title VI complaints does not involve an adversarial process between the complainant and the recipient.... Complainants do not have the burden of proving that their allegations are true.... It is OCR's job to investigate allegations and determine compliance.

Area-specific Agreements...EPA encourages recipients to identify geographic areas where adverse disparate impacts may exist and to enter into agreements with affected residents and stakeholders to eliminate or reduce, to the extent required by Title VI, adverse disparate impacts in those specific areas. ....

Adverse Disparate Impact Analysis...The framework that OCR expects to use for determining whether an adverse disparate impact exists should generally be performed in a step-wise fashion in the order set forth below....

1. **Assess Applicability**...
— Permit actions, including new permits, renewals, and modifications, if the permit causes a net increase in the level of stressors or predicted risks or measures of impact (e.g., an increase in pollutants with no offsetting reductions).

---

35. 42 U.S.C. §2000d-4a.

36. Section 2-2 provides: "Each Federal agency shall conduct its programs, policies, and activities that substantially affect human health or the environment, in a manner that ensures that such programs, policies, and activities do not have the effect of excluding persons (including populations) from participation in, denying persons (including populations) the benefits of, or subjecting persons (including populations) to discrimination under, such programs, policies, and activities, because of their race, color, or national origin." Executive Order 12898, 59 FR 7629 (1994).

— Permit actions, including new permits, renewals, and modifications, that allow existing levels of stressors, predicted risks, or measures of impact to continue unchanged....

There are two situations where OCR will likely close its investigation into allegations of discriminatory effects:

(1) If the complaint alleges discriminatory effects from emissions, including cumulative emissions, and the permit action that triggered the complaint significantly decreases overall emissions[37] at the facility; and

(2) If the complaint alleges discriminatory effects from emissions, including cumulative emissions, and the permit action that triggered the complaint significantly decreases all pollutants of concern named in the complaint or all the pollutants EPA reasonably infers are the potential source of the alleged impact....

2. **Define Scope of Investigation**...

a. Determine the Nature of Stressors and Impacts Considered....

b. Determine Universe of Sources....

3. **Impact Assessment**... Investigatory team develops an assessment to determine whether the alleged discriminatory act may cause or is associated with one or more impacts.... — that there is a plausible mechanism and *exposure route* (e.g., release of a stressor with known *chronic toxicity* effects that may be transported via air to receptors for inhalation)....

Direct link to impacts....

Risk...prediction of potentially significant exposures and risks resulting from stressors created by the permitted activities or other sources....

Toxicity-weighted emissions....

Concentration levels....

4. **Adverse Impact Decision.** Determine whether an estimated risk or measure of impact is significantly adverse.

5. **Characterize Populations and Conduct Comparisons**

Identify and determine the characteristics of the affected population, and conduct an analysis to determine whether a disparity exists between the affected population and an appropriate comparison population in terms of race, color, or national origin, and adverse impact [as a] basis of a finding of non-compliance with EPA's Title VI regulations.

a. Identify and Characterize Affected Population....

b. Comparison to Assess Disparity....

6. **Adverse Disparate Impact Decision**... The final step of the analysis is to determine whether the disparities demonstrated by comparisons in Step 5 are significant under Title VI....

Justification... The recipient will have the opportunity to "justify" the decision to issue the permit notwithstanding the adverse disparate impact, based on a substantial, legitimate justification.... Determining what constitutes an acceptable justification will necessarily be based on the facts of the case. Generally, the recipient would attempt to show that the challenged activity is reasonably necessary to meet a goal that is legitimate, important, and integral to the recipient's institutional mission. For example, because recipients are environmental permitting agencies, OCR expects to consider

---

37. Assessing a significant overall decrease would entail taking into account factors such as total quantity and relative *toxicity* of the emissions reductions.

provision of public health or environmental benefits (e.g., waste water treatment plant) to the affected population from the permitting action to be an acceptable justification because such benefits are generally legitimate, important, and integral to the recipient's mission.

In addition, OCR would also likely consider broader interests, such as economic development, from the permitting action to be an acceptable justification…. However, a justification may be rebutted if EPA determines that a less discriminatory alternative exists….

Less Discriminatory Alternatives. [A] "less discriminatory alternative"…causes less disparate impact than the challenged practice, but is practicable and comparably effective in meeting the needs addressed by the challenged practice…. Practicable *mitigation* measures associated with the permitting action could be considered as less discriminatory alternatives, including, in some cases, modifying permit conditions to lessen or eliminate the demonstrated adverse disparate impacts.

COMMENTARY & QUESTIONS

1. **The significance of the Title VI guidance.** To what situations does the guidance apply, and in what ways does that contrast with past practice? In the draft guidance, EPA recognized that attaching Title VI concerns to permitting greatly expands the federal involvement in environmental justice, moving it from a relatively narrow set of contexts (such as access to public water and sewer facilities and employment) to the heart of the pollution control process. The interim guidance applies not only to the issuance of new permits but also to permit modifications and permit renewals, taking advantage of the special leverage available in the renewal context. In that latter context, the permit holder has already completed its investment in the facility and usually is protecting a productive asset that cannot continue to function if the permit is lost during the renewal process. Given the prominence of cumulative impacts of multiple emitting facilities on minority communities, the ability to obtain pollution control improvements in the renewal context is potentially at least as important as is the new facility-siting context.

2. **Casting a federal shadow on a traditional state prerogative.** To some degree, the Title VI guidance federalizes what was previously a state-controlled area, that of facility siting. Relatively few facilities that pose significant environmental justice issues can be sited without some sort of environmental permit. Under the guidance, state and local agencies receiving federal funds (i.e., virtually all state and local pollution control agencies, and many other governmental entities) are at risk of losing that funding. In many cases, that funding (and the threat of its loss) persuades them to participate in the negotiation process described in the guidance. Contrast with the federal process envisioned here the variety of state siting laws described in Chapter 25.

3. **Are the standards too muddy?** After reading the excerpts from the guidance, can you list the elements of a successful complaint? Taking a different perspective, do permitting agencies and permit seekers know what is in store for them if their actions are shown to have a disparate impact on a minority group? The subject matter does not lend itself to precision, so it is perhaps unfair to treat EPA's effort too harshly.

4. **Are the standards too precise?** The interim guidance has also been criticized from the opposite direction. The claim here is that the revised guidance relies too much on scientific evidence of risk, and other objective, quantifiable information, and too little on the basic but intangible injustices of permitting decisions that have discriminatory effects. See Yang, The Form and Substance of Environmental Justice: The Challenge of Title VI of the Civil Rights Act of 1964 for Environmental Regulation, 29 B.C. Envtl. Aff. L. Rev. 143 (2002). EPA's emphasis on quantitative measures of harm is well illustrated by its first decision based on a Title VI complaint, the *Select Steel* decision. There, EPA concluded that the claimants did not make out a case for an adverse effect (and thus did not have a meritorious case under Title VI) because the NAAQS would not be violated by the steel plant at issue there. Where health-based standards were met, EPA erected a presumption against finding an adverse impact for purposes of Title VI complaints. In re Select Steel, 5R-98-R5 (Oct. 30, 1998).

Knowing what you know now about NAAQSs and their implementation, does EPA's presumption make sense?

5. **Using this guidance document to seek enforceable legal rights and remedies.** Where does the authority to promulgate the guidance come from and how much legal force should it have? Consider first how remote the guidance is from the relevant legislation. Congress, specifically empowered by §5 of the Fourteenth Amendment, passed general anti-discrimination legislation that included Title VI but does not apply to EPA. Thereafter, the President issued Executive Order 12,898, which states in §6-609:

> This order is intended only to improve the internal management of the executive branch and is not intended to, nor does it create any right, benefit, or trust responsibility, substantive or procedural, enforceable at law or equity by a party against the United States, its agencies, its officers, or any person. This order shall not be construed to create any right to judicial review involving the compliance or noncompliance of the United States, its agencies, its officers, or any other person with this order.

That Executive Order provided the predicate for EPA issuance of the guidance. As a concluding statement in the guidance, EPA reiterates the nonbinding nature of the guidance that appeared in the initial footnote. Nevertheless, the guidance states: "Recipients may be able to challenge EPA's finding in court. Moreover, those who believe they have been discriminated against in violation of Title VI or EPA's implementing regulations may challenge a recipient's alleged discriminatory act in court without exhausting their Title VI administrative remedies with EPA." Draft Title VI Guidance at 39,671.

The trouble is the Supreme Court has rejected this kind of remedy in Title VI cases. In Alexander v. Sandoval, 532 U.S. 275 (2001), a Spanish-speaking applicant for a driver's license challenged the Alabama Department of Public Safety's official policy of administering its driver's license examination solely in the English language. The plaintiff cited Title VI and implementing regulations promulgated by the U.S. Department of Transportation. In a 5-4 decision, the Court held that private individuals may sue to enforce §601 of Title VI (the basic statement of rights), but that §601 itself prohibits only *intentional* discrimination. Although the Court acknowledged that regulations promulgated under §602 of Title VI may go beyond prohibiting intentional discrimination to interdict disparate impacts on minority groups, such disparate impact regulations cannot be enforced by private legal action, only by the agency itself. In dissent, Justice Stevens held out the hope that these regulations could be enforced through an action based on 42 U.S.C. §1983, which provides a cause of action for the deprivation of "any rights, privileges, or immunities secured by the Constitution and laws." However, in South Camden Citizens in Action v. Shinn, 274 F.3d 771 (3d Cir. 2001), the Third Circuit rejected this argument. Thus it would appear that only EPA can enforce its environmental justice regulations. For private citizens, freedom from disparate impact in permitting decisions is a right without a judicial remedy in federal court.

6. *South Camden Citizens* and St. Lawrence Cement. The Supreme Court's decision in Alexander v. Sandoval was especially painful for a neighborhood group from South Camden, New Jersey. The group had sued the New Jersey Department of Environmental Protection (NJDEP) for violating EPA regulations by failing to consider the potential adverse, disparate impacts of its decision to grant St. Lawrence Cement's application for air permits to operate its proposed facility in Camden. The proposed plant would grind and process blast furnace slag to sell as an additive to cement. The process emits air pollutants, including mercury, lead, and SO_2. Camden is one of the most depressed cities on the East Coast, and the predominantly African American and Hispanic neighborhood in question already contained two Superfund sites, a solid waste incinerator, and a sewage treatment plant. On the other hand, the new $50 million cement additive plant was to be the first large industrial facility to be built in Camden in over 30 years and, according to company estimates, would inject over $5 million per year into the local economy and create hundreds of jobs. NJDEP claimed that all air quality standards would be met by the emissions limitations in the proposed permit.

Just five days before the Supreme Court handed down Alexander v. Sandoval, Judge Orlofsky had granted a preliminary injunction in favor of the neighborhood group. The victory was short-lived, as the preceding note indicates. Nevertheless, the case remained alive. On remand from the Third Circuit decision denying a cause of action under 42 U.S.C. §1983, Judge Orlofsky held that the neighborhood group had alleged facts that could support a claim directly under Title VI and under the Equal Protection Clause of the Fourteenth Amendment:

> In support of their claim that the NJDEP Defendants purposefully and invidiously discriminated against them on the basis of their race, color, and national origin, the SCCIA Plaintiffs allege facts which, if proven true, would show not only that the operation of the cement grinding facility would have a disparate impact upon the predominantly minority community of Waterfront South, but also that the NJDEP was well-aware of the potential disproportionate and discriminatory burden placed upon that community and failed to take measures to assuage that burden.... A case of intentional discrimination is often based upon the type of circumstantial evidence which the SCCIA Plaintiffs allege..., namely, disparate impact, history of the state action, and foreseeability and knowledge of the discriminatory onus placed upon the complainants. The NJDEP Defendants

disregard the fact that, in addition to alleging disparate impact and knowledge, the SCCIA Plaintiffs also maintain that the NJDEP has historically "engaged in a statewide pattern and practice of granting permits to polluting facilities to operate in communities where most of the residents are African-American and/or Hispanic to a greater extent than in predominately white communities." South Camden Citizens in Action v. New Jersey Dep't of Envt'l Protection, 254 F. Supp. 2d 486 (D.N.J. 2003).

If disparate impact, a historical pattern of permitting facilities in minority neighbor-hoods, and foreseeability and knowledge of discriminatory impact are enough to make out a valid Title VI claim, what remains of the importance of Alexander v. Sandoval in the environmental setting? In considering this question, bear in mind that "no plaintiff ever has succeeded, after the conclusion of all appeals, in proving discriminatory intent in an environmental justice case." Gerrard, Private Lawyers and Environmental Justice, Hum. Rts. Mag. (ABA, Section of Individual Rights and Responsibilities, Fall 2003), available at http://www.abanet.org/irr/hr/fall03/private.html.

7. EPA's record on Title VI complaints. Michael Gerrard is equally doubtful of the potential for EPA's own Title VI process to yield significant benefits for Title VI claimants. After receiving the relevant documents from EPA via the Freedom of Information Act, Gerrard concluded that as of late 2003, of a total of 143 Title VI complaints filed since 1993, 114 had been closed and 29 were still pending (as of November 2003). Most of the cases had been closed due to quite basic defects in the complaints (such as untimely filing). Twenty complaints had proceeded to a decision by EPA. Of these 20, 12 were disposed of based on the *Select Steel* decision's presumption against finding an adverse effect where health-based standards are not violated. Here is Gerrard's assessment of the results of his study:

> To date, citizen complaints to the EPA under Title VI have never been successful, though a few have yielded collateral benefits.... Environmental justice continues to be a potent political argument against the construction or continued operation of hazardous facilities in many communities. These theories have not succeeded in the courts, however, and it now appears that the EPA's complaint procedure is not providing an effective source of redress either, unless some of the 29 cases still pending have different outcomes than the 105 already closed. Gerrard, EPA Dismissal of Civil Rights Complaints, N.Y.L.J., Nov. 28, 2003, at 3, 5.

8. NSR and environmental justice. In a series of recent decisions, EPA has made clear that environmental justice concerns may also be raised under the CAA. In particular, objections to air pollution permits issued under the NSR provisions of the PSD or nonattainment programs may raise such concerns. In coming to this conclusion, EPA has pointed to a heretofore little-noticed provision of the Act, §173(a)(5), which requires that states' NSR permitting programs

> provide that permits to construct and operate may be issued if...an analysis of alternative sites, sizes, production processes, and environmental control tech-niques for such proposed source demonstrates that benefits of the proposed source significantly outweigh the environmental and social costs imposed as a result of its location, construction, or modification. 42 U.S.C. §7503(a)(5).

EPA has specifically held that the "social costs" referred to in §173(a)(5) include disparate impacts on minority communities. EPA, Approval and Promulgation of Implementation Plans; Louisiana; Rescission of the §182(f) and §182(b)(1) Exemptions to the Nitrogen Oxides Control Requirements for the Baton Rouge Ozone Nonattainment Area, 68 Fed. Reg. 23597 (May 5, 2003). Although EPA has yet to reject an NSR permit on the ground that the requirements of §173(a)(5) as they pertain to environmental justice were not met, the decisions recognizing the separate constraints imposed by this provision offer environmental justice advocates another string to their bow in pressing their claims.[38] Notice that here, cost-benefit balancing is being offered as a way to provide *more*, not less, environmental protection.

E. PRESCRIBING THE PATH TO ATTAINMENT

In 1990, after a decade of halting improvement under the 1977 nonattainment provisions, the situation on the ground (or, more aptly, in the ambient air) was better but still unacceptable. Congress found that EPA had been too willing to approve nonattainment SIPs that moved too slowly toward attainment. Public health was perceived as seriously at risk when almost 100 metropolitan areas were still unable to meet the primary NAAQS ozone standard and roughly 40 areas still failed to meet the primary CO standard. Congress took the political initiative and the political heat, and passed legislation that may ultimately be more effective. Congress, in effect, took an inventory of nonattainment areas and then subdivided them according to how far out of attainment they were. Congress then set realistic, firm dates for achieving attainment for each level of nonattainment. It did this on a pollutant-by-pollutant basis giving longer lead times for solving more serious problems of nonattainment. Congress even required that, where necessary, more difficult nonattainment problems be addressed through transportation programs that would make reduction of aggregate mobile source emissions part of the solution. Beyond that, the legislation spelled out specific sanctions — cutoffs of federal highway funds and other federally bestowed benefits — for states that did not comply with the new timetables and required promulgation of a FIP within two years of a state's failure to submit an adequate SIP.

In regard to the most pressing problem, ozone nonattainment, Congress differentiated five degrees of nonattainment: marginal, moderate, serious, severe, and extreme.[39] The amendments set increasingly distant dates for compliance, ranging from 3 years for marginal areas to 20 years for extreme areas. See §181(a), 42 U.S.C. §7511(a). Congress also mandated that SIPs for those areas include an increasingly stringent set of requirements, depending where on the continuum the area of nonattainment fell. See

---

38. As a side light for public trust fans, note that in Louisiana a constitutional provision developed from the public trust doctrine has been used to require, in permitting decisions, (1) an analysis of whether environmental effects have been avoided as much as possible, (2) a cost-benefit analysis showing that the social and economic benefits of the project outweigh its environmental costs, and (3) an analysis of alternative projects, sites, and mitigation measures. See Save Ourselves, Inc. v. Louisiana Envtl. Control Comm'n, 452 So. 2d 1152 (La. 1984) (known as the "IT" decision, after the company involved).

39. A similar, but far simpler two-track system of moderate and serious nonattainment is employed in relation to CO and PM, and attainment deadlines are set for all of the remaining criteria pollutants. See CAA §§186–192, 42 U.S.C. §§7512–7514a.

§182(a)-(e), 42 U.S.C. §7511a(a)-(e). For example, in marginal areas SIPs must include the use of RACT and vehicle maintenance and inspection programs, and offsets must be obtained in a ratio of at least 1.1 to 1, whereas in extreme areas switching to cleaner fuels such as natural gas is required for large emitting sources, high polluting vehicles cannot be used during rush hours, and the general offset requirement is 1.5 to 1.

Coupled with the host of specific nonattainment prescriptions, Congress, by 1990, had a very keen sense of EPA capabilities in implementing programs and built numerous deadlines into the nonattainment amendments in hopes of keeping EPA and the states on track and on time. Frequently in its administration of programs, missed deadlines had landed EPA in court. In most cases, the results were consent decrees pursuant to which EPA agreed to take actions according to judicially approved timetables. With the nonattainment amendments, Congress set deadlines for EPA in its relationship to the states and the SIP process.

Under the amendments, EPA and the states have, at least in part, a mutual interest in easing the process of complying with the new law. In numerous instances both the states and EPA have preferred to delay making the changes required by the nonattainment SIP process. Of necessity, the required provisions of those SIPs will alter the status quo, which generates resistance. Moreover, experience has proved that many of the congressionally required elements of nonattainment SIPs, such as transportation controls, are decidedly unpopular. EPA's efforts to soften the transition to the new regime have often taken the form of the agency using its interpretive power to grant more time to the states. These efforts have met with mixed results when challenged in court. Compare NRDC v. Browner, 57 F.3d 1122 (D.C. Cir. 1995) (upholding EPA's interpretation of how the §110(m) sanctions clock was to be measured, an interpretation that effectively reset the clock at zero whenever a revised proposal was submitted, even if that proposal was ultimately rejected by EPA), with NRDC v. EPA, 22 F.3d 1125 (D.C. Cir. 1994) (disapproving EPA's "conditional approval" procedure for SIPs, which allowed states to meet their SIP deadlines by submitting plans that simply promised to adopt concrete pollution reduction measures within a year).

The following excerpt, also from the Supreme Court's *American Trucking* decision, considers and rejects EPA's proposed approach to handling deadlines and compliance strategies with respect to its revised ozone standard. The opinion presents an opportunity to hone your skills of statutory interpretation in an exceedingly complex regulatory setting.

Whitman v. American Trucking Associations
Supreme Court of the United States, 2001
531 U.S. 457

SCALIA, J.... The final...issue...concern[s] the EPA's authority to implement the revised ozone NAAQS in areas whose ozone levels currently exceed the maximum level permitted by that standard. The CAA designates such areas "nonattainment," §107(d)(1), 42 U.S.C. §7407(d)(1), and it exposes them to additional restrictions over and above the implementation requirements imposed generally by §110 of the CAA. These additional restrictions are found in the five substantive subparts of Part D of Title I, 42 U.S.C. §§7501–7515. Subpart 1 contains general nonattainment regulations that pertain to every pollutant for which a NAAQS exists. Subparts 2 through 5 contain rules tailored to specific individual pollutants. Subpart 2, added by the Clean Air Act Amendments of 1990, addresses ozone. §7511. The dispute before us here, in a nutshell, is whether Subpart 1 alone (as the agency determined), or rather Subpart 2 or some combination of Subparts 1 and 2, controls the implementation of the revised ozone NAAQS in nonattainment areas....

Our approach to the merits of the parties' dispute is the familiar one of *Chevron*. If the statute resolves the question whether Subpart 1 or Subpart 2 (or some combination of the two) shall apply to revised ozone NAAQS, then "that is the end of the matter." But if the statute is "silent or ambiguous" with respect to the issue, then we must defer to a "reasonable interpretation made by the administrator of an agency."... We find the statute to some extent ambiguous. We conclude, however, that the agency's interpretation goes beyond the limits of what is ambiguous and contradicts what in our view is quite clear. We therefore hold the implementation policy unlawful....

Two sections of Subpart 1, (C) and (D), contain switching provisions stating that if the classification of ozone nonattainment areas is "specifically provided for under other provisions of Part D," then those provisions will control.... To determine whether that language *does* apply one must resolve the further textual issue whether some *other* provision, namely Subpart 2, provides for the classification of ozone nonattainment areas....

Does Subpart 2 provide for classifying nonattainment ozone areas under the revised standard? It unquestionably does. The backbone of the subpart is Table 1, printed in §7511(a)(1) and reproduced in the [footnote below],[40] which defines five categories of ozone nonattainment areas and prescribes attainment deadlines for each,...declaring that "each area designated nonattainment for ozone...shall be classified at the time of such designation, under Table 1, by operation of law." And once an area has been classified, "the primary standard attainment date for ozone shall be as expeditiously as practicable but not later than the date provided in Table 1." The EPA argues that..., because the title of §7511(a) reads "Classification and attainment dates for 1989 nonattainment areas," Subpart 2 applies only to areas that were in nonattainment in 1989, and not to areas later designated nonattainment under a revised ozone standard. The suggestion must be rejected, however, because §7511(b)(1) specifically provides for the classification of areas that *were* in attainment in 1989 but have subsequently slipped into nonattainment. It thus makes clear that Subpart 2 is *not* limited solely to 1989 nonattainment areas. This eliminates the interpretive role of the title, which may only "shed light on some ambiguous word or phrase in the statute itself." Carter v. United States, 530 U.S. 255, 267 (2000).

It may well be, as the EPA argues...that some provisions of Subpart 2 are ill fitted to implementation of the revised standard.

These gaps in Subpart 2's scheme prevent us from concluding that Congress clearly intended Subpart 2 to be the exclusive, permanent means of enforcing a revised ozone standard in nonattainment areas. The statute is in our view ambiguous concerning the manner in which

---

40. TABLE 1:

AREA CLASS	PRIMARY STANDARD DESIGN VALUE*	ATTAINMENT DATE **
Marginal	0.121 up to 0.138	3 years after November 15, 1990
Moderate	0.138 up to 0.160	6 years after November 15, 1990
Serious	0.160 up to 0.180	9 years after November 15, 1990
Severe	0.180 up to 0.280	15 years after November 15, 1990
Extreme	0.280 and above	20 years after November 15, 1990

  * The design value is measured in parts per million (ppm).
** The primary standard attainment date is measured from November 15, 1990.

Subpart 1 and Subpart 2 interact with regard to revised ozone standards, and we would defer to the EPA's reasonable resolution of that ambiguity. We cannot defer, however, to the interpretation the EPA has given.

Whatever effect may be accorded the gaps in Subpart 2 as implying some limited applicability of Subpart 1, they cannot be thought to render Subpart 2's carefully designed restrictions on EPA discretion utterly nugatory once a new standard has been promulgated, as the EPA has concluded. The principal distinction between Subpart 1 and Subpart 2 is that the latter eliminates regulatory discretion that the former allowed. While Subpart 1 permits the EPA to establish classifications for nonattainment areas, Subpart 2 classifies areas as a matter of law based on a table. Whereas the EPA has discretion under Subpart 1 to extend attainment dates for as long as 12 years, under Subpart 2 it may grant no more than 2 years' extension. Whereas Subpart 1 gives the EPA considerable discretion to shape nonattainment programs, Subpart 2 prescribes large parts of them by law. Yet, according to the EPA, Subpart 2 was simply Congress's "approach to the implementation of the old 1-hour" standard, and so there was no reason that "the new standard could not simultaneously be implemented under...subpart 1." To use a few apparent gaps in Subpart 2 to render its textually explicit applicability to nonattainment areas under the new standard utterly inoperative is to go over the edge of reasonable interpretation. The EPA may not construe the statute in a way that completely nullifies textually applicable provisions meant to limit its discretion.

The EPA's interpretation making Subpart 2 abruptly obsolete is all the more astonishing because Subpart 2 was obviously written to govern implementation for some time. Some of the elements required to be included in SIPs under Subpart 2 were not to take effect until many years after the passage of the Act. A plan reaching so far into the future was not enacted to be abandoned the next time the EPA reviewed the ozone standard — which Congress knew could happen at any time, since the technical staff papers had already been completed in late 1989. Yet nothing in the EPA's interpretation would have prevented the agency from aborting Subpart 2 the day after it was enacted. Even now, if the EPA's interpretation were correct, some areas of the country could be required to meet the new, more stringent ozone standard in *at most* the same time that Subpart 2 had allowed them to meet the old standard. Los Angeles, for instance, "would be required to attain the revised NAAQS under Subpart 1 no later than the same year that marks the outer time limit for attaining Subpart 2's one-hour ozone standard." An interpretation of Subpart 2 so at odds with its structure and manifest purpose cannot be sustained.

We therefore find the EPA's implementation policy to be unlawful, though not in the precise respect determined by the Court of Appeals. After our remand, and the Court of Appeals' final disposition of this case, it is left to the EPA to develop a reasonable interpretation of the nonattainment implementation provisions insofar as they apply to revised ozone NAAQS....

COMMENTARY & QUESTIONS

1. **A bit of background.** By the time this issue reached the Supreme Court, its most extreme edges had been polished off. In the D.C. Circuit, industry had argued that Subpart 2 prevented EPA from revising the ozone standard at all and, alternatively, that EPA was required to enforce any revised ozone standard in conformity with the deadlines and other dictates of Subpart 2. The court rejected the first argument but accepted the second, stating that "EPA is precluded from enforcing a revised primary ozone NAAQS other than in accordance with the classifications, attainment dates, and control measures set out in Subpart 2." ATA v. EPA, 175 F.3d 1027, 1046 (D.C. Cir. 1999).

To EPA and like-minded participants in the litigation, the ruling made no sense. After all, it was not even possible to classify areas under Subpart 2 under the revised ozone standard. Under Subpart 2, areas were to be classified according to their "design value," which in turn was to be calculated according to the interpretation methodology in effect before November 15, 1990. 42 U.S.C. §7511(a)(1). But that methodology required use of the statistical form of the ozone standard existing in 1990, which was different from the statistical form of the revised standard. Thus EPA could not, within the constraints of Subpart 2, even classify areas under the revised ozone standard. Trying to fit the revised standard within the deadlines of Subpart 2 seemed equally untenable. Many of the deadlines of Subpart 2 had already passed by the time of the litigation in *American Trucking*, yet the D.C. Circuit was instructing EPA to enforce the revised ozone standard only in conformity with those deadlines. These points are undoubtedly what the Supreme Court had in mind when it said, "It may well be, as the EPA argues...that some provisions of Subpart 2 are ill fitted to implementation of the revised standard."

For its part, the D.C. Circuit thought EPA's position had made no sense because it would require areas to comply with a more stringent standard at the same time they were racing to meet the old standard. The court wrote: "Under §181(a) of Subpart 2, Los Angeles, the nation's only Extreme Area, has until 2010 to attain the 0.12 ppm ozone NAAQS, and the possibility of extending that deadline until 2012. That Los Angeles should also have to attain a more stringent ozone standard by that same year, if not earlier, clearly runs counter to the comprehensive enforcement scheme enacted in Subpart 2." 175 F.3d at 1049.

Thus, as the issue came to the Supreme Court, EPA and its supporters thought the appeals court's decision would preclude EPA from developing a reasonable implementation schedule for the revised ozone standard, and they also feared that the decision might preclude EPA from enforcing the revised standard at all until areas had come into compliance with the former standard — a process that would take years. If one had wanted to identify the "environmentalist" position at that time, therefore, one would have pointed to EPA's view that Subpart 1 governed implementation of the revised standard.

2. **Role reversal?** The Supreme Court did not say, as the D.C. Circuit had, that the revised ozone standard could be enforced only in conformity with the deadlines, classifications, and other requirements of Subpart 2. Instead, the Court held that EPA may not render Subpart 2 "utterly nugatory" in implementing the revised standard, and at the same time cautioned that Congress did not intend for Subpart 2 to be "the exclusive, permanent means" of enforcing the revised standard. Does this help environmentalists interested in seeing the revised standard expeditiously enforced more than it helps industry groups interested in putting off enforcement of the standard? Given Subpart 2's exceedingly detailed prescriptions for meeting the ozone NAAQS, doesn't the Court's requirement that EPA consider these prescriptions in enforcing the standard potentially (if ironically) help the environmentalists' cause?

3. **EPA's response on remand.** EPA responded to the Supreme Court's opinion by proposing a "hybrid" plan for implementing the eight-hour ozone standard that

partakes of both Subpart 1 and Subpart 2. Whether an area is governed by Subpart 1 or 2 turns largely on its attainment status under the old one-hour ozone standard. Even areas governed by Subpart 2 are governed only by a framework similar to the statutory Subpart 2; classifications, emission reduction requirements, and attainment dates all are different from those set forth in the statute. Perhaps most notably, attainment dates reach all the way from 2007 to 2024, with many dates in between, for nonattainment areas under EPA's plan. Also significant is EPA's plan to allow states to enter into "early action compacts," under which they will receive a lower (i.e., less stringent) nonattainment classification if they agree to meet the earlier deadline that applies to the lower classification. EPA's plan for transitioning from the former, one-hour standard to the revised, eight-hour standard also appears to leave room for troubling regulatory gaps; for example, once an area is subject to the eight-hour standard and the one-hour standard has been revoked in that area, EPA proposes no longer to require transportation conformity plans under the one-hour standard for that area. EPA's mind-bogglingly complex proposals can be found at http://epa.gov/ttn/naaqs/ozone/o3imp8hr/proprule.html.

F. TRANSBOUNDARY AIRFLOWS

One fundamental argument for federal regulation of pollution is the problem of transboundary pollution, or pollution that travels from one state to another. If, for example, Massachusetts cannot clean up its air without Ohio reducing emissions from its power plants, then federal intervention is needed to broker the dispute.

The original 1970 CAA did little to solve the problem of transboundary pollution. The statute required upwind states to give notice to downwind states of new and proposed major sources that would affect the downwind state's ability to meet the NAAQSs or interfere with the downwind state's PSD program. The adversely affected state could protest to EPA, with EPA becoming the arbiter of the interstate clash of interests. The statute's language seemed to favor the downwind states. To be approved, an upwind state's SIP must

> contain adequate provisions (i) prohibiting...any source or other type of emissions activity within the State from emitting any air pollutant in amounts which will (I) contribute significantly to nonattainment in, or interfere with maintenance by, any other State with respect to any such national primary or secondary ambient air quality standard, or (II) interfere with measures required to be included in the applicable [PSD] implementation plan for any other State.... CAA §110(a)(2) (D)(i).

In practice, however, before the 1990 Amendments to the Act, downwind states won very few concessions from upwind states through appeals to EPA. And they had an even worse record in seeking judicial invalidation of EPA's approval of upwind activities.

Air Pollution Control Dist. v. EPA, 739 F.2d 1071 (6th Cir. 1984), an early leading case in this area, gives a flavor of the difficulty downwind states have experienced. The case involves SO_2 contributions to the Louisville, Kentucky, airshed of a coal-fired power plant located just across the Ohio River in Indiana. For a few months after

Indiana and Kentucky had their initial SIPs approved under the then-new CAA of 1970, the Kentucky and Indiana SIPs required identical SO_2 control efforts for coal-fired power plants, an emission limitation of 1.2 lb. of SO_2 per million British thermal units of heat input (MBTU). Indiana almost immediately won EPA approval for a revised SIP that allowed unregulated SO_2 emissions from coal-fired electric generating facilities. Kentucky, downwind on the other side of the river, held firm to the 1.2 lb./MBTU standard and forced the primary Kentucky SO_2 producer in the region, Louisville Gas & Electric (LG&E), to meet that standard. The court described the contrast in an understated way:

> It can therefore be seen that a significant disparity exists between the permissible emission limits of power plants in Jefferson County, Kentucky and the Gallagher plant in Floyd County, Indiana. LG&E, the primary producer of SO_2 in Jefferson County, spent approximately $138 million installing scrubbers to remove SO_2 from its emissions, while just across the river, Gallagher's SO_2 emissions were completely uncontrolled.[41]

Despite Kentucky's SO_2 control efforts in the Louisville AQCR, it remained a nonattainment area even after LG&E had completed installation of all of the needed emission controls. A petition was lodged with the EPA, seeking relief against the interstate effects of SO_2 pollution from the nearby Indiana plant. EPA concluded that only 3% of the Kentucky SO_2 concentrations that resulted in violations of the NAAQS were attributable to the Gallagher plant. EPA also found, however, that the Gallagher plant contributed large concentrations of SO_2 that were not part of predicted violations of the NAAQS. EPA's own study of the data observed these impacts have "a far more serious potential for limiting growth in Kentucky...." EPA even stated that by 1985, when controls at the LG&E plant would be fully on line, the Gallagher plant "will be the predominate [sic] influence upon air quality in Louisville, Kentucky." Id. at 1078.

EPA denied Kentucky's petition, however, and judicial review in the federal court followed. The court held, first, that EPA had appropriately construed the Act to prohibit only interstate pollution that "significantly contributes" to present violations of the NAAQS or an already established PSD program. In defense of the court's holding, note that 42 U.S.C. §7426 requires notice to downwind states only of new sources in the upwind state that "may significantly contribute" to air quality problems in the downwind state. Also, imagine the results (political and economic) of a conclusion that the CAA forbids all transboundary air pollution.

Second, the court upheld EPA's position that interference with potential growth in the downwind state is not a ground on which relief can be granted in the absence of interference with an established PSD plan or program. The proper accommodation of interstate interests on this question presents a subtle and difficult issue. To grasp the competing positions of Kentucky and the EPA more clearly, imagine what would be the course of events if the Kentucky AQCR involved in the litigation, through additional reductions in emissions, remedies the excessive concentrations of SO_2 in all locations and becomes an attainment area. At that point, Kentucky would be able to adopt a new PSD SIP that allows some new pollution to be introduced if continued compliance with

---

41. 739 F.2d at 1077.

the NAAQSs can be maintained. As the facts set forth above showed, EPA's model of the airshed indicated that there are some parts of the AQCR where, but for the Indiana emissions from the Gallagher plant, there would be substantial room for incremental SO_2 emissions without exceeding the NAAQSs. On this basis, Kentucky claims that Indiana has "stolen its PSD increment" through the failure to limit Gallagher emissions.

In the case as it was litigated, Kentucky made this argument. EPA's response was formalistic and, in light of its own findings in the case, a bit disingenuous. EPA said there could be no present stealing of a PSD increment because no PSD baseline could be set in advance of becoming an attainment area. When attainment occurred, the Kentucky concentrations attributable to the Gallagher plant would not then constitute stealing the increment because those concentrations would be part of the baseline. In this way, regardless of terminology, EPA allows Indiana to dispose of significant SO_2 emissions at Kentucky's expense.

While the EPA position seems palpably unfair to Kentucky, it has the administrative advantage of limiting the need to exercise discretion. It avoids the pitfalls of some vague equity-based approach that would inevitably embroil EPA in bitter interstate disputes involving protracted evidentiary matters concerning the precise extent of interstate pollution. The EPA approach also maintains ambient standards as its central technique, whereas an alternative rule that called for equal pollution control efforts on both sides of the state line would rely more on a mandated technology approach. Although these observations hardly amount to a ringing defense of the EPA position, they give it sufficient rationality to be sustained by a reviewing court applying a deferential standard of review.

COMMENTARY & QUESTIONS

1. **EPA's dilemma.** Do not be too quick to criticize EPA for failing to be more aggressive in these cases. On what principled basis can EPA determine how much pollution can cross state boundaries without constituting an injury to the downwind state? The general movement of air masses and the pollutants they carry is an uncontrollable natural event. A zero transboundary emission limit is unattainable and undesirable. To meet that goal, emissions limits in the upwind state would have to be excessively restrictive. Remember that some NAAQSs are measured in terms of brief sampling-periods, the wind and other atmospheric conditions vary erratically, and virtually all states are both importers and exporters of pollution.

Once EPA is committed to allowing a reasonable amount of pollution to move from a source state to another state, the almost inevitable focus of comparison will be in the relative stringency of regulation of the emissions in the source and recipient state. On that score, the disparity between the uncontrolled emissions at the Gallagher plant and the need to use scrubbers at the LG&E plant may seem to embarrass EPA. Should it? It is possible to argue that EPA is only carrying out the will of Congress. This is a case being resolved using the ambient standards approach that Congress chose for the regulation of conventional air pollutants. The key questions for EPA are whether Indiana is meeting the NAAQSs (without need of regulating Gallagher more stringently) and whether Kentucky is being prevented from meeting the NAAQSs by Indiana emissions. On the record in the case, there is no warrant for EPA to act because the lax Indiana controls are not undermining the operation of the harm-based ambient standards approach. If Congress had intended EPA to insist on an equivalency of interstate effort in emission control, it could have chosen a technology-based approach or a system that relied on uniform emissions control efforts nationwide.

2. **Non-federal remedies.** When §§110 and 126 fail, downwind areas can resort to state law remedies. In Her Majesty the Queen v. City of Detroit, 874 F.2d 332 (6th Cir. 1989), Canada had obtained no satisfaction in a §126 effort to block the construction of a large trash-to-energy incinerator in Detroit, upwind of Windsor, Ontario. Canada, in the name of the Queen, filed an action based on Michigan's Environmental Protection Act. The case was allowed to go forward on that basis. Before a final disposition on the merits, the incinerator was retrofitted to further reduce its emissions.

3. **Experience under the 1990 Amendments.** As a partial response to the unhappy experience of downwind states with their attempts to use §§110 and 126 to block out-of-state pollution, the 1990 Amendments create a new institution called an interstate transport commission. See CAA §176A, 42 U.S.C. §7506a. Such a commission can be formed at EPA's discretion on EPA's own initiative or following a request from an affected state whenever EPA finds there is a significant interstate transport of air pollutants that significantly contribute to an NAAQS violation. If formed, a commission is comprised of two members from each of the interested states and two EPA officials. The commission then assesses the degree of interstate pollution transport and the strategies for mitigating that pollution and makes recommendations to EPA for SIP provisions that will satisfy the interstate control obligations of §7410(a)(2)(D). The 1990 Amendments also created a multistate entity called the Ozone Transport Commission (OTC) and gave EPA the authority to establish a larger entity, the Ozone Transport Advisory Group (OTAG) to consider the movement of NOx and other ozone precursors.

In September 1998, EPA issued an official "call" requiring some states to make significant SIP revisions for ozone control.[42] This "NOx SIP call" requires 22 states and the District of Columbia to submit SIPs that address the regional transport of ground-level ozone. The purpose of the action was to attempt to limit NOx emissions in upwind states from adversely affecting ground level ozone levels in downwind states. This is a complex air quality modeling problem as well as a costly question of subsequent emissions control (NOx upwind vs. VOCs and other ozone precursors downwind).

In 2000, EPA also issued a decision under §126, finding significant interstate contributions to downwind states' failure to attain the ozone NAAQS.

States that found themselves adversely affected by these decisions, which included target reductions on a state-by-state basis, sued to block them. The D.C. Circuit issued two lengthy decisions rejecting the bulk of plaintiffs' challenges to the decisions. See Michigan v. EPA, 213 F.3d 663 (D.C. Cir. 2000); Appalachian Power Co. v. EPA, 249 F.3d 1032 (D.C. Cir. 2001).

---

42. Finding of Significant Contribution and Rulemaking for Certain States in the Ozone Transport Assessment Group Region for Purposes of Reducing Regional Transport of Ozone, Sept. 24, 1998, 63 Fed. Reg. 57356 (Oct. 27, 1998).

Chapter 12

TECHNOLOGY-BASED STANDARD-SETTING: THE CLEAN WATER ACT

A. *An Overview of the Clean Water Act*
B. *The Origin and Evolution of TBELs*
C. *Implementing TBELs through the NPDES Process*
D. *Water Quality-Based Permitting under the CWA*
E. *Controlling Nonpoint Source Pollution without Federal Regulation*
F. *A Complex Hypothetical: The Average River*

A. AN OVERVIEW OF THE CLEAN WATER ACT

The Clean Water Act (CWA), 33 U.S.C. §§1251 et seq., derives from the old Federal Water Pollution Control Act (FWPCA). It was given its modern form in its major amendments of 1972. Like the CAA, the CWA imposes national baseline pollution standards. For the CWA, however, Congress chose a converse approach to the standard-setting methods of the CAA. The CAA primarily employs a strategy of harm-based standard-setting, although it gradually has been moving in the direction of technology-based standard-setting. The CWA, on the other hand, is fundamentally premised on technology-based standard-setting, but in recent years increasingly has included elements of harm-based standard-setting. These tendencies are instructive.

The basic federal "floor" standards under the CWA are effluent limitations based on "Best Available Technology Economically Achievable" (commonly referred to as "BAT"), or one of its variant standards, "Best Conventional Pollutant Control Technology" ("BCT") or "Best Available Demonstrated Control Technology" ("BADT"). Under the CWA's National Pollutant Discharge Elimination System (NPDES), all "point source" dischargers of pollutants[1] (e.g., outfall pipes from factories, municipal sewage treatment plants, vessels) are assigned EPA-promulgated performance standards based on the best water pollution control technology that has been found to be both available and economically achievable industry-by-industry among dischargers performing similar economic activities or using similar mechanical

---

1. The distinction between point and nonpoint source discharges is a critical one and is explored thoroughly below. In general, point source discharges are regulated by the CWA, but nonpoint source discharges are not. The CWA's regulatory mechanism applies to the "discharge of a pollutant," which is defined as "any addition of any pollutant to navigable waters from any point source." §502(12). A "point source" discharges through a discrete and confined conveyance, such as a pipe, ditch, or channel. A nonpoint source produces a diffuse and unconfined discharge, such as overland runoff from a farm or paved surface.

processes.[2] The resulting technology-based effluent limitations are called TBELs. In many cases, compliance with TBELs by point source dischargers located on a particular water-body has enabled the public to return to those waters for fishing and swimming, which is one of the CWA's goals. Waterbodies that can attain the fishable-swimmable criterion through the operation of TBELs alone are called "effluent-limited" waterbodies.

However, situations arise where compliance with TBELs by point source discharg-ers does not produce fishable-swimmable water quality, and additional limits must be applied. These "water quality-limited" stretches (also called impaired waters) may occur where "natural pollution" levels are high (e.g., high concentrations of naturally occurring arsenic and salts in waterbodies of the western United States), intense concentrations of factories or municipal treatment plants overtax the assimilative capacities of receiving waters, past pollution ("legacy pollution") has heavily contami-nated the sediments and water column, or unregulated nonpoint sources, such as large agricultural or silvicultural activities, cause heavy pollutant loadings to nearby water-bodies. Point source dischargers on water quality-limited stretches must meet, in addition to TBELs, more stringent *harm-based* effluent limitations based on achieving fishable-swimmable water quality, wherever that is attainable. These "better-than-best" effluent limitations are customarily referred to as water quality-based effluent limita-tions (WQBELs).

From 1972 to 1987, the major preoccupation of CWA administration was the implementation of TBELs for all point source dischargers. This stage, for the most part, has been reached. Although TBEL implementation remains a high priority for water pollution control agencies, the major focus of water pollution control programs is shifting to WQBEL-setting and implementation. This chapter first analyzes the tradi-tional standard-setting mechanism of the CWA-TBELs and then addresses the comparatively recent developments associated with WQBELs. The chapter concludes with a discussion of nonpoint source pollution control.

The CWA's basic strategy of technology-based standard-setting has made a monu-mental contribution to cleaning up America's surface waterbodies. Major waterbodies that, in the 1960s, were virtual open sewers are now fit for fishing and swimming.[3] The infamous lower Cuyahoga River, which in 1969 was declared a fire hazard and actually caught fire (for the third time) as surface oil and grease was ignited by a spill of hot slag, is now sufficiently safe and attractive (although not yet fishable-swimmable, especially after heavy rains) that the Cleveland Flats area at the river's mouth has been trans-formed from a fetid industrial zone into a waterside entertainment district lined with nightclubs and bistros, with tables on decks at riverside and tie-ups for pleasure boaters.[4] According to EPA estimates, about 60% of the nation's rivers, lakes, and estuar-

---

2. "Performance standard" means that the law requires a certain *result*, without dictating *how* a person must meet it (which would be a "design standard"). Thus although the CWA sets limits for how much of a pollutant can be discharged in a water effluent by figuring out what the best technology would achieve, it is a performance stan-dard because it does not require the polluter to use that technology if it can reach the same result another way, say by reducing the use of polluting materials in the production process.

3. These waterbodies include major stretches of the Delaware, Connecticut, Potomac, Charles, and Tennessee Rivers, Lake Erie, New York City's East River, and Puget Sound.

4. A former EPA Administrator is reputed to have quipped, "the Cuyahoga River may not be fishable and swim-mable, but it is no longer flammable."

ies are now fishable-swimmable, compared with approximately 36% in 1972. This nationwide improvement in water quality has resulted from the reduction of point source discharges by roughly 90%. Despite clear and often dramatic progress in cleaning up America's surface waterbodies, the bad news is that a large percentage of America's waterbodies still do not meet the CWA's fishable-swimmable goal, and nonpoint sources are still largely unregulated.

The following excerpt serves as an introduction to the range of contaminants that degrade water quality and the typical sources of those pollutants.

U.S. Environmental Protection Agency,
National Water Quality Inventory: 1994 Report to Congress
Executive Summary, 7–15

Low Dissolved Oxygen... Dissolved oxygen is a basic requirement for a healthy aquatic ecosystem. Most fish and beneficial aquatic insects "breathe" oxygen dissolved in the water column. Some fish and aquatic organisms (such as carp and sludge worms) are adapted to low oxygen conditions, but the most desirable fish species (such as trout and salmon) suffer if dissolved oxygen concentrations fall below 3 to 4 mg/L (3 to 4 milligrams of oxygen dissolved in 1 liter of water, or 3 to 4 parts of oxygen per million parts of water). Larvae and juvenile fish are more sensitive and require even higher concentrations of oxygen.

Many fish and other aquatic organisms can recover from short periods of low dissolved oxygen availability. However, prolonged episodes of depressed dissolved oxygen concentrations of 2 mg/L or less can result in "dead" waterbodies. Prolonged exposure to low dissolved oxygen conditions can suffocate adult fish or reduce their reproductive survival by suffocating sensitive eggs and larvae or can starve fish by killing aquatic insect larvae and other prey. Low dissolved oxygen concentrations also favor anaerobic bacteria activity that produces noxious gases or foul odors often associated with polluted waterbodies.

Oxygen concentrations in the water column fluctuate under normal conditions, but severe oxygen depletion usually results from human activities that introduce large quantities of biodegradable organic materials into surface waters [measured in terms of biochemical oxygen demand (BOD)]. Biodegradable organic materials contain plant, fish, or animal matter. Leaves, lawn clippings, sewage, manure, shellfish processing waste, milk solids, and other food processing wastes are examples of oxygen-depleting organic materials that enter our surface waters.

In both pristine and polluted waters, beneficial bacteria use oxygen to break apart (or decompose) organic materials. Pollution-containing organic wastes provide a continuous glut of food for the bacteria, which accelerates bacterial activity and population growth. In polluted waters, bacterial consumption of oxygen can rapidly outpace oxygen replenishment from the atmosphere and photosynthesis performed by algae and aquatic plants. The result is a net decline in oxygen concentrations in the water.

Toxic pollutants can indirectly lower oxygen concentrations by killing algae, aquatic weeds, or fish, which provides an abundance of food for oxygen-consuming bacteria. Oxygen depletion can also result from chemical reactions that do not involve bacteria. Some pollutants trigger chemical reactions that place a chemical oxygen demand [COD] on receiving waters.

Other factors (such as temperature and salinity) influence that amount of oxygen dissolved in water. Prolonged hot weather will depress oxygen concentrations and may cause fish kills even in clean waters because warm water cannot hold as much oxygen as cold water. Warm conditions further aggravate oxygen depletion by stimulating bacterial activity and respiration in fish, which consumes oxygen....

Nutrients... Nutrients are essential building blocks for healthy aquatic communities, but excess nutrients (especially nitrogen and phosphorus compounds) overstimulate the growth of aquatic weeds and algae.[5] Excessive growth of these organisms, in turn, can clog navigable waters, interfere with swimming and boating, outcompete submerged aquatic vegetation, and lead to oxygen depletion.

Oxygen concentrations can fluctuate daily during algal blooms, rising during the day as algae perform photosynthesis, and falling at night as algae continue to respire, which consumes oxygen. Beneficial bacteria also consume oxygen as they decompose the abundant organic food supply in dying algae cells.

Lawn and crop fertilizers, sewage, manure, and detergents contain nitrogen and phosphorus, the nutrients most responsible for water quality degradation. Rural areas are vulnerable to ground water contamination from nitrates (a compound containing nitrogen) found in fertilizer and manure. Very high concentrations of nitrate (more than 10 mg/L) in drinking water cause methemoglobinemia, or blue baby syndrome, an inability to fix oxygen in the blood....

Sediment and Siltation... In a water quality context, sediment usually refers to soil particles that enter the water column from eroding land. Sediment consists of particles of all sizes, including fine clay particles, silt, sand, and gravel. Water quality managers use the term "siltation" to describe the suspension and deposition of small particles in waterbodies.

Sediment and siltation can severely alter aquatic communities. Sediment may clog and abrade fish gills, suffocate eggs and aquatic insect larvae on the bottom, and fill in the pore spaces where fish lay eggs. Silt and sediment interfere with recreational activities and aesthetic enjoyment of waterbodies by reducing water clarity and filling in waterbodies. Nutrients and toxic chemicals may attach to sediment particles and ride the particles into surface waters where the pollutants may settle with the sediment or detach and become soluble in the water column.

Rain washes silt and other soil particles off of plowed fields, construction sites, logging sites, urban areas, and strip-mined lands into waterbodies....

Bacteria and Pathogens... Some waterborne bacteria, viruses, and protozoa cause human illnesses that range from typhoid and dysentery to minor respiratory and skin diseases. These organisms may enter waters through a number of routes, including inadequately treated sewage, stormwater drains, septic systems, and sewage dumped overboard from recreational boats. Because it is impossible to test waters for every possible disease-causing organism, States and other jurisdictions usually measure indicator bacteria that are found in great numbers in the stomachs and intestines of warm-blooded animals and people. The presence of indicator bacteria suggests that the waterbody may be contaminated with untreated sewage and that other, more dangerous organisms may be present....[6]

Toxic Organic Chemicals and Metals... Toxic organic chemicals are synthetic compounds that contain carbon, such as polychlorinated biphenyls (PCBs), dioxins, and the pesticide DDT. These synthesized compounds often persist and accumulate in the environment because they do not readily break down in natural ecosystems. Many of these compounds cause cancer in people and birth defects in other predators near the top of the food chain, such as birds and fish.

Metals occur naturally in the environment, but human activities (such as industrial processes and mining) have altered the distribution of metals in the environment. In most

---

5. This process is called eutrophication, or the premature aging of waterbodies. Excessive nutrient discharges are also suspected of creating the conditions under which the *pfisteria piscicida* bacteria has proliferated and killed hundreds of thousands of fish in Chesapeake Bay and the Pamlico River, North Carolina. [Eds.]

6. The most common bacterial indicator is the *E-coli* bacteria. An overabundance of these organisms in a waterbody can trigger beach closings and shutdowns of shellfish beds to harvesting. [Eds.]

reported cases of metals contamination, high concentrations of metals appear in fish tissues rather than the water column because the metals accumulate in greater concentrations in predators near the top of the food chain.[7]

Acidity/Alkalinity pH... Acidity, the concentration of hydrogen ions, drives many chemical reactions in living organisms. The standard measure of acidity is pH, and a pH value of 7 represents a neutral condition. A low pH value (less than 5) indicates acidic conditions; a high pH (greater than 9) indicates alkaline conditions. Many biological processes, such as reproduction, cannot function in acidic or alkaline waters. Acidic conditions also aggravate toxic contamination problems because sediments release toxicants in acidic waters. Common sources of acidity include mine drainage, runoff from mine tailings, and atmospheric deposition.

Habitat Modification/Hydrologic Modification... Habitat modifications include activities in the landscape, on shore, and in waterbodies that alter the physical structure of aquatic ecosystems and have adverse impacts on aquatic life. Examples of habitat modifications include: 1) removal of streamside vegetation that stabilizes the shoreline and provides shade, which moderates instream temperatures; 2) excavation of cobbles from a stream bed that provide nesting habitat for fish; 3) stream burial or destruction; and 4) excessive suburban sprawl that alters the natural drainage patterns by increasing the intensity, magnitude, and energy of runoff waters. Hydrologic modifications alter the flow of water. Examples include channelization, dewatering, damming, and dredging.

Other Pollutants... These include salts and oil and grease. Fresh waters may become unfit for aquatic life and some human uses when they become contaminated by salts. Sources of salinity include irrigation runoff, brine used in oil extraction, road de-icing operations[8], and the intrusion of sea water into ground and surface water in coastal areas. Crude oil and processed petroleum products may be spilled during extraction, processing, or transport or leaked from underground storage tanks.

The Leading Causes of Water Quality Impairment... The five leading causes of water quality impairment, ranked by the areal extent of waterbodies affected,[9] are illustrated in Table 12-1 on the next page.

Where Does This Pollution Come From?... Of the Nation's 615,806 surveyed river miles, 64% have good water quality. Of these waters, 57% fully support their designated uses, and an additional 7% support uses but are threatened and may become impaired if pollution control actions are not taken.

Some form of pollution or habitat degradation prevents the remaining 36% (224,236 miles) of surveyed river miles from fully supporting a healthy aquatic community or human activities all year round. Twenty-two percent of the surveyed river miles have fair water quality that partially supports designated uses. Most of the time, these waters provide adequate habitat

---

7. Excessive concentrations of toxic pollutants frequently result in fish consumption advisory warnings in affected waterbodies. [Eds.]

8. See Chapter 1. [Eds.]

9. Note that pollution by toxic pollutants is not among the top-ranked problems, in terms of miles or acres of waterbodies impacted. However, toxic pollutants may directly and adversely affect human health, especially the health of urban low-income and minority fishers who catch and eat fish from the urban waters that are listed as "toxic hot spots" (see below). [Eds.]

CRITERIA POLLUTANT	AIR QUALITY CONCENTRATION % CHANGE 1977–1996	EMISSIONS % CHANGE 1970–1996
Carbon monoxide	-61%	-31%
Lead	-97%	-98%
Nitrogen Dioxide and NOx (1988–1996 data)	-27%	increased 8%
Ozone	-30%	-38% (VOC)
PM10	Data not available	-73% (includes only direct emissions, not secondary formation from SOx and NOx
Sulfur dioxide	-58%	-39%

FIGURE 12-1

CLEAN AIR ACT AND CLEAN WATER ACT CONTRIBUTIONS TO QUALITY

Source: U.S. EPA, 1996 National Air Quality and Emission Trends Report, R-97-013, January 1998, Table 1-2.

for aquatic organisms and support human activities, but periodic pollution interferes with these activities and/or stresses aquatic life. Fourteen percent of the surveyed river miles have poor water quality that consistently stresses aquatic life and/or prevents people from using the river for activities such as fishing and swimming.

Bacteria pollute 76,397 river miles (which equals 34% of the impaired river miles). Siltation impairs 75,792 river miles (which equals another 34% of the impaired river miles). In addition to siltation and bacteria, nutrients, oxygen-depleting substances, metals, and habitat alterations impact more miles of rivers and streams than other pollutants and processes. Often, several pollutants and processes impact a single river segment. For example, a process, such as removal of shoreline vegetation, may accelerate erosion of sediment and nutrients into a stream.

Agriculture is the most widespread source of pollution in the Nation's surveyed rivers. Agriculture generates pollutants that degrade aquatic life or interfere with public use of 134,557 river miles (which equals 60% of the impaired river miles) in 49 jurisdictions. [There have been] declines in pollution from sewage treatment plants and industrial discharges as a result of sewage treatment plant construction and upgrades and permit controls on industrial discharges. Despite the improvements, municipal sewage treatment plants remain the second most common source of pollution in rivers (impairing 37,443 miles) because population growth increases the burden on our municipal facilities. Urban runoff and storm sewers impair 26,862 river miles (12% of the impaired rivers), resource extraction impairs 24,059 river miles (11% of the impaired rivers), and removal of streamside vegetation impairs 21,706 river miles (10% of the impaired rivers). Hydrologic modifications and habitat alterations are a growing concern. "Natural" sources, such as low flow and soils with arsenic deposits, can prevent waters from supporting uses in the absence of human activities.

Agriculture is [also] the most widespread source of pollution in the Nation's surveyed lakes. Agriculture generates pollutants that degrade aquatic life or interfere with public use of 3.3 million lake acres (which equals 50% of the impaired lake acres). Municipal sewage treatment plants pollute 1.3 million lake acres (19% of the impaired lake acres), urban runoff and storm sewers pollute 1.2 million lake acres (18% of the surveyed lake acres), hydrologic modifications and habitat alterations degrade 832,000 lake acres (12% of the impaired lake acres), and industrial point sources pollute 759,000 lake acres (11% of the impaired lake acres).

Most of the Great Lakes shoreline is polluted by toxic organic chemicals — primarily PCBs — that are often found in fish tissue samples. Toxic organic chemicals impact 98% of the impaired Great Lakes shoreline miles. Other leading causes of impairment include pesticides, affecting 21%; other organic chemicals, affecting 20%; nutrients, affecting 6%; and metals, affecting 6%.

Urban runoff and storm sewers are the most widespread source of pollution in the Nation's surveyed estuarine waters. [These sources] degrade aquatic life or interfere with public use of 4,508 square miles of estuarine waters (which equals 46% of the impaired estuarine waters). Municipal sewage treatment plants pollute 3,827 square miles of estuarine waters (39% of the impaired estuarine waters), agriculture pollutes 3,321 square miles of estuarine waters (34% of the impaired estuarine waters), and industrial discharges pollute 2,609 square miles (27% of the impaired estuarine waters). Urban sources contribute more to the degradation of estuarine waters than agriculture because urban centers are located adjacent to most major estuaries.

COMMENTARY & QUESTIONS

1. **A regulatory paradox.** Since most point source industrial and municipal pollution has been regulated since 1972, today agriculture is the major source of water pollution in most rivers and lakes and a significant source of pollution in estuaries. Many agricultural operations are classified as nonpoint sources of pollution, however, and are thus outside the regulatory scope of the CWA. One of the most contentious issues raised during the debates on reauthorization of the CWA has been whether agriculture should finally be subject to regulation.

2. **We've come a long way, but...** Although significant progress has been made in cleaning up America's waterways, the CWA's statutory goals have not been completely met or its policies thoroughly implemented. The CWA declares:

> The objective of this chapter is to restore and maintain the chemical, physical, and biological integrity of the Nation's waters. In order to achieve this objective it is hereby declared that, consistent with the provisions of this chapter —
>
> (1) it is the national goal that the discharge of pollutants into the navigable waters be eliminated by 1985;
>
> (2) it is the national goal that wherever attainable, an interim goal of water quality which provides for the protection and propagation of fish, shellfish, and wildlife and provides for recreation in and on the water be achieved by July 1, 1983;
>
> (3) it is the national policy that the discharge of toxic pollutants in toxic amounts be prohibited;...
>
> (7) it is the national policy that programs for the control of nonpoint sources of pollution be developed and implemented in an expeditious manner.... 33 U.S.C. §1251.

By "integrity of the Nation's waters" Congress meant their ecological stability, not the revival of a dehumanized state of primeval purity. The Zero-Discharge Goal of subsection (1) is not an enforceable requirement of the CWA but a rebuttable presumption that all discharges are environmentally deleterious and a declaration that pollution prevention is the most desirable form of pollution control. The CWA's enforceable requirements are derived from the "interim goal" of subsection (2).

Despite the manifest and manifold successes of the CWA, approximately half of our nation's waterbodies do not meet the Act's goals.[10] Pollution in some of these waterbodies is effectively incorrigible, due to previous human perturbations and background pollutant levels. But the vast majority of these impaired waters conceivably could be restored to fishability-swimmability and ecological stability. Why are they still dirty?

Unfortunately, the CWA has not been implemented so as to adequately control certain point source discharges from industries and municipal sewerage systems as well as discharges that affect ocean water quality.[11] In addition, the CWA's provisions do not cover: (1) nonpoint sources of pollution, such as most agricultural activities, postconstruction stormwater runoff from suburban residential areas, urban stormwater runoff that is not channeled through pipes or drains, and deposition of air pollutants such as mercury and nutrients (approximately 80% of the mercury and 25% of the nutrients found in U.S. waterbodies are the result of air deposition); (2) point or nonpoint sources of groundwater pollution; (3) hydrologic modifications that disrupt flows, such as dams and flood control devices; (4) water diversions for domestic, industrial, agricultural, and recreational purposes, which frequently result in desiccated waterbodies; (5) destruction of riparian zones through unwise construction, resource extraction, agricultural, silvicultural, and grazing practices; (6) resuspension, due to storms or human disturbances, of pollutants emanating from contaminated sediments; (7) introduction of exotic species of flora and fauna; (8) excessive concentrations of septic systems, which result in pollution of surface and groundwaters; and (9) the expansion of impervious surfaces, which causes not only pollution problems from runoff of sediment and toxic pollutants but also flooding and decreased groundwater recharge. Moreover, the wetlands protection provisions of the CWA, which are discussed in Chapter 25, have proven only moderately successful.

B. THE ORIGIN AND EVOLUTION OF TBELS

U.S. Environmental Protection Agency v. California
United States Supreme Court, 1976
426 U.S. 200

[In this opinion explaining the mechanics of the CWA, the Court held that federal facilities were not required to obtain NPDES permits from states with approved programs, a decision later overridden by Congress in the CWA Amendments of 1977.]

---

10. According to the latest EPA assessment, 39% of assessed rivers and streams, 51% of assessed estuarine square miles, and 46% of assessed lake, pond, and reservoir acres (excluding the Great Lakes) exhibit suboptimal water quality.

11. See the discussions of nonpriority pollutants and combined sewer overflows below. With regard to ocean discharges, see Craig & Miller, Ocean Discharge Criteria and Marine Protection Areas: Ocean Water Quality Protection Under the Clean Water Act, 29 B.C. Envtl. Aff. L. Rev. 1 (2001); Pew Oceans Comm'n, America's Living Oceans: Charting a Course for Sea Change (2003), http://www.pewoceans.org.

WHITE, J. Before it was amended in 1972, the Federal Water Pollution Control Act employed ambient water quality standards specifying the acceptable levels of pollution in a State's inter-state navigable waters as the primary mechanism in its program for the control of water pollution. This program based on water quality standards, which were to serve both to guide performance by polluters and to trigger legal action to abate pollution, proved ineffective. The problems stemmed from the character of the standards themselves, which focused on the tolera-ble effects rather than the preventable causes of water pollution, from the awkwardly shared federal and state responsibility for promulgating such standards, and from the cumbrous enforcement procedures. These combined to make it very difficult to develop and enforce stan-dards to govern the conduct of individual polluters.

Some States developed water quality standards and plans to implement and enforce them, and some relied on discharge permit systems for enforcement. Others did not, and to strengthen the abatement system federal officials revived the Refuse Act of 1899, which prohibits the discharge of any matter into the Nation's navigable waters except with a federal permit. Although this direct approach to water pollution abatement proved helpful, it also was deficient in several respects: the goal of the discharge permit conditions was to achieve water quality stan-dards rather than to require individual polluters to minimize effluent discharge, the permit program was applied only to industrial polluters, some dischargers were required to obtain both federal and state permits, and federal permit authority was shared by two federal agencies.

In 1972, prompted by the conclusion of the Senate Committee on Public Works that "the Federal water pollution control program...has been inadequate in every vital aspect," Congress enacted the Amendments, declaring "the national goal that the discharge of pollutants into the navigable waters be eliminated by 1985." For present purposes the Amendments introduced two major changes in the methods to set and enforce standards to abate and control water pollution. First, the Amendments are aimed at achieving maximum "effluent limitations on point sources," as well as achieving acceptable water quality standards. A point source is "any discernible, confined and discrete conveyance...from which pollutants are or may be discharged." An "effluent limitation" in turn is "any restriction established by a State or the Administrator [of EPA] on quantities, rates, and concentrations of chemical, physical, biological or other constituents which are discharged from point sources...including schedules of compli-ance." Such direct restrictions on discharges facilitate enforcement by making it unnecessary to work backward from an overpolluted body of water to determine which point sources are responsible and which must be abated. In addition, a discharger's performance is now measured against strict technology-based effluent limitations — specified levels of treatment — to which it must conform, rather than against limitations derived from water quality standards to which it and other polluters must collectively conform. Water quality standards are retained as a supplementary basis for effluent limitations, however, so that numerous point sources, despite individual compliance with [technology-based] effluent limitations, may be further regulated to prevent water quality from falling below acceptable levels.

Second, the Amendments establish the NPDES as a means of achieving and enforcing the effluent limitations. Under NPDES, it is unlawful for any person to discharge a pollutant with-out obtaining a permit and complying with its terms. A NPDES permit serves to transform generally applicable effluent limitations and other standards — including those based on water quality — into the obligations (including a timetable for compliance) of the individual discharger, and the Amendments provide for direct administrative and judicial enforcement of permits. With few exceptions, for enforcement purposes a discharger in compliance with the terms and conditions of an NPDES permit is deemed to be in compliance with those sections of the Amendments on which the permit conditions are based. In short, the permit defines, and facilitates compliance with and enforcement of, a preponderance of a discharger's obligations under the Amendments.

NPDES permits are secured, in the first instance, from EPA.... Consonant with its policy "to recognize, preserve, and protect the primary responsibilities and rights of the States to prevent, reduce, and eliminate pollution," Congress also provided that a State may issue NPDES permits "for discharges into navigable waters within its jurisdiction," but only upon EPA approval of the State's proposal to administer its own program. EPA may require modification or revision of a submitted program but when a plan is in compliance with EPA's guidelines...EPA shall approve the program and "suspend the issuance of permits...as to those navigable waters subject to such program."

The EPA retains authority to review operation of a State's permit program. Unless the EPA waives review for particular classes of point sources or for a particular permit application, a State is to forward a copy of each permit application to EPA for review, and no permit may issue if EPA objects that issuance of the permit would be "outside the guidelines and requirements" of the amendments. In addition to this review authority, after notice and opportunity to take action, EPA may withdraw approval of a state permit program which is not being administered in compliance with the [Act as amended]....

COMMENTARY & QUESTIONS

1. **Ineffectuality of prior law.** Before 1972, under the old federal water statute, in more than two decades only one water pollution violation was successfully prosecuted, and in that case more than four years elapsed between the initial enforcement conference and the final consent decree. In those benighted days, desired uses were set by individual states, which classified waterways in categories ranging from Class A (swimming) to Class D (agricultural and industrial use). If a state was satisfied that a particular river need only be aesthetically tolerable and fit for commercial navigation, the law did not afford relief unless the river stank or corroded hulls of ships. The Cuyahoga River was not considered legally objectionable until it caught fire because the state-designated use of that river was waste disposal. See generally Congressional Research Service, Library of Congress, A Legislative History of the Federal Water Pollution Control Act Amendments of 1972 (1973), and Andreen, The Evolution of Water Pollution Control in the United States: State, Local, and Federal Efforts, 1789-1972: Part I, 22 Stan. Envtl. L.J. 145 (2003). See also the *Utilex* case study in Chapter 5.

If the harm-based prior law had failed so miserably, why did Congress, in the 1972 CWA, adopt both technology-based and harm-based controls, superimposing water quality-based controls on a fundamental level of technology-based controls? The answer has to do with congressional politics. The Senate favored replacing the water quality-based approach with progressively stricter technology-based effluent limitations, leading to the ultimate cessation of all discharges. The House, however, believed that a water quality-based approach was still viable. The resulting compromise entails a dual approach, with a harm-based system applicable only where necessary. Several analysts believe that the CWA's many ambiguities can be traced to this original, unsuccessful compromise.

Why did Congress move to a primarily technology-based standard-setting methodology in 1972, when it had embraced an almost totally harm-based strategy in the CAA only two years earlier? The CAA was, in effect, a statute of the 1960s because it extended and strengthened the harm-based Air Quality Act of 1967, which, ironically, followed the ambient standard approach earlier established in the 1965 FWPCA. Between late 1970, when the CAA was being finalized, and the summer of 1971, when the Senate Air and Water Pollution Subcommittee released its technology-based clean water bill (drawn from the new source performance standard section of the 1970 CAA §111), the burgeoning environmental movement had inspired dissatisfaction with the harm-based approach and its philosophy that there exists a right to discharge up to the assimilative capacity of the environment.

2. **Pros and cons of technology-based controls.** Critics of the technology-based approach argue that it is (1) inadequate to protect acutely impacted waterbodies, (2) economically inefficient because it frequently demands "redundant treatment" (i.e., greater treatment than necessary to maintain desired uses for waterbodies), and (3) insufficiently technology-stimulating because it does not encourage industry to develop innovative technology (and in fact may be an example of a "perverse incentive" prompting industries to stifle cleaner technology that might achieve cleaner receiving waters than would be attained through a technology-based standard). The first charge is rebutted, at least theoretically, by the bilevel structure of the CWA, with harm-based standards becoming applicable where technology-based ones do not achieve desired water quality. As for the second objection, defenders of the CWA respond that (1) the harm-based system has not effectively controlled pollution, having instead only exacerbated the race-to-the-bottom because of variable standards from state-to-state (see Chapter 5); (2) BAT standards are significantly simpler and less expensive to administer than harm-based standards; (3) the economic costs of BAT have been exaggerated, and its public health benefits undervalued; and (4) normatively, producers should do the best they can to protect human lives and the ecosystems upon which humans depend.

3. **Frozen technology?** In fact, water quality-based effluent limitations themselves freeze current technology, at least until water quality standards (WQSs) have been violated. To some extent, the charge that BAT standards create perverse incentives by freezing current technology is based on a misunderstanding of the manner in which technology-based standards are implemented in the CWA. There are two types of BAT standards: (1) equipment and design specification standards, and (2) performance standards. The former specifies the precise type of technology that a regulated party must install, whereas the latter establishes a performance standard based on the technology utilized by the best performers in a particular industrial category, but allows the regulated party to meet that standard either by installing the base technology or in any other least-cost way, including using different technology or achieving pollution prevention. As the *Rybachek* opinion excerpted later in this chapter points out, the CWA relies on BAT-based performance standards, not on equipment and design specification standards. Equipment and design specification standards typically are imposed where technology has become standardized and pollutants are difficult to measure, as in drinking water treatment. Several of the CWA's detractors, however, have not

recognized the fact that the CWA relies upon performance standards rather than on equipment and design specification standards.[12]

The CWA's technology-based approach, as originally conceived, can circumvent the perverse incentive to freeze current technology and encourage the development of innovative technology by entrepreneurial ventures both inside and outside the regulated industrial sector. Although technology-based effluent limitations are based on available technology, EPA must review promulgated effluent limitations every five years, with a view toward tightening them to reflect the existence of improved pollution control devices. CWA §301(d). Improved BAT should be reflected in stricter TBELs that are included in five-year permit renewals.[13] In other words, build a better pollutant trap and the regulated dischargers must either beat a path to your door or find some other way to meet the performance standard. Unfortunately, EPA has been so preoccupied with developing its initial technology-based standards that it only recently has begun its five-year reviews of technology-based effluent limitations, partially as a result of congressional prodding through §304(m) of the CWA, added by the Water Quality Act Amendments of 1987, setting deadlines for EPA promulgation of effluent guidelines. In addition, most of EPA's water pollution control resources are currently devoted to TMDL development (see below).

There is evidence that the CWA's strategy of progressively tightening technology-based standards so as ultimately to achieve either significant pollutant reductions or zero-discharge has been realized as to some discharge categories. EPA's final effluent limitation guideline regulations for the pesticide formulating, packaging, and repackaging industry allows dischargers to choose between zero-discharge limits or a pollution prevention alternative. In 1993, EPA proposed a set of "Cluster Rules" for the pulp and paper industry (combining effluent and emissions limitations for both water and air pollution control — counteracting the inefficiencies of the media-specific approach). The water pollution control element of this proposal was based on oxygen delignification, a process that substitutes oxygen for chlorine in the bleaching of paper, thus eliminating the discharge of dioxin, a highly toxic by-product of chlorine bleaching. Goaded by the high cost of complying with this proposed BAT standard, several paper companies began substituting chlorine dioxide for chlorine, which reduced dioxin discharges by approximately 96% at substantially lower cost than oxygen delignification. In 1996, EPA reproposed these regulations and requested comments on both process changes as potential BAT. Finally, in 1997, EPA promulgated BAT standards based on the chlorine dioxide bleaching process. The virtually zero-discharge option was forgone in favor of a slightly less effective alternative that will be less costly to

---

12. See, e.g., Hahn, Getting More Environmental Protection for Less Money: A Practitioner's Guide, 9 Oxford Rev. Econ. Pol'y 112, 116 (1993) ("the technology-based standard, which specifies a particular technology a firm must use to comply with the law,...is used frequently in both air and water regulation in the United States"); Derzko, Using Intellectual Property Law and Regulatory Processes to Foster the Innovation and Diffusion of Environmental Technologies, 20 Harv. Envtl. L. Rev. 3, 18–19 (1996) ("Technology standards require polluting firms to reduce pollution using a certain prescribed technology;...[the CAA and CWA] still operate using technology standards.").

13. Discharge permits have a maximum duration of five years, but, once a renewal application is filed, the original permit remains in effect until renewal. The discharge permit renewal process has traditionally been plagued by severe backlogs, and many dischargers are operating under expired permits.

industry. Moreover, the "Cluster Rules" also include a Voluntary Advanced Technology Incentives Program (VATIP) that provides additional time for meeting effluent limitations if a company submits a viable plan for developing and implementing innovative control technology.

Nevertheless, it is clear that, in general, EPA and state administration of technology-based standard-setting systems discourage technological innovation because (1) in practice, permissible technologies are limited to available ones that meet the standards; (2) governmental permit writers are notoriously risk-averse; (3) multimedia pollution and pollution prevention are rarely considered during the permitting process; and (4) permitting agencies disregard statutory incentives for technological innovation (e.g., CWA §301(k)'s extended compliance schedules). Environmental Law Institute, Barriers to Environmental Technological Innovation (1998). One potential solution to this problem could be allowing sales and trading of pollution control credits earned through compliance beyond minimum standards (see Chapter 14).

4. **Navigable waters.** In the CWA, "discharge of a pollutant" means "any addition of any pollutant to navigable waters from any point source." §502(12). "Navigable waters" is generally defined as "waters of the United States." §502(7). It is well settled that, as far as surface waters are concerned, "waters of the United States" transcends traditional definitions of navigability and is coterminous with the limits of the federal government's Commerce Clause jurisdiction. United States v. Ashland Oil, 504 F.2d 1317 (6th Cir. 1974). Thus wetlands, drainage ditches, mosquito canals, and even intermittent streams are considered waters of the United States. However, man-made waste treat systems, such as treatment ponds or lagoons, are excluded. In United States v. TGR Corp., 171 F.3d 762 (2d Cir. 1999), the court found that an intensely developed brook, into which the defendant had discharged asbestos through a sewer, was waters of the United States (not a municipal waste treatment system) because it was neither man-made nor municipally owned and maintained a viable population of wildlife. In Solid Waste Agency of Northern Cook County v. U.S. Army Corps of Eng'rs, 531 U.S. 159 (2001), the U.S. Supreme Court held that the Corps' rule extending the definition of "navigable waters" under the CWA to include hydrologically "isolated," intrastate wetlands used as habitat by migratory birds exceeded the authority granted to the Corps under §404 of the CWA. See the extended analyses of the SWANCC case in Chapters 6 and 25.

A major unresolved question with regard to the CWA is whether its provisions apply to point source discharges to groundwater. EPA has waffled on this issue, and the courts have split as to whether "tributary groundwater" (groundwater that is hydrologically connected to surface water) is covered by the Act. Contrast Exxon v. Train, 554 F.2d 1310 (5th Cir. 1977) (no groundwater is covered by the CWA), with U.S. Steel v. Train, 556 F.2d 822 (7th Cir. 1977) (groundwater is covered if it is hydrologically connected to surface water). Relying on CWA §510's express authority for states to adopt stricter standards and limitations than those imposed by EPA, a number of states, for example California and New Jersey, require discharge permits for point source dischargers to groundwater. Cal. Water Code §10350(3); N.J. Stat. Ann. §58:10A-3.

5. **Point and nonpoint sources.** A "point source" is "any discernible, confined and discrete conveyance, including but not limited to any pipe, ditch, channel, tunnel, conduit, well, discrete fissure, container, rolling stock, concentrated animal feeding operation, or vessel or other floating craft from which pollutants are or may be discharged. This term does not include agricultural stormwater discharges and return flows from irrigated agriculture." §502(14). A "nonpoint source" is any man-made source, discharging to surface waters, that is not a point source. In general, a nonpoint source is a diffuse, intermittent source of pollutants that does not discharge at a single location but whose pollutants are carried over or through the soil by way of stormflow processes. Nonpoint source pollution generally results from land runoff, atmospheric deposition, drainage, or seepage of contaminants. Major sources of nonpoint pollution include agricultural and silvicultural runoff and runoff from urban areas. In contrast to the high-level technological controls that are most often used to prevent point source pollution, nonpoint sources are best controlled by low-technology Best Management Practices (BMPs) — methods, measures, or practices consisting of structural or nonstructural controls and operation-and-maintenance procedures. BMPs generally involve comparatively inexpensive land use controls and land management practices. They are selected based on site-specific conditions that reflect natural background as well as political, social, economic, and technical feasibility. For example, a set of BMPs to reduce runoff of nutrients, herbicides, and pesticides from a farm into a river might include diminished and staggered applications of these substances, contour plowing, and maintenance of vegetated stream buffers. BMPs are technology-based performance standards, rather than equipment and design specification standards, because nonpoint source control programs offer the discharger a choice from among a menu of BMPs, such as those available to the farmer in the preceding example.

The CWA regulates only point source pollution. In 1972, Congress excluded nonpoint sources from the regulatory ambit of the CWA because (1) point sources were perceived as the primary causes of water pollution, and little was then known about the deleterious impacts of nonpoint source runoff; (2) the BMPs to control nonpoint source pollution call for land use and land management restrictions that generally are implemented by local governments; and (3) nonpoint source pollution being diffuse and sporadic, it is more difficult to ascertain the dischargers and environmental effects of nonpoint source pollution than it is with regard to point sources.

The term "point source" is liberally construed and has been held to include a salmon farm, earth-moving equipment in a wetland, and ponded mine drainage that erodes a channel to a river. Dam releases, which often cause adverse water quality impacts downstream, are treated as nonpoint rather than point sources. In a criminal case involving a co-owner of a blood-testing laboratory who threw vials containing blood contaminated with hepatitis-B virus into the Hudson River, the Second Circuit Court of Appeals held that an individual human being is not a point source within the meaning of the CWA. United States v. Plaza Health Labs., 3 F.3d 643 (2d Cir. 1993), cert. denied, 512 U.S. 1245 (1994).

The Second Circuit has also decided a case that may facilitate the regulation of some agricultural pollution under the CWA. Concerned Area Residents for the Environment

(CARE) v. Southview Farms, 34 F.3d 114 (2d Cir. 1994), cert. denied, 514 U.S. 1082 (1995), was a citizen suit contesting the unpermitted liquid manure spreading operation of a large dairy farm in western New York State. Southview Farms owned 1100 acres and a herd of over 2000 cows. Unlike on older dairy farms, the cows were not pastured but remained in their barns, except during milking. The massive quantities of manure generated by these cows were pumped first into a separator, which drained off the liquid and compressed the solids. The solids were transported to a landfill, while the liquid residue was piped to a four-acre manure storage lagoon and thence to smaller lagoons. The liquid stored in these lagoons was spread over Southview's fields by (1) a center pivot irrigation system, (2) hose systems, and (3) manure spreaders pulled by tractors. Some of the runoff from the manure spreading operations drained into a natural swale, then into a man-made tile drain leading under a stone wall, and finally into a natural ditch that drained into a river. Reversing the district court, which had found the operation to be a nonpoint source, the circuit court held that the manure runoff was a point source because (1) the swale/tile drain/ditch drainage system was a point source, (2) the manure spreading vehicles were point sources, and (3) the defendant was operating a concentrated animal feeding operation (CAFO), which is statutorily defined as a point source. In response to defendant's argument that its manure runoff fell within the CWA's "agricultural stormwater discharge" exemption, the court stated that

> ...there can be no escape from liability for agricultural pollution simply because it occurs on rainy days.... We think the real issue is not whether the discharges occurred during rainfall or were mixed with rain water run-off, but rather whether the discharges were the result of precipitation. Of course, all discharges eventually mix with precipitation run-off in ditches or streams or navigable waters so the fact that the discharge might have been mixed with run-off cannot be determinative.... We think the jury could properly find that the run-off was primarily caused by over-saturation of the fields rather than the rain and that sufficient quantities of manure were present so that run-off could not be classified as "stormwater." 34 F.3d at 120.

The court's finding that the drainage system was a point source is potentially the most important for future cases. Pure sheet-flow runoff is comparatively rare. Most runoff over unpaved surfaces ultimately finds its way to, or creates, gullies or swales that discharge into surface waterbodies. If these are indeed point sources, then agricultural activities that do not comply with BMPs (e.g., for manure spreading or pesticide applications) may be subject to regulation under the CWA because they are not included in the "agricultural stormwater discharge" exemption. EPA and state CAFO permit programs are beginning to substantially reduce water pollution from agricultural operations (see below). The Eleventh Circuit Court of Appeals distinguished *Southview Farms* in Fishermen Against the Destruction of the Environment, Inc. v. Closter Farms, Inc., 300 F.3d 1294 (11th Cir. 2002), where the court decided that the farm's operations fell within both the "agricultural stormwater discharge" and "return flow from irrigation agriculture" exceptions from CWA permitting.

Does pesticide spraying constitute a point source discharge? In Headwaters Inc. v. Talent Irrigation Dist., 243 F.3d 526 (9th Cir. 2001), defendant district argued that its herbicide spraying on irrigation canals was not a point source discharge because EPA had approved the herbicide's label under the Federal Insecticide, Fungicide, and Rodenticide Act (FIFRA — see Chapter 17) and the label did not mention the need to obtain a discharge permit. Thus, claimed the district, CWA permitting had been preempted by FIFRA. The Ninth Circuit disagreed, concluding that "[a] FIFRA label and an NPDES permit serve different purposes." 243 F.3d at 530. (See the discussion of the "different purposes" test in preemption law in Chapter 6.) The Ninth Circuit has also held that aerial spraying of pesticides by the Forest Service directly over streams in National Forests necessitates a discharge permit. League of Wilderness Defenders/Blue Mountain Diversity Project v. Forsgren, 309 F.3d 1181 (9th Cir. 2002).

It appears to be settled that water withdrawals are not point source discharges, even if they might potentially increase the concentration of pollutants in waterbodies. See, e.g., North Carolina v. Federal Energy Reg. Comm'n, 112 F.3d 1175 (D.C. Cir. 1997).

6. **Types of point source dischargers.** Point source dischargers may be either municipal sewage treatment plants (known as Publicly Owned Treatment Works, or POTWs) or industrial or stormwater dischargers. Industrial point source dischargers are either direct dischargers, which discharge directly into waterbodies, or indirect dischargers, which discharge into sewers that lead to POTWs, which then discharge into waterbodies. As is discussed below, the technology-based effluent limitations that an industrial discharger is required to meet are determined by (1) the industrial category in which the discharger is placed, (2) the types of pollutants discharged by its operations, and (3) whether it is an existing or new source of water pollution. Stormwater point source discharges can originate from agricultural, industrial, or municipal sources.

7. **The federal-state partnership.** Forty-five states have been delegated primacy to administer their own counterparts of the NPDES permit program. Alaska, where the *Rybachek* placer mine was located (see below), is one of the few states that has not sought CWA primacy. EPA is authorized by CWA §518 to treat Native American tribes as states for purposes of administering the CWA, and a number of tribes have achieved primacy. In the nonprimacy states, EPA regional offices are administering the program. Nationwide, there are approximately 500,000 water discharge permittees. Do you think that the CWA's safeguards, as described in the EPA v. California opinion, are adequate to prevent a state from treating dischargers leniently in order to attract and retain industry? In particular, given EPA's lack of resources, can EPA effectively review draft state permits? Would an EPA threat to withdraw state program authorization be credible? Can EPA meaningfully exercise its backup enforcement authority under §309 of the CWA? Can state pollution control agencies be significantly influenced by EPA's diminishing ability to award program grants, conduct research, and perform technical assistance activities? See the critique of the purported safeguards of cooperative federalism in Chapter 5.

C. IMPLEMENTING TBELS THROUGH THE NPDES PROCESS

Because environmental issues arise from competing demands on natural resources, environmental lawyers learn to work closely with scientists, engineers, natural resource managers, planners, policy analysts, and social scientists in formulating multidisciplinary, holistic environmental protection strategies for presentation to courts, legislatures, administrative agencies, private corporations, and the general public. The following case is unusual among CWA effluent limitation cases in that it involves a relatively simple technology and is thus intelligible to readers who lack a background in environmental science or chemical engineering, while showing some of the legal complexities involved with technology-based standards under the CWA.

Rybachek v. U.S. Environmental Protection Agency
United States Circuit Court of Appeals for the Ninth Circuit, 1990
904 F.2d 1276

O'SCANNLAIN, J.... Placer mining is one of the four basic methods of mining metal ores; it involves the mining of alluvial or glacial deposits of loose gravel, sand, soil, clay, or mud called "placers." These placers often contain particles of gold and other heavy minerals. Placer miners excavate the gold-bearing material (paydirt) from the placer deposit after removing the surface vegetation and non-gold-bearing gravel (overburden). The gold is then separated from the other materials in the paydirt by a gravity-separation process known as "sluicing."

In the sluicing process, a miner places the ore in an on-site washing plant (usually a sluice box) which has small submerged dams (riffles) attached to its bottom. He causes water to be run over the paydirt in the sluice box; when the heavier materials (including gold) fall, they are caught by the riffles. The lighter sand, dirt, and clay particles are left suspended in the wastewater released from the sluice box.

Placer mining typically is conducted directly in streambeds or on adjacent property. The water usually enters the sluice box through gravity, but may sometimes also enter through the use of pumping equipment. At some point after the process described above, the water in the sluice box is discharged. The discharges from placer mining can have aesthetic and water-quality impacts on waters both in the immediate vicinity and downstream. Toxic metals, including arsenic, cadmium, lead, zinc, and copper, have been found in higher concentration in streams where mining occurs than in non-mining streams.

It is the treatment of the sluice-box discharge water before it re-enters a natural water course that is at the heart of this case.

Statutory Framework... Congress enacted the Clean Water Act to "restore and maintain the chemical, physical, and biological integrity of the Nation's waters." Under the Act, the EPA must impose and enforce technology-based effluent limitations and standards through individual NPDES permits. These permits contain specific terms and conditions as well as numerical discharge limitations, which govern the activities of pollutant dischargers. Through the Clean Water Act, Congress has directed the EPA to incorporate into the permits increasingly stringent technology-based effluent limitations.

Congress specified a number of means for the EPA to impose and to enforce these limitations in NPDES permits. For instance, it requires the Agency to establish effluent limitations requiring dischargers to use the "best practicable control technology currently available" ("BPT") within an industry. These limits are to represent "the average of the best" treatment technology performance in an industrial category. See EPA v. National Crushed Stone Ass'n, 449 U.S. 64 (1980). The EPA is further required to promulgate limitations both for the discharge of toxic pollutants by mandating that an industry use the "best available technology economically achievable" ("BAT") and for discharge of conventional pollutants by requiring the use of the "best conventional pollution control technology" ("BCT"); the congressionally imposed deadline for promulgation of these limitations was March 31, 1989....

In addition, new pollution sources in an industry must meet a separate set of standards, called new-source performance standards ("NSPS"). These standards limit the discharge of pollutants by new sources based on the "best available demonstrated control technology" [BADT]. Finally, the EPA is authorized to establish best management practices ("BMPs") "to control plant site runoff, spillage or leaks, sludge or waste disposal, and drainage from raw material storage" in order to diminish the amount of toxic pollutants flowing into the receiving waters.

Rulemaking History... On November 20, 1985, proceeding under the Clean Water Act, the EPA proposed regulations for placer mining. For most mines processing fewer than 500 cubic yards of ore per day ("yd3/day"), the EPA proposed BPT effluent limitations of 0.2 millilitres per litre ("ml/l") of discharge for settleable solids and 2,000 milligrams per litre ("mg/l") for total suspended solids. For mines processing more than 500 yd3/day of ore, the EPA proposed more stringent BCT and BAT limitations as well as new-source performance standards (NSPS) prohibiting the discharge of processed wastewater. Twice during the rulemaking process, the Agency published notices of new information and requested public comment on additional financial and technical data.

As a result of its studies, the comments received during the review and comment periods, and new studies undertaken in response to the submitted comments, the EPA promulgated final effluent-limitation guidelines and standards on May 24, 1988. The EPA established a BPT limitation, based on simple-settling technology, for settleable solids of 0.2 ml/l for virtually all mines. The final rule also established BAT limitations and NSPS based on recirculation technology, restricting the flow of processed wastewater that could be discharged. In addition, the EPA promulgated five BMPs to control discharges due to mine drainage and infiltration. These regulations were to become effective on July 7, 1988....

The Alaska Miners Association ("AMA") and Stanley and Rosalie Rybachek timely petitioned this court for review of the EPA's regulations. We ordered the petitions consolidated....

The EPA's Authority Under the Clean Water Act... The parties dispute whether placer mining is even subject to regulation under the Clean Water Act. The AMA seizes upon [the CWA's] statutory scheme to argue that placer mining is not subject to regulation under the Clean Water Act for at least two reasons: (1) placer mines do not discharge into "navigable waters"; and (2) placer mining does not "add" pollutants to water within the meaning of the Act.[14] We reject both of these arguments....

The parties agree that placer mines discharge into nearby streams and rivers. These are clearly among the "waters of the United States." Second, we will not strike down the EPA's findings that placer mining discharges pollutants within the meaning of the Act. Placer miners excavate the dirt and gravel in and around waterways, extract any gold, and discharge the dirt and other non-gold material into the water.

---

14. The AMA does not contend that placer mining does not involve a "point source." [This is footnote number 8 in the original — Eds.]

On the one hand, if the material discharged is not from the streambed itself, but from the bank alongside, this is clearly the discharge into navigable waters of a pollutant under the Act. Congress defined "pollutant" as meaning, among other things, "dredged spoil..., rock, sand [and] cellar dirt.".... The term "pollutant" thus encompasses the materials segregated from gold in placer mining. Congress defined "discharge" as "any addition of any pollutant to navigable waters from any point source.".... Because, under this scenario, the material discharged is coming not from the streambed itself, but from outside it, this clearly constitutes an "addition."

And, on the other hand, even if the material discharged originally comes from the streambed itself, such resuspension may be interpreted to be an addition of a pollutant under the Act....

The Final Rule... Petitioners make a host of arguments about the content of the final rule. For instance, they attack the EPA's setting of BPT and BAT limitations. They also allege various errors by the EPA in its promulgation of BMPs and its enunciation of new-source criteria....

Merits of the Limitations... Petitioners challenge the merits of the EPA's regulations on a number of grounds; indeed, virtually every aspect of the regulations is attacked. To the extent the regulations may be divided into component parts (e.g., the BPT limitations, the BAT limitations, and new-source criteria), we address petitioner's arguments along those lines.

Determination of BPT... We turn first to petitioners' argument that the EPA erred in its determination that settling ponds are the best practicable control technology currently available (BPT) within the placer mining industry. There is no dispute that settling ponds are currently available pollution control technology; in fact, the AMA concedes that they are now used by almost all miners. Rather, petitioners contend that the EPA failed to use a "cost-benefit analysis" in determining that settling ponds were BPT for placer mining. They also argue that the EPA failed to consider costs when it set forth BPT limitations governing settleable solids for small mines.

The Clean Water Act controls when and how the EPA should require BPT. Under 33 U.S.C. §1311(b)(1)(A), the Act requires "effluent limitations for point sources...which shall require the application of best practicable control technology currently available [BPT]." Under this section, the EPA is to determine whether a technology is BPT; the factors it considers "shall include...total cost of" the technology "in relation to effluent benefits to be achieved" from it, the age of equipment, engineering aspects, "non-water quality environmental impact...and such other factors as the Administrator deems appropriate."

From this statutory language, it is "plain that, as a general rule, the EPA is required to consider the costs and benefits of proposed technology in its inquiry to determine the BPT." Association of Pacific Fisheries v. EPA, 615 F.2d 794 (9th Cir. 1980). The EPA has broad discretion in weighing these competing factors. It may determine that a technology is not BPT on the basis of this cost-benefit analysis only when the costs are "wholly disproportionate" to the potential effluent-reduction benefits.

We look first to whether the EPA properly considered the costs of BPT and second to whether it properly weighed these costs against the benefits.

First, the record shows that the EPA properly considered costs in conducting the analysis which led to the determination that settling ponds are BPT and to the establishment of BPT effluent limitations for settleable solids. The EPA used a model-mine analysis to estimate the costs to mines of installing settling ponds. The Agency developed several model mines to represent the typical operating and compliance costs that open-cut mines and dredges of various sizes would incur. Commenters attempted to insure that the model-mine analysis reflected actual industry conditions, and the EPA accordingly modified the analysis when it thought it appropriate during the rulemaking. The EPA then determined, for each of its model mines, the incremental costs that would be incurred to construct and operate settling ponds to retain wastewater long enough to achieve a certain settleable solids level. It proceeded to conduct a detailed and complex assessment of the effect of the compliance costs on the mining industry's profits.

The EPA then properly weighed these costs against the benefits of settling ponds. Its data indicated that placer mine wastewater contained high levels of solids and metals that were reduced substantially by simple settling. The upshot of the EPA's analysis was its estimation that installation of settling ponds by open-cut mines industry-wide would remove over four million pounds of solids at a cost of approximately $2.2 million — a removal cost of less than $1 per pound of solids. We would uphold the EPA's determination of BPT.

Determination of BAT: Analysis of Costs... We next confront the AMA's challenge to the EPA's determination that recirculation of process wastewater is the best available technology economically achievable (BAT) in the placer mining industry. By definition, BAT limitations must be both technologically available and economically achievable. We conclude that the EPA's BAT limitations were both and therefore uphold them.

The technological availability of recirculating process wastewater is not in dispute; in fact, placer mines commonly practice it. It is recirculation's economic achievability that petitioners challenge.

In determining the economic achievability of technology, the EPA must consider the "cost" of meeting BAT limitations, but need not compare such cost with the benefits of effluent reduction. The Agency measures costs on a "reasonableness standard"; it has considerable discretion in weighing the technology's costs, which are less-important factors than in setting BPT limitations. The record demonstrates that the EPA weighed the costs that recirculation would impose on gold placer mining....

Total Suspended Solids Limitations... We come to petitioners' claim that the EPA has impermissibly established BAT standards to regulate the discharge of total suspended solids. Petitioners argue that total suspended solids are conventional pollutants and therefore subject to BCT (best conventional pollution control technology), rather than BAT, standards. EPA's adoption of recirculation as BAT to control total suspended solids was arbitrary, petitioners contend, because recirculation could not pass the cost-reasonableness test required in determining BCT.

The EPA declined to establish BCT for total suspended solids because test results indicated that settling technology could not consistently control the level of total suspended solids. Moreover, recirculation failed the BCT cost-reasonableness test.

Petitioners are incorrect in contending that the EPA instead adopted BAT to regulate the level of total suspended solids. The EPA's discussion of BAT in the final rule makes no reference to controlling total suspended solids. Instead, EPA set BAT standards to control the discharge of toxic pollutants — a category which, the parties agree, does not encompass total suspended solids. We therefore reject the contention that the EPA was arbitrary in establishing BAT standards.

Settleable Solids Limitations... Petitioners also claim that settleable solids are a component of total suspended solids and that the EPA should have classified settleable solids as a conventional pollutant rather than a nonconventional pollutant. Petitioners contend that the BAT-based effluent limitations are therefore inappropriate for settleable solids. We disagree.

In the Clean Water Act, Congress classified suspended solids as a conventional pollutant. Congress did not classify settleable solids. We must determine, therefore, whether the EPA's classification of settleable solids as a nonconventional pollutant "is based on a permissible construction of the [CWA]." Chevron U.S.A., Inc. v. EPA, 467 U.S. at 843. This court may not substitute its own construction of the Act if the EPA's interpretation is reasonable.

The EPA argues that because settleable solids were not designated by Congress as either a conventional or a toxic pollutant, they should be considered a nonconventional pollutant under 33 U.S.C. §1311(b)(2)(F). This argument is buttressed by the fact that EPA has subjected settleable solids to BAT-level controls in other regulatory areas. And even if settleable solids should more properly be considered a conventional pollutant, we note that the EPA has determined that settleable solids in placer mining effluent are a toxic pollutant indicator and thus may be subject to BAT-level limitations. We find, therefore, that the EPA's decision to treat settleable solids as a nonconventional pollutant and thus subject to BAT standards was both reasonable and permissible....

Mandating of Technology... The AMA next claims that by forbidding the discharge of any process wastewater, the EPA is mandating that placer miners use recirculation technology. According to the AMA, the EPA's action violates Congress' intent to avoid dictating technologies and to encourage innovation. While admitting that the wastewater flow standards are currently achievable only through certain technology, the EPA responds that the regulations only prescribe limitations reflecting actually achieved wastewater reduction. We agree with the EPA....

The EPA has not mandated use of a particular technology. The Agency first determined that recirculation is BAT for the control of discharges by placer mines of toxic metals and settleable solids. Based on this determination, the EPA established that Zero discharge of process wastewater is achievable and should be the BAT limitation and new-source performance standard. That the standards and limitations are stringent and currently may be achievable only through certain technology is true. However, nothing in the EPA's regulations specifies the use of any particular technology to meet the BAT limitations and new-source performance standards achievable through recirculation. In fact, the EPA has encouraged miners to employ innovative technologies and to seek compliance extensions and alternative BAT limitations under §301(k) of the Act. We find that the EPA's setting of zero-discharge limitations based on recirculation results was within its mandate under the Clean Water Act.

Availability of Variances... Petitioners claim that EPA has contravened Congress' intent by failing to allow miners to obtain variances for site-specific conditions. We first note that this assertion is flatly contradicted by the final rule's express language allowing miners to apply for fundamentally different factor ("FDF") variances for both the BPT and BAT limitations....

Petitioners argue that the EPA's classification of settleable solids as a toxic pollutant indicator will prevent miners from obtaining a variance. Normally, BAT limitations for nonconventional pollutants (here, settleable solids) are subject to modification under §§301(c) and (g) of the Clean Water Act. In this instance, modifications for settleable solids under these provisions are unavailable because settleable solids are considered an indicator of toxic pollutants. This does not mean, however, that no variance in the BAT limitations for settleable solids is available; miners may still apply for an FDF variance under §301(n) of the Act....

COMMENTARY & QUESTIONS

1. **"Addition of any pollutant."** EPA regulations dictate that a discharger is not legally responsible for pollutants that are present in a discharge only by reason of their presence in the discharger's intake water if the intake water is drawn from the same body of water as the receiving water and if the pollutants are not removed by the discharger as part of its normal operations. 40 C.F.R. §122.45(h) (known as the "net/gross credit"). Dam releases are not only considered nonpoint sources of pollution, but their discharges are also not additions of pollutants, even if they adversely affect the temperature or oxygen content of the receiving waters. National Wildlife Fed'n v. Gorsuch, 693 F.2d 156 (D.C. Cir. 1982); but see Committee to Save the Mokelumne River v. East Bay Mun. Util. Dist., 13 F.3d 305 (9th Cir. 1993) (discharges from dam used to collect acid mine drainage from abandoned mine require CWA permits). Aquaculture operations ordinarily are considered to add pollutants such as pesticides, fish feed, fish excrement, and stray fish to receiving waters; but in Association to Protect Hammersley, Eld & Totten Inlets v. Taylor Res., Inc., 299 F.3d 1007 (9th Cir. 2002), excrement from mussels suspended from rafts was not considered addition of a pollutant where the mussels had not been artificially fed or treated with pesticides.

The phrase "addition of any pollutant" has been the source of frequent litigation in cases of wetlands development, involving resuspension and "sidecasting" of dredged or fill material, and situations where water is transferred from one location to another. The wetlands development decisions are discussed in Chapter 25. As for water transfer, the Ninth Circuit Court of Appeals has held that unaltered groundwater — containing "naturally" high quantities of salt and arsenic — produced in association with methane gas exploration and discharged into a river is an addition of a pollutant. Northern Great Plains Res. Council v. Fidelity Exploration & Dev. Co., 325 F.3d 1155 (9th Cir. 2003). Other federal courts have reached similar conclusions in water transfer cases: Miccosukee Tribe v. South Fla. Water Mgmt. Dist., 280 F.3d 1364 (11th Cir. 2002), cert. granted, 123 S. Ct. 2638 (2003); Catskill Mountains Chapter of Trout Unltd. v. City of N.Y., 273 F.3d 481 (2d Cir. 2001); Dubois v. Department of Agric., 102 F.3d 1273 (1st Cir. 1996).

2. **Evolution of categorical technology-based limitations.** When the CWA was enacted in 1972, it contained two phases of technology-based limitations. In the first phase, existing industrial point source dischargers were required to meet effluent limitations based on Best Practicable Control Technology Currently Available (BPT) by 1977. During the second phase, dischargers were to meet stricter effluent limitations based on BAT by 1983. BPT was intended to be primarily "end of pipe" treatment, with process changes required only if they were normal practice within an industry. The factors to be considered in setting BAT limitations were similar to those relied upon in setting BPT-based limitations (and described in the *Rybachek* opinion), except that (1) BAT is based on the single best performer within an industry, rather than on an average of "exemplary plants"; (2) BAT is based on process changes adopted within the industry or reasonably transferable from another industry; and (3) BAT involves a consideration only of the cost of achieving such reduction (cost effectiveness), not comparative benefits and costs, unless compliance costs are "wholly disproportionate" to water qual-

ity benefits. Congress realized that some facilities would be forced to cut back production or even close down as a result of these BAT-based limitations. As in *Rybachek*, BPT-based limitations are generally continued in effect during the three-year BAT compliance period that the CWA mandates for existing dischargers.

EPA adopted a "categorical" approach to setting technology-based effluent limitations. Industries were divided into categories, based on products manufactured, and subcategories, based on processes or raw materials utilized in producing the products (e.g., the dredge-mining subcategory of the placer mining category). Then the BPT and BAT criteria were applied to these categories and subcategories, not to individual plants. EPA's effluent limitation regulations for each industrial subcategory contained maximum daily and monthly average limitations on relevant "parameters" (pollutants) expressed in terms of maximum volume or concentration of parameters in wastewater. These "single number" effluent limitations were uniform for existing plants in a particular subcategory, wherever they were located. EPA cannot establish a subcategory based solely on geographical location. Hundreds of lawsuits by industry and numerous divergences among circuit courts of appeals were resolved in Dupont v. Train, 430 U.S. 12 (1977), in which the Supreme Court upheld EPA's categorical approach but stipulated that EPA must devise a variance for plants that do not fit within an industrial subcategory. This procedure, known as the Fundamentally Different Factors (FDF) variance, was later codified as §301(n) of the CWA. For dischargers receiving an FDF variance (e.g., a placer miner that does not have adequate space for a settling pond) and dischargers for which effluent limitation regulations have not yet been promulgated, effluent limitations are set using Best Professional Judgment (BPJ) in light of the statutory criteria. The water quality of the receiving body of water cannot be considered in setting technology-based effluent limitations. Can a discharger dilute its effluent in order to meet effluent limitations? Weyerhaeuser v. Costle, 590 F.2d 1011 (D.C. Cir. 1978), and other cases make it clear that in-plant dilution is not an acceptable solution to pollution under the CWA. Developers of new sources possess the advantage of being able to build pollution control mechanisms into their original plant designs. Consequently, new sources are required to immediately comply with New Source Performance Standards (NSPS) based on BADT, or zero-discharge where practicable. As in *Rybachek*, NSPS are often equivalent to BAT, but EPA policy is that state-of-the-art technology may be required of new sources where it would be economically infeasible for existing sources to retrofit with such technology. However, having met the relevant NSPS, a new source cannot be required to meet stricter technology-based standards for ten years or the facility's amortization period, whichever comes first. §306.[15]

3. **The midcourse corrections of 1977.** Between 1972 and 1977, the installation of BPT by industry and the decrease in pollution from POTWs had significantly reduced the loadings of so-called "conventional pollutants" (BOD, TSS, pH, fecal coliform, and oil and grease) to America's waterbodies. At the same time, Congress had realized that

---

15. Stricter new source performance standards are sometimes criticized as counterproductive in that they allegedly discourage new plant construction and delay the phaseout of inefficient, polluting older facilities. There is little evidence that this has occurred in the water pollution control area. Competitive pressures militate against the perpetuation of inefficient facilities simply to save on pollution control costs. A greater danger is the offshore migration of dischargers.

toxic pollutants were far more of a problem than had initially been envisioned. Thus a midcourse correction was made in 1977 with regard to conventionals and toxics.

In 1977, convinced that the cost of moving to BAT for conventionals was too high, Congress devised a new standard — BCT — for them. §301(b)(2)(E). BCT includes two cost tests: (1) a comparison between the costs of reducing discharges of conventionals and the resulting water quality benefits, and (2) a comparison between industrial and municipal costs for treating conventionals. §304(b)(2)(B). The congressional supporters of BCT felt that it would produce effluent limitations falling between BPT and BAT, but in practice BCT is similar to BPT.

The CWA's original toxic pollutant control mechanism was a cumbersome pollutant-by-pollutant, harm-based system — modeled after §112 of the CAA — that resulted in little control of toxic water pollutants. Rejecting this exercise in futility, EPA decided to regulate toxic pollutants primarily through BAT-based effluent limitations. EPA's decision was upheld by the famous "Consent Decree of 1976." NRDC v. Train, 8 BNA Env't Rep. Cas. 2120 (often called the "Flannery Decree" after the trial court judge). This decree established timetables for EPA to promulgate effluent limitations, based on BAT, for both direct and indirect discharges from many industrial categories, covering 65 families of compounds that EPA has broken down into 126 "priority pollutants."[16] EPA is authorized to add toxic pollutants to this list by regulation but has not done so. In 1977, Congress codified this methodology for regulating toxics. §§301(b)(2)(C) and 307(a)(1) and (2). As *Rybachek* illustrates, nontoxic pollutants that indicate the presence of toxics ("indicator" or "surrogate" parameters) may be regulated as toxics themselves. 40 C.F.R. §122.44(e)(2)(ii).

In addition to conventional and toxic pollutants, Congress in 1977 created a third class of pollutants called "nonconventional" (or nonconventional/nontoxic) pollutants. §301(b)(2)(F). Ammonia, chlorine, color, iron, and total phenols are some of the designated nonconventional pollutants. Dischargers of nonconventionals are entitled to apply for two variances, the cost-based §301(c) variance and the harm-based §301(g) variance. In *Rybachek*, petitioners unsuccessfully contested EPA's classification of settleable solids, ordinarily a nonconventional pollutant, as a toxic pollutant indicator because such classification rendered the nonconventional pollutant variances unavailable to them. Dischargers of toxics, like dischargers of conventionals, may only apply for FDF variances and §301(k) variances for innovative technology.

Figure 12-1 illustrates the classes of water pollutants with their appropriate technology-based effluent limitations, compliance dates, and available variances.[17]

---

16. The time limits in the consent decree were frequently delayed, and it was not until 1987 that EPA promulgated the last of the effluent limitations guidelines covered by the Flannery Decree. EPA has promulgated effluent limitations guidelines regulations for over 50 industrial categories and will, in the future, promulgate regulations applicable to additional categories. EPA estimates that BAT-based effluent limitations imposed under this program have reduced discharges of priority pollutants from point sources by 99%, but sometimes heavy discharges of toxic nonpriority pollutants from point sources and priority pollutants from nonpoint sources continue.

17. Neither EPA nor a state has the authority to regulate discharges of radioactive materials, which are within the exclusive jurisdiction of the Nuclear Regulatory Commission. Train v. Colorado Pub. Interest Research Group, 426 U.S. 1 (1976). States, however, can control the siting of nuclear power plants through their traditional powers over the need for, and the economic costs of, electrical power. See Pacific Gas & Elec. v. California Energy Res. Conservation & Dev. Comm'n, 461 U.S. 190 (1983).

POLLUTANT TYPE	EFFLUENT LIMITATION	COMPLIANCE DATE	VARIANCES?
Conventional Pollutants (BOD, TSS, etc.)	BCT	3 years after promulgation of standard	FDF: Fundamentally Different Factors variances
Non-Conventionals Non-Toxics (Ammonia, color, etc.)	BAT	3 years after promulgation of standard	FDF: §301(c) and (g) variances based on economics and receiving water quality
Toxics	BAT	3 years after promulgation of standard	FDF: §301(k) 2-year extension for adoption of innovative/alternative technology
Heat	BAT	3 years after promulgation of standard	§316(a)
New Source Discharges	BADT	3 years after promulgation of standard; BPT as interim standard	none 10-year grace period

FIGURE 12-2

TBELS — TECHNOLOGY-BASED EFFLUENT LIMITATIONS

4. **Stormwater discharges.** When the *Rybachek* discharge permit was issued, there was only one point source of stormwater that was being actively regulated under the CWA; §304(e) authorizes EPA to establish BMPs "to control plant site runoff, spillage or leaks, sludge or waste disposal, and drainage from raw material storage" in order to diminish the amount of toxic pollutants flowing into receiving waters. In *Rybachek*, EPA had promulgated five BMPs to control toxic discharges due to mine drainage and infiltration.

In the 1987 CWA Amendments, Congress expanded EPA's jurisdiction to regulate stormwater discharges that are associated with industrial activity and that emanate from municipal separate storm sewer systems (MS4s). CWA §402(p). Currently, there are four major CWA programs regulating stormwater discharges from (1) CAFOs, (2) industrial operations, (3) MS4s, and (4) municipal combined and sanitary sewers.

EPA's final CAFO rules (40 C.F.R. §412) became effective on April 14, 2003. A CAFO is defined as a livestock operation that raises more than a certain minimum number of animals (e.g., 1000 cattle or 125,000 chickens) where manure is disposed of by discharging it into lagoons or treating it and spraying it onto farm fields as fertilizer (as in the *Southview Farms* decision, discussed above). There are currently about 240,000 animal feeding operations (AFOs) in the United States, of which about 15,000 will be classified as CAFOs subject to regulation. If an AFO is not managed properly, during storm events waste lagoons overflow and excess manure applied as fertilizer runs off into waterbodies, frequently leading to widespread nutrient and bacterial contamination.

The regulatory essence of the new CAFO rules is the requirement that CAFOs develop nutrient management plans that set limits on how much manure can be applied and include BMPs for meeting those limits. Nutrient management plans must be approved by states with primacy, or EPA in nonprimacy states, by 2006. States delegated primacy have the authority to design and implement, through either individual or general permits,[18] site-specific requirements containing standards that depend on the size, location, and environmental risks posed by particular CAFOs.

The industrial stormwater permit program covers plant yards, material handling sites, refuse sites, shipping and receiving areas, manufacturing buildings, raw material storage areas, and other areas at industrial sites where toxic materials may be present. The program does not include stormwater from facilities engaged in wholesale, retail, service, or commercial activities. An industrial discharger of stormwater must comply with the terms of a general permit for its industrial category. Each general permit requires the development and implementation of stormwater management plans (SMPs) incorporating pollution prevention BMPs such as planning, reporting, personnel training, preventive maintenance, and good housekeeping. For example, a discharger that experiences runoff from an uncovered outdoor pile of raw materials might either build an enclosure for the pile or move it indoors. SMPs must be reviewed and certified by a registered professional engineer.

The MS4 program has been described by the U.S. General Accounting Office as follows:

> Nonpoint source pollution can result when water, such as precipitation, runs over land surfaces and into bodies of water. Significant nonpoint sources of pollution can include paved urban areas, agricultural practices, forestry, and mining. However, in urban or suburban areas, this runoff generally enters a sewer system that can be regulated as a point source of water pollution. For example, precipitation from rain or snowmelt may run into a [MS4] that eventually discharges into a body of water. The precipitation may also run into a combined sewer system, which carries a combination of storm water runoff, industrial waste, and raw sewage in a single pipe to a sewage treatment facility for discharge after treatment. Lastly, the precipitation may run off of land or paved surfaces directly into nearby receiving waters.... In 1987, the Congress...directed EPA to also control storm water discharges that enter MS4s — essentially requiring EPA to treat such storm water as a point source. MS4s are defined as those sewers that collect and convey storm water; are owned or operated by the federal, state, or local government; and are not part of a publicly owned treatment (sewage) facility.

> To regulate urban storm water runoff, EPA published regulations in 1990 that established the NPDES Storm Water Program and described permit application requirements. According to EPA, the program's objective...is to...reduc[e] the level of runoff pollutants to the maximum extent practicable using best management practices (BMPs).[19]...

---

18. A general permit is an overall permit that is applicable to all members of a particular class of dischargers, e.g., specific CAFOs or small wetlands developers. A general permit contains all the regulatory requirements with which members of the class must comply. A discharger within the class need not obtain an individual permit (unless required by the regulatory authority) but must file a notice of intention to be covered by the general permit and submit plans and monitoring reports as indicated in it. Violators of general permits are subject to enforcement actions in the same manner as violators of individual permits. General permits, where appropriate, conserve the resources of both administrative agencies and dischargers.

19. The "maximum extent practicable" language is the statutory standard, which is not further defined in the CWA. Typical BMPs for MS4s are street sweeping, pet litter control ordinances, and sewer grate cleaning. [Eds.]

The [MS4] program is being implemented in two phases.... First, Phase I of the program requires that municipalities with a population of 100,000 or more obtain a permit for their MS4 system; second, the program requires that [private] entities obtain a permit if they discharge storm water...from construction activities that disturb 5 acres or more of land. Municipalities that meet these conditions must submit a permit application to EPA or the governing regulatory state. In 1990 [when the Phase I regulations became effective], the regulations specifically identified 220 municipalities throughout the United States that were required to apply for a Phase I permit.... Because some permits cover more than one municipality, these permits cover about 1,000 medium and large municipalities nationwide.

The final rule for Phase II of the program was issued in December 1999. Phase II extends Phase I efforts by requiring that a storm water discharge permit must be obtained by (1) operators of all MS4s not already covered by Phase I of the program in urban areas and (2) construction sites that disturb areas equal to or greater than 1 acre and less than 5 acres of land.... Currently, EPA anticipates that about 5,000 municipalities may be subject to permitting requirements under Phase II of the storm water program. These municipalities are required to obtain permits no later than March 10, 2003. GAO, Better Data and Evaluation of Urban Runoff Programs Needed to Assess Effectiveness 6-8 (2001).

EPA's emphasis on BMPs in controlling stormwater discharges from MS4s was upheld in Defenders of Wildlife v. EPA, 197 F.3d 1035 (9th Cir. 1999) (EPA did not act arbitrarily or capriciously in issuing municipalities MS4 discharge permits that included BMPs but not numerical effluent limitations). See also City of Abilene v. EPA, 325 F.3d 657 (5th Cir. 2003) (Phase I regulations upheld against constitutional — including Tenth Amendment — objections). The Phase II regulations were substantially upheld in Environmental Def. Ctr., Inc. v. EPA, 2003 WL 22119563 (9th Cir. 2003) (constitutional objections rejected but rules remanded because notices of intent to be covered by general permits were improperly shielded from EPA review, public disclosure, and administrative hearings).

EPA also regulates combined sewer overflows (CSOs), which are a major source of urban water pollution in general and, in particular, of beach closings and swimming advisories due to high concentrations of pathogens (bacteria and viruses) from untreated municipal sewage. Combined sewer systems, in which stormwater enters pipes already carrying sewage, may overflow when rain or snowmelt entering the system exceeds the system's flow capacity. In the CSO that results, the mixture of untreated sewage and runoff bypasses the POTW and is diverted directly into receiving waters. Nationwide, there are approximately 1100 combined sewer systems, serving about 43 million people. See generally Northwest Envtl. Advocates v. Portland, 56 F.3d 979 (9th Cir. 1995), cert. denied, 518 U.S. 1018 (1996). These combined systems generally serve the older parts of cities in the United States, whereas pipes carrying sewage and stormwater separately generally serve newer parts of cities. Although CSOs are significant point sources of pollution, the CWA does not specifically address them. Because separation of combined sewers is prohibitively expensive, EPA's CSO control requirements focus on BMPs and the development of long-term CSO control plans targeting environmentally sensitive receiving waters.

Sanitary sewer overflows (SSOs) (i.e., overflows of the sewage-carrying components of a separate sewer system) can also result from storm events. SSO regulation has been especially controversial, and EPA's SSO control program is still in its infancy.

5. **Municipal dischargers.** POTWs must also possess NPDES permits containing technology-based effluent limitations. They were required to have met effluent limitations based on "Secondary Treatment" (generally defined as a biological process that achieves 85% removal of conventional pollutants) by 1988. §301(b)(B) and 40 C.F.R. §133. Waivers from secondary treatment are available to POTWs that discharge into deep ocean waters, §301(h), but these waivers are rarely granted. Since 1972, federal monetary subsidies have been available for the construction and upgrading of POTWs and their sewerage systems. These federal incentives were first administered as the Construction Grants Program (CWA Title II), which provided almost $60 billion to municipalities and sewerage authorities in 55 to 85% matching grants for construction and land acquisition. In 1989, the Construction Grants Program was replaced by federal capitalization grants to State Revolving Loan Funds (SRFs). CWA Title VI. Approximately another $20 billion has been granted to the states under this program. However, there is an unmet need for approximately an additional $180 billion in investment for POTWs and sewerage infrastructure upgrades. There is a growing trend toward privatization of POTWs in order to allow for badly needed improvements to municipal wastewater infrastructure that government increasingly is unable to fund.

6. **Indirect dischargers and biosolids disposal.** Toxic and hazardous materials discharged into sanitary and combined sewers compose a substantial percentage of toxic pollutant loadings to waterways:

> A large number of industrial facilities, ranging from pesticide manufacturers to small local electroplaters, discharge toxic wastes to the nation's sewage treatment plants. A 1986 EPA study identified approximately 160,000 industrial and commercial facilities discharging wastes with hazardous constituents to public sewers, representing about 12 percent of the total flow to POTWs.... Secondary treatment alone does not remove these pollutants. While some fraction of organic hazardous constituents is degraded incidentally in the POTW's conventional treatment process, many of these substances evaporate during the treatment (or from the sewer pipes themselves) or wind up in the water or the sludge. None of the metals that go to a treatment plant are degraded: toxic metals pass through the plant into receiving waters or into the sludge generated by the treatment process.
> R. Adler et al., The Clean Water Act 20 Years Later 144–145 (1993).

Section 307 of the CWA requires EPA to promulgate "pretreatment standards" for indirect discharges that interfere with POTW operations, contaminate sludge, or pass untreated through the POTW, causing the POTW to violate its discharge permit. The CWA does not compel indirect dischargers to procure discharge permits, although some states require significant industrial users (SIUs) to obtain permits.

There are two types of national pretreatment standards: "prohibited discharge standards" and "categorical pretreatment standards." 40 C.F.R. §403. Prohibited discharge standards require that pollutants introduced into a POTW not inhibit the POTW's performance. Categorical pretreatment standards set out national discharge limits based on BAT, similar to TBELs for direct dischargers. Categorical pretreatment standards may be supplemented by stricter state or local standards where necessary to enable a POTW to comply with the effluent limitations in its own discharge permit or with an element of its CSO control plan.

Pretreatment standards are primarily enforced by the POTWs themselves — through local sewer connection permits or user agreements — with the states and EPA retaining backup enforcement authority. This system creates a fox-in-the-henhouse situation because POTWs are reluctant to enforce against their own customers unless (1) the indirect discharge disrupts the plant's operations, or (2) the POTW's discharge permit contains effluent limitations for toxics, the permit is being violated, and enforcement action is being taken against the POTW — a rare conjunction of circumstances. Not only has indirect discharge been a significant loophole in the CWA, but it also has been exacerbated by RCRA's exclusion of indirect discharges from its regulatory ambit. See Chapter 18. In Chapter 2, where Allied Chemical and its Life Science Products affiliate had been discharging Kepone directly into the James River, they ultimately opted for indirect discharge into the local POTW.

EPA reports that although toxic loadings to POTWs have decreased by up to 75% through pretreatment, approximately 54% of SIUs are in significant noncompliance with pretreatment standards (compared with a 6% noncompliance rate for direct dischargers), and 39% of POTWs are failing to implement at least one major component of their approved pretreatment programs. These statistics are indicative of problems that have plagued the pretreatment program since 1972. In response, EPA has increased its enforcement efforts against POTWs that are not implementing their approved pretreatment programs.

Biosolids (previously called "sewage sludge," but euphemistically renamed by EPA) are the final residual of the municipal sewage treatment process. Biosolids may be heavily contaminated due to inadequate pretreatment, uncontrolled flushing of household toxics (e.g., drain cleaners and pesticides), toxics entering sewers from road runoff into combined sewers or leaky sanitary sewers, and illegal hazardous waste dumping into municipal sewerage systems. Biosolids contaminated with heavy metals can preclude beneficial use as a soil conditioner on farmland, which EPA now favors as an alternative to disposal in landfills or incineration. CWA §405 establishes a permit system for biosolids disposal and requires EPA to promulgate regulations setting guidelines for biosolids disposal and reuse. EPA's biosolids disposal and reuse regulations have been highly controversial. Farmers are understandably reluctant to accept biosolids for land application because compliance with EPA standards will not insulate a farmer from common law actions brought by neighbors for abnormally dangerous activities resulting in groundwater contamination. See generally Goldfarb et al., Unsafe Sewage Sludge or Beneficial Biosolids?, 26 B.C. Envtl. Aff. L. Rev. 687 (1999).

7. **Drinking water protection.** Ambient water quality and tap water quality are regulated by different federal statutes. Under the Safe Drinking Water Act (SDWA), 42 U.S.C.A. §§300f et seq., EPA is required to promulgate national primary and secondary drinking water regulations applicable to "public water systems," defined as systems that have at least 15 service connections or regularly serve at least 25 individuals at least 60 days per year. Primary drinking water regulations identify potential toxic contaminants

and, for each contaminant, set a maximum contaminant level (MCL) if the contaminant can feasibly be measured or set a treatment technique if it cannot. Secondary drinking water regulations set MCLs for nontoxic contaminants that affect other parameters, for example, color and taste.

The SDWA, like the CWA, relies on technology-based standards. EPA first promulgates Maximum Contaminant Level Goals (MCLGs), which are nonenforceable health goals for public water systems. MCLGs are to be set at levels at which "no known or anticipated adverse effects on the health of persons occur and which allows an adequate margin of safety." Then, EPA promulgates enforceable primary drinking water regulations, including MCLs and monitoring and reporting requirements for dangerous contaminants. MCLs must be set as close to MCLGs as is "feasible," which means "with the use of the best technology, treatment techniques, and other means, which the Administrator finds are generally available (taking costs into consideration)." The SDWA also authorizes federal contributions to state revolving loan funds — modeled on the State Revolving Loan Funds under the CWA — for the construction and upgrade of water purification facilities.

8. **Toxics and the CWA.** Although he believes that "BAT under the Clean Water Act has probably been the most effective pollution control program in the world in terms of producing identifiable abatement," Professor Oliver Houck concludes that EPA's technology-based effluent limitation program is faltering with regard to toxic pollutants. Regulation of Toxic Pollutants Under the Clean Water Act, 21 Envtl. L. Rep. 10528 (1991). EPA has not added any priority pollutants to its list since the consent decree of 1976. According to Houck, "a greater number of individual industries remain unregulated than regulated, and a growing list of toxics have escaped scrutiny and standards."[20] Moreover, in Houck's view:

> Discharge standards have emerged unevenly, with a heavy "zero discharge" hand on such unfortunates as seafood canners and placer mine operators, and a remarkably blind eye to available closed-cycle systems for some of the nation's highest volume dischargers of broad-spectrum toxins [such as petroleum refiners and certain organic chemical producers]. The disparities in these standards reflect nothing more starkly than a disparity in clout. 21 Envtl. L. Rep. at 10539.

Skeptical of the water quality-based approach, Professor Houck recommends that Congress either (1) establish specific deadlines for EPA to promulgate new technology-based effluent limitations, with a zero-discharge "hammer" similar to RCRA's land ban (see Chapter 18); or (2) fix timetables, based on relative risk and reasonable lead times, for the elimination of toxic discharges. What are the potential disadvantages of so closely involving Congress in the intricacies of standard setting? An argument can be made that since Congress possesses a minimum of expertise in the technical aspects of water pollution control, its decisions will be either hopelessly unrealistic or even more politically motivated than EPA's. Under some political scenarios, Professor Houck might be better off with EPA than with Congress.

---

20. A report by the Comptroller General of the United States supports Professor Houck's conclusion. The GAO found that 77% of the discharge of all toxic pollutants across its sample (the vast majority of which were nonpriority pollutants) was uncontrolled. U.S. GAO, Poor Quality Assurance and Limited Pollutant Coverage Undermine EPA's Control of Toxic Substances (1994).

The *Atlantic States* case that follows illustrates the problem of controlling nonpriority toxic pollutants in the context of administering TBELs through the discharge permit of a large, multifaceted industrial operation. The industrial discharge of Kodak and the complexity of the permit in the *Atlantic States* case is more representative of the ordinary discharge permitting context than *Rybachek*. Notice how many pieces of the puzzle that have been studied thus far (e.g., CWA regulations, discharge permits, cooperative federalism, and deferential judicial review) combine to generate the law of water pollution control. Notice also that this litigation arose by way of a citizen suit, one of the approximately 1500 CWA citizen suits that have been filed since 1972. (See Chapters 7 and 21 for analysis of environmental citizen suits.)

Atlantic States Legal Foundation, Inc. v. Eastman Kodak Company
United States Court of Appeals for the Second Circuit, 1993
12 F.3d 353, cert. denied, 513 U.S. 811 (1994)

WINTER, J.: This appeal raises the issue of whether private groups may bring a citizen suit pursuant to §505 of the Clean Water Act to stop the discharge of pollutants not listed in a valid permit issued pursuant to CWA §402. We hold that the discharge of unlisted pollutants is not unlawful under the CWA. We also hold that private groups may not bring such a suit to enforce New York State environmental regulations.

Appellee Eastman Kodak Company ("Kodak") operates an industrial facility in Rochester, New York that discharges wastewater into the Genesee River and Paddy Hill Creek under a State Pollutant Discharge Elimination System ("SPDES") permit issued pursuant to CWA §402. Appellant Atlantic States Legal Foundation, Inc. is a not-for-profit environmental group based in Syracuse, New York.

Kodak operates a wastewater treatment plant at its Rochester facility to purify waste produced in the manufacture of photographic supplies and other laboratory chemicals. The purification plant employs a variety of technical processes to filter harmful pollutants before discharge into the Genesee River at the King's Landing discharge point (designated Outfall 001) pursuant to its SPDES permit.

Kodak first received a federal permit in 1975. At that time, the pertinent regulatory scheme was the NPDES administered directly by the federal Environmental Protection Agency. Subsequently, CWA §402(b-c) delegated authority to the states to establish their own programs in place of the EPA's. As a result, Kodak applied in July 1979 to renew its permit to the New York State Department of Environmental Conservation ("DEC"). The DEC declined to act on Kodak's renewal application, and Kodak's NPDES permit remained in effect. As part of the pending application for a SPDES permit, in April 1982, Kodak provided the DEC with a Form 2C describing estimated discharges of 164 substances from each of its outfalls. Kodak also submitted an Industrial Chemical Survey ("ICS") disclosing the amounts of certain chemicals used in Kodak's facility and whether they might appear in the plant's wastewater. Although the ICS originally requested information on 144 substances, including some broad classes such as "unspecified metals," the DEC restricted the inquiry to chemicals used in excess of specified minimum levels.

On the basis of these disclosures, DEC issued Kodak a SPDES permit, number 000-1643, effective November 1, 1984, establishing specific effluent limitations for approximately 25 pollutants.[21] The permit also included "action levels"[22] for five other pollutants as well as for three of the pollutants for which it had established effluent limits. DEC further required Kodak to conduct a semi-annual scan of "EPA Volatile, Acid and Base/Neutral Fractions and PCBs priority pollutants on a 24-hr. composite sample." In May 1989, Kodak applied to renew the SPDES permit submitting a new Form 2C and ICS, but the 1984 permit will continue to remain in effect until DEC issues a final determination.

On November 14, 1991, Atlantic States filed the complaint in the instant matter. The complaint alleged that Kodak had violated CWA §§301 and 402 by discharging large quantities of pollutants not listed in its SPDES permit.[23] After discovery, Atlantic States moved for partial summary judgment as to Kodak's liability in relation to the post-April 1, 1990 discharge of one or more of 16 of the 27 pollutants listed in the complaint.[24] The 16 pollutants are all listed as toxic chemicals under §313(c) of the Emergency Planning and Community Right-to-Know Act, 42 U.S.C. §11023(c). Atlantic States argued that General Provision 1(b) of the SPDES permit and §301 of the CWA prohibit absolutely the discharge of any pollutant not specifically authorized under Kodak's SPDES permit. Kodak made a cross-motion for summary judgment on the ground that neither the CWA nor the federal regulations implementing it prohibit discharge of pollutants not specifically assigned effluent limitations in an NPDES or SPDES permit.

Atlantic States argues first that the plain language of §301 of the CWA prohibits the discharge of any pollutants not expressly permitted. Section 301(a) reads: "Except as in compliance with this section and §§1312, 1316, 1317, 1328, 1342, and 1344 of this title, the discharge of any pollutant by any person shall be unlawful." This prohibition is tempered, however, by a self-referential host of exceptions that allow the discharge of many pollutants once a polluter has complied with the regulatory program of the CWA. The exception relevant to the instant matter is contained in §402, which outlines the NPDES, and specifies the requirements for suspending the national system with the submission of an approved state program, CWA §402(b-c). Section 402(k) contains the so-called "shield provision" which defines compliance with a NPDES or SPDES permit as compliance with §301 for the purposes of the CWA's enforcement provisions.

---

21. UOD, TKN, Ammonia, BOD sub5, oil & grease, phosphorus, cyanide, cadmium, chromium, copper, iron, lead, nickel, silver (total and ionic), zinc, mercury, chloroform, 4-Chloro-3,5-dimethylphenol, 1,2-Dichloroethane, 1,2-Dichloropropane, N,N-Dimethylaniline, Dichloromethane, Pyridine, and Xylene. [This is footnote 1 in the original. These substances include conventional and toxic pollutants. Most of the toxic parameters are priority pollutants, but some are nonpriority pollutants. — Eds.]

22. If the action level is exceeded, the permittee must undertake a "short-term, high-intensity monitoring program." If levels higher than the action levels are confirmed, the permit is reopened for consideration of revised action levels or effluent limits. [This is footnote 2 in the original. — Eds.]

23. Specifically, the complaint alleged that Kodak had discharged "282,744 pounds of unpermitted pollutants in 1987, 308,537 pounds in 1988, 321,456 pounds in 1989, and 290,121 pounds in 1990," and that Atlantic States believed that Kodak continued to discharge such pollutants. The 27 substances Atlantic States alleged that Kodak discharged were acetonitrile, acetone, carbon tetrachloride, catechol, cyclohexane, dibutyl phthalate, diethanolamine, ethylene glycol, glycol ethers, formaldehyde, hydroquinone, manganese, methanol, methyl ethyl ketone, methyl isobutyl ketone, n-butyl alcohol, nitrobenzene, 1,1,1-trichloroethane, 1,1,2-trichloroethane, 1,4-dioxane, 2-ethoxyethanol, 2-methoxyethanol, tert-butyl alcohol, toluene, and trichloroethylene. [This is footnote 4 in the original. The great majority of these parameters are nonpriority toxic pollutants. — Eds.]

24. Atlantic States' contentions regarding the number and amount of pollutants discharged are not material given our disposition of this matter. Of the 16 substances on which Atlantic States moved for partial summary judgment, seven were listed by Kodak in its permit application, Form 2C, or ICS, or were specifically mentioned in the DEC's 1988 Notice Letter: dibutyl phthalate, ethylene glycol, manganese, 1,4-dioxane, 1,1,1-trichloroethane, 1,1,2-trichloroethane, and toluene. These substances received specific regulatory inquiry. The remaining nine substances appeared on Kodak's Form R's, the source of Atlantic States' information. Kodak must file annual Form Rs, a Toxic Chemical Release Inventory Reporting Form, with both EPA and DEC, pursuant to 42 U.S.C. §11023. Although not listed in Kodak's SPDES permit, these substances were subject to DEC regulation. Even had there been no regulation of the particular substances, Atlantic States would still not have standing to sue unless it could show violations of established regulatory limits. [This is footnote 7 in the original. — Eds.]

The Supreme Court has noted that: "The purpose of [§402(k)] seems to be...to relieve [permit holders] of having to litigate in an enforcement action the question whether their permits are sufficiently strict." E. I. du Pont de Nemours & Co. v. Train, 430 U.S. 112, 138 n. 28 (1977).

Atlantic States' view of the regulatory framework stands that scheme on its head. Atlantic States treats permits as establishing limited permission for the discharge of identified pollutants and a prohibition on the discharge of unidentified pollutants. Viewing the regulatory scheme as a whole, however, it is clear that the permit is intended to identify and limit the most harmful pollutants while leaving the control of the vast number of other pollutants to disclosure requirements. Once within the NPDES or SPDES scheme, therefore, polluters may discharge pollutants not specifically listed in their permits so long as they comply with the appropriate reporting requirements and abide by any new limitations when imposed on such pollutants.

The EPA lists tens of thousands of different chemical substances in the Toxic Substances Control Act Chemical Substance Inventory pursuant to 15 U.S.C. §2607(b). However, the EPA does not demand even information regarding each of the many thousand chemical substances potentially present in a manufacturer's wastewater because "it is impossible to identify and rationally limit every chemical or compound present in a discharge of pollutants." Memorandum from EPA Deputy Assistant Administrator for Water Enforcement Jeffrey G. Miller to Regional Enforcement Director, Region V, at 2 (Apr. 28, 1976). "Compliance with such a permit would be impossible and anybody seeking to harass a permittee need only analyze that permittee's discharge until determining the presence of a substance not identified in the permit." Indeed, at oral argument Atlantic States could provide no principled reason why water itself, which is conceded to be a chemical, would not be considered a "pollutant" under its view of the Act.

The EPA has never acted in any way to suggest that Atlantic States' absolutist and wholly impractical view of the legal effect of a permit is valid. In fact, the EPA's actions and policy statements have frequently contemplated discharges of pollutants not listed under a NPDES or SPDES permit. It has addressed such discharges by amending the permit to list and limit a pollutant when necessary to safeguard the environment without considering pre-amendment discharges to be violations calling for enforcement under the CWA. The EPA thus stated in its comments on proposed 40 C.F.R. §122.68(a), which applied the "application-based" limits approach to implementation of the CWA reporting scheme:

> There is still some possibility...that a [NPDES or SPDES] permittee may discharge a large amount of a pollutant not limited in its permit, and EPA will not be able to take enforcement action against the permittee as long as the permittee complies with the notification requirements [pursuant to the CWA]. 45 Fed. Reg. 33516, 33523 (1980).

The EPA's statement went on to note that this possibility constituted a "regulatory gap," and that, "the final regulations control discharges only of the pollutants listed in the [NPDES or SPDES] permit application, which consist primarily of the listed [priority] toxic pollutants and designated hazardous substances." [The opinion went on to uphold EPA's statutory interpretation using the deferential Chevron v. NRDC, 467 U.S. 837 (1984), standard of review. The decision in favor of Kodak was affirmed.]

COMMENTARY & QUESTIONS

1. **CWA §402(k) and the NPDES permit shield defense.** Is compliance with an NPDES permit a complete defense to *all* claims related to the discharge of pollutants through the regulated outfall? The statutory language of §402(k) links the permit compliance defense only to claims asserting violation of the CWA's effluent limitation provisions.

Common law actions (primarily nuisance) survive despite permit compliance, as do state law-based statutory actions that go beyond the CWA.

2. **Regulating unlisted discharges.** Is it clear that the nine discharged toxic substances that Kodak did not list in its permit application will later be subjected to regulation? Federal law requires that states taking primacy, such as New York in this case, can at any time terminate or modify the permit. CWA §402(b)(1)(C)(iii). More routinely, the revision could be accomplished as part of the five-year periodic renewal process contemplated by §402(b)(1)(B). Even after a state takes primacy, EPA, under §402(i), retains residual enforcement power. Having established that DEC or EPA can force a change in Kodak's discharges, the real question is whether DEC or EPA must act to do so. General administrative law doctrines give the agency a good deal of latitude in enforcement matters (see Chapter 7).

3. **The effluent limitations — BAT and BPJ.** In its ongoing implementation of the CWA, EPA has identified BAT for all 126 toxic pollutants on its priority list, although it has yet to promulgate those limits for all categories of dischargers. As to nonpriority toxic pollutants, regulation of their discharge is to be based on Best Professional Judgment (BPJ).[25] A slightly more comforting view of events in *Atlantic States* can be gleaned from the fact that TBELs are applied to 25 substances, including BAT-level treatments for the priority toxic chemicals, and BPJ for a number of nonpriority toxics. According to experts in the field, the treatments required (whether based on BAT or BPJ) for the toxic chemicals expressly regulated by a complex permit, such as the Kodak permit, will be identical, in a some cases, to the treatments that are appropriate for some of the additional chemicals also present in the discharge but not regulated by the permit. Put differently, chemicals listed in the permits sometimes serve as regulatory surrogates for other chemicals. The matter, however, requires careful case-by-case scrutiny. The toxic combinations may require additional treatments or, worse, present treatment antagonisms rather than treatment synergies.

4. **What did the permit writers know, and when did they know it?** The facts of the case are a bit hard to follow: The complaint alleged unpermitted discharge of 27 pollutants, but the motion for summary judgment limited itself to 16 substances that are all on the EPCRA (Emergency Planning and Community Right-to-Know Act) list of toxic substances. The court observes (in original footnote 7) that 7 of the unlisted 16 substances were included by Kodak on its permit application documents or raised for discussion by DEC. As to those substances, the court is on firm ground in saying the agency knew of them and opted not to regulate them, thereby placing them behind the permit shield. The remaining 9 substances, however, appeared only on the EPCRA Form R. That form is a routine annual report that is filed with a different department within

---

25. BPJ is set on the same basis as BAT but is implemented in the case-by-case context of writing specific permits. In that context, it is easy to imagine that a state permit writer could more easily be persuaded to give greater consideration to the "economically achievable" strand of the BAT standard than might EPA when it establishes its categorical BAT standards. Thus BPJ may tend to demand less stringent controls than those that would obtain if the substance were a priority pollutant regulated by EPA. One favorable aspect of BPJ-based permits is that the CWA's "anti-backsliding" provisions, §402(o), prohibit, with some exceptions, the relaxation of BPJ-based effluent limitations in future permits even if subsequently promulgated effluent limitation regulations might be more lenient.

the state agency. The fact that the Form Rs were filed with DEC is not, without more, a very solid basis for concluding that the permit writers took cognizance of what those forms disclosed.[26]

5. **CWA federalism, devolution, stricter state standards, and citizen suits.** In *Atlantic States* there is a transfer from federal to state primacy, exactly as envisioned by Congress. In portions of the case that were not excerpted here, the plaintiffs argued that linguistic nuances in the New York statutes establishing the SPDES program resulted in SPDES permits having a different impact than federal NPDES permits in regard to unlisted pollutants. States indeed can regulate more stringently than the "federal floor" set by the CWA. Section 510 of the CWA, entitled "State Authority," somewhat elliptically provides that

> ...nothing in this chapter shall (1) preclude or deny the right of any State or political subdivision thereof or interstate agency to adopt or enforce (A) any standard or limitation respecting discharges of pollutants, or (B) any requirement respecting control or abatement of pollution; except if [the state regulation] is less stringent than [the federal regulation imposed by the CWA].

In *Atlantic States*, the court, in dicta, found that the New York SPDES system was not more stringent in limiting the permit shield defense than the NPDES system in this regard. The actual holding on this point is more technical but quite important. The court ruled that a CWA §505 citizen suit cannot be used to enforce claims that are based on those stricter state laws (if the state has indeed enacted stricter-than-federal regulation). This ruling is significant because under the CWA, in §505(d), the court "may award costs of litigation (including reasonable attorney and expert witness fees) to any prevailing, or substantially prevailing party, whenever the court determines such award is appropriate." Such fee-shifting is not generally available under state law.

However, federal citizen suits to enforce more stringent state standards may not be completely foreclosed. The permit shield defense cannot be imposed to block a citizen suit to enforce against a violation of state water quality standards, even if the discharge permit does not include specific WQBELs, as long as the permit generally requires (as most do) that the discharge must be in compliance with applicable water quality standards. See *Northwest Envtl. Advocates*, above. (In addition, most discharge permits contain the language that "discharges of toxics in toxic amounts are prohibited.")

In addition, a large, multifaceted discharger like Kodak might be required to perform expensive and complex ecological monitoring, as in NRDC v. Texaco Ref. & Mktg., Inc., 182 F.3d 904 (3d Cir. 1999) (district court did not abuse its discretion by ordering defendant to implement $500,000 monitoring plan, developed by a court-appointed expert, to monitor receiving waters in order to determine the impact of noncomplying discharges on an estuarine ecosystem).

---

26. Judge Winter adds, at the end of his footnote 7, an even more enigmatic limitation on Atlantic States' ability to bring suit. He asserts that there is no standing to bring suit in regard to discharges of chemicals not revealed to the agency in any fashion unless Atlantic States can also "show violations of established regulatory levels." Recalling the way in which nonpriority toxic pollutants are regulated by the ad hoc generation of BPJ standards, there are no *established* standards for those chemicals. Their discharge would be insulated from attack in a citizen suit if the footnote is correct on this point.

6. **Who should bear the burden of proof regarding toxicity?** Toxicity screening data are unavailable for approximately 90% of the high-volume chemicals utilized by industries in the United States. As for known toxics, the EPCRA list of toxic substances includes nearly 700 substances, and the State of California has listed approximately 300 substances as toxic under its Safe Drinking Water and Toxic Enforcement Act, commonly known as Proposition 65 (discussed in Chapter 10). See Roe, Ready or Not: The Coming Wave of Toxic Chemicals, 29 Ecology L.Q. 623 (2002). Clearly, the CWA's priority pollutant list is profoundly incomplete with regard to identifying toxic parameters discharged into waterbodies. The *Atlantic States* opinion places the burden on state administrative agencies to establish which substances (other than priority pollutants), in which quantities, would constitute an excessive risk when discharged into surface waterbodies. Given the paucity of toxics testing data, the large number of substances that are generally considered to be environmental toxins, and the fiscal crises facing state agencies, perhaps industries such as Kodak should be obligated to demonstrate nontoxicity of nonpriority pollutants before discharging into waterbodies. A similar precautionary approach has been unsuccessfully attempted in the ToSCA (see Chapter 17).

D. WATER QUALITY-BASED PERMITTING UNDER THE CWA

In the 1990s, with the TBEL process a mature and reasonably successful program, WQBELs, which had been on the back burner for 15 years, progressively became the most visible and contentious aspect of point source control under the CWA. Professor Houck has pointed out the irony of this trend:

> At the bottom of these developments is an approach to pollution control — regulating dischargers by their impact on receiving water quality — that never really worked in the first place and is back for another try…. No step in the process worked: use determinations were highly variable, leaving protective states at a distinct disadvantage, and a race-to-the bottom; information on those biological conditions necessary to support aquatic life was spotty and insufficient; impact assessment was equally imprecise, and the chore of tracing impacts from multiple-dischargers was overwhelming; and abatement in the face of these uncertainties was ephemeral and rarely achieved…. One could have legitimate doubts about it this time as well. It is no small irony that the reason the Clean Water Act retained this approach, and directed its use for the upgrade of polluted waters, is that both the states and pollution dischargers insisted on it…. Houck, TMDLs: The Resurrection of Water Quality Standards-Based Regulation under the Clean Water Act, 27 Envtl. L. Rep. 10329, 10330 (1997).

The following case describes the process of setting and implementing WQBELs and illustrates some of the problems that they pose for administrators, dischargers, and concerned citizens.

Sierra Club v. U.S. Environmental Protection Agency
United States Court of Appeals for the Eleventh Circuit, 2003
296 F.3d 1021

CARNES, J. [This litigation involves the interpretation of a consent decree that] resulted from a lawsuit brought by Sierra Club, along with a collection of state and local environmental organizations, against EPA. The plaintiff environmental groups...had sued EPA to force it to establish and implement pollution standards for Georgia waterways. The consent decree that was eventually entered set out a timetable for the establishment of those standards. EPA did establish the standards....

Background: Non-Point Sources, Water Quality Standards, and TMDLs. In addition to originating from point sources, pollution also comes from non-point sources, such as runoff from farmlands, mining activity, housing construction projects, roads, and so on. Non-point sources cannot be regulated by permits because there is no way to trace the pollution to a particular point, measure it, and then set an acceptable level for that point. Therefore, to regulate non-point pollution, the Act requires states to establish water quality standards. 33 U.S.C. §§1313(a)-(c). To determine the water quality standard, a state designates the use for which a given body of water is to be protected (fishing, for example), and then determines the level of water quality needed to safely allow that use. Id. at §1313(c)(2)(A). That level becomes the water quality standard for that body of water.

Things can get complicated. Because of non-point source pollution, achieving the specified water quality standard in a body of water may require more stringent limitations upon point-source discharges than would otherwise be required.... If the regulation of point-source discharges does not achieve the necessary level of water quality, Total Maximum Daily Loads (TMDLs) come into play. Id. at §1313(d)(1)(A), (C). A TMDL is a specification of the maximum amount of a particular pollutant that can pass through a waterbody each day without water quality standards being violated. Id. at §1313(d)(1)(C).

TMDLs must be established for every waterbody within the state for which ordinary technology-based point-source limits will not do enough to achieve the necessary level of water quality. The state must compile a list of these bodies of water in a report and submit it to EPA for approval. (This list is sometimes referred to as "the 303(d) list," because that is the section of the Act which requires each state to prepare the list.) Each body of water on the list is known as a "water quality limited segment" (or "limited segment" for short), and the state must set a TMDL for every pollutant in each limited segment.[27]

Each TMDL serves as the goal for the level of that pollutant in the waterbody to which that TMDL applies, allocating the total "load" — the amount of pollutant introduced into the water — specified in that TMDL among contributing point and non-point sources.[28] The theory is that individual-discharge permits will be adjusted and other measures taken so that the sum of that pollutant in the waterbody is reduced to the level specified by the TMDL. As should be

---

27. Water quality limited segments are also referred to as "impaired waters." [Eds.]

28. The text of §§303(d)(1)(A) and (C) reads:

    (A) Each state shall identify those waters within its boundaries for which the effluent limitations required by [this Act] are not stringent enough to implement any water quality standards applicable to such waters. The state shall establish a priority ranking for such waters, taking into account the severity of the pollution and the uses to be made of such waters.... (C) Each state shall establish for the waters identified in paragraph (1)(A) of this subsection, and in accordance with the priority ranking, the total maximum daily load for those pollutants which the Administrator identifies...as suitable for such calculation. Such load shall be established at a level necessary to implement the applicable water quality standards, with seasonable variations and a margin of safety which takes into account any lack of knowledge concerning the relationship between effluent limitations and water quality. [Eds.]

apparent, TMDLs are central to the Clean Water Act's water-quality scheme because, as one of the plaintiffs puts it, they tie "together point-source and nonpoint-source pollution issues in a manner that addresses the whole health of the water."

The states are primarily responsible for preparing lists of limited segments and their corresponding TMDLs, but EPA has approval authority over those lists. If EPA disapproves a state's list of limited segments, or a TMDL, EPA must issue its own list or TMDL. Some courts have held that a state's failure to timely submit its TMDLs can be taken under certain circumstances by EPA as a constructive submission of no TMDLs, triggering EPA's responsibility to establish its own. See Scott v. City of Hammond, 741 F.2d 992, 996–998 (7th Cir. 1984).... We have not addressed this issue of constructive submission yet, and need not do so in this case because under the consent decree EPA was obligated to issue its own TMDLs according to a prescribed timetable if Georgia continued to fail to establish them.

Once established, TMDLs are implemented through various mechanisms, some of which are provided in the Act, with responsibilities for implementation divided between EPA and the states. Point-source discharges are regulated through the federal permit regime, with TMDLs incorporated into the effluent and technological-based limitations.[29] Although EPA has the authority to issue permits, it has delegated that authority to the states, at least to the majority of them, including Georgia. Even where it has delegated that basic authority, however, EPA does retain the right to include additional limits in NPDES permits when necessary to ensure a congressionally-established standard of water quality.

The Act generally leaves regulation of non-point source discharges through the implementation of TMDLs to the states. It imposes on the states planning responsibilities, including the preparation of a non-point source management plan, commonly referred to as a §319 report. In this report, a state must, among other things, identify waters where water quality standards can reasonably be met only by additional action to control non-point source pollution, and designate the categories and subcategories of non-point sources that contribute to the pollution in those waters. States also have to prepare a management program that identifies "best management practices and measures" to reduce pollution. EPA exercises authority over these programs and must approve them. Once the programs have been approved, EPA may make grants to the states to allow them to implement the plans.

Finally, a state has to prepare a "continuing planning process," which is essentially a plan for how the state is going to clean up pollution. Like the best management program, EPA has to approve or disapprove each state's continuing planning process and, once it has been approved, occasionally review it to ensure it stays consistent with the Act. In preparing its continuing planning process, a state must incorporate established TMDLs.

To summarize, under the Clean Water Act, Georgia has the primary authority and responsibility for issuing permits and controlling nonpoint source pollution in that state. It also has both the authority and the duty to compile the list of limited segments (the §303(d) list), and establish TMDLs for each waterbody on the list. EPA, for its part, has supervisory authority over various reports and plans which the state is required by the Act to produce. EPA can also compile its own list of limited segments and establish its own TMDLs, if the state's efforts are either inadequate or too long delayed.

The Consent Decree and Dispute in this Appeal. By the time Sierra Club sued EPA in 1994, sixteen years after the Act had gone into effect, Georgia had established only two TMDLs for the

---

29. WQBELs become a more stringent level of effluent limitations that supplement TBELs as permit conditions. [Eds.]

approximately 340 limited segments identified in its 303(d) list, and the district court found that neither of those two TMDLs satisfied the requirements of the Act. In the lawsuit, Sierra Club asked the court to force EPA to establish the TMDLs and to implement them, because Georgia had not done so. The district court granted summary judgment for Sierra Club, and entered an injunction requiring the EPA to both establish and implement TMDLs for all Georgia limited segments by June 2001. The injunction directed EPA to "implement (or ensure that the State implements)" TMDLs through the modification, revocation, and re-issuance of permits. It also imposed a number of other requirements on EPA, most of which had to do with making it exercise supervision over Georgia's water quality control efforts. EPA appealed to this Court.

While EPA's appeal was still pending, in July of 1997 the parties agreed upon the terms of a consent decree and persuaded the district court to enter it, which it did in October of 1997. In the consent decree, EPA was ordered to establish TMDLs for the limited segments on Georgia's §303(d) list on a basin approach if Georgia continued to fail to do so. Under a schedule set out in the decree, all TMDLs were to be established by 2004, and additional, more specific deadlines were included. The decree provided that by 1998, EPA was to establish TMDLs for twenty percent of the waterways on Georgia's 1996 list of limited segments. These 1998 TMDLs are the ones that are the subject of this appeal, the ones Sierra Club says EPA should have prepared an implementation plan for, but they are only the first group of TMDLs that EPA was to establish under the terms of the consent decree. The decree also required the EPA to establish TMDLs for the remaining waterbodies on a river basin rotation schedule, if Georgia failed to do so.

The basin rotation schedule was to begin in 1999, with TMDLs proposed for all the basins by 2004. Besides establishing TMDLs, the decree imposed other responsibilities on EPA, including: (1) review of Georgia's continuing planning process, (2) proposal of specific terms for Georgia/EPA Performance Partnership Agreements, (3) biennial review of Georgia's TMDL program, and (4) submission of annual compliance reports to the court and to the plaintiff groups.

EPA proposed 124 TMDLs for Georgia's waterbodies in August of 1997 and attached them to the consent decree which the parties submitted to the district court for its approval. Under the terms of the decree, those TMDLs were to be "established, or finalized" within six months after being proposed. All but eight were timely established by EPA, and even those eight were established after Sierra Club filed a motion to force EPA to do so. Once EPA had established the TMDLs, nothing else was done with them. Georgia did not incorporate the TMDLs into any of its non-point source management plans or reports and did not implement them. As a result, two years after entering into the consent decree, only one of the 124 waterbodies on Georgia's 1996 §303(d) list met water quality standards.

Dissatisfied with the progress made towards clean water in Georgia and with EPA action or lack of it, in February 2000 Sierra Club moved the district court to re-open the decree and to compel EPA to take further action. Specifically, Sierra Club moved the court to order EPA to prepare implementation plans for the 124 TMDLs the agency had established in 1998. EPA argued in response that the decree did not obligate it to prepare implementation plans for or to implement TMDLs, and that the decree should not be modified to impose that responsibility on it.

The district court deferred ruling on Sierra Club's motion because Georgia promised to develop implementation plans for the 124 TMDLs within nine months. Within that time period, Georgia did develop implementation plans for all 124 of those TMDLs. Because the plans which Sierra Club wanted EPA to develop had now been developed by Georgia, EPA moved the court to dismiss as moot Sierra Club's motion to re-open and compel. Sierra Club argued that its motion was not moot, because Georgia's implementation plans were flawed or otherwise unsatisfactory.

The district court denied the EPA's motion to dismiss as moot Sierra Club's motion. In its order, the court ruled that "TMDL implementation plans are required [of EPA] by the Consent Decree." As for the Georgia-prepared plans, the court ruled that EPA had "obligations" to "ensure" those plans were adequate. The order did not, however, declare the Georgia plans insufficient. Instead, it directed EPA and Sierra Club to confer about those plans and attempt to reach an agreement concerning them. If their disagreements could not be resolved by discussion, the order stated, the court would grant either party's request for an evidentiary hearing on the sufficiency of the Georgia plans. EPA appealed the district court's order....

As this Court has explained before, "As a general matter, the rules we use to interpret a consent decree are the same ones we use to interpret a contract — since a consent decree is a form of contract." With a consent decree as with a contract, the first place we look and often the last as well is to the document itself. The consent decree in this case provided that if Georgia failed to establish TMDLs, EPA was required to do so. The decree defined a TMDL as having "the meaning provided at Section 303(d)(1)(C) of the CWA, and 40 C.F.R. §130.2(i), as codified as of the Effective Date of this Decree, or as subsequently amended." Neither the referenced statutory provision nor the referenced regulation includes implementation plans within the meaning of TMDLs.[30] The two are different, and the statute and regulation incorporated into the definition part of the consent decree reflect that difference. A TMDL is defined to be a set measure or prescribed maximum quantity of a particular pollutant in a given waterbody, while an implementation plan is a formal statement of how the level of that pollutant can and will be brought down to or kept under the TMDL.

The consent decree clearly and explicitly places a number of duties on EPA, including the requirement to establish TMDLs on a basin approach if Georgia fails to do so, but it just as clearly does not require EPA to develop implementation plans for those TMDLs once they are established. The decree contains seven pages setting out in detail EPA's obligations under it, and conspicuously absent from the list of those obligations is any mention of implementation plans. Indeed, implementation plans are not mentioned at all anywhere in the 28-page decree. If the parties had intended for the decree to put such an important and substantial responsibility on EPA, they would have spelled that out just they spelled out its responsibility to establish TMDLs.

The district court gave two reasons for finding that implementation plans were required by the consent decree. First, it said that "[u]nder EPA's interpretation of the Consent Decree, TMDLs would be developed with no guarantee that they would ever be implemented. Developing TMDLs without implementing them amounts to an academic endeavor which would have no effect on water quality in Georgia." Or, as Sierra Club restates that concern, unless implementation plans are read into TMDLs, the decree is reduced to "empty formalism." We doubt that, because TMDLs are a necessary step before any implementation plans can be formulated. Interpreting the decree as written gives it meaning, because establishing TMDLs is a meaningful and not necessarily simple step in the process of controlling pollution in Georgia's waterbodies. After all, in sixteen years Georgia had established only two of the hundreds of TMDLs that were necessary, and the adequacy of those two was questionable. The decree put the TMDL task with all of its difficulties on EPA. The responsibility for implementing the TMDLs once they were established was left to Georgia, as it is in the Clean Water Act itself.

The second reason the district court gave for its conclusion that EPA was required by the consent decree to establish implementation plans is that reading that into the decree would further the goal of the Clean Water Act, which is cleaner water. The court stated, "EPA's

---

30. The regulation defines a TMDL as "[t]he sum of the individual [wasteload allocations] for point sources and [load allocations] for non-point sources and natural background." [This is footnote 8 in the original. — Eds.]

interpretation is incompatible with the Clean Water Act goal of improving water quality. Specifically, among the stated objectives of the Clean Water Act is the following: '[I]t is the national policy that programs for the control of nonpoint sources of pollution be developed and implemented in an expeditious manner....'" Of course, the national policy and objectives relating to clean water are most reliably embodied in the Act itself which puts the responsibility for implementation of TMDLs on the states. Logically, the Act cannot be a source of authority for changing the Act's allocation of responsibilities....

This, then is the original relationship between the parties as established by the consent decree: at Sierra Club's insistence EPA was obligated to develop for the State of Georgia TMDLs, as defined by the statutory and regulatory provisions. The order we have before us declared that the consent decree went beyond that and required EPA to develop not just TMDLs but implementation plans for TMDLs. Because the decree as written and entered did not require EPA to prepare implementation plans for the TMDLs, the district court's order requiring EPA to prepare them modified the decree because it changed the legal relationship of the parties by "chang[ing] the command of the earlier injunction."...

Sierra Club contends that there have been changes in both the law and surrounding circumstances which justify the district court's modification of the decree. It points to some guidance documents and a proposed rule published by EPA as proof that the law has changed, but none of those documents or proposals have the effect of law. As for guidance documents, they can modify neither statutes nor regulations. To legally change its regulations, EPA must comply with the rulemaking procedures set out in the Administrative Procedures Act. The method by which guidance documents are created does not even come close to compliance with those procedures.

As for the proposed rule Sierra relies upon, it did not work a change in the law because it has never been implemented and in fact has been withdrawn. EPA proposed the new rule in 1999, see 64 Fed. Reg. 46012 (Aug. 23, 1999), and published it as a final rule in July of 2000, see 65 Fed. Reg. 43586 (July 13, 2000), but it was never implemented. Congress refused to appropriate the necessary funds for implementation, which delayed things, see Pub. L. No. 106-246, 114 Stat. 511, 567 (2000), and then EPA withdrew the proposed rule. See 66 Fed. Reg. 41817 (Aug. 9, 2001). At no time was the new rule ever applied by EPA, and as things stand, the relevant regulations related to the Act are the same as they were in 1997.[31] The statutory and regulatory regime — the applicable law — is the same now as it was when the consent decree was entered. There has been no change.

Nor has there been a change in factual circumstances sufficient to justify the district court's modification of the decree. It is true that the state of Georgia is not currently implementing the TMDLs established by EPA at the rate contemplated by the Act, but Georgia has never carried out its responsibilities under the Act at anywhere near the pace the Act contemplates. Georgia's governmental lethargy in this area is nothing new. Indeed, it was what Sierra Club calls "Georgia's 16 year failure and refusal to develop and implement the [TMDL] process for hundreds of Georgia's rivers, streams, lakes, and estuaries that were not meeting designated standards for fishing, swimming, and drinking," which led to the lawsuit. A decree cannot be justifiably modified based upon the theory of changed factual circumstances when the circumstances simply have not changed....

While the Clean Water Act sets out a process composed of several steps to achieve clean water, the consent decree focuses on bringing about one of those steps, the establishment of

---

31. The "EPA Requirements for Water Quality Planning and Management" are codified at 40 C.F.R. pt. 130. [Eds.]

TMDLs, and it leaves attainment of the Act's ultimate goal of cleaning up the water to the statutory and regulatory scheme which requires compliance by Georgia subject to some oversight by EPA. The consent decree does not supplant the Act itself. Under the decree, Georgia is still responsible for incorporating TMDLs, regardless of whoever establishes them, into its section 303(e) plan; Georgia is still responsible for incorporating TMDLs into its NPDES permits; and Georgia is still responsible for implementing non-point source pollution controls. EPA agreed only to a supervisory role with respect to some of these implementation-related processes, but it did not agree to take over the implementation process. The objective of the consent decree was the establishment of TMDLs, not the much more long-term goal of clean water.... The district court's order denying EPA's motion to dismiss Sierra Club's motion to re-open and compel action is reversed, and this case is remanded for further proceedings consistent with this opinion.

COMMENTARY & QUESTIONS

1. **§303 musical chairs.** Note the elaborate legal and political maneuvering that occurred here. The court of appeals in Sierra Club v. EPA summarized these gambits in another part of its opinion:

> A couple of years after the consent decree had been entered, none of the pollution standards EPA established as a result of the decree had actually been implemented. Upset with the lack of progress, Sierra Club moved the district court to reopen the consent decree and to take action compelling the EPA to develop implementation plans for the standards. EPA took the position that the State of Georgia had the primary responsibility for implementing the standards EPA had established. The district court deferred ruling on Sierra Club's motion pending Georgia's development of the implementation plans. Once Georgia filed with the court what it asserted were the required plans, EPA moved to have Sierra Club's motion to re-open and compel declared moot. Sierra Club responded that Georgia's implementation plans were not adequate and insisted that EPA had the responsibility under the decree for formulating them. The district court denied EPA's mootness motion because it agreed with Sierra Club that the consent decree required EPA to develop implementation plans or to ensure that those Georgia developed were adequate to satisfy the Clean Water Act. 296 F.3d 1023.

The court of appeals then reversed and remanded, holding that the district court had abused its discretion by interpreting the consent decree so as to essentially modify its terms.

Why all these evasions of responsibility? The likely scenario is that just as 90% of the impaired waters nationwide, Georgia's impaired waters were overwhelmingly impacted by nonpoint source pollution, which Georgia lacked the political will to regulate. Since the CWA does not authorize federal jurisdiction over nonpoint sources, EPA could neither regulate these discharges itself nor, consistent with the Tenth Amendment, compel the state of Georgia to do so (see Chapter 6). Nevertheless, during the Clinton Administration, EPA promulgated regulations that required states to include implementation plans in their TMDLs, despite the apparent inability of EPA to compel states to implement these plans. (EPA could threaten to cut off a state's §319 nonpoint source control planning funds, but states generally regarded this threat as an empty one.) These regulations were never implemented because Congress refused to appropriate the necessary funds, and the Bush II Administration later withdrew the regulations.

The trial court judge became impatient with this elaborate exercise in futility and distorted the consent decree between the Sierra Club and EPA to compel EPA to either develop implementation plans for Georgia or else to ensure that Georgia's plans were adequate to meet WQSs, although it is still anybody's guess how the district court envisioned enforcing these plans. Meanwhile, behind the scenes, large nonpoint sources, such as agricultural operations, desirous of continuing their virtual exemption (except for CAFOs) from federal water pollution control law, were facing off in the political arena against large point sources with discharge permits (notably POTWs and large industries), which confronted the formidable prospect of either installing "better-than-best" technology or else limiting operations in order to meet more stringent water quality-based effluent limitations for discharges into waterbodies impaired by both point and nonpoint source pollution.

When will the music stop?

2. **"Things can get complicated."** The first step in the process of setting WQBELs is the establishment of WQSs by a state or by EPA if the state does not develop acceptable standards. A WQS "should, wherever attainable,[32] provide water quality for the protection and propagation of fish, shellfish, and wildlife and for recreation in and on the water...." 40 C.F.R. §130.3. WQSs consist primarily of three components: (1) designated uses, (2) criteria for attaining those uses, and (3) an antidegradation policy (see below). Designated uses ordinarily involve some combination of human recreational (e.g., fishable, swimmable, boatable) and aquatic life maintenance uses; but the designated uses can take a variety of forms. "States may adopt sub-categories of a use and set the appropriate criteria to reflect varying needs of such sub-categories of uses, for instance, to differentiate between cold water and warm water fisheries." 40 C.F.R. §131.10(c). States may also adopt seasonal uses, based on water temperature, flow regimes, and types of aquatic biota present.

Next, a state will develop water quality criteria consistent with attaining the designated uses. Water quality criteria may be expressed either narratively (e.g., "no visible sheen") or numerically, in terms of parts per million of particular parameters in types of waterbodies, or in some other appropriate manner, such as biosurveys. Under §303(c)(B), states must adopt numeric criteria for relevant toxic pollutants, and EPA must publish guidance containing recommended criteria for toxics, but states can adopt less stringent criteria for toxics if they are scientifically defensible.[33] In translating narrative to numerical criteria, states may use "the EPA recommended numeric water quality criteria, but only on a 'case by case basis' and 'supplemented where necessary by other relevant [site-specific] information.'" American Paper Inst. v. EPA, 996 F.2d 346, 350 (D.C. Cir. 1993) (upholding 40 C.F.R. §122.44(d)(1)(vi)). Thus water quality criteria

---

32. The concept of "attainability" is discussed below.

33. See Natural Res. Def. Council v. EPA, 16 F.3d 1395 (4th Cir. 1993) (Virginia adoption of dioxin criterion weaker than EPA guidance upheld as scientifically defensible). Given the scientific uncertainties involved in ascertaining the impacts of pollutants on human health and aquatic life, scientific defensibility, in this area at least, covers a great deal of ground. For example, some states base numeric criteria on a risk level of one excess cancer case per one million people, while others base their criteria on a risk level of one excess cancer case per 100,000 people. See U.S. GAO, Differences Among the States in Issuing Permits Limiting the Discharge of Pollutants 12 (1996).

for particular parameters may differ widely from state to state and from waterbody to waterbody. Additionally, states vary with regard to the types of water quality criteria that they employ. Some states rely almost exclusively on chemical-specific criteria applied to water columns, while other states emphasize biocriteria or sediment quality criteria.

Third, a state must select those "impaired waters" (water quality-limited segments) where WQSs are not currently being met, accompanied by a priority list for state regulatory attention. This step is complicated by the fact that only approximately one-third of the nation's waterbodies have actually been assessed. Moreover, states use different assessment methodologies (e.g., biological, chemical, or physical monitoring) in determining whether a particular waterbody is impaired. U.S. GAO, Inconsistent State Approaches Complicate Nation's Efforts to Identify Its Most Polluted Waters (2002). In some cases, a common body of water shared by two states is listed as impaired by one state and not the other.[34] Despite the fact that the CWA does not regulate nonpoint sources of pollution, waterbodies impaired solely by nonpoint source pollution must be listed as impaired. Pronsolino v. Nastri, 291 F.3d 1123 (9th Cir. 2002), cert. denied, 123 S. Ct. 2573 (2003). EPA guidance suggests that state water quality reports be organized into the following categories: (1) all designated uses are met; (2) some of the uses are met but insufficient data exist to determine if remaining uses are met; (3) insufficient or no data exists to determine if any designated uses are met; (4) water is impaired but a TMDL is not needed; and (5) water is impaired and a TMDL is needed. Many states, however, have adopted different analytical methods and formats for listing impaired waters.

After identifying impaired waters, states must then develop TMDLs for them. A TMDL represents the assimilative or carrying capacity of receiving water for a certain parameter. A TMDL limit is developed for each impaired waterbody as a mechanism for identifying all the contributors to surface water quality impacts and setting implementation goals for load reductions as necessary to meet a WQS. A TMDL for an impaired segment equals the sum of Wasteload Allocations (WLAs) for point sources (i.e., water quality-based effluent limitations), Load Allocations (LAs), representing nonpoint sources and natural background sources, a margin of safety, and a reserve capacity for future growth if the state chooses to set one. As the Sierra Club v. EPA case indicates, TMDLs are generally developed in a rotating, basin-wide manner in accordance with a state's listing of priority impaired waters. TMDL-setting depends on complex mathematical modeling of the assimilative capacity of a waterbody, the movement of a pollutant from various point and nonpoint sources through a watershed, and the effectiveness of control technology and best management practices. Each of these areas is replete with scientific uncertainty:

> There are two significant sources of uncertainty in any water quality management program: epistemic and aleatory uncertainty. Epistemic uncertainty — incomplete knowledge or lack of sufficient data to estimate probabilities — is a by product of

---

34. For example, New Mexico designates its portion of the Rio Grande River as suitable for wading and therefore not impaired from fecal coliform bacteria, while the Texas portion of the Rio Grande is listed as impaired because that state designates the river for swimming.

our reliance on models that relate sources of pollution to human health and biological responses. We are limited by incomplete conceptual understanding of the systems under study, by models that are necessarily simplified representations of the complexity of the natural and socioeconomic systems, as well as by limited data for testing hypotheses and/or simulating the systems.... However, complete certainty in support of water quality management decisions cannot be achieved because of aleatory uncertainty — the inherent variability of natural processes. Aleatory uncertainty arises in systems characterized by randomness.... Not only are waterbodies, watersheds, and their inhabitants characterized by randomness, but they are also open systems in which we cannot know in advance what the boundaries of possible biological outcomes will be. National Research Council, Assessing the TMDL Approach to Water Quality Management 29–30 (2001).

Managing environmental systems where scientific uncertainty is pervasive involves making assumptions with regard to model inputs. In setting TMDLs, states have utilized different water quality models and assumptions regarding mixing zones,[35] measurement of high and low flow conditions, seasonal variations, reserves for margins of safety and economic growth, background concentrations,[36] and data quality.[37] Many states offer site-specific variances from TMDLs. 40 C.F.R. §131.13. Unlike TBELs, WQBELs are not uniform from state to state or waterbody to waterbody. The U.S. GAO found that WQBELs for mercury, a persistent and bioaccumulative pollutant, were 775 times greater at one facility than at a similar facility in another state. Once again, the race of laxity is rearing its ugly head:

> In 1995, an industrial facility in Pennsylvania challenged a discharge limit for arsenic because Pennsylvania's numerical criterion was 2,500 times more stringent than that used by the neighboring state of New York, into which the discharge flowed. (Pennsylvania had updated its water quality standards on the basis of current information on health effects published by EPA.... New York continued to rely on earlier guidance....) Among other things, the discharger argued that having to comply with the more stringent criterion created an economic disadvantage for the company. Eventually, Pennsylvania agreed to reissue the permit with a monitoring requirement for arsenic instead of a discharge limit. The state has also revised its water quality standards using the less stringent criterion. U.S. GAO, State Water Quality Standards Report 9 (1996).

---

35. WQBELs are not measured at the outfall pipe, as are TBELs, but at the outer limits of a mixing zone, within which at least chronic impacts on aquatic life are permitted. Some states have established Zones of Initial Dilution (ZIDs) within mixing zones where acute effects are also tolerated. For judicial discussions of mixing zones, see American Iron & Steel Inst. v. EPA, 115 F.3d 979 (D.C. Cir. 1997) (EPA's prohibition of mixing zones for Bioaccumulative Chemicals of Concern (BCCs) in the Great Lakes system remanded for consideration of economic impacts) (these regulations were repromulgated in 2003), and Granite City Div. of Nat'l Steel Co. v. Illinois Pollution Control Bd., 613 N.E.2d 719 (Ill. Sup. Ct. 1993) (state mixing zone and ZID regulations upheld).

36. Background concentrations are the level of pollutants already present in the receiving waters as a result of naturally occurring pollutants, permitted discharges from upstream, spills, unregulated discharges, etc. "Connecticut, for example, assumes background concentrations of zero in deriving [WQBELs], while Colorado uses actual data. All other things being equal, the discharge limits established by Connecticut will be less stringent than those set by Colorado whenever the actual background concentration is greater than zero." U.S. GAO, Differences Among the States in Issuing Permits Limiting the Discharge of Pollutants 13 (1996). See also Natural Res. Def. Council v. Muszynski, 268 F.3d 91 (2d Cir. 2001) (substantially upholding EPA's approval of New York's determination of seasonal variations, a margin of safety, and the measurement period for setting TMDLs for phosphorous for eight New York City reservoirs).

37. For example, how many exceedances constitute a violation of WQSs? One? More? An average? How should a state determine when older data are still sufficiently representative and valid? Which quality assurance/control protocols should be applied? Where should samples be taken?

Section 303(d) is silent regarding the implementation of TMDLs, beyond requiring that states include them in their continuing planning processes. Moreover, this section not only ignores the economic and technological consequences of TMDLs, but it also lacks a timetable for development of , and compliance with, WLAs and LAs. These lacunae will force states to make difficult tradeoffs between point and nonpoint sources, upstream and downstream dischargers, large and small point sources, industries and POTWs, etc. Or else, in order to avoid these invidious choices, states may descend into "governmental lethargy," as Georgia did. The gaps in §303(d) have also compelled courts to set timetables for TMDL development as a result of lawsuits such as Sierra Club v. EPA. In light of the scientific, legal, economic, and political complexity of implementing §303, is it any wonder that EPA "back burnered" it between 1972 and 1987?

3. **Whole Effluent Testing (WET) as an alternative.** A promising development for setting both WQSs and WQBELs has been the emergence of biomonitoring procedures. Biomonitoring (also known as "whole effluent testing" or "bioassay") is essentially a laboratory simulation of the effects of ambient water quality, or a particular waste stream, on indigenous aquatic biota used as an indicator of the desired quality of an actual waterbody. In conducting a bioassay, a representative aquatic organism is subjected, either for a shorter ("acute bioassay") or longer ("chronic bioassay") period of time, to a sample of a receiving waterbody or a waste stream diluted in a manner that attempts to reproduce ambient conditions. The WQS or WQBEL is then set at a certain percentage (providing a margin of safety) of the concentration of the medium that causes adverse effects on the organism (e.g., for an acute bioassay, 30% of the concentration that kills 50% of the organisms over a 96-hour period). If a discharger exceeds its bioassay-based effluent limitation more than twice during a particular period, it must conduct a pollutant reduction evaluation, the results of which are included as conditions of its discharge permit. Biomonitoring furnishes a useful alternative to a chemical-by-chemical approach to dealing with mixed waste streams. It also provides some indication of how certain levels of water quality will affect ecosystems. However, there is concern that the science of biomonitoring, especially with regard to chronic bioassays, is not sufficiently well developed to support a regulatory program. There is also concern that biomonitoring is "better suited to assuring protection of aquatic life than human health." American Paper Inst. v. EPA, 995 F.2d 346, 350 (D.C. Cir. 1993).[38]

4. **Antidegradation and attainability.** Section 101 of the CWA declares a policy to "restore and maintain" clean water, and antidegradation policies traditionally have been a feature of water pollution control law. Although antidegradation under the CWA is less well developed than its counterpart in the CAA (Prevention of Significant Deterioration, or PSD), Congress in 1987 explicitly recognized that antidegradation is an essential part of the Act. §303(d)(4)(B). But the statutory reference to antidegradation is cryptic; it does not clarify what Congress meant by antidegradation or how this policy is to be implemented.

---

38. EPA's administration of the CWA has been criticized for providing insufficient protection against bioaccumulative substances. See Williamson et al., Gathering Danger: The Urgent Need to Regulate Toxic Substances That Can Bioaccumulate, 20 Ecol. L.Q. 605 (1994).

In 1983, EPA promulgated a set of regulations intended to explicate the antidegradation policy. 40 C.F.R. §131.12. These regulations rest on a distinction between "water quality" and "water uses." Each state must adopt an antidegradation policy and identify methods of applying it where waterbodies are of better quality than fishable-swimmable, for example, if trout can propagate there. The antidegradation policy is divided into three general levels of protection. Tier I establishes the minimum level of fishable-swimmable water quality that must be maintained in every body of water, wherever attainable. Tier II applies to waters whose quality already exceeds the level "necessary to support propagation of fish, shellfish, and wildlife and recreation in and on the water" and only allows a reduction in quality when "necessary to accommodate important economic or social development." For certain exceptionally high-quality bodies of water (e.g., waters in parks, wildlife refuges, and other "waters of exceptional recreational and ecological significance"), Tier III prohibits any degradation of existing water quality, except on a temporary basis. Waters falling into Tier III are designated Outstanding National Resource Waters (ONRWs). Existing water uses are the antidegradation baseline and thus must always be preserved. In effect, these regulations establish a rebuttable presumption that existing water quality, outside of ONRWs, must be maintained, and an irrebuttable presumption that existing water quality in ONRWs, as well as all existing water uses in other waterbodies, must be maintained.

Most states have adopted antidegradation policies, but few have meaningful implementation measures. In the first place, many waterbodies that are subject to antidegradation are threatened by nonpoint source pollution that EPA does not possess the authority to regulate. See American Wildlands v. Browner, 260 F.3d 1192 (10th Cir. 2001) (because EPA lacks the authority to regulate nonpoint sources, EPA's approval of Montana's WQSs, which exempt nonpoint source discharges from antidegradation review, is a permissible construction of the CWA). In the second place, EPA's antidegradation regulations leave implementation almost entirely to the states, which may want to attract development with the inducement of unpolluted segments that will be classified as "effluent limited" (i.e., where WQSs can be met by the imposition of TBELs), thus avoiding the imposition of more stringent WQBELs. EPA can sue a state that has not adopted an acceptable antidegradation policy, but it is doubtful whether EPA can enforce antidegradation in a state that has not adopted such an antidegradation policy or is not enforcing its adopted policy. States have a relatively free hand even as to designating and protecting ONRWs. National Wildlife Fed'n v. EPA, 127 F.3d 1126 (D.C. Cir. 1997). EPA can object to a state discharge permit that allegedly violates the state antidegradation policy, but this rarely occurs. However, suits can be brought in state courts to invalidate discharge permits that violate state antidegradation policies. See Columbus & Franklin County Dist. v. Ohio EPA, 600 N.E.2d 1042 (Ohio Sup. Ct. 1993) (state agency violated antidegradation policy in issuing discharge permit to a POTW).

Section 101 of the CWA establishes a "national goal that wherever attainable, an interim goal of water quality which provides for the protection and propagation of fish, shellfish, and wildlife and provides for recreation in and on the water be achieved by July 1, 1987." What does "wherever attainable" mean? In contrast to antidegradation, attainability applies where a waterbody is of lower quality than the CWA's minimum fishable-swimmable condition. Under EPA regulations (40 C.F.R. §131.10), a use is attainable if it is already being attained. Thus where existing WQSs specify designated uses of a lesser nature than those that are presently being attained, the state must revise its standards upward to reflect the current uses. Second, a use is attainable if it can be achieved by the imposition of technology-based effluent limitations for point sources "and cost-effective and reasonable best management practices for nonpoint source control." Third, a use is deemed attainable unless the state, after a "use attainability analysis" (UAA), can demonstrate that attaining the fishable-swimmable use is not feasible because of specified natural or intractable man-induced conditions, or that "controls more stringent than [the CWA's technology-based effluent limitations] would result in substantial and widespread economic and social impact."[39] How can a definition of attainability be based upon control of nonpoint sources of pollution, when EPA has no authority to regulate them or to compel a state to do so? What is "substantial and widespread economic and social impact"? Few states have found it necessary to petition EPA for the removal of fishable-swimmable uses because of the virtually infinite state flexibility in setting WQSs and implementing WQBELs. The 2001 NRC report cited in note 2 advocates a more frequent reliance on UAAs in order to reduce the number of required TMDLs, but states are reluctant to perform UAAs because they fear that this will be perceived by the public as "writing off" a waterbody by weakening water quality standards.

5. **A spate of §303(d) lawsuits.** After 15 years on the back burner, §303 has become a boiling cauldron. Between 40 and 50 lawsuits similar to Sierra Club v. EPA have been brought against EPA for failing to set TMDLs for states that have not done so. See, e.g., Idaho Sportsmen's Coalition v. EPA, 951 F. Supp. 962 (W.D. Wash. 1996) (EPA ordered to submit a 5-year schedule for developing TMDLs for water quality-limited stretches in Idaho; case dismissed when Idaho agreed to develop TMDLs within 8 years). EPA has issued a policy statement giving states between 8 and 13 years to complete the task of setting TMDLs for appropriate waterbodies. Realistically, however, the job might take far longer.

6. **Interstate water pollution.** Interstate water pollution can be severe, especially in the Mississippi River basin. More than 40% of the phosphorus present in the waterbodies of 16 states in the Mississippi River basin originates in other states. Section 402(d) of the CWA deals with interstate water pollution in the context of issuing discharge permits. In effect, EPA acts as an arbitrator of interstate disputes. This process was described by the U.S. Supreme Court in International Paper Co. v. Ouellette, 479 U.S. 481 (1987):

> While source States have a strong voice in regulating their own pollution, the CWA contemplates a much lesser role for States that share an interstate waterway with the source (the affected States). Even though it may be harmed by the discharges,

---

39. After failing to invalidate their TBELs and then failing to overturn the more stringent WQBELs in their discharge permit, the Rybacheks petitioned the Alaska Department of Environmental Conservation to downgrade ("remove") the water use classifications of streams into which they discharged. The Department, after conducting a UAA, decided not to remove the use classifications applicable to the Rybacheks, and the Alaska Supreme Court upheld the Department. Alaska Dep't of Envtl. Conservation v. Rybachek, 912 P.2d 536 (Alaska 1996).

an affected state only has an advisory role in regulating pollution that originates beyond its borders. Before a federal permit may be issued, each affected State is given notice and the opportunity to object to the proposed standards at a public hearing. An affected State has similar rights to be consulted before the source State issues its own permit; the source State must send notification, and must consider the objections and recommendations submitted by other States before taking action. Significantly, however, an affected State does not have the authority to block the issuance of the permit if it is dissatisfied with the proposed standards. An affected State's only recourse is to apply to the EPA Administrator, who then has the discretion to disapprove the permit if he concludes that the discharges will have an undue impact on interstate waters.... Thus, the Act makes it clear that the affected States occupy a subordinate position to source States in the federal regulatory program. 479 U.S. at 490–491.[40]

When an impasse develops between EPA and a source state with an approved permit program, EPA can retake jurisdiction and issue its own permit. Affected states are given additional power over discharges in source states by an EPA regulation that prohibits the issuance of a discharge permit "when the imposition of conditions cannot ensure compliance with the applicable water quality standards [including antidegradation policies] of all affected states." 40 C.F.R. §122.4(d). In Arkansas v. Oklahoma, 503 U.S. 91 (1992), the Supreme Court upheld this regulation on the ground that federally approved WQSs become federal law that preempts conflicting state regulations. Referring to CWA §402(d), the Court stated that "limits on an affected State's direct participation in a permitting decision, however, do not in any way constrain the EPA's authority to require a point source to comply with downstream water quality standards." 503 U.S. at 106. Since Native American tribes are treated as states by the CWA, if a tribe has been delegated primacy and has established WQSs that have received EPA approval, upstream discharges must comply with the tribal standards. Albuquerque v. EPA, 97 F.3d 415 (10th Cir.), cert. denied, 522 U.S. 965 (1997). But EPA can arbitrate a dispute between a state and a Native American tribe, with EPA retaining the ultimate authority to approve permits and water quality standards. Wisconsin v. Environmental Protection Agency, 266 F.3d 741 (7th Cir. 2001), cert. denied, 535 U.S. 1121 (2002). A second attempt to curtail interstate conflicts over water pollution is CWA §118, added in 1987, which requires EPA to promulgate uniform Water Quality Guidance regulations for the Great Lakes states with regard to WQSs, antidegradation policies, and implementation procedures. It is noteworthy that the increase in litigation and legislation relating to interstate water pollution has occurred primarily because of the resurgence of water quality-based standard-setting and permitting under the CWA.

7. **State water quality certification.** CWA §401 provides that

> Any applicant for a Federal license or permit to conduct any activity...which may result in any discharge into the navigable waters, shall provide the licensing or permitting agency a certification from the State in which the discharge originates or will originate...that any such discharge will comply with [applicable state

---

40. *Ouellette* involved interstate pollution of Lake Champlain. The Vermont plaintiffs eventually prevailed to the extent that their state law nuisance claims were not preempted by the CWA, nor was International Paper allowed to erect a permit defense. The Supreme Court did require, however, that source state nuisance law be applied to the case.

WQSs]. No license or permit shall be granted until the certification required by this section has been obtained or has been waived.... No license or permit shall be granted if certification has been denied by the State.... Any certification provided under this section...shall become a condition on any Federal license or permit subject to the provisions of this section.

Section 401 allows states to veto or place conditions on a federal permit that causes a discharge to navigable waters, such as a U.S. Army Corps of Engineers permit to discharge dredged and fill material or a CWA discharge permit where EPA is the permitting authority.

In Public Util. Dist. No. 1 of Jefferson County & City of Tacoma v. Washington Dep't of Ecology, 511 U.S. 700 (1994), petitioners wanted to build a hydroelectric project on a river possessing exceptionally high-water quality. The project would have appreciably reduced the river's flow and thus would have interfered with the excellent fishery in the river. In order to protect the fishery, respondent state environmental agency included a minimum flow requirement in its §401 certification to the Federal Energy Regulatory Commission (FERC), the federal agency that licenses hydroelectric works under the Federal Power Act. The Supreme Court, in a 7–2 decision, affirmed the Washington Supreme Court's finding that FERC had to honor the minimum flow certification. Justice O'Connor, writing for the majority, reasoned that the state agency had a legal right to protect its WQSs, which included a strong antidegradation requirement for the particular segment involved. In response to petitioners' argument that the CWA is only concerned with water "quality," not water "quantity," Justice O'Connor responded:

> This is an artificial distinction. In many cases, water quantity is closely related to water quality; a sufficient lowering of the water quantity in a body of water could destroy all of its designated uses, be it for drinking water, recreation, navigation, or, as here, as a fishery. In any event, there is recognition in the Clean Water Act itself that reduced stream flow...can constitute water pollution. 511 U.S. at 719.

But the state certification requirement under CWA §401 applies only to point source discharges. In Oregon Nat'l Desert Ass'n v. Dombeck, 172 F.3d 1092 (9th Cir. 1998), cert. denied, 528 U.S. 964 (1999), the court held that private cattle grazing on federal land, subject to a federal grazing permit (see Chapter 24), did not require a state water quality certification because grazing produces nonpoint source pollution that is not regulated by the CWA. *Jefferson County* was distinguished because although flows over dams constitute nonpoint source pollution, dam construction involved discharges of dredged and fill material and the dam's tailrace constituted a point source.

8. **Regulation of "toxic hot spots."** CWA §304(l) establishes a water quality-based system for cleaning up waterbodies impaired by point source discharges of toxic pollutants. For each listed waterbody or segment, a state must develop an individual control strategy that will achieve a reduction "sufficient, in combination with existing controls on point and nonpoint sources of pollution, to achieve the applicable water quality standard as soon as possible, but not later than 3 years after the date of establishment of such strategy." §304(l)(1)(D). See NRDC v. EPA, 915 F.2d 1314 (9th Cir. 1990) (interpreting §304(l)'s listing requirements). But as with the §303 process, EPA's inability to regulate nonpoint sources of toxic pollutants vitiates §304(l).

9. **Whither §303?** The Bush II Administration has downplayed the regulatory potential of TMDLs. EPA's Assistant Administrator for Water, G. Tracy Mehan III, has commented: "I believe TMDLs are a significant example of an information-based environmental policy. To the extent that a TMDL results in bringing stakeholders together in a watershed context, providing them with important information about what's required to achieve water quality standards, I think that's very transformational and very powerful.... I don't think that we need to make the TMDL very prescriptive in regulatory terms...." Quoted in Water Environment and Technology, Nov. 2001, at 24.

The NRC report cited in Commentary note 2, above, concluded that the TMDL process is broken but can be fixed by recognition and reduction of scientific uncertainties, increased use of UAAs, and EPA's standardization of the TMDL process.

The NRC also recommended that TMDLs be subject to "adaptive management." Under the adaptive approach, a TMDL would not be a single precise and final determination, but rather an iterative process of evaluation, action, review, and revision, continually progressing toward water quality compliance. Adaptive management may be an enlightened management strategy, but it is unclear how adaptive management can be reconciled with a legal system that demands predictable and definable outcomes and abhors "moving targets."

Clean water advocates are divided regarding the efficacy of §303. Some, while considering it deeply flawed, believe because it is "the only game in town" that it should be impelled by lawsuits and administrative modifications. Others believe that §303 is irreparable and should be repealed, to be replaced by an extension of the proven technology-based system to nonpoint sources through discharge permits requiring selections from menus of appropriate and site-specific BMPs. The Sierra Club v. EPA court concluded, perhaps cavalierly, that "non-point sources cannot be regulated by permits because there is no way to trace the pollution to a particular point, measure it, and then set an acceptable level for that point." 296 F.3d at 1025.

But the "permit-BMP" approach has functioned quite well in the context of industrial stormwater permitting, covering discharges that would be classified as nonpoint sources if not for congressional inclusion in the CWA.

Meanwhile, despite the scientific uncertainties, implementation shortcomings, inequity between point and nonpoint sources, interstate variability, lack of administrative direction, and unrealistic judicial timetables that beset the §303 process, it is currently monopolizing the limited resources available to EPA and state water pollution control programs. As of the end of 2002, EPA had approved close to 8000 TMDLs out of approximately 40,000 TMDLs that states must develop for their impaired waters. Because states have been compelled to meet unforgiving, litigation-driven phased deadlines for developing TMDLs, many of the TMDLs that have been submitted to, and approved by, EPA are of at best mediocre quality. Some are so superficial that they have been referred to as "cookie cutter" or "haiku" TMDLs. More court battles loom over the adequacy of approved TMDLs.

Whither §303? Benjamin Grumbles, EPA's Deputy Assistant Administrator for Water, has remarked that regulators simply do not know how effective TMDLs will be in the long run. 33 BNA Env't Rep. Curr. Dev. 2424 (2002). This would appear to be an accurate appraisal of the situation.

E. CONTROLLING NONPOINT SOURCE POLLUTION WITHOUT FEDERAL REGULATION

Nonpoint source pollution control is essentially a state function, with EPA and other federal agencies providing incentives such as grants and technical assistance. State nonpoint pollution control laws differ widely with regard to strategy, coverage, institutional structure, enforceability, variances and exemptions, funding, and effectiveness.

> Agriculture is the most problematic area for enforceable mechanisms. Many laws of general applicability...have exceptions for agriculture. Where state laws exist, they often defer to incentives, cost-sharing, and voluntary programs. Nevertheless, about a fifth of the states have some statewide sediment requirements applicable to agriculture, often administered by local governments or soil and water conservation districts. Even more states (about a fourth) authorize individual soil and water conservation districts, as a matter of local option, to adopt enforceable "land use regulations" for the control of erosion and sedimentation. But most of these require approval of landowner referendum, with approval requiring a supermajority (ranging from 66 to 90 percent) in order for such regulations to become effective. Environmental Law Institute, Enforceable State Mechanisms for the Control of Nonpoint Source Water Pollution iii (1997).

One can only imagine how enthusiastically local governments and soil and water conservation districts in agricultural areas will regulate agricultural nonpoint sources.

With regard to agricultural nonpoint source pollution — the major remaining source of water pollution in the United States — "the federal role [has been] indirect, almost passive, and largely ineffective."[41] Nevertheless, a number of provisions of the 1985, 1990, 1996, and 2002 Farm Bills have addressed nonpoint source pollution. The "sodbuster" provision of the 1985 Farm Bill is an example of a "cross-compliance" legislative strategy, where existing subsidies are manipulated to achieve compliance with new requirements. A "sodbuster" — one who farms on highly erodible land not previously in agricultural use — is ineligible for crop subsidies unless she implements a soil conservation plan containing BMPs to control erosion. 16 U.S.C. §§3811–3812. The "swampbuster" provision stops payments to farmers who convert wetlands to croplands. Under the Conservation Reserve Program (CRP), 16 U.S.C. §§3831–3836, the U.S. Department of Agriculture pays producers to temporarily retire environmentally sensitive lands from production. Producers sign ten-year CRP contracts and agree to convert their enrolled acres to approved conservation uses (e.g., vegetated stream buffer strips or plantings of grasses and trees), receiving rental payments in return. After the contracts expire, producers can return these lands to agriculture. Over 35 million acres have been enrolled in the CRP. The Wetlands Reserve Program (WRP) is a voluntary USDA program in which willing sellers receive fair market value to permanently retire wetland acres from farm production. Thirty-year easements can also be

---

41. Gould, Agriculture, Nonpoint Source Pollution, and Federal Law, 23 U.C. Davis L. Rev. 461, 474 (1990).

purchased under this program. Another aspect of the WRP involves cost-sharing with landowners who agree to restore wetlands on cropland. About 1 million acres are under WRP protection in 47 states, primarily in the South. The Environmental Quality Incentives Program (EQIP) authorizes payments to farmers who implement BMPs that are aimed at improving water quality. Other federal subsidy programs provide payments to farmers for grasslands preservation, wildlife habitat protection, and practicing sustainable agriculture.

Reorientation of subsidies and incentive payments to farmers may be marginally helpful in reducing nonpoint source pollution, but they can only scratch the surface of the agricultural nonpoint source pollution problem. Professor Gould believes that antipollution subsidies are appropriate in the agricultural sector because "government has played a major role in the structure of the farm economy, and government programs have indirectly encouraged some of the agricultural practices responsible for agricultural pollution." 23 U.C. Davis L.Rev. at 488. But subsidies and cost-sharing mechanisms cannot be the entire answer because (1) they are dependent upon the vagaries of funding, (2) they pay only part of the cost of pollution control, and (3) "most of the agricultural nonpoint source pollution effects occur off-farm...[and] substantial voluntary efforts by farmers to control this pollution are unlikely." 23 U.C. Davis L.Rev. at 489. Professor Gould concludes that, in most respects, agricultural nonpoint source pollution is a traditional externality, and there is a need for a stronger federal presence if we expect to significantly reduce it. Professor Robert Adler recommends that Congress enact mandatory programs requiring that (1) states create priority lists of watersheds degraded by nonpoint source pollution and agree to restore those watersheds "on a reasonable timetable," and (2) landowners or operators contributing to nonpoint pollution loadings in a target watershed develop site-specific water quality plans and implement them within three-to-five-year time frames. R. Adler et al., The Clean Water Act 20 Years Later Ch. 7 (1993).

A promising mechanism for reducing agricultural nonpoint source pollution, while at the same time counteracting the better-than-best problem, is point/nonpoint source pollution trading. (See Chapter 14 for a more extensive discussion of this device.) In a recent example, the Rahr Malting Co. of Shakopee, Minnesota, wanted to build a plant to treat wastewater from expanded malt production facilities, but the entire nutrient TMDLs for the potential receiving segment of the Minnesota River had been allocated to regional POTWs. The Minnesota Pollution Control Agency (MPCA) arranged a point/nonpoint source trading framework whereby Rahr will fund relatively low-cost BMPs on upstream farmland, leading to reductions in nutrient loadings that will be offset against Rahr's point source discharge of nutrients.

Point/nonpoint source pollution trading is one element of a watershed management strategy, a variety of "place-based" environmental protection. EPA's watershed management program involves awarding federal grant funds for coordinating resource management activities — including CWA water quality-based standard-setting and permitting — within watershed or aquifer recharge area boundaries. This is a "bottom-up" process, involving the participation of watershed stakeholders and the formation of partnerships among federal, state, and local agencies and nongovernmental organizations with interests in the watershed. The stakeholders and partners identify environmental objectives, taking into account the condition of the ecological resource and the economic and social needs of the watershed's population. After a collaborative, consensual management plan has been developed, the governmental partners then coordinate planning, incentives, standard-setting, permitting, monitoring and surveillance, and enforcement in accordance with the watershed plan. If conflicts among stakeholders and partners arise, every attempt is made to resolve them through alternative dispute resolution (see Chapter 21) rather than litigation. The most significant watershed management efforts are being conducted with regard to the Gulf of Mexico, Long Island Sound, the Great Lakes Basin, Chesapeake Bay, Lake Champlain, 28 estuaries in the National Estuary Program, and a number of large lakes in the Clean Lakes Program. CWA §§1267–1270, 1324, 1330. Smaller watershed management processes, focusing primarily on nonpoint source control, are being conducted throughout the nation, under the joint auspices of EPA and USDA. Adler et al. recommend that (1) current watershed management programs be strengthened by raising funding levels and mandating planning deadlines and implementation schedules, and (2) watershed planning and management be instituted for every major watershed in the United States. However, past attempts to establish effective programs based on boundaries other than political ones have not fared particularly well in the United States. See Goldfarb, Watershed Management: Slogan or Solution?, 21 B.C. Envtl. Aff. L. Rev. 483 (1994).

Watershed-wide permitting might facilitate both point/nonpoint source trading and collaborative decisionmaking. For example, a state might develop, on a watershed basis, either a general permit for common point sources or categories of sources, such as POTWs or CAFOs, or an individual permit that covers multiple point sources. This strategy could be effective in those watersheds that are impaired primarily by point source pollution, such as Long Island Sound, which is listed as impaired by excessive nutrients that are emanating mainly from POTWs in Connecticut and New York. But in the majority of impaired watersheds, the source of impairment is agricultural nonpoint sources, and here any point/nonpoint source trading that might occur would have to be implemented outside the scope of the permit system. This highlights a significant problem with point/nonpoint source trading schemes — if the owner or operator of a nonpoint source is not mandated to comply with a pollution control standard, why should she participate in a trade in the first place?

Watershed management is the centerpiece of Bush II Administration's water pollution control program. Assistant Administrator Mehan, in a December 3, 2002, memo to EPA Directors, declared that "the watershed approach should not be seen merely as a special initiative, targeted at just a selected set of places or involving a relatively small group of EPA or state staff. Rather, it should be the fulcrum of our restoration and protection efforts...." But applying the watershed approach to sources of water pollution that lie outside the ambit of the CWA — e.g., agricultural nonpoint sources, air deposition, hydrologic modifications, water diversions, contaminated sediments, invasive species, and inadequately designed and maintained septic systems — will indeed be challenging.

F.   A COMPLEX HYPOTHETICAL: THE AVERAGE RIVER

Here is a cumulative watershed problem, with a series of hypothetical uses named as only law professors could name them, that illustrates many of the CWA's complexities and offers a vehicle for understanding the Act's different sections:

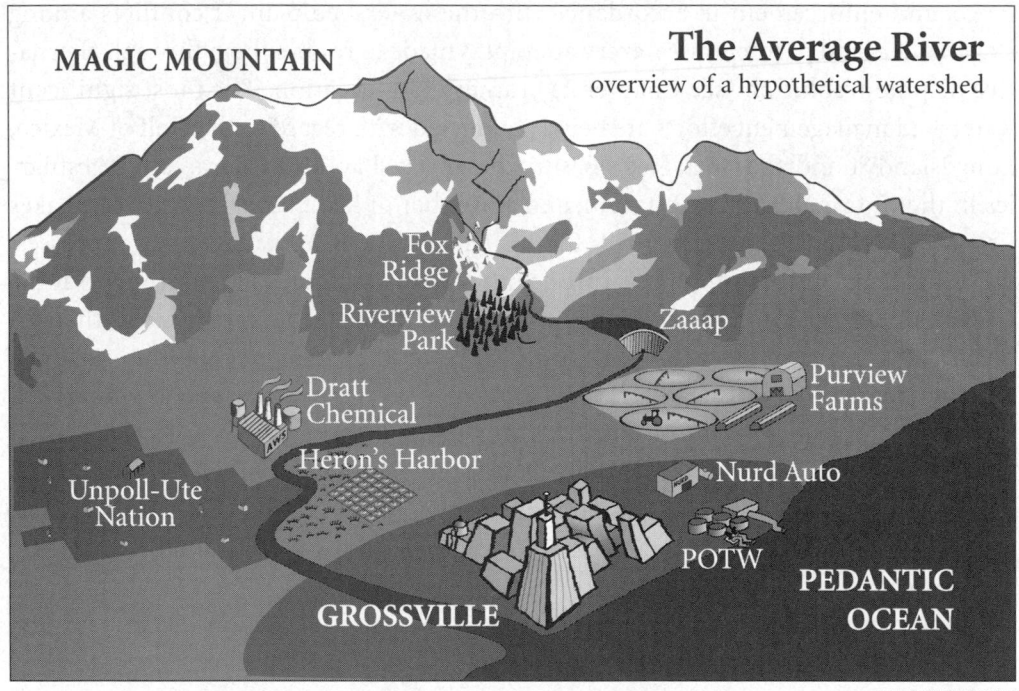

FIGURE 12-3
Here's a cumulative water shed problem with a series of hypothetical uses (named as only a law professor could name them).

The Average River is just that, a hypothetical typical river system. It arises on the slopes of Magic Mountain and flows into the Pedantic Ocean. As shown on the accompanying map, the Average River is also subject to typical threats to its water quality: (1) A second home development, Fox Ridge, with each home serviced by its own on-site septic system, is planned for the lower slopes of Magic Mountain, threatening to degrade the currently pristine water quality found in Riverview Park. (2) Purview Farms, downstream from the park, is a large, multifaceted agricultural enterprise that combines an extensive animal feeding operation (AFO) with irrigated field crops. Purview's operations cause animal waste, fertilizer, pesticide, and sediment residues to flow into the river and infiltrate into groundwater after storm events. In addition, Purview's irrigation water is first diverted from and then channeled back into the river. (3) The Dratt Chemical Co., Inc., discharges BOD, toxic organic chemicals, and phenols from its plant's production and sanitation facilities directly into the river, causing a violation of state-established WQSs — based on fishable-swimmable water quality — downstream of the plant. Dratt also collects its stormwater, which is contaminated by runoff from uncovered raw materials storage piles, and discharges it through a drainage ditch into the river. (4) The Tribal Council of the Unpoll-Ute Indian Nation, which owns a reservation located just below Dratt's discharge points, has approved and submitted to EPA water quality criteria based on a "None Detectable" standard for the parameters discharged by Purview and Dratt. (5) Across the river from the reservation is a wetland area, in which another residential subdivision (Heron's Harbor) is planned. (6) The City of Grossville, population 500,000, is serviced by a POTW that uses secondary treatment but is connected to a combined sewer system that contains 100 "overflow points," which discharge raw sewage mixed with stormwater into the Pedantic Ocean when storm flows exceed the capacity of the sewerage system. (7) Grossville's CSO and sewage treatment problems are exacerbated by the Nurd Auto Co., Inc.'s discharges of heavy metals into the Grossville sewers, and these heavy metals also contaminate the POTW's sewage sludge (biosolids), which is currently being stored in concrete silos at the POTW because ocean dumping — which the POTW once used to dispose of sludge — has been prohibited by federal law, and the high heavy metal levels in the sludge preclude incineration, land application or landfilling. (8) The Zaaap Power Company has applied to the Federal Energy Regulatory Commission (FERC) for a license to construct a hydroelectric power dam on the river between Riverview Park and Purview Farms; if constructed, this facility will add to existing pollution problems by raising water temperatures (depressing dissolved oxygen levels) and causing eutrophication in the reservoir behind the dam, and also by decreasing water flows (providing less dilution) and dissolved oxygen levels below the dam.

How might the CWA apply to each and all of these activities in the Average River watershed? If government does not act effectively to protect the river in these settings, what can citizens do?

Chapter 13

STANDARD-SETTING VIA COST-BENEFIT PROCEDURES

A. *Open-Ended Cost-Benefit Balancing: The Toxic Substances Control Act*
B. *The Practice and Theory of Cost-Benefit Analysis*
C. *Formal Cost-Benefit Analysis: The Safe Drinking Water Act*
D. *Cost-Benefit Analysis at OMB/OIRA*

Cost-benefit analysis occupies a singular position among the alternative regulatory frameworks for environmental problems. It is the only decisionmaking framework that, in theory, could apply to any environmental problem, whether it arises from industrial pollution, natural resource degradation, product hazards, or anything else, and that, in theory, could collect all of the scientific and economic data concerning an environmental problem and use them to develop an economically optimal solution. In theory, therefore, cost-benefit analysis could be to policy analysis what unified field theory is to physics — a dazzling, unifying framework whose ultimate product could be, as wryly put by theoretical physicist Michio Katu, "an equation an inch long that would allow us to read the mind of God."[1]

Perhaps for these reasons, cost-benefit analysis is also a framework that has dominated public policy discussions for decades and has enjoyed a large following among environmental scholars and politicians alike. Yet it is also an approach Congress has rejected as a catch-all decisionmaking framework for environmental policy and has seldom embraced even in discrete regulatory settings. The polarization that characterizes so many environmental disputes is especially severe here: Many opponents of cost-benefit analysis argue that it should never be used in setting environmental policy, while proponents say that it is the only framework that makes any sense.

Regardless of the perspective you ultimately prefer, you must understand the arguments for and against cost-benefit analysis and how it operates in practice. Despite its relative lack of formal recognition in our environmental statutes, cost-benefit analysis in recent years has become exceedingly influential in developing regulatory policy. Mostly, this has been due to the efforts of the Office of Information and Regulatory Affairs (OIRA), within the Office of Management and Budget, to assert greater control over the decisions of executive branch agencies. (We briefly introduced OIRA in Chapter 7.) OIRA uses cost-benefit analysis to assess the appropriateness of agency initiatives, and EPA has been one of its most frequent, and most battered, targets. Thus a

---

1. Available from http://whatis.techtarget.com/definition/0,,sid9_gci554508,00.html.

solid understanding of the theory and workings of cost-benefit analysis is critical in understanding the regulatory process today.

In this chapter, we introduce you to two statutes that contemplate cost-benefit balancing: the Toxic Substances Control Act (ToSCA), and the Safe Drinking Water Act (SDWA), as amended in 1996. These statutes illustrate two very different ways of undertaking cost-benefit balancing. Whereas ToSCA allows quite open-ended balancing of a variety of factors, the SDWA specifically directs EPA's attention to "consumer willingness to pay" in setting drinking water standards. The SDWA is the only federal environmental statute that explicitly contemplates formal cost-benefit analysis based on consumer willingness to pay. See 42 U.S.C. §300g-1(b)(3)(C)(iii). Sandwiched in between our discussions of ToSCA and the SDWA is an introduction to the basic features of formal cost-benefit analysis and to the theoretical arguments for and against basing environmental policy on this approach. At the end of the chapter, we examine OIRA's review of agency initiatives based on cost-benefit analysis.

First, though, it will be helpful to clarify the different types of cost-benefit balancing, and also the difference between cost-benefit balancing and other decisionmaking approaches that take costs into account. Cost-benefit balancing can take one of two forms. First, as in ToSCA, a decisionmaker can be instructed to consider all of the pros and cons of different policy options, and to come up with the most sensible approach in light of these considerations. In this form of cost-benefit balancing, items in the pro and con columns are not necessarily quantified, and many will not be translated into dollar amounts. A second form of cost-benefit balancing is more formal and restrictive; it is also the form of cost-benefit analysis most fashionable in policy circles today and is the approach reflected in the SDWA. It demands quantification and monetization of regulatory considerations wherever possible. Formal cost-benefit analysis is the approach in which tricky questions about the monetary value of human life, endangered species, and the like most frequently enter into the regulatory picture.

It is also important to understand the difference between cost-benefit balancing and other regulatory frameworks that take costs into account. Most environmental standards are set with an eye on costs. As we saw in the discussion of technology-based regulation in Chapter 12, the way costs are taken into account in setting most environmental standards is by using costs (among other factors) to choose the best available means of controlling pollution. The brake on regulation under these laws is the technical and economic feasibility of various methods for controlling pollution.

Cost-benefit analysis, in contrast, attempts to reduce the advantages and disadvantages of regulatory alternatives first to numbers and then, at least in formal cost-benefit analysis, to dollars. The basic idea is that regulatory policies should be evaluated according to their full social consequences and the social utility they produce.

With regard to formal cost-benefit analysis, a further notion is that social consequences, good and bad, should be evaluated according to how much money people are willing to pay to enjoy or to avoid them. Within formal cost-benefit analysis, therefore, the regulator chooses the stopping point for regulation by considering how much the benefits of regulation are "worth" in comparison to the costs, and assesses the worth of the benefits by reference to consumer willingness to pay. Here, then, the brake on regulation is neither economic nor technological feasibility, but limits on the price people are willing to pay for analogous benefits, offered in commercial markets. The difference between formal cost-benefit analysis and other kinds of decisionmaking approaches is not that the latter pay no attention to costs. The difference is that no other decisionmaking approach makes regulatory policy turn on consumer decisions in private market transactions. This feature not only makes cost-benefit analysis unique among the possible regulatory frameworks; it also, as we shall see, makes it unusually contentious.

A. OPEN-ENDED COST-BENEFIT BALANCING: THE TOXIC SUBSTANCES CONTROL ACT

In 1989, after ten years of study, EPA issued a final rule prohibiting the future manufacture, importation, processing, and distribution of asbestos in almost all products. EPA found that only a ban on asbestos would protect against the risks of asbestos posed by all of the stages of its life cycle, including mining, processing, manufacturing, and disposal. EPA estimated that its rule would prevent 202 fatal cancer cases that would have occurred due to exposures occurring in the next 13 years. The agency found that it could not quantify many of the benefits that would be produced by the rule, including asbestosis cases avoided.

Asbestos is a naturally occurring fibrous mineral. Because it resists fire and solvents, it was used widely for insulation, building materials, fireproof clothing, and motor vehicle brake linings. The same properties that made asbestos useful also made it harmful. Asbestos causes mesothelioma, lung cancer, and asbestosis. Thousands of private lawsuits have charged asbestos manufacturers and other companies with exposing workers and others to asbestos, killing or injuring many of them, without warning those exposed. EPA's rulemaking occurred in the midst of the asbestos liability "crisis," which continues to this day.

EPA acted under §6 of ToSCA. ToSCA is one of the principal regulatory efforts to control health risks created by toxic substances. ToSCA tries to manage these risks by regulating the market in toxic substances. (More specifics of ToSCA's statutory design are explored in Chapter 17.) Section 6 of ToSCA sets forth a wide array of regulatory alternatives available to the EPA Administrator ranging from labeling requirements to outright bans. Before embarking on one of these regulatory courses of action, however, the Administrator must first find that "there is a reasonable basis to conclude that the manufacture, processing, distribution in commerce, use, or disposal of a chemical substance or mixture, or that any combination of such activities, presents or will present an unreasonable risk of injury to health or the environment...." 15 U.S.C. §2605(a), ToSCA §6. Then, the Administrator "shall by rule apply one or more of" the regulatory requirements described in §6, "to the extent necessary to protect adequately against such risk using the least burdensome requirements." Id.

ToSCA §6 further provides:

(c) Promulgation of subsection (a) rules. In promulgating any rule under subsection (a) of this section with respect to a chemical substance or mixture, the

Administrator shall consider and publish a statement with respect to — (A) the effects of such substance or mixture on health and the magnitude of the exposure of human beings to such substance or mixture, (B) the effects of such substance or mixture on the environment and the magnitude of the exposure of the environment to such substance or mixture, (C) the benefits of such substance or mixture for various uses and the availability of substitutes for such uses, and (D) the reasonably ascertainable economic consequences of the rule, after consideration of the effect on the national economy, small business, technological innovation, the environment, and public health.

ToSCA also requires that EPA's decisions be reviewed under the "substantial evidence" standard of review. This standard gives courts somewhat more authority to overturn agency decisions than the more forgiving "arbitrary and capricious" standard ordinarily found in environmental cases. In the case that follows, the court first held that EPA had erred in failing to conduct a cost-benefit analysis for every possible regulatory alternative for asbestos, beginning with the least burdensome requirements listed in §6 (such as labeling) and continuing all the way through to the most burdensome (an outright ban). The court then turned to EPA's cost-benefit methodologies and found these, too, wanting.

Corrosion Proof Fittings v. U.S. Environmental Protection Agency
United States Court of Appeals for the Fifth Circuit, 1991
947 F.2d 1201

SMITH, J. ... First, we note that there was some dispute in the record regarding the appropriateness of discounting the perceived benefits of the EPA's rule. In choosing between the calculated costs and benefits, the EPA presented variations in which it discounted only the costs, and counter-variations in which it discounted both the costs and the benefits, measured in both monetary and human injury terms. As between these two variations, we choose to evaluate the EPA's work using its discounted benefits calculations.

Although various commentators dispute whether it ever is appropriate to discount benefits when they are measured in human lives, we note that it would skew the results to discount only costs without according similar treatment to the benefits side of the equation. Adopting the position of the commentators who advocate not discounting benefits would force the EPA similarly not to calculate costs in present discounted real terms, making comparisons difficult. Furthermore, in evaluating situations in which different options incur costs at varying time intervals, the EPA would not be able to take into account that soon-to-be-incurred costs are more harmful than postponable costs. Because the EPA must discount costs to perform its evaluations properly, the EPA also should discount benefits to preserve an apples-to-apples comparison, even if this entails discounting benefits of a non-monetary nature. See What Price Posterity?, The Economist, March 23, 1991, at 73 (explaining use of discount rates for non-monetary goods).

When the EPA does discount costs or benefits, however, it cannot choose an unreasonable time upon which to base its discount calculation. Instead of using the time of injury as the appropriate time from which to discount, as one might expect, the EPA instead used the time of exposure.

The difficulties inherent in the EPA's approach can be illustrated by an example. Suppose two workers will be exposed to asbestos in 1995, with worker X subjected to a tiny amount of asbestos that will have no adverse health effects, and worker Y exposed to massive amounts of asbestos that quickly will lead to an asbestos-related disease. Under the EPA's approach, which takes into account only the time of exposure rather than the time at which any injury manifests itself, both examples would be treated the same. The EPA's approach implicitly assumes that the day on which the risk of injury occurs is the same day the injury actually occurs. Such an approach might be proper when the exposure and injury are one and the same, such as when a person is exposed to an immediately fatal poison, but is inappropriate for discounting toxins in which exposure often is followed by a substantial lag time before manifestation of injuries.[2]

Of more concern to us is the failure of the EPA to compute the costs and benefits of its proposed rule past the year 2000, and its double-counting of the costs of asbestos use. In performing its calculus, the EPA only included the number of lives saved over the next thirteen years, and counted any additional lives saved as simply "unquantified benefits." The EPA and intervenors now seek to use these unquantified lives saved to justify calculations as to which the benefits seem far outweighed by the astronomical costs. For example, the EPA plans to save about three lives with its ban of asbestos pipe, at a cost of $128-227 million (i.e., approximately $43-76 million per life saved). Although the EPA admits that the price tag is high, it claims that the lives saved past the year 2000 justify the price.

Such calculations not only lessen the value of the EPA's cost analysis, but also make any meaningful judicial review impossible. While TSCA contemplates a useful place for unquantified benefits beyond the EPA's calculation, unquantified benefits never were intended as a trump card allowing the EPA to justify any cost calculus, no matter how high.

The concept of unquantified benefits, rather, is intended to allow the EPA to provide a rightful place for any remaining benefits that are impossible to quantify after the EPA's best attempt, but which still are of some concern. But the allowance for unquantified costs is not intended to allow the EPA to perform its calculations over an arbitrarily short period so as to preserve a large unquantified portion.

Unquantified benefits can, at times, permissibly tip the balance in close cases. They cannot, however, be used to effect a wholesale shift on the balance beam. Such a use makes a mockery of the requirements of TSCA that the EPA weigh the costs of its actions before it chooses the least burdensome alternative.[3]

We do not today determine what an appropriate period for the EPA's calculations would be, as this is a matter better left for agency discretion. We do note, however, that the choice of a thirteen-year period is so short as to make the unquantified period so unreasonably large that any EPA reliance upon it must be displaced.

Under the EPA's calculations, a twenty-year-old worker entering employment today still would be at risk from workplace dangers for more than thirty years after the EPA's analysis period had ended. The true benefits of regulating asbestos under such calculations remain

---

2. We also note that the EPA chose to use a real discount rate of 3%. Because historically the real rate of interest has tended to vary between 2% and 4%, this figure was not inaccurate.

3. We thus reject the arguments made by the Natural Resources Defense Council, Inc., and the Environmental Defense Fund, Inc., that the EPA's decision can be justified because the EPA "relied on many serious risks that were understated or not quantified in the final rule," presented figures in which the "benefits are calculated only for a limited time period," and undercounted the risks to the general population from low-level asbestos exposure. In addition, the intervenors argue that the EPA rejected using upper estimates, and that this court now should use the rejected limits as evidence to support the EPA. They thus would have us reject the upper limit concerns when they are not needed, but use them if necessary.

We agree that these all are valid concerns that the EPA legitimately should take into account when considering regulatory action. What we disagree with, however, is the manner in which the EPA incorporated these concerns. By not using such concerns in its quantitative analysis, even where doing so was not difficult, and reserving them as additional factors to buttress the ban, the EPA improperly transformed permissible considerations into determinative factors.

unknown. The EPA cannot choose to leave these benefits high and then use the high unknown benefits as a major factor justifying EPA action.

The final requirement the EPA must satisfy before engaging in any TSCA rulemaking is that it only take steps designed to prevent "unreasonable" risks. In evaluating what is "unreasonable," the EPA is required to consider the costs of any proposed actions and to "carry out this chapter in a reasonable and prudent manner [after considering] the environmental, economic, and social impact of any action." 15 U.S.C. §2601(c).

As the District of Columbia Circuit stated when evaluating similar language governing the Federal Hazardous Substances Act, "the requirement that the risk be 'unreasonable' necessarily involves a balancing test like that familiar in tort law: The regulation may issue if the severity of the injury that may result from the product, factored by the likelihood of the injury, offsets the harm the regulation itself imposes upon manufacturers and consumers." Forester v. CPSC, 559 F.2d 774, 789 (D.C. Cir. 1977). We have quoted this language approvingly when evaluating other statutes using similar language.

That the EPA must balance the costs of its regulations against their benefits further is reinforced by the requirement that it seek the least burdensome regulation. While Congress did not dictate that the EPA engage in an exhaustive, full-scale cost-benefit analysis, it did require the EPA to consider both sides of the regulatory equation, and it rejected the notion that the EPA should pursue the reduction of workplace risk at any cost. See American Textile Mfrs. Inst., 452 U.S. at 510 n. 30 ("unreasonable risk" statutes require "a generalized balancing of costs and benefits" (citing Aqua Slide, 569 F.2d at 839)). Thus, "Congress also plainly intended the EPA to consider the economic impact of any actions taken by it under…TSCA." Chemical Mfrs. Ass'n, 899 F.2d at 348.

Even taking all of the EPA's figures as true, and evaluating them in the light most favorable to the agency's decision (non-discounted benefits, discounted costs, analogous exposure estimates included), the agency's analysis results in figures as high as $74 million per life saved. For example, the EPA states that its ban of asbestos pipe will save three lives over the next thirteen years, at a cost of $128–227 million ($43–76 million per life saved), depending upon the price of substitutes; that its ban of asbestos shingles will cost $23–34 million to save 0.32 statistical lives ($72–106 million per life saved); that its ban of asbestos coatings will cost $46–181 million to save 3.33 lives ($14–54 million per life saved); and that its ban of asbestos paper products will save 0.60 lives at a cost of $4–5 million ($7–8 million per life saved). See 54 Fed. Reg. at 29,484–85. Were the analogous exposure estimates not included, the cancer risks from substitutes such as ductile iron pipe factored in, and the benefits of the ban appropriately discounted from the time of the manifestation of an injury rather than the time of exposure, the costs would shift even more sharply against the EPA's position.

While we do not sit as a regulatory agency that must make the difficult decision as to what an appropriate expenditure is to prevent someone from incurring the risk of an asbestos-related death, we do note that the EPA, in its zeal to ban any and all asbestos products, basically ignored the cost side of the TSCA equation. The EPA would have this court believe that Congress, when it enacted its requirement that the EPA consider the economic impacts of its regulations, thought that spending $200–300 million to save approximately seven lives (approximately $30-40 million per life) over thirteen years is reasonable….

The EPA's willingness to argue that spending $23.7 million to save less than one-third of a life reveals that its economic review of its regulations, as required by TSCA, was meaningless. As the petitioners' brief and our review of EPA caselaw reveals, such high costs are rarely, if ever, used to support a safety regulation. If we were to allow such cavalier treatment of the EPA's duty to consider the economic effects of its decisions, we would have to excise entire sections and phrases from the language of TSCA. Because we are judges, not surgeons, we decline to do so.[4]

COMMENTARY & QUESTIONS

1. **How did the court know how much was too much to save a life?** Is the toothpick comparison persuasive? Would $20 million per life have been too much to spend? $10 million? $5 million? Does the court tell us what standard it is using to judge EPA's rule?

2. **Apples and … apples? Oranges?** Is the court correct in requiring EPA to treat the avoidance of future cancers like an economic benefit that should be discounted to present value? When costs are expressed in dollars and benefits are expressed in human lives, as they were here, is the court correct that we are dealing with apples and apples? Or are we dealing with apples and oranges — goods that cannot be made commensurate through the technical device of discounting? Consider the following observations on the court's ruling:

> One worries about "preserv[ing] an apples-to-apples comparison"…only if one is dealing only with apples. In the asbestos case, the costs were dollars and the benefits were lives. These costs and benefits are the same only if dollars and lives are the same…. The implicit premise of an argument in favor of discounting is that lives can be measured in dollars. Far from being a "value-free and good workable rule,"[5]…the decision to treat future costs and benefits the same — to discount them both and to discount them at the same rate — silently resolves one of the central moral questions of the modern regulatory state. Heinzerling, Regulatory Costs of Mythic Proportions, 107 Yale L.J. 1981, 2053 (1998).

3. **Does discounting miss the point?** Some observers resist the very idea of applying market discount approaches to issues of planetary ecological management. Economist Peter Brown argues:

> There are some things that are not, and should not be, discounted. No one asks, "What is the optimal rate of shredding for the U.S. Constitution?" On the contrary, we assume that we should preserve the historic document for posterity. This is precisely analogous to what many people think we should do with respect to these issues; but all this response demonstrates is that [market accounting] doesn't tell us what the discount rate with respect to these issues should be, or even whether there should be one. [Moreover,] in any situation where there is a long-term asymmetry between costs and benefits, as is the case with global warming, discounting imperils the future by undervaluing it. Although the costs of averting the greenhouse effect are paid in the present, the benefits accrue in the distant future. The discounted value of harms that occur a century from now are insignificant when

---

4. As the petitioners point out, the EPA regularly rejects, as unjustified, regulations that would save more lives at less cost. For example, over the next 13 years, we can expect more than a dozen deaths from ingested toothpicks — a death toll more than twice what the EPA predicts will flow from the quarter-billion-dollar bans of asbestos pipe, shingles, and roof coatings. See L. Budnick, Toothpick-Related Injuries in the United States, 1979 Through 1982, 252 J. Am. Med. Ass'n, Aug. 10, 1984, at 796 (study showing that toothpick-related deaths average approximately one per year).

5. John F. Morrall III, Cotton Dust: An Economist's View, in The Scientific Basis of Health and Safety Regulation 107 (Robert W. Crandall & Lester B. Lave eds., 1981).

compared with the present costs of avoiding them. As D'Arge, Schulze, and Brookshire argue in Carbon Dioxide and Intergenerational Choice, "a complete loss of the world's GNP a hundred years from now would be worth about one million dollars today if discounted by the present prime rate." P. Brown, Greenhouse Economics: Think Before You Count, a Report from the Institute for Philosophy & Public Policy 10, 11 (1991).

4. **Tilting the balance beam.** The court charges that EPA performed its numerical calculations over an "arbitrarily short period so as to preserve a large unquantified portion." Might there be another, less cynical explanation for EPA's choice of a 13-year analytical horizon? Would EPA's predictions about the effects of its rule beyond this period become more or less supportable than predictions about the nearer term?

5. **Trumping quantified costs.** EPA cited substantial unquantified benefits in support of its rule, including not only benefits beyond its 13-year analytical horizon, but also including the avoidance of asbestosis and other harmful effects of asbestos. The court says unquantified benefits can play a role in close cases, but cannot be used to "effect a wholesale shift on the balance beam." Does the statute require the court's result? Does the court's position make sense? If important benefits are unquantified, how do we know whether it is a close case? On the other hand, if unquantified benefits were allowed to trump quantified costs without limit, would there be any meaningful limits on the agency's discretion? Would meaningful judicial review be possible?

6. **The "least burdensome" alternative?** As noted, in a portion of the opinion not excerpted here, the court criticized EPA for its analytical process. The court thought EPA should have started with the least burdensome regulatory alternative available under ToSCA, done a cost-benefit analysis of that alternative, and then continued to a more burdensome alternative (with a full-blown cost-benefit analysis there, too) only if the less onerous alternative failed to bring the risks posed by asbestos down to a reasonable level. The court found this procedural approach required by ToSCA. Do you agree that §6 contemplates this approach? What implications will such an approach have for EPA's ability to respond to toxic threats under ToSCA?

7. **From asbestos to fish sinkers.** The asbestos ban is EPA's first and only ban of a toxic substance under ToSCA's §6. Several years after the ban was overturned, EPA proposed banning lead fish sinkers, popular among avid anglers, due to their harmful effects on water life and on the people who made the sinkers. EPA never finalized this ban. In March 2000, EPA issued an Advance Notice of Proposed Rulemaking seeking public comment on the possibility of banning the fuel additive methyl tertiary butyl ether (MTBE) under ToSCA §6. 65 Fed. Reg. 16094 (Mar. 24, 2000). So far, however, the agency has taken no final action on this matter.

8. **Is ToSCA just like NEPA?** Reread ToSCA's §6(c) carefully. Could you make an argument that this section, like NEPA, merely requires EPA to compile a document describing the costs, benefits, etc., of an action taken under §6 and to consider that document in coming to a decision, but does not require the benefits of the agency's action to be commensurate with the costs? What do you suppose the Fifth Circuit would have made of such an interpretation if EPA had offered it?

9. **The sound of one hand clapping.** Without a monetary value for important regulatory benefits such as saving lives, how is EPA — and then the reviewing court — to decide whether an action is justified under §6? Where costs are stated in dollar terms but benefits are stated in lives and other values, costs take on a role rather like one hand clapping: There is nothing offered in opposition to them, yet it is hard what to make of their presence. For reasons like these, many people who advocate cost-benefit balancing advocate a more formal framework in which, as far as possible, both costs and benefits are reduced to monetary terms.

We turn next to an introduction to the way formal cost-benefit analysis works and the arguments for and against its use in making public policy.

B. THE PRACTICE AND THEORY OF COST-BENEFIT ANALYSIS

Before delving into the theoretical case for and against cost-benefit analysis, it's useful to establish exactly what cost-benefit analysis is and how it works. Here we are discussing formal cost-benefit analysis, in which decisionmakers attempt to reduce as many considerations as possible, first to numbers and then to dollars.

Section 1. HOW COST-BENEFIT ANALYSIS WORKS

Frank Ackerman and Lisa Heinzerling, Pricing the Priceless: Cost-Benefit Analysis of Environmental Protection
150 University of Pennsylvania Law Review 1553 (2002)

…Cost-benefit analysis tries to mimic a basic function of markets by setting an economic standard for measuring the success of the government's projects and programs. That is, cost-benefit analysis seeks to perform, for public policy, a calculation that happens routinely in the private sector. In evaluating a proposed new initiative, how do we know if it is worth doing or not? The answer is much simpler in business than in government.

Private businesses, striving to make money, only produce things that they believe someone is willing to pay for. That is, firms only produce things for which the benefits to consumers, measured by consumers' willingness to pay for them, are expected to be greater than the costs of production. It is technologically possible to produce men's business suits in brightly colored polka dots. Successful producers suspect that no one is willing to pay for such products, and usually stick to at most minor variations on suits in somber, traditional hues. If some firm did happen to produce a polka-dotted business suit, no one would be forced to buy it; the producer would bear the entire loss resulting from the mistaken decision.

Government, in the view of many critics, is in constant danger of drifting toward producing polka dot suits — and making people pay for them. Policies, regulations, and public spending do not face the test of the marketplace; there are no consumers who can withhold their dollars from the government until it produces the regulatory equivalent of navy blue and charcoal gray. There is no single quantitative objective for the public sector comparable to profit maximization for businesses. Even with the best of intentions, critics suggest, government programs can easily go astray for lack of an objective standard by which to judge whether or not they are meeting citizens' needs.

Cost-benefit analysis sets out to do for government what the market does for business: add up the benefits of a public policy and compare them to the costs. The two sides of the ledger raise very different issues.

Estimating Costs. The first step in a cost-benefit analysis is to calculate the costs of a public policy. For example, the government may require a certain kind of pollution control equipment, which businesses must pay for. Even if a regulation only sets a ceiling on emissions, it results in costs that can be at least roughly estimated through research into available technologies and business strategies for compliance.

The costs of protecting human health and the environment through the use of pollution control devices and other approaches are, by their very nature, measured in dollars. Thus, at least in theory, the cost side of cost-benefit analysis is relatively straightforward. (In practice, as we shall see, it is not quite that simple.)

The consideration of the costs of environmental protection is not unique to cost-benefit analysis. Development of environmental regulations has almost always involved consideration of economic costs, with or without formal cost-benefit techniques. What is unique to cost-benefit analysis, and far more problematic, is the other side of the balance, the monetary valuation of the benefits of life, health, and nature itself.

Monetizing Benefits. Since there are no natural prices for a healthy environment, cost-benefit analysis requires the creation of artificial ones. This is the hardest part of the process. Economists create artificial prices for health and environmental benefits by studying what people would be willing to pay for them. One popular method, called "contingent valuation," is essentially a form of opinion poll. Researchers ask a cross-section of the affected population how much they would be willing to pay to preserve or protect something that can't be bought in a store.

Many surveys of this sort have been done, producing prices for things that appear to be priceless. For example, the average American household is supposedly willing to pay $257 to prevent the extinction of bald eagles, $208 to protect humpback whales, and $80 to protect gray wolves.[6] These numbers are quite large: since there are about 100 million households in the country, the nation's total willingness to pay for the preservation of bald eagles alone is ostensibly more than $25 billion.

An alternative method of attaching prices to unpriced things infers what people are willing to pay from observation of their behavior in other markets. To assign a dollar value to risks to human life, for example, economists usually calculate the extra wage — or "wage premium" — that is paid to workers who accept more risky jobs. Suppose that two jobs are comparable, except that one is more dangerous and better paid. If workers understand the risk and voluntarily accept the more dangerous job, then they are implicitly setting a price on risk by accepting the increased risk of death in exchange for increased wages.

What does this indirect inference about wages say about the value of a life? A common estimate in recent cost-benefit analyses is that avoiding a risk that would lead, on average, to one death is worth roughly $6.3 million.[7] This number, in particular, is of great importance in

---

6. Loomis & White, Economic Benefits of Rare and Endangered Species: Summary and Meta-analysis, 18 Ecol. Econ. 197, 199, Table 1 (1996) (figures converted to year 2000 dollars using the consumer price index).

7. The original calculation, based on research by W. Kip Viscusi, can be found in EPA, The Benefits and Costs of the Clean Air Act, 1970 to 1990, 1997, Appendix I. For an example of a subsequent analysis citing the Clean Air Act analysis and adjusting only for inflation, see EPA, Arsenic in Drinking Water Rule: Economic Analysis, EPA Document 815-R-00-026, at 5–23 (Dec. 2000). The arsenic study used $6.1 million in 1999 dollars, which is equivalent to $6.3 million in 2000 dollars.

cost-benefit analyses because avoided deaths are the most thoroughly studied benefits of environmental regulations.

Discounting the Future. One more step requires explanation to complete this quick sketch of cost-benefit analysis. Costs and benefits of a policy frequently occur at different times. Often, costs are incurred today, or in the near future, to prevent harm in the more remote future. When the analysis spans a number of years, future costs and benefits are discounted, or treated as equivalent to smaller amounts of money in today's dollars.

Discounting is a procedure developed by economists in order to evaluate investments that produce future income. The case for discounting begins with the observation that $100, say, received today is worth more than $100 received next year, even in the absence of inflation. For one thing, you could put your money in the bank today and earn a little interest by next year. Suppose that your bank account earns 3% interest. In that case, if you received the $100 today rather than next year, you would earn $3 in interest, giving you a total of $103 next year. Likewise, in order to get $100 next year you only need to deposit $97 today.[8] So, at a 3% discount rate, economists would say that $100 next year has a present value of $97 in today's dollars.

For longer periods of time, the effect is magnified: at a 3% discount rate, $100 twenty years from now has a present value of only $55. The larger the discount rate, and the longer the time intervals involved, the smaller the present value: at a 5% discount rate, for example, $100 twenty years from now has a present value of only $38.

Cost-benefit analysis routinely uses the present value of future benefits. That is, it compares current costs, not to the actual dollar value of future benefits, but to the smaller amount you would have to put into a hypothetical savings account today to obtain those benefits in the future. This application of discounting is essential, and indeed commonplace, for many practical financial decisions. If offered a choice of investment opportunities with payoffs at different times in the future, you can (and should) discount the future payoffs to the present in order to compare them to each other. The important issue for environmental policy, as we shall see, is whether this logic also applies to outcomes far in the future, and to opportunities – like long life and good health – that are not naturally stated in dollar terms....

COMMENTARY & QUESTIONS

1. **Estimating costs.** Estimating the costs of a regulatory intervention is, in principle, the least complex of the steps required for cost-benefit analysis. In practice, however, it turns out to be very difficult to estimate these costs correctly. Empirical studies have demonstrated that costs are often substantially overestimated in advance of regulation. In part, this may be due to the fact that cost estimates often originate from the regulated industries themselves, which have an incentive to overstate costs in order to defeat regulatory initiatives. In addition, regulation often spurs innovation and efficiencies, which in turn lead to lower actual costs than anticipated.[9] One famous example of this phenomenon is the acid rain program of the CAA (discussed in Chapter 14). The actual cost of this program turned out to be approximately one-eighth to one-quarter of industry cost estimates offered before the program was enacted.[10]

---

8. The examples in the text are rounded off to the nearest dollar.

9. For a comprehensive overview and analysis, see McGarity & Ruttenberg, Counting the Cost of Health, Safety, and Environmental Regulation, 80 Tex. L. Rev. 1997 (2002).

10. E. Goodstein, Polluted Data, American Prospect, vol. 8 (Nov.–Dec. 1997).

A more subtle complexity here is that the apparent reasonableness of costs can vary greatly depending on how they are described. EPA's asbestos ban, for example, was expected to cost a total of approximately $460 million — or less than 14 cents per year for each American.[11] At OMB's insistence, however, EPA chose to represent the costs as a ratio of costs to lives saved, on an industry-by-industry basis. This decision is what led the court to find that, in some industries, the ban would cost as much as $106 million per life saved. Which is the correct way to represent costs — on a national basis, on an industry-by-industry basis, as costs per life saved? One court has held that agencies deserve deference in their decisions as to how to represent regulatory costs. American Dental Ass'n v. Martin, 984 F.2d 823, 827 (7th Cir. 1993) (Posner, J.).

2. **Benefits transfer.** Despite the explosion in recent years in economic research on willingness-to-pay for environmental improvements, there remain many gaps in the database. In few cases (perhaps none) are there data on the willingness-to-pay of the very population affected by a regulation for the very regulatory benefit conferred. Thus analysts must try to find an analogous setting in which data exist. When analysts use these data in a different setting from the one in which they arose, this is called "benefits transfer." The most prominent example of benefits transfer in the regulatory context is, as Ackerman and Heinzerling discuss, the practice of using values derived from workers' demand for wage premiums for risky work to infer the value of improvements in environmental quality for the general population.

3. **Monetization and discounting.** The two features of cost-benefit analysis that truly distinguish it from other decisionmaking frameworks are monetization and discounting. Are these features essential to cost-benefit analysis?

Section 2. THE CASE FOR COST-BENEFIT

In American Trucking v. Whitman, a group of prominent economists filed a brief asking the Court to hold that the CAA required EPA to base the NAAQS on cost-benefit analysis. Notably, the economists explicitly declined to address the legal aspects of the case, focusing their arguments solely on policy. The brief's caption read like a Who's Who of American economists and included several Nobel laureates.

American Trucking Associations v. Browner[12]
Brief Amici Curiae of AEI-Brookings Joint Center
for Regulatory Studies, et al.,
in support of American Trucking Associations, et al.
1999 U.S. Briefs 1426

Both the direct benefits and costs of environmental, health, and safety regulations are substantial — estimated to be several hundred billion dollars annually. If these resources were better allocated with the objective of reducing human health risk, scholars have predicted that

---

11. The figure is derived by dividing $460 million by 13 (the number of years in EPA's study period), and dividing this by the approximate U.S. population at the time (250 million).

12. Carol Browner was still the Administrator of EPA when this brief was filed. Christine Todd Whitman became Administrator when George W. Bush assumed office, followed by Mike Leavitt in December, 2003.

tens of thousands more lives could be saved each year.[13] All presidents since Nixon — both Democratic and Republican — have attempted to make environmental, health, and safety regulations more efficient by requiring some form of oversight attempting to balance benefits and costs. President Reagan and President Clinton each crafted an executive order that required an explicit balancing of benefits and costs for major regulations to the extent permitted by law. A comprehensive regulatory impact analysis (RIA) prepared in conformance with President Clinton's Executive Order 12866 was done for the ozone and particulate matter rulemaking, but it played no official or overt part in the decision in this case because of the D.C. Circuit's view that costs must not be considered....

The concern [of amici] is how analytical methods, such as benefit-cost analysis, should be used in regulatory decisionmaking. These methods can help promote the design of better regulations by providing a sensible framework for comparing the alternatives involved in any regulatory choice. Such analysis improves the chances that regulations will be designed to achieve a particular social goal specified by legislators at a lower cost. In addition, they can make the regulatory process more transparent by providing an analytical basis for a decision. Greater transparency in the process, in turn, will help hold regulators and lawmakers more accountable for their decisions.

These analytical methods are neither anti- nor proregulation; they can suggest reasons why it would be desirable to have tighter or more lenient standards depending on the results of an analysis. For example, the benefit-cost analyses in the RIA on particulate matter and ozone could be interpreted as suggesting that the ozone standard should not be lowered while a new PM standard for fine particles should be introduced to protect public health.

Over the past two decades, support has been growing for the proposition that weighing of benefits and costs should play a more central role in regulatory decisionmaking. All three branches of government have recognized the importance of considering benefits and costs in designing regulation.

To address the increase in regulatory activity over the past three decades, the past five presidents and President Clinton have introduced different analytical requirements and oversight mechanisms with varying degrees of success. A central component of later oversight mechanisms was formal economic analysis, which included benefit-cost analysis and cost-effectiveness analysis. Since 1981, presidents have required the preparation of RIAs for a predefined class of significant regulations. President Reagan's Executive Order 12291 required an RIA for each significant regulation whose annual impact on the economy was estimated to exceed $100 million. President Bush used the same executive order. President Clinton's and President Reagan's executive orders require a benefit-cost analysis for significant regulations as well as an assessment of reasonably feasible alternatives to the planned regulation.

Congress has also shown increasing interest in emphasizing the balancing of benefits and costs in regulatory decisions. The Small Business Regulatory Enforcement Fairness Act of 1996 requires agencies to submit final regulations to Congress for review. The regulatory accountability provisions of 1996, 1997, and 1998 require the Office of Management and Budget to assess the benefits and costs of existing federal regulatory programs and to recommend programs or specific regulations to reform or eliminate. The Unfunded Mandates Reform Act of 1995 requires agencies, unless prohibited by law, to choose the most cost-effective regulatory

---

13. See Tammy O. Tengs & John D. Graham, The Opportunity Costs of Haphazard Social Investments in Life-Saving, in Risks, Costs, and Lives Saved: Getting Better Results from Regulation (Robert W. Hahn ed. 1996). (The authors, from the Harvard School of Public Health, calculated that improved priority setting across federal agencies could provide either savings of $31.1 billion from current cost levels with no additional loss of life or savings of 60,200 lives at current cost levels.)

approach or otherwise explain why they have not chosen this alternative.

The courts have also been receptive to the use of benefit-cost analysis in decisionmaking. Indeed, the D.C. Circuit recently held in State of Michigan v. EPA, 213 F.3d 663 (2000), that "it is only where there is 'clear congressional intent to preclude consideration of cost' that we find agencies barred from considering costs." The court went on to cite various cases and legal authorities for the "general view that preclusion of cost consideration requires a rather specific congressional direction." Id. This case and others led Professors Robert H. Frank and Cass R. Sunstein to conclude that "federal law now reflects a kind of default principle: Agencies will consider costs, and thus undertake cost-benefit analysis, if Congress has not unambiguously said that they cannot."[14] ...

Without delving into the legal aspects of the case, we present below why we think the Court should allow the EPA to consider costs in setting standards. In particular, we believe that, as a general principle, regulators should be allowed to consider explicitly the full consequences of their regulatory decisions. These consequences include the regulation's benefits, costs, and any other relevant factors....

Benefit-cost analysis is simply a tool that can aid in making decisions. Most people do a kind of informal benefit-cost analysis when considering the personal pros and cons of their actions in everyday life — more for big decisions, like choosing a college or job or house, than for little ones, like driving to the grocery store. Where decisions, such as federal environmental regulations, are by their nature public rather than private, the government, as a faithful agent of its citizens, should do something similar.

Carefully considering the social benefits and social costs of a course of action makes good sense. Economists and other students of government policy have developed ways of making those comparisons systematic. Those techniques fall under the label benefit-cost analysis. Benefit-cost analysis does not provide the policy answer, but rather defines a useful framework for debate, either by a legislature or, where the legislature has delegated to a specialized agency the responsibility of pursuing a general good, by that agency.

Economists, other policy experts, and the regulatory agencies themselves have produced a large literature on the methods and applications of benefit-cost analysis. There are, and always will be, many uncertainties and disagreements about those methods and their application in particular cases. Nevertheless, a wide consensus exists on certain fundamental matters. In 1996, a group of distinguished economists, including Nobel laureate Kenneth Arrow, were assembled to develop principles for benefit-cost analysis in environmental, health, and safety regulation. Here, we summarize and paraphrase for the Court a number of principles that we think could be helpful in this case, which involves the review of the EPA's NAAQS standard-setting decisions.

A benefit-cost analysis is a useful way of organizing a comparison of the favorable and unfavorable effects of proposed policies. Benefit-cost analysis can help the decisionmaker better understand the implications of a decision. It should be used to inform decisionmakers. Benefit-cost analysis can provide useful estimates of the overall benefits and costs of proposed policies. It can also assess the impacts of proposed policies on consumers, workers, and owners of firms and can identify potential winners and losers.

In many cases, benefit-cost analysis cannot be used to prove that the economic benefits of a decision will exceed or fall short of the costs. Yet benefit-cost analysis should play an important role in informing the decisionmaking process, even when the information on benefits, costs, or

---

14. Robert H. Frank & Cass R. Sunstein, Cost-Benefit Analysis and Relative Position [68 U. Chi. L. Rev. 323, 330 (2001)].

both is highly uncertain, as is often the case with regulations involving the environment, health, and safety.

Economic analysis can be useful in designing regulatory strategies that achieve a desired goal at the lowest possible cost. Too frequently, environmental, health, and safety regulation has used a one-size-fits-all or command-and-control approach. Economic analysis can highlight the extent to which cost savings can be achieved by using alternative, more flexible approaches that reward performance.

Benefit-cost analysis should be required for all major regulatory decisions. The scale of a benefit-cost analysis should depend on both the stakes involved and the likelihood that the resulting information will affect the ultimate decision.

Agencies should not be bound by a strict benefit-cost test, but should be required to consider available benefit-cost analyses. There may be factors other than economic benefits and costs that agencies will want to weigh in decisions, such as equity within and across generations.

Not all impacts of a decision can be quantified or expressed in dollar terms. Care should be taken to ensure that quantitative factors do not dominate important qualitative factors in decisionmaking. A common critique of benefit-cost analysis is that it does not emphasize factors that are not easily quantified or monetized. That critique has merit. There are two principal ways to address it: first, quantify as many factors as are reasonable and quantify or characterize the relevant uncertainties; and second, give due consideration to factors that defy quantification but are thought to be important.

We believe all of the available information should be considered in making any important decision. If costs or other types of data are deliberately left out, the quality of decisionmaking is likely to suffer. In particular, we make one recommendation, closely related to the Arrow et al. principles: The Court should allow the EPA to consider costs in setting NAAQS, so that these costs can then be assessed along with benefits and any other important information....

We believe that this Supreme Court case involving the setting of National Ambient Air Quality Standards could be a historic moment in the making of regulatory policy. This brief has argued that it would be imprudent not to consider costs in the setting of standards. In accordance with Executive Order 12866, we also believe that the full range of benefits and costs should be considered in decisionmaking. Accordingly, this Court should allow the Environmental Protection Agency to consider costs in setting nationwide air quality standards, so that this information can be considered along with benefits and any other relevant factors in setting a standard.

COMMENTARY & QUESTIONS

1. **The result.** As we know from Chapter 11, in *American Trucking* the Supreme Court rejected the economists' pleas, holding that the CAA forbids the consideration of costs in setting the harm-based NAAQSs. In looking for (but not finding) an explicit directive on costs in the text of the statute itself, moreover, the Court arguably created an "anti-cost-benefit default principle" — because costs loom large in any major regulatory endeavor, Congress's failure to mention them explicitly might be taken as a sign, as in *American Trucking*, that it did not want the agency to consider them.

2. **The economists' framework.** How does the economists' description of what they mean by cost-benefit analysis differ from any other decisionmaking framework that takes costs into account — including even that old command-and-control standby,

technology-based regulation? How will quantified and unquantified values be combined in their framework to produce a decision?

3. **Statistical murder?** John Graham, one of the authors of the study relied upon by the AEI amici economists in arguing that a failure to do cost-benefit analysis results in squandered lifesaving opportunities, has called this state of affairs "statistical murder." And indeed, perhaps the most universally compelling case for cost-benefit analysis is one cited by the AEI amici economists in their brief: Unless we perform this analysis, we risk wasting opportunities to save many more thousands of lives every year through redirection of our lifesaving resources. Anyone interested in saving lives must take notice of this argument. It is important to realize, however, that most of the "tens of thousands of lives" that the Tengs-Graham study cited by the AEI amici economists said could be saved by redirecting our lifesaving resources were in the health care field. Only a very small portion of the additional lives saved was due to redirection of environmental priorities. Even there, moreover, Tengs and Graham and their coauthors drastically reduced the apparent lifesaving potential of environmental rules by discounting the regulatory benefits of such rules, using the questionable technique discussed by Ackerman and Heinzerling.

Section 3. THE CASE AGAINST COST-BENEFIT

For the case against cost-benefit analysis, we return to the article that has already described for us how this analysis works.

Frank Ackerman and Lisa Heinzerling, Pricing the Priceless: Cost-Benefit Analysis of Environmental Protection
150 University of Pennsylvania Law Review 1553 (2002)

...Cost-benefit analysis involves the creation of artificial markets for things — like good health, long life, and clean air — that are not bought and sold. It also involves the devaluation of future events through discounting.

So described, the mind-set of the cost-benefit analyst is likely to seem quite foreign. The translation of all good things into dollars and the devaluation of the future are inconsistent with the way many people view the world. Most of us believe that money doesn't buy happiness. Most religions tell us that every human life is sacred; it is obviously illegal, as well as immoral, to buy and sell human lives. Most parents tell their children to eat their vegetables and do their homework, even though the rewards of these onerous activities lie far in the future. Monetizing human lives and discounting future benefits seem at odds with these common perspectives.

The cost-benefit approach also is inconsistent with the way many of us make daily decisions. Imagine performing a new cost-benefit analysis to decide whether to get up and go to work every morning, whether to exercise or eat right on any given day, whether to wash the dishes or leave them in the sink, and so on. Inaction would win far too often — and an absurd amount of effort would be spent on analysis. Most people have long-run goals, commitments, and habits that make such daily balancing exercises either redundant or counterproductive. The same might be true of society as a whole undertaking individual steps in the pursuit of any goal, set for the long haul, that cannot be reached overnight — including, for example, the achievement of a clean environment.

Moving beyond these intuitive responses, we offer in this section a detailed explanation of why cost-benefit analysis of environmental protection fails to live up to the hopes and claims of its advocates. There is no quick fix, because these failures are intrinsic to the methodology, appearing whenever it is applied to any complex environmental problem. In our view, cost-benefit analysis suffers from four fundamental flaws, addressed in the next four subsections:

- The standard economic approaches to valuation are inaccurate and implausible.
- The use of discounting improperly trivializes future harms and the irreversibility of some environmental problems.
- The reliance on aggregate, monetized benefits excludes questions of fairness and morality.
- The value-laden and complex cost-benefit process is neither objective nor transparent.

Dollars Without Sense. Recall that cost-benefit analysis requires the creation of artificial prices for all relevant health and environmental impacts. To weigh the benefits of regulation against the costs, we need to know the monetary value of preventing the extinction of species, preserving many different ecosystems, avoiding all manner of serious health impacts, and even saving human lives. Without such numbers, cost-benefit analysis cannot be conducted.

Artificial prices have been estimated for many, though by no means all, benefits of regulation. As discussed, preventing the extinction of bald eagles reportedly goes for somewhat more than $250 per household. Preventing retardation due to childhood lead poisoning comes in at about $9,000 per lost IQ point in the standard view, or a mere $1,500 per point in Lutter's alternative. Saving a life is ostensibly worth $6.3 million.

This quantitative precision, achieved through a variety of indirect techniques for valuation, comes at the expense of accuracy and even common sense. Though problems arise in many areas of valuation, we will focus primarily on the efforts to attach a monetary value to human life, both because of its importance in cost-benefit analysis and because of its glaring contradictions.

We note, however, that the same kind of problems we are about to discuss affect other valuation issues raised by cost-benefit analysis, such as estimating the value of clean water, biodiversity, or entire ecosystems. The upshot is that cost-benefit analysis is fundamentally incapable of delivering on its promise of more economically efficient decisions about protecting human life, health, and the environment. Absent a credible monetary metric for calculating the benefits of regulation, cost-benefit analysis is inherently unreliable.

There Are No "Statistical" People. What can it mean to say that saving one life is worth $6.3 million? Human life is the ultimate example of a value that is not a commodity, and does not have a price. You cannot buy the right to kill someone for $6.3 million, nor for any other price. Most systems of ethical and religious belief maintain that every life is sacred. If analysts calculated the value of life itself by asking people what it is worth to them (the most common method of valuation of other environmental benefits), the answer would be infinite, as "no finite amount of money could compensate a person for the loss of his life, simply because money is no good to him when he is dead."[15]

The standard response is that a value like $6.3 million is not actually a price on an individual's life or death. Rather, it is a way of expressing the value of small risks of death; for example, it is one million times the value of a one in a million risk. If people are willing to pay $6.30 to avoid a one in a million increase in the risk of death, then the "value of a statistical life" is $6.3 million.

---

15. Broome, Trying to Value a Life, 9 J. Pub. Econ. 91, 92 (1978).

Unfortunately, this explanation fails to resolve the dilemma. It is true that risk (or "statistical life") and life itself are distinct concepts. In practice, however, analysts often ignore the distinction between valuing risk and valuing life.[16] Many regulations reduce risk for a large number of people, and avoid actual death for a much smaller number. A complete cost-benefit analysis should, therefore, include valuation of both of these benefits. However, the standard practice is to calculate a value only for "statistical" life and to ignore life itself.

The confusion between the valuation of risk and the valuation of life itself is embedded in current regulatory practice in another way as well. The Office of Management and Budget — which reviews cost-benefit analyses prepared by federal agencies pursuant to Executive Order — instructs agencies to discount the benefits of life-saving regulations from the moment of avoided death, rather than from the time when the risk of death is reduced.[17] This approach to discounting is plainly inconsistent with the claim that cost-benefit analysis seeks to evaluate risk. When a life-threatening disease — such as cancer — has a long latency period, many years may pass between the time when a risk is imposed and the time of death. If monetary valuations of statistical life represented risk, and not life, then the value of statistical life would be discounted from the date of a change in risk (typically, when a new regulation is enforced) rather than from the much later date of avoided actual death.[18]

In acknowledging the monetary value of reducing risk, economic analysts have contributed to our growing awareness that life-threatening risk itself – and not just the end result of such risk, death — is an injury. But they have blurred the line between risks and actual deaths, by calculating the value of reduced risk while pretending that they have produced a valuation of life itself. The paradox of monetizing the infinite or immeasurable value of human life has not been resolved; it has only been glossed over.

People Care About Other People. Another large problem with the standard approach to valuation of life is that it asks individuals (either directly through surveys, or indirectly through observing wage and job choices) only about their attitudes toward risks to themselves.

A recurring theme in literature suggests that our deepest and noblest sentiments involve valuing someone else's life more highly than our own: think of parents' devotion to their children, soldiers' commitment to those whom they are protecting, lovers' concern for each other. Most spiritual beliefs call on us to value the lives of others — not only those closest to us, but also those whom we have never met.

This point echoes a procedure that has become familiar in other areas of environmental valuation. Economists often ask about existence values: how much is the existence of a wilderness area or an endangered species worth to you, even if you will never personally experience it? If this question makes sense for bald eagles and national parks, it must be at least as important when applied to safe drinking water and working conditions for people we don't know.

What is the existence value of a person you will never meet? How much is it worth to you to prevent a death far away? The answer cannot be deduced solely from your attitudes toward risks to yourself. We are not aware of any attempts to quantify the existence value of the life of a stranger, let alone a relative or a friend, but we are sure that most belief systems affirm that this value is substantial (assuming, of course, that the value of life is a number in the first place).

---

16. For further elaboration, see Heinzerling, The Rights of Statistical People, 24 Harv. Envtl. L. Rev. 189, 203-206 (2000).

17. Economic Analysis of Federal Regulations Under Executive Order 12,866, at pt. III.B.5(a) (Report of Interagency Group Chaired by a Member of the Council of Economic Advisors) (Jan. 11, 1996).

18. Heinzerling, Discounting Our Future, 34 Land & Water L. Rev. 39, 71 (1999); Heinzerling, Discounting Life, 108 Yale L.J. 1911, 1913 (1999).

Voting Is Different From Buying. Cost-benefit analysis, which relies on estimates of individuals' preferences as consumers, also fails to address the collective choice presented to society by most public health and environmental problems.

Valuation of environmental benefits is based on individuals' private decisions as consumers or workers, not on their public values as citizens. However, policies that protect the environment are often public goods, and are not available for purchase in individual portions. In a classic example of this distinction, the philosopher Mark Sagoff found that his students, in their role as citizens, opposed commercial ski development in a nearby wilderness area, but, in their role as consumers, would plan to go skiing there if the development was built.[19] There is no contradiction between these two views: as individual consumers, the students would have no way to express their collective preference for wilderness preservation. Their individual willingness to pay for skiing would send a misleading signal about their views as citizens.

It is often impossible to arrive at a meaningful social valuation by adding up the willingness to pay expressed by individuals. What could it mean to ask how much you personally are willing to pay to clean up a major oil spill? If no one else contributes, the clean-up won't happen regardless of your decision. As the Nobel Prize-winning economist Amartya Sen has pointed out, if your willingness to pay for a large-scale public initiative is independent of what others are paying, then you probably have not understood the nature of the problem.[20] Instead, a collective decision about collective resources is required.

In a similar vein, the philosopher Henry Richardson argues that reliance on the cost-benefit standard forecloses the process of democratic deliberation that is necessary for intelligent decision-making. In his view, attempts to make decisions based on monetary valuation of benefits freeze preferences in advance, leaving no room for the changes in response to new information, rethinking of the issues, and negotiated compromises that lie at the heart of the deliberative process.[21]

Cost-benefit analysis turns public citizens into selfish consumers, and interconnected communities into atomized individuals. In this way, it distorts the question it sets out to answer: how much do we, as a society, value health and the environment?

Numbers Don't Tell Us Everything. A few simple examples illustrate that numerically equal risks are not always equally deserving of regulatory response. The death rate is roughly the same (somewhat less than one in a million) from a day of downhill skiing, from a day of working in the construction industry, or from drinking about 20 liters of water containing 50 parts per billion of arsenic, the old regulatory limit that was recently revised by EPA. This does not mean that society's responsibility to reduce risks is the same in each case.

Most people view risks imposed by others, without an individual's consent, as more worthy of government intervention than risks that an individual knowingly accepts. On that basis, the highest priority among our three examples is to reduce drinking water contamination, a hazard to which no one has consented. The acceptance of a risky occupation such as construction is at best quasi-voluntary — it involves somewhat more individual discretion than the "choice" of public drinking water supplies, but many people go to work under great economic pressure, and with little information about occupational hazards. In contrast, the choice of risky recreational pursuits such as skiing is entirely discretionary; obviously no one is forced to ski. Safety

---

19. Mark Sagoff, The Economy of the Earth: Philosophy, Law, and the Environment (Cambridge University Press 1990).

20. Sen, The Discipline of Cost-Benefit Analysis, 29 J. Legal Stud. 931 (2000).

21. Richardson, The Stupidity of the Cost-Benefit Standard, 29 J. Legal Stud. 971 (2000).

regulation in construction work is thus more urgent than regulation of skiing, despite the equality of numerical risk.

In short, even for ultimate values such as life and death, the social context is decisive in our evaluation of risks. Cost-benefit analysis assumes the existence of generic, acontextual risk, and thereby ignores the contextual information that determines how many people, in practice, think about real risks to real people.

Artificial Prices Are Expensive. Finally, the economic valuation called for by cost-benefit analysis is fundamentally flawed because it demands an enormous volume of consistently updated information, which is beyond the practical capacity of our society to generate.

All attempts at valuation of the environment begin with a problem: the goal is to assign monetary prices to things that have no prices, because they are not for sale. One of the great strengths of the market is that it provides so much information about real prices. For any commodity that is actually bought and sold, prices are communicated automatically, almost costlessly, and with constant updates as needed. To create artificial prices for environmental values, economists have to find some way to mimic the operation of the market. Unfortunately the process is far from automatic, it is certainly not costless, and it has to be repeated every time an updated price is needed.

As a result, there is constant pressure to use outdated or inappropriate valuations. Indeed, there are sound economic reasons for doing so: no one can afford constant updates, and significant savings can be achieved by using valuations created for other cases. In the EPA's original cost-benefit analysis of a revised standard for arsenic in drinking water, a valuation estimated for a case of chronic bronchitis, in a study performed ten years earlier, was used to represent the value of a case of nonfatal bladder cancer.

This is not, we hope and believe, because anyone thinks that bronchitis and bladder cancer are the same disease. The reason is more mundane: no one has performed an analysis of the cost of bladder cancer, and even the extensive analysis of arsenic regulations did not include enough time and money to do so. Therefore, the investigators used an estimated value for a very different disease. The only explanation offered for this procedure was that it had been done before, and the investigators thought nothing better was available.

Use of the bronchitis valuation to represent bladder cancer can charitably be described as grasping at straws. Lacking the time and money to fill in the blank carefully, the economists simply picked a number. This is not remotely close to the level of rigor that is seen throughout the natural science, engineering, and public health portions of the arsenic analysis. Yet it will happen again, for exactly the same reason. It is not a failure of will or intellect, but rather the inescapable limitations of time and budget, that lead to reliance on dated, inappropriate, and incomplete information to fill in the gaps on the benefit side of a cost-benefit analysis.

Trivializing the Future. One of the great triumphs of environmental law is its focus on the future: it seeks to avert harms to people and to natural resources in the future, and not only within this generation, but within future generations as well. Indeed, one of the primary objectives of the National Environmental Policy Act, which has been called our basic charter of environmental protection, is to nudge the nation into "fulfill[ing] the responsibilities of each generation as trustee of the environment for succeeding generations."[22]

Protection of endangered species and ecosystems, reduction of pollution from persistent chemicals such as dioxin and DDT, prevention of long-latency diseases such as cancer,

---

22. 42 U.S.C. §4331(b)(1).

protection of the unborn against the health hazards from exposure to toxins in the womb — all of these protections are afforded by environmental law, and all of them look to the future as well as to the present. Environmental law seeks, moreover, to avoid the unpleasant surprises that come with discontinuities and irreversibility — the kinds of events that outstrip our powers of quantitative prediction. Here, too, environmental law tries to protect the future in addition to the present.

Cost-benefit analysis systematically downgrades the importance of the future in two ways: through the technique of discounting, and through predictive methodologies that take inadequate account of the possibility of catastrophic and irreversible events.

The most common, and commonsense, argument in favor of discounting future human lives saved, illnesses averted, and ecological disasters prevented, is that it is better to suffer a harm later rather than sooner. What's wrong with this argument? A lot, as it turns out.

Do Future Generations Count? The first problem with the later-is-better argument for discounting is that it assumes that one person is deciding between dying or falling ill now, or dying or falling ill later. In that case, virtually everyone would prefer later. But many environmental programs protect the far future, beyond the lifetime of today's decision-makers. Thus the choice implicit in discounting is between preventing harms to the current generation and preventing similar harms to future generations. Seen in this way, discounting looks like a fancy justification for foisting our problems off onto the people who come after us.

The time periods involved in protecting the environment are often enormous — many decades for a wide range of problems, and even many centuries, in the case of climate change, radioactive waste, and other persistent toxins. With time spans this long, discounting at any positive rate will make even global catastrophes seem trivial. At a discount rate of 5 percent, for example, the death of a billion people 500 years from now becomes less serious than the death of one person today.

Does Haste Prevent Waste? The justification of discounting often assumes that environmental problems won't get any worse if we wait to address them. In the market paradigm, buying environmental protection is just like buying any other commodity. You can buy a new computer now or later — and if you don't need it this year, you should probably wait. The technology will undoubtedly keep improving, so next year's models will do more yet cost less. An exactly parallel argument has been made about climate change (and other environmental problems) by some economists: if we wait for further technological progress, we will get more for our climate change mitigation dollars in the future.

If environmental protection was mass-produced by the computer industry, and if environmental problems would agree to stand still indefinitely and wait for us to respond, this might be a reasonable approach. In the real world, however, it is a ludicrous and dangerous strategy.

Too many years of delay may mean that the polar ice cap melts, the spent uranium leaks out of the containment ponds, the hazardous waste seeps into groundwater and basements and backyards — at which point we can't put the genie back in the bottle at any reasonable cost (or perhaps not at all).

Environmentalists often talk of potential "crises," of threats that problems will become suddenly and irreversibly worse. In response to such threats, environmentalists and some governments advocate the so-called "precautionary principle," which calls upon regulators to err on the side of caution and protection when risks are uncertain. Cost-benefit analysts, for the most part, do not assume the possibility of crisis. Their worldview assumes stable problems, with control costs that are stable or declining over time, and thus finds precautionary investment in environmental protection to be a needless expense. Discounting is part of this non-crisis perspective. By implying that the present cost of future environmental harms declines, lockstep, with every year that we look ahead, discounting ignores the possibility of catastrophic and irreversible harms.

For this very reason, some prominent economists have rejected the discounting of intangibles. As William Baumol wrote in an important early article on discounting the benefits of public projects:

> There are important externalities and investments of the public goods variety which cry for special attention. Irreversibilities constitute a prime example. If we poison our soil so that never again will it be the same, if we destroy the Grand Canyon and turn it into a hydroelectric plant, we give up assets which like Goldsmith's bold peasantry, "... their country's pride, when once destroy'd can never be supplied." All the wealth and resources of future generations will not suffice to restore them.[23]

Most cost-benefit analysts do not exhibit this kind of humility about what the future might hold in store for us.

Begging the Question. Extensive discounting of future environmental problems lies at the heart of many recent studies of regulatory costs and benefits that charge "statistical murder." When the costs and benefits of environmental protection are compared to those of safety rules (like requiring fire extinguishers for airplanes) or medical procedures (like vaccinating children against disease), environmental protection almost always comes out the loser. Why is this so?[24]

These studies all discount future environmental benefits by at least 5 percent per year. This has little effect on the evaluation of programs, like auto safety rules requiring seat belts and fire safety rules requiring smoke alarms, that could start saving lives right away. However, for environmental programs like hazardous waste cleanups and control of persistent toxins, that save lives in the future, discounting matters a great deal — especially since, as explained above, the benefits are assumed to occur in the future when deaths are avoided, rather than in the near term when risks are reduced.

By using discounting, analysts assume the answer to the question they purport to be addressing, which is which programs are most worthwhile. The researchers begin with premises that guarantee that programs designed for the long haul — like environmental protection — are not as important as programs that look to the shorter term. When repeated without discounting (or with benefits assumed to occur when risks are reduced), these studies support many more environmental programs, and the cry of "statistical murder" rings hollow.

Citizens and Consumers — Reprise. The issue of discounting illustrates once again the failure of cost-benefit analysis to take into account the difference between citizens and consumers. Many people advocate discounting on the ground that it reflects people's preferences, as expressed in market decisions concerning risk. But again, this omits the possibility that people will have different preferences when they take on a different role. The future seems to matter much more to American citizens than to American consumers, even though they are of course the same people.... Thus private preferences for current over future consumption should not be used to subvert public judgments that future harms are as important as immediate ones.

---

23. Baumol, On the Social Rate of Discount, 58 Am. Econ. Rev. 788, 801 (1968).

24. This discussion draws from Heinzerling, Regulatory Costs of Mythic Proportions, 107 Yale L.J. 1981 (1998); Heinzerling, Five-Hundred Life-Saving Interventions and Their Misuse in the Debate Over Regulatory Reform, Risk (2002); and Heinzerling & Ackerman, The Humbugs of the Anti-Regulatory Movement, 87 Corn. L. Rev. 648 (2002).

Exacerbating Inequality. The third fundamental defect of cost-benefit analysis is that it tends to ignore, and therefore to reinforce, patterns of economic and social inequality. Cost-benefit analysis consists of adding up all the costs of a policy, adding up all the benefits, and comparing the totals. Implicit in this innocuous-sounding procedure is the controversial assumption that it doesn't matter who gets the benefits and who pays the costs. Both benefits and costs are measured simply as dollar totals; those totals are silent on questions of equity and distribution of resources.

Yet in our society, concerns about equity frequently do and should enter into debates over public policy. There is an important difference between spending state tax revenues to improve the parks in rich communities, and spending the same revenues to clean up pollution in poor communities. The value of these two initiatives, measured using cost-benefit analysis, might be the same in both cases, but this does not mean that the two policies are equally urgent or desirable.

The problem of equity runs even deeper. Benefits are typically measured by willingness to pay for environmental improvement, and the rich are able and willing to pay for more than the poor. Imagine a cost-benefit analysis of siting an undesirable facility, such as a landfill or incinerator. Wealthy communities are willing to pay more for the benefit of not having the facility in their backyards; thus the net benefits to society as a whole will be maximized by putting the facility in a low-income area. (Note that wealthy communities do not actually have to pay for the benefit of avoiding the facility; the analysis depends only on the fact that they are willing to pay.)

This kind of logic was made (in)famous in a 1991 memo circulated by Lawrence Summers (former Secretary of the Treasury, now President of Harvard University) when he was the chief economist at the World Bank. Discussing the migration of "dirty industries" to developing countries, Summers' memo explained:

> The measurements of the costs of health impairing pollution depend…on the foregone earnings from increased morbidity and mortality. From this point of view a given amount of health-impairing pollution should be done in the country with the lowest cost, which will be the country with the lowest wages. I think the economic logic behind dumping a load of toxic waste in the lowest wage country is impeccable and we should face up to that.[25]

After this memo became public, Brazil's then-Secretary of the Environment Jose Lutzenburger wrote to Summers:

> Your reasoning is perfectly logical but totally insane…. Your thoughts [provide] a concrete example of the unbelievable alienation, reductionist thinking, social ruthlessness and the arrogant ignorance of many conventional "economists" concerning the nature of the world we live in….[26]

If decisions are based strictly on cost-benefit analysis and willingness to pay, most environmental burdens will end up being imposed on the countries, communities, and individuals with the least resources. This theoretical pattern bears an uncomfortably close resemblance to reality. Cost-benefit methods should not be blamed for existing patterns of environmental injustice; we suspect that pollution is typically dumped on the poor without waiting for formal analysis. Still, cost-benefit analysis rationalizes and reinforces the problem, allowing environmental burdens to flow downhill along the income gradients of an unequal world. It is hard to see this as part of an economically optimal or politically objective method of decision-making.

---

25. Available at http://www.whirledbank.org/ourwords/summers.html.
26. Id.

In short, equity is an important criterion for evaluation of public policy, but it does not fit into the cost-benefit framework. The same is true of questions of rights and morality, principles that are not reducible to monetary terms. Calculations that are acceptable, even common sense, for financial matters can prove absurd or objectionable when applied to moral issues....

Less Objectivity and Transparency. A fourth fundamental flaw of cost-benefit analysis is that it is unable to deliver on the promise of more objective and more transparent decision-making. In fact, in most cases, the use of cost-benefit analysis is likely to deliver less objectivity and less transparency.

For the reasons we have discussed, there is nothing objective about the basic premises of cost-benefit analysis. Treating individuals solely as consumers, rather than as citizens with a sense of moral responsibility to the larger society, represents a distinct and highly contestable worldview. Likewise, the use of discounting reflects judgments about the nature of environmental risks and citizens' responsibilities toward future generations which are, at a minimum, debatable. Because value-laden premises permeate cost-benefit analysis, the claim that cost-benefit analysis offers an "objective" way to make government decisions is simply bogus.

Furthermore, as we have seen, cost benefit analysis relies on a byzantine array of approximations, simplifications, and counterfactual hypotheses. Thus, the actual use of cost-benefit analysis inevitably involves countless judgment calls. People with strong, and clashing, partisan positions will naturally advocate that discretion in the application of this methodology be exercised in favor of their positions, further undermining the claim that cost-benefit analysis is objective.

Perhaps the best way to illustrate how little economic analysis has to contribute, objectively, to the fundamental question of how clean and safe we want our environment to be is to refer again to the controversy over cost-benefit analysis of EPA's regulation of arsenic in drinking water. As Cass Sunstein has recently argued, the available information on the benefits of arsenic reduction supports estimates of net benefits from regulation ranging from less than zero, up to $560 million or more. The number of deaths avoided annually by regulation is, according to Sunstein, between 0 and 112.[27] A procedure that allows such an enormous range of different evaluations of a single rule is certainly not the objective, transparent decision rule that its advocates have advertised.

These uncertainties arise both from the limited knowledge of the epidemiology and toxicology of exposure to arsenic, and from the controversial series of assumptions required for valuation and discounting of costs and (particularly) benefits. As Sunstein explains, a number of different positions, including most of those heard in the recent controversy over arsenic regulation, could be supported by one or another reading of the evidence.

Some analysts might respond that this enormous range of outcomes is not possible if the proper economic assumptions are used; if, for example, human lives are valued at $6 million apiece and discounted at a 5 percent yearly rate (or, depending on the analyst, other favorite numbers). But these assumptions beg fundamental questions about ethics and equity, and one cannot decide whether to embrace them without thinking through the whole range of moral issues they raise. Yet once one has thought through these issues, there is no need then to collapse the complex moral inquiry into a series of numbers. Pricing the priceless merely translates our inquiry into a different, and foreign, language, one with a painfully impoverished vocabulary.

For many of the same reasons, cost-benefit analysis also generally fails to achieve the goal of transparency. Cost-benefit analysis is a complex, resource-intensive, and expert-driven process.

---

27. Sunstein, The Arithmetic of Arsenic, 90 Geo. L.J. 2255 (2002).

It requires a great deal of time and effort to attempt to unpack even the simplest cost-benefit analysis. Few community groups, for example, have access to the kind of scientific and technical expertise that would allow them to evaluate whether, intentionally or unintentionally, the authors of a cost-benefit analysis have unfairly slighted the interests of the community or some of its members. Few members of the public can meaningfully participate in the debates about the use of particular regression analyses or discount rates which are central to the cost-benefit method.

The translation of lives, health, and nature into dollars also renders decision-making about the underlying social values less rather than more transparent. As we have discussed, all of the various steps required to reduce a human life to a dollar value are open to debate and subject to uncertainty. However, the specific dollar values kicked out by cost-benefit analysis tend to obscure these underlying issues rather than encourage full public debate about them....

Economic analysis has had its successes and made its contributions; it has taught us a great deal over the years about how we can most efficiently and cheaply reach a given environmental goal. It has taught us relatively little, however, about what our environmental goals should be. Indeed, while economists have spent three decades wrangling about how much a human life, or a bald eagle, or a beautiful stretch of river, is worth in dollars, ecologists, engineers, and other specialists have gone about the business of saving lives and eagles and rivers, without waiting for formal, quantitative analysis proving that saving these things is worthwhile....

COMMENTARY & QUESTIONS

1. **Doomed, or just needs tinkering?** Are Ackerman and Heinzerling's objections to cost-benefit analysis fundamental, or would refinements to cost-benefit analysis as currently practiced satisfy their concerns?

2. **What's the alternative?** What could take the place of cost-benefit analysis? In their article, Ackerman and Heinzerling suggest that regulatory approaches such as technology-based controls, emissions trading schemes, and disclosure requirements all can (and do) operate without use of cost-benefit analysis, and that they serve as proven alternatives to this analytical framework. Do you agree?

C. FORMAL COST-BENEFIT ANALYSIS: THE SAFE DRINKING WATER ACT

As amended in 1996, the SDWA requires EPA to set maximum contaminant level goals (MCLGs) and maximum contaminant levels (MCLs) for harmful pollutants in drinking water. MCLGs are nonenforceable health goals, set at levels at which "no known or anticipated adverse effects on the health of persons occur and which allow... an adequate margin of safety." 42 U.S.C. §300g-1(b)(4)(A). MCLs are enforceable standards for levels of contaminants in drinking water. In setting an MCL, EPA is to identify the best available control technique for removing the pollutant of concern. EPA is also required to conduct an analysis of the costs and benefits of varying MCLs. If EPA believes that an MCL less stringent than the one achieved through use of the best available control technique is warranted based on EPA's cost-benefit analysis, the agency may set a less stringent standard that "maximizes health risk reductions benefits at a cost that is justified by the benefits." 42 U.S.C. §300g-1(b)(6)(A). The statute specifically provides that "consumer willingness to pay for reductions in health risks from drinking water contaminants" is one of the approaches EPA may identify for "the measurement and valuation of benefits" under the statute. 42 U.S.C. §300g-1(b)(3)(C)(iii).

Arsenic causes cancers of the bladder, lungs, skin, kidneys, nasal passages, liver, and prostate, as well as other cardiovascular, pulmonary, neurological, immunological, and endocrine problems. In 1942, the federal government set a standard of 50 µg/L for arsenic in drinking water. Twenty years later, the U.S. Public Health Services recommended that drinking water should contain no more than 10 µg/L. Three times in 30 years, Congress told EPA to update the 50 µg/L standard. Finally, in January 2001, EPA announced a new standard of 10 µg/L. Less than two months later, the Bush II Administration withdrew this standard — only to accept it again after eight months of further review and debate. The discussion that follows comes from the Clinton-era EPA's preamble to the new arsenic rule. In announcing that it would retain this rule after months of study, the Bush II EPA did not provide a new explanation for its decision (although it did issue a press release).

U.S. Environmental Protection Agency, National Primary Drinking Water Regulations; Arsenic and Clarifications to Compliance and New Source Contaminants Monitoring
66 Fed. Reg. 6976 (Jan. 22, 2001)

Today's rule, with a final MCL of 10 µg/L, reflects the application of several provisions under SDWA, the first of which generally requires that EPA set the MCL for each contaminant as close as feasible to the MCLG, based on available technology and taking costs to large systems into account. The 1996 SDWA amendments also require that the Administrator determine whether or not the quantifiable and nonquantifiable benefits of an MCL justify the quantifiable and nonquantifiable costs. This determination is to be based on the Health Risk Reduction and Cost Analysis (HRRCA) required under section 1412(b)(3)(C). The HRRCA must include consideration of seven analyses: (1) The quantifiable and nonquantifiable benefits from treatment to the new MCL; (2) The quantifiable and nonquantifiable benefits resulting from reductions of co-occurring contaminants; (3) The quantifiable and nonquantifiable costs resulting directly from the MCL; (4) The incremental costs and benefits at the new MCL and alternatives considered; (5) The health risks posed by the contaminant, including risks to vulnerable populations; (6) Any increased risk resulting from compliance, including risks associated with co-occurring contaminants; and (7) Any other relevant factor, including the uncertainties in the analyses and the degree and nature of risk. Finally, the 1996 SDWA amendments provide new discretionary authority for the Administrator to set an MCL less stringent than the feasible level if the benefits of an MCL set at the feasible level would not justify the costs (section 1412(b)(6)) based on the HRRCA analysis.

Today's rule establishing an MCL of 10 µg/L for arsenic is the second time EPA has invoked this new authority. (The first such time was in the final rule for uranium, which was published on December 7, 2000.) In addition to the feasible MCL of 3 µg/L, the Agency evaluated MCL options of 5 µg/L, 10 µg/L, and 20 µg/L…. EPA has determined that a final MCL of 10 µg/L more appropriately meets the relevant statutory criteria referred to above….

The fifth and seventh HRRCA analyses focus on the health risks to be addressed by a new MCL. Estimates of risk levels to the population remaining after the regulation is in place provide a perspective on the level of public health protection and associated benefits. SDWA clearly places a particular focus on public health protection afforded by MCLs. For instance, where EPA decides to use its discretionary authority after a determination that the benefits of an MCL would not justify the costs, section 1412(b)(6) requires EPA to set the MCL at a level that "maximizes health risk reduction benefits at a cost that is justified by the benefits." (EPA does not believe the sixth HRRCA analysis, consideration of increased risk likely to result from compliance is a significant factor in connection with selection of a final MCL; rather, we believe that many of the appropriate technologies for reducing arsenic will reduce many other co-occurring inorganic contaminants as well thereby decreasing, rather than increasing risk.)

The Agency based its evaluation of the risk posed by arsenic at the MCL options of 3 μg/L, 5 μg/L, 10 μg/L and 20 μg/L on a number of considerations, including the bladder cancer risk analysis developed by the National Research Council (NRC) of the National Academy of Sciences (NRC, 1999); the NRC's qualitative assessment of other possible adverse health effects; the lung cancer risk analysis developed by Morales et al. (2000); and findings of other relevant national and international studies. This information included, but was not limited to, findings from epidemiological studies in South America cited in the NRC report (NRC, 1999) and a study of a population exposed to high levels of arsenic in Millard County, Utah conducted by Lewis, et al. (1999). Among the factors EPA considered in choosing the final MCL was Congress' intent that EPA "reduce…[scientific] uncertainty" in promulgating the arsenic regulation reflected in section 1412(b)(12) arsenic research plan provisions and the legislative history on the arsenic provision (S. Rep. 104-169, 104th Cong., 1st Sess. at 39–40).

The uncertainties in the analyses of costs, benefits and risks are also a factor required to be considered in the HRRCA. All assessments of risk are characterized by an amount of uncertainty. Some of this uncertainty can be reduced by collecting more data or data of a different sort. For other types of uncertainty, improved data or assessment methods can allow one to define the degree to which an estimate is likely to be above or below the "true" risk. For the arsenic risk assessment, there are several definable sources of uncertainty that were taken into account. These include, but are not limited to, the following: uncertainty about the exact exposure of individuals in the study population to arsenic in drinking water, water used in cooking, and food; uncertainties associated with applying data from a population in rural Taiwan to the heterogenous population of the U.S. (including differences in health status and diet between the Taiwanese and the U.S. population); and uncertainties concerning precisely how a chemical causes cancer in humans (the mode of action) that affects assessments of the extent and severity of health effects at low doses….

In EPA's judgment, use of a risk range more clearly supports a qualitative consideration and recognition of the uncertainties that are inherent in any risk analysis that substantially relies upon epidemiological information. EPA believes that the health risk analysis presented in…today's rule comprises a plausible range of likely risk associated with various concentrations of arsenic in drinking water. As just suggested, we do not believe it is appropriate to select a central or "best estimate" of the risk, due to the uncertainties associated with the underlying health effects studies and the various plausible assumptions used in considering these uncertainties for our risk analysis….

Under HRRCA analyses one and two, the Agency must consider both quantifiable and nonquantifiable health risk reduction benefits. Benefits considered in our analysis include those about which quantitative information is known and can be monetized as well as those which are more qualitative in nature (such as some of the non-cancer health effects potentially associated with arsenic) and which cannot currently be monetized. Important assumptions inherent in EPA's revised analysis of the benefits estimates include the value of a statistical life and willingness to pay to avoid illness.... EPA considered the relationship of the monetized benefits to the monetized costs for each the regulatory levels it considered. While strict equality of monetized benefits and costs is not a requirement under section 1412(b)(6)(A), this relationship is an important consideration in the regulatory development process....

EPA believes, however, that reliance on only an arithmetic analysis of whether monetized benefits outweigh monetized costs is inconsistent with the statute's instruction to consider both quantifiable and nonquantifiable costs and benefits. The Agency therefore examined and considered qualitative and non-monetized benefits in establishing the final MCL, as well as other factors discussed previously. These benefits are associated with avoiding certain adverse health impacts known to be caused by arsenic at higher concentrations, which may also be associated with low level concentrations, and include skin and prostate cancer as well as cardiovascular, pulmonary, neurological and other non-cancer effects....

Other potential benefits not monetized for today's final rule include customer peace of mind from knowing drinking water has been treated for arsenic and reduced treatment costs for contaminants that may be co-treated with arsenic. (For example, increased use of coagulation and micro filtration by surface water systems will offer benefits with respect to removal of microbial contaminants and disinfection byproducts.) HRRCA analyses three and four require EPA to consider the costs of compliance with the rule and the incremental costs and benefits....

Both our benefits and cost estimates involve ranges, rather than point estimates, due to a variety of factors. Thus, our consideration of costs and benefits involved an examination and comparison of these ranges.... Both total costs and benefits increase as one examines progressively lower (i.e., more stringent) regulatory options compared to higher options. However, the benefits and costs do not increase proportionately across the range of regulatory options as shown by a comparison of net benefits (defined as costs minus benefits). Progressively more stringent regulatory options become considerably more expensive, from a cost standpoint, than the corresponding increases in benefits, as reflected in decreasing net benefits.

The MCL must be set as close as feasible to the MCLG, unless EPA invokes its discretionary authority under section 1412(b)(6) of SDWA to set an alternative MCL, which must then be set at a level that maximizes health risk reduction benefits at a cost that is justified by the benefits.... The MCLG is zero and the feasible level is 3 µg/L. The Agency believes that there are several important considerations in examining the feasible level.

In comparing the benefits and the costs at this level, we note that it has the highest projected total national costs (relative to the other MCL options considered). In addition, while the benefits are highest at this level relative to the other MCL options, both the net benefits and the benefit/cost disparity at the feasible level are the least favorable of the regulatory options considered. For these reasons, we believe benefits of the feasible level do not justify the costs....

Based on substantial public comment, EPA has reexamined the proposed MCL of 5 µg/L. In comparing this level to 10 µg/L, we note that both the net benefits and the benefit-cost relationships are less favorable for 5 µg/L as compared to 10 µg/L. Total national costs at 5 µg/L are also approximately twice the costs of an MCL of 10 µg/L. At 10 µg/L, EPA notes that the lung and bladder cancer risks to the exposed population after the rule's implementation are within the Agency's target risk range for drinking water contaminants of 1×10^{-6} to 1×10^{-4} or below. EPA recognizes that there is uncertainty in this quantification of cancer risk (as well as other health endpoints) and this risk estimate includes a number of assumptions, as discussed previously. EPA did not directly rely on the risk range in selecting the final MCL, since it is not part of the section 1412(b)(6) criteria; however, it is an important consideration, because it has a direct bearing on our estimates of the benefits of the rule.

EPA does not believe an MCL less stringent 10 µg/L is warranted from the standpoint of benefit-cost comparison. While total national costs associated with 20 µg/L are the lowest of the regulatory options considered, benefits are also the lowest of these options. Both regulatory options of 10 µg/L and 20 µg/L have relatively favorable benefit-cost relationships relative to lower regulatory options but are not significantly different from one another based on this comparison metric. However, the incremental, upper-bound benefits at 10 µg/L are more than twice those of 20 µg/L; and 10 µg/L is clearly the more protective level. Thus, we do not believe that an MCL of 20 µg/L would "maximize health risk reduction benefits" as required for an MCL established pursuant to section 1412(b)(6).

Strict parity of monetized costs and monetized benefits is not required to find that the benefits of a particular MCL option are justified under the statutory provisions of section 1412(b)(6) of SDWA. However, EPA believes that, based on comparisons of cost and benefits (using the various benefit-cost comparison tools discussed), the monetized benefits of a regulatory level of 10 µg/L best justify the costs. In addition,…our further qualitative consideration of the various sources of uncertainty in our understanding of arsenic since the proposal (e.g., such as that surrounding the mode of action), has led us to conclude that our estimate of risk (for the risks we have quantified) is most likely an upper bound of risks and that the higher MCL of 10 µg/L is appropriate. Finally,…EPA believes that there are a number of not yet quantified adverse health effects and potentially substantial non-monetized benefits at 10 µg/L that increase the overall benefits at this level.

In summary, based on our reanalysis of costs, benefits, and health risk reduction, and factoring in the uncertainties in these analyses and the degree and nature of risk, EPA believes the final MCL of 10 µg/L represents the level that best maximizes health risk reduction benefits at a cost that is justified by the benefits and that the other regulatory options considered in the proposed rule do not satisfy the statutory requirements of section 1412(b)(6) of SDWA. We are therefore exercising our discretionary authority under the statute to establish an MCL at a level higher than the feasible level and setting that level at 10 µg/L.

ARSENIC STANDARD µG/L	COMPLIANCE COSTS IN MILLIONS (1999 DOLLARS)	HEALTH BENEFITS IN MILLIONS (1999 DOLLARS)	BLADDER AND LUNG CANCER CASES AVOIDED
3	$700–790	$210–490	57–140
5	$420–470	$190–360	51–100
10	$180–210	$140–200	37–56
20	$67–77	$66–75	19–20

FIGURE 13-1

EPA'S ESTIMATES OF THE COSTS AND BENEFITS OF DIFFERENT ARSENIC STANDARDS

Source: EPA, National Primary Drinking Water Regulations; Arsenic and Clarifications to Compliance and New Source Contaminants Monitoring; Final Rules, 66 Fed. Reg. 6976, 7009, 7017 (Jan. 22, 2001) (rounded to two significant figures).

COMMENTARY & QUESTIONS

1. **What explains EPA's decision?** Many scholars have promoted cost-benefit analysis on the ground that it increases objectivity and transparency in regulatory decisionmaking. You will recall from the discussion of Whitman v. American Trucking Ass'ns in

Chapter 7 that a major reason why the D.C. Circuit initially invalidated EPA's imple-mentation of the CAA's NAAQS program was that there was no logical "stopping point" for regulation when economic costs were not taken into account. The court suggested that cost-benefit analysis, if EPA had done it in setting the CAA standards, would have provided such a stopping point. American Trucking Ass'ns v. EPA, 175 F.3d 1027, 1037-1038 (D.C. Cir. 1999). Does the SDWA, as applied to arsenic in drinking water, overcome this problem? Does EPA's cost-benefit analysis identify a logical stopping point for regulation, or does it still leave considerable room for discretion on the part of the agency? Try to develop a justification for one of the alternative MCLs considered by EPA, using the same considerations EPA used in justifying an MCL of 10 µg/L. Can you do it?

2. **Trumping quantified costs: reprise.** At 10 µg/L, EPA thought its arsenic rule would cost about $210 million per year, while producing about $170 million in quantified benefits. The only benefit EPA could quantify was the prevention of bladder and lung cancer, although the agency concluded that many other illnesses were caused by arsenic.

Is this a close case, precluding the trumping of quantified costs by unquantified bene-fits, as in *Corrosion Proof Fittings*? Note that drinking water standards are reviewed under the "arbitrary and capricious" standard of review. Does this justify a different judicial treatment of the arsenic rule, as compared to EPA's asbestos ban? In a challenge to the arsenic rule, the D.C. Circuit upheld the SDWA and the regulation under the Tenth Amendment and Commerce Clause, but did not have the opportunity to review EPA's specific conclusions under general principles of administrative law. Nebraska v. EPA, 331 F.3d 995 (D.C. Cir. 2003).

3. **"The Arithmetic of Arsenic."** In an article with this title, Professor Cass Sunstein argues that the uncertainty of important variables in EPA's analysis — such as the number of cancers prevented by the rule and the monetary value of those illnesses — is so great that EPA could have plausibly concluded that the benefits of the rule spanned a range of $0 to $560 million. Sunstein, The Arithmetic of Arsenic, 90 Geo. L.J. 2255 (2002). Nevertheless, Sunstein argues that cost-benefit analysis is a useful tool in this setting because it limits the influence of irrational perceptions of risk and makes agency decisions more transparent than other regulatory approaches do. Do you agree?

4. **The value of life.** EPA's economic analysis used a value of $6.1 million for each fatal cancer case avoided by the rule. The agency arrived at this figure by considering studies of market decisions about risk. Most of these studies examine how much workers demand in extra wages in exchange for accepting extra workplace risk. EPA's regulation involved latent, passive, involuntary risks of cancer, risks faced by people who had not bargained for such risks, who owned an "entitlement" to be free from risks greater than those remaining after application of the best available control techniques unless EPA chose to depart from an MCL consistent with the best techniques, and who included men, women, and children. The studies on wage premiums for risky work, on the other hand, involved risks of immediate, active accidents among people who (in theory) were paid to take on those risks, and who were mostly men. In light of these contextual

differences, was it sensible for EPA to base regulation of risks from arsenic in drinking water on such data? For an analysis and critique of the concept of "statistical life" that underlies all efforts to value human lives in monetary terms, see Heinzerling, The Rights of Statistical People, 24 Harv. Envtl. L. Rev. 189 (2000).

5. **Willingness to pay…for what?** Another limitation of the studies used to derive the $6.1 million value for a fatality is that they assume that workers and others making marketplace decisions about risk actually know what they're doing. For example, wage premium studies use objective evidence of workers' risks to estimate how much workers are being paid to take on extra risk. But perhaps the workers do not know about the risks, or do not understand their implications. Or, given the difficulties many laypeople have in processing numerical information about risks, perhaps the workers in these studies perceived their risks to be higher or lower than they actually were even if they had information about the numerical risks they faced. Indeed, given the vociferous criticisms of citizens' risk perceptions by Justice Breyer, John Graham, and others, it is a wonder that they accept the wage premium studies at all.

6. **Some arsenic with your bottled water?** One possibility is that, once EPA decided to base its arsenic decision on cost-benefit analysis, EPA was well within reasonable bounds to try to base its arsenic rule on the behavior of actors in private markets, but it erred in choosing the wrong market analogue. Perhaps, rather than looking at wage premiums for risky work, EPA should have considered what the $35 billion global market for bottled water might tell us about "consumer willingness to pay for reductions in health risks from drinking water contaminants." See 42 U.S.C. §300g-1(b)(3)(C)(iii). Market research indicates that consumers are willing to pay from 240 to 10,000 times more for bottled water than for tap water, partly because of their perception that it is safer and healthier. The most stringent standard EPA considered (3 ppb) would have cost the average household at most $9.40 per year. The standard that EPA chose cost even less for the average household. Indeed, households that obtained their water from suppliers serving fewer than 100 households would save more money the lower the standard got. See Heinzerling, Markets for Arsenic, 90 Geo. L.J. 2311, 2311–2312, 2324–2327 (2002). What do these figures suggest about consumer willingness to pay for regulation reducing arsenic in drinking water?

7. **Bladder cancer and chronic bronchitis: are they the same thing?** EPA's $6.1 million figure applied only to fatal cases of bladder cancer. But bladder cancer is often not fatal. "Because the suffering of persons who *survive* cancer was not incorporated into the value of statistical lives calculated from wage premiums, the EPA decided to base the value of reducing survivable cancer on the willingness of individuals to pay to avoid nonfatal cancer. Sadly, the agency lacked any economic studies of the willingness of people to pay to avoid cancer. It instead used a number that some economists had derived for the willingness to pay to avoid chronic bronchitis, which is apparently close enough to nonfatal cancer for government work. That number turned out to be $607,162." McGarity, Professor Sunstein's Fuzzy Math, 90 Geo. L.J. 2341, 2356 (2002). That monetary value for chronic bronchitis was based on responses to a survey conducted in a North Carolina shopping mall, bringing a whole new meaning to the phrase "shoppers rule."

D. COST-BENEFIT ANALYSIS AT OMB/OIRA

The "Contract With America," part of the "Gingrich Revolution" that led to the Republican takeover of the House of Representatives in 1994, was a set of legislative proposals aimed at reducing the burdens of regulations in the United States. One of its most prominent features was a proposal to require cost-benefit analysis as a "super-mandate" to govern policymaking under all of the environmental laws. This proposal was passed by the House of Representatives and was brought to the Senate by Senator Bob Dole and others in May 1995, but ultimately never passed.

Although Congress did not pass the Contract With America's cost-benefit "super-mandate," in 2001 when President George W. Bush came into office, he gave the job of "regulatory czar" within the White House to John Graham, former head of the Harvard Center for Risk Analysis and ardent proponent of cost-benefit analysis. One of Graham's first acts in office was to issue the following memorandum to the heads of executive branch agencies.

> September 20, 2001
> MEMORANDUM FOR THE PRESIDENT'S MANAGEMENT COUNCIL
> FROM: John D. Graham /s/
>   Administrator
> SUBJECT: Presidential Review of Agency Rulemaking by OIRA
>
> Federal regulations can provide cost-effective solutions to many problems. If not properly developed, regulations can lead to an enormous burden on the economy.
>
> In this context, I call your attention to Executive Order No. 12866, "Regulatory Planning and Review." Under this Executive Order, the Administrator of the Office of Information and Regulatory Affairs (OIRA) carries out a regulatory review process on behalf of the President. The President's Chief of Staff, Andrew H. Card, Jr., has directed me to work with the agencies to implement vigorously the principles and procedures in E.O. 12866 until a modified or new Executive Order is issued.
>
> I want to stress that it is my goal to work with you to carry out OIRA's regulatory reviews thoroughly and cooperatively. To help us work together more effectively, I have attached a detailed description of how OIRA carries out this regulatory review, summarizing the principles we follow and the procedures we use. I request that you send this attachment to the appropriate officials in your agency that are responsible for regulatory development.
>
> Working together to apply the regulatory principles in E.O. 12866, I believe we will strengthen the country's regulatory structure. I look forward to working with all of you and your staff.
>
> Attachment:
>
> September 20, 2001
> OMB REGULATORY REVIEW: PRINCIPLES AND PROCEDURES
>
> This attachment describes the general principles and procedures that will be applied by OMB in the implementation of E.O. 12866 and related statutory and executive authority.

OIRA Review of Significant Regulations. E.O. 12866, "Regulatory Planning and Review,"[28] governs OIRA's oversight of agency rulemaking, requiring OIRA review of "significant" agency regulatory actions before they are proposed for public comment, and again before they are issued in final form. The Order defines "regulatory action" broadly to include all substantive action by an agency that is expected to lead to the issuance of a final rule. Over the past several years, OIRA staff have worked with agencies to develop a common understanding of what is meant by a "significant" regulatory action. While OIRA does not formally review non-significant regulatory actions, agencies are expected to ensure that they are consistent with the Order's regulatory principles.

Following agency transmittal to OIRA of a draft rule, OIRA reviews the draft rule for consistency with the regulatory principles stated in the Order, and with the President's policies and priorities. The review determines whether the agency has, in deciding whether and how to regulate, assessed the costs and benefits of available regulatory alternatives (including the alternative of not regulating). Specifically, E.O. 12866 states that, "in choosing among alternative regulatory approaches, agencies should select those approaches that maximize net benefits...." E.O. 12866 further states that, "Each agency shall assess both the costs and the benefits of the intended regulation and, recognizing that some costs and benefits are difficult to quantify, propose or adopt a regulation only upon a reasoned determination that the benefits of the intended regulation justify its costs."

Regulatory Impact Analysis. Agencies must prepare a Regulatory Impact Analysis (RIA) for each regulation that OIRA or the agency designates as "economically significant." Section 3(f)(1) of the Order defines an "economically significant" rule as one likely to "have an annual effect on the economy of $100 million or more or adversely affect in a material way the economy, a sector of the economy, productivity, competition, jobs, the environment, public health or safety, or State, local, or tribal governments or communities."...

The RIA must provide an assessment of benefits, costs, and potentially effective and reasonably feasible alternatives to the planned regulatory action (see section 6(a)(3)(C)). This is submitted to OIRA along with the applicable draft regulatory action. Preparing RIAs helps agencies evaluate the need for and consequences of possible Federal action. By analyzing alternate ways to structure a rule, agencies can select the best option while providing OIRA and the public a broader understanding of the ranges of issues that may be involved. Accordingly, it is important that a draft RIA be reviewed by agency economists, engineers, and scientists, as well as by agency attorneys, prior to submission to OIRA....

Agency submissions to OIRA of economically significant rules shall include RIAs, regardless of the extent to which an agency is permitted by law to consider risks, costs, or benefits in issuing a regulation....

Clearance of Significant Regulatory Actions. In the course of OIRA's review of a draft regulatory action (and accompanying RIA and risk assessment, where applicable), the OIRA Desk Officer will work closely with agency staff. When OIRA has completed its review of a regulatory action, OIRA notifies the agency by telephone that it has concluded review. After receiving notification from OIRA that it has concluded review, the agency may issue the regulatory action.

In the case of a proposed rule, we encourage each agency to provide the public with at least 60 days to comment on proposals (section 6(a)(1)). In the case of a rule subject to statutory or judicial deadlines, OMB will not unilaterally delay publication beyond the deadline. In such cases, the agency must submit the rule to OIRA in a timely fashion, so as to provide a meaningful

---

28. 58 Fed. Reg. 51735 (October 4, 1993).

opportunity for Executive Office review. In cases where time frames are particularly tight due to a statutory or judicial deadline, agencies should consider submitting the draft rule to OIRA for preliminary review at the same time that it is being reviewed by senior agency policymakers.

Public Disclosure of OIRA Communications with Outside Parties. On occasion, parties outside the Executive branch will meet with the OIRA Administrator or his or her designee regarding a rule under review. OIRA will invite representatives of relevant agencies to such meetings and OIRA appreciates having agencies make senior regulatory policy officials available to attend such meetings. In addition, written materials received from those outside the Executive branch are retained for public inspection in OIRA's public docket room and forwarded to the rulemaking agency. It is the responsibility of each agency to place these in the rulemaking docket. These communications are disclosed to the public as described in E.O. 12866, section 6(b)(4).

The "Return" Letter. During the course of OIRA's review of a draft regulation, the Administrator may decide to send a letter to the agency that returns the rule for reconsideration. Such a return may occur if the quality of the agency's analyses is inadequate, if the regulatory standards adopted are not justified by the analyses, if the rule is not consistent with the regulatory principles stated in the Order or with the President's policies and priorities, or if the rule is not compatible with other Executive orders or statutes. As Director Daniels stated in an earlier memorandum, "if OMB determines that more substantial work is needed, OMB will return the draft rule to the agency for improved analysis." Since that memo was issued, OIRA has returned two agency draft rules, in both cases due to analytical problems.

It is important to understand that such a return does not necessarily imply that either OIRA or OMB is opposed to the draft rule. Rather, the return letter will explain why OIRA believes that the rulemaking would benefit from further consideration by the agency.

The "Prompt" Letter. The agencies prepare semi-annual regulatory agendas under E.O. 12866, §4(b), outlining the agencies' foreseeable regulatory priorities. OIRA plans to send, as occasion arises, what will be referred to as "prompt" letters. The purpose of a prompt letter is to suggest an issue that OMB believes is worthy of agency priority. Rather than being sent in response to the agency's submission of a draft rule for OIRA review, a "prompt" letter will be sent on OMB's initiative and will contain a suggestion for how the agency could improve its regulations. For example, the suggestion might be that an agency explore a promising regulatory issue for agency action, accelerate its efforts on an ongoing regulatory matter, or consider rescinding or modifying an existing rule. We will request prompt agency response to "prompt" letters, normally within 30 days....

We are looking forward to working cooperatively with you and your staff to meet our respective statutory obligations and to move the President's programs forward.

COMMENTARY & QUESTIONS

1. **OIRA's legal authority.** What gives OIRA the authority to take the actions it describes in this memo? Suppose a statute forbids cost-benefit balancing in standard-setting. May OIRA return a cost-blind rule to EPA on the ground that it reflects inadequate cost-benefit analysis, or that it conflicts with the President's "programs, policies and priorities"? Suppose a statute requires technology-based regulation, as we have seen the

CWA does. May OIRA require EPA's technology-based rules to be justified by cost-benefit analysis? Would this change the nature of technology-based regulation?

2. **Prompting regulation.** In the Bush II Administration, OIRA for the first time has made a point of announcing that it will not only act to slow down or stop regulations it deems ill advised, but it will also act to "prompt" regulations it considers sensible. On the same day Graham sent this memo to agency heads, for example, he also wrote to the Administrators of OSHA and FDA, pressing them to consider regulating by, respectively, requiring cardiac defibrillators in all workplaces and labeling trans fatty acids in foods. OIRA estimated these rules would save many lives at a reasonable cost and encouraged the relevant agencies to work expeditiously toward that end.

3. **OIRA's new transparency…and its limits.** Under Graham's leadership, OIRA has also increased the transparency of its decisionmaking processes by making many documents available on its Web site, by posting notices of meetings with interested parties on pending agency rulemaking proceedings, and by maintaining a kind of "open door" policy according to which interested parties may seek an audience with decisionmakers at OIRA. Some matters, however, remain opaque. For example, while OIRA does post notices of meetings with parties on pending rules, it does not reveal the substance of the discussions at those meetings, nor does it post notices of meetings with parties on general regulatory matters not embraced by pending rulemaking proceedings. In addition, OIRA has begun to insert itself into the rulemaking process at a very early stage, while the agencies are still formulating their own proposals. In such cases, it is very difficult to identify OIRA's precise influence on the ultimate regulatory product. Even where OIRA has become involved in a proceeding after the agency has developed its own preferred proposal, OIRA's influence on the proposal is denoted on its Web site merely with an obscure "approved: consistent with change" notation on OIRA's notice of its approval of a proposal. In a report on OIRA's regulatory activities issued by the General Accounting Office in 2003, GAO recommended that OIRA take steps to make its influence on agency rules more transparent. GAO, Rulemaking: OMB's Role in Reviews of Agencies' Draft Rules and the Transparency of Those Reviews (Sept. 2003).

4. **Is OIRA's cost-benefit analysis a one-way street?** While OIRA is strict about requiring detailed cost-benefit analysis supporting major regulatory initiatives, it has not been so strict about requiring this analysis for deregulatory actions. EPA's wholesale dismantling of the CAA's "New Source Review" program (discussed in Chapter 11); EPA and the Army Corps of Engineers' reworking of the definition of "fill" material under the CWA to assert that mountaintop removal was an acceptable mining technique (as discussed in Chapter 25); and the Department of the Interior's decision to let the Clinton Administration's roadless area rule — protecting almost 60 million acres of public lands — go undefended by the government in federal court — all of these decisions, and more, having a deregulatory valence were not accompanied by any cost-benefit analysis, and OIRA did not require one.

5. **Is life getting cheaper?** One of the most contentious issues OIRA has faced is how to value the lives saved by regulation. The issue received unusual public attention in the spring of 2003, when OIRA's insistence on incorporating a lower value for elderly lives

in EPA analyses coincided with then-Administrator Whitman's nationwide "listening tour" concerning environmental issues faced by the elderly. At every stop, Whitman was queried about her agency's so-called senior death discount. Ultimately, Whitman vowed not to use the discount anymore. Graham also ordered agencies not to use the specific discount (37%) OIRA had previously insisted on using because he had come to think it was not empirically well grounded. Nevertheless, at the same time, Graham continued to insist that basing regulatory policy on a consideration of the number of life-years saved by regulation made good policy sense.

Chapter 14

MARKET-ENLISTING STATUTORY STRATEGIES: POLLUTION TRADING AND OTHER ECONOMIC INCENTIVES

A. *Clean Air Act Sulfur Dioxide Trading: The "Cap-and-Trade" Poster Child*
B. *More Varied Trading Regimes*
C. *Flawed Trading Systems, and Hot Spots (Adverse Local Effects)*
D. *Trading to Improve Water Quality*

Market incentives and market-based strategies have found, in environmental protection, a somewhat unlikely medium for their expression. Using market incentives to influence polluting behavior is not exactly a new idea in environmental regulation, but has played only a small role until recently.

In a report released in 1997 entitled "Evaluating Economic Instruments for Environmental Policy," the Organisation for Economic Co-operation and Development (OECD) labeled environmental controls "economic" in nature "[when] they affect estimates of costs and benefits of alternative actions open to economic agents."[1] The OECD distinguished four categories of controls: charges and taxes, subsidies, tradeable emissions permits, and deposit refund systems. All of these are represented in contemporary environmental law.

Effluent taxes, such as disposal fees at landfills, have a considerable history and have had the effect of reducing the flow of wastes into the landfills. Subsidies, such as grants for the construction of publicly owned water treatment plants (POTWs), have been an effective staple of the CWA since its inception. More recently, the use of emissions trading systems has become the centerpiece of proposals for major shifts in regulatory policy when combating many of the world's and the United States' most pressing environmental problems, particularly the emission of greenhouse gases and sulfur oxides. Bottle deposit and return laws are in widespread use in the United States and have reduced roadside litter and increased recycling of beverage containers. Still other "economic instruments" such as bounties paid for the delivery of car hulks to metal recyclers,[2] do not fit precisely into any of the categories but are self-evident influences that change behavior in ways that improve environmental quality. This chapter emphasizes trading systems, which are emerging as the economic instrument of primary contemporary interest as an environmental regulatory strategy.

---

1. Organisation for Economic Co-operation and Development, Evaluating Economic Instruments for Environmental Policy 15 (1997).
2. See, e.g., Hughes v. Alexandria Scrap, 426 U.S. 794 (1976).

Market incentives enjoy widespread political and practical appeal. They offer the allure of having the actions of "economic agents" result in improved environmental outcomes that are obtained at lower total social cost than that expected with conventional command-and-control regulatory programs. Moreover, so the claim goes, those more efficient results are obtained without extensive governmental oversight and bureaucracy.

A very simple matrix of behavioral assumptions underlies virtually all of the market incentives-based approaches to environmental regulation. As introduced in Chapter 2, these behavioral assumptions posit firms and individuals as rational profit maximizers reacting to the conditions set by the relevant economic instrument. Taking as an example conventional pollution of air or water by a factory, in the absence of regulation, waste disposal into the commons is a nearly costless activity and is, therefore, the disposal method of choice. If a cost is added to disposal, firms react. The two predominant economic devices that are used to influence disposal decisions are effluent taxes and marketable trading systems.[3] The behavioral assumptions are elementary:

CHARACTERISTICS OF FIRM:	WITH EFFLUENT TAXES:	WITH EMISSIONS TRADING SYSTEMS:
High-cost pollution avoider	Will pay the tax and continue to pollute	Will purchase credits in the market and continue to pollute
Low-cost pollution avoider	Will avoid the tax and reduce pollution	Will sell credits in the market and reduce pollution

FIGURE 14-1

BEHAVIORAL PREMISES OF EFFLUENT TAXES AND EMMISIONS TRADING SYSTEMS

The CAA, beginning with the 1977 Amendments and especially the 1990 Amendments, began an expansion in the use of market-enlisting regulatory regimes, particularly emissions trading, that is nothing short of revolutionary. The 1977 Amendments made possible small-scale trading, such as offsets, netting, banking, and bubbles. The 1990 Amendments added Title IV, an aggressive trading program that is intended to reduce sulfur dioxide (SO_2) emission of electricity generators in the United States by 50% as part of the effort to combat acid rain. By December 1997, emissions trading had emerged at the Kyoto conference on global climate change as the central strategy for managing the emission of greenhouse gases on a global scale. Recently,

---

3. After-the-fact cost internalization, as might be obtained using the common law or CERCLA, is a slightly more attenuated form of effluent tax. The imposition of the cost (liability for damages) is less certain (suit might not be brought, a defense might succeed, etc.), but the expected results of such cases should influence polluting behavior. If the cost of controlling pollution is less than the expected cost of polluting and sometimes paying damages, firms will choose not to pollute. Even then, an effluent tax is likely to operate more efficiently than a damage liability system due to the high transaction costs of imposing damages through a litigation-centered system.

emissions trading has been tried or suggested to manage local air pollution in the Los Angeles area and elsewhere to reduce otherwise unregulated upstream nonpoint source agricultural discharges into rivers and to cap total metals deposition into POTWs so that the resulting sewage sludge is less hazardous.

COMMENTARY & QUESTIONS

1. **Avant-garde.** Trading is the new rage in environmental regulation. An avalanche of commentary on the subject has begun and will continue. One of the most thoughtful and cross-cutting of these is Salzman & Ruhl, Currencies and the Commodification of Environmental Law, 53 Stan. L. Rev. 607 (2000). For a small sampling of the new legal literature on the subject, see id. at 610–611, nn. 4–6. There is also a burgeoning economics literature on trading. See, e.g., Ellerman, Joskow & Harrison, Emissions Trading in the United States: Experience, Lessons and Considerations for Greenhouse Gases (Pew Center on Global Climate Change Report, May 2003) and the sources cited there. The report is available at http://www.pewclimate.org.

2. **Fungibility.** Salzman and Ruhl make a point that bears watching from the outset:

> If one compares trading programs, they all seem to share a basic feature. The CFC, fisheries, and proposed greenhouse gas environmental trading markets [ETMs], for example, all exchange commodities that appear to be fungible. One molecule of CFC, kilo of halibut, or ton of carbon dioxide seems much the same as another, both in terms of identity and impact. It is trading apples for apples (or pork bellies for pork bellies). Thus ETMs are considered a type of commodity market, where environmental credits go to the highest bidder. And for good reason, since the Chicago Board of Trade now sells rights to emit sulfur dioxide alongside pork bellies, orange juice, and grain futures.
>
> Indeed ETMs must assume fungibility — that the things exchanged are sufficiently similar in ways important to the goals of environmental protection — otherwise there would be no assurance that trading ensured environmental protection. While the precondition of fungibility may seem self-evident, this core assumption turns out to be more problematic than it first appears.
>
> As an example of why fungibility matters, consider wetlands mitigation banking. This policy permits developers, once they have taken steps to avoid and minimize wetland loss, to compensate for wetlands that will be destroyed through development by ensuring the restoration of wetlands in another location. The regulations mandate trades that ensure equivalent value and function between destroyed and restored wetlands. In practice, however, most trades are valued in units of acreage. Within very loose guidelines, trades between productive (though soon to be destroyed) wetlands and restored wetlands are approved on an acre-for-acre basis. More sophisticated banks require ratios, trading development on one acre of productive wetlands for, say, restoring four or five acres of wetlands somewhere else. Counting acres may make for easy accounting, but it is poor policy. 53 Stan. L. Rev. at 611–612, footnotes omitted.

3. **Will firms act rationally?** As the behavioral assumption matrix that appears in the text above describes, the economic instruments rely on very simplistic assumptions regarding behavior. Given the knowledge of behavior in complex organizations such as large corporations, is it reasonable to rely on those assumptions? Timothy Malloy, in

Regulating by Incentive: Myths, Models, and Micromarkets, 80 Tex. L. Rev. 531 (2002), describes the situation:

> Environmental regulation is all about using incentives to control behavior. Under direct "command and control" regulation, the government creates specific obligations and generally relies upon the negative incentives of civil and criminal penalties to motivate individuals or organizations to comply with those obligations. Alternatively, the new generation of "market-based" or "incentive-based" regulations typically creates an opportunity rather than (or in addition to) an obligation, offering the positive incentive of increased profits (or reduced costs) in the hope of eliciting the desired behavior. A regulator using either of these two regulatory approaches must identify the appropriate type and level of incentive — be it positive or negative — needed to produce the "correct" response from the target. In crafting and evaluating regulatory incentives, a regulator necessarily relies upon some basic model of how the target makes decisions. If that model is flawed, then the incentive will miss the mark, and the desired behavior may never occur.
>
> Given the importance of accurately predicting responses to regulation, one might expect that regulators and legal scholars alike would carefully select the decision-making models they use. Yet surprisingly little attention is paid to how businesses make choices in the face of government regulation. Many regulators and scholars rely upon a "black-box" model in developing and evaluating environmental regulatory incentives directed at businesses. Although no single, authoritative description of the black-box model exists, most formulations include three major components. First, the model assumes that the organization is a monolithic entity that essentially makes decisions as a natural individual would. Thus, the collective nature of the firm and its internal features are largely ignored. Second, the model assumes that the unitary firm makes decisions rationally. For these purposes, a "rational" person makes decisions by collecting all relevant information, identifying and evaluating all alternatives and their likely outcomes, and selecting the alternative most likely to achieve the person's goals. Third, the traditional formulation of the black-box model assumes that the firm has one dominant goal: maximizing profits. Id at. 531–533, footnotes omitted.

Malloy's article goes on to challenge the black-box model. He posits as more realistic a "resource allocation model" in which the firm's response to an incentive is a function of the firm's "organization and internal processes," not merely a guess based on a simplistic expected cost calculus. If Malloy is correct in his assertion that the regulator should craft a more thorough, unique model of the decisionmaking of each regulated entity, the information demands of using economic instruments (and thereby the transaction costs of this regulatory approach) increase dramatically.

4. **One firm's reduction is another firm's continued pollution.** Why is the society better off if one company which efficiently cuts its pollution by 15 units then just sells those units to a dirty factory somewhere else? The answers are both obvious and subtle — (1) due to the cap, the aggregate loadings of the receiving environmental medium are being reduced and (2) for any given level of allowable loadings, trading should make it possible to reduce pollution to that level at a lower total social cost. Getting to the goal at lower cost means that those savings are available for other productive uses.

A. CLEAN AIR ACT SULFUR DIOXIDE TRADING: THE "CAP-AND-TRADE" POSTER CHILD

In its original 1970 formulation, the CAA did not employ emissions trading. Its key components were the congressionally decreed technology-forcing that demanded a 90% rollback of motor vehicle tailpipe emissions and its harm-based ambient standards approach to stationary air pollution sources that was implemented by the State Implementation Plan (SIP) process.

The CAA Amendments of 1990 signaled the high-visibility embrace of economic instruments by establishing a "cap-and-trade" program that was designed to achieve a 10 million ton per year reduction in SO_2 emissions by the year 2000. At the time, that reduction represented more than 50% of the emissions of SO_2 for the regulated electricity-generating entities when compared with 1980 levels that were used as the baseline for the program. This program addressed concerns additional to those of the health-based primary NAAQS for SO_2. The principal environmental purpose of the cap-and-trade program is to combat downwind acid rain and other forms of acid deposition. The program has obtained the mandated reductions at a cost so low that it surprised many observers. What is less clear is the extent to which the program has alleviated the downwind acidification and whether the reductions were so easily attainable that the program's stunning success can be replicated in other contexts.

U.S. Environmental Protection Agency, Title IV Acid Deposition Program[4]
Implementing the 1990 Clean Air Act: EPA Speaks
77 American Bar Association Journal, February 21, 1991, at 51–57

SO_2 Allowances — Basic Program. The legislation obtains SO_2 emissions reductions from electric utility plants through the use of a market based system of emission allowances. Under this system, "affected units" (essentially all utility boilers that serve generators larger than 25 megawatts (MW)) are allocated allowances in an amount which is based on their past fossil fuel consumption and the emissions rate required by the legislation. An allowance is defined as an authorization allocated to an affected unit, to emit, during or after a specified calendar year, one ton of SO_2. Any new utility units which commence operation after December 31, 1995 are not allocated allowances and must obtain allowances sufficient to cover their emission by January 1, 2000 and thereafter....

Allowance Holding Requirement. Affected sources are required to hold sufficient allowances to cover their level of emissions. Allowances may not be used prior to the calendar year for which they are allocated. Sources may not exceed emission limitations provided in the law unless the owner or operator obtains and holds additional allowances to emit excess tons of SO_2. However, the fact that an affected source holds excess allowances does not entitle it to exceed the National Ambient Air Quality Standard limits.

Penalties for Non-Compliance. Sources whose emissions exceed allowances held will be required to pay $2000 per excess ton, and will be required to offset excess tons the following year.

---

4. Title IV contains both the sulfur dioxide trading program highlighted here and a nitrogen oxide control program that relies on traditional command-and-control performance techniques. See 42 U.S.C. §7651f.

Allowance Usage. Once allocated, allowances can be used by affected sources to cover emissions, banked for future use, or sold to others. Allowances transferred to others are not effective until a written certification of transfer from the parties involved is received and recorded by EPA. No permit alteration is required.

Allowance Tracking. EPA will develop a system for issuing, recording and tracking allowances.

Cap on SO_2 Emissions/Allowances Allocated. Beginning in 2000, the total number of allowances issued by EPA to utility units is, with limited exceptions, not to exceed 8.9 million allowances. This effectively caps emissions and ensures maintenance of the 10 million ton SO_2 reduction.

SO_2 Reduction Program. SO_2 reductions are obtained in two phases. Phase I reductions are required by January 1, 1995 from 111 plants listed in the legislation. These plants have large units — 100 MWs or more — and have high emission rates — 2.5 lbs/mmBTU or more.[5] There will be approximately 265 affected units in these Phase I plants. Phase I plants are located in 21 eastern and midwestern states.

Phase I Allowance Allocations. Phase I affected units will be issued allowances as reflected in the legislation. The allocation was based on a 2.5 lbs/mmBTU emission rate, multiplied by their "baseline," the average fossil fuel consumed during the years 1985, 1986, and 1987.

Phase II Reductions. In Phase II, which begins on January 1, 2000, the emissions limits imposed on Phase I plants are tightened, and emissions limits are imposed on smaller, cleaner plants as well. In general, all utility plants emitting at a rate above 1.2 lbs/mmBTU will have to reduce their emissions to a level equal to 1.2 lbs/mmBTU multiplied by their baseline.

Special Reserve for EPA Allowance Sales and Auctions. EPA is to create an allowance reserve by tapping each affected source's allocation 2.8 percent during 1995–99, and 2.8 percent of the basic Phase II allocation for each year beginning in 2000. These allowances are to be set aside for EPA allowance sales and auctions.

Allowance Sales. A portion of the allowances in the reserve established above are to be put in a direct sale subaccount and sold by EPA in accordance with EPA regulations. The proceeds of the allowance sales are to be returned to the affected units on a pro rata basis.... Unsold allowances are to be transferred to the auction subaccount (discussed below).

EPA Direct Allowance Sales. EPA will offer for sale allowances...[in accordance with a schedule[6]]. They shall be offered at a price of $1500 per allowance (CPI adjusted). Sales are to be made on a first come first served basis subject to the priority for Independent Power Producers.

---

5. The emission rates are measured in pounds of SO_2 emitted per million British thermal units of heat produced (mmBTU). It is widely conceded that fossil fuel fired power plants can, using widely available techniques and technologies, meet a standard of 1.2 lbs/mmBTU. Some plants using both controls and low sulfur fuel achieve rates as low as .3 lbs/mmBTU. [Eds.]

6. The schedule calls for advance sale of 25,000 allowances per year for each year beginning in 1993 and spot sales of an additional 25,000 allowances in 2000 and each year thereafter. Spot sale allowances must be used in the year of the sale unless banked. Advance sale allowances may be used only in the seventh year (or later) following the sale, unless banked. [Eds.]

Allowance Auctions. EPA is to establish a subaccount in the allowance reserve for auctions.... Auctions will be open to any person, and will be carried out by sealed bid, with sales based on bid price. No minimum bid will be established. Auction proceeds will be transferred to affected units contributing to the reserve on a pro rata basis, and allowances held for auction which were not sold at the auction will be returned to contributing affected units on a pro rata basis.[7]

COMMENTARY & QUESTIONS

1. **Key steps in the acid deposition program.** What goes into establishing a trading system? At least five vital building blocks make up the EPA's Title IV efforts to create a market in tradeable emissions allowances for SO_2: (1) the tradeable allowances, (2) the means by which EPA limits their total number, (3) the initial distribution of the allowances, (4) the means by which allowances are redistributed, and (5) the means by which compliance is measured.

2. **Making the reductions of emissions certain to occur.** When enacted, the allowance system appeared likely to reduce SO_2 emissions substantially. The penalties for excess emissions ($2000 per ton) may be inconsequential to a large entity such as a power plant, but the offset requirement for the following year means that the offending firm must obtain allowances and apply them against the previous year's excess emissions in addition to paying the fine. Even if this cost is modest, applying the allowances to "retire" the excess means that the total multiyear pollution remains limited to the number of allowances. As long as (1) the government refuses to increase the number of allowances, (2) the measurement of actual emissions and credits is accurate, and (3) the government enforces the offset requirement, the reductions in a cap-and-trade program are virtually certain to occur.

3. **Knowing the goal.** In Title IV, the goal clearly is to end acid rain, and the trading program is understood to be a means to that end. That will not always be the case. As one commentator puts it, "Market mechanisms will not set our goals for us and may even disguise their absence." Pedersen, The Limits of Market-Based Approaches to Environmental Protection, 24 Envtl. L. Rep. 10173 (1994). Even when the environmental goal is clearly identified, cap-and-trade reduces emissions but does not ensure that the goal is attained.

4. **Has Title IV attained its goal?** The question posed is really two questions, depending on whether the goal is seen as reducing emissions to the "cap" or the improvement of the condition of the affected lakes and rivers. As to the former question, the answer is an unequivocal yes. As to the latter question, the most recent comprehensive study is favorable as well, although there is debate on the subject. See U.S. Environmental Protection Agency, Responses of Surface Water Chemistry to the Clean Air Act Amendments of 1990 (January 2003), available at http://www.epa.gov/ord/htm/ CAAA-2002-report-2col-rev-4.pdf.

---

7. There is also a schedule for the number of allowances to be offered at auction. Like the direct sales schedule it is bifurcated between spot auction of current year allowances and advance auction of allowances good in the seventh year after the auction. In general, 150,000 allowances are offered in the spot auction in each year beginning in 1995 and 100,000 allowances are offered in the advance auction. [Eds.]

B. MORE VARIED TRADING REGIMES

A. Denny Ellerman, Paul L. Joskow, and David Harrison, Jr., Emissions Trading in the United States: Experience, Lessons and Considerations for Greenhouse Gases
Pew Center on Global Climate Change Report
May 2003, at 4–9, 11–18[8]

Three Basic Types of Emissions Trading Programs. Three broad types of emissions trading programs have emerged: reduction credit, averaging, and cap-and-trade programs. Although all share the feature of tradability, the three differ in important respects.

Reduction credit programs provide tradable credits to facilities that reduce emissions more than required by some pre-existing regulation (or other baseline) and allow those credits to be counted towards compliance by other facilities that would face high costs or other difficulties in meeting the regulatory requirements. (These programs sometimes are referred to simply as "credit-based.") Reduction credits are created through an administrative process in which the credits must be pre-certified before they can be traded.

Averaging programs also involve the offsetting of emissions from higher-emitting sources with lower emissions from other sources, so that the average emission *rate* achieves a predetermined level. Like reduction credit programs, averaging programs provide flexibility to individual sources to meet emissions constraints by allowing differences from source-specific standards to be traded between sources. The primary difference between averaging and reduction credit programs is that reduction credits are created (or "certified") through an administrative process, whereas the certification is automatic in averaging programs.

Cap-and-trade programs operate on somewhat different principles. Under a cap-and-trade program, an aggregate cap on emissions is set that defines the total number of emissions "allowances," each of which provides its holder with the right to emit a unit (typically a ton) of emissions. The permits are initially allocated in some way, typically among existing sources. Each source covered by the program must hold permits to cover its emissions, with sources free to buy and sell permits from each other. In contrast to reduction credit programs — but similar to averaging programs — cap-and-trade programs do not require pre-certification of allowances; the allowances are certified when they are distributed initially. Also, cap-and-trade programs limit *total* emissions, a contrast to reduction credit and averaging programs that are not designed to cap emissions.

A trading program might include more than one type of trading mechanism. As discussed below, both the Acid Rain trading program and RECLAIM include reduction credit supplements to the basic cap-and-trade program. In addition, a cap-and-trade program might provide for early reduction credits, which allow firms to get credits for voluntarily reducing emissions prior to the introduction of a cap-and-trade program. The credits allocated can be used to meet requirements once the cap-and-trade program goes into force.

All three types of emissions trading rely on certain factors that constitute preconditions for a successful program. First and most importantly, all three forms assume that an emissions control requirement has been put in place that requires emissions to be reduced to levels below what they otherwise would be. For credit and averaging programs, the requirement will typically be a source-specific standard (e.g., a maximum emissions rate). In a cap-and-trade program the requirement will take the form of an aggregate cap on emissions combined with the provision that each source surrender allowances equal to its emissions. Second, the cost savings achieved by all three forms of trading depend upon variability in the costs of reducing

8. Original references and footnotes are omitted. The report is available at http://www.pewclimate.org.

emissions among emissions sources. Differences in emission control costs across emissions sources create the opportunity to reduce costs through trading. Finally, in all three types of trading programs, the requirements must be both enforceable and enforced. A corollary to this precondition is that there must be accurate measurement of actual emissions or emissions rates—otherwise it would be impossible to enforce the requirements because it would be impossible to determine whether sources were in compliance.

Other Features of Emissions Trading Programs. There are many features that must be specified in an emissions trading program, some of which do not apply to all of the three basic emissions trading types. The following is a list that categorizes the major features of emissions trading programs into two major categories: design issues and implementation issues.

Design Issues. These include the decisions that arise as the program is designed and turned into a specific regulatory program.

Allocation of initial allowances. This issue is only relevant in cap-and-trade programs. Some method is required to distribute the initial allowances. Basic methods include various formulas to distribute initial allowances to participants on the basis of historical information ("grandfathering") or on the basis of updated information ("updating") as well as auctioning of the initial allowances.

Geographic or temporal flexibility or restrictions. This includes the possibility of restricting trades among different parts of the geographic range of the program. It also includes the possibility of banking (i.e., reducing emissions more than required in a given year and "banking" the surplus for future internal use or sale) or borrowing (i.e., reducing less than required in a given year and thus "borrowing," with the borrowed amount made up by reducing more than required in subsequent years).

Emission sources that are required or allowed to participate. This includes specification of the universe of sources that must participate in the trading program. It also includes the possibility of allowing additional sources to opt-in to the program.

Institutions established to facilitate trading. This includes the possibility of encouraging third parties (e.g., brokers) to participate in trading as well as the possibility of setting up an ongoing auction or other institutions to increase liquidity and establish market prices.

Implementation Issues. A number of decisions come into play as the program is implemented.

Certification of permits. This decision applies to reduction credit programs, which require that emission reductions be certified before they can be traded.

Monitoring and reporting of emissions. Methods must be designed to monitor and report emissions from each participating source

Determining compliance and enforcing the trading program. These decisions relate to the means of determining whether sources are in compliance and enforcing the program if sources are out of compliance.

Maintaining and encouraging participation. This relates to decisions made to keep sources in the program and encourage participation of sources whose participation is optional (e.g., those given the opportunity to opt-in)....

Figure 14-2 summarizes the six major programs considered in this paper. The six programs — which represent the bulk of existing experience with emissions trading — include examples of all three basic types. The U.S. EPA has administered most of the programs, although the programs include those administered by states and local air quality agencies as well. The range of experiences represented in these programs, which span about a quarter of a century, provide important insights into the factors that affect the economic and environmental performance of emissions trading in practice....

PROGRAM	AGENCY	TYPE	EMISSIONS	SOURCE	SCOPE
EPA Emissions Trading Program	U.S. EPA	Reduction Credit, Averaging	Various	Stationary	U.S.
Lead-in-Gasoline	U.S. EPA	Averaging	Lead	Gasoline	U.S.
Acid Rain Trading	U.S. EPA	Cap-and-Trade,	SO_2	Electricity	U.S.
RECLAIM	South Coast Air Quality Management District	Cap-and-Trade	NO_x, SO_2	Stationary	Los Angeles Basin
Averaging, Banking, and Trading (ABT)	U.S. EPA	Averaging	Various	Mobile	U.S.
Northeast NO_x Budget Trading	U.S. EPA 12 states, and D.C.	Cap-and-Trade	NO_x	Stationary	Northeastern U.S.

FIGURE 14-2

SUMMARY OF EMISSIONS TRADING PROGRAMS

Experience with EPA Emissions Trading Programs (EPA ET). Starting in the mid-1970s, the U.S. EPA and the states developed four limited emissions trading programs to increase flexibility and reduce the costs of compliance with air emissions standards for stationary sources under the Clean Air Act.

1. *Netting.* Netting allows large new sources and major modifications of existing sources to be exempted from otherwise applicable review procedures if existing emissions elsewhere in the same facility are reduced by a sufficient amount.

2. *Offsets.* The offset policy allows a major new source to locate in an area that does not attain a given National Ambient Air Quality Standard — a non-attainment area — if emissions from an existing source are reduced by at least as much as the new source would contribute (after installation of stringent controls).

3. *Bubble.* The bubble policy allows a firm to combine the limits for several different sources into one combined limit and to determine compliance based on that aggregate limit instead of from each source individually. The name alludes to an imaginary "bubble" placed over the several sources.

4. *Banking.* Under banking, firms that take actions to reduce emissions below the relevant standard can accumulate credits for future internal use or sale.

These four programs — collectively referred to as EPA Emissions Trading or EPA ET — are related by the common objective of providing sources with flexibility to comply with traditional source-specific command-and-control standards while maintaining environmental objectives focused primarily on local air quality. Reliance on these early EPA ET programs has been limited mostly as a result of implementing burdensome regulations that take up 47 pages of multicolumn fine print in the *Federal Register*. In general, the regulations have restricted substantially the applicability of the programs in response to regulatory concerns that the programs would compromise environmental objectives by encouraging "paper credits" or "anyway tons" — credits for emissions reductions that would have been made without the incentives provided by the emissions trading program. Credits must meet detailed criteria to be certified as eligible for trading. Offsets can only be used in certain geographic areas and any "trades" using them are not one-for-one, since the regulations require emissions reductions at the source providing the credit to be greater than the expected increase in emissions by the source using the credit. Potential applications of the bubble policy initially faced even greater hurdles because proposed bubbles had to be approved as revisions to an applicable State Implementation Plan (SIP), a lengthy administrative process that discouraged their use. These and other EPA regulations made efforts to identify and create trading opportunities expensive and uncertain. The result of this process for creating and approving tradable credits, often called certification, is that the EPA ET programs have yielded relatively few trades and low cost savings relative to their potential. The combination of pre-approval requirements and the need to construct customized arrangements for each trade has created substantial transactions costs — often exceeding the market value of the credits. These transaction costs — in effect the result of the lack of a well-defined and standardized commodity to be traded — have been the primary obstacle to more widespread participation in these programs....

Lead-in-Gasoline Program. The averaging program used to regulate lead in gasoline during the mid-1980s provides an example of a much more successful trading program than the early EPA ET programs. The averaging program for lead grew out of EPA's efforts to reduce the lead content of gasoline starting in the early 1970s....

Acid Rain Trading Program. [A remarkable feature of the Acid Rain Program] is the striking reduction of SO$_2$ emissions in the first year of the program. Emissions had been falling steadily throughout the 1980s, even before Title IV was enacted, and they continued to fall at about the same rate during the first half of the 1990s. But the reduction from 1994 to 1995 was far greater than anything that had been seen before, and there can be no doubt that it was caused by Title IV. The only precedent for such a rapid reduction in emissions of this magnitude in the history of the Clean Air Act is the lead phase-down program, which was also implemented by the use of emissions trading and banking.

The reason for the remarkable reduction in emissions in 1995, when the allowable emissions for that year required only a small reduction in emissions, is the availability of "inter-temporal trading" in the form of banking. The prospect of higher marginal abatement costs after 2000 made abating more than required in Phase I an appealing option for smoothing the transition to the more demanding Phase II cap. As a result, the reduction in emissions experienced in Phase I was about twice what would have been required to bring emissions below the level allowed in these years.

Inter-source or "spatial" trading also has been an important feature of the Acid Rain program. Compliance data for each year shows that about one-third of the affected units in Phase I obtained allowances from other units, either by intra-firm transfers or through purchase in the allowance market, to cover emissions in excess of the allowances allocated to those units. Spatial trading has allowed sources with high abatement costs to reduce emissions less — and those with low abatement costs to reduce emissions more — than under a command-and-control mechanism requiring uniform emissions rates, and thus has reduced the overall cost of the mandated emissions reduction.

The purchase and sale of allowances by the owners of affected units has created an active and efficient market for SO_2 allowances. This is evidenced by the single price for allowances at any one point in time regardless of the source of the price quote, by the high volume of inter-firm trades that can be deduced from the allowance registry maintained by EPA, by the low transactions costs associated with trading, and by the development of an active and diverse contract and futures market. The EPA auction has also provided a transparent mechanism to reveal prices, which was very important in the early years when few private transactions were being reported....

The cost savings due to emissions trading in the Acid Rain Program clearly are substantial. Figure 14-3 summarizes estimates of cost savings...attributable to different types of trading, i.e., the savings due to spatial trading in Phase I, banking between Phases I and II, and spatial trading in the more stringent and comprehensive Phase II.

| | ABATEMENT COST WITH TRADING | ABATEMENT COST WITHOUT TRADING | COST SAVINGS FROM EMISSIONS TRADING | | | |
			PHASE I SPATIAL TRADING	BANKING	PHASE II SPATIAL TRADING	TOTAL COST SAVINGS
Average Phase I Year (1995–1999)	735	1,093	358			358
Average Phase II Year (2000–2007)	1,400	3,682		167	2,115	2,282
13-Year Sum	14,875	34,925	1,792	1,339	16,919	20,050

FIGURE 14-3

ABATEMENT COST AND COST SAVINGS FROM TITLE IV EMISSIONS TRADING

Source: Adapted from Ellerman et al. (2000).

Note: All costs are in millions of present-value U.S. 1995 dollars. Estimates are based on economic reasoning assuming reasonably efficient markets based on observed allowance prices and abatement (as explained in Chapter 10 of source). A cost estimate is provided for only the first eight years of Phase II since this is the time period when most of the cost savings from banking were thought likely to be realized.

On average, spatial trading during Phase I reduced annual compliance costs by $358 million per year, a reduction of about 33 percent from the estimated cost of $1,093 million per year under a nontrading regime in which each affected unit limits emissions to the number of allowances received without any trading. During the first eight years of Phase II, the combination of spatial trading and banking is estimated to reduce annual compliance costs by about $2.3 billion per year, a reduction of over 60 percent from a total of about $3.7 billion per year. Over the first 13 years of the program, the ability to trade allowances nationwide across affected units and through time is estimated to reduce compliance costs by a total of $20 billion, a cost reduction of about 57 percent from the assumed command-and-control alternative. This percentage cost saving is similar to that developed by other researchers, although it is less than the percentage cost savings sometimes claimed for emissions trading programs, including the Title IV SO_2 cap-and-trade program.

There are several reasons why the Acid Rain Program has been successful. Of critical importance is the absence of any requirement for regulatory pre-approval of individual trades. Like the Lead Trading Program, the SO_2 program dispensed with the restrictions and cumbersome bureaucracy that characterized the EPA ET program. The lead program took the first step in avoiding the costly process of verifying credits for every transaction by allowing for an automatic crediting of differences from an agreed-upon baseline. Title IV took the further steps of explicitly recognizing the right to emit (albeit at a reduced quantity) and then determining compliance based on an account of *all* emissions, not just the differences from the agreed-upon baseline. These further steps changed the nature of the item traded from an emission reduction, which depends on an agreed upon and non-observable baseline, to emissions that are actually measured — in this case using a continuous emissions monitoring system (CEMS). As was also the case in the Lead Trading Program, the reduced importance of location and timing of emissions facilitated the simpler procedures that made emissions trading successful. In both cases, the reduction in aggregate, cumulative emissions was more important than the precise pattern of reductions at individual sources. Both programs also built in flexibility in the timing of emissions reductions by allowing for banking....

COMMENTARY & QUESTIONS

1. **More trading programs, more economic efficiency.** The Pew Center Report continued its review of the experience obtained with trading programs and found them all successful in obtaining environmental benefits by trading at a lower cost than would have been the case under command-and-control alone. That aspect of trading program success comports with theory. The empirical data also reflect other predictions of the theory, for example, the 1977 EPA trading programs that imposed high transaction costs in the form of trade-specific approvals were far less efficient than the SO_2 program, where there was no trade-specific scrutiny required. Averaging programs, especially when banking (time-shifting) is allowed, had high volumes of trades and reduced costs substantially, with greater cost savings realized in the lead trading program, where inter-firm trades were common, than in the mobile source trading, where fears of revealing proprietary data made intra-firm trading the predominant use of the system.

2. **Which is more impressive, \$20 billion saved by Title IV over 13 years or 57%?** Both figures are impressive, but the percentage cost reduction is the more notable. The monetary savings, as a percentage of the cost of electricity, is miniscule, amounting to less than 2 cents per person per day.

3. **SO_2 emissions reduction success: the virtues of an enforceable cap-and-trade program or low-hanging fruit?** There never was any doubt that Title IV would obtain the mandated reductions in emissions, not just in Phase I but over the life of the program. If cap-and-trade programs are enforceable (accurate measurement and faithful enforcement), they will reduce emissions. This particular cap-and-trade program was almost certain to work easily. The 50% rollback of 10 million tons per year reduction in SO_2 sounds like a monumental improvement, but that level of reductions is not nearly what is achievable at an economically affordable level of effort. In 1990, the known and in-use technology (including fuel switching to low-sulfur coal or the use of scrubbers for high-sulfur coal) was capable of achieving required rates (1.2 lb/mmBTU), and some plants were already operating at rates four times lower than that. As a result, Title IV required no technology-forcing. All Title IV needed was a

small amount of gamesmanship on the part of highly capitalized firms that could choose how best to minimize their long-term costs. Expectations of far higher cost were based on data provided by (guess who) the regulated entities that had two decades of experience fighting against air pollution regulation. Further easing the transition to lower SO_2 emissions was railroad deregulation that greatly reduced the cost of hauling low-sulfur western coal to the East where it could replace high-sulfur eastern coal. This change in the economics of the fuel supply was quite substantial, making low-sulfur fuel the favored choice on a cost per BTU basis. See, e.g., Hahn, The Impact of Economics on Environmental Policy 6 (AEI-Brookings Joint Center for Regulatory Studies, Working Paper No. 99-4, 1999); Schmalensee et al., An Interim Evaluation of Sulfur Dioxide Emissions Trading, 12 J. Econ. Persp. 53 (1998); Stavins, What Can We Learn from the Grand Policy Experiment: Positive and Normative Lessons from the SO_2 Allowance Trading, 12 J. Econ. Persp. 69 (1998).

4. **Hot air credits.** As in most contexts where this term is used, "hot air" is used pejoratively here. In trading regimes, "hot air credits" means credits awarded for activities that do not reduce actual emissions. Such credits not only slow progress toward environmental improvement, but they also undermine the economic incentives in the trading scheme by competing with real credits in the marketplace and depressing credit prices, the signals that influence pollution reduction behavior. Hot air credits are introduced in a variety of ways, such as overestimating the reductions that are associated with a pollution reducing action or setting baseline emissions and allowances at a level that exceeds actual pollution. For example, baselines are frequently set with reference to high-emission years or continuous operation capacity when the reality is more accurately represented by average years and actual operations.

5. **"Anyway" credits.** What is the impact on a trading system that gives credit for emissions reductions that would have happened anyway? For example, in Citizens Against the Refinery's Effects (CARE) v. EPA (discussed in Chapter 11), ozone offsets were given for conduct — road paving that used less expensive and equally suitable water-based asphalt instead of oil-based asphalt — that would have happened anyway. Should reduction credits for reduced pollution be issued to a factory that is closing because it is not profitable? The answer appears to depend on the context and the underlying purposes of the trading program. In the *CARE* case, it seems that Virginia's SIP already created a general obligation to make the change because it required all sources in the state to employ RACT (Reasonably Available Control Technology). Treating that change as an offset seems like a windfall, and it also tends to retard "reasonable further progress toward attainment" (the statutory command for all nonattainment areas) by offsetting new pollution with an anyway credit. The issue for trading, however, is that delving into whether a credit is an anyway credit adds transaction costs (cost of investigation and delay) that compromise the efficiency gains of the trading system. One plausible solution to this problem when designing a cap-and-trade program is to estimate the number of anyway credits and to set the goal in a way that recognizes that some trades will involve anyway credits.

6. **Accountability, measurement, and the cost of measurement.** Measurement of emissions is a necessary element of a workable system. Without accurate measures of

emissions, no trading system can be assured that all of the players have in hand the needed credits to cover their emissions. For large, technologically sophisticated, highly capitalized plants, the cost of monitoring is likely to be a small fraction of the cost of the operation. For example, Title IV required continuous emissions monitoring systems that added about 7% to the cost of Phase I of the program. But this requirement never-theless overcame opposition to the program from environmental groups, which doubted the credibility of "materials balance" methods of estimating emissions based on inputs and design features. Is real-time monitoring a feasible option for small-scale emitters? What would be the cost of monitoring a wood-burning stove as a percentage of the cost of the stove and its wood? How expensive would it be to monitor the hydro-carbon emissions of a dry cleaning establishment or a farmer's on-farm gas tank? When does leaving the small entities out of the trading system undermine the overall program?

7. **Initial allocation.** As a matter of economic theory, building on the famous Coase Theorem, the initial allocation of allowances in the trading system should not adversely affect efficiency. Ellerman et al. address this point in relation to Title IV:

> From the perspective of the performance of the program, i.e., the cost of reducing emissions and the speed with which they were reduced, there is no credible evidence that the initial allocations had any significant effects. This is the case because the allocation process was structured so that the number of allowances a source received was independent of its future output and its future emissions. Id.

In contrast to efficiency, welfare (wealth) effects are impacted by initial allocation of allowances. The allowances are valuable, and their initial distribution enriches its holder if no payment is required.

8. **Emissions trading and the NAAQS.** What is the relationship of Title IV trading of SO_2 credits to attainment of the NAAQS harm-based ambient standard for SO_2? It may overstate the case to deny all relationship, but the two regimes are independent of one another and serve two quite distinct purposes, both of which must be met. There is no warrant to allow a utility to economize on its emissions control expenditures by purchasing credits and increasing its local SO_2 emissions if to do so puts the area in violation of the NAAQS (or other relevant ambient air quality standard, such as a PSD standard). Indeed, local SO_2 problems have led some utilities to invest heavily in controls, making them sellers in the emissions credits market. See Tight Limits in Wisconsin Acid Rain Program May Yield Glut of Allowances, EPA Official Says, 22 BNA Envtl. Rep. 2665 (Apr. 3, 1992).

9. **Can downwind states add requirements that burden the trading system?** Officials in New York State, home to many of the lakes and streams most affected by sulfuric acid deposition, do not believe that Title IV is stringent enough to permit the state's lakes and streams to recover. In 2000, New York enacted a statute that severely penalized in-state firms that sold emission credits to companies located in any of 14 upwind states. In Clean Air Markets Group v. Pataki, 194 F. Supp. 2d 147 (N.D.N.Y. 2003), the U.S. District Court held the law unconstitutional because it violated the Commerce Clause by imposing a burden on interstate commerce that was not justified by its purported purpose of reducing acid deposition and thereby protecting environment and public

health. In the court's view, the statute that was struck down also conflicted with the CAA's chosen method for achieving the goal of air pollution control and thus was preempted by CAA. See generally Chapter 11.

10. **Cheaper, better, faster.** One efficiency claim for trading is that it lowers bureaucratic costs because there is no longer a need to draft detailed plant-specific permits, conduct costly inspections, decide difficult scientific questions relating pollution to harm, and so on. When, if ever, is that claim accurate?

C. FLAWED TRADING SYSTEMS, AND HOTSPOTS (ADVERSE LOCAL EFFECTS)

The South Coast Air Quality Management District (SCAQMD) is a regional state agency (with CAA authority delegated from the U.S. EPA) exercising air pollution control jurisdiction cutting across several county lines in the Los Angeles area. In 1991, SCAQMD voted to institute a tradeable permit system. Known as the Regional Clean Air Incentives Market (RECLAIM), the program covers the area's major stationary sources of nitrogen oxides (NOx) and sulfur oxides (SOx), and aims to reduce the emissions of these compounds each year by an average of 8.3% and 6.8% respectively, through 2003.[9] Thereafter the program expanded to include trading in volatile organic compounds and other emissions linked to ozone formation. This trading system, while widely reported to have achieved significant cost savings over non-trading alternatives, has also, as reflected in the excerpt that follows, been subject to severe criticisms.

Richard Toshiyuki Drury, Michael E. Belliveau, J. Scott Kuhn, and Shipra Bansal, Pollution Trading and Environmental Injustice: Los Angeles' Failed Experiment in Air Quality Policy
9 Duke Environmental Law and Policy Forum 231 (1999)

This article analyzes two of the most developed pollution trading programs in the world — Mobile Source Credits (specifically, the Rule 1610 "car scrapping" program) and RECLAIM. Both programs benefit large industrial polluters in the Los Angeles area, and have been in place for more than five years. Although industry has saved money, these air pollution trading programs have otherwise failed to deliver.

The promises of pollution trading advocates have not come to pass. Pollution trading in Los Angeles has led to concentrated toxic air emission hot-spots that have shackled low-income and minority communities with the region's air pollution. Pollution reductions have been far less than those promised by trading proponents. Furthermore, pollution trading has virtually eliminated public participation in the environmental decision-making process. The lessons learned from the Los Angeles pollution trading experiments should inform decision making in the development and reform of domestic and international emissions trading programs....

Los Angeles: A Test Market for Air Pollution Trading. The Los Angeles, California, region provides an ideal testing ground for environmental policies. Los Angeles' environmental

---

9. See Polesetsky, Will a Market in Air Pollution Clean the Nation's Dirtiest Air? A Study of the South Coast Air Quality Management District's Regional Clean Air Incentives Market, 22 Ecology L.Q. 359, 361 (1995).

problems are severe, its regulatory agencies are sophisticated, its resources are relatively ample, and the region's population is multi-racial and economically diverse....

The South Coast Air Basin, which includes the metropolitan Los Angeles area, suffers the worst air quality in the nation. For example, nearly 6,000 premature deaths caused by particulate air pollution occur in the Los Angeles area each year, representing about a tenth of such fatalities nationwide. Additionally, millions of residents of the region are exposed to unhealthy levels of ground level ozone, which causes aching lungs, wheezing, coughing, headache and permanent lung tissue scarring. Levels of toxic chemicals in the air pose significant risks for causing cancer and other chronic diseases. This dangerous mix of air pollutants, which are emitted by multitudes of factories, cars, and other sources, seriously threatens public health and well being.

A richly diverse, multi-racial and multi-ethnic population lives, works, and plays in the Los Angeles region, raising the environmental justice concern that people of color and poor people are unfairly exposed to more air pollution than others. Therefore, air pollution reduction strategies, including pollution trading programs, should be evaluated not only for their efficacy in reducing air pollution, but also for their effect on achieving environmental justice. Will such programs alleviate or worsen the environmental injustice of disproportionate exposures to air pollution already faced by the most powerless segments of society? The answer to this question is already of pressing importance in Los Angeles and will become increasingly relevant throughout the rest of the country....

Pollution Trading Comes of Age in Los Angeles: From Rule 1610 to RECLAIM and Beyond...
Following a pattern shaped by the policy agenda of the largest industrial polluters, a group of market-based regulations centered on pollution trading have been adopted for the South Coast Air Basin. In 1993, SCAQMD approved the first old vehicle pollution trading program in the country, known as Rule 1610 or the "car scrapping program." Rule 1610 allows stationary source polluters (such as factories and refineries) to avoid installing expensive pollution control equipment if they purchase pollution credits generated by destroying old, high-polluting cars. Ideally, an equal or greater amount of pollution can be reduced at a much lower cost by purchasing and destroying old cars than by forcing stationary sources to install expensive pollution control equipment.

Under Rule 1610, "licensed car scrappers" can purchase and destroy old cars. SCAQMD then grants the scrapper emissions credits based on the projected emissions of the car had it not been destroyed, which may then be sold to stationary source polluters (e.g. factories). The stationary sources use the pollution credits to avoid on-site emission reductions that would be required under the technology-based regulatory regime.[10] Rule 1610 requires polluters to purchase credits representing twenty percent more emission reductions than would be achieved through compliance with technology-based regulations for their plant. Although industrial plants avoid emission reductions, the scrapping of older, high polluting cars should result in greater air quality improvements at a lower cost than regulatory mandates.

SCAQMD then adopted the centerpiece of its pollution trading strategy, the Regional Clean Air Incentives Market (RECLAIM), the world's first urban smog trading program. RECLAIM replaced many of SCAQMD's technology-based regulations aimed at reducing emissions of sulfur oxides (SOx) and nitrogen oxides (NOx). RECLAIM, a "declining cap and trade"

---

10. The RECLAIM Rules of SCAQMD make extensive use of technology-based measures, as well as applying the harm-based SIP regulatory standards. See, e.g., SCAQMD Rule 2005, available at http://www.aqmd.gov/rules/html/r2005.html. [Eds.]

program, mandates annual emission reductions for industry but provides them the flexibility to achieve that goal by either purchasing emission reduction credits or by reducing their own pollution. Under RECLAIM, SCAQMD allocates pollution credits to each major source facility in the region based on its historic level of emissions. Each facility has three options: 1) it can use all of its credits and pollute up to the level they allow; 2) it can reduce its pollution and sell the excess credits to other facilities; or 3) it can increase emissions relative to its initial endowment of credits by buying credits from other facilities. Each year SCAQMD decreases the number of credits allocated by the program, forcing facilities either to decrease their pollution or purchase credits from other facilities. As the number of available credits decreases, their market price should rise, increasing the market incentive for companies to reduce pollution rather than purchase credits. According to its supporters, by 2003 RECLAIM should spur the lowest cost pollution reduction among individual industrial plants and slash aggregate emissions of NOx by seventy-five percent and SOx by sixty percent.

Toward fulfilling industry's goal of indefinitely avoiding emissions reductions at their own plants, SCAQMD aggressively expanded its emissions trading strategy. In April 1997, the SCAQMD Governing Board voted to approve Rule 2506, Area Source Credits (ASCs), which provides for the issuance of marketable credits to entities that voluntarily reduce emissions of NOx and SOx. The resulting ASCs can then be converted to RECLAIM Trading Credits or used as an alternative method of compliance with other SCAQMD regulations. The mobile source pollution trading has expanded beyond Rule 1610 to provide for the issuance of Mobile Source Emission Reduction Credits (MSERCs) for voluntary emission reductions from:

- the repair of emissions-related components in high-emitting vehicles,
- the purchase of clean on-road vehicles, including new, low-emission buses, retrofitting vehicles to low-emission configurations, and purchasing zero-emission vehicles,
- the electrification of truck stops and tour bus stops to prevent engine idling,
- the purchase of low or zero emission off-road vehicles,
- the purchase of clean lawn and garden equipment, such as battery-operated lawn mowers and leaf blowers, and the scrapping of old equipment....

The Harsh Reality: Problems with Pollution Trading in Los Angeles. Evidence indicates that pollution trading programs in Los Angeles are plagued with problems. Although the programs have succeeded in saving money for industry, they have not effectively reduced emissions and have not promoted technology innovation or public participation. Instead, they have further concentrated the region's pollution in lower income communities and given industry a "free ride" from otherwise obligatory emissions reduction schedules.

Toxic Hot-Spots and Environmental Injustice: The Mad Science of Pollution Trading. Pollution trading programs can unfairly concentrate pollution in communities where factories purchase emissions reduction credits rather than reduce actual emissions. These localized health risks from pollution sources, or "toxic hot-spots," tend to be overlooked by policy makers focused on regional air quality concerns. However, the disproportionate burden thrust on communities surrounding major pollution emitters takes its toll in the form of increased risks of toxic exposure and damage to human health. Furthermore, it is environmentally unjust when these communities enduring localized toxic hot-spots are overwhelmingly low income and populated by people of color. Such hot-spots can be worsened when pollution trading programs ignore the differences in chemical hazards posed by the pollutants reduced to earn credits and the pollutants emitted through the purchase of credits. The problem of hot-spots is further complicated by the emission of co-pollutants and precursors, which may increase exposure to certain types of chemicals in downwind communities where pollution is concentrated.

SCAQMD's pollution trading programs have resulted in the creation of toxic hot-spots by concentrating pollution in communities surrounding major sources of pollution. Rule 1610 provides the clearest example. SCAQMD studies indicate that cars destroyed through the Rule 1610 program were registered throughout the air quality management district, a four-county region. Air pollution from these automobiles would have also been distributed throughout this region. By contrast, stationary sources in Los Angeles are densely clustered in only a few communities in this four-county region. As a result of these distribution patterns, Rule 1610 effectively takes pollution formerly distributed throughout the region by automobiles, and concentrates that pollution in the communities surrounding stationary sources.

Most of the emissions credits purchased to avoid stationary source controls have been purchased by four oil companies: Unocal, Chevron, Ultramar and GATX. Of these four companies, three are located close together in the communities of Wilmington and San Pedro; the fourth facility, Chevron, is located nearby in El Segundo. These companies have used pollution credits to avoid installing pollution control equipment that captures toxic gases released during oil tanker loading at their marine terminals. When loading oil tankers, toxic gases are forced out of the tanker and into the air, exposing workers and nearby residents to toxic vapors, including benzene, a known human carcinogen. Thus, by using pollution credits, these companies are allowed to avoid reducing local emissions of hazardous chemicals in exchange for reducing regional auto emissions. As a result of Rule 1610, the four oil companies created a toxic chemical hot-spot around their marine terminals, exposing workers and nearby residents to elevated health risks....

To add insult to injury, the public health risks from the extra pollution concentrated in these neighborhoods constitutes a case of environmental injustice. The demographics of this hot-spot area starkly contrast with that of the metropolitan Los Angeles region. The residents living in San Pedro and Wilmington, which host a majority of the oil companies emitting hazardous toxic chemicals, are overwhelmingly Latino. Furthermore, the racial composition of communities living near three of the marine terminals ranges from 75 to 90 percent people of color, while the entire South Coast Air Basin has a population of only 36 percent people of color....

The hazards of trading extend beyond the shifting of pollution from a dispersed region to more concentrated localized areas; inter-pollutant trading can also create toxic hot-spots. Many trading programs allow facilities to trade pollution credits generated through reductions in a large variety of chemicals. For example, the Rule 1610 program allows pollution credits to be generated through reductions in VOCs. VOCs are a family of over 600 chemical compounds, some of which have high toxicity and some of which have low toxicity. VOC trading raises concerns about the difference in toxicity of VOC emissions from marine terminals compared to VOCs from automobiles. For example, benzene levels may be higher in VOC emissions from marine terminals than from cars, which leads to greater exposure and risks concentrated in the communities around the marine terminals. Benzene exposure can cause leukemia, anemia, respiratory tract irritation, dermatitis, pulmonary edema, and hemorrhaging. Therefore, the Rule 1610 program may allow continued release of highly toxic chemicals into certain communities in exchange for small area-wide reductions in much less toxic chemicals. Yet, no source testing has been required by SCAQMD to accurately characterize the differences in chemical composition and toxicity among VOC emissions subject to trading.

In addition to concerns about variable toxicity, VOCs also exhibit different degrees of reactivity related to their ability to form photochemical smog. These differences in photochemical reactivity have long been recognized in air pollution regulation and have guided priority setting in the control of VOC sources for smog control. In pollution trading programs, however, if highly reactive VOCs are emitted by purchasing credits earned for reducing low reactivity VOCs, then downwind ozone (smog) formation may be increased rather than reduced. This represents another inter-pollutant trading flaw in pollution trading programs that include VOCs.…

Market Incentives Run Amok: Fraud and Manipulation. Air pollution regulatory programs have been plagued with technical uncertainties in accurately accounting for the amount of emissions from different sources. Such concerns exist for both a technology-based approach and an emissions trading approach to regulation. However, for an emissions trading program, accuracy is more important than for technology-based regulations, because an accounting of pollution forms the basis for the number of emissions reduction credits required by each facility. Furthermore, when an emissions trading approach is employed, the incidence of fraud may be greater. Pollution trading programs create stronger incentives to manipulate the numbers and cheat, because credits that are fraudulently created are still worth money. The Los Angeles pollution trading experience with car scrapping has been plagued by a history of under reporting of actual emissions from industry and an over-reporting of claimed emission reductions from cars.…

Rather than measure actual emissions released, companies estimate emissions using emission factors developed by the Western States Petroleum Association. Emissions factors are surrogate estimates of emissions based on activity level. For example, engineers may estimate that a small industrial boiler will release so many pounds of NOx for every barrel of fuel oil burned. Emission factors are hotly argued among technical specialists from different fields and change as new information becomes available. Emissions factors are poor surrogates for actual measurements. With margins of error ranging from fifty percent to one hundred percent, emissions factors are highly uncertain, making claimed emission reduction difficult to verify. They can readily be adjusted to report emissions as being higher or lower, since at best they represent educated guesses of actual emissions. Source testing, which measures actual emissions, was required to ensure compliance with the technology-based emission limits set under Rule 1142 for marine terminals.

Information recently obtained through the Freedom of Information Act reveals that the oil companies did, in fact, measure their emissions. When the actual measurements were compared to reported emissions based on industry emissions factors, striking differences were revealed. Oil companies under-reported their oil tanker emissions by factors between 10 and 1000. As a result, the oil companies purchased between 10 and 1000 times too few credits from scrapping old, high-polluting cars to offset their tanker pollution. This persistent problem was completely overlooked by SCAQMD and was only detected through a time-consuming investigation by Communities for a Better Environment. However, despite this under-reporting, SCAQMD continues to allow the use of emissions factors to underestimate emissions.

Exacerbating the huge gap between actual emissions and credits purchased by polluters, credit generators — the car scrappers — have abused the system. Many of the cars allegedly destroyed through the Rule 1610 program were not, in fact, destroyed, according to Bruce Lohmann, SCAQMD's Chief Inspector for the Rule 1610 program. While the car bodies were crushed, many of the engines which produce the pollution were not. Instead, many of those engines were sold for re-use, despite the fact that pollution credits for destroying the car had been granted by SCAQMD. EPA has refused to approve the Rule 1610 program precisely because car engines are not always destroyed.…

Distortion of the Market: Hot Air and Phantom Reductions. In addition to fraud by market participants, "cap and trade" strategies, like Los Angeles' RECLAIM program, are plagued by a broader form of institutional manipulation. This manipulation takes the form of "phantom reductions" in air emissions — reductions that exist on paper only. Under RECLAIM, allowable emissions have declined each year as required by regulation. However, because emissions reduction credits were initially allocated in an amount significantly inflated above actual emissions, early "reductions" in emissions were illusory. In the first three years of the RECLAIM program, actual industrial NOx emissions have declined by at most three percent, while allowable emissions have been reduced on paper by about thirty percent. In the global context, the term "hot air" has been used to describe the vesting of certain countries like Russia with excess credits. Not only does the trading in hot air credits represent illusory environmental gains, the excess allocation drives down the price of credits, reducing the motivation to invest in actual emission reductions or technological innovation....

According to a SCAQMD audit, over the first three years, RECLAIM has produced barely discernible pollution reductions. In fact, during the first two years of RECLAIM, 1994 and 1995, NOx and SOx emissions reportedly increased compared to 1993. Only in 1996 were emissions reduced, and then by at most three percent from 1993 NOx levels and by less than ten percent from 1993 SOx levels. This pattern contrasts sharply with the time period 1989-1993 when NOx emissions from industrial facilities declined steeply, by approximately thirty-seven percent, as a result of technology-based control regulations....

COMMENTARY & QUESTIONS

1. **The moral trouble with trading.** In a portion of the article that was not excerpted here, its authors take trading to task on several fronts, one of them being moral: "What once was a wrong — polluting — is now a 'right.'" Id. at 269. Is that criticism warranted any more than saying that an NPDES or CAA permit creates rights to pollute? The other moral failing attributed to trading is that of environmental injustice. Most emissions trading systems, especially to the extent that hot spots are not scrupulously avoided, may tend to concentrate pollution in industrialized areas that are home to low-income communities of color. Is that a reason to refuse to permit trading systems? Are there forms of compensation to adversely affected communities that could be melded into trading systems, particularly if a charge were made for initial allocations?

2. **The practical trouble with trading.** Going beyond hot spots, can you construct a list of practical problems that are likely to arise in most trading systems? RECLAIM seems not to have worked to obtain substantial reductions, whereas Title IV had a major effect. Several RECLAIM-specific failings were detailed in the excerpt. There were others, such as "co-pollutant" problems, where the traded pollutant is also an indicator of the presence of numerous other pollutants that are not necessarily eliminated in the trades. In RECLAIM, for example, the off-gassing of tankers unloading emits a host of pollutants that would be captured by hoods that are not in place because of VOC trades for reductions (such as car scrapping) that do not also limit the co-pollutants. Air chemistry also complicates the issue of trading flexibility. RECLAIM allows industrial sources to separately trade two combustion by-products, NOx and SOx. Allowing extra SOx emissions and less NOx emissions may reduce smog, but simultaneously it may introduce fine particulates that are formaldehyde precursors. Is that a safety-improving trade?

Credit modeling is a more general problem. Try to identify all the variables that have to be assumed or measured to determine how much of an emission reduction accompanies the destruction of an older automobile. Should the program try to validate assumptions in trades? That would drive up transaction costs, but investigations of Rule 1610 showed numerous cases of repair to cars that were inoperable solely to prepare them for service as a trading credit and the bounty that would be paid. Another generic criticism of trading is that it tends to stifle innovation. See Driesen, Free Lunch or Cheap Fix? The Emissions Trading Idea and the Climate Change Convention, 26 B.C. Envtl. Aff. L. Rev. 1, 18–35 (1998). Likewise, public participation diminishes in a market system, and monitoring and enforcement seem likely to be less effective than under a typical modern permit system.

3. **Hot spots.** The excerpted article is not alone in decrying hot spots as a major problem in trading schemes. Interestingly, that critique is made by commentators who are associated with more conservative views. For example, in December 2002, Curtis Moore (formerly Republican Counsel to the Senate Environment & Public Works Committee when it was chaired by Sen. Robert Stafford (R Vt.)), on behalf of the Clean Air Trust, stated, "Trading is a policy that ought to be avoided altogether, except in the most narrow and carefully monitored circumstances." 34 BNA Envtl. Rep. 9 (Jan. 3, 2003). The study focused on sulfur dioxide trading and RECLAIM.[11] Jonathan Nash and Richard Revesz suggest the following:

> We propose an alternative that would avoid the violation of ambient standards and formation of hot spots without greatly increasing administrative complexity or introducing excessively high transaction costs. Our idea is to construct a market in tradable emission permits under which trading would be entirely unfettered, with the sole exception that a prospective buyer and seller would have to receive approval before they could consummate their trade. This approval could be accomplished with a database, accessed through a website administered by the government, which would contain emissions data for all sources in the region. When a proposed trade is submitted for approval, the website would temporarily update its saved data to reflect the change in the geographic distribution of emissions that would result from the proposed trade. The website would use an atmospheric dispersion model to predict the impact of the emissions from all the sources in the region — as modified by the proposed trade — on ambient pollution levels at various receptor points. The website would reject any trade resulting in the violation of an applicable ambient standard and would approve all other trades.[12]

Recall the *Cleveland Electric Illuminating* case in Chapter 11, and, in that light, consider the practicality of the Nash and Revesz proposal. That, of course, is an early case, but airshed dispersion modeling remains an inexact art, not a science. Would trading that focuses on effects rather than emissions work any better? For an attempt to describe such a system, see Akers, New Tools for Environmental Justice: Articulating a Net Health Effects Challenge to Emissions Trading Markets, 7 Hastings W.-Nw. J. Envtl. L. & Pol'y 203 (2001).

---

11. See http://www.cleanairtrust.org/release.121902.html for a copy of the report.
12. Nash & Revesz, Markets and Geography: Designing Marketable Permit Schemes to Control Local and Regional Pollutants, 28 Ecol. L.Q. 569, 572–573 (2001).

4. **The consequences of the growing price of ERCs.** Recall the way in which RECLAIM ratchets up its effect, by reducing the cap on NOx and SOx by an average of 8.3% and 6.8%, respectively, per year through 2003. The phase-in allows ample lead time for emission reduction technologies to be planned and implemented more gradually, which probably reduces the cost in comparison to a more abrupt transition. Simple microeconomic theory predicts that as the cap descends it creates an increase in the demand for credits that will result in a higher price being paid to sellers of credits. Moreover, the longer the program is in force, the least-cost methods of supplying credits may be exhausted by the reductions demanded in the early years (the low-hanging fruit phenomenon). This, too, is predicted by microeconomic theory. What happens next, when prices for credits rise because low cost reductions are exhausted but the cap is continuing to decline? Two scenarios emerge — firms that can afford the higher prices of buying credits or installing their own control systems do so and can pass those costs on to their customers. Firms that cannot afford the new price structure become the victims of "Economic Darwinism." Can you predict, in generic terms, which firms will survive and which won't? The principal cleavage is between large and small. Large firms, even inefficient ones, survive because they have greater access to capital markets and other lines of business that can subsidize impacted operations, and they frequently have a greater ability to pass on increased costs to their customers. Are there mechanisms that can be made part of a cap-and-trade system that will ameliorate this effect? Recall here the Title IV program that created a reserve of allowances to be sold by EPA in direct sales and auctions, with some allowances offered to particular classes of users on a preferred basis.

5. **A favorable view of RECLAIM and its emergency suspension in 2000.** In Ellerman, et al., Emissions Trading in the United States: Experience, Lessons and Considerations for Greenhouse Gases (Pew Center on Global Climate Change Report, May 2003), from which excerpts were reproduced previously, the authors give a far more favorable view of RECLAIM. The empirical data they developed depict RECLAIM as an economic instrument that reduced the cost of pollution reduction through active trading, thus making it another "success" story for cap-and-trade. ("The high volume of trading in the RECLAIM program implies significant cost savings relative to command-and-control alternative that it replaced…." Id. at 24.) The focus of that report, on trading as a mechanism for greenhouse gas reduction, allows it to have little concern for hotspots effects and the potential adverse public health consequences of cross-pollutant trades. Greenhouse gas issues are uniquely ones of long-term global dispersion, while hotspots are not a major concern. Thus, for example, that report was more concerned with limits on trading than with hotspots, noting that "[RECLAIM] does not allow banking because of concerns that the ability to use banked emissions might lead to substantial increases of actual emissions in some future year, and thus delay compliance with ambient air quality standards." Id. at 21.

Emphasis on the robustness of trading systems makes the short-term suspension of the RECLAIM program in 2000 a matter of concern. In that year, California experienced massive spikes in prices in the energy sector, due to some combination of deregulation of prices, poor planning, and illegal and collusive behavior by energy suppliers and energy traders. Previous to that year, prices for all vintages of RECLAIM NOx credits had ranged in a band between $1500 and $3000 per ton. In 2000, the energy crisis prompted potential electricity suppliers to maximize output from all available generating sources, including a number of old gas-fired plants for which NOx controls had not been upgraded. This created a spike in demand for vintage 2000 NOx credits, which rose from a high of $4284 in 1999 before the electricity crisis was well perceived, to an average price of $45,000 per credit in 2000, with the highest single price reported to be in excess of $90,000 per credit. Id. at 25. The regulatory response was to suspend temporarily the program for electricity generators, thereby eliminating one factor among many that was contributing to California's electric generation crisis. The results were not as bad as might have been expected.

> In response to the price spikes for NOx RTCs — along with the breach of the cap and the price spikes for electricity linked in part to high NOx prices — electricity generating plants were removed from the RECLAIM program, at least temporarily, in May 2001. The electricity generators were allowed to pay a mitigation fee of $15,000 per ton when they exceeded their caps — with fee revenues used to pay for emission reductions elsewhere — and were placed temporarily under an alternative command-and-control regulatory regime. Thus, an unfortunate outgrowth of the California electricity crisis was the abandonment — at least temporarily — of the use of a successful cap-and-trade program to control electric power emissions.... The increase in demand on electric generating units in 2000 caused emissions to exceed the 2000 cap by about 3,000 tons, or 20 percent; however, the use of allowances from the overlapping 1999 and 2001 cycles reduced the shortfall between NOx emissions and RTCs to 1,110 tons, or about six percent of the 2000 cap, a modest increase given the extraordinary circumstances in 2000. In addition, as noted, the mitigation fees paid by electricity generators are to be used to reduce emissions from other sources and, in any event, the shortfall in emissions will be reflected in decreased future NOx RTC allocations. Thus, the net effect on NOx emissions of the increase in demand in 2000 for NOx allowances is largely to shift a small number of NOx emissions reductions to future years. Moreover, there is no reason to believe that a command-and-control alternative would have performed better under the circumstances. Indeed, since command-and-control mandates typically regulate emission rates — rather than overall emissions — this alternative would likely have resulted in the same emissions increases but without the compensating measures taken as a result of exceeding the RECLAIM NOx cap. Id. at 25–26.

The temporary NOx credit suspension of RECLAIM is an isolated and somewhat extraordinary example. Nonetheless it highlights the need for political will to stay the course in the face of increased costs as an element necessary to the success of a trading program.

6. **Conclusions?** The Drury et al. excerpt lists eight recommendations for urban air quality trading programs:

1. prohibit toxic trading,

2. prohibit trading into overburdened communities,

3. assess and prevent toxic hot spots and discriminatory impacts,

4. prohibit trading out of RACT requirements,

  5. prohibit cross-pollutant trading,

  6. allow affected communities to review and comment on proposed trades,

  7. ban intersource trading between mobile, stationary, and area sources, and

  8. prohibit hot air credits that result from overallocating the baseline.[13]

Are there other recommendations that should be included? Has trading really improved the situation or simply obfuscated the problem by making a complex undertaking wrongly appear simple? The failure of RECLAIM to significantly reduce loadings is troubling. The likelihood that it has increased the level of hazard for identifiable groups of citizens is an indictment. In this regard, RECLAIM is not alone. Other trading programs have similar implementation stories that chronicle their adverse effects on discrete populations. See EPA Ignored Employees' Objections on Louisiana Program, Group Charges, 33 BNA Envtl. Rep. 2401 (Nov. 8, 2002), citing materials marshaled by Public Employees for Environmental Responsibility (PEER). Those materials are available at http://www.peer.org/press/287.html. See also EPA Office of the Inspector General, Open Market Trading Program for Air Emissions Need Strengthening, Report No. 2002-P-00019 (Sept. 30, 2002).

D. TRADING TO IMPROVE WATER QUALITY

U.S. Environmental Protection Agency, Water Quality Trading Policy: Issuance of Final Policy Text
68 Fed. Reg. 1608 (Jan. 13, 2003)

Background and Purpose of the Policy... The application of technology and water quality based requirements through the National Pollutant Discharge Elimination System (NPDES) permit program has achieved and remains critical to success in controlling point source pollution and restoring the nation's waters. Despite these accomplishments approximately 40% of the rivers, 45% of the streams and 50% of the lakes that have been assessed still do not support their designated uses.[14] Sources of pollution such as urban storm water, agricultural runoff and atmospheric deposition continue to threaten our nation's waters. Nutrient and sediment loading from agriculture and storm water are significant contributors to water quality problems such as hypoxia in the Gulf of Mexico and decreased fish populations in Chesapeake Bay. Population growth and development place increasing demands on the environment making it more difficult to achieve and maintain water quality standards.

Finding solutions to these complex water quality problems requires innovative approaches that are aligned with core water programs. Water quality trading is an approach that offers greater efficiency in achieving water quality goals on a watershed basis. It allows one source to meet its regulatory obligations by using pollutant reductions created by another source that has lower pollution control costs. Trading capitalizes on economies of scale and the control cost differentials among and between sources....

---

13. 9 Duke Envtl. L. & Pol'y F. at 283-286.

14. About 33% of the nation's water has been assessed by states and tribes pursuant to Section 305(b) of the Clean Water Act (National Water Quality Inventory: 2000 Report, EPA). The proportion of non-assessed waters that does not meet designated uses is likely lower since assessments tend to be focused in known problem areas. [Eds.]

Water Quality Trading Policy Statement: CWA Requirements. Water quality trading and other market-based programs must be consistent with the CWA.

Trading Areas. All water quality trading should occur within a watershed or a defined area for which a TMDL has been approved. Establishing defined trading areas that coincide with a watershed or TMDL boundary results in trades that affect the same water body or stream segment and helps ensure that water quality standards are maintained or achieved throughout the trading area and contiguous waters.

Pollutants and Parameters Traded. EPA supports trading that involves nutrients (e.g., total phosphorus and total nitrogen) or sediment loads. In addition, EPA recognizes that trading of pollutants other than nutrients and sediments has the potential to improve water quality and achieve ancillary environmental benefits if trades and trading programs are properly designed. EPA believes that such trades may pose a higher level of risk and should receive a higher level of scrutiny to ensure that they are consistent with water quality standards. EPA may support trades that involve pollutants other than nutrients and sediments on a case-by-case basis where prior approval is provided through an NPDES permit, a TMDL or in the context of a watershed plan or pilot trading project that is supported by a state, tribe or EPA. EPA also supports cross-pollutant trading for oxygen-related pollutants where adequate information exists to establish and correlate impacts on water quality. Reducing upstream nutrient levels to offset a downstream biochemical oxygen demand or to improve a depressed in-stream dissolved oxygen level are examples of cross-pollutant trading. EPA does not currently support trading of pollutants considered by EPA to be persistent bioaccumulative toxics (PBTs).... Where state or tribal water quality standards allow for mixing zones, EPA does not support any trading activity that would exceed an acute aquatic life criteria within a mixing zone or a chronic aquatic life or human health criteria at the edge of a mixing zone using design flows specified in the water quality standards.

Baselines for Water Quality Trading. As explained below, the baselines for generating pollution reduction credits should be derived from and consistent with water quality standards. The term pollution reduction credits ("credits"), as used in this policy, means pollutant reductions greater than those required by a regulatory requirement or established under a TMDL. For example, where a TMDL has been approved or established by EPA, the applicable point source waste load allocation or nonpoint source load allocation would establish the baselines for generating credits. For trades that occur where water quality fully supports designated uses, or in impaired waters prior to a TMDL being established, the baseline for point sources should be established by the applicable water quality based effluent limitation, a quantified performance requirement or a management practice derived from water quality standards. In these scenarios the baseline for nonpoint sources should be the level of pollutant load associated with existing land uses and management practices that comply with applicable state, local or tribal regulations....

COMMENTARY & QUESTIONS

1. **Trading as a supplement to regulation.** Note carefully that the Water Quality Trading Policy is treated as an implementation device for the already extant requirements of the CWA. Trading is an economic instrument in the service of independently set water quality goals. In general, industries will be required to meet technology control requirements under the current NPDES program. The major animating force

behind this proposal is the improvement of water quality that is being required by the WQBEL/TMDL/WLA[15] process that is being applied to waters that have not reached the quality required to sustain designated uses through the TBEL[16] process alone. See generally Chapter 12.

2. **Common elements of credible trading programs.** The EPA Water Quality Trading Policy lists and elaborates on the elements of a "credible" trading system. Based on the materials studied thus far, what items should appear in that list? The list is quite ordinary: (1) legal authority, (2) clearly defined units for trade, (3) specific duration of credits, (4) specific quantification of credit producing activity, (5) compliance and enforcement regimes, (6) public participation and information access, and (7) program evaluation. Is there anything unique to water discharge trading that was not an issue in air emissions trading? Consider here a typical river's hydrograph (measure of flow over time). Rivers, the typical receiving body, have marked seasonal variability in flow patterns. What are the implications of that for trading? One way in which the policy addresses this is by calling for tradeable credits to be "expressed in rates or mass per unit time as appropriate to be consistent with the time periods that are used to determine compliance with NPDES permit limitations or other regulatory requirements."

3. **Quantifying and trading nonpoint source loadings and reductions.** The policy calls for using "standardized protocols" in quantification of loads, load reductions, and credits and notes that "where trading involves nonpoint sources, states and tribes should adopt methods to account for the greater uncertainty in estimates of nonpoint source loads and reductions." What steps are available? EPA specifically endorsed several:

> EPA supports a number of approaches to compensate for nonpoint source uncertainty. These include monitoring to verify load reductions, the use of greater than 1:1 trading ratios between nonpoint and point sources, using demonstrated performance values or conservative assumptions in estimating the effectiveness of nonpoint source management practices, using site- or trade-specific discount factors, and retiring a percentage of nonpoint source reductions for each transaction or a predetermined number of credits. Where appropriate, states and tribes may elect to establish a reserve pool of credits that would be available to compensate for unanticipated shortfalls in the quantity of credits that are actually generated. 68 Fed. Reg. 1601, at 1612 (2003).

4. **Estimates of the comparative efficiency of trading.** Is trading likely to result in significant savings, more so than regulatory regimes that seek the same degree of water quality improvement? An EPA study stated:

> EPA estimates that in 1997 annual private point source control costs were about $14 billion and public point source costs were about $34 billion. The National Cost to Implement Total Maximum Daily Loads (TMDLs) Draft Report estimates that flexible approaches to improving water quality could save $900 million annually compared to the least flexible approach. (EPA, August 2001.) Nitrogen trading

---

15. Water Quality Based Effluent Limitation/Total Maximum Daily Load/Waste Load Allocation.
16. Technology-Based Effluent Limitation.

among publicly owned treatment works in Connecticut that discharge into Long Island Sound is expected to achieve the required reductions under a TMDL while saving over $200 million in control costs.[17]

While $900 million per year is surely not chump change, it is less than 2% of the $48 billion the report calculated as being spent on water quality. That data suggest that trading is valuable and worthwhile, but it is not a panacea that vastly diminishes water pollution control costs.

5. **Trading in water effluents is different from trading in air emissions.** The two media exhibit distinctively different mixing qualities that affect trading. Water pollution problems tend to be more restricted geographically, and pollutants tend to disperse less rapidly in water than in air. What does that mean for trading in regard to such things as hot spots, geographic zones for trading, and the number of available participants in the market? Aquatic ecosystems have distinctive characteristics, such as being home to organisms that bioaccumulate many types of pollutants. Such toxic pollutants in this context are called "conservative pollutants." How should the presence of conservative pollutants be figured into setting trading limits? Trading is also proposed for nonconservative pollutants, such as biochemical oxygen demand (BOD). Variables such as water temperature and the presence of differing levels of other pollutants affect the assimilation rate for BOD in a water course. How should that complicating data be reflected in the design of a trading regime?

6. **Colorado's Lake Dillon trading program.** Lake Dillon is a prominent recreation area that also serves as a key staging reservoir in Denver's drinking water system. With several growing communities surrounding the lake, phosphorous pollution is a major concern. In 1984, as part of the first program in the nation of its kind, the Colorado State Water Quality Control Commission authorized pollution trading between point and nonpoint sources. The program was built on a total annual maximum phosphorus load of 4610 kg/yr and allowed point sources to obtain a credit for 1 kg of reduction for every 2 kg of certified reductions obtained from nonpoint sources. The trades were then recorded as part of the NPDES permit of the point source. Although relatively few trades were ever made, the program is considered an important reason for Lake Dillon's continued ability to meet water quality standards. See U.S. Environmental Protection Agency, Draft Trading Update — December 96 Lake Dillon, Colorado, available at http://www.epa.gov/OWOW/watershed/trading/lakedil.htm. Even more varied water effluent trading programs are underway in many parts of the nation. For example, in 2001, the Oregon legislature enacted H.B. 3956 creating an effluent trading program for the Willamette River. The pollutants targeted for trading include "(a) nitrogenous and phosphorous compounds commonly known as nutrients; (b) sediment; (c) temperature; (d) biological oxygen demand; and (e) chemical oxygen demand." §3(2). Implementation of this program, however, has lagged.

7. **Trading selenium in irrigation runoff.** Most nonpoint source trading programs are crafted to allow trading from nonpoint sources to point sources in water quality limited

---

17. EPA, A Retrospective Assessment of the Costs of the Clean Water Act: 1972-1997 (Oct. 2000), available online at http://www.epa.gov/waterscience/economics/costs.pdf.

areas. A pioneering nonpoint-to-nonpoint source trading program has been established that allows the trading of selenium drainage loading among farms in the 97,000 acre Grasslands Drainage Area of the San Joaquin Valley. That arid area relies on irrigation, but the soils are poorly drained and become easily waterlogged. Selenium, which is naturally present in the soils, dissolves in the irrigation water and drains with it, causing serious consequences to wildlife and health risks to humans. As a condition of improving drainage through use of the federally constructed San Luis Drain, Grasslands farmers had to agree to lower selenium levels in the irrigation tail water. A custom-designed trading program was created to assist the farmers in meeting the mandated quality levels. Trades could occur only among farmers; others, such as government agencies or environmental groups, were not allowed to purchase reduction credits. Retroactive trades were allowed to bring noncomplying dischargers into compliance by buying reductions after the fact to avoid the penalties. In part, this was done to offset the lack of contemporaneous knowledge of exactly how much selenium was being discharged. Trades were arranged through bilateral negotiation without aid of brokers or a clearinghouse. Prices were fixed by the parties to the trades, although the comprehensive study of the program compiled by its chief administrator reported that parties had great difficulty in knowing what to charge. The farmers obtained major improvements — a 40% decrease in tail water released and a 48% reduction in selenium loads over a four-year period that began in 1997. The trading program was helpful in achieving those results, although the volume of trades and the prices of them suggest it was not a major factor. In the first three years of operation, there had been 39 trades, involving 605 pounds of monthly selenium load and 128 pounds of annual selenium load, with a total of $14,320 changing hands. See Austin, Designing a Nonpoint Source Selenium Load Trading Program, 25 Harv. Envtl. L. Rev. 337 (2001).

8. **The TMDLs are coming.** Controlling a toxic pollutant such as selenium may, by itself, be sufficiently important to overcome the usual resistance to serious limitation of nonpoint source discharges. Not all other nonpoint source pollution, such as sedimentation and nutrient loading, command the same concern and ability to raise a call to action. For nonpoint source controls and trading to become widespread, some other stimulus may be necessary. In another segment of her article on selenium trading, Susan Austin describes what that might be:

> EPA interprets the TMDL provisions of the CWA to require load allocations for nonpoint sources. The California Farm Bureau and other agricultural and timber interests disagree. The California Farm Bureau argues that nonpoint source regulation should be left to states, while the agricultural and timber industries argue that TMDLs only apply to point sources. In Pronsolino v. Marcus, 91 F. Supp. 2d 1337, 1356 (N.D. Cal. 2000), commonly known as the Garcia River Case, the United States District Court for the Northern District of California considered this issue. The Court held that TMDLs are authorized "without regard to the sources of pollution" and that EPA may withhold grant money from states that refuse to implement TMDLs for nonpoint sources. In light of this ruling, load allocations for many nonpoint sources may become more common. If so, load trading could become an important tool for many nonpoint sources dealing with regulatory caps on a wide variety of discharges. Id. at 342.

9. **Individual take quotas (ITQs).** Trading may be used in many settings, one of the more controversial of which has been as a means of regulating overfishing of commercial fish stocks. In the United States, ITQs are recognized as a fisheries management tool by statute. 16 U.S.C. §1802(21) states as follows: "The term 'individual fishing quota' [IFQ] means a Federal permit under a limited access system to harvest a quantity of fish, expressed by a unit or units representing a percentage of the total allowable catch of a fishery that may be received or held for exclusive use by a person." IFQs can be traded, presumably allowing more efficient fishers to purchase IFQs from less efficient fishers and obtain the needed economies of scale to harvest the fish profitably. IFQs are, in essence a cap-and-trade program. The cap is selected with reference to achieving an environmental goal — in the case of IFQs, a sustainable fishery. Scientific studies are (or should be) relied on to set the cap or allowable harvest to attain the environmental goal. The IFQs represent a right to harvest from the commons; emissions allowances represent a right to dispose to the commons. With IFQs, who are the entities affected? What are the factors influencing the initial distribution of IFQs? What are the alternatives open to a party not having an adequately large IFQ or enough allowances? These last three elements help explain why IFQs are very controversial — they often sound a death knell for a way of life. If a fisher is allocated too small an IFQ, operating a boat becomes uneconomic. Typically, the small family fishers will be the ones forced to sell their IFQs and retire from the industry. Driving out long-time fishing families is a particularly poignant and politically sensitive cost of sustaining the fishery using IFQs.

10. **Trading goes international: Kyoto and more.** Implementing trading schemes on an international level to tackle global problems adds multiple layers of complexity to an already challenging task. International trading of emissions rights was written into the Kyoto Protocol, an international treaty designed to reduce warming of the earth's climate from the "greenhouse" effect discussed in Chapter 26. Implementing those directives proved to be an effort of Herculean proportions. There is no international legislature to establish binding rules, which must be adopted by "consensus" or unanimity among the parties to an international instrument such as the Kyoto Protocol. There is no international executive body to police reporting and compliance. Rather, the international system must rely on self-reporting by states, which have an inherent interest in shading the truth or may have limited technical capabilities. There is, moreover, no international court of general jurisdiction to oversee enforcement or adjudicate disputes. Instead, the parties to the Protocol had to establish their own compliance procedures. In the end, the rules implementing the trading scheme in the Kyoto Protocol — the Marrakesh Accords adopted in November 2001 — run to more than 200 pages of text, every word of it hammered out in a process of consensus formation amongst more than 180 states in 4 years of intense negotiations.[18]

11. **Is mercury a good candidate for either water or air trading?** Mercury is among the hazardous pollutants singled out for special treatment by Congress in the 1990 Amendments to the Clean Air Act. See 43 U.S.C. §§7412(b)(1) and (c)(6). The major sources of mercury in the aquatic environment are airborne deposition of mercury

---

18. See UN Doc. FCCC/CP/2001/13/Adds. 1–4 (2002), http://unfccc.int/cop7/documents/accords_draft.pdf.

released by coal combustion and waterborne discharges from POTWs. One of mercury's important human exposure pathways is through its bioaccumulation in fish consumed by humans. This aspect of mercury's "fate and transport" characteristics, standing alone, suggests that mercury trading has significant potential to create "hotspot" problems. The Bush II Administration nevertheless has proposed mercury trading for both air and water. In regard to water, despite the express language in the January 2003 policy stating that "EPA does not currently support trading of pollutants considered by EPA to be persistent bioaccumulative toxics (PBTs)," a later portion of the EPA policy suggests that "pilot projects may be appropriate where the predominant loads do not come from point sources, trading achieves a substantial reduction of the PBT traded and...trading does not cause an exceedance of an aquatic life or human health criterion." 68 Fed. Reg. at 1610. EPA has announced a pilot trading project along the Sacramento River to reduce mercury discharges to the watershed from unregulated or hard-to-regulate sources.

The proposal for mercury trading in air emissions is surprising because EPA's previous failure to require mercury emissions MACT controls under §7412(d)(2) had been found to violate the clear meaning of the CAA. See National Lime Ass'n v. EPA, 233 F.3d 625 (D.C. Cir. 2000).

Chapter 15

TECHNOLOGY-FORCING STANDARDS

A. *Reducing Auto Emissions Through Technology-Forcing*

B. *International Technology-Forcing: The Phaseout of Ozone-Depleting Substances*

Any of the regulatory strategies analyzed in this coursebook, if sufficiently stringent, might operate to force the development of new technology. This chapter focuses on standards set by legislatures with the direct intent to force the development of new technology — either by limiting releases of a target substance to lower amounts than can be achieved with currently available technology or by banning some or all uses of a substance to force the invention of substitutes. Insofar as government seeks to achieve technology-forcing through a complete prohibition on manufacture or use (sometimes referred to as "sunsetting" a dangerous substance), technology-forcing simultaneously acts as a roadblock to continuation of the commercial activity (see Chapter 16) while encouraging the development of new alternatives. Like roadblock statutes, product bans are crude, blunt instruments that frequently contain mitigating devices in order to gain acceptance by the regulated public. Some of these flexibility mechanisms are lead times for product phaseout, waivers, hardship variances, and sympathetic enforcement. In addition, market-based approaches noted in Chapter 14, such as the use of marketable permits, excise taxes, and governmental purchasing power, can effectively support technology-forcing.

Because the U.S. legal system discourages potential curtailment of economic activity, technology-forcing is often a last regulatory resort. Judge Jasen's recommendation in *Boomer* that the defendant be forced to develop and adopt new pollution control technology was rejected by the majority. The following statement by the Fifth Circuit Court of Appeals in Corrosion Proof Fittings v. EPA, 947 F.2d 1201 (1991),[1] typifies the prevailing judicial skepticism regarding technology-forcing:

> As a general matter we agree with the EPA that a product ban can lead to great innovation, and it is true that an agency [under the Toxic Substances Control Act] as under other regulatory statutes, is empowered to issue safety standards which require improvements in existing technology or which require the development of new technology. As even the EPA acknowledges, however, when no adequate substitutes currently exist, the EPA cannot fail to consider this lack when formulating its own guidelines. Under ToSCA, therefore, the EPA must present a stronger case to justify the ban, as opposed to regulation, of products with no substitutes. 947 F.2d at 1221.

---

1. In this case, the court overturned EPA's ban on the use of asbestos in almost all products.

It appears that administrative technology-forcing will be judicially condoned only where a regulatory agency has exhausted all other regulatory alternatives for controlling a demonstrably intolerable material. See Ethyl Corp. v. EPA, 541 F.2d 1 (D.C. Cir. 1976) (upholding EPA's phaseout of lead in gasoline).

In the relatively few situations where technology-forcing has been attempted, industry has been successful in developing innovative technology that has significantly reduced the environmental threat. In addition to the auto emissions reduction and CFC phaseout case studies presented below, the following regulatory efforts are examples of effective technology-forcing: EPA's prohibition of the commercial distribution and manufacture of PCBs, EPA's phased reduction leading to a prohibition on the use of lead in gasoline (see Ethyl Corp. v. EPA above.), OSHA's drastic reduction in the occupational exposure standard for lead, and the prohibition of phosphate detergents by many state and local governments.[2] It may be that technology-forcing has generally been successful because legislatures and regulatory agencies "hedge their bets" when forcing technology. For example, when Congress enacted the strict 1970 reductions in permissible tailpipe emissions, it was aware that the catalytic converter technology had been developed and subjected to limited testing.

A. REDUCING AUTO EMISSIONS THROUGH TECHNOLOGY-FORCING

The most ambitious and controversial use of technology-forcing as a regulatory strategy to achieve environmental protection goals was the 1970 CAA's Title II, a remarkable example of a drastic, direct, numerical regulatory standard stipulated by the legislature itself, declaring that —

> emissions of carbon monoxide and hydrocarbons from light duty vehicles...manufactured during or after model year 1975 shall...require a reduction of at least 90 per centum from emissions allowable...in model year 1970.[3] CAA §202(b)(1)(a) (1970).

International Harvester v. Ruckelshaus
United States Circuit Court of Appeals
for the District of Columbia Circuit, 1973
478 F.2d 615

LEVENTHAL, C.J.... These consolidated petitions of International Harvester and the three major auto companies, Ford, General Motors, and Chrysler, seek review of a decision by the Administrator [of EPA] denying petitioners' applications...for one year suspensions of the 1975 emissions standards prescribed under the statute for light duty vehicles....

The tension of forces presented by the controversy over automobile emission standards may be focused by two central observations: (1) the automobile is an essential pillar of the American economy. Some 28 per cent of the nonfarm workforce draws its livelihood from the automobile and its products; (2) The automobile has had a devastating impact on the American

---

2. See, e.g., Procter & Gamble Corp. v. Chicago, 509 F.2d 69 (7th Cir. 1975), cert. denied, 421 U.S. 978 (1976) (upholding Chicago's phosphate detergent ban against a dormant Commerce Clause challenge).

3. The Act applied the same specific rollback to nitrogen oxides starting in the 1976 model year.

FIGURE 15-1
A modern urban scene with air pollution caused by automobile emissions. This could be any one of the more than four dozen American cities that are consistently in violation of federal air quality standards due to hydrocarbons, nitrogen oxides, and carbon monoxide produced by automobiles.

environment. As of 1970, authoritative voices stated that "automotive pollution constitutes in excess of 60% of our national air pollution problem" and more than 80 per cent of the air pollutants in concentrated urban areas.

Congressional concern over the problem of automotive emissions dates back to the 1950s, but it was not until the passage of the Clean Air Act in 1965 that Congress established the principle of Federal standards for auto emissions. Under the 1965 act and its successor, the Air Quality Act of 1967, the [Federal authorities] were authorized to promulgate emission limitations commensurate with existing technological feasibility.

The development of emission control technology proceeded haltingly. The Secretary of Health, Education, and Welfare testified in 1967 that "the state of the art has tended to meander along until some sort of regulation took it by the hand and gave it a good pull.... There has been a long period of waiting for it, and it hasn't worked very well."

The legislative background must also take into account the fact that in 1969 the Department of Justice brought suit against the four largest automobile manufacturers on the grounds that they had conspired to delay the development of emission control devices.

On December 31, 1970, Congress grasped the nettle and amended the Clean Air Act to set a statutory standard for required reductions in levels of hydrocarbons (HC) and carbon monoxide (CO) which must be achieved for 1975 models of light duty vehicles. Section 202(b) of the Act...provides that, beginning with the 1975 model year, exhaust emission of HC and CO from light duty vehicles must be reduced at least 90 per cent from the permissible emission levels in the 1970 year. In accordance with the Congressional directives, the Administrator...promulgated regulations limiting HC and CO emissions from 1975 model light duty vehicles to .41 and 3.4 grams per mile respectively....[4]

4. This was a default standard; some car models that were cleaner had even tougher standards. The same regulation also prescribed an interim 3.0 grams per mile 1975 standard for nitrogen oxides (NOx). HC and NOx combine with sunlight to produce photochemical oxidants (ozone), also known as "smog." [Eds.]

Congress was aware that these 1975 standards were "drastic medicine" designed to "force the state of the art." There was, naturally, concern whether the manufacturers would be able to achieve this goal. Therefore, Congress provided...a "realistic escape hatch": the manufacturers could petition the EPA for a one-year suspension of the 1975 requirements, and Congress took the precaution of directing the National Academy of Sciences to undertake an ongoing study of the feasibility of compliance with the emission standards. The "escape hatch" provision addressed itself to the possibility that the NAS study or other evidence might indicate that the standards would be unachievable despite all good faith efforts at compliance.[5] This provision was limited to a one-year suspension....

[The EPA Administrator rejected petitioners' applications for suspensions on the ground that petitioners had not established the unavailability of control technology that could meet the stricter standards. The NAS Report concluded that the necessary control technology was not available.]

Two principal considerations compete for our attention. On the one hand, if suspension is not granted, and the prediction of the EPA that effective technology will be available is proven incorrect, grave economic consequences could ensue.... On the other hand, if suspension is granted, and it later is shown that the Administrator's prediction of feasibility was achievable in 1975 there may be irretrievable ecological costs. It is to this second possibility to which we first turn.

The most authoritative estimate in the record of the ecological costs of a one-year suspension is that of the NAS Report. [The NAS concluded that]

...the effect on total emissions of a one-year suspension with no additional interim standards appears to be small. The effect is not more significant because the emission reduction now required of model year 1974 vehicles, as compared with uncontrolled vehicles (80 percent for HC and 69 percent for CO), is already so substantial.

[The court added that because the technology being tested to meet the 1975 standards would cause fuel economy, acceleration, and "driveability" problems, while adding significantly to the cost of new motor vehicles, "a drop-off in purchase of 1975 cars will result in a prolonged use of older cars with less efficient pollution control devices.... It might even come to pass that total actual emissions (of all cars in use) would be greater under the 1975 than the 1974 standards."]

We also note that it is the belief of many experts — both in and out of the automobile industry — that air pollution cannot be effectively checked until the industry finds a substitute for the conventional automotive power plant — the reciprocating internal combustion (i.e., "piston") engine. According to this view, the conventional unit is a "dirty" engine. While emissions from such a motor can be "cleaned" by various thermal and catalytic converter devices, these devices do nothing to decrease the production of emissions in the engine's combustion chambers. The automobile industry has a multi-billion-dollar investment in the conventional engine, and it has been reluctant to introduce new power plants or undertake major modifications of the conventional one. Thus the bulk of the industry's work on emission control has focused narrowly on converter devices. It is clear from the legislative history that Congress expected the Clean Air Act Amendments to force the industry to broaden the scope of its research — to study new types of engines and new control systems. Perhaps even a one-year suspension does not give the industry sufficient time to develop a new approach to emission control and still meet the absolute deadline of 1976. If so, there will be ample time for the EPA

---

5. The suspension provision also included a criterion that the suspension must be "essential to the public interest or the public health and welfare of the United States." [Eds.]

and Congress, between now and 1976 to reflect on changing the statutory approach. This kind of cooperation, a unique three-way partnership between the legislature, executive, and judiciary, was contemplated by the Congress and is apparent in the provisions of the Act....

If the automobiles of Ford, General Motors and Chrysler cannot meet the 1975 standards..., the Administrator of EPA has the theoretical authority...to shut down the auto industry, as was clearly recognized in the Congressional debate. We cannot put blinders on the facts before us so as to omit awareness of reality that this authority would undoubtedly never be exercised, in light of the fact that approximately 1 out of every 7 jobs in this country is dependent on the production of the automobile. Senator Muskie, the principal sponsor of the bill, stated quite clearly in the debate on the Act that he envisioned the Congress acting if an auto industry shutdown were in sight....

This case is haunted by the irony that what seems to be Ford's technological lead may operate to its grievous detriment, assuming the relaxation-if-necessary [of the standards]. If...any one of the three major companies cannot meet the 1975 standards, it is a likelihood that standards will be set to permit the higher level of emission control achievable by the laggard. This will be the case whether or not the leader has or has not achieved compliance with the 1975 standards. Even if the relaxation is later made industry-wide, the Government's action, in first imposing a standard not generally achievable and then relaxing it, is likely to be detrimental to the leader who has tooled up to meet a higher standard than will ultimately be required.

In some contexts high achievement bestows the advantage that rightly belongs to the leader, of high quality. In this context before us, however, the high achievement in emission control results, under systems presently available, in lessened car performance — an inverse correlation. The competitive disadvantage to the ecological leader presents a forbidding outcome...for which we see no remedy.... [The court remanded the case to EPA for reconsideration of its denial of suspension.]

COMMENTARY & QUESTIONS

1. **Was this really technology-forcing?** Is technology-forcing legislation credible when the bill's sponsor assures his colleagues that the "hammer" (shutdown of large auto manufacturers) will never be allowed to fall? Is it any wonder that the auto industry did not take the threat seriously and instead continued to tinker with add-on devices that would require little modification of existing automobiles and could later be abandoned if Congress changed its mind? In fact, the "three-way partnership" among the legislature, executive branch, and judiciary acted to postpone compliance far beyond the one-year suspension. On remand, EPA granted the extension for both the HC and the CO standards, but promulgated interim standards for 1975 of 1.4 and 15 gpms (grams per mile) respectively.

EPA granted a one-year suspension of the 1976 NOx (nitrogen oxides) standard of 0.2 gpms and set an interim standard of 2 gpms. Through a combination of congressional extensions and congressionally authorized EPA suspensions, the HC and CO standards, based on a 90% rollback, were not finally met until 1980 and 1983 respectively. Congress abandoned the 0.2 gpm NOx standard in 1977 and, in its place, imposed a 1 gpm standard to be met in 1984. By the mid-1980s, the auto industry was willing to accept the standards because market demand was moving toward smaller, less-polluting, and more fuel-efficient vehicles.

Was this an example of successful technology-forcing? Or was the final attainment of the 1975 and 1976 standards merely accidental?[6] Was attainment "too little, too late"?

2. **Why the denial?** Why did EPA deny the one-year suspension, knowing that its decision was in conflict with the prestigious NAS Report and sensing the lack of congressional support for strict deadlines and draconic enforcement? EPA must have realized that its denial would be overturned by a court or Congress (or both, as it turned out). Is it possible that although EPA wanted to censure the auto industry for its failure to make a genuine effort to consider new technology and its alleged conspiracy to suppress new technology, the agency believed that it would have been politically inexpedient to try to prove that the auto industry had violated the requirement of making "all good faith efforts" to meet the standards?

3. **Rewarding the laggard and the risks of leading the way.** Was the court correct in its assumption that a company making good faith efforts to comply with the standards would inevitably be disadvantaged by a standard relaxation dictated by the overall public interest? Whenever standards are set and then reset at different levels, parties that comply quickly may suffer unintended penalties. What if standards are tightened after a company has invested in new technology in order to meet the first change in the standard? What if a rollback approach is taken after one firm has already reduced its emissions? Both situations pose serious interpolluter equity problems that a regulatory scheme should address. (Another approach to this problem is found in §306(d) of the CWA, which provides that a new source of water pollution that has achieved its New Source Performance Standards cannot be subject to stricter standards for ten years or the depreciation or amortization period of the facility, whichever ends first.) What about using incentives such as tax deductions or preferential governmental purchasing to add inducements to early compliance?

4. **The court's balancing test.** Note that the court's cost-benefit analysis followed Talbot Page's recommendation in Chapter 1 that the costs of false negatives be weighed against the costs of false positives in making environmental regulatory decisions. In this case, as analyzed by the court, the cost of a false negative (not granting the suspension when it should have been granted) was relatively high in economic terms, while the cost of a false positive (granting the suspension when it should not have been) was relatively low in environmental terms. Given the broad "public interest" test articulated by Congress, balancing the costs of potential erroneous decisions appears to have been justified. But did the court conduct the balance fairly in light of the fact that the one-year extension was not a firm one, making further slippage predictable?

5. **Types of technology-forcing mechanisms.** Note that, in the case of auto emission controls, Congress itself set the standards based on technology-forcing, instead of delegating standard setting to the experts at EPA. With regard to the phaseout of lead in gasoline, on the other hand, Congress generally delegated to EPA the authority to control or prohibit fuel additives (42 U.S.C. §7545(c)), and EPA did the rest. Why did Congress retain direct control of auto emission standard setting? Because it wanted to

---

6. One serendipitous result of the standards was the EPA phaseout of leaded gasoline; lead poisons the catalytic converter. [Eds.]

ensure that the standards could be modified quickly if they proved to be unachievable? Because it was afraid that EPA would be unable to resist the political power of the auto industry? Because it wanted to take primary credit for responding to this important issue?

6. **The 1990 CAA Amendments, technology-forcing, and auto pollution.** By 1987, emissions of HC, CO, and lead from new cars had dropped by over 95% from uncontrolled levels, and emissions of NOx dropped by over 75%, but increases in automobile use caused ambient air quality standards for ozone to be exceeded in many urban areas.[7] With the lessons of its 1970 technology-forcing effort firmly in mind, in 1990 Congress adopted a more sophisticated but still aggressive technology-forcing strategy to cope with ozone nonattainment problems.

> **Henry Waxman, Gregory Wetstone, and Phillip Barnett, Cars, Fuels and Clean Air: A Review of Title II of the Clean Air Act Amendments of 1990**
> 21 Environmental Law 1947, 1991–2004 (1991)

A major innovation in Title II is the clean-fuel vehicle program, contained in new part C. This program requires the use of a new generation of "clean fuel vehicles" in the most heavily polluted cities. These vehicles, which must meet emission standards eighty percent below today's standards, will often run on clean alternative fuels, such as natural gas, ethanol, or even electricity....

The clean-fuel requirements for light-duty vehicles and light-duty trucks in the final legislation have three central components. First, new sections 242 through 245 establish special emission standards for clean-fuel vehicles. Second, new §246 establishes a program to require the use of clean-fuel vehicles in centrally fueled fleets in polluted cities. Finally, new §249 establishes a large-scale program to introduce clean-fuel vehicles to the passenger car market in California.

Section 242 of the Act requires EPA to set emission standards for clean-fuel vehicles in two years. These standards...mandate a [sixty and later an] eighty percent reduction in exhaust emissions of organic gasses and NOx from today's already controlled levels. They are intended to develop a new generation of clean vehicles, in a fuel-neutral manner. The most heavily polluted cities must reduce aggregate emissions of VOCS [volatile organics] and NOx by sixty to eighty percent from today's levels — and keep them there notwithstanding future economic and population growth — to attain the federal health standard for ozone. This is an immense undertaking, made more immense by the fact that most polluted cities have already adopted most of the obvious control measures. It cannot be accomplished unless vehicle emissions are cut drastically. Indeed, Los Angeles, the most polluted city in the country, cannot achieve attainment by 2010 without the widespread use of zero-emission, electric vehicles.

The standards for clean-fuel vehicles reflect this imperative.... In percent terms, this [eighty percent reduction] is equivalent to the level of technology-forcing required by the 1970 amendments. Under the new clean-fuel standards, organic gas and NOx emissions will be reduced ninety-eight percent below uncontrolled levels.

Meeting these standards will necessitate major advances in vehicles and fuels. Unlike any standards previously established, the final standards appear unachievable by vehicles running on conventional gasoline. They probably can be met by vehicles that use reformulated gasoline,

---

7. Nearly 50% of the U.S. population lives in areas with unhealthy levels of ozone, and approximately half of all ozone is produced by automobiles. [Eds.]

but only if manufacturers develop an additional "preheated" catalyst to capture the emissions that occur during the first seconds of operation. Vehicles built to run on alternative fuels like natural gas, ethanol, or methanol are also likely to meet the standards....

The 1990 amendments establish two programs to require the use of clean-fuel vehicles meeting the [emissions] standards.... One is for fleet vehicles and one is for passenger cars in California.

The fleet program...requires clean-fuel vehicles to be used by the owners of centrally fueled fleets of ten or more vehicles in serious, severe, and extreme ozone nonattainment areas. Examples of centrally fueled fleets are fleets of delivery vans, taxicabs, or school buses that regularly refuel at a common location. When the program is fully phased in, it is expected to cover 250,000 vehicles per year.... By model year 2000, seventy percent of the new vehicles purchased by covered fleet operators must be clean-fuel vehicles.... To ensure that the clean-fuel vehicles run on the clean fuels for which they are designed, the [fleet owners must] fuel the vehicles exclusively with clean fuels....

Ultimately, clean-fuel vehicles must penetrate the passenger-car market to achieve major reductions in air pollution. For this reason, the second clean-fuel program in part C establishes a mandatory pilot program in California that will introduce clean-fuel vehicles to the passenger-car market....

Developing a successful alternative fuels program is often said to pose a "chicken and egg" problem. Car makers argue that they should not be forced to make clean-fuel vehicles until clean fuels are widely available. Oil companies argue the converse: they should not be forced to make clean fuels until clean-fuel vehicles are widely available. Both sides argue that even if the vehicles and fuels are available, there is no guarantee that the consumer will buy them.

The fleet program...tackles this problem through a demand-side approach: it requires fleet operators to buy clean-fuel vehicles and to refuel them with clean fuels. These requirements create a built-in demand that overcomes the "chicken and egg" issue. In the case of the passenger car market, however, it is not practical to mandate that a certain percentage of consumers buy only clean-fuel vehicles. Instead, the California pilot program takes a supply-side approach to ensuring the use of both clean-fuel vehicles and clean fuels.

The California pilot program mandates that vehicle manufacturers produce and sell minimum volumes of clean-fuel vehicles in California. [The California Air Resources Board has determined that two percent of the cars offered for sale in the 1998 model year must be electric, rising to five percent in 2001 and ten percent in 2003.]

The "production mandate" in the California program makes it the obligation of the vehicle manufacturer to ensure that the vehicles find their way into the consumer's garage. The program thus capitalizes on the enormous capacity of manufacturers to influence vehicle purchases. Car companies control the most important factors that affect consumer purchases: they determine how well the vehicle will perform, what its styling will look like, how the vehicle is advertised, and at what price the vehicle will sell. The production mandate forces manufacturers to develop and market a vehicle that consumers will want to buy — which is exactly the incentive that is needed to make the clean-fuel program a success.

COMMENTARY & QUESTIONS

1. **Auto emissions control since 1990.** Once again, implementation of technology-forcing legislation in the auto emissions control area has not gone smoothly. The CAA preempts state regulation of emissions from new automobiles except for California — the only "extreme" ozone nonattainment area — which can

petition EPA for a preemption waiver. Other states may "piggyback" on the California standards under certain conditions.[8] Most of the judicial activity in this area has involved the attempt by several of the 12 northeastern states and the District of Columbia, organized as the Ozone Transport Commission (OTC), to adopt the California standards in whole or part. As indicated above, the California Air Resources Board (CARB) initially determined that 2% of the cars offered for sale in California in the 1998 model year had to be Zero Emission Vehicles (ZEVs) powered by electricity, rising to 5% in 2001 and 10% in 2003 (model year 2004). New York and Massachusetts adopted this program (called California-Low-Emission Vehicle, or CAL-LEV) virtually intact. In 1996, however, CARB, accepting the arguments of the automobile manufacturers that advanced battery technology for practicably fueling electric vehicles was unavailable, repealed the 1998 and 2001 requirements, while retaining the requirement that the manufacturers include ZEVs as 10% of their California sales in 2003. This CAL-LEV modification left New York and Massachusetts, which had adopted the original CARB standards, out on a limb. See, e.g., American Auto. Mfrs. Ass'n v. New York Dep't of Envtl. Protection, 152 F.3d 196 (2d Cir. 1998) (New York's ZEV quotas, replicating California's initial quotas, do not satisfy the "identicality" requirement because California modified its quotas for 1998-2002).

In 2001, CARB, concerned about the marketability of battery-powered electric vehicles, again modified its requirement that major auto manufacturers include ZEVs as 10% of their California auto fleets in 2003. The 2001 rules retained the 10% ZEV target for 2003 but changed the ways by which auto manufacturers could meet it: 2% were required to be full-sized ZEVs, powered by electric batteries or hydrogen fuel cells; another 2% could be natural gas-powered or hybrid vehicles; while the remaining 6% could be a mixture of gasoline-powered Ultra Low-Emission Vehicles (ULEVs). Under pressure from a federal preemption lawsuit brought by automobile manufacturers against the 2001 CAL-LEV modifications, CARB adopted new 2003 ZEV regulations offering two new compliance paths: (1) a "base path" in which 10% of auto fleets sold in California, from 2005 through 2008, must be ZEVs (i.e., a mixture of cars powered by hydrogen or electricity, hybrid electric-gas and hydrogen-gas vehicles, and ULEVs), with a ZEV quota increasing to 11% for the 2009–2011 model years and to 16% in the 2018 model year; and (2) an "alternate path" obligating manufacturers to offer fixed minimum annual quotas of hydrogen fuel cell vehicles in the California market — 250 between 2005 and 2008, 2500 between 2009 and 2011, 25,000 between 2012 and 2014, and 50,000 between 2015 and 2017. Despite CARB's vacillation regarding CAL-LEV standards, four of the OTC states — Maine, Massachusetts, New York, and Vermont — have opted to follow the California regulations.

Has the California preemption waiver created a chaotic implementation climate with regard to the technology-forcing strategies in the 1990 CAA Amendments? Is CARB

---

8. The California preemption waiver and other state "piggyback" provisions can be found at 42 U.S.C. §§7543 and 7589. See also Motor Vehicle Mfrs. Ass'n of the U.S. v. New York State Dep't of Conservation, 15 F.3d 521 (2d Cir. 1993) (substantially upholding New York's adoption of the California program), and Association of Int'l Auto. Mfrs. Inc. v. Massachusetts Dep't of Envtl. Protection, 208 F.3d 1 (1st Cir. 2000) (striking down Massachusetts's adoption of the California ZEV mandates for 1998-2002 for lack of "identicality"). See the discussion of the latter decision and other cases of preemption of state automobile regulations, in Chapter 6.

merely reacting to technological change rather than stimulating it? Will the confusing demands caused by this "moving target" be counterproductive? Should the preemption waiver be repealed? Or has CARB's resolute but mercurial approach to auto pollution control been one factor in persuading the auto industry to develop an entirely new technology — the hydrogen car?

2. The hydrogen car is approaching: Does it need a push? Or is it going too fast? In the long run, automobiles probably will be powered by fuel cells, made with platinum-coated membranes that convert hydrogen and oxygen into electricity and emit only water vapor and hydrogen as residuals. Many of the technological obstacles to introducing an environmentally benign hydrogen-powered internal combustion engine into the commercial automobile market have already been surmounted, except for designing relatively clean hydrogen production systems and viable distribution networks. Hydrogen will be manufactured initially from gasoline or natural gas, which might result in exacerbated greenhouse gas emissions as well as development of natural gas resources located in sensitive environmental areas. (Hydrogen can be created by first producing electricity and then running it through water using a process called electrolysis, which separates the oxygen and hydrogen molecules.)

In his 2003 State of the Union speech, President George W. Bush announced a "FreedomFUEL" initiative to assist in researching and developing technologies for hydrogen fuel production and distribution infrastructure. This new initiative supplements the "FreedomCAR" program, announced in 2002, which was intended to facilitate the development of hydrogen-powered vehicles. The announced goal of these federal subsidy (nearly $2 billion over five years) programs is to make affordable fuel cell vehicles available to the public by 2020.

The Bush II Administration proposals, however, do not guarantee that these vehicles will in fact be available by 2020. Should technology-forcing, in addition to governmental research and development subsidies, be employed in order to develop hydrogen-powered automobiles more quickly? The answer appears to be that technology-forcing is unnecessary because the automobile industry has accepted the inevitable transition from petroleum to hydrogen-powered automobiles. Previous technology-forcing lawmaking has convinced the auto manufacturers (as has the inexorable rise in ozone levels in the cities of the developing world) to abandon their inveterate opposition to technological change in automobile design and instead to maximize the commercial opportunities inherent in hydrogen car development. There is currently fierce international competition to produce and demonstrate hydrogen-powered cars, with every major auto manufacturer — either alone or in consortium with other companies — demonstrating a hydrogen-powered prototype vehicle.

Critics of the Bush II Administration proposals argue that ignoring the emissions and energy use involved in producing and delivering hydrogen fuel undervalues the environmental advantages of hybrid petroleum-electric powered vehicles (HEVs), which are now available. At least until we learn to extract hydrogen from water through the use of green technologies, such as wind and solar power, contend these critics, a hydrogen fuel-cell vehicle is no better than a diesel hybrid in terms of total energy use and greenhouse gas emissions. Moreover, some scientists are concerned that apart from the process of manufacturing hydrogen, the leakage of hydrogen fuel from automobile use might have major adverse environmental impacts. The hydrogen cycle is incompletely understood. Researchers at California Institute of Technology have warned that

> the widespread use of hydrogen fuel cells could have hitherto unknown impacts due to unintended emissions of molecular hydrogen, including an increase in the abundance of water vapor in the stratosphere.... This would cause atmospheric cooling, enhancement of the heterogeneous chemistry that destroys ozone, an increase in noctilucent clouds, and changes in tropospheric chemistry and atmosphere-biosphere interactions. Tromp et al., Potential Environmental Impact of a Hydrogen Economy on the Stratosphere, 300 Science 1740–1742 (2003).

In the short term, perhaps we need technology-forcing and subsidies for the further development and introduction of HEVs, while performing research on (1) "the emissions that could be produced by a hydrogen economy," (2) ways in which "such emissions could be limited and made negligible, although at some cost against which potential environmental impacts must be balanced," and (3) the possibility that soil uptake of increased hydrogen emissions "could entirely compensate for new anthropogenic emissions." Id.

3. **Technology-forcing for fuel efficiency.** Until a hydrogen-powered automobile is widely available, reductions in auto emissions, decreased dependence on foreign oil imports, and petroleum extraction in environmentally sensitive areas can be achieved not only by emissions controls but also by increasing automobile fuel efficiency. During the 1970s, when OPEC placed an oil export embargo on the United States because of political unrest in the Middle East, Congress enacted Corporate Average Fuel Economy (CAFÉ) standards, which required passenger car fleets to achieve an average of 27.5 mpg and light trucks and sport utility vehicles (SUVs) 20.7 mpg. Since Middle Eastern oil has again become abundant and America has become enamored of the SUV (which is classified as a light truck for fuel-efficiency purposes), the average mileage of vehicles sold in the United States has steadily declined. In 1995, after intense lobbying by the auto and petroleum industries and autoworker unions, Congress enacted a ban on federally funded research on increasing automobile fuel efficiency. This ban was lifted in the 2002 appropriations process, at the behest of the Bush II Administration.

In 2001, the National Research Council released a report entitled "Effectiveness and Impacts of Corporate Average Fuel Efficiency Standards," which recommended that the CAFÉ standards be made stricter because the technology exists to significantly improve vehicle fuel efficiency without reducing vehicle size or sacrificing performance. The NRC also recommended that technology-forcing be implemented with a lead time of 10 to 15 years. Opponents of stricter CAFÉ standards argue that past increases in fuel economy have led to smaller, lighter cars with decreased "crashworthiness." Other opponents predict that a tightening of CAFÉ standards would be counterproductive from a pollution control standpoint because benefits would be offset by an increase in vehicle miles traveled caused by lowering the cost of driving.

On April 1, 2003, the National Highway Traffic Safety Administration promulgated a regulation tightening the CAFÉ standard for light trucks by 1.5 mpg over three years —

i.e., from the current 20.7 mpg to 21.0 mpg for model year 2005, 21.6 for model year 2006, and 22.2 mpg for model year 2007. Is this modest change in the fuel-efficiency requirement sufficient to make a difference, or is it relatively cosmetic?

4. **Technology-forcing: the auto verdict?** The congressionally dictated 90% rollbacks in auto emissions certainly caused major disruptions in the automobile industry by derailing ongoing investment planning, rewarding laggards, forcing the companies into expensive last-minute attempts to retool the old design engines rather than being able to take the time to design new ones, and costing as much as $18 billion.[9] On balance, was it a good idea? What would the air in traffic jams probably look like today had Congress imposed a more typical harm-based or technology-based review-and-permit standard? Michael Walsh, former EPA Director of Motor Vehicle Emissions Regulation, has said that "Title II was blunt, but it was the only thing that would work.... Forcing technological development through a 'regulatory hammer' has been and continues to be the only demonstrated way to succeed." Telephone interview, Oct. 16, 1991. It is doubtful whether any regulatory device but the blunt, powerful instrument of technology-forcing would have ultimately achieved results that were virtually unthinkable during the 1970s: the advent of an entirely different, nonpetroleum fuel system for powering automobiles.

B. INTERNATIONAL TECHNOLOGY-FORCING: THE PHASEOUT OF OZONE-DEPLETING SUBSTANCES

The auto emissions case study shows that technology-forcing, which is inherently problematic as a regulatory strategy, becomes increasingly difficult when multiple jurisdictions are involved in setting and implementing standards. If this has been true in the United States, where Congress can preempt state legislation, it is almost inconceivable that technology-forcing could be effective in the international arena, where there is no universal legislature (see Chapters 8 and 26). The improbability of successful international technology-forcing, therefore, underscores the magnificent diplomatic and legal accomplishments of those individuals and nations that negotiated the Montreal Protocol on Substances that Deplete the Ozone Layer.

In 1974 scientists hypothesized that the stratospheric ozone layer protecting the earth from destructive solar ultraviolet radiation was being destroyed by human-generated CFCs (chlorofluorocarbons from refrigeration systems, air conditioners, and other pressurized products). A decade later a huge "hole" — a dramatic seasonal thinning in the ozone layer not predicted by computer models — appeared over Antarctica. Domestic and international environmental law reacted to this threat in three principal legal initiatives:

- Domestic national regulations implementing the international agreements; Amendments to the CAA were adopted in 1977 and 1990 to implement the Protocol in the United States, with other countries adopting analogous policies;

---

9. L. White, The Regulation of Air Pollutant Emissions from Motor Vehicles 64 (1982).

- The 1985 Vienna Convention for the Protection of the Ozone Layer, a so-called framework or umbrella agreement designed to facilitate exchange of information and cooperation in research and to create a setting for further policy discussions among states; and
- The 1987 Montreal Protocol on Substances that Deplete the Ozone Layer, an ancillary agreement to the Vienna Convention that contains substantive regulatory measures to protect the ozone layer.

Despite numerous impediments and setbacks, the legal history of stratospheric ozone has largely been a success story. The U.S. National Oceanic and Atmospheric Administration now reports that the ozone layer is expected to recover by the middle of the twenty-first century. The following excerpt describes both the international negotiation of the Montreal Protocol and the tensions between the U.S. Congress and Executive Branch over the terms of the agreement.

Steven Shimberg, Stratospheric Ozone and Climate Protection: Domestic Legislation and the International Process
21 Environmental Law 2175 (1991)

Ozone is a toxic compound consisting of three oxygen atoms. It is also the only gas in the atmosphere that prevents harmful solar ultraviolet radiation from reaching the surface of the Earth.... Most of the Earth's atmosphere resides in the stratosphere — the region extending from approximately six miles to thirty miles above the Earth's surface. It is this stratospheric ozone layer that serves as Earth's main shield against harmful solar radiation. A decrease in stratospheric ozone produces an increase in the amount of ultraviolet radiation that reaches the Earth. Increased exposure to solar radiation results in increased incidence of skin cancer, cataracts, and may cause suppression of the immune system. Increased ultraviolet radiation has also been shown to damage crops and marine resources.[10]

Prior to anthropogenic influences, the destruction and creation of stratospheric ozone occurred as part of a natural continuing process that maintained a relatively constant amount of ozone in the stratosphere. The introduction of CFCs and similar manufactured substances, however, upset the natural balance of nature. These persistent, stable compounds are not destroyed in the troposphere but survive and rise up into the atmosphere, where the sun's radiation breaks them apart, releasing the chlorine atoms that are integral parts of the molecules. The released chlorine then reacts with ozone to form chlorine monoxide and oxygen, and in the process, destroys ozone molecules.

In addition to the role CFCs play in destroying the stratospheric ozone layer, CFCs are also connected to the global climate change that is predicted to occur as a result of an intensified greenhouse effect.... CFCs are estimated to account for a substantial portion of the problem — from fifteen to twenty percent....

In 1974, Drs. Sherwood Rowland and Mario Molina, from the University of California, published a paper demonstrating how CFCs destroy ozone in the atmosphere.[11] In this country, the original scientific theory prompted Congress to include, in the Clean Air Act Amendments

---

10. At ground level, ozone is a criteria pollutant, regulated as such under the CAA as discussed in Chapter 11. The problem of protecting the stratospheric ozone should be distinguished from that of combating photochemical smog at the Earth's surface. [Eds.]

11. Molina & Rowland, Stratospheric Sink for Chlorofluoromethanes: Chlorine Atom-Catalysed Destruction of Ozone, 249 Nature 810 (1974). Drs. Molina and Rowland received the 1995 Nobel Prize in chemistry for this research. [Eds.]

of 1977, a provision authorizing the Administrator of EPA to regulate "any substance...which in his judgment may reasonably be anticipated to affect the stratosphere, especially ozone in the stratosphere, and such effect may reasonably be anticipated to endanger public health or welfare." In 1978, the EPA and the Food and Drug Administration promulgated a ban on the use of CFCs in most aerosols [e.g., in cans of hair spray or deodorant]. There were [then] no measurements of actual ozone loss, just the scientific theory.

Recognizing the problem, industry began to look for safe substitutes. Progress was being made when, in the early 1980s, Ronald Reagan became President of the United States; the threat of further government regulation subsided; the search for substitutes came to a virtual stand-still; and worldwide use of CFCs continued to grow. Despite the aerosol ban in the United States, nonaerosol uses of CFCs in this country [e.g., in refrigerators and automobile air-conditioners] grew to record high levels and per capita use of CFCs in the United States reached levels that were among the highest in the world. By the middle of the 1980s, the United States was producing approximately 700 million pounds of CFCs each year, roughly one-third of the world total.

In 1985, scientists discovered a significant loss of stratospheric ozone over a large portion of the southern hemisphere. The affected area was approximately the size of North America. This collapse of the stratospheric ozone layer was not predicted by any of the scientific theories or models. Measurements of what had become a seasonal phenomenon revealed losses of greater than fifty percent in the total column of stratospheric and tropospheric ozone and greater than ninety-five percent in stratospheric ozone between an altitude of fifteen to twenty kilometers — nine to twelve miles. The discovery of this "hole" in the stratospheric ozone layer over Antarctica gave renewed impetus to international and domestic efforts to understand and protect the ozone layer....

A new round of international negotiations was scheduled to begin in December 1986.... On February 19, 1987, legislation was introduced in the Senate to impose unilateral controls on the production and use of CFCs and related compounds such as methyl chloroform, carbon tetrachloride, and hydrochlorofluorocarbons (HCFCs). Trade restrictions were included in the bill as a means of forcing other nations to adopt comparable programs to curb CFCs and to avoid placing the domestic industries that would be subject to controls at a competitive disadvantage in the world marketplace [in a manner similar to the Pelly and Packwood Amendments discussed in Chapter 8 – Eds.].

As the international negotiations progressed through the spring and summer of 1987, congressional pressure and the attention of the national news media remained focused on the activities of the U.S. delegation. At a May 1987 congressional hearing, the U.S. negotiators were reminded that they were being watched carefully, encouraged to resist efforts to weaken the U.S. negotiating position, and urged to continue to press for virtual elimination of CFCs. At that hearing, representatives of EPA reviewed the results of a six volume risk assessment that had been prepared by the Agency. They also presented the results of recent studies that showed the overwhelming positive cost-benefit ratio associated with elimination of CFCs and related compounds.

The date of May 29, 1987 represents a watershed for proponents of stringent CFC controls. On that day, the news media published reports of recent efforts by Secretary of the Interior Donald Hodel to revoke the authority of the U.S. delegation to negotiate significant reductions in the production and use of ozone-destroying compounds. The Washington Post's front page headline read: "Administration Ozone Policy May Favor Sunglasses, Hats; Support for Chemical Cutbacks Reconsidered."... The public outcry was prompt and furious. The opponents of mandated reductions in the production and use of ozone destroying compounds had created a backlash that virtually guaranteed the imposition of stringent controls....

In accordance with Article 2, section 2 of the U.S. Constitution, the international negotiations that led to the September 1987 signing of the Montreal Protocol on Substances that Deplete the Ozone Layer (the Protocol) and the June 1990 agreement in London to strengthen the Protocol were conducted by the Executive Branch of the United States Government. Throughout the negotiations, however, the U.S. Congress was proceeding on a parallel track with domestic legislative proposals designed to protect the stratospheric ozone layer — the thin atmospheric shield that safeguards life on Earth from dangerous ultraviolet radiation.

On September 16, 1987, more than two dozen nations concluded negotiations and signed the Montreal Protocol on Substances that Deplete the Ozone Layer. Signatories to the Protocol, including the United States, agreed to respond to the threat of global ozone depletion by imposing limits on consumption — defined as production plus imports minus exports of bulk quantities — of CFCs....

Within two weeks after the Protocol was negotiated and signed..., the causal link between CFCs and the Antarctic ozone "hole" was substantiated. Efforts to reopen the negotiations and strengthen the terms of the agreement began almost immediately. These efforts, and efforts to impose stringent unilateral controls, received an additional push just one day after the Senate voted to approve ratification of the Protocol. On March 15, 1988, the Ozone Trends Panel, a group of more than one hundred scientists from around the world, released an international study on global ozone trends. The Panel's report demonstrated that destruction of the ozone layer was not limited to remote uninhabited portions of Antarctica. Scientists observed and measured losses of ozone on a global scale, including significant losses over densely populated portions of the northern hemisphere. This and similar scientific reports created a new sense of urgency and highlighted the need for controls that went beyond those agreed to as part of the original Protocol.

The Protocol was ratified by a sufficient number of countries to enter into force on the scheduled date of January 1, 1989. Momentum for an international agreement to eliminate CFCs began to build during the spring of 1989. Several nations, including the United States, pledged to support a rapid international phase-out of CFCs. At the same time, momentum was building for the imposition of more stringent unilateral domestic controls.[12]...

In preparation for a diplomatic conference scheduled to be held in London at the end of June 1990, international negotiations to strengthen the Protocol were initiated in the summer of 1989. At the June 1990 diplomatic conference, the second meeting of the parties to the Protocol, an international agreement to strengthen the Protocol was reached.... Despite the new international agreement, Congress proceeded to enact domestic legislation that was more stringent than the newly strengthened Protocol....

The legislative proposals under consideration were more stringent than the proposed Protocol provisions that were being supported by the U.S. delegation to the international negotiations, and were designed to accomplish several objectives: first, to encourage the U.S. delegation to support a more stringent Protocol than it was otherwise prepared to support by creating a serious, viable threat of congressional enactment of more stringent domestic legislation; second, to encourage the delegations of other nations to support a more stringent protocol...by creating a...threat of [U.S.] trade sanctions; third, to eliminate the disproportionately large U.S. contribution to the problems of ozone depletion and global climate change that are created by emissions of chlorofluorocarbons (CFCs) and other ozone-destroying compounds and reestablish the United States as a world leader in matters relating to environmental protection; and finally, to

---

12. In March 1989, the Federal Republic of Germany's Bundestag unanimously decided to proceed with unilateral action and adopted legislation mandating a 95% reduction in production and use of CFCs by 1995.

force domestic industries to develop safe alternatives more quickly than would be required under the terms of the protocol.

The signing of the Protocol on September 16, 1987 was an historic event. It was, however, only "a major half-step forward." Even after the international agreement to strengthen the Protocol was reached at the Second Meeting of the Parties to the Montreal Protocol in London on June 29, 1990, the U.S. Congress proceeded to enact more stringent domestic legislation....

Throughout the effort to enact domestic legislation, [industry] opponents of unilateral action argued that such action would do nothing to help the environment; would put domestic industries at a competitive disadvantage; and would tie the hands of the U.S. government [nego-tiators].... These arguments were soundly rejected when the [U.S. Congress]...passed the 1990 [CAA] Amendments, and on November 15, 1990 President Bush signed the bill that became Public Law 101-549....

The 1990 Amendments include provisions that are more stringent than the Protocol in three major areas: first, the Amendments include an accelerated phase-out schedule for CFCs, halons, and methyl chloroform; second, the new law includes provisions to control and ulti-mately eliminate production and use of HCFCs;[13] and third, it includes provisions to eliminate emissions of ozone-destroying compounds and substitute compounds....

COMMENTARY & QUESTIONS

1. **Lessons from ozone.** The legal history of stratospheric ozone holds many crucial lessons for the future of Earth. The underlying problem originally seemed intractable and immensely costly to tackle. Alternatives to cheap and useful CFCs were not readily at hand, necessitating a leap of faith in industry's innovative capacity to identify substi-tutes. Crafting a solution required a global bargain, delicately balancing the needs of industrialized and developing countries. Fraught with scientific uncertainty, saving the ozone layer required governmental negotiators and scientists to communicate with each other in new and unfamiliar ways. Connections to apparently unrelated issues such as trade created additional complications. Since no state had domestic mecha-nisms in place adequate to the task, all the participating governments were simultaneously creating new domestic environmental law as well. The interplay among all these factors without doubt will characterize the next generations of environmental treaties.

The stratospheric ozone negotiations also invigorated a public culture of global lawmaking. Extensive press coverage of threats to the ozone layer created an unprece-dented sense of public apprehension and urgency. As one of the first major environmental agreements with serious consequences for industry, the ozone negotia-tions became a policy battleground to an extent never before experienced on the international level.[14] The ozone negotiations were also a watershed for vastly expanded

---

13. Some of the compounds that are being promoted as substitutes for CFCs, such as hydrofluorocarbons, may be safe for the ozone layer due to lack of a chlorine molecule, but due to radioactive forcing properties, are expected to contribute to an intensified greenhouse effect....

14 In opposing enhanced controls on CFCs, an industry representative publicly opined that automobile air-conditioners had "come to be regarded" as essential and therefore were untouchable as a matter of public policy. During the drafting sessions on the Protocol, a U.S. negotiator even accused one of the authors, then represent-ing an environmental advocacy organization, of "trying to take refrigerators away from our grandchildren."

participation in international negotiations by environmental organizations — in international parlance NGOs (nongovernmental organizations). Governmental negotiators accustomed to working largely behind closed doors faced new demands for accountability and transparency. Although all of this might go without saying in the United States, active public involvement in international environmental policymaking had been infrequent and sporadic before the ozone negotiations. Now that the debate is largely concluded, and resolved in favor of strict environmental controls, it is all too easy to forget how contentious this issue was during the 1980s — a cautionary lesson about currently controversial threats such as climate warming.

2. **Kick-starting the negotiations into the upper atmosphere.** As noted in the Shimberg excerpt, at the time of the negotiations of the Montreal Protocol, the CAA contained a provision, §157, added in the 1977 Amendments, that expressly anticipated and encouraged cooperative international action on protection of the stratospheric ozone layer.

> §157(b). The Administrator [of EPA] shall propose regulations for the control of any substance which in his judgment may reasonably be anticipated to affect the stratosphere, especially ozone in the stratosphere, if such effect on the stratosphere may reasonably be anticipated to endanger public health or welfare.... Not later than three months after the proposal of such regulations the Administrator shall promulgate such regulations in final form.

In 1980, the Carter Administration, after banning nonessential aerosol uses of CFCs, published an "advance notice of proposed rulemaking" stating that EPA was considering additional controls on other uses of these chemicals. In that notice, EPA stated that "continued world emissions of CFCs (chlorofluorocarbons) are still considered a significant threat to human health and the environment." 45 Fed. Reg. 66726 (Oct. 7, 1980). In 1984, the Natural Resources Defense Council, dissatisfied with the slow pace of further action under the subsequent Reagan Administration, brought suit under this provision to compel domestic regulatory action by EPA. How would you frame the complaint against the Administrator of EPA on behalf of this plaintiff? EPA proposed to settle the lawsuit and subsequently did, publishing a "stratospheric ozone protection plan" in partial response. See 51 Fed. Reg. 1257 (Jan. 10, 1986). How would you structure the settlement agreement to encourage the Executive Branch to obtain the strongest possible international agreement without relinquishing your leverage to require domestic action if international negotiations collapse or produce a poor result? How would you expect this suit and its settlement to affect the international negotiation?

3. **"Frameworking" — the road to Montreal began in Vienna.** Beginning in the late 1970s, ozone negotiators under the auspices of the United Nations Environment Program (UNEP) decided on a two-component process. One piece of work product was a so-called framework multilateral convention. Ancillary agreements, known as "protocols," containing substantive regulatory measures would be appended to the convention. The ozone umbrella treaty evolved into the Vienna Convention for the Protection of the Ozone Layer concluded in March 1985. 26 I.L.M. 1516 (1987). The Vienna Convention itself contains no substantive requirements for regulatory action to protect stratospheric ozone. The negotiation of the Vienna Convention attracted little

public attention, and the agreement might be barely worth notice if the Montreal Protocol had not followed. Negotiations on a CFC protocol, which eventually became the Montreal Protocol, proceeded simultaneously with deliberations on the Convention up to the adoption of the Convention itself in early 1985. The United States even called for a mandatory CFC protocol that all parties to the Convention would have to accept. The principal point of disagreement was a difference in regulatory approach between the European Community (now the European Union) and the so-called Toronto Group of countries, including the United States, Canada, and the Nordic countries. Each side argued that the approach it had already implemented ought to be adopted internationally to the exclusion of the other. The EU limited total production capacity for all uses of CFCs to a level thought to be safe for the ozone layer, approximately a third higher than existing capacity in the mid-1980s. The Toronto Group, on the other hand, had banned nonessential aerosol uses.

Can you make principled arguments for each of these approaches? What are the benefits and disadvantages of each?

When negotiations on the CFC protocol broke down, the Convention alone was adopted. Renegotiation of the protocol after a scheduled one-year cooling off period coincided with an upsurge in public concern about the Antarctic ozone hole, which broke the deadlock and facilitated adoption of the Montreal Protocol in September 1987. In the end, the Montreal Protocol, by requiring substantive reductions in, and ultimately the elimination of, production and consumption of CFCs, proved to be more stringent than either — a case of genuine policymaking on the international level, not just "harmonization" of national regulatory approaches. In structural and legal terms, the legacy of the stratospheric ozone negotiations has been deeply internalized by international policymakers. While not legally required, the framework convention plus protocols model adopted for stratospheric ozone has been routinely, if sometimes slavishly, followed in subsequent multilateral environmental negotiations.

4. **Science in international diplomacy.** Scientific understanding of the stratospheric ozone problem was and is central to the task of crafting a responsive international policy, but diplomatic negotiators rarely have technical scientific training. Consequently, UNEP organized a Coordinating Committee on the Ozone Layer (CCOL) as an institutional link to provide scientific and technical advice to the ozone negotiations. The members of CCOL were scientific experts appointed in their individual and personal capacities. Although some of the individual members might have been employees of national governments, they were expected to operate in a purely collegial, scientific mode. The goal was to create a body that could provide objective and neutral advice on the underlying science to the negotiators who would interpret its policy significance in negotiating instruments such as the Vienna Convention and the Montreal Protocol. The Shimberg excerpt describes subsequent scientific input into the multilateral process, which continues to this day. If you were the chairperson of CCOL, how would you resolve the disputes that inevitably arise between scientists? How would you deal with a scientist who disputed the Rowland-Molina theory and hence the existence of the problem? With a scientist who asserted that the problem was much more severe than the majority view? Despite the potential tensions in such a role, the model

largely worked, with the scientific explanation for such phenomena as the ozone hole, whether provided through CCOL or otherwise, a principal driver in the ozone negotiations, then as now.

5. **Hats, sunglasses, sunscreen, and checks on the Executive Branch.** Initially the Executive Branch was aggressive in the resumed international negotiations on the CFC protocol, advocating deep cuts in production and consumption of compounds that deplete ozone in the stratosphere. As described in the Shimberg excerpt, at a crucial moment the Reagan Administration began to do an about-face. Secretary of the Interior Donald Hodel questioned the need for regulatory interventions, advocating instead that individuals protect themselves from elevated ultraviolet radiation by making use of hats, sunglasses, and sunscreen.[15] This provided an opportunity for some memorable quips — for example, calling the administration's policy the "Ray-Ban Plan," and asking "What does Secretary Hodel want, an entire country that looks like the Blues Brothers?" The President's constitutional role in treaty negotiations puts him in the driver's seat, in the sense that he crafts international law, a function reserved on the domestic level exclusively to the Congress. If that is so, what incentive did Ronald Reagan, or any other President for that matter, have to listen to popular outcry over his conduct of international negotiations?

6. **The delicate interplay between international treaty-making and domestic legislation.** Throughout this case study, Congress was seen as favoring stricter controls on ozone-depleting substances than the Reagan Administration. International agreements, in and of themselves, are not binding on signatory nations; they must be implemented by domestic legislation (see Chapter 8). The U.S. Constitution places the responsibility for negotiating treaties in the Executive Branch but requires ratification by a two-thirds vote of the Senate before a treaty can have the full force and effect of domestic law. In this case, the Senate first ratified the Montreal Protocol and then Congress passed strengthening legislation, which was subsequently signed by a more sympathetic President, George H. W. Bush. One might also imagine a converse situation — like the global warming conventions of the late 1990s — where an administration was more favorably inclined toward a particular treaty than the sitting Congress. In that case, the Senate might refuse to ratify an entire treaty, or else might ratify part of it and reject the rest. Congress might then enact weaker legislation to replace the rejected aspects of the treaty, but the President might veto the bill. Implementing treaties adds another level of complexity to our already elaborate system of checks and balances. Two other valuable studies of the evolution of the Montreal Protocol and national reactions to this process are Benedick, Ozone Diplomacy, Enlarged Edition (1998), and Rowland, Atmospheric Changes Caused by Human Activities: From Science to Regulation, 27 Ecology L.Q. 1261 (2001).

7. **EPA's ambivalent position.** EPA found itself caught between the President and Congress. EPA, along with the FDA, had banned the use of CFCs in consumer aerosol products, but it had not otherwise carried out the broad regulatory authority over

---

15. Peterson, Administration Ozone Policy May Favor Sunglasses, Hats; Support for Chemical Cutbacks Reconsidered, Washington Post, May 29, 1987, at A1.

ozone-depleting substances given to it by Congress in the 1977 CAA Amendments. Most of EPA's efforts in this area had gone into supporting the Executive Branch team attempting to negotiate a Protocol. But, as the scientific evidence supporting the Rowland-Molina thesis mounted, and as Congress and the media began to criticize the Reagan Administration for its timidity regarding ozone-destroying substances, EPA took another tack. At a 1987 congressional hearing, EPA officials testified that the benefits of eliminating CFCs and related compounds would clearly outweigh the costs.

8. **Domestic implementation of the Montreal Protocol.** During the negotiations, the Protocol was expected to be implemented by regulations adopted by EPA under the authority of §157 of the CAA (since repealed and replaced by the 1990 Amendments to the CAA, which are the current legal authority for EPA's regulation of CFCs). Under its Stratospheric Ozone Protection Plan, EPA accepted public comment during the negotiations and prepared an environmental impact statement. Article 2, paragraph 11 of the Montreal Protocol reserves the right to take more stringent measures than provided in that instrument. In responding to the argument of some commenters on EPA's proposed rule that the CAA contained more demanding requirements for the regulation of ozone-depleting chemicals than the Montreal Protocol, the Agency made the following assertion:

> EPA...believes that in deciding whether and how to regulate under §157(b) it may consider other countries' effect on stratospheric ozone and the effect of United States action on other countries' willingness to take regulatory action.... To assess the risk of ozone depletion and the need for regulatory action, EPA must consider other nations' actions affecting the stratosphere. A logical next step in this analysis is what effect United States action could have on other nations' actions now and in the future.... EPA judged that the obvious need for broad international adherence to the Protocol counseled against the United States' deviating from the Protocol, because any significant deviation could lessen other countries' motivation to participate.... Industry commenters also generally agreed with EPA's concern that deviating from the Protocol risked undermining it. They...shared EPA's concern that implementation of more stringent controls would yield little, if any, additional stratospheric protection, while possibly reducing other countries' incentive to join the Protocol. 53 Fed. Reg. 30,566, 30,569, 30,573–74 (Aug. 12, 1988).

What do you think of this argument against unilateral national action as a matter of international strategy? Can you identify counterarguments that might be made by an environmental group advocating stricter unilateral action than required by the Protocol as a domestic strategy? Suppose you are a judge on the U.S. Court of Appeals for the District of Columbia Circuit faced with a petition for review from an environmental organization alleging that EPA's final rule is illegal because it does not require reductions sufficiently stringent to satisfy §157. How, if at all, would the existence of the Montreal Protocol affect your treatment of this petition? Would it make any difference to you that the agreement had or had not entered into force? Would the likelihood of subsequent revisions to the agreement affect your thinking?

9. **International technology-forcing.** The basic approach of the Protocol as adopted in 1987 was to reduce and, in light of the subsequent amendments and adjustments, eventually eliminate production and consumption of CFCs. Because at the time there were

no known substitutes for these cheap, useful, and nontoxic (at least at ground level) chemicals, the Protocol is often cited as an example of a ban designed to create incentives for technological innovation. The 1987 Protocol, however, did not eliminate these chemicals entirely but instead required a 50% reduction in consumption by 1999. Soon after the adoption of the Protocol, the ozone "hole" over Antarctica was connected to CFCs, adding momentum to demands for further reductions and ultimately elimination of these compounds. To some extent, Congress's position was enhanced by Germany's decision, in 1989, to virtually "sunset" all CFCs by 1995 — a far more dramatic reduction than required by the Protocol at that time and on an accelerated schedule by comparison with the international standard. (In 1992, the United States and the remainder of the European Economic Community announced that they would advance their phaseout deadlines to the end of 1995.) In fact, Germany and Japan have utilized technology-forcing to compel the development of "green technologies" that will both prevent domestic pollution and satisfy a growing international demand for minimally polluting industrial processes. See Moore, Green Revolution in the Making, Sierra, Jan./Feb. 1995, at 50. A number of American companies, e.g., Robinair and Trane Company, have also increased their profits by exporting substitutes for CFCs. There has been some discussion in the United States about encouraging technological innovation for pollution prevention through a national "Industrial Policy," but no comprehensive legislation has been enacted on this subject.

10. **Supervising the development of substitutes.** Congress did not leave the development of substitutes entirely to industry. EPA is authorized to certify acceptable substitutes and to prohibit unacceptable ones. Also, industries developing substitutes for banned ozone-depleting substances must notify EPA before introducing substitutes into commerce and also furnish EPA with health and safety data on the substitutes. These notice and reporting requirements were based on provisions in the Federal Insecticide, Fungicide, and Rodenticide Act and the Toxic Substances Control Act (see Chapter 17).

11. **Federal procurement as an incentive.** The federal government is a major consumer of a variety of products, from automobiles to ashtrays. The CAA requires federal agencies to revise their procurement regulations to further the policies of Title VI. Another section of the CAA provides incentives to federal agencies to purchase clean fuel vehicles for their fleets, even if clean fuel vehicles are more expensive than ordinary vehicles (42 U.S.C. §7588). The Resource Conservation and Recovery Act (see Chapter 18) requires federal agencies to procure items composed of the highest percentage of recovered materials practicable or explain why this has not been done (42 U.S.C. §6962). With regard to ozone-depleting chemicals, the U.S. Department of Defense revised its procurement "specs" first to allow, and then to require, use of alternatives to CFC-113 cleaning solvents. See Wexler, New Marching Orders, in Ozone Protection in the United States (Cook ed., 1996).

12. **The judicious use of variances and exemptions.** Congress authorized EPA to grant variances and exemptions to temper the harsh effects of technology-forcing in worthwhile cases (e.g., with regard to essential applications of methyl chloroform where no

substitutes are available) and to allow the production of limited quantities of Class I and II substances for use in medical devices and for export to developing countries that are parties to the Montreal Protocol. Wherever a variance or exemption is authorized, however, it is closely circumscribed as to both the maximum amounts that can be produced for this purpose, as well as the duration of the variance or exemption.

13. **Interpollutant trading and a CFC tax.** Title VI of the 1990 CAA Amendments provides for interpollutant trading in order to achieve reductions of ozone-depleting substances in a least-cost manner. In addition, Congress has imposed an excise tax on these substances, graduated according to the destructive potential of the substance (26 U.S.C. §§4682 et seq.). Pollutant trading and pollution taxes are discussed in Chapter 14. The operation of the interpollutant trading system has helped U.S. companies to meet Protocol requirements without major economic disruptions and at a lower cost than anticipated. Along with environmental benefits, the excise tax has brought in some $2.9 billion in federal revenue in its first five years.

14. **Industry's reaction to technology-forcing.** At first, the Alliance for Responsible CFC Policy, the industrial trade association representing CFC manufacturers and users, argued strongly against a CFC phaseout. But the Alliance reversed its stand after the ozone "hole" was substantiated, and then actually supported the Montreal Protocol. A Texas Instruments plant in McKinney, Texas, which had used CFCs as a solvent to clean lead solder from its circuit boards, achieved compliance with the phaseout by "borrowing" a new soldering process that had been used extensively in Europe but had not yet been adopted in the United States. Using the phaseout as an opportunity to evaluate and install the new technology, the TI engineers found that the new process would leave the circuit boards clean, thus obviating both CFC use and also the disposal of lead-contaminated hazardous wastes. TI's turning of a technology-forcing mandate into a pollution prevention opportunity was facilitated by a unique industry-government coordinating committee entitled the International Cooperative for Ozone Layer Protection (ICOLP). Initiated by EPA, ICOLP's mission was to "promote and coordinate the worldwide exchange of non-proprietary information on alternative technologies, processes, and substances for ozone-depleting solvents." With ICOLP's assistance, other large companies such as Digital Equipment Corp., Ford Motor Co., and IBM were able to phase out their use of CFCs at a relatively modest cost. See Hinrichsen, Fixing the Ozone Hole Is a Work in Progress, The Amicus Journal, Fall 1996, at 35.

E.I. Du Pont de Nemours and Co. discovered the CFC group of chemicals in 1928 and, under the trade name Freon, was its largest manufacturer. Du Pont earned $600 million in revenues from its Freon business in 1987. At the height of its Freon operations, Du Pont maintained 11 Freon plants, including 6 in Europe, Japan, and Latin America, and 5 in the United States. After the 1978 ban on CFC use in consumer aerosols, Du Pont lost one-third of its CFC business and closed several of its Freon manufacturing plants. During the late 1970s, after the publication of Rowland and Molina's findings, Du Pont devoted $3 to $4 million per year to attempts to identify substitutes. However, in the first Reagan Administration years (1980–1984), Du Pont's expenditures for research into Freon substitutes fell to virtually nothing. Since the signing of the Montreal Protocol, Du Pont has reversed course and invested steadily increasing amounts in this area. For example, in 1988 Du Pont spent more than $30 million on research into potential Freon substitutes. Also during that year, Du Pont announced that it would phase out CFC production by 1997. Much of Du Pont's research has focused on HCFCs, which are less stable than — and only 2% as destructive to the ozone layer as — CFCs. But the CAA Amendments of 1990 require a phaseout of HCFCs by 2030, and in 1995, following the United States' lead, the parties to the Protocol agreed that the developed world would phase out HCFC production by 2020, with the developing world to follow by 2040. There are currently no economically achievable substitutes available for HCFCs, but it is widely believed that Du Pont is feverishly conducting research in order to recapture this potentially massive market. See Buchholz et al., Managing Environmental Issues 261 (1992).

Notice the fundamental difference between the cooperative approach to technology-sharing exemplified by ICOLP and the proprietary search for patents illustrated by Du Pont. Both strategies must be pursued if the search for alternatives to ozone-depleting substances is to be successful.

15. **Enforcing technology-forcing.** Technology-forcing creates economic opportunities not only for enterprising entrepreneurs but for unscrupulous criminals as well. Smuggling illegal CFCs into the United States has become a lucrative business because 90% of automobiles in the United States have air-conditioning, compared to about 10% in Europe. Since the late 1980s, new automobiles have utilized an HCFC substitute for CFCs in their air-conditioning systems, but over 50 million older automobile air conditioning systems still rely on CFCs, which are becoming scarce and thus expensive. Also, there is a network of small users, such as garages, among which controls on ozone-depleting substances are difficult to promote, monitor, and enforce. In addition, the U.S. excise tax on CFCs has created an incentive for tax avoidance. It has been widely reported that contraband CFCs are the second largest smuggling problem — next to drugs — for U.S. customs agents along the Mexican border.[16]

16. **Laggards, holdouts, and free riders.** A persistent structural impediment in international law, heavily tilted toward consent and consensus, is how to deal with states that are not parties to a particular agreement. Any state may avoid the obligations of the Montreal Protocol, or any other agreement, merely by refraining from signing and ratifying. In the case of the Montreal Protocol, the problem of nonparties was particularly acute because the parties to the agreement were undertaking expensive obligations in purely economic terms. Nonparties would not incur those costs, putting parties to the agreement at a competitive disadvantage. Article 4 of the Montreal Protocol, entitled "Control of Trade with Non-Parties," addresses this issue. The agreement's trade provisions require parties to the Protocol to prohibit imports from and exports to nonparties of bulk CFCs; products containing CFCs, such as refrigerators and air-conditioners; and products manufactured with CFCs that do not contain them, such as computer chips. At the same time, trade in those products was freely permitted among

---

16. On August 29, 1997, a Florida company was fined $37 million by a federal court for smuggling 4000 tons of CFCs into the United States. Jail sentences were also imposed on three company officials. 28 BNA Env't Rep. Curr. Dev. 839 (1997). At the Ninth Meeting of the Parties to the Montreal Protocol, the parties agreed on a new international licensing system to track trade in CFCs.

parties during the phaseout period. Can you explain why negotiators believed this provision was essential? What would you expect the effect of these requirements to be on relations among parties and nonparties? What beneficial results would you expect for the environment?

17. **COPs and MOPs.** Like its predecessor, the Vienna Convention, the Montreal Protocol is an organic instrument that sets out a framework for future cooperative action by the parties to the instrument. Article 6, entitled "Assessment and Review of Control Measures," specifies periodic reviews of the science with an eye to revising the Protocol. Article 11 calls for regular meetings of the parties to the Protocol (MOPs), which in practice are held simultaneously with the conferences of the parties to the Vienna Convention (COPs). As described in the Shimberg excerpt, the first revisions to the Protocol were adopted in 1990. Even before that, at the first MOP held in 1989, the parties to the then-new Protocol, which had just entered into force, adopted a decision entitled the "Helsinki Declaration on the Protection of The Ozone Layer." This document states that the Protocol parties "agree to phase out the production and the consumption of CFC's controlled by the Montreal Protocol as soon as possible but not later than the year 2000." In other words, the Helsinki Declaration states the same goal as the London amendments and adjustments of a year later. What do you think is the purpose of the Helsinki Declaration? What is the Declaration's legal status? If the Helsinki Declaration accomplished this goal in 1989, what need was there for the London amendments and adjustments? Why would Shimberg not even mention the Helsinki Declaration? Can you identify a legal relationship among the Protocol, the Declaration, and the London adjustments and amendments?

18. **Revising the Protocol and a novel twist.** To date, the periodic reexamination of the Protocol has resulted in five revisions: in 1990 in London, in 1992 in Copenhagen, in 1994 in Vienna, in 1997 in Montreal, and in 1999 in Beijing. Customary international law specifies that an amendment to a multilateral treaty is binding only on those states that indicate their affirmative intent to accept those new obligations, ordinarily through ratification or acceptance of the amendment. In effect, an amendment is a new agreement under international law. The drafters of the Protocol, however, saw that the customary rule is an unattractive option for issues such as stratospheric ozone depletion, in which the scientific knowledge underlying treaty provisions is in a constant state of evolution and reassessing international obligations is often desirable, if not necessary. Under the customary rule, there is a serious risk that repeated amendment of an agreement in light of new scientific developments will result in classes of parties, each with its own configuration of obligations depending upon the amendments to which it has acceded. This danger is particularly grave in the case of complex, delicately balanced regulatory regimes such as the Montreal Protocol, where the costs to state parties are high.

IMPACT OF INTERNATIONAL AGREEMENTS ON CHLORINE LEVELS IN THE STRATOSPHERE

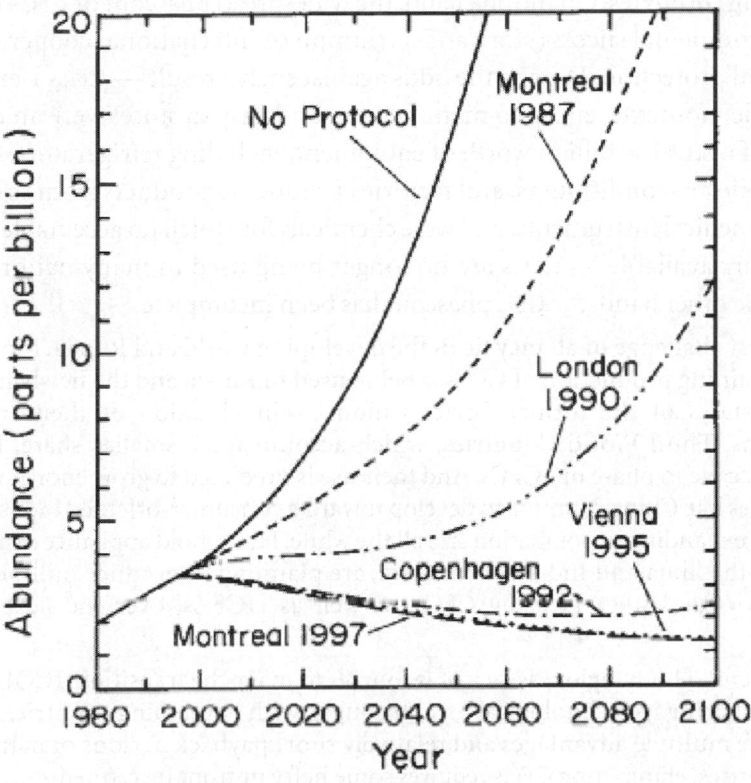

FIGURE 15-2

This figure shows that, because of the long atmospheric lifetimes of CFCs, the 50% reductions called for in the unamended 1987 Protocol would have been useful but insufficient to protect the ozone layer. The assessment and review procedure in the Protocol provided a basis for the parties to the agreement to take the further, more aggressive action incorporated in subsequent revisions.

See http://www.uwmc.uwc.edu/geography/globcat/CL-agreement-impact.htm. See also http://www.niwa.co.nz/shared/faquv8_large.jpg/view.

In a "sleeper" provision little noticed at the time of its drafting, Article 2, Paragraph 9 of the Montreal Protocol modifies the customary rule by providing for "adjustments"— a term otherwise unknown to international law — that are binding on all parties to be adopted by a two-thirds majority vote. There is no opt-out provision, as with the Whaling Convention discussed in Chapter 8. True majority voting of this sort is virtually unknown to the international legal system, which almost always operates by "consensus" or unanimity. Can you see why there is a preference in international relations for acquiescence by every state, in effect giving every country a veto? What drawbacks can you see to the adjustment process? In an approach worthy of Solomon, but understandable in light of the international bias in favor of consensus, the parties to the Protocol split the difference, adopting adjustments on the streamlined, nonconsensus model for those substances already covered by the agreement, but requiring full-blown amendments to add new substances. As of this writing, 185 states are party to the Vienna Convention, 184 to the Protocol, and 164, 145, 91, and 47 to the amendments adopted, respectively, in 1990, 1992, 1997, and 1999.

19. **Developing countries.** On the one hand, the widespread phaseout of CFCs has been a major environmental success story and a triumph of international cooperation for environmental protection. Despite the odds against such a result — CFCs were stable, nonflammable, nontoxic, cheap to manufacture, and easy to store; were an essential component of over $100 billion worth of equipment, including refrigerators, building and automobile air-conditioners, and factories producing products from solvents to insulation to medical instruments; and were chemicals for which no acceptable alternative was readily available — CFCs are no longer being used in many nations of the world.[17] On the other hand, the CFC phaseout has been incomplete:

> The biggest challenge of all may lie in the developing world and Russia. Most of th[e] remaining production of CFCs is being used in Russia and the newly independent states of the former Soviet Union — in violation of their treaty obligations. Third World Countries, which account for a smaller share, have another decade to phase out CFCs. And their use is predicted to grow enormously as countries like China continue to develop toward a consumer-oriented industrial economy; expanding in population size all the while. Household appliance companies in both China and India, for instance, are planning to produce millions of refrigerators and freezers using CFCs, as well as HCFCs, over the next few decades....

> The problem in both regions is lack of resources to make the transition. ICOLP, of course, is sharing its technological breakthroughs with developing countries. But despite the multiple advantages and relatively short payback periods of many of these advances, eliminating CFCs requires some hefty upfront investments....

> Many companies in developing countries cannot raise that kind of capital in the span of a few years. In theory, there is a mechanism in place to help them do it.... One of the provisions hammered out during the [Montreal Protocol negotiating sessions] was a special Multilateral Fund, to be paid for by the industrialized world, which would help poorer countries offset the costs of the phaseout.

> To date, the Fund has financed more than 1,000 projects at a total cost of $440 million. These projects, which are already in place and working, will eliminate 30 percent of all ozone depleters used in the Third World by the turn of the century. Much of the investment has been used to finance suitable alternatives to CFCs, especially as coolants, solvents, and degreasers. "In 1995, we approved $205 million worth of projects to phase out 22,000 metric tons of these chemicals in Third World countries," says Omar El-Arini, head of the fund. "If we kept that up, we could replace all the chemicals the developing countries are committed to phase out by 2010, if they continue their current rate of consumption."

> That last qualification, however, is a big one. It is virtually a given that developing countries will increase their rate of consumption, and that they will need even more help than the framers of the Montreal Protocol originally envisioned. But as the ozone emergency has dropped off the front pages and out of the public's

---

17. According to reliable estimates, global production of CFCs declined from more than one million tons in 1986 to about 250,000 tons in 1995; and production of halons decreased from about 200,000 tons in 1986 to about 40,000 tons in 1995; but production of HCFCs rose sharply during that period. 28 BNA Env't Rep. Curr. Dev. 837–838 (1997) [Eds.].

consciousness, the resolve of the signatories has wavered. The multilateral Fund has been receiving about 20 percent less money than was pledged for 1996. Hinrichsen, Fixing the Ozone Hole Is a Work in Progress, The Amicus Journal, Fall 1996, at 38.

Article 5 of the Protocol responds to the demands of developing countries by giving them a 10-year grace period for implementing the obligations in the Protocol. Why do you think the negotiators might have chosen this particular formula? From the point of view of environmental efficacy, is this a helpful provision or a harmful one? Does it reflect an appropriate balance of competing factors?

Assuming that the international phaseout proceeds according to plan, what will be the ultimate effect on the ozone layer?

> Because it can take up to a decade for a CFC molecule to reach the stratosphere, the ozone that is being destroyed today is very probably, in part, being destroyed by CFCs put into the atmosphere before the first ozone hole was discovered. As a result, CFC concentrations in the stratosphere are expected to double from 1989 to 2000, and decades will pass before we feel effects of the resultant five to twenty percent increase in u.v. radiation. Another source claims that half of the total amount of CFCs produced since 1930 will be produced from now until the phaseout is complete, and yet another source predicts increasing ozone destruction for some 20 years and a return to pre-ozone layer hole concentrations around 2050.... One of the most worrisome aspects of the ozone-hole problem is that the worst is yet to come.... We simply do not know how much damage we have done (or will do) to ourselves, to other species, and to the natural balance among the forces that control the biosphere. We know that some destruction will happen, indeed is happening, but the effects are presently impossible to calculate. Newton and Dillingham, Watersheds 155, 165, 167 (1994)

And finally, the most commonly utilized substitutes for CFCs — HCFCs — are themselves less potent ozone-destroying substances, as well as "greenhouse gases."

Studies by the United Nations Environment Programme and the World Meteorological Organization conclude that the Montreal Protocol has been effective in reducing stratospheric ozone depletion. Ozone depletion is expected to peak over the next several decades but will thereafter begin to abate, and ozone levels should return to levels normal in the mid-1950s by the middle of this century. But these agencies caution that the ozone layer will remain particularly vulnerable for the next decade, and that failure to implement the Montreal Protocol and its successor agreements will delay or even prevent recovery of the ozone layer.

At the Fourteenth Meeting of the Parties to the Montreal Protocol, in November 2002, developed nations agreed to a funding package worth approximately $500 million for reducing the use of ozone depletors in developing nations. China, the world's largest manufacturer and consumer of CFCs, has promised to dismantle its 37 CFC manufacturing plants by 2010. In the United States, EPA promulgated regulations in 2003 (68 Fed. Reg. 2819) to phase out HCFCs in a manner similar to the CFC phaseout program.

20. **The rule of law: confronting scofflaws.** Article 8 of the Protocol directs the MOP to adopt noncompliance procedures "for treatment of Parties found to be in non-compliance." In recognition of the fact that there is little to be done if a state party chooses

flagrantly to violate its international obligations, the Protocol prefers the term "compliance" to the stronger concept of "enforcement." Can you imagine why that might be so? In 1992, the MOP adopted a compliance mechanism, administered by an Implementation Committee, that can be triggered either by a third party or by the noncomplying state itself. Why might a state choose to, in effect, accuse itself of noncompliance? If you were the diplomatic representative of a party admittedly not in compliance, how would you frame your presentation to the Implementation Committee? The first two cases considered by the Implementation Committee concerned Russia and Bulgaria, both of which identified serious impediments to compliance. Nonetheless, the Committee declined to recommend cutting off multilateral aid or trade sanctions, probably the two most serious punishments available to the Committee. Can you imagine why the Implementation Committee might have taken such a lenient approach? If you were representing Russia or Bulgaria, can you make an argument that it would be environmentally counterproductive to sanction your client in that manner?

21. **Technology-forcing reconsidered, and pollution prevention.** Technology-forcing can be a viable mechanism for coping with environmental threats if some or all of the following are features of the problem context or regulatory strategy:

- a substantial, and comparatively clear, environmental threat, and especially a direct threat to public health;
- a credible "hammer" limiting the use of, or banning, a dangerous substance;
- substitutes that are at least theoretically recognized and comparable with regard to costs;
- variance and exemption procedures that are flexible, fair, limited, predictable, and enforceable;
- effective market-enlisting mechanisms, such as tax incentives or disincentives, trading systems, preferential governmental purchasing, and opportunities for private industry;
- clear, generally applicable standards without opt-out possibilities, such as the California preemption waiver;
- supervision of the introduction of substitutes in order to avoid adverse unintended consequences;
- adequate enforcement at all stages of the process;
- agreement between the Executive and Legislative Branches with regard to the need for and the structure of the technology-forcing system finally adopted;
- adequate lead time for compliance;[18]

---

18. See Natural Res. Def. Council v. EPA, 655 F.2d 318, 329 (D.C. Cir. 1981) ("the presence of substantial lead time for development before manufacturers will have to commit themselves to mass production of a chosen prototype gives the agency greater leeway to modify its standards if the actual future course of technology diverges from expectation"). In this case, the court upheld EPA's emissions standards for light-duty diesel vehicles based on "trap-oxidizer" technology, even though a durable model of this device was unavailable. This was not a technology-forcing decision, but one regarding the lead time for compliance with a technology-based standard (see Chapter 12).

- on the international level, differential standards for developed and developing nations, technology-sharing and funding assistance by developed nations for the benefit of developing nations, and effective trade restrictions to track and prevent smuggling.

And note the linkage in both international and domestic environmental law between technology-forcing and pollution prevention strategies: As noted earlier, the more rigorous and predictable that environmental protection standards become, the more industry will be motivated to cut back on the use of polluting processes and the volume of pollutants released to the environment.

Chapter 16

ROADBLOCK STRATEGIES: STARK PROHIBITIONS AND THEIR VIABILITY

A. *An Introduction to Roadblock Statutes*

B. *The Endangered Species Act as a Roadblock Statute*

C. *"Roadblock Bypasses": Subsequent Modifications Can Change the ESA's Stark Standards (and What Lessons Can Be Drawn from That?)*

A. AN INTRODUCTION TO ROADBLOCK STATUTES

"Roadblock" laws — statutory provisions that in stark, direct, easily litigatable flat-out terms declare **"THOU SHALT NOT ..."** — have been a continuing part of the statutory history of environmental law right from the beginning in the 1960s, although they have sometimes been created quite accidentally. They often play a critically important role. There are times when a problem is so complex, so incapable of careful measurement and fine tuning, or so politically difficult to shift away from the old status quo that a stark flat prohibition provision may be necessary to achieve effective environmental protection.

The Endangered Species Act is the prime example used in this chapter, but there are a number of such roadblock statutes in the environmental realm — the 1899 Rivers and Harbors Act, which makes it a crime to dump any refuse into the nation's waters without a permit; the Wilderness Act of 1964, which prohibits virtually all development and motorized uses in declared wildernesses; the Delaney Clause of the Federal Food, Drug, and Cosmetic Act, which banned any food additive that causes cancer in test animals; and other prohibitions that contain very limited exceptions (such as *Overton Park*'s Department of Transportation Act §4(f) provision, the Clean Air Act's Title II prohibition of auto emissions beyond 10% of 1970 levels, and the like).

But are roadblock laws a good idea? They do demonstrate some of the serious potential vices of stark crude strength as well as its virtues. Roadblocks on occasion certainly have been effective. Where would the protection of parklands against highways today be without the roadblock of §4(f), or auto emissions without the stark 90% rollback? For the same reason, however, they may be especially subject to the problems of the unguided missile. The tradeoff for decisive effectiveness is the risk that they may hit too hard, in not exactly the right place, or with disruptive or disproportionate consequences that weren't predicted.

"Eco-pragmatism" is the name given to a lively debate currently going on among a number of legal scholars: Shouldn't environmental statutes be drafted from the very beginning to be less stark and draconian, "seeking the reasonable middle"?[1] Rather than enforcing crude, stringent prohibitions, shouldn't we build eco-pragmatic regulatory programs around standards that incorporate careful balances between ecology and industrial economics? That way, won't these laws have greater "social sustainability," avoiding destructive backlashes?

Roadblocks often evoke an immediate backlash of challenges from the industries they regulate. The standard argument offered by opponents seeking the repeal or dilution of the new law is that it is "extreme" — it is too inflexible and goes too far.

Strict environmental statutes indeed sometimes do go too far and require mellowing. In other cases the opponents of such statutes are transparently trying to avoid effective enforcement of public interest standards in order to maximize their own profits. Figuring out the right degree of stringency for environmental regulation is a very imprecise science.

As it happens, statutes evolve. Over time, many of the strict roadblocks have been softened by compromising amendments, with varying results depending on your point of view. Sometimes this "slippage"[2] or "fine-tuning" modification process consolidates or improves the law's effectiveness, sometimes it reduces it, and sometimes it guts it. The trick is to determine how and when strict environmental protection standards should be imposed in the first place and how they should be maintained over time.

Section 1. THE DELANEY CLAUSE

Take the example of the Delaney Clause. Despite some scientists' skepticism about the usefulness of high-dosage animal tests, the terms of the clause (passed in 1958 at the urging of Rep. James Delaney who had made the provision a personal crusade) declared that

> No [food] additive shall be deemed to be safe if it is found...to induce cancer in man or animal.... 21 U.S.C. §348(c)(3) (1958), FFDCA §409.

In the years after its passage, the Delaney Clause forced the nation's food industry to be far more conscious of potential carcinogenicity, but in some cases the zero-risk ban was clearly too strict. Some cancer-linked additives posed extremely trivial risks of actual harm, arising only in the case of huge overdoses, and were far less dangerous than the toxic but noncarcinogenic additives being used as substitutes. The FDA quietly allowed the use of some additives that posed cancer risks of less than one-in-a-million. When the NRDC blocked the FDA's informal flexibility with an injunction enforcing the statute's absolute ban,[3] Congress and President Clinton decided to overturn the Delaney Clause roadblock, substituting a statutory standard providing that

---

1. Professor Dan Farber prompted the question with Ecopragmatism (1999), which stimulated Professor J. B. Ruhl's Working Both (Positivist) Ends Toward a New (Pragmatist) Middle in Environmental Law, 68 Geo. Wash. L. Rev. 522 (2000); Ruhl, A Manifesto for the Radical Middle, 38 Idaho L. Rev. 385 (2002), and others. For a critical appraisal, see Heinzerling, Pragmatists and Environmentalists, 113 Harv. L. Rev. 1421 (2000).

2. See Farber, Taking Slippage Seriously: Noncompliance and Creative Compliance in Environmental Law, 23 Harv. Envtl. L. Rev. 297 (1999).

3. Les v. Reilly, 968 F.2d 985 (9th Cir. 1992) (EPA had no discretion to permit the use of such food additives).

...as used in this section, the term "safe"...means that the Administrator has determined that there is a *reasonable certainty* that no harm will result from aggregate exposure to the pesticide chemical.... 21 U.S.C. §346a(b)(2)(A)(ii), Food Quality Protection Act of 1996 (FQPA) (emphasis added).

The subsequent effect of this FQPA amendment is subject to debate. Some argue that public health and safety are now undercut by the loosened constraints on the agency; others argue that overall it improves them.[4] Either way, note the strategic shifts that have occurred: The amendment shifts from a clear absolute standard to a subjective balancing — from an objective test litigatable by citizens to a discretionary agency determination of "reasonable" that courts will review deferentially, and from a pluralistic setting where the roadblock norm is enforceable by a wide variety of interested parties, back to a "bipolar" setting where in practical effect the regulatory outcome is primarily determined between industry and the Administrator, whoever that may be. This example of slippage is instructive on several levels.

Section 2. **WEIGHING ROADBLOCKS**

Statutory histories like that of the Delaney Clause open up a range of questions:

- In its strict roadblock form, to what extent does the standard achieve the desired environmental or public health protection? If it is effective, why? Does it overprotect? If so, by how much, and at what relative systemic costs?

- If the roadblock gets amended, is it because the original environmental or public health goal has been found in whole or part to have been wrong-headed from the start? If not, is the new moderated statutory standard as effective as the old in achieving the public's environmental and public health interests? For instance, is it still readily enforceable by citizen plaintiffs if the designated agencies refuse to do it?

- And then there are questions of timing and politics: For legal standards to be effective over spans of years requires an accumulation of political momentum, experience, credibility, acceptance, and support as well as workable technical terminology and enforcement mechanisms. If the roadblock survives over time, how does it do so? What political support has it collected to sustain it? If the roadblock has been moderated by amendments, could the public's environmental and public health interests have been just as well served if it had been legislated this way in the first place? Or was it necessary first to "establish a beachhead," consolidating the standard's political strength as a crude blunt roadblock in order to implant its mandate forcibly into the established political and industrial legal order?

- If the roadblock is amended, is the new format more or less open to public participation and public confidence?

Roadblock statutes may offer a good answer to many environmental problems, but they also raise this chain of important questions.

---

4. The negative argument is that in actual administrative practice the FQPA's word *reasonable* spreads over to modify the *no harm* phrase as well. The positive argument is that the agency now can allow minimalist carcinogens that are far less risky than the alternatives.

As this coursebook has reminded the reader from the outset, every statute is constantly shaped by its political context and the contending forces that surround it. Laws do not necessarily get passed initially because they are right and good, but rather because at one point in time someone marshals a sufficient political mass behind a bill so that a majority of legislators perceive it to be in their self-interest to support, or at least not oppose, it. For environmental laws, this generative political moment typically is forced on the legislative process by outsiders — that is, by opportunistic citizens whose efforts mobilize a politically powerful public fervor or furor in a moment of crisis to demand that something be done.

Once an environmental law is on the books, however, the citizen power blocs that got it passed tend to drift off to other issues, and the question becomes how the provision will take hold and survive in the complex political context of modern government. If a law tends to go up against industrial-political establishments — and most citizen-based environmental statutes do confront major business interests or pork-barrel construction agencies and the insider political structures that serve them — then the sharpness of the law's terms makes a large difference in whether it will ever be effectively implemented. If the bill does not have a continuing public mobilization or some other strong continuing political force behind it, realistically its major chance for effective implementation may be that it is clear and simple enough to be reinforced by citizen lawsuits — a roadblock.

B. THE ENDANGERED SPECIES ACT AS A ROADBLOCK STATUTE

Section 1. THE ESA

The militant environmentalist movement in America today is a new homosocial-ism, communism. What these people are is against private property rights. They are trying to attack capitalism and corporate America in the form of going after timber companies. And they're trying to say that we must preserve these virgin trees because the spotted owl and the rat kangaroo and whatever live in them, and it's the only place they can live, the snail darter and whatever it is.

— Rush Limbaugh, *The Rush Limbaugh Show*, Dec. 7, 1993

The Endangered Species Act of 1973[5] was a revolutionary legal document. It was the first major piece of legislation in any legal system that sought to put teeth into the protection of endangered species domestically and internationally. The ESA has been a model for subsequent wildlife conservation efforts throughout the world. For species that are recognized and listed on the federal Endangered Species List under ESA §4, the Act provides three regulatory approaches to preventing extinction:

- A commercial ban limiting the importation and domestic sale of endangered species and their parts[6]

---

5. 16 U.S.C. §§1531 et seq. (1973, as amended).

6. This ban on the importation or sale of endangered species is a straightforward domestic law implementation of CITES, the Convention on International Trade in Endangered Species, probably the most effective international environmental treaty ever.

- A provision forbidding federal agencies from harming species (ESA §7, the original roadblock hidden within the ESA's text)
- A provision forbidding the killing or taking of endangered species (ESA §9, which also holds a major roadblock)

As to the first, ESA's ban on commercial trade in endangered species, by closing down the U.S. market it provides a partial answer to the threats posed by the worldwide trade in endangered wildlife. Endangered species that have market value, such as leopards, turtles, rare birds, elephants, cacti, and the like, have no protection in the marketplace. Indeed, the market encourages the destruction of many endangered species by raising the exploitation value of each remaining animal as the species approaches extinction. As the market price per skin or rhino horn skyrockets, exploitation of the endangered species becomes almost impossible to stop. Either the Third World countries of origin cannot afford to halt the lucrative trade, or high prices create poaching pressures that subvert any local enforcement efforts. The only way to prevent the elimination of the species is to shut down the market in developed countries. To the extent that the ESA does that, it lessens the pressure on animals hunted to provide fur coats and other luxuries for the American fashion world's cosmopolitan tastes.

Section 7 of the 1973 ESA contained a hidden roadblock, a direct congressional prohibition against federal agency projects and programs that harm endangered species. The strategic resemblance between ESA §7 and NEPA §102 is remarkable. Both provisions got their leverage from targeting the actions of federal agencies. Both contained hidden teeth that subsequently emerged to the surprise of most members of Congress who had voted for them. NEPA, however, only requires procedural compliance. Section 7's roadblock provision was substantive, precise, and mandatory, with specific authorization for enforcement by citizens acting as private attorneys general, setting up a useful case study of the strengths and drawbacks of the roadblock approach.

ESA §9 looks like a straightforward prohibition against "taking" any endangered species, a prohibition that attaches heavy criminal sanctions to the act of killing or capturing endangered animals. But the Department of Interior Fish and Wildlife Service's interpretive rule defines habitat modification or degradation as a "harm" that can constitute an illegal "take."[7] (This makes ecological sense. Habitat alteration is the number one cause of extinction of species on the face of the earth, a far more important threat than hunting and killing.) As a result of the broad agency definition of "harm" under ESA §9, however, the ESA has become a potentially wide-ranging roadblock against private as well as public development, arousing a firestorm of political opposition.

As we'll see later in this chapter, faced with a perceived need for flexibility, Congress ultimately passed amendments somewhat loosening the ESA's roadblocks — the God Committee procedures for §7 in 1978 and the incidental take permit process for §9 in 1982.

---

7. 16 U.S.C. §§1532(19), 1538(a)-(b) (1982); 50 C.F.R. §17.3 (1985).

Section 2. **A FISH, A DAM, AND ESA §7**

The ESA's roadblocks first reached the U.S. Supreme Court in a classic confrontation between a small, endangered fish and the Tennessee Valley Authority's Tellico Dam.

The strict roadblock in the terms of ESA §7 as it was originally written lay camouflaged. When parsed carefully, however, its words absolutely prohibited certain harmful federal agency actions. As you read through the original text of §7 (while noting the clunky prose style that made it unlikely that many members of Congress realized what they were approving), take a pencil and underline the series of words that, pulled together by environmental litigators, created a substantive mandate and several causes of action for citizen lawsuits.

ESA §7, 16 U.S.C. §1536 (1973)

§7. INTERAGENCY COOPERATION. The Secretary [of Interior] shall review other programs administered by him and utilize such programs in furtherance of the purposes of this chapter. All other Federal agencies shall, in consultation with and with the assistance of the Secretary, utilize their authorities in furtherance of the purposes of this chapter by carrying out programs for the conservation of endangered species and threatened species listed pursuant to section 1533 of this title and by taking such action necessary to ensure that actions authorized, funded, or carried out by such agencies do not jeopardize the continued existence of such endangered species or threatened species or result in the destruction or modification of habitat of such species which is determined by the Secretary, after consultation as appropriate with the affected States, to be critical.

The Snail Darter and the Tellico Dam Case. The Supreme Court's dramatic first encounter with ESA §7 arose from a typical environmental controversy between a citizens' group — including farmers, sportsmen, archaeologists, and Cherokee Indians — rallying behind an endangered fish to oppose the Tennessee Valley Authority, a federal, pork-barrel construction agency and its real estate developer allies eager to build TVA's Tellico Dam.[8]

A member of the perch family, the snail darter is a small, brownish fish, rarely more than two-and-a-half inches at maturity, with highly specific habitat requirements: shallow, clean, cool, and rapid-flowing big river habitat with rocky substrates containing small crustaceans, snails, and caddis larvae as food sources. As so often happens, the snail darter was endangered because of habitat alteration. At one time it lived throughout the Alabama-Tennessee-Kentucky river systems between the Appalachians and the Mississippi. Little by little its populations were extirpated by damming. By 1973, TVA and the Army Corps had built more than 60 dams, turning 2500 linear river miles in that relatively flat, gently-rolling region into sluggish, silted, serpentine impoundments and leaving 33 undammed miles of the Little Tennessee River as the darter's last significant habitat.

The river valley was likewise extraordinary in human terms — rolling meadows with 360 family farms on 38,000 acres of some of the richest soils left in the region, unique archaeological

---

8. *Disclosure Notice:* As the length and tone of this section probably reveal, one of the authors was both attorney and a party plaintiff in the snail darter case, beginning in 1974 and continuing up through the Supreme Court and three rounds of congressional review. For images and text on the case, see http://www.law.mercer.edu/elaw/zygplater.html.

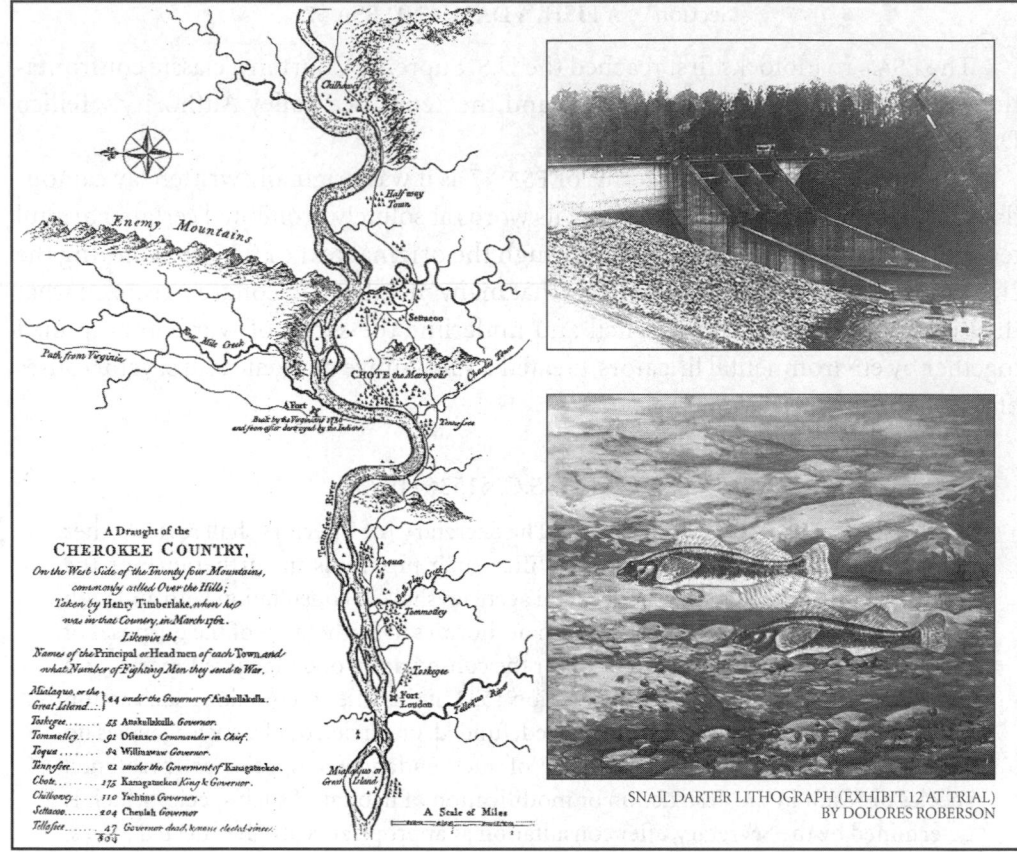

FIGURE 16-1

The Little Tennessee River Valley, the dam, and the snail darter. The river and valley were sacred to the Cherokee, whose towns and sanctuaries appear on the 1762 colonial map. Prior to the Tellico case, TVA had dammed all of the river beyond and through the Enemy (Smoky) Mountains. Tellico Dam, located 14 miles downriver from the bottom of the map, eliminated all of the remaining free-flowing river. The dam structure, as shown, is small (note size of adjacent trees), costing less than $5 million. The darters lived on a broad shallow shoal below the Great Island.

and historical features, and great potential for recreation and tourist development at the edge of the Great Smoky Mountains National Park.

TVA's final dam project was a pork-barrel classic. Since the dam could not be cost-justified for normal dam purposes like power, water supply, or flood control (because it was so small and surrounded by other dams), the agency promoted the project[9] on a novel economic theory. Most of the valley lands were condemned by the agency and bought from the farmers at very low prices, for resale to corporate developers of Timberlake, a model industrial city hypothetically to be funded by federal taxpayers and built by the Boeing Corp. at some point in the future. The reservoir plan claimed these speculative profits of shoreland development, along with recreation gains, as its major "benefit" justifications.

---

9. To control the logrolling tendencies of the congressional pork barrel, all such projects must claim a positive economic benefit-cost ratio, earning at least $1.01 for every $1.00 of federal money spent, albeit estimated over a span of up to 100 years with little or no interest figured in. This requirement prompts highly imaginative agency calculations that wildly expand claimed benefits and trivialize costs. See F. Powledge, Water: The Nature, Uses, and Future of Our Most Precious and Abused Resource 291–302 (1982).

The project calculations made no common sense,[10] and Boeing quickly bowed out saying the project was economically unrealistic. With continuing appropriations from Congress's pork-barrel appropriations committees, however, TVA pressed on. The farmers, fishermen, and environmentalists advanced the usual critical environmental analysis — the project's claimed benefits were wildly exaggerated and unrealistic, the project's direct economic costs were severely underestimated and took no notice of social and ecological costs, and far better alternatives existed that maximized public and natural values but that the project's promoters studiously ignored. The citizens tried to initiate a rational economic review of the project in Congress, in the media, and in the courts through condemnation defenses and a NEPA lawsuit, all without success.

Then in 1973, wading at a wide shoal in the river with a snorkel and facemask, ichthyology professor David Etnier discovered the snail darter. Hiram Hill, a law student, heard about it from Etnier's grad students and wrote an environmental law term paper arguing that Tellico Dam violated ESA §7. The term paper quickly turned into a federal court lawsuit filed by Hill and his professors on behalf of the darter and the river valley's defenders. TVA responded with accelerated construction and bulldozing in the valley, trying to moot the case with a strategy of sunk costs.

As reported in the resulting cascade of raucous stories in the press, the case was consistently portrayed as a simple caricature: the snail darter, a two-inch minnow, discovered at the last possible moment and misused by extremist environmentalists, halting completion of a massive valuable $150 million hydroelectric dam project. This caricature stuck to the case disastrously throughout the following years, but on the factual record every element of that story was wrong.[11]

The citizens carried the case up through the courts. The trial court judge found that the dam would destroy the fish but declined to issue an injunction against the reservoir project. The Sixth Circuit Court of Appeals issued a stay,[12] and the case went to the Supreme Court of the United States.

Tennessee Valley Authority v. Hiram Hill, et al.
United States Supreme Court, 1978
437 U.S. 153

BURGER, C.J. We begin with the premise that operation of the Tellico Dam will either eradicate the known population of snail darters or destroy their critical habitat. Petitioner does not now seriously dispute this fact.

Starting from the above premise, two questions are presented: (a) would TVA be in violation of the Act if it completed and operated the Tellico Dam as planned? (b) if TVA's actions would offend the Act, is an injunction the appropriate remedy for the violation? For the reasons stated hereinafter, we hold that both questions must be answered in the affirmative.

---

10. See the economic verdict of the God Committee in the third part of this chapter.

11. In actual fact, the darter was a perch, closer to three inches long, discovered when only 20% of project costs had been incurred. The citizen opposition centered on farmers and sportsmen as well as on (easygoing, nonextreme) environmentalists. And the dam was small, ca. $5 million in concrete and steel out of a total budget of ca. $150 million, most of which was being spent for land, roads, and bridges. The project was illogical — built for supposed real estate development and recreation, not hydroelectric generation — and was expected to destroy prime farmlands and a beautiful river as well as the darter's prime habitat for no rational public benefit. The existence of the darter as a basis for stopping the dam, the citizens argued, was not a cynical fortuity. Its precarious existence in the Little Tennessee River was caused by the agency's dam programs over the years that made the ecology of the fish a representative barometer of a wide range of threatened public values in the river valley.

12. Hill v. TVA, 549 F.2d 1064 (6th Cir. 1977), reversing 419 F. Supp. 753 (E.D. Tenn. 1976).

It may seem curious to some that the survival of a relatively small number of three-inch fish among all the countless millions of species extant would require the permanent halting of a virtually completed dam for which Congress has expended more than $100 million....

One would be hard pressed to find a statutory provision whose terms were any plainer than those in §7 of the Endangered Species Act. Its very words affirmatively command all federal agencies "to insure that actions authorized, funded, or carried out by them do not jeopardize the continued existence" of an endangered species or "result in the destruction or modification of habitat of such species...." This language admits of no exception. Accepting the Secretary's determinations, as we must, it is clear that TVA's proposed operation of the dam will have precisely the opposite effect, namely the eradication of an endangered species.

Concededly, this view of the Act will produce results requiring the sacrifice of the anticipated benefits of the project and of many millions of dollars in public funds, but close examination of the language, history, and structure of the legislation under review here indicates beyond doubt that Congress intended endangered species to be afforded the highest of priorities.

> The dominant theme pervading all Congressional discussion of the proposed [ESA] was the overriding need to devote whatever effort and resources were necessary to avoid further diminution of national and worldwide wildlife resources. Much of the testimony at the hearings and much debate was devoted to the biological problem of extinction. Senators and Congressmen uniformly deplored the irreplaceable loss to aesthetics, science, ecology, and the national heritage should more species disappear. Coggins, Conserving Wildlife Resources: An Overview of the Endangered Species Act of 1973, 51 N.D. L. Rev. 315, 321 (1975).

The legislative proceedings in 1973 are, in fact, replete with expressions of concern over the risk that might lie in the loss of any endangered species. Typifying these sentiments is the Report of the House Committee on Merchant Marine and Fisheries on HR 37, a bill which contained the essential features of the subsequently enacted Act of 1973; in explaining the need for the legislation, the Report stated:

> As we homogenize the habitats in which these plants and animals evolved, and as we increase the pressure for products that they are in a position to supply (usually unwillingly) we threaten their and our own genetic heritage. The value of this genetic heritage is, quite literally, incalculable. From the most narrow possible point of view, it is in the best interests of mankind to minimize the losses of genetic variations. The reason is simple: they are potential resources. They are keys to puzzles which we cannot solve, and may provide answers to questions which we have not yet learned to ask. To take a homely, but apt, example: one of the critical chemicals in the regulation of ovulations in humans was found in a common plant. Once discovered, and analyzed, humans could duplicate it synthetically, but had it never existed — or had it been driven out of existence before we knew its potentialities — we would never have tried to analyze it in the first place. Who knows, or can say, what potential cures for cancer or other scourges, present or future, may lie locked up in the structures of plants which may yet be undiscovered, much less analyzed?... Sheer self-interest impels us to be cautious. The institutionalization of that caution lies at the heart of HR 37.... H.R. Rep. No. 93–412.

As the examples cited here demonstrate, Congress was concerned about the unknown uses that endangered species might have and about the unforeseeable place such creatures may have in the chain of life on this planet.

In shaping legislation to deal with the problem thus presented, Congress started from the finding that "the two major causes of extinction are hunting, and destruction of natural habitat." Sen. Rep. No. 93-3072 (1973). Of these twin threats, Congress was informed that the greatest was destruction of natural habitats.

It is not for us to speculate, much less act, on whether Congress would have altered its stance had the specific events of this case been anticipated. In any event, we discern no hint in the deliberations of Congress relating to the 1973 Act that would compel a different result than we reach here.

One might dispute the applicability of these examples to the Tellico Dam by saying that in this case the burden on the public through the loss of millions of unrecoverable dollars would greatly outweigh the loss of the snail darter. But neither the Endangered Species Act nor Article III of the Constitution provides federal courts with authority to make such fine utilitarian calculations. On the contrary, the plain language of the Act, buttressed by its legislative history, shows clearly that Congress viewed the value of endangered species as "incalculable." Quite obviously, it would be difficult for a court to balance the loss of a sum certain — even $100 million — against a congressionally declared "incalculable" value, even assuming we had the power to engage in such a weighing process, which we emphatically do not.

Having determined that there is an irreconcilable conflict between operation of the Tellico Dam and the explicit provisions of §7 of the Endangered Species Act, we must now consider what remedy, if any, is appropriate. It is correct, of course, that a federal judge sitting as a chancellor is not mechanically obligated to grant an injunction for every violation of law. [But] once Congress, exercising its delegated powers, has decided the order of priorities in a given area, it is for the Executive to administer the laws and for the courts to enforce them when enforcement is sought.

Here we are urged [in Justices Rehnquist's and Powell's dissents] to view the Endangered Species Act "reasonably," and hence shape a remedy "that accords with some modicum of common sense and the public weal." But is that our function? We have no expert knowledge on the subject of endangered species, much less do we have a mandate from the people to strike a balance of equities on the side of the Tellico Dam. Congress has spoken in the plainest of words, making it abundantly clear that the balance has been struck in favor of affording endangered species the highest of priorities, hereby adopting a policy which it described as "institutionalized caution."

Our individual appraisal of the wisdom or unwisdom of a particular course consciously selected by the Congress is to be put aside in the process of interpreting a statute. Once the meaning of an enactment is discerned and its constitutionality determined, the judicial process comes to an end. We do not sit as a committee of review, nor are we vested with the power of veto. The lines ascribed to Sir Thomas More by Robert Bolt are not without relevance here:

> The law, Roper, the law. I know what's legal, not what's right. And I'll stick to what's legal.... I'm not God. The currents and eddies of right and wrong, which you find such plain-sailing, I can't navigate. I'm no voyager. But in the thickets of the law, oh there I'm a forester.... What would you do? Cut a great road through the law to get after the Devil?.... And when the last law was down, and the Devil turned round on you, where would you hide, Roper, the laws all being flat?... This country's planted thick with laws from coast to coast — Man's laws, not God's — and if you cut them down...d'you really think you could stand upright in the winds that would blow then? Yes, I'd give the Devil benefit of law, for my own safety's sake. R. Bolt, A Man for All Seasons, Act I, 147 (Heinemann ed. 1967).

We agree with the Court of Appeals that in our constitutional system the commitment to the separation of powers is too fundamental for us to pre-empt congressional action by judicially decreeing what accords with "common sense and the public weal." Our Constitution vests such responsibilities in the political branches. Affirmed. POWELL, BLACKMUN, JJ., and REHNQUIST, C.J., dissent.

1. **Is this an "environmental" opinion?** Much of the snail darter majority opinion looks at the ESA to determine, via statutory construction, only the bald questions of whether it applied to the dam and whether a court had to obey the statute. The Court does not provide the citizens with a forum to review the factual merits of the dam and its alternatives, just a roadblock. Justice Burger does echo congressional declarations of the high purposes of endangered species preservation and "institutionalized caution," a critical environmental principle, but when he announced the decision in court he invited Congress to repeal protection for the fish. And the media coverage of the Supreme Court decision predictably chorused the "little fish bites dam" theme, casting the case and plaintiffs in damaging terms of extreme environmentalism. On balance, did the snail darter litigation aid the cause of conservation or undercut it?

2. **Rationales for endangered species protection.** Why might a nation consider it sufficiently important to pass a statute with such patent and latent strengths in an abstract area of natural science? The question is made all the more pointed by the fact that protection of endangered species inevitably causes a head-on confrontation with marketplace politics.

It is easiest to say that the ESA of 1973 was passed to satisfy a vague popular clamor, beginning in the 1960s, to conserve natural resources. Endangered species had the good fortune to be represented by such mediagenic figures as the bald eagle, polar bear, whale, and whooping crane, all of which were sentimentally appealing, fairly remote from market considerations affecting most people, and dramatic or beautiful. Further, there were international conventions ratified by the United States that in broad, hortatory terms expressed an international intention to conserve such species and all endangered and threatened wildlife. Part of the impetus came from the well-organized nationally based conservation groups that have long made the United States a leader in international conservation.

But political pressure and aesthetics alone do not represent a sufficient explanation for why the ESA of 1973 became domestic law. The argument for protection of endangered species represented not only protection of the aesthetic beauties of certain species, but also ecological and philosophical principles asserting the value of the survival of the widest possible number of species, some of them quite homely, in the context of the continuing loss each year of hundreds of species worldwide. In utilitarian terms, preserving endangered species can be directly or indirectly important for the continued survival of human beings. An endangered species may possess chemical or medical properties that will never be discovered if the creatures are rendered extinct. We preserve species because of lessons they may teach us in the future; at some point, "they may reveal a cure for cancer." Another argument is that the more diversity that exists in the natural world, the more adaptable that world is to continuing stresses. This argument reflects a fundamental law of ecology that the more diverse a gene pool or ecosystem, the greater the natural bank of adaptive diversity on which society can draw.

Unfortunately, as repeatedly demonstrated in subsequent hearings on the Act, it is very difficult to show the utility of many species, especially species previously unknown that happen to confront a specific valuable development project. Therefore, beyond the strict utility argument, endangered species protection often draws on a variety of quasi-religious principles emphasizing the sanctity of life. This latter philosophical principle was the most difficult to articulate amidst congressional hearings or agency proceedings, but it reflects an important thread running through the endangered species cases — humans are stewards of their natural environment and ultimately are only constituent members of the community of life of the globe. The ESA, which made no distinction between species that have a commercial value or direct human utility and those that do not, affirmed a variety of abstract interests in protecting species because they were endangered. The statute gave legal value to an abstraction. The survival of species, insofar as possible, was declared a valid and important national goal, backed up with §7's teeth.

The roadblock terms of §7 forced the abstract value of species protection into the heart of the political calculus in a way that traditional review-and-permit regulatory approaches were unlikely to do (in the same way that the parkland protection policy litigated in *Overton Park* needed the absolutism of DoT Act §4(f) to be taken seriously).

Are the ESA's rationales dwarfed by the current reality of global climate change? If it were possible to show that over the next century as many as half of all endangered species were likely to be rendered extinct by global warming, a condition that appears to be human-augmented but quite impervious to legal liability, would the ESA become an obsolete footnote or continue to be a practicable tool, a worthwhile declaration of principle, and a utilitarian canary in a coal mine?

3. **Canaries in a coal mine: the practical utility of endangered species.** Whatever the moral and philosophical arguments for species protection, it is clear that the everyday logic of the political process responds far more readily to practical economic self-interest than to abstract principle; endangered species are generally considered to reflect the latter more than the former. During the Tellico Dam oral argument,[13] Justice Powell skeptically inquired:

> Apart from biological interest, which I do not challenge, what purpose is served, if any, by those little darters? Are they used for food?... Are they suitable for bait?[14]

Many advocates defending strong endangered species protections therefore try to stress human utilitarian reasons for doing so. In the spotted owl debates, environmentalists emphasize the useful function played by the owl in maintaining the ecological and water-cycle balance in Pacific Northwest forests.[15] They tell how the Pacific yew tree (*Taxis brevifolia*), a slow-growing, endangered plant living under the ancient forest

---

13. Transcript of Oral Argument, Apr. 18, 1976, at 43–44.

14. This and the quotation that follows are from Transcript of Oral Argument, Apr. 18, 1976, at 43–44.

15. D. Kelly & G. Braasch, Secrets of the Old Growth Forest 32 (1988). The owl's droppings spread critically important water-storing fungus spores to root systems throughout its habitat.

canopy, is the only known source of taxol, a promising new drug for treating ovarian and breast cancer. Protection of endangered species' habitat protects the critical sources of useful medicines and other products, some of which will remain unknown until future scientists find them, if the trees survive.

But most endangered species will not cure cancer, so utilitarian arguments must range further. The environmentalists answered Justice Powell's question with a utilitarian argument that

> this species turns out to be a highly sensitive indicator of precisely the qualities of the habitat that citizens were fighting about in this case for years before the snail darter was known to exist.

This is the now-familiar "canary in the coal mine" argument. Like the canaries carried down into the mines (because the birds were sensitive to odorless methane coal gas, when they began to asphyxiate, it was time for miners to flee), endangered species can be vivid living indicators of important human concerns. Endangered birdlife and frogs revealed the danger of DDT and other pesticides to humans. The snail darter, like most endangered species, thus acts as a sensitive physical and legal barometer of endangered human values as well as of the ecological qualities in its habitat.[16]

4. **Roadblocks' superior citizen litigatability.** The roadblock character of ESA §7 was important because a looser standard would have been much tougher for citizens to enforce. What exactly was the legal cause of action in TVA v. Hill? Did TVA violate §7's requirements (a) that agencies "shall [carry] out programs for the conservation of endangered species," (b) that agency actions "shall not jeopardize the continued existence of endangered species," and (c) that agency actions "shall not…result in the destruction or modification of [critical] habitat"? The initial "conservation" count (a) is rather vague and open-ended and hasn't been used much by citizen litigants.[17] The latter two provisions are both roadblocks, however, and are the basis of most ESA litigation. As in TVA v. Hill, they often arise concurrently. Thinking like a litigator, which of the two is analytically easier to prove?

What if the operative verb in §7 had been written "may" instead of "shall"? What if the 1973 ESA had retained the phrase from the 1966 ESA, "insofar as practicable and consistent with the [agency's] purposes"? Would the snail darter in either case have reached the Supreme Court? Would endangered species protection today be taken seriously by agencies and industry?

5. **The results of TVA v. Hill's enforcement of the §7 roadblock.** Due in no small measure to its notoriety in the dam-blocking case, ESA §7 became a significant

---

16. See The Embattled Social Utilities of the Endangered Species Act — A Noah Presumption, and a Caution against Putting Gas Masks on the Canaries in the Coal Mine, 27 Envtl. L. 845 (1997).

17. Do agencies have affirmative conservation duties under this clause, which now is generally known as ESA §7(a)? In Carson-Truckee Water Conservancy Dist. v. Clark, 741 F.2d 257 (9th Cir. 1984), the court held that the Department of Interior was required not only to protect existing habitats and endangered species but also to "use programs administered by [the Department] to further the conservation purposes of [the ESA]." The Department must "conserve threatened and endangered species to the extent that they are no longer threatened" and "halt *and reverse* the trend toward species extinction, whatever the cost." 741 F.2d at 262 (the emphasis is the court's). See also Palila v. Hawaii Dep't of Land & Natural Res., 852 F.2d 1106 (9th Cir. 1988). But finding case settings where this vague provision will be enforced is difficult.

regulatory program in the years immediately following the snail darter decision, enjoying substantial increases in its annual budget allocations and a new degree of (sometimes grudging) respect for its regulatory potency from agency bureaucrats and industrial lobbyists. Scientific surveys for endangered species impacts became an accepted part of agency project planning and permit application processes.

The courts since TVA v. Hill generally have been more attentive to the Act's requirements than the national administration. In most cases, courts have strictly interpreted the ESA to the detriment of powerful market forces. Oil well leases have been delayed, a major East Coast refinery was scuttled in part because of endangered species problems, western water reclamation allocations have been changed to favor species protection over industrial and municipal use, and the courts have enforced the Act without reference to the "significance" of the species concerned. How strong would the courts have been in these cases had not the Supreme Court held such a strong line in a highly publicized case poising an "insignificant" species against a purported multimillion dollar project? Judicial experience to date thus offers indications that future cases will be held to a high level of species protection. The snail darter itself may be subject to continued disparagement, and it ultimately did not fare well in congressional pork-barrel politics, but its precedential position seems to have secured protections to its comrades throughout the natural world. Endangered species protection seems likely to be with us for a long time, and the well-publicized roadblock provisions of ESA §7 deserve much of the credit.

6. **Pressures for flexibility.** Strict prohibitions cause forceful backlashes from the interests they regulate. In virtually every case, some affected parties will argue strongly for eliminating the roadblock or opening it up with a variety of discretionary or bureaucratic flexibility devices. In truth, stark roadblocks can sometimes be overinclusive, heavy-handed, and even irrational when applied in the realities of a complex world. Inevitably there will be circumstances in which they may require modification. How and when should flexibility be considered? Pork-barrel agencies and a number of corporate lobbying coalitions began pushing for repeal or amendment of the ESA as soon as the snail darter decision was announced.

7. **Do courts have a role in making flexible adjustments? Statutory violations and equitable balancing.** What if the courts had taken it on themselves to "moderate" the terms of the Act in the process of its judicial application? One way for a roadblock to lose its stringency is if appellate courts say that it need not be enforced if violated. Justice Burger's opinion, however, declared a ringing endorsement of the environmentalists' proposition (and the basis of their empowerment strategy) that if citizens are able to prove a statutory violation, the court must enforce the law without equitable balancing and transfer the debate to the legislative forum. This was a fairly conservative, nonactivist theory of judicial review. It distinguished the traditional three areas of equitable balancing[18] and argued that where statutory violations are concerned, the scope of equitable balancing is restricted to threshold questions (of laches, clean hands,

---

18. A threshold equitable balance to assert standing, a balance of which actions are to be permitted and which proscribed, and a balance to tailor appropriate remedies. See Chapter 3.

and so on) and to the question of which remedy is necessary to effectuate the legislature's substantive prohibition. It does not extend to second-guessing what actions should be prohibited.

Justice Rehnquist wrote a scathing dissent in TVA v. Hill arguing that trial judges, as in this case, should have equitable discretion to override statutory violations, allowing projects to go on. This activist argument raises a basic question about roadblock statutes. When they are violated, who should be able to grant the necessary flexibility — a trial judge "balancing the equities" or Congress? The plaintiffs argued throughout the case that it was perfectly proper for Congress to consider such exemptions. In that way citizens might win the opportunity to have full, rational legislative hearings on the issue, based on the tactical leverage of the injunction.[19] The citizens successfully argued under Hecht v. Bowles, 321 U.S. 321 (1944), that if a violation existed, courts' narrow role is to apply their discretion so as to see that the law was obeyed.

The basic remedy question in the snail darter case — whether courts are bound to enforce statutes when citizens prove violations — continues. Weinberger v. Romero-Barcelo, 456 U.S. 305 (1982) (violation of CWA not so critical as ESA in *Hill*, so no injunction); Amoco Prod. Co. v. Village of Gambell, 480 U.S. 531 (1987) (court implies some judicial flexibility not to enforce laws);[20] cf. Sierra Club v. Marsh, 872 F.2d 497, 500 (1st Cir. 1989) (court could not override statutory violation).

8. **Flexibility through statutory interpretation?** The Supreme Court's opinion in TVA v. Hill included an extensive analysis rejecting the agency's arguments that the statute should be interpreted not to cover the snail darter and the dam — primarily arguments based on retroactivity, implied amendment, and "common sense."

The retroactivity argument urged that since the concrete part of the dam, worth $5 million of the $150 million total, had been built before the ESA was passed, the project could continue even if it would eliminate the endangered species. The Court upheld the citizens' argument that a statute should be applied if it prohibits actions that would cause, as in Justice Holmes's dictum, "the evils that the legislature intended to address." Further, governmental agencies have no vested or civil right to proceed with favorite projects in spite of subsequent federal legislation (see Thorpe v. Housing Auth., 393 U.S. 268 (1969), noted in the *Overton Park* case).

TVA had continued to receive funding for the dam project from the pork-barrel appropriations committees year after year despite the committee's knowledge of the endangered species statutory violation. The agency and appropriations committees also added phrases to the annual funding bills stating the committees' opinion that the Act did not apply, that the Act was frivolous in this setting, and that the importance of the project so exceeded the importance of the endangered species that the project should continue irrespective of any possible statutory violation. TVA argued that

---

19. See Plater, Statutory Violations and Equitable Discretion, 70 Cal. L. Rev. 524, 583-588 (1982).

20. *Gambell* holds that a court may balance the equities so as to allow a violation to continue, although it includes language that "environmental injury, by its nature, can seldom be adequately remedied by money damages and is often permanent or at least of long duration, i.e., irreparable. If such injury is sufficiently likely, therefore, the balance of harms will usually favor the issuance of an injunction to protect the environment." 480 U.S. at 545.

continued funding, plus this legislative intent, constituted an implied amendment, implied repealer, or implied statutory exception to the Act. The Supreme Court disagreed, noting a long line of cases declaring that repeals by implication are suspect, particularly if they are found in appropriations bills, which typically deal with budgetary and financial matters rather than substantive law.

As to common sense in statutory interpretation, at many stages during the course of the litigation, and in the halls of Congress and the agencies, it was argued that a statute should not be applied if it would lead to what the particular observer considered an "absurd" or "extreme" result. As Justice Powell said:

> In my view §7 cannot reasonably be interpreted as applying to a project that is completed or substantially completed when its threat to an endangered species is discovered. Nor can I believe that Congress could have intended this Act to produce the "absurd result" — in the words of the District Court — of this case. 437 U.S. at 196.

The Supreme Court held, however, that even when a statute led to what a court might think was an absurd result, if the facts fit the law, the statute was to be applied as it was written.

9. **Flexibility: remand to Congress.** Throughout the Tellico Dam case, the environmentalists had argued that courts should merely enforce the statute, and the matter then would necessarily be transferred to the legislature. It might not be very convenient to make Congress consider specific legislative resolutions for every conflict that can't be handled in the agencies, but it provides a democratic safety valve and, as in the Tennessee case, can give citizens their first chance to obtain public review of the controversy on the factual and economic merits.

The snail darter case by no means ended with the Supreme Court decision, given the cantankerousness of the contending parties. Congress responded with three series of hearings in the relevant substantive committees, considering whether this extreme application of the law should be reversed. Three times the committees were convinced, much to their surprise, that preservation of the river was not an example of environmental irrationality; no Tellico amendment was passed. The media, however, remained fixated on its "fish-bites-dam" characterization of the case.

10. **Flexibility from an extraordinary tribunal: the God Committee Amendments and the snail darter.** The snail darter's saga continued when Congress was persuaded to create the so-called God Committee, or God Squad, a new statutory flexibility device to calm the avalanche of criticism levied against the "extremism" of the Act revealed by the snail darter decision. Subchapter C of this chapter discusses that part of the darter's story.

11. **ESA procedures: consultation.** The §7 roadblock provision in its original form contained a bare requirement for endangered species "consultation" between Interior and other agencies. When it became clear that §7 was strictly enforceable, the consultation process evolved quickly in agency practice to mediate conflicting interests. By 1979, Department of Interior records showed that more than 4500 potential conflicts between endangered species and federal projects had arisen, and in all but four cases the

agencies were able to adjust project design, timing, or location to accommodate the ESA protections. The formal consultation process has been elaborated and regularized by amendments and regulations. 16 U.S.C. §1536(b)(3) (1978); 50 C.F.R. pt. 402. If agencies or concerned citizens believe that a possible species problem exists, they may ask the Department of Interior to do a Biological Assessment to ascertain if it is so. If the BA finds a threat to endangered species, the project agency requests formal consultation, which triggers a strict time schedule. FWS undertakes active consultation and must issue a Biological Opinion, or Jeopardy Opinion, analyzing the conflict and suggesting alternatives, if necessary, within 90 days. In the aftermath of TVA v. Hill, compliance with these procedures became far more consistent. When a Jeopardy Opinion is issued indicating a threat to a species' continued existence, agencies tend to react to avoid the threat, knowing that if they do not, citizen enforcement is likely to follow.

12. **A tactical footnote on ESA legislative history.** Would it change your view of §7 of the 1973 ESA if you were told that it had been consciously drafted by a legislative aide and several ardent wildlife advocates in a form that would avoid its being recognized as a substantive roadblock statute? If §7, which has become one of the landmark environmental protections in federal law, would never have been passed without a virtually impenetrable verbal camouflage, what does that say about Congress and the legislative process? What does it say about the ethics of the provision's drafters, who successfully slipped it into federal law? Is it a satisfactory excuse that the opponents of environmental protection regularly slip exceptions and destructive undercutting amendments into ongoing legislation?

The tactical questions that arise when environmentalists actively participate in the legislative process continually force thoughtful people to reconsider their philosophy of government, views of public interest advocacy, and ethics.

And the coursebook text at the beginning of this chapter virtually admits that the plaintiffs used the snail darter as a convenient "handle" to raise public issues about farmland, historic values, river recreation, and economics. As Justice Burger said during the oral argument, "the snail darter was discovered, and became a handy handle [for dam opponents] to hold onto.... I'm sure that they just don't want this project!" Was this litigation a misuse of the law, one that moreover selfishly risked the destruction of the ESA itself?

Section 3. SPOTTED OWLS AND ANCIENT FORESTS

Seattle Audubon Society v. John L. Evans (U.S. Forest Service)
and Washington Contract Loggers Association
United States District Court, Western District of Washington, 1991
771 F. Supp. 1081

DWYER, J.... Plaintiffs Seattle Audubon Society, et al. have moved for a permanent injunction prohibiting the sale of logging rights in northern spotted owl [*strix occidentalis caurina*] habitat areas.... The national forests are managed by the Forest Service.... Regulations promulgated under [NFMA, the National Forest Management Act, and the ESA] provide that fish and wildlife shall be managed to maintain viable populations of existing native and desired non-native vertebrate species.... A viable population is "one which has the estimated numbers and distribution of reproductive individuals to insure its continued existence is well distributed in the planning area." To insure viability, habitat must be provided to support at least a minimum number of reproductive individuals.... Since not every species can be monitored, "indicator species" are observed as signs of general wildlife viability. The northern spotted owl is an indicator species....

In recent years logging and development have steadily reduced wildlife habitat in the Pacific Northwest. At the same time many local mills have experienced log shortages. The result is an intensified struggle over the future of the national forests.... In June 1990, the Fish and Wildlife Service...listed the owl as a threatened species under the Endangered Species Act.... On February 26, 1991, Judge Zilly ruled that the FWS had again failed to comply with the law, stating:

> Upon the record presented, this Court finds the Service has failed to discharge its obligations under the Endangered Species Act and its own administrative regulations. Specifically, the Service, acting on behalf of the Secretary of the Interior, abused its discretion when it determined not to designate critical habitat concurrently with the listing of the northern spotted owl, or to explain any basis for concluding that the critical habitat was not determinable. These actions were arbitrary and capricious, and contrary to law. Northern Spotted Owl v. Lujan, 758 F. Supp. 621, 629 (W.D. Wash. 1991).

[In September 1990, without notice, hearing, environmental impact statement, or other rulemaking procedures, the Forest Service announced that it was proceeding with the timber sales, and this court issued a preliminary injunction.]...

The fate of the spotted owl has become a battleground largely because the species is a symbol of the remaining old growth forest. As stated in the Interagency Scientific Committee (ISC) Report:

> Why all the fuss about the status and welfare of this particular bird? The numbers, distribution, and welfare of spotted owls are widely believed to be inextricably tied to mature and old-growth forests. Such forests have been significantly reduced since 1850 (mostly since 1950) by clearing for agriculture, urban development, natural events such as fire and windstorms, and most significantly, by logging in recent decades. Nearly all old growth has been removed on private lands. Most of the remainder is under the management of the BLM, FS, and NPS on Federal lands. As its habitat has declined, the owl has virtually disappeared from some areas and its numbers are decreasing in others.

An old growth forest consists not just of ancient standing trees, but of fallen trees, snags, massive decaying vegetation, and numerous resident plant and animal species, many of which live nowhere else. A great conifer forest originally covered the western parts of Washington, Oregon, and Northern California, from the Cascade and Coast mountains to the sea. Perhaps ten percent of it remains. The spaces protected as parks or wilderness areas are not enough for the survival of the northern spotted owl. The old growth forest sustains a biological community far richer than those of managed forests or tree farms. As testified by Dr. William Ferrell, a forest ecologist: "The most significant implication from our new knowledge regarding old-growth forest ecology is that logging these forests destroys not just trees, but a complex, distinctive, and unique ecosystem." The remaining old growth stands are valued also for their effects on climate, air, and migratory fish runs, and for their beauty. A 1984 Forest Service document summed up the controversy:

> There are at least three main reasons cited for maintaining old growth: wildlife and plant habitat, ecosystem diversity, and preservation of aesthetic qualities. Those opposed to the retention of old growth are primarily concerned with economic factors

FIGURE 16-2

The winged blur in the center right of this ancient forest clearing is a rare daylight image of the northern spotted owl (Strix occidentalis caurina), *perhaps about to strike a red-backed vole. The background shows a fallen "nurse log" which opens a hole in the canopy for sunlight to reach the forest floor, allowing new trees to grow up from the nurse log's decomposing organic matter. The lushness of the decomposition and growth processes in the natural old-growth forests of the Pacific Northwest is supported by rhizoform fungus nodules in the forest's root systems. The fungi provide nutrients and water retention to balance forest moisture throughout the low-precipitation summer season. Red-backed voles live in the nurse logs and specialize in eating the subsoil fungal truffles. The owls eat the voles. The fungi are then transplanted through the forests in owl pellet droppings. Without the owl, the forest's balances of life and water are disrupted.*

and urge rapid conversion of the existing old growth to managed forests of productive, young age classes. Forest Service, Regional Guide for Pacific Northwest Region 3-40 (May 1984).

Through most of the country's history there was little or no logging in the national forests. Intensive logging began with World War II and has accelerated.... Despite increasing concern over the environment, logging sales by the Forest Service have continued on a large scale....

The records of this case...show a remarkable series of violations of the environmental laws.... In the fall of 1990 the Forest Service admitted that [its protocol for logging old growth national forests] was inadequate after all — that it would fail to preserve the northern spotted owl. In seeking a stay of proceedings in this court in 1989 the Forest Service announced its intent to adopt temporary guidelines within thirty days. It did not do that within thirty days, or ever. When directed by Congress to have a revised ROD [record of decision] in place by September 30, 1990, the Forest Service did not even attempt to comply....

The reasons for this pattern of behavior were made clear at the evidentiary hearing. [A Forest Service wildlife biologist testified that] "in every instance there was a considerable — I would emphasize considerable — amount of political pressure to create a plan which was an absolute minimum. That is, which had a very low probability of success and which had a minimum impact on timber harvest...." [Other testimony showed repeated political amendments to the spotted owl plan made in executive offices in Washington.]...

The agency...has the benefit of an [endangered species consultation] opinion letter from the FWS...commenting at length on the ISC strategy and giving recommendations. With the knowledge at hand, there is no reason for the Forest Service to fail to develop quickly a plan to ensure the viability of the spotted owl in the national forests. The northern spotted owl is now threatened with extinction. The ISC Report states:

> We have concluded that the owl is imperiled over significant portions of its range because of continuing losses of habitat from logging and natural disturbances. Current management strategies are inadequate to ensure its viability. Moreover, in some portions of the owl's range, few options for managing habitat remain open, and available alternatives are steadily declining throughout the bird's range....

The population of northern spotted owls continues to decline. "We're going to have to arrest that decline and reverse it," as Dr. Thomas testified. "Spotted owl habitat," also called "suitable habitat," is defined as follows by FWS:

> Suitable owl habitat has moderate to high canopy closure (60 to 80 percent); a multi-layered, multi-species canopy dominated by large (> 30 inches in diameter at breast height (dbh)) overstory trees; a high incidence of large trees with various deformities (e.g., large cavities, broken tops, dwarf-mistletoe infections, and other evidence of decadence); numerous large snags; large accumulations of fallen trees and other woody debris on the ground; and sufficient open space below the canopy for owls to fly.

The Forest Service estimates that an additional 66,000 acres of spotted owl habitat would be destroyed if logging went forward to the extent permitted by the ISC Report over the next sixteen months. That would be in addition to about 400,000 acres of habitat logged in the seven years since the agency began preparing these guidelines, all without having a lawful plan or EIS for the owl's management in place....

Over the past decade many timber jobs have been lost and mills closed in the Pacific Northwest. The main reasons have been modernization of physical plants, changes in product demand, and competition from elsewhere. Supply shortages have also played a part. Those least able to adapt and modernize, and those who have not gained alternative supplies, have been hardest hit by the changes....

Job losses in the wood products industry will continue regardless of whether the northern spotted owl is protected.... The timber industry no longer drives the Pacific Northwest's economy.... The wood products industry now employs about four percent of all workers in Western Oregon, two percent in Western Washington, and six percent in Northern California. Even if some jobs in wood products were affected by protecting owl habitat in the short-term, any effect on the regional economy probably would be small.

The remaining wilderness contributes to the desirability of this region as a site for new industries and their employees. The resulting economic gains, while hard to measure, are genuine and substantial. The FWS has recently noted that preservation of old growth brings economic benefits and amenities "of extremely high value." The court must weigh and consider the public interest in deciding whether to issue an injunction in an environmental case.... The public interest and the balance of equities require the issuance of an injunction directing the Forest Service to comply with the requirements of NFMA, and preventing it from selling additional logging rights in spotted owl habitat until it complies with the law.

COMMENTARY & QUESTIONS

1. **The ESA and the owl.** Note that *Seattle Audubon* is not a pure ESA case. The endangered species issues — primarily raised in parallel lawsuits in the Oregon and Washington district courts[21] — provided the backdrop for *Seattle Audubon*'s NFMA injunction. Judge Dwyer's excerpted opinion reveals the conflicting public interests and the pressures within the federal agencies about the listing of the owl and its critical habitat.

According to the data of the ISC Report, the spotted owl's survival probably would not have been threatened by cutting the 4 billion board feet of timber already sold, but probably would have been by further cutting thereafter. Thus §7's prohibitions would kick in only when the owl's habitat was knowingly brought to the brink of endangerment. Might §7's affirmative conservation provisions support earlier anticipatory protective efforts?

Facing the inevitability of a §7 injunction action, Interior Secretary Lujan took the spotted owl into the God Committee exemption process as noted later in this chapter.

2. **Owl politics and economics.** *Seattle Audubon* describes much of the political backdrop of the spotted owl controversy. The privately owned old-growth forests have long since been largely eliminated, replaced with monoculture (single species) tree farms that are less productive in terms of biomass and have not served to maintain the industry. (They have also drastically reduced plant and wildlife ecosystem diversity.) Timber companies have thus turned to the remaining old-growth public forests to maintain their prosperity, in large part through exports of raw timber to Japan and Korea.

The coalition against the owl is led by the forest products industry's national associations, with its public positions vocally presented in the media by loggers whose jobs appear threatened.[22] The spotted owl issue is often portrayed in the media as a "jobs vs. owls" conflict, but the actual tradeoff is more subtle: The historical backdrop is the timber industry's past broad-scale cutting of private lands, and more than two-thirds of the marketable public forests, with inadequate reforestation.

The economic reality of the conflict, moreover, is a massive program of latent federal subsidies. Federal taxpayers subsidize the timber industry in the following four major ways (in ascending order)

  • The Forest Service sells timber from national forests below regular market price.[23]

---

21. Lane County Audubon v. Jamison, No. 91-6123 (D. Or. Sept. 11, 1991, Jones, J.); Northern Spotted Owl v. Hodel & Northern Spotted Owl v. Lujan, 716 F. Supp. 478, amended by 758 F. Supp. 621 (W.D. Wash. 1988 and 1991, Zilly, J.). Judge Dwyer lifted the injunction in the excerpted case in June 1994 after the federal agency had complied with statutory procedures.

22. The Northwest's loggers have taken a yellow ribbon tied to the truck antenna as their totem, arguing forcefully against environmental accounting and cuts in public subsidies and informally advocating extermination of the spotted owl. With mass gatherings of logging trucks on the roads and in the capitals of the Northwest, the yellow-ribbon timber cutters have forcefully argued their "special five" on timbering: "Shoot an owl, save a job." "I love spotted owls... *fried*." "If it comes down to my family or that bird, that bird's going to suffer." Time, June 25, 1990, at 60. See Plater, Political Tribalism in Natural Resources Management, 11 Pub. Land L. Rev. 1, 11 (1990).

23. The Forest Service sets its auction base price with reference to the *average* potential buyer, rather than the normal appraisal standard of the highest price that would be paid by a willing buyer to a private market seller. See Wolf, National Forest Timber Sales and the Legacy of Gifford Pinchot: Managing a Forest and Making It Pay, 60 U. Colo. L. Rev. 1037 (1989); and Wolf's resource analyses prepared at the request of the House Governmental Operations Subcommittee on Environment, Energy, and Natural Resources, 102d Cong., 1st Sess., Fall 1991.

- The Service spends several hundred million dollars per year on building and maintaining logging roads in rugged terrain (to date the Service has built seven times more road mileage than the entire interstate highway system) and on providing other free services to the industry. In many cases, the timber itself is even sold below the government's own out-of-pocket cash flow costs. During the 1980s, the Service sold 124 billion board feet at a loss of $3.5 billion; for fiscal 1997 alone, the net loss was more than $2.2 billion.[24]

- The Forest Service pays 25% of its gross timber receipts to local communities as payments in lieu of property taxes.[25]

- Fourth, the largest subsidy (unaccounted for in economic analyses) is the subsidy extracted from the economy of nature and the civic-societal economy — the permanent sacrifice of thousands of acres of diverse natural forests, often on fragile, high-elevation steep slopes that otherwise would be available for multiple nonlogging public uses. The logging of old-growth forests leads to severe erosion, wildlife losses, water quality degradation, a tenfold drop in the ecosystem's diversity of species per acre, and other serious long-term effects.[26]

Thus in this, as many other cases, economic analysis can refute the traditional industry argument that we have to choose between economics and ecology. Sound economics are better served by environmentally sensitive planning and management of the forests on principles of sustainability. More jobs can be maintained in the forest industries if clearcutting is replaced by selective-cut harvesting, which maintains forest ecosystems rather than turning public lands into species-depleted, row-planted, monoculture tree farms.

But is it likely that the nation's forest management processes would have forced the timber industry into serious planning and biodiversity conservation efforts if it had not been for the spotted owl ESA roadblock?

3. **Protecting ecosystems instead of just individual species?** The spotted owl is an indicator of the declining health of the old-growth ecosystem, which is characterized by unparalleled biodiversity. If we want to preserve biodiversity, why don't we simply set aside bioreserves instead of indirectly attempting to preserve ecosystems through protection of individual endangered species?

Much scholarly comment has been directed to the preferability of protecting entire ecosystems. The ESA, perhaps mistakenly, wasn't primarily targeted to preserve ecosystem habitats. Are we being fair, not only to ourselves but also to the spotted owls and snail darters of the world, when we use indicator species as legal "handles" to preserve

---

24. If interest is figured in, the 1980s' number is a loss of $6.3 billion. Other services besides providing roads include surveying and inventorying timberlands, fire protection, staff personnel and structures, mapmaking, and disease control. Under cost-accounting analysis, most of the 122 national forests have never earned a penny on timber; in 1990, only 15 showed a cash flow profit. See Wolf's resource analyses, cited supra, at note 23; Knize, The Mismanagement of the National Forests, Atlantic Monthly, Oct. 1991, at 98-101. 1990s net losses averaged over $2 billion per year. See 14 Different Drummer (Spring 1998), at Supp. 1-4.

25. In 1990 this amounted to $327 million. The theory of these payments is that the federal government ought to contribute because it is exempt from state and local property taxation. The Service does not reckon these and many other public costs against revenues in figuring net revenues. See 14 Different Drummer (Spring 1998), at Supp. 1-4.

26. See Young, Tree Slaughter: Your Taxes at Work, Wash. Post, Aug. 13, 1989, at B3; Barlow, Evolution of the NFMA, 8 Envtl. L. 539 (1978).

critical ecosystems? Or does our political system, which functions to muddle through and "satisfice" conflicting demands, militate against attacking the habitat issue directly? If it is difficult to define and prohibit hazards to individual species, how much more difficult would it be to base protections on ecosystems? Does it tell you something that the timber industry has argued that ESA protections should be based on ecosystems to be enforced only at some future date when we know enough to do so? Is the species-oriented ESA only a stopgap measure while we build a political constituency for broader ecosystem and bioreserve protections?

Section 4. ESA §9 AND THE "NO TAKE" PROVISION

The ESA had another lurking roadblock provision, this one potentially even more politically explosive because it potentially hits private land as well as federal agencies.

Babbitt v. Sweet Home Communities for a Great Oregon
Supreme Court of the United States, 1995
515 U.S. 687

STEVENS, J. The Endangered Species Act of 1973 contains a variety of protections designed to save from extinction species that the Secretary of the Interior designates as endangered or threatened....

Section 9(a)(1) of the Endangered Species Act provides the following protection for endangered species:

...With respect to any endangered species of fish or wildlife listed pursuant to section 1533 of this title it is unlawful for any person subject to the jurisdiction of the United States to...(B) take any such species within the United States or the territorial sea of the United States. 16 U.S.C. §1538(a)(1).

Section 3(19) of the Act, 16 U.S.C. §1532(19), defines the statutory term "take":

The term "take" means to harass, harm, pursue, hunt, shoot, wound, kill, trap, capture, or collect, or to attempt to engage in any such conduct.

The Act does not further define the terms it uses to define "take." The Interior Department regulations that implement the statute, however, 50 C.F.R. §17.3, define the statutory term "harm":

"Harm" in the definition of "take" in the Act means an act which actually kills or injures wildlife. Such act may include significant habitat modification or degradation where it actually kills or injures wildlife by significantly impairing essential behavioral patterns, including breeding, feeding, or sheltering....

Respondents in this action are small landowners, logging companies, and families dependent on the forest products industries in the Pacific Northwest and in the Southeast, and organizations that represent their interests. They brought this declaratory judgment action against petitioners...to challenge the statutory validity of the Secretary's regulation defining "harm," particularly the inclusion of habitat modification and degradation in the definition.... Their complaint alleged that application of the "harm" regulation to the red-cockaded woodpecker, an endangered species, and the northern spotted owl, a threatened species, had injured them economically....

We assume respondents have no desire to harm either the red-cockaded woodpecker or the spotted owl; they merely wish to continue logging activities that would be entirely proper if not prohibited by the ESA. On the other hand, we must assume arguendo that those activities will have the effect, even though unintended, of detrimentally changing the natural habitat of both listed species and that, as a consequence, members of those species will be killed or injured. Under respondents' view of the law, the Secretary's only means of forestalling that grave result — even when the actor knows it is certain to occur — is to use his §5 authority to purchase the lands on which the survival of the species depends....

The text of the Act provides three reasons for concluding that the Secretary's interpretation is reasonable.... The dictionary definition of the verb form of "harm" is "to cause hurt or damage; to injure." In the context of the ESA, that definition naturally encompasses habitat modification that results in actual injury or death to members of an endangered or threatened species.... The dictionary definition does not include the word "directly" or suggest in any way that only direct or willful action that leads to injury constitutes "harm."...

Second, the broad purpose of the ESA supports the Secretary's decision to extend protection against activities that cause the precise harms Congress enacted the statute to avoid. In TVA v. Hill, 437 U.S. 153 (1978), we described the Act as "the most comprehensive legislation for the preservation of endangered species ever enacted by any nation"..., among its central purposes is "to provide a means whereby the ecosystems upon which endangered species and threatened species depend may be conserved." "The plain intent of Congress in enacting this statute," we recognized, "was to halt and reverse the trend toward species extinction, whatever the cost. This is reflected not only in the stated policies of the Act, but in literally every section of the statute." Although the §9 "take" prohibition was not at issue in Hill, we took note of that prohibition, placing particular emphasis on the Secretary's inclusion of habitat modification in his definition of "harm."... Respondents...ask us to invalidate the Secretary's understanding of "harm" in every circumstance, even when an actor knows that an activity, such as draining a pond, would actually result in the extinction of a listed species by destroying its habitat....

Third, the fact that Congress in 1982 authorized the Secretary to issue permits for takings that §9(a)(1)(B) would otherwise prohibit, "if such taking is incidental to, and not the purpose of, the carrying out of an otherwise lawful activity," 16 U.S.C. §1539(a)(1)(B), strongly suggests that Congress understood §9(a)(1)(B) to prohibit indirect as well as deliberate takings.... Several of the words that accompany "harm" in the §3 definition of "take," especially "harass," "pursue," "wound," and "kill," refer to actions or effects that do not require direct applications of force.... The statutory context of "harm" suggests that Congress meant that term to serve a particular function in the ESA, consistent with but distinct from the functions of the other verbs used to define "take."...

Our conclusion that the Secretary's definition of "harm" rests on a permissible construction of the ESA gains further support from the legislative history of the statute. The Committee Reports accompanying the bills that became the ESA do not specifically discuss the meaning of "harm," but they make clear that Congress intended "take" to apply broadly to cover indirect as well as purposeful actions. The Senate Report stressed that "'take' is defined...in the broadest possible manner to include every conceivable way in which a person can 'take' or attempt to 'take' any fish or wildlife." The House Report stated that "the broadest possible terms" were used to define restrictions on takings. The House Report underscored the breadth of the "take" definition by noting that it included "harassment, whether intentional or not...." "When Congress has entrusted the Secretary with broad discretion, we are especially reluctant to substitute our views of wise policy for his. See Chevron. In this case, that reluctance accords with our conclusion, based on the text, structure, and legislative history of the ESA, that the Secretary reasonably construed the intent of Congress when he defined "harm" to include "significant habitat modification or degradation that actually kills or injures wildlife."... Reversed.

O'CONNOR, J., concurring.…The challenged regulation is limited to significant habitat modification that causes actual, as opposed to hypothetical or speculative, death or injury to identifiable protected animals.… I do not find it as easy as Justice Scalia does to dismiss the notion that significant impairment of breeding injures living creatures. To raze the last remaining ground on which the piping plover currently breeds, thereby making it impossible for any piping plovers to reproduce, would obviously injure the population (causing the species' extinction in a generation). But by completely preventing breeding, it would also injure the individual living bird, in the same way that sterilizing the creature injures the individual living bird. To "injure" is, among other things, "to impair."… To make it impossible for an animal to reproduce is to impair its most essential physical functions and to render that animal, and its genetic material, biologically obsolete. This, in my view, is actual injury.…

SCALIA, J., joined by REHNQUIST, C.J., and THOMAS, J., dissenting. I think it unmistakably clear that the legislation at issue here (1) forbade the hunting and killing of endangered animals, and (2) provided federal lands and federal funds for the acquisition of private lands, to preserve the habitat of endangered animals. The Court's holding that the hunting and killing prohibition incidentally preserves habitat on private lands imposes unfairness to the point of financial ruin — not just upon the rich, but upon the simplest farmer who finds his land conscripted to national zoological use.… To "take," when applied to wild animals, means to reduce those animals, by killing or capturing, to human control…, a class of acts (not omissions) done directly and intentionally (not indirectly and by accident) to particular animals (not populations of animals).… "Harm" is merely one of 10 prohibitory words…and the other 9 fit the ordinary meaning of "take" perfectly. To "harass, pursue, hunt, shoot, wound, kill, trap, capture, or collect" are all affirmative acts…which are directed immediately and intentionally against a particular animal.…

The regulation…produces a result that no legislature could reasonably be thought to have intended: A large number of routine private activities — farming, for example, ranching, road building, construction and logging — are subjected to strict-liability penalties when they fortuitously injure protected wildlife, no matter how remote the chain of causation.… [Eds. — Justice Scalia, who traditionally is (justifiably) skeptical about excessive reliance upon legislative history, then dismisses the majority's use of congressional committee reports that suggested "take" should be defined in "the broadest possible manner," as an "empty flourish." He focuses on the removal of a habitat destruction ban from one bill and on land acquisition "as the Act's only response to habitat modification by private landowners."]

Habitat modification can constitute a "taking," but only if it results in the killing or harming of individual animals, and only if that consequence is the direct result of the modification. This means that the destruction of privately owned habitat that is essential, not for the feeding or nesting, but for the breeding, of butterflies, would not violate the Act, since it would not harm or kill any living butterfly.… Only action directed at living animals constitutes a "take."… I respectfully dissent.

COMMENTARY & QUESTIONS

1. **What's going on here?** Is this a seminar on statutory interpretation? An administrative law exercise deciding whether to defer to an agency's interpretive regulation? Remember that *Sweet Home* reflects one pitched battle in the ongoing war between western "Wise Use" backers of local sovereignty, resource exploitation corporations, and private property rights activists, on the one hand, and the federal government, environmental

preservationists, and others who think that endangered species law may provide the only effective forum for obtaining overall public accounting of challenged activities, on the other. The defenders won this round, but as Justice O'Connor noted, "Congress may, of course, see fit to revisit this issue. And nothing the Court says today prevents the agency itself from narrowing the scope of its regulation at a later date."

A fervent political backlash was inevitable. The potential consequences of the *Sweet Home* decision are dramatic. Land development, which traditionally has been one of the most unregulated, politically charged economic ventures, can now come under federal government scrutiny forcing intense review of the particular facts of a development site and plan, subject to heavy civil and criminal penalties. The definition of "harm" is subjective and potentially extremely broad ranging, and property that is determined important to endangered species may in effect be frozen.

2. **Statutory interpretation games.** The question is about the meaning of one of ten words — the meaning of "harm" in the statutory definition of "take," as to "harass, harm, pursue, hunt, shoot, wound, kill, trap, capture, or collect." Is this another example of legislative legerdemain — "harm," an environmentally protective phrase, being slipped into a statute by indirection, in this case on the Senate floor after "habitat destruction" had been stricken from the bill in committee? Or is it fairly within the central mandate of the Act?

And what of conflicting canons of interpretation? *Noscitur a sociis*, "a word gathers meaning from the words around it," is one canon that the majority used to establish an interpretive context. On the other hand, *Sweet Home*'s narrow-interpretationists had in mind the stricter *ejusdem generis* — "a word should be defined like the others in the same series, without independent meaning." Given the way lawyers in legislatures write statutes, which canonic interpretation should govern?

3. **Foreseeability and proximate cause.** In order to be subject to the Act's criminal penalties or its most severe civil penalties, one must "knowingly violate" the Act or its implementing regulations. 16 U.S.C. §1540(a)(1) and (b)(1). Congress added "knowingly" in place of "willfully" in 1978 to make "criminal violations of the act a general rather than a specific intent crime." As noted in Chapter 20 on environmental crimes, the courts have imputed scienter requirements to criminal statutes that do not expressly require them. The *Sweet Home* majority said that they "do not agree with the dissent that the regulation covers results that are not 'even foreseeable...no matter how long the chain of causality between modification and injury.' Respondents have suggested no reason why either the 'knowingly violates' or the 'otherwise violates' provision of the statute — or the 'harm' regulation itself — should not be read to incorporate ordinary requirements of proximate causation and foreseeability." Given this constraint, how far in practice can the regulatory definition stretch to burden private parties?

4. **Administrative law: *Chevron* creates a roadblock.** Note that in ESA §9 the roadblock was not created by the statute alone. It required agency elaboration of the meaning of the word "harm," reinforced by *Chevron* deference. The *Sweet Home* majority and dissenting opinions treat the *Chevron* precedent differently. The majority said that "our conclusions that Congress did not unambiguously manifest its intent to adopt

respondents' view, and that the Secretary's interpretation is reasonable, suffice to decide this case. *Chevron.* The latitude the ESA gives the Secretary in enforcing the statute, together with the degree of regulatory expertise necessary to its enforcement, establishes that we owe some degree of deference to the Secretary's reasonable interpretation," citing Breyer, Judicial Review of Questions of Law and Policy, 38 Admin. L. Rev. 363, 373 (1986). In dissent, Justice Scalia, a consistent supporter of broad *Chevron* deference to agencies, argued that here the Secretary's decision need not be deferred to because "the regulation…dispense[s] with a [necessary] proximate-cause requirement…. This Court…may not uphold a regulation by adding to it even the most reasonable of elements it does not contain." Justice Scalia implied that he could ignore *Chevron* deference because he would find either that the agency interpretation was unreasonable or that it violated an express congressional mandate. For the majority, however, the agency's interpretation, backed with *Chevron* deference, created a strong statutory roadblock.

C. "ROADBLOCK BYPASSES": SUBSEQUENT MODIFICATIONS CAN CHANGE THE ESA'S STARK STANDARDS (AND WHAT LESSONS CAN BE DRAWN FROM THAT?)

The realities of legal process have led to a variety of explicit and implicit flexibility mechanisms that may or may not be applied to strict roadblock standards. Each mechanism embodies the perils and potentialities of deviations from a clear rule. Balancing accommodations can be made in the following ways:

- *By private ordering:* When private parties — prompted by idealism, business judgment, public or media pressure, or apprehension about the costs of contesting a civic standard — decide to accept it, they are often able to construct practical and beneficial accommodations to eliminate the conflict.

- *By agency conflict-resolving procedures:* Interior, for example, has successfully resolved hundreds of potential species conflicts through formal or informal ESA §7 interagency "consultation" processes,[27] pushing project agencies to alter harmful elements of their plans to adjust to the needs of species protection; there have been hundreds of similar negotiations with private parties under §9.

- *By administrative interpretations of legal terms or facts:* Agencies can in practice make or break a statute in the vast number of decisions that are made in the daily process of implementation — including how they define the terms of a statute or regulation, such as "harm" in *Sweet Home,* or by findings of fact that acknowledge, or evade, critical elements of the statutory mandate. The degree of transparency of the internal agency process can make a great difference in outcomes.

- *By judicial interpretations of legal terms or facts:* As with agency decisions, the role of courts in enforcement actions and judicial review can vary the strictness given to a roadblock. In the Tellico Dam case, Justices Rehnquist and Powell were

---

27. There is always the possibility, of course, that the agency is diluting the law's standards in order to avoid controversy.

clearly ready to take on the legislative balancing act themselves. Court grants or denials of standing, reviewability, deference, narrow scope of review, and equitable relief can operate sub rosa to strengthen or weaken roadblocks.

- *By "slippage" in administrative process, negative or positive, where agencies allow departures from the strict terms of statutes:* In many cases, the logistics and politics of particular cases are such that administrative accommodations are made for a variety of reasons, salutary or corrosive, and neither official nor citizen strict-enforcement action occurs. In these settings, the practical state of the roadblock law is mutated by default.

- *By legislative amendments that eliminate the roadblock provision:* Faced with roadblocks, affected interests often seek to repeal the obstruction. Thus numerous environmental provisions that blocked industry practices, including wetlands and endangered species protections, were targeted for repeal in the 104th Congress, though unsuccessfully. Marketplace lobbying in the legislatures and agency rulemaking likewise try to rescind the procedures that implement a roadblock (as in Chapter 7's §318, selectively eliminating citizen enforcement of the ESA and forestry laws) or to override laws as applied to particular cases (as in the appropriations rider ultimately repealing the ESA insofar as it prevented TVA from building the Tellico Dam).

- *By legislative amendments that incorporate more or less rigorous balancing mechanisms:* As noted below, the ESA offers prime examples, in the 1978 §7 God Committee exemption amendments and in the 1982 "incidental take" amendments to §9. Private property interests further pushed campaigns at the end of the 1990s to expand the incidental take exemptions to incorporate substantial "habitat conservation plan" bargaining into ESA enforcement, allowing moderate harms to endangered species. If balancing is consigned to agency discretion, the species protection process is likely to be narrowed, if not undercut.

In each and every case, of course, the nature of the balance can vary widely, and opportunities for fudging in each direction are constantly presented. For this reason, no flexibility mechanism can be meaningfully evaluated without realistic consideration of its political context.

ESA §§7 and 9, as originally passed and as upheld by the Supreme Court in *Hill* and *Sweet Home*, both embodied stark statutory roadblock prohibitions. This set up a classic dilemma of democratic process. As noted at the start of this chapter, any stark rule is likely to be a blunt instrument that falls short of perfect rationality; yet without the strength of such a strict clear rule the pressures of marketplace politics can often neutralize the nonmarket-based civic values that the law seeks to protect. The trick is to know when and how strict a statutory standard should be.

Despite public interest arguments showing that preserving the endangered snail darter and spotted owl served the public's overall economic interests, industry lobbyists successfully used *Hill* and the §9 cases leading to *Sweet Home* as "extreme examples" supporting a need for amending the ESA. Congress was persuaded to legislate loophole flexibility provisions for the ESA and thus create potential bypasses around the roadblock statutory provisions. Given the belittling press coverage of the endangered species cases, it was thought that the ESA was politically vulnerable and might be repealed if the statute did not receive a §7 flexibility mechanism in 1978 or a "take" exception provision when the §9 prohibition began to be applied. Whether or not the ESA amendments were necessary, they deserve analysis.

Section 1. ESA §7 GOD COMMITTEE AMENDMENTS

In 1978, in response to a lobbying furor against endangered species regulations, Congress added a major exemption procedure to ESA §7.[28] This exemption created a Cabinet-level review board comprised of the Administrators of EPA and NOAA, the Chair of the Council of Economic Advisors, a state representative, and the Secretaries of Army, Agriculture, and Interior. The Committee soon was dubbed the God Committee (and sometimes even more irreverently, the God Squad) because of its authority to issue ESA exemptions allowing extinction of a species if an agency satisfactorily proved a stringent set of criteria.

> 16 U.S.C. §1536(h)...The Committee shall grant an exemption...if, by a vote of not less than five of its [seven] members voting in person —
>
> (A) it determines on the record [after a full hearing] that —
>
> (i) there are no reasonable and prudent alternatives to the agency action;
>
> (ii) the benefits of such action clearly outweigh the benefits of alternative courses of action consistent with conserving the species or its critical habitat, and such action is in the public interest;
>
> (iii) the action is of regional or national significance; and
>
> (B) it establishes...reasonable mitigation and enhancement measures, including, but not limited to, live propagation, transplantation, and habitat acquisition and improvement....

The amendment stipulated that the Tellico project would be one of the first to be reviewed by the God Committee.

COMMENTARY & QUESTIONS

1. **The God Committee amendment of §7: tough tests or a sellout?** How easy is it for an agency to get an exemption under the God Committee process? Is the amendment a tragic watering down of the ESA or a consolidation of the roadblock's strengths? The drafters' inclusion of two tests seriously examining and weighing alternatives (subparagraphs A(i) and (ii) above)[29] forces the God Committee process to go into the heart of these project-species conflicts. As in NEPA cases, it is clear that one of the alternatives that must be considered is "no action." Thus the God Committee §7's endangered species protections provide a forum to explore objective questions about whether a

---

28. See 16 U.S.C. §1536(e)-(o).

29. Coincidentally, the Senate staffer who produced the first draft of the God Committee amendment with its requirements for scrutinizing project alternatives, like Hank Hill the lead plaintiff, had studied environmental law with an early version of this coursebook in a University of Michigan natural resources course that emphasized the *Overton Park* balance.

project or program makes common sense, questions that often cannot be meaningfully raised anywhere else in the political or judicial system.

The amended standards are quite stringent. Is it likely they would have ended up so strict if there had never been a roadblock in the original 1973 act?

2. **The God Committee in practice: the snail darter gets the third degree.** After four months of intensive fact-finding, the snail darter–Tellico Dam case went before the God Committee. Note how the terms of the exemption review gave the plaintiffs' their first chance to argue their full case before a legal forum charged with making a comprehensive judgment on the full project merits. The river defenders had to make their arguments on the basis of tangible economics rather than intangible ecological values and had to show that, despite the expenditure of millions of dollars, the non-dam alternatives still compared favorably to the dam plan.

In a dramatic showdown, the God Committee unanimously denied an exemption for Tellico on economic grounds.[30] As Charles Schultze, then-Chairman of the Council of Economic Advisors and a member of the Committee said:

> Here is a project that is *95 percent complete*, and if one takes just the cost of finishing it against the [total project] benefits, and does it properly, it doesn't pay,...which says something about the original design!

Committee Chairman Secretary of Interior Cecil Andrus said:

> I hate to see the snail darter get the credit for stopping a project that was so ill-conceived and uneconomic in the first place.

The God Committee suggested that TVA start making alternative plans for the Little Tennessee River.

Is it possible to believe that citizens so lacking in funding, political power, and media clout could have achieved this national-level review of the true merits of a powerful agency's pork-barrel project without a stark clear litigatable statutory provision to enforce?

3. **Denouement for the snail darter.** The God Committee had vindicated the citizens on the merits in every element of their long-running campaign against the project. The possibility lay open for an innovative redevelopment of the valley and its river resource. By coordinating the ecological resources with developable elements of the darter's habitat — prime agricultural lands and the valley's historic, touristic, and recreational assets — the darter saga could show the nation what could be accomplished by heeding endangered species.

It was not to be. For the next four and a half months after the God Committee decision, the citizens worked desperately to begin implementation of alternative planning for the river and the valley. TVA, however, declined to talk with the farmers or environmentalists, and nothing happened. On June 18, 1979, in 42 seconds in a nearly empty House chamber, the appropriations committee slipped a rider onto the ongoing House appropriations bill explicitly overriding the Supreme Court decision and all other federal or

---

30. Decision of Endangered Species Committee, Jan. 23, 1979 (in archives of the Secretary of Interior, sitting as Chair, and the coursebook authors (remarkably, this transcript is unreported)).

state protective laws as they applied to Tellico and ordering the reservoir's immediate completion. Because the amendment was not actually read in the empty chamber, none of the few representatives on the floor other than the committee members knew what was being done. President Jimmy Carter threatened to veto the bill, but then signed it on September 25, 1979, with an abject telephone call thereafter apologizing to the plaintiffs.

The Cherokees then filed another lawsuit based upon the constitutional rights that would be infringed if their most sacred places were destroyed by the reservoir. (Was this an "environmental" suit?) That case died in the courts when an injunction was denied on grounds that Indians could not assert religious rights on land they did not own, and TVA closed the gates to start flooding the valley on November 28, 1979. Ammoneta Sequoyah v. TVA, 480 F. Supp. 608 (E.D. Tenn. 1979), 620 F.2d 1159 (6th Cir.), cert. denied, 449 U.S. 953 (1980).

Of the last major population — 25,000 darters that had lived in the Little Tennessee prior to dam construction — none has survived. Small relict populations have been discovered in several sites downstream, transplants have been successful at two other sites, and the Department of Interior has downlisted the darter to threatened status. The condemned valley lands produced no model industrial city. Today its primary economic activity is the development of upper-income residential communities with a country club and golf courses.[31]

4. **Securing a balance: avoiding sunk cost tactics.** Mechanisms for statutory balancing like the God Committee can easily become politicized tactical battlegrounds. One congressional response to this problem was a later ESA §7(d) amendment. In a host of major cases such as TVA's Tellico Dam and Chapter 7's *Overton Park* case, agencies have tried to accelerate construction in the face of potential statutory constraints, pouring so much concrete or cutting so many trees before a citizen group can finally get to a court hearing that the proponents can then argue that the balance now tips decisively in their favor, or that species preservation and statutory compliance have regrettably become moot. ESA §7(d) was added to prevent just such disingenuity:

> 16 U.S.C. §1536(d). After initiation of consultation…the Federal agency and the permit or license applicant shall not make any irreversible or irretrievable commitment of resources with respect to…agency action which has the effect of foreclosing the formulation or implementation of any reasonable or prudent alternative measures….

This provision is intended to undercut the sunk-cost strategy that can foreclose the God Committee balancing process. It is not well understood, however. See Kopf, Steamrolling §7(d) of the ESA: How Sunk Costs Undermine Environmental Regulations, 23 B.C. Envtl. Aff. L. Rev. 393 (1996); Houck, The "Institutionalization of Caution" under §7 of the Endangered Species Act: What Do You Do When You Don't

---

31. TVA strove to sell the condemned lands for development, but without much success. The first development proposal after two years of stagnation was to create regional toxic waste landfills from the valley lands; the citizens quashed it. Subsequently a small industrial park (smaller than the industrial park included as part of the citizens' non-dam alternative plan) attracted several small businesses. To achieve more development, TVA then transferred a substantial portion of the valley, on a subsidized basis, to a second-home vacation housing developer.

Know?, 12 Envtl. L. Rep. 15001 (1982); and Bays' Legal Fund v. Browner, 828 F. Supp. 102 (D. Mass. 1993) (court ignores ongoing construction despite §7(d), saying $4 billion sewage system could be abandoned later if species threat makes it advisable to do so).

5. **The God Committee after the spotted owl.** For more than a dozen years after the God Committee's rigorous review of the snail darter and its companion *Greyrocks* case, no federal projects sought God Committee exemptions. In 1992 in the spotted owl cases, however, facing inevitable §7 injunction actions, Bush I Administration's Interior Secretary Manuel Lujan decided to seek a Committee exemption for the spotted owl. In a proceeding featuring accusations of improper pressure, God Committee members granted ESA exemptions for 13 timber-cutting contracts. In a citizen challenge of the decision, Portland Audubon Soc'y v. Endangered Species Comm., 984 F.2d 1534, 1538 (9th Cir. 1993), the court noted the environmentalists' contention "that improper ex parte contacts between the White House and members of the Committee tainted the decision-making process.... According to two anonymous administration sources, at least three Committee members had been 'summoned' to the White House and pressured to vote for the exemption...[which] may have changed the vote of at least one Committee member." But because the timber sales were also blocked by NEPA and NFMA injunctions, the court did not issue a final ruling on the validity of the God Committee overrides. Subsequently President Clinton negotiated a Northwest Forests Initiative settling the litigation. See U.S. Forest Service & Bureau of Land Mgmt., Record of Decision for Amendments to Forest Service and Bureau of Land Management Planning Documents Within the Range of the Northern Spotted Owl (1994).

In practice the God Committee's exemption process is perceived as so rigorous and embarrassing that agencies will only rarely even consider undertaking the difficulties of obtaining one. In 2003, when protection for the Rio Grande silvery minnow threatened established water rights, the opponents obtained an appropriations bill rider exemption rather than face the scrutiny and extended procedures of God Committee review.[32] If the God Committee is a bypass to §7's roadblock, it is a tortuous one that does not easily circumvent the obstacle of §7. The net result seems to be a pragmatic compromise that leaves the United States with a potent legal provision protecting endangered species against harm caused by any federal agency actions.

Section 2. ESA §9 PROHIBITION GETS MODIFIED BY THE ESA §10 "INCIDENTAL TAKE" EXEMPTION AMENDMENT

The spotted owl, like the snail darter, aroused strong industry protests about the ESA's alleged irrational extremism. The spotted owl cases, as the later *Sweet Home* case showed, raised issues under the ESA §9 "take" prohibition as well as under ESA §7. In

---

32. See Rio Grande Silvery Minnow v. Keys, 333 F.3d 1109 (10th Cir. 2003) (vacated as moot, 2004 U.S. App. LEXIS 56, Jan. 5, 2004); Energy and Water Development Appropriations Act of 2004, Pub. L. No 108-137 §208(a), 117 Stat. 1827 (Dec. 1, 2003). The latter rider immunized only one federal water supply project from the trial court's intensive analysis and injunction, but the residuum was rendered moot by the end of drought conditions, governmental water use adjustments, and the injunction's own limited duration.

1982, Congress was induced to pass further exemption balance mechanisms to shield certain private property owners from the §9 roadblock. The 1982 amendments created a new §10:[33]

> 16 U.S.C. §1539(a)(1). [Incidental Take] Permits [ITPs]. The Secretary may permit, under such terms and conditions as he shall prescribe — ...
>
> (B) any taking otherwise prohibited by §9 if such taking is incidental to, and not the purpose of, the carrying out of an otherwise lawful activity.
>
> (2)(A) No permit may be issued by the Secretary authorizing any taking referred to in paragraph (1)(B) unless the applicant therefore submits to the Secretary a conservation plan [universally referred to as an "HCP," a habitat conservation plan] that specifies —
>
> (i) the impact which will likely result from such taking;
>
> (ii) what steps the applicant will take to minimize and mitigate such impacts, and the funding that will be available to implement such steps;
>
> (iii) what alternative actions to such taking the applicant considered and the reasons why such alternatives are not being utilized; and
>
> (iv) such other measures that the Secretary may require as being necessary or appropriate for purposes of the plan.
>
> (B) If the Secretary finds, after opportunity for public comment, with respect to a permit application and the related conservation plan that —
>
> (i) the taking will be incidental;
>
> (ii) the applicant will, to the maximum extent practicable, minimize and mitigate the impacts of such taking;
>
> (iii) the applicant will ensure that adequate funding for the plan will be provided;
>
> (iv) the taking will not appreciably reduce the likelihood of the survival and recovery of the species in the wild; and
>
> (v) the measures, if any, required under subparagraph (A)(iv) will be met; and he has received such other assurances as he may require that the plan will be implemented, the Secretary shall issue the permit. The permit shall contain such terms and conditions as the Secretary deems necessary or appropriate....

This incidental take exemption provision theoretically allows the Secretary to modify unnecessary burdens placed on property owners by §9, but it also reflects many of the potential risks that lie in retrenchments from roadblocks.

Was this amendment a good idea? Note the elements that may be quite permissive: Almost any harm to species from habitat destruction will be "incidental" since virtually no market projects set out purposefully to harm species. The requirement that harms to species must be minimized "to the maximum extent practicable" could be a major loophole, interpreted to allow the developer's own practicalities to dominate the balance. The element requiring that "the taking...not appreciably reduce the likelihood of survival and recovery" retreats from the statutory goal of improving the chances for recovery, and "not appreciably" is an indeterminate measure. Ultimately the rationality

---

33. Pub. L. No. 95-632 (1982). The amendments also created a simpler incidental take exemption process for federal agencies, which can apply for and receive an immunity "incidental take statement" without binding promises or a conservation plan. 16 U.S.C. §1536(b)(4)(B) & (C).

of the balance struck under §10 depends completely on the Secretary. If he or she wishes to hold applicants to high standards for HCPs and strict terms for extensive mitigations, and is stringent in setting "such other measures that the Secretary may require as being necessary or appropriate," then the balance may be sufficiently protective of species. If a Secretary doesn't like the Act, however, he or she in practice can use the permissive terms to eviscerate §9. The Secretary's decisions, moreover, are effectively immune from citizen suits, so the amendment rolls the law back to the old bipolar system where the public interest depends totally on bureaucratic enforcement.[34]

For a decade after the incidental take amendments to the §9 roadblock, surprisingly few permits were granted — less than 20 from 1982 to 1994 — but beginning in 1993 the Clinton Administration dramatically accelerated the volume of §10 HCP exemptions, with more than 500 approved by 2002 with 200 pending. Most of the early HCPs covered areas of less than 1000 acres. In applications after 1996, 25 exceeded 10,000 acres in size, 25 exceeded 100,000 acres, and 18 exceeded 500,000 acres. The volume and character of permits mean that it is extremely difficult to gauge how rationally the balancing process works in practice.[35] Some HCPs and §10 permits appear to be biologically sophisticated and carefully balanced to protect the species while accommodating human uses.[36] Others appear to be hapless political capitulations.[37]

> A group of scientists funded by the National Science Foundation released the results of the first comprehensive study of HCPs.... Among the more disturbing findings of the study are these: over three-quarters of the plans lacked such basic information as the population size of species and whether it was growing or shrinking; a third of the plans did not know the life spans of the species at issue; over half did not have adequate monitoring, without which, of course, there is no way to tell whether the measures are working or not; of the 44 plans studied in depth, many prescribed mitigation measures that would do more harm than good. Patrick Parenteau, letter to New England Senators, Mar. 3, 1998.

Nevertheless, a number of committed environmental leaders have urged further regulatory changes to the ESA. Some wish to strengthen protections by encouraging

---

34. The elements of the exemption are determined by relatively unreviewable agency discretion, HCPs are designed to exclude citizen enforceability (the FWS itself expressly proposes that the public not be granted the status of third party beneficiaries (see HCP Handbook App. 9 Template Agreement §14.8.), and the most citizens can do is try to prove that particular exemption shortcomings "jeopardize the existence" of endangered species, a tough burden. The legal opponents are likewise tough: The property owners who take advantage of §10 are unlikely to be the little guys who can least bear the burdens of ESA restrictions and whose limited property holdings have limited impacts. It takes a lot of time, money, biologists, and lawyers to negotiate a §10 exemption, and those who do so will fight to defend their permits.

35. See Hood, Frayed Safety Nets: Conservation Planning under the ESA (1998), Symposium, 27 Envtl. L. 755–877 (1997). A number of studies have concluded that because of political pressures and other constraints, the federal agencies with jurisdiction over endangered species — Interior's Fish and Wildlife Service and Commerce's National Oceanic and Atmospheric Administration — are underprotecting species in their recovery planning under the ESA. Tear et al., Status and Prospects for Success of the Endangered Species Act: A Look at Recovery Plans, Science, Nov. 1993, at 976. Cf. Friends of Endangered Species v. Jantzen, 760 F.2d 976 (9th Cir. 1985) (court holds §10 permit against challenge). *Jantzen*, which involved the California's Mission Blue butterfly, produced an interesting confrontation where an incidental take permit was issued after extensive biological study and mitigation. The court upheld the HCP and permit against challenge, though local citizens remain bitterly critical. *Jantzen* went on to serve as the model for subsequent HCP regulations.

36. The authors have been impressed, for instance, by the Atlantic Coast Piping Plover HCP and Massachusetts's three-year experimental permit allowing restricted dune buggy use of the plover's beach habitat.

37. HCPs and permits allowing large timber companies to cut down nest trees of red-cockaded woodpeckers after waiting 60 days for them to find alternative homes seem to verge on the cynical.

multispecies and ecosystem-wide protections rather than species-by-species regulation.[38] Ecosystem and biodiversity concepts[39] are far more realistic measures of natural habitat qualities than are single-species indicators, but their subtleties make them less feasible as legal concepts. Other environmentalists, traumatized by the close call the ESA barely survived in the 104th Congress and noting that Interior is barely enforcing the politically explosive take prohibitions, urge further preemptive modification of the strictness of §9. Given the dramatic goals of the ESA and the widespread human-based character of species endangerment, it is inevitable that major political conflicts arise in ESA enforcement. It is probably equally inevitable that some agency officials will avoid strong enforcement of their statutory mandate in order to avoid exacerbating the political context. Is this a problem or a solution?

COMMENTARY & QUESTIONS

1. **The §10 incidental take statutory standards.** Where are the legal teeth in the §10 amendment? Note how its legal elements effectively move away from citizen enforceability in courts to a reliance on the energy and judgment of the Secretary of Interior. A tough conservation-minded Secretary could hold the incidental take permit process to a very rigorous standard, but an antiregulationist, business-minded Secretary could apply the terms extremely permissively. In either case, note how subjective the decision is likely to be and therefore, given judicial deference to agency discretion and expertise, not easily reversible in court.

2. **Klamath Basin suckerfish and the expedited federal agency incidental take bypass.** Under the terms of the ESA's incidental take permit amendment, the standard for federal agency exemptions is easier than for private parties. For federal agencies, all that is required to permit takes that hurt members of the species is a biological opinion letter ("incidental take statement") from the Secretary asserting that the action would not jeopardize the species' existence, thus overriding the agency's obligations under both §7 and §9.[40] This process was used in the rancorous Klamath Basin case. In July 2001, a district judge ordered a halt to federal irrigation water diversions because low water conditions caused by several years of drought and increasing small farm withdrawals from the Klamath River severely threatened three endangered species. In the outcry that followed, which of the three affected species — the bald eagle, the coho

---

38. This idea has generic rationality: "By overemphasizing the role of single chemicals, and single media in pollution policy, and of single species in land management policy, we underestimate the interactive effects of chemicals, the cross-media effects of emissions, and the interdependence of habitats." Chertow & Esty, Environmental Policy: The Next Generation, Issues in Sci. & Tech., Fall 1997, at 74. The ecosystem proposals, however, run the practical risk of magnifying what already are very difficult scientific requirements for proposing and defending species protections.

39. "Biodiversity" as a regulatory concept can be difficult to define. It means something more than merely having larger numbers of species: If a road is cut through a wilderness rainforest or tundra, it increases the net number of species but extirpates unique native indicator species. Conservation biologists prefer a concept of "native biodiversity" or "continuum biodiversity" to capture the goal of diverse natural communities evolving as much as possible without anthropogenic disturbances, but the regulatory complexities that would be required have militated five initiatives in that direction. See D. Perlman & G. Adelson, Biodiversity: Exploring Cities in Conservation (1997).

40. ESA §7(b)(4) implicitly authorizes federal agency "incidental takes" based on consultation and a biological opinion letter.

salmon, or the Klamath suckerfish — do you think received the vast majority of press and talk-radio scorn? Bush II Administration's Secretary of Interior Gale Norton quickly issued an incidental take statement permitting irrigation water releases based on a finding that thunderstorms and upstream ranchers' conservation measures would lessen risks to species from low water conditions. Though environmental organizations sought to challenge her order,[41] the subjectivity inherent in the terms of incidental take exemption decisions under ESA §§7 and 10 severely hampered the challenges.

3. **The "critical habitat" roadblock gets bypassed.** Destruction and modification of habitat are the most significant causes of species extinction. Remember that the ESA §7 roadblock provisions forbid not only federal actions that "jeopardize" species existence but also the "destruction or modification of [critical] habitat." The Department of Interior began listing geographic areas in which existing endangered species lived and some further areas into which species populations could re-expand in order to achieve "recovery."

Critical habitat, the second §7 roadblock, however, has been far more of a political football than the "jeopardy" provision. As Professor Parenteau has noted:

> Critical habitat designation has always been controversial. State and local governments may see it as an unwelcome federal intrusion into local land use matters. Private landowners see it as diminishing the value and development potential of their property. Wary of this political minefield, the wildlife agencies have found lots of reasons not to designate critical habitat — not possible, not prudent, not now.[42] Consequently, despite the statutory command that "the Secretary shall designate critical habitat," and shall do so "concurrently" with the listing, only one-fifth of listed species have had critical habitat declared. As with listing decisions, citizens can and do use the ESA's citizen suit provision to challenge the agencies' failure to designate critical habitat. On the other side of the coin, opponents of critical habitat designations have had some success arguing that such designations [require] preparation of an environmental impact statement. Parenteau, Rearranging the Deck Chairs: Endangered Species Act Reforms in an Era of Mass Extinction, 22 Wm. & Mary Envtl. L. & Pol'y Rev. 227, 262–263 (1998).

The potential force of the critical habitat roadblock thus gets bypassed by administrative nonlisting and underenforcement. Critical habitat protection particularly serves the ESA purpose of promoting species recovery, not simply bare survival, in viable sustainable populations. In 1999, however, Secretary Bruce Babbitt's Department of Interior signaled its desire to get out of the habitat-listing business by suggesting that the jeopardy test was all that was necessary:

> We have long believed that, in most circumstances, the designation of "official" critical habitat is... duplicative,...of little additional value for most listed species, yet it consumes large amounts of conservation resources.... For almost all species,

---

41. Pacific Coast Fed'n of Fisherman's Ass'n v. Bureau of Reclamation, N.D. Cal., No. 02-2006SBA (filed Apr. 24, 2002).

42. The 1978 ESA amendments required that critical habitat always be officially listed at the same time as a species is listed, unless the Secretary finds that the geographic area is "not determinable" or listing is "not prudent" or will produce more costs than benefits. ESA §4(b). The amendment was offered by Senator Garn, a staunch foe of the Act, perhaps in the hope that the political and scientific difficulties of listing critical habitat would serve to constrain the listing of species as well. [Eds.]

the adverse modification and jeopardy standards are the same, resulting in critical habitat being an expensive regulatory process that duplicates the protection already provided by the jeopardy standard. 64 Fed. Reg. 31871–74 (June 14, 1999).

Several courts have held, however, that it is improper to conflate and collapse the two protections into one.[43] Given the agency's lack of will, however, the critical habitat roadblock has lost much of its force. Several congressional bills have proposed to conform the law to the agency's unenthusiastic policies, eliminating among others the concurrent listing requirement.

4. **Slippage: administrative flex mechanisms added to the ESA?** Starting in the Clinton years, the Department of Interior, backed by some environmental groups, issued ESA regulations attempting to encourage nonfederal actors to cooperate more in species protection and thus take some heat off the Act. The three main flexibility innovations, each of which has potential pluses and minuses, are these:

- *"No surprises" agreements:* These guarantee landowners that when they fulfill the terms of an HCP they will face no further obligations toward any covered species. If actions under their §10 incidental take permits turn out to harm species, the landowners are immune from liability and any necessary adjustments are paid for by the agency.[44]

- *"Safe harbor" agreements:* These serve landowners owning species habitat who are given "baseline" estimates of the numbers of endangered animals on their land and promised that their responsibilities will not increase if the endangered population's numbers increase; future development activity is allowed to cut the number of animals back to the baseline.[45]

- *"Candidate conservation" agreements (CCAs), and "candidate conservation agreements with assurances" (CCAAs):* These are contracts whereby state and corporate players promise Interior that they will take various measures to protect endangered species that otherwise would be federally listed. In return, Interior agrees not to list, which means the Act is not enforceable for such species, and sometimes gives further no-restrictions assurances.[46]

To this is added the Bush II Administration's moves to lower species protections by nonenforcement of the statute and regulations,[47] nondefense of the ESA in the face of industry challenges,[48] and support of statutory amendments like a blanket amendment

---

43. See Sierra Club v. U.S. Fish & Wildlife Serv., 245 F.3d 434 (5th Cir. 2001); NRDC v. U.S. Dep't of the Interior, 113 F.3d 1121 (9th Cir. 1997).

44. 63 Fed. Reg. 8859 (1998) (to be codified at 50 C.F.R. pt. 222). In each of these administrative contract settings, the backdrop of the Supreme Court's *Winstar* decision means that if an agency violates its assurances, it must pay. See Bosselman, The Statutory and Constitutional Mandate for a No Surprises Policy, 24 Ecology L.Q. 707 (1997), commenting on United States v. Winstar Corp., 518 U.S. 839 (1996).

45. See Announcement of Final Safe Harbor Policy, 64 Fed. Reg. 32,706-32,717 (June 17, 1999) (to be codified at 50 C.F.R. pts. 13 and 17).

46. Under ESA §4, it appears that listing is mandatory if the species is factually endangered, and unfulfilled promises are insufficient to override biological facts.

47. The Bush II Administration was the first to fail to list even a single species or designate any critical habitat in its first two years except under court order, despite a waiting list of over 3000 candidate species, and a lack of designated critical habitat for over three-quarters of those species already listed. See Parenteau, Whatever Industry Wants…: The Bush Environmental Record, 14 Duke Envtl. L. & Pol'y F., No. 2 (2004).

48. See DC Court Rules in Favor of California Homebuilders and Other Development Interests, Earthjustice, Nov. 8, 2002, available at http://www.earthjustice.org/news/display.html?ID=468.

exempting military facilities from various endangered species, marine mammal, and critical habitat protection requirements.[49]

Are we seeing a "slippage" process? And if so, is it constructive or corrosive? Beyond decrying the Bush II Administration's policies, many environmentalists also oppose the Clinton era's ESA regulatory changes as a lowering of the roadblock, amounting to a preemptive capitulation to political threats and a violation of the Act:

> The statute is moving away from a system of regulation by citizen enforcement toward a system of largely closed-door negotiations between agencies and regulated interests, with little meaningful public involvement.... HCP initiatives have seriously weakened safeguards for listed species that were a key feature of the 1982 amendments. Kostyack, Surprise, Envt'l Forum, Mar. 1998 at 19.

> [No surprises] is a reckless policy based on bad science, bad logic, and bad policy,... a recovery strategy that is doomed to fail.... Codifying "no surprises" will mean "no recovery" for many species. Whatever certainty "no surprises" may give to some developers, i.e., those lucky enough to cut their deals early, it will almost certainly take away from others when the plans fail individually and in the aggregate to achieve recovery, and the covered species continue to decline, to be joined perhaps by other species dependent on the same shrinking habitat base.... A more effective way to address landowner concerns is to provide meaningful economic incentives for habitat conservation...including tax credits and financial and technical assistance. Parenteau, A Public Letter to New England Senators, Mar. 3, 1998.

Safe harbor agreements are criticized for achieving only "transitory" protection and for immunizing development that may in fact cut down populations below the initial baseline level.[50]

Candidate conservation agreements are criticized as violations of the Act because, based on mitigation promises that in some cases have been quite minimal, the Secretary agrees not to list species that, on the factual biological record and the terms of the statute, would have to be listed.[51]

The realpolitik counterargument in favor of these administrative flexibility devices is that the Act has been under such brutal attack for its rigidity and harshness that some compromises had to be made. As Professor Holly Doremus has written:

> The Department undertook its flexibility initiatives with the sincere intention of maximizing conservation gains while lowering controversy to a level that would keep the ESA off the political table. It is difficult to know what the political

---

49. Citing a threat to national security the Administration submitted its "Readiness and Range Preservation Initiative" to Congress, requesting exemptions from a number of environmental statutes including the ESA, Marine Mammal Protection Act (MMPA), CAA, RCRA, and CERCLA. 108 Pub. L. No. 136 §318(a), §319(b), 117 Stat. 1392 (2003). The "Military Readiness" amendments created a first categorical ESA exemption, removing protections for critical habitat on military reservations.

50. See Kishida, Safe Harbor Agreements Under the Endangered Species Act, 23 U. Haw. L. Rev. 507, 525-526 (2001). The procedures by which the no-surprises and safe-harbor policies, and the permit security guarantees that underlie them, were adopted have made them vulnerable to court challenge. See Spirit of the Sage Council v. Norton, 2003 U.S. Dist. Lexis 22203 (D.D.C. Dec. 11, 2003) (an extended primer on the administrative adjustment process).

51. See Phelps, Candidate Conservation Agreements under the Endangered Species Act: Prospects and Perils of an Administrative Experiment, 25 B.C. Envtl. Aff. L. Rev. 175 (1997). CCAs and CCAAs are justified as anticipatory implementations of ESA §10(a)(1)(A)'s authority to allow incidental takes, but that authority previously had been thought to require listing prior to immunizing. In some cases, CCAAs have been combined with HCPs for listed species and have allowed substantial habitat losses.

outcome would have been in the absence of those reforms. The reformers...may well be right to congratulate themselves on saving the ESA from repeal or severe weakening during their tenure. Certainly the ESA was a target of the Contract with America Republicans who controlled Congress in the mid-1990s.... [But] agencies are...institutionally disposed to underplay their hand in controversial situations.

Perhaps the Clinton-era ESA reforms...increased the ESA's conservation effectiveness, although...that has yet to be demonstrated. If they did so, however, it was in a curious, Alice-in-Wonderland sort of fashion. The reforms rest on the assumption that the levels of protection facially mandated by the ESA are not practically and politically achievable. By stepping back from that pretense, they are supposed to achieve, in the real world, greater protection than we could expect from vigorous implementation of the ESA. They give up the possibility of strong protection for a higher probability of maintaining a reduced level of protection.[52]

5. **The political context.** Because of a "sunset" provision, every five years the ESA is supposed to go to Congress for reauthorization of its funding, which virtually guarantees its awkward status as a political football. The ESA has not been reauthorized since 1982, surviving on yearly "continuing resolution" funding bills. The ESA, despite broad public support, appears to be much more congressionally embattled than other federal environmental statutes. Why?

With only occasional exceptions, the political marketplace has generally come to accept the validity and permanence of pollution and toxics statutes. Only the ESA is still regularly subjected to plenary denunciations on the floor of Congress; only the ESA faces serious nonreauthorization initiatives; only the ESA was hit by a sweeping one-year listing moratorium.[53] It was the endangered spotted owl that was targeted by a timber cutting rider cynically attached to the Oklahoma bombing relief bill;[54] it is the ESA that has sustained amendments undermining species recovery, its fundamental goal; and it is the ESA that could be undercut instead of reinforced by the regulatory agency's administrative adjustments to species protection regimes.

Why is it that the ESA suffers from this particular precariousness? Pollution and toxics statutes have come to be accepted by agencies and industry, primarily because their direct human utility is intrinsically obvious to public opinion. The societal rationale for endangered species conservation, on the other hand, is generally characterized in terms of philosophy, emotions, and aesthetics — often regarded as heartfelt but not so substantially significant when weighed against the "practical" world of production, payrolls, and profits.

The ESA would clearly gain political strength if it were publicly recognized to fulfill significant utilitarian functions as well. Utility arguments can be made far beyond the

---

52. Doremus, Adaptive Management, the Endangered Species Act, and the Institutional Challenges of "New Age" Environmental Protection, 41 Washburn L.J. 50 (2001). It also can be argued that the main function of ESA §§7 and 9's rigidity is to leverage money out of developers to fund species-conserving compromises.

53. Senator Kay Bailey Hutchinson (R-TX) fronted the successful marketplace campaign for an ESA moratorium. Emergency Supplemental Appropriations and Rescissions for the Department of Defense to Preserve and Enhance Military Readiness Act of 1995..., Pub. L. No. 104-6, 109 Stat. 73, 86 (1995).

54. Pub. L. No. 104-19, §2001 (1995). The same tactic was narrowly avoided when Representative Richard Pombo (R-CA) attempted to attach a rider to a Northwest flood relief bill exempting thousands of water-related public works nationwide from the ESA. H.R. 478, 105th Cong., 1st Sess. (1997); 143 Cong. Rec. H2283-H2313 (1997).

physical or medicinal use of individual species.[55] The predominant cause of endangerment is not hunting or trapping or market harvesting. It is the alteration and destruction of habitat. Because of this, endangered species often play a role serving human utility by identifying problems and triggering protections for habitat areas and conditions that hold threatened human values as well.

The "canary in the coal mine" indicator role is not necessarily the primary nor an omnipresent function of the ESA, but it deserves recognition as a tangible and systemically important function lying within the logic of endangered species protection generally, one that is at least potentially relevant in every case. The ESA's provisions are likely to wax or wane in its current political gauntlets depending on how the various utilities of species protection are publicly perceived.

6. **Anti-ESA agitation,** *Noah's Choice,* **and the future of the ESA.** An impressive marketplace campaign to modify the protections of the ESA was organized through the 1990s,[56] moving at low levels of "Wise Use" rhetoric as well as through industry think tanks — from discredited but incessant stories of how ESA protection for kangaroo rats resulted in property owners' inability to save their homes from wildfires, to sophisticated arguments about "bad science" imprecisions in ESA enforcement, arguments that have gained traction in the hands of Bush II Administration appointees.

Part of the anti-ESA campaign was a beautifully written 1995 book, *Noah's Choice,*[57] ostensibly seeking to set out a rational overall policy assessment of the Act. The book argued that we get very limited tangible benefits from the ESA[58] and noted "perverse incentives" the Act creates for private property interests to subvert its protections. The authors' main argument, as the book's title indicates, is that endangered species pose an inescapable loaded choice: If we as a society want to save species for whatever their charms, we have to ratchet back living standards and pay trillions of dollars; otherwise we must regretfully override endangered species according to whatever course of action is dictated by the marketplace, on the marketplace's own terms.

> It is easy to say that society should extract money from developers and give it to black-capped vireos that need protection. But it is not possible to do this and simultaneously ensure that good housing is available and affordable to everyone. Or good health care, for that matter, or a good education. Embracing the goal of

---

55. "Traditionally, endangered species protection is not viewed as pollution control. It is, however, in a larger sense exactly that. Endangered species are useful, though incomplete, indicators of the health stems and of the earth we share. While the best indicators may often be mollusks, plants and lower life forms, the decline of the bald eagle from the effects of chlorinated hydrocarbons is a good indication of the impact of those chemicals on human life. As water quality becomes inadequate to protect the delta smelt, it will also become inadequate for human uses." Houck, Why Do We Protect Endangered Species, and What Does That Say About Whether Restrictions on Private Property to Protect Them Constitute "Takings"?, 80 Iowa L. Rev. 297, 327–328 (1995).

56. NESARC, the National Endangered Species Act Reform Coalition, a coalition of anti-ESA industries, many of which had participated in the 104th Congress's anti-regulatory jihad, was formed to coordinate a broad front initiative in the ongoing battles of ESA reauthorization.

57. C. Mann & M. Plummer, Noah's Choice: The Future of Endangered Species (1995). See critical discussion in Gasmasks on the Canaries, 27 Envtl. L. 845, 862–865 (1997).

58. "Mann and Plummer's case against the Act is based…on anecdotes and cursory evaluation of evidence of the Act's benefits.… Their mission is accomplished once they reach the conclusion that the Act has no benefits." Rachlinski, Noah by the Numbers: An Empirical Evaluation of the Endangered Species Act, 82 Cornell L. Rev. 356, 357, 359, 365 (1997) (book review). Rachlinski undertakes an extended statistical analysis, essentially refuting the book's premise. 82 Cornell L. Rev. at 379–386.

saving biodiversity and the goals of providing housing, health care, and education, as well as the many other goals we have taken up during the past two hundred years, makes our choices difficult.... To borrow from Freud, what do we humans want? Noah's Choice 26, 213 (1995).

The book was seductively written to frame a version of the classic false tradeoff — the allegedly unavoidable all-or-nothing choice between ecology and economics.[59] National policies on endangered species must be shaped more realistically, taking into account that wise planning usually can avoid conflicts and that species protection often can serve rather than hurt public economic interests (as in the Tellico Dam case, which the book archly mischaracterizes in order to discredit the economics of species protection).

7. **Strict rules or adaptive discretion? Democratic dilemmas in the second generation of environmental law.** In the so-called second generation of environmental law, a number of commentators have preached the need for "adaptive management," in which clear static rules and theories based on preserving a stable natural equilibrium are outmoded, to be scrapped in favor of subjective flexible performance standards. Looking at the original roadblock terms of the ESA — even if they made rational sense in cases such as the darters' or the spotted owls' — isn't it possible that the Act is indeed too stringent? Interior's no-surprises, safe-harbor, and CCA rules reflect the perception that a more modulated balancing is necessary. But this returns us to the old bipolar design of government, where agencies have a monopoly on regulating corporate conduct and citizens are once again outsiders who cannot meaningfully review the exercise of agency discretion. Are you at ease with the old bipolar model, trusting agencies to be guided by the public interest rather than by the blandishments of their political context? Environmental advocates tend to hold onto roadblock prohibitions out of a pragmatic political sense. Given the dangers that agencies will be captured and seduced by the industries they regulate, complex agency balancing processes for setting and applying standards can too easily cause a law's effectiveness to evaporate within the halls of government. The better course, many environmentalists seem to have decided, is to try to retain roadblocks and other easily litigatable standards so as to maintain a continuing role for citizens. Most environmentalists do not trust agencies to strike optimal balances in the long-term interest of the public unless there is an institutionalized counterweight to the blandishments of the regulated. Clear stark statutory commands don't leave much wiggle room, and they subject agencies and regulatees to a tougher level of judicial superintendence so that legal mandates are more likely to be obeyed.

8. **Endangered species in national governance.** It is scarcely surprising that endangered species protection became a target of Bush II Administration anti-regulatory initiatives. Much of the Administration's effort has been located within the administrative process, with cutbacks on listing and enforcement, and in the courts where federal

---

59. Doubts about the book's integrity come from its use of history, including the Tellico case, as well as its authors' linkages to the ESA's industrial opposition. In the book's Chapter 6, "The Awful Beast Is Back," the authors frame the snail darter as a prime example of diseconomic effects of the Act and ignore the case's net economic utilities, although they had been briefed at length on the economic data from the God Committee review.

enforcement has been lackluster.[60] It was the first Administration to fail to list a single species or designate any critical habitat in its first two years except under court order. (There is a waiting list of over 3000 candidate species and a lack of designated critical habitat for over three-quarters of those species already listed.) The Administration has also undertaken legislative initiatives, however, adding provisions undercutting ESA protections in military reservations under its Military Readiness Act and in "fuel reduction" areas targeted for clearcutting under the Healthy Forests Restoration Act of 2003.[61]

It will be interesting to see in the controversies ahead how much we have learned from the whooping crane, the snail darter, and the spotted owl. Will endangered species be listened to as early warning indicators serving to identify larger public issues at stake, or will they be trivialized in the narrowed caricature of localized tradeoffs — "What do you want, owls or jobs?" When the pumps that divert water from northern California's Sacramento River to farms and cities in California's arid south threaten to eliminate the delta smelt (*Hypomesus transpacificus*), or Klamath River water is necessary for protection of endangered salmon and suckerfish,[62] will the question be cast as more "worthless little minnows" versus jobs and progress, or an occasion to raise sensible questions about where most of the water now goes — to massive fiscal and water subsidies for inappropriate agriculture? One such basic question: "Why should we be subsidizing farmers to grow rice and other water-intensive crops in the middle of the desert?"

Like so much of environmental law, endangered species protections can serve as triggering opportunities for reviewing long-term necessities of rational social governance, or can be overwhelmed by the concentrated forces of short-term self-aggrandizement.[63] If the decisional processes ultimately turn on the merits rather than political ploys, endangered species will continue to play their socially useful role — as well as continuing to be prime symbols of a national environmental ethic.

The measure of the current ESA as a roadblock-with-bypasses will be found over time in its further evolution, including the continuing congressional debates over reauthorization. The degree to which full scientific and economic merits are brought to bear in these debates will be critical to the Act's future.

9. **The "roadblock" statutory approach in perspective.** In terms of statutory taxonomy, can any conclusion be drawn about the desirability of roadblocks to fit all the different contexts encountered in environmental law and politics? Were the original ESA §§7 and

---

60. The Administration has hastened to accept administrative or court-approved settlements capitulating to challenges filed against its federal regulations. See 313 F.3d 1094 (9th Cir. 2002) (an agreement between Homebuilders and the Administration to nullify the majority of the 4.1 million acres in California that had been designated as critical habitat for the redlegged frog the previous year). In other cases it has declined to defend the rules altogether. See Parenteau, Whatever Industry Wants…: The Bush Environmental Record, 14 Duke Envtl. L. & Pol'y F., No. 2 (2004).

61. See Pub. L. No. 108-136 §318(a), §319(b), 117 Stat. 1392 (2003), noted above, and Pub. L. No. 108-148, 117 Stat. 1887 (2003).

62. See Gross, A Dying Fish May Force California to Break Its Water Habits, N.Y. Times, Oct. 27, 1991, at A16.

63. Illustrating such obstacles, a Forest Service-Bureau of Reclamation study indicating that management of Northwest forests to protect the spotted owl could actually create more than 15,000 new jobs for former timber workers was suppressed and recalled by the Administration. Leaked copies are available by writing to the Association of Forest Service Employees for Environmental Ethics (AFSEEE), POB 111615, Eugene, OR 97440.

9 roadblocks extreme? Naïve? Necessary? Without them, where would endangered species protection stand today? Would it have been better if the statute had never had roadblock provisions, containing eco-pragmatic flexibility clauses from the start? Professor Jamie Grodsky suggests that starting off at a compromised middle does not necessarily secure the level of protection that results from a process of adjustments to roadblocks.[64]

Flexibility adjustments, of course, can always be found in how a law is administered in agencies and courts, though those avenues raise other issues. Or stark statutes can find adjustment in case-specific legislative amendments, as ultimately occurred in the darter case. If extinction is to be decreed, perhaps it is most appropriate that this be done in the nation's most democratic forum, after debate by elected officials and after considering all factors and balancing all tradeoffs. But legislatures may not be an ideal forum for micromanagement; they are not certain to make judgments in an atmosphere of thoughtful trusteeship. Rather than legislatures, are the protective standards of an environmental statute better entrusted to a system of flexible adjustment by courts, or to administrative agencies with a more or less formal agency process for definition, investigation, application, and enforcement, subject as always to some judicial review?

The ultimate truth is that no effective statute, no matter how constructed, can provide a satisfactory direct answer in every case. No humans (even legally trained humans!) can foresee all the twists and necessities of different settings over time. The question in such cases, if and when regulatory adjustments are determined necessary (which itself is a critically problematic determination), is whether they must derive from a balancing process incorporated into the terms of a statute itself, or should come from social, political, and legal contexts beyond the statutory roadblock.

10. **An international perspective on endangered species and roadblocks.** The ESA was passed by Congress pursuant to CITES, the Convention on International Trade in Endangered Species, Mar. 3, 1973, 27 U.S.T. 1087, which has sometimes been called the world's single most effective international environmental convention.[65] CITES contains no roadblocks resembling those in the ESA.

ESA is the implementing legislation for CITES, the principal international vehicle for conserving endangered species. CITES regulates trade in the form of both importation and exportation of endangered species and specimens. Even before the conclusion of CITES in 1973, the United Kingdom and the United States banned the importation of endangered species in an attempt to leverage conservation policies abroad. The U.S. legislation in particular called upon the Secretary of the Interior to seek an international meeting to agree on a binding treaty regarding endangered species, an initiative

---

64. "The social sustainability of environmental law requires the integration of environmental and economic factors. While this premise is axiomatic, the timing of the integration process may have consequences and merits consideration. Environmental pragmatism should not necessarily be wedded to the notion of starting from a 'deliberate middle,' but should recognize that it may be equally pragmatic to start from a clear rule and adjust, recognizing the feedback loops inherent in the political process, and the various incentive structures operating on regulated entities, outside interest groups, and regulators themselves." Grodsky, The Paradox of (Eco)Pragmatism, 87 Minn. L. Rev. 1037, 1063 (2003).

65. Convention on International Trade in Endangered Species of Wild Flora and Fauna, Mar. 3, 1973, 27 U.S.T. 1087, 993 U.N.T.S. 243 (entered into force July 1, 1975).

that eventually matured into the CITES treaty. As of this writing, 164 states are parties to CITES, which has been in force since 1975. The agreement contains three appendices that are the analogue of listings under ESA:

- Appendix I includes species threatened with extinction. Trade in specimens of these species requires prior permission from both the country of export and the country of import and is allowed only in exceptional circumstances. This is the highest level of protection that applies to the black rhinoceros, all sea turtles, the great apes, big cats like tigers and cheetahs, and endangered whales. It is the closest international analogue to the roadblock strategy of ESA. For instance, when the CITES parties listed the African elephant in Appendix I, the result was effectively a ban on trade in ivory.

- Appendix II includes species not necessarily threatened with extinction, but in which trade must be controlled in order to avoid utilization incompatible with their survival. An export permit, but not an import permit, is required in advance of international commerce in the more than 25,000 species listed in Appendix II.

- Appendix III, the lowest level of protection, contains species that are protected in at least one country, which has asked other CITES parties for assistance in controlling the trade.

Why do you think the drafters of CITES chose trade — importation and exportation — as the juncture at which the roadblock protections of the treaty would attach? What kind of incentive structure does restricting or constricting trade in endangered species create in countries of export? Of import? What would you expect to be the limitations of an approach such as CITES that focuses strictly on trade? How would you propose overcoming those limitations? While CITES has been extraordinarily successful within the scope of its operation, considerations such as these motivated a "second-generation" agreement emphasizing managerial rather than roadblock provisions, the UN Convention on Biological Diversity, May 22, 1992, 31 I.L.M. 822 (1992), which has been signed but not ratified by the United States.

When humans interfere with the Tao,
the sky becomes filthy,
the equilibrium crumbles,
creatures become extinct.

— Lao-tzu, Tao Te Ching, 500 B.C.E

Animals are not brethren, they are not underlings. They are other nations caught with ourselves in the net of life and time.

— Henry Beston

I've know rivers ancient as the world and older than the flow of human blood in human veins. My soul has grown deep like the rivers....

— Langston Hughes

Chapter 17

PRODUCT REGULATION AND MARKET-ACCESS STRATEGIES: PESTICIDES AND TOXICS

A. *Pesticides: The Federal Insecticide, Fungicide, and Rodenticide Act*
B. *Regulating Market Access of Toxics: The Toxic Substances Control Act*

For many years, environmental regulatory strategies in the United States were oriented primarily toward pollution cleanup. More recently, however, these regulatory strategies have targeted pollution prevention as well as pollution control.

At one end of the continuum are regulatory strategies dominated by a desire to minimize "false positives" — regulating only after environmental problems have already appeared. These strategies have resulted in serious and widespread damage to human health and the environment. Good examples of the damage caused by these strategies are our abandoned hazardous waste sites, which can be cleaned up only at a cost running into many billions of dollars.

At the other end of the continuum are regulatory strategies based on the minimization of "false negatives" — regulating in anticipation of environmental problems that have not yet appeared. These strategies, when they are strictly preventive in nature, emphasize stringent precautionary control of a chemical's market access. They would prohibit the introduction of new products, or the further sales of existing products, where products might conceivably be hazardous to human health or the environment. Such broad denials of market access, based exclusively on speculative environmental damage, can have a disabling effect on our system of market enterprise, especially in light of increasing foreign competition. There are many products, moreover, whose palpable economic, health, or environmental benefits outweigh their uncertain environmental risks.

With one exception, federal environmental protection statutes adopting a product regulation strategy have attempted to achieve a balance between the environmental benefits and economic costs of denying market access to a particular product. That single exception was the Delaney Clause of the Federal Food, Drug, and Cosmetic Act (FFDCA), noted in the preceding chapter, which barred any food additive that had been found to induce cancer in humans or animals in any dosage. In the Food Quality Protection Act of 1996 (FQPA),[1] Congress did not comprehensively repeal the Delaney Clause but did remove pesticide residues from its ban by amending the FFDCA's

---

1. 21 U.S.C. §346a.

definition of "food additive" to exclude pesticide chemical residues on raw or processed foods. (The Delaney Clause remains in effect regarding other food additives.) In particular, Congress determined that a pesticide residue on such foods is to be considered unsafe only if the EPA has set a tolerance level for the substance and the residue fails to satisfy that level. The EPA is now allowed to grant a tolerance and register a pesticide upon a finding of safety. As defined in §405 of the FQPA, "safe" means that "there is a reasonable certainty that no harm will result from aggregate exposure to the pesticide chemical residue,"[2] including both dietary and nondietary total exposure. Thus the "zero risk" approach of the former Delaney Clause has been repealed insofar as pesticide residues are concerned, in favor of a standard of "reasonable certainty" that no harm will come from aggregate exposure.[3]

The two most important federal environmental product regulation statutes are the Federal Insecticide, Fungicide, and Rodenticide Act (FIFRA)[4] and the Toxic Substances Control Act (TSCA, or ToSCA).[5] Although these statutes take a similar approach to environmental regulation of toxics, they present instructive differences in practice resulting from their disparate approaches to the triggering mechanisms for regulation and enforcement.

Assume that a manufacturer has invented a potentially useful chemical that can serve as an effective pesticide but that has never been used before. In connection with bringing this new chemical to market, the manufacturer would need to consider the regulatory effect of both FIFRA and ToSCA. Under FIFRA, Congress established the basic framework for pesticide regulation, including the registration of pesticides and the process by which EPA may ban unreasonably dangerous pesticides. Under ToSCA, Congress provided EPA with comprehensive authority to regulate or prohibit the manufacture, distribution, or use of chemicals that pose unreasonable risks, including the authority to require pre-manufacture notification to EPA for new chemicals or significant new uses of existing chemicals.

To a great extent, FIFRA places the burden of going forward — collecting data, establishing testing protocols, testing, and proving safety — on the manufacturer itself under threat of potentially severe legal sanctions. By placing the burden of going forward and proving safety on the manufacturer, FIFRA attempts to provide a comprehensive approach to the pesticide regulation process that regulates environmental toxics from the very outset. By contrast, ToSCA largely places the burden on EPA, not on the manufacturer. ToSCA requires the EPA to establish, by substantial evidence, that chemical testing is necessary and then to set testing protocols. Under ToSCA, EPA uses its statutory authority for "gap-filling," focusing primarily on environmental toxics not otherwise caught up in the regulatory net.

---

2. 21 U.S.C. §346a(b)(2)(A)(ii).

3. As a result of the 1996 Amendments, there has been a lively debate over the extent to which the Delaney Clause was rendered obsolete by Congress's action. See Turner, Delaney Lives! Reports of Delaney's Death Are Greatly Exaggerated, 28 Envtl. L. Rep. 10003 (1998) (concluding that the 1996 Amendments neither remove the protections provided by the Delaney Clause prohibition against adding cancer-causing additives to food nor reflect a public policy rationale or political consensus to do so). For a thorough discussion of the history of the FQPA, see McGarity, Politics by Other Means: Law, Science, and Policy in EPA's Implementation of the Food Quality Protection Act, 53 Admin. L. Rev. 103 (2001).

4. 7 U.S.C. §§135 et seq.

5. 15 U.S.C. §§2601 et seq.

As you consider these laws, analyze which approach is more likely to be effective. For example, consider whether it is the government or the manufacturer that is in the best position to collect data, to engage in chemical testing, or to establish testing protocols. Consider whether it is more efficient for government to regulate a product during the manufacturing process or to wait until after the product has reached the market. Are there phases in the manufacturing process when an industry is more likely to be receptive to and cooperative with governmental regulation? If so, how can government most efficiently take advantage of a manufacturer's profit motive to induce greater cooperation and more effective regulation?

A. PESTICIDES: THE FEDERAL INSECTICIDE, FUNGICIDE, AND RODENTICIDE ACT

Marshall Miller, Federal Regulation of Pesticides, Environmental Law Handbook[6]
284–301 (14th ed. 1997)

The benefits of pesticides, herbicides, rodenticides, and other economic poisons[7] are well known. They have done much to spare us from the ravages of disease, crop infestations, noxious animals, and choking weeds. Over the past two decades, however, beginning with Rachel Carson's *Silent Spring* in 1962, there has been a growing awareness of the hazards, as well as the benefits, of these chemicals, which may be harmful to man and the balance of nature.

The ability to balance these often conflicting effects is hampered by continuing scientific uncertainties. We still lack full understanding of environmental side effects, the sub-cellular mechanism of human carcinogens, and a host of other factors that are important for a proper evaluation of pesticide suitability. Yet scientific progress, especially in the genetic area, has been so rapid over the past decade or two that we are now realizing that many of our previous assumptions have been wrong, or at least oversimplified. The best scientific knowledge is now critical for the agency as it attempts to conduct accelerated reviews of hundreds of chemicals that had been registered earlier under less strict standards.

Public concern regarding pesticides was a principal cause for the rise of the environmental movement in the United States in the late sixties and early seventies, and therefore was probably the single most important reason for the creation of the EPA. While public attention since then has shifted to various other environmental media, the pesticide issue — with its implications for the safety of food supply and of people in the agricultural area — is still central to the public's notion of environmental protection. Indeed, the fluctuation of interest in this topic is often an accurate barometer of public distrust in the official environmental agencies.

In the last few years this distrust has taken a new and different form. EPA is now being criticized not only by the environmentalists for not doing enough, but also by others for ordering unnecessarily costly or extreme measures. At the heart of both views is the belief that the agency's actions are not always firmly based on good science — a skepticism that is of course by no means limited to EPA's pesticide program.

---

6. Mr. Miller is a partner in the Washington, D.C., firm of Baise & Miller.

7. The term "economic poisons" has been applied to pesticides since the 1940s. It reflects the "necessary evil" character of these substances, which FIFRA expresses in its weighing of benefits against costs. As "economic poisons," pesticides can cause adverse effects beyond their target species, thereby resulting in "collateral damage" that must be weighed against the benefits of pesticide use. Rachel Carson's *Silent Spring* was among the first books to recognize the toxics problems caused by pesticide use. [Eds.]

Chemical pesticides have been subject to some degree of federal control since the Insecticide Act of 1910. This Act was primarily concerned with protecting consumers, usually farmers, from ineffective products and deceptive labeling, and it contained neither a federal registration requirement nor any significant safety standards. The relatively insignificant usage of pesticides before World War II made regulation a matter of low priority.

The resulting effects on public health and farm production made pesticides a virtual necessity. The agricultural chemical industry became an influential sector of the economy. In 1947, Congress enacted a more comprehensive statute, the Federal Insecticide, Fungicide, and Rodenticide Act ("FIFRA"). This law required that pesticides distributed in interstate commerce be registered with the United States Department of Agriculture ("USDA"). It also established rudimentary labeling requirements. This Act, like its predecessor, was mostly concerned with product effectiveness; the statute did, however, declare pesticides "misbranded" if they were necessarily harmful to man, animals, or vegetation (except weeds) even when properly used.

Three major defects in the new law soon became evident. First, the registration process was largely an empty formality since the Secretary of Agriculture could not refuse registration even to a chemical he deemed highly dangerous. He could register "under protest," but this had no legal effect on the registrant's ability to manufacture or distribute the product. Second, there was no regulatory control over the use of a pesticide contrary to its label, as long as the label itself complied with statutory requirements. Third, the Secretary's only remedy against a hazardous product was a legal action for misbranding or adulteration, and — this was crucial — the difficult burden of proof was on the government....

In 1964 the USDA persuaded Congress to remedy two of these three defects: the registration system was revised to permit the secretary to refuse to register a new product or to cancel an existing registration, and the burden of proof for safety and effectiveness was placed on the registrant. Those changes considerably strengthened the act, in theory, but made little difference in practice. The Pesticide Registration Division, a section of USDA's Agricultural Research Service, was understaffed...and the division was buried deep in a bureaucracy primarily concerned with promoting agriculture and facilitating the registration of pesticides. The cancellation procedure was seldom if ever used, and there was still no legal sanction against a consumer's applying the chemical for a delisted use.

The growth of the environmental movement in the late 1960s, with its concern about the widespread use of agricultural chemicals, overwhelmed the meager resources of the Pesticide Division. Environmental groups filed a barrage of lawsuits demanding the cancellation or suspension of a host of major pesticides such as DDT, Aldrin-Dieldrin, Mirex and the herbicide 2,4,5-T. This demanding situation demanded a new approach to pesticide regulations.

On December 2, 1970, President Nixon signed Reorganization Order No. 3 creating the Environmental Protection Agency. This Order assigned to EPA the functions and many of the personnel previously under Interior, Agriculture, and other government departments. EPA inherited from USDA not only the Pesticides Division but also the environmental lawsuits against the Secretary of Agriculture....

The Federal Insecticide, Fungicide, and Rodenticide Act (FIFRA), as amended by the Federal Environmental Pesticide Control Act (FEPCA) of October 1972 and the FIFRA amendments of 1975, 1978, 1980, 1988, and 1996, is a complex statute. Terms sometimes have a meaning different from, or even directly contrary to, normal English usage. For example, the term "suspension" really means an immediate ban on a pesticide, while the harsher-sounding term "cancellation" indicates only the initiation of administrative proceedings which can drag on for many years....

All new pesticide products used in the United States, with minor exceptions, must first be registered with EPA. This involves the submittal of the complete formula, a proposed label, and "full description of the tests made and the results thereof upon which the claims are based." The registration is very specific; it is not valid for all formulations or uses of a particular chemical. That is, separate registrations are required for each specific crops and insects on which the pesticide product may be applied, and each use must be supported by research data on safety and efficacy....

The Administrator must approve the registration if the following conditions are met:

(1) Its composition is such as to warrant the proposed claim for it;

(2) Its labeling and other materials required to be submitted comply with the requirements of this act;

(3) It will perform its intended function without unreasonable adverse effects on the environment; and

(4) When used in accordance with widespread and commonly recognized practice it will not generally cause unreasonable adverse effects on the environment.

The operative phrase in the above criteria is "unreasonable adverse effects on the environment," which was added to the act in 1972. This phrase is defined elsewhere in FIFRA as meaning "any unreasonable risk to man or the environment, taking into account the economic, social, and environmental costs and benefits of the use of the pesticide."...

Registrations are for a limited, five-year period; thereafter, they automatically expire unless an interested party petitions for renewal and, if requested by EPA, provides additional data indicating the safety of the product. For the past few years, pre-EPA registrations have been coming up for renewal under much stricter standards than when originally issued....

Until the 1972 reforms, the government had no control over the actual use of a pesticide once it had left a manufacturer or distributor properly labeled. Thus, for example, a chemical which would be perfectly safe for use on a dry field might be environmentally hazardous if applied in a marshy area, and a chemical acceptable for use on one crop might leave dangerous residues on another. EPA's only recourse...was to cancel the entire registration — obviously too unwieldy a weapon to constitute a normal means of enforcement. A second problem was that a...chemical might be too dangerous for general use but could be used safely by trained personnel. There was, however, no legal mechanism for limiting its use only to qualified individuals.

Because of these problems, both environmentalists and the industry agreed that EPA should be given more flexibility than merely the choice between cancelling or approving a pesticide. Congress therefore provided for the classification of pesticides into general and restricted categories, with the latter group available only to Certified Applicators....

While the registration process may be the heart of FIFRA, cancellation represents the cutting edge of the law and attracts the most public attention. Cancellation is used to initiate review of a substance suspected of posing a "substantial question of safety" to man or the environment.

Contrary to the public assumptions, during the pendency of the proceedings the product may be freely manufactured and shipped in commerce. A cancellation order, although final if not challenged within thirty days, usually leads to a public hearing or scientific review committee, or both, and can be quite protracted; this can last a matter of months or years. A recommended decision from the agency hearing examiner (now called the administrative law judge) goes to the Administrator or his delegated representative, the chief agency judicial officer, for a final determination on the cancellation....

A suspension order, despite its misleading name, is an immediate ban on the production and distribution of a pesticide. It is mandated when a product constitutes an "imminent hazard" to man or the environment, and may be invoked at any stage of the cancellation proceeding or even before a cancellation procedure has been initiated....

The purpose of an ordinary suspension is to prevent an imminent hazard during the time required for cancellation or change in classification proceedings. An ordinary suspension proceeding is initiated when the Administrator issues notice to the registrant that he is suspending use of the pesticide and includes the requisite findings as to imminent hazard. The registrant may request an expedited hearing within five days of receipt of the Administrator's notice. If no hearing is requested, the suspension order can take effect immediately thereafter and the order is not reviewable by a court....

The emergency suspension is the strongest action EPA can take under FIFRA. It immediately halts all uses, sales, and distribution of the pesticide. An emergency suspension differs from an ordinary suspension in that it is ex parte. The registrant is not given notice or the opportunity for an expedited hearing prior to the suspension order taking effect. The registrant is, however, entitled to an expedited hearing to determine the propriety of the emergency suspension. The Administrator can only use this procedure when he determines that an emergency exists which does not allow him to hold a hearing before suspending use of a pesticide. This authority has only rarely been invoked....

Environmental Defense Fund v. U.S. Environmental Protection Agency
United States Court of Appeals for the District of Columbia Circuit, 1972
465 F.2d 528

LEVENTHAL, C.J. On December 3, 1970, petitioner Environmental Defense Fund (EDF), a non-profit New York Corporation, petitioned the Environmental Protection Agency under the Federal Insecticide, Fungicide, and Rodenticide Act, for the immediate suspension and ultimate cancellation of all registered uses of aldrin and dieldrin, two chemically similar chlorinated hydrocarbon pesticides. On March 18, 1971, the Administrator of the EPA announced the issuance of "notices of cancellation" for aldrin and dieldrin because of "a substantial question as to the safety of the registered products which has not been effectively countered by the registrant." He declined to order the interim remedy of suspension, pending final decision on cancellation after completion of the pertinent administrative procedure, in light of his decision that "present uses [of aldrin and dieldrin] do not pose an imminent threat to the public such as to require immediate action." EDF filed this petition to review the EPA's failure to suspend the registration....

The EPA's Statement points out that whereas a notice of cancellation is appropriate whenever there is "a substantial question as to the safety of a product," immediate suspension is authorized only in order to prevent an "imminent hazard to the public," and to protect the public by prohibiting shipment of an economic poison "so dangerous that its continued use should not be tolerated during the pendency of the administrative process." The EPA describes its general criteria for suspension as follows:

> This agency will find that an imminent hazard to the public exists when the evidence is sufficient to show that continued registration of an economic poison poses a significant threat of danger to health, or otherwise creates a hazardous situation to the public, that should be corrected immediately to prevent serious injury, and which cannot be permitted to continue during the pendency of administrative proceedings. An "imminent hazard" may be declared at any point in a chain of events which may ultimately result in harm to the public. It is not necessary that the final anticipated injury actually

have occurred prior to a determination that an "imminent hazard" exists. In this connection, significant injury or potential injury to plants or animals alone could justify a finding of imminent hazard to the public from the use of an economic poison. The type, extent, probability and duration of potential or actual injury to man, plants, and animals will be measured in light of the positive benefits accruing from, for example, use of the responsible economic poison in human or animal disease control or food production.

Part II of the Statement of Reasons, captioned "Formulation of Standards," begins with the general standards deemed pertinent to the administration of FIFRA.

EPA points out that, in general, economic poisons, including those under present consideration, are "ecologically crude" — that is, by reason of technology limitations, [they] are toxic to non-target organisms as well as to pest life. Thus continued registration for particular ecologically crude pesticides "are acceptable only to the extent that the benefits accruing from use of a particular economic poison outweigh" the adverse results of effects on non-target species. EPA cites "dramatic steps in disease control" and the gradual amelioration of "the chronic problem of world hunger" as examples of the kind of beneficial effect to be looked for in balancing benefits against harm for specific substances. But it cautions that "triumphs of public health achieved in the past" will not be permitted to justify future registrations, recognizing that fundamentally different considerations are at work in evaluating use of a dangerous pesticide in a developed country such as the United States rather than in a developing non-industrial nation....

Laboratory tests with some substances have raised serious questions regarding carcinogenicity that "deserve particular searching" because carcinogenic effects are generally cumulative and irreversible when discovered. Threats presented by individual substances vary not only as to observed persistence in the environment but also as to environmental mobility — which in turn depends in part on how a particular pesticide is introduced into the environment either by ground insertion or by dispersal directly into the ambient air or water.

Based on the discussion of these general considerations, the EPA concludes that individual decisions on initial or continued registration must depend on a complex administrative calculus, in which the "nature and magnitude of the foreseeable hazards associated with use of a particular product" is weighed against the "nature of the benefit conferred" by its use....

The EDF's main argument [is that] while the Statement of Reasons sets forth, as a matter of EPA policy, that suspension decisions would be made only after the Administrator makes a preliminary assessment of immanency of hazard that includes a balancing of benefit and harm, yet when the EPA discussed aldrin and dieldrin, it inconsistently failed to identify any offsetting benefits, and limited itself to the reference to certain hazards.

The EPA concedes that the "thrust" of the Administrator's analysis related to the absence of any short run major hazards. But it parries that he "did refer to the purposes for which aldrin and dieldrin are used."

In light of his findings with respect to the absence of any foreseeable hazard, there was little need for the Administrator to go into detail in considering — as he had indicated he would do in suspension decisions... — "the positive benefits."

We are not clear that the FIFRA requires separate analysis of benefits at the suspension stage. We are clear that the statute empowers the Administrator to take account of benefits or their absence as affecting imminency of hazard. The Administrator's general decision to follow that course cannot be assailed as unreasonable. The suspension procedures of this agency, though in the abstract designed for emergency situations, seem to us to resemble more closely the judicial proceedings on a contested motion for a preliminary injunction, to prevail during the pendency of the litigation on the merits, rather than proceedings on an ex parte application for an emergency temporary restraining order. The suspension decision is not ordinarily one to be made in a matter of moments, or even hours or days. The statute contemplates at least the kind of ventilation of issues commonly had prior to decisions by courts that govern the relationships of parties pendente lite, during trial on the merits.

Judicial doctrine teaches that a court must consider possibility of success on the merits, the nature and extent of the damage to each of the parties from the granting or denial of the injunction, and where the public interest lies. It was not inappropriate for the Administrator to have chosen a general approach to suspension that permits analysis of similar factors. By definition, a substantial question of safety exists when notices of cancellation issue. If there is no offsetting claim of any benefit to the public, then the EPA has the burden of showing that the substantial safety question does not pose an "imminent hazard" to the public.

EDF is on sound ground in noting that while the EPA's general approach contemplates a decision as to suspension based on a balance of benefit and harm, the later discussion of aldrin and dieldrin relates only to harm.

The Administrator's mere mention of these products' major uses, emphasized by the EPA, cannot suffice as a discussion of benefits, even though the data before him...reflected the view that aldrin-dieldrin pesticides are the only control presently available for some twenty insects which attack corn and for one pest which poses a real danger to citrus orchards....

The interests at stake here are too important to permit the decision to be sustained on the basis of speculative inference as to what the Administrator's findings and conclusions might have been regarding benefits....

Our conclusion that a mere recitation of a pesticide's uses does not suffice as an analysis of benefits is fortified where, as here, there was a submission, by EDF, that alternative pest control mechanisms are available for such use. The analysis of benefit requires some consideration of whether such proposed alternatives are available or feasible, or whether such availability is in doubt.

The importance of an EPA analysis of benefits is underscored by the Administrator's flexibility, in both final decisions and suspension orders, to differentiate between uses of the product. Aldrin and dieldrin are apparently not viewed by the EPA as uniform in their benefit characteristics for all their uses. The Administrator had previously stopped certain uses of the pesticides in question in house paints, and in water use. These actions presumably reflected some evaluation of comparative benefits and hazards. The Administrator's reliance on the "pattern of declining gross use" itself indicates that for some purposes aldrin and dieldrin are or will soon become non-essential. Even assuming the essentiality of aldrin and dieldrin, and of the lack of feasible alternative control mechanisms for certain uses, there may be no corresponding benefit for other uses, which may be curtailed during the suspension period....

We do not say there is an absolute need for analysis of benefits. It might have been possible for EPA to say that although there were no significant benefits from aldrin-dieldrin, the possibility of harm — though substantial enough to present a long-run danger to the public warranting cancellation proceedings — did not present a serious short-run danger that constituted an imminent hazard. EPA's counsel offers this as a justification for its action.

If this is to be said, it must be said clearly, so that it may be reviewed carefully. Logically, there is room for the concept. But we must caution against any approach to the [statutory] term "imminent hazard"...that restricts it to a concept of crisis. It is enough if there is substantial likelihood that serious harm will be experienced during the year or two required in any realistic projection of the administrative process. It is not good practice for an agency to defend an order on the hypothesis that it is valid even assuming there are no benefits, when the reality is that some conclusion of benefits was visualized by the agency. This kind of abstraction pushes argument — and judicial review — to the wall of extremes, when realism calls for an awareness of middle ground.

COMMENTARY & QUESTIONS

1. **The subsequent suspension of aldrin and dieldrin.** The court remanded the matter to EPA for further study. After considering the Advisory Committee Report and further public comments, EPA affirmed its previous decisions to cancel without interim suspension. Twelve months into the cancellation proceeding, the Administrator issued a notice of intent to suspend, and the suspension became final on October 1, 1974. EPA's suspension decision was substantially upheld in EDF v. EPA, 510 F.2d 1292 (D.C. Cir. 1975), where Judge Leventhal, emphasizing that "the responsibility to demonstrate that the benefits outweigh the risks is upon the proponents of continued registration," upheld EPA's finding that alternatives to aldrin-dieldrin were currently available. See also EDF v. EPA, 548 F.2d 998 (D.C. Cir. 1976) (heptachlor and chlordane). For further insight into Judge Leventhal's views, see Leventhal, Environmental Decisionmaking and the Role of the Courts, 122 U. Pa. L. Rev. 509 (1974); Rodgers, Benefits, Costs and Risks: Oversight of Health and Environmental Decisionmaking, 4 Harv. Envtl. L. Rev. 191 (1980).

2. **Emergency suspension.** The aldrin-dieldrin case was an ordinary suspension rather than an emergency suspension. EPA first used the emergency suspension procedure in 1979 when it suspended many uses of 2,4,5-T and Silvex. Emergency suspension is the most potent action available to EPA under FIFRA because it immediately stops all uses, sales, and distribution of the pesticide. In Dow Chem. Co. v. Blum, 469 F. Supp. 892 (E.D. Mich. 1979), a federal district court, upholding EPA's emergency suspension, concluded that whereas an ordinary suspension proceeding is similar to a motion for a preliminary injunction during a lawsuit, the emergency suspension proceeding is similar to an application for a temporary restraining order. An emergency suspension order will be upheld if there is "minimal evidence in the record to support EPA's decision." But see Love v. EPA, 838 F.2d 1059 (9th Cir. 1988), where the emergency suspension of dinoseb in the Northwest was overturned because "EPA's evaluation of the relevant factors under FIFRA was incomplete and rushed and...simply not adequate to justify the emergency suspension...." Registration of dinoseb was later cancelled, but existing stocks were permitted to be used for limited purposes. See Northwest Food Processors Ass'n v. EPA, 886 F.2d 1075 (9th Cir. 1989). Should a reviewing court be more or less deferential to an EPA decision on an ordinary suspension because of the existence of the emergency suspension device? Does the emergency suspension device provide reassurance to courts that EPA can act quickly if further information indicates that suspension is desirable? If so, does the existence of the emergency suspension device affect judges' views pertaining to whether to overturn an ordinary suspension?

Section 102 of the FQPA amended FIFRA to make a material change in the emergency suspension process by allowing a suspension for no more than 90 days without a simultaneous notice of intent to cancel. What concerns was Congress addressing in making this change?

3. **Imminent hazards.** FIFRA operates as a threshold preventive in that it applies "up front" before a potentially dangerous pesticide is introduced into commerce. On the other hand, FIFRA's standards are not pure safety criteria because the economic benefits and costs of regulation are weighed at the registration, cancellation, and suspension stages. Does the "imminent hazard" standard serve as a margin of safety where economic benefits are tangible and potential environmental harms are uncertain? EPA's interpretive statement on "imminent hazard" is highly precautionary, justifying action whenever there is "significant injury or potential injury to plants or animals alone...." Another administrative mechanism for erring on the side of safety is EPA's Special Review process (formerly called Rebuttable Presumption Against Registration, or RPAR), in which evidence developed by EPA or a third party that a pesticide exceeds specified "risk criteria" will raise a presumption against registration or in favor of cancellation or suspension. 40 C.F.R. pt. 154. Moreover, the EDF v. EPA court adds that once a notice of cancellation is issued — if there is no offsetting claim of benefits — then "EPA has the burden of showing that the substantial safety question does not pose an 'imminent hazard' to the public." It seems clear, as the court points out, that "imminent hazard" does not mean "crisis." Operationally it means that the greater the amount of credible evidence EPA has about potential dangers posed by a registered pesticide, the more quickly and easily its use can be discontinued, and the more pronounced benefits must be in order to justify its continued use. How effective is a regulatory scheme that allows a product to be marketed but that makes quick protective withdrawal possible once negative evidence appears? How is negative evidence to be measured or quantified, particularly when scientific uncertainty factors affect benefit-cost analysis? Is it easier for EPA to suspend a pesticide under a "significant threat" standard then under a "crisis" standard of "imminence"?

"Imminent hazard" is one of those all-important statutory terms that defy precise analysis but facilitate administrative and judicial determinations regarding uncertainty and burdens of proof, creating the "common law" of particular statutes. The "imminent hazard" phrase serves a similar function in RCRA (see Chapter 18) and CERCLA (see Chapter 19). Another such term is "endanger." See Ethyl Corp. v. EPA, 541 F.2d 1 (D.C. Cir. 1976).

4. **The role of benefits in a suspension proceeding.** Must benefits be analyzed in a suspension proceeding? Judge Leventhal's opinion is not consistent on this point. Does it depend on whether evidence of available alternatives has been introduced? If there is no short-term danger, why bother analyzing benefits at all? In order to analyze benefits, must they be quantifiable? If not, how do we measure them? Is it possible to distinguish clearly between short- and long-term hazards?

5. **Nonregistration of exports.** Whereas imported pesticides are subject to FIFRA registration requirements, exports are excluded from the regulatory provisions of the Act. Should the federal government permit DDT to be exported to a developing nation where malaria is a serious problem if the pesticide is the only affordable malaria-control alternative? To what extent should the transboundary character of pollution from persistent pesticides be considered in such judgments? Are risk-benefit calculations, as applied to challenged pesticides in the United States, applicable to conditions

faced abroad? If the United States unilaterally regulates pesticide exportation, will other pesticide producing nations gain an unfair competitive advantage? One of Ronald Reagan's first actions as President was to rescind the Carter Administration's ban on export of dangerous pesticides and contaminated pharmaceuticals.

6. **Paying for suspension.** A controversial provision of the 1972 Amendments required EPA to indemnify registrants, formulators, and end users of cancelled or suspended pesticides for remaining stocks that were not permitted to be exhausted. Needless to say, this provision had a chilling effect on cancellations and suspensions. In the 1988 FIFRA Amendments, the indemnity requirement was deleted except for end users (farmers and applicators).[8]

7. **FIFRA and preemption.** There are several issues involved here. First, do FIFRA's labeling requirements preempt private common law tort suits filed in state court based on inadequate labeling ("failure to warn")? Courts are split on this issue, although the general rule is that a license or permit will not insulate a defendant from obligations imposed by common law or other statutes. Thus FIFRA registration is ordinarily no defense to a tort action or to an action demanding compliance with NEPA.[9] The second issue is whether states can impose labeling and packaging requirements stricter than those imposed by EPA under FIFRA. Thus far, courts have upheld more restrictive state pesticide registration requirements.[10] In 1992, in Cipollone v. Liggett Group, 505 U.S. 504 (1992), the Supreme Court decided a preemption case involving health warnings on cigarette packs, addressing the extent to which federal law preempts state common law damages claims brought against cigarette manufacturers. Subsequently, when the FIFRA preemption case of Papas v. Zoecon Corp., 505 U.S. 1215 (1992), reached the Supreme Court, the Court remanded the case to the Eleventh Circuit to decide in light of *Cipollone*. Since that time, however, although a number of federal appellate courts have ruled that FIFRA expressly preempts state law on the issue of labeling,[11] the appellate courts have continued to disagree on the extent to which they will uphold preemption on matters pertaining to product defects, warranties, and product testing.[12] In light of this disagreement among the federal appellate courts, why did Congress choose not to clarify these issues in its latest 1996 Amendments to FIFRA?

Finally, can municipalities ban or limit the use of pesticides registered under FIFRA? The Supreme Court resolved a conflict among the federal circuits by unanimously

---

8. Pub. L. No. 100-532, §501.

9. Compare Chevron Chem. Co. v. Ferebee, 736 F.2d 1529 (D.C. Cir. 1984) (state suit not preempted), with Papas v. Upjohn, 926 F.2d 1019 (11th Cir. 1991) (state suit preempted); Save Our Ecosystems v. Clark, 747 F.2d 1240 (9th Cir. 1984) (FIFRA does not avoid duty to comply with NEPA). See also Howarth, Pre-emption and Punitive Damages: The Conflict Continues Under FIFRA, 136 U. Pa. L. Rev. 1301 (1988) (favoring preemption).

10. See National Agric. Chem. Ass'n v. Rominger, 500 F. Supp. 465 (E.D. Cal. 1980), and New York State Pesticide Coalition v. Jorling, 874 F.2d 115 (2d Cir. 1989); see also D. W. Stever, Law of Chemical Regulation and Hazardous Waste §3.08 (1991), for an interesting discussion of this question.

11. The majority of courts since *Cipollone* have held that common law actions based on inadequate labeling or failure to warn are preempted by FIFRA. See the thorough discussion of this issue by the Kansas Supreme Court in Jenkins v. Amchem Prods., 886 P.2d 869 (Kan. 1994).

12. See, e.g., Arkansas-Platte & Gulf Partnership v. Van Waters & Rogers, Inc., 981 F.2d 1177 (10th Cir. 1993); Papas v. Upjohn Co., 985 F.2d 516 (11th Cir. 1993); Lowe v. Sporicidin Int'l, 47 F.3d 124 (4th Cir. 1995); Worm v. America Cyanamid, 5 F.3d 744 (4th Cir. 1993); King v. E. I. Dupont De Nemours & Co., 996 F.2d 1346 (1st Cir. 1993); Shaw v. Dow Brands, Inc., 994 F.2d 364 (7th Cir. 1993); Bice v. Leslie's Poolmart, Inc., 39 F.3d 887 (8th Cir. 1994).

holding, in Wisconsin Public Intervenor v. Mortier, 501 U.S. 597 (1991), that munici-palities are not preempted by FIFRA from controlling pesticide use:

> FIFRA nowhere seeks to establish an affirmative permit scheme for the actual use of pesticides. It certainly does not equate registration and labeling requirements with a general approval to apply pesticides throughout the Nation without regard to regional and local factors like climate, population, geography, and water supply. Whatever else FIFRA may supplant, it does not occupy the field of pesticide regulation in general or the area of local use permitting in particular. 501 U.S. at 613.

Although the local ordinance upheld in the *Mortier* case involved the legality of a permit requirement for aerial spraying on private lands, the opinion appears to condone local pesticide bans as well.

8. FIFRA as a licensing statute. As commentators have noted, FIFRA creates a unique form of licensing system. See Applegate, The Perils of Unreasonable Risk: Information, Regulatory Policy, and Toxic Substances Control, 91 Colum. L. Rev. 261 (1991) (hereafter "Applegate"). Professor Applegate has written:

> If as a general rule manufacturers can develop toxicology information more cheaply than EPA, or if the cost is more efficiently or equitably borne by them and their customers, then it makes sense to assign the burden of proof to the manufacturer. In regulatory systems, shifting the burden of proof from the government to industry is typically accomplished by enacting a licensing or screening system. In the case of toxic substances, chemical producers would have to demonstrate the safety of their products before these products could be introduced into commerce. Licensing, therefore, not only provides an incentive to development of new information; it also shifts the cost of development away from government to a group that in theory has the capacity to absorb and spread the loss.
>
> Of the toxics statutes, only FIFRA has a true licensing scheme. Before pesticides can be sold, they must be registered and EPA must determine that they do not present an unreasonable risk. The registrant has the initial and continuing burden of demonstrating safety, though EPA has an initial burden of production in a cancellation proceeding and must ultimately be able to support its conclusions by substantial evidence. By placing the burden on the registrant, EPA is able to obtain whatever information it deems necessary to assess whether the chemical poses an unreasonable risk through the simple expedient of specifying data requirements for registration. EPA needs only the most general justification for these requirements, given the breadth of factors relevant to the unreasonable risk determination. Furthermore, the data requirements apply to all pesticides, eliminating the need to demand data on a chemical-by-chemical basis. This technique obviously brings the full profit motive to bear in developing adequate data in an expeditious manner. Applegate at 308–309.

Nevertheless, FIFRA, like all licensing statutes, has two major disadvantages:

> First, the premarket phase of product development is the time when the least information is known about a chemical's long-term effects. Without indications of chronic toxicity, it is hard to justify lengthy, expensive bioassays. Second, a licensing scheme intercepts only new or prospective risks. Since older chemicals are likely to be less well-tested relative to more recently licensed chemicals, the lack of data on existing chemicals constitutes a major gap in an information generation system. This problem can be resolved by a retroactive licensing arrangement like FIFRA's re-registration process.... Recognizing that licensing fails to generate any

information for existing chemicals or post-license information for new ones, FIFRA established a five-year registration period after which reconsideration is necessary. This provision has not generated large amounts of data, however, because EPA has never used the five-year period aggressively for this purpose. Indeed, EPA has lacked sufficient resources to do much more than keep current on new registrations and cancellations. Applegate at 312–313.

These drawbacks in the FIFRA licensing system further emphasize the importance of the cancellation and suspension mechanisms. Ultimately, the best way to prevent pesticide pollution may be Integrated Pest Management (IPM) — placing primary reliance on biological and management controls, with limited applications of pesticides permitted only when absolutely necessary and where least likely to cause environmental damage. Genetic engineering also shows promise in redesigning plants for immunity to traditional pests.

9. **The trouble with FIFRA.** Although FIFRA creates a unique form of licensing, FIFRA nonetheless has come under attack for not effectively protecting public health and the environment against the adverse effects of toxic pesticides. The underlying problem of pesticide policy, manifested in FIFRA, has been to implement a defensible standard of "reasonable risk" that effectively places the burden of proof on pesticide registrants to show that their products' risks are acceptable under FIFRA's cost-benefit framework.

Well over one billion pounds of pesticides are applied annually in the United States, at least 50 million pounds in the Great Lakes Watershed alone. U.S. GAO, Issues Concerning Pesticides Used in the Great Lakes Watershed (June 1993). Pesticides have been shown to cause significant environmental impacts, such as acute or chronic health effects among workers in the manufacturing process, on third parties due to accidents in manufacturing or transport, among applicators and farmworkers, and among consumers due to residues on food; contamination of groundwater due to leaching; contamination of surface waters from farm run-off; poisoning of wildlife; and contamination of the environment due to improper disposal of unused pesticides and their containers. Hornstein, Lessons from Federal Pesticide Regulation on the Paradigms and Politics of Environmental Law Reform, 10 Yale J. Reg. 369, 394–395 (1993) (hereinafter "Hornstein"). Pesticide contamination of groundwater, for example, is a potent threat to human health because nearly 50% of all Americans derive their potable water from groundwater. Many of these are homeowners on private wells who drink untreated groundwater directly from aquifers.

In 1991, the U.S. General Accounting Office evaluated EPA's efforts to deal with the problem of groundwater contamination by pesticides. Pesticides: EPA Could Do More to Minimize Groundwater Contamination (April 1991). In testimony based on that study, a GAO official concluded that

> EPA needs to take more initiative in ensuring that groundwater contamination by pesticides is minimized. Efforts are needed in three areas. First, EPA has been slow in reviewing the scientific studies needed to assess pesticides' potential to leach into groundwater. Therefore, detailed information on the factors that contribute to leaching is not available to pesticide applicators and the pace of reassessing older pesticides has been slowed. Second, while EPA has used the regulatory tools

available[13] in some cases, the agency could do more to help prevent groundwater contamination from worsening. Third, when EPA assesses risks from pesticide residues in food — in order to set residue limits known as tolerances — the agency is not routinely considering the additional exposure that can result from pesticide-contaminated groundwater. As a result, the agency lacks assurance that tolerances for pesticides that leach into groundwater are set low enough to protect public health.

Professor Hornstein attributes these problems, in great measure, to the centrality of risk assessment under FIFRA:

Risk analysis...serves as a procedural device that favors pesticide-using political constituencies in three ways. First, because EPA has no independent method of developing data, risk analysis makes EPA dependent on the data generated by pesticide manufacturers — raising opportunities for various types of bias. Information bias is not limited to cases of data falsification.... The more intractable problems are foot-dragging in submitting data to [EPA] and the ability of industry to shade the way data is presented (without falsification) simply by emphasizing the subtle but genuinely contestable "inference options" on which risk assessments depend. In the mid-70s, an internal EPA audit on the data underlying twenty-three randomly selected pesticides found that "all but one of the tests reviewed were unreliable and inadequate to demonstrate safety" — a level of unreliability that, by 1992, continued for at least some pesticides.... In short, the risk assessment enterprise is so information intensive that it creates strategic incentives to avoid a serious scientific examination of "true" levels of public health and environmental risk.

Second, despite the burden of proof ostensibly shouldered by pesticide manufacturers under FIFRA, the informational demands of risk analysis doom the regulatory process to a perpetual state of slow motion. The [GAO] reported in March 1992 that, "After some 20 years collecting data to reevaluate the health and environmental effects of 19,000 older pesticides, EPA...had reregistered only 2 products. Despite a congressional deadline of 1997 recently set for reregistration, GAO confirms EPA's own projections that the reregistration effort will extend "until early in the next century." Even when EPA chooses to act, the risk analyses required for Special Reviews or cancellation proceedings effectively inoculate manufacturers against timely action. Special Reviews, which were introduced in the mid-1970s to accelerate the cancellation process which then took an average of two years, now themselves average over seven years.... As a practical matter, the burdensomeness of risk analysis has tempered FIFRA's success in shifting the burden of proof to manufacturers.

Third, risk analysis offers the conceptual umbrella of "science" under which numerous non-scientific values can take shelter from public scrutiny and yet prolong the longevity of pesticides that may be neither desirable nor needed.... Hornstein at 436–438.

Thus FIFRA, although it facially requires a manufacturer to bear a more demanding burden of proof than ToSCA, has failed because, in practice, political pressures have caused the same "information bias" in FIFRA that has virtually disabled ToSCA.[14]

---

13. Such as prominent advisories on pesticide labels, prohibitions on use within a specified distance of wells (i.e., well setbacks), prohibitions on use in designated geographic areas, and restricting pesticides' use to certified applicators. [Eds.]

14. Of particular interest to the observation that market access statutes are handicapped by a persistent "information bias" is a line of cases holding that a manufacturer that withholds information from a federal agency is

Are proactive market access statutes inherently ineffectual in a nation that presumes the beneficence of an unregulated market system? Professor Hornstein does not directly ask this question, but he appears to imply a positive answer to it when he argues that FIFRA has "[been] one of the most colossal regulatory failures in Washington" because it does not get at the root causes of excessive pesticide use. American pesticide law "is not a body of law that addresses in any strategic way the underlying prevalence of pesticides in American agriculture, nor is it a body of law designed to minimize pesticide use." Hornstein at 392. He recommends a cause-based approach to pesticide regulation that would emphasize pest control technologies to limit pesticide use without significantly decreasing crop yields or growers' profitability and that would address existing economic incentive structures that lead growers to bypass improved technologies in favor of pesticide use that exceeds economically optimal levels. Professor Hornstein advocates the exploration of various policy options, such as pesticide risk taxes and enhanced "extension" programs, to encourage low-input agriculture.

B. REGULATING MARKET ACCESS OF TOXICS: THE TOXIC SUBSTANCES CONTROL ACT

ToSCA extended the product regulation concept to most new and existing chemicals. Both environmental and industry groups lobbied heavily during congressional deliberations over ToSCA. The result is perhaps the most complex, confusing, and ineffective of all our federal environmental protection statutes.

Ray M. Druley and Girard L. Ordway,
The Toxic Substances Control Act
1–4 (1977)

As summarized by the House Interstate and Foreign Commerce Committee Report, the major provisions of the Act:

- Require manufacturers and processors of potentially harmful chemical substances and mixtures to test the substances or mixtures, as required by rules issued by the Administrator of [EPA], so that their effect on health and the environment may be evaluated.

- Require manufacturers of new chemical substances and manufacturers and processors of existing chemical substances for significant new uses to notify the Administrator ninety days in advance of commercial production.

- Authorize delays or restrictions on the manufacture of a new chemical substance if there is inadequate information to evaluate the health or environmental effects of the substance and if in the absence of such information, the substance may cause or significantly contribute to an unreasonable risk to health or the environment.

- Authorize the Administrator to adopt rules to prohibit the manufacture, processing, or distribution of a chemical substance or mixture, to require labeling, or to regulate the

---

estopped from asserting preemption of packaging and labeling claims. See Roberson v. DuPont, 863 F. Supp. 929 (W.D. Ark. 1994); Burke v. Dow Chem. Co., 797 F. Supp. 1128, 1141 (E.D.N.Y. 1992) (recognizing that allowing preemption would "permit a manufacturer that was...aware of dangers to refrain from informing EPA of needed changes in its product's label and then to hide behind the very label it knew to be inadequate"); and Hurley v. Lederle Lab. Div. of Am. Cyanamid, 863 F.2d 1173 (5th Cir. 1988).

manner of disposal of a chemical substance or mixture for which there is a reasonable basis to conclude that it causes or significantly contributes to an unreasonable risk to health or the environment.

- Authorize the Administrator to obtain injunctive relief from a United States district court to protect the public and the environment from an imminently hazardous chemical substance or mixture.

- Authorize the Administrator to require manufacturers and processors to submit reports and maintain records respecting their commercially produced chemical substances and mixtures, to maintain records respecting adverse health or environmental effects of such substances and mixtures, and to provide available health and safety data on them.

- Require manufacturers and processors of chemical substances and mixtures to immediately notify the Administrator of information indicating that one of their substances or mixtures causes or contributes to a substantial risk to health or the environment.

- Permit administrative inspections to enforce the bill and authorize court actions for seizures of chemical substances and mixtures which have been manufactured or distributed in violation of the requirements of the bill or of rules and orders promulgated under it.

- Permit citizens to bring suits to obtain compliance with the bill.

- Permit federal district courts to order the Administrator to initiate rulemaking proceedings in response to citizen petitions.

- Set up procedural mechanisms to insure that all interested persons have an opportunity to participate in the agency rulemaking proceedings.

- Provide protection for employees who cooperate in the enforcement of the bill.

- Provide for evaluation on a continuing basis of the effects on employment of actions taken under the bill....

Testing and Pre-market Notification... Under the Act, EPA cannot require testing of every chemical. The Act does not regulate all chemicals which pose a risk, but only those which the EPA finds present an "unreasonable" risk of harm to human health or the environment. Accordingly, EPA must first find that there may be a risk or that there may be extensive human or environmental exposure and that information is lacking and testing is necessary. Given these findings, EPA must issue a rule requiring a manufacturer to perform testing and specifying the actual form of testing.

EPA is to issue its testing rules with the advice of an inter-agency committee, which will recommend testing priorities. Although the committee's advice is not binding, EPA is required to publish reasons for not requiring testing of certain specially designated compounds given high priority by the committee.

One of the key provisions of the Act is the section requiring manufacturers to provide EPA with data in advance of marketing. Chemical manufacturers must provide at least a 90-day notice before starting the manufacture of a new chemical or marketing a chemical for a new use as prescribed by EPA.

In order to determine what constitutes a new chemical that must be reported to EPA, EPA must publish an inventory list of chemicals known to be manufactured in the U.S. If a substance is not listed, it is to be considered a new chemical, and its planned production must be reported.

Under certain circumstances EPA can block the marketing of a chemical product pending the completion of testing. If a test order has been issued, test data must be submitted at the same time as the pre-market notification. Because testing may often require several years, this is a much more stringent requirement than simple 90-day notification.

EPA may also publish a hazardous substance list and can even do so by generic names. A manufacturer planning to market a substance included in the list must submit data to show that it is not a hazard for health or the environment.

Finally, if EPA determines upon notification that it has insufficient data on which to base a safety judgment, it may issue a proposed order to block production until testing is completed. The manufacturer may protest this order, and in this case EPA must apply to a federal district court for an injunction in order to block production.

Experimental and research chemicals produced in small quantities are exempt from the premarket notification requirements of the Act.

[ToSCA also does not apply to the following products regulated under other federal laws: firearms and ammunition; food, food additives, and drugs and cosmetics; meat and meat products; eggs and egg products; poultry and poultry products; pesticides; tobacco or tobacco products; and nuclear materials.]

Chemical Manufacturers Association v. U.S. Environmental Protection Agency
United States Court of Appeals for the D.C. Circuit, 1988
859 F.2d 977

WALD, J. Petitioners, Chemical Manufacturers Association and four companies that manufacture chemicals (collectively "CMA"), seek to set aside a rule promulgated by the Environmental Protection Agency. This Final Test Rule was promulgated under §4 of the Toxic Substances Control Act. The final test rule required toxicological testing to determine the health effects of the chemical 2-ethylhexanoic acid ("EHA")....

We uphold EPA's interpretation of TSCA as empowering the Agency to issue a test rule on health grounds where it finds a more-than-theoretical basis for suspecting that the chemical substance in question presents an "unreasonable risk of injury to health." This, in turn, requires the Agency to find a more-than-theoretical basis for concluding that the substance is sufficiently toxic, and human exposure to it is sufficient in amount, to generate an "unreasonable risk of injury to health." We hold, further, that EPA can establish the existence and amount of human exposure on the basis of inferences drawn from the circumstances under which the substance is manufactured and used. EPA must rebut industry-supplied evidence attacking those inferences only if the industry evidence succeeds in rendering the probability of exposure in the amount found by EPA no more than theoretical or speculative. The probability of infrequent or even one-time exposure to individuals can warrant a test rule, so long as there is a more-than-theoretical basis for determining that exposure in such doses presents an "unreasonable risk of injury to health." Finally, we hold that the Agency correctly applied these standards in this case and that its findings are supported by substantial evidence. Consequently, we affirm the Final Test Rule.

TSCA provides for a two-tier system for evaluating and regulating chemical substances to protect against unreasonable risks to human health and the environment. Section 6 of the Act permits EPA to regulate a substance that the Agency has found "presents or will present an unreasonable risk of injury to health or the environment." Section 4 of the Act empowers EPA to require testing of a suspect substance in order to obtain the toxicological data necessary to make a decision whether or not to regulate the substance under §6. The Act provides, not surprisingly, that the level of certainty of risk warranting a §4 test rule is lower than that warranting a §6 regulatory rule. EPA is empowered to require testing where it finds that the manufacture, distribution, processing, use or disposal of a particular chemical substance "may present an unreasonable risk of injury to human health or the environment." The Agency's interpretation of this statutory standard for testing is the central issue in this case.

One of the chief policies underlying the Act is that adequate data should be developed with respect to the effect of chemical substances and mixtures on health and the environment and that the development of such data should be the responsibility of those who manufacture and those who process such chemical substances and mixtures.

The statute establishes an Interagency Testing Committee, comprised of scientists from various federal agencies, to recommend that EPA give certain chemicals "priority consideration" for testing. Under §4, the Agency "shall by rule require that testing [of a particular chemical] be conducted" if three factors are present: (i) activities involving the chemical "may present an unreasonable risk of injury to health or the environment"; (ii) "insufficient data and experience" exist upon which to determine the effects of the chemical on health or environment; and (iii) testing is necessary to develop such data. The companies that manufacture and process the substance are to conduct the tests and submit the data to the Agency. Costs of the testing are to be shared among the companies, either by agreement or by EPA order in the absence of agreement.

A test rule promulgated under §4 is subject to judicial review in a court of appeals.... A test rule may be set aside if it is not "supported by substantial evidence in the rulemaking record...taken as a whole."

EHA is a colorless liquid with a mild odor. It is used exclusively as a chemical intermediate or reactant in the production of metal soaps, peroxyesters and other products used in industrial settings. EHA itself is totally consumed during the manufacture of these products; as a result, no products offered for sale to industry or to consumers contain EHA.

The Interagency Testing Committee first designated EHA for priority consideration for health effects tests on May 29, 1984. The Committee based its recommendation in part on the structural similarity of EHA to chemicals known to cause cancer in test animals and on its finding that insufficient information existed concerning the chronic health effects of EHA. Subsequently, EPA held two public meetings on EHA. During these meetings, in which persons representing the petitioners made appearances, EPA sought information on a variety of issues relating to EHA uses, production and human exposure.

EPA issued a proposed test rule on May 17, 1985. The rule proposed a series of tests to ascertain the health risks of EHA, and it set out proposed standards for the conduct of those tests. EPA based the Proposed Test Rule on a finding that EHA "may present an unreasonable risk" of subchronic toxicity (harm to bodily organs from repeated exposure over a limited period of time), oncogenicity (tumor formation) and developmental toxicity (harm to the fetus.) As to subchronic toxicity, EPA cited studies suggesting that both EHA and chemicals structurally similar to it cause harm to the livers of test animals. As to oncogenicity, EPA cited studies suggesting that chemicals structurally analogous to EHA cause cancer in laboratory animals. As to developmental toxicity, EPA cited studies indicating that both EHA and its chemical analogues have produced fetal malformations in test animals.

The Proposed Test Rule also addressed the question of whether humans are exposed to EHA, a question of critical importance to this case. The Agency acknowledged that, since no finished products contain EHA, consumer exposure is not a concern. It likewise discounted the dangers of worker exposure to EHA vapors. The Agency based its Proposed Test Rule solely on the potential danger that EHA will come in contact with the skin of workers. As evidence of potential dermal exposure, the Agency noted that approximately 400 workers are engaged in the manufacture, transfer, storage and processing of 20 to 25 million pounds of EHA per year.

Further, rebutting claims by industry representatives that gloves are routinely worn during these activities, EPA noted that worker hygiene procedures "can vary widely throughout the industry," that workers are not required by existing federal regulations to wear gloves, and that the industry had not monitored work sites for exposure to EHA.

A public comment period commenced with the publication of the Proposed Test Rule and ended on July 16, 1985. EPA held a public meeting on October 8, 1985, to discuss issues related to the Proposed Test Rule. Industry representatives submitted extensive comments on July 15, 1985, and January 17, 1986. Before publication of the Final Test Rule, EPA received notice of a new study purporting to present further evidence of the potential developmental toxicity of EHA....

EPA published the Final Test Rule for EHA on November 6, 1986. The Rule required a 90-day subchronic toxicity test, a developmental toxicity test, and a pharmacokinetics test.... The pharmacokinetics study required by the rule entailed the oral and dermal administration of EHA to experimental animals at low and high doses. The subchronic toxicity study involved administering EHA to animals in graduated daily doses over a period of 90 days. The developmental toxicity tests entailed administering EHA orally in various doses during the pregnancy of experimental animals. All studies were to be conducted in accordance with EPA standards. Results were to be submitted by certain deadlines, the last of which was 18 months after the effective date of the Final Test Rule....

The [TSCA] requires EPA to promulgate a test rule under §4 if a chemical substance, inter alia, "may present an unreasonable risk of injury to health or the environment." The parties both accept the proposition that the degree to which a particular substance presents a risk to health is a function of two factors: (a) human exposure to the substance, and (b) the toxicity of the substance. See Ausimont U.S.A., Inc. v. EPA, 838 F.2d 93, 96 (3d Cir.1988). They also agree that EPA must make some sort of threshold finding as to the existence of an "unreasonable risk of injury to health." The parties differ, however, as to the manner in which this finding must be made. Specifically, three issues are presented.

The first issue is whether, under §4 of TSCA, EPA must first find that the existence of an "unreasonable risk of injury to health" is more probable than not in order to issue a test rule. CMA argues that the statute requires a more-probable-than-not finding. EPA disagrees, contending that the statute is satisfied where the existence of an "unreasonable risk of injury to health" is a substantial probability — that is, a probability that is more than merely theoretical, speculative, or conjectural.

The second issue is whether, once industry has presented evidence tending to show an absence of human exposure, EPA must rebut it by producing direct evidence of exposure. CMA claims that, when industry evidence casts doubt on the existence of exposure, the burden of production shifts back to EPA, which must produce direct evidence documenting actual instances in which exposure has taken place. EPA, on the other hand, argues that it can make the requisite finding of exposure based solely on inferences drawn from the circumstances under which a chemical substance is manufactured and used.

The third issue is whether the Agency has authority to issue a test rule where any individual's exposure to a substance is an isolated, non-recurrent event. CMA argues that, even if EPA presents direct evidence of exposure, the Act precludes issuance of a test rule where exposure consists only of rare instances involving brief exposure. EPA contends, on the other hand, that the Act does not require in all circumstances a risk of recurrent exposure....

As to the first issue in this case,...both the wording and structure of TSCA reveal that Congress did not expect that EPA would have to document to a certainty the existence of an "unreasonable risk" before it could require testing. This is evident from the two-tier structure of the Act. In order for EPA to be empowered to regulate a chemical substance, the Agency must find that the substance "presents or will present an unreasonable risk of injury to health or the environment." The testing provision at issue here, by contrast, empowers EPA to act at a lower threshold of certainty than that required for regulation. Specifically, testing is warranted if the substance "*may* present an unreasonable risk of injury to health or the environment." Thus, the language of §4 signals that EPA is to make a probabilistic determination of the presence of "unreasonable risk."

The legislative history of TSCA compels a further conclusion. It not only shows that "unreasonable risk" need not be a matter of absolute certainty; it shows the reasonableness of EPA's conclusion that "unreasonable risk" need not be established to a more-probable-than-not degree.

A House Report on the version of the bill that eventually became TSCA underscores the distinction between the §6 standard and the §4 standard. To issue a test rule, EPA need not find that a substance actually does cause or present an "unreasonable risk."

> Such a finding requirement would defeat the purpose of the section, for if the Administrator is able to make such a determination, regulatory action to protect against the risk, not additional testing, is called for. H.R. Rep. No. 1341, 94th Cong., 2d Sess.

The House Report also contains signals indicating that Congress expected EPA to act even when evidence of "unreasonable risk" was less than conclusive. According to that report, the word "may" in §4 was intended to focus the Agency's attention on chemical substances "*about which there is a basis for concern, but about which there is inadequate* information to reasonably predict or determine the effects of the substance or mixture on health or the environment." Id. at 17 (emphasis added). The Conference Committee Report re-emphasized that the statutory language focused the Agency's attention on substances "about which there is a basis for concern." H.R. Conf. Rep. No. 1679, 94th Cong., 2d Sess. 61 (1976).

These indications of congressional intent illustrate that EPA's reading of TSCA is a permissible one. Congress intended to authorize testing where the existence of an "unreasonable risk" could not yet be "reasonably predicted." The Agency's determination that it is empowered to act where the existence of an "unreasonable risk" cannot yet be said to be more probable than not is entirely consistent with that expression of intent. The EPA interpretation is likewise consistent with the level of certainty suggested by the phrase "basis for concern." To accept the CMA's position would require the Agency to gather "adequate" information to make a reasonable prediction or determination of risk before issuing a test rule. To say the least, this is not mandated by the statutory history, which indicates Congress's desire that EPA act on the basis of rational concern even in the absence of "adequate" information that an unreasonable risk existed. Section 4 may permissibly be read to authorize issuance of a test rule on the basis of less than more-probable-than-not evidence about a potentially unreasonable risk to health.

This conclusion is further bolstered by the legislative history underlying §6. If CMA were correct that EPA must make a more-probable-than-not finding of risk under §4's "may present" language, then it would logically follow that §6 — which contains the term "presents or will present an unreasonable risk" — must require an even stronger than more-probable-than-not demonstration of "unreasonable risk." Yet neither §6 nor its legislative history indicate any such super-requirement of certainty. Indeed, §6 states expressly that the Agency need only find a "reasonable basis" to conclude that an "unreasonable risk" exists. A "reasonable basis" requirement is certainly no more demanding than a more-probable-than-not requirement; indeed the phrase suggests a less demanding standard. This interpretation is confirmed by the House Report, which states that an EPA finding of "unreasonable risk" under §6 is not expected to be supported by the same quantum of evidence as is customary in administrative proceedings.... In sum, the standard Congress set for §6 regulation, that the chemical "will present an unreasonable risk," is no more rigorous (and arguably is less rigorous) than a more-probable-than-not finding. It follows as a matter of course that §4's "may present" language demands even less.

Of course, it is also evident from the legislative history that Congress did not intend to authorize EPA to issue test rules on the basis of mere hunches. The House Report states:

> The term "may"...does not permit the Administrator to make a finding respecting probability of a risk on the basis of mere conjecture or speculation, i.e., [that] it may or may not cause a risk. H.R. Rep. No. 1341, at 18.

Congress obviously intended §4 to empower EPA to issue a test rule only after it had found a solid "basis for concern" by accumulating enough information to demonstrate a more-than-theoretical basis for suspecting that an "unreasonable risk" was involved in the use of the chemical....

[Relying on the "more-than-theoretical-basis" test, the court then rejected CMA's other two arguments regarding use of inferences versus direct evidence of exposure and rare versus recurrent exposure. Finally, the court analyzed the evidence submitted by EPA for the Final Test Rule and held that the Agency had produced substantial evidence "to demonstrate not fact, but doubt and uncertainty."]

COMMENTARY & QUESTIONS

1. **An exceptional case.** *Chemical Manufacturers* is an unusual example of ToSCA working smoothly with regard to the promulgation of test rules for existing chemicals. When ToSCA was enacted, some commentators predicted that the statute would be unenforceable because it had been so compromised during the legislative process. Unfortunately, these dire predictions have often been borne out. ToSCA's requirements that EPA promulgate test rules through notice-and-comment rulemaking and support them by substantial evidence, combined with the inadequacy of EPA's budget for ToSCA implementation and intense lobbying by industry, have militated against EPA promulgation of test rules. "By the end of fiscal year 1989, EPA had received full test data for only six chemicals and had not completed review of the data for any." Applegate at 319, citing U.S. GAO, EPA's Chemical Testing Program Has Made Little Progress (April 1990). EPA did not perform its mandatory duty to respond to Interagency Testing Committee (ITC) recommendations until compelled to do so by court order. NRDC v. Costle, 14 BNA Env't Rep. Cas. 1858 (1980). Moreover,

> EPA has historically rarely imposed a testing rule.... The agency has more often found reasons for declining to follow the ITC's testing recommendations. In addition, EPA has followed an administrative practice of entering into Negotiated Testing Agreements (NTAs) with industry trade associations in lieu of issuing test rules, wherever possible. D. W. Stever, The Law of Chemical Regulation and Hazardous Waste 2–8 (1991).

The NTA program was struck down in NRDC v. EPA, 595 F. Supp. 1255 (S.D.N.Y. 1984), partly because it excluded public interest groups. A new process called "testing consent agreements," which provides for public participation, is currently in effect. But ToSCA's cumbersome test rule procedures give EPA and the public little leverage in negotiations with industry.

2. **ToSCA and new chemicals.** ToSCA is no more effective with regard to the introduction of new chemicals into commerce. EPA cannot require the testing of all new chemicals under ToSCA. Unless a test rule is in effect for a component of a new chemical compound, or that component is included on EPA's §5(b)(4) "suspect list," a manufacturer need not submit health and environmental test data unless it has independently developed these data or they are generally available elsewhere. Thus, ToSCA does not require a set of pre-market data on a new chemical. Consequently, only half of all pre-market notifications (PMNs) submitted under ToSCA contain any toxicity information at all, and less than 20% include data on long-term toxicity. Applegate at 303, citing Office of Technology Assessment, The Information Content of Premanufacture Notices (1983). Does ToSCA actually discourage pre-market testing and encourage concealment of information? Or would a manufacturer most likely test a substance prior to manufacture in order to forestall tort liability? For a negative answer to the latter question, see Applegate at 299 ("industry has real incentives to avoid either creating toxic risk data or disclosing the data it already has"), and Lyndon, Information Economics and Chemical Toxicity: Designing Laws to Produce and Use Data, 87 Mich. L. Rev. 1795 (1989).

If EPA does not act to require testing before the expiration of the 90-day PMN period plus an optional additional 90 days, the manufacturer may commence manufacture or distribution. On the other hand, if after receipt of a PMN EPA finds that it has insufficient information on which to base an evaluation of the chemical substance, it may propose a test rule or, after making findings similar to those in §4, may issue a proposed order to prohibit or limit the production of the substance. If the manufacturer formally objects to the proposed order, EPA must seek an injunction in federal district court under §5(e). The strictness of these time constraints and the necessity of resorting to judicial action if a test rule cannot be proposed in time virtually guarantees agency inaction.

3. **FIFRA and ToSCA.** In the congressional proceedings leading to the passage of ToSCA, the Senate preferred a licensing system similar to FIFRA, while the House favored allowing new chemicals to be marketed without notification or registration unless the chemicals or their components appeared on EPA's "suspect list." The emergent ToSCA compromise was based on notification and discretionary intervention by EPA. According to Professor Lyndon, the FIFRA presumption that a substance is unsafe unless the manufacturer proves safety has, in ToSCA, been transformed into a presumption that a substance is safe unless EPA can prove that it is unsafe:

> TSCA's requirement that the EPA issue a rule before requiring testing distinguishes it from food, drug, and pesticide regulations, which mandate production of safety data prior to marketing. The TSCA standard essentially establishes a presumption of safety, which the agency must overcome before it may require further testing of a chemical. Thus, the TSCA's use of strict rulemaking standards inhibits the very information production the statute was written to encourage. 87 Mich. L. Rev. at 1824.

There is a fundamental ToSCA paradox or Catch-22 in regulatory information gathering. Where is EPA to procure the information that it needs to require manufacturers —

who have every incentive to suppress information — to produce health and safety data regarding new and existing chemicals? Does EPA have to know already what it needs to know in order to ask for information about it? Is the necessary information even obtainable, or are there data gaps? See Dernbach, The Unfocused Regulation of Toxic and Hazardous Pollutants, 21 Harv. Envtl. L. Rev. 1, 28 (1997) (noting that no toxicity information is even available for 78% of the 12,860 chemicals that are used in commerce in quantities of more than 1 million pounds per year, and that only minimal toxicity information is available concerning the rest).

4. **Regulation and the common law.** CMA's arguments in opposition to the Final Test Rule were based on common law analogues: (1) the more-probable-than-not test is similar to the "preponderance of the evidence" standard in common law civil litigation, (2) the criticism of EPA's inferences regarding modes of EHA use reflects the burden placed on a common law plaintiff to prove causation-in-fact by a preponderance of the evidence, and (3) the objection to EPA's regulating nonrecurrent exposures echoes a common law defendant's argument that an injunction should not be granted because there is an adequate remedy at law (damages) if the event is unlikely to recur. Administrative agencies, however, are not limited by these common law constraints, as the court reaffirmed in its rejection of CMA's arguments.

5. **The more-than-theoretical-basis test.** Could this standard be used to support a test rule where EPA has not yet explored the toxicity of a chemical but suspects, based on an educated guess, that the substance may be toxic? The more-than-theoretical-basis test probably could not be extended this far, but another section of ToSCA might cover such a situation. Section 4(a)(1)(B) provides that EPA may require testing where

> a chemical substance or mixture is or will be produced in substantial quantities, and (i) it enters or may reasonably be anticipated to enter the environment in substantial quantities or (ii) there is or may be significant or substantial human exposure to such substance or mixture.

In Chemical Mfrs. Ass'n v. EPA, 899 F.2d 344 (5th Cir. 1990) (frequently referred to as *Chemical Manufacturers II*), EPA contended that

> while there is a need to show a potential for exposure in order to make a §4(a)(1)(A) finding ["may present an unreasonable risk of injury to health or the environment"], the exposure threshold is much lower than that under §4(a)(1)(B). This is because the former...finding was intended to focus on those instances where EPA has a scientific basis for suspecting potential toxicity and reflects that the potential for risk to humans may be significant even when the potential for exposure seems small, as, for example, when the chemical is discovered to be hazardous at very low levels. In contrast, the §4(a)(1)(B) finding was intended to allow EPA to require testing, not because of suspicions about the chemical's safety, but because there may be a substantial or significant human exposure to a chemical whose hazards have not been explored. 899 F.2d at 358 n. 20.

The language of §4(a)(1)(B), however, is so ambiguous that this section is of doubtful utility. In *Chemical Manufacturers II*, the Court remanded the test rule to EPA to explain what it meant by "substantial" quantities and human exposure.

6. **The role of economics.** All ToSCA regulatory decisionmaking must balance economic costs against environmental benefits under the "unreasonable risk" standard imported from FIFRA. In addition, §2(c) provides that EPA "shall consider the environmental, economic, and social impact of any action" taken by it under ToSCA. Section 2(b) declares a policy that "authority over chemical substances...be exercised...so as not to impede unduly or create unnecessary economic barriers to technological innovation." Pursuant to §4(b), in specifying tests to be carried out, the EPA shall consider "the relative costs of the various test protocols and the methodologies which may be required." Is it fair to balance tangible and predictable economic costs against intangible and uncertain environmental benefits? The human mind naturally prefers the certain to the uncertain, leading to a "fallacy of numeration." Should the "unreasonable risk" balance be weighted on the side of the environment? Going even further, Professor Applegate recommends that the "unreasonable risk" standard be eliminated from §4:

> Unreasonable risk should be replaced in the §4 context by a more readily satisfied, less complex standard — something, in short, with less baggage. The term "unreasonable" should be dropped. The appropriate level (as opposed to existence) of risk is a policy question and more suitable in the standard-setting stage than in data collection. Under §4, EPA should be exploring policy options, not setting policy. Reasonable restraint by EPA can be assured by the existing provision requiring cost-effective testing and by the usual understanding that the term "risk" standing alone does not include de minimis risks. Applegate at 320.

But is it likely that Congress will repudiate "unreasonable risk," even as to data collection? Congress often prefers standards such as "unreasonable risk," which leave the difficult policy decisions to administrative agencies and courts. Although many critics recommend that Congress allow agencies flexibility in areas of technical expertise and administrative procedure, and the Supreme Court has acknowledged that agencies should be allowed flexibility in setting their own procedures, the trend in Congress is often towards selective micromanagement of deadlines and other goals. In many cases, the result has been agency paralysis, missed deadlines, and bureaucratic frustration.

7. **ToSCA §6.** Under §6 of ToSCA, EPA has authority to regulate existing chemicals that present unreasonable risks to health or the environment. EPA may place controls and restrictions, including outright bans if necessary, upon the manufacture, use, processing, disposal, or distribution of such chemicals. As discussed in *Chemical Manufacturers*, "if the Administrator finds that there is a reasonable basis to conclude that the manufacture, processing, distribution in commerce, use, or disposal of a chemical substance or mixture, or that any combination of such activities, presents or will present an unreasonable risk of injury to health or the environment, the Administrator shall by rule" impose one of the following measures: a prohibition or limitation on the manufacture, processing, or distribution of a substance in general or for specific uses, or an imposition of concentration limits; a requirement as to labeling, public warning, recall, or recordkeeping; or a ban or limitation on a particular form of use or disposal. All other things being equal, however, EPA must regulate under another statute rather than ToSCA §9(b). Although §6, like §4, has not been utilized very often,[15] it does represent a

---

15. U.S. GAO, Toxic Substances: Effectiveness of Unreasonable Risk Standards Unclear 1-2 (1990).

"catchall" or residuary pollution control statute, providing authority to regulate substances or uses that cannot be controlled under other federal pollution control statutes. EPA, for example, initially moved to regulate leaking underground storage tanks under ToSCA §6 until Congress enacted the 1984 RCRA Amendments. See Chapter 18. EPA has also relied on §6 to set soil concentration limits for land application of dioxin-containing pulp and paper sludge. See 56 Fed. Reg. 21802 (May 10, 1991).

8. **The EPA's attempted asbestos ban.** Asbestos is a naturally occurring fibrous material that resists fire and most solvents. For years, it was used as a heat resistant insulator in building materials, in fireproof gloves and clothing, and in motor vehicle brake linings. Asbestos, however, is also a toxic material. Occupational exposure to asbestos dust can cause cancer.

In 1989, after years of review of scientific evidence of asbestos carcinogenity, EPA promulgated a final rule imposing a staged ban on most commercial uses of asbestos. Invoking ToSCA §6, EPA concluded that asbestos exposure "poses an unreasonable risk to human health." This asbestos ban was EPA's first and, to date, only national ban of a toxic substance under ToSCA §6. EPA implemented this ban after it concluded that the ban would, over a 13-year period, save approximately 200 lives otherwise lost to cancer, plus other lives in the future. EPA also estimated that the ban would cost between $450 million to $800 million. EPA estimated that the costs per life saved of the rule ranged between $7 to $8 million (in the asbestos paper product industry) and $72 to $106 million (in the asbestos shingle community).

In its 1991 decision in Corrosion Proof Fittings v. EPA, 947 F.2d 1201 (5th Cir. 1991), the Fifth Circuit held that EPA had presented insufficient evidence to justify the asbestos ban. The Fifth Circuit concluded that EPA had failed to consider all necessary evidence and had failed to give adequate weight to the statutory language in §6, which requires EPA to promulgate the least burdensome, reasonable regulation necessary to protect the environment adequately. In reaching this result, the Fifth Circuit emphasized that, in providing for the regulation of "unreasonable risk" under ToSCA, Congress could not have meant to spend so much money in saving so few lives:

> While we do not sit as a regulatory agency that must make the difficult decision as to what an appropriate expenditure is to prevent someone from incurring the risk of an asbestos-related death, we do note that the EPA, in its zeal to ban any and all asbestos products, basically ignored the cost side of the TSCA equation. The EPA would have this court believe that Congress, when it enacted its requirement that the EPA consider the economic impacts of its regulations, thought that spending $200–300 million to save approximately seven lives (approximately $30–40 million per life) over thirteen years is reasonable....
>
> The EPA's willingness to argue that spending $23.7 million to save less than one-third of a life reveals that its economic review of its regulations, as required by TSCA, was meaningless.... If we were to allow such cavalier treatment of the EPA's duty to consider the economic effects of its decisions, we would have to excise entire sections and phrases from the language of TSCA. Because we are judges, not surgeons, we decline to do so. 947 F.2d at 1222–1223.

Corrosion Proof Fittings highlights the constraints on EPA in assessing risk and in engaging in risk management under §6 of ToSCA. Although EPA has the duty under ToSCA to assess and manage the risk posed by products like asbestos, Congress has imposed statutory limitations upon EPA in carrying out those functions. How is EPA to determine what is the least burdensome, reasonable regulation necessary to protect the environment? How should EPA engage in a cost-benefit risk balancing under §6? Would EPA's attempted asbestos ban have had more likelihood of success if §6 were more like the stark prohibition provisions of the former Delaney Clause?

Is it appropriate for EPA to attempt to justify proposed action under §6 by estimating costs per life saved? The Fifth Circuit in *Corrosion Proof Fittings* seems to suggest that the estimated costs per life saved under EPA's proposed asbestos ban were patently unreasonable. A subsequent study reviewed the economic data relied upon by EPA in support of its asbestos, pesticide, and carcinogenic air pollution regulations, finding that EPA, in effect, had attached a value of $15 million to $45 million to the prevention of one case of cancer. See Van Houtven & Cropper, When Is a Life Too Costly to Save? The Evidence from Environmental Regulations, Resources, Winter 1994, at 6. Recent analysis of the regulatory costs of lives saved, however, raises significant questions as to the validity of the high estimates relied upon by EPA in *Corrosion Proof Fittings* and subsequent studies. See Heinzerling, Regulatory Costs of Mythic Proportions, 107 Yale L.J. 1981, 2038–2040 (1998) (reviewing the data relied upon in numerous studies but concluding that such data indicates a cost per life saved of less than $5 million in most cases). The same analysis also challenges the propriety of "discounting lives" in seeking to estimate the benefits of environmental regulation. Id. at 2043–2056.

9. The PCB Mega Rule. Polychlorinated biphenyls (PCBs) are a class of compounds that were widely used in electrical equipment because of their low flammability, heat capacity, and dielectric properties. Transformers, cooling systems, hydraulic systems, electromagnets, switches, and voltage regulators were the primary types of equipment that contained PCBs.

When Congress enacted ToSCA, it was aware that PCBs were potentially carcinogenic and very persistent in the environment (that is, they decompose slowly). Congress also was aware that PCBs can accumulate in plants, animals, and human tissue and that PCBs have adverse effects on fish and wildlife. As a result, in ToSCA §6(e), Congress determined that PCBs presented an unreasonable risk to human health and the environment and directed EPA to promulgate regulations concerning the use, storage, and disposal of PCBs. EPA issued its first PCB regulations in 1979. See EDF v. EPA, 636 F.2d 1267 (D.C. Cir. 1980) (EPA's PCB regulations overturned and remanded).

In the years since EPA began regulating PCBs, a number of issues arose pertaining to the means and methods of PCB regulation. Rather than address these issues on a piecemeal basis, EPA proposed and subsequently adopted a comprehensive overhaul of its PCB regulations, commonly known as the "PCB Mega Rule." The rule became effective on August 28, 1998. See 63 Fed. Reg. 35,384 (June 29, 1998).

One of the most important changes in the Mega Rule pertains to EPA's reinterpretation of its so-called anti-dilution provision. The anti-dilution provision states that no PCB regulation specifying a concentration can be avoided through dilution. In the past, EPA applied the provision to all cases where dilution has occurred, even if the dilution was accidental. EPA now regulates whether PCBs can be disposed of according to the actual PCB concentration at the time of disposal, thereby reducing disposal costs for large volumes of soil contaminated with low concentrations of PCBs.

EPA also revised its PCB Spill Cleanup Policy, which requires the cleanup of PCBs to certain levels depending upon the spill location, the potential for exposure to residual PCBs remaining after cleanup, the concentration of PCBs initially spilled (high concentration or low), and the nature and size of the population at risk of exposure to residual PCBs. Under the Mega Rule, the EPA now addresses the problem of PCBs in the environment through a single, flexible process. PCBs released into the environment prior to April 18, 1978, will generally be considered disposed of in a manner that does not present a risk of exposure. No further disposal of non-landfilled material will be required unless EPA makes a finding that the released material presents a risk of exposure. If such a finding is made, EPA will then require remediation based on the degree of risk posed by the spill. For spills or releases occurring after April 18, 1978, the PCB Mega Rule provides different methods for remediating the PCB-contamination: (1) remediation in accordance with specific parameters identified in the PCB Mega Rule itself; (2) remediation under a work plan meeting specified performance criteria approved by EPA; and (3) remediation utilizing a risk assessment, under which EPA approves a cleanup consistent with the specific risks posed to the human health and the environment.

EPA has also revised cleanup standards and procedures for PCB bulk product waste. Such PCB waste includes nonliquid bulk wastes such as debris from the demolition of buildings and "fluff" from the shredding of automobiles and household and industrial appliances. PCB bulk product wastes must be disposed of in a ToSCA-approved incinerator or chemical waste landfill if the PCB concentration in the waste is above 50 ppm or in a municipal or industrial solid waste facility if the concentration is less than 50 ppm.

Industry hopes to save millions annually in disposal costs under the PCB Mega Rule. Is the Rule a form of deregulation for high-volume, low PCB-concentration wastes?

10. **Market access statutes and confidentiality.** Given industry's desire to protect trade secrets from competitors, and potential tort plaintiffs' eagerness for access to health and safety testing data, both FIFRA and ToSCA contain extensive provisions regarding confidentiality of information disclosed to EPA. With regard to FIFRA, see Ruckleshaus v. Monsanto, 467 U.S. 986 (1984); as to ToSCA, see McGarity & Shapiro, The Trade Secret Status of Health and Safety Testing Information: Reforming Agency Disclosure Policies, 93 Harv. L. Rev. 837 (1980), and Chevron v. Costle, 443 F. Supp. 1024 (N.D. Cal. 1978.)

11. **The future of ToSCA.** Although ToSCA is currently in eclipse, several commentators agree that it has tremendous potential for achieving environmental protection. Professor Guruswamy sees §3(5) of ToSCA, which defines the term "environment" to include "water, air, land, and the interrelationship which exists among and between water, air, and land and all living things," as the statutory lever for integrating our fragmented, media-specific pollution control statutes. Guruswamy, Integrating Thoughtways: Re-Opening of the Environmental Mind?, 1989 Wis. L. Rev. 463,

523–525. Professor Applegate envisions an amended ToSCA as the key to coordinating and enhancing federal information acquisition regarding toxic substances. In a gloomier vein, Professor Flournoy condemns the basic approaches of all agency decisionmaking with regard to environmental protection and recommends that Congress enact a more sophisticated structure. Flournoy, Legislating Inaction: Asking the Wrong Questions in Protective Environmental Decisionmaking, 15 Harv. Envtl. L. Rev. 327, 382–391 (1991).

Statutes such as ToSCA fail because there is an insufficient political consensus (1) to include provisions that are sufficiently clear and mandatory to be enforceable, and (2) if statutes are indeed clear and enforceable, to fund and enforce them once enacted. Congress is adept at enacting compromise legislation that appears to decide disputes between contending interest groups but does little to change the status quo. Agencies are adept at taking refuge in nonenforcement or "moderated" enforcement of statutes. ToSCA has failed for both reasons. Thus the real problem with ToSCA is not so much a legal one, as some commentators appear to suggest, as a political one. The dilemma that besets ToSCA has not changed since its congressional evolution during the 1970s: As a nation we have been, and still are, unwilling to institutionalize a fully preventive approach to pollution control in the face of the pervasive uncertainty that characterizes environmental decisionmaking. This dilemma recurs in discussions of recent policy shifts toward "pollution prevention." See Pollution Prevention Act of 1990, 42 U.S.C. §§13101 et seq.

12. **Market access beyond toxics: mad cows!** A single picture (of a single cow) may be worth many thousands of (previously futile) words. This is especially true when the picture is broadcast on network news December 24, 2003, and its subject is a cow in Washington (Washington State, of course, not Washington, D.C.) suffering from bovine spongiform encephalitis (BSE or "mad cow" disease). Meat from BSE animals can cause Creutzfeldt-Jacob disease in humans, an untreatable and fatal nervous system wasting disease. The U.S. Department of Agriculture (USDA) oversees many facets of the food supply marketing stream, controlling production and market access of food products to ensure public safety. Not much U.S. regulation was specifically directed at BSE prior to the 1986 BSE outbreak in England that led to destruction of herds and loss of market for English beef. In 1997, regulators sought to avoid similar problems in the U.S. livestock industry by banning animal parts from feed, thereby narrowing BSE's principal exposure pathway into the herds. Additional and more extensive measures, including a ban on meat from "downer cows" (cows unable to walk at the time of arrival at the slaughterhouse but nevertheless processed into food products) were proposed by USDA but were not implemented due to opposition by cattle industry lobbyists. In a most unusual sequence of events, as part of the 2002 Farm Bill, both houses of Congress passed a ban on downer cows, but when the legislation emerged from conference committee, without explanation the downer cow ban had been removed.[16]

---

16. Aubrey, Analysis: Ban on Downer Cows, NPR Morning Edition (Jan. 12, 2004). See Downed Animal Protection Act bills, S. 1298 and H.R. 2519, 108th Cong. (2002). See also Baur v. Veneman, 352 F.3d 625 (2d Cir. 2003) (plaintiff who petitioned USDA to pass ban on use of downed cows for food has standing to seek review of agency's refusal to do so).

Reaction to the discovery of the Washington BSE cow was swift and economically disruptive. Numerous countries, including Japan, a particularly lucrative market for U.S. cattle, placed an immediate ban on imports of beef from this country. Within days, to the applause of the American Beef Council, the USDA's Food Safety and Inspection Service, pursuant to the Federal Meat Inspection Act, 21 U.S.C. §§601 et seq., announced new emergency measures and quickly promulgated an array of new rules. 69 Fed. Reg. 1861–1874 (Jan. 12, 2004). Interestingly, however, the new market access administrative rules do not ban downer cows. Instead they require product-holding procedures (forbidding cattle products to be marketed as "inspected and passed" until after test results are received). The rules also expand a "Specified Risk Material" category for body parts in cattle more than 30 months old that are banned from entering the human food supply. The mad cow issue provides an interesting case study of how risk-regulating market access rules are shaped and implemented in the real world. If there are no more mad cow cases that prolong public attention, will the BSE regulatory issue have temporal staying power ? Will the jury of U.S. public opinion, which did not react fearfully to beef in the marketplace, nevertheless prompt Congress to enact downer cow legislation despite continuing industry opposition? What motivates the beef industry, the USDA, and the eating and voting public? Are their positions driven by objective risk management calculations?

Chapter 18

LIFE-CYCLE WASTE CONTROL STRATEGIES: RCRA'S "CRADLE-TO-GRAVE" REGULATION

A. *Tracking and Controlling the Life Cycle of Hazardous Waste Materials*
B. *The "Land Ban" and the Use of "Hammers" to Control Agency Action*
C. *RCRA Citizen Suits to Obtain Cleanup and Potential Cost Recovery*

Dangerous substances — including PCBs, mercury, arsenic, various petroleum distillates, and a host of others — play vital, even indispensable, roles in producing the material benefits of modern life. They aid in the production of paper, plastics, and other goods; the transmission of electricity; and the powering of motor vehicles. When properly confined, these materials cause little mischief. If released into the environment, however, they pose threats of serious harm to humans, as well as to plants, animals, and natural systems that make up the ecosphere.

As noted in prior chapters, a number of significant statutes play a role in regulating various aspects of the production, use, and disposal of hazardous materials. In connection with hazardous waste contamination and control, however, two federal statutes are key — the Comprehensive Environmental Response, Compensation, and Liability Act (CERCLA or Superfund), 42 U.S.C. §§9601 et seq., and the Resource Conservation and Recovery Act (RCRA), 42 U.S.C. §§6001 et seq. Although these statutes both address the handling and disposal of wastes, they represent disparate, albeit complementary, approaches. CERCLA, studied in Chapter 19, establishes the authority to remediate contamination from past waste disposal practices that now endanger, or threaten to endanger, public health or the environment. CERCLA does so primarily by imposing strict liability on those parties responsible for the release of "hazardous substances" and by creating a "Superfund" to finance actions to clean up such releases. By contrast, RCRA establishes a regulatory program designed to track and control the life cycle of "hazardous wastes" from the time of their initial generation (i.e., the "cradle") to the time of their ultimate disposal (i.e., the "grave"). Rather than focus on past disposal practices, RCRA's "cradle to grave" regulation seeks to eliminate the threats of harm from present and future waste disposal.[1] The principal goal of RCRA is to prevent future Superfund sites.

---

1. Note that the standard "cradle-to-grave" metaphor for RCRA does not mean that RCRA tracks all hazardous materials from creation to disposal. It means only that covered chemical and other waste materials are tracked from the time they become wastes. Other statutes (such as ToSCA) regulate commercial chemicals and other hazardous materials at the stages of manufacture and use (i.e., before they become waste). Still other statutes (such as the CWA, the CAA, OSHA, and EPCRA) regulate the release of hazardous and toxic pollutants from and within industrial facilities. Critics have argued that this panoply of statutory schemes suffers from a lack of focus and harmonization. See Dernbach, The Unfocused Regulation of Toxic and Hazardous Pollutants, 21 Harv. Envtl. L. Rev. 1 (1997).

Because monumental difficulties surround the cleanup of hazardous materials once those materials have already been released into the environment, the life cycle waste control strategies of RCRA — focusing on preventing or limiting the release of hazardous wastes in the first instance — deserve a very high regulatory priority. RCRA establishes a comprehensive, complex, and detailed scheme for regulating hazardous waste management activities that governs the day-to-day operations and waste handling activities of literally hundreds of thousands of corporations and individuals. By regulating all those who (1) generate, (2) transport, or (3) treat, store, or dispose of hazardous wastes, RCRA creates a three-stage regulatory approach that is pervasive and comprehensive. RCRA's broad scope, in fact, was a major factor in the growth of the environmental regulatory community beginning in the early 1980s, as the requirements of RCRA created a demand for environmental consultants, engineers, and lawyers. In its comprehensive approach, RCRA utilizes a variety of regulatory devices, reviewed in preceding chapters, to meet its specific regulatory needs. This chapter explores the substantive content of RCRA, while simultaneously reviewing a variety of statutory approaches considered earlier.

It is important to note that this perspective on RCRA inevitably deemphasizes two important matters. First, although the chapter focuses on hazardous wastes, RCRA as a statute covers much more, including regulation of solid waste generally (a category dominated by nonhazardous industrial waste and municipal waste), underground storage tanks, medical waste, and other categories. Second, although the coverage here focuses solely on the requirements set by federal law, much RCRA enforcement and regulation takes place at the state level. RCRA, like many federal environmental statutes, encourages the states to take primary authority.[2]

A. TRACKING AND CONTROLLING THE LIFE CYCLE OF HAZARDOUS WASTE MATERIALS

RCRA's Subtitle C, regulating hazardous waste, 42 U.S.C. §§6926 et seq., is organized around a pragmatic strategy that can be reduced to the simplest of terms: "If I know where hazardous waste material is, and I know the place is secure, I also know that the material is not loose in the environment causing problems."

In addition to tracking wastes, RCRA and its implementing regulations prescribe waste handling and treatment standards and practices intended to reduce the possibility of escape. This involves equipment, procedure, and design specifications for all parties that play a role in the life cycle of hazardous wastes. In this fashion, generators of waste are regulated, as are transporters and operators of treatment, storage, and disposal (TSD) facilities. RCRA even tries to assure that waste handlers are responsible people who can be trusted with a dangerous assignment, and whose long-term stability can be demonstrated. Administrative effort under RCRA, moreover, has increasingly

---

2. RCRA §3009, 42 U.S.C. §6929. The statute also directs the EPA Administrator to "give a high priority to assisting and cooperating with States in obtaining full authorization of State programs" under Subtitle C. 42 U.S.C. §6902(a)(7).

encouraged policies of "waste minimization," under the assumption that there will be fewer releases if there is less hazardous waste to control.[3]

Section 1. RCRA'S ENACTMENT AND INITIAL IMPLEMENTATION

RCRA was described by one judge called upon to interpret it as a statute of "mind-numbing" complexity.[4] Many forces contributed to its complexity, but EPA's early failure to implement RCRA is surely among the most prominent.

In the years shortly before RCRA's appearance in 1976 (in the form of amendments to the ineffectual Solid Waste Disposal Act), both the CAA and the CWA established major new programs that protected the nation's air and water by mandating the capture and removal of hazardous materials before they were released and thus allowed to pollute these two environmental media. However, the new air and water programs also served to exacerbate an already existing problem — the improper disposal of the hazardous materials extracted from industrial smokestacks and wastewater systems. The disposal and extraction of these hazardous materials was soon determined to be an increasing cause of pollution to other environmental media, in particular the soil and groundwater. Reacting to the need to protect these other environmental media, Congress passed RCRA in an effort to close the circle of environmental regulation.[5]

Although Congress instructed EPA to promulgate regulations promptly, the Carter Administration treated RCRA as a low EPA priority, channeling funds and energy into other issues. Successful citizen suits eventually forced EPA to issue regulations just as the Reagan Administration was taking office. The incoming administration, however, made the environmental area one of the prime targets of its deregulation philosophy and further delayed the promulgation of implementing regulations and the creation of an effective enforcement program. The foot-dragging of EPA in regard to RCRA, coupled with scandals regarding the administration of CERCLA, eroded congressional confidence in EPA. This led, in 1984, to a major legislative effort requiring more vigorous administration of hazardous waste law, under the Hazardous and Solid Waste Amendments of 1984 (HSWA), Pub. L. No. 98-616 (1984). HSWA represented a key turning point in the congressional relationship with EPA. Rather than relying on the EPA to set regulatory parameters and to exercise its discretion in setting and enforcing requirements, Congress became extraordinarily prescriptive and detailed in HSWA, utilizing statutory "hammers" (i.e., the land ban considered later in this chapter) to establish deadlines and limit EPA's discretion. The following article recounts the political climate that surrounded the initial implementation of RCRA.

---

3. The waste reduction strategy also seeks to limit the need for (1) long-term storage of materials for which treatment methods are not yet available, and (2) disposal of the by-products of treatment that may themselves be hazardous materials (such as ash from incineration.) See 42 U.S.C. §6902(a)(6)(b). The Pollution Prevention Act of 1990, 42 U.S.C. §§13101 et seq., confirms and generalizes the waste minimization strategy, applying it to all types of pollution. RCRA also contributes to hazardous waste minimization by making the treatment, storage and disposal of such wastes far more costly, creating a market incentive to waste reduction.

4. American Mining Congress v. EPA, 824 F.2d 1177, 1189 (D.C. Cir. 1987) (Starr, J., writing for the majority).

5. The environmentalist Barry Commoner has admonished that "Everything goes somewhere" in recognition of the fact that every waste treatment process creates a residual that, because it is more concentrated, may be more toxic than the corresponding waste inputs. In passing RCRA, Congress was concerned with the residual hazardous wastes left over from waste treatment under the CAA and the CWA.

James Florio, Congress as Reluctant Regulator:
Hazardous Waste Policy in the 1980s
3 Yale Journal on Regulation 351, 353–376 (1986)[6]

Congress passed the Resource Conservation and Recovery Act, the first federal effort to control the disposal of hazardous waste, in 1976, before the extent and danger of hazardous waste disposal problems became widely known. RCRA created a "cradle to grave" regulatory system for hazardous waste, requiring generators, transporters, and disposers to maintain written records of waste transfers, and establishing standards, procedures, and permit requirements for disposal.

As in most other federal regulatory statutes, including other environmental laws, Congress (in 1976) prescribed goals in broad terms only: what was to be achieved by EPA and when. For example, EPA was directed to develop standards within eighteen months for facilities disposing of hazardous waste and to include provisions for record-keeping; treatment, storage, and disposal methods; requirements for location, design, and construction; contingency plans for accidents; and financial responsibility requirements. The only substantive direction was a requirement that the EPA regulations protect "health and the environment."

Although the task given to EPA was enormously complex — perhaps more complex than anyone, including Congress, understood at the time — the delegation of enormous discretion to EPA was sensible. Prescribing standards for hazardous waste disposal required careful analysis of scientific and economic data and a thorough understanding of the commercial system for hazardous waste disposal. In 1976, the information and analysis necessary for sound formulation of the regulatory details were simply not available to Congress, although enough was known to indicate that considerable hazards did exist.

In our scheme of government, the role of an environmental regulatory agency is to act as the scientific and technical expert in filling in the details of the environmental protection policy enunciated by Congress. Only an executive branch agency possessing sufficient technical expertise, administrative skills, and bureaucratic resources can administer a nationwide regimen for controlling the disposal of hazardous waste. Soon after the enactment of RCRA, EPA learned that the development of hazardous waste regulations would be an enormously difficult task. The complexity of the technical issues involved in determining disposal methods appropriate to the thousands of different chemicals and other wastes, each presenting different dangers, was compounded by the enormous economic impact of controlling the high volume of hazardous waste produced in this country. In the developmental stage of this regulatory system, EPA, like any bureaucracy in a similar situation, moved slowly....

Implementation of the RCRA program began during the Carter Administration. The delays and false starts inherent in the initial implementation of most regulatory efforts were commonplace: EPA quickly fell behind schedule in efforts to issue regulations for permits and standards by the statutory deadlines as it discovered the complexity of the problem and the decisions it faced. EPA's pace under Carter prompted criticism, but its underlying commitment to implementing the statute was not challenged.

In 1981, the situation changed. EPA's nominal efforts to implement the protective provisions of RCRA clearly reflected the Reagan Administration's antipathy for regulation by the federal government and its concern for selection of the least expensive means to dispose of hazardous waste. Indeed, the test at EPA was not whether a regulatory system met the statutory

---

6. In 1986, when Mr. Florio authored this article, he was a member of the House of Representatives from New Jersey and Chairman of the House Subcommittee on Commerce, Transportation, and Tourism, which had jurisdiction over hazardous waste issues.

prescription to protect the environment, but rather whether it met the Administration's ideological regulatory standard. Congress fully expects agencies to exercise delegated discretion in a manner consistent with the Executive's political ideology. Tension between legislative intent and regulatory implementation is inevitable and expected. This tension is usually resolved through a series of small compromises and skirmishes between the legislative and executive branches, often effectuated through Congressional oversight. In the case of EPA and RCRA, however, the Administration's philosophy was more fundamentally at odds with the statute. EPA's implementation of the Administration's philosophy actually subverted the statutory goals by delaying statutorily required action and ignoring technical and scientific information that indicated a need for additional requirements.

In the early 1980's, evidence of the seriousness and scope of the hazardous waste problem mounted while EPA stalled. Congress grew increasingly frustrated with the obvious manipulation practiced by the political appointees at the Agency, as well as with the substantive environmental policy the Agency pursued.

In 1983, five and one-half years after the mandatory deadline for promulgation of RCRA standards and permits, the 98th Congress began a reauthorization process for RCRA. There was still no enforceable system for regulating the disposal of hazardous waste and little prospect for one soon. The problems recognized in 1976 had become common knowledge and, by 1983, evidence of the dangers was even more compelling. Not surprisingly, Congress made clear that it would not allow the delays to continue. Any confidence that EPA could be trusted to act expeditiously had long since evaporated. Witnesses at Congressional hearings urged a legislative solution requiring that disposal firms obtain a permit and meet the federal operating standards.

Congress responded by reauthorizing RCRA with a maze of new deadlines and statutory requirements.... Congressional reluctance to rely on EPA judgments was not limited to technological standards, but extended into all areas of the RCRA program....

In the area of hazardous waste regulation during the 1980's,...the traditional reliance on delegated responsibility...collapsed, with profound implications for the overall regulatory structure. The wide discrepancy between the public's desire for vigorous environmental protection and the Reagan Administration's ideological preference for regulatory relief...forced Congress to produce a new regulatory system that significantly reduces agency discretion.

COMMENTARY & QUESTIONS

The tension between Congress and the executive branch. One axiom of regulatory design is that the implementing agency should not distort or disrupt the policy established by Congress in its enabling legislation. This axiom was apparently violated by EPA in its early approach toward implementing RCRA. Congress's response was to attempt to micromanage RCRA implementation. The advantages and disadvantages of legislative micromanagement are discussed below.

Section 2. RCRA'S ADMINISTRATIVE THICKET: DEFINING HAZARDOUS WASTES

A significant threshold issue under RCRA is defining what materials are to be statutorily regulated as "solid waste" and, further, what solid waste is to be considered "hazardous waste." Congress defined "solid waste" as

> any garbage, refuse, sludge from a waste treatment plant, water supply treatment plant, or air pollution control facility and other discarded material, including

solid, liquid, semisolid, or contained gaseous material resulting from industrial, commercial, mining, and agricultural operations, and from community activities, but does not include solid or dissolved material in domestic sewage, or solid or dissolved materials in irrigation return flows or industrial discharges which are point sources subject to permits under §402 of the Federal Water Pollution Control Act [33 U.S.C. §1342], or source, special nuclear, or byproduct material as defined by the Atomic Energy Act of 1954 [42 U.S.C. §§2011 et seq.]. 42 U.S.C. §6903(27).

Under this portion of the statute, as illustrated in Figure 18-1 below, EPA has promulgated a definition of solid waste that includes abandoned, recycled, and inherently waste-like materials. See 40 C.F.R. §261.2(a)(2). Abandoned materials are those that have been disposed of, burned, incinerated, or accumulated or stored in lieu of being disposed of, burned, or incinerated. See 40 C.F.R. §261.2(b). Recycled materials include sludges, by-products, some commercial chemicals, and scrap metals that have been recycled in various ways. See 40 C.F.R. §261(c). The "inherently waste-like" category is a catch-all that includes materials that are usually treated like waste in that they are usually disposed of, burned, or incinerated. Materials are also classified as inherently waste-like if they contain EPA-listed toxic constituents (see 40 C.F.R. §261, Appendix VIII) that are not ordinarily found in the raw materials for which the toxic-bearing materials are being used as a substitute. See 40 C.F.R. §261.2(d)(2). Further, materials such as dioxin that may pose a substantial hazard to human health and the environment when recycled are likewise defined as inherently waste-like. Id.

By their exclusion from the definition of "solid waste," certain categories of waste are exempted from RCRA by Congress or EPA. These exclusions can have significant environmental consequences because the wastes removed from the RCRA regulatory program include whole categories of hazardous materials whose disposal is largely unregulated. As Figure 18-1 shows, the most important exclusions from the solid waste definition[7] include domestic sewage — alone or in combination with other waste material — that passes through publicly owned treatment works, legal point source discharges, irrigation return flows, and material regulated by the Atomic Energy Act of 1954. In addition, EPA regulations also exempt a number of solid wastes from being considered hazardous wastes. The principal exemptions of this type are household wastes (i.e., the garbage generated at home) and fertilizer used in agricultural operations.[8]

Once material is found to be solid waste, it must further be defined as hazardous waste before the more stringent segments of RCRA Subtitle C are applicable. The statute defines "hazardous waste" as

a solid waste, or combination of solid wastes, which because of its quantity, concentration, or physical, chemical, or infectious characteristics may —

---

7. As reflected in Figure 18-1, the exclusions are listed in 40 C.F.R. §261.4(a).

8. Still further exemptions from Subtitle C were established by Congress with regard to five categories of "special wastes." In general, these wastes are high-volume, low-toxicity material, including certain mining materials that remain largely in place throughout the mining process, cement kiln dust, and certain coal and fuel combustion by-products such as fly ash. For each category of special waste, EPA is required to study the matter and determine whether the exemption from Subtitle C should be made permanent. Pending that determination, special wastes are subject to RCRA regulation on the same basis as most nonhazardous solid waste. RCRA §3001(b)(2)-(3), 42 U.S.C. §6921(b)(2)-(3).

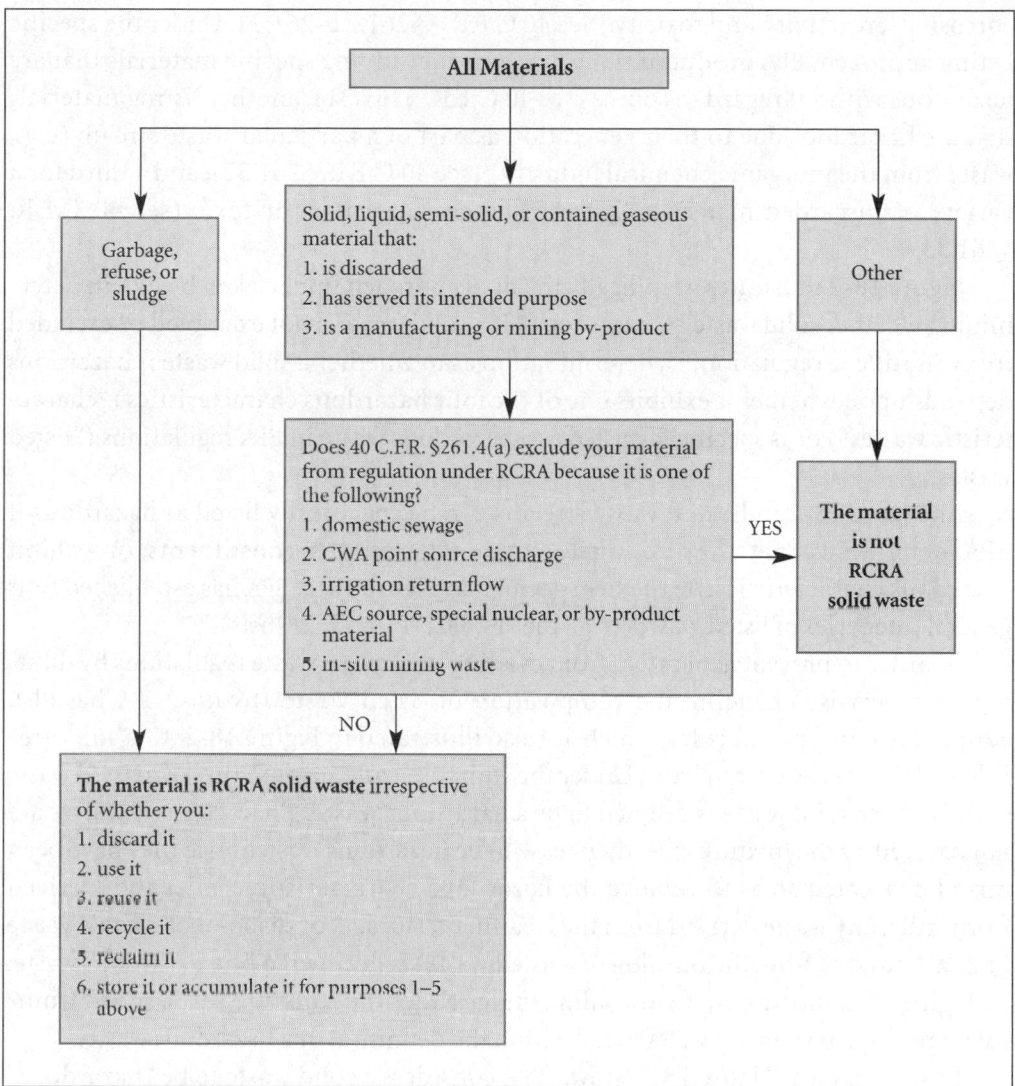

FIGURE 18-1

DEFINITION OF A SOLID WASTE

(A) cause, or significantly contribute to an increase in mortality or an increase in serious irreversible, or incapacitating reversible, illness; or

(B) pose a substantial present or potential hazard to human health or the environment when improperly treated, stored, transported, or disposed of, or otherwise managed. 42 U.S.C. §6903(5).

A separate section of RCRA, 42 U.S.C. §6921(a), directs that EPA promulgate regulations for hazardous wastes taking into account (1) toxicity, persistence, and degradability, (2) the potential of the material to bioaccumulate in plants and animals, and (3) flammability, corrosiveness, and other hazardous characteristics. EPA responded with a dual approach, one that defined material as hazardous waste due to its generic characteristics, and the other listing specifically identified materials or waste streams as hazardous. The characteristics approach relies on four criteria: ignitability, corrosivity, reactivity, and toxicity.[9] See 40 C.F.R. §§261.21–261.24. Under the specific listing approach, EPA produced three lists, one identifying specific materials that are hazardous without regard to source (see 40 C.F.R. §261.31), another listing materials that are hazardous due to their generation as part of a particular waste stream (e.g., waste from the inorganic chemical industry) (see 40 C.F.R. §261.32), and a third for a variety of discarded materials that are acutely hazardous or toxic (see 40 C.F.R. §261.33).

Figure 18-2 illustrates graphically the dual approach undertaken by EPA in determining whether solid waste is "hazardous." If a solid waste is not exempted or excluded from Subtitle C regulation,[10] a determination as to whether a solid waste is hazardous depends upon whether it exhibits one of the four hazardous characteristics ("characteristic wastes") or is specifically listed as a hazardous waste in EPA regulations ("listed wastes").

As Figure 18-2 indicates, waste streams can be specifically listed as hazardous if EPA determines that they routinely contain hazardous constituents or exhibit hazardous characteristics. As further specified in Figure 18-2, EPA has established four general categories of listed wastes (e.g., the "F", "K", "P", and "U" lists).[11]

In order to prevent generators from evading hazardous waste regulations by diluting or otherwise changing the composition of listed waste streams, EPA has also adopted two important rules, which are also illustrated in Figure 18-2: the "mixture" rule and the "derived from" rule. Under the "mixture" rule, any mixture of a listed waste with another solid waste is deemed to be a hazardous waste. Characteristic wastes are not covered by the mixture rule; they cease to be hazardous wastes once they have been mixed or treated so as to remove the hazardous characteristic. Under the "derived from" rule, any waste derived from the treatment, storage, or disposal of a listed waste (e.g., ash residue from the burning of a listed waste) is deemed to be a hazardous waste. As Figure 18-2 illustrates, wastes falling under either the "mixture" or "derived from" rules are also considered by EPA to fall within the definition of a hazardous waste.

In summary, as Figure 18-2 shows, EPA considers a solid waste to be "hazardous" when

- the waste exhibits a hazardous characteristic,
- the waste meets the description of a listed waste,
- the waste is mixed with a listed waste, or
- the waste is derived from the storage, treatment, or disposal of a hazardous waste.

---

9. To assess toxicity, EPA historically utilized a test method called the TCLP (Toxicity Characteristic Leaching Procedure). TCLP is a testing procedure that extracts the toxic constituents from a waste in a manner that EPA believed simulated the leaching action that occurs in landfills. See 40 C.F.R. §261.24, as amended, 55 Fed. Reg. 11862 (Mar. 29, 1990). However, in 1998, the D.C. Circuit held that EPA's use of the TCLP to determine compliance with its treatment standard was arbitrary and capricious because the TCLP failed accurately to predict the actual behavior of hazardous constituents in leachate, in a situation where aluminum waste was treated and disposed of in a landfill. Columbia Falls Aluminum Co. v. EPA, 139 F.3d 914 (D.C. Cir. 1998).

10. The disposal of exempted materials is subject to the much more lenient provisions of RCRA Subtitle D. 40 C.F.R. §261.4(b).

11. The key categories of "listed wastes" list wastes that are (1) hazardous from nonspecific sources (40 C.F.R. §261.31) ("F"), (2) hazardous from specific sources (40 C.F.R. §261.32) ("K"), and (3) acutely hazardous chemical products (40 C.F.R. §261.33) ("P"), or (4) nonacutely hazardous chemical products (40 C.F.R. §261.33(f)) ("U"). EPA has listed hundreds of types of wastes as hazardous by placing them in one of these four categories.

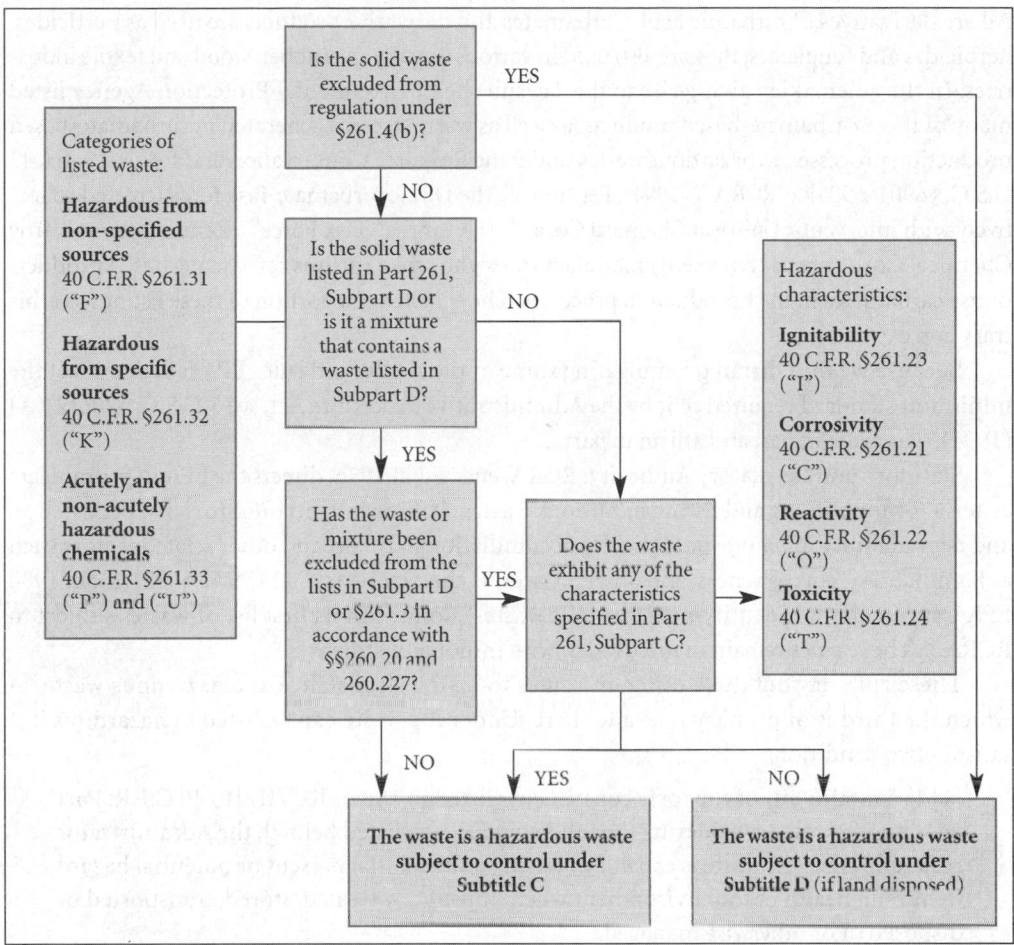

FIGURE 18-2

DEFINITION OF A HAZARDOUS WASTE

To avoid the hazardous waste regulatory system, the waste must be wholly or partially exempted or the hazardous waste status must be terminated.[12]

As the following case illustrates, a decision by EPA identifying particular solid wastes as "hazardous" has significant regulatory and business consequences, often leading to claims that EPA has acted arbitrarily and capriciously in listing compounds as "hazardous wastes."

Dithiocarbamate Task Force v. U.S. Environmental Protection Agency
United States Court of Appeals for the District of Columbia Circuit, 1996
98 F.3d 1394

WILLIAMS, C.J. This consolidated case concerns four classes of carbamate compounds — carbamates proper, carbamoyl oximes, thiocarbamates and dithiocarbamates (collectively "carbamates") — whose similar names reflect similarities in their chemical origins and structures.

---

12. Wastes that have been listed as hazardous must be managed under Subtitle C, unless EPA grants a petition to delist a waste generated at a particular site under §3001(f) of RCRA.

All are derivatives of carbamic acid. Carbamates and derivative products are used as pesticides, herbicides and fungicides; they are also used in various ways by the rubber, wood and textile industries. In the rulemaking giving rise to this lawsuit the Environmental Protection Agency listed many of these carbamate-based products, as well as waste streams generated in carbamate-based production processes, as hazardous wastes under the Resource Conservation and Recovery Act, 42 U.S.C. §6901-6992k ("RCRA") (1994). Petitioners, the Dithiocarbamate Task force (treated collectively with intervenor Uniroyal Chemical Co. as "DTF" or the "Task Force"), Zeneca Inc., and Troy Chemical Corp., are (or represent) manufacturers who make various carbamate-based products or use carbamates in their production processes. They challenge a portion of these listings as arbitrary and capricious.

Because we find that in promulgating some of the challenged rules EPA failed to meet the minimum standard required of it by the Administrative Procedure Act, see 5 U.S.C. §706(2)(A) (1994), we vacate in part and affirm in part....

Statutory and Regulatory Authority: RCRA, enacted in 1976, directs the EPA to promulgate criteria for identifying and listing hazardous wastes, "taking into account toxicity, persistence, and degradability in nature, potential for accumulation in tissue, and other related factors such as flammability, corrosiveness, and other hazardous characteristics." 42 U.S.C. §6921(a). In 1980 EPA issued rules for identifying hazardous wastes, along with its first list of wastes subject to RCRA.... Those rules remain in force today, with minor adjustments.

These rules lay out three different routes to listing a substance as a hazardous waste, of which the third is of primary relevance here. Under it a waste can be listed as hazardous if it satisfies two conditions:

[1] It contains any of the toxic constituents listed in appendix VIII [to 40 C.F.R. Part 261] and [2] after considering the following factors [listed below], the Administrator concludes that the waste is capable of posing a substantial present or potential hazard to human health or the environment when improperly treated, stored, transported or disposed of or otherwise managed....

The first step in the process, adding chemicals to appendix VIII, is to occur "only if [the chemicals] have been shown in scientific studies to have toxic, carcinogenic, mutagenic or teratogenic effects on humans or other life forms." In the second step, the Administrator is to consider the following factors:

(i) The nature of the toxicity presented by the constituent.

(ii) The concentration of the constituent in the waste.

(iii) The potential of the constituent or any toxic degradation product of the constituent to migrate from the waste into the environment under the types of improper management considered in paragraph (a)(3)(vii) of this section.

(iv) The persistence of the constituent or any toxic degradation product of the constituent.

(v) The potential for the constituent or any toxic degradation product of the constituent to degrade into non-harmful constituents and the rate of degradation.

(vi) the degree to which the constituent or any degradation product of the constituent bioaccumulates in ecosystems.

(vii) The plausible types of improper management to which the waste could be subjected.

(viii) The quantities of the waste generated at individual generation sites or on a regional or national basis.

(ix) The nature and severity of the human health and environmental damage that has occurred as a result of the improper management of wastes containing the constituent.

(x) Action taken by other governmental agencies or regulatory programs based on the health or environmental hazard posed by the waste or waste constituent.

(xi) Such other factors as may be appropriate.

Once the EPA decides to list a waste as hazardous, the substance is assigned a particular code and included in the appropriate lists in Subpart D of Part 261. Wastes generated by manufacturing processes are listed in K wastes. Chemical products or manufacturing chemical intermediates that are hazardous if they are discarded or intended to be discarded are listed as P or U wastes, the P designation being reserved for "acute hazardous wastes" of this type. (EPA made 18 P listings in this rulemaking, but none is disputed here.)[13]

Listing has significant consequences. Any hazardous waste is subject to precisely prescribed rules on disposal,...record-keeping (covering both makers and users),...and transport.... In addition, hazardous wastes listed under RCRA or exhibiting one or more of the characteristics of a listed RCRA hazardous waste are considered hazardous substances under the regulatory scheme set up by the Comprehensive Environmental Response, Compensation, and Liability Act ("CERCLA").... CERCLA requires that every release of a hazardous substance above a specified level, known as the reportable quantity ("RQ"), be reported to the National Response Center and to state and local authorities. The EPA set the RQ for all the hazardous wastes we consider here at one pound, the statutory fallback level...pending further study.

The Present Rulemaking: Invoking its authority under 40 C.F.R. §261.11(a)(3), EPA proposed to list six K wastes and 70 P and U wastes, running the gamut of the carbamate industry. In addition, the agency proposed to list four generic U wastes that would cover any substance that could be classified as one of the four kinds of carbamates. The Agency also proposed to add to Appendix VIII of Part 261 each of the chemical constituents that were the basis of the proposed listings, which in the case of the P and U listings were the products or manufacturing chemical intermediates themselves. Proposed Rule: Carbamate Production Identification and Listing of Hazardous Waste, 59 Fed. Reg. 9808 (Mar. 1, 1994).

The final rule differed from the proposal only slightly. In response to comments, the EPA said it would not list the four generic U wastes. It also decided not to make 12 of the proposed U listings because of insufficient toxicity data. Based on a re-analysis of the toxicity data it did have, EPA moved four chemicals from the P listings for acutely hazardous substances to the U listings. The K listings, aside from some tinkering with special exemptions not at issue here, remained essentially unchanged. The result was that 40 carbamate industry products received U listings, 18 received P listings and all 58 were listed on Appendix VIII. In addition, manufacturers involved in each of the four classes of carbamates had at least one production waste stream listed as a K waste. Final Rule: Carbamate Production Identification and Listing of Hazardous Waste, 60 Fed. Reg. 7824, 7825–7827 (Feb. 9, 1995)....

The U Listings: Of the 40 products listed as U wastes, DTF challenges the listing of 17 dithiocarbamates, Zeneca the listing of six of its thiocarbamate products, and Troy the listing of its product, IPBC, U375, a carbamate proper.

Petitioners' first line of attack is on the EPA's adding items to Appendix VIII and listing them pursuant to the 40 C.F.R. §261.11(a)(3), all in one rulemaking rather than two. They do not, however, point to any language in §261.11(a)(3) suggesting any requirement of sequential listing. Nor do they identify any way in which the EPA's consolidated process might jeopardize

---

13. No "F" wastes, or hazardous wastes from nonspecific sources, were involved in this case. [Eds.]

their rights or increase the risk of error. Petitioners also claim that it is unreasonable for EPA to consider aquatic toxicity data, or the harm caused to aquatic environments, in making Appendix VIII listings or the actual hazardous waste listings we consider below. But they point to nothing in the regulations or the statute that prevents EPA from considering the harm to organisms other than mammals or land-based creatures.

Second, petitioners argue that in making the determination necessary in the second step of a §261.11(a)(3) listing — determining "that the waste is capable of posing a substantial present or potential hazard to human health or the environment when improperly treated, stored, transported or disposed of or otherwise managed" — EPA did not consider all of the 11 specified factors. (There are really only ten, since the final factor is a catch-all allowing the Administrator to consider any other factor she finds relevant.) EPA argues both that §261.11(a)(3) does not require the Administrator to consider all ten factors, and that in any event she did consider them.

The theory that §261.11(a)(3) does not require consideration of the ten factors defies the language of the rule, which we have already quoted. Its structure is simple. Given an Appendix VIII listing, the Administrator is to make a determination about "hazard to human health or the environment," and is to do so "after considering" the named factors. EPA, indeed, makes no effort to parse the language to yield a different result. It cites NRDC v. EPA, 25 F.3d. 1063 (D.C. Cir. 1994), in support of its reading, but NRDC merely upheld EPA's discretion to "emphasize or de-emphasize particular factors," id. at 1071, and carefully noted that petitioners there did "not contend that the Administrator failed to consider the relevant factors...." Id.

Moreover, the structure of 40 C.F.R. §261.11(a) forbids EPA's reading. Section 261.11(a)(2), the second of three routes to listing a substance as hazardous, states specific toxicity criteria; if a substance exceeds the specified levels, it is to be listed pure and simple. If EPA were able to list substances that exhibited toxicity below the §261.11(a)(2) thresholds without examining the ten factors and making an overall assessment of the hazards posed by improper management (or doing so only as whimsy moved the agency), the brightline sense of §261.11(a)(2) would be completely undercut. In fact, this rulemaking underscores the structural point. EPA calculated the aquatic toxicity levels for most of the chemicals it listed and found those levels — which were high, but not within the criteria stated in §261.11(a)(2) — to be the most significant factor in its decision to make the listings. See 60 Fed. Reg. at 7838/1.

EPA points to prior statements that §261.11(a)(3) requires it to consider only "appropriate factors," see Identification and Listing of Hazardous Waste, 55 Fed. Reg. 18,726 (May 4, 1990) (technical amendment to 40 C.F.R. §261.11(a)(3)), or "relevant factors," see Identification and Listing of Hazardous Waste, 57 Fed. Reg. 12, 14 (Jan. 2, 1992) (final rule), arguing that these reflect a past practice that is consonant with, and vindicates, the interpretation it asserts here. But neither of these statements adopts the position we understand EPA to argue before us, namely, that it may simply disregard a factor without a word as to why it is irrelevant or unimportant.

Accordingly, despite the great deference we owe an agency in the interpretation of its own regulations,...we must apply the regulation's specific language over the agency's current interpretation. If EPA finds a factor to be irrelevant or unimportant in a particular listing, of course, that finding would be subject to very deferential review. But with no such finding, the court has no reason to suppose that the agency considered each factor, as required by its own regulation.

Almost as an afterthought, EPA argues in its brief that it did consider all the factors in §261.11(a)(3). At oral argument, counsel for EPA acknowledged that EPA did not consider each factor for each of the products listed, but at most considered them in the aggregate, for each of the four classes of chemicals. Where it is reasonable to consider the factors in relation to a class of chemicals, EPA may do so.... [T]hat means essentially that if the known similarities of members of a class are such that it is reasonable to infer the presence of a disputed characteristic throughout the class (not just among members for which it has been shown), the EPA is free to draw that inference. Thus, if the agency is considering a class Ai-n, and members Ai-iv exhibit a specific attribute, and there is reason to believe that they do so because of some trait shared by the whole class, then the agency may draw the inference that all the members of the class exhibit the attribute....

To summarize: EPA's discussion of the quantities of waste is slight and oblique, but we need not consider whether such an inadequacy would require us to vacate the rule. Where EPA falls down completely is on the interlocked topics of other regulatory controls (factor (x)) and mismanagement (factor (vii)). It is tempting to say that the toxicity of these chemicals alone marks them as hazardous, and, of course, in one of the purely colloquial senses of the word, they are. But 40 C.F.R. §261.11(a)(2) gives explicit toxicity benchmarks that are not satisfied here. That relationship underscores what would be true anyway — that a failure on the EPA's part to give serious consideration to the "softer" variables of §261.11(a)(3) tends to turn its application of that section into an exercise in totally standardless discretion. Accordingly, we vacate the challenged U listings as arbitrary and capricious....

COMMENTARY & QUESTIONS

EPA's choice of listing criteria. RCRA §3001, 42 U.S.C. §6921, requires EPA to establish criteria for identifying and listing hazardous waste "taking into account toxicity, persistence, and degradability in nature, potential for accumulation in tissue, and other related factors, such as flammability, corrosiveness, and other hazardous characteristics." The actual listing process, which formed the basis of this lawsuit, was promulgated by EPA as a regulation in 1980; 40 C.F.R. §261.11(a)(3), which EPA relied on in listing the carbamate wastes, established a complex two-step listing process by which EPA must (1) determine whether the waste contains any of the toxic constituents listed in Appendix VIII; and, if it does, (2) find "that the waste is capable of posing a substantial present or potential hazard to human health or the environment when improperly treated, stored, transported, or disposed of or otherwise managed" after consideration of the ten factors listed in 40 C.F.R. §261.11(a)(3). The court held that EPA had been arbitrary and capricious in not explicitly considering two of the ten factors. Is §261.11(a)(3) more demanding than Congress required? Is it more complex than necessary? Why, for example, should a waste not be automatically listed as hazardous if it contains one of the toxic constituents contained in Appendix VIII? Should EPA withdraw §261.11 and repropose it, including a less exacting set of listing criteria? Does it matter if §261.11 is well established (i.e., firms have conformed their business practices to its current operation), or would accounting for such actions tend to ossify environmental regulation? Plainly, if EPA enjoys the authority to promulgate the rule in the first place, EPA enjoys the same authority to alter the rule. But EPA may lack the political will to do so.

Section 3. **REGULATING PARTICIPANTS IN THE HAZARDOUS WASTE LIFE CYCLE**

As noted previously, RCRA divides the universe of persons in the hazardous waste life cycle into three categories: (1) generators of waste, (2) transporters of waste, and (3)

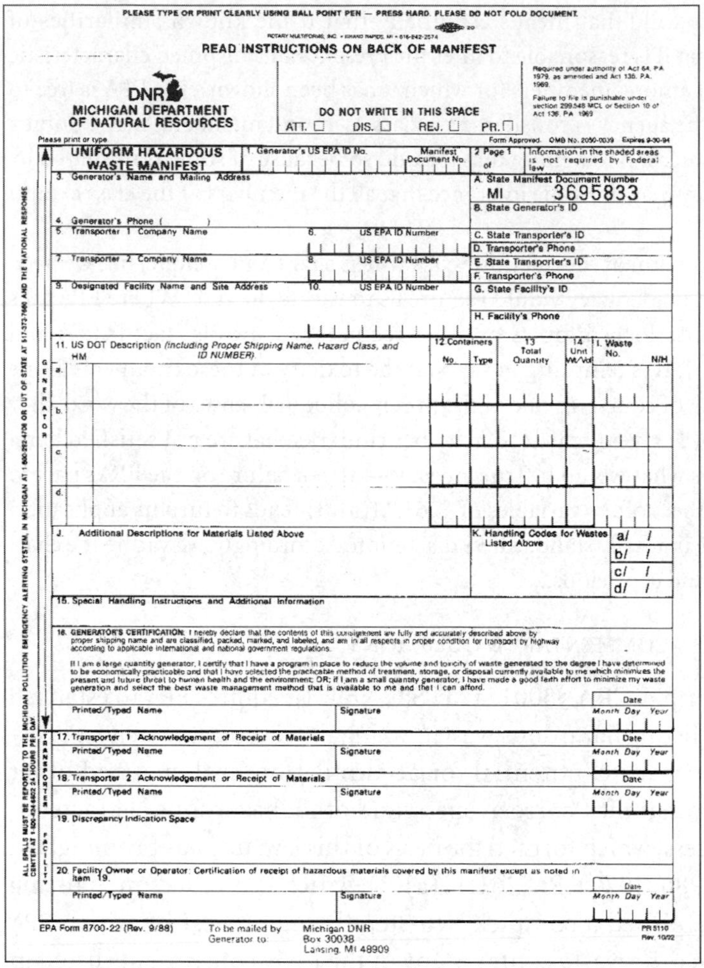

PLEASE TYPE OR PRINT CLEARLY USING BALL POINT PEN — PRESS HARD. PLEASE DO NOT FOLD DOCUMENT.

ROTARY MULTIFORMS, INC. • GRAND RAPIDS, MI • 616-842-2574

READ INSTRUCTIONS ON BACK OF MANIFEST

DNR
MICHIGAN DEPARTMENT OF NATURAL RESOURCES

DO NOT WRITE IN THIS SPACE
ATT. ☐ DIS. ☐ REJ. ☐ PR. ☐

Required under authority of Act 64, P.A. 1979, as amended and Act 136, P.A. 1969.
Failure to file is punishable under section 299.548 MCL or Section 10 of Act 136, P.A. 1969

Please print or type
Form Approved. OMB No. 2050-0039 Expires 9-30-94

UNIFORM HAZARDOUS WASTE MANIFEST
1. Generator's US EPA ID No. | Manifest Document No. | 2. Page 1 of | Information in the shaded areas is not required by Federal law
3. Generator's Name and Mailing Address
A. State Manifest Document Number MI 3695833
B. State Generator's ID
4. Generator's Phone ( )
5. Transporter 1 Company Name | 6. US EPA ID Number | C. State Transporter's ID | D. Transporter's Phone
7. Transporter 2 Company Name | 8. US EPA ID Number | E. State Transporter's ID | F. Transporter's Phone
9. Designated Facility Name and Site Address | 10. US EPA ID Number | G. State Facility's ID | H. Facility's Phone
11. US DOT Description (Including Proper Shipping Name, Hazard Class, and ID NUMBER) HM | 12. Containers No. Type | 13. Total Quantity | 14. Unit Wt/Vol | I. Waste No. N/H
a.
b.
c.
d.
J. Additional Descriptions for Materials Listed Above
K. Handling Codes for Wastes Listed Above a/ / b/ / c/ / d/ /
15. Special Handling Instructions and Additional Information
16. GENERATOR'S CERTIFICATION: I hereby declare that the contents of this consignment are fully and accurately described above by proper shipping name and are classified, packed, marked, and labeled, and are in all respects in proper condition for transport by highway according to applicable international and national government regulations.
If I am a large quantity generator, I certify that I have a program in place to reduce the volume and toxicity of waste generated to the degree I have determined to be economically practicable and that I have selected the practicable method of treatment, storage, or disposal currently available to me which minimizes the present and future threat to human health and the environment; OR, if I am a small quantity generator, I have made a good faith effort to minimize my waste generation and select the best waste management method that is available to me and that I can afford.
Printed/Typed Name | Signature | Date Month Day Year
17. Transporter 1 Acknowledgement of Receipt of Materials
Printed/Typed Name | Signature | Date Month Day Year
18. Transporter 2 Acknowledgement or Receipt of Materials
Printed/Typed Name | Signature | Date Month Day Year
19. Discrepancy Indication Space
20. Facility Owner or Operator: Certification of receipt of hazardous materials covered by this manifest except as noted in Item 19.
Printed/Typed Name | Signature | Date Month Day Year

GENERATOR / TRANSPORTER / FACILITY

ALL SPILLS MUST BE REPORTED TO THE MICHIGAN POLLUTION EMERGENCY ALERTING SYSTEM, IN MICHIGAN AT 1-800-292-4706 OR OUT OF STATE AT 517-373-7660 AND THE NATIONAL RESPONSE CENTER AT 1-800-424-8802 24 HOURS PER DAY.

EPA Form 8700-22 (Rev. 9/88) To be mailed by Generator to: Michigan DNR Box 30038 Lansing, MI 48909 PR 5110 Rev. 10/92

FIGURE 18-3
The Michigan Department of Natural Resources' Uniform Hazardous Waste Manifest

owners and operators of TSD facilities. Of the three groups, only TSD facilities require RCRA permits to operate, but for each of these groups RCRA sets statutory duties that are liberally supplemented by administrative regulation. In general, the very demanding requirements for TSD licensure have limited the number of TSD sites and greatly increased the cost of lawful disposal of hazardous waste.[14]

Although RCRA divides the universe of persons into these three categories, RCRA also links these categories together through the use of a manifest system. The Uniform Hazardous Waste Manifest (the manifest) is the paper trail linking the generator, the transporter, and the TSD for every shipment of hazardous waste from the point of its generation to the point of its ultimate treatment, storage, or disposal. Each time the waste is transferred (e.g., from one transporter to another or from a transporter to a

14. To avoid the possibility that generators will seek to avoid the cost of disposal by storing waste on-site, EPA requires that all but a small portion of a generator's hazardous waste must be consigned for delivery to a TSD facility within 90 days after the date of generation. 40 C.F.R. §262.34 (the "90-day accumulation rule"). A small number of generators have obtained on-site RCRA permits, but the burdens of RCRA regulation and economies of scale have made off-site treatment, storage, and disposal the norm. Small-quantity generators of between 100 kilograms per month and 1000 kilograms per month may store hazardous wastes on site for longer periods than prescribed in the 90-day accumulation rule but must comply with RCRA in virtually all other respects. See 40 C.F.R. §262.34(d)(i).

designated facility), the manifest must be signed to acknowledge the receipt of the waste. A copy of the manifest is retained by each link in the transportation chain and provides verification that waste was delivered where designated or, alternatively, that the waste was not delivered and its whereabouts must be determined.

A manifest form is reproduced in Figure 18-3. Both the use of the manifest and the linkage that it provides among the three discrete sets of participants in the hazardous waste life cycle are key to implementing the controlled tracking system that is at the heart of RCRA.

1. Generators. Generators of hazardous waste are subject to obligations that begin with "recordkeeping practices that accurately identify the quantities...constituents... and the disposition of such wastes." 42 U.S.C. §6922(a)(1). RCRA, and its attendant EPA regulation (40 C.F.R. §262), also require generators to use specific types of containers for hazardous wastes, to label those wastes in a particular fashion, to provide information about the wastes and their characteristics, and to employ the manifest system to track the whereabouts of material until its delivery to a permitted TSD facility. As a review of the manifest form illustrates, the information that must appear on the manifest includes just what you might expect — the name, address, telephone number, and EPA hazardous waste number of the generator, the transporter, and the TSD facility; a carefully quantified description of the materials and the number and types of containers involved; and a series of descriptive names and codes that identify the waste and its hazards in accordance with EPA regulations. The generator must also certify the accuracy of the manifest and that the material was properly prepared for shipment in addition to signing a certificate that states:

> I have a program in place to reduce the volume and toxicity of waste generated to the degree I have determined to be economically practicable and I have selected the method of treatment, storage, or disposal currently available to me which minimizes the present and future threat to human health and the environment. 40 C.F.R. §262, Appendix.

The administrative burden of the proper functioning of the manifest system is largely on the generator, who must obtain from the transporter and TSD facility endorsed copies of the manifest that document proper delivery of the material to the TSD facility within 35 days of the time that the material was consigned for delivery. If successful delivery is not documented within 45 days, the generator must file a report with EPA (or the state where the state program is authorized) advising it of that failure and detailing the generator's efforts to locate the waste. See 40 C.F.R. §262.42.

2. Transporters. Transporters are the least heavily regulated actors in the RCRA hazardous waste life cycle.[15] Their basic obligations under RCRA are to facilitate the operation of the manifest system by making sure (as far as possible) that the manifests are accurate and delivering the material in accordance with the manifests. In the event of a spill, transporters come under additional obligations to minimize the spill's effects and to notify local and federal spill response authorities. Transporters, if they mix

---

15. Transporters, however, are regulated separately by the U.S. Department of Transportation (DOT) pursuant to the Hazardous Materials Transportation Act, 49 U.S.C. §§1801–1812. DOT has promulgated extensive equipment and materials handling specifications under this statute.

dissimilar wastes for shipment in a single container or accept wastes from sources outside of the country, can become liable as generators of wastes for RCRA purposes. Likewise, transporters who store wastes beyond regulatory limits or alter the characteristics of the wastes can become subject to regulation as TSD facilities.

3. TSD facility owners or operators. TSD facilities are the most extensively regulated parties in the RCRA hazardous waste life cycle. The three components of TSD are defined broadly. Treatment includes

> any method, technique, or process, including neutralization, designed to change the physical, chemical, or biological character or composition of any hazardous waste so as to neutralize such waste, or so as to recover energy or material resources from the waste, or so as to render such waste non-hazardous, or less hazardous, safer to transport, store, or dispose of, or amenable for recovery, amenable for storage, or reduced in volume. 40 C.F.R. §260.10.

Storage includes

> the holding of hazardous waste for a temporary period, at the end of which the hazardous waste is treated, disposed of, or stored elsewhere. Id.

Disposal includes

> the discharge, deposit, injection, dumping, spilling, leaking, or placing of any solid waste or hazardous waste into or on any land or water so that such solid waste or hazardous waste or any constituent thereof may enter the environment or be emitted into the air or discharged into any waters, including ground waters. Id.

The obligations of TSD facilities are again predictable. RCRA requires that TSD facilities:

> (1) treat, store, and dispose of wastes in a manner consistent with EPA directives and standards; (2) maintain records of the wastes treated, stored, or disposed of; (3) comply with the requirements of the manifest system; (4) be built to meet certain EPA specified design and siting requirements that seek to ensure safety, such as not being located in flood plains or along earthquake faults; (5) monitor the site for releases of hazardous materials; and (6) take corrective action in the event of a release or threatened release of hazardous materials.[16]

Going further, EPA has set standards for continuity of operations, training personnel, and eventual closure of the facility.

RCRA also requires that TSD operators meet qualifications that touch on issues of financial responsibility, past record of regulatory compliance, and freedom from criminal activity. The financial responsibility standards are intended to avoid the dangers associated with "orphan" sites that have been a major problem in the past. The worry is that a presently solvent and viable TSD operation may become insolvent, leaving behind a potential toxic time bomb that becomes a burden on public resources. The good character and compliance record requirements are aimed at excluding organized crime organizations from the industry and also limiting the class of TSD operators to persons and companies having a good history of regulatory compliance.

---

16. See generally RCRA §3004, 42 U.S.C. §6924. Especially in the early years of RCRA operation, TSD licensing proceeded on a dual track that allowed facilities to obtain "interim" licenses by meeting less stringent standards and to obtain "permanent" status by meeting the full array of Subtitle C regulation. In the 1984 HSWA, Congress set firm deadlines to retire all interim status facilities, the last of which fell due in 1992.

EPA labels the phases of the TSD facility life cycle as operational, closure, and post-closure. In the operational stage, the site is able to accept wastes, for which fees are charged and from which an income stream is generated. Closure is a six-month period that begins when wastes are no longer accepted at the facility, during which time treatment and disposal operations are completed on all wastes that are not going to be relocated to other operating TSD facilities. Closure also includes dismantling and decontaminating equipment and making needed site improvements, such as applying clay capping over hazardous materials that are to be disposed of on-site. Postclosure is a 30-year period following closure during which the TSD facility operator has continuing monitoring, maintenance, and remediation responsibilities.

Both closure and postclosure costs, including costs for relocation of waste, are substantial and pose a special problem that must be addressed by the financial responsibility regulations. By definition, those costs occur at a time when no additional waste is being accepted at the site, and, hence, there is no longer a positive income stream available to meet expenses. Anticipating this situation, as part of licensure, a facility-specific closure plan is required, and its cost is estimated using a "worst case scenario." This figure is adjusted annually to reflect revisions (if any) in the plan itself, and changes in plan costs due to inflation or other factors. The law requires that the TSD operator give a financial assurance in that amount by establishing a closure trust fund during the operational life of the facility, obtaining a surety bond or irrevocable letter of credit, purchasing closure insurance, or, under certain corporate solvency conditions, giving a corporate guarantee. To alleviate problems of TSD operator insolvency that may occur before closure, a second prong of the financial responsibility regulation requires the purchase of liability insurance, or its equivalent, for both sudden and nonsudden accidental releases of hazardous materials.

COMMENTARY & QUESTIONS

1. **RCRA's regulatory scheme as a series of statutory types.** Recall the variety of statutory types studied in preceding chapters. As discussed so far, what kind of statute is RCRA? Although several facets of RCRA have been mentioned only briefly so far in this chapter, RCRA can already be seen to be a composite statute that integrates many taxonomic regulatory mechanisms into a comprehensive, although not complete, hazardous waste management system:

- The manifest system is a form of mandatory disclosure.
- The hammer clauses (i.e., the "land ban" considered later in this chapter) are a form of roadblock statute.
- The TSD licensing procedure is, in part, a form of a traditional review-and-permit statute.
- The financial responsibility requirements are a form of control of market access.
- A number of the congressionally fixed TSD facility design requirements are a form of specific, directly legislated standards.
- The limitation on land-based disposal, making necessary the development of alternative disposal methods, is a form of technology-forcing.

- The TCLP (Toxicity Characteristic Leaching Procedure) test used to define some wastes as hazardous is a form of harm-based ambient standard.

- EPA's land disposal waste treatment regulations are based, in part, on BDAT (Best Demonstrated Available Technology, considered later in this chapter), a form of technology-based regulation.

- In an indirect way, due to the high cost of dealing with hazardous solid waste under Subtitle C, RCRA rewards and encourages waste reduction, thereby serving as a market incentives statute.

- The power of EPA to order corrective action is a form of cleanup statute.

- And, finally, the siting requirements for TSD facilities are a form of land-use control.

The wonder is that this spectrum of approaches has evolved into a coherent overall program.

2. RCRA's impact. Estimates of the amount of hazardous waste generated in the United States vary considerably. According to recent EPA estimates, of the 13 billion tons of industrial, agricultural, commercial, and household wastes generated annually, approximately 279 million tons are "hazardous" as defined by RCRA regulations. EPA estimates also conclude that there has been a historical reduction in the number of facilities where hazardous waste disposal takes place. A 1982 EPA study found that there were in excess of 180,000 facilities at which hazardous waste disposal was occurring prior to RCRA's enactment.[17] By 1986, the number of sites at which legal (RCRA-permitted) disposal of hazardous waste was occurring had dropped below 2000![18] Today, even fewer sites remain problematic. EPA estimates, for example, that approximately 3700 hazardous waste management sites are now subject to RCRA corrective action. Of these, 1700 are high-priority sites targeted for immediate action.[19]

What is so impressive about the reduction in the number of facilities at which hazardous waste disposal is occurring? Recalling the "if I know where it is, I know that it's not somewhere else that's worse" aspect of the RCRA system, it should be clear that herding a substantial portion of the nation's hazardous wastes into RCRA Subtitle C facilities is a vast improvement over past practices. Traditionally, most generators either kept hazardous waste on-site in slag piles, pits, ponds, and lagoons, or shipped it away for disposal at sites that employed the same unsophisticated disposal practices.

3. The cost of RCRA disposal. How expensive has RCRA made the lawful disposal of hazardous waste? Estimates of the cost of building a RCRA-compliant hazardous waste TSD facility range in the tens of millions of dollars for a moderate- to large-sized facility. The process of obtaining a permit alone may cost in excess of $1 million.

These costs, of course, will be passed through to firms that send their wastes to TSD facilities. Nevertheless, by 1984 the total national cost for disposal of hazardous wastes

---

17. See EPA, Surface Impoundment Assessment: National Report (Dec. 29, 1982).

18. See U.S. GAO, Report to the Chairman, Subcommittee on Environment, Energy, and Natural Resources, Committee on Government Operations, House of Representatives, Hazardous Waste – The Cost and Availability of Pollution Insurance 12 (Oct. 1989).

19. See EPA, Reducing Risk from Waste (Sept. 1997).

was only $2.4 billion. When adjusted to constant dollars, this figure represented a 70% increase during the eight-year life span of RCRA. The 1984 cost of disposal represented merely 0.106% of the total value of products shipped by the generators of that waste. For chemical and primary metals, the two most affected industries, the percentages were 0.255% and 0.237%, respectively. Even the advent of land disposal restrictions (LDR) in the 1984 amendments to RCRA were predicted to no more than double the cost of hazardous waste disposal.[20]

What will be the impact of these costs on waste handling practices in the United States? Despite the seemingly small aggregate impact of hazardous waste disposal cost as a percentage of the value of products produced, there appears to be general agreement that the high cost of RCRA disposal is simultaneously an incentive both to dangerous and disruptive illegal dumping and to beneficial waste reduction efforts. Firm RCRA disposal price data is hard to obtain, but analogies can be drawn from the CERCLA cleanup context where disposal costs are quite high. An EPA report found, for example, that the cost of depositing 1 cubic yard of gasoline-contaminated soil in a hazardous waste landfill (i.e., a RCRA Subtitle C permitted facility) ranged between $100 and $200. A 1991 list of disposal costs provided to one of the authors by an industry source listed PCB-contaminated soil as the most expensive for land disposal, costing $470 per ton for disposal.

4. **TSD industry characteristics.** One of the avowed aims of RCRA was to drive undercapitalized firms from the industry, and RCRA seems to have succeeded in this area. A 1989 GAO survey of all nonfederal RCRA-permitted land disposal, land treatment, and surface impoundment facilities indicated that the industry had become the province of large firms.[21] Two-thirds of the over 1200 firms responding to the survey had sales in excess of $11 million per year, half had sales of over $50 million per year, one-third had sales of over $100 million per year, and over 20% had sales of over $500 million per year.[22]

5. **Criticizing RCRA: under-regulation.** More than half of the nation's hazardous waste is outside of the RCRA system. The most significant legal reason for this under-regulation is that Congress and EPA have excluded whole categories of waste from regulation. Why should those categories be exempt from RCRA regulation? Although cost is alleged by some to be the answer, the cost of safe (or at least far safer) disposal is not large in comparison to the value of the finished products of which the wastes are a by-product.

The largest RCRA loophole involves industrial waste[23] not legally defined as "hazardous":

---

20. See J. McCarthy & M. Reisch, Hazardous Waste Fact Book 5-19 (Congressional Research Service No. #87-56 ENR, Jan. 30, 1987).

21. U.S. GAO, Hazardous Waste: The Cost and Availability of Pollution Insurance 15 (Oct. 1989).

22. That same survey found that the purchase of pollution insurance is becoming less common and significantly more expensive for firms choosing that method of satisfying the financial responsibility requirements of RCRA. See Hazardous Waste: An Update on the Cost and Availability of Pollution Insurance (GAO/PEMD-94–161, Sept. 1994).

23. Industrial waste is not specifically defined by RCRA. The category includes more than 90% of the waste streams of factories, foundries, mills, processing plants, refineries, and slaughterhouses. It also includes sludges and other by-products of in-plant waste treatment and those generated by water pollution control facilities. Many of the compounds that are included in this waste stream have chemical constituents similar to hazardous wastes. As an example, off-specification pesticides containing multiple active ingredients fall into the industrial waste category, as does waste containing concentrations of hazardous materials that fall below the EPA thresholds for hazardousness.

There exists a widespread perception that Subtitle D, or nonhazardous waste, is mostly municipal waste. This perception is reinforced by news reports highlighting disposal capacity, ash barges, recycling, and the anticipated publication of EPA's final municipal waste regulations. However, this perception is wrong. Between hazardous waste and municipal waste is a kind of waste that is generated in vastly greater volumes than the other two combined — nonhazardous industrial waste, or simply industrial waste.

The magnitude of the industrial waste problem is overwhelming when it is stated in figures. Nationally, about 211 million tons of municipal waste and approximately 300 million tons of hazardous waste are generated annually. These numbers seem small compared with the 7,600 million tons of industrial waste that are generated and disposed of on-site annually....

Waste that does not meet the legal definition of "hazardous," however, is subject only to EPA's open dump criteria. These criteria apply to only a limited number of waste disposal problems, address many of these problems rather vaguely, and do not apply to treatment, storage, or transportation. 40 C.F.R. §257. RCRA does not expressly require that nonhazardous waste TSD facilities be permitted. Generally, Subtitle D treats all nonhazardous waste the same and only includes specific provisions for municipal waste, household hazardous waste, small-quantity generator hazardous waste, and recycled oil. Industrial waste is not given separate attention. The disparity in regulatory control between hazardous and nonhazardous waste is so great that delisting of a hazardous waste means virtual federal regulatory abandonment. Dernbach, Industrial Waste: Saving the Worst for Last?, 20 Envtl. L. Rep. 10283, 10283–10285 (1990).

Professor Dernbach explains in some detail how dangerous wastes can evade RCRA listing as hazardous and concludes that the sharp divergence in regulation is "inappropriate because of the environmental and public health risks posed by industrial waste." Id. at 10285–10286.

6. **Criticizing RCRA: over-regulation.** Without question, RCRA is a giant step forward from unregulated hazardous waste disposal practices, but RCRA inevitably over-regulates in a way that has unintended results. Dr. Robert Powitz, the Director of Environmental Health and Safety at Wayne State University, posed the following examples in a lecture to law students.

Waste acids can often be combined in a chemical reaction with waste bases to form a salt and water. If performed, this reaction would eliminate the need for transport of two hazardous substances (the acid and the base), having changed them to nonhazardous materials. To do so, however, is to perform treatment under RCRA, which requires the treater to obtain a TSD license that the University cannot afford to obtain. The University estimates that the cost of mere application for a license is in excess of $1 million. The University's annual disposal costs attributable to materials that could be treated safely on campus without major capital investments is in the $50,000 per year range. The alternative is to ship the hazardous material 80 miles through several heavily populated areas to a licensed TSD facility.

A major chemical facility in the suburbs of Detroit, Michigan, produces isocyanate (of Bhopal infamy) as a by-product of plastics production. Isocyanates react readily with water to produce nontoxic by-products. Again, however, to combine them with the water is to engage in treatment and requires a TSD license that the chemical company does not wish to obtain. (Here the hesitancy to seek licensure is less the cost than the desire to avoid being a TSD facility with all of the regulatory burdens that entails.) The lawful disposal requires shipment of isocyanate through residential areas in the vicinity of the plant and highway travel to a facility some 60 miles away.

Do the examples demonstrate that RCRA thwarts its own objectives of increased safety and waste minimization? Should EPA write a blanket exception for safety-enhancing treatment at generators' sites or promulgate certain categorical exceptions from TSD licensure requirements?

7. **Criticizing RCRA: definitional nightmares concerning "hazardous" wastes.** As the Dithiocarbamate Task Force case highlights, one of RCRA's most obvious problems lies in the complex set of definitions and rules that combine to identify what materials qualify as hazardous wastes subject to its stringent regulatory provisions. Some of the complexity is attributable to what wastes are "characteristic" or, as in dithiocarbamate, what wastes are properly "listed" by EPA. Other cases construing RCRA's definition of "hazardous waste" include American Mining Congress v. EPA, 824 F.2d 1177 (D.C. Cir. 1987) (EPA is not authorized to regulate in process recycled materials because they are not "discarded materials"); Horsehead Res. Dev. Co. v. Browner, 16 F.3d 1246 (D.C. Cir. 1994) (EPA can regulate cement kiln dust and combustion residues when they are produced by boilers and industrial furnaces that burn fuel containing hazardous waste); and NRDC v. Hazardous Waste Treatment Council, 25 F.3d 1063 (D.C. Cir. 1994) (used oil need not be listed as a hazardous waste in all circumstances).

Still greater complexity is added by the "mixture" and "derived from" rules. In 1991, a major blow to EPA's RCRA administration occurred when the D.C. Circuit vacated EPA's "mixture" and "derived-from" rules in Shell Oil Co. v. EPA, 950 F.2d 741 (D.C. Cir. 1991). The ground for vacating the rules was a failure by EPA to allow properly for notice and comment, a defect that could be overcome by repeating the process with adequate procedural steps. EPA then re-enacted the rules on an interim basis until new rules could be promulgated with full notice and comment. The interim rules were also challenged in the D.C. Circuit. In response to this challenge, Congress enacted legislation stating that the interim "mixture" and "derived-from" rules "shall not be terminated or withdrawn until revisions are promulgated and become effective." Congress also set a deadline of October 4, 1994, for promulgation of the new rules, but EPA missed the deadline. Faced with lawsuits over failing to meet the deadline, EPA signed a consent decree requiring it to propose a new Hazardous Waste Identification Rule (HWIR).

On December 21, 1995, EPA proposed a new HWIR (60 Fed. Reg. 66344) that would allow listed wastes, as well as wastes subject to the "mixture" and "derived-from" rules, to avoid Subtitle C regulation when their specified hazardous constituents fall below certain levels. EPA proposed "exit levels" for 376 chemical constituents in listed hazardous wastes. Listed hazardous wastes could be exempt from regulation if they do not contain one of the 376 contaminants above its exit level. The exit levels are based on a complex, risk-based system using "one in one million" (for cancer risks) and "no observable toxic effects" (for noncarcinogenic and ecological risks) as end points. The HWIR would be self-executing, meaning that generators could exit Subtitle C without advance approval. Does EPA's HWIR proposal signal a trend away from technology-based regulation of hazardous wastes under RCRA toward a harm-based regulatory approach? If so, will EPA's proposal cure the definitional nightmares that plague the "mixture" and "derived-from" rules? Will EPA's proposal address the under-regulation and over-regulation problems of RCRA? Will it reduce the costs of administering and complying with RCRA? EPA's 1995 proposal is analyzed in Kastner & Goldman, HWIR Could Allow Low Risk Listed Hazardous Waste to Exit RCRA Regulation, Would "Cap" Unnecessary Treatment Under Land Disposal Restrictions Program, 26 BNA Env't Rep. 1623 (1996). Work has continued by the EPA on the issues involved surrounding the issuance of a final HWIR.

8. **Criticizing RCRA: definitional nightmares concerning recycling.** Another definitional quagmire arises in the determination of how to treat recycling. Under existing statutory definitions and EPA regulations, most recycled materials are defined as solid wastes. See 40 C.F.R. §261.2(c). Does subjecting recycled material (if it meets one of the definitions of "hazardous") to rigorous regulation encourage the reuse of those materials, or does it make the use of new raw materials more attractive? To put a damper on recycling would be inconsistent with RCRA's own materials conservation goals. EPA has sought to avoid that dilemma by making its definition of recycled material a term of art that defines some and not other processes as solid waste, and, hence, subject to RCRA Subtitle C if hazardous. For example, using scrap metal as fill material or adding used oil to boiler fuel are defined as recycling, and the material is therefore solid waste. The principle that places these examples on the regulated side of the solid waste line is that they all involve processes that tend to place material into the environment without treatment. By contrast, reclaimed material intended for reuse in the original primary production process in which it was generated is not solid waste. These distinctions reduce the deterrence to recycling but do not eliminate it. Another EPA concern is that materials intended for recycling and reuse may not be used as intended. For example, what if waste oil intended to be resold as boiler fuel finds no buyers due to a dip in energy prices? If that material were not defined as solid waste, its disposal would not be regulated by RCRA. For a more thorough account of the intricacies that confound this area, see Johnson, Recyclable Materials and RCRA's Complicated, Conflicting, and Costly Definition of Solid Waste, 21 Envtl. L. Rep. 10357 (1991); Gaba, Solid Waste and Recycled Materials Under RCRA: Separating Chaff from Wheat, 16 Ecology L.Q. 623 (1989).

9. **When exempt household waste is incinerated, is its hazardous ash exempt too?** According to EPA estimates, almost 300 facilities burn almost 4 million tons of hazardous wastes in incinerators each year. In 1994, the U.S. Supreme Court resolved a split between two of the nation's circuit courts of appeal with regard to whether ash created by the incineration of municipal solid waste can be regulated as hazardous waste under RCRA Subtitle C. Items that would normally qualify as hazardous solid waste, such as discarded batteries, paint, garden care products, and many others, are mixed with other refuse in municipal garbage. Congress foresaw the burden municipalities would face if their entire waste streams had to be disposed of at Subtitle C facilities, and Congress therefore exempted municipal solid waste (MSW) from Subtitle C.

However, when burned, as is common in trash-to-energy incinerators, the ash left after the combustion of MSW would often, depending on its characteristics, be considered a hazardous waste that required RCRA Subtitle C disposal. Perhaps displaying insufficient foresight, Congress did not specify if ash from incineration of MSW is also Subtitle C exempt. The Supreme Court held that the generation of toxic ash is not included within the activities covered by the exemption and thus must be regulated under Subtitle C if the ash possesses the characteristics of hazardous waste. City of Chicago v. EDF, 511 U.S. 328 (1994). As a result, Chicago was no longer able to claim that it was entitled to a cost-saving waste stream exemption. After the Supreme Court's ruling, EPA announced new RCRA permit procedures for "facilities managing ash from waste-to-energy facilities." 59 Fed. Reg. 29372 (Feb. 3, 1995).

10. **Rethinking RCRA.** In their dialogue entitled Rethinking the Resource Conservation and Recovery Act for the 1990s, 21 Envtl. L. Rep. 10063 (1991), Marcia E. Williams and Jonathan Z. Cannon made a series of very technical but very telling criticisms of RCRA as it has developed. One of their most fundamental attacks on RCRA can be stated in simplified form — RCRA makes a great deal turn on the division of wastes into the categories of hazardous and nonhazardous, and then draws that line in a fiendishly complicated way. This leads to a multitude of untoward results. First, because the cost of disposal of hazardous waste is vastly greater than the cost of disposal of nonhazardous waste, generators have immense incentives to contest the categorization decisions. In conjunction with the byzantine definitional rules that are currently in force, a disproportionate amount of both regulatory and enforcement effort is directed to issues of coverage that result in little or no environmental benefit. A related criticism is that the definitional distinctions drawn between hazardous and nonhazardous are too often irrational if one keeps in mind RCRA's goal of reducing the release of dangerous substances. Here, the principal examples are the listing of some compounds as hazardous and the nonlisting of chemically similar compounds having much the same potential for damaging human health and the environment. Moving from the definitional into the regulatory sphere, Williams and Cannon accuse RCRA of severe under- and over-regulation. The under-regulation occurs in regard to the laxity with which nonhazardous wastes are treated. Their point is that many waste streams that are designated as nonhazardous contain substantial quantities of hazardous materials that find their way into the environment. The over-regulation occurs in practices that overestimate risks (such as assuming that all wastes will be totally mismanaged), or in the adoption of anti-dilution rules that are inflexibly applied as rigid "tracking" rules so that wastes remain legally hazardous, even after treatment that produces a by-product that is nonhazardous according to EPA standards.

A somewhat different perspective on RCRA's future focuses on the failure of Subtitle C to address the larger issues of the solid waste problem posed by the need to safely dispose of such vast quantities of material. Taken together, the severity of regulation under Subtitle C, the expense entailed by detoxification of materials under that portion of RCRA, and the laxity of regulation under Subtitle D form an unsatisfactory whole. Too little waste is required to be treated, and the waste that is treated is treated in ways that are too expensive to be used for substantial additional quantities of waste. In the end, long-term land disposal of Subtitle D solid waste imposes risks of "creating new environmental problems in the distant future when and if containment breaks down." Pedersen, The Future of Federal Solid Waste Regulation, 16 Colum. J. Envtl. L. 109, 110 (1991). Pedersen contends that "since our current approach to the solid waste problem has reached its natural limits, market-based approaches provide the best option to induce further reduction of the quantity and toxicity of wastes disposed on land." His article goes on to suggest such things as a deposit on automobiles and other large-item sources of waste (similar to deposits on beverage containers); taxes on disposal of toxic wastes that present major threats of future harm; and a waste disposal allowance system similar to the tradeable emissions credits of the 1990 CAA Amendments.

11. **Reforms to RCRA corrective action.** In light of the continuing barrage of criticism engendered by RCRA, EPA in January 2001 attempted to develop regulatory reforms governing the remediation of existing contamination at industrial facilities that transport, treat, store, and/or dispose of hazardous waste.

The EPA's proposed reforms were intended to enhance the ability to meet cleanup goals that EPA was required by Congress to establish as a means of measuring EPA's performance. To that end, in July 1999, EPA identified 1714 RCRA facilities as "Baseline Facilities" that ostensibly presented the greatest potential both for unacceptable exposure of humans to pollutants and for the uncontrolled migration of pollutants in groundwater. Specifically, the EPA committed to show that, by 2005, 95% of the facilities (1629 of the 1714) will successfully control the potential exposure routes to humans of the pollutants in the contaminated media at these facilities.

To implement these reforms, EPA Headquarters delegated to the Regions the task of formulating policies or guidances that would give substance to the reforms and facilitate the achievement of these goals. However, the initial response of the Regions was sporadic at best. Some Regions, such as Region 5, have implemented programs and policies designed to expedite RCRA cleanups. Other Regions have not publicly identified any RCRA policy or guidance reforms to facilitate RCRA cleanups.

In an effort to accelerate the pace of remediation, EPA announced in January 2001 a second set of reforms designed to facilitate cleanups. In particular, EPA identified 25 pilot projects as "showcase" projects targeted for immediate cleanup, expanded the scope of its reforms to encourage remediation efforts at RCRA facilities to be classified as "brownfields," and announced that it would intensify efforts to engage the public and local communities at corrective action sites. The jury remains out on whether EPA's proposed cleanup reforms will expedite the remediation of existing contamination at targeted industrial facilities.

12. **International shipments.** RCRA is not limited to domestic hazardous wastes. RCRA directs exporters to notify the EPA of the nature of international shipments (e.g., dates, quantity, and description of wastes) at least four weeks prior to shipment. Within 30 days of the receipt of the notification, the State Department, on behalf of the EPA Administrator, must inform the receiving country about the export. The importing country, in turn, must consent (in writing) to accept the waste unless an existing international agreement provides otherwise.

The Clinton Administration recommended a ban on exports of hazardous waste to nations other than Canada and Mexico. The three North American countries routinely ship waste across borders for cheaper and more convenient disposal. The United States ratified the Basel Convention, which sharply limits international shipments of hazardous waste. All told, the United States exports less than 1% of its hazardous wastes (approximately 145,000 tons per year).

13. **Underground storage tank regulation.** Subtitle I of RCRA, 42 U.S.C. §§6991 et seq., establishes a comprehensive regulatory program for Underground Storage Tanks (USTs).[24] RCRA defines a UST as:

Any one or combination of tanks (including underground pipes connected thereto) which is used to contain an accumulation of regulated substances [hazardous substances and petroleum, except for RCRA Subtitle C hazardous wastes], and the volume of which (including the volume of underground pipes connected thereto) is 10 percent or more beneath the surface of the ground. 42 U.S.C. §6991(1).

The UST Program contains the following elements:

- Standards for design, construction, and installation of new tanks
- Requirements for retrofitting existing tanks with anti-corrosion, overfill prevention, and release detection systems
- Operation, maintenance, and inspection requirements
- Release detection, investigation, and reporting requirements
- Corrective action obligations
- Tank closure procedures
- Financial responsibility requirements

A miniature Superfund (the Leaking Underground Storage Tank Trust Fund, financed by a tax on motor fuels) has been created to fund EPA or state cleanups of UST releases. An overview of the federal UST program is provided in Nagle, RCRA Subtitle I: The Federal Underground Storage Tank Program, 24 Envtl. L. Rep. 10057 (1994).

14. **Life cycle assessment in the private sector.** As the following excerpt indicates, life cycle assessment, which underlies RCRA's regulatory strategy, is becoming popular in the private sector:

Life cycle assessment ("LCA") is intended to evaluate as comprehensively as possible "cradle-to-grave" environmental consequences of a product, package, process, or practice. It is supposed to account for energy and material inputs and outputs associated with making, using, and retiring a product, including the environmental risk associated with the life cycle of the product. It could similarly be applied to evaluate processes and practices in manufacturing to account for every resource

---

24. Now called the UST Program. It was originally referred to as the LUST (Leaking Underground Storage Tank) Program. The principal focus of the UST program is the roughly 800,000 petroleum tanks at gasoline stations and other fuel and automotive distribution centers around the country. Designed to protect groundwater from contamination, EPA's regulations govern construction, operation, and closure of tanks to minimize the cause of leaks. The cost of cleaning up current and future tanks has been put at over $35 billion, with an estimated average cost of cleanup put at $100,000 per site. See 25 Envtl. L. Rep. 2290 (1995). Problem tanks typically are those leaking above groundwater supplies or those containing gasoline with MTBE, a toxic additive that travels exceedingly fast through groundwater.

and environmental risk encountered in making, using, and disposing of a product. LCA is thus a tool for identifying material and energy use and the waste released during production, formulation, distribution, consumer use, recycling, and disposal....

[The current technical framework for LCA consists of three distinct but interrelated components:]

- *Life cycle inventory:* An objective, data-based process of quantifying energy and raw material requirements, air emissions, waterborne effluents, solid waste, and other environmental releases incurred throughout the life cycle of a product, process, or activity.
- *Life cycle impact analysis:* A technical, quantitative, or qualitative process to characterize and assess the effects of the environmental loadings identified in the inventory component. The assessment should address both ecological and human health considerations as well as other effects such as habitat modification and noise pollution.
- *Life cycle improvement analysis:* A systematic evaluation of the needs and opportunities to reduce the environmental burden associated with energy and raw materials use and waste emissions throughout the life cycle of a product, process, or activity. This analysis may include both quantitative and qualitative measures of improvements, such as changes in product design, raw materials use, industrial processing, consumer use, and waste management.

Environmental benefits can be realized at each step in the LCA process. For example, the inventory alone may be used to identify opportunities for reducing emissions or the use of energy and materials. The impact analysis and improvement analysis tools, meanwhile, can help ensure optimization of potential reduction strategies and avoidance of unanticipated impacts in improvement programs. Denison, Evaluating Environmental Impacts, in National Academy of Engineering, Industrial Ecology: U.S.-Japan Perspectives 29–30 (1993).

In the light of subsequent paradigm shifts in private-sector thinking, such as LCA, RCRA's life cycle approach was far ahead of its time. RCRA's conceptual framework may ultimately prove as important as its regulatory provisions in stimulating pollution prevention.

B. THE "LAND BAN" AND THE USE OF "HAMMERS" TO CONTROL AGENCY ACTION

The HSWA of 1984[25] made important changes that greatly expanded the reach of federal hazardous waste law. In what may be its most significant feature, the HSWA added stringent regulation of land disposal of hazardous wastes,[26] often referred to as the land ban. In Congress's own words:

---

25. Pub. L. No. 98-616 (1984). For a discussion of the amendments, see Rosbe & Gulley, The Hazardous and Solid Waste Amendments of 1984: A Dramatic Overhaul of the Way America Manages Its Hazardous Wastes, 14 Envtl. L. Rep. 10458, 10459 (1984) (hereinafter cited as Rosbe & Gulley).

26. The term *land disposal* as defined by RCRA includes, but is not limited to, "Any placement of...hazardous waste in a landfill, surface impoundment, waste pile, injection well, land treatment facility, salt dome formation, salt bed formation, or underground mine or cave." RCRA §3004(k), 42 U.S.C. §6924(k).

reliance on land disposal should be minimized or eliminated and land disposal, particularly landfill and surface impoundment, should be the least favored method for managing hazardous wastes.... 42 U.S.C. §6901(b)(7).

As the Florio article above points out in reviewing RCRA's history, Congress feared undue delay if the implementation of its objectives were left to EPA's discretion. Thus Congress placed stringent time deadlines on EPA for the issuance of regulations. To make sure EPA acted promptly, Congress included "hammer clauses" that amounted to direct congressional regulation if EPA failed to act in a timely fashion. Congress took a three-pronged approach to land disposal: (1) it made liquids a particular focus of regulation because of their role in facilitating the migration of hazardous wastes away from disposal sites,[27] (2) it overhauled the means by which solid wastes could be defined as hazardous for purposes of land disposal, and (3) it set specific standards for landfills and surface impoundments that stressed multiple leachate control mechanisms.[28]

To ensure that EPA did not dally in its assigned regulatory tasks, Congress used the threat of a total nationwide ban on land disposal of hazardous waste as a hammer — EPA could avoid the land ban only by promulgating rigorous disposal standards within the allotted time periods. The lists of hazardous wastes were developed in part by Congress and in part by EPA.[29] Before authorizing the land disposal of any listed waste, EPA had to first conclude that a ban on the land disposal of that particular hazardous waste was "not required...to protect human health and the environment for as long as the waste remains hazardous." In making that determination, EPA had to consider "(A) the long-term uncertainties associated with land disposal, (B) the goal of managing hazardous waste in an appropriate manner in the first instance, and (C) the persistence, toxicity, mobility, and propensity to bioaccumulate of such hazardous wastes and their hazardous constituents." 42 U.S.C. §6924(d). Congress also circumscribed EPA's discretion by stating that land disposal could not be allowed unless EPA found that wastes had been treated to levels that "substantially diminish the toxicity of the waste or substantially reduce the likelihood of migration of hazardous constituents from the waste so that short-term and long-term threats to human health and the environment are minimized." 42 U.S.C. §6924(m).

The land ban portended far-reaching changes. As one commentary indicated:

> By these Amendments, Congress effectively has required EPA to phase out most, if not all, methods of land disposal of hazardous wastes. To the extent that any method of land disposal might still be allowed, Congress has shifted the burden to

27. RCRA §3004(c), 42 U.S.C. §6924(c). Uncontainerized liquid hazardous waste was banned from landfills as of May 1985; the placement of nonhazardous liquids in landfills containing hazardous waste was banned as of November 1985; and containerized liquid hazardous waste and free liquid in containers containing other hazardous wastes were minimized as of February 1986.

28. Congress required all systems to have at least two liners, a leachate collection system above and between liners in landfills, and groundwater monitoring. RCRA §3004(o)(1), 42 U.S.C. §6421(o)(1). EPA was also required to promulgate additional design standards that would require leak detection systems to be present in all types of new facilities.

29. Congress adopted the so-called "California list" that identified a number of specific materials at varying concentrations as hazardous. See RCRA §3004(d)(2), 42 U.S.C. §6924(d)(2). In addition, Congress required regulation of certain solvents and dioxins. See RCRA §3004(e), 42 U.S.C. §6924(e). Finally, EPA was to develop a schedule for reviewing all other hazardous wastes. See RCRA §3001, 42 U.S.C. §6921. EPA was given a triparte deadline for completing this process, which led to the description of the EPA regulations as being first third, second third, and third third. See RCRA §3004(g), 42 U.S.C. §6924(g).

EPA to take action before the statutory prohibitions take effect and to industry to urge that EPA act in time. It is doubtful that EPA is capable of meeting the statutory deadlines, even with prodding from industry, unless it can develop simple new procedures for evaluating land disposal methods' protection of health and the environment. Even if EPA develops such procedures, the burden placed on a company to demonstrate "to a reasonable degree of certainty" that there will be "no migration of hazardous constituents" from the unit "for as long as the waste remains hazardous" may be virtually insurmountable. Thus, industry may, instead, elect to invest in incineration and physical-chemical treatment as methods of managing the California list wastes, dioxin-containing wastes, and listed spent solvents rather than attempt to obtain an exception for a method of land disposal for these wastes. With regard to the other listed wastes, industry may decide to focus its efforts on urging EPA to promulgate reasonable treatment standards that would avoid the regulatory prohibitions rather than trying to overcome the burden necessary to obtain an exception. If this happens, Congress will have effectively achieved its goal of forcing the increased use of non-land disposal hazardous waste management methods and the development of new hazardous waste management technology. Whether the waste disposal industry can respond, within the time allowed, to this new technology-forcing imperative with enough effective treatment and incineration capacity to handle the growing hazardous waste load remains to be seen. Rosbe & Gulley at 10463.

To the surprise of many, EPA met many of the HSWA land ban deadlines.[30] What emerged, though, was not a set of substance-specific treatment standards. Instead, EPA relied on a general treatment standard for hazardous waste that requires treatment using BDAT prior to landfilling of the waste.[31]

The BDAT approach creates a problem of inadequate treatment capacity. Especially in the shorter term, there is insufficient capacity nationwide to treat all of the waste that is in need of land-based disposal. As a result, EPA has been forced to issue variances because disposal of untreated hazardous wastes in permitted Subtitle C facilities is preferable to storing the materials in other locations until treatment capacity is increased. Over time the supply of BDAT treatment capacity will grow, although that growth has been severely inhibited by the NIMBY phenomenon and the obstacles it presents to siting hazardous waste treatment facilities.

EPA's move to select BDAT treatment as a precondition for land disposal provoked a legal challenge. Generators feared that they would now be faced with the costly prospect of incineration, even in circumstances where putting untreated waste in landfills would arguably provide adequate protection of human health and the environment.

---

30. See generally Note, An Analysis of the Land Disposal Ban in the 1984 Amendments to the Resource Conservation and Recovery Act, 76 Geo. L.J. 1563 (1988); Williams & Cannon, Rethinking the Resource Recovery and Conservation Act for the 1990s, 21 Envtl. L. Rep. 10063 (1991).

31. EPA had initially proposed to set harm-based treatment standards with reference to limiting health effects to what EPA deemed acceptable levels. See Hazardous Waste Management System: Land Disposal Restriction, 51 Fed. Reg. 1602 (Jan. 14, 1986). Under the proposed methodology, EPA would make a comparative risk assessment that compared the risks of commercially available treatment technologies to the risks of land disposal. Only treatments that resulted in lower risk levels could be selected as treatment standards. This proposal generated substantial adverse comment. Ultimately, EPA adopted the far less problematic strategy for defining treatment standards by reference to BDAT.

Hazardous Waste Treatment Council v. U.S. Environmental Protection Agency
United States Court of Appeals for the District of Columbia Circuit, 1989
886 F.2d 355

Before WALD, C.J., SILBERMAN and D. H. GINSBURG, JJ.

PER CURIAM: RCRA requires EPA to implement the land disposal prohibition in three phases, addressing the most hazardous "listed" wastes first. In accordance with strict statutory deadlines, the Administrator is obligated to specify those methods of land disposal of each listed hazardous waste which "will be protective of human health and the environment." In addition, "[s]imultaneously with the promulgation of regulations...prohibiting...land disposal of a particular hazardous waste, the Administrator" is required to promulgate regulations specifying those levels or methods of treatment, if any, which substantially diminish the toxicity of the waste or substantially reduce the likelihood of migration of hazardous constituents from the waste so that short-term and long-term threats to human health and the environment are minimized. §6924(m).

Section 3004(m) Treatment Standards... In the Proposed Rule, EPA announced its tentative support for a treatment regime embodying both risk-based and technology-based standards. The technology-based standards would be founded upon what EPA determined to be the Best Demonstrated Available Technology ("BDAT"); parallel risk-based or "screening" levels were to reflect "the maximum concentration [of a hazardous constituent] below which the Agency believes there is no regulatory concern for the land disposal program and which is protective of human health and the environment." The Proposed Rule provided that these two sets of standards would be melded in the following manner:

> First, if BDAT standards were more rigorous than the relevant health-screening levels, the latter would be used to "cap the reductions in toxicity and/or mobility that otherwise would result from the application of BDAT treatment[.]" Thus, "treatment for treatment's sake" would be avoided. Second, if BDAT standards were less rigorous than health-screening levels, BDAT standards would govern and the screening level would be used as "a goal for future changes to the treatment standards as new and more efficient treatment technologies become available." Finally, when EPA determined that the use of BDAT would pose a greater risk to human health and the environment than land disposal, or would provide insufficient safeguards against the threats produced by land disposal, the screening level would actually become the 3004(m) treatment standard.

EPA invited public comment on alternative approaches as well. The first alternative identified in the Proposed Rule (and the one ultimately selected by EPA) was based purely on the capabilities of the "best demonstrated available technology."

The Agency received comments supporting both approaches, but ultimately settled on the pure-technology alternative. Of particular importance to EPA's decision were the comments filed by eleven members of Congress, all of whom served as conferees on the 1984 RCRA amendments. As EPA recorded in the preamble to the Final Rule:

> [these] members of Congress argue strongly that [the health screening] approach did not fulfill the intent of the law. They asserted that because of the scientific uncertainty inherent in risk-based decisions, Congress expressly directed the Agency to set treatment standards based on the capabilities of existing technology.

The Agency believes that the technology-based approach adopted in [the] final rule, although not the only approach allowable under the law, best responds to the above stated comments.

874 Chapter 18 ◆ RCRA'S LIFE-CYCLE HAZARDOUS WASTE CONTROLS

EPA also relied on passages in the legislative history supporting an approach under which owners and operators of hazardous waste facilities would be required to use "the best [technology] that has been demonstrated to be achievable." And the agency reiterated that the chief advantage offered by the health-screening approach — avoiding "treatment for treatment's sake" — could "be better addressed through changes in other aspects of its regulatory program." As an example of what parts of the program might be altered, EPA announced that it was "considering the use of its risk-based methodologies to characterize wastes as hazardous pursuant to section 3001 [of RCRA]...."[32]

CMA challenges EPA's adoption of BDAT treatment standards in preference to the approach it proposed initially primarily on the ground that the regulation is not a reasonable interpretation of the statute. CMA obliquely, and Intervenors Edison Electric and the American Petroleum Institute explicitly, argues in the alternative that the agency did not adequately explain its decision to take the course that it did. We conclude, as to CMA's primary challenge, that EPA's decision to reject the use of screening levels is a reasonable interpretation of the statute. We also find, however, that EPA's justification of its choice is so fatally flawed that we cannot, in conscience, affirm it. We therefore grant the petitions for review to the extent of remanding this issue to the agency for a fuller explanation.

Consistency of EPA's Interpretation with RCRA... Our role in evaluating an agency's interpretation of its enabling statute is as strictly circumscribed as it is simply stated: We first examine the statute to ascertain whether it clearly forecloses the course that the agency has taken; if it is ambiguous with respect to that question, we go on to determine whether the agency's interpretation is a reasonable resolution of the ambiguity.

***Chevron* Step 1: Is the Statute Clear?...** CMA reads the statute as requiring EPA to determine the levels of concentration in waste at which the various solvents here at issue are "safe" and to use those "screening levels" as floors below which treatment would not be required. CMA supports its interpretation with the observation that the statute directs EPA to set standards only to the extent that "threats to human health and the environment are minimized." We are unpersuaded, however, that Congress intended to compel EPA to rely upon screening levels in preference to the levels achievable by BDAT.

The statute directs EPA to set treatment standards based upon either "levels or methods" of treatment. Such a mandate makes clear that the choice whether to use "levels" (screening levels) or "methods" (BDAT) lies within the informed discretion of the agency, as long as the result is "that short-term and long-term threats to human health and the environment are minimized." To "minimize" something is, to quote the *Oxford English Dictionary*, to "reduce [it] to the smallest possible amount, extent, or degree." But Congress recognized, in the very amendments here at issue, that there are "long-term uncertainties associated with land disposal," 42 U.S.C. §6924(d)(1)(A). In the face of such uncertainties, it cannot be said that a statute that requires that threats be minimized unambiguously requires EPA to set levels at which it is conclusively presumed that no threat to health or the environment exists.

This is not to say that EPA is free, under §3004(m), to require generators to treat their waste beyond the point at which there is no "threat" to human health or to the environment. That Congress's concern in adopting §3004(m) was with health and the environment would necessarily make it unreasonable for EPA to promulgate treatment standards wholly without regard

---

32. EPA's announcement foreshadowed its subsequent proposed Hazardous Waste Identification Rule, discussed above. [Eds.]

to whether there might be a threat to man or nature. That concern is better dealt with, however, at *Chevron*'s second step; for, having concluded that the statute does not unambiguously and in all circumstances foreclose EPA from adopting treatment levels based upon the levels achievable by BDAT, we must now explore whether the particular levels established by the regulations supply a reasonable resolution of the statutory ambiguity.

***Chevron* Step II: Is EPA's Interpretation Reasonable?...** The screening levels that EPA initially proposed were not those at which the wastes were thought to be entirely safe. Rather, EPA set the levels to reduce risks from the solvents to an "acceptable" level, and it explored, at great length, the manifest (and manifold) uncertainties inherent in any attempt to specify "safe" concentration levels. The agency discussed, for example, the lack of any safe level of exposure to carcinogenic solvents, the extent to which reference dose levels (from which it derived its screening levels) understate the dangers that hazardous solvents pose to particularly sensitive members of the population, the necessarily artificial assumptions that accompany any attempt to model the migration of hazardous wastes from a disposal site, and the lack of dependable data on the effects that solvents have on the liners that bound disposal facilities for the purpose of ensuring that the wastes disposed in a facility stay there. Indeed, several parties made voluminous comments on the Proposed Rule to the effect that EPA's estimates of the various probabilities were far more problematic than even EPA recognized.

CMA suggests, despite these uncertainties, that the adoption of a BDAT treatment regime would result in treatment to "below established levels of hazard." It relies for this proposition almost entirely upon a chart in which it contrasts the BDAT levels with (1) levels EPA has defined as "Maximum Contaminant Levels" (MCLs) under the Safe Drinking Water Act; (2) EPA's proposed "Organic Toxicity Characteristics," threshold levels below which EPA will not list a waste as hazardous by reason of its having in it a particular toxin; and (3) levels at which EPA has recently granted petitions by waste generators to "delist" a particular waste, that is, to remove it from the list of wastes that are deemed hazardous. CMA points out that the BDAT standards would require treatment to levels that are, in many cases, significantly below these "established levels of hazard."

If indeed EPA had determined that wastes at any of the three levels pointed to by CMA posed no threat to human health or the environment, we would have little hesitation in concluding that it was unreasonable for EPA to mandate treatment to substantially lower levels. In fact, however, none of the levels to which CMA compares the BDAT standards purports to establish a level at which safety is assured or "threats to human health and the environment are minimized." Each is a level established for a different purpose and under a different set of statutory criteria than concern us here; each is therefore irrelevant to the inquiry we undertake today....

In sum, EPA's catalog of the uncertainties inherent in the alternative approach using screening levels supports the reasonableness of its reliance upon BDAT instead. Accordingly, finding no merit in CMA's contention that EPA has required treatment to "below established levels of hazard," we find that EPA's interpretation of §3004(m) is reasonable.

To summarize [EPA's explanation for abandoning the combination of using BDAT and screening levels in favor of BDAT alone]: after EPA issued the Proposed Rule, some commenters, including eleven members of Congress, chastised the agency on the ground that the use of screening levels was inconsistent with the intent of the statute. They stated that because of the uncertainties involved, Congress had mandated that BDAT alone be used to set treatment standards. EPA determined that the "best respon[se]" to those comments was to adopt a BDAT standard. It emphasized, however, that either course was consistent with the statute (and that it was therefore not required to use BDAT alone). Finally, it asserted, without explanation, that its major purpose in initially proposing screening levels "may be better addressed through changes in other aspects of its regulatory program," and gave an example of one such aspect that might be changed.

This explanation is inadequate. It should go without saying that members of Congress have no power, once a statute has been passed, to alter its interpretation by post-hoc "explanations" of what it means; there may be societies where "history" belongs to those in power, but ours is not among them. In our scheme of things, we consider legislative history because it is just that: history. It forms the background against which Congress adopted the relevant statute. Post-enactment statements are a different matter, and they are not to be considered by an agency or by a court as legislative history. An agency has an obligation to consider the comments of legislators, of course, but on the same footing as it would those of other commenters; such comments may have, as Justice Frankfurter said in a different context, "power to persuade, if lacking power to control."

It is unclear whether EPA recognized this fundamental point. On the one hand, it suggested that the adoption of a BDAT-only regime "best-respond[ed]" to the comments suggesting that the statute required such a rule. On the other hand, EPA went on at some length to establish that the comments were in error, in that screening levels are permissible under the statute. EPA's "rationale," in other words, is that several members of Congress (among others) urged upon it the claim that Proposition X ("Congress mandated BDAT") requires Result A ("EPA adopts BDAT"), and that although Proposition X is inaccurate, the best response to the commenters is to adopt Result A.

Nor is anything added by EPA's bald assertion that its reason for initially preferring Result B (screening levels) "may be" better served by other changes in the statutory scheme. In its Proposed Rule, EPA had, after extensive analysis of the various alternatives, come to the opposite conclusion. It is insufficient, in that context, for EPA to proceed in a different direction simply on the basis of an unexplained and unelaborated statement that it might have been wrong when it earlier concluded otherwise.... Accordingly, we grant the petitions for review in this respect.

COMMENTARY & QUESTIONS

1. **Politics and judicial review.** In the HWTC case, we catch a rare glimpse of an administrative agency caught in the middle between a Congress and an executive branch with widely different political agendas. An agency must simultaneously attempt to placate both its titular "boss," the Chief Executive, who appoints its leaders and filters its requests for funding, legislative authority, and clearance of proposed regulations, and the legislature that provides its funding and legislative authority, in addition to holding potentially embarrassing oversight hearings. Faced with a Congress enthusiastic about RCRA and an executive branch intent upon turning the statute into symbolic assurance by nonenforcement, EPA, perhaps wisely, decided to procrastinate. The result was congressional frustration and the legislative micromanagement encountered in the HSWA of 1984. EPA's delicate political position was exemplified by its painfully ambiguous and inconsistent explanation of its change in strategy from the Proposed to the Final §3004(m) Rule. The court, although operating under a highly deferential standard of judicial review, forced EPA to take a definite stand on this issue by remanding for the production of a rational and consistent explanation of EPA's position. As in this case, the requirement that an agency produce an adequate record for judicial review

raises the visibility of politicized issues and compels an agency to adopt clear, if not universally popular, positions.

2. **Legislative micromanagement, pro and con.** In this situation, legislative microman-agement appears to have been successful in breaking the political logjam and pushing a reluctant EPA to implement RCRA. But there are possible disadvantages to legislative control of agency regulatory agendas in highly technical areas such as hazardous waste management. In 1986, Congress attempted to goad the Reagan Administration into increasing its sluggish pace of CERCLA cleanups by enacting §116 of CERCLA, 42 U.S.C. §9616, which required EPA to commence specified numbers of remedial investiga-tions/feasibility studies by definite dates, and also to begin remedial actions at the rate of 175 during the first three years after enactment and an additional 200 during the following two years. Given EPA's level of funding and the complexity of the cleanup determinations involved, these timetables proved to have been wildly unrealistic. A similar result occurred when Congress amended the SDWA in 1986 to place EPA on a mandatory timetable for promulgating maximum contaminant goals and maximum contaminant levels for toxic contaminants in drinking water. 42 U.S.C. §300g-1. It appears that legislative micromanagement works best where Congress resorts to a tech-nically crude device such as a hammer clause.

3. **Hammer clauses.** The generally accepted explanation for the presence of hammer clauses in the HSWA is congressional displeasure with the dilatory performance of EPA in the early years of RCRA. Have the hammer clauses proved effective? The short answer is that the hammer clauses and the threat of a true land ban[33] did force EPA into prompt action to provide an alternative that was less disruptive of on-going economic activity. If the RCRA scenario is to serve as a basis for generalization, it seems that hammer clauses work well as long as the contingent legislative regulation (the hammer) is so stringent that the outcome of administrative process is likely to be more favorable to the regulated community.

4. **Is BDAT bad?** In opting for treatment standards founded on BDAT, EPA seems to be locking in existing treatment methods as the future norm, thereby deterring, rather than spurring, advances in the field. A second major criticism of BDAT as the treatment standard is that it trades a land disposal problem for an air pollution problem. This crit-icism arises because incineration is the current BDAT for most types of hazardous waste, and even in the best incinerators many hazardous constituents are not fully destroyed. Beyond that, incineration is not a complete treatment insofar as the ash that remains is itself usually a hazardous material in need of subsequent disposal. Still, BDAT is not without some redeeming features, one of which is its clarity. Once a technology is determined to be the BDAT for the treatment of a hazardous substance, generators and TSD facilities alike know what they must do to comply with the law.

5. **The "no migration" variance.** RCRA authorizes variances to the land ban based on a harm-based review. In order to obtain a variance from BDAT standards, a petitioner must show "to a reasonable degree of certainty, that there will be no migration of

---

33. See, e.g., RCRA §3004(g)(6)(C), 42 U.S.C. §6924(g)(6)(C) (total prohibition on land disposal unless EPA promulgates adequate standards).

hazardous constituents from the disposal unit or injection zone for as long as the wastes remain hazardous." 42 U.S.C. §6924(d)(1). EPA interprets this statutory language to mean that concentrations of hazardous constituents shall not exceed Agency-approved health-based or ecosystem-based levels, in any environmental medium, at the boundary of the unit or injection zone. EPA has set strict ambient standards for granting a "no migration" variance, and few variances have been granted thus far. See Proposed EPA Interpretation of RCRA No Migration Variances, 57 Fed. Reg. 3590 (Aug. 11, 1992). The "no migration" variance is an interesting taxonomic device in that it places the burden of overcoming uncertainty on the applicant, who must show that the fundamental technology-based standard is unnecessary. This approach remedies one of the shortcomings of the pure harm-based approach — the heavy regulatory burden placed on a standard-setting agency to establish harm-based standards under conditions of pervasive scientific uncertainty and political rancor.

6. **Underground injection.** The underground injection of hazardous waste through wells is a form of land disposal that is covered by RCRA and by the Underground Injection Control (UIC) program under Part C of the SDWA, 42 U.S.C. §§300(h) et seq. The UIC regulations (40 C.F.R. pts. 144–148) are primarily concerned with the protection of underground sources of drinking water. The UIC program categorizes hazardous waste injection wells as Class I wells, which receive the highest level of UIC regulation. See 40 C.F.R. §146.61. Although the surface storage and management of hazardous wastes are still subject to RCRA, and although certain closure, corrective action, land disposal, and general RCRA requirements apply to Class I wells, generally the RCRA regulations defer to the UIC regulations for the actual injection process. 40 C.F.R. §264.1(d).

7. **Undersupply of TSD capacity.** Does the combination of a growing universe of generators and the comprehensive regulation of TSD facilities threaten a supply-and-demand imbalance in which more hazardous waste needs to be processed than can be handled by permitted facilities? In the short term, the problem has been finessed by allowing variances to TSD facilities by which they can obtain interim permits even though they are not yet employing BDAT treatment of waste prior to land disposal. Is the variance expedient likely to become a near-permanent fixture in the RCRA program? Another factor in the TSD supply equation is, of course, the NIMBY phenomenon.

Is there any guarantee that there will be adequate disposal capacity? The answer to that question may lie in CERCLA §104(c)(9), 42 U.S.C. §9604(c)(9), which threatens to withhold Superfund remedial actions in states that do not provide disposal capacity for wastes generated within their borders. Under that provision, every state was required to submit, by 1989, a capacity assurance plan (CAP) for EPA approval. These plans must:

> assure the availability of hazardous waste treatment or disposal facilities which —
> (A) have adequate capacity for the destruction, treatment, or secure disposal of all hazardous wastes that are reasonably expected to be generated within the State during the 20-year period following [the giving of the assurance].

These facilities need not be located in-state, but if a CAP calls for interstate shipment of the hazardous waste for treatment, storage, or disposal, the arrangement with the waste-receiving state must be worked out in advance and be evidenced by a formal interstate agreement.

Notice how the CAP requirement is a partial protection for states having RCRA permitted facilities that do not wish to accept out-of-state hazardous wastes deposited in their facilities. Unless the prevailing view of the U.S. Supreme Court changes, the "dormant Commerce Clause" (see Chapter 6) will continue to require that out-of-state waste be accepted. But §104(c)(9) increases the likelihood that most states will develop in-state capacity (or agreements for out-of-state capacity) rather than risk the loss of Superfund money. In the belief that forcing other states to live up to the CAP requirements will slow the flow of hazardous waste into its RCRA permitted facilities, New York has challenged EPA approval of CAPs of other states in the region. New York's challenge attacks CAPs that rely either on New York facilities without having formal agreements with New York or on planned new sites that have not been constructed due to local opposition. See New York Announces Lawsuit Against EPA for Failure to Enforce Capacity Requirement, 22 BNA Env't Rep. 1363 (1991). The CAP requirement loses force to the extent that the expenditure by EPA of CERCLA funds becomes a less significant item than it was in the 1980s heyday of CERCLA cleanups.

8. **The RCRA Subtitle C universe.** In a probing review, EPA identified many trends and problems with its RCRA program. See generally EPA, The Nation's Hazardous Waste Management Program at a Crossroads: The RCRA Implementation Study (July 1990). EPA described the impact of the HSWA as follows:

> HWSA Greatly Expanded the Regulated Universe... To strengthen the nation's shield against hazardous wastes, HWSA established over 70 statutory requirements (often with very tight deadlines) for EPA's action. They can generally be summarized as follows:
>
> - Move away from land disposal as the primary means of hazardous waste management by requiring the treatment of wastes before their final disposal.
> - Reduce the environmental and health risks posed by hazardous waste still managed at land disposal facilities by establishing minimum technology requirements.
> - Close down facilities that cannot safely manage wastes.
> - Decrease and clean up releases to the environment from waste management units by requiring facilities to take corrective action.
> - Issue permits for all treatment, storage, and disposal facilities within prescribed time frames.
> - Close loopholes in the types of wastes and waste management facilities not covered under RCRA.
> - Expand the universe of regulated sources by including generators of small quantities of hazardous wastes.
> - Minimize the amount of wastes being produced.

With this comprehensive sweep of hazardous waste issues, HWSA greatly expanded the magnitude of waste types and waste management facilities requiring regulation. Today the RCRA regulated universe consists of 4700 hazardous waste TSD facilities. Within these facilities are approximately 81,000 waste management units, most of which are units that have received hazardous waste and from which contamination may have spread to the soil and groundwater. In addition to these 4700 facilities are 211,000 facilities that generate hazardous waste. Id. at 7.

The same part of the report also predicted that the continuing expansion of the list of hazardous wastes due to the operation of the TCLP would lead to a further increase in the size of the Subtitle C universe. With more substances considered hazardous, some existing facilities that in the past were not considered to be within RCRA's reach will become covered. The growth in numbers of TSD facilities currently under RCRA regulation is a bit misleading in regard to the longer-term trend. Other data in the report indicate that many of the regulated facilities (almost 3000) are closed (but still regulated) or in the process of closing rather than meeting RCRA's stringent technology-based standards. Id. at 42–43.

9. **The future of overfiling under RCRA.** As noted in Chapter 21, federal law divides the responsibility for enforcing federal environmental regulations between EPA and the states. Generally, state programs that receive formal approval for authorization from EPA may proceed to administer delegated federal environmental programs.

EPA seeks to combine its delegation of authority to the states with retained enforcement for itself. "Overfiling" occurs when the EPA initiates its own enforcement action, even though the state is authorized to administer the federal environmental program and has previously commenced its own enforcement action against the alleged polluter. The effect of EPA overfiling is that an alleged polluter may end up facing two lawsuits and paying penalties twice for the same environmental violation.

Congress has recognized that for the success of its environmental programs (including RCRA, the CAA, and the CWA), state involvement is essential. However, delegation of the federal programs to the states has often been controversial. Overfiling in particular has been criticized as an infringement on states' rights to take appropriate enforcement action free from federal oversight or second-guessing.

The future of overfiling by EPA under RCRA has now been called into question by conflicting decisions of the federal courts of appeal. In Harmon Indus., Inc. v. Browner, 191 F.3d 894 (8th Cir. 1999), the Eighth Circuit held that RCRA precludes EPA from pursuing a duplicate enforcement proceeding, or overfiling, for violation of a state's hazardous waste laws against a facility, when an authorized state has already instituted an enforcement action based upon the same violations. By "harmonizing" state program authorization and federal enforcement provisions within RCRA, *Harmon* found that "Congress intended to grant states the primary role of enforcing their own hazardous waste program(s)," and that the statute "manifests a congressional intent to give EPA a secondary enforcement right" triggered only in those cases where an authorized state fails to act or after EPA rescinds state authorization. Id at 899.

Harmon's prohibition against overfiling was rejected by the Tenth Circuit in United States v. Power Eng'g, 303 F.3d 1232 (10th Cir. 2002), which held that EPA may overfile in federal court after a state brings a state enforcement action under RCRA, even after the state has agreed to settle its enforcement action with the regulated entity. See also

United States v. Elias, 269 F.3d 1003 (9th Cir. 2001), cert. denied, 537 U.S. 812 (2002) (refusing to bar federal criminal prosecution under RCRA, despite prior EPA authorization of state hazardous waste program).

The Tenth Circuit reached its result — that EPA overfiling is permissible — by examining the language, intent, and agency interpretation of RCRA. The Tenth Circuit was not persuaded by the contention that Congress had directly spoken to the precise issue of overfiling. Rather, after its own examination of RCRA, the court found the statute ambiguous. Having concluded that Congress did not directly address the issue of overfiling, the court deferred to EPA's "reasonable" interpretation that overfiling is permissible, relying on *Chevron*.

What is the impact of *Harmon* and *Power Engineering* upon the regulated community? At a minimum, these conflicting decisions create considerable uncertainty. With the specter of EPA overfiling again a looming possibility not only in the Tenth Circuit but also in those circuits that may follow *Power Engineering*, a regulated entity faces potentially duplicative enforcement proceedings, potentially inconsistent corrective measures, and the risk that resolving an environmental dispute under RCRA with the state will not necessarily lead to finality. The question remains: Which governmental agency, the state or EPA, is in charge? Is *Harmon* in eclipse, or is its analysis likely to prevail over that of *Power Engineering*?

In the Tenth Circuit, where *Power Engineering* is controlling, the pragmatic impact is already evident. Before finalizing any RCRA settlement with the state, regulated entities are proactively seeking EPA's sign-off. Otherwise, EPA retains the right to come in after the state settles and seek to impose obligations that the state has negotiated away. Finally, a more fundamental concern remains. If *Harmon* is in eclipse and *Power Engineering* is followed by other circuits, will the regulated community have the incentive to negotiate settlements with the states? If not, will the lack of incentive undercut the efforts by the states to obtain early, nonjudicial resolutions?

C. RCRA CITIZEN SUITS TO OBTAIN CLEANUP AND POTENTIAL COST RECOVERY

CERCLA, studied in Chapter 19, is the traditional vehicle by which cleanups and cost recoveries are obtained. Historically, however, RCRA came first, having been enacted in 1976, followed by CERCLA in 1980. For a time, then, RCRA was the only federal law available for obtaining cleanups, and it was utilized, especially by the federal government, as the basis for seeking the cleanup of contaminated sites.[34]

With the passage of CERCLA, Congress made plain its intent that CERCLA, not RCRA, was the primary vehicle for not only the federal government but also for private parties to obtain cleanups and cost recoveries. RCRA §7002 (citizen suits) was amended to include provisions that forbade suit if CERCLA processes had been invoked. See 42

---

34. An early example of the use of RCRA was United States v. Northeastern Pharm. & Chem. Co. (NEPACCO), 810 F.2d 726 (8th Cir. 1986) (see Chapter 19), initially filed by the federal government under RCRA §7003 and then amended to include counts under the newly passed CERCLA legislation.

U.S.C. §6972(b)(2)(B). However, CERCLA processes cannot always be invoked. This is especially important with respect to releases of petroleum products. Petroleum products are not covered by CERCLA, having been specifically excluded by Congress from CERCLA's definition of "hazardous substances." See 42 U.S.C. §9601(14). RCRA does not have the same limitation, which has led to efforts by parties whose land was contaminated by petroleum releases to seek a remedy under RCRA utilizing its citizen suit provision.

For many years, it appeared that the citizen suit remedy provided by RCRA was limited to abatement of the contamination, not reimbursement for cleanup costs incurred by the RCRA plaintiff. In KFC Western, Inc. v. Meghrig, 49 F.3d 518 (9th Cir. 1995), a private cost recovery action against former service station operators was successfully maintained by a party who had cleaned up a petroleum release on that parcel. Other circuits, however, held that no such cause of action existed under RCRA. The *Meghrig* decision was reviewed and reversed by the Supreme Court in the opinion that follows.

Meghrig v. KFC Western, Inc.
Supreme Court of the United States, 1996
516 U.S. 479

O'CONNOR, J. We consider whether §7002 of the Resource Conservation and Recovery Act of 1976 (RCRA), 42 U.S.C. §6972, authorizes a private cause of action to recover the prior cost of cleaning up toxic waste that does not, at the time of suit, continue to pose an endangerment to health or environment. We conclude that it does not.

Respondent KFC Western, Inc. (KFC), owns and operates a "Kentucky Fried Chicken" restaurant on a parcel of property in Los Angeles. In 1988, KFC discovered during the course of a construction project that the property was contaminated with petroleum. The County of Los Angeles Department of Health Services ordered KFC to attend to the problem, and KFC spent $211,000 removing and disposing of the oil-tainted soil.

Three years later, KFC brought suit under the citizen suit provision of RCRA...seeking to recover these cleanup costs from petitioners Alan and Margaret Meghrig. KFC claimed that the contaminated soil was a "solid waste" covered by RCRA...that it had previously posed an "imminent and substantial endangerment to health or the environment,"...and that the Meghrigs were responsible for "equitable restitution" of KFC's cleanup costs under [the citizen suit provision, 42 U.S.C.] §6972(a) because, as prior owners of the property, they had contributed to the waste's "past or present handling, storage, treatment, transportation, or disposal.".…

RCRA is a comprehensive environmental statute that governs the treatment, storage, and disposal of solid and hazardous waste. Unlike the Comprehensive Environmental Response, Compensation and Liability Act of 1980 (CERCLA), RCRA is not principally designed to effectuate the cleanup of toxic waste sites or to compensate those who have attended to the remediation of environmental hazards. RCRA's primary purpose, rather, is to reduce the generation of hazardous waste and to ensure the proper treatment, storage, and disposal of that waste which is nonetheless generated, "so as to minimize the present and future threat to human health and the environment." 42 U.S.C. §6902(b).…

Two requirements...defeat KFC's suit against the Meghrigs. The first concerns the necessary timing of a citizen suit brought under §6972(a)(1)(B): That section permits a private party to bring suit against certain responsible persons, including former owners, "who ha[ve] contributed or who [are] contributing to the past or present handling, storage, treatment, transportation, or disposal of any solid or hazardous waste which may present an *imminent* and substantial endangerment to health or the environment." (Emphasis added by the Court.) The second defines the remedies a district court can award in a suit brought under §6972(a)(1)(B): Section 6972(a) authorizes district courts "to restrain any person who has contributed or who is contributing to the past or present handling, storage, treatment, transportation, or disposal of any solid or hazardous waste,...*to order such person to take such other action as may be necessary*, or both." (Emphasis added by the Court.)

It is apparent from the two remedies described in §6972(a) that RCRA's citizen suit provision is not directed at providing compensation for past cleanup efforts. Under a plain reading of this remedial scheme, a private citizen suing under §6972(a)(1)(B) could seek a mandatory injunction, i.e., one that orders a responsible party to "take action" by attending to the cleanup and proper disposal of toxic waste, or a prohibitory injunction, i.e., one that "restrains" a responsible party from further violating RCRA. Neither remedy, however, is susceptible of the interpretation adopted by the Ninth Circuit, as neither contemplates the award of past cleanup costs, whether these are denominated "damages" or "equitable restitution."

In this regard, a comparison between the relief available under RCRA's citizen suit provision and that which Congress has provided in the analogous, but not parallel, provisions of CERCLA is telling. CERCLA was passed several years after RCRA went into effect, and it is designed to address many of the same toxic waste problems that inspired the passage of RCRA. Compare 42 U.S.C. §6903(5)...(RCRA definition of "hazardous waste") and §6903(27) (RCRA definition of "solid waste") with §9601(14) (CERCLA provision incorporating certain "hazardous substance[s]," but not the hazardous and solid wastes defined in RCRA, and specifically not petroleum). CERCLA differs markedly from RCRA, however, in the remedies it provides. CERCLA's citizen suit provision mimics §6972(a) in providing district courts with the authority "to order such action as may be necessary to correct the violation" of any CERCLA standard of regulation. 42 U.S.C. §9659 (1988 ed.). But CERCLA expressly permits the Government to recover "all costs of removal or remedial action," §9607(a)(4)(A), and it expressly permits the recovery of any "necessary costs of response, incurred by any...person consistent with the national contingency plan," §9607(a)(4)(B). CERCLA also provides that "[a]ny person may seek contribution from any other person who is liable or potentially liable" for these responses costs. See §9613(f)(1). Congress thus demonstrated in CERCLA that it knew how to provide for the recovery of cleanup costs, and that the language used to define the remedies under RCRA does not provide that remedy.

That RCRA's citizen suit provision was not intended to provide a remedy for past cleanup costs is further apparent from the harm at which it is directed. Section 6972(a)(1)(B) permits a private party to bring suit only upon a showing that the solid or hazardous waste at issue "may present an imminent and substantial endangerment to health or the environment." The meaning of this timing restriction is plain: An endangerment can only be "imminent" if it "threaten[s] to occur immediately," Webster's New International Dictionary of English Language 1245 (2d ed. 1934), and the reference to waste which "may present" imminent harm quite clearly excludes waste that no longer presents such a danger. As the Ninth Circuit itself intimated in Price v. United States Navy, 39 F.3d 1011, 1019 (1994), this language "implies that there must be a threat which is present now, although the impact of the threat may not be felt until later." It follows that §6972(a) was designed to provide a remedy that ameliorates present or obviates the risk of future "imminent" harms, not a remedy that compensates for past cleanup efforts. Cf. §6902(b) (national policy behind RCRA is "to minimize the present and future threat to human health and the environment").

Other aspects of RCRA's enforcement scheme strongly support this conclusion. Unlike CERCLA, RCRA contains no statute of limitations, compare §9613(g)(2) (limitations period in suits under CERCLA §9607), and it does not require a showing that the response costs being sought are reasonable, compare §§9607(a)(4)(A) and (B) (costs recovered under CERCLA must be "consistent with the national contingency plan"). If Congress had intended §6972(a) to function as a cost-recovery mechanism, the absence of these provisions would be striking. Moreover, with one limited exception,...(noting exception to notice requirement "when there is a danger that hazardous waste will be discharged"), a private party may not bring suit under §6972(a)(1)(B) without first giving 90 days' notice to the Administrator of the EPA, to "the State in which the alleged endangerment may occur," and to potential defendants, see §6972(b)(2)(A)(I)-(iii). And no citizen suit can proceed if either the EPA or the State has commenced, and is diligently prosecuting, a separate enforcement action, see §6972(b)(2)(B) and (C). Therefore, if RCRA were designed to compensate private parties for their past cleanup efforts, it would be a wholly irrational mechanism for doing so. Those parties with insubstantial problems, problems that neither the State nor the Federal Government feel compelled to address, could recover their response costs, whereas those parties whose waste problems were sufficiently severe as to attract the attention of Government officials would be left without a recovery....

RCRA does not prevent a private party from recovering its cleanup costs under other federal or state laws, see §6972(f) (preserving remedies under statutory and common law), but the limited remedies described in §6972(a), along with the stark differences between the language of that section and the cost recovery provisions of CERCLA, amply demonstrate that Congress did not intend for a private citizen to be able to undertake a clean up and then proceed to recover its costs under RCRA....

Without considering whether a private party could seek to obtain an injunction requiring another party to pay cleanup costs which arise after a RCRA citizen suit has been properly commenced,...or otherwise recover cleanup costs paid out after the invocation of RCRA's statutory process, we agree with the Meghrigs that a private party cannot recover the cost of a past cleanup effort under RCRA, and that KFC's complaint is defective for the reasons stated by the District Court. Section 6972(a) does not contemplate the award of past cleanup costs, and §6972(a)(1)(B) permits a private party to bring suit only upon an allegation that the contaminated site presently poses an "imminent and substantial endangerment to health or the environment," and not upon an allegation that it posed such an endangerment at some time in the past. The judgment of the Ninth Circuit is reversed.

COMMENTARY & QUESTIONS

1. **Remaining questions regarding the scope of §7002.** Can a private party sue under §7002(a)(1)(B) while an imminent endangerment still exists and obtain restitution of response costs for work taken thereafter? *Meghrig* expressly avoids answering that question. Would the Court be reluctant to provide such a remedy given Congress's failure to do so expressly? How could such a remedy be implied, if, as Justice O'Connor concluded, "Congress thus demonstrated in CERCLA that it knew how to provide for the recovery of cleanup costs, and that the language used to define the remedies under RCRA does not provide that remedy?"

2. **The importance of *Meghrig*.** In advance of the Supreme Court decision in *Meghrig*, one commentator wrote, "The implications of the Ninth Circuit ruling in *KFC Western* are significant. Private parties can now obtain more complete relief under §7002(a)(1)(B) than they can obtain under [CERCLA]." Robertson, Restitution Under RCRA §7002(a)(1)(B): The Courts Finally Grant What Congress Authorized, 25 Envtl.

L. Rep. 10491 (1995). Does the *Meghrig* decision leave a gap in which no remedies are available to recover costs paid to remediate petroleum spills? Probably not. Up until the Ninth Circuit's *Meghrig* decision, RCRA had been on the books for almost 15 years without great fanfare surrounding the lack of a restitutionary remedy. While CERCLA had lacked jurisdiction over petroleum releases and was far too cumbersome in many ways, state common law and statutory remedies for contamination were available, although sometimes open to criticism. See Lopez, Cost Recovery for Petroleum Contamination: Will *RCRA* Citizen Plaintiffs Be Cookin' with KFC or Relegated to a State Law Jungle?, 10 Toxics L. Rep. 946 (1996).

3. **Strategic considerations after *Meghrig*.** After the Supreme Court's decision in *Meghrig*, does a party faced with petroleum contamination on its property have an incentive to sue those responsible for the contamination before undertaking the cleanup? If a party defers cleanup and instead seeks relief from those contributing to an imminent and substantial endangerment, that party may still seek an injunction to require those responsible to participate in the cleanup and may also seek restitution of its prospective cleanup costs. Is the *Meghrig* decision, then, one that provides a strategic incentive to sue first and clean up later, in hopes of recouping cleanup costs? Could such an incentive — to defer cleanups rather than to expedite them — be one that Congress had intended? Attempting to answer these questions, the Seventh Circuit has responded with a resounding "no," holding that a property owner may not recover its cleanup costs under §7002 from the party responsible for the contamination, a decision that the Supreme Court declined to review. See Avondale Fed. Sav. Bank v. Amoco Oil Co., 170 F.3d 692 (7th Cir. 1999), cert. denied, 528 U.S. 922 (1999); see also Albany Bank & Trust Co. v. Exxon Mobil Corp., 310 F.3d 969 (7th Cir. 2002) (holding that investigatory costs are no more recoverable than cleanup costs would be.)

Chapter 19

REMEDIAL LIABILITY STRATEGIES: TOXIC CLEANUPS AND THEIR FUNDING UNDER CERCLA AND STATE PROGRAMS

A. *CERCLA's Liability Rules as Developed through the Judicial Process of Statutory Interpretation*
B. *EPA's Administrative Order Process*
C. *Identifying Sites, Funding, and Setting the Standards for Cleanups*
D. *EPA's Strategy for Cost Recovery and Loss Allocation*

The environmental events that have most galvanized public opinion over the years have been high-profile cases involving the release of hazardous substances into the environment and the resulting threats to public health. Few symbols are as potent as the homes and schools at Love Canal virtually afloat on a toxic stew or working families suffering "the shakes" from Kepone in Hopewell, Virginia, or workers in space suit-like outfits removing PCBs from the newly abandoned ghost town at Times Beach, Missouri. In the face of that degree of public outrage, an almost certain political reaction is to pass laws addressing the subject, not only laws that seek to avert repetition of the calamity, as with Subtitle C of RCRA (see Chapter 18), but also laws that seek to assuage public anger at the parties responsible for the events by making those parties accountable for the results of their actions.

Enacting into law the public desire for an accounting from responsible parties is a natural enough sentiment, but to do so within the constraints imposed by the U.S. Constitution, and to do so effectively, is a more sophisticated proposition. Newly enacted laws that attempt to attach present consequences for past actions have some hurdles to overcome. Not only does Article I §9 of the Constitution state that "No bill of Attainder or ex post facto law shall be passed," but that provision is also complemented by the more general notion that constitutionally guaranteed due process of law requires fair advance notice of what the law requires before sanctions can be imposed for disobedience of the legal command. Beyond the retroactive application of law, crafting a law that holds the "right" actors accountable for acts that have occurred in the distant past raises a host of additional complexities.

In enacting the Comprehensive Environmental Response, Compensation, and Liability Act (CERCLA, popularly named "Superfund"), Congress took on those challenges and more — it imposed retroactive liability on a broad group of actors whom it deemed to be the responsible parties, and it created a system that was intended to secure prompt environmental cleanups of releases of hazardous substances into the environment. At bedrock, CERCLA makes a very serious effort to effectuate the polluter-pays principle (PPP), that is, re-internalizing the costs of environmental harm by imposing an accounting upon those whose actions caused the harm. Its principal method of doing so is to insist on cleanup of the environment in conjunction with a liability scheme that passes the costs of cleanup on to those responsible for the release of the hazardous material into the environment. In effectuating that scheme, CERCLA incorporates devices that ensure that most sites of contamination will be discovered and, thereafter, orchestrates their cleanup and the eventual shifting of the cost to the responsible parties.

CERCLA embodies a particular implementation strategy, that of remedial cost internalization. CERCLA seeks to remediate contamination and to establish liability for past contamination practices that have ongoing environmental consequences. In reviewing CERCLA's remedial implementation strategy, several rather distinct features immediately stand out: (1) the extent to which traditional norms of tort liability are inadequate to obtain remedial cost internalization, (2) the difficulties in equitably applying the PPP to past occurrences that were not monitored with the PPP in mind, and (3) the whole panoply of powers that must be granted to the administering agency to allow for the development of a coherent implementation strategy. Beyond those implementation-based observations, CERCLA's operation and implementation also provide a most instructive case study of statutory evolution.

One of the key and most well-known statutory mechanisms created by Congress in CERCLA is the Superfund itself. After the amendment and reauthorization of CERCLA in 1986,[1] the Superfund operated as a mechanism to ensure that funding would be available to pay for cleanups at the most seriously contaminated sites. The need for the fund part of a Superfund law, however, may not be immediately obvious. After all, if state common law is inadequate to fix liability on the industries that generate, transport, and dispose of hazardous wastes, a federal law imposing liability on a somewhat broader range of potentially responsible parties would seem to be all that is needed. Under such a law, those responsible for hazardous releases could be ordered to undertake a cleanup and to compensate others damaged by their releases. This latter damage calculation would include any cleanup expenses incurred by third parties or government.

The major reasons for the fund component of Superfund are that the responsible parties cannot always be identified — as in the notorious practice of "midnight dumping"— and that responsible parties may be unable to pay the amount of the cleanup costs. The reason that the fund must be "super" is a function of cost. Purging a hazardous waste site of contaminants can be a multimillion dollar undertaking.

The principal statutory mechanisms of CERCLA were succinctly described at the time of its enactment:

> Essentially, CERCLA authorizes governmental responses to actual and threatened releases of a wide range of harmful substances. Parties causing releases of such substances may then be held liable without regard to fault for certain damages resulting from the release, which primarily include government incurred costs for

---

1. Superfund Amendments and Reauthorization Act of 1986 (SARA), Pub. L. No. 99-499, 100 Stat. 1613.

cleanup, removal, and resources restoration. To ensure that such injuries are redressed, the law establishes a $1.6 billion [$8.5 billion, after SARA in 1986] Hazardous Substances Response Fund, financed jointly by industry and the federal government over five years. When polluters are unknown, or are unable or unwilling to provide recompense, a claim for specified damages may be filed against the fund. Payment of claims by the fund then subrogates the fund to the rights of the claimant.[2]

Focusing on specific remedial provisions, CERCLA's provisions retrace the imminent hazard provisions of RCRA[3] and add provisions that relate to recoupment and allocation of cleanup costs already incurred in response to hazardous waste releases.[4]

Although CERCLA's remedial implementation strategy was designed to force cleanups of contaminated sites, that strategy has not always functioned as intended. Perhaps the best example of CERCLA's unintended consequences concerns sites known as "brownfields" — abandoned, idled, or underutilized industrial or commercial sites suffering from environmental contamination. Fearing the broad liability provisions of CERCLA, many prospective purchasers, developers, and lenders historically chose to avoid brownfields redevelopment altogether, with the result that brownfields sites have often become major community and taxpayer burdens. As Chapter 21 details, EPA and the states have recognized that CERCLA's remedial implementation strategy unfortunately has contributed to the perpetuation of brownfields rather than their remediation. As a result, EPA and the states have developed strategies to work more closely with regulated communities to encourage the redevelopment of brownfields. This shift in focus, toward a more flexible and cooperative approach in partnership with the regulated community, signals a new trend in environmental cleanup policies and programs.

A. CERCLA'S LIABILITY RULES AS DEVELOPED THROUGH THE JUDICIAL PROCESS OF STATUTORY INTERPRETATION

Congress expended considerable effort filling in the details of the remedial side of CERCLA but also left many areas in need of judicial interpretation and clarification. Consequently, CERCLA, like RCRA, has become one of the most actively litigated statutes in environmental law. Together, supplemented by state common law tort theories studied in prior chapters, they form the legal basis for determining who will bear the costs associated with the release of hazardous materials on land and into groundwater.[5]

---

2. Comment, Superfund at Square One: Promising Statutory Framework Requires Forceful EPA Implementation, 11 Envtl. L. Rep. 10101 (1981).

3. See CERCLA §106, codified at 42 U.S.C. §9606.

4. See CERCLA §107, codified at 42 U.S.C. §9607. The 1986 Amendments to §107, while adding some material, did not make major changes in the scope and coverage of §107. Its impact with regard to the liability of "innocent purchasers" of realty that is discovered to be contaminated is significantly affected by the amendments to §101(35), wherein the obligations of purchasers to use due diligence to discover the presence of contaminants are spelled out.

5. The release of hazardous materials into the navigable waters (i.e., surface waters) of the United States is governed by the CWA, 33 U.S.C. §§1251 et seq.

Section 1. **THE BASICS OF STATUTORY REMEDIAL LIABILITY FOR CLEANUP OF HAZARDOUS MATERIALS**

42 U.S.C. §9607 [original Act's §107]. **Liability.**

(a) Covered persons; scope; recoverable costs and damages; interest rate; "comparable maturity" date.

Notwithstanding any other provision or rule of law, and subject only to the defenses set forth in subsection (b) of this section —

(1) the owner and operator of a vessel or a facility,

(2) any person who at the time of disposal of any hazardous substance owned or operated any facility at which such hazardous substances were disposed of,

(3) any person who by contract, agreement, or otherwise arranged for disposal or treatment, or arranged with a transporter for transport for disposal or treatment, of hazardous substances owned or possessed by such person, by any other party or entity, at any facility or incineration vessel owned or operated by another party or entity and containing such hazardous substances, and (4) any person who accepts or accepted any hazardous substances for transport to disposal or treatment facilities, incineration vessels or sites selected by such person, from which there is a release, or a threatened release which causes the incurrence of response costs, of a hazardous substance, shall be liable for —

(A) all costs of removal or remedial action incurred by the United States Government or a State or an Indian tribe not inconsistent with the national contingency plan;

(B) any other necessary costs of response incurred by any other person consistent with the national contingency plan;

(C) damages for injury to, destruction of, or loss of natural resources, including the reasonable costs of assessing such injury, destruction, or loss resulting from such a release; and

(D) the costs of any health assessment or health effects study carried out under section 9604(i) of this title....

(b) Defenses... There shall be no liability under subsection (a) of this section for a person otherwise liable who can establish by a preponderance of the evidence that the release or threat of release of a hazardous substance and the damages resulting therefrom were caused solely by —

(1) an act of God;

(2) an act of war;

(3) an act or omission of a third party other than an employee or agent of the defendant, or than one whose act or omission occurs in connection with a contractual relationship, existing directly or indirectly, with the defendant (except where the sole contractual arrangement arises from a published tariff and acceptance for carriage by a common carrier by rail), if the defendant establishes by a preponderance of the evidence that (a) he exercised due care with respect to the hazardous substance concerned, taking into consideration the characteristics of such hazardous substance, in light of all relevant facts and circumstances, and (b) he took precautions against foreseeable acts or omissions of any such third party and the consequences that could foreseeably result from such acts or omissions; or

(4) any combination of the foregoing paragraphs....

(f) Actions involving natural resources; maintenance, scope, etc... (1) Natural resources liability — In the case of an injury to, destruction of, or loss of natural resources under subparagraph (C) of subsection (a) of this section liability shall be to the United States Government and to any State for natural resources within the State or belonging to, managed by, controlled by, or appertaining to such State and to any Indian tribe for natural resources belonging to, managed by, controlled by, or appertaining to such tribe....

A review of CERCLA's definition sections demonstrates that the universe of conduct that might fall within §107 is quite broad and does not explicitly describe the standards of liability that define what conduct is actionable and what is not. This void has been largely filled by the courts. The following excerpt provides a roadmap to some of the early rulings that started to define the operation of CERCLA.

David Rich, Personal Liability for Hazardous Waste Cleanup: An Examination of CERCLA §107
13 Boston College Environmental Affairs Law Review 643, 653–658 (1986)

Section 107 of CERCLA designates certain parties who may be liable for the cleanup costs of a hazardous waste site. Section 107 imposes liability for cleanup costs and damage to natural resources[6] on: (1) past and present owners and operators of hazardous waste facilities; (2) persons who arrange for disposal of hazardous substances to facilities (usually generators); and (3) persons who transport hazardous substances to facilities from which there is a release or a threatened release of toxic chemicals that results in response costs. These responsible parties are liable for three types of costs incurred as a result of a release or a threatened release of hazardous waste: (1) governmental response costs (costs incurred by the federal government to clean up hazardous waste sites); (2) private response costs (costs incurred by other parties consistent with the National Contingency Plan), and (3) damages to natural resources.

Section 107 provides limited defenses. Parties otherwise liable under §107 may escape liability if they can establish that the release or threat of release of hazardous substances and resulting damages were caused by an act of God, an act of war, or an act or omission of a third party other than an employee or agent of the defendants, or one whose act or omission occurs in connection with a contractual relationship with the defendants. The third party exception applies only if defendants both exercised due care with respect to the hazardous substance, and took necessary precautions against acts or omissions by the third party.

Strict Liability... In spite of the comprehensive nature of its hazardous waste cleanup provisions, CERCLA's standards of liability are vague. Congress removed references to strict liability and joint and several liability before the bill's final passage, leaving these matters for judicial interpretation.

The standard of liability under CERCLA is strict liability. Although it does not specifically mention strict liability, §101, CERCLA's definitional section, states that liability under CERCLA "shall be construed to be the standard of liability which obtains under §311 of the Federal Water Pollution Control Act." Although §311 of the Federal Water Pollution Control Act (FWCPA) does not explicitly mention strict liability, courts have inferred such liability from the language of that Act, which subjects certain parties to liability unless they can successfully assert one of

---

6. "Natural resources" under CERCLA means "fish, wildlife, biota, air, water, groundwater, drinking water supplies, and other such resources belonging to, managed by, held in trust by, appertaining to, or otherwise controlled by the United States...any state or local government, or any foreign government." 42 U.S.C. §9601(16).

FIGURE 19-1

An EPA aerial survey photograph of a New England toxic waste storage site. Many drums at this and similar sites are unmarked and leaking; some of the semi-trailers are filled with materials too unstable to be unloaded; site owners lack the resources required to maintain storage integrity or to clean up toxic contamination on the site.

the limited defenses specified. Congress' reference to FWCPA §311 in CERCLA is logical, because the same defenses to liability found in FWCPA §311 also appear in §107 of CERCLA. Courts construing CERCLA have therefore held parties strictly liable for statutory violations.

Joint and Several Liability... Congress also deleted references to joint and several liability from the final version of CERCLA. The original Senate proposal specifically imposed joint and several liability, but this language was deleted from the final version of the bill as part of the "hastily drawn compromise which resulted in the enactment of CERCLA." Federal courts construing liability under CERCLA, however, uniformly have held that CERCLA permits, but does not mandate, joint and several liability. It is therefore within the discretion of the court to impose joint and several liability. Furthermore, some courts have held that joint and several liability should be imposed under CERCLA, unless the defendants can establish that a reasonable basis exists for apportioning the harm against them.[7]

CERCLA's standard of strict liability, coupled with the possibility of joint and several liability, places a heavy burden on defendants. CERCLA does, however, place some constraints on the amount of liability that courts may impose under §107. Section 107 liability is premised upon a governmental response pursuant to §104 and the National Contingency Plan, or a response by another party in accordance with the National Contingency Plan. Both §104 and the National Contingency Plan impose practical limitations on the extent and cost of hazardous waste cleanup operations....

The National Contingency Plan establishes procedures and standards for responding to releases of hazardous substances, pollutants, and contaminants. These procedures include methods for discovering and investigating hazardous substance disposal facilities, for determining the appropriate extent of removal of the substances, for assuring that remedial actions are cost-effective, and for determining priorities among releases or threatened releases. The statute and the National Contingency Plan thus limit the extent of liability under CERCLA §107.

Personal Liability under CERCLA §107... As discussed earlier, CERCLA imposes liability on: (1) past and present owners and operators of hazardous waste facilities; (2) persons who arrange for the transport of hazardous waste; and (3) persons who transport hazardous waste. These parties include individuals as well as corporations. The federal government has sought to hold both corporations and their corporate officers and employees responsible for the costs of hazardous waste cleanup under CERCLA. Although individual defendants have argued that their actions were the actions of the corporation, thereby shielding them from liability under the doctrine of limited liability, this argument has not succeeded. The few district courts to consider this issue have uniformly held that the corporate form does not shield individuals from personal liability where such individuals have exercised personal control over, or have actually been involved in, the disposal of hazardous waste.

COMMENTARY & QUESTIONS

1. **CERCLA and §311 of the Federal Water Pollution Control Act.** Although the Rich excerpt mentions no canons of construction contributing to the interpretation given to CERCLA §107, the "shall be liable" language and reference to §311 of the Federal Water Pollution Control Act (which later evolved into the CWA) led courts initially to look to cases interpreting the CWA as precedent for the interpretation of §107. In §311,

---

7. United States v. Northeastern Pharm. & Chem. Co. (NEPACCO), 579 F. Supp. 823, 844 (W.D. Mo. 1984).

Congress imposed liability on owners and operators of the vessels or facilities causing spills of oil or hazardous substances on navigable waters, requiring owners and operators to pay the government's response costs. Congress also established a $35 million revolving fund, for use by EPA and the Coast Guard when responding to such spills. Section 311 thus provided a model for Congress in developing CERCLA. Following §311, Congress created the Superfund to enable EPA to remediate contaminated sites using federal money and then, under §107, empowered EPA to recover its costs from persons responsible for the contamination.

2. **A common law substitute for Superfund?** What does CERCLA §107 accomplish that the common law could not?[8] The common law can do some of the things that §107 provides. It is quite possible that a common law court would be willing to hold defendants who release hazardous materials into the environment strictly, jointly, and severally liable even in the absence of a statute allowing it. Perhaps the common law might also adopt a relaxed standard of proof of causation similar to that of CERCLA in cases involving concurrent actions of multiple tortfeasors. (In the CERCLA cases, however, the furtherance of legislative policy is a key element underlying judicial willingness to relax traditional tort law standards of proof.) Going further, §107 allows for remedies that would be very difficult to fashion under the common law. The damage assessment of §107(a)(4)(A) is not a traditional damage measure — it assesses the actual costs of environmental remediation (i.e., response costs), not the amount of plaintiffs' loss. Compare, for example, the award of damages paid in *Boomer*. By providing damages for natural resources, §107(a)(4)(C) also moves a step beyond traditional tort law, and §107(a)(4)(D) identifies health studies as an item of recoverable damage, hardly a regular feature of damage awards under the common law.

3. **Joint and several liability in CERCLA cases.** Strategically, joint and several liability is the concept (imported from common law) that makes CERCLA so potent. Courts uniformly interpret CERCLA as manifesting an intent on the part of Congress to allow joint and several liability among potentially responsible parties (PRPs). The consequence of imposing joint and several liability is potentially to shift the entire burden of cleanup onto any identifiable PRP. In deciding whether to impose joint and several liability, the standard view taken by most courts is to decide, on a case-by-case basis, whether harm is sufficiently severable to apportion liability.

United States v. Monsanto, 858 F.2d 160 (4th Cir. 1988) is illustrative. In that case, the Fourth Circuit held that site-owners and generator defendants were jointly and severally liable under §107(a) of CERCLA for the response costs expended by the United States and by South Carolina in removing hazardous wastes from a disposal facility. As to the site-owners' liability, the court found sufficient that they owned the site at the time that the hazardous substances were deposited there. As to the generator defendants' liability, the court found them liable because it was undisputed that (1) they shipped hazardous substances to the facility, (2) hazardous substances "like" those

---

8. CERCLA as a whole does many things that are far beyond the realm of common law possibility. Most obviously, its creation of a national fund from which cleanup expenses can be paid is a mechanism that the common law does not provide. Similarly, the creation of a National Priorities List that identifies and ranks sites as to the need for cleanup action is unthinkable without the intervention of a public law mandate.

present in the generation defendants' waste were found at the facility, and (3) there had been a release of hazardous substances at the site.

Turning next to the issue of apportionment of liability, the Fourth Circuit recognized that CERCLA permits the imposition of joint and several liability in cases of indivisible harm. The court clarified the applicable legal principles by referencing the common law:

> Under common law rules, when two or more persons act independently to cause a single harm for which there is a reasonable basis of apportionment according to the contribution of each, each is held liable only for the portion of harm that he causes. When such persons cause a single and indivisible harm, however, they are held liable jointly and severally for the entire harm. We think these principles, as reflected in the Restatement (Second) of Torts, represent the correct and uniform federal rules applicable to CERCLA cases. 858 F.2d at 171–172.

Applying these principles, the Fourth Circuit rejected the generator defendants' argument that there was a reasonable basis for apportioning the harm. In particular, the court found that the generator defendants presented no evidence showing a relationship between waste volume, the release of hazardous substances, and the harm at the site. Because hazardous substances at the site were commingled, there could be no reasonable apportionment "without some evidence disclosing the individual and interactive qualities of the substances deposited there. Common sense counsels that a million gallons of certain substances could be mixed together without significant consequences, whereas a few pints of others improperly mixed could result in disastrous consequences." 858 F.2d at 172. Because volumetric allocation could not establish the effective contribution of each waste generator to the harm at the site, the court affirmed the imposition of joint and several liability.

4. **The unfairness of joint and several liability.** Is it patently unfair to make a deep-pocket responsible party, such as Monsanto, liable for an entire cleanup when it is demonstrable that it is but one of several causes of the problem? Is it fair to tap the assets of only one of the responsible parties for the entire cost of the cleanup? The Fourth Circuit in its *Monsanto* decision rationalized the initial imposition of potentially unfair allocations in reliance on the later ability of the unfairly burdened party to reallocate some part of the loss by obtaining contribution from fellow joint tortfeasors. Specifically, the court concluded that "the defendants still have the right to sue responsible parties for contribution, and in that action they may assert both legal and equitable theories of cost allocation." 858 F.2d at 173. Although the topic of contribution is considered at length later in this chapter, can you predict why it may prove difficult for parties who pay more than their fair share in a government cleanup action to recover an appropriate amount via contribution?

5. **Divisibility of harm or of costs?** In cases like *Monsanto*, the indivisibility of the environmental harm is the predicate for application of joint and several liability. In United States v. Kramer, 757 F. Supp. 397 (D.N.J. 1991), the generator defendants at a landfill site argued as a defense that the bulk of the anticipated $60 million cleanup cost was attributable to the quantitatively large volume of municipal solid waste and sludge deposited at the site. More narrowly, the nonmunicipal generator defendants sought to limit their liability to an amount that could be calculated arithmetically as the

difference between the cleanup cost with, and without, their waste being present at the site. Why might this approach prove less costly to the nonmunicipal defendants?

Given the limited ability of municipalities to raise large sums of money, an apportionment that left the lion's share of the liability with the municipalities posed a collectability problem for EPA. Historically, EPA limited its efforts to recover a "fair" share from municipalities at sites where other PRPs can be identified and pursued. See EPA's 1989 Interim Policy on CERCLA Settlements Involving Municipalities and Municipal Wastes, 54 Fed. Reg. 51071 (December 12, 1989) (and see the supplemental EPA guidance, reprinted at 28 BNA Env't Rep. 2136 (1998)). As an example, at the Kramer site, EPA did not name the municipalities as defendants in its original complaint, but they remained vulnerable to contribution claims from the named defendants. The federal courts, however, have consistently ruled that municipalities, which unlike the states are not protected by the Eleventh Amendment, may be liable as owners, operators, transporters, and generators of hazardous waste. See Manko & Cozine, The Battle over Municipal Liability under CERCLA Heats Up: An Analysis of Proposed Congressional Amendments to Superfund, 5 Vill. Envtl. L.J. 23 (1994).

6. **Emerging cracks in EPA's joint and several armor.** In United States v. Alcan Aluminum Corp., 990 F.2d 711 (2d Cir. 1993), and in a separate case also entitled United States v. Alcan Aluminum Corp., 964 F.2d 252 (3d Cir. 1992), some modest inroads were made in the unrelenting stream of decisions imposing strict joint and several liability on all PRPs. More significantly of the two, the Third Circuit *Alcan* case ordered the lower court to hear evidence of divisibility of harm. Relying heavily on the Restatement (Second) of Torts §433A, the court set the test for divisibility as follows:

> In sum, on remand, the district court must permit Alcan to attempt to prove that the harm is divisible and that the damages are capable of some reasonable apportionment. We note that the Government need not prove that Alcan's emulsion caused the release or the response costs. On the other hand, if Alcan proves that the emulsion did not or could not, when mixed with other hazardous wastes, contribute to the release and the resultant response costs, then Alcan should not be responsible for any response costs. In this sense, our result thus injects causation into the equation but, as we have already pointed out, places the burden of proof on the defendant instead of the plaintiff. We think that this result is consistent with the statutory scheme and yet recognizes that there must be some reason for the imposition of CERCLA liability. Our result seems particularly appropriate in light of the expansive meaning of "hazardous substance." Of course, if Alcan cannot prove that it should not be liable for any response costs or cannot prove that the harm is divisible and that the damages are capable of some reasonable apportionment, it will be liable for the full claim.... 964 F.2d at 270–271.

The Second Circuit took a similar tack, concluding that based on common law principles, "Alcan may escape any liability for response costs if it either succeeds in proving that its oil emulsion, when mixed with other hazardous wastes, did not contribute to the release and the clean-up costs that followed, or contributed at most to only a divisible portion of the harm." 990 F.2d at 722. Is there now an *Alcan* defense? How many PRPs will be in a position to carry the burden of proof on divisibility and basis for apportionment? Some commentators suggest that only deep-pocket, technically sophisticated PRPs will benefit from *Alcan*. See Harris & Milan, Avoiding Joint and Several Liability Under CERCLA, 23 BNA Env't Rep. 1726 (1992).

A subsequent case, *Bell Petroleum*, went even further than the *Alcan* cases in supporting the argument that PRPs can escape CERCLA joint and several liability. In Bell Petroleum Servs. Inc. v. Sequa Corp., 3 F.3d 899 (5th Cir. 1993), Sequa, one of three successive operators of a chromium plating facility, offered evidence of comparative sales, chrome flake purchases, and electric utility bills, in an effort to show the relative contribution of the three PRPs. The records offered were incomplete and relied on a variety of assumptions in projecting the amount of contamination attributable to each PRP, and the trial court initially ruled that Sequa was jointly and severally liable with the other PRPs. Because the government had previously settled with the other PRPs for $1.1 million out of a total of $1.7 million spent cleaning the site, this left Sequa with a judgment that would require it (on a joint and several basis) to pay $600,000.

On appeal, the Fifth Circuit, engaging in de novo review of the lower court's divisibility ruling, found that Sequa's evidence provided a reasonable basis for apportionment, rendering the imposition of joint and several liability inappropriate, and remanded the case for a determination of Sequa's share of the liability. The trial court interpreted the remand order as requiring obedience not only to the divisibility ruling but also to a particular apportionment of only 4%, entering judgment against Sequa for $68,000. The trial court expressed its view that it could not take into account the full gamut of what it felt were relevant considerations saying it was "convinced that further evidence...would demonstrate Sequa's share of the contamination is much higher." United States v. Bell Petroleum Servs. Inc., MO-88-CA-005 (W.D. Tex. Mar. 11, 1994), discussed at 8 Toxics L. Rep. 1191 (1994). See also Oswald, New Directions in Joint and Several Liability Under CERCLA, 28 U.C. Davis L. Rev. 299 (1995); White & Butler, Applying Cost Causation Principles in Superfund Allocation Cases, 28 Envtl. L. Rep. 10067 (1998).

7. **Administrative order powers.** CERCLA §106 and RCRA §7003 both grant EPA power to issue orders requiring cleanups that address imminent threats to health and the environment caused by the release of hazardous substances into the environment. These sections complement §107 by providing additional remedial options for the EPA. Parties subject to the orders are required to expend resources on the cleanups, sometimes with little hope of shifting the loss to other responsible parties. RCRA §7003 appears in, and is discussed in, the *NEPACCO* case addressed in Part A, Section 3 of this chapter. The extraordinary nature of the CERCLA §106 administrative order power is addressed in Part B.

Section 2. **THE GOVERNMENT'S RELAXED BURDEN OF PROOF OF CAUSATION IN CERCLA CASES**

The material in earlier chapters on toxic tort litigation emphasized the difficulty that plaintiffs encounter in proving that the defendant's activities are the cause in fact of plaintiffs' injuries. Even in a strict liability regime, that same difficulty could scuttle much of CERCLA's effectiveness if the government in every case had to trace each facet of cleanup costs to the actions of a particular PRP. Tracking the actions of a particular PRP in older sites or midnight dumping sites is especially problematic, where the records of what wastes were deposited by whom are sketchy or nonexistent. The courts began to confront this problem within the first years following CERCLA's enactment.

United States v. Wade (*Wade II*)
United States District Court for the Eastern District of Pennsylvania, 1983
577 F. Supp. 1326

[The Wade litigation involved a large disposal site in Chester, Pennsylvania. The site was an extraordinarily high-visibility one, having been the scene of a major fire in 1978 that damaged many of the several thousand tank cars and drums stored on the property. After testing discovered the presence of more than 50 hazardous substances at the site, many of which were leaking into the groundwater and from there into the Delaware River, legal action was instituted.

The Wade site was among the first sites for which the U.S. EPA sought remedies under RCRA and CERCLA. The litigation began in 1979 with the filing of a RCRA §7003 complaint. Shortly after the enactment of CERCLA in 1980, an amended complaint added counts under CERCLA §§106 and 107. The United States sought both injunctive relief as to the cleanup of the site and monetary relief for the response costs incurred by the government and others who had already undertaken steps to begin to seal the site and remove additional wastes still stored there. The parties sued by the United States included the site's owner (Wade), several off-site generators, and some of the transporters who had deposited materials at the site. Earlier litigation had focused on the scope and retroactivity of the major statutes; the excerpted portion of this decision addresses only the issue of proof of causation.]

NEWCOMER, J. This is a civil action brought by the United States against several parties allegedly responsible for the creation of a hazardous waste dump in Chester, Pennsylvania. The government seeks injunctive relief against Melvin R. Wade, the owner of the dump site, ABM Disposal Service, the company which transported the hazardous substances to the site, and Ellis Barnhouse and Franklin P. Tyson, the owners of ABM during the time period at issue ("non-generator defendants"). The government also seeks reimbursement of the costs incurred and to be incurred in cleaning up the site from the non-generator defendants as well as from Apollo Metals, Inc., Congoleum Corporation, Gould, Inc., and Sandvik, Inc. ("generator defendants").

The claims for injunctive relief are brought pursuant to §7003 of the Resource Conservation and Recovery Act of 1976 ("RCRA"), 42 U.S.C. §6973, and §106 of CERCLA, 42 U.S.C. §9606. The claims for monetary relief are based on §107(a) of CERCLA, 42 U.S.C. §9607(a), as well as a common law theory of restitution. Presently before the Court are the government's motions for partial summary judgment on the issue of joint and several liability under §107(a) against each of the defendants....

The generator defendants' motions for summary judgment on the CERCLA claims generally advance two arguments. First, they argue that the government has not and cannot establish the requisite causal relationship between their wastes and the costs incurred by the government in cleaning up the site....

The Causation Argument... Even assuming the government proves that a given defendant's waste was in fact disposed of at the Wade site, the generator defendants argue it must also prove that a particular defendant's actual waste is presently at the site and has been the subject of a removal or remedial measure before that defendant can be held liable. In the alternative, the generator defendants argue that at a minimum the government must link its costs incurred to waste of the sort created by a generator before that generator may be held liable....

Part of the generator defendants' argument revolves around the use of the word "such" in referring to the "hazardous substances" [in CERCLA §107(a)(3)] contained at the dump site or "facility." It could be read to require that the facility contain a particular defendant's waste. On the other hand it could be read merely to require that hazardous substances like those found in a defendant's waste must be present at the site. The legislative history provides no enlightenment on this point. I believe that the less stringent requirement was the one intended by Congress.

The government's experts have admitted that scientific technique has not advanced to a point that the identity of the generator of a specific quantity of waste can be stated with certainty. All that can be said is that a site contains the same kind of hazardous substances as are found in a generator's waste. Thus, to require a plaintiff under CERCLA to "fingerprint" wastes is to eviscerate the statute. Given two possible constructions of a statute, one which renders it useless should be rejected. Generators are adequately protected by requiring a plaintiff to prove that a defendant's waste was disposed of at a site and that the substances that make the defendant's waste hazardous are also present at the site....

I turn now to the generator defendants' contention that the government must link its costs incurred to wastes of the sort created by them.

A reading of the literal language of the statute suggests that the generator defendants read too much into this portion of its causation requirement. Stripping away the excess language, the statute appears to impose liability on a generator who has (1) disposed of its hazardous substances (2) at a facility which now contains hazardous substances of the sort disposed of by the generator (3) if there is a release of that or some other type of hazardous substance (4) which causes the incurrence of response costs. Thus, the release which results in the incurrence of response costs and liability need only be of "a" hazardous substance [the language of CERCLA §107(a)(4)] and not necessarily one contained in the defendant's waste. The only required nexus between the defendant and the site is that the defendant has dumped his waste there and that the hazardous substances found in the defendant's waste are also found at the site. I base my disagreement with defendants' reading in part on the Act's use of "such" to modify "hazardous substance" in paragraph three and the switch to "a" in paragraph four....

Deletion of the causation language contained in the House-passed bill and the Senate draft is not dispositive of the causation issue. Nevertheless, the substitution of the present language for the prior causation requirement evidences a legislative intent which is in accordance with my reading of the Act.

COMMENTARY & QUESTION

Comparison to toxic tort cases. How does the relaxation of the government's burdens in proving causation in CERCLA cases compare with the handling of burden of proof issues in traditional and toxic tort cases that were studied in earlier chapters?

Section 3. THE INDIVIDUAL LIABILITY OF MANAGERIAL OFFICERS

The focus of the Rich excerpt is personal individual liability for §107 recoveries. The typical cases in which this issue arises are those in which a hazardous waste generator, transporter, or disposer is a corporation, and a §107 action seeks to hold individual corporate officers or employees liable (for fiscal or punitive reasons). Their classic defense is to argue limited liability for corporate acts, the protective doctrine that provides such an important incentive to corporate entrepreneurialism. But courts increasingly have allowed application of individual personal liability for corporate officers under CERCLA and other statutes.

Analytically the cases fall into three categories. The first category, occurring most often in small, closely held corporations, involves piercing the corporate veil when corporate structure stands as an impediment to reaching the assets of individuals who have directly profited from the corporation's activities, even though they may not have been personally involved in day-to-day operations. These cases require the sorts of rigorous showings that are required in non-CERCLA veil-piercing cases.

The second class of cases involves officers held liable for their own wrongful personal actions, as, for example, where they themselves personally dumped toxics or directly ordered the illegal act.

The third class of cases involves individuals held liable because of their role as managerial officers, responsible for directing the corporate activity in which violations occurred. Several of these liability theories are explored further in the criminal law materials in Chapter 20, and in the following case arising under CERCLA and RCRA.

United States v. Northeastern Pharmaceutical & Chemical Co. (NEPACCO)
United States Court of Appeals for the Eighth Circuit, 1986
810 F.2d 726, cert. denied, 484 U.S. 848 (1988)

MCMILLIAN, J. Northeastern Pharmaceutical & Chemical Co. (NEPACCO), Edwin Michaels, and John W. Lee appeal from a final judgment entered in the District Court for the Western District of Missouri finding them and Ronald Mills jointly and severally liable for response costs incurred by the government after December 11, 1980, and all future response costs relative to the cleanup of the Denney farm site that are not inconsistent with the national contingency plan (NCP) pursuant to §§104 and 107 of the Comprehensive Environmental Response, Compensation, and Liability Act of 1980 (CERCLA), 42 U.S.C. §§9604, 9607....

The following statement of facts is taken in large part from the district court's excellent memorandum opinion, 579 F. Supp. 823 (W.D. Mo. 1984). NEPACCO was incorporated in 1966.... Although NEPACCO's corporate charter was forfeited in 1976 for failure to maintain an agent for service of process, NEPACCO did not file a certificate of voluntary dissolution with the secretary of state of Delaware. In 1974 its corporate assets were liquidated, and the proceeds were used to pay corporate debts and then distributed to the shareholders. Michaels [had] formed NEPACCO, was a major shareholder, and was its president. Lee was NEPACCO's vice-president, the supervisor of its manufacturing plant located in Verona, Missouri, and also a shareholder. Mills was employed as shift supervisor at NEPACCO's Verona plant.

From April 1970 to January 1972, NEPACCO manufactured the disinfectant hexachlorophene at its Verona plant. NEPACCO leased the plant from Syntex Agribusiness, Inc. (Syntex).... Michaels and Lee knew that NEPACCO's manufacturing process produced various hazardous and toxic byproducts, including 2,4,5-trichlorophenol (TCP), 2,3,7,8-tetrachlorodibenzo-p-dioxin (TCDD or dioxin), and toluene. The waste byproducts were pumped into a holding tank which was periodically emptied by waste haulers. Occasionally, however, excess waste byproducts were sealed in 55-gallon drums and then stored at the plant.

In July 1971 Mills approached NEPACCO plant manager Bill Ray with a proposal to dispose of the waste-filled 55-gallon drums on a farm owned by James Denney located about seven miles south of Verona. Ray visited the Denney farm and discussed the proposal with Lee; Lee approved the use of Mills' services and the Denney farm as a disposal site. In mid-July 1971 Mills and Gerald Lechner dumped approximately 85 of the 55-gallon drums into a large trench on the Denney farm (Denney farm site) that had been excavated by Leon Vaughn. Vaughn then filled in the trench. Only NEPACCO drums were disposed of at the Denney farm site.

In October 1979 the Environmental Protection Agency (EPA) received an anonymous tip that hazardous wastes had been disposed of at the Denney farm. Subsequent EPA investigation confirmed that hazardous wastes had in fact been disposed of at the Denney farm and that the site was not geologically suitable for the disposal of hazardous wastes. Between January and April 1980 the EPA prepared a plan for the cleanup of the Denney farm site and constructed an access road and a security fence. During April 1980 the EPA conducted an on-site investigation, exposed and sampled 13 of the 55-gallon drums, which were found to be badly deteriorated, and took water and soil samples. The samples were found to contain "alarmingly" high concentrations of dioxin, TCP and toluene.

In July 1980 the EPA installed a temporary cap over the trench to prevent the run-off of surface water and to minimize contamination of the surrounding soil and groundwater.... The 55-gallon drums are now stored in a specially constructed concrete bunker on the Denney farm. The drums as stored do not present an imminent and substantial endangerment to health or the environment; however, no plan for permanent disposal has been developed, and the site will continue to require testing and monitoring in the future.

In August 1980 the government filed its initial complaint against NEPACCO, the generator of the hazardous substances; Michaels and Lee, the corporate officers responsible for arranging for the disposal of the hazardous substances; Mills, the transporter of the hazardous substances; and Syntex, the owner and lessor of the Verona plant, seeking injunctive relief and reimbursement of response costs pursuant to RCRA §7003. In August 1982 the government filed an amended complaint adding counts for relief pursuant to CERCLA [which] was enacted after the filing of the initial complaint....

CERCLA Retroactivity: Application of CERCLA to Pre-1980 Acts... Appellants first argue the district court erred in applying CERCLA retroactively, that is, to impose liability for acts committed before its effective date, December 11, 1980. CERCLA §302(a) provides that "[u]nless otherwise provided, all provisions of this chapter shall be effective on December 11, 1980." Appellants argue that CERCLA should not apply to pre-enactment conduct that was neither negligent nor unlawful when committed. Appellants argue that all the conduct at issue occurred in the early 1970s, well before CERCLA became effective. Appellants also argue that there is no language supporting retroactive application in CERCLA's liability section, or in the legislative history. Appellants further argue that because CERCLA imposes a new kind of liability, retroactive application of CERCLA violates due process and the taking clause. We disagree.

The district court correctly found Congress intended CERCLA to apply retroactively. We acknowledge there is a presumption against the retroactive application of statutes. We hold, however, that CERCLA §302(a) is "merely a standard 'effective date' provision that indicates the date when an action can first be brought and when the time begins to run for issuing regulations and doing other future acts mandated by the statute."

Although CERCLA does not expressly provide for retroactivity, it is manifestly clear that Congress intended CERCLA to have retroactive effect. The language used in the key liability provision, CERCLA §107 refers to actions and conditions in the past tense: "any person who at the time of disposal of any hazardous substances owned or operated," CERCLA §107(a)(2), "any person who...arranged with a transporter for transport for disposal," CERCLA §107(a)(3), and "any person who...accepted any hazardous substances for transport to...sites selected by such person," CERCLA §107(a)(4).[9]

Further, the statutory scheme itself is overwhelmingly remedial and retroactive. CERCLA authorizes the EPA to force responsible parties to clean up inactive or abandoned hazardous substance sites, CERCLA §106, and authorizes federal, state and local governments and private parties to clean up such sites and then seek recovery of their response costs from responsible parties, CERCLA §§104, 107. In order to be effective, CERCLA must reach past conduct. CERCLA's backward-looking focus is confirmed by the legislative history. See generally H.R. Rep. No. 1016, 96th Cong., 2d Sess., reprinted in 1980 U.S. Code Cong. & Ad. News 6119 (CERCLA House Report). Congress intended CERCLA "to initiate and establish a comprehensive response and financing mechanism to abate and control the vast problems associated with abandoned and inactive hazardous waste disposal sites."

The district court also correctly found that retroactive application of CERCLA does not violate due process.... Appellants failed to show that Congress acted in an arbitrary and irrational manner. Cleaning up inactive and abandoned hazardous waste disposal sites is a legitimate legislative purpose, and Congress acted in a rational manner in imposing liability for the cost of cleaning up such sites upon those parties who created and profited from the sites and upon the chemical industry as a whole. We hold retroactive application of CERCLA to impose liability upon responsible parties for acts committed before the effective date of the statute does not violate due process.

[The opinion went on to demonstrate at some length that pre-1980 cleanup expenditures, as well as pre-1980 acts of dumping, were covered by CERCLA.]

RCRA: Standard and Scope of §7003 Liability... We have considered the 1984 amendments and the accompanying legislative history and, for the reasons discussed below, we believe the 1984 amendments support the government's arguments about RCRA's standard and scope of liability and retroactivity.

The critical issue is the meaning of the phrase "contributing to." Before its amendment in 1984, RCRA §7003(a), 42 U.S.C. §6973(a), imposed liability upon any person "contributing to" "the handling, storage, treatment, transportation or disposal of any solid or hazardous waste" that "may present an imminent and substantial endangerment to health or the environment." The district court did not find either the statutory language or the statutory framework helpful in determining whether past non-negligent off-site generators and transporters were liable under RCRA §7003(a) (prior to the 1984 amendments). The district court then considered the legislative history of the 1980 amendments because "[t]he legislative history of the [RCRA] as originally enacted contains no specific discussion of the reach of §7003 and no mention of the reasons for its insertion...."

Then, in November 1984, Congress passed and President Reagan signed the 1984 amendments which were described as "clarifying" amendments and specifically addressed the standard and scope of liability of §7003(a). As amended in 1984, RCRA §7003(a), 42 U.S.C. §6973(a) (1986) (new language italicized; deleted language in brackets), now provides in pertinent part:

> Notwithstanding any other provision of this chapter, upon receipt of evidence that the *past or present* handling, storage, treatment, transportation or disposal of any solid waste or hazardous waste may present an imminent and substantial endangerment to

---

9. The court in United States v. South Carolina Recycling & Disposal, Inc., 20 ERC (BNA) 1753, 1760 (D.S.C. 1984), noted that CERCLA does not apply "retroactively" because it does not impose liability for past conduct; rather, CERCLA imposes liability upon those parties responsible for causing certain conditions, that is, the release or threatened release of hazardous substances, that are the present or future results of their past actions.

health or the environment, the Administrator may bring suit on behalf of the United States in the appropriate district court [to immediately restrain any person] *against any person (including any past or present generator, past or present transporter, or past or present owner or operator of a treatment, storage, or disposal facility) who has contributed or who is* contributing to such handling, storage, treatment, transportation or disposal [to stop] *to restrain such person from* such handling, storage, treatment, transportation, or disposal [or to take such other action as may be necessary], *to order such person to take such other action as may be necessary, or both.*

As amended, RCRA §7003(a) specifically applies to past generators and transporters. Congress' intent with respect to the standard of liability under RCRA §7003(a) as amended by the 1984 amendments, is clearly set forth in the accompanying House Conference Report. The House Conference Report also expressly disapproved of the Wade and Waste Industries cases, which were relied upon by the NEPACCO [trial] court, as well as the NEPACCO [trial court] decision itself. The House Conference Report stated:

> Section 7003 focuses on the abatement of conditions threatening health and the environment and not particularly human activity. Therefore, it has *always reached those persons who have contributed in the past or are presently contributing to the endangerment, including but not limited to generators, regardless of fault or negligence.* The amendment, by adding the words "have contributed" is merely intended to clarify the existing authority. Thus, for example, *non-negligent generators whose wastes are no longer being deposited or dumped at a particular site may be ordered to abate the hazard to health or the environment posed by the leaking of the wastes they once generated and which have been deposited on the site.* The amendment reflects the long-standing view that generators and other persons involved in the handling, storage, treatment, transportation or disposal of hazardous wastes must share in the responsibility for the abatement of the hazards arising from their activities. The section was intended and is intended to abate conditions resulting from past activities. Hence, the district court decisions in United States v. Wade, 546 F. Supp. 785 (E.D. Pa. 1982), United States v. Waste Industries, Inc. 556 F. Supp. 1301 (E.D.N.C. 1983), and United States v. Northeastern Pharmaceutical & Chemical Co., 579 F. Supp. 823 (W.D. Mo. 1984), which restricted the application of section 7003, are inconsistent with the authority conferred by the section as initially enacted and with these clarifying amendments. H.R. Conf. Rep. No. 1133, 98th Cong., 2d Sess. 119 (1984) (emphasis added).

Thus, following the 1984 amendments, past off-site generators and transporters are within the scope of RCRA §7003(a). We reverse that part of the district court judgment holding that RCRA does not apply to past non-negligent off-site generators and transporters.

Scope of Liability... The district court found NEPACCO liable as the "owner or operator" of a "facility" (the NEPACCO plant) under CERCLA §107(a)(1) and as a "person" who arranged for the transportation and disposal of hazardous substances under CERCLA §107(a)(3). The district court found Lee liable as a "person" who arranged for the disposal of hazardous substances under CERCLA §107(a)(3) and as an "owner or operator" of the NEPACCO plant under CERCLA §107(a)(1) by "piercing the corporate veil." Id. at 848–849. The district court also found Michaels liable as an "owner or operator" of the NEPACCO plant under CERCLA §107(a)(1).

Appellants concede NEPACCO is liable under CERCLA §107(a)(3) for arranging for the transportation and disposal of hazardous substances at the Denney farm site. Because NEPACCO's assets have already been liquidated and distributed to its shareholders, however, it is unlikely that the government will be able to recover anything from NEPACCO.

Appellants argue (1) they cannot be held liable as "owners or operators" of a "facility" because "facility" refers to the place where hazardous substances are located and they did not own or operate the Denney farm site, (2) Lee cannot be held individually liable for arranging for the transportation and disposal of hazardous substances because he did not "own or possess" the hazardous substances and because he made those arrangements as a corporate officer or employee acting on behalf of NEPACCO, and (3) the district court erred in finding Lee and Michaels individually liable by "piercing the corporate veil." Appellants have not claimed that any of CERCLA's limited affirmative defenses apply to them.

The government argues Lee can be held individually liable without "piercing the corporate veil," under CERCLA §107(a)(3), and that Lee and Michaels can be held individually liable as "contributors" under RCRA §7003(a). For the reasons discussed below, we agree with the government's liability arguments.

Liability Under CERCLA §107(a)(1)... First, appellants argue the district court erred in finding them liable under CERCLA §107(a)(1) as the "owners and operators" of a "facility" where hazardous substances are located. Appellants argue that, regardless of their relationship to the NEPACCO plant, they neither owned nor operated the Denney farm site, and that it is the Denney farm site, not the NEPACCO plant, that is a "facility" for purposes of "owner and operator" liability under CERCLA §107(a)(1). We agree.

CERCLA defines the term "facility" in part as "any site or area where a hazardous substance has been deposited, stored, disposed of, or placed, or otherwise come to be located." CERCLA §101(9)(B); see New York v. Shore Realty Corp., 759 F.2d 1032, 1043 n.15 (2d Cir. 1985). The term "facility" should be construed very broadly to include "virtually any place at which hazardous wastes have been dumped, or otherwise disposed of." United States v. Ward, 618 F. Supp. at 895. In the present case, however, the place where the hazardous substances were disposed of and where the government has concentrated its cleanup efforts is the Denney farm site, not the NEPACCO plant. The Denney farm site is the "facility." Because NEPACCO, Lee and Michaels did not own or operate the Denney farm site, they cannot be held liable as the "owners or operators" of a "facility" where hazardous substances are located under CERCLA §107(a)(1).

Individual Liability Under CERCLA §107(a)(3)... CERCLA §107(a)(3) imposes strict liability upon "any person" who arranged for the disposal or transportation for disposal of hazardous substances. As defined by statute, the term "person" includes both individuals and corporations and does not exclude corporate officers or employees. Congress could have limited the statutory definition of "person" but chose not to do so. Compare CERCLA §101(20)(A)(limiting definition of "owner or operator"). Moreover, construction of CERCLA to impose liability upon only the corporation and not the individual corporate officers and employees who are responsible for making corporate decisions about the handling and disposal of hazardous substances would open an enormous, and clearly unintended, loophole in the statutory scheme.

First, Lee argues he cannot be held individually liable for having arranged for the transportation and disposal of hazardous substances under CERCLA §107(a)(3) because he did not personally own or possess the hazardous substances. Lee argues NEPACCO owned or possessed the hazardous substances.

The government argues Lee "possessed" the hazardous substances within the meaning of CERCLA §107(a)(3) because, as NEPACCO's plant supervisor, Lee had actual "control" over the NEPACCO plant's hazardous substances. We agree. It is the authority to control the handling and disposal of hazardous substances that is critical under the statutory scheme. The district court found that Lee, as plant supervisor, actually knew about, had immediate supervision over, and was directly responsible for arranging for the transportation and disposal of the NEPACCO plant's hazardous substances at the Denney farm site. We believe requiring proof of personal ownership or actual physical possession of hazardous substances as a precondition for liability under CERCLA §107(a)(3) would be inconsistent with the broad remedial purposes of CERCLA.

Next, Lee argues that because he arranged for the transportation and disposal of the hazardous substances as a corporate officer or employee acting on behalf of NEPACCO, he cannot be held individually liable for NEPACCO's violations. Lee also argues the district court erred in disregarding the corporate entity by "piercing the corporate veil" because there was no evidence that NEPACCO was inadequately capitalized, the corporate formalities were not observed, individual and corporate interests were not separate, personal and corporate funds were commingled or corporate property was diverted, or the corporate form was used unjustly or fraudulently.

The government argues Lee can be held individually liable, without "piercing the corporate veil," because Lee personally arranged for the disposal of hazardous substances in violation of CERCLA §107(a)(3). We agree. As discussed below, Lee can be held individually liable because he personally participated in conduct that violated CERCLA; this personal liability is distinct from the derivative liability that results from "piercing the corporate veil." "The effect of piercing a corporate veil is to hold the owner [of the corporation] liable. The rationale for piercing the corporate veil is that the corporation is something less than a bona fide independent entity." Donsco, Inc. v. Casper Corp., 587 F.2d 602, 606 (3d Cir. 1978). Here, Lee is liable because he personally participated in the wrongful conduct and not because he is one of the owners of what may have been a less than bona fide corporation. For this reason, we need not decide whether the district court erred in piercing the corporate veil under these circumstances.

We now turn to Lee's basic argument. Lee argues that he cannot be held individually liable for NEPACCO's wrongful conduct because he acted solely as a corporate officer or employee on behalf of NEPACCO. The liability imposed upon Lee, however, was not derivative but personal. Liability was not premised solely upon Lee's status as a corporate officer or employee. Rather, Lee is individually liable under CERCLA §107(a)(3) because he personally arranged for the transportation and disposal of hazardous substances on behalf of NEPACCO and thus actually participated in NEPACCO's CERCLA violations.

> A corporate officer is individually liable for the torts he [or she] personally commits [on behalf of the corporation] and cannot shield himself [or herself] behind a corpo-ration when he [or she] is an actual participant in the tort. The fact that an officer is acting for a corporation also may make the corporation vicariously or secondarily liable under the doctrine of respondeat superior; it does not however relieve the indi-vidual of his [or her] responsibility. Donsco, Inc. v. Casper Corp., 587 F.2d at 606.

Thus, Lee's personal involvement in NEPACCO's CERCLA violations made him individu-ally liable.

Individual Liability under RCRA §7003(a)... The district court did not reach the question of individual liability under RCRA because it concluded that RCRA did not impose liability upon past non-negligent off-site generators like NEPACCO.... RCRA is applicable to past non-negli-gent off-site generators. The government argues Lee and Michaels are individually liable as "contributors" under RCRA §7003(a). We agree.

RCRA §7003(a) imposes strict liability upon "any person" who is contributing or who has contributed to the disposal of hazardous substances that may present an imminent and substan-tial endangerment to health or the environment. As defined by statute, the term "person" includes both individuals and corporations and does not exclude corporate officers and employees. As with the CERCLA definition of "person," Congress could have limited the RCRA definition of "person" but did not do so. [Again] compare CERCLA §101(20)(A)(limiting definition of "owner and operator"). More importantly, imposing liability upon only the corporation, but not those corporate officers and employees who actually make corporate decisions, would be inconsistent with Congress' intent to impose liability upon the persons who are involved in the handling and disposal of hazardous substances.

Our analysis of the scope of individual liability under the RCRA is similar to our analysis of the scope of individual liability under CERCLA. NEPACCO violated RCRA §7003(a) by "contributing to" the disposal of hazardous substances at the Denney farm site that presented an imminent and substantial endangerment to health and the environment. Thus, Lee and Michaels can be held individually liable if they were personally involved in or directly responsible for corporate acts in violation of RCRA.

We hold Lee and Michaels are individually liable as "contributors" under RCRA §7003(a). Lee actually participated in the conduct that violated RCRA; he personally arranged for the transportation and disposal of hazardous substances that presented an imminent and substantial endangerment to health and the environment. Unlike Lee, Michaels was not personally involved in the actual decision to transport and dispose of the hazardous substances. As NEPACCO's corporate president and as a major NEPACCO shareholder, however, Michaels was the individual in charge of and directly responsible for all of NEPACCO's operations, including those at the Verona plant, and he had the ultimate authority to control the disposal of NEPACCO's hazardous substances. Cf. New York v. Shore Realty Corp., 759 F.2d at 1052-1053 (shareholder-manager held liable under CERCLA).

In summary, we hold Lee individually liable for arranging for the transportation and disposal of hazardous substances in violation of CERCLA §107(a)(3), and Lee and Michaels individually liable for contributing to an imminent and substantial endangerment to health and the environment in violation of RCRA §7003(a)....

Burden of Proof of Response Costs... The district court found appellants had the burden of proving the government's response costs were inconsistent with the NCP, and that response costs that are not inconsistent with the NCP are conclusively presumed to be reasonable and therefore recoverable.

We believe the district court's analysis is correct. CERCLA §107(a)(4)(A) states that the government may recover from responsible parties "all costs of removal or remedial action...not inconsistent with the [NCP]." The statutory language itself establishes an exception for costs that are inconsistent with the NCP, but appellants, as the parties claiming the benefit of the exception, have the burden of proving that certain costs are inconsistent with the NCP and, therefore, not recoverable.... Because determining the appropriate removal and remedial action involves specialized knowledge and expertise, the choice of a particular cleanup method is a matter within the discretion of the EPA. The applicable standard of review is whether the agency's choice is arbitrary and capricious.... Here, appellants failed to show that the government's response costs were inconsistent with the NCP. Appellants also failed to show that the EPA acted arbitrarily and capriciously in choosing the particular method it used to clean up the Denney farm site....

GIBSON, J. (concurring in part and dissenting in part). I concur with the court's opinion except for [those] parts holding that RCRA §7003(a) imposes liability on past off-site nonnegligent generators and transporters and determining that the government could recover its response costs from Lee and Michaels under §7003(a). I respectfully dissent from the court's opinion as to those points.

The majority's analysis of liability under the RCRA focuses exclusively on the legislative history of the 1984 amendments to the RCRA. The majority particularly rely on House Conference Report No. 1133, which singles out the district court's opinion and states that it is "inconsistent with the authority conferred by [§7003] as initially enacted and with these clarifying amendments." H.R. Conf. Rep. No. 1133, 98th Cong., 2d Sess. 119 (1984), reprinted in 1984 U.S. Code Cong. & Ad. News 5649, 5690. The Conference Report also states that §7003 "has always" reached nonnegligent generators and transporters. Id. From these statements, the majority conclude that "the 98th Congress made clear that the intention of the 94th Congress in enacting the RCRA in 1976 had been to impose liability upon past nonnegligent off-site generators and transporters of hazardous waste." Thus, the majority hold that the RCRA as it read prior to the 1984 amendments imposed strict liability upon past generators and transporters and that the district court erred in holding that proof of fault or negligence was necessary for the government to recover its response costs under the RCRA.

I think that the 1984 House Conference Report is nothing more than a blatant effort by members of a later Congress to graft their personal views of the scope of liability under the RCRA onto the original Act. It is bootstrapping, and the majority fail to recognize it as such. The Conference Report characterizes the 1984 amendments as "clarifying" the RCRA. The "clarifying" amendments to §7003, however, did not alter the crucial phrase "contributing to," the construction of which the majority acknowledge as "the critical issue," other than to cast it in both the present and the past tense: "has contributed to or...is contributing." 42 U.S.C. §6973(a). Nor do the amendments supply a definition for this phrase. The amendments to section 7003(a) are directed toward changing the scope of the section to reach past as well as present and future generators and transporters of hazardous waste. I believe this to be a substantive change, rather than a clarification. In any event, because the amendments did not relate to the "contributing to" language, the statements in the House Conference report regarding the standard of liability under §7003(a) — negligence versus strict liability — are wholly gratuitous.

COMMENTARY & QUESTIONS

1. **Private plaintiffs and cleanup legislation.** *NEPACCO*, like many other cases brought under RCRA and CERCLA, features the United States as plaintiff. Private plaintiffs may also sue to enforce those statutes. For example, a subsection of the citizen suit provision of RCRA, 42 U.S.C. §6972(a)(1), authorizes private suits to enforce violation of any of RCRA's regulatory mechanisms, or the imminent hazard provision (see Chapter 18). Still, even with the presence of a citizen suit provision allowing its enforcement, RCRA has been held to create no private cause of action for damages. See, e.g., Walls v. Waste Res. Corp., 761 F.2d 311 (6th Cir. 1985). CERCLA does allow private recovery of response costs, a matter that is considered more fully later in this chapter.

2. **Retroactivity.** The retroactive application of CERCLA continues to be quite perplexing to the courts, on both constitutional and statutory interpretation grounds. One federal court ruled that CERCLA could not be applied retroactively, only to have that decision reversed by the Eleventh Circuit in United States v. Olin Corp., 107 F.3d 1506 (11th Cir. 1997). The Eleventh Circuit concluded that an analysis of CERCLA's purpose, as evinced by its structure and legislative history, supported the view that Congress intended the statute to impose retroactive liability for cleanup of hazardous wastes. The

Eleventh Circuit noted that an essential purpose of CERCLA is to place ultimate responsibility for the cleanup of hazardous wastes on those persons responsible for the waste disposal, finding that this goal could be achieved only through retroactive application of CERCLA's liability provisions. The Eleventh Circuit also rejected the district court's determination that Congress's passage of CERCLA was an invalid exercise of power under the Commerce Clause, instead concluding that the regulation of intrastate, on-site waste disposal is an appropriate element of Congress's broader scheme to protect interstate commerce and industries from pollution.

3. **The strategy of avoiding §107 recoveries.** In *Wade I*, the government sought an injunctive order requiring the defendant generators to clean up the site under CERCLA §106. As noted previously, CERCLA provides for creation of a Superfund from which the government may draw to pay for the cleanup of hazardous waste contamination. The government, when it uses the fund to pay for cleanups, may then sue responsible parties to recoup sums spent and thereby replenish the fund. Given the existence of Superfund cleanup funding and recoupment provisions under §107 and of state law damage remedies, why would EPA seek such an order? Few, if any, of the parties ordered to clean a site are in a position to do the work themselves. Viewed in this light, the order to clean a site looks like an order to pay a contractor to clean the site, which looks like a damage remedy. When first authorized, Superfund had only $1.6 billion available under §107, and the pace of efforts that would have replenished the fund was slow. By obtaining relief under the imminent hazard prongs of RCRA §7003 and CERCLA §106, EPA could bypass the potential cash flow problem facing Superfund cleanups. EPA's position was validated by the fact that CERCLA reimbursement has been very problematic, with only a fraction of the money expended on Superfund cleanups having been recovered and put back into the fund.

4. **The relevance of the views of a subsequent Congress.** Who gets the better of the debate between the majority and the dissent in *NEPACCO* about the relevance of 1984 legislative history to the interpretation of 1980 language? What should not be obscured is that the 1984 Congress was free to adopt prospectively whatever rule it wanted; this is simply an exercise of its constitutional power to legislate granted by Article I. Whatever the state of prior legislation, a later Congress is not required to continue it unchanged. In contrast, what is involved here is the meaning of a provision that the 1980 Congress had enacted as law. Are questions of statutory interpretation to be decided by courts, not subsequent legislatures? What is the relevance of the views of members of a later Congress as evidence of what members of the 1980 Congress actually intended? Are these views legislative history?

5. **Arranging for disposal under CERCLA §107(a)(3).** The most far-reaching development in the *NEPACCO* case is its ruling that holds Michaels personally liable under RCRA §7003 as a person who "contributed" to the disposal of hazardous waste, even though Michaels was not involved in the day-to-day operations of the plant in Verona, Missouri. The key phrases in the court's holding on this point cast a broad net — Michaels was "the individual in charge and directly responsible...and he had ultimate authority to control the disposal of NEPACCO's hazardous substances." But that

description fits almost all chief operating officers of corporations. Looking at CERCLA §107(a)(3), can the "arranging for disposal" language of that liability section be read as broadly? One court has proposed a liability standard based on ability to prevent improper disposal:

> This standard is different, but more stringent on the whole than traditional corporate liability, yet it requires more than mere status as a corporate officer or director.... The test — whether the individual in a close corporation could have prevented or significantly abated the release of hazardous substances — allows the fact-finder to impose liability on a case-by-case basis.... Michigan v. ARCO Indus. Corp., 723 F. Supp. 1214, 1219 (W.D. Mich. 1989).

As discussed later in this chapter, setting appropriate limits on the scope of liability in "ability to control" situations has become an even hotter issue in other contexts. The ARCO Industries standard applies to close corporations, that is, corporations owned and controlled by just a few shareholders. Is there any reason why the same standard would not be equally well suited to determining liability of corporate officers in large publicly held corporations? See also United States v. TIC Inv. Corp., 68 F.3d 1082 (8th Cir. 1995) (holding an officer in a subsidiary corporation liable as an arranger for disposal of hazardous waste as a matter of law, where the officer did not delegate authority and left no room for others to exercise decisionmaking authority or judgment).

6. **Selling hazardous materials as a form of disposal.** Given the breadth of RCRA and CERCLA liability, is it possible that the sale of products that contain hazardous materials such as creosote (a wood preservative that is itself a hazardous substance) can be considered "arranging for disposal" of those materials under §107(a)(3) of CERCLA? Congress did not define the term "arranged" in the statute, and the courts have had to supply a definition. In general, the courts have been quick to reject liability, protecting the sellers of products containing hazardous substances from liability. But is this what Congress intended? See, e.g., Edward Hines Lumber Co. v. Vulcan Materials Co., 685 F. Supp. 651 (N.D. Ill.), aff'd on other grounds, 861 F.2d 155 (7th Cir. 1988); Amcast Indus. Corp. v. Detrex Corp., 2 F.3d 746 (7th Cir. 1993) (rejecting the assertion that any spillage constitutes disposal). See also Gaba, Interpreting §107(a)(3) of CERCLA: When Has a Person "Arranged for Disposal"?, 44 Sw. L.J. 1313 (1991).

7. **Processing hazardous materials through third parties as a form of disposal.** Another important issue under §107(a)(3) of CERCLA is whether companies owning a particular substance may be liable for disposal that occurs when a third party is processing or refining that substance. The decision by the Eighth Circuit in United States v. Aceto Agric. Chems. Corp., 872 F.2d 1373 (8th Cir. 1989) is instructive. There, the Eighth Circuit broadly construed the phase "arranged for disposal" in §107(a)(3) to include manufacturers who sent their pesticide ingredients to a formulator under a tolling agreement, where the formulation activities gave rise to contamination. The manufacturers argued that they could not be said to have "arranged for disposal" of any hazardous substances because they provided only base materials that were to be processed into a valuable product. Nonetheless, in denying a motion to dismiss, the court ruled that the manufacturers were potentially liable as "arrangers" for disposal:

> Defendants nonetheless contend they should escape liability because they had no authority to control Aidex's operations, and our *NEPACCO* decision states "[i]t is the authority to control the handling and disposal of hazardous substances that is critical under the statutory scheme."... In *NEPACCO*, we were confronted with the argument that only individuals who owned or possessed hazardous substances could be liable under CERCLA. We rejected that notion and imposed liability, in addition, on those who had the authority to control the disposal, even without ownership or possession.... Defendants in this case, of course, actually owned the hazardous substances, as well as the work in process. *NEPACCO* does not mandate dismissal of plaintiffs' complaint under these circumstances. 872 F.2d at 1381–1382.

Aceto has led to further analysis of the nature of "arranger" liability. Of particular note, in Morton Int'l v. A. E. Staley Mfg., 343 F.3d 669 (3d Cir. 2003), the Third Circuit dealt with a claim by the owner of a site previously used as a mercury processing plant for contribution from a pipeline company. The owner contended that the pipeline company was responsible for some of the cleanup costs at the site because the pipeline company allegedly "arranged for" the processing of mercury at the facility for many years, resulting in the release of hazardous wastes into the environment. At the outset of its analysis, the Third Circuit recognized that not only did Congress not define the term "arranged for" in CERCLA, but also that the standards adopted for "arranger liability" among the federal circuit courts vary. After reviewing these varying standards, the Third Circuit identified the principal factors necessary, in its view, to establishing the baseline for determining "arranger liability":

> In sum, we conclude that the analysis of "arranger liability" under Section 107(a)(3) should focus on these principal factors: (1) the ownership or possession of a material by the defendant; and (2) the defendant's knowledge that the processing of that material can or will result in the release of hazardous waste; or (3) the defendant's control over the production process. A plaintiff is required to demonstrate ownership or possession, but liability cannot be imposed on that basis alone. A plaintiff is also required to demonstrate either knowledge or control.... [I]t is certainly possible that other factors could be relevant to the analysis in a given case, and we encourage consideration of those as well. 343 F.3d at 678.

Applying this baseline analysis, the Third Circuit remanded for further proceedings because material factual issues remained with respect to the pipeline company's (1) ownership or possession of mercury, (2) knowledge of the environmental hazards of mercury processing at the plant, (3) control over the waste disposal practices at the plant, and (4) shipment of its own "dirty mercury" to the plant. To review the approaches of other federal circuits on "arranger liability," see Geraghty & Miller, Inc. v. Conoco Inc., 234 F.3d 917, 929 (5th Cir.), cert. denied, 533 U.S. 950 (2001); Freeman v. Glaxo Wellcome, Inc., 189 F.3d 160, 164 (2d Cir. 1999); Pneumo Abex Corp. v. High Point, Thomasville & Denton R.R., 142 F.3d 769, 775 (4th Cir. 1998); United States v. Cello-Foil Prods., Inc., 100 F.3d 1227, 1231-1232 (6th Cir. 1996); South Fla. Water Mgmt. Dist. v. Montalvo, 84 F.3d 402, 407 (11th Cir. 1996); Amcast Indus. Corp. v. Detrex Corp., 2 F.3d 746, 751 (7th Cir. 1993); and Jones-Hamilton Co. v. Beazer Materials & Servs., Inc., 973 F.2d 688, 695 (9th Cir. 1992).

8. **Recycling.** Where on the continuum between sale of a useful product and arranging for disposal does recycling fall? In early cases construing CERCLA, most courts ruled

that conventional recycling, even where the recycler paid for the used product, rendered the seller of the used product liable as an "arranger." See, e.g., Chesapeake & Potomac Tel. Co. of Va. v. Peck Iron & Metal Co., Inc., 814 F. Supp. 1269 (E.D. Va. 1992); but see Catellus Dev. Corp. v. United States, 828 F. Supp. 764 (N.D. Cal. 1993) (holding auto parts company not liable for sale of spent batteries to lead reclamation firm that caused release). As a result of these decisions, Congress became concerned that the imposition of arranger liability in the recycling context was working at cross purposes with the desirability of recycling when compared to the use of virgin raw materials. Congress responded with the Superfund Recycling Amendment (SREA), signed into law by President Clinton in November 1999. SREA exempts from liability under §107(a)(4) of CERCLA those persons who "arranged for the recycling" of a "recyclable material." SREA defines "recyclable materials" to include scrap paper, plastic, glass, textiles, rubber, metal, and spent batteries.

Section 4. THE CLASSES OF PARTIES WHO MAY BE HELD LIABLE UNDER CERCLA

CERCLA holds liable all persons or entities classified as "owners or operators" of treatment, storage, or disposal (TSD) facilities and as "generators"[10] and "transporters" of hazardous waste. These latter two terms are easily understood. "Owners or operators" is a more specialized term and is defined as follows by §101(20) of CERCLA:

> (A) The term "owner or operator" means (i) in the case of a vessel, any person owning, operating, or chartering by demise, such vessel, (ii) in the case of an onshore facility or an offshore facility, any person owning or operating such facility, and (iii) in the case of any facility, title or control of which was conveyed due to bankruptcy, foreclosure, tax delinquency, abandonment, or similar means to a unit of State or local government, any person who owned, operated or otherwise controlled activities at such facility immediately beforehand. Such term does not include a person, who, without participating in the management of a vessel or facility, holds indicia of ownership primarily to protect his security interest in the vessel or facility....

> (D) The term "owner or operator" does not include a unit of State or local government which acquired ownership or control involuntarily through bankruptcy, tax delinquency, abandonment, or other circumstances in which the government involuntarily acquires title by virtue of its function as sovereign. The exclusion provided under this paragraph shall not apply to any State or local government which has caused or contributed to the release or threatened release of a hazardous substance from the facility, and such a State or local government shall be subject to the provisions of this chapter in the same manner and to the same extent, both procedurally and substantively, as any nongovernmental entity, including liability under section 9607 of this title.

Despite the presence of an explicit statutory definition, the scope of the "owner or operator" provisions of CERCLA has proved particularly troublesome. The courts have played an important role in delineating the contours of hazardous waste liability through case law interpreting the statutory terms. Three major areas of litigation have emerged.

---

10. Generator liability is traceable to the previously reproduced provision in §107(a)(3) holding liable persons who arranged for disposal of hazardous materials that later are the subject of a removal or remedial action.

The first line of cases focuses on attempts to expand the class of operators. Many of these cases initially concerned the potential liability of lenders who made loans to operators of TSD facilities or to generators. Frequently, when the borrower encountered financial difficulty, the lender attempted to salvage its loan by becoming involved in the operation of the debtor's business. Not surprisingly, the presence of a solvent entity (the lender) participating in the affairs of a financially troubled TSD facility or generator has typically made an inviting target for a CERCLA plaintiff. After years of litigation, as detailed below, EPA sought and obtained a "legislative fix" in the form of an amendment to CERCLA that clarifies the scope of lender liability under the secured creditor exemption of CERCLA, §101(20)(A). [11]

The second line of cases concerns efforts to exonerate innocent purchasers of contaminated parcels from liability. As previously noted, current owners of contaminated property are liable under §107(a) unless they can establish an affirmative defense under §107(b). The first two of the defenses under §107(b) apply only when either an act of God (e.g., pollution caused by an earthquake and a subsequent flood) or an act of war (e.g., pollution caused by wartime bombing) is the sole cause of the release or threatened release and the resulting harm. See §107(b)(1) and (2). To date, these provisions have resulted in little relief for CERCLA defendants. [12] The third affirmative defense, §107(b)(3), applies if a party not in contractual privity with the person asserting the defense is the sole cause of the release or threatened release and the resulting harm. This defense protects property owners against unauthorized "midnight dumping." But under what circumstance does the defense protect predecessors in the chain of title, with whom there will often be a contractual relationship? Congress tried to clarify the third affirmative defense by amendments now codified in §101(35), as discussed more fully below.

The third line of cases focuses less on expanding the class of operators and more on expanding the class of owners. For the most part, these cases concern pinning down who really owns the facility. Here the issues involve corporate structures involving either the relationship of a parent corporation to a subsidiary or corporate succession. [13] These cases, as explained below, initially resulted in substantial disagreement among the federal circuit courts over (1) the circumstances under which a parent corporation will be found liable for environmental conditions caused by its subsidiary or (2) the circumstances under which a successor corporation is responsible for the liabilities of an entity it has taken over.

COMMENTARY & QUESTIONS

1. **The Superfund Amendments and Reauthorization Act of 1986 (SARA).** In 1986, Congress revisited a number of areas of CERCLA in a far-reaching set of amendments

---

11. That part of CERCLA §101(20)(A) known as the "secured creditor exemption" provides: "['Owner' or 'operator'] does not include a person, who, without participating in the management of a vessel or facility, holds indicia of ownership primarily to protect his security interest in the vessel or facility."

12. See, e.g., United States v. Stringfellow, 661 F. Supp. 1053, 1061 (C.D. Cal. 1987) (heavy but foreseeable rains do not constitute an act of God).

13. These issues are not limited to the ownership of TSD facilities but can also arise in the context of deciding who is a generator or transporter.

that also reauthorized the continuing operation of the Superfund system. Pub. L. No. 99-499. SARA, as the 1986 legislation is known, addressed a number of liability issues, usually in ways that confirmed broad judicial interpretations of the liability provisions. As in §101(35), Congress clarified a variety of questions about the scope of the statute. SARA did not cut back on the scope of CERCLA liability. To the contrary, the generally pro-liability posture of SARA led some experts in the field to suggest that its acronym ought to be changed to RACHEL because the Reauthorization Act Confirms How Everyone's Liable. See, e.g., United States v. Kramer, 757 F. Supp. 397 (D.N.J. 1991); Glass, Superfund and SARA: Are There Any Defenses Left?, 12 Harv. Envtl. L. Rev. 385 (1988). In the same vein, one commentator has written, "With only slight exaggeration, one government lawyer has described a [CERCLA] trial as requiring only that the Justice Department lawyer stand up and recite: 'May it please the Court, I represent the government and therefore I win.'" Marzulla, Superfund 1991: How Insurance Firms Can Help Clean Up the Nation's Hazardous Waste, 4 Tex. L. Rev. 685 (1989).

2. **Lender liability and the 1996 Superfund Amendments.** Although CERCLA's secured creditor exemption, §101(20)(A), was designed to protect lenders from strict CERCLA liability, for years there was vigorous litigation over the exemption's proper scope. The chief difficulty concerned the phrase "participating in the management." Some courts held that a lender did not participate in management unless it actually ran the vessel's or facility's operations. See, e.g., In re Bergsoe Metal Corp., 910 F.2d 668 (9th Cir. 1990). In contrast, other courts found creditors liable based simply on their capacity to control a vessel or facility's operations. See, e.g., United States v. Fleet Factors Corp., 901 F.2d 1550 (11th Cir. 1990). In light of these conflicting judicial interpretations, lenders faced great uncertainty concerning their potential exposure.

In attempting to alleviate this confusion, EPA promulgated regulations to define the secured creditor exemption's scope. EPA's lender liability rule, which was issued in April 1992 and codified at 40 C.F.R. §300.1100(c), was short-lived. In response to industry challenges, the D.C. Circuit vacated the rule, holding its promulgation to be beyond EPA's statutory authority. Kelley v. EPA, 15 F.3d 1100 (D.C. Cir. 1994), cert. denied sub nom. American Bankers Ass'n v. Kelley, 513 U.S. 1110 (1995). Two years later, in response to the *Kelley* decision and the continuing uncertainty surrounding the secured creditor exemption, Congress amended CERCLA in the Asset Conservation, Lender Liability, and Deposit Insurance Act, Pub. L. No. 104-208 (the "1996 Act").

The 1996 Act effectively overruled the *Kelley* decision by statutorily reinstating EPA's lender liability rule. The 1996 Act amended CERCLA's definition of "owner or operator" to clarify that most routine lending activities do not constitute "participating in the management" of a vessel or facility. Instead, CERCLA now provides that a lender cannot be liable as an owner or operator unless the lender "actually participates in the management or operational affairs of a vessel or facility." See §101(20)(E)-(G). In addition, the 1996 Act specified that the following activities, routinely performed by lenders in administering a loan, do not amount to "participating in the management" of a vessel or facility: holding, abandoning, or releasing a security interest; including a covenant or warranty of environmental compliance in a loan or security instrument; monitoring or enforcing the terms and conditions of a loan instrument; monitoring or inspecting a facility or vessel; requiring the borrower to address a release or threatened release of hazardous substances; providing financial advice to the borrower or otherwise taking steps to prevent diminution of value of collateral; restructuring or renegotiating the terms of a loan or security interest; exercising available remedies for breach of a condition of the loan; and conducting a response action under the direction of state or federal on-site officials. Id. Perhaps most significantly, the 1996 Act attempted to clarify when creditors may foreclose on property without risking liability. The 1996 Act allows a lender to foreclose and wind up operations as long as it subsequently divests the property at the "earliest practicable, commercially reasonable time, on commercially reasonable terms, taking into account market conditions and legal and regulatory requirements." See §101(20)(E)(ii)(II). For further details on the events leading to the promulgation of the 1996 Act, see EPA Policy on Interpreting CERCLA Provisions, Addressing Lenders and Involuntary Acquisitions by Government Entities, 21 BNA Env't Rep. 5981 (1997).

3. **How the courts make CERCLA liability policy.** After reviewing the preceding notes' forays into the nuts and bolts of CERCLA liability, the prominent role of courts in framing the contours of CERCLA as part of a case-by-case development should be apparent. What is less clear is whether the courts are interpreting statutes or making law. In any event, the courts are not merely engaged in a rote process of statutory interpretation that deduces the intent of Congress through a series of simple logical steps. The process of judicial interpretation frequently calls upon courts to weigh and balance competing policy concerns, giving the process of statutory interpretation much of the same dynamism as the common law. The Sixth Circuit, in a successor liability case, reflected on the role of courts in these terms:

> The Supreme Court has stated that "the authority to construe a statute is fundamentally different from the authority to fashion a new rule or to provide a new remedy which Congress has decided not to adopt." Northwest Airlines, Inc. v. Transport Workers Union of America, 451 U.S. 77, 97 (1981). As Justice Stevens wrote in *Northwest Airlines*, "Broadly worded constitutional and statutory provisions necessarily have been given concrete meaning and application by a process of case-by-case judicial decisions in the common-law tradition." Id. at 95.

> Of course, the line separating statutory interpretation and judicial lawmaking is not always clear and sharp. If a statute is found to be abundantly clear and well defined, a judicial decision that expands or contracts its reach or adds or deletes remedies fashions federal common law. On the other hand, if the court detects only gaps in definitions or descriptions, it may fill these interstices of the statute by exercising its authority to interpret or construe the statute. As the Supreme Court has stated, these two exercises of judicial authority are fundamentally different, and they are subject to different standards. The authority to construe a statute lies at the very heart of judicial power and is not subject to rigorous scrutiny. The rule is otherwise with respect to outright judicial lawmaking, however. Before a federal court may fashion a body of federal common law, it must find either (1) that Congress painted with a broad brush and left it to the courts to "flesh out" the statute by fashioning a body of substantive federal law, or (2) that a federal rule of decision is necessary to protect uniquely federal interests. Anspec Co. v. Johnson Controls, Inc., 922 F.2d 1240, 1245 (6th Cir. 1991).

4. **Would you buy this land?** Assume that you are a commercial investor and are aware of a contaminated parcel that is otherwise well suited for investment. Should you purchase the property? Under CERCLA §101(35), as a purchaser of the property with knowledge of its contamination, you would be liable for cleanup costs as a responsible party. If the sum of the purchase price plus the cost of cleanup is sufficiently low that the parcel freed of contamination is worth more than that sum, the purchase should be consummated. In the case of badly contaminated parcels, however, the cleanup costs alone often dwarf the "clean" market value of the parcel. Those are problem cases for society because one important goal of CERCLA is (or ought to be) the return of contaminated sites to productive use. In the past few years, there has been substantial legislative action seeking to encourage the redevelopment of contaminated brownfields on both the federal and state levels. In late 2001, for example, Congress passed the Small Business Liability Relief and Brownfields Revitalization Act, which was designed to encourage the development and reuse of brownfields, especially where the level of pollution is not so severe that the brownfields are designated as cleanup "priorities" by the EPA or by state environmental agencies. This Act, which signifies a policy of greater regulatory flexibility and cooperation by EPA and the states in the enforcement of the environmental laws, is detailed more fully in Chapter 21.

5. **The "act of a third party" defense.** CERCLA §107(b)(3), set forth in the first section of this chapter, permits a defense when the hazardous release or threatened release is caused solely by the act of a third party with whom the defendant has little or no relation. Section 101(35) in relevant part reads as follows:

(A) The term "contractual relationship," for the purpose of §9607(b)(3) of this title includes, but is not limited to, land contracts, deeds or other instruments transferring title or possession, unless the real property on which the facility concerned is located was acquired by the defendant after the disposal or placement of the hazardous substance on, in, or at the facility, and one or more of the circumstances described in clause (i), (ii), or (iii) is also established by the defendant by a preponderance of the evidence:

(i) At the time the defendant acquired the facility the defendant did not know and had no reason to know that any hazardous substance which is the subject of the release or threatened release was disposed of on, in, or at the facility.

(ii) The defendant is a government entity which acquired the facility by escheat, or through any other involuntary transfer or acquisition, or through the exercise of eminent domain authority by purchase or condemnation.

(iii) The defendant acquired the facility by inheritance or bequest. In addition to establishing the foregoing, the defendant must establish that he has satisfied the requirements of §9607(b)(3)(a) and (b) of this title.

(B) To establish that the defendant had no reason to know, as provided in clause (i) of subparagraph (A) of this paragraph, the defendant must have undertaken, at the time of acquisition, all appropriate inquiry into the previous ownership and uses of the property consistent with good commercial or customary practice in an effort to minimize liability. For purposes of the preceding sentence the court shall take into account any specialized knowledge or experience on the part of the defendant, the relationship of the purchase price to the value of the property if uncontaminated, commonly known or reasonably ascertainable information about the property, the obviousness of the presence or likely presence of contamination at the property, and the ability to detect such contamination by appropriate inspection....

Consider whether that defense is available in the following hypothetical situation: Buyer is considering acquiring a piece of commercial property that shows no obvious signs of contamination. Under what circumstances, if any, will Buyer be free from §107(a)(1) owner's liability if, in the future, it is discovered that previously disposed of hazardous substances are buried under the surface and are releasing toxic contaminants into the groundwater? Does being in the chain of title, without more, vitiate the defense? Or to vitiate the defense, must the contractual relationship relate to the hazardous substances being released? See New York v. Lashins Arcade Co., 91 F.3d 353 (2d Cir. 1996) (holding that a purchaser established a defense to CERCLA liability under §107(b)(3), where the purchase contract did not relate to the hazardous substances or allow the purchaser to exert control over the seller's activities). In this connection, does it matter if a "release" of contaminants is active or, in the alternative, simply the result of prolonged passive migration? See Nurad Inc. v. William E. Hooper & Sons Co., 966 F.2d 837 (4th Cir. 1992); United States v. CDMG Realty Co., 96 F.3d 706 (3d Cir. 1996). For more on the issue of the "due care" required of "innocent" landowners, see Hernan, Due and Don't Care Under CERCLA: An Emerging Standard for Current Owners, 27 Envtl. L. Rep. 10064 (1997); see also Caplan, Escaping CERCLA Liability: The Interim Owner Passive Migration Defense Gains Circuit Recognition, 28 Envtl. L. Rep. 10121 (1998).

6. **Insurance.** CERCLA has created a high-stakes specialized cottage industry in the litigation of defense against claims and the pollution exclusion clause sections of insurance policies. The most readily understood of these cases arise initially when a facility owner PRP receives a PRP letter and looks to its insurer to provide (and pay for) the costs of defending the claim. Later, after being held liable, the PRP seeks indemnification from the insurer. The cases, in the main, involve comprehensive general liability policies (CGL), many of which included a "pollution exclusion" clause that excepted ordinary pollution but covered "sudden and accidental" events. See, e.g., Allstate Ins. Co. v. Klock Oil Co., 426 N.Y.S.2d 603, 604 (N.Y. 1980). Pollutants leaching into groundwater over many years, a typical CERCLA scenario, have proven hard to classify. Intra-insurer conflicts arise because of the durational aspect of the cases — CGL policies cover specific periods of time, but the leaking may have occurred over a period of years, implicating a whole series of insurance policies that may have been issued by different insurers and leading as well to litigation over whether such releases are "sudden and accidental."

7. **Insolvency.** Insolvency issues have led the development of CERCLA into another area of law, that of bankruptcy. A fundamental tension exists between the remedial goals and aspirations of CERCLA and the objectives of bankruptcy law. One goal of bankruptcy law is to distribute the bankrupt's assets fairly among all of the creditors. A second objective is to provide the bankrupt with a fresh start, freed of the previous debts. In contrast, a central concern animating CERCLA is assuring the availability of sufficient resources for the cleanup of hazardous release sites. Accordingly, CERCLA has

a strong interest in making all the bankrupt's assets, both present and future, available to remediate the hazards that the PRP bankrupt has helped to create. This CERCLA-based interest collides with bankruptcy law, when bankruptcy law seeks to protect co-creditors through a fair division of the available assets. Specifically, bankruptcy law gives preference to secured creditors over unsecured creditors, as the government would be in regard to a CERCLA recovery. As a second matter, under normal bankruptcy law, the debtor can expect to be absolved from personal post-bankruptcy obligations relating to CERCLA liabilities. Congress did nothing to broker the competition between these two statutory children, CERCLA and the bankruptcy act, so that task has fallen to the courts. This seemingly narrow area of intersection has its own treatise. See K. R. Heidt, Environmental Obligations in Bankruptcy (2002).

Section 5. CORPORATE LIABILITIES UNDER CERCLA

"The time has come," the walrus said, "to talk of many things...of 'subsids,' parents, shareholders, of cabbages and kings." The courts consistently have construed CERCLA's scope of liability broadly in a variety of contexts that involve scrutinizing a corporation's form. For a number of years, various federal circuits went beyond the traditional common law doctrine that allows for piercing the corporate veil when corporate form is being used as a sham to defraud creditors. To go beyond traditional rules of corporate law in imposing liability on owners of corporations is a very delicate matter because one of the principal assurances of corporate form is that only corporate assets are put at risk by corporate activities; personal assets of a corporation's owners are not supposed to be put at risk. As a matter of policy, adherence to this general principle is quite important. Limited liability invites the formation of new companies that may or may not survive, and is thus vital to economic innovation and dynamism. Shareholder immunity from liability is likewise a vital element in capital formation. Without it, shareholders would be inhibited from purchasing stock as a form of investment in corporations.

Despite these dangers, CERCLA liability was initially extended in certain federal courts beyond the traditional limits of corporate law in a number of disparate settings, as the courts struggled with whether a parent company could be liable under CERCLA by exercising control over its subsidiaries. In June 1998, this issue reached the Supreme Court.

United States v. BestFoods Corporation
Supreme Court of the United States, 1998
524 U.S. 51

[In this case, the U.S. Supreme Court addressed whether a parent corporation that actively participated in and exercised control over the operations of a polluting subsidiary may be held liable. The United States brought the action under §107(a)(2) for the costs of cleaning up industrial waste. The BestFoods Corporation just happened to be the case's first-named defendant; it was an "arranger"; the issue in the case, however, deals with whether a parent corporation, CPC International (which spun off the subsidiary Ott II that "operated" a CERCLA-liable facility in Muskegon, Michigan), is itself an "operator."

The chemical plant involved in the case had been owned by different companies over a 30-year period and had caused substantial contamination. The federal government sued several defendants to recover the money it had spent cleaning up the site. The district court found the parent corporation liable under CERCLA as a former "owner or operator" of the subsidiary's plant because, in part, the parent had appointed its employees as officers and directors of the subsidiary. On appeal, the Sixth Circuit reversed in a 7-6 en banc decision, concluding that where a parent corporation was not directly involved in the operations of a subsidiary's facility as a joint venturer or co-operator, it could not be held liable under CERCLA as an "owner or operator" simply because it exercised corporate oversight of a subsidiary's affairs, except when the requirements of piercing the corporate veil could be met under state law. Thereafter, the Supreme Court granted certiorari.]

SOUTER, J. The United States brought this action for the costs of cleaning up industrial waste generated by a chemical plant. The issue before us, under CERCLA, is whether a parent corporation that actively participated in, and exercised control over, the operations of a subsidiary may, without more, be held liable as an operator of a polluting facility owned or operated by the subsidiary. We answer no, unless the corporate veil may be pierced. But a corporate parent that actively participated in, and exercised control over, the operations of the facility itself may be held directly liable in its own right as an operator of the facility....

III. It is a general principle of corporate law deeply "ingrained in our economic and legal systems" that a parent corporation (so-called because of control through ownership of another corporation's stock) is not liable for the acts of its subsidiaries.... Thus it is hornbook law that "the exercise of the 'control' which stock ownership gives to the stockholders...will not create liability beyond the assets of the subsidiary. That 'control' includes the election of directors, the making of by-laws...and the doing of all other acts incident to the legal status of stockholders. Nor will a duplication of some or all of the directors or executive officers be fatal." Although this respect for corporate distinctions when the subsidiary is a polluter has been severely criticized in the literature,...nothing in CERCLA purports to reject this bedrock principle, and against this venerable common-law backdrop, the congressional silence is audible.... The Government has indeed made no claim that a corporate parent is liable as an owner or an operator under §107 simply because its subsidiary is subject to liability for owning or operating a polluting facility.

But there is an equally fundamental principle of corporate law, applicable to the parent-subsidiary relationship as well as generally, that the corporate veil may be pierced and the shareholder held liable for the corporation's conduct when, inter alia, the corporate form would otherwise be misused to accomplish certain wrongful purposes, most notably fraud, on the shareholder's behalf.... Nothing in CERCLA purports to rewrite this well-settled rule, either. CERCLA is thus like many another congressional enactment in giving no indication "that the entire corpus of state corporation law is to be replaced simply because a plaintiff's cause of action is based upon a federal statute," and the failure of the statute to speak to a matter as fundamental as the liability implications of corporate ownership demands application of the rule that "[i]n order to abrogate a common-law principle, the statute must speak directly to the question addressed by the common law."... The Court of Appeals was accordingly correct in holding that when (but only when) the corporate veil may be pierced, may a parent corporation be charged with derivative CERCLA liability for its subsidiary's actions.

IV. A. If the act rested liability entirely on ownership of a polluting facility, this opinion might end here; but CERCLA liability may turn on operation as well as ownership, and nothing in the statute's terms bars a parent corporation from direct liability for its own actions in operating a facility owned by its subsidiary. As Justice (then-Professor) Douglas noted almost 70 years ago, derivative liability cases are to be distinguished from those in which "the alleged wrong can seemingly be traced to the parent through the conduit of its own personnel and management" and "the parent is directly a participant in the wrong complained of."... In such instances, the parent is directly liable for its own actions.... The fact that a corporate subsidiary happens to own a polluting facility operated by its parent does nothing, then, to displace the rule that the parent "corporation is [itself] responsible for the wrongs committed by its agents in the course of its business,"...and whereas the rules of veil-piercing limit derivative liability for the actions of another corporation, CERCLA's "operator" provision is concerned primarily with direct liability for one's own actions.... It is this direct liability that is properly seen as being at issue here.

Under the plain language of the statute, any person who operates a polluting facility is directly liable for the costs of cleaning up the pollution. See 42 U.S.C. §9607(a)(2). This is so regardless of whether that person is the facility's owner, the owner's parent corporation or business partner, or even a saboteur who sneaks into the facility at night to discharge its poisons out of malice. If any such act of operating a corporate subsidiary's facility is done on behalf of a parent corporation, the existence of the parent-subsidiary relationship under state corporate law is simply irrelevant to the issue of direct liability....

This much is easy to say; the difficulty comes in defining actions sufficient to constitute direct parental "operation." Here of course we may again rue the uselessness of CERCLA's definition of a facility's "operator" as "any person...operating" a facility, 42 U.S.C. §9601(20)(A)(ii), which leaves us to do the best we can to give the term its "ordinary or natural meaning...." So, under CERCLA, an operator is simply someone who directs the workings of, manages, or conducts the affairs of a facility. To sharpen the definition for purposes of CERCLA's concern with environmental contamination, an operator must manage, direct, or conduct operations specifically related to pollution, that is, operations having to do with the leakage or disposal of hazardous waste, or decisions about compliance with environmental regulations.

IV. B. With this understanding, we are satisfied that the Court of Appeals correctly rejected the District Court's analysis of direct liability. But we also think that the appeals court erred in limiting direct liability under the statute to a parent's sole or joint venture operation, so as to eliminate any possible finding that CPC is liable as an operator on the facts of this case.

By emphasizing that "CPC is directly liable under §107(a)(2) as an operator because CPC actively participated in and exerted significant control over Ott II's business and decision-making," 777 F. Supp., at 574, the District Court applied the "actual control" test of whether the parent "actually operated the business of its subsidiary," id., at 573, as several Circuits have employed it....

The well-taken objection to the actual control test, however, is its fusion of direct and indirect liability; the test is administered by asking a question about the relationship between the two corporations (an issue going to indirect liability) instead of a question about the parent's interaction with the subsidiary's facility (the source of any direct liability). If, however, direct liability for the parent's operation of the facility is to be kept distinct from derivative liability for the subsidiary's own operation, the focus of the inquiry must necessarily be different under the two tests. "The question is not whether the parent operates the subsidiary, but rather whether it operates the facility, and that operation is evidenced by participation in the activities of the facility, not the subsidiary. Control of the subsidiary, if extensive enough, gives rise to indirect liability under piercing doctrine, not direct liability under the statutory language.... The District Court was therefore mistaken to rest its analysis on CPC's relationship with Ott II, premising liability on little more than "CPC's 100-percent ownership of Ott II" and "CPC's active participation in, and at times majority control over, Ott II's board of directors." 777 F. Supp., at 575. The analysis should instead have rested on the relationship between CPC and the Muskegon facility itself....

In imposing direct liability..., the District Court failed to recognize that...it is entirely appropriate for directors of a parent corporation to serve as directors of its subsidiary, and that fact alone may not serve to expose the parent corporation to liability for its subsidiary's acts.... This recognition that the corporate personalities remain distinct has its corollary in the "well established principle [of corporate law] that directors and officers holding positions with a parent and its subsidiary can and do 'change hats' to represent the two corporations separately, despite their common ownership." Lusk v. Foxmeyer Health Corp., 129 F.3d 773, 779 (5th Cir. 1997); see also Fisser v. International Bank, 282 F.2d 231, 238 (2d Cir. 1960). Since courts generally presume "that the directors are wearing their 'subsidiary hats' and not their 'parent hats' when acting for the subsidiary"...it cannot be enough to establish liability here that dual officers and directors made policy decisions and supervised activities at the facility. The Government would have to show that, despite the general presumption to the contrary, the officers and directors were acting in their capacities as CPC officers and directors, and not as Ott II officers and directors, when they committed those acts. The District Court made no such inquiry here, however, disregarding entirely this time-honored common law rule.

In sum, the District Court's focus on the relationship between parent and subsidiary (rather than parent and facility), combined with its automatic attribution of the actions of dual officers and directors to the corporate parent, erroneously, even if unintentionally, treated CERCLA as though it displaced or fundamentally altered common law standards of limited liability. Indeed, if the evidence of common corporate personnel acting at management and directorial levels were enough to support a finding of a parent corporation's direct operator liability under CERCLA, then the possibility of resort to veil piercing to establish indirect, derivative liability for the subsidiary's violations would be academic. There would in essence be a relaxed, CERCLA-specific rule of derivative liability that would banish traditional standards and expectations from the law of CERCLA liability. But, as we have said, such a rule does not arise from congressional silence, and CERCLA's silence is dispositive.

We accordingly agree with the Court of Appeals that a participation-and-control test looking to the parent's supervision over the subsidiary, especially one that assumes that dual officers always act on behalf of the parent, cannot be used to identify operation of a facility resulting in direct parental liability. Nonetheless, a return to the ordinary meaning of the word "operate" in the organizational sense will indicate why we think that the Sixth Circuit stopped short when it confined its examples of direct parental operation to exclusive or joint ventures, and declined to find at least the possibility of direct operation by CPC in this case....

Again norms of corporate behavior (undisturbed by any CERCLA provision) are crucial reference points. Just as we may look to such norms in identifying the limits of the presumption that a dual officeholder acts in his ostensible capacity, so here we may refer to them in distinguishing a parental officer's oversight of a subsidiary from such an officer's control over the operation of the subsidiary's facility. "[A]ctivities that involve the facility but which are consistent with the parent's investor status, such as monitoring of the subsidiary's performance, supervision of the subsidiary's finance and capital budget decisions, and articulation of general policies and procedures, should not give rise to direct liability...." The critical question is whether, in degree and detail, actions directed to the facility by an agent of the parent alone are eccentric under accepted norms of parental oversight of a subsidiary's facility.

There is, in fact, some evidence that CPC engaged in just this type and degree of activity at the Muskegon plant. The District Court's opinion speaks of an agent of CPC alone who played a conspicuous part in dealing with the toxic risks emanating from the operation of the plant. G.R.D. Williams worked only for CPC; he was not an employee, officer, or director of Ott II..., and thus, his actions were of necessity taken only on behalf of CPC. The District Court found that "CPC became directly involved in environmental and regulatory matters through the work of...Williams, CPC's governmental and environmental affairs director. Williams...became heavily involved in environmental issues at Ott II." 777 F. Supp., at 561. He "actively participated in and exerted control over a variety of Ott II environmental matters," ibid., and he "issued directives regarding Ott II's responses to regulatory inquiries," id., at 575.

We think that these findings are enough to raise an issue of CPC's operation of the facility through Williams's actions, though we would draw no ultimate conclusion from these findings at this point. Not only would we be deciding in the first instance an issue on which the trial and appellate courts did not focus, but the very fact that the District Court did not see the case as we do suggests that there may be still more to be known about Williams's activities. Indeed, even as the factual findings stand, the trial court offered little in the way of concrete detail for its conclusions about Williams's role in Ott II's environmental affairs, and the parties vigorously dispute the extent of Williams's involvement. Prudence thus counsels us to remand, on the theory of direct operation set out here, for reevaluation of Williams's role, and of the role of any other CPC agent who might be said to have had a part in operating the Muskegon facility....

COMMENTARY & QUESTIONS

1. **Piercing the corporate veil.** Does the *BestFoods* decision simply involve the application of traditional corporate law principles? Justice Souter, writing for a unanimous Supreme Court, began his analysis by emphasizing the general corporate principle of law that a parent corporation is not liable for the acts of its subsidiary simply by virtue of stock ownership or because it exercised supervision over its subsidiary. Justice Souter went on to declare that the CERCLA statute, despite its public purpose of furthering cleanups, did not alter this "bedrock principle." The Supreme Court upheld the Sixth Circuit's ruling that a parent corporation could be held derivatively liable for the acts of its subsidiary only where the corporate veil could be pierced under common law. The common law exceptions to the limited liability principle include the failure of the subsidiary to maintain the corporate formalities and the use of the subsidiary for a fraudulent purpose. Absent proof of one of these traditional exceptions, the common law principle that parent corporations could not be held derivatively liable would control in a CERCLA case.

2. **Operator liability of the parent corporation.** Does the *BestFoods* decision simply involve the application of standard "operator" liability concepts under CERCLA? After analyzing parent corporation liability under corporate law principles, Justice Souter turned to the question of whether CERCLA's creation of "operator" liability expanded the circumstances under which parent corporations may be held liable. Here, the Court began the analysis by focusing on the distinction between "operating" a facility or site and "operating" a subsidiary. In the Supreme Court's analysis, "operator" liability under CERCLA is predicated on the actions that a person or corporation performs directly to operate a facility, not on its control of another company that owns the site. Thus, the Court acknowledged that a parent corporation may be held directly liable under CERCLA where its own employees direct or control environmental activities at a facility,

but not where it simply exercises control of the subsidiary that owns the site through the normal mechanisms of corporate governance. In this respect, the Supreme Court was careful to clarify that a parent corporation does not become an "operator" of a subsidiary's facility through the routine practice of supervising the subsidiary's business. A parent corporation's routine supervision of a subsidiary could include appointing a subsidiary's officers and directors, monitoring its performance, supervising the subsidiary's finances, approving budgets and capital expenditures, and even articulating general policies and procedures for the subsidiary. All of these practices fall within the normal scope of the parent-subsidiary relationship and do not give rise to operator liability under CERCLA. Instead, to incur liability, a parent or its representatives must engage in actions that "are eccentric under the accepted norms of parental oversight of a subsidiary's facility."

3. **Parent corporation liability through the acts of officers and directors.** In assessing the liability arising from actions of officers and directors, does the *BestFoods* decision again simply apply established principles? Justice Souter specifically addressed the question of whether the parent corporation may incur liability through the acts of officers and directors who hold positions in both the parent corporation and its subsidiary. Justice Souter reasoned that it is typical corporate practice for the same individual to hold positions in both companies, and that the general rule is that where a dual office holder acts in the capacity of an officer or director of the subsidiary, the law presumes that the officeholder is acting on behalf of the subsidiary and not the parent. The presumption can be overcome, however, where the dual officeholder acts contrary to the interest of the subsidiary and to the advantage of the parent.

4. **What types of acts are enough for "operator" liability to attach for parent corporations?** The Court indicated that for a parent corporation to be held liable as an operator, it must have acted directly to control the operations of the facility, not to have simply supervised the business of its subsidiary. The Supreme Court identified four situations in which the parent company may be directly liable under CERCLA:

1. where the parent company actually directed operations at a site owned by one of its subsidiaries, such as when a parent had leased property from its subsidiary to conduct its own operations;
2. where a parent corporation participated in a joint venture with its subsidiary;
3. where an officer or director who holds positions in both the parent and the subsidiary abuses his or her position in the subsidiary by making decisions concerning hazardous waste or environmental compliance that, under the norms of corporate behavior, are not in the interest of the subsidiary and are to the advantage of the parent; and
4. where an employee of the parent, who holds no position in the subsidiary, directly controls those operations at the site that involve hazardous substances or environmental compliance.

Are there any other situations in which the parent company may itself be directly liable? What specific type of evidence would be required to establish parental liability?

5. **After *BestFoods*, will it be more difficult to hold parent corporations liable under CERCLA for contamination at their subsidiary's sites?** Much of the evidence upon

which the government has traditionally relied in suing parent corporations is likely insufficient to establish CERCLA liability after *BestFoods*. In the past, the government built many of its cases against parent corporations by showing that the same individuals were officers or directors of both the parent and the subsidiary, that the parent established general policies and practices for the subsidiary to follow, and that the parent's approval was necessary before the subsidiary could make substantial expenditures. Now this evidence will be viewed as indicative of normal parent-subsidiary relationships and, without additional facts, not proof of CERCLA liability. To hold a parent company liable, the government will have to meet either the common law standards of piercing the corporate veil or show that the parent directly controlled environmental activities at the subsidiary's site.

6. **After *BestFoods*, may a parent corporation rely on its own environmental management staff to supervise its subsidiary's compliance without risk of Superfund liability?** The *BestFoods* decision indicates that a parent company may risk CERCLA liability if it assigns its own environmental affairs manager to supervise its subsidiary's compliance, unless that manager also holds a position in the subsidiary. Does this suggest that a parent company should be cautious to make sure that its subsidiary has its own environmental management staff, even if that staff includes individuals who hold dual positions with the parent and the subsidiary?

7. **Successor corporations.** Often one corporation will purchase the productive assets of another, either via merger, through the purchase of stock, or through the purchase of the assets themselves. Corporate law has developed general principles that establish when successor corporations will be held to have purchased the liabilities of their predecessors. EPA has issued the following guidance document that sets forth its general approach to issues of corporate succession:

> In establishing successor liability under CERCLA, the Agency should initially utilize the "continuity of business operation" approach of federal law. However, to provide additional support or an alternative basis for successor corporation liability, the Agency should be prepared to apply the traditional exemptions to the general rule of non-liability in asset acquisitions. EPA Memorandum of Courtney Price, Liability of Corporate Shareholders and Successor Corporations for Abandoned Sites Under [CERCLA] 15–16 (June 13, 1984).

At least one commentator has argued that this position marks a substantial expansion of successor liability because the continuation of the business entity test ignores the nuances of asset transfer that are often a key to determining successor liability under traditional state corporation law. See Wallace, Liability of Corporations and Corporate Officers, Directors, and Shareholders Under Superfund: Should Corporate and Agency Law Concepts Apply?, 14 J. Corp. L. 839, 879–884 (1989). The business continuation standard, instead, has its roots in the modern products liability revolution that has so greatly expanded liability in that realm.

In general, the courts have been receptive to imposing successor liability in CERCLA cases, particularly where the predecessor corporation would have been a PRP at the site. See, e.g., Smith Land & Improvement Corp. v. Celotex Corp., 851 F.2d 86 (3d Cir. 1988); Louisiana-Pacific Corp. v. Asarco, Inc., 909 F.2d 1260 (9th Cir. 1990); United States v.

Mexico Feed & Seed Co., 980 F.2d 478 (8th Cir. 1992); City Envtl. Inc. v. U.S. Chem. Co., 814 F. Supp. 624 (E.D. Mich. 1993); see also Atchison, Topeka & Santa Fe Ry. v. Brown & Bryant Inc., 159 F.3d 358 (9th Cir. 1998) (questioning whether federal rather than state common law should govern successor liability under CERCLA). The traditional corporate law dividing line for liability in these cases is often linked to whether the entity is a mere asset purchaser (nonliability for the past actions of the seller) or a corporate successor (liability). CERCLA has pushed the precedents that are used to recognize corporate successorship to where liability can, at times, be found in cases where it would not have in the past. These areas are usually referred to as "continuing business enterprise" cases and "product line" cases. For a succinct summary of the developments in these areas, as well as an overview of the general distinction between successorship and asset purchases, see Janke & Kuryla, Environmental Liability Risks for Asset Purchasers, 24 BNA Env't Rep. 2237 (1994). The courts generally have also been receptive to efforts by parties to modify successor liability by contract, typically through the use of indemnification agreements. See, e.g., Mardan Corp. v. C.G.C. Music, Ltd., 804 F.2d 1454 (9th Cir. 1986) (upholding claim by purchaser against seller under indemnity agreement); AM Int'l, Inc. v. International Forging Equip. Corp., 982 F.2d 989 (6th Cir. 1993) (ruling that §107(e) of CERCLA does not bar indemnification agreements).

Section 6. PRIVATE LITIGATION UNDER CERCLA §107

Under §107(a)(2)(B), even nongovernmental entities are accorded a remedy to recover for costs that are consistent with the National Contingency Plan (NCP).[14] In this way, CERCLA expressly authorizes private litigants to seek recoveries from PRPs. This cause of action is complementary to causes of action that may exist under the common law, for the allowable scope of recovery relates exclusively to costs that are incurred in the cleanup of a contaminated site. Items such as recovery for personal injuries, or loss of amenity value, remain the province of traditional actions in tort.

The typical scenarios of private §107 actions involve current owners of contaminated property as plaintiffs suing either former occupiers of the property, parties whose wastes were disposed of there, or parties whose wastes have migrated there.[15] In some cases, the current owner will already have been ordered to clean the site by the government; in other cases, the cleanup effort may have preceded governmental involvement. For some time, there was ambiguity about whether costs could be incurred consistent with the NCP in advance of a governmentally initiated investigation or cleanup order and still be recoverable. That issue has been the subject of ongoing debate, as detailed more fully below.

The private cause of action under §107 has four basic elements: the plaintiff must prove that (1) the site in question is a "facility," (2) the defendant is a liable party under CERCLA §107(a), (3) a release or threatened release of a hazardous substance has

---

14. The NCP is discussed more fully below. For present purposes, the NCP can be understood as a set of guidelines framed by the United States that delineate the proper procedures and actions that are to be taken in cleaning up a Superfund site.

15. Adversely affected adjacent landowners are also allowed to sue. See, e.g., Standard Equip., Inc. v. Boeing Co., No. C84-1129 (W.D. Wash. 1986).

occurred at the facility, and (4) the plaintiff has incurred response costs consistent with the NCP in responding to the release or threatened release. Given the broad readings given to CERCLA liability issues, the consistency (with the NCP) requirement has often been the most ardently litigated issue in private §107 suits.[16]

General Elec. Co. v. Litton Indus. Automation Sys., Inc., 920 F.2d 1415 (1990), cert. denied, 499 U.S. 937 (1991), a leading case on consistency with the NCP, concerned the merger by Litton with a former owner and occupant of land now owned by GE. From 1959 to 1962, during the occupancy of the company taken over by Litton, improper disposal of cyanide-based electroplating wastes, sludges, and other pollutants had occurred on the parcel. In the early 1980s, GE and the Missouri Department of Natural Resources (MDNR) investigated the site and decided that no cleanup was necessary. In 1984, GE sold the site to a commercial real estate developer. Shortly thereafter, the MDNR changed its position on the need for a cleanup, at which point GE was threatened with CERCLA lawsuits by both its vendee and MDNR. Negotiations followed in which GE agreed to clean up the site and did so to the satisfaction of MDNR.

Thereafter GE sued Litton under §107. Litton's most vigorous defense was that the cleanup was not consistent with the NCP. The district court ruled in favor of GE, awarding $940,000 as reimbursement for response costs and an additional $419,000 in attorneys' fees. See General Elec. Co. v. Litton Bus. Sys., 715 F. Supp. 949 (W.D. Mo. 1989). In reviewing the critical finding that the costs incurred were consistent with the NCP despite having omitted some detailed requirements mentioned in the NCP, the court wrote:

> We are satisfied that the thorough evaluation that was performed here is consistent with the NCP, specifically with 40 C.F.R. §300.65(b)(2). The site evaluation does not have to comply strictly with the letter of the NCP, but only must be consistent with its requirements. It is not necessary that every factor mentioned by the NCP be dealt with explicitly; thus, for instance, a failure to consider explicitly the weather conditions factor is not fatal to an evaluation's consistency with the NCP. 920 F.2d at 1420.

COMMENTARY & QUESTIONS

1. **The purpose of the consistency requirement.** Why must cleanups be consistent with the NCP to allow recovery in a §107 action? Why isn't the key issue whether the response action was effective? One answer was suggested by counsel for Litton in the oral argument in the Eighth Circuit when he indicated that defendants in private cost recovery suits need protection from parties that voluntarily perform "a Rolls-Royce cleanup when a Volkswagen one would do." See 5 Tex. L. Rev. 651 (1990). (The issue of "Cadillac cleanups" is discussed below.) On the other end of the scale, NCP-consistent cleanups are a means of guaranteeing that the effort is effective. Particularly under the revised NCP, satisfying its requirements would help to ensure an effective cleanup and also involve community sentiment as a factor in the cleanup process.

---

16. See Steinway, Private Cost Recovery Actions Under CERCLA: The Impact of the Consistency Requirements, 4 Tex. L. Rev. 1364 (1990).

2. **Standing in the shoes of the government.** In a private §107 action, should the plaintiff enjoy all of the same advantages (joint and several strict liability with a relaxed standard of causation) as the government does when it sues PRPs? In general, the cases seem to point in that direction. In Dedham Water Co. v. Cumberland Farms Dairy, Inc., 889 F.2d 1146 (1st Cir. 1989), for example, the appeals court reversed a ruling that had required the plaintiff to prove which of two possible sources had caused the contamination of its well that had given rise to CERCLA response costs. The court drew heavily on the liberal liability provisions of CERCLA to find that "a literal reading of the statute imposes liability if releases or threatened releases from defendant's facility cause the plaintiff to incur response costs; it does not say that liability is imposed only if the defendant causes actual contamination of the plaintiff's property." Does it seem odd to hold a party like Cumberland Farms liable when the facts as found by the trial court (and not overturned on appeal) were that two other nearby operations "were 'probable' causes" of the contamination of plaintiff's wells? Is this like the *Wade II* relaxed standard of causation that, in effect, treats all parties whose acts are potential causes of the pollution as being actual causes of the problem?

3. **Private CERCLA lawsuits seeking contribution.** Are all CERCLA §107 private actions in reality claims for contribution? The answer is clearly no because the plaintiff in a §107 suit will at times be a party who is not a PRP, such as an innocent neighbor such as Dedham Water Company. Often, however, the plaintiff will be a PRP who has paid a disproportionate share and seeks to use a §107 action to vindicate the statutory right of contribution created by §113(f)(1). When the suit sounds in contribution, the issue of loss allocation includes assigning a share to the plaintiff, and the rote application of strict joint and several liability of defendants for the entire loss is no longer appropriate. In this context, the differences between private cost recovery and contribution have recently increased in importance. Case law has emerged that distinguishes private cost recovery suits filed under §107(a) from contribution actions filed under §113(f)(1). The principal reason to characterize a suit as one or the other is the posture of the party bringing the suit — is the party an innocent victim of the contamination (§107 available) or a member of the PRP class (only §113 available)? See, e.g., Pinal Creek Group v. Newmont Mining Corp., 118 F.3d 1298 (9th Cir. 1997); Rumpke of Ind., Inc. v. Cummins Engine Co., 107 F.3d 1235 (7th Cir. 1997); United Techs. Corp. v. Browning-Ferris Indus., 33 F.3d 96 (1st Cir. 1994); Akzo Coatings v. Aigner Corp., 30 F.3d 761 (7th Cir. 1994); In re Dant & Russell, 951 F.2d 246 (9th Cir. 1989). With the loss of cost recovery under §107 goes the loss of joint and several liability and a shift to an equitable contribution action in which the plaintiff (and all of the other parties) have to try to persuade the trier of fact of how responsibility ought to be apportioned. But there are other differences as well, including a different and shorter (three years rather than six) statute of limitations. See Araiza, Text, Purpose, and Facts: The Relationship Between CERCLA Sections 107 and 113, 72 Notre Dame L. Rev. 193 (1996); Evans, The Phantom PRP in CERCLA Contribution Litigation: EPA to the Rescue?, 26 BNA Env't Rep. 2109 (1996).

4. **The hotly debated issue of whether contribution exists for voluntary cleanup actions.** On January 9, 2004, the Supreme Court agreed to consider whether a potentially responsible party under CERCLA must first be subject to a CERCLA claim before it

is permitted to bring a §113 contribution claim to recover remediation costs. Section 113, by its express terms, provides that a claim for contribution may be brought "during or following" a claim brought under §106 or under §107. However, the last sentence of §113 provides that "nothing [in Section 113] shall diminish the right...to bring an action for contribution in the absence of a civil action [under CERCLA]." These two provisions seemingly conflict and have caused confusion regarding when it is permissible to bring a CERCLA contribution claim.

In Cooper Industries, Inc. v. Aviall Services, Inc., 312 F.3d 677 (5th Cir. 2002), responding to direction from the Texas environmental agency, Aviall cleaned up contamination on its property. Aviall tried to recover its cleanup costs by suing the property's former owner, Cooper, under §113. A divided Court of Appeals for the Fifth Circuit ruled that a PRP, such as Aviall, may sue at any time to recover response costs. Cooper then asked the Supreme Court to consider the question, and the Supreme Court asked the U.S. Solicitor General to provide his opinion on whether the Court should consider this issue of statutory interpretation. The Solicitor urged the Court to reverse the Fifth Circuit as a matter of statutory construction and to protect the federal courts from the "substantial burden of resolving these complex cases." The Supreme Court granted Cooper's and the Solicitor General's request for a review of this issue.

In its en banc ruling, the Fifth Circuit held that a PRP could bring a §113 action against another PRP even if the plaintiff has not been the subject of a preceding §107 cost recovery action or a §106 order compelling the cleanup. In reaching this result, the full court emphasized that the right to bring a contribution claim had been recognized, based on federal common law, before the statutory authority was created in SARA. Section 113(f) was added in 1986 to reflect the development of the right to contribution. The Fifth Circuit concluded that "it would seem odd that a legislature concerned with clarifying the right to contribution among PRPs...would have...cut back the then prevailing standard for contribution."

Despite a multitude of district court rulings on the issue, *Aviall* was the first appellate decision squarely to decide whether a contribution claim under CERCLA is proper in the absence of a §106 or §107 claim. The regulated community was discouraged by the prospect that, if *Aviall* were decided differently by the Fifth Circuit, a responsible party would not be able to seek contribution unless it was first sued under §107 or faced EPA administrative orders under §106. The Supreme Court will now decide whether Aviall misreads or misinterprets §113(f), on the grounds that §113(f) requires that a PRP face a cost recovery action under §107 or an EPA order under §106 before contribution can be sought under §113(f).

If the Supreme Court rules that a party must be subject to a CERCLA lawsuit before it can bring a CERCLA contribution claim under §113, many PRPs may cease conducting remediation activities without first being required to do so, potentially disrupting "voluntary" remediation programs currently ongoing throughout the country. Moreover, if the Supreme Court were to rule in Cooper's favor, other PRPs in currently pending CERCLA actions would, like Aviall, lose their ability to recover remediation costs under federal law. In light of the negative impact on state remediation programs, would such a ruling by the Supreme Court likely prompt calls for a legislative response by Congress?

5. **A reminder about state law remedies.** Even if it borders on redundancy, it is important to keep in mind the continuing availability of state statutory and common law remedies for environmental harms caused by hazardous materials. Despite the broad federal efforts to govern hazardous groundwater contamination, reflected in both RCRA and CERCLA, Congress was well aware that it was entering a field having a strong tradition of state regulatory and remedial primacy. Both RCRA and CERCLA contain provisions extending authority to states to enact additional more stringent measures.[17] Beyond that, §114(a) of CERCLA provides:

> Nothing in this chapter shall be construed or interpreted as pre-empting any State from imposing any additional liability or requirements with respect to the release of hazardous substances within such State.[18]

6. **Attorneys' fees awards in CERCLA cases.** As with so many CERCLA issues, the recoverability of attorneys' fees as a part of §107(a)(4)(b) response costs is an issue not answered by the statute or its legislative history. The general argument in favor of allowing fee recovery looks at the statutory language as indicating a desire that all costs of remediation are covered, even those that are incurred in obtaining the remedy. At a policy level, the argument stresses that the remedial nature of the statute evidences congressional intent that plaintiffs who have incurred costs of any kind should be made whole. Standing in opposition to these arguments are more traditional notions grounded in the American rule against fee shifting. Eventually, this issue found its way to the U.S. Supreme Court. In Key Tronic Corp. v. United States, 511 U.S. 809 (1994), the Court ruled that CERCLA §107 does not provide for the award of private litigants' attorneys' fees associated with bringing a cost recovery action.

B. EPA'S ADMINISTRATIVE ORDER PROCESS

In creating CERCLA's liability rules, Congress empowered EPA to remediate contaminated sites itself, using federal money, and also allowed EPA to recover its expenditures from persons responsible for the contamination. In passing CERCLA, however, Congress also established another powerful mechanism for use by EPA in seeking to remediate contaminated sites. In CERCLA §106, Congress empowered EPA to bring administrative or judicial enforcement actions against responsible parties to force them to perform the remediation. EPA's administrative order authority provides EPA with perhaps its most potent enforcement tool (see Chapter 21). By its terms,

---

17. RCRA §3009, codified at 24 U.S.C. §6929; CERCLA §114(a), codified at 42 U.S.C. §9614(A).

18. Despite this expressly nonpreemptive character, there are narrow areas of state legislative authority that are preempted by CERCLA and RCRA. These cases arise when states enact their own mini-Superfund laws and fund them via a tax like that used to fund CERCLA. See Exxon Corp. v. Hunt, 475 U.S. 355 (1986). There have also been cases preempting local regulation of RCRA-regulated waste handling facilities. See ENSCO Inc. v. Dumas, 807 F.2d 743 (8th Cir. 1986) (preempting local waste handling regulations that bar methods encouraged by RCRA). The preemption of common law by statutes is generally disfavored; the canon of statutory construction cautions that statutes in derogation of common law are to be narrowly construed.

§106 authorizes EPA to seek relief whenever it determines that a site "may" present "an imminent and substantial endangerment to public health or...the environment." It authorizes EPA to issue "such orders as may be necessary to protect public health and welfare and the environment." The key text is as follows:

42 U.S.C. §9606 [original Act's §106]. **Abatement actions.**

(a) Maintenance, jurisdiction, etc. In addition to any other action taken by a State or local government, when the President determines that there may be an imminent and substantial endangerment to the public health or welfare or the environment because of an actual or threatened release of a hazardous substance from a facility, he may require the Attorney General of the United States to secure such relief as may be necessary to abate such danger or threat, and the district court of the United States in the district in which the threat occurs shall have jurisdiction to grant such relief as the public interest and the equities of the case may require. The President may also, after notice to the affected State, take other action under this section including, but not limited to, issuing such orders as may be necessary to protect public health and welfare and the environment....

(b) Fines; reimbursement. (1) Any person who, without sufficient cause, willfully violates, or fails or refuses to comply with, any order of the President under subsection (a) of this section may...be fined not more than $25,000 for each day in which such violation occurs or such failure to comply continues....

Section 106 is often invoked by EPA to encourage PRPs to do more of the removal and remedial work at sites themselves. When a voluntary agreement to do so cannot be reached (or when a previous agreement is breached), EPA may require PRPs to respond. EPA states its policy as follows:

EPA prefers to obtain private-party response action through the negotiation of settlement agreements with parties willing to do the work. When viable private parties exist and are not willing to reach a timely settlement to undertake work under a consent order or decree, or prior to settlement discussions in appropriate circumstances, the Agency typically will compel private-party response through unilateral orders. If PRPs do not comply with the order, EPA may fund the response or may refer the case for judicial action to compel performance and recover penalties. EPA, OSWER Directive No. 9833.0–1a, at 3 (Mar. 7, 1990).

Section 106(a) administrative orders cannot be disobeyed without substantial risk. Section 106(b)(1) allows EPA to come to court and seek a fine of up to $25,000 per day against "[a]ny person who, without sufficient cause, willfully violates, or fails or refuses to comply with, any order...." Most courts have concluded that, in connection with whether the defendant in a §106 order is a proper PRP, the relevant liability principles, both with respect to the identity of the parties and the applicable standards of liability, are established by §107. See, e.g., United States v. A&F Materials Co., 578 F. Supp. 1249, 1257–1258 (S.D. Ill. 1984).

Alternatively, pursuant to CERCLA §107(c)(3), EPA can undertake the abatement action itself and then sue for reimbursement and statutory punitive damages "in an amount at least equal to, and not more than three times" the amount of the cost of the government action! There is nothing in the statutory language to suggest that EPA cannot seek both the daily penalties and the punitive damages in cases where EPA eventually undertakes the work.

Administrative orders are even more powerful because they are not subject to pre-enforcement review. CERCLA §113(h) explicitly provides that no federal court has jurisdiction "to review any challenges to...any order issued under §9606(a) [CERCLA §106(a)]...." The jurisdictional proviso lists a number of exceptions, only one of which can take place before the required action has been performed. That one exception is a suit brought by EPA to compel a remedial action. See CERCLA §113(h)(5). Courts interpret the law to prevent pre-enforcement review. In so doing, the courts have repeatedly rejected constitutional attacks that challenge the Hobson's choice (take expensive action pursuant to an administrative order that you allege to be illegal, or risk a far more costly array of punitive sanctions if your post-cleanup attack on the order fails) as being a denial of due process. See, e.g., North Shore Gas Co. v. EPA, 753 F. Supp. 1413 (N.D. Ill. 1990), aff'd, 930 F.2d 1239 (7th Cir. 1991); Aminoil, Inc. v. EPA, 599 F. Supp. 69 (N.D. Cal. 1984).

Defense of subsequent suits seeking sanctions for noncompliance with §106(a) orders is also difficult. The defendant-violator has the burden of proving that there was "sufficient cause" for noncompliance. This amounts to proving that either (1) the defendant was not a person to whom the order could have been issued (i.e., was not a PRP), or (2) the actions ordered were inconsistent with the NCP. Making the sufficient cause defense even harder to establish, most courts require that the defendant, by objective evidence, prove that its belief in the invalidity of the order was held reasonably and in good faith. See Donald, Defending Against Daily Fines and Punitive Damages Under CERCLA: The Meaning of "Without Sufficient Cause," 19 Colum. J. Envtl. L. 185 (1994).

Wary of EPA's enforcement priorities and unhappy with the Hobson's choice posed by §106, the regulated community continues to seek ways to thwart the formidable §106 power. The latest challenge came from General Electric, which, amidst great fanfare, sought a declaratory judgment that §106, in tandem with §107(c)(3) and §113(h) of CERCLA, together create a regime that violates due process. GE argued that these sections fail to provide any hearing or other procedural safeguards before EPA issues a §106 order, contrary to fundamental due process requirements. EPA responded by urging dismissal of GE's lawsuit, on the grounds that §113(h) postpones judicial review of any challenges to EPA action — including constitutional challenges to the law itself — until EPA seeks to enforce its remedial actions in court.

In a ruling issued in March 2003, a federal district court granted EPA's motion to dismiss. General Elec. v. Whitman, 257 F. Supp. 2d 8 (D.D.C. 2003). In reaching this result, the district court found that both the language of §113(h) and congressional intent, as discerned in the legislative history, support the finding that judicial review of EPA's enforcement actions may be postponed until EPA brings legal action in a court of law against a potentially responsible party. According to the district court, the language of §113(h) reflects Congress's broad intent to limit judicial review of EPA enforcement actions or orders. The district court noted that Congress employed the term "any" three times in the section to prohibit pre-enforcement judicial review in the most sweeping terms. The court reasoned that to find, as GE argued, that EPA's interpretation of CERCLA is unconstitutional could result in challenges to virtually every other hazardous waste site. Deferring GE's constitutional challenge to a later day, the court concluded that GE's attack upon the statutory scheme did not enable GE to avoid the prohibition on pre-enforcement review.

COMMENTARY & QUESTIONS

1. **EPA's use of its §106 power.** Given the formidable §106 power, it might seem strange that EPA does not always make administrative cleanup orders its remedial method of choice. Walter Mugdan, EPA Deputy Regional Counsel for Region II, listed six reasons why EPA would still prefer to negotiate consent decrees for remedial (as opposed to removal) actions. These included setting the proper tone for the long-term relationship that is entailed in EPA supervision of a PRP-conducted cleanup, rewarding volunteers (by working out fair agreements) and punishing recalcitrants, the congressional policy favoring settlements, judicial supervision of court orders, the availability of CERCLA §122(l) civil penalties, and the availability of CERCLA §122(e)(3)(B) administrative subpoenas to compel testimony and the production of information. See Mugdan, The Use of CERCLA Section 106 Administrative Orders to Secure Remedial Action, in ALI-ABA, Study Materials on Hazardous Wastes, Superfund, and Toxic Substances 601-603 (Oct. 25–27, 1990).

2. **Punitive treble damages.** Despite its presence in CERCLA since original enactment in 1980, the treble damage remedy has not been frequently used. United States v. Parsons, 723 F. Supp. 757 (N.D. Ga. 1989), marked the first time that treble damages had been awarded for noncompliance with a CERCLA §106(a) order.[19] After subsequent litigation over the issue of whether one of the Parsons defendants had made a good faith effort at compliance with the order, the court entered judgment for EPA in the amount of $2,260,173.72, based on proven EPA response costs of $753,391.24. EPA sought reconsideration of the award, arguing that it was entitled to both the response costs and the penalty. The district court ruled against awarding EPA "quadruple" damages. United States v. Parsons, 738 F. Supp. 1436 (N.D. Ga. 1990), but was reversed on appeal, United States v. Parsons, 936 F.2d 336 (11th Cir. 1991) (holding that the federal government could recover four times the amount that EPA spent to clean up a site).

3. **Agency leverage or abuse of power?** The power to seek treble damages is, obviously, a significant tool. In bringing its constitutional challenge, what risks was GE seeking to avoid? Is the district court correct that GE can seek meaningful review after the EPA seeks enforcement of its orders or site remediation is complete? The district court concluded that delaying GE's challenge would not undermine GE's ability to raise it later. But how many years will go by, and how much in the way of resources would GE need to commit to site remediation and cleanup, before a future constitutional challenge could be raised? Does it matter that GE, a large industrial conglomerate with deep pockets, will likely have the staying power to raise its challenge even after cleanup? Would most PRPs have the financial wherewithal to bring such challenges after site

---

19. See EPA Granted Damages for Company's Failure to Obey 106 Order to Perform Response Action, 4 Toxics L. Rep. 515 (1989).

remediation is complete? How much confidence do you have that EPA will use its §106 leverage prudently, without abusing the power that such leverage provides?

4. **Chasing recalcitrant parties.** Does EPA have the power under §106 to pursue recalcitrant parties when other PRPs have previously agreed to perform the necessary response actions? Is EPA entitled to seek "duplicate recovery" on the grounds that recalcitrant parties are also jointly and severally liable? If EPA lacks this power, will recalcitrants be even less willing to join a settling group if the threat of sanctions under §106 no longer looms over them?

5. **The common law, §106, and RCRA corrective action.** What does CERCLA §106 accomplish that the common law does not? Section 106 makes prospective relief routinely available. Under the common law, it is only the extraordinary case that prevents a harm before it happens. Section 106 offers an extrajudicial remedy: EPA can go to court, but it can also issue its own administrative orders against polluters. RCRA §7003 also offers EPA an extrajudicial remedy. Under RCRA §7003, EPA can go to court (as in *NEPACCO*), but EPA can also issue "such orders as may be necessary to protect public health and the environment." However, RCRA corrective action is not governed by the same set of liability rules as CERCLA §106. For example, under RCRA, a party may, in connection with corrective action, move or excavate soil within a corrective action management unit (CAMU) without liability attaching. Movement of waste within a CAMU does not constitute treatment, storage, or disposal of hazardous waste under RCRA, does not constitute "land disposal" triggering RCRA hazardous waste disposal requirements, and does not "produce" hazardous waste implicating RCRA generator requirements. Under CERCLA, by contrast, a party that moves or excavates soils causing a release of hazardous substances, even if in connection with a required cleanup under §106, can nonetheless be held liable either as an operator (under CERCLA §107(a)(2)) or for accepting hazardous substances for transport to sites that it has selected (under CERCLA §107(a)(4)). See, e.g., Kaiser Aluminum & Chem. Corp. v. Ferry, 976 F.2d 1338 (9th Cir. 1992) (holding liable under CERCLA contractor hired to excavate land who spread contaminated soil over uncontaminated soil in the process).

C. IDENTIFYING SITES, FUNDING, AND SETTING THE STANDARDS FOR CLEANUPS

CERCLA not only sets up liability rules enforceable under §106 and §107 but also creates an administrative system for environmental remediation — removing harmful materials improperly dumped into the environment over past years. In this context, what is important are matters of process and execution: identifying sites in need of environmental cleanups, setting priorities among the needed cleanup efforts, planning what actions are needed on a site-by-site basis, and ensuring that planned responses are properly executed. This process begins with a procedure for identifying and ranking the hazards posed by sites of hazardous materials contamination. On the basis of that hazard ranking system (HRS), CERCLA establishes a national priorities list (NPL) that then functions to ensure that the most dangerous sites are remediated first. CERCLA requires EPA to establish a National Contingency Plan (NCP), which is, in essence, a compendium of the standards and procedures for cleanups that will ensure an acceptable result. Cleanups are of two kinds: Removals are short-term measures taken to minimize the dangers to health and the environment from emergency situations, whereas remedial actions are long-term efforts that attempt to rid the site of dangers on a permanent basis.

Generally, CERCLA's cleanup process has worked as expected.[20] The HRS has been used to identify sites and subsequently generate the NPL that serves as the principal means of dictating EPA's cleanup priorities. EPA, through a combination of Superfund money and PRP-funded response and remedial actions, has made progress in the remediation of numerous sites throughout the nation. Nevertheless, the cost and complexity of cleanups has made CERCLA an exciting and intensely fought aspect of hazardous materials regulation. There are literally billions of dollars to be paid by PRPs, as thousands of sites of hazardous material releases are remediated. For many lawyers representing PRPs, the problem is less one of environmental law than it is one of engaging in strategic behavior to minimize both the amount spent on cleanups and the share of the cleanup cost allocated to their clients. EPA, too, is engaged in a strategic process, whereby it seeks to accomplish as much of the massive cleanup job as it can with limited human and material resources.

Cleanup procedures are governed by the NCP. According to CERCLA §105, in the NCP, EPA is to "establish procedures and standards for responding to releases of hazardous substances, pollutants, and contaminants...." The statutorily mandated scope of the NCP includes methodologies that will identify sites in need of remediation, analyze the danger to health and the environment posed by releases and threatened releases, determine the scope and extent of needed remedial measures, and ensure that remedial actions are cost-effective.[21] The NCP must address such mundane matters as the procurement and maintenance of response equipment and the qualifications of private cleanup firms that will be engaged to do the cleanup work on Superfund projects. More politically sensitive matters must also be covered by the NCP. These include the division of authority between the federal, state, and local governments in effectuating the plan and the standards by which innovative cleanup technologies will be judged.[22]

The required priority ranking of sites in order of hazard (i.e., the HRS/NPL process) is also a part of the NCP. In this area, Congress has provided some general directions for EPA. EPA, for example, is required to revise the NPL to reflect new information about existing and additional sites.[23] Similarly, CERCLA specifies that the relative risk assessment under the HRS should include the extent of the population put at risk by the site, the hazard potential of the substances found at the site, the potential to contaminate

---

20. CERCLA's major miscalculation has been its gross underestimation of cleanup costs and recoupment rates. For example, estimates of the total cost for U.S. hazardous waste cleanup fall in the range of $300 to $700 billion. See Passell, Experts Question Staggering Costs of Toxic Cleanups, N.Y. Times (nat'l ed.), Sept. 1, 1991, at 1. Recoupment rates have also not proved promising as a source of funding the program.

21. CERCLA §105(a)(1)-(3), (7), 42 U.S.C. §9605(a)(1)-(3), (7).

22. CERCLA §105(a)(5)-(6), (9)-(10), 42 U.S.C. §9605(a)(5)-(6), (9)-(10).

23. CERCLA §105(a)(8), 42 U.S.C. §9605(a)(8).

groundwater or surface water that is used for either drinking water supply or recreation, the potential for direct human contact, the potential for the destruction of natural resources that affect the human food chain, state preparedness, and "other appropriate factors."[24]

Finally, the statute puts EPA in charge of obtaining the needed cleanups of sites on the NPL in ways that are consistent with the NCP. In this regard, EPA is empowered to (1) undertake cleanups itself, using Superfund monies, and to seek reimbursement from PRPs; (2) issue administrative orders to PRPs directing them to undertake cleanups; (3) seek court orders directing PRPs to undertake cleanups; or (4) use a combination of approaches.

FIGURE 19-2

AVERAGE TIME BETWEEN PRINCIPAL STEPS IN THE SUPERFUND PROCESS

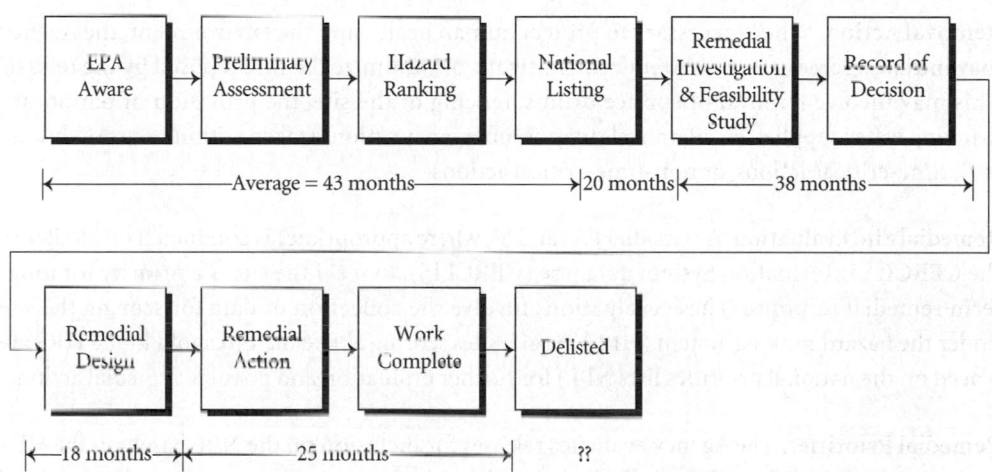

Source: J. P. Acton, Understanding Superfund: A Progress Report 16 (Rand Corporation Institute for Civil Justice, 1989).

After an uneven start,[25] EPA made extensive efforts to regularize Superfund procedures to ensure that all sites receive a thorough investigation and that decisions about remedial actions at each site are made by reference to consistent principles — focusing in each case on a site study document known as a Remedial Investigation/Feasibility Study (RI/FS). After the study and analysis is complete, EPA issues a record of decision (ROD) that selects the principal remedial actions to be taken. An even more detailed remedial design (RD) is prepared and, finally, remedial activity begins. The diagram

---

24. CERCLA §105(a)(8)(A), (c)(2), 42 U.S.C. §9605(a)(8)(A), (c)(2).

25. During the Reagan presidency, when extensive government regulation and intervention was ideological anathema, EPA was not allowed to take an active role under Superfund. In fact, Superfund's misadministration by EPA in the early 1980s was a source of scandal, and several EPA officials were criminally prosecuted and convicted. This period in EPA's CERCLA history is recounted in detail in Mintz, Agencies, Congress, and Regulatory Enforcement: A Review of EPA Hazardous Waste Enforcement Effort, 1970–1987, 18 Envtl. L. 683, 715–43 (1988).

above shows the major steps in the CERCLA process and the average duration of each of those steps.

Lawrence Starfield, The 1990 National Contingency Plan — More Detail and More Structure, But Still a Balancing Act
20 Environmental Law Reporter 10222, 10228–10229, 10236–10241 (1990)

...A Road Map to the CERCLA Site Response Process [Subpart (E) of the NCP]: Site Discovery. The process begins with the discovery of a release by one of several possible mechanisms (e.g., notification requirements under CERCLA §103(a) or (b) under other laws, a petition from a citizen, etc.). In the case of an emergency (e.g., fire, explosion), a removal action will be taken to stabilize the site.

Removal Assessment. In non-emergency situations, the release is evaluated to determine if a removal action is appropriate based on a removal preliminary assessment (PA) and, if appropriate, a removal site inspection (SI).

Removal Action. Where necessary to protect human health and the environment, the Agency may initiate a removal action to prevent, mitigate, or minimize the threat posed by the release. This may involve removal of surface drums, fencing of the site, the provision of temporary drinking water supplies, etc. Removals may be emergency actions (taken within hours of discovery), time-critical actions, or non-time-critical actions.

Remedial Site Evaluation. A remedial PA (and SI, where appropriate) is conducted on all sites in the CERCLA Information System database (CERCLIS), to see if the site is a priority for long-term remedial response. These evaluations involve the collection of data for scoring the site under the hazard ranking system (HRS) model; sites scoring above the threshold in the HRS are placed on the national priorities list (NPL) for further evaluation and possible remedial action.

Remedial Priorities. The Agency evaluates releases for inclusion on the NPL based on the HRS score or one of the other methods for listing outlined in the NCP. The Agency may spend Fund monies for remedial action only at those sites that are on the NPL. ("Fund-financed remedial action" does not include removal action or enforcement action.)

Remedial Investigation/Feasibility Study. The Agency will undertake a remedial investigation and feasibility study (RI/FS) at sites that are, or appear to be, priorities for action (i.e., that are on, or are proposed for listing on, the NPL). The RI/FS, like any other investigation conducted pursuant to CERCLA §104(b), is a removal action under CERCLA §101(23), despite the word remedial in its name.

During the RI, the nature and extent of the threat posed by the contamination is studied; concurrently, alternative approaches are developed as part of the FS for responding to and managing the site problem.

Preliminary Remediation Goal. The first step in developing alternatives during the FS is the establishment of a preliminary goal for the remediation of the site. This goal is initially based on readily available information, such as chemical-specific applicable, relevant and appropriate requirements of other environmental laws (ARARs), or the "point of departure" in the range of acceptable risk. Alternatives are then developed that are capable of attaining the preliminary remediation goal. (The goal may be modified as additional information is developed.)

Screening of Remedial Alternatives. A broad list of alternatives is then reviewed and screened, with the more extreme, impracticable options being eliminated before the detailed analysis of alternatives begins. Alternatives may be eliminated during screening based on effectiveness, implementability, or "grossly excessive" cost.

Analysis of Alternatives Using the Nine Criteria. The Agency then conducts a detailed analysis of the remaining alternatives (usually three to nine [of them], depending on the complexity of the problem). The advantages and disadvantages of the alternatives are studied and compared using the following nine remedy selection criteria:[26]

- Overall protection of human health and the environment,
- Compliance with (or waiver of) the ARARs of other laws,
- Long-term effectiveness and permanence,
- Reduction of toxicity, mobility, or volume through treatment,
- Short-term effectiveness,
- Implementability,
- Cost,
- State acceptance, and
- Community acceptance.

Selection of Remedy. The nine criteria are then used to select the remedy by evaluating them in three functional categories (threshold, balancing, and modifying criteria), in order to reflect the nature and/or timing of their application. The first two criteria — protectiveness and compliance with ARARs — are identified as threshold criteria; only the alternatives that meet those criteria may be carried forward.

Protective, ARAR-compliant alternatives are then "balanced" (i.e., used to evaluate trade-offs) based on the middle five criteria (and the two modifying criteria, to the extent they are known). The Agency then attempts to select the remedial alternative that "utilizes permanent solutions and treatment...to the maximum extent practicable," and is "cost-effective" based on a comparison of the appropriate balancing or modifying criteria. Alternatives are judged cost-effective if their costs are "in proportion" to their overall effectiveness; an alternative is found to achieve the maximum permanence and treatment practicable based on a balancing of the seven nonthreshold criteria, with an emphasis on the factors of "long-term effectiveness and permanence" and "reduction in mobility, toxicity or volume through treatment."

EPA and the state then discuss the remedial options and issue a proposed plan, which sets out the lead agency's recommended alternative. Consistent with CERCLA §117, the public is afforded an opportunity to review and comment on the alternatives studied in the FS and the proposed plan. After review of and response to public comments, and formal consideration of the two modifying criteria (state and community acceptance), the final remedy selection is documented in a record of decision (ROD).

Remedial Design/Remedial Action and Operation and Maintenance. The lead agency then sets about designing, constructing, and implementing the selected remedy. Often, the remedial action plan set out in the ROD will need to be modified in light of information developed during the design phase (e.g., the Agency may learn that more soil is contaminated and needs to be excavated). If the remedial action to be taken differs "significantly" from the remedy selected

---

26. NCP §300.430(e)(9).

in the ROD with respect to scope, performance, or cost, the lead agency will issue an explanation of significant differences (ESD). If the action to be taken "fundamentally alters" the basic features of the remedy selected in the ROD, the lead agency will propose and take comment on a ROD amendment.

Once the remedy is operational and functional (or later, for groundwater restoration remedies), the state undertakes responsibility for funding and carrying out operation and maintenance (O&M) of the remedy.

Deletion from the NPL, Five-Year Review. Once EPA has determined that no further response action is appropriate, the site may be proposed for deletion, or recategorized on the NPL, even where O&M is continuing. Sites at which hazardous substances remain above levels that allow for unlimited use and unrestricted exposure must be reviewed at least every five years after the initiation of the remedy (not merely after completion), consistent with CERCLA §121(c)....

Risk Assessment and Risk Range.... The NCP contemplates the use of risk assessments as an integral part of the process for developing remedial alternatives that are protective of human health and the environment.

Risk analysis begins during the early stages of the RI, when a "baseline risk assessment" is performed to evaluate the risk posed by a site in the absence of any remedial action. It is based on a comparison with this no-action risk level that the lead agency will target levels of risk that will be adequately protective of human health for a particular site. The baseline risk assessment also helps to provide justification for performing remedial action at the site.

Concurrently, the lead agency would begin to set a "preliminary remediation goal" as part of the FS. The preliminary remediation goal is an initial statement of the desired endpoint concentration or risk level, and alternatives are developed that are capable of meeting that goal. It is based on readily available information, such as chemical-specific ARARs (e.g., a drinking water standard), concentrations associated with the reference doses or cancer potency factors, or the point of departure for the Agency's acceptable risk range, discussed below....

Where environmental effects are observed, EPA sets remediation goals based on environmental ARARs (where they exist) and levels based on a site-specific assessment of what is protective of the environment....

The use of a range of acceptable risk is general practice for most government programs. As discussed below in the section on role of cost, it affords the Agency the flexibility to take into account different situations, different kinds of threats, and different kinds of technical remedies. If a single risk level had been adopted (e.g., at the more stringent end of the risk range), fewer alternatives would be expected to pass the protectiveness threshold and qualify for consideration in the balancing phase of the remedy selection process....

Role of Cost. The role of cost in remedy selection has been one of the most hotly disputed issues in the Superfund program. Many PRP groups argue that cost must be a major factor in deciding on an appropriate remedy and note that the requirement to select "cost-effective" remedies appears in CERCLA §121(a) and (b). Many environmentalists and some legislators have argued that cost is given too much emphasis in remedy selection and have posited that cost should be considered only in determining the cost-efficient method for implementing a selected remedy. In effect, they argue that the proper cleanup level for a site should be set, and then a remedy should be selected to attain that level, without consideration of cost....

Cost is specifically considered during the final balancing process, as the Agency attempts to satisfy two statutory mandates of CERCLA §121(b)(1) by identifying the remedial alternative that utilizes "permanent solutions and treatment...to the maximum extent practicable" while being cost-effective. These determinations are intended to be made simultaneously; however, for ease of analysis, they are discussed separately in the NCP.

Cost-Effectiveness. The determination whether a proposed remedial alternative is cost-effective is based on an evaluation of several of the nine criteria. First, overall effectiveness is assessed based on: long-term effectiveness and permanence; reduction of mobility, toxicity, or volume through treatment; and short-term effectiveness. The overall effectiveness is then compared to the cost of the alternative to determine if they are "in proportion" to one another (i.e., does the approach represent a reasonable value for the money?). In making this comparison, the decisionmaker is not directed by the NCP to place special emphasis on the factors of "reduction of toxicity, mobility or volume through treatment" and "long-term effectiveness and permanence," as is required during the assessment of permanence and treatment to the maximum extent practicable (as provided in NCP §300.430(f)(1)(ii)(E)). However, because "effectiveness" is measured based on those two factors (plus short-term effectiveness), an alternative that is high in treatment and permanence will be considered more effective and thus can justify a relatively higher cost (high effectiveness and high cost would be in proportion). The comparison of cost to effectiveness is performed for each alternative individually and for all the alternatives in relation to one another. This latter analysis allows the Agency to identify alternatives that produce an incremental increase in effectiveness for a reasonable increase in cost, based on a comparison of corresponding increases for other alternatives. Several alternatives may be found to be cost-effective....

Cost and Practicability. The statutory requirement to select the alternative (there is only one) that utilizes permanence and treatment to the maximum extent practicable is fulfilled by selecting the protective, ARAR-compliant alternative that provides the best balance of tradeoffs among alternatives based on a review of all the balancing and modifying criteria (if the latter are known). It is a subjective judgment, but the NCP sets out some parameters to help assure consistency in its application. Specifically, the NCP requires that during the balancing process, the factors of long-term effectiveness and permanence and reduction in toxicity, mobility, or volume should be emphasized, and that the "preference for treatment as a principal element" and the "bias against off-site land disposal of untreated wastes" must be considered. This statutory determination is the final step in the process before a remedy is recommended in the proposed plan.

Although cost, as one of the nine criteria, is considered in making this determination, it is not expected to play a major role. The importance of almost every other criterion to this determination is emphasized by the NCP....

Cost as a Screen. Cost may also be considered during one other aspect of the remedy selection process: screening, when alternatives that are deemed not to be viable are eliminated from more thorough consideration. The use of cost at this early stage has also been the subject of considerable comment. Many were concerned that cost would be used to screen out appropriate remedial technologies early in the process before they were given a fair evaluation and without the benefit of public review and comment.

The final NCP has been revised to narrow the circumstances under which cost may be considered when screening alternatives at the start of the evaluation process. Specifically, the final rule provides that a given alternative may be eliminated during screening if it is determined that the cost of the alternative is "grossly excessive" compared with its effectiveness. This provision will allow the Agency to avoid the need to conduct resource-intensive analyses of extreme and unrealistic options, while at the same time not allowing cost to compromise consideration of viable options that may simply be more expensive than other alternatives....

COMMENTARY & QUESTIONS

1. **The slow pace of CERCLA remediation.** Are you surprised at the overall average of 10+ years of time elapsed between EPA's initial discovery of a potential site's existence and completion of cleanup? With the exception of the period of time needed to do the site remediation, all of the stages seem to be longer than necessary, especially the five years that go by at the front end of the process in which the only real activity is making preliminary assessments and obtaining a hazard ranking score. Acton's study suggests a number of factors that may combine to explain the slow pace. These include a lack of aggressiveness by EPA, the complexity of the Superfund program, delays caused while legal interpretations of various portions of the law are obtained, program rigidity, the litigious atmosphere surrounding the program, uncertainty about the efficacy of remedies, and shortages of critical personnel.

Would the pace of Superfund remediation be improved by EPA's adopting standardized procedures to be used at all of the sites? In an apparent effort in this direction, EPA has promulgated model language for use in all consent decrees that govern the RI/FS and the RD/RA processes, in an attempt to reduce transaction time and costs. How does standardized language improve the pace of negotiations? In theory, standardization reduces the number of items that are subject to bargaining and thereby makes it easier for parties to reach agreement. Lawyers for PRPs, however, were quick to criticize the proposals as too one-sided in favor of EPA. They argued that the new terms would deprive PRPs of so many of the benefits of settlement as to have the perverse effect of discouraging settlements.

2. **Lead agencies and PRP-led activities.** Part of the problem that EPA has faced in administering CERCLA is the burden of too much work to be done by too few people. The NCP addresses this problem by allowing EPA to delegate "lead agency" status to a state, political subdivision of a state, or Indian tribe that EPA finds to have adequate ability and enforcement authority (under state or tribal law) to carry out a NCP-consistent removal or remedial action. EPA is also authorized to allow PRPs to conduct many of the phases of the CERCLA process, including, for example, performing the RI/FS,[27] or doing the actual site remediation work. In instances where PRPs take the lead role, EPA remains the official lead agency. The work is done by the PRPs pursuant to a court or administrative order, or in accordance with an express agreement with EPA.

3. **The vital points in the process.** While it is probably fair to say that all of the steps in the remediation process are important, the RI/FS and ROD stages stand out as the points at which the site-specific remedy is selected. Remedy selection determines many of the issues that people care most about. For the affected community, the remedy selection determines the extent to which the hazard will be eliminated. For the PRPs, the remedy

---

27. See CERCLA §104(a), 42 U.S.C. §9604(a).

selection commits the EPA to having a particular type and amount of work done, the cost of which will be borne by the PRPs. By statute, the RI/FS and ROD process is designed to allow input from states and affected communities as well as from PRPs and the EPA itself. Toward that end, the statute authorizes EPA to make grants of up to $50,000 to affected communities for hiring experts to make community participation in the RI/FS and ROD process more effectual.[28]

4. **The forces that govern EPA's NCP-based decisionmaking.** One commentator has suggested that EPA is driven by several factors in addition to the operating legal criteria of the NCP when it makes its decisions about site remediation. These factors include "(a) the large costs that must be borne by either the fund...or responsible parties if complete and thorough cleanups are to be implemented, (b) pressure from the Office of Management and Budget to minimize the costs to American industry, (c) the political need to proceed more quickly with cleanups at Superfund sites because of the perceived failures of the Reagan Administration, (d) the technical complexity of making decisions about health and environmental harm from contaminants that may be left at the site after cleanup, and, (e) the legal requirements of Superfund that structure how these cleanup standards shall be set." Brown, EPA's Resolution of the Conflict Between Cleanup Costs and the Law in Setting Cleanup Standards Under Superfund, 15 Colum. J. Envtl. L. 241 (1990). Assuming that Brown has identified correctly the mix of pressures that govern EPA's decisionmaking, how would they affect remedy selection in a typical case? Using both historical and legal analysis, and an illuminating case study of ROD selection, Brown concludes that the complexity of the technical issues surrounding the post-remedial effects of a remedial plan mask the selection of "remedies that only partially mitigate the impact of the site on the environment" despite legal requirements that the remedy selected must be fully protective of health and environment. Id. at 301. As a cure for this phenomenon, Brown suggests (1) clear congressional definition of "how clean is clean," and (2) allowing RODs that explicitly rely on excessive cost and engineering infeasibility as justifications for selecting a remedy that merely mitigates, but does not completely remediate, environmental harm at the site.

5. **Challenging EPA's decisions.** Congress provided for judicial review of EPA's remedy selection process. The key provisos governing judicial review are a limitation on the scope of review to the administrative record[29] and setting "arbitrary and capricious" as the standard of review.[30] Interested parties can participate in the building of the administrative record,[31] and EPA must give reasonable notice of the proceeding to identifiable interested parties, including PRPs and the affected community. Do these procedures give interested parties a meaningful opportunity to participate in the remedy selection process? See Friedman, Judicial Review Under the Superfund Amendments: Will Parties Have Meaningful Input to the Remedy Selection Process?, 14 Colum. J. Envtl. L. 187 (1989).

---

28. See CERCLA §§104(c)(2), 113(k)(2), 117, 121(f); 42 U.S.C. §§9604(c)(2), 9613(k)(2), 9617, 9621(f).
29. CERCLA §113(j)(1), 42 U.S.C. §9613(j)(1).
30. CERCLA §113(j)(2), 42 U.S.C. §9613(j)(2).
31. CERCLA §113(k), 42 U.S.C. §9613(k).

6. **ARARs as cleanup standards.** ARARs function in a very real sense as cleanup standards, defining how thorough the remedial action must be in its efforts to eliminate environmental hazards at the site. Why does the NCP place so heavy a reliance on ARARs? At a minimum, the borrowing of environmental standards from other areas of the law relieves EPA and the NCP of redundant proceedings concerning contaminant issues that have already been fully determined in other environmental regulatory processes. Simultaneously, by employing the ARARs concept, issues of competing applicability of parallel standards do not arise because there is only one standard to apply.

One of the more perplexing ARARs problems has been whether the exceedingly stringent land disposal regulations of RCRA, the hazardous wastes management statute, are applicable as ARARs at CERCLA sites. Paradoxically, RCRA's treatment standards, if applicable as ARARs, can require EPA to elect a less complete remedial action due to the great cost associated with treatment in accordance with RCRA standards. See Chapter 18.

7. **The "Superfund syndrome."** In a congressionally mandated study of the Superfund process and experience, the Congressional Office of Technology Assessment (OTA) described what it called the "Superfund syndrome":

> Public fears of toxic waste and toxic chemicals set high expectations for Superfund; site communities perceive substantial risks to their health and environment and they want effective and stringent cleanups from EPA, regardless of cost; but communities have experienced slow, incomplete and uncertain cleanups. EPA tries to limit fund-financed cleanups by getting parties held liable for sites to voluntarily pay for cleanups. However, responsible parties often believe that their liabilities are largely unfair, that risks are not as bad as communities think they are, that cleanup objectives are unnecessarily stringent, and, therefore, that they must work hard to minimize their cleanup costs.[32]

Is this snapshot of differing perspectives and attitudes toward Superfund consistent with the picture of it that you have obtained from the materials and your own experience? Can the syndrome be eliminated by small changes at the margin of the Superfund program, or are major changes needed? OTA concluded that fundamental changes were needed in three broad areas: health and environmental protection priorities and goals, workers and technology, and government management.

8. **The staggering cost of "Cadillac" cleanups.** In a provocative article, Peter Passell quotes a noted economist as saying, in reference to how thorough hazardous waste cleanups should be, "Everybody wants a Cadillac as long as someone else is paying."[33] To illustrate the impact of that attitude on CERCLA cleanups, Passell gives the example of the options available for remediating one small (in area) Missouri Superfund site. An expenditure of $71,000 could permanently isolate the contaminants at the site and prevent any exposure from ever reaching the community; an expenditure of $3.6 million could clean up virtually all hazardous material residues and bury any remaining traces under a blanket of clay; an expenditure of $41.5 million could remove and

---

32. Congressional Office of Technology Assessment, Coming Clean: Superfund Problems Can Be Solved... 3 (1984).
33. See Passell, Experts Question Staggering Costs of Toxic Cleanups, N.Y. Times (nat'l ed.), Sept. 1, 1991, at 1, 28.

incinerate the 14,000 tons of contaminated soil and building materials at the site. EPA selected a mix — incineration of the most severely contaminated materials, and clay-lined on-site disposal of the remainder, at a cost of $13.6 million.

Under the NCP, is each of these options sufficiently protective of health and environment? What are the advantages of the more expensive approaches? The most obvious difference between the low-end and high-end choices is that the high end choices return the site to suitability for renewed use. As a matter of social policy, is spending $10 million to reclaim a few acres in Missouri a wise investment of resources? Can the predictable local opposition to anything less than a total cleanup be ignored? Two possibilities raised by economists are to make local citizens help pay for "Cadillac" cleanups, or rebate to local communities a percentage of the difference between such a cleanup and a "merely" functional one.

9. **How much will this cost?** The Congressional Budget Office, in a February 1994 report entitled "The Total Cost of Cleaning Up Nonfederal Superfund Sites," offered a series of estimates of the total outlays likely to be spent at nonfederal Superfund sites. It made low-end, middle, and high-end projections as follows:

FIGURE 19-3

PROJECTION	NUMBER OF NPL SITES	COST (IN 1992 $)	COMPLETED BY YEAR
Low-end	2300	$ 42 billion	2047
Middle	4500	$ 75 billion	2060
High-end	7800	$120 billion	2075

If these figures are not sufficiently disconcerting, remember that they do not include cleanups at federal sites, such as the Rocky Mountain Arsenal, which appear to be multibillion dollar problems in their own right. Also remember that the calculation in 1992 dollars means that future expenditures are inflation-adjusted and discounted, so, for example, the $75 billion mid-range figure represents the present discounted value of actual future outlays of $230 billion (also in 1992 dollars). Perhaps in an effort to underscore the need for a change in Superfund policy, the report expressly states that it assumes no changes in present policy and no limits on authorized spending. It also does not make any adjustment for technological changes that may improve cleanup efficiencies.

10. **And just who is paying?** The staggering amounts of money that are needed for CERCLA cleanups have to come from somewhere, but where? The answer initially was that the polluter-pays principle was going to be invoked with a vengeance. Given the way CERCLA's liability scheme works, especially with the almost inescapable imposition of joint and several liability on PRPs, PRPs now appear likely to pay almost all of the costs. For the most part, the Superfund itself will pay only in those cases where no financially solvent, jointly and severally liable PRPs can be identified. Moreover, recall that the Superfund is funded primarily by a tax on chemical feedstocks, so the chemical industry takes a hit beyond its PRP share and the public at large escapes the cost.

With a small administrative flick of the pen in June 1994, however, the public share suddenly leaped to nearly one-third of the future expense. That major shift in financial burden occurred when the Internal Revenue Service (IRS) issued Revenue Ruling 94-38 concerning the deductibility of CERCLA cleanup costs. See I.R.B. 1994–25 (June 20, 1994). Up until that point, IRS had taken the position that cleanups were to be capitalized as part of the land — that is, the expense of cleanup was to be added to the taxpayer's basis in the asset, its cost of acquiring the land and maintaining its value for sale. Thus, under the previous IRS position, the only effect cleanup expenditures would have on the taxpayer's tax liability would come into play when the land was sold. The profit (if any) on the sale of the land would be less and therefore the tax liability then would be less. Under Revenue Ruling 94-38, however, cleanup costs, except those that are incurred for the construction of an ongoing treatment facility, are now fully deductible under §162 of the Internal Revenue Code as ordinary business expenses of the year in which the costs are incurred. This means that the immediate tax liability of the affected firm is greatly reduced. Consider this example: In 1994, profitable Major Corporation A spends $100,000 on CERCLA cleanup. The present level of the corporate tax is 35%. With the $100,000 now being deductible, A's 1994 net profit is now $100,000 less and its tax liability is $35,000 less. This is money that the federal treasury no longer receives for the benefit of the general public.

11. **CERCLA as the model for the Oil Pollution Act of 1990.** Galvanized into action by the *Exxon-Valdez* oil spill in 1989, Congress enacted the Oil Pollution Act of 1990 (OPA '90),[34] which integrated and strengthened prior federal law covering liability for and cleanup of oil spills. Modeled on CERCLA, OPA '90 establishes a billion dollar Oil Spill Liability Trust Fund financed by the imposition of a five cents per barrel tax on oil delivered at the refinery. Owners and operators of vessels and onshore and offshore facilities are strictly liable for cleanup and natural resource damages, subject to the defenses of (1) act of God, (2) act of war, or (3) negligence of a third party not associated with the owner or operator. Facilities must develop spill prevention, control, and countermeasure (SPCC) plans, have them approved by EPA or the Coast Guard, and implement them, or face heavy civil and criminal penalties. Single-hull tankers are to be phased out, and licensing and supervision of officers and seamen are strengthened. The OPA '90 explicitly does not preempt state oil spill laws.

12. **Natural resource damages.** CERCLA §107(a)(4)(C) provides for the recovery of natural resource damages caused by the release of hazardous materials. The federal government, the states (and their subdivisions), and Indian tribal governments are designated as trustees empowered to sue for those damages by §107(f). While natural resource damage claims have, to date, been secondary to those involving cost recovery, they represent a "sleeping giant" because the potential liability can be enormous.

Section 301(c) of CERCLA authorized the Department of Interior to promulgate regulations for the assessment of natural resource damages, although trustees may seek to establish an alternative measure of damages in any particular case. See 43 C.F.R.

---

34. Pub. L. No. 101-380 (1990).

§11.10.[35] However, a rebuttable presumption of validity attaches to those assessments conducted in accordance with Interior's regulations, and, accordingly, trustees have a significant incentive to conduct their assessments pursuant to Interior's rules.

The most significant issue in the natural resource damages context involves the appropriate measure of damages. In Ohio v. U.S. Dep't of Interior, 880 F.2d 432 (D.C. Cir. 1989), Ohio challenged Interior's regulation providing that natural resource damages shall be the "lesser of" (1) restoration or replacement costs, or (2) lost-use-value. The court invalidated the "lesser of" rule, holding that Congress established a distinct preference for restoration cost as the measure of recovery in natural resource damage cases. The court also concluded, however, that there might be some cases where other considerations — such as infeasibility of restoration or grossly disproportionate cost to use value — might warrant a different standard. Thereafter, in March 1994, Interior issued revisions to its rules, eliminating the "lesser of" rule and replacing it with a requirement that the trustee consider a wide array of "restoration" alternatives and select the most appropriate one. See 43 C.F.R. §11.83. Interior stopped short of requiring significant active restoration in every case. The rule specifically contemplated that included among the "restoration" alternatives to be considered must be one that relies on "natural recovery with minimal management actions." 43 C.F.R. §11.83(c).

The rule listed ten factors to be considered in selecting from among restoration alternatives:

> (1) Technical feasibility; (2) the relationship of the expected costs of the proposed actions to the expected benefits from the restoration, rehabilitation, replacement, and/or acquisition of equivalent resources; (3) cost-effectiveness; (4) the results of any actual or planned response actions; (5) the potential for additional injury resulting from the proposed actions, including long-term and indirect impacts, to the...injured resource or other resources; (6) the natural recovery period; (7) the ability of the resource to recover with or without alternative actions; (8) any potential effects of the action on human health and safety; (9) consistency with applicable Federal and State and tribal policies; and (10) compliance with applicable Federal, State and tribal laws. 43 C.F.R. §11.83(d).

The D.C. Circuit later upheld most elements of Interior's regulations, specifying the procedures that are sufficiently "reliable and valid" for trustees to use in calculating their damage assessments. See Kennecott Utah Copper Corp. v. U.S. Dep't of the Interior, 88 F.3d 1191, 1217 (D.C. Cir. 1996) (upholding Interior's natural resource damage assessment regulations to allow public trustees to consider acquisition of equivalent resources equally with strategies for restoration or replacement of natural resources); General Elec. Co. v. Department of Commerce, 128 F.3d 767 (D.C. Cir. 1997) (upholding NOAA final rule concerning liability for natural resource damages arising from oil spills under OPA).

Although the regulations emerged largely unscathed, the effect of striking down some of the regulatory provisions resulted in Reagan-era provisions of the rule being

---

35. Congress authorized recovery of natural resource damages under both CERCLA and OPA, 42 U.S.C. §9651(c). Under OPA, the National Oceanic and Atmospheric Administration (NOAA) promulgates regulations for natural resource damage assessments.

reinstated. The Clinton Interior Department revised the regulations, releasing a draft proposal in April 1999. Numerous stakeholders objected to the Draft Proposed Rule, including state governments, the Department of Energy, and industry. Interior undertook once again to modify the regulations, finalizing a draft that was sent to the Office of the Federal Register for publication at the end of the Clinton Administration. The draft was not published before the Bush II Administration took office, however, and President Bush withdrew it from publication. DOI did not circulate the revised version of the Draft Proposed Rule to stakeholders outside of government, so the content of the withdrawn Draft Proposed Rule remains uncertain.

Given this history, there is understandable confusion on the part of trustees, responsible parties, and other stakeholders as to what rules actually govern natural resource damage assessments. Moreover, with the *Ohio* and *Kennecott* decisions upholding and vacating portions of natural resource damage assessment rules, coupled with the Draft Proposed Rule's dissemination for two years, trustees' approaches to which rules apply reflect a hodgepodge of various Reagan-era and Clinton-era rules, and a guess at what the Draft Proposed Rule contained. This situation creates uncertainty, which often leads to disagreements about how natural resource damage assessments should proceed. These disagreements in turn add to the time it takes to assess and restore a resource, as well as to the transaction costs for government and responsible parties.

13. **Superfund's scorecard.** In summarizing the impact of Superfund to date, EPA concluded in 2003 that its program has assessed over 44,000 sites; that over 33,000 sites have been removed from the Superfund inventory (i.e., 75%); and that over 11,000 sites remain active with the state assessment program or are on the NPL. In addition, EPA concluded that its removal program has conducted over 7399 removals at over 5000 sites; that 1560 sites were either proposed, final, or deleted from the NPL; that the cumulative value of private party settlements approximated $20.6 billion; and that responsible parties have performed over 70% of nonfederal remedial actions. Although these statistics are impressive, a key question remains: Do the statistics truly reflect progress in cleaning up the environment or are they mere "beancounting" by the EPA without material improvement in environmental quality? That question is explored more fully in Chapter 21, dealing with the success of EPA's enforcement efforts.

14. **The funding and future of Superfund.** To fund the Superfund program, Congress initially established a trust fund to be used to conduct removal and remedial actions, to administer and manage the program, and to identify and oversee responsible parties. Until 1995, the trust fund was financed primarily by a tax on crude oil and certain chemicals and an environment tax on corporations. However, the authority for these taxes expired in December 1995 and has not been reauthorized, with the result that the balance of the trust fund has decreased significantly from more than $2 billion in 1995 to less than $370 million in 2002.

By 2003, as a report by the EPA's Inspector General has now concluded, the Superfund program was short $174.9 million for various cleanup actions at sites across the country. The decline in these revenues has led the Superfund program to rely increasingly on appropriations from the General Fund to supplement the trust fund — from $283 million in 1995 to $676 million in 2002. Annual program expenditures, meanwhile, have remained approximately $1.265 billion, which was the amount appropriated in fiscal 2003.

Meanwhile, as the balance of the trust fund available for future appropriations declines and no reauthorization takes place, hazardous waste sites continue to be placed on the NPL. This is increasingly true of existing military and nuclear sites, most of which involve heavy participation by the federal government. At the same time, after more than two decades of Superfund, many of the worst, most contaminated sites have been identified, and cleanups are either completed or well under way. Today, many of the remaining sites tend to be less contaminated, more localized in character, and are often located in urban areas. Nonetheless, according to EPA's Inspector General, the shortfall in Superfund funding means that "construction at [NPL] sites cannot begin; cleanups are performed in less than an optimal manner; and/or activities are stretched over longer periods of time." Congressional Request on Funding Needs for Non-Federal Superfund Sites (EPA, January 8, 2004).

The cumbersome Superfund process ill fits many of today's sites. The lack of funding and reauthorization also restricts the federal government's remedial role. With Superfund funding running out and reauthorization nowhere on the horizon, hazardous sites are increasingly handled by state-run voluntary cleanup programs that operate without federal funding, with greater PRP input, and with cleanup standards that often take into account the planned future use of the parcel. This trend is more fully addressed in Chapter 21 in relation to brownfields redevelopment. Without question, the states will play a much larger role going forward than they have played in the last 20 years, as a result of these developments. For more on the achievements (or lack thereof) of Superfund on its twentieth anniversary, see John Quarles and Michael W. Steinberg's analysis, The Superfund Program at Its 20th Anniversary, 33 Envtl. L. Rep. 10706 (2001).

D. EPA'S STRATEGY FOR COST RECOVERY AND LOSS ALLOCATION

EPA is charged with many responsibilities in the hazardous waste arena, including its responsibility not only to obtain cleanups at NPL sites but also to ensure that the burden of paying for those cleanups falls on PRPs rather than the Superfund itself. Although it was understood that the Superfund would have to absorb the costs of cleanups of orphan sites where no solvent PRPs could be identified, the mandate to assign the cost of cleanups to the PRPs is a central feature in CERCLA's structure.

The Costs of Cost Recovery. The problems facing EPA in husbanding the monies of the Superfund and running the cost recovery program can be divided into three distinct categories. Perhaps the most rudimentary problem is cash flow. If the average cleanup spans a ten-year period, and EPA is expending funds at a large number of NPL sites from the investigatory stages onward, the fund may get depleted before $107 cost recovery actions can replenish it. Second, years of experience with the cost recovery program have revealed that the program has a surprisingly low rate of recovery. Finally, EPA has a severe staffing problem in both the site management and cost recovery aspects of its operations. The site management staffing problem is simply a lack of sufficient trained and experienced personnel to ensure that sites are cleaned up in the proper manner. The cost recovery staffing problem arises in large part as a result of the nature of CERCLA cases. In most instances, NPL sites involve numerous PRPs with substantial liabilities. The high stakes create a sufficient incentive for PRPs to fight hard to limit their losses on many fronts. They will also be inclined to challenge EPA decisions regarding selection of expensive cleanup measures. PRPs try to minimize EPA's assessment of their contribution to the site, contesting the accuracy of EPA's particular "waste-in" lists,[36] and the identification of materials found at the site as belonging to them rather than some other PRP. Even though PRPs are almost always held to be jointly and severally liable for cost recoveries,[37] they are given a statutory right of contribution[38] and may join their cross-claims for contribution to EPA's cost recovery suit. The effort to sort out comparative responsibility has the potential to make each of the cost recovery suits a quagmire for all involved. Finally, even when the cost allocation issue is absent, experience in all fields of law has shown that complex multiparty litigation invariably imposes massive burdens on all of the parties involved.

Lawsuits prosecuted under RCRA §7003 and CERCLA §§106 and 107 have proven particularly burdensome and expensive to litigate, to the extent that litigation at times proves to be counterproductive. A great deal of money is spent that might otherwise be directed toward remediation of toxic contamination. For example, in United States v. Conservation Chem. Co., 628 F. Supp. 391 (W.D. Mo. 1985), the cost of continuing to litigate the case was estimated to exceed the cost of the proposed remediation at the site. On the basis of that letter, the court allowed time for settlement negotiations, which eventually resulted in an agreement that was upheld over the objections of nonsettling PRPs.

COMMENTARY & QUESTIONS

1. **The likelihood of settlement.** Assume that a site presents a complex groundwater remediation problem. How often will a settlement be achieved? The special facts of the *Conservation Chemical* case noted above and litigation costs substantially in excess of cleanup costs are the hallmarks of a case that should be settled, but how often will that happen? The key factors will include the cost of the cleanup, the sheer number of PRPs, their solvency, the accuracy of the "waste-in" list, and, perhaps, the negotiating strategy of the parties. The high costs of litigation can act as an inducement to settlement. Lowering the total cost, such as by obtaining EPA approval of a PRP-managed cleanup, can also improve the chances of settlement, as noted more fully below. Settling PRPs are

---

36. A "waste-in" list is a computer printout generated by EPA after extensive detective work on each site, collecting much data on who dumped what, based on identifiable barrels, trucking invoices, interviews with workers, corporate records, etc. Based on the list, EPA sends out PRP liability notices, sometimes to hundreds of potentially liable addressees.

37. Recall that courts have found that joint and several liability will not be applied in the event that the PRPs can show that the harm is divisible or that there is an appropriate basis on which to apportion liability.

38. CERCLA §113(f), 42 U.S.C. §9613(f).

protected against additional liability and may seek contribution from nonsettling PRPs.

2. **Settlements and administrative orders as cures for Superfund solvency issues and litigation burdens.** In order to preclude the cash flow and low recovery rate problems, EPA has tried to reduce outlays of monies from the Superfund by increasing the amount of the cleanup work done by the PRPs (or their contractors) rather than by contractors hired by EPA. One means for shifting the costs to PRPs has been to enter into settlements with PRPs in advance of cleanup that place the full anticipated present and future costs on the PRPs. This method of proceeding has the additional advantage of avoiding two types of staffing problems. PRP-led cleanups require EPA oversight, but that is a far more modest task than managing the cleanup. Similarly, by settling in advance of litigation, the burdens of complex litigation are greatly reduced.[39] A second avenue toward increasing the amount of cleanup work done by PRPs is to require that PRPs do the work pursuant to administrative order, a power expressly granted to EPA by Congress. This power is limited to cases where a release or threatened release of hazardous material poses "an imminent and substantial endangerment to public health or welfare or the environment...."[40] Given the nature of Superfund sites, few, if any, do not pose such a danger.

3. **Congressional guidelines for EPA settlements.** Owing to the abuses of the Superfund program in the early years of the Reagan Administration, Congress added extremely detailed provisions when it reauthorized CERCLA in 1986 that were intended to support EPA's pursuit of settlements while keeping a check on EPA to be sure that the settlement process was administered in an evenhanded way. See CERCLA §122. EPA has fully complied with the directive and has promulgated a whole series of guidance documents that announce EPA settlement policies and procedures.

4. **PRP letters — the invitation to the dance.** One of the rituals of Superfund enforcement is the way in which many of EPA's actions are begun. After identifying a site and compiling a list of PRPs, EPA mails letters informing PRPs of their (unhappy) status and inviting them to a forthcoming meeting, usually at a large meeting hall or hotel ballroom near the site. At that meeting, EPA typically presents its waste-in list and a summary of what the agency knows about the site, and then tells the assemblage that they have a few hours to organize themselves into groups for the purpose of negotiating settlements with EPA. The EPA representatives then depart, returning after a few hours to begin discussions with the various newly formed PRP groups. If settlements are not reached within 60 days, the period for negotiation (unless extended for an additional 60 days by EPA) is over, and EPA will file suit or issue administrative orders. Is this reliance on PRPs to organize themselves on such short notice a good procedure to follow in complex Superfund cases? Are brutally short deadlines appropriate and necessary?

---

39. Litigation is not wholly avoided. At times, settlements will be reached after litigation is initiated but before it has matured. At other times, settlements will be reached with less than all of the PRPs, leaving EPA to litigate with the remaining PRPs. See, e.g., O'Neil v. Picillo, below.

40. See CERCLA §106(a), 42 U.S.C. §9606(a). That same subsection authorizes EPA to initiate litigation seeking injunctive relief to the same effect, as discussed in Part B of this chapter.

Of course, if EPA or its state counterpart do not reach settlement and ultimately file suit after undertaking cleanup, recalcitrant PRPs rejecting "the invitation to the dance" may find themselves liable under §107 both for past cleanup costs and for all future costs associated with the site. In the following case, the First Circuit Court of Appeals examines one such situation, where the nonsettling parties fought aggressively, but unsuccessfully, to avoid the onus of joint and several liability.

O'Neil v. Picillo
United States Court of Appeals for the First Circuit, 1989
883 F.2d 176, cert. denied, 493 U.S. 1071 (1990)

COFFIN, J. In July of 1977, the Picillos agreed to allow part of their pig farm in Coventry, Rhode Island to be used as a disposal site for drummed and bulk waste. That decision proved to be disastrous. Thousands of barrels of hazardous waste were dumped on the farm, culminating later that year in a monstrous fire ripping through the site. In 1979, the state and the Environmental Protection Agency (EPA) jointly undertook to clean up the area. What they found, in the words of the district court, were massive trenches and pits "filled with free-flowing, multi-colored, pungent liquid wastes" and thousands of "dented and corroded drums containing a veritable potpourri of toxic fluids." O'Neil v. Picillo, 682 F. Supp. 706, 709, 725 (D.R.I. 1988).

This case involves the State of Rhode Island's attempt to recover the clean-up costs it incurred between 1979 and 1982 and to hold responsible parties liable for all future costs associated with the site. The state's complaint originally named thirty-five defendants, all but five of whom eventually entered into settlements totalling $5.8 million, the money to be shared by the state and EPA. After a month-long bench trial, the district court, in a thorough and well reasoned opinion, found three of the remaining five companies jointly and severally liable under §107 of CERCLA for all of the State's past clean-up costs not covered by settlement agreements, as well as for all costs that may become necessary in the future. The other two defendants obtained judgments in their favor, the court concluding that the state had failed to prove that the waste attributed to those companies was "hazardous," as that term is defined under the Act.

Two of the three companies held liable at trial, American Cyanamid and Rohm & Haas, have taken this appeal. Both are so called "generators" of waste, as opposed to transporters or site owners. See §107(a)(3), 42 U.S.C. §9607. Neither takes issue with the district court's finding that some of their waste made its way to the Picillo site. Rather, they contend that their contribution to the disaster was insubstantial and that it was, therefore, unfair to hold them jointly and severally liable for all of the state's past expenses not covered by settlements....

Joint and Several Liability: Statutory Background... It is by now well settled that Congress intended the federal courts to develop a uniform approach governing the use of joint and several liability in CERCLA actions. The rule adopted by the majority of courts, and the one we adopt, is based on the Restatement 2d of Torts: damages should be apportioned only if the defendant can demonstrate that the harm is divisible.

The practical effect of placing the burden on defendants has been that responsible parties rarely escape joint and several liability, courts regularly finding that where wastes of varying (and unknown) degrees of toxicity and migratory potential commingle, it simply is impossible to determine the amount of environmental harm caused by each party. It has not gone unnoticed that holding defendants jointly and severally liable in such situations may often result in defendants paying for more than their share of the harm. Nevertheless, courts have continued to impose joint and several liability on a regular basis, reasoning that where all of the contributing causes cannot fairly be traced, Congress intended for those proven at least partially culpable to bear the cost of the uncertainty.

In enacting the Superfund Amendments and Reauthorization Act of 1986 (SARA), Congress had occasion to examine this case law. Rather than add a provision dealing explicitly with joint and several liability, it chose to leave the issue with the courts, to be resolved as it had been — on a case by case basis according to the predominant "divisibility" rule first enunciated by the *Chem-Dyne* court [572 F. Supp. 802 (S.D. Ohio 1983)]. Congress did, however, add two important provisions designed to mitigate the harshness of joint and several liability. First, the 1986 Amendments direct the EPA to offer early settlements to defendants who the Agency believes are responsible for only a small portion of the harm, so-called de minimis settlements. See §122(g). Second, the Amendments provide for a statutory cause of action in contribution, codifying what most courts had concluded was implicit in the 1980 Act. See §113(f)(1). Under this section, courts "may allocate response costs among liable parties using such equitable factors as the court determines are appropriate." We note that appellants already have initiated a contribution action against seven parties before the same district court judge who heard this case.

While a right of contribution undoubtedly softens the blow where parties cannot prove that the harm is divisible, it is not a complete panacea since it frequently will be difficult for defendants to locate a sufficient number of additional, solvent parties. Moreover, there are significant transaction costs involved in bringing other responsible parties to court. If it were possible to locate all responsible parties and to do so with little cost, the issue of joint and several liability obviously would be of only marginal significance. We, therefore, must examine carefully appellants' claim that they have met their burden of showing that the harm in this case is divisible....

Removal Costs... The state's removal efforts proceeded in four phases, each phase corresponding roughly to the cleanup of a different trench. The trenches were located in different areas of the site, but neither party has told us the distance between trenches. Appellants contend that it is possible to apportion the state's removal costs because there was evidence detailing (1) the total number of barrels excavated in each phase, (2) the number of barrels in each phase attributable to them, and (3) the total cost associated with each phase. In support of their argument, they point us to a few portions of the record, but for the most part are content to rest on statements in the district court's opinion. Specifically, appellants point to the following two sentences in the opinion: (1) "I find that [American Cyanamid] is responsible for ten drums of toxic hazardous material found at the site"; and (2) as to Rohm & Haas, "I accept the state's estimate [of 49 drums and 303 five-gallon pails]." Appellants then add, without opposition from the government, that the ten barrels of American Cyanamid waste discussed by the district court were found exclusively in Phase II, and that the 303 pails and 49 drums of Rohm & Haas waste mentioned by the court were found exclusively in Phase III. They conclude, therefore, that American Cyanamid should bear only a minute percentage of the $995,697.30 expended by the state during Phase II in excavating approximately 4,500 barrels and no share of the other phases, and that Rohm & Haas should be accountable for only a small portion of the $58,237 spent during Phase III in removing roughly 3,300 barrels and no share of the other phases. We disagree.

The district court's statements concerning the waste attributable to each appellant were based on the testimony of John Leo, an engineer hired by the state to oversee the cleanup. We have reviewed Mr. Leo's testimony carefully. Having done so, we think it inescapably clear that the district court did not mean to suggest that appellants had contributed only 49 and 10 barrels respectively, but rather that those amounts were all that could be positively attributed to appellants.

Mr. Leo testified that out of the approximately 10,000 barrels that were excavated during the four phases, only "three to four hundred of the drums contained markings which could potentially be traced." This is not surprising considering that there had been an enormous fire at the site, that the barrels had been exposed to the elements for a number of years, and that a substantial amount of liquid waste had leaked and eaten away at the outsides of the barrels. Mr. Leo also testified that it was not simply the absence of legible markings that prevented the state from identifying the overwhelming majority of barrels, but also the danger involved in handling the barrels. Ironically, it was appellants themselves who, in an effort to induce Mr. Leo to lower his estimate of the number of barrels attributable to each defendant, elicited much of the testimony concerning the impossibility of accurately identifying all of the waste.[41]

In light of the fact that most of the waste could not be identified, and that the appellants, and not the government, had the burden to account for all of this uncertainty, we think it plain that the district court did not err in holding them jointly and severally liable for the state's past removal costs. Perhaps in this situation the only way appellants could have demonstrated that they were limited contributors would have been to present specific evidence documenting the whereabouts of their waste at all times after it left their facilities. But far from doing so, appellants deny all knowledge of how their waste made its way to the site. Moreover, the government presented evidence that much of Rohm & Haas' waste found at the site came from its laboratory in Spring House, Pennsylvania and that during the relevant years, this lab generated over two thousand drums of waste, all of which were consigned to a single transporter. Under these circumstances, where Rohm & Haas was entrusting substantial amounts of waste to a single transporter who ultimately proved unreliable, we simply cannot conclude, absent evidence to the contrary, that only a handful of the 2,000 or more barrels reached the site.[42]

Appellants have argued ably that they should not have been held jointly and severally liable. In the end, however, we think they have not satisfied the stringent burden placed on them by Congress. As to all other issues, we affirm substantially for the reasons set out by the district court. Appellants should now move on to their contribution action where their burden will be reduced and the district court will be free to allocate responsibility according to any combination of equitable factors it deems appropriate. Indeed, there might be no reason for the district court to place any burden on appellants. If the defendants in that action also cannot demonstrate that they were limited contributors, it is not apparent why all of the parties could not be held jointly and severally liable. However, we leave this judgment to the district court. See, e.g., Developments, Toxic Waste Litigation, 99 Harv. L. Rev. 1458, 1535–1543 (1986). Affirmed.

COMMENTARY & QUESTIONS

1. **The impact of joint and several liability.** Although the proofs in the case are riddled with uncertainty, assume for a moment that the amounts actually contributed to the Picillo site by Cyanamid and Rohm & Haas were little more than the 59 identifiable

---

41. Appellants contend that the state's record keeping was subpar.... In the context of this case, the state's failure to document its work during Phase I was harmless error since Mr. Leo testified that even when the state made an effort to identify the barrels, it could rarely do so.

42. Even if it were possible to determine how many barrels each appellant contributed to the site, we still would have difficulty concluding that the state's removal costs were capable of apportionment.... Appellants have proceeded on the assumption that the cost of removing barrels did not vary depending on their content. This assumption appears untenable given the fact that the state had to take added precautions in dealing with certain particularly dangerous substances.... Moreover...because there was substantial commingling of wastes, we think that any attempt to apportion the costs incurred by the state in removing the contaminated soil would necessarily be arbitrary.

barrels, and that they were present in only one of the four trenches. Those companies are now liable for all past and future costs at the site not paid by other PRPs. Although the court does not make the point explicitly, the unpaid past costs plus all future costs could amount to millions of dollars beyond the $5.8 million already recovered through settlement with other PRPs. (In fact, Cyanamid and Rohm & Haas were subsequently found liable for $3.5 million in addition to $1.5 million they had already paid.[43]) Both Cyanamid and Rohm & Haas are large, well-financed companies and can pay the amount due. To whatever extent that amount (under the present assumptions of limited contribution of materials to the site) is grossly disproportionate to their responsibility for causing the problems at the site, the operation of joint and several liability seems unfair.

The court refers on several occasions to the possibility that subsequent contribution actions by Cyanamid and Rohm & Haas will remedy the unfairness of being held liable for an overly large share of cleanup costs. This may be disingenuous on the part of the court. The possibility of obtaining contribution in this case was limited because the other parties whom EPA identified as PRPs had settled with the government, and these settlements act as a defense to contribution actions.

2. **Problems of uncertainty.** The unfairness in this case appears to be exacerbated by the actions taken by Rhode Island in cleaning up the site in a way that leaves so much uncertainty about whose wastes were actually present at the site. The court, in essence, answers this complaint by claiming that Congress intended PRPs — as the ones who had benefitted from inadequate disposal practices — to bear the risk of occasionally unfair allocations rather than thrusting that risk onto the Superfund. Does the potential unfairness to PRPs of poorly managed cleanups help to explain why the NCP standards for cleanups are so elaborate?

3. **Seeking fairer alternatives.** Even if Cyanamid and Rohm & Haas can justly claim unfairness, are there better alternatives to arming EPA with joint and several liability and placing the burden on PRPs to show divisibility of harm? One family of alternatives, the insistence on the traditional rules of liability, seems to leave EPA and the Superfund without any means by which to shift the loss to PRPs. Forcing EPA to meet traditional cause-in-fact standards, for example, would result in minimal cost recoveries whenever a highly accurate waste-in list doesn't exist. In the end, this burdens the taxpayers who, comparatively speaking, are surely more "innocent" than any of the PRPs. A more promising avenue is to consider ways in which costs that cannot be attributed to any particular PRP might be shared among the PRP group, rather than thrust upon a single PRP using joint and several liability. The law has generally made this attempt in regard to contribution actions, which are studied in the materials that follow.

4. **Contribution among PRPs.** In light of strict liability and the difficulty of proving that the toxic cleanup harm can be apportioned, PRPs increasingly are faced with the certainty that, if sued under CERCLA, they will lose and be held jointly and severally

---

43. The additional liability figure was reported at 5 Toxics L. Rep. 289 (1990). The attorney for the two firms, in a conversation with one of the editors, noted the prior payment as well.

liable for all recoverable costs. In the event that a party pays the entire loss, the appropriate course of action is to seek to shift all or part of the loss to other PRPs via contribution.[44]

Congress directs the courts to apply a federal law of contribution under §113(f)(1) of CERCLA "using such equitable factors as the court determines are appropriate." One of numerous commentators who have addressed this subject summarized federal practice:

> Recent cases suggest that federal courts are creating a federal common law of contribution that follows the Restatement [(Second) of Torts], §886A, and apportions liability according to a modified comparative fault approach that incorporates equitable defenses as to mitigation of damages, and the multi-factor approach suggested by the [unenacted] Gore Amendment [to CERCLA].[45]

The Restatement (Second) of Torts §886A provides generally that in actions for contribution joint tortfeasors cannot be held liable for more than their equitable share. Its key language provides:

> (2) The right of contribution exists only in favor of a tortfeasor who has discharged the entire claim for the harm by paying more than his equitable share of the common liability, and is limited to the amount paid by him in excess of his share. No tortfeasor can be required to make contribution beyond his own equitable share of the liability.

In its commentary on the "method of apportionment," the Restatement identifies two approaches, either pro rata contribution or something along the lines of a comparative fault determination.

The pro rata (equal shares) approach has its roots in the equitable maxim that, "Equality is equity." A pro rata share, moreover, is easy to calculate. The total amount paid in the CERCLA case is divided by the number of parties who were found jointly and severally liable.[46] An equal sharing of costs may be fair in some cases, but the typical CERCLA case involves PRPs having markedly different degrees of responsibility for conditions at the site. Some may have minimal volumes of relatively benign wastes at the site while others have been major contributors to the problem. If the PRP selected by EPA to pay the judgment is in the former category, a pro rata recovery on the contribution claim is unsatisfactory.

---

44. Indemnity may also be a possibility. CERCLA itself creates no general right of indemnification in favor of one responsible party against another. Indemnity is available under traditional common law doctrines, such as granting indemnity pursuant to contractual indemnity agreements or permitting a party that is only passively responsible to seek indemnity from parties that are actively responsible for harm or loss.

45. Comment, Contribution Under CERCLA: Judicial Treatment After SARA, 14 Colum. J. Envtl. L. 267, 278 (1989). [The Gore Amendment, though never enacted, has nevertheless been applied as persuasive analysis by the courts. Eds.] The factors in the Gore Amendment that facilitate a comparative approach include (1) the extent to which the defendant's level of contribution to the problem can be distinguished, (2) the amount of hazardous waste involved, (3) the degree of toxicity of the hazardous waste involved, (4) the degree of involvement by the parties in the generation, transportation, treatment, storage or disposal of the hazardous waste, (5) the degree of care exercised, taking into account the characteristics of the hazardous materials involved, and (6) the degree of cooperation of the party with public officials in working to prevent harm to public health or the environment. See 126 Cong. Rec. 26,781 (1980). See also Garber, Federal Common Law of Contribution under the 1986 CERCLA Amendments, 14 Ecology L.J. 365 (1987); Dubuc & Evans, Recent Developments Under CERCLA: Toward a More Equitable Distribution of Liability, 17 Envtl. L. Rep. 10197 (1987).

46. If some of the jointly liable parties are unable to pay their shares due to insolvency, the usual rule is that the shares of all remaining parties are increased.

To obtain a non-pro rata basis for contribution the party seeking that result has to provide the court with a reasonable alternative basis on which to apportion responsibility. Even using the Gore Amendment factors, that task has a Catch-22 quality about it. Recalling that joint and several liability was imposed initially because of the great difficulty of apportioning responsibility among PRPs, PRPs with only a small share of the responsibility face an unpleasant paradox: They could get contribution (on other than a pro rata basis) if the harm could be apportioned, but they are being held jointly liable precisely because the harm cannot be apportioned.

The availability of contribution, even properly apportioned, is not a panacea for PRPs who have paid more than their "fair share." The PRP who pays the judgment to the government will find that co-PRPs who settled with EPA or the state are immune to suits for contribution. In 1986, Congress added §113(f)(2) to CERCLA establishing the effect of settlement on settling parties' subsequent liability for contribution:

> A person who has resolved its liability to the United States or a State in an administrative or judicially approved settlement shall not be liable for claims for contribution regarding matters addressed in the settlement. Such settlement does not discharge any of the other potentially liable persons unless its terms so provide, but it reduces the potential liability of the others by the amount of the settlement.

5. **Catch-22 revisited.** The seemingly empty promise of non-pro rata contribution described in the text overstates to some extent the problem of apportionment among the PRPs in contribution suits. The rationale for creating a de facto presumption that CERCLA site harms are not divisible in government suits for cost recovery is the congressional policy of imposing the cost of cleanups on PRPs rather than on the Superfund. In the contribution suit, no party comes to the court with a preferred position. All of the PRPs are partly responsible for the harm and none is entitled to preferential treatment as a matter of statutory policy; thus the court in the contribution suit will seek to do whatever is most equitable. In that apportionment setting, it is as if no party has the burden of proof on the apportionment issue.[47]

6. **Congressional intent on encouraging settlements.** Why did Congress grant contribution protection to settling PRPs? The answer has almost nothing to do with contribution and a great deal to do with encouraging settlement. In a settlement, a settling PRP pays only once, an amount that both the PRP and the government think fairly represents the settlor's liability. Absent contribution protection, the settling PRP is at risk of later being held liable for contribution in judgments arising in other subsequent cases, which would reduce the benefits of settling. Settlement without contribution protection would not fix for all time the amount of liability, would not preclude the expense of litigation (e.g., for defense on the merits in contribution actions), and would not offer any respite from the possibility of greater liability that inheres in litigation.

---

47. If this seems unclear, consider the following analogy of the burden of proof to elections. In the government's action, a PRP seeking to be held liable only on a several basis must, because of the congressional policy favoring recoveries by the government, win by a clear majority. In the subsequent contest (the contribution lawsuit) among the PRPs, none of whom enjoy a congressionally favored position, the contest can be won by a mere plurality.

7. **EPA's use of contribution protection as a sword.** Can EPA use §113(f)(2) to coerce parties into settlements? Settling PRPs are free of any contribution responsibility, so if EPA enters into "sweetheart" settlements (i.e., settlements that do not recover a fair proportion of the total liability in relation to the responsibility of settling PRPs for expenses at the site), nonsettling PRPs will inevitably end up paying a disproportionate share. EPA generally does not want to act in ways that are arbitrary and unfair, but making strategic use of legal rules in furtherance of the legitimate policy of seeking to promote settlement is not arbitrary. As discussed in Note 9 below, EPA has been able to make settlements attractive even without offering overlenient terms.

8. **State law analogies, and pitfalls in obtaining contribution.** Although relatively little has been said in this chapter about parallel state cleanup laws — often called spill laws or polluter-pay laws — at times they impose even harsher consequences than CERCLA on parties who pay for cleanups. For example, a New Jersey Supreme Court decision dismissed the appeal of the present owner of a parcel who had cleaned up a toluene contamination site under the New Jersey Environmental Cleanup Responsibility Act,[48] a strict liability statute that requires owners to remedy contamination before they can transfer the parcel. The present owner sought contribution from other parties, including the former owner of the parcel who had contributed to the toluene pollution. The owner was not able to invoke the benefits of strict and joint and several liability in its contribution suit against the past owner.[49] Instead, it had to carry the ordinary common law burdens of proof on the issues of causation and severability of harm in order to recover against the former owner. See Superior Air Prods. v. NL Indus., 522 A.2d 1025 (N.J. Super. Ct. App. Div. 1987), appeal dismissed, No. 32,106 (N.J. Apr. 4, 1991); see also 5 Toxics L. Rep. 1455 (1991).

9. **Strategic EPA behavior in seeking settlements.** EPA can do a great deal to encourage settlement. Consider its tool set: §106 orders, contribution protection, control of the remedy selection process, and, of course, the ability to use Superfund monies to remediate the site and seek to impose §107 liability. Are there policies EPA could adopt that would reward settling PRPs and punish "recalcitrants"? Could EPA manipulate the way it accounts for the possibility of undiscovered pollution or cleanup cost overruns? The short answer to both of these questions is in the affirmative. In fact, EPA has developed explicit policies in this area. PRPs who find these policies unfair to them are most often left with futile lawsuits in which they are challenging a consent decree being entered into by EPA and the settling PRPs. See, e.g., United States v. Cannons Eng'g Corp., 720 F. Supp. 1027 (D. Mass. 1989).

---

48. 13 N.J. Stat. Ann. §13:1K-6 (1983).

49. Had the state been prosecuting the cleanup action under the New Jersey Spill Compensation and Control Act, every "discharger" of contaminants would have been jointly and severally strictly liable. This would have included the former property owner.

PART FOUR

COMPLIANCE, ENFORCEMENT, AND DISPUTE RESOLUTION

When you come to a fork in the road, take it.

— Yogi Berra

"Nature, to be commanded, must be obeyed."

— Francis Bacon, Novum Organum

If a man walks in the woods for love of them half of each day, he is in danger of being regarded as a loafer. But if he spends his days as a speculator, shearing off those woods and making the earth bald before her time, he is deemed an industrious and enterprising citizen.

—Henry David Thoreau (1817–1862)

Chapter 20

ENVIRONMENTAL CRIMINAL LAW

A. *Tactical Rediscovery of Criminal Provisions: The 1899 Refuse Act*
B. *An Increasing Willingness to Prosecute Environmental Crimes*
C. *Criminal Liability: Problems of Knowledge and Intent*
D. *Problems Raised in Corporate and Executive Prosecutions*
E. *Regulatory Prosecutions and the Effect of Federal Sentencing Guidelines*

Criminal punishment is an ancient societal instinct, levying fines, imprisonment, and corporal punishments including death. In legal process terms, the criminal law is often a crude blunt instrument, in comparison to civil remedies, yet even in highly developed modern regulatory systems the force of the criminal law remains an important functional component. In environmental law, despite its highly developed civil and administrative complexity and the growing culture of compliance within the industrial community, the importance of criminal law appears to be increasing rather than shrinking.

Prior to the 1960s, virtually no criminal law was applied to environmental cases. In the 1970s, although statutes such as the federal Refuse Act raised the prospect of criminal fines, and some violators of the newly amended federal Clean Water Act were in fact sanctioned with substantial criminal fines, no one went to jail. By the 1980s, the federal government, and prosecutors in some states, were becoming increasingly sophisticated in using evidence from a variety of sources, including civil litigation, in seeking meaningful criminal sanctions. Typical prosecutions at this time involved false statement cases based upon the failure to report toxic discharges. Still, short of life-threatening acts, prosecutors rarely sought jail time for criminal violations of the environmental laws. By the 1990s, however, criminal prosecution of the environmental laws was much more vigorous. Even when environmental crimes did not directly endanger health or safety, prosecutors were much more likely to seek jail time for those convicted of felonies. Today, it is not unusual for convicted environmental defendants to face actual personal time in jail as well as large punitive fines that cannot be charged to insurance or deducted from income taxes as business expenses.

Criminal law seeks to punish bad actors in order to accomplish several different public policy objectives not so directly involved in civil law:

- incapacitation (the prevention of repeat offenses by holding perpetrators in prison or controlled probation);
- specific deterrence, by making the defendant apprehensive about future conduct;

- general deterrence, by showing other potential culprits that crime does not pay;

- revenge and retribution, through physical and fiscal punishment, for defendants' bad actions; and

- rehabilitation (although in some settings this is merely theoretical).

Regulatory enforcement attorneys consider the utility of potential criminal charges in designing their enforcement agendas, despite the increased difficulties of proof. All the listed rationales for criminal punishment can apply in environmental prosecutions, and to the list should be added the club-in-the-closet function: For environmental regulatory agencies, the background threat of criminal sanctions against violators strongly reinforces negotiations on administrative civil penalties, and compliance.

Criminal prosecutions, more than civil, reflect the governing moral climate of the moment. Criminal law was enlisted in legal efforts to protect the environment when a broadened environmental consciousness infiltrated the general public. Although for some Americans "Throw the bums in jail" was always at least as natural as "Sue the bastards" as a gut reaction to many pollution controversies, only since the 1980s have environmental prosecutions ceased being rare occurrences. They are and probably will remain a small proportion of the environmental litigation total, although the broad availability of criminal punishment remains important practically as well as conceptually. Often criminal proceedings proceed parallel to civil proceedings brought by citizen plaintiffs or the government, with obvious tactical consequences.

The initial rarity of criminal prosecutions for environmental violations was not based upon a lack of criminal law on the books. States have always had general crimes such as battery and homicide that could have been applied, and most of the major federal environmental statutes contain criminal penalty provisions along with civil penalties. Many other state and federal penal laws with potential application to environmental cases, particularly those in the area of public health, still lie virtually unused. Nevertheless, criminal law prosecutions of environmental offenses play a special role in the legal system's response to problems of pollution and environmental quality. Whether that role is ultimately effective or well advised, however, remains the subject of continuing debate.

A. TACTICAL REDISCOVERY OF CRIMINAL PROVISIONS: THE 1899 REFUSE ACT

Here is an illuminating example of how criminal laws lingering on the statute books can have dramatic application in the environmental setting.

In the 1960s, when environmental activists following the lead of Representative Henry Reuss of Wisconsin discovered the 1899 Refuse Act (passed in 1899 as a part of the Federal Rivers and Harbors Appropriation Act of that year), they read its terms with pleased anticipation:

§407. **Deposit of Refuse in Navigable Waters Generally.** It shall not be lawful to throw, discharge, or deposit or cause, suffer, or procure to be thrown, discharged, or deposited either from or out of any ship, barge, or other floating craft of any kind, or from the shore, wharf, manufacturing establishment, or mill of any kind, any refuse matter of any kind or description whatever other than that flowing from streets and sewers and passing therefrom in a liquid state, into any navigable water of the United States, or into any tributary of any navigable water from which the same shall float or be washed into such navigable water, [or] on the bank of any navigable water, where the same shall be liable to be washed into such navigable water...whereby navigation shall or may be impeded or obstructed: Provided, That...the Secretary of the Army, whenever in the judgment of the Chief of Engineers anchorage and navigation will not be injured thereby, may permit the deposit of any material above mentioned in navigable waters, within limits to be defined and under conditions to be prescribed by him....

§411. Penalty for Wrongful Deposit of Refuse: Use of or Injury to Harbor Improvements, and Obstruction of Navigable Waters Generally. Every person and every corporation that shall violate or that shall knowingly aid, abet, authorize, or instigate a violation of the provisions of...this title shall be guilty of a misdemeanor, and on conviction thereof shall be punished by a fine not exceeding $2,500 nor less than $500, or by imprisonment (in the case of a natural person) for not less than thirty days nor more than one year, or by both such fine and imprisonment...one-half of said fine to be paid to the person or persons giving information which shall lead to conviction.

COMMENTARY & QUESTIONS

1. **The Refuse Act in the 1960s.** Upon the discovery of the Refuse Act, a number of prosecutions were begun across the country, as U.S. District Attorneys responded to the 1960s explosion of environmental consciousness in the media and the electorate. In part, the Refuse Act's strategic novelty was due to the fact that it even existed as an actionable pollution statute, not that it was criminal. Most activists in the 1960s had presumed that there were no existing environmental laws with teeth in them, and that legal action would therefore have to await further legislative action. Instead, prosecutors were able to go immediately against a wide range of defendants, from small dumpers to major corporations, obtaining convictions quickly and decisively, and levying substantial fines. The American Chamber of Commerce and the National Association of Manufacturers began to urge repeal of the drastic Refuse Act. The Comprehensive Federal Water Pollution Control Act of 1972 took over most of the Refuse Act's pollution coverage. For a time, however, the Refuse Act was undoubtedly the nation's most direct and effective environmental statute.

2. **Ease of prosecution.** If you were an environmentally minded U.S. Attorney in the 1960s, and the Refuse Act was brought to your attention along with bottles and samples of muck from a particular water pollution outfall pipe, why would you find your case against the suspect dumper so easy to prove? Note first of all the geographical scope of the statute. To what geographical areas does it not apply? To what polluting materials does it apply? Is it clear that it applies to liquid pollutants? All liquid pollutants? And what are the elements of the criminal offense? Virtually no dischargers had obtained a permit from the U.S. Army Corps of Engineers. Not much more had to be proved. The Supreme Court helped by holding, in United States v. Republic Steel, 362 U.S. 482, 491 (1960), that the Act meant what it said in plain words: Pollution was "refuse," and where there were doubts, the Act should be read "charitably in light of the purpose to be

served." (What was the 1899 Act's purpose?) What about the question of criminal mens rea or intent? Section 411 contains the requirement that defendants who aid and abet must be acting "knowingly," but that seems to apply only to aiding and abetting, not to direct violations of §407. To what extent can we punish persons who did not know what they were doing was wrong? What does *knowing* mean? Does it mean that a person was not acting unconsciously? Must a defendant know that she does not have a permit and that federal law requires one? These questions are considered later in this chapter.

3. **Citizen prosecution — qui tam?** If federal (and potentially state) prosecutors decline to prosecute a particular action, for whatever prosecutorial discretion reason, the violation is unlikely to be criminally prosecuted. In some circumstances, citizens attempted to obtain prosecution of particularly egregious polluters by seeking to file qui tam actions themselves against polluters. The qui tam action is a traditional remedy by which a citizen can bring a lawsuit "in the name of the King." Most qui tam suits have failed, but cf. Alameda Conservation Ass'n v. California, 437 F.2d 1087 (9th Cir.), cert. denied, 402 U.S. 908 (1971).

4. **Statutory interpretation issues.** What is "refuse"? Does it include pollution? Yes, said United States v. Standard Oil Co., 384 U.S. 224 (1966). Ultimately even temperature changes came to be regarded as "refuse" and thereby as violations of the statute. What does the Refuse Act thus teach about the life history of statutory enactments? Industrial corporations were the primary targets of Refuse Act prosecutions in the 1960s. Is there any question in your mind what would have happened if someone had told the Congress in 1899 that the statute would be applied against manufacturers producing liquid pollution wastes?

A criminal statute is a potent piece of legislatively created law. It is, however, both a crude blunt instrument and a relatively unguided missile. The words that it embodies continue to be law while surrounding circumstances may change. The legislators who write a statute do not thereafter act as judges determining how it should be applied; the separation of powers sees to that. If the words of the statute are perfectly clear, its application follows, even 70 years after the statute was written. If the citizen activists who pushed prosecutions of the Refuse Act knew that the legislature that had passed the law intended that it have no application to circumstances like pollution, were they being unethical in seeking prosecutions under the Act?

5. **Permits.** Even if prosecutions under the Refuse Act were not certain to follow, many polluters in the 1960s understandably wanted to avoid the possibility of being -prosecuted and started seeking permits from the Corps of Engineers to cover their effluent outfall pipes. Under the terms of the statute, can or must the Corps of Engineers' Chief of Engineers issue permits? Must a permit's issuance or denial be based solely on questions of anchorage and navigation, or can the Corps include other public concerns such as pollution, especially after 1970, when NEPA became law? Must the Corps of Engineers base its permit issuance on considerations of public health and environmental quality? NEPA declared the responsibility of all federal government agencies, including the Corps, to improve environmental quality, said Zabel v. Tabb, 430 F.2d 199 (5th Cir. 1970).

6. **Juries.** In virtually all environmental prosecutions, the defendants will have the right to a jury. Is it any surprise that most of the reported environmental criminal cases are tried to a judge without a jury? In all probability, why did they not request juries in those cases? Jury reactions and verdicts can vary with the environmental setting. How dramatic were the results of the offense? How readily can the jury see itself in the role of victim rather than defendant? What deference attaches to corporate white collar defendants? Is jury nullification — always a possibility in the Anglo-American jury system — a reasonable tactic, or is the jury's hyper-vindictiveness rather to be feared? It depends on the case.

7. **The effectiveness of the Refuse Act.** The effectiveness of the Refuse Act was extraordinary in getting the attention of American polluters. Why does criminal law have this effect? In reality, not many executives can expect to go to jail, and their corporations certainly can be expected to pay any individual fines that corporate officers are assessed in criminal prosecutions. Conviction of a criminal offense, even a misdemeanor, seems to attach some special stigma to corporate officials, unlike civil penalties that are often merely perceived as a cost of doing business. Even though the chance of being convicted may be small, the uncertain possibility is something that no executive lives with easily.

The CWA replaced some of the Refuse Act, but some provisions are still enforced. Ten to fifteen major Refuse Act prosecutions are initiated each year by the Department of Justice, mostly under §407. According to one federal prosecutor, the old statute has major advantages over comparable provisions of the modern CWA. Under the latter statute, for example, defendants can gain immunity from prosecution by self-reporting; the Refuse Act includes no such immunity. The Act continues to serve as an indication of the perils and potential of environmental criminal statutes.

8. **Questioning the effectiveness of criminal prosecutions.** What particular effectiveness does a criminal statute add to the system of pollution laws? Environmental criminal statutes are crude instruments. Often environmental crimes are "accidental." In such cases, is it clear that criminal penalties are appropriate? When do criminal prosecutions constitute overkill? Criminal fines bear no necessary relationship to the amount of harm caused by pollution, and they are not paid into a pollution control fund. Jail sentences can vary widely from judge to judge, although federal sentencing guidelines have reduced the variations between sentences for similar offenses.

Even in the most dramatic cases, criminal prosecutions pose logistical and political problems. The Exxon-Valdez oil spill of March 24, 1989 was the worst oil spill in the history of the United States. It now appears probable that the Alaska spill was not caused only or even primarily by the known alcoholism of the tanker's captain. There appears to have been a consistent corporate shortcutting of safety procedures, cutting back on necessary shipboard personnel to save on payrolls, and perhaps even using financial incentives to encourage ships to run at higher speeds regardless of weather and water conditions. If these and other assertions were proved true and causative, the corporation and its officers would face criminal charges under the Refuse Act §407 and other federal statutes, as well as state laws. But the wreck was not an intentional act; it was "accidental." What further purpose is served by prosecution? What does it say about environmental criminal prosecutions that both the federal and Alaska state governments strenuously avoided criminal trials against Exxon, Alyeska, and their executives?[1]

B. AN INCREASING WILLINGNESS TO PROSECUTE ENVIRONMENTAL CRIMES

People v. Film Recovery Systems, Inc.; Metallic Marketing Systems, Charles Kirschbaum, Daniel Rodriguez, Steven O'Neil

Circuit Court, Cook County, Illinois, Fourth Division
No. 83-11091 (involuntary manslaughter); No. 84-5064 (murder), June 14, 1985

Oral Verdict from the Bench

BANKS, J. This court is being reconvened this afternoon in order for me to render a decision in the case against Film Recovery Systems, Inc., Metallic Marketing Systems, Inc., Steven O'Neil, Charles Kirschbaum, and Daniel Rodriguez.

The record should be clear the defendants are charged with the following offenses: Steven O'Neil, Charles Kirschbaum, and Daniel Rodriguez are charged by way of indictment No. 84 C–5064 with murder as defined in Chapter 38 Section 9-1-a-2, that being "A person who kills an individual without lawful justification commits murder if, in performing the acts which cause the death, such person knows that such acts create a strong probability of death or great bodily harm to the individual or another." Also, the defendants Film Recovery Systems, and Metallic Marketing Systems, Inc. are charged by way of indictment No. 83 C–11091 with involuntary manslaughter and fourteen counts of reckless conduct. Also, Steven O'Neil, Daniel Rodriguez, and Charles Kirschbaum are charged in the same indictment with fourteen counts of reckless conduct.

Before I render a decision in this case, I would like to set forth some of the reasons for my decision. I would like to make it known and make it perfectly clear that the reasons I state are not the total basis for my decision in this case. My decision in this case is based on total review of all evidence presented in this case by both the State and Defense....

During my deliberations and evaluations of all the evidence, let it be known that I never forgot the most important concept in criminal law, that being the defendants are presumed innocent and that it is the burden of the State that they must prove guilt beyond a reasonable doubt.

I hereby make the following findings: No. 1: Stefan Golab died of acute cyanide toxicity. I arrived at that conclusion in the following way: many witnesses testified to the conditions of the air in the plant; not only workers, but independent witnesses as well, such as insurance inspectors, OSHA inspectors, Environmental Protection Agency inspectors, police officers and other service representatives. The testimony of the police investigators is the most important because although we do not know the actual amount of hydrogen cyanide gas in the air on February 10, 1983, the date of the death of Stefan Golab.... The symptoms were classical symptoms, which, according to the Material Safety Data Sheet, would occur if exposed to hydrogen cyanide gas at

---

1. The federal government ultimately negotiated a criminal settlement out of court with Exxon, by which a fine of $100 million was remitted down to $25 million in light of the civil responsibility the defendant had taken on. Captain Hazelwood was not prosecuted under the federal water pollution act because the CWA provides immunity for self-reported acts, and Hazelwood had self-reported the spill when he had radioed the Coast Guard, "Uh…we seem to have got stuck on Bligh Reef, and are losing a little oil…."

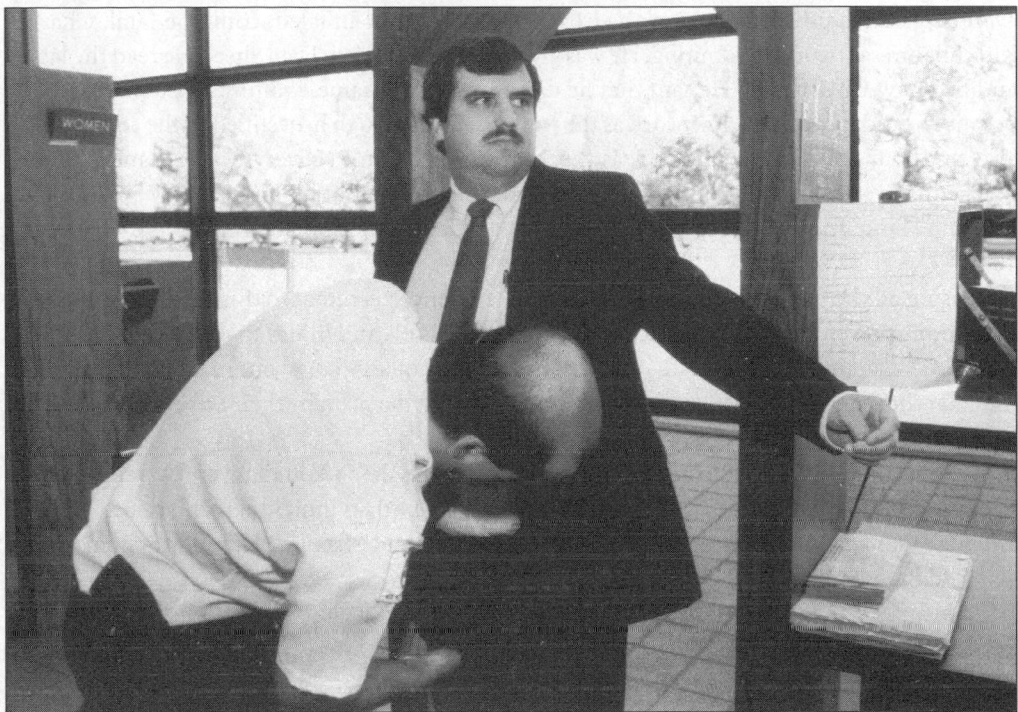

FIGURE 20-1

Former president of Film Recovery Systems Inc., Steven O'Neil, being searched before being sentenced to 25 years in prison for the job-related death of an employee at his Elk Grove Village plant. Prosecutors said O'Neil and two other executives were "motivated by greed and greed alone." Convicted of murder, he theoretically could have faced execution.

high levels — nausea, burning throat, burning eyes, difficulty breathing, plus others.

No. 2: I believe also the Medical Examiner, because in the Medical Examiner and toxicologist reports, the victim had a blood cyanide level of 3.45 micrograms per milliliter, which is a lethal dose and can be fatal. The manufacturer states that sodium cyanide...when mixed with a weak alkali, with water in this case, having a pH of approximately seven, will create hydrogen cyanide gas.

I find that the conditions under which the workers in the plant performed their duties was totally unsafe. There was an insufficient amount of safety equipment present on the premises. There were no safety instructions given to the workers. The workers were not properly warned of the hazards and dangers of working with cyanide. The warning signs were totally inadequate. The warning signs were written in Spanish and English. The warning signs stated the words "poison," or "veneno" meaning poison in Spanish. The problem with that is that...aside from the Spanish and American workers, there was Stefan Golab, plus other Polish workers. The evidence has shown that Stefan Golab did not speak English, could not read or write English, so a sign in Spanish had no benefit to that man at all.

The Cyanogran label...states that there are three ways in which cyanide can be fatal; one being inhalation of the gas hydrogen cyanide, one being ingestion of sodium cyanide, and third, the absorption into the skin of the sodium cyanide.... This was not told to the workers....

I also find the defendants were totally knowledgeable in the dangers which are associated with the use of cyanide.... The defendants knew that the workers were becoming nauseated and vomiting. The workers complained to all three of the defendants. Steven O'Neil knew hydrogen cyanide gas was present. He knew hydrogen cyanide gas, if inhaled, could be fatal. Charles Kirschbaum saw workers vomiting. He was given a Material Safety Data Sheet. He read the label, and he knew what it said. He said that he did not wear the same equipment the workers did because he did not do the same work as the workers, even though he testified to the contrary.... I also find that Steven O'Neil, who was the President of Film Recovery Systems and Metallic Marketing Systems, was in control and exercised control over both Film Recovery Systems and Metallic Marketing Systems before and after the death of Stefan Golab, which was on February 10, 1983.

Using all the facts stated above and all other evidence pertinent to this case, I find that the conditions present in the work place which caused sickness and injury to workers was reckless conduct. I also find that the death of Stefan Golab was not accidental but in fact murder. I also find that the defendants created the conditions present in the plant by their acts of omission and commission....

Therefore, it is the decision of this Court that the defendants Steven O'Neil, Charles Kirschbaum and Daniel Rodriguez are guilty of murder both as individuals and also as officers and high managerial personnel of Film Recovery Systems and Metallic Marketing Systems, Inc. I also find that they are guilty of murder and reckless conduct....

I also find that because of the negligence and reckless behavior of both Film Recovery Systems, Inc. and Metallic Marketing Systems...the corporations are guilty of involuntary manslaughter and fourteen counts of reckless conduct....

Finally, and this is the most important part and most difficult part for a Judge, I believe because the cloak of innocence has been removed from the accused and because the charge of murder, which the defendants have been found guilty of, does not carry probation and carries a minimum of twenty years in the penitentiary, it is my duty to revoke all bail and the defendants shall be remanded to the custody of the Sheriff's Office, awaiting sentencing, and it is the order of this Court that the bonds be revoked.

At this time, gentlemen, I am going to set a date for sentencing....

Steven Ferrey, Hard Time: Criminal Prosecution for Polluters
10.4 Amicus Journal 11 (Fall 1988)

On the surface, it was a model company. It recycled valuable minerals from waste materials, and had a stellar record on hiring minorities. But beyond the facade lurked a darker, more ominous, and deadly story.

Film Recovery Systems...extracted trace amounts of silver from hospitals' discarded X-ray film by using sodium cyanide. In its heyday, the company employed eighty workers and earned about $18 million annually. But in its unventilated workroom, employees hunched over 140 bubbling, foaming cauldrons of sodium cyanide. They were issued no protective gear and were not instructed in safety measures. While manually stirring these vats, sodium cyanide slopped over the sides, soaking the workers' clothing and skin. The air was choked with the fumes of hydrogen cyanide gas.

Film Recovery employed illegal Mexican and Polish immigrant laborers almost exclusively in its silver-recovery process.... Few workers spoke English; even fewer could read. The common antidote for cyanide poisoning, amyl nitrite, was not available at the facility. Even the skull-and-crossbones warning labels on the drums of the cyanide were covered over or obscured by management. One day in February 1983, Stefan Golab, a Polish immigrant, stumbled into the lunchroom, fell to the floor with nausea, and died from acute cyanide poisoning. He was fifty-nine years old....

Jay Magnuson, of the Cook County State's Attorney's Office [who obtained the original indictments] prosecuted Film Recovery President Steven O'Neil, the plant manager, and the foreman, for murder. "Callously, they knowingly maintained an unsafe plant environment that was likely to cause death to workers," Magnuson remarks. "I never had a second thought that they should be convicted for murder."...

Investigators later discovered almost 15 million pounds of cyanide waste from Film Recovery that had been dumped illegally in rented truck trailers parked in other parts of Illinois. The EPA used $4.5 million of taxpayer's funds to clean up this toxic debris. Decontamination of the facility cost the building's landlord $250,000.

[Before Film Recovery,] jail sentences for polluters were unheard of. At worst, the penalty for violating environmental or workplace safety laws was a modest fine. On the remote chance of getting caught, the fines could be rationalized as just another cost of doing business.

But times are changing. Federal and state laws covering hazardous waste, clean air, clean water, and workplace safety impose stiff civil and criminal penalties of up to $25,000 per violation. Like expanding reflections in a carnival mirror, one transgression magnifies into multiple dimensions. A single polluting action can violate several laws simultaneously, and each day of violation is counted by the courts as if it were a new violation. A single act of pollution becomes a serious and compounded felony. "Corporate America will readily take notice of environmental statutes when they start going to jail for their violations," says Glenn Sechen, assistant prosecutor for Cook County. "It simply ceases to be a cost of doing business when it becomes their own necks."

The impact of environmental prosecution has been refocused on individuals. The protective wall between corporate actions and corporate executives is eroding.... The U.S. Department of Justice has brought criminal indictments against 328 individuals and 117 corporations for environmental pollution. The courts have imposed 203 years of jail time and collected $12 million in fines. Sixty-four years of those sentences already have been served. Of those sentenced, about one-third were corporate presidents, 12 percent were vice-presidents, an additional 5 percent were corporate officers, and 20 percent were managers or foremen. Less than 25 percent of those sentenced to jail were the workers who actually released the pollution.

How high in the corporate hierarchy prosecutions reach is a function of employee cooperation in providing evidence against co-workers. An emerging lesson is that the middle of a large corporate ladder can be a perilous place to perch in a company that ignores environmental requirements. At the lower end of the corporation, the "Nuremberg defense" can be an effective escape. Prosecutors are reticent to indict lower-level personnel who claim that they unknowingly were "just following orders" when breaking an environmental law.

Correspondingly, in large corporations, the top-level management may not have direct knowledge of polluting activities. The buck often stops on the desk of middle-level managers, identified by employees as the ones giving the orders to engage in polluting activities. Ironically, a large corporation, with a diffuse management structure and unclear lines of responsibility, may shield executives from potential criminal liability.

In a survey of environmental prosecutions on the East Coast...the typical company cited was small, employing less than fifty persons.... About a quarter are dismissed before a verdict, about half result in guilty pleas by defendants, and of the remaining cases that proceed through a trial, three quarters result in convictions while about a quarter result in acquittals.

Despite successful prosecutorial records in several states, most local prosecutors do not actively pursue criminal environmental polluters. The barriers can be daunting. "Judges understand a smoking gun and a bag of heroin as criminal. They do not understand environmental pollution," laments Lieutenant Gary Long of the Illinois State Police environmental unit — some prosecutors argue privately that criminal court judges, experienced in dealing with common criminals, are uncomfortable with prosecution of executives in Gucci loafers [and with] the very large penalties in environmental statutes ($25,000 per violation per day)....

Problems of proof can be substantial. Documenting the facts and dates of actual polluting activities can prove elusive without help from informants. Allegations against criminal defendants must be proved beyond reasonable doubt. Not all convictions result in jail sentences, and not all jail sentences actually are served. Liberal use of suspended sentences, immediate probation, sentences served on weekends only, and other "innovative" programs mitigate the service of "hard" time. A typical jail sentence is about sixty to ninety days.

Environmental criminals often qualify for treatment that Lynch describes as "commit a crime, go to your room." With jails overcrowded, convicted executives typically fit the profile for release programs: they have ties to the community, references from prominent persons, and are not violent or likely to flee. Consequently, some serve time by wearing an identification bracelet and confining their activities to their homes.

Despite practical problems, criminal prosecution has assumed center stage in environmental enforcement. For an executive, the prospect of incarceration with violent felons focuses the attention like few other sanctions. In return for no jail time, defendants often are willing to plead guilty to violations carrying very large fines.... Until the corporation also can serve time, criminal prosecution of individual corporate executives will remain the most potent weapon in the expanding arsenal of environmental enforcement.

COMMENTARY & QUESTIONS

1. **The aftermath of the *Film Recovery* convictions.** *Film Recovery* was a strategic environmental prosecution because of the dramatic way its precedent-setting homicide charge was covered by the press (the first time in living memory that a corporate executive had been prosecuted for murder in connection with environmental pollution). Less press attention was paid to the aftermath: Judge Banks sentenced Steven O'Neil to 25 years in jail for murder and reckless conduct, but after several unsuccessful appeals urging that the state homicide statute was preempted by the federal OSHA statute, an Illinois appellate court overturned the convictions in 1991. The court held:

> Because the offenses of murder and reckless conduct require mutually exclusive mental states, and because we conclude [that the trial court used the] same evidence of the individual defendants' conduct...to support both offenses and does not establish, separately, each of the requisite mental states, we conclude that the convictions are legally inconsistent. People v. O'Neil, 550 N.E.2d 1090, 1098 (Ill. App. 1991).

Do you see the problem? In most states, murder in the first or second degree requires proof of an intent to kill, while negligent homicide (involuntary manslaughter) and the lesser charge of reckless conduct are based on unintentional harms. The trial judge may have based his verdicts on the wording of part of the Illinois murder statute, which seems to allow a murder conviction without intent to kill if a person "knows that such acts create a strong probability of death or great bodily harm to that individual or another," Chap. 720 Ill. Comp. Stat. 5/9-1, but the appeals court rejected that logic.

To avoid a retrial, the Film Recovery executives cut a deal. On the factual record found in Judge Banks's opinion, in 1993 O'Neil, Kirschbaum, and Rodriguez pleaded guilty to involuntary manslaughter. O'Neil served three years in prison, Kirschbaum got two years in prison, and Rodriguez received two years' probation. Another executive, David McKay, pleaded down to one misdemeanor charge of reckless conduct, and got six months' probation, 100 hours of community service, and a $1000 fine. The new Cook County state's attorney apparently made the deals because he did not believe murder charges were warranted on these environmental facts. Given the murder count, it is not clear why the executives had not also initially been charged with involuntary manslaughter, instead of the lesser reckless conduct. (In this regard, note the remarkably different options available to prosecutors in environmental cases, ranging here from reckless conduct, with simple misdemeanor fines, up to first degree murder for which O'Neil could theoretically have been executed.) With regard to criminal intent, how would you have chosen among the relevant variables of — whether to charge murder, what range of penalties was appropriate, and whether the fact that harm was caused by an indirect environmental exposure lessens the criminality of the act?

The media coverage of *Film Recovery*'s original murder convictions appears to have encouraged prosecution throughout the country for environmental crimes. In Los Angeles, for instance, then District Attorney Ira Reiner made a name for his department by setting up an environmental crime specialty division with 20 attorneys and investigators, prosecuting a wide range of offenses, and L.A. attorneys who specialize in environmental defense work are currently billing in excess of $400 an hour with no market resistance from their frightened clientele. "Clients will say, 'If I'm being sued for dumping toxic wastes, I don't care what it costs to pay the lawyer. I just need to get out of this problem,'" L.A. Times, Sept. 18, 1989, at 1.

In a more recent echo of *Film Recovery*, a district court in Idaho held industrialist Alan Elias, owner of Evergreen Resources, Inc., liable for knowingly exposing a worker to hazardous waste. United States v. Elias, No. CR 98-00070-E-BLW (D. Idaho May 1999). The exposure, which resulted in brain damage to the employee, followed the defendant's order to wash down a 25,000-gallon tank of waste containing phosphoric acid and cyanide. This combination of chemicals produces a gas like that used in the World War II Nazi death camps. Elias was ordered to pay a criminal fine of $5.9 million.

2. *Film Recovery* **and preemption.** What is your assessment of the reliability of law enforcement efforts by the federal OSHA in the Film Recovery case? Should the existence of OSHA preclude other remedies like the state's criminal charges? As Professor Ferrey notes, "The tragedy of Stefan Golab's death is compounded by the fact that OSHA had given the firm a clean bill of health only months before. In the fall of 1982 OSHA inspectors visited the plant, but they never got past the front office, where they saw nothing out of the ordinary in the company's paperwork. They did not walk the additional twenty-five feet beyond the office doors to observe Golab and others hunched over gurgling vats of cyanide. After Golab's death, OSHA inspectors descended on the plant, fining management the seemingly arbitrary and insignificant amount of $4,855. Film Recovery refused to pay, so OSHA reduced it by half, though to this day it has not collected."

Despite an agency's general fecklessness, however, defendants are sometimes successful in persuading courts that the existence of federal statutory remedies precludes and preempts application of general state criminal statutes. See People v. Chicago Magnet Wire, 510 N.E.2d 1173 (Ill. App. 1987) (reversed in 1989 by the Illinois Supreme Court).

3. **Trends in environmental criminal prosecutions.** Environmental prosecutions have been heating up for many years on both the federal and state level, and that trend has continued. During the 1970s, under avowed conservationist Jimmy Carter, only 25 federal environmental prosecutions were commenced. Between 1982 and 1989 under Ronald Reagan's law-and-order policies, there were more than 450 indictments, more than 325 pleas or convictions, almost 100 of them against corporations, with assessed fines of over $13 million (although 20% or more of these appear to have been suspended) and jail terms of more than 200 years (mostly against noncorporate individual offenders), with nearly 65 years of jail time actually being served. Through the Clinton Administration years, the rate of criminal prosecutions continued to rise. The majority of environmental prosecutions, however, unlike *Film Recovery*'s murder indictment, were straightforward regulatory enforcement actions brought by state and federal agencies based on alleged violations of permits and statutory requirements under the CWA, CAA, ESA, and the like, and their state equivalents. To date, in the Bush II Administration, criminal prosecutions have remained a normal part of the administrative arsenal, considered as a necessary backup to regulatory compliance programs. In 2002, EPA made 250 criminal referrals to the Department of Justice (DOJ), a figure slightly decreased from the 256 referrals in 2001. Criminal penalties continued in significance at over $62 million; and criminal sentences also continued apace, totaling 215 years. There continues to be a willingness, as the statistics indicate, to prosecute environmental crimes.

C. CRIMINAL LIABILITY: PROBLEMS OF KNOWLEDGE AND INTENT

Underlying the criminal enforcement of the environmental laws is an implicit question: How much "criminal intent," a.k.a. "mens rea knowledge" or "scienter," must be proved in order to convict a defendant of an environmental crime? Where a statute requires proof of a "knowing" or "willful" violation, how much knowledge does that mean, of what? (And where a statute contains no expressed requirement of knowledge or willfulness, like §411 of the Refuse Act, when can a defendant constitutionally be convicted without any proof of criminal intent?)

United States v. Ahmad
United States Court of Appeals for the Fifth Circuit, 1996
101 F.3d 386

Attique Ahmad appeals his conviction of, and sentence for, criminal violations of the Clean Water Act.... This case arises from the discharge of a large quantity of gasoline into the sewers of Conroe, Texas, in January 1994. In 1992, Ahmad purchased the "Spin-N-Market No. 12," a combination convenience store and gas station.... The Spin-N-Market has two gasoline pumps, each of which is fed by an 8000-gallon underground gasoline tank. Some time after Ahmad bought the station, he discovered that one of the tanks, which held high-octane gasoline, was leaking. This did not pose an immediate hazard, because the leak was at the top of the tank; gasoline could not seep out. The leak did, however, allow water to enter into the tank and contaminate the gas [and] Ahmad was unable to sell from it....

In October 1993, Ahmad hired CTT Environmental Services, a tank testing company, to examine the tank. CTT determined that it contained approximately 800 gallons of water, and the rest mostly gasoline. Jewel McCoy, a CTT employee, testified that she told Ahmad that the leak could not be repaired until the tank was completely emptied, which CTT offered to do for 65 cents per gallon plus $65 per hour of labor. After McCoy gave Ahmad this estimate, he inquired whether he could empty the tank himself. She replied that it would be dangerous and illegal to do so. On her testimony, he responded, "Well, if I don't get caught, what then?"...

On January 25, 1994, Ahmad rented a hand-held motorized water pump from a local hardware store, telling a hardware store employee that he was planning to use it to remove water from his backyard. Victor Fonseca, however, identified Ahmad and the pump, and testified that he had seen Ahmad pumping gasoline into the street. Oscar Alvarez stated that he had seen Ahmad and another person discharging gasoline into a manhole. Tereso Uribe testified that he had confronted Ahmad and asked him what was going on, to which Ahmad responded that he was simply removing the water from the tank.... In all, 5,220 gallons of fluid were pumped from the leaky tank, of which approximately 4,690 gallons were gasoline....

The gasoline discharged onto Lewis Street...entered a storm drain and...flowed through a pipe...into Possum Creek [which] feeds into the San Jacinto River, which eventually flows into Lake Houston. The gasoline that Ahmad discharged into the manhole...entered the city sewage treatment plant.... The plant supervisor ordered that non-essential personnel be evacuated from the plant and called firefighters and a hazardous materials crew to the scene. The Conroe fire department determined the gasoline was creating a risk of explosion and ordered that two nearby schools be evacuated. Although no one was injured as a result of the discharge, fire officials testified at trial that Ahmad had created a "tremendous explosion hazard" that could have led to "hundreds, if not thousands, of deaths and injuries" and millions of dollars of property damage. By 9:00 a.m. on January 26, investigators had traced the source of the gasoline back to the manhole directly in front of the Spin-N-Market.... The investigators questioned Ahmad, who at first denied having operated a pump.... Soon, however, his story changed: He admitted to having used a pump but denied having pumped anything from his tanks.

Ahmad was indicted for three violations of the CWA: knowingly discharging a pollutant from a point source into a navigable water of the United States without a permit, knowingly [discharging into a public sewage works] in violation of a pretreatment standard, and knowingly placing another person in imminent danger of death or serious bodily injury by discharging a pollutant.... 33 U.S.C.A. §1319 says that "any person...commits a felony...who knowingly violates" any of a number of other sections of the CWA [including §§1311(a), 1317(d), and 1319(c)(3) which comprise the three charges].

At trial, Ahmad did not dispute that he had discharged gasoline from the tank or that eventually it had found its way to Possum Creek and the sewage treatment plant. Instead, he contended that his discharge of the gasoline was not "knowing," because he had believed he was discharging water....

The jury instruction on count one stated in relevant part: For you to find Mr. Ahmad guilty of this crime, you must be convinced that the government has proved each of the following beyond a reasonable doubt:

> (1) That on or about the date set forth in the indictment, (2) the defendant knowingly discharged, (3) a pollutant, (4) from a point source, (5) into the navigable waters of the United States, (6) without a permit to do so.

Ahmad contends that the jury should have been instructed that the statutory mens rea — knowledge — was required as to each element of the offenses, rather than only with regard to discharge. The principal issue is to which elements of the offense the modifier "knowingly" applies.... Ahmad argues that within this context, "knowingly violates" should be read to require him knowingly to have acted with regard to each element of the offenses. The government...contends that "knowingly violates" requires it to prove only that Ahmad knew the nature of his acts and that he performed them intentionally. Particularly at issue is whether "knowingly" applies to the...discharge's being a pollutant, for Ahmad's main theory at trial was that he thought he was discharging water, not gasoline....

In Staples v. United States, 511 U.S. 600 (1994), the Court found that statutes criminalizing knowing possession of a machinegun require that defendants know not only that they possess a firearm but that it actually is a machinegun.... Statutory crimes carrying severe penalties are presumed to require that a defendant know the facts that make his conduct illegal.... In United States v. Baytank (Houston), Inc., 934 F.2d 599, we concluded that a conviction for knowing and improper storage of hazardous wastes requires "that the defendant know...factually what he is doing: storing, what is being stored, and that what is being stored factually has the potential for harm to others or the environment, and that he has no permit...." This is directly analogous to the interpretation of the CWA that Ahmad urges upon us. Indeed, we find it eminently sensible that the phrase "knowingly violates" in §1319, when referring to...offenses, should uniformly require knowledge as to each of those elements rather than only one or two. To hold otherwise would require an explanation as to why some elements should be treated differently from others, which neither the parties nor the caselaw seems able to provide....

[Are] CWA violations..."public welfare offenses," under which some regulatory crimes have been held not to require a showing of mens rea[?]... The exception is narrow.... The possession of machineguns fell outside the exception.... [As] Staples held, the key is whether...the defendant [is being punished for acts that are] "traditionally lawful conduct." We hold that the offenses charged...are not public welfare offenses.

At best, the jury charge made it uncertain to which elements "knowingly" applied. At worst, and considerably more likely, it indicated that only the element of discharge need be knowing. The instructions listed each element on a separate line, with the word "knowingly" present only in the line corresponding to the element that something was discharged.... Knowledge was required only as to the fact that something was discharged, and not as to any other fact. In effect, with regard to the other elements of the crimes, the instructions implied that the requisite mens rea was strict liability rather than knowledge....

We conclude that the instructions...withdrew from the jury's consideration facts that it should have been permitted to find or not find.... The district court's instructions...indicate that it thought "knowingly" modified only the element that something was discharged.... Ahmad's defense...was built around the idea that he thought water, rather than gasoline, was being discharged. A rational jury could so have found....

We reverse Ahmad's convictions.

United States v. Weitzenhoff
United States Court of Appeals for the Ninth Circuit, 1993
35 F.3d 1275, cert. denied, 115 S. Ct. 939 (1995)

Michael Weitzenhoff and Thomas Mariani...appeal their convictions for violations of the Clean Water Act...contending that the district court misconstrued the word "knowingly" under §1319....

In 1988 and 1989 Weitzenhoff was the manager and Mariani the assistant manager of the East Honolulu Community Services Sewage Treatment Plant located not far from Sandy Beach, a popular swimming and surfing beach on Oahu. The plant is designed to treat some 4 million gallons of residential wastewater each day....

Weitzenhoff and Mariani instructed two employees at the East Honolulu sewage treatment plant to dispose of waste activated sludge on a regular basis by pumping it from the storage tanks directly into the outfall, that is, directly into the ocean. The sludge thereby bypassed the plant's effluent sampler so that the samples taken and reported to Hawaii's Department of Health and the EPA did not reflect...some 436,000 pounds of pollutant solids being discharged into the ocean.... Most of the discharges occurred during the night.... Inspectors contacted the plant on several occasions in 1988 in response to complaints by lifeguards at Sandy Beach that sewage was being emitted from the outfall, but Weitzenhoff and Mariani repeatedly denied that there was any problem at the plant.... One of the plant employees who participated in the dumping operation testified that Weitzenhoff instructed him not to say anything about the discharges, because if they all stuck together and did not reveal anything, "they [couldn't] do anything to us."...

The district court construed "knowingly" in §1319(c)(2) as requiring only that Weitzenhoff and Mariani were aware that they were discharging the pollutants in question, not that they knew they were violating the terms of the statute or permit. According to appellants, the district court erred in its interpretation of the CWA and in instructing the jury that "the government is not required to prove that the defendant knew that his act or omissions were unlawful...."

As with certain other criminal statutes that employ the term "knowingly," it is not apparent from the face of the statute whether "knowingly" means a knowing violation of the law or simply knowing conduct that is violative of the law.... Our conclusion that "knowingly" does not refer to the legal violation is fortified by decisions interpreting analogous public welfare statutes. The leading case in this area is United States v. International Minerals & Chem. Corp., 402 U.S. 558 (1971). In International Minerals, the Supreme Court construed a statute which made it a crime to "knowingly violate any regulation" promulgated by the ICC...for the safe transport of corrosive liquids. The Court held that the term "knowingly" referred to the acts made criminal rather than a violation of the regulation, and that "regulation" was a shorthand designation for the specific acts or omissions contemplated by the Act. "Where...dangerous or deleterious devices or products or obnoxious waste materials are involved, the probability of regulation is so great that anyone who is aware that he is in possession of them or dealing with them must be presumed to be aware of the regulation."...

Parties such as Weitzenhoff are closely regulated and are discharging waste materials that affect public health. The International Minerals rationale requires that we impute to these parties knowledge of their operating permit.[2] This was recognized by the Court in Staples v. United States, 511 U.S. 600 (1994)...holding...that the government is required to prove that a defendant charged with possession of a machinegun knew that the weapon he possessed had the characteristics that brought it within the statutory definition of a machinegun. But the Court...explicitly contrasted the mere possession of guns to public welfare offenses, which include statutes that regulate "dangerous or deleterious devices or products or obnoxious waste materials," and confirmed the continued vitality of statutes covering public welfare offenses,

---

2. [In] United States v. Speach, 968 F.2d 795, 796-97 [9th Cir. 1992]...we held that 42 U.S.C. §6928(d)(1), which imposes criminal liability on parties who "knowingly transport...hazardous waste...to a facility which does not have a permit," requires that the transporter know that he acted in violation of the statute.... Speach recognizes the general rule that public welfare offenses are not to be construed to require proof that the defendant knew he was violating the law in the absence of clear evidence of contrary congressional intent, and finds only a narrow exception to this general rule...that the defendant was not the permittee but simply the individual who transported waste to the permittee, and...was not...in the best position to know the facility's permit status.

which "regulate potentially harmful or injurious items" and place a defendant on notice that he is dealing with a device or a substance "that places him in responsible relation to a public danger. In such cases Congress intended to place the burden on the defendant to ascertain at his peril whether [his conduct] comes within the inhibition of the statute."...

The dumping of sewage and other pollutants into our nation's waters is precisely the type of activity that puts the discharger on notice that his acts may pose a public danger. Like other public welfare offenses that regulate the discharge of pollutants into the air, the disposal of hazardous wastes, the undocumented shipping of acids, and the use of pesticides on our food, the improper and excessive discharge of sewage causes cholera, hepatitis, and other serious illnesses, and can have serious repercussions for public health and welfare.

The criminal provisions of the CWA are clearly designed to protect the public at large from the potentially dire consequences of water pollution, and as such fall within the category of public welfare legislation.... The government did not need to prove that Weitzenhoff and Mariani knew that their acts violated the permit or the CWA. We affirm both the convictions....

COMMENTARY & QUESTIONS

1. *Ahmad* **and** *Weitzenhoff.* Are these two cases inconsistent? The *Ahmad* court didn't think so, saying that *Weitzenhoff* "was concerned almost exclusively with whether the language of the CWA creates a mistake-of-law defense, [and didn't address the] mistake of fact or the statutory construction issues raised by *Ahmad*." 101 F.3d at 390. If a jury decided that Ahmad truly did not realize that he was discharging gasoline, doesn't the *Ahmad* decision make sense on mistake of fact grounds? (You may suspect that Ahmad actually did know he was discharging gasoline, but the court reminds us that this issue was contested and had not yet been decided by a jury.) Or would it be enough that he knew he was discharging something dangerous or illegal (which McCoy's evidence indicated), which would bring him closer to *Weitzenhoff*? The two cases also clearly reach contrary conclusions about whether CWA violations are "public welfare offenses."

2. **Degrees of knowledge and "intent."** There is a spectrum of interpretation of the different degrees of knowledge that may be applied in cases like these where a statute requires proof that defendants "knowingly" violate its provisions. The range analytically extends from defendants' mere consciousness of the fact of their physical action, to highly specific and willed violation of particular known laws. Here is a rough progression of possible interpretations of what amount of "knowledge" or "scienter" of defendents is required to be proved in order to convict:

(a) "Knowledge" only that they are doing a specific physical action,[3] while not realizing at all that the action happens to fit the description of a crime. (This is the lowest level of "knowledge," only requiring proof that they did the physical act consciously and amounts to liability with no proof of intent. Proof of at least this level of knowledge is probably necessary in every crime.)

(b) Knowledge of the identity of an instrument to some degree of specificity — e.g., knowing that a liquid being discharged is gasoline, or a toxic chemical, or a sludge — without knowing that dumping of such liquids is illegal or possibly harmful.

---

3. Acts of omission add another level of subtlety: Where defendants can violate a law by failing to act, how much in each case do they have to know of the duty to act and how it may be breached?

(c) Knowledge of a specific necessary element of a particular violation, as for discharges under an invalid permit, where defendants say they did not know the permit wasn't valid.

(d) Knowledge, actual or constructive, that such an act might harm individuals or the public (with different degrees of probability ranging from trivial to high likelihood; this often constitutes a negligence-based rather than intent-based culpability).

(e) Knowledge that an act would harm individuals or the public, and specifically intending so to hurt them.

(f) Knowledge that an action is probably illegal because it may harm individuals or the public.

(g) Knowledge that an action is illegal and harmful, but not knowing what specific law is violated (this may also include different degrees of knowledge about degrees of seriousness of the offense, as in acting in the belief that a serious felony is just a trivial misdemeanor).

(h) Knowledge that what they are doing specifically violates a particular provision, e.g., "Hah, what I'm doing here will violate 40 C.F.R. §129.102(b)(3)(i) under 33 U.S.C. §1317(a)(2)!"

Isn't it likely that virtually no defendants will have the highest degree of specialized knowledge? The question is rather where a court will draw the line — based on statutory interpretation, the common law of a statute, and constitutional due process — defining the minimum necessary degree of proof of knowledge.

Courts tend to accept decreased degrees of knowledge when the offense is recognized as a "public welfare offense" and tend to require greater degrees of knowledge, or "specific intent," when penalties are severe and include incarceration. When a court says the prosecution must prove "specific intent," however, it is not necessarily clear which kind of specific intent is being required. Would the *Ahmad* court, after holding that Ahmad had to know his discharge was gasoline (on the mistake-of-fact defense), also require proof that he specifically knew Lake Houston was navigable and that Possum Creek flowed into it? Or that his pump was legally a "point source" (on a mistake-of-law defense)? If not, the court implicitly concedes that not all the elements of a crime must be known by the defendant in order to convict. The Fourth Circuit, however, has implied that strict proof of knowledge of both law and fact elements is required. United States v. Wilson, 133 F.3d 251 (4th Cir. 1997).

3. **Is specific intent a proxy for "knowingly" violating the CWA?** In United States v. Metalite Corp., 2000 U.S. Dist. LEXIS 11507 (S.D. Ind. 2000), a federal district court discussed *Ahmad* and *Wilson* in the context of a mistake-of-fact defense in CWA criminal cases. The indictment charged the defendant Metalite Corp. with "knowingly discharging and causing the discharge of a pollutant, chemical wastes…into waters of the United States" in violation of U.S.C. §1319(c)(2)(A). In rejecting the defendant's argument that the relevant sections of the CWA outline a specific intent crime, the court relied on decisions by five other circuit courts to analyze what constituted a "knowing violation" under the CWA:

BARKER, J.… Although the words "knowingly violate" seem clear in the context of §1319(c)(2)(A) itself, their meaning is less clear when the statute is read as a whole.... When the CWA enforcement provisions are read as a whole, it seems likely that Congress intended "knowingly violates [certain sections]" to be "construed as a shorthand designation for specific acts or omissions which violate the Act.".... The change by the amendment of the CWA's criminal intent language from "willful" to "knowing" suggests Congress did not intend a "knowing violation" to require specific intent of illegality....

None of the five Circuit Court opinions to address the issue of the CWA's mens rea requirement has held that a defendant must know he is violating the law or a permit to be convicted of a knowing violation of the CWA under §1319(c)(2)(A). Most share the view that "requiring the government to prove that a defendant knew he was violating the law or the conditions of a permit would allow defendants to assert a 'mistake of law' defense.".... Drawing on the prevailing law in other circuits as described above, we are persuaded that §1319(c)(2)(A) does not create a specific intent crime and we therefore reject defendants' contentions....

For the reasons stated above, we find that the defendants are not entitled to dismissal of the indictment. We reject defendants' argument that the relevant sections of the CWA outline a specific intent crime and find that the indictment sufficiently communicates the offense being charged, as well as implies the correct scienter requirement, "knowingly," to the offense....

4. Syntax as part of deciding which elements must be "knowingly" violated. In United States v. Hoflin, 880 F.2d 1033 (9th Cir. 1989), a city's Director of Public works was convicted under RCRA §6928(d)(2)(A) of ordering his workers to take 14 barrels filled with waste highway paint to the grounds of the sewage treatment plant, dig a hole, and dump the drums in. Some of the drums were rusted and leaking, and at least one burst open in the process. The hole was not deep enough, so the employees crushed the drums with a front-end loader to make them fit, and they were then covered with sand. Hoflin appealed on the grounds that the jury should have been required to find that he knew the city did not have a permit to dispose of the barrels. RCRA §6928(d)(2)(A) provides:

> (d) Criminal Penalties.... Any person who...(2) knowingly treats, stores or disposes of any hazardous waste identified or listed under this subchapter either — (A) without having obtained a permit...; or (B) in knowing violation of any material condition or requirement of such permit;...shall, upon conviction, be subject to [fines, imprisonment, or both].

The Ninth Circuit interpreted this provision to require only proof that Hoflin knew the paint wastes were hazardous, not to require proof that he knew there wasn't any permit. The Third Circuit, in United States v. Johnson & Towers, Inc., 741 F.2d 662 (3d Cir. 1984), decided the other way — at least as regards prosecution of subordinate employees, the "knowingly" requirement pours over from the first clause of subsection (d)(2) into (d)(2)(a). Which court has the better of the statutory interpretation, in terms of the provision's syntax? (The word *knowing* is left out of the middle clause.)

Do you see also that in cases like *Hoflin* ignorance of the law is no defense? The court did not require proof that Hoflin knew the hazardous dumping was illegal. It used the argument that for regulatory "public welfare" statutes involving grave issues of public health, there is no need to prove mens rea unless statutory terms require it. Does the public welfare offense argument presume that when something is so noxious, everyone must know it is likely to be illegal? Many other environmental statutes besides RCRA would seem to fit this category.

5. **Constitutional dimensions: "void for vagueness."** As in many criminal cases, Weitzenhoff argued that the statute as applied was void for vagueness because it did not clearly give notice of what permit requirements would ground violations. In rejecting the vagueness defense, along with an entrapment claim, the court said, "A defendant is deemed to have fair notice of an offense if a reasonable person of ordinary intelligence would understand that his or her conduct is prohibited by the law in question," and the standard is even easier if the defendants have specialized training:

> Weitzenhoff and Mariani were knowledgeable in the wastewater field and can be expected to have understood what the permit meant. In particular, they should have known that it did not give them license to dump thousands of gallons of partially treated sewage into the ocean on a regular basis. We are further persuaded that appellants had adequate notice of the illegality of their dumping by the considerable pains they took to conceal their activities."

The "void for vagueness" challenge is a serious due process argument, but generally "in the field of regulatory statutes governing business activities, where the acts limited are in a narrow category, greater leeway [in required specificity of notice] is allowed than in statutes applicable to the general public." People v. Martin, 259 Cal. Rptr. 770, 773 (Cal. App. 1989) (a dumper of toxics disputed the specificity of "hazardous wastes"); United States v. Protex, 874 F.2d 740 (10th Cir. 1989) (a chemical company was convicted of "knowing endangerment" of workers who suffered solvent poisoning, under 42 U.S.C.A. §6928(e), of RCRA).

6. **Constitutional dimensions: due process.** Does due process nevertheless require proof of criminal knowledge, intent, or negligent fault, in no-fault crimes where the legislature expressly excludes it?

Contrast two oil spill cases: The Exxon Corporation paid millions of dollars in criminal fines for the unintended *Exxon-Valdez* oil spill, but that penalty did not seem to shock fundamental fairness, perhaps because defendants' behavior showed elements of fault: Exxon should have known its operating practices were unsafe. On the other hand, in United States v. White Fuel Corp., 498 F.2d 619 (1st Cir. 1974), a company had to pay a $1000 fine for violating §407 of the Refuse Act, for oil seepage from a half a million gallon underground leakage under their tank farm abutting Boston Harbor. White Fuel had no warning of the leakage, worked diligently to drain the accumulation, and paid for the cleanup. The court upheld criminal liability because public welfare offenses "are in the nature of neglect where the law requires care, or inaction where it imposes a duty.... The accused, if he does not will the violation, usually is in a position to prevent it with no more care than society might reasonably expect and no more exertion than it might reasonably exact from one who assumed his responsibilities. Morissette v. U.S., 342 U.S. 246, 255–256 (1952)." 498 F.2d at 622. Skepticism of this standard arises in cases like *White Fuel*, where no such neglect and no prior duty were ever proved. When there is truly "no fault" in such cases, isn't there a sense of violated due process? This sense of constitutional unfairness, however, may seem assuaged if (a) the criminal penalty is small, like White Fuel's $1000 fine, and (b) it is a corporation, not a person, that faces criminalization.

Contrast two endangered wildlife cases raising the tougher problem — where individual persons faced no-fault jail time: In United States v. Wulff, 758 F.2d 1121 (6th Cir. 1985), the defendant sold a necklace made of red-tailed hawk and great-horned owl talons to a special agent of the U.S. Fish and Wildlife Service. In United States v. Engler, 806 F.2d 425 (3d Cir. 1986), cert. denied, 481 U.S. 1019 (1987), the defendant was convicted under the same Act for the innocent sale of a protected falcon in interstate commerce. The Migratory Bird Treaty Act (MBTA, 16 U.S.C. §701) provides strict liability for sale of raptors. Without proof of knowledge or intent, defendants "shall be guilty of a felony and fined not more than $2,000 or imprisoned not more than two years, or both...."

Both courts considered the crimes "public welfare offenses," so that proof of criminal intent was not necessarily required by the Constitution. The *Wulff* court, however, found that no-fault convictions violated due process unless "the penalty is relatively small, and conviction does not gravely besmirch" an individual's reputation, quoting a test from Judge Blackmun in Holdridge v. United States, 282 F.2d 302 (8th Cir. 1960). But, it held, the MBTA's fines and two-year jail sentences "were not 'relatively small penalties.' A convicted felon loses his right to vote, his right to sit on a jury and his right to possess a gun, among other civil rights, for the rest of his life."

The *Engler* court, on the other hand, upheld the MBTA conviction, quoting the Supreme Court that "public policy may require in prohibition or punishment of particular acts...that he who shall do them shall do them at his peril and will not be heard to plead good faith or ignorance in defense.... This court cannot set aside legislation because it is harsh. Shevlin-Carpenter v. Minn., 218 U.S. 57, 70 (1910)." 806 F.2d at 434. Engler held that "Due process is not violated by the imposition of strict liability as part of a regulatory measure in the interest of public safety, which may well be premised on the theory that one would hardly be surprised to learn that the prohibited conduct is not an innocent act." Does this imply constructive knowledge? Is the sale of endangered wildlife an act that is obviously not innocent, and an offense against public welfare? Does the prohibition of such sales, as the court said, serve "a national interest of very nearly the first magnitude"? 806 F.2d at 436.

The *Engler* court ridiculed Wulff's "besmirchment" line drawing between felonies and misdemeanors, and went on to add a practical element to the due process balance: "Where the offenses prohibited and made punishable are capable of inflicting widespread injury, and where the requirement of proof of the offender's guilty knowledge and wrongful intent would render enforcement of the prohibition difficult if not impossible, the legislative intent to dispense with mens rea as an element of the offense has justifiable basis." 806 F.2d at 434 (A practical argument in the other direction is that, insofar as a statute is designed to deter proscribed acts, proof of knowing, or at least careless, acts seems logically necessary.)

7. **A scienter requirement balance?** Are some public welfare offenses more dramatic than others, so "less" scienter is required, or in such cases does more "besmirchment" of individual reputation occur, thus requiring proof of "more" scienter? Should distinctions be drawn between protections of endangered birds and protections of human

health against toxic pollution? In *Weitzenhoff*, the court noted that in the *Staples* machine gun case the Supreme Court had acknowledged a changing balance: "The penalty attached to a violation of a criminal statute in the past has been a relevant factor in determining whether the statute defines a public welfare offense.... Public welfare offenses originally involved statutes that provided only light penalties such as fines or short jail sentences, but modern statutes now punish public welfare offenses with much more significant terms of imprisonment." 35 F.3d at 1281.

8. **Strict liability and sentencing options.** In these strict liability crime cases, would you feel differently about convictions that lead only to fines and convictions that could lead to incarceration? Note also that, although fines and imprisonment are the standard criminal sanctions available to environmental prosecutors, injunctions are also available as remedies for many crimes. The field of criminal injunctions is little studied but has particular utility in the field of environmental crimes. Where due process concerns are implicated in no-fault crimes, moreover, the prospective nature of a criminal injunction intrudes far less upon defendant's rights.

D. PROBLEMS RAISED IN CORPORATE AND EXECUTIVE PROSECUTIONS

By the nature of the American economic system, much of the pollution dumped into the air and waters of the United States comes from corporate polluters, especially the most toxic of such waste streams. In *Film Recovery*, the corporation had folded, but in many cases prosecutors target established ongoing corporate enterprises in their tactical gunsights. Successful prosecution of criminal environmental violations always faces an array of difficulties not encountered in civil lawsuits, notably in Fifth Amendment and other limitations on discovery, and the special burden of proof required to prove defendants guilty "beyond a reasonable doubt," not just liable by a simple preponderance of the evidence. These difficulties are particularly pronounced in the case of prosecutions of corporations and corporate executives. In the wake of widely publicized corporate scandals involving Enron and other major corporations, these difficulties in proof are growing in significance as prosecutors strive to get tougher on corporate America.

Section 1. THE FIFTH AMENDMENT AND THE CORPORATION

A corporation can claim Fifth Amendment protections against regulatory takings and violations of procedural due process. Can a corporation take the Fifth, refusing to produce documents that may tend to incriminate it, as a natural person can? The Supreme Court's answer apparently is "no." See Hale v. Henkel, 201 U.S. 43 (1906); United States v. Morton Salt, 338 U.S. 632 (1950); Bellis v. United States, 417 U.S. 85 (1974).

In some cases, the corporation cannot even claim attorney-client privilege. People v. Keuffel & Esser Co., 227 Cal. Rptr. 13 (Cal. Ct. App. 1986) (zinc pollution). In the absence of applicable privileges, the corporation must deliver up documents in its possession even if the documents directly incriminate the individuals who make up the corporation. In such circumstances, by virtue of their corporate positions, corporate officers effectively lose the protections of the Fifth Amendment.

In an effort to motivate corporations to cooperate and avoid harsh sentences, the DOJ traditionally has applied four key factors in determining whether to prosecute criminal violations of the environmental laws: (1) whether the corporation voluntarily discloses its violation, (2) whether the corporation has a pervasive level of noncompliance, (3) whether the corporation establishes preventative measures and compliance programs, and (4) whether the corporation promulgates its own internal disciplinary actions and produces subsequent compliance. EPA has adopted similar criteria in determining whether to pursue investigations for self-disclosed violations identified during voluntary environmental audits.

The purpose of such criteria is essentially the same — to provide significant incentives inducing self-disclosure. Voluntary self-disclosures by corporations may prove very helpful to the corporation in mitigating corporate criminal and civil liabilities. As noted, however, such disclosures may well provide the evidence needed to prosecute corporate officials, whose personal Fifth Amendment rights do not prohibit corporate disclosures.

Increasingly, the DOJ has tried to drive a wedge between the corporations (who are incentivized to turn "state's evidence" and disclose) and their officers and directors (who are often targeted after corporate disclosures). In January 2003, the DOJ released a set of prosecutorial guidelines designed to put increasing pressure on corporations, in response to the recent wave of corporate scandals plaguing corporate America. According to the covering memorandum, "the main focus" of the guidelines "is increased emphasis on and scrutiny of the authenticity of a corporation's cooperation." Of special interest is the guidelines' section on decisions to charge corporations criminally, and the relevance to that decision of a corporation's "timely and voluntary disclosure of wrongdoing and its willingness to cooperate with the government's investigation." To that end, the guidelines note that a key factor prosecutors may weigh is a corporation's "waiver of the attorney-client privilege and work product protections, both with respect to its internal investigations and with respect to communications between specific officers, directors and employees and counsel."

Will these new guidelines materially change the way corporations respond to criminal investigations? Will the guidelines inhibit communications between corporate officials and corporate counsel? The guidelines indicate that, in order for a corporation to be viewed as truly cooperative, it must waive its claims of privilege and hand over to the DOJ all of the documents pertinent to any internal investigation that the corporation conducts. Rather than share information with corporate officials who may be under investigation, a corporation must instead affirmatively turn in those corporate officials who are individually responsible, if it seeks to win favor from the DOJ.

Section 2. DIFFICULTIES IN PROVING COLLECTIVE ACTIVITY CRIMES

The following excerpt notes some of the interesting issues raised by criminal indictments of corporate and individual defendants charged with environmental crimes based upon their collective activities.

William Goldfarb, Kepone: A Case Study
8 Environmental Law 645 (1978)

On May 7, 1976, the Federal grand jury in Richmond, Virginia, handed up two indictments charging Allied, LSP, the City of Hopewell, and six individuals with a total of 1,097 counts (separate offenses) relating to the Kepone incident at Hopewell. Then on July 28th, the grand jury was reconvened to hear further evidence, and the result was a third indictment issued on August 2, 1976.

Indictment #1 charged Allied with 940 alleged violations of the Refuse Act and FWPCA for discharging Kepone, TAIC, and THEIC from Allied's Semi-Works without permits; and one count for an alleged conspiracy to violate control laws among Allied and five of its employees. Each of the individual defendants was also charged with conspiracy to defraud the United States by providing false information regarding the Semi-Works effluent.

Indictment #2 charged Allied, LSP, Hundtofte, Moore, and the City of Hopewell with 153 counts apiece relating to the unlawful discharge of Kepone by LSP into the Hopewell sewer system. In addition, Hopewell was charged with three counts of failure to report the presence of Kepone in its municipal treatment works.

Indictment #3 contained only one count, charging Allied, LSP, Hundtofte, and Moore with conspiracy relating to LSP's discharge of Kepone.

None of the indictments related to conditions within the LSP plant, because no federal law provided for criminal sanctions for such occupational hazards.

The corporate and individual defendants were confronted by the prospect of heavy fines and jail terms if found guilty and accorded maximum sentences. Allied faced a maximum fine of more than $17 million; LSP and its co-owners $3.8 million each; the City of Hopewell $3.9 million; and the alleged co-conspirators $10,000 on each conspiracy count. The more serious potential penalty, however, was imprisonment. The counts for discharging without a permit — 940 counts in Indictment #1 and 153 in Indictment #2 — carried a maximum jail term of one year on each count. The possible penalty on the conspiracy counts was up to five years on each count....

The CWA goes beyond the Refuse Act by explicitly extending liability to a "responsible corporate officer" for the illegal acts of his corporation. LSP as discharger and Hundtofte and Moore as its only officers obviously contravened the CWA by discharging pollutants which interfered with the Hopewell treatment plant, and continuously violating pretreatment standards — all with the knowledge of Hundtofte and Moore. The City of Hopewell was clearly in violation of its own NPDES permit by discharging an unpermitted and unreported substance (Kepone) with knowledge of its presence in the system.

Given the clear-cut direct criminal liability in this case, it is not surprising that the defendants, after having made some unsuccessful preliminary motions, chose to change their pleas from "not guilty" to "nolo contendere" on the direct liability counts[4]....

Virgil Hundtofte was permitted to plead nolo on 79 of the 153 counts of Indictment #2 (the remaining 74 counts were dismissed), and to plead "guilty" to a reduced charge of conspiring to furnish false information to the Federal government. Hundtofte also pleaded nolo to the single

---

4. There are two main reasons for entering a nolo plea. First, carrying less of a stigma than "guilty," it may be part of a plea bargaining process in which a prosecutor agrees that in return for avoiding the delay and expense of a trial he will accept a nolo plea and request the judge to impose a sentence which is lighter than the maximum. Second, the conviction of a defendant after a nolo plea cannot be used as evidence in another legal proceeding arising out of the same set of facts — for example, in a civil action for damages. Had the defendant pleaded or been found guilty, on the other hand, such a conviction would make a prima facie case for the plaintiffs in related civil cases.

conspiracy count of Indictment #3. Hundtofte also consented to appear as a witness for the United States against Allied.

Allied unexpectedly requested permission to plead nolo on 940 counts of Indictment #1. The prosecutor objected vehemently to Allied's request, but Judge Merhige accepted the nolo plea "in the interest of justice." Judge Merhige, in accepting Allied's nolo plea, afforded Allied a profound tactical advantage in subsequent civil suits.

As a result of plea bargaining, all relevant defendants had pleaded nolo to all outstanding counts charging direct violations of pollution control laws.... The ease with which the United States obtained convictions on the counts involving direct violations of law, however, stands in stark contrast to its inability to establish any vicarious liability or conspiracy regarding Allied.

As to vicarious liability, by pretrial motion, Allied sought a ruling dismissing the "conspiracy to provide false information" count on the ground that, as a matter of law, a corporation cannot be in conspiracy with its own employees who are acting within the scope of their authority.... Allied was arguing that it could not be in conspiracy with itself. The court agreed, and dismissed the count as to Allied.

Although the 153 counts of Indictment #2 and the single conspiracy count of Indictment #3 represented less than ten percent of the total number of counts in the three indictments, they were undoubtedly the most controversial and significant from the standpoint of law and public policy since they held Allied responsible for the criminal acts of LSP....

In attempting to hold Allied criminally liable for LSP's discharges, the United States relied upon four legal theories: (1) that LSP was an instrumentality of Allied; (2) that LSP was an agent of Allied; (3) that Allied was an accomplice of LSP; and (4) that Allied and LSP were engaged in a conspiracy to violate pollution control laws.

Under the instrumentality theory, the United States was called upon to prove "actual domination" of LSP by Allied. Somewhat less was necessary to establish an agency relationship: a continuous right of control by Allied (rather than actual domination), along with a consent by LSP to produce Kepone primarily for the benefit of Allied, and at least a tacit acceptance by Allied, if not an explicit condonation, of LSP's unlawful acts. Imposing accomplice liability depended upon proving that Allied "aided and abetted" LSP's illegal discharges. Accomplice liability moves from the realm of control to that of association and assistance, preserving the autonomy of accomplice and perpetrator. It is a kind of vicarious liability that does not require the corporate veil to be pierced. Finally, a conspiracy is a formal or informal agreement to commit another crime. Under a conspiracy theory, Allied and LSP would also be treated as distinct entities.

At the trial, witnesses for the United States, including Hundtofte and Moore, emphasized Allied's close knowledge of Kepone production and toxicity; the relationship of Allied to Hundtofte and Moore; the onesideness of the tolling agreement; Allied's provision of services to LSP — including sampling its effluent on a regular basis, and tours of the LSP plant by Allied's employees and consultants; and Allied's constant urging of LSP to greater Kepone production....

The defense relied on letters from LSP to Allied, allegedly written over a period of years, reassuring Allied that LSP was not discharging in violation of the law. Allied's reasonable reliance on these letters, it was urged, refuted the "instrumentality" and "agency" theories and also precluded the requisite criminal intent to aid and abet LSP's illegal discharges and to agree upon an illegal course of conduct (conspire). Counsel for Allied also highlighted Allied's willingness to pay for LSP's pollution control equipment, claiming that Allied could not have intended to break the law when it was spending money to ensure LSP's compliance.

Without a formal opinion in the case, the court exonerated Allied on all counts involving vicarious liability for LSP. While Judge Merhige's remarks during and after the trial were cryptic, he did indicate that he was not convinced beyond a reasonable doubt of Allied's having possessed the necessary intent upon which to base a conviction, a holding which might encourage corporations to enter into tolling agreements in order to evade the costs of pollution control.

Much greater publicity was accorded to the imposition of the maximum fine on Allied for its own discharges. For its conviction on the 940 counts of Indictment #1 (to which it pleaded "nolo"), Allied was fined $13.2 million. However...Allied sought a reduction in sentence based on its having set aside $8 million to fund the Virginia Environmental Endowment, a nonprofit corporation which would perform research and implement programs to mitigate the environmental effects of Kepone. Judge Merhige then adjusted the fine down to $5 million....

Hundtofte and Moore were fined $25,000 each. LSP received a fine of close to $4 million, a meaningless gesture in light of LSP's lack of assets. The city of Hopewell was fined $10,000....

Did the Kepone sentences actually do justice? Did they achieve the retribution and deterrence (both for the defendants and prospective violators) for which the criminal law strives?... Was Allied's "corporate image" tarnished, as its attorneys claimed prior to sentencing? This argument would deserve greater credence if Allied's operations were more closely related to the general public; but in fact Allied sells almost all of its chemicals to other corporations.... Would it have better served the purposes of the criminal law to have imposed jail terms on some of Allied's executives, and perhaps Hundtofte and Moore? The American public does not look favorably upon the imprisonment of corporate officers for corporate crimes. This explains why jail terms were never a viable alternative in the Kepone case. (Judge Merhige commented early on that "nobody is going to jail in this case.") Moreover, the imprisonment of corporate officers frequently does more harm than good, fostering a "demonology myth" that a few greedy industrialists are responsible for the pollution problem, whereas pollution is a pervasive result of our economic system's "externalization" of certain costs of production. The light fines imposed upon Hundtofte and Moore typify the generous treatment which cooperating corporate officials can expect to receive at the hands of the law.

But is not the function of the criminal law in pollution cases really a symbolic one, to stigmatize an offender so as to achieve deterrence, and to effectuate a catharsis of public outrage?

COMMENTARY & QUESTIONS

1. **The judge, and the absence of a jury.** Where was the jury in this criminal prosecution? Obviously Allied and its indicted executives chose to waive their constitutional right to a jury. Was this a good move? Note the effect of Judge Merhige's rulings on pleadings, on required elements of collective action crimes, and on sentencing, as well as his comments at the early stages of trial ("Nobody is going to jail..."). What effect did these have on the litigative parties? If there had been a jury, would there have been a different judicial posture?

2. **The perils of plea bargaining.** The negotiations between the U.S. Attorney's office and Hundtofte, Moore, and the City of Hopewell illustrate the potential benefits of plea bargaining to both prosecutor and defendants. Note, however, that bargains struck between the parties do not bind the judge. A tough judge could have refused to dismiss the original counts or to allow the lesser pleas, or could have ignored the prosecutors' recommendations for lighter sentences. Judges can go softer on defendants than

the terms of a bargain as well. Judge Merhige felt free to ignore the U.S. Attorney's opposition to Allied's nolo plea, even though it undermined the prosecutors' basis for the prior plea bargains. Can defendants or prosecutors whose plea bargains have not been followed by the trial judge get relief from an appellate court? Not likely because trial judges, within applicable guidelines, have substantial discretion as to whether to accept a plea bargain. In environmental cases, where criminal liability is a relatively novel phenomenon for judges, the reliability of plea bargaining for both sides may be relatively unpredictable.

3. **Allied's vicarious liability.** It is not clear why Judge Merhige dismissed all the vicarious liability counts against Allied. Does it appear that Allied was a stranger to the sloppy operations at Life Science's plant? Did Allied not have the requisite knowledge of what was going on? Should "tolling" and "maquiladora" agreements legally insulate corporate principals from the pollution of their "independent" subcontractors? If the United States had appealed dismissal of the counts holding Allied vicariously liable for LSP's pollution, which argument on the Kepone facts — "instrumentality," "agency," "accomplice," or "conspiracy" — would have appeared strongest?

4. **The Kepone fines and taxes.** Defendant industries that negotiate SEPs (supplemental environmental projects) as setoff alternatives to larger penalties often do so in order to write the sums off on their income tax returns as business expenditures under §162 of the Internal Revenue Code, or as charitable deductions under §170. As noted, Allied agreed with the judge to set up an $8 million Virginia Environmental Endowment, and the fines were then reduced from $13.2 million to $5 million. When Allied deducted the $8 million as a business expense, the IRS balked. When the tax case came to trial almost 20 years later, the court had to decide

> Whether petitioner's payment of $8,000,000 in 1977 to the Virginia Environmental Endowment Fund is deductible under §162(a) as an "ordinary and necessary business expense" or whether such payment is a "fine or similar penalty" [like the $5 million] the deductibility of which is proscribed by §162(f)....

> We accept petitioner's characterization of a "fine or similar penalty" as an involuntary payment [but] in the present case, petitioner made the $8 million payment to the Endowment with the virtual guarantee that the sentencing judge would reduce the criminal fine by at least that amount. Petitioner's characterization of this payment as "voluntary" is simply not borne out by the record as a whole.... We hold that the payment by petitioner to the Endowment was in substance a "fine or similar penalty" within the meaning of §162(f). Allied-Signal, Inc. v. Commissioner, 63 T.C.M. (CCH) 2672 (1992), aff'd without opinion, 54 F.3d 767 (3d Cir. 1995).

If prosecutors negotiating penalties wish to have penalty funds used for onsite remedies rather than merely pouring into the federal treasury, tax deductibility is a settlement incentive. Can such SEPs be made deductible? Does it make a difference if the remediation fund is set up before a judge issues a penalty ruling? Is tax deductibility sound public policy?

Section 3. EXECUTIVE LIABILITY FOR ACTS OR OMISSIONS BY SUBORDINATES

United States v. Park
United States Supreme Court, 1975
421 U.S. 658

BURGER, C.J. Acme Markets, Inc., is a national retail food chain with approximately 36,000 employees, 874 retail outlets, 12 general warehouses, and four special warehouses. Its headquarters, including the office of the president, respondent Park, who is chief executive officer of the corporation, are located in Philadelphia, Pa. In a five-count information filed in the United States District Court for the District of Maryland, the Government charged Acme and respondent with violations of the Federal Food, Drug and Cosmetic Act. Each count of the information alleged that the defendants had received food that had been shipped in interstate commerce and that, while the food was being held for sale in Acme's Baltimore warehouse following shipment in interstate commerce, they caused it to be held in a building accessible to rodents and to be exposed to contamination by rodents. These acts were alleged to have resulted in the food's being adulterated within the meaning of 21 U.S.C. §§342(a)(3) and (4), in violation of 21 U.S.C. §331(k).

Acme pleaded guilty to each count of the information. Respondent pleaded not guilty. The evidence at trial demonstrated that in April 1970 the Food and Drug Administration (FDA) advised respondent by letter of insanitary conditions in Acme's Philadelphia warehouse. In 1971 the FDA found that similar conditions existed in the firm's Baltimore warehouse. An FDA consumer safety officer testified concerning evidence of rodent infestation and other insanitary conditions discovered during a 12-day inspection of the Baltimore warehouse in November and December 1971. He also related that a second inspection of the warehouse had been conducted in March 1972. On that occasion the inspectors found that there had been improvement in the sanitary conditions, but that "there was still evidence of rodent activity in the building and in the warehouse and we found some rodent-contaminated lots of food items."...

The Government's final witness, Acme's vice president for legal affairs and assistant secretary, identified respondent as the president and chief executive officer of the company and read a bylaw prescribing the duties of the chief executive officer. He testified that respondent functioned by delegating "normal operating duties," including sanitation, but that he retained "certain things, which are the big, broad, principles of the operation of the company," and had "the responsibility of seeing that they all work together."

At the close of the Government's case in chief, respondent moved for a judgment of acquittal on the ground that "the evidence in chief has shown that Mr. Park is not personally concerned in this Food and Drug violation." The trial judge denied the motion, stating that United States v. Dotterweich, 320 U.S. 277 (1943), was controlling.

Respondent was the only defense witness. He testified that, although all of Acme's employees were in a sense under his general direction, the company had an "organizational structure for responsibilities for certain functions" according to which different phases of its operation were "assigned to individuals who, in turn, have staff and departments under them." He identified those individuals responsible for sanitation, and related that upon receipt of the January 1972 FDA letter, he had conferred with the vice president for legal affairs, who informed him that the Baltimore division vice president "was investigating the situation immediately and would be taking corrective action and would be preparing a summary of the corrective action to reply to the letter." Respondent stated that he did not "believe there was anything [he] could have done more constructively than what [he] found was being done."

On cross-examination, respondent conceded that providing sanitary conditions for food offered for sale to the public was something that he was "responsible for in the entire operation of the company," and he stated that it was one of many phases of the company that he assigned to "dependable subordinates." Respondent was asked about and, over the objections of his counsel, admitted receiving, the April 1970 letter addressed to him from the FDA regarding insanitary conditions at Acme's Philadelphia warehouse.... Finally, in response to questions concerning the Philadelphia and Baltimore incidents, respondent admitted that the Baltimore problem indicated the system for handling sanitation "wasn't working perfectly" and that as Acme's chief executive officer he was responsible for "any result which occurs in our company."...

The jury found respondent guilty on all counts of the information, and he was subsequently sentenced to pay a fine of $50 on each count.

The Court of Appeals reversed [saying] as "a general proposition, some act of commission or omission is an essential element of every crime."... It reasoned that, although our decision in United States v. Dotterweich, 320 U.S. at 281, had construed the statutory provisions under which respondent was tried to dispense with the traditional element of "awareness of some wrongdoing," the Court had not construed them as dispensing with the element of "wrongful action." The Court of Appeals concluded that...proof of this element was required by due process.... We reverse.

In *Dotterweich* [on similar facts to *Park* concerning contaminated drugs] a jury...convicted Dotterweich, the corporation's president and general manager.... This Court...observed that the Act..."dispenses with the conventional requirement for criminal conduct — awareness of some wrongdoing. In the interest of the larger good it puts the burden of acting at hazard upon a person otherwise innocent but standing in responsible relation to a public danger."... The interpretation given the Act in *Dotterweich*, as holding criminally accountable the persons whose failure to exercise the authority and supervisory responsibility reposed in them by the business organization resulted in the violation complained of, has been confirmed in our subsequent cases.... "The public interest in the purity of its food is so great as to warrant the imposition of the highest standard of care on distributors."... The Act punishes "neglect where the law requires care, or inaction where it imposes a duty." Morissette v. United States, at 255. "The accused, if he does not will the violation, usually is in a position to prevent it with no more care than society might reasonably expect and no more exertion than it might reasonably exact from one who assumed his responsibilities."...

Congress has seen fit to enforce the accountability of responsible corporate agents dealing with products which may affect the health of consumers by penal sanctions cast in rigorous terms, and the obligation of the courts is to give them effect so long as they do not violate the Constitution.

The concept of a "responsible relationship" to, or a "responsible share" in, a violation of the Act indeed imports some measure of blameworthiness; but it is equally clear that the Government establishes a prima facie case when it introduces evidence sufficient to warrant a finding by the trier of the facts that the defendant had, by reason of his position in the corporation, responsibility and authority either to prevent in the first instance, or promptly to correct, the violation complained of, and that he failed to do so.

COMMENTARY & QUESTIONS

1. **Fighting over principles?** Note that this case went up to the Supreme Court of the United States on appeal of a sentence of $50 for each of five counts. Why did Park bother? The corporation itself was also prosecuted but did not attempt to fight the conviction.

2. **Who gets targeted?** The "responsible corporate officer" doctrine. The government, if it had wished, could have prosecuted the actual workers whose acts or omissions had caused the contamination. Many statutes can be so applied, but governmental prosecutors often understandably choose to prosecute higher up the corporate chain of command if they can. The DOJ's environmental crimes division has a policy of prosecuting in each case the highest-ranking corporate officer it can reach. See Starr, Countering Environmental Crimes, 13 B.C. Envtl. Aff. L. Rev. 379 (1986).

The last line in the *Park* excerpt seems to set out an extremely inclusive definition for "responsible corporate officer" liability. Is it really that broad? The presidents of auto companies, for example, clearly have authority to prevent or correct violations of a far-off subsidiary if they are brought to their attention; the question is the interpretation to be given to the word *responsibility*. Two 1991 cases imposed much stricter requirements for the prosecution of corporate executives: In United States v. MacDonald & Watson Waste Oil Co., 933 F.2d 35 (1st Cir. 1991), and United States v. White, 766 F. Supp. 873 (E.D. Wash. 1991), the courts held that, at least for crimes for which knowledge is an element, a mere showing of official responsibility is not an adequate substitute for direct or circumstantial proof of actual knowledge. A recent analysis concluded this:

> No cases under the CWA have held a responsible corporate officer liable merely because of his or her position and it is unlikely that such a holding would occur for violations that require proof of some culpable knowledge. Such a decision may be possible, however, where the violation is based on strict liability or negligence, since there would be no scienter requirement and the conduct of the responsible corporate officer could be portrayed as deficient or negligent in some respect.... Courts have been extremely reticent to punish criminally those with only an attenuated relationship to wrongdoing. Executives must remain wary, however because decisions offering broad definitions of the rule are still being developed, particularly where hazardous substances are involved. D. Carr et al., Environmental Criminal Liability: Avoiding and Defending Enforcement Actions (1995).

The DOJ prosecutorial guidelines advise federal prosecutors to make a particularized scienter showing (direct or circumstantial) even where a statute does not require knowledge.

3. **Defensive organizational responses.** Aware of new liabilities as well as the growing public concern for the environment, many corporations are altering their internal structures to ensure environmental compliance. One common change is creation of a centralized office charged with companywide oversight, to try to ensure that pollution standards are not compromised for the sake of production, particularly given the pressures to cut corners common in times of recession. After Park, would you accept appointment as a major corporation's vice president responsible for pollution control?

4. **Executive liability, civil as well as criminal.** Park demonstrates judicial willingness to extend individual criminal liability far up the corporate executive ladder. Although this chapter focuses on criminal liability, it is appropriate to note the similarities to executive civil liability issues.

As with civil liability, corporate officers can be held criminally liable for their individual acts where they themselves dumped toxics or directly ordered employees to do so (this is obvious but is rarely easy to prove). They also can be held liable, both civilly and criminally, for actions that take place within areas of their corporate responsibility and authority.[5] In some cases, where a corporate officer is in active daily managerial control of the area of corporate activity that caused a statutory violation, liability may reflect an inference that the executive in fact personally ordered, encouraged, or winked at the acts — where these facts cannot be directly proved.[6] See, for example, United States v. Hansen, 262 F.3d 1217 (11th Cir. 2001), discussed in Section E below, where the court upholds the sufficiency of the evidence in affirming the criminal convictions of corporate officers. In other cases, liability appears to be based on a more indirect nexus — the officer's status and general authority over corporate matters. In *Dotterweich*, Justice Frankfurter held that, at least with regard to public health crimes, it is permissible to place the burden on corporate individuals who are in a position to prevent the harm from occurring "rather than to throw the hazard on the innocent public who are wholly helpless." 320 U.S. at 285. In a Vermont case, the court based liability on a finding that "each individual defendant here was either personally involved in corporate acts of Staco, *or was in a position as a corporate officer or majority stockholder to have ultimate control*." Vermont v. Staco Inc., 27 BNA Env't Rep. Cas. 1084 (D.C. Vt. 1988) (emphasis added). In a Ninth Circuit decision, the court sent a clear message that corporate executives, directors, supervisors, and managers of construction projects are personally vulnerable to the risk of criminal prosecutions for CWA violations by those under their supervision. In United States v. Hanousek, 176 F.3d 1116 (9th Cir. 1999), the court affirmed the conviction of a rock-quarrying project supervisor, holding him personally liable for negligent supervision despite the fact that the supervisor was not directly regulated under the Act and did not physically cause the violation. The oil was illegally discharged when a backhoe operator accidentally struck an oil pipeline while working at the site alone at night. Hanousek received a sentence of six months in prison, six months in a halfway house, and six months of supervised release. See also Seymour, Civil and Criminal Liability of Corporate Officers under Federal Environmental Laws, 20 BNA Env't Rptr. 337 (1989). Seymour notes that "even though...actual operating functions had been delegated to subordinate employees who exercised responsibility over the everyday operations of the company, the court...in *Park*...indicated that with the power to delegate comes a corresponding obligation on the part of high-level corporate officers to control the behavior of subordinates...." Failure to discover and correct violations, as well as failure to provide adequate supervision, can be the basis of criminal as well as civil liability. How far up the ladder does such responsibility go? Is the CEO of a Big Three automaker personally liable for an acid spill in one of the company's plating plants in Seattle? The latter, indirect theory of executive responsibility, which comes closest to executive strict liability, raises special problems in the

---

5. The concept of piercing the corporate veil is rarely relevant to the question of officer liability in the criminal setting, where proof of individual responsibility rather than availability of assets is the issue.

6. This may explain the liability found against certain officers in the cases of United States v. Carolawn Co., 21 BNA Env't Rep. Cas. 2124 (D.S.C. 1984); United States v. Pollution Abatement Servs., Inc. of Oswego, 763 F.2d 133 (2d Cir. 1985); and In re BED, EPA No. TSCA-IV-860001 (Dec. 8, 1988).

criminal setting. What if the defendant has no specific knowledge of the illegal acts? The degree to which penal sanctions can then be applied is considered in the following section of this chapter: Some statutes are written without a requirement of proof of knowledge, but constitutional questions arise whether knowledge is nevertheless required. Civil liability is freer of such constraints. Into which liability theory does Park fall, or defendant Michaels's circumstances in *NEPACCO* (see Chapter 19)?

The same defenses that may be available to executives in criminal actions — inability to prevent the violation or ignorance of the violation — are sometimes available in the civil context as well. In any case, criminal sanctions, because of their stigma and potential severity, are generally more credible as deterrents than civil penalties.

5. **Corporate ignorance as a defense.** In *Park* the defendant admitted knowing fairly specifically that there was a violation of federal law that was not being corrected. What if, as in most cases, executives say they did not know that the criminal violation was occurring? How far does the criminal responsibility set out in *Park* and *Dotterweich* extend beyond the facts of those two cases? Could prosecutors — who are continually amazed by how little, according to litigation affidavits, corporate executives know about what really goes on in their factories — base executive criminal liability on a theory of "willful ignorance"? Some executives surely instruct their employees that they "don't want to know" how certain things get done, "just get it done."

In 1991, the California Corporate Criminal Liability Act went into effect, making it a crime whenever a corporation or manager has "actual knowledge" of a serious concealed danger associated with a product or business practice and knowingly fails within 15 days (or immediately, if there is imminent risk of great bodily harm or death) to notify the state occupational safety and health agency and affected employees. Cal. Pen. Code §387. The statute provides that knowledge need not be actual awareness but may simply be possession of facts that would lead a reasonable person to believe that a danger exists.

6. **Probation for corporations.** Note that probation is an available remedy in prosecutions against corporations as well as individuals. Probation, of course, can be used to blunt the force of other remedies when used by sentencing judges to suspend fines and jail sentences so long as probation conditions are not violated. If, on the other hand, judges apply it as a supplement rather than as a substitute for fines and imprisonment, probation allows a court to maintain a watchful eye and tough control over defendants who otherwise might cut corners in future environmental compliance. A court can set out very specific terms for probation, with particular action requirements and performance standards (not to mention community service penance obligations) monitored by a probation officer to whom the defendant corporation must report regularly "like a common criminal." If the terms of probation are violated, the corporate defendants know that further specified penalties will be directly forthcoming. See Gruner, To Let the Punishment Fit the Organization: Sanctioning Corporate Offenders through Corporate Probation, 16 Am. J. Crim. L. 1 (1988).

E. REGULATORY PROSECUTIONS AND THE EFFECT OF FEDERAL SENTENCING GUIDELINES

The U.S. Sentencing Commission, originally set up by the Reagan Administration as part of its law-and-order policy, ended up establishing remarkably stringent Sentencing Guidelines applicable to all federal crimes including environmental crimes, as authorized by the Sentencing Reform Act of 1984, 28 U.S.C. Tit. 58.

The following regulatory prosecution illustrates the modern process of applying a generic sentencing formula under the Guidelines. The prosecution is also noteworthy as a virtual primer in environmental criminal law, involving violations of a panoply of federal environmental statutes (including OSHA, RCRA, CWA, CERCLA, and ESA), the sufficiency of the evidence in support of charges of "knowing endangerment," a *Daubert* motion by the defense seeking to exclude expert testimony, workers exposed to hazardous materials, questionable corporate conduct perpetrated during federal bankruptcy proceedings, and lengthy prison sentences imposed on "responsible corporate officers."

United States v. Hansen

United States Court of Appeals for the Eleventh Circuit, 2001

262 F.3d 1217, cert. denied, 535 U.S. 1111 (2002)

[This case concerned, in pertinent part, the operations of an industrial plant located in Brunswick, Georgia, adjacent to tidal marshes and a creek. The plant was operated continuously year-round and manufactured caustic soda, hydrogen gas, hydrochloric acid, and chlor-alkali bleach. Approximately 150 people worked at the plant and utilized two "cellrooms" (each about the size of a football field and each containing 50 mercury "cells") to produce bleach, soda, gas, and acid, which the plant ultimately sold. The production process generated hazardous wastes, including mercury, mercury-contaminated sludge, wastewater, and caustic wastes. The plant's wastewater treatment system had an NPDES permit to discharge treated wastewater. For a significant period of time, however, the plant discharged more wastewater than permitted, leaked wastewater into the ground, released wastewater into a nearby bodies of water, incurred accidental spills of bleach, allowed employees to be exposed to hazardous materials (some sustaining third degree burns) associated with wastewater on cellroom floors, and lacked adequate funds for cleanup, due in part to the bankruptcy of the plant's parent corporation. EPA estimated that the total cost of cleanup would exceed $50 million. Following a jury trial in federal district court, three corporate officers were convicted of conspiracy to commit environmental crimes and of criminal violations of a variety of federal environmental statutes. This appeal followed.]

PER CURIAM.... The government indicted Christian Hansen, Randall Hansen, Douglas Brent Hanson, and Alfred R. Taylor for conspiracy to commit environmental crimes at the site and various substantive crimes.... The charges included: violating the Clean Water Act...by exceeding the NPDES permit between June 1993 and January 1994..., violating the Resource Conservation and Recovery Act...by storing wastewater on the cellroom floor and permitting some to escape into the environment..., storing wastewater in...tanks [for over 90 days]..., and knowingly endangering employees by exposing them to impermissibly stored wastes and wastewaters,... violating the Comprehensive Environmental Response, Compensation, and Liability Act...by failing to notify the U.S. government of unpermitted releases of chlorine or wastewater into the environment,...and violating the Endangered Species Act...by taking an endangered species, a Wood Stork, as a result of discharging mercury into the marsh, Purvis Creek, and the Turtle River.... Hanson, the former environmental and health and safety [plant] manager, pled guilty to a CERCLA offense...and the offense under the Endangered Species Act,...and testified against [Christian] Hansen, Randall [Hansen], and Taylor....

Hansen was [convicted and] sentenced to 108 months of imprisonment, a fine of $20,000, a special assessment of $2,050, and two years of supervised release.... Randall was [convicted and] sentenced to 46 months of imprisonment, a fine of $20,000, a special assessment of $1,700, and two years of supervised release.... Taylor was [convicted and] sentenced to 78 months of imprisonment, a special assessment of $1,000, and two years of supervised release.... Each defendant appealed, and was allowed to remain on bond pending appeal....

Admission of Expert Witness Testimony. Hansen argues that the district court erred in admitting testimony from government expert witness Daniel Teitelbaum because the government failed to disclose Teitelbaum's checkered history of credibility and the court failed to conduct a hearing regarding the testimony....

The week before trial, Hansen moved for a *Daubert*[7] hearing and to exclude the testimony of expert witnesses regarding certain allegedly scientific conclusions and exhibits.... Teitelbaum testified regarding the plant employees' potential exposure to hazardous substances. Based on his review of "the large number of biological samples," "many interviews," the "documents concerning the health and hygiene program," and other documents, he found "a substantial amount of spillage of sodium hydroxide," "numerous chlorine leaks," and spills and leaks of hydrochloric acid at the plant.... He noted that, because the sodium hydroxide spillage had a very high pH and was quite caustic, contact with the spillage could cause a first- to third-degree burn, or even be lethal.... Teitelbaum explained that exposure to the chlorine leaks could cause "severe injuries to eyes, upper airways, and lungs, and, under some circumstances, death.".... He commented that hydrochloric acid was a "classic poison" which would also cause burns and potential death.... Based on the biological samples, he concluded that the employees were "in danger of death or serious bodily injury.".... Finally, Teitelbaum noted that the data showed the mercury levels in the workers' urine were "between two and five times the acceptable level of excretion, based on the World Health Organization or the NIOSH recommendations."...

At sentencing, the probation officer noted that he had "discredit[ed]" one of Hansen's witnesses "because he was not even at the...Plant" and "did not have firsthand knowledge to see this.".... Hansen's attorney responded that, based on the probation officer's theory, Teitelbaum's testimony should also be discounted "because he never went to the plant before it was shut down.".... The district judge commented that Teitelbaum "made a very credible witness. I think the best witness that the Government had."...

We review for abuse of discretion both the district court's decisions regarding the admission of expert testimony and reliability of an expert...and the denial of a *Daubert* hearing.... Scientific expert testimony is admissible if "(1) the expert is qualified to testify competently regarding the matters he intends to address; (2) the methodology by which the expert reaches his conclusions is sufficiently reliable as determined by the sort of inquiry mandated in *Daubert*; and (3) the testimony assists the trier of fact, through the application of scientific, technical, or specialized expertise, to understand the evidence or to determine a fact in issue.".... In *Daubert*,

---

7. Daubert v. Merrell Dow Pharm., Inc., 509 U.S. 579 (1993). In *Daubert*, the Court held that, when "[f]aced with a proffer of expert scientific testimony,...the trial judge must determine...whether the expert is proposing to testify to (1) scientific knowledge that (2) will assist the trier of fact to understand or determine a fact in issue." Id. at 592.

the Supreme Court suggested a flexible inquiry regarding the methodology considering such factors as "whether it can be (and has been) tested," whether it "has been subjected to peer review and publication," the "known or potential rate of error," "the existence and maintenance of standards controlling the technique's operation, and the degree it is accepted as reliable within the relevant scientific community." 509 U.S. at 591, 593–94.... *Daubert* hearings are not required, but may be helpful in complicated cases involving multiple expert witnesses.... A district court should conduct a *Daubert* inquiry when the opposing party's motion for a hearing is supported by "conflicting medical literature and expert testimony." Tanner v. Westbrook, 174 F.3d 542, 546 (5th Cir. 1999). Consistent with *Daubert*, the evidence must be scientifically related to the disputed facts at issue in the case. Allison v. McGhan Med. Corp., 184 F.3d 1300, 1312 (11th Cir. 1999).

Hansen's motion for a *Daubert* hearing was neither addressed to the charges to which Teitelbaum testified, or his testimony in general, nor supported by the source, substance, or methodology of the challenged testimony. Hansen failed to object to either Teitelbaum's qualification as an expert or his testimony during trial. Teitelbaum's testimony was based on his review of biological samples, interviews, and documents, and assisted the trier of fact in understanding the potential injuries that could result from the conditions at the plant. The district judge did not abuse his discretion by denying the motion or by admitting the testimony....

Insufficiency of the Evidence: Position of Authority. ... The indictment alleged that the defendants, "after learning that the Brunswick facility was disposing of hazardous wastes...without a RCRA permit, continued to operate the Brunswick facility in such a manner as to continue the disposal of these hazardous wastes without expending adequate funds...to prevent the disposal of such hazardous wastes into the environment."... The jury was instructed that the defendants were responsible for the acts of others that they "wilfully directed," "authorized," or aided and abetted by "willfully joining together with [another] person in the commission of a crime...."

a. Hansen.... The testimony at trial indicated that Hansen was aware that wastewater was permitted to flow out the cellroom back door in June 1993, and directed the use of the old...storage tanks for storage of wastewater, including the inadequately treated wastewater from the treatment system, from July through September 1993. Although the acts continued after Hansen left his decision-making position, the acts occurred at his direction. This evidence was sufficient for the jury to reasonably conclude beyond a reasonable doubt that his acts were in furtherance of the violations. The district court did not err in denying Hansen's motion for judgment of acquittal or motion for new trial.

b. Randall. Randall claims that the government presented no evidence that he personally treated, stored, or disposed of a hazardous waste, personally effected a CWA violation, or instructed an agent to do so. He maintains that, under the laws of bankruptcy and corporate governance, he lacked the authority to close the plant or to allocate the funds for the needed capital improvements. He contends that [the plant] needed the bankruptcy court's approval to use the bankruptcy estate's assets, or to obtain a new debt, to perform the needed repairs at the Brunswick plant....

Although Randall claims that his role as Executive Vice-President and acting CEO was limited to financial matters, he also received daily reports about the plant's operations and environmental problems...wrote and received memos regarding specific plant operational problems...received monthly written environmental reports..., and oral environmental reports.... He admitted that [the] bankruptcy was not an excuse for violating environmental laws.... There is no indication that he asked the...Board or the bankruptcy court to close the plant. The evidence indicates that he apparently misled them into believing that environmental compliance was not a problem. After the Georgia [Environmental Protection Department] attempted to revoke the plant's NPDES permit in June 1993, Randall contested the revocation, explaining that the plant's CWA violations were due to a lightning strike and equipment failures, and asserted that "[the plant] has already taken steps to improve the situation.".... This evidence was sufficient for the jury to conclude that Randall's actions were in furtherance of the violations.

 c. Taylor....As project engineer, Taylor was directly involved in responding to the plant's environmental and safety problems and, at Hansen's request, developed a list of short-term solutions to the problems with estimated costs.... Taylor's proposed solutions were subsequently funded....

 Although Taylor left his managerial position, he continued to work in a position in which he directed or authorized acts of the employees on environmental and safety problems. Testimony at trial indicated that, in October 1993, Taylor was aware of the wastewater overflow from the cellrooms, the excess loss of mercury, and the use of the tank cars for wastewater storage, and that he supervised the release of the overflow. This evidence was sufficient for the jury to conclude beyond a reasonable doubt that these acts were in furtherance of the violations. The district court did not err in denying his motion for a new trial.

Hazardous substances or materials. Taylor and Hansen argue that the government failed to prove that the untreated wastewater contained enough mercury and caustic to meet the environmental laws' definition of hazardous substances or materials, or that the untreated wastewater was improperly stored....

 Where there is no sampling of the actual wastes, the government may prove the hazardous nature of the material by inventories, hazardous waste logs, internal memoranda, and trial testimony. United States v. Baytank (Houston), Inc., 934 F.2d 599, 614 (5th Cir. 1991). The government is not required to prove that material is hazardous by EPA testing. United States v. Self, 2 F.3d 1071, 1086 (10th Cir. 1993). We find that the testimony of the former...employees and the wastewater logs were sufficient for the jury to find that the untreated wastewater contained enough mercury and caustic to meet the environmental laws' definition of hazardous substances or materials....

 There was no evidence that suggested that the cellrooms, in which earthen berms were constructed to contain the wastewater, were marked with the date of accumulation or labeled as containing hazardous wastes and thus qualified as "tanks." The testimony and logs indicate that the wastewater, which may have abated in cellroom one during various periods of time, remained in cellroom two and was present for more than 90 days. Therefore, the evidence was sufficient for the jury to find that the wastewater was improperly stored.

Knowing Endangerment Under RCRA. Hansen, Randall, and Taylor argue that the evidence was insufficient to convict them for knowing endangerment. They acknowledge that the government may have shown that they "could have been aware" of the inherent dangers of working in a chlor-alkali plant, but argue that it failed to show that they knew and had an actual belief that the conduct which allegedly violated the environmental laws was substantially certain to cause death or serious bodily injury to others. Specifically, they maintain that, while the evidence showed that the employees were exposed to mercury, the evidence did not show that they were endangered due to any RCRA violation. They contend that the evidence of the employees' exposure to caustic was not sufficient to support the conviction for knowing endangerment. They claim that the government did not show that they had actual knowledge that their conduct in causing the RCRA violation was at that time substantially certain to place the employees in imminent danger of death or serious bodily injury. They also posit that there was no evidence that they were participants in any alleged conspiracy.

For a conviction of knowing endangerment under the RCRA, the government must prove that the defendants knowingly caused the illegal treatment, storage, or disposal of hazardous wastes while knowing that such conduct placed others in imminent danger of death or serious injury. 42 U.S.C. §6928(e).... The evidence showed that Hansen, Randall, and Taylor knew that the conditions of the plant were dangerous and that the conditions posed a serious danger to the employees.... Former employee Wilbur Duane Outhwaite testified that he voiced his opposition to the use of the...storage with Hansen, and that Hansen responded that it was "his decision to make, and he decided to use them."... Acting plant manager Hugh Croom discussed his concerns regarding the dangerous conditions in the cellroom and the danger to the employees with Randall.... Croom and...former employee Outhwaite testified that Randall received daily reports from the plant managers concerning plant operations and "safety problems."... Randall was aware of the water on the cellroom floor and "wouldn't say that [he] wasn't unaware of the hazard," but thought that the walkway was "an acceptable resolution" to "eliminating the hazard to the employees while we worked to dry the cellroom floor."... He conceded that he was aware that the company was cited for willful violation of OSHA safety regulations as a result of water on cellroom floors.... Jesse Jones, a former...employee and a union representative, met with Randall to discuss the employees' safety issues, and Randall promised the needed repairs.... He said that he discussed the safety concerns, specifically "the water condition, the deterioration of the plant with the pipes, the leaks, and the safety equipment[ ]" with Hansen and Taylor.... Between 3 August 1993, and 4 February 1994, Randall was sent 22 reports listing 110 different violations of the NPDES standards.... As...environmental manager, Brent Hanson regularly advised Randall of the plant's environmental problems "whenever he was interested in things" and by monthly reports....

As early as 1988, NIOSH informed Taylor that the plant employees had "extremely high" levels of mercury in their bodies which created "an unacceptably high potential for health effects," and that the mercury- contaminated wastes should be kept in vapor-proof containers.... Despite this, the employees' exposure to high levels of mercury continued. In 1992, Taylor addressed his concerns about "severe safety" problems in a memorandum to Randall.... Taylor was aware that, during the spring of 1993, 23 cellroom employees were removed from their duty in the cellrooms due to their high levels of mercury and that the mercury level in the workplace increased.... Taylor was aware of and concerned by the mercury-contaminated waste which was stored in drums in the cellrooms' basement and which was emitting elevated levels of mercury fumes.... He admitted that the mercury-contaminated mud on the cellroom floors posed a health risk and needed to be monitored.... He testified that, on occasion, he would get into the water wearing protective equipment to make repairs and improvements to the pumps, and admitted that, if the wastewater got onto bare skin and was caustic, "you would start to feel a little burning or a little heat sensation" but that it could be neutralized by washing with the safety solution.... He said that such burns were "not unusual" in a caustic soda manufacturing plant through employee carelessness and equipment failures.

Sentencing Guidelines. We review the district court's factual findings for clear error and its application of the law to those facts de novo....

Downward Departure — Christian Hansen. Hansen argues that the district court erred by concluding that it lacked the authority to depart under [the Federal Sentencing Guidelines]. He maintains that, at a minimum, the district court was ambiguous as to whether it believed that it had the authority to grant a downward departure and that any ambiguity must be resolved in his favor.

At sentencing, Hansen argued, inter alia, that he should be granted a downward departure...because the factors of the case took it outside of the heartland of cases to which the guidelines apply.... He argued that a departure was warranted because the government agencies monitored and knew of the environmental violations, and that this situation was not where Congress intended to impose the high penalties for environmental violations.... After sentencing Hansen, the district judge stated that he "d[id] not really find any actual basis for a departure from the guidelines, even though I might, if I had discretion, found otherwise."...

We "generally may not review the merits of a district court's refusal to grant a downward departure, [but] may conduct a de novo review of a defendant's claim that the district court mistakenly believed it lacked the authority to grant such a departure." United States v. Mignott, 184 F.3d 1288, 1290 (11th Cir. 1999) (per curiam). Where the district court expresses ambivalence about its authority to depart from the guidelines, we review the record to determine the district court's understanding.

Hansen was sentenced after Randall. During Randall's sentencing hearing, the district judge acknowledged his authority to depart.... Hansen's sentencing transcript shows that the district judge permitted extensive discussion of whether the circumstances of Hansen's case were outside the heartland of cases to which the guidelines had been applied, and that neither party argued that the district court lacked the authority to depart downward. There is nothing in the record that shows that the district court misapprehended its authority to depart downward. Therefore, we assume the sentencing court understood its discretionary authority to grant a downward departure but decided not to exercise that authority.... Because the district court understood that it had the authority to depart, we are unable to review the district court's denial of Hansen's request for a downward departure.

Randall Hansen. Randall contends that the district court erred in not granting his requests for a downward departure.... [H]e argues that his case fell outside the heartland of other environmental prosecutions and that he was at all times operating under the authority of the U.S. Bankruptcy Court and upon the advice of his environmental counsel.... [H]e maintains that the district court erred in concluding that financial factors were not a "perceived greater harm" which could trigger a departure and in not understanding that the record supported his belief that a greater environmental, as well as economic, harm would occur at the site and in the community if the plant failed to remain operational.

At Randall's sentencing, the district judge stated:

> The Court acknowledges that it does have authority to depart from the guidelines...if it finds that the circumstances of this case warrant such a departure.[8]... He set forth the requirements for a departure under the guidelines, but found that no departure was warranted under either provision.... We may not review a district court's refusal to

---

8. It appears that, although the district judge did not find that the circumstances warranted a departure, he nonetheless considered Randall's arguments. During the hearing, the district judge continued:

> To consider a departure under this section [§5K2.11], the Court would have to find either that the Defendant committed the crime in order to avoid perceived greater harm or that the Defendant's conduct does not cause or threaten the harm or evil sought to be prevented by the laws prohibiting the offenses at issue.... Defendant has failed to produce evidence, other than his own statement, that closing the...plant would have caused a greater harm [by cutting off the payroll to 300 employees] than allowing it to continue operating in the unsafe manner.... I do not believe that...justifies subjecting the employees and the community to the risk of operating an unsafe chlor-alkali plant.... The guidelines permit a downward departure where the conduct may not cause or threaten the harm or evil sought to be prevented by the law prescribing the offense at issue.... The...Defendant's conduct [however] was the type of conduct which the environmental laws sought to prevent.... And further, I find that there are no factors which take this case outside the heartland of the environmental guidelines. Accordingly, the Court finds that no departure is warranted under 5K2.0 of the guidelines.

grant a downward departure unless the court mistakenly believed that it lacked the authority to grant such a departure.... Despite Randall's argument to the contrary, the district judge indicated his understanding that financial factors could be a "perceived greater harm" by weighing the harms associated with closing the plant and putting 300 employees out of work against keeping the plant open as an unsafe chor-alkali plant and keeping the employees working, but found that the financial factors were not a harm greater than the harms associated with the operation of an unsafe chlor-alkali plant. Because the district court acknowledged that it had the authority to depart, we lack the jurisdiction to review the decision.

Taylor. Taylor also argues that the district court erred by not granting him a downward departure under §§5K2.0 and 5K2.11. As to the request for a departure under §5K2.0, he maintains that his case fell outside the heartland of environmental cases. As to the request for a departure...he contends that he believed that closing the plant would cause a greater environmental harm that continuing operations.

Taylor presented each of his issues at sentencing.... The district judge asked the probation officer to comment on Taylor's requests for a departure, and to specifically address Taylor's cooperation during the cleanup efforts. The probation officer responded that there were no grounds for a downward departure. The district judge commented:

> I am equally bound by the guidelines and by the law. And I do not have much discretion.... And I just cannot find a basis for departure under the guidelines, inasmuch as the facts as found are of the kind contemplated by the Sentencing Commission.

Because there is nothing in the record that indicates that the district court misapprehended its authority to depart downward, we assume that the district court understood its authority to depart and decided not to exercise its discretionary authority. Therefore, we lack jurisdiction to address the district court's decision not to depart.

After reviewing the record and carefully considering the briefs and oral argument, we conclude that the defendants' convictions are supported by the evidence, and that the district court did not err in the evidentiary rulings, the jury instructions, or at sentencing. Accordingly, we affirm.

COMMENTARY & QUESTIONS

1. **The mechanics and strategics of a sentencing formula.** Sentencing in federal criminal cases typically begins with presentence reports (PSRs) prepared by the office of the U.S. Probation Service assigned to the federal court. Normally the sentencing judge takes the PSR's offense level number and simply cross-references that number with the defendant's criminal history category, which then indicates the range of possible sentences within which the trial judge has discretion. Sentencing judges may try to extend the range of their discretion further by pegging the offense level higher or lower than the PSR's recommendation. Under the U.S. Sentencing Guidelines Commentary, for example, a judge can adjust the offense levels for "repetitive discharges" and "disrupting a public utility" up or down by two, based on severity.

What do Sentencing Guidelines look like and how are they applied? Review Figure 20-2. In United States v. Rutana, 18 F.3d 363 (6th Cir. 1994), the defendant had been convicted of dumping highly caustic and acidic wastes into a public sewer system. The calculation of penalty?

FEDERAL SENTENCING TABLE
(stated in months of imprisonment)

Criminal History Category (Criminal History Points)

	Offense Level	I (0 or 1)	II (2 or 3)	III (4,5,6)	IV (7,8,9)	V (10,11,12)	VI (13 or more)
Zone A	1	0–6	0–6	0–6	0–6	0–6	0–6
	2	0–6	0–6	0–6	0–6	0–6	1–7
	3	0–6	0–6	0–6	0–6	2–8	3–9
	4	0–6	0–6	0–6	2–8	4–10	6–12
	5	0–6	0–6	1–7	4–10	6–12	9–15
	6	0–6	1–7	2–8	6–12	9–15	12–18
	7	0–6	2–8	4–10	8–14	12–18	15–21
	8	0–6	4–10	6–12	10–16	15–21	18–24
	9	4–10	6–12	8–14	12–18	18–24	21–27
Zone B	10	6–12	8–14	10–16	15–21	21–27	24–30
Zone C	11	8–14	10–16	12–18	18–24	24–30	27–33
	12	10–16	12–18	15–21	21–27	27–33	30–37
	13	12–18	15–21	18–24	24–30	30–37	33–41
	14	15–21	18–24	21–27	27–33	33–41	37–46
	15	18–24	21–27	24–30	30–37	37–46	41–51
	16	21–27	24–30	27–33	33–41	41–51	46–57
	17	24–30	27–33	30–37	37–46	46–57	51–63
	18	27–33	30–37	33–41	41–51	51–63	57–71
	19	30–37	33–41	37–46	46–57	57–71	63–78
	20	33–41	37–46	41–51	51–63	63–78	70–87
	21	37–46	41–51	46–57	57–71	70–87	77–96
	22	41–51	46–57	51–63	63–78	77–96	84–105
	23	46–57	51–63	57–71	70–87	84–105	92–115
	24	51–63	57–71	63–78	77–96	92–115	100–125
Zone D	25	57–71	63–78	70–87	84–105	100–125	110–137
	26	63–78	70–87	78–97	92–115	110–137	120–150
	27	70–87	78–97	87–108	100–125	120–150	130–162
	28	78–97	87–108	97–121	110–137	130–162	140–175
	29	87–108	97–121	108–135	121–151	140–175	151–188
	30	97–121	108–135	121–151	135–168	151–188	168–210
	31	108–135	121–151	135–168	151–188	168–210	188–235
	32	121–151	135–168	151–188	168–210	188–235	210–262
	33	135–168	151–188	168–210	188–235	210–262	235–293
	34	151–188	168–210	188–235	210–262	235–293	262–327
	35	168–210	188–235	210–262	235–293	262–327	292–365
	36	188–235	210–262	235–293	262–327	292–365	324–405
	37	210–262	235–293	262–327	292–365	324–405	360–life
	38	235–293	262–327	292–365	324–405	360–life	360–life
	39	262–327	292–365	324–405	360–life	360–life	360–life
	40	292–365	324–405	360–life	360–life	360–life	360–life
	41	324–405	360–life	360–life	360–life	360–life	360–life
	42	360–life	360–life	360–life	360–life	360–life	360–life
	43	life	life	life	life	life	life

FIGURE 20-2

THE PRE-SENTENCE REPORT ["PSR"] calculated defendant's offense level of eighteen (18) as follows:

(1) Base offense level of eight (8) for mishandling of hazardous or toxic substances, under U.S.S.G. §2Q1.2(a).

(2) Increase of six (6) levels for repetitive discharge, under U.S.S.G. §2Q1.2(b)(1)(A). [NOTE 5: BASED ON HARMFULNESS OF CONTAMINATION CAN DEPART UP OR DOWNWARD BY 2]

(3) Increase of four (4) levels for disruption of a public utility, under U.S.S.G. §2Q1.2(b)(3). [NOTE 7: 2 UP OR DOWN]

(4) Increase of two (2) levels for playing a leadership role in the activity, under U.S.S.G. §3B1.1(c).

(5) Decrease of two (2) levels for acceptance of responsibility, under U.S.S.G. §3E1.1(a).

This produced a penalty score of 8+6+4+2-2=18; for this the guidelines indicate a term of imprisonment of 27 to 33 months, based upon an offense level of 18 and a criminal history category I; Rutana had no prior offenses. Demonstrating the vagaries of a seemingly objective system, one district judge who initially reviewed the penalty awarded a level 17 sentence, reviewed by a second judge who changed it downward to 8, subsequently revised upward on appeal to 17, and Rutana ultimately settled, agreeing to serve five months in jail and five months home detention, with a $16,700 fine, on a final adjusted offense level of 12.

Why can the offense levels vary so dramatically? In environmental cases, as the *Hansen* decision recognizes, pollution discharges can be very harmful to human health and the environment. In *Hansen*, the court paid particular attention to the expert testimony, concluding that the pollution at issue posed a serious danger to the employees. Judges often seek to tailor criminal remedies to suit the harms caused by pollution and typically place great weight on credible expert testimony. Before the sentencing guidelines took effect, judicial discretion on a case-by-case basis (which is as old as Aristotle's *aequitas*), led to such wide disparities between different courts that Congress decided to force uniformity upon federal sentencing. As *Hansen* illustrates, although judicial discretion did not disappear, it is now definitely constrained.

2. **An array of fudge factors in criminal sentencing.** Because of the guidelines, some further tailoring of remedies now occurs at the beginning of a case, in the prosecution's decisions and plea bargaining over what charges and level-enhancing factual allegations will be made. If you are an EPA or state enforcement attorney, note the range of options you can array against polluters in negotiations on consent agreements. If a defendant will not cut a deal on providing desired information, or a restoration remedy, or funding a SEP supplemental environmental project, filing a complaint for criminal violations poses the threat of locking in a range of severe potential penalties.

The variability in sentencing options that remains available despite the federal guidelines was evident in the aftermath of the *Exxon-Valdez* oil spill. Exxon, as a corporation, could not be imprisoned, so the federal judge was able to take the federal fine of $100 million and remit it down to $25 million, apparently taking into consideration Exxon's acceptance of extensive civil liability. (Criminal fine remittitur is an important and little-studied judicial power.) The federal guidelines, of course, do not apply to state sentences. Captain Hazelwood was convicted by an Alaska state jury of negligent discharge of oil, a misdemeanor, and was sentenced to 90 days in jail and a $1000 fine, but the judge then issued an alternate conditional sentence: He suspended the fine and the jail sentence on condition that Hazelwood complete 12 months of probation, perform 1000 hours of community work, and pay $50,000 in restitution.

3. **"Abuse of trust" under the federal sentencing guidelines.** Under U.S.S.G. §3B1.3, a judge can adjust the offense levels for a violation of a position of trust, so that a defendant is eligible for a two-point enhancement "if the defendant abused a position of public or private trust, or used a special skill, in a manner that significantly facilitated the commission or concealment of the offense." The circuits are split on the issue of what constitutes abuse of a position of trust for purposes of the federal sentencing guidelines. In United States v. Technic Servs., Inc., 314 F.3d 1031 (9th Cir. 2002), the defendant (facing 57 months in prison, a fine of $520,000, 3 years of probation for violations of the CAA and CWA) contended that his sentence had been improperly enhanced by the sentencing enhancements for violation of a position of trust. Defendant was an employee of a private company doing hazardous material remediation work under government contract. The Ninth Circuit held there was no violation of a position of *public* trust and remanded the case for reconsideration whether the defendant's sentence might be enhanced for abuse of a *private* trust. The Ninth Circuit held that, for purposes of §3B1.3, defendant's role was not sufficiently "public." The First and Fourth Circuits, as the court acknowledged, had adopted the broader principle that "reasonable reliance of the public on individuals to comply with the laws they are charged with enforcing may support the inference that a defendant enjoys a position of trust." Id. at 1058.

The *Technic Services* dissent criticized the majority's decision as formalistic, ignoring "the plain reality that he enjoyed a considerable public trust in performing a task that was critical to public health and safety and to the enduring well-being of a delicate environment." Id. at 1059. The dissent also thought it was "patently wrong" to reframe the issue as a violation of private trust since the harms unleashed into the air and water by the defendant's asbestos remediation company were public in their effects on the environment and on public health and welfare. "The trust at issue for the offenses of which [the defendant] was convicted is public, not private." Id.

4. **The continuing strict application of the federal sentencing guidelines.** The courts remain unfriendly to constitutional challenges to the federal sentencing guidelines. Illustrative of this trend is United States v. Strong, 40 Fed. Appx. 214 (7th Cir. 2002). In that case, the defendant (who sought review of concurrent 294-month prison terms for drug trafficking) contended that the application of the criminal history calculations of the federal sentencing guidelines overstated the seriousness of his past criminal conduct, and as a result, his sentences violated both the proportional sentencing requirement of the Eighth Amendment and "due process." The defendant also asserted that the district court should have vacated several of his prior convictions on the grounds that his Sixth Amendment right to the effective assistance of counsel was violated in each proceeding and should have departed downward from the guidelines range.

The Seventh Circuit disagreed and affirmed. The Seventh Circuit found no Eighth Amendment violation, where the defendant received sentences less than the statutory maximums but within the guidelines range and the district court declined to depart downward. Thus the sentences were not "grossly disproportionate." The Seventh Circuit further found no "due process" violation in the sentences imposed on the defendant where his sentences were rationally related to his crimes. As for the claims involving the Sixth Amendment, they were waived for failure to raise them in the district court. The Seventh Circuit concluded by declining to review the district court's discretionary refusal to depart downward from the guidelines, ruling that "we have no jurisdiction to review a district court's discretionary refusal to depart from the sentencing range recommended by the guidelines unless that refusal was based on the district court's erroneous belief that it lacked power to depart." Id. at 219.

5. **A critique of criminalization for environmental injuries.** Professor Herbert Packer has criticized the vagaries of criminal penalties based on evolving concepts of "morality." As to punishment of executives for "economic crimes," he writes that "these are, generally speaking,...uniquely deterrent...sanctions addressed to the law-abiding.... Intimidation...incapacitation [and] rehabilitative effect [are not the reasons for] the imposition of criminal punishment on those pillars of the community who happen to get convicted of economic offenses." He concludes that "it takes a substantial enforcement effort, and the resources required to bring the threat up to its minimal level of credibility might be better expended in noncriminal modes of regulation." See H. Packer, The Limits of the Criminal Sanction 249–259, 356–363 (1968).

This perspective offers a reminder of the special nature of criminal punishment — its costs, consequences, and variable degrees of efficacy. How do you weigh, in each environmental setting, the aptness of criminal sanctions in terms of accomplishing the traditional objectives of penal law noted at the beginning of this chapter — societal revenge and retribution, general deterrence, incapacitation, specific deterrence, and rehabilitation — or is there more to it than that?

6. **Economics.** How about the overview economic analysis that underlies so much of modern environmental law? Environmentalists use legal remedies to make producers take full account of the environmental costs and values, tangible and intangible, imposed by their activities. When environmental prosecutions successfully skewer a polluting defendant and the sentencing guidelines prescribe a jail term, does that necessarily skew the economics of rational accounting, or can it make a nice fit with the rest of the common law and administrative civil remedies in modern environmental legal process?

7. **Ecoguerrillas and the criminal law? The Necessity Defense.** And for a completely different angle on enviro-criminal law, how should the legal system treat activists like EarthFirst! when they spike trees to frustrate legal redwood logging or sabotage highway layouts and electric transmission lines? Is the societal interest "necessity defense" available to override the letter of the law? See California v. McMillan, San Luis Obispo Mun. Ct. 87-D 00518 (1987) (necessity defense applied to defendants in a nuclear protest case), and E. Abbey, The Monkey Wrench Gang (1975).

Chapter 21

EVOLVING PATTERNS OF ENFORCEMENT AND COMPLIANCE

A. THE CONTINUING DEBATE OVER ENVIRONMENTAL ENFORCEMENT STRATEGIES

The effectiveness of environmental enforcement in the United States has been a long-running debate. After the passage in the early 1970s of the CAA and CWA, EPA enforcement initially focused on educating the regulated community, providing technical support, and encouraging compliance. EPA's programs were new, and most of EPA's early initiatives involved assisting the regulated community in developing the training, the expertise, and the tools necessary to achieve compliance with EPA's newly promulgated regulatory schemes. Although Congress armed the EPA with the ability to seek significant sanctions, most penalties sought by the EPA in the early years were modest (in the five-figure range), and the EPA's focus was on negotiated settlements with the regulated community.

This paradigm began to shift by the mid-1970s. By that time, criticism of EPA's effectiveness in enforcement was growing, both in Congress and from an increasingly assertive array of environmental citizen groups. At the same time, EPA was becoming increasingly concerned that, absent meaningful accountability for noncompliance, the regulated community was not significantly motivated to modify its behavior and practices in order to comply with the growing body of environmental regulations and requirements. Concluding that there was a need for more demonstrable environmental progress, EPA began to embrace an enforcement ideology based on the premise that deterrence must be at the heart of an effective regulatory program.

By the late 1970s, EPA's enforcement strategy was fully in place. EPA embraced civil and criminal command-and-control requirements, which were intended to maintain accountability for noncompliance by identifying, prosecuting, and penalizing violators. As environmental enforcement continued through the 1980s, EPA honed its deterrence approach. Armed with tough laws and operating under the watchful eyes of Congress and citizen groups, EPA developed programs involving rigorous inspections of the regulated community coupled with mandatory self-reporting required of violators. Rather than seek out partnerships with the regulated community, EPA's strategy was to maintain an arm's-length approach to enforcement, with the emphasis upon sanctioning violators and deterring other parties from committing violations. EPA assumed that the greater its resources, the higher would be the likelihood that violations would be deterred and that compliance would be achieved. Accordingly, EPA sought, and obtained, more lawyers, investigators, and enforcement personnel. The U.S. Department of Justice (DOJ) was also enlisted to initiate and enforce the growing body of environmental laws.

By the early 1990s, the federal environmental statutes alone exceeded 1300 pages, and the regulations promulgated to implement those statutes were already over 12,000 pages in length. As hundreds of thousands of regulated entities attempted to deal with an increasingly complicated set of federal, state, and local environmental requirements, the nation spent over $700 billion on environmental cleanup efforts. At the same time, approximately 2% of the gross national product was now devoted to pollution control and regulation. The magnitude of these expenditures reflected a major shift in U.S. business priorities. Environmental issues had become a major factor in virtually every significant business decision or transaction. No sale of a business, transfer of real estate, or use of hazardous chemicals could proceed prudently without consideration of the environmental risks, costs, or effects.

What triggered this realignment of U.S. business priorities? Under the traditional enforcement yardsticks employed by EPA — measured in the "bean counting" terms of cases brought and total dollar penalties imposed — EPA contended that its deterrence strategy had caused this shift. EPA touted its enforcement record to Congress and the public as the measure of its success. During fiscal year 1994, for example, EPA reported the initiation of 2249 federal enforcement actions; a total of 430 civil and 200 criminal cases referred to the DOJ for prosecution; criminal charges brought against 250 individuals and corporations; and over $165 million in administrative, civil, and criminal fines.[1]

The significance of EPA's enforcement efforts in this realignment of priorities was nonetheless subject to rigorous debate. By the mid-1990s, there was a growing recognition at EPA, and elsewhere, that EPA's enforcement strategy had major limitations. In particular, critics argued that EPA's deterrence approach focused on punishing violations after they occurred, rather than encouraging systems to prevent violations; relied on governmental enforcement actions rather than enhancing or rewarding private sector compliance; necessarily depended on the limitations of politically influenced enforcement budgets and priorities; and perversely preferred actions yielding high penalties over actions yielding greater impact on environmental quality, thereby confusing means with ends.[2]

Even more significantly, EPA was stung by the criticism that, although its actions in the 1970s and 1980s may have contributed to the shift in U.S. business priorities, by the

---

1. See New Records for Actions, Fines Set by EPA Despite Restructuring Program, 25 BNA Env't Rep. 1501 (1994).
2. See Diamond, Confessions of an Environmental Enforcer, 26 Envtl. L. Rep. 10253 (1996); Garrett, Reinventing EPA Enforcement, Nat. Resources & Env't, Winter 1998, at 180.

1990s EPA's enforcement strategies were actually a drag on environmental progress in the corporate community. By then, many U.S. corporations were reducing emissions and achieving compliance arguably on their own initiative. Critics pointed out that, at a time when corporate environmental focus had progressed to embracing management systems, sustainable development, reuse/recycling, pollution prevention, industry responsible care programs, and international environmental standards, EPA's deterrence approach was still focused on bringing an increasing number of lawsuits in order to collect higher fines. The debate centered on whether EPA was so preoccupied with justifying its budget and proving its enforcement record to Congress that it failed in its central mission to improve environmental quality.

By the mid-1990s, EPA began to reassess its enforcement paradigm and to evaluate whether its approach should be modified once again. To that end, EPA began to consider new initiatives emphasizing compliance assurance and noncompliance prevention. These initiatives were designed to prevent pollution as well as to punish violations after they occurred, to harness market forces proactively (rather than relying solely on command and control), and to seek more partnerships with U.S. business that advance designated environmental priorities. EPA also began a period of greater cooperation with the states. This changing emphasis was most apparent in EPA's increasing efforts to work with the states and the regulated community to redevelop brownfields.

With the advent of the new Bush II Administration in late 2000, the environmental enforcement debate has continued. The Administration has promised a new era of environmental protection, seeking to tie environmental issues to goals including economic growth, protection from regulation, increased energy production, and local control.[3] Critics, in turn, have argued that environmental enforcement is in retreat, citing the Administration's rejection of a treaty on global warming, questioning of rules in forest protection, and pressing for changes in the environmental laws and regulations.[4] Into this picture have now stepped various states that, through their attorneys general, are now planning their own lawsuits over pollution in light of changes in the Administration's enforcement initiatives.[5]

The continuing debate over enforcement strategies, as exemplified by shifting patterns of enforcement, raises important issues pertaining to environmental enforcement, environmental compliance, and their interrelationship:

- How does the existing governmental enforcement process work? What are the key steps in the enforcement process, and what enforcement tools are available and effective?

---

3. "Our approach is to maximize the quality of life in America," said James L. Connaughton, Chairman of the Council on Environmental Quality, "and that means balancing the environmental equation with the natural resource equation, the social equation, and the economic equation." Jehl, On Environmental Rules, Bush Sees a Balance, Critics a Threat, N.Y. Times, Feb. 23, 2003, at 1.

4. "Across the board," said Senator James M. Jeffords, the Vermont independent who was until recently the chairman of the Senate Committee on Environmental and Public Works, "we would be better off doing nothing than doing what the...administration wants to do, which will make things worse than they already are." Id. at 1, 22.

5. "The attorney generals of New York, New Jersey, and Connecticut say they are ready to open a new round of litigation to force [old, coal-fired] power plants to make billions of dollars of pollution-control improvements after a decision by the Bush administration to abandon more than 50 investigations into violations of the Clean Air Act." New Policy at E.P.A., N.Y. Times, Nov. 9, 2003, at 1.

- What is the significance of citizen involvement in environmental enforcement? Do citizen suits prod government to act or provide a credible enforcement alternative when government fails to act?

- If environmental compliance is now a major priority of most companies, what factors caused this shift in business goals? Are there major business events that trigger the need for environmental compliance? What compliance tools are available to U.S. business, and how effective are they? Is U.S. business engaged today in self-generated compliance independent of environmental enforcement, or is it involved because of the continuing enforcement paradigm?

- What is the future of enforcement and compliance? What patterns of enforcement and compliance exist, and what changes are likely to occur?

This chapter explores the scope and effectiveness of environmental enforcement. Since the early, formative days of the 1970s, when EPA and the states first began credibly enforcing the environmental laws, layers of new requirements have made the regulatory structure extremely complicated. Amidst these changes, however, one key constant remains: For environmental regulation to achieve its goals, it must induce compliance. Thus the interplay between environmental enforcement and compliance remains a central inquiry.

B.   THE GOVERNMENTAL ENFORCEMENT PROCESS

Governmental enforcement of the environmental laws cuts across all of the environmental statutes. Although the particular means of enforcement varies from statute to statute, or may be modified as a statute is amended or reauthorized,[6] the governmental enforcement process typically moves violators along toward an inevitable day of reckoning.

Section 1.   PHASES IN THE ENFORCEMENT PROCESS

Joel Mintz, Enforcement at the EPA
13–16 (1995)

At EPA, enforcement cases typically go through three phases; inspection and information gathering, administrative case development, and (if the matter has not yet been resolved) formal litigation. In noncriminal cases, the agency has several primary sources of compliance information: self-monitoring, record keeping and reporting by individual sources of pollution, inspections by government personnel, and the specific complaints of concerned citizens.

Most EPA inspections are announced to the pollution source ahead of time to ensure the presence of vital plant personnel. Inspections may be either "for cause," that is, based on a reasonable suspicion that the inspected source is in violation, or else routinely conducted

---

6. On a variety of occasions, Congress has revised federal statutory enforcement mechanisms. For example, when amending the CAA in 1990, Congress sought to improve the reporting of violations and compliance monitoring. In §113(f) of the CAA, Congress added a bounty provision authorizing EPA to pay up to $10,000 as a reward to anyone providing information leading to a civil penalty or criminal conviction under the Act. 42 U.S.C. §7413(f). To improve monitoring, Congress amended the Act to add the requirement that major sources of air pollution conduct "enhanced monitoring" of their emissions and their pollution control equipment (see CAA §114(a)(3), 42 U.S.C. §7414(a)), a phrase interpreted by EPA to require facilities to develop monitoring protocols that would be incorporated into their Title V permits.

pursuant to a "neutral inspection scheme." Perhaps surprisingly, of the approximately 1,600 individuals who perform EPA inspections, more than 75 percent do so less than 20 percent of the time.

When the agency conducts an investigation on the basis of citizen information, that information may have come from a variety of individuals. Citizen informants often include, for example, disgruntled employees of suspected violators, neighbors, state or local inspectors, environmental citizens organizations, and suspected violators' economic competitors. In potential criminal matters, these sources of information may be replaced — or supplemented — by targeted inspections, conducted under color of search warrant, by EPA criminal investigators and/or special agents of the Federal Bureau of Investigation (FBI), as well as by grand jury proceedings under the auspices of the DOJ.

Once EPA (and/or DOJ) investigators have completed their information gathering, they must determine whether the source in question is in violation of applicable standards and, if so, what type of enforcement response the agency will make. Under most of the relevant federal environmental statutes, EPA has a range of options available to it. It may begin enforcement by issuing a notice of violation to the allegedly violating source, describing the violation and inviting the source to confer informally with agency enforcement personnel. Alternatively, EPA may issue the source an administrative order requiring compliance with applicable requirements and, in some cases, an assessed civil penalty. In addition, EPA is generally authorized to refer enforcement matters to the DOJ for civil action or criminal prosecution. If it deems the circumstances appropriate, the agency may defer to a planned or ongoing enforcement action by state or local environmental officials.

EPA decisions as to which of these various enforcement options to pursue are generally made at the regional level by technically trained personnel working in cooperation with enforcement attorneys. These determinations frequently take account of a number of factors. Regional officials typically consider, among other things, the degree to which the source's discharge or emission exceeds applicable legal requirements, the duration of the violation, the number of previous enforcement actions that have been taken successfully against the same source, any relevant national EPA enforcement policies, the potential deterrence value of the case, the resources available to the agency and DOJ at the time of the decision, EPA's working relationship with interested state and local officials, and the agency's estimation of the enforcement capability of those same officials. These calculations, which are usually made with little public knowledge or participation, have great administrative significance....

At EPA, as at many regulatory agencies and departments, enforcement work involves considerable bargaining. In most instances, bargaining serves the interests and goals of both the agency itself and the regulated enterprises that are subject to enforcement action. From EPA's point of view, the time and energy of its enforcement staff is limited. To accomplish its objectives, it is usually to the agency's advantage to resolve acceptably as many enforcement matters as possible, without resorting to expensive and resource-intensive litigation. Another consideration for agency officials is the bureaucratic wish to retain control over decisions within one's area of responsibility. When compromise is not possible and EPA refers a matter to the DOJ for litigation, some of that control is inevitably relinquished to judges and DOJ attorneys and managers.

Although a number of EPA enforcement cases implicate minor, routine violations that are amenable to prompt resolution, in other matters the enforcement process is laborious and time consuming. For all concerned, these more complex cases involve high stakes and hard choices.

For regulated enterprises, the risks of enforcement sanctions — including the possibility of monetary penalties, mandatory pollution control measures that may be expensive to install and maintain, and even, in some criminal cases, jail time for responsible corporate officials — are very great....

Beyond avoiding or minimizing sanctions, regulated industries have an interest in dispelling uncertainties about their future environmental responsibilities and the costs those responsibilities will entail. In many cases, they are also concerned with preserving (or repairing) their public image as responsible corporate citizens and in reassuring lenders, shareholders, and potential investors of their good faith and freedom from impending open-ended liability. At the same time, regulated enterprises must take care that any settlement they enter into with EPA enforcement officials not harm their firm's competitive standing within its industry. Monies expended on pollution control measures and environmental penalties will not be available for investment in productive manufacturing equipment that can increase corporate profits. As they negotiate with regulators, representatives of industrial firms are thus often mindful of individuals within their companies who focus mostly on the bottom line and see little need for or benefit from corporate environmental expenditure.

For EPA's representatives there are difficult choices as well in enforcement negotiations. Any attempt at standardized decision-making by EPA is confounded by the enormous variety of conditions and circumstances that individual cases involve. The agency's enforcement engineers and attorneys frequently face sensitive decisions with respect to the pollution control measures they will accept, the penalties they will assess, the amount of time they will allow a violator to come into compliance, the legal prerogatives and safeguards they will insist upon, and the appropriateness of avoiding, or terminating, negotiations and referring a matter to the Justice Department for civil or criminal action. These judgments are complex and demanding....

Section 2. THE FLOW OF THE ENFORCEMENT PROCESS

Successful enforcement typically occurs in a setting that balances the formality of the enforcement bureaucracy with the informality that necessarily affects and informs the prosecutorial discretion of environmental authorities. Although a certain degree of flexibility is inherent in the governmental enforcement process, for the most part steps in the process reflect a particular order and manner.

As the flow chart in Figure 21-1 shows, the three phases of enforcement at EPA — (1) inspection and information gathering, (2) administrative case development, and (3) formal litigation — can be illustrated as a series of steps moving violators along a path that, if uninterrupted, will inevitably result in civil or criminal adjudication.

Inspection and information gathering, often triggered by a letter of inquiry from EPA, usually begins the enforcement process. As Figure 21-1 illustrates, the goal of this first phase in the enforcement process is for EPA, as the prime enforcer of the federal environmental statutes, to make a decision concerning whether to proceed with enforcement. Typically, EPA's enforcement decision will be informed by the quality and quantity of information gathered by EPA investigators and technical personnel through site observations, sampling, lab analysis, and other investigative techniques. EPA's ability to gather the information essential to sound enforcement judgments, in part, relies on the mandatory self-monitoring, record keeping, and reporting requirements of various environmental statutes that enable EPA to gather information on regulatory targets.

As part of its enforcement decision, EPA must consider whether EPA or the applicable state should take the enforcement lead. Under many federal environmental statutes, EPA may delegate implementation and enforcement authority to those states that

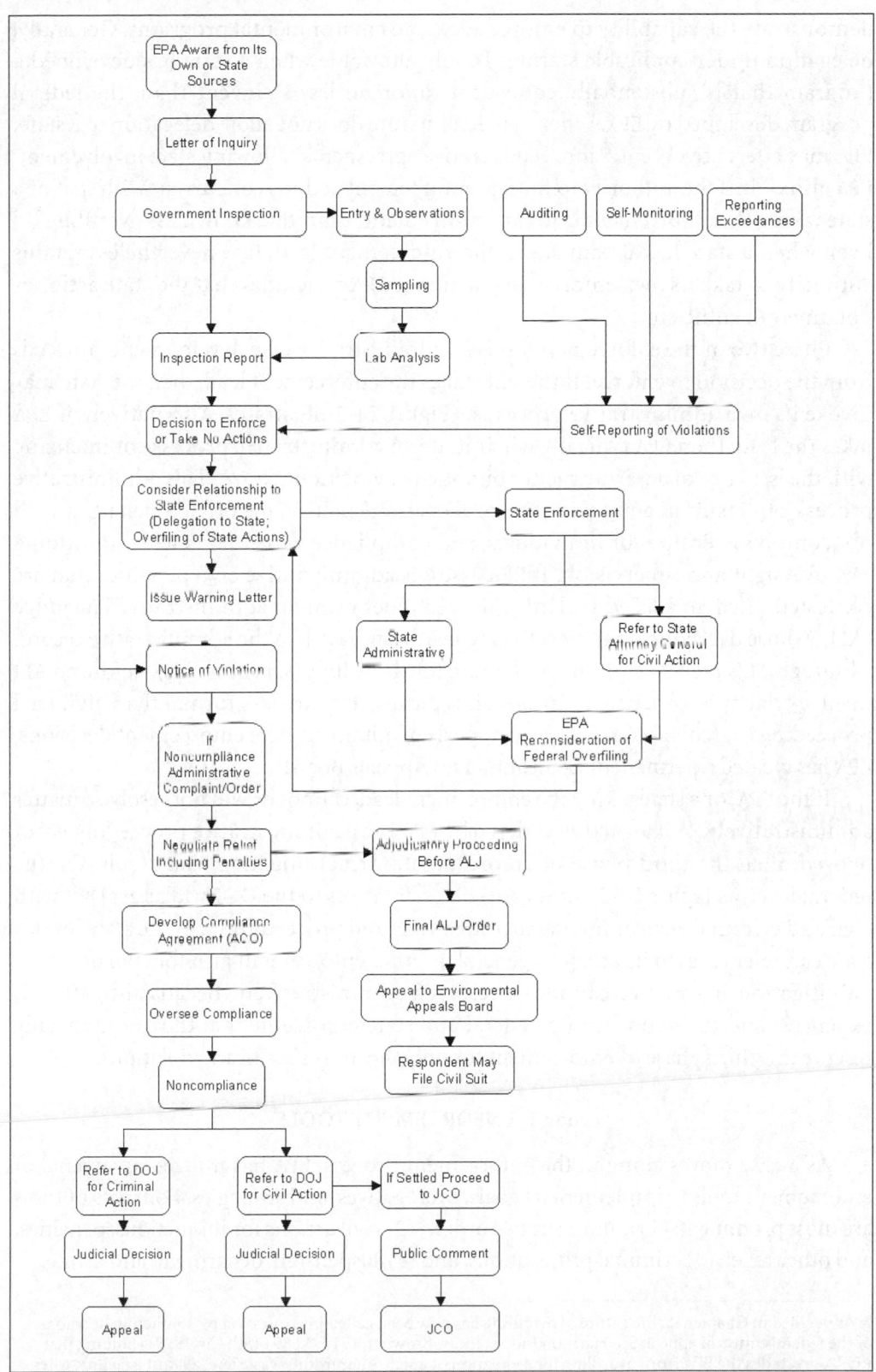

FIGURE 21-1

Overview of Governmental Enforcement of Non-Emergency Air, Water, and Solid Waste Violations

demonstrate the capability to enforce adequate environmental programs. Generally, delegation under applicable statutes is only allowable when a state has developed a program that is substantially equivalent to, or no less stringent than, the federal program developed by EPA. Where a federal statute does not allow delegation to a state, EPA may alternatively enter into "cooperative agreements" allowing state involvement. EPA also claims the authority to initiate enforcement actions concurrent with that of a state taking the enforcement lead (an enforcement technique known as "overfiling").[7] Even when a state has already taken the enforcement lead, EPA nevertheless retains authority to take its own enforcement action if EPA concludes that the state action is not timely or sufficient.

Phase two of the enforcement process, administrative case development, proceeds from the decision to enforce. If the state takes the enforcement lead, then the state may invoke its own administrative process, as Figure 21-1 illustrates. Alternatively, if EPA takes the lead, then EPA typically will initiate an administrative process commencing with the issuance of a warning letter or notice of violation (NOV). This administrative process can result in administrative orders and penalties, negotiated penalties with noncomplying entities or individuals, and compliance agreements with continuing EPA oversight and supervision. If EPA assesses administrative civil penalties that are contested, then an alleged violator can seek relief from an administrative law judge (ALJ), whose decisions are subject to judicial review based on the administrative record. Although ALJs are EPA employees, they are full-time judges. Proceedings before an ALJ involve trial-type procedures, although typically they are less formal than civil trial proceedings in federal court. To hear appeals of administrative enforcement decisions, EPA has created a permanent Environmental Appeals Board.

If the EPA, or a state taking the enforcement lead, cannot or will not resolve a matter administratively, or if an action ordered by EPA in an administrative proceeding is not obeyed, then the third phase of enforcement, formal litigation, can result. On the federal level, as Figure 21-1 shows, EPA can refer cases to the DOJ and assist DOJ with civil and criminal environmental investigations and proceedings. On the state level, a state can refer cases to its attorney general or other enforcement arm for civil or criminal litigation if a matter cannot be resolved administratively. Because litigation is expensive and time-consuming, federal and state enforcement authorities typically reserve this third phase of enforcement for only the most significant violations.

Section 3. ENFORCEMENT TOOLS

As a case moves along in the enforcement process, EPA has utilized an arsenal of enforcement tools to implement its goals, prerogatives, and strategies. Four sets of tools are most prominent: (1) administrative orders; (2) civil actions for injunctions, penalties, and other relief; (3) criminal prosecutions; and (4) suspension, debarment, and listing.

---

7. As detailed in Chapter 18, the future of overfiling has now been called into question by conflicting decisions of the federal courts of appeal. See Harmon Indus., Inc. v. Browner, 191 F.3d 894 (8th Cir. 1999) (holding that RCRA precludes the EPA from overfiling for a violation of a state's hazardous waste laws against a facility, when an authorized state has already instituted an enforcement action for the same violations); and United States v. Power Eng'g, 303 F.3d 1232 (10th Cir. 2002) (holding that EPA may overfile under RCRA, even after a state has agreed to settle its enforcement action against the regulated entity).

Administrative Orders. EPA is increasingly utilizing administrative orders to achieve its enforcement agenda. Administrative orders typically require fewer resources than litigation, can be issued unilaterally, do not require the consent of the alleged violator, and allow EPA to control the direction and outcome of enforcement without DOJ involvement.

Administrative orders have a variety of purposes. They may be issued to gather information, to require compliance, to require remedial action, to suspend or revoke permits, or to assess penalties. Administrative orders also have significant force. Normally, such orders are not subject to pre-enforcement review and accordingly place considerable pressure on alleged violators to comply or suffer significant consequences. Only when EPA attempts to enforce administrative orders are they subject to judicial review.

By their terms, administrative orders can be elaborate and detailed. A typical §106 order issued under CERCLA, for example, may be lengthy and exacting in ordering remedial action activities at a facility to abate an alleged imminent and substantial endangerment presented by the release or threatened release of hazardous substances. Such an order may contain multiple parts and pages, including (1) identification of the parties bound; (2) detailed findings of fact and determinations by EPA pertaining to the conditions at the facility, the responsible parties, and the actions or factors resulting in liability; (3) ordering provisions specifying the work to be performed, requiring EPA approval of engineers and contractors, and further requiring EPA approval of the remedial plan and design; (4) requirements allowing further EPA periodic review; (5) quality assurance provisions imposed by EPA requiring that remedial action be performed to specified standards; (6) provisions allowing EPA future facility access, sampling, and document availability; (7) requirements for periodic progress reports to be made to EPA; and (8) notice outlining penalties for noncompliance.[8]

Violations of administrative orders may result in assessments of civil penalties, often of up to $25,000 for each day of noncompliance for each violation. In determining the amount of the penalty to be assessed, EPA is guided by civil penalty policies. Under its primary policy on civil penalties, EPA calculates the size of the penalty for which it will settle by first considering the gravity of the violation and the economic benefit derived from the violation. Under the gravity component, EPA reviews the seriousness of the violation and the extent to which the violation varies from specified requirements. Under the economic benefit component, EPA determines the gains derived from failure to comply. In calculating the benefits received by the violator from

---

8. A §106 order carries substantial risks for noncompliance, including penalties of three times the amount expended by EPA from the Superfund as a result of a potentially responsible party's (PRP's) failure to comply, without sufficient cause, with the order. For more on §106 orders, see Chapter 19. The notice of penalty provision of a §106 order typically provides:

> The Respondents are advised, pursuant to §106(b) of CERCLA, 42 U.S.C. §9606(b), that willful violation or subsequent failure or refusal to comply with this Order, or any portion thereof, may subject the Respondents to a civil penalty of no more than $25,000 per day for each day in which such violation occurs, or such failure to comply continues. Failure to comply with this Administrative Order, or any portion thereof, without sufficient cause may also subject the Respondents to liability for punitive damages in an amount equal to three times the amount of any costs incurred by the U.S. EPA as a result of the Respondents' failure to take proper action, pursuant to §107(c)(3) of CERCLA, 42 U.S.C. §9607(c)(3).

noncompliance, EPA has utilized a computer model known as the benefit of noncom-pliance (BEN) model. EPA has encouraged state and local agencies to use the BEN model as well, especially in cases where EPA has delegated federal enforcement responsibilities. After calculating the base penalty, EPA may make adjustments in light of willfulness, cooperation, history of noncompliance, and mitigating factors demonstrated by the violator including the violator's ability to pay (a factor in lowering penalties).

Another EPA civil penalty policy is its Supplemental Environmental Project (SEP) Policy, pursuant to which EPA may mitigate a portion of the penalty as a quid pro quo for the violator's undertaking an environmental improvement not otherwise required. SEPs typically are part of a negotiated settlement, utilized as partial offsets to penalties. A SEP precludes the competitive advantage of noncompliance by causing the violator to expend funds on environmental improvements. In negotiating SEPs, EPA will consider whether a penalty should be mitigated by benefits to the environment or the public from a supplemental project, innovation caused by the project, risk reduction to minority or low-income communities, multimedia impacts, and pollution prevention. By encouraging supplemental environmental projects, EPA seeks to produce more envi-ronmentally beneficial enforcement settlements. However, qualifying SEPs must maintain a nexus between the original violation and the supplemental project and are not intended to reward the violator for undertaking activities obviously in its economic self-interest.

An additional enforcement mechanism closely related to SEPs are Environmentally Beneficial Expenditures (EBEs). Enforcement actions frequently result in pretrial consent decrees, which can include polluter-financed EBEs such as donations to purchase critical lands in watersheds where violations have taken place or donations to universities to perform studies.[9]

Civil Actions for Injunctions, Penalties, and Other Relief. In addition to issuing administrative orders to achieve its enforcement goals, EPA, alternatively, can seek a judicial order by requesting DOJ to initiate a civil action in federal court. Because this alternative requires coordination with DOJ, involves the commitment of resources in litigation, and does not allow EPA directly to control the outcome of enforcement, judi-cial enforcement is used less frequently than administrative enforcement.

If EPA issues an administrative order that is not obeyed, EPA must proceed in federal court to secure compliance. Of course, when EPA attempts to enforce adminis-trative orders, such orders are then subject to judicial review, and the statutory provisions prohibiting pre-enforcement review are inapposite.

Once suit is filed in federal court, it may be resolved by settlement in lieu of trial. Normally, DOJ files actions only when DOJ believes, and when the likelihood is, that DOJ will prevail. Consequently, few enforcement cases are tried because most defen-dants find it advantageous to settle such cases. Settlement often reflects the reality that violations may be straightforward or readily proved, using the violator's own discharge monitoring or other reports. Settlements typically are embodied in consent decrees, in

---

9. See Sierra Club v. Electronic Controls Design, 909 F.2d 1350 (9th Cir. 1990), for further discussion of the legal-ity of EBEs.

which the parties agree on a penalty amount and a compliance schedule. DOJ policy requires that all proposed consent decrees be available for public comment prior to entry. In reviewing consent decrees or otherwise deciding whether to impose penalties, courts are not bound by EPA's penalty policies, although such policies may provide useful guidance and receive substantial deference in court. If a consent decree is approved, the court will enter it as an enforceable court order.

Criminal Prosecutions. Environmental criminal prosecution has increased over the years, as noted in Chapter 20. The federal environmental statutes provide for criminal liability for violators and, in certain cases, do not include a requirement of knowledge or other evidence of criminal intent. When determining whether to proceed criminally against an individual or corporation, EPA considers the degree of actual or threatened harm as well as the type and nature of the culpable conduct. On the basis of this review, EPA decides whether to make a referral to DOJ for criminal prosecution. In deciding whether to proceed criminally, DOJ considers, among other factors, voluntary compliance and voluntary disclosure of noncompliance to prosecuting authorities.[10]

Fines as well as incarceration for individuals are available to sanction criminal violators. Statutory provisions as well as U.S. Sentencing Commission Guidelines[11] establish the range of punishment generally available for criminal environmental violations. Although criminal sanctions do not include injunctive orders for compliance or to remedy environmental harm, such requirements may be imposed in connection with fashioning an appropriate penalty under the Sentencing Guidelines. To remedy environmental problems and punish violators, the government can also seek to pursue "parallel" civil and criminal proceedings at the same time, as long as doing so is consistent with due process and other constitutional and statutory protections.

Suspension, Debarment, and Listing. With the increase in civil and criminal enforcement, EPA is now making more use of its contractor listing programs under §508 of the CWA and §306 of the CAA. Under these programs, EPA may suspend (an interim period of probation), debar (a prohibition from contracting for a defined period), or list facilities that are guilty of criminal violations. Being named on the list disqualifies the facility from receiving federal grants or contracts. Such action can be crippling to a violator heavily dependent on such contracts. Until recently, this enforcement power received little attention. Its use by EPA, however, is on the increase, and it provides an additional and important penalty.

COMMENTARY & QUESTIONS

1. **Congressional commitment (or lack thereof) to environmental enforcement.** In the almost 35 years since EPA first began to enforce the federal environmental laws,

---

10. See U.S. Department of Justice, Factors in Decisions on Criminal Prosecutions for Environmental Violations in the Context of Significant Voluntary Compliance or Disclosure Efforts by the Violator, July 1, 1991.

11. U.S. Sentencing Guidelines provide guidance for fines and incarceration and identify appropriate prison terms for individuals, including corporate officers. See U.S. Sentencing Commission Guidelines Manual, Ch. 2Q (guidelines for environmental violations for individuals) and Ch. 8 (guidelines for sentencing organizations), available at http://www.ussc.gov/2003guid/2003guid.pdf.

Congress has repeatedly expanded their scope and reach. At the same time, however, resources committed by Congress to EPA have not kept pace.

> In constant (1982) dollars, EPA's operating budget, which covers all its programs except for the Superfund cleanup program and construction grants for sewage treatment plants, went from $1.7 billion in 1979 down to $1.0 billion in 1983 and rose back up to $1.7 billion again in 1991.

> Yet during this same period, EPA's responsibilities grew enormously. The 1984 Amendments to RCRA, for example, known as the Hazardous and Solid Waste Amendments, significantly broadened EPA's responsibilities for regulating the generation, treatment, storage, and disposal of hazardous waste. The amendments also directed EPA to issue regulations for underground storage tanks. In 1986, the SDWA was amended, requiring EPA to regulate 83 specific drinking water contaminants. In the same year, the Asbestos Hazard Emergency Response Act was passed, requiring EPA to set standards for responding to the presence of asbestos in school buildings and to study the problems of asbestos in other public buildings. The 1980s also saw significant new responsibilities for the EPA under amendments to the CWA, FIFRA, and Superfund legislation (in Title III, EPCRA). Observations on the Environmental Protection Agency's Budget Request for Fiscal Year 1992, Hearing Before the U.S. Senate Comm. on Environment and Public Works, 102d Cong., 1st Sess. (1991) (Statement of Richard L. Hembra, Director, Environmental Protection Issues, Resource, Community, and Economic Development Division, U.S. General Accounting Office).

In the last decade, EPA's budgetary constraints have continued. For example, as noted in Chapter 19, Congress has failed to reauthorize or fund the Superfund. As the EPA Inspector General has concluded, the Superfund program is now short $174.9 million for various cleanup sites across the country, undercutting the effectiveness of the program. EPA, Congressional Request on Funding Needs for Non-Federal Superfund Sites, Jan. 8, 2004.

Given these budgetary constraints on EPA's ability to implement the ambitious statutory agenda passed by Congress, does EPA have the resources and staffing to perform its workload effectively? The lack of resources inhibits enforcement in less dramatic ways as well. For example, low salaries have led experienced professional staff to leave EPA to pursue more lucrative employment opportunities in the private sector. One commentator has observed that "the very frequent replacement of EPA enforcement personnel has substantially denied the Agency a firm foundation of experienced professional staff, as well as a reliable 'institutional memory' that it can rely on as it pursues its enforcement work." Mintz, Rebuttal: EPA Enforcement and the Challenge of Change, 26 Envtl. L. Rep. 10538 (1996).

2. **Enforcement "beans."** EPA has traditionally measured its enforcement success by bean counting — toting up the number of enforcement cases initiated and resolved each fiscal year. Using bean counting to measure success has serious implications for enforcement. Merely counting beans gives as much credit for enforcement based on mandatory self-reporting as for enforcement based on extensive investigation. Counting beans focuses on quantity, not quality, giving as much credit for initiating a case with little hope of improving environmental quality as one that seeks to redress

serious environmental harm. Counting beans favors actions yielding high penalties over actions yielding greater impact on environmental quality.

> Budgetary constraints encourage EPA to put resources into activities that have a measurable payoff. Since current measures of enforcement success place almost exclusive reliance on initiation (and, to a lesser extent, the resolution) of enforcement cases, funding tends to go to activities that will result in production of the much-craved, commodity — the enforcement "bean." [Perversely, compliance] can become a hindrance to the bean harvest, rather than a welcome sign of progress. This doesn't mean that EPA officials encourage violations, but bean counting does tend to isolate enforcement personnel from larger issues of environmental progress. Diamond, Confessions of an Environmental Enforcer, 26 Envtl. L. Rep. 10253 (1996).

Is there any way to measure enforcement progress other than by utilizing the enforcement bean? Because for so many years EPA has reported its enforcement activity as an accomplishment, Congress has grown accustomed to measuring EPA's success by relying on the number of enforcement cases filed. Declining numbers are interpreted as evidence of a less vigilant EPA. When EPA's level of civil enforcement actions dropped in 1995, for example, the agency came under fire for reduced performance.

A related and equally important question is whether bean counting is a real measure of success. By relying for so long on the enforcement bean, EPA "has no comparative basis for evaluating whether this is the best approach to improving environmental protection. Indeed, the Agency cannot say with any level of precision what impact its enforcement cases have had, either on compliance with environmental requirements or on the environment itself. EPA has simply filed its cases, counted up its penalties, and assumed it was making progress." Id.

3. **The latest environmental enforcement beans.** EPA continues to measure its enforcement success by bean counting. Figure 21-2 lists EPA's latest civil and criminal enforcement statistics for the five-year period of 1998 to 2002. Although EPA's statistics provide a widely accepted and readily available means to evaluate its achievements, the central question remains whether enforcement "beans" truly measure environmental progress.

FIGURE 21-2

U.S. ENVIRONMENTAL PROTECTION AGENCY ENFORCEMENT AND COMPLIANCE PROGRAM

Numbers at a Glance Fiscal Years 2002-1998

	FY02	FY01	FY00	FY99	FY98
EPA Inspections	17,668[a]	17,560	20,417	21,847	23,237
Civil Referrals to DoJ	342	327	368	403	411
Civil Judicial Settlements	216	221	219	215	253
Value of Injunctions	$3,931,931,345	$4,453,961,458	$1,562,824,364	$3,424,223,733	$1,978,686,766
Judicial Penalties	$55,571,404	$101,683,157	$54,851,765	$141,211,765	$63,531,731
Administrative Penalties	$25,766,401	$23,782,264	$29,258,502	$25,509,879	$28,263,762
Value of SEPs	$56,458,594	$89,114,956	$55,888,396	$236,768,552	$90,836,361

FIGURE 21-2 *(continued)*

Numbers at a Glance Fiscal Years 2002-1998

	FY02	FY01	FY00	FY99	FY98
Criminal Referrals to DoJ	250	256	236	241	266
Criminal Sentences (years)	215.9	256	146.2	208.3	172.9
Defendants Charged	325	372	360	324	350
Criminal Cases Initiated	674[b]	482	477	471	636
Criminal Penalties	$62,252,318	$94,726,283	$121,974,488	$61,552,874	$92,800,711
Facilities Self-Disclosing Violations	927	1,095	2,190[c]	990	954
Companies Self-Disclosing Violations	500	397	429	260	200
Administrative Penalty Order Complaints	1,441	1,582	1,763	1,654	1,400
Administrative Compliance Orders	1,251	1,494	3,388[d]	1,516	1,721
Total Entities Reached by Compliance Assistance	589,566	551,340	351,287	333,108	246,596
Estimated Pounds of Pollutants Reduced	261,000,000	660,000,000	335,000,000	6,800,000,000[e]	629,000,000
Pounds of Contaminated Soil to Be Treated	513,000,000	1,800,000,000	1,300,000,000	574,000,000	n/a
Gallons of Contaminated Groundwater Treated	2,800,000,000				
Acres of Wetlands to Be Restored	40,000				
Individuals Served by Drinking Water Systems Brought into Compliance	3,150,000				
Superfund Cleanup Enforcement					
Private Party	$627 Million	Over $1.7 billion	Over $1.4 billion		
Orphan Share	$12.5 Million	Over $22.9 million	Over $19.1 billion		
De minimis	20/1,600 Parties	15/Over 1,900			

a. In FY02, OECA adopted a new policy for counting CAA inspections. Under the previous counting method, FY02 inspections would be over 18,000.

b. FY02 includes 190 counterterrorism cases supporting other federal agencies.

c. The increase in facilities involved in Audit Policy settlements was due largely to the Agency's efforts to encourage corporations with multiple facilities to conduct corporate-wide audits and develop corporate compliance systems. EPA reached corporate-wide agreements with the telecommunications and iron and steel sectors.

d. The significant number of administrative settlements in FY00 was due to the first-time enforcement of a new SDWA requirement to submit Consumer Confidence Reports, drinking water quality reports for consumers.

e. In FY99, EPA's settlement with seven major diesel engine manufacturers to resolve claims that they installed illegal computer software on heavy-duty diesel engines resulted in millions of tons of harmful NOx emissions reduced.

4. **The increasing use of SEPs.** EPA is increasingly encouraging the use of SEPs. Under EPA'S SEP Policy, seven specific categories of projects may qualify: (1) public health projects; (2) pollution prevention projects; (3) pollution redirection projects; (4) environmental restoration and protection projects; (5) assessment and audit projects; (6) environmental compliance promotion projects; and (7) emergency planning and preparedness projects. By negotiating a SEP with EPA, a violator may obtain a significant reduction in a proposed penalty by committing to voluntarily perform an environmentally beneficial project. The SEP Policy, however, requires that the final

penalty must still equal or exceed either (a) the economic benefit of noncompliance plus 10% of the gravity component, or (b) 25% of the gravity component only, whichever is greater.

How effective have SEPs become? From EPA's perspective, SEPs are a valuable tool. EPA's use of SEPs peaked in FY99, when EPA executed 197 judicial and administrative settlements valued at over $236 million. By utilizing SEPs, EPA furthers its goals of securing significant environmental or public health improvements while promoting pollution prevention and, where appropriate, environmental justice. From the violator's perspective, SEPs also present an attractive option. Rather than simply paying a civil fine or penalty to the federal treasury, a violator instead can dedicate penalty dollars to local public health or environmental concerns or to improving facility efficiency or operation. Incorporating a SEP into a settlement agreement with EPA can also reduce a violator's civil penalty significantly, even though the guidelines provide for certain thresholds of penalty. Violators can also be creative in proposing SEPs, since the SEP Policy provides for flexibility to incorporate worthwhile projects beyond the seven categories of projects typically allowable.

5. **Calculating civil penalties.** EPA's civil penalty policies, on their face, appear to provide a rational basis for establishing settlement amounts by utilizing what EPA claims are fair and equitable formulas. Those facing civil penalties, however, often encounter a world unto itself, consisting of statute-specific civil penalty policies; gravity of environmental harm calculations; and computer models designed to determine the economic benefit of noncompliance (BEN), the present value of SEPs, and the "ability to pay for environmental liability" (ABEL). See Fuhrman, Almost Always ABEL: EPA Treatment of Ability-to-Pay Issues in Civil Penalty Cases, Toxics L. Rep. 1125 (1997).

As an example, consider the application of the CWA's civil penalty policy. That policy is summarized in the following formula:

Settlement Penalty = Economic Benefit + Gravity Component ± Adjustments

Although the policy provides the appearance of objectivity, consider the following commentary:

> Under the CWA civil penalty policy, a monetary value is placed on gravity through the use of a scoring system in which each point adds $1,000 to the penalty.... EPA personnel are instructed to assign points based on four criteria: the significance of the violation, harm to health and the environment, the number of violations, and the duration of non-compliance. Points are to be assigned for each month in which a violation occurred, and one additional point is to be added for each such month.

> The methodology for quantifying the "significance of the violation" is based on the most significant effluent violation in each month and appears quite quantitative. The CWA policy contains a table that translates the percentage of the exceedance over the allowable level of effluence into a number of points. The point system ranges from zero to 15 points for non-toxic and from zero to 20 for toxic pollutants. Harm to health and the environment is much more difficult to quantify. Nonetheless, the CWA policy allows the attribution of between 10 points and 25 points per month for violations that affect human health. Alternatively, between one point and 10 points may be assigned for impacts on the aquatic environment.

This aspect of the methodology is highly arbitrary, overlaps with the significance of the violation criterion, and avoids the difficult task of identifying and quantifying the harm to human health and natural resources caused by a release of pollutants. It also provides EPA with great flexibility to increase or decrease the monetary value attributed to the gravity component, depending on the attitudes of the litigation team. The guidance for assessing the number of violations is vague. It allows for assigning between zero and five points based on the total number of violations each month, but provides very superficial guidance on how many points should be assigned in a given situation. The discussion of how to assign points for the duration of non-compliance is even more vague. This factor is intended to punish the violator of continuing, long-term violations of an effluent limitation or permit conditions, generally defined as violations continuing for three or more consecutive months. The plaintiffs may identify between zero and five points per month for this category. Given the subjective nature of some of these criteria, two entities in identical situations may receive quite different assessments.

According to the CWA civil penalty policy, after calculating the initial penalty amount (i.e., after adding together the economic benefit and monthly gravity components), this total may be modified by three adjustment factors: the history of non-compliance (which can increase the penalty up to 1.5 times the initial amount), the violator's ability to pay (which may lead to a decrease in the penalty), and litigation considerations (which may also lead to a decrease)....

The penalty policy's discussion of how to treat recalcitrance is so lacking in specifics that almost any outcome can be rationalized within its guidance. The discussion also tells the EPA staff that they may increase the recalcitrance factor during the negotiations if the alleged violator continues to be recalcitrant "with the remedy or with settlement efforts." Clearly, the policy provides leverage for plaintiffs. While recognizing that recalcitrance is an explicit consideration in assessing penalties under most environmental statutes, one can easily criticize the amorphous nature of this part of the guidance. Although it is unlikely that recalcitrance is a factor in all environmental violations, when EPA starts negotiating with an alleged CWA violator, it typically increases the initial penalty at least 50 percent due to alleged recalcitrance. The guidance provides no benchmark for analyzing the appropriate adjustment factor for recalcitrance in a case with a given fact pattern. Fuhrman, Improving EPA's Civil Penalty Policies — And Its Not-So-Gentle BEN Model, 23 Envtl. L. Rep. 874, 876–878 (1994).

In light of questions that can be raised about EPA's economic benefit methodology, does it seem unfair to increase the recalcitrance factor when both parties are negotiating in good faith? The guidance about recalcitrance would be more useful to EPA and the regulated community if it contained examples of situations where the factor was set at specific levels. However, in many cases involving alleged CWA violations, EPA has chosen not to share the basis for its gravity calculations with defendants. This practice preserves the government's flexibility to raise or lower the monetary amount attributed to this factor in settlement negotiations. Does the failure to disclose fuel the perception that the government has not treated the alleged violator objectively and evenhandedly?

6. **EPA's use of enforcement powers: the "any credible evidence" rule.** Generally, there are two types of evidence that can be used to prove CAA violations. The first type is commonly known as the "reference test" method. In simple terms, this is a procedure that provides precise instructions to enforcement officials on how to measure whether

a source is exceeding established emission limits. The second type of evidence is based on the words "any credible evidence" in CAA §113(e), 42 U.S.C. §7413(e). Invoking that statutory language, EPA developed a final rule (effective on April 25, 1997) that allows enforcement officials and citizen groups to expand the types of evidence to be used in proving violations of the statute. This category includes all evidence that is deemed credible as defined by applicable rules of evidence. This evidence might include, for instance, monitoring data that a source has collected for purposes other than enforcement. The key difference between the two types of evidence comes down to whether a party must conduct a specific test that is prescribed by the regulation being enforced, or whether that party can use other available evidence to show a violation has occurred. EPA's "any credible evidence" rule codified the latter approach, expanding the type of evidence that can be used in enforcement actions.

In reviewing EPA's desire to utilize "any credible evidence," consider the following:

EPA first proposed its "any credible evidence" (ACE) rule as part of its enhanced-monitoring rule proposal in October 1993. The ACE rule...amends 40 C.F.R. Parts 51, 52, 60, and 61 to eliminate language that has been read to provide for exclusive reliance on reference test methods as the means of demonstrating compliance with emission limits under the [CAA], and to clarify that credible evidence can be used for compliance determinations.

The ACE...rule...permits a source to certify compliance by using a range of methods, including reference test methods and enhanced monitoring. The...ACE rule requires that SIPs promulgated under the CAA also allow the use of any credible evidence to establish a source's violations....

To understand the issues surrounding ACE, it is necessary to understand the concept of a reference test method and its historic use in EPA and state enforcement under the CAA. Essentially, a reference test method is a specific test method used to determine compliance with a particular EPA emission standard or limitation....

In establishing a reference test method, EPA often specified: (1) training of test personnel; (2) how the test is to be conducted; (3) how test results are to be analyzed; (4) how often tests are to be conducted; and (5) how compliance with the standard is to be determined, using the test results....

However, it is well known today that there are often alternative methods that could theoretically be used to determine compliance, with particular EPA air-quality regulations. For example, in the case of opacity, there are now continuous emission monitors (CEMs) that use lasers to measure the opacity of plumes coming out of a plant stack. The readings produced by these monitors are often more frequent, and in many cases more reliable, than the estimates prepared by even the best-trained human observers called for in the EPA opacity reference test. In addition to CEMs, there are often physical process parameters related to plant emission — such as the temperature, pressure, and speed of gas flows — that can be used to reliably estimate plant emissions of certain pollutants....

The ACE rule...significantly broaden[ed] EPA practice, and citizen-suit enforcement, by permitting compliance with EPA emission standards to be determined through use of "comparable" CEMs data and other measurements such as reliable indirect physical measurement or parametric data. Van Cleve & Holman, Promise and Reality in the Enforcement of the Amended Clean Air Act Part I: EPA's "Any Credible Evidence" and "Compliance Assurance Monitoring" Rules, 27 Envtl. L. Rep. 10097, 10099–10100 (1997).

Has the EPA adopted an overly expansive view of the "any credible evidence" language, as industry contends? Or does the rule simply clarify the existing law, as EPA contends? In light of Congress's strengthening the enforcement capabilities of EPA, the states, and citizens in the 1990 CAA Amendments, did Congress intend that EPA base its broadened regulatory authority and strengthened enforcement program on the best possible data concerning the actual operations of air pollution sources? These issues remain to be clarified in the courts. In August 1998, the D.C. Circuit dismissed an action by industry trade associations challenging ACE, holding that issues concerning whether ACE caused substantive changes in air pollutant standards that required EPA to conduct full rule-making procedures were not ripe for judicial review, but rather must await the application of ACE in the concrete setting of an enforcement action. Clean Air Act Implementation Project v. EPA, 150 F.3d 1200 (D.C. Cir. 1998).

7. **Regulatory creep: the enforceability of EPA informal guidance documents.** Many in the regulated community have experienced firsthand EPA's practice of using informal agency interpretations to broaden the scope of federal regulations. The ever-widening scope of regulation that follows often is referred to as "regulatory creep." However, the D.C. Circuit has now raised significant questions concerning EPA's longstanding practice of expanding the reach of existing rules through informal guidance documents. In Appalachian Power Co. v. EPA, 208 F.3d 1015 (D.C. Cir. 2000), several electric power companies and chemical and petroleum trade associations ("the Petitioners") challenged the validity of portions of a 1998 EPA guidance document entitled "Periodic Monitoring Guidance" ("the Guidance"). The Guidance included the agency's interpretation of 40 C.F.R. §70.6(a)(3)(i)(B) ("the Rule"), one of the implementing regulations for the Title V air permit program. The Rule states that where the applicable air emissions requirement for a facility does not require periodic testing or monitoring, state-issued Title V permits must contain "periodic monitoring sufficient to yield reliable data from the relevant time period that are representative of the source's compliance with the permit." The Petitioners argued that the only purpose of this Rule is to fill the gap when an applicable emissions requirement does not contain any testing or monitoring requirements.

However, the EPA's Guidance interpreted this provision more broadly to allow the state agencies to evaluate applicable requirements and impose a periodic monitoring requirement if the state determines that the monitoring provision in the applicable requirement "does not provide the necessary assurance of compliance." State authorities had invoked this EPA Guidance to require continuous opacity monitors (i.e., 24-hour automated monitoring) of Title V applicants even when the applicable standard specified only a simple visual observation method for ensuring compliance.

The D.C. Circuit agreed with the Petitioners that the plain language of the Rule creates only a gap-filling function and concluded that, as a result, the Guidance necessarily assigns broader authority to state agencies than granted to them in the Rule. In reaching this result, the D.C. Circuit also cited the inconsistency of the Guidance with the 1992 preamble to the Rule. In the preamble, EPA stated that if there is "any federally promulgated requirement with insufficient monitoring, EPA will issue a rulemaking to revise such requirement." 57 Fed. Reg. 32278 (July 21, 1992). As the Court pointed out, the Guidance provides for an altogether different procedure. Under the Guidance, "it is initially up to the States to identify federal standards with deficient monitoring, doubtless with EPA's input, formal or informal. And it is the state and local agencies that must alter the standards by requiring permittees...to comply with more stringent monitoring requirements. Needless to say, EPA's approach...raises serious issues, not the least of which is whether EPA possesses the authority it now purports to delegate." 208 F.3d at 1026. The D.C. Circuit accordingly held that the Guidance's more expansive reading of the Rule could not stand: "[i]n directing state permitting authorities to conduct wide-ranging sufficiency reviews and to enhance the monitoring required in individual permits beyond that contained in State or federal emissions standards...EPA has in effect amended §70.6(a)(3)(i)(B). This it cannot legally do without complying with the rulemaking procedures required by 42 U.S.C. §7607(d) [the APA]." Id. at 1028.

Will this decision aid in challenges to guidance documents related to implementing rules for the CWA, RCRA, CERCLA, and other major federal environmental laws? What steps could EPA undertake to eliminate challenges to its guidance documents?

Section 4. **BROWNFIELDS FEDERALISM AND ITS POLICY OF GREATER FLEXIBILITY AND COOPERATION**

Patterns of environmental enforcement are changing. The area in which the greatest strides have been made is in relation to regulatory developments pertaining to brownfields. As defined by EPA, brownfields are "abandoned, idled, or underused industrial and commercial sites where expansion or redevelopment is complicated by real or perceived environmental contamination that can add cost, time or uncertainty to a redevelopment project."[12]

In the past, redevelopment of brownfields was often avoided for fear of environmental liabilities arising primarily under CERCLA (see Chapter 19), its state equivalents, and RCRA (see Chapter 18). The extensive jurisdictional reach of these statutes, their broad liability provisions, and the fear of federal and state enforcement were all blamed for impeding the redevelopment of many brownfields sites. Historically, prospective purchasers, who often desired to quantify cleanup costs before purchasing a contaminated site, found that governmental entities were unwilling or unable to provide assistance in determining what constitutes an acceptable cleanup. In large part, therefore, brownfields sites sat idle and undeveloped, even if such development were in the public interest. Potential investors, faced with uncertain costs and potential associated legal liabilities, sought development elsewhere, often at pristine rural sites (labeled "greenfields"). Brownfields sites, in turn, became major burdens on the community and taxpayers.

Commencing in the early 1990s, EPA and the states began to recognize that, rather than encouraging brownfields redevelopment, their deterrent enforcement strategies were actually having the opposite effect by discouraging prospective purchasers. In response, federal and state regulatory reforms were announced with the express

---

12. EPA Region 5, Office of Pub. Affairs, Basic Brownfields Fact Sheet (1996). There are an estimated 130,000 to 450,000 contaminated brownfield sites around the country. Current cleanup estimates range up to $650 billion.

purpose of spurring brownfields redevelopment. These reforms reflected (1) a shift from historical reliance on a deterrent and penalty-based enforcement ideology to more flexible initiatives, seeking to induce brownfields development through partnering with the regulated community; and (2) a shift towards increasing cooperation between federal and state enforcement authorities, seeking to harmonize enforcement priorities to allow brownfields development to move forward.

U.S. Environmental Protection Agency,
Brownfields Action Agenda
(1995)

[This agenda had six key reforms, each designed to deal with particular obstacles to brownfields redevelopment.]

1. Prospective purchaser agreements. This reform represents EPA's effort to provide a liability waiver to prospective buyers of brownfields sites. A prospective purchaser agreement is a binding contract entered into between EPA, the owner of a contaminated property, and a prospective purchaser, exonerating the purchaser from any future environmental liability at the site and obligating the EPA not to sue the purchaser for any existing contamination.... Only 16 prospective purchaser agreements were made between 1989 and 1995. In response to pressure for a more flexible, compliance oriented policy, EPA revised its prospective purchaser guidelines in 1995, specifically clarifying and encouraging the use of prospective purchaser agreements. EPA, Announcement and Publication of Guidance on Agreements With Prospective Purchasers of Contaminated Property and Model Prospective Purchaser Agreement, 60 Fed. Reg. 34,792–98 (1995).

2. Delisting sites from the CERCLIS database. To remove the stigma from listing a site on CERCLIS, the national list of CERCLA sites, EPA voluntarily delisted 25,000 (of a total of 38,000) sites for which it plans no further remediation. See CERCLIS Definition Change, 60 Fed. Reg. 16,053 (1995).

3. Other purchaser protections. EPA also issued a guidance document pledging not to pursue innocent landowners with contaminated acquifers and pledging to issue "comfort letters" to those engaged in voluntary cleanups. See U.S. EPA Policy Toward Owners of Property Containing Contaminated Acquifers (Nov. 1995).

4. Land use policy. EPA also promulgated a directive allowing future land uses to be considered in selecting the appropriate remedial action at sites on the National Priorities List. See U.S. EPA, Land Use in the CERCLA Remedy Selection Process, OSWER Directive No. 9355.7-04 (May 25, 1995).

5. Pilot Project Grants. EPA agreed to fund economic redevelopment projects at brownfield sites, in an effort to develop new and more cost-effective cleanup standards. See Superfund: Reports Cite Savings in Remedy Selection Resulting from Superfund Reform at EPA, 27 BNA Env't Rep. 1874 (1997); and

6. Memorandums of Agreement Regarding State Voluntary Cleanups. Certain EPA Regions entered into Memorandums of Agreement (MOAs) with state environmental agencies, providing that EPA will not take enforcement action at sites where private parties have conducted cleanups under the state's direction or under state voluntary cleanup statutes. See ABA, Brownfields Redevelopment: Cleaning Up the Urban Environment 117-25 (Mar. 7, 1996).

COMMENTARY & QUESTIONS

1. **The old horrors of Superfund cleanups.** Chapter 19 reviews how Superfund works or, in the eyes of some critics, how Superfund fails to work. Why was EPA so insistent on rigid, dictatorial cleanups and on harsh bargaining positions in Superfund's earlier years? Many speculative answers are possible. Some relate to the backlash against the Gorsuch-era Superfund nonenforcement in the early Reagan Administration; others relate to the unthinking attitude of EPA as an overzealous agency taking itself too seriously in the exercise of the enormous powers granted by CERCLA §§106 and 107. There are more benign possibilities as well; for example, the change could have been part of a natural agency learning process, through which the agency was able to recognize that a different approach better served the public interest. Most flattering to EPA, it is also possible that the change in course coincided with a change in the nature of the underlying problem and the behavior of the regulated community that had been brought about by EPA's past practices. As to the problem itself, EPA has listed the worst sites on the national priorities list (NPL) and has cleanups well underway at most of them. Sites not on the NPL tend to pose fewer public health hazards and exhibit problems of a more localized nature that do not waken the Love Canal and Times Beach hysteria. Remediation techniques and cleanup methods are better understood and somewhat more efficacious as a result of past experience. Moreover, the regulated entities understand the CERCLA liability scheme better. They are far more adept at estimating their own liabilities under the law, and far more wary of protracted litigation, or strategies of recalcitrance. The combination of less seriously polluted sites and regulated parties ready to negotiate allows EPA the leeway to adopt more flexible approaches.

2. **State law and policy changes affecting enforcement.** Along with federal policy changes, state agencies and state cleanup laws have also changed, perhaps to an even greater degree. Many state laws that mimicked CERCLA were at least as draconian. See Geltman, Recycling Land: Encouraging the Redevelopment of Contaminated Property, 10 Nat. Res. & Env't 3 (Spring 1996). In particular, a majority of the states implemented voluntary cleanup programs or enacted brownfields legislation. These state developments are illustrated in the pie chart set forth in Figure 21-3.

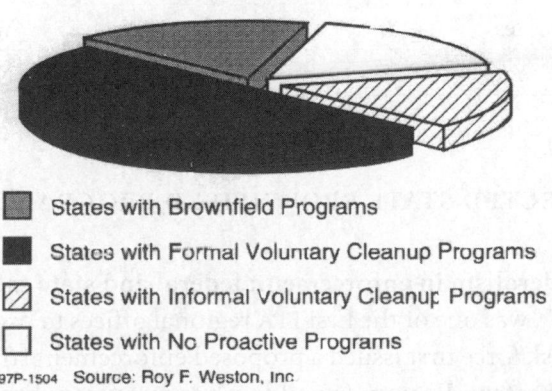

☒ States with Brownfield Programs

■ States with Formal Voluntary Cleanup Programs

▨ States with Informal Voluntary Cleanup Programs

☐ States with No Proactive Programs

97P-1504   Source: Roy F. Weston, Inc.

FIGURE 21-3

STATE BROWNFIELD AND VOLUNTARY CLEANUP PROGRAMS

State brownfields legislation generally has four basic components: (1) risk-based, end-use cleanup standards and voluntary programs; (2) implementation of liability control, comfort, and protection through the use of covenants not to sue; (3) an accelerated program for cleaning up contaminated sites to standards pegged to future property use (so called tiered action objectives); and (4) economic and employment opportunities, particularly for disadvantaged areas, through the cleanup and redevelopment of contaminated sites. Many states have also added unique and potentially important components to their legislative efforts, including tax breaks or incentives for the cost of investigation and remediation associated with an individual site, and financial lender liability protection. This protection often provides for a definition of "owner" that eliminates the lender as a potentially responsible party (PRP).

Looking more closely at examples of how these individual states are tackling the brownfields problem provides some insight into the impact of economic development on enforcement strategies. Figure 21-4 shows selected states and the legislative status and important features of their programs. An interesting aspect of many state initiatives is the impact of neighboring state legislation on their programs, and the "competing" economic development and environmental programs developed in efforts by certain states to become more user-friendly to business.

STATE	BROWNFIELD LEGISLATION	VOLUNTARY PROGRAM	RISK BASED/ END-USE CLEANUP STANDARDS	BUYER LIABILITY PROTECTION	LENDER LIABILITY PROTECTION	TAX INCENTIVES
Pennsylvania	Yes	Yes	Yes	Yes	Yes	Yes
Delaware	Yes	Yes	Yes	Yes	No	Yes
New Jersey	Yes	Yes	Yes	Yes	No	No
Massachusetts	Yes	Yes	Yes	Yes	Yes	Yes
Georgia	Yes	Yes	Partial	No	No	No
Illinois	Yes	Yes	Yes	Yes	Yes	No
Minnesota	Yes	Yes	Yes	Yes	No	No
New York	Yes	Yes	Yes	Yes	No	No
Michigan	Yes	Yes	Yes	Yes	Yes	No
Ohio	Yes	Yes	Yes	Yes	No	No

FIGURE 21-4

STATUS OF SELECTED STATE BROWNFIELD PROGRAMS

3. **Cooperative federalism in enforcement: federal and state memoranda of agreement.** EPA Region V was one of the first EPA regional offices to organize a Brownfields Task Force. This task force first issued a proposed enforcement strategy in 1993–1994. According to this strategy, Region V would seek to encourage brownfields redevelopment based on four basic principles: (1) promote cleanups by encouraging participation in state voluntary cleanup programs; (2) provide information to promote

informed decisionmaking by prospective purchasers and lenders; (3) encourage community participation in the cleanup process; and (4) develop partnerships among Region V states, local governments, and stakeholders. The strategy also delineated specific initiatives, including issuing generic "comfort letters," developing site-specific covenants not to sue, and developing consensus on risk-based cleanup protocols linked to future land use scenarios.

To accomplish these goals, Region V developed a Memorandum of Agreement (MOA) with each of the midwestern states to include language that releases sites remediated successfully under state authority from further attention by Region V. Region V's MOA with the State of Illinois, executed on April 6, 1995, is set forth below.

Superfund Memorandum of Agreement
Illinois Environmental Protection Agency, United States
Environmental Protection Agency, Region V
(1995)

I. Background... The Illinois Environmental Protection Agency ("IEPA") and the United States Environmental Protection Agency, Region V ("Region V") entered a Superfund Memorandum of Agreement (SMOA) effective December 18, 1991. Among other things, the SMOA established operating procedures for general Superfund program coordination and communication between IEPA and Region V.

II. Brownfields... In 1993 IEPA and Region V began developing strategies to promote the remediation and redevelopment of "Brownfield" sites. Both agencies recognize that a key factor to the Brownfields program in Illinois is for both agencies to exercise their authorities and use their resources in ways that are mutually complementary and are not duplicative. Two operational factors are important in this regard. First, the IEPA has successfully operated a voluntary cleanup program since the late 1980s. This program, more formally known as the Pre-Notice Site Cleanup Program ("PNSCP"), provides guidance assistance and oversight by IEPA to owners and operators of sites in Illinois who perform site assessment and remediation in accordance with the practices, and under the approval, of the IEPA. In addition, IEPA has established a consistent cleanup objectives process across all its remediation programs (PWSCP, CERCLA, RCRA, and LUST) which is protective of human health and the environment. Second, USEPA has administered a national site assessment program to assess sites listed on the federal CERCLIS list. This assessment process identifies and prioritizes sites for remediation needs and also establishes a "no further remedial action planned" or NFRAP category of sites. As a result of the success of these two programs, IEPA and Region V have concluded that the principles and procedures set forth in this Addendum will meaningfully assist in the remediation and development of Brownfield sites.

III. Principles... If a site in Illinois has been remediated or investigated under the practices and procedures of the Illinois PNSCP and IEPA has approved the remediation as complete or made a no-action determination upon review of an investigation, consistent with existing information the site will not be expected to require further response actions. Accordingly, Region 5 will not plan or anticipate any federal action under Superfund law unless, in exceptional circumstances, the site poses an imminent threat or emergency situation. Region 5 will also continue to work with Illinois to remove any concerns about federal activity under Superfund so as to encourage appropriate redevelopment.

This Principle does not apply to sites which have been listed on the National Priorities List or sites subject to an order or other enforcement action under Superfund law or sites imminently threatening public health or the environment. Future IEPA activities at the site will be based on the conditions of the remediation approval and whether any imminent threat subsequently arises.

IV. Reporting... On an annual basis IEPA will report to Region V on the number of…sites in the PNSCP, sites entering the PNSCP the previous year, and sites having received approvals by IEPA of full or partial completions in the previous year.…

COMMENTARY & QUESTIONS

1. **How much assurance?** EPA has negotiated agreements on a case-by-case basis with PRPs that include express promises not to go to court and commence enforcement proceedings (covenants not to sue). The MOA does not rise to the level of a covenant not to sue. The MOA does provide prospective purchasers with assurance that, by participating in the Illinois Cleanup Program, they are unlikely to face federal enforcement action. Is that enough assurance to satisfy the PRP's desire to put an upper bound on liability? Also note that the MOA contains exceptions for sites listed on the NPL, for sites already subject to enforcement action under Superfund, and for sites imminently threatening the public health or the environment. Why were these exceptions made? Do the exceptions create "pariah parcels" in the sense that no prospective purchasers will buy such parcels when there are MOA-eligible parcels also available? At a minimum, Region V's MOA encourages prospective purchasers to work more closely with Illinois environmental officials to remediate properties under Illinois law. Does the MOA represent evidence that cooperative federalism is maturing, at least where brownfields are concerned?

2. **Enforcing promises of regulatory forbearance.** As suggested above, a covenant not to sue represents a form of promise by the regulator to exercise its authority in a particular fashion. It is akin to a contract, but is it (or any other promise of regulatory forbearance) enforceable against the government if the government changes its mind? Consent decrees that extinguish liabilities bind government to its promises. See Frew v. Hawkins, 2004 U.S. LEXIS 664 (slip. op. Jan. 14, 2004) (holding that enforcement of a federal consent decree designed to implement a federal statute against state agencies does not violate the Eleventh Amendment, where "the decree vindicates an agreement that the state officials reached to comply with federal law"). But mere promises of the regulator are seldom enforceable. See Toscano, Note, Forbearance Agreements: Invalid Contracts for the Surrender of Sovereignty, 92 Colum. L. Rev. 426 (1992). See also Abrams, Binding Agreements with Governmental Entities, ABA Water L. Conf. Proceedings, Feb. 20, 1998. This landscape may be changing in the wake of United States v. Winstar Corp., 518 U.S. 839 (1996), a case that upheld a governmental promise to bear the risk (i.e., the monetary loss) of a regulatory change it had promised not to make. The reasons that government is free to "change its regulatory mind," even after promising not to do so, have to do with the preservation of sovereignty. Is the enforceability of promises of regulatory forbearance critical to EPA's new policies of more cooperative relations with the regulated community?

3. EPA's rule on brownfield property assessments to avoid liability. A final rule, clarifying how certain owners or purchasers of potentially contaminated property should conduct assessments to avoid Superfund liability, was adopted by the EPA effective June 9, 2003.

Under the rule, EPA clarified the standards to be used by prospective purchasers of brownfields and owners of land contiguous to contaminated sites to assess contamination and identify all prior uses, so that prospective purchasers are not held liable for the pollution.

The EPA developed the rule in response to the Small Business Liability Relief and Brownfields Revitalization Act, 42 U.S.C. §9601 (2000), enacted in January 2002. The Act established new defenses for property owners, provided liability relief to certain kinds of generators, and created a statutory brownfields funding program. The Act also extended financial assistance to states to help establish or administer brownfields or voluntary cleanup programs, and established standards for conducting due diligence. In particular, under the Act, bona fide prospective purchasers and contiguous landowners are protected from Superfund liability as long as they conduct "all appropriate inquiry" into former uses of the land and take other specified steps.

The Act provides that, by the end of 2004, EPA must develop standards for conducting all appropriate inquiry, but that until then, landowners should use an existing standard developed in 1997 by the American Society for Testing and Materials (ASTM). The 1997 standard is known as Standard Practice for Environmental Site Assessment: Phase 1 Environmental Site Assessment Process (E1527-97). However, ASTM, a private, nonprofit standards-writing organization, had updated that standard in 2000, and EPA's final rule clarifies that prospective purchasers and contiguous property owners may also use the 2000 standard in the interim. That standard is known as Assessment Process (E1527-2000). The two versions are not significantly different.

The EPA's final rule, and the Act itself, continue the trend toward brownfields federalism by emphasizing the need for increased cooperation between federal and state enforcement authorities. With certain exceptions identified in the Act, EPA may not bring CERCLA enforcement actions when a cleanup is performed at an "eligible response site" and the state response program meets the minimum standards. An "eligible response site" under §129 of the Act includes sites that fall within the definition of a brownfield site, and those sites that EPA determines are eligible for brownfields assistance on a case-by-case basis. Sites specifically excluded from the definition are NPL sites, and sites where the EPA has conducted or is conducting a preliminary assessment and site inspection whereby it determines, after consultation with the state, that the site is eligible for inclusion on the NPL.

Section 5. ADMINISTRATIVE REFORMS IN ENVIRONMENTAL ENFORCEMENT

Regulatory reforms pertaining to environmental enforcement have repeatedly been proposed from all corners of the political compass and from government itself. In the 1990s, environmental regulation faced frontal assaults by marketplace forces in the 104th Congress, a Clinton Administration program of "Reinventing Government" that continued experiments in negotiated rulemaking, market-enlisting economic incentive programs to change the traditional command-and-control regulatory model, and a number of agency initiatives to simplify regulatory procedures.

The 104th Congress produced a flurry of industry-inspired assaults on environmental regulation. Some, targeting the CWA and ESA, were quite specific; others were quite generic. The House of Representatives, for instance, passed a "regulatory moratorium" drafted by Gordon Gooch, a Project Relief lobbyist for the petrochemical industry, which included as its major provision a freeze and rollback of almost all federal regulations proposed after November 1994. The moratorium was an example of a crude blunt "reform" initiative. Its scope was breathtaking; in fact it suspended a host of rules without knowing what they were. "Regulatory Reform Act" bills were proposed to set up an intricate series of procedural and analytical roadblocks before agencies could put forward environmentally protective regulations, although the 104th Congress bills had fast-track exemptions for pesticide approvals and similar market-permissive rules. The intent of these bills was regulatory "paralysis by analysis." "Property rights" bills provided that regulatory agencies would have to compensate regulated interests if any portion of their property was reduced in value by 20% or more; if the agency did not pay, regulations would be unenforceable. The Unfunded Mandates Reform Act burdened federal-state regulatory systems of "cooperative federalism" by placing procedural hurdles before Congress could delegate regulatory roles to the states.

These political initiatives to change regulatory practices have come to very little, as legislators have discovered that attacks on environmental regulation, once the media covers them, became political hot potatoes, ready to burn anyone who picks them up. With the exception of the unfunded mandates law, marketplace attempts to undercut the regulatory process are either in remission or keeping a lower profile.

Other reform attempts have come from within the executive branch itself — the "Reinventing Government" Executive Order on Regulatory Planning and Review; the EPA's Regulatory Unified Agenda implementations of the Reinventing Government Executive Order; EPA's Project XL Multimedia Permitting; and various Advisory Councils established by EPA under the Federal Advisory Committee Act,[13] including the Common Sense Initiative program, the National Environmental Justice Advisory Council, the Federal Facilities Environmental Restoration Dialogue Committee, and the National Advisory Council for Environmental Policy and Technology (NACEPT).

Project XL: "Multimedia" Permitting. In an attempt to reduce the expensive and lengthy permit process, the EPA has initiated the program known as "Project XL" — a multipurpose environmental permit designed to replace the extreme complexities of some existing procedures. Under the program, the agency issues a single master permit — simplifying the regulatory process by combining or eliminating the need for separate permits in areas such as air, water, and hazardous wastes. The purpose of Project XL is to allow companies freedom to take innovative approaches to pollution control by allowing them to skirt certain regulatory requirements in exchange for setting up an alternative plan that will produce superior overall environmental results. The

---

13. Pub. L. No. 92-463 (1972).

"multimedia" permit is a single, performance-based plan that considers a facility's total net impact on the environment rather than attempting to regulate individual technologies used. The danger, of course, is that in such master permit processes some of the substantive requirements of public and environmental health and safety get compromised. If erosion of norms can be avoided, however, the rationality of the approach militates in favor of the experiment.

EPA's Industry-Specific "Common Sense Initiative." EPA announced in 1994 that it would begin an experiment in cooperation with industry groups to rationalize regulatory approaches where it appeared that equal or greater pollution abatements could be achieved by alternative lower-cost abatement strategies. Targeting the auto, petroleum refining, iron and steel, metal finishing and plating, computer and electronics, and printing industries, the approach presumes that in many cases industry expertise and self-interest will identify protective measures of greater efficiency and oversell net savings. One example is benzene emissions at oil refining facilities. The industry identified the loading stage — the point at which refined petroleum products were being nozzled into tankers or other transport facilities — as generating more ambient benzene emissions than the refining facilities themselves, and these emissions from loading were abatable at far lower cost. EPA proposes to allow that industry to comply with benzene standards by rolling back loading stage emissions rather than requiring the far more difficult and expensive refining process emission cutbacks.

This "common sense initiative" has the potential to improve both the tone and the overall results of our massive command-and-control regulatory systems, but obviously it must take account of the opposing tensions inherent in regulation of economic forces. EPA acceptance of such tradeoffs requires full, comparative, accurate information before and after each tradeoff, and careful implementation and monitoring. A fear on the industry side is that there is no EPA estoppel: The accomplishment of net gains by an industry-suggested alternative does not prevent EPA from coming back later for further incremental improvements under the bypassed restrictions.

Negotiated Rulemaking. A number of regulatory experiments with negotiated rulemaking — "reg-neg" — have taken place in the environmental setting, particularly in EPA and the Department of Interior, under the terms of the Administrative Dispute Resolution Act[14] and the Negotiated Rulemaking Act,[15] passed as amendments to the adjudication section of the APA. See Subchapter D below.

COMMENTARY & QUESTIONS

1. **The quest for efficiency.** EPA's Project XL and Common Sense Initiative have faced problems with the battleground setting of interest-representation regulatory politics. OSHA's attempt to cope with the vast number of rulemakings Congress had required of it foundered on the rocks of judicial review, when the court's requirement of

---

14. Pub. L. No. 101-552 (1990).
15. Pub. L. No. 101-648 (1990).

voluminous individual databases for each proposed new standard proved quite simply to be impossible.

One of the secrets of U.S. government is that legislatures do not give agencies the economic or political capital needed to enforce all the laws on the books. But a will to enforce, coupled with innovative administrative planning, can improve upon the situation. EPA continues to try to make the administrative process "more transparent" so that citizen participation can enter into the bargaining process of regulation. Based on informal communications with OSHA, the agency is giving up a prior attempt to do consolidated "omnibus" rulemaking. See AFL-CIO v. OSHA, 965 F.2d 962 (11th Cir. 1992). EPA, on the other hand, is reportedly proceeding with major new "cluster rule-making" under the CWA, treating classes of industry in the same business in an omnibus process. (EPA's job is easier than OSHA's because its statutory standards under the CWA are based on industrywide BAT rather than the individual safety of each substance standard as with OSHA.)

2. **Other reforms: citizen oversight councils.** Citizen councils, built into governmental regulatory processes, offer interesting innovations for environmental administrative law. Notable examples of citizen councils were created in the aftermath of the *Exxon-Valdez* oil spill. RCACs, Regional Citizens Advisory Councils, generally vested with subpoena powers, bring citizens most directly threatened by environmental hazards into the official public law regulatory process. Faced with the conclusion that official regulatory oversight and enforcement before the Alaska oil spill had been lax and complacent in the face of industry corner-cutting, three models of citizen oversight councils were initiated — a council formed in citizen negotiations with industry; a state-legislated citizens council, chaired by Professor Harry Bader who had helped conceptualize it; and a federal model of citizens council written into law in the Oil Pollution Act of 1990. The first model was incorporated into the third. The state council, after its research began to produce embarrassing evidence of state nonenforcement of pollution laws, was defunded and shut down through the efforts of industry lobbyists. The terms of these innovative administrative experiments are interesting and potentially important far beyond the waters of the Gulf of Alaska. See Oil Pollution Act of 1994, 33 U.S.C. §2732; Alaska Stat. §§24.20.160 et seq. (1990). Citizen councils offer valuable advantages in quality control efforts of both private and governmental resource protection activities, and are designed to be relatively immune from cooptation. These experiments bear continuing study as examples of utilitarian pluralism in government.

3. **"Collaborative governance."** From her study of environmental regulation at OSHA and EPA, Professor Jody Freeman has advocated experiments with "collaborative governance" to respond to the litany of criticisms about the quality, implementability, and legitimacy of rulemaking by agency establishments and cohorts of lobbyists. Collaborative governance would reorient regulatory reform toward joint problem solving and away from controlling discretion. Collaborative governance requires improved mechanisms for problem solving, broad participation, provisional solutions, the sharing of regulatory responsibility across the public-private divide, and flexible, engaged agencies:

Recent experiments with multi-stakeholder decision-making processes, such as regulatory negotiation and Project XL, which offer parties more direct access to, and responsibility for, all stages of the administrative process are promising alternatives to discretion-constraining instruments. They have some potential to facilitate problem solving, produce better-quality rules, and create mechanisms of accountability that take advantage of the capacities of nongovernmental groups. They are not, however, without limitations.... All administrative law reform proposals must cope with the "structural embeddedness" of agencies.... It is still unclear whether a collaborative model that remains dependent upon interest groups can overcome the pathologies of interest-representation, including its strategic-bargaining orientation and its tendency to exclude less-organized interests. Moreover, the potential for a problem-oriented, deliberative dynamic to emerge in the administrative process may be undermined by the reality that "repeat players"...pursue their interests in a wide variety of settings beyond rule making and implementation.... Parties' interactions in the legislative process, litigation, election campaigns, and state and local regulation can hinder collaboration.... Freeman, Collaborative Governance in the Administrative State, 45 UCLA L. Rev. 1 (1997).

Nevertheless Professor Freeman concludes that the destructive and convoluted process of modern lobbyist-dominated interest-representation regulatory politics deserves to be rethought in a more transparent and articulated participatory decisionmaking system.

4. **Sunsets.** Sunsetting provisions are a regulatory reform device with mixed reviews. Much recent public interest legislation has been freighted with a provision suspending funds, authority, or both after a period of years, often five years, thereafter requiring renewal. This approach was touted as making agencies justify their work periodically in a democratic forum. In practice, it typically has been attached to laws such as ESA that do not have sustained marketplace political momentum. This effectively guarantees that environmental protections passed into law have to be defended against assault every five years. Mining, lumbering, and grazing programs on public lands, U.S. Army Corps of Engineers draining and damming programs, and the like never seem to have sunsets attached to them. Administrative law, like the rest of life, is not consistently dominated by civic values or neutral principles, but rather is a continuing reflection of the convoluted tendencies of power coupled with human nature.

C. CITIZEN ENFORCEMENT TO COMPLEMENT GOVERNMENTAL EFFORTS

In the mid-1970s, as chronicled in Chapter 7, a new development emerged in federal environmental law: Private environmental organizations seized the opportunity to enforce major environmental statutes against polluters by invoking the statutes' citizen suit provisions. Beginning in 1970 with the CAA, Congress included citizen suit provisions in virtually all of the major environmental laws.[16] Although the use of citizen

---

16. Citizen suit provisions, for example, appear in CAA §304, CWA §505, ESA §11(g), RCRA §7002, ToSCA §18, and CERCLA §310, and others noted in Chapter 7. There is no citizen suit provision in FIFRA or in MMPA.

suit provisions in federal environmental statutes was new at the time, citizen enforcement was not a new concept. Stockholder derivative suits under the securities laws,
various private rights of action via statutes such as the civil rights acts, and statutory
torts provided precedents for private enforcement of federal environmental statutes.

In enacting the citizen suit provisions of the environmental laws, Congress viewed
the citizen suit both as an efficient policy instrument and as a participatory mechanism, based on Athenian democratic ideals, that would allow concerned citizens to
redress environmental pollution.[17] Citizen suits thus were designed to serve as adjuncts
to federal, state, and local enforcement efforts. In a time of limited resources, when
governmental enforcers cannot always seek compliance from polluters, citizen suits
represent an enforcement safety valve, essentially conferring "private attorney general
status" on the citizenry to sue on behalf of the community at large rather than merely to
redress individual rights involving economic loss. In addition to conferring statutory
authority to prosecute members of the regulated community for certain violations of
the environmental laws, Congress also suspected that there would be occasions when
the executive branch would not perform its responsibilities under the environmental
laws. Accordingly, citizen suit provisions were also enacted to address the concern that
citizen action might be necessary to force government agencies to perform their civic
duties. For these reasons, Congress provided the authority to undertake citizen suits
against public officials (like the Administrator of EPA) based upon the alleged failure to
perform nondiscretionary duties under the environmental laws.

Neither governmental enforcement nor citizen enforcement of the environmental
laws occurs in a vacuum. Citizen enforcement historically has acted as a check on
government, provoking enforcement action or providing an alternative when government fails to act. When business fails to comply with environmental requirements,
governmental and citizen enforcement together can create an impressive threat to business in the marketplace economy. The credibility of that enforcement threat, however,
continues to depend on the relationships, attitudes, and perceptions of the principal
actors, as the following discussion and case point out.

Barry Boyer and Errol Meidinger, Privatizing Regulatory Enforcement: A Preliminary Assessment of Citizen Suits Under Federal Environmental Laws
33 Buffalo Law Review 833, 957–961 (1985)

Despite the fact that private enforcement has eroded administrative control over the
enforcement process, the agencies still retain a dominant position in defining and implementing
enforcement policy. At least at the federal level, the growth of private enforcement is acting as a
competitive spur to government enforcers, prodding them to improve their management tools
for measuring, securing, and overseeing compliance. This increased emphasis on compliance
might well have evolved even without the consistent pressure of private enforcers.... Still, there
is no doubt that private enforcement helped to keep compliance issues high on the agendas of
top agency officials and gave additional urgency to their attempts to abate the most serious
violations.

---

17. Although this assessment is shared by a large majority of legal scholars, not all agree. See Greve, The Private
Enforcement of Environmental Law, 65 Tul. L. Rev. 339 (1990) (arguing that congressional support for private
environmental law enforcement is an outgrowth of interest group politics and contending that citizen suit
provisions are an off-budget entitlement program for the environmental movement).

While citizen suits are prodding the EPA and the state agencies to reassert their control over environmental enforcement, it seems unlikely that the government can wholly recapture its enforcement monopoly. In the short run, compliance rates are not likely to rise to such high levels that private enforcement becomes unnecessary, or unattractive to plaintiff organizations. The sweep of environmental regulations is too broad, the resources available to the agencies for enforcement too modest, and the difficulties of the regulated industries too severe to predict dramatic increases in the compliance rates.... [P]rivate enforcement will probably continue to be a significant force in environmental regulation.

This private enforcement power is tempered by the fact that the agencies will retain the initiative in responding to private enforcers. By deciding how regulations will define compliance, what kinds of monitoring and reporting will be required, how compliance information will be gathered and disseminated, and what levels of noncompliance will be considered significant, the EPA and the state agencies will effectively determine what role private enforcement can play in particular regulatory programs....

The groups bringing the private enforcement actions must be concerned not only about the agencies' response to them, but also about...other potential problems. Most immediate is the need to...make private enforcement a legal and economic success.... Beyond the resource questions, however, is the more fundamental issue of whether private enforcement will be grudgingly accepted or bitterly resisted by the regulated industries and their representatives. Plainly, there is considerable resentment within the regulatory community at having the "rules of the game" changed and at having established relationships and understandings undermined by private enforcement campaigns. There is also widespread skepticism about both the motivations of private enforcers and their legitimacy as surrogates for government.... The direction of development seems to depend less on the inherent characteristics of the citizen suit than on the nature and quality of the relationships that evolve among the major parties....

Assessments of the impacts of third-party interventions like private enforcement depend heavily upon the observer's belief about the substantive desirability of the regulatory program and upon the program's compliance history. If one believes that third-party participation will disrupt the status quo, it then becomes necessary to ask whether that status quo is good or bad, and how and why it developed the way it did. In the case of environmental compliance, the argument that giving increased leverage to single-issue constituency groups might tilt agency policy unduly toward protectionist values implies that the existing system reflects a desirable — or at least acceptable — social equilibrium.... Opportunities for third-party intervention might be better viewed as corrective devices to help keep the agency from straying too far outside the bounds of political consensus.

Comfort Lake Association, Inc. v. Dresel Contracting, Inc.
United States Court of Appeals for the Eighth Circuit, 1998
138 F.3d 351

LOKEN, J. The timing of the various activities underlying this dispute is significant. In the Fall of 1994, the Minnesota Pollution Control Agency issued Dresel and Fain a National Pollution Discharge Elimination System ("NPDES") permit for construction of a Wal-Mart store in Forest Lake, Minnesota. The permit required erosion and sediment control facilities because run-off of pollutants from the construction site threatened the water quality of nearby Comfort Lake and its tributaries. After investigating complaints, MPCA sent Dresel and Fain a warning letter on December 20, 1994, noting permit violations. Dresel and Fain responded in early January 1995, claiming to have properly addressed these problems.

On January 31, Comfort Lake, a non-profit association dedicated to protecting the lake and its tributaries, issued a notice of intent to sue Dresel and Fain over the same NPDES permit violations noted in MPCA's December 20 letter. Under the Clean Water Act, plaintiff must give such a notice of intent to sue to the Administrator of the Environmental Protection Agency, the affected state agency, and the alleged violator at least sixty days before commencing a citizen suit. On April 3, Comfort Lake filed this citizen suit.... Meanwhile, on February 13, MPCA again inspected the construction site, found continuing violations, and issued a Notice of Violation to Dresel and Fain. They responded that the violations were remedied, but after another inspection, MPCA issued a follow-up letter citing specific permit violations and demanding, within ten days, "a detailed schedule for correcting these deficiencies." MPCA issued a second Notice of Violation on May 10, advising Dresel and Fain that the MPCA Board would consider issuing an administrative cease and desist order at its May 23 meeting. On May 19, Dresel and Fain reported full compliance with the permit. MPCA promptly inspected, and a May 22 internal agency memorandum states that the violations had indeed been corrected.

Dresel and Fain completed store construction in November 1995 and applied for termination of the NPDES permit. MPCA terminated the permit on April 11, 1996. MPCA staff negotiated and then proposed to the agency Board a Stipulation Agreement requiring payment of $12,203 in civil penalties for all past violations of the permit, including $6,100 payable to the City of Forest Lake for "a diagnostic study of Comfort Lake." On May 21, 1996, MPCA issued its thirty-four page Findings of Fact, Conclusions of Law and Order approving the Stipulation Agreement over Comfort Lake's opposition. The Stipulation Agreement recites that it...

> covers all alleged NPDES/SDS Permit violations that occurred at the Wal-Mart construction site and that were known by MPCA as of the effective date of this agreement. The alleged violations are considered past violations that have been satisfactorily resolved or corrected. This Agreement contains no remedial or corrective action requirements because construction at the Wal-Mart site has been completed. The NPDES/SDS Permit has been terminated; thus, there is no likelihood that the NPDES/SDS Permit violations will recur at the Wal-Mart site.

Dresel and Fain then renewed their motion for summary judgment. The district court granted that motion, and in a separate order denied Comfort Lake an award of costs and attorney's fees. These appeals followed. Broadly stated, the issues are whether MPCA's enforcement actions preclude Comfort Lake's claims for injunctive relief[18] and civil penalties, and whether the district court abused its discretion in denying an award of costs and attorney's fees.

Is the claim for civil penalties precluded?... Comfort Lake's complaint asked the court to impose civil penalties of $25,000 per day for each Clean Water Act violation. Contending that Dresel and Fain's payment of $12,203 in civil penalties under the MPCA Stipulation Agreement is an insufficient sanction for their permit violations, Comfort Lake argues that its claim for civil penalties should be allowed to proceed even if its claim for injunctive relief is moot. When a claim for injunctive relief becomes moot, a related claim for money relief is not mooted "as long as the parties have a concrete interest, however small, in the outcome of the litigation."

A Clean Water Act citizen suit, including any claim for civil penalties, must be based upon on-going violations, "that is, a reasonable likelihood that a past polluter will continue to pollute in the future." *Gwaltney*, 484 U.S. at 57. Despite this limitation, a number of circuits have concluded that, even if a polluter's voluntary permanent cessation of the alleged violations moots a citizen suit claim for injunctive relief, it does not moot a related claim for civil

---

18. The court found these claims moot. [Eds.]

penalties.... We agree with these decisions. Congress has granted the citizen suit plaintiff standing to seek civil penalties as well as injunctive relief against on-going violations. Plaintiff retains "a concrete interest" in enforcing its penalties claim, even if any penalties recovered from the polluter go to the United States Treasury. When there is no agency enforcement action in the picture, a polluter should not be able to avoid otherwise appropriate civil penalties by dragging the citizen suit plaintiff into costly litigation and then coming into compliance before the lawsuit can be resolved.

However, this is not a case of voluntary compliance mooting the citizen suit's claim for injunctive relief. Here, the on-going violations alleged in Comfort Lake's complaint are moot because of subsequent MPCA enforcement actions that terminated the NPDES permit and assessed Dresel and Fain civil penalties for past violations. The Second Circuit addressed a similar situation in two cases. In *Eastman Kodak*, the state agency extracted $2,000,000 in criminal fines and civil penalties from the polluter. The Second Circuit held that the citizen suit "may not revisit the terms of a settlement reached by competent state authorities" absent proof of a realistic prospect that the alleged violations "will continue notwithstanding the settlement." 933 F.2d at 127 [companion case excerpted in Chapter 12]. But in Atlantic States Legal Found., Inc. v. Pan American Tanning Corp., 993 F.2d 1017, 1022 (2d Cir. 1993), the court held that a citizen suit claim for civil penalties was neither moot nor precluded when the polluter's settlement with a local agency involved a fine of only $6,600 and "did not cover all of the violations plaintiffs allege."

These Second Circuit cases confirm that the problem here is not mootness. Because Comfort Lake satisfied *Gwaltney*'s on-going violation test when its complaint was filed, there remains an actual controversy over its claim for civil penalties for these violations. Rather, the issue is what effect Dresel and Fain's settlement with MPCA has on that claim for civil penalties. Or, to state the question differently, may Comfort Lake collaterally attack MPCA's decision that civil penalties of $12,203 are appropriate for the very same violations alleged in the citizen suit?...

An underlying principle of the Clean Water Act is that "the citizen suit is meant to supplement rather than to supplant" government enforcement action. For example, if EPA or MPCA commences a court enforcement action before or within sixty days after a citizen suit plaintiff's notice of intent to sue, the citizen suit is completely barred. Even when an agency enforcement action is not commenced until after the citizen suit, final judgment in the agency's court action will be a res judicata or collateral estoppel bar to the earlier citizen suit. See United States EPA v. City of Green Forest, 921 F.2d 1394, 1402–1405 (8th Cir. 1990), cert. denied, 502 U.S. 956 (1991).

In addition to court enforcement actions, EPA and many state agencies have statutory authority to proceed by formal administrative action. When EPA "has commenced and is diligently prosecuting" such an administrative action, or when MPCA has commenced and is diligently prosecuting "an action under a State law comparable to this subsection," a subsequent citizen suit for civil penalties is barred. 33 U.S.C. §1319(g)(6). In its initial ruling, the district court held that MPCA's December 1994 non-compliance letter and its February 1995 Notice of Violation did not "commence" an administrative enforcement action, and therefore Comfort Lake's citizen suit was not wholly barred by §1319(g)(6). The Stipulation Agreement between MPCA and Dresel and Fain is not a res judicata or collateral estoppel bar, like the judicially approved consent decree in *Green Forest*. But as a final agency enforcement action, that Agreement is entitled to considerable deference if we are to achieve the Clean Water Act's stated goal of preserving "the primary responsibilities and rights of States to prevent, reduce, and eliminate pollution." 33 U.S.C. §1251(b). Moreover, respondents like Dresel and Fain will be disinclined to resolve disputes by such relatively informal agreements if additional civil penalties may then be imposed in pending citizen suits, thereby depriving MPCA of this resource-conserving enforcement tool. For these reasons, we conclude that an administrative enforcement agreement between EPA or MPCA and the polluter will preclude a pending citizen suit claim for civil penalties if the agreement is the result of a diligently prosecuted enforcement process, however informal.

In this case, MPCA began informal action to enforce the NPDES permit in December 1994, before Comfort Lake issued its notice of intent to sue for the same violations. The agency diligently pursued Dresel and Fain to end permit violations until May 1995, when it concluded compliance had been achieved. After construction was complete, MPCA terminated the permit and negotiated stipulated penalties for past violations. As the district court noted, MPCA extracted a civil penalty that "exceeds penalties imposed in similar cases [and] was derived by looking at factors substantially similar to those which must be considered by a court imposing penalties under" the Clean Water Act. Because MPCA diligently prosecuted its enforcement demands, the civil penalties it elected to extract in settling those demands may not be reconsidered in this citizen suit. While Comfort Lake might have preferred more severe civil penalties, MPCA has the primary responsibility for enforcing the Clean Water Act.

Should attorney's fees have been awarded?... Although Comfort Lake's claims for affirmative relief are foreclosed by the subsequent MPCA enforcement actions, Comfort Lake may still be entitled to an award of costs and a reasonable attorney's fee as a prevailing party under 33 U.S.C. §1365(d) if its citizen suit was the catalyst for agency enforcement action that resulted in the cessation of Clean Water Act violations. However, the district court determined that Comfort Lake was not a catalyst, both because MPCA began enforcing the permit before Comfort Lake's notice of intent to sue, and because Comfort Lake "actually impeded" agency enforcement by suing MPCA in state court and then actively opposing the proposed Stipulation Agreement. This finding of fact is not clearly erroneous. The finding is well supported by the affidavit of MPCA's supervisor in charge of enforcing the NPDES permit, who averred that Comfort Lake impeded and delayed the enforcement process and that "MPCA's enforcement actions would have been the same even in the absence of a citizen's suit by the Comfort Lake Association, except that the enforcement actions would have been completed sooner." Because Comfort Lake was not a prevailing party, the district court properly denied its request for costs and attorney's fees. The judgment of the district court is affirmed.

COMMENTARY & QUESTIONS

1. **Citizen suits and the command-and-control model.** Citizen suits typically do not interfere with the formal processes by which government sets enforcement priorities and balances costs and benefits. Instead, citizen suits implement those decisions by enforcing them. Generally, as in *Comfort Lake*, the government remains the party charged with the policy assessment. The citizen suit, in turn, concerns whether the alleged violator has met the governmental standards, or whether the governmental administrator has carried out the mandatory duties that Congress has prescribed. Nonetheless, citizen suits can affect the command-and-control model. By allowing private enforcement of the goals defined, citizen suits can affect enforcement priorities. Citizen suits can also have the beneficial effect of exposing those priorities to public scrutiny and comment. For example, in the early 1980s, when EPA (under the Anne Gorsuch regime) virtually stopped enforcing the environmental laws, citizen groups

filed hundreds of suits that not only enforced the environmental laws (primarily the CWA at the time) but also exposed EPA's abdication of its enforcement responsibilities.

2. **EPA's inattention to enforcement.** One of the primary rationales for citizen enforcement of the environmental laws is that governmental enforcers do not always have the resources, interest, or will to enforce. Now, over 30 years after the first citizen suit provisions were passed, is EPA paying more attention to enforcement?

A 1996 critique by the U.S. General Accounting Office (GAO) concludes that, at least where water pollution is concerned, EPA is still not paying attention. Pursuant to a congressional request, GAO reviewed EPA's progress in ensuring that facilities comply with federal pollutant discharge requirements, focusing on: (1) the frequency of facilities' violations, (2) the limitations of EPA systems and the effects of these limitations, and (3) EPA plans to correct these violations. GAO found that: (1) EPA compliance data for Fiscal Year 1994 show that 1 in 6 of the nation's 7053 major regulated facilities have significantly violated the discharge limits in their permits; (2) EPA considers facilities to be in significant noncompliance of their discharge levels when discharged pollutants exceed permit limits by 20% or more in a 2- to 6-month period; (3) EPA is unable to identify all of the facilities that violate their discharge limits because the criteria it uses to screen facilities have not remained consistent with the types of discharge limits used in permits; (4) EPA has expanded its criteria for identifying cases of significant noncompliance and assigning priorities of enforcement action in order to identify major facilities that have violated discharge levels in the past; and (5) EPA assessed penalties of about $25 million in 323 cases of CWA violations in 1994, and its studies indicate that very few penalties are assessed for significant violations of daily maximum discharge limits. See Water Pollution: Many Violations Have Not Received Appropriate Enforcement Attention (Letter Report, Mar. 20, 1996, GAO/RCED-96-23).[19]

3. **How much is accomplished by citizen suits?** Quantitatively, it is tempting to give a bean counter's answer based on the number of filings, but the more probing answer lies in estimating the impact of citizen suits and their availability on governmental enforcement performance and voluntary compliance by regulated entities. All such estimates agree that citizen suits have had an immense positive impact on both governmental and regulated entity performance. See, e.g., Maples, Reforming Judicial Interpretation of the Diligent Prosecution Bar: Ensuring an Effective Citizen Role in Achieving the Goals of the Clean Water Act, 16 Va. Envtl. L.J. 195, 203–204 (1996) ("Citizen suits have become so effective that now industry fears them more than negotiation and settlement with the enforcing agency"); Miller, Private Enforcement of Federal Pollution Control Laws Part I, 13 Envtl. L. Rep. 10309 (1983) (concluding that the most celebrated uses of citizen suits have been against EPA for its failures to implement environmental statutes in a timely and complete manner, and that the significance of citizen suits can hardly be doubted); Mann, Polluter-Financed Environmentally Beneficial Expenditures: Effective

---

19. See also H.R. Rep. 1086, 102d Cong., 2d Sess. (Dec. 31, 1992), documenting the snail's pace of regulatory effort under FIFRA, which has no citizen suit provision. Despite a program budget of over $100 million, EPA completed the final re-registrations for only a small fraction of the almost 20,000 registered pesticide end-use products.

Use or Improper Abuse of Citizen Suits Under the Clean Water Act?, 20 Envtl. L. 176, 182–185 (1990) (concluding that citizen suits seeking relief against EPA for failing to perform mandatory duties have had a major impact on shaping implementation of the environmental statutes).

4. Forms of relief available in citizen suits. Under the citizen suit provisions of the environmental laws, private citizens can enforce statutory, regulatory, or permit requirements through suits seeking compliance orders and penalties. In addition to this enforcement type of citizen suit, a mandamus type of action is also available for citizens seeking to require a regulator to comply with his duties under the environmental laws. For example, under the CWA, the EPA Administrator may be sued by citizens "where there is alleged a failure of the Administrator to perform any act or duty...which is not discretionary." CWA §505(a)(1)(2), 33 U.S.C. §1365(a)(1)(2). Significantly, mandamus is not available to require EPA to take enforcement action when a citizen provides EPA with notice of an alleged violation. This point had been the subject of a split in the early cases, particularly because CWA §309(a)(3) provides in pertinent part:

> Whenever on the basis of any information available to him, the Administrator finds that any person is in violation of §1311 [relating to unpermitted discharges]...he *shall* issue an order requiring such person to comply with such section..., or he shall bring a civil action in accordance with subsection (b) of this section. [Emphasis added.]

In what has become a leading case on the issue, Dubois v. Thomas (Administrator of EPA), 820 F.2d 943 (8th Cir. 1987), the court invoked *Chevron* and deferred to EPA's interpretation that claimed discretion not to enforce in spite of the presence of the usually obligatory word "shall." To buttress its position, the court relied on Heckler v. Chaney, 470 U.S. 821, 831 (1985), which said:

> An agency decision not to enforce often involves a complicated balancing of a number of factors which are peculiarly within its expertise. Thus, the agency must not only assess whether a violation has occurred, but whether agency resources are best spent on this violation or another, whether the agency is likely to succeed if it acts, whether the particular enforcement action requested best fits the agency's overall policies, and indeed, whether the agency has enough resources to under-take the action at all. An agency generally cannot act against each technical violation of the statute it is charged with enforcing.

5. Prerequisites to citizen enforcement. Before a citizen suit can proceed, several key statutory and jurisprudential hurdles must be overcome. This should be a familiar topic, having appeared earlier in reviewing the concept of standing (Chapter 7). Beyond standing, additional barriers to citizen suits seek to integrate citizen enforcement with the regulatory regime as administered by governmental officials. First, in order to initiate suit, the citizen must give notice to EPA, the state where the violation occurred, and the alleged violator. Generally, 60 days' notice is required, although the amount of notice can vary for certain kinds of violations. The purpose of notice is to allow the federal government the opportunity to initiate its own suit, precluding the citizen's suit, or to allow the violator to comply and correct its violation. Second, suit must be brought within the applicable statute of limitations, generally viewed, in most citizen suit actions, to be five years. See, e.g. Atlantic States Legal Found. v. Tyson Foods,

Inc., 897 F.2d 1128 (11th Cir. 1990); Sierra Club v. Chevron U.S.A., Inc., 834 F.2d 1517 (9th Cir. 1987). Third, the citizen suit provisions generally specify that if federal or state authorities are diligently prosecuting an action to require compliance, filing of a citizen suit is barred, although citizens may still intervene in federal enforcement actions as of right. This hurdle is designed to prevent citizen suits from infringing on the exercise of enforcement discretion by federal and state authorities. Although a citizen suit is precluded if there is a pending judicial action by a regulatory authority that is being diligently prosecuted, does an administrative action by a regulatory authority also have a preclusive effect on a citizen suit? One court summarized the case law as follows:

> A number of courts have interpreted the statutory language concerning citizen suits when the state has already begun an administrative action. In Baughman v. Bradford Coal Co., 592 F.2d 215 (3d Cir. 1979), the court first held that in certain circumstances an administrative hearing can be the equivalent of a court action. It then held that the court should measure the power of the administrative agency against that of the court to determine whether the administrative action was similar enough to a court action to fall within the statutory language. In Friends of the Earth v. Consolidated Rail Corp., 768 F.2d 57 (2d Cir. 1985), the Second Circuit rejected this rationale, stating it would be inappropriate to expand the statutory language to include administrative enforcement actions. The Ninth Circuit adopted the *Friends of the Earth* rationale, and held that the plain language of the statute provided that only an ongoing action in a court, rather than an administrative agency, would preclude a citizen suit. Sierra Club v. Chevron U.S.A., Inc., 834 F.2d 1517, 1525 (9th Cir. 1987). At least one District Court outside these circuits has followed the *Friends of the Earth* interpretation in Maryland Waste Coalition v. SCM Corp., 616 F. Supp. 1474, 1478-1481 (D. Md. 1985). This Court also adopts the *Friends of the Earth* rationale. Lykins v. Westinghouse Electric Corp., 715 F. Supp. 1357, 1358–1359 (1989). [But see CWA §309(g) (1987), discussed in the *Comfort Lake* case, which codified the *Baughman* rule.]

6. Citizen suit notice. One of the most frequently litigated issues under the citizen suit provisions of the environmental laws is whether to dismiss cases filed by plaintiffs who "jump the gun" and either file suit before passage of the requisite notice period or file a defective notice. In Hallstrom v. Tillamook County, 493 U.S. 20 (1989), the Supreme Court considered whether a case should be dismissed for the complete failure to give notice. Although affirming dismissal, the Court left open whether notice is a jurisdictional prerequisite to suit and how to treat issues of incomplete or defective notice. Should defects in the content and form of notice (as opposed to the timing) result in dismissal? In Dague v. City of Burlington, 935 F.2d 1343 (2d Cir. 1991), the Second Circuit addressed that question in reviewing the RCRA citizen suit requirements, finding that prior notice in suits involving hazardous wastes is of minimal value and that dismissal should not follow for failure to follow technical aspects of notice provisions. In her article, Notice Letters and Notice Pleading, 78 Or. L. Rev. 105 (1999), Robin Craig describes a conflict between the Supreme Court's interpretation of environmental citizen suit notice requirements and the notice pleading standard in Rule 8 of the Federal Rules of Civil Procedure. Whereas under Rule 8 defendants are deemed to have notice of those allegations that a reasonable person would understand the complaint to contain, the Supreme Court's interpretation of citizen suit notice, since Hallstrom v. Tillamook County, has tended to narrow the scope of environmental plaintiffs' claims through requirements such as notice letters, in which plaintiffs must detail every allegation 60 or 90 days prior to filing a complaint. Craig argues that such citizen suit notice standards impermissibly undermine the Federal Rules.

7. **Cessation of violation in a post-*Gwaltney* world.** Gwaltney of Smithfield, Ltd. v. Chesapeake Bay Found., 484 U.S. 49 (1987), the case in which the Supreme Court held that citizen suits under the CWA would not lie for wholly past violations, has become standard fare in the interpretation of citizen suit provisions. As in *Comfort Lake*, courts now carefully inspect the language of the specific provision being considered to see if it refers to past or to current violations, and rule accordingly. After *Gwaltney*, where the relevant citizen suit provision speaks of violation in the present tense, citizens must be prepared to prove at least the likelihood of ongoing violations in order to prevail. See, e.g., Coburn v. Sun Chem. Co., 19 Envtl. L. Rep. 20256 (E.D. Pa. Nov. 9, 1988) (construing "to be in violation" language of RCRA §7002(a)(1)(A) to prevent suit against past owners of parcel allegedly presenting an imminent endangerment while permitting suit against present owner).

The cases in this area tend to be somewhat technical and formalistic in deciding what suffices to constitute allegation of an ongoing violation. First, judgments concerning whether a violation is ongoing are to be made as of the time the complaint is filed. See Atlantic States Legal Found., Inc. v. Tyson Foods, Inc., 897 F.2d 1128 (11th Cir. 1990). Second, a violation will not be considered to be ongoing if remedial measures establish that there is no reasonable prospect for recurrence. See Chesapeake Bay Found. v. Gwaltney of Smithfield, Ltd., 844 F.2d 170 (4th Cir. 1988). Third, plaintiffs, as a pleading matter, need only make a good faith allegation of an ongoing or repeat violation in order to be able to file suit, see Sierra Club v. Union Oil of Cal., 853 F.2d 667 (9th Cir. 1988), but plaintiffs must be able to prove an ongoing or repeat violation in order to prevail at trial. See Carr v. Alta Verde Indus., 924 F.2d 558 (5th Cir. 1991). Finally, ongoing violations can be established by showing that violations continued on or after the filing of a complaint or by producing evidence from which a reasonable trier of fact could find a continuing likelihood that intermittent or sporadic violations would occur. See Connecticut Coastal Fishermen's Ass'n v. Remington Arms Co., 989 F.2d 1305 (2d Cir. 1993).

Of what significance are these technical post-*Gwaltney* decisions? In part, they reflect an attempt by the federal courts to avoid cluttering their dockets with citizen suits. Consider, for example, the following comment on the proliferation of citizen suits under CWA §505:

> The primary reason for the predominance of citizen suits under §505 is the relative ease of uncovering and proving a violation under CWA §402's NPDES program.... [D]ischargers under the program must routinely file discharge monitoring reports [DMRs] with both state regulatory agencies and the EPA. The discharger must certify the accuracy of each DMR and the CWA imposes substantial penalties for false reports. Each DMR must list the actual quantity of waste discharged, as well as the permitted amount that may be discharged. As a consequence, in many instances spotting permit violations is as easy as comparing two numbers on a printout.... The majority of courts have held that DMRs are admissible as evidence of the violations, and have granted summary judgment to citizen plaintiffs based

> solely on DMRs.... Mann, Polluter-Financed Environmentally Beneficial
> Expenditures: Effective Use or Improper Abuse of Citizen Suits Under the Clean
> Water Act?, 20 Envtl. L. 176, 183–184 (1990).

In these circumstances, judicial reliance on jurisprudential mechanisms to limit the
number and scope of citizen suits can be seen as a form of judicial administration, seeking to minimize litigation based on spotting permit violations simply by "comparing
two numbers on a printout." Id.

8. **The *Steel Company* case.** Another post-*Gwaltney* question was resolved by the
Supreme Court itself, as noted in Chapter 7, addressing whether a violator may escape
liability by completing remedial action after receiving notice of a citizens group's intent
to file a suit but before the citizen suit is filed. In Steel Company v. Citizens for a Better
Environment (CBE), 523 U.S. 83 (1998), the Steel Company was charged by a citizens
group with violating the Emergency Planning and Community Right-to-Know Act
(EPCRA), 42 U.S.C. §§11001 et seq., by failing to file timely toxic and hazardous chemical storage and emission reports for past years. By the time the complaint was filed, after
the requisite statutory notice period, the Steel Company had brought its filings up to
date. The Supreme Court held that because none of the relief sought would remedy the
citizen group's alleged injury in fact, there was no standing to maintain the suit, and the
complaint should be dismissed. In particular, the Supreme Court found that none of
the specific items of relief sought — a declaratory judgment that the Steel Company
violated EPCRA; injunctive relief authorizing CBE to make periodic inspections of the
Steel Company's facility and records and requiring the Steel Company to give CBE
copies of its compliance reports; and orders requiring the Steel Company to pay EPCRA
civil penalties to the Treasury and to reimburse CBE's litigation expenses — and no
conceivable relief under the complaint's final general request would serve to reimburse
CBE for losses caused by the Steel Company's late reporting, or to eliminate any effects
of that late reporting upon CBE.

Faced with the prospect of enforcement through citizen efforts, can a company, after
the decision in *Steel Company*, target its compliance to eliminate identified sources
prior to the filing of a citizen suit? If so, citizen enforcement efforts are thereby chilled;
citizens, moreover, then get no reimbursement fees for performing this enforcement
compliance function since the case cannot survive in court. There is a special sense in
which this is a particular problem with EPCRA, where compliance can take the form of
filing reports, rather than installing complex pollution control equipment that may or
may not adequately reduce discharges or emissions. In the EPCRA context, as the
Seventh Circuit noted below in *Steel Company*, to say that industries cannot be sued
when they withhold information from the public about use and release of toxic chemicals until citizens file enforcement notices, if they just provide the overdue information
prior to the lawsuit, raises important questions concerning the significance of citizen
enforcement provisions. "If citizen suits could be fully prevented by 'completing and
submitting' forms, however late, citizens would have no real incentive to incur the costs
of learning about EPCRA, investigating suspected violators, and analyzing information.
[If] citizen suits could only proceed when a violator received notice of intent to sue and
still fails to spend the minimal effort required to fill out the forms and turn them

in,...private citizens would have to absorb much of the cost of [enforcement], with little or no hope of recovering those costs through awards of litigation expenses...." 90 F.3d 1237, 1244–1245 (7th Cir. 1996).

After the *Steel Company* case, in again addressing redressibility, the Supreme Court held that civil penalties for ongoing violations (that have not abated by the time of suit) provide sufficient deterrence to support redressibility. Friends of the Earth, Inc. v. Laidlaw Envtl. Servs., Inc., 528 U.S. 167 (2000).

9. **Defining agency enforcement diligence.** Citizens affected by a polluter's actions often suffer real and immediate consequences as a result of the pollution. Governmental regulators have a different perspective that is shaped by their need to administer the program to achieve its regulatory ends within the constraints of a limited agency budget and under the realities of having to work with the regulated entities on an ongoing basis. Given these differences, cases such as *Comfort Lake* arise in which the citizens assert that the governmental agency is not prosecuting diligently. Some of these citizen suits allege, or at least imply, that the governmental filing is collusive and is intended to shield the polluter from enforcement rather than to seek enforcement. Courts have already had to decide cases, for example, where defendants sought to ensure diligent prosecution for the sole purpose of avoiding a citizen suit. In Friends of the Earth, Inc. v. Laidlaw, 890 F. Supp. 470 (D.S.C. 1995), the defendant requested that its settlement with the state environmental agency and EPA be filed as a lawsuit, so as to avoid the looming citizen suit. The agencies accepted the request on the condition that the defendant cover the expenses. The defendant thereafter funded the filing of a complaint against itself on behalf of the state environmental agency. When the citizen suit was filed two days later, the defendant filed a motion to dismiss based on the diligent prosecution bar. Although the motion was denied, the case warns of the potential misuse of the diligent prosecution bar.

10. **Environmentally Beneficial Expenditures (EBEs).** Note that, in *Comfort Lake*, the negotiated civil penalty included $6100 payable to the City of Forest Lake for a diagnostic study of Comfort Lake. This type of polluter-financed expenditure, frequently appearing in consent decrees in both governmental and citizen enforcement actions, is known as an Environmentally Beneficial Expenditure (EBE). Like SEPs, EBEs are a type of penalty, typically negotiated among the parties, designed to offset the benefits gained through polluting activity by requiring the polluter to expend funds in support of an environmentally beneficial study or activity.

11. **Attorneys' fees and costs under citizen suit provisions.** When citizens embark as "private attorneys general" attempting to enforce existing law in agencies and courts, they often face substantial administrative and financial burdens, and opponents who are either public officials or well-financed corporate entities writing off expenses against revenues. Expert witnesses and attorneys cost money. For plaintiff groups like the citizens in *Overton Park*, this often means having to raise funds through bake sales, raffles, logo t-shirt sales, or hat passing. The larger national environmental groups have substantially greater resources but are confronted with a proportionally broader range of advocacy commitments, and likewise depend upon volunteer contributions.

Environmentalists have turned to both the courts and Congress in attempts to win financial recognition of the role played by private attorneys general. In court, environmentalists face the American rule of fee-shifting; unlike their counterparts under the English rule, prevailing plaintiffs in American courts generally are unable to recover the costs of litigation from defendants. (In part, this explains why punitive damages are often sought in common law litigation.)

The opportunity to recover attorneys' fees and costs is often vital to citizen suit enforcement and, as in *Comfort Lake*, is often a vigorously contested issue. The citizen suit provisions of the CAA allow an award of attorneys' fees and costs where appropriate. See CAA §304(d), 42 U.S.C. §7604(d). Citizen suit provisions of the CWA, RCRA, and CERCLA provide for an award of attorneys' fees and costs to prevailing parties or substantially prevailing parties. See CWA §505(d), 33 U.S.C. §1365(d); RCRA §7002(e), 42 U.S.C. §6972(e); CERCLA §310(f), 42 U.S.C. §9659(f).[20] Environmental fee-shifting provisions are viewed typically as a necessary incentive to environmental enforcement because few private plaintiffs can afford to finance expensive environmental litigation that usually results in nonmonetary benefits to the public at large (rather than damage awards to the individual plaintiffs). Congress accordingly included fee-shifting incentives in various environmental statutes as an incentive to spur enforcement of meritorious claims. Once a plaintiff demonstrates to the court that an award is appropriate, the court may award reasonable attorneys' fees and costs. The appropriate amount of fees is typically calculated as the product of reasonable hours times a reasonable rate, also known as the "lodestar" amount.

Prevailing plaintiffs, however, have often found courts responsive to defendants' attempts to restrict such awards, finding that public interest plaintiffs — since they are supposed to be motivated by civic impulse rather than commercial incentive — should be given less than commercial fee rates. In City of Burlington v. Dague, 505 U.S. 557 (1992), the Supreme Court faced another situation: whether a citizen enforcement fee should be raised above normal hourly rates to take account of the fact that attorneys take a gamble on a zero recovery when they represent citizen plaintiffs enforcing federal law. The Court held that the lodestar amount cannot be adjusted upward to account for the contingency nature of many environmental citizen suits. Citizen groups had fought for upward adjustments to allow the lodestar to be increased by a factor reflecting the contingent risks of bringing suit. Will the Supreme Court's opinion cripple citizen suit enforcement? Absent the right to seek increased fees for contingent risk, will there be an insufficient incentive to bring citizen suits? Some environmental organizations fund significant parts of their environmental public interest watchdog operations on citizen suits, using the lodestar to provide more than public interest salaries and their victories on the merits to pay experts who then work on additional issues. See Axline, Decreasing

---

20. In a variety of federal statutes authorizing citizen suits, as in CWA §505, Congress consistently inserted a fee recovery provision in terms similar to the following:

> §505(d) Litigation costs. The court, in issuing any final order in any action brought pursuant to this section, may award costs of litigation (including reasonable attorney and expert witness fees) to any prevailing or substantially prevailing party, whenever the court determines such award is appropriate. 33 U.S.C. §1365(d).

Incentives to Enforce Environmental Laws: City of Burlington v. Dague, 43 J. Urb. & Contemp. L. 257 (1993).

Environmentalists can also win fees and costs under broad provisions of the Equal Access to Justice Act (EAJA), 28 U.S.C. §2412(d). Prevailing parties, in situations where the reviewing court considers the government agencies' position not "substantially justified," can claim expert witness and attorneys' fees. EAJA litigation extends the realm of fee-shifting even, as in NEPA, where enforced statutes do not specifically grant citizens standing. Where no statute provides for grants of fees, there are several nonstatutory avenues to funding public interest litigation. Under equity principles, U.S. courts have evolved several exceptions to the American rule in addition to private attorney general theories, including where defendants act in bad faith and where the defendants' actions have built up a "common fund" against which plaintiffs' costs can reasonably be assessed. Several state and federal courts initially expanded the private attorney general approach by adding a right to recover attorneys' and expert witness fees when citizen suits prevailed. The Supreme Court, however, in a case arising from environmental efforts to halt or improve the safety of the Trans-Alaska Oil Pipeline, held that federal courts would no longer be permitted to grant expert witness or counsel fees to environmental plaintiffs acting as private attorneys general unless they could prove bad faith, a common fund, or specific statutory authorization for fee awards. Alyeska Pipeline Serv. Co. v. Wilderness Soc'y, 421 U.S. 240 (1975). Although federal courts were thus halted in recognizing fee-shifting in most private attorney general suits, state courts retain the authority to apply their own equity principles, awarding fees to citizens whose efforts enforce the law and defend a public good. See Troutwine, A Primer on Attorneys' Fees Award: Fee Computation under Federal and State Attorneys' Fees Statutes, in PLI, Court Awards of Attorneys' Fees 99–108 (1987); Robertson & Fowler, Recovering Attorneys' Fees from the Government Under the Equal Access to Justice Act, 56 Tul. L. Rev. 903 (1982).

More recently, the Supreme Court addressed yet another issue concerning the award of attorneys' fees involving plaintiffs seeking fees who, even without a formal victory in court, contended that their lawsuit brought about a "voluntary" change in a defendant's conduct, thereby rendering the plaintiffs "prevailing parties." Rejecting the claim that plaintiffs were entitled to fees because their lawsuit was the "catalyst" forcing the defendant to comply, the Supreme Court ruled, in a 5–4 decision, that under statutes awarding fees to "prevailing parties," the plaintiff must be awarded some relief by the court to qualify for fees. Buckhannon Bd. & Care Home Inc. v. West Va. Dep't of Health & Human Servs., 532 U.S. 598 (2001). But see Sierra Club v. EPA, 322 F.3d 718 (D.C. Cir. 2003) (holding that the CAA authorized an award of attorneys' fees to so-called catalyst parties under a statute providing that fees may be awarded by a court "whenever it determines that such award is appropriate").

12. **Attorneys' fees for "prevailing" defendants.** An interesting application of the legal principles concerning attorneys' fees awards occurred on remand in the *Steel Company* case, when the Steel Company filed a petition seeking its attorneys' fees and costs, based

on the contention that it was the prevailing party and was therefore entitled to an award under §326(f) of EPCRA. See 42 U.S.C. §11046(f).

The district court dismissed the petition for lack of jurisdiction. Thereafter the Steel Company appealed to the Seventh Circuit, which in an opinion rendered on October 17, 2000, affirmed the denial of relief to the Steel Company. See 230 F.3d 923 (7th Cir. 2000). The Seventh Circuit held that the Supreme Court's decisions in Pennsylvania v. Delaware Valley Citizens' Council (*Delaware Valley I*), 478 U.S. 546 (1986), and Pennsylvania v. Delaware Valley Citizens' Council (*Delaware Valley II*), 483 U.S. 711 (1987), and in Christiansburg Garment Co. v. EEOC, 434 U.S. 412 (1978), were controlling and precluded awarding attorneys' fees to the Steel Company.

Christiansburg holds that, under 42 U.S.C. §1988 of the Civil Rights Act, prevailing plaintiffs can recover their attorneys' fees from defendants, but prevailing defendants can recover their fees only if the plaintiff's claim was "frivolous" or brought in "bad faith." 434 U.S. at 421. In *Delaware Valley I*, the Supreme Court held that "given the common purpose of both §304(d) [the CAA's fee-shifting provision, 42 U.S.C. §7604(d)] and §1988 [the Civil Rights Act] to promote citizen enforcement of important federal policies, we find no reason not to interpret both provisions governing attorney's fees in the same manner." 478 U.S. at 560. The Supreme Court's follow-up decision in *Delaware Valley II* states that, in applying the fee-shifting provisions of the CAA, "courts should follow the principles and case law governing the award of such fees under 42 U.S.C. §1988." 483 U.S. at 713 n. 1.

Applying these standards, the Seventh Circuit found that the *Delaware Valley I & II* and *Christiansburg* standards are controlling because there is no identifiable feature in the language or structure of §11046(f) (the EPCRA fee-shifting provision) that distinguishes it from the statute (CAA) in *Delaware Valley*. In so holding, the Seventh Circuit joined the Ninth Circuit in concluding that the attorneys' fee-shifting standard should be applied "in the same manner" for both environmental and civil rights laws. See Morris-Smith v. Moulton Niguel Water Dist., 234 F.3d 1277 (9th Cir. 2000); Marbled Murrelet v. Babbitt, 182 F.3d 1091, 1094–1095 (9th Cir. 1999), cert. denied, 528 U.S. 1115 (2000); Washington Wilderness Coalition v. Hecla Mining Co., 156 F.3d 1241 (9th Cir. 1998), cert. denied, 526 U.S. 1004 (1999). The Seventh Circuit then denied the Steel Company's motion for attorneys' fees because CBE's claim was not frivolous:

> A panel of this court held that CBE was entitled to proceed. The Solicitor General supported that decision before the Supreme Court. A suit strong enough to survive an appeal cannot be deemed frivolous even if all nine Justices thought it unavailing.... No one suggests that CBE's claim was frivolous on the merits, however, for the Steel Company concededly filed reports after the statutory deadline. 230 F.3d at 931.

Subsequent to the Seventh Circuit's decision, the Steel Company petitioned the Supreme Court to grant certiorari. The Supreme Court declined to do so.

D. ALTERNATIVE DISPUTE RESOLUTION PROCESSES

Section 1. WHY ALTERNATIVE DISPUTE RESOLUTION?

Environmental law was born and raised in the arena of adversarial combat — the traditional litigation mode in court and agency proceedings. Few argue, however, that the adversarial litigation process is ideal. Environmental enforcement through litigation often proves to be a crude mechanism for achieving resolutions, results in antagonistic relationships, and drains scarce resources in terms of time, money, and energy. Because of its obstacles and inefficiencies, ultimately many disputes never get resolved within the formal mechanisms of the legal system. Because of its practical burdens, the traditional model is often unavailable to those who lack financial and political resources.

Even within traditional adversarial litigation, of course, most disputes are settled out of court through a process of negotiation prior to final judgment. But other options for conflict resolution are increasingly available. A growing movement both within and outside the legal profession is calling for a shift to ADR — alternative dispute resolution mechanisms such as mediation, arbitration, mini-trials, and other procedures. Whether by statutory mandate or pragmatic decision of the parties, many issues that previously would have been handled by litigation or agency enforcement now are resolved through ADR. The trend reemphasizes that the practice of law need not be what many laypersons consider it — an unproductive, insulated mechanism for implementing the more negative elements of human nature — but rather can be a profession that tries to make social relationships and civic mechanisms work.

ADR was first used in the environmental setting (where it is often referred to as "EDR") in the late 1970s.[21] Unlike most litigation models, which are only retrospective or reactive to existing disputes, the ADR approach is forward-looking — designed to anticipate future policy or practical conflicts.[22]

The viability of ADR as an alternative to litigation has caused fierce debate in academic and practice communities. Richard Mays, arguing for expanded environmental use of ADR, notes that in standard EPA enforcement cases, "the average time between discovery of a violation and settlement might easily be three to five years or more. Even after this delay, [all but 5%] of EPA's judicial cases are settled rather than tried."[23] Enormous amounts of time and resources spent on such cases could be reduced dramatically if resolutions were reached through negotiation rather than through the process or threat of litigation.

Not all cases can or should be settled through ADR. Even proponents like Mays agree that adversarial litigation is necessary and appropriate in some cases — for example, if important precedential legal issues need resolution, if injunctions or other court-supervised remedies are necessary and parties lack the time or interest required

---

21. For an overview of major environmental disputes in which ADR methods were used, see A. Talbot, Settling Things (1983), and L. Susskind, L. Bacow & M. Wheeler, Resolving Environmental Regulatory Disputes (1983).

22. This mode has been called "front-loading" or anticipatory consensus-building.

23. May, Alternative Dispute Resolution and Environmental Enforcement: A Noble Experiment or a Lost Cause?, 18 Envtl. L. Rep. 10087, 10088 (1988).

for negotiating settlements, or if, in light of a party's egregious conduct, the public interest requires an open public trial and punishment. These exceptional cases, they argue, however, make up only a small percentage of the total number of environmental suits filed each year.

Some opponents of alternative remedies claim that ADR's purported savings in time and expense are bought at the cost of accuracy, justice, and democratic process. Edward Brunet, a staunch opponent of ADR, claims that "only formal litigation and adjudication provide a mechanism for accurate determination of facts."[24] Brunet maintains that the informality of ADR procedures makes them "weak since they rely on voluntary party exchange of data and do not have an authority figure equivalent to a judge to prevent discovery abuse." In environmental disputes, Brunet claims, the informality of ADR is particularly dangerous. Given the complexity of environmental disputes, "the 'facts' produced in an environmental mediation are likely to be incomplete and inaccurate."

On the other hand, ADR sometimes promotes effective joint fact-finding techniques, producing facts faster and with greater accuracy than traditional discovery. If parties can develop a mutually acceptable fact-finding agenda and methodology, then the traditional "battle of the experts" can be averted and questions shifted from a position-based to a broader interest-based resolution process on the merits.[25]

Section 2. ENVIRONMENTAL ADR

An array of alternative methods is available in the environmental setting to parties seeking to resolve their differences through ADR.

National Institute for Dispute Resolution, Paths to Justice: Major Public Policy Issues of Dispute Resolution
in Administrative Conference of the United States, Sourcebook: Federal Agency Use of Alternative Means of Dispute Resolution 5–47 (1983, 1987)

Some conflict contributes to and, indeed, is essential to a healthy, functioning society. Social change occurs through dispute and controversy. Some observers attribute the long-term stability of the country to its ability to hear and reconcile the disagreements of its diverse population. Thus one should focus not only on avoiding disputes, but also on finding suitable ways of hearing and resolving those that inevitably arise....

Dispute resolution techniques can be arrayed along on a continuum ranging from the most rulebound and coercive to the most informal. Specific techniques differ in many significant ways, including:

- whether participation is voluntary;
- whether parties represent themselves or are represented by counsel;
- whether decisions are made by the disputants or by a third party;

---

24. Brunet, The Costs of Environmental Alternative Dispute Resolution, 18 Envtl. L. Rep. 10515, 10516 (1988). See also Fiss, Against Settlement, 93 Yale L.J. 1073 (1984), and Out of Eden, 94 Yale L.J. 1669 (1985), arguing that, among other major shortcomings, ADR undermines the important law-building, law-applying functions of judicial litigation.

25. See L. Susskind & J. Cruikshank, Breaking the Impasse: Consensual Approaches to Resolving Public Disputes (1987); see also R. Fisher & W. Ury, Getting to Yes (1981).

- whether the procedure employed is formal or informal;
- whether the basis for the decisions is law or some other criteria; and
- whether the settlement is legally enforceable.

At one end of the continuum is adjudication (including both judicial and administrative hearings): parties can be compelled to participate; they are usually represented by counsel; the matter follows specified procedure; the case is decided by a judge in accordance with previously established rules; and the decisions are enforceable by law....

At the other end of the continuum are negotiations in which disputants represent and arrange settlements for themselves: participation is voluntary, and the disputants determine the process to be employed and criteria for making the decision. Somewhere in the middle of the continuum is mediation, in which an impartial party facilitates an exchange among disputants, suggests possible solutions, and otherwise assists the parties in reaching a voluntary agreement....

[Here follows a definitional survey of forms of ADR:]

Arbitration...involves the submission of the dispute to a third party who renders a decision after hearing arguments and reviewing evidence. It is less formal and less complex and often can be concluded more quickly than court proceedings. In its most common form, binding arbitration, the parties select the arbitrator and are bound by the decision, either by prior agreement or by statute.[26] In last-offer arbitration, the arbitrator is required to choose between the final positions of the two parties....

Court-annexed arbitration, a newer development. Judges refer civil suits to arbitrators who render prompt, non-binding decisions. If a party does not accept an arbitrated award, some systems require they better their position at trial by some fixed percentage, or court costs are assessed against them. Even when these decisions are not accepted, they sometimes lead to further negotiations and pretrial settlement.

Conciliation, an informal process in which the third party tries to bring the parties to agreement by lowering tensions, improving communications, interpreting issues, providing technical assistance, exploring potential solutions and bringing about a negotiated settlement, either informally or, in a subsequent step, through formal mediation. Conciliation is frequently used in volatile conflicts and in disputes where the parties are unable, unwilling or unprepared to come to the table to negotiate their differences.

Facilitation, a collaborative process used to help a group of individuals or parties with divergent views reach a goal or complete a task to the mutual satisfaction of the participants. The facilitator functions as a neutral process expert and avoids making substantive contributions, [helping] bring the parties to consensus....

Fact finding, a process used from time to time primarily in public sector collective bargaining. The fact finder, drawing on information provided by the parties and additional research, recommends a resolution of each outstanding issue. It is typically non-binding and paves the way for further negotiations and mediation.

Med-arb, an innovation in dispute resolution under which the med-arbiter is

---

26. In a somewhat surprising 1990 case, representatives of a Phillips 66 petrochemical plant and citizens of a Texas Gulf Coast community agreed to arbitration to resolve a dispute over the company's discharge of polluted waste water into Linnville Bayou. Under the terms of the agreement assenting to arbitration, a panel of three scientists was given binding authority to determine the extent of pollution in the bayou and to set out the best clean-up method. The decision of the arbitration panel could be appealed only to a retired judge, and appeal was limited to the narrow issue of whether the decision was arbitrary.

authorized by the parties to serve first as a mediator and, secondly, as an arbitrator empowered to decide any issues not resolved through mediation.

Mediation, a structured process in which the mediator assists the disputants to reach a negotiated settlement of their differences. Mediation is usually a voluntary process that results in a signed agreement which defines the future behavior of the parties. The mediator uses a variety of skills and techniques to help the parties reach a settlement but is not empowered to render a decision.[27]

The Mini-trial, a privately developed method of helping to bring about a negotiated settlement in lieu of corporate litigation. A typical mini-trial might entail a period of limited discovery after which attorneys present their best case before managers with authority to settle and, most often, a neutral advisor who may be a retired judge or other lawyer. The managers then enter settlement negotiations. They may call on the neutral advisor if they wish to obtain an opinion on how a court might decide the matter.[28]

The Multi-door center (or Multi-door courthouse), a proposal [by Professor Sander] to offer a variety of dispute resolution services in one place with a single intake desk which would screen clients. Under one model, a screening clerk would refer cases for mediation, arbitration, fact-finding, ombudsman or adjudication....

[**Negotiation** is the generic process that recurs in many of these ADR forms. In its simplest incarnation, however, negotiation constitutes discussions between the parties, with no formalized format, ground rules, or third party participation.]

Neighborhood justice centers (NJCs), the title given to...about 180 local centers now operating through the country under the sponsorship of local or state governments, bar associations and foundations.... They are also known as Community Mediation Centers, Citizen Dispute Centers, etc.

Ombudsman, a third party [on the Scandinavian model] who receives and investigates complaints or grievances aimed at an institution by its constituents, clients or employees. The Ombudsman may take actions such as bringing an apparent injustice to the attention of high-level officials, advising the complainant of available options and recourses, proposing a settlement of the dispute or proposing systemic changes in the institution....

Public policy dialogue and negotiation, aimed at bringing together affected representatives of business, public interest groups and government to explore regulatory matters. The dialogue is intended to identify areas of agreement, narrow the areas of disagreement, and identify general areas and specific topics for negotiation. A facilitator guides the process.

[**Reg-neg** is the term given to a process of intensive multiparty negotiations leading to governmental issuance of regulatory rules, noted in the next excerpt.]

Rent-a-judge, the popular name given to a procedure, presently authorized by legislation in six states, in which the court, on stipulation of the parties, can refer a pending lawsuit to a private neutral party for trial with the same effect as though the case were tried in the courtroom before a judge. The verdict can be appealed through the regular court appellate system.

---

27. Mediation has been a particularly successful method for reaching settlement and allocating responsibility among potentially responsible parties in dozens of EPA Superfund toxic waste clean-up cases.

28. Since the mid-1980s, the Army Corps of Engineers has used the mini-trial technique in resolving a number of regulatory environmental disputes.

Section 3. **NEGOTIATED RULEMAKING**

**Lawrence Susskind and Gerard McMahon, The Theory
and Practice of Negotiated Rulemaking**
3 Yale Journal on Regulation 133, 140–141, 142–146 (1985)[29]

Since the late 1970s, advocates of negotiated approaches to rulemaking have argued that the legitimacy of proposed rules could be restored — and time-consuming court challenges avoided — if informal, face-to-face negotiations were used to supplement the traditional review and comment process. Critics, however, have responded quite negatively to what they perceive as the dangers of "deal-making behind closed doors." Nevertheless, proponents of the innovation have persisted, and during the last few years several federal agencies have experimented with negotiated approaches to rulemaking....

Negotiated rulemaking will only be utilized more broadly if it achieves better results than the traditional rulemaking process.... Each party must feel that the negotiated rule serves its interest at least as well as the version of the rule most likely to be developed through conventional process.... A negotiation should yield realistic commitments from all of those involved. A rule that satisfies everyone in principle but cannot be implemented is of little use. Not only is the support of the participants important, but so too is the support of any interested party.... The interests of the parties should be so well-reconciled that no possible joint gains are left unrealized. Changes which would help a party without harming another party should not be missed. If a more elegant method of reconciling conflicting interests of the parties is possible, it will probably emerge once the draft of the agreement is publicized.... The agency should be able to demonstrate that it has upheld its statutory mandate, and the public-at-large should feel satisfied that both the process and outcome were fair.... Relationships among the participants in the negotiations should improve, not deteriorate, as a result of their interactions. The parties should be in a better position to deal with their differences in the future.... The negotiated rule should take account of the best scientific and technological information available at the time of the negotiation.

EPA's Regulatory Negotiation Demonstrations... The notion of using a negotiated approach to rulemaking at EPA first emerged during the Carter Administration.... While the change of Administration slowed the momentum, appointment of Joseph Cannon as Acting Associate Administrator of EPA's Office of Planning and Resource Management in 1981 brought renewed interest.... In February 1983, EPA published a notice in the Federal Register indicating that it intended to pursue the idea of negotiated rulemaking and used solicitation letters to invite interested parties to suggest candidate rules....

In December 1983, David Doniger of the Natural Resources Defense Council (NRDC) formally proposed [rulemaking on CAA motor vehicle emissions] nonconformance penalties [NCPs] as a candidate rule for negotiated rulemaking. Between December 1983 and March 1984, [EPA] found widespread support for negotiating the NCP rule among potential stakeholders. Charles Freed, Director of EPA's Manufacturers Operations Division, the program office responsible for the rule, enthusiastically supported using a negotiated approach, as did the EPA Office of General Counsel and Office of Program Planning and Evaluation. Environmentalists

---

29. Copyright 1985 by Yale Journal on Regulation, Box 401A Yale Station, New Haven, CT 06520; reprinted from Volume 3:133 by permission. Other useful works on reg-neg include Philip Harter's Negotiated Regulations: A Cure for Malaise, 71 Georgetown L. Rev. 1 (1982) and Perritt, Negotiated Rulemaking Before Federal Agencies, 74 Georgetown L. Rev. 1625 (1986). The Administrative Conference has published a useful collection: Negotiated Rulemaking Sourcebook (1990).

were generally supportive, viewing NCPs as a means to accommodate temporary industry needs while holding industry to technology-forcing standards. Smaller manufacturers were somewhat wary of the costs of participating in a negotiated rulemaking and felt that any NCP rule had to preserve their competitiveness. Larger manufacturers generally supported the proposed process and felt that they had adequate staff to participate in the process. In general, all stakeholders felt that the rule was important enough to merit their involvement and that it did not involve the type of "life and death" value questions that would have made negotiation — an unfamiliar process at any rate — appear less workable.

In an April 1984 Federal Register notice, EPA announced its intention to develop an NCP rule using a regulatory negotiation. At an organizational meeting...some twenty participants met to learn more about the proposed process and to discuss how the negotiations would proceed. At that time, EPA announced the creation of a $50,000 resource pool — a fund that any or all of the participants would be able to draw upon to cover the costs of technical studies or other costs related to their participation.

Negotiations began June 14, 1984, and ended October 12, 1984. In order to develop some structure for the process, a negotiation facilitator opened the June session by asking participants to produce a statement of issues reflecting their interests. A final list of ten issues was synthesized to help organize the work of the negotiating committee. Three work groups were formed....

Five one-day negotiating sessions dealing with substantive aspects of the NCP rule and numerous work group sessions dealing with specific technical and administrative issues were held during a four month period. The NCP negotiating committee used over $10,000 to fund an independent study of a proposed engine testing plan. Other collaborative technical work was done by committee members who designed a micro-computer-based spreadsheet model to test the impacts of parameter changes in the penalty formula.

The negotiations were conducted under a Federal Advisory Committee Act (FACA) charter. Notice of the NCP negotiating committee sessions was given in the Federal Register, and meetings were open to the public. The committee eventually reached consensus on all of the issues it originally identified in the first meeting.

In reaching this consensus, EPA's choice of a facilitator was crucial. The ERM-McGlennon team, which had extensive mediation experience, took the lead in generating agreement on a detailed agenda and work schedule, organizing work group meetings at which components of the final version of the regulation were drafted, and convening the full group to review these work group drafts.... [T]he facilitation team initiated caucuses during and outside of meetings, maintained frequent contact with all participants, and intervened quite actively during several of the sessions.

After the last negotiation session on October 12, 1984, in which all the issues were resolved, a four-member subcommittee — consisting of EPA, state, environmental, and industry representatives — was given the responsibility of translating the tentative agreement into a consensus document. A first draft was circulated in mid-October, and comments were solicited. The subcommittee then used several conference calls to prepare the final draft that was signed by the entire committee in December 1984. With the consensus statement signed by all participants, EPA published its notice of proposed rulemaking on March 6, 1985. Only thirteen comments were received during the comment period, all in support of the committee's proposal. The final rule was promulgated without opposition on August 30, 1985....

COMMENTARY & QUESTIONS

1. **Statutory ADR and reg-neg.** In 1990, Congress formally recognized the utility of ADR and negotiated rulemaking, and made them federal policy. The 101st Congress passed the Administrative Dispute Resolution Act, Pub. L. No. 101-552, and the Negotiated Rulemaking Act, Pub. L. No. 101-648, as amendments to the adjudication section of the APA. Under the ADRA, agencies are required to appoint resolution specialists and to develop policy addressing the potential uses of ADR in that agency. The Act does not force agencies to use ADR mechanisms, but each agency must review its litigation and administrative disputes to determine where ADR techniques may be useful. The second statute explicitly establishes the authority of federal regulatory agencies to use negotiated rulemaking and permits the use of federal funds to cover the expenses of private party participants. These policies may give ADR methods new legitimacy and force, although temperaments and practical constraints do not change automatically. FRCP Rules 16 and 68 also promote nonlitigation resolutions in cases filed in federal court.

2. **Technical details.** The EPA reg-neg illustrates several technical issues. It is always a question, for instance, who pays — especially where citizen groups are involved. How many participants are too many? Federal rules may well directly affect thousands. What about the records of an ADR process (this issue applies equally to nonreg-neg cases)? ADR specialists typically try to keep as few records as possible and get the parties to contract to confidentiality, to avoid the disruptive possibility that information may be subpoenaed and used in other more litigious forums. (In some jurisdictions, a nascent "mediation privilege" is being recognized, analogous to an attorney-client privilege.)

And what about the administrative law consequences? Does reg-neg violate the delegation doctrine because nonofficials effectively make the decision?[30] Do split caucuses in reg-neg violate the ban on ex parte contacts with agency decisionmakers?[31] Will courts still feel obliged to scrutinize closely to assure that agencies gave a "hard look" to the facts and law?[32]

3. **Evaluating ADR.** Ultimately, evaluation of ADR depends not only on whether cases reach settlement, but also upon what it is intended to achieve. And different observers have very different views. Justice Burger wanted to unclog the courts. Professor Fiss discerns a questionable political goal "to insulate the status quo from the judiciary."[33] Professors McThenia and Shaffer likewise focus on more holistic goals, quoting Socrates: "Justice is what we discover — you and I — when we walk together, listen together, and even love one another, in our curiosity about what justice is and where justice comes from."[34] (Fiss replied that he's as much for love as anybody, but dispute

---

30. Susskind argues that it doesn't because agency officials have the last word. 3 Yale J. Reg. at 158.

31. Perritt argues that it doesn't, 74 Geo. L. Rev. 1625, 1697 (1986).

32. Susskind argues that the hard look will be satisfied if the reg-neg incorporates notice; equal footing, including funding of citizens; reasonable record; round-robin review of the final draft; full discussion of comments; procedural equality; clear statement of agency negotiation positions; and an opportunity for all parties to sign off on the final rule. 3 Yale J. Reg. at 164. Cf. Wald, Negotiation of Environmental Disputes: A New Role for the Courts?, 10 Colum. J. Envtl. L. 1 (1985).

33. Against Settlement, 94 Yale L.J. 1669, 1670 (1985).

34. For Reconciliation, 94 Yale L.J. 1660, 1665 (1985).

resolution has broader goals and constraints.) Are a governing system's needs adequately fulfilled when the interests of all parties involved in a particular conflict are satisfied, or are there further systemic goals such as establishing precedent?

E. THE IMPETUS TO SELF-GENERATED CORPORATE COMPLIANCE

As noted earlier in this chapter, a critical debate is ongoing concerning whether the deterrent enforcement strategies traditionally used to control pollution should continue to be the highly prescriptive ones inherited from the command-and-control realm or, alternatively, should be "kinder, gentler" ones emphasizing compliance assurance, noncompliance prevention, and alternative dispute resolution. The appropriate role of citizen enforcement has added fuel to this debate.

In recent years, however, with the exponential growth in the scope and complexity of the environmental laws, the debate has entered a new phase. As even those long charged with environmental enforcement have come to recognize, a major change has taken place in the attitudes and business priorities of American business:

> Even the most curmudgeonly old enforcer must recognize...that the general attitudes of the regulated sector have altered over time. Deliberate efforts to evade environmental controls have become rarer (although by no means unknown), the importance attached to compliance has increased, and the resources and management attention devoted to the environmental protection has greatly expanded. Environmental management was once commonly considered a nuisance activity to be conducted and supervised as a corporate backwater function. It has now taken a much more central role, becoming a core part of many companies' management structures. Diamond, Confessions of an Environmental Enforcer, 26 Envtl. L. Rep. 10252, 10254 (1996).

If environmental compliance has now made the transition from a corporate backwater function to a top business priority, what implications does this have for the future of environmental enforcement? If corporations are now reducing emissions and achieving compliance arguably on their own initiative, will this self-generated compliance continue, or is the credible threat of continued governmental and citizen enforcement still required?

Section 1. THE TRIGGERS FOR ENVIRONMENTAL COMPLIANCE

Today, buyers, sellers, borrowers, and lenders almost invariably confront environmental issues when engaging in their regular business activities. While the magnitude of potential liability, and the likelihood of its occurrence, may be greater in certain business sectors (e.g., chemical manufacturers) than in others, the scope of environmental regulation now covers almost every type of property or business. Environmental risks, costs, and benefits have become a factor in virtually every transaction.

Environmental issues typically arise in connection with five key types of business events that trigger attention to the need for environmental compliance in order to avoid environmental liabilities and risks. These five triggers are (1) permitting and reporting, (2) Securities Exchange Commission (SEC) disclosure by public companies, (3) the satisfaction of corporate information needs, (4) borrowing for ongoing business needs, and (5) the purchase or sale of a business or property.

Permitting and Reporting. Hundreds of thousands of dischargers and waste management facilities are subject to the permit programs established under federal and state environmental laws.[35] Permits define and facilitate compliance and enforcement by transforming generally applicable limitations promulgated by governmental enforcers (e.g., "discharges shall be treated in accordance with BAT") into specific obligations, including a timetable for compliance for the individual discharger. Permits thus provide an effective means of assuring that the permittee is on notice of its obligations as spelled out in the permit, that regulators are notified of releases and discharges by permitters as required by the terms of the permit, and that the specific requirements applicable to a particular discharge or activity are identified and clarified.

By applying federal and state requirements to individual pollution sources and hazardous waste management activities, permits play a crucial role, and the inability or failure to obtain a necessary permit can be fatal to business operations. Thus, obtaining permits in the first instance, and then complying with their reporting and other standards, are key events triggering attention to environmental concerns. For these reasons, the need to obtain and comply with permits is taken as a given by business executives today.

SEC Disclosure Requirements for Public Companies. There are two events that may trigger a company's duty to disclose certain of its environmental liabilities under the federal securities laws. First, disclosure may be required as part of a publicly held company's mandated securities filings. See Regulation S-K, 17 C.F.R. pt. 229. Second, disclosure may be required when a company is subject to SEC Rule 10b-5, an anti-fraud rule that usually comes into play as a result of a company selling its securities, such as in a stock purchase agreement in which the company makes representations and warranties concerning its operations, its compliance with laws, and other material facts in the agreement. The importance of compliance with these disclosure obligations is detailed below.

Frank Friedman and David Giannotti, Environmental Self Assessment,
in Environmental Law Institute, Law of Environmental Protection
7-28 to 7-33 (1998)

Publicly held companies must also identify environmental problems to ensure timely and accurate reports under the securities and exchange laws and SEC regulations. An SEC finding that a company failed to disclose environmentally related matters, thereby deceiving investors, could jeopardize the company's ability to raise capital through new stock offerings or debt instruments. It can also result in SEC initiation of costly and time-consuming administrative proceedings. Any such action by the SEC can give rise to shareholders' class actions and derivative suits. Thus, SEC

---

35. Federal statutes creating one or more permit systems include CAA §110(a)(2), 42 U.S.C. §7410(a)(2); CWA §412(b), 33 U.S.C. §1342(b); SDWA §1422(b), 33 U.S.C. §300h-l(b); and RCRA §3006(b), 42 U.S.C. §6929(b). State agencies will issue the permits either when EPA has delegated its authority to implement a program to the state, or when the state has adopted an independent regulatory program.

enforcement of environmental laws and regulations, although indirect, is potentially more powerful than that of direct agency enforcement of environmental laws and regulations. Included within the scope of required SEC reporting are environmentally related matters, such as: (1) two-year estimates of capital expenditures for environmental compliance, or for a longer period if such estimates have been developed and a failure to disclose would be misleading; (2) particular types of environmental proceedings; and (3) circumstances under which companies must disclose their policies or approaches concerning environmental compliance.

With respect to proceedings, any governmental administrative or judicial proceedings arising or known to be contemplated under any federal, state, or local provisions regulating the discharge of materials into the environment or otherwise relating to the protection of the environment must be disclosed if any one of three conditions exist. Any private or governmental proceeding that is material to the business or financial condition of the corporation must be reported. Any private or governmental proceeding for damages, potential monetary sanctions, capital expenditures, deferred charges or charges to income is reportable if the amount involved (exclusive of interest and costs) exceeds 10 percent of the current assets of the corporation. And any governmental proceeding must be reported if monetary sanctions (exclusive of interest and costs) will or reasonably are expected to exceed $100,000....

The SEC's May 1989 interpretative release concerning the disclosure required in Management's Discussion and Analysis of Financial Condition and Results of Operations (MD&A) in SEC filings further details the scope of disclosure. The MD&A release states that "once management knows of a potentially material environmental problem, it must disclose it unless it can determine that the problem is not reasonably likely to cause a material effect, either because the event is not likely to happen or if it does happen, the effect is not likely to be material."[36] Thus, in preparing SEC filings, data developed during routine assessments and assessments made for acquisition and sale of properties becomes important....

The basis for measuring environmental liability is very important and is worth quoting in detail.

In measuring its environmental liability, a registrant should consider available evidence including the registrant's prior experience in remediation of contaminated sites, other companies' cleanup experience, and data released by the Environmental Protection Agency or other organizations. Information necessary to support a reasonable estimate or range of loss may be available prior to the performance of any detailed remediation study. Even in situations in which the registrant has not determined the specific strategy for remediation, estimates of the costs associated with the various alternative remediation strategies considered for a site may be available or reasonably estimable. While the range of costs associated with the alternatives may be broad, the minimum clean-up cost is unlikely to be zero. SEC Staff Accounting Bulletin No. 92....

[The] tightening interpretation of what financial information must be disclosed greatly increases the potential liability exposure for failure to disclose or properly accrue. Legal involvement is critical as these issues are examined....

Corporate Management Information Needs. Environmental considerations are also triggered by a company's corporate management information needs, which can include financial planning, risk management, the setting of appropriate accounting reserves, consideration of new product lines, and the acquisition of appropriate amounts and type of insurance coverage for environmental risk.

---

36. 54 Fed. Reg. at 22427.

Assume, for example, that, in developing a new product line, a company will be developing a product utilizing a new chemical substance. Under ToSCA (see Chapter 17), a company would need to consider whether there may be limitations on the product's use or safety associated with the product's manufacture or processing. Such concerns obviously affect the cost of the product and the ability to market it. Alternatively, assume that a company seeks to establish, under RCRA (see Chapter 18), that it can provide the financial assurance necessary to operate a TSD facility. Evaluation of environmental risks may be essential to establishing that the company qualifies as financially responsible, including covering (through bonds, insurance, and the like) both closure and post-closure costs. As another example, assume that a company is seeking to open another facility. Under the CAA, the company must identify whether the new facility will be in an attainment or nonattainment area, a factor that can affect preconstruction review. Similarly, the company must evaluate whether, under CERCLA (see Chapter 19), the new facility may be near a waste disposal site requiring potential cost and expense of remediation.

As the Frankel article below concludes, sound corporate management especially requires gathering information to address the needs of company auditors. The reporting of environmental contingencies is now a permanent part of the financial landscape within which a business must operate.

Stuart Frankel, Full Disclosure: Financial Statement Disclosures under CERCLA
3 Duke Environmental Law & Policy Forum 57, 65–67 (1993)

Companies typically prepare their financial statements in accordance with Generally Accepted Accounting Principles (GAAP). GAAP is a hierarchy of accounting standards promulgated by various professional accounting bodies, most notably the Financial Accounting Standards Board (FASB) and the American Institute of Certified Public Accountants (AICPA). SFAS-5 is the primary source of guidance available to companies for estimating and disclosing environmental liabilities in their financial statements.

SFAS-5 uses probabilities to determine the likelihood that a loss contingency will eventually be realized. There are three levels of probability at which a contingency may be classified by a business entity:

1. Probable. The future event or events are likely to occur.

2. Reasonably possible. The chance of future event or events occurring is more than remote but less than likely.

3. Remote. The chance of the future event or events occurring is slight.

SFAS-5 delineates appropriate treatment of financial statements based upon each contingency classification. If a loss contingency appears probable and the amount of the loss can be reasonably estimated, the contingency "shall be accrued by a charge to income." This means the estimated amount will be recognized as a loss as well as disclosed in the financial statement. If the loss cannot be estimated but the likelihood of it occurring is probable, the contingency should be disclosed with an explanation of why no estimate can be made. If the loss is reasonably possible, accrual of the expense is not required, but disclosure of the nature of the contingency and an estimate of the potential loss is necessary. Finally, if the contingency is classified as remote, there is generally no impact reflected in financial statements.

In Appendix A to SFAS-5, FASB gives several examples of the application of SFAS-5 to specific situations. With respect to Superfund disclosures, the most appropriate example is set out under the heading "Litigation, Claims, and Assessments." In the discussion, SFAS-5 indicates that the decision to accrue and/or disclose a loss that may result from pending and potential litigation should be based in large part on the "degree of probability of an unfavorable outcome." Several factors are listed that should be considered in assessing the probability of litigation outcome:

> The nature of the litigation, claim, or assessment, the progress of the case..., the opinions or views of legal counsel and other advisers, the experience of the enterprise in similar cases, the experience of other enterprises, and any decision of the enterprise's management as to how the enterprise intends to respond to the lawsuit, claim or assessment....

Once it is determined that an unfavorable litigation outcome is either probable or reasonably possible, the company must derive an estimate for disclosure. In the context of Superfund, that task is even more challenging. Factors such as the number of PRPs, their respective financial resources, joint and several liability, allocation of liability to each PRP, existence of insurance coverage, time frame of the investigation, and related litigation all make the estimation process very difficult and imprecise. Added to the obstacles posed by the estimation process is the fact that companies are generally loath to report information that may attract negative publicity, especially if it is not clear that the loss or other liability will materialize. Consequently, disclosure policies among companies regarding environmental contingencies vary greatly....

Borrowing for Ongoing Business Needs. In order to continue existing operations, to expand to new operations, or to meet capital obligations, companies must consider borrowing to satisfy their ongoing business needs. As a practical matter, without such financing, many private undertakings cannot be pursued.

Lenders typically seek information about environmental issues affecting the property or business that is the subject of the contemplated loan; it is extremely important for both creditworthiness considerations and assessment of potential collateral. Conducting a due diligence investigation, or requiring the borrower to conduct one as a condition precedent to the loan, is often a necessity for assessing, to the extent possible, the value of the property. Likewise, a borrower's ability to repay the loan may be impaired if the borrower must spend significant sums to comply with environmental laws or to clean up historic contamination.

Representations and warranties can be used by a lender to create a mechanism in the event of default should the representation turn out to be false; representations and warranties also can be used to cut off a borrower's ability to make further draws under a revolving credit facility, when something has happened during the term of the loan and the borrower is no longer able to reaffirm the validity of the representations as would be required at the time of the draw request. Also, representations can be used to elicit due diligence information on the target company. Lenders typically require the borrower to provide notice of certain events during the life of the loan (such as receipt of a notice of violation or an information request pertaining to off-site disposal of hazardous substances) to enable the lender to reevaluate its position in light of new events.

In lending for ongoing business needs, lenders are also concerned about their own potential liabilities under the environmental laws. In 1996, after several years of

lobbying by the financial services and real estate industries, Congress adopted significant amendments to CERCLA's security interest exemption in an effort to limit the risks
to lenders arising from the environmental liabilities of their borrowers.[37] Nonetheless,
concerns about lender liability persist, adding additional motivation to lenders' desire
to require their borrowers to engage in environmental compliance.

The Purchase and Sale of a Business or Real Estate. Under CERCLA, and some analogous state laws, present owners of real property may be strictly liable for remediation of
contamination that exists on or beneath, or that flows from, acquired property, despite
their lack of participation in or knowledge of activities that caused the contamination.
Common law damage actions by neighboring landowners based on common law trespass, nuisance, or negligence grounds may also be brought against the present owners
on the theory that they are continuing the tortious interference. In addition, compliance deficiencies and enforcement actions that are directed at ongoing conduct may
become the burden of new owners either of the property or of the operations that are
maintained on the property. Thus, one who acquires a corporation that owns real property or an entity that merges or consolidates with a corporate property owner may, in
appropriate circumstances, succeed to the liabilities of the predecessor.

Identifying, analyzing, and allocating the risks of these potential liabilities among
the parties to the purchase or sale of a business or real estate brings environmental
considerations into virtually every transaction. The assessment and allocation of the
risks of a transaction requires an understanding of both the nature of the environmental liabilities and the types of contract provisions available for incorporation into an
agreement as a mechanism for risk allocation among the parties to the transaction.
Examples of the types of contract provisions available for allocation of financial
responsibility and risk include (1) purchase price adjustments, (2) cost-sharing
arrangements, (3) escrowed monies, (4) representations and warranties, (5) indemnification provisions, and (6) conditions precedent and subsequent to the transaction.

Increasingly, buyers are requiring, as a condition precedent to transactions, that
environmental risks be identified and either eliminated or minimized before a transaction will close. This type of contractual provision implements the buyer's requirement
that, before closing, a property or business come into compliance with the environmental laws, so that the buyer may avoid or limit environmental liability and risk. A
typical example of such a condition precedent to closing, in a real estate transaction in
Illinois, is set forth below.

> **Environmental Remediation…** Seller has advised Purchaser that environmental
> remediation has commenced on the Property. Such remediation shall be subject to
> the following conditions:

---

37. These amendments were codified in the Asset Conservation, Lender Liability, and Deposit Insurance
Protection Act of 1996 (Act), which essentially codified into law EPA's Lender Liability Rule pertaining to the
scope of the secured creditor exemption under CERCLA. See 57 Fed. Reg. 18344 (Apr. 29, 1992). That rule had
not enjoyed smooth going in the courts. In February 1994, the D.C. Circuit struck down that rule, concluding
that Congress made the federal courts, not EPA, the ultimate arbiter of CERCLA's liability provisions. See Kelley
v. EPA, 15 F.3d 1100 (D.C. Cir.), reh'g denied, 25 F.3d 1088 (D.C. Cir. 1994). Thereafter, Congress passed the Act,
which defines what is (and what is not) "participation in management" sufficient to subject a lender to CERCLA
liability. See 42 U.S.C. §9601(20)(E)-(G).

(a) Seller has advised Purchaser that Seller is undertaking remediation of certain hazardous contamination on a portion of the Property, with the goal that, upon completion of such remediation, the Property will not pose a threat to Purchaser's intended use of the Property or to the environment. Seller shall seek to obtain a letter from the Illinois Environmental Protection Agency (IEPA) confirming that no further remediation of said contamination will be necessary with respect to the Property (the IEPA Letter).

(b) Seller shall pay all costs associated with the remediation of the Property. In the event that Seller cannot accomplish the site remediation (including the delivery to Purchaser of the IEPA Letter) by November 1, 1997, Purchaser may elect any of the following options: (i) to terminate the Contract, in which event the escrowee shall release the earnest money and all interest earned thereon to Purchaser immediately and neither party shall have any further obligations or liabilities to each other hereunder; (ii) to waive receipt of the IEPA Letter, provided all site remediation has otherwise been completed and Purchaser has given at least ten (10) business days advance written notice of such waiver; or (iii) to extend in writing the date by which the site remediation may be completed and the IEPA Letter obtained to February 1, 1998.

This contractual provision is a form of self-generated compliance. Buyers are increasingly insisting that businesses and properties that are the target of a transaction come into compliance with federal and state environmental laws before the transaction can proceed. From the buyer's perspective, achieving compliance beforehand is obviously preferable to participating in a transaction that exposes the buyer to potential governmental or citizen enforcement.

COMMENTARY & QUESTIONS

1. **The cooperative agreement between EPA and the SEC.** EPA and the SEC have a cooperative agreement that allows the SEC access to EPA data to audit the adequacy of the data a company releases. Under the agreement, the SEC has offered to perform "full disclosures" of any corporation for EPA, and EPA allows the SEC access to various EPA files. EPA has agreed to provide the SEC with six categories of information on a quarterly basis. See Harrelson, EPA Agrees to Information Exchange with SEC, Inside EPA Superfund Rep., Mar. 28, 1990, at 2. The types of information to be provided are (1) names of parties receiving Superfund notice letters identifying them as potentially liable for the cost of a Superfund cleanup, (2) lists of all filed (but not concluded) RCRA and CERCLA cases, (3) lists of all recently concluded civil cases under federal environmental laws, (4) lists of all filed criminal cases under federal environmental laws, (5) lists of all facilities barred from government contractors under the CWA, and (6) lists of all RCRA facilities subject to cleanup requirements.

What impact does this mutual exchange of information have on the regulated community? In light of the cooperation between EPA and the SEC, should a company take particular steps to ensure that its disclosures to EPA and to the SEC are consistent? What might be the consequences if there were inconsistencies?

2. **The disparity between EPA reporting and SFAS-5 disclosures.** SEC reporting requirements are much more stringent than current GAAP. For an SEC registered company,

there can be a significant disparity between information disclosed in its SEC filings and information disclosed under GAAP in the Notes to the Consolidated Financial Statements. For a company not subject to the SEC reporting requirements, this often means that environmental contingencies either are not disclosed or are underdisclosed in the financial statements. See Frankel, Full Disclosure: Financial Statement Disclosures Under CERCLA, 93 Duke Envtl. L. & Pol'y F. 57, 70–71 (1993).

3. **Private arrangements for loss allocation.** What is the relationship of private agreements that shift or allocate losses and the law's allocation of liability? For example, can a generator PRP escape liability through an indemnity agreement with a transporter or TSD operator, or could a seller, by agreement, agree to assume the CERCLA liability of the facility purchaser? CERCLA §107(e)(1), despite seeming ambiguity, gives a perfectly clear answer, "yes and no." It states:

> No indemnification, holdharmless, or similar agreement or conveyance shall be effective to transfer from [a PRP] to any other person the liability imposed under this section. Nothing in this subsection shall bar any agreement to insure, hold harmless, or indemnify a party to such agreement for liability under this section.

As the courts eventually realized, the statute does not allow private arrangements to limit the legal liability of the parties, which would plainly contravene the statute's policy, but the statute expressly allows the enforcement inter sese of the parties to those private agreements. In short, private arrangements for post-liability loss shifting are allowed and can be enforced. See, e.g., AM Int'l v. International Forging Equip. Corp., 982 F.2d 989 (6th Cir. 1993); Jones-Hamilton v. Beazer Materials & Servs., Inc., 973 F.2d 688 (9th Cir. 1992).

Section 2. DUE DILIGENCE, AUDITS, AND OTHER AVENUES TOWARD VOLUNTARY COMPLIANCE

As business events trigger the need for environmental compliance, companies have increasingly relied on two key tools to evaluate such compliance: environmental due diligence and environmental audits.

Environmental Due Diligence. Due diligence has long been standard practice for companies considering the purchase of the stock, assets, or real estate of a target company. In the environmental context, due diligence essentially involves the examination of a company's compliance with environmental requirements and the assessment of the target's potential or contingent environmental liabilities. The information obtained from the due diligence investigation may be used for different purposes by the various parties to the transaction. For example, due diligence may reveal potential problems that will make a target unattractive to the buyer and suggest abandoning the transaction. Alternatively, it may allow the purchaser to negotiate adjustments to the price, to change the structure of the deal, or to redraft other important contractual provisions,[38] seeking

---

38. In May 1993, the American Society for Testing and Materials (ASTM) promulgated standards for environmental site assessments, or environmental due diligence investigations. The first standard sets out a "Transaction Screen" process for commercial property transactions where environmental problems are unlikely to be of major concern. See ASTM, Standard Practice for Environmental Site Assessment, Transaction Screen Process, E1528-93. The second standard is designed for use in transactions where a more thorough inquiry into environmental issues is necessary. See ASTM, Standard Practice for Environmental Assessments; Phase I Environmental Site Assessment Process, E-527-93.

to satisfy the "appropriate inquiry" requirement of CERCLA's innocent purchaser defense. See CERCLA §101(35)(A), 42 U.S.C. §9601(35)(A). ASTM has also produced a guide to due diligence inquiry, providing checklists for document reviews and question-naires for use in environmental due diligence reviews.

Environmental due diligence also helps a potential lender determine whether to proceed with a loan. It permits a lender to assess whether contingent environmental liabilities may impair a borrower's ability to repay the loan or damage the borrower's credit rating, making it difficult or impossible for the lender to sell the loan. It also enables the lender to identify any environmental contamination that could affect the desirability of foreclosing on property or affect securing the loan. Furthermore, an environmental due diligence investigation can serve to alert the purchaser or lender to present or future environmental problems that may require management or remedial action.

Environmental Audits. Environmental audits are somewhat more formal and extended than due diligence inquiries. EPA defines an environmental audit as a "systematic, documented, periodic and objective review by regulated entities of facility operations and practices related to meeting environmental requirements."[39] An audit represents a "snapshot" of a company's environmental compliance at a moment in time, enabling a company to assess its state of environmental compliance and to iden-tify what, if anything, is necessary to achieve full compliance. Audits generally involve a review of past and present operations; the history of compliance with federal, state, and local environmental laws; permits; waste practices; disclosure and reporting practices; operations and processes; budgets for environmental expenditures; and developing environmental strategies.

EPA generally considers the need for penalties in the context of a company's good faith efforts to comply with environmental laws and regulations. Although the exis-tence of an audit program is not a mitigating factor, EPA may consider honest and genuine efforts of regulated entities to avoid and promptly correct violations discov-ered through audits when fashioning penalties for regulatory violations.

While the existence of an auditing program may have a mitigating effect in enforce-ment proceedings, there is also a risk that an audit report may be used against a company in administrative, civil or criminal enforcement actions. To date, both EPA and DOJ have been unwilling to provide explicit assurances that the results of any audits will not be used as the basis for criminal prosecution. Historically, EPA's position has been that it is free to seek disclosure of internal environmental audit reports on a case-by-case basis.

In July 1991, DOJ issued a long-awaited guidance document entitled "Factors in Decisions on Criminal Prosecutions for Environmental Violations in the Context of Significant Voluntary Disclosure of Compliance Efforts by the Violator." To promote self-auditing, self-policing, and voluntary disclosure of environmental regulation by the regulated community, the DOJ delineated several factors that it will review in

---

39. EPA Environmental Audit Policy Statement, 51 Fed. Reg. 25,004, 25,005 (July 9, 1986).

considering whether, and to what extent, to prosecute criminally under the environmental laws.

In recent years, EPA and DOJ policies have come under close scrutiny. There is great concern in the business community that the risk that environmental audit reports may be used against a company in enforcement proceedings is a disincentive to candid, self-evaluative environmental auditing. As a result, numerous states have enacted statutes establishing a privilege for environmental audit reports and granting immunity from prosecution for violations discovered by an environmental audit and then promptly fixed and reported to appropriate authorities. In general, three conditions must be met under most state audit-privilege laws in order to invoke the privilege or qualify for reduced penalties or immunity: (1) the regulated entity must conduct an audit that uncovers environmental violations, (2) the entity must voluntarily report the violations to authorities within a certain period of time, and (3) the entity must expeditiously correct the violation.

In December 1995, EPA responded to the concerns raised in the business community that environmental audit laws will be used on the federal level to assist in enforcement proceedings. EPA replaced its 1986 Environmental Audit Policy Statement with a new guidance document (effective January 22, 1996) entitled "Incentives for Self-Policing: Discovery, Disclosure, Correction and Prevention of Violations" (Incentives Policy).[40] The Incentives Policy does not provide absolute protection from discovery or an evidentiary privilege. Instead, the policy provides that EPA will not request or use an environmental report to initiate a civil or criminal investigation, but if EPA has an independent reason to believe that a violation has occurred, EPA may seek any information relevant to identifying violations or determining liability or extent of harm. The Incentives Policy provides only that EPA will seek reduced civil fines if certain outcomes are met (e.g., the company discovers the violation through a self-audit, voluntarily discloses the violation within 10 days, corrects the violation promptly, and cooperates with EPA) and will not refer the matter for criminal enforcement if certain other criteria are met (e.g., EPA determines that the violation does not involve a corporate philosophy or practice, or does not involve higher level corporate involvement in, or willful blindness to, the violation).

Rather than aligning with the trend in the states toward developing audit privileges, however, EPA remains staunchly opposed to such privileges. In the Incentives Policy, EPA has stated its opposition to any state legislation that jeopardizes the fundamental interest in assuring that violations of federal law do not threaten the public health or the environment, or make it profitable not to comply. EPA has further stated that it reserves its right to bring independent action against regulated entities for violations of federal law that threaten human health or the environment, reflect criminal conduct, represent repeated noncompliance, or allow one company to make a substantial profit at the expense of its law-abiding competitors. EPA has also requested that some states revise existing audit-privilege laws and has informed certain states that failure to amend privilege and immunity laws may jeopardize their federally delegated authority.

---

40. 60 Fed. Reg. 66706 (Dec. 22, 1995); see also ELR Admin. Mat. I 35639. In addition, on June 3, 1996, EPA issued a policy designed to provide small businesses with an incentive to conduct environmental audits and engage in compliance activities. See 61 Fed. Reg. 27,984 (June 3, 1996).

COMMENTARY & QUESTIONS

1. **EPA and audit privileges.** Critics view EPA's actions limiting the scope of protection it will allow to information discovered through environmental audits as an attempt to coerce states into rescinding, altering, or declining to enact audit-privilege legislation. One pair of commentators has referred to this type of opposition by EPA as "delegation blackmail" because EPA has threatened to rescind delegation of enforcement authority in states where audit privileges immunize many of the violations uncovered in the audit. See Wilkins & Stroman, Delegation Blackmail: EPA's Use of Program Delegation to Combat State Audit Privilege Statutes 11, 16th Annual RCRA/CERCLA and Private Litigation Update, A.B.A. Sec. Nat. Res., Energy & Envtl. L., 25th Annual Conference on Environmental Law (Dec. 12–13, 1996).

2. **The congressional view of state environmental audit privileges.** In the absence of a federal statutory environmental audit privilege, what is the congressional view of audit privileges? Following a series of hearings, members of a House Committee expressed disapproval of EPA's hostility to state audit-privilege laws:

> The greatest burden of environmental enforcement rests in the states, yet testimony received by the Committee suggests that the states may be threatened with the loss of delegation of this responsibility if they do not conform their self-audit laws in ways to meet the specific approval of EPA. The Committee would take a very dim view of such a response on the part of EPA. States should be encouraged to create and implement new, non-adversarial and cost effective alternatives to the traditional "command-and-control" approach for environmental enforcement, such as the self-audit. The Committee strongly urges EPA to allow states — indeed, even assist the states — to go forward in implementing their self-audit laws, giving states the opportunity to demonstrate whether greater flexibility and cooperation will in fact lead to lowering the overall cost of achieving a clean and healthy environment while assuring that legal action remains for those not willing to meet the law. Reprint of House Committee on Appropriations on H.R. 3666, Department of Veterans Affairs and Housing and Urban Development and Independent Agencies 1997 Appropriations Bill, June 18, 1996.

Are the tactics employed by EPA with the states impeding the development of innovative, progressive state programs that could help determine whether greater flexibility and cooperation with industry would lead to improved environmental compliance? Do these tactics represent an appropriate use of enforcement tools for federal management of state environmental agencies?

3. **Citizen groups and environmental audits.** The citizen's right of access to information is often forgotten in the debate over environmental audits. Local citizen groups have fought extensively for greater access to information about corporate environmental compliance, and these groups are reluctant to concede to business any additional control over information on corporate compliance with environmental regulations. Citizen groups view business' desire for self-regulation as a means to avoid environmental disclosure, on the ground that providing business with more secrecy for environmental audits is like the "fox guarding the hen house." Can the views of citizen groups be reconciled with the desire of business to monitor its own compliance with the environmental laws? Could an auditing privilege be fashioned that excludes audits

as admissible evidence in civil suits or government enforcement actions but still allows the results to be available to the public?

4. **Striking the right enforcement balance.** Simply doing business in the United States today involves engaging in activities that trigger material attention to environmental concerns. The development and increasing use of environmental due diligence and auditing, as tools to measure and enhance compliance efforts, reflect these realities. Marketplace priorities are changing. Industry is internalizing new environmental priorities because the business risks and costs of environmental noncompliance are a fundamental factor in business planning. How likely is the prospect of voluntary compliance in the absence of credible threats of governmental or citizen enforcement? There is a growing awareness within the federal government and the states that cooperative approaches with the regulated community have their place in furthering environmental enforcement and compliance. Even if more cooperative approaches are desirable, most agree that cooperation still needs to be tempered by the threat of credible environmental enforcement. Despite the professed desires of business to engage in self-generated compliance, altruism alone does not typically prompt U.S. business to respond. Rather, the ultimate driving force remains the material cost of noncompliance and its adverse effect upon the bottom line. In the words of former EPA Administrator William D. Ruckelshaus, "environmentalism is here to stay" and "paying attention to the environmental impact of technology or processes benefits the bottom line." See Ruckelshaus, Stopping the Pendulum, Envtl. F., Nov./Dec. 1995, at 25–26.

5. **Corporate infighting over environmental principle?** Environmental law creates some unusual twists in corporate law as well as every other part of the field it touches. Imagine a publicly held lumber company run for generations on principles of sustainable silviculture, conserving its mountain acreage, cutting selectively, and enjoying a mutually rewarding partnership with the local communities that supply its workforce. Then comes a Wall Street raider who launches a hostile takeover planning to strip the company of its capital assets and clearcut the forests with no thought of sustainability, to maximize short-term profits, close down the company, and move on. Are there principles of corporate law taking account of such severe environmental consequences that could be mobilized to fend off the raider? See the Pacific Lumber corporate law materials on the coursebook Web site.

6. **New enforcement obstacles: congressional vetoes, and the Data Quality Act.** In recent years a number of new hurdles have been placed before the regulatory process.

In 2000 the Congress, for the first time, exercised a regulatory veto power, striking down an occupational health rule. The Congressional Review Act of 1996[41] allows Congress to rescind regulations less than 60 days old by vote in both chambers, with limited debate and a statutory bar against amendments and filibusters. If the rescission is approved by the President (or enacted over his veto), the regulation is rescinded and the issuing agency is prohibited from issuing any new rule "substantially the same as" the original rule, unless specifically authorized to do so by a subsequent law.[42]

---

41. 5 U.S.C. §§ 801-808 (1996).

42. 5 U.S.C. § 801(b)(2).

The first regulation repealed was OSHA's ergonomic standard intended to prevent repetitive stress injuries to workers. 65 Fed. Reg. 68262 (2000). The regulation had been adopted in the final months of the Clinton Administration, after a full decade of studies and hearings. OSHA had estimated that while the regulation might cost businesses $4.5 billion, it would save them $9 billion a year by eliminating nearly a third of the 1.8 million repetitive stress injuries, and increasing productivity. Industry, however, bitterly opposed the rule. The resolution of disapproval repealing the regulation, supported by the new administration, was passed by party line majorities, without any hearings or committee action, with just an hour of debate in the House.[43]

> Resolved by the Senate and House of Representatives of the United States of America in Congress assembled, that Congress disapproves the rule submitted by the Department of Labor relating to ergonomics (published at 65 Fed. Reg. 68262 (2000)), and such rule shall have no force or effect. Ergonomics Rule Disapproval, Pub. L. No. 107-5, 115 Stat. 7 (2001).

On March 20, 2001, President Bush signed the resolution repealing the health standard.

Other hurdles have emerged from the Bush II Administration's Office of Information and Regulatory Affairs (OIRA, a part of the OMB), which, in addition to requiring cost-benefit analysis for regulatory initiatives and often rejecting them based on this measure (as seen in Chapter 13), constructed a series of restrictive obstacles for regulation — proposing "peer review" standards for agency science that have been widely criticized as bottlenecks by the scientific community itself, and implementing "information quality" review procedures that have unleashed dozens of complaints against agencies charging that the information they use to regulate and inform the public is unreliable. The latter initiative is based on the Data Quality Act (a/k/a "Information Quality Act"), a single-paragraph provision inserted into a massive appropriations bill by an anti-regulationist legislative aide. See Treasury and Government Appropriations Act for Fiscal Year 2001, §515, Pub. L. No. 106-554 (2000); Urstadt, One-Act Farce, Harper's Mag., June 1, 2003, at 52; and Hornstein, Accounting for Science: The Independence of Public Research in the New Subterranean Administrative Law, 66 L. & Contemp. Probs. 229 (2003). In coming years each of these innovations will surely be grist for the political mill in which regulatory policy evolves.

---

43. Steven Greenhouse, House Joins Senate in Repealing Rules on Workplace Injuries, N.Y. Times, March 8, 2001, at A19.

"Redeveloping brownfields is… a great strategy for promoting smart growth. By developing in areas where infrastructure already exists, we can eliminate the need to do so in valuable open spaces."

— Christine Todd Whitman, erstwhile Bush II EPA Administrator, referring to new brownfields initiatives in an EPA Smart Growth program, March 2002

"One of the best ways to arrest urban sprawl is to develop brownfields and make them productive pieces of land, where people can find work and employment. By one estimate, for every one acre of redeveloped brownfields, we save 4.5 acres of open space."

— President George W. Bush, January 11, 2002

PART FIVE

PRIVATE AND PUBLIC RIGHTS AND RESPONSIBILITIES

The law locks up both man and woman
Who steal the goose from off the common,
But lets the greater felon loose
Who steals the common from the goose.

— Old English quatrain

I was always taught as I was growing up that democracy is not something you believe in, not something you hang your hat on. Democracy is something you do.

— Abbie Hoffman, closing argument to jury, in
Commonwealth v. Hoffman, et al.,
Amherst, Mass 1988

Nobody made a greater mistake than he who did nothing because he could only do a little.

— Edmund Burke

Chapter 22

PUBLIC ENVIRONMENTAL RIGHTS AND DUTIES: THE PUBLIC TRUST DOCTRINE

A. *Beyond Direct Threats to Human Health and Property: The Modern Rediscovery of the Public Trust Doctrine*

B. *Applying the Modern Public Trust Doctrine*

C. *Environmental Rights from Constitutions and Statutes*

By the law of nature, these things are common to mankind: the air, running water, the sea, and consequently the shores of the sea....

— Institutes of Emperor Justinian, 2.1.1 (A.D. 529)

So neither can the king intrude upon the common property, thus understood, and appropriate it to himself or to the fiscal purposes of the nation.... The enjoyment of it is a natural right which cannot be infringed or taken away, unless by arbitrary power, and that, in theory at least, [can]not exist in a free government....

— Arnold v. Mundy, 6 N.J.L. 1, 87–88 (1821)

We do not inherit the earth from our fathers. We borrow it from our children.

— David Brower

A. BEYOND DIRECT THREATS TO HUMAN HEALTH AND PROPERTY: THE MODERN REDISCOVERY OF THE PUBLIC TRUST DOCTRINE

The resurrection of the public trust doctrine from relative obscurity is environmental law's unique contribution to the modern legal system, and the trust's continuing background presence is felt throughout the field.

At its heart, environmental law has come to incorporate a set of principles representing and accounting for present and future natural and civic values that lie beyond the daily marketplace and current events. It is perhaps only in environmental law that the legal system directly incorporates measures of long-term societal needs into today's operative norms and doctrinal provisions. The "sustainable development" principle of domestic and global natural resources management is a prime example. The public trust doctrine embodies this perspective and goes further, incorporating societal protections that go beyond strict human utility.

Most environmental cases, of course, are built upon the ultimate social utility of environmental protection. By keeping Allied's Kepone wastes, noted in Chapter 2, out of the river and bay, human and economic health are protected along with natural resources.[1] We protect birds from pesticides in part to protect human genetics. We protect stratospheric ozone and the carbon dioxide functions of global forests on behalf of long-term human and planetary health. But the public trust doctrine, drawing upon ancient roots of heritage legacy principles reflecting themes of continuing intergenerational equity, goes farther.

As noted in Chapter 1, public trust concepts can be found in the protection of endangered species, prevention of significant deterioration (PSD) in air quality far cleaner than necessary for health, restoration of mined lands despite low locational values, safeguards for groundwater purity even where no one uses the groundwater resource, and so on.

Here are some further illustrations of public trust concepts.

The Methuselah Tree. What is lost when an ancient forest is gone, or an ancient tree? A few years ago a geography professor set off on a summer grant project to find the oldest living thing on the face of the earth. What would that be? Not a great whale, not a giant redwood. It seems the oldest living things on earth are bristle-cone pine trees. Bristle-cone pines are not majestic monoliths but rather small scraggly survivors, more than 3000 years old, twisted and gnarled with the winds of time, surviving ice storms, droughts, and wildfires, clinging to a ridge in a federal forest reserve in a remote region of eastern Nevada.

The professor, however, did not have a modern microscopic coring tool for dating trees; the only method he had available to determine a tree's age was to cut it down and count the cross-section rings. So with the approval of the government official in charge of the forest, he found the oldest living thing on the face of the earth and dated it the only way he knew. It was 4990 years old. To be certain he had found the real Methuselah tree, moreover, he also killed and dated the next two oldest living things.

What did we lose by the death of those bristle-cone pine trees? Since the next-oldest one was automatically made the oldest living thing by the professor's actions, what difference did it make? But if you feel something move in the pit of your stomach from the death of the Methuselah tree, it may be the public trust doctrine. If the matter could have been brought to a court in time, seeking to stop the cutting, you would have to find some cause of action in order for an injunction to issue. Analytically the cause of action would probably be, expressly or implicitly, the legal theory of public trust.

Selling Lake Michigan. The classic public trust case in American law arose from a scandalous case of political corruption in the 1890s, when the Illinois state legislature was induced by railroad lawyers to pass a statute selling two square miles of submerged lands along the Chicago waterfront, at a very cheap price, to the Illinois Central

---

1. Nutrient runoffs from chicken-processing plants in the Chesapeake Bay watershed and hog wastes in North Carolina rivers, for instance, have triggered outbreaks of the toxic *Pfisteria piscicida* organism in coastal waters that not only caused the death of hundreds of thousands of fish but also caused human skin lesions and illness. See Environmental Law at Maryland, Summer 1997, at 1.

Railroad Company, which planned to fill and develop the submerged lands for a multi-million dollar profit. When a subsequent (presumably less corrupt) legislature tried to rescind the statute, the state faced the prospect of paying huge compensation awards to get the waterfront back. In Illinois Central R.R. v. Illinois,[2] the Supreme Court had to figure out how to avoid the takings claim without spreading on the public record the unseemly story of how the state had made the deal in the first place. The Court seized upon the unwritten ancient public trust doctrine: The state never had unbridled authority to give away such trust lands in the first place, the Court explained, so the statutory transfer was simply void. Lake Michigan remained a public trust resource owned by all.

The Idaho Shoshone County River Oil-Sheet Case. Can a state require a million-dollar restoration effort to remove a slight oil sheen from a river, if there is no proof and no likelihood of any harm to humans or the ecosystem? In the mid 1990s, it was discovered that a small amount of petroleum was leaching underground from an old railroad switching area into Idaho's St. Joe River, causing a rainbow effect on the downstream water surface. The railroad's corporate successors argued that the sheen did not come from a regulatable "point source" and was totally insignificant. What did it matter that viewed from one angle the water looked a little different, if no other invidious effects could be shown?[3] The State of Idaho, however, prepared a lawsuit "as the trustee of the natural resources within the state...entrusted with the management and protection of said natural resources...and as *parens patriae* [likewise a trusteeship sounding in public trust] on behalf of all residents of the state," alleging injury to, among other things, "ecological" and "aesthetic qualities." Faced with the public trust claim for broad affirmative injunctive relief as well as natural resource damages, the companies ultimately settled, agreeing to fund and carry out a long-term treatment protocol under state oversight.

Natural Resources Damages: *Steuart Transportation*. The public trust doctrine has frequently surfaced, expressly or implicitly, in the blossoming area of natural resources damages. In one typical case, a badly maintained oil barge foundered while being towed, dumping thousands of gallons of crude oil into coastal marshes of the Chesapeake Bay, killing or injuring wildlife and habitat:

> Approximately 30,000 migratory birds allegedly were destroyed as a result of the oil spill.... Steuart contends that...to recover money damages for the loss of property one must establish an ownership interest, and...neither the state nor the federal Government has an ownership interest in migratory waterfowl.... The Commonwealth and the United States, on the other hand, maintain...their right to recover for the loss of migratory waterfowl...upon the sovereign right to protect the public interest in preserving wildlife resources. This sovereign right derives from...the public trust doctrine and the doctrine of parens patriae....

---

2. 146 U.S. 387 (1892). A virtually identical more recent case is Lake Michigan Fed'n v. U.S. Army Corps of Eng'rs, 742 F. Supp. 441 (N.D. Ill. 1990).

3. In fact it seems to the authors, who are troutfishers, that entomologists could have been found to demonstrate a lethal effect on subimago stages of certain aquatic insect species, which would impact the river's food chain.

This Court is of the opinion that both of these doctrines are viable and support the State and the Federal claims for the waterfowl.... Under the public trust doctrine, the State of Virginia and the United States have the right and the duty to protect and preserve the public's interest in natural wildlife resources. Such right does not derive from ownership of the resources but from a duty owing to the people.... In re Steuart Transp. Co., Owner of the Tank Barge STC-101, 495 F. Supp. 38, 40 (E.D. Va. 1980).

Similar natural resources damages were claimed on common law public trust principles after the *Exxon-Valdez* oil spill in Alaska, and in a host of cases under resource damage provisions of several federal pollution statutes.

Three Legal Public Trust Settings. Public trust law, coming from constitutional and statutory sources as well as nonstatutory judicial holdings,[4] is discernable in a wide range of legal settings but can be roughly categorized into three basic legal formats.

- One category might be called "resource-defense" or "prevention-of-derogation" issues, often seen in the water pollution setting but including land-based cases like the bristlecone pines, where human actors threaten to pollute or destroy trust assets.[5]

- A second public trust setting is the "alienation" situation, restricting government attempts to sell public trust assets to a private party, which was the basis of the Illinois Central Chicago waterfront case.[6]

- A third category, "diversion" cases, limits government agency attempts to divert ownership and use of public trust assets from one public use like parkland to other more exploitive uses like construction sites, dumps, or parking lots.[7]

What the public trust doctrine contributes to each setting is an abstract societal interest framed in present and future legacy terms. Its extent is particularly significant, however, in its unique representation of the social and cultural values of natural conditions, going beyond traditional definitions of harm.

The trust's primary remedies are equitable — prohibitory or affirmative restoration injunctions and other orders — but can include monetary damages for remediation or natural resources losses as well.

Joseph L. Sax, Defending the Environment: A Strategy for Citizen Action
163–165 (1970)

Long ago there developed in the law of the Roman Empire a legal theory known as the "doctrine of the public trust." It was founded upon the very sensible idea that certain common

---

4. See Cal. Const. art. XV §§2, 3; Mass. Const. art. IX §1; Pa. Const. art. I §27; Mass. Gen. Laws ch. 214 §7A; Mich. Comp. Laws §§691-1201; Tenn. Code Ann. §70.324.

5. See, e.g., Tenn. Code Ann. §§70.324 et seq.; beyond water resources, see the redwood cases, invoking the trust to protect redwoods against erosion and destruction. Sierra Club v. Department of Interior, 376 F. Supp. 90 (N.D. Cal. 1974); Sierra Club v. Department of Interior, 398 F. Supp. 284 (N.D. Cal. 1975).

6. The classic example of restricted alienability of public trust assets is the *Illinois Central* case noted later in this chapter.

7. An example of the diversion issue is the *Paepke* case reviewing a diversion in Chicago's Washington Park. This case is discussed in Part B of this chapter.

Lying in a grey area between the alienation and diversion categories are cases such as Vermont v. Central Vt. Ry., 571 A.2d 1128 (Vt. 1989), where the state supreme court held that a public utility railroad company's grant of lands on the shores of Lake Champlain would be restricted to public trust uses, where the company, which held title, wanted to undertake resort and commercial development of the lands.

properties, such as rivers, the seashore, and the air, were held by government in trusteeship for the free and unimpeded use of the general public. Our contemporary concerns about "the environment" bear a very close conceptual relationship to this venerable legal doctrine.

Under the Roman law, perpetual use of common properties "was dedicated to the public." As one scholar, R. W. Lee, noted: "In general the shore was not owned by individuals. One test suggests that it was the property of the Roman people. More often it is regarded as owned by no one, the public having undefined rights of use and enjoyment."[8] Similarly in England, according to R. S. Hall, the law developed that "the ownership of the shore, as between the public and the King, has been settled in favor of the King: but…this ownership is, and had been immemorially, liable to certain general rights of egress and regress, for fishing, trading, and other uses claimed and used by his subjects."

American law adopted the general idea of trusteeship but rarely applied it to any but a few sorts of public properties such as shorelands and parks. The content and purpose of the doctrine never received a careful explication, though occasionally a comment can be found in the cases to the effect that it is "inconceivable" that any person would claim a private-property interest in the navigable waters of the United States, assertable against the free and general use of the public at large. And from time to time provisions can be found, as in the Northwest Ordinance of 1787, which stated that "the navigable waters leading into the Mississippi…shall be common highways and forever free…to the citizens of the United States…."

The scattered evidence, taken together, suggests that the idea of a public trusteeship rests upon three related principles. First, that certain interests — like the air and the sea — have such importance to the citizenry as a whole that is would be unwise to make them the subject of private ownership. Second, that they partake so much of the bounty of nature, rather than of individual enterprise, that they should be made freely available to the entire citizenry without regard to economic status. And, finally, that it is a principal purpose of government to promote the interests of the general public rather than to redistribute public goods from broad public uses to restricted private benefit….

Joseph L. Sax, The Public Trust Doctrine in Natural Resource Law: Effective Judicial Intervention
68 Michigan Law Review 471, 489–502 (1970)

The most celebrated public trust case in the American law is the decision of the United States Supreme Court in Illinois Central Railroad Company v. Illinois, 146 U.S. 387 (1892)…. The Court did not actually prohibit the disposition of trust lands to private parties; its holding was much more limited. What a state may not do, the Court said, is to divest itself of authority to govern the whole of an area in which it has responsibility to exercise its police power; to grant almost the entire waterfront of a major city to a private company is, in effect, to abdicate legislative authority over navigation.

But the mere granting of property to a private owner does not ipso facto prevent the exercise of the police power, for states routinely exercise a great deal of regulatory authority over privately owned land. The Court's decision makes sense only because the Court determined that

---

8. The Latin concepts are *res communes* and *res nullius*. The former referred to such things that, while not susceptible to exclusive ownership, can be enjoyed and used by everyone (such as water, air, and light); the latter referred to things that belonged to no one, "either because they were unappropriated by anyone, such as unoccupied lands or wild animals, or things similar to *res sacrae* or *res religiosae* 'to which a religious character prevents any human right of property attaching.'" Coquillette, Mosses from an Old Manse: Another Look at Some Historic Property Cases about the Environment, 64 Cornell L. Rev. 761, 803 n. 196 (1979); Black's Law Dictionary 1304–1305, 1306 (6th ed. 1990). For more from Justinian's Institutes, see Jolowicz, Historical Introduction to the Study of Roman Law 502–503 (2d ed. 1954). [Eds.]

the states have special regulatory obligations over shorelands, obligations which are inconsistent with large-scale private ownership. The Court stated that the title under which Illinois held the navigable waters of Lake Michigan

> is different in character from that which the state holds in lands intended for sale.... It is a title held in trust for the people of the state that they may enjoy the navigation of the waters, carry on commerce over them, and have liberty of fishing therein freed from the obstruction or interference of private parties.

With this language, the Court articulated a principle that has become the central substantive thought in public trust litigation. When a state holds a resource which is available for the free use of the general public, a court will look with considerable skepticism upon *any* governmental conduct which is calculated *either* to reallocate the resource to more restricted uses or to subject public uses to the self-interest of private parties.

The Court in *Illinois Central* did not specify its reasons for adopting the position which it took, but the attitude implicit in the decision is fairly obvious.... While there may be good reason to use governmental resources to benefit some group smaller than the whole citizenry, there is usually some relatively obvious reason for the subsidy, such as a need to assist the farmer or the urban poor. In addition, there is ordinarily some plainly rational basis for the reallocative structure of any such programs — whether it be taxing the more affluent to support the poor or using the tax base of a large community to sustain programs in a smaller unit of government. Although courts are disinclined to examine these issues through a rigorous economic analysis, it seems fair to say that the foregoing observations are consistent with a general view of the function of government. Accordingly, the court's suspicions are naturally aroused when they are faced with a program which seems quite at odds with such a view of government.

In *Illinois Central*, for example, everything seems to have been backwards. There appears to have been no good reason for taxing the general public in order to support a substantial private enterprise in obtaining control of the waterfront. There was no reason to believe that private ownership would have provided incentives for needed developments, as might have been the case with land grants in remote areas of the country; and if the resource was to be maintained for traditional uses, it was unlikely that private management would have produced more efficient or attractive services to the public. Indeed, the public benefits that could have been achieved by private ownership are not easy to identify.

Although the facts of *Illinois Central* were highly unusual — and the grant in that case was particularly egregious — the case remains an important precedent. The model for judicial skepticism it built poses a set of relevant standards for current, less dramatic instances of dubious governmental conduct. For instance, a court should look skeptically at programs which infringe broad public uses in favor of narrower ones. Similarly there should be a special burden of justification on government when such results are brought into question. But *Illinois Central* also raises more far-reaching issues. For example, what are the implications for the workings of the democratic process when such programs, although ultimately found to be unjustifiable, are nonetheless promulgated through democratic institutions? Furthermore, what does the existence of those seeming imperfections in the democratic process imply about the role of the courts, which, *Illinois Central* notwithstanding, are generally reluctant to hold invalid the acts of co-equal branches of government?

The Contemporary Doctrine of the Public Trust: An Instrument for Democratization... The *Illinois Central* problem has had its most significant modern exegesis in Massachusetts. In that state, the Supreme Judicial Court has shown a clear recognition of the potential for abuse which exists whenever power over lands is given to a body which is not directly responsive to the electorate. To counteract the influence which private interest groups may have with administrative agencies and to encourage policy decisions to be made openly at the legislative level, the Massachusetts court has developed a rule that a change in the use of public lands is impermissible without a clear showing of legislative approval.

In Gould v. Greylock Reservation Commission,[9] the Supreme Judicial Court of Massachusetts took the major step in developing the doctrine applicable to changes in the use of lands dedicated to the public interest....

Mount Greylock, about which the controversy centered, is the highest summit of an isolated range which is surrounded by lands of considerably lower elevation. In 1888 a group of citizens, interested in preserving the mountain as an unspoiled natural forest, promoted the creation of an association for the purpose of laying out a public park on it. The state ultimately acquired about 9,000 acres, and the legislature enacted a statute creating the Greylock Reservation Commission and giving it certain of the powers of a park commission. By 1953 the reservation contained a camp ground, a few ski trails, a small lodge, a memorial tower, some TV and radio facilities, and a parking area and garage. In that year, the legislature enacted a statute creating an Authority to construct and operate on Mount Greylock an aerial tramway and certain other facilities, and it authorized the original commission to lease to the Authority "any portion of the Mount Greylock Reservation."

For some time the Authority was unable to obtain the financing necessary to go forward with its desire to build a ski development, but eventually it made an arrangement for the underwriting of revenue bonds. Under that arrangement the underwriters, organized as a joint venture corporation called American Resort Services, were to lease 4,000 acres of the reservation from the Commission. On that land, the management corporation was to build and manage an elaborate ski development, for which it was to receive forty percent of the net operations revenue of the enterprise....

After the arrangements had been made, but before the project went forward, five citizens of the county in which the reservation is located brought an action against both the Greylock Reservation Commission and the Tramway Authority. The plaintiffs brought the suit as beneficiaries of the public trust under which the reservation was said to be held, and they asked that the court declare invalid both the lease of the 4,000 acres of reservation land and the agreement between the Authority and the management corporation. They asked the court to examine the statutes authorizing the project, and to interpret them narrowly to prevent both the extensive development contemplated and the transfer of supervisory powers into the hands of a profit-making corporation. The case seemed an exceedingly difficult one for the plaintiffs, both because the statutes creating the Authority were phrased in extremely general terms, and because legislative grants of power to administrative agencies are usually read quite broadly. Certainly, in light of the statute, it could not be said that the legislature desired Mount Greylock to be preserved in its natural state, nor could the legislature be said to have prohibited leasing agreements with a management agency. Nonetheless, the court held both the lease and the management agreement invalid on the ground that they were in excess of the statutory grant of authority.

Gould cannot be considered merely a conventional exercise in legislative interpretation. It is, rather, a judicial response to a situation in which public powers were being used to achieve a most peculiar purpose.[10] Thus, the critical passage in the decision is that in which the court stated:

---

9. 215 N.E.2d 114 (Mass. 1966).

10. For a confirmation that the "feel" of a case is critical to its decision, the *Gould* case should be compared with People ex rel. Kurcharski v. McGovern, 245 N.E.2d 472 (Ill. 1969). In the latter case, the court upheld recreational developments in a forest preserve, despite a limited statute of authorization, apparently because the public action seemed reasonable and it was the posture of the objector which gave rise to suspicion.

The profit sharing feature and some aspects of the project itself strongly suggest a commercial enterprise. In addition to the absence of any clear or express statutory authorization of as broad a delegation of responsibility by the Authority as is given by the management agreement, we find no express grant to the Authority of power to permit use of public lands and of the Authority's borrowed funds for what seems, in part at least, a commercial venture for private profit.

In coming to this recognition, the court took note of the unusual developments which led to the project. What had begun as authorization to a public agency to construct a tramway had developed into a proposal for an elaborate ski area. Since ski resorts are popular and profitable private enterprises, it seems slightly odd in itself that a state would undertake such a development. Furthermore, the public authority had gradually turned over most of its supervisory powers to a private consortium and had been compelled by economic circumstances to agree to a bargain which heavily favored the private investment house.

It hardly seems surprising, then, that the court questioned why a state should subordinate a public park, serving a useful purpose as relatively undeveloped land, to the demands of private investors for building such a commercial facility. The court, faced with such a situation, could hardly have been expected to have treated the case as if it involved nothing but formal legal issues concerning the state's authority to change the use of a certain tract of land.

Yet the court was unwilling to invalidate an act of the legislature on the sole ground that it involved a modification of the use of public trust land. Instead, the court devised a legal rule which imposed a presumption that the state does not ordinarily intend to divert trust properties in such a manner as to lessen public uses. Such a rule would not require a court to perform the odious and judicially dangerous act of telling a legislature that it is not acting in the public interest, but rather would utilize the court's interpretive powers in accordance with an assumption that the legislature is acting to maintain broad public uses. Under the Massachusetts court rule, that assumption...is to be altered only if the legislature clearly indicates that it has a different view of the public interest....

Although such a rule may seem to be an elaborate example of judicial indirection, it is in fact directly responsive to the central problem of public trust controversies. There must be some means by which a court can keep a check on legislative grants of public lands while ensuring that historical uses may be modified to accommodate contemporary public needs and that the power to make such modifications resides in a branch of government which is responsive to public demands....

While it will seldom be true that a particular governmental act can be termed corrupt, it will often be the case that the whole of the public interest has not been adequately considered by the legislative or administrative officials whose conduct has been brought into question. In those cases, which are at the center of concern with the public trust, there is a strong, if not demonstrable, implication that the acts in question represent a response to limited and self-interested proponents of public action. It is not difficult to perceive the reason for the legislative and administrative actions which give rise to such cases, for public officials are frequently subjected to intensive representations on behalf of interests seeking official concessions to support proposed enterprises. The concessions desired by those interests are often of limited visibility to the general public so that public sentiment is not aroused; but the importance of the grants to those who seek them may lead to extraordinarily vigorous and persistent efforts. It is in these situations that public trust lands are likely to be put in jeopardy and that legislative watchfulness is likely to be at the lowest levels. To send such a case back for express legislative authority is to create through the courts an openness and visibility which is the public's principal protection against overreaching, but which is often absent in the routine political process.

Thus, the courts should intervene to provide the most appropriate climate for democratic policy making.

Gould...provides a useful illustration that it is possible for rather dubious projects to clear all the legislative and administrative hurdles which have been set up to protect the public interest....[11] More significantly, the technique which the court used to confront the basic issues suggests a fruitful mode for carrying on such litigation.

COMMENTARY & QUESTIONS

1. **The history of the public trust doctrine in the United States.** Professor Sax's article can claim the majority of credit for the active presence of the public trust doctrine in American environmental law. (It has been so often cited as the seminal work in the field that Professor Sax was recently introduced at a conference on western public interest law as "Seminal Sax" and received a standing ovation on the point.) But the public trust doctrine did exist earlier in the case law of the United States, waiting to be rediscovered (somewhat like the Refuse Act of 1899). In 1810, in the Pennsylvania case of *Carson v. Glazer*, 2 Binn. 475, the Pennsylvania court asserted the public trust doctrine to affirm that no one could own the rights to fish in a Pennsylvania river as against the public. That case is notable, moreover, not only for the fact that it used the term "trust" in the very modern sense that Sax uses it, but also that the court quite matter of factly extended the traditional trust from navigable waters and ocean waters to inland waterways with no suggestion of navigability. The New Jersey Supreme Court followed in *Arnold v. Mundy*, 6 N.J.L. 1 (1821), asserting that no one could own shell-fishing beds as against the public. Other cases prior to *Illinois Central* had established the same principle. *Martin v. Waddell*, 41 U.S. 367 (1842). Accordingly, there does not seem to be much dispute about the existence of the public trust doctrine within the body of American law. The questions that have arisen about the public trust doctrine do not deny that fact; rather, they debate the terms upon which the trust exists and applies.

---

11. [Sax notes the common problem of agency insulation and the low visibility of official decisions:] After the massive oil leakage off the Santa Barbara coast..., the governmental agency charged with protecting the public interest decided against holding public hearings prior to granting approval for a project because the agency "preferred not to stir the natives up any more than possible [sic]," Interoffice Memo from Eugene W. Standley, Staff Engineer, U.S. Dept. of the Interior, Feb. 15, 1968. When questions were raised, the agency publicly responded by saying, "we feel maximum provision has been made for the local environment and that further delay in the lease sale would not be consistent with the national interest." N.Y. Times, March 25, 1969, at 30, col. 6 (quoting from a letter from the Undersecretary of the Interior to the chairman of the board of supervisors of Santa Barbara County). But the agency privately indicated that "The 'heat' has not died down but we can keep trying to alleviate the fears of the people," id. at col. 3, and noted that pressures were being applied by the oil company whose equipment worth "millions of dollars" was being held "in anticipation."

There are a variety of other ways in which agencies minimize public participation in their deliberations. For example, the duty to hold a public hearing may technically be satisfied by holding a hearing which is "announced" to the public by posting a notice on an obscure bulletin board in a post office. Nashville I-40 Steering Comm. v. Ellington, 387 F.2d 179, 183 (6th Cir. 1967), cert. denied, 390 U.S. 921 (1968). Alternatively, a statutory hearing requirement may simply be ignored, and the argument later made that despite the omission no citizen has legal standing to challenge the agency's action. See D.C. Fed'n of Civic Ass'ns, Inc. v. Airis, 391 F.2d 478 (D.C. Cir. 1968).

[Many courts do not recognize the role of citizens,] e.g., Harrison-Halsted Community Group v. Housing & Home Fin. Agency, 310 F.2d 99, 105 (7th Cir. 1962), cert. denied, 373 U.S. 914 (1963): "The legislature, through its lawfully created agencies, rather than 'interested' citizens, is the guardian of the public needs to be served by social legislation."

2. **The public trust as trust law.** The public trust doctrine is an equitable doctrine that shares its elements with the far more commonly litigated doctrine of private trusts. In both cases, what are the elements of a trust situation? First, there must be the "thing" about which the trust is concerned: the "corpus" or "res," the defined bundle of assets owned and managed under the trust framework. Then there must be a trustee, a person or entity legally charged with responsibilities and rights. Trustees in Anglo-American law actually own the resources in terms of legal title. They accordingly have the right to manage, sell, lease, develop, and so on, the assets, but only insofar as a careful fiduciary would and could so as to protect the existence of the assets and achieve the purposes of the trust. When trustees own a parcel of land in an urban area, as in the case of a number of private or charitable trusts, they may go to an equity court and request permission to sell, lease, or develop the trust property so as to maximize the economic benefits that typically constitute the trust terms in private trusts. The terms of a trust, however, differ from trust to trust and are critically important. When a trust has been set up by the trustor or settlor, the trustees must follow the precise dictates and terms of the trust stipulations. If a trust is mandated to maximize the financial security of family members, then the management of the assets will be judged by the careful economic standards necessary to achieve that end. If the trust is set up to care for a park or an educational institution, then the primary trust standard is to maintain the character of the trust property.

While the legal title of a trust rests with the trustee, the real equitable or beneficial title to the property, enforceable in court, is held by the beneficiaries. In most trusts, the court's enforcement and oversight comes at the request of beneficiaries, any one of whom has standing to call for an accounting from the trustees, in court.

These, then, are the generic elements of a trust. Can you roughly identify how each of them is to be defined in the case of the public trust doctrine? In a public trust, who is the trustee, who are the beneficiaries, what is the corpus, and, perhaps most important, what are the terms? (The identity of the settlor probably depends upon your theological inclinations.)

The public trust's ancient lineage and essential societal role do not mean that it is uncontroversial. For instance, just as environmental conditions do not stop at international borders, note that sometimes, as in the following milestone case, the public trust doctrine does not shy away from private property boundaries.

Marks v. Whitney
Supreme Court of California, 1971
6 Cal. 3d 251, 491 P.2d 374, 98 Cal. Rptr. 790

MCCOMB, J. This is a quiet title action.... A part of Marks' property on the westerly side of Tomales Bay in Marin County is tidelands acquired under an 1874 patent issued pursuant to the Act of March 28, 1868.... A small [strip] of these tidelands adjoins almost the entire shoreline of Whitney's upland property. Marks asserted complete ownership of the tidelands and the right to fill and develop them. Whitney opposed on the ground that this would cut off his rights as a littoral owner and as a member of the public.... He requested a declaration in the decree that Marks' title was burdened with a public trust easement.... The trial court...held that Whitney had no standing to raise the public trust issue and refused to make a finding as to whether the tidelands are so burdened....

This land was patented as tidelands to Marks' predecessor in title [on] May 15, 1874...by the Governor of California "by virtue of authority in me vested" pursuant to "statutes...for the Sale and Conveyance of the Tide Lands belonging to the State by virtue of her sovereignty...."

Regardless of the issue of Whitney's standing to raise this issue the court may take judicial notice of public trust burdens in quieting title to tidelands. This matter is of great public importance, particularly in view of population pressures, demands for recreational property, and the increasing development of seashore and waterfront property....

The title of Marks in these tidelands is burdened with a public easement.... The trial court found that the portion of Marks' lands here under consideration constitutes a part of the tidelands of Tomales Bay.... Tidelands...extend from the Oregon line to Mexico and include the shores of bays and navigable streams as far up as tide water goes and until it meets the lands made swampy by the overflow and seepage of fresh water streams.... The state holds tidelands in trust for public purposes, traditionally delineated in terms of navigation, commerce and fisheries.... They are, therefore, subject to a reserved easement in the state for trust purposes.... Our opinion is that the buyer of land [via] statutes receives the title to the soil, the *jus privatum*, subject to the public right of navigation, and in subordination to the right of the state to take possession and use and improve it for that purpose, as it may deem necessary....

Public trust easements are traditionally defined in terms of navigation, commerce and fisheries. They have been held to include the right to fish, hunt, bathe, swim, to use for boating and general recreation purposes the navigable waters of the state, and to use the bottom of the navigable waters for anchoring, standing, or other purposes. The public has the same rights in and to tidelands.

The public uses to which tidelands are subject are sufficiently flexible to encompass changing public needs. In administering the trust the state is not burdened with an outmoded classification favoring one mode of utilization over another. There is a growing public recognition that one of the most important public uses of the tidelands — a use encompassed within the tidelands trust is the preservation of those lands in their natural state, so that they may serve as ecological units for scientific study, as open space, and as environments which provide food and habitat for birds and marine life, and which favorably affect the scenery and climate of the area. It is not necessary to here define precisely all the public uses which encumber tidelands....

The power of the state to control, regulate and utilize its navigable waterways and the lands lying beneath them, when acting within the terms of the trust, is absolute, except as limited by the paramount supervisory power of the federal government over navigable waters. We are not here presented with any action by the state or the federal government modifying, terminating, altering or relinquishing the *jus publicum* in these tidelands or in the navigable waters covering them. Neither sovereignty is a party to this action. This court takes judicial notice, however, that there has been no official act of either sovereignty to modify or extinguish the public trust servitude upon Marks' tidelands.... In the absence of state or federal action the court may not bar members of the public from lawfully asserting or exercising public trust rights on this privately owned tidelands.

There is absolutely no merit in Marks' contention that as the owner of the jus privatum under this patent he may fill and develop his property, whether for navigational purposes or not; nor in his contention that his past and present plan for development of these tidelands as a marina have caused the extinguishment of the public easement. Reclamation with or without prior authorization from the state does not ipso facto terminate the public trust nor render the issue moot....

The relief sought by Marks resulted in taking away from Whitney rights to which he is entitled as a member of the general public.... Members of the public have been permitted to bring an action to enforce a public right to use a beach access route, to bring an action to quiet title to private and public easements in a public beach, and to bring an action to restrain improper filling of a bay and secure a general declaration of the rights of the people to the waterways and wildlife areas of the bay. Members of the public have been allowed to defend a quiet title action by asserting the right to use a public right of way through private property. They have been allowed to assert the public trust easement for hunting, fishing and navigation in privately owned tidelands as a defense in an action to enjoin such use, and to navigate on shallow navigable waters in small boats....

Whitney had standing to raise this issue. The court could have raised this issue on its own.... Where the interest concerned is one that, as here, constitutes a public burden upon [private] land,...that servitude should be explicitly declared.

COMMENTARY & QUESTIONS

1. **The evolving public trust.** Note how the court matter-of-factly states that "the public uses to which tidelands are subject are sufficiently flexible to encompass changing public needs." The definition of public trust resources and rights is not static but evolves with changing societal concepts of what resources, uses, and values constitute such legacy commons. As constitutional jurisprudence constantly demonstrates, the definition of any significant basic doctrine capable of evolution in ongoing societal contexts is bound to be fascinating and controversial.

2. **How is the public trust a trust?** The public trust doctrine comes into the legal system as a corollary to the familiar field of private trust law. In both cases, there must be a corpus of the trust, resources or assets owned and managed under the trust framework. In Anglo-American law, trustees legally own the resources, with a right to manage, sell, lease, develop, and so on, but only insofar as a careful fiduciary would and could so as to protect the assets and achieve the purposes of the trust. The equitable owners of a trust, however, are its designated beneficiaries, for whom ultimately the trust is to be managed. The terms of a trust, however, differ from trust to trust and are critically important. The public trust as it has developed construes governments as the trustees of public commons, rights, and resources, with a duty to protect the trust in a balanced fiduciary fashion, with only a qualified right to sell, develop, or permit exploitation. The terms of the public trust thus generally reflect a presumption in favor of preservation of the natural and cultural legacy received from past generations, to be passed to the future. The beneficiaries, it then might be said, are all the citizens of the jurisdiction — of the present, the future, and even the past.

3. **Public trust and private property.** Do public trust interests lie latent within private property? In a number of settings the answer appears to be yes, a phenomenon explored below that raises a further range of complications.

B. APPLYING THE MODERN PUBLIC TRUST DOCTRINE

Section 1. **PUBLIC TRUST BALANCING: DIVERSION**

The following modern Illinois case, denying the environmental plaintiffs' claims, involved a proposed diversion of public parkland to a more intensive limited public use. It echoes Sax's analysis of the trust's procedural requirements but also experiments with the process of defining substantive standards.

Paepke v. Building Commission
Supreme Court of Illinois, 1970
46 Ill. 2d 330, 263 N.E.2d 11

BURT, J. Plaintiffs, who are citizens, residents, taxpayers and property owners of the city of Chicago, appeal from an order of the circuit court of Cook County dismissing their complaint by which they sought to prevent defendants, the City of Chicago, the Board of Education of Chicago, and the Chicago Park District, from implementing plans to construct school and recreational facilities in Washington Park. This court has jurisdiction on direct appeal because of the constitutional questions involved....

The Public Building Commission of Chicago, at the request of the Board of Education of the City of Chicago, has undertaken a program involving the construction, alteration, repair, renovation, and rehabilitation of public schools in the city, together with park, recreational, playground, and other related public facilities which will be leased by the Building Commission to the Board of Education, the Chicago Park District, and other governmental agencies....

A site has been designated in Washington Park for the erection of a school-park facility. The Chicago Park District proposes to convey to the Public Building Commission of Chicago for such purposes a total of 3.839 acres located in the northwest portion of the park about 250 feet from the northern boundary. On 2.586 acres of this site the building commission proposes to construct a middle school for approximately 1500 students to be leased to the Board of Education of the City of Chicago. The remaining 1.253 acres would be utilized in the construction of a gymnasium and recreational facilities which will be leased to the Chicago Park District. Construction had started on this site at the time suit was filed but had not proceeded to a point where original use of the land would no longer be possible....

It is plaintiffs' theory that the parks in question are so dedicated that they are held in public trust for use only as park or recreational grounds and that those of them who are property owners adjacent to or in the vicinity of a park dedicated by the acts of 1869 have a private property right to the continuation of the park use of which even the legislature cannot deprive them. They further contend that all plaintiffs who are citizens and residents of any area of the city have a public property right to enforce the public trust existing by reason of the dedication of the parks as aforesaid and to require that no change of park use be permitted because the legislature has not explicitly and openly so provided by statute....

Such dedication having been made by the sovereign, the agencies created by it hold the properties in trust for the uses and purposes specified and for the benefit of the public. See Illinois Central Railroad Co. v. Illinois, 146 U.S. 387 (1892); Sax, The Public Trust Doctrine in Natural Resource Law: Effective Judicial Intervention, 68 Mich. L. Rev. 471–566. [Extensive quotations from Professor Sax's article omitted.]

Have plaintiffs who are property owners adjacent to or in the vicinity of the parks...a *private* property right to continuation of the park use?... This question must be answered in the negative.

The mere dedication by the sovereign of lands to public park uses does not give property owners adjoining or in the vicinity of the park the right to have the use continue unchanged even though, when the park was established, abutting or adjoining owners were assessed for special benefits conferred....

As to the interests of plaintiffs and their standing to bring the action, the trial judge found that they had no rights sufficient to enable them to maintain the action [holding they had no public nuisance or taxpayer standing]. If the public trust doctrine is to have any meaning or vitality at all, however, the members of the public, at least taxpayers who are the beneficiaries of that trust, must have the right and standing to enforce it. To tell them that they must wait upon governmental action is often an effectual denial of the right for all time. The conclusion we have reached is in accord with decisions in other jurisdictions...wherein plaintiffs' rights...in a trust of public lands were enforced without question.

As to...whether there has been a sufficient manifestation of legislative intent to permit the diversion and reallocation contemplated by the plan proposed by defendants, it...is our conclusion [that the] legislation is sufficiently broad, comprehensive and definite to allow the diversion in use involved here.

In passing we think it appropriate to refer to the [substantive balancing] approach developed by the courts of our sister state, Wisconsin, in dealing with diversion problems.... The Supreme Court of Wisconsin [has] approved proposed diversions in the use of public trust lands under conditions which demonstrate (1) that public bodies would control use of the area in question, (2) that the area would be devoted to public purposes and open to the public, (3) the diminution of the area of original use would be small compared with the entire area, (4) that none of the public uses of the original area would be destroyed or greatly impaired and (5) that the disappointment of those wanting to use the area of new use for former purposes is negligible when compared to the greater convenience to be afforded those members of the public using the new facility. We believe that the present plans for Washington Park meet all of these tests....

In conclusion, let it be said that this court is fully aware of the fact that the issues presented in this case illustrate the classic struggle between those members of the public who would preserve our parks and open lands in their pristine purity and those charged with administrative responsibilities who, under the pressures of the changing needs of an increasingly complex society, find it necessary, in good faith and for the public good, to encroach to some extent upon lands heretofore considered inviolate to change. The resolution of this conflict in any given case is for the legislature and not the courts....

COMMENTARY & QUESTIONS

1. **The scope of the trust.** Note here in the *Paepke* case how matter-of-factly the court accepts the assumption that the public trust doctrine, developed in the oceans of the Roman Empire, applies to a public parkland, and that citizens have standing to sue. The public trust doctrine has three strategic advantages over common law remedies: (1) automatic standing (unlike public nuisance, which the lower court in *Paepke* relied on to deny standing); (2) a presumption in favor of public uses, transferring the burden of proof to the public trustee to justify a diversion or alienation; and (3) an ability to avoid sovereign immunity (in this sense at least the public trust clearly acts like a constitutional provision). In fact, there has been little serious argument in the public trust cases over the past decades about whether the public trust doctrine can appropriately be applied to dedicated parklands. The fundamental idea of a park, it appears, is a

long-term special management relationship between land, people, and government. (This may help to explain why Professor Sax's public trust scholarship moved quite naturally into an extensive study of the meaning of parks and wilderness in the twentieth century. See J. Sax, Mountains without Handrails (1981).) What is a "park"? The United States invented the idea of national parks, but there is a continuing debate about what they mean. If the public trust doctrine applies to "parks," does it apply to state or federal forests? Is the concept of "dedication," in some terms, implied or express, the distinguishing factor?

2. **The *Paepke* court's balancing process: a substantive, not merely a procedural standard?** Is the *Paepke* court's holding based on the Wisconsin (substantive) or the Massachusetts (procedural) trust analysis? If, based on Professor Sax's description of the Massachusetts cases, the public trust balance is merely procedural, and all a development-minded legislature would have to do to override the trust would be to pass exceedingly specific authorization for a favored project. (In *Paepke*, in contrast to Sax's prescription, the court did not even require specific authorization: "The legislation is sufficiently broad, comprehensive and definite to allow the diversion.") The *Paepke* case implies, however, that governments also have substantive trusteeship duties as well as procedural requirements — if the court had found that the Wisconsin trust tests were violated, the construction would have been enjoined despite its statutory authorization.

Under the Wisconsin tests, proposed alterations of trust resources will apparently be tested by scrutiny of the actual balance struck between trust obligations and values on one hand and economic or other legislative development motives on the other. The public trust's long-term legacy value is presumed to be primary. Departures from the trust apparently bear the substantive burden of persuasion. When the government is acting as a trustee, it comes before the equity court as a fiduciary subject to special scrutiny.[12] Although courts review the acts of other branches of government deferentially, equity precedents for trust accountings from public officials, as in charitable trusts, argue for less deference.

The standards applied by the *Paepke* court, and the process by which it applied them, have the ring of good common sense. The court recognizes that parklands are important public trust resources and takes seriously, it seems, its role of determining whether the diversion ordered by the governmental process will be permitted to chop a piece out of Washington Park. What do you think of the Wisconsin standards and the way the *Paepke* court applied them to the case? Take the five tests one by one and ask yourself whether they sufficiently capture the protective ideas of the public trust. Is there anything missing that could be added as a litigable standard in *Paepke*?

Why was the city of Chicago diverting this section of parkland to its school department's use? Is this the only place in this area of Chicago where the school board could

---

12. See People ex rel. Scott v. Chicago Park Dist., 360 N.E.2d 773 (Ill. 1977). The Illinois legislature wanted to convey 194.6 acres of submerged lands under Lake Michigan to U.S. Steel — remarkably like the circumstances of *Illinois Central*. Despite a legislative assertion in the bill that the conveyance would result in "the conversion of otherwise useless and unproductive submerged land into an important commercial development to the benefit of the people of the State of Illinois," the court wasn't biting. "The self-serving recitation of a public purpose within a legislative enactment is not conclusive of the existence of such purpose." 360 N.E.2d at 781.

build a new school and facilities? Or is it rather an economic tradeoff? Presumably, since they have the power of eminent domain, the school board and city authorities could take 3.8 acres anywhere in this part of the city. The only problem is cost, because it would surely cost a great deal more to take private property than to grab public property for free. But in every case that motive — saving cash — will result in diversion or destruction of public trust resources. In the *Overton Park* case, analyzed in Chapter 7, the Supreme Court of the United States interpreted a statutory formulation by which the Congress, faced with the same dilemma of automatic tradeoffs, declared that no parkland shall be taken for a federal-aid highway unless there is "no feasible and prudent alternative." Professor Sax clearly would not object to that standard.

For another formulation of the balance, see Payne v. Kassab, 312 A.2d 86, 94 (Pa. Commw. Ct. 1973). The *Payne* court, citing no precedent, asserted that a change in use of public trust parkland must meet three standards: (1) compliance with applicable statutes and regulations, (2) a reasonable effort to minimize environmental "incursions" resulting from the change in use, and (3) benefits must outweigh any resulting harms. The third test is clearly the key to determining whether there will be a meaningful trust balance or a mere conclusory bureaucratic write-off: Will harms be weighed in terms of long-term intangible trust values, or market dollars? Will project benefits be accounted realistically, or in the promoters' hyperbolic terms? Will alternatives be scrupulously weighed against the proposal? Only with a balance weighing the full range of societal legacy values will the sensitive principles of the trust be honored.

And note that the terms of the trust balance, weighing how much, if any, modification is permissible, may be quite different in the three different trust settings of resource derogation, alienation, and diversion.

3. **A diversity of values: environmental justice tradeoffs?** If the City of Chicago was merely trying to save a few dollars and could just as well have condemned private land near the park for its school, that surely should be weighed against the city's proposal. But should the court also consider whether particular proposed alternative locations would disrupt stable, low-income, minority neighborhoods?

Section 2. **PUBLIC TRUST PROTECTIONS AGAINST DEROGATION**

Or what if protection of the public trust resource imposes heavy burdens and expenses on millions of citizens, rich and poor, in a major American city?

National Audubon Society v. Superior Court of Alpine County (*Mono Lake*)
Supreme Court of California, 1983
33 Cal. 3d 419, 658 P.2d 709, 189 Cal. Rptr. 346

[The City of Los Angeles, located in its dry coastal enclave on the southern California coast, has 3 million inhabitants, and continues to grow by over 5% each year. To assure that water supplies critical to its survival and growth would remain available, city officials thought that they had locked up sufficient appropriated/contract water rights in the Sierra Nevada Mountains[13] to last

---

13. The bitter battles over those water rights formed part of the political backdrop for Roman Polanski's movie *Chinatown*.

FIGURE 22-1

Views of Mono Lake; top photograph shows the setting and tufa spires rising from the lake bed. Bottom photograph shows land bridge to Negit Island created by falling water levels in 1979 — because of feeder stream diversions to Los Angeles — allowing invading predators to cross over and destroy the island's nesting population of 38,000 California gulls, three-fourths of the gull's total population in the state.

well into the twenty-first century. Then, using the public trust doctrine, plaintiff environmentalists filed a lawsuit against Los Angeles's water diversions. The case eventually came to the California Supreme Court on a federal trial judge's request for clarification of the state's public trust doctrine.]

BROUSSARD, J.... Mono Lake, the second largest lake in California, sits at the base of the Sierra Nevada escarpment near the eastern entrance to Yosemite National Park. The lake is saline; it contains no fish but supports a large population of brine shrimp which feed vast numbers of nesting and migratory birds. Islands in the lake protect a large breeding colony of California gulls, and the lake itself serves as a haven on the migration route for thousands of Northern Phalarope, Wilson's Phalarope, and Eared Grebe. Towers and spires of tufa on the north and south shores are matters of geological interest and a tourist attraction.

Although Mono Lake receives some water from rain and snow on the lake surface, historically most of its supply came from snowmelt in the Sierra Nevada. Five freshwater streams — Mill, Lee Vining, Walker, Parker and Rush Creeks — arise near the crest of the range and carry the annual runoff to the west shore of the lake. In 1940, however, the state Division of Water Resources granted the Department of Water and Power of the City of Los Angeles (DWP) a permit to appropriate virtually the entire flow of four of the five streams flowing into the lake. DWP promptly constructed facilities to divert about half the flow of these streams into DWP's Owens Valley aqueduct. In 1970 DWP completed a second diversion tunnel, and since that time has taken virtually the entire flow of these streams.... The ultimate effect of continued diversions is a matter of intense dispute, but there seems little doubt that both the scenic beauty and the ecological values of Mono Lake are imperiled....

The case brings together for the first time two systems of legal thought; the appropriative water rights system which since the days of the gold rush has dominated California water law, and the public trust doctrine which, after evolving as a shield for the protection of tidelands, now extends its protective scope to navigable lakes. Ever since we first recognized that the public trust protects environmental and recreational values (Marks v. Whitney, 491 P.2d 374 (1971)), the two systems of legal thought have been on a collision course. Johnson, Public Trust Protection for Stream Flows and Lake Levels, 14 U.C. Davis L. Rev. 233 (1980). They meet in a unique and dramatic setting which highlights the clash of values. Mono Lake is a scenic and ecological treasure of national significance, imperiled by continued diversions of water; yet, the need of Los Angeles for water is apparent, its reliance on rights granted by the board evident, the cost of curtailing diversions substantial.

Attempting to integrate the teachings and values of both the public trust and the appropriative water rights system, we have arrived at certain conclusions which we briefly summarize here. In our opinion, the core of the public trust doctrine is the state's authority as sovereign to exercise a continuous supervision and control over the navigable waters of the state and the lands underlying those waters. This authority applies to the waters tributary to Mono Lake and bars DWP or any other party from claiming a vested right to divert waters once it becomes clear that such diversions harm the interests protected by the public trust. The corollary rule which evolved in tideland and lakeshore cases barring conveyance of rights free of the trust except to serve trust purposes cannot, however, apply without modification to flowing waters. The prosperity and habitability of much of this state requires the diversion of great quantities of water from its streams for purposes unconnected to any navigation, commerce, fishing recreation, or ecological use relating to the source stream. The state must have the power to grant nonvested usufructuary rights to appropriate water even if diversions harm public trust uses. Approval of such diversion without considering public trust values, however, may result in needless destruction of those values. Accordingly, we believe that before state courts and agencies approve water diversions they should consider the effect of such diversions upon interests protected by the public trust, and attempt, so far as feasible, to avoid or minimize any harm to those interests....

DWP expects that its future diversions of about 100,000 acre-feet per year will lower the lake's surface level another 43 feet and reduce its surface area by about 22 square miles over the next 80 to 100 years, at which point the lake will gradually approach environmental equilibrium (the point at which inflow from precipitation, groundwater and nondiverted tributaries equals outflow by evaporation and other means). At this point, according to DWP, the lake will stabilize at a level 6,330 feet above the sea's, with a surface area of approximately 38 square miles. Thus, by DWP's own estimates, unabated diversions will ultimately produce a lake that is about 56 percent smaller on the surface and 42 percent shallower than its natural size.

Plaintiffs consider these projections unrealistically optimistic. They allege that, 50 years hence, the lake will be at least 50 feet shallower than it now is, and hold less than 20 percent of its natural volume. Further, plaintiffs fear that "the lake will not stabilize at this level", but "may continue to reduce in size until it is dried up." Moreover, unlike DWP, plaintiffs believe that the lake's gradual recession indirectly causes a host of adverse environmental impacts. Many of these alleged impacts are related to an increase in the lake's salinity, caused by the decrease in its water volume.

As noted above, Mono Lake has no outlets. The lake loses water only by evaporation and seepage. Natural salts do not evaporate with water, but are left behind. Prior to commencement of the DWP diversions, this naturally rising salinity was balanced by a constant and substantial supply of fresh water from the tributaries. Now, however, DWP diverts most of the fresh water inflow. The resultant imbalance between inflow and outflow not only diminishes the lake's size, but also drastically increases its salinity....

Plaintiffs predict that the lake's steadily increasing salinity, if unchecked, will wreck havoc throughout the local food chain. They contend that the lake's algae, and the brine shrimp and brine flies that feed on it, cannot survive the projected salinity increase. To support this assertion, plaintiffs point to a 50 percent reduction in the shrimp hatch for the spring of 1980 and a startling 95 percent reduction for the spring of 1981. These reductions affirm experimental evidence indicating that brine shrimp populations diminish as the salinity of the water surrounding them increases. DWP admits these substantial reductions, but blames them on factors other than salinity.

DWP's diversions also present several threats to the millions of local and migratory birds using the lake. First, since many species of birds feed on the lake's brine shrimp, any reduction in shrimp population allegedly caused by rising salinity endangers a major avian food source. The Task Force Report considered it "unlikely that any of Mono Lake's major bird species...will persist at the lake if populations of invertebrates disappear."...

The California gull is especially endangered, both by the increase in salinity and by loss of nesting sites. Ninety-five percent of this state's gull population and 25 percent of the total species population nests at the lake. Most of the gulls nest on islands in the lake. As the lake recedes, land between the shore and some of the islands has been exposed, offering such predators as the coyote easy access to the gull nests and chicks. In 1979, coyotes reached Negit Island, once the most popular nesting site, and the number of gull nests at the lake declined sharply. In 1981, 95 percent of the hatched chicks did not survive to maturity. Plaintiffs blame this decline and alarming mortality rate on the predator access created by the land bridges; DWP suggest numerous other causes, such as increased ambient temperatures and human activities, and claims that the joining of some islands with the mainlands is offset by the emergence of new islands due to the lake's recession.

Plaintiffs allege that DWP's diversions adversely affect the human species and its activities as well. First, as the lake recedes, it has exposed more than 18,000 acres of lake bed composed of very fine silt which, once dry, easily becomes airborne in winds. This silt contains a high concentration of alkali and other minerals that irritate the mucous membranes and respiratory systems of humans and other animals. While the precise extent of this threat to the public health has yet to be determined, such threat as exists can be expected to increase with the exposure of additional lake bed. DWP, however, claims that its diversions neither affect the air quality in Mono Basin nor present a hazard to human health.

Furthermore, the lake's recession obviously diminishes its value as an economic, recreational, and scenic resource. Of course, there will be less lake to use and enjoy. The declining shrimp hatch depresses a local shrimping industry. The rings of dry lake bed are difficult to traverse on foot, and thus impair human access to the lake, and reduce the lake's substantial scenic value. Mono Lake has long been treasured as a unique scenic, recreational and scientific resource, but continued diversions threaten to turn it into a desert wasteland like the dry bed of Owens Lake.

[The federal court requested a ruling on an] important issue of California law: "What is the interrelationship of the public trust doctrine and the California water rights system, in the context of the right of the DPW to divert water from Mono Lake pursuant to permits and licenses issued under the California water rights system? In other words, is the public trust doctrine in this context subsumed in the California water rights system, or does it function independently of that system? Stated differently, can the plaintiffs challenge the Department's permits and licenses by arguing that those permits and licenses are limited by the public trust doctrine, or must the plaintiffs challenge the permits and licenses by arguing that the water diversions and uses authorized thereunder are not 'reasonable or beneficial' as required under the California water rights system?..."

[The State Superior] court entered summary judgment against plaintiffs. Its notice of intended ruling stated that "the California water rights system is a comprehensive and exclusive system for determining the legality of the diversions of the City of Los Angeles in the Mono Basin.... The Public Trust Doctrine does not function independently of that system. This Court concludes that as regards the right of the City of Los Angeles to divert waters in the Mono Basin that the Public Trust Doctrine is subsumed in the water rights system of the state."... We set the case for argument....

The Public Trust Doctrine in California... "By the law of nature these things are common to mankind — the air, running water, the sea and consequently the shores of the sea." (Institutes of Justinian 2.1.1.) From this origin in Roman law, the English common law evolved the concept of the public trust, under which the sovereign owns "all of its navigable waterways and the lands lying beneath them 'as trustee of a public trust for the benefit of the people.'" The State of California acquired title as trustee to such lands and waterways upon its admission to the union (see City of Berkeley v. Superior Court (1980) 26 Cal. 3d at 521 and cases there cited). From the earliest days (see Eldridge v. Cowell (1854) 4 Cal. at 87) its judicial decisions have recognized and enforced the trust obligation.

Three aspects of the public trust doctrine require consideration in this opinion: the purpose of the trust; the scope of the trust, particularly as it applies to the nonnavigable tributaries of a navigable lake; and the powers and duties of the state as trustee of the public trust....

The Purpose of the Public Trust... The objective of the public trust has evolved in tandem with the changing public perception of the values and uses of waterways. As we observed in Marks v. Whitney, public trust easements [were] traditionally defined in terms of navigation, commerce and fisheries. They have been held to include the right to fish, hunt, bathe, swim, to use for boating and general recreation purposes the navigable waters of the state, and to use the bottom of the navigable waters for anchoring, standing, or other purposes.

We went on, however, to hold that the traditional triad of uses — navigation, commerce and fishing — did not limit the public interest in the trust res. In language of special importance to the present setting, we stated that —

the public uses to which tidelands are subject are sufficiently flexible to encompass changing public needs.[14] In administering the trust the state is not burdened with an outmoded classification favoring one mode of utilization over another. There is a growing public recognition that one of the most important public uses of the tidelands—a use encompassed within the tidelands trust—is the preservation of those lands in their natural state, so that they may serve as ecological units for scientific study, as open space, and as environments which provide food and habitat for birds and marine life, and which favorably affect the scenery and climate of the area.

Mono Lake is a navigable waterway. It supports a small local industry which harvests brine shrimp for sale as fish food, which endeavor probably qualifies the lake as a "fishery" under the traditional public trust cases. The principal values plaintiffs seek to protect, however, are recreational and ecological — the scenic views of the lake and its shore, the purity of the air, and the use of the lake for nesting and feeding by birds. Under Marks v. Whitney, above, 6 Cal. 3d 251, it is clear that protection of these values is among the purposes of the public trust.

The Scope of the Public Trust... Mono Lake is, as we have said, a navigable waterway. The beds, shores and waters of the lake are without question protected by the public trust. The streams diverted by DWP, however, are not themselves navigable. Accordingly, we must address in this case a question not discussed in any recent public trust case — whether the public trust limits conduct affecting nonnavigable tributaries to navigable waterways....

The principles recognized by [our early public trust dambuilding and stream bed gold mining] decisions apply fully to a case in which diversions from a nonnavigable tributary impair the public trust in a downstream river or lake. "If the public trust doctrine applies to constrain fills which destroy navigation and other public trust uses in navigable waters, it should equally apply to constrain the extraction of water that destroys navigation and other public interests. Both actions result in the same damage to the public interest." Johnson, 14 U.C. Davis L. Rev. at 257–258.... We conclude that the public trust doctrine, as recognized and developed in California decisions, protects navigable waters from harm caused by diversion of nonnavigable tributaries.

Duties and Powers of the State as Trustee... In the following review of the authority and obligations of the state as administrator of the public trust, the dominant theme is the state's sovereign power and duty to exercise continued supervision over the trust. One consequence, of importance to this and many other cases, is that parties acquiring rights in trust property generally hold those rights subject to the trust, and can assert no vested right to use those rights in a manner harmful to the trust.

As we noted recently in City of Berkeley v. Superior Court, 26 Cal. 3d 515, the decision of the United States Supreme Court in *Illinois Central* "remains the primary authority even today,

---

14. "The public trust doctrine, like all common law principles, should not be considered fixed or static, but should be molded and extended to meet changing conditions and needs of the public it was created to benefit." Neptune City v. Avon-by-the-Sea, 294 A.2d 47, 54 (N.J. 1972).

almost nine decades after it was decided." The legislature, it held, did not have the power to convey the entire city waterfront free of trust, thus barring all future legislatures from protecting the public interest. The opinion declares that:

> A grant of all the lands under the navigable waters of a State has never been adjudged to be within the legislative power; and any attempted grant of the kind would be held, if not absolutely void on its face, as subject to revocation. The State can no more abdicate its trust over property in which the whole people are interested, like navigable waters and soils under them...than it can abdicate its police powers in the administration of government and the preservation of the peace. In the administration of government the use of such powers may for a limited period be delegated to a municipality or other body, but there always remains with the State the right to revoke those powers and exercise them in a more direct manner, and one more conformable to its wishes. So with trusts connected with public property, or property of a special character, like lands under navigable waterways, they cannot be placed entirely beyond the direction and control of the State." *Illinois Central*, 146 U.S. at 453–454.

In summary, the foregoing cases amply demonstrate the continuing power of the state as administrator of the public trust, a power which extends to the revocation of previously granted right or to the enforcement of the trust against lands long thought free of the trust. Except for those rare instances in which a grantee may acquire a right to use former trust property free of trust restrictions, the grantee holds subject to the trust, and while he may assert a vested right to the servient estate (the right of use subject to the trust) and to any improvements he erects, he can claim no vested right to bar recognition of the trust or state action to carry out its purposes.

Since the public trust doctrine does not prevent the state from choosing between trust uses, the Attorney General of California, seeking to maximize state power under the trust, argues for a broad concept of trust uses. In his view, "trust uses" encompass all public uses, so that in practical effect the doctrine would impose no restrictions on the state's ability to allocate trust property. We know of no authority which supports this view of the public trust, except perhaps the dissenting opinion in *Illinois Central*. Most decisions and commentators assume that "trust uses" relate to uses and activities in the vicinity of the lake, stream, or tidal reach at issue.... The tideland cases make this point clear: after *City of Berkeley*, no one could contend that the state could grant tidelands free of the trust merely because the grant served some public purpose, such as increasing tax revenues, or because the grantee might put the property to a commercial use....

Thus, the public trust is more than an affirmation of state power to use public property for public purposes. It is an affirmation of the duty of the state to protect the people's common heritage of streams, lakes, marshlands and tidelands, surrendering that right of protection only in rare cases when the abandonment of that right is consistent with the purposes of the trust....

The Relationship Between the Public Trust Doctrine and the California Water Rights System...
As we have seen, the public trust doctrine and the appropriative water rights system administered by the Water Board developed independently of each other. Each developed comprehensive rules and principles which, if applied to the full extent of their scope, would occupy the field of allocation of stream waters to the exclusion of any competing system of legal thought. Plaintiffs, for example, argue that the public trust is antecedent to and thus limits all appropriative water rights, an argument which implies that most appropriative water rights in California were acquired and are presently being used unlawfully. Defendant DWP, on the other hand, argues that the public trust doctrine as to stream waters has been "subsumed" into the appropriative water rights system and, absorbed by that body of law, quietly disappeared:

according to DWP, the recipient of a board license enjoys a vested right in perpetuity to take water without concern for the consequences to the trust.

We are unable to accept either position. In our opinion, both the public trust doctrine and the water rights system embody important precepts which make the law more responsive to the diverse needs and interests involved in the planning and allocation of water resources. To embrace one system of thought and reject the other would lead to an unbalanced structure, one which would either decry as a breach of trust appropriations essential to the economic development of this state, or deny any duty to protect or even consider the values promoted by the public trust. Therefore, seeking an accommodation which will make use of the pertinent principles of both the public trust doctrine and the appropriative water rights system, and drawing upon the history of the public trust and the water rights system, the body of judicial precedent, and the views of expert commentators, we reach the following conclusions:

a. The state as sovereign retains continuing supervisory control over its navigable waters and the lands beneath those waters. This principle, fundamental to the concept of the public trust, applies to rights in flowing waters as well as to rights in tidelands and lakeshores; it prevents any party from acquiring a vested right to appropriate water in a manner harmful to the interests protected by the public trust.

b. As a matter of current and historical necessity, the legislature, acting directly or through an authorized agency such as the Water Board, has the power to grant usufructuary licenses that will permit an appropriator to take water from flowing streams and use that water in a distant part of the state, even though this taking does not promote, and may unavoidably harm, the trust uses at the source stream. The population and economy of this state depend upon the appropriation of vast quantities of water for uses unrelated to in-stream trust values. California's constitution, its statutes, decisions, and commentators all emphasize the need to make efficient use of California's limited water resources: all recognize, at least implicitly, that efficient use requires diverting water from in-stream uses. Now that the economy and population centers of this state have developed in reliance upon appropriated water, it would be disingenuous to hold that such appropriations are and have always been improper to the extent that they harm public trust uses, and can be justified only upon theories of reliance or estoppel.

c. The state has an affirmative duty to take the public trust into account in the planning and allocation of water resources, and to protect public trust uses whenever feasible. Just as the history of this state shows that appropriation may be necessary for efficient use of water despite unavoidable harm to public trust values, it demonstrates that an appropriative water rights system administered without consideration of the public trust may cause unnecessary and unjustified harm to trust interests. As a matter of practical necessity the state may have to approve appropriations despite foreseeable harm to public trust uses. In so doing, however, the state must bear in mind its duty as trustee to consider the effect of the taking on the public trust (see United Plainsmen v. State Water Cons. Comm'n, 247 N.W.2d 457, 462–463 (N.D. 1976)), and to preserve, so far as consistent with the public interest, the uses protected by the trust.

Once the state has approved an appropriation, the public trust imposes a duty of continuing supervision over the taking and use of the appropriated water. In exercising its sovereign power to allocate water resources in the public interest, the state is not confined by past allocation decisions which may be incorrect in light of current knowledge or inconsistent with current needs.

The state accordingly has the power to reconsider allocation decisions even though those decisions were made after due consideration of their effect on the public trust. The case for reconsidering a particular decision, however, is even stronger when that decision failed to weigh and consider public trust uses. In the case before us, the salient fact is that no responsible body has ever determined the impact of diverting the entire flow of the Mono Lake tributaries into the Los Angeles Aqueduct. This is not a case in which the Legislature, the Water Board, or any judicial body has determined that the needs of Los Angeles outweigh the needs of the Mono Basin, that the benefit gained is worth the price. Neither has any responsible body determined whether some lesser taking would better balance the diverse interests. Instead DWP acquired rights to the entire flow in 1940 from a water board which believed it lacked both the power and the duty to protect the Mono Lake environment, and continues to exercise those rights in apparent disregard for the resulting damage to the scenery, ecology, and human uses of Mono Lake.

It is clear that some responsible body ought to reconsider the allocation of the waters of the Mono Basin. No vested rights bar such reconsideration. We recognize the substantial concerns voiced by Los Angeles — the city's need for water, its reliance upon the 1940 board decision, the cost both in terms of money and environmental impact of obtaining water elsewhere. Such concerns must enter into any allocation decision. We hold only that they do not preclude a reconsideration and reallocation which also takes into account the impact of water diversion on the Mono Lake environment....

The federal court inquired first of the interrelationship between the public trust doctrine and the California water rights system, asking whether the "public trust doctrine in this context [is] subsumed in the California water rights system, or...function[s] independently of that system?" Our answer is "neither." The public trust doctrine and the appropriative water rights system are parts of an integrated system of water law. The public trust doctrine serves the function in that integrated system of preserving the continuing sovereign power of the state to protect public trust uses, a power which precludes anyone from acquiring a vested right to harm the public trust, and imposes a continuing duty on the state to take such uses into account in allocating water resources.

Restating its question, the federal court asked: "Can the plaintiffs challenge the Department's permits and licenses by arguing that those permits and licenses are limited by the public trust doctrine, or must the plaintiffs [argue] that the water diversions and uses authorized thereunder are not 'reasonable or beneficial' as required under the California water rights system?" We reply that plaintiffs can rely on the public trust doctrine in seeking reconsideration of the allocation of the waters of the Mono Basin....

This opinion is but one step in the eventual resolution of the Mono Lake controversy. We do not dictate any particular allocation of water. Our objective is to resolve a legal conundrum in which two competing systems of thought — the public trust doctrine and the appropriative water rights system — existed independently of each other, espousing principles which seemingly suggested opposite results. We hope by integrating these two doctrines to clear away the legal barriers which have so far prevented either the Water Board or the courts from taking a new and objective look at the water resources of the Mono Basin. The human and environmental uses of Mono Lake — uses protected by the public trust doctrine — deserve to be taken into account. Such uses should not be destroyed because the state mistakenly thought itself powerless to protect them.

COMMENTARY & QUESTIONS

1. **Scope of the public trust doctrine.** Just what is the public trust resource that is being protected in *Mono Lake*? It clearly has not much to do with navigability. Is it the lake itself that is the public trust asset? If so, is it the lake in its original form, as it is today, or

at some intermediate point? Is it the economic use of the water, based on harvesting brine shrimp? Is it the brine shrimp themselves? The California gulls?

Mono Lake may stand for the proposition that the public trust doctrine is capable of reaching out and encompassing the ecological values of an entire functioning ecosystem. Does this mean all ecosystems, or just those ecosystems fortunate enough to inhabit a photogenic environment?

Note something else striking about *Mono Lake*. The decision apparently applies to *private* rights. True, the water rights to the various streams flowing into Mono Lake are owned by the government of Los Angeles, but it owns them by purchase water rights in the same way that those rights would be obtained and held by a private citizen. Does the public trust lie latent within private property rights? Marks v. Whitney, excerpted above and cited in the main opinion, held precisely that there was an inherent public right in privately owned submerged lands, so that the private property owner was completely restricted unless the government gave permission to fill in the submerged lands and make them economically useful. What if you owned the oldest burr oak tree in Illinois, or the house in which Benjamin Franklin was born, or the land on which the state's oldest church was located, and in each case you wanted to bulldoze the property to make a profitable parking lot? Might the public trust doctrine apply with full force and litigibility to your case as well? What standards would apply?

2. **The terms of the trust balance.** Note that in this case, the state's Attorney General argued against the applicability of the public trust doctrine. Why? Ultimately the court defined a public trust role for the state government that held it to a new and higher standard of decisionmaking. The state could no longer merely be a mechanism of majoritarian politics; it apparently now had enforceable long-term fiduciary obligations to an indefinite constituency including generations unborn.

After the decision in *Mono Lake*, what are the standards by which the public trust balance will be struck to determine how much of Los Angeles's private water rights and how much of Mono Lake's public trust assets will be legally protected? A serious apples and oranges problem presents itself. How can two such disparate public interests be balanced? It is notable, however, that the courts have declared that the public trust doctrine cannot be abrogated, which apparently asserts that the trust obligations, whatever they are, must be substantively fulfilled. After *Mono Lake*, if you were an attorney for the Los Angeles Water Board or, on the other hand, for the environmental coalition, how would you go about preparing for subsequent proceedings in state court to determine what actually would happen to Mono Lake? To what extent in that balance does the lack of prior notice of the trust's existence to owners of the water rights matter to you? Are public trust rights necessarily superior to private property rights, if indeed they conflict? If the trust balance results in a restriction of private water rights, do the losers have a right to compensation for an unconstitutional "taking"? See the next chapter on this.

3. **A reprise on *Mono Lake*.** What further developments in California public trust law followed the decision in *Mono Lake*? The destiny of Mono Lake remains in doubt. The years initially following the California Supreme Court decision were unusually wet and

the level of Mono Lake actually rose.[15] Then there was an extended drought. The court had sent the case back to the Water Board to determine whether and to what extent Los Angeles should cut back its diversions from the Mono Lake tributaries in order to protect public trust values. Even if that task had been undertaken with maximum dispatch, it would have taken years before any final order actually changing the flows into Mono Lake would have been forthcoming. In fact, seven years after the decision, the Water Board has still not completed its investigations and its environmental report. In 1989, officials for the City of Los Angeles and the Mono Lake Committee reached an agreement whereby Los Angeles would abide by a court-set lake level and would give up some of its water rights, in exchange for assistance from the state in finding alternate sources of water. But controversy has continually recurred. An entirely new suit to protect the lake was successfully brought under two obscure provisions of the Fish and Game Code requiring releases from dams sufficient to reestablish and maintain fish populations below the dams.

In the late 1990s, rain levels were again high and the lake level gained. While awaiting the Water Board studies on Mono Lake, the trial court issued a preliminary injunction requiring that the lake be maintained at 6377 feet above sea level, some 2 feet above its existing level but still more than 40 feet below the level it had prior to L.A.'s diversion project. That case has now been expanded to encompass issues other than the balance between public trust and municipal supply needs (the plaintiffs have been concerned that their doctrinal public trust victory might be "balanced away"). One such issue is violation of air quality requirements resulting from blowing dust created by exposure of shoreland flats as the lake level declined. Another is a claim to lake level maintenance on behalf of the U.S. government. The interest of the federal government has come to the fore because in 1984 Congress established a Mono Basin National Forest Scenic Area in order to protect the geological, ecological, and cultural resources of Mono Basin. The Scenic Area statute provides, however, that "nothing in [this law] shall be construed to…affect the present (or prospective) water rights of any person…including the City of Los Angeles." 16 U.S.C. §543c(h). For its part, despite a 1989 negotiated agreement and three trial court rehearings on minimum lake levels, the city continues to oppose the restrictions on withdrawal.

On yet another front, the State of California enacted a statute that makes as much as $60 million available to mitigate the cost to Los Angeles of finding a substitute for the reductions it will eventually bear at Mono Lake. The law anticipates innovations such as conservation, wastewater reclamation, conjunctive use, and groundwater recharge. The idea of the law presumably is that statewide sharing of the costs of finding alternatives will smooth the way to an actual solution of the controversy and keep the legal dispute from continuing indefinitely. To date, the prospect of money has not generated a quick or clear solution.

How will Los Angeles ultimately deal with its loss at Mono Lake? No one knows, and no one yet knows the extent of the potential loss. In an ordinary year, the 10,000 acre-foot

---

15. This update is adapted from J. Sax, R. Abrams & B. Thompson, Legal Control of Water Resources 588–596 (2d ed. 1991).

per year diversion represents about 15% of the city's total water supply. What are the current alternatives facing Los Angeles and other South Coast southern West Coast cities? The adaptation that would produce the least reverberations elsewhere would be reduction of demand through conservation. Alternatively, Los Angeles might purchase the water from other rights owners, most likely agricultural users. The possibility remains, however, that Los Angeles may use its Mono Lake losses to press for new water mega-projects, in which case environmental concerns will simply have been shifted to a new arena.

The opinion in *Mono Lake* has spawned a number of interesting cases exploring the intersection of water rights and the public trust and further defining the balance between water needs and public trust interests that the *Mono Lake* court left for future determination. One case supported the state Water Board's requirement of upstream releases of water to protect the fish and wildlife of the Sacramento-San Joaquin River Delta against saltwater intrusion.[16] A second significant case applied *Mono Lake* to an initial appropriation of water, permitting a requested diversion but imposing strict downstream flow maintenance requirements in order to protect public trust values below the point of diversion, primarily chinook salmon.[17]

The latter court's view of Mono Lake was that it

> encourages and requires the trier of fact to balance and accommodate all legitimate competing interests in a body of water...rather than the "unbalanced structure" that would result from a flat preference for either instream or consumptive values.... Water quality [for municipal use] cannot be excluded from the analysis simply because it does not fit plaintiffs' and intervenors' conception of a public trust value. Neither, however, can the importance of the public trust be diluted by treating it as merely another beneficial use...co-equal with irrigation, power production, and municipal water supply.... Public trust doctrine occupies an exalted position in any judicial or administrative determination of water resource allocation....

The balance, in other words, still remains very unclear. In the arid West, waterfights tend to be long-running battles.

Section 3. HOW FAR DOES THE PUBLIC TRUST DOCTRINE GO?

The public trust doctrine asserts that certain special public rights and duties lie latent within various natural resources, whether publicly or privately owned, with consequences that can be dramatic.

The following case unfolded in 1969, a short distance west of Colorado Springs, where an accident of geology 10 million years ago had created a remarkably rich 6000-acre area of fossil beds. The Florissant Fossil Beds, layer upon layer of paper-thin shales filled with biological artifacts, was a unique and nationally famous archaeological site, featured in many junior high school textbooks. Congress, in desultory fashion, had been discussing whether to purchase the beds in order to create a national monument.

---

16. The "Delta" case, United States v. State Water Res. Control Bd., 227 Cal. Rptr. 161 (Cal. Ct. App. 1986).
17. The "East Bay MUD" case, E.D.F. v. East Bay Mun. Util. Dist., No. 425955 (Super. Ct., Alameda County, Cal., Jan. 2, 1990).

Meanwhile, a group of private developers contracted to purchase the 6000-acre tract. They had determined that in marketplace terms the area's best commercial use lay in subdivision construction, and the bulldozers were poised and ready to roll, to carve roads, driveways, and split-level foundations into the fragile fossil beds.

Defenders of Florissant v. Park Land Development Company
(unreported) Victor J. Yannacone, Jr., Bernard Cohen, and Steven Davison, Environmental Rights and Remedies 47–60 (1972)

**IN THE UNITED STATES DISTRICT COURT
FOR THE DISTRICT OF COLORADO**

DEFENDERS of FLORISSANT, Inc., individually and on behalf of all those entitled to the full benefit use and enjoyment of the national natural resource that is the proposed FLORISSANT FOSSIL BEDS NATIONAL MONUMENT, and all those similarly situated, Plaintiffs, vs. PARK LAND COMPANY, CENTRAL ENTERPRISES, INC., CLAUDE R. BLUE, KENNETH C. WOFFARD; J. R. FONTAN, M. L. BARNES; W. NATE SNARE, A. W. GREGG, R. MITSCHELE, MARILDA NELSON; DELBERT and EMMA WELLS; E. D. KELLY, JOHN BAKER, and their successors in interest, if any, as their interest may appear, Defendants.	)))))))))))))))

NOTICE OF MOTION

PLEASE TAKE NOTICE that the Plaintiffs will move this Court at the United States District Court House, Denver, Colorado, on the 8th day of July, 1969, at half past nine o'clock in the forenoon of that day, or as soon thereafter as counsel can be heard, for an order:

RESTRAINING the Defendants from any actions which may cause serious permanent or irreparable damage to the national natural resource that is the area included within the proposed Florissant Fossil Beds National Monument; or in the alternative,

DIRECTING the immediate hearing on the merits of the Plaintiff's application for a temporary injunction,

TOGETHER with such other and further relief as to the Court shall seem just and proper under the circumstances.

Respectfully submitted,
Victor J. Yannacone, Jr., Attorney for Plaintiff

VERIFIED COMPLAINT

The Plaintiffs, complaining of the Defendants by their attorney, Victor J. Yannacone, Jr., set forth and allege:

1. JURISDICTION: Jurisdiction of this Court is invoked under Title 28 U.S.C. §1331(a), "The district courts shall have original jurisdiction of all civil actions wherein the matter in controversy

exceeds the sum or value of $10,000, exclusive of interest and costs, and arises under the Constitution, laws, or treaties of the United States.":...

2. JURISDICTION: Jurisdiction of this Court is invoked under Title 28 U.S.C. §343(3): "To redress the deprivation, under color of any State law, statute, ordinance, regulation, custom or usage, of any right, privilege or immunity secured by the Constitution of the United States or by any Act of Congress providing for equal rights of citizens or of all persons within jurisdiction of the United States.":...

3. JURISDICTION: This is also a proceeding for Declaratory Judgment under Title 28 U.S.C. §§2201, and 2202, declaring the rights and legal relations of the parties to the matter in controversy, specifically:

(a) That the proposed Florissant Fossil Beds National Monument is a national natural resource.

(b) The right of all the people of the United States in and to the full benefit, use and enjoyment of the unique values of the proposed Florissant Fossil Beds National Monument, without diminution or degradation resulting from any of the activities of the Defendants or their Successors in interest, sought to be restrained herein.

(c) That the degradation of the unique National Natural Resources of the proposed Florissant Fossil Beds National Monument by the Defendants or their Successors in interest violates the rights of the Plaintiffs, guaranteed under the Ninth Amendment of the Constitution of the United States and protected by the due process and equal protection clauses of the Fifth and Fourteenth Amendments of the Constitution of the United States.

4. CLASS ACTION: The Plaintiff is a non-profit, public-benefit corporation duly organized and existing under Colorado law. DEFENDERS OF FLORISSANT, INC. is made up of scientists and other citizens dedicated to the preservation of this natural treasure....

5. THE PROPOSED FLORISSANT FOSSIL BEDS NATIONAL MONUMENT: The proposed national monument comprises an area of 6,000 acres on the east slope of the Rocky Mountains. Located in a region of high recreation use and relatively close to a fast growing metropolitan complex, heavy visitation is expected.

The primary resources are the unique Oligocene lake beds with their plant and insect fossil-bearing layers and related geological features. These resources, combined with a scenic setting and secondary recreational and biological resources, constitute a relatively compact natural unit.

The ancient lake beds of Florissant preserve more species of terrestrial fossils than any other known site in the world. The insect fossils are of primary significance. They represent the evolution and modernization of insects better than any other known site in America. In addition, the fossil plants, emphasized dramatically by the petrified tree stumps and the great variety of leaf fossils, add greatly to the primary values. Fossils of spiders, other invertebrates, fish, and birds also have been found at Florissant.

The beds have been a famous collecting ground by numerous scientists for nearly a century and continue to be of great value for paleontological research.

The present-day vegetation is one of pine-covered hills and grassy meadows. In good years the wildflower display in June and July may be spectacular and is an acknowledged tourist attraction....

Geological History: Subsequent to the birth of the Rocky Mountains, 60 million years, ago, a period of erosion ensued. By Oligocene time, 40 million years ago, the mountains in the Florissant region had been reduced generally to a broad, gently rolling hill land—a piedmont of low relief and moderate elevation.

Volcanic eruptions covered the region with pyroclastics to a depth of 40 to 60 feet or more, and the drainage of the area was blocked, thus forming the Florissant Lake. The rolling slopes and the lakeshore were mantled by many types of deciduous trees and immense Sequoia groves.

Explosive eruptions and mud flows eventually filled the lake. The mud flows engulfed and buried the lakeshore trees which were gradually petrified. Insects, leaves, and other forms of life were carried to the lake bottom and preserved between alternating layers of volcanic ash. The source of the volcanic material appears to have been the Guffey volcano, 15 miles southwest of Florissant....

A number of the tree stumps, including large Sequoias, are exposed at the two commercially operated petrified forest areas. Some of these have been exposed by excavating around them. Many other stumps could be exposed by removing a very shallow over-burden. Some of the exposed stumps have fallen apart as a result of exposure; some are wired together by steel cables.

In addition to the insect, leaf, and wood fossils, the beds contain numerous microfossils. These occur in light-colored diatomited and sapropel laminae which alternate with one another, and in some places with light-colored pumice and graded tuff laminae. Ranking below the fossil insects and leaves in numbers of specimens found here are thin-shelled mollusks, and fresh water fishes. Several bird feathers and a few bird carcasses have been found.

Significance of Geological Resources: These deposits represent a small chapter of the geological history of the earth, but one very closely related to the present. What happened here in Oligocene times — the environment conditions that existed, the life forms that prevailed, the whole story — is written into the Florissant deposits. Scientists have revealed parts of this story; more remains to be told.

The rare quality of the Florissant site lies in the delicacy with which thousands of fragile insects, tree foliage, and other forms of life — completely absent, or extremely rare in most paleontological sites — have been preserved. There is no known locality in the world where so many terrestrial species of one time have been preserved. A total of 144 plant entities or species have been found there. Thirty of these are of uncertain affinity, but the remaining 114 are identifiable with modern species. Approximately 60,000 specimens of insect fossils have been collected here, the site having a world-ranking second only to the Baltic amber sites in Europe. Almost all the fossil butterflies of the new world have come from this site. Even the presence of fresh water diatoms in the Florissant beds is their earliest known occurrence.

The Florissant site has been visited by scientists for nearly a century, and almost all have expressed admiration for the quantity and remarkable perfection of the fossils discovered here. Textbooks of paleontology, historical geology, and entomology cite Florissant as an outstanding locality for fossil insects. Fossil leaves from here are noteworthy and have been described in paleontological and botanical literature. Probably no formation of such limited extent has ever been the subject of as large a body of literature as the Florissant lake beds (226 papers)....

In years of average or better rainfall, the wildflower display in June and July is truly spectacular; every open area is carpeted with paintedcup, many penstemon and crazyweed species, composites, mariposas, harebells, and other varieties. Under the aspens and in wet meadows may be found columbines, pedicularis, iris, shooting-stars, and many others. In August and early September, various sunflowers, groundsels, and fireweed take the place of the earlier flowers, and if there is a late summer rain, frequently this display is as spectacular as the earlier one.

There are many species of large and small mammals, including deer, antelope, elk, mountain lions, bobcats, coyotes, beaver, cottontail and jack rabbits, porcupines, one or more bat species, badgers, goldenmantled ground squirrels, chipmunks, Albert squirrels, white-tailed prairie dog, various mice species, and probably well over 100 bird species. In addition, there are numerous insect and butterfly species....

COURTESY FLORISSANT FOSSIL BEDS
NATIONAL MONUMENT

FIGURE 22-2

*A view of today's Florissant
Fossil Beds National Monument,
showing an area in which ditch
excavations have revealed rich
layering of fossils going back
50 million years.*

6. THE DEFENDANT: That upon information and belief, the defendants, individually and collectively, as their interests may appear, are the owners in fee of lands included within the proposed Florissant Fossil Beds National Monument.

Upon information and belief the defendants individually and collectively as their interests may appear are subject to the exercise of eminent domain by the United States of America upon final action by the Congress of the United States which, upon information and belief, should occur during the current session of the Congress.

7. DEFENDANTS' ACTIONS: That upon information and belief, unless restrained by order of this Court, the Defendants, individually, or their Successors in Interest, will develop the area to be included within the proposed Florissant Fossil Beds National Monument, in such a way as to cause serious, permanent and irreparable damage to the unique national natural resource that is the Florissant Fossil Beds.

That the development of the region of the Florissant Fossil Beds in any way which involves road building, excavation, or covering the fossil beds with permanent dwelling units or building structures, will cause serious permanent and irreparable damage to the unique paleontological resource that is the Florissant Fossil Beds....

That upon information and belief the operation of conventional building construction methods will cause serious permanent and irreparable damage to the unique national paleontological resource represented by the Florissant Fossil Beds.

That the development of the area encompassed within the proposed Florissant Fossil Beds National Monument by Defendants is not compatible with the maintenance of the unique national natural resources, that is the Florissant Fossil Beds.

Upon information and belief, the defendant Park Land Company, Claude R. Blue, Kenneth C. Woffard, J. R. Fontan, and M. L. Barnes, Jointly or severally intend to commence construction operations immediately which will cause serious permanent and irreparable damage to the National Natural Resource which is the Florissant Fossil Beds....

8. EQUITABLE JURISDICTION: That this action is properly brought in equity before this court on the following grounds:

(a) The subject matter of the dispute is equitable in nature. This action is brought for the purpose of restraining the Defendants individually, and their Successors in Interest, from damaging or degrading the unique national natural resource that is, the Florissant Fossil Beds, within the area proposed for inclusion in the Florissant Fossil Beds National Monument. The injury which may be inflicted by the Defendants individually or their successors in Interest, if they are permitted to develop the area without regard for the unique national natural resources represented thereby, will be irreparable, in that it cannot be adequately compensated in damages. The declaratory judgment demanded by the Plaintiffs, together with the equitable relief related thereto are equitable remedies in the substance of character of the rights sought to be enforced or historically, in the province of the Court of Chancery.

(b) There is no adequate remedy at law. The law does not afford any remedy for the contemplated wrong to the American people resulting from the degradation of the unique national natural resources represented by the Florissant Fossil Beds from the development thereof by the Defendants and/or their Successors in Interest, in a way inconsistent with the protection of the paleontological, paleobotanical and palynological resources represented thereby. There is no plain adequate and complete remedy at law as practicable and efficient as the equitable relief sought herein. Nor would the damages sustained by the people of the United States as a result of the improper development of the area by the Defendants or their Successors in Interest, be capable of measurement and determination in any action at law.

9. TRUST: That the Defendants individually and their Successors in Interest, hold the unique national natural resource of the Florissant Fossil Beds, with respect to its paleontological, paleobotanical and palynological values in trust for the full benefit, use and enjoyment of all the people of this generation, and those generations yet unborn.

That the maintenance of this trust is compatible with the proper efficient development of the resource represented by the area encompassed within the proposed Florissant Fossil Beds National Monument area.

That the administrative agencies of the Federal and State governments are incapable of preventing the irreparable damage which will result from the improper development of the region by the Defendants or their Successors in Interest without regard for the protection of the unique paleontological, paleobotanical and palynological values represented by the Florissant Fossil Beds.

That the maintenance of the trust is consistent with private ownership of the property and does not constitute any taking of the Defendant's property.

WHEREFORE, the plaintiffs individually and on behalf of all those entitled to the full benefit, use and enjoyment of the national resource that are the proposed Florissant Fossil Beds National Moment, respectfully pray:

That this Court take jurisdiction of the matter, and that a three judge court be convened to hear and determine this cause as provided by Title 28 U.S. Code, §2281, et seq. and upon such hearing:

(a) Grant judgment declaring the right of the Plaintiff and all others to the full benefit, use and enjoyment of the national natural resources that are the proposed Florissant Fossil Beds National Monument, without any degradation resulting from the improper development thereof by the Defendants and/or their Successors in Interest.

(b) That the Court issue such orders as will protect the unique paleontological, paleobotanical and palynological values encompassed within the Florissant Fossil Beds, pending the final hearing of determination of this action.

(c) That the Court issue such orders as will protect the unique paleontological and palynological values encompassed within the Florissant Fossil Beds.

(d) Together with all such other and further relief as to the Court may seem just, proper, and necessary under the circumstances to protect the unique national natural resources that are in the Florissant Fossil Beds.

(Signed) Victor Yannacone, *Attorney for Plaintiff*

[AFFIDAVIT]
STATE OF COLORADO, CITY AND COUNTY OF DENVER

Estella B. Leopold, being duly sworn deposes and says:

1. That she is a Paleontologist presently employed by the United States Geological Survey, and is personally familiar as a research scientist with the area to be included within the proposed Florissant Fossil Beds National Monument, and in particular the land and area presently being threatened by the activities of the Defendants with respect to excavation and road building.... [Dr. Leopold's affidavit provided detailed description and analysis, and was the source of most of the material set out in the Complaint. The District Court, however, dismissed the action for failure to state a claim upon which relief could be granted. The plaintiffs quickly appealed to the Tenth Circuit for temporary injunctive relief.]

UNITED STATES COURT OF APPEALS FOR THE TENTH CIRCUIT

DEFENDERS OF FLORISSANT, INC., individually) and on behalf of all those entitled to the full) benefit, use and enjoyment of the national) natural resource that is the proposed) FLORISSANT FOSSIL BEDS NATIONAL) MONUMENT, and all those similarly situated,) Plaintiffs,) vs.) PARK LAND COMPANY, et al.) Defendants.)	No. 00341-69

ORDER

Upon reading and filing the application of the plaintiffs herein for a temporary restraining order, together with the transcript of the hearing on the application of plaintiffs for similar relief before the United States District Court, District of Colorado on July 9, 1969, together with the oral application of counsel for the plaintiffs before this Court on this date, including a complete recital of all the efforts by counsel for the plaintiffs to secure the appearance of the defendants, Claude R. Blue and J. R. Thornton, individually and as partners of the Park Land Company, the principal defendant herein, including recital of the substance of the conference held among the parties in the United States District Courthouse...on July 10, 1969...and representations by counsel for the defendants, Robert Johnson of Colorado Springs, that he would not enter a formal appearance under any circumstances in this action at this time, together with telegraphic notice...to which no reply had been received.

AND IT APPEARING TO THE COURT from the representations of counsel and the information contained in the verified complaint and exhibits annexed thereto, the affidavits submitted therewith of Dr. Estella Leopold, Paleontologist for the United States Geological Survey, that the Florissant Fossil Beds represent a unique national natural resource, and that the excavation with road building or other construction equipment of these fossil beds will result in serious, permanent, irreparable damage and render the action for preliminary injunction pending for trial in the United States District Court on July 29, 1969, moot, and it appearing from the uncontradicted statements contained in the transcript of the hearing of July 9, 1969, conducted in the presence of defendants and their counsel and the similar representations of plaintiff's counsel before this Court, and that there will be no damage to the defendants by order of this Court restraining construction activities at the area of the Florissant Fossil Beds,

IT IS ORDERED that the defendants, jointly or severally, individually or collectively, or by their agents, servants or employees, their contract vendees or their successors in interest, be and are hereby restrained from disturbing the soil, or sub-soil or geologic formations at the Florissant Fossil Beds by any physical or mechanical means including, but not limited to excavation, grading, roadbuilding activity or other construction practice until a hearing on the merits of the plaintiff's application for preliminary injunction to be heard in the United States District Court, District of Colorado, on July 29, 1969, at 9:30 a.m.

IT IS FURTHER ORDERED that service of this order shall be made by the United States Marshal on any workman engaged in construction activities at the Florissant Fossil Beds forthwith and that personal service shall also be made on each of the defendants subject to the jurisdiction of the Court.

It is ordered that the effectiveness of the temporary restraining order issued by this court this date is conditioned upon the filing by the plaintiff with the Clerk of the United States District Court for the District of Colorado a cash bond in the amount of $500.00 for the payment of such costs and damages as may be incurred or suffered by any party who is found to have been wrongfully restrained during the period of the temporary restraining order.

> ALFRED P. MURRAH, Chief Judge
> JEAN S. BREITENSTEIN, Judge
> JOHN J. HICKEY, Judge
> United States Court of Appeals
> Dated: July 10, 1969

[On remand, at the hearing for a preliminary injunction, the district court again dismissed the case. On appeal to the Tenth Circuit again, the appellate judges ordered that the above injunction be continued indefinitely, until further order of the Court of Appeals. The federal government authorized eminent domain purchase by a bill signed on August 14, 1969, Pub. L. No. 91-60, and the injunction remained in effect during the time that the federal government was acquiring the lands in question. The fossil beds are now a national monument.]

COMMENTARY & QUESTIONS

1. **The basis of the injunction?** The injunction issued in the Florissant Fossil Beds case (which, it should be noted, is hardly a typical run-of-the-mill environmental case) froze the use of the private land pending possible governmental purchase. What was the basis of the injunction? The court never issued an opinion, so the precise rationale is not clear. An injunction, in modern legal practice, is not itself a cause of action. It requires a

foundation tort or other cause of action in order to be issued. In the course of oral argument in the trial court, the attorney for the fossil beds was asked by the judge what his cause of action was, and he replied that he did not have a clear cause of action. He was dismissed. The Tenth Circuit Court of Appeals panel later asked the same question, and attorney Yannacone replied, more or less, "Your Honors, if I told you that the original U.S. Constitution somehow lay buried there in the fossil beds, would you let the bulldozers roll?" When the court said, "Of course not, we'd issue an injunction," the attorney said, "Whatever you'd use there, I'm using here." Was it, in fact, the public trust?

The complaint uses the word "trust" in substantially the same manner as the public trust doctrine might be applied. Is that the basis of the case? Note that the trustee, according to the plaintiffs' allegation, was not the government but the private owner, certainly a most disgruntled potential trustee.

2. **The balancing process in *Florissant*.** In *Florissant*, the environmentalists were attempting to hold up bulldozing of the fossil bed area until such time as the federal Congress would pony up the money to pay for purchasing it from the owners. Bills were proceeding in both the House and the Senate to that end, but the private developer, with an instinct, perhaps, for playing the role of environmental defendant to the hilt, reportedly announced that it was going to bulldoze some of the fragile areas immediately. The defendant corporation's only concession to the existence of the fossil beds was to offer to sell them to the environmental coalition for a price double what it had itself paid for the property the week before. If the environmentalists would not pay the 100% markup, the defendants clearly wished to proceed quickly because eminent domain proceedings for governmental purchase, as we will see in the next chapter, would pay them fair market value only, which was presumptively the amount that they themselves had just paid for the land. In *Florissant*, the trust balance might have been very different if plaintiffs had sought to freeze the fossil beds permanently from development, without the imminent likelihood of governmental purchase that in fact settled the case. The trust balance in that case may have been a process of weighing the strategic time values of maintaining the status quo, as well as public and private rights.

Does it shock you that these privately owned fossil beds were protected by the court with an injunctive order, freezing them from development, for aesthetic public reasons with no compensation required by the injunction? The following chapter considers such constitutional takings issues at length.

3. **Governmental use of the trust.** Governments have often used the trust doctrine, most often to affirm the existence of their governmental powers to regulate, as in wildlife cases, where the state acts as trustee. In the *Steuart Transportation* oil spill case, for example, countering defendant's argument that neither the federal nor the state government plaintiffs "owned" the birds and ducks destroyed by oil, both governments successfully argued the public trust doctrine to win standing for recovery of damages. The trust can aid in defending against regulatory takings challenges as well. When governments cite the trust in affirming their authority over a matter, however, they may concurrently expand their active liabilities, opening themselves to trust suits by disgruntled environmentalist "beneficiaries." This scenario may help explain the

California Attorney General's hesitation in *Mono Lake*, and why public trust law has generally been developed, like so many other areas of environmental law, through citizen rather than governmental efforts.

4. **Familiarizing the trust.** An initial obstacle to courts' active adoption of public trust theories, understandably, was the fact that many judges had never heard of the trust. Attorneys often faced the task of establishing the existence of the doctrine in their state's common law heritage. Consider the following on researching public trust case law:

> Courts may react hesitantly when faced with potent and unfamiliar legal doctrines introduced into litigation.... The holdings of Supreme Court decisions, especially *Illinois Central*, clearly establish the existence and applicability of the doctrine in all of the states of the Union, while leaving the detailed articulation of the doctrine, in great part, to subsequent state adjudication.

> Often public trust law lies latent in a state's case law. Experience in Tennessee, which is not a leading state in environmental protection, may be indicative: In 1970 the public trust was an unfamiliar principle in Tennessee practice. The drafters of the 1972 water pollution act inserted the public trust concept into that statute (as to water quality only) but the effect of the trust language was not clear. When environmental law classes focused upon the public trust doctrine, however, they came up with a wealth of public trust law starting in the earliest days of statehood. More than 50 cases were found dealing with the trust (often in direct and express terms) in state parklands, lakes and watercourses, wildlife, roads and streets, railroad rights of way, subterranean water, and school lands.

> When the state's regional prison program subsequently proposed a diversion of state forest lands, cutting approximately 50 acres out of the center of a wild public preserve, the student researchers and local attorneys were able to marshal sufficient federal and state case law to convince the court that the trust existed, that citizens had standing as beneficiaries to enforce the trust, and that trust standards had to be complied with prior to any diversion of the resource.[18] Plater, The Non-Statutory Public Trust: Affirmative New Environmental Powers for Attorneys-General, Nat'l Ass'n of Attorneys-General Envtl. Control J., Apr. 1976, at 13–14.

5. **The public trust doctrine: is it amphibious?**[19] As the excerpt from Marks v. Whitney in *Mono Lake* demonstrates, the public trust in water resources has grown far beyond the traditional trust terms of Roman law. To what extent does it apply beyond water-based resources? Parklands are obviously included today, though unknown to Justinian. Why? What is it about parklands that makes them public trust resources? Is it an inherent premise of open, shared public use? During the Pigeon River Forest litigation on the State of Michigan's duty to keep oil wells out of a state forest preserve, West Mich. Envtl. Action Council v. NRC, 275 N.W.2d 538 (Mich. 1978), the Assistant Attorney General, arguing for the oil companies, asked, "Is all publicly-owned land now invested with the public trust, even dumps and highway yards?" It's a good question. If they are not, where is the line to be drawn?

---

18. Marion County v. Luttrell, No. A-3586 (Chancery Ct., Davidson County, Tenn., June 28, 1974). The case was finally resolved extrajudicially, without a statement by higher courts, through local citizens' political pressuring and dynamite threats against development of the forest resource. Citizen standing was also upheld on trust beneficiary principles in State ex rel. SOCM v. Fowinkle, No. A-2914-A (Chancery Ct., Davidson County, Tenn., Nov. 2, 1973).

19. See Scott Reed's article of the same name, 1 J. Envtl. L. & Litig. 107 (1986).

Above the water line, the trust doctrine has been applied, at various times, to parks (*Paepke*, etc.); wildlife and archaeological artifacts (In re Steuart Transp. Co., 495 F. Supp. 38 (E.D. Va. 1980), and Wade v. Kramer, 459 N.E.2d 1025 (Ill. 1984)); beach access over uplands (Matthews v. Bay Head Improvement Ass'n, 471 A.2d 355 (N.J. 1984));[20] stream access, including the right to portage around barriers by traversing adjacent private land (Montana Coalition for Stream Access v. Hildreth, 684 P.2d 1088 (Mont. 1984)); critical upland areas surrounding a redwood forest (Sierra Club v. Department of Interior, 376 F. Supp. 90 (N.D. Cal. 1974); Sierra Club v. Department of Interior, 398 F. Supp. 284 (N.D. Cal. 1975)); trees threatened by resort developments (Irish v. Green, 4 BNA Env't Rep. Cas. 1402 (Mich. Cir. Ct. 1972)); trees damaged by oil spills (Puerto Rico v. S.S. Zoe Colocotroni, 628 F.2d 652 (1st Cir. 1980) (although these were water-based mangrove trees)); perhaps fossil beds, as we have seen; and more.

Take this not-so-hypothetical: What if, after purchasing a painting by the renowned post-Impressionist Paul Cézanne for $800,000, two entrepreneurial MBAs announce that they have decided to cut it up into one-inch squares because their marketing analysis indicates they can sell off the tiny "authentic Cézannes" for more than $1.5 million? See Held, Alteration and Mutilation of Works of Art, 62 S. Atl. Q. 1, 19 (1963) (noting commercial "butchery" chop-jobs on works of Van Eyck, VanderWeyden, and Pollock); The Case of the Dismembered Masterpieces, ARTnews, Sept. 1980, at 68; Cal. Civ. Code §987, Protection of fine art against alteration or destruction (1997); J. L. Sax, Playing Darts with a Rembrandt: Public and Private Rights in Cultural Treasures 85 (1999). Could a public trust be argued here, or public nuisance? Who has standing to sue? What remedy — an injunction pending imminent public purchase, as in *Florissant*? Would the same kind of theory be applicable to the protection of ancient petroglyphs — prehistoric human rock paintings — from willful destruction?

Once started on this road, the trust's complications abound, but the doctrine's recognition of intangible public values undeniably captures a piece of reality, the legal significance of a society's common cultural heritage.

6. The third category of public trust situations. Whenever the trust is used to support antipollution efforts (see Tennessee Water Pollution Control Act, Tenn. Code Ann. §§70.324 et seq., and State v. Amerada Hess, 350 F. Supp. 1060 (D. Md. 1972)), to prevent destruction of trust resources by public or private actors (see the redwood cases in the preceding note), or to recover damages for the destruction of trust assets (see In re Steuart Transp. Co., in the preceding note, or the state of Alaska's oil spill litigation noted in Chapter 3), it is analytically focused on defense of the quality of the resource against derogation rather than protecting the character of ownership. Emperor

---

20. An active case law has developed around the question of public access to beaches, generally asserting the public's rights to use all beaches, sometimes including even the right to go over private land to reach the public beach area. See Matthews v. Bay Head Improvement Ass'n, 471 A.2d 355 (N.J. 1984); Note, Public Trust Doctrine—Beach Access..., 15 Seton Hall L. Rev. 344 (1985); D. Brower, Access to the Nation's Beaches: Legal and Planning Perspectives (1978). Massachusetts and Maine are anomalies, due to the courts' interpretation of a 1647 colonial ordinance issued under authority granted by the King purporting to convey private property grants down to the low water mark, subject only to a public easement for "fyshynge, fowleing, and navigation," but not for beach use. Opinion of the Justices, 313 N.E.2d 561 (Mass. 1974). There is some question whether the King himself possessed such authority.

Justinian, remember, began his list of public trust resources with air, for which issues of ownership are irrelevant but issues of quality essential. In practice, however, the application of the trust analysis in this third resource-defense, or derogation, category parallels the alienation and diversion cases and is the implicit basis for state pollution laws. The issue in each setting is to determine to what extent the qualities of the trust resources are to be preserved and stewarded against short-term exploitation.

7. **The public trust: how far does it go?** The public trust doctrine captures part of the deepest cultural and philosophical conviction that human life, individual and societal, is made up of more than the dictates of a cash register.

Does it cover human-created cultural resources, too? If, as noted above, a person owns the house in which Benjamin Franklin was born, or a rock outcrop with 10,000-year-old rock painting petroglyphs, or an archaeological treasure from ancient India, there is some question under the public trust — and similar emerging international law doctrines like intergenerational equity and common heritage of humankind — that the law can prevent their being destroyed at the whim of an owner.

The trust doctrine is not absolute. Private property rights obviously must be weighed in the trust balance, and the balance struck in the Florissant Fossil Beds case appears to be an appropriate balance. But in some cases the conflict between public rights and private property will produce bitter political confrontations: How far can the system go in regulating private business decisions in favor of protecting cultural and natural values where nobody is going to be hurt except for fossils, or antelope, or a historic battlefield, or ... Where does it stop?

8. **Cultural values beyond market values.** The ultimate measure of a society would seem to be based upon more than just the essential physical needs for survival — to this should be added the full quality of its people's life, and the legacy of ideas, accomplishments, and potentials it seeks to pass on to successor generations. The public trust, whether incorporated in statutes or existing within our nonstatutory jurisprudence, represents and gives legal force to many of the unmarketized present and future social values that often get overlooked in the immediacy of daily life but are part of the ultimate measure.

In emphasizing stewardship, intergenerational equity, and sustainability, the public trust embodies fundamentally conservative principles. If a society is to survive and advance over time, like species competing in the Darwinian process of replicating and prolonging their genetic identity over succeeding generations, it must incorporate present realities and the needs of future generations into its present legal norms. Ethical concepts of environmental stewardship described by ecophilosophers evoke concepts of legacy — nations, like most nondysfunctional families, honoring what they have received from the past, and trying to pass it on, enhanced, to their posterity. The ancient public trust doctrine thus fits well with principles and technologies of sustainability.

9. **What is the public trust and where is it going?** There is little controversy about the existence of the public trust historically in the United States. But what, exactly, is it? Is it a Rawlsian, Lockian, "pre-political" natural right? Is it an implicit constitutional right? Is it intergenerational democracy, mediating resource legacies over the years? Is it

enforceable? Is it merely an administrative law "hard look" doctrine applied to natural resources? Is it like Burke's tree: We honor it for its years of growth, but also because we don't understand exactly whence it comes?

Is the public trust a common law doctrine? If so, how is it that it can overturn a *statutory* enactment, as in *Illinois Central*? Is it a federal or state doctrine? Note that in *Illinois Central*, the doctrine was used by a federal court to overcome the action of a sovereign state. Does the doctrine apply to the federal government as well? In several cases, courts have asserted that the federal government is equally accountable and restricted under the terms of the public trust doctrine. See *Steuart Transportation*, above, and United States v. 1.8 Acres, 523 F. Supp. 120, 124 (D. Mass. 1981). The federal government is a creature of the states by delegation through the Act of Union and the federal Constitution. If the federal government is therefore exercising delegated powers, it would appear straightforward that it cannot have greater rights and fewer limitations than the entities that created it. Is the public trust then a principle of federal common law? A number of courts and commentators have indicated that neither the federal government nor the state governments can act to abolish the public trust doctrine. See Marks v. Whitney, 491 P.2d 374, 380–381 (Cal. 1971). As trustees, the state sovereignties and federal government are bound by the terms of the trust. Is it then a principle of federal constitutional law? If so, where does it lie?

Where is the public trust going? If it is clear that governments — state and perhaps federal — are the trustees, then what is the scope of the assets held in trust? Is it just tidal waters or navigation and fishing in tidal waters? The doctrine has already spread far beyond that locale, as we will see. It clearly applies on dry land as well, but the ultimate scope of the doctrine is not clearly delineated, at least not yet.[21]

But does the public trust require absolute protection of all trust resources? Like standard trust law, variations of the public trust are permissible through a careful fiduciary balancing process. This is more than merely a procedural requirement of specific statutory authorization described by Professor Sax. Simple legislative or referendum majorities are probably not enough to alter trust protections. A substantive trust balance seems necessary under traditional equity standards. After the *Illinois Central* case, the U.S. Supreme Court and state supreme courts have sometimes found that a conscientious substantive balancing of public trust interests permitted alteration of trust assets. In State v. Public Service Comm'n, 81 N.W.2d 71 (Wis. 1957), the issue was the proposed filling of a small percentage of Lake Wingra in the town of Madison, Wisconsin, for the purposes of making a park area more enjoyable and accessible. The court held, after a careful balancing of public trust considerations, that this action would not violate the trust. See also Milwaukee v. State, 214 N.W. 820 (Wis. 1927).

An interesting reprise to *Illinois Central* played out on the Lake Michigan shoreline only a few miles north of the site of the famous case. In Lake Michigan Fed'n v. Army Corps of Eng'rs, 742 F. Supp. 441 (N.D. Ill. 1990), Loyola University proposed an

---

21. See Rieser, Ecological Preservation as a Public Property Right: An Emerging Doctrine in Search of a Theory, 15 Harv. Envtl. L. Rev. 393 (1991); Coastal States Org., Putting the Public Trust to Work (symposium proceedings, 1990) (including a 29-state survey); Symposium, 19 Envtl. L. 425 (1990).

18.5-acre lakefill project that would be owned by the University, with a 35-foot public promenade on the outer rim, and athletic fields on the interior likewise available to the public. The district court held that because the main purpose of the project was for a private interest, the trust land could not be alienated. The court looked solely to the original motivation of the project, rather than balancing the benefits of the public use of the project against the loss of trust land. The University abandoned the project without appealing the decision. Could a trust balancing process have been argued that would have validated the project? See People ex rel. Moloney v. Kirk, 45 N.E. 830 (Ill. 1896).

10. **How will the trust doctrine evolve?** As environmental consciousness grows, public conceptions of public rights inevitably expand, and public and private property expectations follow suit. The United States has been learning to accept the end of the myths of the frontier, of unlimited resources, of the ability to walk away from mistakes to fresh terrain. The public trust doctrine reflects societal realities long accepted in other modern nation states, which have had to deal with problems of limited resources and high population densities. Does the public trust represent a tendency pushing government agencies into less political civic roles? Does it represent a tendency bringing American private property rights closer to those in other industrial nations' legal systems, where property owners generally have "privileges" to develop, rather than relatively unfettered "rights"? Does this prospect worry you? See the next chapter.

Public trust law lies in the deep background of most environmental cases, and at the cutting edge of many. If, as some leaders of the American Bar Association said after the original Earth Day, "Environmental law is what will give the legal profession a soul," it will probably be the public trust doctrine that supplies the conceptual and spiritual compass.

C. ENVIRONMENTAL RIGHTS FROM CONSTITUTIONS AND STATUTES

The public trust doctrine currently is not the only evolving legal principle of environmental stewardship. In a number of states, there have been constitutional or statutory attempts to establish environmental rights and duties, often expressly incorporating the public trust doctrine.

Federal jurisprudence, for its part, has not been a promising seedbed for environmental rights. For a time a number of environmental attorneys held the hope that federal courts could be persuaded to recognize an implicit right to environmental quality lying latent somewhere within the U.S. Constitution. Cases such as Tanner v. Armco Steel[22] put a quick end to this wistful premise, however, and although the idea of federal rights periodically resurfaces,[23] the field of evolving environmental rights has centered on the states.

---

22. 340 F. Supp. 532 (S.D. Tex. 1972).
23. See Krier, The Environment, the Constitution, and the Coupling Fallacy, 32 Mich. L. Quad. Notes 35 (1988), and Soifer, Protecting Posterity, 7 Nova L. Rev. 39, 45 (1982).

Section 1. **STATE CONSTITUTIONAL ENVIRONMENTAL RIGHTS**

A number of states have experimented with constitutional environmental provisions,[24] with significant diversity in their approaches to the declaration of constitutional rights. Some are clear, some unspecific. Some appear to be enforceable by courts and some appear to be mere political posturing. For more on state constitutional provisions, see Howard, State Constitutions and the Environment, 58 Va. L. Rev. 193 (1972).

But just because there is a constitutional right doesn't necessarily mean that one can do anything with it in a court of law. Is the constitutional provision self-enforcing, or does it depend on subsequent legslative action? The following state constitutional provision[25] sets up the following case considering whether state constitutional provisions are self-executing and enforceable.

> The people have a right to clean air, pure water, and to the preservation of the natural, scenic, historic and esthetic values of the environment. Pennsylvania's public natural resources are the common property of all the people, including generations yet to come. As trustee of these resources, the Commonwealth shall conserve and maintain them for the benefit of all the people. Pa. Const. art. 1 §27 (1971).

Commonwealth v. National Gettysburg Tower, Inc.
Supreme Court of Pennsylvania, 1973
454 Pa. 193, 311 A.2d 588

[In this case the Commonwealth of Pennsylvania, acting through and by its Attorney General, sought to enjoin the defendant from erecting a commercial tourism tower more than 300 feet tall that would loom over a portion of the Gettysburg battlefield, based on Article I §27, the state constitution's environmental amendment.[26]]

O'BRIEN J. (joined by POMEROY, J.)... The chancellor, after making detailed findings concerning the location and characteristics of the tower and the neighborhood of the park, concluded that the Commonwealth had failed to show by clear and convincing proof that the natural, scenic, historic or aesthetic values of the Gettysburg environment would be injured by the erection of the tower.... The chancellor first found to be without merit the defense interposed by appellees that Article 1, §27 of the Pennsylvania Constitution — upon which the Commonwealth relied

---

24. See, e.g., Cal. Const. art. 16 §14; Haw. Const. art. 11 §9; Ill. Const. art. 11 §1; La. Const. art. 9 §1; Minn. Const. art. 11 §14; Mont. Const. art. IX; N.M. Const. art. 20 §21; Pa. Const. art. 1 §27.

25. Contrast the Pennsylvania provision with the following:

> The people shall have the right to clean air and water, freedom from excessive and unnecessary noise, and the natural, scenic, historic, and esthetic qualities of their environment; and the protection of the people in their right to the conservation, development and utilization of the agricultural, mineral, forest, water, air and other natural resources is hereby declared to be a public purpose. The general court [legislature] shall have the power to enact legislation necessary or expedient to protect such rights. Mass. Const. art. 49.

> The conservation and development of the natural resources of the state are hereby declared to be of paramount public concern in the interest of the health, safety and general welfare of the people. The legislature shall provide for the protection of the air, water and other natural resources of the state from pollution, impairment and destruction. Mich. Const. art. IV §52.

26. The attorney who represented the Gettysburg developer in this case was the same attorney who had successfully argued trust principles against the development company in the *Florissant Fossil Beds* case.

for the authority of the Attorney General to bring this suit — was not self-executing and, therefore, legislative authority was required before the suit could be brought....

By familiar principles, the appellees, as the owners of the site, may use their property as they please, provided they do not interfere with their neighbors' reasonable enjoyment of their properties and subject to reasonable regulations for the public good imposed under the police power of the State, of which there are none here....

Similarly, there is no statute of the Pennsylvania Legislature, which would authorize the Governor and the Attorney General to initiate actions like the law suit in the instant case. Rather, authority for the Commonwealth's suit is allegedly based entirely upon Article 1, §27 of the State Constitution, ratified by the voters of Pennsylvania on May 18, 1971....

It is the Commonwealth's position that this amendment is self-executing; that the people have been given a right "to the preservation of the natural, scenic, historic and esthetic values of the environment," and "that no further legislation is necessary to vest these rights in the people."

The general principles of law involved in determining whether a particular provision of a constitution is self-executing....

> A Constitution is primarily a declaration of principles of the fundamental law. Its provisions are usually only commands to the legislature to enact laws to carry out the purposes of the framers of the Constitution, or mere restrictions upon the power of the legislature to pass laws, yet it is entirely within the power of those who establish and adopt the Constitution to make any of its provisions self-executing....

> Cooley's Constitutional Limitations (8th ed.), Vol. 1 p. 165 says: "But although none of the provisions of a constitution are to be looked upon as immaterial or merely advisory, there are some which, from the nature of the case, are as incapable of compulsory enforcement as are directory provisions in general. The reason is that, while the purpose may be to establish rights or to impose duties, they do not in and of themselves constitute a sufficient rule by means of which such right may be protected or such duty enforced. In such cases, before the constitutional provision can be made effectual, supplemental legislation must be had; and the provision may be in its nature mandatory to the legislature to enact the needful legislation, though back of it there lies no authority to enforce the command. Sometimes the constitution in terms requires the legislature to enact laws on a particular subject; and here it is obvious that the requirement has only a moral force: the legislature ought to obey it; but the right intended to be given is only assured when the legislation is voluntarily enacted."

> In Davis v. Burke, 179 U.S. 399, 403, the United States Supreme Court said: "Where a constitutional provision is complete in itself it needs no further legislation to put it in force. When it lays down certain general principles, as to enact laws upon a certain subject...or for uniform laws upon the subject of taxation, it may need more specific legislation to make it operative. In other words, it is self-executing only so far as it is susceptible of execution." O'Neill v. White, 22 A.2d at 26–27 (Pa. 1941).

The Commonwealth makes two arguments in support of its contention that §27 of Article 1 is self-executing. We find neither of them persuasive.

First, the Commonwealth emphasizes that the provision in question is part of Article 1 and that no provision of Article 1 has ever been judicially declared to be nonself-executing. The Commonwealth places particular emphasis on the wording of §25 of Article 1. See Erdman v. Mitchell, 56 A. 327 (Pa. 1903). Section 25 of Article 1 reads as follows:

> To guard against transgressions of the high powers which we have delegated, we declare that everything in this article is excepted out of the general powers of government and shall forever remain inviolate.

However, it should be noted that Article 1 is entitled "Declaration of Rights" and all of the first twenty-six sections of Article 1 which state those specific rights must be read as limiting the powers of government to interfere with the rights provided therein.

Section 25 of Article 1 should be read as summarizing the philosophy of the first twenty-four sections of Article 1, particularly when it declares that "...everything in this article is *excepted out of the general powers of government* and shall remain forever inviolate." (Emphasis supplied.)

Unlike the first twenty-six sections of Article 1, §27, the one which concerns us in the instant case, does not merely contain a limitation on the powers of government. True, the first sentence of §27, which states: "The people have a right to clean air, pure water, and to the preservation of the natural, scenic, historic and esthetic values of the environment," can be read as limiting the right of government to interfere with the people's right to "clean air, pure water, and to the preservation of the natural, scenic, historic and esthetic values of the environment." As such, the first part of §27, if read alone, could be read to be self-executing.

But the remaining provisions of §27, rather than limiting the powers of government, expand those powers. These provisions declare that the Commonwealth is the "trustee" of Pennsylvania's "public natural resources" and they give the Commonwealth the power to act "to conserve and maintain them for the benefit of all people." Insofar as the Commonwealth always had a recognized police power to regulate the use of land, and thus could establish standards for clean air and clean water consistent with the requirements

NATIONAL TOWER
Gettysburg, Pa.

GETTYSBURG
"Where history comes alive"
on top of the National Tower

Provisions for handicapped, deaf and blind
Foreign translations available of Sound Program

FIGURE 22-3
A brochure showing the tower, which stood for 25 years before being dismantled in 2000 after a $5 million federal eminent domain acquisition.

of public health, §27 is merely a general reaffirmation of past law. It must be recognized, however, that up until now, aesthetic or historical considerations by themselves have not been considered sufficient to constitute a basis for the Commonwealth's exercise of its police power.

Now for the first time, at least insofar as the state constitution is concerned, the Commonwealth has been given power to act in areas of purely aesthetic or historic concern.

The Commonwealth has cited no example of a situation where a constitutional provision which expanded the powers of government to act against individuals was held to be self-executing.... It should be noted that §27 does not give the powers of a trustee of public natural resources to the *Governor* or to the *Attorney General* but to the *Commonwealth*.

If we were to sustain the Commonwealth's position that the amendment was self-executing, a property owner would not know and would have no way, short of expensive litigation, of finding out what he could do with his property. The fact that the owner contemplated a use similar to others that had not been enjoined would be no guarantee that the Commonwealth would not seek to enjoin his use. Since no executive department has been given authority to determine when to [sue] to protect the environment, there would be no way of obtaining, with respect to a particular use contemplated, an indication of what action the Commonwealth might take before the owner expended what could be significant sums of money for the purchase or the development of the property. We do not believe that the framers of the environmental protection amendment could have intended such an unjust result....

To summarize, we believe that the provisions of §27 of Article 1 of the Constitution merely state the general principle of law that the Commonwealth is trustee of Pennsylvania's public natural resources with power to protect the "natural, scenic, historic and esthetic values" of its environment. If the amendment was self-executing, action taken under it would pose serious problems of constitutionality, under both the equal protection clause and the due process clause of the Fourteenth Amendment. Accordingly, before the environmental protection amendment can be made effective, supplemental legislation will be required to define the values which the amendment seeks to protect and to establish procedures by which the use of private property can be fairly regulated to protect those values....

ROBERTS, J. (concurring). I agree that the order of the Commonwealth Court should be affirmed; however my reasons for affirmance are entirely different from those expressed in the opinion by Mr. Justice O'Brien. I believe that the Commonwealth, even prior to the recent adoption of Article I, Section 27 possessed the inherent sovereign power to protect and preserve for its citizens the natural and historic resources now enumerated in Section 27. The express language of the constitutional amendment merely recites the "inherent and independent rights" of mankind relative to the environment which are "recognized and unalterably established" by Article I, Section 1 of the Pennsylvania Constitution.

Prior to the adoption of Article I, Section 27, it was clear that as sovereign "the state has an interest independent of and behind the titles of its citizens, in all the earth and air within its domain...." Georgia v. Tennessee Copper Co., 206 U.S. 230, 237 (1907). The proposition has long been firmly established that

> it is a fair and reasonable demand on the part of a sovereign that the air over its territory should not be polluted...that the forests on its mountains, be they better or worse, and whatever domestic destruction they have suffered, should not be further destroyed or threatened...that the crops and orchards on its hills should not be endangered.... 206 U.S. at 238.

Parklands and historical sites, as "natural resources," are subject to the same considerations.[27]

Moreover, "it must surely be conceded that, if the health and comfort of the inhabitants of a state are threatened, the state is the proper party to represent and defend them...." Missouri v. Illinois, 180 U.S. 208, 241 (1901). Since natural and historic resources are the common property of the citizens of a state, see McCready v. Virginia, 94 U.S. 391 (1876), the Commonwealth can

---

27. See Snyder v. Bd. Park Comm'rs, 181 N.E. 483, 484 (Ohio 1932): "[W]e...are of the opinion that, to the extent to which a given area possesses elements or features which supply a human need and contribute to the health, welfare, and benefit of a community, and are essential for the well being of such a community and the proper enjoyment of its property devoted to park and recreational purposes, the same constitute natural resources."

— and always could — proceed as parens patriae acting on behalf of the citizens and in the interests of the community,[28] or as trustee of the state's public resources.[29]

However, in my view, the Commonwealth, on this record, has failed to establish its entitlement to the equitable relief it seeks, either on common law or constitutional (prior or subsequent to Section 27) theories.... Moreover, I entertain serious reservations as to the propriety of granting the requested relief in this case in the absence of appropriate and articulated substantive and procedural standards.

MANDERINO, J., joins in this opinion. NIX, J., concurs in the result.

JONES, J., dissenting.... This Court has been given the opportunity to affirm the mandate of the public empowering the Commonwealth to prevent environmental abuses; instead, the Court has chosen to emasculate a constitutional amendment by declaring it not to be self-executing. I am compelled to dissent....

If the amendment was intended only to espouse a policy undisposed to enforcement without supplementing legislation, it would surely have taken a different form. But the amendment is not addressed to the General Assembly. It does not require the legislative creation of remedial measures. Instead, the amendment creates a public trust. The "natural, scenic, historic and aesthetic values of the environment" are the trust res, the Commonwealth, through its executive branch, is the trustee; the *people of this Commonwealth* are the trust beneficiaries. The amendment thus installs the common law public trust doctrine *as a constitutional right to environmental protection* susceptible to enforcement by an action in equity.

Each of the equivalent [environmental protection] amendments [in Illinois, Massachusetts, New York, and Virginia] purports to establish a policy of environmental protection, but either omits the mode of enforcement or explicitly delegates the responsibility for implementation to the legislative branch. The Pennsylvania amendment defines enumerated rights within the scope of existing remedies. It imposes a fiduciary duty upon the Commonwealth to protect the people's "rights to clean air, pure water and to the preservation of the natural, scenic, historical and aesthetic values of the environment." That the language of the amendment is subject to judicial interpretation does not mean that the enactment must remain an *ineffectual constitutional platitude* until such time as the legislature acts.

Because I believe Article 1 §7 is self-executing, I believe that our inquiry should have focused upon the ultimate issue of fact: does the proposed tower violate the rights of the people of the Commonwealth as secured by this amendment?...

The facts indicate that the proposed tower is a metal structure rising 310 feet above the ground. It is shaped like an hourglass; about 90 feet in diameter at the bottom, 30 feet in the middle and 70 feet at the top. The top level will include an observation deck, elevator housings, facilities for warning approaching aircraft and an illuminated American flag. The proposed site of the tower is an area around which the third day of the battle of Gettysburg was fought. It is located immediately south of the Gettysburg National Cemetery.

The Commonwealth presented compelling evidence that the proposed observation tower at Gettysburg would desecrate the natural, scenic, aesthetic and historic values of the Gettysburg environment. The director of the National Park Service, George Hartzog, appeared as a witness for the Commonwealth....

---

28. See Georgia v. Pennsylvania R.R. Co., 324 U.S. 439 (1945); Sparhawk v. Union Passenger Ry. Co., 54 Pa. 401 (1867).

29. Illinois Central R.R. Co. v. Illinois, 146 U.S. 387 (1892); Sax, The Public Trust Doctrine in Natural Resource Law: Effective Judicial Intervention, 68 Mich. L. Rev. 471 (1970).

I described it as a monstrosity. I advised Mr. Ottenstein that between all of the mistakes which I felt the federal government had made here, and all of the mistakes I felt the commercial interests had made here, nevertheless Gettysburg remained a very sacred symbol to the more than 200,000,000 people across the United States, and that an intrusion of this immensity would, in our judgment, be an absolute monstrosity in this kind of environment and I was very much opposed to it.

Mr. Hartzog offered eloquent testimony on the question of the tower's impact upon the Gettysburg environment....

Q. Would it, in your opinion, be possible to measure the damage that would occur to this historic site if that tower were erected?

A. Well, I don't think that you can measure these things in a normal system of values that we articulate in terms of dollars and cents. You measure them more in terms of matters of integrity and understanding and inspiration and involvement. And from this standpoint, I think a monstrous intrusion such as this tower is, into the historical, pastoral scene of the battlefield park and Eisenhower National Site and the National Cemetery and the place where Lincoln spoke, is just destructive of the integrity of its historical value.

Q. And you are saying you can't put a price tag on those values?

A. No, you can't. There is one Yorktown and there is one Gettysburg....

I would enjoin the construction of this tower by the authority of Article 1 §27 of the Pennsylvania Constitution. I dissent!!

EAGEN, J., joins in this opinion.

COMMENTARY & QUESTIONS

1. **A split decision on constitutional enforcement?** As you count the votes on the different merits of this case, how many justices of the state supreme court were of the opinion that the tower did not amount to a violation of law? Clearly the tower won. How many of them, on the other hand, actually held that the constitutional provision was not self-executing? It appears that only the first two justices were convinced that §27 needed further legislative action. This reading of the court is supported by the fact that, like a number of other state high courts, the Pennsylvania Supreme Court subsequently held that §27 of the state constitution is self-executing. Payne v. Kassab, 361 A.2d 263 (Pa. 1976).

2. **The state constitution and the public trust.** Note how the constitutional provision here was intertwined with the public trust doctrine, especially in Justice Roberts's concurrence. How many of the justices appeared to accept that public trust principles were at least theoretically applicable to the private lands surrounding the battlefield? Did §27 add anything to preexisting trust law?

3. **Commercialization, and a parade of horribles.** In hindsight, could you have litigated this case differently so as to have achieved a different result? One way might have been to remind the state supreme court that its decision could well spawn a rash of other towers surrounding the Gettysburg battlefield. If the image of the arrival of a thicket of towers and other tourist attractions (shooting galleries, water slides, cemetery-view ferris wheel rides?) would move the court, could it not draw the line here, enjoining the first tower?

One of the classic problems of public parklands is the way they attract the crassest commercialization to their boundaries — Estes Park at the gateway to the Rockies; West Yellowstone, Montana; and Pigeon Forge at the gateway to the Smokies National Park, with its Dinosaurland, Waterslides, Spaceship rides, Ripley's Believe-It-Or-Not, the Tourist Gardens of Christ, and the only hula dance-porpoise show in the Appalachians. Can the public trust doctrine extend to the surroundings of parklands to protect park resources from the depredations of the tourist marketplace carnival? How about public nuisance? How about legislation? See (as usual) Sax, Helpless Giants: The National Parks and the Regulation of Private Lands, 74 Mich. L. Rev. 239–245 (1976). See also Chapter 24.

4. **The tower came down.** In 2002, the Gettysburg Tower was condemned by the National Park Service and dynamited — in the presence of Secretary of Interior Bruce Babbitt with the accompaniment of a musket volley from a hundred uniformed Union and Confederate soldiers — as the inaugural event in a master plan to restore the battlefield to historical conditions. Aesthetics were not the only reason the tower was loathed by the preservation community. In exchange for an agreement that had provided vehicle access to the privately owned tower, the National Park Service was supposed to receive 5% of the tower's profits to support battlefield maintenance and preservation. Despite ticket sales of more than $300,000 per year, however, the tower's owners insisted they had never made a profit. They sought and received approximately $5 million in just compensation for the tower.

5. **State statutory environmental rights: the Michigan Environmental Protection Act.** The Michigan Environmental Protection Act (MEPA), Mich. Comp. Laws Ann. §§324.1701 et seq. (1970), is a rather unusual approach to environmental regulation. Drafted by Professor Sax, MEPA's central element is the creation of a cause of action whereby any person can file an injunction suit alleging that a challenged private or governmental action will "pollute, impair or destroy" natural resources or the public trust in those resources. If the court finds the facts to be so, the burden switches to the defendant to rebut the claim of resource harm or to prove an affirmative defense. The statute provides a defense if there is no "prudent and feasible alternative" to the action consistent "with the promotion of the public health, safety and welfare in light of the state's paramount concern for the protection of its natural resources from pollution, impairment or destruction." This statute has spawned a number of similar statutes in other states, and a complex caselaw. Materials on MEPA are available on the coursebook Web site.

This noblest patrimony ever yet inherited by any people must be husbanded and preserved with care in such manner that future generations shall not reproach us for having squandered what was justly theirs.

— The Whig Almanac, 1943

The resources of the earth do not exist just to be spent for the comfort, pleasure, or convenience of the generation or two who first learn how to spend them.

David Brower < http://wildnesswithin.com/americanearth.html>

Chapter 23

PRIVATE PROPERTY AND PUBLIC RIGHTS: CONSTITUTIONAL LIMITS ON PHYSICAL AND REGULATORY TAKINGS

A. *Eminent Domain Condemnations*
B. *Inverse Condemnation: A Constitutional Tort?*
C. *Challenges to Regulations as Unconstitutional "Takings"*

How far can government go in imposing public demands on individuals' private property rights? That intensely political question, a central issue of democratic governance, lies latent or explosively obvious within a vast number of environmental issues. Whether by physical appropriations or regulatory restrictions on individual and corporate behavior, the imposition of public values, needs, or whims upon private property and private actions sets up political confrontations of constitutional proportions.

Consider, for instance, this statutory provision in several bills that marketplace lobbyists almost succeeded in pushing through Congress during the mid-1990s:

§3(a) The Federal Government shall compensate an owner of property whose use of any portion of that property has been limited by an agency action, under a specified regulatory law, that diminishes the fair market value of that portion by 20 percent or more. The amount of the compensation shall equal the diminution in value that resulted from the agency action. If the diminution in value of a portion of that property is greater than 50 percent, at the option of the owner, the Federal Government shall buy that portion of the property for its fair market value.[1]

This piece of automatic-compensation legislation from the Contract With America, which was described by its sponsors as "merely codifying existing constitutional rulings," would have had a sweeping effect on federal environmental regulation. It did not pass, but the tension between public and private rights that produced this and similar political battles is a continuing feature of environmental law and policy.

Government agencies are sometimes environmental protectors and sometimes destructive promoters. On one hand, the power of the state can be a strong ally of environmentalists since, in most cases, government actions are backed by substantial public resources and are presumed valid until proven to be unauthorized, arbitrary and

---

1. H.R. 925, Private Property Protection Act, 104th Cong., 1st Sess. (passed by the House Mar. 3, 1995); see also Senate "Omnibus Property Rights Act" bill sponsored by Senator Dole, S. 605 §403, 104th Cong., 1st Sess. (1995). Similar privateering legislation has been introduced in several states; one such bill was signed into law by Governor George W. Bush of Texas. Tex. Gov't Code tit. 10, subtit. A, ch. 2007, subch. A-C, §2007.002; see also Fla. Stat. Ann. tit.VI, ch. 70, §70.001.

capricious, or otherwise invalid. On the other hand, environmentalists opposing particular governmental development projects, such as some marsh drainings and highway sitings, often try to override the presumption of constitutionality that attaches to government agencies' actions.

Local, state, and federal governments each functionally possess, as a basic attribute of sovereignty, the coercive "police power,"[2] the power of government to force anyone within its jurisdiction to do or not to do things that the government believes would affect the health, safety, or general welfare of its citizens. Thus government can prohibit you from dumping pollutants or filling a wetland, force you to sell your land for a public park or parking lot, or regulate your use of wilderness areas and wildlife. The police power includes both physical appropriation and regulatory powers.

Physical appropriations by government — eminent domain condemnations — are difficult to defend against. Environmental cases have begun to develop substantive challenges to physical condemnations, scrutinizing eminent domain decisions (where government accepts the necessity of paying compensation; see Part A below), and imposing liability on government for nuisance-like physical invasions (see Part B on inverse condemnation).[3]

Constitutional attacks against regulations, arguing that environmental restrictions are "invalid regulatory takings" of private property (see Part C), are one of the most pervasive themes of environmental regulation and politics at all levels of government. Almost by definition, civic regulations trying to correct market failures arouse instinctive marketplace resistance.

The constitutional combats between public rights and private property are based on the language of the Fifth Amendment to the U.S. Constitution (as incorporated in the Fourteenth Amendment for state actions and substantially replicated in corresponding provisions in most state constitutions):

> No person shall be...deprived of life, liberty, or property, without due process of law; nor shall private property be taken for public use, without just compensation.

Analytically, this language embodies two different constitutional rights applicable to private property: a right against deprivation without due process (substantive as well as procedural) and a protection against uncompensated "takings." Structurally, these rights are virtually identical.

Virtually all challenges to governmental mandates, whether federal, state, or local, can be subjected to the same five avenues of constitutional attack, four of them substantive and one procedural:

---

2. The police power resides in all state governments by definition, from which it is broadly delegated to local governments for various health, safety, and welfare purposes. The federal government does not possess a general police power, but the federal government exercises such a similar range of powers through its commerce, national defense, property, and other delegated authorities that its exercises of these powers are also at times referred to as "police power" actions.

3. Although the "inverse condemnation" rubric is now sometimes used in claims against regulations as well as against physical acts by government, its application in the regulatory setting follows the tests for regulatory takings rather than the inverse condemnation tests for governmental physical takings. Since governments have the choice, in the event a regulation is found to be a taking, whether to waive or buy, First English Evangelical Lutheran Church of Glendale v. Los Angeles, 482 U.S. 304 (1987), it makes sense to use "inverse condemnation" as a particular cause of action in the physical appropriation context, not as a separate theory of regulatory taking.

The Five Basic Inquiries.[4] Dividing the areas of substantive judicial scrutiny of governmental actions into five separate diagnostic inquiries can clarify many issues of judicial review. These five substantive inquiries are discernible throughout the case law, and appear to encompass all nonstatutory substantive questions typically raised in judicial review of governmental action. Zoning cases, which offer frequent and familiar (if homely) examples of constitutional challenges, provide an area of litigation that helps illustrate issues in all five substantive categories.

1. *Authority.* A challenger to a zoning decision can assert the government's lack of general or specific authority to act. Such a challenge presents an ultra vires question, which clearly is constitutional. Ultra vires challenges involve substantive inquiry because they dispositively review the foundation of the right by which the government constrains private interests in the possession, use, and enjoyment of an individual parcel of property.

In the zoning setting, a plaintiff may attack a municipality by alleging that it has no power to pass a particular zone regulation for lack of sufficient delegated power under the state enabling statute, by alleging preemption of local or state authority, or the like. The same inquiry, of course, can be found in other kinds of cases throughout the range of federal and state regulatory actions arising under the police power and correlative powers ceded to the federal government. This inquiry is analytically a threshold question, not a focus on the particular merits of the governmental act challenged.

2. *Proper Public Purpose.* The second category of challenges addresses proper public purpose. Zoning laws, for example, were originally attacked as not fitting within the "general welfare" component of the police power's classic triad of basic regulatory purposes: health, safety, and welfare. Once Euclid v. Ambler, 272 U.S. 365 (1926), established that the harmony of planned development constituted a proper, generalized public-welfare purpose, the attacks shifted to attempts to define further, particularized, improper purposes. Such narrower "poison purpose" allegations have included, with varying degrees of success, claims that regulations were "purely aesthetic," were for "purely private purposes," were motivated by a desire to drive down land prices for future condemnation, were racially exclusionary or otherwise invidiously intended to discriminate, or, like some motorcycle helmet prohibitions, impermissibly protected individuals against their own rugged wills. Analogous attacks are regularly posed in other regulatory settings as well. This inquiry as to proper public purpose, too, is a form of threshold question, testing the propriety of the governmental objective rather than the nature of the actual decision itself.

3. *Merits Review: Means Rationally Related to Ends.* The third category of challenges involves attacking a governmental action on its merits for lack of rational relationship of means to ends. Where the purposes of challenged governmental actions are perfectly proper, the design of an ordinance or the factual reasoning supporting a decision may nevertheless be insufficiently, illogically or erroneously related to achieving the purposes. Thus zoning acts have been struck down, as applied to specific parcels, when the lines drawn are found to bear no rational nexus to purposes, or when the pattern of

---

4. The text here is developed at greater length in Plater & Norine, Through the Looking Glass of Eminent Domain: Exploring the "Arbitrary and Capricious" Test and Substantive Rationality Review of Governmental Decisions, 16 B.C. Envtl. Aff. L. Rev. 661, 707–712 (1989).

regulation has insufficient supporting data or planning. The floodplain safety zone, for example, cannot rationally be applied to hilltop land; a residential zone cannot be applied to land that could never be used for residences. Analytically, moreover, this third means-end inquiry may also incorporate "least drastic means" and equal protection review. Thus when a zone discriminates against poor people or mobile homes, its distinctions and classifications can be challenged as not rationally related to the purposes of zoning. Beyond zoning, this third inquiry can be widely discerned in judicial declarations that governmental determinations and classifications must "have reasonable relation to a proper legislative purpose, and [be] neither arbitrary nor discriminatory [to satisfy] the requirements of due process," and must "rationally advance...a reasonable and identifiable governmental objective."[5]

4. *Private Burden*. The fourth inquiry, the degree of burden imposed on the individual, is often the emotional heart of substantive review. Its most common manifestation is the allegation of "confiscatory" takings burdens in regulatory cases, asking a question basic to justice and democracy: how far can the collective power of the majority erode the property of the individual for the sake of public well-being? The usual answer in regulatory takings cases is what one of the authors has previously dubbed the "residuum" takings tests.[6] According to these tests, property owners must be left with a beneficial (or "profitable" or "reasonable") remaining use of their regulated property. These various versions of the diminution test require a fair amount of implicit balancing of potential public harms against private property losses, but, if such balancing is done, offer a workable and philosophically defensible test for application far beyond the field of land-use regulation. Of course, when physical appropriation of property is involved under eminent domain, the fourth inquiry is less a balancing than a straightforward measure of governmental payment at fair market value rates to compensate the burdened individual for property rights taken.

5. *Procedural Due Process*. Courts also apply procedural due process requirements. One form considers a contextual balance whether government has given enough process — questions of notice, opportunity to contest issues at a hearing, the quantity of hearing procedures available, the clarity of legal standards to be applied, and the opportunity to obtain review of the application of a law to a particular case. A second form of procedural requirements is owed to the courts themselves. As in *Overton Park*, in order for courts to fulfill their judicial review functions government processes must produce a meaningful reviewable record, showing the basis of official actions and that officials have considered all relevant factors in reaching determinations.

These diagnostic categories are not carved in stone but offer a useful analytical organization that can be applied to the often complex and confusing controversies surrounding the imposition of public power upon private property, as noted in the following materials of this chapter. Do you see why governmental actions that violate Inquiries Number 1, 2, or 3 usually would be declared "void on their face," while violations of the fourth and fifth would usually be voided "as applied" to that particular land?

---

5. Schweiker v. Wilson, 450 U.S. 221, 235 (1981). The latter part of the quotation is clearly directed at establishing a proper public purpose.

6. Plater, The Takings Issue in a Natural Setting: Floodlines and the Police Power, 52 Tex. L. Rev. 201 (1974).

A. EMINENT DOMAIN CONDEMNATIONS

Eminent domain is one important subcomponent of the police power. Governments occasionally use the eminent domain power in the service of environmental goals, for instance to condemn land for parks. More frequently, however, the condemnation power is used in operations that do not take sufficient account of environmental values — cutting highways through wilderness, building publicly owned office towers in low-income neighborhoods, siting regional trash dumps or power plants, creating development parks in bucolic areas to attract industry, or (through delegation of power to private companies), condemning rights of way for power lines, pipelines, ditches, and drains, or taking private lands so that mining companies can operate strip mines. In each case, environmentalists typically are eager to raise some legal questions.

Section 1. **THE DOMAIN OF DEFERENCE**

The power of the public to appropriate private property via condemnation is a universal attribute of sovereign governments, clearly necessary to the functioning of a modern state.[7] As a result, governmental eminent domain decisions in the United States have generally received a most respectful reception in courts, both state and federal. Given that the government concedes that it will pay just compensation for a taking, many courts in effect declare that they have no further questions.[8] The governmental agency's assertions of condemning authority, proper public purpose, and rational choice of means are, in practice, "well-nigh unassailable."[9]

The usual eminent domain case is cut and dried. The condemning entity files a complaint in court against a parcel of land; the "remedy" sought is a court order transferring title. For the condemnation to succeed, the court need only be convinced

1. that the condemning entity, which is normally either a unit of government or a public utility, has the power of eminent domain under the applicable statutes and follows the necessary procedures for its exercise;

2. that the condemnation is for a stated proper public purpose;

3. that the condemnation decision is not "arbitrary and capricious" (or, in some states, whether the condemnation is "necessary," usually an inquiry at the level of "are highways necessary?" rather than "is this particular land essential if a highway is to be built?"); and

---

7. Kohl v. United States, 91 U.S. 367, 371-372 (1875); the following text has been adapted from Plater & Norine, Through the Looking Glass of Eminent Domain: Exploring the "Arbitrary and Capricious" Test and Substantive Rationality Review of Governmental Decisions," 16 B.C. Envtl. Aff. L. Rev. 661, 662-663 (1989) (cited hereafter as Looking Glass).

8. The general invulnerability of eminent domain appears to exist irrespective of which level of condemning authority is involved — federal, state, or local government, or public utility corporation. Analytically, as well, there are no meaningful differences between these condemners. Each must have a proper grant of authority and must satisfy the other three categories of police power tests. Judicial review of the rationality of the condemner's site-selection choice is typically very deferential. In most cases, condemnees cannot require a specific showing why a particular site was not chosen. The Colorado Supreme Court, however, has suggested that public utility condemnations may deserve more scrutiny than governmental takings. Arizona-Colorado Land & Cattle Co. v. District Court, 511 P.2d 23, 24–25 (Colo. 1975).

9. Berman v. Parker, 348 U.S. 26, 35 (1954).

4. that appropriate just compensation will be paid.

The location, amount of land to be taken, and ecological effects of condemnations normally are not open to question. Thus in the vast majority of cases the opponents of condemnation can only stand and fight on the amount of compensation, trying to make the taking more expensive. This tack is practically useless for environmentalists who oppose a condemnation but do not own the subject property. And it is not very satisfying anyway, since money may be small comfort for the unnecessary loss of a beautiful marsh or forest.

Section 2. CHALLENGING AN EMINENT DOMAIN CONDEMNATION

The wonder is that eminent domain condemnation, a governmental power that is so drastic and has such wide-ranging consequences, has been subjected to so little active judicial scrutiny.[10] There are a variety of legal avenues, however, that potentially may be used to open up governmental eminent domain decisions to substantive judicial review, giving challengers the opportunity to nullify condemnations on the merits.

The primary target of such substantive challenges is the question of rationality or arbitrariness. If a court allows property owners a serious hearing on their claim of irrationality, and weighs that defense according to the standard tests of arbitrariness applied in other administrative law settings, substantive challenges can be successful.

One approach is available where property owners can claim that their land serves quasi-public environmental purposes. When one government tries to condemn another governmental entity's property, courts determine the winner under the "paramount public use" balance. Several courts have extended this defense to private lands.[11]

More broadly, some state courts matter-of-factly allow defenses alleging that a particular taking is "unnecessary."[12] Viewed analytically, however, there seem to be compelling arguments for a lessening of deference in federal and state courts generally.

Two hypothetical cases[13] help to set out the legal basis for serious substantive review of condemnation decisions.

A Means-Ends Factual Implausibility Case. Assume that a federal agency with an express statutory mandate to "promote regional economic development" decides to condemn 38,000 acres of farmland to build a regional industrial park for future corporate tenants.[14] The 300+ farm families who own the land typically would respond

---

10. The reason that relatively few condemnations are challenged, though they would appear to present attractive targets for "conservative" opposition, may be that condemnations typically are levied for "establishment" initiatives such as airports and industrial development projects, and the design plans for what property will be taken often avoid land parcels where owners are likely to be able to mount substantial legal defenses.

11. See Texas E. Transmission Co. v. Wildlife Preserves, 225 A.2d 130 (N.J. 1966); Merrill v. City of Manchester, 499 A.2d 216 (N.H. 1985) (the court weighed the "recreational, scenic and ecological importance" of the private land dedicated to open space preservation, against a proposed town industrial park taking); Oxford County Agric. Soc'y v. School Dist., 211 A.2d 893 (Me. 1965); Middlebury Coll. v. Central Power Corp., 143 A. 384 (Vt. 1928).

12. See Plater & Norine, Looking Glass, 16 B.C. Envtl. Aff. L. Rev. at 689–693.

13. The text is adapted from 16 B.C. Envtl. Aff. L. Rev. at 671–677.

14. This hypothetical is, in fact, the case of TVA's Columbia and Tellico Dam Projects. See Chapter 16. By acquiring more than 60 square miles for the Tellico project, only 16,000 acres of which would be flooded, TVA projected that it could resell up to 35 square miles of condemned farmlands to a hypothetical industrial city to be called Timberlake, theoretically to be built by the Boeing Corporation with congressional subsidies.

by making a barrage of complaints — that this is a "land-grab," a taking of private land to be turned over to other private interests, a taking of "excess" land, a "socialistic" governmental land speculation, and so on. Defense attorneys in eminent domain cases turn these verbal complaints into defensive legal arguments, all focusing on alleged improper public purposes and all dead losers.[15]

Assume, however, that the agency previously had used exactly the same rationale to condemn a total of more than 200 square miles of farmland for four other neighboring industrial parks and that virtually no industrial development occurred. These condemnation defendants realistically cannot argue that industrial development is not a proper public policy or public purpose, but they have a further argument: They should now be allowed to try to prove that condemnation of their lands is not rationally related to the accomplishment of the agency's expressed public purpose. That is, whereas a court initially could well have deferred to the agency on its first industrial parks, now that the factual record clearly shows their implausibility, private property owners must be allowed at least a practical chance to challenge the rational basis of such condemnations in court.

The private property owners' defense straightforwardly questions the rational basis of the agency's condemnation: that based on the factual record no governmental official could reasonably believe that the governmental choice of means — condemnation of these lands — would achieve the avowed governmental ends of industrial development. The fundamental problem of modern eminent domain law, however, at least in practical terms, is that under the deferential standard of review applied in condemnation takings the defendants in most federal courts today would not be allowed to take even this first step. The agency's discretion and the rationality of its decisions to condemn, short of lunacy, are supported in court by the strongest presumption of constitutionality.[16]

A Rational Alternatives Case. The second paradigm requires the reviewing court to apply the rationality rule in a contextual setting, reviewing how an agency has chosen between several competing alternatives that admittedly would each achieve the public purpose but are irrational when viewed in context. Poletown Neighborhood Council v. City of Detroit illustrates this paradigm.[17]

Assume that a federal redevelopment agency, working through the auspices of a city government, decides to encourage the construction of a new job-creating,

---

15. Berman v. Parker, 348 U.S. 26, 35 (1954) (declaring that government can condemn private property to give to private redevelopers even if the land was not derelict, so long as the redevelopment served public purposes) effectively killed the public-use eminent domain requirement, though condemnees continue to argue it.

16. Some state courts allow review of the rationality of condemnation decisions, though most have followed the federal courts' extremely deferential example. Use of the federal APA §706 and its state corollaries could help open up such judicial review in the future.

17. See 304 N.W.2d 455 (Mich. 1981) (per curiam); see also Crosby v. Young, 512 F. Supp. 1363, 1374 (E.D. Mich. 1981). For a factual chronicle of Poletown, see *Poletown*, 304 N.W.2d at 464-471 (Ryan, J., dissenting). See J. Wylie, Poletown: Community Betrayed (1989); Bukowczyk, The Decline and Fall of a Detroit Neighborhood: Poletown vs. GM and the City of Detroit, 41 Wash. & Lee L. Rev. 49 (1984); Poletown Lives (documentary film), Information Factory, 3512 Courville St., Detroit MI 48224. General Motors, despite the desperate efforts of property owners and Ralph Nader, successfully induced a federally funded redevelopment condemnation project to give the corporation land in Poletown, a stable, mixed-race, low-income neighborhood of Detroit, to build a Cadillac plant.

DAVID C. TURNLEY, DETROIT FREE PRESS

FIGURE 23-1

Detroit's Poletown area, before and after. General Motors and the city used eminent domain powers to eliminate everything standing on the 465 acres of this integrated low-income residential-commercial neighborhood — the homes of 4,200 people, 144 local businesses, 16 churches, 2 schools, and a hospital — in order to build a Cadillac assembly plant, despite the existence of alternative undeveloped industrial park sites in the area.

manufacturing plant within city limits. It decides to condemn and raze an urban neighborhood of 50 square blocks that contains 1100 homes, 144 businesses, 16 churches
(including 2 cathedrals), 2 schools, and a hospital. The project would cause a substantial amount of personal and commercial distress, all in order to turn over the 500-acre
parcel to a major automobile manufacturer for construction of a Cadillac assembly
plant.

The property owners might, as usual, attack the taking as based on an improper
public purpose — a "private use," for example — and, as usual, would lose. They might
argue further that condemnation payments will never provide sufficient funds for
replacement of their homes and businesses at relocated sites, but, in the absence of
special statutory provisions, this argument also fails because just compensation is
assessed according to the market value of what is taken with no guarantee of relocation
or replacement costs.

Assume further, however, that at the time the officials decided to condemn and raze
the neighborhood at least four other empty industrial sites of 500 acres each are available within city limits with equivalent access to rail, highways, and utilities. The
landowners may now make a further argument: that, given the drastic burden imposed
upon them, and the available alternative sites that cannot be rationally distinguished
from their neighborhood's site (except that they are less expensive to develop given the
cost of condemnation to the city), no official could rationally have chosen to condemn
their homes and businesses rather than go to one of the other four open sites.[18]

Such an argument is not a means-end argument that the condemnation of Parcel A
will not in fact or logic serve the avowed public purpose of industrial development, but
rather that, viewed in the factual context of drastic costs and available alternative sites
at B, C, D, and E, no rational official could have picked A. This version of rationality
review is analytically more complex and difficult, dealing not with basic factual implausibility but with a judicial cost-benefit-alternatives review. In effect, it involves judicial
acknowledgment of a "less-drastic-means" inquiry in review of some governmental
condemnation actions. Deference to governmental decisions is an even greater consideration here, but the fundamental question remains: If to serve the legitimate,
expressed public purpose of industrial development a site must be chosen, but in light
of the disproportionate private and public burdens no rational official could have

---

18. "The Poletown environmental impact statement identified nine potential sites for the Cadillac factory, but,
from the beginning, General Motors' site criteria were so particular to the Poletown site that only it would fit.
The company demanded 'an area of between 450 and 500 acres; a rectangular shape (3/4 mile by 1 mile); access
to a long-haul railroad line; and access to the freeway system.'" 304 N.W.2d at 460 (Fitzgerald, J., dissenting).
Never clarified in the legal battle was the fact that others of the nine potential sites were basically "greenfield"
sites fitting all but the rectangular criterion. In addition, they were also empty of houses, churches, and small
businesses and thus available without the massive disruption of Poletown; but they all were rejected at GM's
insistence, basically because they were not rectangular. Was shape a critical or a superficial requirement? When
Detroit's planning office staffers inquired informally of GM, they were told that the corporation was insisting on
a rectangle so that it could use the same blueprint layout of parking lots and assembly units as at an existing GM
plant in Oklahoma. But could not the design of parking lots be shifted to fit the shape of the existing Detroit
industrial sites? They could, the GM staff said, or a parking structure could be built instead of open lots to
accommodate the plant worker's needs at the less disruptive sites. But GM adamantly refused to consider shifting
the parking lot layout or building a parking structure. The latter could cause congestion, and either would
require a modification of the Oklahoma blueprints, which the company simply declined to do. "'Once we had
decided what we wanted, we would not retrench,' said one GM employee." Plater & Norine, Looking Glass, 16
B.C. Envtl. Aff. L. Rev. at 675, n. 37.

thought that Parcel A was preferable for that legitimate purpose, doesn't a defendant have the right to ask a court to scrutinize the substance of the condemnation decision and rescind it if it fails the test?

These two paradigms present instances in which private property owners would want at least the opportunity to go forward with the burden of proving that a governmental decision is not rational, in terms showing that a rational official could not so have decided. In both these cases, however, the "arbitrary and capricious" standard would be honored in the breach. Federal courts currently do not take on a particularized rational basis scrutiny of governmental condemnation decisions, but instead defer in general terms to the exercise of official discretion, leaving condemnation defendants with no practical substantive review of takings decisions.

The paradigms are admittedly rather extreme examples of eminent domain condemnation, but such cases permit clearer insights into condemnation review. Lest they be thought hyperbolic, moreover, remember that both have actually occurred and may well occur again.

COMMENTARY & QUESTIONS

1. **The legal basis for more active review.** In the *Poletown* case, the arguments made in court for the neighborhood were almost entirely based on challenges to the constitutionality of the public purpose in giving land to a private corporation and, predictably, came to nought. The Supreme Court, however, implicitly accepted a substantive due process test for eminent domain decisions in upholding Hawaii's land reform act: In order to meet constitutional requirements it must be shown that "the Legislature *rationally could have believed* that the [Act] would promote its objective." Hawaii v. Midkiff, 467 U.S. 229, 242 (1984) (O'Connor, J., emphasis in original). Under administrative procedure acts, moreover, courts are directed to review and rescind government agency actions found to be "arbitrary and capricious." 5 U.S.C. §706(a)(2). Administrative law interprets that test far more rigorously than eminent domain case law does, so the door is open for administrative law challenges of agency condemnations and, by extension, of public utility condemnations.

2. **Uncorking judicial review of condemnations.** Is this an area of practice that is about to awaken, after a century of torpor, under the pressures of environmental challenges to governmental condemnation decisions? Once judicial scrutiny is let loose in an area previously characterized by deference, do you realize how difficult it might be later to get the genie back into the bottle? In practical terms, how much would governments be burdened by the necessity of defending their condemnation decisions?

3. **The politics of eminent domain.** The political backdrop to environmentalists' efforts to open up judicial review of condemnation is interesting. On one hand, eminent domain is a longstanding rhetorical bugbear of "conservatives." On the other, those who get hit by government condemnations are rarely the wealthy and powerful, as in highway and pork-barrel water projects. Often, in fact, as in the *Poletown* case, private corporate interests stand foursquare with government in favor of condemnation,

opposing private property owners. Indeed, as in *Poletown*, the business bloc may have initiated and controlled the government's exercise of eminent domain from the start. In Poletown, who were the conservatives and who the liberals? Does anyone still know, in the environmental era, what those labels mean?

B. INVERSE CONDEMNATION: A CONSTITUTIONAL TORT?

At first glance, inverse condemnation scarcely resembles eminent domain. The facts in the following material resemble tort cases, not constitutional law. Governmental actions here result in noise, vibrations, smells, and general disruptions to the neighboring environs.

Why then make these into constitutional cases? The simple answer is: to get around sovereign immunity. If the federal, state, or local government performing a governmental function has not consented to be sued, the immunity doctrine is a defense to tort actions.[19] The right to challenge government action on constitutional grounds, however, remains available.

Why call it "inverse" condemnation? In an ordinary condemnation case, the government decides it wants someone's property and sues to get it. As part of its suit, the government declares its willingness to pay the value of the property as set by the court. But what if, instead of suing to get the property, the government in effect simply goes ahead and takes it physically? In that case, the victim of the taking may sue the government for compensation, and since the government becomes the defendant instead of the plaintiff, the proceeding is called inverse condemnation or "reverse condemnation." The plaintiff is effectively saying, "The government has in reality condemned my property by physically taking it, without admitting it, so I want to sue them in court to make them pay me eminent domain compensation."

Of course, it may be that the reason the government doesn't offer compensation is that it doesn't think what it is doing amounts to condemnation. As in the following case, the government may do something, such as running an airport, without acknowledging significant effects on private property.

In the usual eminent domain case, the amount of compensation is usually the dominant issue. In inverse condemnation cases, however, there is a prior threshold issue: Was there a taking at all?

Thornburg v. Port of Portland
Supreme Court of Oregon, 1962
233 Or. 178, 376 P.2d 100

GOODWIN, J. The issues in their broadest sense concern rights of landowners adjacent to airports and the rights of the public in the airspace near the ground. Specifically, we must decide whether a noise-nuisance can amount to a taking.

The Port of Portland owns and operates the Portland International Airport. It has the power of eminent domain. It has used this power to surround itself with a substantial curtilage,

---

19. The availability and extent of governmental liability, short of constitutional claims, depends on the vagaries of statutory and common law exceptions to immunity.

but its formal acquisition stopped short of the land of the plaintiffs. For the purposes of this case, the parties have assumed that the Port is immune from ordinary tort liability....

The plaintiffs own and reside in a dwelling house located about 6,000 feet beyond the end of one runway and directly under the glide path of aircraft using it. Their land lies about 1,500 feet beyond the end of a second runway, but about 1,000 feet to one side of the glide path of aircraft using that runway. The plaintiffs contend that flights from both runways have resulted in a taking of their property. Their principal complaint is that the noise from jet aircraft makes their land unusable. The jets use a runway the center line of which, if extended, would pass about 1,000 feet to one side of the plaintiffs' land. Some planes pass directly over the plaintiffs' land, but these are not, for the most part, the civilian and military jets which cause the most noise.

The plaintiffs' case proceeded on two theories: (1) Systematic flights directly over their land cause a substantial interference with their use and enjoyment of that land. This interference constitutes a nuisance. Such a nuisance, if persisted in by a private party, could ripen into a prescription. Such a continuing nuisance, when maintained by government, amounts to the taking of an easement, or, more precisely, presents a jury question whether there is a taking. (2) Systematic flights which pass close to their land, even though not directly overhead, likewise constitute the taking of an easement, for the same reasons, and upon the same authority.

The Port of Portland contends that its activities do not constitute the taking of easements in the plaintiffs' land. The Port argues: (1) The plaintiffs have no right to exclude or protest flights directly over their land, if such flights are so high as to be in the public domain, i.e., within navigable airspace as defined by federal law.[20] (2) The plaintiffs have no right to protest flights which do not cross the airspace above their land, since these could commit no trespass in any event. Accordingly, the Port contends, there is no interference with any legally protected interest of the plaintiffs and thus no taking of any property for which the plaintiffs are entitled to compensation. In short, the Port's theory is that the plaintiffs must endure the noise of the nearby airport with the same forbearance that is required of those who live near highways and railroads....

The trial court proceeded as if the rights of the plaintiffs were limited by the imaginary lines that would describe a cube of airspace exactly 500 feet high and bounded on four sides by perpendicular extensions of the surface boundaries of their land. The trial court thus in effect adapted the law of trespass to the issues presented in this case, and held that unless there was a continuing trespass within the described cube of space there could be no recovery. The trial court...adopted the view that even if there was a nuisance, a nuisance could not give rise to a taking....

Since United States v. Causby, 328 U.S. 256 (1946), and particularly since Griggs v. Allegheny County, 369 U.S. 84 (1962), we know that easements can be taken by repeated low-level flights over private land...[and] compensation must be paid to the owners of the lands thus burdened....

It is not so well settled, however, that the easements discussed in the *Causby* and *Griggs* cases are easements to impose upon lands near an airport a servitude of noise. Courts operating upon the theory that repeated trespasses form the basis of the easement have not found it necessary to decide whether a repeated nuisance, which may or may not have been an accompaniment of a trespass, could equally give rise to a servitude upon neighboring land. It must be remembered that in both the *Causby* and *Griggs* cases the flights were virtually at tree-top level. Accordingly, both decisions could perhaps be supported on trespass theories exclusively. Following the

---

20. See Civil Aeronautics Act, 49 U.S.C. §551(a)(7) (1952). One FAA rule fixed 500 feet as the minimum safe altitude over persons, vehicles, and structures. 14 C.F.R. §60.107. Congress has, during all material times, denominated the airspace 500 feet above any person, vessel, vehicle or structure in other than congested areas as navigable airspace which is subject to a public right of transit.

Causby case, several federal district courts held that while repeated flights at low levels directly over private land may amount to a taking for which compensation must be paid, repeated flights nearby but not directly overhead must be endured as mere "damages" which, for various reasons, may not be compensable....

The Tenth Circuit...held...that there must be a trespass before there can be a taking. Batten v. United States, 306 F.2d 580 (10th Cir. 1962). As pointed out in a dissent by Chief Judge Murrah, the interference proven was substantial enough to impose a servitude upon the lands of the plaintiffs, and under the *Causby* and *Griggs* cases equally could have constituted a taking.... We believe the dissenting view in the *Batten* case presents the better-reasoned analysis of the legal principles involved, and that if the majority view in the *Batten* case can be defended it must be defended frankly upon the ground that considerations of public policy justify the result: i.e., that private rights must yield to public convenience in this class of cases....

While not every wrong committed by government will amount to a taking of private property, there are some wrongs which do constitute a taking.... We must decide whether a nuisance can ever constitute a taking.... If the government substantially deprives the owner of the use of his land, such deprivation is a taking for which the government must pay. If, on the other hand, the government merely commits some tort which does not deprive the owner of the use of his land, then there is no taking.

Therefore, unless there is some reason of public policy which bars compensation in cases of governmental nuisance as a matter of law, there is a question, in each case, as a matter of fact, whether or not the governmental activity complained of has resulted in so substantial an interference with use and enjoyment of one's land as to amount to a taking of private property for public use. This factual question, again barring some rule which says we may not ask it, is equally relevant whether the taking is trespassory or by a nuisance. A nuisance can be such an invasion of the rights of a possessor as to amount to a taking, in theory at least, any time a possessor is in fact ousted from the enjoyment of his land....

The plaintiffs concede that single-instance torts, as torts, are not compensable. Inverse condemnation, however, provides the remedy where an injunction would not be in the public interest, and where the continued interference amounts to a taking for which the constitution demands a remedy. In summary, a taking occurs whenever government acts in such a way as substantially to deprive an owner of the useful possession of that which he owns, either by repeated trespasses or by repeated non-trespassory invasions called "nuisance."...

If we accept, as we must upon established principles of the law of servitudes, the validity of the propositions that a noise can be a nuisance; that a nuisance can give rise to an easement; and that a noise coming straight down from above one's land can ripen into a taking if it is persistent enough and aggravated enough, then logically the same kind and degree of interference with the use and enjoyment of one's land can also be a taking even though the noise vector may come from some direction other than the perpendicular.

If a landowner has a right to be free from unreasonable interference caused by noise, as we hold that he has, then when does the noise burden become so unreasonable that the government must pay for the privilege of being permitted to continue to make the noise? Logically, the answer has to be given by the trier of fact.... The balancing of private rights and public necessity is not a novel problem.

Whether expressed in so many words or not, the principle found in the *Causby* [and] *Griggs*...cases is that when the government conducts an activity upon its own land which, after balancing the question of reasonableness, is sufficiently disturbing to the use and enjoyment of neighboring lands to amount to a taking thereof, then the public, and not the subservient landowner, should bear the cost of such public benefit.... The real question was not one of perpendicular extension of surface boundaries into the airspace, but a question of reasonableness based upon nuisance theories. In effect, the inquiry should have been whether the government had undertaken a course of conduct on its own land which, in simple fairness to its neighbors, required it to obtain more land so that the substantial burdens of the activity would fall upon public land, rather than upon that of involuntary contributors who happen to lie in the path of progress....

Logically, it makes no difference to a plaintiff disturbed in the use of his property whether the disturbing flights pass 501 feet or 499 feet above his land. If he is in fact ousted from the legitimate enjoyment of his land, it is to him an academic matter that the planes which have ousted him did not fly below 500 feet. The rule adopted by the majority of the state and federal courts is, then, an arbitrary one. The barring of actions when the flights are above 500 feet is also difficult to reconcile with the theory that recovery should be based upon nuisance concepts rather than upon the trespass theory which we have rejected. Whether a plaintiff is entitled to recover should depend upon the fact of a taking, and not upon an arbitrary rule. The ultimate question is whether there was a sufficient interference with the landowner's use and enjoyment to be a taking.... Congress may very properly declare certain airspace to be in the public domain for navigational purposes, but it does not necessarily follow that rights of navigation may be exercised unreasonably.... There is a point beyond which such power may not be exercised without compensation. *Causby*. The same limitation applies to lesser governmental agencies....

PERRY, J., dissenting.... It should be noted that to reach a reversal of the judgment of the trial court, the majority rely upon the law of nuisance. The majority seem to admit that this has never been the law of this state, but argue that it should be.... Where a flight directly over the land, by reason of noise and vibration, can be said in fact to cause serious interference in the owner's use and enjoyment of the property, it is a trespass, which is a constitutional taking, and requires full compensation. In the matter before us, however, after searching the record, I am unable to find any evidence that would support a judgment of a taking, based on interference with the plaintiffs' use and enjoyment of the land by airplane flights above the 500-foot level....

A nuisance, although a tort, does not contemplate a physical invasion of the property of another, but the use of a person's own property in such a way as to interfere with another's free enjoyment of his property.... Practically all human activities engaged in carrying out a commercial enterprise may interfere with someone's enjoyment of his property. It is the right of an owner of land to use his land in any lawful manner, and it is only when the manner of use creates a grave interference with another's enjoyment of his property that the law will seek to redress this type of wrong. This is a natural requirement of organized society. There must be some give and take to promote the well-being of all. The underlying basis in nuisance law is the common-sense thought that in organized society there must be an adjustment between reasonable use and personal discomfort. No such consideration is involved in the law of trespass.

Trespass of property which, as has been pointed out, effects a taking in a constitutional sense, comprehends a physical invasion of the property either by the person or by causing a physical object to enter upon or over the property of another.... Therefore, it is the taking of an owner's possessory interest in land as compared with interfering with an owner's use and enjoyment of his land that distinguishes a trespass which is a "taking" from a nuisance, which is not.... Nuisance [is based on] the balancing of the interests of owners.... Such considerations are foreign to the law of trespass.... Where a permanent trespass is committed by government, the constitution will not permit a balancing of the value of the taking for the benefit of the public against the interests of an owner. The owner must be fully compensated for his loss....

A nuisance takes none of the title in the property. The full legal title rests in the owner. If the nuisance is abated in any manner, the damage suffered has ended and the land is again restored

to its full value to the owner. On the other hand, if there is a taking, the property right of ownership or some interest therein has been transferred from the owner to the sovereign, and does not
again revert to the original owner even though the use to which the property has been put by the
sovereign ceases....

COMMENTARY & QUESTIONS

1. **Nuisance as a "servitude."** The majority and dissent agree that a plane's physical trespass constitutes the taking of a servitude (more properly labeled an "easement"). They
split over the rather technical point of whether a nuisance can do likewise. The distinction echoes a principle of eminent domain compensation allowing extensive recovery
for "consequential" damages if government has condemned any piece of your real
property, however tiny, but none if no land is taken. Both opinions ignore a fairly well-
established line of cases holding that nuisances can create prescriptive easements to
pollute and that government can take easements that are not permanent. Both recognize that nuisance law involves more balancing than trespass law, although neither is
very clear about intentional nuisance doctrine. To what extent should airport inverse
condemnation cases balance the noise and vibrations suffered by plaintiffs against the
public's need for an airport? Or should any substantial burden on neighbors be
compensated as a cost of doing business? Should it make any difference that government, rather than a private entity, operates the harmful airport?

2. **Extending physical inverse condemnation theories.** There has been some limited
extension of the inverse condemnation remedy beyond airport cases. Compensation
has been ordered for loss of access (where a public road was converted to a limited-
access highway) and loss of light and air (where a bridge or overpass was built alongside
a house), even though no part of the plaintiffs' land or airspace was physically invaded.
The court notes "the forbearance that is required of those who live near highways and
railroads," likewise facing dust, noise, vibrations, flashing lights, and severe losses in
property value. Are these compensable now? If so, the costs could bankrupt public
transit programs.

Inverse condemnation claims can also arise in the wild. Can't it be argued that the
government takes an easement in my property without compensation when it forbids
me from fencing out the antelope that want to eat my grass (giving the antelope an
easement of access over my land), or when I am forbidden to shoot the endangered grey
wolf that still thinks my property is her territory and eats one of my cows every week, or
when the Forest Service adopts a "let-burn" policy for national forests so that my
private trees and vacation cabin are destroyed by fire? See United States v. Lawrence,
848 F.2d 1502 (10th Cir. 1988) (antelope); Christy v. Hodel, 857 F.2d 1324 (9th Cir.
1988) (grizzlies); Winner, Uncle Sam and Forest Fires, 15 Envtl. L. 623 (1985); Keiter &
Holscher, Wolf Recovery under the Endangered Species Act: A Study in Contemporary
Federalism, 11 Pub. Land L. Rev. 19 (1990). This kind of claim has played a major role
in constitutional challenges to "regulatory takings" (as in the next section).

Pushing the inverse condemnation doctrine further, consider the fact that many
Americans are starting to worry about clusters of leukemia and other ailments that

have been correlated in some cases with the presence of high-tension electrical transmission facilities. If clients are worried about high electromagnetic fields (EMFs) on their property caused by utility transmission lines but cannot prove tort liability, can an attorney file an inverse condemnation claim for a "taking" by the public utility company (which has the power of eminent domain) of an "electromagnetic easement" of right of way over their property? See Brodeur, Annals of Radiation: Calamity on Meadow Street, July 9, 1990, New Yorker, at 50. Or likewise against the federal government for low-frequency radio transmissions? Wisconsin v. Weinberger, 745 F.2d 412 (7th Cir. 1984). Or even to use a physical taking argument to circumvent sovereign immunity in tort cases such as Nevin v. United States, 696 F.2d 1229 (9th Cir. 1987), where members of the public were injured by clandestine governmental testing of bacillary and chemical agents in urban public areas? (As to the latter, public notice is now required by law. 52 U.S.C. §1520.)

C. CHALLENGES TO REGULATIONS AS UNCONSTITUTIONAL "TAKINGS"

Section 1. REGULATORY TAKINGS

Determining how far the collective power of the majority can intrude upon individual rights has always been one of the classic problems of democracy. When government regulates private property under the police power, tensions tend to get particularly hot because it does not generally pay for the privilege. Few Americans actively welcome the state's directives about how they should use their land, especially when restrictions get in the way of private profits. In modern America, where rugged frontier individualism lives on in private property doctrines that built the world's greatest economy, environmental regulations may be particularly resented because they are relatively new to the scene, dealing with public "rights" and objectives that the market economy had never heard of before Rachel Carson's *Silent Spring*. Takings challenges can be significant in all areas of government, but nowhere more pressingly and vividly than in the field of environmental protection.

The politics and rhetoric of regulatory takings debates are intense. Takings challenges to environmental statutes and regulations are likely to occur wherever private property rights are impacted, which is to say they arise throughout the field. When a state prohibits development in wetlands, when the federal government prohibits billboards on interstate highways, when a local town council prohibits junkyards, or when a government entity proposes to restrict any of a host of other concerns — automobile pollution, trade in endangered species ivory, use of off-road vehicles on public lands, destruction of historic buildings, biogenetic experimentation and drug development, agricultural pesticides and herbicides, destruction of wildlife and its habitat, air and water pollution, strip mining, throwaway bottles, and so on — in each case the "invalid takings" argument will be heard loudly in the legislative and administrative process. These complaints about government high-handedness are sometimes coupled with a dire warning from lobbyists that if the restriction is passed, those who vote for it as well as the agency regulators may find themselves personally liable for damages for violating the regulatees' civil rights.

Because the legal lines for judging the validity of regulations have been so poorly defined, often the mere threat of a lawsuit raising a takings challenge is enough to dissuade legislators and city councils from passing environmental measures, even where the proposed regulation clearly would comply with judicial takings tests. As Professor Sax has written, "the 'crazy-quilt pattern' of Supreme Court doctrine has effectively been acknowledged by the Court itself, which has developed the habit of introducing its uniformly unsatisfactory opinions in this area with the understatement that 'no rigid rules' or 'set formula' are available to determine where [valid] regulation ends and [invalid] taking begins."[21]

When a restriction is actually challenged in court, the argument typically begins with the allegation of economic loss. (The first three areas of police power tests — authority, proper public purpose, and the restriction's relationship of means to ends — are relevant but usually are in effect conceded.) The attack alleges that even though the restriction does not take physical possession of all or part of the private property (which in virtually all cases would clearly require eminent domain compensation), it so restricts property rights that it amounts to a taking under the Due Process Clause and the eminent domain clause of the Fifth Amendment and their state corollaries. The test is the same under either clause and usually turns in some manner on the amount of property loss, viewed in a vacuum. If a court finds a restriction excessive or confiscatory, the government can accept an equitable remedy nullifying the law as applied to the subject property or agree to pay damages for the invalid taking (which explains why these verdicts are often confusingly referred to as "inverse condemnation" or "eminent domain").[22]

Paradoxically, although courts go to extraordinary lengths to defer to and uphold eminent domain actions, as seen above in Part A, the judicial approach to regulatory acts has been discernibly more critical, especially in the past two decades of the political ascendancy of the Property Rights Movement. In recent years, many courts — when presented with losses of property value, a frequent occurrence in most police power settings — have often shifted the burden to government, ignoring the usual presumption of constitutionality for governmental acts.

President's Council on Environmental Quality, Our Nation's Wetlands
1-2, 19–28, 50 (1978)[23]

Inland and coastal wetlands — only yesterday considered useless — are now seen as valuable endangered natural resources. Estimates of irreversibly altered or destroyed wetlands in the 48 continental states have already reached 40 to 50 percent.... Of California's original 3.5 million

---

21. Sax, Takings and the Police Power, 74 Yale L.J. 36, 37 (1964).

22. The *remedies* sought in regulatory challenges can be the same as in inverse condemnation and eminent domain cases: damages for the taking or injunctions to block the government action. But the substantive elements of the claims are very different in the regulatory and the physical taking settings.

23. Perhaps because wetlands protection was identified as an area of marked controversy between developers and conservationists, this report — produced during the Carter years — was quickly recalled and sequestered in 1981 by the Reagan Administration.

SOUTH FLORIDA WATER MANAGEMENT DISTRICT

FIGURE 23-2

An extensive wetland area, all privately owned lands, lying ready for draining and development. Limited to their natural state, the wetlands have low market value. If drained, they may increase from ten to a hundred times in value.

This wetland overview happens to be the Kissimmee River wetlands of south-central Florida shortly before they were channelized and drained at government expense in 1961 by the Army Corps of Engineers. The drainage project, which had been strongly opposed by environmentalists, created immensely valuable private lands. It also turned out to create a nightmare. The natural meandering streams and wetlands had served as a giant natural filter absorbing and cleaning the water of fertilizer runoffs, other nutrients, and pollution. Without the natural system, Lake Okechobee, a major water source for South Florida, immediately began to choke up with pollution, organic detritus, and eutrophication effects.

Now Corps and Florida officials are attempting to return much of the river system to its original state, hoping to save public water supplies. To restore the river, however, will require $343.6 million (the 1961 channelizing cost less than $30 million); much of the current cost is for governmental compensation payable to private landowners for loss of dryland market values initially created by the public drainage project.

wetland acres, in 1954 only 450,000 remained. In 1959 it was estimated that 45 percent of Connecticut's coastal marshes had been lost since a 1914 survey. At current rates of destruction, it was predicted that only 14 percent might remain by the year 2000. Surveys disclosed that the Rainwater Basin of south-central Nebraska had lost over 80 percent of its marshes by the 1960s. Southeastern Wisconsin had lost 61 percent by 1968. An estimated one-half the wetlands in the prairie pothole region of the United States had been drained by 1950. It is estimated that 35,000 acres of prime prairie wetlands are now being sacrificed each year. A survey conducted by the Fish and Wildlife Service in 1974 revealed that over 40 percent of the potholes existing in 1964 in western Minnesota had been destroyed in that 10-year period....

Many former marshes and swamps are [today] vacation homes and marinas. Other wetlands are used as dumping grounds.... With greater affluence and increased population, the pressures for development of wetlands — for agricultural production, for highways, for residential and commercial building sites, for ports, for marinas, for parking lots, for industries and power plants which require large quantities of cooling water — seem destined to increase....

Clearly it is blatantly wasteful to turn a productive wetland into a dump. But it is harder to assign relative values to leaving a wetland in its natural state or using it for luxurious waterfront dwellings...and highly productive cultivated farmland.... We do know that wetlands are vital fish and wildlife habitats. Two-thirds of the commercially important fish and shellfish harvested along the Atlantic and in the Gulf of Mexico depend on coastal estuaries and their wetlands for food sources, for spawning grounds, for nurseries for the young, or for all these critical purposes; for the Pacific coast, the figure is almost one-half. Wetlands provide essential resting, wintering, and nesting grounds for many species of migratory waterfowl, other waterbirds, and many songbirds. They are among the most productive ecosystems in the world. They are important in maintenance of ground water supplies and water purification. Marshes and swamps along coasts, rivers, and lakes protect shorelines and banks from erosion. Wetlands also have the capacity to store flood waters temporarily and in some instances to reduce the volume and severity of floods. The less tangible values of wetlands may be classified as recreational, educational, scientific, and aesthetic....

There is general recognition of the fact that wetlands are vital to fish and wildlife.... Figures on wetland-dependent fish yields have been the subject of numerous studies. The Georgia Game and Fish Commission estimated the per acre yield of freshwater wetland fish at 75 pounds. In Connecticut's marshy Niantic River, the annual scallop harvest is 15,000 bushels, amounting to 300 pounds per acre per year, which exceeds the beef yield on excellent grazing grounds....

A subject of livelier debate and growing intensity is how wetlands function as pollution filtration systems and as natural flood control mechanisms. The implications of current scientific findings for these subjects are of great interest to ecologists, planners, and engineers. The role of wetlands in reducing the pollution levels in water has recently become one of the most compelling arguments for their preservation. Because wetland ecosystems hold nutrients, they simultaneously act as a pollution filtration system. Water arriving from such "point" sources as waste water treatment plants and from such "nonpoint" sources as runoff from agricultural fields and city streets carries a high level of pollutants, particularly...nitrogen and phosphorus. As the water circulates through a wetland, the plants take up and use these pollutants as nutrients. A study by the Georgia Water Quality Control Board of Mountain Creek, a tributary of the Alcovy River, showed that water heavily polluted with human sewage and chicken offal was designated clean after passing through 2.75 miles of swamp forest. A study of the Tinicum Marsh, located a few miles from the Philadelphia airport...indicated that the marsh significantly improved water quality by increasing the oxygen content and reducing the nutrient load....

Flood protection [is] one of the most innovative practical applications of current findings about wetland functions. [The U.S. Army] Corps of Engineers [determined that wetlands provided] the simplest yet the most innovative of plans for natural flood control in the Massachusetts Charles River watershed.... 20,000 acres of undeveloped wetland...provided the least-cost solution to future flooding [equivalent to] a 55,000 acre-foot reservoir, or extensive walls and dikes...with annual flood control benefits of $1,203,000....

It is difficult to quantify the value of wetlands, and attempts to do so generate considerable disagreement, but because alternative approaches to engineering problems are often judged today by cost-benefit comparisons, such financial estimates are now common. Today a number of ecologists are attempting to apply accounting procedures to wetlands, making financial evaluations of the services which wetlands perform in their natural state and urging that the figures be seriously considered in decisions on uses of water resources. Most quantifiers have concerned themselves solely with wetlands functions. Placing a dollar value on purely aesthetic delight may seem impossible to many scientists, who feel on surer ground pricing wetlands in relation to damage projections or to the known commercial values of estuarine-dependent shellfish....

State of Maine v. Johnson
Supreme Court of Maine, 1970
265 A.2d 711

MARDEN, J. On appeal from an injunction granted under the provisions of 12 M.R.S.A. §§4701-4709, the Wetlands Act, which places restrictions upon the alteration and use of wetlands, as therein defined, without permission from the municipal officers concerned and the State Wetlands Control Board. The Act is a conservation measure under the police power of the State to protect the ecology of areas bordering coastal waters.[24]

The appellants own a tract of land about 220 feet wide and 700 feet long extending across salt water marshes between Atlantic Avenue on the east and the Webhannet River on the west in the Town of Wells. Westerly of the lots fronting on Atlantic Avenue the strip has been subdivided into lots for sale. The easterly 260 feet approximately of the strip has been filled and bears seasonal dwellings. Westerly of this 260 foot development is marsh land flooded at high tide and drained, upon receding tide, into the River by a network of what our Maine historical novelist Kenneth E. Roberts called "eel runs," but referred to in the record as creeks. Similar marsh-land, undeveloped, lies to the north and south of appellants' strip and westerly of the River, all of which makes up a substantial acreage (the extent not given in testimony, but of which we take judicial notice) of marshland known as the Wells Marshes. Appellants' land, by raising the grade above high water by the addition of fill, is adaptable to development for building purposes.

Following the effective date of the Act, an application to the municipal officers, with notice to the Wetlands Control Board, for permission to fill a portion of this land was denied by the

---

24. Pertinent portions of the wetlands act are quoted:

§4701. Prohibition. No person, agency or municipality shall remove, fill, dredge or drain sanitary sewage into, or otherwise alter any coastal waters, as defined herein...without filing written notice of his intention to do so, including such plans as may be necessary to describe the proposed activity, with the municipal officers in the municipality affected and with the Wetlands Control Board.... The municipal officers shall hold a public hearing on the proposal.... For purposes of this chapter, coastal wetland is defined as any swamp, marsh, bog, beach, flat or other contiguous lowland above extreme low water which is subject to tidal action or normal storm flowage at any time excepting periods of maximum storm activity.

§4702. Permits. Permits to undertake the proposed alteration shall be issued by the municipal officers within 7 days of such hearing providing the Wetlands Control Board approves. Such permit may be conditioned upon the applicant amending his proposal to take whatever measures are deemed necessary by either the municipality or the Wetlands Control Board to protect the public interest. Approval may be withheld by either the municipal officers or the board when in the opinion of either body the proposal would threaten the public safety, health or welfare, would adversely affect the value or enjoyment of the property of abutting owners, or would be damaging to the conservation of public or private water supplies or of wildlife or freshwater, estuarine or marine fisheries.

§4704. Appeal. Appeal may be taken to the Superior Court within 30 days after the denial of a permit or the issuance of a conditional permit for the purpose of determining whether the action appealed from so restricts the use of the property as to deprive the owner of the reasonable use thereof, and is therefore an unreasonable exercise of police power, or which constitutes the equivalent of a taking without compensation. The court upon such a finding may set aside the action appealed from.

§4705. Wetlands Control Board. The Wetlands Control Board shall be composed of the Commissioners of Sea and Shore Fisheries and of Inland Fisheries and Game, the Chairman of the Water and Air Environmental Improvement Commission, the Chairman of the State Highway Commission, the Forest Commissioner and the Commissioner of Health and Welfare or their delegates.

§4709. Violations. Violators are subject to fine and/or injunctive process.

Board.... [Subsequently,] fill was deposited on the land in question, as the result of which the State sought an injunction....

The record establishes that the land which the appellants propose to build up by fill and build upon for sale, or to be offered for sale to be built upon, are coastal wetlands within the definition of the Act and that the refusal by the Board to permit the deposit of such fill prevents the development as proposed. The single Justice found that the property is a portion of a salt marsh area, a valuable natural resource of the State, that the highest and best use for the land, so filled, is for housing, and that unfilled it has no commercial value.

The issue is...whether the [wetlands restrictions] so limit the use to plaintiffs of this land that such deprivation of use amounts to a taking of their property without constitutional due process and just compensation.[25]

Due process of law has a dual aspect, procedural and substantive. Procedurally, "notice and opportunity for hearing are of the essence."... The Act meets all requirements of procedural due process.

Substantively, [due process] is "the constitutional guaranty that no person shall be deprived of...property for arbitrary reasons, such a deprivation being constitutionally supportable only if the conduct from which the deprivation flows is proscribed by reasonable legislation (that is, legislation the enactment of which is within the scope of legislative authority) reasonably applied (that is, for a purpose consonant with the purpose of the legislation itself)." 16 Am. Jur. 2d, Constitutional Law §550.

It is this substantive due process which is challenged in the Act.... The constitutionally protected right of property is not unlimited. It is subject to reasonable restraints and regulations in the public interest by means of the legitimate exercise of police power. The exercise of this police power may properly regulate the use of property and if the owner suffers injury "it is either *damnum absque injuria*, or, in the theory of law, he is compensated for it by sharing in the general benefits which the regulations are intended...to secure." The determination of unconstitutional deprivation is difficult and judicial decisions are diverse.... A guiding principle appears in the frequently cited case of Pennsylvania Coal Company v. Mahon, 260 U.S. 393, 413 (1922), where Mr. Justice Holmes declared:

> Government hardly could go on if to some extent values incident to property could not be diminished without paying for every such change in the general law....But obviously the implied limitation must have its limits or the contract and due process clauses are gone....

Confrontation between public interests and private interests is common in the application of zoning laws, with which the Wetlands Act may be analogized, and the great majority of which, upon their facts, are held to be reasonable exercises of the police power. There are, however, zoning restrictions which have been recognized as equivalent to a taking of the property restricted....

Between the public interest in braking and eventually stopping the insidious despoliation of our natural resources which have for so long been taken for granted, on the one hand, and the protection of appellants' property rights on the other, the issue is cast.

Here the single Justice has found that the area of which appellants' land is a part "is a valuable natural resource of the State of Maine and plays an important role in the conservation and development of aquatic and marine life, game birds and waterfowl," which bespeaks the public interest involved and the protection of which is sought by §4702 of the Act. With relation to

---

25. Maine Constitution Article I §6. "He shall not be...deprived of his...property...but by the law of the land." "Section 21. Private property shall not be taken for public uses without just compensation...."

appellants' interest the single Justice found that appellants' land absent the addition of fill "has no commercial value whatever." These findings are supported by the evidence and are conclusive.

As distinguished from conventional zoning for town protection, the area of wetlands representing a "valuable natural resource of the State," of which appellants' holdings are but a minute part, is of state-wide concern. The benefits from its preservation extend beyond town limits and are state-wide. The cost of its preservation should be publicly borne. To leave appellants with commercially valueless land in upholding the restriction presently imposed is to charge them with more than their just share of the cost of this state-wide conservation program, granting fully its commendable purpose.... Their compensation by sharing in the benefits which this restriction is intended to secure is so disproportionate to their deprivation of reasonable use that such exercise of the State's police power is unreasonable.

The application of the wetlands restriction in the terms of the denial of appellants' proposal to fill, and enjoining them from so doing deprives them of the reasonable use of their property and...is both an unreasonable exercise of police power and equivalent to a taking....

Holding, as we do, that the prohibition against the filling of appellants' land, upon the facts peculiar to the case, is an unreasonable exercise of police power, it does not follow that the restriction as to draining sanitary sewage into coastal wetlands is subject to the same infirmity. Additional considerations of health and pollution which are "separable from and independent of" the "fill" restriction may well support validity of the acts in those areas of concern....

K & K Construction, Inc. and JFK Company v. Department of Natural Resources
Supreme Court of Michigan, 1998
456 Mich. 570, cert. denied, 525 U.S. 819 (1998)

CAVANAGH, J. This case requires us to decide whether the denial of a permit to fill wetlands on the plaintiffs' property constitutes a regulatory taking of the property without just compensation. The trial court found that the permit denials effectively rendered part of the plaintiffs' land worthless. The Department of Natural Resources [DNR] was therefore required to compensate the plaintiffs.

Plaintiffs...own eighty-two acres of property...in Waterford Township. JFK is a Michigan limited partnership consisting of the five children of Joseph and Elaine Kosik.... Mr. Kosik and his son are the sole shareholders of K & K Construction [which plans] to build a restaurant and sports complex on the property.

The property consists of four defined parcels, all of which are contiguous. Parcel one consists of approximately fifty-five acres, twenty-seven acres of which are wetlands. It is zoned for commercial use. Parcel two (sixteen acres) is directly south of parcel one. It contains a small portion of the wetlands. Parcel three (9.34 acres) is directly south of parcel two, and does not contain any wetlands. Parcel four (3.4 acres) borders the south side of parcel one, and the east side of parcel two. It is also free of wetlands. Parcels two, three, and four are zoned for multiple family residential housing (R-2). Parcel three has already been developed; parcels two and four have not been developed....

Plaintiffs' original plan...was to build a restaurant and sports complex on forty-two acres of parcel one, and several multiple-family residential structures with a storm-water retention pond on parcels two and four. Pursuant to this plan, plaintiffs applied for a permit to fill part of parcel one in June 1988. The DNR denied the permit, finding that approximately twenty-eight acres of the property were protected wetlands [under the state Wetlands Act, M.C.L. §281.701].... The trial court held that parcel one was the only property relevant to the taking analysis, and that denial of the permit to construct the restaurant and sports complex effectively rendered [that] property commercially worthless. The DNR was required to compensate plaintiffs for the full value....

Faced with a substantial adverse judgment, the DNR attempted to mitigate the loss in value of the property by allowing development to commence [on some of the wetlands]. Even so, the trial court held that the DNR owed plaintiffs damages both for a "temporary" taking of the land that could now be developed...and also for the full value of the [unpermitted parcel one] wetlands.... The trial court ultimately decided that the DNR was liable for approximately $3.5 million for the [unpermitted] wetlands, and approximately $500,000, plus interest for the temporary taking. The Court of Appeals affirmed....

As stated by Justice Holmes, "The general rule at least is, that while property may be regulated to a certain extent, if regulation goes too far it will be recognized as a taking." Pennsylvania Coal Co. v. Mahon, 260 U.S. 393, 415 (1922)....

Regulations effectuate a taking in...two situations: (a) "categorical" taking, where the owner is deprived of "all economically beneficial or productive use of land," Lucas v. South Carolina Coastal Council, 505 U.S. 1003, 1015 (1992); or (b) a taking recognized on the basis of the application of the traditional "balancing test" established in Penn Central v. New York City, 438 U.S. 104 (1978)....

In the former situation...a reviewing court need not apply a case-specific analysis, and the owner should automatically recover for a taking of his property...in the case of a physical invasion of his property by the government (not at issue in this case), or where a regulation forces an owner to "sacrifice all economically beneficial uses [of land] in the name of the common good...." Lucas at 1019.

In the latter situation, the balancing test, a reviewing court must engage in an "ad hoc, factual inquir[y]," centering on three factors: (1) the character of the government's action, (2) the economic effect of the regulation on the property, and (3) the extent by which the regulation has interfered with distinct, investment-backed expectations. Penn Central, 438 U.S. at 124.

The trial court found that the Wetlands Act had effectively eliminated the economically viable use of plaintiffs' land; therefore, plaintiffs were due compensation for a taking of their property. Significantly, the trial court only considered the effect of the regulations on parcel one of plaintiffs' property, finding that parcel one was the only relevant parcel for the taking analysis...which meant that plaintiffs could recover categorically for the taking under...Lucas.

The first step in our analysis is to determine which parcel or parcels owned by plaintiffs are relevant for the taking inquiry. The determination of what is referred to as the "denominator parcel" is important because it often affects the analysis of what economically viable uses remain for a person's property after the regulations are imposed. Plaintiffs urge us to focus our analysis only on parcel one, while defendant argues that we must look at all four of plaintiffs' parcels as a single unit....

One of the fundamental principles of taking jurisprudence is the "nonsegmentation" principle. This principle holds that when evaluating the effect of a regulation on a parcel of property, the effect of the regulation must be viewed with respect to the parcel as a whole. Keystone Bituminous, 480 U.S. 498. Courts should not "divide a single parcel into discrete segments and attempt to determine whether rights in a particular segment have been entirely abrogated." Penn Central, 438 U.S. 130. Rather, we must examine the effect of the regulation on the entire parcel, not just the affected portion of that parcel....[26]

---

26. "Clearly, the quantum of land to be considered is not each individual lot containing wetlands or even the combined area of wetlands. If that were true, the...protection of wetlands via a permit system would, ipso facto, constitute a taking in every case...." Tabb Lakes, Ltd. v. United States, 10 F.3d 796, 802 (C.A. Fed., 1993).

Both permit applications filed by plaintiffs with the DNR contemplated a comprehensive development using part of parcels one, two, and four. In a similar situation, the United States Court of Claims held that a plaintiff may not separate a certain lot of property from others that he owned with regard to his taking claim when he had previously treated them as "a single parcel for purposes of purchase and financing."... We can safely state that the denominator parcel includes parcels one, two, and four.... On remand, we instruct the trial court to determine... whether...all four parcels should be considered in the taking analysis....

The case is remanded to the trial court. On remand, the trial court must determine —

(1) if parcel three of plaintiffs' property should be included in the denominator parcel [according to whether it was conceptually part of the contiguous investment], and

(2) whether the effect of the regulations on the entire denominator parcel resulted in a taking under the balancing test.

[On remand, the trial court adopted the inclusive baseline but did not resolve the case, which in 2004 was still pending in the state courts.]

The next case, *Pennsylvania Coal*, is the classic takings decision cited in both preceding wetlands cases and in virtually every regulatory takings case since 1922. It is the first case in which the 1789 constitutional prohibition on uncompensated physical takings was extended to *nonphysical* regulatory actions.[27] The *Pennsylvania Coal* decision, which raises but does not resolve many of the issues already encountered in the wetlands cases, was, like its author Oliver Wendell Holmes, both eminent and enigmatic.

Pennsylvania Coal Company v. Mahon
Supreme Court of the United States, 1922
260 U.S. 393

HOLMES, J. This is a bill in equity brought by the defendants in error to prevent the Pennsylvania Coal Company from mining under their property in such way as to remove the supports and cause a subsidence of the surface and of their house. The bill sets out a deed executed by the Coal Company in 1878, under which the plaintiffs claim. The deed conveys the surface but in express terms reserves the right to remove all the coal under the same and the grantee takes the premises with the risk and waives all claim for damages that may arise from mining out the coal. But the plaintiffs say that whatever may have been the Coal Company's rights, they were taken away by an Act of Pennsylvania, approved May 27, 1921 (P. L. 1198), commonly known there as the Kohler Act.... The statute forbids the mining of anthracite coal in such a way as to cause the subsidence of, among other things, any structure used as a human habitation [preventing coal companies nearing the end of mining in underground coal seams from quarrying away parts of the supportive "pillars" of coal that are kept in place to hold up the ceilings of working mines, if there are homes, public buildings, roads, lakes, or streams above].... As applied to this case the statute is admitted to destroy previously existing rights of property and contract. The question is whether the police power can be stretched so far.

Government hardly could go on if to some extent values incident to property could not be diminished without paying for every such change in the general law. As long recognized some

---

27. The Founding Fathers quite clearly did not intend that regulations could be takings (see F. Bosselman, D. Callies, and J. Banta, The Taking Issue (1973)) — a fact of constitutional history that gives pause to some who are otherwise strict-constructionists.

values are enjoyed under an implied limitation and must yield to the police power. But obviously the implied limitation must have its limits or the contract and due process clauses are gone. One fact for consideration in determining such limits is the extent of the diminution. When it reaches a certain magnitude, in most if not in all cases there must be an exercise of eminent domain and compensation to sustain the act. So the question depends upon the particular facts. The greatest weight is given to the judgment of the legislature but it always is open to interested parties to contend that the legislature has gone beyond its constitutional power....

This is a case of a single private house. No doubt there is a public interest even in this, as there is in every purchase and sale and in all that happens within the commonwealth. But usually in ordinary private affairs the public interest does not warrant much of this kind of interference. A source of damage to such a house is not a public nuisance even if similar damage is inflicted on others in different places. The damage is not common or public. The extent of the public interest is shown by the statute to be limited, since the statute ordinarily does not apply to land when the surface is owned by the owner of the coal. Furthermore, it is not justified as a protection of personal safety. That could be provided for by notice. Indeed the very foundation of this bill is that the defendant gave timely notice of its intent to mine under the house. On the other hand the extent of the taking is great. It purports to abolish what is recognized in Pennsylvania as an estate in land — a very valuable estate — and what is declared by the Court below to be a contract hitherto binding the plaintiffs. If we were called upon to deal with the plaintiffs' position alone we should think it clear that the statute does not disclose a public interest sufficient to warrant so extensive a destruction of the defendant's constitutionally protected rights.

But the case has been treated as one in which the general validity of the act should be discussed. The Attorney General of the State, the City of Scranton, and the representatives of other extensive interests were allowed to take part in the argument below and have submitted their contentions here. It seems, therefore, to be our duty to go farther in the statement of our opinion, in order that it may be known at once, and that further suits should not be brought in vain. It is our opinion that the act cannot be sustained as an exercise of the police power, so far as it affects the mining of coal under streets or cities in places where the right to mine such coal has been reserved. As said in a Pennsylvania case, "For practical purposes, the right to coal consists in the right to mine it." What makes the right to mine coal valuable is that it can be exercised with profit. To make it commercially impracticable to mine certain coal has very nearly the same effect for constitutional purposes as appropriating or destroying it. This we think that we are warranted in assuming that the statute does.

The protection of private property in the Fifth Amendment presupposes that it is wanted for public use, but provides that it shall not be taken for such use without compensation. A similar assumption is made in the decisions upon the Fourteenth Amendment. When this seemingly absolute protection is found to be qualified by the police power, the natural tendency of human nature is to extend the qualification more and more until at last private property disappears. But that cannot be accomplished in this way under the Constitution of the United States.

The general rule at least is that while property may be regulated to a certain extent, if regulation goes too far it will be recognized as a taking. It may be doubted how far exceptional cases, like the blowing up of a house to stop a conflagration, go — and if they go beyond the general rule, whether they do not stand as much upon tradition as upon principle. In general it is not plain that a man's misfortunes or necessities will justify his shifting the damages to his neighbor's shoulders. We are in danger of forgetting that a strong public desire to improve the public condition is not enough to warrant achieving the desire by a shorter cut than the constitutional way of paying for the change. As we already have said this is a question of degree — and

FIGURE 23-3

Photographs from Scranton, Pennsylvania, showing mine subsidence cave-ins caused by removal of coal pillars beneath the city. The photo above, taken shortly before 1920, was presented to the legislature as part of the city's case for passage of the 1921 Kohler Act, which was declared unconstitutional in Pennsylvania Coal. *The bottom left photograph was taken in the first decade of the century. The residents of the home, Mr. and Mrs. Buckley, escaped safely by ladder up to the surface from their attic window.*

therefore cannot be disposed of by general propositions. But we regard this as going beyond any of the cases decided by this Court. We assume, of course, that the statute was passed upon the conviction that an exigency existed that would warrant it, and we assume that an exigency exists that would warrant the exercise of eminent domain. But the question at bottom is upon whom the loss of the changes desired should fall. So far as private persons or communities have seen fit to take the risk of acquiring only surface rights, we cannot see that the fact that their risk has become a danger warrants the giving to them greater rights than they bought. Decree reversed.

BRANDEIS, J., dissenting.... The right of the owner to use his land is not absolute. He may not so use it as to create a public nuisance, and uses once harmless may, owing to changed conditions, seriously threaten the public welfare. Whenever they do, the Legislature has power to prohibit such uses without paying compensation.... If by mining anthracite coal the owner would necessarily unloose poisonous gases, I suppose no one would doubt the power of the state to prevent the mining without buying his coal fields. And why may not the state, likewise, without paying compensation, prohibit one from digging so deep or excavating so near the surface, as to expose the community to like dangers? In the latter case, as in the former, carrying on the business would be a public nuisance.

It is said that one fact for consideration in determining whether the limits of the police power have been exceeded is the extent of the resulting diminution in value, and that here the restriction destroys existing rights of property and contract. But values are relative. If we are to consider the value of the coal kept in place by the restriction, we should compare it with the value of all other parts of the land. That is, with the value not of the coal alone, but with the value of the whole property. The rights of an owner as against the public are not increased by dividing the interests in his property into surface and subsoil. The sum of the rights in the parts cannot be greater than the rights in the whole.... For aught that appears the value of the coal kept in place by the restriction may be negligible as compared with the value of the whole property, or even as compared with that part of it which is represented by the coal remaining in place and which may be extracted despite the statute.

COMMENTARY & QUESTIONS

1. **The contested elements of regulatory takings cases.** How to define the limit beyond which government regulations on individuals must be compensated? When government authority *physically* appropriates private property, the line normally is passed, a distinction reaffirmed in the 1978 *Loretto* case where a regulation forcing apartment buildings to allot physical space to TV-cable boxes required compensation.[28] And it has been well established that property uses that are nuisances or noxious uses can be abated without compensation.[29] But where the regulatory impact on private property is not physical nor clearly a nuisance, the clarity disappears and a welter of complex issues

---

28. Loretto v. Teleprompter, 458 U.S. 419 (1982). Even this line is not consistent. Justice Holmes acknowledged "exceptional cases, like the blowing up of a house to stop a conflagration," 216 U.S. at 416, and upheld regulations requiring nuisance properties such as diseased cattle or trees to be physically appropriated or destroyed without compensation. See Miller v. Schoene, 276 U.S. 272 (1928).

29. "Since no individual has a right to use his property so as to create a nuisance or otherwise harm others, the State has not 'taken' anything when it asserts its power to enjoin...nuisance-like activity." Stevens, J., in Keystone Bituminous Coal Ass'n v. DeBenedictis, 480 U.S. 470, 491 (1987). See also Penn Central Transp. Co. v. City of N.Y., 438 U.S. 104, 144–146 (1978) (dissent by Rehnquist, J.), citing Mugler v. Kansas, 123 U.S. 623, 668–669 (1887) and Hadacheck v. Sebastian, 239 U.S. 394 (1915).

arises. The three preceding cases serve to raise virtually all the major questions that regularly recur in regulatory takings challenges:

• **Diminution that goes too far?** What is the ultimate legal standard of takings validity? In the preceding wetlands decisions, as in most takings cases, both courts cite Justice Holmes's dictum that "the extent of the diminution" of private property rights is highly significant, and if it goes "too far" the regulation will be an invalid taking. But this standard, though it makes general common sense, is impossible to apply objectively. Asking whether the property owner retains a "reasonable remaining use or value," also a common phrasing of the standard of takings validity, likewise invites subjective judgments. Only recently have these standards been somewhat clarified.

• **Setting the physical baseline for the judicial inquiry into property value diminution: the parcel as a whole?** Since virtually all agree with Holmes that diminution (the degree of private loss caused by a regulation) is relevant to determining regulatory validity, on what physical property baseline is the degree of loss to be calculated — on the property as a whole as Brandeis argued or just on the regulated portion as Holmes held? The latter perspective, a divide-and-conquer definition, dramatically increases the prospects for invalidity. As we will see, the law now favors Brandeis's dissenting view of the conceptual baseline rather than Holmes's.

• **The time baselines.** There are two timing issues: retrospective economic accounting and time-of-purchase notice estoppel. In *Pennsylvania Coal*, the mining company had made huge profits prior to the date that the regulation prohibiting removal of support pillars was passed. Can the reviewing court take the past economic returns from the company's investment into account when weighing the regulation's validity?

Second, are property owners who had bought land, knowing that it was regulated (therefore often paying less for it), thereafter estopped from turning around and seeking to overturn the regulation because it burdens their property value?[30]

• **Investment-backed expectations.** To what extent does constitutional fairness require consideration of the property owner's investment-backed expectations?[31] This issue can support challenged regulations by defining the physical and time baselines broadly, according to the property owner's overall investment planning, and it can reinforce property owners' challenges by emphasizing unfair frustration of reasonable expectations.

• **Measuring land *value* or active *use*?** In virtually all takings reviews, the courts must consider how much economic diminution the private interest has suffered. Generally this measure looks not to how much has been lost but to how much was gained or remains. There is an issue, however, whether this residuum private interest is to be measured in terms of land *value* (if an undevelopable wetland, for instance, nevertheless has market value of $2000 an acre as a buffer or for aesthetics), or whether there must remain an ability to make active commercial *use* of the land. The distinction, only recently clarified, obviously can make a great difference in takings outcomes.

---

30. *K&K*, for instance, reflected both these issues: The wetlands laws were in place when the companies acquired most of their interest in the subject properties, and prior to the government's denial of construction in the wetlands the companies had developed a portion of the acreage at substantial profit.

31. The phrase, as noted below, comes from Michelman, Property, Utility, and Fairness: Comments on the Ethical Foundations of Just Compensation Law, 80 Harv. L. Rev. 1165, 1192 (1967).

• **To balance or not to balance?** In the twentieth century, some takings decisions validated regulations by considering only whether government restrictions had been passed with proper authority. Others looked only at the impacts on private property, making gestalt judgments of whether the restrictions went "too far." Over the years, with occasional departures like the *Lucas* case's exceptional "categorical" rule, the commonsense conviction has grown that constitutional determinations of takings validity require a balancing of both the public and the private rights implicated in a case.

• **How to weigh public rights?** Even if there is now general consensus that takings tests require balancing, how to do so can never be a completely objective technical process. It is far easier to quantify private market value impacts than public interests. As considered below, in weighing this balance do all public benefits of a regulation weigh in its favor, or only those that represent the prevention of harms to the public, and how are these to be measured? Ultimately it will make a great difference which party bears the burden of proof. If properly promulgated government regulations are presumed valid unless the presumption is successfully overridden, they will tend to survive. If private rights are presumed dominant, or the presumption of governmental validity is rebuttable merely by showing economic loss, then regulations generally will fail, unless compensation can be paid. The takings issue tends to force us all to define what we consider to be the proper character and role of government.

• **If a regulation is found to be invalid, what remedy?** If a decision is reached that a regulation impacts too greatly upon private property, further decisions must be made about what form of relief to issue for the excessive taking. One remedy is declaratory nullification of the regulation on its face, or as applied to the property. Another is the payment of compensation by government, as in inverse condemnation cases, while keeping the regulation in force. The government defendant has the choice. A further possibility, noted in *First English* below, is that even if the regulation is voided, government may have to pay "interim damages" for the economic losses suffered during the time that the invalid regulation was on the books. The compensation remedies also raise complex issues of valuation.

2. **"Diminution" — what does it mean?** A continuing quandary begun by Justice Holmes is how diminution of private property interests by regulations is to be measured, even before a court asks whether it has gone "too far." Most courts take evidence of market values as well as of "reasonable remaining use." Market value is the highest price a willing buyer would pay a willing seller for title to a piece of property today. It is usually determined by asking several real estate appraiser witnesses to estimate that price by analyzing "comps" — recent sales of comparable pieces of property in the same vicinity. Some attorneys and courts mistakenly ask for valuation of the "highest and best use," a planning and development concept that is not the same as market value. The *Pennsylvania Coal* diminution principle does not require compensation for every regulatory deflation of a parcel's market value, but only when that reduction goes too far. In practice, that has required quite dramatic private losses, as noted below.

3. **Setting a baseline in wetlands cases: "the parcel as a whole"?** As noted, most wetlands takings cases, like most takings cases generally, focus on the individual landowner's property value diminution, usually asking not how much was taken but

how much remains. Note the games that can be played in determining the "baseline" against which to measure whether there is a reasonable remaining use. If you do a schematic diagram of the *Johnson* case, it rapidly becomes clear that Dr. Johnson made a tidy profit from the earlier sale of the dryland portions of his original property that he had previously sold off for cottages. The court in *Johnson*, like Justice Holmes in *Pennsylvania Coal*, looked *only at the regulated portion* of the property, not the entire parcel, in asking whether a reasonable profitable use remained. At that point, since it looked like a total wipeout, it seemed that no subtle constitutional balance was required.

The *K&K* court, like Justice Brandeis in *Pennsylvania Coal*, suggested that judicial review should weigh the regulations' effect on the plaintiffs' contiguous property as a whole, not merely the regulated portion. Not coincidentally, a focus on the regulated portion alone in wetland cases (and many other environmental settings) typically reveals that the regulation has eliminated virtually all economic value, while a focus on the property owner's parcel as a whole often reveals a substantial profit that has been made in the past or may be made in the future on the property as a whole, rendering the regulation valid. This question of what to consider as the property baseline for judicial review of takings (or the "denominator" of the diminution fraction, as the *K&K* court called it) is considered further in the next section, having been contested and clarified in recent Supreme Court cases.

4. **Balancing?** Judges in wetlands cases are not oblivious to wetlands' ecological values. In *Johnson*, for example, the Maine court noted arguments for protecting wetlands, but it did so only as a basis for establishing that the act served a proper public purpose. Having done so, the *Johnson* opinion focused exclusively on the private loss, without a process of constitutional balancing that would take some account of the public rights in the environmental context. Courts have found it easy to recognize the costs "externalized" onto private property by regulation, but less obvious that there should be a weighing of harms externalized onto the public by private action. Not knowing how to do so, many courts focus primarily on private diminution of value, the market loss figure, and miss the full constitutional context.[32]

K&K, however, reflects the recent trend in takings cases not only in including the plaintiffs' surrounding property in the "denominator" baseline, but also in holding that the constitutional test must include a "balancing of interests." As in the *K&K* decision, courts addressing the constitutional balance often invoke the Supreme Court's *Penn Central* case, noted further in the next section, as it has been subsequently interpreted. In the 2001 *Palazzolo* wetlands case noted below, the Court declared *Penn Central*

---

32. The takings rubric drawn from zoning cases permits extreme results in cases where public harms are discrete and obvious — for instance, striking down floodplain restrictions even where a developer planned to put 300 homes in coastal lowlands repeatedly hit by hurricane flooding. Dooley v. Fairfield, 226 A.2d 509 (Conn. 1967); see Plater, The Takings Issue in a Natural Setting: Floodlines and the Police Power, 52 Tex. L. Rev. 201, 244–252 (1974). In First English Evangelical Lutheran Church v. Los Angeles, 482 U.S. 304 (1987), decided on other grounds, Justice Rehnquist even posited that a floodplain ordinance would be an unconstitutional confiscation because it eliminated the economic value of a canyon floor parcel used as a camp for handicapped children. This amounted to saying that because the market value ignored the dangers, the property owner had a constitutional right to house 200 children in the path of recurring floods or to be compensated fully for the banning of that use.

balancing to be the standard methodology for reviewing regulatory takings challenges. It is still not clear, however, how public and private interests in wetlands are to be weighed against one another. In a New Hampshire coastal wetlands case, the court held that the regulation was "not a [public] appropriation of the property…, but the restraint of an injurious private use…[so] the validity of the state action is determined by balancing the importance of the public benefit which is sought to be promoted against the seriousness of the restriction of a private right sought to be imposed." Sibson v. State, 336 A.2d 239 (N.H. 1976). Are all the "public benefits" noted in the CEQ Wetlands Report above to be balanced, or only public "harms"?

5. **Wetlands as lightning rods.** The nation's largest wetlands protection program is the CWA §404 program. What would have been the effect on the federal wetlands regulation program of applying the regulatory takings compensation provision noted at the beginning of this chapter? Although the press did not understand its significance, can you discern the effect of H.R. 925's §3(a) definition of the property baseline? (Note also that the bill's compensation requirement could have been applied far beyond wetlands protections, to all federal pollution regulations administered by EPA.) Wetlands seem to attract litigation, probably owing to the fact that their virtues are not widely appreciated ("Wetlands? Heck, that there's just an ol' swamp," a grizzled Corps official reportedly said when petitioned to protect an area from channelization) and that most wetlands protections dramatically reduce potential commercial development. Wetlands cases are thus likely to continue to make frequent appearances in the line-up of future takings challenges.

Section 2. **THE U.S. SUPREME COURT'S CLASSIC TAKINGS CASES, AND AN EMERGING CONSENSUS ON TAKINGS BALANCING?**

The cases above directly or indirectly introduce four of the most important environmental regulatory takings cases decided by the Supreme Court. Here are brief summaries of those cases, along with two major recent decisions.

- *Pennsylvania Coal,*[33] in 1922, was, as noted, the first case to hold a regulation invalid as a taking, based on a test of diminution of private property value caused by a state statute prohibiting the mining of coal pillars if surface streets and homes would thereby be destroyed. Justice Holmes said the virtual elimination of each pillar's value was constitutionally excessive.

- *Penn Central*[34] likewise weighed the amount of private diminution loss by viewing plaintiffs' entire property (Grand Central Station, which the Landmark Commission had designated a historic landmark, prohibiting construction above it) and not just the regulated portion (the air space above the terminal).

- *Keystone Bituminous*[35] — on virtually the same facts as *Pennsylvania Coal* — likewise considered private diminution but effectively overruled the way *Pennsylvania Coal* had framed the baseline denominator. Justice Stevens's

---

33. Pennsylvania Coal Co. v. Mahon, 260 U.S. 393 (1922).
34. Penn Central Transp. Co. v. City of N.Y., 438 U.S. 104 (1978).
35. Keystone Bituminous Coal Ass'n v. DeBenedictis, 480 U.S. 470 (1987).

majority opinion viewed the private loss in the context of the entire coalfield, not just the regulated pillars, and upheld the law. *Keystone Bituminous* also assumed that takings review goes beyond a focus on individual loss, incorporating a balancing of public interests through consideration of public harms, "noxiousness," a "nuisance exception," and the like.

- *Lucas*[36] struck down a South Carolina coastal protection act's prohibition of building on barrier beach lots, finding that it rendered the land "valueless." Justice Scalia asserted a "categorical rule" requiring compensation for regulatory wipeout where no economic value remains, although his "categorical" rule allowed exceptions for regulations of nuisance-like public harms.

- In Palazzolo v. Rhode Island,[37] a property owner proposed to build 74 small homes, or alternatively a beach club, on a coastal marsh. Both requests were turned down under a state wetlands regulation. The Court held that Palazzolo had standing to attack the regulation even if he had taken title to the land knowing it was restricted, but refused to apply *Lucas*'s "categorical" rule because the land still retained more than "token" value, and remanded for a judicial balancing of public and private interests, establishing the *Penn Central* balance as the presumptive legal test to be applied in all takings cases other than total wipeouts.

- *Tahoe-Sierra Preservation Council*[38] arose from longstanding governmental attempts to protect the purity of Lake Tahoe from the effects of prolific development in the crater area around the lake. The Court dismissed the property owners' takings lawsuit against a regional planning commission's 32-month construction moratorium. The Court held that the time baseline, like the physical baseline, should be viewed inclusively, not focusing merely upon the regulated time portion; the Court limited the categorical *Lucas* compensation rule to cases where land value was totally wiped out, which could not be shown in *Tahoe*; and the measure of postregulation private rights is to be made in terms of land's remaining market *value*, not a requirement that it retain active market *uses*.

In the half century after *Pennsylvania Coal*, the Supreme Court almost totally avoided reviewing regulatory takings cases. When it did review challenges to land use restrictions, it usually upheld the regulations rather summarily on sketchy ad hoc reasoning.[39] The takings question was recognized as highly political and confusingly subjective, so takings jurisprudence generally was left to bumble along in the state and lower federal courts without Supreme Court guidance, where it exhibited "crazy quilt" inconsistency.[40] Most challenges to regulations were rebuffed but not based on any coherent judicial review standard or methodology.

For years the fundamental logic of the necessity for public-private balancing in takings reviews was not clearly recognized. Most courts tended to avoid acknowledging that public and private rights needed to be considered together. Traditionally, courts

---

36. Lucas v. South Carolina Coastal Council, 505 U.S. 1003, 1015 (1992).
37. Palazzolo v. Rhode Island, 533 U.S. 606, 631 (2001).
38. Tahoe-Sierra Pres. Council v. Tahoe Reg'l Planning Agency, 535 U.S. 302 (2002).
39. See, e.g., Goldblatt v. Town of Hempstead, 369 U.S. 590 (1962), which seems to stand for the simplistic principle, reflected in a long run of cases, that stone quarries are bad.
40. See Sax, Takings and the Police Power, 74 Yale L.J. 36, 37 (1964).

followed the lead set by Justice Holmes in *Pennsylvania Coal* by discussing public rights elements only in the threshold due process inquiry: Is the government pursuing a proper public purpose? If so, this element is checked off affirmatively, and thereafter the public harms at stake often are not given further explicit acknowledgment in a constitutional balance. Many courts thus have weighed private property diminution effects in a constitutional vacuum, without expressly weighing any relativity or proportionality to public interests. Even where courts have discussed both public and private elements, as Justice Holmes did in *Pennsylvania Coal*, they haven't considered them together because no judicial methodology for doing so has been established.

Beginning in the 1970s, the contending forces in the process of government began to identify the courts in general and regulatory takings in particular as strategic battlefields. In his milepost memorandum to the U.S. Chamber of Commerce, just prior to his Court appointment, Justice Powell wrote:

> The judiciary may be the most important instrument for social, economic and political change. Other organizations and groups…have been far more astute in exploiting judicial action than American business…. This is a vast area of opportunity for the Chamber, if it is willing to undertake the role of spokesman for American business and if…business is willing to provide the funds. As with…scholars and speakers, the Chamber would need a highly competent staff…authorized to engage…lawyers of national standing and reputation…to appear as counsel amicus in the Supreme Court. The greatest care should be exercised in selecting the cases in which to participate or the suits to institute. But the opportunity merits the necessary effort.

Beginning in the 1970s, business-oriented foundations such as the Heritage Foundation were created with a focus on property rights as a major part of their programs. Industry-created "public interest law firms" initiated or intervened in a parade of takings cases, and support was given to revisionist legal scholars to construct anti-regulatory conceptions of the proper role of government.[41] In the late 1970s, a theory was developed by Professor Richard Epstein, the most significant voice in the ranks of marketplace-oriented takings scholars, asserting that most government regulations were invalid unless their economic burdens were compensated. Appearing first in the *Wall Street Journal* and later in a 1985 book *Takings*,[42] Epstein's argument asserted that there is a preeminent natural right to property ownership, and that, based on his reinterpretation of the Lockian philosophy, the government has only a very limited right to interfere with such ownership. Property consists of a bundle of rights, including rights of possession, use, disposition, and the right to exclude. Any governmental interference with any of these rights, Epstein said, is a taking that must be compensated, "no matter how small the alteration and no matter how general its application." The Takings Clause of the Constitution, he said, prohibits any and all redistributions of

---

41. The Powell Memorandum is available on the coursebook Web site. See J. Stefanic & R. Delgado, No Mercy, How Conservative Think Tanks and Foundations Changed America's Social Agenda (1996). See also Houck, With Charity for All, 93 Yale L.J. 1415, 1470–1474, 1544–1545 (1984) (chronicling the business community's creation of "public interest law firms," and questioning whether their litigation on behalf of developers qualifies as "public interest law" within the meaning of §501(c)(3) of the U.S. tax code).

42. R. A. Epstein, Takings, Private Property and the Power of Eminent Domain (1985). The author acknowledges "a generous grant from the Institute for Educational Affairs," an industry foundation that launched the Federalist Society. Id. at xi.

wealth, and renders "constitutionally infirm or suspect many of the heralded reforms and institutions of the twentieth century: zoning, rent control, workers' compensation laws, transfer payments, [and] progressive taxation.... It will be said that my position invalidates much of...twentieth century legislation, and so it does."[43] Epstein's takings theories were as widely hailed in business lobbying circles as they were criticized by constitutional scholars.[44] They were featured in a series of vacation seminars for federal judges sponsored by industry-funded foundations and began to appear in judicial majority opinions as well as dissents.

Penn Central:[45] **The Parcel as a Whole and a Three-Factor Ad Hoc Balancing.** The majority of Supreme Court justices, however, resisted the newly energetic property rights assertions when the Court took up the *Penn Central* case. In *Penn Central*, the Court had to determine whether New York City's historic preservation ordinance could block the owners of Grand Central Station from raising a skyscraper in the air rights above the old landmark.

Penn Central raised questions of the takings baseline. The building rights above the terminal were totally eliminated, but the city argued that the diminution analysis should consider the economic value of the terminal itself and of the transferable development rights (TDRs) that the property owners could use for profitable construction credits off-site. Writing for a 6-3 majority, Justice Brennan said:

> Takings jurisprudence does not divide a single parcel into discrete segments and attempt to determine whether rights in a particular segment have been entirely abrogated. In deciding whether a particular governmental action has effected a taking, this Court focuses rather both on the character of the action and on the nature of the interference with rights *in the parcel as a whole*.... 438 U.S. at 130–131 (emphasis added).

And what legal standard should be applied in determining whether a regulatory diminution of property value is excessive?

> This Court, quite simply, has been unable to develop any "set formula" for determining when "justice and fairness" require that economic injuries caused by public action be compensated by the government, rather than remain disproportionately concentrated on a few persons. Indeed, we have frequently observed that whether a particular restriction will be rendered invalid by the government's failure to pay for any losses proximately caused by it depends largely "upon the particular circumstances [in that] case."
>
> In engaging in these essentially ad hoc factual inquiries, the Court's decisions have identified several factors that have particular significance. The *economic impact* of the regulation on the claimant and, particularly, the extent to which the regulation has interfered with distinct *investment-backed expectations* are...relevant considerations. So too is the *character of the governmental action*....

---

43. Id. at x, 57-62, 281.

44. Scholars have criticized *Takings* as a "travesty of constitutional scholarship," shallow, and a failure as a matter of history, logic, philosophy, or textual analysis. Ross, Review, Taking *Takings* Seriously, 80 Nw. U. L. Rev. 1591, 1592 (1987); Grey, The Malthusian Constitution, 41 U. Miami L. Rev. 21, 24 (1986); Sax, Review, *Takings*, 53 U. Chi. L. Rev. 279, 279 (1986); L. H. Tribe, American Constitutional Law §9-6, at 606 n. 6 (2d ed. 1988); Flaherty, History "Lite" in Modern American Constitutionalism, 95 Colum. L. Rev. 523, 556–567 (1995); Kendall & Lord, The Takings Project, 25 B.C. Envtl. Aff. L. Rev. 509, 519–530 (1998).

45. Penn Central Transp. Co. v. City of N.Y., 438 U.S. 104 (1978).

We conclude that the application of New York City's Landmarks Law has not effected a "taking" of appellants' property. The restrictions imposed are substantially related to the promotion of the general welfare and not only permit *reasonable beneficial* use of the landmark site but also afford appellants opportunities further to enhance not only the Terminal site proper but also other properties…. 438 U.S. at 124, 138 (emphasis added).

COMMENTARY & QUESTIONS

1. **The diminution baseline: the parcel as a whole.** It would seem that the *Penn Central* Court had definitively established that diminution is to be weighed on an inclusive baseline, viewing the property as a whole rather than on just the property's regulated portion. The issue, however, did not then go away.

2. **Is the *Penn Central* test a balancing test?** But what is the legal standard that is to be applied to the parcel-as-a-whole baseline? From the above-quoted language, it appeared that the *Penn Central* majority looked to the diminution and applied a form of "reasonable remaining economic value" test, a test drawn from municipal zoning cases in state and federal courts. By using phrases such as "economically viable" and "reasonable beneficial use," the Court was clearly scrutinizing the post-restriction effect on regulated property.

There are a few things to note here. First, the Court doesn't focus its test upon how much value is removed, but how much *remains* — what some scholars have referred to as a residuum approach. Diminution is not measured in terms of numerical amounts or percentages, but in conceptual terms of whether the residuum of property rights existing under the regulation is "reasonable."

Second, for determining what is reasonable, *Penn Central* sets out the three factors — economic impact, investment-backed expectations, and the character of the governmental action — which, though stated in noninclusive form, have become the totemic *Penn Central* triad. But what do they mean? In this triad, the "economic impact" element clearly means diminution; the "investment-backed expectations" clause also implicates diminution, factoring in an added fairness element that considers reasonable marketplace anticipations;[46] but the "character of the governmental action" element seems to extend the court's consideration beyond the private interests at issue.

Third, then, to what extent does *Penn Central* imply a fundamental balancing of public and well as private interests? In subsequent case law, *Penn Central* is invoked repeatedly for its "ad hoc balancing approach,"[47] but the Brennan opinion does not expressly set

---

46. Professor Michelman invented the investment-backed expectations phrase in a book review, Property, Utility, and Fairness: Comments on the Ethical Foundations of Just Compensation Law, 80 Harv. L. Rev. 1165, 1192 (1967), intending it not as a constitutional test but as a policy guide for voluntary compensations. Its utility to takings challengers is evident, and thanks to *Penn Central* it has crossed over beyond its author's intent. Consider this test in the context of Brandeis's poison gas example in *Pennsylvania Coal*: If a landowner discovers, to her dismay, that her land contains poison gas deposits so that it cannot safely be developed, her expectations clearly are frustrated; but is that constitutional injury or merely bad luck? The legislature may well decide to reimburse her as charity, but must it? The expectations may be a factor but are not determinative of takings invalidity.

47. See, e.g., *Tahoe-Sierra*, 535 U.S. at 318 ("[whether] the regulations constitute a taking under the ad hoc balancing approach described in *Penn Central*").

out a balance nor specify any public interests to be weighed. As interpreted in later cases, the "character of the governmental action" factor implies the consideration of public issues — inviting judges to consider whether the government is regulating nuisance-like public harms and distinguishing regulations by their societal objectives. A health and safety law would seem to deserve more weight than a purely aesthetic regulation, as Brandeis implied with the poison gas hypothetical in his *Pennsylvania Coal* dissent. The Brennan opinion mentions only distinctions between physical and regulatory actions. Without a court's consideration of public issues, however, wouldn't its use of the *Penn Central* triad be defining the constitutional "reasonableness" of a regulation's effect in a vacuum?

3. **Dissent in *Penn Central*.** In dissent, Justice Rehnquist launched three arguments that would continue to percolate in subsequent cases. First, he rejected the Brennan majority's parcel-as-a-whole definition of the property baseline upon which diminution should be measured. Focusing on the air rights above the terminal, he noted that the Court had recognized that air rights over an area of land are property for purposes of the Fifth Amendment; and those rights had been completely "destroyed — in a literal sense, 'taken.'" 438 U.S. at 143. The dissent would also have found the regulation unconstitutional under two negative-logic tests. The case law had often rejected takings challenges where the regulated private properties were "nuisances" or "noxious uses," but building a tower above the terminal would be neither and hence, the dissent argued, was an invalid taking. Further, citing a dictum from Justice Holmes that regulations are not invalid if their protections produce a shared "average reciprocity of advantage" for property owners, Justice Rehnquist argued that the reverse is also true — if property owners do not get a reciprocal advantage, the regulation is void. These arguments were wounded but lived to fight another day.

Keystone Bituminous:[48] **Parcel as a Whole, Redux.** In the decade after *Penn Central*, the Reagan Revolution took over Washington and the Court changed with new appointments including William Rehnquist's elevation to Chief Justice. The new political era brought broad new initiatives seeking to roll back the progressive excesses of the 1960s and 1970s. Major attention was paid to changing the constitutional law on regulatory takings. According to President Reagan's Solicitor-General Charles Fried, by no means a liberal, the Reagan White House

> had a specific, aggressive, and it seemed to me, quite radical project in mind: to use the takings clause of the Fifth Amendment as a severe brake on federal and state regulation of business and property.[49]

In their study of the politics of takings law in the last decades of the century, Douglas Kendall and Charles Lord discovered a substantial political backdrop to the appellate decisions in the case reporters, which they described, using Professor Fried's term, as the Takings Project.

---

48. Keystone Bituminous Coal Ass'n v. DeBenedictis, 480 U.S. 470 (1987).
49. C. Fried, Order and Law: Arguing the Reagan Revolution — A Firsthand Account 183 (1991).

What we found is a…campaign by conservatives and libertarians to use the federal judiciary to achieve an anti-regulatory, anti-environmental agenda. Looking first at the courts and judges deciding the most important and influential takings cases, we noted several striking patterns. The vast majority of important victories achieved by developers in takings cases over the last decade have been decided by the same three courts: the United States Supreme Court, the Court of Appeals for the Federal Circuit and the Court of Federal Claims. Moreover, almost without exception, the judges on these courts ruling for developers were appointed to their respective courts by Presidents Reagan and Bush [I]. Finally, the cases themselves showed remarkable activism by the jurists: in many cases, the judges overcame seemingly insurmountable procedural and substantive hurdles to rule in favor of the developers.

Looking a bit deeper, we noted the political, more than the judicial or scholarly, background of many of these same judges and found that the appointment of these politically savvy jurists to their posts resulted, in many instances, from a concerted effort by conservatives and libertarians within the Reagan and Bush administrations to use the court system to further their attack on federal regulations. Even more remarkably, we discovered that the most activist judges on the Federal Circuit and the Court of Federal Claims — the federal courts with exclusive jurisdiction over most takings cases against the federal government —all [had] attended the same, all-expenses-paid, week-long summer seminar at a Montana resort hosted by a property rights group. Finally, we found that the same conservative foundations that funded these Montana seminars also bankroll takings litigation before the Federal Circuit….

The Pacific Legal Foundation (PLF) and a dozen other "public interest" legal foundations located around the country represent developers free-of-charge in takings cases…. Large and powerful lobbies such as the National Association of Home Builders similarly devote significant resources both to litigating takings cases and promoting "procedural reform legislation" in Congress…. Kendall & Lord, The Takings Project: A Critical Analysis and Assessment of the Progress So Far, 25 B.C. Envtl. Aff. L. Rev. 509, 510–511 (1998).

With the ascendancy of Justice Rehnquist, joined in 1986 by Justice Scalia, the Court showed a heightened interest in takings cases. In 1987, the Court granted certiorari in *Keystone Bituminous*, a case that seemed a perfect vehicle for changing the *Penn Central* holding on whether the takings baseline should be the parcel as a whole or just the regulated portion. *Keystone Bituminous* was virtually the same case as *Pennsylvania Coal* — a new Pennsylvania statute required coal companies not to take out underground coal pillars that supported the surface — and *Pennsylvania Coal*, the mother of all takings cases, had clearly focused the diminution exclusively on the restricted pillar portion of the property. The case was argued for the coal companies by Rex Lee, who had been the Reagan Administration's first Solicitor-General.

In *Keystone Bituminous*, however, Justice Stevens (disingenuously denying that he was overruling *Pennsylvania Coal*), held for a narrow 5–4 majority that the takings test should be based on the entire coal field owned by the coal company petitioners, not just on the coal pillars that the companies were required to leave untouched.

Petitioners…claimed that they have been required to leave a bit less than 27 million tons of coal in place…. The total coal in [their] thirteen mines amounts to over 1.46 billion tons. Thus [the Act] requires them to leave less than 2 percent of their coal in place.... Petitioners have sought to narrowly define certain segments of their property and assert that when so defined, the Subsidence Act denies economically viable use.... First, they focus on the specific tons of coal that they must leave in the ground under the Subsidence Act.... Second, they contend that the Commonwealth has taken a separate legal interest in property — the "support estate." The 27 million tons of coal do not constitute a separate segment of property for takings law purposes.... The Court of Appeals...concluded that as a practical matter the support estate is always owned by either the owner of the surface or the owner of the minerals.... Its value is merely a part of the entire bundle of rights possessed by the owner of either the coal or the surface. 480 U.S. at 496–501.

In vigorous dissent, Chief Justice Rehnquist, joined by Justices Powell, O'Connor, and Scalia, focused on the individual coal pillars as "an identifiable and separable property interest" that had been completely taken.

From the relevant perspective — that of the property owners — this interest has been destroyed every bit as much as if the government had proceeded to mine the coal for its own use.... Operation of this [Act] extinguishes the Petitioners' interests in their support estates, making worthless what they purchased as a separate right under Pennsylvania law. Like the restriction on mining particular coal, this complete interference with a property right extinguishes its value, and must be accompanied by just compensation. 480 U.S. at 518.

COMMENTARY & QUESTIONS

1. **The time baseline?** Note that though the *Keystone Bituminous* majority clearly looked at the entire coal field in framing the physical baseline for takings review, it did not make clear whether a court should consider a time baseline including the coal companies' *past* revenues from the coal field in weighing the reasonableness of the regulation's diminution effect. Should it? Note that laws prohibiting the removal of geological support are likely to be passed only after the subsidence problem has become obvious, after most of the coal has already been removed. Should the time baseline be based on "remaining economic value" that exists after the restriction is imposed, or can it consider the entire life of the original coalfield investment? In the latter case, the concept of "investment-backed expectations" would operate to defend rather than undercut the challenged regulation.

2. *Keystone Bituminous*: **Was there a balancing?** *Keystone Bituminous* not only successfully defended the parcel-as-a-whole concept but also asserted clearly that takings cases require a constitutional balance between the public's interests and private regulatory losses. The majority opinion noted:

Many cases before and since *Pennsylvania Coal* have recognized that the nature of the State's action is critical in takings analysis.... In upholding state action [in the tree disease case,] the Court did not consider it necessary to "weigh with nicety the question whether the infected cedars constitute a nuisance according to common law or whether they may be so declared by statute." Rather, it was clear that the State's exercise of its police power to prevent the impending danger was justified, and did not require compensation.... Although a comparison of values before and after a regulatory action is relevant, it is by no means conclusive.... *The question whether a taking has occurred "necessarily requires a weighing of private and public interests."* 480 U.S. at 492 (emphasis added).

This introduces an active consideration of the public harms into a regulatory takings balance, although the terms remain unspecific.

Lucas v. South Carolina Coastal Council:[50] **A Categorical Bombshell.** If takings law seemed to have developed some settled doctrine, that wistful premise was torpedoed in 1992. After *Keystone Bituminous*, the Court had shown an interest in revisiting takings. In *First English*, Justice Rehnquist had fashioned a majority for a remedies-based procedural decision declaring that if a regulation is found invalid, a government may have to pay "interim damages" for the time the law had restricted the property.[51] Although the measure of such damages was and remains unclear, the chilling effect on regulatory agencies around the country was tangible; if a law was eventually found to be an invalid taking, they could not merely rescind it but might face huge interim "rental" charges for restricting the property.[52]

The portents for a major takings assault were fulfilled in the *Lucas* case. A state protection of a barrier beach was challenged by a developer who wanted to build houses on the last two remaining lots on the Isle of Palms shoreline. According to the trial judge's findings, it was a total wipeout: The lots, which unrestricted were worth $1.2 million, were totally "valueless" if regulated.[53] In his majority opinion, Justice Scalia seized upon this seemingly exceptional situation to carve out a "categorical rule" circumventing public-private takings balancing.

> Regulations that leave the owner of land without economically beneficial or productive options for its use — typically, as here, by requiring land to be left substantially in its natural state — carry with them a heightened risk that private property is being pressed into some form of public service under the guise of mitigating serious public harm....
>
> Where the State seeks to sustain regulation that deprives land of all economically beneficial use, we think it may resist compensation only if the logically antecedent inquiry into the nature of the owner's estate shows that the proscribed use interests were not part of his title to begin with....
>
> [As to] regulations that prohibit all economically beneficial use of land: Any limitation so severe cannot be newly legislated or decreed (without compensation), but must inhere in the title itself, in the restrictions that background principles of the State's law of property and nuisance already place upon land ownership,...in other words do no more than duplicate the result that could have been achieved in the [state's] courts. 505 U.S. at 1018, 1027–1029.

---

50. 505 U.S. 1003 (1992).

51. First English Evangelical Lutheran Church of Glendale v. Los Angeles, 482 U.S. 304 (1987). The holding was hypothetical, since the restriction was not found excessive, and remanded.

52. This issue has not been well studied. If interim damages are based on market values before and after, they may be inconsequential since property values tend to increase over time. If, however, a government has to compensate with "rental" for the "use" of property, which, of course, generated no public income, the burden would be devastating, changing the nature of regulatory government to that of a constructive public brokerage house taking in and paying out unmonetizable public interests as if they were cash.

53. When Lucas's attorney began his oral argument by saying the regulated land was worthless, Justice Blackmun leaned over the bench and asked, "Then will he give it to me?" The attorney paused, startled, then replied, "Yes, if you pay the taxes," missing the point that property taxes are assessed on value, and if the land was really valueless the taxes would be zero.

The dissenting opinions feared, presciently, that the *Lucas* decision and the newly created categorical rule would change takings law far beyond the exceptionally rare case of total wipeouts. As Justice Blackmun wrote:

> Today the Court launches a missile to kill a mouse…. My fear is that the Court's new policies will spread beyond the narrow confines of the present case. For that reason, I, like the Court, will give far greater attention to this case than its narrow scope suggests — not because I can intercept the Court's missile, or save the targeted mouse, but because I hope perhaps to limit the collateral damage.… 505 U.S. at 1036–1037.

In a separate opinion, Justice Stevens wrote:

> In my opinion…the categorical rule the Court establishes is an unsound and unwise addition to the law and the Court's formulation of the exception to that rule is too rigid and too narrow…. The categorical rule will likely have one of two effects: Either courts will alter the definition of the "denominator" in the takings "fraction," rendering the Court's categorical rule meaningless, or investors will manipulate the relevant property interests, giving the Court's rule sweeping effect. To my mind, neither of these results is desirable or appropriate, and both are distortions of our takings jurisprudence…. The Court's new rule is unsupported by prior decisions, arbitrary and unsound in practice, and theoretically unjustified. In my opinion, a categorical rule as important as the one established by the Court today should be supported by more history or more reason than has yet been provided…. 505 U.S. at 1064–1067.

COMMENTARY & QUESTIONS

1. **Reading *Lucas*.** The *Lucas* case is a vast, rich accumulation of takings debate. The full text of the five *Lucas* opinions totals 75 pages. Behind the pitched arguments about what substantive takings tests should apply to property value wipeouts — and questions whether this action was truly "ripe" for review, whether the land was truly valueless, and how much a federal court should defer to the findings of state legislatures and supreme courts — lie a concatenation of judicial politics. Had this majority overthrown the *Keystone Bituminous* majority? Did the majority decide this case as an extraordinary total wipeout, or was it framing a test to encourage wider invalidations of regulatory restrictions? Would the votes have been quite different if it had not been such an extreme case?

2. **Takings tests after *Lucas*.** What, if anything, was changed by *Lucas*? Was there now a "bright line" test requiring compensation for regulatory takings, at least for wipeouts? A major exception was apparently built into the test by saying that restrictions must inhere in limits that "background principles of the State's law of property and nuisance already place upon land ownership." But what does this mean? Are the common law precedents existing as of the date of this opinion the limit? Or is there still a balance?

Lucas may have been narrow on its facts, but its forceful rhetoric and attractive clarity invited a subsequent series of anti-regulatory decisions in the lower courts. Many judges were unclear on how much loss had to be shown to trigger categorical *Lucas* compensation. Justice Scalia had used a confusing array of descriptions in addition to "valueless," including where regulation denies "all economically beneficial or productive use of land," all "economically viable use," "all beneficial use," "any reasonable economic use of the lots," "all economically feasible use," or "economically beneficial use of his land." Depending on which trigger phrase was chosen and how it was interpreted, the categorical test could be extremely rare or invoked in a wide range of cases where substantial profits were lost. The latter was often the case,[54] as *Lucas* began to collect as many citations as *Pennsylvania Coal*.

3. Conceptual severance: parcel-as-a-whole baseline games, redux, again? The parcel-as-a-whole baseline debate had been deftly reframed in the literature shortly after *Keystone Bituminous* by an article written by Professor Margaret Radin. "Conceptual severance" was what she dubbed the divide-and-conquer anti-regulatory strategy of defining narrowed baselines in order to increase the chances of finding excessive diminution. Radin, The Liberal Conception of Property: Cross Currents in the Jurisprudence of Takings, 88 Colum. L. Rev. 1667, 1676 (1988). Most scholars agreed with her. Conceptual severance, dividing one original piece of property, one investment, into a series of fractionalized boxes disproportionately burdened by regulations, was a shell game that missed the constitutional point.

In a *Lucas* footnote, however, Justice Scalia attempted to plant a seed in dicta that would reopen the question of the relevant takings baseline. Although *Lucas* did not present a case where only part of the plaintiff's property was restricted, the footnote quickly achieved notoriety among takings scholars for its future potential:

> Regrettably…the rule does not make clear the "property interest" against which the loss of value is to be measured. When, for example, a regulation requires a developer to leave 90% of a rural tract in its natural state, it is unclear whether we would analyze the situation as one in which the owner has been deprived of all economically beneficial use of the burdened portion of the tract, or as one in which the owner has suffered a mere diminution in value of the tract as a whole. (For an extreme — *and, we think, unsupportable* — view of the relevant calculus, see *Penn Central* where the state court examined the diminution in a particular parcel's value produced by a municipal ordinance in light of total value of the takings claimant's other holdings in the vicinity.)… The answer to this difficult question may lie in…whether and to what degree the State's law has accorded legal recognition and protection to the particular interest in land with respect to which the takings claimant alleges a diminution…. 505 U.S. at 1017 n. 7 (emphasis added).

Since Mr. Lucas's land was entirely restricted, however, the point could not become a holding, but the footnote, including the last line clearly referring to *Penn Central*'s air rights and *Keystone Bituminous*'s support estate, appeared to be an invitation to the courts to resurrect Justice Rehnquist's dissents on that point. In the years immediately following *Lucas*, a number of courts, particularly the Claims Court and the Federal Circuit, followed Scalia's lead in footnote 7 to void regulations, even to the point of applying the Rehnquist dissents rather than the holdings in *Penn Central* and *Keystone*.

4. An uncategorical categorical rule? On remand, the *Lucas* case was summarily handled by the South Carolina Supreme Court: Did counsel for the state have any

---

54. Generally overlooked was Justice Scalia's footnote 8, in which he acknowledged that a property owner left with 5% of property value might not be able to invoke the categorical rule. "In at least some cases the landowner with 95% loss will get nothing, while the landowner with total loss will recover in full." 505 U.S. at 1020.

South Carolina cases defining beachfront houses as tortious nuisances? No? Then, without such a state law precedent, the remand court said the categorical rule applied and the only question left was how much compensation needed to be paid. The state had to pay Lucas more than $1.5 million in compensation for property rights, attorneys' fees, and interest.

Is the rule so categorical? "Categorical" means "admitting of no exceptions," and the Scalia opinion provided major fudge factors in its rule, not only opening the takings calculus to definitions of tort and property coming from state case law,[55] but also authorizing the weighing of general nuisance-*like* considerations beyond decided case precedents. For instance:

> the corporate owner of a nuclear generating plant...would not be entitled to compensation...when it is directed to remove all improvements from its land upon discovery that the plant sits astride an earthquake fault. Such regulatory action may well have the effect of eliminating the land's only economically productive use, but it does not proscribe a productive use that was previously permissible under relevant property and nuisance principles. 505 U.S. at 1030.

This concession imports an implicit balance of public harms into the "categorical" rule, and properly so. What happens in cases — such as marginally economic polluting factories, floodplain residential development projects, and the like — where protective regulations would reduce property values to a profitless level, but the properties cause great public harm? Does the Constitution require governments either to pay off owners of such properties, or else allow them a constitutional right to harm the public, if the state has not previously defined the actions as torts? Justice Scalia instead seems to open up even his categorical rule to a dynamic commonsense public-private balance of nuisance-like elements. He also, perhaps inadvertently, opened the rule to public trust issues by incorporating states' definitions of *property* rights as well as tort, as noted below.

Palazzolo v. Rhode Island:[56] Tides Turning on the Rhode Island Coast? Anthony Palazzolo owned approximately 18 acres of predominantly tidal saltmarsh wetland near Westerly, Rhode Island. In 1988, after the denial of several applications to develop the land, Mr. Palazzolo and PLF attorneys filed an inverse condemnation suit seeking $3.15 million in damages based on the estimated value of the subdivision if developed with 70+ houses. The Rhode Island Supreme Court had found that the *Lucas* categorical exception did not apply because the property was not deprived of all economically beneficial use. Undisputed evidence showed that the property had at least $200,000 in development value remaining on upland portions of the property. The state court added that Palazzolo could not recover under the more general *Penn Central* test, saying that, on notice estoppel grounds, he could have had "no reasonable investment-backed expectations that were affected by this regulation" because he knew about the regulatory restrictions on the land when he personally took title.

---

55. The remand's reading of the Scalia decision also overlooked its exception for state *property* restrictions, which would have allowed the public trust doctrine to come into play in support of regulation, as noted in Professor Babcock's analysis below.

56. 533 U.S. 606, 631 (2001).

The U.S. Supreme Court, in an opinion by Justice Kennedy, held that Palazzolo was not estopped from bringing his claim simply because he had acquired legal ownership of the property after Rhode Island's wetlands regulations were enacted. "[Some] enactments," wrote Justice Kennedy, "are unreasonable and do not become less so through passage of time or title." The Court affirmed, however, that *Lucas* did not apply.

> [The Rhode Island Supreme Court] held that all economically beneficial use was not deprived because the uplands portion of the property [one small lot, Lot 19] can still be improved. On this point, we agree with the court's decision. Petitioner accepts the Council's contention and the state trial court's finding that his parcel retains $200,000 in development value under the State's wetlands regulations. He asserts, nonetheless, that he has suffered a total taking and contends the Council cannot sidestep the holding in *Lucas* "by the simple expedient of leaving a landowner a few crumbs of value." A...state may not evade the duty to compensate on the premise that the landowner is left with a token interest. This is not the situation of the landowner in this case, however. A regulation permitting a landowner to build a substantial residence on an 18-acre parcel does not leave the property "economically idle." 533 U.S. at 631–632.

Rejecting applicability of the *Lucas* categorical exception, the Court remanded for a takings review "under the *Penn Central* analysis." But perhaps more significant in *Palazzolo* was the concurring opinion of Justice O'Connor. In her concurrence she made two strategic assertions. She declared, over Justice Scalia's strenuous dissent, that investment-backed expectations could be used to diminish plaintiffs' diminution claims as well as reinforce them — that is, if plaintiffs like Palazzolo have bought land knowing it was restricted, the nature of the investment gamble may serve to offset the amount of market value loss attributable to the regulation. And she reiterated the importance under the *Penn Central* factors of judicial balancing that considered the public concerns that motivated regulations as well as the private rights affected. Justice O'Connor wrote:

> Today's holding does not mean that the timing of the regulation's enactment relative to the acquisition of title is immaterial to the *Penn Central* analysis. Indeed, it would be just as much error to expunge this consideration from the takings inquiry as it would be to accord it exclusive significance. Our polestar...remains the principles set forth in *Penn Central* itself and our other cases that govern partial regulatory takings. Under these cases, interference with investment-backed expectations is one of a number of factors that a court must examine.... [W]e have eschewed "any 'set formula' for determining when 'justice and fairness' require that economic injuries caused by public action be compensated by the government, rather than remain disproportionately concentrated on a few persons." The outcome instead "depends largely upon the particular circumstances [in that] case." We have "identified several factors that have particular significance" in these "essentially ad hoc, factual inquiries." *Penn Central*, 438 U.S. at 124. Two such factors are "[t]he economic impact of the regulation on the claimant and, particularly, the extent to which the regulation has interfered with distinct investment-backed expectations." Another is "the character of the governmental action." The purposes served, as well as the effects produced, by a particular regulation inform the takings analysis. Regulatory takings cases "necessarily entai[l] complex factual assessments of the purposes and economic effects of government actions." 533 U.S. at 633–634.

COMMENTARY & QUESTIONS

1. **Isolating *Lucas*.** The clearest clarification of takings jurisprudence in *Palazzolo* is the narrowing of settings in which the *Lucas* rule can be applied. *Lucas* is now relegated to the category of exceptionally extreme total wipeouts, where property owners are left with a mere "token" of value. The Court makes clear that the standard rule for judging takings validity is the *Penn Central* triad, and very few cases will get *Lucas* treatment.

2. **Express consideration of regulations' public objectives and investment-backed expectation, or "government as thief"?** As noted, Justice O'Connor's concurrence said that the *Penn Central* triad required a balance of the public purposes that had motivated the regulation, as well as saying that a plaintiff's prior knowledge of restrictions at the outset of the investment — what zoning cases call a "self-made hardship" — can be considered when courts assess the degree of diminution.

Justice Scalia reacted by equating regulatory government with a thief. If government can increase its chances of winning the diminution balance by showing that plaintiff developers' investment-backed expectations included knowledge that the land, bought at a reduced cost, was restricted, it would be cheating such property owners of their ability to gamble for the "windfall" of increased market values that would come from voiding the land restrictions.

> There is something to be said (though in my view not much) for...requiring part or all of that windfall to be returned to the naive original owner.... But there is nothing to be said for giving it instead to the government — which...is both the cause of the miscarriage of "fairness" and the only one of the three parties involved in the miscarriage (government, naive original owner, and sharp real estate developer) which acted unlawfully, indeed unconstitutionally. Justice O'Connor would eliminate the windfall by giving the malefactor the benefit of its malefaction. It is rather like [making] a purchaser who bought property at a bargain rate from a thief...turn over the "unjust" profit to the thief. 533 U.S. at 636-637.[57]

3. **An emerging consensus structure for takings reviews?** By the end of the *Palazzolo* decision, it was possible to declare that the basic structure and elements of takings jurisprudence are becoming settled. The parcel-as-a-whole baseline has been repeatedly affirmed. The Court's invocation of the *Penn Central* triad has become the standard takings approach, carrying with it the commonsense principle that constitutional review of regulations requires balanced consideration of both public and private interests. Takings validity cannot be weighed solely in terms of effects on the plaintiffs' private property market values.

Fleshing out the emerging structure, the case law seemed to have arrived at a de facto two-stage takings inquiry.

---

57. In rebuttal, Justice O'Connor footnoted that "Justice Scalia's inapt 'government-as-thief' simile is symptomatic of the larger failing of his opinion, which is that he appears to conflate two questions. The first question is whether the enactment or application of a regulation constitutes a valid exercise of the police power [i.e., whether it had proper authority, proper purpose, and was rationally structured]. The second question is whether the State must compensate a property owner for a diminution in value effected by the State's exercise of its police power [i.e., whether it went 'too far'].... The relative timing of regulatory enactment and title acquisition, of course, does not affect the analysis of whether a State has acted within the scope of these powers in the first place, [which] appears to be the [issue] on which Justice Scalia focuses, but...is not the matter at hand." 533 U.S. at 636 n. **.

The first stage of this "diminution-balancing" approach would draw upon the accepted diminution test as inherited from the zoning cases: Plaintiffs attacking regulations must show that the restrictions eliminate any "reasonable economic value," viewed in terms of the plaintiff's entire contiguous property investment, not just the regulated segment thereof. The definition of "reasonable economic value" remains a subjective contextual task.

If a court determines that regulated property does not have "reasonable economic value," it must move to a second level of consideration, weighing the private loss against public harms. A plaintiff's prima facie case against a regulation must bear the burden of showing not only individual economic loss, but also that the private loss exceeds the public harms that the regulation was designed to prevent. No private loss, in other words, can be constitutionally excessive if it is less than the harms it would impose on others. The second stage balance follows from the proposition that regulations must be deemed constitutionally valid if the costs that an unrestricted property use imposes upon the public would be greater than private diminution losses. As with the "nuisance exception," it is clear that individuals do not have that right.

Here too subjectivity remains, however. What is a public "harm" (and what, on the other hand, is a public "benefit" that government should not receive without paying for it)? And how are these interests to be quantified? These are questions that undoubtedly will be addressed in coming Supreme Court terms, but for the moment it might be noted that the assignment of procedural burdens between regulatory defenders and attackers will provide some indication of outcomes. If government regulations properly promulgated hold a presumption of constitutionality, the subjective burden is placed upon the attackers. If all a plaintiff has to do to shift the burden in takings cases is to show a substantial private loss (and in the past many courts thought that was all that was required to shift the burden), then government is put in the awkward position of having to prove the legitimacy and utility of civic governance in every case. If courts understand that a determination of invalid taking requires findings of both the private and public interests — not only of the private diminution effect, of no reasonable economic use, but also a finding that the public harms avoided or forfended do not exceed the private loss — then the plaintiff's prima facie case against a regulation will require both showings. Given a presumption of validity, the normal requirement is that parties attacking a presumption must offer a full rebuttal in order to shift the burden.

4. **A proportional takings scale.** Understandably, very few courts have wrestled with the details of expressly weighing public harms. In *First English* on remand from the Supreme Court, a California appeals court spoke to the issue. Justice Rehnquist had decided the *First English* remedy question on the hypothesis that prohibiting operation of a church camp in a canyon subject to fatal flash floods might be an unconstitutional deprivation of property rights, but remanded for a substantive balance. In finding the taking valid, the California court subjected the Chief Justice's hypothesis to a common-sense corrective balance:

> If there is a hierarchy of interests the police power serves — and both logic and prior cases suggest there is — then the preservation of life must rank at the top. Zoning restrictions [which require a reasonable remaining economic use] seldom

serve public interests so far up on the scale.... When land use regulations seek to advance what are deemed lesser interests such as aesthetic values of the community they frequently are outweighed by constitutional property rights [but] even these lesser public interests have been deemed sufficient to justify zoning which diminishes — without compensation — the value of individual properties. The zoning regulation challenged in the instant case involves this highest of public interests — the prevention of death and injury. Its enactment was prompted by the loss of life in an earlier flood. And its avowed purpose is to prevent the loss of lives in future floods. Moreover, the lives it seeks to save and the injuries it strives to prevent are not only those on other properties but on appellant's property as well. 210 Cal. App. 3d 1353, 1371 (1989), cert. denied, 493 U.S. 1056 (1990).

Can you say the same about wetlands? A discriminating balancing process requires some proportionality between the degrees of public need and private loss, requiring courts to consider complex physical, ecological, and human relationships, and to distinguish between the different effects of property use. Using this process, the courts are in a far better position to undertake the balancing task at the heart of judicial review.

Tahoe-Sierra Preservation Council v. Tahoe Regional Planning Agency:[58] **Now Some Things Look Much Clearer.** In the *Tahoe-Sierra* case, an association of landowners brought suit against the Tahoe Regional Planning Agency, claiming that temporary moratoria on development (in effect for a total of 32 months) constituted an uncompensated regulatory taking on its face. The trial court agreed with the landowners, and the Ninth Circuit reversed. Propelled by strong pressure from real estate and industrial interests, the case came to the Supreme Court shortly after the Bush II Administration came to Washington. Would the Court's anti-regulatory bloc, buoyed by an antiregulatory administration, once more shift takings case law away from its evolving consensus?

The anticipated rejuggling did not materialize. Pressured by state governors, the Bush II Administration appeared as amici in support of the regulations, and Justice Stevens wrote for a 6–3 majority:

[Petitioners] contend that the mere enactment of a temporary regulation that, while in effect, denies a property owner all viable economic use of her property gives rise to an unqualified constitutional obligation to compensate her for the value of its use during that period.... They face an uphill battle that is made especially steep by their desire for a categorical rule requiring compensation whenever the government imposes such a moratorium on development. Under their proposed rule, there is no need to evaluate the landowners' investment-backed expectations, the actual impact of the regulation on any individual, the importance of the public interest served by the regulation, or the reasons for imposing the temporary restriction [i.e., *Penn Central*-type tests]. For petitioners, it is enough that a regulation imposes a temporary deprivation — no matter how brief — of all economically viable use to trigger a *per se* rule that a taking has occurred.... Our cases do not support their proposed categorical rule....

In our view the answer to the abstract question whether a temporary moratorium effects a taking is neither "yes, always" nor "no, never"; the answer depends upon the particular circumstances of the case. Resisting "the temptation to adopt what

---

58. 535 U.S. 302 (2002).

amount to *per se* rules in either direction," *Palazzolo* (O'Connor, J., concurring), we conclude that the circumstances in this case are best analyzed within the *Penn Central* framework....

Penn Central [made] it clear that even though multiple factors are relevant in the analysis of regulatory takings claims, in such cases we must focus on "the parcel as a whole."... Petitioners [argue] that we can effectively sever a 32-month segment from the remainder of each landowner's fee simple estate, and then ask whether that segment has been taken in its entirety by the moratoria. Of course, defining the property interest taken in terms of the very regulation being challenged is circular. With property so divided, every delay would become a total ban; the moratorium and the normal permit process alike would constitute categorical takings. Petitioners' "conceptual severance" argument is unavailing because it ignores *Penn Central*'s admonition that...we must focus on "the parcel as a whole." "To the extent that any portion of property is taken, that portion is always taken in its entirety; the relevant question, however, is whether the property taken is all, or only a portion of, the parcel in question." 508 U.S. 602, 644. Thus, the District Court erred when it disaggregated petitioners' property into temporal segments.... "Where an owner possesses a full 'bundle' of property rights, the destruction of one 'strand' of the bundle is not a taking...."

More importantly, for reasons set out at some length by Justice O'Connor in her concurring opinion in *Palazzolo*, we are persuaded that the better approach to claims that a regulation has effected a temporary taking "requires careful examination and weighing of all the relevant circumstances...." We conclude, therefore, that the interest in "fairness and justice" will be best served by relying on the familiar *Penn Central* approach when deciding cases like this, rather than by attempting to craft a new categorical rule. Accordingly, the judgment of the Court of Appeals is affirmed. 535 U.S. at 320–342.

The *Tahoe-Sierra* decision, with its reassertion of the parcel-as-a-whole doctrine and the balancing approach, put the anti-regulatory justices on the defensive. In his dissent, joined by Justices Scalia and Thomas, Justice Rehnquist wrote:

The regulation in *Lucas* was the "practical equivalence" of a long-term physical appropriation, i.e., a condemnation, so the Fifth Amendment required compensation. The "practical equivalence," from the landowner's point of view, of a "temporary" ban on all economic use is a forced leasehold.... From petitioners' standpoint, what happened in this case is no different than if the government had taken a...lease of their property.... Because the prohibition on development of nearly six years in this case cannot be said to resemble any "implied limitation" of state property law, it is a taking that requires compensation. 535 U.S. at 330–331, 348–354.

In a separate dissenting opinion, Justice Thomas, joined by Justice Scalia, wrote to address the parcel-as-a-whole issues in the case and to criticize the majority's treatment of the issue:

While this questionable [parcel-as-a-whole] rule[59] has been applied to various alleged regulatory takings, it was, in my view, rejected in the context of temporal

---

59. The majority's decision to embrace the "parcel as a whole" doctrine as settled is puzzling. See, e.g., Palazzolo v. Rhode Island, 533 U.S. 606, 631 (2001) (noting that the Court has "at times expressed discomfort with the logic of [the parcel-as-a-whole] rule"); Lucas v. South Carolina Coastal Council, 505 U.S. 1003, 1016, n. 7 (1992) (recognizing that "uncertainty regarding the composition of the denominator in [the Court's] 'deprivation' fraction has produced inconsistent pronouncements by the Court," and that the relevant calculus is a "difficult question").

deprivations of property by *First English*, which held that temporary and permanent takings "are not different in kind" when a landowner is deprived of all beneficial use of his land. I had thought that *First English* put to rest the notion that the "relevant denominator" is land's infinite life.

A taking is exactly what occurred in this case.... These individuals and families were deprived of the opportunity to build single-family homes as permanent, retirement, or vacation residences on land upon which such construction was authorized when purchased. The Court assures them that "a temporary prohibition on economic use" cannot be a taking because "logically...the property will recover value as soon as the prohibition is lifted." But the "logical" assurance that a "temporary restriction... merely causes a diminution in value" is cold comfort to the property owners in this case or any other.... To my mind,...potential future value bears on the amount of compensation due and has nothing to do with the question whether there was a taking in the first place. 535 U.S. at 355.

COMMENTARY & QUESTIONS

1. **After *Palazzolo* and *Tahoe-Sierra*.** *Palazzolo* and *Tahoe-Sierra* appear to have worked a sea change in takings jurisprudence, leveling what had sometimes seemed a privateering judicial tidal wave in which property rights were overriding civic regulation to a degree never before seen in this (and therefore in any) legal system. Subsequently state courts have generally followed the Supreme Court in casting the takings inquiry as a public-private balance on a parcel-as-a-whole baseline. After these two cases — at least until one or two new Justices are appointed to the Court — it seems that regulatory takings law has found itself centered on a *Penn Central* consensus.

2. ***Lucas* applies only in rare anomalous cases.** *Tahoe-Sierra* makes clear that the *Lucas* test is relegated to only the rarest of cases: It applies only where regulations create total wipeouts. A total wipeout justifies treating a regulation as equivalent to physical appropriations, but total wipeouts will be very rare. "The categorical rule in *Lucas* was carved out for the 'extraordinary case' in which a regulation permanently deprives property of *all* value.... The categorical rule would *not* apply if the diminution in value were 95% instead of 100%." 535 U.S. at 330, 332.

3. **Conceptual severance is dead. No more baseline games: it's the parcel as a whole.** Justice Stevens's *Tahoe-Sierra* opinion seems finally to have re-interred conceptual severance, which had come back to life in spite of his *Keystone Bituminous* majority opinion. The *Tahoe-Sierra* majority, however, does leave room for misunderstanding in one conceptual severance setting. It says, "an interest in real property is defined by the metes and bounds that describe its geographic dimensions and the term of years that describes the temporal aspect of the owner's interest. Both dimensions must be considered if the interest is to be viewed in its entirety." But what if, say, a regulated developer had purchased 1000 separate contiguous one-acre lots, only one of which is subject to the permanent wetlands regulation? According to the investment-backed expectations principle, shouldn't the baseline be all 1000 acres, not just "the metes and bounds" of the separate one-acre wetlands lot? The majority's language overlooked the possibility that the conceptual severance tactic might still work under their metes-and-bounds definition of the parcel as a whole.

4. ***Penn Central* rules!** The *Tahoe-Sierra* majority repeatedly embraced Justice O'Connor's position in *Palazzolo* over Justice Scalia's *Palazzolo* dissent. The *Tahoe-Sierra* decision reemphasizes that, in virtually all cases, *Penn Central* is the test. Courts reviewing a regulation's taking validity under *Penn Central* should examine "a number of factors rather than a simple mathematically precise formula," Justice Stevens said in *Tahoe-Sierra*, quoting as he does so often from Justice O'Connor's concurring *Palazzolo* opinion. Testing the validity of regulations requires *Penn Central*'s "complex factual assessments of the purposes and economic effects of government actions," including "the importance of the public interest served by the regulation, [and] the reasons for imposing the…restriction."

5. **What now is the role of "investment-backed expectations"?** After *Palazzolo* and *Tahoe-Sierra*, it is probably more accurate to ask what are the *roles*, plural, of IBEs (investment-backed expectations). The concept — launched in Professor Frank Michelman's book review[60] and enshrined by *Penn Central* as a constitutional consideration — has become firmly established but cuts both ways. In its initial applications, it was typically used *against* regulatory validity. If property values drop a certain amount owing to a regulation, the constitutional harm is greater if the property owners had invested money without knowledge of the impending restrictions and had their expectations frustrated. IBEs have now developed a role in *supporting* the validity of regulation — in identifying plaintiffs' "self-created hardships" to be weighed in the takings balance and in clarifying the full property baselines upon which that takings balance will be reviewed. Where property owners know of existing or impending regulations at the time of purchase and are gambling that their investment nonetheless will pay off, even though *Palazzolo* made clear that they are not estopped from challenging the regulations, that knowledge can be used to dilute their constitutional claims. IBEs are also relevant to defining the "property baseline" or "denominator" on which plaintiffs' degree of regulatory burden is to be judged. If a land purchase involved buying 1000 acres, only one of which is impacted by severe wetlands restrictions, then the fairness balance of regulatory takings and due process reviews is based on the entire investment, not on a separate segment.

6. **Takings case semantics.** The semantics of takings jurisprudence often had been erratic, imprecise, and poorly thought out. The semantics of the word "categorical" have been mentioned already. The *Palazzolo* and *Tahoe-Sierra* cases clarified some of the basic definitional frames and also perpetuated some of the maladroitnesses:

Semantics (a): "Value" or "use"? Which is to be weighed in the constitutional balance? The *Palazzolo* and *Tahoe-Sierra* decisions forged a major clarification in the definition of what term is to be used to measure the quantum of a property owner's regulatory burden. Must regulated property owners generally realize a reasonable economic "value" or a remaining economic "use" of their property? If the operative term is "value," then the quantum of a regulation's burden will be weighed in the relatively neutral terms of appraised market values. If, on the other hand, value is not enough and

---

60. Property, Utility, and Fairness: Comments on the Ethical Foundations of Just Compensation Law, 80 Harv. L. Rev. 1165 (1967).

property must retain a "use," this terminology implies a much more demanding standard. "Use" raises the implication that the property owner must retain a practical active use, which often will be defined in terms of those uses that the property owner herself is ready and able to undertake. It biases takings reviews in favor of commercially oriented development. Accordingly the *Tahoe-Sierra* dissents by Justices Rehnquist and Thomas bitterly protest the majority's terminology. "The 'temporary' denial of all viable *use* of land for six years [i.e., even if the land retains its *value*] is a taking." This implies that regulations can be invalidated even where property value is unchanged or increases despite a moratorium. The majority's stipulation that value is the issue to be considered seems to make sense, avoiding the subjective imprecisions of the word "use."

Throughout its regulatory takings jurisprudence, the Supreme Court has not been clear or consistent in defining whether it is "use" or "value" that is constitutionally protected. While the Court has often used the words interchangeably, an important distinction should be made. Regulations that potentially offend a use-focused standard likely would pass a value-focused standard since nearly all regulated land retains some financial significance, even if only as a nature preserve or buffer zone for adjacent landowners. The Court's remand on *Penn Central* grounds in *Palazzolo* was framed in terms of value, not use, and the *Tahoe-Sierra* Court said that *Lucas* is to be applied only where there is a "permanent obliteration of the *value* of the fee simple estate" (emphasis added). See B. Crossman, The Use-Value Distinction in Regulatory Takings Law: Which Property Interest Is Protected by the Constitution? (2003) (available on coursebook Web site).

Semantics (b): "Total takings"/"partial takings" and "takings." Like many courts and commentators, the *Tahoe-Sierra* majority unfortunately uses the semantic phrasing of "total takings" and "partial takings." What these phrases are meant to indicate are, respectively, "cases where a total wipeout is alleged, which if proved will trigger a *Lucas* review" and "cases where a total wipeout is not alleged or proved, which therefore will be tested under *Penn Central* diminution-balancing tests." It would be far better if courts and commentators, especially now that *Palazzolo* and *Tahoe-Sierra* have clarified that the vast majority of takings cases should be reviewed under *Penn Central*, referred to these two settings as "the exceptional *Lucas*-type total wipeout claims" on one hand and "standard *Penn Central*-based takings reviews" or "*Penn Central* diminution-balancing reviews" on the other.

Part of the ambiguity in "total takings" and "partial takings" is that the phrasing itself implies presumptive invalidity. For a town counsel to argue that "this is not a total takings case, it's a partial takings case" is to imply that the town admits it has "partially taken" and must pay for the plaintiff's property. But virtually all restrictions on property partially take value by limiting some uses.

The very word "taking" is a phrase that seems already halfway to a finding of invalidity. For those who have limited understanding of the field, if a regulation "takes" property value from a plaintiff, as virtually every plaintiff can show, then isn't it a taking that the Constitution prohibits? This, of course, proves too much. All informed participants in this debate, from whatever ideological perspective, understand that virtually all regulations "take" some value from private property. If my town's zoning prevents me from opening a gas station or convenience store on my residential property, or allows only light manufacturing on my industrial lot, that to at least some small degree diminishes my land's potential market value, the price at which I could sell the land if it were unregulated. But not every taking is an invalid taking. It must overcome the presumption of constitutionality and rise to the level of a constitutionally excessive confiscatory burden on the individual property owner. For reasons of semantic hygiene, it would be preferable for us to use some other wording entirely, like "excessive regulatory burden cases," or consistently use more complete takings phrasing, like "this is a suit claiming an invalid taking." But these alternatives are all awkward mouthfuls compared to "takings," so for the foreseeable future the burden will fall upon the players, particularly the defenders of regulations, to clarify what the phrase "takings" means and entails and what it doesn't.

7. **So, now: how far is too far?** It still isn't very clear, is it, the constitutional takings test line between regulatory restrictions that go too far and not too far?

8. **Are overrides of common law a regulatory taking?** The common law is traditionally aimed at particular localized conditions; police power regulatory permits are typically set with reference to generalized statewide minimum standards in a hurly-burly administrative process and do not purport to be affirmative authorizations of a right to pollute to such levels.

The wood-pulp industry lobby in Alaska got a bill passed in 1994 that effectively repealed the common law tort protections available to private property owners if a factory was in compliance with state permits. If a polluting paper mill, for instance, complied with general statewide emission standards, it could not be sued for its particular local effects on the neighbors. Alaska Stat. §09.45.230. This raises the fascinating constitutional question whether private property due process rights are violated if landowners are stripped of their traditional tort protections. See Hasselman, Alaska's Nuisance Statute Revisited: Federal Substantive Due Process Limits to Common Law Abrogation, 24 B.C. Envtl. Aff. L. Rev. 347 (1997) (concluding after extensive review that it probably does). The amendment also provided a fascinating takings fallback, requiring any industry that availed itself of the shield to cover the state's costs in defending the statute and paying the state's damages owed from any citizens' inverse condemnation challenge against the statute!

9. **Takings as a continuing political target.** As illustrated at the start of this chapter, automatic-compensation regulatory takings bills pushed by industry lobbies continue to surface in the state and federal legislative process, with the potential for dramatic effects on environmental and other regulation. Note that they almost uniformly provide for conceptual severance, not parcel-as-a-whole analysis. They sometimes contain a so-called nuisance exception, but as worded in such bills, these do not provide much of a balance. As Professor Sax has noted, "a nuisance standard operates to restrict regulation to preexisting covered areas, and to impose judicial standards of proof designed for private litigation, rather than for public standards which are often designed to deal with risks to public health and welfare while proof is still uncertain."

Sax, Using Property Rights to Attack Environmental Protection, 14 Pace Envtl. L. Rev. 1 (1996).

Our prediction is that endangered species protections will be the poster child for takings "reform" bills in the legislatures. Antagonism to regulatory restrictions on uses of corporate and individual land in order to protect endangered species has made those wildlife regulations one of the most vulnerable targets of opportunity. ESA §9, in fact, was one of the driving market forces behind the automatic-compensation provisions noted at the beginning of this chapter. Industries have invested a great deal of money and effort to characterize species protections as frivolous and insubstantial, calling for compensation for any regulated portion of property, and inserting amendments for negotiated weakening of species protections where they cause market value losses.[61] Endangered species have been described as good stalking horses for anti-regulatory initiatives in general. It is far easier to trivialize wildlife regulations than to levy direct attacks against pollution abatement regulations.

10. *Metalclad*: **the anti-takings initiative goes international.** Customary international law (see Chapter 26) has long provided a remedy where governments seize, nationalize, or "expropriate" a foreign national's property without compensation — a rough international legal equivalent of traditional takings principles in the United States. The North American Free Trade Agreement (NAFTA) signed by the United States, Mexico, and Canada (see Chapters 8 and 26) was the first international trade agreement to address this issue. NAFTA's Chapter 11 expanded the concept of what "property" was protected by adding the concept that protection now extended to the "investment," and opened the way for challenges to domestic police power regulatory protections of local health, safety, and welfare. (Although international custom did not limit compensability to physical and title expropriations, the previous doctrine barring "creeping expropriations" primarily addressed such nonphysical constraints as predatory taxation, export barriers, and the like rather than police power regulatory protections.)

Soon after NAFTA entered into force, creative trade lawyers began to challenge environmental regulations as international expropriations, beginning with an attack on Canadian health restrictions against a fuel additive, MMT. After Canada settled the challenge for more than $10 million and withdrew the ban, however, a flood of "me-too" challenges followed. Environmentalists and scholars — who until then largely believed that domestic regulations to protect health, safety, and the environment, as an exercise of a country's sovereign police power, were immune from challenge — protested that this NAFTA provision was setting its international standards for takings at a level even stricter than the those in the United States, previously the strictest system by far of property rights protection in the world. Disputes under Chapter 11, moreover, are resolved by commercial arbitration, which, like most arbitrations, has only the rarest ability to be appealed for review by a court. In *Metalclad*, a notable NAFTA case, the NAFTA arbitration panel awarded compensation for a province's denial of a U.S.

---

61. See The Embattled Social Utilities of the Endangered Species Act — A Noah Presumption, and a Caution Against Putting Gas Masks on the Canaries in the Coal Mine, 27 Envtl. L. 845 (1997); Houck, Why Do We Protect Endangered Species, and What Does That Say About Whether Restrictions on Private Property to Protect Them Constitute "Takings"?, 80 Iowa L. Rev. 297 (1995); and Professor Sax's article in the preceding paragraph.

corporation's request to site a hazardous waste disposal facility, because the company had received conflicting signals from Mexican federal and provincial officials. The United Mexican States v. Metalclad Corp., 2001 B.C.S.C. 664 and 1529. In a bizarre twist, the Supreme Court of British Columbia later modified the award at Mexico's request, under a statute authorizing the court to review arbitral awards rendered in that jurisdiction.

Assuming that past experience warrants some concern for mistreatment of foreign investors, and that international legal protections are desirable to encourage foreign investment, to what extent should environmental regulations be subject to international takings challenges? Or should foreign investors be strictly limited to domestic remedies within the foreign jurisdiction? How is the distinction to be made between valid environmental regulations and those that are a mere pretext for harassing foreign businesses? Should foreign investors in the United States be entitled to greater protection than U.S. nationals? Are national courts a good forum for correcting errors in awards, or would an appellate process in NAFTA itself be a preferable solution? These questions frame what may well become an area of passionate debate as anti-regulatory takings issues go international.

11. **Rethinking rights.** The beginning of this chapter notes that extremely rigorous defense of private property rights has been a special characteristic of American democracy, and one of the commonly credited reasons (along with the nation's extraordinary natural wealth available for exploitation) for the American economy's world dominance. In other nations more densely populated and less richly endowed, property rights resemble privileges and are tempered by public rights. In many countries, for instance, landowners have only qualified rights to mineral resources beneath the surface and are forced to share the authority to permit mining, and royalties, with their governments. In most modern nations, it would be unthinkable for property owners to assert a right to destroy permanently the utility and value of their land, but environmental defendants in this country recurringly have made that fundamental claim, as in the coal strip mining controversies.

The awakening communitarian debate about civic responsibilities as counterweights to rights invites further questions about the absolutist nature of the private property assertions so regularly heard contesting regulatory actions by federal, state, and local governments:

> [When rights in general] have a strident and absolutist character, they impoverish political and judicial discourse. They do not admit of compromise. They do not allow room for competing considerations. They impair and even foreclose deliberation. Rooted in 19th century ideas of absolute [private] sovereignty over property, they are ill-adapted to a long discussion of tradeoffs and competing needs. They are, moreover, overly individualistic [and focused on the short-term].... They miss the "dimension of sociality" and posit selfish, isolated individuals asserting what is theirs rather than participating in communal life. Sunstein, Rightalk, New Republic, Sept. 2, 1991, at 33.[62]

---

62. Professor Sunstein is describing Professor Glendon's analysis. M. A. Glendon, Rights Talk: The Impoverishment of Political Discourse (1991). This dimension of communitarian sociability is fine, says the landowner, but why do *I* have to bear the brunt of your high-minded civic protections?

Although the rights-and-responsibilities theorists have sometimes been considered reactionaries, the more sophisticated civic debate they call for cannot be typecast. In the regulatory takings field, for instance, it could do much to temper the average court's preclusive focus on private effects to the exclusion of careful consideration of the public harms that motivate regulation.[63] Coupled with notions of the public trust — and modern acknowledgment of the loss of the mythical American frontier with its boundless resources and ability to absorb mistakes — might it mean that old conceptions of isolated private sovereign rights in land are changing?

Section 3. A TAKINGS ROLE FOR THE PUBLIC TRUST DOCTRINE?

In *Lucas*, Justice Scalia held that, at least where property values were wiped out:

> Any limitation so severe cannot be newly legislated or decreed (without compensation), but must inhere in the title itself, in the restrictions that background principles of the State's law of property and nuisance already place upon land ownership. 505 U.S. at 1029.

Did he inadvertently open the door to an additional consideration of public rights (and perhaps even of the "natural economy") against private marketplace rights by incorporating the public trust doctrine into the takings balance?

Hope Babcock, Has the U.S. Supreme Court Finally Drained the Swamp of Takings Jurisprudence? The Impact of Lucas v. South Carolina Coastal Council on Wetlands and Coastal Barrier Beaches
19 Harvard Environmental Law Review 1 (1994)

Most of the *Lucas* majority opinion focuses on the uses proscribed by state nuisance law. Little attention has been paid to a further source of guidance: state property law [in the public trust doctrine and custom].... As the essence of the...common law doctrine of custom...is the "understandings of our citizens," custom would appear to be one of the *Lucas* Court's "background principles of property" that "inhere[s] in the title itself." As such, it could be used where applicable to support "measures newly enacted by the state in legitimate exercise of its police powers on property impressed with a customary usufruct."...

The public trust doctrine...is considerably more versatile. Unlike custom, the doctrine of public trust has shown enormous vitality and flexibility in the modern era. The *Lucas* decision could give the doctrine even more prominence, as public trust principles may well be employed by government regulators in their attempts to justify their actions under the *Lucas* takings rule....

The relationship between the public trust doctrine and takings jurisprudence has been largely unexplored by the courts.... Courts have commonly given several reasons why exercises of public trust authority should bar a takings claim.... The land in question is not, like ordinary private land held in fee simple absolute, subject to development at the sole whim of the owner, but is impressed with a public trust, which gives the public's representatives an interest and responsibility in its development....

Another reason commonly given is that since private rights attached to the trust resources later than the public's rights, which originated with (or even prior to) sovereignty, private title

---

63. After surveying the cases, Professor Sax observed that, in most cases, there apparently is "a hierarchy [of constitutional values] in which the right to profit stands first, with [only] a grudging exception for exigent public need." Sax, Takings, Private Property, and Public Rights, 81 Yale L.J. 149 n. 7 (1971).

does not include the right to affect trust resources adversely.... It is as though the private property owner of trust lands is merely a custodian of those lands for present and future generations, and the state has an easement over her lands that permanently burdens ownership of them....

Reliance on these doctrines by government regulators to defend against takings claims may...destabilize expectations about property.... Frustrating the expectations of landowners could lead to a backlash not only against the doctrines, but also against the environmental laws which protect wetlands and barrier beaches.

The public trust doctrine [however] helps to harmonize the laws of nature and the law of property, bringing the expectations of landowners into harmony with the needs of nature by infusing an ecological perspective into property law. This is beneficial because the laws of nature are fundamental and irrefutable, unlike the laws of property, which can be changed by legislative or executive fiat.... The doctrines of custom and public trust could thwart the [*Lucas*] decision's preference for private property rights by underscoring the public's superior right to access and use certain resources, but this is not as destabilizing as it sounds because both common law doctrines are a reflection of public expectations....

COMMENTARY & QUESTIONS

1. **The public trust and private property rights.** If public trust rights exist within particular private property, then regulations merely giving effect to a preexisting potential limitation within the private title do not amount to an invalid regulatory taking. You cannot be deprived of what you never really had, and you may never have had an unfettered right to develop. Private property is always held under the risk that some preexisting cloud may upset expectations. When a gravel company is suddenly told that it may not quarry its lands because they are public trust wetlands, as in Potomac Sand & Gravel Co. v. Maryland, 293 A.2d 241 (Md. 1972), the trust doctrine can create unexpected economic losses, anger, and political backlash.

2. **A society's underlying "expectations" in takings balances.** Expectations, both private "investment-backed expectations" and public expectations, play a role in the takings balance, as Professor Babcock notes. Professor Sax, who argued that the *Lucas* case should have considered public trust-like values of "the natural economy" in the takings balance,[64] has argued that the public trust is part of a society's expectations:

> The essence of property law is respect for reasonable expectations. The idea of justice at the root of private property protection calls for identification of those expectations which the legal system ought to recognize. We all appreciate the importance of expectations as an idea of justice, but our concern for expectations has traditionally been confined to private owners.... The central idea of the public trust is preventing the destabilizing disappointment of expectations held in common but without formal recognition such as title. The function of the public trust as a legal doctrine is to protect...public expectations against destabilizing changes, just as we protect conventional private property from such changes.[65]

---

64. Sax, Property Rights and the Economy of Nature: Understanding Lucas v. South Carolina Coastal Council, 45 Stan. L. Rev. 1433 (1993).

65. Sax, Liberating the Public Trust Doctrine from Its Historical Shackles, 14 U.C. Davis L. Rev. 185, 186–194 (1980). A 1988 Supreme Court public trust case turned upon whether a state's assertion that it owned certain tidal wetlands upset "settled private expectations." Philips Petroleum Co. v. Mississippi, 484 U.S. 469 (1988), decided that it did not, in an opinion emphasizing the traditional role of the states in defining their public trust; see also, e.g., Shively v. Bowlby, 152 U.S. 1, 26 (1894).

Sax also argued that a society's expectations about what are unfair impositions on private property change over time.[66] In Sanderson v. Penn Coal,[67] a coal company was mining and dumping its wastes in a river, and a downstream landowner objected, claiming traditional riparian rights and protections under nuisance law. The coal company urged that "the law should be adjusted to the exigencies of the great industrial interests of the Commonwealth and that the production of an indispensable mineral...should not be crippled and endangered by adopting a rule that would make colliers answerable in damages for corrupting a stream." The court held:

> We are of opinion that mere private personal inconvenience...must yield to the necessities of a great public industry, which...subserves a great public interest. To encourage the development of the great natural resources of a country, trifling inconveniences to particular persons must sometimes give way to the necessities of a great community. 6 A. at 459.

In 1886, this ascendancy of marketplace needs did not arouse a horrified reaction in defenders of private property rights. Sax posits that most people are implicitly on notice today that wetlands, beaches, and perhaps even privately owned historic sites may be subjected to future regulation in the public interest.

3. **More from South Carolina.** Remarkably, shortly after *Palazzolo* and *Tahoe-Sierra*, the Supreme Court of South Carolina found that a prohibition on filling tideland below the high water mark issued by the state Coastal Council was not a taking, despite the uncontested fact that the land retained no value as a result of the prohibition. The *McQueen* court found that because the property in question had eroded to the point that it was below the high-water mark, the public trust doctrine granted the state exclusive control over the land for the public benefit, and thus the state could prohibit activity on the land that would threaten public interests such as preserving marine life, water quality, and public access. The *Lucas* background principles of South Carolina's public trust property law absolved the state from having to compensate the plaintiff. According to the court, since the land in question was public trust property, "McQueen's ownership rights do not include the right to backfill or place bulkheads on public trust land and the State need not compensate him for the denial of permits to do what he cannot otherwise do.... Any taking McQueen suffered is not a taking effected by State regulation but by the forces of nature and McQueen's own lack of vigilance in protecting his property." McQueen v. South Carolina Coastal Council, 580 S.E.2d 116 (S.C. 2003).

Section 4. OTHER PROPERTY REGULATION ISSUES: REMEDIES, EXACTIONS, AND INNOCENT LANDOWNER LIABILITY

a. Takings Remedies

The *First English* case, in which land use regulations were ultimately held valid without compensation, earlier had gone to the Supreme Court on the question of what

---

66. Sax, The Limits of Private Rights in Public Waters, 19 Envtl. L. 473 (1989).

67. 6 A. 453 (Pa. 1886). See also Horwitz, The Transformation in the Conception of Property in American Law 1780-1860, 40 U. Chi. L. Rev. 248 (1973).

remedies were theoretically available if a takings challenge succeeds. 482 U.S. 304 (1987). This remedies decision established that if a regulation is finally determined to be an invalid taking, two remedy options are generally available: (1) an equitable injunction or declaration that the regulation is void on its face or as applied to that particular parcel, or (2) payment by the government for the taking under the rubric of "inverse condemnation" applied to regulatory takings. Governments have the choice whether to pay compensation and continue to apply a regulation that has been found to go too far, or to accept its nullification as to the challenger's property, thereby avoiding the need to pay (although temporary interim damages may be assessed).

Governments only rarely will choose to buy off a regulated property owner if regulation has been found to be a taking. If it does so choose, it is not clear how compensation should be measured. Take a zoning example, with regard to a parcel that would have a full fee simple market value of $100,000 if unregulated. Assume that a court is willing to make especially precise findings of fact, and determines that market value after zoning is $20,000 and that is too little, and hence unconstitutional, but that a remaining value of $60,000 would have been constitutional. How much would government have to pay, if it is not taking possession but only maintaining the regulation? $80,000? $40,000?

Even tougher is the question of valuing temporary takings, where the state decides to give up and suspend the regulation's application to the parcel, but the landowner, using the further element of *First English*'s remedy case, demands compensation for the "temporary" taking between the time the regulation was applied and the time that it is suspended. What should the measure of such temporary damages be? If it is the difference in market value, that often will have increased between the time of the initial regulation and the time the regulation is released. Some courts have argued that "rent," or even "lost profits," must be paid by the government. These latter figures can become huge, thereby chilling the exercise of the police power from the start, which may be the point in the first place. What local government wants to undertake an environmental regulation when affected property owners can argue that it confiscates their property and can then force payment of millions in lost profits if a court agrees with them? See Almota Farmer's Elevator & Warehouse Co. v. United States, 409 U.S. 470 (1973) (rental value was used as the measure of damages in a physical appropriation case).

b. Amortization and Offset Alternatives?

One way government can attempt to secure their regulations against takings challenges is by providing a period of delay before enforcement, to allow the property owner to "amortize" and recoup her investment before it is shut down. If state or local governments wish to ban billboards, for example, they may provide a four-year amortization period. The billboard industry, one of the strongest lobbies in the nation, is sure to challenge the ban as a regulatory taking. How is amortization, which has been upheld in a wide variety of other property land use regulations, likely to fare against billboards? See Mayor & Council of New Castle v. Rollins Outdoor Adver., Inc., 459 A.2d 541 (Del. 1983) (three years insufficient); Village of Skokie v. Walton, 456 N.E.2d 293 (Ill. Ct. App. 1983) (seven years OK). Is it relevant that a billboard company has long since written off the billboard in depreciation credits on its tax books for the IRS? National Adver. Co. v. County of Monterey, 464 P.2d 33 (Cal. 1970) (tax depreciation can be considered); Art Neon v. Denver, 488 F.2d 118 (10th Cir. 1973) (amortization need not await depreciation); Modjeska Sign Studios, Inc. v. Berle, 373 N.E.2d 255 (N.Y. 1977) (ditto).

Another possibility is a takings compensation offset. If, for example, the state and federal governments created thousands of acres of private agricultural land out of Florida swamps by channelizing the Kissimmee River at public expense, must they now, 30 years later, pay full dryland market value when they decide that groundwater levels must be raised, returning some of the lands to wetlands (because the loss of marshes turned out to cause massive pollution effects in downstream water supplies and Lake Okeechobee)? Can a state condemning a billboard agree to pay its fair market value minus an offset amount attributable to public expenditures, i.e., excluding all value attributable to the highway? See United States v. Cors, 337 U.S. 325 (1949) (government expropriating a vessel need not pay higher values attributable to demand caused by government program); United States v. Miller, 317 U.S. 369 (1943). Successful offset arguments, however, are rare.

c. Exactions and the *Nollan* and *Dolan* Cases

Physical appropriations by the public, as opposed to mere regulatory prohibitions, are virtually always a taking. See Loretto v. Teleprompter, 458 U.S. 419 (1982). In many so-called exaction cases, however, government regulations have been upheld when they required regulated landowners to provide free property for public parks, public schools, roadways, and the like for public ownership and use, in return for getting development permits, as in subdivision regulation and urban "linkage" programs.

In Nollan v. California Coastal Comm'n, 483 U.S. 825 (1987), the California Coastal Commission had denied the owners of a one-tenth acre lot permission to expand their seashore cabin into a three-bedroom home unless they allowed members of the public using the beach to walk alongside the Nollans' seawall. The Commission said it needed this right-of-way easement for pedestrian passage along the rocky coastline because without it beachgoers would not have a "visual access" visibly linking public sandy beaches north and south of the Nollans' property.[68]

In *Nollan*, the Supreme Court struck down the exaction but held that exactions in general are valid if they (a) occur in a case where the government could constitutionally have denied the entire permit application outright,[69] and (b) if there is a sufficient relationship between the exaction and the regulation — in effect, to assure that the exaction is not arbitrary extortion. The definition of this latter "sufficient relationship"

---

68. This is as hard to visualize as it was to litigate. Apparently the state commission argued that, lacking a declared easement, beachgoers looking along the shore to the next beach would see only private cabins, seawalls, and rocks coming down to the edge of the sea, and would not realize that there was actually an existing narrow path through the rocks on public property (below the high-water mark) along the shore linking the two beaches. By opening up a declared easement, the implied visual barrier would be eliminated.

69. "The Commission argues that a permit condition that serves the same legitimate police-power purpose as a refusal to issue the permit should not be found to be a taking if the refusal to issue the permit would not constitute a taking. We agree." 483 U.S. at 836.

was and is the difficult part. Writing for the Court, Justice Scalia did not question the first step. The Commission apparently could validly have prohibited the application outright because the Nollans had a reasonable remaining use of the cabin as it was. But he rejected the second step:

> The evident constitutional propriety disappears...if the condition substituted for the prohibition utterly fails to further the end advanced as the justification for the prohibition. When that essential nexus is eliminated, [the exaction is void].... Unless the permit condition serves the same governmental purpose as the development ban, the building restriction is not a valid regulation of land use but "an out-and-out plan of extortion...." It is quite impossible to understand how a requirement that people already on public beaches be able to walk across the Nollans' property reduces any obstacles to viewing the beach created by the new house.... 483 U.S. at 837–838. [Police power restrictions on property rights must constitute] a "'substantial advanc[e]'of a legitimate state interest." 483 U.S. at 841.

In *Nollan*, Scalia found there was not a sufficient relationship between the purpose of the regulation (regulation of coastal density, access to the ocean, and so on) and the required lateral easement. He indicated that if the exaction had been to require an easement of visual access across the Nollans' property to the beach from the shore road, that might well have been sufficiently related and acceptable. What is the "essential nexus"? The exaction apparently must have a nexus both to the purpose of the police power regulation and to burdens that would be directly created and imposed upon the public by the proposed development.

In Dolan v. City of Tigard, 512 U.S. 374 (1994), the Supreme Court seized the opportunity to tighten the terms of how much nexus had to be shown in exactions. The city, acting through its Land Use Board of Appeals (LUBA), gave petitioners a discretionary permit to double the size of their electric and plumbing supply store and to expand their parking lot, but required as exaction conditions that they dedicate roughly 10% of their land within the 100-year floodplain for a recreational low-density "greenway" flood area and improvement of storm drainage and, further, that they dedicate an additional 15-foot strip of land adjacent to the floodplain as a pedestrian/bicycle pathway. LUBA found a reasonable relationship between (1) the development and the requirement to dedicate land for a greenway, since the larger building and paved lot would increase the impervious surfaces and thus the runoff into the creek; and (2) the impact of increased traffic from the development and facilitating a bikeway as an alternative means of transportation. The Oregon Supreme Court found that there was a sufficient "nexus." Writing for the majority, Justice Rehnquist disagreed:

> The question for us is whether these findings are constitutionally sufficient to justify the conditions imposed by the city on petitioner's building permit.... We think a term such as "rough proportionality" best encapsulates what we hold to be the requirement of the Fifth Amendment. No precise mathematical calculation is required, but the city must make some sort of individualized determination that the required dedication is related both in nature and extent to the impact of the proposed development....
>
> Keeping the floodplain open and free from development would likely confine the pressures on Fanno Creek created by petitioner's development.... But the city demanded more — it not only wanted petitioner not to build in the floodplain,

but it also wanted petitioner's property along Fanno Creek for its Greenway system.... The difference to petitioner, of course, is the loss of her ability to exclude others. As we have noted, this right to exclude others is "one of the most essential sticks in the bundle of rights that are commonly characterized as property." *Kaiser Aetna*, 444 U.S. at 176. It is difficult to see why recreational visitors trampling along petitioner's floodplain easement are sufficiently related to the city's legitimate interest in reducing flooding problems along Fanno Creek, and the city has not attempted to make any individualized determination to support this part of its request.... We conclude that the findings upon which the city relies do not show the required reasonable relationship between the floodplain easement and the petitioner's proposed new building.

With respect to the pedestrian/bicycle pathway, we have no doubt that the city was correct in finding that the larger retail sales facility proposed by petitioner will increase traffic on the streets of the Central Business District. The city estimates that the proposed development would generate roughly 435 additional trips per day.... But on the record before us, the city has not met its burden of demonstrating that the additional number of vehicle and bicycle trips generated by the petitioner's development reasonably relate to the city's requirement for a dedication of the pedestrian/bicycle pathway easement.... The city must make some effort to quantify its findings in support of the dedication for the pedestrian/bicycle path way beyond the conclusory statement that it could offset some of the traffic demand generated.

Cities have long engaged in the commendable task of land use planning, made necessary by increasing urbanization particularly in metropolitan areas such as Portland. The city's goals of reducing flooding hazards and traffic congestion, and providing for public greenways, are laudable, but there are outer limits to how this may be done. "A strong public desire to improve the public condition [will not] warrant achieving the desire by a shorter cut than the constitutional way of paying for the change." *Pennsylvania Coal*, 260 U.S. at 416. The judgment of the Supreme Court of Oregon is reversed.... 512 U.S. 389–396.

COMMENTARY & QUESTIONS

1. **The battles of *Dolan*: a new essential nexus?** The shadow of the Property Rights Movement loomed behind the pitched battles in the *Nollan* and *Dolan* opinions. Although all the justices in *Dolan* assumed the necessity of a nexus between the exaction and the burdens imposed by the proposed development (by no means previously a foregone conclusion), the strategic question was "how much nexus?" The Rehnquist opinion seemed to say "a lot, more than ever before," but as the four dissenters (Stevens, Souter, Ginsburg, and Blackmun) noted, the quantum required and the lack thereof were not defined.

"Rough proportionality" is a concept that will require a good deal of further judicial elaboration. If the floodplain portion of a proposed housing subdivision could be sold to buyers ignoring flood hazards for $200,000 a lot, would an exaction of a flowage easement preventing home construction have to demonstrate that each built lot would cause roughly $200,000 in discounted risk of death and destruction?

2. **Presumption of constitutionality/burden of proof.** A strategic issue looming even larger than the heightened nexus requirement in these exactions cases is who has the

burden of proving their case. Previously the presumption of constitutionality was presumed to cast the burden on the private party attacking government. The Rehnquist opinion attempted to shift the burden onto government to show the probability that there would be serious effects. While not directly saying they were doing so, the majority justified the shift by saying the city's decision was "adjudicative," for which more evidence was necessary. The vast majority of governmental regulatory actions, however, permits for example, are informal "adjudications." If indeed this case marked a shift toward putting the burden of proof of constitutionality upon regulatory government, its consequences would change the administrative state as we know it. For political reasons, such a judicial shift in presumption is probably more likely to be applied against environmental regulations than generally, as against regulations managing securities markets or ordinances regulating speech or demonstrations.

3. **Other worms in the can.** In presenting Dolan's case, Justice Rehnquist noted that "the city has identified 'no special benefits' conferred on her." Was this a setup for future assertions of his dissenting argument in *Keystone Bituminous* that a regulation is void if it does not give the regulatees a "reciprocity of advantage" roughly proportional to the burdens imposed (as opposed to precedents which used reciprocity only as further evidence to support validity)?

Will there be increasing judicial judgments about what regulations are "necessary"? The majority opinion used a quotation from *Penn Central* about the basic due process requirements of valid regulation: "a use restriction may constitute a taking if not reasonably necessary to the effectuation of a substantial government purpose." In so doing, were they opening up a general inquiry by judges into the wisdom of legislative judgments about how social problems should best be addressed? The temptation toward an activist judiciary is not restricted to the progressive sector.

4. **Predicting the future.** What will be the future effect of *Dolan* on exactions? Faced with the difficulties of negotiating conditions that can be practically defended against *Dolan* challenges, will local governments just deny permits outright, forswearing the flexibility and adjustments previously available under prior exactions law? Can property rights advocates extend Justice Rehnquist's rough proportionality exactions concept to be a requirement in takings cases, so that local governments will bear the burden of convincing courts that the public harms being regulated roughly equal or exceed the private economic burdens imposed, even where reasonable economic uses remain? In Monterey v. Del Monte Dunes Corp., 526 U.S. 687 (1999), the Court rejected such an attempt to extend "rough proportionality" exactions test to the rationality nexus of a regulatory takings case.[70] The politics and law of this debate will continue to be interesting.

---

70. The circuit court had said that "even if the City had a legitimate interest in denying Del Monte's development application, its action must be 'roughly proportional' to furthering that interest. The City's denial [i.e., regulatory, not a physical exaction] must be related 'both in nature and extent to the impact of the proposed development.'" 95 F.3d 1422, 1430 (9th Cir. 1996) (citing *Dolan*). Strangely, the Supreme Court did allow the jury to be given the subtle substantive due process question of whether the regulation "substantially advanced legitimate public interests," perhaps a portent of perplexing developments to come.

d. Substantive Due Process and the Innocent Landowner: *Eastern Enterprises*

In a variety of environmental situations, regulations apply heavy burdens on defendants who can say they themselves did not cause the problem. This often occurs in the case of toxic contamination of land. Most property owners know that they are taking some chances when they buy land; caveat emptor, buyer beware. But the most one thinks is being risked is the amount of the purchase price of the land. Environmental cases have demonstrated that potential liability may be a hundred times the purchase price of the land. This is a setting in which "fairness expectations" are clearly upset. Does that mean the regulations are unconstitutional takings? If not invalid as takings, may they be violations of substantive due process?

For years conventional wisdom had been that the courts should not apply substantive due process to strike down legislation. This truism focused on the Court's reversal of a regressive run of cases where anti-New Deal judges used economic due process to void federal economic recovery legislation. See Ferguson v. Skrupa, 372 U.S. 726, 731, (1963) (noting "our abandonment of the use of the 'vague contours' of the Due Process Clause to nullify laws which a majority of the Court believed to be economically unwise"); see also Williamson v. Lee Optical of Okla., Inc., 348 U.S. 483, 488 (1955) ("The day is gone when this Court uses the Due Process Clause...to strike down...laws, regulatory of business and industrial conditions, because they may be unwise, improvident, or out of harmony with a particular school of thought"). But the courts have nevertheless continued to utilize substantive due process in latent fashion.[71]

Shouldn't courts acknowledge the legitimacy of substantive due process tests of fairness? Assume that your client has purchased a 3-acre piece of land for $60,000 in order to build a greenhouse. She begins digging foundations but suddenly hits 50 leaking unmarked barrels filled with toxic wastes. She notifies the appropriate government agencies, which congratulate her on her forthrightness, and then tell her that the bill for cleanup, for which she is now responsible as an owner under state and federal statutes, will be $1 million! She turns to you and says, "This has got to be unconstitutional." That hypothetical situation was regularly possible under the federal Superfund statute prior to CERCLA's 1986 "innocent landowner" exceptions, and is still possible under some state Superfund statutes and in other statutory settings (for instance, when the CERCLA innocent landowner exception does not apply because EPA finds that the property owner should have been on notice of possible contamination prior to purchase). Is there a viable constitutional argument against the validity of such heavy monetary burdens imposed by regulation, perhaps focusing on the innocent landowner's lack of fault, intent, or "nexus" to the causation of toxic leakage?

---

71. There is an implicit "recognition that substantive due process inquiry is not anathema; it is an established component of the courts' constitutional jurisdiction. Substantive due process occurs in present-day reviews of public purposes, authority, and bad faith, as well as in [reviews of] arbitrariness." Plater & Norine, Exploring the "Arbitrary and Capricious" Test and Substantive Rationality Review of Governmental Decisions, 16 B.C. Envtl. Aff. L. Rev. 661, 697 (1986).

Eastern Enterprises v. Apfel
Supreme Court of the United States, 1998
524 U.S. 498

[A utility company with a subsidiary that had been involved in coal mining prior to passage of the Coal Industry Retiree Health Benefit Act of 1992 challenges the Act's imposition of retroactive liability for payments to former employees (coal miners) and their families suffering the effects of black lung (pneumoconiosis) and associated work-related illnesses. Eastern's invoice for a 12-month period exceeded $5 million and its eventual payments under the Act would total between $50 and $100 million. There is no majority opinion in this case. The voting is 4-1-4: Justice O'Connor, joined by Justices Rehnquist, Scalia, and Thomas, writes for a plurality of the Court in an opinion reying on regulatory takings jurisprudence to invalidate the Act. Justice Kennedy writes a concurrence applying substantive due process as the determinative test, saying that there was no sufficient rational connection between Eastern and the employee benefits that Eastern was retroactively forced to pay. Justice Stevens, joined by Justices Breyer, Souter, and Ginsburg, dissent on the basis of a differing view of the facts surrounding the history of the coal mining industry and the 1992 Coal Act. More importantly for present purposes, Justice Breyer, joined by Justices Stevens, Souter, and Ginsburg, agree with Justice Kennedy that *substantive due process* is the determinative test, which the latter four, however, think had not been violated. So the count supporting the use of substantive due process rather than takings analysis is 5-4.]

O'CONNOR, J., joined by REHNQUIST, C.J., and SCALIA and THOMAS, JJ…. We conclude that the Coal Act, as applied to petitioner Eastern Enterprises, effects an unconstitutional taking…. This case does not present the "classic taking" in which the government directly appropriates private property for its own use…. Our decisions, however, have left open the possibility that legislation might be unconstitutional if it imposes severe retroactive liability on a limited class of parties that could not have anticipated the liability, and the extent of that liability is substantially disproportionate to the parties' experience. We believe that the Coal Act's allocation scheme, as applied to Eastern, presents such a case. We reach that conclusion by applying the three factors that traditionally have informed our regulatory takings analysis [i.e., the *Penn Central* triad: the economic impact of the regulation, the extent to which the regulation interferes with investment-backed expectations, and the character of the governmental action]….

As to the first factor relevant in assessing whether a regulatory taking has occurred, economic impact, there is no doubt that the Coal Act has forced a considerable financial burden upon Eastern…. The Coal Act substantially interferes with Eastern's reasonable investment-backed expectations…. Finally, the nature of the governmental action in this case is quite unusual. That Congress…singles out certain employers to bear a burden that is substantial in amount, based on the employers' conduct far in the past, and unrelated to any commitment that the employers made or to any injury they caused…implicates fundamental principles of fairness…. Accordingly, we conclude that the Coal Act's allocation of liability to Eastern violates the Takings Clause, and…should be enjoined as applied to Eastern….

KENNEDY, J., concurring in the judgment and dissenting in part…. The plurality's Takings Clause analysis…is incorrect and quite unnecessary for decision of the case. I must record my respectful dissent on this issue…. Our cases do not support the plurality's conclusion that the Coal Act takes property. The Coal Act imposes a staggering financial burden on the petitioner, Eastern Enterprises, but it regulates the former mine owner without regard to property. It does not operate upon or alter an identified property interest, and it is not applicable to or measured by a property interest. The Coal Act does not appropriate, transfer, or encumber an estate in land (e.g., a lien on a particular piece of property), a valuable interest in an intangible (e.g., intellectual property), or even a bank account or accrued interest. The law simply imposes an obligation to perform an act, the payment of benefits.... To call this sort of governmental action a taking as a matter of constitutional interpretation is both imprecise and, with all due respect, unwise.

Given that the constitutionality of the Coal Act appears to turn on the legitimacy of Congress' judgment rather than on the availability of compensation,...the more appropriate constitutional analysis arises under general due process principles rather than under the Takings Clause....

When the constitutionality of the Coal Act is tested under the Due Process Clause, it must be invalidated.... Although we have been hesitant to subject economic legislation to due process scrutiny as a general matter, the Court has given careful consideration to due process challenges to legislation with retroactive effects....

While we have upheld the imposition of liability on former employers based on past employment relationships, the statutes at issue were remedial, designed to impose an "actual, measurable cost of [the employer's] business."... Eastern was once in the coal business and employed many of the beneficiaries, but it was not responsible for their expectation of lifetime health benefits or for the perilous financial condition of the 1950 and 1974 Plans which put the benefits in jeopardy. As the plurality opinion discusses in detail, the expectation was created by promises and agreements made long after Eastern left the coal business. Eastern was not responsible for the resulting chaos in the funding mechanism caused by other coal companies leaving the framework of the National Bituminous Coal Wage Agreement.... Application of the Coal Act to Eastern would violate the proper bounds of settled due process principles....

BREYER, J., joined by STEVENS, SOUTER, and GINSBURG, JJ., dissenting.... I agree with Justice Kennedy that the plurality views this case through the wrong legal lens. The Constitution's Takings Clause does not apply. That Clause refers to the taking of "private property...for public use without just compensation...." At the heart of the Clause lies a concern, not with preventing arbitrary or unfair government action, but with providing compensation for legitimate government action that takes "private property" to serve the "public" good. The "private property" upon which the Clause traditionally has focused is a specific interest in physical or intellectual property.... There is no need to torture the Takings Clause to fit this case. The question involved — the potential unfairness of retroactive liability — finds a natural home in the Due Process Clause [that] safeguards citizens from arbitrary or irrational legislation....

To find that the Due Process Clause protects against...fundamental unfairness...is to read the Clause in light of a basic purpose: the fair application of law, which purpose hearkens back to the Magna Carta. It is not to resurrect long-discredited substantive notions of "freedom of contract." Thus, like the plurality I would inquire if the law before us is fundamentally unfair or unjust....

The substantive question before us is whether or not it is fundamentally unfair to require Eastern to make future payments for health care costs of retired miners and their families, on the basis of Eastern's past association with these miners.... I believe...the relationship between Eastern and the payments demanded by the Act is special enough to pass the Constitution's fundamental fairness test. That is, even though Eastern left the coal industry in 1965, the historical circumstances...prevent Eastern from showing that the Act's "reachback" liability provision so frustrates Eastern's reasonable settled expectations as to impose an unconstitutional liability. For one thing, the liability that the statute imposes upon Eastern extends only to miners whom Eastern itself employed.... They are miners whose labor benefited Eastern when they were younger and healthier. Insofar as working conditions created a risk of future health problems for those miners, Eastern created those conditions.... Eastern continued to obtain profits from the coal mining industry long after 1965, for it operated a wholly owned coal-mining subsidiary, Eastern Associated Coal Corp. (EACC), until the late 1980s.... It is not fundamentally unfair for Congress to impose upon Eastern liability for the future health care costs of miners whom it long ago employed — rather than imposing that liability, for example, upon the present industry, coal consumers, or taxpayers....

COMMENTARY & QUESTIONS

1. **The Due Process Clause.** The Due Process Clause offers two distinct protections of property, one directly linked to the phrase "due process" and one containing the Takings Clause. What are the differences? Does Justice O'Connor's opinion conflate the two?

2. **Counting votes and the differing views of the facts.** Given that five Justices agreed that the correct test to apply was substantive due process, how did they see its result differently? In addition to the Kennedy and Breyer opinions, a Stevens dissent, omitted here, argued that Eastern and other coal operators understood that they had enjoyed labor peace because of a shared belief in the fact that the operators would provide benefits to workers in the future as illness and disabilities occurred. On that premise, Eastern had no reasonable expectation of being free of a contingent liability to its workers for future benefits, whether as a result of bargaining or statutory intervention. In support of his view of history, Justice Stevens noted that three different circuits had so found, the Coal Commission was of that view, and so was the Congress that passed the Coal Act.

3. *"Lochnering"* **and fundamental fairness.** One reason that the plurality strives so hard to transmute a relatively vanilla substantive due process claim into a takings claim has a long constitutional history. (A second, less flattering view, is that those four justices are propounding an agenda of judicial activism that intends to limit the scope of legislative action by injecting takings jurisprudence, with all its uncertainty and potential for liability, into new realms.) At the turn of the twentieth century, in a line of cases based on the substantive interpretation of the Due Process Clause as guaranteeing freedom of contract, the Supreme Court struck down whole rafts of state and federal laws designed to protect worker health and safety. This now-much-criticized line of cases was epitomized by Lochner v. New York, 198 U.S. 45 (1905), and modern cases even hinting at resurrecting *Lochner*'s wide-ranging judicial activism in invalidating duly enacted legislation receive a hostile reaction. The plurality plainly did not want to get cast in the role of *Lochner* revivalists and therefore were chary of calling this case a substantive due process case. Justice Kennedy and the dissenters are less afraid of being cast in that light and feel that within the substantive due process realm there are non-*Lochneresque* cases that test legislation to ensure that it passes a "fundamental fairness" test.

4. **Is it fair to Eastern to compel them to pay now?** Retroactivity is, of course, an issue that separates Justice Kennedy from the four dissenters. For Justice Kennedy, the retroactivity of the Coal Act is the key factor. Why? Is retroactivity the problem, or is retroactivity problematic because it identifies a lack of foreseeability or a frustration of justifiable investment-backed expectations?

5. **Applying substantive due process in contaminated land cases.** Does the imposition of severe toxic cleanup burdens on innocent owners of contaminated land, especially those who lack an industry nexus to the original dumping, trigger substantive due process concerns? See Jordan, Substantive Due Process after *Eastern Enterprises*, with New Defenses Based on Lack of Causative Nexus — the Superfund Example, 32 B.C. Envtl. Aff. L. Rev. (forthcoming, 2004). The appropriate test would seem to require some consideration of causation or the lack thereof, evoking the "rational relationship" police power test rather than one testing whether the takings burden is excessive if viewed in the context of public harms. To make noncausative innocent landowners liable for massive cleanup costs presents an obvious fairness problem that, given the heritage of the American bench and bar, may on its own terms be litigatable.[72]

Property is that which is peculiarly yours, whether it is your money, your wife, your children, your house, your car, or your real estate.

— Don Gerdts, founder, Property Rights Council of America
(a Wise Use organization), in Albany Times-Union,
April 11, 1992

---

72. There are a number of situations where burdens are imposed on noncausative parties without recourse. In an acid mine pollution case, Commonwealth v. Barnes & Tucker Co., 371 A.2d 461 (Pa. 1977), the mining company proved that virtually all of the acid mine water draining from its mine came from the past wrongful activities of neighboring coal mines now abandoned. The court nevertheless held the defendant liable to pay for the entire cleanup, perhaps under some sort of theory of "enterprise liability," an approach that has been followed by other courts. A similar situation occurs with the forfeiture of private property used in crimes, even where the property owners are totally innocent, as in Bennis v. Michigan, 516 U.S. 442 (1996), although many consider such cases grossly unfair.

Professor Laitos has pioneered this inquiry into the constitutional invalidity of liability without fault. See Laitos, Causation and the Unconstitutional Conditions Doctrine: Why the City of Tigard's Exaction Was a Taking, 72 U. Denver L. Rev. 893 (1995).

Chapter 24

PUBLIC RESOURCE MANAGEMENT STATUTES

Public resources, whether natural or man-made, are owned by, or held in trust for, all members of a broad community, some of whom use the resources and some of whom do not. Public monuments, beds and banks of navigable waterbodies, fish and wildlife, and public parks are examples of public resources. In order to prevent the tragedy of the commons that threatens resources to which the public has unlimited access, various governmental institutions frequently impose resource management controls, in Hardin's terms of "mutual coercion, mutually agreed upon."[1] Within the borders of the United States, the primary source of such coercion in practice lies in public resource management statutes. Those statutes delegate responsibility, through enabling or organic legislation, to administrative agencies in order to regulate public access and use consistent with legislative goals and requirements. Internationally, where binding legislation is absent, negotiations sometimes lead to international agreements that place restrictions on consenting nations regarding the management of transboundary public resources, such as migratory birds. (See Chapters 8 and 26.)

In each case, subtle and contentious issues are woven into the legal management regime of public resources: Are the resources a legacy for the future or assets for maximization of current economic revenues? Are the resources appropriately consigned to one dominant use, or to be managed for a diversity of uses? Are local citizens specially privileged to use them, or are they for all potential users? What if the activity of one class of resource users interferes with the uses of others? Finally, how are these recurrent political and theoretical questions to be resolved?

Public lands of the state and federal governments exist throughout the United States. Although this chapter focuses primarily on federal lands in the West, where the national government owns almost half the land area, many of the underlying legal issues are relevant throughout the country. The statutes and policy issues explored

---

1. See Garrett Hardin's Tragedy of the Commons in Chapter 1. For a review of contemporary social science research on the commons tragedy and a discussion of possible nonregulatory strategies for addressing the inherent psychological, sociological, and economic obstacles to commons management, see Thompson, Tragically Difficult: The Obstacles to Governing the Commons, 30 Ecology L.Q. 241 (2000).

here, however, have pronounced applicability in the West. This chapter examines the Federal Land Policy and Management Act (FLPMA, pronounced "flipma"), 43 U.S.C. §§1701 et seq., and the federal Bureau of Land Management (BLM), an agency within the U.S. Department of the Interior. Part A of the chapter introduces the federal public lands. Part B presents a brief history of grazing on the public lands and a description and analysis of FLPMA. Part C examines a number of issues raised by one of the keystone public land law cases, Kleppe v. New Mexico, 426 U.S. 529 (1976), analyzing BLM's authority to regulate wild horses on federal land in New Mexico. Part D develops a case study of off-road vehicle (ORV) use on BLM lands. The resource commons can be destroyed by unlimited recreational use, as well as by grazing and other consumptive uses, and the BLM and other federal land management agencies are increasingly called upon to allocate access to their lands among competing recreational groups. Part E examines natural resources planning for public lands, a process that increasingly provides the context for public land use decisions.

As you read this chapter, consider its close relationship to Chapter 9 on NEPA and Chapter 16 on the ESA. NEPA and ESA cases often concern activities planned by federal agencies or their private permittees on federally owned lands. Moreover, land use planning for federal lands, such as that required by FLPMA, is inextricably connected to the preparation of environmental impact documents and mandatory endangered species consultations. In most cases, the land use plan, the negative declaration or environmental impact statement, and the ESA biological assessment are contained in a single document.

A. THE PUBLIC LANDS

The most extensive public resource in the United States is the federal public land system. Almost one-third of the nation's land (over 700 million acres, particularly in the West and Alaska) is owned by the federal government. The federal government owns roughly one-half of all the land in the 11 contiguous western states, including 85% of the State of Nevada and 63% of the State of Utah.[2] These massive federal landholdings persist despite the federal government's spirited attempts, during most of the nineteenth and twentieth centuries, to dispose of the lands obtained in treaties with Great Britain, France, Spain, Russia, and Indian tribes. Between 1781 and 1985, over 1 billion acres of federal public land were sold or granted to homesteaders (287 million acres), railroads (140 million acres), states (72 million acres in the western states), and other persons and entities. The remaining federal public lands are managed, more or less successfully, by numerous federal agencies, some located in different departments of the federal government, with different enabling acts, goals, management philosophies, levels of support and supervision from Congress, and political alliances.

The massive disposal of federal public lands — along with the water, timber, range, and mineral resources associated with them — was, for the most part, implemented in accordance with the "first in time is first in right" (i.e., "first come, first served")

---

2. See G. Coggins, C. Wilkinson & J. Leshy, Federal Public Land and Resources Law (4th ed. 2001) (hereafter cited as Coggins et al.), an invaluable reference work for the study of public land law.

principle. The young United States was intent upon asserting its Manifest Destiny by stimulating settlement and economic development of the West's natural resources as expeditiously as possible. This public land policy engendered an "exploit and run," or "use it or lose it" mentality that was inimical to sustainable resource use, conservation, nonextractive uses such as recreation, and the interests of Native Americans and other indigenous minorities. Withdrawals and reservations for these purposes tended to be sporadic, limited, and unpopular in the West.[3]

The BLM administers 170 million acres of arid or semiarid federal land in the 11 western states pursuant to the congressional directives included in FLPMA. This chapter primarily concentrates on FLPMA and the BLM for several reasons:

- FLPMA is the most unified and comprehensive organic management legislation governing the activities of any federal resource management agency.

- The BLM range lands exhibit a classic tragedy of the commons (destructive overgrazing) caused by the "capture" of a regulatory agency by a single user group and its political allies.[4]

- FLPMA adopts a "multiple use-sustained yield" management standard, the standard that prevails with regard to most of the federal public lands, including the roughly 200 million acres administered by the U.S. Forest Service, located in the Department of Agriculture, in addition to the BLM's own vast holdings.

The BLM lands traditionally have been managed for grazing of private livestock. In 1974, approximately 23,000 western ranches held BLM permits or leases to graze 3.5 million cattle and horses and 4.5 million sheep and goats on BLM lands.[5] This 5% of all American ranchers using approximately 3% of national livestock forage production has had an inordinately strong impact on congressional and BLM policy regarding BLM lands. Some of the reasons for the extraordinary political influence of this segment of the livestock industry are its entrenchment in American mythology, historic dominance over the BLM, consistent single-mindedness, abundant financial resources, and close proximity to information and the BLM field personnel who manage the resource. Locally prominent individuals and interest groups typically have supported the demands of the local livestock industry. Since grazing permits are comparatively permanent privileges, they add great economic value to the ranchers' private "base properties" contiguous to federal permit grazing lands. Consequently, local financial institutions that loan money to ranchers, with grazing permits as security, actively oppose proposals that might have negative effects on the short-term profit margins of

3. The history and modern consequences of the "Disposal Era" are vividly chronicled in Professor Charles Wilkinson's Crossing the Next Meridian (1992). Withdrawals of federal land are proscriptions of particular uses that otherwise would be permitted, such as mining or grazing. Reservations are designations of areas for certain uses, such as Native American reservations or military bases.

4. With regard to public lands suitable for grazing, the BLM has indeed been captured by the grazing industry, but the BLM also manages public lands other than grazing lands. In its management of nongrazing lands, the BLM has often been more environmentally sensitive, with regard to issues such as preservation of biodiversity, than other federal land management agencies (e.g., the National Park Service and the Forest Service). See S. Yaffee, The Wisdom of the Spotted Owl: Policy Lessons for a New Century (1994), and C. Thomas, Bureaucratic Landscapes 277 (2003) ("BLM officials were trying much harder to protect biodiversity than popular stereotypes and academic literature have led us to expect").

5. Coggins, Evans & Lindeberg-Johnson, The Law of Public Rangeland Management I: The Extent and Distribution of Federal Power, 12 Envtl. L. 536, 536–621, 559 (1982) (hereafter cited as Coggins I).

local ranchers — such as cutbacks in grazing allotments in order to revive overgrazed range.

Western state governments also constitute a "public" deeply concerned about BLM management of federal public lands. States cannot impose property taxes on federal property. Instead, they have persuaded Congress to provide annual federal reimbursement payments in lieu of property taxes. These "in lieu payments" are themselves paid from funds generated by fees on private use of federal lands. Western states, for example, receive 12.5% of BLM income from grazing fees.[6] Thus state officials also support continued heavy grazing on BLM lands out of their own institutional fiscal imperatives. Since the 1960s, however, public land law has been revolutionized by the emergence of powerful conservationist and preservationist organizations:

> It is not possible to delineate precisely just who the new parties are or what they represent. In some cases, private landowners have rejected economic benefit to themselves by various forms of development on or adjacent to their property.... Allied to new landowner attitudes is a new aggressiveness on the part of non-consumptive economic users of public lands. Resorts, guides, river outfitters, backpacking equipment manufacturers, and so forth have resisted development of a resource valuable to them as primitive real estate....

> Many of the largest changes have come about through institutional strategies and actions by established and new environmental organizations. Among the most active and effective organizations are the old-line Sierra Club and Wilderness Society, and three newcomers, the Environmental Defense Fund (EDF), the Natural Resources Defense Council (NRDC), and the National Wildlife Federation. Even the traditionally apolitical Audubon Society has found itself lobbying and litigating. These organizations alone — and there are dozens of similar if less visible groups — have wrought legislative change, pursued hundreds of lawsuits...and mobilized considerable public support. Coggins et al. at 6–7.

This new "nonconsumptive use" public, while generally sharing basic preservationist goals, is not monolithic. Local river rafting outfitters, for instance, have occasionally faced off against national kayaking groups over National Park Service (NPS) allocations of permits for trips down the Colorado River.[7]

B. THE BLM, FLPMA, AND GRAZING ON THE PUBLIC LANDS

During the years between 1789 and 1976, when the federal government pursued a policy of disposing of western public lands, a concurrent federal policy was to forestall monopolies by large landholders. Given the relatively unproductive character of the western range, the disposal and antimonopoly policies came into conflict, causing legendary fraud and corruption as well as overgrazing of small holdings.

> Federal land was given to five distinct classes of beneficiaries, but in parcels too small or too scattered to overcome the inherent problems of low vegetative productivity in much of the West. States, railroads, miners, farmers, and ranchers received most of the federal largess.

---

6. Coggins & Lindeberg-Johnson, The Law of Public Rangeland Management II: The Commons and Taylor Act, 13 Envtl. L. 1, 11 (1982) (hereafter cited as Coggins II).

7. See Wilderness Public Rights Fund v. Kleppe, 608 F.2d 1250 (9th Cir. 1979), cert. denied, 446 U.S. 982 (1980).

The federal government gave an enormous amount of public land to the states,...estimated to be 72 million acres in the eleven western states.... Those lands are often still arbitrarily interspersed among private and federal lands.... The railroad land grants continue to obstruct integrated management because they are frequently checkerboarded section-by-section with the public lands.[8] Mining claims are also interspersed, but more randomly. Prospectors who locate a valuable mineral discovery are allowed to take title to the land on which the mineral is found. Agrarian homesteaders claimed hundreds of millions of acres under the various disposition laws, all of which limited the number of acres that could be granted to one individual. Homesteading policy was liberalized many times to accommodate rancher desires for more land, but the effort proved futile in the end: profitable ranching in the Inter mountain West required more land per operation than Congress was willing to grant.[9]

The lands retained by the federal government were those that, as Professor Coggins puts it, "Nobody was willing to buy or steal." Nevertheless, these huge expanses of federal land became immensely valuable as supplementary grazing land to landholders who discovered that their arid lands were profitable only for grazing cattle, and that the relatively small size of their holdings precluded successful ranching operations.

Until 1934, the federal government maintained a laissez-faire attitude toward public lands, perpetuating an unregulated commons that deteriorated into a severely overgrazed range. (In terms of the "three economies," the marketplace economy dominated the range, largely ignoring the needs of the natural economy and the long-term civic-societal interests it served.) A combination of drought and the New Deal prompted a reevaluation of federal range policy, resulting in the Taylor Grazing Act of 1934.[10] Congress had two avowed purposes in enacting the Taylor Act: to end overgrazing and to stabilize the livestock industry. Once again, federal policies that appeared laudable in theory were inconsistent in practice; the Taylor Act did stabilize the livestock industry but did little to alleviate range deterioration.

The Taylor Act had three main components: (1) it authorized the Secretary of the Interior to withdraw the unappropriated public lands from homesteading and organize them into grazing districts; (2) it gave preference in obtaining and renewing grazing permits to adjacent landowners; and (3) it established district advisory boards, composed mainly of ranchers, that had to be consulted before management decisions were made. The unfortunate result was a "captured agency," in which large adjacent ranchers dominated an understaffed Grazing Division (the BLM's predecessor) through advisory boards, gaining for themselves excessive grazing allotments at fees far below market value:

> The first round of grazing permit decisions set a pattern for the next four decades. Adjacent ranchers first received temporary one-year permits. Later hearings to determine carrying capacity for purposes of permit adjustments were conducted

---

8. As an incentive to build the transcontinental railroads, railroad companies were given odd-numbered sections of land within 20 miles on both sides of their rights of way. These odd-numbered sections were later sold to private parties, creating a "checkerboard pattern" of land ownership with the even-numbered federally retained sections. See Figure 24-1. [Eds.]

9. Coggins II at 5–6.

10. 43 U.S.C. §§315 et seq.

by the ranchers through the advisory boards. Ten-year permits — the maximum allowed by statute — soon became the norm.

By early 1936, board representatives and the Grazing Division (which had already issued thousands of permits) worked out rules for preference and fees.... The Division set grazing fees at five cents per month for cows and one cent for sheep. The permits were theoretically limited to "carrying capacity." That term, however, turned out to have a different meaning in practice than in science because capacity was determined (primarily by the stockmen) within the first year or two of Taylor Act administration without benefit of survey or biological opinion. In most districts permits had been issued for many more livestock than the range could properly support. When later scientific information, however inadequate, indicated the need for downward revision, ranchers often effectively opposed cuts.[11]

Instead of affording security to the livestock industry in exchange for responsible grazing practices on public lands, the Taylor Act provided further subsidies to ranchers — primary access to the public lands, preferential permits, federal funds for "range improvements" (fencing, revegetation, etc.), and low grazing fees — to continue their traditional overuse of the federal range resource.

In 1946, the Grazing Division was merged with the General Land Office (an agency with strong disposal inclinations) to form the BLM. There was little change in BLM range policies until 1974, despite a 1970 report of the Public Land Law Review Commission recognizing the deteriorated condition of a substantial amount of BLM lands, implicitly criticizing BLM as a servant of grazing interests (and of the mining and timber industries), and recommending that grazing allotments should be consistent with the productivity of the land.[12] In 1974, a NEPA lawsuit, NRDC v. Morton, 388 F. Supp. 829 (D.D.C. 1974), transformed federal range management. BLM had prepared a programmatic environmental impact statement on its grazing program after the enactment of NEPA in 1970. The NRDC sued, alleging that the programmatic EIS was inadequate because it did not address the site-specific impacts of grazing. The federal district court sided with NRDC, ordering BLM to prepare EISs for each grazing district. Compelled to study rangeland conditions openly and "go public" with its findings, BLM "has had no choice but to reduce allotments down to carrying capacity."[13] NRDC v. Morton also alerted Congress to the deplorable condition of the BLM lands and the failure of the Taylor Act, leading directly to 1976 passage of FLPMA.

George Coggins, The Law of Public Rangeland Management IV: FLPMA, PRIA, and the Multiple Use Mandate
14 Environmental Law 1, 5–6 (1983)[14]

FLPMA does not repeal the major Taylor Act provisions. Instead, the 1976 Act superimposes a new management system, with more diverse goals and emphases. FLPMA requires the multiple use-sustained yield that the BLM has long claimed to practice. The 1976 Act mandates intensive planning; of equal importance, specific management decisions made after the land use plans are completed must accord with the plans. The Act also protects grazing permittees to a

---

11. Coggins II at 58–59.
12. Public Land Law Review Commission, One-Third of the Nation's Land 106–108 (1970).
13. Coggins I at 555.
14. Hereafter cited as Coggins IV.

limited extent. On the whole, however, FLPMA represents a condemnation of past stewardship and requires that the BLM utilize a broader approach to public rangeland management....

FLPMA resolves two fundamental issues: Congress decided to retain the public lands in public ownership and to manage the lands in ways that avoid the "unnecessary or undue degradation" so common in the past.

The framework of FLPMA apparently originated in the 1970 report of the Public Land Law Review Commission (PLLRC). Senator Henry Jackson later claimed that FLPMA embodies the enactment of over 100 PLLRC recommendations into law. In the area of range management, however, the dissimilarities between the report and the final legislation are at least as prominent. The PLLRC recommended that Congress authorize the sale to permittees of lands chiefly valuable for grazing, give ranchers greater security of tenure while requiring them to pay higher fees to use the retained lands, and make livestock grazing the "dominant use of retained lands where appropriate." FLMPA secures permittee tenure in some ways and holds down grazing fee increases, but Congress rejected the generous PLLRC attitude toward ranchers in those other respects. FLMPA adopts the PLLRC recommendations that sought consistency between grazing and land "productivity," that put "priority on the rehabilitation of deteriorated rangeland where possible," that required more administrative flexibility, and that paid more attention to public values, including wildlife. Congress arguably stopped short of adopting the PLLRC recommendation to exclude livestock from "frail lands" and did not make the permittee responsible for the frail condition of the land....

Section 1701(a) of FLPMA declares thirteen sweeping policies. Although it contains some apparent inconsistencies, the section is Congress' most thorough and unambiguous statement of public land policy. The statement is qualified by the proviso in §1701(b) that FLPMA policies are not "effective" until specifically enacted in the Act itself or elsewhere. The courts faced with questions involving §1701(a), however, have uniformly assumed that the policies are binding and effective in the absence of contrary provisions. Whatever their precise legal status, the congressional policies ought to serve as fundamental range management guidelines.

Congress first stated that the public lands will remain in federal ownership unless planning determines that the "national interest" requires disposal of "a particular parcel."... The second policy is that "the national interest will be best realized if the public lands and their resources are periodically and systematically inventoried and their present and future use is projected through a land use planning process coordinated with other Federal and State planning efforts."... [Policies Three to Six involve reviews of existing federal land classifications, restraints on executive withdrawals, encouragement of public participation in BLM decision-making, and judicial review of public land adjudications.]

The seventh congressional statement should be, but has not yet become, the touchstone of public rangeland management. Congress declared that "goals and objectives be established by law as guidelines for public land use planning, and that management be on the basis of multiple use and sustained yield unless otherwise specified by law." Congress specifically enacted these general requirements, but the BLM has neither understood nor carried out these commands.

The eighth statement of policy is a radical departure from all prior rangeland management understanding. Congress required that:

> the public lands be managed in a manner that will protect the quality of scientific, scenic, historical, ecological, environmental, air and atmospheric, water resource, and archeological values; that, where appropriate, will preserve and protect certain public lands in their natural condition; that will provide food and habitat for fish and wildlife and domestic animals; and that will provide for outdoor recreation and human occupancy and use.

Whether or to what extent Congress specifically enacted this goal is unclear. Some sections of FLPMA and other statutes support an argument that this policy binds public land managers, but all the statutory provisions are qualified in some way.

In its ninth policy, Congress sought "fair market value" for public land uses and resources "unless otherwise provided by statute." This policy is definitely not law; not only are grazing fees set at a fraction of market value, but the United States probably does not receive full value for any of the nation's resources.... Congress's tenth policy statement calls for uniform procedures for disposal, exchange, or acquisition of public lands. This policy was enacted in other FLPMA sections.... The eleventh policy seeks rapid protection of "areas of critical environmental concern"; the statute provides that protection.

The twelfth congressional policy balances or counteracts the eighth by emphasizing use instead of preservation. Congress required that "the public lands be managed in a manner which recognizes the Nation's need for domestic sources of minerals, food, timber, and fiber from the public lands."... The thirteenth and final policy calls for equitable reimbursement to states for the local tax burden caused by federal immunity from taxation. This policy was enacted in the Payment in Lieu of Taxes Act of 1976....

For the first time, the BLM is forced by law to develop land use plans in fairly precise ways and, after the plans are promulgated, to act in accordance with the guidelines established in the plans. Section 1711 commands a detailed inventory of all public land resources, and §1712 requires preparation of land use plans for all public land areas.... Section 1732(a) negates any implication that the plans are to be just public relations make-work by making the plans binding on all subsequent multiple use decisions....

FLPMA emphatically rejects the grazing-as-dominant-use tradition in public rangeland management in favor of multiple use-sustained yield principles.... In theory, the standard requires the agency to give all listed resources roughly equal consideration and weight in all decisionmaking. Multiple use-sustained yield is basically a utilitarian principle requiring high-level annual production of all resources in combination.[15] Congress defined both multiple use and sustained yield in sweeping terms. Apparently, however, the legislature never debated precisely how those management concepts were to be applied. Congress assumed instead that the standard was a significant, environmentally-oriented advance over existing authorities. Contrary to the opinions of several commentators, and to BLM predilections, multiple use and sustained yield are more than idle slogans allowing the agency to do as it professionally pleases. If courts begin reviewing multiple use decisions with any depth or insight, the standard as applied through planning processes will reverse the course of public rangeland management....

Before investigating the limitations on management discretion inherent in the multiple use standard, the uses or resources themselves should be defined. In the Multiple Use-Sustained Yield Act (MUSY),[16] the "renewable surface resources" include only "outdoor recreation, range, timber, watershed, and wildlife and fish purposes." In 1976, Congress broadened the list of uses to "renewable and nonrenewable resources including, but not limited to, recreation, range, timber, minerals, watershed, wildlife and fish, and natural scenic, scientific, and historical values."...

Most of the listed resources are "renewable," meaning that they regenerate in some biological or climatological fashion. Although minerals are now included in the list, both hardrock

---

15. Multiple use-sustained yield standards do not necessarily apply to each management unit where multiple use would be inconsistent with the nature of the resource base. In such cases, multiple use-sustained yield must be maintained on the level of some larger, more inclusive planning unit. [Eds.]

16. The Multiple-Use, Sustained Yield Act of 1960, 16 U.S.C. §§528 et seq., along with other statutes, governs the activities of the U.S. Forest Service. [Eds.]

mining and mineral leasing remain primarily governed by other statutes that have given mineral exploitation legal or de facto priority over other uses. Water itself, the key resource, was omitted,[17] probably because water allocation was seen as a state function. Wilderness, or "preservation," is not specifically listed, but is supplied in §1782....

The key to multiple use-sustained yield management as a land management system is in the statutory definition of the two phrases. FLPMA borrows heavily from the MUSY Act:

> 43 U.S.C. §1702...(c) the term "multiple use" means the management of the public lands and their various resource values so that they are utilized in the combination that will best meet the present and future needs of the American people; making the most judicious use of the land for some or all of these resources or related services over areas large enough to provide sufficient latitude for periodic adjustments in use to conform to changing needs and conditions; the use of some land for less than all of the resources; a combination of balanced and diverse resource uses that takes into account the long-term needs of future generations for renewable and nonrenewable resources,...and harmonious and coordinated management of the various resources without permanent impairment of the productivity of the land and the quality of the environment with consideration being given to the relative values of the resources and not necessarily to the combination of uses that will give the greatest economic return or the greatest unit output....
>
> (h) The term "sustained yield" means the achievement and maintenance in perpetuity of a high-level annual or regular periodic output of the various renewable resources of the public lands consistent with multiple use.

The main differences between the 1960 and 1976 definitions, apart from the inclusion of additional resources and values in 1976, are the congressional emphasis on intergenerational equity, the clear directive to achieve long-term conservation, and the requirement of environmental nonimpairment....

[After discussing the numerous discretionary aspects of these statutory definitions, Professor Coggins comments on what he considers to be their enforceable aspects: (1) avoiding impairment of productivity of land and the quality of the environment; and (2) managing for sustained yield.]... This [nonimpairment] standard is fairly precise, and it ought to be enforceable. In a sense, the limitation is a restatement of the watershed value because rangeland productivity requires both water to grow grass and grass to keep the soil in place. "Productivity" is the capacity of the land to support flora and fauna and to furnish "the various renewable resources" in the future. The two key elements in production are soil and water. Therefore, soil and water quality and quantity should be the central focus of public rangeland management attention, but that has not been the case so far.

If the manager were to allow a practice, such as prolonged overgrazing, that causes permanent reductions in future grass production, the nonimpairment limitation would make that action illegal as well as arbitrary. Moreover, when enjoyment of a listed use depends on a rare or unique attribute of an area, the manager must safeguard (or preserve) that attribute to ensure nonimpairment. For example, if a particular vista is especially attractive for hikers or tourists (the "outdoor recreation" resource), actions that seriously and permanently interfere with those scenic qualities arguably violate the nonimpairment standard.... The nonimpairment standard is clear, mandatory and nondiscretionary....

The most significant management limitation in FLPMA is the definition of "sustained yield" in §1702(h). The phrase means *perpetual, high level* annual resource outputs of *all* renewable

---

17. Watershed protection, in multiple use legislation, means preservation of the soil and vegetation conditions necessary to provide adequate supplies of clean water. [Eds.]

resources. Sustained yield is a separate, binding standard that makes continuing resource productivity the highest management criterion. The plain meaning of sustained yield...is that administrators may not sacrifice the future output of any renewable resource in present resource allocations. The "permanent" impairment provision qualifies the sustained yield limitation by ensuring that only serious, longlasting damage is prohibited.... In other words, the agency must plan to accommodate recreation, timber, watershed, wildlife, and natural values, as well as grazing, at high levels in perpetuity, and then act according to that plan....

The search for compatible use combinations at optimum production levels will encounter more conflict than harmony. The main point of multiple use decisionmaking is conflict resolution, with all of the political problems that phrase implies. The manager must try to accommodate all resource uses to the extent possible, giving priority to none — at least on the broad scale — and consideration to all. Sustained yield in compatible combinations does resolve conflicts by theoretically forbidding the optimization of one resource at the expense of others. Such optimization of one resource could leave multiple use decisions vulnerable to attack on sustained yield grounds....

Multiple use-sustained yield management was meant to be more than a "succotash syndrome." Inherent in the concept are detailed and comprehensive commands to force thinking before acting and to mold individual actions into a long-range scheme for the public benefit. FLPMA does not allow the manager to do whatever appears politic or expedient at the time....

COMMENTARY & QUESTIONS

1. **Public land management philosophies.** Multiple use-sustained yield is the management philosophy that applies to BLM lands and national forests managed by the U.S. Forest Service (USFS). Its major rival is "dominant use," a standard recommended by the Public Land Law Review Commission for BLM lands but disavowed by Congress in FLPMA. In a dominant use management system, a primary use is selected for a portion of the public lands; after that, only those secondary uses that are compatible with the dominant use will be allowed there. Where grazing or mining are set as dominant uses, environmental values would be broadly precluded. Given BLM's historic capture by the grazing industry and its supporters, Congress's multiple use directive has been superseded in practice by a de facto dominant use system favoring grazing. Should Congress set grazing as the dominant use on BLM lands? What are the major advantages and disadvantages of multiple use-sustained yield versus dominant use as public land management philosophies?

2. **Multiple use-sustained yield reconsidered.** Despite his earlier enthusiasm for the concept, Professor Coggins has given up on multiple use-sustained yield:

> [Multiple use-sustained yield] is a product of history: it is the latter-day offshoot of Gifford Pinchot's utilitarian maxim, the most benefits for the most people in the long run. Still, however, nobody knows what multiple use really means, but all have opinions. To the resource exploitation industries, multiple use means full speed ahead on the development of all surface and subsurface resources. To the managers on the ground, it means that they are free to decide every question according to their expert judgment without legal standards or judicial review. Neither ever mention sustained yield, except in the context of timber. This commentator once argued that multiple use laws actually meant something — not much, but something — but no court or agency has ever taken that argument seriously.

> Fortunately (from this perspective), multiple use as an operational standard is already dying a slow death, even without statutory repeal or revision.... Multiple use is obsolete.[18]

Professor Michael Blumm concurs that multiple use-sustained yield has failed. In his view, it has resulted, under heavy industry pressure, in the federal agency's "allocation of dominant uses to fulfill [a] preexisting commitment to sustained commodity production."[19]

Other commentators declare the demise of multiple use from entirely different causes:

> Public lands have experienced a fundamental shift in use over the past thirty years. The traditional commodity uses identified with Western folklore — timber, grazing, and mining operations — play a relatively less important role in the modern economy of the West than in past times. For instance,...livestock grazing in the West is down from 17 million head in 1934 to 2 million today....

> The decrease in commodity use parallels an emerging fact about public lands — they are chiefly valuable for non-consumptive uses. Outdoor recreation is a $350 billion industry (in terms of gross national product), with approximately $140 billion attributable to public lands. Consequently, there is a growing demand for public lands from recreational users, and a corresponding commitment towards environmental preservation....

> The emergence of these dominant uses [recreation and preservation] of public lands is a startling development.... Such changes suggest that future conflicts pertaining to public use will not be fought along the traditional lines of commodity versus noncommodity uses. Indeed, that battle has already been largely conceded by commodity developers. Instead, the looming conflict in public land use will be between two former allies — recreation and preservation interests. Such a conflict is particularly likely to arise between low-impact, human-powered recreational users (preservationists) and high-impact, motorized recreational users (recreationists). Laitos & Carr, Transformation on Public Lands, 26 Ecology L.Q. 140, 144–146 (1999).[20]

3. Dominant use management on public lands: mining, logging, wilderness. National Wildlife Refuges are managed by the Fish and Wildlife Service (FWS), of the Department of the Interior, primarily for the benefit of fish and wildlife conservation. A refuge manager may "permit the use of any area within the System for any purpose, including but not limited to hunting, fishing, public recreation and accommodations, and access whenever he determines that such uses are compatible with the major purposes for which such areas were established."[21] Is hunting appropriate in a wildlife refuge? What about ORV or motorboat use? Would dominant use justify opening a wildlife refuge for oil recovery operations that impinge on only a small part of the surface area, but drain a pool of oil that underlies the entire refuge?

---

18. Coggins, Commentary: Overcoming the Unfortunate Legacies of Western Public Land Law, 29 Land & Water L. Rev. 381, 389 (1994).

19. Blumm, Public Choice Theory and The Public Lands: Why "Multiple Use" Failed, 18 Harv. Envtl. L. Rev. 405, 426 (1994).

20. See Part D for an examination of one such conflict in the area of ORV use on public lands.

21. National Wildlife Refuge Administration Act, 16 U.S.C. §668dd(d)(1). This Act was amended by Pub. L. No. 105–57 (1997), which strengthened the conservation mandate of the FWS in National Wildlife Refuges.

Perhaps the best known dominant use statute is the Wilderness Act of 1964, 16 U.S.C. §§1131 et seq. Under the express terms of this statute, all commercial logging and permanent roads and most structures and installations, temporary roads, commercial enterprises, and motorized equipment and forms of transportation are prohibited, but the following secondary uses are explicitly permitted: mining claims; mineral leases, and grazing permits obtained before January 1, 1964; water resources projects approved by the President; commercial services provided by guides, packers, and river runners; and hunting and fishing. Are these secondary uses compatible with a wilderness area, which is defined by the Act as "an area where the earth and its community of life are untrammeled by man, where man is himself a visitor who does not remain," 16 U.S.C. §1131(c)?

Hard-rock mining on public lands represents an extreme form of dominant use. It is still substantially governed by the General Mining Law of 1872, which declares all unreserved public lands open to mineral exploration and extraction.[22] Under this statute, a prospector locating minimum amounts of valuable minerals on public lands can stake a mining claim, exclude other prospectors and interfering recreationists from it, build a house on the property, and use whatever timber exists there for mining purposes. After several years of negligible work, and payment of a modest fee, the locator can be granted a federal patent that will entitle her to outright ownership of the former mining claim. Once a claim has been patented, the owner can do whatever she wants with the property, including using it or selling it for nonmining purposes. At no time is a locator-patentee required to make rental or royalty payments to the United States. Environmental abuses on mining claims and patented lands have been frequent and serious, sometimes resulting in abandoned mines that pose threats to local water supplies.[23]

Although logging in National Forests is ostensibly regulated by the multiple use-sustained yield standard of the National Forest Management Act, 16 U.S.C. §§1600 et seq., many would argue that, like the BLM lands, the National Forests have been managed according to a de facto dominant use for timber production.[24]

Water is the key to other land uses in the arid West, but water allocation is not listed as one of FLPMA's multiple uses because water diversion on federal land has traditionally been governed by state law. West of the Mississippi River, almost all state water allocation laws are based on the "prior appropriation" principle ("first in time is first in right"). Until comparatively recently, environmental protection has been difficult to achieve under western state water allocation systems.[25]

4. **Unenforceable policies and mixed mandates.** FLPMA, like almost every other federal and state statute, has a section (§102) entitled "Declaration of Policy." Section 102(b)

---

22. 30 U.S.C. §§22 et seq. In the Mineral Leasing Act of 1920, 30 U.S.C. §§181 et seq., Congress removed fuel minerals from the ambit of the General Mining Law and established a leasing system, based on competitive bidding, including provisions that authorize the BLM (which also oversees mineral leases on federal lands) to insert environmentally protective provisions in mineral leases.

23. For a portrait and analysis of the General Mining Law in operation, see C. Wilkinson, Crossing the Next Meridian ch. 2 (1992).

24. C. Wilkinson, Crossing the Next Meridian ch. 4; S. Yaffee, The Wisdom of the Spotted Owl (1994); see Part E.

25. See generally J. Sax, R. Abrams & B. Thompson, Legal Control of Water Resources ch. 3 (2d ed. 1991).

states that "the policies of this Act shall become effective only as specific statutory authority for their implementation is enacted by this Act or by subsequent legislation...." As the above excerpt points out, some of FLPMA's policies have been enacted, some have been conditionally enacted, some have not been enacted, and some — e.g., the "fair market value" policy — are being ignored by the BLM. Moreover, FLPMA §102 contains policies encouraging both preservation and consumption. What are the functions of legislative policy statements such as these? Are they intended to mislead an unwary public? Are they media "sound bites"? Do they serve to mollify interest groups that have not received all they wanted? Or are they statements of long-term goals that may or may not now be practicable? In fact, all of these concerns, among others, motivate draftspersons when drafting statutory declarations of policy. Consequently, in reading statutes, one must be sensitive to the difference between hortatory, emotive, and political statements, on the one hand, and enforceable commands on the other.

5. **The public trust and the public lands.** Does the public trust doctrine (see Chapter 22) impose obligations on federal land managers supplementary to those found in their management statutes? Compare Sierra Club v. Department of the Interior, 376 F. Supp. 90 (N.D. Cal. 1974), and Sierra Club v. Department of the Interior, 398 F. Supp. 284 (N.D. Cal. 1975) (the public trust doctrine applies to the activities of the NPS with regard to the management of Redwood National Park), with Sierra Club v. Block, 622 F. Supp. 842 (D. Colo. 1985), vacated on other grounds *sub nom*. Sierra Club v. Yeutter, 911 F. 2d 1405 (10th Cir. 1990) (where Congress has set out statutory duties, they comprise all the responsibilities of a federal land management agency). The public trust doctrine has, however, been applied to a state allocation of water rights that detrimentally affected federal public lands. (See the *Mono Lake* decision in Chapter 22.)

As a remarkable feature of federal public trust powers in public lands management, note the President's inherent stewardship power to withdraw lands into reserves. Teddy Roosevelt withdrew almost 130 million acres from the public domain between 1901 and 1908 to set up wildlife, forest, and oil reserves, a power validated in United States v. Midwest Oil Co., 236 U.S. 459 (1915). The executive apparently has affirmative power to declare such protections unless limited by congressional action (a political process that confronted the Clinton Administration's unilateral extension of rangeland protections).

6. **"Cooperative Management" and the BLM.** In the Public Rangelands Improvement Act of 1978, 32 U.S.C. §§1901 et seq., Congress found that "vast segments" of the public lands were in "unsatisfactory condition" because they were "producing less than their potential" for the multiple uses detailed in FLPMA. The congressional prescription was improved management by the BLM, including discontinuance of grazing on stressed lands and "explor[ation of] innovative grazing management policies and systems which might provide incentives to improve range conditions." Relying on this language, BLM established a Cooperative Management Agreement (CMA) program authorizing BLM to enter into special permit arrangements with selected ranchers who had demonstrated "exemplary rangeland management practices." The purpose of the CMA program was to allow these exemplary ranchers to "manage livestock on the allotment as they determine appropriate" for ten-year periods. "Exemplary practices" were

not defined in the regulation, nor were the agreements required to contain performance standards or any other limiting terms or conditions. If a permittee did not
comply with the nebulous goals of the program, BLM's only remedy was to deny
renewal of the agreement after its ten-year term had elapsed. In NRDC v. Hodel, 618 F.
Supp. 848 (E.D. Cal. 1985), the court, finding that "the CMA program is *not* an experiment, but is a permanent system of permit issuance aimed at a group of favored
permittees," struck down the CMA regulations as inconsistent with BLM's statutory
obligation to "prescribe the manner in and the extent to which livestock practices will
be conducted on public lands."

7. **Grazing fees and other public land use subsidies.** All attempts to raise the grazing fee
to a figure approaching market value (the current federal grazing fee is less than $2 per
cow, per month, in contrast with current forage market rates of over $10 per cow, per
month) have been unsuccessful. Other subsidies for resource use on public lands
include below-cost timber sales from the National Forests, federal payments to timber
companies for logging road construction when they buy timber in the national
forests,[26] extraction of hard-rock minerals from the public lands without paying royalties to the federal government, below-cost sales of water from federally constructed
dams, cost-free water diversions from federal lands, free access to ORVs, and below-cost
fees for public access to National Parks.[27] Are there good reasons for subsidizing
resource use on public lands? Should the USFS sell timber below cost as benign support
for the economies of timber-dependent communities?[28] Should fees for National Park
access be kept low in order to attract low- and middle-income visitors? Should grazing
fees remain low in order to preserve the economic viability of the small rancher?[29]

8. **Recent grazing reform regulations.** On February 22, 1995, the BLM promulgated a
new set of grazing regulations (60 Fed. Reg. 9894–9971, 43 C.F.R. pt. 4100). Among
other provisions, the regulations (1) replace the district advisory boards composed of
ranchers with multi-stakeholder Resource Advisory Councils; and (2) require BLM to
set statewide or regional standards to assure the ecological health of grazing lands, and
to take appropriate management action (e.g., reducing stocking rates or adjusting periods of grazing) where the standards are not being met. Commentary on these
regulations has run the gamut from quite favorable to generally unfavorable.[30]

---

26. In February 1998, the Clinton Administration imposed a moratorium on logging road construction in most
National Forests, even if timber companies are willing to build the roads without federal subsidies. The Bush II
Administration has refused to defend this moratorium in court and is considering whether to suspend the mora-
torium partially or entirely.

27. See generally C. Wilkinson, Crossing the Next Meridian (1992), for a discussion of subsidies for ranchers,
miners, and water users.

28. See the discussion in Anderson, Below-Cost Timber Sales & Community Economic Subsidies: A Conflict of
Values, 5 Md. J. Contemp. Legal Issues 129 (1995).

29. Only 12% of grazing permit holders are listed by the Interior Department as small operators. Ten percent of
permit holders — including the Metropolitan Life Insurance Company (800,000 acres), the Mormon Church,
a Japanese conglomerate, the Nature Conservancy, and some of the wealthiest families in the nation — control
about half of all public grazing land. Egan, Wingtip "Cowboys" in Last Stand to Hold on to Low Grazing Fees,
N.Y. Times, Oct. 29, 1993, at 27.

30. See, e.g., Feller, 'Til The Cows Come Home: The Fatal Flaw in the Clinton Administration's Public Lands
Grazing Policy, 25 Envtl. L. 703 (1995) (Although these regulations are an improvement over the former situation, they reveal a "fatal flaw" in the Clinton Administration's grazing policy — "the failure to admit that
substantial portions of the public lands are poorly suited to livestock production and therefore should be retired

These regulations were substantially upheld in Public Lands Council v. Babbitt, 529 U.S. 728 (2000) (invalidating only a provision authorizing issuance of grazing permits for pure conservation purposes, unrelated to grazing). BLM, however, has not always been enthusiastic about implementing the regulations. See Idaho Watersheds Project v. BLM, 187 F.3d 1035 (9th Cir. 1999) (BLM misinterpreted its own regulations in order to delay substantive action to improve range health).

9. **The more things change....** The BLM continues to defy the dictates of federal law in its regulation of cattle grazing on federal lands in the West. In Idaho Watersheds Project v. Hahn, 307 F.3d 815 (9th Cir. 2002), several environmental groups sued the BLM for, among other things, violating NEPA in the issuance of grazing permits to ranchers grazing cattle on federal lands in the Owyhee Resource Area in southwestern Idaho. The district court held that the BLM had violated NEPA and granted a permanent injunction imposing interim environmental protection conditions (e.g., protection of riparian vegetation) on grazing and imposing a timetable for the BLM to issue new permits in compliance with NEPA. The Ninth Circuit Court of Appeals, in affirming the district court's judgment, extolled the Owyhee Area as "over one million acres of ruggedly beautiful landscape...[including] spectacular and wild canyonlands." In addition, the area "provides habitat for bighorn sheep, elk, mule deer, antelope, peregrine falcon, redband trout, sage grouse, and hundreds of other species. Startling in its ecological diversity, from arid sagebrush desert to lush juniper woodlands, the Owyhee shelters the world's largest population of nesting raptors and a variety of rare and endangered species." Cattle ranching has been a traditional land use in the Owyhee Area: "Ranching families are an important part of the local community with many family members participating actively in civic life as local elected officials, volunteer firefighters, and school board members. Well over four hundred people currently depend on cattle grazing in the Owyhee for their livelihood." 307 F.3d at 821.

But the BLM has managed the Owyhee Area as if cattle grazing were the dominant use of this region:

> Water is life, and the health of the Owyhee depends on the health of its streams. Unfortunately, cattle overgrazing now threatens the life of the Owyhee.... In 1981, the BLM identified livestock overgrazing as a significant problem in the Owyhee and concluded that approximately ninety percent of the Owyhee rangeland was in poor or fair ecological condition. In 1981, the BLM also found over one hundred and forty miles of streams to be in poor condition, due in large part to overgrazing. In 1996, the BLM again examined the health of the streams in the Owyhee and found that ninety-one percent of the stream miles inventoried were in unsatisfactory condition. Despite the BLM's own findings, the BLM failed to address destruction of riparian habitat caused by cattle overgrazing in the fifteen years between 1981 and 1996 and the condition of stream banks in the Owyhee continued to deteriorate during this period....

from grazing in favor of other resources and uses."); Arruda & Watson, The Rise and Fall of Grazing Reform, 32 Land & Water L. Rev. 423 (1997) ("The final regulations weaken the potential of the reforms to improve the range's condition, even though the extent of the regulatory changes has remained substantial."); Pendery, Reforming Livestock Grazing on the Public Domain: Ecosystem Management-Based Standards and Guidelines Blaze a New Path for Range Management, 27 Envtl. L. 513 (1997) ("[The standards] could lead to dramatic changes in livestock grazing over a vast portion of the West.").

In 1997...the BLM issued sixty-eight grazing permits covering about one million acres. The BLM sought to comply with NEPA by filling out pre-printed one page forms for each permit, and stating on the form that the permit complied with the then sixteen-year-old EIS that had been adopted in 1981. Grazing on the allotments covered by these permits continued uninterrupted and continues today. 307 F.3d at 822.

The Ninth Circuit found that "the interim measures imposed by the district court are a fair and balanced interim remedy, giving due regard to protection of the environment and the welfare of the affected ranching families." 307 F.3d at 833.

C. FEDERAL-STATE AND PUBLIC-PRIVATE ISSUES ON THE PUBLIC LANDS

The following Supreme Court decision is the most significant development in over a century of vitriolic litigation regarding federal versus state power and public versus private rights on the public lands, and reflects a chapter in the antifederal "Sagebrush Rebellion." As you read the opinion, consider which legal questions have been definitively settled and which are still open.

Kleppe v. New Mexico
United States Supreme Court, 1976
426 U.S. 529

MARSHALL, J. At issue in this case is whether Congress exceeded its powers under the Constitution in enacting the Wild Free-Roaming Horses and Burros Act, 16 U.S.C. §§1331–1340,...in 1971 to protect "all unbranded and unclaimed horses and burros on public lands in the United States" from "capture, branding, harassment, or death." The Act provides that all such horses and burros on the public lands...are committed to the jurisdiction of the respective Secretaries, who are "directed to protect and manage [the animals] as components of the public lands...in a manner that is designed to achieve and maintain a thriving natural ecological balance on the public lands." If protected horses or burros "stray from public lands onto privately owned land, the owners of such land may inform the nearest Federal marshal or agency of the Secretary, who shall arrange to have the animals removed...."

On February 1, 1974, a New Mexico rancher, Kelley Stephenson, was informed by BLM that several unbranded burros had been seen near Taylor Well, where Stephenson watered his cattle. Taylor Well is on federal property, and Stephenson had access to it and some 8,000 surrounding acres only through a grazing permit.... After BLM made it clear to Stephenson that it would not remove the burros and after he personally inspected the Taylor Well area, Stephenson complained to the [New Mexico] Livestock Board that the burros were interfering with his livestock operation by molesting his cattle and eating their feed. Thereupon the Board rounded up and removed 19 unbranded and unclaimed burros pursuant to the New Mexico Estray Law. Each burro was seized on the public lands of the United States.... On February 18, 1974, the livestock Board, pursuant to its usual practice, sold the burros at public auction. After the sale, BLM asserted jurisdiction under the Act and demanded that the Board recover the animals and return them to the public lands.

On March 4, 1974, appellees [New Mexico public officials] filed a complaint...seeking a declaratory judgment that the [Act] is unconstitutional and an injunction against its enforcement.... [The District Court held the Act unconstitutional and granted the injunction; the Supreme Court reversed.]

The Property Clause of the Constitution provides that "Congress shall have Power to dispose of and make all needful Rules and Regulations respecting the Territory or other Property belonging to the United States." In passing the Wild Free-Roaming Horses and Burros Act, Congress deemed the regulated animals "an integral part of the natural system of the public lands" of the United States, and found that their management was necessary "for the achievement of an ecological balance on the public lands." According to Congress, these animals, if preserved in their native habitats, "contribute to the diversity of life forms within the Nation and enrich the lives of the American people." Indeed, Congress concluded, the wild free-roaming horses and burros "are living symbols of the historic and pioneer spirit of the West." Despite their importance, the Senate Committee found that these animals

> have been cruelly captured and slain and their carcasses used in the production of pet food and fertilizer. They have been used for target practice and harassed for "sport" and profit. In spite of public outrage, this bloody traffic continues unabated, and it is the firm belief of the committee that this senseless slaughter must be brought to an end.

For these reasons, Congress determined to preserve and protect the wild free-roaming horses and burros on the public lands of the United States. The question under the Property Clause is whether this determination can be sustained as a "needful" regulation "respecting" the public lands. In answering this question, we must remain mindful that, while courts must eventually pass upon them, determinations under the Property Clause are entrusted primarily to the judgment of Congress.

Appellees argue that the Act cannot be supported by the Property Clause. They contend that the Clause grants Congress essentially two kinds of power: (1) the power to dispose of and make incidental rules regarding the use of federal property; and (2) the power to protect federal property. According to appellees, the first power is not broad enough to support legislation protecting wild animals that live on federal property; and the second power is not implicated since the Act is designed to protect the animals, which are not themselves federal property, and not the public lands. As an initial matter, it is far from clear that the Act was not passed in part to protect the public lands of the United States[31] or that Congress cannot assert a property interest in the regulated horses and burros superior to that of the State.[32] But we need not consider whether the Act can be upheld on either of these grounds, for we reject appellees' narrow reading of the Property Clause....

In brief...appellees have presented no support for their position that the [Property] Clause grants Congress only the power to dispose of, to make incidental rules regarding the use of, and to protect federal property. This failure is hardly surprising, for the Clause, in broad terms, gives Congress the power to determine what are "needful" rules "respecting" the public lands. And while the furthest reaches of the power granted by the Property Clause have not yet been definitively resolved, we have repeatedly observed that "the power over the public land thus entrusted to Congress is without limitations." United States v. San Francisco, 310 U.S. 16, 29 (1940).

The decided cases have supported this expansive reading. It is the Property Clause, for instance, that provides the basis for governing the territories of the United States. And even over public land within the States, "the general government doubtless has a power over its own

---

31. Congress expressly ordered that the animals were to be managed and protected in order to "achieve and maintain a thriving natural ecological balance on the public lands." [This is footnote 7 in the original.]

32. The Secretary makes no claim here, however, that the United States owns the wild free roaming horses and burros found on public land. [This is footnote 8 in the original.]

property analogous to the police power of the several states, and the extent to which it may go in the exercise of such power is measured by the exigencies of the particular case." Camfield v. United States, 167 U.S. 518, 525 (1897). We have noted, for example, that the Property Clause gives Congress the power over the public lands "to control their occupancy and use, to protect them from trespass and injury, and to prescribe the conditions upon which others may obtain rights in them...." Utah Power & Light Co. v. United States, 243 U.S. 389, 405 (1917).... In short, Congress exercises the powers both of a proprietor and of a legislature over the public domain. Although the Property Clause does not authorize "an exercise of a general control over public policy in a State," it does permit "an exercise of the complete power which Congress has over particular public property entrusted to it." United States v. San Francisco, 310 U.S., at 30. In our view, the "complete power" that Congress has over public lands necessarily includes the power to protect the wildlife living there.

Appellees argue that if we approve the Wild Free-Roaming Horses and Burros Act as a valid exercise of Congress' power under the Property Clause, then we have sanctioned an impermissible intrusion on the sovereignty, legislative authority and police power of the State and have wrongfully infringed upon the State's traditional trustee powers over wild animals. The argument appears to be that Congress could obtain exclusive legislative jurisdiction over the public lands in the State only by state consent, and that in the absence of such consent Congress lacks the power to act contrary to state law. This argument is without merit....

While Congress can acquire exclusive or partial jurisdiction over lands within a State by the State's consent or cession [under the so-called Enclave Clause of the Constitution, Article I §8, cl. 17], the presence or absence of such jurisdiction has nothing to do with Congress' powers under the Property Clause. Absent consent or cession a State undoubtedly retains jurisdiction over federal lands within its territory, but Congress equally surely retains the power to enact legislation respecting those lands pursuant to the Property Clause. And when Congress so acts, the federal legislation necessarily overrides conflicting state laws under the Supremacy Clause. As we said in Camfield v. United States, 167 U.S., at 526, in response to a somewhat different claim, "A different rule would place the public domain of the United States completely at the mercy of state legislation."...

Appellees' fear that the Secretary's position is that "the Property Clause totally exempts federal lands within state borders from state legislative powers, state police powers, and all rights and powers of local sovereignty and jurisdiction of the states," is totally unfounded. The Federal Government does not assert exclusive jurisdiction over the public lands in New Mexico, and the State is free to enforce its criminal and civil laws on those lands. But where those state laws conflict with the Wild Free-Roaming Horses and Burros Act, or with other legislation passed pursuant to the Property Clause, the law is clear: the State laws must recede....

Appellees are concerned that the Act's extension of protection to wild free-roaming horses and burros that stray from public land onto private land will be read to provide federal jurisdiction over every wild horse or burro that at any time sets foot upon federal land. While it is clear that regulations under the Property Clause may have some effect on private lands not otherwise under federal control, Camfield v. United States, 167 U.S. 518 (1897), we do not think it appropriate in this declaratory judgment proceeding to determine the extent, if any, to which the Property Clause empowers Congress to protect animals on private lands or the extent to which such regulation is attempted by the Act....

COMMENTARY & QUESTIONS

1. **The statutory policy.** The Wild Free-Roaming Horses and Burros Act is a statute that causes mixed feelings amongst both ranchers and environmentalists. On one hand these animals, brought from Europe by Spanish and English pioneers, are living symbols of the historic or mythical frontier West and creatures that deserve humane treatment. On the other, they have multiplied so successfully in some niches of their transplanted habitat that they destroy the forage and threaten the survival of native species in the western ecosystem, such as antelope and black-footed ferrets, as well as private livestock.

A vivid, highly focused citizens' campaign — using video footage of dog food suppliers stampeding and butchering terrified wild horses — pushed the statute through Congress, and as law it must be enforced by federal land managers. But the statute does not acknowledge the policy contradictions it presents, with endangered species laws for instance. Some environmentalists have suggested the compromise of inserting IUDs in wild horses and burros (as birth control-laced pigeon food has been advocated in somewhat analogous urban settings), but the issues are likely not to be so easily resolved.

2. **Public land and private land.** Consider a situation where a herd of free-roaming horses and burros strays from public land onto adjacent private land, the rancher informs the BLM, and the BLM fails to remove the animals. The Act specifies that the Secretary "shall arrange to have the animals removed," but it contains no time limitation for BLM action. If the animals injure the private range, can the rancher sue the federal government in inverse condemnation? In Mountain States Legal Found. v. Hodel, 799 F.2d 1423 (10th Cir. 1986), cert. denied, 480 U.S. 951 (1987), the court rejected a takings claim by a grazing association in a similar situation on the grounds that: (1) wild horses are wild animals, not instrumentalities of the federal government; (2) "of the courts that have considered whether damage to private property by protected wildlife constitutes a 'taking,' a clear majority have held that it does not and that the government does not owe compensation"; and (3) the plaintiffs had not shown a deprivation of substantially all economically viable uses of their lands. See also Christy v. Hodel, 857 F.2d 1324 (9th Cir. 1988), cert. denied, 490 U.S. 1114 (1989) (the ESA's protection of grizzly bears did not effect a taking of sheep owner's property where a grizzly bear killed domestic sheep). Federal courts have consistently held that a grazing permit is not a vested property right but merely a revocable privilege, and thus cancellation or substantial modification of a grazing permit cannot constitute a taking of property without just compensation. See, e.g., Federal Lands Legal Consortium v. Agriculture Dep't, 195 F.3d 1190 (10th Cir. 1999).

3. **Helpless giants?** Does the Property Clause give the federal government the authority to regulate activities on state, local, or private lands within ("inholdings") or outside federal landholdings when those activities are interfering with the uses of the federal lands? For example, assume that the FWS seeks an injunction that forbids a promoter from holding rock concerts just outside a National Wildlife Refuge, or that the NPS wants to prevent the construction of a hideously ugly commercial structure adjacent

to — and painfully visible from — a national battlefield.[33] Camfield v. United States, 167 U.S. 518 (1897), cited frequently in *Kleppe*, would appear to authorize the federal government to protect its property against external threats. In *Camfield*, an owner of alternate, odd-numbered sections (purchased from a railroad) effectively fenced off 20,000 acres of federal land by building a zigzag fence on his own property (see Figure 24-1). Declaring that the federal government, under the Property Clause, has the constitutional power to protect its land against nuisances, the Supreme Court held that the fence was a violation of a federal statute prohibiting enclosures of public lands. The Tenth Circuit Court of Appeals has ruled that it is a violation of the Unlawful Enclosures Act to construct a *Camfield*-type fence that effectively excludes pronghorn antelope from their critical winter range on federal land. United States v. Lawrence, 848 F.2d 1502 (10th Cir. 1988), cert. denied, 488 U.S. 980 (1989).

6	5	4	3	2	1
7	8	9	10	11	12
18	17	16	15	14	13
19	20	21	22	23	24
30	29	28	27	26	25
31	32	33	34	35	36

FIGURE 24-1

From Camfield v. United States, 167 U.S. 518 (1897) — illustrating the checkerboard federal/private land ownership pattern, and the strategic fence placement employed by Camfield, shown by the dotted lines, to double his amount of fenced grazing land. The publicly-owned parcels are even-numbered; Camfield's private parcels are odd-numbered.

Since *Camfield*, federal circuit courts of appeals have consistently upheld federal regulation of external threats. See Stupak-Thrall v. United States, 70 F.3d 881 (6th Cir. 1995), and cases cited. The federal land management agencies, however, have been unenthusiastic about exercising these powers. See Sax, Helpless Giants: The National Parks and the Regulation of Private Lands, 75 Mich. L. Rev. 239 (1976). If the federal government has the legal power to regulate external activities, how far does the power extend? Can the NPS promulgate a regulation requiring a large agricultural operation, 50 miles upriver of a national park, to cease discharging nutrients because these pollutants are causing the river in the park to become eutrophic (prematurely aged)?

4. **Access problems.** On checkerboard land grants, can private owners of alternate, odd-numbered sections deny access to recreationists traveling on a BLM-constructed road through sections 14, 22, and 16 (see Figure 24-1) in order to reach a federal reservoir, even though the public road only touches their sections 15, 21, and 23 at the corners? In Leo Sheep Co. v. United States, 440 U.S. 668 (1979), the Supreme Court rejected express or implied easements across private lands, thus requiring the BLM to purchase or condemn road easements. Justice Rehnquist, writing for the majority, distinguished *Camfield* in unconvincing fashion. Isn't the Leo Sheep Company

---

33. The latter example, unfortunately, is not a hypothetical one. See the discussion of the *Gettysburg Tower* case in Chapter 22.

really enclosing public lands? In a condemnation proceeding, would the fair market value of Leo Sheep's land include its proximity to the water supply and recreation provided by the federally funded reservoir?[34]

5. **The "Sagebrush Rebellion" and the "Wise Use" Movement.** Problems caused by interspersed federal and private lands, exacerbated by FLPMA's declaration that the federal lands will generally remain in federal ownership and be managed for multiple use and sustained yield, generated a reaction known as the "Sagebrush Rebellion," one manifestation of which consisted of a number of western states contesting the constitutionality of federal ownership of the public lands. In 1978, the State of Nevada sued the federal government, claiming that federal land ownership was a violation of both Nevada's Tenth Amendment rights and its right to be admitted on an "equal footing" with the original 13 states, in which there is comparatively little federal land. While that case was pending, the Nevada legislature enacted a statute claiming title to most of the federal lands (excepting wildlife refuges and Native American reservations) in the state. The federal district court dismissed Nevada's claim on the merits, Nevada ex rel. Nevada State Bd. of Agric. v. United States, 512 F. Supp. 166 (D. Nev. 1981), aff'd for lack of justiciability, 699 F.2d 486 (9th Cir. 1983). Nye County, Nevada's attempt to assert county ownership of federal lands met the same fate. United States v. Nye County, Nev., 920 F. Supp. 1108 (D. Nev. 1996). The Ninth Circuit Court of Appeals has recently reaffirmed federal ownership of federal public lands. United States v. Gardner, 107 F.3d 1314 (9th Cir. 1996) (involving a defense to an enforcement action for unauthorized grazing on public lands). The so-called Wise Use movement, the loosely organized but high profile anti-environmental and anti-regulatory coalition of mostly western populist groups, funded by industry, continued to pursue the Sagebrush Rebellion agenda of "Local Sovereignty," along with a focus on private property rights, through the media, the political process, and the courts. Although the phrases "Sagebrush Rebellion" and "Wise Use" movement are no longer utilized, the Bush II Administration appears to be more responsive than previous administrations to the demands of the extractive and libertarian interests that espouse these principles.

6. **Public land and ecosystem management.** The Wild Free-Roaming Horses and Burros Act, which deems the animals to be "an integral part of the natural system of the public lands," is Congress's clearest acceptance to date of Aldo Leopold's concept of land as an ecological community rather than a commodity. Increasingly, Americans are looking beyond preservation of particular species or resources (e.g., endangered species or wild and scenic rivers), which is based on a variety of "zoo" mentality, toward preservation of entire ecosystems and their biodiversity.[35] All four of the federal public land management agencies — the BLM, USFS, FWS, and the NPS — have announced that they will implement an ecosystem approach to managing their lands and natural resources. Apart from the primitive character of current ecological data, the most

---

34. For a case holding against the landowner on far more favorable facts, see Branch v. Oconto County, 109 N.W.2d 105 (Wis. 1961).

35. For a critique of the resource-by-resource preservation approach, in the context of the ESA, and an examination of the potential legal means of protecting biodiversity, see Doremus, Patching the Ark: Improving Legal Protection of Biological Diversity, 18 Ecology L.Q. 265 (1991).

obvious impediment to ecosystem management on federal lands is that ecosystems transcend jurisdictional boundaries, not only those of any particular federal land management agency, but also those of the federal government itself:

> While ecosystem management will require unparalleled coordination among federal agencies, disparate missions and planning requirements set forth in federal land management statutes and regulations hamper such efforts. And although ecosystem management will require collaboration and consensus-building among federal and nonfederal parties within most ecosystems, incentives, authorities, interests and limitations embedded in the larger national land and natural resource use framework — many beyond the ability of the federal land management agencies individually or collectively to control and affect — constrain these parties' efforts to work together effectively. U.S. GAO, Ecosystem Management: Additional Actions Needed to Adequately Test a Promising Approach 5 (1994).

Is ecosystem management consistent with a multiple use-sustained yield statutory mandate? What about a dominant use directive?

7. Can states regulate resource extraction and wildlife management on federal lands? In California Coastal Comm'n v. Granite Rock Co., 480 U.S. 572 (1987), the Supreme Court drew a distinction between land use planning and environmental regulation, holding that the National Forest Management Act preempts state land use planning in national forests, but not state environmental regulation.[36] Is there a discernible difference between land use planning and environmental regulation in the context of public lands management?

Except in federal enclaves, such as National Parks, states typically regulate hunting and fishing on federal lands unless the federal government has declared otherwise, as in the Wild Free-Roaming Horses and Burros Act. In a *Kleppe*-like standoff between federal and state wildlife officials, the State of Wyoming challenged the FWS's refusal to permit state officials to vaccinate elk on the National Elk Refuge against brucellosis, a serious disease that threatens not only free-ranging elk but also domestic cattle on neighboring ranches. The Tenth Circuit Court of Appeals held that (1) the Tenth Amendment to the U.S. Constitution does not reserve to the states the absolute right to manage wildlife on federal lands, and (2) the National Wildlife System Improvement Act of 1997 permits federal land management officials to preempt state wildlife management activities in wildlife refuges. Wyoming v. United States, 279 F.3d 1214 (10th Cir. 2002).

D. THE BLM AND OFF-ROAD VEHICLES: A CASE STUDY

The following case study involving BLM management of ORVs illustrates the BLM's political capture by a secondary clientele,[37] the ORV lobby, a powerful coalition of vehicle manufacturers, the petroleum industry, tire manufacturers, and ardent ORV recreationists. Note that excessive recreational use can be as damaging to public natural resources as insensitive extractive uses. It is often said that, as a nation, we are "loving our public lands to death."

---

36. See the discussion of *Granite Rock* in Chapter 6.
37. The BLM's primary "clientele," i.e., regulated industry, is the grazing industry.

David Sheridan, Off-Road Vehicles on Public Lands
7-12 (1979)

Off-road vehicles (ORVs) have damaged every kind of ecosystem found in the United States: sand dunes covered with American Beach grass on Cape Cod; pine and cypress woodlands in Florida; hardwood forests in Indiana; prairie grasslands in Montana; chaparral and sagebrush hills in Arizona; alpine meadows in Colorado; conifer forests in Washington; arctic tundra in Alaska. In some cases the wounds will heal naturally; in others they will not, at least for millennia....

Federal lands have borne a disproportionate share of the damage. State lands are far less extensive; in addition, some states have either prohibited ORV use on their lands (Indiana) or have restricted their use to designated trails (Massachusetts). And the federal government has been more willing to open the lands which it manages for the American public to ORVs than have private landowners....

The ready availability of federal land has profoundly shaped the ORV phenomenon. Per capita ownership of ORVs is significantly higher in areas that possess a lot of public land. The reason is simple: a person is more likely to buy an ORV if he has some place to drive it.... Thus federal land policy has been an important stimulant to ORV growth. Because the federal government has allowed ORVers to consume public resources free of charge, the general public has in a sense subsidized the ORV phenomenon. A second consequence of federal land policy has been to discourage private enterprise from meeting ORVers demand for land. Commercially developed ORV areas are extremely rare....

First and foremost [among environmental costs of ORV use], ORVs eat land. It is because ORVs attack that relatively thin layer of disintegrated rock and organic material to which all earthly life clings — soil — that they can have such a devastating effect on natural resources....

There seem to be two basic soil responses to ORV use. One, sandy and gravelly soils are susceptible to direct quarrying by ORVs, and when stripped of vegetation they are susceptible to rapid erosion processes — usually by rill and gully erosion. Near Santa Cruz, California, for example, ORV trails used for about 6 years are now gullies 8 feet deep. Two, more clay-rich soils are less sensitive to direct mechanical displacement by ORVs, but the rates of erosion of stripped clay-rich soil are much higher under ORV use than under natural conditions. Furthermore, ORV pounding of clay-rich soil causes strong surface seals to form, thereby reducing the infiltration of water. This, in turn, leads to greater rainwater runoff, which causes gullying lower in the drainage.

Once massive soil erosion begins, it will stop only after ORV riding stops and the native vegetation has had a chance to reestablish itself and stabilize the soil. In arid and semiarid areas, recovery is very slow. The same holds true for hilly or mountainous areas which receive heavy rainfall, such as Appalachia or northern California.... In flat, dry areas ORVs expose the soil to another powerful erosional force — the wind. In damp flat areas such as wet prairies or meadows, ORV ruts can turn into drainage ditches — siphoning off water held in the surrounding area.... ORVs destabilize sand dunes, making them more vulnerable to wind erosion and, in the case of coastal dunes, to sea erosion....

A major difficulty with ORVs...is that the terrain which truly challenges the capability of these machines, and which is therefore most attractive to many ORV operators, is exactly that which is most highly sensitive to erosional degradation. This open contradiction between machine capability and land sensitivity is a key issue.

Aside from tearing up soils, ORVs also damage vegetation. They kill plants in several ways. By direct contact — the ORV runs over the plant or brushes against it, breaking off limbs or branches. Sometimes ORV use around a plant so badly erodes the soil that the plant simply collapses from lack of anything to hold onto. Also, ORV soil compaction injures root systems and larger perennials eventually die. In addition, ORVs crush seedlings beneath their wheels or treads as well as seeds germinating on or within the ground. Lastly, on slopes, soil eroded because of ORV use washes to the bottom where it smothers plants that are growing there.

ORVs also disrupt animal life.... They collide with animals, especially smaller mammals and reptiles. By destroying vegetation, they are also destroying animal food and shelter. In addition, ORVs afford hunters and fishermen access to remote, heretofore untouched areas, thereby dramatically increasing the fish and game kills in those areas. The effects of ORV noise on animals, although imperfectly understood, is thought to be very damaging....

Conflicts with Other Users... ORV and snowmobile use of the land conflicts with other human uses of the land [and] the conflicts engendered by these machines can be quite bitter.

Reports from public land managers in nine western states indicate that conflict occurs, upon occasion, between commercial users of the land, such as ranchers, and ORV recreationists. The conflict with grazing, in fact, seems to be more common than with logging or mining. For example, New Mexico BLM director Arthur W. Zimmerman notes that complaints from ranchers have been received concerning trespass, cut fences, broken gates, polluted livestock water, new jeep roads, noise, gully erosion caused by hill climbs, and interference with their livestock operations. The less frequent complaints received from loggers and miners usually concern vandalism of their equipment and property by ORVers.

The most serious conflict arises between ORV operators and nonmotorized picnickers or campers, hikers, backpackers, sightseers, and so on — or between ORVers and persons using the land for educational purposes — students, teachers, researchers. Nonmotorized recreationists do not enjoy their encounters with motorcycles, dune buggies, and four-wheel drive vehicles, numerous studies have shown. The ORV operator, on the other hand, is often quite tolerant, even oblivious, of the person on foot or on horseback.

ORVs, in other words, impair other people's enjoyment or understanding of the outdoors on public land. In terms of public policy, this is a problem equal in importance to ORV damage of the environment.

COMMENTARY & QUESTIONS

1. **Initial federal responses.** To the BLM's credit, it was the first federal agency that recognized the magnitude of the ORV problem on public lands and attempted to do something about it. In 1968, the California state office of the BLM and the Western Regional office of the NPS published a document detailing the damage caused by ORVs in the California Desert and recommending that BLM develop special ORV centers where environmental damage could be kept to a minimum. In 1969, the BLM in California convened an Off-Road Advisory Council composed of ORV organization representatives, environmentalists, ranchers, and businessmen. Despite heated internal disputes, the Council recommended that ORV use not be permitted on highly erodable land, lands typically used for other kinds of public recreation, or sites unique for historic, ecological, or archaeological value. Apparently, these recommendations led the ORV organizations to withdraw their support for the Advisory Council Process and use their contacts in the Interior Department for their own self-interest. In 1971, the Secretary of the Interior formed an ORV task force that whitewashed the ORV problem, recommending further study, state regulation of ORV use, and the development of

private ORV facilities (with no mention of increased federal regulation or subsidies to stimulate the private sector).

By 1972, however, environmental abuse of the public lands by the burgeoning ranks of ORV users was becoming so pronounced that President Nixon issued Executive Order 11644, calling for a unified federal policy toward ORVs on the public lands. E.O. 11644 established a presumption that public lands should be closed to ORV use unless specifically opened by agency regulation, after findings are made under the following criteria:

(1) Areas and trails shall be located to minimize damages to soil, watershed, vegetation, or other resources of the public lands.

(2) Areas and trails shall be located to minimize harassment of wildlife or significant disruption of wildlife habitats.

(3) Areas and trails shall be located to minimize conflicts between off-road vehicle use and other existing or proposed recreational uses of the same or neighboring public lands and to ensure the compatibility of such uses with existing conditions in populated areas, taking into account noise and other factors.

(4) Areas and trails shall not be located in officially designated Wilderness Areas or Primitive Areas. Areas and trails shall be located in areas of the National Park system, Natural Areas, or National Wildlife Refuges and Game Ranges only if the respective agency head determines that off-road vehicle use in such locations will not adversely affect their natural, aesthetic, or scenic values.

2. **BLM backslide.** The BLM regulations implementing E.O. 11644, however, established the opposite presumption, that public lands should be open to ORV use until closed by the management agency because of environmental damage or conflict with other users.[38]

In National Wildlife Fed'n v. Morton, 393 F. Supp. 1286 (D.D.C. 1975), a federal district court overturned the BLM regulations as inconsistent with E.O. 11644, remarking that "BLM has significantly diluted the standards emphatically set forth in Executive Order 11644."

FLPMA, enacted in 1976, was primarily addressed to the grazing issue, and its treatment of ORV use was cursory. Section 601 of FLPMA established a planning process for the 12 million-acre California Desert Conservation Area, one objective of which was that

[§601(4)] The use of all California desert resources can and should be provided for in a multiple use and sustained yield management plan to conserve these resources for future generations, and to provide present and future use and enjoyment, particularly outdoor recreation uses, including the use, where appropriate, of off-road recreational vehicles.

In other words, ORVs were perceived by Congress as just another one of the multiple uses to be accommodated on public lands.

In response to the hesitancy of federal agencies to control ORV use and implement E.O. 11644, President Carter issued E.O. 11989 in 1977.[39] E.O. 11989 reiterated many of the

---

38. In other words, whereas E.O. 11644 minimized false negatives (proactive), the BLM regulations minimized false positives (reactive) (see the Talbot Page essay in Chapter 1).

39. See generally Bleich, Chrome on the Range: Off-Road Vehicles on Public Lands, 15 Ecology L.Q. 159, 166–167 (1988).

provisions of E.O. 11644, but, in addition, ordered agency heads (1) "to develop and issue regulations [governing the] designation of the specific areas and trails on public lands on which the use of off-road vehicles may be permitted," and (2) to immediately ban ORVs where ORV use "will cause or is causing considerable adverse effects." Nevertheless, two days after President Carter signed E.O. 11989, the Interior Department issued a press release interpreting the order as applying only to "fragile areas which are actually threatened with serious damage," disclaiming a general ban on ORV use on public lands, and stressing voluntary action on the part of ORV users. E.O. 11644 had declared that "areas and trails shall be located to minimize [environmental] damages," a highly protective standard. As for closure of existing trails, E.O. 11989 required the agency to prove "considerable adverse effects" in order to close a trail. The BLM, in its California Desert Conservation Area Plan, applied the latter order's looser closure standard, instead of the more protective minimization standard, in its designation of new trails, thus making it far easier to designate ORV routes. This aspect of the plan was struck down in American Motorcyclist Ass'n v. Watt, 543 F. Supp. 789 (C.D. Cal. 1982). The following case involved an attempt by a citizens group to have a particular ORV trail closed.

Sierra Club v. Clark
United States Court of Appeals for the Ninth Circuit, 1985
756 F.2d 686

POOLE, J. Plaintiffs...filed this action seeking review under the APA §706(1), of the failure of the defendants Secretary of the Interior, Director of the BLM, and California State Director of BLM to close Dove Springs Canyon to ORV use. Sierra Club appeals from the district court's denial of their motion for summary judgment, and the grant of the Secretary's motion for summary judgment. We affirm.

Dove Springs Canyon is located in the California Desert Conservation Area.... The Desert Area covers approximately 25 million acres in southeastern California, approximately 12.1 million of which are administered by the BLM. Dove Springs Canyon is comprised of approximately 5500 acres; 3000 acres are designated "open" for unrestricted use of ORVs.

Dove Springs Canyon possesses abundant and diverse flora and fauna. Over 250 species of plants, 24 species of reptiles, and 30 species of birds are found there. It also offers good habitat for the Mojave ground squirrel, the desert kit fox, and the burrowing owl. Because the rich and varied biota is unusual for an area of such low elevation in the Mojave Desert, the canyon was once frequented by birdwatchers and naturalists, as well as hikers and fossil hunters.

Recreational ORV usage of Dove Springs Canyon began in 1965 and became progressively heavier in the ensuing years. By 1971, the Canyon was being used intensively by ORV enthusiasts. It became especially popular because the site's diverse terrain, coupled with relatively easy access, provides outstanding hill-climbing opportunities. By 1979, up to 200 vehicles used the Canyon on a typical weekend; over 500 vehicles used it on a holiday weekend. In 1973, the BLM adopted the Interim Critical Management Program for Recreational Vehicle Use on the California Desert ("Interim Program") which designated Dove Springs Canyon as an ORV Open Area, permitting recreational vehicle travel in the area without restriction.

Extensive ORV usage has been accompanied by severe environmental damage in the form of major surface erosion, soil compaction, and heavy loss of vegetation. The visual aesthetics have markedly declined. The character of the Canyon has been so severely altered that the

FIGURE 24-2
ORV use on public lands. This ridge in California's Jawbone Canyon has been stripped of vegetation by heavy ORV recreational use. The plume of dust marks the uphill run of an all-terrain motorcycle. In the desert, even in cases of low-volume ORV use, noise levels can be deafening, and the tire track ruts made by one machine in one 15-minute run through the fragile ecology of the desert floor may remain visible for more than 50 years.

© 1989 HOWARD WILSHIRE

Canyon is now used almost exclusively for ORV activities.

In July of 1980 Sierra Club petitioned the Secretary of the Interior to close Dove Springs Canyon to ORV use under the authority of Executive Order No. 11644 as amended by Executive Order No. 11989, because of "substantial adverse effects" on the vegetation, soil and wildlife in the Canyon. The Secretary responded that the matter would be addressed in the California Desert Conservation Plan and Final Environmental Impact Statement ("the Final Plan").

The Final Plan approved by the Secretary in December 1980 maintained unrestricted ORV use in Dove Springs of 3000 of the 5500 acres. Sierra Club filed this action on January 6, 1981, alleging that the Secretary's failure to close Dove Springs violated Executive Order No. 11644, as amended by Executive Order No. 11989, and FLPMA §1732(b), which requires the Secretary to prevent "unnecessary or undue degradation of the lands;" and §§1781(b) and (d), which require the Secretary to maintain and conserve resources of the Desert Area under principles of "multiple use and sustained yield."...

The Secretary interprets "considerable adverse effect" to require determining what is "considerable" in the context of the Desert Area as a whole, not merely on a parcel-by-parcel basis. The Secretary contends such a broad interpretation is necessary and is consistent with

§1781(a)(4) which expresses a congressional judgment that ORV use is to be permitted "where appropriate."

Sierra Club argues against the Secretary's interpretation. Sierra Club contends that the interpretation of the Executive Orders set forth by the Council on Environmental Quality (CEQ) in its August 1, 1977 memorandum is entitled to great deference, and that the CEQ's interpretation requires the closure of the canyon. This argument fails on two grounds.

First, the CEQ's interpretation of the Executive Order does not directly conflict with the Secretary's interpretation of the regulation. While it states that "the term 'considerable' should be liberally construed to provide the broadest possible protection reasonably required by this standard," it does not purport to decide whether the term "considerable adverse effects" should be analyzed in the context of the entire Desert Area, or on a site-specific basis. Moreover, the memorandum acknowledges that the responsibility for closing particular areas rests with "responsible federal officials in the field" "[b]ased on their practical experience in the management of the public lands, and their first-hand knowledge of conditions 'on-the-ground.'"

Second, the authority of the CEQ is to maintain a continuing review of the implementation of the Executive Order. The authority of the Secretary, on the other hand, is to promulgate regulations to provide for "administrative designation of the specific areas and trails on public lands on which the use of off-road vehicles may be permitted, and areas in which the use of off-road vehicles may not be permitted." Discretion rests with the Secretary, therefore, to determine whether and to what extent specific areas should be closed to ORV use. Thus, it is the Secretary's interpretation which is entitled to our deference.

Sierra Club argues that even if the CEQ's interpretation of the closure standard is not controlling, the Secretary's interpretation should not be adopted because it is unreasonable. Sierra Club insists that the sacrifice of any area to permanent resource damage is not justified under the multiple use management mandate of §1702(c) that requires multiple use "without permanent impairment of the productivity of the land and the quality of the environment." In further support of its position Sierra Club adverts to the requirement in the Act that the Secretary prevent "unnecessary and undue degradation" of the public lands. In addition, Sierra Club contends, when Congress established the Desert Area it intended the Secretary to fashion a multiple use and sustained yield management plan "to conserve [the California Desert] resources for future generations, and to provide present and future use and enjoyment, particularly outdoor recreational uses, including the use, where appropriate, of off-road recreational vehicles." Sierra Club argues that it is unreasonable for the Secretary to find ORV use "appropriate" when that use violates principles of sustained yield, substantially impairs productivity of renewable resources and is inconsistent with maintenance of environmental quality.

We can appreciate the earnestness and force of Sierra Club's position, and if we could write on a clean slate, would prefer a view which would disallow the virtual sacrifice of a priceless natural area in order to accommodate a special recreational activity. But we are not free to ignore the mandate which Congress wrote into the Act. Sierra Club's interpretation of the regulation would inevitably result in the total prohibition of ORV use because it is doubtful that any discrete area could withstand unrestricted ORV use without considerable adverse effects. However appealing might be such a resolution of the environmental dilemma, Congress has found that ORV use, damaging as it may be, is to be provided "where appropriate." It left determination of appropriateness largely up to the Secretary in an area of sharp conflict. If there is to be a change it must come by way of Congressional reconsideration. The Secretary's interpretation that this legislative determination calls for accommodation of ORV usage in the administrative plan, we must conclude, is not unreasonable and we are constrained to let it stand....

Under the California Desert Conservation Area Plan, approximately 4 percent (485,000 acres) of the total acreage is now open to unrestricted ORV use. Dove Springs itself constitutes only 0.025 percent of BLM administered lands in the Desert Area. Although all parties recognize that the environmental impact of ORV use at Dove Springs is severe, the Secretary's determination that these effects were not "considerable" in the context of the Desert Area as a whole is not arbitrary, capricious, or an abuse of the broad discretion committed to him by an obliging Congress....

COMMENTARY & QUESTIONS

1. **Straw man in the desert.** Do you agree that application of the closure standard to specific portions of the desert, rather than the Desert Area as a whole, would inevitably result in the total prohibition of ORV use in violation of statute? Doesn't this argument assume that there are no qualitative differences among desert sections? Indeed, Sierra Club was arguing that Dove Springs had been a unique ecological resource. (Note the poignancy of the court's use of the past tense in "the Canyon was once frequented by birdwatchers, naturalists, hikers, and fossil hunters.") Do you think that the court might have been implicitly reacting to a perception that the Canyon was already too degraded to support its erstwhile uses?

2. **Another look at multiple use-sustained yield.** Is the *Dove Springs* case simply another indication that the ambiguous multiple use-sustained yield management standard, when added to the deferential "arbitrary and capricious" standard of judicial review (see Chapter 7), places virtually no legal restrictions on federal land managers? Should courts begin to enforce FLPMA's "nonimpairment" and "prevention of unnecessary and undue degradation" criteria in allegedly clear cases such as *Dove Springs*? See Southern Utah Wilderness Alliance v. Norton, 301 F.3d 1217 (10th Cir. 2002), cert. granted, 2003 WL 21691792 (federal court has jurisdiction to determine whether BLM is not properly managing ORV use in Wilderness Study Areas in violation of FLPMA's nonimpairment mandate). Of course, Congress can resolve the problem by clarifying preferable land uses in particular areas.

3. **The enforcement problem.** No public lands management directive can be meaningful if the management agency lacks the resources to enforce it:

> The BLM lacks sufficient personnel to police its domain in anything more than a cursory fashion. Some range managers, for instance, are individually responsible for overseeing activities on a million or more acres. The offenses by nonpermittees — such as taking off-road vehicles into closed areas — are likely to go unpunished for that reason and because the relative triviality of the transgression will discourage use of the prosecutorial apparatus. Coggins IV at 30.

Does the ORV lobby campaign for or against greater funding for BLM enforcement? Can the BLM plead lack of resources as a defense to an action to compel it to perform its FLPMA duties?[40]

Nonenforcement of public land law is a chronic problem with regard to federal landholdings in the West. Illicit activities, such as timber theft, marijuana cultivation,

---

40. See NRDC v. Morton, 388 F. Supp. 829 (D.D.C. 1974), where the court rejected BLM's pleas of poverty in a NEPA case.

unpermitted residences and roads, and unauthorized removal of archaeological relics, as well as illegal ORV use, abound on the public lands. Is the apparent inability of the federal land management agencies to police their lands one reason to either privatize those lands or else allow the states to manage them?

4. **ORVs in the national parks.** The NPS operates with a mixed mandate, to "promote and regulate the use of the Federal areas known as national parks, monuments, and reservations" in order to "conserve the scenery and the natural and historic objects and the wild life therein and to provide for the enjoyment of the same in such manner and by such means as will leave them unimpaired for the enjoyment of future generations." 16 U.S.C. §1. Although the NPS is considered to have a "single use" mission to administer the public lands under its jurisdiction for public recreation, the tension between "promotion" and "regulation" forces the NPS to choose or mediate between users contending for incompatible high- and low-intensity recreational opportunities. This conflict is often reflected in lawsuits contesting "overcommercialization" of national parks.[41]

The NPS has also been involved in ORV litigation, particularly with regard to ORV use in the Cape Cod National Seashore in Massachusetts. In Conservation Law Found. v. Secretary of the Interior, 864 F.2d 954 (1st Cir. 1989), the ORV component of the NPS's Management Plan for the seashore was upheld against claims that it violated the Cape Cod National Seashore Act and the ORV-related executive orders. Obviously impressed by the NPS's environmental research and consequent limitations on ORV routes, the court held that NPS's ORV policy was not arbitrary and capricious or a violation of the Act. The court noted that "the National Park Service has added a number of rangers to improve patrol of the seashore." A contrasting result was reached in Southern Utah Wilderness Alliance v. NPS, 222 F.3d 819 (10th Cir. 2000), where the appellate court reversed and remanded a district court holding that NPS violated federal law in declining to close a streamside road in Canyonlands National Park to ORVs; the court of appeals ruled that the administrative record did not support a conclusion that ORV use would cause permanent impairment of park resources.

Snowmobile use in national parks has become a highly contentious conservation issue. In 2000, under the Clinton Administration, after almost a hundred hearings with several thousand witnesses (most supporting closure), the NPS banned snowmobile use from nearly 30 national parks, recreation areas, and monuments where snowmobiles had previously been permitted. Yellowstone and Grand Teton National Parks — the pinnacle experiences for snowmobilers — were included in the ban. In 2002, the Bush II Administration nullified the NPS's prohibition of snowmobile use in Yellowstone and Grand Teton National Parks.[42] Approximately 1200 snowmobiles would be allowed to enter these parks each day during the 2003–2004 winter seasons. Of these snowmobiles, 80% would be required to be led by commercial guides; the rest

---

41. See, e.g., Friends of Yosemite v. Frizzel, 420 F. Supp. 390 (N.D. Cal. 1976) (plaintiffs' allegation that NPS was breaching the public trust by overcommercializing Yosemite National Park rejected because NPS had not violated a statutory duty).

42. In late 2003 the Administration's action was at least temporarily suspended by federal court litigation. See Fund for Animals, et al. v. Norton, Civ. Action No. 02-2367EGS (D. D.C., Dec. 16, 2003).

would require certifications and reservations. Park areas would be zoned for maximum daily numbers of snowmobiles. All snowmobiles entering these parks would be required to include the best available technology, defined as cleaner-burning four-stroke engines. Is this a workable compromise between two types of recreationists? The new engines are indeed less noisy and polluting than their two-stroke predecessors, but even these new snowmobiles are capable of disturbing wildlife and nonmotorized human enjoyment of park resources. Would the zoning, certification, and escort rules minimize potential conflicts? Are these restrictions enforceable? If so, would they be effectively enforced? In 2003 the Bush Administration regulations embodying these new snowmobile policies were struck down as arbitrary and capricious and violations of NEPA. Fund for Animals v. Norton, 294 F. Supp. 2d 92 (D. D.C. 2003).

The NPS and the USFS have also banned personal watercraft ("jetskis," "jetboats") in 21 National Recreation Areas. See Hells Canyon Alliance v. USFS, 227 F.3d 1170 (9th Cir. 2000) (USFS did not act arbitrarily and capriciously in approving a jetboat ban for three days every other week on the Snake River in Hells Canyon National Recreation Area).

E. PUBLIC LANDS AND RESOURCES PLANNING

Increasingly, statutory planning processes are becoming the locus of public resources management on the federal lands. FLPMA and the National Forest Management Act (NFMA) require formal, participatory land use planning, and the resulting plans are legally binding because on-the-ground-management decisions must be consistent with the adopted plans.[43] Under NFMA,[44] the USFS must prepare Land and Resource Management Plans (LRMPs) for all national forests:

> The LRMP defines the "management direction" for the forest. It constitutes a program for all natural resource management activities and establishes management requirements to be employed in implementing the plan. It identifies the resource management practices, the projected levels of production of goods and services, and the location where various types of resource management may occur. Implementation of the LRMP is achieved through individual site-specific projects and all projects must be consistent with the LRMP. 16 U.S.C. §1604, 36 C.F.R. §219.

But, as the following case indicates, if natural resources planning is to be truly participatory and unbiased, it must not be a post hoc rationalization of previously determined agency policies.

Sierra Club v. Thomas
United States Court of Appeals for the Sixth Circuit, 1997
105 F.3d 248, reversed for lack of ripeness, 523 U.S. 726 (1998)

BOYCE F. MARTIN, JR., C.J.... The Sierra Club and Citizens Council on Conservation and Environmental Control appeal the district court's order granting summary judgment to Jack

---

43. See the discussions of the Coastal Zone Management Act and the Wild and Scenic Rivers Act in Chapter 25 for other examples of "consistency clauses."

44. NFMA planning will be primarily discussed in this section because it has evolved much further than FLPMA planning by the BLM.

Ward Thomas, Chief of the United States Forest Service, and officials of the United States Forest Service, pursuant to the district court's review of the Land and Resource Management Plan for the Wayne National Forest. For the reasons described below, we reverse and remand this matter to the district court for further proceedings consistent with this opinion.

In 1988, the regional forester for the Eastern Division of the United States Forest Service issued a decision, pursuant to the National Forest Management Act, adopting a ten-year plan for Ohio's Wayne National Forest. The plan designated 126,107 acres of the Wayne from which timber could be removed or cut. During the ten-year life of the plan, 7.5 million board feet of timber could be cut per year. The plan designated that eighty percent of all timbering techniques would be "even-aged" management, a harvest technique aimed at creating a regeneration of trees which are essentially the same age. In almost all cases, the even-aged management contemplated clearcutting of the timber. Clearcutting involves the removal of all trees within areas ranging in size from fifteen to thirty acres, and is thus a very sensitive public issue. The Sierra Club appealed the regional forester's decision to the chief of the Forest Service pursuant to the applicable regulations. In 1990, the chief of the Forest Service denied the Sierra Club's appeal and affirmed the plan....

The National Forest Management Act was enacted as a direct result of congressional concern for Forest Service clearcutting practices and the dominant role timber production has historically played in Forest Service policies. Congress was concerned that, if left to its own essentially unbridled devices, the Forest Service would manage the national forests as mere monocultural "tree farms." Procedurally, the Act requires the Forest Service to develop Land and Resource Management Plans for the national forests. This formal planning process was designed to curtail agency discretion and to ensure forest preservation and productivity. Substantively, the Act imposes extensive limitations on timber harvesting by restricting the use of clearcutting to situations in which clearcutting is the optimum method for harvesting....

The Sierra Club contends that the even-aged logging agenda is illegal in that the Forest Service has not complied with the constraints on its choice of even-aged management techniques contained in the National Forest Management Act [because the Forest Service is biased in favor of clearcutting]....

Although it would be impractical to set forth the details of the administrative record here, one example of bias [in favor of clearcutting] is particularly illustrative. The Forest Service argues that its even-aged management plan is based on evidence that timbering will provide new opportunities for recreation that will, in turn, preserve and enhance the diversity of plant and animal communities in the Wayne National Forest. Most recreation does not require timber harvesting, however. Further, as the Forest Service's own records reflect, the Wayne is surrounded by and intermingled with privately-held land which already contains an abundance of diverse plant and animal life. Timbering simply does not promote the kind of recreational activities that are in demand in the Wayne; in fact, recreation like fishing and hiking is harmed by clearcutting. The planners also failed to recognize that cutting is unlikely to stimulate new and valuable forms of recreation because much of the Wayne has already been cut or developed. In that particular environment, clearcutting loses its value.

The National Forest Management Act mandates that the Service ensure that even-aged management practices be used in the national forests only when "consistent with the protection of soil, watershed, fish, wildlife, recreation, and aesthetic resources, and the regeneration of the timber resource." 16 U.S.C. §1604(g)(3)(F)(v). The National Forest Management Act thus contemplates that even-aged management techniques will be used only in exceptional circumstances. Yet, the defendants would utilize even-aged management logging as if it were the statutory rule, rather than the exception. By arbitrarily undervaluing the recreational value of wilderness, the Forest Service created a very distorted picture of the Wayne National Forest. Based on false premises such as these, the Forest Service improperly concluded that clearcutting was necessary.

It is not surprising that the Forest Service came to this conclusion. Created, in part, to ensure a reliable timber supply, the Forest Service has a history of preferring timber production to other uses. Rather than being a neutral process which determines how the national forests can best meet the needs of the American people, forest planning, as practiced by the Forest Service, is a political process replete with opportunities for the intrusion of bias and abuse. Because national forests are located near rural communities, foresters make management decisions to support perceived needs in the communities. By sharing timber proceeds with those communities, the Forest Service strengthens the link between timber sales and the livelihoods of local constituencies. See, Office of Technology Assessment, Forest Service Planning: Accommodating Uses, Producing Outputs, and Sustaining Ecosystems 46 (1992). The resulting dependency of these communities on timber production causes over-harvesting and destructive harvesting methods. The relationship of the Forest Service to the timber industry also constrains the Forest Service's planning freedom. Rural constituencies reliant on timber sale revenues may provoke politicians to place pressure on the Forest Service to sustain that revenue. Consequently, the Forest Service becomes trapped: cutting off timber sales would cause loss of employment and revenue in local communities but continued timber sales risk over-harvesting and below-cost sales.

The Forest Service budgeting process, which allows the Forest Service to keep a percentage of the funds it realizes from timber sales, provides an incentive for the Forest Service to sell timber below cost or at a loss. See Randal O'Toole, Reforming the Forest Service 122 (1988). Also, to maximize its budget, the Forest Service uses expensive timber management and reforestation techniques, such as clearcutting. Again, conflicting interests lead to perverse results: clearcutting provides the Forest Service with a higher congressional subsidy because the Forest Service can request preparation and administrative costs. Consequently, decisions may be made, not because they are in the best interest of the American people but because they benefit the Forest Service's fiscal interest.

Each of these biases undermines even the facial neutrality of the National Forest Management Act. Even when there may be more valuable uses for the land, the above biases and constraints cause the Forest Service to manage primarily to maximize timber outputs....

BATCHELDER, C.J., concurring. ...I write separately because, while I, too, have serious questions and concerns about the management practices and policies of the Forest Service, I do not believe that the majority's largely undocumented broadside against the Forest Service is appropriate. The issue before us is simply whether the Plan was properly promulgated within the appropriate exercise of the agency's discretion and is therefore within the law. We conclude that it is not. Our speculation about the motives and biases of the Forest Service, even if accurate, is unnecessary, and therefore, ought not to be voiced in this opinion.

COMMENTARY & QUESTIONS

1. **"Garbage in, garbage out" planning.** In Citizens for Envtl. Quality v. United States, 731 F. Supp. 970 (D. Colo. 1989), the court threw out a LRMP based on a computer model (FORPLAN) containing artificially limited alternatives:

> From the record, it appears that the Forest Service first established production goals, and then formulated alternatives which would reach those goals through employing data constraints.... We find that this result-based decision making process prevented the Forest Service from establishing a legitimately broad range

of reasonable alternatives as required by the statutory and regulatory scheme....
Defendants' range of alternatives cannot be said to reflect a wide range of goals
since the proposed alternatives each contemplate timber production at a highly
unprofitable level. A broad range of alternatives must also include an alternative
which contemplates timber harvesting at a profitable level even if that level
requires reducing current timber production goals.... From its evaluation, it is clear
that the Forest Service gave a "hard look" only to those alternatives which increased
timber production. 731 F. Supp. at 989–990.

Another variety of "garbage-in, garbage-out" planning occurs when an agency neglects
to compile the data necessary to make a key planning decision. See, e.g., Sierra Club v.
USFS, 168 F.3d 1 (11th Cir.), reh'g denied, 131 F.3d 11 (1999) (USFS approved timber
sales without gathering and considering population data on management indicator
species in violation of the LRMP). Neighbors of Cuddy Mountain v. USFS, 137 F.3d 1372
(9th Cir. 1998), is only one of several federal circuit court decisions holding that USFS
timber sales were inconsistent with applicable LRMPs.

2. **The planning "shell game."** Professor Robert Feller, a keen observer of BLM grazing
management practices, comments that

> Concerned citizens and environmental organizations who urge BLM and the
> Forest Service to assess the appropriateness of grazing on particular parcels of
> public lands find themselves engaged in a bureaucratic shell game in which the
> agencies avoid the issue by sliding it back and forth between their land use planning
> processes and their decision making processes for individual grazing allotments.
> When citizens request that a land use plan include a review of the appropriateness
> of grazing on particular sites or allotments within a planning area, they are typi-
> cally informed that the land use planning process is not designed to address such
> site-specific issues, and that they should raise the issue when allotment manage-
> ment plans (AMPs) are developed for the allotments in question. However, when
> the issue is raised during the development of an AMP or the issuance of a permit
> for an allotment, the agency responds that it is a land use planning issue that should
> have been raised during the development of the applicable land use plan. In fact,
> the issue is never addressed, and grazing continues without ever being seriously
> questioned. Feller, 'Til the Cows Come Home: The Fatal Flaw in the Clinton
> Administration's Public Lands Grazing Policy, 25 Envtl. L. 703, 748 (1995).

At least one federal circuit court has made this shell game even more difficult to win by
denying standing to environmental groups to contest an LRMP because the mere existence of an LRMP, as opposed to a proposal for a site-specific action, does not produce
an imminent injury in fact. Sierra Club v. USFS, 28 F.3d 753 (8th Cir. 1994). This harsh
standing rule has been rejected by the Sixth, Seventh, and Ninth Circuits.[45]

3. **The Aftermath of Sierra Club v. Thomas.** On certiorari the U.S. Supreme Court
vacated the override of the Wayne Forest Plan on pure ripeness grounds. In the Court's
view, the LRMP was not ripe for review because it did not inflict present significant
practical harm on the Sierra Club's interests. Before the USFS permits logging it must

---

45. The court in the principal case above rejected this argument. See also Resources Ltd. v. Robertson, 8 F.3d 1394
(9th Cir. 1993), and Sierra Club v. USFS, 46 F.3d 606 (7th Cir. 1995) ("if the Sierra Club had to wait until the
project level to address general procedural injuries regarding a broad issue like biological diversity, implementation of the forest plan might have progressed too far to permit proper redress").

comply with NEPA and allow public participation, and a court can then review a more specific proposal; with more time, the USFS may correct its own mistakes in implementing the plan; and the Plan is still too abstract for judicial review. Does the Supreme Court ignore the tendency of USFS plans to become "self-fulfilling prophecies" by concretizing agency attitudes and clientele expectations? If a plan is facially illegal, why should it not be immediately invalidated before it causes wasteful sunk costs? Moreover, does this Supreme Court decision place a premium on planning vagueness? If a plan is sufficiently indefinite, it cannot be directly violated and thus may not be ripe for review. Should a reviewing court adopt a compromise position, dismissing generic plan challenges but allowing allegations relating to site-specific injuries caused by plan defects? See Wilderness Soc'y v. USFS, 188 F.3d 1130 (9th Cir. 1999). See also Southern Utah Wilderness Alliance v. Norton, 301 F.3d 1217 (10th Cir. 2002), cert. granted, 2003 WL 21691792. (BLM must carry out specific activities — i.e., monitoring for excessive ORV use and developing ORV management plans — that are promised in Land Use Plans.)

The Sixth Circuit majority opinion in Sierra Club v. Thomas remains a probing criticism of USFS management of logging in national forests. It illuminates administrative realities that have long undercut the civic conservation mandate of government agencies trying to regulate natural resource industries and underscores the need for rational reform of natural resource conservation programs. Only time will tell whether the new natural resources planning processes will bring modern resource management rationality to the public lands or, on the other hand, promote business-as-usual under a different guise.

4. **Theoretical dilemmas underlying public resource management.** This chapter does not provide clear answers to the generic questions with which it began: Are public resources a continuing legacy or current profit-maximizers, assigned to single or multiple uses, to be used for local or nationwide benefit, precluding or harmonizing various competing interests? Statutes such as the Wilderness Act and FLPMA attempt to establish long-term basic principles to guide resource management, which inevitably collide with the pressures of economic interests that focus, as we all do, on the short-term specific.

It doesn't make much difference to the mayor of a small Northwest logging town whether the surrounding mountains are public or private; the old growth forests that remain there are a source for a half dozen more years of economic life for the community on the only terms that are available — clearcutting according to prevailing corporate practice. For as long as these last forests are allowed to be cut, by just so long will local citizens be able to pay their mortgages and taxes and avoid having to go on welfare or move away. The practices of the timber industry, and its failures to implement successful long-term renewable, sustainable timber supply, are matters beyond the control of the community.

What is lost when an ancient forest is gone, beyond a localized depreciation of natural environment? Are there public losses other than those that occur in terms of recreation, tourism, water quality, etc.? What exactly was the value of the old Methusaleh tree in

Chapter 22? Such questions become even more abstract when it isn't the oldest single tree or the last carrier pigeon, but thousands of acres comprising the last 5% of our original natural forest — or when human actions do not destroy the resource but change its setting. Joe Sax once was startled as he climbed up a tortuous ridge in Tennessee to look out over a sprawling, forested, mountain-girded gulf in the Great Smokies National Park, to see a white high-rise Sheraton hotel thrusting up in the middle distance of the valley, built on an inholding within the Park. See J. Sax, Mountains Without Handrails: Reflections on the National Parks (1980); Helpless Giants: The National Parks and the Regulation of Private Lands, 75 Mich. L. Rev. 239 (1976). Like the tower at the Gettysburg battlefield, what kind of experiential or aesthetic issues did this commercial intrusion raise? What is a "wilderness experience"?

Or, for another situation raising a composite of these issues, consider the reintroduction of wolves, grizzlies, and other endangered predator species to areas from which they had previously been exterminated. Montana, Wyoming, Minnesota, and other northern tier states have seen a number of attempts to restore large predators on public lands, especially national parks. For ranchers grazing cattle on nearby public and private rangelands, these ecological experiments represent the height of public policy folly. Keiter & Holscher, Wolf Recovery under the Endangered Species Act: A Study in Contemporary Federalism, 11 Public Land L. Rev. 19 (1990). Killing bears, mountain lions, and wolves seems to be an atavistic human instinct, coupled with a farmer's vivid sense of emotional and economic injury upon finding a calf slaughtered in an early morning meadow. Doesn't a policy to bring back the predators seem irrational? To shoot the animal that killed your calf, however, runs the risk of fine and imprisonment.

At the very least we owe future generations an attempt to clarify what our national public resources policies are.

5. **The Bush II Administration's public land policies.** The Administration of President George W. Bush undertook a dramatic shift in resource policy, returning to 1950s notions of the primacy of extractive industry and high-intensity recreational uses on the public lands. President Bush appointed individuals who had been closely associated with industry to lead the federal land management agencies: Secretary of the Interior Gale Norton, who had served under James Watt during the Reagan Administration; William Geary Myers III, an attorney for the livestock industry, as Solicitor General at Interior; Stephen Griles, an attorney for the mining industry, as head of Interior's Office of Surface Mining; and Mark Rey, a lobbyist for the timber industry, as Chief of the Forest Service. Vice President Cheney, a former industry CEO, has been active as President Bush's chief spokesperson on energy and natural resource matters.

As for public land law, the Interior Department suspended the effectiveness of regulations promulgated during the Clinton Administration that would have established stricter environmental protection standards for hard-rock mining on federal lands. DOI officials attempted to block the phase-out of snowmobile use in Yellowstone and Grand Teton National Parks, suspended the grizzly bear reintroduction program in Idaho, advocated petroleum extraction in the Arctic National Wildlife Refuge, moved to terminate the congressional moratorium on oil drilling on the outer continental shelf, expedited petroleum extraction on other federal lands, refused to list species or critical habitat under the ESA, vacated critical habitat designations for Pacific Salmon, recommended weakening amendments to ESA and NEPA, and opposed Wilderness Act designations in Utah.

In most of its initiatives undercutting natural resource protections, however, the Bush II Administration chose to use administrative rather than legislative means, often in low-profile actions that would move under the radar. A favorite strategem has been, actively or passively, to encourage industries to attack existing federal regulations in court, then either decline to defend the regulations or acquiesce in capitulative settlements. The USFS and the DOJ, for instance, refused to defend against or appeal a federal district court's timber industry injunction invalidating the Clinton Administration's "Roadless Rule" (prohibiting further road construction in national forests).[46] Only because conservation group intervenors stepped in to defend the federal regulation did it survive on appeal. After the Roadless Rule was upheld by the Ninth Circuit, however, the USFS transferred decisions regarding national forest roadbuilding to traditionally pro-development state governors. The USFS has also advocated increased logging in Spotted Owl reserves, in allegedly fire-prone areas in the unique Tongass National Forest in Alaska, and in "salvage logging" situations. Perhaps most important to the long-term integrity of the public lands, the Bush II Administration has attempted to minimize the importance of climate change, and refused to participate in international agreements that would address this issue (see Chapter 26).

Will these Bush II Administration policies be politically acceptable in a West that is changing demographically and economically, where outdoor recreation is frequently considered more valuable than logging, mining, and cattle grazing, or where the solitude provided by low-intensity recreation is often prized more highly than the thrill of motorized pastimes?

6. **Public resources in the nation's waters.** Though this chapter focuses on land-based resources, it is worth noting that most of the resource management issues raised here are also encountered when the question is exploitation of the nation's waters and water-based resources. Water law is an intricately structured and evolving management system for a natural resource that is highly valued, though differently, in the nation's East and West. See J. Sax, B. Thompson, J. Leshy & R. Abrams, Legal Control of Water Resources (3d ed. 2000). As to fisheries, Garrett Hardin wrote in The Tragedy of the Commons that "the oceans of the world continue to suffer from the survival of the philosophy of the commons.... Professing to believe in the 'inexhaustable resources of the oceans,' [we] bring species after species of fish and whales closer to extinction."[47] The difficulties of managing fish stocks and other resources in coastal waters, lakes, and

---

46. See Kootenai v. Veneman, 313 F.3d 1094 (9th Cir. 2002). In this case, the federal government sent an attorney to the trial court, but had him sit in the back of the room as an "observer," not entering an appearance in defense of the regulation as the Boise Cascade lawyers attacked the regulation for insufficient compliance with NEPA. If the judge had not permitted intervention by the citizens' groups, would there have been sufficient representation of a case or controversy to ground Article III federal jurisdiction, or would collusion between the industry and the Administration, with no one defending the targeted regulations, nullify the court's ability to hear the case?

47. Hardin, The Tragedy of the Commons, 162 Sci. 1243, 1245 (1968).

rivers are far more complex than, for example, managing forest resources. You can see and count trees, monitor where they have been cut down, and visually trace the consequences of logging upon surrounding slopes and streams. The process of logging is not a free-for-all where hundreds of loggers have equal access to cut and haul away the resource day or night, and the entities that cut trees are relatively easy to identify and track. By comparison, most bodies of water veil their resources and the process of harvesting them beyond the normal realm of visibility, with management regulations extremely difficult to design and enforce. For an introduction to the fascinating legal dilemmas involved in attempts to restore and sustain fisheries stocks for future generations, see Daniel Pauly and Jay MacLean, In a Perfect Ocean (2003); the Tulane Environmental Law Review Symposium: The Magnuson Fishery Conservation and Management Act — Retrospect and Prospect, 9 Tul. Envtl. L.J. 211–596 (1996); and the Sustainable Fisheries Act of 1996, 16 U.S.C. §1855(h).

As the man said, "Money can always wait."

— Joseph Sax, Defending the Environment, 51 (1970).

We don't want to be a regulatory agency. We want to be a development agency on our national lands.

— Secretary of Interior Manuel Lujan,
speaking to coal executives, N.Y. Times,
29 Nov. 1992 at 30.

It is vain to dream of a wilderness distant from ourselves.

— Henry David Thoreau

Chapter 25

LAND USE-BASED ENVIRONMENTAL PROTECTION STATUTES

A. *The Federal Coastal Zone Management Act*
B. *State Hazardous Waste Facility Siting Statutes*
C. *Critical Area Protection Statutes*
D. *Comprehensive State and Regional Planning and Management*
E. *Traditional Land Use Controls and the Environment: Zoning, Subdivision Regulation, et al.*
F. *The "Smart Growth" Movement and the Environment*

This chapter primarily deals with governmental environmental protection restrictions on private land. Every land use decision has environmental consequences; most environmental protection measures have land use consequences. In fact, it is probable that virtually all the environmental controversies reflected in this book are somehow based on land use decisions. The interrelationships between land use controls and environmental protection mechanisms are so strong that there can be no bright line between environmental law and land use law. In fact, it is not even clear that the two are separate fields.[1]

Although there may be no clear logical or legal distinction between land use and environmental regulation, there certainly is a palpable political distinction between the two. Poll after poll indicates that most people will accept painful sacrifices in the name of environmental protection, while they passionately resist added restrictions on the use of their land. Apparently many Americans do not perceive an inevitable linkage of environmental protection and land use regulation, and treat land purely as a commodity rather than as a natural economy as well. The result is "Sprawl." Sprawl is characterized by dispersed development outside of compact urban and village centers along highways and in the rural countryside, typically with dependency on the automobile, rapid consumption of land and resources, and designation of broad single uses of land within designated industrial, commercial, and residential zones. Nevertheless,

---

1. In California Coastal Comm'n v. Granite Rock Co., 480 U.S. 572 (1987), the Supreme Court awkwardly tried to articulate a distinction between land use regulation and environmental controls:

> The line between environmental regulation and land use planning will not always be bright.... Land use planning in essence chooses particular uses for the land; environmental regulation, at its core, does not mandate particular uses of the land but requires only that, however the land is used, damage to the environment is kept within prescribed limits.... Congress clearly envisioned that although environmental regulation and land use planning may hypothetically overlap in some instances, these two types of activity would in most cases be capable of differentiation. 480 U.S. at 587–588.

Justice Powell and Justice Stevens, however, found this distinction "unsupportable, either as an interpretation of the governing statutes or as a matter of logic..., a distinction...without a rational difference." 480 U.S. at 601, 603.

the increasingly popular "Smart Growth" Movement is pursuing alternatives to traditional, and in many ways environmentally deleterious, urban sprawl development.

The American attitude toward land use is unique. In other parts of the world, land development is not a right but a privilege. Land use decisions are often constrained by comprehensive land use plans that represent the interests of all members of the community, including, in some areas, nonhuman members. In the United States, by contrast, comprehensive land use planning, other than local zoning, is the exception rather than the rule. Governmental restrictions on the unfettered use of private land are strenuously resisted and command a significant degree of constitutional protection, as studied in Chapter 23. In order to avoid stigma, officials in environmental protection agencies at all levels of government often feel compelled to repeat the mantra that they are not regulating land use but protecting the environment. One challenge to environmental law in the twenty-first century will be to implement fair and reasonable systems of land use management without disrupting the powerful political consensus that has supported — against several strong political counterattacks — the manifold environmental improvements since 1970.

The more that environmental and natural resources management policy confronts the impacts of land use on environmental change, the more the area of land use becomes a necessary stage for future rational overview accounting of short- and long-term effects. For example, urban sprawl development takes a heavy toll on environmental quality, especially in coastal zones:

> A trend is emerging in both developed and developing countries: cities from Los Angeles to Jakarta, Indonesia, are rapidly expanding outward, consuming ever greater quantities of land. This urban sprawl, characterized by low-density development and vacant or derelict land, leads to the wasteful use of land resources, higher infrastructure costs, and excessive energy consumption and air pollution because of the greater use of motorized transport. Many criticize urban sprawl for aesthetic reasons as well.

> The United States provides an apt example. Urban population growth there has slowed to less than 1.3 percent per year, yet urban development continues to encroach on surrounding lands as residents abandon inner cities and move to the suburbs. The total amount of land dedicated to urban uses increased from 21 million hectares[2] in 1982 to 26 million hectares in 1992. In one decade, 2,085,945 hectares of forestland, 1,525,314 hectares of cultivated cropland, 943,598 hectares of pastureland, and 774,029 hectares of rangeland were converted to urban uses....

> Coastal ecosystems, including wetlands, tidal flats, salt-water marshes, mangrove swamps, and the flora and fauna that depend on them, are especially threatened by urban land conversion. Already, coastal urban centers are home to almost 1 billion people worldwide and are experiencing unprecedented growth. Much of this growth will take place in developing nations;...[but] even in developed countries such as the United States, some of the highest levels of urban growth are occurring in small coastal cities.[3] Accordingly, urban impacts along the coasts stand to increase markedly in the years ahead.

---

2. A hectare is equal to 2,471 acres. [Eds.]

3. Roughly 75% of the American population lives within 50 miles of an ocean or one of the Great Lakes. [Eds.]

In coastal cities, the higher value placed on shoreline locations increases the economic incentives to develop there. Thus, as coastal cities grow and expand, original coastal habitat is increasingly converted to other uses. Land conversion activities range from draining and filling of marshes and other wetlands to constructing homes or resorts on beaches or dunes, to building seawalls, to undertaking large-scale reclamation projects that extend the shoreline into the sea.... Along the San Francisco Bay, the most highly urbanized estuary in the United States, filling has reduced the areal extent of the bay by one third in the past 150 years. Of the estimated 80,940 hectares of coastal marshes that originally fringed San Francisco Bay, 80 percent have been lost to development. In addition to habitat loss, shoreline development can intensify coastal erosion, alter the hydrology of estuaries, and otherwise disrupt natural processes. The United Nations Environment Programme, World Resources 59–62 (1996).

Many of these urban developments are relatively small and ostensibly insignificant from an environmental standpoint, but when viewed cumulatively and synergistically with similar developments they may have major regional environmental impacts.[4]

Land use restrictions take a variety of forms, falling along a continuum — ranging from processes that raise a strong presumption of nondevelopment to processes that raise a strong presumption of development, with various intermediate gradations. Siting statutes, for example, presume that certain facilities should be sited but in a process that keeps social costs to a minimum. At the other end of the continuum, critical area protection statutes presume that no development should take place in particularly valuable and vulnerable areas unless it is clearly innocuous or else necessary to satisfy a paramount public purpose. Zoning acts and "cooperation" statutes, such as the Coastal Zone Management Act (CZMA) of 1972, 16 U.S.C. §§1451 et seq., fall somewhere between siting and critical area protection legislation on this continuum.

Local governments currently dominate the field of land use controls, using subdivision regulations and zoning. If one pictures land use as a pyramid, local zoning is its broad base; going upward, state land use laws are far fewer, and federal law governing private land use is at the narrow apex. Because this book focuses on legal process techniques, however, this chapter proceeds in inverse order, with local land use controls noted at the end of the chapter.

The CZMA is the first model analyzed, an interesting model of cooperative federalism that addresses both siting and critical area protection, but in a way that encourages state planning rather than imposing federal regulation of private land use decisions. Next, state hazardous waste facility siting statutes are examined as examples of a type of siting process that has been popular, although fraught with major difficulties. Then several varieties of critical area protection statutes are presented: a site-specific permitting model (§404 of the CWA), a single-purpose regional model (the Federal Wild and Scenic Rivers Act), and a comprehensive regional model. Local zoning is then discussed as a means of achieving environmental protection. This chapter ends with an examination of the "Smart Growth" Movement, a set of principles and practices that is substantially changing American land development and management patterns.

---

4. There is a "nibbling effect" when a series of small projects add up to large cumulative impacts.

A. THE FEDERAL COASTAL ZONE MANAGEMENT ACT (CZMA)

Most federal environmental regulation affects the siting of new development and the protection of critical areas in some way. This influence is, for the most part, indirect and implicit. The "Nonattainment" and "PSD" (Prevention of Significant Deterioration) sections of the CAA, for example, provide general rules for attaining and maintaining federally specified ambient air quality standards in particular areas. States then determine the mix of sources that will be permitted to use the available assimilative capacities of the relevant airsheds (see Chapter 11). Similarly, federal water pollution control law requires states to prevent degradation of high-quality waterbodies, but a state may choose to allow lower water quality where "necessary to accommodate important economic or social development" unless Outstanding National Resource Waters are involved. States may also be required to restrict growth in heavily polluted areas where water quality standards are being violated (see Chapter 12). Only rarely, however, does the federal government directly control private land use decisions, as in the ESA (Chapter 16) and in §404 of the CWA (see below). Significantly, it is these direct federal restrictions on private land use that evoke the most highly charged political reactions to federal protection of the environment.

Congress's reluctance to confront private land use explicitly and directly is a function not only of the American public's apparent aversion to land use control, but also of Congress's deference to the traditional state police power to regulate private land use for the public health, safety, and welfare. Under the Tenth Amendment to the U.S. Constitution, all powers not specifically delegated to the federal government or denied to the states are reserved to the states. This fundamental principle of federalism incorporates the state police power over private land use, and the federal government has always trod lightly in this area. Only when other public interests have become compelling has Congress enlisted constitutional powers, such as the Commerce Clause, in aid of regulating land use, albeit indirectly most of the time.

The federal Coastal Zone Management Act (CZMA), 16 U.S.C. §1451 et seq. 1972 does not authorize federal land use controls, but it is explicitly land use legislation. It is fundamentally a planning statute in that it authorizes federal matching grants for the purpose of assisting coastal states, including Great Lakes states, in the development of management programs for the land and water resources of their coastal zones. The CZMA attempts to assure implementation of state coastal management programs in two ways: (1) authorizing the suspension of federal funding if a coastal state fails to adhere to its management program; and (2) mandating that any federal activity within a state's coastal zone be consistent with that state's approved coastal management program. In the following excerpt, Professor J. B. Ruhl summarizes the CZMA and argues that it is an example of a "Cooperation" strategy that is preferable to both the "Coercion" approach (e.g., the ESA and §404) and the "Coordination" model (e.g., NEPA) for the conservation of biodiversity.

**J. B. Ruhl, Biodiversity Conservation and the Ever-Expanding Web of Federal Laws
Regulating Nonfederal Lands: Time for Something Completely Different?**
66 University of Colorado Law Review 555, 616–623 (1995)

The CZMA was enacted in 1972 to promote the "national interest in the effective management, beneficial use, protection, and development of the coastal zone." Ecological protection was paramount among the concerns Congress expressed as reason for addressing the "increasing and competing demands upon the lands and waters of our coastal zone."... Hence, Congress stated as its principal goal for the CZMA "to preserve, protect, develop, and where possible, to restore or enhance, the resources of the Nation's coastal zone for this and succeeding generations."

The approach Congress took in the CZMA, however, is decidedly different from the regulatory structures of the Endangered Species act and §404 of the Clean Water Act. Congress was convinced that "[t]he key to more effective protection and use of the land and water resources of the coastal zone is to encourage the states to exercise their full authority over the lands and waters in the coastal zone." The CZMA does this by establishing a method by which the states, in cooperation with federal and local governments, can establish "unified policies, criteria, standards, methods, and processes for dealing with land and water use decisions of more than local significance." The two CZMA programs for carrying out that objective are the development and approval of coastal management plans ("CMP"s) and the review of federal actions for consistency with established CMPs.

Sections 305 and 306 of the CZMA provide federal grants to the...coastal states for developing and implementing their CMPs. A CMP must be consistent with guidelines established by the Secretary of Commerce, which must require "identification of the means by which the State proposes to exert control over the land uses and water uses" and the "priorities of uses in particular areas." A state's CMP development must be conducted "with the opportunity of full participation by relevant [governmental agencies and private persons]" and must provide "an effective mechanism for continuing consultation and coordination" between those entities. The CMP must define permissible land and water uses in the coastal zone and identify in that regard "areas of particular concern." The CMP also must demonstrate that land and water uses can be controlled and coordinated through either state establishment of standards for local implementation, direct state regulation, state review of all state, local, and private development proposals for consistency with the CMP, or a combination of those three general approaches.

The Secretary's CZMA regulations, promulgated through the National Oceanic and Atmospheric Administration ("NOAA"), elaborate on each of those key statutory elements for CMP development and approval. Significantly, NOAA's rules for special management areas address in detail the "areas of particular concern" feature of the CMP. NOAA's rules recognize that a state's set of controls for the coastal zone may vary throughout the zone in intensity, scope, and detail. NOAA requires that "[w]here these policies are limited and non-specific, greater emphasis should be placed on areas of particular concern [in the CMP] to assure effective management and an adequate degree of program specificity."...

Once a state's CMP is in place, the CZMA requires that all actions carried out by federal agencies directly, or by nonfederal entities requiring some form of federal approval or funding, be concurred with by the state or its designated agency as consistent with the CMP. Significantly, the consistency review requirement applies not only to activities physically located within the CMP boundary, but also to activities outside the boundary which may affect the coastal zone. NOAA's regulations implement a detailed consistency review procedure....

The chief advantage the CZMA presents for promoting biodiversity protection is its flexibility, which operates on many levels. The CZMA allows a state flexibility to adopt the management approach...most consistent with that state's general style of land use regulation and management....

The CZMA also exhibits flexibility in terms of geographic emphasis and intensity of the regulatory program. The program for areas of particular concern allows states to focus regulatory efforts on specified areas in need of close attention, such as those needing intense biodiversity protection. The CZMA also inherently recognizes that land and water uses will occur in the coastal zone and must be accommodated. Hence, rather than requiring a uniform level of regulation throughout the coastal zone ecosystem, the CZMA recognizes that some areas will require more development than others and some will require a greater degree of protection than others. Also, the CZMA recognizes that activities outside the coastal zone boundary may affect coastal resources and thus need to be addressed....

The CZMA's flexibility, however, also imposes burdens in terms of developing and implementing the CMP according to the loosely-stated federal guidelines. The danger exists that goals such as biodiversity protection will become diffusely enforced and thus ineffective as management tools. In that sense, then, if the detailed consistency review procedures are not closely followed, the CZMA could prove ineffective for biodiversity protection in the coastal zone....

The Cooperation model offers some measure of balance between Coercion and Coordination model statutes, holding traits of each. The essence of the Cooperation model is the expression of strong federal goals and policies in the context of a flexible partnership between federal, state, and local interests in seeing to it that the federal policies are implemented in the form of substantive legal requirements. Cooperation model statutes often hold out some form of regulatory carrot or stick, or blend of both, as an incentive for the partners to act together within the framework of the federal goals and policies, but substantive review criteria and outcomes generally are not prescribed. Rather, it is left to the cooperative process to formulate a regulatory response directed at the particular state or local planning area.

The Cooperation model statutes thus are expensive to operate. They involve substantial transaction costs and time as the cooperating partners forge consensus over the final substantive shape of the regulatory policy. But the final result offers promise of achieving the substantive outcome with greater impact than the Coordination model offers, and with greater consensus than the Coercion model offers....

[My] proposal calls for a unified federal biodiversity conservation statute [modeled on the CZMA], the Biological Resources Zone Management Act ("BRZMA"), centered around three stages of biodiversity conservation management: (1) state identification, inventory, and nomination of biological resource zones; (2) local and private development, and federal approval, of biological resource zone management plans; and (3) implementation of the management plan in lieu of the existing federal regulatory structure. The first stage allows states to identify areas of biological resources which are in need of protection and which may present controversial issues if those protective measures are carried out through the existing coercive federal regulations. The second stage allows the local and private entities potentially most at risk of bearing the brunt of federal regulation to develop a comprehensive management plan for the biological resources zone, knowing that it must not only meet their needs, but also the federal objectives of biodiversity conservation. The third stage provides the reward to the state, local, and private interests for their expenditure of time and effort and their commitment to the plan — complete relief from all the headaches of the existing federal structure, including the multiple permitting requirements, inflexible and overlapping regulatory standards, different agencies and policies, and never-ending litigation....

COMMENTARY & QUESTIONS

1. **"Yes, but will they come?"** The linchpin of the BRZMA variation of the Cooperation model is the willingness of states to escape the "coercive" aspects of current regulation by themselves meaningfully regulating land use or effectively directing local land use approval processes. It is not clear that states will appreciate being placed in the potentially unpopular position of superseding closely guarded local powers over land use. In addition, states may also be unwilling to relinquish their politically convenient strategy of scapegoating "The Feds." Industrial and development interests, in general, possess proportionately greater political power at the state level than at the federal level. As a result, state governments frequently find it politically comfortable to satisfy one political constituency by protecting the environment, but simultaneously to placate economic interests by proclaiming that "the Feds made us do it." The BRZMA proposal may give states credit for more political fortitude than they can actually muster.

2. **Resolving interstate resource disputes.** How would the Cooperation model — based on discretionary state participation and individual state planning and management — resolve a dispute where an area of critical environmental concern (e.g., the critical habitat of an endangered species) transcends state lines and the affected states disagree about how the resource should be managed? Under the CZMA, a state may veto any proposed federal activity or permit that is inconsistent with the state's CMP. Since consistency review applies to activities outside the coastal zone boundary (and also, presumably, outside the state) that may affect the coastal zone, neighboring states with approved CMPs might hold conflicting views regarding a proposed federal activity that would impact both their coastal zones. The CZMA provides for override by the Secretary of Commerce of a state veto under certain circumstances. See North Carolina v. Commerce Dep't, 42 BNA Env't Rep. Cas. 1254 (D.D.C. 1995), where the court upheld the Secretary's override of North Carolina's veto of a federal §404 permit for a proposed project by Virginia Beach, Virginia, to withdraw 60 million gallons of drinking water per day from the bi-state Lake Gaston. Under the BRZMA concept, one participating state might be implementing an approved BRZMA management plan, while its neighbor, a nonparticipating state, would be operating under applicable federal law. What if these regulatory schemes produce different results with regard to management of a shared resource? Federal law would probably prevail in such a situation.

3. **Of time and money.** Professor Ruhl recognizes that the Cooperation approach will be expensive and time-consuming. Is such a system compatible with the conservation of endangered species and other unique environmental resources? To use NEPA terms, is it possible that procedural delays and funding shortages might cause "irretrievable commitments of resources"? A Cooperative approach could include exceptions where federal law might preempt the process in emergency situations. Where should the line be drawn between these emergency situations and ordinary situations where the operations of state law may continue unimpeded? What about situations where ostensibly innocuous proposals, taken by themselves, might have extremely deleterious impacts when viewed cumulatively with other completed projects or pending development proposals?

4. **Mixed mandates and diffuse expectations.** Professor Ruhl also understands that the CZMA's guidelines are mainly aspirational, which might render them "diffusely enforced and thus ineffective as management tools." In fact, the CZMA involves a balancing of environmental and economic factors: State coastal management planning must give "full consideration to ecological, cultural, historic, and esthetic values as well as to needs for compatible economic development." 16 U.S.C. §1452(2). Given the equal vagueness of concepts such as "biodiversity," environmentally conscious states, as Professor Ruhl anticipates, might identify and nominate biological resource zones (BRZs) "corresponding to local and regional ecosystems requiring the greatest levels of protection because they are unique, sensitive, or threatened." Other participating states, however, might choose to maximize economic opportunities by nominating few, if any, BRZs. Such interstate economic competition might encourage the "race to the bottom" that provoked the federalization of much of environmental law in the first place (Chapter 5). Thus a substantial federal presence would still be necessary to administer this system. Existing federal law would continue to apply in nonparticipating states. Strong federal oversight would also be necessary to deter participating states from adopting "minimal protection" strategies, and the federal government would have to step in and rescind plan approval in states that are not adequately enforcing their plans. Strong federal oversight is potentially inconsistent with the attempt to provide states with "complete relief from all the headaches of the existing federal structure." Quite the contrary, the BRZMA might simply add another unwelcome layer of bureaucracy to what is already a complex regulatory process or else operate as a Trojan Horse to undercut effective regulation.

5. **Has the CZMA worked?** "As a vehicle for promoting state and local land use planning along coastal America, the CZMA has largely succeeded."[5]

> As for the tough, nasty business of land use regulation, there is evidence that difficult decisions are being made and, at times, against economic and development interests. Spurred forward by CZMA grants of money and authority, some states have passed highly-controversial set-back ordinances, made generous provisions for public access to coastal resources, and banned certain development altogether. On the other hand, states have been almost equally free to look the other way. Id., Houck & Rolland, at 1297–1298.

Nevertheless, this statute has been unsuccessful in curbing what Professor Oliver Houck calls "America's Mad Dash to the Sea." Houck, America's Mad Dash to the Sea, Amicus Journal 21–36 (Summer 1988). According to Professor Houck, "we are expecting state regulation, under the Coastal Zone Management Act, to overcome formidable economic and political pressures without the safeguard of a clear, national mandate." Will the additional "carrot" of a dispensation from existing federal regulations, as advocated by Professor Ruhl, be sufficient to overcome traditional state reluctance to constrain development in coastal zones? When dealing with biodiversity preservation, can we afford to adopt a system in which states are, to a great extent, "free to look the other way"?

---

5. Houck & Rolland, Federalism in Wetlands Regulation: A Consideration of Delegation of Clean Water Act Section 404 and Related Programs to the States, 54 Md. L. Rev. 1242, 1297 (1995).

6. ISTEA, a "Cooperation statute." America's dependence on the automobile, facilitated by massive governmental investments in roads (3 million miles) and interstate highways (45,000 miles), has fostered urban sprawl development, which, in addition to the impacts outlined above, has also led to a lack of affordable housing and the decline of our central cities and their systems of mass transit. In 1991, Congress tentatively responded to this phenomenon by enacting the Intermodal Surface Transportation Efficiency Act, 23 U.S.C. §§134 et seq. (ISTEA, commonly pronounced "Ice-Tea").

Perhaps the most important aspect of ISTEA was its funding flexibility.[6] Whereas federal transportation funding traditionally had been restricted to highway projects, ISTEA made over half of its $155 billion authorization available for any surface transport mode, including construction and maintenance of intracity mass transit systems, bikeways, and pedestrian systems. Second, ISTEA invigorated regional transportation planning by requiring states to develop statewide Transportation Improvement Programs (TIPs) that must be consistent with transportation plans formulated by metropolitan planning organizations (MPOs), with participation by all affected stakeholders. The purpose of this planning process was to promote the development of intermodal transportation systems that "will efficiently maximize mobility of people and goods within and through urbanized areas and minimize transportation-related fuel consumption and air pollution." Planners were required to consider the "overall social, economic, energy, and environmental effects of transportation decisions." Third, TIPs had to be consistent with State Implementation Plans (SIPs) under the CAA (Chapter 11) in order for transportation projects included in TIPs to be eligible for federal funding. The CAA itself bars federal licenses or permits for activities that are inconsistent with SIPs.[7]

ISTEA was reauthorized by the Transportation Equity Act of the 21st Century (TEA-21), Pub. L. No. 105–178 (1998). In addition to retaining the anti-sprawl elements of ISTEA, TEA-21 authorized funding for mitigation of water pollution from road construction or maintenance, restoration of wetlands and other environmental resources impacted by transportation projects, integration of transportation and community planning, and research on the relationship between highway density and ecosystem health. Environmentalists are concerned, however, that a provision of TEA-21 requiring federal agencies to streamline environmental reviews of transportation projects will weaken existing federal agency responsibilities under NEPA (see Chapter 9) and other statutes. The effectiveness of ISTEA is evaluated below.

B. STATE HAZARDOUS WASTE FACILITY SITING STATUTES

All siting statutes presume, to one degree or another, that the facilities involved in the siting process are necessary to society. The purpose of siting statutes is to site these facilities with as little social cost (including environmental cost) and disruption as possible.

---

6. The following summary of ISTEA is, in part, based on Pelham, Innovative Growth Control Measures: The Potential Impacts of Recent Federal Legislation and the *Lucas* Decision, 25 Urb. Law. 881 (1993).
7. 45 U.S.C. §7506(c).

Siting facilities for disposal of solid waste, hazardous waste, and nuclear waste, has become extraordinarily difficult because of the way that LULUs (Locally Undesirable Land Uses) trigger the NIMBY (Not In My Back Yard) syndrome local reaction.[8] Waste management tragedies such as Love Canal, New York, and Times Beach, Missouri — along with the close participation of state and federal government officials in the siting and permitting of some of these misplaced and mismanaged facilities (as in the *Wilsonville* case in Chapter 3) — have created a mood of deep public skepticism about whether waste disposal can be safely performed, and cynicism about whether state or federal governments are sufficiently competent and objective to protect the health and safety of host communities. In addition, local residents harbor reasonable fears that a waste disposal facility will create few jobs, produce little additional tax revenue, over-burden local services (e.g., fire, police) and infrastructure (e.g., roads, sewerage facilities), and negatively affect property values. Any proposal to site a waste disposal facility is met by a generally effective combination of zoning prohibitions, political opposition, media denunciation, lawsuits, and civil disobedience.

Unlike states, municipalities possess no inherent powers. They are capable of exercising only those powers delegated to them by the state governments that created them. Thus even where a state constitution contains a Home Rule provision to the effect that municipalities are responsible for control of land use within their boundaries, the state can legally override municipal decisions to "zone out" particular waste disposal facilities.

A number of states have enacted hazardous waste disposal facility siting statutes relying on Alternative Dispute Resolution (ADR) (see Chapter 21), with regard to providing compensation for host communities and allaying their safety concerns by establishing environmental monitoring and response mechanisms in addition to those required by federal and state laws. Four state hazardous waste facility siting statutes stand out as contrasting types.

Minnesota law gives the community — broadly defined as the county — control over final siting decisions. Minn. Stat. §115A.191. Counties volunteer sites by passing nonbinding Resolutions of Interest, which may be withdrawn at any time before binding site contracts have been signed. Once a county volunteers an environmentally acceptable site, the Minnesota Waste Management Board simultaneously negotiates a siting contract with the county and searches for a private developer to build and operate a facility on the site. During its negotiations with the Board, the county receives up to $4000 per month in local government aid. If a siting contract is ultimately signed, the county receives an additional $150,000 per year for two years. These incentives are in addition to any other payments the county may negotiate with the Board, including tax breaks and other forms of state assistance. Additional compensation mechanisms, however, may require legislative approval.

New Jersey law gives the state Hazardous Waste Facility Siting Commission the power to obtain a site by eminent domain and override local zoning where necessary to site a facility. N.J. Rev. Stat. §13.1E-52-59. After preparing siting criteria, the

---

8. Some other common acronyms inspired by LULU and NIMBY are OOMBY (Out Of My Back Yard), NIFYE (Not In My Front Yard Either), NIMTOO (Not In My Term Of Office), NOPE (Not On Planet Earth), and BANANA (Build Absolutely Nothing Anywhere Near Anything).

Commission searches for the most environmentally acceptable sites. During the latter phases of the siting process, potential host communities are given grant funds to perform their own site suitability studies. Once the site has been chosen, a qualified developer is expected to enter into negotiations with the host community for compensation and safety measures. The host community is entitled to at least 5% of the gross receipts of any facility constructed within its boundaries in order to mitigate the effects of the facility.

In Wisconsin, the developer chooses the site and requests each affected municipality to identify relevant local regulations. Wis. Stat. §144.44. The municipality has the choice of whether to negotiate with the developer. If the municipality chooses not to negotiate, all applicable local regulations enacted within 15 months of the developer's submission of a site feasibility report are preempted. If an affected municipality chooses to negotiate, it must enact a formal siting resolution stating its intent to negotiate and, if necessary, submit to binding arbitration. Arbitrable issues are severely circumscribed. Reimbursement of a community's costs of evaluating a site and participating in the negotiation and arbitration process are limited to $2500. In the arbitration process, each party immediately submits its final offer, and the arbitrator must choose one of these without modification.

In Massachusetts, all post-siting statutes, local permits, and zoning changes promulgated to exclude particular facilities are preempted. Mass. Gen. L. 21D §3-15.The developer initiates the siting process by filing a notice of intent with the state Hazardous Waste Facility Siting Council. The Council may then issue a finding that the proposal is "feasible and deserving" in terms of the developer's financial capability and past management practices, technical feasibility of the proposal, need for the facility, and compliance with state and federal laws. If a feasible and deserving determination is issued, the community, aided by state technical assistance grants, is required to negotiate with the developer and the state. The state is a party to the negotiations because the outcome may include state incentives to a host community. If the negotiations result in impasse, an arbitrator prepares a draft settlement for public comment. The final settlement is submitted to the Council and is subject to judicial review.

COMMENTARY & QUESTIONS

1. **The track record of siting statutes.** In spite of these sophisticated statutes, in fact no major hazardous waste disposal facility has been sited, using the new procedures, in any of these four states or in any of the other approximately eight states that have enacted similar hazardous waste facility siting statutes. The probable reasons for the virtual nonuse of these siting statutes have been the exceptional success of federal environmental statutes — most notably RCRA (see Chapter 18) and EPCRA (see Chapter 21) — in reducing the amounts of hazardous waste generated in the United States, coupled with the inexorable offshore migration of manufacturing facilities. Since the inception of EPCRA's Toxics Release Inventory (TRI) in 1988, hazardous waste releases (including transfers to offsite hazardous waste treatment, storage, and disposal facilities) have declined over 50%. (EPA, TRI, 2003, covering releases during 2001.) Hazardous waste generation in the United States declined 17% between 1993 and 1995. Ironically, the

two most recently constructed hazardous waste incinerators have been located in states without ADR-type siting statutes. See Polumbo v. Waste Techs., 989 F.2d 156 (4th Cir. 1993), and Coalition for Health Concern v. LWD, Inc., 60 F.3d 1188 (6th Cir. 1995) (hazardous waste incinerator sitings in Ohio and Kentucky upheld over public opposition). Professor Barry Rabe and his colleagues describe successful efforts to site hazardous waste disposal facilities in the Canadian provinces of Alberta and Manitoba.[9] First, a moratorium on siting proposals was accompanied by extensive public education as to the problems of hazardous waste management and the potential economic benefits for a host community. Those communities expressing interest were informed that they were free to opt out of the siting process at any time. Those that continued were encouraged to negotiate such factors as site selection and design (within broad site elimination guidelines), type of disposal technology, and impact management (mitigation, compensation, and contingency measures). It is not clear whether participating communities received grants to employ independent experts with regard to these issues. Although negotiations were conducted by local governments, final plebiscites were held to determine community acceptance. Agreements were made with host communities that committed the federal government to (1) restrict out-of-province waste imports to the new facilities, (2) develop transfer and disposal facilities in other provinces, and (3) reduce the volume of wastes being generated and requiring disposal. Responding to fears that private contractors operating these facilities would be unreliable, a "crown corporation" was established to share facility management with private companies, with the entire operation to be overseen by provincial regulatory authorities. Would such a siting system — emphasizing public education and participation, burden sharing, and a substantial federal role in facility management — be successful in the United States? For one thing, restrictions on waste imports from other states would probably be unconstitutional unless specifically approved by Congress (Chapter 6).

2. **Community veto?** The Minnesota siting act gives communities ultimate power to accept or reject hazardous waste disposal facilities. Some commentators believe that given the current NIMBY climate and the probable success of communities that oppose LULUs, this is the most viable way to site hazardous waste disposal facilities:

> A community that feels coerced into having a facility is likely to experience too much anger, fear and outrage about the siting process itself to be concerned about examining the content of the proposal. Guaranteeing a community the right to say no to any proposal it found unacceptable would, by freeing it from the threat of coercion, allow it to explore whether having a facility would be a better option than having none. Given the right to say no, a community might weigh the costs, risks, and benefits of hosting a facility and try to negotiate a package that would be more attractive than maintaining the status quo. E. Schmeidler & P. Sandman, Getting to Maybe 48 (1988).

On the other hand, one could argue that (1) a community possessing a veto will almost certainly exercise it, (2) a developer will not negotiate with a community possessing a veto, (3) local politicians will never take anything but a "hard line" and then complain

---

9. Rabe et al., NIMBY and Maybe: Conflict and Cooperation in the Siting of Low-Level Radioactive Waste Disposal Facilities in the United States and Canada, 24 Envtl. L. 67 (1994).

that "they made us accept the facility," (4) a community will negotiate only if it believes that the facility is inevitable because the state will override its objections, and (5) a community, which bears the concentrated costs of a facility, will be incapable of recognizing the facility's dispersed, statewide benefits.

The New Jersey statute assumes that communities will not negotiate about compensation and mitigation until after the siting decision has been made. How much leverage does a community possess at that point? Has a community by then become so alienated and defensive that it will only dig in its heels and fight? Professor Kent Portney has concluded that political factors militate against state or siting board preemption of local land use authority, even where, as in New Jersey, a siting statute authorizes preemption. K. Portney, Siting Hazardous Waste Treatment Facilities 9, 50–51 (1991).

3. **Choosing the site.** There is general agreement that decisions about the need for hazardous waste disposal facilities and appropriate technologies for these facilities are best made at the state level before making site-specific decisions. But states differ in their approaches to choosing sites. In Minnesota, counties volunteer sites and the state determines the best disposal site from among those volunteered. In New Jersey, the state selects the best sites based on predetermined siting criteria adopted with public participation. In Wisconsin, the developer chooses the site and initiates the siting process by notifying affected municipalities. The state then judges each application against minimum state siting criteria, without comparing other potential sites or determining whether better sites exist. Massachusetts follows a similar procedure, except that the developer first notifies the Council by filing a notice of intent.

Should a developer be permitted to choose a site? Hazardous waste disposal facilities have been disproportionately sited in low-income and minority communities. See Cole, Empowerment as the Key to Environmental Protection: The Need for Environmental Poverty Law, 19 Ecology L.Q. 619, 622 (1992). Would a developer most likely select a disadvantaged community that is poorly organized and desperate for development? Is it necessarily inequitable to locate LULUs in disadvantaged communities, or is the problem one of unequal access to information and political power? As for information, in New Jersey and Massachusetts state grants are available to communities to assist them in collecting information relative to siting. In Wisconsin, however, the municipality must utilize its own resources to evaluate the proposal and, in arbitration, can recover only a maximum of $2500 to cover all costs of negotiation and arbitration. This system would appear to be unfair to a Wisconsin community that bears the burden of showing, among other things, that there are better sites. In this regard, a state might adopt a "best site" or an "available site" strategy. If an available site strategy is chosen, will a state cast its net so wide, in order to assure that a facility will be sited, that its catch will include sites having *Wilsonville*-like problems?

4. **Negotiations: who, what, and when?** In Minnesota, the county proposes a site and negotiates with the state; the developer is not involved in the negotiations. Is the county the proper institution to represent a host municipality? There is a danger here that the state will "give away the store" in its negotiations with local communities and discourage potential developers. Will other municipalities — especially those whose

applications have been rejected — resist the authorization of extraordinary incentives for host communities by opposing the special legislation necessary to enact them?

Negotiation is mandatory in Massachusetts. The state will be part of the negotiations because enhanced state services and benefits are factors that the community and developer may consider. In Wisconsin, an affected municipality is not required to negotiate, but if it does not quickly resolve to negotiate and be subject to arbitration, it loses its power to influence the facility because it cannot "zone out" the facility. (If you were a Wisconsin community, would you swiftly pass a restrictive zoning ordinance and hope that no developer would contact you during the next 15 months?) The developer must negotiate if the municipality resolves to participate in the siting process. Is negotiation that is mandatory (or virtually so as in Wisconsin) a contradiction in terms? Will a party bargain in good faith if it cannot say "no"? The specter of binding arbitration if a siting agreement is not reached — as is the case in both Massachusetts and Wisconsin — will often spur the parties to negotiate in good faith. As a community or a developer, what would your strategy be in Wisconsin, where the arbitrable issues and judicial review are limited, and the arbitrator must accept, as a total package, the "last best offer" of one side or the other? How would that strategy differ in Massachusetts, where the arbitration is wide-ranging and the arbitrator can draft a compromise settlement that is open for public comment and must be approved by the Council, with broad judicial review available?

In Wisconsin, when a community opposes a facility, it passes a siting resolution in order to keep the negotiation option open, but it agrees with the developer to hold negotiations in abeyance while the community fights the site on technical and environmental grounds in separate state licensing proceedings. More tractable communities tend to negotiate and participate in the licensing proceeding simultaneously. The Wisconsin process has resulted in numerous completed siting agreements for projects such as solid waste landfills. None, however, has involved a major offsite hazardous waste disposal facility. Can the success of the Wisconsin siting statute be explained by the fact that its coverage is so inclusive, covering solid waste facilities, on-site facilities, and expansions, as well as new, off-site hazardous waste disposal facilities? Does the expansion of existing facility paradigm overcome the potential stigma of having a facility sited in a community? Or does the community accept the facility because it hasn't the resources to fight the developer, and the arbitrable issues are so circumscribed? Or is it something about the political culture of Wisconsin? Whatever the reason, Wisconsin communities have accepted waste disposal facilities, negotiating for direct payments, property value protection, disposal privileges, extra monitoring, infrastructure subsidies, and public access for surveillance.

The Massachusetts siting act places extensive technical evaluation of the site and the developer's waste disposal technology at the end of the process, rather than at the beginning or concurrent with negotiations, as in Wisconsin. The belated occurrence of technical review has been given as one reason for the failure of the Massachusetts siting act. A different drawback of the Massachusetts process is its excessive complexity. At least five state agencies are closely involved; draft and final reports, public briefings, comment periods, and hearings abound. Negotiations are tripartite, rather than bipartite. Professor Wheeler identifies other flaws in the Massachusetts system as (1) the requirement that communities negotiate, (2) the adversarial nature of the bargaining process — potentially resulting in impasse arbitration — which polarizes the issue and leads to "gunpoint negotiation," and (3) an insufficiently neutral state role in mediation and facilitation, leading to suspicion of the entire process. Wheeler, Negotiating NIMBYs: Learning from the Failure of the Massachusetts Siting Law, 11 Yale J. Reg. 241, 244 (1994).

5. **Other siting recommendations.** Professor Frank B. Cross believes that

> ...one promising approach to public participation in the risk regulation [and facility siting] process is the "citizen panel." Citizen panels are groups of individuals who hear the evidence on the full scope of risk controversies and provide input to decision makers. These panels could be selected randomly almost like a jury panel. After selection, the panels would hear witnesses and evidence to inform themselves about a risk controversy. The panel could then provide input into the government's decision. Cross, The Public Role in Risk Control, 24 Envtl. L. 887, 956 (1994).

Would citizen panels possess the political credibility to overcome intransigent NIMBY reactions? Michael Gerrard implicitly answers "no" when he concludes that the facility siting problem is so intractable that federal intervention is necessary. In his view, potential volunteer host communities do exist, but "single waste myopia," fostered by the fragmentation of hazardous waste regulatory statutes, inhibits a comprehensive approach to hazardous waste disposal. Gerrard recommends that a limited number of centralized treatment and disposal facilities for all nonradioactive hazardous wastes be constructed on already contaminated land, such as Superfund sites and contaminated military bases. Following a federally conducted hazardous waste disposal needs assessment, a Federal Waste Disposal Commission (modeled on the Defense Base Closure and Realignment Commission) would allocate sites to states — based on equity and environmental factors — subject to congressional approval or rejection. Each state would be responsible for developing incentives to attract volunteer communities to accept the allocated sites. If a state fails to site its allocated facilities, the Commission would be authorized to conduct its own preemptive siting process.[10] Would a system such as this be acceptable to the American public, which is cynical about federal policy initiatives? Would it instead be preferable for the federal government to build hazardous waste facilities on federal land or to lease federal land for private disposal operations? Would Gerrard's proposal only exacerbate environmental injustice in that only low-income or minority communities would feel compelled to bid for these LULUs? Why not open the regional LULU allocation process to all LULUs, including prisons, drug treatment facilities, and the like?

6. **Environmental Justice siting debates.** From the beginning, siting of facilities that process, store, or release toxic materials has provided the most dramatic focus for the Environmental Justice Movement, which criticizes the disproportionate cumulative impacts suffered by low-income communities and communities of color. Charles Lee's

---

10. Gerrard, Turning NIMBY on Its Head: A Siting Solution Based on Federal Allocation, State Responsibility, and Local Control, 1995 BNA Env't Rep. Curr. Dev. 2257.

Toxic Wastes and Race in the United States (1987), written for the United Church of Christ Commission for Racial Justice, and Dr. Robert Bullard's Dumping in Dixie: Race, Class & Environmental Quality (1990), presented data showing that risk of exposure to toxic waste hazards appeared to be both quantitatively and qualitatively greater for communities of color and low income than for the general public, a conclusion backed by much subsequent research. Some scholars, however, have criticized the studies' accuracy and argue that even if LULUs disproportionately affect minorities, that is not necessarily the result of racism.

Litigation intended to prove discrimination on the basis of race and poverty in toxics facilities siting decisions has generally been unsuccessful. Courts (unlike EPA, which has issued "discriminatory effect" regulations under Title VI of the 1964 Civil Rights Act[11]) generally require a showing of "discriminatory *intent*," which is most difficult to prove.[12] Is it racism for corporate managers to seek out (1) the most inexpensive land and (2) areas where they will face the least effective political opposition and the most desperate welcome for jobs and economic activity? The correlation of toxics facilities sitings with race and low income thus may well derive from cold marketplace logic rather than discriminatory bias. Moreover, even if the community surrounding a toxics facilities site is not initially low income or of color, market conditions will soon make it so.

Faced with the logic of distributional inequity in exposure to toxics, how can siting processes escape this Catch-22? Some of these issues are raised in Chapter 11. One approach that might be implemented in the state siting processes noted in text above is what Professors Schmeidler and Sandman advocated in Getting to Maybe: community bribery — the ability of poor communities to extort large economic premiums (and hopefully large safety infrastructures) in return for accepting such hazardous land uses. Alternatively, government could play a direct role by taking over toxic disposal functions or, failing this, requiring race and income-conscious protections in licensing the immensely lucrative hazardous waste facilities studied in Chapter 18.

Because of judicial discouragement of environmental injustice lawsuits without showings of discriminatory intent, it is likely that future environmental justice disputes in the toxics facilities siting context will be resolved within federal, state, and local administrative siting and permitting processes. Will proof of discriminatory intent also be demanded in these fora? Additionally, where will representatives of minority and low-income communities acquire the resources to retain the lawyers and expert witnesses that will be necessary in order to support their arguments before local zoning officials

---

11. Title VI of the 1964 federal Civil Rights Act, 42 U.S.C. §2000d, reads:

> No person in the United States shall, on the ground of race, color, or national origin, be excluded from participation in, be denied the benefits of, or be subjected to discrimination under any program or activity receiving Federal financial assistance.

Title VI was long thought not to offer serious remedies for the kinds of problems involved in environmental justice. Since 1993, however, the EPA's Office of Civil Rights has reversed that position and opened investigatory files on more than a dozen major cases alleging violations of Title VI, and EPA regulations, 40 C.F.R. §7.35, and the Browner Guidance have strengthened internal consideration of environmental justice issues.

12. See, e.g., Alexander v. Sandoval, 532 U.S. 275 (2001), and South Camden Citizens in Action v. Shinn, 274 F.3d 771 (3d Cir. 2002), cert. denied, 536 U.S. 939 (2002) (the Civil Rights Act of 1964 does not create a private right of action for judicial enforcement without a showing of discriminatory intent). For the difficulty of proving discriminatory intent, see Arlington Heights v. Metropolitan Hous. Dev. Corp., 429 U.S. 252, 265 (1977).

and state pollution control agency hearing boards? Should the applicant be required to fund local groups' participation in these proceedings? Should such funding be a governmental responsibility? Which governmental units should provide the funding? Which community groups should be entitled to funding, and in what proportions? What if community groups, after making thorough investigations, disagree about whether the facility should be sited? (One group wants the jobs, while another is concerned about declining neighborhood property values.)

At this moment in history, providing relief to environmental justice claimants in toxics facilities siting processes raises many questions that cannot be immediately or definitively answered.

7. **The nuclear waste disposal dilemma.** Disposal of high-level nuclear wastes, primarily produced by commercial nuclear power plants and government defense-related activities, presents an especially complex and contentious siting dilemma. Currently, more than 60,000 metric tons of nuclear waste is being stored in large water-filled pools at 80 power plants in 40 states, raising potential pollution and security threats. Despite the enactment of a federal siting statute, the Nuclear Waste Policy Act (NWPA), 42 U.S.C. §§10101 et seq., there is currently no ultimate disposal facility for high-level nuclear wastes generated by nuclear power plants. See U.S. GAO, Nuclear Waste: Yucca Mountain Project Behind Schedule and Facing Major Uncertainties (1993), and Indiana Michigan Power Co. v. Energy Dep't, 88 F.3d 1272 (D.C. Cir. 1996) (Energy Department was told to provide for disposal of high-level nuclear waste by January 31, 1998; it didn't happen). The Waste Isolation Pilot Plant (WIPP), located in southeastern New Mexico, has begun accepting transuranic waste produced by defense-related activities. As plans for siting temporary and permanent high-level nuclear waste disposal facilities in the Southwest have become bogged down by NIMBY-type, as well as national environmental group, opposition, the Mescalero Apache Tribe of New Mexico and the Goshute Tribe of Central Utah have proposed the construction of interim hazardous waste storage facilities on their lands. See Leonard, Sovereignty, Self-Determination, and Environmental Justice in the Mescalero Apache's Decision to Store Nuclear Waste, 24 B.C. Envtl. Aff. L. Rev. 651 (1997). Leonard sees no easy answer to the question, "Is this an example of large corporations practicing environmental racism or tribes asserting long sought-after autonomy in order to provide schools and services for their people?"

On February 14, 2002, Energy Secretary Spencer Abraham formally recommended to President Bush, pursuant to the NWPA, that the federal government develop Nevada's Yucca Mountain site as a permanent repository for the nation's high-level nuclear waste. The President immediately accepted this recommendation. But three months later, Nevada Governor Kenny Guinn, citing the alleged instability of the site and potential transportation dangers, vetoed President Bush's recommendation. Under the NWPA, Congress must resolve such an impasse, which it did on July 9, 2002, by accepting the Yucca Mountain siting recommendation. The Department of Energy is now authorized to construct the facility, which DOE intends to make operational by 2010. The State of Nevada, having lost its congressional battle to stop the facility, has brought several lawsuits contesting (1) the constitutionality of the NWPA process, (2) the credibility of DOE's evidence in support of the site recommendation, (3) DOE's final environmental impact statement for the proposal, (4) the Nuclear Regulatory Commission's authority to license the project, and (5) EPA's radiation emission standards for the facility. It appears highly unlikely that the Yucca Mountain facility will be operational by 2010.

The Yucca Mountain issue is a surrogate for a renewed debate over the desirability of nuclear-fueled electric power plants, which have been anathema since the 1980s. (See, e.g., the *Pacific Gas & Electric* case in Chapter 6.) Nuclear plants are preferable to their fossil-fueled counterparts because nuclear power generation does not produce greenhouse gases. Nuclear power advocates also argue that contemporary nuclear plants are considerably safer and less expensive than their predecessors. Nevertheless, "Anti-Nuke" spokespersons respond that the extraction, processing, transportation, fission, and waste disposal stages of uranium-derived nuclear power present insurmountable pollution and national security problems.

The facilities siting outlook is no brighter with regard to disposal of low-level radioactive wastes produced by, for example, hospitals and research laboratories. Under the Low-Level Radioactive Waste Policy Act, 42 U.S.C. §§2021(b) et seq., states are required to dispose of their own commercially generated waste, either individually or in interstate compacts. Since the statute was enacted in 1980, ten regional low-level nuclear waste compacts, covering 41 states, have been approved by Congress, but no new disposal facilities have been constructed under any of these compacts. See U.S. GAO, Radioactive Waste: Status of Commercial Low-Level Facilities (1995); McGinnis, Collective Bads: The Case of Low-Level Radioactive Waste Compacts, 34 Nat. Resources J. 563 (1994); New York v. United States, 505 U.S. 144 (1992) (striking down, on Tenth Amendment grounds, portions of the Low-Level Radioactive Waste Policy Act) (see the discussion of this decision in Chapter 6).

C. CRITICAL AREA PROTECTION STATUTES

Section 1. SITE-BY-SITE PERMITTING: §404 OF THE CLEAN WATER ACT

Section 404 of the CWA, 33 U.S.C. §§1344 et seq., governs the discharge of dredged or fill material into waters of the United States. The most environmentally significant and politically controversial use of §404 involves wetlands protection. Wetlands are critically important and exceptionally vulnerable environmental resources:

> Unlike in the past, when wetlands were considered unimportant areas to be filled or drained for various uses, the many important roles that wetlands play are now recognized. Wetlands — which generally include swamps, marshes, bogs, and similar areas — provide vital habitat for fish, waterfowl, and other birds and wildlife. They are also important to commercially valuable fish and shellfish enterprises. In addition, wetlands help maintain water quality and aquatic productivity, aid flood control and erosion control, and provide recreation sites and aesthetically pleasing landscapes.

However, according to estimates, the contiguous 48 states lost approximately 53 percent of their original 221 million acres of wetlands over the 200-year period from the 1780s to the 1980s. [The U.S. Fish and Wildlife Service] estimated that wetlands losses during the period from the mid-1950s to the mid-1970s were about 458,000 acres per year. FWS' most recent estimates covering the years 1974 through 1983 suggest that about 290,000 acres were being lost each year. The Soil Conservation Service [now the Natural Resources Conservation Service] reported that losses of wetlands on nonfederal rural areas in the period from 1982 to 1991 totaled about 120,000 acres per year. U.S. GAO, Wetlands Protection: The Scope of the §404 Program Remains Uncertain 8 (1993).

EPA has estimated that, through the early 1990s, wetlands losses have declined to approximately 90,000 acres per year. EPA, Environmental Indicators of Water Quality in the United States 11 (1996).[13] This decline is due mostly to the fact that prices for agricultural land have decreased so sharply that it is now cheaper for farmers to buy uplands than to convert wetlands to farmland by ditching and diking. Nevertheless, any further loss of wetlands is clearly excessive in light of our explicit national policy of "no net loss" of remaining wetlands.

As the following case indicates, §404 process has profound land use implications.

Bersani v. U.S. Environmental Protection Agency
United States Circuit Court for the Second Circuit, 1988
850 F.2d 36, cert. denied, 489 U.S. 1089 (1989)

TIMBERS, J. Appellants ("Pyramid")...appeal from a judgment entered...granting summary judgment in favor of appellees, the EPA and the United States Army Corps of Engineers, and denying Pyramid's motion for summary judgment.

This case arises out of Pyramid [development company's] attempt to build a shopping mall on certain wetlands in Massachusetts known as Sweeden's Swamp. Acting under the Clean Water Act, EPA vetoed the approval by the Corps of a permit to build the mall because EPA found that an alternative site had been available to Pyramid at the time it entered the market to search for a site for the mall. The alternative site was purchased later by another developer and arguably became unavailable by the time Pyramid applied for a permit to build the mall....

Sweeden's Swamp is a 49.5 acre wetland which is part of an 89 acre site near Interstate 95 in South Attleboro, Massachusetts. Although some illegal dumping and motorbike intrusions have occurred, these activities have been found to have had little impact on the site, which remains a "high-quality red maple swamp" providing wildlife habitat and protecting the area from flooding and pollution.

One of the sections of the Clean Water Act relevant to the instant case is §301(a), which prohibits the discharge of any pollutant, including dredge or fill materials, into the nation's navigable waters, except in compliance with the Act's provisions, including §404. It is undisputed that Sweeden's Swamp is a "navigable water"...and that Pyramid's shopping center proposal will involve the discharge of dredged or fill materials.

Section 404 of the Act, focusing on dredge or fill materials, provides that the United States Army and EPA will share responsibility for implementation of its provisions. EPA and the Corps also share responsibility for enforcing the Act.

---

13. The FWS estimates are slightly higher: 117,000 acres of wetlands lost per year between 1985 and 1995. The FWS credits §404, among other changes in federal law, for the reduction of wetlands losses.

As with virtually all critical areas regulatory programs, applicants seeking permit approval to build a development in the regulated area must submit site plans, various traffic, economic, and environmental analyses, and propose mitigation measures as necessary.

Section 404(a) authorizes the Secretary of the Army, acting through the Corps, to issue permits for the discharge of dredged or fill materials at particular sites. Section 404(b) provides that, subject to §404(c), the Corps must base its decisions regarding permits on guidelines (the "§404(b)(1) guidelines") developed by EPA in conjunction with the Secretary of the Army.

The §404(b)(1) guidelines, published at 40 C.F.R. §230 (1987), are regulations containing the requirements for issuing a permit for discharge of dredged or fill materials. 40 C.F.R. §230.10(a) covers "non-water dependent activities" (i.e., activities that could be performed on non-wetland sites such as building a mall) and provides essentially that the Corps must determine whether an alternative site is available that would cause less harm to the wetlands. Specifically, it provides that "no discharge of dredged or fill material shall be permitted if there is a practicable alternative" to the proposal that would have a "less adverse impact" on the "aquatic ecosystem." It also provides that a practicable alternative may include "an area not presently owned by the applicant which could reasonably be obtained, utilized, expanded, or managed in order to fulfill the basic purpose of the proposed activity." It further provides that "unless clearly demonstrated otherwise," practicable alternatives are (1) "presumed to be available," and (2) "presumed to have less impact on the aquatic ecosystem." Thus, an applicant such as Pyramid must rebut both of these presumptions in order to obtain a permit. Sections 230.10 (c) and (d) require that the Corps not permit any discharge that would contribute to significant degradation of the nation's wetlands and that any adverse impacts must be mitigated through practicable measures.

In addition to following the §404(b)(1) guidelines, the Corps may conduct a "public interest review." 33 C.F.R. §320.4 (1987). This public interest review is not mandatory under §404, unlike consideration of the §404(b) guidelines. In a public interest review, the Corps decision must reflect the "national concern" for protection and use of resources but must also consider the "needs and welfare of the people."

Under §404 of the Act, EPA has veto power over any decision of the Corps to issue a permit. It is this provision that is at the heart of the instant case.

Specifically, §404(c) provides that the Administrator of EPA may prohibit the specification of a disposal site "whenever he determines, after notice and opportunity for public hearings, that the discharge of materials into such area will have an unacceptable adverse effect" on, among other things, wildlife. An "unacceptable adverse effect" is defined in 40 C.F.R. §231.2(e) as an effect that is likely to result in, among other things, "significant loss of or damage to...wildlife habitat...." The burden of proving that the discharge will have an "unacceptable adverse effect" is on EPA.

In short, both EPA and the Corps are responsible for administering the program for granting permits for discharges of pollutants into wetlands under §404. The Corps has the authority to issue permits following the §404(b)(1) guidelines developed by it and EPA; EPA has the authority under §404(c) to veto any permit granted by the Corps. The Corps processes about 11,000 permit applications each year. EPA has vetoed five decisions by the Corps to grant permits....

On appeal, the thrust of Pyramid's argument is a challenge to what it calls EPA's "market entry" theory, i.e. the interpretation by EPA of the relevant regulation, which led EPA to consider the availability of alternative sites at the time Pyramid entered the market for a site, instead of at the time it applied for a permit....

We hold (1) that the market entry theory is consistent with both the regulatory language and past practice; (2) that EPA's interpretation, while not necessarily entitled to deference [because the other federal agency administering §404, the Corps, disagreed with EPA's interpretation], is reasonable; and (3) that EPA's application of the regulation is supported by the administrative record....

The effort to build a mall on Sweeden's Swamp was initiated by Pyramid's predecessor, the Edward J. DeBartolo Corporation. DeBartolo purchased the Swamp some time before April 1982. At the time of this purchase an alternative site was available in North Attleboro (the "North Attleboro site"). Since Massachusetts requires state approval (in addition to federal approval) for projects that would fill wetlands, DeBartolo applied to the Massachusetts Department of Environmental Quality Engineering ("DEQE") for permission to build on Sweeden's Swamp. DEQE denied the application in April, 1982.

Pyramid took over the project in 1983 while the appeal of the DEQE denial was pending. In April 1983, Massachusetts adopted more rigorous standards for approval of permits. The new standards added wildlife habitat as a value of wetlands to be protected and required the absence of a "practicable alternative."...

One of the key issues in dispute in the instant case is just when did Pyramid begin searching for a suitable site for its mall. EPA asserts that Pyramid began to search in the Spring of 1983. Pyramid asserts that it began to search several months later, in September 1983. The difference is crucial because on July 1, 1983 — a date between the starting dates claimed by EPA and Pyramid — a competitor of Pyramid, the New England Development Co. ("NED"), purchased options to buy the North Attleboro site. The site was located upland and could have served as a "practicable alternative" to Sweeden's Swamp, if it had been "available" at the relevant time. Thus, if the relevant time to determine whether an alternative is "available" is the time the applicant is searching for a site (an issue that is hotly disputed), and if Pyramid began to search at a time before NED acquired options on the North Attleboro site, there definitely would have been a "practicable alternative" to Sweeden's Swamp, and the Pyramid application should have been denied. On the other hand, if Pyramid did not begin its search until after NED acquired options on the North Attleboro site, then the site arguably was not "available" and the permit should have been granted....

In August 1984, Pyramid applied under §404(a) to the New England regional division of the Corps (the "NE Corps") for a permit. It sought to fill or alter 32 of the 49.6 acres of the Swamp; to excavate nine acres of uplands to create artificial wetlands; and to alter 13.3 acres of existing wetlands to improve its environmental quality. Later Pyramid proposed to mitigate the adverse impact on the wetlands by creating 36 acres of replacement wetlands in an off-site gravel pit....

In November, 1984, EPA and FWS submitted official comments to the NE Corps recommending denial of the application because Pyramid's proposal was inconsistent with the the §404(b)(1) guidelines. Pyramid had failed (1) to overcome the presumption of the availability of alternatives and (2) to mitigate adequately the adverse impact on wildlife. EPA threatened a §404(c) review. Pyramid then proposed to create additional artificial wetlands at a nearby upland site, a proposal it eventually abandoned.

In January 1985, the NE Corps hired a consultant to investigate the feasibility of Sweeden's Swamp and the North Attleboro site. The consultant reported that either site was feasible but that from a commercial standpoint only one mall could survive in the area. On February 19, 1985, the NE Corps advised Pyramid that denial of its permit was imminent. On May 2, 1985, the NE Corps sent its recommendation to deny the permit to the national headquarters of the Corps. Although the NE Corps ordinarily makes the final decision on whether to grant a permit, see 33 C.F.R. §325.8 (1982), in the instant case, because of the widespread publicity, General John F. Wall, the Director of Civil Works at the national headquarters of the Corps, decided to review the NE Corps' decision. Wall reached a different conclusion. He decided to grant the permit after finding that Pyramid's offsite mitigation proposal would reduce the adverse impacts sufficiently to allow the "practicable alternative" test to be deemed satisfied. He stated:

> In a proper case, mitigation measures can be said to reduce adverse impacts of a proposed activity to the point where there is no "easily identifiable difference in impact" between the proposed activity (including mitigation) versus the alternatives to that activity.

On May 31, 1985, Wall ordered the NE Corps to send Pyramid, EPA and FWS a notice of its intent to grant the permit. The NE Corps complied on June 28, 1985.

On July 23, 1985, EPA's RA [Regional Administrator] initiated a §404(c) review of the Corps decision....

On May 13, 1986, EPA issued its final determination, which prohibited Pyramid from using Sweeden's Swamp. It found (1) that the filling of the Swamp would adversely affect wildlife; (2) that the North Attleboro site could have been available to Pyramid at the time Pyramid investigated the area to search for a site; (3) that considering Pyramid's failure or unwillingness to provide further materials about its investigation of alternative sites, it was uncontested that, at best, Pyramid never checked the availability of the North Attleboro site as an alternative; (4) that the North Attleboro site was feasible and would have a less adverse impact on the wetland environment; and (5) that the mitigation proposal did not make the project preferable to other alternatives because of scientific uncertainty of success....

As EPA has pointed out, the preamble to the §404(b)(1) guidelines states that the purpose of the "practicable alternatives" analysis is "to recognize the specific value of wetlands and to avoid their unnecessary destruction, particularly where practicable alternatives were available in non-aquatic areas to achieve the basic purpose of the proposal." 45 Fed. Reg. 85,338 (1980) (emphasis added). In other words, the purpose is to create an incentive for developers to avoid choosing wetlands when they could choose an alternative upland site. Pyramid's reading of the regulations would thwart this purpose because it would remove the incentive for a developer to search for an alternative site at the time such an incentive is needed, i.e., at the time it is making a decision to select a particular site. If the practicable alternatives analysis were applied to the time of the application for a permit, the developer would have little incentive to search for alternatives, especially if it were confident that alternatives soon would disappear. Conversely, in a case in which alternatives were not available at the time the developer made its selection, but became available by the time of application, the developer's application would be denied even though it could not have explored the alternative site at the time of its decision....

PRATT, C.J., dissenting:...This market entry theory approaches a sensitive environmental problem through a time warp; it ignores the statute's basic purpose and it creates unfair and anomalous results...ignoring the crucial question of whether the site itself should be preserved. Under the market entry theory, developer A would be denied a permit on a specific site because when he entered the market alternatives were available, but latecomer developer B, who entered the market after those alternatives had become unavailable, would be entitled to a permit for developing the same site. In such a case, the theory no longer protects the land but instead becomes a distorted punitive device: it punishes developer A by denying him a permit, but grants developer B a permit for the same property — and the only difference between them is when they "entered the market."

The market entry theory has further problems. In this case, for example, if a Donald Trump had "entered the market" after NED took the option on the North Attleboro site and made it unavailable, under EPA's approach he apparently would have been entitled to a permit to develop Sweeden's Swamp. But after obtaining the permit and the land, could Trump then sell the package to Pyramid to develop? Or could he build the mall and sell the developed site to Pyramid?...

Furthermore, in a business that needs as much predictability as possible, the market entry theory will regrettably inject exquisite vagueness. When does a developer enter the market? When he first contemplates a development in the area? If so, in what area — the neighborhood, the village, the town, the state or the region? Does he enter the market when he first takes some affirmative action? If so, is that when he instructs his staff to research possible sites, when he commits money for more intensive study of those sites, when he contacts a real estate broker, when he first visits a site, or when he makes his first offer to purchase? Without answers to these questions a developer can never know whether to proceed through the expense of contracts, zoning proceedings, and EPA applications....

Since Congress delegated to EPA the responsibility for striking a difficult and sensitive balance among economic and ecological concerns, EPA should do so only after considering the circumstances which exist, not when the developer first conceived of his idea, nor when he entered the market, nor even when he submitted his application; rather, EPA, like a court of equity, should have the full benefit of, and should be required to consider, the circumstances which exist at the time it makes its decision. This is the only method which would allow EPA to make a fully informed decision — as Congress intended — based on whether, at the moment, there is available a site which can provide needed economic and social benefits to the public, without unnecessarily disturbing valuable wetlands.

COMMENTARY & QUESTIONS

1. **Timing theories in *Bersani*.** Should the "practicable alternative" test be applied at the time of "market entry," permit application, or "time of decision"? There are several problems with Judge Pratt's dissenting "time of decision" test. First, there is the question of which of many decision points is applicable. In this case, is it Massachusetts DEQE's original rejection, its subsequent approval, the Corps' original rejection, its subsequent approval, the EPA decision, or the decisions of the two state or two federal courts that considered this matter on judicial review? Second, since the "time of decision" comes rather late in the process, it is doubtful that a developer would take a substantial financial risk in the face of possible permit denial based on distant events that it can neither control nor predict. Third, the developer will have invested so much in project preparation by the time of decision that agencies will be reluctant to deny it a permit based on the availability of a site that has only recently come on the market. But if, as a general matter, the "time of decision" test is problematic, does that mean that the "time of entry" test is necessarily the proper one to apply in all cases? The real issue here is whether the developer, in good faith, considered nonwetland sites. Would it perhaps be better not to adopt a formal timing rule but to encourage the agencies to determine the matter of good faith consideration of alternatives on a case-by-case basis?

2. **The "practicable alternative" test.** Is the §404 "practicable alternative" test a good one? As the dissent points out, this test has nothing to do with the desirability of building in a wetland. Developers, unfortunately, are drawn to wetlands because they are conveniently located, available, and relatively inexpensive. Professor Oliver A. Houck explains that an applicant can manipulate the "practicable alternative" test by defining the project so narrowly that only the proposed site will accommodate it. Houck, Hard

Choices: The Analysis of Alternatives under §404 of the Clean Water Act and Similar Environmental Laws, 60 U. Colo. L. Rev. 773, 788–789, 832–836 (1989). What if Pyramid had proposed a "unique shopping experience in a magnificent aquatic setting"? Since 1989, the Corps has somewhat modified its previous position of deferring to the applicant's statement of purpose and need. Professor Houck considers the *Bersani* decision to be "the most tough-minded [judicial] interpretation of alternatives analysis under §404":

> To the *Bersani* court, then, an alternative to a large commercial development was feasible although it was neither the developer's choice nor the developer's most profitable option; the availability of this alternative would be measured at the time the developer's own, internal choice is being made; and offers of mitigation would not finesse this alternatives analysis but, rather, would follow it to offset losses that could not otherwise be avoided.... The *Bersani* dissent, however, found this result more than remarkable. In its view, the majority mistook §404's "basic purpose," which is not to provide an incentive for developers to avoid choosing wetlands but, rather, to provide a balancing analysis between the "biological integrity" of a wetland area and "commerce and other economic advantages." Alternatives are but a "factor" in this determination. This relatively free-wheeling balancing approach is, of course, reminiscent of the Corps public interest review regulations and has found a secure home in a second line of cases interpreting the alternatives requirement of §404.[14] 60 U. Colo. L. Rev. at 806–807.

Professor Houck concludes that, because the "practicable alternative" test is fatally flawed, §404 should be amended to "make the water dependency test dispositive.... Unless this type of activity needs to be located in waters of the United States, it will not be." Id. at 830.

3. **An uncomfortable partnership.** The sharing of §404 implementation responsibility between the Corps and EPA has been cumbersome and contentious, and the effectiveness of §404 has suffered as a result. The Corps is responsible for permit issuance and initial enforcement, while EPA is authorized to (1) develop the environmental guidelines used to evaluate permit applications, (2) veto proposed permits with unacceptable environmental impacts, (3) oversee state assumption of the §404 program, (4) interpret statutory exemptions, (5) determine the jurisdictional reach of the program, (6) set aside areas where no disposal of fill will be permitted, and (7) enforce in cases where the Corps has not adequately done so. As a primarily construction agency, the Corps has not always been a zealous defender of wetlands:

> The Corps receives about 15,000 individual permit applications annually. Of these 15,000 applications, the Corps issues approximately 10,000 individual permits (67 percent). The Corps denies approximately 500 individual permit applications, or about 3 percent of the applications it receives. The remaining 30 percent, about 4,500 applications, are either withdrawn or qualify for letters of permission or general permits. In addition, the Corps authorizes about 40,000 activities under regional or nationwide general permits each year. U.S. GAO, Wetlands Protection: The Scope of the §404 Program Remains Uncertain 12 (1993).

---

14. See Louisiana Wildlife Fed'n v. York, 761 F.2d 1044 (5th Cir. 1985), and Fund for Animals v. Army Dep't, 85 F.3d 535, 543 (11th Cir. 1996) ("...the Corps'...practicable alternatives analysis is not subject to numerical precision, but instead requires a balancing of the applicant's needs and environmental concerns").

The U.S. GAO also found that Corps enforcement of §404 has been sporadic. EPA, on the other hand, does not possess the resources to adequately supervise the Corps' performance. As of 1993, EPA had used its §404(c) veto power only 11 times since 1979. Only two states, Michigan and New Jersey, have received delegation from EPA to administer the §404 program.[15]

4. **The controversial scope of §404.** EPA regulations define *wetlands* as

> ...those areas that are inundated or saturated by surface or ground water at a frequency and duration sufficient to support, and that under normal circumstances do support, a prevalence of vegatation typically adapted for life in saturated soil conditions. 40 C.F.R. §230(t).

Thus a wetland is an area, including an area constructed by human beings, that exhibits some combination of hydric soils, wetland vegetation, and wetland hydrology. This leaves a great deal of vagueness in the regulatory definition, and the precise identification of individual wetlands depends on interpretive manuals and on-the-ground judgment by Corps and EPA officials. See, e.g., United States v. Deaton, 332 F.3d 698 (4th Cir. 2003) (Corps determination of soil "saturation" by visual observation upheld). Needless to say, the specific criteria to be used in wetlands identification have been the subject of heated political controversy.

The U.S. Supreme Court's decision in Solid Waste Agency of Northern Cook County (SWANNC) v. U.S. Army Corps of Eng'rs, 531 U.S. 159 (2001), has generated the most acrimonious current dispute over the coverage of §404. In that decision, analyzed in detail in Chapter 12, the Court held that the Corps' assertion of jurisdiction over "isolated wetlands" (i.e., those not hydrologically connected to navigable surface waters), based on their function as habitat for migratory waterfowl, exceeded its authority under the CWA. The Court did not reach the constitutional question of whether the protection of migratory birds falls within the Commerce Clause of the U.S. Constitution; it held only that wetlands regulation based solely on use by migratory birds was not included in Congress's CWA delegation of regulatory authority to the Corps.

In ecological terms, *SWANCC* is exceptionally meaningful because the approximately 20 million acres of isolated wetlands in the United States (e.g., prairie potholes, wet meadows, forested wetlands, playas, vernal pools, and wetlands fringing nonnavigable rivers and lakes) constitute nearly 50% of all U.S. wetlands and 70% in states such as South Carolina. There is no difference between the ecological and public health functions performed by isolated wetlands and adjacent wetlands.

SWANCC has shifted the locus of regulating isolated wetlands from the federal government to state and local governments. All coastal states (including Great Lakes states) authorize protection for coastal and estuarine wetlands. With regard to freshwater wetlands, prior to *SWANCC* 14 states had enacted legislation that could be utilized to

---

15. For an analysis of existing delegation programs under §404, see Houck & Rolland, Federalism in Wetlands Regulation: A Consideration of Delegation of Clean Water Act Section 404 and Related Programs to the States, 54 Md. L. Rev. 1242 (1995). The authors argue that if delegation "is done carefully and with the proper mix of federal inducements and safeguards, it could succeed." Id. at 1314.

protect isolated wetlands, and a number of other states (including Wisconsin) have enacted such statutes since *SWANCC*. See Virginia Dep't of Envtl. Quality v. Newdunn Assocs., 344 F.3d 407 (4th Cir. 2003) (describing the relationship between §404 and the Virginia Wetlands Resources Act of 2000, Va. Code Ann. §§62.1–44.3 et seq., which was enacted in response to *SWANCC* precursors in the Fourth Circuit). In other states, wetlands protection is implemented through the cumbersome device of state certification under §401 of the CWA (see Chapter 12). Twenty-one states provide partial protection for wetlands adjacent to tributaries of navigable waters; but 11 states — including some of those with the highest percentages of isolated wetlands — provide no legal protection for freshwater wetlands.

Uncertainties abound regarding the meaning of the *SWANCC* decision. Is a hydrological connection between a wetland and navigable waters necessary in order for the Corps to assert jurisdiction under §404? Or is a "significant nexus" of some other variety, other than use by migratory birds — e.g., an ecological, flooding, recreational, commercial fishing, aquifer recharge, irrigation, industrial water use, or pollution connection — sufficient? If a hydrological connection is necessary, is a groundwater connection acceptable? Is a surface water connection present when a tributary to navigable waters flows for some of its length through a ditch, culvert, pipe, storm sewer, or similar man-made conveyance? Can a stream that flows only intermittently constitute a surface water connection? Does the *SWANCC* holding apply only to §404, or does it also govern jurisdiction under other provisions of the CWA, such as state certifications, effluent discharges and NPDES permits, TMDLs, and oil spill liability and cleanup? (See Chapter 12.)

Federal courts have reached inconsistent results in interpreting *SWANCC*, with conflicts appearing not only among federal circuits but also among district courts within particular circuits. For a review of some of the *SWANCC* judicial crosscurrents, see FD&P Enters., Inc. v. U.S. Army Corps of Eng'rs, 239 F. Supp. 2d 509 (D.N.J. 2003) (holding that a hydrological connection to navigable waters is not the only factor in determining federal jurisdiction under §404). Two federal circuit courts of appeals have recently interpreted *SWANCC* narrowly in decisions upholding Corps jurisdiction over wetlands lying significant distances from navigable waters. In Deaton v. United States, the defendant's wetlands were adjacent to a roadside ditch:

> Water from the roadside ditch takes a winding, thirty-two mile path to the Chesapeake Bay. At the northwest edge of the Deaton's property, the roadside ditch rains into a culvert under Morris Leonard Road. On the other side of the road, the culvert drains into another ditch, known as the John Adkins Prong of Perdue Creek. Perdue Creek flows into the Beaverdam Creek, a natural watercourse with several dams and ponds. Beaverdam Creek is a direct tributary of the Wicomico River, which is navigable. Beaverdam Creek empties into the Wicomico River about eight miles from the Deaton's property. About twenty-five river miles further downstream, the Wicomico River flows into the Chesapeake Bay, a vast body of navigable water.... 332 F.3d at 702.

In United States v. Rapanos, 339 F.3d 447 (6th Cir. 2003), the court, relying heavily on *Deaton*, upheld Corps jurisdiction over wetlands located between 11 and 20 miles from a navigable waterway. These wetlands were connected to a 100-year-old man-made drain, which flowed into a creek, which was tributary to a navigable river.

The Corps is "elevating" problematic jurisdictional cases from its field offices to Washington, which will only exacerbate the permitting delays that have plagued §404's administration. Attempts in Congress to clarify or overturn *SWANCC* have thus far failed.

Land disturbance for agriculture, mining, or residential construction has raised other questions regarding the scope of §404. In United States v. Deaton, 209 F.3d 331 (4th Cir. 2002), the court determined that "sidecasting" — digging ditches with heavy construction equipment in order to drain a wetland and depositing the excavated dirt next to the ditches — is within the ambit of §404; but in National Mining Ass'n v. Army Dep't, 145 F.3d 1399 (D.C. Cir. 1998), the court invalidated the Corps' "Tulloch Rule" regulations, which required a §404 permit where wetlands development caused "incidental fallback" of fill. "Mountaintop removal mining" is a type of surface coal mining practiced in the mountainous eastern coal mining states that involves removing the top of a mountain, ridge, or hill with heavy construction equipment in order to mine a coal seam that runs through the upper fraction of the landform. The "overburden," or waste material generated by mountaintop removal mining, settles into valleys and becomes so-called valley fill, which clogs or destroys waterways located on the valley floors. A Corps determination to regulate mountaintop removal mining under §404, instead of deferring to EPA's stricter water pollution control permitting requirements under §402 of the CWA, was upheld in Kentuckians for the Commonwealth v. Rivenburgh, 317 F.3d 425 (4th Cir. 2003).[16] "Deep ripping" or "deep plowing," when used to convert large portions of a ranch from cattle grazing to orchards, vineyards, and residences, requires a permit under §404 when dirt is charged into wet swales or intermittent drainages that are connected to navigable waters. Borden Ranch P'ship v. Corps of Eng'rs, 537 U.S. 99 (2003), a per curiam affirmance, after a 4-4 vote (Justice Kennedy not participating), of the Ninth Circuit's 2-1 decision, reported at 261 F.3d 810 (2002).

5. **Mitigation of environmental damage.** Typical of §404's administration, Pyramid's mitigation proposals played an important part in the *Bersani* decision. Mitigation, however, continues to be a highly controversial device:

> In the context of existing wetland regulation, mitigation generally refers to avoidance, minimization, and compensation. These steps are frequently applied in a sequential manner. First, a party seeking a permit for a project that affects wetlands must demonstrate that the least environmentally damaging alternative will be used. Second, the permit applicant must develop a plan to minimize the environmental harm from any unavoidable impacts. Finally, the applicant must compensate for or offset any harm done to wetland functions and values which is not avoided or minimized. The applicant satisfies the compensation requirement by enhancing, restoring, creating, or preserving other wetlands that may be located on or off the project site. [There is a] preference for on-site mitigation and for

---

16. Corps regulations define "fill material" based on its effects: Fill is all material that displaces water or changes the bottom elevation of a waterbody except for "waste" (garbage, sewage, or effluent that is regulated under §402 of the CWA). "Overburden from mining or other excavation activities" is expressly included as fill material. 33 C.F.R. §323.2 (2002).

in-kind [restoring the type of wetland function that a development project affects] mitigation, [as well as a preference for] restoration and enhancement, rather than creation or preservation.... Mitigation banking involves mitigating for wetland impacts before an activity causes environmental harm. Mitigation banking occurs when one restores, enhances, creates, or preserves wetlands, thereby generating mitigation credits. A regulatory agency determines the amount and value of the mitigation credits which the credit generator may use to offset the adverse wetland impacts of its own development projects, [or] in a more complex scenario,...a private entity generates credits, which a third party purchases to meet its own unrelated mitigation requirements. Gardner, Banking on Entrepreneurs: Wetlands, Mitigation Banking, and Takings, 81 Iowa L. Rev. 531, 531–537 (1996).

According to Professor Gardner, "[t]he failure of compensatory mitigation is wetland regulation's dirty little secret." Id. at 540. Parties agreeing to perform mitigation often lack the technical or economic resources to fulfill their obligations. Noncompliance is common and enforcement is sporadic. Moreover, scientific uncertainties regarding wetlands ecology militate against the success of mitigation through creation or preservation. Environmentalists also complain that mitigation sends the wrong message to the American public and glosses over the need for humility and restraint with the natural world. Two federal agency reports cast doubt upon the effectiveness of mitigation efforts under §404 and suggest means of improving this process, including better data collection and enforcement. National Research Council, Compensating for Wetland Losses under the Clean Water Act (2001), and U.S. GAO, Wetlands Protection Assessments Needed to Determine Effectiveness of In-Lieu Fee Mitigation, USGAO-01-325 (2001). A New Jersey study concludes that only 78% of the freshwater wetland acreage lost to development at 75 New Jersey sites studied has been replaced with newly constructed wetlands, despite a requirement of New Jersey law that degraded or destroyed wetlands be replaced at a 2-1 ratio. New Jersey Dep't of Environmental Protection, Creating Indicators of Wetland Status (Quantity and Quality): Freshwater Wetland Mitigation in New Jersey (2002).

6. Evaluation of §404 as an example of site-by-site permitting. Section 404 undoubtedly has been successful in preserving some wetlands from development, but the site-by-site approach, as illustrated by §404, nevertheless has significant disadvantages as a critical area protection mechanism. To reiterate a point made above, §404 applies only to the deposit of dredged or fill material in wetlands; it does not apply to all wetland development activities. See, e.g., Save Our Community v. EPA, 971 F.2d 1155 (5th Cir. 1992), where a permit was not required for draining a wetland.[17] Neither does §404 apply to activities on neighboring nonwetland areas that lead to impairment of wetlands functions. Second, §404 administration is replete with statutory exemptions (e.g., for many agricultural activities) and general permits (both nationwide and regional) that limit the scope of the program. See 40 C.F.R. §323.3 (Activities Not Requiring Permits), and 33 C.F.R. §330 (Corps of Engineers Nationwide Permit

---

17. The use of mechanized earth-moving equipment to conduct landclearing, drainage, ditching, channelization, in-stream mining, or other development activities in wetlands (at least in "adjacent wetlands") is covered by §404, unless only "incidental fallback" results. But wetlands drainage without utilizing heavy equipment (e.g., through hydraulic conveyance devices such as pipes, hoses, or tile drains) is not subject to §404 permitting.

Program Regulations). Of the approximately 50,000 projects that are currently covered by §404 permits, roughly 35,000 are operating under either nationwide or regional permits, which entail a minimum of paperwork and are desultorily enforced. Nationwide permits involving discharge of dredged or fill material into headwaters wetlands and construction of single-family homes in wetlands have been especially controversial. Third, cumulative impacts of past, proposed, and potential projects are also systematically neglected in the §404 permitting process. The U.S. GAO Report cited above in Note 5 commented, "case files we reviewed indicated that Corps districts generally considered the impacts of projects on a case-by-case basis, and that cumulative impacts were sporadically addressed...." This is plainly a matter of Corps choice, for Buttrey v. United States, 690 F.2d 1170 (5th Cir. 1982), indicates that the Corps is authorized to, and sometimes does, consider cumulative impacts in making §404 permitting decisions. Thorough critical area protection can be assured only through a preventive land use planning and management program administered by an institution that possesses jurisdiction over an area that includes the entire resource to be protected. In the wetlands context, one commentator has suggested that EPA could achieve biodiversity protection through the §404 process by "exercis[ing] its *advance* veto authority, which can be used to protect relatively intact ecosystems in advance of a 404 permit application." Fischman, Biological Diversity and Environmental Protection: Authorities to Reduce Risk, 22 Envtl. L. 435, 496 (1992). Whether EPA will have the political leverage to exercise this authority is another matter entirely.

Section 2. SINGLE-PURPOSE REGIONAL CRITICAL AREA PROTECTION:

The federal Wild and Scenic Rivers Act. The federal Wild and Scenic Rivers Act of 1968 (WSRA), 16 U.S.C. §§1271 et seq., is a prime example of congressional cynicism toward federal control over private lands. This statute has been somewhat effective in protecting certain values on segments of designated rivers on federal lands. It has done little, however, to protect rivers and riverine ecosystems from incompatible private development. See generally Raffensperger & Tarlock, The Wild and Scenic Rivers Act at 25: The Need for a New Focus, 4 Rivers 81 (1993).

The scope of the WSRA is limited to designated "Wild," "Scenic," and "Recreational" Rivers, with their "immediate environments," defined as narrow corridors extending approximately one-quarter mile from the ordinary high-water mark on both sides of the rivers. Wider watershed impacts of development on private lands outside the management corridors, such as polluted runoff caused by residential development or agricultural operations, are beyond the WSRA's scope. Both the federal and the state designation processes of the WSRA, are so cumbersome that they actually discourage the addition of any but the least controversial rivers to the system. Nevertheless, once a river is admitted to the system, certain tangible protections do follow. Most important, a "roadblock" is placed in the way not only of FERC licensing of any dam "on or directly affecting" a designated river, but also in the way of any other federal agency that proposes to assist in any way "in the construction of any water resources project that would have a direct and adverse effect on the values for which such river was established...." §1278. Rivers that flow through federal land receive special protection under the WSRA. Federal agencies that manage lands "which include, border upon, or are adjacent to" any designated river — including lands outside the management corridor — "shall take such action respecting management policies, regulations, contracts, [and] plans, affecting such lands...as may be necessary to protect such rivers...." §1283.

In the politically unlikely situation that the prevailing political climate would permit the designation of a segment containing sizeable tracts of private land were designated wild and scenic, the Act has no teeth to restrain disruptive development. The WSRA provides no federal regulatory authority in designated corridors and land acquisition power is sharply limited. The federal government is barred from acquiring, by any means, more than approximately 15% of land within a corridor, and lands owned by a state may be acquired only by donation. As supplements to the WSRA, many states and local governments also administer programs to protect wild and scenic rivers, but these programs, like the WSRA, are strongly hampered by the pervasive aversion to governmental land use decisions.

D. COMPREHENSIVE STATE AND REGIONAL PLANNING AND MANAGEMENT

Comprehensive state and regional planning and management systems, including protections of environmentally critical areas, have emerged only sporadically across the United States, except for federal lands as noted in the preceding chapter. Regional land use planning and management is clearly the exception to the American rule of local control over land use decisions. Bi-state land use commissions have been established for Lake Tahoe and the Columbia River Gorge.[18] Other states have established substate regional land use planning and permitting agencies to supervise development along the California Coast, in the Hackensack Meadowlands and Pinelands of New Jersey, and in the Adirondack Mountains of New York State.[19] Additionally, some established regional institutions, such as the Delaware River Basin Commission and the South Florida Water Management District, perform land use planning and management functions with conservation as one of their goals.

In practice, regional planning and management are often necessary for rational resolution of problems that extend beyond village limits, but regional coordination (if it has any teeth) threatens both existing governmental institutions and development interests.[20] There is, moreover, a justifiable fear that new regional institutions and regional planning by existing institutions will be expensive and cumbersome. Local "Home Rule" land use powers are closely guarded perquisites. It will be interesting to see what coordination mechanisms will be adopted in the future to reconcile local land use control with the necessity to protect regional environmental values.

---

18. Pub. L. No. 91-148, and 16 U.S.C. §§544 et seq. On the subject of the Lake Tahoe area land use planning and management system, see Tahoe-Sierra Preservation Council, Inc. v. Tahoe Regional Planning Agency, 535 U.S. 302 (2002), discussed in Chapter 23.
19. Cal. Pub. Res. Code §30601; N.J. Stat. Ann. §13:17-6; and N.Y. Exec. Law §800; N.Y. Const. Art. 14 §1.
20. The 1970s campaigns to create regional "councils of governments" (COGs) appear to have foundered on these twin shoals.

Nine states — Florida, Georgia, Maine, Maryland, New Jersey, Oregon, Rhode Island, Vermont, and Washington — have enacted comprehensive growth management statutes that require local master plans and zoning ordinances to be consistent with state plans that emphasize protection of natural resources.[21] See F. Bosselman, The Quiet Revolution in Land Use Control (1972).

Oregon has implemented one of the most interesting state-level land use systems. The Comprehensive Land Use Planning Coordination Act, Or. Rev. Stat., tit. 19, ch. 197 (1973), sets up a state Land Conservation and Development Commission (LCDC) with authority to establish statewide land use planning goals. The LCDC adopted 19 statewide goals categorized into 4 broad areas: (1) goals related to planning procedures; (2) conservation goals related to farm lands, forest lands, and natural resources; (3) development goals related to housing, transportation, and public facilities and services; and (4) coastal resource goals. These guidelines are not law, but each local entity must adopt a comprehensive plan and land use regulations implementing the goals, and they must be approved ("acknowledged") by the LCDC. Any "land conservation and development action" must be consistent with the plans and local regulations. If there is no approved plan or regulations, the state guidelines can be applied directly. See Note, 31 Willamette L. Rev. 449 (1995). Oregon's land use planning system combines statewide standards with implementation by local agencies in local regulatory programs that are initially approved and subsequently monitored by the state agency — in a process remarkably like the federal EPA's relationship to state SIPs under the CAA.

E. TRADITIONAL LAND USE CONTROLS AND THE ENVIRONMENT: ZONING, SUBDIVISION REGULATION, ET AL.

In day-to-day practice, the overwhelming majority of land use management occurs at the local level, predominantly through local government regulation (the focus of this part of the chapter) counterbalanced by the constitutional protection afforded to landowners to protect their property rights from unreasonable governmental interference (Chapter 23). Local land use law is quite variable from jurisdiction to jurisdiction and thus cannot be treated in more than cursory fashion in this textbook.

Section 1. SUBDIVISION REGULATIONS

A variety of environmental problems commonly arise throughout the United States when subdividers take large parcels of land (often farms or ranches purchased in large blocks) and divide them up legally into many small lots (often a quarter of an acre or less) to be resold subject to a master recorded deed ("plat"). The problems posed by subdivisions can be severe. Developers too often lack design sophistication, ignoring topography so that various roads and lots lie at steep angles. Physical site disruption

---

21. For a useful review of these statutes, see Wickersham, The Quiet Revolution Continues: The Emerging New Model for State Growth Management Statutes, 18 Harv. Envtl. L. Rev. 489, 524-529 (1994). On Vermont's elaborate statewide land use review and permit legislation, Act 250 [10 Vt. Stat. Ann. §6086(a)(1-10)], see the two-volume treatise edited by Richard Brooks, Toward Community Sustainability: Vermont's Act 250 (1997).

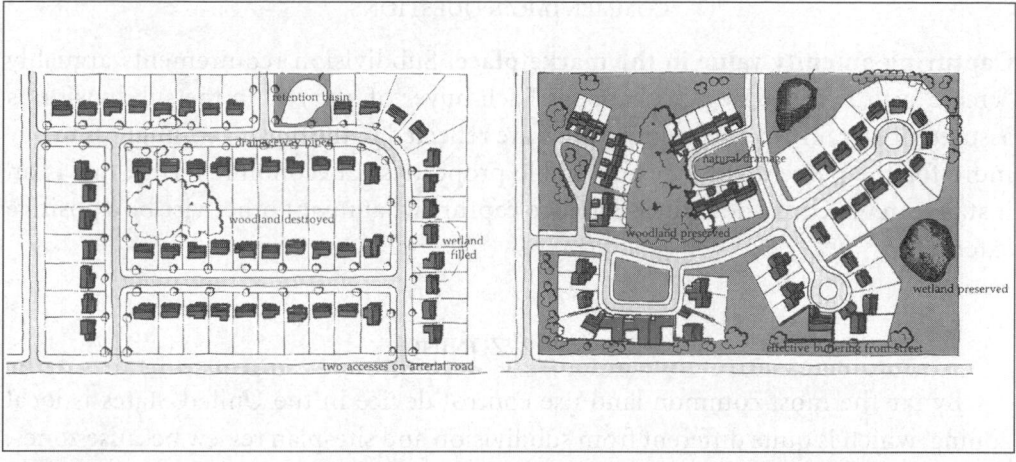

FIGURE 25-1

Same parcel of land, two development alternatives: Standard subdivision design covering maximal area with diminished utility, or "performance" design retaining natural features, more amenities, less roadway, same or greater population, higher unit prices. Reprinted with permission from Lane Kendig, et al., Performance Zoning, 1980 American Planning Association, Suite 1600, 122 S. Michigan Ave., Chicago IL 60603. Applying the same principles across a broader geographical area promotes effective anti-sprawl Smart Growth development patterns.

and other problems can occur: For example, erosion and septic overflows from high-density uses frequently cause degradation of lakes and rivers.

Subdivision regulations work by focusing on the registration of the master deed plat: Before a master plat subdividing a parcel into lots can be recorded, the ordinance requires that it meet a variety of legal requirements — e.g., sewerage, utilities, and road criteria — often expressed in the form of certificates annexed to the master plat itself.

To these basic requirements, which have obvious environmental consequences, communities have started adding more sophisticated subdivision requirements: e.g., erosion and sedimentation control standards, dedication of park land and other "exactions" offsetting burdens imposed on the community,[22] certified landscape architects' plans with analyses of groundwater flows and slope configurations, and the like.[23] Subdivision regulations can also require that developers put enforceable restrictive covenants and other private law devices on the master deed, such as requirements for open space protection, density controls, and other use restrictions, which are specifically enforceable both by the local government, as a third party beneficiary, and also by other lot owners. The more carefully such ordinances are drafted, the more they assure that developments will be harmonious with their surrounding environment. These ordinances frequently enhance the profitability of developments. They may be more acceptable to the developer than other forms of land use regulation because they bear a clear relationship to the value of parcels in the subdivision.

---

22. Exactions may have takings implications. See Chapter 23.

23. Design standards can encourage site plans that "cluster" residential structures to preserve the maximum amount of amenities and useful space for the inhabitants of the subdivision, rather than cutting up the parcel into the allowable number of standardized front, back, and side lots covering the site like a checkerboard.

COMMENTARY & QUESTIONS

Capturing amenity value in the marketplace. Subdivision requirements arguably "create" value. How does this happen? Each buyer of a parcel in the subdivision is assured of certain amenity values, which are reflected in the buyer's willingness to pay more for the parcel than for comparable properties. In economic terms, this is an instance in which the developer is able to capture what might otherwise be a positive externality.

Section 2. ZONING

By far the most common land use control device in the United States is local zoning, which is quite different from subdivision and site-plan review because zones, included in a Master Plan, apply to every square inch of the jurisdiction and set out a comprehensive set of land use district designations specifying, before the fact, which uses will automatically be allowed and which excluded. The most common form of zone ordinance is the "Euclidean" model, named for Village of Euclid v. Ambler Realty Co., 272 U.S. 365 (1926), the case that established zoning's general validity.[24]

Zoning directly affects private property decisions, which explains why, from its inception, it has stirred up a hornet's nest of opposition. Nevertheless, because the land-use problems of American communities have become so much more complex and pressing since World War II, zoning has become an unloved but widespread phenomenon. Of major American cities, only Houston has refused to employ zoning, and has apparently paid the price in chaotic land-development patterns.

Zoning implicitly incorporates some environmental values. If a zone planning agency knows which way the political wind is blowing, it will not locate residential areas downwind from its industrial zone districts. "Densities" (concentrations of permitted structures) designated for various districts may have direct consequences for local quality of life. The districting process, however, must build upon existing political systems, and in many cases "Home Rule" laws induce each community to perceive itself as a separate little city-state, with prime residential areas, industrial zones to capture tax base, no waste-disposal sites, and no coordination on a county or regional basis to determine how and where larger settlement and economic development patterns should be located.

Over the years, a variety of other environmental regulations have often been grafted as overlays to basic zoning ordinances, capitalizing upon zoning's established political and legal acceptability. Thus when some communities wanted to protect wetlands or flood plains, they added overlay categories to their zone maps; land in any district that had the characteristics of flood plain or wetland had to comply with the

---

24. The Euclidean model requires: (1) a comprehensive plan, adopted by the community, analyzing existing land uses and specifying future community development desires; (2) a separate zone ordinance creating a catalogue of zone district categories, defining the range of permitted uses, densities, and structural characteristics in each category; (3) an official zone map, incorporated as part of the ordinance, mapping out the districts on the ground; and, finally, (4) a zone enforcement agency, acting to interpret and apply the zone requirements throughout the community, and reviewing and determining enforcement issues, special exceptions, and variances as required.

added requirements. Some communities have added "open space" overlays or green belt requirements, erosion and sedimentation restrictions, historic preservation controls, and similar modern environmental resource protections to the basic zone ordinance and map.

Over time, as local zoning increasingly reflects the growing sophistication of the land use planning and landscape architecture specialties, more and more environmentally oriented elements will be incorporated in the initial planning and the subsequent implementation of zone ordinances.

COMMENTARY & QUESTIONS

1. **The local basis of zoning.** The federal government, as noted earlier, generally stays far away from regulating land use. State governments also typically avoid direct land use regulation, leaving it up to the lowest level of government — local government — with a few exceptions.[25] Efforts to set up regional land use controls have largely failed, due to the balkanized nature of intergovernmental relations and the traditional norms of local government home rule.

Consider the range of legal problems and political turmoil that would be engendered by shifting particularized land use control decisions to the state or regional levels. How would one draw rational jurisdictional lines? According to river drainage watersheds? Airsheds? Metropolitan-based market areas? Zoning replays a traditional question of democracy: To what extent should single communities be able to operate as isolated units?

Along with the drawbacks of fracturing land use controls into tens of thousands of small, uncoordinated jurisdictions, there are corresponding advantages. In addition to its widespread acceptance, zoning reflects local knowledge of the community and landscape in which it applies. It can often serve as a useful vehicle for carrying modern environmental ideas into practical land development practice.

2. **TDRs.** A number of local governments have set up creative systems of TDRs, transferable development rights, to give developers and the public a measure of design flexibility. Much like the markets in tradeable pollution credits noted in Chapter 14, TDRs represent unused development density at one site that can be transferred and sold to other sites that wish to build beyond standard regulatory limits.

> TDR programs aim to direct development away from environmentally sensitive land to land more suitable for development by creating a market for development rights. Logistically, TDR programs achieve this result by quantifying the development potential of sensitive properties ("sending sites"), and providing that this development potential may be sold to landowners to increase building density in areas suitable for development ("receiving sites"). Good v. United States, 39 Fed. Cl. 81, 107 (1997).

New York City has a complex system of TDRs, featured in the *Penn Central* case, 438 U.S. 104 (1978) (see Chapter 23), where the Supreme Court held that the value of

---

25. Hawaii and Maine have state-based land use regulatory systems that, at least in theory, cover the entire state.

TDRs is relevantly weighed in regulatory takings challenges. The technique has state- and federal-level corollaries, notably the CAA's sale of sulfur oxides credits (see Chapter 11), and notable potential for further applications. The theory was charted out in Professor John Costonis's Development Rights Transfers: An Exploratory Essay, 83 Yale L.J. 75 (1973); for a current environmental TDR primer, see McEleney, Using Transferable Development Rights to Preserve Vanishing Landscapes and Landmarks, 1995 Ill. B.J. 634.

A particularly interesting environmental application of TDRs has been implemented in the Lake Tahoe Basin. The Tahoe Regional Planning Agency, created through a bi-state compact between Nevada and California, seeks to prevent overdevelopment of the watershed in order to reduce erosion and sewage discharges into the lake. Under the terms of its integrated Basin management plan, designed to protect the lake's remarkably pure waters, owners of restricted parcels may sell TDRs within the Basin, even across the state line. See Fink, Structuring a Program for the Lake Tahoe Basin, 18 Ecology L.Q. 485 (1991); Suitum v. Tahoe Regional Planning Agency, 520 U.S. 725 (1997); Lazarus, Litigating Suitum..., 12 J. Land Use & Envtl. L. 179 (1995). One challenge, in both constitutional and planning terms, is to assure a sufficient array of transfer-importing sites to maintain a market, while assuring that the TDR transfers serve and not undermine the public values sought to be protected in the base regulation.

3. **Impact fees.** This evolving device resembles subdivision exactions. Impact fees respond to the problem that developers often locate high-density developments without sufficient regard to the public's costs of providing utilities and amenities. Impact fees are a self-defense mechanism, analyzing the imposed costs and requiring that they be paid in advance. Impact fees can defray costs of added parks and recreation facilities, schools, drainage and sewer construction, roads and other transportation infrastructure, groundwater recharge facilities, and an infinitely expandable range of other imposed costs.[26] In economic terms, what role do impact fees play? Do they force the project proponent to internalize costs, or are they instead merely a form of governmental extortion? Like other land use devices currently applied at the local level, impact fees can mobilize the expertise and defensive instincts of local communities. They hold larger intercommunity and regional potential as well.

F. THE "SMART GROWTH" MOVEMENT AND THE ENVIRONMENT

"The best developers have visions that extend beyond the single site or project to what makes a better neighborhood, a better community, and a better quality of life."

National Governors' Association, 2000

There is a growing realization among the American public that urban sprawl development — the post–World War II American ideal — can be inimical to a desirable quality of life and a sustainable environmental and economic future. The "Smart Growth" Movement is one expression of public frustration with urban sprawl

---

26. See Blasser & Kentopp, Impact Fees: The Second Generation, 38 J. Urb. & Contemp. L. 55 (1990).

development. In the following excerpt, the author describes the basic tenets of "Smart Growth" and assays the potential of "Smart Growth" to change American patterns of land development and use.

Oliver A. Pollard III, Smart Growth: The Promise, Politics, and Potential Pitfalls of Emerging Growth Management Strategies
19 Virginia Environmental Law Journal 247 (2000)

...Although growth can bring jobs, wealth, tax revenues, and amenities, more people are recognizing the link between accelerating suburban sprawl and pervasive problems such as traffic congestion, overcrowded schools, deteriorating neighborhoods, air and water pollution, higher taxes, and communities that are being transformed by changing development and population patterns, regardless of whether they are declining or struggling to deep pace with growth....

Current land use and transportation policies have become a major issue of environmental concern as evidence of the heavy toll sprawling development patterns take on the environment continues to mount. Virtually every environmental problem — from air and water pollution to the destruction of wetlands and wildlife habitat, from global climate change to overflowing landfills — has been linked to the land consumption and pollution that result from current land use and transportation patterns....

A more nuanced view of economic development is emerging. Citizens and politicians increasingly recognize that they face choices about the pace, scale, and location of development they wish to permit and attract. There is also greater recognition that development decisions are not merely the result of the free market, but are influenced by a broad range of federal, state, and local policies. Further, in a more mobile, information-based economy, it is increasingly evident that the quality of life in an area can have a significant impact on its ability to attract and retain businesses. These changing views of development have sparked efforts throughout the country to capture the benefits of economic growth while minimizing the costs;... Many of these strategies are being lumped together under the label "smart growth."...

The goals of smart growth [are] to balance economic development and limit sprawl by channeling growth to areas that have already been developed; to revitalize and prevent the decline of existing urban and suburban areas; to promote more compact urban form; to protect open space, farmland, forests, and environmentally sensitive areas from suburban encroachment; to reduce the public cost of providing infrastructure and services to new development by making more efficient use of existing resources; to protect the natural environment; and to provide affordable housing....

In contrast [to state growth management acts], smart growth approaches, at least at this point in the evolution of the concept, do not place as much emphasis on regulation to shape long-term growth patterns. Land use controls, such as zoning codes, and environmental regulations remain important, but smart growth typically seeks to supplement these provisions using incentives rather than additional regulation. The model state smart growth statute is Maryland's Priority Funding Areas Act [Md. Ann Code State Fin. & Procurement Act §5-7B-01 to §5-7B-10), which was part of a broader "Smart Growth and Neighborhood Conservation" initiative. This statute does not identify specific measures local governments must adopt. Instead, it targets the flow of state funds for "growth related" projects (such as highways and water and sewer lines) to existing communities and to additional areas where growth is planned as long as these additional areas meet minimum state criteria for average residential density and for provision of public water and sewer. Development is not prohibited outside the designated growth areas, but by limiting state financial assistance outside of these areas, the statute creates a strong incentive for localities to guide growth to existing communities. The premise is that guiding growth to areas with existing infrastructure is more efficient than incurring the expense of building new infrastructure to serve development in outlying areas. In addition, encouraging the revitalization of existing communities both strengthens these communities and reduces pressure on undeveloped areas by providing attractive, alternative places to live and work.

In general, the smart growth approach tends to be less proscriptive and less regulatory-intensive than previous growth management efforts. It tends to discourage, rather than to forbid, undesired development....

A second, related distinction between smart growth and more traditional growth management approaches is that smart growth focuses more on the role federal, state, and local government policies and practices play in influencing land use development patterns.

Although the causes of scattered development patterns are numerous and complex, a cornerstone of the smart growth approach is the recognition that public investments (such as funding for highways and water and sewer lines), regulatory policies (such as zoning and street design requirements), and tax policies (such as estate taxes and the tax treatment of easements) strongly influence the pace, scale, and location of development....

Subsidies distort market and individual behavior. There are a host of federal, state, and local public subsidies that arguably have fueled sprawling development for decades,[27] including transportation funding policies that emphasize highway construction; public funding for water and sewer extensions that open new land in outlying areas to development; cash payments and tax breaks to lure new businesses to outlying areas; mortgage policies that subsidize and favor single-family suburban homes; tax deductions for mortgage interest and property taxes; and school construction spending that favors building new schools in new suburban areas over expanding and renovating existing structures....

The smart growth approach seeks to limit or eliminate subsidies that fuel development in outlying areas and undermine existing cities, towns, and suburbs, and to use government expenditures and tax policy to promote more sensible growth patterns in two ways: First, development is guided toward existing communities, encouraging more concentrated, pedestrian- or transit-friendly development within these communities. Measures that promote this objective include providing incentives for infill development, historic preservation, and the development of abandoned industrial sites or "brownfields;"[28] directing government funds for roads, water, sewer, and other infrastructure to existing communities; and allocating a higher percentage of transportation funding to transit, bicycling, and pedestrian projects....

Second, smart growth investments seek to preserve open space, farmland, and environmental areas through tools such as the purchase of property or development rights, or by providing tax incentives for private donations of agricultural or conservation easements....

Smart growth also focuses on the detrimental role governmental regulations can play in driving development to the outskirts of existing communities.... Smart growth...reexamin[es] growth management tools that have been employed in the past and reduc[es] or revis[es] certain planning and zoning requirements that have been found to promote sprawling development.

Instead of refining and extending zoning and planning, advocates for more sensible growth patterns have often called for streamlining or eliminating requirements such as single-use zoning, minimum lot size, setback, parking, and street width standards that are at the heart of

---

27. For an example of the encouragement, by public subsidies, of sprawl development in an environmentally sensitive coastal area, see the discussion of the *Lucas* case in Chapter 23. [Eds.]
28. See Chapter 21. [Eds.]

most zoning codes. Perhaps most strikingly, the bedrock principle of zoning — the segregation of commercial and residential uses into different geographic areas — is increasingly being identified as a culprit driving wasteful, low-density development; such separation requires people to use automobiles to get to work or to shopping areas, to reach a park or a school, or to conduct most other activities....

Political and Policy Obstances to Smarter Growth. Despite the popular support smart growth has enjoyed, it will be difficult to make the fundamental changes in deeply entrenched land use and transportation policies, processes, perceptions, and agencies that are necessary to achieve more sensible growth. The inertia of fifty years of land use and transportation policies that have favored scattered development will not be easy to overcome; bureaucracies are resistant to change, and powerful corporate and other financial interests have an enormous stake in continuing current policies and practices.

Efforts to shift decades of transportation policies emphasizing road building offer an instructive example. Congress made fundamental changes to federal transportation law when it adopted the landmark [ISTEA].[29] Among other things, ISTEA placed greater emphasis on maintaining the existing transportation system, allowing states to spend a larger share of the federal funds they receive on a broader range of transportation options (such as mass transit), increased local authority over transportation decisions, and dedicated transportation funds to air quality improvements in areas that do not meet the requirements of the Clean Air Act.... Yet the practical impact of ISTEA has been limited: although some states broadened the focus of their transportation programs as envisioned..., most have continued to focus on building and expanding roads as the response to their transportation problems and have limited the local role in transportation decisionmaking....

Another factor that may limit the prospects for success of smart growth measures is that growth problems rarely respect political boundaries. Scattered development patterns, as well as the traffic congestion, environmental degradation, fiscal stresses, and other problems that accompany them, tend to be regional in nature, extending beyond the boundaries of any one locality. Consequently, many growth problems are best addressed through regional solutions that federal, state and local smart growth measures may not provide.

Although there is evidence of increasing cooperation among localities as they realize that sprawl problems cross political boundaries, localities are often unwilling to cooperate with one another, jealously guarding their autonomy. Even if localities were to agree to a more sensible growth approach and limit development to areas where there is existing infrastructure, this would not eliminate the competition for new development among localities, particularly since most localities are dependent upon real estate taxes as a primary revenue source....

Some critics argue...that sprawling development is part of a larger problem of unsustainable consumption that smart growth does not address. That charge is that smart growth accepts the dominant growth paradigm in American society that drives unsustainable consumption, rather than addressing deeper issues such as the appropriate rate of population growth and the implications of a lifestyle that consumes a vastly disproportionate share of the world's natural resources. Smart growth thus might lead to more compact development on smaller lot sizes, for example, but the core smart growth concepts would not limit the number of lots created, nor would they limit the amount of material goods possessed, resources used, or waste generated by residents of these more compact areas....

---

29. See the discussion of ISTEA above in the Commentary & Questions following Professor Ruhl's article. [Eds.]

A...criticism of smart growth on equity grounds is that tools to guide growth may be used to stop or slow growth, intentionally or unintentionally limiting the availability of affordable housing. As a result, it can be argued that smart growth may not merely preserve the good life for those who already have it, but deny the good life to those who do not....

COMMENTARY & QUESTIONS

1. **Smart growth and the takings issue.** Which aspects of smart growth might raise constitutional takings questions? (See Chapter 23.) Would your property be "taken" if a change in the local zoning ordinance abolishes "single-use" zoning in your neighborhood and thus significantly reduces your property value?

2. **Are we ready for smart growth?** Identify the economic and political constituencies for current sprawl growth patterns. Is this an invincible political coalition? What economic mechanisms might encourage these interests to support smart growth? For example, might transferrable development rights for development in smart growth areas be distributed to real estate companies that have purchased farmland and are holding it for development? How might municipalities be encouraged to relinquish their devotion to "Home Rule" and participate in regional growth management strategies? Could new revenue-sharing strategies be devised that would discourage the race-to-the-bottom that often accompanies the "rateables game"?

3. **Can we afford smart growth?** Smart growth could be expensive. For example, government must either purchase open space outright or else purchase or lease development rights from landowners. How will these expenditures be funded? Open space taxes? If so, who should be required to pay them?

4. **Is smart growth really smart?** In the long run, will smart growth only reinforce our current glorification of unsustainable and inequitable concepts of economic growth? Or should "growth" be redefined in order to include quality of life concerns, such as environmental protection?

Environmentalists should make good urbanists, since they understand systems, diversity, connectivity and interdependence.

— Caryl Terrell

There are two types of environmentalists: those who understand that the city is part of the environment and those who do not.

—Paul Soglin, Mayor of Madison, Wisconsin

The compact neighborhood is the true architecture of nature…. The loss of a forest or a farm is justified only if it is replaced by a village. A subdivision and a shopping center is not an even trade.

— Andres Duany

FIGURE 26-1

The Grinnell Glacier in Glacier National Park, photographed from the same vantage point in 1910, 1931, and 1997 (top to bottom at left), as average temperatures around the globe continue to rise by small increments over the decades. Having receded 3,100 feet in a century, the glacier is expected to disappear within 30 years.

GLACIER NATIONAL PARK ARCHIVE

"*Earth averaged 57.9 degrees, or 1.6 degrees hotter, in the 1990s than in 1860. Atmospheric carbon dioxide now measures 360 ppm; that's 30 percent higher than at the start of the industrial era, higher, in fact, than in the past 160,000 years. In half a century, that could double.... Atmospheric layers of gases (water vapor, methane, nitrous oxide and carbon dioxide) let in sunlight, then trap heat.... Trouble comes when humans artificially pump up the volume to unnatural levels. Concentrating carbon dioxide...trap[s] more heat. Can we 'think global, act local' regarding climate change? No. But we can invert the slogan to think about what we may lose locally, then act at a global forum." Bruce Babbitt, Park's Retreating Glaciers Signal a Climate Warning, Denver Post, November 16, 1997, at H-08. Cf. T.M. Moore, Climate of Fear: Why We Shouldn't Worry about Global Warming (1997).*

Chapter 26

INTERNATIONAL AND COMPARATIVE ENVIRONMENTAL LAW

A. *Customary International Law*
B. *International Conferences and Soft Law*
C. *Comparative Environmental Law*
D. *Multilateral Environmental Agreements*
E. *International Institutions*

This coursebook began with the metaphor of Spaceship Earth, emphasizing the interconnectedness of the planet's geophysical, ecological, and human components, and the law. Slowly circling the globe, an observing eye could catalog a depressingly long list of planetary environmental threats, more daunting than the problems encountered in any single nation. International environmental governance, however, is not just public international law on the level of relations between nation-states and within international organizations. Just as global environmental problems are built by an aggregation of dozens or billions of individual actions, the legal responses to global problems must inevitably draw upon multiple levels of law and governance — national, subnational, and supra-national forces intersecting with the marketplace, governments and "transgovernmental" linkages, and citizen groups.

Like domestic environmental law, the global setting presents the same tensions and interconnections between the dominant marketplace economy, the economy of Nature, and civic-societal imperatives for sustainability, but on an almost incomprehensibly immense scale. Sustainable development, one of the most important "emerging principles" of international environmental law, is becoming a dominant focusing concept for law and policymaking at national, regional, and local levels as well. As the First Law of Ecology says, everything is connected to everything else.

Over the past two decades, environmental organizations — known in international jargon as NGOs (nongovernmental organizations) — have played an increasingly prominent role in an area previously reserved almost exclusively to states[1] and governments. Environmental activists from every corner of the world have become increasingly energized in publicizing international environmental issues,[2] in lobbying for international rules to protect the global environment, and in utilizing newly created mechanisms for enforcing those rules at the international and domestic levels.

---

1. The word "state" is the standard term in international jurisprudence for a country or nation-state.
2. See, e.g., Wirth, Legitimacy, Accountability, and Partnership: A Model for Advocacy on Third World Environmental Issues, 100 Yale L.J. 2645 (1991).

At the same time, international environmental law has increasingly penetrated into national legal systems, as we saw in Chapter 8, which over time promotes coherence and consistency in environmental law and policy from one state to another. International environmental law is no longer confined strictly to rights and obligations exercised by states, but increasingly is a vehicle for crafting international standards and enforceable national policies simultaneously. International environmental law has established new directions and precedents that have profoundly affected how states deal with each other in every aspect of international relations.

While pessimism about the fate of the world in general, and the environment in particular, may be the order of the day in the United States and abroad, lawyers and others with legal training are uniquely well positioned to alter the trajectory of the future. Notwithstanding the serious challenges facing us as a planet, there is reason for optimism about the potential for meaningful solutions. This chapter presents international environmental law and policy not as an abstract, amorphous, and enormous problem — although it is all of those. Instead, we proceed from the perspective that complex interrelated international linkages can be demystified and mastered by identifying the forces that drive them and the junctures at which they can be effectively influenced. Just as previous generations of lawyers, activists, advocates, and environmental professionals molded the domestic law of the environment from next to nothing, the international environmental lawyers of the present and future face the exhilarating opportunity and profound responsibility of shaping the world to come.

A. CUSTOMARY INTERNATIONAL LAW

Transboundary pollution is the simplest form of international environmental problem. Toxic by-products from a manufacturing process in one state may cause harm in another state because a factory may be located at or near the border between the two countries. Typically such situations involve the transmission of a physical pollutant into a passive, and perhaps unknowing, "victim" state. The international setting, however, raises complexities that are not encountered in a purely domestic context like the United States. What standards apply to the activity, if any? Does the victim state have the authority to enforce that standard, or any rights at all? What about impacts on private parties, including landowners and citizens, in the victim state? Just such a situation arose in the early twentieth century along the western border between the United States and Canada.

Trail Smelter Arbitration (United States v. Canada)
3 U.N.R.I.A.A. 1965 (1941)

[A privately owned metal smelter operating in Trail, British Columbia, had been belching sulfur dioxide fumes into Washington State, causing considerable damage to orchards and other property on the U.S. side of the border. No private remedy was available to the injured U.S. citizens: The courts of British Columbia did not have jurisdiction to hear the case because the injury was physically located across the border, and the courts of Washington lacked jurisdiction because the polluters had no business presence in their state. The United States intervened — somewhat unusually because the case did not directly concern the interests or conduct of either national government — filing what amounted to a novel international nuisance claim. At first, the issue was referred for study to the International Joint Commission, a standing international organization established under a 1909 treaty on boundary waters between the United States and Canada. In 1931 the Commission identified a figure of U.S. $350,000 in accrued damages, together with a finding expressing the Tribunal's expectation that further harm would not occur. Canada accepted the report, but the United States did not. The two countries negotiated an agreement to settle the dispute, a type of international legal instrument often known by the French term *compromis*. The *compromis* referred the disagreement to a three-member arbitral tribunal established specifically to deal with this case, consisting of one Canadian, one American, and a Belgian national. Article III of the *compromis* instructed the arbitral tribunal to decide the following four questions:

1. Whether damage caused by the Trail Smelter in the State of Washington has occurred since the first day of January 1932, and, if so, what indemnity should be paid therefor?

2. In the event of the answer to the first part of the preceding question being in the affirmative, whether the Trail Smelter should be required to refrain from causing damage in the State of Washington in the future and, if so, to what extent?

3. In the light of the answer to the preceding question, what measures or regime, if any, should be adopted or maintained by the Trail Smelter?

4. What indemnity or compensation, if any, should be paid on account of any decision or decisions rendered by the Tribunal pursuant to the preceding two questions?

Article IV of the *compromis* stated: "The Tribunal shall apply the law and practice followed in dealing with cognate question in the United States of America as well as international law and practice, and shall give consideration to the desire of the high contracting parties to reach a solution just to all parties concerned." In 1938 the tribunal rendered a preliminary decision establishing interim restrictions for the smelter's operation and issued the following final decision in 1941.[3]]

Decision of the Tribunal. The first problem which arises is whether the question should be answered on the basis of the law followed in the United States or on the basis of international law. The Tribunal, however, finds that this problem need not be solved here as the law followed in the United States in dealing with the quasi-sovereign rights of the States of the Union, in the matter of air pollution, whilst more definite, is in conformity with the general rules of international law....

No case of air pollution dealt with by an international tribunal has been brought to the attention of the Tribunal nor does the Tribunal know of any such case. The nearest analogy is that of water pollution. But, here also, no decision of an international tribunal has been cited or has been found.

There are, however, as regards both air pollution and water pollution, certain decisions of the Supreme Court of the United States which may legitimately be taken as a guide in this field of international law, for it is reasonable to follow by analogy, in international cases, precedents established by that court in dealing with controversies between States of the Union or with other controversies concerning the quasi-sovereign rights of such States, where no contrary rule prevails in international law and no reason for rejecting such precedents can be adduced from the limitations of sovereignty inherent in the Constitution of the United States.

---

3. See Read, The Trail Smelter Dispute, 1 Can. Y.B. Int'l L. 213 (1963); Rubin, Pollution by Analogy: The Trail Smelter Arbitration, 50 Or. L. Rev. 259 (1971). The citation for the 1938 order is 3 U.N.R.I.A.A. 1905 (1938).

In the suit of the State of Missouri v. the State of Illinois (200 U.S. 496, 521) concerning the pollution, within the boundaries of Illinois, of the Illinois River, an affluent of the Mississippi flowing into the latter where it forms the boundary between that State and Missouri, an injunction was refused. "Before this court ought to intervene," said the court, "the case should be of serious magnitude, clearly and fully proved, and the principle to be applied should be one which the court is prepared deliberately to maintain against all considerations on the other side." The court found that the practice complained of was general along the shores of the Mississippi River at that time, that it was followed by Missouri itself and that thus a standard was set up by the defendant which the claimant was entitled to invoke.

As the claims of public health became more exacting and methods for removing impurities from the water were perfected, complaints ceased. It is significant that Missouri sided with Illinois when the other riparians of the Great Lakes' system sought to enjoin it to desist from diverting the waters of that system into that of the Illinois and Mississippi for the very purpose of disposing of the Chicago sewage....

What the Supreme Court says there of its power under the Constitution equally applies to the extraordinary power granted this Tribunal under the Convention. What is true between States of the Union is, at least, equally true concerning the relations between the United States and the Dominion of Canada.

In another recent case concerning water pollution (283 U.S. 473), the complainant was successful. The City of New York was enjoined, at the request of the State of New Jersey, to desist, within a reasonable time limit, from the practice of disposing of sewage by dumping it into the sea, a practice which was injurious to the coastal waters of New Jersey in the vicinity of her bathing resorts.

In the matter of air pollution itself, the leading decisions are those of the Supreme Court in the State of Georgia v. Tennessee Copper Company and Ducktown Sulphur, Copper and Iron Company, Limited. Although dealing with a suit against private companies, the decisions were on questions cognate to those here at issue. Georgia stated that it had in vain sought relief from the State of Tennessee, on whose territory the smelters were located, and the court defined the nature of the suit by saying: "This is a suit by a State for an injury to it in its capacity of quasi-sovereign. In that capacity, the State has an interest independent of and behind the titles of its citizens, in all the earth and air within its domain."

On the question whether an injunction should be granted or not, the court said (206 U.S. 230):

> It [the State] has the last word as to whether its mountains shall be stripped of their forests and its inhabitants shall breathe pure air.... It is not lightly to be presumed to give up quasi-sovereign rights for pay and...if that be its choice, it may insist that an infraction of them shall be stopped. This court has not quite the same freedom to balance the harm that will be done by an injunction against that of which the plaintiff complains, that it would have in deciding between two subjects of a single political power. Without excluding the considerations that equity always takes into account...it is a fair and reasonable demand on the part of a sovereign that the air over its territory should not be polluted on a great scale by sulphurous acid gas, that the forests on its mountains, be they better or worse, and whatever domestic destruction they may have suffered, should not be further destroyed or threatened by the act of persons beyond its control, that the crops and orchards on its hills should not be endangered from the same source.... Whether Georgia, by insisting upon this claim, is doing more harm than good to her own citizens, is for her to determine. The possible disaster to those outside the State must be accepted as a consequence of her standing upon her extreme rights.

Later on, however, when the court actually framed an injunction, in the case of the Ducktown Company (237 U.S. 474, 477) (an agreement on the basis of an annual compensation was reached with the most important of the two smelters, the Tennessee Copper Company), they did not go beyond a decree "adequate to diminish materially the present probability of damage to its (Georgia's) citizens."

Great progress in the control of fumes has been made by science in the last few years and this progress should be taken into account.

The Tribunal, therefore, finds that the above decisions, taken as a whole, constitute an adequate basis for its conclusions, namely, that, under the principles of international law, as well as of the law of the United States, no State has the right to use or permit the use of its territory in such a manner as to cause injury by fumes in or to the territory of another or the properties or persons therein, when the case is of serious consequence and the injury is established by clear and convincing evidence....

Considering the circumstances of the case, the Tribunal holds that the Dominion of Canada is responsible in international law for the conduct of the Trail Smelter. Apart from the undertakings in the Convention, it is, therefore, the duty of the Government of the Dominion of Canada to see to it that this conduct should be in conformity with the obligation of the Dominion under international law as herein determined.

COMMENTARY & QUESTIONS

1. **Customary international law.** In Chapter 8, we encountered treaties as the international equivalent of contracts between states that create law for the parties to them. The *Trail Smelter* arbitration relies on the other principal kind or "source" of international law, known as "custom." Unlike the law in the United States and many other countries, customary international law is not based on a text in the form of a constitution or a statute. Rather, customary international law accumulates over time through a pattern of practice of states based on a sense of legal right or obligation (*opinio juris*). States adopt patterns of behaviors in dealing with other states that are in those states' mutual interests. As those patterns are reinforced over time and states come to rely on them as predicting future state behavior, those habits crystallize into legally enforceable norms or rules. The legal status of the high seas as a global commons, beyond the jurisdictional reach of any state, is originally of customary origin, arising because all states have an interest in freedom of the seas to facilitate global commerce. At a more micro level, for obvious practical reasons it became a uniform customary legal rule that ships passing on the right had priority. Proving the existence of a customary rule involves two steps. The first is identifying the pattern of state behavior. While the pattern need not be universal without departures, it must be discernibly consistent. Second, the pattern must be motivated by a sense of legal obligation. The evidence of both factors can be drawn from various actions and inactions by states that are not ordinarily considered lawmaking, including statements of government officials in press releases and news conferences, actions of regulatory authorities in an enforcement setting, and news stories reporting factual events. If you were representing the United States, how would you confirm the existence of a customary rule governing a situation like that encountered in the *Trail Smelter* arbitration? If you were representing Canada, how would you attempt to demonstrate the absence of a rule? What are the

relative advantages and disadvantages of custom as opposed to treaties as legal vehicles for making international environmental law? Although customary law would appear to develop slowly, that is not necessarily so. So long as acceptance of a new principle is widespread, the law may change quite quickly, a phenomenon sometimes called "instant custom."[4]

2. **State responsibility for internationally wrongful acts.** International claims typically are framed in terms of "state responsibility." The regime of state responsibility is the approximate international analogue of a tort system, with the important distinction that the law applies to, and can be invoked by, states and not private actors such as individuals or corporations. As with many international environmental issues, the real parties in interest in the *Trail Smelter* dispute are not states, but individuals. On their behalf, how could you overcome the doctrine that international law does not regulate the behavior of the Canadian smelter because the owner of the smelter is not a "subject" of international law? Similarly, how would you establish standing (*locus standi*), given that your client is an individual and not a state? The international system deals with these structural problems through a legal construct known as "espousal." In principle, the Tribunal in the *Trail Smelter* arbitration is not adjudicating a dispute between two private parties, but between two states — the United States and Canada. The claimant state, in this case the United States, has espoused the claim of the Washington landowners, in effect adopting the injuries of its nationals as its own. If you represent the Washington landowners, what difficulties might you have in persuading the U.S. government to "espouse" your clients' claims or to resolve them satisfactorily once espoused? If you represent the government of Canada, what arguments might you make that Canada ought not be responsible for the behavior of private parties under its jurisdiction, such as the smelter at Trail?

3. **International adjudication.** Like the law of treaties, customary international law governs relations between states even if there is no obvious forum in which to apply it. The United States could have asserted an international "claim" against Canada through bilateral diplomatic channels even if Canada had refused to agree to establish an arbitral tribunal. In a domestic setting, we think of taking disputes to court as the norm. In the international system, in which there are no courts of general jurisdiction, that is not necessarily the case. In the *Trail Smelter* arbitration, the two governments took the step of contractually agreeing to arbitrate the dispute before a neutral, impartial tribunal and to accept the result as binding. In international jurisprudence, opinions of international courts and tribunals like the one in this dispute are evidence of the state of the law. But international tribunals, in contrast to common law courts, cannot make international law, which is created strictly by states and a few other subjects of international law, including international organizations. The International Court of Justice (ICJ), sitting in The Hague, Netherlands, has a strictly delimited scope of law that it can

---

4. As discussed below in regard to the Rio UNCED and similar conclaves, international conference statements endorsed by most or all states on the planet may rapidly change the law. As a nonenvironmental example, widespread acceptance of, or at least acquiescence in, the need for the military operations in Afghanistan after the terrorist attacks of September 11, 2001, arguably tended to solidify the proposition that states have an obligation to refrain from harboring terrorists — a principle not widely understood as international law before then.

apply.[5] Taken together with the requirement for espousal, the hurdles to binding international dispute settlement of transboundary pollution issues such as sulfur fumes from a smelter in British Columbia are high indeed. Based on your insights from domestic environmental law, what recommendations could you make to modify international law to facilitate binding resolution of international pollution controversies, consistent with the basic principle that only states may make international law?

4. **The rule of the *Trail Smelter*.** Before the *Trail Smelter* decision, as noted by the Tribunal, international law appeared to provide no rule of decision dealing with harm to a private party in one jurisdiction by a private party in another. The *Trail Smelter* arbitration is consequently most famous for articulating the rule that "under the principles of international law, as well as of the law of the United States, no State has the right to use or permit the use of its territory in such a manner as to cause injury by fumes in or to the territory of another or the properties or persons therein, when the case is of serious consequence and the injury is established by clear and convincing evidence." This teaching is similar to the common law maxim *sic utere tuo ut alienum non laedas* — one should use one's own property so as not to injure that of another. According to the Tribunal, what is the source of this customary rule? Why does the Tribunal rely on cases from the United States? How convincing do you consider its reasoning? Comparing the Tribunal's articulation of this principle to the tasks that the U.S. and Canadian governments assigned the Tribunal in the *compromis*, how would you characterize the famous language as an analytical matter? To what extent is this "principle" necessary to the tasks the Tribunal was instructed to perform? If you are representing the polluting state, Ruritania, in a different dispute initiated by the "victim" state of Fredonia, how might you argue that the rule of the *Trail Smelter* is not good law? If it does apply to Ruritania and Fredonia, how might you envisage distinguishing that situation from that in the *Trail Smelter* dispute? What do you think of the wisdom of the *Trail Smelter* rule from an international environmental policy point of view? What are the benefits of the rule? What might be its drawbacks? How would you evaluate it from an economic perspective? Is it effective as a rule of environmental protection?

B. INTERNATIONAL CONFERENCES AND SOFT LAW

Customary international law of the *Trail Smelter* variety may be too slow in evolving to meet the urgent environmental threats of the twenty-first century. Based on a pattern of often unilateral actions, and frequently reflecting existing power relationships among the international community, customary principles often leave little room for bargaining and deal-making of the sort necessary to engage many or all states in a

---

5. According to Article 36 of the Statute of the International Court of Justice, a multilateral agreement appended to the Charter of the United Nations, the ICJ may obtain jurisdiction over a "contentious" case by (1) special agreement or *compromis*; (2) a clause in a treaty specifying that disputes arising under the agreement may be referred to the Court; or (3) the prior general consent of a state to the Court's exercise of jurisdiction in all cases or particular classes of cases, the misleadingly named "compulsory" jurisdiction of the Court. Article 65 also authorizes the ICJ, unlike federal courts in the United States, to issue advisory opinions.

collective solution to a common problem. As demonstrated by the *Trail Smelter* rule, the content of customary norms may be vague or uncertain, or formulated as adjective tests — attributes that are not necessarily helpful when the practical, real-world need may be, for example, emissions reductions of a specified amount. Because the existence of a customary rule depends on a pattern of state behavior that may be difficult to discern, the very existence of a customary norm may be subject to dispute. International agreements, as discussed in Chapter 8, overcome many of these impediments but are themselves subject to other weaknesses due to the twin downward drags of consent and consensus that characterize most international processes.

Jump-starting progress on international environmental policy at high-profile, global meetings is a recent response to these problems. The first of these events, the United Nations Conference on the Human Environment held in Stockholm, Sweden, in 1972, is generally considered the catalytic event signaling the internationalization of environmental policy and law. Delegations representing 114 of the then-131 UN member states participated in the 1972 event. The Stockholm Conference advocated the creation of a new UN effort that became the United Nations Environment Program (UNEP), virtually the sole international institution whose mission is strictly environmental. More generally, the Stockholm Conference left a lasting legacy as a clarion call for cooperative action on environmental problems of international and even global concern.

The Stockholm meeting adopted a conference declaration containing 26 principles and an action plan including 109 recommendations for future implementation at the international level. Unlike a formal international agreement like those discussed in Chapter 8, the Stockholm Declaration does not have identifiable parties, did not have an identifiable date for entry into force, and was not subject to ratification. The Stockholm Declaration is an advisory statement of purpose — so-called soft law, in contrast to binding or "hard" legal obligations contained in bilateral or multilateral treaties or whose origin is custom. Although frequently encountered, the term "soft law" is itself an oxymoron because international law governs only binding obligations, whose origin is typically treaty or custom. In the international system, nonbinding standards or expectations are not law at all.

The Stockholm Declaration is an example of a very large number of these nonbinding international instruments, whose form may vary significantly but that nonetheless set out normative expectations for behavior by states. Conference declarations like the Stockholm Declaration, recommendations, guidelines and principles adopted by international organizations, and multi- and bilateral summit statements are but a few of the vehicles for governments to undertake commitments or to create expectations that are politically significant but not legally binding.

Nonbinding documents may serve a number of purposes. Perhaps the most important function of soft law is consciously to establish normative expectations — to be contrasted with binding obligations, which in principle are the realm of "hard" law. Nonbinding instruments often function as "good practice standards," phrased in terms of advisory "shoulds" rather than obligatory "shalls." While not creating formal international legal obligations, these advisory instruments can nonetheless establish widely accepted standards for desirable or sound state practice. Adjectives typically applied to this category of instruments include "hortatory," "precatory," and "aspirational."

On the twentieth anniversary of the Stockholm Conference nearly to the day, the United Nations Conference on Environment and Development (UNCED), the so-called Earth Summit, was held in Rio de Janeiro, Brazil, in 1992. The Earth Summit was expressly planned as a successor to the Stockholm Conference. Continuity was assured by the selection of Maurice Strong, Secretary General of the Stockholm Conference, to serve in the same capacity for UNCED. More than 180 countries sent delegations to the Rio meeting, which, due to the presence of over 100 heads of state or government, was the largest summit-level conference to that date. Like the earlier Stockholm meeting, the Rio conference was preceded by extensive preparatory meetings. The principal theme of UNCED was reconciling environmental protection and economic development, an approach encapsulated in the term "sustainable development."

While there is no agreed definition for "sustainable development," a widely accepted description was provided by a precursor body, the World Commission on Environment and Development:

> Sustainable development is development that meets the needs of the present without compromising the ability of future generations to meet their own needs. It contains within it two key concepts:
>
> • the concept of "needs," in particular the essential needs of the world's poor, to which overriding priority should be given; and
>
> • the idea of limitations imposed by the state of technology and social organization on the environment's ability to meet present and future needs.

UNCED produced four major pieces of "deliverables" (international parlance for lasting work products). Two major multilateral conventions were opened for signature at the Earth Summit: the United Nations Framework Convention on Climate Change, discussed in Section D below, and a Convention on Biological Diversity. The nonbinding Rio Declaration on Environment and Development, consisting of 27 principles, originally planned as an "Earth Charter," was purposefully crafted as a successor to the Stockholm Declaration. The nonbinding Agenda 21, the action plan for the future adopted at UNCED, is the analogue of the Stockholm action plan.[6]

Rio Declaration on Environment and Development
31 I.L.M. 876 (1992)

The United Nations Conference on Environment and Development...

Reaffirming the Declaration of the United Nations Conference on the Human Environment, adopted at Stockholm on 16 June 1972, and seeking to build upon it...

Proclaims that:

---

6. See generally Wirth, The Rio Declaration on Environment and Development: Two Steps Forward and One Back, or Vice Versa?, 29 Ga. L. Rev. 599 (1994); Kovar, A Short Guide to the Rio Declaration, 4 Colum. J. Int'l Envtl. L. & Pol'y 119 (1993). The text of the Rio Declaration was drafted in private toward the end of the preparatory meetings leading up to UNCED by a small group of seven industrialized and seven developing countries, with the direct input of Preparatory Committee chairman Tommy Koh from Singapore. That text was adopted by the Rio conference without alteration.

Principle 1. Human beings are at the centre of concerns for sustainable development. They are entitled to a healthy and productive life in harmony with nature.

Principle 2. States have, in accordance with the Charter of the United Nations and the principles of international law, the sovereign right to exploit their own resources pursuant to their own environmental and developmental policies, and the responsibility to ensure that activities within their jurisdiction or control do not cause damage to the environment of other States or of areas beyond the limits of national jurisdiction.

Principle 3. The right to development must be fulfilled so as to equitably meet developmental and environmental needs of present and future generations.

Principle 4. In order to achieve sustainable development, environmental protection shall constitute an integral part of the development process and cannot be considered in isolation from it....

Principle 6. The special situation and needs of developing countries, particularly the least developed and those most environmentally vulnerable, shall be given special priority. International actions in the field of environment and development should also address the interests and needs of all countries.

Principle 7. States shall cooperate in a spirit of global partnership to conserve, protect and restore the health and integrity of the Earth's ecosystem. In view of the different contributions to global environmental degradation, States have common but differentiated responsibilities. The developed countries acknowledge the responsibility that they bear in the international pursuit of sustainable development in view of the pressures their societies place on the global environment and of the technologies and financial resources they command....

Principle 10. Environmental issues are best handled with the participation of all concerned citizens, at the relevant level. At the national level, each individual shall have appropriate access to information concerning the environment that is held by public authorities, including information on hazardous materials and activities in their communities, and the opportunity to participate in decision-making processes. States shall facilitate and encourage public awareness and participation by making information widely available. Effective access to judicial and administrative proceedings, including redress and remedy, shall be provided....

Principle 12. States should cooperate to promote a supportive and open international economic system that would lead to economic growth and sustainable development in all countries, to better address the problems of environmental degradation. Trade policy measures for environmental purposes should not constitute a means of arbitrary or unjustifiable discrimination or a disguised restriction on international trade. Unilateral actions to deal with environmental challenges outside the jurisdiction of the importing country should be avoided. Environmental measures addressing transboundary or global environmental problems should, as far as possible, be based on an international consensus....

Principle 14. States should effectively cooperate to discourage or prevent the relocation and transfer to other States of any activities and substances that cause severe environmental degradation or are found to be harmful to human health.

Principle 15. In order to protect the environment, the precautionary approach shall be widely applied by States according to their capabilities. Where there are threats of serious or irreversible damage, lack of full scientific certainty shall not be used as a reason for postponing cost-effective measures to prevent environmental degradation.

Principle 16. National authorities should endeavour to promote the internalization of environmental costs and the use of economic instruments, taking into account the approach that the polluter should, in principle, bear the cost of pollution, with due regard to the public interest and without distorting international trade and investment.

Principle 17. Environmental impact assessment, as a national instrument, shall be undertaken for proposed activities that are likely to have a significant adverse impact on the environment and are subject to a decision of a competent national authority....

COMMENTARY & QUESTIONS

1. **What's soft law good for?** Nonbinding principles and declarations such as the Stockholm and Rio Declarations are not necessarily second-best alternatives to hard or binding law. Soft law is different in kind from treaties and custom and sometimes facilitates better compliance. Because the obligations are perceived as requiring a lower level of commitment on the part of states, a soft instrument may be appropriate in controversial situations in which a high degree of consensus is impossible to obtain. What other situations can you identify in which a soft law approach might be particularly desirable? What might be the benefits of employing a soft approach as opposed to hard law? The benefits? What criteria would you apply in determining whether a particular subject matter ought to be addressed through a hard or soft instrument? On occasion, the position of the United States with respect to soft law instruments has been to treat them as de facto hard. That is, the United States will not agree to a multilateral soft law document like the Stockholm Declaration unless the United States is able, and prepared, to implement that instrument fully. Does this policy tend to further the purposes of soft law by giving greater weight to such instruments? Or does it tend to undermine the advantages of the soft approach?

2. ***Trail Smelter* revisited: Stockholm Principle 21, first among equals.** The *Trail Smelter*'s rule governing transboundary pollution reappeared in 1972 as Principle 21 of the Stockholm Declaration, which specifies that

> States have, in accordance with the Charter of the United Nations and the principles of international law, the sovereign right to exploit their own resources pursuant to their own environmental policies, and the responsibility to ensure that activities within their jurisdiction or control do not cause damage to the environment of other States or of areas beyond the limits of national jurisdiction.

How does this formulation of the basic rule governing transboundary pollution differ from the *Trail Smelter*'s language? What does the first clause in Principle 21 — "the sovereign right to exploit their own resources pursuant to their own environmental policies" — mean when juxtaposed with the second — "the responsibility to ensure that activities within their jurisdiction or control do not cause damage to the environment of other States or of areas beyond the limits of national jurisdiction"? Does the Principle give with one hand and take away with the other? How viable do you think this rule is as an aspirational principle in international relations?

Stockholm's Principle 21, although originally framed as a nonbinding exhortation, over time has been accepted as a substantive rule of customary international law, the only one of the Stockholm Declaration's 26 principles to have achieved that status. Can you explain as an analytical matter how a nonbinding principle can metamorphose into binding customary international law? From a policy point of view, what do you think of Principle 21 as a binding directive of international law creating rights for aggrieved states? Would you regard Principle 21 as sufficient to serve as the central organizing doctrine of international environmental law and policy, as has sometimes been asserted? Is it adequate for that purpose, or is it perhaps underinclusive in the sense of failing to address some important international issues? If not Principle 21, what should be the overarching goal or goals of international environmental law?

3. **Stockholm Principle 21 goes Latin.** Stockholm Principle 21 reappears in substantially similar — but not identical — form as Principle 2 of the Rio Declaration. The change in language relates to the expansion in the later text of states' "sovereign right to exploit their own resources pursuant to their own environmental *and developmental policies....*" Since 1972, innumerable international authorities, including binding treaties and nonbinding principles and guidelines, allude to and incorporate Principle 21 by reference. The addition of the phrase "and developmental" in Rio might be taken to disrupt and skew the already delicate balance between the two clauses somewhat uncomfortably juxtaposed in Stockholm Principle 21, inconsistent with at least some post-Stockholm codifications and reaffirmations of the earlier Principle. Alternatively, maybe the drafters of Rio Principle 2 simply updated the Stockholm formulation. If Stockholm Principle 21 was customary law before the Rio Conference, as many scholars have asserted, of what legal significance is the modification to that Principle in the Rio Declaration? What arguments can you make to support the position that Rio Principle 2 is now binding law? Or that, alternatively, Rio Principle 2 fails to displace Stockholm Principle 21, which continues to be the statement of governing international law? (Welcome to the ambiguities of international law.)

4. **Precaution, principle or approach?** Concepts of "precaution," with roots in domestic approaches such as the German *Vorsorgeprinzip,*[7] have rapidly become the subject of a wide variety of international instruments. Rio Principle 15 codified a perspective that has gained considerable currency in recent years. This exhortation to "precautious" decisionmaking is characteristic of a recent upsurge in the importance of "principles" such as sustainable development in international environmental law and policy. Even the terminology employed — for instance, references to "the precautionary principle" as opposed to "a precautionary approach"— can be an occasion for vigorous international disagreements. The United States, for example, has asserted that "the precautionary principle" is an invitation to disregard science, while at the same time supporting "a precautionary approach." The European Union, for its part, has forcefully argued for the acceptance of "principle" over "approach," asserting that a principle enjoys a higher status than an approach. What is the status of the precautionary principle in international law? Of other principles such as sustainable development? How would you approach these questions from an analytical point of view?

5. **Precaution at home in the United States.** Consider the following classic statement of precaution in domestic environmental law:

> Where a statute is precautionary in nature, the evidence difficult to come by, uncertain, or conflicting because it is on the frontiers of scientific knowledge, the regulations designed to protect the public health, and the decision that of an expert

---

7. *Vorsorgeprinzip* is the straightforward German phrase for "precautionary principle."

administrator, we will not demand rigorous step-by-step proof of cause and effect. Such proof may be impossible to obtain if the precautionary purpose of the statute is to be served. Ethyl Corp. v. EPA, 541 F.2d 1, 28 (D.C. Cir. 1976) (en banc).

What domestic regulatory approaches would you describe as precautionary? What regulatory approaches to the environment employed in U.S. law would not qualify as precautionary?

6. **The Rio Declaration and U.S. law.** One of the purposes of the Rio Declaration is to catalyze the development of national legislation. Based on your study of the domestic environmental law of the United States in the previous portions of this coursebook, to what extent would you say that our domestic environmental law conforms to the requirements of the Rio Declaration? Specifically, by reference to Rio Principle 3, does U.S. law assure the goal of "equitably meet[ing] developmental and environmental needs of present and future generations?" Principle 4's standard that "environmental protection shall constitute an integral part of the development process and cannot be considered in isolation from it"? Principle 14's exhortation to "discourage or prevent the relocation and transfer to other States of any activities and substances that cause severe environmental degradation or are found to be harmful to human health"? Principle 10 addresses public participation in the processes of environmental law. Principle 16 is an international formulation of the basic principle of environmental economics asserting the need to internalize environmental externalities, in a precept known as the Polluter Pays Principle. Similarly, Principle 17 generalizes the National Environmental Policy Act to the international level, where the analogous methodology is known as "environmental impact assessment." To what extent would you say that the expectations of these principles have been met by the United States? As an environmental advocate at the domestic level, how might you use the Rio Declaration to argue for changes to domestic law? See Stumbling Toward Sustainability (John C. Dernbach ed., 2002).

7. **What is "sustainability" anyway?** International environmental law has been criticized for lack of any readily identifiable, coherent central principles. "Sustainable development," the central theme of the 1992 UNCED, probably comes closest to a broad-gauge theme. Despite numerous attempts, however, there has yet to be a consensus statement of the meaning of this amorphous term, with many diverse interests projecting their own agendas onto it. As used in the 1987 report of the World Commission on Environment and Development, the term suggests confining development options to those that preserve environmental integrity. As articulated in the Rio Declaration from the Earth Summit, however, the term seems to suggest an entirely different sort of approach that balances economic and environmental interests, trading one off against the other. What should be the overarching goal or goals of international environmental law and policy? If not sustainable development, prohibitions on transboundary pollution, or the precautionary principle, then what?

8. **The 2002 Johannesburg summit.** Another of these global events, the World Summit on Sustainable Development (WSSD), the so-called "Rio + 10" meeting, a ten-year follow-up to UNCED, was held in Johannesburg, South Africa, in 2002. The WSSD was intended to be different in kind from its predecessors, the 1972 Stockholm Conference and the 1992 Earth Summit. Instead of serving as an agenda-setting vehicle, the

emphasis at the WSSD was on effectiveness in implementation. Delegates from 193 countries attended the Summit, which was addressed by some 100 world leaders. The work product from the WSSD includes two types of deliverables: (1) intergovernmentally negotiated instruments of a character similar to the Rio Declaration, including a political declaration and a plan of implementation intended to focus on priorities for the near term; and (2) partnerships of various kinds, including both intergovernmental and public-private partnerships, the latter involving governments and international organizations, the private sector, NGOs, and scientific communities. As of this writing, 232 partnerships have been registered with the UN Commission for Sustainable Development after conforming to criteria adopted by the Summit. Although the mega-meeting format now seems to be a standard fixture in the multilateral arena, the apparently modest goals of WSSD, the equivocal public and policy response to it, and its low profile in the press suggest that these global summits may be less important than in the past as vehicles for creating international environmental law and policy.

C. COMPARATIVE ENVIRONMENTAL LAW

Triggering positive developments in national law and policy by setting aspirational good practice standards is a central goal of the Rio Declaration and many other nonbinding instruments. To date, this approach has had little impact in the United States, where national legislative priorities established by Congress and domestic agencies such as EPA tend to be interpreted as establishing not only minimum standards but also maximum expectations for private parties such as industry. While the United States can lay claim to taking an early lead as a pacesetter in shaping and molding environmental policy early in the development of the modern environmental era, other countries more recently have been crucibles for domestic implementation of more up-to-date innovations in environmental policy like sustainability and precaution. For example, the constitutions of a number of states — including Brazil, Chile, Ecuador, Honduras, Nicaragua, Peru, Portugal, South Korea, and Spain — explicitly pronounce an individual right to a clean and healthy environment. Comparative approaches, examining foreign law and policy, have much to teach us here in the United States as we move into the dizzyingly globalized world of the twenty-first century.

International law and comparative law are two very different enterprises, although many internationally focused jurists concern themselves with both. International law governs relationships at the level of nation-states and international organizations such as the United Nations. Comparative law instead considers what goes on *within* states. Comparisons between foreign legal traditions and our own in some cases can shed light on deeper structural dynamics common to both; in others, comparisons explain divergences in terms of differing legal traditions or cultures. The methods and skills of comparative analysis are also useful to attorneys practicing between different states in a federal system like ours. Different legal systems naturally find themselves addressing domestic implementation of common principles or international agreements quite differently. The following case, an example of "social action litigation," deals with urban air pollution in India, a country where environmental law is a constitutional issue.

Mehta v. Union of India
2 Law Reports of India 1 (2002)

[The Constitution of India directs that

> The State shall endeavour to protect and improve the environment and to safeguard the forests and wild life of the country.... It further shall be the duty of every citizen of India...to protect and improve the natural environment including forests, lakes, rivers and wild life, and to have compassion for living creatures. Article 51A, Fundamental Duties.

M. C. Mehta, a public interest lawyer practicing by himself, filed suit against the government of India in 1986 challenging unhealthy levels of air pollution in Delhi. As the case dragged on over the years, orders issued by the Supreme Court of India between 1986 and 1996 resulted in the introduction of unleaded gasoline, catalytic converters, low-sulfur diesel fuel, and government vehicles fired by compressed natural gas (CNG). A special committee established during the course of the litigation under India's Environment (Protection) Act of 1986 recommended a conversion of all buses to CNG, and the Environment Pollution (Prevention and Control) Authority, India's version of the U.S. EPA, adopted a binding direction implementing the recommendation. As part of the relief in the case, the Court in 1998 ordered the conversion of all buses in Delhi to CNG by a deadline of January 31, 2002, a target that had been delayed by the court twice before. The government requested yet another extension of the deadline, claiming shortage of CNG and disruption of bus service to the public. In response, the Court issued the following extraordinary order, imposing a fine of 500 rupees per day per bus on diesel bus operators from the original deadline and literally overnight removing as many as 6000 diesel-fueled buses from the streets of Delhi.]

Decision of the Court. Articles 39(e), 47 and 48A [of the Indian Constitution] by themselves and collectively cast a duty on the State to secure the health of the people, improve public health and protect and improve the environment. It was by reason of the lack of effort on the part of the enforcement agencies, notwithstanding adequate laws being in place, that this Court has been concerned with the state of air pollution in the capital of this country. Lack of concern or effort on the part of various governmental agencies had resulted in spiralling pollution levels. The quality of air was steadily decreasing and no effective steps were being taken by the administration in this behalf. It was by reason of the failure to discharge its constitutional obligations, and with a view to protect the health of the present and future generations, that this Court, for the first time, on 23rd September, 1986, directed the Delhi Administration to file an affidavit specifying steps taken by it for controlling pollution emission of smoke, noise, etc. from vehicles plying in Delhi.

The concern of this Court in passing various orders since 1986 has only been one, namely, to protect the health of the people of Delhi..., [although to avoid] disruption in bus services...and unnecessary hardship...this Court has been extending the time with regard to the conversion of commercial vehicles.... Action has been taken by the [Government] of India which leaves us with no doubt that its intention, clearly, is to frustrate the orders passed by this Court with regard to conversion of commercial vehicles to CNG. The manner in which it has sought to achieve this object is to try and dis-credit CNG as the proper fuel and, secondly, to represent to this Court that CNG is in short supply and, thirdly, delay the setting of adequate dispensing stations.

One of the principles underlying environmental law is that of sustainable development. This principle requires such development to take place which is ecologically sustainable. The two essential features of sustainable development are the precautionary principle and the polluter pays principle.

The "precautionary principle" was elucidated thus by this Court in Vellore Citizens' Welfare Forum vs. Union of India and Others, (1996) 5 SCC 647, inter alia, as follows: The State Government and the statutory authorities must anticipate, prevent and attack the causes of environmental degradation. Where there are threats of serious and irreversible damage, lack of scientific certainty should not be used as a reason for postponing measures to prevent environmental degradation. The "onus of proof" is on the actor or the developer to show that his action is environmentally benign. It cannot be gainsaid that permission to use automobiles has environmental implications, and thus any "auto policy" framed by the Government must, therefore, of necessity conform to the Constitutional principles as well as over-riding statutory duties can upon the Government under the EPA. The "auto policy" must, therefore, focus upon measures to

(a) "Anticipate, prevent and attack" the cause of environmental degradation in this field. (b) In the absence of adequate information, lean in favour of environmental protection by refusing rather than permitting activities likely to be detrimental. (c) Adopt the "precautionary principle" and thereby ensure that unless an activity is proved to be environmentally benign in real and practical terms, it is to be presumed to be environmentally harmful. (d) Make informed recommendations which balance the needs of transportation with the need to protect the environment and reverse the large scale degradation that has resulted over the years, priority being given to the environment over economic issues.

The plea of the Government that CNG is in short supply, and that it is unable to supply adequate quantity is incorrect, and this is clearly a deliberate attempt to frustrate the orders passed by this Court....

During the course of arguments, literature was filed in Court giving data from cities all over the world which co-relates increased air pollution with increase in cardiovascular and respiratory diseases and also shows the carcinogenic nature of Respirable Particulate Matter (RSPM). The scientific studies indicate that air pollution leads to considerable levels of mortality and morbidity. Fine particulate matter, or RSPM-PM10 (i.e. matter less than 10 microns in size), is particularly dangerous.

The Journal of American Medical Association (JAMA) has published in its recent issue the findings of a study involving over 500,000 people, conducted over 16 years, in different cities of the US. The researchers find that fine particle related pollution leads to lung cancer and cardiopulmonary mortality. Their research indicates that with an increase of every 10 microgramme per cum (mg/cum) of fine particles, the risk of lung cancer increases by 8 per cent.

The USEPA has mandated that annual average levels of PM 2.5 particles in the air should not exceed 15 mg/cum. The Indian annual national average standard for PM10 is 60 mg/cum, but most cities, including Delhi register PM10 levels above 150–200 mg/cum on an annual basis....

The increase in respiratory diseases specially amongst the children should normally be a cause of concern for any responsible government. The precautionary principle enshrined in the concept of sustainable development would have expected the government and the health authorities to take appropriate action and arrest the air pollution. However, children do not agitate or hold rallies and, therefore, their sound is not heard and the only concern of the Government now appears to be is to protect the financial health of the polluters, including the oil companies who by present international desirable standards produce low quality petrol and diesel at the cost of public health. The statistics show that the continuing air pollution is having a more devastating effect on the people than what was caused by the Bhopal gas tragedy....

Under these circumstances, it becomes the duty of this Court to direct such steps being taken as are necessary for cleaning the air so that the future generations do not suffer from ill-health.

It was repeatedly contended on behalf of the Union of India that no other city in the world had introduced CNG buses at the scale directed by this Court. Both the State Government and the Union of India had urged that the CNG technology was still evolving and experimental. It is no doubt true that most of the cities of the industrialised world do not have large numbers of CNG buses, but the share of natural gas buses, needed to meet the stringent norms in the future, are growing. The data filed indicates that in the United States, CNG buses account for 18 per cent of the current bus orders and 28 per cent of the potential orders. Under pressure to clean up the air because of the approaching Olympic Games in 2004, Beijing has resorted to an alternative fuel strategy. Latest figures from Beijing indicates that there will be 18,000 buses fuelled by CNG, LPG and electricity in that city. By 1999, Beijing had 1300 CNG buses and the numbers are growing rapidly to meet the Olympic deadline. Similarly, the Ministry of Environment in South Korea, partly to meet the targets in time for World Cup Soccer, aims to induct 20,000 natural gas buses in its fleet and already 3000 such buses are plying. From the aforesaid, it is clear that the alternative fuel of CNG, LPG and electricity is a preferred technology which critically polluted cities like Delhi need as a leapfrogging technological option....

[The request] of the Union of India for extension of time to run diesel buses is dismissed.... It is made clear, and it is obvious in our constitutional setup, that orders and directions of this Court cannot be nullified or modified or in any way altered by any administrative decision of the Central or the State Governments. The administrative decision to continue to ply diesel buses is, therefore, clearly in violation of this Court's orders.

COMMENTARY & QUESTIONS

1. **Judicial activism in other jurisdictions.** The Supreme Court of India has been described as "India's main catalyst of environmental reform." From a U.S. viewpoint, the Court's approach in this case is highly unusual. The Court appears to decide many scientific questions for itself, or at least feels comfortable evaluating the public policy significance of scientific data. The Court unashamedly scolds the government of India, overruling governmental determinations, substituting its conclusions for those of the government, and accusing governmental authorities of outright deception. The Court's order, in addition to removing diesel buses from the streets of Delhi, instructed the government to give preference to CNG vehicles throughout India, directed the government to make a minimum amount of CNG available to Delhi, required the city of Delhi to phase out 800 diesel buses per month, and ordered that permits of bus owners cancelled for nonconversion to CNG be reallocated to "weaker sections of society." These are all attributes that we associate with judicial activism. Is this an appropriate role for courts to play? If you think so, what limits would you identify for the judicial function?

2. **Constitutionalization of environmental law.** Over the years, there have been proposals for an environmental amendment to the U.S. Constitution, but they have never gained much momentum. Would you consider a constitutional amendment along the lines of the constitution of India to be a useful addition to U.S. environmental jurisprudence? What might be some of the drawbacks to such an approach? The constitutions of some U.S. states contain environmental guarantees. For example, the

Virginia Constitution establishes a conservation policy of the Commonwealth "[t]o the end that the people have clean air, pure water, and the use and enjoyment for recreation of adequate public lands, waters, and other natural resources...." Many state constitutional provisions, however, have been held to be nonjusticiable, meaning that they cannot be enforced in court. See, e.g., Robb v. Shockoe Slip Found., 324 S.E.2d 674, 676 n.2, 677 (Va. 1985). The provisions cited by the Supreme Court in the first sentence of its order, which fall under the heading "Directive Principles of State Policy," according to the Indian Constitution "shall not be enforced by any court, but the principles therein laid down are nevertheless fundamental in the governance of the country and it shall be the duty of the State to apply these principles in making laws." The Court does not seem to consider this an impediment to relying on these constitutional provisions in its order. Can you craft an argument on behalf of the citizen plaintiff in this case that overcomes the apparent prohibition on judicial application of these constitutional principles? See H. Steiner & P. Alston, International Human Rights in Context: Law, Politics, Morals 283–284 (2d ed. 2000).

3. **International environmental law in national courts.** The Supreme Court of India refers to principles of precaution and sustainability familiar from the Rio Declaration, a nonbinding soft law instrument. What role do those principles play in the Court's reasoning, and how do they affect the outcome in the case? As an analytical matter, how did they metamorphose from nonbinding international exhortations to enforceable domestic rules of decision against which the Court measures the performance of the Indian government?

4. **Regional impacts outside India.** Actions in one jurisdiction can lead by example, spurring other states to apply laws and policies that have worked elsewhere. The *Mehta* decision has already had this effect in other countries of South Asia. The Supreme Court of Bangladesh is requiring classes of vehicles there to use CNG. In July 2003, the Lahore High Court established the Lahore Clean Air Commission (LCAC) for the State of Punjab, Pakistan, which will advise the court about measures to improve urban air quality. The LCAC will recommend, among other measures, that public transportation vehicles now using diesel fuel convert to the use of CNG. What does this case have to teach us here in the United States about air pollution policy and law, or environmental law more generally?

5. **Who is M. C. Mehta?** In early 1984, M. C. Mehta, a public interest attorney, visited the Taj Mahal for the first time. He saw that the famed monument's marble had turned yellow and was pitted as a result of pollutants from nearby industries. This spurred Mehta to file his first environmental case in the Supreme Court of India. The following year, Mehta learned that the Ganges River, considered to be the holiest river in India and used by millions of people every day for bathing and drinking water, caught fire due to industrial effluents in the river. Once again Mehta filed a petition in the Supreme Court against the polluting factories, and the scope of the case was broadened to include all the industries and municipalities in the river basin.

For years, every Friday a courtroom has been set aside just for Mehta's cases. In 1993, after a decade of court battles and threats from factory owners, the Supreme Court ordered 212 small factories surrounding the Taj Mahal to close because they had not installed pollution control devices. Another 300 factories were put on notice to do the same. While the Ganges cases continue to be heard every week, 5000 factories along the river were directed to install pollution control devices and 300 factories were closed. Approximately 250 towns and cities in the Ganges Basin have been ordered to set up sewage treatment plants.

Mehta has won additional precedent-setting suits against industries that generate hazardous waste and has succeeded in obtaining a court order to make lead-free gasoline available. He has also been working to ban intensive shrimp farming and other damaging activities along India's 7000-kilometer coast. Mehta has succeeded in getting new environmental policies initiated and has brought environmental protection into India's constitutional framework. He has almost singlehandedly obtained about 40 landmark judgments and numerous orders from the Supreme Court against polluters, a record that may be unequaled by any other environmental lawyer in the world.[8]

D. MULTILATERAL ENVIRONMENTAL AGREEMENTS

Some problems of the international environment are immensely challenging to address with only the simple model of transboundary pollution set out above in *Trail Smelter*. Harm may be long term and diffuse, instead of palpable and substantial as in the smelter dispute. It may be difficult to prove relationships between emissions in one state and impacts in another, or there may be multiple sources from a multiplicity of states, as is the case with acid precipitation in Europe. Some environmental risks even threaten the entire globe. Scientific evidence may be equivocal, or scientific opinion divided or in a state of evolution, which should suggest the application of precautionary methodology. Such challenges are truly multilateral and require the cooperation of all states in implementing solutions.

Although complex challenges often call for creative use of some or all of the legal and policy tools discussed so far, many of them are unsuited to serious global environmental challenges requiring concrete policy responses. Customary law is of limited utility in response to urgent, controversial threats. Global summits, while useful for elevating the profile of international environmental hazards, have largely become "talking shops" for articulating aspirational goals and general principles. The adoption of national laws and policies, while helpful, must be coordinated multilaterally to address threats of global proportions.

Multilateral agreements consequently have become the principal workhorse of international law and policy. Chapter 8 assesses the effect of environmental treaties as domestic law in the United States. Chapter 15 traces the history of the international negotiations to protect the stratospheric ozone layer. This section analyzes the equally complex operation of multilateral environmental agreements to prevent disruption of the earth's climate from the phenomenon of global warming to illustrate the

---

8. Information from the Web site of the Goldman Environmental Prize, awarded annually to six "environmental heroes," and received by Mr. Mehta in 1996. See http://www.goldmanprize.org.

innumerable opportunities and frustrating challenges encountered in protecting our fragile planet.

Climate change is perhaps the most daunting of the global threats currently facing humankind. Human activities since the Industrial Revolution have dramatically altered the composition of the global atmosphere. A number of gases, emitted in small but significant amounts, absorb infrared radiation reflected from the surface of the earth, causing average temperature to rise. The impact of these changes is highly unpredictable, but almost certainly detrimental to both the health of ecosystems and quality of life for human beings.

Emissions of carbon dioxide (CO_2) are the single largest cause of elevated temperatures from the greenhouse effect. According to ice-coring and organic material dating data, concentrations of atmospheric CO_2 over the past 20 million years up to the start of the Industrial Revolution varied between 190 and 280 parts per million (ppm) which, together with water vapor in the atmosphere, produced the pre-industrial high and low equilibrium temperatures of the planet. In the last century, however, atmospheric CO_2 levels have increased by about 31% to reach a current unprecedentedly high level of approximately 370 ppm, continuing to rise by about 10 ppm per year![9] (Elevated CO_2 concentrations result primarily from the intensified burning of fossil fuels — coal, oil, and natural gas — which liberates the chemical in varying amounts; coal burning releases the most CO_2, while the combustion of equivalent quantities of natural gas and oil results in only about 57% and 83% as much CO_2, respectively.) High levels of atmospheric carbon dioxide over the aeons have presaged periods of rapid erratic climate shifts and global warming.

The world's forests are vast storehouses or "sinks" for carbon. Worldwide loss of forest cover releases this vast stockpile of carbon into the atmosphere as CO_2, aggravating the greenhouse problem. Deforestation in Third World countries is particularly severe, with the destruction of tropical forests in developing countries such as Brazil and Indonesia exceeding 27 million acres annually from activities such as burning, logging, and conversion to agricultural and pastureland.

The accumulation in the atmosphere of CO_2, methane, and other greenhouse gases could have sweeping and far-reaching effects on the earth's climate. By as early as the year 2030, the heat-retaining capacity of the atmosphere may have doubled in relation to pre-industrial concentrations of CO_2. By 2100, the annual global mean surface temperatures may have risen by as much as 1.4° to 5.8° C. — 2.5° to 10.5° F. The absolute magnitude of these temperatures, as well as the rapidity of temperature change, will exceed any ever experienced previously in human history.

The effects of a greenhouse-driven climate disruption will be characterized with complete certainty only after significant damage has already occurred. However, among the most dramatic effects likely to ensue from greenhouse warming is an unprecedented rise in sea level resulting from thermal expansion of the oceans and

---

9. See Pearce, Ice Ages Key to Understanding Change, Boston Globe, August 26, 2003 at D-1. Methane, the principal component of natural gas, is another significant climate-modifying chemical. Average global concentrations of methane were approximately 1750 ppb in 2000. Animal husbandry and rice cultivation have been identified as major sources of increased methane emissions. Coal mining and landfills are also significant sources, with large potential for rapid growth in the future.

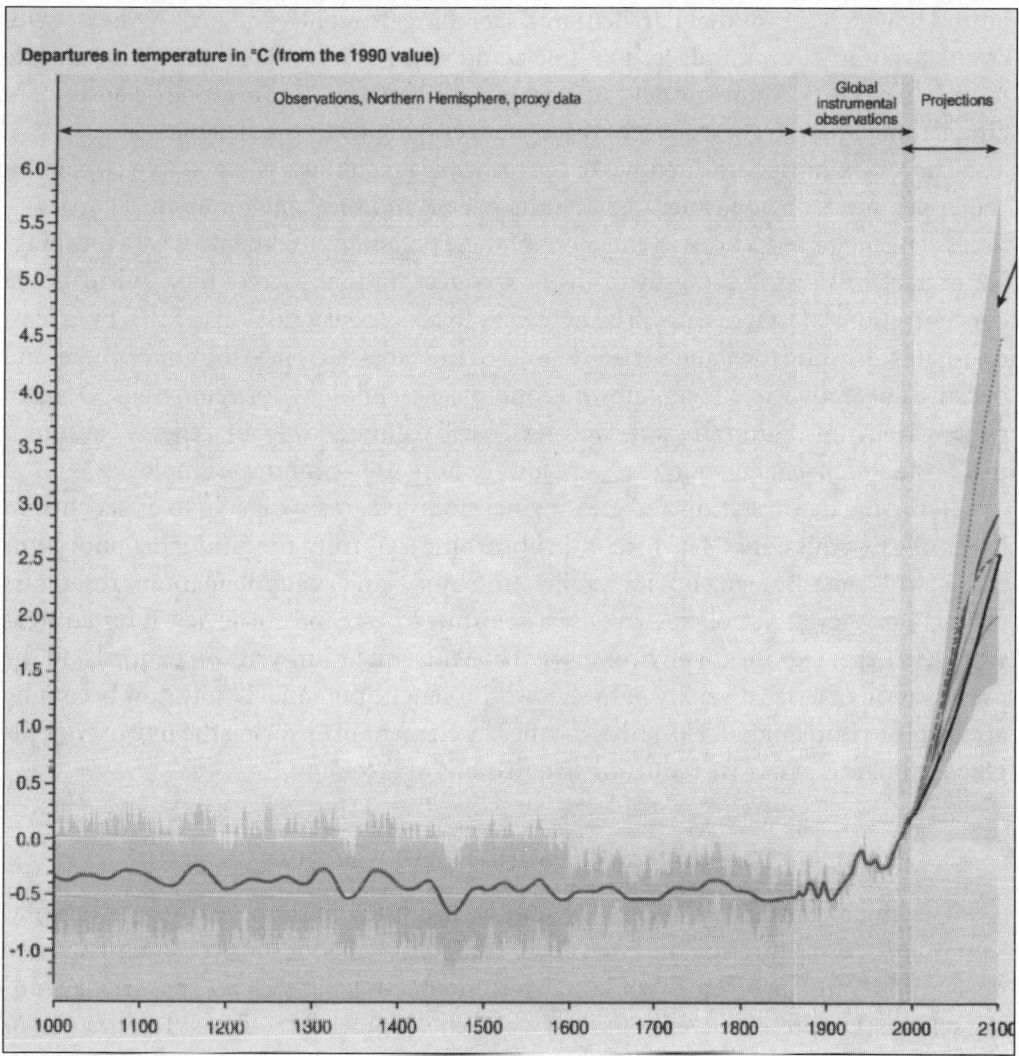

FIGURE 26-2

Variations of the Earth's surface temperature: years 1000 to 2100. The 7 different curves show 7 different projections based on a range of potential scenarios from most to least severe foreseeable atmospheric conditions. Intergovernmental Panel on Climate Change, Climate Change 2001: Synthesis Report Summary for Policymakers 34 (2001), available at http://www.ipcc.ch/pub/un/ syreng/spm.pdf.

melting of glaciers and polar ice. Over the twentieth century, the average global sea level increased less than 2 mm. By contrast, by 2100 the sea level rise will accelerate considerably, producing a total increase of up to 3 feet, depending on the degree of global warming that occurs.

The dramatic anticipated increases in global temperature are virtually certain to cause a wide variety of modifications in regional climates, affecting agriculture in particular. Forests, many of them economically productive, could begin to die off if they prove unable to adjust to rapidly shifting climatic zones. Regions of agricultural productivity could shift. Computer models predict continental drying in middle latitudes, which means that parched soils, scorching droughts, and massive heat waves could become commonplace. Extreme temperatures have been shown to elevate human mortality. Some models also project disruptions in atmospheric and ocean circulation patterns. The impact of these changes is highly unpredictable.

The long atmospheric lifetimes of the principal greenhouse gases — CO_2 remains in the upper atmosphere for decades after its release and methane for about 11 years — necessitate major reductions in emissions of these pollutants in order to have a meaningful impact in slowing the growth in their concentration. Merely to stabilize global concentrations of CO_2 gas, it will be necessary to cut global emissions of CO_2 by at least one-half.[10] Burning fossil fuels releases most of the excess CO_2 into the atmosphere, and because currently there is no known economical technology for removing CO_2 from waste-gas streams, cutting back releases of CO_2 will require a lower total energy consumption and a shift in energy sources toward low- or non- CO_2-emitting technologies.

Reversing deforestation and creating new forested areas will help to offset current levels of CO_2 emissions. New forests, in absorbing CO_2 from the air during photosynthesis, will contribute to climate stabilization by serving as supplementary reservoirs for carbon. Aggressive policies to conserve existing forests and create new forested areas will yield other significant environmental benefits, including erosion control and the preservation of a rich diversity of species whose genetic potential is only now becoming accessible to humankind. Nevertheless, the key element in ensuring the integrity of the global climate is a massive reduction in emissions of greenhouse gasses.

Section 1. THE GLOBAL WARMING FRAMEWORK CONVENTION

The global warming problem is a model case study in the formation of international consensus through international conferences, nonbinding statements and declarations, and involvement of nongovernmental stakeholders and experts, including scientists, representatives of industry, and environmental activists. The first major juncture in the public debate was a report prepared with support from the International Council of Scientific Unions, the UNEP, and the World Meteorological Organization (WMO). UNEP and WMO followed up with informal meetings of independent experts, cosponsored by a Swedish think tank. Several other important studies were prepared or coauthored by U.S. EPA.

In response to mounting concerns about the integrity of the global climate, UNEP and WMO created the Intergovernmental Panel on Climate Change (IPCC) with a mandate to study the climate change issue primarily from a scientific perspective. The principal activities of the IPCC, which met for the first time in November 1988, were and are divided among three working groups: a scientific one that addresses the causes

---

10. To understand why major *cuts* in *emissions* are required merely to *stabilize* ambient *concentrations*, it helps to analogize the earth's atmosphere to a home or apartment into which a stove is leaking gas. Opening the window — the equivalent of natural removal processes for carbon dioxide and methane — will alleviate the problem somewhat. However, if gas continues to gush from the stove — corresponding to emissions of polluting chemicals — faster than it leaves through the window, there will still be a net accumulation of gas, resulting in an increase in concentration. In the case of greenhouse gases, natural decomposition occurs very slowly, particularly by comparison with the rate at which pollutants have been released into the environment, a figure that has increased dramatically since the Industrial Revolution.

of climate change (Working Group I); one that studies the social and environmental impact of climate change (Working Group II); and one that addresses response options for limiting greenhouse gas emissions and mitigating the effects of climate change (Working Group III).

Now literally thousands of scientists from all over the world participate in IPCC activities, and the institution's broadly international character and consensus decision-making processes account for much of its well-earned perception of legitimacy and impartiality. The IPCC's most recent report, published in 2001, reinforces the urgency of the threats to the global climate, underscoring that "Earth's climate system has demonstrably changed on both global and regional scales since the pre-industrial era, with some of these changes attributable to human activities."

The IPCC's First Assessment Report, released in 1990, provided much of the scientific basis for subsequent international work on the global warming problem, much of which took place during the run-up to UNCED. A major international meeting hosted by the Government of Canada in 1988 called for a "reduc[tion in] CO_2 emissions by approximately 20 percent of 1988 levels by the year 2005" as an initial goal. An international meeting attended by 17 heads of state or government in The Hague in 1989 called for nonconsensus decisionmaking procedures similar to those in the Montreal Protocol to deal with urgent environmental problems. The Second World Climate Conference held in Geneva in 1990, like many others, affirmed the importance of precaution in dealing with the threatened climate warming. Simultaneously, global warming featured prominently in such established fora as the UN General Assembly and the annual meetings at the head-of-state level of the Group of Seven (G-7) (now the G-8, including Russia) industrialized countries, which includes many of the world's largest emitters of CO_2 and other greenhouse gases.

The UN Framework Convention on Climate Change (FCCC) was one of the two global treaties to emerge from the 1992 Earth Summit. Following the framework convention-plus-protocols model that appeared to be successful in addressing stratospheric ozone, the Convention is primarily a procedural vehicle for further cooperation on scientific matters and identification of policy options. Reflecting the need perceived by at least some states for "targets and timetables," the Convention also includes a goal for industrialized countries of limiting greenhouse gas emissions to 1990 levels.[11] Another important feature of the framework-convention-with protocols model found in the FCCC is a requirement for periodic review of the science and policy related to protection of the global climate at an annual conference of the parties (COP).

The yearly COPs have since served as the institutional juncture at which major new pieces of the climate regime have been put in place, for instance the Kyoto Protocol adopted at COP-3. Virtually every state on the planet sends a reasonable level of representation to what continues to be an occasion for vigorous policy debate. The annual COPs have also acquired a larger cultural significance, with COP-8 held in Delhi, India, in 2002, attracting more than 1600 individuals representing more than 200 nongovernmental organizations from all over the world. On an even higher level of generality, the

---

11. As noted above, even if this goal were achieved, it would have little beneficial effect on the climate system.

annual COPs are an occasion for the entire world to debate an important component of the future well-being of the planet, with extensive press coverage and intense public attention. While the negotiations leading to the Rio Convention attracted some attention in this vein, the interest in what might very well be perceived as a routine international meeting has now become staggering.

Apart from the United States, which is the single largest national emitter of greenhouse gases, developing countries are probably the biggest "hot spot" in the climate regime. While developing countries have caused little of the existing problem, as economic development accelerates, Third World countries may account for the preponderance of greenhouse gas emissions by the middle of this century. An international solution that provides incentives for the participation of developing countries while fairly distributing the responsibility for implementing solutions is essential to a successful global strategy for combating greenhouse warming. Both the Convention and the subsequent Kyoto Protocol exempt developing countries from substantive control and reduction obligations, but it is clear that that situation will not be suitable for the long term. At the same time, the Convention and Protocol recognize the special needs of developing countries for external assistance to fund adaptation, mitigation, and emission reduction efforts.

As of this writing, 188 states — virtually every one on the planet, including the United States — are parties to the Convention. For a negotiating history of the Convention, see Bodansky, The United Nations Framework Convention on Climate Change: A Commentary, 18 Yale J. Int'l L. 451 (1993).

United Nations Framework Convention on Climate Change
31 I.L.M. 851 (1992)

The Parties to this Convention… Have agreed as follows…

Article 2. Objective. The ultimate objective of this Convention and any related legal instruments that the Conference of the Parties may adopt is to achieve, in accordance with the relevant provisions of the Convention, stabilization of greenhouse gas concentrations in the atmosphere at a level that would prevent dangerous anthropogenic interference with the climate system. Such a level should be achieved within a time-frame sufficient to allow ecosystems to adapt naturally to climate change, to ensure that food production is not threatened and to enable economic development to proceed in a sustainable manner.

Article 3. Principles. In their actions to achieve the objective of the Convention and to implement its provisions, the Parties shall be guided, inter alia, by the following:

1. The Parties should protect the climate system for the benefit of present and future generations of humankind, on the basis of equity and in accordance with their common but differentiated responsibilities and respective capabilities. Accordingly, the developed country Parties should take the lead in combating climate change and the adverse effects thereof.

2. The specific needs and special circumstances of developing country Parties, especially those that are particularly vulnerable to the adverse effects of climate change, and of those Parties, especially developing country Parties, that would have to bear a disproportionate or abnormal burden under the Convention, should be given full consideration.

3. The Parties should take precautionary measures to anticipate, prevent or minimize the causes of climate change and mitigate its adverse effects. Where there are threats of serious or

irreversible damage, lack of full scientific certainty should not be used as a reason for postponing such measures, taking into account that policies and measures to deal with climate change should be cost-effective so as to ensure global benefits at the lowest possible cost. To achieve this, such policies and measures should take into account different socio-economic contexts, be comprehensive, cover all relevant sources, sinks and reservoirs of greenhouse gases and adaptation, and comprise all economic sectors. Efforts to address climate change may be carried out cooperatively by interested Parties.

4. The Parties have a right to, and should, promote sustainable development. Policies and measures to protect the climate system against human-induced change should be appropriate for the specific conditions of each Party and should be integrated with national development programmes, taking into account that economic development is essential for adopting measures to address climate change.

5. The Parties should cooperate to promote a supportive and open international economic system that would lead to sustainable economic growth and development in all Parties, particularly developing country Parties, thus enabling them better to address the problems of climate change. Measures taken to combat climate change, including unilateral ones, should not constitute a means of arbitrary or unjustifiable discrimination or a disguised restriction on international trade.

Article 4. Commitments.... 2. The developed country Parties and other Parties included in Annex I commit themselves specifically as provided for in the following:

(a) Each of these Parties shall adopt national policies and take corresponding measures on the mitigation of climate change, by limiting its anthropogenic emissions of greenhouse gases and protecting and enhancing its greenhouse gas sinks and reservoirs. These policies and measures will demonstrate that developed countries are taking the lead in modifying longer-term trends in anthropogenic emissions consistent with the objective of the Convention, recognizing that the return by the end of the present decade to earlier levels of anthropogenic emissions of carbon dioxide and other greenhouse gases not controlled by the Montreal Protocol would contribute to such modification, and taking into account the differences in these Parties' starting points and approaches, economic structures and resource bases, the need to maintain strong and sustainable economic growth, available technologies and other individual circumstances, as well as the need for equitable and appropriate contributions by each of these Parties to the global effort regarding that objective. These Parties may implement such policies and measures jointly with other Parties and may assist other Parties in contributing to the achievement of the objective of the Convention and, in particular, that of this subparagraph.

(b) In order to promote progress to this end, each of these Parties shall communicate, within six months of the entry into force of the Convention for it and periodically thereafter, and in accordance with Article 12, detailed information on its policies and measures referred to in subparagraph (a) above, as well as on its resulting projected anthropogenic emissions by sources and removals by sinks of greenhouse gases not controlled by the Montreal Protocol for the period referred to in subparagraph (a), with the aim of returning individually or jointly to their 1990 levels these anthropogenic emissions of carbon dioxide and other greenhouse gases not controlled by the Montreal Protocol. This information will be reviewed by the Conference of the Parties, at its first session and periodically thereafter, in accordance with Article 7....

7. The extent to which developing country Parties will effectively implement their commitments under the Convention will depend on the effective implementation by developed country Parties of their commitments under the Convention related to financial resources and transfer

of technology and will take fully into account that economic and social development and poverty eradication are the first and overriding priorities of the developing country Parties.

COMMENTARY & QUESTIONS

1. **Soft or hard law — which is more environmentally friendly?** A major international meeting hosted by the Government of Canada in 1988 and attended by more than 300 individuals from 46 countries, including government officials, scientists, and representatives of industry and environmental organizations, adopted a nonbinding recommendation for a "reduc[tion in] CO_2 emissions by approximately 20 percent of 1988 levels by the year 2005" as an initial goal. The Convention, by contrast, requires at most stabilization of emissions of greenhouse gases from industrialized countries at 1990 levels, a less ambitious target. After the adoption of the Convention, what is left of the earlier commitment? Was it just a waste of time or — considering the carbon emissions associated with the air travel that many delegates used to get there — worse than nothing? What insight does the relationship between the two instruments provide into the relationship between hard and soft law?

2. **The Convention and the Rio Declaration.** Article 3 of the Convention, entitled "Principles," was considered very important by many delegations and was extensively scrutinized and reworked during the negotiations. What is the relationship between the "principles" of Article 3 and the "obligations" of Article 4? Of what practical utility, if any, are Articles 2 and 3? Many provisions in the Convention, and Article 3 in particular, have exact analogues in the Rio Declaration, which was adopted more or less simultaneously. Compare, for instance, Rio Principle 15 with Convention Article 3, paragraph 3, both of which deal with precaution. Negotiations on the Convention, however, were complete by the time serious discussions on the Rio Declaration had begun. What is the legal relationship between the two instruments? Of what significance are the divergences in language between the Rio Principles and the Convention in treatment of the same subject matter, such as precaution? Can you imagine a scenario in which each influenced the development of the other?

3. **The Convention as substantive law.** At the time it was negotiated, the principal policy debate over the FCCC concerned the question of "targets and timetables" — that is, to what extent the Convention would contain substantive policy measures or be confined to the framework or "umbrella" role for which the Vienna Convention on ozone depletion was the model. The result was the language in Article 4.2(a) and (b). Predictably, states have interpreted this hard-fought language as either mandatory or hortatory, depending on their domestic policies. Based strictly on the language of these two provisions, can you argue that the Convention articulates a binding target of stabilizing emissions of greenhouse gases by the year 2000? Alternatively, how would you argue that this is a nonbinding "soft" target, identified as helpful guidance for states to aim for, but not enforceable under international law?

4. **The Convention as U.S. law.** As discussed below, since the adoption of the Kyoto Protocol, the debate over the binding character of the Convention's stabilization goal is largely irrelevant for all parties to the Convention save one — the United States, which

has stated its intent not to become a party to the Protocol. Recall that under Article VI of the Constitution, ratified treaties such as the UNFCCC are "the supreme Law of the Land." A U.S. EPA routine report submitted in 2002 to the Convention Secretariat, the professional staff serving the parties to the agreement, identified numerous consequences of global warming that were "likely, very likely, or projected" to occur, including temperature increases of up to 9° F; rises in sea level of up to 35 inches; loss of sensitive ecosystems such as barrier islands, alpine meadows, coral reefs, and coastal wetlands; and dramatic increases in heat indices during the summer that could trigger heat-related illnesses and deaths. Several months later, Massachusetts, Connecticut, and Maine filed suit against EPA, alleging that the Agency had violated the CAA by failing to list CO_2 as a pollutant under §108. Massachusetts v. Whitman, Civ. No. 3:03CV984 (PCD) (D. Mass. filed June 4, 2003). Assuming you are a lawyer for the plaintiff states, how would you weave together the Convention and the CAA as legal authorities to obtain the desired relief? If you represent EPA, what defenses would you raise to the states' suit? Even if the states are successful in securing the listing of CO_2 as a pollutant, to what extent would you expect the CAA to serve as a successful vehicle for reducing carbon emissions from the United States? What other goals do you think the states might have? What legal theories other than a violation of the CAA might they have employed?

Section 2. THE KYOTO PROTOCOL

In 1997, the parties to the FCCC adopted the Kyoto Protocol, which sets out commitments by 21 industrialized states (plus the European Community), as well as by 11 states undergoing the process of transition to a market economy (such as the formerly socialist countries allied with the Soviet Union), to limit or reduce their emissions of greenhouse gases — carbon dioxide, methane, and others. During the first commitment period, which covers the years 2008 to 2012, the required reductions average about 5% and range as high as 8% for particular countries, measured by reference to 1990 levels. The Protocol also anticipates additional reductions in a second and subsequent commitment periods, although the specific obligations have not yet been negotiated. One of the Kyoto Protocol's principal innovations is to allow trading of emissions entitlements so as to reduce the cost of compliance for individual countries and for the world as a whole. The novelty of emissions trading on so grand a scale, coupled with other unresolved implementation issues, led to an immediate round of further negotiations.

The Protocol anticipates an initial allocation of "assigned amount units" (AAUs) corresponding to the legally binding cap for those states that have substantive obligations under the agreement. Article 17 of the Protocol then establishes that rights to emit may be traded among this group. Second, Article 6 of the Protocol permits the parties with reduction obligations to undertake cooperative projects that reduce emissions of greenhouse gases in other similarly situated countries and to obtain credit for those reductions, an option known as "joint implementation" (JI). Like AAUs, the resulting "emissions reduction units" (ERUs) are tradable. Third, Article 12 of the Protocol establishes a "clean development mechanism" (CDM), which provides a basis for parties with reduction obligations to implement their reduction commitments by undertaking projects in developing countries, which have no obligations under the Protocol. The resulting "certified emissions reductions units" (CERs) may also be traded. CERs, which are generated by activities in developing countries that do not have emissions targets under the Protocol, are unusual in that they may increase the total number of AAUs.

In March 2001, at a crucial juncture near completion of negotiations on the Kyoto implementing rules, the Bush Administration announced that, notwithstanding the previous administration's signature of the Protocol, the United States — the country with the highest emissions of CO_2 in the world — did not intend to ratify it. Soon thereafter, the IPCC released its Third Assessment Report, concluding "there is new and stronger evidence that most of the warming observed over the last 50 years is attributable to human activities." Undaunted and unabashed, the Bush Administration requested the U.S. National Academy of Sciences to review the IPCC's work product. Instead of contradicting the Panel's conclusions, the National Academy reaffirmed them, thereby negating any inference that the panel's conclusions had been politically motivated and, incidentally, further embarrassing the United States. While the Bush Administration could hardly deny the seriousness of the global-warming problem after the National Academy's report, or the scientific basis for the conclusion that human activities are adversely affecting the world's climate, President Bush nonetheless reiterated his opposition to the Kyoto Protocol mere days after the document's release.

Notwithstanding the dire advance predictions that the Kyoto Protocol was "dead" as a result of the U.S. pullout, a major breakthrough occurred in the negotiations in mid-2001, and the Marrakesh Accords containing the final rules — a document approaching 200 pages in length — were adopted later that year. As a condition precedent for entry into force, the Protocol requires 55 ratifications representing 55% of total carbon dioxide emissions from industrialized countries in 1990; emissions of CO_2 from the United States account for slightly more than 36% of that number for that year. Notwithstanding the setback in the form of the U.S. withdrawal, there is a substantial possibility that those conditions will be met and the Protocol will become operational in the near future.[12] The following article considers the Protocol's subsequent trajectory.

Daniel Bodansky, U.S. Climate Policy After Kyoto: Elements for Success
Carnegie Foundation for International Peace Policy Brief, April 2002

With the U.S. withdrawal from the Kyoto Protocol and the agreement's likely entry into force, it appears that the United States and the rest of the world will go their separate ways on climate change. The United States now faces a stark choice: Do nothing, join Kyoto, or come up with a policy of its own. The first option would be unwise, environmentally and politically. The second would require an embarrassing flip-flop by the Bush administration. This leaves the third option: proposing a credible U.S. approach separate from Kyoto....

In addressing climate change, success will not go to the swiftest policy but to the most durable. How can the United States build such a regime? The answer is to start small and add

---

12. As of this writing, Russia — whose ratification of the Kyoto Protocol after the U.S. withdrawal is essential for entry into force — had issued equivocal announcements concerning its intention to become a party to the instrument. In contrast to the United States, however, Russia may be bluffing, trying to up the stakes as a quid pro quo for ratifying.

complexity and ambition step by step. By beginning with achievable goals, a regime will be able to build on a foundation of success rather than failure. By not trying to do everything at once, it will be able to learn from experience and to develop institutional capacity over time.

Starting small has three dimensions, relating to the number of countries involved, the stringency of the commitments, and the complexity of the procedural and institutional mechanisms. Kyoto started big in every way: It is a global agreement, which establishes potentially tough commitments (at least before the United States dropped out) and quite complex implementation mechanisms. Alternatives to Kyoto should be more modest in all three respects.

Initially, U.S. climate policy should focus on domestic actions. In part, this is a necessity, because other countries will be reluctant to entertain international alternatives as long as Kyoto appears on track. But it also reflects an important lesson of the U.S. rejection of Kyoto, namely, that climate policy should start at home: All the international attention in the world will not overcome failure to develop a domestic political consensus. The most obvious and desirable starting point would be a domestic emissions trading system covering a significant segment of the U.S. economy—for example, carbon emissions from electric utilities. This option has received by far the most attention, is economically efficient, and commands some support in the Cabinet if not the White House....

One way to address the cost issue is by expressing the emissions target not in absolute terms, but relative to economic output, like the voluntary target announced recently by President Bush to reduce the level of emissions relative to gross domestic product by 18 percent during the next decade. Such a target could be credible if it required a real reduction in emissions from what is expected to occur anyway—a test the Bush target fails.

An alternative approach that provides even greater protection against excessive costs is a so-called safety valve, which caps the overall costs of compliance and thereby provides economic predictability. A safety valve controls compliance costs by setting a maximum price on carbon: If the emissions trading price reached this preagreed level, emissions targets would be relaxed. It thus combines positive features of both price- and quantity-based approaches to pollution control. Like quantity-based instruments such as emission targets, a safety valve provides a minimum level of emissions reductions if the price remains low. But like price-based instruments such as pollution taxes, a safety valve provides economic predictability by setting an upper bound on potential costs.

A domestic emissions trading program could easily incorporate international components over time. An initial step would be to provide credits for actions to reduce emissions in other countries, where reductions might be achievable at lower costs. A further option would be an agreement with like-minded states—for example, Latin American countries that are also interested in market-based approaches such as emissions trading. Such an agreement could coexist with Kyoto, because it would simply provide supplementary actions and mechanisms. Developing countries would have an interest in joining because they could make money from selling surplus emissions reductions to the United States.

In the long term, of course, a purely regional approach will not suffice—a global regime will be needed. But starting with a few like-minded countries such as Colombia, Costa Rica, and Mexico would have several advantages over the Kyoto process. Hard-line developing countries would not be able to prevent more moderate developing states from joining, as they are able to do under Kyoto, so the regime would begin to break down Kyoto's rigid, debilitating divide between industrial and developing countries.

The countries involved could design the system more coherently, because they would not need to compromise with states holding opposing views. And their common views would give them greater trust in one another, making them more willing to entrust international institutions with the necessary decision-making authority. For these reasons, regional human rights agreements have tended to be more effective then global regimes. Starting small, with fewer states, would provide a better opportunity to build a system with a sound architecture and strong institutions that could eventually merge with Kyoto or replace it.

A small group of states would be reluctant to make stringent commitments by themselves, for fear that this would put them at a competitive disadvantage vis-à-vis countries without comparable targets. They would likely want to begin with modest targets, so that they could gauge the costs of compliance before deciding how much further to proceed. However, beginning with modest, achievable targets would be an advantage rather than a drawback....

What distinguishes the Kyoto targets is their legally binding character. This is an asset that must be carefully nurtured. Like the emperor's new clothes, it is largely a state of mind. Once a state breaks the taboo by violating a target, countries may conclude that the legally binding nature of the target did not mean much after all. That is why, in the early days of a legal regime, it is important to start with relatively easy commitments. As the regime gains a track record of success, a culture of compliance develops....

A regional agreement could also incorporate a safety valve, to remove the cost uncertainties that have plagued the Kyoto negotiations. These uncertainties have created a dilemma for states: Either choose emissions targets that are definitely affordable but extremely weak, or agree to stronger targets that create significant economic risks. A safety valve would allow states to have the best of both worlds: strong targets with a guarantee that costs will not become excessive. And it would help contain the pressure toward noncompliance, thus protecting the agreement's legal authority.

Finally, a new international approach to climate need not do everything at once. It should establish the principle that climate policy should comprehensively address all the sources and sinks of greenhouse gases. But its operational rules could focus initially on the simplest parts of the problem—in particular, carbon dioxide emissions from energy—leaving more complex issues until later. As long as the emissions targets are moderate, this should not pose a problem. What drove the United States to push for the inclusion of six gases and carbon sinks was the need to have every possible means to achieve what were regarded as extremely tough targets. More modest targets could be achieved solely through reductions in carbon emissions.

COMMENTARY & QUESTIONS

1. **Common but (highly) differentiated responsibilities.** Parties to the Kyoto Protocol are divided into three categories roughly as follows: (1) industrialized, (2) industrialized and in transition to a market economy, and (3) developing. The first two groups are the Annex I parties with substantive commitments under the agreement. Bodansky refers to this as a "rigid, debilitating divide between industrial and developing countries." Why are these groups of states treated differently under the Protocol, with developing countries having essentially no obligations whatsoever? Was the absence of a quantified commitment a political imperative needed to "buy" the participation of the developing nations? Some countries have indicated an interest in joining the Annex I grouping and accepting quantified emissions reductions under the Kyoto Protocol. Why might a state choose to take on obligations that it otherwise would not have had? What incentives does the Protocol create for such a move? How might those incentives be enhanced?

2. **Safeguards for international trading.** International emissions trading of the scale anticipated by the Kyoto Protocol and the Marrakesh Accords has never been attempted before. The Montreal Protocol authorizes limited reassignment of rights to emit the chlorofluorocarbons and other gases controlled by that agreement, but the scale is not even close to that anticipated by the Kyoto Protocol. The U.S. CAA Amendments of 1990 provide for extensive trading of rights to emit sulfur dioxide, but that scheme is embedded in a municipal legal setting with much more obvious mechanisms for verification, compliance, and enforcement. What assurances would you want to see in the Kyoto/Marrakesh scheme to assure the integrity of the trading process, in particular so as to assure the value of the traded rights? How should those guarantees be implemented at the international level?

3. **Giving credit only for the road that would not have been taken.** In several places in the Marrakesh Accords, credits are limited to those "emission reductions or removals that are additional to any that would have occurred without the project." Why is that an important concept? Recall the *Citizens Against the Refinery's Effects* case, Chapter 11, where the plaintiffs objected to granting offsets for a pollution reducing change in road paving practice that involved a cost saving rather than a cost increase. Will it be easy to ascertain what steps would have been taken without the incentive provided by the emissions trading mechanisms?

4. **Baseline choices and the over-creation of credits.** The choice of 1990 as the date for baseline emissions creates a vast oversupply of AAUs — colloquially known as "hot air" — for some counties, notably Russia, as a result of substantially decreased economic activity following the end of the Cold War. Trading of "hot air" is not subject to the "would not have happened anyway" limitation. Does that mean that tradable credits will be in too great a supply to spur real reductions in industrialized nations? Was the grant of these seemingly excess AAUs a political imperative needed to "buy" the participation of these states?

5. **Heavy weather for the Protocol in the United States.** The Clinton Administration negotiated the Kyoto Protocol during a period in which both houses of the Congress were controlled by Republicans who were quite vocal in their skepticism about the agreement. How would you go about negotiating an international agreement against such a backdrop? What kinds of considerations might you take into account, and what would you do to assuage congressional opposition? Before the diplomatic conference that adopted the Kyoto Protocol, the Senate adopted a bipartisan resolution sponsored by Senators Byrd and Hagel, which specifies that

> the United States should not be a signatory to any protocol to, or other agreement regarding, the United Nations Framework Convention on Climate Change of 1992, at negotiations in Kyoto in December 1997, or thereafter, which would... mandate new commitments to limit or reduce greenhouse gas emissions for the Annex I Parties, unless the protocol or other agreement also mandates new specific scheduled commitments to limit or reduce greenhouse gas emissions for Developing Country Parties within the same compliance period, or would result in serious harm to the economy of the United States.

How would you suggest responding to those concerns given the current status of the Protocol? How might the United States subsequently become a party to the Protocol, notwithstanding the hostile posture of the Bush II Administration?

6. **No pain, no gain.** Bodansky makes a beguiling argument extolling the virtues of aiming low: having like-minded nations take easily accomplished small steps toward reducing greenhouse gas emissions. Is his argument a form of surrender to global warming as inevitable if meaningful reductions prove to be the least bit expensive? Predicting the cost curve of the needed reductions is assuredly complex and uncertain, but recalling that it is necessary to obtain at least a global 50% reduction from 1990 emission levels merely to stabilize greenhouse gas concentrations eases the predictive task — it will be expensive. Is there an unspoken premise in Bodansky's position that envisions the imposition of ever more stringent reductions over time that will be enforceable because a "culture of compliance" has developed in response to the easy small steps that were previously taken? What, if anything, suggests that when it comes time for the real pain (economic cost of substantial reductions) that the politics, domestic U.S or global, will be any different?

7. **Of international law and the tragedy of the commons.** As so succinctly stated by Garrett Hardin, the solution to the tragedy of the commons is "mutual coercion, mutually agreed upon." Bodansky suggests that the nations populating the global commons may agree to mutual coercion but are unlikely to endure its economic consequences if they are significant, thereby rendering the threat of coercion as illusory as the Emperor's New Clothes. To a large degree, he suggests that each nation's continued obedience to a strong international environmental regime remains a political choice that is pragmatically made by each nation. Is U.S. domestic environmental law really any different? In the United States, environmental laws can be repealed, weakened, or go unenforced, but most of the evidence to date suggests that compliance is the norm and broad-scale evisceration by any of those means is infrequent.

8. **Business as unusual.** In January 2003, a group of 14 greenhouse gas emitters in the United States announced the voluntary formation of the Chicago Climate Exchange for the trading of emissions credits for the reduction of greenhouse gasses. The players include such entities as American Electric Power Company, the largest emitter of greenhouse gases in the United States, General Motors, and a number of other prominent multinational corporations. They have required of themselves a 4% reduction of greenhouse gas emissions over a five-year period, using trading as a means by which companies that reduce by greater than that amount can sell credits to companies that fail to meet that requirement. Enforcement will be taken by the group on the same basis as traders in the mercantile exchanges enforce trading rules. Why would these companies impose requirements on themselves when the Bush Administration has chosen to leave greenhouse emissions unregulated? A news article by Andrew Revkin reporting on the behind the scenes activities of Bush Administration officials suggests one explanation:

> In an aggressive effort to show that President Bush's voluntary climate strategy can work, senior administration officials are traveling the country collecting written promises from industries to curb emissions of gases linked to global warming. White House officials, insisting on concrete commitments measured in tons of

gases, have rejected written offers from some industry groups to take nonspecific actions, several industry officials said. The administration and industry leaders plan to unveil a broad array of pledges at the White House on Feb. 6 [2003]. This is the administration's latest and most intensive effort to demonstrate that voluntarily controlling emissions can make mandatory reductions unnecessary. Mr. Bush has said such reductions will harm the economy. The effort has no teeth, officials and company representatives say, other than the growing realization in industry that without measurable success from voluntary reductions, it will become ever harder in coming years to stave off legislation requiring companies to act. Senators of both parties introduced such legislation in Congress this month, and states are acting on their own as well. The administration's intent, once all the industries' commitments are tallied, is to meet Mr. Bush's stated goal: an 18 percent reduction, by 2012, in emissions of greenhouse gases for each unit of gross domestic product. Overall emissions would continue to grow, but more slowly.... The administration's push has intensified as criticisms of its cautious climate policies have increased, and more aggressive alternatives have been proposed. Revkin, U.S. Is Pressuring Industries to Cut Greenhouse Gases, N.Y. Times, Jan. 20, 2003, at A1.

9. **Getting worse before it gets better.** What will it take to change the current U.S. policy? In some areas of environmental law, major strengthening of the law followed a galvanizing event, such as Love Canal or the loss of fish in Lake Erie. With climate change, calamities that could muster the political will to comply with a painfully strict emissions reduction regime are not difficult to envision. Will it be the inundation of coastal areas? Will it be diseased and dying mountainside forests whose trees are now rooted in locally changed climates that their species cannot endure? Will it be a decade of unrelenting midcontinent drought? Will it be documentary films chronicling the loss of a photogenic species, such as the polar bears, whose food chain or breeding patterns have become insupportable? It is easy to envision not only environmental catastrophes that would follow climate change but also the difficulty or impossibility of their reversal. This argues strongly that policymakers should adopt the views of Talbot Page (see Chapter 1) that would have them proactively manage so grave an "environmental risk" even in the face of expense and uncertainty.

10. **Role of the press.** Because there is no court of general jurisdiction to engage in judicial review of the actions of government, in international environmental law and policy the "court of public opinion" assumes relatively greater importance than in the domestic setting. The media are major factors in shaping public opinion on the environment. In Europe, the press routinely connects extreme weather events such as the extreme heat wave during the summer of 2003, which claimed hundreds of lives in Paris alone, with greenhouse warming. In the United States, by contrast, the admitted uncertainties linking the causes of the phenomenon with local effects have tended to discourage reporting from this perspective. Which do you consider the more responsible approach, and why?

11. **National implementation of the Protocol.** As one point of reference, implementing legislation for the Kyoto Protocol in Japan, which has a 6% reduction target under the Protocol:

- specifies emission reduction targets for different greenhouse gases and sectors, and targets for the use of sinks, for emissions reductions by innovative technologies, and for additional efforts by various sectors;

- identifies the roles of central and local government policies to implement or augment those measures;

- calls for a comprehensive review of Japan's implementation of the Protocol in 2004 and 2007, with revisions as necessary to achieve the 6% reduction target;

- establishes a Global Warming Prevention Headquarters, to be headed by the Prime Minister, for the purpose of drafting the Kyoto Target Achievement Plan and supervising its implementation;

- instructs the central government and local governments to implement policies and measures under the Forest and Forestry Plan with the aim of achieving the target of the use of sinks stipulated by the Kyoto Target Achievement Plan;

- calls for the central government to study the way to use the Kyoto Mechanisms and to take necessary measures for their use; and

- establishes other positions and institutions, including Global Warming Prevention Activities Advisers, local centers to promote and enhance global warming prevention activities, and a Local Partnership Council.

What, if anything, does the Japanese experience have to teach us here in the United States concerning implementation of the Protocol?

E. INTERNATIONAL INSTITUTIONS

International environmental agreements such as the UNFCCC and the Kyoto Protocol exist in a larger international legal universe in which they are embedded within other international institutions and commitments. As an emerging environmental problem like global warming begins to penetrate the consciousness of the public, environmental activists, and governmental decisionmakers, tensions or even outright clashes between public policy goals as pursued by other mission-oriented international institutions may appear – a problem antiseptically dubbed "multilateral coherence" in international bureaucratese. Friction with two international institutions created to promote economic development, the World Bank and the World Trade Organization, has provoked fierce criticism of those institutions from environmental NGOs and equally vigorous defenses by the institutions themselves and constituencies whose interests they promote. The First Law of Ecology — everything is connected to everything else — applies not only to ecosystems but also to international institutions such as the Bank and the WTO.

Section 1. THE WORLD BANK

One of the World Bank's principal functions, according to its constitutive multilateral treaty, is "to promote economic development, increase productivity and thus raise standards of living in the less-developed areas of the world…in particular by providing financing to meet their important developmental requirements." Similar international institutions, designed on the model of the World Bank — including the Inter-American Development Bank, the African Development Bank, the Asian Development

Bank, and the European Bank for Reconstruction and Development — perform similar functions on a regional basis.

The World Bank consists of a number of "windows," each of which technically is a separate international organization established by a distinct treaty entitled the "Articles of Agreement." The two most important of these windows are the International Bank for Reconstruction and Development (IBRD), established in 1945, which lends roughly at prevailing market rates of interest; and the International Development Association (IDA), established in 1965, which lends to the very poorest countries in the form of concessional "credits" that carry very low interest rates or no interest whatsoever. As of this writing, the IBRD has 184 member states and IDA a similar number. In fiscal year 2002, the IBRD and IDA together approved 229 loans and credits totaling U.S. $19.5 billion, many of which financed major development projects. The IBRD and IDA together are often known simply as the "World Bank."

The IBRD and IDA share common institutions within the Bank. One Governor, ordinarily that country's finance minister, represents each member state at the Bank. The U.S. Governor is the Secretary of the Treasury. The Board of Governors meets as a body only once a year and in practice gives only very general guidance to the Bank's professional staff. Twenty four Executive Directors, appointed or elected by member country governments, have offices physically located in the World Bank headquarters complex in Washington and exercise day-to-day authority on behalf of the Governors by approving staff proposals for individual loans. The United States, Japan, Germany, the United Kingdom, France, China, Saudi Arabia, and Russia each have a single Executive Director. Other Executive Directors represent groups of states, some of them quite odd, for example, the Netherlands, Armenia, Bulgaria, Cyprus, Georgia, Israel, Moldova, Romania, and Ukraine. The individual commonly identified as the Executive Director for Canada also represents most of the Caribbean countries.

The Board of Executive Directors takes decisions by weighted majority voting. Votes are allocated according to a formula that depends on the number of a member state's shares and its capital contribution to the institution. So, among the current IBRD members, the United States now exercises somewhat more than 17% of the total voting power in the IBRD, nearly three times as much as the next largest shareholder, Japan. No single shareholder holds enough votes unilaterally to direct the Bank as an institution to take a particular action, including the approval or rejection of a particular lending proposal. Both the IBRD and IDA Articles of Agreement prohibit political activity by specifying that "[t]he [Bank] and its officers shall not interfere in the political affairs of any member; nor shall they be influenced in their decisions by the political character of the member or members concerned. Only economic considerations shall be relevant to their decisions, and these considerations shall be weighed impartially in order to achieve the purposes stated [in the Articles of Agreement]."

Only the governments of member states may borrow from the IBRD and IDA, which do not lend to private parties. Loan agreements between borrowing country governments on the one hand and the IBRD or IDA on the other have the status of binding treaties under international law. Loan agreements may contain certain promises or "conditions" that the borrowing country government agrees to perform in return for the loan — including, of course, repayment of the loan proceeds — but perhaps other requirements as well. In recent years, the Bank's increasing tendency to include environmental or "green" conditionality in its lending program has created some friction with borrowing country governments.

The World Bank's professional staff, headed by the President of the Bank, is somewhat analogous to the secretariat of other international organizations. Bank staff work for the international institution of the World Bank and do not represent the interests of their own national governments. Bank staff are specifically charged with the operational task of preparing or "appraising" specific loan proposals for approval by the Bank's Board of Executive Directors. Lending proposals must be agreed between the professional staff and the borrowing country government before presentation to the Board of Executive Directors for subsequent approval. Bank staff may choose not to pursue negotiations on a loan proposal, or negotiations between the borrowing country government and the Bank may break down. For either of these reasons, a particular loan proposal may not reach the Board.

In the fall of 1993, in response to continued criticism about the Bank's environmental performance, the World Bank's Board of Executive Directors adopted a resolution creating a new Inspection Panel. The Panel is intended to serve as a vehicle for ensuring full implementation by Bank staff of Bank Operational Directives (ODs) and other internal Bank policies. The Panel provides new opportunities for private parties — principally NGOs — to initiate proceedings to encourage performance of international standards. NGOs may seek review of both failures by the Bank's professional staff to observe that institution's own internal standards and inadequate supervision by Bank staff on the implementation of loan covenants by borrowing country governments. The new Panel consists of three independent experts appointed in their personal capacities. Although created as an investigatory body, many of its pronouncements have an adjudicatory character. By creating rights of access for NGOs, the Panel is a major innovation in public international law. The Inspection Panel is also the first time an international institution has created a mechanism for independent oversight of its own operations.

Nonetheless, the resolution creating the Panel establishes some potentially significant limitations to its authority. Only organizations, and not individuals, may file a "request for inspection." The Panel is confined to considering "failure of the Bank to follow its operational policies and procedures with respect to the design, appraisal and/or implementation of a project financed by the Bank." These internal Bank standards, which govern such issues as the prior evaluation of environmental impacts, involuntary resettlement, and indigenous peoples, do not necessarily reflect customary norms in areas such as human rights. The Panel, after receiving a request for inspection, may proceed only with the subsequent approval of the Bank's Board of Executive Directors. Despite these weaknesses, the new Inspection Panel creates entirely new formal opportunities for nonstate actors to assure compliance with international standards, both by the Bank's professional staff and, indirectly, by borrowing country governments.

In June 1999, the International Campaign for Tibet, a U.S. NGO, filed a request for inspection of the Bank's proposed Western Poverty Reduction Project in China. The request challenged one component of the $311 million project located in Qinghai

Province, which included resettling nearly 58,000 subsistence farmers earning about $60 a year from the hillsides of eastern Qinghai (the "move-out" area) to a new irrigation project involving construction of a new 400-foot high dam (the "move-in" area). The requesters complained that the project would involve the relocation of other ethnic groups into a traditionally Tibetan area and that the project would have adverse environmental effects. The Panel reported its findings less than a year after receiving the request.

Inspection Panel's Report and Findings on the Qinghai Project: Executive Summary
World Bank RQ99/3 (2000)

If there is no alternative there can be no choice.... One of the most noticeable and significant weaknesses of the [environmental] assessments [EAs] is that investment and project alternatives are neither identified nor systematically compared. For all practical purposes, the Environmental Assessment avoids consideration of alternatives, both for poverty reduction in the Move-out areas and for sites in the Move-in area. From the documentation, it is not possible to deduce whether the Qinghai Project as proposed is the best way for the Bank to meet the Project's objectives or to ensure that the Bank's safeguard policies are being respected.

Management failed to ensure that those responsible for the EA understood their brief to include an examination of alternatives to resettlement in both the Move-out and Move-in areas. Instead, the Panel found that they understood the main purpose of their studies to be to assist the optimal resettlement of around 60,000 people from the Move-out area into the Balong-Xiangride Irrigation area. The same is true of the Social Assessment. There is no systematic study of *in situ* alternatives to resettlement, or of alternative resettlement sites, or of alternative development plans for the national minorities affected within the Move-in area.

Why the Bank accepted Assessments conducted in such circumscribed and limiting manner is unclear. Whatever the reasons, the Panel finds that the Assessments do not make any meaningful analysis of realistic project alternatives as required by Bank policy.

One of the most important decisions (perhaps the most crucial) that Management must make concerning the environmental assessment of any project is the category of the assessment that will be undertaken. Under OD 4.01 [on environmental assessment], this critical judgement is made in the first instance by the Task Manager (now Task Team Leader), with the concurrence of the regional environment unit. The project is assigned to Category "A," in which case a full Environment Assessment (EA) is required, or a Category "B," in which case a full EA is not required, but an environmental analysis is, or a Category "C," in which case no environmental analysis is required.... The OD further provides that a full EA is required if a project is likely to have significant adverse impacts that may be sensitive, irreversible, and diverse.... This critical decision of the category of the EA is made at a very early stage in the project cycle, but the OD permits a later revision of the category as new information becomes available....

The initial decision to assign "B," taken on January 8, 1998, was made before the Task Team leader, or any other Bank official associated with the decision, had an opportunity to visit the Move-in area.... The first Bank official involved in the decision to visit the Project site was the consultant who was engaged to be responsible for the environmental impact assessment aspects of the Project. Following his visit, on March 13, 1998, he raised a number of issues with senior staff and recommended the re-classification of the Qinghai component as an "A." Senior staff responded at length, citing reasons why it should remain a "B." Management was aware of the A/B debate, but did not intervene. The Project concept Document meeting of April 14, 1998, in effect confirmed a "B."...

After reviewing the screening process, the Panel finds that management's decision to classify the project as a "B" was not in compliance with OD 4.01. Several components of the Project fall within the illustrative list of "A" projects in Annex E, i.e., dams and reservoirs, irrigation, and resettlement. And the impacts qualify as "sensitive" since vulnerable ethnic minorities are affected and involuntary resettlement is involved....

The proposed in-migration to Dulan county will more than double its population. The proposed new towns will each have populations five times as large as Xiangride, the nearest established town to the main irrigation site. This will lead to further induced development, on which OD 4.01 lays great stress. The dam, irrigation and resettlement parts of the Qinghai Project are treated as though they were to take place in a regional vacuum. The potential impact of this development on the network of social, commercial and political interactions that exists in Dulan county and Xiangride Township has not been considered. There is no indication of how these communities and their populations will be affected, for better or worse, by the Project. Without this assessment, the Bank's policy goal of enhancing Project benefits has no substance or meaning.

The EA and other Project documents fail to consider the appropriateness of implanting large-scale irrigated agriculture in this Region. It does not examine its suitability or viability in comparison with the traditional forms of land use, including agropastoralism, sedentary pastoralism, semi-sedentary pastoralism (semi-nomadism), and migratory pastoralism involving the herding of sheep and other animals. There appears simply to be an assumption that irrigated agriculture is "a good thing" without consideration of alternatives and relative costs....

The information on the biodiversity of the area is very sketchy and inadequate. It does not incorporate an assessment of the diversity encountered with regard to distribution, frequency/rarity and conservation status.... Extensive exploitation of oil, natural gas and minerals is carried out in parts of the Qaidam basin and test drillings have been undertaken near the Project area. No mention is made in the EA of the general economic importance of oil and minerals in the Province, or its possible effects on the Project areas, or of any drilling activities in the Region.

Given the scale of absolute habitat conversion in the Project area, involving 19,000 hectares of land that will be irrigated, and construction developments such as the dam, canals, townships, villages and roads — all adding up to an estimated 21,444 hectares — it cannot be asserted with confidence that possible critical natural habitats will not be lost. The necessary baseline information is not available in the Assessment. The Panel is therefore of the view that the Project is in contravention of the Bank's policy OP 4.04, in regard to the significant conversion of critical natural habitats.

The Panel finds that the Environmental Assessment of the Qinghai Project is not in compliance with Bank policies as set out in OD 4.01.

COMMENTARY & QUESTIONS

1. **Environmental impact assessment and foreign aid.** The Bank's loan preparation process is governed by a series of instruments known as Operational Policies (OPs), Bank Procedures (BPs), and Good Practices (GPs). In principle, the first two categories are binding and the third advisory, but the force of the instruments may vary depending on their terms. Two of those instruments, OP 4.01 and BP 4.01, require environmental assessments to be conducted as part of the loan appraisal process. This process is the equivalent of NEPA in the United States or environmental impact assessment as

specified in Principle 17 of the Rio Declaration. Indeed, the Inspection Panel's report reads very much like a U.S. court opinion in NEPA cases involving judicial review of federal agency action, as in Chapter 9. The U.S. bilateral assistance agency, the Agency for International Development, has similar requirements. As described by the Inspection Panel, the World Bank — like the regional development banks for Latin America, Asia, and Eastern Europe and the former Soviet Union — categorizes projects according to the magnitude of their impacts and pegs the detail of the analysis to that determination. A setting involving external financing presents somewhat different financing from a purely domestic project. For example, the Bank's policies specify that the borrowing country government is responsible for carrying out the EA, including hiring consultants, while Bank staff exercise an oversight role. What might be the weak links in the multilateral aid process from the point of view of the environment? From the point of view of an individual in a borrowing country whose livelihood might be affected by a Bank-financed project?

2. **Unilateralism at the World Bank.** In 1987 the United States, in response to concerns about the World Bank's environmental performance, adopted new legislation address-ing the role of environment in the United States' future participation in the World Bank. The legislation is specifically targeted at the U.S. Executive Director to the World Bank and the Department of the Treasury, to which the U.S. Executive Director reports. For example, 22 U.S.C. §262m-7, the so-called Pelosi Amendment, establishes stan-dards of performance in the area of environmental impact assessment by the multilateral development banks as a condition of favorable votes by the U.S. Executive Director to those institutions. Partially as a result of the legislation, but also on his own initiative, in 1988 then-Secretary of the Treasury James Baker issued instructions to the U.S. Executive Director to the World Bank concerning the manner in which the United States would exercise its vote within that institution on projects that could affect tropi-cal forests. The World Bank's staff and other countries have on occasion vehemently protested the congressional legislation and Baker instructions as unilateral attempts to leverage change at the Bank. In particular, these actions of both the Congress and the executive branch have been labeled by the Bank's professional staff as "inconsistent with multilateralism." What arguments can you make in support of that assertion? As a representative of U.S. Department of the Treasury, how would you respond?

3. **Foreign aid for the global environment.** Article 11 of the UNFCCC, entitled "Financial Mechanism," responds to the demands of developing countries during the negotiation of the Climate Convention for additional resources to facilitate their contri-butions to reducing global warming. Paragraph 1 of that provision specifies that the operation of the financial mechanism "shall be entrusted to one or more existing inter-national entities," a reference to the Global Environment Facility (GEF). The GEF is a multilateral entity whose projects are developed and implemented by the World Bank, the United Nations Development Program, and the United Nations Environment Program. It provides developing countries with grant and concessional (low or zero interest) funding in four areas — climate change, stratospheric ozone depletion, biolog-ical diversity, and international waters. The GEF has allocated $4 billion in grants and leveraged an additional $12 billion in co-financing from other sources, including

bilateral donors such as the U.S. Agency for International Development, to support more than 1000 projects in over 140 developing countries and former socialist states. In August 2002, donors pledged nearly $3 billion more to fund the work of the GEF for the following four years. Notwithstanding its environmentally beneficial mission, the GEF has come under criticism from developing countries as reflecting the priorities of wealthy, industrialized donor countries and from environmentalists and human rights advocates as nothing more than a fig leaf that masks the much larger problem of environmentally and socially harmful projects like that in China. What factors would you identify as key to effective deployment of environmentally beneficial aid, and how would you structure a multilateral institution to reflect them? Or is it impossible, as some have asserted, for foreign aid to reduce global environmental threats?

4. **The Inspection Panel fights for independence.** The interim juncture of the inspection process at which the Bank's Board of Executive Directors must approve a request for inspection before the inspection may go forward created a great deal of tension between the Board and the Panel. Members of the Panel were publicly and vocally critical of the Bank Management's attempts to circumvent or hobble the Panel. In at least two cases, Bank Management cited remedial action plans identified by the borrower as reasons for disapproving a request for inspection. In a third, it authorized only a limited "desk study" investigation confined to information already available at the Bank's headquarters in Washington. Not coincidentally, these cases involved large and influential borrowers, Brazil and India. See The World Bank Inspection Panel: The First Four Years (1994–1998) (A. Umaña ed., 1998); Bissell, Recent Practice of the Inspection Panel of the World Bank, 91 Am. J. Int'l L. 741 (1997). In the end, the Board accepted a "tacit approval" or "nonobjection" procedure in which the Board is deemed to have consented to the Panel's recommendation to proceed with an investigation unless that recommendation is expressly disapproved by the Board. The Panel, however, is still confined to considering only compliance with internal Bank policies, a factor some critics have identified as creating an incentive to weaken those requirements. On behalf of an NGO submitting a request for inspection, what arguments could you make that the Panel nonetheless must consider customary international legal norms, multilateral treaties of general application, and widely accepted nonbinding instruments such as the Rio Declaration?

5. **Are alternatives to the Bank worse?** In response to the Inspection Panel's report, China announced that it intended to go forward with the Qinghai component of the Western Poverty Reduction Project without Bank funding. The Chinese Executive Director stated that "[i]t is unacceptable to my authorities that other Bank shareholders would insist on imposing additional conditions on Management's recommendations.... China will therefore turn to its own resources to implement the Qinghai Component of the project, and in its own way.... [C]ompliance policies have been interpreted by some to an extreme and used for political purposes.... From the very start, the whole process has been under enormous political pressure." Bank staff have often asserted that the environmental and human rights goals are better served by having the Bank involved in major projects such as the Western Poverty Reduction Project, even if some concessions to borrowing country governments are necessary.

If the Bank pulls out, they say, there will be no external checks to assure that even mini-mal standards are met. Do you agree with this argument? If not, how would you respond to it?

Section 2. **THE WORLD TRADE ORGANIZATION**

Free trade is not a principle, it is an expedient.

— Benjamin Disraeli, Speech on import duties, April 25, 1843

Until the mid-1990s, the principal multilateral instrument governing trade rela-tionships among states was the General Agreement on Tariffs and Trade (GATT). The GATT was adopted soon after World War II to encourage liberalized trade relations among states. Originally a formal International Trade Organization (ITO) was envi-sioned to be established by what came to be known as the Havana Charter. In the event, there was no agreement on the establishment of a new international organization, and the agreement now known as the GATT was provisionally agreed. Over time, it acquired the status of a de facto international organization, with a secretariat located in Geneva.

The basic obligations or "disciplines" found in the GATT that relate to environ-ment, described in greater detail in Chapter 8, are

the most-favored nation (MFN) obligation in Article I, which prohibits discrimi-nation among imported products on the basis of their national origin;

the national treatment requirement in Article III, which prohibits discrimination between foreign products and "like" domestic products; and

a prohibition on quantitative restrictions in Article XI, which precludes numerical restrictions on imports and exports.

Article XX of the GATT contains a number of exemptions from the General Agreement for specific categories of national measures that otherwise would violate these three basic disciplines. Of particular importance in the fields of environment and public health are two express exceptions: one in paragraph (b) for measures "necessary to protect human, animal or plant life or health"; and another in paragraph (g) for measures "relating to the conservation of exhaustible natural resources if such measures are made effective in conjunction with restrictions on domestic production or consumption."

The potential for these international obligations substantially to constrain domes-tic environmental policies hit home in 1991 when a GATT dispute settlement panel issued its report reviewing a challenge initiated by Mexico. The challenge objected to a U.S. ban on importation of tuna that had been caught through the use of fishing prac-tices that injure and kill dolphins. In the Eastern Tropical Pacific Ocean (ETP), schools of tuna often travel below pods of air-breathing dolphin, which are visible at or just below the surface of the water as they break the surface to breathe and leap into the air. Taking advantage of this relationship, tuna fishing fleets from several nations, including the United States and numerous South and Central American nations such as Ecuador, Mexico, Panama, and Venezuela, typically targeted the visible dolphin herds to locate schools of yellowfin tuna below. In a practice known as "setting on dolphin," fishing boats encircle pods of air-breathing dolphin with a "purse-seine" net to capture the tuna below. Setting on dolphin entangles many dolphin in the nets above the tuna, holding them below the surface so they cannot breathe, resulting in widespread injury and death to dolphin. Although dolphin-safe netting devices and methods exist, they cost more and require more attention, so that unregulated fishing fleets have tended to continue slaughtering dolphin to catch tuna.

In response to this problem, the U.S. Marine Mammal Protection Act (MMPA), enacted in 1972, establishes industrywide practices for tuna harvesting designed to prevent the incidental "taking" of marine mammals, specifically various species of dolphins. The law prohibits the incidental taking of marine mammals by U.S. fishermen unless a permit has been issued by the National Marine Fisheries Service (NMFS) of the National Oceanic and Atmospheric Administration (NOAA), located within the Department of Commerce. Under the permitting program, no more than 20,500 dolphins may be incidentally killed or injured each year by the U.S. fleet fishing in the ETP. These provisions apply as well to all entities and vessels subject to U.S. jurisdiction, on the high seas and in U.S. territory, including the territorial sea of the United States and the U.S. exclusive economic zone.

The U.S. fleet is generally in compliance with these requirements. Foreign fleets not subject to U.S. jurisdiction, however, have had considerably higher dolphin mortality rates. To address this problem, the MMPA contains provisions that apply specifically to imports of tuna and that require the U.S. Customs Service to "ban the importation of commercial fish or products from fish which have been caught with commercial fishing technology which results in the incidental kill or incidental serious injury of ocean mammals in excess of United States standards." Dissatisfied with executive branch inaction with respect to foreign tuna, Congress amended the statute in 1984 and 1988 with increasingly specific requirements that require that the harvesting country's tuna fleet does not exceed 1.25 times the average taking rate for U.S. vessels.

By 1990, the Secretary of Commerce had neither issued findings of comparability nor banned tuna imports from the offending nations. Frustrated with this delay, the Earth Island Institute, a private environmental organization, brought suit in the U.S. District Court for the Northern District of California to compel the executive branch to comply with the MMPA. The court enjoined executive branch officials from permitting further tuna imports into the United States because no findings of comparability had been made. Earth Island Inst. v. Mosbacher, 746 F. Supp. 964 (N.D. Cal. 1990). The court's order affected tuna imports from Ecuador, Mexico, Panama, Vanuatu, and Venezuela. Panama and Ecuador later prohibited their fleets from setting on dolphin and were consequently exempted from the embargo. Mexico did not, and a ban on imports of Mexican tuna took effect in 1991. Mexico then challenged the ban in the GATT.

The GATT's dispute resolution mechanisms first encourage contracting parties to the General Agreement to settle differences through consultation and negotiation. If negotiations and consultations are unsuccessful, as they were in this case, an aggrieved party may submit a complaint requesting appointment of a panel of experts to hear the dispute. The panel constituted to consider Mexico's complaint issued the following report, the most controversial in its history, prompting a representative of the Humane Society of the United States to utter the plaintive rhetorical question, "How many more of these gentle creatures will have to die in the name of free trade?"

United States — Restrictions on Imports of Tuna
30 I.L.M. 1594 (1991)

The Panel...concluded that...the United States import prohibition would not meet the requirements of Article III [requiring national treatment of "like" products, in this case tuna]. Article III:4 calls for a comparison of the treatment of imported tuna as a product with that of domestic tuna as a product. Regulations governing the taking of dolphins incidental to the taking of tuna could not possibly affect tuna as a product. Article III:4 therefore obliges the United States to accord treatment to Mexican tuna no less favourable than that accorded to United States tuna, whether or not the incidental taking of dolphins by Mexican vessels corresponds to that of United States vessels....

The Panel noted that the United States had argued that its direct embargo under the MMPA could be justified under Article XX(b) or Article XX(g).... The Panel recalled that previous panels had established that Article XX is a limited and conditional exception from obligations under other provisions of the General Agreement, and not a positive rule establishing obligations in itself. Therefore, the practice of panels has been to interpret Article XX narrowly, to place the burden on the party invoking Article XX to justify its invocation, and not to examine Article XX exceptions unless invoked....

The Panel proceeded to examine whether Article XX(b) or Article XX(g) could justify the MMPA provisions on imports of certain yellowfin tuna and yellowfin tuna products, and the import ban imposed under these provisions. The Panel noted that Article XX provides that:

> "Subject to the requirement that such measures are not applied in a manner which would constitute a means of arbitrary or unjustifiable discrimination between countries where the same conditions prevail, or a disguised restriction on international trade, nothing in this Agreement shall be construed to prevent the adoption or enforcement by any contracting party of measures...
>
> (b) necessary to protect human, animal or plant life or health;...
>
> (g) relating to the conservation of exhaustible natural resources if such measures are made effective in conjunction with restrictions on domestic production or consumption...."

The Panel noted that the United States considered the prohibition of imports of certain yellowfin tuna and certain yellowfin tuna products from Mexico, and the provisions of the MMPA on which this prohibition is based, to be justified by Article XX(b) because they served solely the purpose of protecting dolphin life and health and were "necessary" within the meaning of that provision because, in respect of the protection of dolphin life and health outside its jurisdiction, there was no alternative measure reasonably available to the United States to achieve this objective. Mexico considered that Article XX(b) was not applicable to a measure imposed to protect the life or health of animals outside the jurisdiction of the contracting party taking it and that the import prohibition imposed by the United States was not necessary because alternative means consistent with the General Agreement were available to it to protect dolphin lives or health, namely international co-operation between the countries concerned.

The Panel noted that the basic question raised by these arguments, namely whether Article XX(b) covers measures necessary to protect human, animal or plant life or health outside the jurisdiction of the contracting party taking the measure, is not clearly answered by the text of that provision. It refers to life and health protection generally without expressly limiting that protection to the jurisdiction of the contracting party concerned. The Panel therefore decided to analyze this issue in the light of the drafting history of Article XX(b), the purpose of this provision, and the consequences that the interpretations proposed by the parties would have for the operation of the General Agreement as a whole....

The Panel...noted that Article XX(b) allows each contracting party to set its human, animal or plant life or health standards. The conditions set out in Article XX(b) which limit resort to this exception, namely that the measure taken must be "necessary" and not "constitute a means of arbitrary or unjustifiable discrimination or a disguised restriction on international trade," refer to the trade measure requiring justification under Article XX(b), not however to the life or health standard chosen by the contracting party.... The Panel considered that if the broad interpretation of Article XX(b) suggested by the United States were accepted, each contracting party could unilaterally determine the life or health protection policies from which other contracting parties could not deviate without jeopardizing their rights under the General Agreement. The General Agreement would then no longer constitute a multilateral framework for trade among all contracting parties but would provide legal security only in respect of trade between a limited number of contracting parties with identical internal regulations.

The Panel considered that the United States' measures, even if Article XX(b) were interpreted to permit extrajurisdictional protection of life and health, would not meet the requirement of necessity set out in that provision. The United States had not demonstrated to the Panel — as required of the party invoking an Article XX exception — that it had exhausted all options reasonably available to it to pursue its dolphin protection objectives through measures consistent with the General Agreement, in particular through the negotiation of international cooperative arrangements, which would seem to be desirable in view of the fact that dolphins roam the waters of many states and the high seas. Moreover, even assuming that an import prohibition were the only resort reasonably available to the United States, the particular measure chosen by the United States could in the Panel's view not be considered to be necessary within the meaning of Article XX(b). The United States linked the maximum incidental dolphin taking rate which Mexico had to meet during a particular period in order to be able to export tuna to the United States to the taking rate actually recorded for United States fishermen during the same period. Consequently, the Mexican authorities could not know whether, at a given point of time, their policies conformed to the United States' dolphin protection standards. The Panel considered that a limitation on trade based on such unpredictable conditions could not be regarded as necessary to protect the health or life of dolphins.

On the basis of the above considerations, the Panel found that the United States' direct import prohibition imposed on certain yellowfin tuna and certain yellowfin tuna products of Mexico and the provisions of the MMPA under which it is imposed could not be justified under the exception in Article XX(b).

[For similar reasons, the Panel found that the exception in Article XX(g) for the conservation of exhaustible natural resources was inapplicable.]

The Panel wished to underline that its task was limited to the examination of this matter "in the light of the relevant GATT provisions," and therefore did not call for a finding on the appropriateness of the United States' and Mexico's conservation policies as such.

The Panel wished to note the fact, made evident during its consideration of this case, that the provisions of the General Agreement impose few constraints on a contracting party's implementation of domestic environmental policies.... [However,] a contracting party may not restrict imports of a product merely because it originates in a country with environmental policies different from its own. The Panel further recalled its finding that the import restrictions examined in this dispute, imposed to respond to differences in environmental regulation of producers, could not be justified under the exceptions in Articles XX(b) or XX(g). These exceptions did not specify criteria limiting the range of life or health protection policies, or resource conservation policies, for the sake of which they could be invoked. It seemed evident to the Panel that, if the [GATT] were to permit import restrictions in response to differences in environmental policies under the General Agreement, they would need to impose limits on the range of policy differences justifying such responses and to develop criteria so as to prevent abuse....

These considerations led the Panel to the view that the adoption of its report would affect neither the rights of individual contracting parties to pursue their internal environmental policies and to co-operate with one another in harmonizing such policies, nor the right of the [GATT parties] acting jointly to address international environmental problems which can only be resolved through measures in conflict with the present rules of the General Agreement.

COMMENTARY & QUESTIONS

1. **Process and production methods (PPMs).** In the first paragraph of its report quoted above, the GATT Panel makes a distinction between the content of an imported product and the method by which it is produced — so-called process and production methods (PPMs) — even when a manufacturing process creates environmental externalities. If tuna from Mexico had been tainted with mercury, for example, it would not be a "like" product by comparison with uncontaminated tuna. According to the Panel, however, tuna caught by methods that harm dolphin is comparable to dolphin-safe tuna. The Panel's conclusion necessarily means that states of import may not discriminate among products based on manufacturing methodologies that do not cause environmental harm within the state of import's jurisdiction. How did the Panel justify this conclusion? According to the Panel, what harm would result to the international trading system if the United States had been permitted to discriminate against dolphin-unsafe tuna? Do you agree or disagree with the Panel's conclusion? If you disagree, how would you respond to the Panel's concern about the adverse effects on international trade?

2. **An escape valve for the environment.** The bulk of the excerpt above is devoted to the Panel's analysis of Article XX of the GATT, which permits the United States to attempt to justify the tuna embargo despite the fact that it violates the basic GATT disciplines. At the time the GATT was adopted, protection of the environment was not widely understood as a basis for national policies. Consequently, environmentally related measures are most likely to fall under the exceptions in Article XX(b) addressing "human, animal or plant life or health" or in Article XX(g) dealing with "conservation of exhaustible natural resources." As with the U.S. arguments concerning the "likeness" of dolphin-safe and dolphin-unsafe tuna, the United States lost on this point, meaning that it lost the overall dispute. According to the Panel, why do neither of these two exceptions justify the tuna embargo? Accepting this conclusion at least for the sake of argument, what alternatives would be available to the United States to protect dolphin outside its jurisdiction? How do those alternatives compare with the trade ban in their effectiveness in protecting dolphin?

3. **Baptists, bootleggers, and Flipper.** One of the GATT Panel's concerns seems to be the willingness of the United States to utilize a trade ban to achieve its conservation purposes when less coercive approaches might have accomplished a similar result without disadvantaging Mexico or foreign fishing interests. If you were a representative of the U.S. tuna fishing industry, which had already been subjected to regulatory

requirements that limited dolphin "bycatch" (unwanted species caught incidentally and dumped at sea), why might you find a ban on imports of tuna from countries that did not have comparable requirements a particularly attractive alternative? Trade policy analysts sometimes speak of "Baptist-bootlegger" coalitions, referring to political dynamics during the era of prohibition when both teetotalers and smugglers supported a ban on alcohol, one group out of principle and the other motivated by self-interest. The United States in defending the tuna ban argued that its purpose was benign (i.e., aimed at protecting dolphins) and not protectionist (i.e., designed to protect the domestic tuna industry from foreign competition). Should this have made a difference to the Panel? If so, what should be the role of intent in analyzing the validity of a trade barrier such as the tuna ban? How would you go about determining the intent of Congress in passing the MMPA? As a matter of principle, why might a GATT panel conclude, as it did, that intent is immaterial and that the relevant question is the effect of the measure?

4. **PPMs in the World Trade Organization.** In the GATT system, panel reports such as that on the U.S. tuna embargo did not have legal effect unless they were adopted by consensus by the GATT Council, which represented all the GATT "contracting parties." Mexico declined to present the tuna report to the GATT Council, presumably because of concerns that the intense public outcry over the most publicized panel report ever could threaten then-ongoing negotiations with the United States and Canada over the North American Free Trade Agreement (NAFTA). The European Union and the Netherlands then challenged a secondary embargo designed to prevent "tuna laundering," with a result similar to Mexico's challenge. United States — Restrictions on Imports of Tuna, 33 I.L.M. 839 (1994). Because both reports remained unadopted at the end of 1994, when the GATT as a legal matter ceased to exist, neither is a definitive statement of GATT law. One of the principal innovations in the World Trade Organization (WTO), which came into existence as the successor to the GATT on January 1, 1995, was the dispute settlement process through the creation of a standing Appellate Body that could consider appeals of panel decisions on questions of law. It was no longer possible, as in the GATT, for a losing party with political clout such as the United States unilaterally to block the adoption of an adverse panel report. The WTO Appellate Body confronted the issue of PPMs in a dispute very similar to the tuna/dolphin case, which was initiated by India, Malaysia, Pakistan, and Thailand concerning a U.S. ban on importation of shrimp harvested by methods that harm endangered sea turtles. The new Appellate Body concluded that the shrimp ban, like the tuna embargo, violated the trading rights of the complainants and the obligations of the United States. In contrast to both tuna panels, however, the Appellate Body strongly suggested that the deficiencies in the U.S. scheme were not inherent in the "extraterritorial" reach of the import ban but instead could be corrected through a more careful design and implementation of the program. After the U.S. State Department amended its guidelines for implementation of the program, the Appellate Body held the ban consistent with GATT/WTO rules. United States — Import Prohibition of Certain Shrimp and Shrimp Products, available at http://www.wto.org/english/tratop_e/dispu_e/dispu_subjects_index_e.htm#bkmk116.

5. **Unilateralism versus multilateralism.** The MMPA, like the Pelly and Packwood Amendments described in Chapter 8, is an example of a unilateral measure taken to fill gaps in, and to reinforce, international cooperative regimes such as the Inter-American Tropical Tuna Commission, which has the authority to regulate tuna on a multilateral basis. The executive branch embargoed tuna imports from Mexico only after two amendments to the MMPA and a court order obtained by a domestic environmental organization. With the ban in place, the U.S. government continued to negotiate with Mexico and other governments in an attempt to identify an alternative to the ban. Soon after the imposition of the tuna embargo, ten states, negotiating under the auspices of the Inter-American Tropical Tuna Commission, entered into an agreement to reduce dolphin mortality, the so-called La Jolla Agreement. This instrument was intended to phase down the maximum permissible take of dolphins in the Eastern Pacific Ocean to 5000 in 1999 while continuing to allow the practice of dolphin sets. In October 1995, a configuration of states similar to those parties to the La Jolla Agreement adopted the Declaration of Panama, which anticipated further binding international commitments with the goal of eliminating dolphin mortality and further tightened standards beyond those identified in the earlier La Jolla Agreement. After Congress amended the MMPA, the embargoes were lifted after the State Department's finding that an agreement meeting the requirements of the legislation is in effect for countries that are in compliance with the agreement — as of this writing, virtually all countries with vessels setting on dolphins in the region. Is this what the tuna panel had in mind when it referred to "the negotiation of international cooperative arrangements"? What practical difference is there between approaching Mexico in the first instance about the possibility of an international agreement and proposing negotiations against the backdrop of a ban already in place? Which is better for dolphins, a unilateral embargo or a multilateral agreement such as the La Jolla Agreement or the Panama Declaration? As a representative of the Earth Island Institute, how would you decide whether such a multilateral agreement made sufficient progress such that your organization could support lifting the embargo? As a government official, what incentive would you have to consult with the Earth Island Institute during negotiations with Mexico and other countries? In the event, the Panama Declaration seriously divided the U.S. conservation community.

6. **WTO dispute settlement and democratic participation.** In contrast to the opportunities for public input into the legislative, administrative, and judicial fora in which this dispute was treated on the domestic level, but consistent with standard GATT procedures, the documents and oral proceedings in the case were not accessible to the public. Dispute settlement in GATT did not allow for participation by private parties such as the Earth Island Institute. According to anecdotal reports, the Earth Island Institute's lawyer was shut out and forced to wait in the corridor while the Panel heard arguments from Mexico and the United States. Ten other GATT parties and the European Union nonetheless were permitted to make written submissions to the Panel, all of which were critical of the ban, arguing that it violated the GATT. The Uruguay Round made some changes toward a more transparent process in the WTO, principally by permitting — although not requiring — publication of nonconfidential summaries of parties' written submissions to panels and the Appellate Body. The Appellate Body's jurisprudence

has moved toward a more open process, principally by creating entry points for submissions by NGOs in a role analogous to amici curiae in domestic courts. The WTO Council, however, has expressed virtually unanimous dissatisfaction with this practice. In contrast with many other international organizations such as UNEP, NGO "observers" are still excluded from formal negotiating sessions of new WTO agreements. As a representative of the Earth Island Institute, what are the costs if members of the public — including NGOs, industry, and private citizens — are excluded from WTO panels, the Appellate Body, and the negotiation of new agreements? What principled arguments can you make in support of the proposition that trade agreement negotiation and dispute settlement processes, unlike multilateral environmental agreements, should not be conducted "in a fishbowl"? How might the potential adverse effects from greater transparency be minimized or eliminated?

7. **Greening the WTO.** The trade and environment debate highlights competing visions of the interrelationship between these two aspirational goals, both of which are intended to promote human welfare. One perspective is that excessively zealous attempts to address environmental and public health measures as potential nontariff trade barriers may excessively constrain legitimate national regulatory measures through a process of "deregulation from abroad." From this perspective, trade-based restrictions on environmental measures may justify or promote a downward spiral — a race-to-the-bottom — toward weak, least common denominator domestic regulatory standards or chill the adoption of new regulatory measures out of fear of a trade-based challenge. An alternative view is that trade promotes wealth, which in turn becomes available for "investment" in environmental protection. According to this view, "[p]rotectionist practices might well be viewed as generally promoting environmental degradation because they provide no incentive to use resources efficiently. Free trade might justifiably be viewed as promoting environmental protection, because countries will generate more wealth with which to protect the environment." Weiss, Environment and Trade as Partners in Sustainable Development: A Commentary, 86 Am. J. Int'l L. 728, 729–730 (1992). Principle 12 of the Rio Declaration, reproduced in Section B above, is a response to the GATT tuna-dolphin decision of the previous year. What proposals could you make for reconciling environmental and trade policy? One solution that has been proposed is to treat environmental laxity — the failure of certain countries to require compliance with minimum international environmental standards — as an impermissible de facto "subsidy" that can be offset through at-the-border measures such as tariffs. This would appear to be consistent with Rio Principle 16, which encourages states to "promote the internalization of environmental costs and the use of economic instruments, taking into account the approach that the polluter should, in principle, bear the cost of pollution, with due regard to the public interest and without distorting international trade and investment." What do you think of such a proposal? How might it be written into GATT/WTO rules? What difficulties could you imagine in implementing it, and how might they be resolved?

At the beginning of the twenty-first century, international environmental law is at a crossroads. Over the past 20 years or so, major strides have been made in encouraging a sense of accountability and global democracy in decisionmaking, largely through the inclusion of NGOs and members of the public at large. Institutions such as the World Bank Inspection Panel and the Commission for Environmental Cooperation's citizen submission process even seem like international analogues of domestic citizen suits. Major, complex new agreements have been negotiated to deal with such pressing global problems as climate warming, species loss, and desertification. Indeed, international environmental policy is at the forefront of many progressive innovations that prefigure more general trends in public international law. More generally, an awareness of the magnitude of international environmental threats has risen among the public world-wide.

At the same time, there is evidence of dysfunction in the system, partially but not solely attributable to the recent chilly attitude of the U.S. government toward multilateralism. Despite the great activity in drafting new international environmental treaties in recent years, international environmental law has not been accompanied by a commensurate level of institutional growth. The result has been a lack of coordination and a high degree of fragmentation.

The mission of only one international organization, the UN Environment Program (UNEP), is exclusively environmental. Numerous other international organizations established for a variety of other purposes have also played significant roles on international environmental challenges: the International Maritime Organization (IMO), under whose auspices a number of marine pollution agreements have been negotiated; the Organization for Economic Co-operation and Development (OECD), which in the past has been a principal forum for discussing transboundary pollution and is now working on the environment-and-trade nexus; and the UN Food and Agriculture Organization (FAO), which has played a major role in work on pesticides at the international level. Even more institutional decentralization has taken place as the secretariats for environmental agreements have increasingly acquired an independent character and been located far from one another.

Overcoming the inertial drag of an international system based on consent and consensus and rigorously tied to short-term national interests — this is a fundamental challenge for the new century. Looking back a quarter century from now — and, with the help of a new generation of creative international lawyers, perhaps sooner — we may well view developments that now seem innovative as merely primitive precursors of an effective, comprehensive international system to come that will protect this fragile planet, the only one we have.

It suddenly struck me that that tiny pea, pretty and blue, was the Earth. I put up my thumb and shut one eye, and my thumb blotted out the planet Earth. I didn't feel like a giant. I felt very, very small.

—Astronaut Neil Armstrong

Afterword

FACING THE FUTURE

For two reasons, our generation will bear a heavier responsibility for the future of planet Earth than any generation before it has. First, we know better — having gained access to an unprecedented wealth of new scientific information and a vastly improved capacity for analysis and prediction. Second, we can do better — having accumulated enough experience, technological and institutional, to take the necessary…action.

— Peter Sand[1]

Predicting the future of environmental law — a field characterized by diverse legal approaches to scientific uncertainty — is itself a risky venture. Environmental law has evolved in response to unexpected and unsettling discoveries and events. Rachel Carson's identification of the pernicious effects of DDT on food webs led directly to major revisions of the Federal Insecticide, Fungicide, and Rodenticide Act; the Environmental Defense Fund's discovery of toxic chemicals in the lower Mississippi River, which serves as the potable water supply for New Orleans, was instrumental in the enactment of the Safe Drinking Water Act; the *Kepone* debacle resulted in developments in common law and criminal law, and was partially responsible for the passage of the Resource Conservation and Recovery Act; and the *Exxon-Valdez* disaster stimulated the passage of the Oil Pollution Act and prompted innovations in other areas of law as well. Why should the future of environmental law be any more predictable than its first decades?

Figuratively speaking, environmental law, as both a stimulant and manifestation of environmental policy, undergoes tidal fluctuations: Periods of incoming tides, when resort to environmental litigation, legislation, and regulation rises in response to focused popular concerns about environmental quality, alternate with outgoing tides, when diminished attention to environmental concerns combines with trepidations about the economic costs of environmental protection. Some of these tidal fluctuations are every bit as extreme as Bay of Fundy tides. During such periods, the "environmentalist versus anti-environmentalist" political rhetoric becomes heated, and proposed changes in environmental law become stridently controversial. During times of more moderate political tides, environmental law is characterized by the "fine-tuning" of existing law. More extreme times, as in the Bush II presidency, are characterized by strong environmental outgoing currents, including outspoken rejections of previously accepted environmental legal principles such as the need for international cooperation in the solution of transnational environmental problems. We can only speculate about

---

1. Sand, Lessons Learned in Global Environmental Governance, 18 B.C. Envtl. Aff. L. Rev. 1 (1990).

the political direction and intensity of future conflicts regarding environmental law, but we can predict with relative certainty that the alternating political crosscurrents in this area will continue, and the basic themes articulated in this coursebook will not become mere whisps of nostalgia.

A number of comparatively recent but substantial legal trends are likely to continue into the foreseeable future. Some of these developments have been discussed in previous chapters: the dynamic growth of toxic tort law; the application of corporate, contract, and property law concepts to environmental issues; the increasing interactions between common law and statutes; the evolution of environmental criminal law; the unfolding of the public trust doctrine; the tension and competition between federal and state governments; the wrangling over competing uses of public lands; the increasingly sophisticated implementation of market incentives for pollution control; new types of environmental land use mechanisms; the increased use of ADR; and the emergence of international environmental law.

There will be further amendments, extensions, applications, administrative and judicial interpretations, and enforcement (and nonenforcement) of existing environmental statutes. Congress may enact a limited number of new federal statutes — perhaps appearing as amendments to existing acts — that cover areas ignored or inadequately addressed by prior federal legislation, like groundwater pollution, indoor air pollution, and protection of biodiversity. Even though the emphasis during the next 20 years of environmental law will probably be on the implementation, fine-tuning, and interpretation of existing federal statutes, we must always be prepared for the revelations or catastrophes that galvanize the creation of new environmental law. And if the federal government shows increasing laxity in its approach to environmental protection, then — as in the field of civil rights — the cutting edge of the law will move to state legislatures and courts, and to the international realm.

In a world currently facing enormous environmental challenges, moreover, merely staying in the same place is — like Alice in the looking-glass world — inevitably to fall behind. Although the emphasis during the next twenty years of environmental law should be on the full implementationof existing statutes and the identification of effective responses to new challenges like global warming, that is unlikely to happen in a climate in which existing structures and laws are repeatedly under challenge. We must always be prepared for the revelations or catastrophes that galvanize the creation of new environmental law, not looking backward with a siege mentality to preserve the accomplishments of the past.

A Triad of Environmental Challenges. Professor Arnold Rietze pointed out that global environmental degradation can be traced and categorized in three spheres of human activity — population, consumption, and pollution. Of the three, only the last (which is perhaps least important) has received major attention.[2]

Population. Currently the earth supports between 5 and 6 billion people. Because population grows exponentially, unless we have a global nuclear war or widespread

---

2. Reitze, Environmental Policy — It Is Time for a New Beginning, 14 Colum. J. Envtl. L. 111 (1989).

famine and disease, by 2100 the earth's population will be 10.4 billion — more than twice that in 1988. Most of the increase will take place in the impoverished Third World.

Lester R. Brown of the Worldwatch Institute describes the environmental consequences of what has been called the Population Bomb:

> Ecologists looking at biological indicators...see rising human demand, driven by population growth and rising affluence, surpassing the carrying capacity of local forests, grasslands, and soils in country after country. They see sustainable yield thresholds of the economy's natural support systems being breached throughout the Third World. And as a result, they see the natural resource base diminishing even as population growth is expanding.... Continuing rapid population growth and spreading environmental degradation have trapped hundreds of millions in a downward spiral of falling incomes and growing hunger. With the number of people caught in this life-threatening cycle increasing each year, the world may soon be forced to reckon with the consequence of years of population policy neglect.[3]

But population control runs afoul of deep-seated moral and religious convictions and human instincts, and comes close to being an intractable challenge.

Consumption. Critics of our inefficient, wasteful, consumption-oriented "throwaway" society advocate modes of sustainable economic activity that maintain a long-term equilibrium between production and ecological integrity.

William Ruckelshaus, a former EPA Administrator and now the Chief Executive Officer of the world's largest waste handling firm, notes the shift toward concepts of sustainability:

> Sustainability is a nascent doctrine that economic growth and development must take place, and be maintained over time, within limits set by ecology in the broadest sense — by the interrelations of human beings and their works, the biosphere, and the physical and chemical laws that govern it. The doctrine of sustainability holds that the spread of a reasonable level of prosperity and security to the less developed nations is essential to protecting ecological balance and hence essential to the continued prosperity of the wealthy nations. It follows that environmental protection and economic development are complementary rather than antagonistic processes....[4]

For Ruckelshaus, the fundamental principles of a sustainable economy would be to recognize that:

- The human species is part of nature. Its existence depends on its ability to draw sustenance from a finite world; its continuance depends on its ability to abstain from destroying the natural systems that regenerate this world....
- Economic activity must account for the [full] environmental costs of production....
- The maintenance of a liveable global environment depends on the sustainable development of the entire human family.

---

3. Worldwatch Institute, Population: The Neglected Issue, State of the World 1991, 15–18.
4. Toward a Sustainable World, 261 Sci. Am. (No. 1) 166, 167–168 (1989).

Globally, as the Brundtland Commission declared, the concept of sustainable development is not just an aesthetic good; it is a necessary principle for long-term survivability. It involves not only the prevention of global threats such as global warming and ozone depletion, but also the assurance that citizens of less developed nations will receive equitable material treatment.[5]

Sustainability also means a commitment to maximizing biodiversity, both because other species may be necessary for human well-being and because all species are essential participants in ecological integrity. Sustainability cannot be achieved without conservation — of resources, of energy, and of a quality existence for all species on earth. Reaching a state of sustainability will certainly require the moderation of the wasteful modes of life that have become instinctive in some affluent nations.

Pollution. Pollution control efforts will become increasingly proactive, emphasizing pollution prevention rather than the infernal complexities of end-of-pipe command-and-control systems and cleanup liability.

The Pollution Prevention Act of 1990[6] illustrates that trend. Its basic premise is that source reduction "is fundamentally different and more desirable than waste management and pollution control." It envisions source reduction as a win win opportunity for EPA and the regulated community because of "significant opportunities for industry to reduce or prevent pollution at the source through cost-effective changes in production, operation, and raw material use." These changes, in turn, ensure "reduced raw material, pollution control, and liability costs as well as help to protect the environment and reduce risks to worker health and safety." The most forceful language in the statute is its unequivocal declaration of policy:

> The Congress hereby declares it to be the national policy of the United States that pollution should be prevented or reduced at the source whenever feasible; pollution that cannot be prevented should be recycled in an environmentally safe manner whenever feasible; pollution that cannot be prevented or recycled should be treated in an environmentally safe manner whenever feasible; and disposal or other release into the environment should be employed only as a last resort and should be conducted in an environmentally safe manner.

Thus far, pollution prevention has been hortatory rather than mandatory, but EPA possesses the legal authority to include pollution prevention requirements in permits and enforcement settlements; agencies in other nations are already far along that trail.

EVOLVING PRINCIPLES AND PROCESSES

Sustainable Development. Sustainable development is a powerful guiding concept carried into the new millennium. It is both a progressive and a conservative principle, compelling to any human analysis concerned beyond the shortest short term. We owe it

---

5. Adlai Stevenson, who supplied the image of Spaceship Earth with which the Introduction to this casebook began more than a thousand pages ago, continued by saying:

> We cannot maintain it half fortunate, half miserable, half confident, half dispairing, half slave to the ancient enemies of mankind, half free in a liberation of resources undreamed of until this day. No craft, no crew, can travel safely with such vast contradictions. On their resolution depends the survival of us all.

6. Pub. L. No. 101-508, Title VI, §§6601-6610, 42 U.S.C. §§13101–13119.

to ourselves and our posterity to improve the quality of life on earth, to steward the legacy of the resources we inherit, and to preserve, not destroy, the environmental birthright of future generations for the needs and profits of today. Healthy societal economic systems are founded upon healthy and sustainable ecological system cycles of soil, water, air, and living communities — human and all the others. Development must not be based upon an erosive diminution of global assets but rather on governance systems of indefinitely extendable human sustenance and life quality, in balance with the resource capacity of the planet's environments.

Integrated Environmental Planning and Management. Throughout this book we provide examples of the traditional, incremental, medium-specific, and site-specific approaches to environmental protection. We can no longer afford, however — either in an economic or an environmental sense — to hold to this narrow and reactive style of environmental management. The resulting array of laws is in too many ways an unco-ordinated, unruly mess that is ineffective or, even worse, counterproductive.

A more integrated approach is inevitably necessary. An integrated overview would consider the cumulative impacts and multimedia exposures threatened by a potential polluting or resource-depleting activity or series of activities, facilitating more accurate assessments of risk, with attendant improvements in setting environmental protection priorities and issuing permits. The most salient problem with integrated environmental control is implementation. Institutions capable of making the necessary holistic assess-ments are not yet in existence, and the track record of governmental central management systems does not inspire confidence. The inertia and institutional investments of the present fragmented systems assure that any fundamental reorienting will meet with specific resistance. But principles of integrated overview are ultimately unavoidable and eventually must be built into the diverse mechanisms that drive our societies.

Institutionalized Caution. Institutionalized caution — a principle enunciated in the ESA that also serves more broadly as a general reminder of the importance of looking before we leap — implies a functional and effective planning process. NEPA prescribes a basic form of that rational process, although most of the inside players still resist taking the medicine.

Meaningful environmental planning systems must be established in both the public and private sectors, and at all levels of government — local, state, interstate, national, regional, and international. The design and implementation of these innova-tive modes of environmental planning will constitute one of the profound and difficult challenges facing humankind during the twenty-first century.

Citizen Action. Citizen environmentalists over the years have all too often felt like Cassandra. The daughter of King Priam of Troy rejected the seductive blandishments of Apollo, and in retaliation the god burdened her with a terrible curse: She would accu-rately see the future — the impending onslaughts of storms, droughts, death lurking in the belly of the Trojan horse — but she would not be heeded.

Modern environmentalists' warnings about ecological dangers — acid rain, leukemia from hazardous wastes, the diminishing legacy of natural resources, pollution-caused health and welfare costs — have been important, as are environmentalism's systemic process warnings about narrow-minded decisionmaking, inattention to noneconomic values, erosions of civic responsibility and governmental integrity, regressions in the state of the federal courts, the low level of the national information process, and many more. Despite chronic inertia and resistance within corporate and governmental establishments, there has been a significant increase in popular dismay about systemic environmental problems. Environmental concerns can no longer be dismissively caricatured as just a whimsical aesthetic fad, and the minions of the media, though typically superficial and erratic, know that it is important to try to tell the story.

Environmental law, which was built by citizen efforts in legislatures, courts, and agencies, will continue to assure that citizens play a fundamental role in the governance of our society. Because environmental law has become such a major presence in the law books and in public awareness, environmentalism is not likely ever to go away, nor ever again to be the lonely domain of a tiny group of unheard seers.

The Common Heritage of Humankind. Our environment is indeed a global public trust. We have inherited from predecessor generations the responsibility for managing and shepherding it for our descendants and all other life forms. The principles of intergenerational equity advanced by Edith Brown Weiss suggest that rights and responsibilities of ecological stewardship are owed across political borders and the boundaries of time, ultimately as a matter of law as well as ethics. If we are to fulfill this fiduciary responsibility successfully, we must overcome what one of the authors of this book has referred to as a modern form of divisive tribalism:

> As the problems of managing the economy and ecology...become ever more complex, subtly-interrelated, pressured and demanding, our processes of legal and political governance might be expected to become more integrative and comprehensive in scope. Instead, however, there often appears to be a contrary dysfunctional tendency. The more complex and stressed an issue becomes, the more its political actors retreat into a narrow, insulated factionalism that can be viewed as a form of latter-day tribalism.[7]

In framing environmental problems, it might help to conceive of humans and all other forms of life as members of a global tribe, a comprehensive and integrated social unit that transcends the incessant territorial skirmishing of fragmented factions.

The ancient Greeks understood that the core philosophical problem is how to maintain a balance between the individual and the community, between unity and diversity. To this environmentalists add explicitly what the Greeks implicitly understood — that the human community is itself a component part of a larger community of living systems, of earth, water, air, and spirit. We must learn to retain the energy and richness of our disparate individual diversities, while creating the national, international, and intergenerational cooperation necessary for 10 billion human beings to live in relative harmony, crafting a sustainable future for the planet and its natural systems, including us.

Facing the future it seems that fundamentally we're all in this together.

---

7. A Modern Political Tribalism in Natural Resources Management, 11 Pub. Land L. Rev. 1, 3 (1990).

"Not that the story need be long, but it will take a long while to make it short."

— H.D. Thoreau, Letter to Mr. B. (1857)

REFERENCE MATERIALS

ACKNOWLEDGMENT OF PERMISSIONS TO REPRINT

The authors gratefully acknowledge the cooperation and generosity of many authors and publishers who consented to have portions of their works excerpted and reprinted in this book. The works are listed here in alphabetical order by last name of first author. Photographs and charts are acknowledged where they appear in the text.

Bruce A. Ackerman and Richard B. Stewart, Comment: Reforming Environmental Law, 37 Stanford Law Review 1333. Reprinted material first appeared in 37 Stanford Law Review at page 1333. Copyright © 1985 by the Board of Trustees of Leland Stanford Junior University. Reprinted by permission of the copyright holder, the authors, and Fred B. Rothman Company.

Hope Babcock, Has the U.S. Supreme Court Finally Drained the Swamp of Takings Jurisprudence? — The Impact of Lucas v. South Carolina Coastal Commission on Wetlands and Coastal Barrier Beaches, 19 Harvard Environmental Law Review 1 (1994).

Patricia Birnie, Whaling: End of an Era, International Whaling Regulation, 1985. Copyright 1985, Oceana Publications, reprinted with permission.

Daniel Bodansky, U.S. Climate Policy After Kyoto. Reprinted by permission of the publisher, from U.S. Climate Policy After Kyoto: Elements for Success (Washington, DC: Carnegie Endowment for International Peace, 2002). www.ceip.org

B. Boyer and E. Meidinger, Privatizing Regulatory Enforcement: A Preliminary Assessment of Citizen Suits Under Federal Environmental Laws, 33 Buffalo Law Review 833, 957-961 (1985). Reprinted by permission.

Rachel Carson, Silent Spring (1962). Copyright © 1962 by Rachel L. Carson. Reprinted by permission of Houghton Mifflin Company. All rights reserved.

Coggins, Charles, The Law of Public Rangeland Management IV: FLPMA, PRIA, and the Multiple Use Mandate, 14 Environmental Law 1 (1983). Reprinted by permission of Environmental Law.

Ray Druley & Girard Ordway, The Toxic Substance Control Act, pages 1-4 (1977). ©1977 by the Bureau of National Affairs, Inc., Washington, D.C. 20037. Reprinted by permission.

A. Denny Ellerman, Richard Schmalensee, Paul L. Joskow, Juan Pablo Montero, Elizabeth M. Bailey, Emissions Trading Under the U.S. Acid Rain Program: Evaluation of Compliance Costs and Allowance Market Performance (MIT, 1997). Reprinted by permission.

Steven Ferrey, Hard Time Criminal Prosecution For Polluters. © 1988, The Amicus Journal, a publication of the Natural Resources Defense Council, reprinted with permission.

James Florio, Congress as Reluctant Regulator: Hazardous Waste Policy in the 1980's; 3 Yale J. on Reg. 351, 353-376 (1986). Reprinted by permission.

Stuart Frankel, Full Disclosure: Financial Statement Disclosures under CERCLA; 3 Duke Environmental Law & Policy Forum 57, 65-67 (1993) Reprinted by permission.

Frank Friedman and David Giannotti, Environmental Self Assessment, in Law of Environmental Protection; Environmental Law Institute, 7-28 to 7-33 (1998). Reprinted by permission.

A GLOSSARY OF ACRONYMS AND ABBREVIATIONS IN ENVIRONMENTAL PRACTICE

Page numbers, where they appear, are references to a description of that term in the text.

For further references, see the Tables of Authorities and Index.

AAU — Assigned Amount Units, 1283

ABEL — Ability to pay for environmental liability (ABEL), 1013

ACE — Any Credible Evidence rule (CAA), 1015

ACO — Administrative Consent Order, 1005

ACRS — Advisory Committee on Reactor Safeguards, 419

ADEC — Alaska Dept. Envtl. Conserv., 338

ADR — Alternate Dispute Resolution, 1042

ADRA — Administrative Dispute Resolution Act, 1048

AEC — Atomic Energy Commission (now NRC), 400

AFO — Animal Feeding Operation, 644

AID — U.S. Agency for International Development, 410

ALJ — Administrative Law Judge, 1006

AMPs — Allotment management plans (grazing), 1211

ANPR — Advanced Notice of Proposed Rulemaking, 532

APA — Administrative Procedures Act, 377

AQCR — Air Quality Control Regions (CAA), 559

AR — Attributable Risk, 241

ARARs — Applicable, Relevant, Appropriate Requirements (CERCLA), 934

ASCs — Area Source Credits (CAA), 729

ASTM — American Society for Testing and Materials, 1023

ATA — American Trucking Ass'n, Whitman v., 568

BACT — Best Available Control Technology, 553

BADT — Best Available Demonstrated Control Technology (CWA), 620, 637

BANANA — Build Absolutely Nothing Anywhere Near Anybody (See NIMBY), 1225, n. 8

BAT — Best Available Technology, 484

BAT — Best Available Technology Economically Achievable (CWA), 428, 620

BCC — (Bioaccumulative Chemical of Concern), 664, n. 35

BCT — Best Conventional Control Technology (CWA), 620, 637

BDAT — Best Demonstrated Available Technology (RCRA), 862

BECC — Border Envtl Coop Comm., (NAFTA)

BEN — Economic benefit of noncompliance (EPA), 1008

BLM — Bureau of Land Management (DoI), 1179

BMP — Best Management Practices, 633, 637

BNA — Bureau of National Affairs

BOD — Biological Oxygen Demand (CWA), 622

CSO | Combined Sewer Overflows (CWA), 646

CWA | Clean Water Act (FWPCA), 67, 620

CZMA | Coastal Zone Management Act, 68, 1218

DEC | Department of Environmental Conservation (various states), 125

DEIS | Draft Environmental Impact Statement (NEPA), 506, 511

DEP | Department of Environmental Protection (various states), 331

DEQ | Department of Environmental Quality (various states), 1236

DHEC | Department of Health and Environmental Conservation

DMRs | Discharge Monitoring Reports (CWA), 1036

DNR | Department of Natural Resources, 1133

DoA | U.S. Department of Agriculture

DoI | U.S. Department of Interior

DoJ | U.S. Department of Justice, 1000

DoT | U.S. Department of Transportation, 392

DWP | Department of Water and Power (state-level), 1082

EA | Environmental Assessment (NEPA), 492

EAJA | Equal Access to Justice Act, 1040

EBEs | Environmentally Beneficial Expenditures (CWA), 1038

EC | European Community

ECJ | European Court of Justice

ECOS | Economic Council of the States, 311

ECRA | Envt'l Cleanup Resp. Act (N.J.)

EDF | Environmental Defense Fund, now Environmental Defense, 1181

EIA | Environmental Impact Assessment, 523

EIS | Environmental Impact Statement (NEPA), 68, 471

EJ | Environmental justice

ELI | Environmental Law Institute

ELP | Environmental Leadership Program

ELR | Environmental Law Reporter (by ELI)

EO | Executive Order

EPA | U.S. Environmental Protection Agency, 50, 300

EPCRA | Emergency Planning and Community Right-to-Know Act, 67, 528

EPCRTKA | EPCRA, See EPCRA

EQIP | Environmental Quality Incentives Program, 672

ERC | Emission Reduction Credits (CAA)

ERC | BNA Environmental Reporter — Cases, 734

ERDA | Energy Research and Development Administration, 400

ERUs | Emissions Reduction Units, 1283

ESA | Endangered Species Act, 69, 775

ESD | Explanation of significant differences (CERCLA), 936

FAA | Federal Aeronautics Commission, 503

FACA | Federal Advisory Committee Act, 1047

FACE | For a Cleaner Environment (Woburn citizen group), 203

FASB | Financial Accounting Standards Board, 1052

FCCC | UN Framework Convention on Climate Change, 1279

FDA | U.S. Food and Drug Administration, 542

FDF | Fundamentally Different Factors (FDF) (CWA), 642

OMB — Office of Management and Budget (executive offices of the President) 477, 551

ONRW — Outstanding National Resource Waters, 666

OOMBY — Out Of My Back Yard (See NIMBY), 1225, n. 8

OPA — Oil Pollution Act of 1990, 942

ORV — Off-Road Vehicle, 1179

OSHA — Occupational Safety and Health Act; Occupational Safety and Health Administration, 54, 68

OSWER — Office of Solid Waste and Energy Response, 928, 1018

OTA — Office of Technology Assessment (congressional), 940

OTAG — Ozone Transport Advisory Group, 619

OTC — Ozone Transport Commission (mobile sources), 751

PA — Preliminary Assessment (CERCLA), 924

PG & E — Pacific Gas & Electric

PCBs — Polychlorinated biphenyls, 116

PCSD — President's Council on Sustainable Development

PIL — Public Interest Litigation

PLLRC — Public Land Law Review Commission, 1184

PM — Particulate Matter, 552, 564

PMNs — Premarket Notifications (ToSCA), 837

PNSCP — Pre-Notice Site Cleanup Program (CERCLA), 1021

POCLAD — Program on Corporations, Law, and Democracy, 58

POTW — Publicly Owned Treatment Works (CWA), 53, 635

PPA — Pollution Prevention Act, 68

PPP — Polluter-Pays Principle (CERCLA), 887

PRIA — Public Rangelands Improvement Act, 1183

PRP — Potentially Responsible Party (Superfund), 893

PSD — Prevention of Significant Deterioration, 555

QALYs — Quality-Adjusted Life Years [QALYs], 567

QNCR — EPA's Quarterly Noncompliance Reports, e.g. on water pollution permit violations

RAC — Resource Advisory Council

RACHEL — Reauthorization Act Confirms How Everyone's Liable (SARA's unofficial alternate name), 912

RACM — Reasonably Available Control Measurements (CAA), 599

RACT — Reasonably Available Control Technology (CAA), 556

RAM — Real-time Air-quality-simulator Model, 585

RAP — Refuse Act Program permit

RARE I, II, III — Roadless Areas Review and Evaluation (Wilderness Act)

RCACs — Regional Citizens Advisory Councils, 1026

RCRA — Resource Conservation and Recovery Act, 67, 845

RD — Remedial Design (CERCLA), 933

RECLAIM — Regional Clean Air Incentives Market, 727

RIA — Regulatory Impact Analysis, 708

RI/FS — Remedial Investing/Feasibility Study (CERCLA), 933

ROD — Record of Decision, 933

RPAR — Rebuttable Presumption Against Registration (ToSCA), 825

RQ — Reportable Quantity (CERCLA), 855

RR — Relative Risk, 241

RRA — Resource Recovery Act

TABLE OF CASES

TABLE OF AUTHORITIES — BOOKS, ARTICLES, MONOGRAPHS, &C.

TABLE OF AUTHORITIES — STATUTES, REGULATIONS, TREATIES, CONSTITUTIONAL PROVISIONS, ETC.

STATUTORY CAPSULE APPENDIX: SUMMARIES OF MAJOR FEDERAL AND STATE ENVIRONMENTAL STATUTES

and citations to major international accords

Dates first given in the capsule descriptions are dates of first significant enactment. Later significant amendments may be noted. Statutory section references may use the familiar original act numbers, as noted in a number of annual publications of Selected Environmental Law Statutes. State statutes are alphabetized by state; citations to treaties and conventions are listed in a separate section below. For many statutes and treaties, page references to coursebook text are in the Glossary of Acronyms, the Table of Statutory Authorities, and the Index in these reference pages.

INDEX — STATE & FEDERAL STATUTES — U.S. (STATUTORY CAPSULES BELOW)

INDEX — SOME INTERNATIONAL TREATIES, CONVENTIONS, AND RESOLUTIONS

(Access citations below)

STATE AND FEDERAL STATUTORY CAPSULES

APA

Administrative Procedure Act, 5 U.S.C.A. §501 et seq. (1946). Passed virtually unanimously in 1946, the APA is the basic format statute for federal agencies' procedures for making law that affects persons outside the agencies (Title 5), and judicial review thereof (Title 7). It is binding on all federal agencies, and used as a model by most state administrative procedure codes and state courts' review thereof. Title 5 sets out some of the minimum procedural structures for rulemaking and adjudication (both can be done formally, with full TTP, trial-type-process, or informally), and the implicit basis for citizen participation therein. Informal rulemaking under §553 can be requested by any individual under §553(e). Agencies promulgate rules informally by notice-and-comment, with a Fed.Register Notice of Proposed Rulemaking, receipt and processing of written comments, and subsequent publication of a Notice of Final Rulemaking. Further formalization of rulemaking processes occurs with the voluntary or mandatory addition of hearings and other TTP. Title 7 creates a "generous review provisions" that should be given "a hospitable reception" in the reviewing courts. Abbott Labs, See Chapter Seven, 377–383. A valuable authoritative contemporaneous legal interpretation of all provisions of the APA is the U.S. Dep't of Justice, Attorney General's Manual on the APA (1946, reissued 1979). Amendments in the 1960s and '70s added the Freedom of Information Act (§552) and the [less effective] Government-in-the-Sunshine Open Meetings Act (§552a).

CAA

Clean Air Act, 42 U.S.C.A. §§7521 et seq. (1970). Originally passed as 1970 Amendments to a weak prior federal law, the Clean Air Act (CAA) is the leading example of a modern federal regulatory statute governing an environmental medium. Extensively amended in 1977 and 1990, it comprises several coordinated programs that address the major sources of air pollution in the United States. More specifically, it has programs that separately address stationary sources (Title I) and mobile sources of air pollution (Title II); it also has a separate program that addresses the control of hazardous air pollutants (§112). As the first statute of its kind it was and remains the principal model of what is usually referred to as a "command and control" statute. Title II controls mobile source pollution by setting maximum allowable tailpipe emissions for each type of vehicle (autos, light duty trucks, etc.), on a pollutant-by-pollutant basis as a function of the number of miles driven. For stationary sources, the CAA sets standards for emitters on a source-by-source basis, reverse engineered from a planning process that begins with National Ambient Air Quality Standards (NAAQSs)(health-based primary standards, and welfare [property and environment]-based secondary standards) that must be attained for the most common air pollutants. CAA, as a cooperative federalism statute, offers states the leading regulatory role so long as they enact and enforce programs that meet the federally mandated quality standards, under State Implementation Plans (SIPs) that prescribe the allowable emissions from stationary sources that will insure NAAQS attainment. Special sub-programs govern SIPs in areas of "nonattainment" of NAAQS quality levels, and areas to be regulated to prevent significant deterioration (PSD). As of 1990 the CAA implements a large scale emissions trading program for sulfur dioxide emissions as part of the effort to combat acid deposition from long range transport of that pollutant. A second major trading program to combat the effects of NOx pollution is in its formative stages.

Prop. 65

California "Proposition 65," Safe Drinking Water and Toxic Enforcement Act of 1986, Cal. Health & Safety Code §§25249 ff. (1990). All private businesses with more than ten employees must provide warnings with regard to consumer product exposures, occupational exposures, and environmental exposures to over 650 listed carcinogenic, mutagenic, and teratogenic substances. Carcinogens that pose "no significant risk" of contracting cancer and reproductive toxicants below a maximum risk level are exempted from the warning requirements. Warnings are required to be "clear and reasonable." Although Proposition 65 warnings have, in general, been inconspicuous and uninformative, the statute has been successful in achieving significant product reformulation and pollution prevention because of industry concerns about tort liability and consumer reactions to warnings.

CERCLA, (Superfund)

Comprehensive Environmental Response, Compensation, and Liability Act, 42 U.S.C.A. §9601 et seq. (1980). Major amendment and reauthorization in 1986 known as the Superfund Amendments and Reauthorization Act (SARA). CERCLA is administered by EPA. Under CERCLA, Congress established the authority to remediate contamination from past waste disposal practices that now endanger, or threaten to endanger, public health or the environment. CERCLA does so primarily (1) by imposing strict liability on those parties responsible for the release of hazardous substances (§107); (2) by creating a "Superfund" to finance actions to clean up such releases (§111); and (3) by imposing the cleanup costs upon the parties who generated and handled hazardous substances. (§§107, 113.) CERCLA also empowers EPA to bring administrative or judicial enforcement actions against responsible parties to force them to perform site remediation. (§106.) In addition to establishing liability rules, CERCLA creates an administrative system to identify sites in need of environmental cleanups, to set priorities among cleanup efforts, to ensure that actions are taken on a site-by-site basis, and to require that planned responses are properly executed. (§105, 121.) CERCLA provides for civil and criminal penalties (CERCLA §103(b), (c), and (d)(2)), natural resource damages (§107(a)(4)(c)), and citizen enforceability (§310).

CWA

Clean Water Act, 33 U.S.C.A. §1251 et seq. (1972). Originally passed as 1972 Amendments to a weak prior federal law (FWPCA: the Federal Water Pollution Control Act), significantly amended in 1977 and 1987. Authorizes EPA to establish national, uniform technology-based effluent limitations for point sources of pollution (e.g., factories and sewage treatment plants) discharging to waters of the United States, broadly defined to include wetlands. On waterways where technology based limitations do not meet water quality standards based on fishable-swimmable quality, more stringent water quality-based effluent limitations must be imposed. Effluent limitations are enforced through the National Pollutant Discharge Eliminations System permit program, which has been delegated to 39 states. CWA §404 of the establishes another major permit program governing discharge of dredged and fill material into wetlands and other waters. The CWA does not apply to agricultural nonpoint source pollution (runoff), which accounts for approximately half of the water pollution in the United States. CWA §309 includes a wide range of civil and criminal enforcement mechanisms; and §505 contains a frequently-used citizen suit provision.

CZMA

Costal Zone Management Act of 1972, 16 U.S.C.A. §1451 et seq. (1972). A federal land-use planning statute that authorizes federal matching grants for assisting coastal states, including Great Lakes states, in the development of management programs for the land and water resources of their coastal zones. Once NOAA has approved a state's coastal management program as complying with minimum federal standards, additional federal matching funds become available for administering the program. CZMA contains a "consistency clause" mandating that any federal activity within a state's coastal zone be consistent with that state's approved coastal management program. CZMA §1455b, added in 1990, requires a state with an approved coastal management program to submit a Coastal Nonpoint Pollution Control Program for developing and implementing management measures to control coastal nonpoint source pollution.

EPCRA

Emergency Planning and Community Right to Know Act, 42 U.S.C.A. §1100 et seq. (1986). Establishes the Toxic Release Inventory ("TRI"), which requires certain manufacturing facilities to file annual reports with EPA that identify their use and release of one or more of 650 listed toxic chemicals above yearly threshold amounts. Results of this reporting are available on the Internet ("TOXNET"). Provides for a network of state and local emergency planning committees to facilitate preparation and implementation of emergency response plans.

ESA

Endangered Species Act, 16 U.S.C.A. §1531 et seq. (1973). Legislated in furtherance of C.I.T.E.S., the Convention on International Trade in Endangered Species. ESA is administered by DoI's Fish & Wildlife Service and Commerce's National Marine Fisheries Service. Under ESA§4 the Services place endangered and threatened species on the federal endangered species list, and prepare recovery plans. Under ESA§7 all federal agencies are forbidden to "jeopardize the existence" or destroy "critical habitat" of listed species, and must enter "consultation" with the Services when a Service's Biological Assessment shows that conflicts exist. Agencies can try to get "incidental take" exemptions from the Secretaries. By 1978 amendment a Cabinet-level "God Committee" is given power to issue exemptions after stringent findings of necessity and lack of alternatives. ESA§9 prohibits the "taking" of species by anyone, interpreted to include habitat destruction, thus reaching onto private property interests. By 1982 amendment ESA§10 allows petitioners to get exemptions via "incidental take" permits from the Secretaries, after going through procedures, including HCPs (habitat conservation plans), that can attach strict controls to private project actions if the Secretary so desires. ESA§11 provides severe criminal and civil penalties, and citizen enforceability.

FDCA

Federal Food, Drug, and Cosmetics Act, 21 U.S.C.A. §301 et seq. (1938). The FFDCA is administered by the Food and Drug Administration (FDA, in the Dep't of Health and Human Services). The FFDCA prohibits the introduction or delivery into interstate commerce of any food, drug, device, or cosmetic that is adulterated or misbranded. The FFDCA regulates the occurrence of pesticide residues on raw agricultural commodities. The Delaney Clause §409 prohibits additives that cause cancer when ingested by humans or animals, and until the FQPA of 1996 this was interpreted to include slightly carcinogenic pesticide residues in processed food as well. FFDCA violators face civil and criminal penalties.

FIFRA

Federal Insecticide, Fungicide, Rodenticide Act, 7 U.S.C.A. §135 et seq. (1972). In 1972, Congress passed the Federal Environmental Pesticide Control Act, which amended the first version of FIFRA passed in 1947 by establishing the basic framework for pesticide regulation. FIFRA is administered by EPA. FIFRA requires any person distributing, selling, offering, or receiving any pesticide to register with EPA (§3). EPA will grant registration upon the determination that (i) the pesticide is effective as claimed, (ii) the labeling and other data supplied by the manufacturer meet federal standards, and (iii) the pesticide will not cause unreasonable risks to humans or the environment, taking into account the economic, social, and environmental costs and benefits of intended use. Registrations must also be followed by establishing official tolerance levels that set the maximum permissible exposure for each chemical. Once granted, registrations act as perpetual licenses to market, although they can be cancelled or suspended upon an appropriate showing that a pesticide poses a substantial risk of safety or imminent hazard to man or the environment (§6). Other major amendments to FIFRA were passed in 1975, 1978, 1980, 1988, and 1996, which, in substance, shifted the statutory emphasis from labeling and efficacy to health and the environment and provided EPA with greater flexibility in controlling dangerous chemicals. FIFRA provides civil and criminal penalties (§14) but has no citizen enforceability provision.

Florida "Critical Areas" Act

Florida Environmental Land and Water Management Act of 1972, Fla. Stat. Ch. 380.06 (1972). The state legislature may designate certain environmental resources as "areas of critical concern." After designation, local development plans and regulations must be consistent with development principles established by the State Planning Agency. If local plans or regulations are not consistent with these principles, the State Administration Commission can override local authority and promulgate binding land-use plans and regulations for the area. Four areas, including the Big Cypress Swamp and the Florida Keys, have been designated to date. "Developments of regional impact" must be reviewed by Regional Planning Agencies if the relevant municipal plans and regulations have not been declared to be consistent with statewide planning goals.

FLPMA

Federal Land Policy and Management Act, 43 U.S.C.A. §1701 et seq. (1976). The current organic act for the Bureau of Land Management (BLM) in the Department of the Interior. Applies a multiple use, sustained yield management standard — including scenic, historic, ecological, and environmental uses — to a land-use planning process for allocating private access to the public lands, especially for grazing. Declares that the public lands will remain in public ownership, except where the national interest requires disposal or exchange. FLPMA establishes uniform disposal and exchange procedures. Although declaring that "fair market value" will be charged for private use of public lands, FLPMA, in practice, continues the preferential system of grazing permits and low grazing fees included in the Taylor Grazing Act of 1936.

FWPCA

Federal Water Pollution Control Act, see CWA

FOIA

Freedom of Information Act, 5 U.S.C.A. §552 (1966). Provides that each agency state and publish in the Federal Register descriptions of its organization; location where the public may obtain information, make requests, or obtain decisions; nature of all formal and informal procedures; rules of procedure; statements of general policy adopted by the agency; and each amendment, revision, or repeal of the foregoing. Each agency shall make available for public inspection and duplication final opinions and orders made in the adjudication of cases; statements of policy not published in the Federal Register; and administrative staff manuals and instructions to staff that affect a member of the public. Fees for the furnishing of documents are limited to reasonable standard charges. Upon any request for records, each agency has ten days after the receipt of any request to determine whether to comply. Each agency has twenty days to determine whether to grant judicial review. Time limits may be extended only under "unusual circumstances." A request for records cannot be extended to matters (1) kept secret in the interest of national defense or foreign policy; (2) related solely to the internal personnel rules and practices of an agency; (3) specifically exempted from disclosure by statute; (4) trade secrets and commercial or financial information obtained from a person; (5) interagency or intra-agency memorandums or letters not generally available to the public; (6) disclosure of files which would constitute an unwarranted invasion of personal privacy; (7) records or information compiled for law enforcement purposes to the extent that the production of those records would interfere with an investigation or proceedings of law; (8) contained in or related to examination, operating, or condition reports prepared by or for the use of an agency responsible for the regulation or supervision of financial institutions; or (9) geological and geophysical information and data concerning wells.

FQPA

Food Quality Protection Act of 1996, Pub. L. No. 104–170, 110 Stat. 1489 (1996). Administered by EPA. Significantly amended both FIFRA and the Federal Food, Drug, and Cosmetic Act ("FFDCA"). Under FQPA, Congress did not comprehensively repeal the Delaney Clause, but did remove pesticide residues from its ambit by amending the FFDCA's definition of "food additive" (the Delaney Clause applies only to food additives) to exclude pesticide residues on raw or processed foods. In particular, Congress determined that a pesticide residue on such food is only to be considered unsafe if EPA has set a tolerance level for the substance and the residue fails to satisfy that level. The EPA is now allowed to grant a tolerance and register a pesticide upon a finding of safety (FQPA §405). Liberalized appeal rights for citizens is part of the compromise struck in eliminating the food additive ban.

HMTA

Hazardous Materials Transportation Act, 49 U.S.C.A. §§5101 et seq. (1976). HMTA is administered by the Department of Transportation. HMTA covers the transportation of all types of hazardous materials, regardless of whether they are raw materials, chemical intermediates, finished products or wastes. In particular, HMTA governs the safety aspects of transportation, and requires the specification of containers, warning signs, and the like, complementing RCRA. §3003(b) provides that RCRA transporter regulations are to be consistent with DOT regulations under HMTA when the transportation of hazardous waste is subject to both Acts.

Hazardous Substances Act, see RCRA

MMPA

Marine Mammal Protection Act of 1972, 13 U.S.C.A. § 1361 et seq. (1972). Devised in response to a Congressional finding that some marine mammals were in danger of depletion or extinction. These mammals were found important to the ecosystem and warranted protection for the health and stability of the marine ecosystem rather than for commercial exploitation. The Secretaries of Commerce and of the Interior bear the responsibilities of this Act for their respective groups of mammals. Title I declares a permanent moratorium on the "taking" and importation of marine mammals or their products. Exceptions to this moratorium include (1) the "taking" of marine mammals for subsistence or for the manufacture of native clothing or crafts by Alaskan natives; (2) the "taking" of marine mammals for scientific research; and (3) additional one-year exceptions for those who might otherwise suffer undue economic hardship. Before the imposition of regulations, public hearings and publications of information are required. This Act directs the Secretary of Treasury to ban the importation of fish or products caught in a manner that causes death or injury in excess of federal standards. Regulations are issued with regard to the "taking" and importation of marine mammals. Violation of regulations and provisions of this Act results in either civil penalties, criminal penalties, or both, but the Act provides no citizen enforcement provision. Commerce and Interior Secretaries are responsible for enforcement, with assistance from the Coast Guard and state officers.

MEPA

Michigan Environmental Protection Act, M.C.L.A. §§1701 et seq. (1970). MEPA represented the legislative embodiment of Professor Joseph Sax' efforts to open up the process of environmental regulation and law to citizen initiatives. In 1994, the law was recodified in a process that intended no substantive changes, but which removed some of MEPA's broad language of citizen enforcement. Along with broad citizen standing provisions, MEPA has two extraordinary substantive aspects: it invites the courts of Michigan to create a common law of environmental quality under the aegis of the statute (which has been done), and it grants courts the authority to ignore or revise administrative standards that the court finds inadequately protective of the public trust in the state's air, water, and natural resources. The limitation of relief to injunctive relief and not awarding attorney's fees to successful plaintiffs are the most probable explanations of why the statute has not been used in large numbers of cases.

Mining Act of 1872

General Mining Law of 1872, 30 U.S.C.A. §22 ff. (1872). Governs hardrock mining on federal land. Declared all non-withdrawn federal land open to hardrock mineral exploration and extraction, without requiring payment of a fee to the United States. Established the system of "discovery — location — patent": (1) staking a mining claim entitles the claimant to an exclusive property right against all but the United States; (2) once a valuable mineral is located in a barely profitable quantity, the property right can be excercised even against the United States; and (3) after several years of negligible work and payment of a modest fee, the claimant can be granted a federal patent that gives her outright ownership of the former claim. Until fairly recently, federal land management agencies claimed to possess no statutory authority to regulate the environmental abuses caused by hardrock mining. Thus, abandoned and polluting mines are frequently encountered in the West.

Mineral Leasing Act of 1920

30 U.S.C.A. §181 ff. (1920). One of several federal statutes — including the Federal Coal Leasing Amendments of 1975, 30 U.S.C.A. §1201 et seq. — that removed fuel minerals from the ambit of the General Mining Law, and established a leasing system administered by the BLM. This statute required competitive bidding for oil leases on federal lands, including the outer continental shelf, and reasonable royalty payments to the federal government. The BLM is authorized to include lease provisions protecting the environment against potential damage caused by extraction and road-construction.

NEPA

National Environmental Policy Act of 1969, 42 U.S.C.A. §4321 et seq. (1970). NEPA §102(2)(c) requires all federal agencies proposing to undertake major actions that might significantly affect the human environment to prepare and circulate Environmental Impact Statements ("EISs"). Under CEQ's NEPA regulations, Draft EISs ("DEISs") must be made available to the public and other federal agencies possessing expertise regarding the proposal. The proposing ("lead") agency may not make irretrievable commitments of resources during the comment period and for 90 days after the publication of the Final Environmental Impact Statement ("FEIS"). NEPA does not contain a citizen suit provision, but the courts have recognized a lawsuit for violation of NEPA's "procedural" obligations — i.e., the responsibility of the lead agency to make full disclosure of the proposal's alternatives and environmental impacts, as well as the agency's balancing process between environmental protection and economic development. Once full disclosure has been made, an agency decision to implement a proposal cannot be overturned in court unless it is found to be arbitrary and capricious.

NFMA

National Forest Management Act, 16 U.S.C.A. 1600 et seq. (1976). Applies a multiple use, sustained yield standard to management of the National Forests by the Forest Service (in the Department of Agriculture). Establishes a planning program requiring the development of Land and Resource

Management Plans ("LRMPs"), with which site-specific activities, such as timber sales, must be consistent. NFMA sets vague guidelines, replete with exceptions, for timber harvesting in general, and clearcutting in particular.

New Jersey ECRA

Environmental Cleanup Responsibility Act, N.J.S.A. 13: 1K-6 ff. (1983). This statute administered by the New Jersey Department of Environmental Protection ("DEP") ensures that when industrial properties are sold, any contamination will be discovered and remediated. ECRA applies only to industrial establishments with SIC Code numbers from 22 to 39 (industrial manufacturing), 46–49 (utilities), 51 (nondurable goods wholesaling), and 76 (miscellaneous repair services). ECRA is triggered by transactions such as sale, long-term lease, merger, bankruptcy, or closure. Prior to completing the transaction, the owner or operator must notify DEP, which determines the nature of site sampling that must take place before the transaction may be closed. The owner/operator must submit to DEP the sampling results, along with data regarding the history of the site, environmental permits and violations since 1960, hazardous materials stored onsite, etc. Depending on the condition of the site, the owner/operator must then submit a Negative Declaration or Cleanup (Closure) Plan to DEP for approval. If cleanup is necessary, DEP enters into an Administrative Consent Order with the owner/operator that sets cleanup schedules and ensures that financing (e.g., surety bonds) will be available for the cleanup. Owners and operators are strictly and jointly and severally liable for ECRA compliance. If ECRA is violated, DEP may void the transaction. However, ECRA has proven to be virtually self-executing in that financial institutions will not become involved in transactions that are not ECRA-compliant.

New York: Forever Wild provision

Forever Wild provision, McKinney's N.Y. Const. Art. 14, § 1, (1894, amended 1995). This provision dictates that the lands of the state, now owned or later acquired, constituting the Adirondack Park forest preserve as now fixed by law, shall be forever kept as wild forest lands. These lands will not be leased, sold or exchanged, or be taken by any corporation, public or private, nor shall the timber be sold, removed or destroyed. A citizen may bring a suit alleging a violation of this provision pursuant to Article 14 §5.

OPA '90

Oil Pollution Act of 1990, 33 U.S.C.A. §§ 2701 et seq. (1990). First passed in 1990. Modelled on CERCLA, OPA is administered by EPA, in conjunction with the U.S. Coast Guard and the National Oceanic and Atmospheric Administration. Under OPA, Congress imposed strict liability upon owners or operators of vessels or facilities that discharge oil upon waters subject to United States jurisdiction, for cleanup costs and damages caused by such discharges (OPA §1002). However, Congress exempted cargo owners from such liability (OPA §1002). Facilities must develop spill prevention, control, and countermeasure ("SPCC") plans, have them approved by EPA or the Coast Guard, and implement them, or face heavy civil and criminal penalties. OPA '90 explicitly does not preempt state oil spill cleanup laws. Congress also placed limitations on the extent of liability. Under OPA §1004, Congress increased the federal liability limit eight-fold (to $1,200 per gross ton) over the cap previously provided in §311 of the Clean Water Act. Congress also created a $1 billion Oil Spill Liability Trust Fund to pay for cleanup costs in excess of the liability limit, with up to $500 million available for payments for damages to natural resources (OPA §1012). Congress further disavowed any intent to preempt state liability requirements with respect to oil spill and removal activities (OPA §1018). OPA provides for civil and criminal penalties (OPA §§4301–4303) for natural resource damages (OPA §1006).

Oregon LCDC Act

Oregon State Land Use Act of 1973, Or Rev. Stat. §197 (1973). Established a seven member Land Conservation and Development Commission ("LCDC"). All municipalities and counties must prepare comprehensive land-use plans, and adopt and enforce zoning ordinances that are consistent with the statewide planning principles set by the LCDC. Nonconforming local plans or regulations may be rejected by the LCDC.

OSHA

Occupational Health and Safety Act, 29 U.S.C.A. §651 et seq. (1970). Under OSHA, employers are required to furnish a workplace free from recognized hazards that cause or are likely to cause death or serious physical harm to employees (§5). This act charged the Secretary of Labor with the responsibility of promulgating national consensus safety standards and established federal safety standards (§6). An employer may apply to the Secretary of Labor for a "temporary order" granting a variance from a standard or any provision under this section, establishing that (1) he is unable to comply with a standard because of an unavailability of professional or technical personnel, materials and equipment needed to come into compliance with the standard, or because necessary construction or alteration of facilities cannot be completed by the effective date, (2) he is taking all available steps to safeguard his employees against the hazards covered by the standard, and (3) he has an effective program for coming into compliance with the standard as quickly as practicable. The Secretary of Labor can establish emergency standards when employees are exposed to grave dangers from toxic materials or new hazards. Under §8, federal inspections and investigations of working conditions are authorized. Employees can request an inspection if they believe a safety or health violation exists in the workplace. If an employer is in violation of a standard, a federal inspector is authorized to issue a citation (§9). Section 17 outlines civil penalties for serious violations and willful or repeated violations. The Secretary of Labor can approve a state plan to develop and enforce standards if the plan is found in compliance with OSHA (§18).

P2 Act

Pollution Prevention Act, 42 U.S.C. 13101 et seq. (1990). The P2 Act establishes pollution prevention as a national objective, and declares a hierarchy of waste reduction strategies: pollution prevention is the highest priority, followed, in order of declining desirability, by recycling, treatment, and disposal. EPA is authorized to study, report on, and fund pollution prevention efforts, but the Act does not make pollution prevention mandatory.

RCRA

Resource Conservation and Recovery Act of 1976, 42 U.S.C.A. §6901–6992(k) (1976). RCRA is administered by EPA. RCRA Subtitle C directs EPA to establish regulations ensuring the safe management of hazardous waste from "cradle to grave," in order to eliminate endangerment from present and future waste disposal (§3001)("non-hazardous" waste is much less regulated, under Subtitle D). RCRA was reauthorized and substantially amended by the Hazardous and Solid Waste Amendments of 1984 (HWSA), which imposed new technology-based standards on landfills handling hazardous wastes, required the phaseout of land disposal for certain untreated wastes, and increased federal authority over disposal of nonhazardous solid wastes. In creating "cradle to grave" regulation over hazardous waste, RCRA attempts to regulate all aspects of the life cycle of hazardous waste. RCRA does so by creating a tracking system that follows hazardous waste from the time of generation through treatment, storage, and disposal(§3002–4). RCRA also authorizes EPA to engage in corrective action that can prevent or remedy the release of hazardous wastes (§7003). EPA is authorized to seek significant civil and criminal penalties (§3008). RCRA also provides for citizen enforceability (§7002).

Refuse Act

Refuse Act/Rivers and Harbors Appropriations Act of 1899, Pub. L. 97–322, 33 U.S.C.A. §40ff (1899). A statute passed at the end of the 19th century to facilitate the Corps of Engineers' mission to keep navigation channels free of obstruction. §407 forbade deposit without a permit of refuse in (or on the banks of so as to be washed into) any navigable river or any tributary thereto, which covers virtually the entire U.S. Other sections required permits for physical alterations to watercourses. §411 sets criminal penalties, and a reward for informants who report violations. When in the 20th century the word "refuse" came to be commonly defined to include pollution, the Act became the first effective public law weapon against pollution. Its enforcement federalized the field and changed the way industry regarded pollution. To moderate some of the harshness of the Refuse Act, Congress passed the Clean Water Act of 1972 with far tougher standards than otherwise would have been likely, repalcing some but not all of the Refuse Act's authority in the field. Federal prosecutors use the Act in cases of grave intentional discharges into water bodies.

SDWA

Safe Drinking Water Act, 42 U.S.C.A. §3007 et seq. (1974). The SDWA regulates purveyors of potable water. It authorizes EPA to promulgate technology-based primary and secondary drinking water regulations, containing maximum contaminant levels ("MCLs"), applicable to public water systems, defined as systems that provide water to at least 25 individuals. Primary enforcement responsibility under the SDWA is delegated to states. The SDWA bans new installations of lead drinking water pipes, protects "sole source aquifers" from inconsistent federal actions, and contains a major regulatory program applicable to underground injection of hazardous wastes. With regard to funding, the SDWA authorizes federal grants to states for (1) improving state drinking water regulation, (2) establishing revolving loan funding mechanisms for low-interest loans to upgrade public water systems, and (3) facilitating state planning for the protection of wellhead areas.

SMCRA

Surface Mining Control and Reclamation Act, 30 U.S.C.A. §1201 et seq. (1977). SMCRA established the Office of Surface Mining Reclamation and Enforcement in the Department of Interior, charged with administering the Act's regulatory and reclamation programs, and providing grants and technical assistance to the states. Title IV establishes a self-supporting Abandoned Mine Reclamation Fund to restore land adversely affected by past uncontrolled mining operations. Titles IV and V provide that the state and federal governments are jointly responsibile for acquiring lands and enforcing environmental protection regulations required by the Act. Under Title V, performance standards are set for environmental protection to be met by all major surface mining operations for coal. Title VI protects certain lands regarded as unsuitable for suface mining.

SWDA

Solid Waste Disposal Act of 1965, 42 U.S.C.A. §6901 et seq., see RCRA

ToSCA

Toxic Substance Control Act, 15 U.S.C.A. §2601 et seq. (1976). ToSCA is administered by EPA, and places on manufacturers the responsibility to provide data on the health and environmental effects of chemical substances, and provides EPA with comprehensive authority to prohibit the manufacture, distribution, or use of chemical substances that pose unreasonable risks. ToSCA also requires premanufacture notification of EPA for new chemicals or significant new uses of chemicals. To implement these goals, EPA has the authority (1) to require the testing of chemicals (ToSCA §4), (2) to require the premanufacture review of new chemical substances (ToSCA §5), (3) to limit or prohibit manufacture, use, distribution, and disposal of chemicals (ToSCA §6), and (4) to require recordkeeping and reporting (ToSCA §8). ToSCA provides for civil and criminal penalties (ToSCA §16) as well as citizen enforceability (ToSCA §20.)

Vermont Act 250

Vermont State Land Use and Development Act of 1970, Vt. Stat. Ann. Tit. 10 §6001 et seq. (1970). All developers of public or private construction projects of more than ten acres, and residential units of more than ten units, must obtain a project permit from one of nine regional Environmental District Commissions ("EDCs"). A permit may be denied if it is "detrimental to the public health, safety, or general welfare." The burden is on the applicant to prove that the project will not cause undue environmental degradation. Project opponents bear the burden of proving unreasonable burden on infrastructure or damage to aesthetic or historic sites. A developer must obtain an EDC permit before applying for other necessary local development permits. See Richard Brooks' two-volume treatise, Toward Community Sustainability: Vermont's Act 250 (1997).

Watershed Act

Watershed Protection and Flood Prevention Act, 16 U.S.C.A. §1001 et seq. (1954). The Act initiates a program where the Secretary of Agriculture cooperates with States and local agencies in the construction and financing of comprehensive soil conservation, flood-prevention and water control projects for small watersheds (§3). Under §4, the Secretary of Agriculture is permitted to determine the "proportionate share" of federal assistance that local organizations would receive for such projects. Under §5, the President issues rules and regulations necessary to carry out the purposes of the Act, and coordinates the projects under this Act with existing programs.

WSRA

Wild and Scenic Rivers Act, 16 U.S.C.A. 1271 et seq. (1968). The WSRA establishes the Dep't of Interior's Federal Wild and Scenic Rivers System, including approximately 10,000 miles of designated wild, scenic, and recreational rivers and their corridors within one-quarter mile of each river bank. Dams are prohibited on designated rivers and their tributaries, and all federal activities must be consistent with the river's wild and scenic character. Federal lands abutting designated rivers must also be managed in a consistent manner. The WSRA contains no authority for federal regulation of private activities within the corridor of a designated river, and federal condemnation powers within the corridor are severely limited.

Wilderness Act of 1964

16 U.S.C.A. §1131 et seq. (1964). Establishes the Wilderness System, including extensive Wilderness Areas where all commercial logging and permanent roads and most structures and installations, temporary roads, commercial enterprises, mining, grazing, and use of motorized equipment are prohibited. The following secondary uses are permitted: logging to control insect infestations and fires; mineral exploration; mining claims, mineral leases, and grazing permits obtained before January 1, 1964; commercial services provided by guides, packers, and river runners; and hunting and fishing. The Departments of Interior and Agriculture are the primary agencies. Each addition to the Wilderness System must be made by specific congressional enactment.

SOME INTERNATIONAL TREATIES, CONVENTIONS, AND RESOLUTIONS — CITATIONS

Agenda 21, see Report of the UNCED at Rio de Janeiro, June 3–14, 1992.

United Nations Conference on Environment and Development, Agenda 21, U.N. Doc. A/CONF. 151/26 (1992); reprinted in The Earth Summit: The United Nations Conference on Environment and Development (UNCED) 125–508 (Stanley P. Johnson ed. 1993). See also for annotations, Agenda 21: Earth's Action Plan Annotated (Nicholas A. Robinson ed. 1993)

Basel Convention on the Control of Transboundary Movements of Hazardous Wastes and Their Disposal, Mar. 22, 1989.

United Nations Environment Programme, UNEP/IG.80/3, March 22, 1989; reprinted in 28 I.L.M. 657 (1989).

Convention on Biological Diversity, see Report of the UNCED at Rio de Janeiro, June 3–14, 1992.

United Nations Convention on Biological Diversity, June 5, 1992, S. Treaty Doc. 20 (1993); reprinted in 31 I.L.M. 818 (1992).

Convention on International Trade in Endangered Species of Wild Fauna and Flora (CITES), March 3, 1973. 27 U.S.T. 1087, 999 U.N.T.S. 243; reprinted in 12 I.L.M. 1085 (1973).

Desertification Convention

International Convention to Combat Desertification in Those Countries Experiencing Serious Drought and/or Desertification, Particularly in Africa, June, 17, 1994, U.N. General Assembly Doc. A/AC. 241/15/Rev. 7 (1994); reprinted in 33 I.L.M. 1328 (1994).

European Community Directive on the Assessment on the Effects of Certain Public and Private Projects on the Environment

Directive on the Assessment on the Effects of Certain Public and Private Projects on the Environment, Council Directive 85/337/EEC, 1985 O.J. (L 175/40); 28 Official Journal of E.C. 40 (1985) L-175.

General Agreement on Tariffs and Trade (GATT), Oct. 30, 1947.

T.I.A.S. No. 1700, 61-V Stat. All, 4 Bevans 639, 55 U.N.T.S. 18: Arts. I, III, IX, XI, XX.

Kyoto Protocol on Global Warming

Kyoto Protocol to the FCCC, FCCC Conference of the Parties, 3d Sess., UN Doc. FCCC/CP/1997/L.7/
Add.1 (Dec. 10, 1997); reprinted in 37 I.L.M. 22 (1998). Final version was issued as part of the Third Conference of the Parties Report, UN Doc. FCCC/CP/1997/7/Add.2.

Montreal Protocol

Montreal Protocol on Substances That Deplete the Ozone Layer, Sept. 16, 1987, S. Treaty Doc. No. 100-10 (1987); reprinted in 26 I.L.M. 1550. Pursuant to Vienna Convention for the Protection of the Ozone Layer

Vienna Convention for the Protection of the Ozone Layer, Mar. 22, 1985, U.N. Doc. UNEP/Ig.53/Rev.1, S.Treaty Doc. No. 99-9, 99th Cong., 1st Sess. (1985), T.I.A.S. 11097; reprinted in 26 I.L.M. 1529.

NAFTA (Side Agreement)

The North American Agreement on Environmental Cooperation (environmental side agreement to NAFTA), Sept. 8–14, 1993, 32 I.L.M. 1482(1993).

POPS Convention

The Stockholm Convention on Persistent Organic Pollutants, May 22, 2001, 40 I.L.M. 532 (2001.

OECD Polluter-Pays OECD Doc. C(72) 128

OECD Council Recommendations on Guiding Principles Concerning International Economic Aspects of Environmental Policies, adopted May 26, 1972, OECD Doc. C(72)128, Annex A(a) in Organisation For Economic Co-operation and Development, OECD and the Environment 24 (1986). Also available at 1972 WL 24710 (Int'l Envtl L. Library).

Resolution on Large-Scale Pelagic Driftnet Fishing and Its Impact on the Living Marine Resources of the World's Oceans and Seas

G.A. Res. 46/215, U.N. GAOR, 46th Sess., U.N. Doc. A/RES/46/215 (1992), Dec. 20, 1991; reprinted in 31 I.L.M. 241 (1992).

Rio Declaration on Environment and Development, June 13, 1992.

UNCED Doc. A/CONF.151/5/Rev. 1, June 13, 1992; reprinted in 31 I.L.M. 874 (1992); and Agenda 21.

Stockholm Declaration of 1972

Stockholm Declaration of the United Nations Conference on the Human Environment, June 16, 1972, Principle 21, U.N. Doc. A/Conf. 48/14 (1972), 11 I.L.M. 1416 (1972).

Straddling Fish Stocks Convention

Agreement for the Implementation of the United Nations Convention of the Law of the Sea of 10 December 1988, Relating to the Conservation and Management of Straddling Fish Stocks and Highly Migratory Fish Stocks, U.N. GAOR, 6th Sess., pt. x, art. 34, U.N. Doc. A/CONF.164/37 (1995), reprinted in 34 I.L.M. 1542 (1995).

Treaty on the Non-Proliferation of Nuclear Weapons, July 1, 1968.

21 U.S.T. 483, 729 U.N.T.S. 161; reprinted in 7 I.L.M. 811 (1968): Art. III.

UNCLOS, United Nations Convention on the Law of the Sea, Oct. 7, 1982.

United Nations, Official Text of the United Nations Convention on the Law of the Sea with Annexes and Index, U.N. Sales No. E83.v.5 (1983); see also U.N. Doc. A/Conf.62/122; reprinted in 21 I.L.M. 1261 (1982).

INDEX

See separate Tables for cases, statutes, books, and articles.